Congressional Roll Call 2012

REFERENCE

Congressional Roll Call 2012

A Chronology and Analysis of Votes in the House and Senate
112th Congress, Second Session

Los Angeles | London | New Delhi
Singapore | Washington DC

Los Angeles | London | New Delhi
Singapore | Washington DC

FOR INFORMATION:

CQ Press

An Imprint of SAGE Publications, Inc.

2455 Teller Road

Thousand Oaks, California 91320

E-mail: order@sagepub.com

SAGE Publications Ltd.

1 Oliver's Yard

55 City Road

London EC1Y 1SP

United Kingdom

SAGE Publications India Pvt. Ltd.

B 1/I 1 Mohan Cooperative Industrial Area

Mathura Road, New Delhi 110 044

India

SAGE Publications Asia-Pacific Pte. Ltd.

3 Church Street

#10-04 Samsung Hub

Singapore 049483

Cover image © Getty Images/Visions of America/Joe Sohm

Printed in the United States of America

Library of Congress Cataloging-in-Publication Data

ISBN 978-1-4522-7778-3 (pbk.)

This book is printed on acid-free paper.

SFI label applies to text stock

Developmental Editor: Andrew Boney

Editorial Assistant: Josh Benjamin

Production Editor: David C. Felts

Typesetter: C&M Digitals (P) Ltd.

Cover Designer: Michael Dubowe

Marketing Managers: Carmel Schrire

13 14 15 16 17 10 9 8 7 6 5 4 3 2 1

Table of Contents

Editor's Note

Written and compiled by the editors and journalists at CQ Roll Call, *Congressional Roll Call 2012* provides a member-by-member survey and analysis of votes of the House of Representatives and Senate during the second session of the 112th Congress.

An introductory legislative summary is followed by three sections. The first contains CQ Roll Call's special voting studies. These studies examine the voting behavior of members of Congress, including congressional support of the president's position on specific votes and the percentage of all recorded votes on which members voted or took stands. Summaries and charts of the key votes are included in the second section.

The third section of the book contains a compilation of roll call votes in the House and Senate in 2012, and includes indexes of the roll call votes and the bills on which roll call votes were taken.

INTRODUCTION

Partisan Combat Prevailed in 112th, Fiscal Cliff Narrowly Avoided

THE MOST SIGNIFICANT moment in the second session of the 112th Congress came on the last day, when lawmakers narrowly avoided taking the country over what was known as the fiscal cliff.

The fiscal cliff was a combination of huge tax increases and automatic, across-the-board spending cuts scheduled to take effect at the start of 2013. A last-minute deal averted the tax crisis but put off the sequester for only three months.

Much of the regular session was relatively uneventful, with both parties spending a great deal of their time in futile battles devoted to disparaging their opponents and positioning themselves for the November election.

The public noticed: The average approval rating for the year in Gallup's polls was 15 percent, the lowest since the pollster had begun asking Americans their opinions of lawmaker performance 38 years earlier. With the Republican House and Democratic Senate unable to agree on policy matters, a fewer-than-usual number of bills landed on President Barack Obama's desk. A total of 193 bills became public law, including 150 signed before the session adjourned — by far the lowest election-year total of the decade.

Some of the more significant legislation was cleared during the lame-duck session following Obama's decisive Nov. 6 re-election victory.

Much of the dysfunction took place in the House, where Speaker John A. Boehner of Ohio struggled to keep both the tea party advocates on his right flank and the more moderate wing of the Republican Party unified. On more than one occasion, he gave up on a House bill because he could not solidify the support of his caucus. He could rarely count on Democrats, even if he had wanted to. An exception was the fiscal-cliff legislation, which he ended up forcing through the House by relying on Democrats to make up for Republican defectors.

On the other hand, the GOP majority was able to unite on most bills, many of them meant to showcase Republican positions that had little if any support from Democrats and no hope in the Senate.

The partisanship was reflected in the relatively large number of votes on which members of each party stuck with their own caucus. An annual study by CQ Roll Call (formerly Congressional Quarterly) found that in 72.8 percent of the 657 roll call votes taken in the House, a majority of one party voted against a majority of the other, the highest rate in a presidential election year since CQ began doing the study. The overall percentage of so-called party unity in the House for the two sessions of the 112th Congress was

the highest since 1953.

In the Democratic Senate, Majority Leader Harry Reid of Nevada largely followed the "Hastert rule," a practice of bringing to the floor only bills that he could pass by a majority of his own party. Party unity was reflected in 60 percent of the roll call votes cast. Reid also sought to cast Republicans as the party of "no" by bringing up bills he knew they would reject by denying him the 60-vote supermajority needed to prevent a filibuster.

A steady stream of retirements throughout the year signaled members' dissatisfaction, with a number of departing lawmakers citing the paralyzing partisanship in Congress. One of the most prominent examples was moderate Republican Olympia J. Snowe of Maine, who announced in February that, rather than seek another term, she would try to effect change from the outside. "Unfortunately, I do not realistically expect the partisanship of recent years in the Senate to change over the short term," she said.

BUDGET AND SPENDING

• **Budget.** Obama kicked off the fiscal 2013 congressional budget season Feb. 13 with a proposal that was slightly more than the $3.796 trillion in outlays enacted for fiscal 2012. The plan complied with a $1.047 trillion cap for fiscal 2013 discretionary budget authority set under the hard-fought negotiations that produced the 2011 Budget Control Act (PL 112-25). The White House said if Obama's budget were accepted in full, it would serve as an alternative to the pending automatic spending cuts that were on the minds of many in Congress. *(Budget act, 2011 Almanac, p. 3-11)*

In late March, the House adopted a fiscal 2013 budget resolution, written by Budget Chairman Paul D. Ryan, R-Wis., that would have limited discretionary appropriations to $1.028 trillion — $19 billion below the cap set in 2011. All of the new cuts would have come from domestic spending. The measure, which also included a number of GOP policy initiatives, was uniformly rejected by Democrats and did not get beyond a procedural challenge in the Senate. For the second year in a row, the Senate Budget Committee did not approve a budget resolution.

While the budget resolution does not become law, it would have set common House-Senate tax and spending guidelines for the year.

• **Appropriations.** Although Democrats and Republicans agreed on few other matters, they joined forces in September to suspend the fiscal 2013 appropriations process and clear legislation that continued existing spending through March 27, 2013.

Leaders: 112th Congress, 2nd Session

SENATE

President of the Senate: Vice President Joseph R. Biden Jr.
President Pro Tempore: Daniel K. Inouye, D-Hawaii*

DEMOCRATIC LEADERS

Majority Leader . . . . Harry Reid, Nev.	Steering and Outreach
Majority Whip . . . . Richard J. Durbin, Ill.	Committee Chairman. . . . . .Mark Begich, Alaska
Conference Vice Chairman . . . . Charles E. Schumer, N.Y.	Chief Deputy Whip . . . . .Barbara Boxer, Calif.
Policy Committee Chairman . . . . . . Charles E. Schumer, N.Y.	Democratic Senatorial Campaign
Conference Secretary . . . . Patty Murray, Wash.	Committee Chairwoman . . . . . .Patty Murray, Wash.

REPUBLICAN LEADERS

Minority Leader . . . . Mitch McConnell, Ky.	Conference Vice Chairman . . . . . .Roy Blunt, Mo.
Minority Whip . . . . Jon Kyl, Ariz.	Chief Deputy Whip . . . . .Richard M. Burr, N.C.
Conference Chairman . . . . John Thune, S.D.	National Republican Senatorial
Policy Committee Chairman . . . . . . John Barrasso, Wyo.	Committee Chairman. . . . . .John Cornyn, Texas

HOUSE

Speaker of the House: John A. Boehner, R-Ohio

REPUBLICAN LEADERS

Majority Leader . . . . Eric Cantor, Va.	Policy Committee Chairman . . . . .Tom Price, Ga.
Majority Whip . . . . Kevin McCarthy, Calif.	Chief Deputy Whip . . . . .Peter Roskam, Ill.
Conference Chairman . . . . Jeb Hensarling, Texas	National Republican Congressional
Conference Vice Chairwoman . . . . . Cathy McMorris Rodgers,	Committee Chairman. . . . . .Pete Sessions, Texas
Wash.	Conference Secretary . . . . .John Carter, Texas

DEMOCRATIC LEADERS

Minority Leader . . . . Nancy Pelosi, Calif.	Democratic Congressional Campaign
Minority Whip . . . . Steny H. Hoyer, Md.	Committee Chairman. . . . . .Steve Israel, N.Y.
Assistant Leader . . . . James E. Clyburn, S.C.	Steering and Policy Committee
Caucus Chairman . . . . John B. Larson, Conn.	Co-Chairwoman. . . . . .Rosa DeLauro, Conn.
Caucus Vice Chairman. . . . . Xavier Becerra, Calif.	Co-Chairman . . . . .George Miller, Calif.
Senior Chief Deputy Whip . . . . John Lewis, Ga.	

* Died Dec. 17, 2012; succeeded by Patrick J. Leahy, D-Vt.

The agreement was negotiated by the White House and a bipartisan congressional leadership team. Both parties wanted to avoid any chance of a government shutdown before the election and remove partisan fights over appropriations from the expected year-end clash over the fiscal cliff.

None of the 12 fiscal 2013 spending bills cleared. The House passed all but the controversial Labor-Health and Human Services-Education bill, while the Senate passed five. The continuing resolution (PL 112-175) increased spending by 0.6 percent for most federal programs and agencies.

MAKING IT INTO LAW

Despite the partisan combat, lawmakers did succeed in sending the president several notable bills that were signed into law.

- **Unemployment benefits.** One of the first orders of business at the start of the year was completing legislation that renewed federal emergency unemployment benefits and extended a reduction in employees' Social Security payroll tax rates to 4.2 percent from 6.2 percent. The bill (PL 112-96) also blocked a sharp scheduled drop in reimbursement rates for doctors who served Medicare patients.

The provisions had produced a deadlock at the end of 2011 that ended in an agreement to sort them out at the start of 2012. The gridlock finally ended in February, when political leaders agreed that the 10-month cost of the payroll tax cut extension would not be offset but found enough savings to pay for the rest of the bill. By most accounts, the debate over the payroll tax cut bruised Republicans, who had insisted on offsetting spending cuts and resisted attempts by Democrats to pay for the extension with a popular "millionaire's surtax."

The unemployment benefits and "doc fix" were subsequently extended through 2013 as part of the fiscal-cliff agreement, but the payroll tax holiday was allowed to expire at the end of 2012.

- **Federal Aviation Administration.** Congress cleared an FAA reauthorization bill in February (PL 112-95) that added slots for long-distance flights at Ronald Reagan Washington National Airport and left in place a National Mediation Board ruling, strongly opposed by Republicans, that made it easier for airline and railroad workers to unionize. Senate Democrats had flatly rejected a provision in the original House version of the bill that would have rescinded the rule. The measure also set deadlines to accelerate completion of the updated air traffic control system known as NextGen.

- **Surface transportation.** After a battle of almost three years

and a series of ups and downs during the session, lawmakers reached agreement on a two-year surface transportation bill before breaking for the July Fourth recess. Known as the Moving Ahead for Progress in the 21st Century Act, or MAP-21, the measure (PL 112-141) reauthorized federal highway, transit and other surface transportation programs through fiscal 2014 at existing levels, with some inflationary increases, and allowed the collection of revenue and the expenditure of money from the Highway Trust Fund.

The agreement gave the White House a jobs bill, which it had sought, while enabling Republicans to scale back federal regulation of transportation projects, in part by speeding up environmental reviews.

Boehner had championed a five-year version that would have significantly modified federal highway and transit programs, including the elimination of dedicated funding for mass transit projects. It would have covered part of the growing shortfall in Highway Trust Fund financing by dedicating new revenues from a proposed increase in domestic oil and gas production. But, with many tea party conservatives skeptical that infrastructure was worth spending more than was in the Highway Trust Fund, Boehner could not find enough support in his fractured caucus to bring the bill to the floor. The final legislation, negotiated between the two chambers, contained enough sweeteners for conservatives that it got through the House and became law.

• **Student loans.** Students and their families got a one-year reprieve from a scheduled increase in student loan interest rates in legislation that was attached to the transportation bill. The popular measure extended the existing 3.4 percent rate through June 2013. Without the bill, the rate would have reverted to 6.8 percent on July 1, affecting an estimated 7.4 million undergraduate students who had federally subsidized Stafford loans.

Obama called on Congress to extend the student loan interest rate and publicly campaigned for it on college campuses. Republicans initially rejected the idea, calling it a campaign ploy, but came on board after GOP presidential candidate Mitt Romney agreed that Congress should keep the interest rate low. A compromise reached in the Senate paid the cost by making changes in pension law and shortening the time frame for the interest subsidies.

• **FDA user fees.** Congress easily cleared legislation allowing the Food and Drug Administration to continue collecting the fees that supported the approval process for prescription drugs and medical devices. The bill also created two new user fee programs, one for generic drugs and the other for generic biologic drugs.

The five-year authorization (PL 112-144) made numerous changes to the user fee programs and required drugmakers to notify the FDA of expected shortages of certain critical drugs. However, it did not include Senate-passed provisions to create a national drug-tracking and -tracing system.

• **Iran sanctions.** Lawmakers pushed through two rounds of legislation toughening economic sanctions against Iran in hope of forcing that country's government to end its alleged nuclear-weapons program. Congress cleared the first measure (PL 112-158) just before the August recess. Leading sanctions hawks in the Senate, who said the bill did not go far enough, succeeded in attaching additional sanctions to the 2013 defense authorization bill (PL 112-329), which cleared in December.

Shortly before the August bill cleared, Obama imposed new sanctions of his own through an executive order.

• **Stock Act.** In the aftermath of a story on "60 Minutes" suggesting that members of Congress might have used knowledge gained in the course of their duties to profit in the stock market, Congress cleared the Stop Trading on Congressional Knowledge Act (PL 112-105).

Initially drafted as a bill to state explicitly that Securities and Exchange Commission rules banning insider trading applied to members of Congress, the legislation grew into a rewrite of financial-disclosure requirements that applied not only to lawmakers and congressional staff but also to officials and senior staff throughout the government.

UNFINISHED BILLS

• **Farm bill.** One of the biggest pieces of legislation left unfinished at the end of the session was a huge, multiyear bill to reauthorize and modify federal farm and nutrition programs. The Senate passed a five-year farm bill in June, but a separate version approved by the House Agriculture Committee never made it to the floor. House GOP leaders said they did not have the votes — largely because conservative members wanted even deeper cuts to food stamps, officially known as the Supplemental Nutrition Assistance Program, than were proposed in the bill. The House bill would have cut funding for the program by three times the reduction in the Senate version.

Leaders of the House and Senate Agriculture committees pushed until the bitter end to clear a reauthorization bill, which would have allowed Congress to influence agriculture and nutrition policy. They said they had reached an agreement that would extend the farm bill through 2013, with some changes. But in the end, negotiators on the fiscal-cliff package included a simple extension of existing law, which sent the Agriculture committees back to the drawing boards for the 113th Congress.

• **Postal Service.** Despite agreement on both sides of the aisle that action was needed to save the cash-strapped Postal Service from financial losses that threatened its operations, lawmakers were unable to complete legislation. Partly because of the steep drop in the volume of first-class mail due to the use of the Internet, the quasi-governmental agency lost $15.9 billion in fiscal 2012 and defaulted in August 2012 on a $5.5 billion payment needed to cover future retiree health costs.

The Senate passed a bill in April, but a version approved in a House committee the previous year did not reach the floor. Both legislative proposals fell short of changes Postmaster General Patrick R. Donahoe said he needed in order to cut operating costs. Differences between the two bills included how much authority the Postal Service should have to overhaul its operations, whether to end Saturday mail delivery, and whether to allow the USPS to recoup overpayments made to its federal retirement account and use that money to provide retirement incentives to about 100,000 employees.

• **Cybersecurity.** Bipartisan alarm over the threat of cyberattacks was not enough for Democrats and Republicans to narrow their differences over the proper scope and nature of federal involvement in strengthening the defenses of vital, privately owned computer networks. The House passed a series of smaller bills that did not propose any new rules for businesses. One measure offered incentives to businesses to share threat information with the federal

Highlights: 112th Congress, Second Session

CONGRESS DID

- Reauthorize surface transportation, federal aviation and flood insurance programs.
- Permanently extend personal income tax rates for all except those with incomes of more than $400,000 for individuals and $450,000 for couples; permanently tied to inflation the level at which the alternative minimum tax took effect; and permanently reset the estate tax rate to 40 percent from 35 percent for the portion of estates worth more than $5 million, tying to inflation the amount that was exempt.
- Extend unemployment benefits for many long-term jobless workers through 2013.
- Delay until March 1 an across-the-board sequester of $109 billion from all federal agencies that had been scheduled to take effect Jan. 2, reducing it to $85 billion for the remainder of the year.
- Reauthorize defense programs for fiscal 2013.
- Establish normal trade relations with Russia.
- Toughen sanctions on Iran.
- Impose new disclosure requirements for financial transactions on officials in Congress and the Executive Branch.
- Hold Eric H. Holder Jr. in contempt of Congress, the first time the House (or either chamber) had officially taken such a step against an attorney general.
- Extend through 2017 a warrantless-surveillance program for foreign targets communicating with people in the United States.

CONGRESS DID NOT

- Enact any of the 12 regular appropriations bills for fiscal 2013 or agree to a full-year continuing appropriations resolution, leaving spending decisions for the year to the 113th Congress.
- Raise the $16.4 trillion federal debt ceiling, which, according to the Treasury Department, was reached on Dec. 31.
- Appropriate $60.4 billion in disaster aid sought by the Obama administration for communities in the Northeast damaged by Superstorm Sandy in October.
- Repeal significant provisions of the 2010 health care overhaul.
- Improve cybersecurity by strengthening the defenses of privately owned computer networks.
- Reauthorize or overhaul federal farm assistance programs.
- Find a source of money for federal transportation programs.
- Roll back provisions of the 2010 Dodd-Frank overhaul of financial-service-industry regulations.
- Reauthorize the Elementary and Secondary Education Act, known as No Child Left Behind.
- Overhaul the Postal Service.
- Block proposed EPA regulations.
- Reauthorize the Violence Against Women Act.
- Overhaul federal immigration policy.
- Expedite the permitting process for the Keystone XL pipeline from Canada to the Gulf Coast.

government, but the legislation ran afoul of privacy advocates who said it did not do enough to protect the data of U.S. citizens whose information could be passed along to the Pentagon.

Solid GOP opposition blocked Reid from winning cloture on a more comprehensive Senate measure, backed by the White House, that would have created a set of voluntary industry security standards for critical infrastructure and provided incentives for businesses to meet them. Republicans argued that the voluntary standards could become mandatory in practice.

- **Violence against women.** Both chambers passed bills to reauthorize the Violence Against Women Act. But after months of arguing, they could not agree on a Senate provision that would have extended the law's protections to tribal lands. The Senate bill, passed in April, also included provisions to cover gay and lesbian victims and to grant more visas to illegal immigrants who were victims of domestic violence. The House passed a version in May that included new visa application benchmarks for illegal immigrants who were victims of violent crimes and who assisted with law enforcement investigations.

- **Storm aid.** The Senate passed a bill to provide $60.4 billion for recovery efforts from Superstorm Sandy, but Boehner put off further action until early 2013. The delay infuriated members from New York and New Jersey, whose states suffered devastating damage from the Oct. 29 storm, and brought unusually harsh criticism of Boehner from members of his own caucus.

Facing the bipartisan backlash from Northeastern lawmakers, Boehner quickly announced that a vote on an initial aid installment would be held on the first legislative day of the 113th Congress, with a subsequent package considered by Jan. 15.

GOP PRIORITIES THAT FELL SHORT

A number of GOP-sponsored bills and amendments that prevailed in the House were rejected or never taken up by the Democratic Senate but gave House Republicans a chance to take a stand on GOP policy priorities.

In addition to trying to cut appropriations below the Budget Control Act caps, House Republicans passed a slew of measures to alter the budget process, including bills to require the Congressional Budget Office to take into account how legislation might affect economic growth in calculating the resulting revenue or cost — a method known as dynamic scoring — and a measure to give the president line-item veto authority over discretionary spending.

Other GOP legislation would have repealed, defunded or ratcheted back Obama's signature 2010 health care overhaul, including abolishing an independent panel charged with curbing Medicare spending growth. The attempts came both before and after a historic Supreme Court ruling in June that the overhaul could go forward largely as written, although states could opt out of a provision that expanded the state-federal Medicaid program for the poor without losing all of their federal Medicaid funds.

Republicans took their opposition to "Obamacare" on the road as a central issue in their fall campaign, but Obama's victory largely took the wind out of their sails.

The House GOP energy agenda also included efforts to ease regulations and expand the availability of new federal lands for drilling, including areas off the coastal United States, in the Gulf of Mexico and in Alaska's Arctic National Wildlife Refuge. The House also passed a package of measures that would have rolled back fuel economy standards, barred regulation of greenhouse gas emissions

112th Congress, Second Session: By the Numbers

The second session of the 112th Congress began at noon Jan. 3, 2012, and kept going until a few minutes before noon, Jan. 3, 2013. (The Senate never adjourned sine die.) Both chambers conducted significant legislative business after Dec. 31 for the first time since 1970. Following are statistical highlights of the two chambers over the past decade.

		2012	2011	2010	2009	2008	2007	2006	2005	2004	2003	2002
Days in session	Senate	153	170	158	191	184	190	138	159	133	167	149
	House	152	175	127	159	119	164	101	140	110	133	123
Time in session *(hours)*	Senate	930	1,102	1,075	1,421	989	1,376	1,028	1,222	1,032	1,454	1,043
	House	725	993	879	1,247	890	1,248	850	1,067	879	1,015	772
Average length of daily session *(hours)*	Senate	6.1	6.5	6.8	7.4	5.4	7.2	7.4	7.7	7.8	8.7	7.0
	House	4.8	5.7	6.9	7.8	7.5	7.6	8.4	7.6	8.0	7.6	6.3
Public laws enacted [1]		150	90	258	125	280	180	313	169	300	198	241
Bills and resolutions introduced	Senate	2,014	2,447	1,506	3,380	1,590	3,033	2,302	2,618	1,318	2,398	1,558
	House	3,381	4,456	3,098	5,699	3,225	6,194	2,451	5,703	2,338	4,616	2,711
	Total	5,395	6,903	4,604	9,079	4,815	9,227	4,753	8,321	3,656	7,014	4,269
Roll calls	Senate [2]	251	235	299	397	215	442	279	366	216	459	253
	House [2]	656 [3]	945 [3]	660	987	688	1,177	539	669	543	675	483
	House [4]	657 [3]	948 [3]	664	991	690	1,186	541	671	544	677	484
	Total [4]	908	1,183 [3]	963	1,388	905	1,628	820	1,037	760	1,136	737
Vetoes		0	0	1	1	4	7 [5]	1	0	0	0	0

[1] Bills signed into law during congressional session. [2] Votes only; excludes quorum calls. [3] Excludes one roll call vote that was vitiated. [4] Includes House quorum calls. [5] Includes pocket vetoes.
SOURCE: Congressional Record

and ceded authority over coal waste to the states. Republican said the bills would combat what they called Obama's "war on coal."

The 2010 Dodd-Frank regulatory overhaul of the financial services industry was another Republican target, with bills to delay, modify or repeal parts of the law. Although some of those bills had support from House Democrats, they, too, were ignored in the Senate.

THE ELECTION

The Nov. 6 election, which had loomed over both sessions of the 112th Congress, ended in a decisive victory for Obama, dashing Republican hopes that Romney would be the next occupant of the White House. As a subsequent March 2013 article in the conservative magazine Commentary lamented: "Obama won going away, defeating Romney by 126 electoral votes (332 to Romney's 206) and winning the popular vote by nearly 5 million. In the Senate, which many had thought likely to fall to Republican control, the GOP lost two seats; in the House, it managed to hold its majority, but at the loss of eight seats."

The campaign featured two very different visions of how to push the sluggish economic recovery forward and particularly how to create jobs. Romney called for slashing government spending to cut the deficit while rolling back regulation, which he said hobbled businesses. He spoke out for tax cuts for all Americans, including the wealthy, whom Republicans called the "job creators."

Obama called for increasing taxes on the wealthy while cutting them for the middle class and portrayed Romney as being out of touch with the needs of ordinary Americans and seeking to protect the rich. He said that investments in such things as education and infrastructure were crucial to America's future and should be balanced with deficit reduction.

The outcome of the presidential race opened a lengthy period of soul-searching for Republicans, with some members of their party saying they were out of touch with the coalition of young people, women, blacks and Hispanics that put Obama over the top. But the party remained deeply divided over the proper remedy. The Commentary article, titled "How to Save the Republican Party," noted that "a hundred paths diverge and a thousand voices have been heard."

Republicans' net loss of just eight seats in the House left them with a healthy majority of 233 seats to 200 for the Democrats. Their casualty list was short, given Obama's relatively easy re-election, and conservatives quickly said that while Obama had won the presidency, they had won their districts and would reflect the views of their constituents.

In the Senate, where the Democratic majority increased to 53-45, no Democratic incumbent was defeated, and the party lost only the seat of departing Sen. Ben Nelson of Nebraska. Also, Democrats won two Republican-held seats and added another vote when Maine independent Angus King chose to caucus with the party.

The overall outcome left the government divided and provided little hope that the partisan gridlock would give way anytime soon.

THE LAME DUCK

Several important bills that had stalled before the election came back to life in the lame-duck session that followed the election.
- **Defense authorization.** In one of its final acts of the year, Congress cleared a measure (PL 112-329) authorizing $633.3 billion in

discretionary spending for national defense programs, approving more money and more weapons than the Defense Department sought. The bulk of the authorization — $527.5 billion — was for the base Pentagon budget. The amount was $2.1 billion more than Obama requested. The rest of the bill consisted of $88.5 billion for the war in Afghanistan and other overseas contingencies, virtually the same as requested, although other funds in the bill could also be used. The agreement also authorized $17.4 billion for nuclear defense activities carried out by the Energy Department, about $400 million less than requested. Overall, the total was $1.7 billion more than the president's request.

Lawmakers were able to limit the number of controversial provisions in the bill and managed to complete a final House-Senate conference in a little more than three days. But despite the relative comity in the effort, there were difficult issues. In particular, lawmakers tangled over detention policies up until the end of the conference, finally dropping a provision in the Senate version that was billed as a guarantee against indefinite incarceration of U.S. citizens captured in the United States in the war on terrorism. The final law still included some tough detainee language, largely from the House bill.

● **FISA reauthorization.** In a victory for Obama and Senate Select Intelligence Chairwoman Dianne Feinstein, D-Calif., Congress cleared a five-year renewal of a post-Sept. 11 foreign-intelligence law in the final days of the session (PL 112-238). The bill extended through 2017 expiring provisions of the 2008 Foreign Intelligence Surveillance Act, which gave the intelligence community authority to conduct wiretaps of certain foreigners communicating with people in the United States without obtaining individual warrants.

The measure cleared over the objections of mostly Democratic opponents, who said that the reauthorization was too long and did not do enough to ensure the rights of individual Americans.

● **Intelligence reauthorization.** Shortly before the end of the year, Congress cleared a fiscal 2013 intelligence bill (PL 112-277) that authorized funding for 16 U.S. intelligence agencies, including the Office of the Director of National Intelligence, the CIA and the National Security Agency. Leaders of the Intelligence committees worked to make the legislation relatively non-controversial, but near the end of the process, the bill became caught up in a dispute among senators over efforts to crack down on leaks of classified information after a spate of high-profile spy operation disclosures over the summer. In the end, lawmakers agreed to delete the most controversial provisions, opening the way for the bill to clear.

THE FISCAL CLIFF

After months of negotiations that stretched through the winter holidays, lawmakers meeting on New Year's Day 2013 finally reached agreement with Obama on a bill (PL 112-240) to raise taxes on the wealthiest Americans and put off automatic, across-the-board spending cuts until March 1, 2013. The package averted the fiscal cliff of higher taxes and spending reductions that threatened to tumble the economy back into recession. The bill also extended benefits for long-term unemployed workers for another year, kept farm assistance programs operating through the end of fiscal 2013 and deferred for a year the cut in reimbursement rates for doctors who served Medicare patients.

The more than $500 billion in pending tax increases was a result of the Jan. 1 expiration of individual income tax cuts and other reductions enacted under President George W. Bush in 2001 and 2003. The $109 billion in automatic spending cuts had been ordered under the 2011 Budget Control Act — itself the product of cliffhanger negotiations — after a committee created by the act failed to agree on an alternative plan to reduce the deficit by $1.2 trillion over 10 years. The sequester was due to take effect Jan. 2.

House Republicans, led by Boehner, demanded deep spending cuts, the extension of all the Bush-era tax cuts regardless of income, and no tax increases. Democrats, led by Obama, proposed extending the tax cuts for everyone but the wealthiest Americans, no changes in entitlement program benefits and smaller spending cuts.

Negotiations began in earnest after Thanksgiving, with Obama and Boehner eager to reach agreement but reluctant to give much of any ground. At one point, with the talks stalled, Boehner tried to have the House pass what he called a Plan B — a tax cut extension for all but those earning $1 million or more a year. House Republicans balked, and Boehner left it to Senate Minority Leader Mitch McConnell of Kentucky to try to work out a deal with the White House led by Vice President Joseph R. Biden Jr.

An agreement reached on New Year's Eve and cleared the next day permanently extended the 2001 and 2003 tax rates and other tax benefits for virtually all taxpayers, while allowing the top tax rate to rise to 39.6 percent from 35 percent on annual income of more than $400,000 for individuals and $450,000 for couples. Among other key provisions, the law extended reduced tax rates on capital gains and dividend income for those with taxable income of less than $400,000 for individuals and $450,000 for couples, while for those above those levels the rate was 20 percent, up from 15 percent.

The higher taxes on the wealthy were very unpopular with conservative Republicans, and party leaders vowed they would not consider any additional tax increases and would focus solely on spending cuts in the new year as they looked ahead to negotiations on the sequester and funding for the rest of fiscal 2013.

According to a Gallup survey taken Dec. 21-22, just 26 percent of respondents approved of the efforts by Republican leaders to work with Obama on a fiscal deal, compared with 54 percent who said they approved of Obama's approach to Republicans.

The temporary nature of the sequester deal, combined with the expiration of fiscal 2013 government funding on March 27, 2013, and a need to raise the debt limit at about that time were seen as major impediments for Obama, who hoped to achieve new immigration and job creation legislation in the 113th Congress. ∎

VOTE STUDIES

Blaming GOP for Low Success Rate, Obama Draws Victory From Defeat

I F 2012 SEEMED LIKE A YEAR marked by futile battles between President Barack Obama and Republicans in Congress, that's because it was. Obama signed fewer new laws than any president this century, or in the half-century before that.

For all that, Congress was given much of the blame. Its average approval rating for the year in Gallup's polls was 15 percent, the lowest since the pollsters began asking Americans their opinions of lawmaker performance 38 years earlier. Because the Republican House and Democratic Senate could not agree on policy matters, few bills landed on Obama's desk.

But Obama also had a poor record when it came to those votes on Capitol Hill on which he spoke out. The president got his way on just 54 percent of the votes where he made his preference known, the lowest success score of his presidency, according to an analysis of congressional voting patterns by CQ Roll Call. In just 11 of the 60 years since Congressional Quarterly began studying the twin subjects of presidential success on Capitol Hill and support for the president's position by individual lawmakers had the occupant of the White House done worse.

The context was important. Obama foresaw many of the losses. He knew that Republicans in the House would rarely vote his way, and they didn't, setting a record for low individual support for a president. Obama also knew that Democrats in the Senate would often be unable to overcome GOP filibusters in an election year, and on 14 of the 16 votes in the Senate where he took a stand and lost, he had a majority of the chamber but not the 60-vote supermajority required.

When Senate votes on presidential nomination votes were excluded from the tally of votes in both chambers where the president weighed in, he lost on two-thirds of them.

Still, Obama won the year's biggest prizes, his re-election and the post-election fiscal-cliff deal that raised taxes on the wealthy. That suggested the role of presidential positioning could be changing. If presidents of previous decades issued statements on bills to help forge compromise and resolve policy disputes, Obama's statements came to serve a more political purpose. And Obama used his pulpit deftly.

"Putting forward ideas without regard to their ability to pass Congress enabled him to run against Congress," said Frances E. Lee, a political scientist at the University of Maryland. "With Congress as unpopular as it is, it was a good strategy."

In the past, presidential success in congressional policy fights had been linked to re-election. Since CQ began its voting study in 1953, Republican presidents who earned a second term boasted decent success scores in their re-election years. In 2004, George W. Bush got his way on 73 percent of the votes where he expressed a view, compared with the 60-year average presidential-success score of 68 percent. Ronald Reagan in 1984 and Richard Nixon in 1972 won on 66 percent of the votes on which they weighed in, despite dealing with chambers controlled by the other party. Dwight D. Eisenhower's 1956 tally was 70 percent.

The two Democrats who won second full terms in the post-World War II era — Bill Clinton and Obama — were exceptions to the rule.

Both faced similar circumstances. In 1996, Clinton confronted a Republican House and Senate that were eager to smite him. His success score that year was 55 percent. In 2012, Obama's party held a six-seat margin in a Senate where 60 votes were routinely required to move legislation, while Republicans in the House had a majority

CQ Vote Study Guide

CQ Roll Call (previously Congressional Quarterly) has analyzed the voting behavior of members of Congress since 1945. The three principal vote studies currently produced — presidential support, party unity and voting participation — have been conducted in a consistent manner since 1953. This is how the studies are done:

Selecting votes CQ Roll Call bases its vote studies on all floor votes for which members were asked to vote "yea" or "nay." In 2012, there were 657 such roll call votes in the House and 251 in the Senate. The House total excludes quorum calls (there was one in 2012) because they require only that members vote "present." (The House total for 2012 also excludes one vote that was vitiated after it occurred.)

The House total includes votes on procedural matters, including votes to approve the Journal (12 in 2012). The Senate total includes votes to instruct the sergeant at arms to request members' presence in the chamber (although there were no such votes in 2012).

The presidential support and party unity studies are based on votes selected from the total according to the criteria explained on pages B-8 and B-18.

Individual scores Members' scores in the following charts are based only on the votes each member actually cast. This makes individual support and opposition scores add to 100 percent. The same method is used to identify the leading scorers on pages B-5 and B-17.

Overall scores To maintain consistency with previous years, calculations of average scores by chamber and party are based on all eligible votes, whether or not all members cast a "yea" or "nay." As a result, the failure of lawmakers to participate in a roll call vote reduces chamber and party average support and opposition scores. And those averages are not strictly comparable with individual member scores, which are calculated differently. (Methodology, 1987 Almanac, p. 22-C)

Rounding Scores in the tables for the full House and Senate membership are rounded to the nearest percentage point, although rounding does not raise any score to 100 percent or reduce any score to zero. Scores for the leaders in presidential and party support are reported to one decimal point to rank them more precisely.

Obama's Success Rate His Lowest Yet

President Barack Obama's success rate on votes on which he took a clear position declined in 2012, as often happened in a president's fourth year. He won on fewer than 20 percent of House votes — the lowest for any president except George W. Bush in 2007 — although he held his own in the Senate, winning almost 80 percent of the time. The data in the graphic combine House and Senate figures.

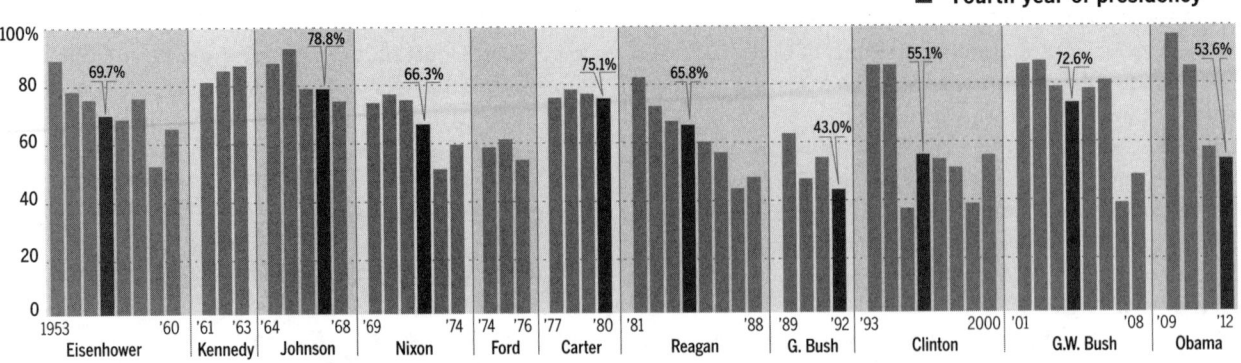

■ **Fourth year of presidency**

that ranged from 48 to 51 seats. It was a recipe for gridlock. Yet both Clinton and Obama garnered rising approval ratings throughout their re-election years and won re-election by wide margins.

CHOOSING HIS BATTLES

Obama picked his fights carefully. In 2012, the president or his surrogates expressed a preference on 61 House votes. In the Senate, where the rules made it much harder to even bring bills to the floor, the policy votes on which Obama expressed a view were even more sporadic. There were just 39 such votes in 2012. The chamber took an additional 40 votes on presidential nominees, where Obama had an obvious position.

The reaction on Capitol Hill was predictable. The average House Republican lawmaker voted the president's way on only 10 of those votes. That rate of support — 17 percent — was the lowest for House Republicans since CQ began tracking presidential positions. (The record low for House Democrats was an average 7 percent support score for Bush in 2007.)

The rare instances of GOP support came on matters, such as the payroll tax cut in February or the agreement to extend normal trade status to Russia in November, that Republicans were in no position to oppose. Both of those bills passed overwhelmingly.

By contrast, Senate Democrats set an all-time high in their support for a president. The average Senate Democrat voted the way Obama wanted on 73 of the 79 votes where he had stated a preference, a rate of 93 percent. Senate Republicans backed Obama 47 percent of the time.

Party leaders in the House echoed this new reality. Republicans were indifferent to policy pronouncements from the president, while Democrats rarely needed persuading.

"We try to write and pass the best legislation possible," House Speaker John A. Boehner of Ohio said. "The president's support or opposition doesn't change that."

House Minority Leader Nancy Pelosi of California offered an opposite view. "The president knows our views, shares our values, and we respect his leadership," she said. "Democrats in the House may not have the gavel, but we have unity."

For rank-and-file lawmakers as well, the guiding principle was politics, not policy, Lee said. Presidential positions made it harder for members of the opposite party to sign on, even on proposals that seemed to fit their ideological perspective. For members of the president's party, a presidential position served as an inducement to get in line, even when the vote might require an explanation.

Why else did so many Republicans vote for Bush's 2002 "No Child Left Behind" law increasing federal aid for elementary and secondary education? Or why did they pass his expensive new Medicare drug benefit in 2004? Both had become anathema to many Republicans.

Mixed Success

Support for President Barack Obama's positions among Senate Democrats fell just short of a record and hit a new low among House Republicans. Across both chambers, the president got his way just over half the time.

Share of votes on which the president took a clear position:

House
9.3% down from 2011
61 out of 657

Senate
31.5% down from 2011
79 out of 251

Average for both chambers: **15.4%**

How often the president won:

House
19.7% second lowest on record
12 out of 61

Senate
79.7% down from 2011
63 out of 79

Average for both chambers: **53.6%**

Average chamber presidential support scores:

House
D **77%** down from 2011
R **17%** lowest on record

Senate
D **93%** second highest on record
R **47%** down from 2011

Leading Scorers: Presidential Support

Support indicates those who voted in 2012 most often for President Barack Obama's position, when it was clearly known. **Opposition** shows those who voted most often against his position. Lawmakers who left office or who missed half or more of the votes are not listed. Scores are reported in this list only to one decimal point; members with identical scores are listed alphabetically. *(Complete scores, pp. B-10, B-12)*

SENATE

SUPPORT

Democrats		Republicans		Democrats		Republicans	
Johnson, S.D.	98.7%	Snowe, Maine	80.3%	Manchin, W.Va.	15.2%	DeMint, S.C.	83.9%
Kerry, Mass.	98.7	Brown, Mass.	78.5	Webb, Va.	11.7	Lee, Utah	83.1
Klobuchar, Minn.	98.7	Collins, Maine	78.5	Landrieu, La.	10.4	Paul, Ky.	66.2
Nelson, Fla.	98.7	Murkowski, Alaska	68.9	Nelson, Neb.	10.3	Vitter, La.	59.1
Schumer, N.Y.	98.7	Lugar, Ind.	66.2	Pryor, Ark.	8.9	Cornyn, Texas	59.0
Shaheen, N.H.	98.7	Alexander, Tenn.	62.2	Baucus, Mont.	7.6	Risch, Idaho	59.0
Rockefeller, W.Va.	98.6	Hoeven, N.D.	60.0	Harkin, Iowa	6.8	Coburn, Okla.	58.7
Cantwell, Wash.	97.5	Hutchison, Texas	57.9	Begich, Alaska	6.7	Hatch, Utah	58.5
Carper, Del.	97.5	McCain, Ariz.	56.9	Casey, Pa.	5.3	Toomey, Pa.	57.9
Coons, Del.	97.5	Graham, S.C.	56.6	Merkley, Ore.	5.2	Inhofe, Okla.	56.2
Feinstein, Calif.	97.5	Ayotte, N.H.	56.4	Mikulski, Md.	5.2	Rubio, Fla.	56.2
Gillibrand, N.Y.	97.5	Corker, Tenn.	56.4	Whitehouse, R.I.	5.2	Chambliss, Ga.	55.6
5 senators	97.4	Cochran, Miss.	54.4	Tester, Mont.	5.1	Burr, N.C.	54.8

OPPOSITION

HOUSE

SUPPORT

Democrats		Republicans		Democrats		Republicans	
Pelosi, Calif.	94.9%	Amash, Mich.	50.8%	McIntyre, N.C.	82.1%	Burton, Ind.	90.2%
Sherman, Calif.	93.4	Paul, Texas	44.7	Peterson, Minn.	75.4	Forbes, Va.	90.0
DeGette, Colo.	93.2	Johnson, Ill.	42.6	Barrow, Ga.	70.5	Bonner, Ala.	89.7
Honda, Calif.	93.2	Campbell, Calif.	38.6	Matheson, Utah	68.9	Landry, La.	89.1
Yarmuth, Ky.	93.0	Gibson, N.Y.	37.7	Boren, Okla.	67.9	Blackburn, Tenn.	88.5
Lewis, Ga.	92.9	Jones, N.C.	36.1	Kissell, N.C.	67.2	DesJarlais, Tenn.	88.5
Bass, Calif.	92.7	Bass, N.H.	33.3	Ross, Ark.	63.2	Foxx, N.C.	88.5
Deutch, Fla.	92.7	McClintock, Calif.	33.3	Donnelly, Ind.	61.4	Lankford, Okla.	88.5
Neal, Mass.	92.7	Dold, Ill.	31.1	Cuellar, Texas	52.5	Palazzo, Miss.	88.5
Velázquez, N.Y.	92.7	Duncan Jr., Tenn.	30.0	Chandler, Ky.	51.7	Roby, Ala.	88.5
Wasserman Schultz, Fla.	92.6	Hayworth, N.Y.	29.5	Owens, N.Y.	51.7	Rogers, Ala.	88.5
Slaughter, N.Y.	92.3	Huelskamp, Kan.	27.9	Altmire, Pa.	50.0	Bachus, Ala.	88.3
Hirono, Hawaii	91.8	Mulvaney, S.C.	27.9	Bishop, Ga.	46.6	Gingrey, Ga.	88.3
Quigley, Ill.	91.8	Labrador, Idaho	27.6	Shuler, N.C.	46.0	Harris, Md.	88.3
McGovern, Mass.	91.7	Bilbray, Calif.	27.1	Boswell, Iowa	45.9	Hunter, Calif.	88.3
Welch, Vt.	91.7	Fitzpatrick, Pa.	26.7	Hochul, N.Y.	45.9	King, Iowa	88.3
4 members	91.5	LaTourette, Ohio	26.3	Cardoza, Calif.	41.9	Kingston, Ga.	88.3
		Ros-Lehtinen, Fla.	26.2	Costa, Calif.	41.8	Neugebauer, Texas	88.3

OPPOSITION

Likewise, why had Democrats mostly laid down their swords on the drone strikes overseas that targeted American citizens or the eavesdropping by government agents on phone calls originating abroad but sometimes involving Americans? When Bush was president, they criticized him for similar policies.

In September 2011, Obama addressed a joint session of Congress to offer new jobs legislation. The proposals in it, he noted, were ones that had won bipartisan support in the past. But when the Senate brought up the ideas, including tax cuts for companies that hired new workers or brought jobs back from overseas, Republicans blocked them.

Meanwhile, when the House brought up legislation to reauthorize the warrantless wiretapping program that Bush had started to go after terrorists overseas, Obama urged his party's lawmakers to support it. Four in 10 House Democrats did. In the Senate, it was six in 10, in spite of opposition from civil-liberties groups.

Most policy votes, however, tracked traditional party divisions. Obama sparred with House Republicans repeatedly, rejecting their efforts to force him to approve an oil pipeline connecting Canada's tar sands region with American refiners in Texas. He called out the GOP again when it moved to quash Education Department rules regulating for-profit colleges and to repeal part of the 2010 health care law. He rejected their efforts to make it more difficult for individuals to

Presidential Position Votes Decline in 2012

The share of roll call votes on which President Barack Obama took a clear position fell slightly in 2012 in both chambers, while the absolute number of presidential support votes fell more substantially in a year in which roll calls declined. The president took a position on 9.3 percent of House votes and on not quite one-third of Senate roll calls (15.5 percent when nominations are excluded).

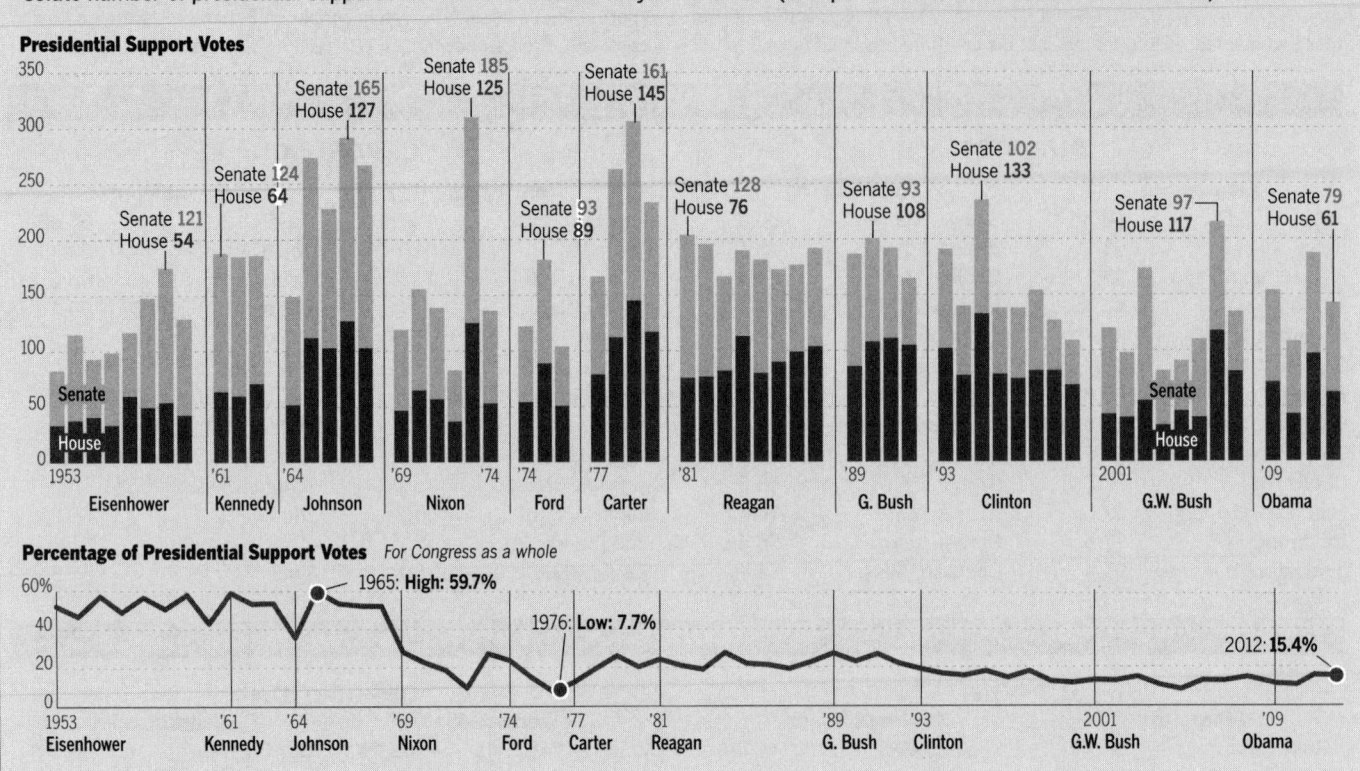

sue their doctors for medical malpractice and to replace the spending sequester Congress created in 2011 with a new plan that would take more from domestic programs and less from defense. They fought over a GOP plan to cut tax rates for individuals and corporations.

Each time Obama asked House members to vote no, Democrats did and Republicans ignored him. But with a Democratic Senate standing in the way, the president prevailed.

60-VOTE THRESHOLD

Unlike in the House, the president tended to get his way in the Senate. That helped Obama raise the debt ceiling and extend a payroll tax break. Obama's losses almost all came when Republicans filibustered, as they did over his jobs package, or when Senate leaders agreed that 60 votes would be required for passage to avoid a filibuster.

In the House, Obama commanded considerable loyalty from Democrats. But with little hope of affecting the outcome of votes and an election pending, Democratic representatives felt freer than in years past to buck the president. House Democrats took Obama's side 77 percent of the time — a very high tally historically — but still his lowest level of support in four years.

The votes revealed a spread among different House Democratic factions. Members of the Progressive Caucus stuck with Obama 87 percent of the time, while fiscally conservative Blue Dogs did on only 56 percent of the votes.

Meanwhile, even as they set a record for their lack of support for the president, House Republicans did occasionally agree. Besides the payroll tax and Russia trade votes, the GOP supported legislation, ultimately enacted, to require additional disclosure of stock trades by members of Congress. The issue took on urgency for both parties after the CBS News program "60 Minutes" ran an exposé in November 2011 alleging that members of Congress had boosted the value of their portfolios using insider knowledge.

Rare, though, were House votes on which Obama got his way in defiance of most Republicans. That only happened twice. The New Year's Day vote to avert the fiscal cliff was the only one of consequence, when Boehner brought up a bill that raised tax rates on the wealthy in defiance of two-thirds of his caucus. He and a minority of Republicans voted with almost every Democrat to pass it.

The other vote came in September, when Republicans fell short of the two-thirds majority needed to pass a bill under suspension of the rules. The measure — intended to replace an existing visa lottery for people from countries with historically low rates of immigration with a new system favoring foreign scientists, engineers and technology workers — passed easily when Boehner brought it up again two months later under normal procedures. Yet like so many other bills passed by the House in 2012, the Senate ignored it.

In the end, Congress didn't pass many laws. But as far as Obama was concerned, the major impasses — over his jobs bill and immigration policy as well as taxes — involved issues he wanted to emphasize to voters in November.

Partisan voting had become more common in Congress since the early 1990s and had become closely linked to the votes on which the

president expressed his preference. Of the policy votes where Obama weighed in, eight in 10 divided the parties.

FEWER MODERATES

Experts pointed to several causes. Regional differences in ideology had wiped out most Southern Democrats and Northeastern Republicans. Redistricting made House seats safe for one party or the other but opened incumbents to primary challenges from the right.

Jason Grumet, president of the Bipartisan Policy Center, a think tank that sought to help lawmakers find common ground, argued that a breakdown in interpersonal relationships among lawmakers was a major factor, a result perhaps of the pressure they felt to spend more time at home, away from Washington, and easier transportation to and from the Capitol that enabled them to get away more often.

At the same time, those moderates still in Congress tended to represent swing districts and, as a result, were in constant electoral danger. The 2010 election wiped out half of the Blue Dog Coalition of fiscally conservative House Democrats. And while the 2012 election wasn't the political tidal wave of 2010, more than 20 percent of the remaining Blue Dogs were defeated, and others retired. By contrast, members of the Progressive Caucus lost at only a 4 percent rate.

Republican moderates also took a beating. Charles Bass of New Hampshire, the former head of the moderate Republican Main Street Partnership who sided with Obama on a third of the votes where the president expressed a view, went down. So did Roscoe G. Bartlett of Maryland, Brian P. Bilbray of California, Nan Hayworth of New York, and Robert Dold and Joe Walsh of Illinois, all of whom had voted with Obama more often than most of their peers.

It wasn't always this way. Bipartisan coalitions were powerful forces in the first four decades following World War II. "Any given president, even a minority party president, could put together a winning coalition on floor votes from moderate and cross-pressure sections of the other party," said Jon R. Bond, a political science professor at Texas A&M University. "Nixon and Reagan did this to great effect."

But Bond said that as the ranks of moderates dwindled, those who remained were less willing to cross their party leaders. "When 20 [percent] or 25 percent of a party caucus are moderates, they have enough critical mass to stand up. With more homogenous party caucuses, the president is not going to lose as many votes from his own party."

Tensions within the GOP on its right flank led to some anomalies: two libertarian-leaning House Republicans, Justin Amash of Michigan and Ron Paul of Texas, ended up among the president's most frequent supporters on roll call votes, usually because Obama had objected to spending cuts and they voted against the reduction, saying their party was not cutting enough.

If bucking the party line was a political anvil, it followed that presidential positions on bills served less to persuade the opposite party than to motivate members of the president's own party and activists at home.

Steven Schier, a political scientist at Carleton College, said that as the presidential statement of policy shifted away from any persuasive purpose, its content had also changed. Presidential statements were more strident than they used to be, he contended, and rarely signaled a willingness to compromise. As a result, they reinforced partisan divisions more than they broke them down.

"It's signaling to the Democratic base that he is in sync with them," Schier said. "Why take the risk of alienating your base when your statement is unlikely to convince anyone?"

A primary example was the annual defense authorization bill.

Obama repeatedly threatened vetoes, principally over provisions denying his ability to shutter the prison camp at Guantánamo Bay, Cuba, and to bring alleged terrorists to the United States for trial.

With lawmakers of both parties aligned against him, Obama always went on to sign the law. But the veto threat signaled to liberals that Obama's failure to close the prison was Congress' fault, not his.

Lee said a presidential statement made compromise less likely. "When presidents take a stand on issues, those areas systemically become more controversial in Congress, on partisan lines, than they typically are," she said. "When presidents really want to cut a deal, their best strategy is to keep what they are offering quiet" from the public.

If there was a persuasive purpose in a presidential statement of policy, it was an indirect one, Schier said: Interest groups that gained motivation from a statement from Obama might have more influence over GOP representatives and senators than Obama himself did.

Signals sent by the president to Democratic lawmakers on whom he could rely also could yield tangible changes in bills, said John J. Pitney Jr., a political science professor at Claremont McKenna College in California. If they took issue with specific provisions of a bill, for instance, allies of the president might propose an amendment to fix the problem. Likewise, if a bill was missing an element crucial to the president, an ally might propose an amendment to add it."

For much of the year, Republicans were free to ignore the president's wishes and allow bills to die. But on must-pass measures, such as the defense authorization and the fiscal-cliff-averting tax increases, compromise was crucial and presidential positions sent signals to Republicans about where compromise might lie. In the end, both sides reached accommodations.

For instance, when Obama threatened to veto the defense authorization bill over the Guantánamo Bay language, the House and Senate votes on the bill were among Obama's losses. In the end, however, Congress agreed to a small compromise, removing language that would have permanently barred the president from bringing detainees at Guantánamo back to the United States for trial, while extending the ban for another year. It was enough. Obama signed the law, but reiterated his misgivings in a signing statement and pledged, vaguely, to ignore provisions that interfered with his constitutional authority.

The president was more successful on the fiscal-cliff votes at the end of the 112th Congress. His hard-line stance demanding that Congress allow tax rates to rise on wealthy Americans ultimately forced the hand of Republicans who were fearful of taking blame for allowing even broader tax increases and cuts in defense spending.

Still, if politicians once took signals from elections and gave newly elected presidents honeymoons to pursue their goals, the fiscal-cliff debate showed those days were over. Bush enjoyed a honeymoon after his 2000 win, signing laws cutting taxes and overhauling federal education policy in his first year in office, both with bipartisan support. But he enjoyed no such leeway after his re-election in 2004, despite his famous pledge to use his "political capital" to overhaul Social Security.

Obama never got a honeymoon after his landslide victory in 2008. His stimulus bill got not a single GOP vote in the House and was enacted only after Maine's two moderate Republican senators, Susan Collins and Olympia J. Snowe, and Pennsylvania's Arlen Specter signed on. Two months later, Specter bolted the GOP. In 2012, Snowe decided not to seek re-election. She cited the Senate's "dysfunction and political polarization" as her reason. ■

Presidential Support Background

CQ Roll Call editors select presidential support votes each year based on clear statements by the president or authorized spokesmen. **Success** scores show the percentage of the selected votes on which the president prevailed. **Support** shows the percentage of roll call votes on which members of Congress voted in agreement with the president's position.

Presidential Success by Issues

	Defense/Foreign Policy		Domestic		Economic Affairs		Overall	
	2012	2011	2012	2011	2012	2011	2012	2011
House	0%	65.0%	11.1%	16.4%	53.3%	50.0%	19.7%	31.6%
Senate	25.0	0	68.2	85.7	61.5	73.9	79.7	84.3
Congress	7.1	61.9	32.8	29.3	57.1	64.9	53.6	57.1

Economic affairs includes votes on taxes, trade, omnibus and some supplemental spending bills, which may fund both domestic and defense and foreign policy programs. Confirmation votes in the Senate are included only in the chamber's overall scores.

Average Presidential Support Scores

	House		Senate			House		Senate	
	Democrats	Republicans	Democrats	Republicans		Democrats	Republicans	Democrats	Republicans
Eisenhower					**Reagan**				
1954	44%	71%	38%	73%	1981	42%	68%	49%	80%
1955	53	60	56	72	1982	39	64	43	74
1956	52	72	39	72	1983	28	70	42	73
1957	49	54	51	69	1984	34	60	41	76
1958	44	67	44	67	1985	30	67	35	75
1959	40	68	38	72	1986	25	65	37	78
1960	44	59	43	66	1987	24	62	36	64
Kennedy					1988	25	57	47	68
1961	73	37	65	36	**G. Bush**				
1962	72	42	63	39	1989	36	69	55	82
1963	72	32	63	44	1990	25	63	38	70
Johnson					1991	34	72	41	83
1964	74	38	61	45	1992	25	71	32	73
1965	74	41	64	48	**Clinton**				
1966	63	37	57	43	1993	77	39	87	29
1967	69	46	61	53	1994	75	47	86	42
1968	64	51	48	47	1995	75	22	81	29
Nixon					1996	74	38	83	37
1969	48	57	47	66	1997	71	30	85	60
1970	53	66	45	60	1998	74	26	82	41
1971	47	72	40	64	1999	73	23	84	34
1972	47	64	44	66	2000	73	27	89	46
1973	35	62	37	61	**G.W. Bush**				
1974	46	65	39	57	2001	31	86	66	94
Ford					2002	32	82	71	89
1974	41	51	39	55	2003	26	89	48	94
1975	38	63	47	68	2004	30	80	60	91
1976	32	63	39	62	2005	24	81	38	86
Carter					2006	31	85	51	85
1977	63	42	70	52	2007	7	72	37	78
1978	60	36	66	41	2008	16	64	34	70
1979	64	34	68	47	**Obama**				
1980	63	40	62	45	2009	90	26	92	50
					2010	84	29	94	41
					2011	80	22	92	53
					2012	77	17	93	47

2012 Presidential Position Votes

The following is a list of the 61 House and 79 Senate roll call votes in 2012 on which the president took a clear position, based on his statements or those of authorized spokespersons. A victory is a vote on which the president's position prevailed.

HOUSE

Defense and Foreign Policy

VOTE NUMBER DESCRIPTION

10 Defeats

266	Detainee policy
280	Nuclear weapons
281	Defense spending
288	Nuclear weapons
291	Defense policy
489	Defense spending
491	Nuclear weapons
493	Nuclear weapons
497	Health care
498	Defense spending

Domestic Policy

VOTE NUMBER DESCRIPTION

4 Victories

47	Insider trading
306	Domestic spending
569	Domestic surveillance
590	Immigration policy

32 Defeats

18	Health care
71	Energy policy
79	Education policy
91	Environmental policy
126	Health care
138	Telecommunications policy
170	Transportation policy
192	Cybersecurity
195	Education policy
235	Same-sex marriage
249	Domestic spending
258	Legal affairs
305	Domestic spending
308	Environmental regulation
342	Domestic spending
361	Health care
363	Immigration policy
370	Domestic spending
387	Public lands
410	Energy policy
441	Legal affairs
442	Legal affairs
450	Domestic spending
460	Health care
468	Mining regulation
487	Same-sex marriage
511	Energy policy
512	Energy policy
536	Regulatory policy
603	Energy regulation
613	Immigration policy
655	Federal employees

Economic Affairs and Trade

VOTE NUMBER DESCRIPTION

8 Victories

46	Line-item veto
72	Economic stimulus
110	Small-business capital
132	Small-business capital
224	Trade policy
579	Omnibus spending
608	Trade policy
659	Tax rates

7 Defeats

4	Debt limit
177	Economic stimulus
247	Sequester replacement
545	Tax rates
552	Tax overhaul
577	Sequester replacement
644	Sequester replacement

House Success Score

Victories	12
Defeats	49
Total	61
Success rate	**19.7%**

SENATE

Defense and Foreign Policy

VOTE NUMBER DESCRIPTION

1 Victory

206	Defense policy

3 Defeats

212	Detainee policy
219	Disabilities treaty
221	Defense policy

Domestic Policy

VOTE NUMBER DESCRIPTION

15 Victories

14	Insider trading
24	Heath care
30	Environmental regulation
34	Energy policy
48	Transportation policy
56	Insider trading
68	Labor policy
87	Legal affairs
111	Health care
112	Education policy
139	Environmental regulation
164	Farm policy
168	Health care
236	Domestic surveillance
248	Disaster aid

7 Defeats

89	Education policy
113	Education policy
115	Labor policy
180	Campaign finance
187	Cybersecurity
193	Job training
204	Public lands

Economic Affairs and Trade

VOTE NUMBER DESCRIPTION

8 Victories

2	Debt limit
22	Economic stimulus
55	Small-business capital
96	Trade policy
184	Tax rates
199	Omnibus spending
223	Trade policy
251	Tax rates

5 Defeats

63	Energy policy
65	Tax rates
177	Economic stimulus
181	Tax policy
227	Bank regulation

Nominations

VOTE NUMBER DESCRIPTION

39 Victories

1	John M. Gerrard
16	Cathy Ann Bencivengo
19	Adalberto Jose Jordan
21	Jesse M. Furman
23	Margo Kitsy Brodie
26	Mary Elizabeth Phillips
27	Thomas Owen Rice
49	Gina Marie Groh
50	Michael Walter Fitzgerald
57	David Nuffer
58	Ronnie Abrams
61	Miranda Du
62	Susie Morgan
64	Stephanie Dawn Thacker
67	Brian C. Wimes
83	Gregg Jeffrey Costa
88	Jacqueline H. Nguyen
90	John J. Tharp Jr.
102	Jeremy C. Stein
103	Jerome H. Powell
104	Paul J. Watford
114	Timothy S. Hillman
116	Jeffrey J. Helmick
118	Andrew D. Hurwitz (cloture)
121	Mari Carmen Aponte (cloture)
122	Mary Geiger Lewis
167	Robin S. Rosenbaum
173	John Thomas Fowlkes Jr.
178	Kevin McNulty
182	Michael A. Shipp
189	Gershwin A. Drain
190	Stephanie Marie Rose
217	Paul William Grimm
222	Michael P. Shea
224	Mark E. Walker
226	John E. Dowdell
228	Lorna G. Schofield
249	William Joseph Baer
250	Carol J. Galante

1 Defeat

186	Robert E. Bacharach (cloture)

Senate Success Score

Victories	63
Defeats	16
Total	79
Success rate	**79.7%**
Success rate without nominations	**61.5%**

HOUSE

1. Presidential Support. Percentage of recorded votes cast in 2012 on which President Barack Obama took a position and on which the member voted "yea" or "nay" in agreement with the president's position. Failure to vote does not lower an individual's score.

2. Presidential Opposition. Percentage of recorded votes cast in 2012 on which President Barack Obama took a position and on which the member voted "yea" or "nay" in disagreement with the president's position. Failure to vote does not lower an individual's score.

3. Participation in Presidential Support Votes. Percentage of recorded votes in 2012 on which President Barack Obama took a position and for which the member was eligible and present and voted "yea" or "nay." There were a total of 61 such recorded votes in the House.

[1] Ron Barber, D-Ariz., was sworn in June 19, 2012, to fill the vacancy created by the Jan. 25 resignation of fellow Democrat Gabrielle Giffords. Giffords was eligible for one presidential support vote in 2012; Barber was eligible for 28 presidential support votes.

[2] Dennis Cardoza, D-Calif., resigned Aug. 15, 2012. The last vote for which he was eligible was vote 556. Cardoza was eligible for 51 presidential support votes in 2012.

[3] Bob Filner, D-Calif., resigned Dec. 3, 2012. The last vote for which he was eligible was vote 613. Filner was eligible for 58 presidential support votes in 2012.

[4] Jesse L. Jackson Jr., D-Ill., resigned Nov. 21, 2012. The last vote for which he was eligible was vote 608. Jackson was eligible for 57 presidential support votes in 2012.

[5] Thomas Massie, R-Ky., was sworn in Nov. 13, 2012, to fill the vacancy created by the July 31 resignation of fellow Republican Geoff Davis. Davis was eligible for 49 presidential support votes in 2012; Massie was eligible for 5 presidential support votes.

[6] David A. Curson, D-Mich., was sworn in Nov. 13, 2012, to fill the vacancy created by the July 6 resignation of Republican Thaddeus McCotter. McCotter was eligible for 38 presidential support votes in 2012; Curson was eligible for five presidential support votes.

[7] Donald M. Payne Jr., D-N.J., was sworn in Nov. 15, 2012, to fill the vacancy created by the March 6 death of his father, fellow Democrat Donald M. Payne. The elder Payne was eligible for eight presidential support votes in 2012; Payne Jr. was eligible for five presidential support votes.

[8] The speaker votes only at his discretion.

[9] Suzanne Bonamici, D-Ore., was sworn in Feb. 7, 2012, to fill the vacancy created by the Aug. 3, 2011, resignation of fellow Democrat David Wu. Bonamici was eligible for 59 presidential support votes in 2012. (Wu was not eligible for any votes in 2012.)

[10] Suzan DelBene, D-Wash., was sworn in Nov. 13, 2012, to fill the vacancy created by the March 20 resignation of fellow Democrat Jay Inslee. Inslee was eligible for nine presidential support votes in 2012; DelBene was eligible for five presidential support votes.

	1	2	3			1	2	3
ALABAMA					**COLORADO**			
1 Bonner	10	90	95		1 DeGette	93	7	97
2 Roby	11	89	100		2 Polis	91	9	89
3 Rogers	11	89	100		3 Tipton	16	84	100
4 Aderholt	13	87	100		4 Gardner	13	87	100
5 Brooks	20	80	100		5 Lamborn	13	87	98
6 Bachus	12	88	98		6 Coffman	15	85	98
7 Sewell	79	21	95		7 Perlmutter	85	15	98
ALASKA					**CONNECTICUT**			
AL Young	14	86	93		1 Larson	86	14	97
ARIZONA					2 Courtney	89	11	100
1 Gosar	20	80	90		3 DeLauro	87	13	100
2 Franks	16	84	100		4 Himes	85	15	100
3 Quayle	17	83	98		5 Murphy	88	12	93
4 Pastor	82	18	100		**DELAWARE**			
5 Schweikert	25	75	98		AL Carney	80	20	97
6 Flake	24	76	97		**FLORIDA**			
7 Grijalva	88	12	95		1 Miller	17	83	97
8 Giffords[1]	—	—	0		2 Southerland	18	82	100
8 Barber[1]	70	30	96		3 Brown	88	12	80
ARKANSAS					4 Crenshaw	13	87	100
1 Crawford	17	83	98		5 Nugent	18	82	100
2 Griffin	15	85	100		6 Stearns	18	82	100
3 Womack	15	85	100		7 Mica	15	85	100
4 Ross	37	63	93		8 Webster	15	85	100
CALIFORNIA					9 Bilirakis	19	81	93
1 Thompson	90	10	100		10 Young	18	82	92
2 Herger	13	87	90		11 Castor	86	14	97
3 Lungren	18	82	100		12 Ross	15	85	100
4 McClintock	33	67	98		13 Buchanan	23	77	100
5 Matsui	90	10	98		14 Mack	19	81	79
6 Woolsey	87	13	90		15 Posey	18	82	100
7 Miller, George	91	9	93		16 Rooney	13	87	100
8 Pelosi	95	5	97		17 Wilson	90	10	97
9 Lee	84	16	92		18 Ros-Lehtinen	26	74	97
10 Garamendi	77	23	92		19 Deutch	93	7	90
11 McNerney	79	21	100		20 Wasserman Schultz	93	7	89
12 Speier	87	13	85		21 Diaz-Balart	22	78	97
13 Stark	87	13	90		22 West	15	85	100
14 Eshoo	90	10	100		23 Hastings	88	12	93
15 Honda	93	7	97		24 Adams	15	85	100
16 Lofgren	85	15	100		25 Rivera	20	80	98
17 Farr	90	10	95		**GEORGIA**			
18 Cardoza[2]	58	42	61		1 Kingston	12	88	98
19 Denham	21	79	100		2 Bishop	53	47	95
20 Costa	58	42	90		3 Westmoreland	17	83	98
21 Nunes	15	85	97		4 Johnson	84	16	95
22 McCarthy	15	85	95		5 Lewis	93	7	92
23 Capps	90	10	100		6 Price	20	80	100
24 Gallegly	15	85	85		7 Woodall	17	83	98
25 McKeon	15	85	95		8 Scott, A.	13	87	100
26 Dreier	18	82	100		9 Graves	16	84	100
27 Sherman	93	7	100		10 Broun	21	79	93
28 Berman	86	14	92		11 Gingrey	12	88	98
29 Schiff	90	10	98		12 Barrow	28	72	100
30 Waxman	87	13	98		13 Scott, D.	87	13	92
31 Becerra	88	12	97		**HAWAII**			
32 Chu	86	14	97		1 Hanabusa	87	13	98
33 Bass	93	7	90		2 Hirono	92	8	80
34 Roybal-Allard	91	9	93		**IDAHO**			
35 Waters	91	9	92		1 Labrador	27	73	95
36 Hahn	84	16	95		2 Simpson	15	85	95
37 Richardson	83	17	95		**ILLINOIS**			
38 Napolitano	85	15	89		1 Rush	87	13	92
39 Sánchez, Linda	91	9	95		2 Jackson[4]	90	10	51
40 Royce	25	75	100		3 Lipinski	61	39	97
41 Lewis	19	81	75		4 Gutierrez	89	11	93
42 Miller, Gary	15	85	90		5 Quigley	92	8	100
43 Baca	79	21	92		6 Roskam	16	84	100
44 Calvert	15	85	97		7 Davis	87	13	89
45 Bono Mack	16	84	93		8 Walsh	23	77	93
46 Rohrabacher	21	79	100		9 Schakowsky	90	10	97
47 Sanchez, Loretta	85	15	90		10 Dold	31	69	100
48 Campbell	39	61	93		11 Kinzinger	18	82	98
49 Issa	15	85	95		12 Costello	65	35	85
50 Bilbray	27	73	97		13 Biggert	22	78	98
51 Filner[3]	75	25	41		14 Hultgren	17	83	98
52 Hunter	12	88	98		15 Johnson	43	57	100
53 Davis	83	17	98					

KEY	**Republicans**	Democrats

	1	2	3
16 Manzullo	19	81	95
17 Schilling	14	86	95
18 Schock	19	81	97
19 Shimkus	18	82	98
INDIANA			
1 Visclosky	76	24	97
2 Donnelly	39	61	93
3 Stutzman	13	87	97
4 Rokita	15	85	98
5 Burton	10	90	84
6 Pence	16	84	93
7 Carson	88	12	93
8 Bucshon	15	85	98
9 Young	13	87	100
IOWA			
1 Braley	84	16	93
2 Loebsack	70	30	100
3 Boswell	54	46	100
4 Latham	15	84	100
5 King	12	88	98
KANSAS			
1 Huelskamp	28	72	100
2 Jenkins	16	84	93
3 Yoder	13	87	100
4 Pompeo	13	87	100
KENTUCKY			
1 Whitfield	17	83	98
2 Guthrie	15	85	100
3 Yarmuth	93	7	93
4 Davis[5]	15	85	96
4 Massie[5]	40	60	100
5 Rogers	16	84	100
6 Chandler	48	52	98
LOUISIANA			
1 Scalise	15	85	100
2 Richmond	89	11	93
3 Landry	11	89	90
4 Fleming	15	85	100
5 Alexander	17	83	98
6 Cassidy	17	83	95
7 Boustany	15	85	100
MAINE			
1 Pingree	86	14	97
2 Michaud	83	17	98
MARYLAND			
1 Harris	12	88	98
2 Ruppersberger	74	26	95
3 Sarbanes	85	15	97
4 Edwards	88	12	93
5 Hoyer	88	12	98
6 Bartlett	22	78	95
7 Cummings	86	14	95
8 Van Hollen	91	9	97
MASSACHUSETTS			
1 Olver	86	14	97
2 Neal	93	7	90
3 McGovern	92	8	98
4 Frank	89	11	93
5 Tsongas	88	12	97
6 Tierney	85	15	100
7 Markey	90	10	97
8 Capuano	83	17	97
9 Lynch	85	15	100
10 Keating	83	17	98
MICHIGAN			
1 Benishek	18	82	100
2 Huizenga	17	83	97
3 Amash	51	49	100
4 Camp	17	83	98
5 Kildee	83	17	98
6 Upton	15	85	100
7 Walberg	15	85	100
8 Rogers	15	85	98
9 Peters	90	10	98
10 Miller	18	82	100
11 McCotter[6]	18	82	100
11 Curson[6]	100	0	100
12 Levin	90	10	97
13 Clarke	90	10	97
14 Conyers	88	12	95
15 Dingell	85	15	97
MINNESOTA			
1 Walz	71	29	97
2 Kline	18	82	100
3 Paulsen	17	83	97
4 McCollum	86	14	93

	1	2	3
5 Ellison	91	9	92
6 Bachmann	15	85	98
7 Peterson	25	75	100
8 Cravaack	16	84	100
MISSISSIPPI			
1 Nunnelee	13	87	98
2 Thompson	85	15	90
3 Harper	16	84	100
4 Palazzo	11	89	100
MISSOURI			
1 Clay	89	11	87
2 Akin	16	84	62
3 Carnahan	88	12	93
4 Hartzler	13	87	98
5 Cleaver	89	11	93
6 Graves	13	87	98
7 Long	13	87	98
8 Emerson	17	83	98
9 Luetkemeyer	18	82	100
MONTANA			
AL Rehberg	15	85	100
NEBRASKA			
1 Fortenberry	19	81	93
2 Terry	16	84	100
3 Smith	15	85	100
NEVADA			
1 Berkley	73	27	98
2 Amodei	20	80	92
3 Heck	18	82	100
NEW HAMPSHIRE			
1 Guinta	17	83	93
2 Bass	33	67	98
NEW JERSEY			
1 Andrews	85	15	97
2 LoBiondo	25	75	100
3 Runyan	20	80	97
4 Smith	23	77	98
5 Garrett	20	80	98
6 Pallone	88	12	98
7 Lance	16	84	100
8 Pascrell	85	15	87
9 Rothman	89	11	93
10 Payne[7]	100	0	37
10 Payne Jr.[7]	100	0	100
11 Frelinghuysen	22	78	98
12 Holt	87	13	98
13 Sires	86	14	93
NEW MEXICO			
1 Heinrich	85	15	90
2 Pearce	18	82	98
3 Luján	89	11	100
NEW YORK			
1 Bishop	78	22	89
2 Israel	86	14	93
3 King	15	85	97
4 McCarthy	81	19	97
5 Ackerman	84	16	90
6 Meeks	89	11	89
7 Crowley	90	10	98
8 Nadler	88	12	97
9 Turner	18	82	100
10 Towns	86	14	82
11 Clarke	88	12	95
12 Velázquez	93	7	90
13 Grimm	18	82	98
14 Maloney	86	14	93
15 Rangel	87	13	75
16 Serrano	91	9	95
17 Engel	86	14	95
18 Lowey	89	11	89
19 Hayworth	28	72	100
20 Gibson	38	62	100
21 Tonko	86	14	97
22 Hinchey	84	16	95
23 Owens	48	52	98
24 Hanna	21	79	100
25 Buerkle	19	81	87
26 Hochul	54	46	100
27 Higgins	80	20	98
28 Slaughter	92	8	64
29 Reed	18	82	100
NORTH CAROLINA			
1 Butterfield	88	12	95
2 Ellmers	16	84	100
3 Jones	36	64	100
4 Price	90	10	98

	1	2	3
5 Foxx	11	89	100
6 Coble	22	78	89
7 McIntyre	18	82	92
8 Kissell	33	67	100
9 Myrick	15	85	97
10 McHenry	15	85	95
11 Shuler	54	46	82
12 Watt	90	10	95
13 Miller	87	13	100
NORTH DAKOTA			
AL Berg	15	85	100
OHIO			
1 Chabot	15	85	100
2 Schmidt	12	88	95
3 Turner	13	87	100
4 Jordan	15	85	100
5 Latta	16	84	100
6 Johnson	18	82	100
7 Austria	13	87	97
8 Boehner[8]	33	67	5
9 Kaptur	84	16	95
10 Kucinich	85	15	89
11 Fudge	88	12	95
12 Tiberi	16	84	100
13 Sutton	83	17	95
14 LaTourette	26	74	93
15 Stivers	20	80	84
16 Renacci	20	80	100
17 Ryan	85	15	98
18 Gibbs	16	84	100
OKLAHOMA			
1 Sullivan	14	86	92
2 Boren	32	68	87
3 Lucas	18	82	100
4 Cole	16	84	100
5 Lankford	11	89	100
OREGON			
1 Bonamici[9]	91	9	100
2 Walden	16	84	100
3 Blumenauer	89	11	89
4 DeFazio	77	23	100
5 Schrader	74	26	100
PENNSYLVANIA			
1 Brady	83	17	95
2 Fattah	84	16	95
3 Kelly	18	82	100
4 Altmire	50	50	98
5 Thompson	16	84	100
6 Gerlach	16	84	100
7 Meehan	21	79	100
8 Fitzpatrick	27	73	98
9 Shuster	13	87	97
10 Marino	19	81	85
11 Barletta	20	80	100
12 Critz	61	39	100
13 Schwartz	91	9	97
14 Doyle	88	12	93
15 Dent	20	80	100
16 Pitts	20	80	100
17 Holden	63	37	93
18 Murphy	18	82	98
19 Platts	23	77	98
RHODE ISLAND			
1 Cicilline	91	9	97
2 Langevin	90	10	98
SOUTH CAROLINA			
1 Scott	18	82	100
2 Wilson	16	84	100
3 Duncan	13	87	100
4 Gowdy	16	84	100
5 Mulvaney	28	72	100
6 Clyburn	85	15	90
SOUTH DAKOTA			
AL Noem	12	88	95
TENNESSEE			
1 Roe	16	84	100
2 Duncan	30	70	98
3 Fleischmann	15	85	89
4 DesJarlais	11	89	100
5 Cooper	70	30	98
6 Black	13	87	97
7 Blackburn	11	89	100
8 Fincher	15	85	100
9 Cohen	88	12	98

	1	2	3
TEXAS			
1 Gohmert	22	78	98
2 Poe	16	84	100
3 Johnson, S.	15	85	98
4 Hall	13	87	98
5 Hensarling	15	85	100
6 Barton	18	82	98
7 Culberson	14	86	93
8 Brady	18	82	100
9 Green, A.	83	17	97
10 McCaul	17	83	98
11 Conaway	15	85	100
12 Granger	13	87	97
13 Thornberry	16	84	100
14 Paul	45	55	62
15 Hinojosa	86	14	93
16 Reyes	88	12	82
17 Flores	13	87	97
18 Jackson Lee	85	15	75
19 Neugebauer	12	88	98
20 Gonzalez	86	14	95
21 Smith	18	82	98
22 Olson	15	85	100
23 Canseco	13	87	97
24 Marchant	15	85	95
25 Doggett	87	13	100
26 Burgess	20	80	97
27 Farenthold	16	84	100
28 Cuellar	47	53	100
29 Green, G.	75	25	97
30 Johnson, E.	86	14	95
31 Carter	13	87	100
32 Sessions	17	83	97
UTAH			
1 Bishop	17	83	93
2 Matheson	31	69	100
3 Chaffetz	17	83	98
VERMONT			
AL Welch	92	8	98
VIRGINIA			
1 Wittman	20	80	100
2 Rigell	20	80	100
3 Scott	81	19	97
4 Forbes	10	90	98
5 Hurt	16	84	100
6 Goodlatte	18	82	100
7 Cantor	17	83	95
8 Moran	82	18	100
9 Griffith	20	80	100
10 Wolf	22	78	97
11 Connolly	83	17	98
WASHINGTON			
1 Inslee[10]	87	13	89
1 DelBene[10]	80	20	100
2 Larsen	85	15	100
3 Herrera Beutler	23	77	100
4 Hastings	20	80	100
5 McMorris Rodgers	18	82	100
6 Dicks	82	18	98
7 McDermott	84	16	100
8 Reichert	22	78	98
9 Smith	87	13	98
WEST VIRGINIA			
1 McKinley	13	87	100
2 Capito	15	85	100
3 Rahall	64	36	100
WISCONSIN			
1 Ryan	13	87	97
2 Baldwin	88	12	93
3 Kind	80	20	97
4 Moore	91	9	92
5 Sensenbrenner	24	76	97
6 Petri	15	85	100
7 Duffy	17	83	98
8 Ribble	21	79	100
WYOMING			
AL Lummis	24	76	97

SENATE

1. **Presidential Support.** Percentage of recorded votes cast in 2012 on which President Barack Obama took a position and on which the senator voted "yea" or "nay" in agreement with the president's position. Failure to vote does not lower an individual's score.

2. **Presidential Opposition.** Percentage of recorded votes cast in 2012 on which the president took a position and on which the senator voted "yea" or "nay" in disagreement with the president's position. Failure to vote does not lower an individual's score.

3. **Participation in Presidential Support Votes.** Percentage of recorded votes in 2012 on which the president took a position and for which the senator was eligible and present and voted "yea" or "nay." There were a total of 79 such recorded votes in the Senate.

	1	2	3		1	2	3
ALABAMA				**MONTANA**			
Shelby	47	53	99	Baucus	92	8	100
Sessions	48	52	100	Tester	95	5	99
ALASKA				**NEBRASKA**			
Murkowski	69	31	94	Nelson	90	10	99
Begich	93	7	95	Johanns	52	48	99
ARIZONA				**NEVADA**			
McCain	57	43	91	Reid	95	5	100
Kyl	52	48	99	Heller	54	46	89
ARKANSAS				**NEW HAMPSHIRE**			
Pryor	91	9	100	Shaheen	99	1	99
Boozman	46	54	99	Ayotte	56	44	99
CALIFORNIA				**NEW JERSEY**			
Feinstein	97	3	100	Lautenberg	95	5	83
Boxer	96	4	91	Menendez	97	3	99
COLORADO				**NEW MEXICO**			
Udall	97	3	96	Bingaman	96	4	97
Bennet	97	3	99	Udall	96	4	100
CONNECTICUT				**NEW YORK**			
Lieberman	96	4	96	Schumer	99	1	99
Blumenthal	97	3	96	Gillibrand	97	3	100
DELAWARE				**NORTH CAROLINA**			
Carper	97	3	100	Burr	45	55	92
Coons	97	3	100	Hagan	96	4	97
FLORIDA				**NORTH DAKOTA**			
Nelson	99	1	99	Conrad	96	4	97
Rubio	44	56	92	Hoeven	60	40	95
GEORGIA				**OHIO**			
Chambliss	44	56	91	Brown	96	4	100
Isakson	45	55	97	Portman	49	51	94
HAWAII				**OKLAHOMA**			
Inouye[1]	97	3	86	Inhofe	44	56	92
Schatz[1]	80	20	100	Coburn	41	59	95
Akaka	96	4	97	**OREGON**			
IDAHO				Wyden	96	4	97
Crapo	46	54	99	Merkley	95	5	97
Risch	41	59	99	**PENNSYLVANIA**			
ILLINOIS				Casey	95	5	95
Durbin	96	4	100	Toomey	42	58	96
Kirk	—	—	0	**RHODE ISLAND**			
INDIANA				Reed	95	5	100
Lugar	66	34	97	Whitehouse	95	5	97
Coats	54	46	99	**SOUTH CAROLINA**			
IOWA				Graham	57	43	96
Grassley	49	51	100	DeMint	16	84	78
Harkin	93	7	94	**SOUTH DAKOTA**			
KANSAS				Johnson	99	1	100
Roberts	47	53	96	Thune	50	50	96
Moran	52	48	92	**TENNESSEE**			
KENTUCKY				Alexander	62	38	94
McConnell	48	52	100	Corker	56	44	99
Paul	34	66	97	**TEXAS**			
LOUISIANA				Hutchison	58	42	96
Landrieu	90	10	97	Cornyn	41	59	99
Vitter	41	59	83	**UTAH**			
MAINE				Hatch	41	59	82
Snowe	80	20	96	Lee	17	83	97
Collins	78	22	100	**VERMONT**			
MARYLAND				Leahy	96	4	97
Mikulski	95	5	97	Sanders	88	12	96
Cardin	96	4	100	**VIRGINIA**			
MASSACHUSETTS				Webb	88	12	97
Kerry	99	1	97	Warner	96	4	99
Brown	78	22	100	**WASHINGTON**			
MICHIGAN				Murray	96	4	99
Levin	96	4	100	Cantwell	97	3	100
Stabenow	96	4	99	**WEST VIRGINIA**			
MINNESOTA				Rockefeller	99	1	90
Klobuchar	99	1	100	Manchin	85	15	100
Franken	96	4	99	**WISCONSIN**			
MISSISSIPPI				Kohl	97	3	99
Cochran	54	46	100	Johnson	47	53	99
Wicker	50	50	96	**WYOMING**			
MISSOURI				Enzi	47	53	96
McCaskill	96	4	92	Barrasso	48	52	100
Blunt	47	53	99				
KEY **Republicans** Democrats *Independents*							

[1] Sen. Brian Schatz, D-Hawaii, was sworn in Dec. 27, 2012, to fill the seat vacated by the Dec. 17 death of fellow Democrat Daniel K. Inouye. Inouye was eligible for 74 presidential support votes in 2012; Schatz was eligible for five presidential support votes.

Unity Votes Reflect Polarization

AT THE END OF HIS FIRST TERM as speaker, John A. Boehner, R-Ohio, struggled under blankets of criticism piled on from both the left and right. Fellow Republicans and conservative commentators lamented that he had done too little to unify his own House caucus behind the tea party principles that had swept them into power. Democrats complained that Boehner had become so worried about his right flank that he had spurned all efforts at compromise while turning his chamber into nothing more than a forum for party-galvanizing posturing.

The numbers gave more credence to the latter complaint. Although no single-year records for measurable partisanship were broken in 2012, the data for the two years of the 112th Congress reveal the House — back under GOP control after four years under the Democrats — to have been a place where party unity was stronger (and on more varied display) than at any time since 1953. That is when CQ Roll Call (previously Congressional Quarterly) began analyzing votes in which a majority of Republicans voted one way and most Democrats voted the other way as an empirical means of gauging the level of polarization at the Capitol.

According to the study, 72.8 percent of the 657 House roll call votes taken in 2012 divided the parties, the highest incidence of such party unity votes ever in a presidential election year. In the Senate, 59.8 percent of 251 votes split along party lines, the most in a presidential election year since 1996.

Most of the roll calls arranged by Senate Majority Leader, D-Nev., exposed a clear ideological divide between his caucus and the GOP. As a result, the majority prevailed far more often than not and senators of both parties reliably aligned themselves with their caucuses on eight or nine of every 10 votes.

"It is more partisan in Congress, but I think this is a polarized country," said Rep. Tom Cole of Oklahoma, a deputy whip and former campaign chairman. Cole was the first Republican to argue after the November election that the GOP should accept the offer from Democrats to extend the 2001 and 2003 tax cuts for household income less than $250,000 a year — a campaign promise from President Barack Obama. That ran counter to the Republican position at the time to extend the cuts for all taxpayers.

"There really are sharp differences" between the parties, Cole said. "With all due respect to the president, he is probably the most liberal president in my lifetime and this is probably the most conservative conference in my lifetime. They really do disagree over big issues, and the debate is not going to disappear."

The desire for Republicans to offer their own agenda was also the result of the competition to win and hold majorities in both chambers, said Frances E. Lee, a political science professor at the University of Maryland who wrote about the ebb and flow of partisanship. "It's important to keep in mind the extent to which party conflict is driven by party control of institutions," Lee said. "That is a real change. Before 1980, Republicans really thought of themselves as a permanent minority. When Republicans won the Senate in 1980, that was a surprise. That let them know that they could aspire to congressional majorities, and you began to see House Republicans pursue a different strategy, less accommodating."

The consequence was a changed dynamic and permanent entrenchment of more partisan behavior, she said. "This strategy has become universal now, and both parties use it because both parties can see a path back to power," Lee said. "So, the political incentives to do a deal, which would have the effect of blurring the differences between the parties, are less."

BOEHNER'S MAJORITY RULE

What became clear from the party unity statistics was that Boehner almost always abided by what was commonly referred to as the "Hastert rule" — the policy of Republican Speaker J. Dennis Hastert of Illinois, who during his time in charge (1999 through 2006) decreed that no legislation would be put before the House unless a majority of the majority wanted it there. That almost always meant the bill would pass, because the bulk of the votes came from most of the Republicans.

The continuation — even intensification — of that practice was reflected in 2012 voting patterns. The percentage of party unity votes in the House was higher only twice since Dwight D. Eisenhower took office. Once was the first year of the 112th Congress, when the figure was 75.8 percent. The only other year in the post-World War II era when more than two-thirds of the House's business was conducted on a mostly party-line basis was 1995, the year Republicans took control for the first time in 40 years. That year, party unity votes occurred 73.2 percent of the time.

The most prominent exception to all the polarization came on the final roll call vote of the 112th Congress, when Boehner abandoned the Hastert rule and allowed the tax-raising, fiscal-cliff-averting bill that embraced a Senate-White House compromise to become law.

Polarized Still

Democrats maintained their high levels of party unity in both chambers in 2012, while Republicans voted together somewhat less often than the year before. The majority's success rate on votes that split the two parties declined in both chambers.

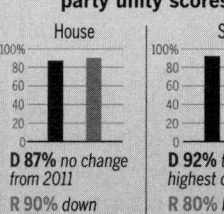

Frequency of party unity votes:

House
72.8% third highest on record
478 out of 657

Senate
59.8% up from 2011
150 out of 251

Average for both chambers: 69.2%

How often the majority won:

House Republicans
86.0% down from 2011
411 out of 478

Senate Democrats
68.7% down from 2011
103 out of 150

Average for both chambers: 81.8%

Average chamber party unity scores:

House
D 87% no change from 2011
R 90% down from 2011

Senate
D 92% ties highest on record
R 80% lowest since 1994

Unity Vote Frequency Stays High in House, Rises in Senate

Both the number and frequency of Senate roll call votes in which a majority of Democrats opposed a majority of Republicans rose somewhat from 2011 — although the percentage of these party unity votes stayed well below a historic level. In the House, the number of unity votes slumped along with the overall number of roll calls, but the frequency of partisan votes, 72.8 percent, held just below the record set in 2011.

Party Unity Votes

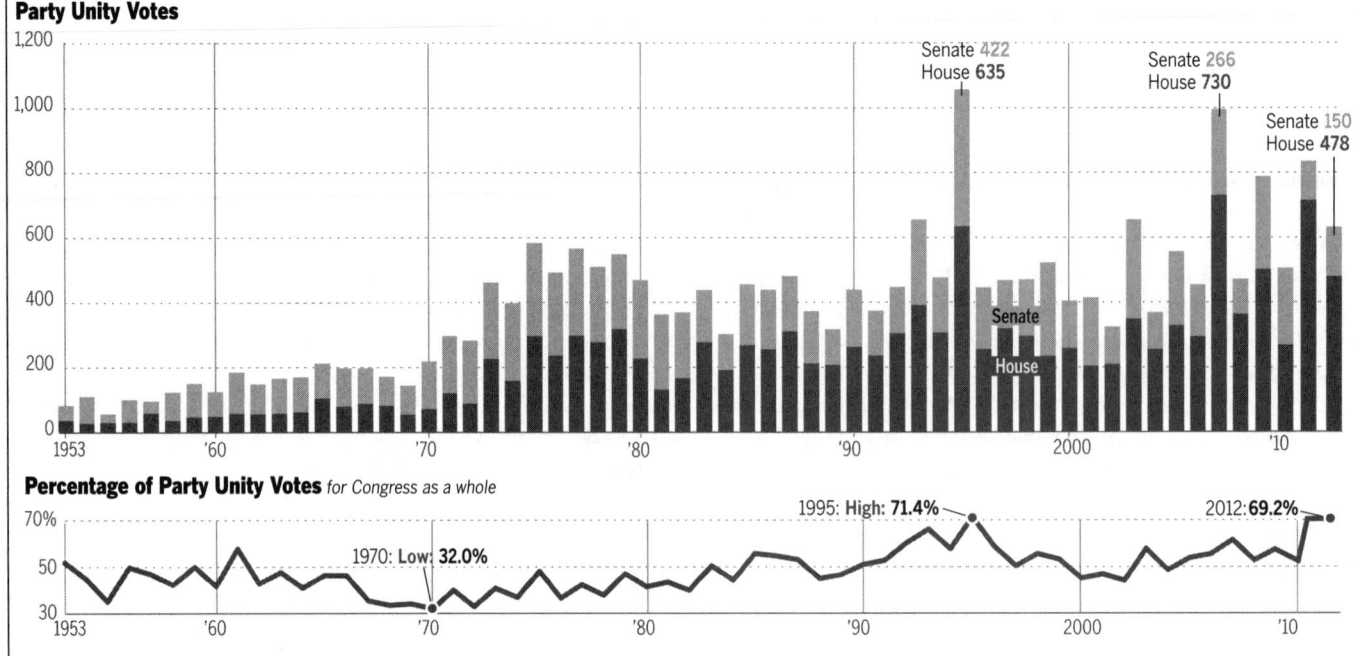

Percentage of Party Unity Votes *for Congress as a whole*

That New Year's Day vote cleared legislation to postpone across-the-board spending cuts for two months and to increase taxes on more well-to-do Americans by about $600 billion over the following decade. Only a third of Republicans voted "yes," and the measure was sent to Obama's desk because 90 percent of his fellow Democrats went along.

It left the impression with many people both inside and outside the House Republican Conference that the speaker would take a different approach the following year, when there would be eight people fewer in his caucus, a re-elected president and a Senate that would be more Democratic than in the previous two years.

But the likelihood of a sea change seemed remote given the House GOP's tendency to prefer victory. Republicans won 86 percent of House party unity votes in 2012 — a GOP success rate bested only four times in the previous six decades. One of those years was 2011, Boehner's first on the job, when Republicans recorded victories on 88.5 percent of party-splitting votes. The record for the GOP was 88.8 percent in 2003.

The Republican victory percentage was so high in 2011 in large part because GOP leaders arranged votes by the week on legislation they knew would pass with minimal, if any, crossing of party lines — even though they were just as certain that the bills would be ignored by the Democratic Senate. These included votes to repeal the 2010 financial industry regulatory overhaul law, votes to relax all manner of environmental and energy regulations, and — most famously — more than 30 votes to repeal or deny funding for all or part of the 2010 health care overhaul that was Obama's signature achievement. Getting those bills enacted was hardly the Republican high command's objective. To the contrary, drawing a contrast with Obama seemed the order of the day.

"A lot of the votes that the House took were deliberately designed to be partisan votes," said American Enterprise Institute scholar Norman J. Ornstein, who in 2012 dubbed the 112th the "worst Congress ever" in a magazine article. "These were not things where you were laying down a marker in order to get a law enacted. So 31 votes on repealing the Affordable Care Act, those are not votes where you are going to put out something that the Senate might respond to where you could go to a conference. They are not votes designed to attract Democrats."

PROMOTING THE BRAND

Republicans were not surprised that few of their initiatives became law, said Sarah Binder, a political scientist at George Washington University and the Brookings Institution. Floor votes were "an opportunity for House Republicans to cast the party's reputation, mold the brand name," she said. "They are trying to make clear what Republicans stand for and the way they do that is by creating these voting records to trumpet positions the House Republicans have taken."

The votes also helped to define the party for GOP presidential candidate Mitt Romney, especially early in the year. The House vote to embrace the budget blueprint championed by Wisconsin Rep. Paul D. Ryan made it hard for Romney to distance himself from it, and he ended up picking Ryan as his running mate.

Probably the biggest reason for Boehner's high success rate was his fealty to the Hastert rule. Never before the end of 2012 did he had he allowed the House to vote on legislation that he knew would divide his caucus into warring factions and pass with a Democratic majority.

In 2012, Boehner was pilloried by Democrats over a bill

Lawmakers Mostly Stay True to Their Caucuses

House and Senate Democrats voted on average with their caucuses in 2012 at the same rates as in 2011. And House Republicans were almost as consistent, voting on average with their caucus only slightly less often than in 2011. Only Senate Republicans showed a noteworthy departure from the partisan norm; their average party unity score fell from 86 percent the previous year to 80 percent.

Average party unity scores

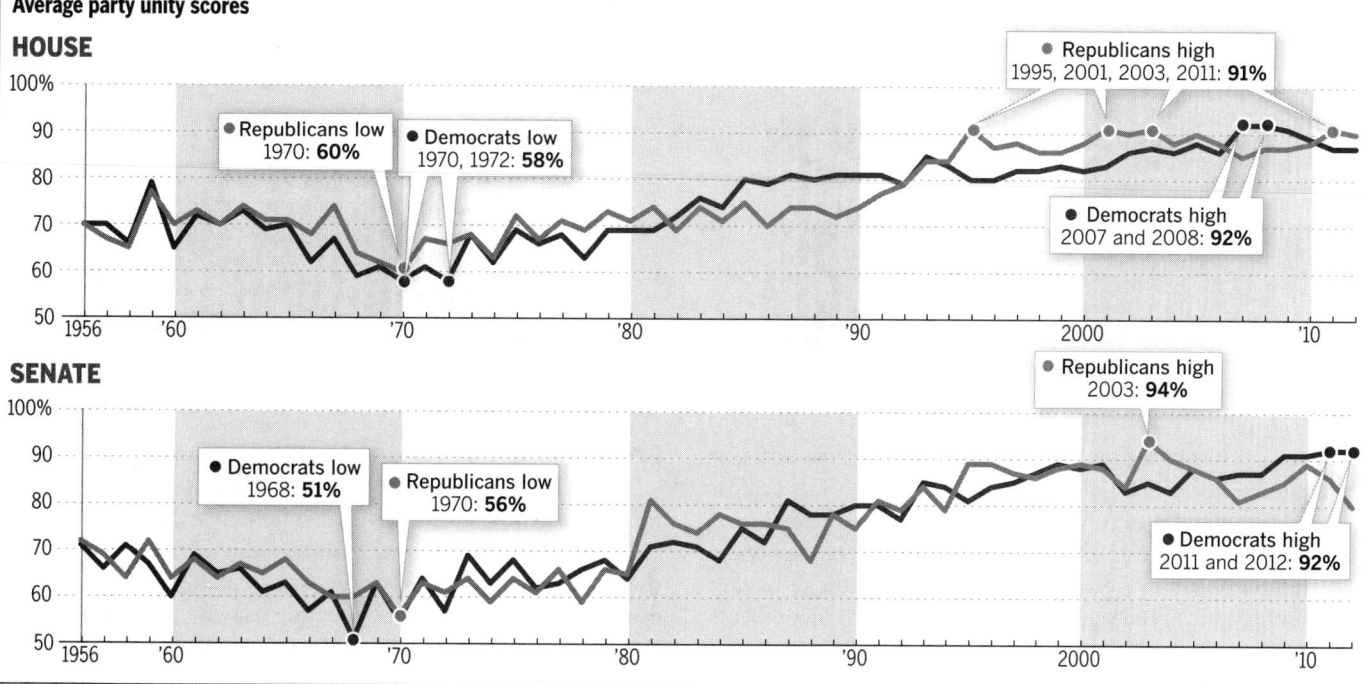

reauthorizing highway and other surface transportation programs after he delayed passage because of push-back from conservatives who believed it would lead to too much spending. Similarly, Boehner never brought up a long-term reauthorization of farm programs, because of conservative complaints that the measure did not cut food stamp spending sufficiently. Other measures that might have drawn bipartisan support and were sidetracked by partisan concerns included reauthorization of the Violence Against Women Act and a bill to overhaul the Postal Service.

Transportation programs had long received bipartisan support, but with Republicans looking to take a stand on spending across the budget, it was no longer an easy lift. A self-imposed moratorium on earmarks, pushed through by House Republicans and reluctantly agreed to by Senate Democrats for the 112th Congress, also played a role in delaying passage of the highway bill, as earmarks had previously been used to entice cooperation across party lines.

After failing to rally Republicans around a $260 billion, five-year highway measure, Boehner won passage in April of a three-month extension of existing law that became the legislative vehicle for a conference with the Senate, which wanted a five-year bill. A two-year compromise that did not include a long-term financing mechanism became law in June.

Agriculture policy typically was also bipartisan, but in 2012 House Republicans resisted the urge to compromise. The Senate passed a five-year reauthorization of farm programs in June, but House GOP leaders declined to bring to the floor an Agriculture Committee-approved measure. They were afraid they did not have enough Republican votes. As a result, Congress passed a one-year

extension of existing law as part of the fiscal-cliff tax measure — averting a crisis in rising milk prices and other consequences of the expiration of the farm law.

Congressional redistricting practices that created safe seats for both parties and lessened the need to appeal to independent voters exacerbated the polarization in 2012. And it was a pattern that seemed likely to persist.

"It's become quite an effective device for building homogenous districts that provide even more pressure on members of Congress to hew to one end or the other of the political spectrum," said Scott Keeter, director of survey research at the Pew Research Center.

The November election, under newly drawn district lines in most states, plainly reflected the one-party dominance of most districts and marked the departure from the House, through retirement or defeat, of another cluster of the already-dwindling group of moderate Democrats and Republicans. Almost half of the three dozen House members with the lowest party unity scores in 2012 — by definition, those most willing to cross party lines — were gone by the 113th Congress. Ten of the Democrats and seven of the Republicans left at the end of the 112th Congress.

SENATORS ON THE SPOT

In the Senate, Reid almost always followed a rubric similar to Boehner's for directing legislative business in a way that favored the political goals of his fellow Democrats. Not surprisingly, casting everything in a partisan light worked as just well for Minority Leader Mitch McConnell of Kentucky.

Senators were called to answer roll calls 251 times in 2012,

Majority Thwarted More Often in Both Chambers

The majority party's success rate on votes that split the two parties declined in both chambers in 2012. House Republicans got their way on 86 percent of party unity votes, down from 88.5 percent in 2011. Senate Democrats won 68.7 percent of the time, down from 72.5 percent in 2011 and down from a chamber record of 92.3 percent in 2009, when the caucus had a supermajority.

Majority party victory percentages *on party unity votes*

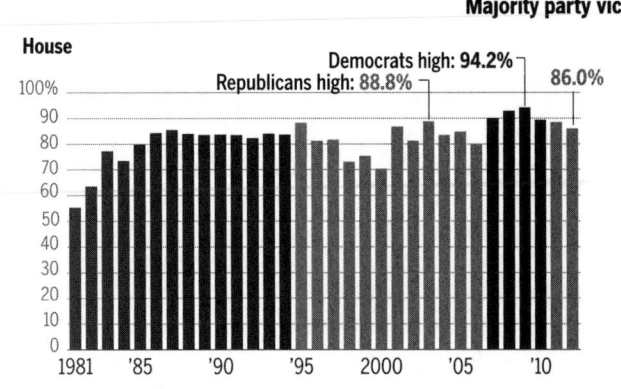

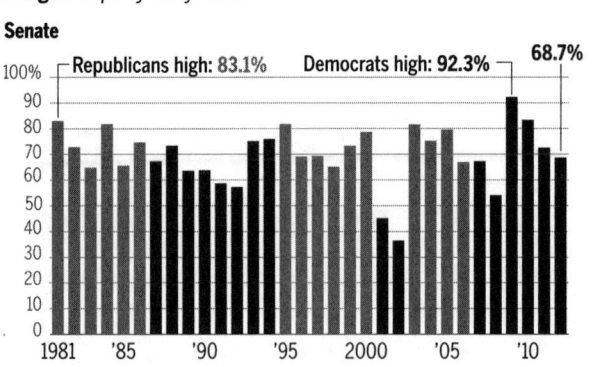

less than half as often as in the House. But 150 of those votes, or almost three out of five, pitted a majority of Democrats against a majority of Republicans. While not a record, that frequency of party unity votes was significantly higher than the year before — a reflection of Reid's interest in defining for voters the difference between his caucus colleagues — including the two incumbents viewed as ripest for defeat, Claire McCaskill of Missouri and Jon Tester of Montana, both of whom were re-elected — and the Republicans. Notably, the votes also were designed in part to expose two vulnerable Republican senators, Scott P. Brown of Massachusetts, who lost, and Dean Heller from Reid's home state of Nevada, who won.

Those two were among a group of six Republican senators who departed from their party's majority on at least a third of party unity votes. Those defections pushed the average Senate GOP unity score down to 80 percent, the lowest since 1994.

Only two Democrats — McCaskill and Joe Manchin III of West Virginia — opposed their party's majority more than a fifth of the time. As a result, the average Senate Democratic unity score held for a second year at a record 92 percent.

Nonetheless, rules that led to a significant number of Senate votes requiring a 60-vote majority limited Reid's winning percentage on party unity votes. The Democrats' success score dropped for a third straight year in 2012 to 68.7 percent. When the Senate Democratic Caucus briefly had a 60-seat majority in 2009, the party

prevailed on a record 92.3 percent of all unity votes.

"If you look at the Senate over the last year, you see it driven as much as anything — with some exceptions, like the transportation bill and the farm bill — by the famous Mitch McConnell dictum: the Senate Republicans' priority was to make Barack Obama a one-term president," Ornstein said. "Having a whole series of bipartisan votes where the president could declare victory wasn't going to cut it."

At the same time, the limited range of floor debates and the generally foreordained outcomes infuriated Senate leaders on both sides, although for mirror-image reasons. Democrats said there were so few signs of collaboration because the Republicans showed a historic level of disinterest in deal-making. Republicans said what was historic was the way the Democrats had abrogated their responsibility to govern.

"We have never, ever in the history of the United States Senate run into such a consistent strategy of obstruction by one party," Democratic Whip Richard J. Durbin of Illinois said on the floor just before the election. McConnell countered soon after: "Never before have a president and a majority party in the Senate done so little to address challenges as great as the ones our nation faces right now — never."

One thing was clear. The partisan posture evident in the previous decade and particularly during the 112th Congress showed little sign of changing. ∎

Leading Scorers: Party Unity

Support indicates those who voted most often with a majority of their party against a majority of the other party in 2012. **Opposition** shows those who voted most often against their party. Lawmakers who left office or who missed half or more of the votes are not listed. Scores are reported only in this list to one decimal point; members with identical scores are listed alphabetically. *(Complete scores, pp. B-20, B-22)*

SENATE

SUPPORT

Democrats		Republicans	
Udall, N.M.	100.0%	Cornyn, Texas	98.0%
Cardin, Md.	98.7	Johnson, Wis.	95.3
Franken, Minn.	98.0	Risch, Idaho	94.0
Murray, Wash.	98.0	Burr, N.C.	93.8
Blumenthal, Conn.	97.9	Chambliss, Ga.	93.8
Reed, R.I.	97.3	DeMint, S.C.	93.5
Schumer, N.Y.	97.3	Kyl, Ariz.	93.3
Shaheen, N.H.	97.3	McConnell, Ky.	93.3
Gillibrand, N.Y.	97.3	Toomey, Pa.	93.2
Boxer, Calif.	97.0	Crapo, Idaho	92.6
Inouye, Hawaii	96.9	Sessions, Ala.	92.6
Lautenberg, N.J.	96.9	Hatch, Utah	92.4
2 senators	98.3	Inhofe, Okla.	92.2

OPPOSITION

Democrats		Republicans	
Manchin, W.Va.	24.0%	Brown, Mass.	61.7%
McCaskill, Mo.	22.4	Collins, Maine	61.3
Webb, Va.	17.7	Snowe, Maine	56.2
Nelson, Neb.	16.7	Murkowski, Alaska	49.3
Pryor, Ark.	14.7	Heller, Nev.	34.8
Warner, Va.	13.9	Hoeven, N.D.	33.1
Landrieu, La.	12.8	Lugar, Ind.	30.9
Hagan, N.C.	12.7	Cochran, Miss.	28.0
Carper, Del.	11.3	Blunt, Mo.	21.3
Baucus, Mont.	9.3	Johanns, Neb.	19.5
Casey, Pa.	8.7	Moran, Kan.	19.4
Nelson, Fla.	8.7	Grassley, Iowa	17.3
Stabenow, Mich.	8.7	Alexander, Tenn.	16.8

HOUSE

SUPPORT

Democrats		Republicans	
Nadler, N.Y.	99.1%	Akin, Mo.	99.3%
Neal, Mass.	99.1	Jenkins, Kan.	99.1
Filner, Calif.	99.0	Pence, Ind.	99.1
Pallone, N.J.	98.9	Conaway, Texas	99.0
McGovern, Mass.	98.9	Pompeo, Kan.	99.0
Markey, Mass.	98.9	Gingrey, Ga.	98.9
Woolsey, Calif.	98.9	Lamborn, Colo.	98.9
Ellison, Mich.	98.9	Mack, Fla.	98.8
Velázquez, N.Y.	98.8	Black, Tenn.	98.7
Becerra, Calif.	98.7	Blackburn, Tenn.	98.7
Conyers, Mich.	98.7	Gowdy, S.C.	98.7
Lewis, Ga.	98.7	Hensarling, Texas	98.7
McDermott, Wash.	98.7	Kline, Minn.	98.7
Olver, Mass.	98.7	Olson, Texas	98.7
Schakowsky, Ill.	98.7	Graves, Mo.	98.5
Slaughter, N.Y.	98.7	Quayle, Ariz.	98.5
Stark, Calif.	98.7	Wilson, S.C.	98.5
2 members	98.5	Issa, Calif.	98.3

OPPOSITION

Democrats		Republicans	
Matheson, Utah	68.2%	Gibson, N.Y.	38.0%
Boren, Okla.	63.2	Jones, N.C.	35.2
Ross, Ark.	54.6	Dold, Ill.	25.8
Peterson, Minn.	54.0	Johnson, Ill.	25.7
McIntyre, N.C.	51.9	Bass, N.H.	23.8
Shuler, N.C.	50.0	Fitzpatrick, Pa.	23.1
Barrow, Ga.	49.2	Paul, Texas	21.2
Donnelly, Ind.	45.1	LoBiondo, N.J.	20.3
Kissell, N.C.	43.5	LaTourette, Ohio	18.8
Costa, Calif.	35.9	Smith, N.J.	18.5
Altmire, Pa.	32.8	Gerlach, Pa.	18.1
Owens, N.Y.	32.1	Hayworth, N.Y.	18.0
Cuellar, Texas	31.9	Platts, Pa.	18.0
Chandler, Ky.	30.4	Dent, Pa.	16.7
Cardoza, Calif.	28.0	Meehan, Pa.	16.5
Bishop, Ga.	25.5	Reichert, Wash.	15.6
Hochul, N.Y.	25.3	Hanna, N.Y.	15.2
Critz, Pa.	24.9	Amash, Mich.	15.1

Party Unity Background

Roll call votes used for the party unity study were all those on which a majority of Democrats opposed a majority of Republicans. **Support** indicates the percentage of the time that members voted in agreement with the majority of their party on such party unity votes. **Opposition** indicates the percentage of the time that members voted against the majority of their party. In calculations of average scores by party and chamber, a member's failure to vote lowers the score for the group. The tables below also show the number of party unity votes on which each party was victorious and the number of instances in which either party voted unanimously.

Average Party Unity Scores by Chamber

		SUPPORT		OPPOSITION	
		2012	2011	2012	2011
HOUSE	Democrats	87%	87%	8%	9%
	Republicans	90	91	7	6
SENATE	Democrats	92	92	7	6
	Republicans	80	86	16	11
CONGRESS	Democrats	87	87	8	9
	Republicans	89	91	7	6

Victories in Party Unity Votes

	HOUSE		SENATE		CONGRESS	
YEAR	DEMOCRATS	REPUBLICANS	DEMOCRATS	REPUBLICANS	DEMOCRATS	REPUBLICANS
2012	67	411	103	47	170	458
2011	82	634	87	33	169	667
2010	236	28	196	39	432	67
2009	473	29	264	22	737	51
2008	342	25	60	51	402	76
2007	658	72	179	87	837	159
2006	59	236	53	107	112	343
2005	50	278	47	182	97	460
2004	42	213	28	85	70	298
2003	39	310	56	250	95	560
2002	39	170	42	73	81	243
2001	27	177	95	115	122	292
2000	77	182	31	114	108	296
1999	58	177	77	211	135	388
1998	80	216	61	114	141	330
1997	58	261	46	104	104	365
1996	48	208	59	132	107	340
1995	74	561	77	345	151	906

Unanimous Voting by Parties

	HOUSE		SENATE		CONGRESS	
YEAR	DEMOCRATS	REPUBLICANS	DEMOCRATS	REPUBLICANS	DEMOCRATS	REPUBLICANS
2012	40	99	60	19	100	118
2011	76	209	55	31	131	240
2010	10	91	67	106	77	197
2009	29	144	79	74	108	218
2008	66	96	30	19	96	115
2007	170	177	102	35	272	212
2006	70	62	34	30	104	92
2005	82	91	69	59	151	150
2004	70	77	3	31	73	108
2003	94	109	32	130	126	239
2002	37	54	12	23	49	77
2001	1	66	37	55	38	121
2000	1	67	52	19	53	86
1999	11	59	100	63	111	122
1998	8	42	46	33	54	75
1997	11	63	35	38	46	101
1996	10	32	35	47	45	79
1995	17	159	63	104	80	263

Party Unity History

The table below on the left shows how frequently during roll call votes a majority of Democrats aligned against a majority of Republicans. The tables in the center and at right show the average party unity support score for each party in each chamber.

YEAR	Frequency of Unity Votes		House Average Scores		Senate Average Scores	
	HOUSE	SENATE	DEMOCRATS	REPUBLICANS	DEMOCRATS	REPUBLICANS
2012	72.8%	59.8%	87	90	92	80
2011	75.8	51.1	87	91	92	86
2010	40.0	78.6	89	88	91	89
2009	50.9	72.0	91	87	91	85
2008	53.3	51.6	92	87	87	83
2007	62.0	60.2	92	85	87	81
2006	54.5	57.3	86	88	86	86
2005	49.0	62.6	88	90	88	88
2004	47.0	52.3	86	88	83	90
2003	51.7	66.7	87	91	85	94
2002	43.3	45.5	86	90	83	84
2001	40.2	55.3	83	91	89	88
2000	43.2	48.7	82	88	88	89
1999	47.3	62.8	83	86	89	88
1998	55.5	55.7	82	86	87	86
1997	50.4	50.3	82	88	85	87
1996	56.4	62.4	80	87	84	89
1995	73.2	68.8	80	91	81	89
1994	61.8	51.7	83	84	84	79
1993	65.5	67.1	85	84	85	84
1992	64.5	53.0	79	79	77	79
1991	55.1	49.3	81	77	80	81
1990	49.1	54.3	81	74	80	75
1989	56.3	35.3	81	72	78	78
1988	47.0	42.5	80	74	78	68
1987	63.7	40.7	81	74	81	75
1986	56.5	52.3	79	70	72	76
1985	61.0	49.6	80	75	75	76
1984	47.1	40.0	74	71	68	78
1983	55.6	43.7	76	74	71	74
1982	36.4	43.4	72	69	72	76
1981	37.4	47.8	69	74	71	81
1980	37.6	45.8	69	71	64	65
1979	47.3	46.7	69	73	68	66
1978	33.2	45.2	63	69	66	59
1977	42.2	42.4	68	71	63	66
1976	35.9	37.2	66	67	62	61
1975	48.4	47.8	69	72	68	64
1974	29.4	44.3	62	63	63	59
1973	41.8	39.9	68	68	69	64
1972	27.1	36.5	58	66	57	61
1971	37.8	41.6	61	67	64	63
1970	27.1	35.2	58	60	55	56
1969	31.1	36.3	61	62	63	63
1968	35.2	32.0	59	64	51	60
1967	36.3	34.6	67	74	61	60
1966	41.5	50.2	62	68	57	63
1965	52.2	41.9	70	71	63	68
1964	54.9	35.7	69	71	61	65
1963	48.7	47.2	73	74	66	67
1962	46.0	41.1	70	70	65	64
1961	50.0	62.3	72	73	69	68
1960	52.7	36.7	65	70	60	64
1959	55.2	47.9	79	77	67	72
1958	39.8	43.5	66	65	71	64
1957	59.0	35.5	70	67	66	69
1956	43.8	53.1	70	70	71	72
1955	40.8	29.9				

Tallying Party Unity Votes

In the House in 2012, the two parties aligned against each other on 478 of 657 roll call votes, or 72.8 percent of the time — the second highest frequency of unity votes ever for the chamber, down a bit from 2011. In the Senate, the parties opposed each other on 150 of 251 roll calls, or 59.8 percent of the time — an increase from 2011 but still well below the record 78.6 percent in 2010. A list of roll call votes that pitted majorities of the two parties against each other is available upon request from CQ Roll Call.

Calculations of average scores by chamber and party are based on all eligible "yea" or "nay" votes, whether or not all members participated. Under this methodology, average support and opposition scores are reduced when members choose not to vote. Because individual member scores are based on the number of votes cast, party and chamber averages are not strictly comparable to individual member scores. (*Complete member scores, pp. B-20, B-22*)

Also, in the member score tables, Sens. Joseph I. Lieberman, I-Conn., and Bernard Sanders, I-Vt., are treated as if they are Democrats when calculating their support and opposition scores. Their votes were not used to determine which roll calls were party unity votes, and they are not included in the Democratic Party averages for the Senate.

HOUSE

1. Party Unity. Percentage of recorded party unity votes in 2012 on which a member voted "yea" or "nay" in agreement with a majority of his or her party. (Party unity votes are those on which a majority of voting Democrats opposed a majority of voting Republicans.) Percentages are based on votes cast; thus, failure to vote does not lower a member's score.

2. Party Opposition. Percentage of recorded party unity votes in 2012 on which a member voted "yea" or "nay" in disagreement with a majority of his or her party. Percentages are based on votes cast; thus, failure to vote does not lower a member's score.

3. Participation in Party Unity Votes. Percentage of the House party unity votes in 2012 for which a member was eligible and present and voted "yea" or "nay." There were a total of 478 such recorded votes.

[1] Ron Barber, D-Ariz., was sworn in June 19, 2012, to fill the vacancy created by the Jan. 25 resignation of fellow Democrat Gabrielle Giffords. Giffords was eligible for two party unity votes in 2012; Barber was eligible for 199 party unity votes.

[2] Dennis Cardoza, D-Calif., resigned Aug. 15, 2012. The last vote for which he was eligible was vote 556. Cardoza was eligible for 426 party unity votes in 2012.

[3] Bob Filner, D-Calif., resigned Dec. 3, 2012. The last vote for which he was eligible was vote 613. Filner was eligible for 467 party unity votes in 2012.

[4] Jesse L. Jackson Jr., D-Ill., resigned Nov. 21, 2012. The last vote for which he was eligible was vote 608. Jackson was eligible for 464 party unity votes in 2012.

[5] Thomas Massie, R-Ky., was sworn in Nov. 13, 2012, to fill the vacancy created by the July 31 resignation of fellow Republican Geoff Davis. Davis was eligible for 412 party unity votes in 2012; Massie was eligible for 16 party unity votes.

[6] David A. Curson, D-Mich., was sworn in Nov. 13, 2012, to fill the vacancy created by the July 6 resignation of Republican Thaddeus McCotter. McCotter was eligible for 343 party unity votes in 2012; Curson was eligible for 16 party unity votes.

[7] Donald M. Payne Jr., D-N.J., was sworn in Nov. 15, 2012, to fill the vacancy created by the March 6 death of his father, fellow Democrat Donald M. Payne. Payne was eligible for 70 party unity votes in 2012; Payne Jr. was eligible for 15 party unity votes.

[8] The speaker votes only at his discretion.

[9] Suzanne Bonamici, D-Ore., was sworn in Feb. 7, 2012, to fill the vacancy created by the Aug. 3, 2011, resignation of fellow Democrat David Wu. Bonamici was eligible for 453 party unity votes in 2012. (Wu was not eligible for any votes in 2012.)

[10] Suzan DelBene, D-Wash., was sworn in Nov. 13, 2012, to fill the vacancy created by the March 20 resignation of fellow Democrat Jay Inslee. Inslee was eligible for 83 party unity votes in 2012; DelBene was eligible for 16 party unity votes.

	1	2	3
ALABAMA			
1 **Bonner**	92	8	95
2 **Roby**	92	8	99
3 **Rogers**	91	9	99
4 **Aderholt**	89	11	99
5 **Brooks**	96	4	100
6 **Bachus**	91	9	93
7 Sewell	92	8	96
ALASKA			
AL **Young**	88	12	94
ARIZONA			
1 **Gosar**	97	3	94
2 **Franks**	97	3	99
3 **Quayle**	99	1	99
4 Pastor	91	9	99
5 **Schweikert**	97	3	99
6 **Flake**	96	4	97
7 Grijalva	98	2	98
8 Giffords [1]	—	—	0
8 Barber [1]	88	12	98
ARKANSAS			
1 **Crawford**	91	9	99
2 **Griffin**	95	5	99
3 **Womack**	89	11	100
4 Ross	45	55	93
CALIFORNIA			
1 Thompson	96	4	99
2 **Herger**	98	2	92
3 **Lungren**	91	9	99
4 **McClintock**	92	8	99
5 Matsui	98	2	99
6 Woolsey	99	1	94
7 Miller, George	96	4	97
8 Pelosi	98	2	96
9 Lee	98	2	92
10 Garamendi	90	10	94
11 McNerney	90	10	99
12 Speier	96	4	88
13 Stark	99	1	95
14 Eshoo	95	5	99
15 Honda	98	2	93
16 Lofgren	93	7	97
17 Farr	97	3	98
18 Cardoza [2]	72	28	60
19 **Denham**	93	7	98
20 Costa	64	36	96
21 **Nunes**	94	6	99
22 **McCarthy**	97	3	95
23 Capps	97	3	100
24 **Gallegly**	91	9	86
25 **McKeon**	92	8	94
26 **Dreier**	92	8	99
27 Sherman	95	5	99
28 Berman	96	4	91
29 Schiff	95	5	99
30 Waxman	98	2	98
31 Becerra	99	1	96
32 Chu	98	2	96
33 Bass	97	3	86
34 Roybal-Allard	98	2	95
35 Waters	97	3	92
36 Hahn	97	3	93
37 Richardson	93	7	97
38 Napolitano	98	2	86
39 Sánchez, Linda	98	2	90
40 **Royce**	94	6	99
41 **Lewis**	94	6	69
42 **Miller, Gary**	95	5	89
43 Baca	92	8	94
44 **Calvert**	91	9	98
45 **Bono Mack**	93	7	95
46 **Rohrabacher**	95	5	98
47 Sanchez, Loretta	96	4	91
48 **Campbell**	92	8	93
49 **Issa**	98	2	98
50 **Bilbray**	87	13	99
51 Filner [3]	99	1	43
52 **Hunter**	97	3	99
53 Davis	94	6	99
KEY Republicans Democrats			

	1	2	3
COLORADO			
1 DeGette	98	2	98
2 Polis	89	11	95
3 **Tipton**	90	10	99
4 **Gardner**	97	3	100
5 **Lamborn**	99	1	95
6 **Coffman**	93	7	99
7 Perlmutter	85	15	99
CONNECTICUT			
1 Larson	96	4	99
2 Courtney	94	6	99
3 DeLauro	98	2	100
4 Himes	90	10	99
5 Murphy	93	7	94
DELAWARE			
AL Carney	89	11	99
FLORIDA			
1 **Miller**	97	3	93
2 **Southerland**	96	4	99
3 Brown	92	8	95
4 **Crenshaw**	89	11	99
5 **Nugent**	96	4	99
6 **Stearns**	96	4	99
7 **Mica**	96	4	99
8 **Webster**	94	6	99
9 **Bilirakis**	96	4	96
10 **Young**	90	10	93
11 Castor	96	4	99
12 **Ross**	97	3	99
13 **Buchanan**	94	6	99
14 **Mack**	99	1	70
15 **Posey**	96	4	99
16 **Rooney**	97	3	99
17 Wilson	98	2	97
18 **Ros-Lehtinen**	86	14	99
19 Deutch	98	2	98
20 Wasserman Schultz	97	3	94
21 **Diaz-Balart**	86	14	97
22 **West**	93	7	99
23 Hastings	97	3	98
24 **Adams**	97	3	100
25 **Rivera**	88	12	98
GEORGIA			
1 **Kingston**	95	5	99
2 Bishop	75	25	99
3 **Westmoreland**	97	3	99
4 Johnson	98	2	95
5 Lewis	99	1	93
6 **Price**	97	3	99
7 **Woodall**	96	4	99
8 **Scott, A.**	98	2	99
9 **Graves**	97	3	99
10 **Broun**	94	6	94
11 **Gingrey**	99	1	97
12 Barrow	51	49	100
13 Scott, D.	93	7	97
HAWAII			
1 Hanabusa	95	5	99
2 Hirono	98	2	80
IDAHO			
1 **Labrador**	93	7	94
2 **Simpson**	88	12	99
ILLINOIS			
1 Rush	97	3	89
2 Jackson [4]	97	3	53
3 Lipinski	79	21	98
4 Gutierrez	98	2	93
5 Quigley	96	4	99
6 **Roskam**	95	5	99
7 Davis	97	3	91
8 **Walsh**	94	6	95
9 Schakowsky	99	1	98
10 **Dold**	74	26	99
11 **Kinzinger**	91	9	97
12 Costello	80	20	91
13 **Biggert**	86	14	99
14 **Hultgren**	96	4	99
15 **Johnson**	74	26	93

	1	2	3
16 Manzullo	96	4	95
17 Schilling	92	8	98
18 Schock	89	11	97
19 Shimkus	91	9	97
INDIANA			
1 Visclosky	92	8	97
2 Donnelly	55	45	90
3 Stutzman	97	3	97
4 Rokita	98	2	99
5 Burton	98	2	87
6 Pence	99	1	91
7 Carson	94	6	90
8 Bucshon	95	5	99
9 Young	97	3	99
IOWA			
1 Braley	94	6	97
2 Loebsack	87	13	99
3 Boswell	79	21	100
4 Latham	87	13	99
5 King	97	3	98
KANSAS			
1 Huelskamp	95	5	100
2 Jenkins	99	1	94
3 Yoder	97	3	99
4 Pompeo	99	1	100
KENTUCKY			
1 Whitfield	91	9	97
2 Guthrie	95	5	100
3 Yarmuth	97	3	97
4 Davis[5]	90	10	97
4 Massie[5]	87	13	100
5 Rogers	89	11	99
6 Chandler	69	31	99
LOUISIANA			
1 Scalise	98	2	99
2 Richmond	94	6	95
3 Landry	97	3	92
4 Fleming	98	2	99
5 Alexander	91	9	97
6 Cassidy	96	4	97
7 Boustany	97	3	99
MAINE			
1 Pingree	99	1	99
2 Michaud	91	9	99
MARYLAND			
1 Harris	95	5	99
2 Ruppersberger	88	12	95
3 Sarbanes	98	2	99
4 Edwards	97	3	98
5 Hoyer	94	6	98
6 Bartlett	90	10	98
7 Cummings	97	3	96
8 Van Hollen	97	3	99
MASSACHUSETTS			
1 Olver	99	1	95
2 Neal	99	1	93
3 McGovern	99	1	99
4 Frank	96	4	96
5 Tsongas	97	3	95
6 Tierney	98	2	99
7 Markey	99	1	97
8 Capuano	99	1	99
9 Lynch	91	9	99
10 Keating	96	4	99
MICHIGAN			
1 Benishek	95	5	99
2 Huizenga	97	3	96
3 Amash	85	15	100
4 Camp	94	6	99
5 Kildee	96	4	99
6 Upton	93	7	100
7 Walberg	98	2	99
8 Rogers	96	4	99
9 Peters	95	5	99
10 Miller	93	7	99
11 McCotter[6]	92	8	99
11 Curson[6]	94	6	100
12 Levin	97	3	99
13 Clarke	98	2	99
14 Conyers	99	1	95
15 Dingell	93	7	98
MINNESOTA			
1 Walz	85	15	98
2 Kline	99	1	100
3 Paulsen	95	5	99
4 McCollum	98	2	97

	1	2	3
5 Ellison	99	1	94
6 Bachmann	97	3	96
7 Peterson	46	54	98
8 Cravaack	93	7	99
MISSISSIPPI			
1 Nunnelee	97	3	99
2 Thompson	92	8	94
3 Harper	92	8	99
4 Palazzo	96	4	99
MISSOURI			
1 Clay	97	3	93
2 Akin	99	1	64
3 Carnahan	97	3	96
4 Hartzler	97	3	99
5 Cleaver	95	5	94
6 Graves	99	1	98
7 Long	97	3	99
8 Emerson	91	9	99
9 Luetkemeyer	96	4	99
MONTANA			
AL Rehberg	89	11	99
NEBRASKA			
1 Fortenberry	90	10	95
2 Terry	93	7	99
3 Smith	98	2	99
NEVADA			
1 Berkley	89	11	99
2 Amodei	95	5	95
3 Heck	89	11	100
NEW HAMPSHIRE			
1 Guinta	95	5	95
2 Bass	76	24	99
NEW JERSEY			
1 Andrews	94	6	95
2 LoBiondo	80	20	100
3 Runyan	85	15	98
4 Smith	81	19	99
5 Garrett	98	2	97
6 Pallone	99	1	99
7 Lance	93	7	100
8 Pascrell	97	3	87
9 Rothman	97	3	89
10 Payne[7]	100	0	30
10 Payne Jr.[7]	100	0	93
11 Frelinghuysen	87	13	99
12 Holt	98	2	99
13 Sires	95	5	94
NEW MEXICO			
1 Heinrich	91	9	93
2 Pearce	94	6	97
3 Luján	93	7	99
NEW YORK			
1 Bishop	93	7	93
2 Israel	95	5	98
3 King	86	14	98
4 McCarthy	91	9	99
5 Ackerman	96	4	85
6 Meeks	96	4	87
7 Crowley	97	3	96
8 Nadler	99	1	96
9 Turner	90	10	97
10 Towns	95	5	87
11 Clarke	98	2	92
12 Velázquez	99	1	88
13 Grimm	87	13	98
14 Maloney	98	2	98
15 Rangel	97	3	72
16 Serrano	98	2	96
17 Engel	94	6	95
18 Lowey	97	3	95
19 Hayworth	82	18	99
20 Gibson	62	38	99
21 Tonko	98	2	99
22 Hinchey	98	2	93
23 Owens	68	32	99
24 Hanna	85	15	98
25 Buerkle	97	2	97
26 Hochul	75	25	100
27 Higgins	95	5	99
28 Slaughter	99	1	63
29 Reed	89	11	99
NORTH CAROLINA			
1 Butterfield	95	5	92
2 Ellmers	97	3	95
3 Jones	65	35	95
4 Price	97	3	99

	1	2	3
5 Foxx	97	3	100
6 Coble	96	4	86
7 McIntyre	48	52	95
8 Kissell	57	43	99
9 Myrick	97	3	93
10 McHenry	98	2	94
11 Shuler	50	50	82
12 Watt	97	3	97
13 Miller	96	4	99
NORTH DAKOTA			
AL Berg	91	9	98
OHIO			
1 Chabot	97	3	99
2 Schmidt	95	5	94
3 Turner	88	12	99
4 Jordan	97	3	98
5 Latta	96	4	100
6 Johnson	95	5	99
7 Austria	91	9	96
8 Boehner[8]	67	33	1
9 Kaptur	94	6	94
10 Kucinich	96	4	87
11 Fudge	96	4	99
12 Tiberi	89	11	99
13 Sutton	93	7	97
14 LaTourette	81	19	95
15 Stivers	91	9	83
16 Renacci	92	8	99
17 Ryan	92	8	99
18 Gibbs	95	5	100
OKLAHOMA			
1 Sullivan	97	3	90
2 Boren	37	63	99
3 Lucas	89	11	99
4 Cole	89	11	99
5 Lankford	97	3	99
OREGON			
1 Bonamici[9]	98	2	100
2 Walden	92	8	100
3 Blumenauer	97	3	96
4 DeFazio	91	9	99
5 Schrader	82	18	99
PENNSYLVANIA			
1 Brady	97	3	99
2 Fattah	96	4	97
3 Kelly	91	9	99
4 Altmire	67	33	99
5 Thompson	87	13	99
6 Gerlach	82	18	99
7 Meehan	83	17	99
8 Fitzpatrick	77	23	99
9 Shuster	91	9	99
10 Marino	93	7	88
11 Barletta	89	11	100
12 Critz	75	25	99
13 Schwartz	95	5	99
14 Doyle	95	5	96
15 Dent	83	17	100
16 Pitts	95	5	97
17 Holden	77	23	89
18 Murphy	93	7	99
19 Platts	82	18	96
RHODE ISLAND			
1 Cicilline	98	2	98
2 Langevin	95	5	99
SOUTH CAROLINA			
1 Scott	98	2	100
2 Wilson	99	1	99
3 Duncan	98	2	99
4 Gowdy	99	1	99
5 Mulvaney	94	6	99
6 Clyburn	93	7	95
SOUTH DAKOTA			
AL Noem	93	7	97
TENNESSEE			
1 Roe	97	3	99
2 Duncan	89	11	99
3 Fleischmann	97	3	96
4 DesJarlais	96	4	99
5 Cooper	81	19	99
6 Black	99	1	98
7 Blackburn	99	1	99
8 Fincher	97	3	98
9 Cohen	97	3	97

	1	2	3
TEXAS			
1 Gohmert	94	6	93
2 Poe	96	4	99
3 Johnson, S.	97	3	97
4 Hall	95	5	99
5 Hensarling	99	1	100
6 Barton	94	6	99
7 Culberson	95	5	89
8 Brady	98	2	99
9 Green, A.	88	12	99
10 McCaul	97	3	98
11 Conaway	99	1	100
12 Granger	89	11	95
13 Thornberry	97	3	100
14 Paul	79	21	57
15 Hinojosa	92	8	94
16 Reyes	93	7	91
17 Flores	98	2	97
18 Jackson Lee	94	6	79
19 Neugebauer	98	2	99
20 Gonzalez	88	12	96
21 Smith	96	4	99
22 Olson	99	1	99
23 Canseco	98	2	98
24 Marchant	97	3	96
25 Doggett	95	5	96
26 Burgess	95	5	97
27 Farenthold	97	3	99
28 Cuellar	68	32	99
29 Green, G.	78	22	98
30 Johnson, E.	94	6	94
31 Carter	90	10	99
32 Sessions	98	2	98
UTAH			
1 Bishop	96	4	94
2 Matheson	32	68	100
3 Chaffetz	96	4	97
VERMONT			
AL Welch	95	5	98
VIRGINIA			
1 Wittman	94	6	100
2 Rigell	93	7	99
3 Scott	95	5	99
4 Forbes	95	5	99
5 Hurt	97	3	99
6 Goodlatte	95	5	99
7 Cantor	98	2	90
8 Moran	94	6	99
9 Griffith	92	8	99
10 Wolf	86	14	99
11 Connolly	91	9	99
WASHINGTON			
1 Inslee[10]	91	9	94
1 DelBene[10]	94	6	100
2 Larsen	90	10	99
3 Herrera Beutler	89	11	99
4 Hastings	90	10	100
5 McMorris Rodgers	97	3	99
6 Dicks	92	8	93
7 McDermott	99	1	99
8 Reichert	84	16	95
9 Smith	93	7	98
WEST VIRGINIA			
1 McKinley	88	12	99
2 Capito	88	12	99
3 Rahall	81	19	100
WISCONSIN			
1 Ryan	97	3	93
2 Baldwin	97	3	95
3 Kind	88	12	88
4 Moore	98	2	88
5 Sensenbrenner	93	7	99
6 Petri	93	7	99
7 Duffy	96	4	99
8 Ribble	95	5	99
WYOMING			
AL Lummis	96	4	98

SENATE

1. Party Unity. Percentage of recorded party unity votes in 2012 on which a senator voted "yea" or "nay" in agreement with a majority of his or her party. (Party unity votes are those on which a majority of voting Democrats opposed a majority of voting Republicans.) Percentages are based on votes cast; thus, failure to vote does not lower a member's score.

2. Party Opposition. Percentage of recorded party unity votes in 2012 on which a senator voted "yea" or "nay" in disagreement with a majority of his or her party. Percentages are based on votes cast; thus, failure to vote does not lower a member's score.

3. Participation in Party Unity Votes. Percentage of the Senate party unity votes in 2012 for which a senator was eligible and present and voted "yea" or "nay." There were a total of 150 such recorded votes.

	1	2	3		1	2	3
ALABAMA				**MONTANA**			
Shelby	90	10	99	Baucus	91	9	100
Sessions	93	7	99	Tester	92	8	100
ALASKA				**NEBRASKA**			
Murkowski	51	49	97	Nelson	83	17	100
Begich	93	7	99	Johanns	81	19	99
ARIZONA				**NEVADA**			
McCain	88	12	98	Reid	94	6	99
Kyl	93	7	99	Heller	65	35	92
ARKANSAS				**NEW HAMPSHIRE**			
Pryor	85	15	100	Shaheen	97	3	100
Boozman	86	14	99	Ayotte	86	14	99
CALIFORNIA				**NEW JERSEY**			
Feinstein	93	7	99	Lautenberg	97	3	86
Boxer	97	3	88	Menendez	97	3	99
COLORADO				**NEW MEXICO**			
Udall	93	7	99	Bingaman	96	4	98
Bennet	92	8	99	Udall	100	0	99
CONNECTICUT				**NEW YORK**			
Lieberman	89	11	99	Schumer	97	3	100
Blumenthal	98	2	97	Gillibrand	97	3	99
DELAWARE				**NORTH CAROLINA**			
Carper	89	11	100	**Burr**	94	6	97
Coons	95	5	100	Hagan	87	13	100
FLORIDA				**NORTH DAKOTA**			
Nelson	91	9	100	Conrad	93	7	99
Rubio	90	10	97	Hoeven	67	33	99
GEORGIA				**OHIO**			
Chambliss	94	6	97	Brown	97	3	99
Isakson	92	8	99	**Portman**	86	14	99
HAWAII				**OKLAHOMA**			
Inouye[1]	97	3	96	**Inhofe**	92	8	94
Schatz[1]	100	0	100	**Coburn**	92	8	97
Akaka	97	3	99	**OREGON**			
IDAHO				Wyden	95	5	95
Crapo	93	7	99	Merkley	95	5	99
Risch	94	6	99	**PENNSYLVANIA**			
ILLINOIS				Casey	91	9	99
Durbin	97	3	100	**Toomey**	93	7	98
Kirk	—	—	0	**RHODE ISLAND**			
INDIANA				Reed	97	3	100
Lugar	69	31	99	Whitehouse	95	5	99
Coats	89	11	100	**SOUTH CAROLINA**			
IOWA				Graham	86	14	99
Grassley	83	17	100	DeMint	93	7	83
Harkin	97	3	97	**SOUTH DAKOTA**			
KANSAS				Johnson	95	5	99
Roberts	86	14	97	**Thune**	88	12	96
Moran	81	19	96	**TENNESSEE**			
KENTUCKY				**Alexander**	83	17	95
McConnell	93	7	100	**Corker**	86	14	99
Paul	92	8	99	**TEXAS**			
LOUISIANA				**Hutchison**	83	17	97
Landrieu	87	13	99	**Cornyn**	98	2	100
Vitter	89	11	93	**UTAH**			
MAINE				**Hatch**	92	8	87
Snowe	44	56	97	**Lee**	91	9	99
Collins	39	61	100	**VERMONT**			
MARYLAND				Leahy	97	3	98
Mikulski	95	5	100	*Sanders*	97	3	99
Cardin	99	1	100	**VIRGINIA**			
MASSACHUSETTS				Webb	82	18	98
Kerry	94	6	99	Warner	86	14	91
Brown	38	62	99	**WASHINGTON**			
MICHIGAN				Murray	98	2	98
Levin	96	4	100	Cantwell	97	3	100
Stabenow	91	9	100	**WEST VIRGINIA**			
MINNESOTA				Rockefeller	96	4	94
Klobuchar	93	7	100	Manchin	76	24	100
Franken	98	2	100	**WISCONSIN**			
MISSISSIPPI				Kohl	92	8	99
Cochran	72	28	100	**Johnson**	95	5	99
Wicker	85	15	99	**WYOMING**			
MISSOURI				**Enzi**	91	9	99
McCaskill	78	22	95	**Barrasso**	89	11	100
Blunt	79	21	100				

KEY   **Republicans**   Democrats   *Independents*

[1] Sen. Brian Schatz, D-Hawaii, was sworn in Dec. 27, 2012, to fill the seat vacated by the Dec. 17 death of fellow Democrat Daniel K. Inouye. Inouye was eligible for 133 party unity votes in 2012; Schatz was eligible for 16 party unity votes.

Still Showing Up in an Election Year

Just before 11 p.m. on New Year's Day, a mere 37 hours before the Constitution would dissolve the 112th Congress, the House banged the gavel down on its last vote. Even though members had been called back from their districts on a holiday, and there was little controversy left about a bill to skirt the fiscal cliff, more than 98 percent of them showed up to cast ballots.

In some ways, the vote — a well-attended, last-minute, half-resolution of a self-imposed deadline — perfectly represented the just-finished Congress. Both chambers worked down to the wire, taking the second-most election year votes in three decades, and boasting the fourth-highest election year participation rate on record, 95.4 percent. Yet, while second sessions generally produce more laws than their opening years, only 193 public laws were enacted, by far the lowest election year total of the previous decade.

The enthusiasm and a flurry of activity that arrived with the 112th Congress was quickly dampened by the realities of a divided government, leaders who pleaded for patience and practicality, and the need to go back home, raise money and get re-elected in a presidential election year amid record-low approval ratings of the institution.

SCHEDULING HELPED VOTING NUMBERS

How were members of both chambers able to cast so many votes while maintaining a reasonably high rate of participation?

First, leaders made it easy to vote. Knowing that absentee rates double near weekends, leaders scheduled 93 percent of votes to fall Tuesdays through Fridays. In the House, the average workday lasted a decade-low 4.8 hours.

Leaders gave rank-and-file lawmakers plenty of time to campaign. Eighty percent of House votes occurred in the six months from February through July; this total was close to 75 percent in the Senate. The members of the 112th spent all of August electioneering, returned for eight days in September to keep the government funded, then left with another 46 days to campaign.

The Senate had 251 roll call votes, in line with the average over the previous decade. The chamber's 96.6 percent average participation rate was the same as in 2010, despite losing a full percentage point because of the absence of Illinois Republican Sen. Mark S. Kirk, who spent the year rehabilitating from a January stroke. Four years after America's first presidential election that pitted two sitting senators against each other, 2012 marked the only presidential election year in which no senators were distracted by their own presidential run.

The House held 657 roll call votes, not counting one quorum call and one vitiated vote. This was its fifth-highest election year vote total on record. The chamber's average participation rate was 95.3 percent, the fourth-highest in an election year. That was in spite of Texas Republican Ron Paul, who missed almost half his votes while campaigning for president, and Illinois Democrat Jesse L. Jackson Jr., who missed an equal percentage while undergoing mental health treatment before resigning in November. ■

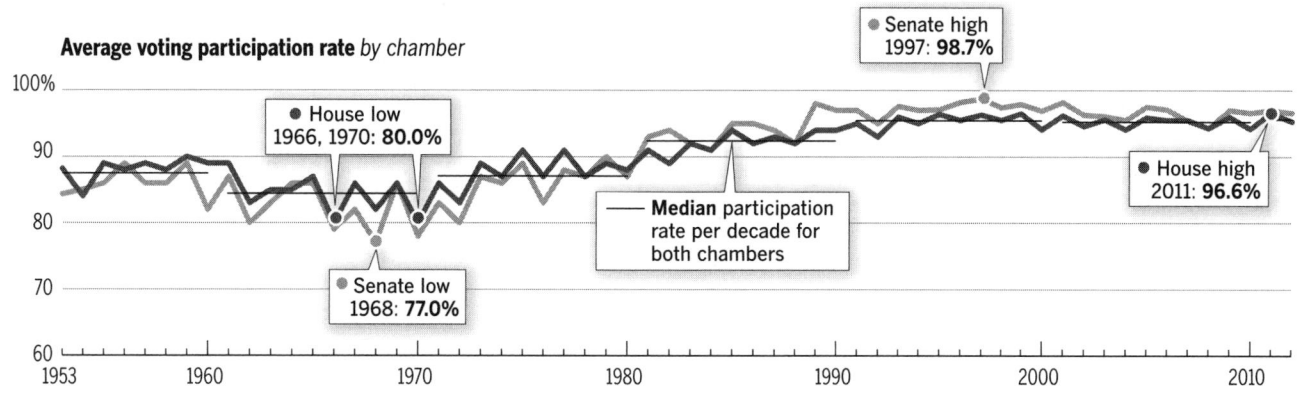

Participation Down in Both Chambers in 2012

The average House member cast a "yea" or "nay" vote 95.3 percent of the time on roll calls in 2012, down from a record 96.6 percent in 2011. The participation rate for senators ticked down as well, to 96.6 percent, while remaining higher than the House rate for the fourth straight year. After climbing in the 1970s and 1980s, voting participation has remained fairly consistent in both chambers for the past two decades, hovering around 95 percent in the House and 96 percent in the Senate.

Average voting participation rate *by chamber*

- Senate high 1997: **98.7%**
- House low 1966, 1970: **80.0%**
- House high 2011: **96.6%**
- Median participation rate per decade for both chambers
- Senate low 1968: **77.0%**

Voting Participation History

These tables show the number of roll call votes in each chamber and in Congress as a whole since 1954, as well as the frequency with which lawmakers on average cast "yea" or "nay" votes. Participation in floor votes has ranged around 95 percent over the past two decades.

YEAR	House ROLL CALL VOTES	House RATE	Senate ROLL CALL VOTES	Senate RATE	Congress as a Whole ROLL CALL VOTES	Congress as a Whole RATE
2012	657	95.3%	251	96.6%	908	95.4%
2011	945	96.6	235	97.0	1,180	96.6
2010	660	94.2	299	96.6	959	94.4
2009	987	96.0	397	97.0	1,384	96.1
2008	688	94.3	215	94.3	903	94.3
2007	1,177	95.5	442	95.0	1,619	95.4
2006	541	95.5	279	97.1	820	95.7
2005	669	95.9	366	97.4	1,035	96.1
2004	543	94.1	216	95.5	759	94.2
2003	675	95.6	459	96.1	1,134	95.7
2002	483	94.6	253	96.3	736	94.8
2001	507	96.2	380	98.2	887	96.5
2000	600	94.1	298	96.9	898	94.4
1999	609	96.5	374	97.9	983	96.6
1998	533	95.5	314	97.4	847	95.7
1997	633	96.3	298	98.7	931	96.5
1996	454	95.5	306	98.2	760	95.8
1995	867	96.4	613	97.1	1,480	96.5
1994	497	95.0	329	97.0	826	95.0
1993	597	96.0	395	97.6	992	96.0
1992	473	93.0	270	95.0	743	93.4
1991	428	95.0	280	97.0	708	95.0
1990	536	94.0	326	97.0	862	95.0
1989	368	94.0	312	98.0	680	95.0
1988	451	92.0	379	92.0	830	92.0
1987	488	93.0	420	94.0	908	93.0
1986	451	92.0	354	95.0	805	93.0
1985	439	94.0	381	95.0	820	94.0
1984	408	91.0	275	91.0	683	91.0
1983	498	92.0	371	92.0	869	92.0
1982	459	89.0	465	94.0	924	90.0
1981	353	91.0	483	93.0	836	92.0
1980	604	88.0	531	87.0	1,135	87.0
1979	672	89.0	497	90.0	1,169	89.0
1978	834	87.0	516	87.0	1,350	87.0
1977	706	91.0	635	88.0	1,341	90.0
1976	661	87.0	688	83.0	1,349	86.0
1975	612	91.0	602	89.0	1,214	91.0
1974	537	87.0	544	86.0	1,081	87.0
1973	541	89.0	594	87.0	1,135	89.0
1972	329	83.0	532	80.0	861	82.0
1971	320	86.0	423	83.0	743	85.0
1970	266	80.0	418	78.0	684	79.0
1969	177	86.0	245	86.0	422	86.0
1968	233	82.0	281	77.0	514	80.0
1967	245	86.0	315	82.0	560	85.0
1966	193	80.0	235	79.0	428	79.0
1965	201	87.0	258	86.0	459	87.0
1964	113	85.0	305	86.0	418	85.0
1963	119	85.0	229	83.0	348	84.0
1962	124	83.0	224	80.0	348	82.0
1961	116	89.0	204	87.0	320	88.0
1960	93	89.0	207	82.0	300	87.0
1959	87	90.0	215	89.0	302	89.0
1958	93	88.0	200	86.0	293	87.0
1957	100	89.0	107	86.0	207	88.0
1956	73	88.0	130	89.0	203	88.0
1955	76	89.0	87	86.0	163	88.0

Perfect Records Of Attendance

As is typical in an election year, voting participation dropped in both chambers. Despite this, the count of those with perfect attendance on roll call votes increased: Fifteen House members and 13 senators cast a "yea" or a "nay" on every recorded vote.

Perfect Attendance, House

Democrats
John Barrow of Georgia
Jim Matheson of Utah

Republicans
Sandy Adams of Florida
Lou Barletta of Pennsylvania
K. Michael Conaway of Texas
Charlie Dent of Pennsylvania
Virginia Foxx of North Carolina
Brett Guthrie of Kentucky
Joe Heck of Nevada
Leonard Lance of New Jersey
Bob Latta of Ohio
Frank A. LoBiondo of New
   Jersey
Mike Pompeo of Kansas
Fred Upton of Michigan
Steve Womack of Arkansas

*(Four other House members —
Suzanne Bonamici, D-Ore.;
David A. Curson, D-Mich.; Suzan
DelBene, D-Wash.; and Thomas
Massie, R-Ky. — recorded perfect
attendance but weren't eligible for
all votes in 2012.)*

Perfect Attendance, Senate

Democrats
Max Baucus of Montana
Maria Cantwell of Washington
Thomas R. Carper of Delaware
Chris Coons of Delaware
Richard J. Durbin of Illinois
Amy Klobuchar of Minnesota
Carl Levin of Michigan
Joe Manchin III of West Virginia
Mark Pryor of Arkansas

Republicans
Thad Cochran of Mississippi
Susan Collins of Maine
Charles E. Grassley of Iowa
Mitch McConnell of Kentucky

*(One other senator, Brian Schatz,
D-Hawaii, recorded perfect
attendance but wasn't eligible for
all votes in 2012.)*

SENATE

1. Voting Participation. Percentage of recorded votes in 2012 on which a senator was eligible and present, and voted "yea" or "nay." There were a total of 251 such recorded votes.

Voting participation excluding motions to instruct. Typically, CQ Roll Call also calculates Senate voting percentages by excluding votes on motions to instruct the sergeant at arms to request the attendance of absent senators. In 2012, there were no such votes, so this study was eliminated for the past year only.

Absences because of illness. CQ Roll Call no longer designates members who missed votes because of illness. In the past, notations to that effect were based on official statements published in the Congressional Record, but these were found to be inconsistently used.

Rounding. Scores are rounded to the nearest percentage point, except that no scores are rounded up to 100 percent. Senators with a 100 percent score participated in all recorded votes for which they were eligible.

State / Senator		State / Senator	
ALABAMA		**MONTANA**	
Shelby	99	Baucus	100
Sessions	99	Tester	99
ALASKA		**NEBRASKA**	
Murkowski	96	Nelson	99
Begich	97	Johanns	99
ARIZONA		**NEVADA**	
McCain	97	Reid	99
Kyl	99	Heller	90
ARKANSAS		**NEW HAMPSHIRE**	
Pryor	100	Shaheen	99
Boozman	98	Ayotte	99
CALIFORNIA		**NEW JERSEY**	
Feinstein	99	Lautenberg	86
Boxer	88	Menendez	99
COLORADO		**NEW MEXICO**	
Udall	97	Bingaman	98
Bennet	98	Udall	99
CONNECTICUT		**NEW YORK**	
Lieberman	98	Schumer	99
Blumenthal	96	Gillibrand	99
DELAWARE		**NORTH CAROLINA**	
Carper	100	Burr	95
Coons	100	Hagan	99
FLORIDA		**NORTH DAKOTA**	
Nelson	99	Conrad	98
Rubio	95	Hoeven	98
GEORGIA		**OHIO**	
Chambliss	96	Brown	99
Isakson	99	Portman	98
HAWAII		**OKLAHOMA**	
Inouye[1]	92	Inhofe	93
Schatz[1]	100	Coburn	95
Akaka	98	**OREGON**	
IDAHO		Wyden	95
Crapo	98	Merkley	99
Risch	99	**PENNSYLVANIA**	
ILLINOIS		Casey	98
Durbin	100	Toomey	98
Kirk	0	**RHODE ISLAND**	
INDIANA		Reed	99
Lugar	99	Whitehouse	99
Coats	99	**SOUTH CAROLINA**	
IOWA		Graham	99
Grassley	100	DeMint	83
Harkin	96	**SOUTH DAKOTA**	
KANSAS		Johnson	99
Roberts	98	Thune	96
Moran	95	**TENNESSEE**	
KENTUCKY		Alexander	95
McConnell	100	Corker	99
Paul	98	**TEXAS**	
LOUISIANA		Hutchison	96
Landrieu	98	Cornyn	99
Vitter	91	**UTAH**	
MAINE		Hatch	86
Snowe	98	Lee	98
Collins	100	**VERMONT**	
MARYLAND		Leahy	98
Mikulski	99	Sanders	97
Cardin	99	**VIRGINIA**	
MASSACHUSETTS		Webb	98
Kerry	98	Warner	94
Brown	99	**WASHINGTON**	
MICHIGAN		Murray	98
Levin	100	Cantwell	100
Stabenow	99	**WEST VIRGINIA**	
MINNESOTA		Rockefeller	91
Klobuchar	100	Manchin	100
Franken	99	**WISCONSIN**	
MISSISSIPPI		Kohl	99
Cochran	100	Johnson	99
Wicker	98	**WYOMING**	
MISSOURI		Enzi	99
McCaskill	96	Barrasso	99
Blunt	99		

KEY — Republicans · Democrats · Independents

[1] Sen. Brian Schatz, D-Hawaii, was sworn in Dec. 27, 2012, to fill the seat vacated by the Dec. 17 death of fellow Democrat Daniel K. Inouye. Inouye was eligible for 228 votes in 2012; Schatz was eligible for 20 votes.

HOUSE

1. Voting Participation.
Percentage of recorded votes in 2012 on which a representative was eligible and present, and voted "yea" or "nay." There were a total of 657 such recorded votes. Quorum calls, although they are included in the House list of recorded roll calls, are not counted as votes because lawmakers are asked only to respond "present." There was one recorded quorum call in 2012. In addition, the result of one vote (No. 327) was vitiated after it occurred, further reducing the count of actual votes from the total number of roll calls.

2. Voting Participation (without Journal votes).
Percentage of recorded votes in 2012 on which a representative was eligible and present, and voted "yea" or "nay." There were a total of 645 such recorded votes in this version of the study, which excludes 12 votes on motions to approve the House Journal.

Absences because of illness. CQ Roll Call no longer designates members who missed votes because of illness. In the past, notations to that effect were based on official statements published in the Congressional Record, but these were found to be inconsistently used.

Rounding. Scores are rounded to the nearest percentage point, except that no scores are rounded up to 100 percent. Members with a 100 percent score participated in all recorded votes for which they were eligible.

[1] Ron Barber, D-Ariz., was sworn in June 19, 2012, to fill the vacancy created by the Jan. 25 resignation of fellow Democrat Gabrielle Giffords. Giffords was eligible for 10 votes in 2012; Barber was eligible for 278 votes.

[2] Dennis Cardoza, D-Calif., resigned Aug. 15, 2012. The last vote for which he was eligible was vote 556. Cardoza was eligible for 554 votes in 2012.

[3] Bob Filner, D-Calif., resigned Dec. 3, 2012. The last vote for which he was eligible was vote 613. Filner was eligible for 611 votes in 2012.

[4] Jesse L. Jackson Jr., D-Ill., resigned Nov. 21, 2012. The last vote for which he was eligible was vote 608. Jackson was eligible for 606 votes in 2012.

[5] Thomas Massie, R-Ky., was sworn in Nov. 13, 2012, to fill the vacancy created by the July 31 resignation of fellow Republican Geoff Davis. Davis was eligible for 537 votes in 2012; Massie was eligible for 55 votes.

[6] David A. Curson, D-Mich., was sworn in Nov. 13, 2012, to fill the vacancy created by the July 6 resignation of Republican Thaddeus McCotter. McCotter was eligible for 449 votes in 2012; Curson was eligible for 55 votes.

[7] Donald M. Payne Jr., D-N.J., was sworn in Nov. 15, 2012, to fill the vacancy created by the March 6 death of his father, fellow Democrat Donald M. Payne. Payne was eligible for 94 votes in 2012; Payne Jr. was eligible for 54 votes.

[8] The speaker votes only at his discretion.

[9] Suzanne Bonamici, D-Ore., was sworn in Feb. 7, 2012, to fill the vacancy created by the Aug. 3, 2011, resignation of fellow Democrat David Wu. Bonamici was eligible for 622 votes in 2012. (Wu was not eligible for any votes in 2012.)

[10] Suzan DelBene, D-Wash., was sworn in Nov. 13, 2012, to fill the vacancy created by the March 20 resignation of fellow Democrat Jay Inslee. Inslee was eligible for 110 votes in 2012; DelBene was eligible for 55 votes.

	1	2		1	2
ALABAMA			**COLORADO**		
1 **Bonner**	93	93	1 **DeGette**	97	97
2 **Roby**	98	98	2 **Polis**	95	94
3 **Rogers**	99	99	3 **Tipton**	99	99
4 **Aderholt**	99	99	4 **Gardner**	99	100
5 **Brooks**	99	99	5 **Lamborn**	95	95
6 **Bachus**	94	94	6 **Coffman**	99	99
7 **Sewell**	95	95	7 Perlmutter	97	97
ALASKA			**CONNECTICUT**		
AL **Young**	94	94	1 Larson	98	98
ARIZONA			2 Courtney	99	99
1 **Gosar**	91	91	3 DeLauro	99	99
2 **Franks**	98	98	4 Himes	99	99
3 **Quayle**	99	99	5 Murphy	92	92
4 Pastor	97	98	**DELAWARE**		
5 **Schweikert**	99	99	AL Carney	99	99
6 **Flake**	95	95	**FLORIDA**		
7 Grijalva	94	94	1 **Miller**	94	94
8 Giffords [1]	10	11	2 **Southerland**	99	99
8 Barber [1]	97	97	3 Brown	93	93
ARKANSAS			4 **Crenshaw**	99	99
1 **Crawford**	99	99	5 **Nugent**	99	99
2 **Griffin**	98	98	6 **Stearns**	99	99
3 **Womack**	100	100	7 **Mica**	99	99
4 Ross	93	93	8 **Webster**	99	99
CALIFORNIA			9 **Bilirakis**	96	96
1 Thompson	99	99	10 **Young**	91	92
2 **Herger**	92	92	11 Castor	98	98
3 **Lungren**	99	99	12 **Ross**	99	99
4 **McClintock**	99	99	13 **Buchanan**	98	98
5 Matsui	99	99	14 **Mack**	68	67
6 Woolsey	93	93	15 **Posey**	99	99
7 Miller, George	94	94	16 **Rooney**	99	99
8 Pelosi	96	96	17 Wilson	97	97
9 Lee	92	92	18 **Ros-Lehtinen**	98	98
10 Garamendi	95	95	19 Deutch	96	97
11 McNerney	99	99	20 Wasserman Schultz	94	94
12 Speier	86	86	21 **Diaz-Balart**	97	97
13 Stark	91	91	22 **West**	99	99
14 Eshoo	99	99	23 Hastings	97	98
15 Honda	94	94	24 **Adams**	100	100
16 Lofgren	97	97	25 **Rivera**	96	96
17 Farr	97	97	**GEORGIA**		
18 Cardoza [2]	60	60	1 **Kingston**	98	98
19 **Denham**	98	98	2 Bishop	98	98
20 Costa	95	95	3 **Westmoreland**	99	99
21 **Nunes**	97	98	4 Johnson	94	94
22 **McCarthy**	95	95	5 Lewis	92	92
23 Capps	99	99	6 **Price**	99	99
24 **Gallegly**	85	85	7 **Woodall**	99	99
25 **McKeon**	93	93	8 **Scott, A.**	99	99
26 **Dreier**	99	99	9 **Graves**	99	99
27 Sherman	98	98	10 **Broun**	94	94
28 Berman	89	89	11 **Gingrey**	95	96
29 Schiff	99	99	12 Barrow	100	100
30 Waxman	97	97	13 Scott, D.	97	97
31 Becerra	95	95	**HAWAII**		
32 Chu	96	96	1 Hanabusa	99	99
33 Bass	87	87	2 Hirono	78	78
34 Roybal-Allard	94	94	**IDAHO**		
35 Waters	93	93	1 **Labrador**	93	93
36 Hahn	92	92	2 **Simpson**	98	98
37 Richardson	97	97	**ILLINOIS**		
38 Napolitano	87	87	1 Rush	87	87
39 Sánchez, Linda	90	90	2 Jackson [4]	54	54
40 **Royce**	99	99	3 Lipinski	96	96
41 Lewis	70	69	4 Gutierrez	88	88
42 **Miller, Gary**	88	88	5 Quigley	99	99
43 Baca	91	91	6 **Roskam**	99	99
44 **Calvert**	98	98	7 Davis	91	91
45 **Bono Mack**	90	90	8 **Walsh**	95	95
46 **Rohrabacher**	94	94	9 Schakowsky	98	98
47 Sanchez, Loretta	89	89	10 **Dold**	98	98
48 **Campbell**	89	89	11 **Kinzinger**	97	97
49 **Issa**	98	98	12 Costello	88	88
50 **Bilbray**	97	97	13 **Biggert**	99	99
51 Filner [3]	41	41	14 **Hultgren**	99	99
52 **Hunter**	99	99	15 Johnson	84	85
53 Davis	99	99			

KEY   **Republicans**   Democrats

	1	2
16 Manzullo	93	93
17 Schilling	96	97
18 Schock	95	95
19 Shimkus	97	97
INDIANA		
1 Visclosky	96	96
2 Donnelly	89	90
3 Stutzman	97	97
4 Rokita	98	99
5 Burton	84	85
6 Pence	85	85
7 Carson	91	91
8 Bucshon	98	98
9 Young	99	99
IOWA		
1 Braley	96	96
2 Loebsack	98	98
3 Boswell	99	99
4 Latham	99	99
5 King	98	98
KANSAS		
1 Huelskamp	99	99
2 Jenkins	95	95
3 Yoder	99	99
4 Pompeo	100	100
KENTUCKY		
1 Whitfield	96	96
2 Guthrie	100	100
3 Yarmuth	95	96
4 Davis[5]	95	96
4 Massie[5]	100	100
5 Rogers	99	99
6 Chandler	97	97
LOUISIANA		
1 Scalise	99	99
2 Richmond	94	94
3 Landry	88	88
4 Fleming	99	99
5 Alexander	97	97
6 Cassidy	96	96
7 Boustany	99	99
MAINE		
1 Pingree	98	99
2 Michaud	99	99
MARYLAND		
1 Harris	99	99
2 Ruppersberger	94	94
3 Sarbanes	99	99
4 Edwards	97	97
5 Hoyer	98	98
6 Bartlett	94	94
7 Cummings	97	97
8 Van Hollen	98	98
MASSACHUSETTS		
1 Olver	95	95
2 Neal	92	92
3 McGovern	99	99
4 Frank	93	93
5 Tsongas	95	96
6 Tierney	98	99
7 Markey	96	96
8 Capuano	99	99
9 Lynch	97	97
10 Keating	99	99
MICHIGAN		
1 Benishek	99	99
2 Huizenga	97	97
3 Amash	98	100
4 Camp	99	99
5 Kildee	99	99
6 Upton	100	100
7 Walberg	98	99
8 Rogers	99	99
9 Peters	99	99
10 Miller	99	99
11 McCotter[6]	98	98
11 Curson[6]	100	100
12 Levin	99	99
13 Clarke	99	99
14 Conyers	95	95
15 Dingell	96	96
MINNESOTA		
1 Walz	98	98
2 Kline	99	99
3 Paulsen	99	99
4 McCollum	97	97

	1	2
5 Ellison	94	94
6 Bachmann	94	94
7 Peterson	98	98
8 Cravaack	98	99
MISSISSIPPI		
1 Nunnelee	96	96
2 Thompson	94	94
3 Harper	99	99
4 Palazzo	99	99
MISSOURI		
1 Clay	94	93
2 Akin	63	63
3 Carnahan	96	96
4 Hartzler	99	99
5 Cleaver	93	93
6 Graves	98	98
7 Long	99	99
8 Emerson	99	99
9 Luetkemeyer	99	99
MONTANA		
AL Rehberg	99	99
NEBRASKA		
1 Fortenberry	94	94
2 Terry	99	99
3 Smith	99	99
NEVADA		
1 Berkley	98	98
2 Amodei	94	94
3 Heck	100	100
NEW HAMPSHIRE		
1 Guinta	95	95
2 Bass	96	97
NEW JERSEY		
1 Andrews	95	95
2 LoBiondo	100	100
3 Runyan	98	98
4 Smith	98	98
5 Garrett	98	98
6 Pallone	99	99
7 Lance	100	100
8 Pascrell	85	85
9 Rothman	88	88
10 Payne[7]	32	33
10 Payne, Jr.[7]	98	98
11 Frelinghuysen	99	99
12 Holt	99	99
13 Sires	93	93
NEW MEXICO		
1 Heinrich	92	92
2 Pearce	98	98
3 Luján	97	97
NEW YORK		
1 Bishop	93	93
2 Israel	97	97
3 King	97	97
4 McCarthy	97	97
5 Ackerman	83	83
6 Meeks	87	87
7 Crowley	97	97
8 Nadler	95	95
9 Turner	97	97
10 Towns	82	82
11 Clarke	93	93
12 Velázquez	89	89
13 Grimm	98	98
14 Maloney	95	94
15 Rangel	72	73
16 Serrano	96	96
17 Engel	95	95
18 Lowey	94	94
19 Hayworth	99	99
20 Gibson	99	99
21 Tonko	99	99
22 Hinchey	92	92
23 Owens	97	99
24 Hanna	96	96
25 Buerkle	96	96
26 Hochul	99	99
27 Higgins	98	98
28 Slaughter	63	62
29 Reed	99	99
NORTH CAROLINA		
1 Butterfield	91	91
2 Ellmers	95	96
3 Jones	94	94
4 Price	99	99

	1	2
5 Foxx	100	100
6 Coble	86	85
7 McIntyre	94	94
8 Kissell	97	97
9 Myrick	93	93
10 McHenry	93	93
11 Shuler	78	78
12 Watt	95	95
13 Miller	99	99
NORTH DAKOTA		
AL Berg	99	99
OHIO		
1 Chabot	99	99
2 Schmidt	94	94
3 Turner	98	98
4 Jordan	97	98
5 Latta	100	100
6 Johnson	99	99
7 Austria	93	93
8 Boehner[8]	1	1
9 Kaptur	93	93
10 Kucinich	88	88
11 Fudge	98	98
12 Tiberi	98	98
13 Sutton	97	97
14 LaTourette	94	94
15 Stivers	85	85
16 Renacci	99	99
17 Ryan	98	98
18 Gibbs	99	99
OKLAHOMA		
1 Sullivan	89	89
2 Boren	93	93
3 Lucas	99	99
4 Cole	99	99
5 Lankford	99	99
OREGON		
1 Bonamici[9]	100	100
2 Walden	99	99
3 Blumenauer	94	94
4 DeFazio	98	98
5 Schrader	97	98
PENNSYLVANIA		
1 Brady	99	99
2 Fattah	97	97
3 Kelly	99	99
4 Altmire	98	98
5 Thompson	99	99
6 Gerlach	98	98
7 Meehan	97	97
8 Fitzpatrick	99	99
9 Shuster	98	98
10 Marino	86	87
11 Barletta	100	100
12 Critz	98	98
13 Schwartz	99	99
14 Doyle	96	96
15 Dent	100	100
16 Pitts	97	97
17 Holden	88	88
18 Murphy	99	99
19 Platts	93	93
RHODE ISLAND		
1 Cicilline	97	97
2 Langevin	98	98
SOUTH CAROLINA		
1 Scott	99	99
2 Wilson	99	99
3 Duncan	99	99
4 Gowdy	99	99
5 Mulvaney	99	99
6 Clyburn	95	95
SOUTH DAKOTA		
AL Noem	97	97
TENNESSEE		
1 Roe	99	99
2 Duncan	99	99
3 Fleischmann	95	95
4 DesJarlais	99	99
5 Cooper	99	99
6 Black	98	98
7 Blackburn	99	99
8 Fincher	97	97
9 Cohen	96	96

	1	2
TEXAS		
1 Gohmert	90	92
2 Poe	98	98
3 Johnson, S.	95	95
4 Hall	98	98
5 Hensarling	99	99
6 Barton	98	98
7 Culberson	89	89
8 Brady	96	96
9 Green, A.	98	98
10 McCaul	98	98
11 Conaway	100	100
12 Granger	95	95
13 Thornberry	99	99
14 Paul	54	54
15 Hinojosa	93	93
16 Reyes	86	87
17 Flores	95	95
18 Jackson Lee	81	81
19 Neugebauer	99	99
20 Gonzalez	94	94
21 Smith	99	99
22 Olson	99	99
23 Canseco	97	97
24 Marchant	94	94
25 Doggett	95	95
26 Burgess	97	97
27 Farenthold	99	99
28 Cuellar	99	99
29 Green, G.	97	97
30 Johnson, E.	95	95
31 Carter	98	98
32 Sessions	98	98
UTAH		
1 Bishop	94	95
2 Matheson	100	100
3 Chaffetz	97	98
VERMONT		
AL Welch	97	97
VIRGINIA		
1 Wittman	99	99
2 Rigell	99	99
3 Scott	98	98
4 Forbes	97	98
5 Hurt	99	99
6 Goodlatte	98	98
7 Cantor	91	91
8 Moran	97	97
9 Griffith	99	99
10 Wolf	99	99
11 Connolly	99	99
WASHINGTON		
1 Inslee[10]	90	91
1 DelBene[10]	100	100
2 Larsen	99	99
3 Herrera Beutler	99	99
4 Hastings	99	99
5 McMorris Rodgers	98	98
6 Dicks	91	91
7 McDermott	99	99
8 Reichert	95	95
9 Smith	97	97
WEST VIRGINIA		
1 McKinley	99	99
2 Capito	99	99
3 Rahall	99	99
WISCONSIN		
1 Ryan	93	93
2 Baldwin	95	95
3 Kind	97	97
4 Moore	88	87
5 Sensenbrenner	99	99
6 Petri	99	99
7 Duffy	98	99
8 Ribble	99	99
WYOMING		
AL Lummis	97	98

KEY VOTES

Two Dozen Votes Illustrate What a Do-Nothing Congress Actually Did

FOR A LEGISLATIVE SESSION roundly criticized for accomplishing relatively little, Congress took a surprising number of votes in 2012 that proved to be important either because of their ultimate outcome or because of the ways in which they embellished the overall political landscape.

As had frequently been the case in the previous decade or so, lawmakers regularly answered the bells to participate in roll call votes designed mostly to make a partisan point and to distinguish the positions of the two parties — rather than to accomplish some larger legislative purpose. Even so, among the 13 Senate votes and the 11 House votes selected by the editors at CQ Roll Call as the key votes of the year, several stand out as particularly noteworthy.

The most significant were the last recorded votes in each chamber. On New Year's Day of 2013, first the Senate and then the House voted to raise taxes on wealthy Americans and postpone $109 billion in automatic spending cuts as a way to avert the economic consequences of sending the government over the fiscal cliff. The likelihood of either chamber taking such a step was considered quite low for much of the year. In fact, it might be said that the true key vote of the year was the one cast collectively by the country on Nov. 6, which re-elected President Barack Obama to a second term.

With his future position ensured — and with taxes having been a centerpiece of the campaign — the president was able to pressure Republicans to accept a fiscal-cliff deal mostly on his terms.

In fact, the president took a position on almost all of the key votes in 2012.

There were cases in which Obama actually worked with Republicans, resulting in important policy shifts and yielding notable votes.

Attributes of a Key Vote

Since its 1945 founding, CQ Roll Call (previously Congressional Quarterly) has selected a series of key votes for both the House and Senate on major issues of the year.

A vote is judged to be key by the extent to which it represents:

- a matter of major controversy.
- a matter of presidential or political power.
- a matter of potentially great impact on the nation and the lives of Americans.

For each group of related votes on an issue in each chamber, one key vote is usually chosen — one that, in the opinion of CQ Roll Call editors, was most important in determining the outcome of the issue for the year or best reflected the views of individual lawmakers on that issue.

In March, both chambers cooperated with the president to relax the rules governing capital formation by small enterprises. Late in the year, both chambers voted, at the behest of the White House, to eliminate a Cold War–era barrier to normal trade relations with Russia.

At the same time, a few key votes in 2012 amounted to real defeats for the president. Those included a somewhat bipartisan vote by the House in June to find Attorney General Eric H. Holder Jr. in contempt for not cooperating with the chamber's inquiry into the Fast and Furious gun-tracking program involving Mexican drug cartels, and one by the Senate in November that limited the president's maneuvering room on the detainee prison at Guantánamo Bay, Cuba.

Obama also fell short in December of corralling the 67 votes he needed in the Senate to ratify an international treaty on the rights of people with disabilities that was modeled on U.S. law. Eight Republicans joined the 53 members of the Democratic caucus to support the treaty, but that was not enough.

In several cases, the president took his lumps from House Republicans but in ways that did not amount to an actual defeat. The chamber voted in April to offset the cost of low interest rates on college loans in a way that the White House opposed, but the House plan was abandoned in the Senate. Similar showcase votes occurred in July on health care, in November on immigration and in December on the spending sequester. In each case, however, the House position proved irrelevant in the end, other than to demonstrate differences between the parties.

The stories of the 24 key votes chosen for 2012 appear on the following pages.

HOUSE VOTES

72 Temporary Payroll Tax Cut

Passage of a bill to extend a Social Security payroll tax cut, unemployment benefits and Medicare payments to physicians.

After months of twists and turns, the House cleared the way in February for an extension of a payroll tax cut through the end of 2012, reducing the tax burden for the vast majority of households during a period of tepid economic growth.

The vote came relatively quickly and easily once House Republican leaders abandoned their demand that the cost of the tax cut be offset by spending cuts, a harbinger of the political dynamic later in the year that dogged action on fiscal-cliff and Superstorm Sandy legislation.

Before then, House and Senate leaders had been involved in protracted negotiations, highlighted by a short-term extension of the tax break and other temporary policies at the end of 2011 (PL 112-78). The 2 percentage point reduction in the 6.2 percent Social Security payroll tax on employees was first enacted in late 2010 (PL 111-312) as a response to the lingering recession.

Lawmakers attempted to resolve their differences in 2012 through a House-Senate conference committee. The panel, led by Republican Dave Camp of Michigan, chairman of the House Ways and Means Committee, featured civil discussions but saw little progress until Republicans made their crucial concession. Even then, lawmakers still needed to pay for an extension of long-term unemployment benefits and a Medicare fix to prevent payment cuts to doctors. One solution — a reduction in contributions to federal worker pensions — angered some Democrats, particularly those from Maryland, but not enough to derail the bill.

By the end, many Republicans were eager to move on from the payroll tax debate. The push for a deficit-neutral bill had come largely from House Republican freshmen, who disliked the tax break for its associations with stimulus spending and President Barack Obama. Nevertheless, Republican leaders came to realize that a fight over the payroll tax cut was not helping them politically, as Democrats relentlessly attacked them for obstructing tax relief for low- and middle-income families.

The final House vote on the payroll tax cut extension was 293-132. Among Republicans, the split was 146-91 in a solid but less-than-enthusiastic show of support for House Speaker John A. Boehner of Ohio.

After the Senate cleared the bill and Obama signed it (PL 112-96), the themes of the payroll tax cut debate lingered through the November elections, with Republicans fighting against the impression that they cared more about the rich than the middle class. However, the tax cut was not renewed at the end of the year, as Democrats decided to fight for other priorities.

HOUSE PASSED HR 3630 on Feb. 17, **293-132:** R 146-91; D 147-41. *(House vote 72, p. C-18; unemployment benefits, p. 7-8; Medicare physician payments, p. 9-4)*

132 Small-Business Startups

Passage of legislation to loosen securities regulations on smaller businesses in order to attract capital and foster job growth.

The vote was the culmination of a monthslong bipartisan push to ease financial regulations for some companies in the hope of spurring job creation. In a rare instance of agreement, congressional Republicans and the Obama administration concurred to boost the sluggish economy, and the vote showed the power of such an agreement.

Business leaders had long maintained that certain Securities and Exchange Commission rules should be relaxed to better reflect changing investment practices and to reduce regulatory costs for smaller companies. In September 2011, President Barack Obama joined that chorus when he urged Congress to "cut away the red tape that prevents too many rapidly growing startup companies from raising capital and going public."

In November 2011, the House passed several measures intended to do just that. One bill would have exempted registration with the SEC for companies that planned to sell $50 million in shares as part of a public offering — up from the existing threshold of $5 million. Another would have lifted an SEC ban on small, privately held companies using advertisements to solicit investors. A third bill would have permitted companies to employ "crowdfunding," or the use of social media and the Internet, to raise capital from the public without having to register with the SEC.

Although some senators introduced companion measures, the broader deregulation effort largely fell off the radar until House Majority Leader Eric Cantor, R-Va., bundled these bills together, as well as a few others, into a single piece of legislation. The bill, named the Jumpstart Our Business Startups Act, or JOBS Act, included new provisions to raise the threshold for the number of shareholders a company or bank could have before triggering SEC registration. It also included provisions to allow certain companies to sell shares to the public without complying with some audit requirements in the 2002 Sarbanes-Oxley law (PL 107-204).

On March 8, with Obama's endorsement, the House passed the measure 390-23. The Senate initially balked at the bill, which top securities experts and regulators had warned would leave the typical investor vulnerable to fraud. With Obama behind the legislation, though, the pressure on the Senate to act was enormous. Several attempts to add consumer protections were defeated; the lone amendment adopted, offered by Oregon Democrat Jeff Merkley, required individuals acting as crowdfunding intermediaries to register with the SEC.

The Senate then passed the amended bill, sending it back to the House, where it was quickly cleared (PL 112-106).

HOUSE CLEARED HR 3606 on March 27, **380-41:** R 235-0; D 145-41. *(House vote 132, p. C-18; Senate vote 55, p. C-15)*

151 Fiscal 2013 Budget Resolution

Adoption of a fiscal 2013 budget resolution written by House Republicans that called for significant spending cuts over a decade, new budgetary controls and a transition of Medicare from a fee-for-service entitlement to a premium support program for private insurance coverage.

The House and Senate once again were unable to agree on a budget resolution for fiscal 2013. The House adoption of a blueprint written

by Budget Chairman and GOP vice presidential nominee Paul D. Ryan of Wisconsin demonstrated both the stark partisan divide in the chamber and the determination of some Republicans to make deeper spending cuts than those required under the terms of a hard-fought 2011 debt limit deal (PL 112-25).

House leaders had to work harder to round up Republican votes for their fiscal 2013 budget resolution than they did for the fiscal 2012 edition. Although the tax and spending blueprint differed little from the previous year's offering, it did not call for spending cuts deep enough for some conservatives. No Democrat voted for the plan.

Dubbed "The Path to Prosperity" for the second consecutive year, the budget resolution (H Con Res 112) included a higher discretionary spending limit — $1.028 trillion — than many conservatives favored. That figure represented a middle ground between a smaller figure favored by conservatives and the $1.047 trillion discretionary limit imposed by the debt limit law. The plan was projected to reduce spending by $4 trillion over a decade. It assumed an overhaul of Medicare and Medicaid and simplification of the tax code.

The resolution would have led to a balanced budget by 2040. Some conservatives wanted a plan for achieving that goal in 10 years.

By the time the House voted, most GOP conservatives had accepted the discretionary cap, although some did so grudgingly. Six more Republicans voted against the budget resolution, however, than had opposed the fiscal 2012 version. The Republican dissenters included Budget Committee members Justin Amash of Michigan and Tim Huelskamp of Kansas, who were subsequently removed from the panel for the 113th Congress in a signal to others not to abandon the party on important votes.

The proposed Medicare rewrite was not particularly controversial among Republicans. The plan borrowed from a bipartisan measure offered by Ryan and Oregon Democratic Sen. Ron Wyden. Unlike the House's fiscal 2012 budget resolution, the Ryan-Wyden proposal in the fiscal 2013 version would have given seniors the option of choosing traditional Medicare or private health care coverage plans starting in 2023.

Another provision that enjoyed widespread support among Republicans was a reconciliation instruction directing House committees to find at least $261 billion in 10-year savings from mandatory programs as an alternative to most of the $109 billion in automatic spending cuts that were then scheduled to begin Jan. 2, 2013, under the debt limit law.

Because Ryan's budget faced solid Democratic opposition in the Senate, it once again had no chance of becoming a template for fiscal policy.

HOUSE ADOPTED H Con Res 112 on March 29, **228-191:** R 228-10; D 0-181. (*House vote 151, p. C-18; budget resolution, p. 4-9*)

195   Student Loans

Passage of a bill that would provide a one-year reprieve from a scheduled increase in student loan interest rates.

With President Barack Obama traveling the country in the spring to chastise Republicans for not renewing a 3.4 percent interest rate for subsidized college loans, House GOP leaders hastily responded with a remedy typical in this hyperpartisan age: a one-year extension of the interest rate, but with the estimated $6 billion cost to be paid for with money from the president's health care overhaul. That, of

course, was anathema to Obama; he called the bill a "politically motivated proposal and not a serious response" and said he would veto it if it reached him.

The subsequent maneuvering led to a House vote that illustrated not only the almost-routine opposition Obama faced in the midst of a presidential campaign, but also the fissures within each party. The GOP bill lost 30 Republican votes and would have been defeated had not 13 Democrats voted for it.

Congress had addressed the rising cost of college in a 2007 law (PL 110-84) that, among other things, started lowering the interest rate for subsidized Stafford Loans made to undergraduate students, to 3.4 percent from 6.8 percent. Because of the cost, though, the special rate was set to expire July 1, 2012. On that date, the rate would immediately revert to 6.8 percent.

Obama called for the lower rate to be extended. Republicans initially resisted, calling the idea a campaign ploy, but they shifted their stance after GOP presidential candidate Mitt Romney, a month away from wrapping up the nomination, agreed that Congress should preserve the low rate.

The problem was how to cover the budgetary cost. The House Republican bill would have drawn the money from the Prevention and Public Health Fund, created by the 2010 health care law (PL 111-148, PL 111-152), which provided money for programs designed to prevent tobacco use, obesity, heart disease, strokes and cancer.

Judy Biggert, R-Ill., the bill's sponsor, said the money for disease prevention was "nothing more than an open-ended fund that has no clear oversight or purpose." Other Republicans called it a slush fund for Health and Human Services Secretary Kathleen Sebelius.

Democrats who voted with Republicans on the bill included Collin C. Peterson of Minnesota, who had opposed Obama's health care overhaul, and his fellow Minnesotan Tim Walz, who issued a statement afterward in which he wrote, "While I strongly disagree with how this bill is paid for, I will not let politics get in the way of keeping college affordable." Democrat Timothy H. Bishop of New York explained to constituents that he expected the offsets in the bill to be changed in conference.

Some Democrats responded with a separate bill (HR 4816) that would have paid for the one-year loan rate extension by ending tax subsidies for oil and gas companies.

By the time the House Republican bill passed on April 27, the battle had already moved to the Senate, where a compromise was eventually worked out to extend the low interest rate for a year and to pay for it by changing two provisions of pension law and by shortening the time period for which students were eligible for the subsidized loans. Because these offsets raised more money than the loan bill cost, the language was added to a revenue-short highway and transit authorization bill that was passed in late June.

HOUSE PASSED HR 4628 on April 27, **215-195:** R 202-30; D 13-165. (*House vote 195, p. C-20; student loans, p. 9-7*)

270   Indefinite Detention of Terrorism Suspects

Rejection of an amendment to the defense authorization bill to ban indefinite detention of terrorism suspects captured in the United States.

When the House debated the fiscal 2013 defense authorization bill (HR 4310), its members had to decide between competing amendments on the detention of terrorism suspects. The split in the votes

illustrated divisions over the issue of the Guantánamo Bay, Cuba, detention facility and over civil liberties in general, particularly within the tea party movement. One amendment, offered by Louie Gohmert, R-Texas, was adopted, and a version of it became law. The other, by Adam Smith, D-Wash., and Justin Amash, R-Mich., was more ambitious in scope and drew a more politically diverse group of supporters, but ultimately it was rejected.

The Smith amendment brought together not only unlikely allies such as Smith and Amash but also groups as far apart as the liberal American Civil Liberties Union and the conservative Young Americans for Liberty. The amendment would have banned the indefinite detention of suspected terrorists without charge or trial if they were apprehended within the United States — something the Obama administration said it would never do. A similar amendment was offered to the Senate version of the bill and adopted on the floor, but it was left out of the final conference agreement.

The Smith amendment also split tea party Republicans, some of whom backed it because they considered indefinite detention an example of government overreach. Others favored the Gohmert amendment, which stated broadly that Americans detained in the United States on terrorism charges are entitled to all constitutional protections. Backers of the Smith amendment decried the Gohmert amendment as a do-nothing smokescreen that just restated rights already guaranteed. Republican leaders, though, rallied their troops behind it as an alternative to the Smith amendment. They also whipped up opposition to the Smith amendment by arguing that it would allow not just Americans but also foreign suspects the right to a trial in civilian courts that did not exist in law.

The Gohmert amendment, in modified form, appeared in the final conference agreement on the defense authorization measure.

HOUSE REJECTED the Smith amendment to HR 4310 on May 18, **182-238:** R 19-219; D 163-19. *(House vote 270, p. C-20; Senate vote 212, p. C-16; defense authorization, p. 6-3)*

441 Holder Contempt Resolution

Adoption of a resolution that cited Attorney General Eric H. Holder Jr. for contempt of Congress.

The House made history June 28 when it held Attorney General Eric H. Holder Jr. in contempt of Congress; it was the first time the nation's top law enforcement officer had faced that sanction.

Republicans brought the resolution (H Res 711) to the floor after Holder refused to provide documents sought by the House Oversight and Government Reform Committee pertaining to a law enforcement operation known as Fast and Furious, in which the Justice Department lost track of thousands of guns it had hoped to trace to drug cartels in Mexico. Two of those guns were later discovered at the murder scene of a U.S. Border Patrol agent in Arizona, prompting Republicans to launch a monthslong investigation into the operation and the Justice Department's handling of it.

Holder previously had testified about the operation before the Oversight panel and turned over thousands of pages of documents to its investigators, but he stopped short of providing everything the committee had sought. Instead, he invoked executive privilege before a committee hearing June 20, arguing that the documents

he was withholding could legally be shielded from congressional review. That prompted a contempt vote along party lines in the Oversight panel, with the full House following eight days later.

On the floor, all but two Republicans supported the contempt resolution, and nearly half of the House Democratic Caucus boycotted the vote, underscoring the intensely partisan nature of the resolution, which passed 255-67. Republicans accused Holder of ignoring congressional oversight powers, while Democrats defended him and said that the GOP had set up the vote to gain an advantage in a presidential election year. The National Rifle Association, which had long called on Holder to resign over the Fast and Furious scandal, scored the vote and gave lower marks to lawmakers who voted against the resolution.

Legally, the contempt resolution had little effect. Holder remained in office, while the House later sued him in federal court, hoping to obtain the documents it wanted through a judicial order.

HOUSE PASSED H Res 711 on June 28, **255-67:** R 238-2; D 17-65. *(House vote 441, p. C-20; Holder contempt resolution, p. 10-3)*

460 Repeal of Health Care Overhaul

Passage of a bill to repeal the 2010 health care law.

In the lead-up to the Supreme Court's ruling on the 2010 health care law, House Republicans said they would move to repeal whatever was left if the justices did not strike down the overhaul in its entirety. So once the high court announced its decision largely upholding the law, GOP leaders scheduled a vote on full repeal.

The symbolic response was a way to reiterate Republicans' commitment to undoing the overhaul and put lawmakers on the record once again before the November election. House Republicans had passed a measure (HR 2) in January 2011 to repeal the law, with support from three Democrats, but that bill never advanced in the Democrat-led Senate.

"By passing our repeal bill in July, we will give the Senate and Mr. Obama a second opportunity to follow the will of the American people," Speaker John A. Boehner, R-Ohio, wrote in the opinion section of the July 5 edition of The Washington Times.

In its June 28 decision, the Supreme Court ruled that the law's requirement that most individuals maintain health coverage or pay a penalty fell under Congress' taxing power, and Republicans seized on the tax label as a new line of attack. They also maintained, as the House began consideration of the bill July 10, that the overhaul stifled job growth and raised health care costs.

But Democrats criticized the GOP for not offering its own proposal to replace the law and slammed the vote as political theater and a waste of time. "The last thing the Congress should do is refight old political battles and take a massive step backward by repealing basic protections that provide security for the middle class," the Obama administration said in a July 9 statement threatening to veto the measure.

When the House passed the legislation July 11, five Democrats joined a unified Republican caucus in support of repeal: Dan Boren of Oklahoma, Mike McIntyre of North Carolina and Mike Ross of Arkansas — the three Democrats who voted for the 2011 repeal bill — as well as Larry Kissell of North Carolina and Jim Matheson of Utah.

As expected, the Senate never took up the bill or anything similar to it, and the effort died with the end of the 112th Congress.

HOUSE PASSED HR 6079 on July 11, **244-185**: R 239-0; D 5-185. *(House vote 460, p. C-20; health care law, p. 9-3)*

608 U.S.-Russia Trade Relations

Passage of legislation to establish permanent normal trade relations with Russia and Moldova. The bill also provided sanctions against individuals involved in human rights violations in Russia.

Efforts by business groups and the Obama administration to persuade Congress to normalize trade relations permanently with Russia began a year earlier, after the World Trade Organization agreed to accept Russian membership. The step was a requirement for the United States to be able to take full advantage of the lower trade barriers that came with Russia joining the WTO.

Mindful of China's poor trade record even after it was granted permanent normal trade relations with the United States, though, many lawmakers were initially reluctant to normalize trade relations with Russia. To do so would mean certifying that Russia was in full compliance with the Jackson-Vanik amendment, a Cold War measure (PL 93-618) prohibiting normal trade with any communist country that restricted emigration. In reality, since 1992 successive presidents had waived the restrictions of Jackson-Vanik and allowed normal trade with Russia, although only Congress could lift the law formally.

Human rights advocates in Congress also opposed improving trade ties with Russia without new methods to counteract the sorts of human rights violations that Russian President Vladimir V. Putin had been accused of and that had grown in number since Putin won a third term as president, earlier in 2012.

In order to win support from those and other lawmakers, the Obama administration agreed to borrow human rights provisions from bills that were approved in June by the Senate Foreign Relations and House Foreign Affairs committees and add them to the trade measure. They were named for attorney and anti-corruption activist Sergei Magnitsky, who died while in Russian police custody. The House language would sanction Russian human rights violators tied to the Magnitsky case, while the Senate version was more expansive, potentially targeting human rights violators anywhere in the world.

Those moves won the support of top lawmakers in both parties and cleared the way for legislative progress. Both the House Ways and Means and Senate Finance committees approved bills in July, with virtually no opposition.

Proponents of lifting Jackson-Vanik had hoped to pass the bill before, or shortly after, Russia joined the WTO. But congressional leaders were initially wary of bringing the measure to the floor. Organized labor had expressed some opposition to the bill, which might have siphoned off Democratic votes. Meanwhile, House GOP leaders did not want to force their incumbents to take a vote shortly before the 2012 elections that might make them appear soft on Putin.

After Congress returned from the elections, the obstacles to the bill appeared to melt away in the lame-duck session. Bearing the limited human rights provisions, the bill breezed through the House, with the support of nearly all Republicans and the vast majority of Democrats. House passage set up the Senate's vote to clear the bill for the president only a few weeks later.

HOUSE PASSED HR 6156 on Nov. 16, **365-43**: R 227-6; D 138-37. *(House vote 608, p. C-20; Senate vote 223, p. C-17; Russia trade relations, p. 6-13)*

613 STEM Visa Program

Passage of a bill that would create a visa program for foreign graduates of U.S. colleges and universities in high-tech fields.

Less than a month after Latino voters helped President Barack Obama win a second term, backing him over GOP challenger Mitt Romney by a nearly 3-to-1 margin, House Republicans set up a floor vote on a measure they said showed their willingness to work with Democrats on immigration — and perhaps win over some of those Latino voters.

In fact, the vote on the bill, which was to provide 55,000 additional green cards for highly skilled foreign-born graduates of American universities, laid down initial markers for an immigration debate that would unfold into 2013.

After the election, Speaker John A. Boehner of Ohio and other House Republicans made clear that they preferred an incremental, "step-by-step" approach to immigration that could involve a series of small immigration bills, such as the high-tech visa legislation. The Obama administration and many congressional Democrats wanted a comprehensive overhaul of immigration law.

That is why the White House said it opposed the House's high-tech visa bill, even though the administration generally backed the bill's underlying goal of admitting skilled workers. "The administration," explained a White House statement, "does not support narrowly tailored proposals that do not meet the president's long-term objectives with respect to comprehensive immigration reform."

The so-called STEM bill — referring to the science, technology, engineering and mathematics specialists the measure was to benefit — had been seen as an area of potential compromise in the tricky political terrain of immigration. Both parties had expressed support for the idea, and the sponsor, Rep. Lamar Smith, R-Texas, had negotiated with Sen. Charles E. Schumer, D-N.Y., for months in an effort to find common ground.

When it came time to vote, though, the House measure did not attract the support of Democrats, who said the Republican legislation pitted one group of immigrants against another by creating the additional visas for STEM workers by eliminating a separate "diversity" visa program that offered green cards through a lottery system.

Democrats also maintained that the bill did not do enough to keep families together throughout the immigration process and said that it would decrease overall immigration levels, since the number of high-tech visas available under the measure would have exceeded the number of beneficiaries.

The House passed the bill on a largely party-line vote, with Republicans accusing Democrats of blocking a broadly popular measure they said would have benefited businesses and boosted job creation. The Senate did not take up the issue before the end of the session.

HOUSE PASSED HR 6429 on Nov. 30, **245-139**: R 218-5; D 27-134. *(House vote 613, p. C-22)*

644 Sequester Replacement

Passage of a bill to replace the across-the-board spending cuts with a reduction in discretionary appropriations caps and $300 billion in other savings over 10 years.

With conservative Republicans balking at an attempt by Speaker John A. Boehner of Ohio to avert economic damage from the fiscal cliff by raising income taxes on people making more than $1 million a year, GOP party leaders offered a last-minute budgetary sweetener that they hoped would ease passage of the tax measure.

Boehner had hoped his tax bill would win support from a majority of his caucus and show the White House and congressional Democrats that Republicans were closing ranks against all but the smallest, most targeted tax increases. Democrats were pushing to raise taxes on households making $250,000 or more.

Despite Boehner's public statements that the tax bill would pass, conservatives remained unconvinced, objecting that the measure did not include any spending cuts. House leaders proposed the separate spending-reduction bill (HR 6684) at the last minute, during a Rules Committee meeting the night before the tax measure was to come to the floor. Although the goal was to win votes for the tax measure, the vote on the spending measure provided stark evidence not only of the deep partisan divide in the chamber but also of the difficulties Boehner had in rallying his caucus.

Angry Democrats staged a walkout of a Dec. 19 Rules panel meeting, accusing Republicans of forcing the spending bill to the floor right before the holiday recess in order to appease conservatives and to pressure Senate Democrats. The bill made it through the committee with only Republican votes.

"What I suspect is that you're going to stick this country with this dog, and you're going to take off," said Rep. Louise M. Slaughter, D-N.Y., the ranking Democrat on the Rules Committee. Referring to the Senate majority leader from Nevada, she said, "And you're going to say to Harry Reid, 'Well, screw you, Harry. You don't want to take up this bill? Well, tough.'"

The new measure was modeled on legislation that passed the House in May on a close vote, 218-199. The measure would have replaced the $98 billion automatic spending cut scheduled to start in January 2013 with a $19 billion reduction in spending caps and a $300 billion cut in entitlement spending over 10 years. The automatic cuts under the sequester had been required as part of an August 2011 spending deal that raised the debt ceiling (PL 112-25), but both parties had since tried to find ways to forestall them.

On Dec. 20, House leaders called up the spending bill before considering the tax proposal. The sequester replacement measure passed even more narrowly than before, 215-209, with 21 Republicans joining all Democrats in voting against it. More important, the spending measure did little to build GOP enthusiasm for Boehner's tax increase and, as a result, did not succeed in its original purpose. After spending hours trying to whip up conservative votes for the tax measure, House leaders admitted defeat and pulled the bill from the floor.

HOUSE PASSED HR 6684 on Dec. 20, **215-209:** R 215-21; D 0-188. *(House vote 644, p. C-22; Senate vote 251, p. C-17; fiscal cliff, p. 7-3)*

659 Tax Rate Extensions

Passage of legislation to extend most income tax rates set in 2001 and 2003 while allowing taxes for top-bracket taxpayers to rise.

Concluding a long battle over the extension of the George W. Bush administration's tax cuts, the Republican-controlled House voted to allow an income tax increase that many in the GOP opposed. While most expiring tax cuts were extended at a huge cost, an increased rate for top-bracket taxpayers provided a victory for President Barack Obama as he prepared to begin his second term.

The vote settled some of the most urgent tax issues that had loomed over Congress and the administration in previous years, but it pushed into the next Congress a broader tax overhaul that Republicans and Democrats alike said was needed.

Obama had long supported extending income tax cuts for earnings up to $250,000 for couples while allowing tax rates to revert to higher Clinton administration levels for those above that threshold. After Obama's re-election, it was clear that Republicans, who had staunchly resisted any tax increase, would have to give ground. House Speaker John A. Boehner, R-Ohio, said after the election that he would go along with up to $800 billion in new revenue, although the money, he said, should come from the curtailment of tax breaks rather than from tax rate increases.

Boehner and Obama resumed the fiscal negotiations they had pursued but ultimately abandoned during the 2011 debt limit debate. The goal for the renewed talks was to reach an agreement that would reduce the deficit by approximately $2 billion over 10 years. The two leaders came close in terms of spending and revenue targets but, once again, could not agree on specifics.

Boehner decided to advance a Plan B approach, which would have increased the tax rate only on income above $1 million. But the speaker abandoned that proposal when it appeared that a majority of Republicans would vote against it. After that embarrassment, Boehner left it to Senate leaders to negotiate a compromise.

A deal was struck between Senate Minority Leader Mitch McConnell, R-Ky., and White House negotiators, led by Vice President Joseph R. Biden Jr., to increase the top tax rate from 35 percent to 39.6 percent on joint income above $450,000. The resulting legislation also delayed automatic spending cuts for two months, extended federal benefits for the long-term unemployed for a year, kept farm programs operating through fiscal 2013 and deferred for a year a scheduled cut in Medicare payments to doctors.

The bill (HR 8) was passed on a bipartisan vote in the Senate, but House Republicans were a tougher sell. After considering a plan to amend the bill and send it back to the Senate, Republican leaders found enough GOP votes to clear the measure, with the support of House Democrats.

Although Democrats wondered whether they could have gotten a better deal by driving a harder bargain, Republicans emerged from the fight angry, somewhat disorganized and eager to cut spending in future budget battles.

HOUSE CLEARED HR 8 on Jan. 1, 2013, **257-167:** R 85-151; D 172-16. *(House vote 659, p. C-22; Senate vote 251, p. C-17; fiscal cliff, p. 7-3)*

SENATE VOTES

24 Religious Exemptions for Health Care

Rejection of an amendment to allow health insurance plans to deny coverage for provisions of medical services that run counter to the plan sponsor or employer's religious beliefs.

The narrow vote against the amendment from Missouri Republican Roy Blunt effectively doused Republicans' plans to continue fighting an Obama administration rule requiring insurance coverage of contraceptive services without sharing costs. It also served as one of the few times in 2012 that the Senate directly voted on modifying the 2010 health care overhaul. By opposing the amendment, Senate Democrats showed they would continue to defend the law.

For weeks in early 2012, Republicans' opposition to the rule gained headlines and national attention. The debate tapped into several contentious areas: the health care law, women's health issues and religious freedom.

GOP leaders maintained that the rule violated religious freedoms of employers that did not qualify as religious institutions, which were exempt from its requirements. Supporters, meanwhile, defended it as necessary to protect women's health and an important part of the health care law's coverage of preventive services.

In early February, House Speaker John A. Boehner, R-Ohio, made a rare floor speech pledging to undo the rule and put the Energy and Commerce Committee in charge of finding a legislative way to reverse it.

Blunt introduced a proposal that would have allowed health plans to deny coverage for services that were against the plan sponsor's or employer's religious beliefs, similar to a House measure from Rep. Jeff Fortenberry, R-Neb. Blunt offered his measure as an amendment to a highway funding bill Feb. 9, but Senate Majority Leader Harry Reid, D-Nev., blocked it.

The next day, the administration clarified its rule to say that religiously affiliated hospitals, charities and other institutions would not have to pay for coverage of contraception and that their insurance plans would offer it directly to employees instead.

Republicans, however, vowed to fight on, saying the modification was insufficient. A few days later, Reid changed his position and said he would allow the vote on the Blunt amendment.

The Senate turned back the amendment 51-48 on March 1, with Maine Republican Olympia J. Snowe joining most Democrats in opposition and three Democrats — Bob Casey of Pennsylvania, Ben Nelson of Nebraska and Joe Manchin III of West Virginia — supporting it.

Following that vote, the contraception issue lost momentum. House leaders never brought legislation to the floor or held a committee markup on the issue. Fortenberry acknowledged in March that progress had stalled, although he still pushed for action on his bill.

By May, a senior Senate leadership aide was urging Republicans to stay away from the contraception fight. GOP leaders let the issue drop, and the debate then moved to several legal challenges.

SENATE AGREED to a motion to table the Blunt, R-Mo., amendment to the Reid, D-Nev., amendment to S 1813 on March 1, **51-48:** D 48-3; R 1-45; I 2-0. *(Senate vote 24, p. C-15; health care law, p. 9-3)*

34 Keystone XL Pipeline

Rejection of an amendment to the surface transportation authorization bill that would have required immediate federal approval of the Keystone XL oil pipeline from Canada without further executive branch review.

President Barack Obama survived a test of his power in March when the Senate narrowly defeated an attempt to strip him of authority to review the Keystone XL pipeline project. While a majority of senators supported the proposal by North Dakota Republican John Hoeven, the 56-42 vote fell short of a 60-vote threshold set by unanimous consent.

The vote had more of a political than a practical impact on the project, since TransCanada, the company developing the pipeline between Canada's tar sands and Gulf Coast refineries, was trying at the time to map a new route that would skirt environmentally sensitive areas in Nebraska. Citing Nebraska's concerns, Obama had deferred a decision until after the election.

Republicans were determined not to let the president duck the politically tough decision. A GOP-backed rider on a payroll tax cut law enacted late in 2011 had required the government to make a final decision on the pipeline by Feb. 21, 2012. Obama rejected the application, saying the deadline was unrealistic, although he invited the project developer to reapply when it had completed its revised plan. Hoeven's amendment was designed to reverse that decision by allowing Trans-Canada to begin construction without waiting for Nebraska to approve the new route — and without further review by the State Department, which was required to approve such projects crossing the U.S. border.

Hoeven's amendment put Obama in a difficult position. A coalition of business and labor groups was pressing him to sign off on the project because it would create jobs. But the president faced furious opposition from environmental groups important to his re-election. Those groups contended that expanding oil production in Alberta's vast tar sands would accelerate global warming.

The outcome remained uncertain as debate on the amendment began. The Senate dispatched, with a 33-65 vote, Oregon Democrat Ron Wyden's competing proposal to set a 90-day deadline for a presidential decision and to bar the export of any oil transported through the pipeline. The focus turned to whether Hoeven could attract enough Democrats to reach the 60-vote threshold agreed to by both parties.

Hoeven, a former governor of a state in the midst of an oil and natural-gas boom, said on the Senate floor that the vote offered a "clear choice" between energy security and continued reliance on oil from unstable parts of the world. In response to assertions that the amendment would improperly usurp executive authority, Hoeven secured an opinion from the nonpartisan Congressional Research Service that affirmed Congress' constitutional authority to approve the project.

Eleven Democrats joined all 45 Republican senators present in voting for the amendment. Democratic supporters of the measure included senators from states that produced fossil fuels, such as Finance Chairman Max Baucus of Montana and Budget Chairman Kent Conrad of North Dakota, as well as some from Republican-leaning Southern states, such as Kay Hagan of North Carolina and Mark Pryor of Arkansas.

The vote still left supporters of the amendment four votes shy of what they needed. Keystone remained a political talking point as the 2012 political campaign unfolded, but the Senate showdown in March marked the last serious legislative attempt that year to challenge Obama's authority to decide the issue.

SENATE REJECTED the Keystone pipeline amendment to a surface transportation authorization (S 1813) on March 8, **56-42:** D 11-40; R 45-0; I 0-2. *(Senate vote 34, p. C-15; Keystone XL pipeline, p. 8-3)*

55 Small-Business Startups

Passage of legislation to loosen securities regulations on smaller businesses to encourage capital formation and foster job growth.

The Senate's lopsided vote to pass bipartisan House legislation to ease financial rules for companies with the hope of spurring job creation belied the misgivings of a number of lawmakers and took place only after the Senate rejected attempts by Democrats to add protections for consumers.

Securities experts and regulators worried that by raising the threshold for federal regulation of companies — for instance, by allowing them to sell $50 million in stock, rather than $5 million, before having to register with the Securities and Exchange Commission — and lifting other regulations for small companies, Congress would leave investors vulnerable to fraud.

President Barack Obama's endorsement of the legislation, though, made it difficult for congressional Democrats to head off or amend the bill. In September 2011, Obama had urged Congress to "cut away the red tape that prevents too many rapidly growing startup companies from raising capital and going public."

The bill that the House passed, 390-23, on March 8 with Obama's blessing was actually a bundle of several measures designed to ease regulation and help smaller companies raise capital. Assembled by House Majority Leader Eric Cantor of Virginia and called the Jumpstart Our Business Startups Act, or JOBS Act, it included new language to raise the threshold for the number of shareholders a company or bank could have before triggering SEC registration. It also included provisions to allow certain companies to sell shares to the public without complying with some audit requirements in the 2002 Sarbanes-Oxley law (PL 107-204).

The Senate initially balked at the bill. Democratic leaders in the Senate promised to introduce their own version, which they said would also help smaller companies raise capital but would include enhanced protections for consumers.

However, a few days later, Senate Democrats reversed course and decided not to advance their own bill, largely because of the overwhelming vote for passage in the House and the president's support for the measure. Still, some Senate Democrats, including Jack Reed of Rhode Island, Carl Levin of Michigan and Jeff Merkley of Oregon, sought to delay the fast-moving measure in hopes of making changes.

The Senate considered several amendments to the bill, but they were mostly felled by GOP opposition. A broad substitute amendment sponsored by the Democratic critics was rejected, as was an amendment to reauthorize the Export-Import Bank. The Senate also rejected a Reed amendment that would have required more companies to register with the SEC. The Senate did adopt one amendment, sponsored by Merkley, to require individuals acting as

"crowdfunding" intermediaries to register with the SEC.

The Senate then passed the amended bill with unanimous GOP backing and an almost even division among Democrats. That paved the way for the House to clear the bill for Obama's signature the following week (PL 112-106).

SENATE PASSED HR 3606 on March 22, **73-26:** R 46-0; D 26-25; I 1-1. *(Senate vote 55, p. C-15; House vote 132, p. C-18; Export-Import Bank, p. 7-9)*

68 Union Election Rules

Rejection of a GOP bid to block a federal rule speeding up union elections.

In a year that otherwise saw little action on labor legislation, this Senate vote served as an important election season statement from both parties on the issue of union organizing. Republicans used the vote to try to protect businesses and bash the Obama administration, while Democrats sided with their labor union allies.

The April 24 Senate vote was on a GOP-sponsored joint resolution aimed at blocking a National Labor Relations Board rule that would speed up union elections by postponing voter eligibility lawsuits until after the workers' vote. According to the NLRB, employers could stall a unionization vote for months by filing such lawsuits.

During debate before the vote, Republicans maintained that the rule would result in "ambush elections" that would deny employers their First Amendment right to speak to their employees and try to persuade them not to vote for a union. Republicans also depicted the rule as the administration's latest attempt to curry favor with unions, whose fundraising prowess was helping President Barack Obama as he campaigned for re-election.

The NLRB "seems hell-bent on changing processes across the board more for a political reason than a substantive reason," Lindsey Graham, R-S.C, said during floor debate. Michael B. Enzi, R-Wyo., the resolution's sponsor, called the rule "reckless," adding: "It's kind of like Thelma and Louise driving off a cliff. I, for one, do not want to see the NLRB driving the economy off a cliff."

Democrats, however, strongly supported the NLRB rule, saying it was a common-sense fix to ensure fair and timely elections. Tom Harkin, D-Iowa, called the resolution a "Republican assault on unions," adding that Republicans were using the new rule as an "election year political football."

The White House threatened to veto the measure if it got that far, saying in a statement that it was "committed to supporting the right of workers to join and participate in a union and bargain for fair wages, benefits and a safe workplace." The resolution "attacks these bedrock values," the statement said.

Interest groups heavily lobbied senators in advance of the vote. On one side were business groups, including the U.S. Chamber of Commerce and the National Retail Federation; on the other were unions, including the AFL-CIO.

In the end, the Senate rejected the measure by a simple majority, 45-54. Lisa Murkowski of Alaska was the only Republican to vote no. The House did not take up its companion resolution.

The NLRB rule went into effect on April 30, but business groups challenged it in court. In May, a federal judge at the U.S. District Court for the District of Columbia ruled the NLRB's action invalid because only two board members voted on the rule and at least three were needed for a quorum.

SENATE REJECTED S J Res 36 on April 24, **45-54:** D 0-51; R 45-1; I 0-2. *(Senate vote 68, p. C-15)*

98 Fiscal 2013 Budget Resolution

Rejection of a motion to take up a fiscal 2013 budget resolution adopted by the House that called for significant spending cuts over a decade, new budgetary controls and a future change in how Medicare provided health care for seniors.

The Senate Democratic majority's rejection of the fiscal 2013 budget blueprint written by House Republicans, a near replay of what happened a year earlier, reinforced the stark differences between the two parties' fiscal policies and signaled that Congress would once again be unable to agree on an annual budget resolution.

With Democratic leaders refusing for a third year in a row to bring any budget resolution to the floor, Republicans charged that, once again, Democrats were afraid to lay out their own spending plans. Budget Chairman Kent Conrad, D-N.D., said a budget resolution was unnecessary because the 2011 debt limit law (PL 112-25) set the annual discretionary-spending cap that a budget resolution would normally provide.

All Democrats and the Senate's two independents voted against taking up the House budget resolution, mirroring the united opposition to it among House Democrats. Five Senate Republicans voted against consideration of the House proposal.

Dubbed "The Path to Prosperity," the fiscal 2013 budget resolution (H Con Res 112) written by House Budget Chairman and eventual GOP vice presidential nominee Paul D. Ryan, R-Wis., proposed a discretionary spending limit of $1.028 trillion, $19 billion below the $1.047 trillion cap in the debt limit law. That discrepancy in the two caps resulted in the House and Senate proceeding on different appropriations tracks, with the Senate marking up bills at the higher limit and the House sticking with its lower cap. The House eventually acceded to the $1.047 trillion limit in a six-month stopgap funding measure (PL 112-75) that funded government operations through March 27, 2013.

The Ryan budget proposed to reduce spending by $4 trillion over a decade, in part by converting Medicaid to a block grant. A proposed Medicare change would have given seniors the option of taking subsidies for private insurance rather than the traditional fee-for-service program beginning in 2023. The premium support proposal was based on a plan crafted by Ryan and Oregon Democratic Sen. Ron Wyden. Wyden, however, denounced the plan as differing from his concept in important respects.

SENATE REJECTED a motion to proceed to H Con Res 112 on May 16, **41-58:** R 41-5; D 0-51; I 0-2. *(Senate vote 98, p. C-15; House vote 151, p. C-18; budget resolution, p. 4-9)*

164 Farm Bill Reauthorization

Passage of a five-year reauthorization of farm and nutrition programs.

Some groups had privately begun doubting Congress could produce a five-year farm bill in 2012 before Senate Agriculture Chairwoman Debbie Stabenow moved her bill to the floor in June. It was an unusual action, because the House Agriculture Committee traditionally had been the first to write the bill that sets policy for agriculture, nutrition, conservation, rural development and other areas.

But Stabenow, D-Mich., hoped to build pressure for action in the House with a bipartisan vote in her chamber. She said her House counterpart, Frank D. Lucas, R-Okla., faced an unfavorable environment for taking the lead in writing a farm bill.

In April, Stabenow and the committee's ranking Republican, Pat Roberts of Kansas, took less than five hours to move the bill (S 3240) through the panel despite opposition from several Southern members. The Southerners said the legislation's new insurance-like revenue protection plan disproportionately favored Midwest growers. To help fund the plan, Stabenow and Roberts shifted much of the $5 billion a year in annual direct payments to the new revenue plan. The legislation would have created a separate program for cotton farmers to address a World Trade Organization ruling that the United States needed to change its cotton subsidy program to comply with trade rules. In that ruling, Brazil won the right to impose more than $800 million in retaliatory import taxes against U.S. industries such as automobiles and financial services.

On the floor, the bill idled after cloture was invoked June 7. Over the course of six days, Stabenow and Roberts were largely able to defeat amendments on changes to the sugar program and the Supplemental Nutrition Assistance Program that they thought could stall the bill in the Senate or cause problems in negotiations with the House on a compromise measure.

The Senate passed the bill June 21 on a 64-35 vote. Forty-six Democrats and 16 Republicans voted for the legislation, while 30 Republicans and five Democrats voted against it.

Even with Stabenow's and Roberts' efforts, the measure turned out to be the only long-term reauthorization of farm programs to pass a chamber. The House Agriculture Committee approved its bill (HR 6083) in July, but Republican leaders kept the bill off the floor. Conservatives said the proposed level of cuts to SNAP was not enough — and Democrats said it was too high — so House leaders knew they could not get enough support for the measure to pass. In the end, lawmakers settled Jan. 1, 2013, on a one-year extension of the 2008 law, which had been allowed to expire in September, a rare occurrence in farm bill history.

SENATE PASSED S 3240 on June 21, **64-35:** D 46-5; R 16-30; I 2-0. *(Senate vote 164, p. C-16; farm bill, p. 3-3)*

187 Cybersecurity Standards

Rejection of a motion to end debate on a bill that would have created cybersecurity standards for industry.

The vote was a rebuff to the Obama administration and Senate Democratic leaders, who had made the cybersecurity legislation a top national security priority, and a sign of the power of business groups such as the U.S. Chamber of Commerce that shared ideological common ground with the majority of Senate Republicans on the issue. Although both sides acknowledged the dire nature of the threat, they became hung up over the proper role of the government in how best to defend computer networks from attack, dooming any congressional action on cybersecurity.

At the beginning of 2012, a group of mostly Senate Democrats working at the behest of Senate Majority Leader Harry Reid, D-Nev., produced a bill that would have created mandatory security standards for the nation's most vital digital infrastructure that was owned by the private sector. The White House endorsed the legislation, but once

business groups came out in opposition to the bill, calling it inflexible and expensive, its authors were forced to modify it toward a more voluntary approach where businesses would receive incentives such as liability protection for adopting security standards.

That change was enough to clear the path to floor debate. But while the Obama administration accepted the watered-down measure, it was not enough to win over Republicans and business lobbyists, who contended that the voluntary standards could become mandatory in practice and that the incentives were not enough in exchange. Although the two sides worked behind closed doors to find a compromise, they could not, and in the meantime a large stack of amendments piled up, some of them unrelated to cybersecurity. Republicans filibustered the bill absent an agreement on amendments, and while a handful of GOP senators voted to invoke cloture Aug. 2, Democrats fell short of the 60 votes needed to move forward and blamed business lobbying for the bill's demise.

Republicans said the Senate could have taken up a House-passed bill that was centered on fostering information sharing about cybersecurity threats between businesses and the federal government. The bill had come out of the House with some Democratic support. But backers of the Senate bill, which also contained information-sharing provisions, said any legislation without security standards for industry was woefully inadequate. Although Reid made a second attempt to end debate on the bill in November, it was never expected to succeed; the vote in August sealed the fate of cybersecurity legislation for the year.

SENATE REJECTED a motion to invoke cloture on S 3414 on Aug. 2, **52-46:** R 5-40; D 45-6; I 2-0. *(Senate vote 187, p. C-16; cybersecurity, p. 6-8)*

212 Guantánamo Bay Detainees

Approval of an amendment to the fiscal 2013 defense authorization bill blocking transfer of Guantánamo Bay detainees to the United States.

The vote exemplified one of the major reasons President Barack Obama was unable to close the Guantánamo Bay Naval Base detention center in Cuba: Even a Senate controlled by his own party was willing to tie Obama's hands on the methods with which he could move detainees out of the facility. The amendment attracted significant Democratic support, despite Armed Services Chairman Carl Levin, D-Mich., labeling it "veto bait."

If Obama was to close Guantánamo — which he said was a symbol that served as a terrorist recruitment tool in the Arab world — he needed to be able to either ship detainees to other countries or conduct trials that freed or convicted them but kept them elsewhere during their sentences. The amendment to the defense authorization bill offered by Kelly Ayotte, R-N.H., would have blocked several of those options, such as trial in federal court or detention in a domestic prison.

Ayotte said it was too dangerous to have ex-Guantánamo detainees on U.S. soil and that the Guantánamo facility was ample for the United States' needs. But many Democrats said there were already terrorists kept safely in U.S. prisons and that Ayotte's amendment would place too many restrictions on the executive branch.

However, nine Democrats still voted for the amendment, along with every Republican present and one independent, Joseph I. Lieberman of Connecticut, giving it more than enough votes to succeed.

Republicans used the debate over Guantánamo to portray Democrats as soft on national security, and Democrats who lacked safe seats and emphasized national security issues or represented states that leaned right tended to vote with Republicans on the issue.

A similar but more restrictive amendment was adopted to the defense authorization measure in the House. It would have mandated that all detainee trials be conducted at Guantánamo. Both the Ayotte amendment and the House amendment were left out of the final version of the bill to avoid a threatened White House veto.

SENATE ADOPTED the Ayotte amendment to the fiscal 2013 defense authorization bill (S 3254, HR 4310) on Nov. 29, **54-41:** D 9-40; R 44-0; I 1-1. *(Senate vote 212, p. C-16; House vote 270, p. C-20; defense authorization, p. 6-3)*

215 Iran Sanctions

Adoption of an amendment to the fiscal 2013 defense authorization bill to blacklist Iran's energy and shipping sectors.

The White House succeeded in watering down Congress' latest Iran sanctions initiative. But lawmakers demonstrated their determination to press for a tougher policy toward Iran by forcing a reluctant administration to accept another round of sanctions. A Senate amendment containing the new sanctions was adopted without a dissenting vote.

The measure, attached to the annual defense authorization bill, was intended to put additional economic pressure on Tehran as it mulled a new round of diplomatic negotiations on its nuclear program.

Sens. Robert Menendez, D-N.J., and Mark S. Kirk, R-Ill., who sponsored the amendment to the defense bill, initially considered restrictions that would have effectively imposed an international trade embargo by requiring all countries to reduce non-petroleum sales to Iran significantly. The senators also wanted to force other countries to freeze Iranian foreign-currency reserves.

The administration warned that such moves could cause a diplomatic backlash. And with the help of Armed Services Chairman Carl Levin, D-Mich., the manager of the defense bill; Foreign Relations Chairman John Kerry, D-Mass.; and Banking Chairman Tim Johnson, D-S.D., the White House persuaded Kirk and Menendez to delete or dilute some of their toughest language.

The measure barred all transactions with Tehran's energy, shipping and shipbuilding sectors and its ports, as well as sales to Iran of metals including graphite, aluminum, steel and metallurgical coal used in those sectors and in other manufacturing. The law also sanctioned Iran's state broadcaster and its president, as well as anyone found to be diverting some humanitarian goods, for human rights violations.

The legislation continued to allow countries to buy oil from Iran if they demonstrated every 180 days that they had significantly reduced their purchases. As amended, the president could waive the restriction for 120 days if a nation "faced exceptional circumstances that prevented it from significantly reducing purchases."

The Senate provisions survived almost entirely intact in the final version of the defense authorization bill (PL 112-239). After modifying the amendment before it was offered, its supporters were not interested in seeing it changed very much in conference with the House.

Much of the new sanctions language came from proposals left out of legislation that President Barack Obama reluctantly signed into law in August. That law expanded sanctions targeting financial institutions, including Iran's Central Bank, that Tehran used to facilitate its oil trade and maintain its economy. It also went after the National Iranian Oil Company and the National Iranian Tanker Company, the state-run oil and shipping conglomerates, and companies that did business with them.

SENATE ADOPTED the Menendez amendment to S 3254, Nov. 30, **94-0:** R 43-0; D 49-0; I 2-0. *(Senate vote 215, p. C-16; Iran sanctions, p. 6-10)*

219 International Treaty on Disability Rights

Refusal to ratify a multilateral treaty that sought to bring foreign disabilities rights laws up to U.S. standards.

Although outnumbered, conservative Republicans in the Senate, backed by outside groups such as Heritage Action, retained enough voting power to prevent ratification of a popular multilateral treaty modeled on the Americans with Disabilities Act that the Senate had passed two decades earlier with just eight dissenting votes.

Thirty-eight Republicans voted against the U.N. Convention on the Rights of Persons with Disabilities, enough to deny the treaty the two-thirds majority necessary for ratification. The dissenters said the treaty was unnecessary and that it might compromise U.S. sovereignty, with international tribunals intruding in domestic policy on issues such as child care and abortion.

As the Senate prepared for debate after Thanksgiving, one critic, Republican Mike Lee of Utah, said opponents had the votes to block the treaty. Even the presence on the floor of 89-year-old former Sen. Robert Dole, the Kansas Republican who drove the ADA through the Senate in 1990, did not change the outcome.

Senate Foreign Relations Chairman John Kerry of Massachusetts, who shepherded the bill through his committee by a 13-6 vote, declared it "one of the saddest days I've seen in almost 28 years in the Senate."

"It needs to be a wake-up call about a broken institution," Kerry said. "Today the dysfunction hurt veterans and the disabled, and that's unacceptable."

The treaty would have brought other countries up to U.S. standards on the treatment of those with disabilities. It had been widely supported by disability rights groups and veterans organizations, as well as former officials from both Republican and Democratic administrations. Republican Sens. John McCain of Arizona and John Barrasso of Wyoming were leading backers.

But Heritage Action, an advocacy arm of the Heritage Foundation, warned senators that it would keep score of those who backed the treaty. Many Republicans, in fact, had signed a letter to Majority Leader Harry Reid, D-Nev., that they would oppose any treaty taken up during the lame duck-session of Congress that followed the November election.

Just one of the 36 GOP senators who signed that letter, Scott P. Brown of Massachusetts, voted for the disability treaty.

SENATE REJECTED ratification of Treaty Doc 112-7 on Dec. 4, **61-38:** D 51-0; R 8-38; I 2-0. *(Senate vote 219, p. C-16)*

223 U.S.-Russia Trade Relations

Passage of legislation to establish permanent normal trade relations with Russia and Moldova. The bill also provided sanctions against individuals involved in human rights violations in Russia.

The historic vote to lift Cold War-era trade restrictions on Russia, after nearly four decades, was a big win for U.S. business and the Obama administration, which had begun lobbying Congress to take the step soon after the World Trade Organization approved Russia's membership in December 2011.

For U.S. businesses to take full advantage of the lowered trade barriers that came with Russia's joining the WTO, the United States had to establish permanent normal trade relations and lift the 1974 sanctions known as Jackson-Vanik, which had targeted communist countries that restricted Jewish emigration.

Although the step had broad support, relations with Russia were still sensitive, on Capitol Hill at least. Senate leaders wanted to wait for the House to act, and House leaders were wary of bringing the bill to the floor before the November elections for fear it might make lawmakers look soft on Russian President Vladimir V. Putin.

To win the backing of lawmakers concerned about human rights violations during Putin's tenure, the administration agreed to support attaching provisions to the legislation that would sanction human rights violators. The Senate Foreign Relations and Finance committees approved language that would have targeted such violators anywhere in the world and named the provision for attorney and anti-corruption activist Sergei Magnitsky, who died while in Russian police custody.

Proponents of the bill, who argued that it would boost U.S. exports and create jobs, had hoped it would pass before or shortly after Russia formally joined the WTO in August 2012.

Early in the lame-duck session, the House took up the measure and passed it easily. The bill included human rights provisions that differed from those backed by the Senate committees, imposing sanctions only on human rights violators who were tied to the Magnitsky case.

Despite concerns from Sen. Benjamin L. Cardin, a Maryland Democrat, and other human rights advocates, the Senate took up the measure a few weeks later. The Senate then passed the bill without trying to amend it, and it was cleared for the president's signature with overwhelming bipartisan support.

SENATE PASSED HR 6156 on Dec. 6, **92-4:** R 46-0; D 45-3; I 1-1. *(Senate vote 223, p. C-17; House vote 608, p. C-20; Russia trade relations, p. 6-13)*

248 Sandy Emergency Relief

Passage of a $60.4 billion supplemental emergency aid package for mid-Atlantic communities damaged by Superstorm Sandy in late October.

In 17 of the 22 budget years from fiscal 1989 through 2010, lawmakers appropriated supplemental funds to help communities hit by natural disasters, according to the Congressional Research Service.

But the willingness to shell out extra money for disaster relief had decreased significantly in the previous few years, for several reasons. First, Congress had greatly increased its initial appropriations for the Disaster Relief Fund in the hope of being able to avoid the need for emergency appropriations bills. More significant, though, was a growing anti-spending culture, especially in the House, that no longer tolerated extra appropriations without offsetting cuts in programs elsewhere.

Robert B. Aderholt, R-Ala., chairman of the House Homeland Security Appropriations Subcommittee, said during the summer that funding disaster relief through supplementals "is simply an irresponsible gimmick," as it put spending outside of budget caps.

And so Congress essentially ignored devastation in 2012 from an active tornado season, wildfires in Colorado and intense summer thunderstorms from the Midwest to the mid-Atlantic. But when a superstorm named Sandy rocked the East Coast, destroying homes and businesses from Delaware to Connecticut, lawmakers were hard-pressed to look the other way. Governors and mayors demanded federal assistance, and President Barack Obama promised it — to the tune of $60 billion.

Even though such legislation usually started in the House, the Senate took the lead, using a House-passed appropriations bill from 2011. After two weeks of debate on the $60.4 billion recovery package, the Senate passed it before leaving town for Christmas.

Of course, passage was not as simple as Democratic leaders had hoped it would be. Patrick J. Toomey, a Pennsylvania Republican, succeeded in stripping the emergency designation from $3.4 billion to be provided for longer-term Army Corps of Engineers projects intended to better protect communities from future storms. Maryland Democrat Barbara A. Mikulski called this a "dangerous precedent" and noted that cuts would be needed elsewhere in the federal budget to make up for the Army Corps spending. Toomey argued that such spending for longer-term projects should be provided through the regular appropriations process.

Democrats did beat back a perhaps bigger threat, which came in the form of a pared-down alternative offered by Indiana Republican Dan Coats. His $23.8 billion measure addressed the immediate needs of communities pummeled by the storm and would have had a better chance for passage in the House. But Coats' alternative failed to gain traction. Four Republicans — Olympia J. Snowe and Susan Collins of Maine, Rand Paul of Kentucky, and Scott P. Brown of Massachusetts — broke ranks to join Democrats in defeating Coats' alternative.

In the end, a dozen Republicans joined Democrats in the 62-32 vote to pass the Sandy recovery bill, with much of the GOP support coming from members from hurricane-prone Gulf Coast states.

The solid vote and bipartisan outcome also sent a message to House leaders that, this time at least, the public cry for disaster relief outweighed party politics, even when it came to spending more than $60 billion.

Speaker John A. Boehner of Ohio tried to ignore that message, choosing to conclude the 112th Congress without taking up the Senate disaster aid bill. But a loud, public and immediate uproar from Northeastern Republicans, particularly New York Rep. Peter T.

King and New Jersey Gov. Chris Christie, led the speaker to retreat quickly. Boehner scheduled a vote on Jan. 4, 2013 — the second day of the 113th Congress — on flood insurance provisions of the Senate bill and another on Jan. 15, on disaster relief money.

SENATE PASSED HR 1 on Dec. 28, **62-32:** D 48-0; R 12-32; I 2-0. *(Senate vote 248, p. C-17; disaster aid, p. 2-16)*

251   Tax Rates Extension   ■

Passage of a bill to extend a host of tax cuts while allowing taxes to rise on high-income earners.

After talks broke down for the last time between President Barack Obama and House Speaker John A. Boehner, R-Ohio, it was left to the Senate to take a lead role in averting the full brunt of what had become known as the fiscal cliff.

The eventual compromise was largely crafted by Senate Minority Leader Mitch McConnell, R-Ky., and Vice President Joseph R. Biden Jr. after negotiations between McConnell and Senate Majority Leader Harry Reid, D-Nev., also reached a dead end.

The bill allowed, for the first time in two decades, the top marginal tax rate to rise on family income of more than $450,000 while permanently extending lower tax rates on income below that threshold. The top tax rates on capital gains, dividends and large estates also were allowed to go up.

To satisfy the constitutional requirement that revenue measures originate in the House, the Senate voted on the McConnell-Biden measure as a substitute amendment to a House-passed tax bill.

The order of events was considered important because House Republicans were never going to vote for a tax increase, or even allow a bill to come to the floor, unless the Senate acted first.

Once an agreement had been reached at the leadership level, the Senate vote was a formality. In the early morning hours of Jan. 1, 2013, the legislation was passed 89-8, with even some staunch conservatives such as Patrick J. Toomey, R-Pa., and Jeff Sessions, R-Ala., voting "yea" because they saw the legislation as the only way to avoid a broader tax increase.

The lopsided vote made it even more difficult for House leaders to stall on the bill. Hours later, after a day of closed-door strategy meetings and vote counting, GOP leaders allowed a vote on the Senate-passed bill, and allowed the measure to clear without a majority of Republicans supporting it.

SENATE PASSED HR 8 on Jan. 1, 2013, **89-8:** D 47-3; R 40-5; I 2-0. *(Senate vote 251, p. C-17; House vote 659, p. C-22; fiscal cliff, p. 7-3)* ■

IN THE SENATE | By Vote Number

24. **S 1813. Surface Transportation Authorization/Religious Exemptions for Health Care.** Murray, D-Wash., motion to table (kill) the Blunt, R-Mo., amendment to the Reid, D-Nev., amendment. The Blunt amendment would allow health insurance plans to deny coverage for medical services that run counter to the plan sponsor's or employer's religious beliefs. It also would establish a private right of legal action for enforcement of the coverage exemptions. The Reid amendment would add safety, revenue and public transit titles to a bill that would authorize federal highway programs for two years. Motion agreed to 51-48: D 48-3; R 1-45; I 2-0. A "yea" was a vote in support of the president's position. March 1, 2012. *(Story, p. C-9)*

34. **S 1813. Surface Transportation Authorization/Keystone XL Pipeline.** Hoeven, R-N.D., amendment that would provide for approval of the Keystone XL pipeline between Canada and Gulf Coast refineries. It would require that the route for the pipeline in Nebraska be submitted by the state of Nebraska. It also would provide for certain environmental protections. Rejected 56-42: D 11-40; R 45-0; I 0-2. (By unanimous consent, the Senate agreed to raise the majority requirement for adoption of the Hoeven amendment to 60 votes.) A "nay" was a vote in support of the president's position. March 8, 2012. *(Story, p. C-9)*

55. **HR 3606. Small-Business Startups/Passage.** Passage of the bill that would define "emerging growth companies" and exempt them from certain independent auditing requirements. It would increase from $5 million to $50 million the annual public offering threshold for companies to be exempt from full Securities and Exchange Commission filing requirements and raise the number of shareholders that would trigger mandatory SEC registration from 750 to 2,000. It also would raise to 2,000 the number of shareholders that would trigger a requirement for SEC registration for a bank. The bill would lift an SEC ban that prevents small, privately held companies from using advertisements to solicit investors and allow companies to sell up to $1 million worth of securities. As amended, it also would require anyone acting as a "crowdfunding" intermediary to register with securities regulators. Passed 73-26: D 26-25; R 46-0; I 1-1. A "yea" was a vote in support of the president's position. March 22, 2012. *(Story, p. C-10)*

68. **S J Res 36. Union Election Rules/Motion to Proceed.** Enzi, R-Wyo., motion to proceed to the joint resolution that would disapprove of a National Labor Relations Board rule regarding union elections. Motion rejected 45-54: D 0-51; R 45-1; I 0-2. A "nay" was a vote in support of the president's position. April 24, 2012. *(Story, p. C-10)*

98. **H Con Res 112. House Fiscal 2013 Budget Resolution/Motion to Proceed.** Conrad, D-N.D., motion to proceed to the concurrent resolution that would allow $2.794 trillion in new budget authority for fiscal 2013, not including off-budget accounts. Motion rejected 41-58: D 0-51; R 41-5; I 0-2. May 16, 2012. *(Story, p. C-11)*

	24	34	55	68	98			24	34	55	68	98
ALABAMA							**MONTANA**					
Shelby	N	Y	Y	Y	Y		Baucus	Y	Y	N	N	N
Sessions	N	Y	Y	Y	Y		Tester	Y	Y	N	N	N
ALASKA							**NEBRASKA**					
Murkowski	N	Y	Y	N	Y		Nelson	N	N	Y	N	N
Begich	Y	Y	N	N	N		**Johanns**	N	Y	Y	Y	Y
ARIZONA							**NEVADA**					
McCain	N	Y	Y	Y	Y		Reid	Y	N	Y	N	N
Kyl	N	Y	Y	Y	Y		**Heller**	N	Y	Y	Y	N
ARKANSAS							**NEW HAMPSHIRE**					
Pryor	Y	Y	Y	N	N		Shaheen	Y	N	Y	N	N
Boozman	N	Y	Y	Y	Y		**Ayotte**	N	Y	Y	Y	Y
CALIFORNIA							**NEW JERSEY**					
Feinstein	Y	N	N	N	N		Lautenberg	Y	N	N	N	N
Boxer	Y	N	N	N	N		Menendez	Y	N	N	N	N
COLORADO							**NEW MEXICO**					
Udall	Y	N	Y	N	N		Bingaman	Y	N	Y	N	N
Bennet	Y	N	Y	N	N		Udall	Y	N	N	N	N
CONNECTICUT							**NEW YORK**					
Lieberman	Y	N	Y	N	N		Schumer	Y	N	Y	N	N
Blumenthal	Y	N	N	N	N		Gillibrand	Y	N	N	N	N
DELAWARE							**NORTH CAROLINA**					
Carper	Y	N	Y	N	N		**Burr**	N	Y	Y	Y	Y
Coons	Y	N	Y	N	N		Hagan	Y	Y	Y	N	N
FLORIDA							**NORTH DAKOTA**					
Nelson	Y	N	Y	N	N		Conrad	Y	Y	N	N	N
Rubio	N	Y	Y	Y	Y		**Hoeven**	N	Y	Y	Y	Y
GEORGIA							**OHIO**					
Chambliss	N	Y	Y	Y	Y		Brown	Y	N	N	N	N
Isakson	N	Y	Y	Y	Y		**Portman**	N	Y	Y	Y	Y
HAWAII							**OKLAHOMA**					
Inouye	Y	N	Y	N	N		**Inhofe**	N	Y	Y	Y	Y
Akaka	Y	N	N	N	N		**Coburn**	N	Y	Y	Y	Y
IDAHO							**OREGON**					
Crapo	N	Y	Y	Y	Y		Wyden	Y	N	Y	N	N
Risch	N	Y	Y	Y	Y		Merkley	Y	N	N	N	N
ILLINOIS							**PENNSYLVANIA**					
Durbin	Y	N	N	N	N		Casey	N	Y	Y	N	N
Kirk	?	?	?	?	?		**Toomey**	N	Y	Y	Y	Y
INDIANA							**RHODE ISLAND**					
Lugar	N	Y	Y	Y	Y		Reed	Y	N	N	N	N
Coats	N	Y	Y	Y	Y		Whitehouse	Y	N	N	N	N
IOWA							**SOUTH CAROLINA**					
Grassley	N	Y	Y	Y	Y		**Graham**	N	Y	Y	Y	Y
Harkin	Y	N	N	N	N		**DeMint**	N	Y	Y	Y	Y
KANSAS							**SOUTH DAKOTA**					
Roberts	N	Y	Y	Y	Y		Johnson	Y	N	Y	N	N
Moran	N	Y	Y	Y	Y		**Thune**	N	?	Y	Y	Y
KENTUCKY							**TENNESSEE**					
McConnell	N	Y	Y	Y	Y		**Alexander**	N	Y	Y	Y	Y
Paul	N	Y	Y	Y	N		**Corker**	N	Y	Y	Y	Y
LOUISIANA							**TEXAS**					
Landrieu	Y	Y	N	N	N		**Hutchison**	N	Y	Y	Y	Y
Vitter	N	Y	Y	Y	Y		**Cornyn**	N	Y	Y	Y	Y
MAINE							**UTAH**					
Snowe	Y	Y	Y	N	N		**Hatch**	N	Y	Y	Y	Y
Collins	N	Y	Y	N	N		**Lee**	N	Y	Y	Y	Y
MARYLAND							**VERMONT**					
Mikulski	Y	N	N	N	N		Leahy	Y	N	N	N	N
Cardin	Y	N	N	N	N		*Sanders*	Y	N	N	N	N
MASSACHUSETTS							**VIRGINIA**					
Kerry	Y	N	Y	N	N		Webb	Y	Y	Y	N	N
Brown	N	Y	Y	Y	N		Warner	Y	N	Y	N	N
MICHIGAN							**WASHINGTON**					
Levin	Y	N	Y	N	N		Murray	Y	N	N	N	N
Stabenow	Y	N	Y	N	N		Cantwell	Y	N	Y	N	N
MINNESOTA							**WEST VIRGINIA**					
Klobuchar	Y	N	Y	N	N		Rockefeller	Y	N	N	N	N
Franken	Y	N	N	N	N		Manchin	N	Y	N	N	N
MISSISSIPPI							**WISCONSIN**					
Cochran	N	Y	Y	Y	Y		Kohl	Y	N	Y	N	N
Wicker	N	Y	Y	Y	Y		**Johnson**	N	Y	Y	Y	Y
MISSOURI							**WYOMING**					
McCaskill	Y	Y	N	N	N		**Enzi**	N	Y	Y	Y	Y
Blunt	N	Y	Y	Y	Y		**Barrasso**	N	Y	Y	Y	Y

KEY	**Republicans**	Democrats	*Independents*	
Y Voted for (yea)		X Paired against		C Voted "present" to avoid possible conflict of interest
# Paired for		– Announced against		
+ Announced for		P Voted "present"		? Did not vote or otherwise make a position known
N Voted against (nay)				

IN THE SENATE | By Vote Number

164. **S 3240. Farm Programs/Passage.** Passage of the bill that would reauthorize federal farm and nutrition programs for five years, including crop subsidies, food stamps, conservation, rural development and foreign food aid programs, for a total projected cost of roughly $969 billion over the next decade. It would reauthorize the Supplemental Nutrition Assistance Program. The bill would eliminate direct and countercyclical payments and replace them with a new supplemental coverage option that would allow producers to purchase additional crop insurance coverage. The bill would make any person with a non-farm adjusted gross income of more than $750,000 ineligible for payments from commodity programs, currently capped at $50,000, pending a study to determine the impact on costs. Passed 64-35: D 46-5; R 16-30; I 2-0. (By unanimous consent, the Senate agreed to raise the majority requirement for passage of the bill to 60 votes.) A "yea" was a vote in support of the president's position. June 21, 2012. *(Story, p. C-11)*

187. **S 3414. Cybersecurity Standards/Cloture.** Motion to invoke cloture (thus limiting debate) on the bill that would create voluntary security standards for vital digital infrastructure. Three-fifths of the total Senate (60) is required to invoke cloture. Motion rejected 52-46: D 45-6; R 5-40; I 2-0. A "yea" was a vote in support of the president's position. Aug. 2, 2012. *(Story, p. C-11)*

212. **S 3254. Fiscal 2013 Defense Authorization/Guantánamo Bay Detainees.** Ayotte, R-N.H., amendment that would prohibit the transfer of detainees from Guantánamo Bay, Cuba, military facilities to the United States. Adopted 54-41: D 9-40; R 44-0; I 1-1. A "nay" was a vote in support of the president's position. Nov. 29, 2012. *(Story, p. C-12)*

215. **S 3254. Fiscal 2013 Defense Authorization/Iran Sanctions.** Menendez, D-N.J., amendment that would bar all transactions with Iran's energy, shipping and shipbuilding sectors and its ports. It would ban the sale to Iran of certain metals, including graphite, aluminum, steel and metallurgical coal, which are used in those sectors and in other industrial processes. Adopted 94-0: D 49-0; R 43-0; I 2-0. Nov. 30, 2012. *(Story, p. C-12)*

219. **Treaty Doc 112-7. Convention on the Rights of Persons With Disabilities/Adoption.** Adoption of the resolution of ratification of the Convention on the Rights of Persons with Disabilities (Treaty Doc 112-7), which would establish global standards for the treatment of people with disabilities. The resolution would state that current U.S. law fulfills or exceeds the obligations of the treaty. Rejected 61-38: D 51-0; R 8-38; I 2-0. (A two-thirds majority of those present and voting, 66 in this case, is required for adoption of resolutions of ratification.) A "yea" was a vote in support of the president's position. Dec. 4, 2012. *(Story, p. C-13)*

	164	187	212	215	219			164	187	212	215	219
ALABAMA							**MONTANA**					
Shelby	N	N	Y	Y	N		Baucus	Y	N	Y	Y	Y
Sessions	N	N	Y	Y	N		Tester	Y	N	N	Y	Y
ALASKA							**NEBRASKA**					
Murkowski	N	N	Y	Y	Y		Nelson	Y	Y	Y	Y	Y
Begich	Y	Y	N	Y	Y		Johanns	Y	N	Y	Y	N
ARIZONA							**NEVADA**					
McCain	N	N	Y	Y	Y		Reid	Y	N	N	Y	Y
Kyl	N	N	Y	Y	N		Heller	N	N	?	+	N
ARKANSAS							**NEW HAMPSHIRE**					
Pryor	N	N	Y	Y	Y		Shaheen	Y	Y	N	Y	Y
Boozman	N	N	Y	Y	N		Ayotte	N	N	Y	Y	Y
CALIFORNIA							**NEW JERSEY**					
Feinstein	Y	Y	N	Y	Y		Lautenberg	N	Y	N	Y	Y
Boxer	Y	Y	N	Y	Y		Menendez	Y	Y	N	Y	Y
COLORADO							**NEW MEXICO**					
Udall	Y	Y	N	Y	Y		Bingaman	Y	Y	N	Y	Y
Bennet	Y	Y	N	Y	Y		Udall	Y	Y	N	Y	Y
CONNECTICUT							**NEW YORK**					
Lieberman	Y	Y	Y	Y	Y		Schumer	Y	Y	N	Y	Y
Blumenthal	Y	Y	N	Y	Y		Gillibrand	Y	Y	N	Y	Y
DELAWARE							**NORTH CAROLINA**					
Carper	Y	Y	N	Y	Y		Burr	N	N	Y	Y	N
Coons	Y	Y	N	Y	Y		Hagan	Y	Y	N	Y	Y
FLORIDA							**NORTH DAKOTA**					
Nelson	Y	Y	N	Y	Y		Conrad	Y	Y	N	Y	Y
Rubio	N	?	Y	Y	N		**Hoeven**	Y	N	Y	Y	N
GEORGIA							**OHIO**					
Chambliss	N	N	Y	Y	N		Brown	Y	Y	N	Y	Y
Isakson	N	N	Y	Y	N		**Portman**	N	N	Y	Y	N
HAWAII							**OKLAHOMA**					
Inouye	Y	Y	Y	Y	Y		**Inhofe**	N	N	Y	Y	N
Akaka	Y	Y	N	Y	Y		**Coburn**	N	N	Y	Y	N
IDAHO							**OREGON**					
Crapo	N	N	Y	Y	N		Wyden	Y	N	?	?	Y
Risch	N	N	Y	Y	N		Merkley	Y	N	Y	Y	Y
ILLINOIS							**PENNSYLVANIA**					
Durbin	Y	Y	N	Y	Y		Casey	Y	Y	N	Y	Y
Kirk	?	?	?	?	?		**Toomey**	N	N	Y	Y	N
INDIANA							**RHODE ISLAND**					
Lugar	Y	Y	Y	Y	Y		Reed	N	Y	N	Y	Y
Coats	Y	Y	Y	Y	N		Whitehouse	N	Y	N	Y	Y
IOWA							**SOUTH CAROLINA**					
Grassley	Y	N	Y	Y	N		**Graham**	N	N	Y	Y	N
Harkin	Y	Y	N	Y	Y		**DeMint**	N	N	?	Y	N
KANSAS							**SOUTH DAKOTA**					
Roberts	Y	N	Y	Y	N		Johnson	Y	Y	N	Y	Y
Moran	Y	N	Y	Y	N		**Thune**	Y	N	Y	Y	N
KENTUCKY							**TENNESSEE**					
McConnell	N	N	Y	Y	N		**Alexander**	Y	N	Y	+	N
Paul	N	N	Y	Y	N		**Corker**	N	N	Y	Y	N
LOUISIANA							**TEXAS**					
Landrieu	N	Y	Y	Y	Y		**Hutchison**	Y	N	Y	Y	N
Vitter	N	N	Y	Y	N		**Cornyn**	N	N	Y	Y	N
MAINE							**UTAH**					
Snowe	Y	Y	Y	Y	Y		**Hatch**	N	N	Y	?	N
Collins	Y	Y	Y	Y	Y		**Lee**	N	N	Y	Y	N
MARYLAND							**VERMONT**					
Mikulski	Y	Y	N	Y	Y		Leahy	Y	Y	N	Y	Y
Cardin	Y	Y	N	Y	Y		*Sanders*	Y	Y	N	Y	Y
MASSACHUSETTS							**VIRGINIA**					
Kerry	Y	Y	N	Y	Y		Webb	Y	Y	Y	Y	Y
Brown	Y	Y	Y	Y	Y		Warner	Y	Y	N	Y	Y
MICHIGAN							**WASHINGTON**					
Levin	Y	Y	N	Y	Y		Murray	Y	Y	N	Y	Y
Stabenow	Y	Y	Y	Y	Y		Cantwell	Y	Y	N	Y	Y
MINNESOTA							**WEST VIRGINIA**					
Klobuchar	Y	Y	N	Y	Y		Rockefeller	Y	Y	?	?	Y
Franken	Y	Y	N	Y	Y		Manchin	Y	Y	Y	Y	Y
MISSISSIPPI							**WISCONSIN**					
Cochran	N	N	Y	Y	N		Kohl	Y	Y	N	Y	Y
Wicker	N	N	Y	Y	N		**Johnson**	N	N	Y	Y	N
MISSOURI							**WYOMING**					
McCaskill	Y	Y	N	Y	Y		**Enzi**	Y	N	Y	Y	N
Blunt	Y	N	Y	Y	N		**Barrasso**	Y	N	Y	Y	Y

KEY **Republicans** Democrats *Independents*

Y	Voted for (yea)	X	Paired against
#	Paired for	−	Announced against
+	Announced for	P	Voted "present"
N	Voted against (nay)		

C Voted "present" to avoid possible conflict of interest

? Did not vote or otherwise make a position known

IN THE SENATE | By Vote Number

223. **HR 6156. Russia Trade Relations/Passage.** Passage of the bill that would establish permanent normal trade relations with Russia and Moldova and end Jackson-Vanik restrictions on both economies. The bill also would provide sanctions against persons involved in human rights violations in Russia. Passed (thus cleared for the president) 92-4: D 45-3; R 46-0; I 1-1. A "yea" was a vote in support of the president's position. Dec. 6, 2012. *(Story, p. C-13)*

248. **HR 1. Disaster Supplemental/Passage.** Passage of the bill that would provide $60.4 billion in emergency spending for communities hit by Superstorm Sandy, including an additional $9.7 billion in borrowing authority for the National Flood Insurance Program, $13 billion for mitigation projects, $11.5 billion for the Federal Emergency Management Agency's Disaster Relief Fund and $10.8 billion to the Federal Transit Administration to rebuild public transit systems. As amended, the bill would provide $17 billion for the Community Development Fund, with $500 million designated for regions that suffered major disasters or for "small, economically distressed areas" with less-severe calamities in 2011 and 2012. It would allow the transfer of previously appropriated foreign affairs funds to pay for increased security at U.S. embassies and other overseas posts. Passed 62-32: D 48-0; R 12-32; I 2-0. (Prior to passage the Reid, D-Nev., substitute amendment was adopted by voice vote.) A "yea" was a vote in support of the president's position. Dec. 28, 2012. *(Story, p. C-13)*

251. **HR 8. Tax Rates Extensions/Passage.** Passage of the bill that permanently would extend the 2001 and 2003 tax rates for individual income below $400,000 and joint-filer income below $450,000. Rates for income above those thresholds would rise to 39.6 percent from 35 percent. It also would permanently extend the tax rates on dividends and capital gains for individual income below $400,000 and joint-filer income below $450,000. Rates for the dividends and capital gains taxes would rise to 20 percent for income above those thresholds. The measure would delay the automatic, across-the-board cuts known as sequester for two months. Half of the sequester delay would be offset by discretionary cuts, split between defense and nondefense, and the other half offset by revenue raised through the voluntary transfer of traditional IRAs to Roth IRAs, which would tax retirement savings when transferred. It also would tax individual estates valued at more than $5 million and joint estates valued at more than $10 million at 40 percent. It would permanently "patch" the alternative minimum tax to account for inflation. Unemployment insurance would be extended through 2013. The bill would block scheduled cuts to Medicare physician payment rates and extend for five years tax credits included in the 2009 stimulus law including the child tax credit and the earned income tax credit. It would allow the 2 percent payroll tax holiday to expire. It also would extend the Milk Income Loss Contract program at current rates. Passed 89-8: D 47-3; R 40-5; I 2-0. (By unanimous consent, the Senate agreed to raise the majority requirement for passage of the bill to 60 votes.) A "yea" was a vote in support of the president's position. Jan. 1, 2013 (in the session that began and the Congressional Record dated Dec. 31, 2012). *(Story, p. C-14)*

	223	248	251
ALABAMA			
Shelby	Y	Y	N
Sessions	Y	N	Y
ALASKA			
Murkowski	Y	Y	Y
Begich	Y	Y	Y
ARIZONA			
McCain	Y	N	Y
Kyl	Y	N	Y
ARKANSAS			
Pryor	Y	Y	Y
Boozman	Y	N	Y
CALIFORNIA			
Feinstein	Y	Y	Y
Boxer	Y	?	Y
COLORADO			
Udall	Y	Y	Y
Bennet	Y	Y	N
CONNECTICUT			
Lieberman	Y	Y	Y
Blumenthal	Y	Y	Y
DELAWARE			
Carper	Y	Y	N
Coons	Y	Y	Y
FLORIDA			
Nelson	Y	Y	Y
Rubio	Y	N	N
GEORGIA			
Chambliss	Y	N	Y
Isakson	Y	N	Y
HAWAII			
Inouye *	?		
Schatz *		Y	Y
Akaka	Y	Y	Y
IDAHO			
Crapo	Y	N	Y
Risch	Y	?	Y
ILLINOIS			
Durbin	Y	Y	Y
Kirk	?	?	?
INDIANA			
Lugar	Y	Y	Y
Coats	Y	N	Y
IOWA			
Grassley	Y	N	N
Harkin	Y	Y	N
KANSAS			
Roberts	Y	N	Y
Moran	Y	N	Y
KENTUCKY			
McConnell	Y	N	Y
Paul	Y	N	N
LOUISIANA			
Landrieu	Y	Y	Y
Vitter	Y	Y	Y
MAINE			
Snowe	Y	Y	Y
Collins	Y	Y	Y
MARYLAND			
Mikulski	Y	Y	Y
Cardin	Y	Y	Y
MASSACHUSETTS			
Kerry	Y	Y	Y
Brown	Y	Y	Y
MICHIGAN			
Levin	N	Y	Y
Stabenow	Y	Y	Y
MINNESOTA			
Klobuchar	Y	Y	Y
Franken	Y	Y	Y
MISSISSIPPI			
Cochran	Y	Y	Y
Wicker	Y	Y	Y
MISSOURI			
McCaskill	Y	Y	Y
Blunt	Y	N	Y

	223	248	251
MONTANA			
Baucus	Y	Y	Y
Tester	Y	Y	Y
NEBRASKA			
Nelson	Y	Y	Y
Johanns	Y	N	Y
NEVADA			
Reid	Y	Y	Y
Heller	Y	Y	Y
NEW HAMPSHIRE			
Shaheen	Y	Y	Y
Ayotte	Y	N	Y
NEW JERSEY			
Lautenberg	Y	?	?
Menendez	Y	Y	Y
NEW MEXICO			
Bingaman	Y	Y	Y
Udall	Y	Y	Y
NEW YORK			
Schumer	Y	Y	Y
Gillibrand	Y	Y	Y
NORTH CAROLINA			
Burr	Y	N	Y
Hagan	Y	Y	Y
NORTH DAKOTA			
Conrad	+	Y	Y
Hoeven	Y	Y	Y
OHIO			
Brown	Y	Y	Y
Portman	Y	N	Y
OKLAHOMA			
Inhofe	Y	N	Y
Coburn	Y	N	Y
OREGON			
Wyden	Y	Y	Y
Merkley	Y	Y	Y
PENNSYLVANIA			
Casey	Y	Y	Y
Toomey	Y	N	Y
RHODE ISLAND			
Reed	N	Y	Y
Whitehouse	N	Y	Y
SOUTH CAROLINA			
Graham	Y	N	Y
DeMint	Y	?	?
SOUTH DAKOTA			
Johnson	Y	Y	Y
Thune	Y	N	Y
TENNESSEE			
Alexander	Y	N	Y
Corker	Y	N	Y
TEXAS			
Hutchison	Y	Y	Y
Cornyn	Y	N	Y
UTAH			
Hatch	Y	N	Y
Lee	Y	N	N
VERMONT			
Leahy	Y	Y	Y
Sanders	N	Y	Y
VIRGINIA			
Webb	Y	Y	Y
Warner	Y	?	Y
WASHINGTON			
Murray	Y	Y	Y
Cantwell	Y	Y	Y
WEST VIRGINIA			
Rockefeller	?	Y	Y
Manchin	Y	Y	Y
WISCONSIN			
Kohl	Y	Y	Y
Johnson	Y	N	Y
WYOMING			
Enzi	Y	N	Y
Barrasso	Y	N	Y

*Brian Schatz, D-Hawaii, was sworn in Dec. 27, 2012, to fill the vacancy created by the Dec. 17 death of fellow Democrat Daniel K. Inouye. The last vote for which Inouye was eligible was vote 228; the first vote for which Schatz was eligible was vote 232.

IN THE HOUSE | By Vote Number

72. **HR 3630. Payroll Tax Relief Extension/Conference Report.**
Adoption of the conference report on the bill that would extend the 4.2 percent employee payroll tax rate through 2012. It also would renew long-term unemployment benefits into January 2013, with three stages of reductions. The current Medicare reimbursement rate for physicians would be preserved through 2012, preventing a scheduled 27.4 percent payment cut. The cost of the legislation would be partially offset by requiring larger pension payments from newly hired federal employees and from lawmakers, by auctioning blocks of electromagnetic spectrum used by television broadcasters, and by reducing funds for certain programs tied to the 2010 health care overhaul. Adopted (thus sent to the Senate) 293-132: R 146-91; D 147-41. A "yea" was a vote in support of the president's position. Feb. 17, 2012. (Story, p. C-4)

132. **HR 3606. Small-Business Startups/Motion to Concur.** Bachus, R-Ala., motion to suspend the rules and concur in the Senate amendment to the bill that would define "emerging-growth companies" and exempt them from certain independent auditing requirements. It would increase from $5 million to $50 million the annual public-offering threshold for companies to be exempt from full Securities and Exchange Commission filing requirements and raise the number of shareholders that would trigger mandatory SEC registration from 750 to 2,000. It would raise to 2,000 the number of shareholders that would trigger a requirement for SEC registration for a bank. The bill would lift an SEC ban that prevents small, privately held companies from using advertisements to solicit investors and allow companies to sell up to $1 million worth of securities without registering with the SEC. It also would require anyone acting as a "crowd funding" intermediary to register with securities regulators. Motion agreed to (thus clearing the bill for the president) 380-41: R 235-0; D 145-41. A two-thirds majority of those present and voting (281 in this case) is required for passage under suspension of the rules. A "yea" was a vote in support of the president's position. March 27, 2012. (Story, p. C-4)

151. **H Con Res 112. Fiscal 2013 Budget Resolution/Adoption.**
Adoption of the concurrent resolution that would provide $2.793 trillion in new budget authority for fiscal 2013, not including off-budget accounts. It calls for limiting discretionary appropriations to $1.028 trillion in 2013 and for major cuts in nondefense discretionary and mandatory spending over the next 10 years. It would assume significant future savings by restructuring Medicare into a "premium support" system beginning in 2023, converting Medicaid and the food stamp program into block grants to states and repealing the 2010 health care overhaul. It calls for an overhaul of the tax code, under which the alternative minimum tax would be repealed, the six current individual income tax brackets would be consolidated into two, tax credits and deductions would be eliminated or curtailed, and the corporate tax code modified to reduce the top rate from 35 percent to 25 percent and converted into a "territorial" tax system in which U.S. companies would pay tax only on income earned in the United States. It also would direct the Budget Committee to report a bill that would repeal the sequestration of discretionary spending set for January 2013 by the 2011 debt limit law and direct six House committees to find substitute savings from mandatory programs. Adopted 228-191: R 228-10; D 0-181. March 29, 2012. (Story, p. C-4)

[1] Ron Barber, D-Ariz., was sworn in June 19, 2012, to fill the vacancy created by the Jan. 25 resignation of fellow Democrat Gabrielle Giffords. The last vote for which Giffords was eligible was vote 11; the first vote for which Barber was eligible was vote 382.

[2] David A. Curson, D-Mich., was sworn in Nov. 13, 2012, to fill the vacancy created by the July 6 resignation of Republican Thaddeus McCotter. The last vote for which McCotter was eligible was vote 451; the first vote for which Curson was eligible was vote 605.

[3] Donald M. Payne Jr., D-N.J., was sworn in Nov. 15, 2012, to fill the vacancy created by the March 6 death of his father, fellow Democrat Donald M. Payne. The last vote for which the elder Payne was eligible was vote 97; the first vote for which Payne Jr. was eligible was vote 606.

[4] The speaker votes only at his discretion.

[5] Suzanne Bonamici, D-Ore., was sworn in Feb. 7, 2012, to fill the vacancy created by the Aug. 3, 2011, resignation of fellow Democrat David Wu. Wu was not eligible for any votes in 2012; the first vote for which Bonamici was eligible was vote 37.

[6] Suzan DelBene, D-Wash., was sworn in Nov. 13, 2012, to fill the vacancy created by the March 20 resignation of fellow Democrat Jay Inslee. The last vote for which Inslee was eligible was vote 111; the first vote for which DelBene was eligible was vote 605.

	72	132	151
ALABAMA			
1 Bonner	N	Y	Y
2 Roby	N	Y	Y
3 Rogers	N	Y	Y
4 Aderholt	N	Y	Y
5 Brooks	N	Y	Y
6 Bachus	N	Y	Y
7 Sewell	Y	Y	N
ALASKA			
AL Young	Y	Y	Y
ARIZONA			
1 Gosar	?	Y	Y
2 Franks	N	Y	Y
3 Quayle	N	Y	Y
4 Pastor	Y	N	N
5 Schweikert	Y	Y	Y
6 Flake	N	Y	Y
7 Grijalva	Y	N	N
8 Vacant[1]			
ARKANSAS			
1 Crawford	Y	Y	Y
2 Griffin	Y	Y	Y
3 Womack	Y	Y	Y
4 Ross	Y	Y	N
CALIFORNIA			
1 Thompson	N	Y	N
2 Herger	Y	Y	Y
3 Lungren	Y	Y	Y
4 McClintock	N	Y	Y
5 Matsui	Y	Y	N
6 Woolsey	N	N	N
7 Miller, George	Y	N	N
8 Pelosi	Y	Y	?
9 Lee	N	N	N
10 Garamendi	Y	Y	N
11 McNerney	Y	Y	N
12 Speier	Y	Y	N
13 Stark	Y	N	N
14 Eshoo	Y	Y	N
15 Honda	Y	Y	N
16 Lofgren	Y	Y	N
17 Farr	N	Y	N
18 Cardoza	N	Y	N
19 Denham	Y	Y	Y
20 Costa	Y	Y	N
21 Nunes	Y	Y	Y
22 McCarthy	Y	Y	Y
23 Capps	Y	Y	N
24 Gallegly	N	Y	Y
25 McKeon	Y	Y	Y
26 Dreier	Y	Y	Y
27 Sherman	Y	Y	N
28 Berman	Y	N	N
29 Schiff	Y	Y	N
30 Waxman	Y	N	N
31 Becerra	Y	N	N
32 Chu	Y	Y	N
33 Bass	Y	Y	N
34 Roybal-Allard	Y	Y	N
35 Waters	Y	Y	N
36 Hahn	Y	Y	N
37 Richardson	Y	Y	N
38 Napolitano	Y	N	N
39 Sánchez, Linda	Y	Y	N
40 Royce	N	Y	Y
41 Lewis	Y	Y	Y
42 Miller, Gary	Y	Y	Y
43 Baca	Y	Y	N
44 Calvert	Y	Y	Y
45 Bono Mack	?	Y	Y
46 Rohrabacher	N	Y	Y
47 Sanchez, Loretta	Y	Y	N
48 Campbell	?	Y	Y
49 Issa	Y	Y	Y
50 Bilbray	Y	Y	Y
51 Filner	N	N	–
52 Hunter	Y	Y	Y
53 Davis	Y	Y	N

	72	132	151
COLORADO			
1 DeGette	Y	Y	N
2 Polis	Y	Y	N
3 Tipton	Y	Y	Y
4 Gardner	N	Y	Y
5 Lamborn	N	Y	Y
6 Coffman	Y	Y	Y
7 Perlmutter	Y	Y	N
CONNECTICUT			
1 Larson	Y	Y	N
2 Courtney	Y	Y	N
3 DeLauro	Y	Y	N
4 Himes	Y	Y	N
5 Murphy	Y	Y	N
DELAWARE			
AL Carney	Y	Y	N
FLORIDA			
1 Miller	N	Y	Y
2 Southerland	Y	Y	Y
3 Brown	+	Y	N
4 Crenshaw	Y	Y	Y
5 Nugent	N	Y	Y
6 Stearns	Y	Y	Y
7 Mica	N	Y	Y
8 Webster	Y	Y	Y
9 Bilirakis	Y	Y	Y
10 Young	Y	Y	Y
11 Castor	Y	Y	N
12 Ross	N	Y	Y
13 Buchanan	Y	Y	Y
14 Mack	Y	?	?
15 Posey	N	Y	Y
16 Rooney	Y	Y	Y
17 Wilson	N	Y	N
18 Ros-Lehtinen	Y	Y	Y
19 Deutch	Y	N	N
20 Wasserman Schultz	Y	Y	N
21 Diaz-Balart	Y	+	Y
22 West	N	Y	Y
23 Hastings	N	Y	N
24 Adams	N	Y	Y
25 Rivera	Y	Y	Y
GEORGIA			
1 Kingston	N	Y	Y
2 Bishop	Y	Y	N
3 Westmoreland	Y	Y	Y
4 Johnson	N	N	N
5 Lewis	Y	Y	N
6 Price	Y	Y	Y
7 Woodall	N	Y	Y
8 Scott, A.	N	Y	Y
9 Graves	N	Y	Y
10 Broun	N	Y	?
11 Gingrey	N	Y	Y
12 Barrow	Y	Y	N
13 Scott, D.	Y	Y	N
HAWAII			
1 Hanabusa	Y	Y	N
2 Hirono	Y	Y	N
IDAHO			
1 Labrador	N	Y	Y
2 Simpson	N	Y	Y
ILLINOIS			
1 Rush	Y	Y	N
2 Jackson	Y	?	?
3 Lipinski	Y	Y	N
4 Gutierrez	N	Y	N
5 Quigley	Y	Y	N
6 Roskam	Y	Y	Y
7 Davis, D.	N	Y	N
8 Walsh	Y	Y	Y
9 Schakowsky	Y	N	N
10 Dold	Y	Y	Y
11 Kinzinger	N	Y	N
12 Costello	N	Y	N
13 Biggert	Y	Y	Y
14 Hultgren	Y	Y	Y
15 Johnson	N	Y	Y

KEY   **Republicans**   Democrats

Y Voted for (yea)	X Paired against	C Voted "present" to avoid possible conflict of interest
# Paired for	– Announced against	
+ Announced for	P Voted "present"	? Did not vote or otherwise make a position known
N Voted against (nay)		

	72	132	151
16 Manzullo	Y	Y	Y
17 Schilling	Y	Y	Y
18 Schock	Y	Y	Y
19 Shimkus	Y	Y	Y
INDIANA			
1 Visclosky	N	N	N
2 Donnelly	Y	Y	N
3 Stutzman	Y	Y	Y
4 Rokita	N	Y	Y
5 Burton	N	Y	Y
6 Pence	Y	Y	Y
7 Carson	Y	Y	N
8 Bucshon	Y	Y	Y
9 Young	Y	Y	Y
IOWA			
1 Braley	Y	Y	N
2 Loebsack	Y	Y	N
3 Boswell	Y	Y	N
4 Latham	Y	Y	Y
5 King	N	Y	Y
KANSAS			
1 Huelskamp	Y	Y	N
2 Jenkins	Y	Y	Y
3 Yoder	Y	Y	Y
4 Pompeo	N	Y	Y
KENTUCKY			
1 Whitfield	N	Y	N
2 Guthrie	Y	Y	Y
3 Yarmuth	Y	Y	Y
4 Davis	Y	Y	Y
5 Rogers	Y	Y	Y
6 Chandler	Y	Y	N
LOUISIANA			
1 Scalise	Y	Y	Y
2 Richmond	Y	Y	N
3 Landry	N	?	Y
4 Fleming	N	Y	Y
5 Alexander	Y	Y	Y
6 Cassidy	N	Y	Y
7 Boustany	N	Y	Y
MAINE			
1 Pingree	N	N	?
2 Michaud	Y	Y	N
MARYLAND			
1 Harris	N	Y	Y
2 Ruppersberger	Y	Y	N
3 Sarbanes	N	N	N
4 Edwards	N	N	N
5 Hoyer	N	Y	N
6 Bartlett	Y	Y	Y
7 Cummings	N	N	N
8 Van Hollen	N	Y	N
MASSACHUSETTS			
1 Olver	Y	N	N
2 Neal	Y	?	N
3 McGovern	Y	Y	N
4 Frank	Y	Y	N
5 Tsongas	Y	Y	N
6 Tierney	Y	N	N
7 Markey	Y	N	N
8 Capuano	N	N	N
9 Lynch	N	Y	N
10 Keating	Y	Y	N
MICHIGAN			
1 Benishek	Y	Y	Y
2 Huizenga	Y	Y	Y
3 Amash	N	N	N
4 Camp	Y	Y	Y
5 Kildee	Y	N	N
6 Upton	Y	Y	Y
7 Walberg	N	Y	Y
8 Rogers	Y	Y	Y
9 Peters	Y	Y	N
10 Miller	Y	Y	Y
11 McCotter[2]	N	Y	Y
12 Levin	Y	Y	N
13 Clarke	Y	Y	N
14 Conyers	Y	Y	N
15 Dingell	Y	N	N
MINNESOTA			
1 Walz	Y	Y	N
2 Kline	Y	Y	Y
3 Paulsen	Y	Y	Y
4 McCollum	Y	N	N

	72	132	151
5 Ellison	N	Y	N
6 Bachmann	N	Y	Y
7 Peterson	N	Y	N
8 Cravaack	Y	Y	Y
MISSISSIPPI			
1 Nunnelee	Y	Y	Y
2 Thompson	Y	Y	N
3 Harper	Y	Y	Y
4 Palazzo	Y	Y	Y
MISSOURI			
1 Clay	N	N	N
2 Akin	N	+	Y
3 Carnahan	Y	Y	N
4 Hartzler	Y	Y	Y
5 Cleaver	N	Y	N
6 Graves	N	Y	Y
7 Long	Y	Y	Y
8 Emerson	Y	Y	Y
9 Luetkemeyer	Y	Y	Y
MONTANA			
AL Rehberg	Y	Y	N
NEBRASKA			
1 Fortenberry	N	Y	Y
2 Terry	N	Y	Y
3 Smith	Y	Y	Y
NEVADA			
1 Berkley	Y	Y	N
2 Amodei	Y	Y	Y
3 Heck	Y	Y	Y
NEW HAMPSHIRE			
1 Guinta	Y	Y	Y
2 Bass	Y	Y	Y
NEW JERSEY			
1 Andrews	Y	Y	N
2 LoBiondo	Y	Y	Y
3 Runyan	Y	Y	Y
4 Smith	Y	Y	Y
5 Garrett	N	Y	Y
6 Pallone	Y	Y	N
7 Lance	Y	Y	Y
8 Pascrell	Y	Y	N
9 Rothman	Y	Y	N
10 Payne[3]	?		
11 Frelinghuysen	Y	Y	Y
12 Holt	Y	N	N
13 Sires	Y	Y	N
NEW MEXICO			
1 Heinrich	Y	Y	N
2 Pearce	N	Y	Y
3 Luján	Y	Y	N
NEW YORK			
1 Bishop	Y	Y	N
2 Israel	Y	Y	N
3 King	Y	Y	Y
4 McCarthy	Y	Y	N
5 Ackerman	N	Y	N
6 Meeks	Y	Y	?
7 Crowley	Y	Y	N
8 Nadler	Y	N	N
9 Turner	Y	Y	Y
10 Towns	Y	Y	N
11 Clarke	N	N	N
12 Velázquez	Y	Y	N
13 Grimm	Y	Y	Y
14 Maloney, C.	Y	Y	N
15 Rangel	?	?	?
16 Serrano	Y	Y	N
17 Engel	Y	?	N
18 Lowey	Y	Y	N
19 Hayworth	Y	Y	Y
20 Gibson	Y	Y	N
21 Tonko	Y	Y	N
22 Hinchey	Y	N	?
23 Owens	Y	Y	N
24 Hanna	Y	Y	Y
24 Maffei			
25 Buerkle	N	Y	Y
26 Hochul	Y	Y	N
27 Higgins	Y	Y	N
28 Slaughter	Y	Y	N
29 Reed	Y	Y	Y
NORTH CAROLINA			
1 Butterfield	Y	Y	N
2 Ellmers	Y	Y	Y
3 Jones	Y	Y	Y
4 Price	Y	Y	N

	72	132	151
5 Foxx	N	Y	Y
6 Coble	Y	Y	Y
7 McIntyre	Y	Y	N
8 Kissell	Y	Y	N
9 Myrick	Y	Y	Y
10 McHenry	Y	Y	Y
11 Shuler	?	Y	N
12 Watt	Y	Y	?
13 Miller	Y	Y	N
NORTH DAKOTA			
AL Berg	Y	Y	Y
OHIO			
1 Chabot	N	Y	Y
2 Schmidt	N	Y	Y
3 Turner	Y	Y	Y
4 Jordan	Y	Y	Y
5 Latta	Y	Y	Y
6 Johnson	Y	Y	Y
7 Austria	Y	Y	Y
8 Boehner[4]			
9 Kaptur	Y	Y	N
10 Kucinich	Y	N	N
11 Fudge	N	N	N
12 Tiberi	Y	Y	Y
13 Sutton	Y	Y	N
14 LaTourette	Y	Y	Y
15 Stivers	Y	Y	Y
16 Renacci	Y	Y	Y
17 Ryan	N	Y	N
18 Gibbs	Y	Y	Y
OKLAHOMA			
1 Sullivan	N	Y	Y
2 Boren	Y	Y	N
3 Lucas	Y	Y	Y
4 Cole	Y	Y	Y
5 Lankford	N	Y	Y
OREGON			
1 Bonamici[5]	Y	Y	N
2 Walden	Y	Y	Y
3 Blumenauer	Y	Y	N
4 DeFazio	N	Y	N
5 Schrader	N	Y	N
PENNSYLVANIA			
1 Brady	Y	N	N
2 Fattah	Y	N	N
3 Kelly	Y	Y	Y
4 Altmire	Y	Y	N
5 Thompson	Y	Y	Y
6 Gerlach	Y	Y	Y
7 Meehan	Y	Y	Y
8 Fitzpatrick	Y	Y	Y
9 Shuster	Y	Y	Y
10 Marino	Y	Y	Y
11 Barletta	Y	Y	Y
12 Critz	Y	Y	N
13 Schwartz	Y	Y	N
14 Doyle	Y	N	N
15 Dent	Y	Y	Y
16 Pitts	Y	Y	Y
17 Holden	Y	N	N
18 Murphy	Y	Y	Y
19 Platts	Y	Y	N
RHODE ISLAND			
1 Cicilline	Y	Y	N
2 Langevin	Y	Y	N
SOUTH CAROLINA			
1 Scott	Y	Y	Y
2 Wilson	N	Y	Y
3 Duncan	N	Y	Y
4 Gowdy	N	Y	Y
5 Mulvaney	N	Y	Y
6 Clyburn	Y	Y	N
SOUTH DAKOTA			
AL Noem	N	Y	Y
TENNESSEE			
1 Roe	N	Y	Y
2 Duncan	Y	Y	Y
3 Fleischmann	Y	Y	Y
4 DesJarlais	N	Y	Y
5 Cooper	N	Y	N
6 Black	N	Y	Y
7 Blackburn	N	Y	Y
8 Fincher	Y	Y	Y
9 Cohen	Y	N	N

	72	132	151
TEXAS			
1 Gohmert	N	Y	Y
2 Poe	N	Y	Y
3 Johnson, S.	Y	Y	Y
4 Hall	N	Y	Y
5 Hensarling	Y	Y	Y
6 Barton	N	Y	N
7 Culberson	Y	Y	Y
8 Brady	Y	Y	Y
9 Green, A.	Y	Y	N
10 McCaul	Y	Y	Y
11 Conaway	Y	Y	Y
12 Granger	N	Y	Y
13 Thornberry	N	Y	Y
14 Paul	?	Y	?
15 Hinojosa	Y	Y	N
16 Reyes	N	Y	N
17 Flores	Y	?	Y
18 Jackson Lee	Y	Y	N
19 Neugebauer	N	Y	Y
20 Gonzalez	Y	Y	N
21 Smith	Y	Y	Y
22 Olson	N	Y	Y
23 Canseco	Y	Y	Y
24 Marchant	Y	?	Y
25 Doggett	Y	Y	N
26 Burgess	N	Y	Y
27 Farenthold	N	Y	Y
28 Cuellar	Y	Y	N
29 Green, G.	Y	N	N
30 Johnson, E.	N	N	N
31 Carter	N	Y	Y
32 Sessions	N	Y	Y
UTAH			
1 Bishop	N	Y	Y
2 Matheson	Y	Y	N
3 Chaffetz	N	Y	Y
VERMONT			
AL Welch	N	Y	N
VIRGINIA			
1 Wittman	Y	Y	Y
2 Rigell	Y	Y	Y
3 Scott	N	N	N
4 Forbes	N	Y	Y
5 Hurt	Y	Y	Y
6 Goodlatte	N	Y	Y
7 Cantor	Y	Y	Y
8 Moran	N	Y	N
9 Griffith	N	Y	Y
10 Wolf	N	Y	Y
11 Connolly	N	Y	N
WASHINGTON			
1 Inslee[6]	Y		
2 Larsen	Y	Y	N
3 Herrera Beutler	Y	Y	Y
4 Hastings	Y	Y	Y
5 McMorris Rodgers	Y	Y	Y
6 Dicks	Y	Y	?
7 McDermott	N	N	N
8 Reichert	Y	Y	Y
9 Smith	N	Y	N
WEST VIRGINIA			
1 McKinley	N	Y	N
2 Capito	Y	Y	Y
3 Rahall	Y	Y	N
WISCONSIN			
1 Ryan	N	Y	Y
2 Baldwin	Y	Y	N
3 Kind	N	Y	N
4 Moore	Y	Y	N
5 Sensenbrenner	N	Y	Y
6 Petri	N	Y	Y
7 Duffy	Y	Y	Y
8 Ribble	Y	Y	Y
WYOMING			
AL Lummis	N	Y	Y

IN THE HOUSE | By Vote Number

195. **HR 4628. Student Loan Interest Rates/Passage.** Passage of the bill that would extend for one year, through June 30, 2013, the 3.4 percent interest rate for federally subsidized undergraduate student loans. It would be offset by repealing the Prevention and Public Health Fund established by the health care overhaul and rescinding unobligated amounts in the fund. Passed 215-195: R 202-30; D 13-165. A "nay" was a vote in support of the president's position. April 27, 2012. *(Story, p. C-5)*

270. **HR 4310. Fiscal 2013 Defense Authorization/Guantánamo Detention Facility.** Smith, D-Wash., amendment that would strike language from the bill that would provide the authority to transfer individuals captured within the United States, territories or other locations to military authorities and prevent the indefinite detention of such individuals at Guantánamo Bay, Cuba. Rejected in Committee of the Whole 182-238: R 19-219; D 163-19. May 18, 2012. *(Story, p. C-5)*

441. **H Res 711. Holder Contempt Resolution/Adoption.** Adoption of the resolution that would cite Attorney General Eric H. Holder Jr. for contempt of Congress for refusing to comply with the subpoena issued by the House Oversight and Government Reform Committee to provide documents to the committee regarding the "Operation Fast and Furious" gun-tracking program. Adopted 255-67: R 238-2; D 17-65. A "nay" was a vote in support of the president's position. June 28, 2012. *(Story, p. C-6)*

460. **HR 6079. Repeal of Health Care Overhaul/Passage.** Passage of the bill that would repeal the 2010 health care overhaul, which requires most individuals to buy health insurance by 2014, makes changes to government health care programs and sets new requirements for health insurers. The bill would restore the provisions of law amended or repealed by the health care overhaul and would repeal certain provisions of the health care reconciliation law. Passed 244-185: R 239-0; D 5-185. A "nay" was a vote in support of the president's position. July 11, 2012. *(Story, p. C-6)*

608. **HR 6156. Russia Trade Relations/Passage.** Passage of the bill that would establish permanent normal trade relations with Russia and Moldova and end Jackson-Vanik restrictions on both economies. The bill also would provide sanctions against people involved in human rights violations in Russia. Passed 365-43: R 227-6; D 138-37. A "yea" was a vote in support of the president's position. Nov. 16, 2012. *(Story, p. C-7)*

[1] Ron Barber, D-Ariz., was sworn in June 19, 2012, to fill the vacancy created by the Jan. 25 resignation of fellow Democrat Gabrielle Giffords. The last vote for which Giffords was eligible was vote 11; the first vote for which Barber was eligible was vote 382.

[2] Dennis Cardoza, D-Calif., resigned Aug. 15, 2012. The last vote for which he was eligible was vote 556.

[3] Thomas Massie, R-Ky., was sworn in Nov. 13, 2012, to fill the vacancy created by the July 31 resignation of fellow Republican Geoff Davis. The last vote for which Davis was eligible was vote 539; the first vote for which Massie was eligible was vote 605.

[4] David A. Curson, D-Mich., was sworn in Nov. 13, 2012, to fill the vacancy created by the July 6 resignation of Republican Thaddeus McCotter. The last vote for which McCotter was eligible was vote 451; the first vote for which Curson was eligible was vote 605.

[5] Donald M. Payne Jr., D-N.J., was sworn in Nov. 15, 2012, to fill the vacancy created by the March 6 death of his father, fellow Democrat Donald M. Payne. The last vote for which the elder Payne was eligible was vote 97; the first vote for which Payne Jr. was eligible was vote 606.

[6] The speaker votes only at his discretion.

[7] Suzan DelBene, D-Wash., was sworn in Nov. 13, 2012, to fill the vacancy created by the March 20 resignation of fellow Democrat Jay Inslee. The last vote for which Inslee was eligible was vote 111; the first vote for which DelBene was eligible was vote 605.

	195	270	441	460	608
ALABAMA					
1 Bonner	Y	N	Y	?	Y
2 Roby	Y	N	Y	Y	Y
3 Rogers	Y	?	Y	Y	Y
4 Aderholt	Y	N	Y	Y	Y
5 Brooks	Y	N	Y	Y	Y
6 Bachus	Y	N	Y	Y	Y
7 Sewell	N	N	?	N	Y
ALASKA					
AL Young	Y	N	Y	Y	Y
ARIZONA					
1 Gosar	N	?	Y	Y	Y
2 Franks	N	N	Y	Y	Y
3 Quayle	N	N	Y	Y	Y
4 Pastor	N	Y	N	N	Y
5 Schweikert	N	N	Y	Y	Y
6 Flake	N	N	Y	Y	Y
7 Grijalva	N	Y	?	N	N
8 Barber[1]			N	N	Y
ARKANSAS					
1 Crawford	Y	N	Y	Y	Y
2 Griffin	Y	N	Y	Y	Y
3 Womack	Y	N	Y	Y	Y
4 Ross	N	N	Y	Y	Y
CALIFORNIA					
1 Thompson	N	Y	N	N	Y
2 Herger	Y	N	Y	Y	Y
3 Lungren	Y	N	Y	Y	Y
4 McClintock	N	Y	Y	Y	Y
5 Matsui	N	Y	?	N	Y
6 Woolsey	N	Y	?	N	-
7 Miller, George	N	Y	N	N	Y
8 Pelosi	N	Y	?	N	Y
9 Lee	N	Y	?	N	N
10 Garamendi	N	Y	?	N	Y
11 McNerney	N	Y	N	N	Y
12 Speier	N	?	N	N	Y
13 Stark	N	Y	?	N	N
14 Eshoo	N	Y	N	N	Y
15 Honda	N	Y	?	N	Y
16 Lofgren	N	Y	N	N	N
17 Farr	?	Y	N	N	Y
18 Cardoza[2]	?	?	?	N	
19 Denham	Y	N	Y	Y	Y
20 Costa	+	Y	?	N	Y
21 Nunes	?	N	Y	Y	Y
22 McCarthy	Y	N	Y	Y	Y
23 Capps	N	Y	N	N	Y
24 Gallegly	Y	N	Y	Y	?
25 McKeon	Y	N	Y	Y	Y
26 Dreier	Y	N	Y	Y	Y
27 Sherman	N	Y	N	N	Y
28 Berman	N	Y	N	N	Y
29 Schiff	N	Y	?	N	Y
30 Waxman	N	Y	N	N	Y
31 Becerra	N	Y	?	N	Y
32 Chu	N	Y	?	N	N
33 Bass	N	Y	?	N	Y
34 Roybal-Allard	N	Y	?	N	Y
35 Waters	N	Y	?	N	N
36 Hahn	N	Y	?	N	N
37 Richardson	N	Y	?	N	Y
38 Napolitano	N	Y	?	N	N
39 Sánchez, Linda	N	Y	?	N	Y
40 Royce	Y	N	Y	Y	Y
41 Lewis	Y	N	?	Y	Y
42 Miller, Gary	Y	N	Y	Y	Y
43 Baca	N	Y	?	N	N
44 Calvert	Y	N	Y	Y	Y
45 Bono Mack	Y	N	Y	Y	Y
46 Rohrabacher	Y	N	Y	Y	Y
47 Sanchez, Loretta	N	?	N	N	Y
48 Campbell	Y	N	Y	Y	Y
49 Issa	Y	N	Y	Y	Y
50 Bilbray	Y	N	Y	Y	Y
51 Filner	-	+	?	N	?
52 Hunter	Y	N	Y	Y	Y
53 Davis	N	Y	?	N	Y

	195	270	441	460	608
COLORADO					
1 DeGette	N	Y	?	N	Y
2 Polis	N	Y	?	N	Y
3 Tipton	Y	Y	Y	Y	Y
4 Gardner	Y	N	Y	Y	Y
5 Lamborn	N	N	Y	Y	Y
6 Coffman	Y	N	Y	Y	Y
7 Perlmutter	N	Y	N	N	Y
CONNECTICUT					
1 Larson	N	Y	?	N	Y
2 Courtney	N	Y	N	N	Y
3 DeLauro	N	Y	N	N	N
4 Himes	N	Y	N	N	Y
5 Murphy	N	Y	N	N	Y
DELAWARE					
AL Carney	N	Y	?	N	Y
FLORIDA					
1 Miller	N	N	Y	Y	Y
2 Southerland	Y	N	Y	Y	Y
3 Brown	N	Y	?	N	Y
4 Crenshaw	Y	N	Y	Y	Y
5 Nugent	Y	N	Y	Y	Y
6 Stearns	Y	N	Y	Y	Y
7 Mica	Y	N	Y	Y	Y
8 Webster	Y	N	Y	Y	Y
9 Bilirakis	Y	N	Y	Y	Y
10 Young	Y	N	Y	Y	Y
11 Castor	N	Y	?	N	Y
12 Ross	Y	N	Y	Y	Y
13 Buchanan	Y	N	Y	Y	Y
14 Mack	Y	N	Y	Y	Y
15 Posey	Y	N	Y	Y	Y
16 Rooney	Y	N	Y	Y	Y
17 Wilson	N	Y	?	N	N
18 Ros-Lehtinen	Y	N	Y	Y	Y
19 Deutch	N	Y	N	N	Y
20 Wasserman Schultz	N	Y	N	N	Y
21 Diaz-Balart	Y	N	Y	Y	Y
22 West	Y	N	Y	Y	Y
23 Hastings	N	Y	?	N	Y
24 Adams	Y	N	Y	Y	Y
25 Rivera	Y	N	Y	Y	Y
GEORGIA					
1 Kingston	?	N	Y	Y	Y
2 Bishop	N	N	?	N	?
3 Westmoreland	N	N	Y	Y	Y
4 Johnson	N	Y	?	N	Y
5 Lewis	N	Y	?	N	Y
6 Price	N	Y	Y	Y	Y
7 Woodall	N	N	Y	Y	Y
8 Scott, A.	Y	N	Y	Y	Y
9 Graves	N	N	Y	Y	Y
10 Broun	N	Y	Y	Y	Y
11 Gingrey	N	Y	Y	Y	Y
12 Barrow	Y	N	Y	N	Y
13 Scott, D.	N	Y	?	N	Y
HAWAII					
1 Hanabusa	N	Y	?	N	Y
2 Hirono	?	Y	N	N	Y
IDAHO					
1 Labrador	N	Y	Y	Y	Y
2 Simpson	Y	N	Y	Y	Y
ILLINOIS					
1 Rush	N	Y	?	N	?
2 Jackson	N	Y	?	?	?
3 Lipinski	Y	N	P	N	N
4 Gutierrez	N	Y	?	N	Y
5 Quigley	N	Y	N	N	Y
6 Roskam	Y	N	Y	Y	Y
7 Davis, D.	N	Y	?	N	Y
8 Walsh	N	Y	Y	Y	Y
9 Schakowsky	N	Y	-	N	Y
10 Dold	Y	N	Y	Y	Y
11 Kinzinger	Y	N	Y	Y	Y
12 Costello	N	?	N	N	?
13 Biggert	Y	N	Y	Y	Y
14 Hultgren	Y	N	Y	Y	Y
15 Johnson	Y	N	Y	Y	Y

KEY   **Republicans**   Democrats

Y Voted for (yea)	X Paired against	C Voted "present" to avoid possible conflict of interest
# Paired for	- Announced against	
+ Announced for	P Voted "present"	? Did not vote or otherwise make a position known
N Voted against (nay)		

	195	270	441	460	608
16 Manzullo	Y	N	Y	Y	Y
17 Schilling	Y	N	Y	Y	Y
18 Schock	Y	N	Y	Y	Y
19 Shimkus	Y	Y	Y	Y	Y
INDIANA					
1 Visclosky	N	Y	N	N	N
2 Donnelly	Y	N	Y	N	Y
3 Stutzman	Y	N	Y	Y	Y
4 Rokita	Y	N	Y	Y	Y
5 Burton	Y	N	Y	Y	Y
6 Pence	Y	N	Y	Y	+
7 Carson	N	Y	?	N	Y
8 Bucshon	Y	N	Y	Y	Y
9 Young	Y	N	Y	Y	Y
IOWA					
1 Braley	N	Y	N	N	Y
2 Loebsack	N	Y	N	N	Y
3 Boswell	N	Y	Y	N	Y
4 Latham	Y	N	Y	Y	Y
5 King	Y	N	Y	Y	Y
KANSAS					
1 Huelskamp	N	Y	Y	Y	Y
2 Jenkins	?	N	Y	Y	Y
3 Yoder	Y	N	Y	Y	Y
4 Pompeo	Y	N	Y	Y	Y
KENTUCKY					
1 Whitfield	Y	N	Y	Y	Y
2 Guthrie	Y	N	Y	Y	Y
3 Yarmuth	N	Y	?	N	?
4 Davis[3]	+	N	Y	Y	
Massie[3]					Y
5 Rogers	Y	N	Y	Y	Y
6 Chandler	N	N	Y	N	Y
LOUISIANA					
1 Scalise	Y	N	Y	Y	Y
2 Richmond	N	Y	?	N	Y
3 Landry	Y	N	Y	Y	Y
4 Fleming	Y	N	Y	Y	Y
5 Alexander	Y	N	Y	Y	Y
6 Cassidy	?	N	Y	Y	Y
7 Boustany	Y	N	Y	Y	Y
MAINE					
1 Pingree	N	Y	?	N	N
2 Michaud	N	Y	N	N	Y
MARYLAND					
1 Harris	Y	N	Y	Y	Y
2 Ruppersberger	N	N	?	N	Y
3 Sarbanes	N	Y	?	N	Y
4 Edwards	N	Y	?	N	Y
5 Hoyer	N	Y	?	N	Y
6 Bartlett	Y	Y	Y	Y	?
7 Cummings	N	Y	?	N	Y
8 Van Hollen	N	Y	?	N	Y
MASSACHUSETTS					
1 Olver	N	Y	?	N	Y
2 Neal	N	Y	?	N	Y
3 McGovern	N	Y	?	N	Y
4 Frank	N	Y	?	N	Y
5 Tsongas	N	Y	N	N	Y
6 Tierney	N	Y	N	N	N
7 Markey	N	Y	?	N	Y
8 Capuano	N	Y	?	N	Y
9 Lynch	N	Y	N	N	Y
10 Keating	N	Y	?	N	N
MICHIGAN					
1 Benishek	Y	N	Y	Y	Y
2 Huizenga	N	N	Y	Y	Y
3 Amash	N	Y	Y	Y	Y
4 Camp	?	N	Y	Y	Y
5 Kildee	N	Y	?	N	N
6 Upton	Y	N	Y	Y	N
7 Walberg	N	N	Y	Y	Y
8 Rogers	Y	N	Y	N	Y
9 Peters	N	Y	?	N	Y
10 Miller	Y	N	Y	Y	Y
11 McCotter[4]	Y	N			
11 Curson[4]					Y
12 Levin	N	N	?	N	Y
13 Clarke	N	Y	?	N	N
14 Conyers	N	Y	?	N	Y
15 Dingell	N	Y	N	N	Y
MINNESOTA					
1 Walz	Y	Y	N	N	Y
2 Kline	Y	N	Y	Y	Y
3 Paulsen	Y	N	Y	Y	Y
4 McCollum	N	Y	?	N	N

	195	270	441	460	608
5 Ellison	N	N	?	N	Y
6 Bachmann	Y	N	Y	Y	Y
7 Peterson	Y	N	Y	N	Y
8 Cravaack	Y	N	Y	Y	Y
MISSISSIPPI					
1 Nunnelee	Y	N	Y	Y	Y
2 Thompson	N	Y	?	N	N
3 Harper	Y	N	Y	Y	Y
4 Palazzo	Y	N	Y	Y	Y
MISSOURI					
1 Clay	N	?	?	N	Y
2 Akin	Y	N	Y	Y	Y
3 Carnahan	N	Y	?	N	Y
4 Hartzler	Y	N	Y	Y	Y
5 Cleaver	N	Y	?	N	Y
6 Graves	Y	N	Y	Y	Y
7 Long	Y	N	Y	Y	Y
8 Emerson	Y	N	Y	Y	Y
9 Luetkemeyer	Y	N	Y	Y	Y
MONTANA					
AL Rehberg	Y	Y	Y	Y	Y
NEBRASKA					
1 Fortenberry	Y	N	Y	Y	Y
2 Terry	Y	N	Y	Y	Y
3 Smith	Y	N	Y	Y	Y
NEVADA					
1 Berkley	N	Y	N	N	Y
2 Amodei	Y	?	Y	Y	Y
3 Heck	Y	N	Y	Y	Y
NEW HAMPSHIRE					
1 Guinta	Y	N	Y	Y	Y
2 Bass	Y	N	Y	Y	Y
NEW JERSEY					
1 Andrews	N	Y	?	N	Y
2 LoBiondo	Y	N	Y	Y	N
3 Runyan	Y	N	Y	Y	Y
4 Smith	Y	N	Y	Y	Y
5 Garrett	N	N	Y	Y	Y
6 Pallone	N	Y	?	N	N
7 Lance	Y	N	Y	Y	Y
8 Pascrell	N	+	?	N	Y
9 Rothman	N	Y	N	N	?
10 Payne[5]					Y
11 Frelinghuysen	Y	N	Y	Y	Y
12 Holt	N	Y	N	N	?
13 Sires	?	Y	?	N	Y
NEW MEXICO					
1 Heinrich	N	Y	N	N	?
2 Pearce	Y	N	Y	Y	Y
3 Luján	N	Y	N	N	Y
NEW YORK					
1 Bishop	Y	Y	N	N	Y
2 Israel	N	Y	?	N	Y
3 King	Y	N	Y	Y	Y
4 McCarthy	N	N	?	N	Y
5 Ackerman	N	Y	?	N	Y
6 Meeks	N	Y	?	N	Y
7 Crowley	N	Y	?	N	Y
8 Nadler	N	Y	N	N	N
9 Turner	Y	N	Y	Y	Y
10 Towns	?	Y	?	N	?
11 Clarke	N	Y	?	N	N
12 Velázquez	N	Y	?	N	N
13 Grimm	Y	N	Y	Y	Y
14 Maloney, C.	N	Y	?	N	?
15 Rangel	?	Y	?	N	Y
16 Serrano	N	Y	?	N	N
17 Engel	N	Y	?	N	Y
18 Lowey	N	Y	?	N	Y
19 Hayworth	Y	N	Y	Y	Y
20 Gibson	Y	Y	Y	Y	Y
21 Tonko	N	Y	?	N	Y
22 Hinchey	N	Y	?	N	N
23 Owens	Y	N	Y	N	Y
24 Hanna	Y	N	Y	Y	Y
24 Maffei					
25 Buerkle	Y	N	Y	Y	Y
26 Hochul	Y	Y	N	N	Y
27 Higgins	Y	Y	N	N	Y
28 Slaughter	–	+	N	N	Y
29 Reed	Y	N	Y	Y	Y
NORTH CAROLINA					
1 Butterfield	N	Y	?	N	Y
2 Ellmers	Y	N	Y	Y	Y
3 Jones	Y	Y	Y	Y	N
4 Price	N	Y	?	N	Y

	195	270	441	460	608
5 Foxx	N	N	Y	Y	Y
6 Coble	N	N	Y	Y	Y
7 McIntyre	Y	N	Y	N	Y
8 Kissell	Y	N	Y	Y	Y
9 Myrick	Y	N	Y	Y	Y
10 McHenry	?	N	Y	Y	Y
11 Shuler	N	Y	N	N	?
12 Watt	N	Y	?	N	Y
13 Miller	N	Y	N	N	Y
NORTH DAKOTA					
AL Berg	Y	N	Y	Y	Y
OHIO					
1 Chabot	Y	N	Y	Y	Y
2 Schmidt	Y	N	Y	Y	Y
3 Turner	Y	N	Y	Y	Y
4 Jordan	Y	N	Y	Y	Y
5 Latta	Y	N	Y	Y	Y
6 Johnson	Y	N	Y	Y	Y
7 Austria	Y	N	Y	Y	Y
8 Boehner[6]	Y				
9 Kaptur	N	Y	?	N	N
10 Kucinich	N	Y	?	N	N
11 Fudge	N	Y	?	N	N
12 Tiberi	Y	N	Y	Y	Y
13 Sutton	N	Y	N	N	N
14 LaTourette	Y	N	N	Y	N
15 Stivers	Y	N	Y	Y	Y
16 Renacci	Y	N	Y	Y	Y
17 Ryan	N	Y	N	N	N
18 Gibbs	Y	N	Y	Y	Y
OKLAHOMA					
1 Sullivan	Y	N	Y	Y	?
2 Boren	Y	N	Y	Y	?
3 Lucas	Y	N	Y	Y	Y
4 Cole	Y	N	Y	Y	Y
5 Lankford	Y	N	Y	Y	Y
OREGON					
1 Bonamici	N	Y	N	N	Y
2 Walden	Y	N	Y	Y	Y
3 Blumenauer	?	Y	N	N	Y
4 DeFazio	N	Y	N	N	N
5 Schrader	N	Y	N	N	Y
PENNSYLVANIA					
1 Brady	N	Y	?	N	?
2 Fattah	N	Y	?	N	Y
3 Kelly	Y	N	Y	Y	Y
4 Altmire	N	Y	Y	N	Y
5 Thompson	Y	N	Y	Y	Y
6 Gerlach	Y	N	Y	Y	Y
7 Meehan	Y	N	Y	Y	Y
8 Fitzpatrick	Y	N	Y	Y	?
9 Shuster	Y	N	Y	Y	Y
10 Marino	?	N	Y	Y	Y
11 Barletta	Y	N	Y	Y	Y
12 Critz	N	Y	Y	N	Y
13 Schwartz	N	Y	N	N	Y
14 Doyle	N	Y	?	N	N
15 Dent	Y	N	Y	Y	Y
16 Pitts	Y	N	Y	Y	Y
17 Holden	?	Y	N	N	?
18 Murphy	N	N	Y	Y	Y
19 Platts	Y	N	Y	Y	Y
RHODE ISLAND					
1 Cicilline	N	Y	?	N	N
2 Langevin	N	Y	N	N	Y
SOUTH CAROLINA					
1 Scott	Y	N	Y	Y	Y
2 Wilson	N	N	Y	Y	Y
3 Duncan	N	N	Y	Y	Y
4 Gowdy	N	N	Y	Y	Y
5 Mulvaney	N	N	Y	Y	Y
6 Clyburn	N	Y	?	N	Y
SOUTH DAKOTA					
AL Noem	Y	N	Y	Y	Y
TENNESSEE					
1 Roe	Y	N	Y	Y	Y
2 Duncan	Y	Y	Y	Y	Y
3 Fleischmann	Y	N	Y	Y	Y
4 DesJarlais	Y	N	Y	Y	Y
5 Cooper	N	Y	N	N	Y
6 Black	N	N	Y	Y	Y
7 Blackburn	Y	N	Y	Y	Y
8 Fincher	N	N	Y	Y	Y
9 Cohen	N	Y	N	N	Y

	195	270	441	460	608
TEXAS					
1 Gohmert	Y	N	Y	Y	Y
2 Poe	Y	N	Y	Y	Y
3 Johnson, S.	Y	N	Y	Y	Y
4 Hall	Y	N	Y	Y	Y
5 Hensarling	Y	N	Y	Y	Y
6 Barton	Y	N	Y	Y	Y
7 Culberson	Y	N	Y	Y	Y
8 Brady	Y	N	Y	Y	Y
9 Green, A.	N	Y	?	N	Y
10 McCaul	Y	N	Y	Y	Y
11 Conaway	Y	N	Y	Y	Y
12 Granger	Y	N	Y	Y	Y
13 Thornberry	Y	N	Y	Y	Y
14 Paul	?	Y	Y	Y	N
15 Hinojosa	?	Y	?	N	Y
16 Reyes	N	Y	?	N	Y
17 Flores	Y	N	Y	Y	Y
18 Jackson Lee	N	Y	?	N	+
19 Neugebauer	N	N	Y	Y	Y
20 Gonzalez	N	Y	?	N	Y
21 Smith	Y	N	Y	Y	Y
22 Olson	Y	N	Y	Y	Y
23 Canseco	+	N	Y	Y	Y
24 Marchant	Y	N	Y	Y	Y
25 Doggett	N	Y	N	N	Y
26 Burgess	Y	N	Y	Y	Y
27 Farenthold	Y	N	Y	Y	Y
28 Cuellar	N	N	N	N	Y
29 Green, G.	N	Y	N	N	N
30 Johnson, E.	N	Y	?	N	Y
31 Carter	Y	N	Y	Y	Y
32 Sessions	Y	N	Y	Y	Y
UTAH					
1 Bishop	Y	Y	Y	Y	Y
2 Matheson	Y	N	Y	Y	Y
3 Chaffetz	Y	N	Y	Y	Y
VERMONT					
AL Welch	N	Y	N	N	Y
VIRGINIA					
1 Wittman	Y	N	Y	Y	Y
2 Rigell	Y	N	N	Y	Y
3 Scott	N	Y	?	N	Y
4 Forbes	Y	N	Y	Y	?
5 Hurt	Y	N	Y	Y	Y
6 Goodlatte	Y	N	Y	Y	Y
7 Cantor	Y	N	Y	Y	Y
8 Moran	N	Y	N	N	Y
9 Griffith	Y	Y	Y	Y	Y
10 Wolf	Y	N	Y	Y	?
11 Connolly	N	Y	N	N	Y
WASHINGTON					
1 DelBene[7]					Y
2 Larsen	N	Y	N	N	Y
3 Herrera Beutler	Y	N	Y	Y	Y
4 Hastings	Y	N	Y	Y	Y
5 McMorris Rodgers	Y	N	Y	Y	Y
6 Dicks	N	Y	N	N	Y
7 McDermott	N	Y	N	N	Y
8 Reichert	Y	N	Y	Y	Y
9 Smith	N	Y	N	N	Y
WEST VIRGINIA					
1 McKinley	Y	N	Y	Y	Y
2 Capito	Y	N	Y	Y	Y
3 Rahall	N	Y	N	N	N
WISCONSIN					
1 Ryan	Y	N	Y	Y	Y
2 Baldwin	N	Y	N	N	Y
3 Kind	N	Y	N	N	Y
4 Moore	N	Y	?	N	Y
5 Sensenbrenner	Y	Y	Y	Y	Y
6 Petri	Y	Y	Y	Y	Y
7 Duffy	Y	N	Y	Y	Y
8 Ribble	Y	Y	Y	Y	Y
WYOMING					
AL Lummis	Y	N	Y	Y	Y

IN THE HOUSE | By Vote Number

613. **HR 6429. STEM Visa Program/Passage.** Passage of the bill that would create a new visa program under which foreign students earning advanced degrees in science, technology, engineering or mathematics at eligible U.S. colleges and universities could remain in the United States to work in those fields. The bill would eliminate the Diversity Visa Program and would reallocate 55,000 visas to the new STEM visa program. It would allow spouses and children of STEM graduates to reside in the United States without work authorization after a one-year waiting period. Passed 245-139: R 218-5; D 27-134. A "nay" was a vote in support of the president's position. Nov. 30, 2012. *(Story, p. C-7)*

644. **HR 6684. Sequester Replacement/Passage.** Passage of the bill that would cancel the automatic cuts from discretionary programs set to occur in January 2013 and replace the sequester with a $19 billion reduction in the discretionary cap for fiscal 2013 and savings from mandatory programs totaling more than $300 billion over 10 years. It also would eliminate the separate cap on defense spending for the year to allow for higher spending levels. Passed 215-209: R 215-21; D 0-188. A "nay" was a vote in support of the president's position. Dec. 20, 2012. *(Story, p. C-8)*

659. **HR 8. Tax Rates Extensions/Motion to Concur.** Camp, R-Mich., motion to concur in the Senate amendments to the bill that permanently would extend the 2001 and 2003 tax rates for individual income below $400,000 and joint-filer income below $450,000. Rates for income above those thresholds would rise from 35 percent to 39.6 percent. It also would permanently extend the tax rates on dividends and capital gains for individual income below $400,000 and joint-filer income below $450,000. Rates for the dividends and capital gains taxes would rise to 20 percent for income above those thresholds. The measure would delay the automatic, across-the-board cuts known as sequester for two months. Half of the sequester delay would be offset by discretionary cuts, split between defense and non-defense programs, and the other half offset by revenue raised through the voluntary transfer of traditional IRAs to Roth IRAs, which would tax retirement savings when transferred. The measure also would tax individual estates valued at more than $5 million and joint estates valued at more than $10 million at 40 percent. It permanently would "patch" the alternative minimum tax to account for inflation. Unemployment insurance would be extended through 2013. The bill would block scheduled cuts to Medicare physician payment rates and extend for five years tax credits included in the 2009 stimulus law, including the child tax credit and the earned-income tax credit. It would allow the 2 percent payroll tax holiday to expire. It also would extend the Milk Income Loss Contract program at current rates. Motion agreed to (thus clearing the bill for the president) 257-167: R 85-151; D 172-16. A "yea" was a vote in support of the president's position. Jan. 1, 2013. *(Story, p. C-8)*

	613	644	659
ALABAMA			
1 Bonner	?	Y	N
2 Roby	Y	Y	N
3 Rogers	Y	Y	N
4 Aderholt	Y	Y	N
5 Brooks	Y	Y	N
6 Bachus	Y	Y	N
7 Sewell	N	N	Y
ALASKA			
AL Young	?	Y	Y
ARIZONA			
1 Gosar	Y	Y	N
2 Franks	Y	Y	N
3 Quayle	Y	Y	N
4 Pastor	N	N	Y
5 Schweikert	?	N	N
6 Flake	Y	Y	N
7 Grijalva	N	N	Y
8 Barber	+	N	Y
ARKANSAS			
1 Crawford	Y	Y	N
2 Griffin	Y	Y	N
3 Womack	Y	Y	Y
4 Ross	Y	N	Y
CALIFORNIA			
1 Thompson	N	N	Y
2 Herger	+	Y	Y
3 Lungren	Y	Y	Y
4 McClintock	?	Y	N
5 Matsui	N	N	Y
6 Woolsey	N	N	?
7 Miller, George	N	N	Y
8 Pelosi	N	N	Y
9 Lee	N	N	Y
10 Garamendi	Y	N	Y
11 McNerney	Y	N	Y
12 Speier	?	N	Y
13 Stark	?	?	?
14 Eshoo	N	N	Y
15 Honda	N	N	Y
16 Lofgren	N	N	Y
17 Farr	N	N	Y
18 Vacant			
19 Denham	N	Y	Y
20 Costa	N	N	Y
21 Nunes	Y	Y	N
22 McCarthy	Y	Y	N
23 Capps	N	N	Y
24 Gallegly	?	Y	Y
25 McKeon	Y	Y	Y
26 Dreier	Y	Y	Y
27 Sherman	N	N	Y
28 Berman	?	N	Y
29 Schiff	N	N	Y
30 Waxman	N	N	Y
31 Becerra	N	N	N
32 Chu	Y	N	Y
33 Bass	N	N	Y
34 Roybal-Allard	–	N	Y
35 Waters	N	N	Y
36 Hahn	N	N	Y
37 Richardson	?	N	Y
38 Napolitano	N	N	Y
39 Sánchez, Linda	N	N	Y
40 Royce	Y	Y	Y
41 Lewis	Y	Y	?
42 Miller, Gary	Y	Y	Y
43 Baca	N	N	Y
44 Calvert	Y	Y	Y
45 Bono Mack	Y	Y	Y
46 Rohrabacher	Y	Y	Y
47 Sanchez, Loretta	N	N	Y
48 Campbell	N	Y	N
49 Issa	Y	Y	N
51 Filner[1]			
50 Bilbray	?	Y	Y
52 Hunter	Y	Y	N
53 Davis	N	N	Y

	613	644	659
COLORADO			
1 DeGette	?	N	Y
2 Polis	N	N	Y
3 Tipton	Y	Y	N
4 Gardner	Y	Y	N
5 Lamborn	Y	Y	N
6 Coffman	Y	Y	N
7 Perlmutter	N	N	Y
CONNECTICUT			
1 Larson	N	N	Y
2 Courtney	N	N	Y
3 DeLauro	N	N	N
4 Himes	Y	N	Y
5 Murphy	?	N	Y
DELAWARE			
AL Carney	Y	N	Y
FLORIDA			
1 Miller	Y	Y	N
2 Southerland	Y	Y	N
3 Brown	N	N	Y
4 Crenshaw	Y	Y	N
5 Nugent	Y	Y	N
6 Stearns	Y	Y	N
7 Mica	Y	Y	N
8 Webster	Y	Y	N
9 Bilirakis	Y	Y	N
10 Young	Y	Y	Y
11 Castor	N	N	Y
12 Ross	Y	Y	N
13 Buchanan	Y	Y	Y
14 Mack	Y	Y	N
15 Posey	Y	Y	N
16 Rooney	Y	Y	N
17 Wilson	N	N	Y
18 Ros-Lehtinen	Y	Y	Y
19 Deutch	N	N	Y
20 Wasserman Schultz	N	N	Y
21 Diaz-Balart	Y	Y	Y
22 West	Y	Y	N
23 Hastings	?	N	Y
24 Adams	Y	Y	N
25 Rivera	Y	?	N
GEORGIA			
1 Kingston	Y	Y	N
2 Bishop	N	N	Y
3 Westmoreland	Y	Y	N
4 Johnson	N	N	Y
5 Lewis	?	N	?
6 Price	Y	Y	N
7 Woodall	Y	Y	N
8 Scott, A.	Y	Y	N
9 Graves	Y	N	N
10 Broun	Y	N	N
11 Gingrey	Y	Y	N
12 Barrow	Y	N	N
13 Scott, D.	N	N	Y
HAWAII			
1 Hanabusa	N	N	Y
2 Hirono	N	N	Y
IDAHO			
1 Labrador	Y	N	N
2 Simpson	+	Y	Y
ILLINOIS			
1 Rush	?	N	Y
2 Vacant[2]			
3 Lipinski	Y	N	Y
4 Gutierrez	N	N	Y
5 Quigley	N	N	Y
6 Roskam	Y	Y	N
7 Davis, D.	N	N	Y
8 Walsh	Y	N	N
9 Schakowsky	N	N	Y
10 Dold	Y	Y	Y
11 Kinzinger	Y	Y	Y
12 Costello	?	?	Y
13 Biggert	Y	Y	Y
14 Hultgren	Y	Y	N
15 Johnson	Y	N	Y

KEY   Republicans   Democrats

Y Voted for (yea)	X Paired against	C Voted "present" to avoid possible conflict of interest
# Paired for	– Announced against	
+ Announced for	P Voted "present"	? Did not vote or otherwise make a position known
N Voted against (nay)		

[1] Bob Filner, D-Calif., resigned Dec. 3, 2012. The last vote for which he was eligible was vote 613.

[2] Jesse L. Jackson Jr., D-Ill., resigned Nov. 21, 2012. The last vote for which he was eligible was vote 608.

[3] The speaker votes only at his discretion.

		613	644	659
16	**Manzullo**	+	Y	Y
17	**Schilling**	Y	Y	N
18	**Schock**	Y	Y	Y
19	**Shimkus**	Y	Y	Y
INDIANA				
1	Visclosky	–	N	N
2	Donnelly	Y	N	Y
3	**Stutzman**	Y	Y	N
4	**Rokita**	Y	Y	N
5	**Burton**	?	Y	?
6	**Pence**	–	Y	N
7	Carson	N	N	Y
8	**Bucshon**	Y	Y	N
9	**Young**	Y	Y	N
IOWA				
1	Braley	N	N	Y
2	Loebsack	N	N	Y
3	Boswell	Y	N	Y
4	**Latham**	Y	Y	N
5	**King**	Y	Y	N
KANSAS				
1	**Huelskamp**	Y	N	N
2	**Jenkins**	Y	Y	N
3	**Yoder**	Y	Y	N
4	**Pompeo**	Y	Y	N
KENTUCKY				
1	**Whitfield**	Y	N	N
2	**Guthrie**	Y	Y	N
3	Yarmuth	N	N	Y
4	**Massie**	Y	N	N
5	**Rogers**	Y	Y	Y
6	Chandler	?	N	Y
LOUISIANA				
1	**Scalise**	Y	Y	N
2	Richmond	N	N	Y
3	**Landry**	Y	N	N
4	**Fleming**	Y	Y	N
5	**Alexander**	Y	Y	Y
6	**Cassidy**	Y	N	N
7	**Boustany**	Y	Y	N
MAINE				
1	Pingree	N	N	Y
2	Michaud	Y	N	Y
MARYLAND				
1	**Harris**	Y	Y	N
2	Ruppersberger	Y	N	Y
3	Sarbanes	N	N	Y
4	Edwards	–	N	Y
5	Hoyer	N	N	Y
6	**Bartlett**	Y	Y	N
7	Cummings	N	N	Y
8	Van Hollen	N	N	Y
MASSACHUSETTS				
1	Olver	N	N	Y
2	Neal	N	N	Y
3	McGovern	N	N	Y
4	Frank	N	N	Y
5	Tsongas	N	N	Y
6	Tierney	N	N	Y
7	Markey	N	N	Y
8	Capuano	N	N	Y
9	Lynch	N	N	Y
10	Keating	N	N	Y
MICHIGAN				
1	**Benishek**	Y	Y	Y
2	**Huizenga**	Y	Y	N
3	**Amash**	Y	N	N
4	**Camp**	Y	Y	Y
5	Kildee	N	N	Y
6	**Upton**	Y	Y	Y
7	**Walberg**	Y	Y	N
8	**Rogers**	Y	Y	Y
9	Peters	N	N	Y
10	**Miller**	Y	Y	N
11	Curson	N	N	Y
12	Levin	N	N	Y
13	Clarke	N	N	Y
14	Conyers	N	N	Y
15	Dingell	N	N	Y
MINNESOTA				
1	Walz	N	N	Y
2	**Kline**	Y	Y	Y
3	**Paulsen**	Y	Y	N
4	McCollum	N	N	Y

		613	644	659
5	Ellison	N	N	Y
6	**Bachmann**	Y	Y	N
7	Peterson	Y	N	N
8	**Cravaack**	Y	Y	N
MISSISSIPPI				
1	**Nunnelee**	Y	Y	N
2	Thompson	N	N	Y
3	**Harper**	Y	Y	N
4	**Palazzo**	Y	Y	N
MISSOURI				
1	Clay	N	N	Y
2	**Akin**	?	Y	N
3	Carnahan	?	N	Y
4	**Hartzler**	Y	Y	N
5	Cleaver	N	N	Y
6	**Graves**	Y	Y	–
7	**Long**	Y	Y	N
8	**Emerson**	Y	Y	Y
9	**Luetkemeyer**	Y	Y	Y
MONTANA				
AL	**Rehberg**	Y	Y	N
NEBRASKA				
1	**Fortenberry**	Y	Y	Y
2	**Terry**	Y	Y	N
3	**Smith**	Y	Y	N
NEVADA				
1	Berkley	N	N	Y
2	**Amodei**	Y	Y	N
3	**Heck**	Y	Y	Y
NEW HAMPSHIRE				
1	**Guinta**	Y	Y	N
2	**Bass**	Y	Y	Y
NEW JERSEY				
1	Andrews	N	N	Y
2	**LoBiondo**	Y	N	Y
3	**Runyan**	Y	Y	Y
4	**Smith**	Y	Y	Y
5	**Garrett**	Y	Y	N
6	Pallone	N	N	Y
7	**Lance**	Y	Y	Y
8	Pascrell	N	N	Y
9	Rothman	?	N	Y
10	Payne	N	N	Y
11	**Frelinghuysen**	+	Y	Y
12	Holt	N	N	Y
13	Sires	N	N	Y
NEW MEXICO				
1	Heinrich	N	N	Y
2	**Pearce**	Y	Y	N
3	Luján	N	N	Y
NEW YORK				
1	Bishop	N	N	Y
2	Israel	N	N	Y
3	**King**	Y	Y	N
4	McCarthy	N	N	Y
5	Ackerman	N	N	Y
6	Meeks	N	N	Y
7	Crowley	N	N	Y
8	Nadler	N	N	Y
9	**Turner**	Y	Y	Y
10	Towns	?	N	Y
11	Clarke	N	N	Y
12	Velázquez	–	N	Y
13	**Grimm**	Y	Y	N
14	Maloney, C.	N	N	Y
15	Rangel	N	N	Y
16	Serrano	N	N	Y
17	Engel	N	N	Y
18	Lowey	N	N	Y
19	**Hayworth**	Y	Y	N
20	**Gibson**	Y	Y	N
21	Tonko	N	N	Y
22	Hinchey	N	N	Y
23	Owens	–	N	Y
24	**Hanna**	Y	Y	Y
24	Maffei			
25	**Buerkle**	Y	Y	–
26	Hochul	Y	N	Y
27	Higgins	N	N	Y
28	Slaughter	–	N	Y
29	**Reed**	Y	Y	N
NORTH CAROLINA				
1	Butterfield	N	N	Y
2	**Ellmers**	Y	Y	N
3	**Jones**	N	N	Y
4	Price	N	N	Y

		613	644	659
5	**Foxx**	Y	Y	N
6	**Coble**	Y	Y	N
7	McIntyre	Y	N	N
8	Kissell	Y	N	Y
9	**Myrick**	Y	Y	N
10	**McHenry**	Y	Y	N
11	Shuler	?	N	Y
12	Watt	?	N	Y
13	Miller	N	N	N
NORTH DAKOTA				
AL	**Berg**	Y	Y	N
OHIO				
1	**Chabot**	Y	Y	N
2	**Schmidt**	?	Y	N
3	**Turner**	Y	Y	N
4	**Jordan**	Y	Y	N
5	**Latta**	Y	Y	Y
6	**Johnson**	Y	Y	Y
7	**Austria**	Y	Y	N
8	**Boehner**[3]			Y
9	Kaptur	N	N	Y
10	Kucinich	N	N	Y
11	Fudge	N	N	Y
12	**Tiberi**	Y	Y	N
13	Sutton	?	N	Y
14	**LaTourette**	Y	Y	N
15	**Stivers**	Y	Y	N
16	**Renacci**	Y	Y	N
17	Ryan	N	N	Y
18	**Gibbs**	Y	Y	N
OKLAHOMA				
1	**Sullivan**	Y	Y	Y
2	Boren	?	N	Y
3	**Lucas**	Y	Y	Y
4	**Cole**	Y	Y	Y
5	**Lankford**	Y	Y	N
OREGON				
1	Bonamici	N	N	Y
2	**Walden**	Y	Y	Y
3	Blumenauer	Y	N	N
4	DeFazio	Y	N	N
5	Schrader	Y	N	N
PENNSYLVANIA				
1	Brady	N	N	Y
2	Fattah	?	N	Y
3	**Kelly**	Y	Y	Y
4	Altmire	Y	N	Y
5	**Thompson**	Y	Y	Y
6	**Gerlach**	Y	Y	Y
7	**Meehan**	Y	Y	Y
8	**Fitzpatrick**	Y	N	Y
9	**Shuster**	Y	Y	Y
10	**Marino**	Y	Y	Y
11	**Barletta**	N	Y	Y
12	Critz	N	N	Y
13	**Schwartz**	+	N	Y
14	Doyle	N	N	Y
15	**Dent**	Y	Y	Y
16	**Pitts**	Y	Y	Y
17	Holden	N	N	Y
18	**Murphy**	Y	Y	Y
19	**Platts**	Y	N	Y
RHODE ISLAND				
1	Cicilline	N	N	Y
2	Langevin	N	N	Y
SOUTH CAROLINA				
1	**Scott**	Y	Y	N
2	**Wilson**	Y	Y	N
3	**Duncan**	Y	Y	N
4	**Gowdy**	Y	Y	N
5	**Mulvaney**	Y	Y	N
6	Clyburn	N	N	Y
SOUTH DAKOTA				
AL	**Noem**	Y	Y	Y
TENNESSEE				
1	**Roe**	Y	Y	N
2	**Duncan**	Y	N	N
3	**Fleischmann**	Y	Y	N
4	**DesJarlais**	Y	Y	N
5	Cooper	Y	N	N
6	**Black**	+	Y	N
7	**Blackburn**	Y	Y	N
8	**Fincher**	Y	Y	N
9	Cohen	Y	N	Y

		613	644	659
TEXAS				
1	**Gohmert**	Y	N	N
2	**Poe**	Y	Y	N
3	**Johnson, S.**	Y	?	N
4	**Hall**	Y	Y	N
5	**Hensarling**	Y	Y	N
6	**Barton**	Y	Y	N
7	**Culberson**	?	?	N
8	**Brady**	Y	Y	Y
9	Green, A.	N	N	Y
10	**McCaul**	Y	Y	N
11	**Conaway**	Y	Y	N
12	**Granger**	Y	Y	N
13	**Thornberry**	Y	Y	Y
14	**Paul**	Y	N	?
15	Hinojosa	N	N	Y
16	Reyes	?	?	Y
17	**Flores**	Y	Y	N
18	Jackson Lee	N	N	Y
19	**Neugebauer**	Y	Y	N
20	Gonzalez	N	N	Y
21	**Smith**	?	Y	Y
22	**Olson**	Y	Y	N
23	**Canseco**	Y	Y	N
24	**Marchant**	Y	Y	N
25	Doggett	N	N	Y
26	**Burgess**	Y	Y	N
27	**Farenthold**	Y	Y	N
28	Cuellar	Y	N	Y
29	Green, G.	N	N	Y
30	Johnson, E.	N	N	Y
31	**Carter**	Y	Y	N
32	**Sessions**	Y	Y	Y
UTAH				
1	**Bishop**	Y	P	N
2	Matheson	Y	N	N
3	**Chaffetz**	Y	Y	N
VERMONT				
AL	Welch	N	N	Y
VIRGINIA				
1	**Wittman**	Y	Y	N
2	**Rigell**	Y	Y	N
3	Scott	N	N	N
4	**Forbes**	Y	Y	N
5	**Hurt**	Y	Y	N
6	**Goodlatte**	Y	Y	N
7	**Cantor**	Y	Y	N
8	Moran	Y	N	N
9	**Griffith**	Y	Y	N
10	**Wolf**	Y	N	N
11	Connolly	N	N	Y
WASHINGTON				
1	DelBene	N	N	Y
2	Larsen	N	N	Y
3	**Herrera Beutler**	Y	N	Y
4	Hastings	N	Y	Y
5	**McMorris Rodgers**	Y	Y	Y
6	Dicks	N	N	Y
7	McDermott	N	N	N
8	**Reichert**	Y	Y	Y
9	Smith	–	N	N
WEST VIRGINIA				
1	**McKinley**	Y	Y	N
2	**Capito**	Y	Y	N
3	Rahall	N	N	Y
WISCONSIN				
1	**Ryan**	Y	Y	Y
2	Baldwin	?	N	Y
3	Kind	Y	N	Y
4	Moore	N	N	Y
5	**Sensenbrenner**	Y	Y	N
6	**Petri**	Y	Y	N
7	**Duffy**	Y	Y	N
8	**Ribble**	Y	Y	Y
WYOMING				
AL	**Lummis**	Y	Y	N

HOUSE
ROLL CALL
VOTES

House Roll Call Index
By Bill Number

IN THE HOUSE | By Vote Number

1. Procedural Matter/Quorum Call.* A quorum was present with 378 members responding (56 members did not respond). Jan. 17, 2012.

2. H J Res 98. Debt Limit Disapproval/Previous Question. Scott, R-S.C., motion to order the previous question (thus ending debate and the possibility of amendment) on adoption of the rule (H Res 515) that would provide for a motion to proceed to a joint resolution disapproving of the president's exercise of authority to raise the borrowing limit, even if the joint resolution has not been reported to the House. Motion agreed to 238-176: R 235-0; D 3-176. (Subsequently, the rule was adopted by voice vote.) Jan. 18, 2012.

3. Procedural Motion/Journal. Approval of the House Journal of Tuesday, Jan. 17, 2012. Approved 292-120: R 197-37; D 95-83. Jan. 18, 2012.

4. H J Res 98. Debt Limit Disapproval/Passage. Passage of the joint resolution that would disapprove of a request by the president for a $1.2 trillion debt limit increase. Current law provides for a $1.2 trillion increase in the debt limit upon certification from the president that the debt is within $100 billion of the debt limit unless a disapproval measure is enacted. Passed 239-176: R 233-1; D 6-175. A "nay" was a vote in support of the president's position. Jan. 18, 2012.

		2	3	4
ALABAMA				
1	**Bonner**	Y	Y	Y
2	**Roby**	Y	Y	Y
3	**Rogers**	Y	Y	Y
4	**Aderholt**	Y	Y	Y
5	**Brooks**	Y	Y	Y
6	**Bachus**	Y	?	Y
7	Sewell	N	Y	N
ALASKA				
AL	**Young**	Y	Y	Y
ARIZONA				
1	**Gosar**	Y	Y	Y
2	**Franks**	Y	Y	Y
3	**Quayle**	Y	N	Y
4	Pastor	N	N	N
5	**Schweikert**	Y	Y	Y
6	**Flake**	Y	Y	Y
7	Grijalva	N	N	N
8	Giffords	?	?	?
ARKANSAS				
1	**Crawford**	Y	N	Y
2	**Griffin**	Y	N	Y
3	**Womack**	Y	Y	Y
4	Ross	N	Y	N
CALIFORNIA				
1	Thompson	N	N	N
2	**Herger**	Y	Y	Y
3	**Lungren**	Y	Y	Y
4	**McClintock**	Y	Y	Y
5	Matsui	N	Y	N
6	Woolsey	N	Y	N
7	Miller, George	N	Y	N
8	Pelosi	?	N	N
9	Lee	N	N	N
10	Garamendi	N	N	N
11	McNerney	N	Y	N
12	Speier	?	?	?
13	Stark	N	Y	N
14	Eshoo	N	Y	N
15	Honda	N	N	N
16	Lofgren	N	Y	N
17	Farr	?	?	?
18	Cardoza	?	?	?
19	**Denham**	Y	Y	Y
20	Costa	N	N	N
21	**Nunes**	Y	Y	Y
22	**McCarthy**	Y	Y	Y
23	Capps	N	N	N
24	**Gallegly**	Y	Y	Y
25	**McKeon**	Y	Y	Y
26	**Dreier**	Y	Y	N
27	Sherman	N	Y	N
28	Berman	N	Y	N
29	Schiff	N	Y	N
30	Waxman	N	Y	N
31	Becerra	N	Y	N
32	Chu	N	Y	N
33	Bass	N	N	N
34	Roybal-Allard	N	Y	N
35	Waters	N	Y	N
36	Hahn	N	N	N
37	Richardson	N	Y	N
38	Napolitano	N	Y	N
39	Sánchez, Linda	N	N	N
40	**Royce**	Y	Y	Y
41	**Lewis**	Y	Y	Y
42	**Miller, Gary**	Y	Y	Y
43	Baca	N	Y	N
44	**Calvert**	Y	Y	Y
45	**Bono Mack**	Y	Y	Y
46	**Rohrabacher**	Y	N	Y
47	Sanchez, Loretta	N	N	N
48	**Campbell**	?	?	?
49	**Issa**	Y	Y	Y
50	**Bilbray**	Y	N	Y
51	Filner	–	–	–
52	**Hunter**	Y	N	Y
53	Davis	N	Y	N

		2	3	4
COLORADO				
1	DeGette	N	Y	N
2	Polis	N	N	N
3	**Tipton**	Y	N	Y
4	**Gardner**	Y	N	Y
5	**Lamborn**	Y	Y	Y
6	**Coffman**	Y	N	Y
7	Perlmutter	N	Y	N
CONNECTICUT				
1	Larson	N	Y	N
2	Courtney	N	N	N
3	DeLauro	N	Y	N
4	Himes	N	N	N
5	Murphy	N	Y	N
DELAWARE				
AL	Carney	N	Y	N
FLORIDA				
1	**Miller**	Y	Y	Y
2	**Southerland**	Y	Y	Y
3	Brown	N	Y	?
4	**Crenshaw**	Y	Y	Y
5	**Nugent**	Y	Y	Y
6	**Stearns**	Y	Y	Y
7	**Mica**	Y	Y	Y
8	**Webster**	Y	Y	Y
9	**Bilirakis**	Y	Y	Y
10	**Young**	Y	Y	Y
11	Castor	N	N	N
12	**Ross**	Y	Y	Y
13	**Buchanan**	Y	Y	Y
14	**Mack**	Y	Y	Y
15	**Posey**	Y	Y	Y
16	**Rooney**	Y	N	Y
17	Wilson	N	Y	N
18	**Ros-Lehtinen**	Y	Y	Y
19	Deutch	N	Y	N
20	Wasserman Schultz	N	Y	N
21	**Diaz-Balart**	Y	Y	Y
22	**West**	Y	Y	Y
23	Hastings	N	N	N
24	**Adams**	Y	N	Y
25	**Rivera**	Y	Y	Y
GEORGIA				
1	**Kingston**	Y	Y	Y
2	Bishop	N	Y	N
3	**Westmoreland**	Y	Y	Y
4	Johnson	N	N	N
5	Lewis	N	N	N
6	**Price**	Y	Y	Y
7	**Woodall**	Y	N	Y
8	**Scott, A.**	Y	Y	Y
9	**Graves**	Y	Y	Y
10	**Broun**	Y	Y	Y
11	**Gingrey**	Y	Y	Y
12	Barrow	N	N	Y
13	Scott, D.	N	Y	N
HAWAII				
1	Hanabusa	N	Y	N
2	Hirono	N	Y	N
IDAHO				
1	**Labrador**	Y	Y	Y
2	**Simpson**	Y	Y	?
ILLINOIS				
1	Rush	N	N	N
2	Jackson	N	N	N
3	Lipinski	N	N	N
4	Gutierrez	N	Y	N
5	Quigley	N	Y	N
6	**Roskam**	Y	Y	Y
7	Davis	N	N	N
8	**Walsh**	Y	N	P
9	Schakowsky	N	N	N
10	**Dold**	Y	N	Y
11	**Kinzinger**	Y	Y	Y
12	Costello	N	N	N
13	**Biggert**	Y	Y	Y
14	**Hultgren**	Y	Y	Y
15	**Johnson**	Y	Y	Y

KEY   **Republicans**   Democrats

Y Voted for (yea)	**X** Paired against	**C** Voted "present" to avoid possible conflict of interest
# Paired for	**–** Announced against	
+ Announced for	**P** Voted "present"	**?** Did not vote or otherwise make a position known
N Voted against (nay)		

* CQ does not include quorum calls in its vote charts.

		2	3	4
16	Manzullo	Y	Y	Y
17	Schilling	Y	Y	Y
18	Schock	Y	Y	Y
19	Shimkus	Y	Y	Y
INDIANA				
1	Visclosky	N	N	N
2	Donnelly	N	N	N
3	Stutzman	Y	Y	Y
4	Rokita	Y	Y	Y
5	Burton	Y	Y	Y
6	Pence	Y	Y	Y
7	Carson	N	N	N
8	Bucshon	Y	Y	Y
9	Young	Y	Y	Y
IOWA				
1	Braley	N	N	N
2	Loebsack	N	Y	N
3	Boswell	N	Y	N
4	Latham	Y	N	Y
5	King	Y	Y	Y
KANSAS				
1	Huelskamp	Y	Y	Y
2	Jenkins	Y	Y	Y
3	Yoder	Y	N	Y
4	Pompeo	Y	Y	Y
KENTUCKY				
1	Whitfield	Y	Y	Y
2	Guthrie	Y	Y	Y
3	Yarmuth	N	Y	N
4	Davis	Y	Y	Y
5	Rogers	Y	Y	Y
6	Chandler	N	Y	N
LOUISIANA				
1	Scalise	Y	Y	Y
2	Richmond	N	Y	N
3	Landry	P	Y	P
4	Fleming	Y	Y	Y
5	Alexander	Y	Y	Y
6	Cassidy	Y	?	Y
7	Boustany	Y	Y	Y
MAINE				
1	Pingree	N	Y	N
2	Michaud	N	Y	N
MARYLAND				
1	Harris	Y	Y	Y
2	Ruppersberger	N	Y	N
3	Sarbanes	N	N	N
4	Edwards	N	Y	N
5	Hoyer	N	N	N
6	Bartlett	Y	Y	?
7	Cummings	N	N	N
8	Van Hollen	N	Y	N
MASSACHUSETTS				
1	Olver	N	N	N
2	Neal	N	N	N
3	McGovern	N	N	N
4	Frank	N	?	N
5	Tsongas	N	N	N
6	Tierney	N	N	N
7	Markey	N	N	N
8	Capuano	N	N	N
9	Lynch	N	N	N
10	Keating	N	N	N
MICHIGAN				
1	Benishek	Y	N	Y
2	Huizenga	Y	Y	Y
3	Amash	Y	P	Y
4	Camp	Y	Y	Y
5	Kildee	N	Y	N
6	Upton	Y	Y	Y
7	Walberg	Y	Y	Y
8	Rogers	Y	Y	Y
9	Peters	N	N	N
10	Miller	Y	Y	Y
11	McCotter	Y	Y	Y
12	Levin	N	N	N
13	Clarke	N	N	N
14	Conyers	N	N	N
15	Dingell	N	N	N
MINNESOTA				
1	Walz	N	Y	N
2	Kline	Y	Y	Y
3	Paulsen	Y	Y	Y
4	McCollum	N	Y	N

		2	3	4
5	Ellison	N	N	N
6	Bachmann	Y	Y	Y
7	Peterson	N	N	N
8	Cravaack	Y	N	Y
MISSISSIPPI				
1	Nunnelee	Y	Y	Y
2	Thompson	N	N	N
3	Harper	Y	Y	Y
4	Palazzo	Y	Y	Y
MISSOURI				
1	Clay	N	Y	N
2	Akin	Y	Y	Y
3	Carnahan	?	N	N
4	Hartzler	Y	Y	Y
5	Cleaver	N	N	N
6	Graves	Y	Y	Y
7	Long	Y	Y	Y
8	Emerson	Y	Y	Y
9	Luetkemeyer	Y	Y	Y
MONTANA				
AL	Rehberg	Y	Y	Y
NEBRASKA				
1	Fortenberry	Y	Y	Y
2	Terry	N	Y	N
3	Smith	Y	Y	Y
NEVADA				
1	Berkley	?	?	?
2	Amodei	Y	Y	Y
3	Heck	Y	N	Y
NEW HAMPSHIRE				
1	Guinta	Y	Y	Y
2	Bass	Y	Y	Y
NEW JERSEY				
1	Andrews	N	N	N
2	LoBiondo	Y	N	Y
3	Runyan	Y	Y	Y
4	Smith	Y	Y	Y
5	Garrett	Y	N	Y
6	Pallone	N	N	N
7	Lance	Y	Y	Y
8	Pascrell	N	N	N
9	Rothman	N	N	N
10	Payne	?	?	N
11	Frelinghuysen	Y	Y	Y
12	Holt	N	N	N
13	Sires	N	Y	N
NEW MEXICO				
1	Heinrich	?	?	?
2	Pearce	Y	Y	Y
3	Luján	N	Y	N
NEW YORK				
1	Bishop	N	N	N
2	Israel	N	N	N
3	King	Y	Y	Y
4	McCarthy	N	Y	N
5	Ackerman	N	Y	N
6	Meeks	N	Y	N
7	Crowley	N	Y	N
8	Nadler	N	Y	N
9	Turner	Y	Y	Y
10	Towns	N	N	N
11	Clarke	N	N	N
12	Velázquez	N	N	N
13	Grimm	?	Y	Y
14	Maloney	N	Y	N
15	Rangel	N	Y	N
16	Serrano	N	Y	N
17	Engel	N	Y	N
18	Lowey	N	Y	N
19	Hayworth	Y	Y	Y
20	Gibson	Y	N	Y
21	Tonko	N	Y	N
22	Hinchey	?	?	?
23	Owens	N	Y	N
24	Hanna	Y	N	Y
25	Buerkle	Y	Y	Y
26	Hochul	N	Y	N
27	Higgins	N	N	N
28	Slaughter	N	N	N
29	Reed	Y	N	Y
NORTH CAROLINA				
1	Butterfield	N	Y	N
2	Ellmers	Y	Y	Y
3	Jones	Y	Y	Y
4	Price	N	Y	N

		2	3	4
5	Foxx	Y	Y	Y
6	Coble	Y	Y	Y
7	McIntyre	N	Y	N
8	Kissell	N	Y	N
9	Myrick	Y	Y	Y
10	McHenry	Y	Y	Y
11	Shuler	N	N	N
12	Watt	N	Y	N
13	Miller	N	N	N
NORTH DAKOTA				
AL	Berg	Y	Y	Y
OHIO				
1	Chabot	Y	Y	Y
2	Schmidt	Y	Y	Y
3	Turner	Y	Y	Y
4	Jordan	Y	Y	Y
5	Latta	Y	Y	Y
6	Johnson	Y	N	Y
7	Austria	Y	Y	Y
8	Boehner			
9	Kaptur	N	Y	N
10	Kucinich	N	N	N
11	Fudge	N	N	N
12	Tiberi	Y	Y	Y
13	Sutton	N	N	N
14	LaTourette	Y	Y	Y
15	Stivers	Y	N	Y
16	Renacci	Y	N	Y
17	Ryan	N	Y	N
18	Gibbs	Y	N	Y
OKLAHOMA				
1	Sullivan	Y	Y	Y
2	Boren	N	Y	Y
3	Lucas	Y	Y	Y
4	Cole	Y	Y	Y
5	Lankford	Y	Y	Y
OREGON				
1	Vacant			
2	Walden	Y	Y	Y
3	Blumenauer	N	Y	N
4	DeFazio	N	N	N
5	Schrader	N	Y	N
PENNSYLVANIA				
1	Brady	N	N	N
2	Fattah	N	?	N
3	Kelly	Y	Y	Y
4	Altmire	N	Y	N
5	Thompson	Y	Y	Y
6	Gerlach	Y	N	Y
7	Meehan	Y	Y	Y
8	Fitzpatrick	Y	N	Y
9	Shuster	Y	Y	Y
10	Marino	?	?	?
11	Barletta	Y	Y	Y
12	Critz	N	Y	N
13	Schwartz	N	Y	N
14	Doyle	N	N	N
15	Dent	Y	N	Y
16	Pitts	Y	Y	Y
17	Holden	N	N	N
18	Murphy	Y	Y	Y
19	Platts	Y	Y	Y
RHODE ISLAND				
1	Cicilline	N	Y	N
2	Langevin	N	Y	N
SOUTH CAROLINA				
1	Scott	Y	Y	Y
2	Wilson	Y	Y	Y
3	Duncan	Y	Y	Y
4	Gowdy	Y	Y	Y
5	Mulvaney	Y	Y	Y
6	Clyburn	N	N	N
SOUTH DAKOTA				
AL	Noem	?	?	+
TENNESSEE				
1	Roe	Y	Y	Y
2	Duncan	Y	Y	Y
3	Fleischmann	Y	Y	Y
4	DesJarlais	Y	Y	Y
5	Cooper	N	Y	N
6	Black	Y	Y	Y
7	Blackburn	Y	Y	Y
8	Fincher	Y	Y	Y
9	Cohen	N	Y	N

		2	3	4
TEXAS				
1	Gohmert	Y	?	Y
2	Poe	Y	N	Y
3	Johnson, S.	Y	Y	Y
4	Hall	Y	Y	Y
5	Hensarling	Y	Y	Y
6	Barton	Y	Y	Y
7	Culberson	Y	Y	Y
8	Brady	Y	Y	Y
9	Green, A.	N	Y	N
10	McCaul	Y	Y	Y
11	Conaway	Y	N	Y
12	Granger	Y	Y	Y
13	Thornberry	Y	Y	Y
14	Paul	Y	Y	Y
15	Hinojosa	N	Y	N
16	Reyes	?	?	?
17	Flores	Y	Y	Y
18	Jackson Lee	N	Y	N
19	Neugebauer	Y	Y	Y
20	Gonzalez	N	Y	N
21	Smith	Y	Y	Y
22	Olson	?	Y	Y
23	Canseco	Y	Y	Y
24	Marchant	Y	Y	Y
25	Doggett	N	N	N
26	Burgess	Y	N	Y
27	Farenthold	Y	Y	Y
28	Cuellar	N	N	N
29	Green, G.	N	N	N
30	Johnson, E.	N	+	N
31	Carter	Y	Y	Y
32	Sessions	Y	Y	Y
UTAH				
1	Bishop	Y	Y	Y
2	Matheson	Y	Y	Y
3	Chaffetz	Y	Y	Y
VERMONT				
AL	Welch	N	Y	N
VIRGINIA				
1	Wittman	Y	Y	Y
2	Rigell	Y	Y	Y
3	Scott	N	Y	N
4	Forbes	Y	Y	Y
5	Hurt	Y	Y	Y
6	Goodlatte	Y	Y	Y
7	Cantor	Y	Y	Y
8	Moran	N	Y	N
9	Griffith	Y	Y	Y
10	Wolf	Y	Y	Y
11	Connolly	N	Y	N
WASHINGTON				
1	Inslee	?	?	?
2	Larsen	N	N	N
3	Herrera Beutler	Y	N	Y
4	Hastings	Y	Y	Y
5	McMorris Rodgers	Y	Y	Y
6	Dicks	N	Y	N
7	McDermott	N	N	N
8	Reichert	Y	Y	Y
9	Smith	N	Y	N
WEST VIRGINIA				
1	McKinley	Y	Y	Y
2	Capito	Y	Y	Y
3	Rahall	N	N	N
WISCONSIN				
1	Ryan	Y	Y	Y
2	Baldwin	N	N	N
3	Kind	N	N	N
4	Moore	N	N	N
5	Sensenbrenner	Y	Y	Y
6	Petri	Y	Y	Y
7	Duffy	Y	N	Y
8	Ribble	Y	Y	Y
WYOMING				
AL	Lummis	Y	Y	Y

IN THE HOUSE | By Vote Number

5. **HR 3117. Electronic Duck Stamp/Passage.** Wittman, R-Va., motion to suspend the rules and pass the bill that would grant the Interior Department permanent authority to authorize states to issue electronic duck stamps, digital versions of a federal migratory-bird hunting license that also helps fund conservation efforts. States would be required to remit to the Interior Department the face value of the stamp as well as the federal portion of any additional fees. Motion agreed to 373-1: R 214-1; D 159-0. A two-thirds majority of those present and voting (250 in this case) is required for passage under suspension of the rules. Jan. 23, 2012.

6. **HR 1141. Rota Forest Sites Study/Passage.** Wittman, R-Va., motion to suspend the rules and pass the bill that would direct the Interior Department to study the feasibility and suitability of designating certain forest sites on Rota, Commonwealth of the Northern Mariana Islands, as a unit of the National Park System. Motion agreed to 278-100: R 116-100; D 162-0. A two-thirds majority of those present and voting (252 in this case) is required for passage under suspension of the rules. Jan. 23, 2012.

7. **H Res 516. Fiscal 2013 Budget Importance/Adoption.** Ryan, R-Wis., motion to suspend the rules and adopt the resolution that would declare the sense of the House that the adoption of a fiscal 2013 federal budget is of national importance. Motion agreed to 410-1: R 234-0; D 176-1. A two-thirds majority of those present and voting (274 in this case) is required for adoption under suspension of the rules. Jan. 24, 2012.

8. **HR 2070. World War II Memorial Prayer Plaque/Passage.** Johnson, R-Ohio, motion to suspend the rules and pass the bill that would direct the Interior Department to install in the area of the World War II Memorial in Washington, D.C., a plaque or inscription with the words of a prayer said to the nation by President Franklin D. Roosevelt on June 6, 1944, the morning of D-Day. The agency would not be allowed to use federal funds for the plaque, but could solicit private contributions. Motion agreed to 386-26: R 233-0; D 153-26. A two-thirds majority of those present and voting (275 in this case) is required for passage under suspension of the rules. Jan. 24, 2012.

9. **HR 3630. Year-End Extensions/Motion to Instruct.** Capps, D-Calif., motion to instruct conferees to file a conference report by Feb. 17, 2012, on a bill (HR 3630) that would extend the 4.2 percent employee payroll tax rate, Medicare payment rates to doctors and workers' eligibility for certain expanded unemployment benefits. Motion agreed to 397-16: R 218-16; D 179-0. Jan. 24, 2012.

10. **HR 1022. Buffalo Soldiers Study/Passage.** Johnson, R-Ohio, motion to suspend the rules and pass the bill that would direct the Interior Department to study options for commemorating the role of the Buffalo Soldiers, a group of African-American troops, in the early days of the National Park System. Motion agreed to 338-70: R 159-70; D 179-0. A two-thirds majority of those present and voting (272 in this case) is required for passage under suspension of the rules. Jan. 25, 2012.

11. **HR 3801. Ultralight Aircraft Smuggling/Passage.** Reichert, R-Wash., motion to suspend the rules and pass the bill that would subject individuals who smuggle drugs into the United States using certain light, one-person aircraft to the same penalties that apply to smuggling with other aircraft. Ultralight vehicles would be included under this aviation smuggling ban, subjecting their operators to the same penalties for violations. Motion agreed to 408-0: R 227-0; D 181-0. A two-thirds majority of those present and voting (272 in this case) is required for passage under suspension of the rules. Jan. 25, 2012.

	5	6	7	8	9	10	11
ALABAMA							
1 Bonner	?	?	Y	Y	Y	N	Y
2 Roby	Y	Y	Y	Y	Y	Y	Y
3 Rogers	Y	Y	Y	Y	N	Y	Y
4 Aderholt	Y	N	Y	N	N	N	Y
5 Brooks	Y	Y	Y	Y	Y	Y	Y
6 Bachus	Y	Y	Y	Y	Y	Y	Y
7 Sewell	Y	Y	Y	Y	Y	Y	Y
ALASKA							
AL Young	Y	Y	Y	Y	Y	?	?
ARIZONA							
1 Gosar	?	?	?	?	?	?	?
2 Franks	Y	N	Y	Y	Y	Y	Y
3 Quayle	Y	N	Y	Y	N	N	Y
4 Pastor	Y	Y	Y	Y	Y	Y	Y
5 Schweikert	Y	Y	Y	Y	Y	Y	Y
6 Flake	?	?	Y	Y	N	N	Y
7 Grijalva	?	?	Y	N	Y	Y	Y
8 Giffords	?	?	?	?	?	?	Y
ARKANSAS							
1 Crawford	Y	Y	Y	Y	Y	Y	Y
2 Griffin	Y	N	Y	Y	Y	Y	Y
3 Womack	Y	Y	Y	Y	Y	Y	Y
4 Ross	Y	Y	Y	Y	Y	Y	Y
CALIFORNIA							
1 Thompson	Y	Y	Y	Y	Y	Y	Y
2 Herger	Y	Y	Y	Y	Y	Y	?
3 Lungren	Y	Y	Y	Y	Y	Y	Y
4 McClintock	Y	Y	Y	Y	N	Y	Y
5 Matsui	Y	Y	Y	Y	Y	Y	Y
6 Woolsey	Y	Y	Y	N	Y	Y	Y
7 Miller, George	+	+	+	+	+	Y	Y
8 Pelosi	Y	Y	Y	Y	Y	Y	Y
9 Lee	Y	Y	Y	N	Y	Y	Y
10 Garamendi	Y	Y	Y	Y	Y	Y	Y
11 McNerney	Y	Y	Y	Y	Y	Y	Y
12 Speier	?	Y	?	Y	Y	Y	Y
13 Stark	Y	Y	Y	N	Y	Y	Y
14 Eshoo	Y	Y	Y	Y	Y	Y	Y
15 Honda	Y	Y	N	N	Y	Y	Y
16 Lofgren	Y	Y	Y	Y	Y	Y	Y
17 Farr	?	?	?	?	?	?	?
18 Cardoza	Y	Y	Y	Y	Y	Y	Y
19 Denham	?	?	Y	Y	Y	Y	Y
20 Costa	?	Y	Y	Y	Y	Y	Y
21 Nunes	Y	Y	Y	Y	Y	Y	Y
22 McCarthy	Y	Y	Y	Y	Y	Y	Y
23 Capps	Y	Y	Y	Y	Y	Y	Y
24 Gallegly	?	?	Y	Y	Y	Y	Y
25 McKeon	?	?	Y	Y	Y	Y	Y
26 Dreier	Y	Y	Y	Y	Y	Y	Y
27 Sherman	+	+	Y	Y	Y	Y	Y
28 Berman	?	?	?	?	?	?	?
29 Schiff	Y	Y	Y	Y	Y	Y	Y
30 Waxman	Y	Y	Y	Y	Y	Y	Y
31 Becerra	Y	Y	Y	?	Y	Y	Y
32 Chu	Y	Y	Y	N	Y	Y	Y
33 Bass	Y	Y	Y	Y	Y	Y	Y
34 Roybal-Allard	Y	Y	Y	Y	Y	Y	Y
35 Waters	Y	Y	Y	Y	Y	?	Y
36 Hahn	Y	Y	Y	Y	Y	Y	Y
37 Richardson	Y	Y	Y	Y	Y	Y	Y
38 Napolitano	Y	Y	Y	Y	Y	Y	Y
39 Sánchez, Linda	?	?	?	?	?	Y	Y
40 Royce	Y	N	Y	Y	Y	Y	Y
41 Lewis	Y	Y	Y	Y	Y	Y	Y
42 Miller, Gary	Y	Y	Y	Y	Y	Y	Y
43 Baca	Y	Y	Y	Y	Y	Y	Y
44 Calvert	Y	Y	Y	Y	Y	Y	Y
45 Bono Mack	?	?	Y	Y	Y	Y	Y
46 Rohrabacher	Y	Y	Y	Y	Y	Y	Y
47 Sanchez, Loretta	Y	Y	Y	Y	Y	Y	Y
48 Campbell	Y	N	Y	N	Y	?	?
49 Issa	Y	Y	Y	Y	Y	Y	Y
50 Bilbray	Y	Y	Y	Y	Y	Y	Y
51 Filner	+	+	Y	Y	Y	Y	Y
52 Hunter	Y	Y	Y	Y	Y	Y	Y
53 Davis	Y	Y	Y	Y	Y	Y	Y

	5	6	7	8	9	10	11
COLORADO							
1 DeGette	Y	Y	Y	Y	Y	Y	Y
2 Polis	Y	Y	N	Y	Y	Y	Y
3 Tipton	Y	N	Y	Y	N	Y	Y
4 Gardner	Y	N	Y	Y	N	Y	Y
5 Lamborn	Y	Y	Y	Y	Y	Y	Y
6 Coffman	Y	N	Y	Y	Y	Y	Y
7 Perlmutter	Y	Y	Y	Y	Y	Y	Y
CONNECTICUT							
1 Larson	Y	Y	Y	Y	Y	Y	Y
2 Courtney	Y	Y	Y	Y	Y	Y	Y
3 DeLauro	Y	Y	Y	Y	Y	Y	Y
4 Himes	Y	Y	Y	Y	Y	Y	Y
5 Murphy	Y	Y	Y	Y	Y	Y	Y
DELAWARE							
AL Carney	Y	Y	Y	Y	Y	Y	Y
FLORIDA							
1 Miller	Y	N	Y	Y	Y	Y	Y
2 Southerland	Y	N	Y	Y	Y	Y	Y
3 Brown	Y	Y	Y	Y	Y	Y	Y
4 Crenshaw	Y	Y	Y	Y	Y	Y	Y
5 Nugent	Y	N	Y	Y	Y	Y	Y
6 Stearns	Y	N	Y	Y	Y	N	Y
7 Mica	Y	N	Y	Y	Y	Y	Y
8 Webster	?	?	Y	Y	Y	Y	Y
9 Bilirakis	Y	Y	Y	Y	Y	Y	Y
10 Young	Y	Y	Y	Y	Y	Y	Y
11 Castor	Y	Y	Y	Y	Y	Y	Y
12 Ross	Y	N	Y	Y	N	Y	Y
13 Buchanan	Y	Y	Y	Y	Y	Y	Y
14 Mack	?	?	?	?	?	?	?
15 Posey	Y	N	Y	Y	Y	Y	Y
16 Rooney	Y	Y	Y	Y	Y	Y	Y
17 Wilson	Y	Y	Y	Y	Y	Y	Y
18 Ros-Lehtinen	Y	Y	Y	Y	Y	?	?
19 Deutch	Y	Y	Y	Y	Y	Y	Y
20 Wasserman Schultz	Y	Y	Y	Y	Y	Y	Y
21 Diaz-Balart	Y	Y	Y	Y	Y	Y	Y
22 West	Y	Y	Y	Y	Y	Y	Y
23 Hastings	Y	Y	Y	Y	Y	Y	Y
24 Adams	Y	N	Y	Y	Y	Y	Y
25 Rivera	Y	Y	Y	Y	Y	?	?
GEORGIA							
1 Kingston	Y	N	Y	Y	Y	N	Y
2 Bishop	Y	Y	?	?	Y	Y	Y
3 Westmoreland	Y	N	Y	Y	Y	N	Y
4 Johnson	Y	Y	Y	Y	Y	Y	Y
5 Lewis	Y	Y	Y	Y	Y	Y	Y
6 Price	Y	Y	Y	Y	Y	N	Y
7 Woodall	Y	Y	Y	Y	Y	Y	Y
8 Scott, A.	Y	Y	Y	Y	Y	Y	Y
9 Graves	Y	N	Y	Y	Y	N	Y
10 Broun	Y	N	Y	Y	Y	N	Y
11 Gingrey	?	?	Y	Y	Y	Y	Y
12 Barrow	Y	Y	Y	Y	Y	Y	Y
13 Scott, D.	Y	Y	Y	Y	Y	Y	Y
HAWAII							
1 Hanabusa	Y	Y	Y	Y	Y	Y	Y
2 Hirono	Y	Y	Y	Y	?	Y	Y
IDAHO							
1 Labrador	Y	Y	Y	Y	Y	Y	Y
2 Simpson	Y	Y	Y	Y	Y	Y	Y
ILLINOIS							
1 Rush	?	?	?	Y	Y	Y	Y
2 Jackson	Y	Y	Y	N	Y	Y	Y
3 Lipinski	Y	Y	Y	Y	Y	Y	Y
4 Gutierrez	+	+	Y	N	Y	Y	Y
5 Quigley	Y	Y	Y	Y	Y	Y	Y
6 Roskam	Y	?	Y	Y	Y	Y	Y
7 Davis	?	?	Y	Y	Y	Y	Y
8 Walsh	Y	N	Y	Y	Y	N	Y
9 Schakowsky	Y	Y	Y	Y	Y	Y	Y
10 Dold	+	Y	Y	Y	Y	Y	Y
11 Kinzinger	Y	N	Y	Y	Y	N	Y
12 Costello	Y	Y	Y	Y	Y	Y	Y
13 Biggert	Y	Y	Y	Y	Y	Y	Y
14 Hultgren	Y	N	Y	Y	Y	N	Y
15 Johnson	+	+	Y	Y	Y	Y	Y

KEY   **Republicans**   Democrats

Y Voted for (yea)	X Paired against	C Voted "present" to avoid possible conflict of interest
# Paired for	− Announced against	
+ Announced for	P Voted "present"	? Did not vote or otherwise make a position known
N Voted against (nay)		

	5	6	7	8	9	10	11
16 **Manzullo**	Y	N	Y	Y	Y	N	Y
17 **Schilling**	Y	N	Y	Y	Y	Y	Y
18 **Schock**	Y	Y	Y	Y	Y	Y	Y
19 **Shimkus**	Y	Y	Y	Y	Y	Y	Y
INDIANA							
1 Visclosky	Y	Y	Y	Y	Y	Y	Y
2 Donnelly	Y	Y	Y	Y	Y	Y	Y
3 **Stutzman**	Y	N	Y	Y	N	N	Y
4 **Rokita**	Y	Y	Y	Y	Y	N	Y
5 **Burton**	Y	Y	?	?	?	?	?
6 **Pence**	?	?	Y	Y	Y	N	Y
7 Carson	Y	Y	Y	Y	Y	Y	Y
8 **Bucshon**	Y	N	Y	Y	Y	N	Y
9 **Young**	Y	N	Y	Y	Y	N	Y
IOWA							
1 Braley	Y	Y	Y	Y	Y	+	+
2 Loebsack	Y	Y	Y	Y	Y	+	+
3 Boswell	Y	Y	Y	Y	Y	Y	Y
4 **Latham**	Y	N	Y	Y	Y	Y	Y
5 **King**	Y	N	Y	Y	Y	Y	Y
KANSAS							
1 **Huelskamp**	Y	N	Y	Y	Y	N	Y
2 **Jenkins**	Y	Y	Y	Y	Y	Y	Y
3 **Yoder**	Y	Y	Y	Y	N	Y	Y
4 **Pompeo**	Y	N	Y	Y	Y	N	Y
KENTUCKY							
1 **Whitfield**	?	?	Y	Y	Y	Y	Y
2 **Guthrie**	Y	Y	Y	Y	Y	Y	Y
3 Yarmuth	Y	Y	Y	Y	Y	Y	Y
4 **Davis**	Y	Y	Y	Y	Y	Y	Y
5 **Rogers**	Y	Y	Y	Y	Y	Y	Y
6 Chandler	Y	Y	Y	Y	Y	Y	Y
LOUISIANA							
1 **Scalise**	Y	N	Y	Y	Y	N	Y
2 Richmond	Y	Y	Y	Y	Y	Y	Y
3 **Landry**	Y	Y	Y	Y	Y	N	Y
4 **Fleming**	Y	Y	Y	Y	Y	Y	Y
5 **Alexander**	?	?	Y	Y	Y	N	Y
6 **Cassidy**	Y	N	Y	Y	Y	N	Y
7 **Boustany**	Y	Y	Y	Y	Y	Y	Y
MAINE							
1 Pingree	Y	Y	Y	Y	Y	Y	Y
2 Michaud	Y	Y	Y	Y	Y	Y	Y
MARYLAND							
1 **Harris**	Y	Y	Y	Y	Y	N	Y
2 Ruppersberger	Y	Y	Y	Y	Y	Y	Y
3 Sarbanes	Y	Y	Y	Y	Y	Y	Y
4 Edwards	Y	Y	Y	N	Y	Y	Y
5 Hoyer	Y	Y	Y	Y	Y	Y	Y
6 **Bartlett**	Y	Y	Y	Y	Y	Y	Y
7 Cummings	Y	Y	Y	Y	Y	Y	Y
8 Van Hollen	Y	Y	Y	Y	Y	Y	Y
MASSACHUSETTS							
1 Olver	Y	Y	Y	Y	Y	Y	Y
2 Neal	Y	Y	Y	Y	Y	Y	Y
3 McGovern	Y	Y	Y	Y	Y	Y	Y
4 Frank	Y	Y	?	Y	Y	Y	Y
5 Tsongas	Y	Y	Y	Y	Y	Y	Y
6 Tierney	Y	Y	Y	Y	Y	Y	Y
7 Markey	?	?	Y	Y	Y	Y	Y
8 Capuano	Y	Y	Y	Y	Y	Y	Y
9 Lynch	Y	Y	Y	Y	Y	Y	Y
10 Keating	Y	Y	Y	Y	Y	Y	Y
MICHIGAN							
1 **Benishek**	Y	N	Y	Y	Y	N	Y
2 **Huizenga**	Y	N	Y	Y	Y	N	Y
3 **Amash**	Y	N	Y	Y	N	N	Y
4 **Camp**	Y	Y	Y	Y	Y	Y	Y
5 Kildee	Y	Y	Y	Y	Y	Y	Y
6 **Upton**	Y	Y	Y	Y	Y	Y	Y
7 **Walberg**	Y	N	Y	Y	Y	N	Y
8 **Rogers**	Y	Y	Y	Y	Y	Y	Y
9 Peters	Y	Y	Y	Y	Y	Y	Y
10 **Miller**	Y	N	Y	Y	Y	Y	Y
11 **McCotter**	Y	N	Y	Y	Y	Y	Y
12 Levin	Y	Y	Y	Y	Y	Y	Y
13 Clarke	Y	Y	Y	Y	Y	Y	Y
14 Conyers	Y	Y	Y	N	?	Y	Y
15 Dingell	Y	Y	Y	Y	Y	Y	Y
MINNESOTA							
1 Walz	Y	Y	Y	Y	Y	Y	Y
2 **Kline**	Y	N	Y	Y	Y	N	Y
3 **Paulsen**	Y	N	Y	Y	Y	Y	Y
4 McCollum	Y	Y	Y	Y	Y	Y	Y

	5	6	7	8	9	10	11
5 Ellison	Y	Y	Y	N	Y	Y	Y
6 **Bachmann**	Y	N	Y	Y	N	N	Y
7 Peterson	Y	Y	Y	Y	Y	Y	Y
8 **Cravaack**	Y	Y	Y	Y	Y	Y	Y
MISSISSIPPI							
1 **Nunnelee**	Y	N	Y	Y	Y	N	Y
2 Thompson	Y	Y	Y	Y	Y	Y	Y
3 **Harper**	Y	Y	Y	Y	Y	Y	Y
4 **Palazzo**	Y	N	Y	Y	Y	N	Y
MISSOURI							
1 Clay	Y	Y	Y	N	Y	Y	Y
2 **Akin**	Y	N	Y	?	Y	N	Y
3 Carnahan	Y	Y	Y	Y	Y	Y	Y
4 **Hartzler**	Y	N	Y	Y	Y	Y	Y
5 Cleaver	Y	Y	Y	Y	Y	Y	Y
6 **Graves**	Y	Y	Y	Y	Y	N	Y
7 **Long**	Y	Y	Y	Y	N	Y	Y
8 **Emerson**	Y	Y	Y	Y	Y	?	Y
9 **Luetkemeyer**	Y	N	Y	Y	Y	Y	+
MONTANA							
AL **Rehberg**	Y	Y	Y	Y	Y	Y	Y
NEBRASKA							
1 **Fortenberry**	Y	Y	Y	Y	Y	Y	Y
2 **Terry**	Y	N	Y	Y	Y	N	Y
3 **Smith**	Y	Y	Y	Y	Y	Y	Y
NEVADA							
1 Berkley	?	?	Y	Y	Y	Y	Y
2 **Amodei**	Y	Y	Y	Y	Y	Y	Y
3 **Heck**	Y	Y	Y	Y	Y	Y	Y
NEW HAMPSHIRE							
1 **Guinta**	?	Y	Y	Y	Y	Y	Y
2 **Bass**	Y	Y	Y	Y	Y	Y	Y
NEW JERSEY							
1 Andrews	Y	Y	Y	Y	Y	Y	Y
2 **LoBiondo**	Y	N	Y	Y	Y	Y	Y
3 **Runyan**	Y	Y	Y	Y	Y	Y	Y
4 **Smith**	Y	Y	Y	Y	Y	Y	Y
5 **Garrett**	Y	N	Y	Y	Y	N	Y
6 Pallone	Y	Y	Y	Y	Y	Y	Y
7 **Lance**	Y	N	Y	Y	Y	Y	Y
8 Pascrell	+	+	Y	Y	Y	Y	Y
9 Rothman	Y	Y	Y	Y	Y	Y	Y
10 Payne	Y	Y	Y	N	Y	?	Y
11 **Frelinghuysen**	Y	Y	Y	Y	Y	Y	Y
12 Holt	Y	Y	Y	Y	Y	Y	Y
13 Sires	Y	Y	Y	Y	Y	Y	Y
NEW MEXICO							
1 Heinrich	Y	Y	Y	Y	Y	Y	Y
2 **Pearce**	Y	N	Y	Y	Y	N	Y
3 Luján	Y	Y	Y	Y	Y	Y	Y
NEW YORK							
1 Bishop	Y	Y	Y	Y	Y	Y	Y
2 Israel	Y	Y	Y	Y	Y	Y	Y
3 **King**	Y	Y	Y	Y	Y	Y	Y
4 McCarthy	Y	Y	Y	Y	Y	Y	Y
5 Ackerman	Y	Y	Y	Y	Y	?	?
6 Meeks	Y	Y	Y	Y	Y	Y	Y
7 Crowley	Y	Y	Y	Y	Y	Y	Y
8 Nadler	Y	Y	Y	N	Y	Y	Y
9 **Turner**	+	+	Y	Y	Y	Y	Y
10 Towns	?	?	Y	Y	Y	Y	Y
11 Clarke	Y	Y	Y	N	Y	Y	Y
12 Velázquez	Y	Y	Y	N	Y	Y	Y
13 **Grimm**	Y	Y	Y	Y	Y	Y	Y
14 Maloney	+	+	Y	N	Y	Y	Y
15 Rangel	Y	Y	Y	N	Y	Y	Y
16 Serrano	Y	Y	Y	N	Y	Y	Y
17 Engel	Y	Y	Y	Y	Y	Y	Y
18 Lowey	Y	Y	Y	Y	Y	Y	Y
19 **Hayworth**	Y	N	Y	Y	Y	Y	Y
20 **Gibson**	Y	N	Y	Y	Y	Y	Y
21 Tonko	Y	Y	Y	Y	Y	Y	Y
22 Hinchey	?	?	?	?	?	?	?
23 Owens	Y	Y	Y	Y	Y	Y	Y
24 **Hanna**	Y	Y	Y	Y	Y	Y	Y
25 **Buerkle**	Y	N	Y	Y	Y	N	Y
26 Hochul	Y	Y	Y	Y	Y	Y	Y
27 Higgins	Y	Y	Y	Y	Y	Y	Y
28 Slaughter	?	?	?	?	?	?	?
29 **Reed**	Y	N	Y	Y	Y	Y	Y
NORTH CAROLINA							
1 Butterfield	?	?	Y	Y	Y	Y	Y
2 **Ellmers**	Y	Y	Y	Y	Y	N	Y
3 **Jones**	Y	Y	Y	Y	Y	Y	Y
4 Price	Y	Y	Y	Y	Y	Y	Y

	5	6	7	8	9	10	11
5 **Foxx**	Y	N	Y	Y	Y	Y	Y
6 **Coble**	Y	N	Y	Y	Y	N	Y
7 McIntyre	Y	Y	Y	Y	Y	Y	Y
8 Kissell	Y	Y	Y	Y	Y	Y	Y
9 **Myrick**	Y	Y	Y	Y	Y	N	Y
10 **McHenry**	Y	Y	Y	Y	Y	N	Y
11 Shuler	?	?	Y	Y	Y	Y	Y
12 Watt	?	?	?	?	?	?	?
13 Miller	Y	Y	Y	Y	Y	Y	Y
NORTH DAKOTA							
AL **Berg**	Y	Y	Y	Y	Y	Y	Y
OHIO							
1 **Chabot**	Y	N	Y	Y	Y	Y	Y
2 **Schmidt**	Y	N	Y	Y	Y	Y	Y
3 **Turner**	Y	Y	Y	Y	Y	Y	Y
4 **Jordan**	Y	N	Y	Y	Y	N	Y
5 **Latta**	Y	N	Y	Y	Y	Y	Y
6 **Johnson**	Y	N	Y	Y	Y	N	Y
7 **Austria**	?	?	Y	Y	Y	Y	Y
8 **Boehner**							
9 Kaptur	?	?	Y	Y	Y	Y	Y
10 Kucinich	?	?	Y	Y	Y	Y	Y
11 Fudge	Y	Y	Y	N	Y	Y	Y
12 **Tiberi**	Y	N	Y	Y	Y	Y	Y
13 Sutton	Y	Y	Y	Y	Y	Y	Y
14 **LaTourette**	?	?	?	?	?	?	?
15 **Stivers**	Y	N	Y	Y	Y	Y	Y
16 **Renacci**	Y	N	Y	Y	Y	N	Y
17 Ryan	Y	Y	Y	Y	Y	Y	Y
18 **Gibbs**	Y	N	Y	Y	Y	N	Y
OKLAHOMA							
1 **Sullivan**	Y	Y	Y	Y	Y	N	Y
2 Boren	Y	Y	Y	Y	Y	Y	Y
3 **Lucas**	Y	Y	Y	Y	Y	Y	Y
4 **Cole**	Y	Y	Y	Y	Y	Y	Y
5 **Lankford**	Y	Y	Y	Y	Y	Y	Y
OREGON							
1 Vacant							
2 **Walden**	Y	Y	Y	Y	Y	N	Y
3 Blumenauer	Y	Y	Y	N	Y	Y	Y
4 DeFazio	?	?	?	?	?	?	?
5 Schrader	Y	Y	?	?	?	Y	Y
PENNSYLVANIA							
1 Brady	?	?	Y	Y	Y	Y	Y
2 Fattah	Y	Y	Y	Y	Y	Y	Y
3 **Kelly**	Y	Y	Y	Y	Y	Y	Y
4 Altmire	Y	Y	Y	Y	Y	Y	Y
5 **Thompson**	Y	N	Y	Y	Y	Y	Y
6 **Gerlach**	Y	Y	Y	Y	Y	Y	Y
7 **Meehan**	Y	N	Y	Y	Y	Y	Y
8 **Fitzpatrick**	Y	N	Y	Y	Y	N	Y
9 **Shuster**	Y	N	Y	Y	Y	N	Y
10 **Marino**	Y	Y	Y	Y	Y	Y	Y
11 **Barletta**	Y	Y	Y	Y	Y	Y	Y
12 Critz	Y	Y	Y	Y	Y	Y	Y
13 Schwartz	Y	Y	Y	Y	Y	Y	Y
14 Doyle	Y	Y	Y	Y	Y	Y	Y
15 **Dent**	Y	Y	Y	Y	Y	Y	Y
16 **Pitts**	Y	N	Y	Y	Y	Y	Y
17 Holden	Y	Y	Y	Y	Y	Y	Y
18 **Murphy**	Y	Y	Y	Y	Y	Y	Y
19 **Platts**	?	?	Y	Y	Y	Y	Y
RHODE ISLAND							
1 Cicilline	Y	Y	Y	Y	Y	Y	Y
2 Langevin	Y	Y	Y	Y	Y	Y	Y
SOUTH CAROLINA							
1 **Scott**	Y	N	Y	Y	Y	Y	Y
2 **Wilson**	Y	Y	Y	Y	Y	Y	Y
3 **Duncan**	Y	N	Y	Y	Y	N	Y
4 **Gowdy**	Y	N	Y	Y	Y	Y	Y
5 **Mulvaney**	Y	N	Y	Y	Y	N	Y
6 Clyburn	?	?	Y	Y	Y	Y	Y
SOUTH DAKOTA							
AL **Noem**	?	?	Y	Y	Y	Y	Y
TENNESSEE							
1 **Roe**	Y	Y	Y	Y	Y	Y	Y
2 **Duncan**	Y	N	Y	Y	Y	Y	Y
3 **Fleischmann**	Y	N	Y	Y	Y	Y	Y
4 **DesJarlais**	Y	N	Y	Y	Y	N	Y
5 Cooper	Y	Y	Y	Y	Y	Y	Y
6 **Black**	Y	N	Y	Y	Y	Y	Y
7 **Blackburn**	Y	N	Y	Y	N	N	Y
8 **Fincher**	Y	Y	Y	Y	Y	Y	Y
9 Cohen	Y	Y	Y	N	Y	Y	Y

	5	6	7	8	9	10	11
TEXAS							
1 **Gohmert**	Y	N	Y	Y	Y	Y	Y
2 **Poe**	Y	N	Y	Y	Y	Y	Y
3 **Johnson, S.**	Y	N	Y	Y	Y	Y	Y
4 **Hall**	Y	N	Y	Y	Y	Y	Y
5 **Hensarling**	Y	Y	Y	Y	Y	N	Y
6 **Barton**	Y	Y	Y	Y	Y	Y	Y
7 **Culberson**	?	?	?	?	?	?	?
8 **Brady**	?	?	?	?	?	?	?
9 Green, A.	Y	Y	Y	Y	Y	Y	Y
10 **McCaul**	Y	Y	Y	Y	Y	Y	Y
11 **Conaway**	Y	N	Y	Y	Y	N	Y
12 **Granger**	Y	N	Y	Y	Y	Y	?
13 **Thornberry**	Y	N	Y	Y	Y	N	Y
14 **Paul**	?	?	?	?	?	?	?
15 Hinojosa	Y	Y	Y	Y	Y	Y	Y
16 Reyes	Y	Y	Y	?	Y	Y	Y
17 **Flores**	Y	N	Y	Y	Y	N	Y
18 Jackson Lee	Y	Y	Y	Y	Y	Y	Y
19 **Neugebauer**	Y	N	Y	Y	N	N	Y
20 Gonzalez	Y	Y	Y	Y	Y	Y	Y
21 **Smith**	Y	Y	Y	Y	Y	Y	Y
22 **Olson**	Y	N	Y	Y	Y	Y	Y
23 **Canseco**	Y	Y	Y	Y	Y	Y	Y
24 **Marchant**	?	?	Y	Y	Y	N	Y
25 Doggett	Y	Y	Y	Y	Y	Y	Y
26 **Burgess**	Y	N	Y	Y	Y	N	Y
27 **Farenthold**	Y	N	Y	Y	Y	N	Y
28 Cuellar	Y	Y	Y	Y	Y	Y	Y
29 Green, G.	Y	Y	Y	Y	Y	Y	Y
30 Johnson, E.	Y	Y	Y	Y	Y	Y	Y
31 **Carter**	?	?	Y	Y	Y	N	Y
32 **Sessions**	Y	N	Y	Y	Y	Y	Y
UTAH							
1 **Bishop**	Y	Y	Y	Y	Y	Y	Y
2 Matheson	Y	Y	Y	Y	Y	Y	Y
3 **Chaffetz**	Y	Y	Y	Y	Y	Y	Y
VERMONT							
AL Welch	Y	Y	P	Y	Y	Y	Y
VIRGINIA							
1 **Wittman**	Y	Y	Y	Y	Y	Y	Y
2 **Rigell**	Y	Y	Y	Y	Y	Y	Y
3 Scott	Y	Y	Y	N	Y	Y	Y
4 **Forbes**	Y	N	Y	Y	Y	Y	Y
5 **Hurt**	Y	Y	Y	Y	Y	N	Y
6 **Goodlatte**	Y	N	Y	Y	Y	N	Y
7 **Cantor**	Y	Y	Y	Y	Y	Y	Y
8 Moran	?	Y	Y	N	Y	Y	Y
9 **Griffith**	Y	Y	Y	Y	Y	Y	Y
10 **Wolf**	Y	Y	Y	Y	N	Y	Y
11 Connolly	Y	Y	Y	Y	Y	Y	Y
WASHINGTON							
1 Inslee	?	?	Y	Y	Y	Y	Y
2 Larsen	Y	Y	Y	Y	Y	Y	Y
3 **Herrera Beutler**	Y	Y	Y	Y	Y	Y	Y
4 **Hastings**	Y	Y	Y	Y	Y	Y	Y
5 **McMorris Rodgers**	Y	Y	Y	Y	Y	Y	Y
6 Dicks	Y	Y	Y	Y	Y	Y	Y
7 McDermott	Y	Y	Y	N	?	Y	Y
8 **Reichert**	Y	Y	Y	Y	Y	Y	Y
9 Smith	+	+	Y	Y	Y	Y	Y
WEST VIRGINIA							
1 **McKinley**	Y	Y	Y	Y	N	Y	Y
2 **Capito**	Y	Y	Y	Y	Y	Y	Y
3 Rahall	Y	Y	Y	Y	Y	Y	?
WISCONSIN							
1 **Ryan**	Y	Y	Y	Y	Y	Y	Y
2 Baldwin	?	?	Y	Y	Y	Y	Y
3 Kind	+	+	Y	Y	Y	Y	Y
4 Moore	Y	Y	Y	Y	Y	Y	Y
5 **Sensenbrenner**	N	N	Y	Y	Y	Y	Y
6 **Petri**	Y	Y	Y	Y	Y	Y	Y
7 **Duffy**	Y	Y	Y	Y	Y	Y	Y
8 **Ribble**	Y	Y	Y	Y	Y	Y	Y
WYOMING							
AL **Lummis**	Y	N	Y	Y	N	Y	Y

IN THE HOUSE | By Vote Number

12. **H Res 522. Long-Term-Care Program Repeal/Rule.** Adoption of the rule (H Res 522) that would provide for House floor consideration of the bill that would repeal the Community Living Assistance Services and Supports (CLASS) program authorized as part of the 2010 health care overhaul. Adopted 251-157: R 233-0; D 18-157. Jan. 31, 2012.

13. **HR 1173. Long-Term-Care Program Repeal/Macroeconomic Effects Study.** Jackson Lee, D-Texas, amendment that would prevent the CLASS program repeal from taking effect until the Congressional Budget Office conducts a study on the macroeconomic effects of individuals not having long-term care on federal, state and local governments, and the Department of Health and Human Services conducts a study regarding what best practices are necessary to create a sustainable long-term care program. Rejected in Committee of the Whole 161-263: R 1-236; D 160-27. Feb. 1, 2012.

14. **HR 1173. Long-Term-Care Program Repeal/Long-Term-Care Insurance.** Jackson Lee, D-Texas, amendment that would prevent the CLASS program repeal from taking effect until the Health and Human Services Department certifies that at least 60 percent of U.S. individuals ages 25 or older have private long-term care insurance. Rejected in Committee of the Whole 157-264: R 0-235; D 157-29. Feb. 1, 2012.

15. **HR 1173. Long-Term-Care Program Repeal/Medicaid Spending Increase.** Deutch, D-Fla., amendment that would prevent the CLASS program repeal from taking effect until the U.S. comptroller general certifies that failure to implement the program will not cause an increase in state or federal Medicaid spending. Rejected in Committee of the Whole 164-260: R 0-237; D 164-23. Feb. 1, 2012.

16. **HR 1173. Long-Term-Care Program Repeal/Program Authority.** Deutch, D-Fla., amendment that would prevent the CLASS program repeal from taking effect until the Department of Health and Human Services determines whether it has authority to implement the program and what statutory changes or waivers would be required. Rejected in Committee of the Whole 160-264: R 0-239; D 160-25. Feb. 1, 2012.

17. **HR 1173. Long-Term-Care Program Repeal/Recommit.** Garamendi, D-Calif., motion to recommit the bill to the Energy and Commerce Committee with instructions that it be reported back immediately with an amendment that would prevent the repeal of the CLASS program from taking effect until the Department of Health and Human Services certifies that a national voluntary insurance program is in effect for purchasing community-living assistance services and supports for individuals who have Alzheimer's disease, chronic diabetes, heart disease or advanced stages of cancer, a disability or traumatic injury or any other serious disease or health condition. Motion rejected 175-247: R 0-236; D 175-11. Feb. 1, 2012.

	12	13	14	15	16	17
ALABAMA						
1 Bonner	Y	N	N	N	N	N
2 Roby	Y	N	N	N	N	N
3 Rogers	Y	N	N	N	N	N
4 Aderholt	Y	N	N	N	N	?
5 Brooks	Y	N	N	N	N	N
6 Bachus	Y	N	N	N	N	N
7 Sewell	N	Y	Y	Y	Y	Y
ALASKA						
AL Young	?	N	N	N	N	N
ARIZONA						
1 Gosar	Y	N	N	N	N	N
2 Franks	Y	N	N	–	N	N
3 Quayle	Y	N	N	N	N	N
4 Pastor	N	Y	Y	Y	Y	Y
5 Schweikert	Y	N	N	N	N	N
6 Flake	Y	N	N	N	N	N
7 Grijalva	?	Y	Y	Y	Y	Y
8 Vacant*						
ARKANSAS						
1 Crawford	Y	N	N	N	N	N
2 Griffin	Y	N	N	N	N	N
3 Womack	Y	N	N	N	N	N
4 Ross	Y	N	N	N	N	N
CALIFORNIA						
1 Thompson	N	Y	Y	Y	Y	Y
2 Herger	Y	N	N	N	N	N
3 Lungren	Y	N	N	N	N	N
4 McClintock	Y	N	N	N	N	N
5 Matsui	N	Y	Y	Y	Y	Y
6 Woolsey	N	Y	Y	Y	Y	Y
7 Miller, George	N	Y	Y	Y	Y	Y
8 Pelosi	N	Y	Y	Y	Y	Y
9 Lee	N	Y	Y	Y	Y	Y
10 Garamendi	Y	Y	Y	Y	Y	Y
11 McNerney	N	Y	Y	Y	Y	Y
12 Speier	N	N	Y	Y	Y	?
13 Stark	N	Y	Y	Y	Y	Y
14 Eshoo	N	Y	Y	Y	Y	Y
15 Honda	N	Y	Y	Y	Y	Y
16 Lofgren	N	N	Y	Y	Y	Y
17 Farr	N	N	Y	Y	Y	Y
18 Cardoza	N	N	N	Y	Y	Y
19 Denham	Y	N	N	N	N	N
20 Costa	N	N	N	N	N	Y
21 Nunes	Y	N	N	N	N	N
22 McCarthy	Y	N	N	N	N	N
23 Capps	N	Y	Y	Y	Y	Y
24 Gallegly	Y	N	N	N	N	N
25 McKeon	Y	N	N	N	N	N
26 Dreier	Y	N	N	N	N	N
27 Sherman	N	Y	Y	Y	Y	Y
28 Berman	N	Y	Y	Y	Y	Y
29 Schiff	N	Y	Y	Y	Y	Y
30 Waxman	N	Y	Y	Y	Y	Y
31 Becerra	N	Y	Y	Y	Y	Y
32 Chu	N	Y	Y	Y	Y	Y
33 Bass	N	Y	Y	Y	Y	Y
34 Roybal-Allard	N	?	?	?	?	?
35 Waters	N	Y	?	Y	Y	Y
36 Hahn	N	Y	Y	Y	Y	Y
37 Richardson	N	Y	Y	Y	Y	Y
38 Napolitano	N	Y	Y	Y	Y	Y
39 Sánchez, Linda	N	Y	Y	Y	Y	Y
40 Royce	Y	N	?	N	N	N
41 Lewis	Y	N	N	N	N	N
42 Miller, Gary	Y	N	N	N	N	N
43 Baca	N	Y	Y	Y	Y	Y
44 Calvert	Y	N	N	N	N	N
45 Bono Mack	?	N	N	N	N	N
46 Rohrabacher	Y	?	N	N	N	N
47 Sanchez, Loretta	N	Y	Y	Y	Y	Y
48 Campbell	Y	N	N	N	N	N
49 Issa	Y	N	?	N	N	N
50 Bilbray	Y	N	N	N	N	N
51 Filner	–	+	+	+	+	+
52 Hunter	Y	N	N	N	N	N
53 Davis	N	N	N	Y	Y	Y
COLORADO						
1 DeGette	N	Y	Y	Y	Y	Y
2 Polis	N	Y	Y	Y	Y	Y
3 Tipton	Y	N	N	N	N	N
4 Gardner	Y	N	N	N	N	N
5 Lamborn	Y	N	N	N	N	N
6 Coffman	Y	N	N	N	N	N
7 Perlmutter	N	N	N	Y	N	Y
CONNECTICUT						
1 Larson	N	Y	Y	Y	Y	Y
2 Courtney	N	Y	Y	Y	Y	Y
3 DeLauro	N	Y	Y	Y	Y	Y
4 Himes	N	N	N	N	N	Y
5 Murphy	Y	N	N	N	N	Y
DELAWARE						
AL Carney	Y	Y	N	N	N	Y
FLORIDA						
1 Miller	Y	N	N	N	N	N
2 Southerland	Y	N	N	N	N	N
3 Brown	?	Y	Y	Y	Y	Y
4 Crenshaw	Y	N	N	N	N	N
5 Nugent	Y	N	N	N	N	N
6 Stearns	Y	N	N	N	N	N
7 Mica	Y	N	N	N	N	N
8 Webster	Y	N	N	N	N	N
9 Bilirakis	Y	N	N	N	N	N
10 Young	Y	N	N	N	N	N
11 Castor	N	N	Y	Y	Y	Y
12 Ross	Y	N	N	N	N	N
13 Buchanan	Y	N	N	N	N	N
14 Mack	?	?	?	?	?	?
15 Posey	Y	N	N	N	N	N
16 Rooney	Y	N	N	N	N	N
17 Wilson	N	Y	Y	Y	Y	Y
18 Ros-Lehtinen	Y	N	N	N	N	N
19 Deutch	N	Y	Y	Y	Y	Y
20 Wasserman Schultz	?	Y	Y	Y	Y	Y
21 Diaz-Balart	Y	N	N	N	N	N
22 West	Y	N	N	N	N	N
23 Hastings	N	Y	Y	Y	Y	Y
24 Adams	Y	N	N	N	N	N
25 Rivera	Y	N	N	N	N	N
GEORGIA						
1 Kingston	?	N	N	N	N	N
2 Bishop	N	Y	Y	Y	Y	Y
3 Westmoreland	Y	N	N	N	N	N
4 Johnson	N	Y	Y	Y	Y	Y
5 Lewis	N	Y	Y	Y	Y	Y
6 Price	Y	N	N	N	N	N
7 Woodall	Y	N	N	N	N	N
8 Scott, A.	Y	N	N	N	N	N
9 Graves	Y	N	N	N	N	N
10 Broun	Y	N	N	N	N	N
11 Gingrey	Y	N	N	N	N	N
12 Barrow	N	Y	Y	Y	Y	Y
13 Scott, D.	N	Y	Y	Y	Y	Y
HAWAII						
1 Hanabusa	N	Y	Y	Y	Y	Y
2 Hirono	N	Y	Y	Y	Y	Y
IDAHO						
1 Labrador	Y	N	N	N	N	N
2 Simpson	Y	N	N	N	N	N
ILLINOIS						
1 Rush	?	Y	Y	Y	Y	Y
2 Jackson	N	Y	Y	Y	Y	Y
3 Lipinski	Y	N	N	N	N	N
4 Gutierrez	–	Y	Y	Y	?	Y
5 Quigley	N	Y	Y	Y	Y	Y
6 Roskam	Y	N	N	N	N	N
7 Davis	N	Y	Y	Y	Y	Y
8 Walsh	Y	N	N	N	N	?
9 Schakowsky	N	Y	Y	Y	Y	Y
10 Dold	Y	N	N	N	N	N
11 Kinzinger	Y	N	N	N	N	N
12 Costello	N	Y	Y	Y	Y	Y
13 Biggert	Y	N	N	N	N	N
14 Hultgren	Y	N	N	N	N	N
15 Johnson	Y	N	N	N	N	N

KEY	**Republicans**	Democrats
Y Voted for (yea)	**X** Paired against	**C** Voted "present" to avoid possible conflict of interest
# Paired for	**-** Announced against	
+ Announced for	**P** Voted "present"	**?** Did not vote or otherwise make a position known
N Voted against (nay)		

*Rep. Gabrielle Giffords, D-Ariz., resigned effective Jan. 25, 2012. The last vote for which she was eligible was vote 11.

	12	13	14	15	16	17
16 **Manzullo**	Y	N	N	N	N	N
17 **Schilling**	Y	N	N	N	N	N
18 **Schock**	Y	N	N	N	N	N
19 **Shimkus**	Y	N	N	N	N	N
INDIANA						
1 Visclosky	–	Y	Y	Y	Y	Y
2 Donnelly	Y	N	N	N	N	N
3 **Stutzman**	Y	N	N	N	N	N
4 **Rokita**	Y	N	N	N	N	N
5 **Burton**	?	N	N	N	N	N
6 **Pence**	Y	N	N	N	N	N
7 Carson	N	+	+	+	+	+
8 **Bucshon**	Y	N	N	N	N	N
9 **Young**	Y	N	N	N	N	N
IOWA						
1 Braley	N	N	Y	Y	Y	Y
2 Loebsack	N	Y	Y	Y	Y	Y
3 Boswell	N	Y	Y	Y	Y	Y
4 **Latham**	Y	N	N	N	N	N
5 **King**	Y	N	N	N	N	N
KANSAS						
1 **Huelskamp**	Y	N	N	N	N	N
2 **Jenkins**	Y	N	N	N	N	N
3 **Yoder**	Y	N	N	N	N	N
4 **Pompeo**	Y	N	N	N	N	N
KENTUCKY						
1 **Whitfield**	Y	N	N	N	N	N
2 **Guthrie**	Y	N	N	N	N	N
3 Yarmuth	N	Y	Y	Y	Y	Y
4 **Davis**	Y	N	N	N	N	N
5 **Rogers**	Y	N	N	N	N	N
6 Chandler	Y	N	N	N	N	N
LOUISIANA						
1 **Scalise**	Y	N	N	N	N	N
2 Richmond	N	Y	Y	Y	Y	Y
3 **Landry**	Y	N	N	N	N	N
4 **Fleming**	Y	N	N	N	N	N
5 **Alexander**	Y	N	N	N	N	N
6 **Cassidy**	Y	N	N	N	N	N
7 **Boustany**	Y	N	N	N	N	N
MAINE						
1 Pingree	?	Y	Y	Y	Y	Y
2 Michaud	N	Y	Y	Y	Y	Y
MARYLAND						
1 **Harris**	Y	N	N	N	N	N
2 Ruppersberger	N	Y	Y	Y	Y	Y
3 Sarbanes	N	Y	Y	Y	Y	Y
4 Edwards	N	Y	Y	Y	Y	Y
5 Hoyer	N	Y	Y	Y	N	Y
6 **Bartlett**	Y	N	N	N	N	N
7 Cummings	N	Y	Y	Y	Y	Y
8 Van Hollen	N	Y	Y	Y	Y	Y
MASSACHUSETTS						
1 Olver	N	Y	Y	Y	Y	Y
2 Neal	N	Y	Y	Y	Y	Y
3 McGovern	N	Y	Y	Y	Y	Y
4 Frank	?	Y	Y	Y	Y	Y
5 Tsongas	N	Y	Y	Y	Y	Y
6 Tierney	N	Y	Y	Y	Y	Y
7 Markey	N	Y	Y	Y	Y	Y
8 Capuano	N	Y	Y	Y	Y	Y
9 Lynch	N	Y	N	Y	N	Y
10 Keating	N	Y	Y	Y	Y	Y
MICHIGAN						
1 **Benishek**	Y	N	N	N	N	N
2 **Huizenga**	Y	N	N	N	N	N
3 **Amash**	Y	N	N	N	N	N
4 **Camp**	Y	N	N	N	N	N
5 Kildee	Y	Y	Y	Y	Y	Y
6 **Upton**	Y	N	N	N	N	N
7 **Walberg**	Y	N	N	N	N	N
8 **Rogers**	Y	N	N	N	N	N
9 Peters	N	Y	Y	Y	Y	Y
10 **Miller**	Y	N	N	N	N	N
11 **McCotter**	Y	N	N	N	N	N
12 Levin	N	Y	Y	Y	Y	Y
13 Clarke	N	Y	Y	Y	Y	Y
14 Conyers	N	Y	Y	Y	Y	Y
15 Dingell	N	Y	Y	Y	Y	Y
MINNESOTA						
1 Walz	N	Y	Y	Y	Y	Y
2 **Kline**	Y	N	N	N	N	N
3 **Paulsen**	Y	N	N	N	N	N
4 McCollum	N	Y	Y	Y	Y	Y

	12	13	14	15	16	17
5 Ellison	N	Y	Y	Y	Y	Y
6 **Bachmann**	Y	N	N	N	N	N
7 Peterson	N	N	N	N	N	Y
8 **Cravaack**	Y	N	N	N	N	N
MISSISSIPPI						
1 **Nunnelee**	Y	N	N	N	N	N
2 Thompson	N	Y	Y	Y	Y	Y
3 **Harper**	Y	N	N	N	N	N
4 **Palazzo**	Y	N	N	N	N	N
MISSOURI						
1 Clay	N	Y	Y	Y	Y	Y
2 **Akin**	Y	N	N	N	N	N
3 Carnahan	N	Y	Y	Y	Y	Y
4 **Hartzler**	Y	N	N	N	N	N
5 Cleaver	N	Y	N	Y	Y	Y
6 **Graves**	Y	N	N	N	N	N
7 **Long**	Y	N	N	N	N	N
8 **Emerson**	Y	N	N	N	N	N
9 **Luetkemeyer**	Y	N	N	N	N	N
MONTANA						
AL **Rehberg**	Y	N	N	N	N	N
NEBRASKA						
1 **Fortenberry**	Y	N	N	N	N	N
2 **Terry**	Y	N	N	N	N	N
3 **Smith**	Y	N	N	N	N	N
NEVADA						
1 Berkley	N	N	N	N	N	Y
2 **Amodei**	Y	N	N	N	N	N
3 **Heck**	Y	N	N	N	N	N
NEW HAMPSHIRE						
1 **Guinta**	Y	N	N	N	N	N
2 **Bass**	Y	N	N	N	N	N
NEW JERSEY						
1 Andrews	N	Y	Y	Y	Y	Y
2 **LoBiondo**	Y	N	N	N	N	N
3 **Runyan**	Y	N	N	N	N	N
4 **Smith**	Y	Y	N	N	N	N
5 **Garrett**	Y	N	N	N	N	N
6 Pallone	N	Y	Y	Y	Y	Y
7 **Lance**	Y	N	N	N	N	N
8 Pascrell	N	Y	Y	Y	Y	Y
9 Rothman	N	Y	Y	Y	Y	Y
10 Payne	N	Y	Y	Y	Y	Y
11 **Frelinghuysen**	Y	N	N	N	N	N
12 Holt	N	Y	Y	Y	Y	Y
13 Sires	N	Y	Y	Y	Y	Y
NEW MEXICO						
1 Heinrich	N	Y	Y	Y	Y	Y
2 **Pearce**	Y	N	N	N	N	N
3 Luján	N	Y	Y	Y	Y	Y
NEW YORK						
1 Bishop	N	Y	N	N	Y	Y
2 Israel	N	Y	Y	Y	Y	Y
3 **King**	Y	N	N	N	N	N
4 McCarthy	N	N	Y	Y	Y	Y
5 Ackerman	N	Y	Y	Y	Y	Y
6 Meeks	N	Y	Y	Y	Y	Y
7 Crowley	N	Y	Y	Y	Y	Y
8 Nadler	N	Y	Y	Y	Y	Y
9 **Turner**	Y	N	N	N	N	N
10 Towns	N	Y	Y	Y	Y	Y
11 Clarke	N	Y	Y	Y	Y	Y
12 Velázquez	N	Y	Y	Y	Y	Y
13 **Grimm**	Y	N	N	N	N	N
14 Maloney	N	Y	Y	Y	Y	Y
15 Rangel	N	Y	Y	Y	Y	Y
16 Serrano	N	Y	Y	Y	Y	Y
17 Engel	?	Y	Y	Y	Y	Y
18 Lowey	N	Y	Y	Y	Y	Y
19 **Hayworth**	Y	N	N	N	N	N
20 **Gibson**	Y	N	N	N	N	N
21 Tonko	N	Y	Y	Y	Y	Y
22 Hinchey	?	?	?	?	?	?
23 Owens	N	Y	N	N	N	N
24 **Hanna**	Y	N	N	N	N	N
25 **Buerkle**	Y	N	N	N	N	N
26 Hochul	N	Y	N	N	N	N
27 Higgins	?	Y	Y	Y	Y	Y
28 Slaughter	N	Y	Y	Y	Y	Y
29 **Reed**	Y	N	N	N	N	N
NORTH CAROLINA						
1 Butterfield	?	Y	Y	Y	Y	Y
2 **Ellmers**	Y	N	N	N	N	N
3 **Jones**	Y	N	N	N	N	N
4 Price	N	Y	Y	Y	Y	Y

	12	13	14	15	16	17
5 **Foxx**	Y	N	N	N	N	N
6 **Coble**	Y	N	N	N	N	N
7 McIntyre	Y	N	N	N	N	Y
8 Kissell	Y	Y	Y	Y	Y	Y
9 **Myrick**	Y	N	N	N	N	N
10 **McHenry**	Y	N	N	N	N	N
11 Shuler	Y	N	N	N	N	N
12 Watt	N	Y	Y	Y	Y	Y
13 Miller	N	Y	Y	Y	Y	Y
NORTH DAKOTA						
AL **Berg**	Y	N	N	N	N	N
OHIO						
1 **Chabot**	Y	N	N	N	N	N
2 **Schmidt**	Y	N	N	N	N	N
3 **Turner**	Y	N	N	N	N	N
4 **Jordan**	Y	N	N	N	N	N
5 **Latta**	Y	N	N	N	N	N
6 **Johnson**	Y	N	N	N	N	N
7 **Austria**	Y	N	N	N	N	N
8 **Boehner**						
9 Kaptur	?	Y	Y	Y	Y	Y
10 Kucinich	N	Y	Y	Y	Y	Y
11 Fudge	N	Y	Y	Y	Y	Y
12 **Tiberi**	Y	N	N	N	N	N
13 Sutton	N	Y	Y	Y	Y	Y
14 **LaTourette**	Y	?	N	?	N	N
15 **Stivers**	Y	N	N	N	N	N
16 **Renacci**	Y	N	N	N	N	N
17 Ryan	N	Y	Y	Y	Y	Y
18 **Gibbs**	Y	N	N	N	N	N
OKLAHOMA						
1 **Sullivan**	Y	N	?	N	N	N
2 Boren	Y	N	N	N	N	N
3 **Lucas**	Y	N	N	N	N	N
4 **Cole**	Y	N	N	N	N	N
5 **Lankford**	Y	N	N	N	N	?
OREGON						
1 Vacant						
2 **Walden**	Y	N	N	N	N	N
3 Blumenauer	N	Y	Y	Y	Y	Y
4 DeFazio	N	N	Y	N	N	Y
5 Schrader	Y	N	Y	N	N	N
PENNSYLVANIA						
1 Brady	N	Y	Y	Y	Y	Y
2 Fattah	N	Y	Y	Y	Y	Y
3 **Kelly**	Y	N	N	N	N	N
4 Altmire	N	Y	N	Y	Y	Y
5 **Thompson**	Y	N	N	N	N	N
6 **Gerlach**	Y	N	N	N	N	N
7 **Meehan**	Y	N	N	N	N	N
8 **Fitzpatrick**	Y	N	N	N	N	N
9 **Shuster**	Y	N	N	N	N	N
10 **Marino**	Y	N	N	N	N	N
11 **Barletta**	Y	N	N	N	N	N
12 Critz	N	Y	Y	Y	Y	Y
13 Schwartz	N	Y	Y	Y	Y	Y
14 Doyle	N	Y	Y	Y	Y	Y
15 **Dent**	Y	N	N	N	N	N
16 **Pitts**	Y	N	N	N	N	N
17 Holden	N	Y	Y	Y	Y	Y
18 **Murphy**	Y	N	N	N	N	N
19 **Platts**	?	N	N	N	N	N
RHODE ISLAND						
1 Cicilline	N	Y	Y	Y	Y	Y
2 Langevin	N	Y	Y	Y	Y	Y
SOUTH CAROLINA						
1 **Scott**	Y	N	N	N	N	N
2 **Wilson**	Y	N	N	N	N	N
3 **Duncan**	Y	N	N	N	N	N
4 **Gowdy**	Y	N	N	N	N	N
5 **Mulvaney**	Y	N	N	N	N	N
6 Clyburn	N	Y	Y	Y	Y	Y
SOUTH DAKOTA						
AL **Noem**	Y	N	N	N	N	N
TENNESSEE						
1 **Roe**	Y	N	N	N	N	N
2 **Duncan**	Y	N	N	N	N	N
3 **Fleischmann**	Y	N	N	N	N	N
4 **DesJarlais**	Y	N	N	N	N	N
5 Cooper	N	Y	N	N	N	Y
6 **Black**	Y	N	N	N	N	N
7 **Blackburn**	Y	N	N	N	N	N
8 **Fincher**	Y	N	N	N	N	N
9 Cohen	N	Y	Y	Y	Y	Y

	12	13	14	15	16	17
TEXAS						
1 **Gohmert**	Y	N	N	N	N	N
2 **Poe**	Y	N	N	N	N	N
3 **Johnson, S.**	Y	N	N	N	N	N
4 **Hall**	Y	N	N	N	N	N
5 **Hensarling**	Y	N	N	N	N	N
6 **Barton**	Y	N	N	N	N	N
7 **Culberson**	Y	N	N	N	N	N
8 **Brady**	Y	N	N	N	N	N
9 Green, A.	N	Y	Y	Y	Y	Y
10 **McCaul**	Y	N	N	N	N	N
11 **Conaway**	Y	N	N	N	N	N
12 **Granger**	Y	N	N	N	N	N
13 **Thornberry**	Y	N	N	N	N	N
14 **Paul**	?	?	?	?	?	?
15 Hinojosa	N	Y	Y	Y	Y	Y
16 Reyes	N	Y	Y	Y	Y	Y
17 **Flores**	Y	N	?	N	N	N
18 Jackson Lee	N	Y	Y	Y	Y	Y
19 **Neugebauer**	Y	N	N	N	N	N
20 Gonzalez	N	Y	Y	Y	?	Y
21 **Smith**	Y	N	N	N	N	N
22 **Olson**	Y	N	N	N	N	N
23 **Canseco**	Y	N	N	N	N	N
24 **Marchant**	Y	N	N	N	N	N
25 Doggett	N	Y	Y	Y	Y	Y
26 **Burgess**	Y	N	N	N	N	N
27 **Farenthold**	Y	N	N	N	N	N
28 Cuellar	?	Y	N	N	Y	Y
29 Green, G.	N	Y	N	Y	Y	Y
30 Johnson, E.	N	Y	Y	Y	Y	Y
31 **Carter**	Y	N	N	N	N	N
32 **Sessions**	Y	N	N	N	N	N
UTAH						
1 **Bishop**	Y	N	N	N	N	N
2 Matheson	Y	N	N	N	N	N
3 **Chaffetz**	?	N	N	N	N	N
VERMONT						
AL Welch	Y	Y	Y	Y	Y	Y
VIRGINIA						
1 **Wittman**	Y	N	N	N	N	N
2 **Rigell**	Y	N	N	N	N	N
3 Scott	N	Y	Y	Y	Y	Y
4 **Forbes**	Y	N	N	N	N	N
5 **Hurt**	Y	N	N	N	N	N
6 **Goodlatte**	Y	N	N	N	N	N
7 **Cantor**	Y	N	N	N	N	N
8 Moran	N	Y	Y	Y	Y	Y
9 **Griffith**	Y	N	N	N	N	N
10 **Wolf**	Y	N	N	N	N	N
11 Connolly	N	Y	Y	Y	Y	Y
WASHINGTON						
1 Inslee	?	Y	Y	Y	Y	Y
2 Larsen	N	Y	N	Y	N	Y
3 **Herrera Beutler**	Y	N	N	N	N	N
4 **Hastings**	Y	N	N	N	N	N
5 **McMorris Rodgers**	Y	N	N	N	N	N
6 Dicks	Y	Y	Y	Y	Y	Y
7 McDermott	N	Y	Y	Y	Y	Y
8 **Reichert**	Y	N	N	N	N	N
9 Smith	N	Y	Y	Y	Y	Y
WEST VIRGINIA						
1 **McKinley**	Y	N	N	N	N	N
2 **Capito**	Y	N	N	N	N	N
3 Rahall	N	Y	Y	Y	Y	Y
WISCONSIN						
1 **Ryan**	Y	N	N	N	N	N
2 Baldwin	N	Y	Y	Y	Y	Y
3 Kind	Y	N	N	N	N	Y
4 Moore	N	Y	Y	Y	Y	Y
5 **Sensenbrenner**	Y	N	N	N	N	N
6 **Petri**	Y	N	N	N	N	N
7 **Duffy**	Y	N	N	N	N	N
8 **Ribble**	Y	N	N	N	N	N
WYOMING						
AL **Lummis**	Y	N	N	N	N	N

IN THE HOUSE | By Vote Number

18. HR 1173. Long-Term-Care Program Repeal/Passage. Passage of the bill that would repeal the Community Living Assistance Services and Supports (CLASS) program authorized as part of the 2010 health care overhaul. It also would shift funding for the National Clearinghouse for Long-Term Care Information from a mandatory appropriation to an authorization. Passed 267-159: R 239-0; D 28-159. A "nay" was a vote in support of the president's position. Feb. 1, 2012.

19. HR 3835. Pay Freeze Extension/Passage. Ross, R-Fla., motion to suspend the rules and pass the bill that would extend an existing pay freeze on federal employees for an additional year, through Dec. 31, 2013, and apply the same pay freeze to members of Congress. Motion agreed to 309-117: R 237-2; D 72-115. A two-thirds majority of those present and voting (284 in this case) is required for passage under suspension of the rules. Feb. 1, 2012.

20. HR 3567. TANF Benefit Restrictions/Passage. Boustany, R-La., motion to suspend the rules and pass the bill that would require states to ensure that Temporary Assistance for Needy Families (TANF) program benefits are not used to purchase alcohol, for casino gambling or in strip clubs or other adult entertainment venues. States that do not meet the requirement within two years could be subject to 5 percent cuts in their annual TANF funding. Motion agreed to 395-27: R 236-1; D 159-26. A two-thirds majority of those present and voting (282 in this case) is required for passage under suspension of the rules. Feb. 1, 2012.

21. HR 3578, HR 3582. Budget Baseline and Dynamic Scoring/ Previous Question. Woodall, R-Ga., motion to order the previous question (thus ending debate and possibility of amendment) on adoption of the rule (H Res 534) that would provide for House floor consideration of a bill (HR 3578) that would prevent the Congressional Budget Office (CBO) from incorporating inflation increases into its projected spending baselines and a bill (HR 3582) that would require CBO to take into account the effects that bills might have on economic growth, a calculation known as "dynamic scoring." Motion agreed to 238-177: R 236-1; D 2-176. Feb. 2, 2012.

22. HR 3578, HR 3582. Budget Baseline and Dynamic Scoring/Rule. Adoption of the rule (H Res 534) that would provide for House floor consideration of a bill (HR 3578) that would prevent CBO from incorporating inflation increases into its projected spending baselines and a bill (HR 3582) that would require CBO to take into account the effects that bills might have on economic growth, a calculation known as "dynamic scoring." Adopted 238-179: R 235-0; D 3-179. Feb. 2, 2012.

23. HR 3630. Year-End Extensions/Motion to Instruct. Michaud, D-Maine, motion to instruct conferees to recede from House language that would allow states to use unemployment insurance funds for re-employment demonstration projects. The bill would extend the 4.2 percent employee payroll tax rate, Medicare payment rates to doctors and workers' eligibility for certain expanded unemployment benefits. Motion rejected 184-236: R 4-233; D 180-3. Feb. 2, 2012.

	18	19	20	21	22	23
ALABAMA						
1 Bonner	Y	Y	Y	Y	Y	N
2 Roby	Y	Y	Y	Y	Y	N
3 Rogers	Y	Y	Y	Y	Y	N
4 Aderholt	Y	Y	Y	?	Y	N
5 Brooks	Y	Y	Y	Y	Y	N
6 Bachus	Y	Y	Y	Y	Y	N
7 Sewell	N	N	Y	N	N	Y
ALASKA						
AL Young	Y	N	Y	Y	Y	Y
ARIZONA						
1 Gosar	Y	Y	Y	Y	Y	N
2 Franks	Y	Y	Y	Y	Y	N
3 Quayle	Y	Y	Y	Y	Y	N
4 Pastor	N	N	Y	N	N	Y
5 Schweikert	Y	Y	Y	Y	Y	N
6 Flake	Y	Y	Y	Y	Y	N
7 Grijalva	N	N	N	N	N	Y
8 Vacant						
ARKANSAS						
1 Crawford	Y	Y	Y	Y	Y	N
2 Griffin	Y	Y	Y	Y	Y	N
3 Womack	Y	Y	Y	Y	Y	N
4 Ross	Y	Y	Y	N	N	Y
CALIFORNIA						
1 Thompson	N	N	Y	N	N	Y
2 Herger	Y	Y	?	Y	Y	N
3 Lungren	Y	Y	Y	Y	Y	N
4 McClintock	Y	Y	Y	Y	Y	N
5 Matsui	N	N	Y	N	N	Y
6 Woolsey	N	N	N	N	N	Y
7 Miller, George	N	N	Y	N	N	Y
8 Pelosi	N	N	Y	N	N	Y
9 Lee	N	N	N	N	N	Y
10 Garamendi	N	Y	Y	N	N	Y
11 McNerney	N	Y	Y	N	N	Y
12 Speier	N	Y	Y	N	N	Y
13 Stark	N	N	N	N	N	Y
14 Eshoo	N	Y	Y	N	N	Y
15 Honda	N	N	N	?	N	Y
16 Lofgren	N	Y	Y	N	N	Y
17 Farr	N	N	Y	N	N	Y
18 Cardoza	N	N	Y	N	N	Y
19 Denham	Y	Y	Y	Y	Y	N
20 Costa	N	N	Y	N	N	Y
21 Nunes	Y	Y	Y	Y	Y	N
22 McCarthy	Y	Y	Y	Y	Y	N
23 Capps	N	Y	Y	N	N	Y
24 Gallegly	Y	Y	Y	Y	Y	N
25 McKeon	Y	Y	Y	Y	Y	N
26 Dreier	Y	Y	Y	Y	Y	N
27 Sherman	N	N	Y	N	N	Y
28 Berman	N	N	Y	N	N	Y
29 Schiff	N	Y	Y	N	N	Y
30 Waxman	N	N	Y	N	N	Y
31 Becerra	N	N	Y	N	N	Y
32 Chu	N	Y	Y	N	N	Y
33 Bass	N	N	N	N	N	Y
34 Roybal-Allard	?	?	?	?	?	?
35 Waters	N	N	N	N	N	Y
36 Hahn	N	N	Y	N	N	Y
37 Richardson	N	Y	Y	N	N	Y
38 Napolitano	N	N	Y	N	N	Y
39 Sánchez, Linda	N	N	N	N	N	Y
40 Royce	Y	Y	Y	Y	Y	N
41 Lewis	Y	Y	Y	Y	Y	N
42 Miller, Gary	Y	Y	Y	Y	Y	N
43 Baca	N	N	Y	N	N	Y
44 Calvert	Y	Y	Y	Y	Y	N
45 Bono Mack	Y	Y	Y	Y	Y	N
46 Rohrabacher	Y	Y	Y	Y	Y	N
47 Sanchez, Loretta	N	Y	Y	N	N	Y
48 Campbell	Y	Y	Y	Y	Y	N
49 Issa	Y	Y	Y	Y	Y	N
50 Bilbray	Y	Y	Y	Y	Y	N
51 Filner	–	–	–	–	–	+
52 Hunter	Y	Y	Y	Y	Y	N
53 Davis	N	N	Y	N	N	Y
COLORADO						
1 DeGette	N	N	Y	N	N	Y
2 Polis	N	Y	Y	N	N	Y
3 Tipton	Y	Y	Y	Y	Y	N
4 Gardner	Y	Y	Y	Y	Y	N
5 Lamborn	Y	Y	Y	Y	Y	N
6 Coffman	Y	Y	Y	Y	Y	N
7 Perlmutter	Y	Y	Y	N	N	Y
CONNECTICUT						
1 Larson	N	N	Y	N	N	Y
2 Courtney	N	N	Y	N	N	Y
3 DeLauro	N	N	Y	N	N	Y
4 Himes	Y	Y	Y	N	N	Y
5 Murphy	Y	Y	Y	N	N	Y
DELAWARE						
AL Carney	Y	Y	Y	N	N	Y
FLORIDA						
1 Miller	Y	Y	Y	Y	Y	N
2 Southerland	Y	Y	Y	Y	Y	N
3 Brown	N	N	Y	N	N	Y
4 Crenshaw	Y	Y	Y	Y	Y	N
5 Nugent	Y	Y	Y	Y	Y	N
6 Stearns	Y	Y	Y	Y	Y	N
7 Mica	Y	Y	Y	Y	Y	N
8 Webster	Y	Y	Y	Y	Y	N
9 Bilirakis	Y	Y	Y	Y	Y	N
10 Young	Y	Y	Y	Y	Y	N
11 Castor	N	Y	Y	N	N	Y
12 Ross	Y	Y	Y	Y	Y	N
13 Buchanan	Y	Y	Y	Y	Y	N
14 Mack	?	?	?	?	?	?
15 Posey	Y	Y	Y	Y	Y	N
16 Rooney	Y	Y	Y	Y	Y	N
17 Wilson	N	N	N	N	N	Y
18 Ros-Lehtinen	Y	Y	Y	Y	Y	N
19 Deutch	N	N	Y	N	N	Y
20 Wasserman Schultz	N	Y	Y	N	N	Y
21 Diaz-Balart	Y	Y	Y	Y	Y	N
22 West	Y	Y	Y	Y	Y	N
23 Hastings	N	N	Y	N	N	Y
24 Adams	Y	Y	Y	Y	Y	N
25 Rivera	Y	Y	Y	Y	Y	N
GEORGIA						
1 Kingston	Y	Y	Y	Y	Y	N
2 Bishop	N	Y	Y	N	N	Y
3 Westmoreland	Y	Y	Y	Y	Y	N
4 Johnson	N	N	Y	N	N	Y
5 Lewis	N	N	Y	N	N	Y
6 Price	Y	Y	Y	Y	Y	N
7 Woodall	Y	Y	Y	Y	Y	N
8 Scott, A.	Y	Y	Y	Y	Y	N
9 Graves	Y	Y	Y	Y	Y	N
10 Broun	Y	Y	Y	Y	Y	N
11 Gingrey	Y	Y	Y	Y	Y	N
12 Barrow	Y	Y	Y	N	N	Y
13 Scott, D.	N	Y	Y	N	N	Y
HAWAII						
1 Hanabusa	N	Y	Y	N	N	Y
2 Hirono	N	N	Y	N	–	Y
IDAHO						
1 Labrador	Y	Y	Y	Y	Y	N
2 Simpson	Y	Y	Y	Y	Y	N
ILLINOIS						
1 Rush	N	N	N	N	N	Y
2 Jackson	N	N	Y	N	N	Y
3 Lipinski	Y	Y	Y	N	N	Y
4 Gutierrez	N	N	N	N	N	Y
5 Quigley	N	Y	Y	N	N	Y
6 Roskam	Y	Y	Y	Y	Y	N
7 Davis	N	N	N	N	N	Y
8 Walsh	Y	Y	Y	Y	Y	N
9 Schakowsky	N	N	N	N	N	Y
10 Dold	Y	Y	Y	Y	Y	N
11 Kinzinger	Y	Y	Y	Y	Y	N
12 Costello	N	Y	Y	N	N	Y
13 Biggert	Y	Y	Y	Y	Y	N
14 Hultgren	Y	Y	Y	Y	Y	N
15 Johnson	Y	Y	Y	Y	Y	N

KEY — Republicans, Democrats

Y	Voted for (yea)	X Paired against
#	Paired for	– Announced against
+	Announced for	P Voted "present"
N	Voted against (nay)	C Voted "present" to avoid possible conflict of interest
		? Did not vote or otherwise make a position known

	18	19	20	21	22	23
16 **Manzullo**	Y	Y	Y	Y	Y	N
17 **Schilling**	Y	Y	Y	Y	Y	N
18 **Schock**	Y	Y	Y	Y	Y	N
19 **Shimkus**	Y	Y	Y	Y	Y	N
INDIANA						
1 Visclosky	N	N	Y	N	N	Y
2 Donnelly	Y	Y	Y	N	N	Y
3 **Stutzman**	Y	Y	Y	Y	Y	N
4 **Rokita**	Y	Y	Y	Y	Y	N
5 **Burton**	Y	Y	Y	Y	Y	N
6 **Pence**	Y	Y	Y	Y	Y	N
7 Carson	–	+	+	–	–	+
8 **Bucshon**	Y	Y	Y	Y	Y	N
9 **Young**	Y	Y	Y	Y	Y	N
IOWA						
1 Braley	N	Y	Y	–	N	Y
2 Loebsack	Y	Y	Y	N	N	Y
3 Boswell	Y	Y	Y	N	N	Y
4 **Latham**	Y	Y	Y	Y	Y	N
5 **King**	Y	Y	Y	Y	Y	N
KANSAS						
1 **Huelskamp**	Y	Y	Y	Y	Y	N
2 **Jenkins**	Y	Y	Y	Y	Y	?
3 **Yoder**	Y	Y	Y	Y	Y	N
4 **Pompeo**	Y	Y	Y	Y	Y	N
KENTUCKY						
1 **Whitfield**	Y	Y	Y	Y	Y	N
2 **Guthrie**	Y	Y	Y	Y	Y	N
3 Yarmuth	N	Y	Y	N	N	Y
4 **Davis**	Y	Y	Y	Y	?	N
5 **Rogers**	Y	Y	Y	Y	Y	N
6 Chandler	Y	Y	Y	N	N	Y
LOUISIANA						
1 **Scalise**	Y	Y	Y	Y	Y	N
2 Richmond	N	N	Y	N	N	Y
3 **Landry**	Y	Y	Y	Y	Y	N
4 **Fleming**	Y	Y	Y	Y	Y	N
5 **Alexander**	Y	Y	Y	Y	Y	N
6 **Cassidy**	Y	Y	Y	Y	Y	N
7 **Boustany**	Y	Y	Y	Y	Y	N
MAINE						
1 Pingree	N	Y	Y	N	N	Y
2 Michaud	N	Y	Y	N	N	Y
MARYLAND						
1 **Harris**	Y	Y	Y	Y	Y	N
2 Ruppersberger	N	Y	Y	N	N	Y
3 Sarbanes	N	N	Y	N	N	Y
4 Edwards	N	N	N	N	N	Y
5 Hoyer	N	N	Y	N	N	Y
6 **Bartlett**	Y	N	Y	Y	Y	Y
7 Cummings	N	N	Y	N	N	Y
8 Van Hollen	N	N	Y	N	N	Y
MASSACHUSETTS						
1 Olver	N	N	N	?	N	Y
2 Neal	N	N	Y	N	N	Y
3 McGovern	N	N	N	N	N	Y
4 Frank	N	N	N	N	N	Y
5 Tsongas	N	Y	Y	N	N	N
6 Tierney	N	Y	Y	N	N	Y
7 Markey	N	N	N	N	N	Y
8 Capuano	N	N	Y	N	N	Y
9 Lynch	N	N	Y	N	N	Y
10 Keating	N	Y	Y	N	N	Y
MICHIGAN						
1 **Benishek**	Y	Y	Y	Y	Y	N
2 **Huizenga**	Y	Y	Y	Y	Y	N
3 **Amash**	Y	Y	N	Y	Y	N
4 **Camp**	Y	Y	Y	Y	Y	N
5 Kildee	N	N	Y	N	N	Y
6 **Upton**	Y	Y	Y	Y	Y	N
7 **Walberg**	Y	Y	Y	Y	Y	N
8 **Rogers**	Y	Y	Y	Y	Y	N
9 Peters	N	N	Y	N	N	Y
10 **Miller**	Y	Y	Y	Y	Y	N
11 **McCotter**	Y	Y	Y	Y	Y	N
12 Levin	N	N	Y	N	N	Y
13 Clarke	N	N	Y	N	N	Y
14 Conyers	N	N	N	N	N	Y
15 Dingell	N	N	Y	N	N	Y
MINNESOTA						
1 Walz	N	Y	Y	N	N	Y
2 **Kline**	Y	Y	Y	Y	Y	N
3 **Paulsen**	Y	Y	Y	Y	Y	N
4 McCollum	N	N	Y	N	N	Y

	18	19	20	21	22	23
5 Ellison	N	N	N	N	N	Y
6 **Bachmann**	Y	Y	Y	Y	Y	N
7 Peterson	Y	Y	Y	N	N	Y
8 **Cravaack**	Y	Y	Y	Y	Y	N
MISSISSIPPI						
1 **Nunnelee**	Y	Y	Y	Y	Y	N
2 Thompson	N	N	Y	N	N	Y
3 **Harper**	Y	Y	Y	Y	Y	N
4 **Palazzo**	Y	Y	Y	Y	Y	N
MISSOURI						
1 Clay	N	N	N	N	N	Y
2 **Akin**	Y	Y	Y	Y	+	N
3 Carnahan	N	N	Y	N	N	Y
4 **Hartzler**	Y	Y	Y	Y	Y	N
5 Cleaver	N	N	Y	N	N	Y
6 **Graves**	Y	Y	Y	Y	Y	N
7 **Long**	Y	Y	Y	Y	Y	N
8 **Emerson**	Y	Y	Y	Y	Y	N
9 **Luetkemeyer**	Y	Y	Y	Y	Y	N
MONTANA						
AL **Rehberg**	Y	Y	Y	Y	Y	N
NEBRASKA						
1 **Fortenberry**	Y	Y	Y	Y	Y	N
2 **Terry**	Y	Y	Y	Y	Y	N
3 **Smith**	Y	Y	Y	Y	Y	N
NEVADA						
1 Berkley	Y	Y	Y	N	N	Y
2 **Amodei**	Y	Y	Y	Y	Y	N
3 **Heck**	Y	Y	Y	Y	Y	N
NEW HAMPSHIRE						
1 **Guinta**	Y	Y	Y	Y	Y	N
2 **Bass**	Y	Y	Y	Y	Y	N
NEW JERSEY						
1 Andrews	N	Y	Y	N	N	Y
2 **LoBiondo**	Y	Y	Y	Y	Y	N
3 **Runyan**	Y	Y	Y	Y	Y	N
4 **Smith**	Y	Y	Y	?	?	N
5 **Garrett**	Y	Y	Y	Y	Y	N
6 Pallone	N	N	Y	N	N	Y
7 **Lance**	Y	Y	Y	Y	Y	N
8 Pascrell	N	N	Y	N	N	Y
9 Rothman	N	N	Y	?	?	?
10 Payne	N	N	N	N	N	Y
11 **Frelinghuysen**	Y	Y	Y	Y	Y	N
12 Holt	N	N	N	N	N	Y
13 Sires	N	N	Y	?	?	?
NEW MEXICO						
1 Heinrich	N	Y	Y	N	N	Y
2 **Pearce**	Y	Y	Y	Y	Y	Y
3 Luján	N	Y	Y	N	N	Y
NEW YORK						
1 Bishop	Y	Y	Y	N	N	Y
2 Israel	N	Y	Y	?	?	?
3 **King**	Y	Y	Y	Y	Y	N
4 McCarthy	N	N	Y	N	N	Y
5 Ackerman	N	N	Y	N	N	Y
6 Meeks	N	N	Y	N	N	Y
7 Crowley	N	N	Y	N	N	Y
8 Nadler	N	N	N	Y	N	Y
9 **Turner**	Y	Y	Y	Y	Y	N
10 Towns	N	N	Y	N	N	Y
11 Clarke	N	N	N	N	N	Y
12 Velázquez	N	N	Y	N	N	Y
13 **Grimm**	Y	Y	Y	Y	Y	N
14 Maloney	N	N	Y	N	N	Y
15 Rangel	N	N	Y	N	N	Y
16 Serrano	N	N	Y	N	N	Y
17 Engel	N	N	Y	N	N	Y
18 Lowey	N	Y	Y	N	N	Y
19 **Hayworth**	Y	Y	Y	Y	Y	N
20 **Gibson**	Y	Y	Y	Y	Y	N
21 Tonko	N	Y	Y	N	N	Y
22 Hinchey	?	?	?	?	?	?
23 Owens	Y	Y	Y	N	N	Y
24 **Hanna**	Y	Y	Y	Y	Y	N
25 **Buerkle**	Y	Y	Y	Y	Y	N
26 Hochul	Y	Y	Y	N	N	Y
27 Higgins	Y	Y	Y	N	N	Y
28 Slaughter	N	Y	Y	N	N	Y
29 **Reed**	Y	Y	Y	Y	Y	N
NORTH CAROLINA						
1 Butterfield	N	N	Y	N	N	Y
2 **Ellmers**	Y	Y	Y	Y	Y	N
3 **Jones**	Y	Y	Y	Y	Y	N
4 Price	N	N	Y	N	N	Y

	18	19	20	21	22	23
5 **Foxx**	Y	Y	Y	Y	Y	N
6 **Coble**	Y	Y	Y	Y	Y	N
7 McIntyre	Y	Y	Y	N	N	Y
8 Kissell	N	Y	Y	N	Y	Y
9 **Myrick**	Y	Y	Y	Y	Y	N
10 **McHenry**	Y	Y	Y	Y	Y	N
11 Shuler	Y	Y	Y	N	N	Y
12 Watt	N	N	Y	N	N	Y
13 Miller	N	N	Y	N	N	Y
NORTH DAKOTA						
AL **Berg**	Y	Y	Y	Y	Y	N
OHIO						
1 **Chabot**	Y	Y	Y	Y	Y	N
2 **Schmidt**	Y	Y	Y	Y	Y	N
3 **Turner**	Y	Y	Y	Y	Y	N
4 **Jordan**	Y	Y	Y	Y	Y	N
5 **Latta**	Y	Y	Y	Y	Y	N
6 **Johnson**	Y	Y	Y	Y	Y	N
7 **Austria**	Y	Y	Y	Y	Y	N
8 **Boehner**						
9 Kaptur	N	Y	Y	?	?	?
10 Kucinich	N	N	Y	N	N	Y
11 Fudge	N	N	Y	N	N	Y
12 **Tiberi**	Y	Y	Y	Y	Y	N
13 Sutton	N	Y	Y	N	N	Y
14 **LaTourette**	Y	Y	Y	Y	?	N
15 **Stivers**	Y	Y	Y	Y	Y	N
16 **Renacci**	Y	Y	Y	Y	Y	N
17 Ryan	N	Y	Y	N	N	Y
18 **Gibbs**	Y	Y	Y	Y	Y	N
OKLAHOMA						
1 **Sullivan**	Y	Y	Y	Y	Y	N
2 Boren	Y	Y	Y	N	Y	Y
3 **Lucas**	Y	Y	Y	Y	Y	N
4 **Cole**	Y	Y	Y	Y	Y	N
5 **Lankford**	Y	Y	Y	Y	Y	N
OREGON						
1 Vacant						
2 **Walden**	Y	Y	Y	Y	Y	N
3 Blumenauer	Y	N	Y	N	N	Y
4 DeFazio	Y	Y	Y	N	N	Y
5 Schrader	Y	Y	Y	N	N	Y
PENNSYLVANIA						
1 Brady	N	N	Y	N	N	Y
2 Fattah	N	N	Y	N	N	Y
3 **Kelly**	Y	Y	Y	Y	Y	N
4 Altmire	N	Y	Y	N	N	Y
5 **Thompson**	Y	Y	Y	Y	Y	N
6 **Gerlach**	Y	Y	Y	Y	Y	N
7 **Meehan**	Y	Y	Y	Y	Y	N
8 **Fitzpatrick**	Y	Y	Y	Y	Y	N
9 **Shuster**	Y	Y	Y	Y	Y	N
10 **Marino**	Y	Y	Y	Y	Y	N
11 **Barletta**	Y	Y	Y	Y	Y	N
12 Critz	N	Y	Y	N	N	Y
13 Schwartz	N	Y	Y	N	N	Y
14 Doyle	N	N	Y	N	N	Y
15 **Dent**	Y	Y	Y	Y	Y	N
16 **Pitts**	Y	Y	Y	Y	Y	N
17 Holden	N	N	Y	N	N	Y
18 **Murphy**	Y	Y	Y	Y	Y	N
19 **Platts**	Y	Y	Y	Y	Y	N
RHODE ISLAND						
1 Cicilline	N	Y	Y	N	N	Y
2 Langevin	N	Y	Y	?	N	Y
SOUTH CAROLINA						
1 **Scott**	Y	Y	Y	Y	Y	N
2 **Wilson**	Y	Y	Y	Y	Y	N
3 **Duncan**	Y	Y	Y	Y	Y	N
4 **Gowdy**	Y	Y	Y	Y	Y	N
5 **Mulvaney**	Y	Y	Y	Y	Y	N
6 Clyburn	N	N	Y	?	N	Y
SOUTH DAKOTA						
AL **Noem**	Y	Y	Y	Y	Y	N
TENNESSEE						
1 **Roe**	Y	Y	Y	Y	Y	N
2 **Duncan**	Y	Y	Y	Y	Y	N
3 **Fleischmann**	Y	Y	Y	Y	Y	N
4 **DesJarlais**	Y	Y	Y	Y	Y	N
5 Cooper	Y	Y	Y	N	N	Y
6 **Black**	Y	Y	Y	Y	Y	N
7 **Blackburn**	Y	Y	Y	Y	Y	N
8 **Fincher**	Y	Y	Y	Y	Y	N
9 Cohen	N	N	Y	N	N	Y

	18	19	20	21	22	23
TEXAS						
1 **Gohmert**	Y	Y	Y	Y	Y	N
2 **Poe**	Y	Y	Y	Y	Y	N
3 **Johnson, S.**	Y	Y	Y	Y	Y	N
4 **Hall**	Y	Y	Y	Y	Y	Y
5 **Hensarling**	Y	Y	Y	Y	Y	N
6 **Barton**	Y	Y	Y	Y	Y	N
7 **Culberson**	Y	Y	Y	Y	Y	N
8 **Brady**	Y	Y	Y	Y	Y	N
9 Green, A.	N	N	Y	N	N	Y
10 **McCaul**	Y	Y	Y	Y	Y	N
11 **Conaway**	Y	Y	Y	Y	Y	N
12 **Granger**	Y	Y	Y	Y	Y	N
13 **Thornberry**	Y	Y	Y	Y	Y	N
14 **Paul**	?	?	?	?	?	?
15 Hinojosa	N	N	Y	N	N	Y
16 Reyes	N	N	Y	N	N	Y
17 **Flores**	Y	Y	Y	Y	Y	?
18 Jackson Lee	N	N	N	N	N	Y
19 **Neugebauer**	Y	Y	Y	Y	Y	N
20 Gonzalez	N	N	Y	N	N	Y
21 **Smith**	Y	Y	Y	Y	Y	N
22 **Olson**	Y	Y	Y	Y	Y	N
23 **Canseco**	Y	Y	Y	Y	Y	N
24 **Marchant**	Y	Y	Y	Y	Y	N
25 Doggett	N	N	Y	N	N	Y
26 **Burgess**	Y	Y	Y	Y	Y	N
27 **Farenthold**	Y	Y	Y	Y	Y	N
28 Cuellar	Y	Y	Y	N	N	Y
29 Green, G.	N	Y	Y	N	N	Y
30 Johnson, E.	N	N	Y	N	N	Y
31 **Carter**	Y	Y	Y	Y	Y	N
32 **Sessions**	Y	Y	Y	Y	Y	N
UTAH						
1 **Bishop**	Y	Y	Y	Y	Y	N
2 Matheson	Y	Y	Y	Y	Y	N
3 **Chaffetz**	Y	Y	Y	Y	Y	N
VERMONT						
AL Welch	N	N	Y	N	N	Y
VIRGINIA						
1 **Wittman**	Y	Y	Y	Y	Y	N
2 **Rigell**	Y	Y	Y	Y	Y	N
3 Scott	N	N	N	N	N	Y
4 **Forbes**	Y	Y	Y	Y	Y	N
5 **Hurt**	Y	Y	Y	Y	Y	N
6 **Goodlatte**	Y	Y	Y	Y	Y	N
7 **Cantor**	Y	Y	Y	Y	Y	N
8 Moran	N	N	Y	N	N	Y
9 **Griffith**	Y	Y	Y	Y	Y	N
10 **Wolf**	Y	Y	Y	N	Y	N
11 Connolly	N	N	Y	N	N	Y
WASHINGTON						
1 Inslee	N	Y	Y	N	N	Y
2 Larsen	Y	N	Y	N	N	Y
3 **Herrera Beutler**	Y	Y	Y	Y	Y	N
4 **Hastings**	Y	Y	Y	Y	Y	N
5 **McMorris Rodgers**	Y	Y	+	Y	Y	N
6 Dicks	N	N	?	N	N	Y
7 McDermott	N	N	Y	N	N	Y
8 **Reichert**	Y	Y	Y	Y	Y	N
9 Smith	N	N	Y	N	N	Y
WEST VIRGINIA						
1 **McKinley**	Y	Y	Y	Y	Y	N
2 **Capito**	Y	Y	Y	Y	Y	N
3 Rahall	N	Y	Y	N	N	Y
WISCONSIN						
1 **Ryan**	Y	Y	Y	Y	Y	N
2 Baldwin	N	Y	Y	N	N	Y
3 Kind	Y	Y	Y	N	N	Y
4 Moore	N	N	–	N	N	Y
5 **Sensenbrenner**	Y	Y	Y	Y	Y	N
6 **Petri**	Y	Y	Y	Y	Y	N
7 **Duffy**	Y	Y	Y	Y	Y	N
8 **Ribble**	Y	Y	Y	Y	Y	N
WYOMING						
AL **Lummis**	Y	Y	Y	Y	Y	N

IN THE HOUSE | By Vote Number

24. **HR 3582. Dynamic Scoring/Tax Cut Impacts.** Peters, D-Mich., amendment that would add a section detailing the macroeconomic impact of the 2001 and 2003 tax cuts to the bill's findings. Rejected in Committee of the Whole 174-244: R 0-237; D 174-7. Feb. 2, 2012.

25. **HR 3582. Dynamic Scoring/Appropriations Analysis.** Connolly, D-Va., amendment that would require the Congressional Budget Office to prepare macroeconomic impact analyses of appropriations bills. Rejected in Committee of the Whole 177-237: R 4-231; D 173-6. Feb. 2, 2012.

26. **HR 3582. Dynamic Scoring/Income Inequality.** Fudge, D-Ohio, amendment that would add "income inequality" to the major economic variables used to determine the economic impact of legislation. Rejected in Committee of the Whole 171-243: R 2-234; D 169-9. Feb. 2, 2012.

27. **HR 3582. Dynamic Scoring/HUB Zones.** Jackson Lee, D-Texas, amendment that would require the Congressional Budget Office to include the potential impact on Historically Underutilized Business (HUB) zones as part of its macroeconomic analysis. Rejected in Committee of the Whole 173-243: R 5-231; D 168-12. Feb. 2, 2012.

28. **HR 3582. Dynamic Scoring/Substitute.** Cicilline, D-R.I., substitute amendment that would require the Congressional Budget Office to include in its official cost estimates of legislation an estimate of the number of jobs that would be created, sustained or lost in carrying out the proposed bill for each year over a five-year period. Rejected in Committee of the Whole 174-245: R 0-238; D 174-7. Feb. 2, 2012.

29. **HR 3582. Dynamic Scoring/Recommit.** Boswell, D-Iowa, motion to recommit the bill to the Budget Committee with instructions that it be reported back immediately with an amendment that would require the Congressional Budget Office to prepare for each major bill or resolution reported by any congressional committee, except for Appropriations, an impact analysis of the budgetary effects of the measure on Medicare beneficiaries and the Social Security and Medicare Trust Funds. Motion rejected 183-237: R 2-237; D 181-0. Feb. 2, 2012.

30. **HR 3582. Dynamic Scoring/Passage.** Passage of the bill that would require the Congressional Budget Office to prepare supplements to their cost estimates that include a macroeconomic impact analysis of the budgetary effects of major pieces of legislation, a calculation known as "dynamic scoring." The bill would exclude appropriations measures from the dynamic-scoring requirement. Passed 242-179: R 238-0; D 4-179. Feb. 2, 2012.

	24	25	26	27	28	29	30
ALABAMA							
1 Bonner	N	N	N	N	N	N	Y
2 Roby	N	N	N	N	N	N	Y
3 Rogers	N	N	N	N	N	N	Y
4 Aderholt	N	N	N	N	N	N	Y
5 Brooks	N	N	N	N	N	N	Y
6 Bachus	N	N	N	N	N	N	Y
7 Sewell	Y	Y	Y	Y	Y	?	N
ALASKA							
AL Young	N	N	N	N	N	N	Y
ARIZONA							
1 Gosar	N	N	N	N	N	N	Y
2 Franks	N	N	N	N	N	N	Y
3 Quayle	N	N	N	N	N	N	Y
4 Pastor	Y	Y	Y	Y	Y	Y	N
5 Schweikert	N	N	N	N	N	N	Y
6 Flake	N	N	N	N	N	N	Y
7 Grijalva	Y	Y	Y	Y	Y	Y	N
8 Vacant							
ARKANSAS							
1 Crawford	N	N	N	N	N	N	Y
2 Griffin	N	N	N	N	N	N	Y
3 Womack	N	N	N	N	N	N	Y
4 Ross	N	Y	Y	Y	Y	Y	N
CALIFORNIA							
1 Thompson	Y	Y	Y	Y	Y	Y	N
2 Herger	N	N	N	N	N	N	Y
3 Lungren	N	N	N	N	N	N	Y
4 McClintock	N	N	N	N	N	N	Y
5 Matsui	Y	Y	Y	Y	Y	Y	N
6 Woolsey	Y	Y	Y	Y	Y	Y	N
7 Miller, George	Y	Y	Y	Y	Y	Y	N
8 Pelosi	Y	Y	Y	Y	Y	Y	N
9 Lee	Y	Y	Y	Y	Y	Y	N
10 Garamendi	Y	Y	?	Y	Y	Y	N
11 McNerney	Y	Y	Y	Y	Y	Y	N
12 Speier	Y	Y	Y	Y	Y	Y	N
13 Stark	Y	Y	Y	Y	Y	Y	N
14 Eshoo	Y	Y	Y	Y	Y	Y	N
15 Honda	Y	Y	Y	Y	Y	Y	N
16 Lofgren	Y	Y	Y	Y	Y	Y	N
17 Farr	Y	Y	Y	Y	Y	Y	N
18 Cardoza	?	?	?	?	?	?	?
19 Denham	N	N	N	N	N	N	Y
20 Costa	Y	Y	N	N	Y	Y	N
21 Nunes	N	N	N	N	N	N	Y
22 McCarthy	N	N	N	N	N	N	Y
23 Capps	Y	Y	Y	Y	Y	Y	N
24 Gallegly	N	N	N	N	N	N	Y
25 McKeon	N	N	N	N	N	N	Y
26 Dreier	N	N	N	N	N	N	Y
27 Sherman	Y	Y	+	Y	Y	Y	N
28 Berman	Y	Y	Y	Y	Y	Y	N
29 Schiff	Y	Y	Y	Y	Y	Y	N
30 Waxman	Y	Y	Y	Y	Y	Y	N
31 Becerra	Y	Y	Y	Y	Y	Y	N
32 Chu	Y	Y	Y	Y	Y	Y	N
33 Bass	Y	Y	Y	Y	Y	Y	N
34 Roybal-Allard	?	?	?	?	?	?	?
35 Waters	Y	Y	Y	?	Y	Y	N
36 Hahn	Y	Y	Y	Y	Y	Y	N
37 Richardson	Y	Y	Y	Y	Y	Y	N
38 Napolitano	Y	Y	Y	?	Y	Y	N
39 Sánchez, Linda	Y	Y	Y	Y	Y	Y	N
40 Royce	N	N	N	N	N	N	Y
41 Lewis	N	N	N	N	N	N	Y
42 Miller, Gary	N	N	N	N	N	N	Y
43 Baca	Y	Y	Y	Y	Y	Y	N
44 Calvert	N	N	N	N	N	N	Y
45 Bono Mack	N	N	N	N	N	N	Y
46 Rohrabacher	N	N	N	N	N	N	Y
47 Sanchez, Loretta	Y	Y	Y	Y	Y	Y	N
48 Campbell	N	N	N	N	N	N	Y
49 Issa	N	N	N	N	N	N	Y
50 Bilbray	N	N	N	N	N	N	Y
51 Filner	+	+	+	+	+	+	-
52 Hunter	N	N	N	N	N	N	Y
53 Davis	Y	Y	Y	Y	Y	Y	N

	24	25	26	27	28	29	30
COLORADO							
1 DeGette	Y	Y	Y	Y	Y	Y	N
2 Polis	Y	Y	Y	Y	Y	Y	N
3 Tipton	N	N	N	N	N	N	Y
4 Gardner	N	N	N	N	N	N	Y
5 Lamborn	N	N	N	N	N	N	Y
6 Coffman	N	N	N	N	N	N	Y
7 Perlmutter	Y	Y	Y	Y	Y	Y	N
CONNECTICUT							
1 Larson	Y	Y	Y	Y	Y	Y	N
2 Courtney	Y	Y	Y	Y	Y	Y	N
3 DeLauro	Y	Y	Y	Y	Y	Y	N
4 Himes	Y	Y	Y	Y	Y	Y	N
5 Murphy	Y	Y	Y	Y	Y	Y	N
DELAWARE							
AL Carney	Y	Y	Y	N	Y	Y	N
FLORIDA							
1 Miller	N	N	N	N	N	N	Y
2 Southerland	N	N	N	N	N	N	Y
3 Brown	Y	Y	Y	Y	Y	Y	N
4 Crenshaw	N	N	N	N	N	N	Y
5 Nugent	N	N	N	N	N	N	Y
6 Stearns	N	N	N	N	N	N	Y
7 Mica	N	N	N	N	N	N	Y
8 Webster	N	N	N	N	N	N	Y
9 Bilirakis	N	N	N	N	N	N	Y
10 Young	N	N	N	N	N	N	Y
11 Castor	Y	Y	Y	Y	Y	Y	N
12 Ross	N	N	N	N	N	N	Y
13 Buchanan	N	N	N	N	N	N	Y
14 Mack	?	?	?	?	?	?	?
15 Posey	N	N	N	N	N	N	Y
16 Rooney	N	N	N	N	N	N	Y
17 Wilson	Y	Y	Y	Y	Y	Y	N
18 Ros-Lehtinen	N	N	N	N	?	N	Y
19 Deutch	Y	Y	Y	Y	Y	Y	N
20 Wasserman Schultz	Y	Y	Y	Y	Y	Y	N
21 Diaz-Balart	N	N	N	N	N	N	Y
22 West	N	N	N	N	N	N	Y
23 Hastings	Y	Y	Y	Y	Y	Y	N
24 Adams	N	N	N	N	N	N	Y
25 Rivera	N	N	N	N	N	N	Y
GEORGIA							
1 Kingston	N	N	N	N	N	N	Y
2 Bishop	Y	Y	Y	Y	Y	Y	N
3 Westmoreland	N	N	N	N	N	N	Y
4 Johnson	Y	Y	Y	Y	Y	Y	N
5 Lewis	Y	Y	Y	Y	Y	Y	N
6 Price	N	N	N	N	N	N	Y
7 Woodall	N	N	N	N	N	N	Y
8 Scott, A.	N	N	N	N	N	N	Y
9 Graves	N	N	N	N	N	N	Y
10 Broun	N	N	N	?	N	N	Y
11 Gingrey	N	N	N	N	N	N	Y
12 Barrow	N	Y	Y	Y	N	Y	N
13 Scott, D.	Y	Y	Y	Y	Y	Y	N
HAWAII							
1 Hanabusa	Y	Y	Y	Y	Y	Y	N
2 Hirono	Y	Y	Y	Y	Y	Y	N
IDAHO							
1 Labrador	N	N	N	N	N	N	Y
2 Simpson	N	N	N	N	N	N	Y
ILLINOIS							
1 Rush	Y	Y	Y	Y	Y	Y	N
2 Jackson	Y	Y	Y	Y	Y	Y	N
3 Lipinski	Y	Y	Y	N	Y	Y	N
4 Gutierrez	Y	?	Y	Y	Y	Y	N
5 Quigley	Y	Y	Y	Y	Y	Y	N
6 Roskam	N	N	N	N	N	N	Y
7 Davis	Y	Y	Y	Y	Y	Y	N
8 Walsh	N	N	N	N	N	N	Y
9 Schakowsky	Y	Y	Y	Y	Y	Y	N
10 Dold	N	N	N	N	N	N	Y
11 Kinzinger	N	N	N	N	N	N	Y
12 Costello	Y	Y	Y	Y	Y	Y	N
13 Biggert	N	N	N	N	N	N	Y
14 Hultgren	N	N	N	N	N	N	Y
15 Johnson	N	Y	N	N	N	N	Y

	24	25	26	27	28	29	30
16 **Manzullo**	N	N	N	N	N	N	Y
17 **Schilling**	N	N	Y	Y	N	N	Y
18 **Schock**	N	?	N	N	N	N	Y
19 **Shimkus**	N	N	N	N	N	N	Y
INDIANA							
1 Visclosky	Y	Y	Y	Y	Y	Y	N
2 Donnelly	Y	Y	N	N	Y	Y	N
3 **Stutzman**	N	N	N	N	N	N	Y
4 **Rokita**	N	N	N	N	N	N	Y
5 **Burton**	N	N	N	N	N	N	Y
6 **Pence**	N	N	N	N	N	N	Y
7 Carson	+	+	+	+	+	+	–
8 **Bucshon**	N	N	N	N	N	N	Y
9 **Young**	N	N	N	N	N	N	Y
IOWA							
1 Braley	Y	Y	Y	Y	Y	Y	N
2 Loebsack	Y	Y	Y	Y	Y	Y	N
3 Boswell	Y	Y	Y	Y	Y	Y	N
4 **Latham**	N	N	N	N	N	Y	Y
5 **King**	N	N	N	N	N	N	Y
KANSAS							
1 **Huelskamp**	N	N	N	N	N	N	Y
2 **Jenkins**	N	N	N	N	N	N	Y
3 **Yoder**	N	N	N	N	N	N	?
4 **Pompeo**	N	N	N	N	N	N	Y
KENTUCKY							
1 **Whitfield**	N	N	N	N	N	N	Y
2 **Guthrie**	N	N	N	N	N	N	Y
3 Yarmuth	Y	Y	Y	Y	Y	Y	N
4 **Davis**	N	N	N	N	N	N	Y
5 **Rogers**	N	N	N	N	N	N	Y
6 Chandler	Y	Y	Y	Y	Y	Y	N
LOUISIANA							
1 **Scalise**	N	N	N	N	N	N	Y
2 Richmond	Y	Y	Y	Y	Y	Y	N
3 **Landry**	N	N	N	N	N	N	Y
4 **Fleming**	N	N	N	N	N	N	Y
5 **Alexander**	N	N	N	N	N	N	Y
6 **Cassidy**	–	N	N	N	N	N	Y
7 **Boustany**	N	N	N	N	N	N	Y
MAINE							
1 Pingree	Y	Y	Y	Y	Y	Y	N
2 Michaud	Y	Y	Y	Y	Y	Y	N
MARYLAND							
1 **Harris**	N	N	N	Y	N	N	Y
2 Ruppersberger	?	Y	Y	Y	Y	Y	N
3 Sarbanes	Y	Y	Y	Y	Y	Y	N
4 Edwards	Y	Y	Y	Y	Y	Y	N
5 Hoyer	Y	Y	Y	Y	Y	?	N
6 **Bartlett**	N	N	N	Y	N	N	Y
7 Cummings	Y	Y	Y	Y	Y	Y	N
8 Van Hollen	Y	Y	Y	Y	Y	Y	N
MASSACHUSETTS							
1 Olver	Y	Y	Y	Y	Y	Y	N
2 Neal	Y	Y	Y	Y	Y	Y	N
3 McGovern	Y	Y	Y	Y	Y	Y	N
4 Frank	Y	Y	Y	Y	Y	Y	N
5 Tsongas	Y	Y	Y	Y	Y	Y	N
6 Tierney	Y	Y	Y	Y	Y	Y	N
7 Markey	Y	Y	Y	Y	Y	Y	N
8 Capuano	Y	?	Y	Y	Y	Y	N
9 Lynch	Y	Y	Y	Y	Y	Y	N
10 Keating	Y	Y	Y	Y	Y	Y	N
MICHIGAN							
1 **Benishek**	N	N	N	N	N	N	Y
2 **Huizenga**	N	N	N	N	N	N	Y
3 **Amash**	N	N	N	N	N	N	Y
4 **Camp**	N	N	N	N	N	N	Y
5 Kildee	Y	Y	Y	Y	Y	Y	N
6 **Upton**	N	N	N	N	N	N	Y
7 **Walberg**	N	N	N	N	N	N	Y
8 **Rogers**	N	N	N	N	N	N	Y
9 Peters	Y	Y	Y	Y	Y	Y	N
10 **Miller**	N	N	N	N	N	N	Y
11 **McCotter**	N	N	N	N	N	N	Y
12 Levin	Y	Y	Y	Y	Y	Y	N
13 Clarke	Y	Y	Y	Y	Y	Y	N
14 Conyers	Y	Y	Y	Y	Y	Y	N
15 Dingell	Y	Y	Y	Y	Y	Y	N
MINNESOTA							
1 Walz	Y	Y	Y	Y	Y	Y	N
2 **Kline**	N	N	N	N	N	N	Y
3 **Paulsen**	N	N	N	N	N	N	Y
4 McCollum	Y	Y	Y	Y	Y	Y	N

	24	25	26	27	28	29	30
5 Ellison	Y	Y	Y	Y	Y	Y	N
6 **Bachmann**	N	N	N	N	N	N	Y
7 Peterson	N	N	N	N	N	Y	N
8 **Cravaack**	N	N	N	N	N	N	Y
MISSISSIPPI							
1 **Nunnelee**	N	N	N	N	N	N	Y
2 Thompson	Y	Y	Y	Y	Y	Y	N
3 **Harper**	N	N	N	N	N	N	Y
4 **Palazzo**	N	N	N	N	N	N	Y
MISSOURI							
1 Clay	Y	Y	Y	Y	Y	Y	N
2 **Akin**	N	N	N	N	N	N	Y
3 Carnahan	Y	?	Y	Y	Y	Y	N
4 **Hartzler**	N	N	N	N	N	N	Y
5 Cleaver	Y	Y	Y	Y	Y	Y	N
6 **Graves**	N	N	N	N	N	N	Y
7 **Long**	N	N	N	N	N	N	Y
8 **Emerson**	N	N	N	N	N	N	Y
9 **Luetkemeyer**	N	N	N	N	N	N	Y
MONTANA							
AL **Rehberg**	N	N	N	N	N	N	Y
NEBRASKA							
1 **Fortenberry**	N	N	N	N	N	N	Y
2 **Terry**	N	N	N	N	N	N	Y
3 **Smith**	N	N	N	N	N	N	Y
NEVADA							
1 Berkley	Y	Y	Y	Y	Y	Y	N
2 **Amodei**	N	N	N	N	N	N	Y
3 **Heck**	N	N	N	N	N	N	Y
NEW HAMPSHIRE							
1 **Guinta**	N	N	N	N	N	N	Y
2 **Bass**	N	N	N	N	N	N	Y
NEW JERSEY							
1 Andrews	Y	Y	Y	Y	Y	Y	N
2 **LoBiondo**	N	N	N	N	N	N	Y
3 **Runyan**	N	N	N	N	N	N	Y
4 **Smith**	N	N	N	N	N	N	Y
5 **Garrett**	N	N	N	N	N	N	Y
6 Pallone	Y	Y	Y	Y	Y	Y	N
7 **Lance**	N	N	N	N	N	N	Y
8 Pascrell	+	+	+	+	+	+	–
9 Rothman	?	?	?	?	?	?	?
10 Payne	Y	Y	Y	Y	?	Y	N
11 **Frelinghuysen**	N	N	N	N	N	N	Y
12 Holt	Y	Y	Y	Y	Y	Y	N
13 Sires	?	?	?	?	?	?	?
NEW MEXICO							
1 Heinrich	Y	Y	Y	Y	Y	Y	N
2 **Pearce**	N	N	N	N	N	N	Y
3 Luján	Y	Y	Y	Y	Y	Y	N
NEW YORK							
1 Bishop	Y	Y	Y	Y	Y	Y	N
2 Israel	Y	Y	Y	Y	Y	Y	N
3 **King**	N	N	N	N	N	N	Y
4 McCarthy	Y	Y	Y	Y	Y	Y	N
5 Ackerman	Y	Y	Y	Y	Y	Y	N
6 Meeks	Y	Y	Y	Y	Y	Y	N
7 Crowley	Y	Y	Y	Y	Y	Y	N
8 Nadler	Y	Y	Y	Y	Y	Y	N
9 **Turner**	N	N	N	N	N	N	Y
10 Towns	Y	Y	Y	Y	Y	Y	N
11 Clarke	Y	Y	Y	Y	Y	Y	N
12 Velázquez	Y	Y	Y	Y	Y	Y	N
13 **Grimm**	N	N	N	N	N	N	Y
14 Maloney	Y	Y	Y	Y	Y	Y	N
15 Rangel	Y	Y	Y	Y	Y	Y	N
16 Serrano	Y	Y	Y	Y	Y	Y	N
17 Engel	Y	Y	Y	Y	Y	Y	N
18 Lowey	Y	Y	Y	Y	Y	Y	N
19 **Hayworth**	N	N	N	N	N	N	Y
20 **Gibson**	N	N	Y	N	N	N	Y
21 Tonko	Y	Y	Y	Y	Y	Y	N
22 Hinchey	?	?	?	?	?	?	?
23 Owens	Y	Y	N	Y	Y	Y	N
24 **Hanna**	N	N	N	N	N	N	Y
25 **Buerkle**	N	N	N	N	N	N	Y
26 Hochul	Y	Y	Y	Y	Y	Y	N
27 Higgins	Y	Y	Y	Y	Y	Y	N
28 Slaughter	Y	Y	Y	Y	Y	Y	N
29 **Reed**	N	N	N	N	N	N	Y
NORTH CAROLINA							
1 Butterfield	Y	Y	Y	Y	Y	Y	N
2 **Ellmers**	N	N	N	N	N	N	Y
3 **Jones**	N	Y	N	Y	N	Y	Y
4 Price	Y	Y	Y	Y	Y	Y	N

	24	25	26	27	28	29	30
5 **Foxx**	N	N	N	N	N	N	Y
6 **Coble**	N	N	N	N	N	N	Y
7 McIntyre	N	N	N	N	Y	Y	Y
8 Kissell	Y	Y	Y	Y	Y	Y	N
9 **Myrick**	N	N	N	N	N	N	Y
10 **McHenry**	N	N	N	N	N	N	Y
11 Shuler	Y	N	N	N	N	Y	N
12 Watt	Y	Y	Y	Y	Y	Y	N
13 Miller	Y	Y	?	Y	Y	Y	N
NORTH DAKOTA							
AL **Berg**	–	–	–	–	N	N	Y
OHIO							
1 **Chabot**	N	N	N	N	N	N	Y
2 **Schmidt**	N	N	N	N	N	N	Y
3 **Turner**	N	N	N	N	N	N	Y
4 **Jordan**	N	N	N	N	N	N	Y
5 **Latta**	N	N	N	N	N	N	Y
6 **Johnson**	N	N	N	N	N	N	Y
7 **Austria**	N	N	N	N	N	N	Y
8 **Boehner**							
9 Kaptur	?	?	?	?	?	Y	N
10 Kucinich	Y	Y	Y	Y	Y	Y	N
11 Fudge	Y	Y	Y	Y	Y	Y	N
12 **Tiberi**	N	N	N	N	N	N	Y
13 Sutton	Y	Y	Y	Y	Y	Y	N
14 **LaTourette**	N	?	N	N	N	N	Y
15 **Stivers**	N	N	N	N	N	N	Y
16 **Renacci**	N	N	N	N	N	N	Y
17 Ryan	Y	Y	Y	Y	Y	Y	N
18 **Gibbs**	N	N	N	N	N	N	Y
OKLAHOMA							
1 **Sullivan**	N	N	?	N	N	N	Y
2 Boren	N	N	N	N	N	Y	Y
3 **Lucas**	N	N	N	N	N	N	Y
4 **Cole**	N	N	N	N	N	N	Y
5 **Lankford**	N	N	N	N	N	N	Y
OREGON							
1 Vacant							
2 **Walden**	N	N	N	N	N	N	Y
3 Blumenauer	Y	Y	Y	Y	Y	Y	N
4 DeFazio	Y	Y	Y	Y	Y	Y	N
5 Schrader	Y	Y	Y	N	Y	Y	N
PENNSYLVANIA							
1 Brady	Y	Y	Y	Y	Y	Y	N
2 Fattah	Y	Y	Y	Y	Y	Y	N
3 **Kelly**	N	N	N	N	N	N	Y
4 Altmire	Y	Y	Y	Y	Y	Y	N
5 **Thompson**	N	N	N	N	N	N	Y
6 **Gerlach**	N	N	N	N	N	N	Y
7 **Meehan**	N	N	N	N	N	N	Y
8 **Fitzpatrick**	N	Y	N	N	N	N	Y
9 **Shuster**	N	N	N	N	N	N	Y
10 **Marino**	N	N	N	N	N	N	Y
11 **Barletta**	N	N	N	Y	N	N	Y
12 Critz	Y	Y	Y	Y	Y	Y	N
13 Schwartz	Y	Y	Y	Y	Y	Y	N
14 Doyle	Y	Y	Y	Y	Y	Y	N
15 **Dent**	N	N	N	N	N	N	Y
16 **Pitts**	N	N	N	N	N	N	Y
17 Holden	Y	Y	Y	Y	Y	Y	N
18 **Murphy**	N	N	N	N	N	N	Y
19 **Platts**	N	N	N	N	N	N	Y
RHODE ISLAND							
1 Cicilline	Y	Y	Y	Y	Y	Y	N
2 Langevin	Y	Y	Y	Y	Y	Y	N
SOUTH CAROLINA							
1 **Scott**	N	N	N	N	N	N	Y
2 **Wilson**	N	N	N	N	N	N	Y
3 **Duncan**	N	N	N	N	N	N	Y
4 **Gowdy**	N	N	N	N	N	N	Y
5 **Mulvaney**	N	N	N	N	N	N	Y
6 Clyburn	Y	Y	Y	Y	Y	Y	N
SOUTH DAKOTA							
AL **Noem**	N	N	N	N	N	N	Y
TENNESSEE							
1 **Roe**	N	N	N	N	N	N	Y
2 **Duncan**	N	N	N	N	N	N	Y
3 **Fleischmann**	N	N	N	N	N	N	Y
4 **DesJarlais**	N	N	N	N	N	N	Y
5 Cooper	Y	N	N	N	N	Y	N
6 **Black**	N	N	N	N	N	N	Y
7 **Blackburn**	N	N	N	N	N	N	Y
8 **Fincher**	N	N	N	N	N	N	Y
9 Cohen	Y	Y	Y	Y	Y	Y	N

	24	25	26	27	28	29	30
TEXAS							
1 **Gohmert**	N	N	N	N	N	N	Y
2 **Poe**	N	N	N	N	N	N	Y
3 **Johnson, S.**	N	N	N	N	N	N	Y
4 **Hall**	N	N	N	N	N	N	Y
5 **Hensarling**	N	N	N	N	N	N	Y
6 **Barton**	N	N	N	N	N	N	Y
7 **Culberson**	N	N	N	N	N	N	Y
8 **Brady**	N	N	N	N	N	N	Y
9 Green, A.	Y	Y	Y	Y	Y	Y	N
10 **McCaul**	N	N	N	N	N	N	Y
11 **Conaway**	N	N	N	N	N	N	Y
12 **Granger**	N	N	N	N	N	N	Y
13 **Thornberry**	N	N	N	N	N	N	Y
14 **Paul**	?	?	?	?	?	?	?
15 Hinojosa	Y	Y	Y	Y	Y	Y	N
16 Reyes	Y	Y	Y	Y	Y	Y	N
17 **Flores**	N	N	N	N	N	N	Y
18 Jackson Lee	Y	Y	Y	Y	Y	Y	N
19 **Neugebauer**	N	N	N	N	N	N	Y
20 Gonzalez	Y	Y	Y	Y	Y	Y	N
21 **Smith**	N	N	N	N	N	N	Y
22 **Olson**	N	N	N	N	N	N	Y
23 **Canseco**	N	?	?	?	N	N	Y
24 **Marchant**	N	N	N	N	N	N	Y
25 Doggett	Y	Y	Y	Y	Y	Y	N
26 **Burgess**	N	N	N	N	N	N	Y
27 **Farenthold**	N	N	N	N	N	N	Y
28 Cuellar	N	Y	Y	Y	Y	Y	N
29 Green, G.	Y	Y	Y	Y	Y	Y	N
30 Johnson, E.	Y	Y	Y	Y	Y	Y	N
31 **Carter**	N	N	N	N	N	N	Y
32 **Sessions**	N	N	N	N	N	N	Y
UTAH							
1 **Bishop**	N	N	N	N	N	N	Y
2 Matheson	N	N	N	N	N	Y	Y
3 **Chaffetz**	N	N	N	N	N	N	Y
VERMONT							
AL Welch	Y	Y	Y	Y	Y	Y	N
VIRGINIA							
1 **Wittman**	N	N	N	N	N	N	Y
2 **Rigell**	N	N	N	N	N	N	Y
3 Scott	Y	Y	Y	Y	Y	Y	N
4 **Forbes**	N	N	N	N	N	N	Y
5 **Hurt**	N	N	N	N	N	N	Y
6 **Goodlatte**	N	N	N	N	N	N	Y
7 **Cantor**	N	N	N	N	N	N	Y
8 Moran	Y	Y	Y	Y	Y	Y	N
9 **Griffith**	N	N	N	N	N	N	Y
10 **Wolf**	N	N	N	N	N	N	Y
11 Connolly	Y	Y	Y	Y	Y	Y	N
WASHINGTON							
1 Inslee	Y	Y	Y	Y	Y	Y	N
2 Larsen	Y	Y	Y	Y	Y	Y	N
3 **Herrera Beutler**	N	N	N	N	N	N	Y
4 **Hastings**	N	N	N	N	N	N	Y
5 **McMorris Rodgers**	N	N	N	N	N	N	Y
6 Dicks	Y	Y	?	Y	Y	Y	N
7 McDermott	Y	Y	Y	Y	Y	Y	N
8 **Reichert**	N	N	N	N	N	N	Y
9 Smith	Y	Y	Y	Y	Y	Y	N
WEST VIRGINIA							
1 **McKinley**	N	N	N	N	N	N	Y
2 **Capito**	N	N	N	N	N	N	Y
3 Rahall	Y	Y	Y	Y	Y	Y	N
WISCONSIN							
1 **Ryan**	N	N	N	N	N	N	Y
2 Baldwin	Y	Y	Y	Y	Y	Y	N
3 Kind	Y	Y	Y	N	Y	Y	N
4 Moore	Y	Y	Y	Y	Y	Y	N
5 **Sensenbrenner**	N	N	N	N	N	N	Y
6 **Petri**	N	N	N	N	N	N	Y
7 **Duffy**	N	N	N	N	N	N	Y
8 **Ribble**	N	N	N	N	N	N	Y
WYOMING							
AL **Lummis**	N	N	N	N	N	N	Y

IN THE HOUSE | By Vote Number

31. HR 3578. Budget Baseline/Recommit. Tierney, D-Mass., motion to recommit the bill to the Budget Committee with instructions to report it back immediately with an amendment that would require the Congressional Budget Office to maintain current funding levels in inflation-adjusted terms for Pell grants and education programs for students; health and all discretionary spending that provides benefits for seniors; job, health and all discretionary spending that provides benefits to veterans and health research. Motion rejected 177-238: R 0-235; D 177-3. Feb. 3, 2012.

32. HR 3578. Budget Baseline/Passage. Passage of the bill that would amend current law governing the development of budget baselines to remove the assumption that discretionary spending will increase each year by the level of inflation. It would require the Congressional Budget Office to prepare an annual alternative baseline that shows the projected spending, revenue, deficits and debt that would occur if current tax policy was maintained. Passed 235-177: R 231-0; D 4-177. Feb. 3, 2012.

33. HR 658. FAA Reauthorization/Conference Report. Adoption of the conference report on the bill that would authorize $15.9 billion annually for federal aviation programs through fiscal 2015. The measure would increase the proportion of eligible members of the National Mediation Board needed to petition for new union elections from 35 percent to 50 percent. It would increase by 16 the number of slots permitted for long-distance flights in and out of Ronald Reagan Washington National Airport. Adopted (thus sent to the Senate) 248-169: R 224-12; D 24-157. Feb. 3, 2012.

34. HR 1734. Civilian Property Realignment/Rule. Adoption of the rule (H Res 537) to provide for House floor consideration of the bill that would establish an independent Civilian Property Realignment Commission to identify opportunities for the federal government to reduce its inventory of civilian real property and reduce its costs. Adopted 233-155: R 226-0; D 7-155. Feb. 6, 2012.

35. HR 1162. Quileute Land Designation/Passage. Hastings, R-Wash., motion to suspend the rules and pass the bill that would provide the Quileute American Indian Tribe with roughly 785 acres for Olympia National Park, to be held in trust for the benefit of the tribe. Motion agreed to 381-7: R 220-7; D 161-0. A two-thirds majority of those present and voting (259 in this case) is required for passage under suspension of the rules. Feb. 6, 2012.

36. HR 1734. Civilian Property Realignment/Property Exclusion. Connolly, D-Va., amendment that would allow the General Services Administration to exclude property from any transactions determined to be suitable for assignment to the Interior Department for transfer to a state or municipality for use as a public park or recreation area. Rejected in Committee of the Whole 191-230: R 11-227; D 180-3. Feb. 7, 2012.

Member	31	32	33	34	35	36
ALABAMA						
1 Bonner	N	Y	Y	?	?	N
2 Roby	N	Y	Y	Y	Y	N
3 Rogers	N	Y	Y	Y	Y	N
4 Aderholt	N	Y	Y	Y	Y	N
5 Brooks	N	Y	Y	Y	Y	N
6 Bachus	N	Y	Y	Y	N	N
7 Sewell	Y	N	N	N	Y	Y
ALASKA						
AL Young	N	Y	Y	?	?	N
ARIZONA						
1 Gosar	N	Y	Y	Y	Y	N
2 Franks	N	+	N	Y	Y	N
3 Quayle	N	Y	Y	Y	Y	N
4 Pastor	Y	N	N	N	Y	Y
5 Schweikert	N	Y	Y	Y	Y	N
6 Flake	N	Y	Y	Y	Y	N
7 Grijalva	Y	N	N	?	?	Y
8 Vacant						
ARKANSAS						
1 Crawford	N	Y	Y	Y	Y	N
2 Griffin	N	Y	Y	Y	Y	N
3 Womack	N	Y	Y	Y	Y	N
4 Ross	Y	N	Y	Y	Y	Y
CALIFORNIA						
1 Thompson	Y	N	N	N	Y	Y
2 Herger	N	Y	Y	Y	N	N
3 Lungren	N	Y	Y	Y	Y	N
4 McClintock	N	Y	Y	Y	Y	N
5 Matsui	Y	N	N	N	Y	Y
6 Woolsey	Y	N	N	N	Y	Y
7 Miller, George	Y	N	N	N	Y	Y
8 Pelosi	Y	N	N	N	Y	Y
9 Lee	Y	N	N	N	Y	Y
10 Garamendi	Y	N	N	N	Y	Y
11 McNerney	Y	N	N	?	?	?
12 Speier	?	?	?	N	Y	Y
13 Stark	Y	N	N	N	Y	Y
14 Eshoo	Y	N	N	N	Y	Y
15 Honda	Y	N	–	N	Y	Y
16 Lofgren	Y	N	N	N	Y	Y
17 Farr	Y	?	N	N	Y	Y
18 Cardoza	?	?	?	?	?	Y
19 Denham	N	Y	Y	Y	Y	N
20 Costa	Y	N	Y	Y	Y	Y
21 Nunes	N	Y	Y	Y	Y	N
22 McCarthy	N	Y	Y	Y	Y	N
23 Capps	Y	N	N	N	Y	Y
24 Gallegly	N	Y	Y	Y	Y	N
25 McKeon	N	Y	Y	Y	Y	N
26 Dreier	N	Y	Y	Y	Y	N
27 Sherman	Y	N	N	N	Y	Y
28 Berman	Y	N	N	N	Y	Y
29 Schiff	Y	N	N	N	Y	Y
30 Waxman	Y	N	N	N	Y	Y
31 Becerra	Y	N	N	N	Y	Y
32 Chu	Y	N	N	N	Y	Y
33 Bass	Y	N	N	N	Y	Y
34 Roybal-Allard	Y	N	N	N	?	Y
35 Waters	Y	N	N	N	Y	Y
36 Hahn	?	?	?	N	Y	Y
37 Richardson	Y	N	N	N	Y	Y
38 Napolitano	Y	N	N	N	Y	Y
39 Sánchez, Linda	Y	N	N	N	Y	Y
40 Royce	N	Y	Y	Y	Y	N
41 Lewis	N	Y	Y	Y	Y	N
42 Miller, Gary	N	?	Y	Y	Y	N
43 Baca	Y	N	N	N	Y	Y
44 Calvert	N	Y	Y	Y	Y	N
45 Bono Mack	N	Y	Y	Y	Y	N
46 Rohrabacher	N	Y	Y	?	?	N
47 Sanchez, Loretta	Y	N	N	N	Y	Y
48 Campbell	N	Y	Y	?	?	N
49 Issa	?	?	?	Y	Y	Y
50 Bilbray	N	Y	Y	Y	Y	N
51 Filner	+	–	–	–	+	Y
52 Hunter	N	Y	Y	Y	Y	N
53 Davis	Y	N	Y	N	Y	Y
COLORADO						
1 DeGette	Y	N	N	N	Y	Y
2 Polis	?	N	Y	N	Y	Y
3 Tipton	N	Y	Y	Y	Y	N
4 Gardner	N	Y	Y	Y	Y	N
5 Lamborn	N	Y	N	Y	Y	N
6 Coffman	N	Y	Y	Y	Y	N
7 Perlmutter	Y	N	Y	N	Y	Y
CONNECTICUT						
1 Larson	Y	N	N	N	Y	Y
2 Courtney	Y	N	N	N	Y	Y
3 DeLauro	Y	N	N	N	Y	Y
4 Himes	Y	N	N	N	Y	Y
5 Murphy	Y	N	N	Y	Y	Y
DELAWARE						
AL Carney	Y	N	N	N	Y	Y
FLORIDA						
1 Miller	N	Y	Y	Y	Y	N
2 Southerland	N	Y	Y	Y	Y	N
3 Brown	Y	N	N	N	Y	Y
4 Crenshaw	N	Y	Y	Y	Y	N
5 Nugent	N	Y	Y	Y	Y	N
6 Stearns	N	Y	Y	Y	Y	N
7 Mica	N	Y	Y	Y	Y	N
8 Webster	N	Y	Y	Y	Y	N
9 Bilirakis	N	Y	Y	Y	Y	N
10 Young	N	Y	Y	Y	Y	N
11 Castor	Y	N	N	N	Y	Y
12 Ross	N	Y	Y	Y	Y	N
13 Buchanan	N	Y	Y	Y	Y	N
14 Mack	?	?	?	?	?	?
15 Posey	N	Y	Y	Y	Y	N
16 Rooney	N	Y	Y	?	?	N
17 Wilson	Y	N	N	N	Y	Y
18 Ros-Lehtinen	N	Y	Y	Y	Y	N
19 Deutch	Y	N	N	N	Y	Y
20 Wasserman Schultz	Y	N	N	N	Y	Y
21 Diaz-Balart	N	Y	Y	Y	Y	N
22 West	N	Y	Y	Y	Y	N
23 Hastings	Y	N	N	N	Y	Y
24 Adams	N	Y	Y	Y	Y	N
25 Rivera	N	Y	Y	Y	Y	N
GEORGIA						
1 Kingston	N	Y	Y	?	?	N
2 Bishop	Y	N	Y	N	Y	Y
3 Westmoreland	N	Y	Y	Y	Y	N
4 Johnson	Y	N	N	N	Y	Y
5 Lewis	Y	N	N	N	Y	Y
6 Price	N	Y	Y	?	Y	N
7 Woodall	N	Y	Y	Y	N	N
8 Scott, A.	N	Y	Y	Y	Y	N
9 Graves	N	Y	Y	Y	Y	N
10 Broun	N	N	Y	Y	Y	N
11 Gingrey	N	Y	Y	Y	Y	N
12 Barrow	N	Y	N	Y	Y	Y
13 Scott, D.	Y	N	Y	N	Y	Y
HAWAII						
1 Hanabusa	Y	N	Y	N	Y	Y
2 Hirono	Y	N	Y	N	Y	Y
IDAHO						
1 Labrador	N	Y	N	Y	Y	N
2 Simpson	N	Y	Y	Y	Y	N
ILLINOIS						
1 Rush	Y	N	N	N	Y	Y
2 Jackson	Y	N	N	N	Y	Y
3 Lipinski	Y	N	Y	?	?	?
4 Gutierrez	Y	N	N	?	?	Y
5 Quigley	Y	N	Y	N	Y	Y
6 Roskam	N	Y	Y	Y	Y	N
7 Davis	Y	N	N	N	Y	Y
8 Walsh	N	Y	Y	Y	Y	N
9 Schakowsky	Y	N	N	N	Y	Y
10 Dold	N	Y	Y	Y	Y	Y
11 Kinzinger	N	Y	Y	?	?	N
12 Costello	Y	N	Y	N	Y	Y
13 Biggert	N	Y	Y	Y	Y	N
14 Hultgren	N	Y	Y	Y	Y	N
15 Johnson	N	Y	Y	+	+	Y

KEY — Republicans (bold), Democrats

Y Voted for (yea)	X Paired against	C Voted "present" to avoid possible conflict of interest
# Paired for	– Announced against	? Did not vote or otherwise make a position known
+ Announced for	P Voted "present"	
N Voted against (nay)		

	31	32	33	34	35	36
16 **Manzullo**	N	Y	Y	Y	Y	N
17 **Schilling**	N	Y	Y	Y	Y	N
18 **Schock**	N	Y	Y	Y	Y	N
19 **Shimkus**	N	Y	Y	Y	Y	N
INDIANA						
1 Visclosky	Y	N	N	N	Y	Y
2 Donnelly	Y	N	N	N	Y	N
3 **Stutzman**	N	Y	N	Y	Y	?
4 **Rokita**	N	Y	Y	Y	Y	N
5 **Burton**	?	Y	Y	Y	Y	N
6 **Pence**	N	Y	Y	?	?	N
7 Carson	+	–	+	N	Y	Y
8 **Bucshon**	N	Y	Y	Y	Y	N
9 **Young**	N	Y	Y	Y	Y	N
IOWA						
1 Braley	Y	N	N	N	Y	Y
2 Loebsack	Y	N	N	N	Y	Y
3 Boswell	Y	N	Y	N	Y	Y
4 **Latham**	N	Y	Y	Y	Y	N
5 **King**	N	Y	Y	Y	Y	N
KANSAS						
1 **Huelskamp**	N	Y	Y	Y	Y	N
2 **Jenkins**	N	Y	Y	Y	Y	N
3 **Yoder**	N	Y	Y	Y	Y	N
4 **Pompeo**	N	Y	Y	Y	Y	N
KENTUCKY						
1 **Whitfield**	N	Y	Y	Y	Y	N
2 **Guthrie**	N	Y	Y	Y	Y	N
3 Yarmuth	Y	N	N	?	?	Y
4 **Davis**	N	Y	Y	Y	Y	N
5 **Rogers**	N	Y	Y	Y	Y	N
6 Chandler	Y	N	N	N	Y	Y
LOUISIANA						
1 **Scalise**	N	Y	Y	Y	Y	N
2 Richmond	Y	N	N	N	Y	Y
3 **Landry**	N	Y	Y	Y	Y	N
4 **Fleming**	N	Y	Y	Y	Y	N
5 **Alexander**	N	Y	Y	Y	Y	N
6 **Cassidy**	N	Y	Y	Y	Y	N
7 **Boustany**	N	Y	Y	Y	Y	N
MAINE						
1 Pingree	Y	N	N	N	Y	Y
2 Michaud	Y	N	N	N	Y	Y
MARYLAND						
1 **Harris**	N	Y	Y	Y	Y	N
2 Ruppersberger	?	N	N	N	Y	Y
3 Sarbanes	Y	N	N	N	Y	Y
4 Edwards	Y	N	N	N	Y	Y
5 Hoyer	Y	N	N	N	Y	Y
6 **Bartlett**	N	Y	Y	Y	Y	N
7 Cummings	Y	N	N	N	Y	Y
8 Van Hollen	Y	N	N	–	+	Y
MASSACHUSETTS						
1 Olver	Y	N	N	N	Y	Y
2 Neal	Y	N	N	?	?	?
3 McGovern	Y	N	N	N	Y	Y
4 Frank	Y	N	N	N	Y	Y
5 Tsongas	Y	N	N	N	Y	Y
6 Tierney	Y	N	N	N	Y	Y
7 Markey	Y	N	N	N	Y	Y
8 Capuano	Y	N	N	N	Y	Y
9 Lynch	Y	N	N	?	?	Y
10 Keating	Y	N	N	N	Y	Y
MICHIGAN						
1 **Benishek**	N	Y	Y	Y	Y	N
2 **Huizenga**	N	Y	Y	Y	N	N
3 **Amash**	N	Y	N	Y	N	N
4 **Camp**	N	Y	Y	Y	Y	N
5 Kildee	Y	N	N	N	Y	Y
6 **Upton**	N	Y	Y	Y	Y	N
7 **Walberg**	N	Y	Y	Y	Y	N
8 **Rogers**	N	Y	Y	Y	Y	N
9 Peters	Y	N	N	N	Y	Y
10 **Miller**	N	Y	Y	Y	Y	N
11 **McCotter**	N	Y	Y	Y	Y	N
12 Levin	Y	N	N	N	Y	Y
13 Clarke	Y	N	N	N	Y	Y
14 Conyers	Y	N	N	?	?	Y
15 Dingell	Y	N	N	N	Y	Y
MINNESOTA						
1 Walz	Y	N	N	N	Y	Y
2 **Kline**	N	Y	Y	Y	Y	N
3 **Paulsen**	N	Y	Y	Y	Y	N
4 McCollum	Y	N	N	N	Y	Y

	31	32	33	34	35	36
5 Ellison	Y	N	N	?	?	+
6 **Bachmann**	N	Y	Y	Y	Y	N
7 Peterson	N	N	N	N	Y	N
8 **Cravaack**	N	Y	Y	Y	Y	N
MISSISSIPPI						
1 **Nunnelee**	N	Y	Y	Y	Y	N
2 Thompson	Y	N	N	N	Y	Y
3 **Harper**	N	Y	Y	Y	Y	N
4 **Palazzo**	N	Y	Y	Y	N	N
MISSOURI						
1 Clay	Y	N	N	N	Y	Y
2 **Akin**	N	Y	Y	Y	Y	N
3 Carnahan	Y	N	Y	N	Y	?
4 **Hartzler**	N	Y	Y	Y	Y	N
5 Cleaver	Y	N	N	N	Y	Y
6 **Graves**	N	+	Y	Y	Y	N
7 **Long**	N	Y	Y	Y	Y	N
8 **Emerson**	N	Y	Y	Y	Y	N
9 **Luetkemeyer**	N	Y	Y	Y	Y	N
MONTANA						
AL **Rehberg**	N	Y	Y	Y	Y	N
NEBRASKA						
1 **Fortenberry**	?	?	?	Y	Y	N
2 **Terry**	N	Y	Y	Y	Y	N
3 **Smith**	N	Y	Y	Y	Y	N
NEVADA						
1 Berkley	Y	N	Y	N	Y	Y
2 **Amodei**	N	Y	Y	Y	Y	N
3 **Heck**	N	Y	Y	Y	Y	N
NEW HAMPSHIRE						
1 **Guinta**	N	Y	Y	Y	Y	N
2 **Bass**	N	Y	Y	Y	Y	Y
NEW JERSEY						
1 Andrews	Y	N	N	N	Y	Y
2 **LoBiondo**	N	Y	Y	Y	Y	N
3 **Runyan**	N	Y	Y	Y	Y	N
4 **Smith**	N	?	Y	Y	Y	N
5 **Garrett**	N	Y	Y	Y	Y	N
6 Pallone	Y	N	N	N	Y	Y
7 **Lance**	N	Y	Y	Y	Y	N
8 Pascrell	Y	N	N	–	+	Y
9 Rothman	Y	N	N	?	?	Y
10 Payne	Y	N	N	?	?	?
11 **Frelinghuysen**	N	Y	Y	Y	Y	N
12 Holt	Y	N	N	N	Y	Y
13 Sires	?	?	?	?	?	?
NEW MEXICO						
1 Heinrich	?	?	?	N	Y	Y
2 **Pearce**	N	Y	Y	Y	Y	N
3 Luján	Y	N	N	N	Y	Y
NEW YORK						
1 Bishop	Y	N	N	N	Y	Y
2 Israel	Y	N	N	N	Y	Y
3 **King**	N	Y	Y	Y	Y	N
4 McCarthy	Y	N	N	N	Y	Y
5 Ackerman	Y	N	N	N	Y	Y
6 Meeks	Y	N	N	?	?	Y
7 Crowley	Y	N	N	N	Y	Y
8 Nadler	Y	N	N	?	?	Y
9 **Turner**	N	Y	Y	Y	Y	N
10 Towns	Y	N	N	?	?	Y
11 Clarke	Y	N	N	N	Y	Y
12 Velázquez	Y	N	N	N	Y	Y
13 **Grimm**	N	Y	Y	Y	Y	N
14 Maloney	Y	N	N	N	Y	Y
15 Rangel	Y	N	N	N	Y	Y
16 Serrano	Y	N	N	N	Y	Y
17 Engel	Y	N	N	?	?	Y
18 Lowey	Y	N	N	?	?	Y
19 **Hayworth**	N	Y	Y	Y	Y	N
20 **Gibson**	N	Y	Y	Y	Y	N
21 Tonko	Y	N	N	N	Y	Y
22 Hinchey	?	?	?	N	Y	Y
23 Owens	Y	N	N	?	?	Y
24 **Hanna**	N	Y	Y	Y	Y	N
25 **Buerkle**	N	Y	Y	?	?	N
26 Hochul	Y	N	N	N	Y	Y
27 Higgins	Y	N	N	N	Y	Y
28 Slaughter	Y	N	N	N	Y	Y
29 **Reed**	N	Y	Y	Y	Y	N
NORTH CAROLINA						
1 Butterfield	Y	N	N	N	Y	Y
2 **Ellmers**	N	Y	Y	Y	Y	N
3 **Jones**	N	Y	Y	Y	Y	Y
4 Price	Y	N	N	N	Y	Y

	31	32	33	34	35	36
5 **Foxx**	N	Y	Y	Y	Y	N
6 **Coble**	N	Y	Y	Y	Y	N
7 McIntyre	Y	Y	Y	Y	Y	Y
8 Kissell	Y	N	N	Y	Y	Y
9 **Myrick**	N	Y	Y	Y	Y	N
10 **McHenry**	N	Y	Y	Y	Y	N
11 Shuler	?	?	?	?	?	Y
12 Watt	Y	N	N	N	Y	Y
13 Miller	Y	N	N	?	?	Y
NORTH DAKOTA						
AL **Berg**	N	Y	Y	Y	Y	N
OHIO						
1 **Chabot**	N	Y	Y	Y	Y	N
2 **Schmidt**	N	Y	Y	Y	Y	N
3 **Turner**	?	?	?	Y	Y	N
4 **Jordan**	N	Y	Y	Y	Y	N
5 **Latta**	N	Y	Y	Y	Y	N
6 **Johnson**	N	Y	Y	Y	Y	N
7 **Austria**	N	Y	Y	Y	Y	N
8 **Boehner**						
9 Kaptur	Y	N	N	N	Y	Y
10 Kucinich	Y	N	N	N	Y	Y
11 Fudge	Y	N	N	N	Y	Y
12 **Tiberi**	N	Y	Y	Y	Y	N
13 Sutton	Y	N	N	N	Y	Y
14 **LaTourette**	N	Y	Y	Y	Y	N
15 **Stivers**	N	Y	Y	Y	Y	N
16 **Renacci**	N	Y	Y	Y	Y	N
17 Ryan	Y	N	N	N	Y	?
18 **Gibbs**	N	Y	Y	Y	Y	N
OKLAHOMA						
1 **Sullivan**	N	Y	Y	Y	Y	N
2 Boren	Y	N	Y	Y	Y	Y
3 **Lucas**	N	Y	Y	Y	Y	N
4 **Cole**	N	Y	Y	Y	Y	–
5 **Lankford**	N	Y	Y	Y	Y	N
OREGON						
1 Vacant						
2 **Walden**	N	Y	Y	Y	Y	N
3 Blumenauer	Y	N	N	N	Y	Y
4 DeFazio	Y	N	N	N	Y	Y
5 Schrader	Y	N	Y	N	Y	Y
PENNSYLVANIA						
1 Brady	Y	N	N	N	Y	Y
2 Fattah	Y	N	N	N	Y	Y
3 **Kelly**	N	Y	Y	Y	Y	N
4 Altmire	Y	N	N	N	Y	Y
5 **Thompson**	N	Y	Y	Y	Y	N
6 **Gerlach**	N	Y	Y	Y	Y	Y
7 **Meehan**	N	Y	Y	Y	Y	N
8 **Fitzpatrick**	N	Y	Y	Y	Y	Y
9 **Shuster**	N	Y	Y	Y	Y	N
10 **Marino**	N	Y	Y	Y	Y	N
11 **Barletta**	N	Y	Y	Y	Y	N
12 Critz	Y	N	N	N	Y	Y
13 Schwartz	Y	N	N	N	Y	Y
14 Doyle	Y	N	N	N	Y	Y
15 **Dent**	N	Y	Y	Y	Y	N
16 **Pitts**	N	Y	Y	Y	Y	N
17 Holden	Y	N	N	N	Y	Y
18 **Murphy**	N	Y	Y	Y	Y	N
19 **Platts**	N	Y	Y	Y	Y	Y
RHODE ISLAND						
1 Cicilline	Y	N	N	N	Y	Y
2 Langevin	Y	N	N	N	Y	Y
SOUTH CAROLINA						
1 **Scott**	N	Y	N	Y	Y	N
2 **Wilson**	N	Y	Y	Y	Y	N
3 **Duncan**	N	Y	N	Y	Y	N
4 **Gowdy**	N	Y	N	Y	Y	N
5 **Mulvaney**	N	Y	N	Y	Y	N
6 Clyburn	Y	N	N	?	?	Y
SOUTH DAKOTA						
AL **Noem**	N	Y	Y	Y	Y	N
TENNESSEE						
1 **Roe**	N	Y	Y	Y	Y	N
2 **Duncan**	N	Y	Y	Y	Y	N
3 **Fleischmann**	N	Y	Y	Y	Y	N
4 **DesJarlais**	N	Y	Y	Y	Y	N
5 Cooper	Y	N	Y	N	Y	Y
6 **Black**	N	Y	Y	Y	Y	N
7 **Blackburn**	N	Y	Y	Y	Y	N
8 **Fincher**	N	Y	Y	Y	Y	N
9 Cohen	Y	N	N	N	Y	Y

	31	32	33	34	35	36
TEXAS						
1 **Gohmert**	N	Y	N	Y	Y	N
2 **Poe**	N	Y	Y	?	?	N
3 **Johnson, S.**	N	Y	Y	Y	Y	N
4 **Hall**	N	Y	Y	Y	Y	N
5 **Hensarling**	N	Y	Y	Y	Y	N
6 **Barton**	N	Y	Y	Y	Y	N
7 **Culberson**	N	Y	Y	Y	Y	N
8 **Brady**	N	Y	Y	Y	Y	N
9 Green, A.	Y	N	N	N	Y	Y
10 **McCaul**	N	Y	Y	Y	Y	N
11 **Conaway**	N	Y	Y	Y	Y	N
12 **Granger**	N	Y	Y	Y	Y	N
13 **Thornberry**	N	Y	Y	Y	Y	N
14 **Paul**	?	?	?	?	?	?
15 Hinojosa	Y	N	N	N	Y	Y
16 Reyes	Y	N	N	?	?	Y
17 **Flores**	N	Y	Y	Y	Y	N
18 Jackson Lee	Y	N	N	N	Y	Y
19 **Neugebauer**	N	Y	Y	Y	Y	N
20 Gonzalez	Y	N	N	N	Y	Y
21 **Smith**	N	Y	Y	Y	Y	N
22 **Olson**	N	Y	Y	Y	Y	N
23 **Canseco**	N	Y	Y	Y	Y	N
24 **Marchant**	N	Y	Y	?	?	Y
25 Doggett	Y	N	N	N	Y	Y
26 **Burgess**	N	Y	Y	Y	Y	N
27 **Farenthold**	N	Y	Y	Y	Y	N
28 Cuellar	Y	N	Y	N	Y	Y
29 Green, G.	Y	Y	N	N	Y	Y
30 Johnson, E.	Y	N	Y	N	Y	Y
31 **Carter**	N	?	Y	Y	Y	N
32 **Sessions**	N	Y	Y	Y	Y	N
UTAH						
1 **Bishop**	N	Y	Y	Y	Y	N
2 Matheson	N	Y	Y	Y	Y	N
3 **Chaffetz**	N	Y	Y	Y	Y	Y
VERMONT						
AL Welch	Y	N	N	N	Y	Y
VIRGINIA						
1 **Wittman**	N	Y	Y	Y	Y	N
2 **Rigell**	N	Y	Y	Y	Y	N
3 Scott	Y	N	N	N	Y	Y
4 **Forbes**	N	Y	Y	Y	Y	N
5 **Hurt**	N	Y	Y	Y	N	N
6 **Goodlatte**	N	Y	Y	Y	N	N
7 **Cantor**	N	Y	Y	Y	Y	N
8 Moran	Y	N	N	?	?	Y
9 **Griffith**	N	Y	Y	Y	N	N
10 **Wolf**	N	Y	Y	Y	Y	Y
11 Connolly	Y	N	N	N	Y	Y
WASHINGTON						
1 Inslee	Y	N	N	?	?	Y
2 Larsen	Y	N	N	N	Y	Y
3 **Herrera Beutler**	N	Y	Y	Y	Y	N
4 **Hastings**	N	Y	Y	Y	Y	N
5 **McMorris Rodgers**	N	Y	Y	Y	Y	Y
6 Dicks	Y	N	N	N	Y	Y
7 McDermott	Y	N	N	N	Y	Y
8 **Reichert**	N	Y	Y	Y	Y	N
9 Smith	Y	N	N	–	+	Y
WEST VIRGINIA						
1 **McKinley**	N	Y	Y	Y	Y	N
2 **Capito**	N	Y	Y	Y	Y	N
3 Rahall	Y	N	Y	N	Y	Y
WISCONSIN						
1 **Ryan**	N	Y	Y	Y	Y	N
2 Baldwin	Y	N	N	N	Y	Y
3 Kind	Y	N	N	N	Y	Y
4 Moore	Y	N	N	N	Y	Y
5 **Sensenbrenner**	N	Y	N	Y	Y	N
6 **Petri**	N	Y	Y	Y	Y	N
7 **Duffy**	N	Y	Y	Y	Y	N
8 **Ribble**	N	Y	Y	Y	Y	N
WYOMING						
AL **Lummis**	N	Y	Y	Y	Y	N

IN THE HOUSE | By Vote Number

37. **HR 1734. Civilian Property Realignment/Recommit.** Michaud, D-Maine, motion to recommit the bill to the Transportation and Infrastructure Committee with instructions that it be reported back immediately with an amendment that would exempt certain properties owned by the Veterans Affairs Department or used in connection with providing services for veterans from consideration by the new Civilian Property Realignment Commission. Motion rejected 186-238: R 1-237; D 185-1. Feb. 7, 2012.

38. **HR 1734. Civilian Property Realignment/Passage.** Passage of the bill that would establish an independent Civilian Property Realignment Commission that would make recommendations to the president about federal properties, including public buildings, occupied grounds or leased space to be consolidated, sold, exchanged or redeveloped. Congress would be required to take a vote on the commission's recommendations. Passed 259-164: R 238-1; D 21-163. Feb. 7, 2012.

39. **HR 3581. Calculation of Federal Loans and Loan Guarantees/ Rule.** Adoption of the rule (H Res 539) to provide for House floor consideration of the bill that would change the way costs of federal loans and loan guarantees are calculated for budget purposes. Adopted 239-181: R 235-0; D 4-181. Feb. 7, 2012.

40. **HR 3581. Calculation of Federal Loans and Loan Guarantees/ Commission.** Tonko, D-N.Y., amendment that would delay the implementation of the bill's provisions until a six-member commission of budgeting and accounting experts provides recommendations to Congress on the best way to accurately account for the cost of federal credit programs. Congress would be required to vote on the recommendations, which would supersede the bill's requirements if enacted. Rejected in Committee of the Whole 187-238: R 2-236; D 185-2. Feb. 7, 2012.

41. **HR 3581. Calculation of Federal Loans and Loan Guarantees/ Recommit.** Walz, D-Minn., motion to recommit the bill to the Budget Committee with instructions that it be reported back immediately with an amendment that would exempt loans for students or veterans from appearing more expensive for budget purposes due to changes in the underlying bill. Motion rejected 190-238: R 1-238; D 189-0. Feb. 7, 2012.

42. **HR 3581. Calculation of Federal Loans and Loan Guarantees/ Passage.** Passage of the bill that would change the way costs of federal loans and loan guarantees are calculated for budget purposes. It would require costs of federal credit programs to be measured on a "fair-value basis," which incorporates a premium for market risk that more closely reflects the cost of loans offered in the private market. The bill would increase discretionary spending caps to accommodate resulting cost increases. It would require Fannie Mae and Freddie Mac to be included in the federal budget and require departments and agencies to make publicly available the justifications used to prepare their annual budget requests. Passed 245-180: R 238-2; D 7-178. Feb. 7, 2012.

	37	38	39	40	41	42
ALABAMA						
1 **Bonner**	N	Y	Y	N	N	Y
2 **Roby**	N	Y	Y	N	N	Y
3 **Rogers**	N	Y	Y	N	N	Y
4 **Aderholt**	N	Y	Y	N	N	Y
5 **Brooks**	N	Y	Y	N	N	Y
6 **Bachus**	N	Y	Y	N	N	Y
7 Sewell	Y	N	N	Y	Y	N
ALASKA						
AL **Young**	N	Y	?	N	N	Y
ARIZONA						
1 **Gosar**	N	Y	Y	N	N	Y
2 **Franks**	N	Y	Y	N	N	Y
3 **Quayle**	N	Y	+	N	N	Y
4 Pastor	Y	N	N	Y	Y	N
5 **Schweikert**	N	Y	Y	N	N	Y
6 **Flake**	N	Y	Y	N	N	Y
7 Grijalva	Y	N	N	Y	Y	N
8 Vacant						
ARKANSAS						
1 **Crawford**	N	Y	Y	N	N	Y
2 **Griffin**	N	Y	Y	N	N	Y
3 **Womack**	N	Y	Y	N	N	Y
4 Ross	Y	Y	N	Y	Y	N
CALIFORNIA						
1 Thompson	Y	N	N	Y	Y	N
2 **Herger**	N	Y	Y	N	N	Y
3 **Lungren**	N	Y	Y	N	N	Y
4 **McClintock**	N	Y	Y	N	N	Y
5 Matsui	Y	N	N	Y	Y	N
6 Woolsey	Y	N	N	Y	Y	N
7 Miller, George	Y	N	N	Y	Y	N
8 Pelosi	Y	N	N	Y	Y	N
9 Lee	Y	N	N	Y	Y	N
10 Garamendi	Y	N	N	Y	Y	N
11 McNerney	?	?	?	?	Y	N
12 Speier	Y	N	Y	Y	Y	N
13 Stark	Y	N	N	Y	Y	N
14 Eshoo	Y	N	N	Y	Y	N
15 Honda	Y	N	N	Y	Y	N
16 Lofgren	Y	N	N	Y	Y	N
17 Farr	Y	N	N	Y	Y	N
18 Cardoza	Y	Y	N	Y	Y	N
19 **Denham**	N	Y	Y	N	N	Y
20 Costa	Y	Y	N	Y	Y	N
21 **Nunes**	N	Y	Y	N	N	Y
22 **McCarthy**	N	Y	Y	N	N	Y
23 Capps	Y	N	N	Y	Y	N
24 **Gallegly**	N	Y	Y	N	N	Y
25 **McKeon**	N	Y	Y	N	N	Y
26 **Dreier**	N	Y	Y	N	N	Y
27 Sherman	Y	N	N	Y	Y	N
28 Berman	Y	N	N	Y	Y	N
29 Schiff	Y	N	N	Y	Y	N
30 Waxman	Y	N	N	Y	Y	N
31 Becerra	Y	N	N	Y	Y	N
32 Chu	Y	N	N	Y	Y	N
33 Bass	Y	?	N	Y	Y	N
34 Roybal-Allard	Y	N	N	Y	Y	N
35 Waters	Y	N	N	Y	Y	N
36 Hahn	Y	N	N	Y	Y	N
37 Richardson	Y	N	N	Y	Y	N
38 Napolitano	Y	N	N	Y	Y	N
39 Sánchez, Linda	N	N	N	Y	Y	N
40 **Royce**	N	Y	Y	N	N	Y
41 **Lewis**	N	Y	Y	N	N	Y
42 **Miller, Gary**	N	Y	Y	N	N	Y
43 Baca	Y	N	N	Y	Y	N
44 **Calvert**	N	Y	Y	N	N	Y
45 **Bono Mack**	N	Y	Y	N	N	Y
46 **Rohrabacher**	N	Y	Y	N	N	Y
47 Sanchez, Loretta	Y	N	N	Y	Y	N
48 **Campbell**	N	Y	Y	N	N	Y
49 **Issa**	N	Y	Y	N	N	Y
50 **Bilbray**	N	Y	Y	N	N	Y
51 Filner	Y	N	N	Y	Y	N
52 **Hunter**	N	Y	Y	N	N	Y
53 Davis	Y	N	N	Y	Y	N

	37	38	39	40	41	42
COLORADO						
1 DeGette	Y	N	N	Y	Y	N
2 Polis	Y	N	Y	Y	Y	N
3 **Tipton**	N	Y	Y	N	N	Y
4 **Gardner**	N	Y	Y	N	N	Y
5 **Lamborn**	N	Y	Y	N	N	Y
6 **Coffman**	N	Y	Y	N	N	Y
7 Perlmutter	Y	Y	N	Y	Y	N
CONNECTICUT						
1 Larson	Y	N	N	Y	Y	N
2 Courtney	Y	N	N	Y	Y	N
3 DeLauro	Y	N	N	Y	Y	N
4 Himes	Y	Y	N	Y	Y	N
5 Murphy	Y	N	?	Y	Y	N
DELAWARE						
AL Carney	Y	N	N	Y	Y	N
FLORIDA						
1 **Miller**	N	Y	Y	N	N	Y
2 **Southerland**	N	Y	Y	N	N	Y
3 Brown	Y	N	N	Y	Y	N
4 **Crenshaw**	N	Y	Y	N	N	Y
5 **Nugent**	N	Y	Y	N	N	Y
6 **Stearns**	N	Y	Y	N	N	Y
7 **Mica**	N	Y	Y	N	N	Y
8 **Webster**	N	Y	Y	N	N	Y
9 **Bilirakis**	N	Y	Y	N	N	Y
10 **Young**	N	Y	Y	N	N	Y
11 Castor	Y	N	N	Y	Y	N
12 **Ross**	N	Y	Y	N	N	Y
13 **Buchanan**	N	Y	Y	N	N	Y
14 **Mack**	N	Y	Y	N	N	Y
15 **Posey**	N	Y	Y	N	N	Y
16 **Rooney**	N	Y	Y	N	N	Y
17 Wilson	Y	N	N	Y	Y	?
18 **Ros-Lehtinen**	N	Y	Y	N	N	Y
19 Deutch	Y	N	N	Y	Y	N
20 Wasserman Schultz	Y	N	N	Y	Y	N
21 **Diaz-Balart**	N	Y	Y	N	N	Y
22 **West**	N	Y	Y	N	N	Y
23 Hastings	Y	N	N	Y	Y	N
24 **Adams**	N	Y	Y	N	N	Y
25 **Rivera**	N	Y	Y	N	N	Y
GEORGIA						
1 **Kingston**	N	Y	Y	N	N	Y
2 Bishop	Y	N	N	Y	Y	N
3 **Westmoreland**	N	Y	Y	N	N	Y
4 Johnson	Y	N	N	Y	Y	N
5 Lewis	Y	N	N	Y	Y	N
6 **Price**	N	Y	Y	N	N	Y
7 **Woodall**	?	Y	Y	N	N	Y
8 **Scott, A.**	N	Y	Y	N	N	Y
9 **Graves**	N	Y	Y	N	N	Y
10 **Broun**	N	N	Y	N	N	Y
11 **Gingrey**	N	Y	Y	N	N	Y
12 Barrow	Y	Y	N	Y	Y	N
13 Scott, D.	Y	N	Y	Y	Y	N
HAWAII						
1 Hanabusa	Y	N	N	Y	Y	N
2 Hirono	Y	?	N	Y	Y	N
IDAHO						
1 **Labrador**	N	Y	Y	N	N	Y
2 **Simpson**	N	Y	Y	N	N	Y
ILLINOIS						
1 Rush	Y	N	N	Y	Y	N
2 Jackson	Y	N	N	Y	Y	N
3 Lipinski	Y	N	N	Y	Y	N
4 Gutierrez	Y	N	N	Y	Y	?
5 Quigley	Y	N	N	Y	Y	N
6 **Roskam**	N	Y	Y	N	N	Y
7 Davis	Y	N	N	Y	Y	N
8 Walsh	N	Y	Y	N	N	Y
9 Schakowsky	Y	N	N	Y	Y	N
10 **Dold**	N	Y	Y	N	N	Y
11 **Kinzinger**	N	Y	Y	N	N	Y
12 Costello	Y	N	N	Y	Y	N
13 **Biggert**	N	Y	Y	N	N	Y
14 **Hultgren**	N	Y	Y	N	N	Y
15 **Johnson**	N	Y	Y	N	N	Y

KEY   **Republicans**   Democrats

Y Voted for (yea)	**X** Paired against	**C** Voted "present" to avoid possible conflict of interest
# Paired for	**–** Announced against	
+ Announced for	**P** Voted "present"	**?** Did not vote or otherwise make a position known
N Voted against (nay)		

*Rep. Suzanne Bonamici, D-Ore., was sworn in Feb. 7, 2012, to fill the seat vacated by the Aug. 3, 2011, resignation of fellow Democrat David Wu. The first vote for which Bonamici was eligible was vote 37.

	37	38	39	40	41	42
16 **Manzullo**	N	Y	Y	N	N	Y
17 **Schilling**	N	Y	Y	N	N	Y
18 **Schock**	N	Y	Y	N	N	Y
19 **Shimkus**	N	Y	Y	N	N	Y
INDIANA						
1 Visclosky	Y	N	N	Y	Y	N
2 Donnelly	Y	Y	N	Y	Y	N
3 **Stutzman**	N	Y	Y	N	N	Y
4 **Rokita**	N	Y	Y	N	N	Y
5 **Burton**	N	Y	Y	N	N	Y
6 **Pence**	N	Y	Y	N	N	Y
7 Carson	Y	N	N	Y	Y	N
8 **Bucshon**	N	Y	Y	N	N	Y
9 **Young**	N	Y	Y	N	N	Y
IOWA						
1 Braley	Y	N	N	Y	Y	N
2 Loebsack	Y	N	N	Y	Y	N
3 Boswell	Y	N	N	Y	Y	N
4 **Latham**	N	Y	Y	N	N	Y
5 **King**	N	Y	Y	N	N	Y
KANSAS						
1 **Huelskamp**	N	Y	Y	N	N	Y
2 **Jenkins**	N	Y	Y	N	N	Y
3 **Yoder**	N	Y	Y	N	N	Y
4 **Pompeo**	N	Y	Y	N	N	Y
KENTUCKY						
1 **Whitfield**	N	Y	Y	N	N	Y
2 **Guthrie**	N	Y	Y	N	N	Y
3 Yarmuth	Y	N	N	Y	Y	N
4 **Davis**	N	Y	Y	N	N	Y
5 **Rogers**	N	Y	Y	N	N	Y
6 Chandler	Y	N	N	Y	Y	N
LOUISIANA						
1 **Scalise**	N	Y	Y	N	N	Y
2 Richmond	Y	N	N	Y	Y	N
3 **Landry**	N	Y	Y	N	N	Y
4 **Fleming**	N	Y	Y	N	N	Y
5 **Alexander**	N	Y	Y	N	?	Y
6 **Cassidy**	N	Y	Y	N	N	Y
7 **Boustany**	N	Y	Y	N	N	Y
MAINE						
1 Pingree	Y	N	N	Y	Y	N
2 Michaud	Y	Y	N	Y	Y	N
MARYLAND						
1 **Harris**	N	Y	Y	N	N	Y
2 Ruppersberger	Y	N	N	Y	Y	N
3 Sarbanes	Y	N	N	Y	Y	N
4 Edwards	Y	N	N	?	?	?
5 Hoyer	Y	N	N	Y	Y	N
6 **Bartlett**	N	Y	Y	N	N	Y
7 Cummings	Y	N	N	Y	Y	N
8 Van Hollen	Y	N	N	Y	Y	N
MASSACHUSETTS						
1 Olver	Y	N	N	?	Y	N
2 Neal	?	?	N	Y	Y	N
3 McGovern	Y	N	N	Y	Y	N
4 Frank	Y	N	N	Y	Y	N
5 Tsongas	Y	N	N	Y	Y	N
6 Tierney	Y	N	N	Y	Y	?
7 Markey	Y	N	N	Y	Y	N
8 Capuano	Y	N	N	Y	Y	N
9 Lynch	Y	N	N	Y	Y	N
10 Keating	Y	N	N	Y	Y	N
MICHIGAN						
1 **Benishek**	N	Y	Y	N	N	Y
2 **Huizenga**	N	Y	Y	N	N	Y
3 **Amash**	N	Y	Y	N	N	Y
4 **Camp**	N	Y	Y	N	N	Y
5 Kildee	Y	N	N	Y	Y	N
6 **Upton**	N	Y	Y	N	N	Y
7 **Walberg**	N	Y	Y	N	N	Y
8 **Rogers**	N	Y	Y	N	N	Y
9 Peters	Y	N	N	Y	Y	N
10 **Miller**	N	Y	Y	N	N	Y
11 **McCotter**	N	Y	Y	N	N	Y
12 Levin	Y	N	N	Y	Y	N
13 Clarke	Y	N	N	Y	Y	N
14 Conyers	Y	N	N	Y	Y	N
15 Dingell	Y	N	N	Y	Y	N
MINNESOTA						
1 Walz	Y	N	N	Y	Y	N
2 **Kline**	N	Y	Y	N	N	Y
3 **Paulsen**	N	Y	Y	N	N	Y
4 McCollum	Y	N	N	Y	Y	N

	37	38	39	40	41	42
5 Ellison	+	–	–	+	+	–
6 **Bachmann**	N	Y	Y	N	N	Y
7 Peterson	Y	N	N	N	Y	N
8 **Cravaack**	N	Y	Y	N	N	Y
MISSISSIPPI						
1 **Nunnelee**	N	Y	Y	N	N	Y
2 Thompson	Y	N	N	Y	Y	?
3 **Harper**	N	Y	Y	N	N	Y
4 **Palazzo**	N	Y	Y	N	N	Y
MISSOURI						
1 Clay	Y	N	N	Y	Y	N
2 **Akin**	N	Y	Y	N	N	Y
3 Carnahan	?	?	N	Y	Y	N
4 **Hartzler**	N	Y	Y	N	N	Y
5 Cleaver	Y	N	N	Y	Y	N
6 **Graves**	N	Y	Y	N	N	Y
7 **Long**	N	Y	Y	N	N	Y
8 **Emerson**	N	Y	Y	N	N	Y
9 **Luetkemeyer**	N	Y	Y	N	N	Y
MONTANA						
AL **Rehberg**	N	Y	Y	N	N	Y
NEBRASKA						
1 **Fortenberry**	N	Y	?	N	N	Y
2 **Terry**	N	Y	Y	N	N	Y
3 **Smith**	N	Y	?	N	N	Y
NEVADA						
1 Berkley	Y	Y	N	Y	Y	N
2 **Amodei**	N	Y	Y	N	N	Y
3 **Heck**	N	Y	Y	N	N	Y
NEW HAMPSHIRE						
1 **Guinta**	N	Y	Y	N	N	Y
2 **Bass**	N	Y	Y	N	N	Y
NEW JERSEY						
1 Andrews	Y	N	N	Y	Y	N
2 **LoBiondo**	N	Y	Y	N	N	Y
3 **Runyan**	N	Y	Y	N	N	Y
4 **Smith**	N	Y	Y	N	N	Y
5 **Garrett**	N	Y	Y	N	N	Y
6 Pallone	Y	N	N	Y	Y	N
7 **Lance**	N	Y	Y	N	N	Y
8 Pascrell	Y	N	N	Y	Y	N
9 Rothman	Y	N	N	Y	Y	N
10 Payne	?	?	?	?	?	?
11 **Frelinghuysen**	N	Y	Y	N	N	Y
12 Holt	Y	N	N	Y	Y	N
13 Sires	?	?	?	Y	Y	N
NEW MEXICO						
1 Heinrich	Y	N	N	Y	Y	N
2 **Pearce**	N	Y	Y	N	N	Y
3 Luján	Y	N	N	Y	Y	N
NEW YORK						
1 Bishop	Y	Y	N	Y	Y	N
2 Israel	Y	N	N	Y	Y	N
3 **King**	N	Y	Y	N	N	Y
4 McCarthy	Y	N	N	Y	Y	N
5 Ackerman	Y	N	N	Y	Y	N
6 Meeks	Y	N	N	Y	Y	N
7 Crowley	Y	N	N	Y	Y	N
8 Nadler	Y	N	N	Y	Y	N
9 **Turner**	N	Y	Y	N	N	Y
10 Towns	Y	N	N	Y	Y	N
11 Clarke	Y	N	N	Y	Y	N
12 Velázquez	Y	N	N	Y	Y	N
13 **Grimm**	N	Y	Y	N	N	Y
14 Maloney	Y	Y	N	Y	Y	N
15 Rangel	Y	N	N	Y	Y	N
16 Serrano	Y	N	N	Y	Y	N
17 Engel	Y	N	N	Y	Y	N
18 Lowey	Y	N	N	Y	Y	N
19 **Hayworth**	N	Y	Y	N	N	Y
20 **Gibson**	N	Y	Y	N	Y	Y
21 Tonko	Y	N	N	Y	Y	N
22 Hinchey	Y	N	N	Y	Y	N
23 Owens	Y	Y	N	Y	Y	Y
24 **Hanna**	N	?	Y	N	N	Y
25 **Buerkle**	N	Y	Y	N	N	Y
26 Hochul	Y	Y	N	Y	Y	N
27 Higgins	Y	N	N	Y	Y	N
28 Slaughter	Y	N	N	Y	Y	N
29 **Reed**	N	Y	Y	N	N	Y
NORTH CAROLINA						
1 Butterfield	Y	N	N	Y	Y	N
2 **Ellmers**	N	Y	?	N	N	Y
3 **Jones**	Y	Y	Y	N	Y	Y
4 Price	Y	N	N	Y	Y	N

	37	38	39	40	41	42
5 **Foxx**	N	Y	Y	N	N	Y
6 **Coble**	N	Y	Y	N	N	N
7 McIntyre	Y	Y	N	Y	Y	N
8 Kissell	Y	Y	N	Y	Y	Y
9 **Myrick**	N	Y	Y	N	N	Y
10 **McHenry**	N	Y	Y	N	N	Y
11 Shuler	Y	N	N	Y	Y	N
12 Watt	Y	N	N	Y	Y	N
13 Miller	Y	N	N	Y	Y	N
NORTH DAKOTA						
AL **Berg**	N	Y	Y	N	N	Y
OHIO						
1 **Chabot**	N	Y	Y	N	N	Y
2 **Schmidt**	N	Y	Y	N	N	Y
3 **Turner**	N	Y	Y	N	N	Y
4 **Jordan**	N	Y	Y	N	N	Y
5 **Latta**	N	Y	Y	N	N	Y
6 **Johnson**	N	Y	Y	N	N	Y
7 **Austria**	N	Y	Y	N	N	Y
8 **Boehner**						
9 Kaptur	Y	N	N	Y	Y	N
10 Kucinich	Y	N	N	Y	Y	N
11 Fudge	Y	N	N	Y	Y	N
12 **Tiberi**	N	Y	Y	N	N	Y
13 Sutton	Y	N	?	Y	Y	N
14 **LaTourette**	N	Y	Y	?	N	Y
15 **Stivers**	N	Y	Y	N	N	Y
16 **Renacci**	N	Y	Y	N	N	Y
17 Ryan	Y	N	N	Y	Y	N
18 **Gibbs**	N	Y	Y	N	N	Y
OKLAHOMA						
1 **Sullivan**	N	Y	Y	N	N	Y
2 Boren	Y	Y	N	Y	Y	N
3 **Lucas**	N	Y	Y	N	N	Y
4 **Cole**	N	Y	Y	N	N	Y
5 **Lankford**	N	Y	Y	N	N	Y
OREGON						
1 Bonamici*	Y	N	N	Y	Y	N
2 **Walden**	N	Y	Y	N	N	Y
3 Blumenauer	Y	N	N	Y	Y	N
4 DeFazio	Y	N	N	Y	Y	Y
5 Schrader	Y	Y	N	Y	Y	N
PENNSYLVANIA						
1 Brady	Y	N	N	Y	Y	N
2 Fattah	Y	N	N	Y	Y	N
3 **Kelly**	N	Y	Y	N	N	Y
4 Altmire	Y	N	Y	Y	Y	N
5 **Thompson**	N	Y	Y	N	N	Y
6 **Gerlach**	N	Y	Y	N	N	Y
7 **Meehan**	N	Y	Y	N	N	Y
8 **Fitzpatrick**	N	Y	Y	N	N	Y
9 **Shuster**	N	Y	Y	N	N	Y
10 **Marino**	N	Y	Y	N	N	Y
11 **Barletta**	N	Y	Y	N	N	Y
12 Critz	Y	N	N	Y	Y	N
13 Schwartz	Y	N	N	Y	Y	N
14 Doyle	Y	N	N	Y	Y	N
15 **Dent**	N	Y	Y	N	N	Y
16 **Pitts**	N	Y	Y	N	N	Y
17 Holden	Y	N	N	Y	Y	N
18 **Murphy**	N	Y	Y	N	N	Y
19 **Platts**	N	Y	Y	N	N	Y
RHODE ISLAND						
1 Cicilline	Y	N	N	Y	Y	N
2 Langevin	Y	N	N	Y	Y	N
SOUTH CAROLINA						
1 **Scott**	N	Y	Y	N	N	Y
2 **Wilson**	N	Y	Y	N	N	Y
3 **Duncan**	N	Y	Y	N	N	Y
4 **Gowdy**	N	Y	Y	N	N	Y
5 **Mulvaney**	N	Y	Y	?	N	Y
6 Clyburn	Y	N	N	Y	Y	N
SOUTH DAKOTA						
AL **Noem**	N	Y	Y	N	N	Y
TENNESSEE						
1 **Roe**	N	Y	Y	N	N	Y
2 **Duncan**	N	Y	Y	N	N	Y
3 **Fleischmann**	N	Y	Y	N	N	Y
4 **DesJarlais**	N	Y	Y	N	N	Y
5 Cooper	Y	Y	N	Y	Y	Y
6 **Black**	N	Y	Y	N	N	Y
7 **Blackburn**	N	Y	Y	N	N	Y
8 **Fincher**	N	Y	Y	N	N	Y
9 Cohen	Y	N	N	Y	Y	N

	37	38	39	40	41	42
TEXAS						
1 **Gohmert**	N	Y	Y	N	N	Y
2 **Poe**	N	Y	Y	N	N	Y
3 **Johnson, S.**	N	Y	Y	N	N	Y
4 **Hall**	N	Y	Y	N	N	Y
5 **Hensarling**	N	Y	Y	N	N	Y
6 **Barton**	N	Y	Y	N	N	Y
7 **Culberson**	N	Y	Y	N	N	Y
8 **Brady**	N	Y	Y	N	N	Y
9 Green, A.	Y	N	N	Y	Y	N
10 **McCaul**	N	Y	Y	N	N	Y
11 **Conaway**	N	Y	Y	N	N	Y
12 **Granger**	N	Y	Y	N	N	Y
13 **Thornberry**	N	Y	Y	N	N	Y
14 **Paul**	?	?	?	?	?	?
15 Hinojosa	Y	N	N	Y	Y	N
16 Reyes	Y	N	N	Y	Y	N
17 **Flores**	N	Y	Y	N	N	Y
18 Jackson Lee	Y	N	N	Y	Y	N
19 **Neugebauer**	N	Y	Y	N	N	Y
20 Gonzalez	Y	N	N	Y	Y	N
21 **Smith**	N	Y	Y	N	N	Y
22 **Olson**	N	Y	Y	N	N	Y
23 **Canseco**	N	Y	Y	N	N	Y
24 **Marchant**	N	Y	Y	N	N	Y
25 Doggett	Y	N	N	Y	Y	N
26 **Burgess**	N	Y	Y	N	N	Y
27 **Farenthold**	N	Y	Y	N	N	Y
28 Cuellar	Y	N	N	Y	Y	Y
29 Green, G.	Y	N	N	Y	Y	N
30 Johnson, E.	Y	N	N	Y	Y	N
31 **Carter**	N	Y	Y	N	N	Y
32 **Sessions**	N	Y	Y	N	N	Y
UTAH						
1 **Bishop**	N	Y	Y	N	N	Y
2 Matheson	Y	Y	Y	Y	Y	N
3 **Chaffetz**	N	Y	Y	N	N	Y
VERMONT						
AL Welch	Y	N	N	Y	Y	N
VIRGINIA						
1 **Wittman**	N	Y	Y	N	N	Y
2 **Rigell**	N	Y	Y	N	N	Y
3 Scott	Y	N	N	Y	Y	N
4 **Forbes**	N	Y	Y	N	N	Y
5 **Hurt**	–	Y	Y	N	N	Y
6 **Goodlatte**	N	Y	Y	N	N	Y
7 **Cantor**	N	Y	Y	N	N	Y
8 Moran	Y	N	N	Y	Y	N
9 **Griffith**	N	Y	Y	N	N	Y
10 **Wolf**	N	Y	Y	N	N	Y
11 Connolly	Y	N	?	Y	Y	N
WASHINGTON						
1 Inslee	Y	N	N	Y	Y	N
2 Larsen	Y	Y	N	Y	Y	N
3 **Herrera Beutler**	N	Y	Y	N	N	Y
4 **Hastings**	N	Y	Y	N	N	Y
5 **McMorris Rodgers**	N	Y	Y	N	N	Y
6 Dicks	Y	N	N	Y	Y	N
7 McDermott	Y	N	N	Y	Y	N
8 **Reichert**	N	Y	Y	N	N	Y
9 Smith	Y	N	N	Y	Y	N
WEST VIRGINIA						
1 **McKinley**	N	Y	Y	N	N	Y
2 **Capito**	N	Y	Y	N	N	Y
3 Rahall	Y	N	N	Y	Y	N
WISCONSIN						
1 **Ryan**	N	Y	Y	N	N	Y
2 Baldwin	Y	N	N	Y	Y	N
3 Kind	Y	N	N	Y	Y	N
4 Moore	Y	N	N	Y	Y	N
5 **Sensenbrenner**	N	Y	Y	N	N	Y
6 **Petri**	N	Y	Y	Y	N	Y
7 **Duffy**	N	Y	Y	N	N	Y
8 **Ribble**	N	Y	Y	N	N	Y
WYOMING						
AL **Lummis**	N	Y	Y	N	N	Y

IN THE HOUSE | By Vote Number

43. **HR 3521. Expedited Line-Item Veto/Previous Question.**
Woodall, R-Ga., motion to order the previous question (thus ending debate and possibility of amendment) on adoption of the rule (H Res 540) that would provide for House floor consideration of a bill that would grant the president expedited rescission authority over discretionary spending in enacted appropriations bills, which would subject to an expedited up-or-down vote in Congress. Motion agreed to 240-184: R 234-1; D 6-183. Feb. 8, 2012.

44. **HR 3521. Expedited Line-Item Veto/Rule.** Adoption of the rule (H Res 540) to provide for House floor consideration of the bill that would grant the president expedited rescission authority over discretionary spending items in enacted appropriations bills, which would be subject to an expedited up-or-down vote in Congress. Adopted 238-175: R 228-1; D 10-174. Feb. 8, 2012.

45. **HR 3521. Expedited Line-Item Veto/Army Corps of Engineers.**
Alexander, R-La., amendment that would prohibit the president from proposing rescission to funds appropriated to the Army Corps of Engineers. Rejected in Committee of the Whole 128-300: R 46-193; D 82-107. Feb. 8, 2012.

46. **HR 3521. Expedited Line-Item Veto/Passage.** Passage of the bill that would grant the president expedited rescission authority over discretionary spending items in enacted appropriations bills, which would be subject to an expedited up-or-down vote in Congress. Proposed rescissions would take effect only if Congress passes, and the president signs, a measure specifically approving the spending cuts. The expedited authority would expire Dec. 15, 2015. Passed 254-173: R 197-41; D 57-132. A "yea" was a vote in support of the president's position. Feb. 8, 2012.

47. **S 2038. Congressional Insider-Trading Ban/Passage.** Smith, R-Texas, motion to suspend the rules and pass the bill that would clarify that members of Congress, officials and senior staff of the legislative, executive and judicial branches of the U.S. government are covered by current regulations that bar the use of non-public information for trading stocks and bonds. It would require lawmakers and other covered officials to report publicly any stock or securities transaction within 45 days of when the transaction occurs. The measure adds new provisions barring lawmakers and other covered officials from participating in initial stock offerings on a favored basis. Motion agreed to 417-2: R 232-2; D 185-0. A two-thirds majority of those present and voting (280 in this case) is required for passage under suspension of the rules. A "yea" was a vote in support of the president's position. Feb. 9, 2012.

48. **HR 3630. Year-End Extensions/Motion to Instruct.** Bishop, D-N.Y., motion to instruct conferees to file a conference report by Feb. 17, 2012, on the bill that would extend the 4.2 percent employee payroll tax rate, Medicare payment rates to doctors and workers' eligibility for certain expanded unemployment benefits. Motion agreed to 405-15: R 220-15; D 185-0. Feb. 9, 2012.

	43	44	45	46	47	48
ALABAMA						
1 Bonner	Y	Y	N	N	Y	Y
2 Roby	+	+	N	N	Y	Y
3 Rogers	Y	Y	Y	N	Y	N
4 Aderholt	Y	Y	N	N	Y	Y
5 Brooks	Y	Y	N	Y	Y	Y
6 Bachus	Y	Y	Y	N	Y	Y
7 Sewell	N	–	Y	N	Y	Y
ALASKA						
AL Young	Y	N	Y	N	?	Y
ARIZONA						
1 Gosar	Y	Y	N	Y	Y	Y
2 Franks	Y	?	N	Y	Y	Y
3 Quayle	Y	Y	N	Y	Y	N
4 Pastor	N	N	Y	N	Y	Y
5 Schweikert	Y	Y	N	Y	Y	Y
6 Flake	Y	Y	N	Y	Y	N
7 Grijalva	N	N	N	N	Y	Y
8 Vacant						
ARKANSAS						
1 Crawford	Y	Y	Y	Y	Y	Y
2 Griffin	Y	Y	N	Y	Y	Y
3 Womack	Y	Y	N	Y	Y	Y
4 Ross	Y	Y	Y	Y	Y	Y
CALIFORNIA						
1 Thompson	N	N	Y	N	Y	Y
2 Herger	Y	Y	N	Y	Y	Y
3 Lungren	Y	Y	N	Y	Y	Y
4 McClintock	Y	Y	N	Y	Y	N
5 Matsui	N	N	Y	N	Y	Y
6 Woolsey	N	N	Y	N	Y	Y
7 Miller, George	N	?	N	Y	Y	Y
8 Pelosi	N	N	N	Y	Y	Y
9 Lee	N	N	N	N	Y	Y
10 Garamendi	N	N	Y	N	Y	Y
11 McNerney	N	N	Y	N	Y	Y
12 Speier	N	N	N	N	Y	Y
13 Stark	N	N	N	N	Y	Y
14 Eshoo	N	N	Y	Y	Y	Y
15 Honda	N	N	N	N	Y	Y
16 Lofgren	N	N	N	N	Y	Y
17 Farr	N	N	N	N	Y	Y
18 Cardoza	N	N	Y	N	?	?
19 Denham	Y	Y	N	Y	Y	Y
20 Costa	N	N	Y	N	Y	Y
21 Nunes	Y	?	N	Y	Y	Y
22 McCarthy	Y	Y	N	Y	Y	Y
23 Capps	N	N	Y	Y	Y	Y
24 Gallegly	Y	Y	N	Y	Y	Y
25 McKeon	Y	Y	N	Y	Y	Y
26 Dreier	Y	Y	N	Y	Y	Y
27 Sherman	N	N	N	N	Y	Y
28 Berman	N	N	N	N	Y	Y
29 Schiff	N	N	N	N	Y	Y
30 Waxman	N	N	N	N	Y	Y
31 Becerra	N	N	N	N	Y	Y
32 Chu	N	–	Y	N	Y	Y
33 Bass	N	N	N	Y	Y	Y
34 Roybal-Allard	N	N	Y	N	Y	Y
35 Waters	N	N	N	N	Y	Y
36 Hahn	N	N	N	N	Y	Y
37 Richardson	N	N	Y	N	Y	Y
38 Napolitano	N	N	N	N	Y	Y
39 Sánchez, Linda	N	N	N	N	Y	Y
40 Royce	Y	Y	N	Y	Y	Y
41 Lewis	Y	Y	Y	N	Y	Y
42 Miller, Gary	Y	Y	Y	Y	Y	Y
43 Baca	N	N	N	N	Y	Y
44 Calvert	Y	Y	Y	N	Y	Y
45 Bono Mack	Y	Y	Y	Y	Y	Y
46 Rohrabacher	Y	Y	N	Y	Y	Y
47 Sanchez, Loretta	N	N	N	N	Y	Y
48 Campbell	Y	Y	N	Y	N	N
49 Issa	Y	Y	Y	Y	Y	Y
50 Bilbray	Y	Y	N	Y	Y	Y
51 Filner	N	N	N	N	Y	Y
52 Hunter	Y	Y	N	Y	N	Y
53 Davis	N	N	Y	N	Y	Y

	43	44	45	46	47	48
COLORADO						
1 DeGette	N	N	N	N	Y	Y
2 Polis	N	?	N	Y	Y	Y
3 Tipton	Y	Y	N	Y	Y	Y
4 Gardner	Y	Y	N	Y	Y	Y
5 Lamborn	Y	Y	N	Y	Y	Y
6 Coffman	Y	Y	N	Y	Y	Y
7 Perlmutter	N	Y	Y	Y	Y	Y
CONNECTICUT						
1 Larson	N	N	Y	N	Y	Y
2 Courtney	N	N	Y	N	Y	Y
3 DeLauro	N	N	Y	N	Y	Y
4 Himes	N	N	N	N	Y	Y
5 Murphy	N	N	N	N	Y	Y
DELAWARE						
AL Carney	N	N	N	Y	?	?
FLORIDA						
1 Miller	Y	Y	N	Y	Y	Y
2 Southerland	Y	Y	N	Y	Y	Y
3 Brown	N	N	Y	N	Y	Y
4 Crenshaw	Y	Y	N	Y	Y	Y
5 Nugent	Y	Y	N	Y	Y	Y
6 Stearns	Y	Y	N	Y	Y	Y
7 Mica	Y	+	N	Y	Y	Y
8 Webster	Y	Y	N	Y	Y	Y
9 Bilirakis	Y	Y	N	Y	Y	Y
10 Young	Y	Y	N	Y	Y	Y
11 Castor	N	N	Y	Y	Y	Y
12 Ross	Y	Y	N	Y	Y	Y
13 Buchanan	Y	Y	N	Y	Y	Y
14 Mack	Y	Y	Y	Y	Y	Y
15 Posey	Y	Y	N	Y	Y	Y
16 Rooney	Y	Y	Y	N	Y	Y
17 Wilson	N	N	Y	Y	Y	Y
18 Ros-Lehtinen	Y	Y	N	Y	Y	Y
19 Deutch	N	N	N	N	Y	Y
20 Wasserman Schultz	N	N	Y	N	Y	Y
21 Diaz-Balart	Y	Y	Y	Y	Y	Y
22 West	Y	Y	Y	Y	Y	Y
23 Hastings	N	N	N	N	Y	Y
24 Adams	Y	Y	N	Y	Y	Y
25 Rivera	Y	Y	N	Y	Y	Y
GEORGIA						
1 Kingston	Y	Y	Y	Y	Y	Y
2 Bishop	N	N	Y	N	Y	Y
3 Westmoreland	Y	Y	N	Y	–	Y
4 Johnson	N	N	N	N	Y	Y
5 Lewis	N	N	N	N	Y	Y
6 Price	Y	Y	N	Y	Y	Y
7 Woodall	Y	Y	N	Y	N	Y
8 Scott, A.	Y	Y	N	Y	Y	Y
9 Graves	Y	Y	N	Y	Y	Y
10 Broun	Y	Y	N	Y	Y	Y
11 Gingrey	Y	Y	N	Y	Y	Y
12 Barrow	N	Y	Y	Y	Y	Y
13 Scott, D.	N	N	N	N	Y	Y
HAWAII						
1 Hanabusa	N	N	Y	N	Y	Y
2 Hirono	N	N	N	N	Y	Y
IDAHO						
1 Labrador	Y	Y	N	N	Y	Y
2 Simpson	Y	Y	N	N	Y	Y
ILLINOIS						
1 Rush	N	N	Y	N	Y	Y
2 Jackson	N	N	Y	N	Y	Y
3 Lipinski	N	N	Y	N	Y	Y
4 Gutierrez	N	N	Y	N	Y	Y
5 Quigley	N	Y	N	Y	Y	Y
6 Roskam	Y	Y	N	Y	Y	Y
7 Davis	N	N	N	N	Y	Y
8 Walsh	Y	Y	N	Y	Y	Y
9 Schakowsky	N	N	N	N	Y	Y
10 Dold	Y	Y	N	Y	Y	Y
11 Kinzinger	Y	Y	N	Y	Y	Y
12 Costello	N	N	Y	Y	Y	Y
13 Biggert	Y	Y	N	Y	Y	Y
14 Hultgren	Y	Y	N	Y	Y	Y
15 Johnson	Y	Y	N	Y	Y	Y

	43	44	45	46	47	48
16 **Manzullo**	Y	Y	N	Y	Y	Y
17 **Schilling**	Y	Y	Y	Y	Y	Y
18 **Schock**	Y	Y	N	Y	Y	Y
19 **Shimkus**	Y	Y	Y	Y	Y	Y
INDIANA						
1 Visclosky	N	N	N	N	Y	Y
2 Donnelly	N	Y	N	Y	Y	Y
3 **Stutzman**	Y	?	N	Y	Y	N
4 **Rokita**	Y	Y	N	Y	Y	Y
5 **Burton**	Y	Y	N	N	?	?
6 **Pence**	Y	Y	N	Y	Y	Y
7 Carson	N	N	N	N	Y	Y
8 **Bucshon**	Y	Y	N	Y	Y	Y
9 **Young**	Y	Y	N	Y	Y	Y
IOWA						
1 Braley	N	N	N	N	Y	Y
2 Loebsack	N	N	Y	Y	Y	Y
3 Boswell	N	N	Y	Y	Y	Y
4 **Latham**	Y	Y	Y	Y	Y	Y
5 **King**	Y	Y	Y	N	Y	Y
KANSAS						
1 **Huelskamp**	Y	Y	N	Y	Y	N
2 **Jenkins**	Y	Y	N	Y	Y	Y
3 **Yoder**	Y	Y	N	Y	Y	N
4 **Pompeo**	Y	Y	N	Y	Y	Y
KENTUCKY						
1 **Whitfield**	Y	Y	N	N	Y	Y
2 **Guthrie**	Y	Y	N	Y	Y	Y
3 Yarmuth	N	N	N	N	Y	Y
4 **Davis**	Y	Y	N	Y	Y	Y
5 **Rogers**	Y	Y	Y	N	Y	Y
6 Chandler	N	N	N	Y	Y	Y
LOUISIANA						
1 **Scalise**	Y	Y	Y	Y	Y	Y
2 Richmond	N	N	Y	N	Y	Y
3 **Landry**	Y	Y	Y	N	Y	Y
4 **Fleming**	Y	Y	N	Y	Y	Y
5 **Alexander**	?	Y	Y	N	Y	Y
6 **Cassidy**	?	?	?	?	Y	Y
7 **Boustany**	Y	Y	Y	N	Y	Y
MAINE						
1 Pingree	N	N	N	N	Y	Y
2 Michaud	N	N	N	Y	?	?
MARYLAND						
1 **Harris**	Y	Y	Y	Y	Y	Y
2 Ruppersberger	N	?	Y	Y	Y	Y
3 Sarbanes	N	N	Y	N	Y	Y
4 Edwards	N	N	N	N	?	?
5 Hoyer	N	N	N	N	Y	Y
6 **Bartlett**	Y	Y	N	Y	Y	Y
7 Cummings	N	N	Y	N	Y	Y
8 Van Hollen	N	N	N	Y	Y	Y
MASSACHUSETTS						
1 Olver	N	N	N	N	Y	Y
2 Neal	N	N	N	N	Y	Y
3 McGovern	N	N	Y	N	Y	Y
4 Frank	N	N	N	N	Y	Y
5 Tsongas	N	N	N	Y	Y	Y
6 Tierney	N	N	Y	N	Y	Y
7 Markey	N	N	Y	N	Y	Y
8 Capuano	N	N	Y	N	Y	Y
9 Lynch	N	N	N	N	Y	Y
10 Keating	N	N	Y	N	Y	Y
MICHIGAN						
1 **Benishek**	Y	Y	N	Y	Y	Y
2 **Huizenga**	Y	Y	N	Y	Y	Y
3 **Amash**	Y	Y	N	N	Y	N
4 **Camp**	Y	Y	N	Y	Y	Y
5 Kildee	N	N	N	N	Y	Y
6 **Upton**	Y	Y	N	Y	Y	Y
7 **Walberg**	Y	Y	N	Y	Y	Y
8 **Rogers**	Y	Y	N	Y	?	Y
9 Peters	N	N	Y	Y	Y	Y
10 **Miller**	Y	+	N	Y	Y	Y
11 **McCotter**	Y	Y	N	Y	Y	Y
12 Levin	N	N	N	N	Y	Y
13 Clarke	N	N	N	N	Y	Y
14 Conyers	N	N	N	N	Y	Y
15 Dingell	N	N	N	N	Y	Y
MINNESOTA						
1 Walz	N	N	Y	N	Y	Y
2 **Kline**	Y	Y	N	Y	Y	Y
3 **Paulsen**	Y	Y	N	Y	Y	Y
4 McCollum	N	N	N	N	Y	Y

	43	44	45	46	47	48
5 Ellison	N	N	N	N	Y	Y
6 **Bachmann**	Y	Y	N	Y	Y	N
7 Peterson	Y	N	Y	N	Y	Y
8 **Cravaack**	Y	Y	N	Y	Y	Y
MISSISSIPPI						
1 **Nunnelee**	Y	Y	Y	N	Y	Y
2 Thompson	N	N	N	N	?	?
3 **Harper**	Y	Y	Y	Y	Y	Y
4 **Palazzo**	Y	Y	Y	N	Y	Y
MISSOURI						
1 Clay	N	N	N	N	Y	Y
2 **Akin**	?	?	N	Y	Y	Y
3 Carnahan	N	N	N	Y	Y	Y
4 **Hartzler**	N	Y	N	Y	Y	Y
5 Cleaver	N	N	N	N	Y	Y
6 **Graves**	Y	Y	N	Y	Y	Y
7 **Long**	Y	Y	N	+	Y	N
8 **Emerson**	Y	Y	Y	N	Y	Y
9 **Luetkemeyer**	Y	Y	N	Y	Y	Y
MONTANA						
AL **Rehberg**	Y	Y	Y	Y	Y	Y
NEBRASKA						
1 **Fortenberry**	Y	Y	Y	Y	Y	Y
2 **Terry**	Y	Y	Y	Y	Y	?
3 **Smith**	Y	Y	N	Y	Y	Y
NEVADA						
1 Berkley	N	N	N	N	Y	Y
2 **Amodei**	Y	Y	N	Y	Y	Y
3 **Heck**	Y	Y	N	Y	Y	Y
NEW HAMPSHIRE						
1 **Guinta**	Y	Y	N	Y	Y	Y
2 **Bass**	Y	Y	N	Y	Y	Y
NEW JERSEY						
1 Andrews	N	N	N	Y	Y	Y
2 **LoBiondo**	Y	Y	Y	Y	Y	Y
3 **Runyan**	Y	Y	Y	Y	Y	Y
4 **Smith**	Y	Y	N	Y	Y	Y
5 **Garrett**	Y	Y	N	Y	Y	Y
6 Pallone	N	N	Y	N	Y	Y
7 **Lance**	Y	Y	N	Y	Y	Y
8 Pascrell	N	N	Y	N	Y	Y
9 Rothman	N	N	Y	N	Y	Y
10 Payne	?	?	?	?	Y	Y
11 **Frelinghuysen**	Y	Y	N	Y	Y	Y
12 Holt	N	N	N	N	Y	Y
13 Sires	N	N	Y	N	Y	Y
NEW MEXICO						
1 Heinrich	N	N	N	Y	Y	Y
2 **Pearce**	?	Y	N	Y	Y	Y
3 Luján	N	N	Y	N	Y	Y
NEW YORK						
1 Bishop	N	N	Y	Y	Y	Y
2 Israel	N	N	N	Y	Y	Y
3 **King**	Y	Y	Y	Y	Y	Y
4 McCarthy	N	N	Y	Y	Y	Y
5 Ackerman	N	N	N	N	Y	Y
6 Meeks	N	N	N	N	Y	Y
7 Crowley	N	N	N	N	Y	Y
8 Nadler	N	N	Y	N	Y	Y
9 **Turner**	Y	Y	Y	Y	Y	Y
10 Towns	N	N	N	N	Y	Y
11 Clarke	N	N	N	N	Y	Y
12 Velázquez	N	N	N	N	Y	Y
13 **Grimm**	Y	Y	Y	Y	Y	Y
14 Maloney	N	N	Y	N	Y	Y
15 Rangel	N	N	N	N	Y	Y
16 Serrano	N	N	N	N	Y	Y
17 Engel	N	N	N	N	Y	Y
18 Lowey	N	N	N	N	Y	Y
19 **Hayworth**	Y	Y	N	Y	Y	Y
20 **Gibson**	Y	Y	N	Y	Y	Y
21 Tonko	N	N	N	N	Y	Y
22 Hinchey	N	N	Y	N	Y	Y
23 Owens	N	N	N	Y	Y	Y
24 **Hanna**	Y	Y	N	Y	Y	Y
25 **Buerkle**	Y	Y	N	Y	Y	Y
26 Hochul	N	Y	N	Y	Y	Y
27 Higgins	N	N	N	Y	Y	Y
28 Slaughter	N	N	N	N	Y	Y
29 **Reed**	Y	Y	N	Y	Y	Y
NORTH CAROLINA						
1 Butterfield	N	?	Y	N	Y	Y
2 **Ellmers**	Y	Y	N	Y	Y	Y
3 **Jones**	Y	Y	Y	N	Y	Y
4 Price	N	N	Y	N	Y	Y

	43	44	45	46	47	48
5 **Foxx**	Y	Y	N	Y	Y	Y
6 **Coble**	Y	Y	Y	Y	Y	Y
7 McIntyre	N	Y	+	+	Y	Y
8 Kissell	N	Y	N	Y	Y	Y
9 **Myrick**	Y	Y	N	Y	Y	Y
10 **McHenry**	Y	Y	N	Y	Y	Y
11 Shuler	Y	N	N	Y	Y	Y
12 Watt	N	N	Y	N	Y	Y
13 Miller	N	N	N	N	Y	Y
NORTH DAKOTA						
AL **Berg**	Y	Y	N	Y	Y	Y
OHIO						
1 **Chabot**	Y	Y	N	Y	Y	Y
2 **Schmidt**	Y	Y	N	Y	Y	Y
3 **Turner**	Y	Y	N	Y	Y	Y
4 **Jordan**	Y	Y	N	Y	Y	Y
5 **Latta**	Y	Y	N	Y	Y	Y
6 **Johnson**	Y	Y	N	Y	Y	Y
7 **Austria**	Y	Y	Y	N	Y	Y
8 **Boehner**						
9 Kaptur	N	N	N	N	Y	Y
10 Kucinich	N	N	Y	N	Y	Y
11 Fudge	N	N	N	N	?	?
12 **Tiberi**	Y	Y	N	Y	Y	Y
13 Sutton	N	N	Y	N	Y	Y
14 **LaTourette**	Y	Y	Y	N	Y	Y
15 **Stivers**	Y	Y	N	Y	Y	Y
16 **Renacci**	Y	Y	N	Y	Y	Y
17 Ryan	N	N	Y	N	Y	Y
18 **Gibbs**	Y	Y	N	Y	Y	Y
OKLAHOMA						
1 **Sullivan**	Y	Y	N	Y	Y	Y
2 Boren	Y	Y	N	Y	Y	Y
3 **Lucas**	Y	Y	N	Y	Y	Y
4 **Cole**	Y	+	Y	N	Y	Y
5 **Lankford**	Y	Y	N	Y	Y	Y
OREGON						
1 Bonamici*	N	N	N	Y	Y	Y
2 **Walden**	Y	Y	N	Y	Y	Y
3 Blumenauer	?	?	?	?	?	?
4 DeFazio	N	N	Y	Y	Y	Y
5 Schrader	N	N	N	Y	Y	Y
PENNSYLVANIA						
1 Brady	N	N	Y	N	Y	Y
2 Fattah	?	N	Y	N	Y	Y
3 **Kelly**	Y	Y	N	Y	Y	Y
4 Altmire	N	N	Y	Y	Y	Y
5 **Thompson**	Y	Y	N	N	Y	Y
6 **Gerlach**	Y	Y	N	Y	Y	Y
7 **Meehan**	Y	?	Y	Y	Y	Y
8 **Fitzpatrick**	Y	Y	Y	Y	Y	Y
9 **Shuster**	Y	Y	Y	N	?	?
10 **Marino**	Y	Y	N	Y	Y	Y
11 **Barletta**	Y	Y	Y	Y	Y	Y
12 Critz	N	N	Y	N	Y	Y
13 Schwartz	N	N	Y	Y	Y	Y
14 Doyle	N	N	Y	N	Y	Y
15 **Dent**	Y	Y	N	Y	Y	Y
16 **Pitts**	Y	Y	N	Y	Y	Y
17 Holden	N	N	Y	N	Y	Y
18 **Murphy**	Y	Y	N	Y	Y	Y
19 **Platts**	Y	Y	N	Y	+	+
RHODE ISLAND						
1 Cicilline	N	N	N	Y	Y	Y
2 Langevin	N	N	N	Y	Y	Y
SOUTH CAROLINA						
1 **Scott**	Y	Y	N	Y	Y	Y
2 **Wilson**	Y	Y	N	Y	Y	Y
3 **Duncan**	Y	Y	N	N	Y	Y
4 **Gowdy**	Y	Y	N	Y	Y	Y
5 **Mulvaney**	Y	Y	N	Y	Y	Y
6 Clyburn	N	N	Y	N	Y	Y
SOUTH DAKOTA						
AL **Noem**	Y	Y	N	Y	Y	Y
TENNESSEE						
1 **Roe**	Y	Y	N	Y	Y	Y
2 **Duncan**	Y	Y	N	Y	Y	Y
3 **Fleischmann**	Y	Y	N	Y	Y	Y
4 **DesJarlais**	Y	Y	N	Y	Y	Y
5 Cooper	N	N	N	Y	Y	Y
6 **Black**	Y	Y	N	Y	Y	Y
7 **Blackburn**	Y	Y	N	Y	Y	N
8 **Fincher**	Y	Y	N	Y	Y	Y
9 Cohen	N	N	N	N	Y	Y

	43	44	45	46	47	48
TEXAS						
1 **Gohmert**	Y	Y	N	Y	Y	Y
2 **Poe**	Y	Y	N	Y	Y	Y
3 **Johnson, S.**	Y	Y	N	Y	Y	Y
4 **Hall**	Y	Y	N	Y	Y	Y
5 **Hensarling**	Y	Y	N	Y	Y	Y
6 **Barton**	Y	Y	N	Y	Y	Y
7 **Culberson**	Y	Y	Y	Y	Y	Y
8 **Brady**	Y	Y	N	Y	Y	Y
9 Green, A.	N	N	Y	N	Y	Y
10 **McCaul**	Y	Y	N	Y	Y	Y
11 **Conaway**	Y	Y	N	Y	Y	Y
12 **Granger**	Y	Y	Y	N	Y	Y
13 **Thornberry**	Y	Y	N	Y	Y	Y
14 **Paul**	?	?	?	?	?	?
15 Hinojosa	N	N	N	N	Y	Y
16 Reyes	N	N	Y	N	Y	Y
17 **Flores**	Y	Y	N	Y	Y	Y
18 Jackson Lee	N	N	Y	N	Y	Y
19 **Neugebauer**	Y	Y	N	Y	Y	N
20 Gonzalez	N	N	Y	N	Y	Y
21 **Smith**	Y	Y	N	Y	Y	Y
22 **Olson**	Y	Y	N	Y	Y	Y
23 **Canseco**	Y	Y	N	Y	Y	Y
24 **Marchant**	Y	Y	N	Y	Y	Y
25 Doggett	N	N	N	Y	Y	Y
26 **Burgess**	Y	Y	N	Y	Y	Y
27 **Farenthold**	Y	Y	N	Y	Y	Y
28 Cuellar	N	N	N	Y	Y	Y
29 Green, G.	N	N	Y	N	Y	Y
30 Johnson, E.	N	N	Y	N	Y	Y
31 **Carter**	Y	Y	N	N	Y	Y
32 **Sessions**	Y	Y	N	Y	Y	Y
UTAH						
1 **Bishop**	Y	Y	N	Y	Y	Y
2 Matheson	Y	Y	N	Y	Y	Y
3 **Chaffetz**	Y	Y	N	Y	Y	Y
VERMONT						
AL Welch	N	N	N	Y	Y	Y
VIRGINIA						
1 **Wittman**	Y	Y	N	Y	Y	Y
2 **Rigell**	Y	Y	N	Y	Y	Y
3 Scott	N	N	N	N	Y	Y
4 **Forbes**	Y	Y	N	Y	Y	Y
5 **Hurt**	Y	Y	N	Y	Y	Y
6 **Goodlatte**	Y	Y	N	Y	Y	Y
7 **Cantor**	Y	Y	N	Y	Y	Y
8 Moran	N	N	N	N	Y	Y
9 **Griffith**	Y	Y	N	N	Y	Y
10 **Wolf**	Y	Y	N	N	Y	N
11 Connolly	N	N	N	Y	Y	Y
WASHINGTON						
1 Inslee	N	N	N	Y	Y	Y
2 Larsen	N	N	N	Y	Y	Y
3 **Herrera Beutler**	Y	?	Y	N	Y	Y
4 **Hastings**	Y	Y	N	Y	Y	Y
5 **McMorris Rodgers**	Y	Y	N	Y	Y	Y
6 Dicks	N	N	Y	N	Y	Y
7 McDermott	N	N	N	N	Y	Y
8 **Reichert**	Y	Y	N	Y	Y	Y
9 Smith	N	N	N	Y	Y	Y
WEST VIRGINIA						
1 **McKinley**	Y	Y	N	Y	Y	Y
2 **Capito**	Y	Y	N	Y	Y	Y
3 Rahall	N	N	Y	N	Y	Y
WISCONSIN						
1 **Ryan**	Y	Y	N	Y	Y	Y
2 Baldwin	N	N	N	N	Y	Y
3 Kind	Y	Y	N	Y	Y	Y
4 Moore	N	N	Y	N	Y	Y
5 **Sensenbrenner**	Y	Y	N	Y	Y	Y
6 **Petri**	Y	Y	N	Y	Y	Y
7 **Duffy**	Y	Y	N	Y	Y	Y
8 **Ribble**	Y	Y	N	Y	Y	?
WYOMING						
AL **Lummis**	Y	Y	N	Y	Y	N

IN THE HOUSE | By Vote Number

49. Procedural Motion/Journal. Approval of the House Journal of Monday, Feb. 13, 2012. Approved 303-89: R 176-44; D 127-45. Feb. 14, 2012.

50. HR 7. Surface Transportation Reauthorization/Previous Question. Webster, R-Fla., motion to order the previous question (thus ending debate and possibility of amendment) on adoption of the rule (H Res 547) that would provide for House floor consideration of a bill (HR 3408) consisting of the energy titles of a surface transportation package and a bill (HR 3813) consisting of federal employee pension modification provisions of the package, as well as general debate on a bill (HR 7) that would reauthorize surface transportation programs through fiscal 2016. Motion agreed to 229-181: R 227-0; D 2-181. Feb. 15, 2012.

51. HR 7. Surface Transportation Reauthorization/Rule. Adoption of the rule (H Res 547) that would provide for House floor consideration of a bill (HR 3408) consisting of the energy titles of a surface transportation package and a bill (HR 3813) consisting of federal employee pension modification provisions of the package, as well as general debate on a bill (HR 7) that would reauthorize surface transportation programs through fiscal 2016 and extend the Highway Trust Fund. The rule would require that the text of the energy and pension measures, as amended and passed by the House, be added back to the surface transportation bill upon engrossment of that legislation. Adopted 235-186: R 232-4; D 3-182. Feb. 5, 2012.

52. HR 2079. John J. Cook Post Office/Passage. Kelly, R-Pa., motion to suspend the rules and pass the bill that would designate a post office in East Rockaway, N.Y., as the "John J. Cook Post Office." Motion agreed to 418-2: R 233-2; D 185-0. A two-thirds majority of those present and voting (280 in this case) is required for passage under suspension of the rules. Feb. 15, 2012.

53. HR 3247. Lance Cpl. Matthew P. Pathenos Post Office Building/Passage. Kelly, R-Pa., motion to suspend the rules and pass the bill that would designate a post office in Chesterfield, Mo., as the "Lance Cpl. Matthew P. Pathenos Post Office Building." Motion agreed to 419-0: R 235-0; D 184-0. A two-thirds majority of those present and voting (280 in this case) is required for passage under suspension of the rules. Feb. 15, 2012.

54. HR 3248. Cpl. Drew W. Weaver Post Office Building/Passage. Kelly, R-Pa., motion to suspend the rules and pass the bill that would designate a post office in St. Charles, Mo., as the "Cpl. Drew W. Weaver Post Office Building." Motion agreed to 412-0: R 233-0; D 179-0. A two-thirds majority of those present and voting (275 in this case) is required for passage under suspension of the rules. Feb. 15, 2012.

	49	50	51	52	53	54
ALABAMA						
1 **Bonner**	Y	Y	Y	Y	Y	Y
2 **Roby**	Y	Y	Y	Y	Y	Y
3 **Rogers**	Y	Y	Y	Y	Y	Y
4 **Aderholt**	Y	Y	Y	Y	Y	Y
5 **Brooks**	Y	Y	Y	Y	Y	Y
6 **Bachus**	Y	Y	Y	Y	Y	Y
7 Sewell	Y	N	N	Y	Y	Y
ALASKA						
AL **Young**	N	Y	Y	Y	Y	Y
ARIZONA						
1 **Gosar**	?	Y	Y	Y	Y	Y
2 **Franks**	Y	Y	Y	Y	Y	Y
3 **Quayle**	N	Y	Y	Y	Y	Y
4 Pastor	N	N	N	Y	Y	Y
5 **Schweikert**	Y	Y	Y	Y	Y	Y
6 **Flake**	Y	Y	N	Y	Y	Y
7 Grijalva	?	N	N	Y	Y	Y
8 Vacant						
ARKANSAS						
1 **Crawford**	Y	Y	Y	Y	Y	Y
2 **Griffin**	N	Y	Y	Y	Y	Y
3 **Womack**	Y	Y	Y	Y	Y	Y
4 Ross	Y	N	N	Y	Y	Y
CALIFORNIA						
1 Thompson	N	N	N	Y	Y	Y
2 **Herger**	Y	Y	Y	Y	Y	?
3 **Lungren**	Y	Y	Y	Y	Y	Y
4 **McClintock**	Y	Y	Y	Y	Y	Y
5 Matsui	N	N	N	Y	Y	Y
6 Woolsey	Y	–	N	Y	Y	Y
7 Miller, George	Y	N	N	Y	Y	Y
8 Pelosi	Y	N	N	Y	Y	Y
9 Lee	N	N	N	Y	Y	Y
10 Garamendi	Y	N	N	Y	Y	Y
11 McNerney	Y	N	N	Y	Y	Y
12 Speier	Y	N	N	Y	Y	Y
13 Stark	Y	N	N	Y	Y	Y
14 Eshoo	Y	N	N	Y	Y	Y
15 Honda	Y	N	N	Y	Y	Y
16 Lofgren	Y	N	N	Y	Y	Y
17 Farr	Y	N	N	Y	Y	Y
18 Cardoza	?	?	N	Y	Y	Y
19 **Denham**	Y	Y	Y	Y	Y	Y
20 Costa	N	N	N	Y	Y	Y
21 **Nunes**	Y	Y	Y	Y	Y	Y
22 **McCarthy**	Y	Y	Y	Y	Y	Y
23 Capps	Y	N	N	Y	Y	Y
24 **Gallegly**	Y	Y	Y	Y	Y	Y
25 **McKeon**	Y	Y	Y	Y	Y	Y
26 **Dreier**	Y	Y	Y	Y	Y	Y
27 Sherman	Y	N	N	Y	Y	Y
28 Berman	Y	N	N	Y	Y	Y
29 Schiff	Y	N	N	Y	Y	Y
30 Waxman	Y	N	N	Y	Y	Y
31 Becerra	Y	–	–	+	+	+
32 Chu	Y	N	N	Y	Y	Y
33 Bass	Y	N	N	Y	Y	Y
34 Roybal-Allard	Y	N	N	Y	Y	Y
35 Waters	Y	N	?	Y	Y	Y
36 Hahn	Y	N	N	Y	Y	Y
37 Richardson	Y	N	N	Y	Y	Y
38 Napolitano	Y	N	N	Y	Y	Y
39 Sánchez, Linda	N	N	N	Y	Y	Y
40 **Royce**	Y	Y	Y	Y	Y	Y
41 **Lewis**	Y	Y	Y	Y	Y	Y
42 **Miller, Gary**	Y	Y	Y	Y	Y	Y
43 Baca	Y	N	N	Y	Y	Y
44 **Calvert**	Y	Y	Y	Y	Y	Y
45 **Bono Mack**	Y	Y	Y	Y	Y	Y
46 **Rohrabacher**	?	Y	Y	Y	Y	Y
47 Sanchez, Loretta	?	N	N	Y	Y	Y
48 **Campbell**	?	?	?	?	?	?
49 **Issa**	Y	Y	Y	Y	Y	Y
50 **Bilbray**	Y	Y	Y	Y	Y	Y
51 Filner	+	N	N	+	Y	Y
52 **Hunter**	Y	Y	Y	Y	Y	Y
53 Davis	Y	N	N	Y	Y	+

	49	50	51	52	53	54
COLORADO						
1 DeGette	Y	N	N	Y	Y	Y
2 Polis	Y	N	N	Y	Y	Y
3 **Tipton**	N	Y	Y	Y	Y	Y
4 **Gardner**	?	Y	Y	Y	Y	Y
5 **Lamborn**	Y	Y	Y	Y	Y	Y
6 **Coffman**	N	Y	Y	Y	Y	Y
7 Perlmutter	Y	N	N	Y	Y	Y
CONNECTICUT						
1 Larson	Y	N	N	Y	Y	Y
2 Courtney	N	N	N	Y	Y	Y
3 DeLauro	Y	N	N	Y	Y	Y
4 Himes	Y	N	N	Y	Y	Y
5 Murphy	Y	N	N	Y	Y	Y
DELAWARE						
AL Carney	Y	N	N	Y	Y	Y
FLORIDA						
1 **Miller**	N	Y	Y	Y	Y	Y
2 **Southerland**	Y	Y	Y	Y	Y	Y
3 Brown	Y	N	N	Y	Y	Y
4 **Crenshaw**	N	Y	Y	Y	Y	Y
5 **Nugent**	Y	Y	Y	Y	Y	Y
6 **Stearns**	Y	Y	Y	Y	Y	Y
7 **Mica**	Y	Y	Y	Y	Y	Y
8 **Webster**	Y	Y	Y	Y	Y	Y
9 **Bilirakis**	Y	Y	Y	Y	Y	Y
10 **Young**	?	?	?	?	?	?
11 Castor	N	N	N	Y	Y	Y
12 **Ross**	Y	Y	N	Y	Y	Y
13 **Buchanan**	Y	Y	Y	Y	Y	Y
14 **Mack**	Y	Y	Y	Y	Y	Y
15 **Posey**	Y	Y	Y	Y	Y	Y
16 **Rooney**	Y	Y	Y	Y	Y	Y
17 Wilson	Y	N	N	Y	Y	Y
18 **Ros-Lehtinen**	Y	Y	Y	Y	Y	Y
19 Deutch	Y	N	N	Y	Y	Y
20 Wasserman Schultz	Y	N	N	Y	Y	Y
21 **Diaz-Balart**	Y	?	Y	Y	Y	Y
22 **West**	Y	Y	Y	Y	Y	Y
23 Hastings	N	N	N	Y	Y	Y
24 **Adams**	N	Y	N	Y	Y	Y
25 **Rivera**	Y	Y	Y	Y	Y	Y
GEORGIA						
1 **Kingston**	Y	Y	Y	Y	Y	Y
2 Bishop	Y	N	N	Y	Y	Y
3 **Westmoreland**	Y	Y	Y	Y	Y	Y
4 Johnson	Y	N	N	Y	Y	Y
5 Lewis	Y	N	N	Y	Y	Y
6 **Price**	Y	Y	Y	Y	Y	Y
7 **Woodall**	N	Y	Y	Y	Y	Y
8 **Scott, A.**	Y	Y	Y	Y	Y	Y
9 **Graves**	Y	Y	Y	Y	Y	Y
10 **Broun**	Y	Y	Y	Y	Y	Y
11 **Gingrey**	Y	Y	Y	Y	Y	Y
12 Barrow	Y	N	N	Y	Y	Y
13 Scott, D.	Y	N	N	Y	Y	Y
HAWAII						
1 Hanabusa	Y	N	N	Y	Y	Y
2 Hirono	?	N	N	Y	?	?
IDAHO						
1 **Labrador**	Y	Y	Y	Y	Y	Y
2 **Simpson**	Y	Y	Y	Y	Y	Y
ILLINOIS						
1 Rush	?	N	N	Y	Y	Y
2 Jackson	Y	N	N	Y	Y	Y
3 Lipinski	Y	N	N	Y	Y	Y
4 Gutierrez	+	N	N	Y	Y	Y
5 Quigley	Y	N	N	Y	Y	Y
6 **Roskam**	Y	Y	Y	Y	Y	Y
7 Davis	?	N	N	Y	Y	Y
8 **Walsh**	?	Y	Y	Y	Y	Y
9 Schakowsky	N	N	N	Y	Y	Y
10 **Dold**	N	Y	Y	Y	Y	Y
11 **Kinzinger**	Y	Y	Y	Y	Y	Y
12 Costello	N	N	N	Y	Y	Y
13 **Biggert**	Y	Y	Y	Y	Y	Y
14 **Hultgren**	Y	Y	Y	Y	Y	Y
15 **Johnson**	?	+	+	+	+	+

	49	50	51	52	53	54
16 **Manzullo**	Y	Y	Y	Y	Y	Y
17 **Schilling**	N	Y	Y	Y	Y	Y
18 **Schock**	N	Y	Y	Y	Y	?
19 **Shimkus**	Y	Y	Y	Y	Y	Y
INDIANA						
1 Visclosky	N	N	N	Y	Y	Y
2 Donnelly	N	N	N	Y	Y	Y
3 **Stutzman**	Y	Y	Y	Y	Y	Y
4 **Rokita**	Y	Y	Y	Y	Y	Y
5 **Burton**	?	Y	Y	Y	Y	Y
6 **Pence**	Y	Y	Y	Y	Y	Y
7 Carson	Y	N	N	Y	Y	Y
8 **Bucshon**	Y	Y	Y	Y	Y	Y
9 **Young**	Y	Y	Y	Y	Y	Y
IOWA						
1 Braley	Y	N	N	Y	Y	Y
2 Loebsack	Y	N	N	Y	Y	Y
3 Boswell	Y	N	N	Y	Y	Y
4 **Latham**	N	Y	Y	Y	Y	Y
5 **King**	Y	Y	Y	Y	Y	Y
KANSAS						
1 **Huelskamp**	Y	Y	Y	Y	?	Y
2 **Jenkins**	Y	Y	Y	Y	Y	Y
3 **Yoder**	N	Y	Y	Y	Y	Y
4 **Pompeo**	Y	Y	Y	Y	Y	Y
KENTUCKY						
1 **Whitfield**	Y	Y	Y	Y	Y	Y
2 **Guthrie**	Y	Y	Y	Y	Y	Y
3 Yarmuth	Y	N	N	Y	Y	Y
4 **Davis**	N	Y	Y	Y	Y	Y
5 **Rogers**	Y	Y	Y	Y	Y	Y
6 Chandler	N	N	N	Y	Y	Y
LOUISIANA						
1 **Scalise**	Y	Y	Y	Y	Y	Y
2 Richmond	Y	N	N	Y	Y	Y
3 **Landry**	Y	Y	Y	Y	Y	Y
4 **Fleming**	Y	Y	Y	Y	Y	Y
5 **Alexander**	Y	Y	Y	Y	Y	Y
6 **Cassidy**	Y	Y	Y	Y	Y	Y
7 **Boustany**	Y	Y	Y	Y	Y	Y
MAINE						
1 Pingree	Y	N	N	Y	Y	Y
2 Michaud	Y	N	N	Y	Y	Y
MARYLAND						
1 **Harris**	Y	Y	Y	N	Y	Y
2 Ruppersberger	Y	N	N	Y	Y	?
3 Sarbanes	N	N	N	Y	Y	Y
4 Edwards	Y	N	N	Y	Y	Y
5 Hoyer	N	N	N	Y	Y	Y
6 **Bartlett**	Y	Y	Y	Y	Y	Y
7 Cummings	Y	N	N	Y	Y	Y
8 Van Hollen	Y	N	N	Y	Y	Y
MASSACHUSETTS						
1 Olver	N	N	N	Y	Y	Y
2 Neal	N	N	N	Y	Y	?
3 McGovern	N	N	N	Y	Y	Y
4 Frank	Y	N	N	Y	Y	Y
5 Tsongas	?	N	N	Y	Y	Y
6 Tierney	Y	N	N	Y	Y	Y
7 Markey	N	N	N	Y	Y	Y
8 Capuano	N	N	N	Y	Y	Y
9 Lynch	N	N	N	Y	Y	Y
10 Keating	Y	N	N	Y	Y	Y
MICHIGAN						
1 **Benishek**	N	Y	Y	Y	Y	Y
2 **Huizenga**	Y	Y	Y	Y	Y	Y
3 **Amash**	P	Y	Y	Y	Y	Y
4 **Camp**	Y	Y	Y	Y	Y	Y
5 Kildee	Y	N	N	Y	Y	Y
6 **Upton**	Y	Y	Y	Y	Y	Y
7 **Walberg**	N	Y	Y	Y	Y	Y
8 **Rogers**	Y	Y	Y	Y	Y	Y
9 Peters	N	N	N	Y	Y	Y
10 **Miller**	Y	Y	Y	Y	Y	Y
11 **McCotter**	N	Y	Y	Y	Y	Y
12 Levin	Y	N	N	Y	Y	Y
13 Clarke	Y	N	N	Y	Y	Y
14 Conyers	Y	N	N	Y	Y	Y
15 Dingell	Y	N	N	Y	Y	Y
MINNESOTA						
1 Walz	Y	N	N	Y	Y	Y
2 **Kline**	Y	Y	Y	Y	Y	Y
3 **Paulsen**	Y	Y	Y	Y	Y	Y
4 McCollum	Y	N	N	Y	Y	Y

	49	50	51	52	53	54
5 Ellison	Y	N	N	Y	Y	Y
6 **Bachmann**	Y	Y	Y	Y	Y	Y
7 Peterson	N	N	Y	Y	Y	Y
8 **Cravaack**	N	Y	Y	Y	Y	Y
MISSISSIPPI						
1 **Nunnelee**	Y	Y	Y	Y	Y	Y
2 Thompson	N	N	N	Y	Y	Y
3 **Harper**	Y	Y	Y	Y	Y	Y
4 **Palazzo**	Y	Y	Y	?	Y	Y
MISSOURI						
1 Clay	Y	N	N	Y	Y	Y
2 **Akin**	Y	Y	Y	Y	Y	Y
3 Carnahan	Y	N	N	Y	Y	Y
4 **Hartzler**	N	?	Y	Y	Y	Y
5 Cleaver	N	N	N	Y	Y	Y
6 **Graves**	N	Y	Y	Y	Y	Y
7 **Long**	Y	Y	Y	Y	Y	Y
8 **Emerson**	Y	Y	Y	Y	Y	Y
9 **Luetkemeyer**	Y	?	Y	Y	Y	Y
MONTANA						
AL **Rehberg**	Y	Y	Y	Y	Y	Y
NEBRASKA						
1 **Fortenberry**	Y	Y	Y	Y	Y	Y
2 **Terry**	N	Y	Y	Y	Y	Y
3 **Smith**	Y	Y	Y	Y	Y	Y
NEVADA						
1 Berkley	Y	N	N	Y	Y	Y
2 **Amodei**	Y	Y	Y	Y	Y	Y
3 **Heck**	N	Y	Y	Y	Y	Y
NEW HAMPSHIRE						
1 **Guinta**	?	?	?	?	?	?
2 **Bass**	Y	Y	Y	Y	Y	Y
NEW JERSEY						
1 Andrews	Y	N	N	Y	Y	Y
2 **LoBiondo**	N	Y	Y	Y	Y	Y
3 **Runyan**	Y	Y	Y	Y	Y	Y
4 **Smith**	Y	Y	Y	Y	Y	Y
5 **Garrett**	N	Y	Y	Y	Y	Y
6 Pallone	Y	–	N	Y	Y	Y
7 **Lance**	Y	Y	Y	Y	Y	Y
8 Pascrell	+	N	N	Y	Y	Y
9 Rothman	Y	N	N	Y	Y	Y
10 Payne	?	?	?	?	?	?
11 **Frelinghuysen**	Y	Y	Y	Y	Y	Y
12 Holt	Y	N	N	Y	Y	Y
13 Sires	?	N	N	Y	Y	Y
NEW MEXICO						
1 Heinrich	?	N	N	Y	Y	Y
2 **Pearce**	N	Y	Y	Y	Y	Y
3 Luján	Y	N	N	Y	Y	Y
NEW YORK						
1 Bishop	N	N	N	Y	Y	Y
2 Israel	Y	N	N	Y	Y	Y
3 **King**	Y	Y	Y	Y	Y	Y
4 McCarthy	Y	N	N	Y	Y	Y
5 Ackerman	Y	N	N	Y	Y	Y
6 Meeks	?	N	N	Y	Y	Y
7 Crowley	Y	N	N	Y	Y	Y
8 Nadler	Y	N	N	Y	Y	Y
9 **Turner**	Y	Y	Y	Y	Y	Y
10 Towns	N	N	N	Y	Y	Y
11 Clarke	N	N	N	Y	Y	Y
12 Velázquez	N	N	N	Y	Y	Y
13 **Grimm**	Y	Y	Y	Y	Y	Y
14 Maloney	Y	N	N	Y	Y	Y
15 Rangel	?	?	?	?	?	?
16 Serrano	?	?	?	?	?	?
17 Engel	Y	N	N	Y	Y	Y
18 Lowey	Y	N	N	Y	Y	Y
19 **Hayworth**	Y	Y	Y	Y	Y	Y
20 **Gibson**	N	Y	Y	Y	Y	Y
21 Tonko	Y	N	N	Y	Y	Y
22 Hinchey	Y	N	N	Y	Y	Y
23 Owens	Y	N	N	Y	Y	Y
24 **Hanna**	N	Y	Y	Y	Y	Y
25 **Buerkle**	Y	Y	Y	Y	Y	Y
26 Hochul	Y	N	N	Y	Y	Y
27 Higgins	Y	N	N	Y	Y	Y
28 Slaughter	N	N	N	Y	Y	Y
29 **Reed**	N	Y	Y	Y	Y	Y
NORTH CAROLINA						
1 Butterfield	?	N	N	Y	Y	Y
2 **Ellmers**	Y	Y	Y	Y	Y	Y
3 **Jones**	Y	Y	Y	Y	Y	Y
4 Price	Y	N	N	Y	Y	Y

	49	50	51	52	53	54
5 **Foxx**	N	Y	Y	Y	Y	Y
6 **Coble**	Y	Y	Y	Y	Y	Y
7 McIntyre	Y	N	N	Y	Y	Y
8 Kissell	Y	N	Y	Y	Y	Y
9 **Myrick**	Y	Y	Y	Y	Y	Y
10 **McHenry**	Y	Y	Y	Y	Y	Y
11 Shuler	?	N	N	Y	Y	Y
12 Watt	Y	N	N	Y	Y	?
13 Miller	Y	N	N	Y	Y	Y
NORTH DAKOTA						
AL **Berg**	Y	Y	Y	Y	Y	Y
OHIO						
1 **Chabot**	Y	Y	Y	Y	Y	Y
2 **Schmidt**	Y	Y	Y	Y	Y	Y
3 **Turner**	Y	Y	Y	Y	Y	Y
4 **Jordan**	+	Y	Y	Y	Y	Y
5 **Latta**	Y	Y	Y	Y	Y	Y
6 **Johnson**	N	Y	Y	Y	Y	Y
7 **Austria**	?	Y	Y	Y	Y	Y
8 **Boehner**						
9 Kaptur	Y	N	N	Y	Y	Y
10 Kucinich	N	N	N	Y	Y	Y
11 Fudge	Y	N	N	Y	Y	Y
12 **Tiberi**	?	Y	Y	Y	Y	Y
13 Sutton	N	N	N	Y	Y	Y
14 **LaTourette**	?	Y	Y	Y	Y	Y
15 **Stivers**	?	Y	Y	Y	Y	Y
16 **Renacci**	N	?	Y	Y	Y	Y
17 Ryan	N	N	N	Y	Y	Y
18 **Gibbs**	Y	Y	Y	Y	Y	Y
OKLAHOMA						
1 **Sullivan**	Y	Y	Y	Y	Y	Y
2 Boren	N	Y	N	Y	Y	Y
3 **Lucas**	Y	Y	Y	Y	Y	Y
4 **Cole**	Y	Y	Y	Y	Y	Y
5 **Lankford**	Y	Y	Y	Y	Y	Y
OREGON						
1 Bonamici	Y	N	N	Y	Y	Y
2 **Walden**	Y	Y	Y	Y	Y	Y
3 Blumenauer	Y	N	N	Y	Y	Y
4 DeFazio	N	N	N	Y	Y	Y
5 Schrader	Y	N	N	Y	Y	Y
PENNSYLVANIA						
1 Brady	N	N	N	Y	Y	Y
2 Fattah	Y	N	N	Y	Y	Y
3 **Kelly**	Y	Y	Y	Y	Y	Y
4 Altmire	Y	N	N	Y	Y	Y
5 **Thompson**	Y	Y	Y	Y	Y	Y
6 **Gerlach**	?	Y	Y	Y	Y	Y
7 **Meehan**	Y	Y	Y	Y	Y	Y
8 **Fitzpatrick**	N	Y	Y	Y	Y	Y
9 **Shuster**	Y	Y	Y	Y	Y	Y
10 **Marino**	Y	Y	Y	Y	Y	Y
11 **Barletta**	Y	Y	Y	Y	Y	Y
12 Critz	N	N	N	Y	Y	Y
13 Schwartz	Y	N	N	Y	Y	Y
14 Doyle	Y	N	N	Y	Y	Y
15 **Dent**	Y	Y	Y	Y	Y	Y
16 **Pitts**	Y	?	Y	Y	Y	Y
17 Holden	Y	N	N	Y	Y	Y
18 **Murphy**	N	Y	Y	Y	Y	Y
19 **Platts**	Y	Y	Y	Y	Y	Y
RHODE ISLAND						
1 Cicilline	Y	N	N	Y	Y	Y
2 Langevin	Y	N	N	Y	Y	Y
SOUTH CAROLINA						
1 **Scott**	Y	Y	Y	Y	Y	Y
2 **Wilson**	Y	Y	Y	Y	Y	Y
3 **Duncan**	Y	Y	Y	Y	Y	Y
4 **Gowdy**	Y	Y	Y	Y	Y	Y
5 **Mulvaney**	Y	Y	Y	Y	Y	?
6 Clyburn	Y	N	N	Y	Y	Y
SOUTH DAKOTA						
AL **Noem**	?	Y	Y	Y	Y	Y
TENNESSEE						
1 **Roe**	Y	Y	Y	Y	Y	Y
2 **Duncan**	Y	Y	Y	Y	Y	Y
3 **Fleischmann**	Y	Y	Y	Y	Y	Y
4 **DesJarlais**	Y	Y	Y	Y	Y	Y
5 Cooper	Y	N	N	Y	Y	Y
6 **Black**	Y	Y	Y	Y	Y	Y
7 **Blackburn**	Y	?	Y	Y	Y	Y
8 **Fincher**	Y	Y	Y	Y	Y	Y
9 Cohen	Y	N	N	Y	Y	?

	49	50	51	52	53	54
TEXAS						
1 **Gohmert**	?	Y	Y	Y	Y	Y
2 **Poe**	N	Y	Y	Y	Y	Y
3 **Johnson, S.**	Y	Y	Y	Y	Y	Y
4 **Hall**	Y	Y	Y	Y	Y	Y
5 **Hensarling**	Y	Y	Y	Y	Y	Y
6 **Barton**	Y	Y	Y	Y	Y	Y
7 **Culberson**	?	Y	Y	Y	Y	Y
8 **Brady**	Y	Y	Y	Y	Y	Y
9 Green, A.	Y	N	N	Y	Y	Y
10 **McCaul**	Y	Y	Y	Y	Y	Y
11 **Conaway**	N	Y	Y	Y	Y	Y
12 **Granger**	Y	Y	Y	Y	Y	Y
13 **Thornberry**	Y	Y	Y	Y	Y	Y
14 **Paul**	?	?	?	?	?	?
15 Hinojosa	Y	N	N	Y	Y	Y
16 Reyes	Y	N	N	Y	Y	Y
17 **Flores**	N	Y	Y	Y	Y	Y
18 Jackson Lee	Y	N	N	Y	Y	Y
19 **Neugebauer**	Y	Y	Y	Y	Y	Y
20 Gonzalez	Y	N	N	Y	Y	Y
21 **Smith**	Y	Y	Y	Y	Y	Y
22 **Olson**	Y	Y	Y	Y	Y	Y
23 **Canseco**	Y	?	Y	Y	Y	Y
24 **Marchant**	N	Y	Y	Y	Y	Y
25 Doggett	?	?	?	?	?	?
26 **Burgess**	N	Y	Y	Y	Y	Y
27 **Farenthold**	Y	Y	Y	Y	Y	Y
28 Cuellar	Y	N	N	Y	Y	Y
29 Green, G.	N	N	N	Y	?	?
30 Johnson, E.	Y	N	N	Y	Y	Y
31 **Carter**	Y	Y	Y	Y	Y	Y
32 **Sessions**	N	Y	Y	Y	Y	Y
UTAH						
1 **Bishop**	Y	Y	Y	Y	Y	Y
2 Matheson	N	Y	Y	Y	Y	Y
3 **Chaffetz**	Y	Y	Y	Y	Y	Y
VERMONT						
AL Welch	Y	N	N	Y	Y	Y
VIRGINIA						
1 **Wittman**	N	Y	Y	Y	Y	Y
2 **Rigell**	Y	Y	Y	N	Y	Y
3 Scott	?	N	N	Y	Y	Y
4 **Forbes**	N	Y	Y	Y	Y	Y
5 **Hurt**	Y	Y	Y	Y	Y	Y
6 **Goodlatte**	Y	Y	Y	Y	Y	Y
7 **Cantor**	Y	Y	Y	Y	Y	Y
8 Moran	Y	N	N	Y	Y	Y
9 **Griffith**	Y	Y	Y	Y	Y	Y
10 **Wolf**	N	Y	N	Y	Y	Y
11 Connolly	Y	N	N	Y	Y	Y
WASHINGTON						
1 Inslee	Y	N	N	Y	Y	Y
2 Larsen	Y	N	N	Y	Y	Y
3 **Herrera Beutler**	N	Y	Y	Y	Y	Y
4 **Hastings**	Y	Y	Y	Y	Y	Y
5 **McMorris Rodgers**	Y	Y	Y	Y	Y	Y
6 Dicks	Y	N	N	Y	Y	Y
7 McDermott	N	N	N	Y	Y	Y
8 **Reichert**	Y	Y	Y	Y	Y	Y
9 Smith	Y	N	N	Y	Y	Y
WEST VIRGINIA						
1 **McKinley**	Y	Y	Y	Y	Y	Y
2 **Capito**	Y	?	Y	Y	Y	Y
3 Rahall	N	N	N	Y	Y	Y
WISCONSIN						
1 **Ryan**	Y	Y	Y	Y	Y	Y
2 Baldwin	N	N	N	Y	Y	Y
3 Kind	N	N	N	Y	Y	Y
4 Moore	N	?	?	?	?	?
5 **Sensenbrenner**	Y	Y	Y	Y	Y	Y
6 **Petri**	Y	Y	Y	Y	Y	Y
7 **Duffy**	?	?	Y	Y	Y	Y
8 **Ribble**	Y	Y	Y	Y	Y	Y
WYOMING						
AL **Lummis**	Y	Y	Y	Y	Y	Y

IN THE HOUSE | By Vote Number

55. HR 3408. Expansion of Oil and Gas Production/Keystone XL Pipeline Review. Eshoo, D-Calif., amendment that would require the Federal Energy Regulatory Commission to review the results of the Pipeline and Hazardous Materials Safety Administration study, as required by a 2012 pipeline safety law, before issuing a permit for the Keystone XL pipeline. Rejected in Committee of the Whole 173-249: R 2-231; D 171-18. Feb. 15, 2012.

56. HR 3408. Expansion of Oil and Gas Production/Domestic Use of Oil from Keystone XL. Markey, D-Mass., amendment that would ensure that if the Keystone XL pipeline is built, the oil that it transports to the Gulf of Mexico and the fuels made from that oil remain in the United States. It would allow the president to waive the requirement if exports would not increase U.S. dependence on oil or fuels that the U.S. buys from hostile or unstable nations and if exports would not lead to price increases for refiners or consumers or to a net loss of oil or fuels consumed in the United States, or if exports are needed to comply with an international treaty or other agreement. Rejected in Committee of the Whole 173-254: R 9-230; D 164-24. Feb. 15, 2012.

57. HR 3408. Expansion of Oil and Gas Production/Keystone XL Eminent Domain Restriction. Rush, D-Ill., amendment that would prohibit issuing a permit for construction or operation of the Keystone XL pipeline without conditions that restrict the ability of the permit recipient from initiating or threatening to initiate proceedings to invoke the power of eminent domain against the will of a property owner. Rejected in Committee of the Whole 149-276: R 3-235; D 146-41. Feb. 15, 2012.

58. HR 3408. Expansion of Oil and Gas Production/Iron and Steel in Construction of Keystone XL Pipeline. Doyle, D-Pa., amendment that would require that a permit for the Keystone XL pipeline not be issued or deemed issued unless the permit applicant can certify and provide adequate documentation to the Federal Energy Regulatory Commission that at least 75 percent of the iron and steel to be used in the U.S. portion of the pipeline is produced in North America. Rejected in Committee of the Whole 193-234: R 14-225; D 179-9. Feb. 15, 2012.

59. HR 3408. Expansion of Oil and Gas Production/Shale Oil Leasing Program. Polis, D-Colo., amendment that would strike language in the bill that would direct the Interior Department to conduct a shale oil leasing program. Rejected in Committee of the Whole 160-265: R 2-235; D 158-30. Feb. 15, 2012.

60. HR 3408. Expansion of Oil and Gas Production/Southern California Oil and Gas Drilling. Capps, D-Calif., amendment that would strike from the bill provisions that would allow the sale of gas and oil leases in the Southern California Planning Area in the Santa Maria and Santa Barbara/Ventura basins. It also would remove language that would provide for the sharing of revenue generated by lease sales on the outer continental shelf. Rejected in Committee of the Whole 160-267: R 2-237; D 158-30. Feb. 15, 2012.

	55	56	57	58	59	60
ALABAMA						
1 Bonner	?	N	N	N	N	N
2 Roby	N	N	N	N	N	N
3 Rogers	N	N	N	N	N	N
4 Aderholt	N	N	N	N	N	N
5 Brooks	N	N	N	N	N	N
6 Bachus	N	N	N	N	N	N
7 Sewell	Y	Y	Y	Y	Y	N
ALASKA						
AL Young	N	N	N	N	N	N
ARIZONA						
1 Gosar	N	N	N	N	N	N
2 Franks	N	N	N	N	N	N
3 Quayle	N	N	N	N	N	N
4 Pastor	Y	Y	Y	Y	N	Y
5 Schweikert	N	N	N	N	N	N
6 Flake	N	N	N	N	N	N
7 Grijalva	Y	N	Y	Y	Y	Y
8 Vacant						
ARKANSAS						
1 Crawford	N	N	N	N	N	N
2 Griffin	N	N	N	N	N	N
3 Womack	N	N	N	N	N	N
4 Ross	N	N	N	N	N	N
CALIFORNIA						
1 Thompson	Y	Y	Y	Y	Y	Y
2 Herger	N	N	N	N	N	N
3 Lungren	N	N	N	N	N	N
4 McClintock	N	N	N	N	N	N
5 Matsui	Y	Y	Y	Y	Y	Y
6 Woolsey	Y	Y	Y	Y	Y	Y
7 Miller, George	Y	Y	Y	Y	Y	Y
8 Pelosi	Y	Y	Y	Y	Y	Y
9 Lee	Y	Y	Y	Y	Y	Y
10 Garamendi	Y	Y	Y	Y	Y	Y
11 McNerney	Y	Y	Y	Y	Y	Y
12 Speier	Y	Y	Y	Y	Y	Y
13 Stark	Y	Y	Y	Y	Y	Y
14 Eshoo	Y	Y	Y	Y	Y	Y
15 Honda	Y	Y	Y	Y	Y	Y
16 Lofgren	Y	Y	Y	Y	Y	Y
17 Farr	Y	Y	Y	Y	Y	Y
18 Cardoza	Y	N	N	Y	Y	Y
19 Denham	N	N	N	N	N	N
20 Costa	N	N	N	Y	Y	Y
21 Nunes	N	N	N	N	N	N
22 McCarthy	N	N	N	N	N	N
23 Capps	Y	Y	Y	Y	Y	Y
24 Gallegly	N	N	N	N	N	N
25 McKeon	N	N	N	N	N	N
26 Dreier	N	N	N	N	N	N
27 Sherman	Y	Y	Y	Y	Y	Y
28 Berman	Y	Y	Y	Y	Y	Y
29 Schiff	Y	Y	Y	Y	Y	Y
30 Waxman	Y	Y	Y	Y	Y	Y
31 Becerra	Y	Y	Y	Y	Y	Y
32 Chu	Y	Y	Y	Y	Y	Y
33 Bass	Y	Y	Y	Y	Y	Y
34 Roybal-Allard	Y	Y	Y	Y	Y	Y
35 Waters	Y	Y	Y	Y	Y	Y
36 Hahn	Y	Y	Y	N	Y	Y
37 Richardson	Y	Y	Y	N	Y	Y
38 Napolitano	Y	Y	Y	Y	Y	Y
39 Sánchez, Linda	Y	Y	Y	Y	Y	Y
40 Royce	N	N	N	N	N	N
41 Lewis	?	N	N	N	N	N
42 Miller, Gary	N	N	N	N	N	N
43 Baca	Y	Y	Y	Y	Y	Y
44 Calvert	N	N	N	N	N	N
45 Bono Mack	N	N	N	N	N	N
46 Rohrabacher	N	N	N	N	N	N
47 Sanchez, Loretta	Y	Y	Y	Y	Y	Y
48 Campbell	?	?	?	?	?	?
49 Issa	N	N	N	N	N	N
50 Bilbray	Y	Y	Y	Y	Y	N
51 Filner	Y	Y	Y	Y	Y	Y
52 Hunter	N	N	N	N	N	N
53 Davis	Y	Y	Y	Y	Y	Y

	55	56	57	58	59	60
COLORADO						
1 DeGette	Y	Y	Y	Y	Y	Y
2 Polis	Y	Y	Y	N	Y	Y
3 Tipton	N	N	N	N	N	N
4 Gardner	N	N	N	N	N	N
5 Lamborn	N	N	N	N	N	N
6 Coffman	N	N	N	N	N	N
7 Perlmutter	Y	Y	N	Y	Y	Y
CONNECTICUT						
1 Larson	Y	Y	Y	Y	Y	Y
2 Courtney	Y	Y	Y	Y	Y	Y
3 DeLauro	Y	Y	Y	Y	Y	Y
4 Himes	Y	N	Y	Y	Y	Y
5 Murphy	Y	Y	Y	Y	Y	Y
DELAWARE						
AL Carney	Y	Y	Y	Y	Y	Y
FLORIDA						
1 Miller	N	N	N	N	N	N
2 Southerland	N	N	N	N	N	N
3 Brown	Y	Y	Y	Y	Y	Y
4 Crenshaw	N	N	N	N	N	N
5 Nugent	N	N	N	N	N	N
6 Stearns	N	N	N	N	N	N
7 Mica	N	N	N	N	N	N
8 Webster	N	N	N	N	N	N
9 Bilirakis	N	N	N	N	N	N
10 Young	N	Y	N	Y	N	N
11 Castor	Y	Y	Y	Y	Y	Y
12 Ross	N	N	N	N	N	N
13 Buchanan	N	N	N	N	N	N
14 Mack	N	N	N	N	N	N
15 Posey	N	N	N	N	N	N
16 Rooney	N	N	N	N	N	N
17 Wilson	Y	Y	Y	Y	Y	Y
18 Ros-Lehtinen	N	N	N	N	N	N
19 Deutch	Y	Y	Y	Y	Y	Y
20 Wasserman Schultz	Y	Y	Y	Y	Y	Y
21 Diaz-Balart	N	N	N	N	N	N
22 West	Y	Y	Y	Y	Y	Y
23 Hastings	Y	Y	Y	Y	Y	Y
24 Adams	N	N	N	N	N	N
25 Rivera	N	N	N	N	N	N
GEORGIA						
1 Kingston	N	N	N	N	N	N
2 Bishop	Y	Y	N	Y	Y	Y
3 Westmoreland	N	N	?	N	N	N
4 Johnson	Y	Y	Y	Y	Y	Y
5 Lewis	Y	Y	Y	Y	Y	Y
6 Price	N	N	N	N	N	N
7 Woodall	N	N	N	N	N	N
8 Scott, A.	N	N	N	N	N	N
9 Graves	N	N	N	N	N	N
10 Broun	N	N	N	N	N	N
11 Gingrey	N	N	N	N	N	N
12 Barrow	N	Y	N	Y	Y	Y
13 Scott, D.	Y	Y	Y	Y	Y	Y
HAWAII						
1 Hanabusa	Y	Y	Y	Y	Y	Y
2 Hirono	Y	Y	Y	Y	Y	Y
IDAHO						
1 Labrador	N	N	N	N	N	N
2 Simpson	N	N	N	N	N	N
ILLINOIS						
1 Rush	Y	Y	Y	Y	Y	Y
2 Jackson	Y	Y	Y	Y	Y	Y
3 Lipinski	N	Y	N	Y	Y	Y
4 Gutierrez	Y	Y	Y	Y	Y	Y
5 Quigley	Y	Y	Y	Y	Y	Y
6 Roskam	N	N	N	N	N	N
7 Davis	Y	Y	Y	Y	Y	Y
8 Walsh	N	N	N	N	N	N
9 Schakowsky	Y	Y	Y	Y	Y	Y
10 Dold	N	N	N	N	N	N
11 Kinzinger	N	N	N	N	N	N
12 Costello	Y	N	Y	N	Y	Y
13 Biggert	N	N	N	N	N	N
14 Hultgren	N	N	N	N	N	N
15 Johnson	N	N	N	N	N	Y

KEY Republicans Democrats

Y Voted for (yea)	**X** Paired against
# Paired for	**–** Announced against
+ Announced for	**P** Voted "present"
N Voted against (nay)	

C Voted "present" to avoid possible conflict of interest

? Did not vote or otherwise make a position known

	55	56	57	58	59	60
16 **Manzullo**	N	N	N	N	N	N
17 **Schilling**	N	N	N	N	N	N
18 **Schock**	N	N	N	N	N	N
19 **Shimkus**	N	N	N	N	N	N
INDIANA						
1 Visclosky	Y	Y	N	Y	Y	Y
2 Donnelly	N	Y	N	Y	N	N
3 **Stutzman**	N	N	N	N	N	N
4 **Rokita**	N	N	N	N	N	N
5 **Burton**	N	N	N	N	N	N
6 **Pence**	N	N	N	N	N	N
7 Carson	Y	Y	Y	Y	Y	Y
8 **Bucshon**	N	N	N	N	N	N
9 **Young**	N	N	N	N	N	N
IOWA						
1 Braley	Y	Y	N	Y	Y	Y
2 Loebsack	Y	Y	Y	Y	N	Y
3 Boswell	Y	Y	Y	Y	N	N
4 **Latham**	N	N	N	N	N	N
5 **King**	N	N	N	N	N	N
KANSAS						
1 **Huelskamp**	N	N	N	N	N	N
2 **Jenkins**	N	N	N	N	N	N
3 **Yoder**	N	N	N	N	N	N
4 **Pompeo**	N	N	N	N	N	N
KENTUCKY						
1 **Whitfield**	N	N	N	N	N	N
2 **Guthrie**	N	N	N	N	N	N
3 Yarmuth	Y	Y	Y	Y	Y	N
4 **Davis**	N	N	N	N	N	N
5 **Rogers**	N	N	N	N	N	N
6 Chandler	N	Y	N	Y	N	N
LOUISIANA						
1 **Scalise**	N	N	N	N	N	N
2 Richmond	Y	N	Y	Y	Y	Y
3 **Landry**	N	N	N	N	N	N
4 **Fleming**	N	N	N	N	N	N
5 **Alexander**	N	N	N	N	N	N
6 **Cassidy**	N	N	N	N	N	N
7 **Boustany**	N	N	N	N	N	N
MAINE						
1 Pingree	Y	Y	Y	Y	Y	Y
2 Michaud	Y	Y	Y	Y	Y	N
MARYLAND						
1 **Harris**	Y	N	N	N	N	N
2 Ruppersberger	Y	Y	Y	Y	N	Y
3 Sarbanes	Y	Y	Y	Y	Y	Y
4 Edwards	Y	Y	Y	Y	Y	Y
5 Hoyer	Y	Y	Y	Y	Y	Y
6 **Bartlett**	N	N	N	N	N	N
7 Cummings	Y	Y	Y	Y	Y	Y
8 Van Hollen	Y	Y	Y	Y	Y	Y
MASSACHUSETTS						
1 Olver	Y	Y	Y	Y	Y	Y
2 Neal	Y	Y	Y	Y	Y	Y
3 McGovern	Y	Y	Y	Y	Y	Y
4 Frank	Y	N	N	Y	Y	Y
5 Tsongas	Y	Y	Y	Y	Y	Y
6 Tierney	Y	Y	Y	Y	Y	Y
7 Markey	Y	Y	Y	Y	Y	Y
8 Capuano	Y	Y	Y	Y	Y	Y
9 Lynch	N	Y	N	Y	Y	Y
10 Keating	Y	Y	Y	Y	Y	Y
MICHIGAN						
1 **Benishek**	N	N	N	N	N	N
2 **Huizenga**	N	N	N	N	N	N
3 **Amash**	N	N	Y	N	N	N
4 **Camp**	N	N	N	N	N	N
5 Kildee	Y	Y	Y	Y	Y	Y
6 **Upton**	N	N	N	N	N	N
7 **Walberg**	N	N	N	N	N	N
8 **Rogers**	N	N	N	N	N	N
9 Peters	Y	Y	Y	Y	Y	Y
10 **Miller**	N	N	N	N	N	N
11 **McCotter**	N	N	N	N	N	N
12 Levin	Y	Y	Y	Y	Y	Y
13 Clarke	Y	N	Y	Y	Y	Y
14 Conyers	Y	Y	Y	Y	Y	Y
15 Dingell	Y	N	Y	Y	Y	N
MINNESOTA						
1 Walz	N	Y	N	Y	Y	N
2 **Kline**	N	N	N	N	N	N
3 **Paulsen**	N	N	N	N	N	N
4 McCollum	Y	Y	Y	Y	Y	Y

	55	56	57	58	59	60
5 Ellison	Y	Y	Y	Y	Y	Y
6 **Bachmann**	N	N	N	N	N	N
7 Peterson	N	N	N	N	N	N
8 **Cravaack**	N	N	N	N	N	N
MISSISSIPPI						
1 **Nunnelee**	N	N	N	N	N	N
2 Thompson	Y	N	Y	Y	N	N
3 **Harper**	N	N	N	N	N	N
4 **Palazzo**	–	N	N	N	N	N
MISSOURI						
1 Clay	Y	Y	Y	Y	Y	Y
2 **Akin**	N	N	N	N	N	N
3 Carnahan	Y	Y	Y	Y	Y	Y
4 **Hartzler**	N	N	N	N	N	N
5 Cleaver	Y	Y	Y	Y	Y	Y
6 **Graves**	N	N	N	N	N	N
7 **Long**	N	N	N	N	N	N
8 **Emerson**	N	N	N	N	N	N
9 **Luetkemeyer**	N	N	N	N	N	N
MONTANA						
AL **Rehberg**	N	N	N	N	N	N
NEBRASKA						
1 **Fortenberry**	?	N	Y	Y	N	N
2 **Terry**	N	N	N	N	N	N
3 **Smith**	N	N	N	N	N	N
NEVADA						
1 Berkley	Y	Y	Y	Y	Y	Y
2 **Amodei**	N	N	N	N	N	N
3 **Heck**	N	N	N	N	N	N
NEW HAMPSHIRE						
1 **Guinta**	N	N	N	N	N	N
2 **Bass**	N	N	N	N	N	N
NEW JERSEY						
1 Andrews	Y	Y	Y	Y	Y	Y
2 **LoBiondo**	N	Y	N	Y	N	N
3 **Runyan**	N	N	N	Y	N	N
4 **Smith**	N	N	N	N	N	N
5 **Garrett**	N	N	N	N	N	N
6 Pallone	Y	Y	Y	Y	Y	Y
7 **Lance**	N	N	N	N	N	N
8 Pascrell	Y	Y	Y	Y	Y	Y
9 Rothman	Y	Y	Y	Y	Y	Y
10 Payne	?	?	?	?	?	?
11 **Frelinghuysen**	N	N	N	N	N	N
12 Holt	Y	Y	Y	Y	Y	Y
13 Sires	Y	Y	Y	Y	Y	Y
NEW MEXICO						
1 Heinrich	Y	Y	Y	Y	Y	Y
2 **Pearce**	N	N	N	N	N	N
3 Luján	Y	Y	Y	Y	Y	Y
NEW YORK						
1 Bishop	Y	Y	Y	Y	Y	Y
2 Israel	Y	Y	Y	Y	Y	Y
3 **King**	N	Y	N	N	N	N
4 McCarthy	Y	Y	Y	Y	Y	Y
5 Ackerman	Y	Y	Y	Y	Y	Y
6 Meeks	Y	Y	Y	Y	Y	Y
7 Crowley	Y	Y	Y	Y	Y	Y
8 Nadler	Y	Y	Y	Y	Y	Y
9 **Turner**	N	Y	N	N	N	N
10 Towns	Y	Y	Y	Y	Y	Y
11 Clarke	Y	Y	Y	Y	Y	Y
12 Velázquez	Y	Y	Y	Y	Y	Y
13 **Grimm**	N	N	N	N	N	N
14 Maloney	Y	Y	Y	Y	Y	Y
15 Rangel	?	?	?	?	?	?
16 Serrano	?	?	?	?	?	?
17 Engel	Y	Y	Y	Y	Y	Y
18 Lowey	Y	Y	Y	Y	Y	Y
19 **Hayworth**	N	N	N	N	N	N
20 **Gibson**	Y	Y	Y	Y	N	N
21 Tonko	Y	Y	Y	Y	Y	Y
22 Hinchey	Y	Y	Y	Y	Y	Y
23 Owens	N	Y	N	Y	N	Y
24 **Hanna**	N	N	N	N	N	N
25 **Buerkle**	N	N	N	N	N	N
26 Hochul	Y	Y	N	Y	N	N
27 Higgins	Y	Y	N	Y	Y	Y
28 Slaughter	Y	+	+	+	+	+
29 **Reed**	N	N	N	N	N	N
NORTH CAROLINA						
1 Butterfield	Y	Y	Y	Y	Y	Y
2 **Ellmers**	N	N	N	N	N	N
3 **Jones**	N	Y	N	Y	N	N
4 Price	Y	Y	Y	Y	Y	Y

	55	56	57	58	59	60
5 **Foxx**	N	N	N	N	N	N
6 **Coble**	N	N	N	N	N	N
7 McIntyre	Y	Y	N	Y	N	N
8 Kissell	Y	Y	Y	Y	N	Y
9 **Myrick**	N	N	N	N	N	N
10 **McHenry**	N	N	N	N	N	N
11 Shuler	N	Y	N	Y	Y	N
12 Watt	Y	Y	Y	Y	Y	Y
13 Miller	Y	Y	N	Y	Y	Y
NORTH DAKOTA						
AL **Berg**	N	N	N	N	N	N
OHIO						
1 **Chabot**	N	N	N	N	N	N
2 **Schmidt**	N	N	N	N	N	N
3 **Turner**	N	N	N	N	N	N
4 **Jordan**	N	N	N	N	N	N
5 **Latta**	N	N	N	N	N	N
6 **Johnson**	N	N	N	Y	N	N
7 **Austria**	N	N	N	N	N	N
8 **Boehner**						
9 Kaptur	Y	Y	Y	Y	Y	Y
10 Kucinich	Y	Y	Y	Y	Y	Y
11 Fudge	Y	Y	Y	Y	Y	Y
12 **Tiberi**	N	N	N	N	N	N
13 Sutton	Y	Y	Y	Y	Y	Y
14 **LaTourette**	N	N	N	Y	N	N
15 **Stivers**	N	N	N	Y	N	N
16 **Renacci**	N	N	N	Y	N	N
17 Ryan	Y	Y	Y	Y	Y	Y
18 **Gibbs**	N	N	N	N	N	N
OKLAHOMA						
1 **Sullivan**	?	N	N	N	N	N
2 Boren	N	N	N	N	N	N
3 **Lucas**	N	N	N	N	N	N
4 **Cole**	N	N	N	N	N	N
5 **Lankford**	N	N	N	N	N	N
OREGON						
1 Bonamici	Y	Y	Y	Y	Y	Y
2 **Walden**	N	N	N	N	N	N
3 Blumenauer	Y	Y	N	Y	Y	Y
4 DeFazio	Y	Y	Y	Y	Y	Y
5 Schrader	Y	Y	Y	Y	Y	Y
PENNSYLVANIA						
1 Brady	Y	Y	N	Y	Y	Y
2 Fattah	Y	Y	N	Y	Y	Y
3 **Kelly**	N	N	N	N	N	N
4 Altmire	N	Y	N	Y	N	N
5 **Thompson**	N	N	N	N	N	N
6 **Gerlach**	N	Y	N	N	N	N
7 **Meehan**	N	N	N	Y	N	N
8 **Fitzpatrick**	N	Y	N	Y	N	N
9 **Shuster**	N	N	N	N	?	N
10 **Marino**	N	N	N	N	N	N
11 **Barletta**	N	N	N	N	N	N
12 Critz	N	N	N	Y	N	N
13 Schwartz	Y	Y	Y	Y	Y	Y
14 Doyle	Y	N	N	Y	Y	Y
15 **Dent**	N	N	N	Y	N	N
16 **Pitts**	N	N	N	N	N	N
17 Holden	Y	Y	N	Y	N	N
18 **Murphy**	N	N	N	N	N	N
19 **Platts**	N	Y	N	N	N	N
RHODE ISLAND						
1 Cicilline	Y	Y	Y	Y	Y	Y
2 Langevin	Y	Y	Y	Y	Y	Y
SOUTH CAROLINA						
1 **Scott**	N	N	N	N	N	N
2 **Wilson**	N	N	N	N	N	N
3 **Duncan**	N	N	N	N	N	N
4 **Gowdy**	N	N	N	N	N	N
5 **Mulvaney**	N	N	N	N	N	N
6 Clyburn	Y	Y	Y	Y	Y	Y
SOUTH DAKOTA						
AL **Noem**	N	N	N	N	N	N
TENNESSEE						
1 **Roe**	N	N	N	N	N	N
2 **Duncan**	N	N	N	N	N	N
3 **Fleischmann**	N	N	N	N	N	N
4 **DesJarlais**	N	N	N	N	N	N
5 Cooper	N	N	N	N	Y	N
6 **Black**	N	N	N	N	N	N
7 **Blackburn**	N	N	N	N	N	N
8 **Fincher**	N	N	N	N	N	N
9 Cohen	Y	Y	Y	Y	Y	Y

	55	56	57	58	59	60
TEXAS						
1 **Gohmert**	N	N	N	N	N	N
2 **Poe**	N	N	N	N	N	N
3 **Johnson, S.**	N	N	N	N	N	N
4 **Hall**	N	N	N	N	N	N
5 **Hensarling**	N	N	N	N	N	N
6 **Barton**	N	N	N	N	N	N
7 **Culberson**	N	N	N	N	N	N
8 **Brady**	N	N	N	N	?	N
9 Green, A.	Y	Y	N	Y	N	N
10 **McCaul**	N	N	N	N	N	N
11 **Conaway**	N	N	N	N	N	N
12 **Granger**	N	N	N	N	N	N
13 **Thornberry**	N	N	N	N	N	N
14 **Paul**	?	?	?	?	?	?
15 Hinojosa	Y	N	Y	Y	N	N
16 Reyes	N	Y	Y	Y	Y	Y
17 **Flores**	?	N	N	N	N	N
18 Jackson Lee	Y	Y	N	Y	N	N
19 **Neugebauer**	N	N	N	N	N	N
20 Gonzalez	Y	N	N	Y	N	N
21 **Smith**	N	N	N	N	N	N
22 **Olson**	N	N	N	N	N	N
23 **Canseco**	N	N	N	N	N	N
24 **Marchant**	N	N	N	N	N	N
25 Doggett	Y	Y	?	Y	Y	Y
26 **Burgess**	N	N	N	N	N	N
27 **Farenthold**	N	N	N	N	N	N
28 Cuellar	Y	N	N	N	N	N
29 Green, G.	N	N	N	Y	N	N
30 Johnson, E.	Y	Y	Y	Y	Y	Y
31 **Carter**	N	N	N	N	N	N
32 **Sessions**	N	N	N	N	N	N
UTAH						
1 **Bishop**	N	N	N	N	N	N
2 Matheson	N	N	N	N	N	N
3 **Chaffetz**	N	N	N	N	N	N
VERMONT						
AL Welch	Y	Y	Y	Y	Y	Y
VIRGINIA						
1 **Wittman**	N	N	N	N	N	N
2 **Rigell**	N	N	N	N	N	N
3 Scott	Y	N	Y	Y	Y	Y
4 **Forbes**	N	N	N	N	N	N
5 **Hurt**	N	N	N	N	N	N
6 **Goodlatte**	N	N	N	N	N	N
7 **Cantor**	N	N	N	N	N	N
8 Moran	Y	Y	Y	Y	Y	Y
9 **Griffith**	N	N	N	N	N	N
10 **Wolf**	N	N	N	N	N	N
11 Connolly	Y	Y	Y	Y	Y	Y
WASHINGTON						
1 Inslee	Y	N	N	Y	Y	Y
2 Larsen	Y	N	N	Y	Y	Y
3 **Herrera Beutler**	N	N	N	N	N	N
4 **Hastings**	N	N	N	N	N	N
5 **McMorris Rodgers**	N	N	N	N	N	N
6 Dicks	Y	Y	Y	Y	N	Y
7 McDermott	Y	Y	Y	Y	Y	Y
8 **Reichert**	N	N	N	N	Y	Y
9 Smith	Y	Y	Y	Y	Y	Y
WEST VIRGINIA						
1 **McKinley**	N	N	N	N	N	N
2 **Capito**	N	N	N	N	N	N
3 Rahall	Y	Y	N	Y	Y	Y
WISCONSIN						
1 **Ryan**	N	N	N	N	N	N
2 Baldwin	Y	Y	Y	Y	Y	Y
3 Kind	Y	Y	Y	Y	N	Y
4 Moore	Y	Y	Y	Y	Y	Y
5 **Sensenbrenner**	N	N	N	N	N	N
6 **Petri**	N	N	N	N	N	N
7 **Duffy**	N	N	N	N	N	N
8 **Ribble**	N	N	N	N	N	N
WYOMING						
AL **Lummis**	N	N	N	N	N	N

IN THE HOUSE | By Vote Number

61. HR 3408. Expansion of Oil and Gas Production/East Coast Offshore Drilling. Bishop, D-N.Y., amendment that would prohibit oil and natural gas lease sales in any area of the outer continental shelf if any of the states of New York, New Jersey, Connecticut, Rhode Island, Massachusetts, New Hampshire or Maine is affected. Rejected in Committee of the Whole 169-257: R 7-232; D 162-25. Feb. 15, 2012.

62. HR 3408. Expansion of Oil and Gas Production/Revenue-Sharing Cap Increase. Landry, R-La., amendment that would raise the annual cap on offshore energy revenue that Gulf Coast states may share to $750 million starting in fiscal 2023. It would keep the current $500 million cap in place through fiscal 2022. Adopted in Committee of the Whole 266-159: R 228-10; D 38-149. Feb. 15, 2012.

63. HR 3408. Expansion of Oil and Gas Production/Oil Spill Estimate. Deutch, D-Fla., amendment that would require a person to include in the application for a drilling lease an estimate of the economic impact, including job losses, resulting from a worst-case discharge of oil from facilities operating under the lease. Rejected in Committee of the Whole 188-236: R 14-225; D 174-11. Feb. 15, 2012.

64. HR 3408. Expansion of Oil and Gas Production/Drilling off Northern California Coast. Thompson, D-Calif., amendment that would clarify that offshore drilling would not be allowed in areas west of Marin, Sonoma, Mendocino, Humboldt or Del Norte counties in California. Rejected in Committee of the Whole 167-253: R 5-229; D 162-24. Feb. 16, 2012.

65. HR 3408. Expansion of Oil and Gas Production/Safety Standards. Hanabusa, D-Hawaii, amendment that would require offshore oil and gas leases issued under the bill to meet certain safety standards. Rejected in Committee of the Whole 189-228: R 12-220; D 177-8. Feb. 16, 2012.

66. HR 3408. Expansion of Oil and Gas Production/Renewable-Energy Projects. Hastings, R-Wash., amendment that would require federal agencies in reviewing proposals and considering public comment for renewable-energy projects on federal land and waters to consider only the proposed action or an alternative of no action during the environmental review process. Adopted in Committee of the Whole 250-171: R 232-4; D 18-167. Feb. 16, 2012.

	61	62	63	64	65	66
ALABAMA						
1 Bonner	N	Y	N	N	N	Y
2 Roby	N	Y	N	N	N	Y
3 Rogers	N	Y	N	N	N	Y
4 Aderholt	N	Y	N	N	N	Y
5 Brooks	N	Y	N	N	N	Y
6 Bachus	N	Y	N	N	N	Y
7 Sewell	Y	Y	Y	Y	Y	N
ALASKA						
AL Young	N	Y	N	N	N	Y
ARIZONA						
1 Gosar	N	Y	N	?	N	Y
2 Franks	N	Y	N	N	N	Y
3 Quayle	N	Y	N	N	N	Y
4 Pastor	Y	Y	Y	Y	Y	N
5 Schweikert	N	Y	N	N	N	Y
6 Flake	N	Y	N	N	N	Y
7 Grijalva	Y	N	Y	Y	Y	N
8 Vacant						
ARKANSAS						
1 Crawford	N	Y	N	N	N	Y
2 Griffin	N	Y	N	N	N	Y
3 Womack	N	Y	N	N	N	Y
4 Ross	N	Y	N	N	N	Y
CALIFORNIA						
1 Thompson	Y	N	Y	Y	Y	N
2 Herger	N	Y	N	N	N	Y
3 Lungren	N	Y	N	N	N	Y
4 McClintock	N	Y	N	N	N	Y
5 Matsui	Y	N	Y	Y	Y	N
6 Woolsey	Y	N	Y	Y	Y	N
7 Miller, George	Y	N	Y	Y	Y	N
8 Pelosi	Y	N	Y	Y	Y	N
9 Lee	Y	N	Y	Y	Y	N
10 Garamendi	Y	Y	Y	Y	Y	N
11 McNerney	Y	N	Y	Y	Y	N
12 Speier	Y	N	Y	Y	Y	N
13 Stark	Y	N	Y	Y	Y	N
14 Eshoo	Y	N	Y	Y	Y	N
15 Honda	Y	N	Y	Y	Y	N
16 Lofgren	Y	N	Y	Y	Y	N
17 Farr	Y	N	Y	Y	Y	N
18 Cardoza	Y	N	Y	Y	Y	Y
19 Denham	N	Y	N	N	N	Y
20 Costa	N	N	N	N	N	N
21 Nunes	N	Y	N	N	N	Y
22 McCarthy	N	Y	N	N	N	Y
23 Capps	Y	N	Y	Y	Y	N
24 Gallegly	N	Y	N	N	N	Y
25 McKeon	N	Y	N	N	N	Y
26 Dreier	N	Y	N	N	N	Y
27 Sherman	Y	N	Y	Y	Y	N
28 Berman	Y	N	Y	Y	Y	N
29 Schiff	Y	N	Y	Y	Y	N
30 Waxman	Y	N	Y	Y	Y	N
31 Becerra	Y	N	Y	Y	Y	N
32 Chu	Y	N	Y	Y	Y	N
33 Bass	Y	N	Y	Y	Y	N
34 Roybal-Allard	Y	N	Y	Y	Y	N
35 Waters	Y	N	Y	Y	Y	N
36 Hahn	Y	N	Y	Y	Y	N
37 Richardson	Y	Y	Y	Y	Y	N
38 Napolitano	Y	N	Y	Y	Y	N
39 Sánchez, Linda	Y	N	Y	Y	Y	N
40 Royce	N	Y	N	N	N	Y
41 Lewis	N	Y	N	N	N	Y
42 Miller, Gary	N	Y	N	N	N	Y
43 Baca	Y	N	Y	N	Y	Y
44 Calvert	N	Y	N	N	N	Y
45 Bono Mack	N	Y	N	?	?	?
46 Rohrabacher	N	Y	N	N	N	Y
47 Sanchez, Loretta	Y	N	Y	?	?	?
48 Campbell	?	?	?	?	?	?
49 Issa	N	Y	N	N	N	Y
50 Bilbray	N	Y	N	N	N	Y
51 Filner	Y	N	Y	Y	Y	N
52 Hunter	N	Y	N	N	N	Y
53 Davis	Y	N	Y	Y	Y	N

	61	62	63	64	65	66
COLORADO						
1 DeGette	Y	N	Y	Y	Y	N
2 Polis	Y	N	Y	Y	Y	N
3 Tipton	N	N	N	N	N	Y
4 Gardner	N	Y	N	N	N	Y
5 Lamborn	N	Y	N	N	N	Y
6 Coffman	N	Y	N	N	N	Y
7 Perlmutter	Y	N	Y	Y	Y	Y
CONNECTICUT						
1 Larson	Y	Y	Y	Y	Y	N
2 Courtney	Y	N	Y	Y	Y	N
3 DeLauro	Y	N	Y	Y	Y	N
4 Himes	Y	N	?	Y	Y	N
5 Murphy	Y	N	Y	Y	Y	N
DELAWARE						
AL Carney	Y	N	Y	Y	Y	N
FLORIDA						
1 Miller	N	Y	N	N	N	Y
2 Southerland	N	Y	N	N	N	Y
3 Brown	Y	Y	Y	Y	Y	N
4 Crenshaw	N	Y	N	N	N	Y
5 Nugent	N	Y	N	N	N	Y
6 Stearns	N	Y	N	N	N	Y
7 Mica	N	Y	N	N	N	Y
8 Webster	N	Y	N	N	N	Y
9 Bilirakis	N	Y	N	–	N	Y
10 Young	N	Y	N	Y	Y	N
11 Castor	Y	N	Y	Y	Y	N
12 Ross	N	Y	N	N	N	Y
13 Buchanan	N	Y	N	?	N	Y
14 Mack	N	Y	N	?	?	?
15 Posey	N	Y	N	N	N	Y
16 Rooney	N	Y	N	N	N	Y
17 Wilson	Y	Y	Y	Y	Y	N
18 Ros-Lehtinen	N	Y	N	Y	Y	Y
19 Deutch	Y	N	Y	Y	Y	N
20 Wasserman Schultz	Y	N	Y	Y	Y	N
21 Diaz-Balart	N	Y	N	N	N	Y
22 West	N	Y	N	N	N	Y
23 Hastings	Y	N	Y	Y	Y	N
24 Adams	N	Y	N	N	N	Y
25 Rivera	N	Y	N	N	N	Y
GEORGIA						
1 Kingston	N	Y	N	N	N	Y
2 Bishop	N	Y	Y	N	Y	Y
3 Westmoreland	N	Y	N	N	N	Y
4 Johnson	Y	N	Y	Y	Y	N
5 Lewis	Y	N	Y	Y	Y	N
6 Price	N	Y	N	N	N	Y
7 Woodall	N	Y	N	N	N	Y
8 Scott, A.	N	Y	N	N	N	Y
9 Graves	Y	Y	N	N	N	Y
10 Broun	N	Y	N	N	N	Y
11 Gingrey	N	?	N	N	N	Y
12 Barrow	N	N	N	Y	Y	Y
13 Scott, D.	Y	Y	Y	Y	Y	N
HAWAII						
1 Hanabusa	Y	Y	Y	Y	Y	N
2 Hirono	Y	N	Y	Y	Y	N
IDAHO						
1 Labrador	N	Y	N	N	N	Y
2 Simpson	N	Y	N	N	N	Y
ILLINOIS						
1 Rush	Y	Y	Y	Y	Y	N
2 Jackson	Y	Y	Y	Y	Y	N
3 Lipinski	Y	N	Y	Y	Y	N
4 Gutierrez	Y	N	Y	Y	Y	N
5 Quigley	Y	N	Y	Y	Y	N
6 Roskam	N	Y	N	N	N	Y
7 Davis	Y	Y	Y	Y	Y	N
8 Walsh	N	Y	N	N	N	Y
9 Schakowsky	Y	N	Y	Y	Y	N
10 Dold	N	Y	N	Y	Y	N
11 Kinzinger	N	Y	N	N	N	Y
12 Costello	Y	N	Y	Y	Y	N
13 Biggert	N	N	N	N	N	Y
14 Hultgren	N	Y	N	N	N	Y
15 Johnson	N	N	N	N	N	Y

KEY   Republicans   Democrats

Y Voted for (yea)	X Paired against	C Voted "present" to avoid possible conflict of interest
# Paired for	– Announced against	
+ Announced for	P Voted "present"	? Did not vote or otherwise make a position known
N Voted against (nay)		

	61	62	63	64	65	66
16 **Manzullo**	N	Y	N	N	N	Y
17 **Schilling**	N	Y	N	N	N	Y
18 **Schock**	N	Y	N	N	N	Y
19 **Shimkus**	N	Y	N	N	N	Y
INDIANA						
1 Visclosky	Y	N	Y	Y	Y	N
2 Donnelly	N	N	Y	N	N	Y
3 **Stutzman**	N	Y	N	N	N	Y
4 **Rokita**	N	Y	N	N	N	Y
5 **Burton**	N	Y	N	N	N	Y
6 **Pence**	N	Y	N	N	N	Y
7 Carson	Y	N	Y	Y	Y	N
8 **Bucshon**	N	Y	N	N	N	Y
9 **Young**	N	Y	N	N	N	Y
IOWA						
1 Braley	N	N	Y	Y	Y	N
2 Loebsack	N	N	Y	Y	Y	Y
3 Boswell	N	N	Y	N	Y	Y
4 **Latham**	N	Y	N	N	N	Y
5 **King**	N	Y	N	N	N	Y
KANSAS						
1 **Huelskamp**	N	Y	N	N	N	Y
2 **Jenkins**	N	Y	N	N	N	Y
3 **Yoder**	N	Y	N	N	N	Y
4 **Pompeo**	N	Y	N	N	N	Y
KENTUCKY						
1 **Whitfield**	N	Y	N	N	N	Y
2 **Guthrie**	N	Y	N	N	N	Y
3 Yarmuth	N	N	Y	Y	Y	N
4 **Davis**	N	Y	N	N	N	Y
5 **Rogers**	N	Y	N	N	N	Y
6 Chandler	Y	N	Y	N	Y	N
LOUISIANA						
1 **Scalise**	N	Y	N	N	N	Y
2 Richmond	Y	Y	Y	Y	Y	N
3 **Landry**	N	Y	N	N	N	Y
4 **Fleming**	N	Y	N	N	N	Y
5 **Alexander**	N	Y	N	N	N	Y
6 **Cassidy**	N	Y	N	N	N	Y
7 **Boustany**	N	Y	N	N	N	Y
MAINE						
1 Pingree	Y	N	Y	Y	Y	N
2 Michaud	N	Y	Y	N	Y	N
MARYLAND						
1 **Harris**	N	Y	N	N	?	N
2 Ruppersberger	Y	N	Y	Y	Y	N
3 Sarbanes	Y	N	Y	Y	Y	N
4 Edwards	Y	N	Y	Y	Y	N
5 Hoyer	Y	N	Y	Y	Y	N
6 **Bartlett**	N	Y	N	N	N	Y
7 Cummings	Y	Y	Y	Y	Y	N
8 Van Hollen	Y	N	Y	Y	Y	N
MASSACHUSETTS						
1 Olver	Y	N	Y	Y	Y	N
2 Neal	Y	N	Y	Y	Y	N
3 McGovern	Y	N	Y	Y	Y	N
4 Frank	Y	N	Y	Y	Y	N
5 Tsongas	Y	N	Y	Y	Y	N
6 Tierney	Y	N	Y	Y	Y	N
7 Markey	Y	N	Y	Y	Y	N
8 Capuano	Y	N	Y	Y	Y	N
9 Lynch	Y	N	Y	Y	Y	N
10 Keating	Y	N	Y	Y	Y	N
MICHIGAN						
1 **Benishek**	N	Y	N	N	N	Y
2 **Huizenga**	N	Y	N	N	N	Y
3 **Amash**	N	Y	N	N	N	N
4 **Camp**	N	Y	N	N	N	Y
5 Kildee	Y	N	Y	Y	Y	N
6 **Upton**	N	Y	N	N	N	Y
7 **Walberg**	N	Y	N	N	N	Y
8 **Rogers**	N	Y	N	N	N	Y
9 Peters	Y	N	Y	Y	Y	N
10 **Miller**	N	N	N	N	N	Y
11 **McCotter**	N	Y	N	N	N	Y
12 Levin	Y	N	Y	Y	Y	N
13 Clarke	Y	N	Y	Y	Y	N
14 Conyers	Y	N	Y	Y	Y	N
15 Dingell	Y	N	Y	Y	Y	N
MINNESOTA						
1 Walz	N	N	Y	N	Y	N
2 **Kline**	N	Y	N	N	N	Y
3 **Paulsen**	N	Y	N	N	Y	Y
4 McCollum	Y	N	Y	Y	Y	N

	61	62	63	64	65	66
5 Ellison	Y	N	Y	Y	Y	N
6 **Bachmann**	N	Y	N	N	N	Y
7 Peterson	N	N	N	N	N	Y
8 **Cravaack**	N	Y	N	N	N	Y
MISSISSIPPI						
1 **Nunnelee**	N	Y	N	N	N	Y
2 Thompson	Y	Y	Y	Y	Y	N
3 **Harper**	N	Y	N	N	N	Y
4 **Palazzo**	N	Y	N	N	N	Y
MISSOURI						
1 Clay	Y	Y	Y	Y	Y	N
2 **Akin**	N	Y	N	N	N	Y
3 Carnahan	Y	N	Y	Y	Y	N
4 **Hartzler**	N	Y	N	N	N	Y
5 Cleaver	+	+	+	?	?	?
6 **Graves**	N	Y	N	N	N	Y
7 **Long**	N	Y	N	N	N	Y
8 **Emerson**	N	Y	N	N	N	Y
9 **Luetkemeyer**	N	Y	N	N	N	Y
MONTANA						
AL **Rehberg**	N	Y	N	N	N	Y
NEBRASKA						
1 **Fortenberry**	N	Y	N	N	N	Y
2 **Terry**	N	Y	N	N	N	Y
3 **Smith**	N	Y	N	N	N	Y
NEVADA						
1 Berkley	Y	N	Y	Y	Y	N
2 **Amodei**	N	Y	N	N	N	Y
3 **Heck**	N	Y	N	N	N	Y
NEW HAMPSHIRE						
1 **Guinta**	N	Y	N	N	N	Y
2 **Bass**	N	N	N	N	N	N
NEW JERSEY						
1 Andrews	Y	N	Y	Y	Y	N
2 **LoBiondo**	Y	N	Y	N	Y	Y
3 **Runyan**	Y	Y	N	N	N	Y
4 **Smith**	Y	N	Y	N	Y	Y
5 **Garrett**	N	Y	N	N	N	Y
6 Pallone	Y	N	Y	Y	Y	N
7 **Lance**	Y	Y	N	N	N	Y
8 Pascrell	Y	N	Y	Y	Y	?
9 Rothman	Y	N	Y	Y	Y	N
10 Payne	?	?	?	?	?	?
11 **Frelinghuysen**	Y	Y	N	N	N	Y
12 Holt	Y	N	Y	Y	Y	N
13 Sires	Y	N	Y	Y	Y	N
NEW MEXICO						
1 Heinrich	Y	N	Y	Y	Y	N
2 **Pearce**	N	Y	N	N	N	Y
3 Luján	Y	N	Y	Y	Y	N
NEW YORK						
1 Bishop	Y	N	Y	Y	Y	N
2 Israel	Y	N	Y	Y	Y	N
3 **King**	N	Y	N	N	N	Y
4 McCarthy	Y	N	Y	N	Y	N
5 Ackerman	Y	N	Y	Y	Y	N
6 Meeks	Y	N	Y	Y	Y	N
7 Crowley	Y	N	Y	Y	Y	N
8 Nadler	Y	N	Y	Y	Y	N
9 **Turner**	N	Y	N	N	N	Y
10 Towns	Y	Y	Y	Y	Y	N
11 Clarke	Y	Y	Y	Y	Y	N
12 Velázquez	Y	N	Y	Y	Y	N
13 **Grimm**	N	Y	N	N	N	Y
14 Maloney	Y	N	?	Y	Y	N
15 Rangel	?	?	?	?	?	?
16 Serrano	?	?	?	?	?	?
17 Engel	Y	N	Y	Y	Y	N
18 Lowey	Y	N	Y	Y	Y	N
19 **Hayworth**	N	N	N	N	N	Y
20 **Gibson**	N	N	Y	N	Y	Y
21 Tonko	Y	N	Y	Y	Y	N
22 Hinchey	Y	N	Y	Y	Y	N
23 Owens	Y	N	Y	Y	Y	N
24 **Hanna**	N	Y	N	N	Y	Y
25 **Buerkle**	N	Y	N	N	N	Y
26 Hochul	Y	N	Y	N	Y	N
27 Higgins	Y	N	Y	Y	Y	N
28 Slaughter	+	−	+	Y	Y	N
29 **Reed**	N	Y	N	N	N	Y
NORTH CAROLINA						
1 Butterfield	Y	N	Y	Y	Y	N
2 **Ellmers**	N	Y	N	N	N	Y
3 **Jones**	N	Y	Y	Y	N	Y
4 Price	Y	N	Y	Y	Y	N

	61	62	63	64	65	66
5 **Foxx**	N	Y	N	N	N	Y
6 **Coble**	N	Y	N	Y	N	Y
7 McIntyre	N	Y	Y	N	Y	Y
8 Kissell	Y	Y	Y	Y	Y	Y
9 **Myrick**	N	Y	N	N	N	Y
10 **McHenry**	N	Y	N	N	N	Y
11 Shuler	N	N	N	?	?	?
12 Watt	Y	N	Y	Y	Y	N
13 Miller	Y	N	Y	Y	Y	N
NORTH DAKOTA						
AL **Berg**	N	Y	N	N	N	Y
OHIO						
1 **Chabot**	N	Y	N	N	N	Y
2 **Schmidt**	N	Y	N	N	N	Y
3 **Turner**	N	Y	N	N	N	Y
4 **Jordan**	N	Y	N	N	N	Y
5 **Latta**	N	Y	N	N	N	Y
6 **Johnson**	N	Y	N	N	N	Y
7 **Austria**	N	Y	N	?	?	?
8 **Boehner**						
9 Kaptur	Y	N	Y	Y	Y	N
10 Kucinich	Y	N	Y	Y	Y	N
11 Fudge	Y	Y	Y	Y	Y	N
12 **Tiberi**	N	Y	N	N	N	Y
13 Sutton	Y	N	Y	Y	Y	N
14 **LaTourette**	N	Y	N	N	N	Y
15 **Stivers**	N	Y	N	N	N	Y
16 **Renacci**	N	Y	N	N	N	Y
17 Ryan	Y	N	Y	Y	Y	N
18 **Gibbs**	N	Y	N	N	N	Y
OKLAHOMA						
1 **Sullivan**	N	Y	N	N	?	Y
2 Boren	N	Y	N	N	N	Y
3 **Lucas**	N	Y	N	N	N	Y
4 **Cole**	N	Y	N	N	N	Y
5 **Lankford**	N	Y	N	N	N	Y
OREGON						
1 Bonamici	Y	N	Y	Y	Y	N
2 **Walden**	N	Y	N	N	N	Y
3 Blumenauer	Y	N	Y	Y	Y	N
4 DeFazio	Y	N	Y	Y	Y	N
5 Schrader	Y	N	Y	Y	Y	Y
PENNSYLVANIA						
1 Brady	Y	N	Y	Y	Y	N
2 Fattah	Y	N	Y	Y	Y	N
3 **Kelly**	N	Y	N	N	N	Y
4 Altmire	N	Y	Y	N	Y	Y
5 **Thompson**	N	Y	N	N	N	Y
6 **Gerlach**	N	Y	N	N	N	Y
7 **Meehan**	N	Y	Y	N	N	Y
8 **Fitzpatrick**	N	Y	Y	N	Y	Y
9 **Shuster**	N	Y	N	N	N	Y
10 **Marino**	N	Y	N	N	N	Y
11 **Barletta**	N	Y	N	N	N	Y
12 Critz	N	N	Y	N	N	N
13 Schwartz	Y	N	Y	Y	Y	N
14 Doyle	Y	N	Y	Y	Y	N
15 **Dent**	N	Y	Y	N	Y	Y
16 **Pitts**	N	Y	N	N	N	Y
17 Holden	N	N	Y	N	Y	N
18 **Murphy**	N	Y	N	N	N	Y
19 **Platts**	N	Y	N	N	N	Y
RHODE ISLAND						
1 Cicilline	Y	N	Y	Y	Y	N
2 Langevin	Y	N	Y	Y	Y	N
SOUTH CAROLINA						
1 **Scott**	N	Y	N	N	N	Y
2 **Wilson**	N	Y	N	N	N	Y
3 **Duncan**	N	Y	N	N	N	Y
4 **Gowdy**	N	Y	N	N	N	Y
5 **Mulvaney**	N	Y	N	N	?	Y
6 Clyburn	Y	Y	Y	Y	Y	N
SOUTH DAKOTA						
AL **Noem**	N	Y	N	N	N	Y
TENNESSEE						
1 **Roe**	N	Y	N	N	N	Y
2 **Duncan**	N	Y	N	N	N	Y
3 **Fleischmann**	N	Y	N	N	N	Y
4 **DesJarlais**	N	Y	N	N	N	Y
5 Cooper	N	N	Y	N	Y	N
6 **Black**	N	Y	N	N	N	Y
7 **Blackburn**	N	Y	N	N	N	Y
8 **Fincher**	N	Y	N	N	N	Y
9 Cohen	Y	Y	Y	Y	?	N

	61	62	63	64	65	66
TEXAS						
1 **Gohmert**	N	Y	Y	N	N	Y
2 **Poe**	N	Y	N	N	N	Y
3 **Johnson, S.**	N	Y	N	N	N	Y
4 **Hall**	N	Y	N	N	N	Y
5 **Hensarling**	N	Y	N	N	N	Y
6 **Barton**	N	Y	N	N	N	Y
7 **Culberson**	N	Y	N	N	N	Y
8 **Brady**	N	Y	N	N	N	Y
9 Green, A.	N	Y	Y	N	Y	N
10 **McCaul**	N	Y	N	N	N	Y
11 **Conaway**	N	Y	N	N	N	Y
12 **Granger**	N	Y	N	N	N	Y
13 **Thornberry**	N	Y	N	N	N	Y
14 **Paul**	?	?	?	?	?	?
15 Hinojosa	Y	Y	Y	Y	Y	N
16 Reyes	Y	Y	Y	Y	Y	Y
17 **Flores**	N	Y	N	N	N	Y
18 Jackson Lee	Y	Y	Y	Y	Y	N
19 **Neugebauer**	N	Y	N	N	N	Y
20 Gonzalez	N	Y	N	Y	Y	N
21 **Smith**	N	Y	N	N	N	Y
22 **Olson**	N	Y	N	N	N	Y
23 **Canseco**	N	Y	N	N	N	Y
24 **Marchant**	N	Y	N	N	N	Y
25 Doggett	Y	Y	Y	Y	Y	N
26 **Burgess**	N	Y	N	N	N	Y
27 **Farenthold**	N	Y	N	N	N	Y
28 Cuellar	N	Y	Y	N	Y	N
29 Green, G.	N	Y	N	N	N	N
30 Johnson, E.	Y	Y	Y	Y	Y	N
31 **Carter**	N	Y	N	N	N	Y
32 **Sessions**	N	Y	N	N	N	Y
UTAH						
1 **Bishop**	N	Y	N	N	N	Y
2 Matheson	N	Y	N	N	N	Y
3 **Chaffetz**	N	Y	N	N	N	Y
VERMONT						
AL Welch	Y	N	Y	Y	Y	N
VIRGINIA						
1 **Wittman**	N	Y	N	N	N	Y
2 **Rigell**	N	Y	N	N	N	Y
3 Scott	Y	N	Y	Y	Y	N
4 **Forbes**	N	Y	N	N	N	Y
5 **Hurt**	N	Y	N	N	N	Y
6 **Goodlatte**	N	Y	N	N	N	Y
7 **Cantor**	N	Y	N	N	N	Y
8 Moran	Y	N	Y	Y	Y	N
9 **Griffith**	N	Y	N	N	N	Y
10 **Wolf**	N	Y	N	N	N	Y
11 Connolly	Y	N	Y	Y	Y	N
WASHINGTON						
1 Inslee	Y	N	Y	Y	Y	N
2 Larsen	Y	N	N	Y	Y	N
3 **Herrera Beutler**	N	Y	N	N	N	Y
4 **Hastings**	N	Y	N	N	N	Y
5 **McMorris Rodgers**	N	Y	N	N	N	Y
6 Dicks	Y	N	Y	Y	Y	N
7 McDermott	Y	N	Y	Y	Y	N
8 **Reichert**	Y	Y	Y	Y	Y	Y
9 Smith	Y	N	Y	Y	Y	N
WEST VIRGINIA						
1 **McKinley**	N	Y	N	N	N	Y
2 **Capito**	N	Y	N	N	N	Y
3 Rahall	Y	N	Y	Y	Y	N
WISCONSIN						
1 **Ryan**	N	Y	N	N	N	Y
2 Baldwin	Y	N	Y	Y	Y	N
3 Kind	N	N	N	N	Y	N
4 Moore	Y	N	Y	Y	Y	N
5 **Sensenbrenner**	N	Y	N	N	N	Y
6 **Petri**	N	Y	N	N	N	Y
7 **Duffy**	N	Y	N	N	N	Y
8 **Ribble**	N	Y	N	N	N	Y
WYOMING						
AL **Lummis**	N	N	N	N	N	Y

IN THE HOUSE | By Vote Number

67. HR 3408. **Expansion of Oil and Gas Production/Natural-Gas Export.** Markey, D-Mass., amendment that would bar the export of natural gas produced from leases issued under the bill. Rejected in Committee of the Whole 168-254: R 9-227; D 159-27. Feb. 16, 2012.

68. HR 3408. **Expansion of Oil and Gas Production/Royalties.** Markey, D-Mass., amendment that would require companies that hold leases for oil and gas production in the Gulf of Mexico without paying royalties to renegotiate the leases to pay royalties before bidding on new leases issued under the bill. Rejected in Committee of the Whole 183-238: R 14-222; D 169-16. Feb. 16, 2012.

69. HR 3408. **Expansion of Oil and Gas Production/Geothermal Exploration.** Labrador, R-Idaho, amendment that would allow geothermal exploration test projects that meet certain requirements to be excluded from certain federal environmental review requirements. Adopted in Committee of the Whole 244-177: R 230-5; D 14-172. Feb. 16, 2012.

70. HR 3408. **Expansion of Oil and Gas Production/Recommit.** Castor, D-Fla., motion to recommit the bill to the Natural Resources Committee with instructions to report it back immediately with an amendment that would bar federal or state permits or leases for new oil and gas slant, directional, or offshore drilling within five miles of the Great Lakes or the Florida Everglades. Motion rejected 176-241: R 2-232; D 174-9. Feb. 16, 2012.

71. HR 3408. **Expanded Oil and Gas Production/Passage.** Passage of the bill that would open up a portion of Alaska's Arctic National Wildlife Refuge to oil and gas exploration and production and expand lease sales to include areas off the coast of southern California, in the eastern and central Gulf of Mexico, the Virginia coastline and near Bristol Bay, Alaska. The bill also would provide for approval of the 1,700-mile Canadian tar sands Keystone XL pipeline and shift permitting authority for the project from the State Department to the Federal Energy Regulatory Commission. As amended, it would establish a trust fund for Gulf Coast restoration efforts. Passed 237-187: R 216-21; D 21-166. A "nay" was a vote in support of the president's position. Feb. 16, 2012.

72. HR 3630. **Payroll Tax Relief Extension/Conference Report.** Adoption of the conference report on the bill that would extend the 4.2 percent employee payroll tax rate through 2012. It also would renew long-term unemployment benefits into January 2013, with three stages of reductions. The current Medicare reimbursement rate for physicians would be preserved through 2012, preventing a scheduled 27.4 percent payment cut. The cost of the legislation would be partially offset by requiring larger pension payments from newly hired federal employees and from lawmakers, by auctioning blocks of electromagnetic spectrum used by television broadcasters, and by reducing funds for certain programs tied to the 2010 health care overhaul. Adopted (thus sent to the Senate) 293-132: R 146-91; D 147-41. A "yea" was a vote in support of the president's position. Feb. 17, 2012.

	67	68	69	70	71	72
ALABAMA						
1 **Bonner**	N	N	Y	N	Y	N
2 **Roby**	N	N	Y	N	Y	N
3 **Rogers**	N	N	Y	N	Y	N
4 **Aderholt**	N	N	Y	N	Y	N
5 **Brooks**	N	N	Y	N	Y	N
6 **Bachus**	N	N	Y	N	Y	N
7 Sewell	Y	Y	N	Y	N	Y
ALASKA						
AL **Young**	N	N	Y	N	Y	Y
ARIZONA						
1 **Gosar**	N	N	Y	N	Y	?
2 **Franks**	N	N	Y	N	Y	N
3 **Quayle**	N	N	Y	N	Y	N
4 Pastor	Y	Y	N	Y	N	Y
5 **Schweikert**	N	N	Y	N	Y	Y
6 **Flake**	N	N	Y	N	Y	N
7 Grijalva	Y	Y	N	Y	N	Y
8 Vacant						
ARKANSAS						
1 **Crawford**	N	N	Y	N	Y	Y
2 **Griffin**	N	N	Y	N	Y	Y
3 **Womack**	N	N	Y	N	Y	Y
4 Ross	N	N	Y	N	Y	Y
CALIFORNIA						
1 Thompson	Y	Y	N	Y	N	N
2 **Herger**	N	N	Y	N	Y	Y
3 **Lungren**	N	N	Y	?	Y	Y
4 **McClintock**	N	N	Y	N	Y	N
5 Matsui	Y	Y	N	Y	N	Y
6 Woolsey	Y	Y	N	Y	N	N
7 Miller, George	Y	Y	N	Y	N	N
8 Pelosi	Y	Y	N	Y	N	Y
9 Lee	Y	Y	N	Y	N	N
10 Garamendi	Y	Y	N	Y	N	Y
11 McNerney	Y	Y	N	Y	N	Y
12 Speier	Y	Y	N	Y	N	Y
13 Stark	Y	Y	N	Y	N	Y
14 Eshoo	Y	Y	N	Y	N	Y
15 Honda	Y	Y	N	?	N	Y
16 Lofgren	Y	Y	N	Y	N	Y
17 Farr	Y	Y	N	Y	N	N
18 Cardoza	N	N	Y	Y	N	Y
19 **Denham**	N	N	Y	N	Y	Y
20 Costa	N	N	Y	N	Y	Y
21 **Nunes**	N	N	Y	N	Y	Y
22 **McCarthy**	N	N	Y	N	Y	Y
23 Capps	Y	Y	N	Y	N	Y
24 **Gallegly**	N	N	Y	N	Y	N
25 **McKeon**	N	N	Y	N	Y	Y
26 **Dreier**	N	N	Y	N	Y	Y
27 Sherman	Y	Y	N	Y	N	Y
28 Berman	Y	Y	N	Y	N	Y
29 Schiff	Y	Y	N	Y	N	Y
30 Waxman	Y	Y	N	Y	N	Y
31 Becerra	Y	Y	N	Y	N	Y
32 Chu	Y	Y	N	?	N	Y
33 Bass	Y	Y	N	Y	N	Y
34 Roybal-Allard	Y	Y	N	Y	N	Y
35 Waters	Y	Y	N	Y	N	Y
36 Hahn	Y	Y	N	Y	N	Y
37 Richardson	Y	Y	Y	Y	N	Y
38 Napolitano	Y	Y	N	Y	N	Y
39 Sánchez, Linda	Y	Y	N	Y	N	Y
40 **Royce**	N	N	Y	N	Y	N
41 **Lewis**	N	N	Y	N	Y	Y
42 **Miller, Gary**	N	N	Y	N	Y	Y
43 Baca	N	Y	N	Y	N	Y
44 **Calvert**	N	N	Y	N	Y	Y
45 **Bono Mack**	?	?	?	?	?	?
46 **Rohrabacher**	N	N	Y	N	Y	N
47 Sanchez, Loretta	?	?	?	?	?	Y
48 **Campbell**	?	?	?	?	?	?
49 **Issa**	N	N	Y	N	Y	Y
50 **Bilbray**	N	N	Y	N	Y	Y
51 Filner	Y	Y	N	Y	N	N
52 **Hunter**	N	N	Y	N	Y	Y
53 Davis	Y	Y	N	Y	N	Y

	67	68	69	70	71	72
COLORADO						
1 DeGette	Y	Y	N	Y	N	Y
2 Polis	Y	Y	Y	Y	N	Y
3 **Tipton**	N	N	Y	N	Y	Y
4 **Gardner**	N	N	Y	N	Y	N
5 **Lamborn**	N	N	Y	N	Y	N
6 **Coffman**	N	N	Y	N	Y	Y
7 Perlmutter	N	Y	N	Y	N	Y
CONNECTICUT						
1 Larson	Y	Y	N	Y	N	Y
2 Courtney	N	Y	N	Y	N	Y
3 DeLauro	Y	Y	N	Y	N	Y
4 Himes	N	Y	N	Y	N	Y
5 Murphy	Y	Y	N	Y	N	Y
DELAWARE						
AL Carney	Y	Y	N	Y	N	Y
FLORIDA						
1 **Miller**	N	N	Y	N	N	N
2 **Southerland**	N	N	Y	N	N	+
3 Brown	Y	Y	N	Y	N	+
4 **Crenshaw**	N	N	Y	N	Y	Y
5 **Nugent**	N	N	Y	N	Y	N
6 **Stearns**	N	N	Y	N	Y	N
7 **Mica**	N	N	Y	N	Y	N
8 **Webster**	N	N	Y	N	Y	Y
9 **Bilirakis**	N	N	Y	N	N	Y
10 **Young**	N	Y	N	Y	N	Y
11 Castor	Y	Y	N	Y	N	Y
12 **Ross**	N	N	Y	N	Y	N
13 **Buchanan**	N	Y	N	N	N	Y
14 **Mack**	?	?	?	?	?	Y
15 **Posey**	N	N	Y	Y	Y	N
16 **Rooney**	N	N	Y	N	Y	Y
17 Wilson	Y	Y	N	Y	N	N
18 **Ros-Lehtinen**	N	Y	N	N	N	Y
19 Deutch	Y	Y	N	Y	N	Y
20 Wasserman Schultz	Y	Y	N	Y	N	Y
21 **Diaz-Balart**	N	N	Y	N	N	Y
22 **West**	N	N	Y	N	N	N
23 Hastings	N	N	Y	N	N	N
24 **Adams**	N	N	Y	N	N	N
25 **Rivera**	N	N	Y	N	Y	Y
GEORGIA						
1 **Kingston**	N	N	Y	N	Y	N
2 Bishop	Y	Y	Y	Y	Y	Y
3 **Westmoreland**	N	N	Y	N	Y	Y
4 Johnson	Y	Y	N	Y	N	N
5 Lewis	Y	Y	N	Y	N	Y
6 **Price**	N	N	Y	N	Y	N
7 **Woodall**	N	N	Y	N	Y	N
8 **Scott, A.**	N	N	Y	N	Y	N
9 **Graves**	N	N	Y	N	Y	N
10 **Broun**	N	N	Y	N	Y	N
11 **Gingrey**	N	N	Y	N	Y	N
12 Barrow	Y	N	Y	N	Y	Y
13 Scott, D.	Y	Y	N	Y	N	Y
HAWAII						
1 Hanabusa	Y	Y	N	Y	N	Y
2 Hirono	Y	Y	N	Y	N	Y
IDAHO						
1 **Labrador**	N	N	Y	N	Y	N
2 **Simpson**	N	N	Y	N	Y	N
ILLINOIS						
1 Rush	Y	Y	N	Y	N	Y
2 Jackson	Y	Y	N	Y	N	Y
3 Lipinski	N	Y	N	Y	N	N
4 Gutierrez	Y	Y	N	Y	N	N
5 Quigley	Y	Y	N	Y	N	Y
6 **Roskam**	N	N	Y	N	Y	Y
7 Davis	Y	Y	N	Y	N	Y
8 **Walsh**	N	N	Y	N	Y	Y
9 Schakowsky	Y	Y	N	Y	N	Y
10 **Dold**	Y	Y	N	N	N	Y
11 **Kinzinger**	N	N	Y	N	Y	Y
12 Costello	N	Y	N	Y	N	Y
13 **Biggert**	N	N	Y	N	Y	Y
14 **Hultgren**	N	N	Y	N	Y	Y
15 **Johnson**	N	N	?	N	N	N

	67	68	69	70	71	72
16 **Manzullo**	N	N	Y	N	Y	Y
17 **Schilling**	N	N	Y	N	Y	Y
18 **Schock**	N	N	Y	N	Y	Y
19 **Shimkus**	N	N	Y	N	Y	Y
INDIANA						
1 Visclosky	Y	Y	N	Y	N	N
2 Donnelly	Y	N	Y	Y	Y	Y
3 **Stutzman**	N	N	Y	N	Y	Y
4 **Rokita**	N	N	Y	N	Y	N
5 **Burton**	N	N	Y	N	Y	N
6 **Pence**	N	N	Y	N	Y	Y
7 Carson	Y	Y	N	Y	N	Y
8 **Bucshon**	N	N	Y	N	Y	Y
9 **Young**	N	N	Y	N	Y	Y
IOWA						
1 Braley	Y	Y	N	Y	N	Y
2 Loebsack	Y	Y	N	Y	N	Y
3 Boswell	Y	Y	Y	N	Y	Y
4 **Latham**	N	N	Y	N	Y	Y
5 **King**	N	N	Y	N	Y	N
KANSAS						
1 **Huelskamp**	N	N	Y	N	Y	Y
2 **Jenkins**	N	N	Y	N	Y	Y
3 **Yoder**	N	N	Y	N	Y	Y
4 **Pompeo**	N	N	Y	N	Y	N
KENTUCKY						
1 **Whitfield**	N	N	Y	N	Y	N
2 **Guthrie**	N	N	Y	N	Y	Y
3 Yarmuth	Y	Y	N	Y	N	Y
4 **Davis**	N	N	Y	N	Y	Y
5 **Rogers**	N	N	Y	N	Y	Y
6 Chandler	Y	Y	N	Y	N	Y
LOUISIANA						
1 **Scalise**	N	N	Y	N	Y	Y
2 Richmond	N	Y	N	Y	Y	Y
3 **Landry**	N	N	Y	N	Y	N
4 **Fleming**	N	N	Y	N	Y	N
5 **Alexander**	N	N	Y	N	Y	Y
6 **Cassidy**	N	N	Y	N	Y	N
7 **Boustany**	N	N	Y	N	Y	N
MAINE						
1 Pingree	Y	Y	N	Y	N	N
2 Michaud	Y	Y	N	Y	N	Y
MARYLAND						
1 **Harris**	N	N	Y	N	Y	N
2 Ruppersberger	Y	Y	N	Y	N	Y
3 Sarbanes	Y	Y	N	Y	N	N
4 Edwards	Y	Y	N	Y	N	N
5 Hoyer	N	Y	N	Y	N	N
6 **Bartlett**	N	Y	Y	N	Y	Y
7 Cummings	Y	Y	N	Y	N	N
8 Van Hollen	Y	Y	N	Y	N	N
MASSACHUSETTS						
1 Olver	Y	Y	N	Y	N	Y
2 Neal	Y	?	N	Y	N	Y
3 McGovern	Y	Y	N	Y	N	Y
4 Frank	N	Y	N	Y	N	Y
5 Tsongas	Y	Y	N	Y	N	Y
6 Tierney	Y	Y	N	Y	N	Y
7 Markey	Y	Y	N	Y	N	Y
8 Capuano	Y	Y	N	Y	N	N
9 Lynch	Y	Y	N	Y	N	N
10 Keating	Y	Y	N	Y	N	Y
MICHIGAN						
1 **Benishek**	N	N	Y	N	Y	Y
2 **Huizenga**	N	N	Y	N	Y	Y
3 **Amash**	N	N	N	N	Y	N
4 **Camp**	N	N	Y	N	Y	Y
5 Kildee	Y	Y	N	Y	N	Y
6 **Upton**	N	N	Y	N	Y	Y
7 **Walberg**	N	N	Y	N	Y	N
8 **Rogers**	N	N	Y	N	Y	Y
9 Peters	Y	Y	N	Y	N	Y
10 **Miller**	N	N	Y	N	Y	Y
11 **McCotter**	N	N	Y	N	Y	N
12 Levin	Y	Y	N	Y	N	Y
13 Clarke	N	Y	N	Y	N	Y
14 Conyers	Y	Y	N	Y	N	Y
15 Dingell	N	Y	N	Y	N	Y
MINNESOTA						
1 Walz	Y	Y	N	Y	N	Y
2 **Kline**	N	N	Y	N	Y	Y
3 **Paulsen**	N	N	Y	N	N	Y
4 McCollum	Y	Y	N	Y	N	Y

	67	68	69	70	71	72
5 Ellison	Y	Y	N	Y	N	N
6 **Bachmann**	N	N	Y	N	Y	N
7 Peterson	N	N	Y	N	Y	N
8 **Cravaack**	N	N	Y	N	Y	Y
MISSISSIPPI						
1 **Nunnelee**	N	N	Y	N	Y	Y
2 Thompson	N	N	N	Y	N	Y
3 **Harper**	N	N	Y	N	Y	Y
4 **Palazzo**	N	N	Y	N	Y	Y
MISSOURI						
1 Clay	Y	Y	N	Y	N	N
2 **Akin**	N	N	Y	N	Y	N
3 Carnahan	Y	Y	N	Y	N	Y
4 **Hartzler**	N	N	Y	N	Y	Y
5 Cleaver	+	+	–	+	–	N
6 **Graves**	N	N	Y	N	Y	N
7 **Long**	N	N	Y	N	Y	Y
8 **Emerson**	N	N	Y	N	Y	Y
9 **Luetkemeyer**	N	N	Y	N	Y	Y
MONTANA						
AL **Rehberg**	N	N	Y	N	Y	Y
NEBRASKA						
1 **Fortenberry**	N	Y	Y	N	Y	N
2 **Terry**	N	N	Y	N	Y	N
3 **Smith**	N	N	Y	N	Y	Y
NEVADA						
1 Berkley	Y	Y	N	Y	N	Y
2 **Amodei**	N	N	Y	N	Y	Y
3 **Heck**	N	N	Y	N	Y	Y
NEW HAMPSHIRE						
1 **Guinta**	N	N	Y	N	Y	Y
2 **Bass**	N	N	Y	N	N	Y
NEW JERSEY						
1 Andrews	Y	Y	N	Y	N	Y
2 **LoBiondo**	Y	Y	N	N	N	Y
3 **Runyan**	N	N	N	N	Y	Y
4 **Smith**	Y	Y	N	N	N	Y
5 **Garrett**	N	N	Y	N	Y	N
6 Pallone	Y	Y	N	Y	N	Y
7 **Lance**	N	N	Y	N	Y	Y
8 Pascrell	Y	Y	N	Y	N	Y
9 Rothman	Y	Y	N	Y	N	Y
10 Payne	?	?	?	?	?	?
11 **Frelinghuysen**	N	N	Y	N	N	Y
12 Holt	Y	Y	N	Y	N	Y
13 Sires	Y	Y	N	Y	N	Y
NEW MEXICO						
1 Heinrich	Y	Y	N	Y	N	Y
2 **Pearce**	N	N	Y	N	Y	N
3 Luján	Y	Y	N	Y	N	Y
NEW YORK						
1 Bishop	Y	Y	N	Y	N	Y
2 Israel	Y	Y	N	Y	N	Y
3 **King**	N	N	Y	N	Y	Y
4 McCarthy	Y	Y	N	Y	N	Y
5 Ackerman	Y	Y	N	Y	N	N
6 Meeks	Y	Y	N	Y	N	Y
7 Crowley	Y	Y	N	Y	N	Y
8 Nadler	Y	Y	N	Y	N	Y
9 **Turner**	N	N	Y	N	Y	Y
10 Towns	Y	Y	N	Y	N	Y
11 Clarke	Y	Y	N	?	N	N
12 Velázquez	Y	Y	N	Y	N	Y
13 **Grimm**	N	N	Y	N	Y	Y
14 Maloney	Y	Y	N	Y	N	Y
15 Rangel	?	?	?	?	?	?
16 Serrano	?	?	+	Y	N	Y
17 Engel	Y	Y	N	Y	N	Y
18 Lowey	Y	Y	N	Y	N	Y
19 **Hayworth**	Y	N	Y	N	N	Y
20 **Gibson**	Y	Y	Y	N	Y	Y
21 Tonko	Y	Y	N	Y	N	Y
22 Hinchey	Y	Y	N	Y	N	Y
23 Owens	Y	Y	N	Y	Y	Y
24 **Hanna**	N	N	Y	N	Y	Y
25 **Buerkle**	N	N	Y	N	Y	N
26 Hochul	Y	Y	N	Y	Y	Y
27 Higgins	Y	Y	N	Y	N	Y
28 Slaughter	Y	Y	N	Y	N	Y
29 **Reed**	N	N	Y	N	Y	Y
NORTH CAROLINA						
1 Butterfield	N	Y	N	?	N	Y
2 **Ellmers**	N	N	Y	N	Y	Y
3 **Jones**	Y	Y	Y	N	Y	Y
4 Price	Y	Y	N	Y	N	Y

	67	68	69	70	71	72
5 **Foxx**	N	N	Y	N	Y	N
6 **Coble**	N	N	Y	N	Y	Y
7 McIntyre	Y	Y	Y	Y	Y	Y
8 Kissell	Y	Y	Y	Y	Y	Y
9 **Myrick**	N	N	Y	N	Y	Y
10 **McHenry**	N	N	Y	N	Y	Y
11 Shuler	?	?	?	?	?	?
12 Watt	Y	Y	N	Y	N	Y
13 Miller	Y	Y	N	Y	N	Y
NORTH DAKOTA						
AL **Berg**	N	N	Y	N	Y	Y
OHIO						
1 **Chabot**	N	N	Y	N	Y	N
2 **Schmidt**	N	N	Y	N	Y	N
3 **Turner**	N	N	Y	N	Y	Y
4 **Jordan**	N	N	Y	N	Y	N
5 **Latta**	N	N	Y	N	Y	Y
6 **Johnson**	N	N	Y	N	Y	Y
7 **Austria**	?	?	?	?	?	Y
8 **Boehner**					Y	
9 Kaptur	Y	Y	N	Y	N	Y
10 Kucinich	Y	Y	N	Y	N	Y
11 Fudge	Y	Y	N	Y	N	N
12 **Tiberi**	N	N	Y	N	Y	Y
13 Sutton	Y	Y	N	Y	N	Y
14 **LaTourette**	N	N	Y	N	Y	Y
15 **Stivers**	N	N	Y	N	Y	Y
16 **Renacci**	N	N	Y	N	Y	Y
17 Ryan	N	Y	N	Y	N	N
18 **Gibbs**	N	N	Y	N	Y	Y
OKLAHOMA						
1 **Sullivan**	N	N	Y	N	Y	N
2 Boren	N	N	Y	N	Y	Y
3 **Lucas**	N	N	Y	N	Y	Y
4 **Cole**	N	N	Y	N	Y	Y
5 **Lankford**	N	N	Y	N	Y	N
OREGON						
1 Bonamici	Y	Y	N	Y	N	Y
2 **Walden**	N	N	Y	N	Y	Y
3 Blumenauer	N	Y	N	Y	N	Y
4 DeFazio	Y	Y	N	Y	N	N
5 Schrader	Y	Y	N	Y	N	N
PENNSYLVANIA						
1 Brady	Y	Y	N	Y	N	Y
2 Fattah	Y	Y	N	Y	N	Y
3 **Kelly**	N	N	Y	N	Y	Y
4 Altmire	Y	N	N	Y	Y	Y
5 **Thompson**	N	N	Y	N	Y	Y
6 **Gerlach**	Y	Y	Y	N	Y	Y
7 **Meehan**	N	N	Y	N	Y	Y
8 **Fitzpatrick**	Y	Y	Y	N	Y	Y
9 **Shuster**	N	N	Y	N	Y	Y
10 **Marino**	N	N	Y	N	Y	Y
11 **Barletta**	N	N	Y	N	Y	Y
12 Critz	N	Y	N	Y	Y	Y
13 Schwartz	Y	Y	N	Y	N	Y
14 Doyle	N	Y	N	Y	N	Y
15 **Dent**	N	Y	Y	N	Y	Y
16 **Pitts**	N	N	Y	N	Y	Y
17 Holden	Y	Y	N	Y	N	Y
18 **Murphy**	N	N	Y	N	Y	Y
19 **Platts**	Y	Y	Y	N	Y	Y
RHODE ISLAND						
1 Cicilline	Y	Y	N	Y	N	Y
2 Langevin	Y	Y	N	Y	N	Y
SOUTH CAROLINA						
1 **Scott**	N	N	Y	N	Y	Y
2 **Wilson**	N	N	Y	N	Y	N
3 **Duncan**	N	N	Y	N	Y	N
4 **Gowdy**	N	N	Y	N	Y	N
5 **Mulvaney**	N	N	Y	N	Y	N
6 Clyburn	Y	Y	N	Y	N	Y
SOUTH DAKOTA						
AL **Noem**	N	N	Y	N	Y	N
TENNESSEE						
1 **Roe**	N	N	Y	N	Y	N
2 **Duncan**	N	N	Y	N	Y	N
3 **Fleischmann**	N	N	Y	N	Y	Y
4 **DesJarlais**	N	N	Y	N	Y	N
5 Cooper	Y	Y	N	Y	Y	N
6 **Black**	N	N	Y	N	Y	N
7 **Blackburn**	N	N	Y	N	Y	N
8 **Fincher**	N	N	Y	N	Y	Y
9 Cohen	Y	Y	N	Y	N	Y

	67	68	69	70	71	72
TEXAS						
1 **Gohmert**	N	N	Y	N	Y	N
2 **Poe**	N	N	Y	N	Y	N
3 **Johnson, S.**	N	N	Y	N	Y	Y
4 **Hall**	N	N	Y	N	Y	N
5 **Hensarling**	N	N	Y	N	Y	Y
6 **Barton**	N	N	Y	N	Y	N
7 **Culberson**	N	N	Y	N	Y	Y
8 **Brady**	N	N	Y	N	Y	Y
9 Green, A.	Y	N	N	Y	Y	Y
10 **McCaul**	N	N	Y	N	Y	Y
11 **Conaway**	N	N	Y	N	Y	Y
12 **Granger**	N	N	Y	N	Y	N
13 **Thornberry**	N	N	Y	N	Y	N
14 **Paul**	?	?	?	?	?	?
15 Hinojosa	N	N	N	Y	Y	Y
16 Reyes	Y	Y	N	Y	N	N
17 **Flores**	N	N	Y	N	Y	Y
18 Jackson Lee	Y	N	N	Y	N	Y
19 **Neugebauer**	N	N	Y	N	Y	N
20 Gonzalez	N	N	N	Y	N	Y
21 **Smith**	N	N	Y	?	Y	Y
22 **Olson**	N	N	Y	N	Y	N
23 **Canseco**	N	N	Y	N	Y	Y
24 **Marchant**	N	N	Y	N	Y	Y
25 Doggett	Y	Y	N	Y	N	Y
26 **Burgess**	N	N	Y	N	Y	N
27 **Farenthold**	N	N	Y	N	Y	N
28 Cuellar	N	N	N	N	Y	Y
29 Green, G.	N	N	N	N	Y	Y
30 Johnson, E.	Y	Y	N	Y	N	N
31 **Carter**	N	N	Y	N	Y	N
32 **Sessions**	N	N	Y	N	Y	N
UTAH						
1 **Bishop**	N	N	Y	N	Y	N
2 Matheson	N	N	Y	N	Y	Y
3 **Chaffetz**	N	N	Y	N	Y	N
VERMONT						
AL Welch	Y	Y	N	Y	N	N
VIRGINIA						
1 **Wittman**	N	N	Y	N	Y	Y
2 **Rigell**	N	N	Y	N	Y	Y
3 Scott	Y	Y	N	Y	N	N
4 **Forbes**	N	N	Y	N	Y	N
5 **Hurt**	N	N	Y	N	Y	Y
6 **Goodlatte**	N	N	Y	N	Y	N
7 **Cantor**	N	N	Y	N	Y	Y
8 Moran	Y	Y	N	Y	N	N
9 **Griffith**	N	N	Y	N	Y	N
10 **Wolf**	N	N	Y	N	Y	N
11 Connolly	Y	Y	N	Y	N	N
WASHINGTON						
1 Inslee	Y	Y	N	Y	N	Y
2 Larsen	N	Y	N	Y	N	Y
3 **Herrera Beutler**	N	N	Y	N	Y	Y
4 **Hastings**	N	N	Y	N	Y	Y
5 **McMorris Rodgers**	N	N	Y	N	Y	Y
6 Dicks	Y	Y	N	Y	N	Y
7 McDermott	Y	Y	N	Y	N	N
8 **Reichert**	N	N	Y	N	N	Y
9 Smith	Y	Y	N	Y	N	N
WEST VIRGINIA						
1 **McKinley**	N	N	Y	N	Y	N
2 **Capito**	N	N	Y	N	Y	Y
3 Rahall	Y	Y	N	Y	N	Y
WISCONSIN						
1 **Ryan**	N	N	Y	N	Y	N
2 Baldwin	Y	Y	N	Y	N	Y
3 Kind	Y	Y	N	Y	N	N
4 Moore	Y	Y	N	Y	N	Y
5 **Sensenbrenner**	N	N	Y	N	Y	N
6 **Petri**	N	N	Y	N	Y	N
7 **Duffy**	N	N	Y	N	Y	Y
8 **Ribble**	N	N	Y	N	Y	Y
WYOMING						
AL **Lummis**	N	N	Y	N	Y	N

IN THE HOUSE | By Vote Number

73. **HR 347. Federal-Property Trespassing Violations/Passage.** Smith, R-Texas, motion to suspend the rules and concur in the Senate amendment to the bill that would extend violations associated with trespassing in secured areas on federal property to those found trespassing on White House grounds or the vice president's official residence. Motion agreed to 388-3: R 224-2; D 164-1. A two-thirds majority of those present and voting (261 in this case) is required for passage under suspension of the rules. Feb. 27, 2012.

74. **HR 2117. For-Profit College Regulations/Rule.** Adoption of the rule (H Res 563) that would provide for House floor consideration of the bill (HR 2117) that would rescind Education Department regulations that define a "credit hour" and set minimum requirements that all higher education institutions must meet to be considered authorized by a state. Adopted 244-171: R 234-0; D 10-171. Feb. 28, 2012.

75. **HR 2117. For-Profit College Regulations/Student Complaints.** Grijalva, D-Ariz., amendment that would strike language that would repeal Education Department regulations requiring states to have a process to hear and take action on student complaints regarding institutions in order for the institution to be considered state-authorized. Rejected in Committee of the Whole 170-247: R 0-236; D 170-11. Feb. 28, 2012.

76. **HR 2117. For-Profit College Regulations/Credit-Hour Rules.** Bishop, D-N.Y., amendment that would strike language from the bill that would bar the Education secretary from establishing or enforcing any new rules to define the term "credit hour." Rejected in Committee of the Whole 160-255: R 1-232; D 159-23. Feb. 28, 2012.

77. **HR 2117. For-Profit College Regulations/Waste, Fraud and Abuse Prevention.** Polis, D-Colo., amendment that would require the Education Department to submit a plan to Congress on how the agency will prevent waste, fraud and abuse of federal financial aid dollars by institutions of higher education. Rejected in Committee of the Whole 199-217: R 21-214; D 178-3. Feb. 28, 2012.

78. **HR 2117. For-Profit College Regulations/Recommit.** Capps, D-Calif., motion to recommit the bill to the Education and the Workforce Committee with instructions to report it back immediately with an amendment that would clarify that nothing in the bill would limit the Education secretary from promulgating or enforcing regulations to reduce the cost of higher education for students. It also would clarify that the Education secretary may create or enforce regulations related to student assistance in any year that the interest rate for federal Stafford loans used to purchase credit hours is higher than 3.4 percent. Motion rejected 176-241: R 0-233; D 176-8. Feb. 28, 2012.

	73	74	75	76	77	78
ALABAMA						
1 Bonner	Y	Y	N	N	N	N
2 Roby	Y	Y	N	N	N	N
3 Rogers	Y	Y	N	N	N	N
4 Aderholt	Y	Y	N	N	N	N
5 Brooks	Y	Y	N	N	N	N
6 Bachus	Y	Y	N	N	N	N
7 Sewell	Y	N	Y	Y	Y	Y
ALASKA						
AL Young	?	?	?	?	?	?
ARIZONA						
1 Gosar	Y	Y	?	N	N	N
2 Franks	?	Y	N	N	N	N
3 Quayle	Y	Y	N	N	N	N
4 Pastor	Y	N	Y	Y	Y	Y
5 Schweikert	Y	Y	N	N	N	N
6 Flake	Y	Y	N	N	N	N
7 Grijalva	?	N	Y	Y	Y	Y
8 Vacant						
ARKANSAS						
1 Crawford	Y	Y	N	N	N	N
2 Griffin	Y	Y	N	N	N	N
3 Womack	Y	Y	N	N	N	N
4 Ross	Y	Y	N	N	Y	Y
CALIFORNIA						
1 Thompson	Y	N	Y	Y	Y	Y
2 Herger	Y	Y	N	N	N	N
3 Lungren	Y	?	N	N	N	N
4 McClintock	Y	Y	N	N	Y	N
5 Matsui	Y	N	Y	Y	Y	Y
6 Woolsey	+	N	Y	Y	Y	Y
7 Miller, George	Y	N	Y	Y	Y	Y
8 Pelosi	Y	N	Y	Y	Y	Y
9 Lee	+	-	+	+	+	+
10 Garamendi	Y	N	Y	Y	Y	Y
11 McNerney	Y	N	Y	Y	Y	Y
12 Speier	?	N	Y	Y	Y	Y
13 Stark	?	N	Y	Y	Y	Y
14 Eshoo	Y	N	Y	Y	Y	Y
15 Honda	Y	N	Y	Y	Y	Y
16 Lofgren	Y	N	Y	Y	Y	Y
17 Farr	Y	N	Y	Y	Y	Y
18 Cardoza	Y	?	?	?	?	?
19 Denham	Y	Y	N	N	N	N
20 Costa	Y	N	Y	Y	N	Y
21 Nunes	Y	Y	N	N	N	N
22 McCarthy	Y	Y	N	N	N	N
23 Capps	Y	N	Y	Y	Y	Y
24 Gallegly	Y	Y	N	N	N	N
25 McKeon	Y	Y	N	N	N	N
26 Dreier	Y	Y	N	N	N	N
27 Sherman	Y	N	Y	Y	Y	Y
28 Berman	Y	N	Y	Y	Y	Y
29 Schiff	Y	N	Y	Y	Y	Y
30 Waxman	Y	?	Y	Y	Y	Y
31 Becerra	Y	N	Y	Y	Y	Y
32 Chu	Y	N	Y	Y	Y	Y
33 Bass	Y	N	Y	Y	Y	Y
34 Roybal-Allard	Y	N	Y	Y	Y	Y
35 Waters	Y	N	Y	Y	Y	Y
36 Hahn	Y	N	Y	Y	Y	Y
37 Richardson	Y	N	Y	Y	Y	Y
38 Napolitano	Y	N	Y	Y	Y	Y
39 Sánchez, Linda	Y	N	Y	Y	Y	Y
40 Royce	Y	Y	N	N	N	N
41 Lewis	Y	Y	N	N	N	N
42 Miller, Gary	Y	Y	N	N	N	N
43 Baca	Y	N	Y	Y	Y	Y
44 Calvert	Y	Y	N	N	N	N
45 Bono Mack	Y	Y	N	N	N	N
46 Rohrabacher	Y	Y	N	N	N	N
47 Sanchez, Loretta	Y	N	Y	Y	Y	Y
48 Campbell	?	Y	N	N	N	N
49 Issa	Y	Y	N	N	N	N
50 Bilbray	?	Y	N	N	N	N
51 Filner	+	N	Y	Y	Y	Y
52 Hunter	Y	Y	N	N	N	N
53 Davis	Y	N	Y	Y	Y	Y

	73	74	75	76	77	78
COLORADO						
1 DeGette	Y	N	Y	Y	Y	Y
2 Polis	Y	N	Y	N	Y	Y
3 Tipton	Y	Y	N	N	Y	N
4 Gardner	Y	Y	N	N	Y	N
5 Lamborn	Y	Y	N	N	N	N
6 Coffman	Y	Y	N	N	Y	N
7 Perlmutter	Y	?	Y	Y	Y	Y
CONNECTICUT						
1 Larson	Y	N	Y	Y	Y	Y
2 Courtney	Y	N	Y	Y	Y	Y
3 DeLauro	Y	N	Y	Y	Y	Y
4 Himes	Y	N	Y	Y	Y	Y
5 Murphy	Y	Y	Y	Y	Y	Y
DELAWARE						
AL Carney	Y	N	Y	Y	Y	Y
FLORIDA						
1 Miller	Y	Y	N	N	N	N
2 Southerland	Y	Y	N	N	N	N
3 Brown	?	N	Y	Y	Y	Y
4 Crenshaw	Y	Y	N	N	N	N
5 Nugent	Y	Y	N	N	N	N
6 Stearns	Y	Y	N	N	N	N
7 Mica	Y	Y	N	N	N	N
8 Webster	Y	Y	N	N	N	N
9 Bilirakis	Y	Y	N	N	N	N
10 Young	Y	Y	N	N	N	N
11 Castor	Y	N	Y	Y	Y	Y
12 Ross	Y	Y	N	N	N	N
13 Buchanan	Y	Y	N	N	N	N
14 Mack	Y	Y	N	N	N	N
15 Posey	Y	Y	N	N	N	N
16 Rooney	Y	+	N	N	N	N
17 Wilson	Y	N	Y	Y	Y	Y
18 Ros-Lehtinen	Y	Y	N	N	N	N
19 Deutch	Y	N	Y	Y	Y	Y
20 Wasserman Schultz	Y	N	Y	Y	Y	Y
21 Diaz-Balart	Y	Y	N	N	N	N
22 West	Y	Y	N	N	N	N
23 Hastings	Y	N	Y	Y	Y	Y
24 Adams	Y	Y	N	N	N	N
25 Rivera	Y	Y	N	N	N	N
GEORGIA						
1 Kingston	?	Y	N	N	Y	N
2 Bishop	Y	N	Y	Y	Y	Y
3 Westmoreland	Y	Y	N	N	N	N
4 Johnson	Y	N	Y	Y	Y	Y
5 Lewis	Y	N	Y	Y	Y	Y
6 Price	Y	Y	N	N	N	N
7 Woodall	Y	Y	N	N	N	N
8 Scott, A.	Y	Y	N	N	N	N
9 Graves	Y	Y	N	N	N	N
10 Broun	N	Y	N	N	N	N
11 Gingrey	Y	Y	N	N	N	N
12 Barrow	Y	N	Y	Y	Y	Y
13 Scott, D.	Y	N	Y	Y	Y	Y
HAWAII						
1 Hanabusa	Y	N	Y	Y	Y	Y
2 Hirono	?	N	Y	Y	Y	Y
IDAHO						
1 Labrador	Y	Y	N	N	N	N
2 Simpson	Y	Y	N	N	N	N
ILLINOIS						
1 Rush	?	N	Y	Y	Y	Y
2 Jackson	+	-	+	+	+	+
3 Lipinski	Y	N	Y	Y	Y	Y
4 Gutierrez	?	N	Y	Y	Y	Y
5 Quigley	Y	N	Y	Y	Y	Y
6 Roskam	Y	Y	N	N	N	N
7 Davis	Y	N	?	Y	Y	Y
8 Walsh	Y	Y	N	N	N	N
9 Schakowsky	Y	N	Y	Y	Y	Y
10 Dold	Y	Y	N	N	N	N
11 Kinzinger	Y	Y	N	N	N	N
12 Costello	Y	N	Y	Y	Y	Y
13 Biggert	Y	Y	N	Y	N	N
14 Hultgren	Y	Y	N	N	N	N
15 Johnson	+	Y	N	N	N	N

KEY   **Republicans**   Democrats

Y	Voted for (yea)	
#	Paired for	
+	Announced for	
N	Voted against (nay)	

X	Paired against
-	Announced against
P	Voted "present"

C	Voted "present" to avoid possible conflict of interest
?	Did not vote or otherwise make a position known

	73	74	75	76	77	78
16 **Manzullo**	Y	Y	N	N	N	N
17 **Schilling**	Y	Y	N	N	Y	N
18 **Schock**	Y	Y	N	N	N	N
19 **Shimkus**	Y	Y	N	N	N	N
INDIANA						
1 Visclosky	Y	N	Y	Y	Y	Y
2 Donnelly	Y	Y	N	Y	Y	Y
3 **Stutzman**	Y	Y	N	N	N	N
4 **Rokita**	Y	Y	N	N	N	N
5 **Burton**	Y	Y	N	N	N	N
6 **Pence**	Y	Y	N	N	N	N
7 Carson	Y	N	Y	Y	Y	Y
8 **Bucshon**	Y	Y	N	N	N	N
9 **Young**	Y	Y	N	N	N	N
IOWA						
1 Braley	Y	N	Y	Y	Y	Y
2 Loebsack	Y	N	Y	N	Y	Y
3 Boswell	Y	N	Y	Y	Y	Y
4 **Latham**	Y	Y	N	N	N	N
5 **King**	Y	Y	N	N	N	N
KANSAS						
1 **Huelskamp**	Y	Y	N	N	N	N
2 **Jenkins**	Y	Y	N	N	N	N
3 **Yoder**	Y	Y	N	N	N	N
4 **Pompeo**	Y	Y	N	N	N	N
KENTUCKY						
1 **Whitfield**	Y	Y	N	N	N	N
2 **Guthrie**	Y	Y	N	N	N	N
3 Yarmuth	Y	N	Y	Y	Y	?
4 **Davis**	Y	Y	N	N	N	N
5 **Rogers**	Y	Y	N	N	N	N
6 Chandler	Y	N	Y	N	Y	Y
LOUISIANA						
1 **Scalise**	Y	Y	N	N	N	N
2 Richmond	Y	N	Y	Y	Y	Y
3 **Landry**	?	?	?	?	?	?
4 **Fleming**	Y	Y	N	N	N	N
5 **Alexander**	Y	Y	N	N	N	N
6 **Cassidy**	Y	Y	N	N	N	–
7 **Boustany**	Y	Y	N	N	N	N
MAINE						
1 Pingree	Y	N	Y	Y	Y	Y
2 Michaud	Y	Y	Y	Y	Y	Y
MARYLAND						
1 **Harris**	Y	Y	N	N	N	N
2 Ruppersberger	Y	N	Y	Y	?	Y
3 Sarbanes	Y	N	Y	Y	Y	Y
4 Edwards	Y	N	Y	Y	Y	Y
5 Hoyer	Y	N	Y	Y	Y	Y
6 **Bartlett**	Y	Y	N	N	N	N
7 Cummings	Y	N	Y	Y	Y	Y
8 Van Hollen	Y	N	Y	Y	Y	Y
MASSACHUSETTS						
1 Olver	Y	N	Y	Y	Y	Y
2 Neal	Y	N	Y	Y	Y	Y
3 McGovern	Y	N	Y	Y	Y	Y
4 Frank	Y	N	Y	Y	N	Y
5 Tsongas	Y	N	Y	Y	Y	Y
6 Tierney	?	N	Y	Y	Y	Y
7 Markey	Y	N	Y	Y	Y	Y
8 Capuano	Y	N	Y	Y	Y	Y
9 Lynch	Y	?	?	Y	Y	Y
10 Keating	Y	N	Y	Y	Y	Y
MICHIGAN						
1 **Benishek**	Y	Y	N	N	N	N
2 **Huizenga**	Y	Y	N	N	N	N
3 **Amash**	N	Y	N	N	N	N
4 **Camp**	Y	Y	N	N	N	N
5 Kildee	Y	N	Y	Y	Y	Y
6 **Upton**	Y	Y	N	N	Y	N
7 **Walberg**	Y	Y	N	N	N	N
8 **Rogers**	Y	Y	N	N	N	N
9 Peters	Y	N	Y	Y	Y	Y
10 **Miller**	Y	Y	N	N	Y	N
11 **McCotter**	Y	Y	N	N	N	N
12 Levin	Y	N	Y	Y	Y	Y
13 Clarke	Y	N	Y	Y	Y	Y
14 Conyers	Y	N	Y	Y	Y	Y
15 Dingell	?	N	Y	Y	Y	Y
MINNESOTA						
1 Walz	Y	N	N	N	Y	Y
2 **Kline**	Y	Y	N	N	N	N
3 **Paulsen**	Y	Y	N	N	Y	N
4 McCollum	Y	N	Y	Y	?	Y

	73	74	75	76	77	78
5 Ellison	N	N	Y	Y	Y	Y
6 **Bachmann**	Y	Y	N	N	N	N
7 Peterson	Y	N	Y	N	Y	N
8 **Cravaack**	Y	Y	N	N	N	N
MISSISSIPPI						
1 **Nunnelee**	Y	Y	N	N	N	N
2 Thompson	Y	N	Y	Y	Y	Y
3 **Harper**	Y	Y	N	N	N	N
4 **Palazzo**	Y	Y	N	N	N	N
MISSOURI						
1 Clay	?	?	?	?	?	?
2 **Akin**	+	+	–	–	–	–
3 Carnahan	?	?	Y	?	?	Y
4 **Hartzler**	Y	Y	N	N	N	N
5 Cleaver	?	?	?	?	?	?
6 **Graves**	Y	Y	N	N	N	N
7 **Long**	Y	Y	N	N	N	N
8 **Emerson**	Y	Y	N	N	N	N
9 **Luetkemeyer**	Y	Y	N	N	N	N
MONTANA						
AL **Rehberg**	Y	Y	N	N	N	N
NEBRASKA						
1 **Fortenberry**	Y	Y	N	N	N	N
2 **Terry**	Y	Y	N	?	N	N
3 **Smith**	Y	Y	N	N	N	N
NEVADA						
1 Berkley	Y	N	Y	Y	Y	Y
2 **Amodei**	?	Y	N	N	N	N
3 **Heck**	Y	Y	N	N	N	N
NEW HAMPSHIRE						
1 **Guinta**	Y	Y	N	N	N	N
2 **Bass**	Y	Y	N	N	N	N
NEW JERSEY						
1 Andrews	Y	N	Y	N	N	Y
2 **LoBiondo**	Y	Y	N	N	N	N
3 **Runyan**	Y	Y	N	N	N	N
4 **Smith**	Y	Y	N	N	N	?
5 **Garrett**	Y	Y	N	N	N	N
6 Pallone	Y	N	Y	Y	Y	Y
7 **Lance**	Y	Y	N	N	Y	N
8 Pascrell	+	N	Y	?	Y	Y
9 Rothman	Y	N	Y	Y	Y	Y
10 Payne	?	?	?	?	?	?
11 **Frelinghuysen**	Y	Y	N	N	N	N
12 Holt	Y	Y	Y	N	Y	Y
13 Sires	Y	N	Y	N	Y	N
NEW MEXICO						
1 Heinrich	Y	N	Y	Y	Y	Y
2 **Pearce**	Y	Y	N	N	N	N
3 Luján	Y	N	Y	Y	Y	Y
NEW YORK						
1 Bishop	Y	Y	Y	Y	Y	Y
2 Israel	Y	N	Y	Y	Y	Y
3 **King**	Y	Y	N	N	N	N
4 McCarthy	Y	N	Y	Y	Y	Y
5 Ackerman	Y	N	Y	Y	Y	Y
6 Meeks	Y	N	Y	Y	Y	Y
7 Crowley	Y	N	Y	Y	Y	Y
8 Nadler	Y	N	Y	Y	Y	Y
9 **Turner**	Y	Y	N	N	N	N
10 Towns	?	N	N	N	Y	Y
11 Clarke	?	N	Y	Y	Y	Y
12 Velázquez	Y	N	Y	Y	Y	Y
13 **Grimm**	Y	Y	?	N	N	N
14 Maloney	Y	N	Y	Y	Y	Y
15 Rangel	?	?	?	?	?	?
16 Serrano	Y	N	Y	Y	Y	Y
17 Engel	Y	N	Y	N	Y	Y
18 Lowey	Y	N	Y	Y	Y	Y
19 **Hayworth**	Y	Y	N	N	N	N
20 **Gibson**	Y	Y	N	N	Y	N
21 Tonko	Y	N	Y	Y	Y	Y
22 Hinchey	Y	N	Y	Y	Y	Y
23 Owens	Y	N	N	N	Y	N
24 **Hanna**	Y	Y	N	N	Y	N
25 **Buerkle**	Y	Y	N	N	N	N
26 Hochul	Y	N	Y	N	Y	Y
27 Higgins	Y	N	Y	Y	Y	Y
28 Slaughter	Y	N	Y	Y	Y	Y
29 **Reed**	Y	Y	N	N	N	N
NORTH CAROLINA						
1 Butterfield	Y	N	Y	Y	Y	Y
2 **Ellmers**	Y	Y	N	N	N	N
3 **Jones**	Y	Y	N	N	N	N
4 Price	Y	N	Y	Y	Y	Y

	73	74	75	76	77	78
5 **Foxx**	Y	Y	N	N	N	N
6 **Coble**	Y	Y	N	N	N	N
7 McIntyre	Y	Y	Y	N	Y	Y
8 Kissell	Y	Y	Y	N	Y	Y
9 **Myrick**	Y	Y	N	N	N	N
10 **McHenry**	Y	Y	N	N	N	N
11 Shuler	?	Y	Y	N	N	Y
12 Watt	Y	N	Y	Y	Y	Y
13 Miller	Y	N	Y	Y	Y	Y
NORTH DAKOTA						
AL **Berg**	Y	Y	N	N	N	N
OHIO						
1 **Chabot**	Y	Y	N	N	N	N
2 **Schmidt**	Y	Y	N	N	N	N
3 **Turner**	Y	Y	N	N	N	N
4 **Jordan**	Y	Y	N	N	N	N
5 **Latta**	Y	Y	N	N	N	N
6 **Johnson**	Y	Y	N	N	N	N
7 **Austria**	Y	Y	N	N	N	N
8 **Boehner**						
9 Kaptur	?	N	?	?	?	Y
10 Kucinich	?	N	Y	Y	Y	Y
11 Fudge	Y	N	Y	Y	Y	Y
12 **Tiberi**	Y	Y	N	N	N	N
13 Sutton	Y	N	Y	Y	Y	Y
14 **LaTourette**	Y	Y	N	N	N	N
15 **Stivers**	Y	Y	N	N	N	N
16 **Renacci**	Y	Y	N	N	N	N
17 Ryan	Y	N	Y	Y	Y	Y
18 **Gibbs**	Y	Y	N	N	N	N
OKLAHOMA						
1 **Sullivan**	Y	Y	N	N	N	N
2 Boren	Y	N	N	N	Y	Y
3 **Lucas**	Y	Y	N	N	N	N
4 **Cole**	Y	Y	N	N	N	N
5 **Lankford**	Y	?	N	N	N	?
OREGON						
1 Bonamici	Y	N	N	Y	Y	Y
2 **Walden**	Y	Y	N	N	N	N
3 Blumenauer	Y	N	Y	Y	Y	Y
4 DeFazio	Y	N	Y	Y	Y	Y
5 Schrader	Y	N	N	N	Y	N
PENNSYLVANIA						
1 Brady	Y	N	Y	Y	Y	Y
2 Fattah	Y	N	Y	Y	Y	Y
3 **Kelly**	Y	Y	N	N	N	N
4 Altmire	Y	N	Y	Y	Y	Y
5 **Thompson**	Y	Y	N	N	N	N
6 **Gerlach**	Y	Y	N	N	Y	N
7 **Meehan**	Y	Y	N	N	Y	N
8 **Fitzpatrick**	Y	Y	N	N	Y	N
9 **Shuster**	Y	Y	N	?	N	N
10 **Marino**	?	Y	N	N	N	N
11 **Barletta**	Y	Y	N	N	N	N
12 Critz	Y	N	N	N	Y	Y
13 Schwartz	Y	N	Y	Y	Y	Y
14 Doyle	Y	N	Y	Y	Y	Y
15 **Dent**	Y	Y	N	N	Y	N
16 **Pitts**	Y	Y	N	N	N	N
17 Holden	Y	N	Y	N	Y	Y
18 **Murphy**	Y	Y	N	N	N	N
19 **Platts**	?	Y	N	N	N	N
RHODE ISLAND						
1 Cicilline	Y	N	Y	Y	Y	Y
2 Langevin	?	N	Y	Y	Y	Y
SOUTH CAROLINA						
1 **Scott**	Y	Y	N	N	N	N
2 **Wilson**	Y	Y	N	N	N	N
3 **Duncan**	Y	Y	N	N	N	N
4 **Gowdy**	Y	Y	N	N	N	N
5 **Mulvaney**	Y	Y	N	N	N	N
6 Clyburn	Y	N	Y	Y	Y	Y
SOUTH DAKOTA						
AL **Noem**	Y	Y	N	N	N	N
TENNESSEE						
1 **Roe**	Y	Y	N	N	N	N
2 **Duncan**	Y	Y	N	?	?	N
3 **Fleischmann**	Y	Y	N	N	N	N
4 **DesJarlais**	Y	Y	N	N	N	N
5 Cooper	Y	N	Y	Y	Y	Y
6 **Black**	Y	Y	N	N	N	N
7 **Blackburn**	Y	Y	N	N	N	N
8 **Fincher**	Y	Y	N	N	N	N
9 Cohen	Y	N	Y	Y	Y	Y

	73	74	75	76	77	78
TEXAS						
1 **Gohmert**	Y	Y	N	N	N	N
2 **Poe**	Y	Y	N	N	N	N
3 **Johnson, S.**	Y	Y	N	N	N	N
4 **Hall**	Y	Y	N	N	N	?
5 **Hensarling**	Y	Y	N	N	N	N
6 **Barton**	Y	Y	N	Y	N	N
7 **Culberson**	?	Y	N	N	N	N
8 **Brady**	Y	Y	N	?	N	N
9 Green, A.	Y	N	Y	Y	Y	Y
10 **McCaul**	Y	Y	N	N	N	N
11 **Conaway**	Y	Y	N	N	N	N
12 **Granger**	Y	Y	N	N	N	N
13 **Thornberry**	?	Y	N	N	N	N
14 **Paul**	?	Y	N	N	N	N
15 Hinojosa	Y	N	+	Y	Y	Y
16 Reyes	Y	N	Y	Y	Y	Y
17 **Flores**	Y	Y	N	N	N	N
18 Jackson Lee	Y	N	Y	Y	Y	Y
19 **Neugebauer**	Y	Y	N	N	N	N
20 Gonzalez	Y	N	Y	Y	Y	Y
21 **Smith**	Y	Y	N	N	N	N
22 **Olson**	Y	Y	N	N	N	N
23 **Canseco**	Y	Y	N	N	N	N
24 **Marchant**	?	Y	N	N	N	N
25 Doggett	Y	N	Y	Y	Y	Y
26 **Burgess**	Y	Y	N	N	N	N
27 **Farenthold**	Y	Y	N	N	N	N
28 Cuellar	Y	N	Y	Y	Y	Y
29 Green, G.	Y	N	Y	Y	Y	Y
30 Johnson, E.	Y	N	Y	Y	Y	Y
31 **Carter**	Y	Y	N	N	N	N
32 **Sessions**	Y	Y	N	N	N	N
UTAH						
1 **Bishop**	Y	Y	N	N	N	N
2 Matheson	Y	Y	N	N	Y	N
3 **Chaffetz**	Y	Y	N	N	N	N
VERMONT						
AL Welch	Y	N	Y	Y	Y	Y
VIRGINIA						
1 **Wittman**	Y	Y	N	N	N	N
2 **Rigell**	Y	Y	N	N	Y	N
3 Scott	Y	N	Y	Y	Y	Y
4 **Forbes**	Y	Y	N	N	N	N
5 **Hurt**	Y	Y	N	N	N	N
6 **Goodlatte**	Y	Y	N	N	N	N
7 **Cantor**	Y	Y	N	?	?	N
8 Moran	Y	N	Y	Y	Y	Y
9 **Griffith**	Y	Y	N	N	N	N
10 **Wolf**	Y	Y	N	N	N	N
11 Connolly	Y	N	Y	Y	Y	Y
WASHINGTON						
1 Inslee	?	N	Y	N	Y	Y
2 Larsen	Y	N	Y	Y	Y	Y
3 **Herrera Beutler**	Y	Y	N	N	N	N
4 **Hastings**	Y	Y	N	N	N	N
5 **McMorris Rodgers**	Y	?	N	N	N	?
6 Dicks	Y	N	Y	Y	Y	Y
7 McDermott	Y	N	Y	Y	Y	Y
8 **Reichert**	Y	Y	N	N	?	N
9 Smith	?	N	Y	Y	Y	Y
WEST VIRGINIA						
1 **McKinley**	Y	Y	N	N	N	N
2 **Capito**	Y	Y	N	N	Y	N
3 Rahall	Y	N	Y	Y	Y	Y
WISCONSIN						
1 **Ryan**	Y	Y	N	N	N	N
2 Baldwin	Y	N	Y	Y	Y	Y
3 Kind	Y	N	Y	Y	Y	Y
4 Moore	Y	N	Y	Y	Y	Y
5 **Sensenbrenner**	Y	Y	N	N	N	N
6 **Petri**	Y	Y	N	N	N	N
7 **Duffy**	Y	Y	N	N	N	N
8 **Ribble**	Y	Y	N	N	N	N
WYOMING						
AL **Lummis**	Y	Y	N	N	N	N

IN THE HOUSE | By Vote Number

79. **HR 2117. For-Profit College Regulations/Passage.** Passage of the bill that would rescind Education Department regulations that define a credit hour and set minimum requirements that all higher education institutions must meet to be considered authorized by a state. It also would bar the Education secretary from establishing or enforcing any new rules to define the term "credit hour." Passed 303-114: R 234-0; D 69-114. A "nay" was a vote in support of the president's position. Feb. 28, 2012.

80. **HR 1837. California Water Resources/Previous Question.** Bishop, R-Utah, motion to order the previous question (thus ending debate and possibility of amendment) on adoption of the rule (H Res 566) that would provide for House floor consideration of the bill that would change California water-supply practices around the San Joaquin Valley. Motion agreed to 241-178: R 235-1; D 6-177. Feb. 29, 2012.

81. **HR 1837. California Water Resources/Rule.** Adoption of the rule (H Res 566) that would provide for House floor consideration of the bill that would change California water-supply practices around the San Joaquin Valley. Adopted 245-173: R 236-0; D 9-173. Feb. 29, 2012.

82. **Procedural Motion /Journal.** Approval of the House Journal of Tuesday, Feb. 28, 2012. Approved 283-127: R 176-52; D 107-75. Feb. 29, 2012.

83. **HR 1837. California Water Resources/Jobs and Revenue Impact.** Thompson, D-Calif., amendment that would prevent portions of the bill relating to conservation and environmental regulations from taking effect unless the Interior Department, in consultation with the Agriculture, Commerce and Labor departments, certifies that the bill would not result in the loss of agriculture- or fishery-related jobs or revenue within counties north of the Sacramento-San Joaquin River Delta. Rejected in Committee of the Whole 178-239: R 2-231; D 176-8. Feb. 29, 2012.

84. **HR 1837. California Water Resources/Drinking-Water Supply Impact.** McNerney, D-Calif., amendment that would prevent portions of the bill relating to conservation and environmental regulations from taking effect until the Interior Department determines that there would be no harmful effects on the drinking water supplies for residents of the five California delta-area counties. Rejected in Committee of the Whole 178-242: R 1-236; D 177-6. Feb. 29, 2012.

	79	80	81	82	83	84
ALABAMA						
1 Bonner	Y	Y	Y	Y	N	N
2 Roby	Y	Y	Y	Y	N	N
3 Rogers	Y	Y	Y	Y	N	N
4 Aderholt	Y	Y	Y	Y	N	N
5 Brooks	Y	Y	Y	Y	N	N
6 Bachus	Y	Y	Y	Y	N	N
7 Sewell	Y	N	N	Y	Y	Y
ALASKA						
AL Young	?	Y	Y	N	N	N
ARIZONA						
1 Gosar	Y	Y	Y	Y	N	N
2 Franks	Y	Y	Y	Y	N	N
3 Quayle	Y	Y	Y	Y	N	N
4 Pastor	Y	N	N	N	Y	Y
5 Schweikert	Y	Y	Y	Y	N	N
6 Flake	Y	Y	Y	Y	N	N
7 Grijalva	N	N	N	N	Y	Y
8 Vacant						
ARKANSAS						
1 Crawford	+	Y	Y	Y	N	N
2 Griffin	Y	Y	Y	N	N	N
3 Womack	Y	Y	Y	Y	N	N
4 Ross	Y	Y	Y	Y	N	N
CALIFORNIA						
1 Thompson	N	N	N	N	Y	Y
2 Herger	Y	Y	Y	Y	N	N
3 Lungren	Y	Y	Y	Y	N	N
4 McClintock	Y	Y	Y	Y	N	N
5 Matsui	N	N	N	Y	Y	Y
6 Woolsey	N	?	?	?	Y	Y
7 Miller, George	N	N	N	Y	Y	Y
8 Pelosi	N	N	N	Y	?	Y
9 Lee	–	–	–	+	+	+
10 Garamendi	N	N	N	Y	Y	Y
11 McNerney	N	N	N	Y	Y	Y
12 Speier	N	N	N	Y	Y	Y
13 Stark	N	N	N	Y	Y	Y
14 Eshoo	N	N	N	Y	Y	Y
15 Honda	N	N	N	Y	Y	Y
16 Lofgren	N	N	N	Y	Y	Y
17 Farr	N	N	N	Y	Y	Y
18 Cardoza	?	Y	Y	N	N	N
19 Denham	Y	Y	Y	Y	N	N
20 Costa	Y	Y	Y	N	N	N
21 Nunes	Y	Y	Y	Y	N	N
22 McCarthy	Y	Y	Y	Y	N	N
23 Capps	N	N	N	Y	Y	Y
24 Gallegly	Y	Y	Y	Y	N	N
25 McKeon	Y	Y	Y	Y	N	N
26 Dreier	Y	Y	Y	Y	N	N
27 Sherman	N	?	N	Y	Y	Y
28 Berman	N	N	N	?	Y	Y
29 Schiff	N	N	N	Y	Y	Y
30 Waxman	N	N	N	Y	Y	Y
31 Becerra	N	N	N	Y	Y	Y
32 Chu	N	N	N	N	Y	Y
33 Bass	N	?	?	?	?	?
34 Roybal-Allard	N	N	N	Y	Y	Y
35 Waters	N	N	N	N	Y	Y
36 Hahn	N	N	N	Y	Y	Y
37 Richardson	N	N	N	Y	Y	Y
38 Napolitano	N	N	N	Y	Y	Y
39 Sánchez, Linda	N	N	N	N	Y	Y
40 Royce	Y	Y	Y	Y	N	N
41 Lewis	Y	Y	Y	Y	N	N
42 Miller, Gary	Y	Y	Y	Y	N	N
43 Baca	Y	N	N	Y	Y	Y
44 Calvert	Y	Y	Y	Y	N	N
45 Bono Mack	Y	Y	Y	Y	N	N
46 Rohrabacher	Y	Y	Y	Y	N	N
47 Sanchez, Loretta	N	N	N	Y	Y	Y
48 Campbell	Y	Y	Y	Y	N	N
49 Issa	Y	Y	Y	Y	N	N
50 Bilbray	Y	Y	Y	Y	N	N
51 Filner	N	N	N	N	Y	Y
52 Hunter	?	Y	Y	N	N	N
53 Davis	N	N	N	Y	Y	+

	79	80	81	82	83	84
COLORADO						
1 DeGette	N	N	N	Y	Y	Y
2 Polis	Y	N	N	Y	Y	Y
3 Tipton	Y	Y	Y	N	N	N
4 Gardner	Y	Y	Y	Y	N	N
5 Lamborn	Y	Y	Y	Y	N	N
6 Coffman	Y	Y	Y	Y	N	N
7 Perlmutter	Y	N	N	Y	Y	Y
CONNECTICUT						
1 Larson	N	N	N	Y	Y	Y
2 Courtney	N	N	N	Y	Y	Y
3 DeLauro	N	N	N	Y	Y	Y
4 Himes	N	N	N	Y	Y	Y
5 Murphy	–	N	N	Y	Y	Y
DELAWARE						
AL Carney	Y	N	N	Y	Y	Y
FLORIDA						
1 Miller	Y	Y	Y	Y	N	N
2 Southerland	Y	Y	Y	N	N	N
3 Brown	N	N	N	Y	Y	Y
4 Crenshaw	Y	Y	Y	Y	N	N
5 Nugent	Y	Y	Y	Y	N	N
6 Stearns	Y	Y	Y	Y	N	N
7 Mica	Y	Y	Y	Y	N	N
8 Webster	Y	Y	Y	Y	N	N
9 Bilirakis	Y	Y	Y	Y	N	N
10 Young	Y	Y	Y	Y	N	N
11 Castor	N	N	N	Y	Y	Y
12 Ross	Y	Y	Y	Y	N	N
13 Buchanan	Y	Y	Y	Y	N	N
14 Mack	Y	Y	Y	Y	N	N
15 Posey	Y	Y	Y	Y	N	N
16 Rooney	Y	Y	Y	Y	N	N
17 Wilson	N	N	N	Y	Y	Y
18 Ros-Lehtinen	Y	?	?	?	N	N
19 Deutch	N	N	N	Y	Y	Y
20 Wasserman Schultz	N	N	N	Y	Y	Y
21 Diaz-Balart	Y	Y	Y	Y	?	N
22 West	Y	Y	Y	Y	N	N
23 Hastings	N	N	N	N	Y	Y
24 Adams	Y	Y	Y	Y	N	N
25 Rivera	Y	Y	?	Y	N	N
GEORGIA						
1 Kingston	Y	Y	Y	Y	N	N
2 Bishop	Y	N	N	Y	Y	Y
3 Westmoreland	Y	Y	Y	Y	N	N
4 Johnson	N	N	N	Y	Y	Y
5 Lewis	N	N	N	N	Y	Y
6 Price	Y	Y	Y	Y	N	N
7 Woodall	Y	Y	Y	Y	N	N
8 Scott, A.	Y	Y	Y	Y	N	N
9 Graves	Y	Y	Y	Y	N	N
10 Broun	Y	Y	Y	Y	N	N
11 Gingrey	Y	Y	Y	Y	N	N
12 Barrow	Y	N	N	Y	Y	Y
13 Scott, D.	N	N	N	Y	Y	Y
HAWAII						
1 Hanabusa	Y	N	N	Y	Y	Y
2 Hirono	N	N	N	Y	Y	Y
IDAHO						
1 Labrador	Y	Y	Y	Y	N	N
2 Simpson	Y	Y	Y	Y	N	N
ILLINOIS						
1 Rush	N	N	N	N	?	?
2 Jackson	–	N	N	N	Y	Y
3 Lipinski	Y	N	N	Y	Y	Y
4 Gutierrez	N	N	N	N	Y	Y
5 Quigley	N	N	N	Y	Y	Y
6 Roskam	Y	Y	Y	Y	N	N
7 Davis	N	N	N	N	Y	Y
8 Walsh	Y	Y	Y	N	N	N
9 Schakowsky	N	N	N	N	?	+
10 Dold	Y	Y	Y	N	N	N
11 Kinzinger	Y	Y	Y	N	N	N
12 Costello	N	N	N	Y	Y	Y
13 Biggert	Y	Y	Y	Y	N	N
14 Hultgren	Y	Y	Y	Y	N	N
15 Johnson	Y	Y	Y	Y	N	N

KEY   **Republicans**   Democrats

Y Voted for (yea)	X Paired against
# Paired for	– Announced against
+ Announced for	P Voted "present"
N Voted against (nay)	

C Voted "present" to avoid possible conflict of interest

? Did not vote or otherwise make a position known

	79	80	81	82	83	84
16 **Manzullo**	Y	Y	Y	Y	N	N
17 **Schilling**	Y	Y	Y	N	N	N
18 **Schock**	Y	Y	Y	Y	N	N
19 **Shimkus**	Y	Y	Y	Y	N	N
INDIANA						
1 Visclosky	Y	N	N	N	Y	Y
2 Donnelly	Y	N	N	N	Y	Y
3 **Stutzman**	Y	Y	Y	Y	N	N
4 **Rokita**	Y	Y	Y	Y	N	N
5 **Burton**	Y	Y	Y	Y	N	N
6 **Pence**	Y	Y	Y	Y	N	N
7 Carson	Y	N	N	Y	Y	Y
8 **Bucshon**	Y	Y	Y	Y	N	N
9 **Young**	Y	Y	Y	Y	N	N
IOWA						
1 Braley	Y	N	–	Y	Y	Y
2 Loebsack	Y	N	N	Y	Y	Y
3 Boswell	Y	N	N	N	Y	Y
4 **Latham**	Y	Y	Y	N	N	N
5 **King**	Y	Y	Y	Y	N	N
KANSAS						
1 **Huelskamp**	Y	Y	Y	?	N	N
2 **Jenkins**	Y	Y	Y	Y	N	N
3 **Yoder**	Y	Y	Y	N	N	N
4 **Pompeo**	Y	Y	Y	Y	N	N
KENTUCKY						
1 **Whitfield**	Y	Y	Y	Y	N	N
2 **Guthrie**	Y	Y	Y	Y	N	N
3 Yarmuth	N	N	N	Y	Y	Y
4 **Davis**	Y	Y	Y	N	?	N
5 **Rogers**	Y	Y	Y	Y	N	?
6 Chandler	Y	N	N	N	Y	Y
LOUISIANA						
1 **Scalise**	Y	Y	Y	Y	N	N
2 Richmond	N	N	N	N	Y	Y
3 **Landry**	?	Y	Y	Y	N	N
4 **Fleming**	Y	Y	Y	?	N	N
5 **Alexander**	Y	Y	Y	Y	N	N
6 **Cassidy**	Y	Y	Y	Y	N	N
7 **Boustany**	Y	Y	Y	Y	?	N
MAINE						
1 Pingree	N	N	N	N	Y	Y
2 Michaud	Y	N	N	Y	Y	Y
MARYLAND						
1 **Harris**	Y	Y	Y	Y	N	N
2 Ruppersberger	Y	N	?	Y	Y	Y
3 Sarbanes	N	N	N	N	Y	Y
4 Edwards	N	N	N	Y	Y	Y
5 Hoyer	N	N	N	N	Y	Y
6 **Bartlett**	Y	Y	Y	Y	N	N
7 Cummings	N	N	N	N	Y	Y
8 Van Hollen	N	N	N	Y	Y	Y
MASSACHUSETTS						
1 Olver	N	N	N	N	Y	Y
2 Neal	N	N	N	N	Y	Y
3 McGovern	N	N	N	N	Y	Y
4 Frank	N	N	N	Y	Y	Y
5 Tsongas	N	N	N	Y	Y	Y
6 Tierney	N	N	N	N	Y	?
7 Markey	N	N	N	N	Y	Y
8 Capuano	Y	N	N	N	Y	Y
9 Lynch	N	N	N	N	Y	Y
10 Keating	N	N	N	N	Y	Y
MICHIGAN						
1 **Benishek**	Y	Y	Y	N	N	N
2 **Huizenga**	Y	Y	Y	Y	N	N
3 **Amash**	Y	Y	Y	P	N	N
4 **Camp**	Y	Y	Y	Y	N	N
5 Kildee	N	N	N	Y	Y	Y
6 **Upton**	Y	Y	Y	Y	N	N
7 **Walberg**	Y	Y	Y	N	Y	N
8 **Rogers**	Y	Y	Y	Y	N	N
9 Peters	N	N	N	N	Y	Y
10 **Miller**	Y	Y	Y	Y	N	N
11 **McCotter**	Y	Y	Y	N	N	N
12 Levin	N	N	N	Y	Y	Y
13 Clarke	N	N	N	N	Y	Y
14 Conyers	N	N	N	N	Y	Y
15 Dingell	N	N	N	Y	Y	Y
MINNESOTA						
1 Walz	Y	N	N	Y	Y	Y
2 **Kline**	Y	Y	Y	Y	N	N
3 **Paulsen**	Y	Y	Y	Y	N	N
4 McCollum	N	N	N	Y	Y	Y

	79	80	81	82	83	84
5 Ellison	N	N	N	Y	Y	Y
6 **Bachmann**	Y	Y	Y	Y	N	N
7 Peterson	Y	N	Y	N	N	N
8 **Cravaack**	Y	Y	Y	N	N	N
MISSISSIPPI						
1 **Nunnelee**	Y	Y	Y	Y	N	N
2 Thompson	Y	N	N	N	Y	Y
3 **Harper**	Y	Y	Y	?	N	N
4 **Palazzo**	Y	Y	Y	Y	?	N
MISSOURI						
1 Clay	?	N	N	N	Y	Y
2 **Akin**	+	Y	Y	?	N	N
3 Carnahan	N	N	N	Y	Y	Y
4 **Hartzler**	Y	Y	Y	Y	N	N
5 Cleaver	?	N	N	N	Y	Y
6 **Graves**	Y	Y	Y	N	N	N
7 **Long**	Y	Y	Y	Y	N	N
8 **Emerson**	Y	Y	Y	N	N	N
9 **Luetkemeyer**	Y	Y	Y	Y	N	N
MONTANA						
AL **Rehberg**	Y	Y	Y	Y	N	N
NEBRASKA						
1 **Fortenberry**	Y	Y	Y	Y	N	N
2 **Terry**	Y	Y	Y	N	N	N
3 **Smith**	Y	Y	Y	Y	N	N
NEVADA						
1 Berkley	Y	N	N	Y	Y	Y
2 **Amodei**	Y	Y	Y	Y	N	N
3 **Heck**	Y	Y	Y	N	N	N
NEW HAMPSHIRE						
1 **Guinta**	Y	Y	Y	Y	N	N
2 **Bass**	Y	Y	Y	Y	N	N
NEW JERSEY						
1 Andrews	Y	N	N	N	Y	Y
2 **LoBiondo**	Y	Y	Y	N	N	N
3 **Runyan**	Y	Y	Y	Y	N	N
4 **Smith**	Y	Y	Y	Y	N	N
5 **Garrett**	Y	Y	Y	N	N	N
6 Pallone	N	N	N	N	Y	Y
7 **Lance**	Y	Y	Y	N	N	N
8 Pascrell	Y	N	N	Y	Y	Y
9 Rothman	N	N	N	Y	Y	Y
10 Payne	?	?	?	?	?	?
11 **Frelinghuysen**	Y	Y	Y	Y	N	N
12 Holt	Y	N	N	N	Y	Y
13 Sires	Y	N	N	N	Y	Y
NEW MEXICO						
1 Heinrich	N	N	N	Y	Y	Y
2 **Pearce**	Y	Y	Y	N	N	N
3 Luján	N	N	N	Y	Y	Y
NEW YORK						
1 Bishop	N	N	N	N	Y	Y
2 Israel	?	N	N	N	Y	Y
3 **King**	Y	Y	Y	Y	N	N
4 McCarthy	Y	N	N	Y	Y	Y
5 Ackerman	N	?	?	?	Y	Y
6 Meeks	N	N	N	Y	Y	Y
7 Crowley	N	?	?	Y	Y	Y
8 Nadler	N	?	?	?	?	?
9 **Turner**	Y	Y	Y	Y	N	N
10 Towns	Y	N	N	Y	Y	Y
11 Clarke	N	N	N	N	Y	Y
12 Velázquez	N	N	N	N	Y	Y
13 **Grimm**	Y	Y	Y	Y	N	N
14 Maloney	N	N	N	Y	Y	Y
15 Rangel	?	?	?	?	?	?
16 Serrano	N	N	N	Y	Y	Y
17 Engel	Y	N	N	Y	Y	Y
18 Lowey	Y	N	N	Y	Y	Y
19 **Hayworth**	Y	Y	Y	Y	N	N
20 **Gibson**	Y	Y	Y	N	N	Y
21 Tonko	Y	N	N	Y	Y	Y
22 Hinchey	Y	N	N	N	Y	Y
23 Owens	Y	N	N	P	Y	Y
24 **Hanna**	Y	Y	Y	N	N	N
25 **Buerkle**	Y	Y	Y	Y	N	N
26 Hochul	Y	N	N	Y	Y	Y
27 Higgins	Y	N	N	Y	Y	Y
28 Slaughter	N	N	N	N	Y	Y
29 **Reed**	Y	Y	Y	N	N	N
NORTH CAROLINA						
1 Butterfield	Y	N	N	Y	Y	Y
2 **Ellmers**	Y	Y	Y	Y	N	N
3 **Jones**	Y	N	Y	N	Y	N
4 Price	N	N	N	Y	Y	Y

	79	80	81	82	83	84
5 **Foxx**	Y	Y	Y	N	N	N
6 **Coble**	Y	Y	Y	Y	N	N
7 McIntyre	Y	N	Y	Y	Y	Y
8 Kissell	Y	Y	Y	Y	Y	Y
9 **Myrick**	Y	?	Y	Y	N	N
10 **McHenry**	+	Y	Y	Y	N	N
11 Shuler	Y	N	Y	N	N	Y
12 Watt	N	N	N	Y	Y	Y
13 Miller	N	N	N	Y	Y	Y
NORTH DAKOTA						
AL **Berg**	Y	Y	Y	Y	N	N
OHIO						
1 **Chabot**	Y	Y	Y	Y	N	N
2 **Schmidt**	Y	Y	Y	Y	?	N
3 **Turner**	Y	Y	Y	N	N	N
4 **Jordan**	Y	Y	Y	N	N	N
5 **Latta**	Y	Y	Y	Y	N	N
6 **Johnson**	Y	Y	Y	N	N	N
7 **Austria**	Y	Y	Y	Y	N	N
8 **Boehner**						
9 Kaptur	N	N	N	Y	Y	Y
10 Kucinich	N	N	N	N	Y	Y
11 Fudge	N	N	N	N	Y	Y
12 **Tiberi**	Y	Y	Y	Y	N	N
13 Sutton	Y	N	N	Y	Y	Y
14 **LaTourette**	Y	Y	Y	Y	N	N
15 **Stivers**	Y	Y	Y	N	N	N
16 **Renacci**	Y	Y	Y	N	N	N
17 Ryan	Y	N	N	N	Y	Y
18 **Gibbs**	Y	Y	Y	N	N	N
OKLAHOMA						
1 **Sullivan**	Y	Y	Y	Y	N	N
2 Boren	Y	Y	Y	Y	N	N
3 **Lucas**	Y	Y	Y	Y	N	N
4 **Cole**	Y	Y	Y	Y	N	N
5 **Lankford**	Y	Y	Y	Y	N	N
OREGON						
1 Bonamici	Y	N	N	Y	Y	Y
2 **Walden**	Y	Y	Y	Y	N	N
3 Blumenauer	N	N	N	Y	Y	Y
4 DeFazio	Y	N	N	N	Y	Y
5 Schrader	Y	N	N	Y	Y	Y
PENNSYLVANIA						
1 Brady	N	N	N	N	Y	Y
2 Fattah	N	N	N	N	Y	Y
3 **Kelly**	Y	Y	Y	Y	N	N
4 Altmire	Y	N	N	Y	Y	Y
5 **Thompson**	Y	Y	Y	Y	N	N
6 **Gerlach**	Y	Y	Y	Y	N	N
7 **Meehan**	Y	Y	Y	Y	N	N
8 **Fitzpatrick**	Y	Y	Y	N	N	N
9 **Shuster**	Y	Y	Y	Y	N	N
10 **Marino**	Y	Y	Y	Y	N	N
11 **Barletta**	Y	Y	Y	Y	N	N
12 Critz	Y	N	N	N	Y	Y
13 Schwartz	N	N	N	Y	Y	Y
14 Doyle	Y	N	N	N	Y	Y
15 **Dent**	Y	Y	Y	Y	N	N
16 **Pitts**	Y	Y	Y	Y	N	N
17 Holden	Y	N	N	N	Y	Y
18 **Murphy**	Y	Y	Y	N	N	N
19 **Platts**	Y	Y	Y	Y	N	N
RHODE ISLAND						
1 Cicilline	N	N	N	Y	Y	Y
2 Langevin	N	N	N	Y	Y	Y
SOUTH CAROLINA						
1 **Scott**	Y	Y	Y	Y	N	N
2 **Wilson**	Y	Y	Y	Y	N	N
3 **Duncan**	Y	Y	Y	Y	N	N
4 **Gowdy**	Y	Y	Y	Y	N	N
5 **Mulvaney**	Y	Y	Y	Y	N	N
6 Clyburn	Y	N	N	N	Y	Y
SOUTH DAKOTA						
AL **Noem**	Y	Y	Y	Y	N	N
TENNESSEE						
1 **Roe**	Y	Y	Y	N	N	N
2 **Duncan**	Y	Y	Y	Y	N	N
3 **Fleischmann**	Y	Y	Y	Y	N	N
4 **DesJarlais**	Y	Y	Y	Y	N	N
5 Cooper	N	N	N	Y	Y	Y
6 **Black**	Y	Y	Y	Y	N	N
7 **Blackburn**	Y	Y	Y	Y	N	N
8 **Fincher**	Y	Y	Y	Y	N	N
9 Cohen	N	N	N	Y	Y	Y

	79	80	81	82	83	84
TEXAS						
1 **Gohmert**	Y	Y	Y	?	?	?
2 **Poe**	Y	Y	Y	N	N	N
3 **Johnson, S.**	Y	Y	Y	Y	N	N
4 **Hall**	?	Y	Y	Y	N	N
5 **Hensarling**	Y	Y	Y	Y	N	N
6 **Barton**	Y	Y	Y	Y	N	N
7 **Culberson**	Y	Y	Y	Y	N	N
8 **Brady**	Y	Y	Y	Y	N	N
9 Green, A.	N	N	N	Y	Y	Y
10 **McCaul**	Y	Y	Y	Y	N	N
11 **Conaway**	Y	Y	Y	N	N	N
12 **Granger**	Y	Y	Y	Y	N	N
13 **Thornberry**	Y	Y	Y	Y	N	N
14 **Paul**	Y	?	?	?	?	?
15 Hinojosa	N	N	N	Y	Y	Y
16 Reyes	Y	N	N	Y	Y	Y
17 **Flores**	Y	Y	Y	?	N	N
18 Jackson Lee	N	N	N	N	Y	Y
19 **Neugebauer**	Y	Y	Y	Y	N	N
20 Gonzalez	N	N	N	Y	Y	Y
21 **Smith**	Y	Y	Y	Y	N	N
22 **Olson**	Y	Y	Y	Y	N	N
23 **Canseco**	Y	Y	Y	Y	N	N
24 **Marchant**	Y	Y	Y	Y	N	N
25 Doggett	N	N	N	Y	Y	Y
26 **Burgess**	Y	Y	Y	N	N	N
27 **Farenthold**	Y	Y	Y	Y	N	N
28 Cuellar	Y	N	N	Y	Y	Y
29 Green, G.	N	N	N	Y	Y	Y
30 Johnson, E.	N	N	N	N	Y	Y
31 **Carter**	Y	Y	Y	Y	N	N
32 **Sessions**	Y	Y	Y	Y	N	N
UTAH						
1 **Bishop**	Y	Y	Y	?	N	N
2 Matheson	Y	Y	Y	N	N	N
3 **Chaffetz**	Y	Y	Y	Y	N	N
VERMONT						
AL Welch	Y	N	N	Y	Y	Y
VIRGINIA						
1 **Wittman**	Y	Y	Y	N	N	N
2 **Rigell**	Y	Y	Y	Y	N	N
3 Scott	N	N	N	Y	Y	Y
4 **Forbes**	Y	Y	Y	Y	N	N
5 **Hurt**	Y	Y	Y	Y	N	N
6 **Goodlatte**	Y	+	+	?	N	N
7 **Cantor**	Y	?	?	?	?	?
8 Moran	N	N	N	Y	Y	Y
9 **Griffith**	Y	Y	Y	Y	N	N
10 **Wolf**	Y	Y	Y	Y	N	N
11 Connolly	Y	N	N	Y	Y	Y
WASHINGTON						
1 Inslee	Y	N	N	N	Y	Y
2 Larsen	Y	N	N	Y	Y	Y
3 **Herrera Beutler**	Y	Y	Y	N	N	N
4 **Hastings**	Y	Y	Y	Y	N	N
5 **McMorris Rodgers**	Y	Y	Y	Y	N	N
6 Dicks	Y	N	N	N	Y	Y
7 McDermott	N	N	N	N	Y	Y
8 **Reichert**	Y	Y	Y	Y	N	N
9 Smith	Y	N	N	Y	Y	Y
WEST VIRGINIA						
1 **McKinley**	Y	Y	Y	Y	N	N
2 **Capito**	Y	Y	Y	Y	N	N
3 Rahall	Y	N	N	N	Y	Y
WISCONSIN						
1 **Ryan**	Y	Y	Y	Y	N	N
2 Baldwin	Y	N	N	N	Y	Y
3 Kind	Y	N	N	N	Y	Y
4 Moore	Y	N	N	N	Y	Y
5 **Sensenbrenner**	Y	Y	Y	Y	N	N
6 **Petri**	Y	Y	Y	Y	N	N
7 **Duffy**	Y	Y	Y	N	N	N
8 **Ribble**	Y	Y	Y	N	N	N
WYOMING						
AL **Lummis**	Y	Y	Y	?	N	N

IN THE HOUSE | By Vote Number

85. **HR 1837. California Water Resources/Agricultural-Producer Water Supply.** McNerney, D-Calif., amendment that would prevent portions of the bill relating to conservation and environmental regulations from taking effect until the Interior Department determines there would be no harmful effects on water supplies for agricultural producers of the five California delta-area counties. Rejected in Committee of the Whole 177-243: R 1-234; D 176-9. Feb. 29, 2012.

86. **HR 1837. California Water Resources/Water Service Contract Renewal.** Garamendi, D-Calif., amendment that would strike a section of the bill that would permit contract renewals upon the request of the contractor. The amendment would maintain Interior Department authority over contract renewals. Rejected in Committee of the Whole 181-243: R 2-236; D 179-7. Feb. 29, 2012.

87. **HR 1837. California Water Resources/Water Service Charges.** Napolitano, D-Calif., amendment that would stipulate that charges for delivered water include interest as determined by the Treasury secretary based on average market yields. Rejected in Committee of the Whole 174-250: R 1-237; D 173-13. Feb. 29, 2012.

88. **HR 1837. California Water Resources/Water Conservation and Environmental Projects.** Garamendi, D-Calif., amendment that would strike a section in the bill that would limit the water dedicated to conservation and reduce water allocated for environmental projects by 25 percent in subsequent years if resources are not made available. Rejected in Committee of the Whole 178-247: R 0-239; D 178-8. Feb. 29, 2012.

89. **HR 1837. California Water Resources/Central Valley Project.** Markey, D-Mass., amendment that would require all Central Valley projects to operate within any applicable state and federal statutory requirements and be based on the best available science. Rejected in Committee of the Whole 180-244: R 1-236; D 179-8. Feb. 29, 2012.

	85	86	87	88	89
ALABAMA					
1 Bonner	N	N	N	N	N
2 Roby	N	N	N	N	N
3 Rogers	N	N	N	N	N
4 Aderholt	N	N	N	N	N
5 Brooks	N	N	N	N	N
6 Bachus	N	N	N	N	N
7 Sewell	Y	Y	Y	Y	Y
ALASKA					
AL Young	N	N	N	N	N
ARIZONA					
1 Gosar	N	N	N	N	N
2 Franks	N	N	N	N	N
3 Quayle	N	N	N	N	N
4 Pastor	Y	Y	Y	Y	Y
5 Schweikert	N	N	N	N	N
6 Flake	N	N	N	N	N
7 Grijalva	Y	Y	Y	Y	Y
8 Vacant					
ARKANSAS					
1 Crawford	N	N	N	N	N
2 Griffin	N	N	N	N	N
3 Womack	N	N	N	N	N
4 Ross	N	N	N	N	N
CALIFORNIA					
1 Thompson	Y	Y	Y	Y	Y
2 Herger	N	N	N	N	N
3 Lungren	N	N	N	N	N
4 McClintock	N	N	N	N	N
5 Matsui	Y	Y	Y	Y	Y
6 Woolsey	Y	Y	Y	Y	Y
7 Miller, George	Y	Y	Y	Y	Y
8 Pelosi	Y	Y	Y	Y	Y
9 Lee	+	+	+	+	+
10 Garamendi	Y	Y	Y	Y	Y
11 McNerney	Y	Y	N	Y	Y
12 Speier	Y	Y	Y	Y	Y
13 Stark	Y	Y	Y	Y	Y
14 Eshoo	Y	Y	Y	Y	Y
15 Honda	Y	Y	Y	Y	Y
16 Lofgren	Y	Y	Y	Y	Y
17 Farr	Y	Y	Y	Y	Y
18 Cardoza	N	N	N	N	N
19 Denham	N	N	N	N	N
20 Costa	N	N	N	N	N
21 Nunes	N	N	N	N	N
22 McCarthy	N	N	N	N	N
23 Capps	Y	Y	Y	Y	Y
24 Gallegly	N	N	N	N	N
25 McKeon	N	N	N	N	N
26 Dreier	N	N	N	N	N
27 Sherman	Y	Y	Y	Y	Y
28 Berman	Y	Y	Y	Y	Y
29 Schiff	Y	Y	Y	Y	Y
30 Waxman	Y	Y	Y	Y	Y
31 Becerra	Y	Y	Y	Y	Y
32 Chu	Y	Y	Y	Y	Y
33 Bass	?	?	?	?	?
34 Roybal-Allard	Y	Y	Y	Y	Y
35 Waters	Y	Y	Y	Y	Y
36 Hahn	Y	Y	Y	Y	Y
37 Richardson	Y	Y	Y	Y	Y
38 Napolitano	Y	Y	Y	Y	Y
39 Sánchez, Linda	Y	Y	Y	Y	Y
40 Royce	N	N	N	N	N
41 Lewis	N	N	N	N	N
42 Miller, Gary	N	N	N	N	N
43 Baca	Y	Y	Y	Y	Y
44 Calvert	N	N	N	N	N
45 Bono Mack	N	N	N	N	N
46 Rohrabacher	N	N	N	N	N
47 Sanchez, Loretta	Y	Y	Y	Y	Y
48 Campbell	N	N	N	N	N
49 Issa	N	N	N	N	N
50 Bilbray	N	N	N	N	N
51 Filner	Y	Y	Y	Y	Y
52 Hunter	N	N	N	N	N
53 Davis	Y	Y	Y	Y	Y

	85	86	87	88	89
COLORADO					
1 DeGette	Y	Y	Y	Y	Y
2 Polis	Y	Y	Y	Y	Y
3 Tipton	N	N	N	N	N
4 Gardner	N	N	N	N	N
5 Lamborn	N	N	N	N	N
6 Coffman	N	N	N	N	N
7 Perlmutter	N	Y	N	Y	Y
CONNECTICUT					
1 Larson	Y	Y	Y	Y	Y
2 Courtney	Y	Y	Y	Y	Y
3 DeLauro	Y	Y	Y	Y	Y
4 Himes	Y	Y	Y	Y	Y
5 Murphy	Y	Y	Y	Y	Y
DELAWARE					
AL Carney	Y	Y	Y	Y	Y
FLORIDA					
1 Miller	N	N	N	N	N
2 Southerland	N	N	N	N	N
3 Brown	Y	Y	Y	Y	Y
4 Crenshaw	N	N	N	N	N
5 Nugent	N	N	N	N	N
6 Stearns	N	N	N	N	N
7 Mica	N	N	N	N	N
8 Webster	N	N	N	N	N
9 Bilirakis	N	N	N	N	N
10 Young	N	N	N	N	N
11 Castor	Y	Y	Y	Y	Y
12 Ross	N	N	N	N	N
13 Buchanan	N	N	N	N	N
14 Mack	N	N	N	N	N
15 Posey	N	N	N	N	N
16 Rooney	N	N	N	N	N
17 Wilson	Y	Y	Y	Y	Y
18 Ros-Lehtinen	N	N	N	N	N
19 Deutch	Y	Y	Y	Y	Y
20 Wasserman Schultz	Y	Y	Y	Y	Y
21 Diaz-Balart	N	N	N	N	N
22 West	N	N	N	N	N
23 Hastings	Y	Y	Y	Y	Y
24 Adams	N	N	N	N	N
25 Rivera	N	N	N	N	N
GEORGIA					
1 Kingston	N	N	N	N	N
2 Bishop	N	Y	N	N	N
3 Westmoreland	N	N	N	N	N
4 Johnson	Y	Y	Y	Y	Y
5 Lewis	Y	Y	Y	Y	Y
6 Price	N	N	N	N	N
7 Woodall	N	N	N	N	N
8 Scott, A.	N	N	N	N	N
9 Graves	N	N	N	N	N
10 Broun	N	N	N	N	N
11 Gingrey	N	N	N	N	N
12 Barrow	Y	Y	N	Y	Y
13 Scott, D.	Y	Y	Y	Y	Y
HAWAII					
1 Hanabusa	Y	Y	Y	Y	Y
2 Hirono	Y	Y	Y	Y	Y
IDAHO					
1 Labrador	N	N	N	N	N
2 Simpson	N	N	N	N	N
ILLINOIS					
1 Rush	?	?	?	?	Y
2 Jackson	Y	Y	Y	Y	Y
3 Lipinski	Y	Y	Y	Y	Y
4 Gutierrez	Y	Y	Y	Y	Y
5 Quigley	Y	Y	Y	Y	Y
6 Roskam	N	N	N	N	N
7 Davis	Y	Y	Y	Y	Y
8 Walsh	N	N	N	N	N
9 Schakowsky	+	Y	Y	Y	Y
10 Dold	N	N	N	N	N
11 Kinzinger	N	N	N	N	N
12 Costello	Y	Y	Y	Y	Y
13 Biggert	N	N	N	N	N
14 Hultgren	N	N	N	N	N
15 Johnson	N	Y	N	N	N

KEY **Republicans** Democrats

Y Voted for (yea)	X Paired against	C Voted "present" to avoid possible conflict of interest
# Paired for	− Announced against	
+ Announced for	P Voted "present"	? Did not vote or otherwise make a position known
N Voted against (nay)		

	85	86	87	88	89
16 Manzullo	N	N	N	N	N
17 Schilling	N	N	N	N	N
18 Schock	N	N	N	N	N
19 Shimkus	N	N	N	N	N
INDIANA					
1 Visclosky	Y	Y	Y	Y	Y
2 Donnelly	Y	Y	Y	Y	Y
3 Stutzman	N	N	N	N	N
4 Rokita	N	N	N	N	N
5 Burton	N	N	N	N	N
6 Pence	N	N	N	N	N
7 Carson	Y	Y	Y	Y	Y
8 Bucshon	N	N	N	N	N
9 Young	N	N	N	N	N
IOWA					
1 Braley	Y	Y	Y	Y	Y
2 Loebsack	Y	Y	Y	Y	Y
3 Boswell	Y	Y	Y	Y	Y
4 Latham	N	N	N	N	N
5 King	N	N	N	N	N
KANSAS					
1 Huelskamp	N	N	N	N	N
2 Jenkins	N	N	N	N	N
3 Yoder	N	N	N	N	N
4 Pompeo	N	N	N	N	N
KENTUCKY					
1 Whitfield	N	N	N	N	N
2 Guthrie	N	N	N	N	N
3 Yarmuth	Y	Y	Y	Y	Y
4 Davis	N	N	N	N	N
5 Rogers	N	N	N	N	N
6 Chandler	Y	Y	Y	Y	Y
LOUISIANA					
1 Scalise	N	N	N	N	N
2 Richmond	Y	Y	Y	Y	Y
3 Landry	N	N	N	N	N
4 Fleming	N	N	N	N	N
5 Alexander	N	N	N	N	N
6 Cassidy	N	N	N	N	N
7 Boustany	N	N	N	N	N
MAINE					
1 Pingree	Y	Y	Y	Y	Y
2 Michaud	Y	Y	Y	Y	Y
MARYLAND					
1 Harris	N	N	N	N	N
2 Ruppersberger	Y	Y	Y	Y	Y
3 Sarbanes	Y	Y	Y	Y	Y
4 Edwards	Y	Y	Y	Y	Y
5 Hoyer	Y	Y	Y	Y	Y
6 Bartlett	N	N	N	N	N
7 Cummings	Y	Y	Y	Y	Y
8 Van Hollen	Y	Y	Y	Y	Y
MASSACHUSETTS					
1 Olver	Y	Y	Y	Y	Y
2 Neal	Y	Y	Y	Y	Y
3 McGovern	Y	Y	Y	Y	Y
4 Frank	Y	Y	Y	Y	Y
5 Tsongas	Y	Y	Y	Y	Y
6 Tierney	Y	Y	Y	Y	Y
7 Markey	Y	Y	Y	Y	Y
8 Capuano	Y	Y	Y	Y	Y
9 Lynch	Y	Y	Y	Y	Y
10 Keating	Y	Y	Y	Y	Y
MICHIGAN					
1 Benishek	N	N	N	N	N
2 Huizenga	N	N	N	N	N
3 Amash	N	N	N	N	N
4 Camp	N	N	N	N	N
5 Kildee	Y	Y	Y	Y	Y
6 Upton	N	N	N	N	N
7 Walberg	N	N	N	N	N
8 Rogers	N	N	N	N	N
9 Peters	Y	Y	Y	Y	Y
10 Miller	N	N	N	N	N
11 McCotter	N	N	N	N	N
12 Levin	Y	Y	Y	Y	Y
13 Clarke	Y	Y	Y	Y	Y
14 Conyers	Y	Y	Y	Y	Y
15 Dingell	Y	Y	Y	Y	Y
MINNESOTA					
1 Walz	Y	Y	N	Y	Y
2 Kline	N	N	N	N	N
3 Paulsen	N	N	N	N	N
4 McCollum	Y	Y	Y	Y	Y

	85	86	87	88	89
5 Ellison	Y	Y	Y	Y	Y
6 Bachmann	N	N	N	N	N
7 Peterson	N	N	N	N	N
8 Cravaack	N	N	N	N	N
MISSISSIPPI					
1 Nunnelee	N	N	N	N	N
2 Thompson	Y	Y	Y	Y	Y
3 Harper	N	N	N	N	N
4 Palazzo	N	N	N	N	N
MISSOURI					
1 Clay	Y	Y	Y	Y	Y
2 Akin	N	N	N	N	N
3 Carnahan	Y	Y	Y	Y	Y
4 Hartzler	N	N	N	N	N
5 Cleaver	Y	Y	Y	Y	Y
6 Graves	N	N	N	N	N
7 Long	N	N	N	N	N
8 Emerson	N	N	N	N	N
9 Luetkemeyer	N	N	N	N	N
MONTANA					
AL Rehberg	N	N	N	N	N
NEBRASKA					
1 Fortenberry	?	N	N	N	N
2 Terry	N	N	N	N	N
3 Smith	N	N	N	N	N
NEVADA					
1 Berkley	Y	Y	Y	Y	Y
2 Amodei	N	N	N	N	N
3 Heck	N	N	N	N	N
NEW HAMPSHIRE					
1 Guinta	N	N	N	N	N
2 Bass	N	N	N	N	N
NEW JERSEY					
1 Andrews	Y	Y	Y	Y	Y
2 LoBiondo	N	N	N	N	N
3 Runyan	N	N	N	N	N
4 Smith	?	N	N	N	N
5 Garrett	N	N	N	N	N
6 Pallone	Y	Y	Y	Y	Y
7 Lance	N	N	N	N	N
8 Pascrell	Y	Y	Y	Y	Y
9 Rothman	Y	Y	Y	Y	Y
10 Payne	?	?	?	?	?
11 Frelinghuysen	N	N	N	N	N
12 Holt	Y	Y	Y	Y	Y
13 Sires	Y	Y	Y	Y	Y
NEW MEXICO					
1 Heinrich	Y	Y	Y	Y	Y
2 Pearce	N	N	N	N	N
3 Luján	Y	Y	Y	Y	Y
NEW YORK					
1 Bishop	Y	Y	Y	Y	Y
2 Israel	Y	Y	Y	Y	Y
3 King	N	N	N	N	N
4 McCarthy	Y	Y	Y	Y	Y
5 Ackerman	Y	Y	Y	Y	Y
6 Meeks	Y	Y	Y	Y	Y
7 Crowley	Y	Y	Y	Y	Y
8 Nadler	?	?	?	?	?
9 Turner	N	N	N	N	N
10 Towns	Y	Y	Y	Y	Y
11 Clarke	Y	Y	Y	Y	Y
12 Velázquez	Y	Y	Y	Y	Y
13 Grimm	N	N	N	N	N
14 Maloney	Y	Y	Y	Y	Y
15 Rangel	?	?	?	?	?
16 Serrano	Y	Y	Y	Y	Y
17 Engel	Y	Y	Y	Y	Y
18 Lowey	Y	Y	Y	Y	Y
19 Hayworth	N	N	N	N	N
20 Gibson	Y	N	N	N	N
21 Tonko	Y	Y	Y	Y	Y
22 Hinchey	Y	Y	Y	Y	Y
23 Owens	Y	Y	Y	Y	Y
24 Hanna	N	Y	N	N	N
25 Buerkle	N	N	N	N	N
26 Hochul	Y	Y	Y	Y	Y
27 Higgins	Y	Y	Y	Y	Y
28 Slaughter	Y	Y	Y	Y	Y
29 Reed	N	N	N	N	N
NORTH CAROLINA					
1 Butterfield	Y	Y	Y	Y	Y
2 Ellmers	N	N	N	N	N
3 Jones	N	N	N	N	N
4 Price	Y	Y	Y	Y	Y

	85	86	87	88	89
5 Foxx	N	N	N	N	N
6 Coble	N	N	N	N	N
7 McIntyre	Y	Y	Y	Y	Y
8 Kissell	Y	Y	Y	Y	Y
9 Myrick	N	N	N	N	N
10 McHenry	N	N	N	N	N
11 Shuler	Y	Y	N	Y	Y
12 Watt	Y	Y	Y	Y	Y
13 Miller	Y	Y	Y	Y	Y
NORTH DAKOTA					
AL Berg	N	N	N	N	N
OHIO					
1 Chabot	N	N	N	N	N
2 Schmidt	N	N	N	N	N
3 Turner	N	N	N	N	N
4 Jordan	N	N	N	N	N
5 Latta	N	N	N	N	N
6 Johnson	N	N	N	N	N
7 Austria	N	N	N	N	N
8 Boehner					
9 Kaptur	Y	Y	Y	Y	Y
10 Kucinich	Y	Y	Y	Y	Y
11 Fudge	Y	Y	Y	Y	Y
12 Tiberi	N	N	N	N	N
13 Sutton	Y	Y	Y	Y	Y
14 LaTourette	N	N	N	N	N
15 Stivers	N	N	N	N	N
16 Renacci	N	N	N	N	N
17 Ryan	Y	Y	Y	Y	Y
18 Gibbs	N	N	N	N	N
OKLAHOMA					
1 Sullivan	N	N	N	N	N
2 Boren	N	N	N	N	N
3 Lucas	N	N	N	N	N
4 Cole	N	N	N	N	N
5 Lankford	N	N	N	N	N
OREGON					
1 Bonamici	Y	Y	Y	Y	Y
2 Walden	N	N	N	N	N
3 Blumenauer	Y	Y	Y	Y	Y
4 DeFazio	Y	Y	Y	Y	Y
5 Schrader	Y	Y	Y	Y	Y
PENNSYLVANIA					
1 Brady	Y	Y	Y	Y	Y
2 Fattah	Y	Y	Y	Y	Y
3 Kelly	N	N	N	N	N
4 Altmire	Y	Y	Y	Y	N
5 Thompson	N	N	N	N	N
6 Gerlach	N	N	N	N	N
7 Meehan	N	N	N	N	N
8 Fitzpatrick	N	N	N	N	N
9 Shuster	N	N	N	N	N
10 Marino	N	N	N	N	N
11 Barletta	N	N	N	N	N
12 Critz	Y	Y	Y	Y	Y
13 Schwartz	Y	Y	Y	Y	Y
14 Doyle	Y	Y	Y	Y	Y
15 Dent	N	N	N	N	N
16 Pitts	?	N	N	N	N
17 Holden	Y	Y	Y	Y	Y
18 Murphy	N	N	N	N	N
19 Platts	N	N	N	N	N
RHODE ISLAND					
1 Cicilline	Y	Y	Y	Y	Y
2 Langevin	Y	Y	Y	Y	Y
SOUTH CAROLINA					
1 Scott	N	N	N	N	N
2 Wilson	N	N	N	N	N
3 Duncan	N	N	N	N	N
4 Gowdy	N	N	N	N	N
5 Mulvaney	N	N	N	N	N
6 Clyburn	Y	Y	Y	Y	Y
SOUTH DAKOTA					
AL Noem	N	N	N	N	N
TENNESSEE					
1 Roe	N	N	N	N	N
2 Duncan	N	N	N	N	N
3 Fleischmann	N	N	N	N	N
4 DesJarlais	N	N	N	N	N
5 Cooper	N	N	Y	N	Y
6 Black	N	N	N	N	N
7 Blackburn	N	N	N	N	N
8 Fincher	N	N	N	N	N
9 Cohen	Y	Y	Y	Y	Y

	85	86	87	88	89
TEXAS					
1 Gohmert	?	?	?	N	N
2 Poe	N	N	N	N	N
3 Johnson, S.	N	N	N	N	N
4 Hall	N	N	N	N	N
5 Hensarling	N	N	N	N	N
6 Barton	N	N	Y	N	N
7 Culberson	N	N	N	N	N
8 Brady	N	N	N	N	N
9 Green, A.	Y	Y	Y	Y	Y
10 McCaul	N	N	N	N	N
11 Conaway	N	N	N	N	N
12 Granger	N	N	N	N	N
13 Thornberry	N	N	N	N	N
14 Paul	?	?	?	?	?
15 Hinojosa	Y	Y	Y	Y	Y
16 Reyes	Y	Y	Y	Y	Y
17 Flores	N	N	N	N	N
18 Jackson Lee	Y	Y	Y	Y	Y
19 Neugebauer	N	N	N	N	N
20 Gonzalez	Y	Y	Y	Y	Y
21 Smith	N	N	N	N	N
22 Olson	N	N	N	N	N
23 Canseco	N	N	N	N	N
24 Marchant	N	N	N	N	N
25 Doggett	Y	Y	Y	Y	Y
26 Burgess	N	N	N	N	N
27 Farenthold	N	N	N	N	N
28 Cuellar	Y	Y	Y	Y	Y
29 Green, G.	Y	Y	Y	Y	Y
30 Johnson, E.	Y	Y	Y	Y	Y
31 Carter	N	N	N	N	N
32 Sessions	N	N	N	N	N
UTAH					
1 Bishop	N	N	N	N	N
2 Matheson	N	N	N	N	N
3 Chaffetz	N	N	N	N	N
VERMONT					
AL Welch	Y	Y	Y	Y	Y
VIRGINIA					
1 Wittman	N	N	N	N	N
2 Rigell	N	N	N	N	?
3 Scott	Y	Y	Y	Y	Y
4 Forbes	N	N	N	N	N
5 Hurt	N	N	N	N	N
6 Goodlatte	N	N	N	N	N
7 Cantor	?	?	?	?	?
8 Moran	Y	Y	Y	Y	Y
9 Griffith	N	N	N	N	N
10 Wolf	N	N	N	N	N
11 Connolly	Y	Y	Y	Y	Y
WASHINGTON					
1 Inslee	Y	Y	N	Y	Y
2 Larsen	Y	Y	Y	Y	Y
3 Herrera Beutler	N	N	N	N	N
4 Hastings	N	N	N	N	N
5 McMorris Rodgers	N	N	N	N	N
6 Dicks	Y	Y	Y	Y	Y
7 McDermott	Y	Y	Y	Y	Y
8 Reichert	N	N	N	N	N
9 Smith	Y	Y	Y	Y	Y
WEST VIRGINIA					
1 McKinley	N	N	N	N	N
2 Capito	N	N	N	N	N
3 Rahall	Y	Y	Y	Y	Y
WISCONSIN					
1 Ryan	N	N	N	N	N
2 Baldwin	Y	Y	Y	Y	Y
3 Kind	Y	Y	Y	Y	Y
4 Moore	Y	Y	Y	Y	Y
5 Sensenbrenner	N	N	N	N	N
6 Petri	N	N	N	N	N
7 Duffy	N	N	N	N	N
8 Ribble	N	N	N	N	?
WYOMING					
AL Lummis	N	N	N	N	N

IN THE HOUSE | By Vote Number

90. **HR 1837. California Water Resources/Recommit.** Garamendi, D-Calif., motion to recommit the bill to the House Natural Resources Committee with instructions to report it back immediately with an amendment that would clarify that nothing in the bill would pre-empt or supersede state laws, including state water laws. Motion rejected 178-248: R 0-239; D 178-9. Feb. 29, 2012.

91. **HR 1837. California Water Resources/Passage.** Passage of the bill that would change California water supply practices around the San Joaquin Valley. It would require the Interior Department to increase the total water delivery capability of the Central Valley Project by 800,000 acre-feet of water by Sept. 30, 2016. It also would repeal provisions of the San Joaquin River Restoration Settlement Act and would impose an alternative set of water flow requirements. It also would limit the enforcement or consideration of environmental rules under the National Environmental Policy Act and the Endangered Species Act. Passed 246-175: R 236-1; D 10-174. A "nay" was a vote in support of the president's position. Feb. 29, 2012.

92. **H Res 562. Civil Rights Oral History Compilation/Adoption.** Adoption of the resolution that would direct the Office of the Historian to compile oral histories from current and former members of the House who participated in the historic 1965 Selma to Montgomery, Ala., march and subsequent annual marches and who were involved in the civil rights movement in general. Adopted 418-0: R 235-0; D 183-0. March 1, 2012.

93. **S 1134. St. Croix River Crossing Project/Passage.** Petri, R-Wis., motion to suspend the rules and pass the bill that would authorize federal participation or assistance for the construction of a bridge over the St. Croix River between Wisconsin and Minnesota. The bill would condition federal support for the project on mitigation measures to promote conservation, recreation and aesthetic enhancement along the river. Motion agreed to, thus clearing the bill for the president, 339-80: R 219-16; D 120-64. A two-thirds majority of those present and voting (280 in this case) is required for passage under suspension of the rules. March 1, 2012.

94. **H Res 556. Religious Persecution in Iran/Adoption.** Pitts, R-Pa., motion to suspend the rules and adopt the resolution that would condemn the government of Iran for its ongoing and systemic violations of the human rights of the Iranian people, including state-sponsored persecution of religious minorities. It also would call for the Iranian government to exonerate and immediately release Youcef Nadarkhani and all other individuals held or charged on account of their religion. Motion agreed to 417-1: R 234-0; D 183-1. A two-thirds majority of those present and voting (279 in this case) is required for adoption under suspension of the rules. March 1, 2012.

	90	91	92	93	94
ALABAMA					
1 Bonner	N	Y	Y	Y	Y
2 Roby	N	Y	Y	Y	Y
3 Rogers	N	Y	Y	Y	Y
4 Aderholt	N	Y	Y	Y	Y
5 Brooks	N	Y	Y	Y	Y
6 Bachus	N	Y	Y	Y	Y
7 Sewell	Y	N	Y	Y	Y
ALASKA					
AL Young	N	Y	Y	Y	Y
ARIZONA					
1 Gosar	N	Y	Y	Y	Y
2 Franks	N	Y	+	Y	Y
3 Quayle	N	Y	Y	Y	Y
4 Pastor	Y	N	Y	Y	Y
5 Schweikert	N	Y	Y	Y	Y
6 Flake	N	Y	Y	Y	Y
7 Grijalva	Y	N	Y	N	Y
8 Vacant					
ARKANSAS					
1 Crawford	N	Y	Y	Y	Y
2 Griffin	N	Y	Y	Y	Y
3 Womack	N	Y	Y	Y	Y
4 Ross	N	Y	Y	Y	Y
CALIFORNIA					
1 Thompson	Y	N	Y	N	Y
2 Herger	N	Y	Y	Y	Y
3 Lungren	N	Y	Y	Y	Y
4 McClintock	N	Y	Y	Y	Y
5 Matsui	Y	N	Y	N	Y
6 Woolsey	Y	N	Y	N	Y
7 Miller, George	Y	N	Y	Y	Y
8 Pelosi	Y	N	Y	Y	Y
9 Lee	+	–	Y	N	Y
10 Garamendi	Y	N	Y	N	Y
11 McNerney	Y	N	Y	Y	Y
12 Speier	Y	N	Y	N	Y
13 Stark	Y	N	Y	N	Y
14 Eshoo	Y	N	Y	Y	Y
15 Honda	Y	N	Y	N	Y
16 Lofgren	Y	N	Y	N	Y
17 Farr	Y	N	Y	Y	Y
18 Cardoza	N	Y	?	?	?
19 Denham	N	Y	Y	N	Y
20 Costa	N	Y	Y	Y	Y
21 Nunes	N	Y	Y	Y	Y
22 McCarthy	N	Y	Y	Y	Y
23 Capps	Y	N	Y	N	N
24 Gallegly	N	Y	Y	Y	Y
25 McKeon	N	Y	Y	Y	Y
26 Dreier	N	Y	Y	Y	Y
27 Sherman	Y	N	Y	N	Y
28 Berman	Y	N	Y	N	Y
29 Schiff	Y	N	Y	N	Y
30 Waxman	Y	N	Y	N	Y
31 Becerra	Y	N	Y	N	Y
32 Chu	Y	N	Y	N	Y
33 Bass	?	?	Y	N	Y
34 Roybal-Allard	Y	N	Y	N	Y
35 Waters	Y	N	Y	N	Y
36 Hahn	Y	N	Y	N	Y
37 Richardson	Y	N	Y	Y	Y
38 Napolitano	Y	N	Y	N	Y
39 Sánchez, Linda	Y	N	?	Y	Y
40 Royce	N	Y	Y	Y	Y
41 Lewis	N	Y	Y	Y	Y
42 Miller, Gary	N	Y	Y	Y	Y
43 Baca	Y	Y	Y	Y	Y
44 Calvert	N	Y	Y	Y	Y
45 Bono Mack	N	Y	Y	Y	Y
46 Rohrabacher	N	Y	Y	Y	Y
47 Sanchez, Loretta	Y	N	Y	Y	Y
48 Campbell	N	Y	?	?	?
49 Issa	N	Y	Y	Y	Y
50 Bilbray	N	Y	Y	Y	Y
51 Filner	Y	N	Y	Y	Y
52 Hunter	N	Y	Y	Y	Y
53 Davis	Y	N	Y	Y	Y

	90	91	92	93	94
COLORADO					
1 DeGette	Y	N	Y	N	Y
2 Polis	Y	N	Y	N	Y
3 Tipton	N	Y	Y	Y	Y
4 Gardner	N	Y	Y	Y	Y
5 Lamborn	N	Y	Y	Y	Y
6 Coffman	N	Y	Y	Y	Y
7 Perlmutter	Y	N	Y	Y	Y
CONNECTICUT					
1 Larson	Y	N	Y	Y	Y
2 Courtney	Y	N	Y	Y	Y
3 DeLauro	Y	N	Y	N	Y
4 Himes	Y	N	Y	Y	Y
5 Murphy	Y	N	Y	N	?
DELAWARE					
AL Carney	Y	N	Y	Y	Y
FLORIDA					
1 Miller	N	Y	Y	Y	Y
2 Southerland	N	Y	Y	Y	Y
3 Brown	Y	N	Y	N	Y
4 Crenshaw	N	Y	Y	Y	Y
5 Nugent	N	Y	Y	Y	Y
6 Stearns	N	Y	Y	Y	Y
7 Mica	N	Y	Y	Y	Y
8 Webster	N	Y	Y	Y	Y
9 Bilirakis	N	Y	Y	Y	Y
10 Young	N	Y	Y	N	Y
11 Castor	Y	N	Y	Y	Y
12 Ross	N	Y	Y	Y	Y
13 Buchanan	N	Y	Y	N	Y
14 Mack	N	Y	Y	Y	Y
15 Posey	N	Y	Y	Y	Y
16 Rooney	N	Y	Y	Y	Y
17 Wilson	Y	N	Y	Y	Y
18 Ros-Lehtinen	N	Y	Y	Y	Y
19 Deutch	Y	N	Y	N	Y
20 Wasserman Schultz	Y	N	Y	N	Y
21 Diaz-Balart	N	Y	Y	Y	Y
22 West	N	Y	Y	Y	Y
23 Hastings	Y	N	Y	Y	Y
24 Adams	N	Y	Y	Y	Y
25 Rivera	N	Y	Y	Y	Y
GEORGIA					
1 Kingston	N	Y	Y	Y	Y
2 Bishop	Y	Y	Y	Y	Y
3 Westmoreland	N	Y	Y	Y	Y
4 Johnson	Y	N	Y	N	Y
5 Lewis	Y	N	Y	N	Y
6 Price	N	Y	Y	Y	Y
7 Woodall	N	Y	Y	Y	Y
8 Scott, A.	N	Y	Y	Y	Y
9 Graves	N	Y	Y	Y	Y
10 Broun	N	Y	Y	Y	Y
11 Gingrey	N	Y	Y	Y	Y
12 Barrow	Y	N	Y	Y	Y
13 Scott, D.	Y	N	Y	Y	Y
HAWAII					
1 Hanabusa	Y	N	Y	N	Y
2 Hirono	Y	N	Y	N	Y
IDAHO					
1 Labrador	N	Y	Y	Y	Y
2 Simpson	N	Y	Y	N	Y
ILLINOIS					
1 Rush	Y	N	Y	Y	Y
2 Jackson	Y	N	Y	Y	Y
3 Lipinski	Y	N	Y	Y	Y
4 Gutierrez	Y	N	Y	Y	Y
5 Quigley	Y	N	Y	N	Y
6 Roskam	N	Y	Y	Y	Y
7 Davis	Y	N	Y	Y	Y
8 Walsh	N	Y	Y	Y	?
9 Schakowsky	Y	N	Y	Y	Y
10 Dold	N	Y	Y	Y	Y
11 Kinzinger	N	Y	Y	Y	Y
12 Costello	Y	N	Y	Y	Y
13 Biggert	N	Y	Y	N	Y
14 Hultgren	N	Y	Y	N	Y
15 Johnson	N	Y	Y	N	Y

	90	91	92	93	94
16 **Manzullo**	N	Y	Y	Y	Y
17 **Schilling**	N	Y	Y	Y	Y
18 **Schock**	N	Y	Y	Y	Y
19 **Shimkus**	N	Y	?	?	?
INDIANA					
1 Visclosky	Y	N	Y	Y	Y
2 Donnelly	Y	N	Y	Y	Y
3 **Stutzman**	N	Y	N	Y	N
4 **Rokita**	N	Y	Y	Y	Y
5 **Burton**	N	Y	Y	Y	Y
6 **Pence**	N	Y	Y	Y	Y
7 Carson	Y	N	Y	Y	Y
8 **Bucshon**	N	Y	Y	Y	Y
9 **Young**	N	Y	Y	Y	Y
IOWA					
1 Braley	Y	N	Y	Y	Y
2 Loebsack	Y	N	Y	Y	Y
3 Boswell	Y	N	Y	Y	Y
4 **Latham**	N	Y	Y	Y	Y
5 **King**	N	Y	Y	Y	Y
KANSAS					
1 **Huelskamp**	N	Y	Y	Y	Y
2 **Jenkins**	N	Y	Y	Y	Y
3 **Yoder**	N	Y	Y	Y	Y
4 **Pompeo**	N	Y	Y	Y	Y
KENTUCKY					
1 **Whitfield**	N	?	Y	Y	Y
2 **Guthrie**	N	Y	Y	Y	Y
3 Yarmuth	Y	N	Y	N	Y
4 **Davis**	N	Y	Y	Y	Y
5 **Rogers**	N	Y	Y	Y	Y
6 Chandler	Y	N	Y	Y	Y
LOUISIANA					
1 **Scalise**	N	Y	Y	Y	Y
2 Richmond	Y	N	Y	Y	Y
3 **Landry**	N	Y	Y	Y	?
4 **Fleming**	N	Y	Y	Y	Y
5 **Alexander**	N	Y	Y	Y	Y
6 **Cassidy**	N	Y	Y	Y	Y
7 **Boustany**	N	Y	Y	Y	Y
MAINE					
1 Pingree	Y	N	Y	Y	Y
2 Michaud	Y	N	Y	Y	Y
MARYLAND					
1 **Harris**	N	Y	Y	Y	Y
2 Ruppersberger	Y	N	Y	Y	Y
3 Sarbanes	Y	N	Y	N	Y
4 Edwards	Y	N	Y	N	Y
5 Hoyer	Y	N	Y	Y	Y
6 **Bartlett**	N	Y	Y	Y	Y
7 Cummings	Y	N	Y	Y	Y
8 Van Hollen	Y	N	Y	Y	Y
MASSACHUSETTS					
1 Olver	Y	N	?	Y	Y
2 Neal	Y	N	Y	Y	Y
3 McGovern	Y	N	Y	Y	Y
4 Frank	Y	N	Y	Y	Y
5 Tsongas	Y	N	Y	Y	Y
6 Tierney	Y	N	Y	Y	Y
7 Markey	Y	N	Y	N	Y
8 Capuano	Y	N	Y	Y	Y
9 Lynch	Y	N	Y	Y	Y
10 Keating	Y	N	Y	N	Y
MICHIGAN					
1 **Benishek**	N	Y	Y	Y	Y
2 **Huizenga**	N	Y	Y	Y	Y
3 **Amash**	N	N	N	N	Y
4 **Camp**	N	Y	Y	Y	Y
5 Kildee	Y	N	Y	Y	Y
6 **Upton**	N	Y	Y	Y	Y
7 **Walberg**	N	Y	Y	Y	Y
8 **Rogers**	N	Y	Y	Y	Y
9 Peters	Y	N	Y	Y	Y
10 **Miller**	N	Y	Y	Y	Y
11 **McCotter**	N	Y	Y	Y	Y
12 Levin	Y	N	Y	Y	Y
13 Clarke	Y	N	Y	Y	Y
14 Conyers	Y	N	Y	Y	Y
15 Dingell	Y	N	Y	Y	Y
MINNESOTA					
1 Walz	Y	N	Y	Y	Y
2 **Kline**	N	Y	Y	Y	Y
3 **Paulsen**	N	Y	Y	Y	Y
4 McCollum	Y	N	Y	N	Y

	90	91	92	93	94
5 Ellison	Y	N	Y	N	Y
6 **Bachmann**	N	Y	Y	Y	Y
7 Peterson	N	Y	Y	Y	Y
8 **Cravaack**	N	Y	Y	Y	Y
MISSISSIPPI					
1 **Nunnelee**	N	Y	Y	Y	Y
2 Thompson	Y	N	Y	Y	Y
3 **Harper**	N	Y	Y	Y	Y
4 **Palazzo**	N	Y	Y	Y	Y
MISSOURI					
1 Clay	Y	N	Y	Y	Y
2 **Akin**	N	Y	Y	?	Y
3 Carnahan	Y	N	Y	Y	Y
4 **Hartzler**	N	Y	Y	Y	Y
5 Cleaver	Y	N	+	+	+
6 **Graves**	N	Y	Y	Y	Y
7 **Long**	N	Y	Y	Y	Y
8 **Emerson**	N	Y	Y	Y	Y
9 **Luetkemeyer**	N	Y	Y	Y	Y
MONTANA					
AL **Rehberg**	N	Y	Y	Y	Y
NEBRASKA					
1 **Fortenberry**	N	Y	Y	Y	Y
2 **Terry**	N	Y	Y	Y	Y
3 **Smith**	N	Y	Y	Y	Y
NEVADA					
1 Berkley	Y	N	Y	Y	Y
2 **Amodei**	N	Y	Y	Y	Y
3 **Heck**	N	Y	Y	Y	Y
NEW HAMPSHIRE					
1 **Guinta**	N	Y	Y	Y	Y
2 **Bass**	N	Y	Y	Y	Y
NEW JERSEY					
1 Andrews	Y	N	Y	N	Y
2 **LoBiondo**	N	Y	Y	Y	Y
3 **Runyan**	N	Y	Y	Y	Y
4 **Smith**	N	Y	Y	Y	Y
5 **Garrett**	N	Y	Y	Y	Y
6 Pallone	Y	N	Y	N	Y
7 **Lance**	N	Y	Y	Y	Y
8 Pascrell	Y	N	Y	Y	Y
9 Rothman	Y	N	Y	Y	Y
10 Payne	?	?	?	?	?
11 **Frelinghuysen**	N	Y	Y	Y	Y
12 Holt	Y	N	Y	N	Y
13 Sires	Y	N	Y	Y	Y
NEW MEXICO					
1 Heinrich	Y	N	Y	N	Y
2 **Pearce**	N	Y	Y	Y	Y
3 Luján	Y	N	Y	N	Y
NEW YORK					
1 Bishop	Y	N	Y	N	Y
2 Israel	Y	N	Y	N	Y
3 **King**	N	Y	Y	Y	Y
4 McCarthy	Y	N	Y	Y	Y
5 Ackerman	Y	N	Y	N	Y
6 Meeks	Y	?	?	?	?
7 Crowley	Y	N	Y	Y	Y
8 Nadler	?	?	?	?	?
9 **Turner**	N	Y	Y	Y	Y
10 Towns	Y	N	Y	Y	Y
11 Clarke	Y	N	Y	Y	Y
12 Velázquez	Y	N	Y	N	Y
13 **Grimm**	N	Y	Y	Y	Y
14 Maloney	Y	N	Y	N	Y
15 Rangel	?	?	?	?	?
16 Serrano	Y	N	Y	N	Y
17 Engel	Y	N	Y	Y	Y
18 Lowey	Y	N	Y	Y	Y
19 **Hayworth**	N	Y	Y	N	Y
20 **Gibson**	N	Y	Y	Y	Y
21 Tonko	Y	N	Y	Y	Y
22 Hinchey	Y	N	Y	N	Y
23 Owens	Y	N	Y	Y	Y
24 **Hanna**	N	Y	Y	Y	Y
25 **Buerkle**	N	Y	Y	Y	Y
26 Hochul	Y	N	Y	N	Y
27 Higgins	Y	N	Y	Y	Y
28 Slaughter	Y	N	Y	N	Y
29 **Reed**	N	Y	Y	Y	Y
NORTH CAROLINA					
1 Butterfield	Y	N	Y	N	Y
2 **Ellmers**	N	Y	Y	Y	Y
3 **Jones**	N	Y	Y	Y	Y
4 Price	Y	N	Y	N	Y

	90	91	92	93	94
5 **Foxx**	N	Y	Y	Y	Y
6 **Coble**	N	Y	Y	Y	Y
7 McIntyre	Y	?	Y	Y	Y
8 Kissell	N	Y	Y	Y	Y
9 **Myrick**	N	Y	Y	Y	Y
10 **McHenry**	N	Y	Y	Y	Y
11 Shuler	N	P	Y	Y	Y
12 Watt	Y	N	Y	Y	Y
13 Miller	Y	N	Y	N	Y
NORTH DAKOTA					
AL **Berg**	N	Y	Y	Y	Y
OHIO					
1 **Chabot**	N	Y	Y	N	Y
2 **Schmidt**	N	Y	Y	N	Y
3 **Turner**	N	Y	Y	Y	Y
4 **Jordan**	N	Y	Y	Y	Y
5 **Latta**	N	Y	Y	Y	Y
6 **Johnson**	N	Y	Y	Y	Y
7 **Austria**	N	Y	Y	Y	Y
8 **Boehner**					
9 Kaptur	Y	N	?	?	?
10 Kucinich	Y	N	Y	N	Y
11 Fudge	Y	N	Y	Y	Y
12 **Tiberi**	N	Y	Y	Y	Y
13 Sutton	Y	N	Y	Y	Y
14 **LaTourette**	N	Y	Y	Y	Y
15 **Stivers**	N	Y	Y	Y	Y
16 **Renacci**	N	Y	Y	Y	Y
17 Ryan	Y	N	Y	Y	Y
18 **Gibbs**	N	Y	Y	Y	Y
OKLAHOMA					
1 **Sullivan**	N	Y	Y	Y	Y
2 Boren	N	Y	Y	Y	Y
3 **Lucas**	N	Y	Y	Y	Y
4 **Cole**	N	Y	Y	Y	Y
5 **Lankford**	N	Y	Y	Y	Y
OREGON					
1 Bonamici	Y	N	Y	N	Y
2 **Walden**	N	Y	Y	Y	Y
3 Blumenauer	Y	N	Y	N	Y
4 DeFazio	Y	N	Y	N	Y
5 Schrader	Y	N	Y	Y	Y
PENNSYLVANIA					
1 Brady	Y	N	Y	Y	Y
2 Fattah	Y	N	Y	Y	Y
3 **Kelly**	N	Y	Y	Y	Y
4 Altmire	N	Y	Y	Y	Y
5 **Thompson**	N	Y	Y	Y	Y
6 **Gerlach**	N	Y	Y	Y	Y
7 **Meehan**	N	Y	Y	Y	Y
8 **Fitzpatrick**	N	Y	Y	N	Y
9 **Shuster**	N	Y	Y	Y	Y
10 **Marino**	N	Y	Y	Y	Y
11 **Barletta**	N	Y	Y	Y	Y
12 Critz	Y	N	Y	Y	Y
13 Schwartz	Y	N	Y	Y	Y
14 Doyle	Y	N	Y	Y	Y
15 **Dent**	N	Y	Y	Y	Y
16 **Pitts**	N	Y	Y	Y	Y
17 Holden	Y	N	Y	Y	Y
18 **Murphy**	N	+	Y	N	Y
19 **Platts**	N	Y	Y	Y	Y
RHODE ISLAND					
1 Cicilline	Y	N	Y	N	Y
2 Langevin	Y	N	Y	N	Y
SOUTH CAROLINA					
1 **Scott**	N	Y	Y	Y	Y
2 **Wilson**	N	Y	Y	Y	Y
3 **Duncan**	N	Y	Y	Y	Y
4 **Gowdy**	N	Y	Y	Y	Y
5 **Mulvaney**	N	Y	Y	Y	Y
6 Clyburn	Y	N	Y	Y	Y
SOUTH DAKOTA					
AL **Noem**	N	Y	Y	Y	Y
TENNESSEE					
1 **Roe**	N	Y	Y	Y	Y
2 **Duncan**	N	Y	Y	Y	Y
3 **Fleischmann**	N	Y	Y	Y	Y
4 **DesJarlais**	N	Y	Y	Y	Y
5 Cooper	Y	N	Y	Y	Y
6 **Black**	N	Y	Y	Y	Y
7 **Blackburn**	N	Y	Y	Y	Y
8 **Fincher**	N	Y	Y	N	Y
9 Cohen	Y	N	Y	N	Y

	90	91	92	93	94
TEXAS					
1 **Gohmert**	N	Y	Y	Y	Y
2 **Poe**	N	Y	Y	Y	Y
3 **Johnson, S.**	N	Y	Y	Y	Y
4 **Hall**	N	Y	Y	Y	Y
5 **Hensarling**	N	Y	Y	Y	Y
6 **Barton**	N	Y	Y	Y	Y
7 **Culberson**	N	Y	Y	Y	Y
8 **Brady**	N	Y	Y	Y	Y
9 Green, A.	Y	N	Y	Y	Y
10 **McCaul**	N	Y	Y	Y	Y
11 **Conaway**	N	Y	Y	Y	Y
12 **Granger**	N	Y	Y	Y	Y
13 **Thornberry**	N	Y	Y	Y	Y
14 **Paul**	?	?	?	?	?
15 Hinojosa	Y	N	Y	Y	Y
16 Reyes	Y	N	Y	Y	Y
17 Flores	N	Y	Y	Y	Y
18 Jackson Lee	Y	N	Y	Y	Y
19 **Neugebauer**	N	Y	Y	Y	Y
20 Gonzalez	Y	N	Y	Y	Y
21 **Smith**	N	Y	Y	Y	Y
22 **Olson**	N	Y	Y	Y	Y
23 **Canseco**	N	Y	Y	Y	Y
24 **Marchant**	N	Y	Y	Y	Y
25 Doggett	Y	N	Y	N	Y
26 **Burgess**	N	Y	Y	Y	Y
27 **Farenthold**	N	Y	Y	Y	Y
28 Cuellar	Y	N	Y	Y	Y
29 Green, G.	Y	N	Y	+	Y
30 Johnson, E.	Y	N	Y	N	Y
31 **Carter**	N	Y	Y	Y	Y
32 **Sessions**	N	Y	Y	Y	Y
UTAH					
1 **Bishop**	N	Y	Y	Y	Y
2 **Matheson**	N	Y	Y	Y	Y
3 **Chaffetz**	N	Y	Y	Y	Y
VERMONT					
AL Welch	Y	N	Y	N	Y
VIRGINIA					
1 **Wittman**	N	Y	Y	Y	Y
2 **Rigell**	N	Y	Y	Y	Y
3 Scott	Y	N	Y	Y	Y
4 **Forbes**	N	Y	Y	Y	Y
5 **Hurt**	N	Y	Y	Y	Y
6 **Goodlatte**	N	Y	?	?	?
7 **Cantor**	?	?	Y	Y	Y
8 Moran	Y	N	Y	N	Y
9 **Griffith**	N	Y	Y	Y	Y
10 **Wolf**	N	Y	Y	Y	Y
11 Connolly	Y	N	Y	Y	Y
WASHINGTON					
1 Inslee	Y	N	Y	Y	Y
2 Larsen	Y	N	Y	Y	Y
3 **Herrera Beutler**	N	Y	Y	Y	Y
4 **Hastings**	N	Y	Y	Y	Y
5 **McMorris Rodgers**	N	Y	?	?	?
6 Dicks	Y	N	Y	N	Y
7 McDermott	Y	N	Y	N	Y
8 **Reichert**	N	Y	Y	Y	Y
9 Smith	Y	N	Y	Y	Y
WEST VIRGINIA					
1 **McKinley**	N	Y	Y	Y	Y
2 **Capito**	N	Y	Y	Y	Y
3 Rahall	Y	N	Y	Y	Y
WISCONSIN					
1 **Ryan**	N	Y	Y	Y	Y
2 Baldwin	Y	N	Y	N	Y
3 Kind	Y	N	Y	Y	Y
4 Moore	Y	N	Y	Y	Y
5 **Sensenbrenner**	N	Y	Y	Y	Y
6 **Petri**	N	Y	Y	Y	Y
7 **Duffy**	N	Y	Y	Y	Y
8 **Ribble**	N	Y	Y	Y	Y
WYOMING					
AL **Lummis**	N	Y	Y	Y	Y

IN THE HOUSE | By Vote Number

95. **HR 3637. Roy Schallern Rood Post Office Building/Passage.** Farenthold, R-Texas, motion to suspend the rules and pass the bill that would designate a post office in Jupiter, Fla., as the "Roy Schallern Rood Post Office Building." Motion agreed to 362-2: R 217-2; D 145-0. A two-thirds majority of those present and voting (243 in this case) is required for passage under suspension of the rules. March 5, 2012.

96. **HR 4105. Countervailing Duties/Passage.** Camp, R-Mich., motion to suspend the rules and pass the bill that would clarify that the Commerce Department has the authority to impose countervailing duties on imports from non-market economy countries. Motion agreed to 370-39: R 194-39; D 176-0. A two-thirds majority of those present and voting (273 in this case) is required for passage under suspension of the rules. March 6, 2012.

97. **HR 2842. Hydropower Projects/Previous Question.** Bishop, R-Utah, motion to order the previous question (thus ending debate and the possibility of amendment) on adoption of the rule (H Res 570) that would provide for House floor consideration of the bill that would authorize the Interior Department to enter into contracts for the construction and operation of hydropower facilities on man-made water conduits such as tunnels, canals and ditches. Motion agreed to 232-177: R 228-0; D 4-177. March 6, 2012.

98. **HR 2842. Hydropower Projects/Environmental-Review Requirements.** Napolitano, D-Calif., amendment that would strike language from the bill that would exempt small hydropower projects on conduits from federal environmental review requirements under the National Environmental Policy Act. Rejected in Committee of the Whole 168-253: R 0-238; D 168-15. March 7, 2012.

99. **HR 2842. Hydropower Projects/Recommit.** Garamendi, D-Calif., motion to recommit the bill to the House Natural Resources Committee with instructions to report it back immediately with an amendment that would require that all materials used in hydropower construction projects authorized by the bill be manufactured in the United States. Motion rejected 182-237: R 1-235; D 181-2. March 7, 2012.

100. **HR 2842. Hydropower Projects/Passage.** Passage of the bill that would authorize the Interior Department to enter into contracts for the construction and operation of hydropower facilities on man-made water conveyances such as tunnels, canals and ditches. The bill also would exempt small hydropower projects on such conduits from federal environmental review requirements under the National Environmental Policy Act. Passed 265-154: R 237-0; D 28-154. March 7, 2012.

*Rep. Donald M. Payne, D-N.J., died March 6, 2012. The last vote for which he was eligible was vote 95.

	95	96	97	98	99	100
ALABAMA						
1 **Bonner**	?	Y	Y	N	N	Y
2 **Roby**	Y	Y	Y	N	N	Y
3 **Rogers**	Y	Y	Y	N	N	Y
4 **Aderholt**	Y	Y	Y	N	N	Y
5 **Brooks**	Y	Y	Y	N	N	Y
6 **Bachus**	Y	Y	Y	N	N	Y
7 Sewell	Y	Y	N	Y	Y	N
ALASKA						
AL **Young**	Y	Y	?	N	N	Y
ARIZONA						
1 **Gosar**	?	N	Y	N	N	Y
2 **Franks**	?	N	Y	N	N	Y
3 **Quayle**	Y	N	Y	N	N	Y
4 Pastor	Y	Y	N	Y	Y	N
5 **Schweikert**	Y	N	Y	N	N	Y
6 **Flake**	Y	N	Y	N	N	Y
7 Grijalva	?	Y	N	Y	Y	N
8 Vacant						
ARKANSAS						
1 **Crawford**	Y	Y	Y	N	N	Y
2 **Griffin**	Y	Y	Y	N	N	Y
3 **Womack**	Y	Y	Y	N	N	Y
4 Ross	?	Y	Y	N	Y	Y
CALIFORNIA						
1 Thompson	Y	Y	N	Y	Y	N
2 **Herger**	Y	Y	Y	N	N	Y
3 **Lungren**	Y	Y	Y	N	N	Y
4 **McClintock**	Y	N	Y	N	N	Y
5 Matsui	Y	Y	N	Y	Y	N
6 Woolsey	?	Y	N	Y	Y	N
7 Miller, George	?	Y	N	Y	Y	N
8 Pelosi	Y	Y	N	?	Y	N
9 Lee	Y	Y	N	Y	Y	N
10 Garamendi	Y	Y	N	Y	Y	N
11 McNerney	Y	Y	N	Y	Y	N
12 Speier	?	?	?	Y	Y	N
13 Stark	Y	Y	N	Y	Y	N
14 Eshoo	Y	Y	N	Y	Y	N
15 Honda	Y	Y	N	Y	Y	N
16 Lofgren	Y	Y	N	Y	Y	N
17 Farr	Y	Y	N	Y	Y	N
18 Cardoza	?	?	?	N	Y	Y
19 **Denham**	Y	Y	Y	N	N	Y
20 Costa	Y	Y	N	N	Y	Y
21 **Nunes**	Y	Y	Y	N	N	Y
22 **McCarthy**	Y	Y	Y	N	N	Y
23 Capps	Y	Y	N	Y	Y	N
24 **Gallegly**	Y	Y	Y	N	N	Y
25 **McKeon**	Y	Y	Y	N	N	Y
26 **Dreier**	Y	Y	Y	N	N	Y
27 Sherman	?	Y	N	Y	Y	N
28 Berman	Y	Y	N	Y	Y	N
29 Schiff	Y	Y	N	Y	Y	N
30 Waxman	?	Y	N	Y	Y	N
31 Becerra	Y	Y	N	Y	Y	N
32 Chu	Y	Y	N	Y	Y	N
33 Bass	Y	Y	N	Y	Y	N
34 Roybal-Allard	Y	Y	N	Y	Y	N
35 Waters	?	Y	N	Y	Y	N
36 Hahn	Y	Y	N	Y	Y	N
37 Richardson	Y	Y	N	Y	Y	N
38 Napolitano	Y	Y	N	Y	Y	N
39 Sánchez, Linda	Y	Y	N	Y	Y	N
40 **Royce**	?	Y	Y	N	N	Y
41 **Lewis**	Y	Y	Y	N	N	Y
42 **Miller, Gary**	Y	Y	Y	N	N	Y
43 Baca	Y	Y	N	Y	Y	N
44 **Calvert**	Y	Y	Y	N	N	Y
45 **Bono Mack**	Y	Y	Y	N	N	Y
46 **Rohrabacher**	Y	Y	Y	N	N	Y
47 Sanchez, Loretta	?	Y	N	Y	Y	N
48 **Campbell**	?	?	?	N	N	Y
49 **Issa**	Y	Y	Y	N	N	Y
50 **Bilbray**	Y	Y	Y	N	N	Y
51 Filner	Y	Y	N	Y	Y	N
52 **Hunter**	Y	Y	Y	N	N	Y
53 Davis	Y	Y	N	Y	Y	N

	95	96	97	98	99	100
COLORADO						
1 DeGette	Y	Y	N	Y	Y	N
2 Polis	Y	Y	N	N	Y	Y
3 **Tipton**	Y	Y	Y	N	N	Y
4 **Gardner**	N	Y	Y	N	N	Y
5 **Lamborn**	Y	N	Y	N	N	Y
6 **Coffman**	Y	Y	Y	N	N	Y
7 Perlmutter	?	+	N	Y	Y	Y
CONNECTICUT						
1 Larson	Y	Y	N	Y	Y	N
2 Courtney	Y	Y	N	Y	Y	N
3 DeLauro	Y	Y	N	Y	Y	N
4 Himes	Y	Y	N	Y	Y	N
5 Murphy	?	Y	N	Y	Y	N
DELAWARE						
AL Carney	Y	Y	N	Y	Y	Y
FLORIDA						
1 **Miller**	+	–	+	N	N	Y
2 **Southerland**	Y	N	Y	N	N	Y
3 Brown	?	Y	N	Y	Y	N
4 **Crenshaw**	Y	Y	Y	N	N	Y
5 **Nugent**	Y	N	Y	N	N	Y
6 **Stearns**	Y	N	Y	N	N	Y
7 **Mica**	Y	Y	Y	N	N	Y
8 **Webster**	Y	Y	Y	N	N	Y
9 **Bilirakis**	Y	Y	Y	N	N	Y
10 **Young**	?	Y	Y	N	N	Y
11 Castor	Y	Y	N	Y	Y	N
12 **Ross**	Y	Y	Y	N	N	Y
13 **Buchanan**	Y	Y	Y	N	N	Y
14 **Mack**	Y	N	Y	N	N	Y
15 **Posey**	Y	Y	Y	N	N	Y
16 **Rooney**	Y	Y	Y	N	N	Y
17 Wilson	Y	Y	N	Y	Y	N
18 **Ros-Lehtinen**	Y	Y	Y	N	N	Y
19 Deutch	?	Y	N	Y	Y	N
20 Wasserman Schultz	Y	Y	N	Y	Y	N
21 **Diaz-Balart**	Y	Y	Y	N	N	Y
22 **West**	Y	Y	Y	N	N	Y
23 Hastings	Y	Y	N	Y	Y	N
24 **Adams**	Y	Y	Y	N	N	Y
25 **Rivera**	Y	Y	Y	N	N	Y
GEORGIA						
1 **Kingston**	Y	N	Y	N	N	Y
2 Bishop	Y	Y	N	Y	Y	Y
3 **Westmoreland**	?	Y	Y	N	N	Y
4 Johnson	?	Y	N	Y	Y	?
5 Lewis	?	Y	N	Y	Y	N
6 **Price**	Y	Y	N	Y	N	Y
7 **Woodall**	Y	Y	Y	N	?	Y
8 **Scott, A.**	Y	Y	Y	N	N	Y
9 **Graves**	Y	N	Y	N	N	Y
10 **Broun**	Y	N	Y	N	N	Y
11 **Gingrey**	Y	Y	Y	N	N	Y
12 Barrow	Y	Y	N	N	Y	Y
13 Scott, D.	Y	Y	N	Y	Y	N
HAWAII						
1 Hanabusa	Y	Y	N	Y	Y	N
2 Hirono	?	Y	N	Y	Y	N
IDAHO						
1 **Labrador**	?	?	?	?	?	?
2 **Simpson**	?	Y	Y	N	N	Y
ILLINOIS						
1 Rush	Y	Y	N	Y	Y	N
2 Jackson	Y	Y	N	Y	Y	N
3 Lipinski	Y	Y	N	Y	Y	N
4 Gutierrez	?	Y	N	Y	Y	N
5 Quigley	Y	Y	N	Y	Y	N
6 **Roskam**	Y	Y	?	N	N	Y
7 Davis	?	?	N	Y	Y	N
8 **Walsh**	Y	N	Y	N	N	Y
9 Schakowsky	Y	Y	N	Y	Y	N
10 **Dold**	Y	Y	Y	N	N	Y
11 **Kinzinger**	Y	Y	Y	N	N	Y
12 **Costello**	Y	Y	Y	N	N	Y
13 **Biggert**	Y	Y	Y	N	N	Y
14 **Hultgren**	Y	Y	Y	N	N	Y
15 **Johnson**	+	Y	Y	N	N	Y

KEY **Republicans** Democrats

Y Voted for (yea)	X Paired against	C Voted "present" to avoid possible conflict of interest
# Paired for	– Announced against	
+ Announced for	P Voted "present"	? Did not vote or otherwise make a position known
N Voted against (nay)		

	95	96	97	98	99	100
16 **Manzullo**	?	Y	Y	N	N	Y
17 **Schilling**	Y	Y	Y	N	N	Y
18 **Schock**	Y	Y	Y	N	N	Y
19 **Shimkus**	Y	Y	Y	N	N	Y
INDIANA						
1 Visclosky	?	+	–	?	?	?
2 Donnelly	?	Y	N	N	Y	Y
3 **Stutzman**	Y	Y	Y	N	N	Y
4 **Rokita**	Y	Y	Y	N	N	Y
5 **Burton**	?	Y	Y	N	N	Y
6 **Pence**	Y	Y	Y	N	N	Y
7 Carson	Y	Y	N	Y	Y	N
8 **Bucshon**	Y	Y	Y	N	N	Y
9 **Young**	Y	Y	Y	N	N	Y
IOWA						
1 Braley	Y	Y	N	Y	Y	N
2 Loebsack	Y	Y	N	N	Y	Y
3 Boswell	Y	Y	N	N	Y	Y
4 **Latham**	Y	Y	Y	N	N	Y
5 **King**	Y	?	?	N	N	Y
KANSAS						
1 **Huelskamp**	Y	N	Y	N	N	Y
2 **Jenkins**	Y	Y	Y	N	N	Y
3 **Yoder**	Y	N	Y	N	N	Y
4 **Pompeo**	Y	N	Y	N	N	Y
KENTUCKY						
1 **Whitfield**	Y	Y	Y	N	N	Y
2 **Guthrie**	Y	Y	Y	N	N	Y
3 Yarmuth	Y	Y	N	Y	Y	N
4 **Davis**	Y	Y	Y	N	N	?
5 **Rogers**	Y	Y	Y	N	N	Y
6 Chandler	Y	Y	Y	Y	Y	N
LOUISIANA						
1 **Scalise**	Y	N	Y	N	N	Y
2 Richmond	?	Y	N	Y	Y	N
3 **Landry**	Y	Y	Y	N	N	Y
4 **Fleming**	Y	N	Y	N	N	Y
5 **Alexander**	Y	Y	Y	N	N	Y
6 **Cassidy**	Y	Y	Y	N	N	Y
7 **Boustany**	Y	Y	Y	N	N	Y
MAINE						
1 Pingree	?	Y	N	Y	Y	N
2 Michaud	Y	Y	N	Y	Y	N
MARYLAND						
1 **Harris**	Y	N	Y	N	N	Y
2 Ruppersberger	?	Y	N	Y	Y	N
3 Sarbanes	Y	Y	N	Y	Y	N
4 Edwards	Y	Y	N	Y	Y	N
5 Hoyer	Y	Y	N	Y	Y	N
6 **Bartlett**	Y	Y	Y	N	N	Y
7 Cummings	Y	Y	N	Y	Y	?
8 Van Hollen	Y	Y	N	Y	Y	N
MASSACHUSETTS						
1 Olver	Y	Y	N	Y	Y	N
2 Neal	Y	Y	N	Y	Y	N
3 McGovern	Y	Y	N	Y	Y	N
4 Frank	Y	Y	N	Y	Y	N
5 Tsongas	?	Y	N	Y	Y	N
6 Tierney	Y	Y	N	Y	Y	N
7 Markey	Y	Y	N	Y	Y	N
8 Capuano	Y	Y	N	Y	Y	N
9 Lynch	?	Y	N	Y	Y	N
10 Keating	Y	Y	N	Y	Y	N
MICHIGAN						
1 **Benishek**	Y	Y	Y	N	N	Y
2 **Huizenga**	Y	Y	Y	N	N	Y
3 **Amash**	Y	N	Y	N	N	Y
4 **Camp**	Y	Y	Y	N	N	Y
5 Kildee	Y	Y	N	Y	Y	N
6 **Upton**	Y	Y	Y	N	N	Y
7 **Walberg**	Y	Y	Y	N	?	Y
8 **Rogers**	Y	Y	Y	N	N	Y
9 Peters	Y	Y	N	Y	Y	N
10 **Miller**	Y	Y	Y	N	N	Y
11 **McCotter**	?	?	?	N	N	Y
12 Levin	Y	Y	N	Y	Y	N
13 Clarke	Y	Y	N	Y	Y	N
14 Conyers	Y	Y	N	Y	Y	N
15 Dingell	Y	Y	N	Y	Y	N
MINNESOTA						
1 Walz	Y	Y	N	Y	Y	N
2 **Kline**	Y	Y	Y	N	N	Y
3 **Paulsen**	Y	Y	Y	N	N	Y
4 McCollum	Y	Y	N	Y	Y	N
5 Ellison	Y	Y	N	Y	Y	N
6 **Bachmann**	Y	N	Y	N	N	Y
7 Peterson	Y	Y	N	N	?	Y
8 **Cravaack**	N	Y	Y	N	N	Y
MISSISSIPPI						
1 **Nunnelee**	Y	Y	Y	N	N	Y
2 Thompson	Y	Y	N	N	Y	N
3 **Harper**	Y	Y	Y	N	N	Y
4 **Palazzo**	Y	Y	Y	N	N	Y
MISSOURI						
1 Clay	Y	Y	N	Y	Y	N
2 **Akin**	Y	Y	Y	N	N	Y
3 Carnahan	Y	Y	N	Y	Y	N
4 **Hartzler**	Y	Y	Y	N	N	Y
5 Cleaver	Y	Y	N	Y	Y	N
6 **Graves**	Y	Y	Y	N	N	Y
7 **Long**	Y	Y	Y	N	N	Y
8 **Emerson**	Y	Y	Y	N	N	Y
9 **Luetkemeyer**	Y	Y	Y	N	N	Y
MONTANA						
AL **Rehberg**	Y	Y	Y	N	N	Y
NEBRASKA						
1 **Fortenberry**	Y	Y	Y	N	N	Y
2 **Terry**	Y	Y	Y	N	N	Y
3 **Smith**	Y	Y	Y	N	N	Y
NEVADA						
1 Berkley	Y	Y	N	Y	Y	Y
2 **Amodei**	Y	Y	Y	N	N	Y
3 **Heck**	Y	Y	Y	N	N	Y
NEW HAMPSHIRE						
1 **Guinta**	Y	Y	Y	N	N	Y
2 **Bass**	Y	Y	Y	N	N	Y
NEW JERSEY						
1 Andrews	Y	Y	N	Y	Y	N
2 **LoBiondo**	Y	Y	Y	N	N	Y
3 **Runyan**	Y	Y	Y	N	N	Y
4 **Smith**	Y	Y	Y	N	N	Y
5 **Garrett**	Y	N	Y	N	N	Y
6 Pallone	Y	Y	N	Y	Y	N
7 **Lance**	Y	N	Y	N	N	Y
8 Pascrell	Y	Y	N	Y	Y	N
9 Rothman	Y	Y	N	Y	Y	N
10 Payne*	?					
11 **Frelinghuysen**	Y	Y	Y	N	N	Y
12 Holt	Y	Y	N	Y	Y	N
13 Sires	Y	Y	N	Y	Y	N
NEW MEXICO						
1 Heinrich	Y	Y	N	Y	Y	N
2 **Pearce**	Y	N	Y	N	N	Y
3 Luján	Y	Y	N	Y	Y	Y
NEW YORK						
1 Bishop	?	?	N	Y	Y	N
2 Israel	Y	Y	N	Y	Y	N
3 **King**	Y	Y	Y	N	N	Y
4 McCarthy	Y	Y	N	Y	Y	N
5 Ackerman	Y	Y	N	Y	Y	N
6 Meeks	Y	Y	N	Y	Y	N
7 Crowley	Y	Y	N	Y	Y	N
8 Nadler	?	Y	N	Y	Y	N
9 **Turner**	Y	Y	Y	N	N	Y
10 Towns	?	Y	N	Y	Y	N
11 Clarke	+	Y	N	Y	Y	N
12 Velázquez	?	Y	N	Y	Y	N
13 **Grimm**	Y	Y	Y	N	N	Y
14 Maloney	Y	Y	N	Y	Y	N
15 Rangel	?	?	?	?	?	?
16 Serrano	?	Y	N	Y	Y	N
17 Engel	?	Y	N	Y	Y	N
18 Lowey	?	Y	N	Y	Y	N
19 **Hayworth**	Y	Y	Y	N	N	Y
20 **Gibson**	Y	Y	?	N	N	Y
21 Tonko	Y	Y	N	Y	Y	N
22 Hinchey	Y	Y	N	Y	Y	N
23 Owens	Y	Y	N	N	N	Y
24 **Hanna**	Y	Y	Y	N	N	Y
25 **Buerkle**	Y	Y	Y	N	N	Y
26 Hochul	Y	Y	N	Y	Y	N
27 Higgins	Y	Y	N	Y	Y	N
28 Slaughter	Y	Y	N	Y	Y	N
29 **Reed**	Y	Y	Y	N	N	Y
NORTH CAROLINA						
1 Butterfield	Y	Y	N	Y	Y	N
2 **Ellmers**	Y	Y	Y	N	N	Y
3 **Jones**	Y	Y	Y	N	Y	Y
4 Price	Y	Y	N	Y	Y	N
5 **Foxx**	Y	Y	Y	N	N	Y
6 **Coble**	Y	Y	?	N	N	Y
7 McIntyre	Y	Y	N	Y	Y	Y
8 Kissell	Y	Y	N	Y	Y	Y
9 **Myrick**	Y	Y	Y	N	N	Y
10 **McHenry**	Y	Y	Y	N	N	Y
11 Shuler	Y	Y	N	?	?	?
12 Watt	Y	Y	N	?	?	?
13 Miller	Y	Y	N	Y	Y	N
NORTH DAKOTA						
AL **Berg**	Y	Y	Y	N	N	Y
OHIO						
1 **Chabot**	Y	Y	Y	N	N	Y
2 **Schmidt**	Y	N	Y	?	?	?
3 **Turner**	?	Y	Y	N	N	Y
4 **Jordan**	?	N	Y	N	N	Y
5 **Latta**	Y	Y	Y	N	N	Y
6 **Johnson**	Y	Y	Y	N	N	Y
7 **Austria**	Y	Y	Y	N	N	Y
8 **Boehner**						
9 Kaptur	?	?	?	Y	Y	N
10 Kucinich	?	?	?	Y	Y	N
11 Fudge	?	?	?	Y	Y	N
12 **Tiberi**	Y	Y	Y	N	N	Y
13 Sutton	Y	Y	N	Y	Y	N
14 **LaTourette**	Y	Y	?	N	N	Y
15 **Stivers**	Y	Y	Y	N	N	Y
16 **Renacci**	Y	Y	Y	N	N	Y
17 Ryan	Y	Y	N	Y	Y	N
18 **Gibbs**	Y	Y	Y	N	N	Y
OKLAHOMA						
1 **Sullivan**	Y	Y	Y	N	N	Y
2 Boren	Y	Y	Y	N	Y	Y
3 **Lucas**	Y	Y	Y	N	N	Y
4 **Cole**	Y	Y	Y	N	N	Y
5 **Lankford**	Y	Y	Y	N	N	Y
OREGON						
1 Bonamici	Y	Y	N	Y	Y	N
2 **Walden**	Y	Y	Y	N	N	Y
3 Blumenauer	Y	Y	N	Y	Y	N
4 DeFazio	Y	Y	N	Y	Y	N
5 Schrader	Y	Y	N	Y	Y	Y
PENNSYLVANIA						
1 Brady	Y	Y	N	Y	Y	N
2 Fattah	Y	?	N	Y	Y	N
3 **Kelly**	Y	Y	Y	N	N	Y
4 Altmire	Y	Y	N	Y	Y	N
5 **Thompson**	Y	Y	Y	N	N	Y
6 **Gerlach**	Y	Y	Y	N	N	Y
7 **Meehan**	Y	Y	Y	N	N	Y
8 **Fitzpatrick**	Y	Y	Y	N	N	Y
9 **Shuster**	?	Y	Y	N	N	Y
10 **Marino**	Y	Y	Y	N	N	Y
11 **Barletta**	Y	Y	Y	N	N	Y
12 Critz	Y	Y	N	Y	Y	N
13 Schwartz	Y	+	N	Y	Y	N
14 Doyle	?	Y	N	Y	Y	N
15 **Dent**	Y	Y	Y	N	N	Y
16 **Pitts**	Y	Y	Y	N	N	Y
17 Holden	Y	Y	N	Y	Y	N
18 **Murphy**	Y	Y	Y	N	N	Y
19 **Platts**	Y	Y	Y	N	N	Y
RHODE ISLAND						
1 Cicilline	Y	Y	N	Y	Y	N
2 Langevin	Y	Y	N	Y	Y	N
SOUTH CAROLINA						
1 **Scott**	Y	N	Y	N	N	Y
2 **Wilson**	Y	Y	?	N	N	Y
3 **Duncan**	Y	N	Y	N	N	Y
4 **Gowdy**	Y	Y	Y	N	N	Y
5 **Mulvaney**	Y	N	Y	N	N	Y
6 Clyburn	Y	Y	N	Y	Y	N
SOUTH DAKOTA						
AL **Noem**	Y	Y	Y	N	N	Y
TENNESSEE						
1 **Roe**	Y	Y	Y	N	N	Y
2 **Duncan**	Y	Y	Y	N	N	Y
3 **Fleischmann**	?	Y	Y	N	N	Y
4 **DesJarlais**	Y	Y	Y	N	N	Y
5 Cooper	Y	Y	N	Y	Y	N
6 **Black**	Y	Y	Y	N	N	Y
7 **Blackburn**	Y	Y	Y	N	N	Y
8 **Fincher**	Y	N	Y	N	N	Y
9 Cohen	Y	Y	N	Y	Y	N
TEXAS						
1 **Gohmert**	?	?	?	N	N	Y
2 **Poe**	Y	Y	Y	N	N	Y
3 **Johnson, S.**	Y	Y	Y	N	N	Y
4 **Hall**	Y	N	Y	N	N	Y
5 **Hensarling**	Y	N	Y	N	N	Y
6 **Barton**	Y	Y	Y	N	N	Y
7 **Culberson**	Y	Y	Y	N	N	Y
8 **Brady**	Y	Y	Y	N	N	Y
9 Green, A.	Y	Y	N	Y	Y	N
10 **McCaul**	Y	Y	Y	N	N	Y
11 **Conaway**	Y	Y	Y	N	N	Y
12 **Granger**	Y	Y	Y	N	N	Y
13 **Thornberry**	Y	Y	Y	N	N	Y
14 **Paul**	?	?	?	?	?	?
15 Hinojosa	?	?	?	?	?	?
16 Reyes	?	Y	N	Y	Y	N
17 **Flores**	Y	N	Y	N	N	Y
18 Jackson Lee	Y	Y	N	Y	Y	N
19 **Neugebauer**	Y	Y	Y	N	N	Y
20 Gonzalez	Y	Y	N	Y	Y	N
21 **Smith**	Y	Y	Y	N	N	Y
22 **Olson**	Y	Y	Y	N	N	Y
23 **Canseco**	Y	N	Y	N	N	Y
24 **Marchant**	Y	Y	Y	N	N	Y
25 Doggett	?	?	?	Y	Y	N
26 **Burgess**	Y	N	Y	N	N	Y
27 **Farenthold**	Y	Y	Y	N	N	Y
28 Cuellar	Y	Y	N	Y	Y	Y
29 Green, G.	Y	Y	N	Y	Y	?
30 Johnson, E.	Y	Y	N	Y	Y	N
31 **Carter**	Y	Y	Y	N	N	Y
32 **Sessions**	Y	Y	Y	N	N	Y
UTAH						
1 **Bishop**	Y	?	Y	N	N	Y
2 Matheson	Y	Y	Y	N	Y	Y
3 **Chaffetz**	Y	N	Y	N	N	Y
VERMONT						
AL Welch	Y	Y	N	Y	Y	Y
VIRGINIA						
1 **Wittman**	?	Y	Y	N	N	Y
2 **Rigell**	N	Y	Y	N	N	Y
3 Scott	Y	Y	N	Y	Y	N
4 **Forbes**	?	Y	Y	N	N	Y
5 **Hurt**	Y	Y	Y	N	N	Y
6 **Goodlatte**	Y	Y	Y	N	N	Y
7 **Cantor**	Y	Y	Y	N	N	Y
8 Moran	?	Y	N	Y	Y	N
9 **Griffith**	Y	Y	Y	N	N	Y
10 **Wolf**	Y	Y	Y	N	N	Y
11 Connolly	Y	Y	N	Y	Y	N
WASHINGTON						
1 Inslee	?	Y	N	?	Y	N
2 Larsen	Y	Y	N	Y	Y	N
3 **Herrera Beutler**	Y	Y	Y	N	N	Y
4 **Hastings**	Y	Y	Y	N	N	Y
5 **McMorris Rodgers**	Y	Y	Y	N	N	Y
6 Dicks	?	Y	N	Y	?	N
7 McDermott	Y	Y	N	Y	Y	N
8 **Reichert**	Y	Y	Y	N	N	Y
9 Smith	Y	Y	N	Y	Y	N
WEST VIRGINIA						
1 **McKinley**	Y	Y	Y	N	N	Y
2 **Capito**	Y	Y	Y	N	N	Y
3 Rahall	?	Y	N	Y	Y	N
WISCONSIN						
1 **Ryan**	Y	Y	Y	N	N	Y
2 Baldwin	Y	Y	N	Y	Y	N
3 Kind	Y	Y	N	Y	Y	N
4 Moore	?	?	?	?	?	?
5 **Sensenbrenner**	Y	Y	Y	N	N	Y
6 **Petri**	Y	Y	Y	N	N	Y
7 **Duffy**	Y	Y	Y	N	N	Y
8 **Ribble**	Y	Y	Y	N	N	Y
WYOMING						
AL **Lummis**	Y	Y	Y	N	N	Y

IN THE HOUSE | By Vote Number

101. HR 3606. Small-Business Startups/Previous Question.
Sessions, R-Texas, motion to order the previous question (thus ending debate and the possibility of amendment) on the rule (H Res 572) that would provide for House floor consideration of the bill regarding certain rules related to small businesses. Motion agreed to 244-177: R 235-1; D 9-176. March 7, 2012.

102. HR 3606. Small-Business Startups/Rule.
Adoption of the rule (H Res 572) that would provide for House floor consideration of the bill that would define "emerging growth companies" and exempt them from certain independent auditing requirements. The rule also would provide for the automatic adoption of a substitute amendment that would add provisions to modify Securities and Exchange Commission reporting and registration requirements for small businesses. Adopted 252-166: R 235-0; D 17-166. March 7, 2012.

103. HR 3606. Small-Business Startups/Qualifying Threshold.
Himes, D-Conn., amendment that would lower the threshold from $1 billion to $750 million for a business to qualify as an emerging growth company. It also would eliminate the requirement that emerging growth companies cannot have more than $700 million in publicly traded shares. Rejected in Committee of the Whole 164-245: R 1-232; D 163-13. March 7, 2012.

104. HR 3606. Small-Business Startups/Executive Compensation.
Ellison, D-Minn., amendment that would strike language from the bill that would exempt emerging growth companies from required shareholder votes on executive compensation and on executive compensation known as "golden parachutes." Rejected in Committee of the Whole 169-244: R 3-232; D 166-12. March 7, 2012.

105. HR 3606. Small-Business Startups/Broker-Dealer Reports.
Waters, D-Calif., amendment that would require research reports to be filed with the Securities and Exchange Commission (SEC) if a broker or dealer is underwriting an initial public offering (IPO) for an emerging growth company and providing research to the public about the IPO. It also would require that communications before or after an offering between emerging growth companies and potential investors be filed with the SEC. Rejected in Committee of the Whole 161-259: R 0-237; D 161-22. March 7, 2012.

	101	102	103	104	105
ALABAMA					
1 Bonner	Y	Y	N	N	N
2 Roby	Y	Y	N	N	N
3 Rogers	Y	Y	N	N	N
4 Aderholt	Y	Y	N	N	N
5 Brooks	Y	Y	N	N	N
6 Bachus	Y	Y	?	N	N
7 Sewell	N	N	?	Y	Y
ALASKA					
AL Young	Y	Y	N	N	N
ARIZONA					
1 Gosar	Y	Y	N	N	N
2 Franks	Y	Y	N	N	N
3 Quayle	Y	Y	N	N	N
4 Pastor	N	N	Y	Y	Y
5 Schweikert	Y	Y	N	N	N
6 Flake	Y	Y	N	N	N
7 Grijalva	N	N	Y	Y	Y
8 Vacant					
ARKANSAS					
1 Crawford	Y	Y	N	N	N
2 Griffin	Y	Y	N	N	N
3 Womack	Y	Y	N	N	N
4 Ross	Y	Y	N	N	N
CALIFORNIA					
1 Thompson	N	N	Y	Y	Y
2 Herger	Y	Y	N	N	N
3 Lungren	Y	Y	N	N	N
4 McClintock	Y	Y	N	N	N
5 Matsui	N	N	Y	Y	Y
6 Woolsey	N	N	?	?	?
7 Miller, George	N	N	Y	Y	Y
8 Pelosi	N	N	?	?	Y
9 Lee	N	N	Y	Y	Y
10 Garamendi	N	N	Y	Y	N
11 McNerney	N	N	Y	Y	Y
12 Speier	N	N	Y	Y	Y
13 Stark	N	N	Y	Y	Y
14 Eshoo	N	N	Y	Y	Y
15 Honda	N	N	Y	Y	Y
16 Lofgren	N	N	Y	Y	Y
17 Farr	N	N	Y	Y	Y
18 Cardoza	N	N	N	N	N
19 Denham	Y	Y	N	?	?
20 Costa	N	N	N	N	N
21 Nunes	Y	Y	N	N	N
22 McCarthy	Y	Y	N	N	N
23 Capps	N	N	Y	Y	Y
24 Gallegly	Y	Y	N	N	N
25 McKeon	Y	Y	N	N	N
26 Dreier	Y	Y	N	N	N
27 Sherman	N	N	Y	Y	Y
28 Berman	N	N	Y	Y	Y
29 Schiff	N	N	Y	Y	Y
30 Waxman	N	N	Y	Y	Y
31 Becerra	N	N	Y	Y	Y
32 Chu	N	N	Y	Y	Y
33 Bass	N	N	Y	Y	Y
34 Roybal-Allard	N	N	Y	Y	Y
35 Waters	N	N	Y	Y	Y
36 Hahn	N	N	Y	Y	Y
37 Richardson	N	Y	Y	Y	Y
38 Napolitano	N	N	Y	Y	Y
39 Sánchez, Linda	N	N	Y	Y	Y
40 Royce	Y	Y	N	N	N
41 Lewis	Y	Y	N	N	N
42 Miller, Gary	Y	Y	N	N	N
43 Baca	N	N	Y	Y	Y
44 Calvert	Y	Y	N	N	N
45 Bono Mack	Y	Y	N	N	N
46 Rohrabacher	Y	Y	N	N	N
47 Sanchez, Loretta	N	N	Y	Y	Y
48 Campbell	Y	Y	N	N	N
49 Issa	Y	Y	N	N	N
50 Bilbray	Y	Y	N	N	N
51 Filner	N	N	+	+	+
52 Hunter	Y	Y	N	N	N
53 Davis	N	N	Y	Y	Y

	101	102	103	104	105
COLORADO					
1 DeGette	N	N	Y	Y	Y
2 Polis	N	N	Y	N	Y
3 Tipton	Y	Y	N	N	N
4 Gardner	Y	Y	N	N	N
5 Lamborn	Y	Y	N	N	N
6 Coffman	Y	Y	N	N	N
7 Perlmutter	N	N	Y	Y	Y
CONNECTICUT					
1 Larson	N	N	Y	Y	Y
2 Courtney	N	N	Y	Y	Y
3 DeLauro	N	N	Y	Y	Y
4 Himes	N	Y	Y	N	Y
5 Murphy	N	Y	Y	Y	Y
DELAWARE					
AL Carney	N	Y	N	N	N
FLORIDA					
1 Miller	Y	Y	N	N	N
2 Southerland	Y	Y	N	N	N
3 Brown	N	N	Y	Y	Y
4 Crenshaw	Y	Y	N	N	N
5 Nugent	Y	Y	N	N	N
6 Stearns	Y	Y	N	N	N
7 Mica	Y	Y	N	N	N
8 Webster	Y	Y	N	N	N
9 Bilirakis	Y	Y	N	N	N
10 Young	Y	Y	N	N	N
11 Castor	N	N	Y	Y	Y
12 Ross	Y	Y	N	N	N
13 Buchanan	Y	Y	N	N	N
14 Mack	Y	Y	N	N	N
15 Posey	Y	Y	N	N	N
16 Rooney	Y	Y	N	N	N
17 Wilson	N	N	Y	Y	Y
18 Ros-Lehtinen	Y	Y	N	N	N
19 Deutch	N	N	Y	Y	Y
20 Wasserman Schultz	N	N	Y	Y	Y
21 Diaz-Balart	Y	Y	N	N	N
22 West	Y	Y	N	N	N
23 Hastings	N	N	Y	Y	Y
24 Adams	Y	Y	N	N	N
25 Rivera	Y	Y	N	N	N
GEORGIA					
1 Kingston	Y	Y	N	N	N
2 Bishop	N	N	Y	Y	Y
3 Westmoreland	Y	Y	N	N	N
4 Johnson	N	N	Y	Y	Y
5 Lewis	N	N	Y	Y	Y
6 Price	Y	Y	N	N	N
7 Woodall	Y	Y	N	N	N
8 Scott, A.	Y	Y	N	N	N
9 Graves	Y	Y	N	N	N
10 Broun	Y	Y	N	N	N
11 Gingrey	Y	Y	N	N	N
12 Barrow	N	N	Y	Y	Y
13 Scott, D.	N	N	Y	Y	Y
HAWAII					
1 Hanabusa	N	N	Y	Y	Y
2 Hirono	N	N	Y	Y	Y
IDAHO					
1 Labrador	?	?	?	?	?
2 Simpson	Y	Y	N	N	N
ILLINOIS					
1 Rush	N	N	Y	?	Y
2 Jackson	N	N	Y	Y	Y
3 Lipinski	N	Y	Y	Y	Y
4 Gutierrez	N	N	Y	?	Y
5 Quigley	N	Y	Y	Y	Y
6 Roskam	Y	Y	?	N	N
7 Davis	N	N	?	?	?
8 Walsh	Y	Y	N	N	N
9 Schakowsky	N	N	Y	Y	Y
10 Dold	Y	Y	N	N	N
11 Kinzinger	Y	Y	N	N	N
12 Costello	N	N	Y	Y	Y
13 Biggert	Y	Y	N	N	N
14 Hultgren	Y	Y	N	N	N
15 Johnson	Y	Y	N	N	N

KEY   Republicans   Democrats

Y Voted for (yea)	X Paired against	C Voted "present" to avoid possible conflict of interest
# Paired for	– Announced against	
+ Announced for	P Voted "present"	? Did not vote or otherwise make a position known
N Voted against (nay)		

	101	102	103	104	105
16 **Manzullo**	Y	Y	N	N	N
17 **Schilling**	Y	Y	N	N	N
18 **Schock**	Y	Y	N	?	N
19 **Shimkus**	Y	Y	N	N	N
INDIANA					
1 Visclosky	?	?	?	?	?
2 Donnelly	N	Y	Y	Y	Y
3 **Stutzman**	Y	Y	N	N	N
4 **Rokita**	Y	Y	N	N	N
5 **Burton**	Y	Y	?	N	N
6 **Pence**	Y	Y	N	N	N
7 Carson	N	N	N	Y	Y
8 **Bucshon**	Y	Y	N	N	N
9 **Young**	Y	Y	N	N	N
IOWA					
1 Braley	N	N	+	Y	Y
2 Loebsack	N	N	Y	Y	Y
3 Boswell	N	N	Y	Y	Y
4 **Latham**	Y	Y	N	N	N
5 **King**	Y	Y	N	N	N
KANSAS					
1 **Huelskamp**	Y	Y	N	N	N
2 **Jenkins**	Y	Y	N	N	N
3 **Yoder**	Y	Y	N	N	N
4 **Pompeo**	Y	Y	N	N	N
KENTUCKY					
1 **Whitfield**	Y	Y	N	N	N
2 **Guthrie**	Y	Y	N	N	N
3 Yarmuth	N	N	Y	Y	Y
4 **Davis**	?	Y	N	N	N
5 **Rogers**	Y	Y	N	N	N
6 Chandler	N	N	Y	Y	Y
LOUISIANA					
1 **Scalise**	Y	Y	N	N	N
2 Richmond	N	N	Y	Y	Y
3 **Landry**	Y	Y	N	N	N
4 **Fleming**	Y	Y	N	N	N
5 **Alexander**	Y	Y	N	N	N
6 **Cassidy**	Y	Y	N	N	N
7 **Boustany**	Y	Y	N	N	N
MAINE					
1 Pingree	N	N	Y	Y	Y
2 Michaud	N	Y	Y	Y	Y
MARYLAND					
1 **Harris**	Y	Y	N	N	N
2 Ruppersberger	N	N	Y	Y	Y
3 Sarbanes	N	N	Y	Y	Y
4 Edwards	N	N	Y	Y	Y
5 Hoyer	N	N	Y	Y	Y
6 **Bartlett**	Y	Y	N	N	N
7 Cummings	N	N	Y	Y	Y
8 Van Hollen	N	N	Y	Y	Y
MASSACHUSETTS					
1 Olver	N	N	Y	Y	Y
2 Neal	N	N	Y	Y	Y
3 McGovern	N	N	Y	Y	Y
4 Frank	N	N	Y	Y	Y
5 Tsongas	N	N	Y	Y	Y
6 Tierney	N	N	Y	Y	Y
7 Markey	N	N	?	Y	Y
8 Capuano	N	N	Y	Y	Y
9 Lynch	N	N	Y	Y	Y
10 Keating	N	N	Y	Y	Y
MICHIGAN					
1 **Benishek**	Y	Y	N	N	N
2 **Huizenga**	Y	Y	N	N	N
3 **Amash**	Y	Y	N	N	N
4 **Camp**	Y	Y	N	N	N
5 Kildee	N	N	Y	Y	Y
6 **Upton**	Y	Y	N	N	N
7 **Walberg**	Y	Y	N	N	N
8 **Rogers**	Y	Y	N	N	N
9 Peters	N	N	N	Y	Y
10 **Miller**	Y	Y	N	N	N
11 **McCotter**	Y	Y	N	N	N
12 Levin	N	N	Y	Y	Y
13 Clarke	N	N	Y	Y	Y
14 Conyers	N	N	Y	Y	Y
15 Dingell	N	N	Y	Y	Y
MINNESOTA					
1 Walz	N	N	Y	Y	Y
2 **Kline**	Y	Y	N	N	N
3 **Paulsen**	Y	Y	N	N	N
4 McCollum	N	N	Y	Y	Y

	101	102	103	104	105
5 Ellison	N	N	Y	Y	Y
6 **Bachmann**	Y	Y	N	N	N
7 **Peterson**	Y	Y	Y	N	N
8 **Cravaack**	Y	Y	N	N	N
MISSISSIPPI					
1 **Nunnelee**	Y	Y	N	N	N
2 Thompson	N	N	Y	Y	Y
3 **Harper**	Y	Y	N	N	N
4 **Palazzo**	Y	Y	N	N	N
MISSOURI					
1 Clay	N	N	Y	Y	Y
2 **Akin**	Y	Y	N	N	N
3 Carnahan	N	N	?	Y	Y
4 **Hartzler**	Y	Y	N	N	N
5 Cleaver	N	N	Y	Y	Y
6 **Graves**	Y	Y	N	N	N
7 **Long**	Y	Y	N	N	N
8 **Emerson**	Y	Y	N	N	N
9 **Luetkemeyer**	Y	Y	N	N	N
MONTANA					
AL **Rehberg**	Y	Y	N	N	N
NEBRASKA					
1 **Fortenberry**	Y	Y	N	N	N
2 **Terry**	Y	Y	N	N	N
3 **Smith**	Y	Y	N	N	N
NEVADA					
1 Berkley	N	N	Y	Y	Y
2 **Amodei**	Y	Y	N	N	N
3 **Heck**	Y	Y	N	N	N
NEW HAMPSHIRE					
1 **Guinta**	Y	Y	N	N	N
2 **Bass**	Y	Y	N	N	N
NEW JERSEY					
1 Andrews	N	N	Y	Y	Y
2 **LoBiondo**	Y	Y	N	N	N
3 **Runyan**	Y	?	N	N	N
4 **Smith**	Y	Y	N	N	N
5 **Garrett**	Y	Y	N	N	N
6 Pallone	N	N	Y	Y	Y
7 **Lance**	Y	Y	N	N	N
8 Pascrell	N	N	Y	Y	Y
9 Rothman	N	N	Y	Y	Y
10 Vacant					
11 **Frelinghuysen**	Y	Y	N	N	N
12 Holt	N	N	Y	Y	Y
13 Sires	N	N	Y	Y	Y
NEW MEXICO					
1 Heinrich	N	N	Y	Y	Y
2 **Pearce**	Y	Y	N	N	N
3 Luján	N	N	Y	Y	Y
NEW YORK					
1 Bishop	N	N	Y	Y	Y
2 Israel	N	N	Y	Y	Y
3 **King**	Y	Y	N	N	N
4 McCarthy	N	N	Y	Y	N
5 Ackerman	N	N	Y	Y	Y
6 Meeks	N	N	Y	Y	Y
7 Crowley	N	N	N	Y	N
8 Nadler	N	N	Y	Y	Y
9 **Turner**	Y	Y	N	N	N
10 Towns	N	N	Y	Y	Y
11 Clarke	N	N	Y	Y	Y
12 Velázquez	N	?	Y	Y	Y
13 **Grimm**	Y	Y	N	N	N
14 Maloney	N	N	Y	Y	Y
15 Rangel	?	?	?	?	?
16 Serrano	N	N	Y	Y	Y
17 Engel	N	N	Y	Y	Y
18 Lowey	N	N	Y	Y	Y
19 **Hayworth**	Y	Y	N	N	N
20 **Gibson**	Y	Y	Y	N	N
21 Tonko	N	N	Y	Y	Y
22 Hinchey	N	N	Y	Y	Y
23 Owens	N	N	Y	Y	Y
24 **Hanna**	Y	Y	N	N	N
25 **Buerkle**	Y	Y	N	N	N
26 **Hochul**	Y	Y	Y	Y	Y
27 Higgins	N	N	Y	Y	Y
28 Slaughter	N	N	Y	Y	Y
29 **Reed**	Y	Y	N	N	N
NORTH CAROLINA					
1 Butterfield	N	N	Y	Y	Y
2 **Ellmers**	Y	Y	N	N	N
3 **Jones**	N	Y	N	N	N
4 Price	N	N	Y	Y	Y

	101	102	103	104	105
5 **Foxx**	Y	Y	N	N	N
6 **Coble**	Y	Y	N	N	N
7 McIntyre	N	Y	Y	Y	Y
8 Kissell	N	Y	N	N	?
9 **Myrick**	Y	Y	N	N	N
10 **McHenry**	Y	Y	N	N	N
11 Shuler	?	?	N	N	N
12 Watt	?	?	Y	Y	Y
13 Miller	N	N	Y	Y	Y
NORTH DAKOTA					
AL **Berg**	Y	Y	N	N	N
OHIO					
1 **Chabot**	Y	Y	N	N	N
2 **Schmidt**	?	?	?	?	?
3 **Turner**	Y	Y	N	N	N
4 **Jordan**	Y	Y	N	N	N
5 **Latta**	Y	Y	N	N	N
6 **Johnson**	Y	Y	N	N	N
7 **Austria**	Y	Y	N	N	N
8 **Boehner**					
9 Kaptur	N	N	Y	Y	Y
10 Kucinich	N	N	N	Y	Y
11 Fudge	N	N	Y	Y	Y
12 **Tiberi**	Y	Y	?	N	N
13 Sutton	N	N	Y	Y	Y
14 **LaTourette**	Y	Y	N	N	N
15 **Stivers**	Y	Y	N	N	N
16 **Renacci**	Y	Y	N	N	N
17 Ryan	N	N	Y	Y	Y
18 **Gibbs**	Y	Y	N	N	N
OKLAHOMA					
1 **Sullivan**	Y	Y	N	N	N
2 **Boren**	Y	Y	N	N	N
3 **Lucas**	Y	Y	N	N	N
4 **Cole**	Y	Y	N	N	N
5 **Lankford**	Y	Y	N	N	N
OREGON					
1 Bonamici	N	N	Y	Y	Y
2 **Walden**	Y	Y	N	N	N
3 Blumenauer	N	N	Y	Y	Y
4 DeFazio	N	N	Y	Y	Y
5 Schrader	N	Y	?	?	N
PENNSYLVANIA					
1 Brady	N	N	Y	Y	Y
2 Fattah	N	N	Y	Y	Y
3 **Kelly**	Y	Y	–	N	N
4 Altmire	N	N	Y	Y	N
5 **Thompson**	Y	Y	N	N	N
6 **Gerlach**	Y	Y	N	N	N
7 **Meehan**	Y	Y	N	N	N
8 **Fitzpatrick**	Y	Y	N	N	N
9 **Shuster**	Y	Y	N	?	N
10 **Marino**	Y	Y	N	N	N
11 **Barletta**	Y	Y	N	N	N
12 Critz	N	N	Y	Y	Y
13 Schwartz	N	N	+	+	Y
14 Doyle	N	N	Y	Y	Y
15 **Dent**	Y	Y	N	N	N
16 **Pitts**	Y	Y	N	N	N
17 Holden	N	N	Y	Y	N
18 **Murphy**	Y	Y	N	N	N
19 **Platts**	Y	Y	N	N	N
RHODE ISLAND					
1 Cicilline	N	N	Y	Y	Y
2 Langevin	N	N	Y	Y	Y
SOUTH CAROLINA					
1 **Scott**	Y	Y	N	N	N
2 **Wilson**	Y	Y	N	N	N
3 **Duncan**	Y	Y	N	N	N
4 **Gowdy**	Y	Y	N	N	N
5 **Mulvaney**	Y	Y	N	N	N
6 Clyburn	N	N	Y	Y	Y
SOUTH DAKOTA					
AL **Noem**	Y	Y	N	N	N
TENNESSEE					
1 **Roe**	Y	Y	N	N	N
2 **Duncan**	Y	Y	N	Y	N
3 **Fleischmann**	Y	Y	N	N	N
4 **DesJarlais**	Y	Y	N	N	N
5 Cooper	N	N	Y	Y	Y
6 **Black**	Y	Y	N	N	N
7 **Blackburn**	Y	Y	N	N	N
8 **Fincher**	Y	Y	N	N	N
9 Cohen	N	N	?	?	Y

	101	102	103	104	105
TEXAS					
1 **Gohmert**	Y	Y	N	N	N
2 **Poe**	Y	Y	N	N	N
3 **Johnson, S.**	Y	Y	N	N	N
4 **Hall**	Y	Y	N	N	N
5 **Hensarling**	Y	Y	N	N	N
6 **Barton**	Y	Y	N	N	N
7 **Culberson**	Y	Y	N	N	N
8 **Brady**	Y	?	N	N	N
9 Green, A.	N	N	Y	Y	Y
10 **McCaul**	Y	Y	N	N	N
11 **Conaway**	Y	Y	N	N	N
12 **Granger**	Y	Y	N	N	N
13 **Thornberry**	Y	Y	N	N	N
14 **Paul**	?	?	?	?	?
15 Hinojosa	?	?	?	?	?
16 Reyes	N	N	Y	Y	Y
17 **Flores**	Y	Y	N	N	N
18 Jackson Lee	N	N	Y	Y	Y
19 **Neugebauer**	Y	Y	N	N	N
20 Gonzalez	N	N	Y	Y	Y
21 **Smith**	Y	Y	N	N	N
22 **Olson**	Y	Y	N	N	N
23 **Canseco**	Y	Y	N	N	N
24 **Marchant**	Y	Y	N	N	N
25 Doggett	N	N	Y	Y	Y
26 **Burgess**	Y	Y	N	N	N
27 **Farenthold**	Y	Y	N	N	N
28 Cuellar	Y	N	Y	Y	Y
29 Green, G.	Y	N	Y	Y	Y
30 Johnson, E.	N	N	Y	Y	Y
31 **Carter**	Y	Y	N	N	N
32 **Sessions**	Y	Y	N	N	N
UTAH					
1 **Bishop**	Y	Y	N	N	N
2 Matheson	Y	Y	N	Y	N
3 **Chaffetz**	Y	Y	N	N	N
VERMONT					
AL Welch	N	N	N	Y	Y
VIRGINIA					
1 **Wittman**	Y	Y	N	N	N
2 **Rigell**	Y	Y	N	N	N
3 Scott	N	N	Y	Y	Y
4 **Forbes**	Y	Y	N	N	N
5 **Hurt**	?	Y	N	N	N
6 **Goodlatte**	Y	Y	N	N	N
7 **Cantor**	Y	Y	N	N	N
8 Moran	N	N	Y	Y	Y
9 **Griffith**	Y	Y	N	N	N
10 **Wolf**	Y	Y	N	N	N
11 Connolly	N	N	N	N	N
WASHINGTON					
1 Inslee	N	N	Y	Y	Y
2 Larsen	N	N	Y	Y	N
3 **Herrera Beutler**	Y	Y	N	N	N
4 **Hastings**	Y	Y	N	N	N
5 **McMorris Rodgers**	Y	Y	N	N	N
6 Dicks	N	N	Y	Y	Y
7 McDermott	N	?	Y	Y	Y
8 **Reichert**	Y	Y	N	N	N
9 Smith	N	N	Y	N	N
WEST VIRGINIA					
1 **McKinley**	Y	Y	N	N	N
2 **Capito**	Y	?	N	N	N
3 Rahall	N	N	Y	Y	Y
WISCONSIN					
1 **Ryan**	Y	Y	N	N	N
2 Baldwin	N	N	Y	Y	Y
3 Kind	Y	Y	N	N	N
4 Moore	?	?	?	?	?
5 **Sensenbrenner**	Y	Y	N	N	N
6 **Petri**	Y	Y	N	N	N
7 **Duffy**	Y	Y	N	N	N
8 **Ribble**	Y	Y	N	N	N
WYOMING					
AL **Lummis**	Y	Y	N	N	N

IN THE HOUSE | By Vote Number

106. **HR 3606. Small-Business Startups/Oil and Gas Price Speculation.** Connolly, D-Va., amendment that would require the Securities and Exchange Commission to study and report to Congress on the impact of financial speculation of domestic oil and gasoline prices on the ability of emerging growth companies to raise capital. Rejected in Committee of the Whole 185-236: R 12-225; D 173-11. March 7, 2012.

107. **HR 3606. Small-Business Startups/Employer Disclosures.** Peters, D-Mich., amendment that would require publicly traded companies to disclose on an annual basis the total number of employees they have in each country and the percentage increase or decrease in employment in each country. It would exempt emerging growth companies from the requirement and give new public companies five years to comply. Rejected in Committee of the Whole 175-239: R 3-230; D 172-9. March 8, 2012.

108. **HR 3606. Small-Business Startups/IPO Report.** Capps, D-Calif., amendment that would require the Securities and Exchange Commission to issue a report to Congress within one year of the bill's enactment on the increase in initial public offerings that resulted from the bill, including specific increases in filings by manufacturing and high-technology companies. Rejected in Committee of the Whole 172-236: R 5-226; D 167-10. March 8, 2012.

109. **HR 3606. Small-Business Startups/Recommit.** Eshoo, D-Calif., motion to recommit the bill to the House Financial Services Committee with instructions to report it back immediately with an amendment that would require "emerging growth companies" to disclose publicly and to the Federal Election Commission any political expenditures or contributions made during a fiscal year. Motion rejected 170-244: R 1-232; D 169-12. March 8, 2012.

110. **HR 3606. Small-Business Startups/Passage.** Passage of the bill that would define "emerging growth companies" and exempt them from certain independent auditing requirements. As amended, a company would lose its emerging-growth status if it has issued more than $1 billion in non-convertible debt over the prior three years. The bill includes provisions to increase from $5 million to $50 million the annual public offering threshold for companies to be exempt from full Securities and Exchange Commission (SEC) filing requirements and raise the number of shareholders that would trigger mandatory SEC registration from 500 to 2,000. Passed 390-23: R 232-0; D 158-23. A "yea" was a vote in support of the president's position. March 8, 2012.

	106	107	108	109	110
ALABAMA					
1 Bonner	N	?	?	?	?
2 Roby	N	N	N	N	Y
3 Rogers	N	N	N	N	Y
4 Aderholt	N	N	N	N	Y
5 Brooks	N	N	N	N	Y
6 Bachus	N	N	N	N	Y
7 Sewell	Y	Y	Y	Y	Y
ALASKA					
AL Young	N	N	N	N	Y
ARIZONA					
1 Gosar	N	N	N	N	Y
2 Franks	N	N	N	N	Y
3 Quayle	N	N	N	N	Y
4 Pastor	Y	Y	Y	Y	Y
5 Schweikert	N	N	N	N	Y
6 Flake	N	N	N	N	Y
7 Grijalva	Y	Y	Y	Y	Y
8 Vacant					
ARKANSAS					
1 Crawford	N	N	N	N	Y
2 Griffin	N	N	N	N	Y
3 Womack	N	N	N	N	Y
4 Ross	N	N	N	N	Y
CALIFORNIA					
1 Thompson	Y	Y	Y	Y	Y
2 Herger	N	N	N	N	Y
3 Lungren	N	N	N	N	Y
4 McClintock	N	N	N	N	Y
5 Matsui	Y	Y	Y	Y	Y
6 Woolsey	?	Y	Y	Y	Y
7 Miller, George	Y	Y	Y	Y	Y
8 Pelosi	Y	Y	Y	Y	Y
9 Lee	Y	Y	Y	Y	N
10 Garamendi	Y	?	?	?	?
11 McNerney	Y	Y	Y	Y	Y
12 Speier	Y	Y	Y	Y	Y
13 Stark	Y	Y	Y	Y	Y
14 Eshoo	Y	Y	Y	Y	Y
15 Honda	Y	Y	Y	Y	Y
16 Lofgren	Y	Y	Y	Y	Y
17 Farr	Y	Y	Y	Y	Y
18 Cardoza	N	?	?	?	?
19 Denham	?	N	N	N	Y
20 Costa	N	N	?	N	Y
21 Nunes	N	N	N	N	Y
22 McCarthy	N	N	N	N	Y
23 Capps	Y	Y	Y	Y	Y
24 Gallegly	N	N	N	N	Y
25 McKeon	N	N	N	N	Y
26 Dreier	N	N	N	N	Y
27 Sherman	Y	Y	Y	Y	Y
28 Berman	Y	Y	Y	Y	Y
29 Schiff	Y	Y	Y	Y	Y
30 Waxman	Y	Y	Y	Y	N
31 Becerra	Y	Y	Y	Y	Y
32 Chu	Y	Y	Y	Y	Y
33 Bass	Y	Y	Y	Y	N
34 Roybal-Allard	Y	Y	Y	Y	Y
35 Waters	Y	Y	Y	Y	Y
36 Hahn	Y	Y	Y	Y	Y
37 Richardson	Y	Y	Y	Y	Y
38 Napolitano	Y	Y	Y	Y	N
39 Sánchez, Linda	Y	Y	Y	Y	Y
40 Royce	N	N	N	N	Y
41 Lewis	N	N	N	N	Y
42 Miller, Gary	N	?	?	?	?
43 Baca	Y	Y	Y	Y	N
44 Calvert	N	N	N	N	Y
45 Bono Mack	N	N	N	N	Y
46 Rohrabacher	N	N	N	N	Y
47 Sanchez, Loretta	Y	Y	Y	Y	Y
48 Campbell	N	N	N	N	Y
49 Issa	N	N	N	N	Y
50 Bilbray	N	N	N	N	Y
51 Filner	+	+	+	+	–
52 Hunter	N	N	N	N	Y
53 Davis	Y	Y	Y	Y	Y

	106	107	108	109	110
COLORADO					
1 DeGette	Y	Y	Y	Y	Y
2 Polis	Y	Y	Y	Y	Y
3 Tipton	N	N	N	N	Y
4 Gardner	N	N	N	N	Y
5 Lamborn	N	N	N	N	Y
6 Coffman	N	N	Y	N	Y
7 Perlmutter	Y	Y	Y	Y	Y
CONNECTICUT					
1 Larson	Y	Y	Y	Y	Y
2 Courtney	Y	Y	Y	Y	Y
3 DeLauro	Y	Y	Y	Y	Y
4 Himes	N	N	N	Y	Y
5 Murphy	Y	Y	Y	Y	Y
DELAWARE					
AL Carney	N	Y	Y	N	Y
FLORIDA					
1 Miller	N	N	N	N	Y
2 Southerland	N	N	N	N	Y
3 Brown	Y	Y	Y	Y	Y
4 Crenshaw	N	N	N	N	Y
5 Nugent	N	N	N	N	Y
6 Stearns	N	N	N	N	Y
7 Mica	N	N	N	N	Y
8 Webster	N	N	N	N	Y
9 Bilirakis	N	N	N	N	Y
10 Young	Y	N	N	N	Y
11 Castor	Y	Y	Y	Y	Y
12 Ross	N	N	N	N	Y
13 Buchanan	N	N	N	N	Y
14 Mack	N	N	N	N	Y
15 Posey	N	N	N	N	Y
16 Rooney	N	N	N	N	Y
17 Wilson	Y	Y	Y	Y	Y
18 Ros-Lehtinen	N	N	N	N	Y
19 Deutch	Y	Y	Y	Y	Y
20 Wasserman Schultz	Y	Y	Y	Y	Y
21 Diaz-Balart	N	N	N	N	Y
22 West	N	N	N	N	Y
23 Hastings	Y	Y	Y	Y	Y
24 Adams	N	N	N	N	Y
25 Rivera	N	N	N	N	Y
GEORGIA					
1 Kingston	N	N	N	N	Y
2 Bishop	Y	Y	Y	Y	Y
3 Westmoreland	N	N	N	N	Y
4 Johnson	Y	?	?	Y	N
5 Lewis	Y	Y	Y	Y	Y
6 Price	N	N	N	N	Y
7 Woodall	N	N	N	N	Y
8 Scott, A.	N	N	N	N	Y
9 Graves	N	N	N	N	Y
10 Broun	N	N	N	N	Y
11 Gingrey	N	N	N	N	Y
12 Barrow	Y	Y	Y	N	Y
13 Scott, D.	Y	Y	Y	Y	Y
HAWAII					
1 Hanabusa	Y	Y	Y	Y	Y
2 Hirono	Y	Y	Y	Y	Y
IDAHO					
1 Labrador	?	?	?	?	?
2 Simpson	N	N	N	N	Y
ILLINOIS					
1 Rush	Y	Y	Y	Y	Y
2 Jackson	Y	Y	Y	Y	Y
3 Lipinski	Y	Y	Y	Y	Y
4 Gutierrez	Y	Y	Y	Y	Y
5 Quigley	Y	Y	Y	Y	Y
6 Roskam	N	N	N	N	Y
7 Davis	?	?	?	?	?
8 Walsh	N	N	N	N	Y
9 Schakowsky	Y	Y	Y	Y	N
10 Dold	N	N	N	N	Y
11 Kinzinger	N	N	N	N	Y
12 Costello	Y	Y	Y	Y	Y
13 Biggert	N	N	N	N	Y
14 Hultgren	N	N	N	N	Y
15 Johnson	N	N	N	N	Y

KEY	**Republicans**	Democrats		
Y Voted for (yea)		X Paired against		C Voted "present" to avoid possible conflict of interest
# Paired for		– Announced against		
+ Announced for		P Voted "present"		? Did not vote or otherwise make a position known
N Voted against (nay)				

	106	107	108	109	110
16 Manzullo	N	N	N	N	Y
17 Schilling	N	N	N	N	Y
18 Schock	N	N	N	N	Y
19 Shimkus	N	N	N	N	Y
INDIANA					
1 Visclosky	?	+	+	+	+
2 Donnelly	Y	Y	Y	Y	Y
3 Stutzman	N	N	N	N	Y
4 Rokita	N	N	N	N	Y
5 Burton	N	N	N	N	Y
6 Pence	N	N	N	N	Y
7 Carson	Y	Y	Y	Y	Y
8 Bucshon	N	N	N	N	Y
9 Young	N	N	N	N	Y
IOWA					
1 Braley	Y	Y	Y	Y	Y
2 Loebsack	Y	Y	Y	Y	Y
3 Boswell	Y	Y	Y	Y	Y
4 Latham	N	N	N	N	Y
5 King	N	N	N	N	Y
KANSAS					
1 Huelskamp	N	N	N	N	Y
2 Jenkins	N	N	N	N	Y
3 Yoder	N	N	N	N	Y
4 Pompeo	N	N	N	N	Y
KENTUCKY					
1 Whitfield	N	N	N	N	Y
2 Guthrie	N	N	N	N	Y
3 Yarmuth	Y	Y	Y	Y	Y
4 Davis	N	N	N	N	Y
5 Rogers	N	N	N	N	Y
6 Chandler	Y	Y	N	N	Y
LOUISIANA					
1 Scalise	N	N	N	N	Y
2 Richmond	Y	Y	Y	Y	Y
3 Landry	N	?	?	?	?
4 Fleming	N	N	N	N	Y
5 Alexander	N	N	N	N	Y
6 Cassidy	N	N	N	N	Y
7 Boustany	N	N	N	N	Y
MAINE					
1 Pingree	Y	Y	Y	Y	N
2 Michaud	Y	Y	Y	Y	Y
MARYLAND					
1 Harris	N	N	N	N	Y
2 Ruppersberger	Y	Y	Y	Y	Y
3 Sarbanes	Y	Y	Y	Y	N
4 Edwards	Y	Y	Y	Y	N
5 Hoyer	Y	Y	?	Y	Y
6 Bartlett	N	N	?	N	Y
7 Cummings	Y	Y	Y	Y	Y
8 Van Hollen	Y	Y	Y	Y	Y
MASSACHUSETTS					
1 Olver	Y	Y	Y	Y	N
2 Neal	Y	Y	Y	Y	Y
3 McGovern	Y	Y	Y	Y	Y
4 Frank	Y	Y	Y	Y	Y
5 Tsongas	Y	Y	Y	Y	Y
6 Tierney	Y	Y	Y	Y	Y
7 Markey	Y	Y	Y	Y	N
8 Capuano	Y	Y	Y	Y	N
9 Lynch	Y	Y	Y	Y	Y
10 Keating	Y	Y	Y	Y	Y
MICHIGAN					
1 Benishek	N	N	N	N	Y
2 Huizenga	N	N	N	N	Y
3 Amash	N	N	N	N	Y
4 Camp	N	N	N	N	Y
5 Kildee	Y	Y	Y	Y	N
6 Upton	N	N	N	N	Y
7 Walberg	N	N	N	N	Y
8 Rogers	N	N	N	N	Y
9 Peters	Y	Y	Y	Y	Y
10 Miller	N	N	N	N	Y
11 McCotter	N	N	N	N	Y
12 Levin	Y	Y	Y	Y	Y
13 Clarke	Y	Y	Y	Y	Y
14 Conyers	Y	Y	Y	Y	N
15 Dingell	Y	Y	Y	Y	N
MINNESOTA					
1 Walz	Y	Y	Y	Y	Y
2 Kline	N	N	N	N	Y
3 Paulsen	Y	N	N	N	Y
4 McCollum	Y	Y	Y	Y	Y

	106	107	108	109	110
5 Ellison	Y	Y	Y	Y	Y
6 Bachmann	N	N	N	N	Y
7 Peterson	N	N	N	N	Y
8 Cravaack	N	N	N	N	Y
MISSISSIPPI					
1 Nunnelee	N	N	N	N	Y
2 Thompson	Y	?	?	?	?
3 Harper	N	N	N	N	Y
4 Palazzo	N	N	N	N	Y
MISSOURI					
1 Clay	Y	Y	Y	Y	Y
2 Akin	N	N	N	N	Y
3 Carnahan	Y	Y	Y	Y	Y
4 Hartzler	N	N	N	N	Y
5 Cleaver	Y	Y	Y	Y	Y
6 Graves	N	N	N	N	Y
7 Long	N	N	N	N	Y
8 Emerson	N	N	N	N	Y
9 Luetkemeyer	N	N	N	N	Y
MONTANA					
AL Rehberg	N	N	N	N	Y
NEBRASKA					
1 Fortenberry	Y	N	N	N	Y
2 Terry	N	N	N	N	Y
3 Smith	N	N	N	N	Y
NEVADA					
1 Berkley	Y	Y	Y	Y	Y
2 Amodei	N	N	N	N	Y
3 Heck	N	N	N	N	Y
NEW HAMPSHIRE					
1 Guinta	N	N	N	N	Y
2 Bass	N	N	N	N	Y
NEW JERSEY					
1 Andrews	Y	Y	Y	Y	Y
2 LoBiondo	N	N	N	N	Y
3 Runyan	N	N	N	N	Y
4 Smith	N	N	N	N	Y
5 Garrett	N	N	N	N	Y
6 Pallone	Y	Y	Y	Y	Y
7 Lance	N	N	N	N	Y
8 Pascrell	Y	Y	Y	Y	Y
9 Rothman	Y	Y	Y	Y	Y
10 Vacant					
11 Frelinghuysen	N	N	N	N	Y
12 Holt	Y	Y	Y	Y	N
13 Sires	Y	Y	Y	Y	Y
NEW MEXICO					
1 Heinrich	Y	Y	Y	Y	Y
2 Pearce	N	N	N	N	Y
3 Luján	Y	Y	Y	Y	Y
NEW YORK					
1 Bishop	Y	Y	Y	Y	Y
2 Israel	Y	Y	Y	Y	Y
3 King	N	N	N	N	Y
4 McCarthy	Y	Y	Y	Y	Y
5 Ackerman	Y	Y	Y	Y	Y
6 Meeks	Y	Y	Y	Y	Y
7 Crowley	Y	Y	Y	Y	Y
8 Nadler	Y	Y	Y	Y	Y
9 Turner	N	N	N	N	Y
10 Towns	Y	Y	Y	Y	Y
11 Clarke	Y	Y	Y	Y	Y
12 Velázquez	Y	Y	Y	Y	Y
13 Grimm	N	N	N	N	Y
14 Maloney	Y	Y	Y	?	?
15 Rangel	?	?	?	?	?
16 Serrano	Y	Y	Y	Y	Y
17 Engel	Y	Y	Y	Y	Y
18 Lowey	Y	Y	Y	Y	Y
19 Hayworth	N	N	N	N	Y
20 Gibson	Y	Y	Y	Y	Y
21 Tonko	Y	Y	Y	Y	Y
22 Hinchey	Y	Y	Y	Y	N
23 Owens	Y	Y	Y	Y	Y
24 Hanna	N	Y	N	N	Y
25 Buerkle	N	N	N	N	Y
26 Hochul	Y	Y	Y	Y	Y
27 Higgins	Y	Y	Y	Y	Y
28 Slaughter	Y	Y	Y	Y	Y
29 Reed	N	N	N	N	Y
NORTH CAROLINA					
1 Butterfield	Y	Y	Y	Y	Y
2 Ellmers	N	N	N	N	Y
3 Jones	Y	Y	Y	Y	Y
4 Price	Y	Y	Y	Y	Y

	106	107	108	109	110
5 Foxx	N	N	N	N	Y
6 Coble	N	N	N	N	Y
7 McIntyre	Y	Y	Y	Y	Y
8 Kissell	Y	Y	Y	Y	Y
9 Myrick	N	N	N	N	Y
10 McHenry	N	N	N	N	Y
11 Shuler	N	N	N	N	Y
12 Watt	Y	Y	Y	Y	N
13 Miller	Y	Y	Y	Y	N
NORTH DAKOTA					
AL Berg	N	N	N	N	Y
OHIO					
1 Chabot	N	N	N	N	Y
2 Schmidt	?	?	?	?	?
3 Turner	N	N	N	N	Y
4 Jordan	N	N	N	N	Y
5 Latta	N	N	N	N	Y
6 Johnson	Y	N	N	N	Y
7 Austria	N	N	N	N	Y
8 Boehner					
9 Kaptur	Y	Y	Y	Y	Y
10 Kucinich	Y	Y	Y	Y	N
11 Fudge	Y	Y	Y	Y	Y
12 Tiberi	N	N	N	N	Y
13 Sutton	Y	Y	Y	Y	Y
14 LaTourette	N	N	?	N	Y
15 Stivers	N	N	N	N	Y
16 Renacci	N	N	N	N	Y
17 Ryan	Y	Y	Y	Y	Y
18 Gibbs	N	N	N	N	Y
OKLAHOMA					
1 Sullivan	N	N	N	N	Y
2 Boren	N	N	N	N	Y
3 Lucas	N	N	N	N	Y
4 Cole	N	N	N	N	Y
5 Lankford	N	N	N	N	Y
OREGON					
1 Bonamici	Y	Y	Y	Y	Y
2 Walden	N	N	N	N	Y
3 Blumenauer	Y	Y	Y	Y	Y
4 DeFazio	Y	Y	Y	Y	Y
5 Schrader	Y	Y	N	N	Y
PENNSYLVANIA					
1 Brady	Y	Y	Y	Y	Y
2 Fattah	Y	Y	Y	Y	Y
3 Kelly	N	N	N	N	Y
4 Altmire	Y	Y	Y	Y	Y
5 Thompson	N	N	N	N	Y
6 Gerlach	Y	N	N	N	Y
7 Meehan	N	N	N	N	Y
8 Fitzpatrick	Y	N	N	N	Y
9 Shuster	N	N	N	N	Y
10 Marino	N	N	N	N	Y
11 Barletta	N	N	N	N	Y
12 Critz	Y	Y	Y	Y	Y
13 Schwartz	Y	Y	Y	Y	Y
14 Doyle	Y	Y	Y	Y	Y
15 Dent	N	N	N	N	Y
16 Pitts	N	N	N	N	Y
17 Holden	Y	Y	Y	Y	Y
18 Murphy	N	N	N	N	Y
19 Platts	Y	N	N	N	Y
RHODE ISLAND					
1 Cicilline	Y	Y	Y	Y	Y
2 Langevin	Y	Y	Y	Y	Y
SOUTH CAROLINA					
1 Scott	N	N	N	N	Y
2 Wilson	N	N	N	N	Y
3 Duncan	N	N	N	N	Y
4 Gowdy	N	N	N	N	Y
5 Mulvaney	N	N	N	N	Y
6 Clyburn	Y	Y	Y	Y	Y
SOUTH DAKOTA					
AL Noem	N	N	N	N	Y
TENNESSEE					
1 Roe	N	N	N	N	Y
2 Duncan	N	Y	N	N	?
3 Fleischmann	N	N	N	N	Y
4 DesJarlais	N	N	N	N	Y
5 Cooper	N	N	N	N	Y
6 Black	N	N	N	N	Y
7 Blackburn	N	N	N	N	Y
8 Fincher	N	N	N	N	Y
9 Cohen	Y	Y	Y	Y	Y

	106	107	108	109	110
TEXAS					
1 Gohmert	N	N	N	N	Y
2 Poe	N	N	N	N	Y
3 Johnson, S.	N	N	N	N	Y
4 Hall	N	N	N	N	Y
5 Hensarling	N	N	N	N	Y
6 Barton	N	N	N	N	Y
7 Culberson	N	?	?	?	?
8 Brady	N	N	N	N	Y
9 Green, A.	Y	Y	Y	Y	Y
10 McCaul	N	N	N	N	Y
11 Conaway	N	N	N	N	Y
12 Granger	N	N	N	N	Y
13 Thornberry	N	N	N	N	Y
14 Paul	?	?	?	?	?
15 Hinojosa	?	?	?	?	?
16 Reyes	Y	Y	Y	Y	Y
17 Flores	N	N	N	N	Y
18 Jackson Lee	Y	Y	Y	Y	Y
19 Neugebauer	N	?	?	?	?
20 Gonzalez	Y	Y	Y	Y	Y
21 Smith	N	N	N	N	Y
22 Olson	N	N	N	N	Y
23 Canseco	N	N	N	N	Y
24 Marchant	N	N	N	N	Y
25 Doggett	Y	Y	?	Y	Y
26 Burgess	Y	N	N	N	Y
27 Farenthold	N	N	N	N	Y
28 Cuellar	N	N	Y	Y	Y
29 Green, G.	Y	Y	Y	Y	Y
30 Johnson, E.	Y	Y	Y	Y	Y
31 Carter	N	N	N	N	Y
32 Sessions	N	N	N	N	Y
UTAH					
1 Bishop	N	N	N	N	Y
2 Matheson	N	N	Y	N	Y
3 Chaffetz	N	N	N	N	Y
VERMONT					
AL Welch	Y	Y	Y	Y	Y
VIRGINIA					
1 Wittman	N	N	N	N	Y
2 Rigell	N	N	N	N	Y
3 Scott	Y	Y	Y	Y	Y
4 Forbes	N	N	N	N	Y
5 Hurt	N	N	N	N	Y
6 Goodlatte	N	N	N	N	Y
7 Cantor	N	N	N	N	Y
8 Moran	Y	Y	?	Y	Y
9 Griffith	Y	N	N	N	Y
10 Wolf	N	N	N	N	Y
11 Connolly	Y	Y	Y	Y	Y
WASHINGTON					
1 Inslee	Y	Y	Y	Y	Y
2 Larsen	Y	Y	Y	Y	Y
3 Herrera Beutler	N	N	N	N	Y
4 Hastings	N	N	N	N	Y
5 McMorris Rodgers	N	N	N	N	Y
6 Dicks	Y	Y	Y	Y	Y
7 McDermott	Y	Y	Y	Y	N
8 Reichert	N	N	N	N	Y
9 Smith	Y	Y	N	Y	Y
WEST VIRGINIA					
1 McKinley	N	N	N	N	Y
2 Capito	N	N	N	N	Y
3 Rahall	Y	Y	Y	Y	Y
WISCONSIN					
1 Ryan	N	N	N	N	Y
2 Baldwin	Y	Y	Y	Y	Y
3 Kind	Y	Y	Y	Y	Y
4 Moore	?	?	?	?	?
5 Sensenbrenner	Y	N	N	N	Y
6 Petri	N	N	N	N	Y
7 Duffy	N	N	N	N	Y
8 Ribble	N	N	N	N	Y
WYOMING					
AL Lummis	N	N	N	N	Y

IN THE HOUSE | By Vote Number

111. **HR 3992. Israeli Non-Immigrant Visas/Passage.** Smith, R-Texas, motion to suspend the rules and pass the bill that would allow Israeli nationals to apply for E-2 non-immigrant investor visas as long as Israel provides reciprocal treatment to U.S. nationals. Motion agreed to 371-0: R 218-0; D 153-0. A two-thirds majority of those present and voting (248 in this case) is required for passage. March 19, 2012.

112. **HR 2087. Virginia Land Deeds Restrictions/Question of Consideration.** Question of whether the House should consider the rule (H Res 587) to provide for House floor consideration of the bill that would require the Interior secretary to remove all public use and recreation deed restrictions on conveyed land in Accomack County, Va., within 90 days of enactment. Agreed to consider 227-172: R 226-0; D 1-172. (Grijalva, D-Ariz., had raised a point of order that the rule would violate clause 9(b) of House Rule 21, regarding disclosure of earmarks.) March 20, 2012.

113. **HR 2087. Virginia Land Deeds Restrictions/Rule.** Adoption of the rule (H Res 587) that would provide for House floor consideration of the bill that would remove deed restrictions on a parcel of land in Accomack County, Va. Adopted 232-170: R 227-0; D 5-170. March 20, 2012.

114. **HR 665. Excess Federal Property/Passage.** Chaffetz, R-Utah, motion to suspend the rules and pass the bill that would establish a pilot program for the expedited disposal of excess federal real property through public auctions with net profits to be used for deficit reduction and aid to the homeless. The program would terminate five years after the date of enactment. Passed 403-0: R 227-0; D 176-0. A two-thirds majority of those present and voting (269 in this case) is required for passage. March 20, 2012.

	111	112	113	114
ALABAMA				
1 Bonner	Y	Y	Y	Y
2 Roby	Y	Y	Y	Y
3 Rogers	Y	Y	Y	Y
4 Aderholt	Y	Y	Y	Y
5 Brooks	Y	Y	Y	Y
6 Bachus	?	?	?	?
7 Sewell	Y	N	N	Y
ALASKA				
AL Young	Y	Y	Y	Y
ARIZONA				
1 Gosar	Y	Y	Y	Y
2 Franks	Y	Y	Y	Y
3 Quayle	Y	Y	Y	Y
4 Pastor	Y	N	N	Y
5 Schweikert	Y	Y	Y	Y
6 Flake	Y	Y	Y	Y
7 Grijalva	?	N	N	Y
8 Vacant				
ARKANSAS				
1 Crawford	?	Y	Y	Y
2 Griffin	Y	Y	Y	Y
3 Womack	Y	Y	Y	Y
4 Ross	Y	N	N	Y
CALIFORNIA				
1 Thompson	Y	N	N	Y
2 Herger	Y	Y	Y	Y
3 Lungren	Y	Y	Y	Y
4 McClintock	Y	Y	Y	Y
5 Matsui	Y	N	N	Y
6 Woolsey	+	N	N	Y
7 Miller, George	Y	N	N	Y
8 Pelosi	Y	N	N	Y
9 Lee	+	−	−	+
10 Garamendi	Y	N	N	Y
11 McNerney	Y	N	N	Y
12 Speier	+	N	N	Y
13 Stark	Y	?	N	Y
14 Eshoo	Y	N	N	Y
15 Honda	?	?	N	Y
16 Lofgren	?	N	N	Y
17 Farr	?	N	N	Y
18 Cardoza	Y	N	N	Y
19 Denham	Y	Y	Y	Y
20 Costa	Y	N	N	Y
21 Nunes	Y	Y	Y	Y
22 McCarthy	Y	Y	Y	Y
23 Capps	Y	N	N	Y
24 Gallegly	Y	Y	Y	Y
25 McKeon	Y	Y	Y	Y
26 Dreier	Y	Y	Y	Y
27 Sherman	Y	N	N	Y
28 Berman	Y	N	N	Y
29 Schiff	Y	N	N	Y
30 Waxman	Y	N	N	Y
31 Becerra	Y	N	N	Y
32 Chu	Y	N	N	Y
33 Bass	Y	?	N	Y
34 Roybal-Allard	Y	N	N	Y
35 Waters	Y	N	N	Y
36 Hahn	Y	N	N	Y
37 Richardson	Y	N	N	Y
38 Napolitano	Y	N	N	Y
39 Sánchez, Linda	Y	N	N	Y
40 Royce	Y	Y	Y	Y
41 Lewis	?	?	?	?
42 Miller, Gary	Y	Y	Y	?
43 Baca	Y	N	N	Y
44 Calvert	Y	Y	Y	Y
45 Bono Mack	?	?	?	?
46 Rohrabacher	?	Y	Y	Y
47 Sanchez, Loretta	?	N	N	Y
48 Campbell	?	Y	Y	Y
49 Issa	Y	Y	Y	Y
50 Bilbray	Y	Y	Y	Y
51 Filner	+	N	N	Y
52 Hunter	Y	Y	Y	Y
53 Davis	Y	N	N	Y

	111	112	113	114
COLORADO				
1 DeGette	Y	N	N	Y
2 Polis	?	N	N	Y
3 Tipton	Y	Y	Y	Y
4 Gardner	Y	Y	Y	Y
5 Lamborn	Y	Y	Y	Y
6 Coffman	Y	Y	Y	Y
7 Perlmutter	Y	N	N	Y
CONNECTICUT				
1 Larson	Y	?	N	Y
2 Courtney	Y	N	N	Y
3 DeLauro	Y	N	N	Y
4 Himes	Y	N	N	Y
5 Murphy	?	N	N	Y
DELAWARE				
AL Carney	Y	N	N	Y
FLORIDA				
1 Miller	Y	Y	Y	Y
2 Southerland	Y	Y	Y	Y
3 Brown	Y	N	?	Y
4 Crenshaw	Y	Y	Y	Y
5 Nugent	Y	Y	Y	Y
6 Stearns	Y	Y	Y	Y
7 Mica	Y	Y	Y	Y
8 Webster	Y	Y	Y	Y
9 Bilirakis	Y	Y	Y	Y
10 Young	?	Y	Y	Y
11 Castor	Y	N	N	Y
12 Ross	Y	Y	Y	Y
13 Buchanan	Y	Y	Y	Y
14 Mack	?	Y	Y	Y
15 Posey	Y	Y	Y	Y
16 Rooney	Y	Y	Y	Y
17 Wilson	+	N	N	Y
18 Ros-Lehtinen	Y	Y	Y	Y
19 Deutch	Y	N	N	Y
20 Wasserman Schultz	Y	N	N	Y
21 Diaz-Balart	Y	Y	Y	Y
22 West	Y	Y	Y	Y
23 Hastings	Y	N	N	Y
24 Adams	Y	Y	Y	Y
25 Rivera	Y	Y	Y	Y
GEORGIA				
1 Kingston	Y	Y	Y	Y
2 Bishop	?	N	N	Y
3 Westmoreland	Y	Y	Y	Y
4 Johnson	Y	N	?	?
5 Lewis	?	N	N	Y
6 Price	Y	Y	Y	Y
7 Woodall	Y	Y	Y	Y
8 Scott, A.	Y	Y	Y	Y
9 Graves	Y	Y	Y	Y
10 Broun	Y	Y	Y	Y
11 Gingrey	?	Y	Y	Y
12 Barrow	Y	N	N	Y
13 Scott, D.	Y	N	N	Y
HAWAII				
1 Hanabusa	Y	N	N	Y
2 Hirono	Y	−	N	Y
IDAHO				
1 Labrador	Y	Y	Y	Y
2 Simpson	Y	Y	Y	Y
ILLINOIS				
1 Rush	?	?	?	?
2 Jackson	?	?	?	?
3 Lipinski	?	?	?	?
4 Gutierrez	+	N	N	Y
5 Quigley	Y	N	N	Y
6 Roskam	Y	Y	Y	Y
7 Davis	?	?	?	?
8 Walsh	?	?	?	?
9 Schakowsky	Y	N	N	Y
10 Dold	+	?	?	+
11 Kinzinger	+	?	?	+
12 Costello	Y	N	N	Y
13 Biggert	Y	Y	Y	Y
14 Hultgren	Y	Y	Y	Y
15 Johnson	+	Y	Y	Y

*Rep. Jay Inslee, D-Wash., resigned effective March 20, 2012. The last vote for which he was eligible was vote 111.

	111	112	113	114
16 **Manzullo**	?	?	?	?
17 **Schilling**	+	Y	Y	Y
18 **Schock**	?	?	?	?
19 **Shimkus**	Y	Y	Y	Y
INDIANA				
1 Visclosky	Y	N	N	Y
2 Donnelly	?	N	N	Y
3 **Stutzman**	Y	Y	Y	Y
4 **Rokita**	Y	Y	Y	Y
5 **Burton**	Y	Y	Y	Y
6 **Pence**	Y	Y	Y	Y
7 Carson	Y	N	N	Y
8 **Bucshon**	Y	Y	Y	Y
9 **Young**	Y	Y	Y	Y
IOWA				
1 Braley	Y	N	N	Y
2 Loebsack	Y	N	N	Y
3 Boswell	Y	N	N	Y
4 **Latham**	Y	Y	Y	Y
5 **King**	Y	Y	Y	Y
KANSAS				
1 **Huelskamp**	Y	Y	Y	Y
2 **Jenkins**	Y	Y	Y	Y
3 **Yoder**	Y	Y	Y	Y
4 **Pompeo**	Y	Y	Y	Y
KENTUCKY				
1 **Whitfield**	Y	Y	Y	Y
2 **Guthrie**	Y	Y	Y	Y
3 Yarmuth	?	?	?	?
4 **Davis**	Y	Y	Y	Y
5 **Rogers**	Y	Y	Y	Y
6 Chandler	Y	N	N	?
LOUISIANA				
1 **Scalise**	Y	Y	Y	Y
2 Richmond	?	N	N	Y
3 **Landry**	Y	Y	Y	Y
4 **Fleming**	Y	Y	Y	Y
5 **Alexander**	Y	Y	Y	Y
6 **Cassidy**	Y	Y	Y	Y
7 **Boustany**	Y	Y	Y	Y
MAINE				
1 Pingree	Y	N	N	Y
2 Michaud	Y	N	Y	Y
MARYLAND				
1 **Harris**	Y	Y	Y	Y
2 Ruppersberger	Y	N	N	Y
3 Sarbanes	Y	N	N	Y
4 Edwards	Y	N	N	Y
5 Hoyer	Y	N	N	Y
6 **Bartlett**	Y	Y	Y	Y
7 Cummings	Y	N	N	Y
8 Van Hollen	Y	?	?	?
MASSACHUSETTS				
1 Olver	Y	N	N	Y
2 Neal	Y	N	N	Y
3 McGovern	Y	N	N	Y
4 Frank	Y	N	N	Y
5 Tsongas	Y	N	N	Y
6 Tierney	Y	N	N	Y
7 Markey	?	N	N	?
8 Capuano	Y	N	N	Y
9 Lynch	Y	N	N	Y
10 Keating	Y	N	N	Y
MICHIGAN				
1 **Benishek**	Y	Y	Y	Y
2 **Huizenga**	Y	Y	Y	Y
3 **Amash**	Y	Y	Y	Y
4 **Camp**	Y	Y	Y	Y
5 Kildee	Y	N	N	Y
6 **Upton**	Y	Y	Y	Y
7 **Walberg**	Y	Y	Y	Y
8 **Rogers**	Y	Y	Y	Y
9 Peters	Y	N	N	Y
10 **Miller**	Y	Y	Y	Y
11 **McCotter**	Y	Y	Y	Y
12 Levin	Y	N	N	Y
13 Clarke	Y	N	N	Y
14 Conyers	Y	N	N	Y
15 Dingell	?	N	N	Y
MINNESOTA				
1 Walz	Y	N	N	Y
2 **Kline**	Y	Y	Y	Y
3 **Paulsen**	Y	Y	Y	Y
4 McCollum	Y	N	N	Y

	111	112	113	114
5 Ellison	?	N	N	Y
6 **Bachmann**	Y	Y	Y	Y
7 Peterson	Y	N	N	Y
8 **Cravaack**	Y	Y	Y	Y
MISSISSIPPI				
1 **Nunnelee**	Y	Y	Y	Y
2 Thompson	Y	N	N	Y
3 **Harper**	Y	Y	Y	Y
4 **Palazzo**	Y	Y	Y	Y
MISSOURI				
1 Clay	Y	N	N	Y
2 **Akin**	+	+	+	+
3 Carnahan	Y	N	N	Y
4 **Hartzler**	Y	?	Y	Y
5 Cleaver	Y	N	N	Y
6 **Graves**	Y	Y	Y	Y
7 **Long**	Y	Y	Y	Y
8 **Emerson**	Y	Y	Y	Y
9 **Luetkemeyer**	Y	Y	Y	Y
MONTANA				
AL **Rehberg**	Y	Y	Y	Y
NEBRASKA				
1 **Fortenberry**	Y	Y	Y	Y
2 **Terry**	?	Y	Y	Y
3 **Smith**	Y	Y	Y	Y
NEVADA				
1 Berkley	Y	N	N	Y
2 **Amodei**	Y	?	Y	Y
3 **Heck**	Y	Y	Y	Y
NEW HAMPSHIRE				
1 **Guinta**	Y	Y	Y	Y
2 **Bass**	Y	Y	Y	Y
NEW JERSEY				
1 Andrews	Y	N	N	Y
2 **LoBiondo**	Y	Y	Y	Y
3 **Runyan**	Y	Y	Y	Y
4 **Smith**	Y	Y	Y	Y
5 **Garrett**	Y	Y	Y	Y
6 Pallone	Y	N	N	Y
7 **Lance**	Y	Y	Y	Y
8 Pascrell	+	N	N	Y
9 Rothman	Y	N	N	Y
10 Vacant				
11 **Frelinghuysen**	Y	Y	Y	Y
12 Holt	Y	N	N	Y
13 Sires	?	N	N	Y
NEW MEXICO				
1 Heinrich	?	N	N	Y
2 **Pearce**	Y	Y	Y	Y
3 Luján	Y	N	N	Y
NEW YORK				
1 Bishop	Y	N	N	Y
2 Israel	Y	N	N	Y
3 **King**	Y	Y	Y	Y
4 McCarthy	Y	?	N	Y
5 Ackerman	Y	N	N	Y
6 Meeks	Y	N	N	Y
7 Crowley	Y	N	N	Y
8 Nadler	Y	N	N	Y
9 **Turner**	?	Y	Y	Y
10 Towns	?	N	N	Y
11 Clarke	Y	N	N	Y
12 Velázquez	?	?	?	?
13 **Grimm**	Y	Y	Y	Y
14 Maloney	Y	N	N	Y
15 Rangel	?	?	?	?
16 Serrano	Y	N	N	Y
17 Engel	Y	N	N	Y
18 Lowey	Y	N	N	Y
19 **Hayworth**	Y	Y	Y	Y
20 **Gibson**	Y	Y	Y	Y
21 Tonko	Y	N	N	Y
22 Hinchey	?	N	N	Y
23 Owens	Y	N	N	Y
24 **Hanna**	Y	Y	Y	Y
25 **Buerkle**	Y	Y	Y	Y
26 Hochul	Y	N	N	Y
27 Higgins	Y	N	N	Y
28 Slaughter	Y	N	N	Y
29 **Reed**	?	Y	Y	Y
NORTH CAROLINA				
1 Butterfield	Y	N	N	Y
2 **Ellmers**	Y	Y	Y	Y
3 **Jones**	Y	Y	Y	Y
4 Price	Y	N	N	Y

	111	112	113	114
5 **Foxx**	Y	Y	Y	Y
6 **Coble**	Y	Y	Y	Y
7 McIntyre	Y	N	Y	Y
8 **Kissell**	Y	Y	Y	Y
9 **Myrick**	Y	Y	Y	Y
10 **McHenry**	Y	Y	Y	Y
11 Shuler	?	N	N	Y
12 Watt	Y	N	N	Y
13 Miller	Y	N	N	Y
NORTH DAKOTA				
AL **Berg**	Y	Y	Y	Y
OHIO				
1 **Chabot**	Y	Y	Y	Y
2 **Schmidt**	Y	Y	Y	Y
3 **Turner**	Y	Y	Y	Y
4 **Jordan**	Y	Y	Y	Y
5 **Latta**	Y	Y	Y	Y
6 **Johnson**	Y	Y	Y	Y
7 **Austria**	Y	Y	Y	Y
8 **Boehner**				
9 Kaptur	Y	N	N	Y
10 Kucinich	Y	N	N	Y
11 Fudge	Y	N	N	Y
12 **Tiberi**	Y	Y	Y	Y
13 Sutton	Y	N	N	Y
14 **LaTourette**	Y	Y	Y	Y
15 **Stivers**	Y	Y	Y	Y
16 **Renacci**	Y	Y	Y	Y
17 Ryan	Y	N	N	Y
18 **Gibbs**	Y	Y	Y	Y
OKLAHOMA				
1 **Sullivan**	Y	Y	Y	Y
2 Boren	Y	N	N	Y
3 **Lucas**	Y	Y	Y	Y
4 **Cole**	Y	Y	Y	Y
5 **Lankford**	Y	Y	Y	Y
OREGON				
1 Bonamici	Y	N	N	Y
2 **Walden**	Y	Y	Y	Y
3 Blumenauer	Y	N	N	Y
4 DeFazio	Y	N	N	Y
5 Schrader	Y	N	N	Y
PENNSYLVANIA				
1 Brady	?	N	N	Y
2 Fattah	Y	N	N	Y
3 **Kelly**	Y	Y	Y	Y
4 Altmire	Y	N	N	Y
5 **Thompson**	Y	Y	?	Y
6 **Gerlach**	Y	Y	Y	Y
7 **Meehan**	Y	Y	?	?
8 **Fitzpatrick**	Y	Y	Y	Y
9 **Shuster**	Y	Y	Y	Y
10 **Marino**	?	?	?	?
11 **Barletta**	Y	Y	Y	Y
12 Critz	Y	N	N	Y
13 Schwartz	Y	N	N	Y
14 Doyle	Y	N	N	Y
15 **Dent**	Y	Y	Y	Y
16 **Pitts**	Y	Y	Y	Y
17 Holden	Y	N	N	Y
18 **Murphy**	Y	Y	Y	Y
19 **Platts**	Y	Y	Y	Y
RHODE ISLAND				
1 Cicilline	Y	N	N	Y
2 Langevin	Y	N	?	Y
SOUTH CAROLINA				
1 **Scott**	Y	Y	Y	Y
2 **Wilson**	Y	Y	Y	Y
3 **Duncan**	Y	Y	Y	Y
4 **Gowdy**	Y	Y	Y	Y
5 **Mulvaney**	Y	Y	Y	Y
6 Clyburn	Y	N	N	Y
SOUTH DAKOTA				
AL **Noem**	Y	?	Y	Y
TENNESSEE				
1 **Roe**	Y	Y	Y	Y
2 **Duncan**	Y	Y	Y	Y
3 **Fleischmann**	Y	Y	Y	Y
4 **DesJarlais**	Y	Y	Y	Y
5 Cooper	Y	N	N	Y
6 **Black**	Y	Y	Y	Y
7 **Blackburn**	Y	Y	Y	Y
8 **Fincher**	Y	Y	Y	Y
9 Cohen	Y	N	N	Y

	111	112	113	114
TEXAS				
1 **Gohmert**	Y	Y	Y	Y
2 **Poe**	Y	Y	Y	Y
3 **Johnson, S.**	Y	Y	Y	Y
4 **Hall**	Y	Y	Y	Y
5 **Hensarling**	Y	Y	Y	Y
6 **Barton**	Y	Y	Y	Y
7 **Culberson**	Y	Y	Y	Y
8 **Brady**	Y	?	Y	Y
9 Green, A.	Y	N	N	Y
10 **McCaul**	Y	Y	Y	Y
11 **Conaway**	Y	Y	Y	Y
12 **Granger**	Y	Y	Y	Y
13 **Thornberry**	Y	Y	Y	Y
14 **Paul**	?	?	?	?
15 Hinojosa	Y	N	N	Y
16 Reyes	Y	N	N	Y
17 **Flores**	Y	Y	Y	Y
18 Jackson Lee	Y	N	N	Y
19 **Neugebauer**	Y	Y	Y	Y
20 Gonzalez	?	?	?	?
21 **Smith**	Y	Y	Y	Y
22 **Olson**	Y	Y	Y	Y
23 **Canseco**	Y	Y	Y	Y
24 **Marchant**	?	Y	Y	Y
25 **Doggett**	?	?	?	?
26 **Burgess**	Y	Y	Y	Y
27 **Farenthold**	Y	Y	Y	Y
28 Cuellar	Y	N	N	Y
29 Green, G.	Y	N	N	Y
30 Johnson, E.	Y	N	N	Y
31 **Carter**	Y	Y	Y	Y
32 **Sessions**	Y	Y	+	+
UTAH				
1 **Bishop**	Y	Y	Y	Y
2 Matheson	Y	N	Y	Y
3 **Chaffetz**	Y	Y	Y	Y
VERMONT				
AL Welch	Y	N	N	Y
VIRGINIA				
1 **Wittman**	Y	Y	Y	Y
2 **Rigell**	Y	Y	Y	Y
3 Scott	Y	N	N	Y
4 **Forbes**	Y	Y	Y	Y
5 **Hurt**	Y	Y	Y	Y
6 **Goodlatte**	Y	Y	Y	Y
7 **Cantor**	Y	Y	Y	Y
8 Moran	?	N	N	Y
9 **Griffith**	Y	Y	Y	Y
10 **Wolf**	Y	Y	Y	Y
11 Connolly	Y	N	N	Y
WASHINGTON				
1 Inslee*	Y			
2 Larsen	Y	N	N	Y
3 **Herrera Beutler**	Y	Y	Y	Y
4 **Hastings**	Y	Y	Y	Y
5 **McMorris Rodgers**	Y	Y	Y	Y
6 Dicks	?	N	N	Y
7 McDermott	Y	N	N	Y
8 **Reichert**	Y	Y	Y	Y
9 Smith	Y	N	N	Y
WEST VIRGINIA				
1 **McKinley**	Y	Y	Y	Y
2 **Capito**	Y	Y	Y	Y
3 Rahall	Y	N	N	Y
WISCONSIN				
1 **Ryan**	Y	Y	Y	Y
2 Baldwin	Y	N	?	Y
3 Kind	Y	N	N	Y
4 Moore	Y	N	N	Y
5 **Sensenbrenner**	Y	Y	Y	Y
6 **Petri**	Y	Y	Y	Y
7 **Duffy**	Y	Y	Y	Y
8 **Ribble**	Y	Y	Y	Y
WYOMING				
AL **Lummis**	Y	Y	Y	Y

IN THE HOUSE | By Vote Number

115. **HR 2087. Virginia Land Deeds Restrictions/Land Price and Appraisal.** Grijalva, D-Ariz., amendment that would require Accomack County, Va., to pay fair market value for the land and require an independent appraisal of the land prior to sale. Rejected in Committee of the Whole 178-226: R 5-220; D 173-6. March 20, 2012.

116. **HR 2087. Virginia Land Deeds Restrictions/Recommit.** Sanchez, Loretta, D-Calif., motion to recommit the bill to the House Natural Resources Committee with instructions to report it back immediately with an amendment that would prevent the sale, lease or rental of the conveyed land in Accomack County, Va., to an adult entertainment facility or to a foreign government that might pose a security threat to the NASA Wallops Flight Facility. Motion rejected 180-226: R 1-224; D 179-2. March 20, 2012.

117. **HR 2087. Virginia Land Deeds Restrictions/Passage.** Passage of the bill that would require the Interior secretary to remove all public use and recreation deed restrictions on conveyed land in Accomack County, Va., within 90 days of the bill's enactment. Passed 240-164: R 223-3; D 17-161. March 20, 2012.

118. **HR 5. IPAB Repeal and Medical-Malpractice Lawsuits/Previous Question.** Nugent, R-Fla., motion to order the previous question (thus ending debate and the possibility of amendment) on the rule (H Res 591) that would provide for House floor consideration of the bill that would repeal the Independent Payment Advisory Board, set limits on some damages in medical-malpractice lawsuits and set a statute of limitations on filing health care lawsuits. Motion agreed to 231-179: R 229-1; D 2-178. March 21, 2012.

	115	116	117	118
ALABAMA				
1 Bonner	N	N	Y	Y
2 Roby	N	N	Y	Y
3 Rogers	N	N	Y	Y
4 Aderholt	N	N	Y	Y
5 Brooks	N	N	Y	Y
6 Bachus	?	?	?	?
7 Sewell	Y	Y	N	N
ALASKA				
AL Young	N	N	Y	Y
ARIZONA				
1 Gosar	N	N	Y	Y
2 Franks	N	N	Y	Y
3 Quayle	N	N	Y	Y
4 Pastor	Y	Y	N	N
5 Schweikert	N	N	Y	Y
6 Flake	N	N	Y	Y
7 Grijalva	Y	Y	N	N
8 Vacant				
ARKANSAS				
1 Crawford	N	N	Y	Y
2 Griffin	N	N	Y	Y
3 Womack	N	N	Y	Y
4 Ross	Y	Y	N	N
CALIFORNIA				
1 Thompson	Y	Y	N	N
2 Herger	N	N	Y	Y
3 Lungren	N	N	Y	Y
4 McClintock	N	N	Y	Y
5 Matsui	Y	Y	N	N
6 Woolsey	Y	Y	N	N
7 Miller, George	Y	Y	N	N
8 Pelosi	Y	Y	N	N
9 Lee	+	+	–	?
10 Garamendi	Y	Y	N	?
11 McNerney	Y	Y	N	N
12 Speier	Y	Y	N	N
13 Stark	Y	Y	N	N
14 Eshoo	Y	Y	N	N
15 Honda	Y	Y	N	N
16 Lofgren	Y	Y	N	N
17 Farr	Y	Y	N	N
18 Cardoza	Y	Y	N	?
19 Denham	N	N	Y	Y
20 Costa	Y	Y	N	N
21 Nunes	N	N	Y	Y
22 McCarthy	N	N	Y	Y
23 Capps	Y	Y	N	N
24 Gallegly	N	N	Y	Y
25 McKeon	N	N	Y	Y
26 Dreier	N	N	Y	Y
27 Sherman	Y	Y	N	N
28 Berman	Y	Y	N	N
29 Schiff	Y	Y	N	N
30 Waxman	Y	Y	N	N
31 Becerra	Y	Y	N	N
32 Chu	Y	Y	N	N
33 Bass	?	Y	N	N
34 Roybal-Allard	Y	Y	N	N
35 Waters	Y	Y	N	N
36 Hahn	N	Y	N	N
37 Richardson	Y	Y	N	N
38 Napolitano	Y	Y	N	N
39 Sánchez, Linda	Y	Y	?	N
40 Royce	N	N	Y	Y
41 Lewis	?	?	?	Y
42 Miller, Gary	N	N	Y	Y
43 Baca	Y	Y	N	N
44 Calvert	N	N	Y	Y
45 Bono Mack	?	?	?	?
46 Rohrabacher	N	N	Y	Y
47 Sanchez, Loretta	Y	Y	N	N
48 Campbell	N	N	Y	Y
49 Issa	N	N	Y	Y
50 Bilbray	N	N	Y	Y
51 Filner	Y	Y	N	N
52 Hunter	N	N	Y	Y
53 Davis	Y	Y	N	N

	115	116	117	118
COLORADO				
1 DeGette	Y	Y	N	N
2 Polis	Y	Y	N	N
3 Tipton	N	N	?	Y
4 Gardner	N	N	Y	Y
5 Lamborn	N	N	Y	Y
6 Coffman	N	N	Y	Y
7 Perlmutter	Y	Y	?	N
CONNECTICUT				
1 Larson	Y	Y	N	N
2 Courtney	Y	Y	N	N
3 DeLauro	Y	Y	N	N
4 Himes	Y	Y	N	N
5 Murphy	Y	Y	N	N
DELAWARE				
AL Carney	Y	Y	N	N
FLORIDA				
1 Miller	N	N	Y	Y
2 Southerland	N	N	Y	Y
3 Brown	Y	Y	N	N
4 Crenshaw	N	N	Y	Y
5 Nugent	N	N	Y	Y
6 Stearns	N	N	Y	Y
7 Mica	N	N	Y	Y
8 Webster	N	N	Y	Y
9 Bilirakis	N	N	Y	Y
10 Young	N	N	Y	Y
11 Castor	Y	Y	N	N
12 Ross	N	N	Y	Y
13 Buchanan	N	N	Y	Y
14 Mack	N	N	Y	Y
15 Posey	N	N	Y	Y
16 Rooney	N	N	Y	Y
17 Wilson	Y	Y	N	N
18 Ros-Lehtinen	N	N	Y	Y
19 Deutch	Y	Y	N	N
20 Wasserman Schultz	Y	Y	N	N
21 Diaz-Balart	N	N	Y	Y
22 West	N	N	Y	Y
23 Hastings	Y	Y	N	N
24 Adams	N	N	Y	Y
25 Rivera	N	N	Y	Y
GEORGIA				
1 Kingston	N	N	Y	Y
2 Bishop	Y	Y	N	N
3 Westmoreland	N	N	Y	Y
4 Johnson	Y	Y	N	?
5 Lewis	Y	Y	N	N
6 Price	N	N	Y	Y
7 Woodall	Y	N	Y	Y
8 Scott, A.	N	N	Y	Y
9 Graves	N	N	Y	Y
10 Broun	N	N	Y	Y
11 Gingrey	N	N	Y	Y
12 Barrow	N	Y	Y	N
13 Scott, D.	Y	Y	Y	N
HAWAII				
1 Hanabusa	Y	Y	Y	N
2 Hirono	Y	Y	N	N
IDAHO				
1 Labrador	N	N	Y	Y
2 Simpson	N	N	Y	Y
ILLINOIS				
1 Rush	?	?	?	N
2 Jackson	?	?	?	?
3 Lipinski	?	?	?	N
4 Gutierrez	Y	Y	N	N
5 Quigley	Y	Y	N	N
6 Roskam	N	N	Y	Y
7 Davis	?	?	?	?
8 Walsh	?	?	?	Y
9 Schakowsky	Y	Y	N	N
10 Dold	+	?	+	Y
11 Kinzinger	?	?	+	?
12 Costello	Y	Y	N	N
13 Biggert	N	N	Y	Y
14 Hultgren	N	N	Y	Y
15 Johnson	N	N	Y	P

KEY **Republicans** Democrats

Y Voted for (yea)	X Paired against	C Voted "present" to avoid possible conflict of interest
# Paired for	– Announced against	
+ Announced for	P Voted "present"	? Did not vote or otherwise make a position known
N Voted against (nay)		

	115	116	117	118
16 Manzullo	?	?	?	?
17 Schilling	N	N	Y	Y
18 Schock	?	?	?	Y
19 Shimkus	N	N	Y	Y
INDIANA				
1 Visclosky	Y	Y	N	N
2 Donnelly	Y	Y	N	N
3 Stutzman	N	N	Y	Y
4 Rokita	N	N	Y	Y
5 Burton	Y	N	Y	Y
6 Pence	N	N	Y	Y
7 Carson	Y	Y	N	N
8 Bucshon	N	N	Y	Y
9 Young	N	N	Y	Y
IOWA				
1 Braley	Y	Y	N	N
2 Loebsack	Y	Y	N	N
3 Boswell	Y	Y	Y	N
4 Latham	N	N	Y	Y
5 King	N	N	Y	Y
KANSAS				
1 Huelskamp	N	N	Y	Y
2 Jenkins	N	N	Y	Y
3 Yoder	N	N	Y	Y
4 Pompeo	N	N	Y	Y
KENTUCKY				
1 Whitfield	N	N	Y	Y
2 Guthrie	N	N	Y	Y
3 Yarmuth	?	?	?	N
4 Davis	N	N	Y	Y
5 Rogers	N	N	Y	Y
6 Chandler	Y	Y	Y	N
LOUISIANA				
1 Scalise	N	N	Y	Y
2 Richmond	Y	Y	N	N
3 Landry	N	N	Y	Y
4 Fleming	N	N	Y	Y
5 Alexander	N	N	Y	Y
6 Cassidy	N	N	Y	Y
7 Boustany	N	N	Y	Y
MAINE				
1 Pingree	Y	Y	N	N
2 Michaud	N	Y	Y	N
MARYLAND				
1 Harris	N	N	Y	Y
2 Ruppersberger	Y	Y	Y	Y
3 Sarbanes	Y	Y	N	N
4 Edwards	Y	Y	N	N
5 Hoyer	Y	Y	N	N
6 Bartlett	N	N	Y	Y
7 Cummings	Y	Y	N	N
8 Van Hollen	Y	Y	N	N
MASSACHUSETTS				
1 Olver	Y	Y	N	N
2 Neal	Y	Y	N	N
3 McGovern	Y	Y	N	N
4 Frank	Y	Y	N	N
5 Tsongas	Y	Y	N	N
6 Tierney	Y	Y	N	N
7 Markey	?	Y	N	N
8 Capuano	Y	Y	N	N
9 Lynch	Y	Y	N	N
10 Keating	Y	Y	N	N
MICHIGAN				
1 Benishek	N	N	Y	Y
2 Huizenga	N	N	Y	Y
3 Amash	Y	N	N	Y
4 Camp	N	N	Y	Y
5 Kildee	Y	Y	N	N
6 Upton	N	N	Y	Y
7 Walberg	N	N	Y	Y
8 Rogers	N	N	Y	Y
9 Peters	Y	Y	N	N
10 Miller	N	N	Y	Y
11 McCotter	N	N	Y	Y
12 Levin	Y	Y	N	N
13 Clarke	Y	Y	N	N
14 Conyers	Y	Y	N	N
15 Dingell	Y	Y	N	N
MINNESOTA				
1 Walz	Y	Y	N	N
2 Kline	N	N	Y	Y
3 Paulsen	N	N	Y	Y
4 McCollum	Y	Y	N	N

	115	116	117	118
5 Ellison	Y	Y	N	N
6 Bachmann	N	N	Y	Y
7 Peterson	Y	Y	N	N
8 Cravaack	N	N	Y	Y
MISSISSIPPI				
1 Nunnelee	N	N	Y	Y
2 Thompson	Y	Y	N	?
3 Harper	N	N	Y	Y
4 Palazzo	N	N	Y	Y
MISSOURI				
1 Clay	Y	Y	N	N
2 Akin	–	–	+	Y
3 Carnahan	Y	Y	N	N
4 Hartzler	N	N	Y	Y
5 Cleaver	Y	Y	?	N
6 Graves	N	N	Y	Y
7 Long	N	N	Y	Y
8 Emerson	N	N	Y	Y
9 Luetkemeyer	N	N	Y	Y
MONTANA				
AL Rehberg	N	N	Y	Y
NEBRASKA				
1 Fortenberry	N	N	Y	Y
2 Terry	N	N	Y	N
3 Smith	N	N	Y	Y
NEVADA				
1 Berkley	N	Y	Y	N
2 Amodei	N	N	Y	Y
3 Heck	N	N	Y	Y
NEW HAMPSHIRE				
1 Guinta	N	N	Y	Y
2 Bass	N	N	?	Y
NEW JERSEY				
1 Andrews	Y	Y	N	N
2 LoBiondo	N	N	Y	Y
3 Runyan	N	N	Y	Y
4 Smith	N	N	Y	Y
5 Garrett	N	N	Y	Y
6 Pallone	Y	Y	N	N
7 Lance	N	N	Y	Y
8 Pascrell	Y	Y	N	N
9 Rothman	Y	Y	N	N
10 Vacant				
11 Frelinghuysen	N	N	Y	Y
12 Holt	Y	Y	N	N
13 Sires	Y	Y	N	N
NEW MEXICO				
1 Heinrich	Y	Y	Y	N
2 Pearce	N	N	Y	Y
3 Luján	Y	Y	N	N
NEW YORK				
1 Bishop	Y	Y	N	N
2 Israel	Y	Y	N	N
3 King	N	N	Y	Y
4 McCarthy	Y	Y	N	N
5 Ackerman	Y	Y	N	N
6 Meeks	Y	Y	N	N
7 Crowley	Y	Y	N	N
8 Nadler	Y	Y	N	N
9 Turner	N	N	Y	Y
10 Towns	Y	Y	N	N
11 Clarke	Y	Y	N	N
12 Velázquez	Y	Y	N	N
13 Grimm	N	N	Y	Y
14 Maloney	Y	Y	N	N
15 Rangel	?	?	?	?
16 Serrano	Y	Y	N	N
17 Engel	Y	Y	N	N
18 Lowey	Y	Y	N	N
19 Hayworth	N	N	Y	Y
20 Gibson	N	N	Y	Y
21 Tonko	Y	Y	N	N
22 Hinchey	Y	Y	N	N
23 Owens	Y	Y	N	N
24 Hanna	N	N	Y	Y
25 Buerkle	N	N	Y	Y
26 Hochul	Y	Y	N	N
27 Higgins	Y	Y	N	N
28 Slaughter	Y	Y	N	N
29 Reed	N	N	Y	+
NORTH CAROLINA				
1 Butterfield	Y	Y	N	N
2 Ellmers	N	N	Y	Y
3 Jones	N	Y	Y	Y
4 Price	Y	Y	N	N

	115	116	117	118
5 Foxx	N	N	Y	Y
6 Coble	N	N	Y	Y
7 McIntyre	Y	Y	Y	N
8 Kissell	Y	Y	Y	N
9 Myrick	N	N	Y	Y
10 McHenry	N	N	Y	Y
11 Shuler	N	Y	N	N
12 Watt	Y	Y	N	N
13 Miller	Y	Y	N	N
NORTH DAKOTA				
AL Berg	N	N	Y	Y
OHIO				
1 Chabot	N	N	Y	Y
2 Schmidt	N	N	Y	Y
3 Turner	N	N	Y	Y
4 Jordan	N	N	Y	Y
5 Latta	N	N	Y	Y
6 Johnson	N	N	Y	Y
7 Austria	N	N	Y	Y
8 Boehner				
9 Kaptur	Y	Y	N	N
10 Kucinich	Y	Y	N	N
11 Fudge	Y	Y	N	N
12 Tiberi	N	?	Y	Y
13 Sutton	Y	Y	N	N
14 LaTourette	N	N	Y	Y
15 Stivers	N	N	Y	Y
16 Renacci	N	N	Y	Y
17 Ryan	Y	Y	N	N
18 Gibbs	N	N	Y	Y
OKLAHOMA				
1 Sullivan	N	N	Y	Y
2 Boren	Y	Y	Y	N
3 Lucas	N	N	Y	Y
4 Cole	N	N	Y	Y
5 Lankford	N	N	Y	Y
OREGON				
1 Bonamici	Y	Y	N	N
2 Walden	N	N	Y	Y
3 Blumenauer	Y	Y	N	N
4 DeFazio	Y	Y	N	N
5 Schrader	Y	Y	Y	N
PENNSYLVANIA				
1 Brady	Y	Y	N	N
2 Fattah	Y	Y	N	N
3 Kelly	N	N	Y	Y
4 Altmire	Y	Y	N	N
5 Thompson	N	N	Y	Y
6 Gerlach	N	N	Y	Y
7 Meehan	?	?	?	Y
8 Fitzpatrick	Y	N	Y	Y
9 Shuster	N	N	Y	Y
10 Marino	?	?	?	?
11 Barletta	N	N	Y	Y
12 Critz	Y	Y	N	N
13 Schwartz	Y	Y	N	N
14 Doyle	Y	Y	N	N
15 Dent	N	N	Y	Y
16 Pitts	N	N	Y	Y
17 Holden	Y	Y	N	N
18 Murphy	N	N	Y	Y
19 Platts	?	N	Y	Y
RHODE ISLAND				
1 Cicilline	Y	Y	N	N
2 Langevin	Y	Y	N	N
SOUTH CAROLINA				
1 Scott	N	N	Y	Y
2 Wilson	N	N	Y	Y
3 Duncan	N	N	Y	Y
4 Gowdy	N	N	Y	Y
5 Mulvaney	N	N	Y	Y
6 Clyburn	Y	Y	N	N
SOUTH DAKOTA				
AL Noem	N	N	Y	Y
TENNESSEE				
1 Roe	N	N	Y	Y
2 Duncan	N	N	Y	Y
3 Fleischmann	N	N	Y	Y
4 DesJarlais	N	N	Y	Y
5 Cooper	Y	Y	N	N
6 Black	N	N	Y	Y
7 Blackburn	N	N	Y	Y
8 Fincher	N	N	Y	Y
9 Cohen	Y	Y	N	N

	115	116	117	118
TEXAS				
1 Gohmert	N	?	Y	Y
2 Poe	N	N	Y	Y
3 Johnson, S.	N	N	Y	Y
4 Hall	N	N	Y	Y
5 Hensarling	N	N	Y	Y
6 Barton	N	N	Y	Y
7 Culberson	N	N	Y	Y
8 Brady	N	N	Y	Y
9 Green, A.	Y	Y	N	N
10 McCaul	N	N	Y	Y
11 Conaway	N	N	Y	Y
12 Granger	N	N	Y	Y
13 Thornberry	N	N	Y	Y
14 Paul	?	?	?	?
15 Hinojosa	Y	Y	N	N
16 Reyes	Y	Y	N	N
17 Flores	N	N	Y	Y
18 Jackson Lee	Y	Y	N	N
19 Neugebauer	N	N	Y	Y
20 Gonzalez	?	?	?	?
21 Smith	N	N	Y	Y
22 Olson	N	N	Y	Y
23 Canseco	N	N	Y	Y
24 Marchant	N	N	Y	?
25 Doggett	?	?	?	N
26 Burgess	?	?	?	Y
27 Farenthold	N	N	Y	Y
28 Cuellar	Y	Y	N	?
29 Green, G.	Y	Y	N	N
30 Johnson, E.	Y	Y	N	N
31 Carter	N	N	Y	Y
32 Sessions	–	–	+	Y
UTAH				
1 Bishop	N	N	Y	Y
2 Matheson	Y	Y	N	Y
3 Chaffetz	N	N	Y	?
VERMONT				
AL Welch	Y	Y	N	N
VIRGINIA				
1 Wittman	N	N	Y	Y
2 Rigell	N	N	Y	Y
3 Scott	N	N	Y	N
4 Forbes	N	N	Y	Y
5 Hurt	N	N	Y	Y
6 Goodlatte	N	N	Y	Y
7 Cantor	?	N	Y	Y
8 Moran	Y	Y	Y	N
9 Griffith	N	N	Y	Y
10 Wolf	N	N	Y	Y
11 Connolly	Y	Y	N	N
WASHINGTON				
1 Vacant				
2 Larsen	Y	Y	Y	N
3 Herrera Beutler	N	N	Y	Y
4 Hastings	N	N	Y	Y
5 McMorris Rodgers	N	N	Y	Y
6 Dicks	Y	Y	N	N
7 McDermott	Y	Y	N	N
8 Reichert	N	N	Y	Y
9 Smith	Y	Y	N	N
WEST VIRGINIA				
1 McKinley	N	N	Y	Y
2 Capito	N	N	Y	Y
3 Rahall	Y	Y	N	N
WISCONSIN				
1 Ryan	N	N	Y	Y
2 Baldwin	Y	Y	N	N
3 Kind	Y	Y	N	N
4 Moore	Y	Y	N	N
5 Sensenbrenner	N	N	Y	Y
6 Petri	N	N	Y	Y
7 Duffy	N	N	Y	Y
8 Ribble	N	N	Y	Y
WYOMING				
AL Lummis	N	N	Y	Y

IN THE HOUSE | By Vote Number

119. **HR 5. IPAB Repeal and Medical-Malpractice Lawsuits/Rule.**
Adoption of the rule (H Res 591) that would provide for House floor consideration of the bill that would repeal the Independent Payment Advisory Board (IPAB), set limits on some damages in medical-malpractice lawsuits and set a statute of limitations on filing health care lawsuits. The rule also would provide for the automatic adoption of a substitute amendment that would add the IPAB provisions to the underlying bill. Adopted 233-182: R 228-4; D 5-178. March 21, 2012.

120. **HR 886. U.S. Marshals Service Anniversary Coin/Passage.**
Stivers, R-Ohio, motion to suspend the rules and concur in the Senate amendment to the bill that would direct Treasury to mint and issue coins to commemorate the 225th anniversary of the U.S. Marshals Service. The Senate amendment would require the Treasury secretary to ensure that issuing the coins would not result in a net cost to the federal government. Motion agreed to 409-2: R 227-1; D 182-1. A two-thirds majority of those present and voting (274 in this case) is required for passage under suspension of the rules. March 21, 2012.

121. **Procedural Motion/Journal.** Approval of the House Journal of Tuesday, March 20, 2012. Approved 308-101: R 179-47; D 129-54. March 21, 2012.

122. **HR 5. IPAB Repeal and Medical-Malpractice Lawsuits/Health Care Costs.** Woodall, R-Ga., amendment that would strike findings in the bill regarding current health care access and costs, interstate commerce and federal spending. Adopted in Committee of the Whole 234-173: R 223-5; D 11-168. March 22, 2012.

		119	120	121	122
ALABAMA					
1	**Bonner**	Y	Y	Y	Y
2	**Roby**	Y	Y	Y	Y
3	**Rogers**	Y	Y	Y	Y
4	**Aderholt**	Y	Y	Y	Y
5	**Brooks**	Y	Y	Y	Y
6	**Bachus**	?	?	?	?
7	Sewell	N	Y	Y	N
ALASKA					
AL	**Young**	Y	Y	N	Y
ARIZONA					
1	**Gosar**	Y	Y	Y	Y
2	**Franks**	Y	Y	Y	Y
3	**Quayle**	Y	Y	N	Y
4	Pastor	N	Y	N	N
5	**Schweikert**	?	Y	Y	Y
6	**Flake**	Y	Y	Y	Y
7	Grijalva	N	Y	N	N
8	Vacant				
ARKANSAS					
1	**Crawford**	Y	Y	Y	Y
2	**Griffin**	Y	Y	N	Y
3	**Womack**	Y	Y	Y	Y
4	Ross	N	Y	Y	Y
CALIFORNIA					
1	Thompson	N	Y	N	N
2	**Herger**	Y	Y	Y	Y
3	**Lungren**	Y	Y	Y	Y
4	**McClintock**	Y	Y	Y	Y
5	Matsui	N	Y	Y	N
6	Woolsey	N	Y	Y	N
7	Miller, George	N	Y	N	N
8	Pelosi	N	Y	N	N
9	Lee	?	?	?	-
10	Garamendi	N	Y	Y	N
11	McNerney	N	Y	Y	N
12	Speier	N	Y	Y	N
13	Stark	N	Y	N	N
14	Eshoo	N	Y	Y	N
15	Honda	N	Y	N	N
16	Lofgren	N	Y	Y	N
17	Farr	N	Y	Y	N
18	Cardoza	N	Y	Y	N
19	**Denham**	Y	Y	Y	Y
20	Costa	N	Y	N	N
21	**Nunes**	Y	Y	Y	Y
22	**McCarthy**	Y	Y	Y	Y
23	Capps	N	Y	Y	N
24	**Gallegly**	Y	Y	Y	Y
25	**McKeon**	Y	Y	Y	Y
26	**Dreier**	Y	Y	Y	Y
27	Sherman	N	Y	Y	N
28	Berman	N	Y	Y	N
29	Schiff	N	Y	Y	N
30	Waxman	N	Y	Y	N
31	Becerra	N	Y	Y	N
32	Chu	N	Y	N	N
33	Bass	N	Y	?	N
34	Roybal-Allard	N	Y	Y	N
35	Waters	N	Y	N	N
36	Hahn	N	Y	Y	N
37	Richardson	N	Y	Y	N
38	Napolitano	N	Y	Y	N
39	Sánchez, Linda	N	Y	N	N
40	**Royce**	Y	Y	Y	Y
41	**Lewis**	Y	Y	Y	Y
42	**Miller, Gary**	Y	Y	Y	Y
43	Baca	N	Y	Y	N
44	**Calvert**	Y	Y	Y	Y
45	**Bono Mack**	?	?	?	?
46	**Rohrabacher**	Y	Y	Y	Y
47	Sanchez, Loretta	N	Y	Y	N
48	**Campbell**	Y	Y	Y	N
49	**Issa**	Y	Y	Y	Y
50	**Bilbray**	Y	Y	N	N
51	Filner	N	Y	N	N
52	**Hunter**	Y	Y	N	Y
53	Davis	N	Y	Y	N

		119	120	121	122
COLORADO					
1	DeGette	N	Y	Y	N
2	Polis	N	N	Y	N
3	**Tipton**	Y	Y	N	Y
4	**Gardner**	Y	Y	N	Y
5	**Lamborn**	Y	Y	Y	Y
6	**Coffman**	Y	Y	N	Y
7	Perlmutter	N	Y	Y	N
CONNECTICUT					
1	Larson	N	Y	N	N
2	Courtney	N	Y	N	N
3	DeLauro	N	Y	Y	N
4	Himes	N	Y	N	N
5	Murphy	N	Y	Y	N
DELAWARE					
AL	Carney	N	Y	Y	N
FLORIDA					
1	**Miller**	Y	Y	N	Y
2	**Southerland**	Y	Y	Y	Y
3	Brown	N	Y	Y	?
4	**Crenshaw**	Y	Y	Y	Y
5	**Nugent**	Y	Y	Y	Y
6	**Stearns**	Y	Y	Y	Y
7	**Mica**	Y	Y	Y	Y
8	**Webster**	Y	Y	Y	Y
9	**Bilirakis**	Y	Y	Y	Y
10	**Young**	Y	Y	Y	Y
11	Castor	N	Y	N	N
12	**Ross**	Y	Y	Y	Y
13	**Buchanan**	Y	Y	Y	Y
14	**Mack**	Y	Y	Y	Y
15	**Posey**	Y	Y	Y	Y
16	**Rooney**	Y	Y	N	Y
17	Wilson	N	Y	Y	N
18	**Ros-Lehtinen**	Y	Y	N	Y
19	Deutch	N	Y	Y	N
20	Wasserman Schultz	N	Y	Y	N
21	**Diaz-Balart**	Y	Y	Y	Y
22	**West**	Y	Y	Y	Y
23	Hastings	N	Y	Y	N
24	**Adams**	Y	Y	N	Y
25	**Rivera**	Y	Y	Y	Y
GEORGIA					
1	**Kingston**	Y	Y	Y	Y
2	Bishop	N	Y	N	N
3	**Westmoreland**	Y	Y	Y	Y
4	Johnson	N	Y	Y	N
5	Lewis	N	Y	Y	N
6	**Price**	Y	Y	Y	Y
7	**Woodall**	Y	Y	N	Y
8	**Scott, A.**	Y	Y	Y	Y
9	**Graves**	Y	Y	Y	Y
10	**Broun**	Y	Y	Y	Y
11	**Gingrey**	Y	?	Y	Y
12	Barrow	N	Y	Y	N
13	Scott, D.	N	Y	Y	N
HAWAII					
1	Hanabusa	N	Y	Y	N
2	Hirono	N	Y	Y	N
IDAHO					
1	**Labrador**	Y	Y	Y	Y
2	**Simpson**	Y	Y	Y	Y
ILLINOIS					
1	Rush	N	Y	Y	N
2	Jackson	?	?	?	?
3	Lipinski	N	Y	Y	N
4	Gutierrez	N	Y	Y	N
5	Quigley	N	Y	Y	N
6	**Roskam**	Y	Y	Y	Y
7	Davis	?	?	?	?
8	**Walsh**	Y	Y	N	Y
9	Schakowsky	N	Y	N	N
10	**Dold**	Y	+	N	N
11	**Kinzinger**	?	?	?	+
12	Costello	N	Y	N	N
13	**Biggert**	Y	Y	Y	Y
14	**Hultgren**	Y	Y	Y	Y
15	Johnson	P	Y	Y	Y

KEY Republicans Democrats

Y Voted for (yea)	**X** Paired against	**C** Voted "present" to avoid possible conflict of interest
# Paired for	**–** Announced against	**?** Did not vote or otherwise make a position known
+ Announced for	**P** Voted "present"	
N Voted against (nay)		

	119	120	121	122
16 Manzullo	?	?	?	?
17 Schilling	Y	Y	N	Y
18 Schock	Y	Y	Y	N
19 Shimkus	Y	Y	Y	Y
INDIANA				
1 Visclosky	N	Y	N	N
2 Donnelly	N	Y	N	N
3 Stutzman	Y	Y	Y	Y
4 Rokita	Y	Y	?	Y
5 Burton	Y	Y	Y	Y
6 Pence	Y	Y	Y	Y
7 Carson	N	Y	N	N
8 Bucshon	Y	Y	Y	Y
9 Young	Y	Y	?	Y
IOWA				
1 Braley	N	Y	Y	Y
2 Loebsack	N	Y	Y	N
3 Boswell	N	Y	N	N
4 Latham	Y	Y	N	Y
5 King	Y	Y	Y	Y
KANSAS				
1 Huelskamp	Y	Y	Y	Y
2 Jenkins	Y	Y	Y	Y
3 Yoder	Y	Y	N	Y
4 Pompeo	Y	Y	Y	Y
KENTUCKY				
1 Whitfield	Y	?	Y	Y
2 Guthrie	Y	Y	Y	Y
3 Yarmuth	N	Y	Y	N
4 Davis	Y	Y	Y	Y
5 Rogers	Y	Y	Y	Y
6 Chandler	N	Y	Y	N
LOUISIANA				
1 Scalise	Y	Y	Y	Y
2 Richmond	N	Y	Y	N
3 Landry	Y	Y	Y	Y
4 Fleming	Y	Y	Y	Y
5 Alexander	Y	Y	Y	Y
6 Cassidy	Y	Y	Y	Y
7 Boustany	Y	Y	Y	Y
MAINE				
1 Pingree	N	Y	Y	N
2 Michaud	N	Y	Y	N
MARYLAND				
1 Harris	Y	Y	Y	Y
2 Ruppersberger	N	Y	Y	Y
3 Sarbanes	N	Y	N	N
4 Edwards	N	Y	Y	N
5 Hoyer	N	Y	Y	N
6 Bartlett	Y	Y	Y	Y
7 Cummings	N	Y	Y	N
8 Van Hollen	N	Y	Y	N
MASSACHUSETTS				
1 Olver	N	Y	N	N
2 Neal	N	Y	N	N
3 McGovern	N	Y	N	N
4 Frank	N	Y	Y	N
5 Tsongas	N	Y	Y	N
6 Tierney	N	Y	N	N
7 Markey	N	Y	N	N
8 Capuano	N	Y	N	N
9 Lynch	N	Y	N	N
10 Keating	N	Y	N	N
MICHIGAN				
1 Benishek	Y	Y	N	Y
2 Huizenga	Y	Y	N	Y
3 Amash	Y	N	P	Y
4 Camp	Y	Y	Y	Y
5 Kildee	N	Y	Y	N
6 Upton	Y	Y	Y	Y
7 Walberg	Y	Y	Y	Y
8 Rogers	Y	Y	?	Y
9 Peters	N	Y	N	N
10 Miller	Y	Y	Y	Y
11 McCotter	Y	Y	N	Y
12 Levin	N	Y	Y	N
13 Clarke	N	Y	Y	N
14 Conyers	N	Y	N	N
15 Dingell	N	Y	Y	N
MINNESOTA				
1 Walz	N	Y	Y	N
2 Kline	Y	Y	Y	Y
3 Paulsen	Y	Y	Y	Y
4 McCollum	N	Y	Y	N

	119	120	121	122
5 Ellison	N	Y	Y	N
6 Bachmann	Y	Y	Y	Y
7 Peterson	Y	Y	N	N
8 Cravaack	Y	Y	N	Y
MISSISSIPPI				
1 Nunnelee	Y	Y	Y	Y
2 Thompson	?	?	N	?
3 Harper	Y	Y	Y	Y
4 Palazzo	Y	Y	Y	Y
MISSOURI				
1 Clay	N	Y	Y	N
2 Akin	Y	Y	Y	Y
3 Carnahan	N	Y	Y	N
4 Hartzler	Y	Y	Y	Y
5 Cleaver	N	Y	Y	N
6 Graves	Y	Y	N	Y
7 Long	Y	Y	Y	Y
8 Emerson	Y	Y	Y	Y
9 Luetkemeyer	Y	Y	Y	Y
MONTANA				
AL Rehberg	Y	Y	Y	Y
NEBRASKA				
1 Fortenberry	Y	Y	Y	Y
2 Terry	N	Y	Y	N
3 Smith	Y	Y	Y	Y
NEVADA				
1 Berkley	N	Y	Y	N
2 Amodei	Y	Y	N	Y
3 Heck	Y	Y	N	Y
NEW HAMPSHIRE				
1 Guinta	Y	Y	Y	Y
2 Bass	Y	Y	Y	Y
NEW JERSEY				
1 Andrews	N	Y	N	N
2 LoBiondo	Y	Y	N	Y
3 Runyan	Y	Y	Y	Y
4 Smith	Y	Y	Y	Y
5 Garrett	Y	Y	Y	Y
6 Pallone	N	Y	N	N
7 Lance	Y	Y	Y	Y
8 Pascrell	N	Y	Y	N
9 Rothman	N	Y	N	N
10 Vacant				
11 Frelinghuysen	Y	?	Y	Y
12 Holt	N	Y	N	N
13 Sires	N	Y	Y	N
NEW MEXICO				
1 Heinrich	N	Y	Y	N
2 Pearce	Y	Y	Y	Y
3 Luján	N	Y	Y	N
NEW YORK				
1 Bishop	N	Y	N	N
2 Israel	N	Y	N	N
3 King	Y	Y	Y	Y
4 McCarthy	N	Y	Y	N
5 Ackerman	N	Y	Y	?
6 Meeks	N	Y	Y	N
7 Crowley	N	Y	Y	N
8 Nadler	N	Y	N	N
9 Turner	Y	Y	Y	Y
10 Towns	N	Y	Y	N
11 Clarke	N	Y	Y	N
12 Velázquez	N	Y	Y	N
13 Grimm	Y	Y	Y	Y
14 Maloney	N	Y	Y	N
15 Rangel	?	?	?	?
16 Serrano	N	Y	Y	N
17 Engel	N	Y	Y	?
18 Lowey	N	Y	Y	?
19 Hayworth	Y	Y	Y	Y
20 Gibson	Y	Y	N	Y
21 Tonko	N	Y	Y	N
22 Hinchey	N	Y	N	N
23 Owens	N	Y	P	N
24 Hanna	Y	Y	Y	Y
25 Buerkle	Y	Y	Y	Y
26 Hochul	N	Y	Y	N
27 Higgins	N	Y	Y	N
28 Slaughter	N	Y	N	N
29 Reed	Y	Y	N	Y
NORTH CAROLINA				
1 Butterfield	N	Y	Y	N
2 Ellmers	Y	Y	Y	Y
3 Jones	Y	Y	Y	Y
4 Price	N	Y	Y	N

	119	120	121	122
5 Foxx	Y	Y	N	Y
6 Coble	Y	Y	Y	Y
7 McIntyre	Y	Y	N	?
8 Kissell	Y	Y	Y	Y
9 Myrick	Y	Y	Y	Y
10 McHenry	Y	Y	Y	Y
11 Shuler	N	Y	N	Y
12 Watt	N	Y	Y	N
13 Miller	N	Y	Y	N
NORTH DAKOTA				
AL Berg	Y	Y	Y	Y
OHIO				
1 Chabot	Y	Y	Y	Y
2 Schmidt	Y	Y	Y	Y
3 Turner	Y	Y	Y	Y
4 Jordan	Y	Y	Y	Y
5 Latta	Y	Y	Y	Y
6 Johnson	Y	Y	N	Y
7 Austria	Y	Y	Y	?
8 Boehner				
9 Kaptur	N	Y	Y	N
10 Kucinich	N	Y	Y	N
11 Fudge	N	Y	N	N
12 Tiberi	Y	Y	Y	Y
13 Sutton	N	Y	Y	N
14 LaTourette	Y	Y	Y	Y
15 Stivers	Y	Y	N	Y
16 Renacci	Y	Y	N	Y
17 Ryan	N	Y	N	N
18 Gibbs	Y	Y	Y	Y
OKLAHOMA				
1 Sullivan	Y	Y	Y	Y
2 Boren	Y	Y	Y	N
3 Lucas	Y	Y	Y	Y
4 Cole	Y	Y	Y	Y
5 Lankford	Y	Y	Y	Y
OREGON				
1 Bonamici	N	Y	Y	N
2 Walden	Y	Y	Y	Y
3 Blumenauer	N	Y	Y	N
4 DeFazio	N	Y	Y	N
5 Schrader	N	Y	Y	N
PENNSYLVANIA				
1 Brady	N	Y	N	N
2 Fattah	N	Y	Y	N
3 Kelly	Y	Y	Y	Y
4 Altmire	N	Y	Y	N
5 Thompson	Y	Y	Y	Y
6 Gerlach	Y	Y	N	Y
7 Meehan	Y	Y	N	Y
8 Fitzpatrick	Y	Y	N	Y
9 Shuster	Y	Y	?	Y
10 Marino	?	?	?	?
11 Barletta	Y	Y	Y	Y
12 Critz	N	Y	N	N
13 Schwartz	N	Y	Y	N
14 Doyle	N	Y	N	N
15 Dent	Y	Y	N	Y
16 Pitts	Y	Y	Y	Y
17 Holden	N	Y	Y	N
18 Murphy	Y	Y	Y	Y
19 Platts	Y	Y	Y	?
RHODE ISLAND				
1 Cicilline	N	Y	Y	N
2 Langevin	N	Y	Y	N
SOUTH CAROLINA				
1 Scott	Y	Y	Y	Y
2 Wilson	Y	Y	Y	Y
3 Duncan	Y	P	Y	Y
4 Gowdy	Y	Y	Y	Y
5 Mulvaney	Y	P	Y	Y
6 Clyburn	N	Y	N	N
SOUTH DAKOTA				
AL Noem	Y	Y	Y	Y
TENNESSEE				
1 Roe	Y	Y	N	Y
2 Duncan	N	Y	Y	Y
3 Fleischmann	Y	Y	Y	Y
4 DesJarlais	Y	Y	N	Y
5 Cooper	N	Y	Y	N
6 Black	Y	Y	Y	Y
7 Blackburn	Y	Y	Y	Y
8 Fincher	Y	Y	Y	Y
9 Cohen	N	Y	Y	N

	119	120	121	122
TEXAS				
1 Gohmert	N	Y	P	Y
2 Poe	N	Y	N	Y
3 Johnson, S.	Y	Y	Y	Y
4 Hall	Y	Y	Y	Y
5 Hensarling	Y	Y	Y	Y
6 Barton	Y	Y	Y	Y
7 Culberson	Y	Y	Y	Y
8 Brady	Y	Y	Y	Y
9 Green, A.	N	Y	Y	N
10 McCaul	Y	Y	Y	Y
11 Conaway	Y	Y	N	Y
12 Granger	Y	Y	Y	Y
13 Thornberry	Y	Y	Y	Y
14 Paul	?	?	?	?
15 Hinojosa	N	Y	Y	N
16 Reyes	N	Y	N	N
17 Flores	Y	Y	Y	Y
18 Jackson Lee	–	Y	N	N
19 Neugebauer	Y	Y	?	Y
20 Gonzalez	?	?	?	?
21 Smith	Y	Y	Y	Y
22 Olson	Y	Y	Y	Y
23 Canseco	Y	Y	?	Y
24 Marchant	Y	Y	N	?
25 Doggett	N	Y	Y	N
26 Burgess	Y	Y	N	Y
27 Farenthold	Y	Y	Y	Y
28 Cuellar	N	Y	N	Y
29 Green, G.	N	+	N	N
30 Johnson, E.	N	Y	Y	N
31 Carter	Y	Y	Y	Y
32 Sessions	Y	Y	Y	Y
UTAH				
1 Bishop	Y	Y	Y	?
2 Matheson	Y	Y	Y	Y
3 Chaffetz	?	?	?	?
VERMONT				
AL Welch	N	Y	Y	N
VIRGINIA				
1 Wittman	Y	Y	Y	Y
2 Rigell	Y	Y	Y	Y
3 Scott	N	Y	Y	N
4 Forbes	Y	Y	N	Y
5 Hurt	Y	Y	Y	Y
6 Goodlatte	Y	Y	Y	Y
7 Cantor	Y	Y	Y	Y
8 Moran	N	Y	Y	N
9 Griffith	Y	Y	Y	P
10 Wolf	Y	Y	Y	Y
11 Connolly	N	Y	Y	N
WASHINGTON				
1 Vacant				
2 Larsen	N	Y	Y	N
3 Herrera Beutler	Y	Y	N	Y
4 Hastings	Y	Y	Y	Y
5 McMorris Rodgers	Y	Y	Y	Y
6 Dicks	N	Y	Y	N
7 McDermott	N	Y	N	N
8 Reichert	Y	Y	Y	Y
9 Smith	N	Y	Y	N
WEST VIRGINIA				
1 McKinley	Y	Y	P	Y
2 Capito	Y	Y	Y	Y
3 Rahall	N	Y	N	N
WISCONSIN				
1 Ryan	Y	Y	Y	Y
2 Baldwin	N	Y	N	N
3 Kind	N	Y	Y	N
4 Moore	N	Y	Y	N
5 Sensenbrenner	Y	Y	Y	P
6 Petri	Y	Y	Y	Y
7 Duffy	Y	Y	N	Y
8 Ribble	Y	Y	N	Y
WYOMING				
AL Lummis	Y	Y	Y	Y

IN THE HOUSE | By Vote Number

123. **HR 5. IPAB Repeal and Medical-Malpractice Lawsuits/ Enactment Delay.** Bonamici, D-Ore., amendment that would delay the date of the bill's enactment until the Health and Human Services secretary submits to Congress a report on the potential effects of the bill on health care premiums. Rejected in Committee of the Whole 179-228: R 4-224; D 175-4. March 22, 2012.

124. **HR 5. IPAB Repeal and Medical-Malpractice Lawsuits/Civil Liability Protection.** Stearns, R-Fla., amendment that would extend the bill's medical liability damage caps to include medical professionals who volunteer at federally declared disaster sites. Adopted in Committee of the Whole 251-157: R 224-4; D 27-153. March 22, 2012.

125. **HR 5. IPAB Repeal and Medical-Malpractice Lawsuits/ Recommit.** Loebsack, D-Iowa, motion to recommit the bill to the Ways and Means and Energy and Commerce committees with instructions to report it back immediately with an amendment to clarify that the bill could not be construed as eliminating guaranteed health benefits for seniors or people with disabilities, establishing a Medicare voucher program, reducing benefits or raising premiums for seniors and people with disabilities. Motion rejected 180-229: R 1-228; D 179-1. March 22, 2012.

126. **HR 5. IPAB Repeal and Medical-Malpractice Lawsuits/Passage.** Passage of the bill that would repeal the provisions of the 2010 health care overhaul laws that established the Independent Payment Advisory Board (IPAB) responsible for curbing Medicare costs. It would restore previous law provisions to maintain the current Medicare spending review process. The bill also would impose caps on some damages in malpractice lawsuits, limit attorney fees and establish a statute of limitations for filing health care lawsuits. Passed 223-181: R 216-10; D 7-171. A "nay" was a vote in support of the president's position. March 22, 2012.

	123	124	125	126
ALABAMA				
1 **Bonner**	N	Y	N	Y
2 **Roby**	N	Y	N	Y
3 **Rogers**	N	Y	N	Y
4 **Aderholt**	N	Y	N	Y
5 **Brooks**	N	Y	N	Y
6 **Bachus**	?	?	?	?
7 Sewell	Y	N	Y	N
ALASKA				
AL **Young**	N	Y	N	Y
ARIZONA				
1 **Gosar**	N	Y	N	Y
2 **Franks**	N	Y	N	Y
3 **Quayle**	N	Y	N	Y
4 Pastor	Y	N	Y	N
5 **Schweikert**	N	Y	N	Y
6 **Flake**	N	Y	N	Y
7 Grijalva	Y	N	Y	N
8 Vacant				
ARKANSAS				
1 **Crawford**	N	Y	N	Y
2 **Griffin**	N	Y	N	Y
3 **Womack**	N	Y	N	Y
4 Ross	Y	Y	Y	N
CALIFORNIA				
1 Thompson	Y	N	Y	N
2 **Herger**	N	Y	N	Y
3 **Lungren**	N	Y	N	Y
4 **McClintock**	N	Y	N	Y
5 Matsui	Y	N	Y	N
6 Woolsey	Y	N	Y	N
7 Miller, George	Y	N	Y	N
8 Pelosi	Y	N	Y	N
9 Lee	+	−	+	−
10 Garamendi	Y	Y	Y	N
11 McNerney	Y	N	Y	N
12 Speier	Y	N	Y	N
13 Stark	Y	N	Y	N
14 Eshoo	Y	N	Y	N
15 Honda	Y	N	Y	N
16 Lofgren	Y	N	Y	N
17 Farr	Y	N	Y	N
18 Cardoza	Y	Y	Y	Y
19 **Denham**	N	Y	N	Y
20 Costa	Y	Y	Y	N
21 **Nunes**	N	Y	N	Y
22 **McCarthy**	N	Y	N	Y
23 Capps	Y	N	Y	N
24 **Gallegly**	N	Y	N	Y
25 **McKeon**	N	Y	N	Y
26 **Dreier**	N	Y	N	Y
27 Sherman	Y	N	Y	N
28 Berman	Y	N	Y	N
29 Schiff	Y	N	Y	N
30 Waxman	Y	N	Y	N
31 Becerra	Y	N	Y	N
32 Chu	Y	N	Y	N
33 Bass	Y	N	Y	N
34 Roybal-Allard	Y	N	Y	N
35 Waters	Y	N	Y	N
36 Hahn	Y	N	Y	N
37 Richardson	Y	N	Y	N
38 Napolitano	Y	N	Y	N
39 Sánchez, Linda	Y	N	Y	N
40 **Royce**	N	Y	N	Y
41 **Lewis**	N	Y	N	Y
42 **Miller, Gary**	N	Y	N	Y
43 Baca	Y	N	Y	N
44 **Calvert**	N	Y	N	Y
45 **Bono Mack**	?	?	?	?
46 **Rohrabacher**	N	Y	N	Y
47 Sanchez, Loretta	Y	N	Y	N
48 **Campbell**	N	Y	N	Y
49 **Issa**	N	Y	N	Y
50 **Bilbray**	N	Y	N	Y
51 Filner	Y	N	Y	N
52 **Hunter**	N	Y	N	Y
53 Davis	Y	N	Y	N

	123	124	125	126
COLORADO				
1 DeGette	Y	N	Y	N
2 Polis	Y	Y	Y	N
3 **Tipton**	N	Y	N	Y
4 **Gardner**	N	Y	N	Y
5 **Lamborn**	N	Y	N	Y
6 **Coffman**	N	Y	N	Y
7 Perlmutter	Y	Y	Y	N
CONNECTICUT				
1 Larson	Y	N	Y	N
2 Courtney	Y	N	Y	N
3 DeLauro	Y	N	Y	N
4 Himes	Y	N	Y	N
5 Murphy	Y	N	Y	N
DELAWARE				
AL Carney	Y	N	Y	N
FLORIDA				
1 **Miller**	N	Y	N	Y
2 **Southerland**	N	Y	N	Y
3 Brown	?	?	?	?
4 **Crenshaw**	N	Y	N	Y
5 **Nugent**	N	Y	N	Y
6 **Stearns**	N	Y	N	Y
7 **Mica**	N	Y	N	Y
8 **Webster**	N	Y	N	N
9 **Bilirakis**	N	Y	N	Y
10 **Young**	N	Y	N	Y
11 Castor	Y	N	Y	?
12 **Ross**	N	Y	N	Y
13 **Buchanan**	N	Y	N	Y
14 **Mack**	N	Y	N	Y
15 **Posey**	N	Y	N	Y
16 **Rooney**	N	Y	N	Y
17 Wilson	Y	N	Y	N
18 **Ros-Lehtinen**	N	Y	N	Y
19 Deutch	Y	N	Y	N
20 Wasserman Schultz	Y	N	Y	N
21 **Diaz-Balart**	N	Y	N	Y
22 **West**	N	Y	N	Y
23 Hastings	Y	N	Y	N
24 **Adams**	N	Y	N	Y
25 **Rivera**	N	Y	N	Y
GEORGIA				
1 **Kingston**	N	Y	N	Y
2 Bishop	Y	N	Y	N
3 **Westmoreland**	N	Y	N	Y
4 Johnson	Y	N	Y	N
5 Lewis	Y	N	Y	N
6 **Price**	N	Y	N	Y
7 **Woodall**	N	Y	N	P
8 **Scott, A.**	N	Y	N	Y
9 **Graves**	N	Y	N	Y
10 **Broun**	N	N	N	P
11 **Gingrey**	N	Y	N	Y
12 Barrow	Y	N	Y	N
13 Scott, D.	Y	N	Y	N
HAWAII				
1 Hanabusa	Y	N	Y	N
2 Hirono	Y	N	Y	N
IDAHO				
1 **Labrador**	N	Y	N	Y
2 **Simpson**	N	Y	N	Y
ILLINOIS				
1 Rush	Y	N	Y	N
2 Jackson	?	?	?	?
3 Lipinski	Y	N	Y	N
4 Gutierrez	Y	N	Y	?
5 Quigley	Y	N	Y	N
6 **Roskam**	N	Y	N	Y
7 Davis	?	?	?	?
8 **Walsh**	N	Y	N	Y
9 Schakowsky	Y	N	Y	N
10 **Dold**	N	Y	N	Y
11 **Kinzinger**	−	+	?	+
12 Costello	Y	N	Y	N
13 **Biggert**	N	Y	N	Y
14 **Hultgren**	N	Y	N	Y
15 **Johnson**	Y	N	N	N

KEY	Republicans	Democrats
Y Voted for (yea)	X Paired against	C Voted "present" to avoid possible conflict of interest
# Paired for	− Announced against	
+ Announced for	P Voted "present"	? Did not vote or otherwise make a position known
N Voted against (nay)		

	123	124	125	126
16 Manzullo	?	?	?	?
17 Schilling	N	Y	N	Y
18 Schock	N	Y	N	Y
19 Shimkus	N	Y	N	Y
INDIANA				
1 Visclosky	Y	N	Y	N
2 Donnelly	Y	N	Y	N
3 Stutzman	N	Y	N	Y
4 Rokita	N	Y	N	Y
5 Burton	N	Y	N	Y
6 Pence	N	Y	N	Y
7 Carson	Y	Y	Y	N
8 Bucshon	N	Y	N	Y
9 Young	N	Y	N	Y
IOWA				
1 Braley	Y	N	Y	N
2 Loebsack	Y	N	Y	N
3 Boswell	Y	N	Y	N
4 Latham	N	Y	N	Y
5 King	N	Y	N	P
KANSAS				
1 Huelskamp	N	Y	N	Y
2 Jenkins	N	Y	N	Y
3 Yoder	N	Y	N	Y
4 Pompeo	N	Y	N	Y
KENTUCKY				
1 Whitfield	N	Y	N	Y
2 Guthrie	N	Y	N	Y
3 Yarmuth	Y	N	Y	N
4 Davis	N	Y	N	Y
5 Rogers	N	Y	N	Y
6 Chandler	Y	N	Y	N
LOUISIANA				
1 Scalise	N	Y	N	Y
2 Richmond	Y	N	Y	N
3 Landry	N	Y	N	Y
4 Fleming	N	Y	N	Y
5 Alexander	N	Y	N	Y
6 Cassidy	N	Y	N	Y
7 Boustany	N	Y	N	Y
MAINE				
1 Pingree	Y	N	Y	N
2 Michaud	Y	N	Y	N
MARYLAND				
1 Harris	N	Y	N	Y
2 Ruppersberger	Y	Y	Y	N
3 Sarbanes	Y	N	Y	N
4 Edwards	Y	N	Y	N
5 Hoyer	Y	N	Y	N
6 Bartlett	N	Y	P	Y
7 Cummings	Y	N	Y	N
8 Van Hollen	Y	N	Y	N
MASSACHUSETTS				
1 Olver	Y	N	Y	N
2 Neal	Y	N	Y	N
3 McGovern	Y	N	Y	N
4 Frank	?	Y	Y	N
5 Tsongas	Y	N	Y	N
6 Tierney	Y	N	Y	N
7 Markey	Y	N	Y	N
8 Capuano	Y	N	Y	N
9 Lynch	Y	Y	Y	N
10 Keating	Y	N	Y	N
MICHIGAN				
1 Benishek	N	Y	N	Y
2 Huizenga	N	Y	N	Y
3 Amash	N	N	N	N
4 Camp	N	Y	N	Y
5 Kildee	Y	N	Y	N
6 Upton	N	Y	N	Y
7 Walberg	N	Y	N	Y
8 Rogers	N	Y	N	Y
9 Peters	Y	N	Y	N
10 Miller	N	Y	N	Y
11 McCotter	N	Y	N	Y
12 Levin	Y	N	Y	N
13 Clarke	Y	N	Y	N
14 Conyers	Y	N	Y	N
15 Dingell	Y	N	Y	N
MINNESOTA				
1 Walz	Y	N	Y	N
2 Kline	N	Y	N	Y
3 Paulsen	N	Y	N	Y
4 McCollum	Y	N	Y	N

	123	124	125	126
5 Ellison	Y	N	Y	N
6 Bachmann	N	Y	N	Y
7 Peterson	N	N	Y	Y
8 Cravaack	N	Y	N	Y
MISSISSIPPI				
1 Nunnelee	N	Y	N	Y
2 Thompson	?	?	?	?
3 Harper	Y	Y	N	Y
4 Palazzo	N	Y	N	Y
MISSOURI				
1 Clay	Y	N	Y	N
2 Akin	N	Y	N	Y
3 Carnahan	Y	N	Y	N
4 Hartzler	N	Y	N	Y
5 Cleaver	Y	N	Y	N
6 Graves	N	Y	N	Y
7 Long	N	Y	N	Y
8 Emerson	N	Y	N	Y
9 Luetkemeyer	N	Y	N	Y
MONTANA				
AL Rehberg	N	Y	N	Y
NEBRASKA				
1 Fortenberry	N	Y	N	Y
2 Terry	?	?	N	N
3 Smith	N	Y	N	Y
NEVADA				
1 Berkley	Y	Y	Y	N
2 Amodei	N	Y	N	Y
3 Heck	N	Y	N	Y
NEW HAMPSHIRE				
1 Guinta	N	Y	N	Y
2 Bass	N	Y	N	Y
NEW JERSEY				
1 Andrews	Y	N	Y	N
2 LoBiondo	N	Y	N	Y
3 Runyan	N	Y	N	Y
4 Smith	N	Y	N	Y
5 Garrett	N	Y	N	Y
6 Pallone	Y	N	Y	N
7 Lance	N	Y	N	Y
8 Pascrell	Y	N	Y	N
9 Rothman	Y	N	Y	N
10 Vacant				
11 Frelinghuysen	N	Y	N	Y
12 Holt	Y	N	Y	N
13 Sires	Y	N	Y	N
NEW MEXICO				
1 Heinrich	Y	N	Y	N
2 Pearce	N	Y	N	Y
3 Luján	Y	N	Y	N
NEW YORK				
1 Bishop	Y	N	Y	N
2 Israel	Y	N	Y	N
3 King	Y	N	Y	N
4 McCarthy	Y	N	Y	N
5 Ackerman	?	?	?	?
6 Meeks	Y	N	Y	N
7 Crowley	Y	N	Y	N
8 Nadler	Y	N	Y	N
9 Turner	N	Y	N	Y
10 Towns	Y	N	Y	N
11 Clarke	Y	N	Y	N
12 Velázquez	Y	N	Y	N
13 Grimm	N	Y	N	Y
14 Maloney	Y	N	Y	N
15 Rangel	?	?	?	?
16 Serrano	Y	N	Y	N
17 Engel	Y	N	Y	N
18 Lowey	?	?	?	?
19 Hayworth	N	Y	N	Y
20 Gibson	Y	Y	N	Y
21 Tonko	Y	N	Y	N
22 Hinchey	Y	N	Y	N
23 Owens	Y	N	Y	N
24 Hanna	N	Y	N	Y
25 Buerkle	N	Y	N	Y
26 Hochul	Y	Y	Y	Y
27 Higgins	Y	N	Y	N
28 Slaughter	Y	Y	Y	N
29 Reed	N	Y	N	Y
NORTH CAROLINA				
1 Butterfield	Y	Y	Y	N
2 Ellmers	N	Y	N	Y
3 Jones	N	Y	Y	Y
4 Price	Y	N	Y	N

	123	124	125	126
5 Foxx	N	Y	N	Y
6 Coble	N	Y	N	Y
7 McIntyre	?	?	?	?
8 Kissell	N	Y	Y	Y
9 Myrick	N	Y	N	Y
10 McHenry	Y	Y	N	Y
11 Shuler	Y	Y	N	N
12 Watt	Y	N	Y	N
13 Miller	Y	N	Y	N
NORTH DAKOTA				
AL Berg	N	Y	N	Y
OHIO				
1 Chabot	N	Y	N	Y
2 Schmidt	N	Y	N	Y
3 Turner	N	Y	N	Y
4 Jordan	N	Y	N	Y
5 Latta	N	Y	N	Y
6 Johnson	N	Y	N	Y
7 Austria	?	?	?	?
8 Boehner				
9 Kaptur	Y	N	Y	N
10 Kucinich	Y	N	Y	N
11 Fudge	Y	N	Y	N
12 Tiberi	N	Y	N	Y
13 Sutton	Y	N	Y	N
14 LaTourette	N	Y	N	Y
15 Stivers	N	Y	N	Y
16 Renacci	N	Y	N	Y
17 Ryan	Y	N	Y	N
18 Gibbs	N	Y	N	Y
OKLAHOMA				
1 Sullivan	N	Y	N	Y
2 Boren	N	Y	Y	Y
3 Lucas	N	Y	N	Y
4 Cole	N	Y	N	Y
5 Lankford	N	Y	N	Y
OREGON				
1 Bonamici	Y	N	Y	N
2 Walden	N	Y	N	Y
3 Blumenauer	Y	N	Y	N
4 DeFazio	Y	Y	Y	N
5 Schrader	Y	Y	Y	N
PENNSYLVANIA				
1 Brady	Y	N	Y	N
2 Fattah	Y	Y	Y	N
3 Kelly	N	Y	N	Y
4 Altmire	Y	N	Y	N
5 Thompson	N	Y	N	Y
6 Gerlach	N	Y	N	Y
7 Meehan	N	Y	N	Y
8 Fitzpatrick	N	Y	N	Y
9 Shuster	N	Y	N	Y
10 Marino	?	?	?	?
11 Barletta	N	Y	N	Y
12 Critz	Y	N	Y	N
13 Schwartz	Y	N	Y	N
14 Doyle	Y	N	Y	N
15 Dent	N	Y	N	Y
16 Pitts	N	Y	N	Y
17 Holden	Y	N	Y	N
18 Murphy	N	Y	N	Y
19 Platts	?	Y	N	Y
RHODE ISLAND				
1 Cicilline	Y	N	Y	N
2 Langevin	Y	N	Y	N
SOUTH CAROLINA				
1 Scott	N	Y	N	Y
2 Wilson	N	Y	N	Y
3 Duncan	N	Y	N	Y
4 Gowdy	N	Y	N	Y
5 Mulvaney	N	Y	N	Y
6 Clyburn	Y	N	Y	N
SOUTH DAKOTA				
AL Noem	N	Y	N	Y
TENNESSEE				
1 Roe	N	Y	N	Y
2 Duncan	N	Y	N	N
3 Fleischmann	N	Y	N	Y
4 DesJarlais	N	Y	N	Y
5 Cooper	Y	N	Y	N
6 Black	N	Y	N	Y
7 Blackburn	N	Y	N	Y
8 Fincher	N	Y	N	Y
9 Cohen	Y	N	Y	N

	123	124	125	126
TEXAS				
1 Gohmert	N	?	N	N
2 Poe	N	N	N	N
3 Johnson, S.	N	Y	N	Y
4 Hall	N	Y	N	Y
5 Hensarling	N	Y	N	Y
6 Barton	N	Y	N	Y
7 Culberson	N	Y	N	Y
8 Brady	N	Y	N	Y
9 Green, A.	Y	N	Y	N
10 McCaul	N	Y	N	Y
11 Conaway	N	Y	N	Y
12 Granger	N	Y	N	Y
13 Thornberry	N	Y	N	Y
14 Paul	?	?	?	?
15 Hinojosa	Y	N	Y	N
16 Reyes	Y	Y	Y	N
17 Flores	N	Y	N	Y
18 Jackson Lee	Y	N	Y	N
19 Neugebauer	N	Y	N	Y
20 Gonzalez	?	?	?	?
21 Smith	N	Y	N	Y
22 Olson	N	Y	N	Y
23 Canseco	N	Y	N	Y
24 Marchant	?	?	?	?
25 Doggett	Y	N	Y	N
26 Burgess	N	Y	N	Y
27 Farenthold	N	Y	N	Y
28 Cuellar	Y	Y	Y	N
29 Green, G.	Y	Y	Y	N
30 Johnson, E.	Y	N	Y	N
31 Carter	N	Y	N	Y
32 Sessions	N	Y	N	Y
UTAH				
1 Bishop	?	?	?	?
2 Matheson	N	Y	Y	Y
3 Chaffetz	?	?	?	?
VERMONT				
AL Welch	Y	N	Y	N
VIRGINIA				
1 Wittman	N	Y	N	Y
2 Rigell	N	Y	N	Y
3 Scott	Y	N	Y	N
4 Forbes	N	Y	N	Y
5 Hurt	N	Y	N	Y
6 Goodlatte	N	Y	N	Y
7 Cantor	N	Y	N	Y
8 Moran	Y	Y	Y	N
9 Griffith	N	N	N	N
10 Wolf	N	Y	N	Y
11 Connolly	Y	Y	Y	N
WASHINGTON				
1 Vacant				
2 Larsen	Y	Y	Y	N
3 Herrera Beutler	N	Y	N	Y
4 Hastings	N	Y	N	Y
5 McMorris Rodgers	N	Y	N	Y
6 Dicks	Y	N	Y	N
7 McDermott	Y	N	Y	N
8 Reichert	N	Y	N	Y
9 Smith	Y	N	Y	N
WEST VIRGINIA				
1 McKinley	N	Y	N	Y
2 Capito	N	Y	N	Y
3 Rahall	Y	N	Y	N
WISCONSIN				
1 Ryan	N	Y	N	Y
2 Baldwin	Y	N	Y	N
3 Kind	Y	N	Y	N
4 Moore	Y	N	Y	N
5 Sensenbrenner	P	P	P	P
6 Petri	N	Y	N	Y
7 Duffy	N	Y	N	+
8 Ribble	N	Y	N	Y
WYOMING				
AL Lummis	N	Y	N	Y

IN THE HOUSE | By Vote Number

127. **HR 2779. Inter-Affiliate Swaps Exemption/Passage.** Garrett, R-N.J., motion to suspend the rules and pass the bill that would exclude from the definition of "swap" any agreement, contract or transaction entered between affiliated entities under the common control of the same parent company. This would exempt affiliate swap transactions from clearing and execution requirements, margin and capital requirements, and reporting requirements other than reporting directly to the Securities and Exchange Commission or the Commodity Futures Trading Commission. Motion agreed to 357-36: R 223-0; D 134-36. A two-thirds majority of those present and voting (262 in this case) is required for passage. March 26, 2012.

128. **HR 2682. Derivatives End-User Exemption/Passage.** Garrett, R-N.J., motion to suspend the rules and pass the bill that would exempt non-financial companies that use derivatives to hedge risk from having to meet Commodity Futures Trading Commission and Securities and Exchange Commission margin requirements mandated in the 2010 financial regulatory overhaul law. Motion agreed to 370-24: R 224-0; D 146-24. A two-thirds majority of those present and voting (263 in this case) is required for passage under suspension of the rules. March 26, 2012.

129. **Procedural Motion/Journal.** Approval of the House Journal of Thursday, March 22, 2012. Approved 310-80: R 182-39; D 128-41. March 26, 2012.

130. **HR 3309. Federal Communications Commission Rulemaking/ Previous Question.** Webster, R-Fla., motion to order the previous question (thus ending debate and the possibility of amendment) on adoption of the rule (H Res 595) that would provide for House floor consideration of the bill that would modify requirements for the Federal Communications Commission rule-making process. Motion agreed to 236-182: R 235-0; D 1-182. March 27, 2012.

131. **HR 3309. Federal Communications Commission Rulemaking/ Rule.** Adoption of the rule (H Res 595) that would provide for House floor consideration of the bill that would modify requirements for the Federal Communications Commission rule-making process. Adopted 242-177: R 235-0; D 7-177. March 27, 2012.

132. **HR 3606. Small-Business Startups/Motion to Concur.** Bachus, R-Ala., motion to suspend the rules and concur in the Senate amendment to the bill that would define "emerging-growth companies" and exempt them from certain independent auditing requirements. It would increase from $5 million to $50 million the annual public offering threshold for companies to be exempt from full Securities and Exchange Commission filing requirements and raise the number of shareholders that would trigger mandatory SEC registration from 750 to 2,000. It would raise to 2,000 the number of shareholders that would trigger a requirement for SEC registration for a bank. The bill would lift an SEC ban that prevents small, privately held companies from using advertisements to solicit investors and allow companies to sell up to $1 million worth of securities without registering with the SEC. It also would require anyone acting as a "crowdfunding" intermediary to register with securities regulators. Motion agreed to (thus clearing the bill for the president) 380-41: R 235-0; D 145-41. A two-thirds majority of those present and voting (263 in this case) is required for passage under suspension of the rules. A "yea" was a vote in support of the president's position. March 27, 2012.

	127	128	129	130	131	132
ALABAMA						
1 Bonner	Y	Y	Y	Y	Y	Y
2 Roby	Y	Y	Y	Y	Y	Y
3 Rogers	Y	Y	Y	Y	Y	Y
4 Aderholt	Y	Y	Y	Y	Y	Y
5 Brooks	Y	Y	Y	Y	Y	Y
6 Bachus	Y	Y	Y	Y	Y	Y
7 Sewell	Y	Y	Y	N	N	Y
ALASKA						
AL Young	Y	Y	N	Y	Y	Y
ARIZONA						
1 Gosar	?	Y	Y	Y	Y	Y
2 Franks	Y	Y	Y	Y	Y	Y
3 Quayle	Y	Y	N	Y	Y	Y
4 Pastor	Y	Y	N	N	N	N
5 Schweikert	Y	Y	Y	Y	Y	Y
6 Flake	Y	Y	Y	Y	Y	Y
7 Grijalva	N	N	N	N	N	N
8 Vacant						
ARKANSAS						
1 Crawford	Y	Y	Y	Y	Y	Y
2 Griffin	Y	Y	N	Y	Y	Y
3 Womack	Y	Y	Y	Y	Y	Y
4 Ross	Y	Y	Y	N	Y	Y
CALIFORNIA						
1 Thompson	Y	Y	N	N	N	Y
2 Herger	Y	Y	Y	Y	Y	Y
3 Lungren	Y	Y	Y	Y	Y	Y
4 McClintock	Y	Y	Y	Y	Y	Y
5 Matsui	Y	Y	Y	N	N	Y
6 Woolsey	Y	Y	Y	N	N	N
7 Miller, George	Y	N	N	N	N	N
8 Pelosi	Y	Y	Y	N	N	Y
9 Lee	N	N	N	N	N	N
10 Garamendi	N	Y	Y	N	N	Y
11 McNerney	Y	Y	Y	N	N	Y
12 Speier	Y	Y	Y	N	N	Y
13 Stark	Y	N	N	N	N	N
14 Eshoo	Y	Y	Y	N	N	Y
15 Honda	Y	Y	N	N	N	Y
16 Lofgren	Y	Y	Y	N	N	Y
17 Farr	Y	Y	Y	N	N	Y
18 Cardoza	Y	Y	Y	N	N	Y
19 Denham	Y	Y	Y	Y	Y	Y
20 Costa	?	?	Y	N	N	Y
21 Nunes	Y	Y	Y	Y	Y	Y
22 McCarthy	Y	Y	Y	Y	Y	Y
23 Capps	Y	Y	Y	N	N	Y
24 Gallegly	Y	Y	Y	Y	Y	Y
25 McKeon	Y	Y	Y	Y	Y	Y
26 Dreier	Y	Y	Y	Y	Y	Y
27 Sherman	Y	Y	Y	N	N	Y
28 Berman	N	N	Y	N	N	N
29 Schiff	Y	Y	Y	N	N	Y
30 Waxman	Y	Y	Y	N	N	N
31 Becerra	N	Y	Y	N	N	Y
32 Chu	Y	Y	N	N	N	Y
33 Bass	Y	Y	Y	N	N	Y
34 Roybal-Allard	Y	Y	Y	N	N	Y
35 Waters	Y	Y	N	N	N	Y
36 Hahn	Y	Y	Y	N	N	Y
37 Richardson	Y	Y	Y	N	N	Y
38 Napolitano	Y	Y	Y	N	N	N
39 Sánchez, Linda	Y	Y	N	N	N	Y
40 Royce	Y	Y	Y	Y	Y	Y
41 Lewis	Y	Y	Y	Y	Y	Y
42 Miller, Gary	Y	Y	Y	Y	Y	Y
43 Baca	Y	Y	Y	N	N	Y
44 Calvert	Y	Y	Y	Y	Y	Y
45 Bono Mack	Y	Y	Y	N	N	Y
46 Rohrabacher	?	?	?	Y	Y	Y
47 Sanchez, Loretta	Y	Y	N	N	N	Y
48 Campbell	?	?	?	Y	Y	Y
49 Issa	Y	Y	Y	Y	Y	Y
50 Bilbray	Y	Y	Y	Y	Y	Y
51 Filner	N	N	N	N	N	N
52 Hunter	Y	Y	N	Y	Y	Y
53 Davis	Y	Y	Y	N	N	Y

	127	128	129	130	131	132
COLORADO						
1 DeGette	Y	Y	Y	N	N	Y
2 Polis	Y	Y	Y	N	N	Y
3 Tipton	Y	Y	N	Y	Y	Y
4 Gardner	Y	Y	N	Y	Y	Y
5 Lamborn	Y	Y	Y	Y	Y	Y
6 Coffman	Y	Y	N	Y	Y	Y
7 Perlmutter	Y	Y	Y	N	N	Y
CONNECTICUT						
1 Larson	N	Y	Y	N	N	Y
2 Courtney	N	Y	Y	N	N	Y
3 DeLauro	N	Y	Y	N	N	Y
4 Himes	Y	Y	Y	N	N	Y
5 Murphy	Y	Y	Y	N	N	Y
DELAWARE						
AL Carney	Y	Y	Y	N	N	Y
FLORIDA						
1 Miller	Y	Y	Y	Y	Y	Y
2 Southerland	Y	Y	Y	Y	Y	Y
3 Brown	?	?	?	N	N	Y
4 Crenshaw	Y	Y	Y	Y	Y	Y
5 Nugent	?	?	?	Y	Y	Y
6 Stearns	Y	Y	Y	Y	Y	Y
7 Mica	Y	Y	Y	Y	Y	Y
8 Webster	Y	Y	Y	Y	Y	Y
9 Bilirakis	Y	Y	Y	Y	Y	Y
10 Young	Y	Y	Y	Y	Y	Y
11 Castor	Y	Y	N	N	N	Y
12 Ross	Y	Y	Y	Y	Y	Y
13 Buchanan	Y	Y	Y	Y	Y	Y
14 Mack	?	?	?	?	?	?
15 Posey	Y	Y	Y	Y	Y	Y
16 Rooney	Y	Y	N	Y	Y	Y
17 Wilson	Y	Y	Y	–	N	Y
18 Ros-Lehtinen	Y	Y	Y	Y	Y	Y
19 Deutch	N	Y	N	N	N	Y
20 Wasserman Schultz	Y	Y	Y	N	N	Y
21 Diaz-Balart	Y	Y	Y	Y	Y	+
22 West	Y	Y	Y	Y	Y	Y
23 Hastings	Y	Y	Y	N	N	Y
24 Adams	Y	Y	N	Y	Y	Y
25 Rivera	?	?	?	Y	Y	Y
GEORGIA						
1 Kingston	Y	Y	Y	Y	Y	Y
2 Bishop	Y	Y	Y	N	N	Y
3 Westmoreland	Y	Y	Y	Y	Y	Y
4 Johnson	?	?	?	N	N	N
5 Lewis	Y	Y	N	?	?	Y
6 Price	Y	Y	Y	Y	Y	Y
7 Woodall	Y	Y	N	?	?	Y
8 Scott, A.	Y	Y	Y	Y	Y	Y
9 Graves	Y	Y	Y	Y	Y	Y
10 Broun	Y	Y	Y	N	N	Y
11 Gingrey	Y	Y	Y	Y	Y	Y
12 Barrow	Y	Y	Y	N	N	Y
13 Scott, D.	Y	Y	Y	N	N	Y
HAWAII						
1 Hanabusa	Y	Y	Y	N	N	Y
2 Hirono	N	N	Y	N	N	Y
IDAHO						
1 Labrador	Y	Y	Y	Y	Y	Y
2 Simpson	Y	Y	Y	Y	Y	Y
ILLINOIS						
1 Rush	?	?	?	N	N	Y
2 Jackson	?	?	?	?	?	?
3 Lipinski	Y	Y	Y	N	N	Y
4 Gutierrez	?	?	?	N	N	Y
5 Quigley	Y	Y	Y	N	N	Y
6 Roskam	Y	Y	Y	Y	Y	Y
7 Davis	N	Y	Y	N	N	Y
8 Walsh	Y	Y	N	Y	Y	Y
9 Schakowsky	N	Y	N	N	N	N
10 Dold	Y	Y	N	Y	Y	Y
11 Kinzinger	Y	Y	Y	Y	Y	Y
12 Costello	Y	Y	N	N	N	Y
13 Biggert	Y	Y	Y	Y	Y	Y
14 Hultgren	Y	Y	Y	Y	Y	Y
15 Johnson	+	+	?	Y	Y	Y

KEY   **Republicans**   Democrats

Y Voted for (yea)	X Paired against	C Voted "present" to avoid possible conflict of interest
# Paired for	– Announced against	
+ Announced for	P Voted "present"	? Did not vote or otherwise make a position known
N Voted against (nay)		

	127	128	129	130	131	132
16 **Manzullo**	Y	Y	N	Y	Y	Y
17 **Schilling**	Y	Y	Y	Y	Y	Y
18 **Schock**	Y	Y	Y	Y	Y	Y
19 **Shimkus**	Y	Y	Y	Y	Y	Y
INDIANA						
1 Visclosky	Y	Y	N	N	N	N
2 Donnelly	?	?	?	N	Y	Y
3 **Stutzman**	Y	Y	Y	Y	Y	Y
4 **Rokita**	Y	Y	Y	Y	Y	Y
5 **Burton**	Y	Y	Y	Y	Y	Y
6 **Pence**	Y	Y	Y	Y	Y	Y
7 Carson	Y	Y	Y	N	N	Y
8 **Bucshon**	Y	Y	Y	Y	Y	Y
9 **Young**	Y	Y	Y	Y	Y	Y
IOWA						
1 Braley	Y	Y	Y	N	N	Y
2 Loebsack	Y	Y	Y	N	N	Y
3 Boswell	Y	Y	N	N	N	Y
4 **Latham**	Y	Y	Y	Y	Y	Y
5 **King**	Y	Y	Y	Y	Y	Y
KANSAS						
1 **Huelskamp**	Y	Y	Y	Y	Y	Y
2 **Jenkins**	Y	Y	Y	Y	Y	Y
3 **Yoder**	Y	Y	N	Y	Y	Y
4 **Pompeo**	Y	Y	Y	Y	Y	Y
KENTUCKY						
1 **Whitfield**	Y	Y	Y	Y	Y	Y
2 **Guthrie**	Y	Y	Y	Y	Y	Y
3 Yarmuth	Y	Y	Y	N	N	Y
4 **Davis**	Y	Y	Y	Y	Y	Y
5 **Rogers**	Y	Y	Y	Y	Y	Y
6 Chandler	Y	Y	Y	N	N	Y
LOUISIANA						
1 **Scalise**	Y	Y	Y	Y	Y	Y
2 Richmond	Y	Y	Y	N	N	Y
3 **Landry**	?	?	?	?	?	?
4 **Fleming**	Y	Y	Y	Y	Y	Y
5 **Alexander**	Y	Y	Y	Y	Y	Y
6 **Cassidy**	Y	Y	Y	Y	Y	Y
7 **Boustany**	Y	Y	Y	Y	Y	Y
MAINE						
1 Pingree	N	Y	Y	N	N	N
2 Michaud	Y	Y	Y	N	N	Y
MARYLAND						
1 **Harris**	Y	Y	N	Y	Y	Y
2 Ruppersberger	Y	Y	Y	N	N	Y
3 Sarbanes	N	Y	N	N	N	N
4 Edwards	Y	Y	Y	N	N	N
5 Hoyer	Y	Y	N	N	N	Y
6 **Bartlett**	Y	Y	Y	Y	Y	Y
7 Cummings	Y	Y	Y	N	N	N
8 Van Hollen	Y	Y	Y	N	N	Y
MASSACHUSETTS						
1 Olver	Y	Y	N	N	N	N
2 Neal	?	?	?	?	?	?
3 McGovern	Y	N	N	N	N	Y
4 Frank	Y	Y	Y	N	N	Y
5 Tsongas	Y	Y	Y	N	N	Y
6 Tierney	N	N	Y	N	N	N
7 Markey	N	N	N	N	N	N
8 Capuano	Y	Y	N	N	N	N
9 Lynch	Y	Y	N	N	N	Y
10 Keating	Y	Y	Y	N	N	Y
MICHIGAN						
1 **Benishek**	Y	Y	N	Y	Y	Y
2 **Huizenga**	Y	Y	N	Y	Y	Y
3 **Amash**	Y	Y	P	Y	Y	Y
4 **Camp**	Y	Y	Y	Y	Y	Y
5 Kildee	N	N	Y	N	N	N
6 **Upton**	Y	Y	Y	Y	Y	Y
7 **Walberg**	Y	Y	N	Y	Y	Y
8 **Rogers**	Y	Y	Y	Y	Y	Y
9 Peters	Y	Y	N	N	N	Y
10 **Miller**	Y	Y	Y	Y	Y	Y
11 **McCotter**	Y	Y	N	Y	Y	Y
12 Levin	Y	Y	Y	N	N	Y
13 Clarke	Y	Y	Y	N	N	Y
14 Conyers	N	N	P	N	N	Y
15 Dingell	N	N	Y	N	N	N
MINNESOTA						
1 Walz	Y	Y	Y	N	N	Y
2 **Kline**	Y	Y	Y	Y	Y	Y
3 **Paulsen**	Y	Y	Y	Y	Y	Y
4 McCollum	Y	Y	Y	N	N	N

	127	128	129	130	131	132
5 Ellison	Y	Y	Y	N	N	Y
6 **Bachmann**	Y	Y	Y	Y	Y	Y
7 Peterson	Y	Y	N	N	N	Y
8 **Cravaack**	Y	Y	N	Y	Y	Y
MISSISSIPPI						
1 **Nunnelee**	Y	Y	Y	Y	Y	Y
2 Thompson	?	?	?	N	N	Y
3 **Harper**	Y	Y	Y	Y	Y	Y
4 **Palazzo**	Y	Y	Y	Y	Y	Y
MISSOURI						
1 Clay	Y	Y	Y	N	N	N
2 **Akin**	+	+	+	+	+	+
3 Carnahan	Y	Y	Y	N	N	Y
4 **Hartzler**	Y	Y	Y	Y	Y	Y
5 Cleaver	Y	Y	Y	N	N	Y
6 **Graves**	Y	Y	Y	Y	Y	Y
7 **Long**	Y	Y	Y	Y	Y	Y
8 **Emerson**	Y	Y	Y	Y	Y	Y
9 **Luetkemeyer**	Y	Y	Y	Y	Y	Y
MONTANA						
AL **Rehberg**	Y	Y	Y	Y	Y	Y
NEBRASKA						
1 **Fortenberry**	Y	Y	Y	Y	Y	Y
2 **Terry**	Y	Y	N	Y	Y	Y
3 **Smith**	Y	Y	Y	Y	Y	Y
NEVADA						
1 Berkley	Y	Y	Y	N	N	Y
2 **Amodei**	Y	Y	Y	Y	Y	Y
3 **Heck**	Y	Y	N	Y	Y	Y
NEW HAMPSHIRE						
1 **Guinta**	Y	Y	Y	Y	Y	Y
2 **Bass**	Y	Y	Y	Y	Y	Y
NEW JERSEY						
1 Andrews	Y	Y	N	N	N	Y
2 **LoBiondo**	Y	Y	N	Y	Y	Y
3 **Runyan**	Y	Y	Y	Y	Y	Y
4 **Smith**	Y	Y	Y	Y	Y	Y
5 **Garrett**	Y	Y	N	Y	Y	Y
6 Pallone	Y	Y	Y	N	N	Y
7 **Lance**	Y	Y	Y	Y	Y	Y
8 Pascrell	?	?	?	N	N	Y
9 Rothman	Y	Y	Y	N	N	Y
10 Vacant						
11 **Frelinghuysen**	Y	Y	Y	Y	Y	Y
12 Holt	N	Y	Y	N	N	N
13 Sires	Y	Y	Y	N	N	Y
NEW MEXICO						
1 Heinrich	+	+	+	N	N	Y
2 **Pearce**	Y	Y	Y	Y	Y	Y
3 Luján	Y	Y	Y	N	N	Y
NEW YORK						
1 Bishop	Y	Y	N	N	N	Y
2 Israel	Y	Y	N	N	N	Y
3 **King**	Y	Y	Y	Y	Y	Y
4 McCarthy	+	+	+	N	N	Y
5 Ackerman	Y	Y	Y	N	N	Y
6 Meeks	Y	Y	Y	N	N	Y
7 Crowley	Y	Y	Y	N	N	Y
8 Nadler	N	N	Y	N	N	N
9 **Turner**	Y	Y	Y	Y	Y	Y
10 Towns	?	?	?	N	N	Y
11 Clarke	Y	Y	Y	N	N	N
12 Velázquez	N	N	N	N	N	Y
13 **Grimm**	Y	Y	Y	Y	Y	Y
14 Maloney	Y	Y	Y	N	N	Y
15 Rangel	?	?	?	?	?	?
16 Serrano	N	N	Y	N	N	Y
17 Engel	Y	Y	Y	?	?	?
18 Lowey	Y	Y	Y	N	N	Y
19 **Hayworth**	Y	Y	Y	Y	Y	Y
20 **Gibson**	Y	Y	N	Y	Y	Y
21 Tonko	Y	Y	Y	N	N	Y
22 Hinchey	N	N	Y	N	N	N
23 Owens	Y	Y	P	N	N	Y
24 **Hanna**	Y	Y	N	Y	Y	Y
25 **Buerkle**	?	?	?	Y	Y	Y
26 Hochul	Y	Y	Y	N	N	Y
27 Higgins	Y	Y	Y	N	N	Y
28 Slaughter	Y	Y	N	N	N	Y
29 **Reed**	Y	Y	N	Y	Y	Y
NORTH CAROLINA						
1 Butterfield	Y	Y	Y	N	N	Y
2 **Ellmers**	Y	Y	Y	Y	Y	Y
3 **Jones**	Y	?	Y	Y	Y	Y
4 Price	Y	Y	Y	N	N	Y

	127	128	129	130	131	132
5 **Foxx**	Y	Y	N	Y	Y	Y
6 **Coble**	Y	Y	Y	Y	Y	Y
7 McIntyre	+	+	+	N	N	Y
8 Kissell	?	?	?	N	Y	Y
9 **Myrick**	Y	Y	Y	Y	Y	Y
10 **McHenry**	Y	Y	Y	Y	Y	Y
11 Shuler	Y	Y	N	N	Y	Y
12 Watt	Y	Y	Y	?	N	Y
13 Miller	N	N	Y	N	N	Y
NORTH DAKOTA						
AL **Berg**	Y	Y	Y	Y	Y	Y
OHIO						
1 **Chabot**	Y	Y	Y	Y	Y	Y
2 **Schmidt**	Y	Y	Y	Y	Y	Y
3 **Turner**	Y	Y	Y	Y	Y	Y
4 **Jordan**	Y	Y	Y	Y	Y	Y
5 **Latta**	Y	Y	Y	Y	Y	Y
6 **Johnson**	Y	Y	N	Y	Y	Y
7 **Austria**	Y	Y	Y	Y	Y	Y
8 **Boehner**						
9 Kaptur	N	N	Y	N	N	Y
10 Kucinich	N	N	N	N	N	N
11 Fudge	N	Y	Y	N	N	N
12 **Tiberi**	Y	Y	Y	Y	Y	Y
13 Sutton	Y	Y	Y	N	N	Y
14 **LaTourette**	Y	Y	Y	Y	Y	Y
15 **Stivers**	Y	Y	Y	Y	Y	Y
16 **Renacci**	Y	Y	N	Y	Y	Y
17 Ryan	Y	Y	N	N	N	Y
18 **Gibbs**	Y	Y	?	Y	Y	Y
OKLAHOMA						
1 **Sullivan**	Y	Y	Y	Y	Y	Y
2 Boren	Y	Y	Y	N	Y	Y
3 **Lucas**	Y	Y	Y	Y	Y	Y
4 **Cole**	Y	Y	Y	Y	Y	Y
5 **Lankford**	Y	Y	Y	Y	Y	Y
OREGON						
1 Bonamici	N	Y	Y	N	N	Y
2 **Walden**	Y	Y	N	Y	Y	Y
3 Blumenauer	Y	Y	Y	N	?	Y
4 DeFazio	N	Y	N	N	N	Y
5 Schrader	Y	Y	Y	N	N	Y
PENNSYLVANIA						
1 Brady	Y	Y	N	N	N	N
2 Fattah	Y	Y	N	N	N	Y
3 **Kelly**	?	?	?	Y	Y	Y
4 Altmire	Y	Y	Y	N	N	Y
5 **Thompson**	Y	Y	Y	Y	Y	Y
6 **Gerlach**	Y	Y	Y	Y	Y	Y
7 **Meehan**	?	Y	N	Y	Y	Y
8 **Fitzpatrick**	Y	Y	N	Y	Y	Y
9 **Shuster**	Y	Y	Y	Y	Y	Y
10 **Marino**	Y	Y	Y	Y	Y	Y
11 **Barletta**	Y	Y	Y	Y	Y	Y
12 Critz	Y	Y	Y	N	N	Y
13 Schwartz	Y	Y	Y	N	N	Y
14 Doyle	?	?	?	N	N	N
15 **Dent**	Y	Y	Y	Y	Y	Y
16 **Pitts**	Y	Y	Y	Y	Y	Y
17 Holden	Y	Y	N	N	N	N
18 **Murphy**	Y	Y	Y	Y	Y	Y
19 **Platts**	Y	Y	Y	Y	Y	Y
RHODE ISLAND						
1 Cicilline	Y	N	Y	N	N	Y
2 Langevin	N	N	Y	N	N	Y
SOUTH CAROLINA						
1 **Scott**	Y	Y	Y	Y	Y	Y
2 **Wilson**	Y	Y	Y	Y	Y	Y
3 **Duncan**	Y	Y	Y	Y	Y	Y
4 **Gowdy**	Y	Y	Y	Y	Y	Y
5 **Mulvaney**	Y	Y	Y	Y	Y	Y
6 Clyburn	Y	Y	Y	N	N	Y
SOUTH DAKOTA						
AL **Noem**	Y	Y	Y	Y	Y	Y
TENNESSEE						
1 **Roe**	Y	Y	Y	Y	Y	Y
2 **Duncan**	Y	Y	Y	Y	Y	Y
3 **Fleischmann**	Y	Y	Y	Y	Y	Y
4 **DesJarlais**	Y	Y	Y	Y	Y	Y
5 Cooper	Y	Y	Y	N	N	Y
6 **Black**	Y	Y	Y	Y	Y	Y
7 **Blackburn**	Y	Y	Y	Y	Y	Y
8 **Fincher**	Y	Y	N	Y	Y	Y
9 Cohen	N	N	Y	N	N	N

	127	128	129	130	131	132
TEXAS						
1 **Gohmert**	Y	Y	P	Y	?	Y
2 **Poe**	Y	Y	N	Y	Y	Y
3 **Johnson, S.**	Y	Y	Y	Y	Y	Y
4 **Hall**	Y	Y	Y	Y	Y	Y
5 **Hensarling**	Y	Y	Y	Y	Y	Y
6 **Barton**	Y	Y	Y	Y	Y	Y
7 **Culberson**	Y	Y	Y	Y	Y	Y
8 **Brady**	Y	Y	Y	Y	Y	Y
9 Green, A.	Y	Y	Y	N	N	Y
10 **McCaul**	Y	Y	?	Y	Y	Y
11 **Conaway**	Y	Y	N	Y	Y	Y
12 **Granger**	Y	Y	Y	Y	Y	Y
13 **Thornberry**	Y	Y	Y	Y	Y	Y
14 **Paul**	?	?	?	Y	Y	Y
15 Hinojosa	Y	Y	Y	N	N	Y
16 Reyes	?	?	?	N	N	Y
17 **Flores**	?	?	?	?	?	?
18 Jackson Lee	+	+	–	N	N	Y
19 **Neugebauer**	Y	Y	Y	Y	Y	Y
20 Gonzalez	Y	Y	Y	N	N	Y
21 **Smith**	Y	Y	Y	Y	Y	Y
22 **Olson**	Y	Y	Y	Y	Y	Y
23 **Canseco**	Y	Y	Y	Y	Y	Y
24 **Marchant**	?	?	?	?	?	?
25 Doggett	N	Y	Y	N	N	Y
26 **Burgess**	Y	Y	N	Y	Y	Y
27 **Farenthold**	Y	Y	Y	Y	Y	Y
28 Cuellar	Y	Y	Y	N	N	Y
29 Green, G.	Y	Y	N	N	N	N
30 Johnson, E.	Y	Y	Y	N	N	N
31 **Carter**	Y	Y	Y	Y	Y	Y
32 **Sessions**	Y	Y	Y	Y	Y	Y
UTAH						
1 **Bishop**	?	?	?	Y	Y	Y
2 Matheson	Y	Y	Y	Y	Y	Y
3 **Chaffetz**	Y	Y	Y	Y	Y	Y
VERMONT						
AL Welch	N	Y	Y	N	N	Y
VIRGINIA						
1 **Wittman**	Y	Y	Y	Y	Y	Y
2 **Rigell**	Y	Y	Y	Y	Y	Y
3 Scott	N	Y	Y	N	N	N
4 **Forbes**	?	?	?	Y	Y	Y
5 **Hurt**	Y	Y	Y	Y	Y	Y
6 **Goodlatte**	Y	Y	Y	Y	Y	Y
7 **Cantor**	Y	Y	Y	Y	Y	Y
8 Moran	Y	Y	Y	N	N	Y
9 **Griffith**	Y	Y	Y	Y	Y	Y
10 **Wolf**	Y	Y	Y	Y	Y	Y
11 Connolly	Y	Y	Y	N	N	Y
WASHINGTON						
1 Vacant						
2 Larsen	Y	Y	Y	N	N	Y
3 **Herrera Beutler**	Y	Y	N	Y	Y	Y
4 **Hastings**	Y	Y	Y	Y	Y	Y
5 **McMorris Rodgers**	Y	Y	Y	Y	Y	Y
6 Dicks	?	?	?	N	N	Y
7 McDermott	N	Y	Y	N	N	N
8 **Reichert**	?	?	?	Y	Y	Y
9 Smith	Y	Y	Y	N	N	Y
WEST VIRGINIA						
1 **McKinley**	Y	Y	Y	Y	Y	Y
2 **Capito**	Y	Y	Y	Y	Y	Y
3 Rahall	Y	Y	N	N	N	Y
WISCONSIN						
1 **Ryan**	Y	Y	Y	Y	Y	Y
2 Baldwin	Y	Y	N	N	N	Y
3 Kind	Y	Y	Y	N	N	Y
4 Moore	Y	Y	Y	N	N	Y
5 **Sensenbrenner**	Y	Y	Y	Y	Y	Y
6 **Petri**	Y	Y	Y	Y	Y	Y
7 **Duffy**	Y	Y	Y	Y	Y	Y
8 **Ribble**	Y	Y	N	Y	Y	Y
WYOMING						
AL **Lummis**	Y	Y	Y	Y	Y	Y

IN THE HOUSE | By Vote Number

133. **HR 3298. Veterans Housing Assistance/Passage.** Biggert, R-Ill., motion to suspend the rules and pass the bill that would establish a special assistant for veterans affairs within the Department of Housing and Urban Development to help provide rental assistance for homeless veterans. Motion agreed to 414-5: R 230-5; D 184-0. A two-thirds majority of those present and voting (280 in this case) is required for passage under suspension of the rules. March 27, 2012.

134. **HR 3309. Federal Communications Commission Rulemaking/Baby Monitor Labeling Rules.** Crowley, D-N.Y., amendment that would require that new or revised Federal Communications Commission rules on baby monitors mandate the packaging of an analog baby monitor to display a warning label stating that sounds or images shown by the monitor could be easily seen or heard by potential intruders outside the home. Rejected in Committee of the Whole 196-219: R 18-216; D 178-3. March 27, 2012.

135. **HR 3309. Federal Communications Commission Rulemaking/Political-Ad Disclosures.** Eshoo, D-Calif., amendment that would require entities sponsoring media political programming to disclose the identity of any donor that has contributed $10,000 or more to the group in an election reporting cycle. Broadcasters would have to include the information in files available for public inspection. Rejected in Committee of the Whole 179-238: R 5-230; D 174-8. March 27, 2012.

136. **HR 3309. Federal Communications Commission Rulemaking/Rural Broadband Access.** Owens, D-N.Y., amendment that would specify that nothing in the bill would prohibit the Federal Communications Commission from implementing rules to ensure broadband access in rural areas. Rejected in Committee of the Whole 194-222: R 13-220; D 181-2. March 27, 2012.

137. **HR 3309. Federal Communications Commission Rulemaking/Recommit.** Perlmutter, D-Colo., motion to recommit the bill to the House Energy and Commerce Committee and report it back immediately with an amendment that would clarify that nothing in the bill would prohibit the Federal Communications Commission from adopting or amending rules to protect online privacy, including rules that prohibit licensees or regulated entities from mandating that job applicants or employees disclose confidential passwords to social networking websites. Motion rejected 184-236: R 1-234; D 183-2. March 27, 2012.

138. **HR 3309. Federal Communications Commission Rulemaking/Passage.** Passage of the bill that would modify requirements for the Federal Communications Commission rule-making process. Rules with an economic impact of at least $100 million would need to include an identification and analysis of specific market failure or consumer harm as well as a determination that the benefits justify the cost. The FCC could only conditionally approve line and license transfers, such as those relating to corporate mergers and acquisitions, if the commission tailored them to address specific harm that could result from the transaction. Passed 247-174: R 235-0; D 12-174. A "nay" was a vote in support of the president's position. March 27, 2012.

	133	134	135	136	137	138
ALABAMA						
1 Bonner	Y	N	N	N	N	Y
2 Roby	Y	N	N	N	N	Y
3 Rogers	Y	N	N	N	N	Y
4 Aderholt	Y	N	N	N	N	Y
5 Brooks	Y	N	N	N	N	Y
6 Bachus	Y	N	N	N	N	Y
7 Sewell	Y	Y	Y	Y	Y	N
ALASKA						
AL Young	Y	N	N	N	N	Y
ARIZONA						
1 Gosar	Y	N	N	N	N	Y
2 Franks	Y	N	N	N	N	Y
3 Quayle	Y	N	N	N	N	Y
4 Pastor	Y	Y	Y	Y	Y	N
5 Schweikert	Y	N	N	N	N	Y
6 Flake	N	N	N	N	N	Y
7 Grijalva	Y	Y	Y	Y	Y	N
8 Vacant						
ARKANSAS						
1 Crawford	Y	N	N	N	N	Y
2 Griffin	Y	N	N	N	N	Y
3 Womack	Y	N	N	N	N	Y
4 Ross	Y	Y	Y	Y	Y	Y
CALIFORNIA						
1 Thompson	Y	Y	Y	Y	Y	N
2 Herger	Y	N	N	N	N	Y
3 Lungren	Y	N	N	N	N	Y
4 McClintock	Y	N	N	N	N	Y
5 Matsui	Y	Y	Y	Y	Y	N
6 Woolsey	Y	Y	Y	Y	Y	N
7 Miller, George	Y	Y	Y	Y	Y	N
8 Pelosi	Y	Y	Y	Y	Y	N
9 Lee	Y	Y	Y	Y	Y	N
10 Garamendi	Y	Y	Y	Y	Y	N
11 McNerney	Y	Y	Y	Y	Y	N
12 Speier	Y	Y	Y	Y	Y	N
13 Stark	Y	Y	Y	Y	Y	N
14 Eshoo	Y	Y	Y	Y	Y	N
15 Honda	Y	Y	Y	Y	Y	N
16 Lofgren	Y	Y	Y	Y	Y	N
17 Farr	Y	Y	Y	Y	Y	N
18 Cardoza	Y	Y	N	Y	Y	N
19 Denham	Y	N	N	N	N	Y
20 Costa	Y	Y	Y	Y	Y	N
21 Nunes	Y	N	N	N	N	Y
22 McCarthy	Y	N	N	N	N	Y
23 Capps	Y	Y	Y	Y	Y	N
24 Gallegly	Y	N	N	N	N	Y
25 McKeon	Y	N	N	N	N	Y
26 Dreier	Y	N	N	N	N	Y
27 Sherman	Y	Y	Y	Y	Y	N
28 Berman	Y	Y	Y	Y	Y	N
29 Schiff	Y	Y	Y	Y	Y	N
30 Waxman	Y	Y	Y	Y	Y	N
31 Becerra	Y	Y	Y	Y	Y	N
32 Chu	Y	Y	Y	Y	Y	N
33 Bass	Y	Y	Y	Y	Y	N
34 Roybal-Allard	Y	Y	Y	Y	Y	N
35 Waters	Y	Y	Y	Y	Y	N
36 Hahn	Y	Y	Y	Y	Y	N
37 Richardson	Y	?	Y	Y	Y	N
38 Napolitano	Y	Y	Y	Y	Y	N
39 Sánchez, Linda	Y	Y	Y	Y	Y	N
40 Royce	Y	N	N	N	N	Y
41 Lewis	Y	N	N	N	N	Y
42 Miller, Gary	Y	N	N	N	N	Y
43 Baca	Y	Y	Y	Y	Y	N
44 Calvert	Y	N	N	N	N	Y
45 Bono Mack	Y	N	N	N	N	Y
46 Rohrabacher	Y	N	N	?	N	Y
47 Sanchez, Loretta	Y	Y	Y	Y	Y	N
48 Campbell	Y	N	N	N	N	Y
49 Issa	Y	N	N	N	N	Y
50 Bilbray	Y	Y	Y	Y	Y	N
51 Filner	Y	Y	Y	Y	Y	N
52 Hunter	Y	N	N	N	N	Y
53 Davis	Y	Y	Y	Y	Y	N

	133	134	135	136	137	138
COLORADO						
1 DeGette	Y	Y	Y	Y	Y	N
2 Polis	Y	N	Y	Y	Y	N
3 Tipton	Y	N	N	N	N	Y
4 Gardner	Y	N	N	N	N	Y
5 Lamborn	Y	?	N	N	N	Y
6 Coffman	Y	N	N	Y	N	Y
7 Perlmutter	Y	Y	Y	Y	Y	N
CONNECTICUT						
1 Larson	Y	Y	+	Y	Y	N
2 Courtney	Y	Y	Y	Y	Y	N
3 DeLauro	Y	Y	Y	Y	Y	N
4 Himes	Y	Y	Y	Y	Y	N
5 Murphy	Y	Y	Y	Y	Y	N
DELAWARE						
AL Carney	Y	Y	Y	Y	Y	N
FLORIDA						
1 Miller	Y	N	N	N	N	Y
2 Southerland	Y	N	N	N	N	Y
3 Brown	Y	Y	Y	Y	Y	N
4 Crenshaw	Y	N	N	N	N	Y
5 Nugent	Y	N	N	N	N	Y
6 Stearns	Y	N	N	N	N	Y
7 Mica	Y	N	N	N	N	Y
8 Webster	Y	N	N	N	N	Y
9 Bilirakis	Y	N	N	N	N	Y
10 Young	Y	N	N	N	N	Y
11 Castor	Y	Y	Y	Y	Y	N
12 Ross	Y	N	N	N	N	Y
13 Buchanan	Y	N	N	N	N	Y
14 Mack	?	?	?	?	?	?
15 Posey	Y	N	N	N	N	Y
16 Rooney	Y	N	N	N	N	Y
17 Wilson	Y	?	Y	Y	Y	N
18 Ros-Lehtinen	Y	N	N	N	N	Y
19 Deutch	Y	Y	Y	Y	Y	N
20 Wasserman Schultz	Y	Y	Y	Y	Y	N
21 Diaz-Balart	Y	–	–	–	–	+
22 West	Y	N	N	N	N	Y
23 Hastings	Y	Y	Y	Y	Y	N
24 Adams	Y	N	N	N	N	Y
25 Rivera	Y	N	N	N	N	Y
GEORGIA						
1 Kingston	Y	N	N	N	N	Y
2 Bishop	Y	Y	Y	Y	Y	N
3 Westmoreland	Y	N	N	N	N	Y
4 Johnson	Y	Y	Y	Y	Y	N
5 Lewis	Y	Y	Y	Y	Y	N
6 Price	Y	N	N	N	N	Y
7 Woodall	Y	N	N	N	N	Y
8 Scott, A.	Y	N	N	N	N	Y
9 Graves	Y	N	N	N	N	Y
10 Broun	N	N	N	N	N	Y
11 Gingrey	Y	N	N	N	N	Y
12 Barrow	Y	Y	Y	Y	Y	N
13 Scott, D.	Y	Y	Y	Y	Y	N
HAWAII						
1 Hanabusa	Y	Y	Y	Y	Y	N
2 Hirono	Y	Y	Y	Y	Y	N
IDAHO						
1 Labrador	Y	N	N	N	N	Y
2 Simpson	Y	N	N	N	N	Y
ILLINOIS						
1 Rush	Y	?	Y	Y	Y	N
2 Jackson	?	?	?	?	?	?
3 Lipinski	Y	Y	Y	Y	Y	N
4 Gutierrez	Y	Y	Y	Y	Y	N
5 Quigley	Y	Y	Y	Y	Y	N
6 Roskam	Y	N	N	N	N	Y
7 Davis	Y	Y	Y	Y	Y	N
8 Walsh	Y	N	N	N	N	Y
9 Schakowsky	Y	Y	Y	Y	Y	N
10 Dold	Y	Y	N	Y	N	Y
11 Kinzinger	Y	N	N	N	N	Y
12 Costello	Y	Y	Y	Y	Y	N
13 Biggert	Y	N	N	N	N	Y
14 Hultgren	Y	N	N	N	N	Y
15 Johnson	Y	N	N	N	N	Y

KEY   **Republicans**   Democrats

Y Voted for (yea)	**X** Paired against	**C** Voted "present" to avoid possible conflict of interest
# Paired for	**–** Announced against	
+ Announced for	**P** Voted "present"	**?** Did not vote or otherwise make a position known
N Voted against (nay)		

	133	134	135	136	137	138
16 **Manzullo**	Y	N	Y	N	N	Y
17 **Schilling**	Y	N	N	N	N	Y
18 **Schock**	Y	N	N	N	N	Y
19 **Shimkus**	Y	N	N	N	N	Y
INDIANA						
1 Visclosky	Y	Y	Y	Y	Y	N
2 Donnelly	Y	Y	Y	Y	Y	Y
3 **Stutzman**	Y	N	N	N	N	Y
4 **Rokita**	Y	N	N	N	N	Y
5 **Burton**	Y	N	N	N	N	Y
6 **Pence**	Y	N	N	N	N	Y
7 Carson	Y	Y	Y	Y	Y	N
8 **Bucshon**	Y	N	N	N	N	Y
9 **Young**	Y	N	N	N	N	Y
IOWA						
1 Braley	Y	Y	Y	Y	Y	N
2 Loebsack	Y	Y	Y	Y	Y	N
3 Boswell	?	Y	Y	Y	Y	N
4 **Latham**	Y	Y	N	N	N	Y
5 **King**	Y	N	N	N	N	Y
KANSAS						
1 **Huelskamp**	N	N	N	N	N	Y
2 **Jenkins**	Y	N	N	N	N	Y
3 **Yoder**	Y	N	N	N	N	Y
4 **Pompeo**	Y	N	N	N	N	Y
KENTUCKY						
1 **Whitfield**	Y	N	N	N	N	Y
2 **Guthrie**	Y	N	N	N	N	Y
3 Yarmuth	Y	Y	Y	Y	Y	N
4 **Davis**	Y	N	N	N	N	Y
5 **Rogers**	Y	N	N	N	N	Y
6 Chandler	Y	Y	Y	Y	Y	N
LOUISIANA						
1 **Scalise**	Y	N	N	N	N	Y
2 Richmond	Y	Y	Y	Y	Y	N
3 **Landry**	?	N	N	N	N	Y
4 **Fleming**	Y	N	N	N	N	Y
5 **Alexander**	Y	N	N	Y	N	Y
6 **Cassidy**	Y	N	N	N	N	Y
7 **Boustany**	Y	N	N	N	N	Y
MAINE						
1 Pingree	Y	Y	Y	Y	Y	N
2 Michaud	Y	N	Y	Y	Y	N
MARYLAND						
1 **Harris**	Y	N	N	N	N	Y
2 Ruppersberger	Y	?	?	?	?	?
3 Sarbanes	Y	Y	Y	Y	Y	N
4 Edwards	Y	Y	Y	Y	Y	N
5 Hoyer	Y	Y	Y	Y	Y	N
6 **Bartlett**	Y	Y	N	N	N	Y
7 Cummings	Y	Y	Y	Y	Y	N
8 Van Hollen	Y	Y	Y	Y	Y	N
MASSACHUSETTS						
1 Olver	Y	Y	Y	Y	Y	N
2 Neal	?	Y	Y	Y	Y	N
3 McGovern	Y	Y	Y	Y	Y	N
4 Frank	Y	Y	Y	N	Y	N
5 Tsongas	Y	Y	Y	Y	Y	N
6 Tierney	Y	Y	Y	Y	Y	N
7 Markey	Y	Y	Y	Y	Y	N
8 Capuano	Y	Y	Y	Y	Y	N
9 Lynch	Y	Y	Y	Y	Y	N
10 Keating	Y	Y	Y	Y	Y	N
MICHIGAN						
1 **Benishek**	Y	N	N	N	N	Y
2 **Huizenga**	+	N	N	N	N	Y
3 **Amash**	N	N	N	N	N	Y
4 **Camp**	Y	N	N	N	N	Y
5 Kildee	Y	Y	Y	Y	Y	N
6 **Upton**	Y	N	N	N	N	Y
7 **Walberg**	Y	N	N	N	N	Y
8 **Rogers**	Y	N	N	N	N	Y
9 Peters	Y	Y	Y	Y	Y	N
10 **Miller**	Y	N	N	N	N	Y
11 **McCotter**	Y	N	N	N	N	Y
12 Levin	Y	Y	Y	Y	Y	N
13 Clarke	Y	Y	Y	Y	Y	N
14 Conyers	Y	Y	Y	Y	Y	N
15 Dingell	Y	Y	Y	Y	Y	N
MINNESOTA						
1 Walz	Y	Y	Y	Y	Y	N
2 **Kline**	Y	N	N	N	N	Y
3 **Paulsen**	Y	Y	N	N	N	Y
4 McCollum	Y	Y	Y	Y	Y	N

	133	134	135	136	137	138
5 Ellison	Y	Y	Y	Y	Y	N
6 **Bachmann**	Y	N	N	N	N	Y
7 Peterson	Y	Y	N	Y	Y	Y
8 **Cravaack**	Y	N	N	N	N	Y
MISSISSIPPI						
1 **Nunnelee**	Y	N	N	N	N	Y
2 Thompson	Y	Y	Y	Y	Y	N
3 **Harper**	Y	N	N	N	N	Y
4 **Palazzo**	Y	N	N	N	N	Y
MISSOURI						
1 Clay	Y	Y	Y	Y	Y	N
2 **Akin**	+	–	–	–	–	+
3 Carnahan	Y	Y	Y	Y	Y	N
4 **Hartzler**	Y	N	N	N	N	Y
5 Cleaver	Y	Y	Y	Y	Y	N
6 **Graves**	Y	N	N	N	N	Y
7 **Long**	Y	N	N	N	N	Y
8 **Emerson**	Y	N	N	N	N	Y
9 **Luetkemeyer**	Y	N	N	N	N	Y
MONTANA						
AL **Rehberg**	Y	N	N	N	N	Y
NEBRASKA						
1 **Fortenberry**	Y	Y	N	N	N	Y
2 **Terry**	Y	N	N	N	N	Y
3 **Smith**	Y	N	N	N	N	Y
NEVADA						
1 Berkley	Y	Y	Y	Y	+	N
2 **Amodei**	Y	Y	N	N	N	Y
3 **Heck**	Y	Y	N	N	N	Y
NEW HAMPSHIRE						
1 **Guinta**	Y	N	N	Y	N	Y
2 **Bass**	Y	N	N	N	N	Y
NEW JERSEY						
1 Andrews	Y	Y	Y	Y	Y	N
2 **LoBiondo**	Y	Y	N	Y	N	Y
3 **Runyan**	Y	Y	N	N	N	Y
4 **Smith**	Y	Y	N	N	N	Y
5 **Garrett**	Y	N	N	N	N	Y
6 Pallone	Y	Y	Y	Y	Y	N
7 **Lance**	Y	N	N	N	N	Y
8 Pascrell	Y	Y	Y	Y	Y	N
9 Rothman	Y	Y	Y	Y	Y	N
10 Vacant						
11 **Frelinghuysen**	Y	N	N	?	N	Y
12 Holt	Y	Y	Y	Y	Y	N
13 Sires	Y	Y	Y	Y	Y	N
NEW MEXICO						
1 Heinrich	Y	Y	Y	Y	Y	N
2 **Pearce**	Y	N	N	N	N	Y
3 Luján	Y	Y	Y	Y	Y	N
NEW YORK						
1 Bishop	Y	Y	Y	Y	Y	N
2 Israel	Y	Y	Y	Y	Y	N
3 **King**	Y	Y	N	N	N	Y
4 McCarthy	Y	Y	Y	Y	Y	N
5 Ackerman	Y	Y	Y	Y	Y	N
6 Meeks	Y	Y	Y	Y	Y	?
7 Crowley	Y	Y	Y	Y	Y	N
8 Nadler	Y	Y	Y	Y	Y	N
9 **Turner**	Y	N	N	N	N	Y
10 Towns	Y	Y	Y	Y	Y	N
11 Clarke	Y	Y	Y	Y	Y	N
12 Velázquez	Y	Y	Y	Y	Y	N
13 **Grimm**	Y	N	N	N	N	Y
14 Maloney	Y	N	Y	Y	Y	N
15 Rangel	?	?	?	?	?	?
16 Serrano	Y	Y	Y	Y	Y	N
17 Engel	?	Y	Y	Y	?	N
18 Lowey	Y	Y	Y	Y	Y	N
19 **Hayworth**	Y	N	N	N	N	Y
20 **Gibson**	Y	Y	N	Y	N	Y
21 Tonko	Y	Y	Y	Y	Y	N
22 Hinchey	Y	Y	Y	Y	Y	N
23 Owens	Y	Y	Y	Y	N	Y
24 **Hanna**	Y	N	N	Y	N	Y
25 **Buerkle**	Y	N	N	Y	N	Y
26 Hochul	Y	Y	N	Y	Y	Y
27 Higgins	Y	Y	Y	Y	Y	N
28 Slaughter	Y	Y	Y	Y	Y	N
29 **Reed**	Y	N	N	N	N	Y
NORTH CAROLINA						
1 Butterfield	Y	Y	Y	Y	Y	N
2 **Ellmers**	Y	N	N	N	N	Y
3 **Jones**	Y	Y	Y	Y	Y	Y
4 Price	Y	?	?	?	Y	N

	133	134	135	136	137	138
5 **Foxx**	Y	N	N	N	N	Y
6 **Coble**	Y	N	N	N	N	Y
7 McIntyre	Y	Y	Y	Y	Y	Y
8 Kissell	Y	Y	Y	Y	Y	N
9 **Myrick**	Y	N	N	N	N	Y
10 **McHenry**	Y	N	N	N	N	Y
11 Shuler	Y	Y	N	Y	N	Y
12 Watt	Y	Y	Y	Y	Y	N
13 Miller	Y	Y	Y	Y	Y	N
NORTH DAKOTA						
AL **Berg**	Y	N	N	N	N	Y
OHIO						
1 **Chabot**	Y	N	N	N	N	Y
2 **Schmidt**	Y	N	N	N	N	Y
3 **Turner**	Y	N	N	N	N	Y
4 **Jordan**	Y	N	N	N	N	Y
5 **Latta**	Y	N	N	N	N	Y
6 **Johnson**	Y	N	N	N	N	Y
7 **Austria**	Y	N	N	N	N	Y
8 **Boehner**						
9 Kaptur	Y	Y	Y	?	Y	N
10 Kucinich	Y	Y	Y	Y	Y	N
11 Fudge	Y	Y	Y	Y	Y	N
12 **Tiberi**	Y	N	N	N	N	Y
13 Sutton	Y	Y	Y	Y	Y	N
14 **LaTourette**	Y	N	N	N	N	Y
15 **Stivers**	Y	N	N	N	N	Y
16 **Renacci**	Y	N	N	N	N	Y
17 Ryan	Y	Y	Y	Y	Y	N
18 **Gibbs**	Y	N	N	N	N	Y
OKLAHOMA						
1 **Sullivan**	Y	N	N	N	N	Y
2 Boren	Y	Y	N	Y	Y	Y
3 **Lucas**	Y	N	N	N	N	Y
4 **Cole**	Y	N	N	N	N	Y
5 **Lankford**	Y	N	N	N	N	Y
OREGON						
1 Bonamici	Y	Y	Y	Y	Y	N
2 **Walden**	Y	N	N	N	N	Y
3 Blumenauer	Y	Y	Y	Y	Y	N
4 DeFazio	Y	Y	Y	Y	Y	N
5 Schrader	Y	Y	N	Y	Y	Y
PENNSYLVANIA						
1 Brady	Y	Y	Y	Y	Y	N
2 Fattah	Y	Y	Y	Y	Y	N
3 **Kelly**	Y	N	N	N	N	Y
4 Altmire	Y	Y	Y	Y	Y	N
5 **Thompson**	Y	N	N	N	N	Y
6 **Gerlach**	Y	N	N	Y	N	Y
7 **Meehan**	Y	N	N	N	N	Y
8 **Fitzpatrick**	Y	Y	N	N	N	Y
9 **Shuster**	Y	N	N	N	N	Y
10 **Marino**	Y	N	N	N	N	Y
11 **Barletta**	Y	N	N	N	N	Y
12 Critz	Y	Y	Y	Y	Y	N
13 Schwartz	Y	Y	Y	Y	Y	N
14 Doyle	Y	Y	Y	Y	Y	N
15 **Dent**	Y	Y	N	Y	N	Y
16 **Pitts**	Y	N	N	N	N	Y
17 Holden	Y	Y	Y	Y	Y	N
18 **Murphy**	Y	N	N	N	N	Y
19 **Platts**	Y	N	Y	N	N	Y
RHODE ISLAND						
1 Cicilline	Y	Y	Y	Y	Y	N
2 Langevin	Y	Y	Y	Y	Y	N
SOUTH CAROLINA						
1 **Scott**	Y	N	N	N	N	Y
2 **Wilson**	Y	N	N	N	N	Y
3 **Duncan**	Y	N	N	N	N	Y
4 **Gowdy**	Y	N	N	N	N	Y
5 **Mulvaney**	Y	N	N	N	N	Y
6 Clyburn	Y	Y	Y	Y	Y	N
SOUTH DAKOTA						
AL **Noem**	Y	N	N	N	N	Y
TENNESSEE						
1 **Roe**	Y	N	N	N	N	Y
2 **Duncan**	Y	N	N	N	N	Y
3 **Fleischmann**	Y	N	N	N	N	Y
4 **DesJarlais**	Y	N	N	N	N	Y
5 Cooper	Y	Y	N	Y	Y	N
6 **Black**	Y	N	N	N	N	Y
7 **Blackburn**	Y	N	N	N	N	Y
8 **Fincher**	Y	N	N	N	N	Y
9 Cohen	Y	Y	Y	Y	Y	N

	133	134	135	136	137	138
TEXAS						
1 **Gohmert**	Y	N	N	Y	N	Y
2 **Poe**	Y	N	N	N	N	Y
3 **Johnson, S.**	Y	N	N	N	N	Y
4 **Hall**	Y	N	N	N	N	Y
5 **Hensarling**	Y	N	N	N	N	Y
6 **Barton**	Y	N	Y	N	N	Y
7 **Culberson**	Y	N	N	N	N	Y
8 **Brady**	Y	N	N	N	N	Y
9 Green, A.	Y	Y	Y	Y	Y	N
10 **McCaul**	Y	N	N	N	N	Y
11 **Conaway**	Y	N	N	N	N	Y
12 **Granger**	Y	N	N	N	N	Y
13 **Thornberry**	Y	N	N	N	N	Y
14 **Paul**	N	?	?	?	?	?
15 Hinojosa	Y	Y	+	Y	Y	N
16 Reyes	Y	Y	Y	Y	Y	N
17 **Flores**	?	?	?	?	?	?
18 Jackson Lee	Y	?	?	?	Y	N
19 **Neugebauer**	Y	N	N	N	N	Y
20 Gonzalez	Y	Y	Y	Y	Y	N
21 **Smith**	Y	N	N	N	N	Y
22 **Olson**	Y	N	N	N	N	Y
23 **Canseco**	Y	N	N	N	N	Y
24 **Marchant**	?	?	?	?	?	?
25 Doggett	Y	Y	Y	Y	Y	N
26 **Burgess**	Y	Y	N	N	N	Y
27 **Farenthold**	Y	N	N	N	N	Y
28 Cuellar	Y	Y	Y	Y	Y	Y
29 Green, G.	Y	Y	Y	Y	Y	N
30 Johnson, E.	Y	Y	Y	Y	Y	N
31 **Carter**	Y	N	N	N	N	Y
32 **Sessions**	Y	N	N	N	N	Y
UTAH						
1 **Bishop**	Y	N	N	N	N	Y
2 Matheson	Y	Y	Y	N	Y	Y
3 **Chaffetz**	Y	N	N	N	N	Y
VERMONT						
AL Welch	Y	+	+	+	Y	N
VIRGINIA						
1 **Wittman**	Y	Y	N	Y	N	Y
2 **Rigell**	Y	N	N	N	N	Y
3 Scott	Y	Y	Y	Y	Y	N
4 **Forbes**	Y	N	N	N	N	Y
5 **Hurt**	Y	N	N	N	N	Y
6 **Goodlatte**	Y	N	N	N	N	Y
7 **Cantor**	Y	N	N	N	N	Y
8 Moran	Y	Y	Y	Y	Y	N
9 **Griffith**	Y	Y	N	N	N	Y
10 **Wolf**	Y	N	N	N	N	Y
11 Connolly	Y	Y	Y	Y	Y	N
WASHINGTON						
1 Vacant						
2 Larsen	Y	Y	Y	Y	Y	N
3 **Herrera Beutler**	Y	N	N	N	N	Y
4 **Hastings**	Y	N	N	N	N	Y
5 **McMorris Rodgers**	Y	N	N	N	N	Y
6 Dicks	?	Y	Y	Y	Y	N
7 McDermott	Y	Y	Y	Y	Y	N
8 **Reichert**	Y	N	N	N	N	Y
9 Smith	Y	Y	Y	Y	Y	N
WEST VIRGINIA						
1 **McKinley**	Y	N	N	N	N	Y
2 **Capito**	Y	N	N	N	N	Y
3 Rahall	Y	Y	Y	Y	Y	N
WISCONSIN						
1 **Ryan**	Y	N	N	N	N	Y
2 Baldwin	Y	Y	Y	Y	Y	N
3 Kind	Y	Y	Y	Y	Y	N
4 Moore	Y	Y	Y	Y	Y	N
5 **Sensenbrenner**	Y	N	N	N	N	Y
6 **Petri**	Y	N	N	N	N	Y
7 **Duffy**	Y	N	N	N	N	Y
8 **Ribble**	Y	N	N	Y	N	Y
WYOMING						
AL **Lummis**	Y	N	N	N	N	Y

IN THE HOUSE | By Vote Number

139. **H Con Res 112. Fiscal 2013 Budget Resolution/Previous Question.** Woodall, R-Ga., motion to order the previous question (thus ending debate and the possibility of amendment) on the rule (H Res 597) which would provide for House floor consideration of the concurrent resolution that would set broad spending and revenue targets for the next 10 years. Motion agreed to 235-183: R 234-0; D 1-183. March 28, 2012.

140. **H Con Res 112. Fiscal 2013 Budget Resolution/Rule.** Adoption of the rule (H Res 597) that would provide for House floor consideration of the concurrent resolution that would set broad spending and revenue targets for the next 10 years. The rule also would allow the House to consider a measure related to extending surface transportation programs under suspension of the rules on the legislative day of Thursday, March 29, 2012. Adopted 241-184: R 236-3; D 5-181. March 28, 2012.

141. **HR 1339. National Guard Birthplace/Passage.** Platts, R-Pa., motion to suspend the rules and pass the bill that would designate Salem, Mass., as the birthplace of the National Guard. Motion agreed to 413-6: R 227-6; D 186-0. A two-thirds majority of those present and voting (280 in this case) is required for passage under suspension of the rules. March 28, 2012.

142. **Procedural Motion/Journal.** Approval of the House Journal of Tuesday, March 27, 2012. Approved 300-111: R 178-55; D 122-56. March 28, 2012.

143. **H Con Res 112. Fiscal 2013 Budget Resolution/President's Budget Substitute.** Mulvaney, R-S.C., substitute amendment that would provide $2.981 trillion in new budget authority in fiscal 2013, not including off-budget accounts. It would assume the replacement of the $1.2 trillion sequestration scheduled under the 2011 debt limit law with $517 billion in mandatory savings over the next 10 years and assume changes to the tax code that would raise more than $1.5 trillion. It would assume the expiration of the 2001 and 2003 tax cuts for single taxpayers with incomes over $200,000 ($250,000 for married couples), and would include $364 billion in savings from Medicare, Medicaid and other health programs. Rejected in Committee of the Whole 0-414: R 0-239; D 0-175. March 28, 2012.

144. **H Con Res 112. Fiscal 2013 Budget Resolution/Congressional Black Caucus Substitute.** Cleaver, D-Mo., substitute amendment that would provide $3.128 trillion in new budget authority in fiscal 2013, not including off-budget accounts. It would assume the cancellation of the sequestration and cap fiscal 2013 defense spending at $554 billion. It would call for increased spending for education and job training. It would assume additional revenue, including most of the proposals in the president's budget as well as changes to the treatment of capital gains and dividends. It would call for increased funding for transportation projects, health care services and veterans' benefits and services. Rejected in Committee of the Whole 107-314: R 0-239; D 107-75. March 28, 2012.

	139	140	141	142	143	144
ALABAMA						
1 Bonner	Y	Y	Y	Y	N	N
2 Roby	Y	Y	Y	Y	N	N
3 Rogers	Y	Y	Y	Y	N	N
4 Aderholt	Y	Y	Y	Y	N	N
5 Brooks	Y	Y	Y	Y	N	N
6 Bachus	Y	Y	Y	Y	N	N
7 Sewell	N	N	Y	Y	?	Y
ALASKA						
AL Young	Y	Y	Y	N	N	N
ARIZONA						
1 Gosar	Y	Y	Y	Y	N	N
2 Franks	Y	Y	Y	Y	N	N
3 Quayle	Y	Y	Y	N	N	N
4 Pastor	N	N	Y	Y	N	Y
5 Schweikert	Y	Y	Y	Y	N	N
6 Flake	Y	Y	Y	N	N	N
7 Grijalva	N	N	Y	N	?	Y
8 Vacant						
ARKANSAS						
1 Crawford	Y	Y	Y	Y	N	N
2 Griffin	Y	Y	Y	N	N	N
3 Womack	Y	Y	Y	Y	N	N
4 Ross	N	N	Y	Y	N	N
CALIFORNIA						
1 Thompson	N	N	Y	N	N	N
2 Herger	Y	Y	Y	Y	N	N
3 Lungren	Y	Y	Y	Y	N	N
4 McClintock	Y	Y	Y	Y	N	N
5 Matsui	N	N	Y	Y	N	N
6 Woolsey	N	N	Y	Y	N	Y
7 Miller, George	–	N	Y	N	N	N
8 Pelosi	N	N	Y	Y	N	N
9 Lee	N	N	Y	N	N	Y
10 Garamendi	N	N	Y	N	N	N
11 McNerney	N	N	Y	Y	N	N
12 Speier	N	N	Y	Y	N	N
13 Stark	N	N	Y	N	N	Y
14 Eshoo	N	N	Y	Y	N	N
15 Honda	N	N	Y	N	N	Y
16 Lofgren	N	N	Y	Y	N	N
17 Farr	N	N	Y	Y	N	Y
18 Cardoza	N	N	Y	P	?	?
19 Denham	Y	Y	Y	Y	N	N
20 Costa	N	N	Y	N	N	N
21 Nunes	Y	Y	Y	Y	N	N
22 McCarthy	Y	Y	Y	Y	N	N
23 Capps	N	N	Y	Y	N	N
24 Gallegly	Y	Y	Y	Y	N	N
25 McKeon	Y	Y	Y	Y	N	N
26 Dreier	Y	Y	Y	?	N	N
27 Sherman	N	N	Y	Y	N	N
28 Berman	N	N	Y	Y	N	N
29 Schiff	N	N	Y	Y	N	N
30 Waxman	N	N	Y	Y	N	Y
31 Becerra	N	N	Y	Y	N	Y
32 Chu	N	N	Y	N	N	Y
33 Bass	N	N	Y	?	N	Y
34 Roybal-Allard	N	N	Y	Y	N	Y
35 Waters	N	N	Y	Y	N	Y
36 Hahn	N	N	Y	Y	N	Y
37 Richardson	N	N	Y	Y	N	Y
38 Napolitano	N	N	Y	Y	N	Y
39 Sánchez, Linda	N	N	Y	?	N	Y
40 Royce	Y	Y	Y	Y	N	N
41 Lewis	Y	Y	Y	Y	N	N
42 Miller, Gary	Y	Y	Y	Y	N	N
43 Baca	N	N	Y	Y	N	Y
44 Calvert	Y	Y	Y	Y	N	N
45 Bono Mack	Y	Y	Y	Y	N	N
46 Rohrabacher	Y	Y	Y	Y	N	N
47 Sanchez, Loretta	N	N	Y	N	N	Y
48 Campbell	Y	Y	Y	Y	N	N
49 Issa	Y	Y	Y	Y	N	N
50 Bilbray	Y	Y	Y	Y	N	N
51 Filner	–	–	+	–	–	+
52 Hunter	Y	Y	Y	N	N	N
53 Davis	N	N	Y	Y	N	N

	139	140	141	142	143	144
COLORADO						
1 DeGette	N	N	Y	Y	N	N
2 Polis	N	N	Y	N	N	N
3 Tipton	Y	Y	Y	N	N	N
4 Gardner	Y	Y	Y	N	N	N
5 Lamborn	Y	Y	Y	Y	N	N
6 Coffman	Y	Y	Y	N	N	N
7 Perlmutter	N	N	Y	N	N	N
CONNECTICUT						
1 Larson	N	N	Y	Y	–	Y
2 Courtney	N	N	Y	Y	N	N
3 DeLauro	N	N	Y	Y	N	N
4 Himes	N	N	Y	N	N	N
5 Murphy	N	N	Y	Y	N	N
DELAWARE						
AL Carney	N	N	Y	Y	N	N
FLORIDA						
1 Miller	Y	Y	Y	N	N	N
2 Southerland	Y	Y	Y	N	N	N
3 Brown	N	N	Y	N	N	Y
4 Crenshaw	Y	Y	Y	N	N	N
5 Nugent	Y	Y	Y	N	N	N
6 Stearns	+	Y	Y	N	N	N
7 Mica	Y	Y	Y	N	N	N
8 Webster	Y	Y	Y	N	N	N
9 Bilirakis	Y	Y	Y	N	N	N
10 Young	Y	Y	Y	N	N	N
11 Castor	N	N	Y	N	N	Y
12 Ross	Y	Y	Y	N	N	N
13 Buchanan	Y	Y	Y	Y	N	N
14 Mack	?	?	?	?	?	?
15 Posey	Y	Y	Y	Y	N	N
16 Rooney	Y	Y	P	N	N	N
17 Wilson	N	N	Y	N	N	Y
18 Ros-Lehtinen	Y	Y	Y	N	N	N
19 Deutch	N	N	Y	Y	?	?
20 Wasserman Schultz	N	N	Y	N	N	Y
21 Diaz-Balart	Y	Y	Y	Y	N	N
22 West	Y	Y	Y	N	N	N
23 Hastings	N	N	Y	?	N	Y
24 Adams	Y	Y	Y	N	N	N
25 Rivera	Y	Y	Y	Y	N	N
GEORGIA						
1 Kingston	Y	Y	Y	Y	N	N
2 Bishop	N	N	Y	Y	N	Y
3 Westmoreland	Y	Y	Y	N	N	N
4 Johnson	N	N	Y	Y	N	Y
5 Lewis	N	N	Y	N	N	Y
6 Price	Y	Y	Y	N	N	N
7 Woodall	Y	Y	Y	N	N	N
8 Scott, A.	Y	Y	Y	N	N	N
9 Graves	Y	Y	Y	N	N	N
10 Broun	Y	Y	Y	N	N	N
11 Gingrey	Y	Y	Y	P	N	N
12 Barrow	N	N	Y	Y	N	N
13 Scott, D.	N	N	Y	Y	N	Y
HAWAII						
1 Hanabusa	N	N	Y	Y	N	Y
2 Hirono	N	N	Y	Y	N	Y
IDAHO						
1 Labrador	Y	Y	Y	Y	N	N
2 Simpson	Y	N	Y	Y	N	N
ILLINOIS						
1 Rush	N	N	Y	N	N	Y
2 Jackson	?	?	?	?	?	?
3 Lipinski	N	N	Y	Y	N	N
4 Gutierrez	N	N	Y	N	N	Y
5 Quigley	N	N	Y	Y	N	N
6 Roskam	Y	Y	Y	Y	N	N
7 Davis	N	N	Y	N	N	Y
8 Walsh	Y	Y	Y	N	N	N
9 Schakowsky	N	N	Y	N	N	Y
10 Dold	Y	Y	Y	N	N	N
11 Kinzinger	Y	Y	Y	N	N	N
12 Costello	N	N	Y	N	N	N
13 Biggert	Y	Y	Y	N	N	N
14 Hultgren	Y	Y	Y	Y	N	N
15 Johnson	Y	Y	Y	Y	N	N

	139	140	141	142	143	144
16 **Manzullo**	Y	Y	Y	N	N	N
17 **Schilling**	Y	Y	Y	N	N	N
18 **Schock**	Y	Y	Y	Y	N	N
19 **Shimkus**	?	Y	Y	Y	N	N
INDIANA						
1 Visclosky	N	N	Y	N	N	N
2 Donnelly	N	N	Y	N	N	N
3 **Stutzman**	Y	Y	Y	Y	N	N
4 **Rokita**	Y	Y	Y	Y	N	N
5 **Burton**	Y	Y	Y	Y	N	N
6 **Pence**	Y	Y	Y	Y	N	N
7 Carson	N	N	Y	Y	N	Y
8 **Bucshon**	Y	Y	Y	Y	N	N
9 **Young**	Y	Y	Y	Y	N	N
IOWA						
1 Braley	N	N	Y	Y	N	N
2 Loebsack	N	N	Y	N	N	N
3 Boswell	N	N	Y	N	N	N
4 **Latham**	Y	Y	Y	N	N	N
5 **King**	Y	Y	Y	Y	N	N
KANSAS						
1 **Huelskamp**	Y	Y	Y	N	N	N
2 **Jenkins**	Y	Y	Y	Y	N	N
3 **Yoder**	Y	Y	Y	N	N	N
4 **Pompeo**	Y	Y	Y	Y	N	N
KENTUCKY						
1 **Whitfield**	Y	Y	Y	Y	N	N
2 **Guthrie**	Y	Y	Y	Y	N	N
3 Yarmuth	N	N	Y	Y	N	Y
4 **Davis**	Y	Y	Y	?	N	N
5 **Rogers**	Y	Y	Y	Y	N	N
6 Chandler	N	Y	Y	N	N	N
LOUISIANA						
1 **Scalise**	Y	Y	Y	Y	N	N
2 Richmond	N	N	Y	N	N	Y
3 **Landry**	Y	Y	Y	N	N	N
4 **Fleming**	Y	Y	Y	Y	N	N
5 **Alexander**	Y	Y	Y	Y	N	N
6 **Cassidy**	Y	Y	Y	Y	N	N
7 **Boustany**	Y	Y	Y	Y	N	N
MAINE						
1 Pingree	N	N	Y	Y	N	Y
2 Michaud	N	N	Y	Y	N	N
MARYLAND						
1 **Harris**	Y	Y	Y	N	N	N
2 Ruppersberger	N	N	Y	Y	N	N
3 Sarbanes	N	N	Y	N	N	Y
4 Edwards	N	N	Y	N	N	Y
5 Hoyer	N	N	Y	N	N	Y
6 **Bartlett**	Y	Y	Y	Y	N	N
7 Cummings	N	N	Y	N	N	Y
8 Van Hollen	N	N	Y	?	N	Y
MASSACHUSETTS						
1 Olver	N	N	Y	N	N	Y
2 Neal	N	N	Y	N	N	Y
3 McGovern	N	N	Y	N	N	Y
4 Frank	N	N	Y	Y	N	Y
5 Tsongas	N	N	Y	Y	N	Y
6 Tierney	N	N	Y	N	N	Y
7 Markey	N	N	Y	N	N	Y
8 Capuano	N	N	Y	N	N	Y
9 Lynch	N	N	Y	N	N	Y
10 Keating	N	N	Y	Y	N	N
MICHIGAN						
1 **Benishek**	?	Y	P	N	N	N
2 **Huizenga**	Y	Y	Y	N	N	N
3 **Amash**	Y	Y	N	P	N	N
4 **Camp**	Y	Y	Y	Y	N	N
5 Kildee	N	N	Y	Y	N	Y
6 **Upton**	Y	Y	Y	Y	N	N
7 **Walberg**	Y	Y	Y	Y	N	N
8 **Rogers**	Y	Y	Y	Y	N	N
9 Peters	N	N	Y	N	N	N
10 **Miller**	Y	Y	Y	Y	N	N
11 **McCotter**	Y	Y	Y	N	N	N
12 Levin	N	N	Y	Y	N	N
13 Clarke	N	N	Y	Y	N	Y
14 Conyers	N	N	Y	Y	N	Y
15 Dingell	N	N	Y	Y	N	N
MINNESOTA						
1 Walz	N	N	Y	Y	N	N
2 **Kline**	Y	Y	Y	Y	N	N
3 **Paulsen**	Y	Y	Y	N	N	N
4 McCollum	N	N	Y	Y	N	Y
5 Ellison	N	N	Y	Y	N	Y
6 **Bachmann**	Y	Y	Y	Y	N	N
7 Peterson	N	N	Y	N	N	N
8 **Cravaack**	Y	Y	Y	N	N	N
MISSISSIPPI						
1 **Nunnelee**	Y	Y	Y	Y	N	N
2 Thompson	N	N	Y	N	N	Y
3 **Harper**	Y	Y	Y	Y	N	N
4 **Palazzo**	Y	Y	Y	Y	N	N
MISSOURI						
1 Clay	N	N	Y	Y	?	?
2 **Akin**	Y	Y	Y	Y	N	N
3 Carnahan	N	N	Y	Y	N	Y
4 **Hartzler**	Y	Y	Y	N	N	N
5 Cleaver	N	N	Y	?	N	Y
6 **Graves**	Y	Y	Y	N	N	N
7 **Long**	Y	Y	Y	Y	N	N
8 **Emerson**	Y	Y	Y	Y	N	N
9 **Luetkemeyer**	Y	Y	Y	Y	N	N
MONTANA						
AL **Rehberg**	Y	Y	Y	Y	N	N
NEBRASKA						
1 **Fortenberry**	Y	Y	Y	Y	N	N
2 **Terry**	Y	Y	Y	N	N	N
3 **Smith**	Y	Y	Y	Y	N	N
NEVADA						
1 Berkley	N	N	Y	Y	N	N
2 **Amodei**	Y	Y	Y	Y	N	N
3 **Heck**	Y	Y	Y	N	N	N
NEW HAMPSHIRE						
1 **Guinta**	Y	Y	Y	Y	N	N
2 **Bass**	Y	N	Y	Y	N	N
NEW JERSEY						
1 Andrews	N	N	Y	N	N	Y
2 **LoBiondo**	Y	Y	Y	Y	N	N
3 **Runyan**	Y	Y	Y	Y	N	N
4 **Smith**	Y	Y	Y	Y	N	N
5 **Garrett**	Y	Y	Y	N	N	N
6 Pallone	N	N	Y	N	N	Y
7 **Lance**	Y	Y	Y	Y	N	N
8 Pascrell	N	N	Y	Y	N	Y
9 Rothman	N	N	Y	Y	N	Y
10 Vacant						
11 **Frelinghuysen**	Y	Y	Y	Y	N	N
12 Holt	N	N	Y	Y	N	Y
13 Sires	N	N	Y	Y	N	Y
NEW MEXICO						
1 Heinrich	N	N	Y	Y	N	N
2 **Pearce**	Y	Y	Y	Y	N	N
3 Luján	N	N	Y	Y	N	N
NEW YORK						
1 Bishop	N	N	Y	N	N	N
2 Israel	N	N	Y	N	?	Y
3 **King**	Y	Y	Y	Y	N	N
4 McCarthy	N	N	Y	Y	N	N
5 Ackerman	N	N	Y	Y	N	Y
6 Meeks	?	?	?	?	?	?
7 Crowley	N	N	Y	Y	N	Y
8 Nadler	N	N	Y	Y	N	Y
9 **Turner**	Y	Y	Y	N	N	N
10 Towns	N	N	Y	Y	?	?
11 Clarke	N	N	Y	Y	N	Y
12 Velázquez	N	N	Y	N	N	Y
13 **Grimm**	Y	Y	Y	Y	N	N
14 Maloney	N	N	Y	Y	N	N
15 Rangel	?	?	?	?	?	?
16 Serrano	N	N	Y	Y	N	Y
17 Engel	N	N	Y	Y	N	Y
18 Lowey	N	N	Y	Y	N	N
19 **Hayworth**	Y	Y	Y	Y	N	N
20 **Gibson**	Y	Y	Y	N	N	N
21 Tonko	N	N	Y	Y	N	Y
22 Hinchey	N	N	Y	Y	N	Y
23 Owens	N	N	Y	P	N	N
24 **Hanna**	Y	Y	Y	N	N	N
25 **Buerkle**	Y	Y	Y	N	N	N
26 Hochul	N	N	Y	Y	N	N
27 Higgins	N	N	Y	Y	N	N
28 Slaughter	N	N	Y	N	N	Y
29 **Reed**	Y	Y	Y	N	N	N
NORTH CAROLINA						
1 Butterfield	N	N	Y	Y	N	Y
2 **Ellmers**	Y	Y	Y	Y	N	N
3 **Jones**	Y	Y	Y	Y	N	N
4 Price	N	N	Y	Y	N	Y
5 **Foxx**	Y	Y	Y	N	N	N
6 **Coble**	Y	Y	Y	Y	N	N
7 McIntyre	N	N	Y	Y	N	N
8 Kissell	N	Y	Y	Y	N	N
9 **Myrick**	Y	Y	Y	Y	N	N
10 **McHenry**	Y	Y	Y	Y	N	N
11 Shuler	Y	Y	Y	N	?	N
12 Watt	N	N	Y	Y	N	Y
13 Miller	N	N	Y	Y	N	Y
NORTH DAKOTA						
AL **Berg**	Y	Y	Y	Y	N	N
OHIO						
1 **Chabot**	Y	Y	Y	Y	N	N
2 **Schmidt**	Y	Y	Y	Y	N	N
3 **Turner**	Y	Y	Y	N	N	N
4 **Jordan**	Y	Y	Y	Y	N	N
5 **Latta**	Y	Y	Y	Y	N	N
6 **Johnson**	Y	Y	Y	N	N	N
7 **Austria**	Y	Y	Y	Y	N	N
8 **Boehner**						
9 Kaptur	N	N	Y	Y	?	Y
10 Kucinich	N	N	Y	N	N	N
11 Fudge	N	N	Y	Y	N	Y
12 **Tiberi**	Y	Y	Y	Y	N	N
13 Sutton	N	N	Y	Y	N	Y
14 **LaTourette**	Y	N	Y	Y	N	N
15 **Stivers**	Y	Y	Y	N	N	N
16 **Renacci**	Y	Y	Y	N	N	N
17 Ryan	N	N	Y	N	?	Y
18 **Gibbs**	Y	Y	Y	Y	N	N
OKLAHOMA						
1 **Sullivan**	Y	Y	?	Y	N	N
2 Boren	N	N	Y	Y	N	N
3 **Lucas**	Y	Y	Y	Y	N	N
4 **Cole**	Y	Y	Y	Y	N	N
5 **Lankford**	Y	Y	Y	Y	N	N
OREGON						
1 Bonamici	N	N	Y	Y	N	N
2 **Walden**	Y	Y	Y	Y	N	N
3 Blumenauer	N	N	Y	Y	N	Y
4 DeFazio	N	N	Y	N	N	Y
5 Schrader	N	N	Y	Y	N	N
PENNSYLVANIA						
1 Brady	N	N	Y	N	N	Y
2 Fattah	N	N	Y	?	N	Y
3 **Kelly**	Y	Y	Y	Y	N	N
4 Altmire	N	N	Y	Y	N	N
5 **Thompson**	Y	Y	Y	Y	N	N
6 **Gerlach**	Y	Y	Y	N	N	N
7 **Meehan**	Y	Y	Y	Y	N	N
8 **Fitzpatrick**	Y	Y	Y	N	N	N
9 **Shuster**	Y	Y	Y	Y	N	N
10 **Marino**	Y	Y	Y	Y	N	N
11 **Barletta**	Y	Y	Y	Y	N	N
12 Critz	N	N	Y	Y	N	N
13 Schwartz	N	N	Y	Y	N	N
14 Doyle	N	N	Y	Y	N	Y
15 **Dent**	Y	Y	Y	N	N	N
16 **Pitts**	Y	Y	Y	Y	N	N
17 Holden	N	N	Y	Y	N	N
18 **Murphy**	Y	Y	Y	Y	N	N
19 **Platts**	Y	Y	Y	Y	N	N
RHODE ISLAND						
1 Cicilline	N	N	Y	Y	N	N
2 Langevin	N	N	Y	Y	N	N
SOUTH CAROLINA						
1 **Scott**	Y	Y	Y	Y	N	N
2 **Wilson**	Y	Y	Y	Y	N	N
3 **Duncan**	Y	Y	Y	Y	N	N
4 **Gowdy**	Y	Y	Y	Y	N	N
5 **Mulvaney**	Y	Y	Y	Y	N	N
6 Clyburn	N	N	Y	N	N	Y
SOUTH DAKOTA						
AL **Noem**	Y	Y	Y	Y	N	N
TENNESSEE						
1 **Roe**	?	Y	Y	N	N	N
2 **Duncan**	Y	Y	Y	Y	N	N
3 **Fleischmann**	Y	Y	Y	Y	N	N
4 **DesJarlais**	Y	Y	Y	Y	N	N
5 Cooper	N	Y	Y	Y	N	N
6 **Black**	Y	Y	Y	Y	N	N
7 **Blackburn**	Y	Y	Y	Y	N	N
8 **Fincher**	Y	Y	Y	Y	N	N
9 Cohen	N	N	Y	Y	N	Y
TEXAS						
1 **Gohmert**	Y	Y	Y	?	N	N
2 **Poe**	Y	Y	Y	N	N	N
3 **Johnson, S.**	Y	Y	Y	Y	N	N
4 **Hall**	Y	Y	Y	Y	N	N
5 **Hensarling**	Y	Y	Y	Y	N	N
6 **Barton**	Y	Y	Y	Y	N	N
7 **Culberson**	Y	Y	Y	Y	N	N
8 **Brady**	Y	Y	Y	Y	N	N
9 Green, A.	N	N	Y	Y	N	Y
10 **McCaul**	Y	Y	Y	Y	N	N
11 **Conaway**	Y	Y	Y	N	N	N
12 **Granger**	Y	Y	Y	Y	N	N
13 **Thornberry**	Y	Y	Y	Y	N	N
14 **Paul**	?	?	?	?	?	?
15 Hinojosa	N	N	Y	Y	N	Y
16 Reyes	N	N	Y	N	N	N
17 **Flores**	Y	Y	Y	Y	N	N
18 Jackson Lee	N	N	Y	N	N	Y
19 **Neugebauer**	Y	Y	Y	Y	N	N
20 Gonzalez	?	N	Y	Y	N	N
21 **Smith**	Y	Y	Y	Y	N	N
22 **Olson**	Y	Y	Y	Y	N	N
23 **Canseco**	Y	Y	Y	Y	N	N
24 **Marchant**	Y	Y	Y	Y	N	N
25 Doggett	N	N	Y	N	N	N
26 **Burgess**	Y	Y	Y	N	N	N
27 **Farenthold**	Y	Y	Y	Y	N	N
28 Cuellar	N	N	Y	Y	N	N
29 Green, G.	N	N	Y	N	N	Y
30 Johnson, E.	N	N	Y	Y	N	Y
31 **Carter**	Y	Y	Y	Y	N	N
32 **Sessions**	Y	Y	Y	Y	N	N
UTAH						
1 **Bishop**	Y	Y	Y	Y	N	N
2 Matheson	N	Y	Y	N	N	N
3 **Chaffetz**	Y	Y	Y	Y	N	N
VERMONT						
AL Welch	N	N	Y	Y	N	Y
VIRGINIA						
1 **Wittman**	Y	Y	P	Y	N	N
2 **Rigell**	Y	Y	Y	Y	N	N
3 Scott	N	N	Y	Y	N	Y
4 **Forbes**	Y	Y	P	N	N	N
5 **Hurt**	Y	Y	N	Y	N	N
6 **Goodlatte**	+	Y	N	Y	N	N
7 **Cantor**	Y	Y	?	Y	N	N
8 Moran	N	N	Y	Y	N	Y
9 **Griffith**	Y	Y	N	Y	N	N
10 **Wolf**	Y	Y	N	Y	N	N
11 Connolly	N	N	Y	Y	N	Y
WASHINGTON						
1 Vacant						
2 Larsen	N	N	Y	Y	N	N
3 **Herrera Beutler**	Y	Y	Y	N	N	N
4 **Hastings**	Y	Y	Y	Y	N	N
5 **McMorris Rodgers**	Y	Y	Y	Y	N	N
6 Dicks	N	N	Y	Y	N	N
7 McDermott	N	N	Y	N	N	Y
8 **Reichert**	Y	Y	Y	Y	N	N
9 Smith	N	N	Y	Y	N	Y
WEST VIRGINIA						
1 **McKinley**	Y	Y	N	N	N	N
2 **Capito**	Y	Y	Y	?	N	N
3 Rahall	N	N	Y	N	N	N
WISCONSIN						
1 **Ryan**	Y	Y	Y	Y	N	N
2 Baldwin	N	N	Y	N	N	N
3 Kind	N	N	Y	N	N	N
4 Moore	N	N	Y	N	N	Y
5 **Sensenbrenner**	Y	Y	Y	Y	N	N
6 **Petri**	Y	Y	Y	Y	N	N
7 **Duffy**	Y	Y	Y	N	N	N
8 **Ribble**	Y	Y	Y	N	N	N
WYOMING						
AL **Lummis**	Y	Y	Y	Y	N	N

IN THE HOUSE | By Vote Number

145. H Con Res 112. Fiscal 2013 Budget Resolution/Bipartisan Budget Substitute.
Cooper, D-Tenn., substitute amendment that would provide $2.87 trillion in new budget authority in fiscal 2013, not including off-budget accounts. It would call for $4 trillion in deficit reduction through spending cuts and revenue increases. It would call for a comprehensive overhaul of the tax code to simplify the system and reduce marginal tax rates, as well as changes to the health care system that would achieve savings of $485 billion through 2021. It would direct the Budget Committee to report a bill that would repeal the sequester and direct seven House committees to find savings in fiscal 2013 through 2021. Rejected in Committee of the Whole 38-382: R 16-223; D 22-159. March 28, 2012.

146. HR 4281. Surface Transportation Extension/Previous Question.
Webster, R-Fla., motion to order the previous question (thus ending debate and the possibility of amendment) on the rule (H Res 600) that would provide for House floor consideration of the bill that would extend the authorization for surface transportation programs for three months, through June 30. Motion agreed to 237-178: R 236-0; D 1-178. March 29, 2012.

147. HR 4281. Surface Transportation Extension/Passage.
Passage of the bill that would extend the authorization for surface transportation programs, including federal aid highway, mass transit and safety programs, for three months, through June 30. It also would extend the authority to spend money from the Highway Trust Fund through June 30. The bill would authorize appropriations for federal aid highway programs equal to three-fourths of the amount authorized in fiscal 2011. It would allow for the obligation of $7.8 billion for transit programs and limit the amount that would be derived from the Mass Transit Account to $6.3 billion. It would authorize funding for highway safety programs administered by the National Highway Traffic Safety Administration and for truck safety activities of the Federal Motor Carrier Safety Administration. Passed 266-158: R 229-10; D 37-148. March 29, 2012.

148. H Con Res 112. Fiscal 2013 Budget Resolution/Congressional Progressive Caucus Budget Substitute.
Honda, D-Calif., substitute amendment that would provide $3.309 trillion in new budget authority in fiscal 2013, not including off-budget accounts. The substitute would assume increased tax revenue, in part by indexing the alternative minimum tax for 10 years, maintaining the current top tax brackets until 2017, creating a progressive estate tax and taxing capital gains and qualified dividends as ordinary income. It also would assume the enactment of a public option for health care and prevention of a cut in Medicare physician payments. It would assume the elimination of corporate tax breaks for oil, gas and coal companies. It also would assume no funding for military activities in Afghanistan in 2014 but would call for funding in 2013 for redeployment out of the region. It would accommodate investments for job creation, early childhood, K-12 and special education, energy and alternative-fuel vehicle research, housing, and research and development. It also would accommodate a six-year surface transportation authorization. Rejected in Committee of the Whole 78-346: R 0-239; D 78-107. March 29, 2012.

	145	146	147	148
ALABAMA				
1 **Bonner**	N	Y	Y	N
2 **Roby**	N	Y	Y	N
3 **Rogers**	N	Y	Y	N
4 **Aderholt**	N	Y	Y	N
5 **Brooks**	N	Y	Y	N
6 **Bachus**	N	Y	Y	N
7 Sewell	N	N	Y	N
ALASKA				
AL **Young**	Y	?	Y	N
ARIZONA				
1 **Gosar**	N	Y	Y	N
2 **Franks**	N	Y	Y	N
3 **Quayle**	N	Y	Y	N
4 Pastor	N	N	Y	Y
5 **Schweikert**	N	Y	N	N
6 **Flake**	N	Y	N	N
7 Grijalva	N	N	N	Y
8 Vacant				
ARKANSAS				
1 **Crawford**	N	Y	Y	N
2 **Griffin**	N	Y	Y	N
3 **Womack**	N	Y	Y	N
4 Ross	N	N	N	N
CALIFORNIA				
1 Thompson	N	N	N	N
2 **Herger**	N	Y	Y	N
3 **Lungren**	N	Y	Y	N
4 **McClintock**	N	Y	N	N
5 Matsui	N	N	N	N
6 Woolsey	N	N	N	Y
7 Miller, George	N	N	N	N
8 Pelosi	N	N	N	N
9 Lee	N	N	N	Y
10 Garamendi	N	N	Y	N
11 McNerney	N	N	N	N
12 Speier	N	?	N	N
13 Stark	N	N	N	Y
14 Eshoo	N	N	N	N
15 Honda	N	N	N	Y
16 Lofgren	N	N	N	Y
17 Farr	N	N	N	Y
18 Cardoza	?	N	N	N
19 **Denham**	N	Y	Y	N
20 Costa	Y	N	N	N
21 **Nunes**	N	Y	Y	N
22 **McCarthy**	N	Y	Y	N
23 Capps	N	N	Y	N
24 **Gallegly**	N	Y	Y	N
25 **McKeon**	N	Y	Y	N
26 **Dreier**	N	Y	Y	N
27 Sherman	N	N	N	N
28 Berman	N	N	N	N
29 Schiff	N	N	N	N
30 Waxman	N	N	N	Y
31 Becerra	N	N	N	Y
32 Chu	N	N	N	Y
33 Bass	N	N	Y	Y
34 Roybal-Allard	N	N	N	Y
35 Waters	N	N	N	Y
36 Hahn	N	N	N	Y
37 Richardson	N	N	N	Y
38 Napolitano	N	N	N	Y
39 Sánchez, Linda	N	N	N	Y
40 **Royce**	N	Y	Y	N
41 **Lewis**	N	Y	Y	N
42 **Miller, Gary**	N	Y	Y	N
43 Baca	N	N	N	N
44 **Calvert**	N	Y	Y	N
45 **Bono Mack**	N	Y	Y	N
46 **Rohrabacher**	N	Y	Y	N
47 Sanchez, Loretta	N	?	N	N
48 **Campbell**	N	Y	N	N
49 **Issa**	N	Y	Y	N
50 **Bilbray**	N	Y	Y	N
51 Filner	–	–	–	+
52 **Hunter**	N	Y	Y	N
53 Davis	N	N	N	N

	145	146	147	148
COLORADO				
1 DeGette	N	N	N	N
2 Polis	Y	N	N	N
3 **Tipton**	N	Y	Y	N
4 **Gardner**	N	Y	Y	N
5 **Lamborn**	N	Y	Y	N
6 **Coffman**	N	Y	Y	N
7 Perlmutter	Y	N	N	N
CONNECTICUT				
1 Larson	N	N	N	N
2 Courtney	N	N	N	N
3 DeLauro	N	N	N	N
4 Himes	Y	N	N	N
5 Murphy	N	N	N	N
DELAWARE				
AL Carney	Y	N	N	N
FLORIDA				
1 **Miller**	N	Y	Y	N
2 **Southerland**	N	Y	Y	N
3 Brown	N	N	N	Y
4 **Crenshaw**	N	Y	Y	N
5 **Nugent**	N	Y	Y	N
6 **Stearns**	N	Y	Y	N
7 **Mica**	N	Y	Y	N
8 **Webster**	N	Y	Y	N
9 **Bilirakis**	N	Y	Y	N
10 **Young**	N	Y	Y	N
11 Castor	N	N	N	N
12 **Ross**	N	Y	Y	N
13 **Buchanan**	N	Y	Y	N
14 **Mack**	?	?	?	?
15 **Posey**	N	Y	Y	N
16 **Rooney**	N	Y	Y	N
17 Wilson	N	N	N	Y
18 **Ros-Lehtinen**	N	Y	Y	N
19 Deutch	?	N	N	Y
20 Wasserman Schultz	N	N	N	N
21 **Diaz-Balart**	N	Y	Y	N
22 **West**	N	Y	Y	N
23 Hastings	N	N	N	Y
24 **Adams**	N	Y	Y	N
25 **Rivera**	N	Y	Y	N
GEORGIA				
1 **Kingston**	N	Y	Y	N
2 Bishop	N	N	Y	N
3 **Westmoreland**	N	Y	Y	N
4 Johnson	N	N	N	Y
5 Lewis	N	N	N	Y
6 **Price**	N	Y	Y	N
7 **Woodall**	N	?	Y	N
8 **Scott, A.**	N	Y	Y	N
9 **Graves**	N	Y	Y	N
10 **Broun**	N	Y	N	N
11 **Gingrey**	N	Y	Y	N
12 Barrow	N	N	Y	N
13 Scott, D.	N	N	Y	Y
HAWAII				
1 Hanabusa	N	N	N	N
2 Hirono	N	N	N	Y
IDAHO				
1 **Labrador**	N	Y	Y	N
2 **Simpson**	Y	Y	Y	N
ILLINOIS				
1 Rush	N	N	N	Y
2 Jackson	?	?	?	?
3 Lipinski	Y	N	N	N
4 Gutierrez	N	N	N	Y
5 Quigley	Y	N	N	N
6 **Roskam**	N	Y	Y	N
7 Davis	N	N	N	Y
8 **Walsh**	N	Y	Y	N
9 Schakowsky	N	N	N	Y
10 **Dold**	Y	Y	N	N
11 **Kinzinger**	N	Y	Y	N
12 **Costello**	N	?	N	N
13 **Biggert**	N	Y	Y	N
14 **Hultgren**	N	Y	Y	N
15 **Johnson**	Y	Y	Y	N

KEY   Republicans   Democrats

Y Voted for (yea)	X Paired against
# Paired for	– Announced against
+ Announced for	P Voted "present"
N Voted against (nay)	

C Voted "present" to avoid possible conflict of interest

? Did not vote or otherwise make a position known

		145	146	147	148
16	Manzullo	N	Y	Y	N
17	Schilling	N	Y	Y	N
18	Schock	N	Y	Y	N
19	Shimkus	Y	Y	Y	N
INDIANA					
1	Visclosky	Y	N	N	N
2	Donnelly	N	N	Y	N
3	Stutzman	N	Y	Y	N
4	Rokita	N	Y	Y	N
5	Burton	N	Y	Y	N
6	Pence	N	Y	Y	N
7	Carson	N	N	Y	Y
8	Bucshon	N	Y	Y	N
9	Young	N	Y	Y	N
IOWA					
1	Braley	N	N	Y	N
2	Loebsack	N	N	Y	N
3	Boswell	Y	N	Y	N
4	Latham	N	Y	Y	N
5	King	N	Y	Y	N
KANSAS					
1	Huelskamp	N	Y	Y	N
2	Jenkins	N	Y	Y	N
3	Yoder	N	Y	Y	N
4	Pompeo	N	Y	Y	N
KENTUCKY					
1	Whitfield	N	Y	Y	N
2	Guthrie	N	Y	Y	N
3	Yarmuth	N	N	N	N
4	Davis	N	Y	Y	N
5	Rogers	N	Y	Y	N
6	Chandler	N	N	Y	N
LOUISIANA					
1	Scalise	N	Y	Y	N
2	Richmond	N	N	N	N
3	Landry	N	Y	Y	N
4	Fleming	N	Y	Y	N
5	Alexander	N	Y	Y	N
6	Cassidy	N	Y	Y	N
7	Boustany	N	Y	Y	N
MAINE					
1	Pingree	N	N	N	Y
2	Michaud	N	N	N	N
MARYLAND					
1	Harris	N	Y	Y	N
2	Ruppersberger	N	N	Y	N
3	Sarbanes	N	N	N	N
4	Edwards	N	N	N	Y
5	Hoyer	N	N	Y	N
6	Bartlett	N	Y	Y	N
7	Cummings	N	N	N	N
8	Van Hollen	N	N	Y	N
MASSACHUSETTS					
1	Olver	N	N	N	Y
2	Neal	N	N	N	N
3	McGovern	N	N	N	N
4	Frank	N	N	N	Y
5	Tsongas	N	N	Y	N
6	Tierney	N	N	N	N
7	Markey	N	N	N	Y
8	Capuano	N	N	N	Y
9	Lynch	N	N	Y	N
10	Keating	N	N	N	N
MICHIGAN					
1	Benishek	N	Y	Y	N
2	Huizenga	N	Y	Y	N
3	Amash	N	Y	N	N
4	Camp	N	Y	Y	N
5	Kildee	N	N	N	Y
6	Upton	N	Y	Y	N
7	Walberg	N	Y	Y	N
8	Rogers	N	Y	Y	N
9	Peters	N	N	N	N
10	Miller	N	Y	Y	N
11	McCotter	N	Y	Y	N
12	Levin	N	N	N	N
13	Clarke	N	N	N	Y
14	Conyers	N	N	N	N
15	Dingell	N	N	N	N
MINNESOTA					
1	Walz	N	N	Y	N
2	Kline	N	Y	Y	N
3	Paulsen	N	Y	Y	N
4	McCollum	N	N	N	Y

		145	146	147	148
5	Ellison	N	N	N	Y
6	Bachmann	N	Y	Y	N
7	Peterson	Y	N	Y	N
8	Cravaack	N	Y	Y	N
MISSISSIPPI					
1	Nunnelee	N	Y	Y	N
2	Thompson	N	N	N	N
3	Harper	N	Y	Y	N
4	Palazzo	N	Y	Y	N
MISSOURI					
1	Clay	N	N	N	Y
2	Akin	N	Y	Y	N
3	Carnahan	N	N	N	N
4	Hartzler	N	Y	Y	N
5	Cleaver	N	N	N	Y
6	Graves	N	Y	Y	N
7	Long	N	Y	Y	N
8	Emerson	N	Y	Y	N
9	Luetkemeyer	N	Y	Y	N
MONTANA					
AL	Rehberg	N	Y	Y	N
NEBRASKA					
1	Fortenberry	N	Y	Y	N
2	Terry	N	Y	Y	N
3	Smith	N	Y	Y	N
NEVADA					
1	Berkley	N	N	N	N
2	Amodei	N	Y	Y	N
3	Heck	N	Y	Y	N
NEW HAMPSHIRE					
1	Guinta	N	Y	Y	N
2	Bass	Y	Y	Y	N
NEW JERSEY					
1	Andrews	Y	N	N	Y
2	LoBiondo	N	Y	Y	N
3	Runyan	N	Y	Y	N
4	Smith	N	Y	Y	N
5	Garrett	N	Y	Y	N
6	Pallone	N	N	N	Y
7	Lance	N	Y	Y	N
8	Pascrell	N	N	N	Y
9	Rothman	N	N	N	Y
10	Vacant				
11	Frelinghuysen	N	Y	Y	N
12	Holt	N	N	N	Y
13	Sires	N	N	N	N
NEW MEXICO					
1	Heinrich	N	N	N	N
2	Pearce	N	Y	Y	N
3	Luján	N	N	N	N
NEW YORK					
1	Bishop	N	N	Y	N
2	Israel	N	N	Y	N
3	King	N	Y	Y	N
4	McCarthy	N	N	Y	N
5	Ackerman	N	N	N	N
6	Meeks	?	?	?	?
7	Crowley	N	N	N	N
8	Nadler	N	N	N	Y
9	Turner	N	Y	Y	N
10	Towns	?	?	?	?
11	Clarke	N	N	N	Y
12	Velázquez	N	N	N	Y
13	Grimm	N	Y	Y	N
14	Maloney	N	N	N	N
15	Rangel	?	?	?	?
16	Serrano	N	N	N	Y
17	Engel	N	?	N	N
18	Lowey	N	N	N	N
19	Hayworth	N	Y	Y	N
20	Gibson	Y	Y	Y	N
21	Tonko	N	N	N	Y
22	Hinchey	N	N	N	Y
23	Owens	N	N	N	N
24	Hanna	N	Y	Y	N
25	Buerkle	Y	Y	Y	N
26	Hochul	N	N	Y	N
27	Higgins	N	N	N	Y
28	Slaughter	N	N	N	Y
29	Reed	Y	Y	Y	N
NORTH CAROLINA					
1	Butterfield	N	N	N	N
2	Ellmers	N	Y	Y	N
3	Jones	N	Y	Y	N
4	Price	N	N	N	Y

		145	146	147	148
5	Foxx	N	Y	Y	N
6	Coble	N	Y	Y	N
7	McIntyre	N	N	Y	N
8	Kissell	N	N	Y	N
9	Myrick	N	Y	Y	N
10	McHenry	N	Y	Y	N
11	Shuler	Y	Y	Y	N
12	Watt	Y	N	Y	N
13	Miller	N	N	N	Y
NORTH DAKOTA					
AL	Berg	N	Y	Y	N
OHIO					
1	Chabot	N	Y	Y	N
2	Schmidt	N	Y	N	N
3	Turner	N	Y	Y	N
4	Jordan	N	Y	N	N
5	Latta	N	Y	Y	N
6	Johnson	N	Y	Y	N
7	Austria	N	Y	Y	N
8	Boehner				
9	Kaptur	N	N	N	Y
10	Kucinich	N	N	Y	N
11	Fudge	N	N	N	Y
12	Tiberi	N	Y	Y	N
13	Sutton	N	N	N	Y
14	LaTourette	Y	Y	Y	N
15	Stivers	N	Y	Y	N
16	Renacci	N	Y	Y	N
17	Ryan	N	N	N	Y
18	Gibbs	N	Y	Y	N
OKLAHOMA					
1	Sullivan	N	Y	Y	N
2	Boren	Y	N	N	N
3	Lucas	N	Y	Y	N
4	Cole	N	Y	Y	N
5	Lankford	N	Y	Y	N
OREGON					
1	Bonamici	N	N	N	N
2	Walden	N	Y	Y	N
3	Blumenauer	N	N	N	Y
4	DeFazio	N	N	N	N
5	Schrader	Y	N	Y	N
PENNSYLVANIA					
1	Brady	N	N	N	Y
2	Fattah	Y	N	N	Y
3	Kelly	N	Y	Y	N
4	Altmire	N	N	N	N
5	Thompson	N	Y	Y	N
6	Gerlach	N	Y	Y	N
7	Meehan	Y	Y	Y	N
8	Fitzpatrick	N	Y	Y	N
9	Shuster	N	Y	Y	N
10	Marino	N	Y	Y	N
11	Barletta	N	Y	Y	N
12	Critz	N	N	N	N
13	Schwartz	Y	N	N	N
14	Doyle	N	N	N	Y
15	Dent	Y	Y	Y	N
16	Pitts	N	Y	Y	N
17	Holden	N	N	N	N
18	Murphy	N	Y	Y	N
19	Platts	Y	Y	Y	N
RHODE ISLAND					
1	Cicilline	N	N	N	N
2	Langevin	N	N	N	N
SOUTH CAROLINA					
1	Scott	N	Y	Y	N
2	Wilson	N	Y	Y	N
3	Duncan	N	Y	Y	N
4	Gowdy	N	Y	Y	N
5	Mulvaney	N	Y	Y	N
6	Clyburn	Y	N	N	Y
SOUTH DAKOTA					
AL	Noem	N	Y	Y	N
TENNESSEE					
1	Roe	N	Y	Y	N
2	Duncan	N	Y	Y	N
3	Fleischmann	N	Y	Y	N
4	DesJarlais	N	Y	Y	N
5	Cooper	Y	N	N	N
6	Black	N	+	Y	N
7	Blackburn	N	Y	Y	N
8	Fincher	N	Y	Y	N
9	Cohen	N	N	N	Y

		145	146	147	148
TEXAS					
1	Gohmert	N	Y	Y	N
2	Poe	N	Y	Y	N
3	Johnson, S.	N	Y	Y	N
4	Hall	N	Y	Y	N
5	Hensarling	N	Y	Y	N
6	Barton	N	Y	Y	N
7	Culberson	N	Y	Y	N
8	Brady	N	Y	Y	N
9	Green, A.	N	N	N	Y
10	McCaul	N	Y	Y	N
11	Conaway	N	Y	Y	N
12	Granger	N	Y	Y	N
13	Thornberry	N	Y	Y	N
14	Paul	?	?	?	?
15	Hinojosa	N	N	N	N
16	Reyes	N	N	N	N
17	Flores	N	Y	Y	N
18	Jackson Lee	N	–	Y	Y
19	Neugebauer	N	Y	Y	N
20	Gonzalez	N	N	N	N
21	Smith	N	Y	Y	N
22	Olson	N	Y	Y	N
23	Canseco	N	Y	Y	N
24	Marchant	N	Y	Y	N
25	Doggett	N	N	N	N
26	Burgess	N	Y	Y	N
27	Farenthold	N	Y	Y	N
28	Cuellar	Y	N	N	N
29	Green, G.	N	N	Y	N
30	Johnson, E.	N	N	N	N
31	Carter	N	Y	Y	N
32	Sessions	N	Y	Y	N
UTAH					
1	Bishop	N	Y	Y	N
2	Matheson	N	N	Y	N
3	Chaffetz	N	Y	Y	N
VERMONT					
AL	Welch	N	N	N	Y
VIRGINIA					
1	Wittman	N	Y	Y	N
2	Rigell	N	Y	Y	N
3	Scott	N	N	N	N
4	Forbes	N	Y	Y	N
5	Hurt	N	Y	Y	N
6	Goodlatte	N	Y	Y	N
7	Cantor	N	Y	Y	N
8	Moran	P	N	N	Y
9	Griffith	N	Y	Y	N
10	Wolf	Y	Y	Y	N
11	Connolly	P	N	Y	N
WASHINGTON					
1	Vacant				
2	Larsen	Y	N	N	N
3	Herrera Beutler	N	Y	Y	N
4	Hastings	N	Y	Y	N
5	McMorris Rodgers	N	Y	Y	N
6	Dicks	N	N	N	N
7	McDermott	N	N	N	Y
8	Reichert	N	Y	Y	N
9	Smith	N	N	Y	N
WEST VIRGINIA					
1	McKinley	N	Y	Y	N
2	Capito	N	Y	Y	?
3	Rahall	N	N	N	N
WISCONSIN					
1	Ryan	N	Y	Y	N
2	Baldwin	N	N	N	N
3	Kind	Y	N	N	N
4	Moore	N	?	N	Y
5	Sensenbrenner	N	Y	Y	N
6	Petri	Y	Y	Y	N
7	Duffy	N	Y	Y	N
8	Ribble	N	Y	Y	N
WYOMING					
AL	Lummis	Y	Y	Y	N

IN THE HOUSE | By Vote Number

149. **H Con Res 112. Fiscal 2013 Budget Resolution/Republican Study Committee Substitute.** Garrett, R-N.J., substitute amendment that would provide $2.663 trillion in new budget authority for fiscal 2013, not including off-budget accounts. It would limit non-defense discretionary spending for fiscal 2013 to $931 billion. It would assume a health care overhaul that would, beginning in 2023, transform Medicare into a health insurance program that provides premium subsidies to enrollees to help offset the cost of health insurance policies. It also would assume conversion of the federal share of Medicaid spending into a block grant to states that would be level-funded at $267 billion per year for the next 10 years. It would assume an overhaul of the tax code that would eliminate the estate tax, allow taxpayers to switch to a system with two tax brackets and cut the corporate tax rate to 25 percent. Rejected in Committee of the Whole 136-285: R 136-104; D 0-181. March 29, 2012.

150. **H Con Res 112. Fiscal 2013 Budget Resolution/Democratic Substitute.** Van Hollen, D-Md., substitute amendment that would provide $2.966 trillion in new budget authority for fiscal 2013, not including off-budget accounts. In fiscal 2013, it would cap discretionary spending at $1.047 trillion, including $546 billion for defense spending. It would assume the replacement of the $1.2 trillion sequestration scheduled under the 2011 debt limit law with deficit reduction from targeted spending cuts and revenue increases. It would reduce the deficit to below 3 percent of gross domestic product for every year after 2014 and assume permanent extension of the 2001 and 2003 tax cuts for the middle class and the elimination of a variety of corporate tax breaks. It would assume full implementation of the 2010 health care overhaul and accommodate funding for surface transportation, first-responder and veterans jobs and a temporary tax credit for new hiring and wage increases. Rejected in Committee of the Whole 163-262: R 0-240; D 163-22. March 29, 2012.

151. **H Con Res 112. Fiscal 2013 Budget Resolution/Adoption.** Adoption of the concurrent resolution that would provide $2.793 trillion in new budget authority for fiscal 2013, not including off-budget accounts. It calls for limiting discretionary appropriations to $1.028 trillion in 2013 and for major cuts in non-defense discretionary and mandatory spending over the next 10 years. It would assume significant future savings by restructuring Medicare into a "premium support" system beginning in 2023, converting Medicaid and the food stamp program into block grants to states, and repealing the 2010 health care overhaul. It calls for an overhaul of the tax code, under which the alternative minimum tax would be repealed, the six current individual income tax brackets would be consolidated into two, tax credits and deductions would be eliminated or curtailed, and the corporate tax code modified to reduce the top rate to 25 percent from 35 percent and converted into a "territorial" tax system in which U.S. companies would pay tax only on income earned in the United States. It also would direct the Budget Committee to report a bill that would repeal the sequestration of discretionary spending set for January 2013 by the 2011 debt limit law and direct six House committees to find substitute savings from mandatory programs. Adopted 228-191: R 228-10; D 0-181. March 29, 2012.

	149	150	151
ALABAMA			
1 Bonner	N	N	Y
2 Roby	N	N	Y
3 Rogers	N	N	Y
4 Aderholt	N	N	Y
5 Brooks	Y	N	Y
6 Bachus	N	N	Y
7 Sewell	N	Y	N
ALASKA			
AL Young	N	N	Y
ARIZONA			
1 Gosar	Y	N	Y
2 Franks	Y	N	Y
3 Quayle	Y	N	Y
4 Pastor	N	Y	N
5 Schweikert	Y	N	Y
6 Flake	Y	N	Y
7 Grijalva	N	Y	N
8 Vacant			
ARKANSAS			
1 Crawford	N	N	Y
2 Griffin	Y	N	Y
3 Womack	N	N	Y
4 Ross	N	N	N
CALIFORNIA			
1 Thompson	N	Y	N
2 Herger	Y	N	Y
3 Lungren	N	N	Y
4 McClintock	Y	N	Y
5 Matsui	N	Y	N
6 Woolsey	N	Y	N
7 Miller, George	N	Y	N
8 Pelosi	N	Y	?
9 Lee	N	Y	N
10 Garamendi	N	Y	N
11 McNerney	N	Y	N
12 Speier	N	Y	N
13 Stark	N	Y	N
14 Eshoo	N	Y	N
15 Honda	N	Y	N
16 Lofgren	N	Y	N
17 Farr	N	Y	N
18 Cardoza	N	Y	N
19 Denham	N	N	Y
20 Costa	N	N	N
21 Nunes	N	N	Y
22 McCarthy	N	N	Y
23 Capps	N	Y	N
24 Gallegly	N	N	Y
25 McKeon	N	N	Y
26 Dreier	N	N	Y
27 Sherman	N	Y	N
28 Berman	N	Y	N
29 Schiff	N	Y	N
30 Waxman	P	Y	N
31 Becerra	N	Y	N
32 Chu	N	Y	N
33 Bass	N	Y	N
34 Roybal-Allard	N	Y	N
35 Waters	N	Y	N
36 Hahn	N	Y	N
37 Richardson	N	Y	N
38 Napolitano	N	Y	N
39 Sánchez, Linda	N	Y	N
40 Royce	Y	N	Y
41 Lewis	N	N	Y
42 Miller, Gary	Y	N	Y
43 Baca	N	Y	N
44 Calvert	N	N	Y
45 Bono Mack	N	N	Y
46 Rohrabacher	Y	N	Y
47 Sanchez, Loretta	N	Y	N
48 Campbell	Y	N	Y
49 Issa	Y	N	Y
50 Bilbray	N	N	Y
51 Filner	–	+	–
52 Hunter	Y	N	Y
53 Davis	N	Y	N

	149	150	151
COLORADO			
1 DeGette	N	Y	N
2 Polis	P	Y	N
3 Tipton	Y	N	Y
4 Gardner	Y	N	Y
5 Lamborn	Y	N	Y
6 Coffman	Y	N	Y
7 Perlmutter	N	Y	N
CONNECTICUT			
1 Larson	N	Y	N
2 Courtney	N	Y	N
3 DeLauro	N	Y	N
4 Himes	N	N	N
5 Murphy	N	Y	N
DELAWARE			
AL Carney	N	Y	N
FLORIDA			
1 Miller	N	N	Y
2 Southerland	N	N	Y
3 Brown	N	Y	N
4 Crenshaw	N	N	Y
5 Nugent	N	N	Y
6 Stearns	Y	N	Y
7 Mica	Y	N	Y
8 Webster	N	N	Y
9 Bilirakis	N	N	Y
10 Young	N	Y	N
11 Castor	N	Y	N
12 Ross	Y	N	Y
13 Buchanan	N	N	Y
14 Mack	?	?	?
15 Posey	Y	N	Y
16 Rooney	Y	N	Y
17 Wilson	N	Y	N
18 Ros-Lehtinen	N	N	Y
19 Deutch	N	Y	N
20 Wasserman Schultz	N	Y	N
21 Diaz-Balart	N	N	Y
22 West	Y	N	Y
23 Hastings	N	Y	N
24 Adams	Y	N	Y
25 Rivera	Y	N	Y
GEORGIA			
1 Kingston	Y	N	Y
2 Bishop	N	Y	N
3 Westmoreland	Y	N	Y
4 Johnson	N	Y	N
5 Lewis	N	Y	N
6 Price	Y	N	Y
7 Woodall	Y	N	Y
8 Scott, A.	Y	N	Y
9 Graves	Y	N	Y
10 Broun	Y	N	?
11 Gingrey	Y	N	Y
12 Barrow	N	N	N
13 Scott, D.	N	Y	N
HAWAII			
1 Hanabusa	N	Y	N
2 Hirono	N	Y	N
IDAHO			
1 Labrador	Y	N	Y
2 Simpson	Y	N	Y
ILLINOIS			
1 Rush	N	Y	N
2 Jackson	?	?	?
3 Lipinski	N	N	Y
4 Gutierrez	N	Y	N
5 Quigley	N	Y	N
6 Roskam	N	N	Y
7 Davis	N	Y	N
8 Walsh	Y	N	Y
9 Schakowsky	N	Y	N
10 Dold	N	N	Y
11 Kinzinger	N	N	Y
12 Costello	N	Y	N
13 Biggert	N	N	Y
14 Hultgren	Y	N	Y
15 Johnson	Y	N	Y

KEY   Republicans   Democrats

Y Voted for (yea)
\# Paired for
\+ Announced for
N Voted against (nay)

X Paired against
– Announced against
P Voted "present"

C Voted "present" to avoid possible conflict of interest

? Did not vote or otherwise make a position known

	149	150	151			149	150	151			149	150	151			149	150	151
16 Manzullo	Y	N	Y		5 Ellison	N	Y	N		5 Foxx	Y	N	Y		**TEXAS**			
17 Schilling	N	N	Y		6 Bachmann	Y	N	Y		6 Coble	Y	N	Y		1 Gohmert	Y	N	Y
18 Schock	N	N	Y		7 Peterson	N	N	N		7 McIntyre	N	N	N		2 Poe	Y	N	Y
19 Shimkus	Y	N	Y		8 Cravaack	N	N	Y		8 Kissell	N	N	N		3 Johnson, S.	Y	N	Y
INDIANA					**MISSISSIPPI**					9 Myrick	Y	N	Y		4 Hall	Y	N	Y
1 Visclosky	N	N	N		1 Nunnelee	Y	N	Y		10 McHenry	Y	N	Y		5 Hensarling	Y	N	Y
2 Donnelly	N	N	N		2 Thompson	N	Y	N		11 Shuler	N	N	N		6 Barton	Y	N	N
3 Stutzman	Y	N	Y		3 Harper	Y	N	Y		12 Watt	N	Y	?		7 Culberson	Y	N	Y
4 Rokita	Y	N	Y		4 Palazzo	Y	N	Y		13 Miller	N	Y	N		8 Brady	Y	N	Y
5 Burton	Y	N	Y		**MISSOURI**					**NORTH DAKOTA**					9 Green, A.	N	Y	N
6 Pence	Y	N	Y		1 Clay	N	Y	N		AL Berg	N	N	Y		10 McCaul	Y	N	Y
7 Carson	N	Y	N		2 Akin	Y	N	Y		**OHIO**					11 Conaway	Y	N	Y
8 Bucshon	Y	N	Y		3 Carnahan	N	Y	N		1 Chabot	Y	N	Y		12 Granger	Y	N	Y
9 Young	N	N	Y		4 Hartzler	Y	N	Y		2 Schmidt	Y	N	Y		13 Thornberry	Y	N	Y
IOWA					5 Cleaver	N	Y	N		3 Turner	N	N	Y		14 Paul	Y	N	?
1 Braley	N	Y	N		6 Graves	Y	N	Y		4 Jordan	Y	N	Y		15 Hinojosa	N	Y	N
2 Loebsack	N	N	N		7 Long	Y	N	Y		5 Latta	Y	N	Y		16 Reyes	N	Y	N
3 Boswell	N	Y	N		8 Emerson	N	N	Y		6 Johnson	N	N	Y		17 Flores	Y	N	Y
4 Latham	N	N	Y		9 Luetkemeyer	N	N	Y		7 Austria	Y	N	Y		18 Jackson Lee	N	Y	N
5 King	Y	N	Y		**MONTANA**					8 Boehner					19 Neugebauer	Y	N	Y
KANSAS					AL Rehberg	N	N	N		9 Kaptur	N	Y	N		20 Gonzalez	N	Y	N
1 Huelskamp	Y	N	N		**NEBRASKA**					10 Kucinich	N	N	N		21 Smith	Y	N	Y
2 Jenkins	Y	N	Y		1 Fortenberry	N	N	Y		11 Fudge	N	Y	N		22 Olson	Y	N	Y
3 Yoder	Y	N	Y		2 Terry	N	N	Y		12 Tiberi	N	N	Y		23 Canseco	N	N	Y
4 Pompeo	Y	N	Y		3 Smith	N	N	Y		13 Sutton	N	Y	N		24 Marchant	Y	N	Y
KENTUCKY					**NEVADA**					14 LaTourette	N	N	Y		25 Doggett	N	Y	N
1 Whitfield	N	N	N		1 Berkley	N	Y	N		15 Stivers	N	N	Y		26 Burgess	Y	N	Y
2 Guthrie	N	N	Y		2 Amodei	Y	N	Y		16 Renacci	N	N	Y		27 Farenthold	Y	N	Y
3 Yarmuth	N	Y	N		3 Heck	N	N	Y		17 Ryan	N	Y	N		28 Cuellar	N	Y	N
4 Davis	N	N	Y		**NEW HAMPSHIRE**					18 Gibbs	N	N	Y		29 Green, G.	N	N	N
5 Rogers	N	N	Y		1 Guinta	Y	N	Y		**OKLAHOMA**					30 Johnson, E.	N	Y	N
6 Chandler	N	N	N		2 Bass	N	N	Y		1 Sullivan	Y	N	Y		31 Carter	N	N	Y
LOUISIANA					**NEW JERSEY**					2 Boren	N	N	N		32 Sessions	Y	N	Y
1 Scalise	Y	N	Y		1 Andrews	N	Y	N		3 Lucas	N	N	Y		**UTAH**			
2 Richmond	N	Y	N		2 LoBiondo	N	N	Y		4 Cole	Y	N	Y		1 Bishop	Y	N	Y
3 Landry	Y	N	Y		3 Runyan	N	N	Y		5 Lankford	Y	N	Y		2 Matheson	N	N	N
4 Fleming	Y	N	Y		4 Smith	N	N	Y		**OREGON**					3 Chaffetz	Y	N	Y
5 Alexander	N	N	Y		5 Garrett	Y	N	Y		1 Bonamici	N	Y	N		**VERMONT**			
6 Cassidy	Y	N	Y		6 Pallone	N	Y	N		2 Walden	N	N	Y		AL Welch	N	Y	N
7 Boustany	Y	N	Y		7 Lance	Y	N	Y		3 Blumenauer	N	Y	N		**VIRGINIA**			
MAINE					8 Pascrell	N	Y	N		4 DeFazio	N	N	N		1 Wittman	N	N	Y
1 Pingree	N	Y	?		9 Rothman	N	Y	N		5 Schrader	N	N	N		2 Rigell	Y	N	Y
2 Michaud	N	Y	N		10 Vacant					**PENNSYLVANIA**					3 Scott	N	Y	N
MARYLAND					11 Frelinghuysen	N	N	Y		1 Brady	N	Y	N		4 Forbes	N	N	Y
1 Harris	Y	N	Y		12 Holt	N	Y	N		2 Fattah	P	Y	N		5 Hurt	N	N	Y
2 Ruppersberger	N	Y	N		13 Sires	N	Y	N		3 Kelly	N	N	Y		6 Goodlatte	Y	N	Y
3 Sarbanes	N	Y	N		**NEW MEXICO**					4 Altmire	N	Y	N		7 Cantor	N	N	Y
4 Edwards	N	Y	N		1 Heinrich	N	Y	N		5 Thompson	Y	N	Y		8 Moran	N	Y	N
5 Hoyer	N	Y	N		2 Pearce	Y	N	Y		6 Gerlach	N	N	Y		9 Griffith	Y	N	Y
6 Bartlett	Y	N	Y		3 Luján	N	Y	N		7 Meehan	N	N	Y		10 Wolf	N	N	Y
7 Cummings	N	Y	N		**NEW YORK**					8 Fitzpatrick	N	N	Y		11 Connolly	N	Y	N
8 Van Hollen	N	Y	N		1 Bishop	N	Y	N		9 Shuster	Y	N	Y		**WASHINGTON**			
MASSACHUSETTS					2 Israel	N	Y	N		10 Marino	N	N	Y		1 Vacant			
1 Olver	N	Y	N		3 King	N	N	Y		11 Barletta	N	N	Y		2 Larsen	N	Y	N
2 Neal	N	Y	N		4 McCarthy	N	Y	N		12 Critz	N	Y	N		3 Herrera Beutler	N	N	Y
3 McGovern	N	Y	N		5 Ackerman	N	Y	N		13 Schwartz	N	Y	N		4 Hastings	N	N	Y
4 Frank	N	Y	N		6 Meeks	?	?	?		14 Doyle	N	Y	N		5 McMorris Rodgers	Y	N	Y
5 Tsongas	N	Y	N		7 Crowley	N	Y	N		15 Dent	N	N	Y		6 Dicks	N	Y	?
6 Tierney	N	Y	N		8 Nadler	N	Y	N		16 Pitts	Y	N	Y		7 McDermott	N	Y	N
7 Markey	N	Y	N		9 Turner	N	N	Y		17 Holden	N	Y	N		8 Reichert	N	N	Y
8 Capuano	N	Y	N		10 Towns	?	?	N		18 Murphy	Y	N	Y		9 Smith	N	Y	N
9 Lynch	N	Y	N		11 Clarke	N	Y	N		19 Platts	N	N	N		**WEST VIRGINIA**			
10 Keating	N	Y	N		12 Velázquez	N	Y	N		**RHODE ISLAND**					1 McKinley	N	N	N
MICHIGAN					13 Grimm	N	N	Y		1 Cicilline	N	Y	N		2 Capito	N	N	Y
1 Benishek	N	N	Y		14 Maloney	?	Y	N		2 Langevin	N	Y	N		3 Rahall	N	Y	N
2 Huizenga	Y	N	Y		15 Rangel	?	?	?		**SOUTH CAROLINA**					**WISCONSIN**			
3 Amash	Y	N	N		16 Serrano	N	Y	N		1 Scott	Y	N	Y		1 Ryan	N	N	Y
4 Camp	N	N	Y		17 Engel	N	Y	N		2 Wilson	Y	N	Y		2 Baldwin	N	Y	N
5 Kildee	N	Y	N		18 Lowey	N	Y	N		3 Duncan	Y	N	Y		3 Kind	N	N	N
6 Upton	Y	N	Y		19 Hayworth	N	N	Y		4 Gowdy	Y	N	Y		4 Moore	N	Y	N
7 Walberg	Y	N	Y		20 Gibson	N	N	Y		5 Mulvaney	Y	N	Y		5 Sensenbrenner	Y	N	Y
8 Rogers	N	N	Y		21 Tonko	N	Y	N		6 Clyburn	N	Y	N		6 Petri	N	N	Y
9 Peters	N	Y	N		22 Hinchey	N	Y	?		**SOUTH DAKOTA**					7 Duffy	N	N	Y
10 Miller	N	N	Y		23 Owens	N	Y	N		AL Noem	N	N	Y		8 Ribble	Y	N	Y
11 McCotter	Y	N	Y		24 Hanna	N	N	Y		**TENNESSEE**					**WYOMING**			
12 Levin	N	Y	N		25 Buerkle	Y	N	Y		1 Roe	Y	N	Y		AL Lummis	Y	N	Y
13 Clarke	N	Y	N		26 Hochul	N	N	Y		2 Duncan	N	N	N					
14 Conyers	N	Y	N		27 Higgins	N	Y	N		3 Fleischmann	Y	N	Y					
15 Dingell	N	Y	N		28 Slaughter	N	Y	N		4 DesJarlais	Y	N	Y					
MINNESOTA					29 Reed	N	N	Y		5 Cooper	N	N	N					
1 Walz	N	Y	N		**NORTH CAROLINA**					6 Black	Y	N	Y					
2 Kline	Y	N	Y		1 Butterfield	N	Y	N		7 Blackburn	Y	N	Y					
3 Paulsen	N	N	Y		2 Ellmers	Y	N	Y		8 Fincher	Y	N	Y					
4 McCollum	N	Y	N		3 Jones	N	N	Y		9 Cohen	N	Y	N					
					4 Price	N	Y	N										

IN THE HOUSE | By Vote Number

152. **HR 3001. Raoul Wallenberg Congressional Gold Medal/Passage.** Luetkemeyer, R-Mo., motion to suspend the rules and pass the bill that would award a posthumous Congressional Gold Medal to Raoul Wallenberg, a Swedish businessman who helped rescue thousands of Jews from Nazi-occupied Hungary near the end of World War II. Motion agreed to 377-0: R 216-0; D 161-0. A two-thirds majority of those present and voting (252 in this case) is required for passage under suspension of the rules. April 16, 2012.

153. **HR 4040. Jack Nicklaus Congressional Gold Medal/Passage.** Luetkemeyer, R-Mo., motion to suspend the rules and pass the bill that would award the Congressional Gold Medal to golfer Jack Nicklaus in recognition of his service to the nation in promoting excellence and good sportsmanship. Motion agreed to 373-4: R 213-4; D 160-0. A two-thirds majority of those present and voting (252 in this case) is required for passage under suspension of the rules. April 16, 2012.

154. **HR 4089. Sportsmen's Land Access/Question of Consideration.** Question of whether the House should consider the rule (H Res 614) that would provide for House floor consideration of the bill that would allow fishing, hunting and shooting on certain public lands. The rule, upon adoption, also would deem the House budget resolution (H Con Res 112) as the final budget resolution. Agreed to consider 234-175: R 233-0; D 1-175. (Moore, D-Wis., had raised a point of order that the rule would violate clause 426(a) of the Congressional Budget Act, regarding unfunded mandates.) April 17, 2012.

155. **HR 4089. Sportsmen's Land Access/Previous Question.** Bishop, R-Utah, motion to order the previous question (thus ending debate and the possibility of amendment) on the rule (H Res 614) that would provide for House floor consideration of a bill to allow fishing, hunting and shooting on certain public lands. Motion agreed to 235-179: R 234-1; D 1-178. April 17, 2012.

156. **HR 4089. Sportsmen's Land Access/Rule.** Adoption of the rule (H Res 614) that would provide for House floor consideration of the bill that would allow fishing, hunting and shooting on certain public lands. The rule, upon adoption, also would deem the House budget resolution (H Con Res 112) as the final budget resolution. Adopted 228-184: R 228-4; D 0-180. April 17, 2012.

157. **HR 1815. Lena Horne Congressional Gold Medal/Passage.** Luetkemeyer, R-Mo., motion to suspend the rules and pass the bill that would authorize the posthumous award of the Congressional Gold Medal to entertainer and activist Lena Horne in recognition of her achievements and contributions to American culture and the civil rights movement. Motion agreed to 410-2: R 230-2; D 180-0. A two-thirds majority of those present and voting (275 in this case) is required for passage under suspension of the rules. April 17, 2012.

158. **HR 4089. Sportsmen's Land Access/National Park Service Land.** Holt, D-N.J., amendment that would modify the bill to exclude all national park lands managed by the National Park Service from being opened to recreational hunting or shooting activities unless statute specifically permits such activities on specifically designated park lands. Rejected in Committee of the Whole 152-260: R 6-228; D 146-32. April 17, 2012.

	152	153	154	155	156	157	158
ALABAMA							
1 Bonner	Y	Y	Y	Y	Y	Y	N
2 Roby	Y	Y	Y	Y	Y	Y	N
3 Rogers	Y	Y	Y	Y	Y	Y	N
4 Aderholt	Y	Y	Y	Y	Y	Y	N
5 Brooks	Y	Y	Y	Y	Y	Y	N
6 Bachus	Y	Y	Y	Y	Y	Y	N
7 Sewell	Y	Y	N	N	N	Y	Y
ALASKA							
AL Young	Y	Y	Y	Y	?	Y	N
ARIZONA							
1 Gosar	Y	Y	Y	Y	Y	Y	N
2 Franks	+	Y	Y	Y	Y	Y	N
3 Quayle	Y	Y	Y	Y	Y	Y	N
4 Pastor	Y	Y	N	N	N	Y	Y
5 Schweikert	Y	Y	Y	Y	Y	Y	N
6 Flake	Y	Y	Y	Y	Y	Y	N
7 Grijalva	?	?	N	N	N	Y	Y
8 Vacant							
ARKANSAS							
1 Crawford	Y	Y	Y	Y	Y	Y	N
2 Griffin	Y	Y	Y	Y	Y	Y	N
3 Womack	Y	Y	Y	Y	Y	Y	N
4 Ross	Y	Y	N	N	N	Y	N
CALIFORNIA							
1 Thompson	Y	Y	N	N	N	Y	Y
2 Herger	Y	Y	Y	Y	Y	Y	N
3 Lungren	Y	Y	Y	Y	Y	Y	N
4 McClintock	Y	Y	Y	Y	Y	Y	N
5 Matsui	Y	Y	N	N	N	Y	Y
6 Woolsey	Y	Y	N	N	N	Y	Y
7 Miller, George	Y	Y	N	N	N	Y	Y
8 Pelosi	Y	Y	N	N	N	Y	Y
9 Lee	Y	Y	N	N	N	Y	Y
10 Garamendi	Y	Y	N	N	N	Y	?
11 McNerney	Y	Y	N	N	N	Y	Y
12 Speier	Y	Y	N	N	N	Y	Y
13 Stark	Y	Y	N	N	N	Y	Y
14 Eshoo	Y	Y	N	N	N	Y	Y
15 Honda	Y	Y	N	N	N	Y	Y
16 Lofgren	Y	?	N	N	N	Y	Y
17 Farr	Y	Y	N	N	N	Y	Y
18 Cardoza	Y	Y	?	?	?	Y	N
19 Denham	Y	Y	?	Y	Y	Y	N
20 Costa	Y	Y	N	N	N	Y	N
21 Nunes	Y	Y	Y	Y	Y	Y	N
22 McCarthy	Y	Y	Y	Y	Y	Y	N
23 Capps	Y	Y	N	N	N	Y	Y
24 Gallegly	Y	Y	Y	?	?	?	N
25 McKeon	Y	Y	Y	Y	Y	Y	N
26 Dreier	Y	Y	Y	Y	Y	Y	N
27 Sherman	Y	Y	N	N	N	Y	Y
28 Berman	Y	Y	N	N	N	Y	Y
29 Schiff	+	+	N	N	N	Y	Y
30 Waxman	Y	Y	N	N	N	Y	Y
31 Becerra	Y	Y	N	N	N	Y	Y
32 Chu	Y	Y	N	N	N	Y	Y
33 Bass	Y	Y	N	N	N	Y	Y
34 Roybal-Allard	Y	Y	N	N	N	Y	Y
35 Waters	?	?	N	N	N	Y	Y
36 Hahn	Y	Y	N	N	N	Y	Y
37 Richardson	Y	Y	N	N	N	Y	Y
38 Napolitano	+	+	–	–	–	+	?
39 Sánchez, Linda	Y	Y	N	N	N	Y	Y
40 Royce	Y	Y	Y	Y	Y	Y	N
41 Lewis	?	?	Y	Y	?	Y	N
42 Miller, Gary	Y	Y	Y	Y	Y	Y	N
43 Baca	Y	Y	N	N	N	Y	N
44 Calvert	Y	Y	Y	Y	Y	Y	N
45 Bono Mack	Y	Y	Y	Y	Y	Y	N
46 Rohrabacher	?	?	Y	Y	Y	Y	N
47 Sanchez, Loretta	Y	Y	N	N	N	Y	Y
48 Campbell	?	?	Y	Y	Y	Y	N
49 Issa	Y	Y	Y	Y	Y	Y	N
50 Bilbray	Y	Y	Y	Y	Y	Y	N
51 Filner	+	+	–	–	–	+	+
52 Hunter	Y	Y	Y	Y	Y	Y	N
53 Davis	Y	Y	N	N	N	Y	Y

	152	153	154	155	156	157	158
COLORADO							
1 DeGette	Y	Y	N	N	N	Y	?
2 Polis	Y	Y	N	N	N	Y	Y
3 Tipton	?	?	Y	Y	Y	Y	N
4 Gardner	Y	Y	Y	Y	Y	Y	N
5 Lamborn	Y	Y	Y	Y	Y	Y	N
6 Coffman	Y	Y	Y	Y	Y	Y	N
7 Perlmutter	?	Y	N	N	N	Y	N
CONNECTICUT							
1 Larson	Y	Y	N	N	N	Y	Y
2 Courtney	Y	Y	N	N	N	Y	Y
3 DeLauro	Y	Y	N	N	N	Y	Y
4 Himes	Y	Y	N	N	N	Y	Y
5 Murphy	?	?	N	N	N	Y	Y
DELAWARE							
AL Carney	Y	Y	?	N	N	Y	Y
FLORIDA							
1 Miller	+	Y	Y	Y	Y	Y	N
2 Southerland	Y	Y	Y	Y	Y	Y	N
3 Brown	Y	Y	N	N	N	Y	Y
4 Crenshaw	?	?	Y	Y	Y	Y	N
5 Nugent	Y	Y	Y	Y	Y	Y	N
6 Stearns	Y	Y	Y	Y	Y	Y	N
7 Mica	Y	Y	Y	Y	N	Y	N
8 Webster	Y	Y	Y	Y	Y	Y	N
9 Bilirakis	Y	Y	Y	Y	Y	Y	N
10 Young	?	?	Y	Y	Y	Y	N
11 Castor	Y	Y	N	N	N	Y	Y
12 Ross	Y	Y	Y	Y	Y	Y	N
13 Buchanan	Y	Y	Y	Y	Y	Y	N
14 Mack	Y	Y	Y	Y	Y	Y	N
15 Posey	Y	Y	Y	Y	Y	Y	N
16 Rooney	Y	Y	Y	Y	Y	Y	N
17 Wilson	Y	Y	N	N	N	Y	Y
18 Ros-Lehtinen	?	?	Y	Y	Y	Y	N
19 Deutch	Y	Y	N	N	N	Y	Y
20 Wasserman Schultz	Y	Y	N	N	N	Y	Y
21 Diaz-Balart	Y	Y	Y	Y	Y	Y	N
22 West	Y	Y	Y	Y	Y	Y	N
23 Hastings	Y	Y	N	N	N	Y	Y
24 Adams	Y	Y	Y	Y	Y	Y	N
25 Rivera	Y	Y	Y	Y	Y	Y	N
GEORGIA							
1 Kingston	Y	Y	Y	Y	Y	Y	N
2 Bishop	Y	Y	N	N	N	Y	N
3 Westmoreland	Y	Y	Y	Y	Y	Y	N
4 Johnson	Y	Y	N	N	N	Y	Y
5 Lewis	Y	Y	N	?	?	Y	Y
6 Price	Y	Y	Y	Y	Y	Y	N
7 Woodall	Y	Y	Y	Y	Y	Y	N
8 Scott, A.	Y	Y	Y	Y	Y	Y	N
9 Graves	Y	Y	Y	Y	Y	Y	N
10 Broun	Y	Y	Y	Y	Y	Y	N
11 Gingrey	Y	Y	Y	Y	Y	Y	N
12 Barrow	Y	Y	N	N	N	Y	N
13 Scott, D.	Y	Y	N	N	N	Y	Y
HAWAII							
1 Hanabusa	Y	Y	N	N	N	Y	Y
2 Hirono	Y	Y	?	N	N	Y	Y
IDAHO							
1 Labrador	?	?	Y	Y	Y	Y	N
2 Simpson	Y	Y	Y	Y	Y	Y	N
ILLINOIS							
1 Rush	?	Y	N	N	N	Y	Y
2 Jackson	Y	Y	N	N	N	Y	Y
3 Lipinski	Y	Y	N	N	N	Y	Y
4 Gutierrez	+	+	N	N	N	Y	Y
5 Quigley	Y	Y	N	N	N	Y	Y
6 Roskam	Y	Y	Y	Y	Y	Y	N
7 Davis	Y	Y	N	?	N	Y	Y
8 Walsh	Y	Y	Y	?	Y	Y	N
9 Schakowsky	Y	Y	N	N	N	Y	Y
10 Dold	Y	Y	Y	Y	Y	Y	Y
11 Kinzinger	Y	Y	Y	Y	Y	Y	N
12 Costello	?	?	?	?	?	?	N
13 Biggert	Y	Y	Y	Y	Y	Y	N
14 Hultgren	Y	Y	Y	Y	Y	Y	N
15 Johnson	+	+	+	Y	Y	Y	Y

KEY   **Republicans**   Democrats

Y	Voted for (yea)	X	Paired against	C	Voted "present" to avoid possible conflict of interest
#	Paired for	–	Announced against		
+	Announced for	P	Voted "present"	?	Did not vote or otherwise make a position known
N	Voted against (nay)				

	152	153	154	155	156	157	158
16 **Manzullo**	Y	Y	Y	Y	Y	Y	N
17 **Schilling**	Y	Y	Y	Y	Y	Y	N
18 **Schock**	Y	Y	Y	Y	Y	Y	N
19 **Shimkus**	Y	Y	Y	Y	Y	Y	N
INDIANA							
1 Visclosky	Y	Y	N	N	N	Y	Y
2 Donnelly	Y	Y	N	N	N	Y	N
3 **Stutzman**	?	?	Y	Y	Y	Y	N
4 **Rokita**	Y	Y	Y	Y	Y	Y	N
5 **Burton**	Y	Y	?	Y	?	Y	N
6 **Pence**	Y	Y	Y	Y	Y	Y	N
7 Carson	Y	Y	N	N	N	Y	Y
8 **Bucshon**	Y	Y	Y	Y	Y	Y	N
9 **Young**	Y	Y	Y	Y	Y	Y	N
IOWA							
1 Braley	Y	Y	N	N	N	Y	+
2 Loebsack	Y	Y	N	N	N	Y	Y
3 Boswell	Y	Y	N	N	N	Y	N
4 **Latham**	Y	Y	Y	Y	Y	?	N
5 **King**	Y	Y	Y	Y	Y	Y	–
KANSAS							
1 **Huelskamp**	Y	Y	Y	Y	Y	Y	N
2 **Jenkins**	Y	Y	Y	Y	Y	Y	N
3 **Yoder**	Y	Y	Y	Y	Y	Y	N
4 **Pompeo**	Y	Y	Y	Y	Y	Y	N
KENTUCKY							
1 **Whitfield**	Y	Y	?	Y	Y	Y	N
2 **Guthrie**	Y	Y	Y	Y	Y	Y	N
3 Yarmuth	Y	Y	N	N	N	Y	Y
4 **Davis**	Y	Y	Y	Y	Y	Y	N
5 **Rogers**	Y	Y	Y	Y	Y	Y	N
6 Chandler	Y	Y	N	N	N	Y	N
LOUISIANA							
1 **Scalise**	Y	Y	Y	Y	Y	Y	N
2 Richmond	Y	Y	N	N	N	Y	Y
3 **Landry**	?	?	Y	Y	Y	Y	N
4 **Fleming**	Y	Y	Y	Y	Y	Y	N
5 **Alexander**	Y	Y	Y	Y	Y	Y	N
6 **Cassidy**	+	P	Y	Y	Y	Y	N
7 **Boustany**	Y	Y	Y	Y	Y	Y	N
MAINE							
1 Pingree	Y	Y	N	N	N	Y	Y
2 Michaud	Y	Y	N	N	N	Y	N
MARYLAND							
1 **Harris**	Y	Y	Y	Y	Y	Y	N
2 Ruppersberger	Y	Y	N	N	N	Y	Y
3 Sarbanes	Y	Y	N	N	N	Y	Y
4 Edwards	+	+	N	N	N	Y	Y
5 Hoyer	Y	Y	N	N	N	Y	Y
6 **Bartlett**	Y	Y	Y	Y	Y	Y	N
7 Cummings	?	?	?	N	N	Y	Y
8 Van Hollen	Y	Y	N	N	N	Y	Y
MASSACHUSETTS							
1 Olver	Y	Y	N	N	N	Y	Y
2 Neal	Y	Y	N	N	N	Y	Y
3 McGovern	Y	Y	N	N	N	Y	?
4 Frank	?	?	N	N	N	Y	?
5 Tsongas	Y	Y	N	N	N	Y	Y
6 Tierney	Y	Y	N	N	N	Y	Y
7 Markey	Y	Y	N	N	N	Y	Y
8 Capuano	Y	Y	N	N	N	Y	Y
9 Lynch	Y	Y	N	N	N	Y	Y
10 Keating	Y	Y	N	N	N	Y	Y
MICHIGAN							
1 **Benishek**	Y	Y	Y	Y	Y	Y	N
2 **Huizenga**	Y	Y	Y	Y	Y	Y	N
3 **Amash**	Y	N	Y	Y	Y	N	N
4 **Camp**	Y	Y	Y	Y	Y	Y	N
5 Kildee	Y	Y	N	N	N	Y	Y
6 **Upton**	Y	Y	Y	Y	Y	Y	N
7 **Walberg**	Y	Y	?	Y	Y	Y	N
8 **Rogers**	Y	Y	Y	Y	Y	Y	N
9 Peters	Y	Y	N	N	N	Y	Y
10 **Miller**	Y	Y	Y	Y	Y	Y	N
11 **McCotter**	Y	Y	Y	Y	Y	Y	N
12 Levin	Y	Y	N	N	N	Y	Y
13 Clarke	Y	Y	N	N	N	Y	Y
14 Conyers	Y	Y	N	N	N	Y	Y
15 Dingell	Y	Y	N	N	N	Y	Y
MINNESOTA							
1 Walz	Y	Y	N	N	N	Y	N
2 **Kline**	Y	Y	Y	Y	Y	Y	N
3 **Paulsen**	Y	Y	Y	Y	Y	Y	Y
4 McCollum	Y	Y	N	N	N	Y	Y

	152	153	154	155	156	157	158
5 Ellison	Y	Y	N	N	N	Y	Y
6 **Bachmann**	Y	Y	Y	Y	Y	Y	N
7 Peterson	Y	Y	N	N	N	Y	N
8 **Cravaack**	Y	Y	Y	Y	Y	Y	N
MISSISSIPPI							
1 **Nunnelee**	Y	Y	Y	Y	Y	Y	N
2 Thompson	Y	Y	N	N	N	Y	N
3 **Harper**	Y	Y	Y	Y	Y	Y	N
4 **Palazzo**	Y	Y	Y	Y	Y	Y	N
MISSOURI							
1 Clay	Y	Y	N	N	N	Y	Y
2 **Akin**	Y	Y	Y	?	?	?	N
3 Carnahan	Y	Y	N	N	N	Y	Y
4 **Hartzler**	Y	Y	Y	Y	Y	Y	N
5 Cleaver	Y	Y	N	N	N	Y	Y
6 **Graves**	Y	Y	Y	Y	Y	Y	N
7 **Long**	Y	Y	Y	Y	Y	Y	N
8 **Emerson**	Y	Y	Y	Y	Y	Y	N
9 **Luetkemeyer**	Y	Y	Y	Y	Y	Y	N
MONTANA							
AL **Rehberg**	Y	Y	Y	Y	Y	Y	N
NEBRASKA							
1 **Fortenberry**	Y	Y	Y	Y	Y	Y	N
2 **Terry**	Y	Y	Y	Y	?	Y	N
3 **Smith**	Y	Y	Y	Y	Y	Y	N
NEVADA							
1 Berkley	Y	Y	N	N	N	Y	Y
2 **Amodei**	Y	Y	Y	Y	Y	Y	N
3 **Heck**	Y	Y	Y	Y	Y	Y	N
NEW HAMPSHIRE							
1 **Guinta**	Y	Y	Y	Y	Y	Y	N
2 **Bass**	Y	Y	Y	Y	Y	Y	N
NEW JERSEY							
1 Andrews	?	?	?	?	?	?	?
2 **LoBiondo**	Y	Y	Y	Y	Y	Y	N
3 **Runyan**	Y	Y	Y	Y	Y	Y	N
4 **Smith**	Y	Y	Y	Y	Y	Y	N
5 **Garrett**	Y	Y	Y	Y	Y	Y	N
6 Pallone	Y	Y	N	N	N	Y	Y
7 **Lance**	Y	Y	Y	Y	Y	Y	N
8 Pascrell	?	?	N	N	N	Y	Y
9 Rothman	Y	Y	N	N	N	Y	Y
10 Vacant							
11 **Frelinghuysen**	Y	Y	Y	Y	Y	Y	N
12 Holt	Y	?	N	N	N	Y	Y
13 Sires	Y	Y	N	N	N	Y	Y
NEW MEXICO							
1 Heinrich	Y	Y	N	N	N	Y	Y
2 **Pearce**	Y	Y	Y	Y	Y	Y	N
3 Luján	Y	Y	N	N	N	Y	Y
NEW YORK							
1 Bishop	Y	Y	N	N	N	Y	Y
2 Israel	Y	Y	N	N	N	Y	Y
3 **King**	Y	Y	Y	Y	Y	Y	N
4 McCarthy	Y	Y	N	N	N	Y	Y
5 Ackerman	Y	Y	N	N	N	Y	Y
6 Meeks	Y	Y	N	N	N	Y	Y
7 Crowley	Y	Y	N	N	N	Y	Y
8 Nadler	Y	Y	N	N	N	Y	Y
9 **Turner**	Y	Y	Y	Y	Y	Y	N
10 Towns	?	?	N	N	N	Y	Y
11 Clarke	Y	Y	N	N	N	Y	Y
12 Velázquez	?	?	N	N	N	Y	Y
13 **Grimm**	Y	Y	Y	Y	Y	Y	N
14 Maloney	Y	Y	N	N	N	Y	Y
15 Rangel	?	?	?	?	?	?	?
16 Serrano	Y	Y	N	N	N	Y	Y
17 Engel	Y	Y	N	N	N	Y	Y
18 Lowey	Y	Y	N	N	N	Y	Y
19 **Hayworth**	Y	Y	Y	Y	Y	Y	N
20 **Gibson**	Y	Y	Y	Y	Y	Y	N
21 Tonko	Y	Y	N	N	N	Y	Y
22 Hinchey	?	?	N	N	N	Y	Y
23 Owens	Y	Y	N	N	N	Y	N
24 **Hanna**	?	?	Y	Y	Y	Y	N
25 **Buerkle**	Y	Y	Y	Y	Y	Y	N
26 Hochul	Y	Y	N	N	N	Y	N
27 Higgins	Y	Y	N	N	N	Y	Y
28 Slaughter	?	?	?	?	?	?	?
29 **Reed**	Y	Y	Y	Y	Y	Y	N
NORTH CAROLINA							
1 Butterfield	?	?	N	N	N	Y	Y
2 **Ellmers**	Y	Y	Y	Y	Y	Y	N
3 **Jones**	?	?	Y	N	N	Y	N
4 Price	Y	Y	N	N	N	Y	Y

	152	153	154	155	156	157	158
5 **Foxx**	Y	Y	Y	Y	Y	Y	N
6 **Coble**	Y	Y	Y	Y	Y	Y	N
7 McIntyre	+	+	–	–	+	+	–
8 Kissell	Y	Y	N	N	N	Y	N
9 **Myrick**	Y	Y	Y	Y	Y	Y	N
10 **McHenry**	Y	Y	Y	Y	Y	Y	N
11 Shuler	?	?	Y	Y	N	Y	N
12 Watt	Y	Y	N	N	N	Y	Y
13 Miller	Y	Y	N	N	N	Y	Y
NORTH DAKOTA							
AL **Berg**	Y	Y	Y	Y	Y	Y	N
OHIO							
1 **Chabot**	Y	Y	Y	Y	Y	Y	N
2 **Schmidt**	?	?	Y	Y	Y	Y	N
3 **Turner**	Y	Y	Y	Y	Y	Y	N
4 **Jordan**	Y	Y	Y	Y	Y	Y	N
5 **Latta**	Y	Y	Y	Y	Y	Y	N
6 **Johnson**	Y	Y	Y	Y	Y	Y	N
7 **Austria**	?	?	?	Y	Y	Y	N
8 **Boehner**							
9 Kaptur	?	?	N	N	N	Y	Y
10 Kucinich	Y	Y	N	N	N	Y	Y
11 Fudge	Y	Y	N	N	N	Y	Y
12 **Tiberi**	Y	Y	Y	Y	Y	Y	N
13 Sutton	Y	Y	N	N	N	Y	Y
14 **LaTourette**	Y	Y	Y	Y	Y	Y	N
15 **Stivers**	Y	Y	Y	Y	Y	Y	N
16 **Renacci**	Y	Y	Y	Y	Y	Y	N
17 Ryan	Y	Y	N	N	N	Y	N
18 **Gibbs**	Y	Y	Y	Y	Y	Y	N
OKLAHOMA							
1 **Sullivan**	Y	Y	Y	Y	Y	Y	N
2 Boren	?	?	N	N	N	Y	N
3 **Lucas**	Y	Y	Y	Y	Y	Y	N
4 **Cole**	Y	Y	Y	Y	Y	Y	N
5 **Lankford**	Y	Y	Y	Y	Y	Y	N
OREGON							
1 Bonamici	Y	Y	N	N	N	Y	Y
2 **Walden**	Y	Y	Y	Y	Y	Y	N
3 Blumenauer	Y	Y	N	N	N	Y	N
4 DeFazio	Y	Y	N	N	N	Y	Y
5 Schrader	Y	Y	N	N	N	Y	N
PENNSYLVANIA							
1 Brady	Y	Y	N	N	N	Y	Y
2 Fattah	Y	Y	N	N	N	Y	Y
3 **Kelly**	Y	Y	Y	Y	Y	Y	N
4 Altmire	Y	Y	N	N	N	Y	N
5 **Thompson**	Y	Y	Y	Y	Y	Y	N
6 **Gerlach**	Y	Y	Y	Y	Y	Y	Y
7 **Meehan**	Y	Y	Y	Y	Y	Y	N
8 **Fitzpatrick**	Y	Y	Y	Y	Y	Y	N
9 **Shuster**	Y	Y	Y	Y	Y	Y	N
10 **Marino**	?	?	?	?	?	?	?
11 **Barletta**	Y	Y	Y	Y	Y	Y	N
12 Critz	?	?	N	N	N	Y	N
13 Schwartz	Y	Y	N	N	N	Y	Y
14 Doyle	Y	Y	N	N	N	Y	Y
15 **Dent**	Y	Y	Y	Y	Y	Y	N
16 **Pitts**	Y	Y	Y	?	?	?	?
17 Holden	Y	Y	N	N	N	Y	N
18 **Murphy**	Y	Y	Y	Y	Y	Y	N
19 **Platts**	Y	Y	Y	Y	Y	Y	Y
RHODE ISLAND							
1 Cicilline	Y	?	N	N	N	Y	Y
2 Langevin	Y	Y	N	N	N	Y	Y
SOUTH CAROLINA							
1 **Scott**	Y	Y	Y	Y	Y	Y	N
2 **Wilson**	Y	Y	Y	Y	Y	Y	N
3 **Duncan**	Y	Y	Y	Y	Y	+	N
4 **Gowdy**	Y	Y	Y	Y	Y	?	N
5 **Mulvaney**	Y	Y	Y	Y	Y	Y	N
6 Clyburn	Y	Y	N	N	N	Y	Y
SOUTH DAKOTA							
AL **Noem**	?	?	Y	Y	Y	Y	N
TENNESSEE							
1 **Roe**	Y	Y	Y	Y	Y	Y	N
2 **Duncan**	Y	Y	Y	Y	Y	Y	N
3 **Fleischmann**	Y	Y	Y	Y	Y	Y	N
4 **DesJarlais**	Y	Y	Y	Y	Y	Y	N
5 Cooper	Y	Y	N	N	N	Y	Y
6 **Black**	Y	Y	Y	Y	Y	Y	N
7 **Blackburn**	Y	Y	Y	Y	Y	Y	N
8 **Fincher**	Y	Y	?	?	?	?	–
9 Cohen	+	+	–	–	–	+	Y

	152	153	154	155	156	157	158
TEXAS							
1 **Gohmert**	Y	Y	Y	Y	Y	Y	N
2 **Poe**	Y	Y	Y	Y	Y	Y	N
3 **Johnson, S.**	?	?	Y	Y	Y	Y	N
4 **Hall**	Y	Y	Y	Y	Y	Y	N
5 **Hensarling**	Y	Y	Y	Y	Y	Y	N
6 **Barton**	?	?	Y	Y	N	Y	N
7 **Culberson**	?	?	Y	Y	Y	Y	N
8 **Brady**	Y	Y	Y	Y	Y	Y	N
9 Green, A.	Y	Y	N	N	N	Y	Y
10 **McCaul**	Y	Y	Y	Y	Y	Y	?
11 **Conaway**	Y	Y	Y	Y	Y	Y	N
12 **Granger**	Y	Y	Y	Y	Y	Y	N
13 **Thornberry**	Y	Y	Y	Y	Y	Y	N
14 **Paul**	?	?	Y	Y	Y	N	?
15 Hinojosa	Y	Y	N	N	N	Y	Y
16 Reyes	Y	Y	N	N	N	Y	Y
17 **Flores**	Y	?	Y	Y	Y	Y	N
18 Jackson Lee	Y	Y	N	N	N	Y	Y
19 **Neugebauer**	Y	Y	Y	Y	Y	Y	N
20 Gonzalez	Y	Y	N	N	N	Y	Y
21 **Smith**	Y	Y	Y	Y	Y	Y	N
22 **Olson**	Y	Y	Y	Y	Y	Y	N
23 **Canseco**	Y	Y	Y	Y	Y	Y	N
24 **Marchant**	Y	Y	Y	Y	Y	?	N
25 Doggett	?	?	?	N	N	Y	Y
26 **Burgess**	?	?	Y	Y	Y	Y	N
27 **Farenthold**	Y	Y	Y	Y	Y	Y	N
28 Cuellar	Y	Y	N	N	N	Y	N
29 Green, G.	Y	Y	N	N	N	Y	N
30 Johnson, E.	Y	Y	N	N	N	Y	Y
31 **Carter**	Y	Y	Y	Y	Y	Y	N
32 **Sessions**	Y	Y	Y	Y	Y	Y	N
UTAH							
1 **Bishop**	Y	Y	Y	Y	Y	Y	N
2 Matheson	Y	Y	N	N	N	Y	N
3 **Chaffetz**	Y	N	Y	Y	Y	Y	N
VERMONT							
AL Welch	Y	Y	N	N	N	Y	Y
VIRGINIA							
1 **Wittman**	Y	Y	Y	Y	Y	Y	N
2 **Rigell**	Y	N	Y	Y	Y	Y	N
3 Scott	Y	Y	?	N	N	Y	Y
4 **Forbes**	Y	Y	Y	Y	Y	Y	N
5 **Hurt**	Y	Y	Y	Y	Y	Y	N
6 **Goodlatte**	Y	Y	Y	Y	Y	Y	N
7 **Cantor**	Y	Y	Y	Y	Y	Y	N
8 Moran	Y	Y	N	N	N	Y	Y
9 **Griffith**	Y	Y	Y	Y	Y	Y	N
10 **Wolf**	Y	Y	Y	Y	Y	Y	N
11 Connolly	Y	Y	N	N	N	Y	Y
WASHINGTON							
1 Vacant							
2 Larsen	Y	Y	N	N	N	Y	Y
3 **Herrera Beutler**	Y	Y	Y	Y	Y	Y	N
4 **Hastings**	Y	Y	Y	Y	Y	Y	N
5 **McMorris Rodgers**	Y	Y	Y	Y	Y	Y	?
6 Dicks	?	?	N	N	N	Y	?
7 McDermott	Y	Y	N	N	N	Y	Y
8 **Reichert**	Y	Y	Y	Y	Y	Y	Y
9 Smith	Y	Y	N	N	N	Y	Y
WEST VIRGINIA							
1 **McKinley**	Y	Y	Y	Y	Y	Y	N
2 **Capito**	Y	Y	Y	Y	Y	Y	N
3 Rahall	Y	Y	N	N	N	Y	N
WISCONSIN							
1 **Ryan**	Y	Y	Y	Y	Y	Y	N
2 Baldwin	Y	Y	N	N	N	Y	Y
3 Kind	Y	Y	N	N	N	Y	N
4 Moore	Y	Y	N	N	N	Y	N
5 **Sensenbrenner**	Y	Y	Y	Y	Y	Y	N
6 **Petri**	Y	Y	Y	Y	Y	Y	N
7 **Duffy**	Y	Y	Y	Y	Y	Y	N
8 **Ribble**	Y	N	Y	Y	Y	Y	N
WYOMING							
AL **Lummis**	Y	Y	Y	Y	Y	Y	N

IN THE HOUSE | By Vote Number

159. HR 4089. **Sportsmen's Land Access/Applicability Conditions.**
Grijalva, D-Ariz., amendment that would prevent provisions in the bill that require federal land management officials to facilitate the use of public lands for recreational hunting, fishing and shooting from taking effect unless the total amount of federal land made available for those activities is less than 75 percent of federal lands. Rejected in Committee of the Whole 138-279: R 2-234; D 136-45. April 17, 2012.

160. HR 4089. **Sportsmen's Land Access/Polar Bear Trophy Importation.** Peters, D-Mich., amendment that would strike language from the bill that would require the Interior secretary to issue importation permits to hunters for polar bear trophies taken in Canada before the bears were listed as threatened under the Endangered Species Act. Rejected in Committee of the Whole 155-262: R 10-226; D 145-36. April 17, 2012.

161. HR 4089. **Sportsmen's Land Access/Wilderness Activity Prohibition.** Heinrich, D-N.M., amendment that would clarify that the bill would not permit oil and gas development, mining, logging or motorized activity within any federal land that is designated as wilderness. Rejected in Committee of the Whole 176-244: R 8-228; D 168-16. April 17, 2012.

162. HR 4089. **Sportsmen's Land Access/National Monument Designation.** Foxx, R-N.C., amendment that would require the federal government to consult with states and obtain state approval when designating federal land as a monument location or seeking to restrict certain public use activities on national monument lands. Adopted in Committee of the Whole 223-198: R 216-21; D 7-177. April 17, 2012.

163. HR 4089. **Sportsmen's Land Access/Recommit.** Tierney, D-Mass., motion to recommit the bill to the Natural Resources Committee and report it back immediately with an amendment that would authorize funds for the Commodity Futures Trading Commission for oversight of the oil market to combat speculation and market manipulation. It also would prohibit members of Congress from participating in hunting, fishing or recreational shooting activities on federal lands paid for by a registered lobbyist or foreign agent. Motion rejected 160-261: R 1-236; D 159-25. April 17, 2012.

164. HR 4089. **Sportsmen's Land Access/Passage.** Passage of the bill that would open lands under the jurisdiction of the Bureau of Land Management and the U.S. Forest Service, including wilderness lands, for recreational fishing, hunting and shooting unless the managing federal agency acts to close lands to such activities. Under the bill, agencies could block or limit access to land to ensure resource conservation, public safety and national security. As amended, the bill would include shooting ranges in the list of valid uses of public land. It also would open, with certain exceptions, national monument land under the Bureau of Land Management's jurisdiction for recreational shooting and limit the EPA's authority to regulate bullets, angling lures and other hunting equipment under its jurisdiction. Passed 274-146: R 235-2; D 39-144. April 17, 2012.

	159	160	161	162	163	164
ALABAMA						
1 Bonner	N	N	N	Y	N	Y
2 Roby	N	N	N	Y	N	Y
3 Rogers	N	N	N	Y	N	Y
4 Aderholt	N	N	N	Y	N	Y
5 Brooks	N	N	N	Y	N	Y
6 Bachus	N	N	N	Y	N	Y
7 Sewell	N	Y	Y	N	Y	N
ALASKA						
AL Young	N	N	N	Y	N	Y
ARIZONA						
1 Gosar	N	N	N	Y	N	Y
2 Franks	N	N	N	Y	N	Y
3 Quayle	N	N	N	Y	N	Y
4 Pastor	Y	Y	Y	N	Y	N
5 Schweikert	N	?	N	Y	N	Y
6 Flake	N	N	N	Y	N	Y
7 Grijalva	N	Y	Y	N	Y	N
8 Vacant						
ARKANSAS						
1 Crawford	N	N	N	Y	N	Y
2 Griffin	N	N	N	Y	N	Y
3 Womack	N	N	N	Y	N	Y
4 Ross	N	N	N	Y	N	Y
CALIFORNIA						
1 Thompson	N	N	Y	N	Y	Y
2 Herger	N	N	N	Y	N	Y
3 Lungren	N	N	N	Y	N	Y
4 McClintock	N	N	N	Y	N	Y
5 Matsui	Y	Y	Y	N	Y	N
6 Woolsey	Y	Y	Y	N	Y	N
7 Miller, George	N	Y	Y	N	Y	N
8 Pelosi	Y	Y	Y	N	Y	N
9 Lee	Y	Y	Y	N	Y	N
10 Garamendi	Y	Y	Y	N	Y	Y
11 McNerney	Y	Y	Y	N	Y	N
12 Speier	Y	Y	Y	N	Y	N
13 Stark	Y	Y	Y	N	Y	N
14 Eshoo	Y	Y	Y	N	Y	N
15 Honda	Y	Y	Y	N	Y	N
16 Lofgren	Y	Y	Y	N	Y	N
17 Farr	Y	Y	Y	N	Y	N
18 Cardoza	N	N	Y	N	N	Y
19 Denham	N	N	N	Y	N	Y
20 Costa	N	N	Y	N	N	Y
21 Nunes	N	N	N	Y	N	Y
22 McCarthy	N	N	N	Y	N	Y
23 Capps	Y	Y	Y	N	Y	N
24 Gallegly	N	Y	N	Y	N	Y
25 McKeon	N	N	N	Y	N	Y
26 Dreier	N	N	N	Y	N	Y
27 Sherman	Y	Y	Y	N	Y	N
28 Berman	Y	Y	Y	N	Y	N
29 Schiff	Y	Y	Y	N	Y	N
30 Waxman	Y	Y	Y	N	Y	N
31 Becerra	Y	Y	Y	N	Y	N
32 Chu	Y	Y	Y	N	Y	N
33 Bass	Y	Y	Y	N	Y	N
34 Roybal-Allard	Y	Y	Y	N	Y	N
35 Waters	Y	Y	Y	N	Y	N
36 Hahn	Y	Y	Y	N	Y	N
37 Richardson	Y	Y	Y	N	Y	N
38 Napolitano	?	?	?	?	+	-
39 Sánchez, Linda	Y	Y	Y	N	Y	N
40 Royce	N	N	N	Y	N	Y
41 Lewis	N	N	N	Y	N	Y
42 Miller, Gary	N	N	N	Y	N	Y
43 Baca	N	Y	N	N	N	Y
44 Calvert	N	N	N	Y	N	Y
45 Bono Mack	N	Y	N	Y	N	Y
46 Rohrabacher	N	N	N	Y	N	Y
47 Sanchez, Loretta	Y	Y	Y	N	Y	N
48 Campbell	N	Y	N	Y	N	Y
49 Issa	N	N	N	Y	N	Y
50 Bilbray	N	N	N	Y	N	Y
51 Filner	+	+	+	-	+	-
52 Hunter	N	N	N	Y	N	Y
53 Davis	Y	Y	Y	N	N	N

	159	160	161	162	163	164
COLORADO						
1 DeGette	Y	Y	Y	N	Y	N
2 Polis	Y	Y	Y	N	Y	N
3 Tipton	N	N	N	Y	N	Y
4 Gardner	N	N	N	Y	N	Y
5 Lamborn	N	N	N	Y	N	Y
6 Coffman	N	N	N	Y	N	Y
7 Perlmutter	N	Y	Y	N	Y	N
CONNECTICUT						
1 Larson	Y	Y	Y	N	Y	N
2 Courtney	N	Y	Y	N	Y	N
3 DeLauro	Y	Y	Y	N	Y	N
4 Himes	N	Y	Y	N	Y	N
5 Murphy	Y	Y	Y	N	Y	N
DELAWARE						
AL Carney	Y	N	Y	N	Y	N
FLORIDA						
1 Miller	N	N	N	Y	N	Y
2 Southerland	N	N	N	Y	N	Y
3 Brown	Y	Y	Y	N	Y	N
4 Crenshaw	N	N	N	Y	N	Y
5 Nugent	N	N	N	Y	N	Y
6 Stearns	N	N	N	Y	N	Y
7 Mica	N	N	N	Y	N	Y
8 Webster	N	N	N	Y	N	Y
9 Bilirakis	N	N	N	Y	N	Y
10 Young	N	N	N	Y	N	Y
11 Castor	Y	Y	Y	N	Y	N
12 Ross	N	N	N	Y	N	Y
13 Buchanan	N	N	N	Y	N	Y
14 Mack	N	N	N	Y	N	Y
15 Posey	N	N	N	Y	N	Y
16 Rooney	N	N	N	Y	N	Y
17 Wilson	Y	Y	Y	N	Y	N
18 Ros-Lehtinen	N	N	N	Y	N	Y
19 Deutch	Y	Y	Y	N	Y	N
20 Wasserman Schultz	Y	Y	Y	N	Y	N
21 Diaz-Balart	N	N	N	Y	N	Y
22 West	N	N	N	N	N	Y
23 Hastings	Y	Y	Y	N	Y	N
24 Adams	N	N	N	Y	N	Y
25 Rivera	N	N	N	Y	N	Y
GEORGIA						
1 Kingston	N	N	N	Y	N	Y
2 Bishop	N	N	N	N	N	Y
3 Westmoreland	N	N	N	Y	N	Y
4 Johnson	Y	Y	Y	N	Y	N
5 Lewis	Y	Y	Y	N	Y	N
6 Price	N	N	N	Y	N	Y
7 Woodall	N	N	N	Y	N	Y
8 Scott, A.	N	N	N	Y	N	Y
9 Graves	N	N	N	Y	N	Y
10 Broun	N	N	N	Y	N	Y
11 Gingrey	N	N	N	Y	N	Y
12 Barrow	N	N	N	N	N	Y
13 Scott, D.	Y	Y	Y	N	Y	N
HAWAII						
1 Hanabusa	Y	Y	Y	N	Y	N
2 Hirono	Y	Y	Y	N	Y	N
IDAHO						
1 Labrador	N	N	N	Y	N	Y
2 Simpson	N	N	N	N	N	Y
ILLINOIS						
1 Rush	Y	Y	Y	N	Y	N
2 Jackson	Y	Y	Y	N	Y	N
3 Lipinski	N	Y	Y	N	Y	Y
4 Gutierrez	Y	Y	Y	N	Y	N
5 Quigley	Y	Y	Y	N	Y	N
6 Roskam	N	N	N	Y	N	Y
7 Davis	Y	Y	Y	N	Y	N
8 Walsh	N	N	N	Y	N	Y
9 Schakowsky	Y	Y	Y	N	Y	N
10 Dold	N	Y	Y	N	N	N
11 Kinzinger	N	N	N	Y	N	Y
12 Costello	N	N	Y	N	Y	N
13 Biggert	N	N	N	Y	N	Y
14 Hultgren	N	N	N	Y	N	Y
15 Johnson	Y	Y	Y	N	N	N

KEY Republicans   Democrats

Y Voted for (yea)	X Paired against
# Paired for	- Announced against
+ Announced for	P Voted "present"
N Voted against (nay)	

C Voted "present" to avoid possible conflict of interest

? Did not vote or otherwise make a position known

	159	160	161	162	163	164
16 **Manzullo**	N	N	N	Y	N	Y
17 **Schilling**	N	N	N	Y	N	Y
18 **Schock**	N	N	N	Y	N	Y
19 **Shimkus**	N	N	N	Y	N	Y
INDIANA						
1 Visclosky	Y	Y	Y	N	Y	N
2 Donnelly	N	N	N	N	N	Y
3 **Stutzman**	N	N	N	Y	N	Y
4 **Rokita**	N	N	N	Y	N	Y
5 **Burton**	N	N	N	Y	N	Y
6 **Pence**	N	N	N	Y	N	Y
7 Carson	Y	Y	Y	N	Y	Y
8 **Bucshon**	N	N	N	Y	N	Y
9 **Young**	N	N	N	Y	N	Y
IOWA						
1 Braley	Y	Y	Y	N	Y	N
2 Loebsack	N	Y	Y	N	Y	Y
3 Boswell	N	N	N	Y	N	Y
4 **Latham**	N	N	N	Y	N	Y
5 **King**	N	N	N	Y	N	Y
KANSAS						
1 **Huelskamp**	N	N	N	Y	N	Y
2 **Jenkins**	N	N	N	Y	N	Y
3 **Yoder**	N	N	N	Y	N	Y
4 **Pompeo**	N	N	N	Y	N	Y
KENTUCKY						
1 **Whitfield**	N	N	N	Y	N	Y
2 **Guthrie**	N	N	N	Y	N	Y
3 Yarmuth	Y	Y	Y	N	Y	N
4 **Davis**	N	N	N	Y	N	Y
5 **Rogers**	N	N	N	Y	N	Y
6 Chandler	N	N	N	N	N	Y
LOUISIANA						
1 **Scalise**	N	N	N	Y	N	Y
2 Richmond	N	Y	Y	N	Y	Y
3 **Landry**	N	N	?	Y	N	Y
4 **Fleming**	N	N	N	Y	N	Y
5 **Alexander**	N	N	N	Y	N	Y
6 **Cassidy**	N	N	N	Y	N	Y
7 **Boustany**	N	N	N	Y	N	Y
MAINE						
1 Pingree	Y	Y	Y	N	Y	N
2 Michaud	N	N	Y	N	N	Y
MARYLAND						
1 **Harris**	N	N	N	Y	N	Y
2 Ruppersberger	Y	Y	Y	N	Y	N
3 Sarbanes	Y	Y	Y	N	Y	N
4 Edwards	Y	Y	Y	N	Y	N
5 Hoyer	?	Y	Y	N	Y	N
6 **Bartlett**	N	Y	N	Y	N	Y
7 Cummings	Y	Y	Y	N	Y	N
8 Van Hollen	Y	Y	Y	N	Y	N
MASSACHUSETTS						
1 Olver	Y	Y	Y	N	Y	N
2 Neal	Y	Y	Y	N	Y	N
3 McGovern	Y	Y	Y	N	Y	N
4 Frank	Y	Y	Y	N	Y	?
5 Tsongas	Y	Y	Y	N	Y	N
6 Tierney	Y	Y	Y	N	Y	N
7 Markey	Y	Y	Y	N	Y	N
8 Capuano	Y	Y	Y	N	Y	N
9 Lynch	Y	Y	Y	N	Y	N
10 Keating	Y	Y	Y	N	Y	N
MICHIGAN						
1 **Benishek**	N	N	N	Y	N	Y
2 **Huizenga**	N	N	N	Y	N	Y
3 **Amash**	N	N	N	Y	N	Y
4 **Camp**	N	N	N	Y	N	Y
5 Kildee	Y	Y	Y	N	Y	N
6 **Upton**	N	N	N	Y	N	Y
7 **Walberg**	N	N	N	Y	N	Y
8 **Rogers**	N	N	N	Y	N	Y
9 Peters	Y	Y	Y	N	Y	N
10 **Miller**	N	N	N	N	N	Y
11 **McCotter**	N	N	N	Y	N	Y
12 Levin	Y	Y	Y	N	Y	N
13 Clarke	Y	Y	Y	N	Y	N
14 Conyers	Y	Y	Y	N	Y	N
15 Dingell	Y	N	Y	N	Y	N
MINNESOTA						
1 Walz	N	N	Y	N	N	Y
2 **Kline**	N	N	N	Y	N	Y
3 **Paulsen**	N	N	N	N	N	Y
4 McCollum	Y	Y	Y	N	Y	N

	159	160	161	162	163	164
5 Ellison	Y	Y	Y	N	Y	N
6 **Bachmann**	N	N	N	Y	N	Y
7 Peterson	N	N	N	Y	N	Y
8 **Cravaack**	N	N	N	Y	N	Y
MISSISSIPPI						
1 **Nunnelee**	N	N	N	Y	N	Y
2 Thompson	N	N	Y	N	Y	Y
3 **Harper**	N	N	N	Y	N	Y
4 **Palazzo**	N	N	N	Y	N	Y
MISSOURI						
1 Clay	Y	Y	Y	N	Y	N
2 **Akin**	N	N	N	Y	N	Y
3 Carnahan	Y	Y	Y	N	Y	N
4 **Hartzler**	N	N	N	Y	N	Y
5 Cleaver	Y	Y	Y	N	Y	N
6 **Graves**	N	N	N	Y	N	Y
7 **Long**	N	N	N	Y	N	Y
8 **Emerson**	N	N	N	Y	N	Y
9 **Luetkemeyer**	N	N	N	Y	N	Y
MONTANA						
AL **Rehberg**	N	N	N	Y	N	Y
NEBRASKA						
1 **Fortenberry**	N	N	N	N	N	Y
2 **Terry**	N	N	N	Y	N	Y
3 **Smith**	N	N	N	Y	N	Y
NEVADA						
1 Berkley	Y	Y	Y	N	Y	N
2 **Amodei**	N	N	N	Y	N	Y
3 **Heck**	N	N	N	Y	N	Y
NEW HAMPSHIRE						
1 **Guinta**	N	N	N	N	N	Y
2 **Bass**	N	N	Y	N	N	Y
NEW JERSEY						
1 Andrews	?	?	?	?	?	?
2 **LoBiondo**	N	N	N	N	N	Y
3 **Runyan**	N	N	N	Y	N	Y
4 **Smith**	N	N	N	N	N	Y
5 **Garrett**	N	N	N	Y	N	Y
6 Pallone	Y	Y	Y	N	Y	N
7 **Lance**	N	N	N	Y	N	Y
8 Pascrell	Y	Y	Y	N	Y	N
9 Rothman	Y	Y	Y	N	Y	N
10 Vacant						
11 **Frelinghuysen**	N	Y	N	Y	N	Y
12 Holt	Y	Y	Y	N	Y	N
13 Sires	Y	Y	Y	N	Y	N
NEW MEXICO						
1 Heinrich	N	N	Y	N	N	Y
2 **Pearce**	N	N	N	Y	N	Y
3 Luján	N	N	Y	N	Y	N
NEW YORK						
1 Bishop	Y	Y	Y	N	Y	N
2 Israel	Y	Y	Y	N	Y	N
3 **King**	N	N	N	N	N	Y
4 McCarthy	Y	Y	Y	N	Y	N
5 Ackerman	Y	Y	Y	N	Y	N
6 Meeks	Y	Y	Y	N	Y	N
7 Crowley	Y	Y	Y	N	Y	N
8 Nadler	Y	Y	Y	N	Y	N
9 **Turner**	N	N	Y	Y	N	Y
10 Towns	Y	Y	Y	N	Y	N
11 Clarke	Y	Y	Y	N	Y	N
12 Velázquez	Y	Y	Y	N	Y	N
13 **Grimm**	N	N	N	N	N	Y
14 Maloney	Y	Y	Y	N	Y	N
15 Rangel	?	?	?	?	?	?
16 Serrano	Y	Y	Y	N	Y	N
17 Engel	Y	Y	Y	N	Y	N
18 Lowey	Y	?	Y	N	Y	N
19 **Hayworth**	N	N	Y	N	N	Y
20 **Gibson**	N	N	Y	N	N	Y
21 Tonko	Y	Y	Y	N	Y	N
22 Hinchey	Y	Y	Y	N	Y	N
23 Owens	N	N	N	N	N	Y
24 **Hanna**	N	N	N	N	N	Y
25 **Buerkle**	N	N	N	Y	N	Y
26 Hochul	N	N	N	N	N	Y
27 Higgins	Y	Y	Y	N	Y	N
28 Slaughter	?	?	?	?	?	?
29 **Reed**	N	N	N	Y	N	Y
NORTH CAROLINA						
1 Butterfield	Y	Y	Y	N	Y	N
2 **Ellmers**	N	N	N	Y	N	Y
3 **Jones**	N	N	N	Y	Y	Y
4 Price	Y	Y	Y	N	Y	N

	159	160	161	162	163	164
5 **Foxx**	N	N	N	Y	N	Y
6 **Coble**	N	N	N	Y	N	Y
7 McIntyre	–	–	+	+	–	+
8 Kissell	N	N	N	Y	N	Y
9 **Myrick**	N	N	N	Y	N	Y
10 **McHenry**	N	N	N	Y	N	Y
11 Shuler	N	N	N	N	N	Y
12 Watt	Y	Y	Y	N	Y	N
13 Miller	Y	Y	Y	N	Y	N
NORTH DAKOTA						
AL **Berg**	N	N	N	Y	N	Y
OHIO						
1 **Chabot**	N	N	N	Y	N	Y
2 **Schmidt**	N	N	N	Y	N	Y
3 **Turner**	N	N	N	Y	N	Y
4 **Jordan**	N	N	N	Y	N	Y
5 **Latta**	N	N	N	Y	N	Y
6 **Johnson**	N	N	N	Y	N	Y
7 **Austria**	N	N	N	Y	N	Y
8 **Boehner**						
9 Kaptur	Y	?	Y	N	Y	N
10 Kucinich	Y	Y	Y	N	Y	N
11 Fudge	Y	Y	Y	N	Y	N
12 **Tiberi**	N	N	N	Y	N	Y
13 Sutton	Y	Y	Y	N	Y	N
14 **LaTourette**	N	N	N	Y	N	Y
15 **Stivers**	N	N	N	Y	N	Y
16 **Renacci**	N	N	N	Y	N	Y
17 Ryan	N	N	Y	N	Y	Y
18 **Gibbs**	N	N	N	Y	N	Y
OKLAHOMA						
1 **Sullivan**	–	N	N	Y	N	Y
2 Boren	N	N	N	Y	N	Y
3 **Lucas**	N	N	N	Y	N	Y
4 **Cole**	N	N	N	Y	N	Y
5 **Lankford**	N	N	N	Y	N	Y
OREGON						
1 Bonamici	Y	Y	Y	N	Y	N
2 **Walden**	N	N	N	Y	N	Y
3 Blumenauer	Y	Y	Y	N	Y	N
4 DeFazio	N	N	Y	N	Y	Y
5 Schrader	N	N	Y	N	N	Y
PENNSYLVANIA						
1 Brady	Y	Y	Y	N	Y	N
2 Fattah	Y	Y	Y	N	Y	N
3 **Kelly**	N	N	N	Y	N	Y
4 Altmire	N	N	N	N	N	Y
5 **Thompson**	N	N	N	Y	N	Y
6 **Gerlach**	N	N	N	N	N	Y
7 **Meehan**	N	N	N	Y	N	Y
8 **Fitzpatrick**	N	Y	N	N	N	Y
9 **Shuster**	N	N	N	Y	N	Y
10 **Marino**	?	?	?	?	?	?
11 **Barletta**	N	N	N	Y	N	Y
12 Critz	N	N	Y	N	N	Y
13 Schwartz	Y	Y	Y	N	Y	N
14 Doyle	Y	Y	Y	N	Y	N
15 **Dent**	N	N	N	Y	N	Y
16 **Pitts**	?	?	?	?	?	?
17 Holden	N	N	Y	N	Y	Y
18 **Murphy**	N	N	N	Y	N	Y
19 **Platts**	N	Y	N	N	N	Y
RHODE ISLAND						
1 Cicilline	Y	Y	Y	N	Y	N
2 Langevin	Y	Y	Y	N	Y	N
SOUTH CAROLINA						
1 **Scott**	N	N	N	Y	N	Y
2 **Wilson**	N	N	N	Y	N	Y
3 **Duncan**	N	N	N	Y	N	Y
4 **Gowdy**	N	N	N	Y	N	Y
5 **Mulvaney**	N	N	N	Y	N	Y
6 Clyburn	Y	Y	Y	N	Y	N
SOUTH DAKOTA						
AL **Noem**	N	N	N	Y	N	Y
TENNESSEE						
1 **Roe**	N	N	N	Y	N	Y
2 **Duncan**	N	N	N	Y	N	Y
3 **Fleischmann**	N	N	N	Y	N	Y
4 **DesJarlais**	N	N	N	Y	N	Y
5 Cooper	N	N	Y	N	N	Y
6 **Black**	N	N	N	Y	N	Y
7 **Blackburn**	N	N	N	Y	N	Y
8 **Fincher**	–	–	–	+	–	+
9 Cohen	?	Y	Y	N	Y	N

	159	160	161	162	163	164
TEXAS						
1 **Gohmert**	N	N	N	Y	N	Y
2 **Poe**	N	N	N	Y	N	Y
3 **Johnson, S.**	N	N	N	Y	N	Y
4 **Hall**	N	N	N	Y	N	Y
5 **Hensarling**	N	N	N	Y	N	Y
6 **Barton**	N	N	N	Y	N	Y
7 **Culberson**	N	N	N	Y	N	Y
8 **Brady**	N	N	N	Y	N	Y
9 Green, A.	Y	Y	Y	Y	Y	N
10 **McCaul**	N	N	N	Y	N	Y
11 **Conaway**	N	N	N	Y	N	Y
12 **Granger**	N	N	N	Y	N	Y
13 **Thornberry**	N	N	N	Y	N	Y
14 **Paul**	?	?	?	?	?	?
15 Hinojosa	Y	Y	Y	N	Y	N
16 Reyes	Y	Y	Y	N	Y	N
17 **Flores**	N	N	N	Y	N	Y
18 Jackson Lee	Y	Y	Y	N	Y	N
19 **Neugebauer**	N	N	N	Y	N	Y
20 Gonzalez	Y	Y	Y	N	Y	N
21 **Smith**	N	N	N	Y	N	Y
22 **Olson**	N	N	N	Y	N	Y
23 **Canseco**	N	N	N	Y	N	Y
24 **Marchant**	N	N	N	Y	N	Y
25 Doggett	Y	Y	Y	N	Y	N
26 **Burgess**	N	N	N	Y	N	Y
27 **Farenthold**	N	N	N	Y	N	Y
28 Cuellar	N	N	N	N	N	Y
29 Green, G.	N	N	N	N	Y	Y
30 Johnson, E.	Y	Y	Y	N	Y	N
31 **Carter**	N	N	N	Y	N	Y
32 **Sessions**	N	N	N	Y	N	Y
UTAH						
1 **Bishop**	N	N	N	Y	N	Y
2 Matheson	N	N	N	Y	N	Y
3 **Chaffetz**	N	N	N	Y	N	Y
VERMONT						
AL Welch	N	Y	Y	N	Y	Y
VIRGINIA						
1 **Wittman**	N	N	N	Y	N	Y
2 **Rigell**	N	N	N	Y	N	Y
3 Scott	Y	Y	Y	N	Y	N
4 **Forbes**	N	N	N	Y	N	Y
5 **Hurt**	N	N	N	Y	N	Y
6 **Goodlatte**	N	N	N	Y	N	Y
7 **Cantor**	N	N	N	Y	N	Y
8 Moran	Y	Y	Y	N	Y	N
9 **Griffith**	N	N	N	Y	N	Y
10 **Wolf**	N	N	N	Y	N	Y
11 Connolly	Y	Y	Y	N	Y	N
WASHINGTON						
1 Vacant						
2 Larsen	N	Y	Y	N	Y	N
3 **Herrera Beutler**	N	N	N	Y	N	Y
4 **Hastings**	N	N	N	Y	N	Y
5 **McMorris Rodgers**	N	N	N	Y	N	Y
6 Dicks	?	?	Y	N	Y	N
7 McDermott	Y	Y	Y	N	Y	N
8 **Reichert**	N	Y	Y	N	N	Y
9 Smith	Y	Y	Y	N	Y	N
WEST VIRGINIA						
1 **McKinley**	N	N	N	Y	N	Y
2 **Capito**	N	N	N	Y	N	Y
3 Rahall	N	N	Y	N	Y	Y
WISCONSIN						
1 **Ryan**	N	N	N	Y	N	Y
2 Baldwin	Y	Y	Y	N	Y	N
3 Kind	N	N	Y	N	N	Y
4 Moore	Y	Y	Y	N	Y	N
5 **Sensenbrenner**	N	N	N	Y	N	Y
6 **Petri**	N	N	N	Y	N	Y
7 **Duffy**	N	N	N	Y	N	Y
8 **Ribble**	N	N	N	Y	N	Y
WYOMING						
AL **Lummis**	N	N	N	Y	N	Y

IN THE HOUSE | By Vote Number

165. **HR 4348. Surface Transportation Extension/Previous Question.** Foxx, R-N.C., motion to order the previous question (thus ending debate and the possibility of amendment) on the rule (H Res 619) that would provide for House floor consideration of a three-month extension of surface transportation programs. Motion agreed to 243-180: R 239-0; D 4-180. April 18, 2012.

166. **HR 4348. Surface Transportation Extension/Rule.** Adoption of the rule (H Res 619) that would provide for House floor consideration of a three-month extension of surface transportation programs. Adopted 246-177: R 239-0; D 7-177. April 18, 2012.

167. **Procedural Motion/Journal.** Approval of the House Journal of Tuesday, April 17, 2012. Approved 295-118: R 174-60; D 121-58. April 18, 2012.

168. **HR 4348. Surface Transportation Extension/Environmental Permits and Review.** Ribble, R-Wis., amendment that would exempt from federal environmental permitting requirements any reconstruction project for a road, highway or bridge that was damaged during an emergency declared by a state governor or the president. It also would permit the use of state environmental review standards in cases where local standards meet or exceed federal standards and would require that all environmental reviews be completed within 270 days of a project announcement. Adopted in Committee of the Whole 255-165: R 237-1; D 18-164. April 18, 2012.

169. **HR 4348. Surface Transportation Extension/Recommit.** Polis, D-Colo., motion to recommit the bill to the House Transportation and Infrastructure Committee and report it back immediately with an amendment that would prohibit the use of Highway Trust Fund revenue for the construction of highways in foreign countries and rescind $12.3 million in funds available for a road in Canada. It also would prohibit funding targeted at building a new Birmingham, Ala., highway. Motion rejected 176-242: R 1-237; D 175-5. April 18, 2012.

170. **HR 4348. Surface Transportation Extension/Passage.** Passage of the bill that would extend the authorization for surface transportation programs, including federal aid highway, mass transit and safety programs, for three months through Sept. 30, 2012. It also would extend the authority to spend money from the Highway Trust Fund through the same period. It would transfer authority to approve the Keystone XL pipeline project from the State Department to the Federal Energy Regulatory Commission which would be required to issue the permit within 30 days of receiving an application. As amended, the bill would ease federal environmental permitting requirements for highway construction projects and provide states with more authority over environmental reviews. Passed 293-127: R 224-14; D 69-113. A "nay" was a vote in support of the president's position. April 18, 2012.

171. **HR 2453. Mark Twain Commemorative Coins/Passage.** Luetkemeyer, R-Mo., motion to suspend the rules and pass the bill that would direct the Treasury Department to mint and issue $5 gold coins and $1 silver coins commemorating author Mark Twain. Motion agreed to 408-4: R 228-4; D 180-0. A two-thirds majority of those present and voting (275 in this case) is required for passage under suspension of the rules. April 18, 2012.

	165	166	167	168	169	170	171
ALABAMA							
1 Bonner	Y	Y	Y	Y	N	Y	Y
2 Roby	Y	Y	Y	Y	N	Y	Y
3 Rogers	Y	Y	Y	Y	N	Y	Y
4 Aderholt	Y	Y	Y	Y	N	Y	Y
5 Brooks	Y	Y	Y	Y	N	N	Y
6 Bachus	Y	Y	Y	Y	N	Y	Y
7 Sewell	N	N	Y	N	N	Y	Y
ALASKA							
AL Young	Y	N	N	Y	N	Y	Y
ARIZONA							
1 Gosar	Y	Y	Y	Y	N	Y	Y
2 Franks	Y	Y	Y	Y	N	Y	Y
3 Quayle	Y	Y	N	Y	N	N	Y
4 Pastor	N	N	N	N	Y	Y	Y
5 Schweikert	Y	Y	Y	Y	N	N	Y
6 Flake	Y	Y	Y	?	?	?	?
7 Grijalva	N	N	N	N	Y	N	?
8 Vacant							
ARKANSAS							
1 Crawford	Y	Y	Y	Y	N	Y	Y
2 Griffin	Y	Y	N	Y	N	N	Y
3 Womack	Y	Y	Y	Y	N	N	Y
4 Ross	N	N	Y	N	Y	N	Y
CALIFORNIA							
1 Thompson	N	N	N	N	Y	N	Y
2 Herger	Y	Y	Y	Y	N	Y	Y
3 Lungren	Y	Y	Y	Y	N	Y	Y
4 McClintock	Y	Y	Y	Y	N	N	Y
5 Matsui	N	N	N	N	Y	N	Y
6 Woolsey	N	N	N	N	Y	N	Y
7 Miller, George	N	N	N	N	Y	N	Y
8 Pelosi	N	N	Y	N	?	N	Y
9 Lee	N	N	N	N	Y	N	Y
10 Garamendi	N	N	N	N	Y	N	Y
11 McNerney	N	N	N	N	?	N	Y
12 Speier	N	N	N	N	Y	N	Y
13 Stark	N	N	N	N	Y	N	Y
14 Eshoo	N	N	?	N	Y	Y	Y
15 Honda	N	N	N	N	?	N	Y
16 Lofgren	N	N	?	N	Y	Y	Y
17 Farr	N	N	N	N	Y	N	Y
18 Cardoza	N	Y	N	?	Y	Y	Y
19 Denham	Y	Y	Y	Y	N	Y	Y
20 Costa	N	Y	N	Y	Y	Y	Y
21 Nunes	Y	Y	Y	Y	N	Y	Y
22 McCarthy	Y	Y	Y	Y	N	Y	Y
23 Capps	N	N	Y	N	Y	N	Y
24 Gallegly	Y	Y	Y	Y	N	Y	Y
25 McKeon	Y	Y	Y	Y	N	Y	Y
26 Dreier	Y	Y	Y	Y	N	Y	Y
27 Sherman	N	N	N	N	Y	N	Y
28 Berman	N	N	Y	N	Y	N	Y
29 Schiff	N	N	N	N	Y	N	Y
30 Waxman	N	N	N	N	Y	N	Y
31 Becerra	N	N	N	N	Y	N	Y
32 Chu	N	N	N	N	Y	N	Y
33 Bass	N	N	N	N	Y	N	Y
34 Roybal-Allard	N	N	Y	N	Y	N	Y
35 Waters	N	N	?	N	Y	N	Y
36 Hahn	N	N	Y	N	Y	N	Y
37 Richardson	N	N	Y	N	Y	Y	Y
38 Napolitano	–	–	?	–	+	–	+
39 Sánchez, Linda	N	N	N	N	Y	N	Y
40 Royce	Y	Y	Y	Y	N	Y	Y
41 Lewis	Y	Y	Y	Y	N	Y	Y
42 Miller, Gary	Y	Y	Y	Y	N	Y	Y
43 Baca	N	Y	Y	Y	N	Y	Y
44 Calvert	Y	Y	Y	Y	N	Y	Y
45 Bono Mack	Y	Y	Y	Y	N	Y	Y
46 Rohrabacher	Y	Y	Y	Y	N	Y	Y
47 Sanchez, Loretta	N	N	Y	N	Y	?	?
48 Campbell	Y	Y	Y	Y	N	N	Y
49 Issa	Y	Y	Y	Y	N	Y	Y
50 Bilbray	Y	Y	Y	Y	N	Y	Y
51 Filner	–	–	–	–	+	–	+
52 Hunter	Y	Y	Y	Y	N	Y	Y
53 Davis	N	N	Y	N	Y	N	Y

	165	166	167	168	169	170	171
COLORADO							
1 DeGette	N	N	Y	N	Y	N	Y
2 Polis	N	N	Y	N	Y	N	Y
3 Tipton	Y	Y	N	Y	N	Y	Y
4 Gardner	Y	Y	N	Y	N	Y	Y
5 Lamborn	Y	Y	Y	Y	N	Y	Y
6 Coffman	Y	N	Y	Y	N	Y	Y
7 Perlmutter	N	N	Y	N	Y	Y	?
CONNECTICUT							
1 Larson	N	N	N	N	Y	Y	Y
2 Courtney	N	N	N	N	Y	N	Y
3 DeLauro	N	N	Y	N	Y	N	Y
4 Himes	N	N	N	N	Y	N	Y
5 Murphy	N	N	Y	N	Y	N	Y
DELAWARE							
AL Carney	N	N	Y	N	Y	N	Y
FLORIDA							
1 Miller	Y	Y	N	Y	N	Y	Y
2 Southerland	Y	Y	Y	Y	N	Y	Y
3 Brown	N	N	Y	N	Y	Y	Y
4 Crenshaw	Y	Y	Y	Y	N	Y	Y
5 Nugent	Y	Y	N	Y	N	Y	N
6 Stearns	Y	Y	Y	Y	N	Y	Y
7 Mica	Y	Y	N	Y	N	Y	Y
8 Webster	Y	Y	Y	Y	N	Y	Y
9 Bilirakis	Y	Y	Y	Y	N	Y	Y
10 Young	Y	Y	Y	Y	N	Y	Y
11 Castor	N	N	N	N	Y	N	Y
12 Ross	Y	Y	Y	Y	N	Y	Y
13 Buchanan	Y	Y	Y	Y	N	Y	Y
14 Mack	Y	Y	Y	Y	N	Y	Y
15 Posey	Y	Y	Y	Y	N	Y	Y
16 Rooney	Y	Y	Y	Y	N	Y	Y
17 Wilson	N	N	Y	N	Y	N	Y
18 Ros-Lehtinen	Y	Y	Y	Y	N	Y	Y
19 Deutch	N	N	Y	N	Y	N	Y
20 Wasserman Schultz	N	N	Y	N	Y	N	Y
21 Diaz-Balart	Y	Y	Y	Y	N	Y	Y
22 West	Y	Y	Y	Y	N	Y	Y
23 Hastings	N	N	N	N	Y	N	Y
24 Adams	Y	Y	N	Y	N	Y	Y
25 Rivera	Y	Y	+	Y	N	Y	Y
GEORGIA							
1 Kingston	Y	Y	Y	Y	N	Y	Y
2 Bishop	N	N	Y	Y	Y	Y	Y
3 Westmoreland	Y	Y	Y	Y	N	Y	Y
4 Johnson	N	N	Y	N	Y	N	Y
5 Lewis	N	N	N	N	Y	N	Y
6 Price	Y	Y	Y	Y	N	Y	Y
7 Woodall	Y	Y	N	Y	N	Y	Y
8 Scott, A.	Y	Y	Y	Y	N	Y	Y
9 Graves	Y	Y	Y	Y	N	N	Y
10 Broun	Y	Y	Y	Y	N	N	Y
11 Gingrey	Y	Y	Y	Y	N	Y	Y
12 Barrow	N	N	Y	Y	Y	Y	Y
13 Scott, D.	N	N	Y	N	Y	N	Y
HAWAII							
1 Hanabusa	N	N	Y	N	Y	N	Y
2 Hirono	N	N	Y	N	Y	N	Y
IDAHO							
1 Labrador	Y	Y	?	Y	N	N	Y
2 Simpson	Y	Y	Y	Y	N	Y	Y
ILLINOIS							
1 Rush	N	N	N	N	Y	Y	Y
2 Jackson	N	N	N	N	Y	Y	Y
3 Lipinski	N	N	Y	N	Y	Y	Y
4 Gutierrez	N	N	N	N	Y	N	Y
5 Quigley	N	N	Y	N	Y	N	Y
6 Roskam	Y	Y	Y	Y	N	Y	Y
7 Davis	N	N	N	N	Y	Y	Y
8 Walsh	Y	Y	Y	N	Y	N	Y
9 Schakowsky	N	N	N	N	Y	N	Y
10 Dold	Y	Y	N	Y	N	Y	Y
11 Kinzinger	Y	Y	Y	Y	N	Y	Y
12 Costello	N	N	Y	N	Y	Y	Y
13 Biggert	Y	Y	N	Y	N	Y	Y
14 Hultgren	Y	Y	Y	Y	N	Y	Y
15 Johnson	Y	Y	N	Y	N	Y	Y

KEY   **Republicans** (bold)   Democrats

Y Voted for (yea)	X Paired against	C Voted "present" to avoid possible conflict of interest
# Paired for	– Announced against	? Did not vote or otherwise make a position known
+ Announced for	P Voted "present"	
N Voted against (nay)		

	165	166	167	168	169	170	171
16 **Manzullo**	Y	Y	N	Y	N	Y	Y
17 **Schilling**	Y	Y	N	Y	N	Y	Y
18 **Schock**	Y	Y	Y	Y	N	Y	Y
19 **Shimkus**	Y	Y	Y	Y	N	Y	Y
INDIANA							
1 Visclosky	N	N	N	N	Y	N	Y
2 Donnelly	Y	N	N	Y	Y	Y	Y
3 **Stutzman**	Y	Y	Y	Y	N	Y	Y
4 **Rokita**	Y	Y	Y	Y	N	Y	Y
5 **Burton**	Y	Y	Y	Y	N	Y	Y
6 **Pence**	Y	Y	Y	Y	N	Y	Y
7 Carson	N	N	Y	N	Y	Y	Y
8 **Bucshon**	Y	Y	Y	Y	N	Y	Y
9 **Young**	Y	Y	Y	Y	N	Y	Y
IOWA							
1 Braley	N	N	Y	N	Y	Y	Y
2 Loebsack	N	N	Y	N	Y	Y	?
3 Boswell	N	N	N	Y	Y	Y	Y
4 **Latham**	Y	Y	N	Y	N	Y	Y
5 **King**	Y	Y	Y	Y	N	Y	Y
KANSAS							
1 **Huelskamp**	Y	Y	N	Y	N	Y	Y
2 **Jenkins**	Y	Y	Y	Y	N	Y	Y
3 **Yoder**	Y	Y	N	Y	N	Y	Y
4 **Pompeo**	Y	Y	Y	Y	N	Y	Y
KENTUCKY							
1 **Whitfield**	Y	Y	Y	Y	N	Y	Y
2 **Guthrie**	Y	Y	Y	Y	N	Y	Y
3 Yarmuth	N	N	Y	N	Y	Y	Y
4 **Davis**	Y	Y	Y	Y	N	Y	Y
5 **Rogers**	Y	Y	Y	Y	N	Y	Y
6 Chandler	N	N	N	Y	Y	Y	Y
LOUISIANA							
1 **Scalise**	Y	Y	Y	Y	N	Y	Y
2 Richmond	N	N	Y	N	Y	Y	Y
3 **Landry**	Y	Y	Y	Y	N	Y	Y
4 **Fleming**	Y	Y	Y	Y	N	Y	Y
5 **Alexander**	Y	Y	Y	Y	N	Y	Y
6 **Cassidy**	Y	Y	Y	Y	N	Y	Y
7 **Boustany**	Y	Y	Y	Y	N	Y	Y
MAINE							
1 Pingree	N	N	?	?	?	?	?
2 Michaud	N	N	Y	N	Y	Y	Y
MARYLAND							
1 **Harris**	Y	Y	N	Y	N	Y	Y
2 Ruppersberger	N	N	Y	N	Y	Y	Y
3 Sarbanes	N	N	N	N	Y	N	Y
4 Edwards	N	N	Y	N	Y	N	Y
5 Hoyer	N	N	N	N	Y	N	Y
6 **Bartlett**	Y	Y	Y	Y	N	Y	Y
7 Cummings	N	N	Y	N	Y	N	Y
8 Van Hollen	N	N	Y	N	Y	N	Y
MASSACHUSETTS							
1 Olver	N	N	N	N	Y	N	Y
2 Neal	N	N	N	N	Y	N	Y
3 McGovern	N	N	N	N	Y	N	Y
4 Frank	N	N	Y	N	Y	N	Y
5 Tsongas	N	N	Y	N	Y	N	Y
6 Tierney	N	N	Y	N	Y	N	Y
7 Markey	N	N	Y	N	Y	N	Y
8 Capuano	N	N	N	N	Y	N	Y
9 Lynch	N	N	N	N	Y	Y	Y
10 Keating	N	N	N	N	Y	Y	Y
MICHIGAN							
1 **Benishek**	Y	Y	N	Y	N	Y	Y
2 **Huizenga**	Y	Y	Y	Y	N	Y	Y
3 **Amash**	Y	Y	P	N	N	N	N
4 **Camp**	Y	Y	Y	Y	N	Y	Y
5 Kildee	N	N	Y	N	Y	N	Y
6 **Upton**	Y	Y	Y	Y	N	Y	Y
7 **Walberg**	Y	Y	?	Y	N	Y	Y
8 **Rogers**	Y	Y	Y	Y	N	Y	Y
9 Peters	N	N	N	N	Y	N	Y
10 **Miller**	Y	Y	Y	Y	N	Y	Y
11 **McCotter**	Y	Y	N	Y	N	Y	?
12 Levin	N	N	Y	N	Y	N	Y
13 Clarke	N	N	Y	N	Y	N	Y
14 Conyers	N	N	Y	N	Y	N	Y
15 Dingell	N	N	Y	N	Y	N	Y
MINNESOTA							
1 Walz	N	N	Y	N	Y	Y	Y
2 **Kline**	Y	Y	Y	Y	N	Y	Y
3 **Paulsen**	Y	Y	N	Y	N	Y	Y
4 McCollum	N	N	Y	N	Y	N	Y

	165	166	167	168	169	170	171
5 Ellison	N	N	Y	N	Y	N	Y
6 **Bachmann**	Y	Y	Y	Y	N	Y	Y
7 Peterson	N	N	N	Y	N	Y	Y
8 **Cravaack**	Y	Y	N	Y	N	Y	Y
MISSISSIPPI							
1 **Nunnelee**	Y	Y	Y	Y	N	Y	Y
2 Thompson	N	N	N	N	Y	Y	Y
3 **Harper**	Y	Y	Y	Y	N	Y	Y
4 **Palazzo**	Y	Y	Y	Y	N	Y	Y
MISSOURI							
1 Clay	N	N	Y	N	Y	N	Y
2 **Akin**	Y	Y	Y	Y	N	Y	Y
3 Carnahan	N	N	Y	N	Y	?	Y
4 **Hartzler**	Y	Y	N	Y	N	Y	Y
5 Cleaver	N	N	Y	N	Y	N	Y
6 **Graves**	Y	Y	N	Y	N	Y	Y
7 **Long**	Y	Y	Y	Y	N	Y	Y
8 **Emerson**	Y	Y	Y	Y	N	Y	Y
9 **Luetkemeyer**	Y	Y	N	Y	N	Y	Y
MONTANA							
AL **Rehberg**	Y	Y	Y	Y	N	Y	Y
NEBRASKA							
1 **Fortenberry**	Y	Y	Y	Y	N	Y	Y
2 **Terry**	Y	Y	N	Y	N	Y	Y
3 **Smith**	Y	Y	Y	Y	N	Y	Y
NEVADA							
1 Berkley	N	N	Y	N	Y	N	Y
2 **Amodei**	Y	Y	Y	Y	N	Y	Y
3 **Heck**	Y	Y	N	Y	N	Y	Y
NEW HAMPSHIRE							
1 **Guinta**	Y	Y	Y	Y	N	Y	Y
2 **Bass**	Y	Y	Y	Y	N	N	Y
NEW JERSEY							
1 Andrews	?	?	?	?	?	?	?
2 **LoBiondo**	Y	Y	N	Y	N	Y	Y
3 **Runyan**	Y	Y	Y	Y	N	Y	Y
4 **Smith**	Y	Y	Y	Y	N	Y	Y
5 **Garrett**	Y	Y	Y	Y	N	Y	?
6 Pallone	N	N	N	N	Y	N	Y
7 **Lance**	Y	Y	Y	Y	N	Y	Y
8 Pascrell	N	N	Y	N	Y	Y	Y
9 Rothman	N	N	Y	N	Y	Y	Y
10 Vacant							
11 **Frelinghuysen**	Y	Y	Y	Y	N	Y	Y
12 Holt	N	N	Y	N	Y	N	Y
13 Sires	N	N	Y	N	Y	Y	Y
NEW MEXICO							
1 Heinrich	N	N	Y	N	Y	N	Y
2 **Pearce**	Y	Y	N	Y	N	Y	Y
3 Luján	N	N	Y	N	Y	N	Y
NEW YORK							
1 Bishop	N	N	Y	N	Y	Y	Y
2 Israel	N	N	N	N	Y	N	Y
3 **King**	Y	Y	Y	Y	N	Y	?
4 McCarthy	N	N	Y	N	Y	Y	Y
5 Ackerman	N	N	Y	N	Y	N	Y
6 Meeks	N	N	Y	N	Y	N	Y
7 Crowley	N	N	Y	N	Y	N	Y
8 Nadler	N	N	Y	N	Y	N	Y
9 **Turner**	Y	Y	Y	Y	N	Y	Y
10 Towns	N	N	N	N	Y	N	Y
11 Clarke	N	N	N	N	Y	N	Y
12 Velázquez	N	N	N	N	Y	N	Y
13 **Grimm**	Y	Y	Y	Y	N	Y	Y
14 Maloney	N	N	N	N	Y	N	Y
15 Rangel	?	?	?	?	?	?	?
16 Serrano	N	N	Y	N	Y	N	Y
17 Engel	N	N	Y	N	Y	N	Y
18 Lowey	N	N	Y	N	Y	N	Y
19 **Hayworth**	Y	Y	Y	Y	N	Y	Y
20 **Gibson**	Y	Y	N	Y	N	Y	Y
21 Tonko	N	N	Y	N	Y	N	Y
22 Hinchey	N	N	Y	N	Y	N	Y
23 Owens	N	N	P	N	N	Y	Y
24 **Hanna**	Y	Y	N	Y	N	Y	Y
25 **Buerkle**	Y	Y	Y	Y	N	Y	Y
26 Hochul	N	N	Y	N	Y	Y	Y
27 Higgins	N	N	Y	N	Y	Y	Y
28 Slaughter	?	?	?	?	?	?	?
29 **Reed**	Y	Y	N	Y	N	Y	Y
NORTH CAROLINA							
1 Butterfield	N	N	Y	N	Y	N	Y
2 **Ellmers**	Y	Y	Y	Y	N	Y	Y
3 **Jones**	Y	Y	N	Y	N	Y	Y
4 Price	N	N	Y	N	Y	N	Y

	165	166	167	168	169	170	171
5 **Foxx**	Y	Y	N	Y	N	Y	Y
6 **Coble**	Y	Y	Y	Y	N	Y	Y
7 McIntyre	N	Y	Y	Y	Y	Y	Y
8 Kissell	N	Y	Y	Y	Y	Y	Y
9 **Myrick**	Y	Y	Y	Y	N	Y	Y
10 **McHenry**	Y	Y	Y	Y	N	Y	Y
11 Shuler	Y	Y	N	N	Y	Y	Y
12 Watt	N	N	Y	N	Y	Y	Y
13 Miller	N	N	Y	N	Y	N	Y
NORTH DAKOTA							
AL **Berg**	Y	Y	Y	Y	N	Y	Y
OHIO							
1 **Chabot**	Y	Y	Y	Y	N	Y	Y
2 **Schmidt**	Y	Y	Y	Y	N	Y	Y
3 **Turner**	Y	Y	N	Y	N	Y	Y
4 **Jordan**	Y	Y	Y	Y	N	N	Y
5 **Latta**	Y	Y	Y	Y	N	Y	Y
6 **Johnson**	Y	Y	N	Y	N	Y	Y
7 **Austria**	Y	Y	Y	Y	N	Y	Y
8 **Boehner**							
9 Kaptur	?	?	?	?	?	?	?
10 Kucinich	N	N	N	N	Y	N	Y
11 Fudge	N	N	Y	N	Y	N	Y
12 **Tiberi**	Y	Y	N	Y	N	Y	Y
13 Sutton	N	N	N	N	Y	N	Y
14 **LaTourette**	Y	Y	Y	Y	N	Y	Y
15 **Stivers**	Y	Y	N	Y	N	Y	Y
16 **Renacci**	Y	Y	N	Y	N	Y	Y
17 Ryan	N	N	Y	N	Y	Y	Y
18 **Gibbs**	Y	Y	Y	Y	N	Y	Y
OKLAHOMA							
1 **Sullivan**	Y	Y	Y	Y	N	Y	Y
2 Boren	Y	Y	N	Y	N	Y	Y
3 **Lucas**	Y	Y	Y	Y	N	Y	Y
4 **Cole**	Y	Y	Y	Y	N	Y	?
5 **Lankford**	Y	Y	Y	Y	N	Y	Y
OREGON							
1 Bonamici	N	N	Y	N	Y	N	Y
2 **Walden**	Y	Y	N	Y	N	Y	Y
3 Blumenauer	N	N	Y	N	Y	N	Y
4 DeFazio	N	N	N	N	Y	Y	Y
5 Schrader	N	N	Y	N	Y	Y	Y
PENNSYLVANIA							
1 Brady	N	N	N	N	Y	Y	Y
2 Fattah	N	Y	Y	N	Y	Y	Y
3 **Kelly**	Y	Y	Y	Y	N	Y	Y
4 Altmire	N	N	N	Y	Y	Y	Y
5 **Thompson**	Y	Y	Y	Y	N	Y	Y
6 **Gerlach**	Y	Y	N	Y	N	Y	Y
7 **Meehan**	Y	Y	N	Y	N	Y	Y
8 **Fitzpatrick**	Y	Y	N	Y	N	Y	Y
9 **Shuster**	Y	Y	Y	Y	N	Y	Y
10 **Marino**	?	?	?	?	?	?	?
11 **Barletta**	Y	Y	Y	Y	N	Y	Y
12 Critz	N	N	N	Y	Y	Y	Y
13 Schwartz	N	N	Y	N	Y	Y	Y
14 Doyle	N	N	Y	N	Y	Y	Y
15 **Dent**	Y	Y	N	Y	N	Y	Y
16 **Pitts**	Y	Y	Y	Y	N	Y	Y
17 Holden	N	N	N	N	Y	Y	Y
18 **Murphy**	Y	Y	Y	Y	N	Y	Y
19 **Platts**	Y	Y	Y	Y	N	Y	Y
RHODE ISLAND							
1 Cicilline	N	N	Y	N	Y	N	Y
2 Langevin	N	N	N	N	Y	N	Y
SOUTH CAROLINA							
1 **Scott**	Y	Y	Y	Y	N	Y	Y
2 **Wilson**	Y	Y	Y	Y	N	Y	Y
3 **Duncan**	Y	Y	Y	Y	N	Y	P
4 **Gowdy**	Y	Y	Y	Y	N	Y	Y
5 **Mulvaney**	Y	Y	N	Y	N	N	P
6 Clyburn	N	N	N	N	Y	Y	Y
SOUTH DAKOTA							
AL **Noem**	Y	Y	Y	Y	N	Y	Y
TENNESSEE							
1 **Roe**	Y	Y	N	Y	N	Y	Y
2 **Duncan**	Y	Y	Y	Y	N	Y	Y
3 **Fleischmann**	Y	Y	Y	Y	N	Y	Y
4 **DesJarlais**	Y	Y	N	Y	N	Y	Y
5 Cooper	N	N	Y	N	Y	Y	Y
6 **Black**	Y	Y	Y	Y	N	Y	Y
7 **Blackburn**	Y	Y	Y	Y	N	Y	Y
8 **Fincher**	Y	Y	Y	Y	N	Y	Y
9 Cohen	N	N	Y	N	Y	N	Y

	165	166	167	168	169	170	171
TEXAS							
1 **Gohmert**	Y	Y	?	Y	N	Y	Y
2 **Poe**	Y	Y	N	Y	N	Y	Y
3 **Johnson, S.**	Y	Y	Y	Y	N	Y	Y
4 **Hall**	Y	Y	N	Y	N	Y	Y
5 **Hensarling**	Y	Y	Y	Y	N	Y	Y
6 **Barton**	Y	Y	Y	Y	N	Y	Y
7 **Culberson**	Y	Y	Y	Y	N	Y	Y
8 **Brady**	Y	Y	Y	Y	N	Y	N
9 Green, A.	N	N	Y	N	Y	Y	Y
10 **McCaul**	Y	Y	Y	Y	N	Y	Y
11 **Conaway**	Y	Y	N	Y	N	Y	Y
12 **Granger**	Y	Y	Y	Y	N	Y	Y
13 **Thornberry**	Y	Y	Y	Y	N	Y	Y
14 **Paul**	?	?	?	?	?	?	?
15 Hinojosa	N	N	Y	N	Y	N	Y
16 Reyes	N	N	Y	N	Y	N	Y
17 **Flores**	Y	Y	Y	Y	N	Y	Y
18 Jackson Lee	N	N	N	N	Y	Y	Y
19 **Neugebauer**	Y	Y	Y	Y	N	Y	Y
20 Gonzalez	N	N	Y	N	Y	N	Y
21 **Smith**	Y	Y	Y	Y	N	Y	Y
22 **Olson**	Y	Y	Y	Y	N	Y	Y
23 **Canseco**	Y	Y	Y	Y	N	Y	Y
24 **Marchant**	Y	Y	Y	Y	N	Y	Y
25 Doggett	N	N	Y	N	Y	N	Y
26 **Burgess**	Y	Y	N	Y	N	Y	Y
27 **Farenthold**	Y	Y	Y	Y	N	Y	Y
28 Cuellar	N	N	Y	Y	Y	Y	Y
29 Green, G.	N	N	N	Y	Y	Y	Y
30 Johnson, E.	N	N	Y	N	Y	Y	Y
31 **Carter**	Y	Y	Y	Y	N	Y	Y
32 **Sessions**	Y	Y	Y	Y	N	Y	Y
UTAH							
1 **Bishop**	Y	Y	Y	Y	N	Y	Y
2 Matheson	Y	N	N	Y	Y	Y	Y
3 **Chaffetz**	Y	Y	Y	Y	N	Y	Y
VERMONT							
AL Welch	N	N	Y	N	Y	N	Y
VIRGINIA							
1 **Wittman**	Y	Y	N	Y	N	Y	Y
2 **Rigell**	Y	Y	N	Y	N	Y	N
3 Scott	N	N	Y	N	Y	N	Y
4 **Forbes**	Y	Y	N	Y	N	Y	Y
5 **Hurt**	Y	Y	Y	Y	N	Y	Y
6 **Goodlatte**	Y	Y	Y	Y	N	Y	Y
7 **Cantor**	Y	Y	Y	Y	N	Y	Y
8 Moran	N	N	Y	N	Y	N	Y
9 **Griffith**	Y	Y	Y	Y	N	Y	Y
10 **Wolf**	Y	Y	Y	Y	N	Y	Y
11 Connolly	N	N	Y	N	Y	N	Y
WASHINGTON							
1 Vacant							
2 Larsen	N	N	Y	N	Y	N	Y
3 **Herrera Beutler**	Y	Y	N	Y	N	Y	Y
4 **Hastings**	Y	Y	Y	Y	N	Y	Y
5 **McMorris Rodgers**	Y	Y	Y	Y	N	Y	Y
6 Dicks	N	N	Y	N	Y	Y	Y
7 McDermott	N	N	N	N	Y	N	Y
8 **Reichert**	Y	Y	N	Y	N	Y	Y
9 Smith	N	N	Y	N	Y	N	Y
WEST VIRGINIA							
1 **McKinley**	Y	Y	Y	Y	N	Y	Y
2 **Capito**	Y	Y	Y	Y	N	Y	Y
3 Rahall	N	N	Y	N	Y	Y	Y
WISCONSIN							
1 **Ryan**	Y	Y	Y	Y	N	Y	Y
2 Baldwin	N	N	N	N	Y	N	Y
3 Kind	N	N	N	N	Y	N	Y
4 Moore	N	N	Y	N	Y	N	Y
5 **Sensenbrenner**	Y	Y	Y	Y	N	N	Y
6 **Petri**	Y	Y	Y	Y	N	Y	Y
7 **Duffy**	Y	Y	N	Y	N	Y	Y
8 **Ribble**	Y	Y	N	Y	N	Y	Y
WYOMING							
AL **Lummis**	Y	Y	Y	Y	N	Y	Y

IN THE HOUSE | By Vote Number

172. **HR 9. Small-Business Tax Deduction/Previous Question.**
Sessions, R-Texas, motion to order the previous question (thus ending debate and the possibility of amendment) on the rule (H Res 620) that would provide for House floor consideration of a bill that would allow businesses with fewer than 500 employees to deduct 20 percent of their net domestic business income from their taxable income. Motion agreed to 234-179: R 229-0; D 5-179. April 19, 2012.

173. **HR 9. Small-Business Tax Deduction/Rule.** Adoption of the rule (H Res 620) that would provide for House floor consideration of a bill that would allow businesses with fewer than 500 employees to deduct 20 percent of their net domestic business income from their taxable income. Adopted 234-178: R 227-0; D 7-178. April 19, 2012.

174. **Procedural Motion/Journal.** Approval of the House Journal of Wednesday, April 18, 2012. Approved 290-118: R 175-51; D 115-67. April 19, 2012.

175. **HR 9. Small-Business Tax Deduction/Substitute.** Levin, D-Mich., substitute amendment that would replace the text of the bill with language that would allow small businesses with fewer than 500 employees to deduct 20 percent of their taxable income, not to exceed 100 percent of the amounts they spend on capital investments in 2012. Rejected in Committee of the Whole 175-236: R 0-229; D 175-7. April 19, 2012.

176. **HR 9. Small-Business Tax Deduction/Recommit.** Deutch, D-Fla., motion to recommit the bill to the House Ways and Means Committee and report it back immediately with an amendment that would make income from prostitution, pornography, drug trafficking, lobbying, golf courses that discriminate based on sex or race, or taxpayers who violate Iran sanctions ineligible for the tax deduction. It also would require members of Congress claiming the deduction to disclose the deduction amount and type of business income it came from. Motion rejected 179-229: R 1-227; D 178-2. April 19, 2012.

177. **HR 9. Small-Business Tax Deduction/Passage.** Passage of the bill that would allow businesses with fewer than 500 employees a 20 percent deduction on their taxable income in 2012. A business would be eligible for the deduction if it had fewer than 500 full-time equivalent employees in calendar year 2010 or 2011. If the business was not in existence in those years, the threshold would apply to 2012. The bill would limit the deduction to 50 percent of certain W-2 wages paid by the business. Passed 235-173: R 217-10; D 18-163. A "nay" was a vote in support of the president's position. April 19, 2012.

		172	173	174	175	176	177
ALABAMA							
1	Bonner	Y	Y	Y	N	N	Y
2	Roby	Y	Y	Y	N	N	Y
3	Rogers	Y	Y	Y	N	N	Y
4	Aderholt	Y	Y	Y	N	N	Y
5	Brooks	Y	Y	Y	N	N	Y
6	Bachus	Y	Y	Y	N	N	Y
7	Sewell	–	N	Y	Y	?	N
ALASKA							
AL	Young	?	?	?	N	N	Y
ARIZONA							
1	Gosar	?	?	?	?	?	?
2	Franks	Y	Y	Y	N	N	Y
3	Quayle	Y	Y	N	N	N	Y
4	Pastor	N	N	N	Y	N	N
5	Schweikert	Y	Y	Y	N	N	Y
6	Flake	?	?	?	?	?	?
7	Grijalva	N	N	N	Y	Y	N
8	Vacant						
ARKANSAS							
1	Crawford	Y	Y	Y	N	N	Y
2	Griffin	Y	Y	N	N	N	Y
3	Womack	Y	Y	Y	N	N	Y
4	Ross	Y	Y	Y	N	Y	Y
CALIFORNIA							
1	Thompson	N	N	N	Y	N	N
2	Herger	Y	Y	Y	N	N	Y
3	Lungren	Y	Y	Y	N	N	Y
4	McClintock	Y	Y	Y	N	N	N
5	Matsui	N	N	N	Y	Y	N
6	Woolsey	N	N	Y	Y	Y	N
7	Miller, George	N	N	N	Y	Y	N
8	Pelosi	N	N	Y	Y	Y	N
9	Lee	N	N	N	Y	Y	N
10	Garamendi	N	N	Y	Y	Y	Y
11	McNerney	N	N	N	Y	Y	N
12	Speier	N	N	Y	Y	Y	N
13	Stark	N	N	N	Y	Y	N
14	Eshoo	N	N	Y	Y	Y	N
15	Honda	N	N	Y	Y	Y	N
16	Lofgren	N	N	Y	Y	Y	N
17	Farr	N	N	Y	Y	Y	N
18	Cardoza	N	N	N	Y	Y	N
19	Denham	Y	Y	Y	N	N	Y
20	Costa	N	N	N	Y	Y	N
21	Nunes	Y	Y	Y	?	?	?
22	McCarthy	Y	Y	Y	N	N	Y
23	Capps	N	N	Y	Y	Y	N
24	Gallegly	Y	Y	Y	N	N	Y
25	McKeon	Y	Y	Y	N	N	Y
26	Dreier	Y	Y	Y	N	N	Y
27	Sherman	N	N	Y	Y	?	N
28	Berman	N	N	Y	Y	Y	N
29	Schiff	N	N	Y	Y	Y	N
30	Waxman	N	N	Y	Y	Y	N
31	Becerra	N	N	Y	Y	Y	N
32	Chu	N	N	N	Y	Y	N
33	Bass	N	N	N	Y	Y	N
34	Roybal-Allard	N	N	Y	Y	Y	N
35	Waters	N	N	N	?	Y	N
36	Hahn	N	N	Y	Y	Y	N
37	Richardson	N	N	Y	Y	Y	N
38	Napolitano	–	–	?	+	+	–
39	Sánchez, Linda	N	N	N	Y	Y	N
40	Royce	Y	Y	Y	N	N	Y
41	Lewis	Y	Y	Y	N	N	Y
42	Miller, Gary	Y	Y	Y	N	N	Y
43	Baca	N	N	Y	Y	Y	N
44	Calvert	Y	Y	Y	N	N	Y
45	Bono Mack	Y	Y	Y	N	N	Y
46	Rohrabacher	Y	Y	Y	N	N	Y
47	Sanchez, Loretta	N	N	N	Y	Y	N
48	Campbell	Y	Y	Y	N	N	Y
49	Issa	Y	Y	Y	N	N	Y
50	Bilbray	Y	Y	Y	N	N	Y
51	Filner	–	–	–	+	+	–
52	Hunter	Y	Y	Y	N	N	Y
53	Davis	N	N	Y	Y	Y	N

		172	173	174	175	176	177
COLORADO							
1	DeGette	N	N	Y	Y	Y	N
2	Polis	N	N	Y	Y	Y	N
3	Tipton	Y	Y	Y	N	N	Y
4	Gardner	Y	Y	N	N	N	Y
5	Lamborn	Y	Y	Y	N	N	Y
6	Coffman	Y	Y	N	N	N	Y
7	Perlmutter	N	N	Y	Y	Y	?
CONNECTICUT							
1	Larson	N	N	Y	Y	Y	N
2	Courtney	N	N	N	Y	Y	N
3	DeLauro	N	N	Y	Y	Y	N
4	Himes	N	N	Y	Y	Y	N
5	Murphy	N	N	Y	Y	Y	N
DELAWARE							
AL	Carney	N	N	Y	Y	Y	N
FLORIDA							
1	Miller	Y	Y	N	N	N	Y
2	Southerland	Y	Y	Y	N	N	Y
3	Brown	N	N	Y	Y	Y	N
4	Crenshaw	Y	Y	Y	N	N	Y
5	Nugent	Y	Y	N	N	N	Y
6	Stearns	Y	Y	N	N	N	Y
7	Mica	Y	Y	Y	N	N	Y
8	Webster	Y	Y	Y	N	N	Y
9	Bilirakis	Y	Y	Y	N	N	Y
10	Young	?	?	?	?	?	?
11	Castor	N	N	N	Y	Y	N
12	Ross	Y	Y	Y	N	N	Y
13	Buchanan	Y	Y	Y	N	N	Y
14	Mack	Y	Y	N	N	N	Y
15	Posey	Y	Y	Y	N	N	Y
16	Rooney	Y	Y	N	N	N	Y
17	Wilson	N	N	Y	Y	Y	N
18	Ros-Lehtinen	Y	Y	N	N	N	Y
19	Deutch	N	N	Y	Y	Y	N
20	Wasserman Schultz	N	N	Y	Y	Y	N
21	Diaz-Balart	Y	Y	Y	N	N	Y
22	West	Y	Y	Y	N	N	Y
23	Hastings	N	N	Y	Y	Y	N
24	Adams	Y	Y	N	N	N	Y
25	Rivera	Y	Y	Y	N	N	Y
GEORGIA							
1	Kingston	Y	Y	Y	N	N	Y
2	Bishop	N	N	Y	Y	Y	N
3	Westmoreland	Y	Y	Y	N	N	Y
4	Johnson	N	N	Y	Y	Y	N
5	Lewis	N	N	N	Y	Y	N
6	Price	Y	Y	N	N	N	Y
7	Woodall	Y	Y	N	N	N	Y
8	Scott, A.	Y	Y	Y	N	N	Y
9	Graves	Y	Y	N	N	N	Y
10	Broun	Y	Y	N	N	N	Y
11	Gingrey	Y	Y	Y	N	N	Y
12	Barrow	N	N	Y	Y	N	Y
13	Scott, D.	N	N	Y	Y	Y	N
HAWAII							
1	Hanabusa	N	N	Y	Y	Y	N
2	Hirono	N	N	Y	Y	Y	N
IDAHO							
1	Labrador	Y	Y	Y	N	N	N
2	Simpson	Y	Y	Y	N	N	Y
ILLINOIS							
1	Rush	N	N	N	Y	Y	N
2	Jackson	N	N	N	Y	Y	N
3	Lipinski	N	N	Y	Y	Y	N
4	Gutierrez	N	N	Y	Y	Y	N
5	Quigley	N	N	Y	Y	Y	N
6	Roskam	Y	Y	Y	N	N	Y
7	Davis	N	N	Y	Y	Y	N
8	Walsh	?	?	?	?	?	?
9	Schakowsky	N	N	Y	Y	Y	N
10	Dold	Y	Y	N	N	N	Y
11	Kinzinger	Y	Y	Y	N	N	Y
12	Costello	N	N	N	Y	Y	N
13	Biggert	Y	Y	N	N	N	Y
14	Hultgren	Y	Y	Y	N	N	Y
15	Johnson	Y	Y	Y	N	N	Y

	172	173	174	175	176	177
16 **Manzullo**	+	+	–	–	–	+
17 **Schilling**	Y	Y	N	N	N	Y
18 **Schock**	Y	?	N	N	N	Y
19 **Shimkus**	Y	Y	Y	N	N	Y
INDIANA						
1 Visclosky	N	N	N	Y	Y	N
2 Donnelly	N	Y	N	Y	Y	Y
3 **Stutzman**	Y	Y	Y	N	N	Y
4 **Rokita**	Y	Y	Y	N	N	Y
5 **Burton**	?	?	?	?	?	?
6 **Pence**	Y	Y	Y	N	N	Y
7 Carson	N	N	Y	Y	Y	N
8 **Bucshon**	Y	Y	Y	N	N	Y
9 **Young**	Y	Y	Y	N	N	Y
IOWA						
1 Braley	?	?	?	?	?	?
2 Loebsack	N	N	Y	Y	Y	Y
3 Boswell	N	N	N	Y	Y	Y
4 **Latham**	Y	Y	N	N	N	Y
5 **King**	Y	Y	Y	N	N	Y
KANSAS						
1 **Huelskamp**	Y	Y	N	N	N	Y
2 **Jenkins**	Y	Y	Y	N	N	Y
3 **Yoder**	Y	Y	N	N	N	Y
4 **Pompeo**	Y	Y	Y	N	N	Y
KENTUCKY						
1 **Whitfield**	Y	Y	Y	N	N	Y
2 **Guthrie**	Y	Y	Y	N	N	Y
3 Yarmuth	N	N	Y	Y	Y	N
4 **Davis**	Y	Y	?	N	N	Y
5 **Rogers**	Y	Y	Y	N	N	Y
6 Chandler	N	N	N	Y	Y	Y
LOUISIANA						
1 **Scalise**	Y	Y	Y	N	N	Y
2 Richmond	N	N	N	Y	Y	N
3 **Landry**	Y	Y	Y	N	?	?
4 **Fleming**	Y	Y	Y	N	N	Y
5 **Alexander**	Y	Y	Y	N	N	Y
6 **Cassidy**	Y	Y	Y	N	N	Y
7 **Boustany**	Y	Y	Y	N	N	Y
MAINE						
1 Pingree	N	N	Y	Y	Y	N
2 Michaud	N	N	Y	Y	Y	N
MARYLAND						
1 **Harris**	Y	Y	Y	N	N	Y
2 Ruppersberger	N	N	Y	Y	Y	Y
3 Sarbanes	N	N	N	Y	Y	N
4 Edwards	N	N	Y	Y	Y	N
5 Hoyer	N	N	N	Y	Y	N
6 **Bartlett**	Y	Y	Y	N	N	Y
7 Cummings	N	N	?	Y	Y	N
8 Van Hollen	N	N	Y	Y	Y	N
MASSACHUSETTS						
1 Olver	N	N	N	Y	Y	N
2 Neal	N	N	N	Y	Y	N
3 McGovern	N	N	Y	Y	Y	N
4 Frank	N	N	Y	Y	Y	N
5 Tsongas	N	N	Y	Y	Y	N
6 Tierney	N	N	Y	Y	Y	N
7 Markey	N	N	N	Y	Y	N
8 Capuano	N	N	N	Y	Y	N
9 Lynch	N	N	N	Y	Y	N
10 Keating	N	N	N	Y	Y	N
MICHIGAN						
1 **Benishek**	Y	Y	N	N	N	Y
2 **Huizenga**	Y	Y	Y	N	N	Y
3 **Amash**	Y	Y	P	N	N	N
4 **Camp**	Y	Y	Y	N	N	Y
5 Kildee	N	N	Y	Y	Y	N
6 **Upton**	Y	Y	Y	N	N	Y
7 **Walberg**	Y	Y	N	N	N	Y
8 **Rogers**	Y	Y	Y	N	N	Y
9 Peters	N	N	N	Y	Y	N
10 **Miller**	Y	Y	Y	N	N	Y
11 **McCotter**	Y	Y	N	N	N	Y
12 Levin	N	N	Y	Y	Y	N
13 Clarke	N	N	Y	Y	Y	N
14 Conyers	N	N	Y	Y	Y	N
15 Dingell	N	N	Y	Y	Y	N
MINNESOTA						
1 Walz	N	N	Y	Y	Y	Y
2 **Kline**	Y	Y	Y	N	N	Y
3 **Paulsen**	Y	Y	N	N	N	Y
4 McCollum	N	N	Y	Y	Y	N

	172	173	174	175	176	177
5 Ellison	N	N	Y	Y	Y	N
6 **Bachmann**	Y	Y	Y	N	N	Y
7 Peterson	N	N	N	N	N	N
8 **Cravaack**	Y	Y	N	N	N	Y
MISSISSIPPI						
1 **Nunnelee**	Y	Y	Y	N	N	Y
2 Thompson	N	N	N	?	?	?
3 **Harper**	Y	Y	Y	N	N	Y
4 **Palazzo**	Y	Y	Y	N	N	Y
MISSOURI						
1 Clay	N	N	Y	Y	Y	N
2 **Akin**	Y	Y	Y	N	N	Y
3 Carnahan	N	N	Y	Y	Y	N
4 **Hartzler**	Y	Y	N	N	N	Y
5 Cleaver	N	N	N	Y	Y	N
6 **Graves**	Y	Y	N	N	N	Y
7 **Long**	Y	Y	Y	N	N	Y
8 **Emerson**	Y	Y	Y	N	N	Y
9 **Luetkemeyer**	Y	Y	N	N	N	Y
MONTANA						
AL **Rehberg**	Y	Y	Y	N	N	Y
NEBRASKA						
1 **Fortenberry**	Y	Y	Y	N	N	N
2 **Terry**	Y	Y	N	N	N	Y
3 **Smith**	Y	Y	Y	N	N	Y
NEVADA						
1 Berkley	N	N	Y	Y	Y	N
2 **Amodei**	Y	Y	Y	N	N	Y
3 **Heck**	Y	Y	N	N	N	Y
NEW HAMPSHIRE						
1 **Guinta**	?	?	?	?	?	?
2 **Bass**	?	?	?	?	?	?
NEW JERSEY						
1 Andrews	N	N	N	Y	Y	N
2 **LoBiondo**	Y	Y	N	N	N	Y
3 **Runyan**	Y	Y	Y	N	N	Y
4 **Smith**	Y	Y	Y	N	N	Y
5 **Garrett**	Y	Y	N	N	N	Y
6 Pallone	N	N	N	Y	Y	N
7 **Lance**	Y	Y	Y	N	N	Y
8 Pascrell	N	N	Y	Y	Y	N
9 Rothman	N	N	Y	Y	Y	N
10 Vacant						
11 **Frelinghuysen**	Y	Y	Y	N	N	Y
12 Holt	N	N	Y	Y	Y	N
13 Sires	N	N	N	Y	Y	N
NEW MEXICO						
1 Heinrich	N	N	Y	Y	Y	N
2 **Pearce**	Y	Y	Y	N	N	Y
3 Luján	N	N	Y	Y	Y	N
NEW YORK						
1 Bishop	N	N	N	Y	Y	Y
2 Israel	N	N	N	Y	Y	N
3 **King**	Y	Y	Y	N	N	Y
4 McCarthy	N	N	Y	Y	Y	N
5 Ackerman	N	N	Y	Y	Y	N
6 Meeks	N	N	N	Y	Y	N
7 Crowley	N	N	Y	Y	Y	N
8 Nadler	N	N	Y	Y	Y	N
9 **Turner**	Y	Y	Y	N	N	Y
10 Towns	N	N	Y	Y	Y	N
11 Clarke	N	N	N	Y	Y	N
12 Velázquez	N	N	N	Y	Y	N
13 **Grimm**	Y	Y	Y	N	N	Y
14 Maloney	N	N	Y	Y	Y	N
15 Rangel	?	?	?	?	?	?
16 Serrano	N	N	Y	Y	Y	N
17 Engel	N	N	Y	Y	Y	N
18 Lowey	N	N	Y	Y	Y	N
19 **Hayworth**	Y	Y	Y	N	N	Y
20 **Gibson**	Y	Y	N	N	N	Y
21 Tonko	N	N	Y	Y	Y	N
22 Hinchey	N	N	Y	Y	Y	N
23 Owens	N	N	P	Y	Y	Y
24 **Hanna**	Y	Y	N	N	N	Y
25 **Buerkle**	Y	Y	Y	N	N	Y
26 Hochul	N	N	Y	Y	Y	Y
27 Higgins	N	N	Y	Y	Y	N
28 Slaughter	?	?	?	?	?	?
29 **Reed**	Y	Y	N	N	N	Y
NORTH CAROLINA						
1 Butterfield	N	N	Y	Y	Y	N
2 **Ellmers**	Y	Y	Y	N	N	Y
3 **Jones**	Y	Y	Y	N	Y	Y
4 Price	N	N	Y	Y	Y	N

	172	173	174	175	176	177
5 **Foxx**	Y	Y	N	N	N	Y
6 **Coble**	Y	Y	Y	N	N	Y
7 McIntyre	Y	Y	Y	N	Y	Y
8 Kissell	N	Y	Y	Y	Y	Y
9 **Myrick**	Y	Y	Y	N	N	Y
10 **McHenry**	Y	Y	Y	N	N	Y
11 Shuler	Y	Y	N	N	Y	N
12 Watt	N	N	Y	Y	Y	N
13 Miller	N	N	Y	Y	Y	N
NORTH DAKOTA						
AL **Berg**	Y	Y	Y	N	N	Y
OHIO						
1 **Chabot**	Y	Y	Y	N	N	Y
2 **Schmidt**	Y	Y	Y	N	N	Y
3 **Turner**	Y	Y	Y	N	N	Y
4 **Jordan**	Y	Y	Y	N	N	Y
5 **Latta**	Y	Y	Y	N	N	Y
6 **Johnson**	Y	Y	N	N	N	Y
7 **Austria**	Y	Y	Y	N	N	Y
8 **Boehner**						
9 Kaptur	N	N	Y	Y	Y	N
10 Kucinich	N	N	N	Y	Y	N
11 Fudge	N	N	N	Y	Y	N
12 **Tiberi**	Y	Y	Y	N	N	Y
13 Sutton	N	N	Y	Y	Y	Y
14 **LaTourette**	Y	Y	Y	N	N	N
15 **Stivers**	Y	Y	N	N	N	Y
16 **Renacci**	Y	Y	N	N	N	Y
17 Ryan	N	N	N	Y	Y	N
18 **Gibbs**	Y	Y	Y	N	N	Y
OKLAHOMA						
1 **Sullivan**	Y	Y	Y	N	N	Y
2 Boren	Y	Y	Y	N	Y	Y
3 **Lucas**	Y	Y	Y	N	N	Y
4 **Cole**	Y	Y	Y	N	N	Y
5 **Lankford**	Y	Y	Y	N	N	Y
OREGON						
1 Bonamici	N	N	Y	Y	Y	N
2 **Walden**	Y	Y	Y	N	N	Y
3 Blumenauer	N	N	Y	Y	Y	N
4 DeFazio	N	N	N	Y	Y	N
5 Schrader	N	N	?	?	Y	N
PENNSYLVANIA						
1 Brady	N	N	N	Y	Y	N
2 Fattah	N	N	N	Y	Y	N
3 **Kelly**	Y	Y	Y	N	N	Y
4 Altmire	N	N	N	Y	Y	N
5 **Thompson**	Y	Y	Y	N	N	Y
6 **Gerlach**	Y	Y	N	N	N	Y
7 **Meehan**	Y	Y	N	N	N	Y
8 **Fitzpatrick**	Y	Y	N	N	N	Y
9 **Shuster**	Y	Y	Y	N	N	Y
10 **Marino**	?	?	?	?	?	?
11 **Barletta**	Y	Y	Y	N	N	Y
12 Critz	N	N	N	Y	Y	N
13 Schwartz	N	N	Y	Y	Y	N
14 Doyle	N	N	Y	Y	Y	N
15 **Dent**	Y	Y	N	N	N	Y
16 **Pitts**	Y	Y	Y	N	N	Y
17 Holden	N	N	Y	Y	Y	N
18 **Murphy**	Y	Y	Y	N	N	Y
19 **Platts**	Y	Y	Y	N	N	Y
RHODE ISLAND						
1 Cicilline	N	N	Y	Y	Y	N
2 Langevin	N	N	N	Y	Y	N
SOUTH CAROLINA						
1 **Scott**	Y	Y	Y	N	N	Y
2 **Wilson**	Y	Y	Y	N	N	Y
3 **Duncan**	Y	Y	Y	N	N	Y
4 **Gowdy**	Y	Y	Y	N	N	Y
5 **Mulvaney**	Y	Y	Y	N	N	N
6 Clyburn	N	N	N	Y	?	?
SOUTH DAKOTA						
AL **Noem**	Y	Y	Y	N	N	Y
TENNESSEE						
1 **Roe**	Y	Y	Y	N	N	Y
2 **Duncan**	Y	Y	Y	N	N	Y
3 **Fleischmann**	Y	Y	Y	N	N	Y
4 **DesJarlais**	Y	Y	N	N	N	Y
5 Cooper	N	N	Y	Y	Y	N
6 **Black**	Y	Y	Y	N	N	Y
7 **Blackburn**	Y	Y	Y	N	N	Y
8 **Fincher**	Y	Y	Y	N	N	Y
9 Cohen	N	N	N	Y	Y	N

	172	173	174	175	176	177
TEXAS						
1 **Gohmert**	Y	Y	P	N	N	Y
2 **Poe**	Y	Y	N	N	N	Y
3 **Johnson, S.**	Y	Y	Y	N	N	Y
4 **Hall**	Y	Y	Y	N	N	Y
5 **Hensarling**	Y	Y	Y	N	N	Y
6 **Barton**	Y	Y	Y	N	N	Y
7 **Culberson**	Y	Y	Y	N	N	Y
8 **Brady**	Y	Y	Y	N	N	Y
9 Green, A.	N	N	Y	Y	Y	N
10 **McCaul**	Y	Y	Y	N	N	Y
11 **Conaway**	Y	Y	N	N	N	Y
12 **Granger**	Y	Y	Y	N	N	Y
13 **Thornberry**	Y	Y	Y	N	N	Y
14 **Paul**	?	?	?	?	?	?
15 Hinojosa	N	N	Y	Y	Y	N
16 Reyes	N	N	Y	Y	Y	N
17 **Flores**	Y	Y	Y	N	N	Y
18 Jackson Lee	N	N	N	Y	Y	N
19 **Neugebauer**	Y	Y	Y	N	N	Y
20 Gonzalez	N	N	Y	Y	Y	N
21 **Smith**	Y	Y	Y	N	N	Y
22 **Olson**	Y	Y	Y	N	N	Y
23 **Canseco**	Y	Y	Y	N	N	Y
24 **Marchant**	Y	Y	Y	N	N	Y
25 Doggett	N	N	Y	Y	Y	N
26 **Burgess**	Y	Y	N	N	N	Y
27 **Farenthold**	Y	Y	Y	N	N	Y
28 Cuellar	N	N	Y	Y	Y	Y
29 Green, G.	N	N	N	Y	+	–
30 Johnson, E.	N	N	Y	Y	Y	N
31 **Carter**	Y	Y	Y	N	N	Y
32 **Sessions**	Y	Y	Y	N	N	Y
UTAH						
1 **Bishop**	?	?	?	?	?	?
2 Matheson	Y	Y	N	N	Y	Y
3 **Chaffetz**	Y	Y	Y	N	N	Y
VERMONT						
AL Welch	N	N	Y	Y	Y	N
VIRGINIA						
1 **Wittman**	Y	Y	N	N	N	Y
2 **Rigell**	Y	Y	N	N	N	Y
3 Scott	N	N	Y	Y	Y	N
4 **Forbes**	Y	Y	N	N	N	Y
5 **Hurt**	Y	Y	Y	N	N	Y
6 **Goodlatte**	Y	Y	Y	N	N	Y
7 **Cantor**	Y	Y	Y	N	N	Y
8 Moran	N	N	Y	Y	Y	N
9 **Griffith**	Y	?	Y	N	N	Y
10 **Wolf**	Y	Y	Y	N	N	P
11 Connolly	N	N	Y	Y	Y	N
WASHINGTON						
1 Vacant						
2 Larsen	N	N	Y	Y	Y	N
3 **Herrera Beutler**	Y	Y	N	N	N	Y
4 **Hastings**	Y	Y	Y	N	N	Y
5 **McMorris Rodgers**	Y	Y	Y	N	N	Y
6 Dicks	N	N	Y	Y	Y	N
7 McDermott	N	N	N	Y	Y	N
8 **Reichert**	Y	Y	N	N	N	Y
9 Smith	N	N	Y	Y	Y	N
WEST VIRGINIA						
1 **McKinley**	Y	Y	Y	N	N	Y
2 **Capito**	Y	Y	Y	N	N	Y
3 Rahall	N	N	N	Y	Y	N
WISCONSIN						
1 **Ryan**	Y	Y	Y	N	N	Y
2 Baldwin	N	N	N	Y	Y	N
3 Kind	N	N	N	Y	Y	N
4 Moore	N	N	Y	Y	Y	N
5 **Sensenbrenner**	Y	Y	Y	N	N	Y
6 **Petri**	Y	Y	Y	N	N	Y
7 **Duffy**	Y	Y	N	N	N	Y
8 **Ribble**	Y	Y	N	N	N	N
WYOMING						
AL **Lummis**	Y	Y	Y	N	N	N

IN THE HOUSE | By Vote Number

178. **HR 2157. Inyo National Forest Land Exchange/Passage.** Bishop, R-Utah, motion to suspend the rules and pass the bill that would convey 20 acres of land within the Inyo National Forest in California, in exchange for non-federal lands owned by the Mammoth Mountain ski area outside the forest boundaries. The bill would allow the Agriculture secretary to accept a cash equalization payment in excess of 25 percent to complete the exchange. Motion agreed to 376-2: R 217-2; D 159-0. A two-thirds majority of those present and voting (252 in this case) is required for passage under suspension of the rules. April 24, 2012.

179. **HR 4348. Surface Transportation Extension/Motion to Instruct.** Rahall, D-W.Va., motion to instruct conferees to recede from the House's disagreement with a Senate-passed version of the measure that would authorize federal highway, highway safety and public transit programs at $109 billion over two years. Motion rejected 181-242: R 1-238; D 180-4. April 25, 2012.

180. **HR 3336. Swap Dealer Exclusions/Passage.** Lucas, R-Okla., motion to suspend the rules and pass the bill that would exclude certain financial institutions regulated by the Commodity Futures Trading Commission from being classified as swap dealers under the 2010 financial regulatory overhaul law. To be excluded, depository institutions and farm credit institutions would have to limit the use of swaps to transactions that help customers manage risk on a loan made by the institution or that offset risks arising from the swaps made with customers. Motion agreed to 312-111: R 239-0; D 73-111. A two-thirds majority of those present and voting (282 in this case) is required for passage under suspension of the rules. April 25, 2012.

181. **HR 1038. Coconino National Forest Land Exchange/Passage.** Bishop, R-Utah, motion to suspend the rules and pass the bill that would authorize the Agriculture secretary to convey two parcels of land located within the Coconino National Forest in Arizona to the landowners holding interests in the adjacent land. Motion agreed to 421-1: R 237-1; D 184-0. A two-thirds majority of those present and voting (282 in this case) is required for passage under suspension of the rules. April 25, 2012.

	178	179	180	181
ALABAMA				
1 Bonner	Y	N	Y	Y
2 Roby	Y	N	Y	Y
3 Rogers	Y	N	Y	Y
4 Aderholt	Y	N	Y	Y
5 Brooks	Y	N	Y	Y
6 Bachus	Y	N	Y	Y
7 Sewell	Y	Y	Y	Y
ALASKA				
AL Young	Y	N	Y	Y
ARIZONA				
1 Gosar	Y	N	Y	Y
2 Franks	Y	N	Y	Y
3 Quayle	Y	N	Y	Y
4 Pastor	Y	Y	Y	Y
5 Schweikert	Y	N	Y	Y
6 Flake	Y	N	Y	Y
7 Grijalva	Y	Y	N	Y
8 Vacant				
ARKANSAS				
1 Crawford	Y	N	Y	Y
2 Griffin	+	N	Y	Y
3 Womack	Y	N	Y	Y
4 Ross	Y	Y	Y	Y
CALIFORNIA				
1 Thompson	Y	Y	N	Y
2 **Herger**	Y	N	Y	Y
3 **Lungren**	Y	N	Y	Y
4 **McClintock**	?	N	Y	Y
5 Matsui	Y	Y	N	Y
6 Woolsey	Y	Y	N	Y
7 Miller, George	Y	Y	N	Y
8 Pelosi	Y	Y	N	Y
9 Lee	Y	Y	N	Y
10 Garamendi	?	Y	N	Y
11 McNerney	Y	Y	Y	Y
12 Speier	Y	Y	N	Y
13 Stark	Y	Y	N	Y
14 Eshoo	Y	Y	N	Y
15 Honda	Y	Y	Y	Y
16 Lofgren	?	Y	N	Y
17 Farr	Y	Y	Y	Y
18 Cardoza	?	Y	Y	Y
19 **Denham**	Y	N	Y	Y
20 Costa	Y	Y	Y	Y
21 **Nunes**	Y	N	Y	Y
22 **McCarthy**	Y	N	Y	Y
23 Capps	Y	Y	N	Y
24 **Gallegly**	Y	N	Y	Y
25 **McKeon**	Y	N	Y	Y
26 **Dreier**	Y	N	Y	Y
27 Sherman	Y	Y	N	Y
28 Berman	Y	Y	N	Y
29 Schiff	+	Y	Y	Y
30 Waxman	Y	Y	N	Y
31 Becerra	Y	Y	N	Y
32 Chu	Y	Y	N	Y
33 Bass	Y	Y	Y	Y
34 Roybal-Allard	?	Y	Y	Y
35 Waters	Y	Y	N	Y
36 Hahn	Y	Y	Y	Y
37 Richardson	Y	Y	Y	Y
38 Napolitano	Y	Y	N	Y
39 Sánchez, Linda	Y	Y	N	Y
40 **Royce**	Y	N	Y	Y
41 **Lewis**	Y	N	Y	Y
42 **Miller, Gary**	Y	N	Y	Y
43 Baca	Y	Y	Y	Y
44 **Calvert**	Y	N	Y	Y
45 **Bono Mack**	?	N	Y	Y
46 **Rohrabacher**	Y	N	Y	Y
47 Sanchez, Loretta	Y	Y	Y	Y
48 **Campbell**	?	N	Y	Y
49 **Issa**	Y	N	Y	Y
50 **Bilbray**	Y	N	Y	Y
51 Filner	+	+	-	+
52 **Hunter**	Y	N	Y	Y
53 Davis	+	Y	N	Y

	178	179	180	181
COLORADO				
1 DeGette	?	Y	N	Y
2 Polis	Y	Y	Y	Y
3 Tipton	Y	N	Y	Y
4 Gardner	Y	N	Y	Y
5 Lamborn	Y	N	Y	Y
6 Coffman	Y	N	Y	Y
7 Perlmutter	Y	Y	N	Y
CONNECTICUT				
1 Larson	Y	Y	N	Y
2 Courtney	Y	Y	N	Y
3 DeLauro	Y	Y	N	Y
4 Himes	Y	Y	Y	Y
5 Murphy	Y	Y	N	Y
DELAWARE				
AL Carney	Y	Y	Y	Y
FLORIDA				
1 Miller	Y	N	Y	Y
2 Southerland	Y	N	Y	Y
3 Brown	Y	Y	Y	Y
4 Crenshaw	Y	N	Y	Y
5 Nugent	Y	N	Y	Y
6 Stearns	Y	N	Y	Y
7 Mica	Y	N	Y	Y
8 Webster	Y	N	Y	Y
9 Bilirakis	Y	N	Y	Y
10 Young	?	N	Y	Y
11 Castor	Y	Y	Y	Y
12 Ross	Y	N	Y	Y
13 Buchanan	Y	N	Y	Y
14 Mack	Y	N	Y	Y
15 Posey	Y	N	Y	Y
16 Rooney	Y	N	Y	Y
17 Wilson	Y	Y	N	Y
18 Ros-Lehtinen	Y	N	Y	Y
19 Deutch	Y	Y	N	Y
20 Wasserman Schultz	?	Y	N	Y
21 Diaz-Balart	Y	N	Y	Y
22 West	Y	N	Y	Y
23 Hastings	Y	Y	N	Y
24 Adams	Y	N	Y	Y
25 Rivera	Y	N	Y	Y
GEORGIA				
1 Kingston	Y	N	Y	Y
2 Bishop	Y	Y	Y	Y
3 Westmoreland	Y	N	Y	Y
4 Johnson	Y	Y	N	Y
5 Lewis	Y	Y	N	Y
6 Price	Y	N	Y	Y
7 Woodall	Y	N	Y	Y
8 Scott, A.	Y	N	Y	Y
9 Graves	Y	N	Y	Y
10 Broun	Y	N	Y	Y
11 Gingrey	Y	N	Y	Y
12 Barrow	Y	N	Y	Y
13 Scott, D.	Y	Y	Y	Y
HAWAII				
1 Hanabusa	Y	Y	Y	Y
2 Hirono	?	Y	N	Y
IDAHO				
1 Labrador	Y	N	Y	Y
2 Simpson	?	N	Y	Y
ILLINOIS				
1 Rush	Y	Y	N	Y
2 Jackson	Y	Y	N	Y
3 Lipinski	Y	N	Y	Y
4 Gutierrez	?	Y	N	Y
5 Quigley	Y	Y	Y	Y
6 Roskam	Y	N	Y	Y
7 Davis	Y	Y	N	Y
8 Walsh	Y	N	Y	Y
9 Schakowsky	Y	Y	N	Y
10 Dold	Y	N	Y	Y
11 Kinzinger	Y	Y	Y	Y
12 Costello	Y	Y	Y	Y
13 Biggert	Y	N	Y	Y
14 Hultgren	Y	N	Y	Y
15 Johnson	+	N	Y	Y

KEY   **Republicans**   Democrats

Y Voted for (yea)	X Paired against	C Voted "present" to avoid possible conflict of interest
# Paired for	- Announced against	
+ Announced for	P Voted "present"	? Did not vote or otherwise make a position known
N Voted against (nay)		

		178	179	180	181
16	Manzullo	Y	N	Y	Y
17	Schilling	Y	N	Y	Y
18	Schock	Y	N	Y	Y
19	Shimkus	Y	N	Y	Y
INDIANA					
1	Visclosky	Y	Y	N	Y
2	Donnelly	?	Y	Y	Y
3	Stutzman	Y	N	Y	Y
4	Rokita	Y	N	Y	Y
5	Burton	Y	N	Y	Y
6	Pence	?	N	Y	Y
7	Carson	Y	Y	Y	Y
8	Bucshon	?	N	Y	Y
9	Young	Y	N	Y	Y
IOWA					
1	Braley	Y	Y	N	Y
2	Loebsack	?	?	?	?
3	Boswell	Y	Y	Y	Y
4	Latham	Y	N	Y	Y
5	King	Y	N	Y	Y
KANSAS					
1	Huelskamp	Y	N	Y	Y
2	Jenkins	Y	N	Y	Y
3	Yoder	Y	N	Y	Y
4	Pompeo	Y	N	Y	Y
KENTUCKY					
1	Whitfield	Y	N	Y	Y
2	Guthrie	Y	N	Y	Y
3	Yarmuth	?	Y	N	Y
4	Davis	Y	N	Y	Y
5	Rogers	Y	N	Y	Y
6	Chandler	Y	Y	Y	Y
LOUISIANA					
1	Scalise	Y	N	Y	Y
2	Richmond	Y	Y	Y	Y
3	Landry	?	N	Y	Y
4	Fleming	Y	N	Y	Y
5	Alexander	Y	N	Y	Y
6	Cassidy	Y	N	Y	Y
7	Boustany	Y	N	Y	Y
MAINE					
1	Pingree	Y	Y	N	Y
2	Michaud	Y	Y	N	Y
MARYLAND					
1	Harris	Y	N	Y	Y
2	Ruppersberger	Y	Y	Y	Y
3	Sarbanes	Y	Y	N	Y
4	Edwards	Y	Y	N	Y
5	Hoyer	Y	Y	N	Y
6	Bartlett	Y	N	Y	Y
7	Cummings	Y	Y	N	Y
8	Van Hollen	Y	Y	N	Y
MASSACHUSETTS					
1	Olver	Y	Y	N	Y
2	Neal	Y	Y	N	Y
3	McGovern	Y	Y	N	Y
4	Frank	Y	Y	N	Y
5	Tsongas	Y	Y	N	Y
6	Tierney	Y	Y	N	Y
7	Markey	Y	Y	N	Y
8	Capuano	Y	Y	N	Y
9	Lynch	Y	Y	N	Y
10	Keating	Y	Y	Y	Y
MICHIGAN					
1	Benishek	Y	N	Y	Y
2	Huizenga	Y	N	Y	Y
3	Amash	N	N	Y	N
4	Camp	Y	N	Y	Y
5	Kildee	Y	Y	N	Y
6	Upton	Y	N	Y	Y
7	Walberg	Y	N	Y	Y
8	Rogers	Y	N	Y	Y
9	Peters	Y	Y	Y	Y
10	Miller	Y	N	Y	Y
11	McCotter	Y	N	Y	Y
12	Levin	Y	Y	N	Y
13	Clarke	Y	Y	Y	Y
14	Conyers	Y	Y	N	Y
15	Dingell	Y	Y	N	Y
MINNESOTA					
1	Walz	Y	Y	Y	Y
2	Kline	Y	N	Y	Y
3	Paulsen	Y	N	Y	Y
4	McCollum	Y	Y	N	Y

		178	179	180	181
5	Ellison	Y	Y	N	Y
6	Bachmann	Y	N	Y	Y
7	Peterson	Y	N	Y	Y
8	Cravaack	Y	N	Y	Y
MISSISSIPPI					
1	Nunnelee	Y	N	Y	Y
2	Thompson	Y	Y	Y	Y
3	Harper	Y	N	Y	Y
4	Palazzo	Y	N	Y	Y
MISSOURI					
1	Clay	Y	Y	N	Y
2	Akin	?	N	Y	+
3	Carnahan	Y	Y	Y	Y
4	Hartzler	Y	N	Y	Y
5	Cleaver	Y	Y	N	Y
6	Graves	Y	N	Y	Y
7	Long	Y	N	Y	Y
8	Emerson	Y	N	Y	Y
9	Luetkemeyer	Y	N	Y	Y
MONTANA					
AL	Rehberg	Y	N	Y	Y
NEBRASKA					
1	Fortenberry	Y	N	Y	Y
2	Terry	Y	N	Y	Y
3	Smith	Y	N	Y	Y
NEVADA					
1	Berkley	Y	Y	Y	Y
2	Amodei	Y	N	Y	Y
3	Heck	Y	N	Y	Y
NEW HAMPSHIRE					
1	Guinta	Y	N	Y	Y
2	Bass	Y	Y	Y	Y
NEW JERSEY					
1	Andrews	Y	Y	Y	Y
2	LoBiondo	Y	N	Y	Y
3	Runyan	Y	N	Y	Y
4	Smith	Y	N	Y	Y
5	Garrett	Y	N	Y	Y
6	Pallone	Y	Y	N	Y
7	Lance	Y	N	Y	Y
8	Pascrell	+	Y	N	Y
9	Rothman	Y	Y	N	Y
10	Vacant				
11	Frelinghuysen	Y	N	Y	Y
12	Holt	Y	Y	N	Y
13	Sires	Y	Y	Y	Y
NEW MEXICO					
1	Heinrich	Y	Y	N	Y
2	Pearce	Y	N	Y	Y
3	Luján	Y	Y	N	Y
NEW YORK					
1	Bishop	Y	Y	N	Y
2	Israel	?	Y	Y	Y
3	King	Y	N	Y	Y
4	McCarthy	Y	Y	Y	Y
5	Ackerman	?	Y	N	Y
6	Meeks	Y	Y	N	Y
7	Crowley	Y	Y	N	Y
8	Nadler	Y	Y	N	Y
9	Turner	Y	N	Y	Y
10	Towns	Y	Y	N	Y
11	Clarke	Y	Y	N	Y
12	Velázquez	Y	Y	N	Y
13	Grimm	Y	N	Y	Y
14	Maloney	Y	Y	N	Y
15	Rangel	?	?	?	?
16	Serrano	Y	Y	N	Y
17	Engel	Y	Y	N	Y
18	Lowey	?	?	?	?
19	Hayworth	Y	N	Y	Y
20	Gibson	Y	N	Y	Y
21	Tonko	Y	Y	N	Y
22	Hinchey	Y	Y	N	Y
23	Owens	Y	Y	N	Y
24	Hanna	Y	N	Y	Y
25	Buerkle	Y	N	Y	Y
26	Hochul	Y	Y	Y	Y
27	Higgins	Y	Y	Y	Y
28	Slaughter	+	+	−	+
29	Reed	Y	N	Y	Y
NORTH CAROLINA					
1	Butterfield	?	Y	Y	Y
2	Ellmers	Y	N	Y	Y
3	Jones	Y	N	Y	Y
4	Price	Y	Y	N	Y

		178	179	180	181
5	Foxx	Y	N	Y	Y
6	Coble	Y	N	Y	Y
7	McIntyre	Y	Y	Y	Y
8	Kissell	Y	N	Y	Y
9	Myrick	Y	N	Y	Y
10	McHenry	Y	N	Y	Y
11	Shuler	Y	Y	Y	Y
12	Watt	Y	Y	N	Y
13	Miller	?	Y	N	Y
NORTH DAKOTA					
AL	Berg	Y	N	Y	Y
OHIO					
1	Chabot	Y	N	Y	Y
2	Schmidt	Y	N	Y	Y
3	Turner	Y	N	Y	Y
4	Jordan	Y	N	Y	Y
5	Latta	Y	N	Y	Y
6	Johnson	Y	N	Y	Y
7	Austria	Y	N	Y	Y
8	Boehner				
9	Kaptur	?	Y	N	Y
10	Kucinich	Y	Y	N	Y
11	Fudge	Y	Y	N	Y
12	Tiberi	Y	N	Y	Y
13	Sutton	Y	Y	Y	Y
14	LaTourette	Y	N	Y	Y
15	Stivers	Y	N	Y	Y
16	Renacci	Y	N	Y	Y
17	Ryan	Y	Y	N	Y
18	Gibbs	Y	N	Y	Y
OKLAHOMA					
1	Sullivan	Y	N	Y	Y
2	Boren	Y	Y	Y	Y
3	Lucas	Y	N	Y	Y
4	Cole	Y	N	Y	Y
5	Lankford	Y	N	Y	Y
OREGON					
1	Bonamici	Y	Y	N	Y
2	Walden	Y	N	Y	Y
3	Blumenauer	Y	Y	N	Y
4	DeFazio	Y	Y	N	Y
5	Schrader	?	Y	Y	Y
PENNSYLVANIA					
1	Brady	?	Y	N	Y
2	Fattah	Y	Y	N	Y
3	Kelly	Y	N	Y	Y
4	Altmire	Y	Y	Y	Y
5	Thompson	Y	N	Y	Y
6	Gerlach	+	N	Y	Y
7	Meehan	Y	N	Y	Y
8	Fitzpatrick	Y	N	Y	Y
9	Shuster	Y	N	Y	Y
10	Marino	?	?	?	?
11	Barletta	Y	N	Y	Y
12	Critz	?	Y	Y	Y
13	Schwartz	?	Y	Y	Y
14	Doyle	?	Y	Y	Y
15	Dent	Y	N	Y	Y
16	Pitts	Y	N	Y	Y
17	Holden	?	?	?	?
18	Murphy	?	Y	Y	Y
19	Platts	?	N	Y	Y
RHODE ISLAND					
1	Cicilline	Y	Y	N	Y
2	Langevin	Y	Y	Y	Y
SOUTH CAROLINA					
1	Scott	Y	N	Y	Y
2	Wilson	Y	N	Y	Y
3	Duncan	Y	N	Y	Y
4	Gowdy	Y	N	Y	Y
5	Mulvaney	N	N	Y	Y
6	Clyburn	Y	Y	Y	Y
SOUTH DAKOTA					
AL	Noem	Y	N	Y	Y
TENNESSEE					
1	Roe	Y	N	Y	Y
2	Duncan	Y	N	Y	Y
3	Fleischmann	Y	N	Y	Y
4	DesJarlais	Y	N	Y	Y
5	Cooper	Y	Y	Y	Y
6	Black	Y	N	Y	Y
7	Blackburn	Y	N	Y	Y
8	Fincher	Y	N	Y	Y
9	Cohen	Y	Y	N	Y

		178	179	180	181
TEXAS					
1	Gohmert	?	N	Y	Y
2	Poe	Y	N	Y	Y
3	Johnson, S.	?	N	Y	Y
4	Hall	Y	N	Y	Y
5	Hensarling	?	N	Y	Y
6	Barton	?	N	Y	Y
7	Culberson	Y	N	Y	Y
8	Brady	Y	N	Y	Y
9	Green, A.	Y	Y	N	Y
10	McCaul	Y	N	Y	Y
11	Conaway	Y	N	Y	Y
12	Granger	Y	N	Y	Y
13	Thornberry	Y	N	Y	Y
14	Paul	?	?	?	?
15	Hinojosa	Y	Y	Y	Y
16	Reyes	?	Y	Y	Y
17	Flores	Y	N	Y	Y
18	Jackson Lee	Y	Y	N	Y
19	Neugebauer	Y	N	Y	Y
20	Gonzalez	Y	Y	N	Y
21	Smith	Y	N	Y	Y
22	Olson	Y	N	Y	Y
23	Canseco	Y	N	Y	Y
24	Marchant	?	N	Y	Y
25	Doggett	Y	Y	N	Y
26	Burgess	Y	N	Y	Y
27	Farenthold	Y	N	Y	Y
28	Cuellar	Y	Y	Y	Y
29	Green, G.	Y	Y	Y	Y
30	Johnson, E.	Y	Y	N	Y
31	Carter	Y	N	Y	Y
32	Sessions	+	N	Y	Y
UTAH					
1	Bishop	Y	N	Y	Y
2	Matheson	Y	Y	Y	Y
3	Chaffetz	Y	N	Y	Y
VERMONT					
AL	Welch	Y	Y	N	Y
VIRGINIA					
1	Wittman	Y	N	Y	Y
2	Rigell	Y	N	Y	Y
3	Scott	Y	Y	N	Y
4	Forbes	Y	N	Y	Y
5	Hurt	Y	N	Y	Y
6	Goodlatte	Y	N	Y	Y
7	Cantor	Y	N	Y	Y
8	Moran	?	Y	N	Y
9	Griffith	Y	N	Y	Y
10	Wolf	Y	N	Y	Y
11	Connolly	Y	Y	Y	Y
WASHINGTON					
1	Vacant				
2	Larsen	Y	Y	Y	Y
3	Herrera Beutler	Y	N	Y	Y
4	Hastings	Y	N	Y	Y
5	McMorris Rodgers	Y	N	Y	Y
6	Dicks	Y	Y	N	Y
7	McDermott	Y	Y	N	Y
8	Reichert	Y	N	Y	Y
9	Smith	Y	Y	N	Y
WEST VIRGINIA					
1	McKinley	Y	N	Y	Y
2	Capito	Y	N	Y	Y
3	Rahall	Y	Y	Y	Y
WISCONSIN					
1	Ryan	Y	N	Y	Y
2	Baldwin	Y	Y	N	Y
3	Kind	Y	Y	Y	Y
4	Moore	Y	Y	Y	Y
5	Sensenbrenner	Y	N	Y	Y
6	Petri	Y	N	Y	Y
7	Duffy	Y	N	Y	Y
8	Ribble	Y	N	Y	Y
WYOMING					
AL	Lummis	Y	N	Y	Y

IN THE HOUSE | By Vote Number

182. HR 3523, HR 4628. **Cybersecurity and Student Loans/Previous Question.** Nugent, R-Fla., motion to order the previous question (thus ending debate and the possibility of amendment) on the rule (H Res 631) that would provide for House floor consideration of a bill (HR 3523) that would provide for cyberthreat information sharing between the private sector and the federal intelligence community and a bill (HR 4628) that would extend the current student loan interest rates for one year. Motion agreed to 241-179: R 236-0; D 5-179. April 26, 2012.

183. HR 3523, HR 4628. **Cybersecurity and Student Loans/Rule.** Adoption of the rule (H Res 631) that would provide for House floor consideration of a bill (HR 3523) that would provide for cyberthreat information sharing between the private sector and the federal intelligence community and a bill (HR 4628) that would extend the current student loan interest rates for one year. The rule also would allow for consideration of three cybersecurity measures under suspension of the rules at any time through the legislative day of April 27, 2012. Adopted 236-185: R 234-1; D 2-184. April 26, 2012.

184. HR 3523. **Cybersecurity Information Sharing/Critical Infrastructure.** Langevin, D-R.I., amendment that would make critical infrastructure owners and operators eligible to participate in the information-sharing program to be created by the bill. Rejected in Committee of the Whole 167-243: R 11-222; D 156-21. April 26, 2012.

185. HR 3523. **Cybersecurity Information Sharing/FOIA Requests.** Rogers, R-Mich., amendment that would clarify that providing information to the federal government as allowed by the bill does not affect requirements to provide information subject to the Freedom of Information Act. Adopted in Committee of the Whole 412-0: R 233-0; D 179-0. April 26, 2012.

186. HR 3523. **Cybersecurity Information Sharing/Information Use.** Quayle, R-Ariz., amendment that would limit the way the government could use information on cyberthreats obtained from the private sector. It would allow the federal government to use the information for cybersecurity purposes generally, and to investigate and prosecute cybersecurity crimes and threats involving possible death or serious bodily harm, to protect minors from child pornography or other sexual crimes and to protect national security. Adopted in Committee of the Whole 410-3: R 231-2; D 179-1. April 26, 2012.

187. HR 3523. **Cybersecurity Information Sharing/Personal Information.** Amash, R-Mich., amendment that would prohibit the federal government from using personal information from library records, firearms sales records, tax returns and education or medical records received from private entities. Adopted in Committee of the Whole 415-0: R 234-0; D 181-0. April 26, 2012.

	182	183	184	185	186	187
ALABAMA						
1 Bonner	Y	Y	N	Y	Y	Y
2 Roby	Y	Y	N	Y	Y	Y
3 Rogers	Y	Y	N	Y	Y	Y
4 Aderholt	Y	Y	N	Y	Y	Y
5 Brooks	Y	Y	N	Y	Y	Y
6 Bachus	Y	Y	N	Y	Y	Y
7 Sewell	N	N	Y	Y	Y	Y
ALASKA						
AL Young	Y	Y	N	Y	Y	Y
ARIZONA						
1 Gosar	Y	Y	N	Y	Y	Y
2 Franks	Y	Y	N	Y	Y	Y
3 Quayle	Y	Y	N	Y	Y	Y
4 Pastor	N	N	Y	Y	Y	Y
5 Schweikert	Y	Y	N	Y	Y	Y
6 Flake	Y	Y	N	Y	Y	Y
7 Grijalva	N	N	Y	Y	Y	Y
8 Vacant						
ARKANSAS						
1 Crawford	Y	Y	N	Y	Y	Y
2 Griffin	Y	Y	N	Y	Y	Y
3 Womack	Y	Y	N	Y	Y	Y
4 Ross	N	N	N	Y	Y	Y
CALIFORNIA						
1 Thompson	N	N	Y	Y	Y	Y
2 Herger	Y	Y	N	Y	Y	Y
3 Lungren	Y	Y	Y	Y	Y	Y
4 McClintock	Y	Y	N	N	N	Y
5 Matsui	N	N	Y	Y	Y	Y
6 Woolsey	N	N	Y	Y	Y	Y
7 Miller, George	N	N	Y	Y	Y	Y
8 Pelosi	N	N	Y	Y	Y	Y
9 Lee	N	N	Y	Y	Y	Y
10 Garamendi	N	N	N	Y	Y	Y
11 McNerney	N	N	N	Y	Y	Y
12 Speier	N	N	Y	Y	Y	Y
13 Stark	N	N	Y	Y	Y	Y
14 Eshoo	N	N	N	Y	Y	Y
15 Honda	N	N	Y	Y	Y	Y
16 Lofgren	N	N	Y	Y	N	Y
17 Farr	N	N	Y	Y	Y	Y
18 Cardoza	N	N	?	Y	Y	Y
19 Denham	Y	Y	N	Y	Y	Y
20 Costa	N	N	Y	Y	Y	Y
21 Nunes	Y	Y	N	Y	Y	Y
22 McCarthy	Y	Y	N	Y	Y	Y
23 Capps	N	N	Y	Y	Y	Y
24 Gallegly	Y	Y	N	Y	Y	Y
25 McKeon	Y	Y	N	Y	Y	Y
26 Dreier	Y	Y	N	Y	Y	Y
27 Sherman	N	N	N	Y	Y	Y
28 Berman	N	N	Y	Y	Y	Y
29 Schiff	N	N	Y	Y	Y	Y
30 Waxman	?	N	Y	Y	Y	Y
31 Becerra	N	N	Y	Y	Y	Y
32 Chu	N	N	Y	Y	Y	Y
33 Bass	N	N	Y	Y	Y	Y
34 Roybal-Allard	N	N	Y	Y	Y	Y
35 Waters	?	N	Y	Y	Y	Y
36 Hahn	N	N	Y	Y	Y	Y
37 Richardson	N	N	Y	Y	Y	Y
38 Napolitano	N	N	N	Y	Y	Y
39 Sánchez, Linda	N	N	Y	Y	Y	Y
40 Royce	Y	Y	N	Y	Y	Y
41 Lewis	Y	Y	N	Y	Y	Y
42 Miller, Gary	Y	Y	N	Y	Y	Y
43 Baca	N	N	N	Y	Y	Y
44 Calvert	Y	Y	N	Y	Y	Y
45 Bono Mack	Y	Y	N	Y	Y	Y
46 Rohrabacher	Y	Y	N	Y	Y	Y
47 Sanchez, Loretta	N	N	Y	Y	Y	Y
48 Campbell	Y	Y	N	Y	Y	Y
49 Issa	Y	Y	N	Y	Y	Y
50 Bilbray	Y	Y	N	Y	Y	Y
51 Filner	–	–	+	+	+	+
52 Hunter	Y	Y	N	Y	Y	Y
53 Davis	N	N	Y	Y	Y	Y

	182	183	184	185	186	187
COLORADO						
1 DeGette	N	N	Y	Y	Y	Y
2 Polis	N	N	Y	Y	Y	Y
3 Tipton	Y	Y	N	Y	Y	Y
4 Gardner	Y	Y	N	Y	Y	Y
5 Lamborn	Y	Y	N	Y	Y	Y
6 Coffman	Y	Y	Y	Y	Y	Y
7 Perlmutter	N	N	Y	Y	Y	Y
CONNECTICUT						
1 Larson	N	N	Y	Y	Y	Y
2 Courtney	N	N	N	Y	Y	Y
3 DeLauro	N	N	Y	Y	Y	Y
4 Himes	N	N	Y	Y	Y	Y
5 Murphy	N	N	?	Y	Y	Y
DELAWARE						
AL Carney	N	N	Y	Y	Y	Y
FLORIDA						
1 Miller	Y	Y	N	Y	Y	Y
2 Southerland	Y	Y	N	Y	Y	Y
3 Brown	N	N	Y	Y	Y	Y
4 Crenshaw	Y	Y	N	Y	Y	Y
5 Nugent	Y	Y	N	Y	Y	Y
6 Stearns	Y	Y	N	Y	Y	Y
7 Mica	Y	Y	N	Y	Y	Y
8 Webster	Y	Y	N	Y	Y	Y
9 Bilirakis	Y	Y	N	Y	Y	Y
10 Young	Y	Y	N	Y	Y	Y
11 Castor	N	N	Y	Y	Y	Y
12 Ross	Y	Y	N	Y	Y	Y
13 Buchanan	Y	Y	N	Y	Y	Y
14 Mack	Y	Y	N	Y	Y	Y
15 Posey	Y	Y	N	Y	Y	Y
16 Rooney	Y	Y	N	Y	Y	Y
17 Wilson	N	N	Y	Y	Y	Y
18 Ros-Lehtinen	Y	Y	N	Y	Y	Y
19 Deutch	N	N	Y	Y	Y	Y
20 Wasserman Schultz	N	N	Y	Y	Y	Y
21 Diaz-Balart	Y	Y	N	Y	Y	Y
22 West	Y	Y	N	Y	Y	Y
23 Hastings	N	N	Y	Y	Y	Y
24 Adams	Y	Y	N	Y	Y	Y
25 Rivera	Y	Y	N	Y	Y	Y
GEORGIA						
1 Kingston	Y	Y	N	Y	Y	Y
2 Bishop	N	N	Y	Y	Y	Y
3 Westmoreland	Y	Y	N	Y	Y	Y
4 Johnson	N	N	?	?	?	?
5 Lewis	N	N	Y	Y	Y	Y
6 Price	Y	Y	N	Y	Y	Y
7 Woodall	Y	Y	Y	Y	Y	Y
8 Scott, A.	Y	Y	N	Y	Y	Y
9 Graves	Y	Y	N	Y	Y	Y
10 Broun	Y	Y	N	Y	Y	Y
11 Gingrey	Y	Y	N	Y	Y	Y
12 Barrow	N	N	N	Y	Y	Y
13 Scott, D.	N	N	?	Y	Y	Y
HAWAII						
1 Hanabusa	N	N	Y	Y	Y	Y
2 Hirono	N	N	?	?	?	?
IDAHO						
1 Labrador	Y	Y	N	Y	Y	Y
2 Simpson	Y	Y	N	Y	Y	Y
ILLINOIS						
1 Rush	N	N	Y	Y	Y	Y
2 Jackson	N	N	Y	Y	Y	Y
3 Lipinski	N	N	Y	Y	Y	Y
4 Gutierrez	N	N	Y	Y	Y	Y
5 Quigley	N	N	Y	Y	Y	Y
6 Roskam	Y	Y	N	Y	Y	Y
7 Davis	N	N	Y	Y	Y	Y
8 Walsh	Y	Y	N	Y	Y	Y
9 Schakowsky	N	N	Y	Y	Y	Y
10 Dold	Y	Y	N	Y	Y	Y
11 Kinzinger	Y	Y	N	Y	Y	Y
12 Costello	N	N	N	Y	Y	Y
13 Biggert	Y	Y	N	Y	Y	Y
14 Hultgren	Y	Y	N	Y	Y	Y
15 Johnson	Y	Y	N	Y	Y	Y

	182	183	184	185	186	187
16 **Manzullo**	Y	Y	N	Y	Y	Y
17 **Schilling**	Y	Y	N	Y	Y	Y
18 **Schock**	Y	Y	N	Y	Y	Y
19 **Shimkus**	Y	Y	N	Y	Y	Y
INDIANA						
1 Visclosky	N	N	Y	Y	Y	Y
2 Donnelly	N	N	N	Y	Y	Y
3 **Stutzman**	Y	Y	N	Y	Y	Y
4 **Rokita**	Y	Y	N	Y	Y	Y
5 **Burton**	Y	Y	N	Y	Y	Y
6 **Pence**	Y	Y	?	?	?	?
7 Carson	N	N	Y	Y	Y	Y
8 **Bucshon**	Y	Y	?	?	?	?
9 **Young**	Y	Y	N	Y	Y	Y
IOWA						
1 Braley	N	N	Y	Y	Y	Y
2 Loebsack	N	N	Y	Y	Y	Y
3 Boswell	N	N	Y	Y	Y	Y
4 **Latham**	Y	Y	N	Y	Y	Y
5 **King**	Y	Y	N	Y	Y	Y
KANSAS						
1 **Huelskamp**	Y	Y	N	Y	Y	Y
2 **Jenkins**	Y	Y	N	Y	Y	Y
3 **Yoder**	Y	Y	N	Y	Y	Y
4 **Pompeo**	Y	Y	N	Y	Y	Y
KENTUCKY						
1 **Whitfield**	Y	Y	N	Y	Y	Y
2 **Guthrie**	Y	Y	N	Y	Y	Y
3 Yarmuth	N	N	Y	Y	Y	Y
4 **Davis**	?	?	?	?	?	?
5 **Rogers**	Y	Y	N	Y	Y	Y
6 Chandler	N	N	Y	Y	Y	Y
LOUISIANA						
1 **Scalise**	Y	Y	N	Y	Y	Y
2 Richmond	N	N	Y	Y	Y	Y
3 **Landry**	Y	Y	N	?	Y	Y
4 **Fleming**	Y	Y	N	Y	Y	Y
5 **Alexander**	Y	Y	N	Y	Y	Y
6 **Cassidy**	Y	Y	N	Y	Y	Y
7 **Boustany**	Y	Y	N	Y	Y	Y
MAINE						
1 Pingree	N	N	Y	Y	Y	Y
2 Michaud	N	N	Y	Y	Y	Y
MARYLAND						
1 **Harris**	Y	Y	N	Y	Y	Y
2 Ruppersberger	N	N	Y	Y	Y	Y
3 Sarbanes	N	N	Y	Y	Y	Y
4 Edwards	N	N	Y	Y	Y	Y
5 Hoyer	N	N	Y	Y	Y	Y
6 **Bartlett**	Y	Y	N	Y	Y	Y
7 Cummings	N	N	Y	Y	Y	Y
8 Van Hollen	N	N	Y	Y	Y	Y
MASSACHUSETTS						
1 Olver	N	N	Y	Y	Y	Y
2 Neal	N	N	Y	Y	Y	Y
3 McGovern	N	N	Y	Y	Y	Y
4 Frank	N	N	Y	Y	Y	Y
5 Tsongas	N	N	Y	Y	Y	Y
6 Tierney	N	N	Y	Y	Y	Y
7 Markey	N	N	Y	Y	Y	Y
8 Capuano	N	N	Y	Y	Y	Y
9 Lynch	N	N	Y	Y	Y	Y
10 Keating	N	N	Y	Y	Y	Y
MICHIGAN						
1 **Benishek**	Y	Y	N	Y	Y	Y
2 **Huizenga**	Y	Y	N	Y	Y	Y
3 **Amash**	Y	Y	N	Y	Y	Y
4 **Camp**	Y	Y	N	Y	Y	Y
5 Kildee	N	N	Y	Y	Y	Y
6 **Upton**	Y	Y	N	Y	Y	Y
7 **Walberg**	Y	Y	N	Y	Y	Y
8 **Rogers**	Y	Y	N	Y	Y	Y
9 Peters	N	N	Y	Y	Y	Y
10 **Miller**	Y	Y	N	Y	Y	Y
11 **McCotter**	Y	Y	N	Y	Y	Y
12 Levin	N	N	Y	Y	Y	Y
13 Clarke	N	N	Y	Y	Y	Y
14 Conyers	N	N	Y	Y	Y	Y
15 Dingell	N	N	Y	Y	Y	Y
MINNESOTA						
1 Walz	N	N	Y	Y	Y	Y
2 **Kline**	Y	Y	N	Y	Y	Y
3 **Paulsen**	Y	Y	N	Y	Y	Y
4 McCollum	N	N	Y	Y	Y	Y

	182	183	184	185	186	187
5 Ellison	N	N	Y	Y	Y	Y
6 **Bachmann**	Y	Y	N	Y	Y	Y
7 Peterson	N	N	N	Y	Y	Y
8 **Cravaack**	Y	Y	N	Y	Y	Y
MISSISSIPPI						
1 **Nunnelee**	Y	Y	N	Y	Y	Y
2 Thompson	N	N	Y	Y	Y	Y
3 **Harper**	Y	Y	N	Y	Y	Y
4 **Palazzo**	Y	Y	N	Y	Y	Y
MISSOURI						
1 Clay	N	N	Y	Y	Y	Y
2 **Akin**	Y	Y	N	Y	Y	Y
3 Carnahan	N	N	Y	Y	Y	Y
4 **Hartzler**	Y	Y	N	Y	Y	Y
5 Cleaver	N	N	Y	Y	Y	Y
6 **Graves**	Y	Y	N	Y	Y	Y
7 **Long**	Y	Y	N	Y	Y	Y
8 **Emerson**	Y	Y	N	Y	Y	Y
9 **Luetkemeyer**	Y	Y	N	Y	Y	Y
MONTANA						
AL **Rehberg**	Y	Y	N	Y	Y	Y
NEBRASKA						
1 **Fortenberry**	Y	Y	N	Y	Y	Y
2 **Terry**	Y	Y	N	Y	Y	Y
3 **Smith**	Y	Y	N	Y	Y	Y
NEVADA						
1 Berkley	N	N	Y	Y	Y	Y
2 **Amodei**	Y	Y	N	Y	Y	Y
3 **Heck**	Y	Y	N	Y	Y	Y
NEW HAMPSHIRE						
1 **Guinta**	Y	Y	N	Y	Y	Y
2 **Bass**	Y	Y	N	Y	Y	Y
NEW JERSEY						
1 Andrews	N	N	Y	Y	Y	Y
2 **LoBiondo**	Y	Y	N	Y	Y	Y
3 **Runyan**	Y	Y	N	Y	Y	Y
4 **Smith**	Y	Y	N	Y	Y	Y
5 **Garrett**	Y	Y	N	Y	Y	Y
6 Pallone	N	N	Y	Y	Y	Y
7 **Lance**	Y	Y	N	Y	Y	Y
8 Pascrell	N	N	Y	Y	Y	Y
9 Rothman	N	N	Y	Y	Y	Y
10 Vacant						
11 **Frelinghuysen**	Y	Y	N	Y	Y	Y
12 Holt	N	N	Y	Y	Y	Y
13 Sires	N	N	?	?	?	?
NEW MEXICO						
1 Heinrich	N	N	Y	Y	Y	Y
2 **Pearce**	Y	Y	N	Y	Y	Y
3 Luján	N	N	Y	Y	Y	Y
NEW YORK						
1 Bishop	N	N	Y	Y	Y	Y
2 Israel	N	N	Y	Y	Y	Y
3 **King**	Y	Y	Y	Y	Y	Y
4 McCarthy	N	N	N	Y	Y	Y
5 Ackerman	N	N	Y	Y	Y	Y
6 Meeks	N	N	Y	Y	Y	Y
7 Crowley	N	N	N	Y	Y	Y
8 Nadler	N	N	Y	Y	Y	Y
9 **Turner**	Y	Y	Y	Y	Y	Y
10 Towns	N	N	Y	Y	Y	Y
11 Clarke	N	N	?	?	Y	Y
12 Velázquez	N	N	Y	Y	Y	Y
13 **Grimm**	Y	Y	Y	Y	Y	Y
14 Maloney	N	N	?	?	?	?
15 Rangel	?	?	?	?	?	?
16 Serrano	N	N	Y	Y	Y	Y
17 Engel	N	N	Y	Y	Y	Y
18 Lowey	N	N	Y	Y	Y	Y
19 **Hayworth**	Y	Y	N	Y	Y	Y
20 **Gibson**	Y	Y	Y	Y	Y	Y
21 Tonko	N	N	Y	Y	Y	Y
22 Hinchey	N	N	Y	Y	Y	Y
23 Owens	N	N	Y	Y	Y	Y
24 **Hanna**	Y	Y	N	Y	Y	Y
25 **Buerkle**	Y	Y	N	Y	Y	Y
26 Hochul	N	N	Y	Y	Y	Y
27 Higgins	N	N	Y	Y	Y	Y
28 Slaughter	–	–	+	+	+	+
29 **Reed**	Y	Y	N	Y	Y	Y
NORTH CAROLINA						
1 Butterfield	N	N	Y	Y	Y	Y
2 **Ellmers**	Y	Y	N	Y	Y	Y
3 **Jones**	Y	N	N	Y	Y	Y
4 Price	N	N	Y	Y	Y	Y

	182	183	184	185	186	187
5 **Foxx**	Y	Y	N	Y	Y	Y
6 **Coble**	Y	Y	N	Y	Y	Y
7 McIntyre	N	N	Y	Y	Y	Y
8 Kissell	N	N	Y	Y	Y	Y
9 **Myrick**	Y	Y	N	Y	Y	Y
10 **McHenry**	?	?	?	?	?	?
11 Shuler	Y	Y	Y	Y	Y	Y
12 Watt	N	N	Y	Y	Y	Y
13 Miller	N	N	Y	Y	Y	Y
NORTH DAKOTA						
AL **Berg**	Y	Y	N	Y	Y	Y
OHIO						
1 **Chabot**	Y	Y	N	Y	Y	Y
2 **Schmidt**	Y	Y	N	Y	Y	Y
3 **Turner**	Y	Y	N	Y	Y	Y
4 **Jordan**	Y	Y	N	Y	Y	Y
5 **Latta**	Y	Y	N	Y	Y	Y
6 **Johnson**	Y	Y	N	Y	Y	Y
7 **Austria**	Y	Y	N	Y	Y	Y
8 **Boehner**						
9 Kaptur	N	N	Y	Y	Y	Y
10 Kucinich	N	N	Y	Y	Y	Y
11 Fudge	N	N	Y	Y	Y	Y
12 **Tiberi**	Y	Y	N	Y	Y	Y
13 Sutton	N	N	Y	Y	Y	Y
14 **LaTourette**	Y	Y	N	Y	Y	Y
15 **Stivers**	Y	Y	N	Y	Y	Y
16 **Renacci**	Y	Y	N	Y	Y	Y
17 Ryan	N	N	Y	Y	Y	Y
18 **Gibbs**	Y	Y	N	Y	Y	Y
OKLAHOMA						
1 **Sullivan**	?	?	N	Y	?	Y
2 Boren	Y	N	Y	Y	Y	Y
3 **Lucas**	Y	Y	N	Y	Y	Y
4 **Cole**	Y	Y	N	Y	Y	Y
5 **Lankford**	Y	Y	N	Y	Y	Y
OREGON						
1 Bonamici	N	N	Y	Y	Y	Y
2 **Walden**	Y	Y	N	Y	Y	Y
3 Blumenauer	N	N	?	?	?	?
4 DeFazio	N	N	Y	Y	Y	Y
5 Schrader	N	N	N	?	?	Y
PENNSYLVANIA						
1 Brady	N	N	N	Y	Y	Y
2 Fattah	N	N	Y	Y	Y	Y
3 **Kelly**	Y	Y	N	Y	Y	Y
4 Altmire	N	N	N	Y	Y	Y
5 **Thompson**	Y	Y	N	Y	Y	Y
6 **Gerlach**	Y	Y	N	Y	Y	Y
7 **Meehan**	Y	Y	Y	Y	Y	Y
8 **Fitzpatrick**	Y	Y	N	Y	Y	Y
9 **Shuster**	Y	Y	N	Y	Y	Y
10 **Marino**	?	?	?	?	?	?
11 **Barletta**	Y	Y	N	Y	Y	Y
12 Critz	N	N	Y	Y	Y	Y
13 Schwartz	N	N	Y	Y	Y	Y
14 Doyle	N	N	Y	Y	Y	Y
15 **Dent**	Y	Y	Y	Y	Y	Y
16 **Pitts**	Y	Y	N	Y	Y	Y
17 Holden	?	?	?	?	?	?
18 **Murphy**	Y	Y	N	Y	Y	Y
19 **Platts**	Y	Y	N	Y	Y	Y
RHODE ISLAND						
1 Cicilline	N	N	Y	Y	Y	Y
2 Langevin	N	N	Y	Y	Y	Y
SOUTH CAROLINA						
1 **Scott**	Y	Y	N	Y	Y	Y
2 **Wilson**	Y	Y	N	Y	Y	Y
3 **Duncan**	Y	Y	N	Y	Y	Y
4 **Gowdy**	Y	Y	N	Y	Y	Y
5 **Mulvaney**	Y	Y	N	Y	Y	Y
6 Clyburn	N	N	Y	Y	Y	Y
SOUTH DAKOTA						
AL **Noem**	Y	Y	N	Y	Y	Y
TENNESSEE						
1 **Roe**	Y	Y	N	Y	Y	Y
2 **Duncan**	Y	Y	N	Y	Y	Y
3 **Fleischmann**	Y	Y	N	Y	Y	Y
4 **DesJarlais**	Y	Y	N	Y	Y	Y
5 Cooper	N	N	Y	Y	Y	Y
6 **Black**	Y	Y	N	Y	Y	Y
7 **Blackburn**	Y	Y	N	Y	Y	Y
8 **Fincher**	Y	Y	N	Y	Y	Y
9 Cohen	N	N	Y	Y	Y	Y

	182	183	184	185	186	187
TEXAS						
1 **Gohmert**	Y	Y	N	Y	N	Y
2 **Poe**	Y	Y	N	Y	Y	Y
3 **Johnson, S.**	Y	Y	N	Y	Y	Y
4 **Hall**	Y	Y	N	Y	Y	Y
5 **Hensarling**	Y	Y	N	Y	Y	Y
6 **Barton**	Y	Y	N	Y	Y	Y
7 **Culberson**	Y	Y	N	Y	Y	Y
8 **Brady**	Y	Y	Y	Y	Y	Y
9 Green, A.	N	N	Y	Y	Y	Y
10 **McCaul**	Y	Y	N	Y	Y	Y
11 **Conaway**	Y	Y	N	Y	Y	Y
12 **Granger**	Y	Y	N	Y	Y	Y
13 **Thornberry**	Y	Y	Y	Y	Y	Y
14 **Paul**	?	?	?	?	?	?
15 Hinojosa	N	N	N	Y	Y	Y
16 Reyes	N	N	Y	Y	Y	Y
17 **Flores**	Y	Y	N	Y	Y	Y
18 Jackson Lee	N	N	Y	Y	Y	Y
19 **Neugebauer**	Y	Y	N	Y	Y	Y
20 Gonzalez	N	N	Y	Y	Y	Y
21 **Smith**	Y	Y	N	Y	Y	Y
22 **Olson**	Y	Y	N	Y	Y	Y
23 **Canseco**	Y	Y	?	?	?	?
24 **Marchant**	Y	Y	N	Y	Y	Y
25 Doggett	N	N	Y	Y	Y	Y
26 **Burgess**	Y	Y	N	Y	Y	Y
27 **Farenthold**	Y	Y	N	Y	Y	Y
28 Cuellar	Y	N	Y	Y	Y	Y
29 Green, G.	Y	N	N	Y	Y	Y
30 Johnson, E.	N	N	Y	Y	Y	Y
31 **Carter**	Y	Y	N	Y	Y	Y
32 **Sessions**	Y	?	N	Y	Y	Y
UTAH						
1 **Bishop**	Y	Y	N	Y	Y	Y
2 Matheson	Y	Y	N	Y	Y	Y
3 **Chaffetz**	Y	Y	N	Y	Y	Y
VERMONT						
AL Welch	N	N	N	Y	Y	Y
VIRGINIA						
1 **Wittman**	Y	Y	N	Y	Y	Y
2 **Rigell**	Y	Y	N	Y	Y	Y
3 Scott	N	N	Y	Y	Y	Y
4 **Forbes**	Y	Y	N	Y	Y	Y
5 **Hurt**	Y	Y	N	Y	Y	Y
6 **Goodlatte**	Y	Y	N	Y	Y	Y
7 **Cantor**	Y	Y	?	Y	Y	Y
8 Moran	N	N	Y	Y	Y	Y
9 **Griffith**	Y	Y	N	Y	Y	Y
10 **Wolf**	Y	Y	N	Y	Y	Y
11 Connolly	N	N	Y	Y	Y	Y
WASHINGTON						
1 Vacant						
2 Larsen	N	N	Y	Y	Y	Y
3 **Herrera Beutler**	Y	Y	N	Y	Y	Y
4 **Hastings**	Y	Y	N	Y	Y	Y
5 **McMorris Rodgers**	Y	Y	N	Y	Y	Y
6 Dicks	N	N	Y	Y	Y	Y
7 McDermott	N	N	Y	Y	Y	Y
8 **Reichert**	Y	Y	N	Y	Y	Y
9 Smith	N	N	Y	Y	Y	Y
WEST VIRGINIA						
1 **McKinley**	Y	Y	N	Y	Y	Y
2 **Capito**	Y	Y	N	Y	Y	Y
3 Rahall	N	N	N	Y	Y	Y
WISCONSIN						
1 **Ryan**	Y	Y	N	Y	Y	Y
2 Baldwin	N	N	Y	Y	Y	Y
3 Kind	N	N	Y	Y	Y	Y
4 Moore	N	N	Y	Y	Y	Y
5 **Sensenbrenner**	Y	Y	N	Y	Y	Y
6 **Petri**	Y	Y	N	Y	Y	Y
7 **Duffy**	Y	Y	N	Y	Y	Y
8 **Ribble**	Y	Y	N	Y	Y	Y
WYOMING						
AL **Lummis**	Y	Y	N	Y	Y	Y

IN THE HOUSE | By Vote Number

188. **HR 3523. Cybersecurity Information Sharing/Impact on Information Sharing.** Mulvaney, R-S.C., amendment that would allow the government to undertake efforts to limit the impact cyberthreat information sharing would have on privacy and civil liberties. It also would prohibit the federal government from retaining or using information shared by certain cybersecurity providers for purposes not allowed by the bill. Adopted in Committee of the Whole 416-0: R 234-0; D 182-0. April 26, 2012.

189. **HR 3523. Cybersecurity Information Sharing/Cyberthreat Information.** Goodlatte, R-Va., amendment that would narrow the definitions of what information could be identified, obtained and shared under the bill. The information would have to be linked to threats to the integrity, confidentiality or availability of government or private networks or to efforts to degrade, disrupt or destroy those systems or to gain unauthorized access to extract information. Adopted in Committee of the Whole 414-1: R 233-0; D 181-1. April 26, 2012.

190. **HR 3523. Cybersecurity Information Sharing/Sunset Date.** Mulvaney, R-S.C., amendment that would sunset the provisions of the bill five years after the date of enactment. Adopted in Committee of the Whole 413-3: R 233-1; D 180-2. April 26, 2012.

191. **HR 3523. Cybersecurity Information Sharing/Recommit.** Perlmutter, D-Colo., motion to recommit the bill to the House Intelligence Committee and report it back immediately with an amendment that would prohibit employers or the federal government from requiring that job applicants or employees disclose confidential passwords to social networking websites without a court order. It also would prohibit the government from establishing a national firewall to control access to and use of the Internet. Motion rejected 183-233: R 1-233; D 182-0. April 26, 2012.

192. **HR 3523. Cybersecurity Information Sharing/Passage.** Passage of the bill that would require the director of national intelligence (DNI) to establish procedures to promote information sharing between the federal intelligence community and the private sector. It would require the DNI to issue guidelines for temporary or permanent security clearances to allow the government to share classified cybersecurity threat intelligence with certified entities. Passed 248-168: R 206-28; D 42-140. A "nay" was a vote in support of the president's position. April 26, 2012.

	188	189	190	191	192
ALABAMA					
1 Bonner	Y	Y	Y	N	Y
2 Roby	Y	Y	Y	N	Y
3 Rogers	Y	Y	Y	N	Y
4 Aderholt	Y	Y	Y	N	Y
5 Brooks	Y	Y	Y	N	N
6 Bachus	Y	Y	Y	N	Y
7 Sewell	Y	Y	Y	Y	N
ALASKA					
AL Young	Y	Y	Y	N	Y
ARIZONA					
1 Gosar	Y	Y	Y	N	N
2 Franks	Y	Y	Y	N	Y
3 Quayle	Y	Y	Y	N	Y
4 Pastor	Y	Y	Y	Y	N
5 Schweikert	Y	Y	Y	N	N
6 Flake	Y	Y	Y	N	Y
7 Grijalva	Y	Y	Y	Y	N
8 Vacant					
ARKANSAS					
1 Crawford	Y	Y	Y	N	Y
2 Griffin	Y	Y	Y	N	Y
3 Womack	Y	Y	Y	N	Y
4 Ross	Y	Y	Y	Y	Y
CALIFORNIA					
1 Thompson	Y	Y	Y	Y	Y
2 Herger	Y	Y	Y	N	Y
3 Lungren	Y	Y	Y	N	Y
4 McClintock	Y	Y	Y	N	N
5 Matsui	Y	Y	Y	Y	N
6 Woolsey	Y	Y	Y	Y	N
7 Miller, George	Y	Y	Y	Y	N
8 Pelosi	Y	Y	Y	Y	N
9 Lee	Y	Y	Y	Y	N
10 Garamendi	Y	Y	Y	Y	Y
11 McNerney	Y	Y	Y	Y	N
12 Speier	Y	Y	Y	Y	N
13 Stark	Y	Y	Y	Y	N
14 Eshoo	Y	Y	Y	Y	N
15 Honda	Y	Y	Y	Y	N
16 Lofgren	Y	N	Y	Y	N
17 Farr	Y	Y	Y	Y	N
18 Cardoza	Y	Y	Y	Y	Y
19 Denham	Y	Y	Y	N	Y
20 Costa	Y	Y	Y	Y	Y
21 Nunes	Y	Y	Y	N	Y
22 McCarthy	Y	Y	Y	N	Y
23 Capps	Y	Y	Y	Y	N
24 Gallegly	Y	Y	Y	N	Y
25 McKeon	Y	Y	Y	N	Y
26 Dreier	Y	Y	Y	N	Y
27 Sherman	Y	Y	Y	Y	N
28 Berman	Y	Y	Y	Y	N
29 Schiff	Y	Y	Y	Y	N
30 Waxman	Y	Y	Y	Y	N
31 Becerra	Y	Y	Y	Y	N
32 Chu	Y	Y	Y	Y	N
33 Bass	Y	Y	Y	Y	N
34 Roybal-Allard	Y	Y	Y	Y	N
35 Waters	Y	Y	Y	Y	N
36 Hahn	Y	Y	Y	Y	N
37 Richardson	Y	Y	Y	Y	N
38 Napolitano	Y	Y	Y	Y	N
39 Sánchez, Linda	Y	Y	Y	Y	N
40 Royce	Y	Y	Y	N	Y
41 Lewis	Y	Y	Y	N	Y
42 Miller, Gary	Y	Y	Y	N	Y
43 Baca	Y	Y	Y	Y	Y
44 Calvert	Y	Y	Y	N	Y
45 Bono Mack	Y	Y	Y	N	Y
46 Rohrabacher	Y	Y	Y	N	N
47 Sanchez, Loretta	Y	Y	Y	Y	N
48 Campbell	Y	Y	Y	N	Y
49 Issa	Y	Y	Y	N	Y
50 Bilbray	Y	Y	Y	N	Y
51 Filner	+	+	+	+	–
52 Hunter	Y	Y	Y	N	Y
53 Davis	Y	Y	Y	Y	N

	188	189	190	191	192
COLORADO					
1 DeGette	Y	Y	Y	Y	N
2 Polis	Y	Y	Y	Y	N
3 Tipton	Y	Y	Y	N	Y
4 Gardner	Y	Y	Y	N	Y
5 Lamborn	Y	Y	Y	N	Y
6 Coffman	Y	Y	Y	N	Y
7 Perlmutter	Y	Y	Y	Y	N
CONNECTICUT					
1 Larson	Y	Y	Y	Y	N
2 Courtney	Y	Y	Y	Y	N
3 DeLauro	Y	Y	Y	Y	N
4 Himes	Y	Y	Y	Y	N
5 Murphy	Y	Y	Y	Y	N
DELAWARE					
AL Carney	Y	Y	Y	Y	Y
FLORIDA					
1 Miller	Y	Y	Y	N	Y
2 Southerland	Y	Y	Y	N	Y
3 Brown	Y	Y	Y	Y	N
4 Crenshaw	Y	Y	Y	N	Y
5 Nugent	Y	Y	Y	N	Y
6 Stearns	Y	Y	Y	N	Y
7 Mica	Y	Y	Y	N	Y
8 Webster	Y	Y	Y	N	Y
9 Bilirakis	Y	Y	Y	N	Y
10 Young	Y	Y	Y	N	Y
11 Castor	Y	Y	Y	Y	Y
12 Ross	Y	Y	Y	N	Y
13 Buchanan	Y	Y	Y	N	Y
14 Mack	Y	Y	Y	N	N
15 Posey	Y	Y	Y	N	Y
16 Rooney	Y	Y	Y	N	Y
17 Wilson	Y	Y	Y	Y	N
18 Ros-Lehtinen	Y	Y	Y	N	Y
19 Deutch	Y	Y	Y	Y	N
20 Wasserman Schultz	Y	Y	Y	Y	N
21 Diaz-Balart	Y	Y	Y	N	Y
22 West	Y	Y	Y	N	Y
23 Hastings	Y	Y	Y	Y	N
24 Adams	Y	Y	Y	N	Y
25 Rivera	Y	Y	Y	N	Y
GEORGIA					
1 Kingston	Y	Y	Y	N	Y
2 Bishop	Y	Y	Y	Y	Y
3 Westmoreland	Y	Y	Y	N	Y
4 Johnson	Y	Y	Y	Y	N
5 Lewis	Y	Y	Y	Y	N
6 Price	Y	Y	Y	N	Y
7 Woodall	Y	Y	Y	N	Y
8 Scott, A.	Y	Y	Y	N	Y
9 Graves	Y	Y	Y	N	Y
10 Broun	Y	Y	Y	N	Y
11 Gingrey	Y	Y	Y	N	Y
12 Barrow	Y	Y	Y	Y	Y
13 Scott, D.	Y	Y	Y	Y	Y
HAWAII					
1 Hanabusa	Y	Y	Y	Y	Y
2 Hirono	?	?	?	?	?
IDAHO					
1 Labrador	Y	Y	Y	N	Y
2 Simpson	Y	Y	Y	N	N
ILLINOIS					
1 Rush	Y	Y	Y	Y	N
2 Jackson	Y	Y	Y	Y	N
3 Lipinski	Y	Y	Y	Y	Y
4 Gutierrez	Y	Y	Y	Y	N
5 Quigley	Y	Y	Y	Y	N
6 Roskam	Y	Y	Y	N	Y
7 Davis	Y	Y	Y	Y	N
8 Walsh	Y	Y	Y	N	N
9 Schakowsky	Y	Y	Y	Y	N
10 Dold	Y	Y	Y	N	Y
11 Kinzinger	Y	Y	Y	N	Y
12 Costello	Y	Y	Y	Y	N
13 Biggert	Y	Y	Y	N	Y
14 Hultgren	Y	Y	Y	N	Y
15 Johnson	Y	Y	Y	N	N

KEY Republicans Democrats

Y Voted for (yea)	X Paired against
# Paired for	– Announced against
+ Announced for	P Voted "present"
N Voted against (nay)	

C   Voted "present" to avoid possible conflict of interest

?   Did not vote or otherwise make a position known

Member	188	189	190	191	192
16 Manzullo	Y	Y	Y	N	Y
17 Schilling	Y	Y	Y	N	Y
18 Schock	Y	Y	Y	N	Y
19 Shimkus	Y	Y	Y	N	Y
INDIANA					
1 Visclosky	Y	Y	Y	Y	N
2 Donnelly	Y	Y	Y	Y	Y
3 Stutzman	Y	Y	Y	N	Y
4 Rokita	Y	Y	Y	N	Y
5 Burton	Y	Y	Y	N	Y
6 Pence	?	?	?	?	?
7 Carson	Y	Y	Y	Y	N
8 Bucshon	?	?	?	?	?
9 Young	Y	Y	Y	N	Y
IOWA					
1 Braley	Y	Y	Y	Y	N
2 Loebsack	Y	Y	Y	Y	N
3 Boswell	Y	Y	Y	Y	N
4 Latham	Y	Y	Y	N	Y
5 King	Y	Y	Y	N	Y
KANSAS					
1 Huelskamp	Y	Y	Y	N	Y
2 Jenkins	Y	Y	Y	N	Y
3 Yoder	Y	Y	Y	N	Y
4 Pompeo	Y	Y	Y	N	Y
KENTUCKY					
1 Whitfield	Y	Y	Y	N	Y
2 Guthrie	Y	Y	Y	N	Y
3 Yarmuth	Y	Y	Y	N	Y
4 Davis	?	?	?	?	?
5 Rogers	Y	Y	Y	N	Y
6 Chandler	Y	Y	Y	Y	Y
LOUISIANA					
1 Scalise	Y	Y	Y	N	Y
2 Richmond	Y	Y	Y	Y	N
3 Landry	Y	Y	Y	N	N
4 Fleming	Y	Y	Y	N	N
5 Alexander	Y	Y	Y	N	Y
6 Cassidy	Y	Y	Y	N	Y
7 Boustany	Y	Y	Y	N	Y
MAINE					
1 Pingree	Y	Y	Y	Y	N
2 Michaud	Y	Y	Y	Y	N
MARYLAND					
1 Harris	Y	Y	Y	N	Y
2 Ruppersberger	Y	Y	Y	Y	Y
3 Sarbanes	Y	Y	Y	Y	N
4 Edwards	Y	Y	Y	Y	N
5 Hoyer	Y	Y	Y	Y	N
6 Bartlett	Y	Y	Y	N	Y
7 Cummings	Y	Y	Y	Y	N
8 Van Hollen	Y	Y	Y	Y	N
MASSACHUSETTS					
1 Olver	Y	Y	Y	Y	N
2 Neal	Y	Y	Y	Y	N
3 McGovern	Y	Y	Y	Y	N
4 Frank	Y	Y	Y	Y	N
5 Tsongas	Y	Y	Y	Y	N
6 Tierney	Y	Y	Y	Y	N
7 Markey	Y	Y	Y	Y	N
8 Capuano	Y	Y	Y	Y	N
9 Lynch	Y	Y	Y	Y	N
10 Keating	Y	Y	Y	Y	N
MICHIGAN					
1 Benishek	Y	Y	Y	N	Y
2 Huizenga	Y	Y	Y	N	Y
3 Amash	Y	Y	Y	N	Y
4 Camp	Y	Y	Y	N	Y
5 Kildee	Y	Y	Y	N	Y
6 Upton	Y	Y	Y	N	Y
7 Walberg	Y	Y	Y	N	Y
8 Rogers	Y	Y	Y	N	Y
9 Peters	Y	Y	Y	N	Y
10 Miller	Y	Y	Y	N	Y
11 McCotter	Y	Y	Y	N	Y
12 Levin	Y	Y	Y	Y	N
13 Clarke	Y	Y	Y	Y	N
14 Conyers	Y	Y	Y	Y	N
15 Dingell	Y	Y	N	N	N
MINNESOTA					
1 Walz	Y	Y	Y	Y	N
2 Kline	Y	Y	Y	N	Y
3 Paulsen	Y	Y	Y	N	Y
4 McCollum	Y	Y	Y	Y	N
5 Ellison	Y	Y	Y	Y	N
6 Bachmann	Y	Y	Y	N	Y
7 Peterson	Y	Y	Y	Y	Y
8 Cravaack	Y	Y	Y	N	Y
MISSISSIPPI					
1 Nunnelee	Y	Y	Y	N	Y
2 Thompson	Y	Y	Y	Y	N
3 Harper	Y	Y	Y	N	Y
4 Palazzo	Y	Y	Y	N	Y
MISSOURI					
1 Clay	Y	Y	Y	Y	N
2 Akin	Y	?	Y	N	N
3 Carnahan	Y	Y	Y	Y	N
4 Hartzler	Y	Y	Y	N	Y
5 Cleaver	Y	Y	Y	Y	N
6 Graves	Y	Y	Y	N	Y
7 Long	Y	Y	Y	N	Y
8 Emerson	Y	Y	Y	N	N
9 Luetkemeyer	Y	Y	Y	N	Y
MONTANA					
AL Rehberg	Y	Y	Y	N	N
NEBRASKA					
1 Fortenberry	Y	Y	Y	N	Y
2 Terry	Y	Y	Y	N	Y
3 Smith	Y	Y	Y	N	Y
NEVADA					
1 Berkley	Y	Y	Y	Y	N
2 Amodei	Y	Y	Y	N	Y
3 Heck	Y	Y	Y	N	Y
NEW HAMPSHIRE					
1 Guinta	Y	Y	Y	N	Y
2 Bass	Y	Y	Y	N	Y
NEW JERSEY					
1 Andrews	Y	Y	Y	Y	N
2 LoBiondo	Y	Y	Y	N	Y
3 Runyan	Y	Y	Y	N	Y
4 Smith	Y	Y	Y	N	Y
5 Garrett	Y	Y	Y	N	Y
6 Pallone	Y	Y	Y	Y	N
7 Lance	Y	Y	Y	N	Y
8 Pascrell	Y	Y	Y	Y	N
9 Rothman	Y	Y	Y	Y	N
10 Vacant					
11 Frelinghuysen	Y	Y	Y	N	Y
12 Holt	Y	Y	Y	Y	N
13 Sires	?	?	?	?	?
NEW MEXICO					
1 Heinrich	Y	Y	Y	Y	N
2 Pearce	Y	Y	Y	N	N
3 Luján	Y	Y	Y	Y	N
NEW YORK					
1 Bishop	Y	Y	Y	Y	Y
2 Israel	Y	Y	Y	Y	Y
3 King	Y	Y	Y	N	Y
4 McCarthy	Y	Y	Y	Y	N
5 Ackerman	Y	Y	Y	Y	N
6 Meeks	Y	Y	Y	Y	N
7 Crowley	Y	Y	Y	Y	N
8 Nadler	Y	Y	Y	Y	N
9 Turner	Y	Y	N	N	Y
10 Towns	Y	Y	Y	Y	Y
11 Clarke	Y	Y	Y	Y	N
12 Velázquez	Y	Y	Y	Y	N
13 Grimm	Y	Y	Y	N	Y
14 Maloney	?	?	?	?	?
15 Rangel	?	?	?	?	?
16 Serrano	Y	Y	Y	Y	N
17 Engel	Y	Y	Y	Y	N
18 Lowey	Y	Y	Y	Y	N
19 Hayworth	Y	Y	Y	N	Y
20 Gibson	Y	Y	Y	N	N
21 Tonko	Y	Y	Y	Y	N
22 Hinchey	Y	Y	Y	Y	N
23 Owens	Y	Y	Y	Y	Y
24 Hanna	Y	Y	Y	N	Y
25 Buerkle	Y	Y	Y	N	Y
26 Hochul	Y	Y	Y	Y	Y
27 Higgins	Y	Y	Y	Y	N
28 Slaughter	?	+	+	+	−
29 Reed	Y	Y	Y	N	Y
NORTH CAROLINA					
1 Butterfield	Y	Y	Y	Y	Y
2 Ellmers	Y	Y	Y	N	Y
3 Jones	Y	Y	Y	N	Y
4 Price	Y	Y	Y	Y	N
5 Foxx	Y	Y	Y	N	Y
6 Coble	Y	Y	Y	N	Y
7 McIntyre	Y	Y	Y	Y	Y
8 Kissell	Y	Y	Y	Y	Y
9 Myrick	Y	Y	Y	N	Y
10 McHenry	?	?	?	?	?
11 Shuler	Y	Y	Y	Y	Y
12 Watt	Y	Y	Y	Y	N
13 Miller	Y	Y	Y	N	
NORTH DAKOTA					
AL Berg	Y	Y	Y	N	Y
OHIO					
1 Chabot	Y	Y	Y	N	Y
2 Schmidt	Y	Y	Y	N	Y
3 Turner	Y	Y	Y	N	Y
4 Jordan	Y	Y	Y	N	Y
5 Latta	Y	Y	Y	N	Y
6 Johnson	Y	Y	Y	N	Y
7 Austria	Y	Y	Y	N	Y
8 Boehner					
9 Kaptur	Y	Y	Y	Y	N
10 Kucinich	Y	Y	Y	Y	N
11 Fudge	Y	Y	Y	Y	N
12 Tiberi	Y	Y	Y	N	Y
13 Sutton	Y	Y	Y	Y	N
14 LaTourette	Y	Y	Y	N	Y
15 Stivers	Y	Y	Y	N	Y
16 Renacci	Y	Y	Y	N	Y
17 Ryan	Y	Y	Y	Y	N
18 Gibbs	Y	Y	Y	N	Y
OKLAHOMA					
1 Sullivan	Y	Y	Y	N	Y
2 Boren	Y	Y	Y	Y	Y
3 Lucas	Y	Y	Y	N	Y
4 Cole	Y	Y	Y	N	Y
5 Lankford	Y	Y	Y	N	Y
OREGON					
1 Bonamici	Y	Y	Y	Y	N
2 Walden	Y	Y	Y	N	Y
3 Blumenauer	?	?	?	?	?
4 DeFazio	Y	Y	Y	Y	N
5 Schrader	Y	Y	N	Y	Y
PENNSYLVANIA					
1 Brady	Y	Y	Y	Y	N
2 Fattah	Y	Y	Y	Y	N
3 Kelly	Y	Y	Y	N	Y
4 Altmire	Y	Y	Y	N	Y
5 Thompson	Y	Y	Y	N	Y
6 Gerlach	Y	Y	Y	N	Y
7 Meehan	Y	Y	Y	N	Y
8 Fitzpatrick	Y	Y	Y	N	Y
9 Shuster	Y	Y	Y	N	Y
10 Marino	?	?	?	?	?
11 Barletta	Y	Y	Y	N	Y
12 Critz	Y	Y	Y	Y	Y
13 Schwartz	Y	Y	Y	Y	N
14 Doyle	Y	Y	Y	Y	N
15 Dent	Y	Y	Y	N	Y
16 Pitts	Y	Y	Y	N	Y
17 Holden	?	?	?	?	?
18 Murphy	Y	Y	Y	N	Y
19 Platts	Y	Y	Y	N	Y
RHODE ISLAND					
1 Cicilline	Y	Y	Y	Y	N
2 Langevin	Y	Y	Y	Y	Y
SOUTH CAROLINA					
1 Scott	Y	Y	Y	N	Y
2 Wilson	Y	Y	Y	N	Y
3 Duncan	Y	Y	Y	N	Y
4 Gowdy	Y	Y	Y	N	Y
5 Mulvaney	Y	Y	Y	N	Y
6 Clyburn	Y	Y	Y	Y	Y
SOUTH DAKOTA					
AL Noem	Y	Y	Y	N	Y
TENNESSEE					
1 Roe	Y	Y	Y	N	Y
2 Duncan	Y	Y	Y	N	Y
3 Fleischmann	Y	Y	Y	N	Y
4 DesJarlais	Y	Y	Y	N	Y
5 Cooper	Y	Y	Y	Y	N
6 Black	Y	Y	Y	N	Y
7 Blackburn	Y	Y	Y	N	Y
8 Fincher	Y	Y	Y	N	Y
9 Cohen	Y	Y	Y	Y	N
TEXAS					
1 Gohmert	Y	Y	Y	N	N
2 Poe	Y	Y	Y	N	N
3 Johnson, S.	Y	Y	Y	N	Y
4 Hall	Y	Y	Y	N	N
5 Hensarling	Y	Y	Y	N	Y
6 Barton	Y	Y	Y	N	N
7 Culberson	Y	Y	Y	N	Y
8 Brady	Y	Y	Y	N	Y
9 Green, A.	Y	Y	Y	Y	N
10 McCaul	Y	Y	Y	N	Y
11 Conaway	Y	Y	Y	N	Y
12 Granger	Y	Y	Y	N	Y
13 Thornberry	Y	Y	Y	N	Y
14 Paul	?	?	?	?	?
15 Hinojosa	Y	Y	Y	Y	N
16 Reyes	Y	Y	Y	Y	N
17 Flores	Y	Y	Y	N	Y
18 Jackson Lee	Y	Y	Y	Y	N
19 Neugebauer	Y	Y	Y	N	Y
20 Gonzalez	Y	Y	Y	Y	Y
21 Smith	Y	Y	Y	N	Y
22 Olson	Y	Y	Y	N	Y
23 Canseco	?	?	?	?	?
24 Marchant	Y	Y	Y	N	Y
25 Doggett	Y	Y	Y	Y	N
26 Burgess	Y	Y	Y	N	Y
27 Farenthold	Y	Y	Y	N	N
28 Cuellar	Y	Y	Y	Y	Y
29 Green, G.	Y	Y	Y	Y	N
30 Johnson, E.	Y	Y	Y	Y	N
31 Carter	Y	Y	Y	N	Y
32 Sessions	Y	Y	Y	N	Y
UTAH					
1 Bishop	Y	Y	Y	N	N
2 Matheson	Y	Y	Y	Y	Y
3 Chaffetz	Y	Y	Y	N	Y
VERMONT					
AL Welch	Y	Y	Y	Y	N
VIRGINIA					
1 Wittman	Y	Y	Y	N	Y
2 Rigell	Y	Y	Y	N	N
3 Scott	Y	Y	Y	Y	N
4 Forbes	Y	Y	Y	N	Y
5 Hurt	Y	Y	Y	N	Y
6 Goodlatte	Y	Y	Y	N	Y
7 Cantor	Y	Y	Y	N	Y
8 Moran	Y	Y	Y	Y	N
9 Griffith	Y	Y	Y	N	Y
10 Wolf	Y	Y	Y	N	Y
11 Connolly	Y	Y	Y	Y	Y
WASHINGTON					
1 Vacant					
2 Larsen	Y	Y	Y	Y	Y
3 Herrera Beutler	Y	Y	Y	N	Y
4 Hastings	Y	Y	Y	N	Y
5 McMorris Rodgers	Y	Y	Y	N	Y
6 Dicks	Y	Y	Y	Y	N
7 McDermott	Y	Y	Y	Y	N
8 Reichert	Y	Y	Y	N	Y
9 Smith	Y	Y	Y	Y	Y
WEST VIRGINIA					
1 McKinley	Y	Y	Y	N	Y
2 Capito	Y	Y	Y	N	Y
3 Rahall	Y	Y	Y	Y	N
WISCONSIN					
1 Ryan	Y	Y	Y	N	Y
2 Baldwin	Y	Y	Y	Y	N
3 Kind	Y	Y	Y	Y	N
4 Moore	Y	Y	Y	Y	N
5 Sensenbrenner	Y	Y	Y	N	N
6 Petri	Y	Y	Y	N	Y
7 Duffy	Y	Y	Y	N	Y
8 Ribble	Y	Y	Y	N	Y
WYOMING					
AL Lummis	Y	Y	Y	N	Y

IN THE HOUSE | By Vote Number

193. **HR 2096. Cybersecurity Research and Development Plan/ Passage.** McCaul, R-Texas, motion to suspend the rules and pass the bill that would require agencies of the Networking and Information Technology Research and Development program to develop, update and implement a strategic plan for cybersecurity research and development. It also would reauthorize cybersecurity programs at the National Science Foundation and direct the National Institute of Technology and Standards to develop cybersecurity standards for the federal government. Motion agreed to 395-10: R 220-10; D 175-0. A two-thirds majority of those present and voting (270 in this case) is required for passage under suspension of the rules. April 27, 2012.

194. **HR 4628. Student Loan Interest Rates/Recommit.** Capps, D-Calif., motion to recommit the bill to the House Education and the Workforce and the House Energy and Commerce committees and report it back immediately with an amendment specifying that nothing in the bill would endorse, promote or result in a reduction or increased cost for health insurance for women and children. Motion rejected 178-231: R 0-231; D 178-0. April 27, 2012.

195. **HR 4628. Student Loan Interest Rates/Passage.** Passage of the bill that would extend for one year — through June 30, 2013 — the 3.4 percent interest rate for federally subsidized undergraduate student loans. It would be offset by repealing the Prevention and Public Health Fund established by the health care overhaul law and rescinding unobligated amounts in the fund. Passed 215-195: R 202-30; D 13-165. A "nay" was a vote in support of the president's position. April 27, 2012.

196. **H Con Res 105. King Kamehameha Celebration/Adoption.** Harper, R-Miss., motion to suspend the rules and adopt the concurrent resolution that would authorize the use of Emancipation Hall in the Capitol Visitor Center on June 24, 2012, for an event to celebrate the birth of King Kamehameha, who unified the Hawaiian Islands in the early 1800s. Motion agreed to 376-0: R 213-0; D 163-0. A two-thirds majority of those present and voting (251 in this case) is required for adoption under suspension of the rules. May 7, 2012.

197. **H Con Res 117. National Peace Officers' Memorial Service/ Adoption.** Denham, R-Calif., motion to suspend the rules and adopt the concurrent resolution that would authorize the use of the Capitol grounds for the 31st annual National Peace Officers' Memorial Service to honor law enforcement officers who died in the line of duty during 2011. Motion agreed to 377-0: R 216-0; D 161-0. A two-thirds majority of those present and voting (252 in this case) is required for adoption under suspension of the rules. May 7, 2012.

	193	194	195	196	197
ALABAMA					
1 Bonner	Y	N	Y	?	?
2 Roby	Y	N	Y	Y	Y
3 Rogers	Y	N	Y	Y	Y
4 Aderholt	Y	N	Y	Y	Y
5 Brooks	Y	N	Y	Y	Y
6 Bachus	Y	N	Y	Y	Y
7 Sewell	Y	Y	N	Y	Y
ALASKA					
AL Young	Y	N	Y	Y	Y
ARIZONA					
1 Gosar	Y	N	N	?	?
2 Franks	Y	N	N	Y	Y
3 Quayle	Y	N	N	Y	Y
4 Pastor	+	Y	N	Y	Y
5 Schweikert	Y	N	N	Y	Y
6 Flake	N	N	N	?	?
7 Grijalva	Y	Y	N	?	?
8 Vacant					
ARKANSAS					
1 Crawford	Y	N	Y	Y	Y
2 Griffin	Y	N	Y	Y	Y
3 Womack	Y	N	Y	Y	Y
4 Ross	Y	Y	N	Y	Y
CALIFORNIA					
1 Thompson	Y	Y	N	Y	Y
2 Herger	Y	N	Y	Y	Y
3 Lungren	Y	N	Y	Y	Y
4 McClintock	Y	N	N	Y	Y
5 Matsui	Y	Y	N	Y	Y
6 Woolsey	Y	Y	N	Y	Y
7 Miller, George	Y	Y	N	Y	Y
8 Pelosi	Y	Y	N	Y	Y
9 Lee	Y	Y	N	Y	Y
10 Garamendi	Y	Y	N	Y	Y
11 McNerney	Y	Y	N	Y	Y
12 Speier	Y	Y	N	?	?
13 Stark	Y	Y	N	Y	Y
14 Eshoo	Y	Y	N	Y	Y
15 Honda	Y	Y	N	Y	Y
16 Lofgren	Y	Y	N	Y	Y
17 Farr	?	?	?	Y	Y
18 Cardoza	?	?	?	?	?
19 Denham	Y	N	Y	Y	Y
20 Costa	Y	Y	+	Y	Y
21 Nunes	?	?	?	Y	Y
22 McCarthy	Y	N	Y	?	?
23 Capps	Y	Y	N	Y	Y
24 Gallegly	Y	N	Y	?	Y
25 McKeon	Y	N	Y	Y	Y
26 Dreier	Y	N	Y	Y	Y
27 Sherman	Y	Y	N	Y	Y
28 Berman	Y	Y	N	Y	Y
29 Schiff	Y	Y	N	Y	Y
30 Waxman	Y	Y	N	Y	Y
31 Becerra	Y	Y	N	Y	Y
32 Chu	Y	Y	N	Y	Y
33 Bass	Y	Y	N	Y	Y
34 Roybal-Allard	Y	Y	N	Y	Y
35 Waters	Y	Y	N	Y	Y
36 Hahn	Y	Y	N	Y	Y
37 Richardson	Y	Y	N	Y	Y
38 Napolitano	Y	Y	N	Y	Y
39 Sánchez, Linda	Y	Y	N	Y	Y
40 Royce	Y	N	Y	Y	Y
41 Lewis	Y	N	Y	Y	Y
42 Miller, Gary	Y	N	Y	Y	Y
43 Baca	Y	Y	N	Y	Y
44 Calvert	Y	N	Y	Y	Y
45 Bono Mack	Y	N	Y	Y	Y
46 Rohrabacher	Y	N	Y	?	?
47 Sanchez, Loretta	Y	Y	N	?	?
48 Campbell	Y	N	Y	Y	Y
49 Issa	Y	N	Y	Y	Y
50 Bilbray	Y	N	Y	Y	Y
51 Filner	+	+	–	+	+
52 Hunter	Y	N	Y	Y	Y
53 Davis	Y	Y	N	Y	Y

	193	194	195	196	197
COLORADO					
1 DeGette	Y	Y	N	Y	Y
2 Polis	Y	Y	N	Y	Y
3 Tipton	Y	N	Y	Y	Y
4 Gardner	Y	N	Y	Y	Y
5 Lamborn	Y	N	N	?	?
6 Coffman	Y	N	Y	Y	Y
7 Perlmutter	Y	Y	N	?	?
CONNECTICUT					
1 Larson	Y	Y	N	Y	Y
2 Courtney	Y	Y	N	Y	Y
3 DeLauro	Y	Y	N	Y	Y
4 Himes	Y	Y	N	Y	Y
5 Murphy	Y	Y	N	?	?
DELAWARE					
AL Carney	Y	Y	N	Y	Y
FLORIDA					
1 Miller	Y	N	Y	Y	Y
2 Southerland	Y	N	Y	Y	Y
3 Brown	Y	Y	N	?	?
4 Crenshaw	Y	N	Y	Y	Y
5 Nugent	Y	N	Y	Y	Y
6 Stearns	Y	N	Y	Y	Y
7 Mica	Y	N	Y	Y	Y
8 Webster	Y	N	Y	Y	Y
9 Bilirakis	Y	N	Y	Y	Y
10 Young	Y	N	Y	Y	Y
11 Castor	Y	Y	N	Y	Y
12 Ross	Y	N	Y	Y	Y
13 Buchanan	Y	N	Y	Y	Y
14 Mack	Y	N	Y	?	?
15 Posey	Y	N	Y	Y	Y
16 Rooney	Y	N	Y	Y	Y
17 Wilson	Y	Y	N	Y	Y
18 Ros-Lehtinen	Y	N	Y	Y	Y
19 Deutch	Y	Y	N	Y	Y
20 Wasserman Schultz	?	Y	N	Y	Y
21 Diaz-Balart	Y	N	Y	Y	Y
22 West	Y	N	Y	Y	Y
23 Hastings	Y	Y	N	Y	Y
24 Adams	Y	N	Y	Y	Y
25 Rivera	Y	N	Y	Y	Y
GEORGIA					
1 Kingston	?	?	?	Y	Y
2 Bishop	Y	Y	N	Y	Y
3 Westmoreland	Y	N	N	Y	Y
4 Johnson	Y	Y	N	Y	Y
5 Lewis	Y	Y	N	Y	Y
6 Price	Y	N	N	Y	Y
7 Woodall	Y	N	Y	Y	Y
8 Scott, A.	Y	Y	Y	Y	Y
9 Graves	N	N	N	Y	Y
10 Broun	N	N	N	Y	Y
11 Gingrey	Y	N	Y	Y	Y
12 Barrow	Y	Y	N	Y	Y
13 Scott, D.	Y	Y	N	Y	Y
HAWAII					
1 Hanabusa	Y	Y	N	Y	Y
2 Hirono	?	?	?	Y	Y
IDAHO					
1 Labrador	N	N	N	?	?
2 Simpson	Y	N	Y	Y	Y
ILLINOIS					
1 Rush	Y	Y	N	?	?
2 Jackson	Y	Y	N	Y	Y
3 Lipinski	Y	Y	Y	Y	Y
4 Gutierrez	Y	Y	N	+	+
5 Quigley	Y	Y	N	Y	Y
6 Roskam	Y	N	Y	Y	Y
7 Davis	Y	Y	N	Y	Y
8 Walsh	N	N	N	Y	Y
9 Schakowsky	Y	Y	N	Y	Y
10 Dold	Y	N	Y	Y	Y
11 Kinzinger	Y	N	Y	Y	Y
12 Costello	Y	Y	N	Y	Y
13 Biggert	Y	N	Y	Y	Y
14 Hultgren	Y	N	Y	Y	Y
15 Johnson	Y	N	Y	+	+

	193	194	195	196	197
16 Manzullo	Y	N	Y	?	?
17 Schilling	Y	N	Y	Y	Y
18 Schock	Y	N	Y	Y	Y
19 Shimkus	Y	N	Y	Y	Y
INDIANA					
1 Visclosky	Y	Y	N	Y	Y
2 Donnelly	Y	Y	Y	Y	Y
3 Stutzman	Y	N	Y	Y	Y
4 Rokita	Y	N	Y	Y	Y
5 Burton	Y	N	Y	?	?
6 Pence	Y	N	Y	?	?
7 Carson	Y	Y	N	+	+
8 Bucshon	Y	N	Y	Y	Y
9 Young	Y	N	Y	Y	Y
IOWA					
1 Braley	Y	Y	N	Y	Y
2 Loebsack	Y	Y	N	Y	Y
3 Boswell	Y	Y	N	Y	Y
4 Latham	Y	N	Y	Y	Y
5 King	Y	N	Y	Y	Y
KANSAS					
1 Huelskamp	Y	N	N	Y	Y
2 Jenkins	?	?	?	Y	Y
3 Yoder	Y	N	Y	Y	Y
4 Pompeo	Y	N	Y	Y	Y
KENTUCKY					
1 Whitfield	Y	N	Y	Y	Y
2 Guthrie	Y	N	Y	Y	Y
3 Yarmuth	Y	Y	N	Y	Y
4 Davis	+	−	+	Y	Y
5 Rogers	Y	N	Y	Y	Y
6 Chandler	Y	Y	N	Y	Y
LOUISIANA					
1 Scalise	Y	N	Y	?	?
2 Richmond	Y	Y	N	?	?
3 Landry	Y	N	Y	?	?
4 Fleming	Y	N	Y	Y	Y
5 Alexander	Y	N	Y	Y	Y
6 Cassidy	?	?	?	Y	Y
7 Boustany	Y	N	Y	Y	Y
MAINE					
1 Pingree	Y	Y	N	Y	Y
2 Michaud	Y	Y	N	Y	Y
MARYLAND					
1 Harris	Y	N	Y	Y	Y
2 Ruppersberger	Y	Y	N	?	?
3 Sarbanes	Y	Y	N	Y	Y
4 Edwards	Y	Y	N	Y	Y
5 Hoyer	Y	Y	N	?	?
6 Bartlett	Y	N	Y	Y	Y
7 Cummings	Y	Y	N	Y	Y
8 Van Hollen	Y	Y	N	Y	Y
MASSACHUSETTS					
1 Olver	Y	Y	N	?	?
2 Neal	Y	Y	N	Y	Y
3 McGovern	Y	Y	N	Y	Y
4 Frank	Y	Y	N	?	?
5 Tsongas	Y	Y	N	Y	Y
6 Tierney	Y	Y	N	Y	Y
7 Markey	Y	Y	N	Y	Y
8 Capuano	Y	Y	N	Y	Y
9 Lynch	Y	Y	N	Y	Y
10 Keating	Y	Y	N	Y	Y
MICHIGAN					
1 Benishek	Y	N	Y	Y	Y
2 Huizenga	Y	N	Y	Y	Y
3 Amash	N	N	N	Y	Y
4 Camp	?	?	?	Y	Y
5 Kildee	Y	Y	N	Y	Y
6 Upton	Y	N	Y	Y	Y
7 Walberg	Y	N	Y	Y	Y
8 Rogers	Y	N	Y	Y	Y
9 Peters	Y	Y	N	Y	Y
10 Miller	Y	N	Y	Y	Y
11 McCotter	Y	Y	N	Y	Y
12 Levin	Y	Y	N	Y	Y
13 Clarke	Y	Y	N	Y	Y
14 Conyers	Y	Y	N	Y	Y
15 Dingell	Y	Y	N	Y	Y
MINNESOTA					
1 Walz	Y	Y	Y	Y	Y
2 Kline	Y	N	Y	Y	Y
3 Paulsen	Y	N	Y	Y	Y
4 McCollum	Y	Y	N	Y	Y

	193	194	195	196	197
5 Ellison	Y	Y	N	Y	+
6 Bachmann	Y	N	Y	Y	Y
7 Peterson	Y	Y	Y	Y	Y
8 Cravaack	Y	N	Y	Y	Y
MISSISSIPPI					
1 Nunnelee	Y	N	Y	Y	Y
2 Thompson	Y	Y	N	Y	Y
3 Harper	Y	N	Y	Y	Y
4 Palazzo	Y	N	Y	Y	+
MISSOURI					
1 Clay	Y	Y	N	Y	Y
2 Akin	Y	N	Y	Y	Y
3 Carnahan	Y	Y	N	Y	Y
4 Hartzler	Y	N	Y	Y	Y
5 Cleaver	Y	Y	N	Y	Y
6 Graves	Y	N	Y	Y	Y
7 Long	Y	N	Y	Y	Y
8 Emerson	Y	N	Y	Y	Y
9 Luetkemeyer	Y	N	Y	Y	Y
MONTANA					
AL Rehberg	Y	N	Y	Y	Y
NEBRASKA					
1 Fortenberry	Y	N	Y	Y	Y
2 Terry	Y	N	Y	Y	Y
3 Smith	Y	N	Y	Y	Y
NEVADA					
1 Berkley	Y	Y	N	Y	Y
2 Amodei	Y	N	Y	Y	Y
3 Heck	Y	N	Y	Y	Y
NEW HAMPSHIRE					
1 Guinta	Y	N	Y	Y	Y
2 Bass	Y	N	Y	Y	Y
NEW JERSEY					
1 Andrews	Y	Y	N	Y	?
2 LoBiondo	Y	N	Y	Y	Y
3 Runyan	Y	N	Y	Y	Y
4 Smith	Y	N	Y	Y	Y
5 Garrett	Y	N	N	Y	Y
6 Pallone	Y	Y	N	Y	Y
7 Lance	Y	N	Y	Y	Y
8 Pascrell	Y	Y	N	+	+
9 Rothman	Y	Y	N	?	?
10 Vacant					
11 Frelinghuysen	Y	N	Y	Y	Y
12 Holt	Y	Y	N	Y	Y
13 Sires	?	?	?	Y	Y
NEW MEXICO					
1 Heinrich	Y	Y	N	Y	Y
2 Pearce	Y	N	Y	Y	Y
3 Luján	Y	Y	N	Y	Y
NEW YORK					
1 Bishop	Y	Y	Y	Y	Y
2 Israel	Y	Y	N	Y	Y
3 King	Y	N	Y	Y	Y
4 McCarthy	Y	Y	N	Y	Y
5 Ackerman	Y	Y	N	?	?
6 Meeks	Y	Y	N	Y	Y
7 Crowley	Y	Y	N	Y	Y
8 Nadler	Y	Y	N	Y	Y
9 Turner	Y	N	Y	Y	Y
10 Towns	?	?	?	?	?
11 Clarke	Y	Y	N	Y	Y
12 Velázquez	Y	Y	N	Y	Y
13 Grimm	Y	N	Y	Y	Y
14 Maloney	Y	Y	N	?	?
15 Rangel	?	?	?	Y	Y
16 Serrano	Y	Y	N	Y	Y
17 Engel	Y	Y	N	Y	Y
18 Lowey	Y	Y	N	Y	Y
19 Hayworth	Y	N	Y	Y	Y
20 Gibson	Y	N	Y	Y	Y
21 Tonko	Y	Y	N	Y	Y
22 Hinchey	Y	Y	N	Y	Y
23 Owens	Y	Y	Y	Y	Y
24 Hanna	Y	N	Y	?	?
25 Buerkle	Y	N	Y	Y	Y
26 Hochul	Y	Y	N	Y	Y
27 Higgins	Y	Y	N	Y	Y
28 Slaughter	+	+	−	+	+
29 Reed	Y	N	Y	Y	Y
NORTH CAROLINA					
1 Butterfield	Y	Y	N	?	?
2 Ellmers	Y	N	Y	?	?
3 Jones	Y	N	Y	?	?
4 Price	Y	Y	N	?	?

	193	194	195	196	197
5 Foxx	Y	N	Y	Y	Y
6 Coble	Y	N	N	?	?
7 McIntyre	Y	Y	Y	Y	Y
8 Kissell	Y	Y	Y	Y	Y
9 Myrick	Y	N	Y	Y	Y
10 McHenry	?	?	?	?	?
11 Shuler	Y	Y	N	Y	Y
12 Watt	?	Y	N	Y	Y
13 Miller	Y	Y	N	Y	Y
NORTH DAKOTA					
AL Berg	Y	N	Y	Y	Y
OHIO					
1 Chabot	Y	N	Y	Y	Y
2 Schmidt	Y	N	Y	Y	Y
3 Turner	Y	N	Y	Y	Y
4 Jordan	Y	N	Y	+	+
5 Latta	Y	N	Y	Y	Y
6 Johnson	Y	N	Y	Y	Y
7 Austria	Y	N	Y	Y	Y
8 Boehner		Y			
9 Kaptur	Y	Y	N	Y	Y
10 Kucinich	Y	Y	N	?	?
11 Fudge	Y	Y	N	Y	Y
12 Tiberi	Y	N	Y	?	?
13 Sutton	Y	Y	N	Y	Y
14 LaTourette	Y	N	Y	Y	Y
15 Stivers	Y	N	Y	Y	Y
16 Renacci	Y	N	Y	Y	Y
17 Ryan	Y	Y	N	Y	?
18 Gibbs	Y	N	Y	Y	Y
OKLAHOMA					
1 Sullivan	Y	N	Y	Y	Y
2 Boren	Y	Y	Y	Y	Y
3 Lucas	Y	N	Y	Y	Y
4 Cole	Y	N	Y	Y	Y
5 Lankford	Y	N	Y	Y	Y
OREGON					
1 Bonamici	Y	Y	N	Y	Y
2 Walden	Y	N	Y	Y	Y
3 Blumenauer	?	?	?	Y	Y
4 DeFazio	Y	Y	N	Y	Y
5 Schrader	Y	Y	N	Y	Y
PENNSYLVANIA					
1 Brady	Y	Y	N	Y	Y
2 Fattah	Y	Y	N	Y	Y
3 Kelly	Y	N	Y	Y	Y
4 Altmire	Y	Y	N	Y	Y
5 Thompson	Y	N	Y	Y	Y
6 Gerlach	Y	N	Y	Y	Y
7 Meehan	Y	N	Y	Y	Y
8 Fitzpatrick	Y	N	Y	Y	Y
9 Shuster	Y	N	Y	Y	Y
10 Marino	?	?	?	Y	Y
11 Barletta	Y	N	Y	Y	Y
12 Critz	?	Y	N	Y	Y
13 Schwartz	Y	Y	N	Y	Y
14 Doyle	Y	Y	N	Y	Y
15 Dent	Y	N	Y	Y	Y
16 Pitts	Y	N	Y	Y	Y
17 Holden	?	?	?	Y	Y
18 Murphy	Y	N	N	?	Y
19 Platts	Y	N	Y	?	?
RHODE ISLAND					
1 Cicilline	Y	Y	N	Y	Y
2 Langevin	Y	Y	N	Y	Y
SOUTH CAROLINA					
1 Scott	Y	N	Y	Y	Y
2 Wilson	Y	N	Y	Y	Y
3 Duncan	Y	N	Y	Y	Y
4 Gowdy	Y	N	Y	Y	Y
5 Mulvaney	N	N	Y	Y	Y
6 Clyburn	Y	Y	N	Y	Y
SOUTH DAKOTA					
AL Noem	Y	N	Y	Y	Y
TENNESSEE					
1 Roe	Y	N	Y	Y	Y
2 Duncan	N	N	Y	Y	Y
3 Fleischmann	Y	N	Y	Y	Y
4 DesJarlais	Y	N	Y	Y	Y
5 Cooper	Y	Y	N	Y	Y
6 Black	Y	N	Y	Y	Y
7 Blackburn	Y	N	Y	Y	Y
8 Fincher	Y	N	Y	Y	Y
9 Cohen	Y	Y	N	Y	Y

	193	194	195	196	197
TEXAS					
1 Gohmert	?	N	Y	Y	Y
2 Poe	Y	N	Y	?	?
3 Johnson, S.	Y	N	Y	Y	Y
4 Hall	Y	N	Y	Y	Y
5 Hensarling	Y	N	Y	Y	Y
6 Barton	Y	N	Y	Y	Y
7 Culberson	Y	N	Y	Y	Y
8 Brady	Y	N	Y	Y	Y
9 Green, A.	Y	Y	N	Y	Y
10 McCaul	Y	N	Y	Y	Y
11 Conaway	Y	N	Y	Y	Y
12 Granger	Y	N	Y	Y	Y
13 Thornberry	Y	N	Y	Y	Y
14 Paul	?	?	?	?	?
15 Hinojosa	?	?	?	?	?
16 Reyes	Y	Y	N	Y	Y
17 Flores	Y	N	Y	?	Y
18 Jackson Lee	Y	Y	N	Y	Y
19 Neugebauer	Y	N	Y	Y	Y
20 Gonzalez	Y	Y	N	Y	Y
21 Smith	Y	N	Y	Y	Y
22 Olson	Y	N	Y	Y	Y
23 Canseco	+	−	+	Y	Y
24 Marchant	Y	N	Y	Y	Y
25 Doggett	Y	?	N	Y	Y
26 Burgess	Y	N	Y	Y	Y
27 Farenthold	Y	N	Y	Y	Y
28 Cuellar	Y	Y	N	Y	Y
29 Green, G.	Y	Y	N	Y	Y
30 Johnson, E.	Y	Y	N	?	?
31 Carter	Y	N	Y	Y	Y
32 Sessions	Y	N	Y	Y	Y
UTAH					
1 Bishop	Y	N	Y	Y	Y
2 Matheson	Y	Y	Y	Y	Y
3 Chaffetz	Y	N	Y	Y	Y
VERMONT					
AL Welch	Y	Y	N	Y	Y
VIRGINIA					
1 Wittman	Y	N	Y	Y	Y
2 Rigell	Y	N	Y	Y	Y
3 Scott	Y	Y	N	Y	Y
4 Forbes	Y	N	Y	Y	Y
5 Hurt	Y	N	Y	Y	Y
6 Goodlatte	Y	N	Y	Y	Y
7 Cantor	Y	N	Y	Y	Y
8 Moran	Y	Y	N	Y	Y
9 Griffith	N	N	Y	Y	Y
10 Wolf	Y	N	Y	Y	Y
11 Connolly	Y	Y	N	Y	Y
WASHINGTON					
1 Vacant					
2 Larsen	Y	Y	N	Y	Y
3 Herrera Beutler	Y	N	Y	Y	Y
4 Hastings	Y	N	Y	Y	Y
5 McMorris Rodgers	Y	N	Y	Y	Y
6 Dicks	Y	Y	N	Y	Y
7 McDermott	Y	Y	N	Y	Y
8 Reichert	Y	N	Y	Y	Y
9 Smith	Y	Y	N	Y	Y
WEST VIRGINIA					
1 McKinley	Y	N	Y	Y	Y
2 Capito	Y	N	Y	Y	Y
3 Rahall	Y	Y	N	Y	Y
WISCONSIN					
1 Ryan	Y	N	Y	Y	Y
2 Baldwin	Y	Y	N	Y	Y
3 Kind	Y	Y	N	?	?
4 Moore	Y	Y	N	?	?
5 Sensenbrenner	N	N	Y	Y	Y
6 Petri	Y	N	Y	Y	Y
7 Duffy	Y	N	Y	Y	Y
8 Ribble	Y	N	Y	Y	Y
WYOMING					
AL Lummis	Y	N	Y	?	?

IN THE HOUSE | By Vote Number

198. **H Con Res 118. D.C. Special Olympics Law Enforcement Torch Run/Adoption.** Denham, R-Calif., motion to suspend the rules and adopt the concurrent resolution that would authorize the use of the Capitol grounds for the District of Columbia Special Olympics Law Enforcement Torch Run. Motion agreed to 375-0: R 215-0; D 160-0. A two-thirds majority of those present and voting (250 in this case) is required for adoption under suspension of the rules. May 7, 2012.

199. **HR 5326. Fiscal 2013 Commerce-Justice-Science Appropriations/ Previous Question.** Woodall, R-Ga., motion to order the previous question (thus ending debate and the possibility of amendment) on the rule (H Res 643) that would provide for House floor consideration of the bill that would provide $51.1 billion in fiscal 2013 for the Commerce and Justice departments, NASA and other agencies. Motion agreed to 235-174: R 231-0; D 4-174. May 8, 2012.

200. **HR 5326. Fiscal 2013 Commerce-Justice-Science Appropriations/ Rule.** Adoption of the rule (H Res 643) that would provide for House floor consideration of the bill that would provide $51.1 billion in fiscal 2013 for the Commerce and Justice departments, NASA and other agencies. The rule also would waive through the legislative day of May 10, 2012, the two-thirds requirement to consider a rule on the same day it is reported from the Rules Committee. The waiver would apply only to measures related to budget reconciliation. Adopted 228-181: R 228-0; D 0-181. May 8, 2012.

201. **Procedural Motion/Journal.** Approval of the House Journal of Monday, May 7, 2012. Approved 296-108: R 175-53; D 121-55. May 8, 2012.

202. **HR 5326. Fiscal 2013 Commerce-Justice-Science Appropriations/ Trade Administration and USTR Funding.** Peters, D-Mich., amendment that would increase by $9 million the amount provided for the International Trade Administration's operations and administration and reduce by $17 million the amount provided for science, aeronautics, exploration, space operations, and education research and development activities. It also would increase the amount provided for salaries and expenses for the Office of the U.S. Trade Representative by $1.8 million. Rejected in Committee of the Whole 141-261: R 14-216; D 127-45. May 8, 2012.

	198	199	200	201	202
ALABAMA					
1 Bonner	?	?	?	?	?
2 Roby	Y	Y	Y	Y	N
3 Rogers	Y	Y	Y	Y	N
4 Aderholt	Y	Y	Y	Y	N
5 Brooks	Y	Y	Y	Y	N
6 Bachus	Y	Y	Y	Y	N
7 Sewell	Y	N	N	Y	N
ALASKA					
AL Young	Y	Y	Y	N	N
ARIZONA					
1 Gosar	?	Y	Y	Y	N
2 Franks	Y	Y	Y	Y	N
3 Quayle	Y	Y	Y	N	N
4 Pastor	Y	N	N	N	N
5 Schweikert	Y	Y	Y	Y	N
6 Flake	?	Y	Y	Y	N
7 Grijalva	?	N	N	Y	Y
8 Vacant					
ARKANSAS					
1 Crawford	Y	Y	Y	N	N
2 Griffin	Y	Y	Y	N	N
3 Womack	Y	Y	Y	N	N
4 Ross	Y	N	N	Y	Y
CALIFORNIA					
1 Thompson	Y	N	N	N	Y
2 Herger	Y	Y	Y	Y	N
3 Lungren	Y	Y	Y	Y	N
4 McClintock	Y	Y	Y	Y	N
5 Matsui	Y	N	N	Y	Y
6 Woolsey	Y	N	N	Y	Y
7 Miller, George	Y	N	N	N	Y
8 Pelosi	Y	N	N	Y	?
9 Lee	Y	N	N	N	?
10 Garamendi	Y	N	N	Y	Y
11 McNerney	Y	N	N	Y	Y
12 Speier	?	N	N	N	Y
13 Stark	Y	N	N	?	Y
14 Eshoo	Y	N	N	Y	N
15 Honda	Y	N	N	Y	—
16 Lofgren	Y	N	N	Y	N
17 Farr	Y	N	N	Y	N
18 Cardoza	?	N	N	N	?
19 Denham	Y	Y	Y	N	N
20 Costa	Y	?	N	N	Y
21 Nunes	Y	Y	Y	Y	N
22 McCarthy	?	Y	Y	Y	N
23 Capps	Y	N	N	Y	Y
24 Gallegly	Y	Y	Y	Y	N
25 McKeon	Y	Y	Y	Y	N
26 Dreier	Y	Y	Y	Y	N
27 Sherman	Y	N	N	Y	Y
28 Berman	Y	N	N	Y	Y
29 Schiff	Y	N	N	Y	N
30 Waxman	Y	N	N	Y	N
31 Becerra	Y	N	N	Y	?
32 Chu	Y	N	Y	Y	Y
33 Bass	Y	N	N	N	Y
34 Roybal-Allard	Y	N	N	Y	Y
35 Waters	Y	N	N	N	N
36 Hahn	Y	N	N	N	N
37 Richardson	Y	N	N	Y	Y
38 Napolitano	Y	N	N	Y	Y
39 Sánchez, Linda	Y	N	N	N	Y
40 Royce	Y	?	?	Y	N
41 Lewis	Y	Y	Y	Y	N
42 Miller, Gary	Y	Y	Y	Y	N
43 Baca	Y	N	N	Y	Y
44 Calvert	Y	Y	Y	Y	N
45 Bono Mack	Y	Y	Y	Y	N
46 Rohrabacher	?	Y	Y	Y	N
47 Sanchez, Loretta	?	N	N	N	Y
48 Campbell	Y	Y	Y	Y	N
49 Issa	Y	Y	Y	Y	N
50 Bilbray	Y	Y	Y	Y	N
51 Filner	+	—	—	—	—
52 Hunter	Y	Y	Y	N	N
53 Davis	Y	N	N	Y	Y

	198	199	200	201	202
COLORADO					
1 DeGette	Y	N	N	Y	Y
2 Polis	Y	N	N	Y	N
3 Tipton	Y	Y	Y	N	N
4 Gardner	Y	Y	Y	N	N
5 Lamborn	?	Y	Y	N	N
6 Coffman	Y	Y	Y	N	N
7 Perlmutter	?	N	N	Y	Y
CONNECTICUT					
1 Larson	Y	N	N	Y	Y
2 Courtney	Y	N	N	N	Y
3 DeLauro	Y	N	N	?	Y
4 Himes	Y	N	N	Y	Y
5 Murphy	?	N	N	Y	Y
DELAWARE					
AL Carney	Y	N	N	Y	Y
FLORIDA					
1 Miller	Y	Y	Y	N	N
2 Southerland	Y	Y	Y	Y	N
3 Brown	?	N	N	N	Y
4 Crenshaw	Y	Y	Y	Y	N
5 Nugent	Y	Y	Y	N	N
6 Stearns	Y	Y	Y	Y	N
7 Mica	Y	Y	Y	Y	N
8 Webster	Y	Y	Y	N	N
9 Bilirakis	Y	Y	Y	Y	N
10 Young	Y	Y	Y	Y	N
11 Castor	Y	N	N	N	N
12 Ross	Y	Y	Y	N	N
13 Buchanan	Y	Y	Y	N	N
14 Mack	?	Y	Y	Y	N
15 Posey	Y	Y	Y	N	N
16 Rooney	Y	Y	Y	N	N
17 Wilson	Y	N	N	N	N
18 Ros-Lehtinen	Y	Y	Y	N	N
19 Deutch	Y	N	N	Y	Y
20 Wasserman Schultz	Y	N	N	N	N
21 Diaz-Balart	Y	Y	Y	Y	N
22 West	Y	Y	Y	Y	N
23 Hastings	Y	N	N	N	Y
24 Adams	Y	Y	Y	N	N
25 Rivera	Y	Y	Y	Y	N
GEORGIA					
1 Kingston	Y	Y	Y	Y	N
2 Bishop	Y	N	N	Y	Y
3 Westmoreland	Y	Y	Y	Y	N
4 Johnson	Y	N	N	Y	?
5 Lewis	Y	N	N	N	N
6 Price	Y	Y	Y	Y	N
7 Woodall	Y	Y	Y	N	N
8 Scott, A.	Y	Y	Y	N	N
9 Graves	Y	Y	Y	N	N
10 Broun	Y	Y	Y	N	N
11 Gingrey	Y	Y	Y	Y	N
12 Barrow	Y	N	N	Y	Y
13 Scott, D.	Y	N	N	Y	Y
HAWAII					
1 Hanabusa	Y	N	N	Y	Y
2 Hirono	Y	N	N	Y	?
IDAHO					
1 Labrador	?	Y	Y	Y	N
2 Simpson	Y	Y	Y	Y	N
ILLINOIS					
1 Rush	?	N	N	N	Y
2 Jackson	Y	N	N	N	Y
3 Lipinski	Y	N	N	Y	Y
4 Gutierrez	+	N	N	Y	Y
5 Quigley	Y	N	N	Y	Y
6 Roskam	Y	Y	Y	Y	N
7 Davis	Y	N	N	N	N
8 Walsh	Y	Y	Y	N	N
9 Schakowsky	Y	—	N	N	Y
10 Dold	Y	Y	Y	N	Y
11 Kinzinger	Y	Y	Y	Y	N
12 Costello	?	N	N	N	Y
13 Biggert	Y	Y	Y	Y	Y
14 Hultgren	Y	Y	Y	Y	N
15 Johnson	+	Y	Y	Y	N

KEY   **Republicans**   Democrats

Y Voted for (yea)	X Paired against	C Voted "present" to avoid possible conflict of interest
# Paired for	– Announced against	
+ Announced for	P Voted "present"	? Did not vote or otherwise make a position known
N Voted against (nay)		

	198	199	200	201	202
16 Manzullo	?	Y	Y	N	N
17 Schilling	Y	Y	Y	N	Y
18 Schock	Y	Y	Y	Y	N
19 Shimkus	Y	Y	Y	Y	N
INDIANA					
1 Visclosky	Y	N	N	N	Y
2 Donnelly	Y	?	?	?	?
3 Stutzman	Y	Y	Y	Y	N
4 Rokita	Y	Y	Y	Y	N
5 Burton	?	Y	Y	Y	N
6 Pence	?	+	+	+	−
7 Carson	+	−	−	+	+
8 Bucshon	Y	Y	Y	Y	N
9 Young	Y	Y	Y	Y	N
IOWA					
1 Braley	?	N	N	Y	Y
2 Loebsack	Y	N	N	Y	Y
3 Boswell	Y	N	N	N	Y
4 Latham	Y	Y	Y	N	N
5 King	Y	Y	Y	Y	N
KANSAS					
1 Huelskamp	Y	Y	Y	Y	N
2 Jenkins	Y	Y	Y	Y	?
3 Yoder	Y	Y	Y	N	N
4 Pompeo	Y	Y	Y	Y	N
KENTUCKY					
1 Whitfield	Y	Y	Y	Y	?
2 Guthrie	Y	Y	Y	Y	N
3 Yarmuth	Y	N	N	?	Y
4 Davis	Y	Y	Y	Y	N
5 Rogers	Y	Y	Y	Y	N
6 Chandler	Y	N	N	N	Y
LOUISIANA					
1 Scalise	?	Y	Y	Y	N
2 Richmond	Y	N	N	Y	Y
3 Landry	?	Y	Y	Y	N
4 Fleming	Y	Y	Y	Y	N
5 Alexander	Y	Y	Y	Y	N
6 Cassidy	Y	Y	Y	Y	N
7 Boustany	Y	Y	Y	Y	N
MAINE					
1 Pingree	Y	N	N	Y	Y
2 Michaud	Y	N	N	Y	Y
MARYLAND					
1 Harris	Y	Y	Y	N	N
2 Ruppersberger	?	−	N	Y	N
3 Sarbanes	Y	N	N	N	N
4 Edwards	Y	N	N	N	N
5 Hoyer	?	N	N	N	N
6 Bartlett	Y	Y	Y	Y	N
7 Cummings	Y	N	N	Y	Y
8 Van Hollen	Y	N	N	Y	N
MASSACHUSETTS					
1 Olver	?	N	N	N	Y
2 Neal	Y	N	N	N	Y
3 McGovern	Y	N	N	N	Y
4 Frank	?	N	N	Y	Y
5 Tsongas	Y	N	N	Y	Y
6 Tierney	Y	N	N	Y	Y
7 Markey	Y	N	N	Y	Y
8 Capuano	Y	N	N	N	Y
9 Lynch	Y	N	N	Y	Y
10 Keating	Y	N	N	Y	Y
MICHIGAN					
1 Benishek	Y	Y	Y	N	Y
2 Huizenga	Y	Y	Y	Y	N
3 Amash	Y	Y	Y	P	N
4 Camp	Y	Y	Y	Y	?
5 Kildee	Y	N	N	Y	Y
6 Upton	Y	Y	Y	Y	N
7 Walberg	?	Y	Y	N	N
8 Rogers	Y	Y	Y	Y	N
9 Peters	Y	N	N	N	Y
10 Miller	Y	Y	Y	Y	Y
11 McCotter	Y	Y	Y	N	Y
12 Levin	Y	N	N	Y	Y
13 Clarke	Y	N	N	Y	Y
14 Conyers	Y	N	N	N	Y
15 Dingell	Y	N	N	Y	Y
MINNESOTA					
1 Walz	Y	N	N	Y	Y
2 Kline	Y	Y	Y	Y	N
3 Paulsen	Y	Y	Y	N	N
4 McCollum	Y	N	N	Y	Y

	198	199	200	201	202
5 Ellison	Y	N	N	N	Y
6 Bachmann	Y	Y	Y	Y	N
7 Peterson	Y	N	N	N	Y
8 Cravaack	Y	Y	Y	N	Y
MISSISSIPPI					
1 Nunnelee	Y	Y	Y	Y	N
2 Thompson	Y	N	N	N	Y
3 Harper	Y	Y	Y	Y	N
4 Palazzo	Y	?	?	?	N
MISSOURI					
1 Clay	Y	N	N	Y	Y
2 Akin	Y	Y	Y	Y	N
3 Carnahan	Y	N	N	Y	Y
4 Hartzler	Y	Y	Y	Y	N
5 Cleaver	Y	N	N	N	Y
6 Graves	Y	Y	Y	N	N
7 Long	Y	Y	Y	Y	N
8 Emerson	Y	Y	Y	Y	N
9 Luetkemeyer	Y	Y	Y	Y	N
MONTANA					
AL Rehberg	Y	Y	Y	Y	N
NEBRASKA					
1 Fortenberry	Y	Y	Y	Y	Y
2 Terry	Y	Y	Y	N	N
3 Smith	Y	Y	Y	Y	N
NEVADA					
1 Berkley	Y	N	N	Y	Y
2 Amodei	Y	Y	Y	Y	N
3 Heck	Y	Y	Y	Y	N
NEW HAMPSHIRE					
1 Guinta	Y	Y	Y	N	N
2 Bass	Y	Y	Y	Y	N
NEW JERSEY					
1 Andrews	?	N	N	N	Y
2 LoBiondo	Y	Y	Y	Y	N
3 Runyan	Y	Y	Y	Y	N
4 Smith	Y	Y	Y	Y	N
5 Garrett	Y	Y	Y	N	N
6 Pallone	Y	N	N	N	Y
7 Lance	Y	Y	Y	Y	N
8 Pascrell	+	N	N	Y	+
9 Rothman	?	N	N	Y	?
10 Vacant					
11 Frelinghuysen	Y	Y	Y	Y	N
12 Holt	Y	N	N	N	Y
13 Sires	Y	N	N	N	Y
NEW MEXICO					
1 Heinrich	Y	N	N	Y	Y
2 Pearce	Y	Y	Y	Y	N
3 Luján	Y	N	N	?	Y
NEW YORK					
1 Bishop	Y	N	N	N	Y
2 Israel	Y	N	N	Y	Y
3 King	Y	Y	Y	N	Y
4 McCarthy	Y	N	N	N	Y
5 Ackerman	?	N	N	Y	Y
6 Meeks	?	N	N	Y	N
7 Crowley	Y	N	N	Y	Y
8 Nadler	Y	N	N	Y	Y
9 Turner	Y	Y	Y	Y	N
10 Towns	?	N	N	Y	Y
11 Clarke	Y	N	N	Y	Y
12 Velázquez	Y	N	N	Y	Y
13 Grimm	Y	Y	Y	Y	N
14 Maloney	?	N	N	N	Y
15 Rangel	Y	N	N	Y	Y
16 Serrano	Y	N	N	N	Y
17 Engel	Y	N	N	N	Y
18 Lowey	Y	N	N	N	Y
19 Hayworth	Y	Y	Y	Y	N
20 Gibson	Y	?	?	?	?
21 Tonko	Y	−	−	+	Y
22 Hinchey	Y	N	N	Y	Y
23 Owens	Y	N	N	P	Y
24 Hanna	?	Y	Y	N	Y
25 Buerkle	Y	Y	Y	Y	N
26 Hochul	Y	N	N	Y	Y
27 Higgins	Y	N	N	Y	Y
28 Slaughter	+	−	−	−	+
29 Reed	Y	Y	Y	Y	N
NORTH CAROLINA					
1 Butterfield	?	?	?	?	?
2 Ellmers	?	?	?	?	?
3 Jones	?	?	?	?	?
4 Price	Y	N	N	Y	Y

	198	199	200	201	202
5 Foxx	Y	Y	Y	N	N
6 Coble	?	Y	Y	N	N
7 McIntyre	Y	N	N	Y	N
8 Kissell	Y	N	N	Y	Y
9 Myrick	Y	Y	+	Y	N
10 McHenry	?	?	?	?	?
11 Shuler	Y	Y	N	N	N
12 Watt	Y	N	N	Y	Y
13 Miller	Y	N	N	Y	Y
NORTH DAKOTA					
AL Berg	Y	Y	Y	Y	N
OHIO					
1 Chabot	Y	Y	Y	Y	N
2 Schmidt	Y	Y	Y	Y	N
3 Turner	Y	Y	Y	Y	N
4 Jordan	+	Y	Y	N	N
5 Latta	Y	Y	Y	Y	N
6 Johnson	Y	Y	Y	Y	N
7 Austria	Y	Y	Y	Y	N
8 Boehner					
9 Kaptur	Y	N	N	Y	Y
10 Kucinich	?	?	?	?	?
11 Fudge	Y	N	N	N	Y
12 Tiberi	?	Y	Y	Y	N
13 Sutton	Y	N	N	Y	Y
14 LaTourette	Y	Y	Y	Y	N
15 Stivers	Y	Y	Y	N	N
16 Renacci	Y	Y	Y	N	N
17 Ryan	Y	N	N	N	Y
18 Gibbs	Y	Y	Y	Y	N
OKLAHOMA					
1 Sullivan	Y	Y	Y	Y	N
2 Boren	Y	Y	N	Y	Y
3 Lucas	Y	Y	Y	Y	N
4 Cole	Y	Y	Y	Y	N
5 Lankford	Y	Y	Y	?	N
OREGON					
1 Bonamici	Y	N	N	Y	Y
2 Walden	Y	Y	Y	N	N
3 Blumenauer	Y	N	N	Y	Y
4 DeFazio	Y	N	N	Y	Y
5 Schrader	Y	N	N	Y	Y
PENNSYLVANIA					
1 Brady	Y	N	N	N	Y
2 Fattah	Y	N	N	N	Y
3 Kelly	Y	Y	Y	Y	N
4 Altmire	Y	N	N	Y	Y
5 Thompson	Y	Y	Y	Y	N
6 Gerlach	Y	Y	Y	Y	N
7 Meehan	Y	Y	+	Y	N
8 Fitzpatrick	Y	Y	Y	Y	N
9 Shuster	Y	Y	Y	Y	N
10 Marino	Y	Y	Y	Y	N
11 Barletta	Y	Y	Y	Y	N
12 Critz	Y	N	N	Y	Y
13 Schwartz	Y	N	N	Y	Y
14 Doyle	Y	N	N	N	Y
15 Dent	Y	Y	Y	N	Y
16 Pitts	Y	Y	Y	Y	N
17 Holden	Y	N	N	N	N
18 Murphy	Y	Y	Y	Y	N
19 Platts	?	Y	Y	Y	N
RHODE ISLAND					
1 Cicilline	Y	N	N	Y	Y
2 Langevin	Y	N	N	Y	Y
SOUTH CAROLINA					
1 Scott	Y	Y	Y	Y	N
2 Wilson	Y	Y	Y	Y	N
3 Duncan	Y	Y	Y	Y	N
4 Gowdy	Y	Y	Y	Y	N
5 Mulvaney	Y	Y	Y	N	Y
6 Clyburn	Y	N	N	Y	N
SOUTH DAKOTA					
AL Noem	Y	Y	Y	Y	N
TENNESSEE					
1 Roe	Y	Y	Y	Y	N
2 Duncan	Y	Y	Y	Y	N
3 Fleischmann	Y	Y	Y	Y	N
4 DesJarlais	Y	Y	Y	Y	N
5 Cooper	Y	N	N	Y	Y
6 Black	Y	Y	Y	Y	N
7 Blackburn	Y	Y	Y	Y	N
8 Fincher	Y	Y	Y	Y	N
9 Cohen	Y	N	N	Y	Y

	198	199	200	201	202
TEXAS					
1 Gohmert	Y	Y	Y	P	N
2 Poe	?	Y	Y	N	N
3 Johnson, S.	Y	Y	Y	Y	N
4 Hall	Y	Y	Y	Y	N
5 Hensarling	Y	Y	Y	Y	N
6 Barton	Y	Y	Y	Y	N
7 Culberson	Y	Y	Y	Y	N
8 Brady	Y	Y	Y	Y	N
9 Green, A.	Y	N	N	Y	Y
10 McCaul	Y	Y	Y	Y	N
11 Conaway	Y	Y	Y	N	N
12 Granger	Y	Y	Y	Y	N
13 Thornberry	Y	Y	Y	Y	N
14 Paul	?	Y	Y	Y	N
15 Hinojosa	?	?	?	?	Y
16 Reyes	Y	N	N	Y	Y
17 Flores	Y	Y	Y	Y	N
18 Jackson Lee	Y	N	N	Y	Y
19 Neugebauer	Y	Y	Y	Y	N
20 Gonzalez	Y	N	N	Y	Y
21 Smith	Y	Y	Y	Y	N
22 Olson	Y	Y	Y	Y	N
23 Canseco	Y	Y	Y	Y	N
24 Marchant	Y	Y	Y	Y	N
25 Doggett	Y	N	N	Y	Y
26 Burgess	Y	Y	Y	N	N
27 Farenthold	Y	Y	Y	Y	N
28 Cuellar	Y	Y	Y	N	Y
29 Green, G.	Y	N	N	N	Y
30 Johnson, E.	Y	N	N	Y	Y
31 Carter	Y	Y	Y	Y	N
32 Sessions	Y	Y	Y	Y	N
UTAH					
1 Bishop	Y	Y	Y	Y	N
2 Matheson	Y	Y	N	N	N
3 Chaffetz	Y	Y	?	?	N
VERMONT					
AL Welch	Y	N	N	Y	Y
VIRGINIA					
1 Wittman	Y	Y	Y	Y	N
2 Rigell	Y	Y	Y	Y	N
3 Scott	Y	N	N	Y	Y
4 Forbes	Y	Y	Y	Y	N
5 Hurt	Y	Y	Y	Y	N
6 Goodlatte	Y	Y	Y	Y	N
7 Cantor	Y	?	?	?	?
8 Moran	Y	N	N	Y	N
9 Griffith	Y	Y	Y	N	Y
10 Wolf	Y	Y	Y	Y	N
11 Connolly	Y	N	N	Y	Y
WASHINGTON					
1 Vacant					
2 Larsen	Y	N	N	Y	Y
3 Herrera Beutler	Y	Y	Y	N	N
4 Hastings	Y	Y	Y	Y	N
5 McMorris Rodgers	Y	Y	Y	Y	N
6 Dicks	Y	N	N	Y	Y
7 McDermott	Y	N	N	N	Y
8 Reichert	Y	?	?	?	?
9 Smith	Y	N	N	Y	Y
WEST VIRGINIA					
1 McKinley	Y	Y	Y	Y	N
2 Capito	Y	Y	Y	Y	N
3 Rahall	Y	N	N	N	Y
WISCONSIN					
1 Ryan	Y	Y	Y	Y	N
2 Baldwin	Y	N	N	N	Y
3 Kind	?	N	N	N	Y
4 Moore	?	?	?	?	?
5 Sensenbrenner	Y	Y	Y	Y	N
6 Petri	Y	Y	Y	Y	N
7 Duffy	Y	Y	Y	Y	N
8 Ribble	Y	Y	Y	N	N
WYOMING					
AL Lummis	?	Y	Y	Y	N

IN THE HOUSE | By Vote Number

203. HR 5326. Fiscal 2013 Commerce-Justice-Science Appropriations/ **Spending Reduction.** Broun, R-Ga., amendment that would reduce by about 3 percent the amounts provided in the bill for various administrative and salaries and expenses accounts and direct $874.6 million to the bill's spending-reduction account. Rejected in Committee of the Whole 137-270: R 133-100; D 4-170. May 8, 2012.

204. HR 5326. Fiscal 2013 Commerce-Justice-Science Appropriations/ **International Trade Administration Funding.** McClintock, R-Calif., amendment that would reduce by $277.8 million the amount provided for International Trade Administration operations and administration and direct the same amount to the bill's spending-reduction account. Rejected in Committee of the Whole 121-287: R 121-112; D 0-175. May 8, 2012.

205. HR 5326. Fiscal 2013 Commerce-Justice-Science Appropriations/ **Economic Development Assistance Grants.** Michaud, D-Maine, amendment that would increase funding by $38 million for economic development assistance program grants under the Economic Development Administration, offset by reducing funds for periodic censuses and programs by the same amount. Rejected in Committee of the Whole 190-218: R 48-185; D 142-33. May 8, 2012.

206. HR 5326. Fiscal 2013 Commerce-Justice-Science Appropriations/ **Economic Development Administration Salaries and Expenses.** Scalise, R-La., amendment that would reduce funding for Economic Development Administration salaries and expenses by $7.5 million and also reduce funding for the Commerce Department's management account by $10.7 million. The amendment would direct $18.2 million to the bill's spending-reduction account. Rejected in Committee of the Whole 174-233: R 172-61; D 2-172. May 8, 2012.

207. HR 5326. Fiscal 2013 Commerce-Justice-Science Appropriations/ **Economic Development Administration Grants.** Pompeo, R-Kan., amendment that would eliminate $182 million in Economic Development Administration (EDA) program grants and $37.5 million in EDA salaries and expenses and direct $219.5 million to the bill's spending-reduction account. Rejected in Committee of the Whole 129-279: R 129-104; D 0-175. May 8, 2012.

208. HR 5326. Fiscal 2013 Commerce-Justice-Science Appropriations/ **Advanced Manufacturing Technology Consortia.** Quayle, R-Ariz., amendment that would reduce by $21 million the amount provided for industrial technology services at the National Institute of Standards and Technology (NIST) and direct that amount to the bill's spending-reduction account. It would strike a requirement that $21 million be allocated for NIST's Advanced Manufacturing Technology Consortia. Rejected in Committee of the Whole 147-259: R 147-86; D 0-173. May 8, 2012.

209. HR 5326. Fiscal 2013 Commerce-Justice-Science Appropriations/ **National Oceanic and Atmospheric Administration Operations and Research.** Harris, R-Md., amendment that would reduce by $542,000 the amount provided for National Oceanic and Atmospheric Administration (NOAA) operations, research and facilities, and direct the same amount to the bill's spending reduction account. Adopted in Committee of the Whole 219-189: R 216-17; D 3-172. May 8, 2012.

	203	204	205	206	207	208	209
ALABAMA							
1 **Bonner**	?	?	?	?	?	?	?
2 **Roby**	N	N	N	Y	N	Y	Y
3 **Rogers**	N	N	N	N	N	N	Y
4 **Aderholt**	N	N	N	N	N	N	Y
5 **Brooks**	Y	Y	N	Y	Y	Y	Y
6 **Bachus**	N	N	Y	N	Y	Y	Y
7 Sewell	N	N	Y	N	N	N	N
ALASKA							
AL **Young**	Y	N	N	Y	N	Y	N
ARIZONA							
1 **Gosar**	Y	Y	N	Y	Y	Y	Y
2 **Franks**	Y	Y	N	Y	Y	Y	Y
3 **Quayle**	Y	Y	N	Y	Y	Y	Y
4 Pastor	N	N	N	N	N	N	N
5 **Schweikert**	Y	Y	N	Y	Y	Y	Y
6 **Flake**	Y	Y	N	Y	Y	Y	Y
7 Grijalva	N	N	N	N	N	N	N
8 Vacant							
ARKANSAS							
1 **Crawford**	N	N	Y	N	N	N	Y
2 **Griffin**	N	N	Y	N	N	N	Y
3 **Womack**	N	N	Y	N	N	N	Y
4 Ross	N	N	Y	N	N	N	N
CALIFORNIA							
1 Thompson	N	N	Y	N	N	N	N
2 **Herger**	Y	Y	N	Y	Y	Y	Y
3 **Lungren**	N	N	N	Y	N	Y	Y
4 **McClintock**	Y	Y	N	Y	Y	Y	Y
5 Matsui	N	N	Y	N	N	N	N
6 Woolsey	N	N	Y	N	N	N	N
7 Miller, George	N	N	Y	N	N	N	N
8 Pelosi	N	N	Y	N	N	N	N
9 Lee	?	N	Y	N	N	N	N
10 Garamendi	N	N	Y	N	N	N	N
11 McNerney	N	N	Y	N	N	N	N
12 Speier	N	N	Y	N	N	N	N
13 Stark	N	N	Y	N	N	N	N
14 Eshoo	N	N	Y	N	N	N	N
15 Honda	–	–	–	–	–	–	–
16 Lofgren	N	N	N	N	N	N	N
17 Farr	N	N	Y	N	N	N	N
18 Cardoza	?	?	?	?	?	?	?
19 **Denham**	N	Y	Y	N	N	Y	Y
20 Costa	N	N	N	N	N	N	N
21 **Nunes**	N	N	N	N	N	N	N
22 **McCarthy**	N	N	N	Y	N	Y	Y
23 Capps	N	N	N	N	N	N	N
24 **Gallegly**	N	N	N	N	N	N	N
25 **McKeon**	N	N	N	N	N	N	Y
26 **Dreier**	N	N	N	Y	N	Y	Y
27 Sherman	N	N	Y	N	N	N	N
28 Berman	N	N	Y	N	N	N	N
29 Schiff	N	N	Y	N	N	N	N
30 Waxman	N	N	N	N	N	N	N
31 Becerra	?	?	?	?	?	?	?
32 Chu	?	?	?	?	?	?	?
33 Bass	N	N	Y	N	N	N	N
34 Roybal-Allard	N	N	Y	N	N	?	N
35 Waters	N	N	Y	N	N	N	N
36 Hahn	N	N	Y	N	N	N	N
37 Richardson	N	N	Y	N	N	N	N
38 Napolitano	N	N	N	N	N	N	N
39 Sánchez, Linda	N	N	Y	N	N	N	N
40 Royce	Y	Y	N	Y	Y	Y	Y
41 Lewis	N	N	N	N	N	N	N
42 **Miller, Gary**	N	Y	N	Y	Y	Y	N
43 Baca	N	N	Y	N	N	N	N
44 **Calvert**	N	N	N	Y	N	N	N
45 **Bono Mack**	N	Y	N	Y	N	Y	Y
46 **Rohrabacher**	Y	Y	N	Y	Y	Y	Y
47 Sanchez, Loretta	Y	Y	N	N	N	N	N
48 **Campbell**	Y	Y	N	Y	Y	Y	Y
49 **Issa**	Y	Y	N	Y	Y	Y	Y
50 **Bilbray**	N	N	N	N	N	N	N
51 Filner	–	–	+	–	–	–	–
52 **Hunter**	Y	Y	N	Y	Y	Y	Y
53 Davis	N	N	Y	N	N	N	N

	203	204	205	206	207	208	209
COLORADO							
1 DeGette	N	N	Y	N	N	N	N
2 Polis	Y	N	Y	N	N	N	N
3 **Tipton**	Y	Y	N	Y	Y	N	Y
4 **Gardner**	Y	Y	N	Y	Y	Y	Y
5 **Lamborn**	Y	Y	N	Y	Y	Y	Y
6 **Coffman**	Y	Y	N	Y	Y	Y	Y
7 Perlmutter	N	N	N	N	N	N	N
CONNECTICUT							
1 Larson	N	N	Y	N	N	N	N
2 Courtney	N	N	Y	N	N	N	N
3 DeLauro	N	N	Y	N	N	N	N
4 Himes	N	N	Y	N	N	N	N
5 Murphy	N	N	Y	N	N	N	N
DELAWARE							
AL Carney	N	N	Y	N	N	N	N
FLORIDA							
1 **Miller**	Y	Y	N	Y	Y	Y	Y
2 **Southerland**	Y	Y	N	Y	N	Y	Y
3 Brown	N	N	Y	N	N	N	N
4 **Crenshaw**	N	N	N	N	N	N	Y
5 **Nugent**	Y	Y	N	Y	Y	Y	Y
6 **Stearns**	Y	Y	N	Y	Y	Y	Y
7 **Mica**	Y	N	Y	Y	Y	Y	Y
8 **Webster**	Y	Y	N	Y	N	Y	Y
9 **Bilirakis**	Y	Y	N	Y	Y	Y	Y
10 **Young**	N	N	N	Y	Y	Y	Y
11 Castor	N	N	Y	N	N	N	N
12 **Ross**	Y	Y	N	Y	Y	Y	Y
13 **Buchanan**	Y	N	N	Y	N	N	Y
14 **Mack**	Y	Y	N	Y	Y	Y	Y
15 **Posey**	Y	Y	N	Y	Y	Y	Y
16 **Rooney**	Y	Y	N	Y	Y	Y	Y
17 Wilson	N	N	Y	N	N	N	N
18 **Ros-Lehtinen**	N	N	N	N	N	N	Y
19 Deutch	N	N	Y	N	N	N	N
20 Wasserman Schultz	N	N	Y	N	N	N	N
21 **Diaz-Balart**	N	N	N	N	N	N	Y
22 **West**	Y	N	N	Y	N	Y	Y
23 Hastings	N	N	Y	N	N	N	N
24 **Adams**	Y	N	Y	Y	Y	Y	Y
25 **Rivera**	N	N	N	N	N	N	Y
GEORGIA							
1 **Kingston**	N	N	Y	Y	Y	N	Y
2 Bishop	N	N	N	N	N	N	N
3 **Westmoreland**	N	Y	N	Y	Y	N	Y
4 Johnson	N	N	Y	N	N	N	N
5 Lewis	N	N	N	N	N	N	N
6 **Price**	N	Y	N	Y	Y	Y	Y
7 **Woodall**	Y	Y	N	Y	Y	Y	Y
8 **Scott, A.**	Y	N	N	Y	Y	Y	Y
9 **Graves**	Y	Y	N	Y	Y	Y	Y
10 **Broun**	Y	Y	N	Y	Y	Y	Y
11 **Gingrey**	Y	Y	N	Y	Y	Y	Y
12 Barrow	N	N	Y	N	N	N	N
13 Scott, D.	N	N	Y	N	N	N	N
HAWAII							
1 Hanabusa	N	N	Y	N	N	N	N
2 Hirono	?	?	?	?	?	?	?
IDAHO							
1 **Labrador**	Y	Y	N	Y	Y	Y	Y
2 **Simpson**	N	N	N	N	N	N	Y
ILLINOIS							
1 Rush	?	?	?	?	?	?	?
2 Jackson	N	N	N	N	N	N	N
3 Lipinski	N	N	Y	N	N	N	N
4 Gutierrez	N	N	N	N	N	N	N
5 Quigley	N	N	Y	N	N	N	N
6 **Roskam**	N	N	Y	Y	Y	Y	Y
7 Davis	N	N	Y	N	N	N	N
8 **Walsh**	Y	Y	N	Y	Y	Y	Y
9 Schakowsky	N	N	N	N	N	N	N
10 **Dold**	N	N	Y	N	N	N	N
11 **Kinzinger**	N	N	N	N	N	N	Y
12 Costello	N	N	Y	N	N	N	N
13 **Biggert**	N	N	Y	N	N	N	N
14 **Hultgren**	Y	Y	N	Y	Y	N	Y
15 **Johnson**	Y	Y	N	Y	Y	Y	N

	203	204	205	206	207	208	209
16 **Manzullo**	Y	N	Y	Y	N	N	Y
17 **Schilling**	Y	N	Y	Y	N	N	Y
18 **Schock**	N	N	Y	N	N	N	Y
19 **Shimkus**	Y	Y	N	Y	N	N	Y
INDIANA							
1 Visclosky	N	N	Y	N	N	N	N
2 Donnelly	?	?	?	?	?	?	?
3 **Stutzman**	N	Y	N	Y	Y	Y	Y
4 **Rokita**	Y	Y	N	Y	Y	Y	Y
5 **Burton**	Y	Y	N	Y	Y	Y	Y
6 **Pence**	+	?	–	?	+	+	+
7 Carson	–	–	+	–	–	–	–
8 **Bucshon**	N	N	N	N	N	N	Y
9 **Young**	Y	Y	N	Y	Y	Y	Y
IOWA							
1 Braley	N	N	Y	N	N	N	N
2 Loebsack	N	N	Y	N	N	N	N
3 Boswell	N	N	Y	N	N	N	N
4 **Latham**	N	N	Y	N	N	N	Y
5 **King**	Y	Y	N	Y	Y	Y	Y
KANSAS							
1 **Huelskamp**	Y	Y	N	Y	Y	Y	Y
2 **Jenkins**	Y	Y	N	Y	Y	Y	Y
3 **Yoder**	Y	Y	N	Y	Y	Y	Y
4 **Pompeo**	Y	Y	N	Y	Y	Y	Y
KENTUCKY							
1 **Whitfield**	?	?	?	?	?	?	?
2 **Guthrie**	Y	N	N	Y	Y	Y	Y
3 Yarmuth	N	N	Y	N	N	N	N
4 **Davis**	Y	N	N	N	N	N	Y
5 **Rogers**	N	N	Y	N	N	N	Y
6 Chandler	N	N	Y	N	N	N	N
LOUISIANA							
1 **Scalise**	Y	Y	N	Y	Y	Y	Y
2 Richmond	N	N	N	N	N	N	N
3 **Landry**	Y	Y	Y	Y	Y	Y	Y
4 **Fleming**	Y	Y	N	Y	Y	Y	Y
5 **Alexander**	N	N	Y	N	N	Y	Y
6 **Cassidy**	N	Y	N	Y	Y	Y	Y
7 **Boustany**	Y	Y	Y	Y	Y	Y	Y
MAINE							
1 Pingree	N	N	Y	N	N	N	N
2 Michaud	N	N	Y	N	N	N	N
MARYLAND							
1 **Harris**	Y	N	Y	Y	N	Y	Y
2 Ruppersberger	N	N	Y	N	N	N	N
3 Sarbanes	N	N	Y	N	N	N	N
4 Edwards	N	N	N	N	N	N	N
5 Hoyer	N	N	Y	N	N	N	N
6 **Bartlett**	N	N	N	N	N	N	Y
7 Cummings	N	N	Y	N	N	N	N
8 Van Hollen	N	N	N	N	N	N	N
MASSACHUSETTS							
1 Olver	N	N	Y	N	N	N	N
2 Neal	N	N	Y	N	N	N	N
3 McGovern	N	N	Y	N	N	N	N
4 Frank	Y	N	Y	N	N	N	N
5 Tsongas	N	N	Y	N	N	N	N
6 Tierney	N	N	Y	N	N	N	N
7 Markey	N	N	N	N	N	N	N
8 Capuano	N	N	Y	N	N	N	N
9 Lynch	N	N	Y	N	N	N	N
10 Keating	N	N	Y	N	N	N	N
MICHIGAN							
1 **Benishek**	Y	N	Y	Y	N	Y	Y
2 **Huizenga**	Y	Y	N	Y	Y	Y	Y
3 **Amash**	Y	Y	N	Y	Y	Y	Y
4 **Camp**	N	N	N	Y	Y	Y	Y
5 Kildee	N	N	Y	N	N	N	N
6 **Upton**	Y	Y	N	Y	N	Y	Y
7 **Walberg**	Y	Y	N	Y	Y	Y	Y
8 **Rogers**	Y	N	N	Y	Y	Y	Y
9 Peters	N	N	Y	N	N	N	N
10 **Miller**	Y	N	N	Y	N	Y	Y
11 **McCotter**	N	N	Y	Y	Y	Y	Y
12 Levin	N	N	Y	N	N	N	N
13 Clarke	N	N	Y	N	N	N	N
14 Conyers	N	N	N	N	N	N	N
15 Dingell	N	N	Y	N	N	N	N
MINNESOTA							
1 Walz	N	N	Y	N	N	N	N
2 **Kline**	Y	N	N	Y	Y	Y	Y
3 **Paulsen**	N	N	Y	Y	N	Y	Y
4 McCollum	N	N	Y	N	N	N	N

	203	204	205	206	207	208	209
5 Ellison	N	N	Y	N	N	N	N
6 **Bachmann**	Y	N	N	Y	Y	Y	Y
7 Peterson	N	N	Y	N	N	N	N
8 **Cravaack**	N	Y	N	Y	N	N	Y
MISSISSIPPI							
1 **Nunnelee**	N	Y	N	Y	Y	Y	Y
2 Thompson	N	N	Y	N	N	N	N
3 **Harper**	Y	Y	N	Y	Y	Y	Y
4 **Palazzo**	N	Y	N	Y	Y	N	Y
MISSOURI							
1 Clay	N	N	N	N	N	N	N
2 **Akin**	Y	Y	N	Y	Y	Y	Y
3 Carnahan	N	N	Y	N	N	N	N
4 **Hartzler**	Y	Y	N	Y	N	N	Y
5 Cleaver	N	N	Y	N	N	N	N
6 **Graves**	Y	N	N	Y	N	Y	Y
7 **Long**	Y	Y	N	Y	Y	Y	Y
8 **Emerson**	Y	Y	N	Y	N	N	Y
9 **Luetkemeyer**	Y	N	Y	Y	N	Y	Y
MONTANA							
AL **Rehberg**	N	N	Y	N	N	N	Y
NEBRASKA							
1 **Fortenberry**	Y	N	N	Y	N	Y	Y
2 **Terry**	Y	Y	N	Y	Y	Y	Y
3 **Smith**	Y	N	N	Y	N	Y	Y
NEVADA							
1 Berkley	N	N	Y	N	N	N	N
2 **Amodei**	Y	Y	N	Y	Y	Y	Y
3 **Heck**	N	N	Y	N	N	N	Y
NEW HAMPSHIRE							
1 **Guinta**	N	Y	Y	N	N	N	Y
2 **Bass**	N	N	Y	N	N	N	N
NEW JERSEY							
1 Andrews	N	N	N	N	N	N	N
2 **LoBiondo**	Y	N	Y	N	N	N	N
3 **Runyan**	Y	N	N	Y	N	N	Y
4 **Smith**	N	N	N	N	N	N	Y
5 **Garrett**	Y	Y	N	Y	Y	Y	Y
6 Pallone	N	N	Y	N	N	N	N
7 **Lance**	N	Y	N	Y	Y	Y	Y
8 Pascrell	–	–	+	–	–	–	–
9 Rothman	?	?	?	?	?	?	?
10 Vacant							
11 **Frelinghuysen**	N	N	N	N	N	N	Y
12 Holt	N	N	Y	N	N	N	N
13 Sires	N	N	Y	N	N	N	N
NEW MEXICO							
1 Heinrich	N	N	Y	N	N	N	N
2 **Pearce**	N	Y	N	N	N	N	Y
3 Luján	N	N	Y	N	N	N	N
NEW YORK							
1 Bishop	N	N	Y	N	N	N	N
2 Israel	N	N	Y	N	N	N	N
3 **King**	N	N	N	N	N	N	N
4 McCarthy	N	N	Y	N	N	N	N
5 Ackerman	N	N	Y	N	N	N	N
6 Meeks	N	N	Y	N	N	N	N
7 Crowley	N	N	Y	N	N	N	N
8 Nadler	N	N	Y	N	N	N	N
9 **Turner**	N	N	N	N	N	N	Y
10 Towns	Y	N	Y	N	N	N	N
11 Clarke	N	N	Y	N	N	N	N
12 Velázquez	N	N	N	N	N	N	N
13 **Grimm**	N	N	Y	N	N	N	Y
14 Maloney	N	N	N	?	N	N	N
15 Rangel	N	N	Y	N	N	N	N
16 Serrano	N	N	N	N	N	N	N
17 Engel	N	N	Y	N	N	N	N
18 Lowey	N	N	N	N	N	N	N
19 **Hayworth**	N	N	N	N	N	N	N
20 **Gibson**	N	N	Y	Y	N	N	N
21 Tonko	N	N	Y	N	N	N	N
22 Hinchey	N	N	Y	N	N	N	N
23 Owens	N	N	Y	N	N	N	Y
24 **Hanna**	N	N	Y	Y	N	N	N
25 **Buerkle**	Y	Y	N	Y	Y	Y	Y
26 Hochul	N	N	Y	Y	N	N	Y
27 Higgins	N	N	Y	N	N	N	N
28 Slaughter	–	–	+	–	–	–	–
29 **Reed**	N	N	Y	N	N	N	Y
NORTH CAROLINA							
1 Butterfield	?	?	?	?	?	?	?
2 **Ellmers**	?	?	?	?	?	?	?
3 **Jones**	?	?	?	?	?	?	?
4 Price	N	N	Y	N	N	N	N

	203	204	205	206	207	208	209
5 **Foxx**	Y	Y	N	Y	Y	Y	Y
6 **Coble**	Y	Y	N	Y	Y	N	Y
7 McIntyre	N	N	Y	N	N	N	N
8 Kissell	N	N	Y	N	N	N	N
9 **Myrick**	Y	Y	N	Y	Y	Y	Y
10 **McHenry**	?	?	?	?	?	?	?
11 Shuler	N	N	Y	N	N	N	N
12 Watt	N	N	Y	N	N	N	N
13 Miller	N	N	Y	N	N	N	N
NORTH DAKOTA							
AL **Berg**	N	N	Y	N	N	N	Y
OHIO							
1 **Chabot**	Y	Y	N	Y	Y	Y	Y
2 **Schmidt**	Y	Y	N	Y	Y	Y	Y
3 **Turner**	N	N	Y	N	N	N	Y
4 **Jordan**	Y	Y	N	Y	Y	Y	Y
5 **Latta**	N	N	N	Y	N	N	Y
6 **Johnson**	Y	N	Y	Y	N	N	Y
7 **Austria**	N	N	Y	N	N	N	Y
8 **Boehner**							
9 Kaptur	N	N	Y	N	N	N	N
10 Kucinich	?	?	?	?	?	?	?
11 Fudge	N	N	N	N	N	N	N
12 **Tiberi**	N	Y	Y	Y	Y	Y	Y
13 Sutton	N	N	Y	N	N	N	N
14 **LaTourette**	N	N	Y	N	N	N	Y
15 **Stivers**	N	N	Y	Y	N	N	Y
16 **Renacci**	N	N	Y	N	N	N	Y
17 Ryan	N	N	Y	N	N	N	N
18 **Gibbs**	N	N	N	N	N	N	Y
OKLAHOMA							
1 **Sullivan**	Y	Y	N	Y	Y	Y	Y
2 Boren	N	N	Y	N	N	N	N
3 **Lucas**	N	N	N	N	N	N	Y
4 **Cole**	N	N	N	N	N	N	Y
5 **Lankford**	N	Y	N	Y	N	Y	Y
OREGON							
1 Bonamici	N	N	Y	N	N	N	N
2 **Walden**	Y	N	N	Y	N	Y	Y
3 Blumenauer	N	N	Y	N	N	N	N
4 DeFazio	N	N	Y	N	N	N	N
5 Schrader	N	N	N	N	N	N	N
PENNSYLVANIA							
1 Brady	N	N	Y	N	N	N	N
2 Fattah	N	N	Y	N	N	N	N
3 **Kelly**	N	N	Y	N	N	N	Y
4 Altmire	N	N	Y	N	N	N	N
5 **Thompson**	Y	N	Y	N	N	N	Y
6 **Gerlach**	N	N	N	N	N	N	Y
7 **Meehan**	N	N	N	N	N	N	N
8 **Fitzpatrick**	Y	N	Y	Y	N	N	Y
9 **Shuster**	N	N	N	N	Y	Y	Y
10 **Marino**	N	N	Y	Y	N	N	Y
11 **Barletta**	N	N	N	N	N	N	Y
12 Critz	N	N	Y	N	N	N	N
13 Schwartz	N	N	Y	N	N	N	N
14 Doyle	N	N	Y	N	N	N	N
15 **Dent**	N	N	N	N	N	N	Y
16 **Pitts**	N	N	N	Y	N	N	Y
17 Holden	N	N	Y	N	N	N	N
18 **Murphy**	Y	N	N	Y	N	Y	Y
19 **Platts**	N	N	N	N	N	N	Y
RHODE ISLAND							
1 Cicilline	N	N	Y	N	N	N	N
2 Langevin	N	N	Y	N	N	?	N
SOUTH CAROLINA							
1 **Scott**	Y	Y	N	Y	Y	Y	Y
2 **Wilson**	Y	Y	N	Y	Y	Y	Y
3 **Duncan**	Y	Y	N	Y	Y	Y	Y
4 **Gowdy**	Y	Y	N	Y	Y	Y	Y
5 **Mulvaney**	Y	Y	N	Y	Y	Y	Y
6 Clyburn	N	N	Y	N	N	N	N
SOUTH DAKOTA							
AL **Noem**	N	N	Y	N	N	N	Y
TENNESSEE							
1 **Roe**	N	N	N	Y	N	N	Y
2 **Duncan**	Y	Y	Y	Y	N	Y	Y
3 **Fleischmann**	Y	N	N	Y	Y	Y	Y
4 **DesJarlais**	N	N	N	N	N	N	Y
5 Cooper	N	N	Y	N	N	N	N
6 **Black**	Y	Y	N	Y	Y	Y	Y
7 **Blackburn**	Y	N	N	Y	Y	Y	Y
8 **Fincher**	Y	Y	N	Y	N	Y	Y
9 Cohen	N	N	Y	N	N	N	N

	203	204	205	206	207	208	209
TEXAS							
1 **Gohmert**	Y	Y	N	Y	Y	Y	Y
2 **Poe**	Y	N	N	Y	Y	Y	Y
3 **Johnson, S.**	N	N	N	Y	Y	Y	Y
4 **Hall**	N	N	N	Y	N	Y	Y
5 **Hensarling**	Y	Y	N	Y	Y	Y	Y
6 **Barton**	N	Y	N	Y	N	Y	Y
7 **Culberson**	N	Y	N	Y	Y	Y	Y
8 **Brady**	Y	N	N	Y	Y	Y	Y
9 Green, A.	N	N	Y	N	N	N	N
10 **McCaul**	N	N	N	Y	Y	Y	Y
11 **Conaway**	Y	Y	N	Y	Y	Y	Y
12 **Granger**	N	N	N	N	Y	Y	Y
13 **Thornberry**	Y	Y	N	Y	Y	Y	Y
14 **Paul**	Y	Y	Y	Y	Y	Y	Y
15 Hinojosa	N	N	N	N	N	N	N
16 Reyes	N	N	N	N	N	N	N
17 **Flores**	Y	Y	N	Y	Y	Y	Y
18 Jackson Lee	N	N	Y	N	N	N	N
19 **Neugebauer**	Y	Y	N	Y	Y	Y	Y
20 Gonzalez	N	N	N	N	N	N	N
21 **Smith**	Y	Y	N	Y	Y	Y	Y
22 **Olson**	Y	Y	N	Y	Y	N	Y
23 **Canseco**	N	Y	N	Y	Y	Y	Y
24 **Marchant**	Y	N	N	Y	Y	Y	Y
25 Doggett	N	N	N	N	N	N	N
26 **Burgess**	Y	Y	N	Y	Y	Y	Y
27 **Farenthold**	Y	Y	N	Y	Y	Y	Y
28 Cuellar	N	N	Y	Y	N	N	N
29 Green, G.	N	N	Y	N	N	N	N
30 Johnson, E.	N	N	Y	N	N	N	N
31 **Carter**	Y	N	N	N	Y	Y	Y
32 **Sessions**	N	Y	N	Y	Y	Y	Y
UTAH							
1 **Bishop**	Y	Y	N	Y	Y	Y	Y
2 Matheson	N	N	Y	N	N	N	Y
3 **Chaffetz**	Y	Y	N	Y	Y	Y	Y
VERMONT							
AL Welch	N	N	Y	N	N	N	N
VIRGINIA							
1 **Wittman**	N	N	N	Y	Y	Y	Y
2 **Rigell**	N	N	N	Y	Y	Y	Y
3 Scott	N	N	Y	N	N	N	N
4 **Forbes**	N	N	N	Y	Y	Y	Y
5 **Hurt**	Y	Y	N	Y	Y	Y	Y
6 **Goodlatte**	Y	Y	Y	Y	Y	Y	Y
7 **Cantor**	?	?	?	?	?	?	?
8 Moran	N	N	N	N	N	N	N
9 **Griffith**	Y	Y	Y	Y	N	Y	Y
10 **Wolf**	N	N	N	N	N	N	Y
11 Connolly	N	N	Y	N	N	N	N
WASHINGTON							
1 Vacant							
2 Larsen	N	N	Y	N	N	N	N
3 **Herrera Beutler**	N	Y	N	Y	N	N	N
4 **Hastings**	N	Y	N	Y	N	N	Y
5 **McMorris Rodgers**	Y	Y	N	Y	Y	Y	Y
6 Dicks	N	N	Y	N	N	N	N
7 McDermott	N	N	Y	N	N	N	N
8 **Reichert**	?	?	?	?	?	?	?
9 Smith	N	N	Y	N	N	N	N
WEST VIRGINIA							
1 **McKinley**	N	N	N	N	N	N	Y
2 **Capito**	N	N	Y	N	N	N	Y
3 Rahall	N	N	Y	N	N	N	N
WISCONSIN							
1 **Ryan**	Y	Y	N	Y	Y	Y	Y
2 Baldwin	N	N	Y	N	N	N	N
3 Kind	N	N	Y	N	N	N	N
4 Moore	?	?	?	?	?	?	?
5 **Sensenbrenner**	Y	Y	N	Y	Y	Y	Y
6 **Petri**	Y	Y	N	Y	Y	Y	Y
7 **Duffy**	Y	Y	N	Y	Y	N	Y
8 **Ribble**	Y	Y	N	Y	Y	Y	Y
WYOMING							
AL **Lummis**	Y	Y	N	Y	Y	Y	Y

IN THE HOUSE | By Vote Number

210. HR 5326. Fiscal 2013 Commerce-Justice-Science Appropriations/ **National Oceanic and Atmospheric Administration.** Grimm, R-N.Y., amendment that would reduce by $18 million the amount provided for National Oceanic and Atmospheric Administration (NOAA) operations, research, and facilities and increase by the same amount funding provided for the Office of Justice Programs. It would stipulate that the additional funds be used for regional information sharing activities. Adopted in Committee of the Whole 209-199: R 163-70; D 46-129. May 8, 2012.

211. HR 5326. Fiscal 2013 Commerce-Justice-Science Appropriations/ **Pacific Salmon Populations.** Broun, R-Ga., amendment that would reduce by $15 million the amount provided for expenses associated with the restoration of Pacific salmon populations and direct the funds to the bill's spending-reduction account. Rejected in Committee of the Whole 168-239: R 163-70; D 5-169. May 8, 2012.

212. HR 5326. Fiscal 2013 Commerce-Justice-Science Appropriations/ **Byrne Memorial Justice Assistance Grants.** Runyan, R-N.J., amendment that would reduce by $22.4 million the amount provided for administrative expenses at the Justice Department and increase by the same amount funds provided for state and local law enforcement assistance programs. It would stipulate that the additional funding be used for the Edward Byrne Memorial Justice Assistance Grant program. Adopted in Committee of the Whole 325-81: R 227-6; D 98-75. May 8, 2012.

213. HR 5326. Fiscal 2013 Commerce-Justice-Science Appropriations/ **Court-Appointed Special Advocate Program.** Davis, D-Ill., amendment that would decrease by $10 million the amount provided for the state criminal-alien assistance program and increase by the same amount the funds provided for the court-appointed special advocate program. Rejected in Committee of the Whole 99-311: R 3-229; D 96-82. May 8, 2012.

214. HR 5326. Fiscal 2013 Commerce-Justice-Science Appropriations/ **Community Oriented Policing Services Program Funding.** Grimm, R-N.Y., amendment that would increase by $126 million the amount provided for the Community Oriented Policing Services Program and stipulate that the additional funding be used for grants for the hiring and rehiring of career law enforcement officers. It would reduce by the same amount funding provided for science, aeronautics, exploration, space operations, and education research and development activities. Adopted in Committee of the Whole 206-204: R 61-171; D 145-33. May 8, 2012.

215. HR 5326. Fiscal 2013 Commerce-Justice-Science Appropriations/ **Bureau of Prisons and Federal Prison Industries.** Huizenga, R-Mich., amendment that would strike language from the bill that would bar the use of funds in the bill for a public-private sector competition within the Bureau of Prisons and Federal Prison Industries. Rejected in Committee of the Whole 199-211: R 193-38; D 6-173. May 8, 2012.

216. HR 5326. Fiscal 2013 Commerce-Justice-Science Appropriations/ **Equal Employment Opportunity Commission Funding.** Johnson, D-Ga., amendment that would reduce by $26 million the amount provided for science, aeronautics, exploration, space operations and education research and development activities. It also would increase by $7.1 million the amount provided for expenses of the Equal Employment Opportunity Commission. Rejected in Committee of the Whole 96-314: R 4-229; D 92-85. May 9, 2012 (in the session that began and the Congressional Record dated May 8, 2012).

	210	211	212	213	214	215	216
ALABAMA							
1 Bonner	?	?	?	N	N	Y	N
2 Roby	Y	Y	Y	N	N	Y	N
3 Rogers	Y	N	Y	N	N	Y	N
4 Aderholt	N	N	Y	N	N	Y	N
5 Brooks	Y	Y	Y	N	N	Y	N
6 Bachus	Y	N	Y	N	N	N	N
7 Sewell	N	N	Y	Y	Y	N	N
ALASKA							
AL Young	Y	N	Y	N	N	Y	N
ARIZONA							
1 Gosar	Y	Y	Y	N	N	Y	N
2 Franks	Y	Y	Y	N	N	Y	N
3 Quayle	Y	Y	Y	N	N	Y	N
4 Pastor	N	N	N	N	Y	N	Y
5 Schweikert	Y	Y	Y	N	N	Y	N
6 Flake	Y	Y	Y	N	N	Y	Y
7 Grijalva	N	N	N	N	Y	N	Y
8 Vacant							
ARKANSAS							
1 Crawford	N	N	Y	N	Y	Y	N
2 Griffin	N	N	Y	N	N	Y	N
3 Womack	N	N	Y	N	N	Y	N
4 Ross	N	N	Y	N	Y	N	N
CALIFORNIA							
1 Thompson	N	N	Y	N	Y	N	N
2 Herger	Y	Y	Y	N	N	Y	N
3 Lungren	Y	N	Y	N	N	Y	N
4 McClintock	N	Y	N	N	N	Y	N
5 Matsui	N	N	Y	N	Y	N	N
6 Woolsey	N	N	N	Y	Y	N	Y
7 Miller, George	N	N	N	Y	Y	N	Y
8 Pelosi	N	N	N	N	Y	N	N
9 Lee	N	N	N	Y	N	N	Y
10 Garamendi	N	N	N	N	Y	N	N
11 McNerney	N	N	Y	N	Y	N	N
12 Speier	N	N	N	N	Y	N	Y
13 Stark	N	N	N	Y	N	Y	N
14 Eshoo	N	N	Y	N	Y	N	N
15 Honda	—	—	—	—	—	—	—
16 Lofgren	N	N	Y	N	N	N	N
17 Farr	N	N	N	Y	N	N	Y
18 Cardoza	?	?	?	?	?	?	?
19 Denham	Y	N	Y	N	Y	?	N
20 Costa	Y	N	?	Y	Y	Y	N
21 Nunes	Y	Y	Y	N	N	Y	N
22 McCarthy	Y	Y	Y	N	N	Y	N
23 Capps	N	N	N	Y	N	N	N
24 Gallegly	Y	Y	Y	N	N	Y	N
25 McKeon	Y	N	Y	N	N	Y	N
26 Dreier	N	N	Y	N	?	Y	N
27 Sherman	N	N	Y	N	N	N	N
28 Berman	N	N	N	N	N	N	N
29 Schiff	N	N	Y	N	N	Y	N
30 Waxman	N	N	N	N	?	N	N
31 Becerra	?	?	?	N	Y	N	Y
32 Chu	?	?	?	Y	N	N	N
33 Bass	N	N	Y	N	N	N	Y
34 Roybal-Allard	N	N	N	Y	N	Y	N
35 Waters	N	N	N	Y	Y	N	N
36 Hahn	N	N	Y	Y	Y	N	Y
37 Richardson	Y	N	Y	N	Y	N	Y
38 Napolitano	N	N	N	N	Y	N	N
39 Sánchez, Linda	N	N	N	Y	Y	N	Y
40 Royce	Y	Y	Y	N	N	Y	N
41 Lewis	Y	N	Y	N	N	Y	N
42 Miller, Gary	Y	N	Y	N	N	Y	N
43 Baca	N	N	N	N	Y	N	Y
44 Calvert	Y	N	Y	N	N	Y	N
45 Bono Mack	Y	Y	Y	N	N	Y	N
46 Rohrabacher	N	Y	Y	N	N	Y	N
47 Sanchez, Loretta	Y	N	Y	N	Y	N	Y
48 Campbell	N	Y	N	N	N	Y	N
49 Issa	Y	Y	Y	N	Y	Y	N
50 Bilbray	N	N	Y	N	N	N	N
51 Filner	—	—	—	—	+	—	+
52 Hunter	Y	Y	Y	N	N	Y	N
53 Davis	N	N	N	N	Y	N	N

	210	211	212	213	214	215	216
COLORADO							
1 DeGette	N	N	Y	Y	Y	N	Y
2 Polis	N	N	N	Y	N	N	N
3 Tipton	N	N	N	N	Y	N	N
4 Gardner	N	Y	Y	N	N	Y	N
5 Lamborn	Y	Y	Y	N	N	Y	N
6 Coffman	N	N	Y	N	N	Y	N
7 Perlmutter	Y	N	Y	N	N	N	N
CONNECTICUT							
1 Larson	Y	N	Y	N	Y	N	Y
2 Courtney	Y	N	Y	N	Y	N	N
3 DeLauro	Y	N	Y	N	Y	N	N
4 Himes	Y	N	Y	N	Y	N	Y
5 Murphy	Y	N	Y	N	N	N	Y
DELAWARE							
AL Carney	N	N	N	N	Y	N	N
FLORIDA							
1 Miller	Y	Y	Y	N	N	Y	N
2 Southerland	Y	Y	Y	N	N	Y	N
3 Brown	N	N	N	Y	Y	N	N
4 Crenshaw	N	N	Y	N	N	Y	N
5 Nugent	Y	Y	Y	N	N	Y	N
6 Stearns	Y	Y	Y	N	N	Y	N
7 Mica	Y	Y	Y	N	N	Y	N
8 Webster	N	Y	Y	N	N	Y	N
9 Bilirakis	N	Y	Y	N	N	Y	N
10 Young	N	N	Y	N	N	Y	N
11 Castor	N	N	N	Y	Y	N	Y
12 Ross	Y	Y	Y	N	N	Y	N
13 Buchanan	Y	N	Y	N	N	Y	N
14 Mack	Y	Y	Y	N	N	Y	N
15 Posey	N	Y	Y	N	N	Y	N
16 Rooney	Y	Y	Y	N	N	Y	N
17 Wilson	N	?	N	Y	Y	N	N
18 Ros-Lehtinen	N	Y	N	N	N	Y	N
19 Deutch	N	N	Y	Y	Y	N	N
20 Wasserman Schultz	N	N	N	N	Y	N	N
21 Diaz-Balart	N	Y	Y	N	N	Y	N
22 West	Y	Y	Y	N	Y	Y	N
23 Hastings	N	N	N	Y	Y	N	N
24 Adams	Y	Y	Y	N	N	Y	N
25 Rivera	N	N	Y	N	N	N	N
GEORGIA							
1 Kingston	N	N	Y	N	N	Y	N
2 Bishop	N	N	Y	Y	Y	N	Y
3 Westmoreland	Y	Y	Y	N	N	Y	N
4 Johnson	N	N	Y	Y	Y	N	Y
5 Lewis	N	N	N	Y	Y	N	N
6 Price	Y	Y	Y	N	N	Y	N
7 Woodall	Y	Y	Y	N	N	Y	N
8 Scott, A.	Y	Y	Y	N	Y	Y	N
9 Graves	Y	Y	Y	N	N	Y	N
10 Broun	Y	Y	Y	N	N	Y	N
11 Gingrey	Y	Y	Y	N	N	Y	N
12 Barrow	N	Y	Y	N	Y	N	Y
13 Scott, D.	N	N	N	Y	Y	N	Y
HAWAII							
1 Hanabusa	N	N	Y	Y	Y	N	Y
2 Hirono	?	?	?	Y	Y	N	Y
IDAHO							
1 Labrador	N	Y	Y	N	N	Y	N
2 Simpson	N	N	Y	N	N	Y	N
ILLINOIS							
1 Rush	?	?	?	?	?	?	?
2 Jackson	N	N	N	Y	Y	N	Y
3 Lipinski	N	N	Y	N	N	N	N
4 Gutierrez	N	N	N	Y	Y	N	?
5 Quigley	N	N	N	Y	Y	N	Y
6 Roskam	Y	Y	Y	N	N	Y	N
7 Davis	N	N	Y	Y	Y	N	Y
8 Walsh	Y	Y	Y	N	N	Y	N
9 Schakowsky	N	N	Y	Y	Y	N	Y
10 Dold	N	N	Y	N	Y	Y	N
11 Kinzinger	Y	Y	Y	N	N	Y	N
12 Costello	N	N	Y	N	N	N	N
13 Biggert	Y	N	Y	N	N	Y	N
14 Hultgren	Y	Y	Y	N	N	Y	N
15 Johnson	N	Y	Y	Y	Y	Y	Y

KEY   Republicans   Democrats

Y Voted for (yea)	X Paired against	C Voted "present" to avoid possible conflict of interest
# Paired for	– Announced against	
+ Announced for	P Voted "present"	? Did not vote or otherwise make a position known
N Voted against (nay)		

MINNESOTA	210	211	212	213	214	215	216
16 **Manzullo**	Y	N	Y	N	N	Y	N
17 **Schilling**	Y	Y	Y	N	Y	Y	N
18 **Schock**	Y	N	Y	N	N	Y	N
19 **Shimkus**	N	N	Y	N	N	N	N
INDIANA							
1 Visclosky	N	N	N	Y	N	N	Y
2 Donnelly	?	?	?	?	?	?	?
3 **Stutzman**	Y	Y	Y	N	N	Y	N
4 **Rokita**	N	Y	Y	N	N	Y	N
5 **Burton**	Y	Y	Y	N	N	Y	N
6 **Pence**	+	+	+	–	–	?	–
7 Carson	+	–	–	+	+	–	+
8 **Bucshon**	Y	Y	Y	N	Y	Y	N
9 **Young**	N	Y	Y	N	Y	Y	N
IOWA							
1 Braley	Y	N	Y	N	Y	N	Y
2 Loebsack	Y	N	Y	N	Y	N	Y
3 Boswell	Y	N	Y	N	Y	N	Y
4 **Latham**	Y	N	Y	N	N	Y	N
5 **King**	Y	Y	Y	N	N	Y	N
KANSAS							
1 **Huelskamp**	Y	Y	Y	N	N	Y	N
2 **Jenkins**	Y	Y	Y	N	N	Y	N
3 **Yoder**	N	Y	Y	N	N	Y	N
4 **Pompeo**	N	Y	Y	N	N	Y	N
KENTUCKY							
1 **Whitfield**	?	?	?	N	N	Y	N
2 **Guthrie**	Y	Y	Y	N	N	Y	N
3 Yarmuth	Y	N	Y	Y	Y	N	Y
4 **Davis**	Y	Y	Y	N	N	Y	N
5 **Rogers**	N	N	Y	N	N	N	N
6 Chandler	N	N	?	N	Y	N	N
LOUISIANA							
1 **Scalise**	Y	Y	Y	N	N	Y	N
2 Richmond	N	N	Y	Y	Y	N	Y
3 **Landry**	Y	Y	Y	Y	N	Y	N
4 **Fleming**	Y	N	Y	N	Y	Y	N
5 **Alexander**	Y	N	Y	N	N	Y	N
6 **Cassidy**	N	Y	Y	N	N	Y	N
7 **Boustany**	Y	Y	Y	N	N	Y	N
MAINE							
1 Pingree	N	N	Y	Y	Y	N	Y
2 Michaud	Y	N	Y	Y	Y	N	Y
MARYLAND							
1 **Harris**	N	Y	Y	N	N	Y	N
2 Ruppersberger	Y	N	N	N	Y	N	N
3 Sarbanes	N	N	N	?	Y	N	Y
4 Edwards	N	N	N	Y	N	N	N
5 Hoyer	Y	N	N	N	N	N	N
6 **Bartlett**	N	N	Y	N	N	?	N
7 Cummings	N	N	N	Y	Y	N	N
8 Van Hollen	N	N	Y	Y	N	N	N
MASSACHUSETTS							
1 Olver	N	N	Y	N	N	N	N
2 Neal	N	N	N	Y	Y	N	N
3 McGovern	N	N	Y	Y	Y	N	N
4 Frank	N	N	Y	Y	Y	Y	Y
5 Tsongas	N	N	Y	N	Y	N	Y
6 Tierney	N	N	Y	Y	Y	N	Y
7 Markey	N	N	Y	Y	Y	N	?
8 Capuano	N	N	Y	Y	Y	N	Y
9 Lynch	Y	N	Y	Y	Y	N	Y
10 Keating	N	N	Y	Y	Y	N	Y
MICHIGAN							
1 **Benishek**	Y	N	Y	N	N	Y	N
2 **Huizenga**	Y	Y	Y	N	N	Y	N
3 **Amash**	N	Y	N	N	N	Y	N
4 **Camp**	Y	Y	Y	N	N	Y	N
5 Kildee	N	N	Y	Y	Y	N	N
6 **Upton**	Y	Y	Y	N	Y	Y	N
7 **Walberg**	Y	Y	Y	N	N	Y	N
8 **Rogers**	Y	Y	Y	N	N	Y	N
9 Peters	N	N	N	Y	Y	N	Y
10 **Miller**	Y	Y	Y	N	Y	Y	N
11 **McCotter**	N	N	Y	N	Y	Y	N
12 Levin	N	N	N	Y	Y	N	Y
13 Clarke	Y	N	Y	Y	Y	N	Y
14 Conyers	N	N	N	Y	Y	N	Y
15 Dingell	N	N	Y	Y	Y	N	N
MINNESOTA							
1 Walz	Y	N	Y	N	Y	N	N
2 **Kline**	Y	N	Y	N	N	Y	N
3 **Paulsen**	Y	N	Y	N	Y	Y	N
4 McCollum	N	N	N	Y	N	N	Y

	210	211	212	213	214	215	216
5 Ellison	N	N	N	Y	Y	N	Y
6 **Bachmann**	Y	Y	Y	–	–	+	–
7 Peterson	Y	N	Y	N	Y	N	N
8 **Cravaack**	Y	Y	Y	N	Y	Y	N
MISSISSIPPI							
1 **Nunnelee**	N	Y	Y	N	N	Y	N
2 Thompson	N	N	N	Y	Y	N	Y
3 **Harper**	Y	Y	Y	N	N	N	N
4 **Palazzo**	Y	Y	Y	N	N	Y	N
MISSOURI							
1 Clay	N	N	Y	Y	Y	N	Y
2 **Akin**	Y	Y	Y	N	N	Y	N
3 Carnahan	N	N	Y	Y	Y	N	Y
4 **Hartzler**	Y	Y	Y	N	Y	Y	N
5 Cleaver	Y	N	Y	Y	N	N	N
6 **Graves**	Y	Y	Y	N	N	Y	N
7 **Long**	N	Y	N	N	N	Y	N
8 **Emerson**	Y	N	Y	N	Y	N	N
9 **Luetkemeyer**	Y	Y	Y	N	Y	Y	N
MONTANA							
AL **Rehberg**	Y	Y	Y	N	Y	Y	N
NEBRASKA							
1 **Fortenberry**	Y	N	Y	N	Y	Y	N
2 **Terry**	Y	N	Y	N	Y	Y	N
3 **Smith**	Y	Y	Y	N	N	Y	N
NEVADA							
1 Berkley	Y	N	Y	N	Y	N	Y
2 **Amodei**	Y	Y	Y	N	N	Y	N
3 **Heck**	Y	Y	Y	N	Y	Y	N
NEW HAMPSHIRE							
1 **Guinta**	Y	Y	Y	N	Y	Y	N
2 **Bass**	Y	N	Y	N	Y	N	N
NEW JERSEY							
1 Andrews	N	N	Y	Y	Y	N	N
2 **LoBiondo**	Y	N	Y	N	Y	N	N
3 **Runyan**	Y	N	Y	N	Y	N	N
4 **Smith**	Y	Y	Y	N	Y	N	N
5 **Garrett**	Y	Y	Y	N	N	Y	N
6 Pallone	N	N	Y	Y	Y	N	N
7 **Lance**	Y	Y	Y	N	Y	Y	N
8 Pascrell	+	–	+	Y	Y	N	Y
9 Rothman	?	?	?	?	?	?	?
10 Vacant							
11 **Frelinghuysen**	Y	N	Y	N	Y	Y	N
12 Holt	N	N	Y	Y	Y	N	N
13 Sires	Y	N	Y	N	Y	N	Y
NEW MEXICO							
1 Heinrich	N	N	Y	N	N	N	N
2 **Pearce**	N	Y	Y	N	N	Y	N
3 Luján	Y	N	Y	N	Y	N	N
NEW YORK							
1 Bishop	N	N	Y	N	Y	N	N
2 Israel	N	N	Y	N	Y	N	Y
3 **King**	Y	N	Y	N	Y	N	N
4 McCarthy	N	N	Y	N	Y	N	Y
5 Ackerman	Y	N	N	N	Y	N	Y
6 Meeks	Y	N	N	Y	Y	N	Y
7 Crowley	Y	N	N	Y	Y	N	Y
8 Nadler	N	N	N	Y	Y	N	Y
9 **Turner**	Y	Y	Y	N	Y	N	N
10 Towns	Y	N	N	Y	Y	N	Y
11 Clarke	N	N	N	Y	N	N	Y
12 Velázquez	N	N	N	Y	Y	N	Y
13 **Grimm**	Y	N	Y	N	Y	N	N
14 Maloney	N	N	N	Y	Y	N	N
15 Rangel	Y	N	N	Y	Y	N	Y
16 Serrano	N	N	N	Y	Y	N	Y
17 Engel	N	N	N	N	Y	N	N
18 Lowey	N	N	N	N	Y	N	Y
19 **Hayworth**	Y	N	Y	N	Y	Y	N
20 **Gibson**	Y	Y	Y	N	Y	N	N
21 Tonko	Y	N	N	Y	Y	N	Y
22 Hinchey	N	N	N	Y	Y	N	N
23 Owens	N	N	N	Y	Y	N	Y
24 **Hanna**	N	N	Y	N	N	Y	N
25 **Buerkle**	Y	Y	Y	N	N	Y	N
26 Hochul	Y	N	Y	N	Y	N	N
27 Higgins	N	N	N	N	Y	N	Y
28 Slaughter	–	–	–	–	+	–	–
29 **Reed**	Y	Y	Y	N	Y	Y	N
NORTH CAROLINA							
1 Butterfield	?	?	?	?	?	?	?
2 **Ellmers**	?	?	?	?	?	?	?
3 **Jones**	?	?	?	?	?	?	?
4 Price	N	N	Y	Y	Y	N	Y

	210	211	212	213	214	215	216
5 **Foxx**	N	Y	Y	N	N	Y	N
6 **Coble**	Y	N	Y	N	Y	Y	N
7 McIntyre	N	Y	Y	N	Y	N	N
8 Kissell	Y	N	Y	N	Y	N	N
9 **Myrick**	Y	Y	Y	N	Y	Y	N
10 **McHenry**	?	?	?	?	?	?	?
11 Shuler	N	N	Y	N	Y	N	N
12 Watt	N	N	N	Y	N	N	Y
13 Miller	N	N	N	Y	Y	N	Y
NORTH DAKOTA							
AL **Berg**	Y	Y	Y	N	Y	Y	N
OHIO							
1 **Chabot**	Y	Y	Y	N	Y	N	N
2 **Schmidt**	Y	Y	Y	N	N	N	N
3 **Turner**	Y	Y	Y	N	Y	Y	N
4 **Jordan**	Y	Y	Y	N	N	Y	N
5 **Latta**	Y	Y	Y	N	N	Y	N
6 **Johnson**	Y	Y	Y	N	Y	Y	N
7 **Austria**	Y	N	Y	N	Y	N	N
8 **Boehner**							
9 Kaptur	N	N	Y	Y	N	N	N
10 Kucinich	?	?	?	?	?	?	?
11 Fudge	N	N	N	Y	N	N	N
12 **Tiberi**	Y	Y	Y	N	Y	Y	N
13 Sutton	Y	N	Y	N	Y	N	N
14 **LaTourette**	N	N	Y	N	Y	N	N
15 **Stivers**	Y	N	Y	N	Y	Y	N
16 **Renacci**	Y	Y	Y	N	Y	Y	N
17 Ryan	N	N	Y	N	Y	N	Y
18 **Gibbs**	Y	Y	Y	N	N	Y	N
OKLAHOMA							
1 **Sullivan**	Y	N	Y	N	N	Y	N
2 Boren	N	N	Y	N	Y	N	N
3 **Lucas**	N	N	Y	N	N	N	N
4 **Cole**	N	N	Y	N	N	Y	N
5 **Lankford**	N	Y	Y	N	N	Y	N
OREGON							
1 Bonamici	N	N	Y	Y	Y	N	N
2 **Walden**	Y	N	Y	N	N	Y	N
3 Blumenauer	N	N	N	Y	Y	N	N
4 DeFazio	N	N	Y	N	Y	N	N
5 Schrader	N	N	Y	Y	Y	N	Y
PENNSYLVANIA							
1 Brady	Y	N	Y	Y	Y	N	Y
2 Fattah	N	N	N	Y	N	N	Y
3 **Kelly**	Y	Y	Y	N	Y	Y	N
4 Altmire	N	N	Y	N	Y	N	N
5 **Thompson**	Y	Y	Y	N	Y	Y	N
6 **Gerlach**	Y	Y	Y	N	Y	N	N
7 **Meehan**	Y	Y	Y	N	Y	N	N
8 **Fitzpatrick**	Y	N	Y	Y	Y	N	Y
9 **Shuster**	Y	N	Y	N	N	Y	N
10 **Marino**	Y	Y	Y	N	Y	N	N
11 **Barletta**	Y	Y	Y	N	Y	Y	N
12 Critz	Y	N	Y	N	Y	N	Y
13 Schwartz	Y	N	Y	N	Y	N	N
14 Doyle	N	N	Y	Y	Y	N	Y
15 **Dent**	Y	Y	Y	N	Y	Y	N
16 **Pitts**	N	Y	Y	N	N	N	N
17 Holden	Y	N	Y	N	Y	N	Y
18 **Murphy**	Y	N	Y	N	Y	Y	N
19 **Platts**	Y	Y	Y	N	Y	N	N
RHODE ISLAND							
1 Cicilline	N	N	Y	Y	Y	N	Y
2 Langevin	N	N	Y	Y	Y	N	Y
SOUTH CAROLINA							
1 **Scott**	Y	Y	Y	N	N	Y	N
2 **Wilson**	Y	Y	Y	N	N	Y	N
3 **Duncan**	Y	Y	Y	N	N	Y	N
4 **Gowdy**	Y	Y	Y	N	N	Y	N
5 **Mulvaney**	Y	Y	Y	N	N	Y	N
6 Clyburn	N	N	N	Y	N	N	N
SOUTH DAKOTA							
AL **Noem**	N	Y	Y	N	N	Y	N
TENNESSEE							
1 **Roe**	Y	Y	Y	N	N	Y	N
2 **Duncan**	Y	Y	Y	N	Y	Y	N
3 **Fleischmann**	Y	Y	Y	N	N	Y	N
4 **DesJarlais**	N	N	Y	N	Y	Y	N
5 Cooper	Y	N	N	Y	N	N	Y
6 **Black**	Y	Y	Y	N	N	Y	N
7 **Blackburn**	N	Y	Y	N	N	Y	N
8 **Fincher**	Y	Y	Y	N	N	Y	N
9 Cohen	N	N	Y	Y	Y	N	Y

	210	211	212	213	214	215	216
TEXAS							
1 **Gohmert**	Y	Y	Y	N	N	Y	N
2 **Poe**	Y	Y	Y	N	N	N	N
3 **Johnson, S.**	N	Y	Y	N	N	N	N
4 **Hall**	N	Y	Y	N	N	Y	N
5 **Hensarling**	Y	Y	Y	N	N	N	N
6 **Barton**	N	Y	Y	N	N	Y	N
7 **Culberson**	N	Y	Y	N	N	N	N
8 **Brady**	Y	Y	Y	N	N	Y	N
9 Green, A.	N	Y	N	Y	N	N	N
10 **McCaul**	Y	Y	Y	?	N	Y	N
11 **Conaway**	Y	Y	Y	N	N	Y	N
12 **Granger**	N	Y	Y	N	N	Y	N
13 **Thornberry**	N	Y	Y	N	N	Y	N
14 **Paul**	N	Y	Y	?	?	?	?
15 Hinojosa	N	N	Y	N	Y	N	N
16 Reyes	N	N	N	N	N	N	N
17 **Flores**	N	Y	Y	N	N	Y	N
18 Jackson Lee	N	N	N	Y	N	N	N
19 **Neugebauer**	Y	Y	Y	N	N	Y	N
20 Gonzalez	N	N	N	N	N	N	N
21 **Smith**	N	Y	Y	N	N	N	N
22 **Olson**	N	Y	Y	N	N	Y	N
23 **Canseco**	Y	Y	Y	N	N	N	N
24 **Marchant**	N	Y	Y	N	N	Y	N
25 Doggett	N	N	Y	N	Y	N	Y
26 **Burgess**	Y	Y	N	N	N	Y	N
27 **Farenthold**	N	Y	Y	N	N	Y	N
28 Cuellar	Y	N	Y	N	Y	N	N
29 Green, G.	N	Y	Y	Y	N	N	N
30 Johnson, E.	N	N	N	Y	N	N	N
31 **Carter**	N	Y	Y	N	N	Y	N
32 **Sessions**	Y	Y	Y	N	N	Y	N
UTAH							
1 **Bishop**	Y	Y	Y	N	N	Y	N
2 Matheson	N	Y	Y	N	Y	N	N
3 **Chaffetz**	N	N	Y	N	N	Y	N
VERMONT							
AL Welch	N	N	N	Y	Y	N	Y
VIRGINIA							
1 **Wittman**	Y	Y	Y	N	N	Y	N
2 **Rigell**	Y	Y	Y	N	N	Y	N
3 Scott	N	N	Y	Y	N	N	N
4 **Forbes**	Y	Y	Y	N	N	Y	N
5 **Hurt**	Y	Y	Y	N	N	Y	N
6 **Goodlatte**	Y	Y	Y	N	N	N	N
7 **Cantor**	?	?	?	?	?	?	?
8 Moran	N	N	N	Y	Y	N	N
9 **Griffith**	Y	Y	Y	N	Y	N	N
10 **Wolf**	N	N	Y	N	N	N	N
11 Connolly	Y	N	N	N	Y	Y	N
WASHINGTON							
1 Vacant							
2 Larsen	Y	N	Y	Y	Y	N	N
3 **Herrera Beutler**	N	N	Y	N	Y	Y	N
4 **Hastings**	N	N	Y	N	N	Y	N
5 **McMorris Rodgers**	Y	N	Y	N	Y	Y	N
6 Dicks	N	N	N	N	Y	N	N
7 McDermott	N	N	N	Y	Y	N	Y
8 **Reichert**	?	?	?	?	?	?	?
9 Smith	Y	N	Y	Y	Y	Y	Y
WEST VIRGINIA							
1 **McKinley**	N	N	Y	N	N	N	N
2 **Capito**	Y	N	Y	N	N	Y	N
3 Rahall	Y	N	Y	N	Y	N	N
WISCONSIN							
1 **Ryan**	Y	Y	Y	N	N	Y	N
2 Baldwin	Y	N	Y	Y	Y	N	Y
3 Kind	Y	N	Y	N	Y	N	Y
4 Moore	?	?	?	?	?	?	?
5 **Sensenbrenner**	Y	Y	Y	N	N	Y	N
6 **Petri**	Y	N	Y	N	N	Y	N
7 **Duffy**	Y	N	Y	N	N	Y	N
8 **Ribble**	Y	Y	Y	N	N	Y	N
WYOMING							
AL **Lummis**	N	Y	N	N	N	Y	N

IN THE HOUSE | By Vote Number

217. HR 5326. Fiscal 2013 Commerce-Justice-Science Appropriations/ **National Science Foundation Funding.** Flake, R-Ariz., amendment that would reduce by $1.2 billion the amount provided for activities at the National Science Foundation and direct the same amount to the spending-reduction account. Rejected in Committee of the Whole 121-291: R 121-112; D 0-179. May 9, 2012 (in the session that began and the Congressional Record dated May 8, 2012).

218. HR 5326. Fiscal 2013 Commerce-Justice-Science Appropriations/ **Legal Services Corporation Funding.** Westmoreland, R-Ga., amendment that would reduce by $128 million the amount provided for payment to the Legal Services Corporation and direct the same amount to the bill's spending-reduction account. Rejected in Committee of the Whole 165-246: R 163-69; D 2-177. May 9, 2012 (in the session that began and the Congressional Record dated May 8, 2012).

219. HR 5326. Fiscal 2013 Commerce-Justice-Science Appropriations/ **Legal Services Corporation Funding.** Scott, R-Ga., amendment that would eliminate all funding in the bill for payments to the Legal Services Corporation and direct $328 million to the bill's spending-reduction account. Rejected in Committee of the Whole 122-289: R 122-110; D 0-179. May 9, 2012 (in the session that began and the Congressional Record dated May 8, 2012).

220. HR 5326. Fiscal 2013 Commerce-Justice-Science Appropriations/ **State Immigration Lawsuits.** Black, R-Tenn., amendment that would bar the use of funds in the bill for the attorney general to originate or join in any lawsuit that seeks to overturn, enjoin or invalidate certain state immigration laws. Adopted in Committee of the Whole 238-173: R 226-6; D 12-167. May 9, 2012 (in the session that began and the Congressional Record dated May 8, 2012).

221. HR 5326. Fiscal 2013 Commerce-Justice-Science Appropriations/ **One Percent Funding Reduction.** Blackburn, R-Tenn., amendment that would reduce the amounts that would be provided in the bill by 1 percent. It would exclude from that reduction any amounts required under current law. Rejected in Committee of the Whole 160-251: R 156-77; D 4-174. May 9, 2012 (in the session that began and the Congressional Record dated May 8, 2012).

222. HR 5326. Fiscal 2013 Commerce-Justice-Science Appropriations/ **Spending Reduction.** Broun, R-Ga., amendment that would reduce by 12.2 percent the amounts provided in the bill. It would exempt from that reduction funds made available for the U.S. Marshal Service, the FBI and NASA. Rejected in Committee of the Whole 105-307: R 105-128; D 0-179. May 9, 2012 (in the session that began and the Congressional Record dated May 8, 2012).

223. HR 5326. Fiscal 2013 Commerce-Justice-Science Appropriations/ **Fishery Conservation and Management.** Southerland, R-Fla., amendment that would bar the use of funds in the bill for any new limited-access privilege program to harvest fish for any fishery under the jurisdiction of the South Atlantic, Mid-Atlantic, New England or Gulf of Mexico Fishery Management Council. It would exempt programs that have already been developed, approved or implemented. Adopted in Committee of the Whole 220-191: R 197-35; D 23-156. May 9, 2012 (in the session that began and the Congressional Record dated May 8, 2012).

	217	218	219	220	221	222	223
ALABAMA							
1 Bonner	N	N	N	Y	N	N	Y
2 Roby	Y	Y	N	Y	N	N	N
3 Rogers	N	N	N	Y	N	N	Y
4 Aderholt	N	N	N	Y	N	N	Y
5 Brooks	Y	Y	Y	Y	Y	Y	Y
6 Bachus	N	N	N	Y	N	N	Y
7 Sewell	N	N	N	N	N	N	N
ALASKA							
AL Young	N	Y	N	Y	Y	Y	Y
ARIZONA							
1 Gosar	Y	Y	Y	Y	Y	Y	Y
2 Franks	Y	Y	Y	Y	Y	Y	Y
3 Quayle	Y	Y	Y	Y	Y	Y	Y
4 Pastor	N	N	N	N	N	N	N
5 Schweikert	Y	Y	Y	Y	Y	Y	Y
6 Flake	Y	Y	Y	Y	Y	Y	Y
7 Grijalva	N	N	N	N	N	N	N
8 Vacant							
ARKANSAS							
1 Crawford	N	N	N	Y	N	N	Y
2 Griffin	N	N	N	Y	N	N	Y
3 Womack	N	N	N	Y	N	N	Y
4 Ross	N	N	N	Y	N	N	N
CALIFORNIA							
1 Thompson	N	N	N	N	N	N	N
2 Herger	Y	Y	Y	Y	N	N	?
3 Lungren	N	Y	N	Y	N	N	Y
4 McClintock	Y	Y	Y	Y	Y	Y	Y
5 Matsui	N	N	N	N	N	N	N
6 Woolsey	N	N	N	N	N	N	N
7 Miller, George	N	N	N	N	N	N	N
8 Pelosi	N	N	N	N	N	N	N
9 Lee	N	N	N	N	N	N	N
10 Garamendi	N	N	N	N	N	N	N
11 McNerney	N	N	N	N	N	N	N
12 Speier	N	N	N	N	N	N	N
13 Stark	N	N	N	N	N	N	N
14 Eshoo	N	N	N	N	N	N	N
15 Honda	–	–	–	–	–	–	–
16 Lofgren	N	N	N	N	N	N	N
17 Farr	N	N	N	N	N	N	N
18 Cardoza	?	?	?	?	?	?	?
19 Denham	Y	Y	Y	?	N	N	Y
20 Costa	N	N	N	N	N	N	N
21 Nunes	N	Y	Y	Y	Y	Y	Y
22 McCarthy	Y	Y	Y	Y	N	Y	Y
23 Capps	N	N	N	N	N	N	N
24 Gallegly	N	Y	Y	Y	N	N	Y
25 McKeon	N	Y	Y	Y	N	N	Y
26 Dreier	N	N	Y	N	Y	Y	Y
27 Sherman	N	N	N	N	N	N	N
28 Berman	N	N	N	N	N	N	N
29 Schiff	N	N	N	N	N	N	N
30 Waxman	N	N	N	N	N	N	N
31 Becerra	N	N	N	N	N	N	N
32 Chu	N	N	N	N	N	N	N
33 Bass	N	N	N	N	N	N	N
34 Roybal-Allard	N	N	N	N	N	N	N
35 Waters	N	N	N	N	N	N	N
36 Hahn	N	N	N	N	N	N	N
37 Richardson	N	N	N	N	N	N	N
38 Napolitano	N	N	N	N	N	N	N
39 Sánchez, Linda	N	N	N	N	N	N	N
40 Royce	Y	Y	Y	Y	Y	Y	Y
41 Lewis	N	N	N	N	N	N	Y
42 Miller, Gary	Y	Y	Y	Y	Y	Y	Y
43 Baca	N	N	N	N	N	N	N
44 Calvert	N	Y	N	Y	N	N	Y
45 Bono Mack	Y	Y	N	Y	N	N	Y
46 Rohrabacher	Y	Y	Y	Y	Y	Y	Y
47 Sanchez, Loretta	N	N	N	N	N	N	N
48 Campbell	Y	Y	Y	Y	Y	Y	Y
49 Issa	Y	Y	Y	Y	Y	Y	Y
50 Bilbray	N	Y	Y	Y	N	N	N
51 Filner	–	–	–	–	–	–	–
52 Hunter	Y	Y	Y	Y	Y	Y	Y
53 Davis	N	N	N	N	N	N	N
COLORADO							
1 DeGette	N	N	N	N	N	N	N
2 Polis	N	N	N	Y	N	N	N
3 Tipton	N	Y	N	Y	Y	Y	Y
4 Gardner	Y	Y	Y	Y	Y	Y	Y
5 Lamborn	Y	Y	Y	Y	Y	Y	Y
6 Coffman	Y	Y	Y	Y	Y	Y	Y
7 Perlmutter	N	N	N	N	N	N	N
CONNECTICUT							
1 Larson	N	N	N	N	N	N	N
2 Courtney	N	N	N	N	N	N	Y
3 DeLauro	N	N	N	N	N	N	N
4 Himes	N	N	N	N	N	N	N
5 Murphy	N	N	N	N	N	N	N
DELAWARE							
AL Carney	N	N	N	N	N	N	N
FLORIDA							
1 Miller	Y	Y	Y	Y	Y	Y	Y
2 Southerland	Y	Y	Y	Y	Y	Y	Y
3 Brown	N	N	N	N	N	N	N
4 Crenshaw	N	N	N	Y	N	N	Y
5 Nugent	Y	Y	Y	Y	Y	Y	Y
6 Stearns	Y	Y	Y	Y	Y	Y	Y
7 Mica	Y	Y	Y	Y	Y	Y	Y
8 Webster	Y	Y	N	Y	N	N	Y
9 Bilirakis	Y	Y	N	Y	N	N	Y
10 Young	Y	Y	N	Y	N	N	Y
11 Castor	N	N	N	N	N	N	N
12 Ross	Y	Y	Y	Y	Y	Y	Y
13 Buchanan	N	Y	N	Y	N	N	Y
14 Mack	Y	Y	Y	Y	Y	Y	Y
15 Posey	Y	Y	Y	Y	N	N	Y
16 Rooney	Y	Y	Y	Y	Y	N	Y
17 Wilson	N	N	N	N	N	N	N
18 Ros-Lehtinen	N	N	N	N	N	N	N
19 Deutch	N	N	N	N	N	N	N
20 Wasserman Schultz	N	N	N	N	N	N	N
21 Diaz-Balart	N	N	N	N	N	N	N
22 West	Y	Y	N	Y	N	N	Y
23 Hastings	N	N	N	N	N	N	N
24 Adams	Y	Y	Y	Y	Y	Y	Y
25 Rivera	N	N	N	N	N	N	Y
GEORGIA							
1 Kingston	Y	Y	N	Y	N	N	N
2 Bishop	N	N	N	N	N	N	N
3 Westmoreland	Y	Y	Y	Y	Y	Y	Y
4 Johnson	N	N	N	N	N	N	N
5 Lewis	N	N	N	N	N	N	N
6 Price	N	Y	N	Y	N	N	Y
7 Woodall	Y	Y	Y	Y	Y	Y	Y
8 Scott, A.	Y	Y	Y	Y	N	N	Y
9 Graves	Y	Y	Y	Y	N	N	Y
10 Broun	Y	Y	Y	Y	Y	Y	Y
11 Gingrey	Y	Y	Y	Y	Y	N	Y
12 Barrow	N	Y	N	Y	N	N	Y
13 Scott, D.	N	N	N	N	N	N	N
HAWAII							
1 Hanabusa	N	N	N	N	N	N	N
2 Hirono	N	N	N	N	N	N	N
IDAHO							
1 Labrador	Y	Y	Y	Y	Y	Y	Y
2 Simpson	N	N	N	Y	N	N	Y
ILLINOIS							
1 Rush	?	?	?	?	?	?	?
2 Jackson	N	N	N	N	N	N	N
3 Lipinski	N	N	N	N	N	N	N
4 Gutierrez	N	N	N	N	N	N	N
5 Quigley	N	N	N	N	N	N	N
6 Roskam	N	Y	N	Y	N	N	Y
7 Davis	N	N	N	N	N	N	N
8 Walsh	Y	Y	Y	Y	Y	Y	Y
9 Schakowsky	N	N	N	N	N	N	N
10 Dold	N	N	N	N	N	N	Y
11 Kinzinger	N	N	N	Y	N	N	Y
12 Costello	N	N	N	N	N	N	N
13 Biggert	N	N	N	Y	N	N	Y
14 Hultgren	N	Y	N	Y	N	N	Y
15 Johnson	N	N	N	Y	N	N	N

KEY   **Republicans**   Democrats

Y	Voted for (yea)	X	Paired against	C	Voted "present" to avoid possible conflict of interest
#	Paired for	–	Announced against		
+	Announced for	P	Voted "present"	?	Did not vote or otherwise make a position known
N	Voted against (nay)				

	217	218	219	220	221	222	223
16 **Manzullo**	Y	Y	Y	Y	Y	Y	Y
17 **Schilling**	N	Y	Y	Y	Y	N	Y
18 **Schock**	N	Y	Y	Y	N	N	Y
19 **Shimkus**	Y	N	Y	Y	Y	Y	N
INDIANA							
1 Visclosky	N	N	N	N	N	N	N
2 Donnelly	?	?	?	?	?	?	?
3 **Stutzman**	Y	Y	Y	Y	Y	Y	Y
4 **Rokita**	Y	Y	?	Y	Y	Y	Y
5 **Burton**	Y	Y	Y	Y	Y	Y	Y
6 **Pence**	+	+	+	+	+	+	+
7 Carson	–	–	–	–	–	–	–
8 **Bucshon**	Y	Y	N	Y	N	N	N
9 **Young**	Y	Y	Y	Y	Y	Y	Y
IOWA							
1 Braley	N	N	N	N	N	N	N
2 Loebsack	N	N	N	N	N	N	N
3 Boswell	N	N	N	N	N	N	N
4 **Latham**	N	N	N	Y	N	N	Y
5 **King**	Y	Y	Y	Y	Y	Y	Y
KANSAS							
1 **Huelskamp**	Y	Y	Y	Y	Y	Y	Y
2 **Jenkins**	Y	Y	Y	Y	Y	N	Y
3 **Yoder**	Y	Y	Y	Y	Y	N	Y
4 **Pompeo**	Y	Y	Y	Y	Y	Y	Y
KENTUCKY							
1 **Whitfield**	N	Y	N	Y	Y	N	Y
2 **Guthrie**	N	N	N	Y	Y	N	Y
3 Yarmuth	N	N	N	N	N	N	N
4 **Davis**	N	N	N	Y	Y	N	Y
5 **Rogers**	N	N	N	Y	N	N	Y
6 Chandler	N	N	N	Y	N	N	N
LOUISIANA							
1 **Scalise**	Y	Y	Y	Y	Y	Y	Y
2 Richmond	N	N	N	N	N	N	N
3 **Landry**	Y	Y	Y	Y	Y	Y	Y
4 **Fleming**	Y	Y	Y	Y	Y	Y	Y
5 **Alexander**	N	N	N	Y	N	N	Y
6 **Cassidy**	N	N	N	Y	Y	N	Y
7 **Boustany**	Y	Y	Y	Y	Y	Y	Y
MAINE							
1 Pingree	N	N	N	N	N	N	N
2 Michaud	N	N	N	N	N	N	N
MARYLAND							
1 **Harris**	Y	Y	Y	Y	Y	Y	Y
2 Ruppersberger	N	N	N	N	N	N	N
3 Sarbanes	N	N	N	N	N	N	N
4 Edwards	N	N	N	N	N	N	N
5 Hoyer	N	N	N	N	N	N	N
6 **Bartlett**	N	N	N	Y	Y	N	Y
7 Cummings	N	N	N	N	N	N	N
8 Van Hollen	N	N	N	N	N	N	N
MASSACHUSETTS							
1 Olver	N	N	N	N	N	N	N
2 Neal	N	N	N	N	N	N	Y
3 McGovern	N	N	N	N	N	N	Y
4 Frank	N	N	N	N	N	N	Y
5 Tsongas	N	N	N	N	N	N	Y
6 Tierney	N	N	N	N	N	N	Y
7 Markey	N	N	N	N	N	N	N
8 Capuano	N	N	N	N	N	N	Y
9 Lynch	N	N	N	Y	Y	N	Y
10 Keating	N	N	N	N	N	N	Y
MICHIGAN							
1 **Benishek**	N	Y	Y	Y	Y	Y	Y
2 **Huizenga**	Y	Y	Y	Y	Y	Y	Y
3 **Amash**	Y	Y	Y	Y	Y	Y	Y
4 **Camp**	N	Y	N	Y	Y	N	Y
5 Kildee	N	N	N	N	N	N	N
6 **Upton**	Y	Y	N	Y	Y	N	Y
7 **Walberg**	Y	Y	Y	Y	Y	Y	Y
8 **Rogers**	N	Y	Y	Y	Y	N	Y
9 Peters	N	N	N	N	N	N	N
10 **Miller**	N	Y	N	Y	Y	Y	Y
11 **McCotter**	N	Y	N	Y	Y	N	Y
12 Levin	N	N	N	N	N	N	N
13 Clarke	N	N	N	N	N	N	N
14 Conyers	N	N	N	N	N	N	N
15 Dingell	N	N	N	N	N	N	N
MINNESOTA							
1 Walz	N	N	N	N	N	N	N
2 **Kline**	Y	Y	Y	Y	Y	N	Y
3 **Paulsen**	N	Y	Y	Y	Y	N	Y
4 McCollum	N	N	N	N	N	N	N

	217	218	219	220	221	222	223
5 Ellison	N	N	N	N	N	N	N
6 **Bachmann**	+	+	+	+	+	+	+
7 Peterson	N	N	N	Y	N	N	N
8 **Cravaack**	N	N	N	Y	N	N	Y
MISSISSIPPI							
1 **Nunnelee**	N	Y	Y	Y	Y	Y	Y
2 Thompson	N	N	N	N	?	N	N
3 **Harper**	N	N	N	Y	Y	N	N
4 **Palazzo**	N	Y	N	Y	Y	N	Y
MISSOURI							
1 Clay	N	N	N	N	N	N	N
2 **Akin**	Y	Y	Y	Y	Y	Y	Y
3 Carnahan	N	N	N	N	N	N	N
4 **Hartzler**	Y	Y	N	Y	Y	Y	Y
5 Cleaver	N	N	N	N	N	N	N
6 **Graves**	Y	Y	N	Y	Y	Y	Y
7 **Long**	Y	Y	Y	Y	Y	Y	Y
8 **Emerson**	N	N	N	Y	N	N	N
9 **Luetkemeyer**	N	N	N	Y	Y	N	Y
MONTANA							
AL **Rehberg**	Y	Y	Y	Y	N	N	Y
NEBRASKA							
1 **Fortenberry**	Y	N	N	Y	Y	N	N
2 **Terry**	N	N	N	Y	Y	N	N
3 **Smith**	Y	Y	Y	Y	Y	N	Y
NEVADA							
1 Berkley	N	N	N	N	N	N	N
2 **Amodei**	N	Y	N	Y	Y	N	Y
3 **Heck**	N	N	N	Y	N	N	Y
NEW HAMPSHIRE							
1 **Guinta**	N	Y	Y	Y	N	N	Y
2 **Bass**	N	N	N	Y	N	N	N
NEW JERSEY							
1 Andrews	N	N	N	N	N	N	N
2 **LoBiondo**	N	Y	N	Y	N	N	Y
3 **Runyan**	N	N	N	Y	N	N	Y
4 **Smith**	N	Y	N	Y	N	N	Y
5 **Garrett**	Y	Y	Y	Y	Y	Y	Y
6 Pallone	N	N	N	N	N	N	Y
7 **Lance**	Y	Y	N	Y	Y	Y	N
8 Pascrell	N	N	N	N	N	N	N
9 Rothman	?	?	?	?	?	?	?
10 Vacant							
11 **Frelinghuysen**	N	N	N	Y	N	N	Y
12 Holt	N	N	N	N	N	N	N
13 Sires	N	N	N	N	N	N	Y
NEW MEXICO							
1 Heinrich	N	N	N	N	N	N	N
2 **Pearce**	N	Y	Y	Y	Y	N	Y
3 Luján	N	N	N	N	N	N	N
NEW YORK							
1 Bishop	N	N	N	N	N	N	Y
2 Israel	N	N	N	N	N	N	N
3 **King**	N	Y	N	Y	N	N	Y
4 McCarthy	N	N	N	N	N	N	Y
5 Ackerman	N	N	N	N	N	N	N
6 Meeks	N	N	N	N	N	N	N
7 Crowley	N	N	N	N	N	N	N
8 Nadler	N	N	N	N	N	N	N
9 **Turner**	N	Y	N	Y	N	N	Y
10 Towns	N	N	N	N	N	N	N
11 Clarke	N	N	N	N	N	N	N
12 Velázquez	N	N	N	N	N	N	N
13 **Grimm**	N	N	N	Y	N	N	Y
14 Maloney	N	N	N	N	N	N	N
15 Rangel	N	N	N	N	N	N	N
16 Serrano	N	N	N	N	N	N	N
17 Engel	N	N	N	N	N	N	N
18 Lowey	N	N	N	N	N	N	N
19 **Hayworth**	N	N	N	Y	N	N	N
20 **Gibson**	N	N	N	Y	N	N	Y
21 Tonko	N	N	N	N	N	N	N
22 Hinchey	N	N	N	N	N	N	N
23 Owens	N	N	N	N	N	N	N
24 **Hanna**	N	N	N	Y	N	N	N
25 **Buerkle**	Y	Y	Y	Y	Y	Y	N
26 Hochul	N	N	N	N	N	N	N
27 Higgins	N	N	N	N	N	N	N
28 Slaughter	–	–	–	–	–	–	–
29 **Reed**	N	N	N	Y	N	N	Y
NORTH CAROLINA							
1 Butterfield	?	?	?	?	?	?	?
2 **Ellmers**	?	?	?	?	?	?	?
3 **Jones**	?	?	?	?	?	?	?
4 Price	N	N	N	N	N	N	N

	217	218	219	220	221	222	223
5 **Foxx**	Y	Y	Y	Y	Y	Y	N
6 **Coble**	Y	Y	N	Y	Y	Y	Y
7 McIntyre	N	Y	N	Y	N	N	Y
8 Kissell	N	N	N	Y	N	N	N
9 **Myrick**	N	Y	Y	Y	Y	Y	Y
10 **McHenry**	?	?	?	?	?	?	?
11 Shuler	N	N	N	Y	N	N	N
12 Watt	N	N	N	N	N	N	N
13 Miller	N	N	N	N	N	N	N
NORTH DAKOTA							
AL **Berg**	N	Y	Y	Y	N	N	Y
OHIO							
1 **Chabot**	Y	Y	Y	Y	Y	Y	Y
2 **Schmidt**	Y	Y	Y	Y	Y	Y	Y
3 **Turner**	N	N	N	Y	N	N	Y
4 **Jordan**	Y	Y	Y	Y	Y	Y	Y
5 **Latta**	Y	Y	N	Y	Y	Y	Y
6 **Johnson**	N	Y	Y	Y	Y	N	Y
7 **Austria**	N	N	N	Y	Y	N	Y
8 **Boehner**							
9 Kaptur	N	N	N	N	N	N	N
10 Kucinich	?	?	?	?	?	?	?
11 Fudge	N	N	N	N	N	N	N
12 **Tiberi**	N	Y	N	Y	N	N	N
13 Sutton	N	N	N	N	N	N	N
14 **LaTourette**	N	N	N	Y	N	N	N
15 **Stivers**	N	Y	N	Y	N	N	Y
16 **Renacci**	N	N	N	Y	N	N	Y
17 Ryan	N	N	N	N	N	N	N
18 **Gibbs**	N	Y	Y	Y	N	N	N
OKLAHOMA							
1 **Sullivan**	Y	N	N	Y	Y	Y	Y
2 Boren	N	N	N	Y	N	N	N
3 **Lucas**	N	N	N	Y	N	N	Y
4 **Cole**	N	N	N	Y	N	N	N
5 **Lankford**	N	Y	N	Y	Y	N	Y
OREGON							
1 Bonamici	N	N	N	N	N	N	N
2 **Walden**	Y	N	N	Y	Y	N	Y
3 Blumenauer	N	N	N	N	N	N	N
4 DeFazio	N	N	N	N	N	N	Y
5 Schrader	N	N	N	N	N	N	N
PENNSYLVANIA							
1 Brady	N	N	N	N	N	N	N
2 Fattah	N	N	N	N	N	N	N
3 **Kelly**	Y	Y	Y	Y	Y	N	Y
4 Altmire	N	N	N	Y	N	N	N
5 **Thompson**	N	N	N	Y	N	N	Y
6 **Gerlach**	N	N	N	Y	N	N	Y
7 **Meehan**	N	N	N	N	N	N	Y
8 **Fitzpatrick**	Y	N	N	Y	Y	Y	N
9 **Shuster**	Y	Y	N	Y	Y	N	N
10 **Marino**	N	Y	Y	Y	N	N	Y
11 **Barletta**	N	N	N	Y	N	N	Y
12 Critz	N	N	N	N	N	N	Y
13 Schwartz	N	N	N	N	N	N	N
14 Doyle	N	N	N	N	N	N	Y
15 **Dent**	N	N	N	Y	N	N	Y
16 **Pitts**	Y	Y	Y	Y	Y	N	Y
17 Holden	N	N	N	N	N	N	N
18 **Murphy**	N	Y	Y	Y	Y	N	Y
19 **Platts**	N	N	N	Y	N	N	Y
RHODE ISLAND							
1 Cicilline	N	N	N	N	N	N	N
2 Langevin	N	N	N	N	N	N	N
SOUTH CAROLINA							
1 **Scott**	Y	Y	Y	Y	Y	Y	Y
2 **Wilson**	Y	Y	Y	Y	Y	Y	Y
3 **Duncan**	Y	Y	Y	Y	Y	Y	Y
4 **Gowdy**	Y	Y	Y	Y	Y	Y	Y
5 **Mulvaney**	Y	Y	Y	Y	Y	Y	Y
6 Clyburn	N	N	N	N	N	N	N
SOUTH DAKOTA							
AL **Noem**	N	Y	Y	Y	N	N	Y
TENNESSEE							
1 **Roe**	N	N	N	Y	Y	N	Y
2 **Duncan**	Y	N	N	Y	Y	Y	Y
3 **Fleischmann**	N	N	N	Y	Y	Y	Y
4 **DesJarlais**	Y	Y	Y	Y	Y	Y	Y
5 Cooper	N	N	N	N	Y	N	N
6 **Black**	Y	Y	Y	Y	Y	Y	Y
7 **Blackburn**	Y	Y	Y	Y	Y	Y	Y
8 **Fincher**	Y	Y	Y	Y	Y	Y	Y
9 Cohen	N	N	N	N	N	N	N

	217	218	219	220	221	222	223
TEXAS							
1 **Gohmert**	Y	?	N	Y	Y	Y	Y
2 **Poe**	Y	N	N	Y	Y	Y	Y
3 **Johnson, S.**	N	Y	Y	Y	N	N	N
4 **Hall**	N	Y	N	Y	N	N	Y
5 **Hensarling**	Y	Y	Y	Y	Y	Y	Y
6 **Barton**	N	Y	Y	Y	Y	N	Y
7 **Culberson**	N	Y	Y	Y	Y	N	Y
8 **Brady**	Y	Y	Y	Y	Y	Y	Y
9 Green, A.	N	N	N	N	N	N	Y
10 **McCaul**	N	Y	N	Y	Y	N	Y
11 **Conaway**	Y	Y	Y	Y	Y	Y	Y
12 **Granger**	N	Y	Y	Y	N	N	N
13 **Thornberry**	Y	Y	Y	Y	Y	Y	Y
14 **Paul**	?	?	?	?	?	?	?
15 Hinojosa	N	N	N	N	N	N	N
16 Reyes	N	N	N	N	N	N	Y
17 **Flores**	N	Y	Y	Y	Y	Y	Y
18 Jackson Lee	N	N	N	N	N	N	N
19 **Neugebauer**	Y	Y	Y	Y	Y	Y	Y
20 Gonzalez	N	N	N	N	N	N	N
21 **Smith**	N	N	N	Y	N	N	Y
22 **Olson**	Y	Y	Y	Y	Y	Y	Y
23 **Canseco**	Y	Y	Y	Y	Y	Y	Y
24 **Marchant**	Y	N	N	Y	Y	Y	Y
25 Doggett	N	N	N	N	N	N	N
26 **Burgess**	N	Y	Y	Y	Y	Y	Y
27 **Farenthold**	Y	N	N	Y	Y	N	N
28 Cuellar	N	N	N	N	N	N	N
29 Green, G.	N	N	N	N	N	N	Y
30 Johnson, E.	N	N	N	N	N	N	N
31 **Carter**	N	Y	Y	Y	N	N	N
32 **Sessions**	Y	Y	N	Y	Y	Y	Y
UTAH							
1 **Bishop**	Y	Y	Y	Y	Y	Y	Y
2 Matheson	N	N	N	Y	Y	N	Y
3 **Chaffetz**	Y	Y	Y	Y	Y	Y	Y
VERMONT							
AL Welch	N	N	N	N	N	N	Y
VIRGINIA							
1 **Wittman**	N	Y	N	Y	Y	N	N
2 **Rigell**	Y	N	N	Y	Y	N	N
3 Scott	N	N	N	N	N	N	N
4 **Forbes**	N	N	N	Y	N	N	N
5 **Hurt**	Y	Y	Y	Y	Y	Y	N
6 **Goodlatte**	Y	Y	Y	Y	Y	Y	N
7 **Cantor**	?	?	?	?	?	?	?
8 Moran	N	N	N	N	N	N	N
9 **Griffith**	Y	Y	N	Y	Y	Y	N
10 **Wolf**	N	N	N	Y	N	N	Y
11 Connolly	N	N	N	N	N	N	N
WASHINGTON							
1 Vacant							
2 Larsen	N	N	N	N	N	N	N
3 **Herrera Beutler**	N	N	N	Y	N	N	Y
4 **Hastings**	N	Y	Y	Y	N	N	N
5 **McMorris Rodgers**	N	Y	N	Y	Y	N	N
6 Dicks	N	N	N	N	N	N	N
7 McDermott	N	N	N	N	N	N	N
8 **Reichert**	?	?	?	?	?	?	?
9 Smith	N	N	N	N	N	N	N
WEST VIRGINIA							
1 **McKinley**	N	N	N	Y	N	N	Y
2 **Capito**	N	N	N	Y	N	N	N
3 Rahall	N	N	N	Y	N	N	N
WISCONSIN							
1 **Ryan**	Y	Y	Y	Y	Y	Y	Y
2 Baldwin	N	N	N	N	N	N	N
3 Kind	N	N	N	N	N	N	N
4 Moore	?	?	?	?	?	?	?
5 **Sensenbrenner**	Y	Y	Y	Y	Y	Y	Y
6 **Petri**	Y	Y	Y	Y	Y	Y	Y
7 **Duffy**	N	Y	Y	Y	Y	N	Y
8 **Ribble**	Y	Y	Y	Y	Y	Y	Y
WYOMING							
AL **Lummis**	Y	Y	N	Y	Y	Y	Y

IN THE HOUSE | By Vote Number

224. **HR 2072. Export-Import Bank Reauthorization/Passage.** Miller, R-Calif., motion to suspend the rules and pass the bill that would reauthorize through Sept. 30, 2014, the charter for the U.S. Export-Import Bank. The bill would incrementally increase to $140 billion the cap on outstanding loans, guarantees and insurance that the bank is authorized to have at any given time. Motion agreed to 330-93: R 147-93; D 183-0. A two-thirds majority of those present and voting (282 in this case) is required for passage under suspension of the rules. A "yea" was a vote in support of the president's position. May 9, 2012.

225. **HR 4133. U.S.-Israel Relations/Passage.** Ros-Lehtinen, R-Fla., motion to suspend the rules and pass the bill that would express the sense of Congress that the United States should assist in the defense of Israel, including providing Israel the military capabilities necessary to deter and defend itself against any threats. The bill also would extend until Sept. 30, 2015, the U.S. government guarantee of loans taken out by the state of Israel. Motion agreed to 411-2: R 236-1; D 175-1. A two-thirds majority of those present and voting (276 in this case) is required for passage under suspension of the rules. May 9, 2012.

226. **HR 5326. Fiscal 2013 Commerce-Justice-Science Appropriations/ Fraudulent Statements.** Chaffetz, R-Utah, amendment that would bar the use of funds in the bill to violate laws against knowingly and willfully issuing fraudulent statements to Congress. Adopted in Committee of the Whole 381-41: R 239-0; D 142-41. May 9, 2012.

227. **HR 5326. Fiscal 2013 Commerce-Justice-Science Appropriations/ Prosecutors and Public Defenders Loan Repayment Program.** Tierney, D-Mass., amendment that would increase by $10 million the amount provided in the bill for the John R. Justice Prosecutors and Public Defenders Program, which provides loan repayment assistance for state and federal public defenders and state prosecutors. The amendment would reduce by the same amount the funding in the bill for NASA's Mars Next Decade program. Rejected in Committee of the Whole 160-260: R 34-203; D 126-57. May 9, 2012.

228. **HR 5326. Fiscal 2013 Commerce-Justice-Science Appropriations/ Health Care Litigation.** Blackburn, R-Tenn., amendment that would bar the use of funds in the bill for defending against any action challenging a provision of the 2010 health care law or any of the health-care-related provisions in the corresponding reconciliation law. Adopted in Committee of the Whole 229-194: R 220-17; D 9-177. May 9, 2012.

229. **HR 5326. Fiscal 2013 Commerce-Justice-Science Appropriations/ Secret-Ballot Union Elections.** Duncan, R-S.C., amendment that would bar the use of funds in the bill for litigation against states on behalf of the National Labor Relations Board with respect to secret-ballot union elections. Adopted in Committee of the Whole 232-192: R 225-13; D 7-179. May 9, 2012.

230. **HR 5326. Fiscal 2013 Commerce-Justice-Science Appropriations/ Residential-Mortgage Settlements.** Garrett, R-N.J., amendment that would bar the use of funds for the Justice Department to be a party to a single-state or multistate court settlement agreement where funds are removed from any residential-mortgage-backed securitization trust. Adopted in Committee of the Whole 238-185: R 233-4; D 5-181. May 9, 2012.

	224	225	226	227	228	229	230
ALABAMA							
1 Bonner	Y	Y	Y	N	Y	Y	Y
2 Roby	Y	Y	Y	N	Y	Y	Y
3 Rogers	Y	Y	Y	N	Y	Y	Y
4 Aderholt	Y	Y	Y	N	Y	Y	Y
5 Brooks	Y	Y	Y	N	Y	Y	Y
6 Bachus	Y	Y	?	?	?	?	?
7 Sewell	Y	Y	Y	N	N	N	N
ALASKA							
AL Young	Y	Y	Y	N	Y	N	Y
ARIZONA							
1 Gosar	N	Y	Y	N	Y	Y	Y
2 Franks	N	Y	Y	N	Y	Y	Y
3 Quayle	N	Y	Y	N	Y	Y	Y
4 Pastor	Y	Y	Y	N	N	N	N
5 Schweikert	N	Y	Y	N	Y	Y	Y
6 Flake	N	Y	Y	N	Y	Y	Y
7 Grijalva	Y	Y	Y	N	N	N	N
8 Vacant							
ARKANSAS							
1 Crawford	Y	Y	Y	Y	Y	Y	Y
2 Griffin	N	Y	Y	N	Y	Y	Y
3 Womack	Y	Y	Y	N	Y	Y	Y
4 Ross	Y	Y	Y	Y	Y	Y	Y
CALIFORNIA							
1 Thompson	Y	Y	Y	N	N	N	N
2 Herger	N	Y	Y	N	Y	Y	Y
3 Lungren	Y	Y	Y	N	N	Y	Y
4 McClintock	N	Y	Y	N	Y	Y	Y
5 Matsui	Y	Y	N	N	N	N	N
6 Woolsey	Y	P	N	Y	N	N	N
7 Miller, George	Y	Y	?	Y	N	N	N
8 Pelosi	Y	Y	?	?	N	N	N
9 Lee	Y	P	N	N	N	N	N
10 Garamendi	Y	?	?	?	N	N	N
11 McNerney	Y	Y	Y	N	N	N	N
12 Speier	Y	Y	Y	N	N	N	N
13 Stark	Y	P	N	Y	N	N	N
14 Eshoo	Y	+	Y	N	N	N	N
15 Honda	Y	Y	N	N	N	N	N
16 Lofgren	Y	Y	Y	N	N	N	N
17 Farr	Y	Y	Y	N	N	N	N
18 Cardoza	Y	Y	Y	Y	N	N	N
19 Denham	Y	Y	Y	N	Y	Y	Y
20 Costa	Y	Y	?	Y	N	N	N
21 Nunes	Y	Y	Y	N	Y	Y	Y
22 McCarthy	Y	Y	Y	N	Y	Y	Y
23 Capps	Y	Y	Y	N	N	N	N
24 Gallegly	Y	Y	Y	N	Y	Y	Y
25 McKeon	Y	Y	Y	N	Y	Y	Y
26 Dreier	Y	Y	Y	N	Y	Y	Y
27 Sherman	Y	Y	Y	N	N	N	N
28 Berman	Y	Y	Y	N	N	N	N
29 Schiff	Y	Y	Y	N	N	N	N
30 Waxman	Y	Y	Y	N	N	N	N
31 Becerra	Y	Y	N	N	N	N	N
32 Chu	Y	Y	N	N	N	N	N
33 Bass	Y	Y	Y	N	N	N	N
34 Roybal-Allard	Y	Y	Y	N	N	N	N
35 Waters	Y	Y	N	N	N	N	N
36 Hahn	Y	Y	N	N	N	N	N
37 Richardson	Y	Y	N	N	N	N	N
38 Napolitano	Y	Y	N	N	N	N	N
39 Sánchez, Linda	Y	Y	Y	N	N	N	N
40 Royce	N	Y	Y	N	Y	Y	Y
41 Lewis	Y	Y	Y	N	Y	Y	Y
42 Miller, Gary	Y	Y	Y	N	Y	Y	Y
43 Baca	Y	Y	Y	N	N	N	N
44 Calvert	Y	Y	Y	N	Y	Y	Y
45 Bono Mack	Y	Y	Y	N	Y	Y	Y
46 Rohrabacher	N	Y	Y	N	Y	Y	Y
47 Sanchez, Loretta	Y	Y	Y	N	N	N	N
48 Campbell	Y	Y	Y	N	Y	Y	Y
49 Issa	Y	Y	Y	N	N	Y	Y
50 Bilbray	Y	Y	Y	N	Y	Y	Y
51 Filner	+	+	+	+	–	–	–
52 Hunter	N	Y	Y	N	Y	Y	Y
53 Davis	Y	Y	Y	N	N	N	N
COLORADO							
1 DeGette	Y	Y	N	Y	N	N	N
2 Polis	Y	Y	Y	N	N	N	N
3 Tipton	N	Y	Y	N	Y	Y	Y
4 Gardner	N	Y	Y	N	Y	Y	Y
5 Lamborn	N	Y	Y	N	Y	Y	Y
6 Coffman	N	Y	Y	N	Y	Y	Y
7 Perlmutter	Y	Y	Y	N	N	N	N
CONNECTICUT							
1 Larson	Y	Y	Y	N	N	N	N
2 Courtney	Y	Y	Y	N	N	N	N
3 DeLauro	Y	Y	Y	N	N	N	N
4 Himes	Y	Y	Y	N	N	N	N
5 Murphy	Y	Y	Y	N	N	N	N
DELAWARE							
AL Carney	Y	Y	Y	N	N	N	N
FLORIDA							
1 Miller	N	Y	Y	–	Y	Y	Y
2 Southerland	N	Y	Y	N	Y	Y	Y
3 Brown	Y	Y	Y	N	N	N	N
4 Crenshaw	Y	Y	Y	N	Y	Y	Y
5 Nugent	N	Y	Y	N	Y	Y	Y
6 Stearns	N	Y	Y	N	Y	Y	Y
7 Mica	Y	Y	Y	N	Y	Y	Y
8 Webster	N	Y	Y	N	Y	Y	Y
9 Bilirakis	Y	Y	Y	N	Y	Y	Y
10 Young	Y	Y	Y	Y	Y	Y	Y
11 Castor	Y	Y	Y	N	N	N	N
12 Ross	N	Y	Y	N	Y	Y	Y
13 Buchanan	Y	Y	Y	N	Y	Y	Y
14 Mack	Y	Y	Y	N	Y	Y	Y
15 Posey	N	Y	Y	N	Y	Y	Y
16 Rooney	N	Y	Y	N	Y	Y	Y
17 Wilson	Y	Y	Y	N	N	N	N
18 Ros-Lehtinen	Y	Y	Y	N	N	N	N
19 Deutch	Y	Y	Y	N	N	N	N
20 Wasserman Schultz	Y	Y	Y	N	N	N	N
21 Diaz-Balart	Y	Y	Y	N	Y	Y	Y
22 West	N	Y	Y	N	Y	Y	Y
23 Hastings	Y	Y	Y	N	N	N	N
24 Adams	N	Y	Y	N	Y	Y	Y
25 Rivera	Y	Y	Y	N	Y	Y	Y
GEORGIA							
1 Kingston	N	Y	Y	N	Y	Y	Y
2 Bishop	Y	Y	Y	N	N	N	N
3 Westmoreland	N	Y	Y	N	Y	Y	Y
4 Johnson	Y	N	Y	N	N	N	N
5 Lewis	Y	Y	N	N	N	N	N
6 Price	N	Y	Y	N	Y	Y	Y
7 Woodall	N	Y	Y	N	Y	Y	Y
8 Scott, A.	N	Y	Y	N	Y	Y	Y
9 Graves	N	Y	Y	N	Y	Y	Y
10 Broun	N	Y	Y	N	Y	Y	Y
11 Gingrey	N	Y	Y	N	Y	Y	Y
12 Barrow	Y	Y	Y	Y	Y	N	N
13 Scott, D.	?	Y	N	Y	N	N	N
HAWAII							
1 Hanabusa	Y	Y	Y	Y	N	N	N
2 Hirono	Y	Y	Y	Y	N	N	N
IDAHO							
1 Labrador	N	Y	Y	Y	Y	Y	Y
2 Simpson	Y	Y	Y	N	Y	Y	Y
ILLINOIS							
1 Rush	Y	Y	Y	N	N	N	N
2 Jackson	Y	Y	N	N	N	N	N
3 Lipinski	Y	Y	Y	N	N	N	N
4 Gutierrez	Y	Y	Y	N	N	N	N
5 Quigley	Y	Y	Y	N	N	N	N
6 Roskam	Y	Y	Y	N	Y	Y	Y
7 Davis	Y	Y	N	N	N	N	N
8 Walsh	Y	Y	Y	N	Y	Y	Y
9 Schakowsky	Y	Y	N	N	N	N	N
10 Dold	Y	Y	Y	N	N	Y	Y
11 Kinzinger	Y	Y	Y	N	Y	Y	Y
12 Costello	Y	Y	Y	N	N	N	N
13 Biggert	Y	Y	Y	N	N	Y	N
14 Hultgren	Y	Y	Y	N	Y	Y	Y
15 Johnson	N	Y	Y	N	Y	N	Y

KEY	**Republicans**	Democrats		
Y	Voted for (yea)	X	Paired against	C Voted "present" to avoid possible conflict of interest
#	Paired for	–	Announced against	
+	Announced for	P	Voted "present"	? Did not vote or otherwise make a position known
N	Voted against (nay)			

	224	225	226	227	228	229	230
16 **Manzullo**	Y	Y	Y	N	Y	Y	Y
17 **Schilling**	Y	Y	Y	N	Y	N	Y
18 **Schock**	Y	Y	Y	N	Y	N	Y
19 **Shimkus**	Y	Y	Y	N	Y	Y	Y
INDIANA							
1 Visclosky	Y	Y	Y	Y	N	N	N
2 Donnelly	?	?	?	?	?	?	?
3 **Stutzman**	N	Y	Y	N	Y	Y	Y
4 **Rokita**	N	Y	Y	N	Y	Y	Y
5 **Burton**	Y	?	Y	N	Y	Y	Y
6 **Pence**	Y	Y	Y	Y	Y	Y	Y
7 Carson	Y	P	N	Y	N	N	N
8 **Bucshon**	Y	Y	Y	N	Y	Y	Y
9 **Young**	N	Y	Y	N	Y	Y	Y
IOWA							
1 Braley	Y	Y	Y	Y	N	N	N
2 Loebsack	Y	Y	Y	Y	N	N	N
3 Boswell	Y	Y	Y	Y	N	N	N
4 **Latham**	Y	Y	Y	N	Y	Y	Y
5 **King**	N	Y	Y	N	Y	Y	Y
KANSAS							
1 **Huelskamp**	N	Y	Y	N	Y	Y	Y
2 **Jenkins**	N	Y	Y	N	Y	Y	Y
3 **Yoder**	Y	Y	Y	N	Y	Y	Y
4 **Pompeo**	N	Y	Y	N	Y	Y	Y
KENTUCKY							
1 **Whitfield**	Y	Y	Y	N	Y	Y	Y
2 **Guthrie**	Y	Y	Y	N	Y	Y	Y
3 Yarmuth	Y	Y	Y	Y	N	N	N
4 **Davis**	Y	Y	Y	Y	Y	Y	Y
5 **Rogers**	Y	Y	Y	N	Y	Y	Y
6 Chandler	Y	Y	Y	Y	Y	N	N
LOUISIANA							
1 **Scalise**	N	Y	Y	N	Y	Y	Y
2 Richmond	Y	Y	Y	N	N	N	N
3 **Landry**	N	Y	Y	N	Y	Y	Y
4 **Fleming**	N	Y	Y	N	Y	Y	Y
5 **Alexander**	Y	Y	Y	N	Y	Y	Y
6 **Cassidy**	Y	Y	Y	N	Y	Y	Y
7 **Boustany**	Y	Y	Y	N	Y	Y	Y
MAINE							
1 Pingree	Y	Y	Y	Y	N	N	N
2 Michaud	Y	Y	Y	Y	N	N	N
MARYLAND							
1 **Harris**	N	Y	Y	Y	Y	Y	Y
2 Ruppersberger	Y	Y	Y	N	N	N	N
3 Sarbanes	Y	Y	Y	Y	N	N	N
4 Edwards	Y	P	N	N	N	N	N
5 Hoyer	Y	Y	Y	N	N	N	N
6 **Bartlett**	Y	Y	Y	Y	Y	Y	Y
7 Cummings	Y	Y	Y	Y	N	N	N
8 Van Hollen	Y	Y	Y	N	N	N	N
MASSACHUSETTS							
1 Olver	Y	Y	Y	Y	N	N	N
2 Neal	Y	Y	Y	Y	N	N	N
3 McGovern	Y	Y	Y	Y	N	N	N
4 Frank	Y	Y	Y	Y	N	N	N
5 Tsongas	Y	Y	Y	Y	N	N	N
6 Tierney	Y	Y	Y	Y	N	N	N
7 Markey	Y	Y	Y	Y	N	N	N
8 Capuano	Y	Y	Y	Y	N	N	N
9 Lynch	Y	Y	Y	Y	N	N	N
10 Keating	Y	Y	Y	Y	N	N	N
MICHIGAN							
1 **Benishek**	Y	Y	Y	N	Y	Y	Y
2 **Huizenga**	N	Y	Y	N	Y	Y	Y
3 **Amash**	N	Y	Y	N	Y	Y	Y
4 **Camp**	Y	Y	Y	Y	Y	Y	Y
5 Kildee	Y	Y	Y	Y	N	N	N
6 **Upton**	N	Y	Y	Y	Y	Y	Y
7 **Walberg**	N	Y	Y	N	Y	Y	Y
8 **Rogers**	Y	Y	Y	N	Y	Y	Y
9 Peters	Y	Y	Y	Y	N	N	N
10 **Miller**	Y	Y	Y	N	N	Y	Y
11 **McCotter**	Y	Y	Y	N	Y	N	Y
12 Levin	Y	Y	Y	Y	N	N	N
13 Clarke	Y	Y	Y	Y	N	N	N
14 Conyers	Y	Y	N	Y	N	N	N
15 Dingell	Y	N	N	Y	N	N	N
MINNESOTA							
1 Walz	Y	Y	Y	N	N	N	N
2 **Kline**	Y	Y	Y	N	Y	Y	Y
3 **Paulsen**	N	Y	Y	N	Y	Y	Y
4 McCollum	Y	P	N	Y	N	N	N

	224	225	226	227	228	229	230
5 Ellison	Y	P	Y	Y	N	N	N
6 **Bachmann**	–	+	+	–	+	+	+
7 Peterson	Y	Y	Y	N	Y	N	N
8 **Cravaack**	Y	Y	Y	N	Y	Y	Y
MISSISSIPPI							
1 **Nunnelee**	N	Y	Y	N	Y	Y	Y
2 Thompson	Y	Y	Y	Y	N	N	N
3 **Harper**	Y	Y	Y	N	Y	Y	Y
4 **Palazzo**	N	Y	Y	N	Y	Y	Y
MISSOURI							
1 Clay	Y	Y	Y	Y	N	N	N
2 **Akin**	N	Y	Y	N	Y	Y	Y
3 Carnahan	Y	Y	Y	Y	N	N	N
4 **Hartzler**	Y	Y	Y	N	N	N	Y
5 Cleaver	Y	Y	N	?	N	N	N
6 **Graves**	Y	Y	Y	N	Y	Y	Y
7 **Long**	Y	Y	Y	N	Y	Y	Y
8 **Emerson**	Y	Y	Y	N	Y	Y	Y
9 **Luetkemeyer**	Y	Y	Y	N	Y	N	Y
MONTANA							
AL **Rehberg**	Y	Y	Y	N	Y	Y	Y
NEBRASKA							
1 **Fortenberry**	Y	Y	Y	N	N	Y	Y
2 **Terry**	Y	Y	Y	N	Y	Y	Y
3 **Smith**	Y	Y	Y	N	Y	Y	Y
NEVADA							
1 Berkley	Y	Y	Y	Y	N	N	N
2 **Amodei**	Y	Y	Y	N	Y	Y	Y
3 **Heck**	N	Y	Y	N	Y	Y	Y
NEW HAMPSHIRE							
1 **Guinta**	Y	Y	Y	Y	Y	Y	Y
2 **Bass**	N	Y	Y	N	Y	Y	Y
NEW JERSEY							
1 Andrews	Y	Y	N	Y	N	N	N
2 **LoBiondo**	Y	Y	Y	Y	Y	N	Y
3 **Runyan**	Y	Y	Y	N	Y	N	Y
4 **Smith**	Y	Y	Y	Y	Y	N	Y
5 **Garrett**	N	Y	Y	N	Y	Y	Y
6 Pallone	Y	Y	Y	Y	N	N	N
7 **Lance**	N	Y	Y	N	Y	Y	Y
8 Pascrell	Y	Y	N	Y	N	N	N
9 Rothman	Y	Y	N	Y	N	N	N
10 Vacant							
11 **Frelinghuysen**	Y	Y	Y	N	Y	Y	Y
12 Holt	Y	Y	Y	Y	N	N	N
13 Sires	Y	Y	Y	Y	N	N	N
NEW MEXICO							
1 Heinrich	Y	Y	Y	Y	N	N	N
2 **Pearce**	Y	Y	Y	N	Y	Y	Y
3 Luján	Y	Y	Y	Y	N	N	N
NEW YORK							
1 Bishop	Y	Y	Y	Y	N	N	N
2 Israel	Y	Y	Y	Y	N	N	N
3 **King**	Y	Y	Y	N	Y	Y	Y
4 McCarthy	Y	Y	Y	Y	N	N	N
5 Ackerman	Y	Y	Y	Y	N	N	N
6 Meeks	Y	Y	N	Y	N	N	N
7 Crowley	Y	Y	N	Y	N	N	N
8 Nadler	Y	Y	Y	Y	N	N	N
9 **Turner**	Y	Y	Y	N	Y	Y	Y
10 Towns	Y	Y	Y	Y	N	N	N
11 Clarke	Y	Y	N	N	N	N	N
12 Velázquez	Y	Y	Y	Y	N	N	N
13 **Grimm**	Y	Y	Y	Y	Y	N	Y
14 Maloney	Y	Y	Y	Y	N	N	N
15 Rangel	Y	Y	N	Y	N	N	N
16 Serrano	Y	Y	Y	Y	N	N	N
17 Engel	Y	Y	Y	Y	N	N	N
18 Lowey	Y	Y	Y	N	N	N	N
19 **Hayworth**	Y	Y	Y	Y	Y	Y	Y
20 **Gibson**	Y	Y	Y	Y	N	Y	Y
21 Tonko	Y	Y	Y	Y	N	N	N
22 Hinchey	Y	Y	N	N	N	N	N
23 Owens	Y	Y	Y	Y	N	N	N
24 **Hanna**	N	Y	Y	N	Y	Y	Y
25 **Buerkle**	Y	Y	Y	N	Y	Y	Y
26 Hochul	Y	Y	Y	Y	N	N	N
27 Higgins	Y	Y	Y	Y	N	N	N
28 Slaughter	+	+	–	+	–	–	–
29 **Reed**	Y	Y	Y	N	Y	Y	Y
NORTH CAROLINA							
1 Butterfield	Y	Y	N	N	N	N	N
2 **Ellmers**	Y	Y	Y	N	Y	Y	Y
3 **Jones**	N	P	Y	Y	Y	Y	N
4 Price	Y	Y	Y	Y	N	N	N

	224	225	226	227	228	229	230
5 **Foxx**	N	Y	Y	N	N	Y	Y
6 **Coble**	Y	Y	Y	N	Y	Y	Y
7 McIntyre	Y	Y	Y	Y	Y	Y	N
8 Kissell	Y	Y	Y	Y	Y	N	Y
9 **Myrick**	Y	Y	Y	Y	Y	Y	Y
10 **McHenry**	N	Y	Y	N	Y	Y	Y
11 Shuler	Y	Y	Y	Y	Y	Y	Y
12 Watt	Y	Y	N	Y	N	N	N
13 Miller	Y	Y	Y	N	N	N	N
NORTH DAKOTA							
AL **Berg**	Y	Y	Y	N	Y	Y	Y
OHIO							
1 **Chabot**	N	Y	Y	N	Y	Y	Y
2 **Schmidt**	N	Y	Y	N	?	?	?
3 **Turner**	Y	Y	Y	N	Y	Y	Y
4 **Jordan**	N	Y	Y	N	Y	Y	Y
5 **Latta**	N	Y	Y	N	Y	Y	Y
6 **Johnson**	Y	Y	Y	N	Y	Y	Y
7 **Austria**	Y	Y	Y	N	Y	Y	Y
8 **Boehner**							
9 Kaptur	Y	Y	N	N	N	N	N
10 Kucinich	?	?	?	?	?	?	?
11 Fudge	Y	Y	N	N	N	N	N
12 **Tiberi**	Y	Y	Y	N	Y	Y	Y
13 Sutton	+	Y	Y	N	N	N	N
14 **LaTourette**	Y	Y	Y	N	N	N	Y
15 **Stivers**	Y	+	Y	N	Y	Y	Y
16 **Renacci**	Y	Y	Y	N	Y	Y	Y
17 Ryan	Y	Y	Y	Y	N	N	N
18 **Gibbs**	Y	Y	Y	N	Y	Y	Y
OKLAHOMA							
1 **Sullivan**	N	Y	Y	?	Y	Y	?
2 Boren	Y	Y	Y	N	Y	Y	Y
3 **Lucas**	Y	Y	Y	N	Y	Y	Y
4 **Cole**	Y	Y	Y	N	Y	Y	Y
5 **Lankford**	N	Y	Y	N	Y	Y	Y
OREGON							
1 Bonamici	Y	Y	Y	Y	N	N	N
2 **Walden**	Y	Y	Y	Y	Y	Y	Y
3 Blumenauer	Y	P	Y	Y	N	N	N
4 DeFazio	Y	Y	Y	Y	N	N	N
5 Schrader	Y	Y	Y	Y	N	N	N
PENNSYLVANIA							
1 Brady	Y	Y	Y	Y	N	N	N
2 Fattah	Y	Y	Y	N	N	N	N
3 **Kelly**	Y	Y	Y	N	Y	Y	Y
4 Altmire	Y	Y	Y	Y	N	N	N
5 **Thompson**	Y	Y	Y	N	Y	Y	Y
6 **Gerlach**	Y	Y	Y	Y	Y	Y	Y
7 **Meehan**	Y	Y	Y	Y	N	Y	N
8 **Fitzpatrick**	Y	Y	Y	Y	Y	Y	Y
9 **Shuster**	Y	Y	Y	N	Y	Y	Y
10 **Marino**	Y	Y	Y	N	Y	Y	Y
11 **Barletta**	Y	Y	Y	N	Y	Y	Y
12 Critz	Y	Y	Y	Y	N	N	N
13 Schwartz	Y	Y	Y	Y	N	N	N
14 Doyle	Y	Y	Y	Y	N	N	N
15 **Dent**	Y	Y	Y	Y	Y	Y	Y
16 **Pitts**	Y	Y	Y	N	Y	Y	Y
17 Holden	Y	Y	Y	Y	N	N	N
18 **Murphy**	Y	Y	Y	N	Y	Y	Y
19 **Platts**	Y	Y	Y	Y	Y	Y	Y
RHODE ISLAND							
1 Cicilline	Y	Y	Y	Y	N	N	N
2 Langevin	Y	Y	Y	Y	N	N	N
SOUTH CAROLINA							
1 **Scott**	Y	Y	Y	Y	Y	Y	Y
2 **Wilson**	Y	Y	Y	Y	Y	Y	Y
3 **Duncan**	N	Y	Y	Y	Y	Y	Y
4 **Gowdy**	Y	Y	Y	Y	Y	Y	Y
5 **Mulvaney**	N	Y	Y	Y	Y	Y	Y
6 Clyburn	Y	Y	N	N	N	N	N
SOUTH DAKOTA							
AL **Noem**	N	Y	Y	N	Y	Y	Y
TENNESSEE							
1 **Roe**	Y	Y	Y	N	Y	Y	Y
2 **Duncan**	N	Y	Y	N	Y	Y	Y
3 **Fleischmann**	N	Y	Y	N	Y	Y	Y
4 **DesJarlais**	Y	Y	Y	N	Y	Y	Y
5 Cooper	Y	Y	Y	Y	N	N	N
6 **Black**	N	Y	Y	N	Y	Y	Y
7 **Blackburn**	N	Y	Y	N	Y	Y	Y
8 **Fincher**	N	Y	Y	N	Y	Y	Y
9 Cohen	Y	Y	N	Y	N	N	N

	224	225	226	227	228	229	230
TEXAS							
1 **Gohmert**	N	Y	Y	N	Y	Y	Y
2 **Poe**	N	Y	Y	N	Y	Y	Y
3 **Johnson, S.**	N	Y	Y	N	Y	Y	Y
4 **Hall**	N	Y	Y	N	Y	Y	Y
5 **Hensarling**	N	Y	Y	N	Y	Y	Y
6 **Barton**	Y	Y	Y	N	Y	Y	Y
7 **Culberson**	N	Y	Y	N	Y	Y	Y
8 **Brady**	Y	Y	Y	N	Y	Y	Y
9 Green, A.	Y	Y	Y	N	N	N	N
10 **McCaul**	Y	Y	Y	N	?	Y	Y
11 **Conaway**	N	Y	Y	N	Y	Y	Y
12 **Granger**	Y	Y	Y	N	Y	Y	Y
13 **Thornberry**	Y	Y	Y	N	Y	Y	Y
14 **Paul**	N	N	Y	N	Y	Y	Y
15 Hinojosa	Y	Y	N	Y	N	N	N
16 Reyes	Y	Y	Y	N	N	N	N
17 **Flores**	Y	Y	Y	N	Y	Y	Y
18 Jackson Lee	Y	Y	Y	N	N	N	N
19 **Neugebauer**	N	Y	Y	N	Y	Y	Y
20 Gonzalez	Y	Y	Y	N	N	N	N
21 **Smith**	Y	Y	Y	N	Y	Y	Y
22 **Olson**	Y	Y	Y	N	Y	Y	Y
23 **Canseco**	N	Y	Y	N	Y	Y	Y
24 **Marchant**	N	Y	Y	N	Y	Y	Y
25 Doggett	Y	Y	Y	Y	N	N	N
26 **Burgess**	N	Y	Y	N	N	Y	Y
27 **Farenthold**	N	Y	Y	N	Y	Y	Y
28 Cuellar	Y	Y	Y	N	N	Y	Y
29 Green, G.	+	Y	Y	N	N	N	N
30 Johnson, E.	Y	Y	Y	N	N	N	N
31 **Carter**	Y	Y	Y	N	Y	Y	Y
32 **Sessions**	Y	Y	Y	N	Y	Y	Y
UTAH							
1 **Bishop**	Y	Y	Y	N	Y	Y	Y
2 Matheson	Y	Y	Y	Y	Y	Y	N
3 **Chaffetz**	N	Y	Y	N	N	Y	Y
VERMONT							
AL Welch	Y	Y	Y	Y	N	N	N
VIRGINIA							
1 **Wittman**	Y	Y	Y	N	Y	Y	Y
2 **Rigell**	Y	Y	Y	N	N	Y	Y
3 Scott	Y	Y	Y	Y	N	N	N
4 **Forbes**	N	Y	Y	N	Y	Y	Y
5 **Hurt**	Y	Y	Y	N	Y	Y	Y
6 **Goodlatte**	Y	Y	Y	Y	Y	Y	Y
7 **Cantor**	Y	Y	Y	N	Y	Y	Y
8 Moran	Y	Y	N	Y	N	N	N
9 **Griffith**	Y	Y	Y	N	Y	Y	Y
10 **Wolf**	Y	Y	Y	N	Y	Y	Y
11 Connolly	Y	Y	Y	Y	N	N	N
WASHINGTON							
1 Vacant							
2 Larsen	Y	Y	Y	Y	N	N	N
3 **Herrera Beutler**	Y	Y	Y	Y	Y	Y	Y
4 **Hastings**	Y	Y	Y	N	Y	Y	Y
5 **McMorris Rodgers**	Y	Y	Y	N	Y	Y	Y
6 Dicks	Y	Y	N	N	N	N	N
7 McDermott	Y	Y	N	Y	N	N	N
8 **Reichert**	Y	Y	Y	Y	Y	Y	Y
9 Smith	Y	Y	Y	Y	N	N	N
WEST VIRGINIA							
1 **McKinley**	Y	Y	Y	Y	Y	N	Y
2 **Capito**	Y	Y	Y	N	Y	Y	Y
3 Rahall	Y	Y	Y	Y	N	N	N
WISCONSIN							
1 **Ryan**	N	Y	Y	N	N	Y	Y
2 Baldwin	Y	Y	Y	Y	N	N	N
3 Kind	Y	Y	Y	Y	N	N	N
4 Moore	Y	Y	Y	Y	N	N	N
5 **Sensenbrenner**	N	Y	Y	N	N	Y	Y
6 **Petri**	N	Y	Y	N	Y	Y	Y
7 **Duffy**	Y	Y	Y	N	Y	Y	Y
8 **Ribble**	Y	Y	Y	N	Y	Y	Y
WYOMING							
AL **Lummis**	Y	Y	Y	N	Y	Y	Y

IN THE HOUSE | By Vote Number

231. HR 5326. Fiscal 2013 Commerce-Justice-Science Appropriations/ **Voter Identification Laws.** Schweikert, R-Ariz., amendment that would bar the use of funds in the bill for the Justice Department to litigate against state laws that require voter identification. Adopted in Committee of the Whole 232-190: R 231-7; D 1-183. May 9, 2012.

232. HR 5326. Fiscal 2013 Commerce-Justice-Science Appropriations/ **American Community Survey.** Webster, R-Fla., amendment that would bar the use of funds in the bill for conducting the Commerce Department's American Community Survey, which gathers demographic information to help determine how federal and state funds are distributed each year. Adopted in Committee of the Whole 232-190: R 228-10; D 4-180. May 9, 2012.

233. HR 5326. Fiscal 2013 Commerce-Justice-Science Appropriations/ **Alternative-Fuels Procurement.** Flores, R-Texas, amendment that would bar the use of funds in the bill to enforce a law that prohibits government procurement and acquisition of alternative fuels, including those produced from unconventional petroleum sources, for uses other than research or testing unless the contract certifies that the greenhouse gas emissions generated from producing and burning those fuels are less than or equal to conventional fuel emissions. Adopted in Committee of the Whole 250-173: R 235-3; D 15-170. May 9, 2012.

234 HR 5326. Fiscal 2013 Commerce-Justice-Science Appropriations/ **National Ocean Policy.** Flores, R-Texas, amendment that would bar the use of funds in the bill to implement an executive order calling for a national ocean policy that would protect, maintain and restore the health of ocean, coastal and Great Lakes ecosystems. Adopted in Committee of the Whole 246-174: R 229-8; D 17-166. May 9, 2012.

235. HR 5326. Fiscal 2013 Commerce-Justice-Science Appropriations/ **Defense of Marriage Act.** Huelskamp, R-Kan., amendment that would bar the use of funds in the bill for activities that would violate the Defense of Marriage Act of 1996, which defines marriage as the union of one man and one woman and stipulates that states are not required to grant the benefits of marriage to same-sex couples. Adopted in Committee of the Whole 245-171: R 229-7; D 16-164. A "nay" was a vote in support of the president's position. May 9, 2012.

236. HR 5326. Fiscal 2013 Commerce-Justice-Science Appropriations/ **Sea Turtle Conservation.** Landry, R-La., amendment that would bar the use of funds in the bill to implement a proposed National Oceanic and Atmospheric Administration rule to require all skimmer trawls, pusher-head trawls and wing nets to use turtle-excluder devices. Adopted in Committee of the Whole 218-201: R 208-28; D 10-173. May 9, 2012.

237. HR 5326. Fiscal 2013 Commerce-Justice-Science Appropriations/ **NOAA Fisheries Enforcement Asset Forfeiture Fund.** Gardner, R-Colo., amendment that would bar the use of funds in the bill to pay the salary of any Commerce Department officer or employee who uses money in the National Oceanic and Atmospheric Administration's Fisheries Enforcement Asset Forfeiture Fund for activities not specifically authorized by law. Adopted in Committee of the Whole 357-68: R 239-1; D 118-67. May 9, 2012.

	231	232	233	234	235	236	237
ALABAMA							
1 Bonner	Y	Y	Y	Y	Y	Y	Y
2 Roby	Y	Y	Y	Y	Y	Y	Y
3 Rogers	Y	Y	Y	Y	Y	Y	Y
4 Aderholt	Y	Y	Y	Y	Y	Y	Y
5 Brooks	Y	Y	Y	Y	Y	Y	Y
6 Bachus	?	?	?	?	Y	Y	Y
7 Sewell	N	N	N	N	N	N	Y
ALASKA							
AL Young	Y	Y	Y	Y	Y	Y	Y
ARIZONA							
1 Gosar	Y	Y	Y	Y	Y	Y	Y
2 Franks	Y	Y	Y	Y	Y	+	Y
3 Quayle	Y	Y	Y	+	Y	Y	Y
4 Pastor	N	N	N	N	N	N	N
5 Schweikert	Y	Y	Y	Y	Y	Y	Y
6 Flake	Y	Y	Y	Y	Y	Y	Y
7 Grijalva	N	N	N	N	N	N	N
8 Vacant							
ARKANSAS							
1 Crawford	Y	Y	Y	Y	Y	Y	Y
2 Griffin	Y	Y	Y	Y	Y	Y	Y
3 Womack	Y	Y	Y	Y	Y	Y	Y
4 Ross	N	N	Y	Y	Y	Y	Y
CALIFORNIA							
1 Thompson	N	N	N	N	N	N	N
2 Herger	Y	Y	Y	Y	Y	Y	Y
3 Lungren	Y	Y	Y	Y	Y	Y	Y
4 McClintock	Y	Y	Y	Y	Y	Y	Y
5 Matsui	N	N	N	N	N	N	Y
6 Woolsey	N	N	N	N	N	N	N
7 Miller, George	N	N	N	N	N	N	N
8 Pelosi	N	N	N	N	N	N	Y
9 Lee	N	N	N	N	N	N	N
10 Garamendi	N	N	N	N	N	N	N
11 McNerney	N	N	N	N	N	N	Y
12 Speier	N	N	N	N	N	N	N
13 Stark	N	N	N	N	N	N	N
14 Eshoo	N	N	N	N	N	N	N
15 Honda	N	N	N	N	N	N	Y
16 Lofgren	N	N	N	N	N	N	N
17 Farr	N	N	N	N	N	N	N
18 Cardoza	N	N	N	N	N	N	N
19 Denham	Y	Y	Y	Y	Y	Y	Y
20 Costa	N	N	N	N	N	N	Y
21 Nunes	Y	Y	Y	Y	Y	Y	Y
22 McCarthy	Y	Y	Y	Y	Y	Y	Y
23 Capps	N	N	N	N	N	N	Y
24 Gallegly	Y	Y	Y	Y	Y	Y	Y
25 McKeon	Y	Y	Y	Y	Y	Y	Y
26 Dreier	Y	Y	Y	Y	Y	Y	Y
27 Sherman	N	N	N	N	N	N	N
28 Berman	N	N	N	N	N	?	N
29 Schiff	N	N	N	N	N	N	Y
30 Waxman	N	N	N	N	N	N	N
31 Becerra	N	N	N	N	N	N	Y
32 Chu	N	N	N	N	N	N	Y
33 Bass	N	N	N	N	N	N	Y
34 Roybal-Allard	N	N	N	N	N	N	Y
35 Waters	N	N	N	N	N	?	N
36 Hahn	N	N	N	N	N	N	N
37 Richardson	N	N	N	?	N	N	N
38 Napolitano	N	N	N	?	N	N	Y
39 Sánchez, Linda	N	N	N	N	N	N	N
40 Royce	Y	Y	Y	Y	Y	Y	Y
41 Lewis	Y	Y	Y	Y	N	Y	Y
42 Miller, Gary	Y	Y	Y	Y	Y	Y	Y
43 Baca	N	N	N	N	N	N	Y
44 Calvert	Y	Y	Y	Y	Y	Y	Y
45 Bono Mack	Y	Y	Y	Y	N	Y	Y
46 Rohrabacher	Y	Y	Y	Y	Y	Y	Y
47 Sanchez, Loretta	N	N	N	N	N	N	Y
48 Campbell	Y	Y	Y	Y	Y	Y	Y
49 Issa	Y	Y	Y	Y	Y	Y	Y
50 Bilbray	Y	N	N	Y	Y	N	Y
51 Filner	-	-	-	-	-	-	-
52 Hunter	Y	Y	Y	Y	Y	Y	Y
53 Davis	N	N	N	N	N	N	N
COLORADO							
1 DeGette	N	N	N	N	N	N	Y
2 Polis	N	N	N	N	N	N	Y
3 Tipton	Y	Y	Y	Y	Y	Y	Y
4 Gardner	Y	Y	Y	Y	Y	Y	Y
5 Lamborn	Y	Y	Y	Y	Y	Y	Y
6 Coffman	Y	Y	Y	Y	Y	Y	Y
7 Perlmutter	N	N	N	N	N	N	Y
CONNECTICUT							
1 Larson	N	N	N	N	N	N	Y
2 Courtney	N	N	N	N	N	N	Y
3 DeLauro	N	N	N	N	N	N	Y
4 Himes	N	N	N	N	N	N	Y
5 Murphy	N	N	N	N	N	N	Y
DELAWARE							
AL Carney	N	N	N	N	N	N	Y
FLORIDA							
1 Miller	Y	Y	Y	Y	Y	Y	Y
2 Southerland	Y	Y	Y	Y	Y	Y	Y
3 Brown	N	N	N	N	N	N	N
4 Crenshaw	Y	Y	Y	Y	Y	Y	Y
5 Nugent	Y	Y	Y	Y	Y	Y	Y
6 Stearns	Y	Y	Y	N	Y	Y	Y
7 Mica	Y	Y	Y	Y	Y	Y	Y
8 Webster	Y	Y	Y	Y	Y	Y	Y
9 Bilirakis	Y	Y	Y	Y	Y	Y	Y
10 Young	Y	Y	Y	Y	Y	Y	Y
11 Castor	N	N	N	N	N	N	Y
12 Ross	Y	Y	Y	Y	Y	Y	Y
13 Buchanan	Y	Y	Y	Y	Y	Y	Y
14 Mack	Y	Y	Y	Y	Y	Y	Y
15 Posey	Y	Y	Y	Y	Y	Y	Y
16 Rooney	Y	Y	Y	Y	Y	Y	Y
17 Wilson	N	N	N	?	N	N	Y
18 Ros-Lehtinen	Y	Y	Y	Y	N	Y	Y
19 Deutch	N	N	N	N	N	N	N
20 Wasserman Schultz	N	N	N	N	N	N	N
21 Diaz-Balart	Y	Y	Y	Y	Y	Y	Y
22 West	Y	Y	Y	Y	Y	Y	Y
23 Hastings	N	N	N	N	N	N	N
24 Adams	Y	Y	Y	Y	Y	Y	Y
25 Rivera	Y	Y	Y	Y	Y	N	Y
GEORGIA							
1 Kingston	Y	Y	Y	Y	Y	Y	Y
2 Bishop	N	N	N	N	Y	N	Y
3 Westmoreland	Y	Y	Y	Y	Y	Y	Y
4 Johnson	N	N	N	N	N	N	N
5 Lewis	N	N	N	N	N	N	Y
6 Price	Y	Y	Y	Y	Y	Y	Y
7 Woodall	Y	Y	Y	Y	Y	Y	Y
8 Scott, A.	Y	Y	Y	Y	Y	Y	Y
9 Graves	Y	Y	Y	Y	Y	Y	Y
10 Broun	Y	Y	Y	Y	Y	Y	Y
11 Gingrey	Y	Y	Y	Y	Y	Y	Y
12 Barrow	N	N	N	N	N	N	Y
13 Scott, D.	N	N	N	N	N	N	N
HAWAII							
1 Hanabusa	N	N	N	N	N	N	Y
2 Hirono	N	N	N	N	N	N	N
IDAHO							
1 Labrador	Y	Y	Y	Y	Y	Y	Y
2 Simpson	Y	Y	Y	Y	Y	Y	Y
ILLINOIS							
1 Rush	N	N	N	N	N	N	N
2 Jackson	N	N	N	N	N	N	N
3 Lipinski	N	N	N	N	Y	N	N
4 Gutierrez	N	N	N	N	N	N	Y
5 Quigley	N	N	N	N	N	N	Y
6 Roskam	Y	Y	Y	Y	Y	Y	Y
7 Davis	N	N	N	N	N	N	N
8 Walsh	Y	Y	Y	Y	Y	Y	Y
9 Schakowsky	N	N	N	N	N	N	N
10 Dold	Y	Y	Y	Y	N	Y	Y
11 Kinzinger	Y	Y	Y	Y	Y	Y	Y
12 Costello	N	N	Y	N	Y	N	Y
13 Biggert	N	N	Y	N	Y	Y	Y
14 Hultgren	Y	Y	Y	Y	Y	Y	Y
15 Johnson	Y	Y	N	Y	N	Y	Y

KEY   Republicans   Democrats

Y	Voted for (yea)	X	Paired against	C	Voted "present" to avoid possible conflict of interest
#	Paired for	-	Announced against		
+	Announced for	P	Voted "present"	?	Did not vote or otherwise make a position known
N	Voted against (nay)				

	231	232	233	234	235	236	237
16 **Manzullo**	Y	Y	Y	Y	Y	Y	Y
17 **Schilling**	Y	Y	Y	Y	Y	Y	Y
18 **Schock**	Y	Y	Y	Y	Y	Y	Y
19 **Shimkus**	Y	Y	Y	Y	Y	Y	Y
INDIANA							
1 Visclosky	N	N	N	N	N	N	N
2 Donnelly	?	?	?	?	?	?	?
3 **Stutzman**	Y	Y	Y	Y	Y	Y	Y
4 **Rokita**	Y	Y	Y	Y	Y	Y	Y
5 **Burton**	Y	Y	Y	Y	Y	Y	Y
6 **Pence**	Y	Y	Y	Y	Y	Y	Y
7 Carson	N	N	N	N	N	N	N
8 **Bucshon**	Y	Y	Y	Y	Y	Y	Y
9 **Young**	Y	Y	Y	Y	Y	Y	Y
IOWA							
1 Braley	N	N	N	N	?	N	Y
2 Loebsack	N	N	N	N	N	N	Y
3 Boswell	N	N	N	N	N	N	Y
4 **Latham**	Y	Y	Y	Y	Y	Y	Y
5 **King**	Y	Y	Y	Y	Y	Y	Y
KANSAS							
1 **Huelskamp**	Y	Y	Y	Y	Y	Y	Y
2 **Jenkins**	Y	Y	Y	Y	Y	Y	Y
3 **Yoder**	Y	Y	Y	Y	Y	Y	Y
4 **Pompeo**	Y	Y	Y	Y	Y	Y	Y
KENTUCKY							
1 **Whitfield**	Y	Y	Y	Y	Y	N	Y
2 **Guthrie**	Y	Y	N	Y	Y	Y	Y
3 Yarmuth	N	N	N	N	?	N	Y
4 **Davis**	Y	Y	Y	Y	Y	Y	Y
5 **Rogers**	Y	Y	Y	Y	Y	Y	Y
6 Chandler	N	N	Y	N	Y	N	Y
LOUISIANA							
1 **Scalise**	Y	Y	Y	Y	Y	Y	Y
2 Richmond	N	N	N	N	N	N	Y
3 **Landry**	Y	Y	Y	Y	Y	Y	Y
4 **Fleming**	Y	Y	Y	Y	Y	Y	Y
5 **Alexander**	Y	Y	Y	Y	Y	Y	Y
6 **Cassidy**	Y	Y	Y	Y	Y	Y	Y
7 **Boustany**	Y	Y	Y	Y	Y	Y	Y
MAINE							
1 Pingree	N	N	N	N	N	N	Y
2 Michaud	N	N	N	N	N	N	Y
MARYLAND							
1 **Harris**	Y	Y	Y	Y	Y	Y	Y
2 Ruppersberger	N	N	N	N	N	N	Y
3 Sarbanes	N	N	N	N	N	N	Y
4 Edwards	N	N	N	N	N	N	N
5 Hoyer	N	N	N	N	N	N	Y
6 **Bartlett**	Y	Y	Y	Y	Y	Y	Y
7 Cummings	N	N	N	N	N	N	N
8 Van Hollen	N	N	N	N	N	N	Y
MASSACHUSETTS							
1 Olver	N	?	N	N	N	N	N
2 Neal	N	N	N	N	N	N	Y
3 McGovern	N	N	N	N	N	N	Y
4 Frank	N	N	N	N	N	N	Y
5 Tsongas	N	N	N	N	N	N	Y
6 Tierney	N	N	N	N	N	N	Y
7 Markey	N	N	N	N	N	N	Y
8 Capuano	N	N	N	N	N	N	Y
9 Lynch	N	N	N	N	N	N	Y
10 Keating	N	N	N	N	N	N	Y
MICHIGAN							
1 **Benishek**	Y	Y	Y	Y	Y	Y	Y
2 **Huizenga**	Y	Y	Y	Y	Y	Y	Y
3 **Amash**	N	Y	Y	Y	Y	Y	Y
4 **Camp**	Y	Y	Y	Y	Y	Y	Y
5 Kildee	N	N	N	N	N	N	Y
6 **Upton**	Y	Y	Y	Y	Y	N	Y
7 **Walberg**	Y	Y	Y	Y	Y	Y	Y
8 **Rogers**	Y	Y	Y	Y	Y	Y	Y
9 Peters	N	N	N	N	N	N	Y
10 **Miller**	Y	Y	Y	Y	Y	Y	Y
11 **McCotter**	Y	Y	Y	Y	Y	Y	Y
12 Levin	N	N	N	N	N	N	Y
13 Clarke	N	N	N	N	N	N	Y
14 Conyers	N	N	N	N	N	N	N
15 Dingell	N	N	N	N	N	N	Y
MINNESOTA							
1 Walz	N	N	N	N	N	N	N
2 **Kline**	Y	Y	Y	Y	Y	Y	Y
3 **Paulsen**	Y	Y	Y	Y	Y	Y	Y
4 McCollum	N	N	N	N	N	N	N

	231	232	233	234	235	236	237
5 Ellison	N	N	N	N	N	N	N
6 **Bachmann**	+	+	+	+	Y	Y	Y
7 Peterson	N	N	N	Y	Y	Y	Y
8 **Cravaack**	Y	Y	Y	Y	Y	Y	Y
MISSISSIPPI							
1 **Nunnelee**	Y	Y	Y	Y	Y	Y	Y
2 Thompson	N	N	N	N	N	N	N
3 **Harper**	Y	Y	Y	Y	Y	Y	Y
4 **Palazzo**	Y	Y	Y	Y	Y	Y	Y
MISSOURI							
1 Clay	N	N	N	N	N	N	N
2 **Akin**	Y	Y	Y	Y	Y	Y	Y
3 Carnahan	N	N	N	N	–	N	Y
4 **Hartzler**	Y	Y	Y	Y	Y	Y	Y
5 Cleaver	N	N	N	N	N	N	N
6 **Graves**	Y	Y	Y	Y	Y	Y	Y
7 **Long**	Y	Y	Y	Y	Y	Y	Y
8 **Emerson**	Y	Y	Y	Y	Y	Y	Y
9 **Luetkemeyer**	Y	Y	Y	Y	Y	Y	Y
MONTANA							
AL **Rehberg**	Y	Y	Y	Y	Y	Y	Y
NEBRASKA							
1 **Fortenberry**	Y	Y	Y	Y	Y	N	Y
2 **Terry**	Y	Y	Y	Y	N	N	Y
3 **Smith**	Y	Y	Y	Y	Y	Y	Y
NEVADA							
1 Berkley	N	N	N	N	N	N	Y
2 **Amodei**	Y	Y	Y	Y	Y	Y	Y
3 **Heck**	Y	Y	Y	Y	Y	Y	Y
NEW HAMPSHIRE							
1 **Guinta**	Y	Y	Y	Y	Y	Y	Y
2 **Bass**	Y	Y	Y	N	Y	Y	Y
NEW JERSEY							
1 Andrews	N	N	N	N	N	N	N
2 **LoBiondo**	Y	Y	Y	Y	Y	N	Y
3 **Runyan**	Y	Y	Y	Y	Y	Y	Y
4 **Smith**	Y	Y	Y	Y	Y	N	Y
5 **Garrett**	Y	Y	Y	Y	Y	Y	Y
6 Pallone	N	N	N	N	N	N	Y
7 **Lance**	Y	Y	Y	Y	Y	Y	Y
8 Pascrell	N	N	N	N	N	N	Y
9 Rothman	N	N	N	N	N	N	Y
10 Vacant							
11 **Frelinghuysen**	Y	Y	Y	Y	Y	Y	Y
12 Holt	N	N	N	N	N	N	Y
13 Sires	N	N	N	N	N	N	N
NEW MEXICO							
1 Heinrich	N	N	N	N	N	N	Y
2 **Pearce**	Y	Y	Y	Y	Y	Y	Y
3 Luján	N	N	N	N	N	N	Y
NEW YORK							
1 Bishop	N	N	N	Y	N	N	Y
2 Israel	N	N	N	N	N	N	Y
3 **King**	Y	Y	Y	Y	Y	Y	Y
4 McCarthy	N	N	N	N	N	N	Y
5 Ackerman	N	N	N	N	N	N	N
6 Meeks	N	N	N	N	?	?	?
7 Crowley	N	N	N	N	N	N	N
8 Nadler	N	N	N	N	N	N	N
9 **Turner**	Y	Y	Y	Y	Y	Y	Y
10 Towns	N	N	N	N	N	N	N
11 Clarke	N	N	N	N	N	N	N
12 Velázquez	N	N	N	N	N	N	N
13 **Grimm**	Y	Y	Y	Y	Y	N	Y
14 Maloney	N	N	N	N	N	N	Y
15 Rangel	N	N	N	N	N	N	N
16 Serrano	N	N	N	N	N	N	N
17 Engel	N	N	N	N	N	N	Y
18 Lowey	N	N	N	N	N	N	Y
19 **Hayworth**	N	N	Y	N	N	N	Y
20 **Gibson**	N	N	Y	Y	N	Y	Y
21 Tonko	N	N	N	N	N	N	Y
22 Hinchey	N	N	N	N	N	N	N
23 Owens	N	N	N	Y	N	N	Y
24 **Hanna**	Y	Y	Y	Y	N	N	Y
25 **Buerkle**	Y	Y	Y	Y	Y	N	Y
26 Hochul	N	Y	N	Y	N	Y	Y
27 Higgins	N	N	N	N	N	N	Y
28 Slaughter	–	–	–	–	–	–	+
29 **Reed**	Y	Y	Y	Y	Y	Y	Y
NORTH CAROLINA							
1 Butterfield	N	N	N	N	N	N	N
2 **Ellmers**	Y	Y	Y	Y	Y	Y	Y
3 **Jones**	Y	Y	Y	N	Y	Y	Y
4 Price	N	N	N	N	N	N	N

	231	232	233	234	235	236	237
5 **Foxx**	Y	Y	Y	Y	Y	Y	Y
6 **Coble**	Y	Y	Y	Y	Y	Y	Y
7 McIntyre	N	N	N	N	Y	Y	Y
8 Kissell	N	Y	Y	Y	Y	Y	Y
9 **Myrick**	Y	Y	Y	Y	Y	Y	Y
10 **McHenry**	Y	N	Y	Y	Y	Y	Y
11 Shuler	N	N	N	Y	Y	Y	Y
12 Watt	N	N	N	N	N	N	N
13 Miller	?	N	N	N	N	N	N
NORTH DAKOTA							
AL **Berg**	Y	Y	Y	Y	Y	Y	Y
OHIO							
1 **Chabot**	Y	Y	Y	Y	Y	Y	Y
2 **Schmidt**	?	?	?	?	Y	Y	Y
3 **Turner**	Y	N	Y	Y	Y	Y	Y
4 **Jordan**	Y	Y	Y	Y	Y	Y	Y
5 **Latta**	Y	Y	Y	Y	Y	Y	Y
6 **Johnson**	Y	Y	Y	Y	Y	?	Y
7 **Austria**	Y	Y	Y	Y	Y	Y	Y
8 **Boehner**							
9 Kaptur	N	N	N	N	N	N	Y
10 Kucinich	?	?	?	?	?	?	?
11 Fudge	N	N	N	N	N	N	N
12 **Tiberi**	Y	Y	Y	Y	Y	N	Y
13 Sutton	N	N	N	N	N	N	Y
14 **LaTourette**	Y	Y	Y	N	N	N	N
15 **Stivers**	Y	Y	Y	Y	Y	Y	Y
16 **Renacci**	Y	Y	Y	Y	Y	Y	Y
17 Ryan	N	N	Y	N	N	N	Y
18 **Gibbs**	Y	Y	Y	Y	Y	Y	Y
OKLAHOMA							
1 **Sullivan**	Y	Y	Y	Y	Y	?	Y
2 Boren	N	Y	Y	Y	Y	Y	Y
3 **Lucas**	Y	Y	Y	Y	Y	Y	Y
4 **Cole**	Y	Y	Y	Y	Y	Y	Y
5 **Lankford**	Y	Y	Y	Y	Y	Y	Y
OREGON							
1 Bonamici	N	N	N	N	N	N	N
2 **Walden**	Y	Y	Y	Y	Y	N	Y
3 Blumenauer	N	N	N	N	N	N	Y
4 DeFazio	N	N	N	N	N	N	Y
5 Schrader	N	N	N	N	N	N	Y
PENNSYLVANIA							
1 Brady	N	N	N	N	N	N	Y
2 Fattah	N	N	N	N	N	N	N
3 **Kelly**	Y	Y	Y	Y	Y	Y	Y
4 Altmire	Y	N	Y	Y	N	N	Y
5 **Thompson**	Y	N	Y	Y	Y	Y	Y
6 **Gerlach**	Y	N	Y	Y	Y	N	Y
7 **Meehan**	N	Y	Y	Y	Y	Y	Y
8 **Fitzpatrick**	Y	Y	Y	N	Y	N	Y
9 **Shuster**	Y	Y	Y	Y	Y	Y	Y
10 **Marino**	Y	Y	Y	Y	Y	Y	Y
11 **Barletta**	Y	Y	Y	Y	Y	Y	Y
12 Critz	N	N	Y	Y	Y	N	Y
13 Schwartz	N	N	N	N	N	N	Y
14 Doyle	N	N	Y	N	N	N	Y
15 **Dent**	Y	N	Y	Y	Y	N	Y
16 **Pitts**	Y	Y	Y	Y	Y	Y	Y
17 Holden	N	N	Y	Y	Y	N	Y
18 **Murphy**	Y	Y	Y	Y	Y	N	Y
19 **Platts**	Y	Y	Y	Y	Y	N	Y
RHODE ISLAND							
1 Cicilline	N	N	N	N	N	N	Y
2 Langevin	N	N	N	N	?	N	Y
SOUTH CAROLINA							
1 **Scott**	Y	Y	Y	Y	Y	Y	Y
2 **Wilson**	Y	Y	Y	Y	Y	Y	Y
3 **Duncan**	Y	Y	Y	Y	Y	Y	Y
4 **Gowdy**	Y	Y	Y	Y	Y	Y	Y
5 **Mulvaney**	Y	Y	Y	Y	Y	Y	Y
6 Clyburn	N	N	N	N	N	N	Y
SOUTH DAKOTA							
AL **Noem**	Y	Y	Y	Y	Y	Y	Y
TENNESSEE							
1 **Roe**	Y	Y	Y	Y	Y	Y	Y
2 **Duncan**	Y	Y	Y	Y	Y	Y	Y
3 **Fleischmann**	Y	Y	Y	Y	Y	Y	Y
4 **DesJarlais**	Y	Y	Y	Y	Y	Y	Y
5 Cooper	N	N	N	N	N	N	Y
6 **Black**	Y	Y	Y	Y	Y	Y	Y
7 **Blackburn**	Y	Y	Y	Y	Y	Y	Y
8 **Fincher**	Y	Y	Y	Y	Y	Y	Y
9 Cohen	N	N	N	N	N	N	N

	231	232	233	234	235	236	237
TEXAS							
1 **Gohmert**	Y	Y	Y	Y	Y	Y	Y
2 **Poe**	Y	Y	Y	Y	Y	Y	Y
3 **Johnson, S.**	Y	Y	Y	Y	Y	Y	Y
4 **Hall**	Y	Y	Y	Y	Y	Y	Y
5 **Hensarling**	Y	Y	Y	Y	Y	Y	Y
6 **Barton**	Y	Y	Y	Y	Y	Y	Y
7 **Culberson**	Y	Y	Y	Y	Y	Y	Y
8 **Brady**	Y	Y	Y	Y	Y	Y	Y
9 Green, A.	N	N	N	Y	N	N	Y
10 **McCaul**	Y	Y	Y	Y	?	?	Y
11 **Conaway**	Y	Y	Y	Y	Y	Y	Y
12 **Granger**	Y	Y	Y	Y	Y	Y	Y
13 **Thornberry**	Y	Y	Y	Y	Y	Y	Y
14 **Paul**	Y	Y	Y	Y	Y	Y	Y
15 Hinojosa	N	N	N	N	N	N	Y
16 Reyes	N	N	N	N	N	N	Y
17 **Flores**	Y	Y	Y	Y	Y	Y	Y
18 Jackson Lee	N	N	N	N	N	N	Y
19 **Neugebauer**	Y	Y	Y	Y	Y	Y	Y
20 Gonzalez	N	N	N	N	N	N	N
21 **Smith**	Y	Y	Y	Y	Y	Y	Y
22 **Olson**	Y	Y	Y	Y	Y	Y	Y
23 **Canseco**	Y	Y	Y	Y	Y	Y	Y
24 **Marchant**	Y	Y	Y	Y	Y	Y	Y
25 Doggett	N	N	N	N	N	N	Y
26 **Burgess**	Y	Y	Y	Y	Y	Y	Y
27 **Farenthold**	Y	Y	Y	Y	Y	Y	Y
28 Cuellar	N	N	Y	Y	Y	N	Y
29 Green, G.	N	Y	Y	Y	N	N	Y
30 Johnson, E.	N	N	N	N	N	N	Y
31 **Carter**	Y	Y	Y	Y	Y	Y	Y
32 **Sessions**	Y	Y	Y	Y	Y	Y	Y
UTAH							
1 **Bishop**	Y	Y	Y	?	Y	Y	Y
2 Matheson	N	N	Y	Y	Y	Y	Y
3 **Chaffetz**	Y	Y	Y	Y	Y	Y	Y
VERMONT							
AL Welch	?	?	?	?	N	N	N
VIRGINIA							
1 **Wittman**	Y	Y	Y	Y	Y	Y	Y
2 **Rigell**	N	Y	Y	Y	Y	Y	Y
3 Scott	N	N	N	N	N	N	N
4 **Forbes**	N	Y	Y	Y	Y	Y	Y
5 **Hurt**	Y	Y	Y	Y	Y	Y	Y
6 **Goodlatte**	Y	Y	Y	Y	Y	Y	Y
7 **Cantor**	Y	Y	Y	Y	?	?	?
8 Moran	N	N	N	N	N	N	Y
9 **Griffith**	Y	Y	Y	Y	Y	N	Y
10 **Wolf**	Y	Y	Y	Y	Y	Y	Y
11 Connolly	N	N	N	N	?	N	Y
WASHINGTON							
1 Vacant							
2 Larsen	N	N	N	N	N	N	Y
3 **Herrera Beutler**	Y	Y	Y	Y	Y	Y	Y
4 **Hastings**	Y	Y	Y	Y	Y	Y	Y
5 **McMorris Rodgers**	Y	Y	Y	Y	Y	Y	Y
6 Dicks	N	N	N	N	N	N	Y
7 McDermott	N	N	N	N	N	N	Y
8 **Reichert**	Y	Y	Y	Y	?	Y	Y
9 Smith	N	N	N	N	N	N	Y
WEST VIRGINIA							
1 **McKinley**	Y	Y	Y	Y	Y	Y	Y
2 **Capito**	Y	Y	Y	Y	Y	N	Y
3 Rahall	N	N	Y	Y	Y	N	Y
WISCONSIN							
1 **Ryan**	Y	Y	Y	Y	Y	Y	Y
2 Baldwin	N	N	N	N	N	N	N
3 Kind	N	N	N	N	N	N	Y
4 Moore	N	N	N	N	N	N	N
5 **Sensenbrenner**	Y	Y	Y	Y	Y	Y	Y
6 **Petri**	Y	Y	Y	Y	Y	Y	Y
7 **Duffy**	Y	Y	Y	Y	Y	Y	Y
8 **Ribble**	Y	Y	Y	Y	Y	Y	Y
WYOMING							
AL **Lummis**	Y	Y	Y	Y	?	Y	Y

IN THE HOUSE | By Vote Number

238. HR 5326. Fiscal 2013 Commerce-Justice-Science Appropriations/ **State Medical-Marijuana Laws.** Rohrabacher, R-Calif., amendment that would bar the Justice Department from using funds provided in the bill to prevent certain states and the District of Columbia from implementing laws authorizing the use, distribution, possession or cultivation of medical marijuana. Rejected in Committee of the Whole 163-262: R 28-212; D 135-50. May 9, 2012.

239. HR 5326. Fiscal 2013 Commerce-Justice-Science Appropriations/ **Justice Department Antitrust Regional Field Offices.** Lewis, D-Ga., amendment that would bar the use of funds in the bill to close the Justice Department's antitrust division regional field offices. Rejected in Committee of the Whole 189-235: R 12-227; D 177-8. May 9, 2012.

240. HR 5326. Fiscal 2013 Commerce-Justice-Science Appropriations/ **Discrimination Laws.** Holt, D-N.J., amendment that would bar the Justice Department from using funds in the bill for activities that would violate the Fifth and Fourteenth amendments to the U.S. Constitution as well as laws against unlawful police practices and discrimination on the basis of race, sex, ethnicity or religion. Rejected in Committee of the Whole 193-232: R 16-224; D 177-8. May 9, 2012.

241. HR 5326. Fiscal 2013 Commerce-Justice-Science Appropriations/ **Climate Change Education.** Cravaack, R-Minn., amendment that would bar the use of funds in the bill to carry out the National Science Foundation's Climate Change Education Partnership program. Adopted in Committee of the Whole 238-188: R 230-10; D 8-178. May 9, 2012.

242. HR 5326. Fiscal 2013 Commerce-Justice-Science Appropriations/ **Business Investments.** Flake, R-Ariz., amendment that would bar the use of funds in the bill for the Commerce Department's SelectUSA program, which coordinates and helps direct foreign business investments in the United States. Rejected in Committee of the Whole 209-217: R 206-34; D 3-183. May 9, 2012.

243. HR 5326. Fiscal 2013 Commerce-Justice-Science Appropriations/ **NSF Political Science Program.** Flake, R-Ariz., amendment that would bar the use of funds in the bill to carry out the National Science Foundation's Political Science Program, which supports scientific research that advances knowledge and understanding of citizenship, government and politics. Adopted in Committee of the Whole 218-208: R 213-27; D 5-181. May 9, 2012.

244. HR 5652. Budget Sequestration Replacement/Previous **Question.** Woodall, R-Ga., motion to order the previous question (thus ending debate and the possibility of amendment) on the rule (H Res 648) that would provide for House floor consideration of the bill that would replace the $98 billion in automatic discretionary spending cuts scheduled to go into effect in January 2013 with a $19 billion reduction in the discretionary cap for fiscal 2013 and with reconciliation savings that would cut about $310 billion over a decade from mandatory spending. Motion agreed to 237-177: R 232-0; D 5-177. May 10, 2012.

	238	239	240	241	242	243	244
ALABAMA							
1 **Bonner**	N	N	N	Y	N	Y	Y
2 **Roby**	N	N	N	Y	Y	Y	Y
3 **Rogers**	N	N	N	Y	Y	Y	Y
4 **Aderholt**	N	N	N	Y	N	N	Y
5 **Brooks**	N	N	N	Y	Y	Y	Y
6 **Bachus**	N	N	N	Y	Y	Y	Y
7 Sewell	N	Y	Y	N	N	N	N
ALASKA							
AL **Young**	Y	N	N	Y	N	Y	?
ARIZONA							
1 **Gosar**	N	N	N	Y	Y	Y	Y
2 **Franks**	N	N	N	Y	Y	Y	Y
3 **Quayle**	N	N	N	Y	Y	Y	Y
4 **Pastor**	N	Y	Y	N	N	N	N
5 **Schweikert**	N	N	N	Y	Y	Y	Y
6 **Flake**	Y	N	N	Y	Y	Y	Y
7 **Grijalva**	Y	Y	Y	N	N	N	N
8 **Vacant**							
ARKANSAS							
1 **Crawford**	N	N	N	Y	Y	Y	Y
2 **Griffin**	N	N	N	Y	Y	Y	Y
3 **Womack**	N	N	N	Y	Y	Y	Y
4 Ross	N	Y	Y	Y	N	N	Y
CALIFORNIA							
1 Thompson	Y	Y	Y	N	N	N	N
2 **Herger**	N	N	N	Y	Y	Y	Y
3 **Lungren**	N	N	N	Y	Y	Y	Y
4 **McClintock**	Y	N	N	Y	Y	Y	Y
5 Matsui	Y	Y	Y	N	N	N	N
6 Woolsey	Y	Y	Y	N	N	N	N
7 Miller, George	Y	Y	Y	N	N	N	N
8 Pelosi	Y	Y	Y	N	N	N	N
9 Lee	Y	Y	Y	N	N	N	N
10 Garamendi	Y	Y	N	N	N	N	N
11 McNerney	Y	Y	Y	N	N	N	N
12 Speier	Y	Y	Y	N	N	N	N
13 Stark	Y	Y	Y	N	N	N	N
14 Eshoo	Y	Y	Y	N	N	N	N
15 Honda	Y	Y	Y	N	N	N	N
16 Lofgren	Y	Y	Y	N	N	N	N
17 Farr	Y	Y	Y	N	N	N	N
18 Cardoza	N	Y	Y	N	N	N	N
19 **Denham**	N	N	N	Y	Y	Y	Y
20 Costa	N	Y	Y	N	N	N	N
21 **Nunes**	N	N	N	Y	Y	Y	Y
22 **McCarthy**	N	N	N	Y	Y	Y	Y
23 Capps	Y	Y	Y	N	N	N	N
24 **Gallegly**	N	N	N	Y	Y	Y	Y
25 **McKeon**	N	N	N	Y	Y	Y	Y
26 **Dreier**	N	N	N	Y	N	Y	Y
27 Sherman	Y	Y	Y	N	N	N	N
28 Berman	Y	Y	Y	N	N	N	N
29 Schiff	Y	Y	Y	N	N	N	N
30 Waxman	Y	Y	Y	N	N	N	N
31 Becerra	Y	Y	Y	N	N	N	N
32 Chu	Y	Y	Y	N	N	N	N
33 Bass	Y	Y	Y	N	N	N	N
34 Roybal-Allard	Y	Y	Y	N	N	N	N
35 Waters	N	Y	Y	N	N	N	?
36 Hahn	Y	Y	Y	N	N	N	N
37 Richardson	Y	Y	Y	N	N	N	N
38 Napolitano	Y	Y	Y	N	N	N	N
39 Sánchez, Linda	Y	Y	Y	N	N	N	N
40 **Royce**	Y	N	N	Y	Y	Y	Y
41 **Lewis**	N	N	N	Y	Y	Y	Y
42 **Miller, Gary**	N	N	N	Y	Y	Y	Y
43 Baca	N	Y	Y	N	N	N	N
44 **Calvert**	N	N	N	Y	Y	Y	Y
45 **Bono Mack**	N	N	N	Y	Y	Y	Y
46 **Rohrabacher**	Y	N	N	Y	Y	Y	Y
47 Sanchez, Loretta	Y	Y	Y	N	N	N	N
48 **Campbell**	Y	N	N	Y	Y	Y	Y
49 **Issa**	N	N	N	Y	Y	Y	Y
50 **Bilbray**	N	N	N	Y	Y	Y	Y
51 Filner	+	+	+	–	–	–	–
52 **Hunter**	N	N	N	Y	Y	Y	Y
53 Davis	Y	Y	Y	N	N	N	N

	238	239	240	241	242	243	244
COLORADO							
1 DeGette	Y	Y	Y	N	N	N	N
2 Polis	Y	Y	Y	N	N	N	N
3 **Tipton**	N	N	Y	Y	Y	N	Y
4 **Gardner**	N	N	N	Y	Y	Y	Y
5 **Lamborn**	N	N	N	Y	Y	Y	Y
6 **Coffman**	N	N	N	Y	Y	Y	Y
7 Perlmutter	Y	Y	Y	N	N	N	N
CONNECTICUT							
1 Larson	Y	Y	Y	N	N	N	N
2 Courtney	Y	Y	Y	N	N	N	N
3 DeLauro	Y	Y	Y	N	N	N	N
4 Himes	Y	Y	Y	N	N	N	N
5 Murphy	Y	Y	Y	N	N	N	N
DELAWARE							
AL Carney	Y	Y	Y	N	N	Y	N
FLORIDA							
1 **Miller**	N	N	N	Y	Y	Y	Y
2 **Southerland**	N	N	N	Y	Y	Y	Y
3 Brown	N	Y	Y	N	N	N	N
4 **Crenshaw**	N	N	N	Y	Y	Y	Y
5 **Nugent**	N	N	N	Y	Y	Y	Y
6 **Stearns**	N	N	N	Y	Y	Y	Y
7 **Mica**	N	N	N	Y	Y	Y	Y
8 **Webster**	N	N	N	Y	Y	Y	Y
9 **Bilirakis**	N	N	N	Y	Y	Y	Y
10 **Young**	N	Y	N	Y	Y	Y	Y
11 Castor	Y	Y	Y	N	N	N	N
12 **Ross**	N	N	N	Y	Y	Y	Y
13 **Buchanan**	N	N	N	Y	Y	Y	Y
14 **Mack**	N	N	N	Y	Y	Y	?
15 **Posey**	N	N	N	Y	Y	Y	Y
16 **Rooney**	N	N	N	Y	Y	Y	Y
17 Wilson	Y	Y	Y	N	N	N	N
18 **Ros-Lehtinen**	N	N	N	Y	Y	Y	Y
19 Deutch	Y	Y	Y	N	N	N	N
20 Wasserman Schultz	N	Y	Y	N	N	N	N
21 **Diaz-Balart**	N	N	N	Y	Y	Y	Y
22 **West**	N	N	N	Y	Y	Y	Y
23 Hastings	Y	Y	Y	N	N	N	N
24 **Adams**	N	N	N	Y	Y	Y	Y
25 **Rivera**	N	N	Y	N	Y	N	Y
GEORGIA							
1 **Kingston**	N	N	N	Y	Y	Y	Y
2 Bishop	N	Y	Y	N	N	N	N
3 **Westmoreland**	N	N	N	Y	Y	Y	Y
4 Johnson	Y	Y	Y	N	N	N	?
5 Lewis	Y	Y	Y	N	N	N	N
6 **Price**	N	N	N	Y	Y	Y	Y
7 **Woodall**	N	N	N	Y	Y	Y	Y
8 **Scott, A.**	N	N	N	Y	Y	Y	Y
9 **Graves**	Y	N	N	Y	Y	Y	Y
10 **Broun**	Y	N	N	Y	Y	Y	Y
11 **Gingrey**	N	N	N	Y	Y	Y	Y
12 **Barrow**	N	Y	Y	N	N	Y	N
13 Scott, D.	N	Y	Y	N	N	N	N
HAWAII							
1 Hanabusa	Y	Y	Y	N	N	N	N
2 Hirono	Y	Y	Y	N	N	N	N
IDAHO							
1 **Labrador**	N	N	N	Y	Y	Y	Y
2 **Simpson**	N	N	N	Y	Y	Y	Y
ILLINOIS							
1 Rush	Y	Y	Y	N	N	N	N
2 Jackson	Y	Y	Y	N	N	N	N
3 Lipinski	N	Y	Y	N	N	N	N
4 Gutierrez	Y	Y	Y	N	N	N	N
5 Quigley	Y	Y	Y	N	N	N	N
6 **Roskam**	N	N	N	Y	Y	Y	Y
7 Davis	Y	Y	Y	N	N	N	N
8 **Walsh**	Y	N	N	Y	Y	Y	Y
9 Schakowsky	Y	Y	Y	N	N	N	N
10 **Dold**	N	N	N	N	N	N	Y
11 **Kinzinger**	N	N	N	Y	Y	Y	Y
12 Costello	N	Y	Y	N	N	N	N
13 **Biggert**	N	N	N	Y	N	N	Y
14 **Hultgren**	N	N	N	Y	Y	Y	Y
15 Johnson	Y	N	Y	N	Y	N	Y

KEY	**Republicans**	Democrats		
Y	Voted for (yea)	X	Paired against	C Voted "present" to avoid possible conflict of interest
#	Paired for	–	Announced against	
+	Announced for	P	Voted "present"	? Did not vote or otherwise make a position known
N	Voted against (nay)			

	238	239	240	241	242	243	244
16 **Manzullo**	N	N	N	Y	N	Y	Y
17 **Schilling**	N	N	N	Y	Y	Y	Y
18 **Schock**	N	N	N	Y	Y	Y	Y
19 **Shimkus**	N	N	N	Y	N	Y	Y
INDIANA							
1 Visclosky	Y	Y	Y	N	N	N	N
2 Donnelly	?	?	?	?	?	?	?
3 **Stutzman**	N	N	N	Y	Y	Y	?
4 **Rokita**	N	N	N	Y	Y	Y	Y
5 **Burton**	Y	N	N	Y	Y	Y	Y
6 **Pence**	N	N	N	Y	Y	Y	Y
7 Carson	Y	Y	Y	N	N	N	N
8 **Bucshon**	N	N	N	Y	Y	Y	Y
9 **Young**	Y	N	Y	Y	Y	N	Y
IOWA							
1 Braley	N	Y	Y	N	N	N	N
2 Loebsack	Y	Y	Y	N	N	N	N
3 Boswell	N	Y	Y	N	N	N	N
4 **Latham**	N	N	N	Y	Y	N	Y
5 **King**	N	N	N	Y	Y	Y	Y
KANSAS							
1 **Huelskamp**	N	N	N	Y	Y	Y	Y
2 **Jenkins**	N	N	N	Y	Y	Y	Y
3 **Yoder**	N	N	N	Y	Y	Y	Y
4 **Pompeo**	N	N	N	Y	Y	Y	Y
KENTUCKY							
1 **Whitfield**	N	N	N	Y	N	Y	Y
2 **Guthrie**	N	N	N	Y	Y	Y	Y
3 Yarmuth	Y	Y	Y	N	N	N	N
4 **Davis**	N	N	N	Y	Y	Y	Y
5 **Rogers**	N	N	N	Y	Y	Y	Y
6 Chandler	N	Y	Y	N	N	N	N
LOUISIANA							
1 **Scalise**	N	N	N	Y	Y	Y	Y
2 Richmond	N	Y	Y	N	N	N	N
3 **Landry**	N	N	N	Y	Y	Y	Y
4 **Fleming**	N	N	N	Y	Y	Y	Y
5 **Alexander**	N	N	N	Y	Y	Y	Y
6 **Cassidy**	N	N	N	Y	Y	Y	Y
7 **Boustany**	N	N	N	Y	Y	Y	Y
MAINE							
1 Pingree	Y	Y	Y	N	N	N	N
2 Michaud	Y	Y	Y	N	N	N	N
MARYLAND							
1 **Harris**	N	N	N	Y	Y	Y	Y
2 Ruppersberger	N	Y	Y	N	N	N	N
3 Sarbanes	Y	Y	Y	N	N	N	N
4 Edwards	Y	Y	Y	N	N	N	N
5 Hoyer	Y	Y	Y	N	N	N	N
6 **Bartlett**	N	N	N	N	Y	N	Y
7 Cummings	N	Y	Y	N	N	N	N
8 Van Hollen	Y	Y	Y	N	N	N	N
MASSACHUSETTS							
1 Olver	Y	Y	Y	N	N	N	N
2 Neal	Y	Y	Y	N	N	N	N
3 McGovern	Y	Y	Y	N	N	N	N
4 Frank	Y	N	Y	N	N	N	N
5 Tsongas	Y	Y	Y	N	N	N	N
6 Tierney	Y	N	Y	N	N	N	N
7 Markey	Y	Y	Y	N	N	N	N
8 Capuano	Y	N	Y	N	N	N	N
9 Lynch	N	Y	Y	N	N	N	?
10 Keating	N	N	Y	N	N	N	N
MICHIGAN							
1 **Benishek**	Y	N	N	Y	Y	Y	Y
2 **Huizenga**	N	N	N	Y	Y	Y	Y
3 **Amash**	Y	N	Y	Y	Y	Y	Y
4 **Camp**	N	N	Y	Y	Y	Y	Y
5 Kildee	N	Y	Y	N	N	N	N
6 **Upton**	Y	N	N	Y	Y	Y	Y
7 **Walberg**	N	N	N	Y	Y	Y	Y
8 **Rogers**	N	N	N	Y	Y	Y	Y
9 Peters	Y	Y	Y	N	N	N	N
10 **Miller**	N	N	N	Y	Y	Y	Y
11 **McCotter**	N	N	N	Y	Y	Y	Y
12 Levin	N	Y	Y	N	N	N	N
13 Clarke	Y	Y	Y	N	N	N	N
14 Conyers	Y	Y	Y	N	N	N	N
15 Dingell	N	Y	Y	N	N	N	N
MINNESOTA							
1 Walz	Y	Y	Y	N	N	N	N
2 **Kline**	N	N	N	Y	Y	Y	Y
3 **Paulsen**	N	N	N	Y	Y	Y	Y
4 McCollum	Y	Y	Y	N	N	N	N

	238	239	240	241	242	243	244
5 Ellison	Y	Y	Y	N	N	N	N
6 **Bachmann**	N	N	N	Y	Y	Y	Y
7 Peterson	N	Y	Y	Y	N	N	N
8 **Cravaack**	N	N	N	Y	Y	Y	Y
MISSISSIPPI							
1 **Nunnelee**	N	N	N	Y	Y	Y	Y
2 Thompson	Y	Y	Y	N	N	N	N
3 **Harper**	N	N	N	Y	N	Y	Y
4 **Palazzo**	N	N	N	Y	Y	Y	Y
MISSOURI							
1 Clay	Y	Y	Y	N	N	N	N
2 **Akin**	N	N	N	Y	Y	Y	Y
3 Carnahan	Y	Y	Y	N	N	N	N
4 **Hartzler**	N	N	N	Y	Y	Y	Y
5 Cleaver	N	Y	Y	N	N	N	N
6 **Graves**	N	N	N	Y	Y	Y	Y
7 **Long**	N	N	N	Y	Y	Y	Y
8 **Emerson**	N	N	N	Y	Y	Y	Y
9 **Luetkemeyer**	N	N	Y	Y	Y	Y	Y
MONTANA							
AL **Rehberg**	Y	N	N	Y	Y	Y	Y
NEBRASKA							
1 **Fortenberry**	N	N	N	Y	Y	Y	Y
2 **Terry**	N	N	N	Y	N	Y	Y
3 **Smith**	N	N	N	Y	Y	Y	Y
NEVADA							
1 Berkley	Y	Y	Y	N	N	N	N
2 **Amodei**	Y	N	N	Y	Y	Y	Y
3 **Heck**	Y	N	N	Y	Y	Y	Y
NEW HAMPSHIRE							
1 **Guinta**	N	N	N	Y	Y	Y	Y
2 **Bass**	Y	N	N	N	Y	Y	Y
NEW JERSEY							
1 Andrews	Y	Y	Y	N	N	N	N
2 **LoBiondo**	N	N	N	Y	N	Y	Y
3 **Runyan**	N	N	N	Y	Y	Y	Y
4 **Smith**	N	N	N	Y	N	Y	Y
5 **Garrett**	Y	N	N	Y	Y	Y	Y
6 Pallone	Y	Y	Y	N	N	N	N
7 **Lance**	N	N	N	Y	Y	Y	Y
8 Pascrell	Y	Y	Y	N	N	N	N
9 Rothman	Y	Y	Y	N	N	N	N
10 Vacant							
11 **Frelinghuysen**	N	N	N	Y	Y	Y	Y
12 Holt	Y	Y	Y	N	N	N	N
13 Sires	Y	Y	Y	N	N	N	N
NEW MEXICO							
1 Heinrich	Y	Y	Y	N	N	N	N
2 **Pearce**	N	N	N	Y	Y	Y	Y
3 Luján	Y	Y	Y	N	N	N	N
NEW YORK							
1 Bishop	Y	Y	Y	N	N	N	N
2 Israel	Y	Y	Y	N	N	Y	N
3 **King**	N	N	N	Y	N	N	Y
4 McCarthy	Y	Y	N	N	N	N	N
5 Ackerman	Y	Y	Y	N	N	N	N
6 Meeks	?	?	?	N	N	N	N
7 Crowley	Y	Y	Y	N	N	N	N
8 Nadler	Y	Y	Y	N	N	N	N
9 **Turner**	N	Y	N	Y	N	Y	Y
10 Towns	Y	Y	Y	N	N	N	N
11 Clarke	Y	Y	Y	N	N	N	N
12 Velázquez	Y	Y	Y	N	N	N	N
13 **Grimm**	Y	N	N	Y	N	N	Y
14 Maloney	Y	Y	Y	N	N	N	N
15 Rangel	Y	Y	Y	N	N	N	N
16 Serrano	Y	Y	Y	N	N	N	N
17 Engel	Y	Y	Y	N	N	N	N
18 Lowey	Y	Y	Y	N	N	N	N
19 **Hayworth**	Y	N	N	N	Y	N	Y
20 **Gibson**	N	Y	N	N	N	N	Y
21 Tonko	Y	Y	Y	N	N	N	N
22 Hinchey	Y	Y	Y	N	N	N	?
23 Owens	N	N	Y	N	N	Y	N
24 **Hanna**	Y	N	N	N	Y	N	Y
25 **Buerkle**	N	N	N	Y	Y	Y	Y
26 Hochul	N	N	N	N	N	N	N
27 Higgins	Y	Y	N	N	N	N	N
28 Slaughter	+	+	+	–	–	–	–
29 **Reed**	N	N	N	Y	Y	Y	Y
NORTH CAROLINA							
1 Butterfield	Y	Y	Y	N	N	N	N
2 **Ellmers**	N	N	N	Y	Y	Y	Y
3 **Jones**	N	N	N	N	Y	Y	Y
4 Price	Y	Y	Y	N	N	N	N

	238	239	240	241	242	243	244
5 **Foxx**	N	N	N	Y	Y	Y	Y
6 **Coble**	N	N	N	Y	Y	Y	Y
7 McIntyre	N	N	Y	Y	Y	N	Y
8 Kissell	N	Y	Y	N	N	N	Y
9 **Myrick**	N	N	N	Y	Y	Y	Y
10 **McHenry**	N	N	N	Y	Y	Y	Y
11 Shuler	N	Y	N	N	N	N	N
12 Watt	Y	Y	Y	N	N	N	N
13 Miller	N	Y	Y	N	N	N	N
NORTH DAKOTA							
AL **Berg**	N	N	N	Y	N	Y	Y
OHIO							
1 **Chabot**	N	N	N	Y	Y	Y	Y
2 **Schmidt**	N	N	N	Y	Y	Y	Y
3 **Turner**	N	N	N	Y	Y	N	Y
4 **Jordan**	N	N	N	Y	Y	Y	Y
5 **Latta**	N	N	N	Y	Y	Y	Y
6 **Johnson**	N	N	N	Y	Y	Y	Y
7 **Austria**	N	N	N	Y	Y	Y	Y
8 **Boehner**							
9 Kaptur	N	Y	Y	N	N	N	N
10 Kucinich	?	?	?	?	?	?	N
11 Fudge	Y	Y	Y	N	N	N	N
12 **Tiberi**	N	Y	N	Y	N	N	Y
13 Sutton	Y	Y	Y	N	N	N	N
14 **LaTourette**	Y	Y	Y	Y	N	Y	Y
15 **Stivers**	N	Y	N	Y	N	N	Y
16 **Renacci**	N	Y	N	Y	Y	N	Y
17 Ryan	Y	Y	Y	N	N	N	N
18 **Gibbs**	N	N	N	Y	Y	Y	Y
OKLAHOMA							
1 **Sullivan**	N	?	N	Y	Y	Y	Y
2 Boren	N	Y	N	Y	N	N	Y
3 **Lucas**	N	N	N	Y	N	N	Y
4 **Cole**	N	N	N	Y	N	N	Y
5 **Lankford**	N	N	N	Y	Y	Y	Y
OREGON							
1 Bonamici	Y	Y	Y	N	N	N	N
2 **Walden**	N	N	N	Y	Y	Y	Y
3 Blumenauer	Y	Y	Y	N	N	N	N
4 DeFazio	Y	Y	Y	N	N	N	N
5 Schrader	N	Y	Y	N	N	N	N
PENNSYLVANIA							
1 Brady	Y	Y	Y	N	N	N	N
2 Fattah	Y	Y	Y	N	N	N	N
3 **Kelly**	N	N	N	Y	Y	N	Y
4 Altmire	N	Y	N	N	N	N	N
5 **Thompson**	N	N	N	Y	N	N	Y
6 **Gerlach**	N	Y	Y	Y	Y	Y	Y
7 **Meehan**	N	Y	N	Y	Y	Y	Y
8 **Fitzpatrick**	N	Y	N	Y	Y	N	Y
9 **Shuster**	N	N	N	Y	Y	Y	Y
10 **Marino**	N	N	N	Y	Y	Y	Y
11 **Barletta**	N	N	N	Y	Y	Y	Y
12 Critz	Y	Y	Y	Y	N	N	N
13 Schwartz	N	Y	Y	N	N	N	N
14 Doyle	Y	Y	Y	N	N	N	N
15 **Dent**	N	Y	N	Y	Y	N	Y
16 **Pitts**	N	N	N	Y	N	Y	Y
17 Holden	Y	Y	Y	N	N	N	N
18 **Murphy**	N	N	N	Y	Y	Y	Y
19 **Platts**	N	Y	Y	N	Y	N	Y
RHODE ISLAND							
1 Cicilline	Y	Y	Y	N	N	N	N
2 Langevin	Y	Y	Y	N	N	N	N
SOUTH CAROLINA							
1 **Scott**	N	N	N	Y	Y	Y	Y
2 **Wilson**	N	N	N	Y	Y	Y	Y
3 **Duncan**	N	N	N	Y	Y	Y	Y
4 **Gowdy**	N	N	N	Y	Y	Y	Y
5 **Mulvaney**	Y	N	Y	Y	Y	Y	Y
6 Clyburn	N	Y	Y	N	N	N	N
SOUTH DAKOTA							
AL **Noem**	N	N	N	Y	Y	Y	?
TENNESSEE							
1 **Roe**	N	N	N	Y	Y	Y	Y
2 **Duncan**	N	N	N	Y	Y	Y	Y
3 **Fleischmann**	N	N	N	Y	Y	Y	Y
4 **DesJarlais**	N	N	N	Y	Y	Y	Y
5 Cooper	N	Y	Y	N	N	N	N
6 **Black**	N	N	N	Y	Y	Y	Y
7 **Blackburn**	N	N	N	Y	Y	Y	Y
8 **Fincher**	N	N	N	Y	Y	Y	Y
9 Cohen	Y	Y	Y	N	N	N	N

	238	239	240	241	242	243	244
TEXAS							
1 **Gohmert**	N	N	N	Y	Y	Y	Y
2 **Poe**	N	N	N	Y	Y	Y	Y
3 **Johnson, S.**	N	N	N	Y	Y	Y	Y
4 **Hall**	N	N	N	Y	Y	Y	Y
5 **Hensarling**	N	N	N	Y	Y	Y	Y
6 **Barton**	N	N	N	Y	Y	Y	Y
7 **Culberson**	N	N	N	Y	Y	Y	Y
8 **Brady**	N	N	N	Y	Y	Y	Y
9 Green, A.	Y	Y	Y	N	N	N	N
10 **McCaul**	N	N	N	Y	Y	Y	?
11 **Conaway**	N	N	N	Y	Y	Y	Y
12 **Granger**	N	N	N	Y	Y	Y	?
13 **Thornberry**	N	N	N	Y	Y	Y	Y
14 **Paul**	Y	N	Y	Y	Y	Y	?
15 Hinojosa	N	Y	Y	N	N	N	N
16 Reyes	N	Y	Y	N	N	N	N
17 **Flores**	N	N	N	Y	Y	Y	Y
18 Jackson Lee	Y	Y	Y	N	N	N	N
19 **Neugebauer**	N	N	N	Y	Y	Y	Y
20 Gonzalez	N	Y	Y	N	N	N	N
21 **Smith**	N	N	N	Y	N	Y	Y
22 **Olson**	N	N	N	Y	Y	Y	Y
23 **Canseco**	N	N	N	Y	Y	Y	Y
24 **Marchant**	N	N	N	Y	N	Y	Y
25 Doggett	Y	Y	Y	N	N	N	N
26 **Burgess**	N	N	N	Y	Y	Y	?
27 **Farenthold**	N	N	N	Y	Y	Y	Y
28 Cuellar	N	Y	Y	N	N	N	N
29 Green, G.	N	Y	Y	N	N	Y	N
30 Johnson, E.	Y	Y	Y	N	N	N	N
31 **Carter**	N	N	N	Y	Y	Y	Y
32 **Sessions**	N	N	N	Y	Y	Y	Y
UTAH							
1 **Bishop**	N	N	N	Y	Y	Y	Y
2 Matheson	N	N	N	N	N	N	Y
3 **Chaffetz**	N	N	N	Y	Y	Y	Y
VERMONT							
AL Welch	Y	Y	Y	N	N	N	N
VIRGINIA							
1 **Wittman**	N	N	N	Y	Y	Y	Y
2 **Rigell**	N	N	Y	Y	Y	Y	Y
3 Scott	Y	Y	Y	N	N	N	N
4 **Forbes**	N	N	N	Y	Y	Y	Y
5 **Hurt**	N	N	N	Y	Y	N	+
6 **Goodlatte**	N	N	N	Y	Y	Y	Y
7 **Cantor**	?	?	?	?	?	?	Y
8 Moran	Y	Y	Y	N	N	N	N
9 **Griffith**	N	N	N	Y	Y	Y	Y
10 **Wolf**	N	N	N	Y	Y	Y	Y
11 Connolly	Y	Y	Y	N	N	N	N
WASHINGTON							
1 Vacant							
2 Larsen	N	Y	Y	N	N	N	N
3 **Herrera Beutler**	N	N	N	Y	N	Y	Y
4 **Hastings**	N	N	N	Y	Y	Y	Y
5 **McMorris Rodgers**	N	N	N	Y	Y	Y	Y
6 Dicks	N	Y	Y	N	N	N	?
7 McDermott	Y	Y	Y	N	N	N	N
8 **Reichert**	N	N	N	N	N	N	Y
9 Smith	Y	Y	Y	N	N	N	N
WEST VIRGINIA							
1 **McKinley**	N	N	N	Y	Y	Y	Y
2 **Capito**	N	N	N	Y	N	Y	Y
3 Rahall	N	Y	Y	Y	N	N	N
WISCONSIN							
1 **Ryan**	N	N	N	Y	Y	Y	Y
2 Baldwin	Y	Y	Y	N	N	N	N
3 Kind	N	Y	Y	N	N	N	N
4 Moore	Y	Y	Y	N	N	N	N
5 **Sensenbrenner**	N	N	Y	Y	Y	Y	Y
6 **Petri**	Y	N	Y	Y	Y	Y	Y
7 **Duffy**	N	N	Y	Y	Y	Y	Y
8 **Ribble**	Y	N	Y	Y	Y	Y	Y
WYOMING							
AL **Lummis**	Y	N	N	Y	Y	Y	Y

IN THE HOUSE | By Vote Number

245. **HR 5652. Budget Sequestration Replacement/Rule.** Adoption of the rule (H Res 648) that would provide for House floor consideration of a bill that would replace the $98 billion in automatic discretionary spending cuts scheduled to go into effect in January 2013 with a $19 billion reduction in the discretionary cap for fiscal 2013 and with reconciliation savings that would cut about $310 billion over a decade from mandatory spending. Adopted 233-183: R 232-0; D 1-183. May 10, 2012.

246. **HR 5652. Budget Sequestration Replacement/Recommit.** Loebsack, D-Iowa, motion to recommit the bill to the House Budget Committee and report it back immediately with an amendment that would make former members of Congress who are registered lobbyists earning more than $1 million annually ineligible to receive retirement benefits under the Civil Service Retirement System or Federal Employees Retirement System. It also would require that members of Congress contribute more toward their retirement benefits and prohibit lawmakers from making contributions to retirement benefits with accrued or accumulated leave. Motion rejected 170-232: R 2-228; D 168-4. May 10, 2012.

247. **HR 5652. Budget Sequestration Replacement/Passage.** Passage of the bill that would cancel $98 billion in automatic discretionary spending cuts that would go into effect in January 2013. It would replace the sequester with a $19 billion reduction in the discretionary cap for fiscal 2013 and with reconciliation savings from mandatory programs recommended by six House committees. It also would eliminate the separate cap on defense spending for the year to allow for higher spending levels. The bill would modify mandatory programs to save $19.7 billion through fiscal 2013 and about $310 billion over 10 years. Passed 218-199: R 218-16; D 0-183. A "nay" was a vote in support of the president's position. May 10, 2012.

248. **HR 5326. Fiscal 2013 Commerce-Justice-Science Appropriations/Recommit.** Nadler, D-N.Y., motion to recommit the bill to the House Appropriations Committee and report it back immediately with an amendment that would increase by $20.5 million the amount provided in the bill for programs that aid in the prevention and prosecution of acts of violence against women. It would reduce by the same amount general administrative funding for the Commerce and Justice departments and the Office of Science and Technology. Motion rejected 181-233: R 1-232; D 180-1. May 10, 2012.

249. **HR 5326. Fiscal 2013 Commerce-Justice-Science Appropriations/Passage.** Passage of the bill that would provide $51.1 billion in fiscal 2013 for the departments of Commerce and Justice and other agencies such as NASA and the National Science Foundation. It would provide $7.7 billion for the Commerce Department and $27.4 billion for the Justice Department. The bill would provide $17.4 billion for NASA, $7.3 billion for the National Science Foundation, $5 billion for the National Oceanic Atmospheric Administration and $2.9 billion for the Patent and Trademark Office offset by fees. Passed 247-163: R 224-8; D 23-155. A "nay" was a vote in support of the president's position. May 10, 2012.

	245	246	247	248	249
ALABAMA					
1 Bonner	Y	N	Y	N	Y
2 Roby	Y	N	Y	N	Y
3 Rogers	Y	N	Y	N	Y
4 Aderholt	Y	N	Y	?	Y
5 Brooks	Y	N	Y	N	Y
6 Bachus	?	N	Y	N	Y
7 Sewell	N	Y	N	Y	N
ALASKA					
AL Young	?	N	Y	N	Y
ARIZONA					
1 Gosar	Y	N	Y	N	Y
2 Franks	Y	N	Y	N	N
3 Quayle	Y	N	Y	N	Y
4 Pastor	N	Y	N	Y	N
5 Schweikert	Y	N	Y	N	Y
6 Flake	Y	N	Y	N	N
7 Grijalva	N	Y	N	Y	N
8 Vacant					
ARKANSAS					
1 Crawford	Y	N	Y	N	Y
2 Griffin	Y	N	Y	N	Y
3 Womack	Y	N	Y	N	Y
4 Ross	N	Y	N	Y	N
CALIFORNIA					
1 Thompson	N	Y	N	Y	N
2 Herger	Y	N	Y	N	Y
3 Lungren	Y	N	Y	N	Y
4 McClintock	Y	N	Y	N	N
5 Matsui	N	Y	N	Y	N
6 Woolsey	N	Y	N	Y	N
7 Miller, George	N	Y	N	Y	N
8 Pelosi	N	Y	N	Y	N
9 Lee	N	Y	N	Y	N
10 Garamendi	N	Y	N	Y	N
11 McNerney	N	Y	N	Y	N
12 Speier	N	Y	N	Y	N
13 Stark	N	Y	N	Y	N
14 Eshoo	N	Y	N	Y	N
15 Honda	N	Y	N	Y	N
16 Lofgren	N	Y	N	Y	N
17 Farr	N	Y	N	Y	N
18 Cardoza	N	N	N	?	?
19 Denham	Y	N	Y	N	Y
20 Costa	N	Y	N	Y	Y
21 Nunes	Y	N	Y	N	Y
22 McCarthy	Y	N	Y	N	Y
23 Capps	N	Y	N	Y	N
24 Gallegly	Y	N	Y	N	?
25 McKeon	Y	N	Y	N	Y
26 Dreier	Y	N	Y	N	Y
27 Sherman	N	Y	N	Y	N
28 Berman	?	?	?	?	?
29 Schiff	N	Y	N	Y	N
30 Waxman	N	P	N	Y	N
31 Becerra	N	Y	N	Y	N
32 Chu	N	Y	N	Y	N
33 Bass	N	Y	N	Y	N
34 Roybal-Allard	N	Y	N	Y	N
35 Waters	N	Y	N	Y	N
36 Hahn	N	Y	N	Y	N
37 Richardson	N	Y	N	Y	N
38 Napolitano	N	+	–	+	–
39 Sánchez, Linda	N	Y	N	Y	N
40 Royce	Y	N	Y	?	Y
41 Lewis	Y	N	Y	N	Y
42 Miller, Gary	Y	N	Y	N	Y
43 Baca	N	Y	N	Y	?
44 Calvert	Y	N	Y	N	Y
45 Bono Mack	Y	N	Y	N	Y
46 Rohrabacher	Y	P	Y	N	Y
47 Sanchez, Loretta	N	Y	N	Y	N
48 Campbell	Y	N	Y	N	N
49 Issa	Y	N	Y	N	Y
50 Bilbray	Y	N	Y	N	Y
51 Filner	–	+	–	+	–
52 Hunter	Y	N	Y	N	Y
53 Davis	N	Y	N	Y	N

	245	246	247	248	249
COLORADO					
1 DeGette	N	N	N	Y	N
2 Polis	N	Y	N	Y	N
3 Tipton	Y	N	Y	N	Y
4 Gardner	Y	N	Y	N	Y
5 Lamborn	Y	N	Y	N	Y
6 Coffman	Y	N	Y	N	Y
7 Perlmutter	N	Y	N	Y	Y
CONNECTICUT					
1 Larson	N	Y	N	Y	N
2 Courtney	N	Y	N	Y	N
3 DeLauro	N	Y	N	Y	N
4 Himes	N	Y	N	Y	N
5 Murphy	N	Y	N	Y	N
DELAWARE					
AL Carney	N	Y	N	Y	Y
FLORIDA					
1 Miller	Y	N	Y	N	Y
2 Southerland	Y	N	Y	N	Y
3 Brown	N	P	N	Y	Y
4 Crenshaw	Y	N	Y	N	Y
5 Nugent	Y	N	Y	N	Y
6 Stearns	Y	N	Y	N	Y
7 Mica	Y	N	Y	N	Y
8 Webster	Y	N	Y	N	Y
9 Bilirakis	Y	N	Y	N	Y
10 Young	Y	N	Y	N	Y
11 Castor	N	Y	N	Y	N
12 Ross	Y	N	Y	N	Y
13 Buchanan	Y	N	Y	N	Y
14 Mack	?	?	?	?	?
15 Posey	Y	N	Y	N	Y
16 Rooney	Y	N	Y	N	Y
17 Wilson	N	Y	N	Y	N
18 Ros-Lehtinen	Y	N	Y	N	Y
19 Deutch	N	Y	N	Y	N
20 Wasserman Schultz	N	Y	N	Y	N
21 Diaz-Balart	Y	N	Y	N	Y
22 West	Y	N	Y	N	Y
23 Hastings	N	Y	N	Y	N
24 Adams	Y	N	Y	N	Y
25 Rivera	Y	N	Y	N	Y
GEORGIA					
1 Kingston	Y	N	Y	N	Y
2 Bishop	N	Y	N	Y	Y
3 Westmoreland	Y	N	Y	N	Y
4 Johnson	?	?	N	Y	N
5 Lewis	N	Y	N	Y	N
6 Price	Y	N	Y	N	Y
7 Woodall	Y	N	Y	N	Y
8 Scott, A.	Y	N	Y	N	Y
9 Graves	Y	N	Y	N	Y
10 Broun	?	?	Y	N	N
11 Gingrey	Y	N	Y	N	Y
12 Barrow	N	Y	N	Y	Y
13 Scott, D.	N	Y	N	Y	N
HAWAII					
1 Hanabusa	N	Y	N	Y	N
2 Hirono	N	Y	N	Y	N
IDAHO					
1 Labrador	Y	N	N	N	Y
2 Simpson	Y	N	Y	N	Y
ILLINOIS					
1 Rush	N	P	N	Y	N
2 Jackson	N	P	N	Y	N
3 Lipinski	N	Y	N	Y	Y
4 Gutierrez	N	Y	N	Y	N
5 Quigley	N	Y	N	Y	N
6 Roskam	Y	N	Y	N	Y
7 Davis	N	Y	N	Y	N
8 Walsh	Y	N	Y	N	Y
9 Schakowsky	N	Y	N	Y	N
10 Dold	Y	N	Y	N	Y
11 Kinzinger	Y	N	Y	N	Y
12 Costello	N	Y	N	Y	?
13 Biggert	Y	N	Y	N	Y
14 Hultgren	Y	N	Y	N	Y
15 Johnson	Y	N	N	N	Y

	245	246	247	248	249
16 Manzullo	Y	N	Y	N	Y
17 Schilling	Y	N	Y	N	Y
18 Schock	Y	N	Y	N	Y
19 Shimkus	Y	N	Y	N	Y
INDIANA					
1 Visclosky	N	Y	N	Y	Y
2 Donnelly	?	?	?	?	?
3 Stutzman	?	?	?	?	?
4 Rokita	Y	N	Y	N	Y
5 Burton	Y	N	Y	N	?
6 Pence	Y	N	Y	N	Y
7 Carson	N	Y	N	Y	?
8 Bucshon	Y	N	Y	N	Y
9 Young	Y	N	Y	N	Y
IOWA					
1 Braley	N	Y	N	Y	N
2 Loebsack	N	Y	N	Y	N
3 Boswell	N	Y	N	Y	Y
4 Latham	Y	N	Y	N	Y
5 King	Y	N	Y	N	Y
KANSAS					
1 Huelskamp	Y	N	Y	N	Y
2 Jenkins	Y	N	Y	N	Y
3 Yoder	Y	N	Y	N	Y
4 Pompeo	Y	N	Y	N	Y
KENTUCKY					
1 Whitfield	Y	N	N	N	Y
2 Guthrie	Y	N	Y	N	Y
3 Yarmuth	N	Y	N	Y	N
4 Davis	Y	N	Y	N	Y
5 Rogers	Y	N	Y	N	Y
6 Chandler	N	Y	N	Y	N
LOUISIANA					
1 Scalise	Y	N	Y	N	Y
2 Richmond	N	Y	N	Y	N
3 Landry	Y	N	Y	N	Y
4 Fleming	Y	N	Y	N	Y
5 Alexander	Y	N	Y	N	Y
6 Cassidy	Y	N	Y	N	Y
7 Boustany	Y	N	Y	N	Y
MAINE					
1 Pingree	N	Y	N	Y	N
2 Michaud	N	Y	N	Y	N
MARYLAND					
1 Harris	Y	N	Y	N	Y
2 Ruppersberger	N	Y	N	Y	Y
3 Sarbanes	N	Y	N	Y	N
4 Edwards	N	Y	N	Y	N
5 Hoyer	N	P	N	Y	N
6 Bartlett	Y	N	N	N	Y
7 Cummings	N	Y	N	Y	N
8 Van Hollen	N	Y	N	Y	N
MASSACHUSETTS					
1 Olver	N	Y	N	Y	N
2 Neal	N	Y	N	Y	N
3 McGovern	N	Y	N	Y	N
4 Frank	N	Y	N	Y	N
5 Tsongas	N	Y	N	Y	N
6 Tierney	N	Y	N	Y	N
7 Markey	N	Y	N	+	N
8 Capuano	N	?	?	Y	N
9 Lynch	N	Y	N	Y	N
10 Keating	N	Y	N	Y	N
MICHIGAN					
1 Benishek	Y	N	Y	N	Y
2 Huizenga	Y	N	Y	N	Y
3 Amash	Y	N	N	N	N
4 Camp	Y	N	Y	N	Y
5 Kildee	N	Y	N	Y	N
6 Upton	Y	N	Y	N	Y
7 Walberg	Y	N	Y	N	Y
8 Rogers	Y	N	Y	N	Y
9 Peters	N	Y	N	Y	N
10 Miller	Y	N	Y	N	Y
11 McCotter	Y	N	Y	N	Y
12 Levin	N	Y	N	Y	N
13 Clarke	N	Y	N	Y	N
14 Conyers	N	Y	N	Y	N
15 Dingell	N	Y	N	Y	N
MINNESOTA					
1 Walz	N	Y	N	Y	N
2 Kline	Y	N	Y	N	Y
3 Paulsen	Y	?	?	?	?
4 McCollum	N	Y	N	Y	N

	245	246	247	248	249
5 Ellison	N	N	N	N	N
6 Bachmann	Y	N	Y	N	Y
7 Peterson	N	Y	N	Y	Y
8 Cravaack	Y	N	Y	N	Y
MISSISSIPPI					
1 Nunnelee	Y	N	Y	N	Y
2 Thompson	N	Y	N	Y	N
3 Harper	Y	N	Y	N	Y
4 Palazzo	Y	N	Y	N	Y
MISSOURI					
1 Clay	N	Y	N	Y	N
2 Akin	Y	N	Y	N	Y
3 Carnahan	N	Y	N	Y	N
4 Hartzler	Y	N	Y	N	Y
5 Cleaver	N	P	N	Y	N
6 Graves	Y	N	Y	N	Y
7 Long	Y	N	Y	N	Y
8 Emerson	Y	N	Y	N	Y
9 Luetkemeyer	Y	N	Y	N	Y
MONTANA					
AL Rehberg	Y	N	Y	N	Y
NEBRASKA					
1 Fortenberry	Y	N	Y	N	Y
2 Terry	Y	N	Y	N	Y
3 Smith	Y	N	Y	N	Y
NEVADA					
1 Berkley	N	Y	N	Y	Y
2 Amodei	Y	N	Y	N	Y
3 Heck	Y	N	Y	N	Y
NEW HAMPSHIRE					
1 Guinta	Y	N	Y	N	Y
2 Bass	Y	N	N	N	Y
NEW JERSEY					
1 Andrews	N	Y	N	Y	N
2 LoBiondo	Y	N	N	N	Y
3 Runyan	Y	N	Y	N	Y
4 Smith	Y	N	Y	N	Y
5 Garrett	Y	N	Y	N	Y
6 Pallone	N	Y	N	Y	N
7 Lance	Y	N	Y	N	Y
8 Pascrell	N	Y	N	Y	N
9 Rothman	N	Y	N	Y	N
10 Vacant					
11 Frelinghuysen	Y	N	Y	N	Y
12 Holt	N	Y	N	Y	N
13 Sires	N	?	N	Y	N
NEW MEXICO					
1 Heinrich	N	?	?	?	?
2 Pearce	Y	N	Y	N	Y
3 Luján	N	Y	N	N	N
NEW YORK					
1 Bishop	N	Y	N	Y	Y
2 Israel	N	Y	N	Y	N
3 King	Y	N	Y	N	Y
4 McCarthy	N	Y	N	Y	N
5 Ackerman	N	Y	N	Y	Y
6 Meeks	N	?	N	Y	N
7 Crowley	N	Y	N	Y	N
8 Nadler	N	Y	N	Y	N
9 Turner	Y	N	Y	N	Y
10 Towns	N	Y	N	Y	N
11 Clarke	N	P	N	Y	N
12 Velázquez	N	Y	N	Y	N
13 Grimm	Y	N	Y	N	Y
14 Maloney	N	Y	N	Y	N
15 Rangel	N	Y	N	Y	N
16 Serrano	N	Y	N	Y	N
17 Engel	N	Y	N	Y	N
18 Lowey	N	Y	N	Y	N
19 Hayworth	Y	N	Y	N	Y
20 Gibson	Y	N	N	N	Y
21 Tonko	N	Y	N	Y	N
22 Hinchey	?	Y	N	Y	N
23 Owens	N	Y	N	Y	N
24 Hanna	Y	N	Y	N	Y
25 Buerkle	Y	N	Y	N	Y
26 Hochul	N	Y	N	Y	Y
27 Higgins	N	Y	N	Y	Y
28 Slaughter	-	+	-	+	-
29 Reed	Y	N	Y	N	Y
NORTH CAROLINA					
1 Butterfield	N	Y	N	Y	N
2 Ellmers	Y	N	Y	N	Y
3 Jones	Y	Y	N	Y	Y
4 Price	N	Y	N	Y	N

	245	246	247	248	249
5 Foxx	Y	N	Y	N	Y
6 Coble	Y	Y	Y	N	Y
7 McIntyre	N	Y	?	?	?
8 Kissell	N	Y	N	Y	Y
9 Myrick	Y	N	Y	N	Y
10 McHenry	Y	N	Y	N	Y
11 Shuler	Y	N	N	Y	Y
12 Watt	N	P	N	Y	N
13 Miller	N	Y	N	Y	N
NORTH DAKOTA					
AL Berg	Y	N	Y	N	Y
OHIO					
1 Chabot	Y	N	Y	N	Y
2 Schmidt	Y	N	Y	N	Y
3 Turner	Y	N	Y	N	Y
4 Jordan	Y	N	Y	N	Y
5 Latta	Y	N	Y	N	Y
6 Johnson	Y	N	Y	N	Y
7 Austria	?	N	Y	N	Y
8 Boehner					
9 Kaptur	N	Y	N	Y	N
10 Kucinich	N	Y	N	Y	N
11 Fudge	N	P	N	Y	N
12 Tiberi	Y	N	Y	N	Y
13 Sutton	N	Y	N	Y	N
14 LaTourette	Y	N	Y	N	Y
15 Stivers	Y	N	Y	N	Y
16 Renacci	Y	N	Y	N	Y
17 Ryan	N	Y	N	Y	N
18 Gibbs	Y	N	Y	N	Y
OKLAHOMA					
1 Sullivan	Y	N	Y	N	Y
2 Boren	N	Y	N	Y	Y
3 Lucas	Y	N	Y	N	Y
4 Cole	Y	N	Y	N	Y
5 Lankford	Y	N	Y	N	Y
OREGON					
1 Bonamici	N	Y	N	Y	N
2 Walden	Y	N	Y	N	Y
3 Blumenauer	N	Y	N	Y	N
4 DeFazio	N	Y	N	Y	N
5 Schrader	N	Y	N	Y	N
PENNSYLVANIA					
1 Brady	N	Y	N	Y	N
2 Fattah	N	Y	N	Y	Y
3 Kelly	Y	N	Y	N	Y
4 Altmire	N	Y	N	Y	N
5 Thompson	Y	N	Y	N	Y
6 Gerlach	Y	N	Y	N	Y
7 Meehan	Y	N	Y	N	Y
8 Fitzpatrick	Y	N	N	N	Y
9 Shuster	Y	N	Y	N	Y
10 Marino	Y	N	Y	N	Y
11 Barletta	Y	N	Y	N	Y
12 Critz	N	Y	N	Y	N
13 Schwartz	N	Y	N	Y	N
14 Doyle	N	Y	N	Y	N
15 Dent	Y	N	Y	N	Y
16 Pitts	Y	N	Y	N	Y
17 Holden	N	Y	N	Y	N
18 Murphy	Y	N	Y	N	Y
19 Platts	Y	N	N	N	Y
RHODE ISLAND					
1 Cicilline	N	Y	N	Y	N
2 Langevin	N	Y	N	Y	N
SOUTH CAROLINA					
1 Scott	Y	N	Y	N	Y
2 Wilson	Y	N	Y	N	Y
3 Duncan	Y	?	Y	N	Y
4 Gowdy	Y	N	Y	N	Y
5 Mulvaney	Y	N	Y	N	Y
6 Clyburn	N	Y	N	Y	N
SOUTH DAKOTA					
AL Noem	?	?	?	?	?
TENNESSEE					
1 Roe	Y	N	Y	N	Y
2 Duncan	Y	N	N	N	N
3 Fleischmann	Y	N	Y	N	Y
4 DesJarlais	Y	N	Y	N	Y
5 Cooper	N	Y	N	Y	-
6 Black	Y	N	Y	N	Y
7 Blackburn	Y	N	Y	N	Y
8 Fincher	Y	N	Y	N	Y
9 Cohen	N	Y	N	Y	N

	245	246	247	248	249
TEXAS					
1 Gohmert	Y	N	N	N	Y
2 Poe	Y	N	Y	N	Y
3 Johnson, S.	Y	N	Y	N	Y
4 Hall	Y	N	Y	N	Y
5 Hensarling	Y	N	Y	N	Y
6 Barton	Y	N	Y	N	?
7 Culberson	Y	N	Y	N	Y
8 Brady	Y	N	Y	N	Y
9 Green, A.	N	Y	N	Y	N
10 McCaul	Y	N	Y	N	Y
11 Conaway	Y	N	Y	N	Y
12 Granger	Y	N	Y	N	Y
13 Thornberry	Y	N	Y	N	Y
14 Paul	?	?	?	?	?
15 Hinojosa	N	Y	N	Y	N
16 Reyes	N	Y	N	Y	N
17 Flores	Y	?	Y	N	Y
18 Jackson Lee	N	Y	N	Y	N
19 Neugebauer	Y	N	Y	N	Y
20 Gonzalez	N	Y	N	Y	N
21 Smith	Y	N	Y	N	Y
22 Olson	Y	N	Y	N	Y
23 Canseco	Y	N	Y	N	Y
24 Marchant	Y	N	Y	N	Y
25 Doggett	N	Y	N	Y	N
26 Burgess	?	?	?	?	?
27 Farenthold	Y	N	Y	N	Y
28 Cuellar	N	Y	N	Y	N
29 Green, G.	N	Y	N	Y	N
30 Johnson, E.	N	Y	N	Y	N
31 Carter	Y	N	Y	N	Y
32 Sessions	Y	N	Y	N	Y
UTAH					
1 Bishop	Y	N	Y	N	Y
2 Matheson	N	Y	N	Y	N
3 Chaffetz	Y	N	Y	N	Y
VERMONT					
AL Welch	N	Y	N	Y	N
VIRGINIA					
1 Wittman	Y	N	Y	N	Y
2 Rigell	Y	N	Y	N	Y
3 Scott	N	Y	N	Y	N
4 Forbes	Y	N	Y	N	Y
5 Hurt	Y	N	Y	N	Y
6 Goodlatte	Y	N	Y	N	Y
7 Cantor	Y	N	Y	N	Y
8 Moran	N	Y	N	Y	N
9 Griffith	Y	N	Y	N	Y
10 Wolf	Y	N	N	N	Y
11 Connolly	N	Y	N	Y	N
WASHINGTON					
1 Vacant					
2 Larsen	N	Y	N	Y	N
3 Herrera Beutler	Y	N	N	N	Y
4 Hastings	Y	N	Y	N	Y
5 McMorris Rodgers	Y	N	Y	N	Y
6 Dicks	N	Y	N	Y	Y
7 McDermott	N	Y	N	Y	N
8 Reichert	Y	N	Y	N	Y
9 Smith	N	Y	N	Y	N
WEST VIRGINIA					
1 McKinley	Y	N	Y	N	Y
2 Capito	Y	N	Y	N	Y
3 Rahall	N	Y	N	Y	N
WISCONSIN					
1 Ryan	Y	N	Y	N	Y
2 Baldwin	N	Y	N	Y	N
3 Kind	N	Y	N	Y	N
4 Moore	N	Y	N	Y	N
5 Sensenbrenner	Y	P	P	N	Y
6 Petri	Y	N	Y	N	Y
7 Duffy	Y	N	Y	N	Y
8 Ribble	Y	N	Y	N	Y
WYOMING					
AL Lummis	Y	N	Y	N	N

IN THE HOUSE | By Vote Number

250. **HR 365. National Blue Alert Plan/Passage.** Smith, R-Texas, motion to suspend the rules and pass the bill that would direct the attorney general to establish a national Blue Alert communications network within the Justice Department to disseminate information when a law enforcement officer is seriously injured or killed in the line of duty. Motion agreed to 394-1: R 222-1; D 172-0. A two-thirds majority of those present and voting (264 in this case) is required for passage under suspension of the rules. May 15, 2012.

251. **HR 3874. Black Hills Forest Cemeteries/Passage.** Bishop, R-Utah, motion to suspend the rules and pass the bill, as amended, that would direct the Agriculture secretary to convey parcels of National Forest System land located in Black Hills National Forest, S.D., containing nine cemeteries to local communities. Motion agreed to 400-1: R 224-1; D 176-0. A two-thirds majority of those present and voting (268 in this case) is required for passage under suspension of the rules. May 15, 2012.

252. **HR 205. American Indian Land Leases/Passage.** Bishop, R-Utah, motion to suspend the rules and pass the bill that would allow American Indian tribes to enter into leases of their lands held in trust by the federal government without approval from the Bureau of Indian Affairs. Motion agreed to 400-0: R 225-0; D 175-0. A two-thirds majority of those present and voting (267 in this case) is required for passage under suspension of the rules. May 15, 2012.

253. **HR 4310. Violence Against Women Act Reauthorization and Fiscal 2013 Defense Authorization/Question of Consideration.** Question of whether the House should consider the rule (H Res 656) that would provide for House floor consideration of a bill (HR 4970) that would reauthorize grant and assistance programs under the Violence Against Women Act (VAWA) through fiscal 2017 and provide one hour of general debate for a bill (HR 4310) to authorize fiscal 2013 funding for Defense Department and national security programs. Agreed to consider 239-183: R 236-0; D 3-183. (Moore, D-Wis., had raised a point of order that the rule would violate clause 426(a) of the Congressional Budget Act, regarding unfunded mandates.) May 16, 2012.

254. **HR 4310. Violence Against Women Act Reauthorization and Fiscal 2013 Defense Authorization/Previous Question.** Foxx, R-N.C., motion to order the previous question (thus ending debate and the possibility of amendment) on the rule (H Res 656) that would provide for House floor consideration of a bill (HR 4970) that would reauthorize grant and assistance programs under the Violence Against Women Act through fiscal 2017 and provide one hour of general debate for a bill (HR 4310) to authorize fiscal 2013 funding for Defense Department and national security programs. Motion agreed to 235-187: R 234-1; D 1-186. May 16, 2012.

255. **H Res 656. Violence Against Women Act Reauthorization and Fiscal 2013 Defense Authorization/Rule.** Adoption of the rule that would provide for House floor consideration of a bill that would reauthorize grant and assistance programs under the Violence Against Women Act through fiscal 2017. The rule also would provide one hour of general debate for a bill (HR 4310) to authorize fiscal 2013 funding for Defense Department and national security programs. Adopted 235-186: R 234-2; D 1-184. May 16, 2012.

256. **HR 4119. Border Tunnel Smuggling/Passage.** Smith, R-Texas, motion to suspend the rules and pass the bill that would make attempting to or conspiring to use, finance or construct a tunnel to be used for smuggling a criminal offense. Motion agreed to 416-4: R 233-3; D 183-1. A two-thirds majority of those present and voting (280 in this case) is required for passage under suspension of the rules. May 16, 2012.

	250	251	252	253	254	255	256
ALABAMA							
1 Bonner	Y	Y	Y	Y	Y	Y	Y
2 Roby	Y	Y	Y	Y	Y	Y	Y
3 Rogers	Y	Y	Y	Y	Y	Y	Y
4 Aderholt	Y	Y	Y	Y	Y	Y	Y
5 Brooks	Y	Y	Y	Y	Y	Y	Y
6 Bachus	Y	Y	Y	Y	Y	Y	Y
7 Sewell	Y	Y	Y	N	N	N	Y
ALASKA							
AL Young	Y	Y	Y	Y	Y	P	Y
ARIZONA							
1 Gosar	Y	Y	Y	Y	Y	Y	Y
2 Franks	+	+	+	Y	Y	Y	Y
3 Quayle	Y	Y	Y	Y	Y	Y	Y
4 Pastor	Y	Y	Y	N	N	N	Y
5 Schweikert	Y	Y	Y	Y	Y	Y	Y
6 Flake	?	?	?	Y	Y	Y	Y
7 Grijalva	Y	Y	Y	N	N	N	Y
8 Vacant							
ARKANSAS							
1 Crawford	+	+	+	Y	Y	Y	Y
2 Griffin	Y	Y	Y	Y	Y	Y	Y
3 Womack	Y	Y	Y	Y	Y	Y	Y
4 Ross	Y	Y	Y	N	N	N	Y
CALIFORNIA							
1 Thompson	Y	Y	Y	N	N	N	Y
2 Herger	Y	Y	Y	Y	N	Y	Y
3 Lungren	Y	Y	Y	Y	Y	Y	Y
4 McClintock	Y	Y	Y	Y	Y	Y	Y
5 Matsui	Y	Y	Y	N	N	N	Y
6 Woolsey	Y	Y	Y	N	N	N	Y
7 Miller, George	Y	Y	Y	N	N	N	Y
8 Pelosi	?	Y	Y	N	N	N	Y
9 Lee	Y	Y	Y	N	N	N	Y
10 Garamendi	Y	Y	Y	N	N	N	Y
11 McNerney	Y	Y	Y	N	N	N	Y
12 Speier	?	?	?	N	N	N	Y
13 Stark	Y	Y	Y	N	N	N	Y
14 Eshoo	Y	Y	Y	N	N	N	Y
15 Honda	Y	Y	Y	N	N	N	Y
16 Lofgren	Y	Y	Y	N	N	N	Y
17 Farr	Y	Y	Y	N	N	N	Y
18 Cardoza	?	?	?	N	N	N	Y
19 Denham	Y	Y	Y	Y	Y	Y	Y
20 Costa	Y	Y	Y	N	N	N	Y
21 Nunes	Y	Y	Y	Y	Y	Y	Y
22 McCarthy	Y	Y	Y	Y	Y	Y	Y
23 Capps	Y	Y	Y	N	N	N	Y
24 Gallegly	Y	Y	Y	Y	Y	Y	Y
25 McKeon	Y	Y	Y	Y	Y	Y	Y
26 Dreier	Y	Y	Y	Y	Y	Y	Y
27 Sherman	Y	Y	Y	N	N	N	Y
28 Berman	Y	Y	Y	N	N	N	Y
29 Schiff	Y	Y	Y	N	N	N	Y
30 Waxman	Y	Y	Y	N	N	N	Y
31 Becerra	Y	Y	Y	N	N	N	Y
32 Chu	Y	Y	Y	N	N	N	Y
33 Bass	Y	Y	Y	N	N	N	Y
34 Roybal-Allard	Y	Y	Y	N	N	N	Y
35 Waters	Y	Y	Y	N	N	N	Y
36 Hahn	Y	Y	Y	N	N	N	Y
37 Richardson	Y	Y	Y	N	N	N	Y
38 Napolitano	Y	Y	Y	N	N	N	Y
39 Sánchez, Linda	Y	Y	Y	N	N	N	Y
40 Royce	Y	Y	Y	Y	Y	Y	Y
41 Lewis	Y	Y	Y	Y	Y	Y	Y
42 Miller, Gary	Y	Y	Y	Y	Y	Y	Y
43 Baca	Y	Y	Y	N	N	N	Y
44 Calvert	Y	Y	Y	Y	Y	Y	Y
45 Bono Mack	Y	Y	Y	Y	Y	Y	Y
46 Rohrabacher	?	?	?	Y	Y	Y	Y
47 Sanchez, Loretta	Y	Y	Y	N	N	N	Y
48 Campbell	?	Y	Y	Y	Y	Y	Y
49 Issa	Y	Y	Y	Y	Y	Y	Y
50 Bilbray	Y	Y	Y	Y	Y	Y	Y
51 Filner	+	+	+	-	-	-	+
52 Hunter	Y	Y	Y	Y	Y	Y	Y
53 Davis	Y	Y	Y	N	N	N	Y
COLORADO							
1 DeGette	Y	Y	Y	N	N	N	Y
2 Polis	Y	Y	Y	N	N	N	Y
3 Tipton	Y	Y	Y	Y	Y	Y	Y
4 Gardner	Y	Y	Y	Y	Y	Y	Y
5 Lamborn	Y	Y	Y	Y	Y	Y	Y
6 Coffman	Y	Y	Y	Y	Y	Y	Y
7 Perlmutter	Y	Y	Y	N	?	?	?
CONNECTICUT							
1 Larson	Y	Y	Y	N	N	N	Y
2 Courtney	Y	Y	Y	N	N	N	Y
3 DeLauro	Y	Y	Y	N	N	N	Y
4 Himes	Y	Y	Y	N	N	N	Y
5 Murphy	Y	Y	Y	N	N	N	Y
DELAWARE							
AL Carney	Y	Y	Y	N	N	N	Y
FLORIDA							
1 Miller	Y	Y	Y	Y	Y	Y	Y
2 Southerland	Y	Y	Y	Y	Y	Y	Y
3 Brown	?	?	?	N	N	N	Y
4 Crenshaw	Y	Y	Y	Y	Y	Y	Y
5 Nugent	Y	Y	Y	Y	Y	Y	Y
6 Stearns	Y	Y	Y	Y	Y	Y	Y
7 Mica	Y	Y	Y	Y	Y	Y	Y
8 Webster	Y	Y	Y	Y	Y	Y	Y
9 Bilirakis	Y	Y	Y	Y	Y	Y	Y
10 Young	Y	Y	Y	?	Y	Y	Y
11 Castor	Y	Y	Y	N	N	N	Y
12 Ross	Y	Y	Y	Y	Y	Y	Y
13 Buchanan	Y	Y	Y	Y	Y	Y	Y
14 Mack	Y	Y	Y	Y	Y	Y	Y
15 Posey	Y	Y	Y	Y	Y	Y	Y
16 Rooney	Y	Y	Y	Y	Y	Y	Y
17 Wilson	Y	Y	Y	N	N	N	Y
18 Ros-Lehtinen	Y	Y	Y	N	N	N	Y
19 Deutch	Y	Y	Y	N	N	N	Y
20 Wasserman Schultz	Y	Y	Y	N	N	N	Y
21 Diaz-Balart	Y	Y	Y	Y	Y	Y	Y
22 West	Y	Y	Y	Y	Y	Y	Y
23 Hastings	Y	Y	Y	N	N	N	Y
24 Adams	Y	Y	Y	Y	Y	Y	Y
25 Rivera	Y	Y	Y	Y	Y	Y	Y
GEORGIA							
1 Kingston	Y	Y	Y	Y	Y	Y	Y
2 Bishop	Y	Y	Y	N	N	N	Y
3 Westmoreland	Y	Y	Y	Y	Y	Y	Y
4 Johnson	Y	Y	Y	N	N	N	Y
5 Lewis	Y	Y	Y	N	N	N	Y
6 Price	Y	Y	Y	Y	Y	Y	Y
7 Woodall	Y	Y	Y	Y	Y	Y	Y
8 Scott, A.	Y	Y	Y	Y	Y	Y	Y
9 Graves	Y	Y	Y	Y	Y	Y	Y
10 Broun	Y	Y	Y	Y	Y	Y	N
11 Gingrey	Y	Y	Y	Y	Y	Y	Y
12 Barrow	Y	Y	Y	N	N	N	Y
13 Scott, D.	Y	Y	Y	N	N	N	Y
HAWAII							
1 Hanabusa	Y	Y	Y	N	N	N	Y
2 Hirono	Y	Y	Y	N	N	N	Y
IDAHO							
1 Labrador	?	?	?	?	?	?	?
2 Simpson	Y	Y	Y	Y	Y	Y	Y
ILLINOIS							
1 Rush	Y	Y	Y	N	N	N	Y
2 Jackson	Y	Y	Y	N	N	N	Y
3 Lipinski	Y	Y	Y	N	N	N	Y
4 Gutierrez	Y	Y	Y	N	N	N	Y
5 Quigley	Y	Y	Y	N	N	N	Y
6 Roskam	Y	Y	Y	Y	Y	Y	Y
7 Davis	Y	Y	Y	N	N	N	Y
8 Walsh	Y	Y	Y	Y	Y	Y	Y
9 Schakowsky	Y	Y	Y	N	N	N	Y
10 Dold	+	+	+	Y	Y	Y	Y
11 Kinzinger	Y	Y	Y	Y	Y	Y	Y
12 Costello	Y	Y	Y	N	N	N	Y
13 Biggert	Y	Y	Y	Y	Y	Y	Y
14 Hultgren	Y	Y	Y	Y	Y	Y	Y
15 Johnson	+	+	+	Y	Y	Y	Y

KEY Republicans   Democrats

Y Voted for (yea)	X Paired against
# Paired for	- Announced against
+ Announced for	P Voted "present"
N Voted against (nay)	

C Voted "present" to avoid possible conflict of interest

? Did not vote or otherwise make a position known

	250	251	252	253	254	255	256
16 **Manzullo**	Y	?	?	Y	Y	Y	Y
17 **Schilling**	Y	Y	Y	Y	Y	Y	Y
18 **Schock**	Y	Y	Y	Y	Y	Y	Y
19 **Shimkus**	Y	Y	Y	Y	Y	Y	Y
INDIANA							
1 Visclosky	Y	Y	Y	N	N	N	Y
2 Donnelly	Y	Y	Y	N	N	N	Y
3 **Stutzman**	?	Y	Y	Y	Y	Y	Y
4 **Rokita**	Y	Y	Y	Y	Y	Y	Y
5 **Burton**	Y	Y	Y	+	+	+	+
6 **Pence**	Y	Y	Y	Y	Y	Y	Y
7 Carson	Y	Y	Y	N	N	N	Y
8 **Bucshon**	Y	Y	Y	Y	Y	Y	Y
9 **Young**	Y	Y	Y	Y	Y	Y	Y
IOWA							
1 Braley	?	Y	Y	N	N	N	Y
2 Loebsack	Y	Y	Y	N	N	N	Y
3 Boswell	Y	Y	Y	N	N	N	Y
4 **Latham**	Y	Y	Y	Y	Y	Y	Y
5 **King**	Y	Y	Y	?	Y	N	Y
KANSAS							
1 **Huelskamp**	Y	Y	Y	Y	Y	Y	Y
2 **Jenkins**	Y	Y	Y	Y	Y	Y	Y
3 **Yoder**	Y	Y	Y	Y	Y	Y	Y
4 **Pompeo**	Y	Y	Y	Y	Y	Y	Y
KENTUCKY							
1 **Whitfield**	Y	Y	Y	Y	Y	Y	Y
2 **Guthrie**	Y	Y	Y	Y	Y	Y	Y
3 Yarmuth	+	+	+	N	N	–	+
4 **Davis**	Y	Y	Y	Y	Y	Y	Y
5 **Rogers**	Y	Y	Y	Y	Y	Y	Y
6 Chandler	Y	Y	Y	?	N	N	Y
LOUISIANA							
1 **Scalise**	Y	Y	Y	Y	Y	Y	Y
2 Richmond	?	?	?	N	N	N	Y
3 **Landry**	?	?	?	Y	Y	Y	Y
4 **Fleming**	Y	Y	Y	Y	Y	Y	Y
5 **Alexander**	Y	Y	Y	Y	Y	Y	Y
6 **Cassidy**	?	?	?	?	?	?	?
7 **Boustany**	+	+	+	Y	Y	Y	Y
MAINE							
1 Pingree	Y	Y	Y	N	N	N	Y
2 Michaud	Y	Y	Y	N	N	N	Y
MARYLAND							
1 **Harris**	Y	Y	Y	Y	Y	Y	Y
2 Ruppersberger	Y	Y	?	N	N	N	Y
3 Sarbanes	Y	Y	Y	N	N	N	Y
4 Edwards	Y	Y	Y	N	N	N	Y
5 Hoyer	Y	Y	Y	N	N	N	Y
6 **Bartlett**	Y	Y	Y	Y	Y	Y	Y
7 Cummings	Y	Y	Y	N	N	N	Y
8 Van Hollen	Y	Y	Y	N	N	N	Y
MASSACHUSETTS							
1 Olver	Y	Y	Y	N	N	N	Y
2 Neal	Y	Y	Y	N	N	N	Y
3 McGovern	Y	Y	Y	N	N	N	Y
4 Frank	?	?	?	N	N	N	Y
5 Tsongas	Y	Y	Y	N	N	N	Y
6 Tierney	Y	Y	Y	N	N	N	Y
7 Markey	Y	Y	Y	N	N	N	Y
8 Capuano	Y	Y	Y	N	N	N	Y
9 Lynch	Y	Y	Y	N	N	N	Y
10 Keating	Y	Y	Y	N	N	N	Y
MICHIGAN							
1 **Benishek**	Y	Y	Y	Y	Y	Y	Y
2 **Huizenga**	Y	Y	Y	Y	Y	Y	Y
3 **Amash**	N	N	Y	Y	Y	Y	N
4 **Camp**	Y	Y	Y	Y	Y	Y	Y
5 Kildee	Y	Y	Y	N	N	N	Y
6 **Upton**	Y	Y	Y	Y	Y	Y	Y
7 **Walberg**	Y	Y	Y	Y	Y	Y	Y
8 **Rogers**	Y	Y	Y	Y	Y	Y	Y
9 Peters	Y	Y	Y	N	N	N	Y
10 **Miller**	Y	Y	Y	Y	Y	Y	Y
11 **McCotter**	Y	Y	Y	Y	Y	Y	Y
12 Levin	Y	Y	Y	N	N	N	Y
13 Clarke	Y	Y	Y	N	N	N	Y
14 Conyers	?	Y	Y	N	N	N	Y
15 Dingell	Y	Y	Y	N	N	N	Y
MINNESOTA							
1 Walz	Y	Y	Y	N	N	N	Y
2 **Kline**	Y	Y	Y	Y	Y	Y	Y
3 **Paulsen**	Y	Y	Y	Y	Y	Y	Y
4 McCollum	Y	Y	Y	N	N	N	Y
5 Ellison	Y	Y	Y	N	N	N	Y
6 **Bachmann**	Y	Y	Y	Y	Y	Y	Y
7 Peterson	Y	Y	Y	Y	N	N	Y
8 **Cravaack**	Y	Y	Y	Y	Y	Y	Y
MISSISSIPPI							
1 **Nunnelee**	Y	Y	Y	Y	Y	Y	Y
2 Thompson	Y	Y	Y	N	N	N	Y
3 **Harper**	Y	Y	Y	Y	Y	Y	Y
4 **Palazzo**	Y	Y	Y	Y	Y	Y	Y
MISSOURI							
1 Clay	Y	Y	Y	N	N	N	Y
2 **Akin**	Y	Y	Y	Y	?	Y	Y
3 Carnahan	Y	Y	Y	N	N	N	Y
4 **Hartzler**	Y	Y	Y	Y	Y	Y	Y
5 Cleaver	Y	Y	Y	N	N	N	Y
6 **Graves**	Y	Y	Y	Y	Y	Y	Y
7 **Long**	Y	Y	Y	Y	Y	Y	Y
8 **Emerson**	Y	Y	Y	Y	Y	Y	Y
9 **Luetkemeyer**	+	+	+	Y	?	Y	Y
MONTANA							
AL **Rehberg**	Y	Y	Y	Y	Y	Y	Y
NEBRASKA							
1 **Fortenberry**	Y	Y	Y	Y	Y	Y	Y
2 **Terry**	Y	Y	Y	Y	Y	Y	Y
3 **Smith**	Y	Y	Y	Y	Y	Y	Y
NEVADA							
1 Berkley	Y	Y	Y	N	N	N	Y
2 **Amodei**	Y	Y	Y	Y	Y	Y	Y
3 **Heck**	Y	Y	Y	Y	Y	Y	Y
NEW HAMPSHIRE							
1 **Guinta**	Y	Y	Y	Y	Y	Y	Y
2 **Bass**	Y	Y	Y	Y	Y	Y	Y
NEW JERSEY							
1 Andrews	Y	Y	Y	?	N	N	Y
2 **LoBiondo**	Y	Y	Y	Y	Y	Y	Y
3 **Runyan**	Y	Y	Y	Y	Y	Y	Y
4 **Smith**	Y	Y	Y	Y	Y	Y	Y
5 **Garrett**	Y	Y	Y	Y	Y	Y	Y
6 Pallone	Y	Y	Y	N	N	N	Y
7 **Lance**	Y	Y	Y	Y	Y	Y	Y
8 Pascrell	Y	Y	Y	N	N	N	Y
9 Rothman	Y	Y	Y	N	N	N	Y
10 Vacant							
11 **Frelinghuysen**	Y	Y	Y	Y	Y	Y	Y
12 Holt	Y	Y	Y	N	N	N	Y
13 Sires	Y	Y	Y	N	N	N	Y
NEW MEXICO							
1 Heinrich	Y	Y	Y	N	N	N	Y
2 **Pearce**	Y	Y	Y	Y	Y	Y	Y
3 Luján	Y	Y	Y	N	N	N	Y
NEW YORK							
1 Bishop	Y	Y	Y	N	N	N	Y
2 Israel	Y	Y	Y	N	N	N	Y
3 **King**	Y	Y	Y	Y	Y	Y	Y
4 McCarthy	Y	Y	Y	N	N	N	Y
5 Ackerman	?	?	?	N	N	N	Y
6 Meeks	Y	Y	Y	N	N	N	Y
7 Crowley	Y	Y	Y	N	N	N	Y
8 Nadler	Y	Y	Y	N	N	N	Y
9 **Turner**	Y	Y	Y	Y	Y	Y	Y
10 Towns	Y	Y	Y	N	N	N	Y
11 Clarke	Y	Y	Y	N	N	N	Y
12 Velázquez	Y	Y	Y	N	N	N	Y
13 **Grimm**	Y	Y	Y	Y	Y	Y	Y
14 Maloney	Y	Y	Y	N	N	N	Y
15 Rangel	Y	Y	Y	N	N	N	Y
16 Serrano	Y	Y	Y	N	N	N	Y
17 Engel	Y	Y	Y	N	N	N	Y
18 Lowey	Y	Y	Y	N	N	N	Y
19 **Hayworth**	Y	Y	Y	Y	Y	Y	Y
20 **Gibson**	Y	Y	Y	Y	Y	Y	Y
21 Tonko	Y	Y	Y	N	N	N	Y
22 Hinchey	?	?	?	N	N	N	Y
23 Owens	Y	Y	Y	N	N	N	Y
24 **Hanna**	Y	Y	Y	Y	Y	Y	Y
25 **Buerkle**	Y	Y	Y	Y	Y	Y	Y
26 Hochul	Y	Y	Y	N	N	N	Y
27 Higgins	Y	Y	Y	N	N	N	Y
28 Slaughter	?	?	?	?	?	?	?
29 **Reed**	Y	Y	Y	Y	Y	Y	Y
NORTH CAROLINA							
1 Butterfield	Y	Y	Y	N	N	N	Y
2 **Ellmers**	Y	Y	Y	Y	Y	Y	Y
3 **Jones**	Y	Y	Y	Y	Y	Y	Y
4 Price	Y	Y	Y	N	N	N	Y
5 **Foxx**	Y	Y	Y	Y	Y	Y	Y
6 **Coble**	Y	Y	Y	Y	Y	Y	Y
7 McIntyre	+	+	+	N	N	N	Y
8 Kissell	Y	Y	Y	N	N	N	Y
9 **Myrick**	Y	Y	Y	Y	Y	Y	Y
10 **McHenry**	Y	Y	Y	Y	Y	Y	Y
11 Shuler	?	?	?	Y	Y	Y	Y
12 Watt	Y	Y	Y	N	N	N	Y
13 Miller	Y	Y	Y	N	N	N	Y
NORTH DAKOTA							
AL **Berg**	Y	Y	Y	Y	Y	Y	Y
OHIO							
1 **Chabot**	Y	Y	Y	Y	Y	Y	Y
2 **Schmidt**	Y	Y	Y	Y	Y	Y	Y
3 **Turner**	Y	Y	Y	Y	Y	Y	?
4 **Jordan**	Y	Y	Y	Y	Y	Y	Y
5 **Latta**	Y	Y	Y	Y	Y	Y	Y
6 **Johnson**	Y	Y	Y	Y	Y	Y	Y
7 **Austria**	Y	Y	Y	Y	Y	Y	Y
8 **Boehner**							
9 Kaptur	Y	Y	Y	N	N	N	Y
10 Kucinich	Y	Y	Y	N	N	N	Y
11 Fudge	?	?	?	N	N	N	Y
12 **Tiberi**	Y	Y	Y	Y	Y	Y	Y
13 Sutton	Y	Y	Y	N	N	N	Y
14 **LaTourette**	Y	Y	Y	Y	Y	Y	Y
15 **Stivers**	Y	Y	Y	Y	Y	Y	Y
16 **Renacci**	Y	Y	Y	Y	Y	Y	Y
17 Ryan	Y	Y	Y	N	N	N	Y
18 **Gibbs**	Y	Y	Y	Y	Y	Y	Y
OKLAHOMA							
1 **Sullivan**	Y	Y	Y	Y	Y	Y	Y
2 Boren	Y	Y	Y	N	N	N	?
3 **Lucas**	Y	Y	Y	Y	Y	Y	Y
4 **Cole**	Y	Y	Y	Y	Y	Y	Y
5 **Lankford**	Y	Y	Y	Y	Y	Y	Y
OREGON							
1 Bonamici	Y	Y	Y	N	N	N	Y
2 **Walden**	Y	Y	Y	Y	Y	Y	Y
3 Blumenauer	Y	Y	Y	N	N	N	Y
4 DeFazio	Y	Y	Y	N	N	N	Y
5 Schrader	Y	Y	Y	N	N	N	Y
PENNSYLVANIA							
1 Brady	Y	Y	Y	N	N	N	Y
2 Fattah	Y	Y	Y	N	N	N	Y
3 **Kelly**	Y	Y	Y	Y	Y	Y	Y
4 Altmire	Y	Y	Y	N	N	?	?
5 **Thompson**	Y	Y	Y	Y	Y	Y	Y
6 **Gerlach**	Y	Y	Y	Y	Y	?	?
7 **Meehan**	Y	Y	Y	Y	Y	Y	Y
8 **Fitzpatrick**	Y	Y	Y	Y	Y	Y	Y
9 **Shuster**	Y	Y	Y	Y	Y	Y	Y
10 **Marino**	Y	Y	Y	Y	Y	Y	Y
11 **Barletta**	Y	Y	Y	Y	Y	Y	Y
12 Critz	Y	Y	Y	N	N	N	Y
13 Schwartz	Y	Y	Y	N	N	N	Y
14 Doyle	Y	Y	Y	N	N	N	Y
15 **Dent**	Y	Y	Y	Y	Y	Y	Y
16 **Pitts**	Y	Y	Y	?	Y	Y	Y
17 Holden	Y	Y	Y	N	N	N	Y
18 **Murphy**	Y	Y	Y	Y	Y	Y	Y
19 **Platts**	Y	Y	Y	Y	Y	Y	Y
RHODE ISLAND							
1 Cicilline	Y	Y	Y	N	N	N	Y
2 Langevin	+	Y	Y	N	N	N	Y
SOUTH CAROLINA							
1 **Scott**	?	Y	Y	Y	Y	Y	Y
2 **Wilson**	Y	Y	Y	Y	Y	Y	Y
3 **Duncan**	Y	Y	Y	Y	Y	Y	Y
4 **Gowdy**	Y	Y	Y	Y	Y	Y	Y
5 **Mulvaney**	Y	Y	Y	Y	Y	Y	Y
6 Clyburn	Y	Y	Y	N	N	N	Y
SOUTH DAKOTA							
AL **Noem**	Y	Y	Y	Y	Y	Y	Y
TENNESSEE							
1 **Roe**	Y	Y	Y	Y	Y	Y	Y
2 **Duncan**	Y	Y	Y	Y	Y	Y	Y
3 **Fleischmann**	Y	Y	Y	Y	Y	Y	Y
4 **DesJarlais**	Y	Y	Y	Y	Y	Y	Y
5 Cooper	Y	Y	Y	N	N	N	Y
6 **Black**	Y	Y	Y	Y	Y	N	Y
7 **Blackburn**	Y	Y	Y	Y	Y	Y	Y
8 **Fincher**	+	+	+	Y	Y	Y	Y
9 Cohen	+	+	+	N	N	N	Y
TEXAS							
1 **Gohmert**	Y	Y	Y	Y	Y	Y	Y
2 **Poe**	?	?	?	Y	Y	Y	Y
3 **Johnson, S.**	Y	Y	Y	Y	Y	Y	Y
4 **Hall**	Y	Y	Y	Y	Y	Y	Y
5 **Hensarling**	Y	Y	Y	Y	Y	Y	Y
6 **Barton**	Y	Y	Y	Y	Y	Y	Y
7 **Culberson**	Y	Y	Y	Y	Y	Y	Y
8 **Brady**	Y	Y	Y	Y	Y	Y	Y
9 Green, A.	Y	Y	Y	N	N	N	Y
10 **McCaul**	Y	Y	Y	Y	Y	Y	Y
11 **Conaway**	Y	Y	Y	Y	Y	Y	Y
12 **Granger**	Y	Y	Y	Y	Y	Y	Y
13 **Thornberry**	Y	Y	Y	Y	Y	Y	Y
14 **Paul**	?	?	?	Y	Y	Y	N
15 Hinojosa	Y	Y	Y	N	N	N	Y
16 Reyes	Y	Y	Y	N	N	N	Y
17 **Flores**	?	?	?	Y	Y	Y	Y
18 Jackson Lee	Y	Y	Y	N	N	N	Y
19 **Neugebauer**	Y	Y	Y	Y	Y	Y	Y
20 Gonzalez	Y	Y	Y	N	N	N	Y
21 **Smith**	Y	Y	Y	Y	Y	Y	Y
22 **Olson**	Y	Y	Y	Y	Y	Y	Y
23 **Canseco**	Y	Y	Y	Y	Y	Y	Y
24 **Marchant**	Y	Y	Y	Y	Y	Y	Y
25 Doggett	Y	Y	Y	N	N	N	Y
26 **Burgess**	Y	Y	Y	Y	Y	Y	Y
27 **Farenthold**	Y	Y	Y	Y	Y	Y	Y
28 Cuellar	Y	Y	Y	N	N	N	Y
29 Green, G.	Y	Y	Y	N	N	N	Y
30 Johnson, E.	Y	Y	Y	N	N	N	Y
31 **Carter**	Y	Y	Y	Y	Y	Y	Y
32 **Sessions**	Y	Y	Y	Y	Y	Y	Y
UTAH							
1 **Bishop**	Y	Y	Y	Y	Y	Y	Y
2 Matheson	Y	Y	Y	N	N	N	Y
3 **Chaffetz**	Y	Y	Y	Y	Y	Y	Y
VERMONT							
AL Welch	Y	Y	Y	N	N	N	Y
VIRGINIA							
1 **Wittman**	Y	Y	Y	Y	Y	Y	Y
2 **Rigell**	Y	Y	Y	Y	Y	Y	Y
3 Scott	Y	Y	Y	N	N	N	N
4 **Forbes**	Y	Y	Y	Y	Y	Y	Y
5 **Hurt**	Y	Y	Y	Y	Y	Y	Y
6 **Goodlatte**	Y	Y	Y	Y	Y	Y	Y
7 **Cantor**	Y	Y	Y	Y	Y	Y	Y
8 Moran	Y	Y	Y	N	N	N	Y
9 **Griffith**	Y	Y	Y	Y	Y	Y	Y
10 **Wolf**	Y	Y	Y	Y	Y	Y	Y
11 Connolly	Y	Y	Y	N	N	N	Y
WASHINGTON							
1 Vacant							
2 Larsen	Y	Y	Y	N	N	N	Y
3 **Herrera Beutler**	Y	Y	Y	Y	Y	Y	Y
4 **Hastings**	Y	Y	Y	Y	Y	Y	Y
5 **McMorris Rodgers**	Y	Y	Y	Y	Y	Y	Y
6 Dicks	Y	Y	Y	N	N	N	Y
7 McDermott	Y	Y	Y	N	N	N	Y
8 **Reichert**	Y	Y	Y	Y	Y	Y	Y
9 Smith	Y	Y	Y	N	N	N	Y
WEST VIRGINIA							
1 **McKinley**	Y	Y	Y	Y	Y	Y	Y
2 **Capito**	Y	Y	Y	Y	Y	Y	Y
3 Rahall	Y	Y	Y	N	N	N	Y
WISCONSIN							
1 **Ryan**	Y	Y	Y	Y	Y	Y	Y
2 Baldwin	Y	Y	Y	N	N	N	Y
3 Kind	Y	Y	Y	N	N	N	Y
4 Moore	Y	Y	Y	N	N	N	Y
5 **Sensenbrenner**	Y	Y	Y	Y	Y	Y	Y
6 **Petri**	Y	Y	Y	Y	Y	Y	Y
7 **Duffy**	Y	Y	Y	Y	Y	Y	Y
8 **Ribble**	Y	Y	Y	Y	Y	Y	Y
WYOMING							
AL **Lummis**	Y	Y	Y	Y	Y	Y	Y

IN THE HOUSE | By Vote Number

257. HR 4970. Violence Against Women Act Reauthorization/ **Recommit.** Moore, D-Wis., motion to recommit the bill to the House Judiciary Committee and report it back immediately with an amendment that would stipulate that nothing in the bill would eliminate, reduce or limit confidentiality protections in current law to shield domestic violence victims from future violence. Motion rejected 187-236: R 2-236; D 185-0. May 16, 2012.

258. HR 4970. Violence Against Women Act Reauthorization/ **Passage.** Passage of the bill that would authorize $660 million per year through fiscal 2017 to reauthorize and modify grant and assistance programs enacted under the Violence Against Women Act. The bill would authorize funds for law enforcement training programs, prosecution and victim services. It also would impose mandatory criminal penalties for certain aggravated sexual crimes, modify visa programs for immigrant victims of domestic violence and make changes to current law protections for housing services provided to victims of violence and abuse. Passed 222-205: R 216-23; D 6-182. A "nay" was a vote in support of the president's position. May 16, 2012.

259. HR 4310. Fiscal 2013 Defense Authorization/Previous **Question.** Bishop, R-Utah, motion to order the previous question (thus ending debate and the possibility of amendment) on adoption of the rule (H Res 661) that would provide for further House floor consideration of the bill that would authorize fiscal 2013 funding for Defense Department and national security programs. Motion agreed to 236-182: R 233-3; D 3-179. May 17, 2012.

260. H Res 661. Fiscal 2013 Defense Authorization/Rule. Adoption of the rule (H Res 661) that would provide for further House floor consideration of the bill that would authorize fiscal 2013 funding for Defense Department and national security programs. Adopted 244-178: R 236-4; D 8-174. May 17, 2012.

261. H Res 568. Iranian Nuclear Weapons Capability/Adoption. Ros-Lehtinen, R-Fla., motion to suspend the rules and adopt the resolution that would express support for an increase in economic and diplomatic pressure on Iran to prevent the country from acquiring nuclear weapons capability. It also would press for an agreement with the government of Iran that includes suspension of all uranium enrichment activities, complete cooperation with the International Atomic Energy Agency and a permanent agreement that verifiably assures that Iran's nuclear program is peaceful. Motion agreed to 401-11: R 235-4; D 166-7. A two-thirds majority of those present and voting (275 in this case) is required for adoption under suspension of the rules. May 17, 2012.

262. HR 5740. National Flood Insurance Program Reauthorization/ **Passage.** Biggert, R-Ill., motion to suspend the rules and pass the bill that would extend through June 30, 2012, authorization for the National Flood Insurance Program. The bill would allow homeowners to purchase private flood insurance to satisfy the program's mandatory flood insurance coverage as long as the insurance meets federal coverage requirements. Motion agreed to 402-18: R 221-17; D 181-1. A two-thirds majority of those present and voting (280 in this case) is required for passage under suspension of the rules. May 17, 2012.

	257	258	259	260	261	262
ALABAMA						
1 Bonner	N	Y	Y	Y	Y	Y
2 Roby	N	Y	Y	Y	Y	Y
3 Rogers	N	Y	Y	Y	Y	Y
4 Aderholt	N	Y	Y	Y	Y	Y
5 Brooks	N	Y	Y	Y	Y	Y
6 Bachus	N	Y	Y	Y	Y	Y
7 Sewell	Y	N	N	N	Y	Y
ALASKA						
AL Young	N	Y	Y	Y	Y	Y
ARIZONA						
1 Gosar	N	N	Y	Y	Y	Y
2 Franks	N	Y	Y	Y	Y	N
3 Quayle	N	Y	Y	Y	Y	N
4 Pastor	Y	N	N	N	Y	Y
5 Schweikert	N	Y	Y	Y	Y	N
6 Flake	N	Y	Y	Y	Y	N
7 Grijalva	Y	N	N	N	Y	Y
8 Vacant						
ARKANSAS						
1 Crawford	N	Y	Y	Y	Y	Y
2 Griffin	N	Y	Y	Y	Y	Y
3 Womack	N	Y	Y	Y	Y	Y
4 Ross	Y	N	Y	Y	Y	Y
CALIFORNIA						
1 Thompson	Y	N	N	N	Y	Y
2 Herger	N	Y	Y	Y	Y	Y
3 Lungren	N	Y	Y	Y	Y	Y
4 McClintock	N	N	Y	Y	Y	N
5 Matsui	Y	N	N	N	Y	Y
6 Woolsey	Y	N	N	N	N	Y
7 Miller, George	Y	N	?	?	?	?
8 Pelosi	Y	N	N	N	N	Y
9 Lee	Y	N	N	N	N	Y
10 Garamendi	Y	N	N	N	Y	Y
11 McNerney	Y	N	N	N	Y	Y
12 Speier	Y	N	N	P	Y	Y
13 Stark	Y	N	N	N	N	Y
14 Eshoo	Y	N	N	N	Y	Y
15 Honda	Y	N	N	P	N	Y
16 Lofgren	Y	N	N	N	Y	Y
17 Farr	Y	N	N	N	Y	Y
18 Cardoza	Y	N	N	N	Y	Y
19 Denham	N	Y	Y	Y	Y	Y
20 Costa	Y	N	N	N	Y	Y
21 Nunes	N	Y	Y	Y	Y	Y
22 McCarthy	N	Y	Y	Y	Y	Y
23 Capps	Y	N	N	N	Y	Y
24 Gallegly	N	Y	Y	Y	Y	Y
25 McKeon	N	Y	Y	Y	Y	Y
26 Dreier	N	Y	Y	Y	Y	Y
27 Sherman	Y	N	N	N	Y	Y
28 Berman	Y	N	N	N	Y	Y
29 Schiff	Y	N	N	N	Y	Y
30 Waxman	Y	N	N	N	Y	Y
31 Becerra	Y	N	N	N	Y	Y
32 Chu	Y	N	N	N	Y	Y
33 Bass	Y	N	N	N	Y	Y
34 Roybal-Allard	Y	N	N	N	Y	Y
35 Waters	Y	N	N	N	Y	Y
36 Hahn	Y	N	N	N	Y	Y
37 Richardson	Y	N	N	N	Y	Y
38 Napolitano	Y	N	N	N	Y	Y
39 Sánchez, Linda	?	N	N	N	Y	Y
40 Royce	N	Y	Y	Y	Y	Y
41 Lewis	N	Y	Y	Y	Y	Y
42 Miller, Gary	N	Y	Y	Y	Y	Y
43 Baca	Y	N	N	N	Y	Y
44 Calvert	N	Y	Y	Y	Y	Y
45 Bono Mack	N	Y	Y	Y	Y	Y
46 Rohrabacher	N	Y	Y	Y	Y	Y
47 Sanchez, Loretta	Y	N	?	?	?	?
48 Campbell	N	Y	Y	N	Y	Y
49 Issa	N	Y	?	Y	Y	Y
50 Bilbray	N	Y	Y	Y	Y	Y
51 Filner	+	–	–	–	+	+
52 Hunter	N	Y	Y	Y	Y	Y
53 Davis	Y	N	N	N	Y	Y

	257	258	259	260	261	262
COLORADO						
1 DeGette	Y	N	N	N	Y	Y
2 Polis	Y	N	N	N	Y	Y
3 Tipton	N	Y	Y	Y	Y	Y
4 Gardner	N	Y	Y	Y	Y	Y
5 Lamborn	N	Y	Y	Y	Y	Y
6 Coffman	N	Y	Y	Y	Y	Y
7 Perlmutter	Y	N	N	N	Y	Y
CONNECTICUT						
1 Larson	Y	N	N	N	Y	Y
2 Courtney	Y	N	N	N	Y	Y
3 DeLauro	Y	N	N	N	Y	Y
4 Himes	Y	N	N	N	Y	Y
5 Murphy	Y	N	N	N	Y	Y
DELAWARE						
AL Carney	Y	N	N	N	Y	Y
FLORIDA						
1 Miller	N	Y	Y	Y	Y	Y
2 Southerland	N	Y	?	Y	Y	Y
3 Brown	Y	N	N	N	Y	Y
4 Crenshaw	N	Y	Y	Y	Y	Y
5 Nugent	N	Y	Y	Y	Y	Y
6 Stearns	N	Y	Y	Y	Y	Y
7 Mica	N	Y	Y	Y	Y	Y
8 Webster	N	Y	Y	Y	Y	Y
9 Bilirakis	N	Y	Y	Y	Y	Y
10 Young	N	Y	Y	Y	Y	Y
11 Castor	Y	N	N	N	Y	Y
12 Ross	N	Y	Y	Y	Y	N
13 Buchanan	N	Y	Y	Y	Y	Y
14 Mack	N	Y	Y	Y	Y	N
15 Posey	N	Y	Y	Y	Y	Y
16 Rooney	N	Y	Y	Y	Y	Y
17 Wilson	Y	N	N	N	Y	Y
18 Ros-Lehtinen	N	N	Y	Y	Y	Y
19 Deutch	Y	N	N	N	Y	Y
20 Wasserman Schultz	Y	N	?	?	?	?
21 Diaz-Balart	N	N	Y	Y	Y	Y
22 West	N	Y	Y	Y	Y	Y
23 Hastings	Y	N	N	N	Y	Y
24 Adams	N	Y	Y	Y	Y	Y
25 Rivera	N	N	Y	Y	Y	Y
GEORGIA						
1 Kingston	N	Y	Y	Y	Y	Y
2 Bishop	Y	N	N	N	Y	Y
3 Westmoreland	N	Y	Y	Y	Y	Y
4 Johnson	?	N	N	N	P	Y
5 Lewis	Y	N	N	N	Y	Y
6 Price	N	Y	Y	Y	Y	Y
7 Woodall	N	Y	Y	Y	Y	Y
8 Scott, A.	N	Y	Y	Y	Y	Y
9 Graves	N	Y	Y	Y	Y	N
10 Broun	N	N	Y	Y	Y	N
11 Gingrey	N	Y	Y	Y	Y	Y
12 Barrow	Y	Y	N	N	Y	Y
13 Scott, D.	Y	N	N	N	Y	Y
HAWAII						
1 Hanabusa	Y	N	N	N	Y	Y
2 Hirono	Y	N	N	N	Y	Y
IDAHO						
1 Labrador	?	?	Y	Y	Y	Y
2 Simpson	N	Y	Y	Y	Y	Y
ILLINOIS						
1 Rush	Y	N	N	N	Y	Y
2 Jackson	Y	N	N	N	Y	Y
3 Lipinski	Y	N	N	N	Y	Y
4 Gutierrez	Y	N	N	N	Y	Y
5 Quigley	Y	N	N	N	Y	Y
6 Roskam	N	Y	Y	Y	Y	Y
7 Davis	Y	N	N	N	Y	Y
8 Walsh	N	Y	Y	Y	Y	N
9 Schakowsky	Y	N	N	N	Y	Y
10 Dold	N	N	Y	Y	Y	Y
11 Kinzinger	N	Y	Y	Y	Y	Y
12 Costello	Y	N	?	?	?	?
13 Biggert	N	N	Y	Y	Y	Y
14 Hultgren	N	Y	Y	Y	Y	Y
15 Johnson	N	Y	Y	Y	Y	Y

KEY   **Republicans**   Democrats

Y Voted for (yea)	**X** Paired against	**C** Voted "present" to avoid possible conflict of interest
# Paired for	**–** Announced against	
+ Announced for	**P** Voted "present"	**?** Did not vote or otherwise make a position known
N Voted against (nay)		

	257	258	259	260	261	262
16 **Manzullo**	N	Y	Y	Y	Y	Y
17 **Schilling**	N	Y	Y	Y	Y	Y
18 **Schock**	N	Y	Y	Y	Y	?
19 **Shimkus**	N	Y	Y	Y	Y	Y
INDIANA						
1 Visclosky	Y	N	N	N	Y	N
2 Donnelly	Y	N	Y	Y	Y	Y
3 **Stutzman**	N	Y	Y	Y	Y	Y
4 **Rokita**	N	Y	Y	Y	Y	Y
5 **Burton**	Y	Y	Y	Y	Y	Y
6 **Pence**	N	Y	Y	Y	Y	Y
7 Carson	Y	N	N	N	Y	Y
8 **Bucshon**	N	Y	Y	Y	Y	Y
9 **Young**	N	Y	Y	Y	Y	Y
IOWA						
1 Braley	Y	N	N	N	Y	Y
2 Loebsack	Y	N	N	N	Y	Y
3 Boswell	Y	N	N	N	Y	Y
4 **Latham**	N	Y	Y	Y	Y	Y
5 **King**	N	Y	Y	Y	Y	Y
KANSAS						
1 **Huelskamp**	N	N	Y	Y	Y	Y
2 **Jenkins**	N	Y	Y	Y	Y	Y
3 **Yoder**	N	Y	Y	Y	Y	Y
4 **Pompeo**	N	Y	Y	Y	Y	Y
KENTUCKY						
1 **Whitfield**	N	Y	Y	Y	Y	Y
2 **Guthrie**	N	Y	Y	Y	Y	Y
3 Yarmuth	Y	N	N	N	Y	Y
4 **Davis**	N	N	Y	Y	N	Y
5 **Rogers**	N	Y	Y	Y	Y	Y
6 Chandler	Y	N	N	N	Y	Y
LOUISIANA						
1 **Scalise**	N	Y	?	Y	Y	Y
2 Richmond	Y	N	N	N	Y	Y
3 **Landry**	?	Y	Y	Y	Y	Y
4 **Fleming**	N	Y	Y	Y	Y	Y
5 **Alexander**	N	Y	Y	Y	Y	Y
6 **Cassidy**	?	?	Y	Y	Y	Y
7 **Boustany**	N	Y	Y	Y	Y	Y
MAINE						
1 Pingree	Y	N	N	N	Y	Y
2 Michaud	Y	N	N	N	Y	Y
MARYLAND						
1 **Harris**	N	Y	Y	Y	Y	Y
2 Ruppersberger	Y	N	N	N	Y	Y
3 Sarbanes	Y	N	N	N	Y	Y
4 Edwards	Y	N	N	N	Y	Y
5 Hoyer	Y	N	N	N	Y	Y
6 **Bartlett**	N	N	Y	Y	Y	Y
7 Cummings	Y	N	N	N	Y	Y
8 Van Hollen	Y	N	N	N	Y	Y
MASSACHUSETTS						
1 Olver	Y	N	N	N	N	Y
2 Neal	Y	N	N	N	Y	Y
3 McGovern	Y	N	N	N	Y	Y
4 Frank	Y	N	N	N	Y	Y
5 Tsongas	Y	N	N	N	Y	Y
6 Tierney	Y	N	N	N	Y	Y
7 Markey	Y	N	N	N	Y	Y
8 Capuano	Y	N	N	N	Y	Y
9 Lynch	Y	N	N	N	Y	Y
10 Keating	Y	N	N	N	Y	Y
MICHIGAN						
1 **Benishek**	N	Y	Y	Y	Y	Y
2 **Huizenga**	N	Y	Y	Y	Y	Y
3 **Amash**	N	N	Y	Y	N	N
4 **Camp**	N	Y	Y	Y	Y	Y
5 Kildee	Y	N	N	N	Y	Y
6 **Upton**	N	Y	Y	Y	Y	Y
7 **Walberg**	N	Y	Y	Y	Y	Y
8 **Rogers**	N	Y	Y	Y	Y	Y
9 Peters	Y	N	N	N	Y	Y
10 **Miller**	N	Y	Y	Y	Y	N
11 **McCotter**	N	Y	Y	Y	Y	Y
12 Levin	Y	N	N	N	Y	Y
13 Clarke	Y	N	N	N	Y	Y
14 Conyers	Y	N	N	N	P	Y
15 Dingell	Y	N	N	N	Y	Y
MINNESOTA						
1 Walz	Y	N	N	N	Y	Y
2 **Kline**	N	Y	Y	Y	Y	Y
3 **Paulsen**	N	Y	Y	Y	Y	Y
4 McCollum	Y	N	N	N	P	Y

	257	258	259	260	261	262
5 Ellison	Y	N	N	N	P	Y
6 **Bachmann**	N	Y	Y	Y	Y	Y
7 Peterson	Y	Y	N	N	Y	Y
8 **Cravaack**	N	Y	Y	Y	Y	Y
MISSISSIPPI						
1 **Nunnelee**	N	Y	?	Y	Y	Y
2 Thompson	Y	N	N	N	Y	Y
3 **Harper**	N	Y	Y	Y	Y	Y
4 **Palazzo**	N	Y	Y	Y	Y	Y
MISSOURI						
1 Clay	Y	N	N	N	Y	Y
2 **Akin**	N	Y	Y	Y	Y	Y
3 Carnahan	Y	N	N	N	Y	Y
4 **Hartzler**	N	Y	Y	Y	Y	Y
5 Cleaver	Y	N	N	N	Y	Y
6 **Graves**	N	Y	Y	Y	Y	Y
7 **Long**	N	Y	Y	Y	Y	Y
8 **Emerson**	N	Y	Y	Y	Y	Y
9 **Luetkemeyer**	N	Y	Y	Y	Y	Y
MONTANA						
AL **Rehberg**	N	Y	Y	Y	Y	Y
NEBRASKA						
1 **Fortenberry**	N	Y	Y	Y	Y	Y
2 **Terry**	N	Y	Y	Y	Y	Y
3 **Smith**	N	Y	Y	Y	Y	Y
NEVADA						
1 Berkley	Y	Y	N	N	Y	Y
2 **Amodei**	N	Y	?	?	?	?
3 **Heck**	N	Y	Y	Y	Y	Y
NEW HAMPSHIRE						
1 **Guinta**	N	Y	Y	Y	Y	Y
2 **Bass**	N	N	Y	Y	Y	Y
NEW JERSEY						
1 Andrews	Y	N	N	N	Y	Y
2 **LoBiondo**	N	Y	Y	Y	Y	Y
3 **Runyan**	N	Y	Y	Y	Y	Y
4 **Smith**	N	Y	Y	Y	Y	Y
5 **Garrett**	N	N	Y	Y	Y	Y
6 Pallone	Y	N	N	N	Y	Y
7 **Lance**	N	Y	Y	Y	Y	Y
8 Pascrell	Y	N	–	–	+	+
9 Rothman	Y	N	N	N	Y	Y
10 Vacant						
11 **Frelinghuysen**	N	Y	Y	Y	Y	Y
12 Holt	Y	N	N	N	Y	Y
13 Sires	Y	N	N	N	Y	Y
NEW MEXICO						
1 Heinrich	Y	N	N	N	Y	Y
2 **Pearce**	N	Y	Y	Y	Y	Y
3 Luján	Y	N	N	N	Y	Y
NEW YORK						
1 Bishop	Y	N	N	N	Y	Y
2 Israel	Y	N	N	N	Y	Y
3 **King**	N	Y	Y	Y	Y	Y
4 McCarthy	Y	N	N	N	Y	Y
5 Ackerman	Y	N	N	N	Y	Y
6 Meeks	Y	N	N	N	Y	Y
7 Crowley	Y	N	N	N	Y	Y
8 Nadler	Y	N	N	N	Y	Y
9 **Turner**	N	Y	Y	Y	Y	Y
10 Towns	Y	N	N	N	Y	Y
11 Clarke	Y	N	N	N	Y	Y
12 Velázquez	Y	N	N	N	Y	Y
13 **Grimm**	N	Y	Y	Y	Y	Y
14 Maloney	Y	N	N	N	Y	Y
15 Rangel	Y	N	N	N	Y	Y
16 Serrano	Y	N	N	N	Y	Y
17 Engel	Y	N	N	N	Y	Y
18 Lowey	Y	N	N	N	Y	Y
19 **Hayworth**	N	Y	Y	Y	Y	Y
20 **Gibson**	N	Y	N	N	Y	Y
21 Tonko	Y	N	N	N	Y	Y
22 Hinchey	Y	N	N	N	Y	Y
23 Owens	Y	N	N	Y	Y	Y
24 **Hanna**	N	N	Y	Y	Y	Y
25 **Buerkle**	N	Y	Y	Y	Y	Y
26 Hochul	Y	N	N	N	Y	Y
27 Higgins	Y	N	N	N	Y	Y
28 Slaughter	?	?	?	?	?	?
29 **Reed**	N	Y	Y	Y	Y	N
NORTH CAROLINA						
1 Butterfield	Y	N	N	N	Y	Y
2 **Ellmers**	N	Y	Y	Y	Y	Y
3 Jones	Y	Y	N	N	Y	Y
4 Price	Y	N	N	N	Y	Y

	257	258	259	260	261	262
5 **Foxx**	N	Y	Y	Y	Y	Y
6 **Coble**	N	Y	Y	Y	Y	Y
7 McIntyre	Y	Y	N	Y	Y	Y
8 Kissell	Y	N	N	Y	Y	Y
9 **Myrick**	N	Y	Y	Y	Y	Y
10 **McHenry**	N	Y	Y	Y	Y	Y
11 Shuler	Y	N	N	Y	Y	Y
12 Watt	Y	N	N	N	Y	Y
13 Miller	Y	N	N	N	Y	Y
NORTH DAKOTA						
AL **Berg**	N	N	Y	Y	Y	Y
OHIO						
1 **Chabot**	N	Y	Y	Y	Y	Y
2 **Schmidt**	N	Y	Y	Y	Y	Y
3 **Turner**	N	Y	Y	Y	Y	Y
4 **Jordan**	N	Y	Y	Y	Y	Y
5 **Latta**	N	Y	Y	Y	Y	Y
6 **Johnson**	N	Y	Y	Y	Y	Y
7 **Austria**	N	Y	Y	Y	Y	Y
8 **Boehner**						
9 Kaptur	Y	N	N	N	Y	Y
10 Kucinich	Y	N	N	N	N	Y
11 Fudge	Y	N	N	N	Y	Y
12 **Tiberi**	N	Y	Y	Y	Y	Y
13 Sutton	Y	N	N	N	Y	Y
14 **LaTourette**	N	N	Y	Y	Y	Y
15 **Stivers**	N	Y	Y	Y	Y	Y
16 **Renacci**	N	Y	Y	Y	Y	Y
17 Ryan	Y	N	N	N	Y	Y
18 **Gibbs**	N	Y	Y	Y	Y	Y
OKLAHOMA						
1 **Sullivan**	N	Y	Y	Y	Y	Y
2 Boren	Y	Y	N	Y	Y	Y
3 **Lucas**	N	Y	Y	Y	Y	Y
4 **Cole**	N	Y	Y	Y	Y	Y
5 **Lankford**	N	Y	Y	Y	Y	Y
OREGON						
1 Bonamici	Y	N	N	N	Y	Y
2 **Walden**	N	Y	Y	Y	Y	Y
3 Blumenauer	Y	N	N	N	N	Y
4 DeFazio	Y	N	N	N	P	Y
5 Schrader	Y	N	N	N	Y	Y
PENNSYLVANIA						
1 Brady	Y	N	N	N	Y	Y
2 Fattah	Y	N	N	N	Y	Y
3 **Kelly**	N	Y	Y	Y	Y	Y
4 Altmire	Y	N	N	N	Y	Y
5 **Thompson**	N	Y	Y	Y	Y	Y
6 **Gerlach**	N	Y	Y	Y	Y	Y
7 **Meehan**	N	N	Y	Y	Y	Y
8 **Fitzpatrick**	N	Y	Y	Y	Y	Y
9 **Shuster**	N	Y	Y	Y	Y	Y
10 **Marino**	N	Y	Y	Y	Y	Y
11 **Barletta**	N	Y	Y	Y	Y	Y
12 Critz	Y	N	N	N	Y	Y
13 Schwartz	Y	N	N	N	Y	Y
14 Doyle	Y	N	N	N	Y	Y
15 **Dent**	N	Y	Y	Y	Y	Y
16 **Pitts**	N	Y	Y	Y	Y	Y
17 Holden	Y	N	?	?	?	?
18 **Murphy**	N	Y	Y	Y	Y	Y
19 **Platts**	N	N	Y	Y	Y	Y
RHODE ISLAND						
1 Cicilline	Y	N	N	N	Y	Y
2 Langevin	Y	N	N	N	Y	Y
SOUTH CAROLINA						
1 **Scott**	N	Y	Y	Y	Y	Y
2 **Wilson**	N	Y	Y	Y	Y	Y
3 **Duncan**	N	Y	Y	Y	Y	Y
4 **Gowdy**	N	Y	Y	Y	Y	Y
5 **Mulvaney**	N	Y	Y	Y	Y	Y
6 Clyburn	Y	N	N	N	Y	Y
SOUTH DAKOTA						
AL **Noem**	N	Y	Y	Y	Y	Y
TENNESSEE						
1 **Roe**	N	Y	Y	Y	Y	Y
2 **Duncan**	N	Y	Y	Y	N	N
3 **Fleischmann**	N	Y	Y	Y	Y	Y
4 **DesJarlais**	N	Y	Y	Y	Y	Y
5 Cooper	Y	N	N	N	Y	Y
6 **Black**	N	Y	Y	Y	Y	Y
7 **Blackburn**	N	Y	Y	Y	Y	Y
8 **Fincher**	N	Y	Y	Y	Y	Y
9 Cohen	Y	N	N	N	Y	Y

	257	258	259	260	261	262
TEXAS						
1 **Gohmert**	N	Y	Y	Y	?	Y
2 **Poe**	N	N	Y	Y	Y	Y
3 **Johnson, S.**	N	Y	Y	Y	Y	Y
4 **Hall**	N	Y	Y	Y	Y	Y
5 **Hensarling**	N	Y	Y	Y	Y	Y
6 **Barton**	N	Y	Y	Y	Y	Y
7 **Culberson**	N	Y	Y	Y	Y	Y
8 **Brady**	N	Y	Y	Y	Y	Y
9 Green, A.	Y	N	N	N	Y	Y
10 **McCaul**	N	Y	Y	Y	Y	Y
11 **Conaway**	N	Y	Y	Y	Y	Y
12 **Granger**	N	Y	Y	Y	Y	Y
13 **Thornberry**	N	Y	Y	Y	Y	Y
14 **Paul**	N	N	N	N	N	N
15 Hinojosa	?	N	N	N	Y	Y
16 Reyes	Y	N	N	N	Y	Y
17 **Flores**	N	Y	Y	Y	Y	Y
18 Jackson Lee	Y	N	N	N	Y	Y
19 **Neugebauer**	N	Y	Y	Y	Y	Y
20 Gonzalez	Y	N	N	N	Y	Y
21 **Smith**	N	Y	Y	Y	Y	Y
22 **Olson**	N	Y	Y	Y	Y	Y
23 **Canseco**	N	Y	Y	Y	Y	Y
24 **Marchant**	N	Y	Y	Y	Y	Y
25 Doggett	Y	N	N	N	Y	Y
26 **Burgess**	N	Y	Y	Y	Y	Y
27 **Farenthold**	N	Y	Y	Y	Y	Y
28 Cuellar	Y	N	N	N	Y	Y
29 Green, G.	Y	N	N	N	Y	Y
30 Johnson, E.	Y	N	N	N	P	Y
31 **Carter**	N	Y	Y	Y	Y	Y
32 **Sessions**	N	Y	Y	Y	Y	Y
UTAH						
1 **Bishop**	N	Y	Y	Y	Y	Y
2 Matheson	Y	Y	Y	Y	Y	Y
3 **Chaffetz**	N	Y	Y	Y	Y	Y
VERMONT						
AL Welch	Y	N	N	N	Y	Y
VIRGINIA						
1 **Wittman**	N	Y	Y	Y	Y	Y
2 **Rigell**	N	Y	Y	Y	Y	Y
3 Scott	Y	N	N	N	Y	Y
4 **Forbes**	N	Y	Y	Y	Y	Y
5 **Hurt**	N	Y	Y	Y	Y	Y
6 **Goodlatte**	N	Y	Y	Y	Y	Y
7 **Cantor**	N	Y	Y	Y	Y	Y
8 Moran	Y	N	N	N	Y	Y
9 **Griffith**	N	Y	Y	Y	Y	Y
10 **Wolf**	N	N	Y	Y	Y	Y
11 Connolly	Y	N	N	N	Y	Y
WASHINGTON						
1 Vacant						
2 Larsen	Y	N	N	N	Y	Y
3 **Herrera Beutler**	N	Y	Y	Y	Y	Y
4 **Hastings**	N	Y	Y	Y	Y	?
5 **McMorris Rodgers**	N	Y	Y	Y	Y	Y
6 Dicks	Y	N	N	N	Y	Y
7 McDermott	Y	N	N	N	N	Y
8 **Reichert**	N	Y	Y	Y	Y	Y
9 Smith	Y	N	N	N	Y	Y
WEST VIRGINIA						
1 **McKinley**	N	Y	Y	Y	Y	Y
2 **Capito**	N	Y	Y	Y	Y	Y
3 Rahall	Y	N	N	N	Y	Y
WISCONSIN						
1 **Ryan**	N	Y	Y	Y	Y	Y
2 Baldwin	Y	N	N	N	Y	Y
3 Kind	Y	N	N	N	Y	Y
4 Moore	Y	N	N	N	P	Y
5 **Sensenbrenner**	N	Y	Y	Y	Y	N
6 **Petri**	N	Y	Y	Y	Y	N
7 **Duffy**	N	Y	Y	Y	Y	Y
8 **Ribble**	N	Y	Y	Y	Y	Y
WYOMING						
AL **Lummis**	N	Y	Y	Y	Y	Y

IN THE HOUSE | By Vote Number

263. HR 4310. Fiscal 2013 Defense Authorization/Pakistan **Assistance.** Rohrabacher, R-Calif., amendment that would bar the use of funds in the bill for assistance for Pakistan in fiscal 2013. Rejected in Committee of the Whole 84-335: R 69-169; D 15-166. May 17, 2012.

264. HR 4310. Fiscal 2013 Defense Authorization/Afghanistan Troop **Withdrawal.** Lee, D-Calif., amendment that would limit the use of funds provided for operations in Afghanistan to the purpose of facilitating a safe and orderly withdrawal of forces. Rejected in Committee of the Whole 113-303: R 12-224; D 101-79. May 17, 2012.

265. HR 4310. Fiscal 2013 Defense Authorization/Coalition Support **Fund.** Connolly, D-Va., amendment that would prevent the disbursement of funds to the Coalition Support Fund until the Defense Department certifies that Pakistan has opened ground-line communication, is allowing NATO to move supplies through Pakistan into Afghanistan and is supporting the removal of U.S. equipment from Afghanistan. Adopted in Committee of the Whole 412-1: R 232-0; D 180-1. May 17, 2012.

266. HR 4310. Fiscal 2013 Defense Authorization/Detainee Trials. Rooney, R-Fla., amendment that would direct the Defense Department to hold detainee trials in the U.S. military facility at Guantánamo Bay, Cuba, and not in the United States. Adopted in Committee of the Whole 249-171: R 227-11; D 22-160. A "nay" was a vote in support of the president's position. May 17, 2012.

267. HR 4310. Fiscal 2013 Defense Authorization/Labor **Agreements.** Bartlett, R-Md., amendment that would prohibit government agencies, when awarding federal construction contracts, from requiring or prohibiting contractors to enter into labor agreements or from awarding or withholding contracts on the basis of contractor decisions regarding such agreements. The provision would not apply to contracts awarded before the bill's enactment. Adopted in Committee of the Whole 211-209: R 210-28; D 1-181. May 17, 2012.

268. HR 4310. Fiscal 2013 Defense Authorization/Long-Range **Nuclear Bomber.** Markey, D-Mass., amendment that would strike language in the bill that would require the Air Force to ensure that the next generation long-range strike bomber is capable of carrying strategic nuclear weapons once it is operable. It also would reduce funding in the bill by $292 million and bar the Defense Department from using any funds authorized in fiscal 2013 through fiscal 2023 for the research, development, testing and evaluation or procurement of a new long-range nuclear-capable bomber. Rejected in Committee of the Whole 112-308: R 11-227; D 101-81. May 17, 2012.

269. HR 4310. Fiscal 2013 Defense Authorization/Missile Defense **System.** Polis, D-Colo., amendment that would reduce the amount for the ground-based midcourse missile defense system by $403 million and require those funds be used for deficit reduction. Rejected in Committee of the Whole 165-252: R 13-223; D 152-29. May 17, 2012.

	263	264	265	266	267	268	269
ALABAMA							
1 Bonner	N	N	Y	Y	Y	N	N
2 Roby	N	N	Y	Y	Y	N	N
3 Rogers	N	N	Y	Y	Y	N	N
4 Aderholt	N	N	Y	Y	Y	N	N
5 Brooks	N	N	Y	Y	Y	N	N
6 Bachus	N	N	Y	Y	Y	N	N
7 Sewell	N	N	Y	Y	N	N	Y
ALASKA							
AL Young	N	N	Y	Y	N	N	N
ARIZONA							
1 Gosar	N	N	Y	Y	Y	N	N
2 Franks	Y	N	Y	Y	Y	N	N
3 Quayle	N	N	Y	Y	Y	N	N
4 Pastor	N	Y	Y	N	N	N	Y
5 Schweikert	Y	N	Y	Y	Y	N	N
6 Flake	N	N	Y	Y	Y	N	N
7 Grijalva	N	Y	Y	N	N	Y	Y
8 Vacant							
ARKANSAS							
1 Crawford	N	N	Y	Y	Y	N	N
2 Griffin	N	N	Y	Y	Y	N	N
3 Womack	N	N	Y	Y	Y	N	N
4 Ross	N	N	Y	Y	N	N	N
CALIFORNIA							
1 Thompson	N	Y	Y	N	N	Y	Y
2 Herger	N	N	Y	Y	Y	N	N
3 Lungren	N	N	Y	Y	Y	N	N
4 McClintock	Y	Y	Y	N	Y	N	N
5 Matsui	N	Y	Y	N	N	Y	Y
6 Woolsey	N	Y	Y	N	N	Y	Y
7 Miller, George	N	Y	?	N	N	Y	Y
8 Pelosi	N	N	Y	N	N	Y	Y
9 Lee	N	Y	Y	N	N	Y	Y
10 Garamendi	N	Y	Y	N	N	Y	Y
11 McNerney	N	N	Y	N	N	N	Y
12 Speier	N	Y	Y	N	N	Y	Y
13 Stark	Y	Y	Y	N	N	Y	Y
14 Eshoo	N	Y	Y	N	N	Y	Y
15 Honda	N	Y	Y	N	N	Y	Y
16 Lofgren	N	Y	Y	N	N	Y	Y
17 Farr	N	Y	Y	N	N	Y	Y
18 Cardoza	?	?	?	?	?	?	?
19 Denham	Y	N	Y	Y	Y	N	N
20 Costa	N	N	Y	Y	N	N	N
21 Nunes	N	N	Y	Y	Y	N	N
22 McCarthy	N	N	Y	Y	Y	N	N
23 Capps	N	Y	Y	N	N	Y	Y
24 Gallegly	N	N	Y	Y	Y	N	N
25 McKeon	N	N	Y	Y	Y	N	N
26 Dreier	N	N	Y	Y	Y	N	N
27 Sherman	N	N	Y	N	N	N	Y
28 Berman	N	N	Y	N	N	N	Y
29 Schiff	N	N	Y	N	N	N	Y
30 Waxman	N	Y	Y	N	N	Y	Y
31 Becerra	N	Y	Y	N	N	Y	Y
32 Chu	N	Y	Y	N	N	Y	Y
33 Bass	N	Y	Y	N	N	Y	Y
34 Roybal-Allard	N	N	Y	N	N	N	?
35 Waters	N	Y	Y	N	N	Y	Y
36 Hahn	N	Y	Y	N	N	Y	Y
37 Richardson	N	Y	Y	N	N	N	N
38 Napolitano	Y	Y	Y	N	N	Y	Y
39 Sánchez, Linda	N	Y	Y	N	N	Y	Y
40 Royce	Y	N	Y	Y	Y	N	N
41 Lewis	N	?	Y	Y	Y	N	N
42 Miller, Gary	N	N	Y	Y	Y	N	N
43 Baca	N	N	Y	N	N	N	Y
44 Calvert	N	N	Y	Y	Y	N	N
45 Bono Mack	Y	N	Y	Y	Y	N	N
46 Rohrabacher	Y	Y	Y	Y	Y	N	N
47 Sanchez, Loretta	?	?	?	?	?	?	?
48 Campbell	N	Y	Y	Y	Y	N	N
49 Issa	N	N	Y	Y	Y	N	N
50 Bilbray	N	N	Y	Y	Y	N	N
51 Filner	+	+	+	–	–	+	+
52 Hunter	Y	N	Y	Y	Y	N	N
53 Davis	N	N	Y	N	N	N	Y

	263	264	265	266	267	268	269
COLORADO							
1 DeGette	N	Y	Y	N	N	Y	Y
2 Polis	N	Y	Y	N	N	Y	Y
3 Tipton	N	N	Y	Y	Y	N	N
4 Gardner	N	N	Y	Y	Y	N	N
5 Lamborn	N	N	Y	Y	Y	N	N
6 Coffman	N	N	Y	Y	Y	N	N
7 Perlmutter	N	N	Y	N	N	Y	Y
CONNECTICUT							
1 Larson	N	Y	Y	N	N	N	Y
2 Courtney	N	N	Y	N	N	N	Y
3 DeLauro	N	Y	Y	N	N	N	Y
4 Himes	N	Y	Y	N	N	N	Y
5 Murphy	N	Y	Y	N	N	N	Y
DELAWARE							
AL Carney	N	N	Y	N	N	N	Y
FLORIDA							
1 Miller	Y	N	Y	Y	Y	N	N
2 Southerland	N	N	Y	Y	Y	N	N
3 Brown	N	N	Y	N	N	N	N
4 Crenshaw	N	N	Y	Y	Y	N	N
5 Nugent	Y	N	Y	Y	Y	N	N
6 Stearns	Y	N	Y	Y	Y	N	N
7 Mica	N	N	Y	Y	Y	N	N
8 Webster	N	N	Y	Y	Y	N	N
9 Bilirakis	Y	N	Y	Y	Y	N	N
10 Young	N	N	Y	Y	Y	N	N
11 Castor	N	N	Y	N	N	N	Y
12 Ross	N	N	Y	Y	Y	N	N
13 Buchanan	Y	N	Y	Y	Y	N	N
14 Mack	Y	N	Y	Y	Y	N	N
15 Posey	Y	N	Y	Y	Y	N	N
16 Rooney	Y	N	Y	Y	Y	N	N
17 Wilson	N	?	Y	N	N	Y	Y
18 Ros-Lehtinen	N	N	Y	Y	Y	N	N
19 Deutch	N	Y	Y	N	N	N	Y
20 Wasserman Schultz	?	?	?	?	?	?	?
21 Diaz-Balart	N	N	Y	Y	N	N	N
22 West	N	N	Y	Y	Y	N	N
23 Hastings	N	Y	Y	N	N	N	Y
24 Adams	Y	N	Y	Y	Y	N	N
25 Rivera	N	N	Y	Y	Y	N	N
GEORGIA							
1 Kingston	N	N	Y	Y	Y	N	N
2 Bishop	N	N	Y	N	N	N	N
3 Westmoreland	Y	N	Y	Y	Y	N	N
4 Johnson	N	N	Y	N	N	N	Y
5 Lewis	N	Y	Y	N	N	N	Y
6 Price	Y	N	Y	Y	Y	N	N
7 Woodall	Y	N	Y	Y	Y	N	N
8 Scott, A.	Y	N	Y	Y	Y	N	N
9 Graves	Y	N	Y	Y	Y	N	N
10 Broun	Y	N	Y	Y	Y	N	N
11 Gingrey	Y	N	Y	Y	Y	N	N
12 Barrow	N	N	Y	Y	N	N	N
13 Scott, D.	N	N	Y	N	N	N	N
HAWAII							
1 Hanabusa	N	Y	Y	N	N	N	N
2 Hirono	N	Y	Y	N	N	Y	Y
IDAHO							
1 Labrador	N	N	Y	Y	Y	N	Y
2 Simpson	N	N	Y	Y	Y	N	N
ILLINOIS							
1 Rush	Y	Y	Y	N	N	Y	Y
2 Jackson	Y	Y	Y	N	N	Y	Y
3 Lipinski	N	N	Y	N	N	N	N
4 Gutierrez	N	Y	Y	N	N	Y	Y
5 Quigley	N	Y	Y	N	N	Y	Y
6 Roskam	N	N	Y	Y	Y	N	N
7 Davis	Y	Y	Y	N	N	Y	Y
8 Walsh	Y	Y	Y	N	N	Y	N
9 Schakowsky	N	Y	Y	N	N	Y	Y
10 Dold	N	N	Y	N	N	N	N
11 Kinzinger	Y	N	Y	Y	N	N	N
12 Costello	?	?	?	?	?	?	?
13 Biggert	?	?	?	?	?	?	?
14 Hultgren	Y	N	Y	Y	N	N	N
15 Johnson	Y	Y	Y	N	N	N	N

KEY **Republicans** Democrats

Y Voted for (yea)
Paired for
+ Announced for
N Voted against (nay)

X Paired against
– Announced against
P Voted "present"

C Voted "present" to avoid possible conflict of interest
? Did not vote or otherwise make a position known

	263	264	265	266	267	268	269
16 **Manzullo**	N	N	Y	Y	Y	N	N
17 **Schilling**	Y	N	?	Y	Y	N	N
18 **Schock**	N	N	?	Y	N	N	N
19 **Shimkus**	N	N	Y	Y	N	N	N
INDIANA							
1 Visclosky	N	Y	Y	N	N	N	Y
2 Donnelly	N	N	Y	Y	N	N	N
3 **Stutzman**	Y	N	Y	Y	Y	N	N
4 **Rokita**	Y	N	Y	Y	Y	N	N
5 **Burton**	N	N	Y	Y	Y	N	N
6 **Pence**	N	?	?	?	?	?	?
7 Carson	N	Y	Y	N	N	Y	Y
8 **Bucshon**	N	N	Y	Y	Y	N	N
9 **Young**	N	N	Y	Y	Y	N	N
IOWA							
1 Braley	N	Y	Y	N	N	Y	Y
2 Loebsack	N	Y	Y	N	N	Y	Y
3 Boswell	N	Y	Y	N	N	Y	Y
4 **Latham**	N	N	Y	Y	Y	N	N
5 **King**	Y	N	Y	Y	Y	N	N
KANSAS							
1 **Huelskamp**	Y	N	Y	Y	Y	N	N
2 **Jenkins**	Y	N	Y	Y	Y	N	N
3 **Yoder**	Y	N	Y	Y	Y	N	N
4 **Pompeo**	N	N	Y	Y	Y	N	N
KENTUCKY							
1 **Whitfield**	N	N	Y	Y	Y	N	N
2 **Guthrie**	N	N	Y	Y	Y	N	N
3 Yarmuth	N	Y	Y	N	N	Y	Y
4 **Davis**	N	N	Y	Y	Y	N	N
5 **Rogers**	N	N	Y	Y	Y	N	N
6 Chandler	N	N	Y	Y	N	N	N
LOUISIANA							
1 **Scalise**	N	N	Y	Y	Y	N	N
2 Richmond	N	N	Y	N	N	Y	Y
3 **Landry**	Y	N	Y	Y	Y	N	?
4 **Fleming**	N	N	Y	Y	Y	N	N
5 **Alexander**	N	N	Y	Y	Y	N	N
6 **Cassidy**	N	Y	Y	Y	Y	N	N
7 **Boustany**	N	N	Y	Y	Y	N	N
MAINE							
1 Pingree	N	Y	Y	N	N	Y	Y
2 Michaud	N	Y	Y	N	N	Y	Y
MARYLAND							
1 **Harris**	N	N	Y	Y	Y	N	N
2 Ruppersberger	N	N	Y	N	N	N	N
3 Sarbanes	N	N	Y	N	N	Y	Y
4 Edwards	N	Y	Y	N	N	Y	Y
5 Hoyer	N	N	Y	N	N	N	Y
6 **Bartlett**	N	N	Y	Y	Y	N	N
7 Cummings	N	Y	Y	N	N	Y	Y
8 Van Hollen	N	N	Y	N	N	Y	Y
MASSACHUSETTS							
1 Olver	N	Y	Y	N	N	Y	Y
2 Neal	N	Y	Y	N	N	Y	Y
3 McGovern	N	Y	Y	N	N	Y	Y
4 Frank	N	Y	Y	N	N	Y	Y
5 Tsongas	N	Y	Y	N	N	Y	Y
6 Tierney	N	Y	Y	N	N	Y	Y
7 Markey	N	Y	Y	N	N	Y	Y
8 Capuano	N	Y	Y	N	N	Y	Y
9 Lynch	Y	N	Y	Y	N	Y	Y
10 Keating	Y	Y	Y	N	N	Y	Y
MICHIGAN							
1 **Benishek**	Y	Y	Y	Y	Y	N	N
2 **Huizenga**	N	N	Y	Y	Y	N	Y
3 **Amash**	Y	Y	Y	N	Y	Y	Y
4 **Camp**	N	N	Y	Y	Y	N	N
5 Kildee	N	N	Y	N	N	N	Y
6 **Upton**	Y	N	Y	Y	Y	N	Y
7 **Walberg**	N	N	?	Y	Y	N	N
8 **Rogers**	N	N	Y	Y	Y	N	N
9 Peters	N	N	Y	Y	N	Y	Y
10 **Miller**	N	N	Y	Y	Y	N	N
11 **McCotter**	N	N	Y	Y	N	N	N
12 Levin	N	N	Y	N	N	N	Y
13 Clarke	N	Y	Y	N	N	Y	Y
14 Conyers	N	Y	Y	N	N	Y	Y
15 Dingell	N	N	Y	N	N	N	Y
MINNESOTA							
1 Walz	N	N	Y	N	N	Y	Y
2 **Kline**	N	N	Y	Y	Y	N	N
3 **Paulsen**	N	N	Y	Y	Y	N	N
4 McCollum	N	N	Y	N	N	Y	Y

	263	264	265	266	267	268	269
5 Ellison	N	Y	Y	N	N	Y	Y
6 **Bachmann**	N	N	Y	Y	Y	N	N
7 Peterson	N	N	Y	Y	N	N	N
8 **Cravaack**	Y	N	?	Y	N	N	N
MISSISSIPPI							
1 **Nunnelee**	N	N	Y	Y	Y	N	N
2 Thompson	N	Y	Y	N	N	N	N
3 **Harper**	N	N	Y	Y	Y	N	N
4 **Palazzo**	N	N	Y	Y	Y	N	N
MISSOURI							
1 Clay	N	Y	Y	N	N	Y	Y
2 **Akin**	N	N	Y	Y	Y	N	N
3 Carnahan	N	N	Y	N	N	N	Y
4 **Hartzler**	N	N	Y	Y	Y	N	N
5 Cleaver	N	Y	Y	N	N	Y	Y
6 **Graves**	N	N	Y	Y	Y	N	N
7 **Long**	N	N	Y	Y	Y	N	N
8 **Emerson**	N	N	Y	Y	N	N	N
9 **Luetkemeyer**	N	N	Y	Y	Y	N	N
MONTANA							
AL **Rehberg**	N	N	Y	Y	Y	N	N
NEBRASKA							
1 **Fortenberry**	N	N	Y	Y	Y	N	N
2 **Terry**	N	N	Y	Y	Y	N	N
3 **Smith**	N	N	Y	Y	Y	N	N
NEVADA							
1 Berkley	N	N	Y	Y	N	Y	N
2 **Amodei**	?	?	?	?	?	?	?
3 **Heck**	N	N	Y	Y	Y	N	N
NEW HAMPSHIRE							
1 **Guinta**	N	N	Y	Y	Y	N	N
2 **Bass**	N	N	Y	Y	Y	N	N
NEW JERSEY							
1 Andrews	N	N	Y	N	N	N	Y
2 **LoBiondo**	Y	N	Y	Y	N	N	N
3 **Runyan**	Y	N	Y	Y	N	N	N
4 **Smith**	N	N	Y	Y	N	Y	N
5 **Garrett**	Y	N	Y	Y	Y	N	N
6 Pallone	Y	Y	Y	N	N	Y	Y
7 **Lance**	N	N	Y	Y	N	N	N
8 Pascrell	–	+	+	–	–	+	+
9 Rothman	Y	Y	Y	N	N	Y	Y
10 Vacant							
11 **Frelinghuysen**	N	N	Y	Y	Y	N	N
12 Holt	N	Y	Y	N	N	Y	Y
13 Sires	N	Y	Y	N	N	N	Y
NEW MEXICO							
1 Heinrich	N	N	Y	N	N	N	Y
2 **Pearce**	N	N	Y	Y	Y	N	N
3 Luján	N	N	Y	N	N	N	Y
NEW YORK							
1 Bishop	N	N	Y	Y	N	Y	Y
2 Israel	N	N	Y	N	N	N	Y
3 **King**	N	N	Y	Y	N	N	N
4 McCarthy	N	N	Y	N	N	N	N
5 Ackerman	N	N	Y	N	N	N	Y
6 Meeks	N	Y	Y	N	N	N	Y
7 Crowley	N	Y	Y	N	N	Y	Y
8 Nadler	N	Y	Y	N	N	Y	Y
9 **Turner**	N	N	Y	Y	Y	N	N
10 Towns	N	Y	Y	N	N	Y	Y
11 Clarke	N	Y	Y	N	N	Y	Y
12 Velázquez	N	Y	Y	N	N	Y	Y
13 **Grimm**	N	N	?	Y	N	N	N
14 Maloney	N	Y	Y	N	N	Y	Y
15 Rangel	N	Y	Y	N	N	Y	Y
16 Serrano	N	Y	Y	N	N	Y	Y
17 Engel	N	N	Y	N	N	N	Y
18 Lowey	N	N	Y	N	N	N	Y
19 **Hayworth**	N	N	Y	Y	Y	N	N
20 **Gibson**	Y	N	Y	Y	N	Y	N
21 Tonko	N	Y	Y	N	N	Y	Y
22 Hinchey	N	Y	Y	N	N	Y	Y
23 Owens	N	N	Y	Y	N	N	Y
24 **Hanna**	N	N	Y	Y	Y	N	N
25 **Buerkle**	N	N	Y	Y	Y	N	N
26 Hochul	N	N	Y	N	N	N	Y
27 Higgins	N	Y	Y	N	N	Y	Y
28 Slaughter	?	?	?	?	?	?	?
29 **Reed**	Y	N	Y	Y	Y	N	N
NORTH CAROLINA							
1 Butterfield	N	N	Y	N	N	N	Y
2 **Ellmers**	N	N	Y	Y	Y	N	N
3 **Jones**	N	Y	Y	N	N	N	N
4 Price	N	N	Y	N	N	N	Y

	263	264	265	266	267	268	269
5 **Foxx**	Y	N	Y	Y	Y	N	N
6 **Coble**	N	N	Y	Y	Y	N	N
7 McIntyre	N	N	Y	Y	N	N	N
8 Kissell	Y	N	Y	Y	N	N	N
9 **Myrick**	N	N	Y	Y	Y	N	N
10 **McHenry**	N	N	Y	Y	Y	N	N
11 Shuler	N	N	Y	Y	N	N	N
12 Watt	N	Y	Y	N	N	N	Y
13 Miller	N	N	Y	N	N	N	Y
NORTH DAKOTA							
AL **Berg**	N	N	Y	Y	Y	N	N
OHIO							
1 **Chabot**	N	N	Y	Y	Y	N	N
2 **Schmidt**	N	N	Y	Y	Y	N	N
3 **Turner**	N	N	Y	Y	N	N	N
4 **Jordan**	Y	N	Y	Y	Y	N	N
5 **Latta**	N	N	Y	Y	Y	N	N
6 **Johnson**	N	N	Y	Y	Y	N	N
7 **Austria**	N	N	Y	Y	Y	N	N
8 **Boehner**							
9 Kaptur	N	?	Y	N	N	N	Y
10 Kucinich	N	Y	N	N	N	Y	Y
11 Fudge	N	Y	Y	N	N	Y	Y
12 **Tiberi**	Y	N	Y	Y	Y	N	N
13 Sutton	N	N	Y	N	N	N	Y
14 **LaTourette**	N	N	Y	Y	N	N	?
15 **Stivers**	N	N	Y	Y	Y	N	N
16 **Renacci**	N	N	Y	Y	Y	N	N
17 Ryan	N	N	Y	N	N	N	N
18 **Gibbs**	N	N	Y	Y	Y	N	N
OKLAHOMA							
1 **Sullivan**	N	?	Y	Y	Y	N	N
2 Boren	N	N	Y	Y	Y	N	N
3 **Lucas**	N	N	Y	Y	Y	N	N
4 **Cole**	N	N	Y	Y	Y	N	N
5 **Lankford**	N	N	Y	Y	Y	N	N
OREGON							
1 Bonamici	N	Y	Y	N	N	Y	Y
2 **Walden**	N	N	Y	Y	Y	N	Y
3 Blumenauer	N	Y	Y	N	N	Y	Y
4 DeFazio	Y	Y	Y	N	N	Y	Y
5 Schrader	N	Y	Y	N	N	N	Y
PENNSYLVANIA							
1 Brady	N	Y	Y	N	N	N	Y
2 Fattah	N	Y	Y	N	N	Y	Y
3 **Kelly**	?	N	Y	Y	Y	N	N
4 Altmire	N	N	Y	Y	N	N	N
5 **Thompson**	N	N	Y	Y	Y	N	N
6 **Gerlach**	Y	N	Y	Y	Y	N	N
7 **Meehan**	N	N	Y	N	N	N	N
8 **Fitzpatrick**	N	N	Y	Y	Y	N	N
9 **Shuster**	N	N	Y	Y	Y	N	N
10 **Marino**	N	N	Y	Y	Y	N	N
11 **Barletta**	N	N	Y	Y	Y	N	N
12 Critz	N	N	Y	N	N	N	Y
13 Schwartz	N	N	Y	N	N	Y	Y
14 Doyle	N	Y	Y	N	N	Y	Y
15 **Dent**	N	N	Y	Y	Y	N	N
16 **Pitts**	N	N	Y	Y	Y	N	N
17 Holden	?	?	?	?	?	?	?
18 **Murphy**	N	N	Y	Y	N	N	N
19 **Platts**	N	N	Y	Y	Y	N	N
RHODE ISLAND							
1 Cicilline	N	Y	Y	N	N	N	Y
2 Langevin	N	N	Y	N	N	N	Y
SOUTH CAROLINA							
1 **Scott**	Y	N	Y	Y	Y	N	N
2 **Wilson**	N	N	Y	Y	Y	N	N
3 **Duncan**	Y	N	Y	Y	Y	N	N
4 **Gowdy**	Y	N	Y	Y	Y	N	N
5 **Mulvaney**	Y	N	Y	Y	Y	Y	Y
6 Clyburn	N	N	Y	N	N	N	Y
SOUTH DAKOTA							
AL **Noem**	N	N	Y	Y	Y	N	N
TENNESSEE							
1 **Roe**	N	N	Y	Y	Y	N	N
2 **Duncan**	Y	Y	Y	Y	Y	N	Y
3 **Fleischmann**	N	N	Y	Y	Y	N	N
4 **DesJarlais**	Y	N	Y	Y	Y	N	N
5 Cooper	N	N	Y	Y	N	N	Y
6 **Black**	Y	N	Y	Y	Y	N	N
7 **Blackburn**	N	N	Y	Y	Y	N	N
8 **Fincher**	Y	N	Y	Y	Y	N	N
9 Cohen	Y	Y	Y	N	N	Y	Y

	263	264	265	266	267	268	269
TEXAS							
1 **Gohmert**	Y	N	Y	Y	Y	N	N
2 **Poe**	Y	N	Y	Y	Y	N	N
3 **Johnson, S.**	N	N	Y	Y	Y	N	N
4 **Hall**	N	N	?	Y	Y	N	N
5 **Hensarling**	N	N	Y	Y	Y	N	N
6 **Barton**	N	N	Y	Y	Y	N	N
7 **Culberson**	Y	N	Y	Y	Y	N	N
8 **Brady**	N	N	Y	Y	Y	N	N
9 Green, A.	N	N	Y	N	N	N	N
10 **McCaul**	N	N	Y	Y	Y	N	N
11 **Conaway**	N	N	Y	Y	Y	N	N
12 **Granger**	N	N	Y	Y	Y	N	N
13 **Thornberry**	N	N	Y	Y	Y	N	N
14 **Paul**	Y	Y	Y	N	Y	Y	Y
15 Hinojosa	N	N	Y	N	N	Y	Y
16 Reyes	N	N	Y	N	N	N	Y
17 **Flores**	N	N	Y	Y	Y	N	N
18 Jackson Lee	N	Y	Y	N	N	Y	Y
19 **Neugebauer**	N	N	Y	Y	Y	N	N
20 Gonzalez	N	N	Y	N	N	N	Y
21 **Smith**	N	N	Y	Y	Y	N	N
22 **Olson**	N	N	Y	Y	Y	N	N
23 **Canseco**	N	N	Y	Y	Y	N	N
24 **Marchant**	N	N	Y	Y	Y	N	N
25 Doggett	Y	N	Y	N	N	Y	Y
26 **Burgess**	N	N	Y	Y	Y	N	N
27 **Farenthold**	Y	N	Y	N	Y	N	N
28 Cuellar	?	N	Y	Y	N	N	N
29 Green, G.	Y	N	Y	Y	N	N	N
30 Johnson, E.	N	Y	Y	N	N	N	N
31 **Carter**	N	N	Y	Y	Y	N	N
32 **Sessions**	N	N	Y	Y	Y	N	N
UTAH							
1 **Bishop**	N	N	Y	Y	Y	N	N
2 Matheson	N	N	Y	Y	N	N	Y
3 **Chaffetz**	N	N	Y	Y	Y	N	N
VERMONT							
AL Welch	N	Y	Y	N	N	Y	Y
VIRGINIA							
1 **Wittman**	N	N	Y	Y	Y	N	N
2 **Rigell**	Y	N	Y	Y	Y	N	N
3 Scott	N	Y	Y	N	N	N	Y
4 **Forbes**	N	N	Y	Y	Y	N	N
5 **Hurt**	N	N	Y	Y	Y	N	N
6 **Goodlatte**	N	N	Y	Y	Y	N	Y
7 **Cantor**	N	N	Y	Y	Y	N	N
8 Moran	N	Y	Y	N	N	N	Y
9 **Griffith**	N	N	Y	N	Y	Y	Y
10 **Wolf**	N	N	Y	Y	Y	N	N
11 Connolly	N	N	Y	N	N	N	N
WASHINGTON							
1 Vacant							
2 Larsen	N	N	Y	N	N	N	Y
3 **Herrera Beutler**	Y	N	Y	Y	Y	N	N
4 **Hastings**	N	N	Y	Y	Y	N	N
5 **McMorris Rodgers**	N	N	Y	Y	Y	N	N
6 Dicks	N	N	Y	N	N	N	N
7 McDermott	N	Y	Y	N	N	Y	Y
8 **Reichert**	N	N	Y	Y	N	N	N
9 Smith	N	N	Y	N	N	N	Y
WEST VIRGINIA							
1 **McKinley**	N	N	Y	Y	N	N	N
2 **Capito**	N	N	Y	Y	Y	N	N
3 Rahall	N	Y	Y	N	N	Y	Y
WISCONSIN							
1 **Ryan**	N	N	Y	Y	Y	N	N
2 Baldwin	Y	Y	Y	N	N	Y	Y
3 Kind	N	N	Y	N	N	Y	Y
4 Moore	N	Y	Y	N	N	Y	Y
5 **Sensenbrenner**	Y	N	Y	Y	Y	Y	N
6 **Petri**	Y	Y	Y	N	Y	Y	Y
7 **Duffy**	Y	N	Y	Y	Y	N	N
8 **Ribble**	Y	N	Y	N	Y	N	Y
WYOMING							
AL **Lummis**	Y	N	Y	Y	Y	N	N

IN THE HOUSE | By Vote Number

270. HR 4310. Fiscal 2013 Defense Authorization/Guantánamo Detention Facility. Smith, D-Wash., amendment that would strike language from the bill that would provide the authority to transfer individuals captured within the United States, territories or other locations to military authorities and prevent the indefinite detention of such individuals at Guantánamo Bay, Cuba. Rejected in Committee of the Whole 182-238: R 19-219; D 163-19. May 18, 2012.

271. HR 4310. Fiscal 2013 Defense Authorization/Detainee Rights. Gohmert, R-Texas, amendment that would clarify that the bill and the 2001 authorization for use of military force do not deny the writ of habeas corpus or deny any constitutional rights for persons detained in the United States under the use of force authorization who are entitled to such rights. Adopted in Committee of the Whole 243-173: R 230-7; D 13-166. May 18, 2012.

272. HR 4310. Fiscal 2013 Defense Authorization/Contractor Authority. Coffman, R-Colo., amendment that would allow contractor personnel to perform functions currently restricted to Defense Department civilian employees and would repeal the prohibition against public-private competition for certain Defense Department functions. Rejected in Committee of the Whole 209-211: R 209-29; D 0-182. May 18, 2012.

273. HR 4310. Fiscal 2013 Defense Authorization/Air National Guard Units. Keating, D-Mass., amendment that would bar the use of funds authorized by the bill for the Air Force in fiscal 2013 to transfer, reduce or eliminate any Air National Guard units supporting an Air and Space Operations Center or an Air Force Forces staff. It would allow the Defense secretary to waive the limitation 30 days after submitting written certification to Congress that the waiver is necessary to meet an emergency national security requirement. It also would increase by $36.5 million the amount authorized for the Air National Guard and reduce by the same amount the authorization for the Ballistic Missile Defense Midcourse Defense Segment. Rejected in Committee of the Whole 192-229: R 25-214; D 167-15. May 18, 2012.

274. HR 4310. Fiscal 2013 Defense Authorization/Enlistment Age Cap Elimination. Broun, R-Ga., amendment that would permit qualified and able-bodied individuals older than 42 to enlist in the U.S. military. Rejected in Committee of the Whole 164-256: R 94-145; D 70-111. May 18, 2012.

275. HR 4310. Fiscal 2013 Defense Authorization/Military Promotion Determinations. Carson, D-Ind., amendment that would prohibit military promotion boards from using information regarding an individual seeking mental health or addiction treatment services when making a promotion determination. It would require information regarding this prohibition be made available to servicemembers and direct the Defense secretary to establish a process to exclude certain individuals from the prohibition. Rejected in Committee of the Whole 180-241: R 12-227; D 168-14. May 18, 2012.

	270	271	272	273	274	275
ALABAMA						
1 Bonner	N	Y	Y	N	N	N
2 Roby	N	Y	Y	N	N	N
3 Rogers	?	Y	N	N	N	N
4 Aderholt	N	Y	Y	N	Y	N
5 Brooks	N	Y	Y	N	Y	N
6 Bachus	N	Y	Y	N	Y	N
7 Sewell	N	N	N	Y	N	Y
ALASKA						
AL Young	N	Y	N	N	Y	N
ARIZONA						
1 Gosar	?	?	?	?	?	?
2 Franks	N	Y	Y	N	Y	N
3 Quayle	N	Y	Y	N	Y	N
4 Pastor	Y	N	N	Y	Y	Y
5 Schweikert	N	N	Y	N	Y	N
6 Flake	N	Y	Y	N	N	N
7 Grijalva	Y	N	N	Y	N	Y
8 Vacant						
ARKANSAS						
1 Crawford	N	Y	Y	N	N	N
2 Griffin	N	Y	Y	N	N	N
3 Womack	N	Y	Y	N	N	N
4 Ross	N	N	Y	N	Y	N
CALIFORNIA						
1 Thompson	Y	N	N	Y	Y	Y
2 Herger	N	Y	Y	N	N	N
3 Lungren	N	Y	Y	N	N	N
4 McClintock	Y	N	Y	N	Y	N
5 Matsui	Y	N	N	Y	Y	Y
6 Woolsey	Y	N	N	Y	N	Y
7 Miller, George	Y	N	N	Y	Y	Y
8 Pelosi	Y	N	N	Y	N	Y
9 Lee	Y	N	N	Y	Y	Y
10 Garamendi	Y	N	N	Y	Y	Y
11 McNerney	Y	N	N	Y	N	Y
12 Speier	?	?	?	?	?	?
13 Stark	Y	N	N	N	Y	Y
14 Eshoo	Y	N	N	Y	Y	Y
15 Honda	Y	N	N	Y	N	Y
16 Lofgren	Y	N	N	Y	Y	Y
17 Farr	Y	N	N	Y	Y	Y
18 Cardoza	?	?	?	?	?	?
19 Denham	N	Y	Y	N	N	N
20 Costa	N	Y	N	Y	Y	N
21 Nunes	N	Y	Y	N	N	N
22 McCarthy	N	Y	Y	N	N	N
23 Capps	Y	N	N	Y	N	Y
24 Gallegly	N	Y	Y	N	N	N
25 McKeon	N	Y	Y	N	N	N
26 Dreier	N	Y	Y	N	N	N
27 Sherman	Y	N	Y	Y	Y	Y
28 Berman	Y	N	N	Y	Y	Y
29 Schiff	Y	N	Y	Y	Y	Y
30 Waxman	Y	N	N	Y	Y	Y
31 Becerra	Y	N	N	Y	N	Y
32 Chu	Y	N	N	Y	N	N
33 Bass	Y	N	N	Y	Y	Y
34 Roybal-Allard	Y	N	N	Y	N	Y
35 Waters	Y	N	N	Y	Y	Y
36 Hahn	Y	N	N	Y	Y	Y
37 Richardson	Y	N	N	Y	Y	Y
38 Napolitano	Y	N	N	Y	Y	Y
39 Sánchez, Linda	Y	N	N	N	N	Y
40 Royce	N	Y	Y	N	N	N
41 Lewis	N	Y	Y	N	N	N
42 Miller, Gary	N	Y	Y	N	N	N
43 Baca	Y	N	N	Y	Y	Y
44 Calvert	N	Y	Y	N	N	N
45 Bono Mack	N	Y	Y	N	N	N
46 Rohrabacher	N	Y	Y	N	Y	N
47 Sanchez, Loretta	?	?	?	?	?	?
48 Campbell	N	Y	Y	N	N	Y
49 Issa	N	Y	Y	N	N	N
50 Bilbray	N	Y	Y	N	N	N
51 Filner	+	–	+	+	–	+
52 Hunter	N	Y	Y	N	N	N
53 Davis	Y	N	N	N	N	N

	270	271	272	273	274	275
COLORADO						
1 DeGette	Y	N	N	N	N	Y
2 Polis	Y	N	N	Y	Y	Y
3 Tipton	Y	Y	Y	N	Y	N
4 Gardner	N	Y	Y	N	N	N
5 Lamborn	N	Y	Y	N	N	N
6 Coffman	N	Y	Y	N	N	N
7 Perlmutter	Y	N	N	Y	N	N
CONNECTICUT						
1 Larson	Y	N	N	Y	N	Y
2 Courtney	Y	N	N	Y	N	Y
3 DeLauro	Y	N	N	Y	N	Y
4 Himes	Y	N	N	Y	N	Y
5 Murphy	Y	N	N	Y	N	Y
DELAWARE						
AL Carney	Y	N	N	Y	Y	Y
FLORIDA						
1 Miller	N	Y	Y	N	Y	N
2 Southerland	N	Y	Y	N	N	N
3 Brown	N	Y	N	Y	N	N
4 Crenshaw	N	Y	Y	N	N	N
5 Nugent	N	Y	Y	N	N	N
6 Stearns	N	Y	Y	N	N	N
7 Mica	N	Y	Y	Y	N	N
8 Webster	N	Y	Y	N	N	N
9 Bilirakis	N	Y	Y	N	N	N
10 Young	N	Y	Y	Y	N	N
11 Castor	Y	N	N	Y	N	Y
12 Ross	N	Y	Y	N	Y	N
13 Buchanan	N	Y	Y	N	Y	N
14 Mack	N	Y	Y	N	N	N
15 Posey	N	Y	Y	N	N	N
16 Rooney	N	Y	Y	N	Y	N
17 Wilson	Y	N	N	Y	N	Y
18 Ros-Lehtinen	N	Y	?	N	Y	N
19 Deutch	Y	N	N	Y	N	Y
20 Wasserman Schultz	Y	N	N	Y	N	Y
21 Diaz-Balart	N	Y	Y	N	N	N
22 West	N	Y	Y	N	N	N
23 Hastings	Y	N	N	Y	N	Y
24 Adams	N	Y	Y	N	Y	N
25 Rivera	N	Y	Y	N	N	N
GEORGIA						
1 Kingston	N	Y	Y	N	Y	N
2 Bishop	N	N	N	N	N	Y
3 Westmoreland	N	Y	Y	N	N	N
4 Johnson	Y	N	N	Y	N	Y
5 Lewis	Y	N	N	Y	N	Y
6 Price	N	Y	Y	N	Y	N
7 Woodall	N	Y	Y	N	Y	N
8 Scott, A.	N	Y	N	N	N	N
9 Graves	N	Y	Y	N	Y	N
10 Broun	Y	Y	Y	N	Y	N
11 Gingrey	N	Y	Y	N	Y	N
12 Barrow	N	N	N	N	Y	N
13 Scott, D.	Y	N	N	Y	N	Y
HAWAII						
1 Hanabusa	Y	N	N	Y	N	Y
2 Hirono	Y	N	N	Y	N	Y
IDAHO						
1 Labrador	Y	Y	Y	N	Y	N
2 Simpson	N	Y	Y	N	Y	N
ILLINOIS						
1 Rush	Y	N	N	Y	Y	Y
2 Jackson	Y	N	N	Y	N	Y
3 Lipinski	N	Y	N	N	N	Y
4 Gutierrez	Y	N	N	Y	N	Y
5 Quigley	Y	N	N	N	Y	Y
6 Roskam	N	Y	Y	N	N	N
7 Davis	Y	N	N	Y	Y	Y
8 Walsh	N	Y	N	Y	Y	Y
9 Schakowsky	Y	N	N	Y	Y	Y
10 Dold	N	Y	Y	N	N	N
11 Kinzinger	N	Y	N	N	N	N
12 Costello	?	?	?	?	?	?
13 Biggert	N	Y	Y	N	N	N
14 Hultgren	N	Y	Y	N	Y	N
15 Johnson	Y	N	N	Y	N	N

	270	271	272	273	274	275
16 **Manzullo**	N	Y	Y	N	Y	N
17 **Schilling**	N	Y	N	Y	Y	N
18 **Schock**	N	Y	Y	N	N	N
19 **Shimkus**	Y	Y	Y	N	N	N
INDIANA						
1 Visclosky	Y	N	N	Y	N	Y
2 Donnelly	N	Y	N	Y	N	Y
3 **Stutzman**	N	Y	Y	Y	Y	N
4 **Rokita**	N	Y	Y	N	Y	N
5 **Burton**	N	Y	Y	N	Y	N
6 **Pence**	N	Y	Y	N	N	N
7 Carson	Y	N	N	Y	N	Y
8 **Bucshon**	N	Y	Y	N	N	N
9 **Young**	N	Y	Y	N	Y	N
IOWA						
1 Braley	Y	N	N	Y	Y	Y
2 Loebsack	Y	N	N	Y	N	Y
3 Boswell	Y	N	N	Y	Y	Y
4 **Latham**	N	Y	Y	N	Y	N
5 **King**	N	Y	Y	N	Y	N
KANSAS						
1 **Huelskamp**	Y	N	Y	N	Y	N
2 **Jenkins**	N	Y	Y	N	N	N
3 **Yoder**	N	Y	Y	N	Y	N
4 **Pompeo**	N	Y	Y	N	N	N
KENTUCKY						
1 **Whitfield**	N	Y	Y	N	Y	N
2 **Guthrie**	N	Y	Y	N	N	N
3 Yarmuth	Y	N	N	Y	N	Y
4 **Davis**	N	Y	Y	N	N	N
5 **Rogers**	N	Y	Y	N	N	N
6 Chandler	N	N	N	Y	N	Y
LOUISIANA						
1 **Scalise**	N	Y	Y	Y	N	N
2 Richmond	Y	N	N	Y	N	Y
3 **Landry**	N	Y	Y	N	Y	N
4 **Fleming**	N	Y	Y	Y	N	N
5 **Alexander**	N	Y	Y	Y	N	N
6 **Cassidy**	N	Y	Y	N	Y	N
7 **Boustany**	N	Y	Y	Y	N	N
MAINE						
1 Pingree	Y	N	N	Y	N	Y
2 Michaud	Y	N	N	Y	N	Y
MARYLAND						
1 **Harris**	N	Y	Y	N	Y	Y
2 Ruppersberger	N	N	N	Y	N	Y
3 Sarbanes	Y	N	N	Y	Y	Y
4 Edwards	Y	N	N	Y	N	Y
5 Hoyer	Y	N	N	Y	N	Y
6 **Bartlett**	Y	Y	Y	N	N	N
7 Cummings	Y	N	N	Y	Y	Y
8 Van Hollen	Y	N	N	Y	N	Y
MASSACHUSETTS						
1 Olver	Y	N	N	Y	N	Y
2 Neal	Y	N	N	Y	N	Y
3 McGovern	Y	N	N	Y	N	Y
4 Frank	Y	N	N	Y	Y	Y
5 Tsongas	Y	N	N	Y	N	Y
6 Tierney	Y	N	N	Y	N	Y
7 Markey	Y	N	N	Y	N	Y
8 Capuano	Y	N	N	Y	Y	Y
9 Lynch	Y	Y	N	Y	Y	N
10 Keating	Y	N	N	Y	Y	Y
MICHIGAN						
1 **Benishek**	N	Y	Y	N	Y	N
2 **Huizenga**	N	Y	Y	N	Y	N
3 **Amash**	Y	N	Y	N	Y	N
4 **Camp**	N	Y	Y	N	Y	N
5 Kildee	Y	N	N	Y	N	Y
6 **Upton**	N	Y	Y	Y	Y	Y
7 **Walberg**	N	Y	Y	N	Y	N
8 **Rogers**	N	Y	Y	N	Y	N
9 Peters	Y	N	N	Y	N	Y
10 **Miller**	N	Y	Y	N	N	N
11 **McCotter**	N	Y	N	N	Y	N
12 Levin	N	N	N	Y	N	Y
13 Clarke	Y	N	N	Y	Y	Y
14 Conyers	Y	N	N	Y	N	Y
15 Dingell	Y	N	N	Y	N	Y
MINNESOTA						
1 Walz	Y	Y	N	Y	N	N
2 **Kline**	N	Y	Y	N	N	N
3 **Paulsen**	N	+	Y	N	N	N
4 McCollum	Y	N	N	Y	Y	Y

	270	271	272	273	274	275
5 Ellison	N	N	N	Y	Y	Y
6 **Bachmann**	N	Y	Y	Y	N	N
7 Peterson	N	Y	N	Y	Y	Y
8 **Cravaack**	N	Y	Y	N	N	N
MISSISSIPPI						
1 **Nunnelee**	N	?	Y	Y	N	N
2 Thompson	Y	N	N	Y	N	Y
3 **Harper**	N	Y	Y	Y	N	N
4 **Palazzo**	N	Y	Y	N	N	N
MISSOURI						
1 Clay	?	?	?	?	?	?
2 **Akin**	N	Y	Y	N	N	N
3 Carnahan	Y	N	N	Y	Y	Y
4 **Hartzler**	N	Y	Y	N	N	N
5 Cleaver	Y	N	N	Y	N	Y
6 **Graves**	N	Y	Y	N	N	N
7 **Long**	N	Y	Y	N	N	N
8 **Emerson**	N	Y	N	N	N	N
9 **Luetkemeyer**	N	Y	Y	Y	N	N
MONTANA						
AL **Rehberg**	Y	Y	Y	N	N	N
NEBRASKA						
1 **Fortenberry**	N	Y	Y	N	N	N
2 **Terry**	N	Y	Y	N	N	N
3 **Smith**	N	Y	Y	N	N	N
NEVADA						
1 Berkley	Y	N	N	Y	N	Y
2 **Amodei**	?	?	?	?	?	?
3 **Heck**	N	Y	Y	N	N	N
NEW HAMPSHIRE						
1 **Guinta**	N	Y	Y	Y	N	N
2 **Bass**	N	Y	N	N	Y	N
NEW JERSEY						
1 Andrews	Y	N	N	Y	N	Y
2 **LoBiondo**	N	Y	N	Y	Y	N
3 **Runyan**	N	Y	N	N	N	Y
4 **Smith**	N	Y	N	N	Y	N
5 **Garrett**	N	Y	Y	N	Y	N
6 Pallone	Y	N	N	Y	Y	Y
7 **Lance**	N	Y	Y	N	N	N
8 Pascrell	+	−	−	+	+	+
9 Rothman	Y	N	N	Y	Y	Y
10 Vacant						
11 **Frelinghuysen**	N	Y	Y	N	N	N
12 Holt	Y	N	N	Y	N	Y
13 Sires	Y	N	N	Y	Y	Y
NEW MEXICO						
1 Heinrich	Y	N	N	Y	Y	Y
2 **Pearce**	N	Y	Y	N	Y	N
3 Luján	Y	N	N	Y	Y	Y
NEW YORK						
1 Bishop	Y	N	N	Y	N	Y
2 Israel	Y	N	N	Y	Y	Y
3 **King**	N	Y	Y	N	N	N
4 McCarthy	N	Y	N	Y	N	Y
5 Ackerman	Y	N	N	Y	N	Y
6 Meeks	Y	N	N	Y	Y	Y
7 Crowley	Y	N	N	Y	Y	Y
8 Nadler	Y	N	N	Y	N	Y
9 **Turner**	N	Y	Y	N	Y	N
10 Towns	Y	N	N	Y	Y	Y
11 Clarke	Y	N	N	Y	N	Y
12 Velázquez	Y	N	N	Y	N	Y
13 **Grimm**	N	Y	N	N	N	N
14 Maloney	Y	N	N	Y	N	Y
15 Rangel	Y	?	N	Y	Y	Y
16 Serrano	Y	N	N	Y	Y	Y
17 Engel	Y	N	N	Y	Y	Y
18 Lowey	Y	N	N	Y	N	Y
19 **Hayworth**	N	Y	Y	N	Y	N
20 **Gibson**	Y	Y	N	Y	Y	Y
21 Tonko	Y	N	N	Y	N	Y
22 Hinchey	Y	N	N	Y	N	Y
23 Owens	N	N	N	Y	N	Y
24 **Hanna**	N	Y	Y	N	N	N
25 **Buerkle**	N	Y	Y	N	N	N
26 Hochul	Y	N	N	Y	N	Y
27 Higgins	Y	N	N	Y	N	Y
28 Slaughter	?	?	?	?	?	?
29 **Reed**	N	Y	Y	N	N	N
NORTH CAROLINA						
1 Butterfield	Y	N	N	Y	Y	Y
2 **Ellmers**	N	Y	Y	N	N	N
3 **Jones**	Y	N	N	Y	Y	N
4 Price	Y	N	N	Y	N	Y

	270	271	272	273	274	275
5 **Foxx**	N	Y	Y	N	N	Y
6 **Coble**	N	Y	N	N	Y	N
7 McIntyre	N	Y	N	N	Y	Y
8 Kissell	N	Y	N	N	Y	N
9 **Myrick**	N	Y	Y	N	N	N
10 **McHenry**	N	Y	Y	N	N	N
11 Shuler	Y	Y	N	Y	N	N
12 Watt	Y	N	N	N	Y	Y
13 Miller	Y	N	N	Y	N	Y
NORTH DAKOTA						
AL **Berg**	N	Y	Y	N	N	N
OHIO						
1 **Chabot**	N	Y	Y	N	Y	N
2 **Schmidt**	N	Y	Y	N	Y	N
3 **Turner**	N	Y	N	N	N	N
4 **Jordan**	N	Y	Y	N	Y	N
5 **Latta**	N	Y	Y	N	N	N
6 **Johnson**	N	Y	Y	N	Y	N
7 **Austria**	N	Y	Y	N	N	N
8 **Boehner**						
9 Kaptur	Y	N	N	Y	N	Y
10 Kucinich	Y	N	N	Y	Y	Y
11 Fudge	Y	N	N	Y	N	Y
12 **Tiberi**	N	Y	Y	Y	Y	N
13 Sutton	Y	?	N	Y	N	Y
14 **LaTourette**	N	Y	N	N	Y	N
15 **Stivers**	N	Y	Y	N	Y	N
16 **Renacci**	N	Y	Y	N	N	N
17 Ryan	Y	N	N	Y	?	Y
18 **Gibbs**	N	Y	Y	N	N	N
OKLAHOMA						
1 **Sullivan**	N	Y	Y	N	Y	N
2 Boren	N	N	N	N	N	N
3 **Lucas**	N	Y	N	N	Y	N
4 **Cole**	N	Y	N	N	N	N
5 **Lankford**	N	Y	Y	N	Y	N
OREGON						
1 Bonamici	Y	N	N	Y	Y	Y
2 **Walden**	N	Y	Y	Y	Y	Y
3 Blumenauer	Y	N	N	Y	N	Y
4 DeFazio	Y	N	N	Y	Y	Y
5 Schrader	Y	N	N	Y	N	N
PENNSYLVANIA						
1 Brady	Y	N	N	Y	N	Y
2 Fattah	Y	N	N	Y	N	Y
3 **Kelly**	N	Y	Y	N	N	N
4 Altmire	Y	N	N	Y	N	Y
5 **Thompson**	N	Y	Y	Y	Y	Y
6 **Gerlach**	N	Y	N	N	N	N
7 **Meehan**	N	Y	N	Y	N	N
8 **Fitzpatrick**	N	Y	N	Y	N	N
9 **Shuster**	N	Y	N	N	N	N
10 **Marino**	N	Y	Y	N	N	N
11 **Barletta**	N	Y	Y	N	N	N
12 Critz	Y	N	N	Y	N	Y
13 Schwartz	Y	N	N	Y	N	Y
14 Doyle	Y	N	N	Y	N	Y
15 **Dent**	N	Y	Y	Y	Y	N
16 **Pitts**	N	Y	Y	N	N	N
17 Holden	Y	N	N	Y	N	Y
18 **Murphy**	N	Y	N	N	N	N
19 **Platts**	N	Y	N	N	N	N
RHODE ISLAND						
1 Cicilline	Y	N	N	Y	Y	Y
2 Langevin	Y	N	N	Y	Y	Y
SOUTH CAROLINA						
1 **Scott**	N	Y	Y	N	Y	N
2 **Wilson**	N	Y	Y	N	N	N
3 **Duncan**	N	Y	Y	N	Y	N
4 **Gowdy**	N	Y	Y	N	Y	N
5 **Mulvaney**	N	Y	Y	N	Y	N
6 Clyburn	Y	N	N	Y	N	Y
SOUTH DAKOTA						
AL **Noem**	N	Y	Y	N	N	N
TENNESSEE						
1 **Roe**	N	Y	Y	N	N	N
2 **Duncan**	Y	Y	Y	N	Y	N
3 **Fleischmann**	N	Y	Y	N	N	N
4 **DesJarlais**	N	Y	Y	N	N	N
5 Cooper	Y	N	N	N	N	Y
6 **Black**	N	Y	Y	N	N	N
7 **Blackburn**	N	Y	Y	N	N	N
8 **Fincher**	N	Y	Y	N	N	N
9 Cohen	Y	N	N	Y	Y	Y

	270	271	272	273	274	275
TEXAS						
1 **Gohmert**	N	Y	Y	N	Y	N
2 **Poe**	N	Y	Y	Y	Y	N
3 **Johnson, S.**	N	Y	Y	N	N	N
4 **Hall**	N	Y	Y	N	N	N
5 **Hensarling**	N	Y	Y	N	N	N
6 **Barton**	N	Y	Y	N	Y	N
7 **Culberson**	N	Y	Y	N	N	N
8 **Brady**	N	Y	Y	N	Y	N
9 Green, A.	Y	N	N	Y	N	Y
10 **McCaul**	N	Y	Y	N	Y	N
11 **Conaway**	N	Y	Y	N	N	N
12 **Granger**	N	Y	Y	N	N	N
13 **Thornberry**	N	Y	Y	N	N	N
14 **Paul**	Y	N	N	Y	Y	Y
15 Hinojosa	Y	N	N	Y	N	Y
16 Reyes	Y	N	N	N	Y	Y
17 **Flores**	N	Y	Y	N	N	N
18 Jackson Lee	Y	N	N	Y	Y	Y
19 **Neugebauer**	N	Y	Y	N	Y	N
20 Gonzalez	Y	N	N	Y	Y	Y
21 **Smith**	N	Y	Y	N	N	N
22 **Olson**	N	Y	Y	N	N	N
23 **Canseco**	N	Y	Y	N	N	N
24 **Marchant**	N	Y	Y	N	N	N
25 Doggett	Y	N	N	Y	Y	Y
26 **Burgess**	N	Y	Y	N	Y	N
27 **Farenthold**	N	Y	Y	N	N	N
28 Cuellar	N	Y	N	Y	N	Y
29 Green, G.	Y	N	N	Y	Y	Y
30 Johnson, E.	Y	N	N	Y	N	Y
31 **Carter**	N	Y	Y	N	N	N
32 **Sessions**	N	Y	Y	N	N	N
UTAH						
1 **Bishop**	Y	Y	N	N	Y	N
2 Matheson	N	Y	N	N	N	Y
3 **Chaffetz**	N	Y	N	N	N	N
VERMONT						
AL Welch	Y	N	N	Y	N	N
VIRGINIA						
1 **Wittman**	N	Y	Y	N	N	N
2 **Rigell**	N	Y	Y	N	N	N
3 Scott	Y	N	N	Y	Y	Y
4 **Forbes**	N	Y	Y	N	N	N
5 **Hurt**	N	Y	Y	N	N	N
6 **Goodlatte**	N	Y	Y	N	N	N
7 **Cantor**	N	Y	Y	N	N	N
8 Moran	Y	N	N	Y	Y	Y
9 **Griffith**	Y	N	Y	N	N	N
10 **Wolf**	N	Y	N	N	Y	N
11 Connolly	Y	N	N	Y	Y	Y
WASHINGTON						
1 Vacant						
2 Larsen	Y	N	N	Y	N	Y
3 **Herrera Beutler**	N	Y	Y	N	Y	Y
4 **Hastings**	N	Y	Y	N	N	N
5 **McMorris Rodgers**	N	Y	Y	N	Y	N
6 Dicks	Y	N	N	Y	N	Y
7 McDermott	Y	?	N	Y	N	Y
8 **Reichert**	N	Y	Y	N	N	N
9 Smith	Y	N	N	Y	N	Y
WEST VIRGINIA						
1 **McKinley**	N	Y	Y	N	Y	N
2 **Capito**	N	Y	Y	N	N	N
3 Rahall	Y	Y	N	Y	N	Y
WISCONSIN						
1 **Ryan**	N	Y	Y	N	N	N
2 Baldwin	Y	N	N	Y	Y	Y
3 Kind	Y	N	N	Y	N	Y
4 Moore	Y	N	N	Y	Y	Y
5 **Sensenbrenner**	Y	Y	Y	N	Y	N
6 **Petri**	Y	Y	Y	N	Y	N
7 **Duffy**	N	Y	Y	N	N	N
8 **Ribble**	Y	Y	Y	N	Y	N
WYOMING						
AL **Lummis**	N	Y	Y	N	N	N

IN THE HOUSE | By Vote Number

276. HR 4310. Fiscal 2013 Defense Authorization/Mortgage Protections. Cummings, D-Md., amendment that would repeal the sunset for mortgage security protections under the Servicemembers Civil Relief Act and expand the program to include service members serving in a contingency operation, surviving spouses of service members whose deaths are service-connected, and veterans who are totally disabled at the time of discharge. It also would increase fines for mortgage violations of the Servicemembers Civil Relief Act. Adopted in Committee of the Whole 394-27: R 212-27; D 182-0. May 18, 2012.

277. HR 4310. Fiscal 2013 Defense Authorization/Naval Vessel Maintenance. Sablan, D-N. Marianas, amendment that would include the Northern Mariana Islands as an eligible location, in addition to the United States and Guam, for the overhaul, repair and maintenance of naval vessels and other vessels under the jurisdiction of the Navy. Rejected in Committee of the Whole 118-303: R 30-209; D 88-94. May 18, 2012.

278. HR 4310. Fiscal 2013 Defense Authorization/Nuclear-Weapons Deployment to South Korea. Johnson, D-Ga., amendment that would include congressional findings language stating that the deployment of tactical nuclear weapons to South Korea would destabilize the Western Pacific region and would not be in the national security interests of the United States. Rejected in Committee of the Whole 160-261: R 5-234; D 155-27. May 18, 2012.

279. HR 4310. Fiscal 2013 Defense Authorization/Nuclear-Weapons Reduction Reports. Johnson, D-Ga., amendment that would require the Defense Department and the Joint Chiefs of Staff to report to Congress by Jan. 15, 2013, on whether nuclear weapons reductions pursuant to the New START agreement are in the national security interests of the United States and whether such reductions should continue. Rejected in Committee of the Whole 175-245: R 4-234; D 171-11. May 18, 2012.

280. HR 4310. Fiscal 2013 Defense Authorization/Nuclear-Weapons Reduction. Price, R-Ga., amendment that would prohibit the president from unilaterally entering into any agreement that would decrease the size of the U.S. nuclear arsenal to a level less than described in the New START agreement. Adopted in Committee of the Whole 241-179: R 233-5; D 8-174. A "nay" was a vote in support of the president's position. May 18, 2012.

281. HR 4310. Fiscal 2013 Defense Authorization/Defense Sequester Elimination. Rigell, R-Va., amendment that would eliminate the automatic budget cuts, known as a sequester, in discretionary defense-related spending. The elimination of the sequester would be conditional upon making corresponding reductions elsewhere in the budget over five years. The amendment would reduce the cap on domestic discretionary spending by $19.1 billion in fiscal 2013. Adopted in Committee of the Whole 220-201: R 218-21; D 2-180. A "nay" was a vote in support of the president's position. May 18, 2012.

	276	277	278	279	280	281
ALABAMA						
1 Bonner	Y	N	N	N	Y	Y
2 Roby	Y	N	N	N	Y	Y
3 Rogers	Y	N	N	N	Y	Y
4 Aderholt	Y	N	N	N	Y	Y
5 Brooks	Y	N	N	N	Y	Y
6 Bachus	Y	N	N	N	Y	Y
7 Sewell	Y	N	Y	Y	N	N
ALASKA						
AL Young	Y	Y	N	N	Y	Y
ARIZONA						
1 Gosar	?	?	?	?	?	?
2 Franks	N	N	N	N	Y	Y
3 Quayle	Y	N	N	N	Y	Y
4 Pastor	Y	Y	Y	Y	N	N
5 Schweikert	Y	N	N	N	Y	Y
6 Flake	N	N	N	N	Y	Y
7 Grijalva	Y	Y	Y	Y	N	N
8 Vacant						
ARKANSAS						
1 Crawford	Y	N	N	N	Y	Y
2 Griffin	Y	N	N	N	Y	Y
3 Womack	Y	N	N	N	Y	Y
4 Ross	Y	N	N	N	N	N
CALIFORNIA						
1 Thompson	Y	Y	Y	Y	N	N
2 Herger	Y	N	N	N	Y	Y
3 Lungren	Y	Y	N	N	Y	Y
4 McClintock	N	N	N	N	Y	Y
5 Matsui	Y	Y	Y	Y	N	N
6 Woolsey	Y	Y	Y	Y	N	N
7 Miller, George	Y	Y	Y	Y	N	N
8 Pelosi	Y	Y	Y	Y	N	N
9 Lee	Y	Y	Y	Y	N	N
10 Garamendi	Y	Y	Y	Y	N	N
11 McNerney	Y	Y	Y	Y	N	N
12 Speier	?	?	?	?	?	?
13 Stark	Y	Y	Y	Y	N	N
14 Eshoo	Y	Y	Y	Y	N	N
15 Honda	Y	Y	Y	Y	N	N
16 Lofgren	Y	Y	Y	Y	N	N
17 Farr	Y	Y	Y	Y	N	N
18 Cardoza	?	?	?	?	?	?
19 Denham	Y	Y	N	N	Y	Y
20 Costa	Y	N	N	Y	N	N
21 Nunes	Y	N	N	N	Y	Y
22 McCarthy	Y	N	N	N	Y	Y
23 Capps	Y	N	Y	N	N	N
24 Gallegly	Y	N	N	N	Y	Y
25 McKeon	Y	N	N	N	Y	Y
26 Dreier	Y	Y	N	N	Y	Y
27 Sherman	Y	N	Y	Y	N	N
28 Berman	Y	N	Y	Y	N	N
29 Schiff	Y	Y	Y	Y	N	N
30 Waxman	Y	N	Y	Y	N	N
31 Becerra	Y	Y	Y	Y	N	N
32 Chu	Y	Y	Y	Y	N	N
33 Bass	Y	N	Y	Y	N	N
34 Roybal-Allard	Y	Y	Y	Y	N	N
35 Waters	Y	Y	Y	Y	N	N
36 Hahn	Y	Y	Y	Y	N	N
37 Richardson	Y	Y	N	Y	N	N
38 Napolitano	Y	Y	Y	Y	N	N
39 Sánchez, Linda	Y	Y	Y	Y	N	N
40 Royce	Y	N	N	N	Y	Y
41 Lewis	Y	N	N	N	Y	Y
42 Miller, Gary	Y	N	N	N	Y	Y
43 Baca	Y	Y	Y	Y	N	N
44 Calvert	Y	N	N	N	Y	Y
45 Bono Mack	Y	N	N	N	Y	Y
46 Rohrabacher	Y	Y	N	N	Y	Y
47 Sanchez, Loretta	?	?	?	?	?	?
48 Campbell	Y	N	N	N	N	N
49 Issa	Y	N	N	?	Y	Y
50 Bilbray	Y	Y	N	N	Y	Y
51 Filner	+	−	+	+	−	−
52 Hunter	Y	N	N	N	Y	Y
53 Davis	Y	N	Y	Y	N	N

	276	277	278	279	280	281
COLORADO						
1 DeGette	Y	N	Y	Y	N	N
2 Polis	Y	Y	Y	Y	N	N
3 Tipton	Y	N	N	N	Y	Y
4 Gardner	Y	N	N	N	Y	Y
5 Lamborn	Y	N	N	N	Y	Y
6 Coffman	Y	N	N	N	Y	Y
7 Perlmutter	Y	Y	N	N	N	N
CONNECTICUT						
1 Larson	Y	Y	Y	Y	N	N
2 Courtney	Y	Y	Y	Y	N	N
3 DeLauro	Y	N	Y	Y	N	N
4 Himes	Y	Y	Y	Y	N	N
5 Murphy	Y	N	Y	Y	N	N
DELAWARE						
AL Carney	Y	N	Y	Y	N	N
FLORIDA						
1 Miller	Y	N	N	N	Y	Y
2 Southerland	Y	N	N	N	Y	Y
3 Brown	Y	Y	Y	Y	N	N
4 Crenshaw	N	N	N	N	Y	Y
5 Nugent	Y	N	N	N	Y	Y
6 Stearns	Y	N	N	N	Y	Y
7 Mica	Y	N	N	N	Y	Y
8 Webster	Y	N	N	N	Y	Y
9 Bilirakis	Y	N	N	N	Y	Y
10 Young	Y	N	N	N	Y	Y
11 Castor	Y	N	Y	Y	N	N
12 Ross	Y	N	N	N	Y	Y
13 Buchanan	Y	N	N	N	Y	Y
14 Mack	Y	N	N	N	Y	Y
15 Posey	Y	N	N	N	Y	Y
16 Rooney	Y	Y	N	N	Y	Y
17 Wilson	Y	N	Y	Y	N	N
18 Ros-Lehtinen	Y	N	Y	Y	N	N
19 Deutch	Y	N	Y	N	N	N
20 Wasserman Schultz	Y	N	Y	Y	N	N
21 Diaz-Balart	Y	N	N	N	Y	Y
22 West	Y	N	N	N	Y	Y
23 Hastings	Y	N	Y	Y	N	N
24 Adams	Y	N	N	N	Y	Y
25 Rivera	Y	N	N	Y	Y	Y
GEORGIA						
1 Kingston	N	Y	N	N	Y	Y
2 Bishop	Y	N	N	N	N	N
3 Westmoreland	Y	N	N	N	Y	Y
4 Johnson	Y	N	Y	Y	N	N
5 Lewis	Y	N	Y	Y	N	N
6 Price	Y	N	N	N	Y	Y
7 Woodall	Y	Y	N	N	Y	Y
8 Scott, A.	N	N	N	N	Y	Y
9 Graves	N	N	N	N	Y	Y
10 Broun	Y	N	N	N	Y	Y
11 Gingrey	Y	Y	N	N	Y	Y
12 Barrow	Y	N	N	N	Y	Y
13 Scott, D.	Y	Y	Y	Y	N	N
HAWAII						
1 Hanabusa	Y	N	Y	Y	N	N
2 Hirono	Y	N	Y	Y	N	N
IDAHO						
1 Labrador	N	N	N	N	Y	Y
2 Simpson	Y	N	N	Y	N	N
ILLINOIS						
1 Rush	Y	Y	Y	Y	N	N
2 Jackson	Y	Y	Y	Y	N	N
3 Lipinski	Y	N	N	N	N	N
4 Gutierrez	Y	Y	Y	Y	N	N
5 Quigley	Y	N	Y	Y	N	N
6 Roskam	Y	N	N	N	Y	Y
7 Davis	Y	Y	Y	Y	N	N
8 Walsh	Y	N	N	N	Y	Y
9 Schakowsky	Y	Y	Y	Y	N	N
10 Dold	Y	N	N	N	Y	Y
11 Kinzinger	Y	N	N	N	Y	Y
12 Costello	?	?	?	?	?	?
13 Biggert	Y	N	N	N	Y	Y
14 Hultgren	Y	Y	N	N	Y	Y
15 Johnson	Y	N	?	Y	N	N

KEY Republicans Democrats

Y Voted for (yea)	**X** Paired against	**C** Voted "present" to avoid possible conflict of interest
# Paired for	**−** Announced against	
+ Announced for	**P** Voted "present"	**?** Did not vote or otherwise make a position known
N Voted against (nay)		

	276	277	278	279	280	281
16 **Manzullo**	Y	Y	N	N	Y	Y
17 **Schilling**	Y	N	N	N	Y	Y
18 **Schock**	Y	N	N	N	Y	Y
19 **Shimkus**	Y	N	N	N	Y	Y
INDIANA						
1 Visclosky	Y	Y	Y	Y	N	N
2 Donnelly	Y	N	N	Y	N	N
3 **Stutzman**	Y	N	N	N	Y	Y
4 **Rokita**	N	N	N	N	Y	Y
5 **Burton**	Y	N	N	N	Y	Y
6 **Pence**	Y	N	N	N	Y	Y
7 Carson	Y	Y	Y	Y	N	N
8 **Bucshon**	Y	N	N	N	Y	Y
9 **Young**	Y	Y	N	N	Y	Y
IOWA						
1 Braley	Y	N	Y	Y	N	N
2 Loebsack	Y	N	Y	Y	N	N
3 Boswell	Y	N	Y	Y	N	N
4 **Latham**	Y	Y	N	N	Y	Y
5 **King**	Y	N	N	N	Y	Y
KANSAS						
1 **Huelskamp**	N	N	N	N	Y	Y
2 **Jenkins**	N	N	N	N	Y	Y
3 **Yoder**	Y	N	N	N	Y	Y
4 **Pompeo**	N	N	N	N	Y	Y
KENTUCKY						
1 **Whitfield**	Y	N	N	N	Y	Y
2 **Guthrie**	Y	N	N	N	Y	Y
3 Yarmuth	Y	N	Y	Y	N	N
4 **Davis**	Y	N	N	N	Y	Y
5 **Rogers**	Y	N	N	N	Y	Y
6 Chandler	Y	N	N	Y	N	N
LOUISIANA						
1 **Scalise**	Y	N	N	N	Y	Y
2 Richmond	Y	N	Y	Y	N	N
3 **Landry**	Y	N	N	N	Y	Y
4 **Fleming**	Y	N	N	N	Y	Y
5 **Alexander**	Y	N	N	N	Y	Y
6 **Cassidy**	Y	N	N	N	Y	Y
7 **Boustany**	Y	N	N	N	Y	Y
MAINE						
1 Pingree	Y	Y	Y	Y	N	N
2 Michaud	Y	Y	Y	Y	N	N
MARYLAND						
1 **Harris**	Y	Y	N	N	Y	Y
2 Ruppersberger	Y	N	Y	Y	N	N
3 Sarbanes	Y	N	Y	Y	N	N
4 Edwards	Y	Y	Y	Y	N	N
5 Hoyer	Y	Y	Y	Y	N	N
6 **Bartlett**	Y	N	N	N	Y	N
7 Cummings	Y	Y	Y	Y	N	N
8 Van Hollen	Y	N	Y	Y	N	N
MASSACHUSETTS						
1 Olver	Y	N	Y	Y	N	N
2 Neal	Y	Y	Y	Y	N	N
3 McGovern	Y	Y	Y	Y	N	N
4 Frank	Y	Y	N	Y	N	N
5 Tsongas	Y	N	Y	Y	N	N
6 Tierney	Y	Y	Y	Y	N	N
7 Markey	Y	N	Y	Y	N	N
8 Capuano	Y	Y	Y	Y	N	N
9 Lynch	Y	N	Y	Y	N	N
10 Keating	Y	N	N	Y	N	N
MICHIGAN						
1 **Benishek**	Y	Y	N	N	Y	Y
2 **Huizenga**	Y	N	N	N	Y	Y
3 **Amash**	N	Y	Y	N	N	N
4 **Camp**	Y	N	N	N	Y	Y
5 Kildee	Y	N	Y	Y	N	N
6 **Upton**	Y	N	N	N	Y	Y
7 **Walberg**	Y	N	N	N	Y	Y
8 **Rogers**	Y	N	N	N	Y	Y
9 Peters	Y	N	Y	Y	N	N
10 **Miller**	Y	N	N	N	Y	Y
11 **McCotter**	Y	Y	N	N	Y	Y
12 Levin	Y	N	Y	Y	N	N
13 Clarke	Y	N	Y	Y	N	N
14 Conyers	Y	N	Y	Y	N	N
15 Dingell	Y	N	Y	Y	N	N
MINNESOTA						
1 Walz	Y	Y	Y	N	N	N
2 **Kline**	Y	N	N	N	Y	Y
3 **Paulsen**	Y	N	N	N	Y	Y
4 McCollum	Y	N	Y	Y	N	N
5 Ellison	Y	Y	Y	Y	N	N
6 **Bachmann**	Y	N	N	N	Y	Y
7 Peterson	Y	Y	N	N	Y	N
8 **Cravaack**	Y	N	N	N	Y	Y
MISSISSIPPI						
1 **Nunnelee**	Y	N	N	N	Y	Y
2 Thompson	Y	Y	Y	Y	N	N
3 **Harper**	Y	N	N	N	Y	Y
4 **Palazzo**	Y	N	N	N	Y	Y
MISSOURI						
1 Clay	?	?	?	?	?	?
2 **Akin**	Y	N	N	N	Y	Y
3 Carnahan	Y	N	Y	Y	N	N
4 **Hartzler**	Y	N	N	N	Y	Y
5 Cleaver	Y	N	Y	Y	N	N
6 **Graves**	Y	N	N	N	Y	Y
7 **Long**	Y	N	N	N	Y	Y
8 **Emerson**	Y	N	N	N	Y	Y
9 **Luetkemeyer**	Y	N	N	N	Y	Y
MONTANA						
AL **Rehberg**	Y	N	N	N	Y	Y
NEBRASKA						
1 **Fortenberry**	Y	N	N	N	Y	Y
2 **Terry**	Y	N	N	N	Y	Y
3 **Smith**	N	N	N	N	Y	Y
NEVADA						
1 Berkley	Y	N	N	Y	N	N
2 **Amodei**	?	?	?	?	?	?
3 **Heck**	Y	Y	N	N	Y	Y
NEW HAMPSHIRE						
1 **Guinta**	Y	N	N	N	Y	Y
2 **Bass**	Y	N	N	N	Y	Y
NEW JERSEY						
1 Andrews	Y	N	Y	Y	N	N
2 **LoBiondo**	Y	N	N	N	Y	Y
3 **Runyan**	Y	N	N	N	Y	Y
4 **Smith**	Y	N	N	N	Y	Y
5 **Garrett**	N	N	N	N	Y	N
6 Pallone	Y	Y	Y	Y	N	N
7 **Lance**	Y	N	N	N	Y	Y
8 Pascrell	+	–	+	+	–	–
9 Rothman	Y	N	Y	Y	N	N
10 Vacant						
11 **Frelinghuysen**	Y	N	N	N	Y	Y
12 Holt	Y	Y	Y	Y	N	N
13 Sires	Y	Y	Y	Y	N	N
NEW MEXICO						
1 Heinrich	Y	Y	Y	Y	N	N
2 **Pearce**	Y	N	N	N	Y	Y
3 Luján	Y	Y	Y	Y	N	N
NEW YORK						
1 Bishop	Y	Y	Y	Y	N	N
2 Israel	Y	N	Y	Y	N	N
3 **King**	Y	N	N	N	Y	Y
4 McCarthy	Y	N	Y	Y	N	N
5 Ackerman	Y	N	Y	Y	N	N
6 Meeks	Y	Y	Y	Y	N	N
7 Crowley	Y	Y	Y	Y	N	N
8 Nadler	Y	N	Y	Y	N	N
9 **Turner**	Y	N	N	N	Y	Y
10 Towns	Y	Y	Y	Y	N	N
11 Clarke	Y	Y	Y	Y	N	N
12 Velázquez	Y	Y	Y	Y	N	N
13 **Grimm**	Y	N	N	N	Y	Y
14 Maloney	Y	N	Y	Y	N	N
15 Rangel	Y	N	Y	Y	N	N
16 Serrano	Y	Y	Y	Y	N	N
17 Engel	Y	Y	N	Y	N	N
18 Lowey	Y	N	Y	Y	N	N
19 **Hayworth**	Y	N	N	N	Y	Y
20 **Gibson**	Y	Y	N	N	Y	Y
21 Tonko	Y	N	Y	Y	N	N
22 Hinchey	Y	Y	Y	Y	N	N
23 Owens	Y	Y	N	N	N	N
24 **Hanna**	Y	N	N	N	Y	Y
25 **Buerkle**	Y	N	N	N	Y	Y
26 Hochul	Y	N	Y	Y	N	N
27 Higgins	Y	N	Y	Y	N	N
28 Slaughter	?	?	?	?	?	?
29 **Reed**	Y	N	N	N	Y	Y
NORTH CAROLINA						
1 Butterfield	Y	N	Y	Y	N	N
2 **Ellmers**	Y	N	N	N	Y	Y
3 **Jones**	Y	Y	Y	Y	Y	N
4 Price	Y	Y	Y	Y	N	N
5 **Foxx**	Y	N	N	N	Y	Y
6 **Coble**	Y	N	N	N	Y	Y
7 McIntyre	Y	N	Y	Y	Y	Y
8 Kissell	Y	Y	Y	Y	Y	N
9 **Myrick**	N	N	N	N	Y	Y
10 **McHenry**	Y	N	N	N	Y	Y
11 Shuler	Y	N	N	N	Y	N
12 Watt	Y	Y	N	N	N	N
13 Miller	Y	N	Y	Y	N	N
NORTH DAKOTA						
AL **Berg**	Y	N	N	N	Y	Y
OHIO						
1 **Chabot**	Y	N	N	N	Y	Y
2 **Schmidt**	Y	N	N	N	Y	Y
3 **Turner**	Y	N	N	N	Y	Y
4 **Jordan**	Y	N	N	N	Y	Y
5 **Latta**	Y	N	N	N	Y	Y
6 **Johnson**	Y	N	N	N	Y	Y
7 **Austria**	Y	N	N	N	Y	Y
8 **Boehner**						
9 Kaptur	Y	Y	N	Y	N	N
10 Kucinich	Y	Y	Y	Y	N	N
11 Fudge	Y	N	Y	Y	N	N
12 **Tiberi**	Y	N	N	N	Y	Y
13 Sutton	Y	N	Y	Y	N	N
14 **LaTourette**	Y	N	N	N	Y	N
15 **Stivers**	Y	N	N	N	Y	Y
16 **Renacci**	Y	N	N	N	Y	Y
17 Ryan	Y	N	Y	Y	N	N
18 **Gibbs**	Y	N	N	N	Y	Y
OKLAHOMA						
1 **Sullivan**	Y	N	N	N	Y	Y
2 Boren	Y	N	N	N	N	N
3 **Lucas**	Y	N	N	N	Y	Y
4 **Cole**	Y	N	N	N	Y	Y
5 **Lankford**	Y	N	N	N	Y	Y
OREGON						
1 Bonamici	Y	N	Y	Y	N	N
2 **Walden**	Y	N	N	N	Y	Y
3 Blumenauer	Y	N	Y	Y	N	N
4 DeFazio	Y	N	Y	Y	N	N
5 Schrader	Y	Y	Y	Y	N	N
PENNSYLVANIA						
1 Brady	Y	N	Y	Y	N	N
2 Fattah	Y	N	Y	Y	N	N
3 **Kelly**	Y	N	N	N	Y	Y
4 Altmire	Y	Y	N	Y	N	N
5 **Thompson**	Y	N	N	N	Y	Y
6 **Gerlach**	Y	N	N	N	Y	Y
7 **Meehan**	Y	N	N	N	Y	Y
8 **Fitzpatrick**	Y	N	N	N	Y	N
9 **Shuster**	Y	N	N	N	Y	Y
10 **Marino**	Y	N	N	N	Y	Y
11 **Barletta**	Y	N	N	N	Y	Y
12 Critz	Y	N	Y	Y	N	N
13 Schwartz	Y	Y	Y	Y	N	N
14 Doyle	Y	N	Y	Y	N	N
15 **Dent**	Y	N	N	N	Y	N
16 **Pitts**	Y	Y	N	N	Y	Y
17 Holden	Y	N	Y	Y	N	N
18 **Murphy**	Y	N	N	N	Y	Y
19 **Platts**	Y	N	N	N	Y	Y
RHODE ISLAND						
1 Cicilline	Y	N	Y	Y	N	N
2 Langevin	Y	N	Y	Y	N	N
SOUTH CAROLINA						
1 **Scott**	N	N	N	N	Y	N
2 **Wilson**	Y	N	N	N	Y	Y
3 **Duncan**	N	N	N	N	Y	Y
4 **Gowdy**	Y	N	N	N	Y	Y
5 **Mulvaney**	N	Y	N	N	N	N
6 Clyburn	Y	Y	Y	Y	N	N
SOUTH DAKOTA						
AL **Noem**	Y	N	N	N	Y	Y
TENNESSEE						
1 **Roe**	Y	N	N	N	Y	Y
2 **Duncan**	Y	N	N	N	Y	N
3 **Fleischmann**	Y	N	N	N	Y	Y
4 **DesJarlais**	Y	N	N	N	Y	Y
5 Cooper	Y	N	Y	Y	N	N
6 **Black**	Y	N	N	N	Y	Y
7 **Blackburn**	Y	N	N	N	Y	Y
8 **Fincher**	Y	N	N	N	Y	Y
9 Cohen	Y	Y	Y	Y	N	N
TEXAS						
1 **Gohmert**	Y	N	N	N	Y	Y
2 **Poe**	Y	Y	N	N	Y	N
3 **Johnson, S.**	Y	N	N	N	Y	Y
4 **Hall**	Y	N	N	N	Y	Y
5 **Hensarling**	N	N	N	N	Y	Y
6 **Barton**	Y	N	N	N	Y	N
7 **Culberson**	Y	N	N	N	Y	Y
8 **Brady**	Y	N	N	N	Y	Y
9 Green, A.	Y	Y	N	Y	N	N
10 **McCaul**	Y	N	N	N	Y	Y
11 **Conaway**	Y	N	N	N	Y	Y
12 **Granger**	Y	N	N	N	Y	Y
13 **Thornberry**	Y	N	N	N	Y	Y
14 **Paul**	N	Y	Y	Y	N	N
15 Hinojosa	Y	Y	Y	Y	N	N
16 Reyes	Y	Y	Y	Y	N	N
17 **Flores**	N	N	N	N	Y	Y
18 Jackson Lee	Y	Y	Y	Y	N	N
19 **Neugebauer**	N	N	N	N	Y	Y
20 Gonzalez	Y	Y	Y	Y	N	N
21 **Smith**	Y	N	N	N	Y	Y
22 **Olson**	Y	N	N	N	Y	Y
23 **Canseco**	Y	N	N	N	Y	Y
24 **Marchant**	Y	N	N	N	Y	Y
25 Doggett	Y	N	Y	Y	N	N
26 **Burgess**	Y	N	N	N	Y	Y
27 **Farenthold**	Y	N	N	N	Y	Y
28 Cuellar	Y	Y	N	Y	Y	N
29 Green, G.	Y	Y	N	Y	N	N
30 Johnson, E.	Y	Y	Y	Y	N	N
31 **Carter**	Y	N	N	N	Y	Y
32 **Sessions**	N	Y	N	N	Y	Y
UTAH						
1 **Bishop**	Y	Y	N	N	Y	Y
2 Matheson	Y	N	N	Y	Y	N
3 **Chaffetz**	N	N	N	N	Y	Y
VERMONT						
AL Welch	Y	Y	Y	Y	N	N
VIRGINIA						
1 **Wittman**	Y	N	N	N	Y	Y
2 **Rigell**	Y	N	Y	Y	Y	Y
3 Scott	Y	N	Y	Y	N	N
4 **Forbes**	Y	N	N	N	Y	Y
5 **Hurt**	Y	N	N	N	Y	Y
6 **Goodlatte**	Y	N	N	N	Y	Y
7 **Cantor**	Y	N	N	N	Y	Y
8 Moran	Y	Y	Y	Y	N	N
9 **Griffith**	Y	N	N	N	Y	Y
10 **Wolf**	Y	N	N	N	Y	N
11 Connolly	Y	N	N	Y	N	N
WASHINGTON						
1 Vacant						
2 Larsen	Y	N	Y	Y	N	N
3 **Herrera Beutler**	Y	N	N	N	Y	N
4 **Hastings**	N	N	N	N	Y	Y
5 **McMorris Rodgers**	Y	N	N	N	Y	Y
6 Dicks	Y	N	N	Y	N	N
7 McDermott	Y	N	Y	Y	N	N
8 **Reichert**	Y	N	N	N	Y	Y
9 Smith	Y	N	Y	Y	N	N
WEST VIRGINIA						
1 **McKinley**	Y	N	N	N	Y	Y
2 **Capito**	Y	N	N	N	Y	Y
3 Rahall	Y	Y	Y	Y	N	N
WISCONSIN						
1 **Ryan**	Y	N	N	N	Y	Y
2 Baldwin	Y	Y	Y	Y	N	N
3 Kind	Y	N	Y	Y	N	N
4 Moore	Y	Y	Y	Y	N	N
5 **Sensenbrenner**	Y	N	N	N	Y	Y
6 **Petri**	Y	N	N	N	Y	Y
7 **Duffy**	Y	N	N	N	Y	Y
8 **Ribble**	Y	Y	N	N	Y	Y
WYOMING						
AL **Lummis**	N	N	N	N	Y	Y

IN THE HOUSE | By Vote Number

282. HR 4310. Fiscal 2013 Defense Authorization/Department **Spending Reductions.** Lee, D-Calif., amendment that would direct the president to make $8 billion in reductions to the amounts authorized by the bill. It would exempt military, reserve and National Guard personnel accounts and the Defense Health Program from the reductions. Rejected in Committee of the Whole 170-252: R 16-223; D 154-29. May 18, 2012.

283. HR 4310. Fiscal 2013 Defense Authorization/Ocean Affairs **Organizations.** Duncan, R-S.C., amendment that would bar any funds authorized by the bill from being made available for any institution or organization established by the U.N. Convention on the Law of the Sea. Adopted in Committee of the Whole 229-193: R 228-11; D 1-182. May 18, 2012.

284. HR 4310. Fiscal 2013 Defense Authorization/Combat **Brigades in Europe.** Coffman, R-Colo., amendment that would authorize the president to remove all brigade combat teams that are permanently stationed in Europe and replace them with a rotational force. Adopted in Committee of the Whole 226-196: R 63-176; D 163-20. May 18, 2012.

285. HR 4310. Fiscal 2013 Defense Authorization/Iran Special **Envoy.** Lee, D-Calif., amendment that would require the president, in consultation with the secretary of State, to appoint a special envoy to ease tensions and normalize relations between the United States and Iran. It also would recommend that it should be U.S. policy to prevent Iran from acquiring a nuclear weapon. Rejected in Committee of the Whole 77-344: R 2-236; D 75-108. May 18, 2012.

286. HR 4310. Fiscal 2013 Defense Authorization/Nuclear **Non-Proliferation Activities.** Franks, R-Ariz., amendment that would restrict the availability of funds for nuclear non-proliferation activities with the Russian Federation until 30 days after the Energy, State and Defense secretaries certify to Congress that Russia is no longer providing support to the Syrian government's suppression of the Syrian people or transferring equipment and technology to Syria, Iran, or North Korea that could be used to make weapons of mass destruction. Adopted in Committee of the Whole 241-181: R 229-10; D 12-171. May 18, 2012.

287. HR 4310. Fiscal 2013 Defense Authorization/Domestic **Uranium Enrichment.** Pearce, R-N.M., amendment that would strike provisions in the bill that would authorize $150 million for the development of domestic uranium enrichment. Rejected in Committee of the Whole 121-300: R 45-194; D 76-106. May 18, 2012.

	282	283	284	285	286	287
ALABAMA						
1 Bonner	N	Y	N	N	Y	N
2 Roby	N	Y	N	N	Y	N
3 Rogers	N	Y	N	N	Y	N
4 Aderholt	N	Y	N	N	Y	N
5 Brooks	N	Y	Y	N	Y	N
6 Bachus	N	Y	N	N	Y	N
7 Sewell	Y	N	Y	N	N	N
ALASKA						
AL Young	N	N	N	N	Y	N
ARIZONA						
1 Gosar	?	?	?	?	?	?
2 Franks	N	Y	N	N	Y	N
3 Quayle	N	Y	N	N	Y	N
4 Pastor	Y	N	Y	Y	N	N
5 Schweikert	N	Y	N	N	Y	N
6 Flake	N	Y	N	N	Y	Y
7 Grijalva	Y	N	Y	Y	N	Y
8 Vacant						
ARKANSAS						
1 Crawford	N	Y	N	N	Y	N
2 Griffin	N	Y	N	N	Y	N
3 Womack	N	Y	N	N	Y	N
4 Ross	N	N	N	N	Y	N
CALIFORNIA						
1 Thompson	Y	N	Y	Y	N	N
2 Herger	N	Y	N	N	Y	N
3 Lungren	N	Y	Y	N	N	N
4 McClintock	Y	Y	Y	N	Y	Y
5 Matsui	Y	N	Y	N	N	Y
6 Woolsey	Y	N	Y	N	N	Y
7 Miller, George	Y	N	Y	Y	N	N
8 Pelosi	Y	N	Y	N	N	Y
9 Lee	Y	N	Y	Y	N	N
10 Garamendi	Y	N	Y	Y	N	Y
11 McNerney	Y	N	N	N	N	Y
12 Speier	?	?	?	?	?	?
13 Stark	Y	N	Y	Y	N	Y
14 Eshoo	Y	N	Y	Y	N	N
15 Honda	Y	N	Y	Y	N	Y
16 Lofgren	Y	N	Y	Y	N	Y
17 Farr	Y	N	Y	Y	N	Y
18 Cardoza	?	?	?	?	?	?
19 Denham	N	Y	N	N	Y	N
20 Costa	N	N	N	N	N	N
21 Nunes	N	Y	Y	N	Y	N
22 McCarthy	N	Y	N	N	Y	N
23 Capps	Y	N	Y	Y	N	Y
24 Gallegly	N	Y	N	N	Y	N
25 McKeon	N	Y	N	N	Y	N
26 Dreier	N	Y	N	N	Y	N
27 Sherman	Y	N	Y	N	N	Y
28 Berman	N	N	Y	N	N	N
29 Schiff	Y	N	Y	N	N	N
30 Waxman	Y	N	Y	Y	N	Y
31 Becerra	Y	N	Y	Y	N	Y
32 Chu	Y	N	Y	Y	N	Y
33 Bass	Y	N	Y	Y	N	Y
34 Roybal-Allard	Y	N	Y	Y	N	Y
35 Waters	Y	N	Y	Y	N	Y
36 Hahn	Y	N	Y	Y	N	Y
37 Richardson	Y	N	Y	Y	N	N
38 Napolitano	Y	N	Y	Y	N	Y
39 Sánchez, Linda	Y	N	Y	Y	N	Y
40 Royce	Y	Y	Y	N	Y	N
41 Lewis	N	Y	N	N	Y	N
42 Miller, Gary	N	Y	N	N	Y	N
43 Baca	Y	N	Y	N	N	N
44 Calvert	N	Y	N	N	Y	N
45 Bono Mack	N	Y	N	N	Y	N
46 Rohrabacher	Y	Y	Y	N	Y	N
47 Sanchez, Loretta	?	?	?	?	?	?
48 Campbell	Y	Y	Y	N	N	Y
49 Issa	N	Y	N	N	Y	N
50 Bilbray	N	Y	Y	N	Y	N
51 Filner	+	–	+	+	–	+
52 Hunter	N	Y	N	N	Y	N
53 Davis	Y	N	N	N	N	Y
COLORADO						
1 DeGette	Y	N	Y	Y	N	N
2 Polis	Y	N	Y	Y	N	Y
3 Tipton	N	Y	N	N	Y	N
4 Gardner	N	Y	N	N	Y	N
5 Lamborn	N	Y	N	N	Y	N
6 Coffman	N	Y	Y	?	Y	Y
7 Perlmutter	Y	N	Y	N	N	Y
CONNECTICUT						
1 Larson	N	N	Y	N	N	N
2 Courtney	N	N	N	N	N	Y
3 DeLauro	Y	N	Y	N	N	N
4 Himes	Y	N	Y	N	N	Y
5 Murphy	Y	N	Y	N	N	N
DELAWARE						
AL Carney	Y	N	Y	N	N	N
FLORIDA						
1 Miller	N	Y	N	N	Y	N
2 Southerland	N	Y	Y	N	Y	N
3 Brown	Y	N	Y	N	N	N
4 Crenshaw	N	Y	N	N	Y	N
5 Nugent	N	Y	N	N	Y	N
6 Stearns	Y	Y	N	N	Y	N
7 Mica	N	Y	N	N	Y	N
8 Webster	N	Y	Y	N	Y	N
9 Bilirakis	N	Y	N	N	Y	Y
10 Young	N	Y	N	N	Y	N
11 Castor	Y	N	Y	N	N	N
12 Ross	N	Y	N	N	Y	N
13 Buchanan	N	Y	N	N	Y	N
14 Mack	N	Y	N	N	Y	N
15 Posey	N	Y	N	N	Y	Y
16 Rooney	N	Y	N	N	Y	N
17 Wilson	Y	N	Y	N	N	N
18 Ros-Lehtinen	N	Y	N	N	N	N
19 Deutch	Y	N	Y	N	N	N
20 Wasserman Schultz	Y	N	N	N	N	N
21 Diaz-Balart	N	Y	N	N	N	N
22 West	N	Y	N	N	Y	N
23 Hastings	Y	N	Y	N	N	N
24 Adams	N	Y	Y	N	Y	N
25 Rivera	N	Y	N	N	Y	N
GEORGIA						
1 Kingston	N	Y	Y	N	Y	Y
2 Bishop	Y	N	Y	Y	Y	N
3 Westmoreland	N	Y	N	N	Y	N
4 Johnson	Y	N	Y	Y	N	?
5 Lewis	Y	N	Y	N	N	N
6 Price	N	Y	Y	N	Y	N
7 Woodall	N	Y	N	N	Y	Y
8 Scott, A.	N	Y	N	N	Y	N
9 Graves	N	Y	N	N	Y	N
10 Broun	N	Y	N	N	Y	Y
11 Gingrey	N	Y	N	N	Y	Y
12 Barrow	N	N	N	N	Y	N
13 Scott, D.	Y	N	Y	N	N	N
HAWAII						
1 Hanabusa	N	N	Y	N	N	N
2 Hirono	Y	N	Y	N	N	N
IDAHO						
1 Labrador	Y	Y	Y	N	Y	Y
2 Simpson	N	Y	N	N	Y	N
ILLINOIS						
1 Rush	Y	N	Y	Y	N	N
2 Jackson	Y	N	Y	Y	N	Y
3 Lipinski	N	N	Y	N	N	N
4 Gutierrez	Y	N	Y	Y	N	N
5 Quigley	Y	N	Y	N	N	N
6 Roskam	N	Y	N	N	Y	N
7 Davis	Y	N	Y	Y	N	Y
8 Walsh	Y	Y	Y	N	Y	N
9 Schakowsky	Y	N	Y	N	N	Y
10 Dold	N	N	N	N	Y	N
11 Kinzinger	N	Y	N	N	Y	N
12 Costello	?	?	?	?	?	?
13 Biggert	N	Y	N	N	Y	N
14 Hultgren	N	Y	N	N	Y	Y
15 Johnson	N	Y	N	N	Y	N

	282	283	284	285	286	287
16 **Manzullo**	N	Y	N	N	Y	N
17 **Schilling**	N	Y	N	N	Y	N
18 **Schock**	N	N	N	N	Y	N
19 **Shimkus**	N	Y	N	N	Y	Y
INDIANA						
1 Visclosky	Y	N	Y	N	N	Y
2 Donnelly	N	N	Y	N	N	N
3 **Stutzman**	Y	Y	Y	N	Y	N
4 **Rokita**	N	Y	Y	N	Y	Y
5 **Burton**	N	Y	N	N	Y	N
6 **Pence**	N	Y	N	N	Y	N
7 Carson	Y	N	Y	N	N	N
8 **Bucshon**	N	Y	N	N	Y	N
9 **Young**	N	Y	N	N	Y	N
IOWA						
1 Braley	Y	N	Y	N	N	N
2 Loebsack	N	N	Y	N	N	N
3 Boswell	Y	N	N	N	N	N
4 **Latham**	N	Y	N	N	Y	N
5 **King**	N	Y	N	N	Y	Y
KANSAS						
1 **Huelskamp**	N	Y	Y	N	Y	Y
2 **Jenkins**	N	Y	Y	N	Y	N
3 **Yoder**	N	Y	Y	N	Y	N
4 **Pompeo**	N	Y	N	N	Y	N
KENTUCKY						
1 **Whitfield**	N	Y	N	N	Y	N
2 **Guthrie**	N	Y	Y	N	Y	N
3 Yarmuth	Y	N	Y	N	N	N
4 **Davis**	N	Y	N	N	Y	N
5 **Rogers**	N	Y	N	N	Y	N
6 Chandler	N	N	Y	N	Y	N
LOUISIANA						
1 **Scalise**	N	Y	N	N	Y	N
2 Richmond	Y	N	Y	Y	N	N
3 **Landry**	N	Y	Y	N	Y	N
4 **Fleming**	N	Y	N	N	Y	N
5 **Alexander**	N	Y	N	N	Y	N
6 **Cassidy**	N	Y	N	N	Y	Y
7 **Boustany**	N	Y	N	N	Y	N
MAINE						
1 Pingree	Y	N	Y	Y	N	Y
2 Michaud	Y	N	Y	N	N	Y
MARYLAND						
1 **Harris**	N	Y	Y	N	Y	N
2 Ruppersberger	N	N	Y	N	N	N
3 Sarbanes	Y	N	Y	N	N	Y
4 Edwards	Y	N	Y	Y	N	Y
5 Hoyer	Y	N	N	N	N	N
6 **Bartlett**	N	Y	Y	N	Y	N
7 Cummings	Y	N	Y	Y	N	Y
8 Van Hollen	Y	N	Y	N	N	N
MASSACHUSETTS						
1 Olver	Y	N	Y	Y	N	Y
2 Neal	Y	N	Y	N	N	Y
3 McGovern	Y	N	Y	Y	N	Y
4 Frank	Y	N	Y	N	N	Y
5 Tsongas	Y	N	Y	N	N	Y
6 Tierney	Y	N	Y	N	N	Y
7 Markey	Y	N	Y	N	N	Y
8 Capuano	Y	N	Y	Y	N	Y
9 Lynch	Y	N	Y	N	N	N
10 Keating	Y	N	Y	N	N	Y
MICHIGAN						
1 **Benishek**	N	Y	Y	N	Y	N
2 **Huizenga**	N	Y	Y	N	Y	Y
3 **Amash**	Y	Y	Y	N	Y	Y
4 **Camp**	N	Y	Y	N	Y	N
5 Kildee	Y	N	Y	N	N	N
6 **Upton**	N	Y	Y	N	Y	N
7 **Walberg**	N	Y	N	N	Y	Y
8 **Rogers**	N	Y	Y	N	Y	N
9 Peters	Y	N	Y	N	Y	N
10 **Miller**	N	Y	N	N	Y	N
11 **McCotter**	N	Y	N	N	Y	N
12 Levin	Y	N	N	N	N	Y
13 Clarke	Y	N	Y	N	N	N
14 Conyers	Y	N	Y	Y	N	Y
15 Dingell	Y	N	Y	N	N	N
MINNESOTA						
1 Walz	Y	N	Y	Y	N	N
2 **Kline**	N	Y	N	N	Y	N
3 **Paulsen**	N	Y	N	N	Y	Y
4 McCollum	Y	N	Y	Y	N	N
5 Ellison	Y	N	Y	Y	N	Y
6 **Bachmann**	N	Y	N	N	Y	N
7 Peterson	Y	N	N	N	Y	N
8 **Cravaack**	N	Y	Y	N	Y	N
MISSISSIPPI						
1 **Nunnelee**	N	Y	N	N	Y	N
2 Thompson	Y	N	Y	Y	N	N
3 **Harper**	N	N	N	N	Y	N
4 **Palazzo**	N	Y	N	N	Y	N
MISSOURI						
1 Clay	Y	N	N	Y	N	N
2 **Akin**	N	Y	N	N	Y	N
3 Carnahan	Y	N	Y	N	N	N
4 **Hartzler**	N	Y	N	N	Y	N
5 Cleaver	Y	N	Y	Y	N	N
6 **Graves**	N	Y	N	N	Y	Y
7 **Long**	N	Y	N	N	Y	N
8 **Emerson**	N	Y	N	N	Y	N
9 **Luetkemeyer**	N	Y	N	N	Y	N
MONTANA						
AL **Rehberg**	N	Y	N	N	Y	N
NEBRASKA						
1 **Fortenberry**	N	Y	N	N	Y	N
2 **Terry**	N	Y	N	N	Y	N
3 **Smith**	N	Y	N	N	Y	Y
NEVADA						
1 Berkley	N	N	N	N	N	Y
2 **Amodei**	?	?	?	?	?	?
3 **Heck**	N	Y	N	N	N	N
NEW HAMPSHIRE						
1 **Guinta**	N	Y	N	N	Y	N
2 **Bass**	N	Y	N	N	Y	N
NEW JERSEY						
1 Andrews	Y	N	Y	N	N	N
2 **LoBiondo**	N	Y	N	N	Y	N
3 **Runyan**	N	Y	N	N	Y	N
4 **Smith**	N	Y	Y	N	Y	N
5 **Garrett**	N	Y	Y	N	Y	N
6 Pallone	Y	N	Y	N	N	Y
7 **Lance**	N	Y	N	N	Y	Y
8 Pascrell	+	–	+	–	–	–
9 Rothman	Y	N	Y	N	N	N
10 Vacant						
11 **Frelinghuysen**	N	Y	N	N	N	N
12 Holt	Y	N	Y	Y	N	Y
13 Sires	Y	N	Y	N	N	N
NEW MEXICO						
1 Heinrich	N	N	Y	Y	N	Y
2 **Pearce**	N	Y	N	N	Y	Y
3 Luján	Y	N	Y	Y	N	Y
NEW YORK						
1 Bishop	Y	N	Y	N	N	N
2 Israel	Y	N	Y	N	N	Y
3 **King**	N	Y	N	N	Y	N
4 McCarthy	Y	N	Y	N	N	N
5 Ackerman	Y	N	Y	N	N	N
6 Meeks	Y	N	Y	N	N	N
7 Crowley	Y	N	Y	N	N	N
8 Nadler	Y	N	Y	N	N	Y
9 **Turner**	N	Y	N	N	Y	N
10 Towns	Y	N	N	Y	N	N
11 Clarke	Y	N	Y	Y	N	N
12 Velázquez	Y	N	Y	N	N	N
13 **Grimm**	N	Y	N	N	Y	N
14 Maloney	Y	N	Y	N	N	Y
15 Rangel	Y	N	Y	N	N	Y
16 Serrano	Y	N	Y	Y	N	Y
17 Engel	Y	N	N	N	N	N
18 Lowey	Y	N	Y	N	N	N
19 **Hayworth**	N	N	N	N	Y	N
20 **Gibson**	N	Y	N	N	Y	N
21 Tonko	Y	N	Y	Y	N	Y
22 Hinchey	Y	N	Y	Y	N	Y
23 Owens	N	N	Y	N	N	N
24 **Hanna**	N	Y	N	N	N	N
25 **Buerkle**	N	Y	N	N	Y	N
26 Hochul	N	N	Y	N	N	N
27 Higgins	Y	N	Y	N	N	Y
28 Slaughter	?	?	?	?	?	?
29 **Reed**	N	Y	N	N	Y	N
NORTH CAROLINA						
1 Butterfield	Y	N	Y	N	N	N
2 **Ellmers**	N	Y	N	N	Y	N
3 **Jones**	Y	Y	Y	Y	Y	Y
4 Price	Y	N	Y	Y	N	N
5 **Foxx**	N	Y	N	N	Y	N
6 **Coble**	N	Y	Y	N	Y	N
7 McIntyre	N	N	N	N	Y	N
8 Kissell	N	N	Y	N	N	N
9 **Myrick**	N	Y	N	N	Y	N
10 **McHenry**	N	Y	N	N	Y	N
11 Shuler	N	N	N	N	Y	N
12 Watt	Y	N	Y	Y	N	Y
13 Miller	Y	N	N	Y	N	N
NORTH DAKOTA						
AL **Berg**	N	Y	N	N	Y	N
OHIO						
1 **Chabot**	N	Y	Y	N	Y	N
2 **Schmidt**	N	Y	N	N	Y	N
3 **Turner**	N	Y	N	N	Y	N
4 **Jordan**	N	Y	Y	N	Y	N
5 **Latta**	N	Y	N	N	Y	N
6 **Johnson**	N	Y	N	N	Y	N
7 **Austria**	N	Y	N	N	Y	N
8 **Boehner**						
9 Kaptur	N	N	Y	Y	N	N
10 Kucinich	Y	N	Y	Y	N	Y
11 Fudge	Y	N	Y	Y	N	N
12 **Tiberi**	N	Y	Y	N	Y	N
13 Sutton	Y	N	Y	N	N	N
14 **LaTourette**	N	Y	N	N	Y	N
15 **Stivers**	N	N	Y	N	Y	N
16 **Renacci**	N	N	N	N	Y	N
17 Ryan	Y	N	Y	Y	N	N
18 **Gibbs**	N	Y	N	N	Y	N
OKLAHOMA						
1 **Sullivan**	N	Y	N	N	Y	N
2 Boren	N	N	N	N	Y	N
3 **Lucas**	N	Y	N	N	Y	N
4 **Cole**	N	Y	N	N	Y	N
5 **Lankford**	N	Y	N	N	Y	Y
OREGON						
1 Bonamici	Y	N	Y	N	N	Y
2 **Walden**	N	Y	Y	N	Y	N
3 Blumenauer	Y	N	Y	Y	N	Y
4 DeFazio	Y	N	Y	Y	N	Y
5 Schrader	Y	N	Y	N	N	N
PENNSYLVANIA						
1 Brady	Y	N	Y	N	N	N
2 Fattah	Y	N	Y	Y	N	N
3 **Kelly**	N	Y	N	N	Y	N
4 Altmire	N	N	N	N	N	N
5 **Thompson**	N	Y	Y	N	Y	Y
6 **Gerlach**	N	Y	N	N	Y	N
7 **Meehan**	N	Y	Y	N	Y	N
8 **Fitzpatrick**	N	Y	N	N	N	N
9 **Shuster**	N	Y	N	N	Y	N
10 **Marino**	N	Y	N	N	Y	N
11 **Barletta**	N	N	N	N	Y	N
12 Critz	N	N	Y	N	N	N
13 Schwartz	Y	N	Y	N	N	Y
14 Doyle	Y	N	Y	Y	N	N
15 **Dent**	N	Y	N	N	N	N
16 **Pitts**	N	Y	N	N	Y	N
17 Holden	Y	N	Y	N	N	N
18 **Murphy**	N	Y	N	N	Y	N
19 **Platts**	N	Y	N	N	Y	N
RHODE ISLAND						
1 Cicilline	Y	N	Y	N	N	Y
2 Langevin	Y	N	Y	N	N	N
SOUTH CAROLINA						
1 **Scott**	N	Y	N	N	Y	N
2 **Wilson**	N	Y	N	N	Y	N
3 **Duncan**	N	Y	Y	N	Y	N
4 **Gowdy**	N	Y	N	N	Y	N
5 **Mulvaney**	Y	Y	Y	N	Y	N
6 Clyburn	Y	N	Y	Y	N	N
SOUTH DAKOTA						
AL **Noem**	N	Y	N	N	Y	N
TENNESSEE						
1 **Roe**	N	Y	N	N	Y	N
2 **Duncan**	Y	Y	Y	Y	Y	N
3 **Fleischmann**	N	Y	N	N	Y	N
4 **DesJarlais**	N	Y	N	N	Y	N
5 Cooper	N	N	Y	N	N	N
6 **Black**	N	Y	N	N	Y	N
7 **Blackburn**	N	Y	N	N	Y	N
8 **Fincher**	N	Y	N	N	Y	N
9 Cohen	Y	N	Y	Y	N	N
TEXAS						
1 **Gohmert**	N	Y	Y	N	Y	Y
2 **Poe**	N	Y	Y	N	Y	N
3 **Johnson, S.**	N	Y	N	N	Y	N
4 **Hall**	N	Y	N	N	Y	N
5 **Hensarling**	N	Y	N	N	Y	N
6 **Barton**	N	Y	N	N	Y	Y
7 **Culberson**	N	Y	N	N	Y	N
8 **Brady**	N	Y	N	N	Y	N
9 Green, A.	Y	N	Y	N	N	N
10 **McCaul**	N	Y	N	N	Y	Y
11 **Conaway**	N	Y	N	N	Y	Y
12 **Granger**	N	N	N	N	Y	N
13 **Thornberry**	N	Y	N	N	Y	N
14 **Paul**	Y	Y	Y	N	N	Y
15 Hinojosa	Y	N	Y	N	N	N
16 Reyes	N	N	Y	N	N	N
17 **Flores**	N	Y	N	N	Y	N
18 Jackson Lee	Y	N	Y	N	N	N
19 **Neugebauer**	N	Y	N	N	Y	Y
20 Gonzalez	Y	N	Y	N	N	N
21 **Smith**	N	Y	N	N	Y	N
22 **Olson**	N	Y	N	N	Y	Y
23 **Canseco**	N	Y	N	N	Y	Y
24 **Marchant**	N	Y	N	N	Y	Y
25 Doggett	Y	N	Y	Y	N	Y
26 **Burgess**	N	Y	N	N	Y	Y
27 **Farenthold**	N	Y	N	N	Y	Y
28 Cuellar	N	N	Y	N	Y	N
29 Green, G.	Y	Y	Y	N	N	N
30 Johnson, E.	Y	N	Y	Y	N	N
31 **Carter**	N	Y	N	N	Y	Y
32 **Sessions**	N	Y	Y	N	Y	N
UTAH						
1 **Bishop**	N	Y	N	N	Y	Y
2 Matheson	N	N	Y	N	Y	Y
3 **Chaffetz**	N	Y	N	N	Y	Y
VERMONT						
AL Welch	Y	N	Y	Y	N	Y
VIRGINIA						
1 **Wittman**	N	Y	N	N	Y	N
2 **Rigell**	N	Y	Y	N	Y	N
3 Scott	N	N	Y	Y	N	N
4 **Forbes**	N	Y	N	N	Y	N
5 **Hurt**	N	Y	N	N	Y	N
6 **Goodlatte**	N	Y	Y	N	Y	N
7 **Cantor**	N	Y	N	N	Y	N
8 Moran	Y	N	Y	Y	N	N
9 **Griffith**	N	Y	Y	N	Y	N
10 **Wolf**	N	Y	N	N	Y	N
11 Connolly	N	N	Y	N	N	N
WASHINGTON						
1 Vacant						
2 Larsen	Y	N	N	N	N	Y
3 **Herrera Beutler**	N	Y	N	N	Y	N
4 **Hastings**	N	Y	N	N	Y	N
5 **McMorris Rodgers**	N	Y	N	N	Y	Y
6 Dicks	Y	N	Y	N	N	N
7 McDermott	Y	N	Y	Y	N	Y
8 **Reichert**	N	Y	N	N	Y	N
9 Smith	Y	N	Y	N	N	N
WEST VIRGINIA						
1 **McKinley**	N	Y	N	N	Y	N
2 **Capito**	N	Y	N	N	Y	N
3 Rahall	Y	N	Y	Y	N	Y
WISCONSIN						
1 **Ryan**	N	Y	Y	N	Y	N
2 Baldwin	Y	N	Y	Y	N	Y
3 Kind	Y	N	Y	N	N	N
4 Moore	Y	N	Y	Y	N	N
5 **Sensenbrenner**	N	Y	Y	N	N	N
6 **Petri**	N	Y	Y	N	Y	N
7 **Duffy**	N	Y	N	N	Y	N
8 **Ribble**	Y	Y	Y	N	Y	N
WYOMING						
AL **Lummis**	N	Y	Y	N	Y	Y

IN THE HOUSE | By Vote Number

288. **HR 4310. Fiscal 2013 Defense Authorization/Nuclear Delivery Systems.** Rehberg, R-Mont., amendment that would bar the use of funds authorized by the bill for the reduction, conversion or decommission of any strategic delivery system pursuant to the New START agreement unless the president certifies that reductions in the Russia's arsenal are needed for compliance with New START limits and that Russia is not developing or deploying nuclear delivery systems not covered by New START limits. Adopted in Committee of the Whole 238-162: R 225-3; D 13-159. A "nay" was a vote in support of the president's position. May 18, 2012.

289. **HR 4310. Fiscal 2013 Defense Authorization/U.S. and Israeli Leak Investigation.** Price, R-Ga., amendment that would require the Justice Department to investigate possible violations of federal law regarding leaks of sensitive information involving U.S. and Israeli military, intelligence and operational capabilities. Adopted in Committee of the Whole 379-38: R 234-2; D 145-36. May 18, 2012.

290. **HR 4310. Fiscal 2013 Defense Authorization/Recommit.** Garamendi, D-Calif., motion to recommit the bill to the House Armed Services Committee and report it back immediately with an amendment that would bar naval and other U.S. flagged vessels from being overhauled, repaired or maintained in shipyards outside the U.S. or Guam. Voyage repairs in foreign shipyards would not be prohibited. The bill would allow the Defense secretary to waive the prohibition in cases of national security or urgent repair. Motion rejected 182-236: R 2-236; D 180-0. May 18, 2012.

291. **HR 4310. Fiscal 2013 Defense Authorization/Passage.** Passage of the bill that would authorize $642.7 billion in discretionary funding for defense programs in fiscal 2013, including $554 billion in base funding for the Defense Department and for Energy Department national security programs and $88.5 billion in contingency funds for the war in Afghanistan and the general war on terrorism. It includes $236.1 billion for operations and maintenance accounts, $109.4 billion for procurement and $149.7 billion for military personnel. The bill would authorize $10.8 billion for military construction and family housing, $32.8 billion for the Defense Health Program and a 1.7 percent pay raise for military personnel. As amended, the bill would prohibit the transfer of detainees from Guantánamo Bay, Cuba, to the United States and other countries and limit the president's ability to decommission nuclear weapons, as required by the New START agreement with Russia. Passed 299-120: R 222-16; D 77-104. A "nay" was a vote in support of the president's position. May 18, 2012.

292. **HR 4348. Surface Transportation Extension/Motion to Instruct.** Barrow, D-Ga., motion to instruct House conferees to insist on House-passed provisions that would transfer the authority to approve the Keystone XL pipeline project from the State Department to the Federal Energy Regulatory Commission (FERC), and provide that if FERC does not approve the pipeline within 30 days it be deemed approved. Motion agreed to 261-152: R 235-1; D 26-151. May 18, 2012.

293. **HR 4348. Surface Transportation Extension/Motion to Instruct.** Rahall, D-W.Va., motion to instruct House conferees to agree to a Senate-passed provision relating to Buy American requirements, which generally mandate that the materials for federally funded highway, transit and rail projects be produced in the United States. Motion agreed to 245-169: R 69-166; D 176-3. May 18, 2012.

	288	289	290	291	292	293
ALABAMA						
1 Bonner	Y	Y	N	Y	Y	N
2 Roby	Y	Y	N	Y	Y	N
3 Rogers	Y	Y	N	Y	Y	N
4 Aderholt	Y	Y	N	Y	Y	Y
5 Brooks	Y	Y	N	Y	Y	Y
6 Bachus	Y	Y	N	Y	Y	Y
7 Sewell	N	Y	Y	Y	Y	N
ALASKA						
AL Young	Y	N	N	Y	Y	N
ARIZONA						
1 Gosar	?	?	?	?	?	?
2 Franks	Y	Y	N	Y	Y	N
3 Quayle	Y	Y	N	Y	Y	N
4 Pastor	N	Y	Y	Y	N	Y
5 Schweikert	Y	Y	N	N	Y	N
6 Flake	Y	Y	N	Y	Y	N
7 Grijalva	N	N	Y	N	N	Y
8 Vacant						
ARKANSAS						
1 Crawford	Y	Y	N	Y	Y	N
2 Griffin	Y	Y	N	Y	Y	N
3 Womack	Y	Y	N	Y	Y	N
4 Ross	Y	Y	Y	Y	Y	Y
CALIFORNIA						
1 Thompson	N	Y	Y	N	N	Y
2 Herger	Y	Y	N	Y	Y	N
3 Lungren	Y	Y	N	Y	Y	N
4 McClintock	Y	Y	N	N	Y	N
5 Matsui	N	Y	Y	N	N	Y
6 Woolsey	–	Y	Y	N	N	Y
7 Miller, George	N	Y	Y	N	N	Y
8 Pelosi	N	Y	Y	N	N	Y
9 Lee	N	N	Y	N	N	Y
10 Garamendi	N	Y	Y	N	N	Y
11 McNerney	N	Y	Y	Y	N	Y
12 Speier	?	?	?	?	?	?
13 Stark	N	N	Y	N	N	Y
14 Eshoo	N	Y	Y	N	N	Y
15 Honda	N	N	Y	N	N	Y
16 Lofgren	N	Y	Y	N	N	Y
17 Farr	?	Y	+	N	N	Y
18 Cardoza	?	?	?	?	?	?
19 Denham	Y	Y	N	Y	Y	N
20 Costa	?	Y	Y	Y	?	Y
21 Nunes	Y	Y	N	Y	Y	N
22 McCarthy	Y	Y	N	Y	Y	N
23 Capps	N	Y	Y	N	N	Y
24 Gallegly	Y	Y	N	Y	Y	N
25 McKeon	Y	Y	N	Y	Y	N
26 Dreier	Y	Y	N	Y	Y	N
27 Sherman	N	N	Y	N	N	Y
28 Berman	N	N	Y	N	N	Y
29 Schiff	N	Y	Y	N	N	Y
30 Waxman	?	Y	Y	N	N	Y
31 Becerra	N	N	Y	N	N	Y
32 Chu	N	Y	Y	N	N	Y
33 Bass	N	Y	Y	N	N	Y
34 Roybal-Allard	N	Y	Y	N	N	Y
35 Waters	N	N	Y	N	N	Y
36 Hahn	N	Y	Y	N	N	Y
37 Richardson	N	Y	Y	N	N	Y
38 Napolitano	N	Y	Y	N	N	Y
39 Sánchez, Linda	N	Y	Y	N	N	Y
40 Royce	Y	Y	N	N	Y	N
41 Lewis	?	?	N	Y	Y	N
42 Miller, Gary	Y	Y	N	Y	Y	N
43 Baca	N	Y	Y	Y	Y	Y
44 Calvert	Y	Y	N	N	Y	N
45 Bono Mack	Y	Y	N	Y	Y	N
46 Rohrabacher	Y	Y	N	Y	Y	N
47 Sanchez, Loretta	?	?	?	?	?	?
48 Campbell	Y	Y	N	N	Y	N
49 Issa	Y	Y	N	Y	Y	N
50 Bilbray	Y	Y	N	Y	Y	Y
51 Filner	–	+	+	–	–	+
52 Hunter	Y	Y	N	Y	Y	N
53 Davis	N	Y	Y	Y	Y	Y

	288	289	290	291	292	293
COLORADO						
1 DeGette	N	Y	Y	N	N	Y
2 Polis	N	Y	Y	N	N	N
3 Tipton	Y	Y	N	Y	Y	N
4 Gardner	Y	Y	N	Y	Y	N
5 Lamborn	Y	Y	N	Y	Y	N
6 Coffman	Y	Y	N	Y	Y	N
7 Perlmutter	N	Y	Y	Y	Y	Y
CONNECTICUT						
1 Larson	N	Y	Y	Y	N	Y
2 Courtney	N	Y	Y	N	N	Y
3 DeLauro	N	Y	Y	N	N	Y
4 Himes	N	Y	Y	N	N	Y
5 Murphy	N	Y	Y	N	N	Y
DELAWARE						
AL Carney	N	Y	Y	Y	N	Y
FLORIDA						
1 Miller	Y	Y	N	Y	Y	N
2 Southerland	Y	Y	N	Y	Y	N
3 Brown	N	N	Y	N	N	Y
4 Crenshaw	Y	Y	N	Y	Y	N
5 Nugent	Y	Y	N	N	Y	N
6 Stearns	Y	Y	N	Y	Y	N
7 Mica	Y	Y	N	Y	Y	N
8 Webster	Y	Y	N	Y	Y	N
9 Bilirakis	?	Y	N	Y	Y	N
10 Young	Y	Y	N	Y	Y	N
11 Castor	N	Y	Y	N	N	Y
12 Ross	Y	Y	N	Y	Y	N
13 Buchanan	Y	Y	N	Y	Y	N
14 Mack	Y	Y	N	Y	Y	N
15 Posey	Y	Y	N	Y	Y	N
16 Rooney	Y	Y	N	Y	Y	N
17 Wilson	N	Y	Y	N	N	Y
18 Ros-Lehtinen	Y	Y	N	Y	Y	Y
19 Deutch	N	Y	Y	N	N	Y
20 Wasserman Schultz	N	N	Y	N	N	Y
21 Diaz-Balart	Y	Y	N	Y	Y	Y
22 West	Y	Y	N	Y	Y	N
23 Hastings	N	Y	Y	N	N	Y
24 Adams	Y	Y	N	Y	Y	Y
25 Rivera	Y	Y	N	Y	Y	Y
GEORGIA						
1 Kingston	Y	Y	N	Y	Y	N
2 Bishop	N	Y	Y	Y	Y	Y
3 Westmoreland	Y	Y	N	Y	Y	N
4 Johnson	?	N	Y	N	N	Y
5 Lewis	N	N	Y	N	N	Y
6 Price	Y	Y	N	Y	Y	N
7 Woodall	Y	Y	N	Y	Y	N
8 Scott, A.	Y	Y	N	Y	Y	N
9 Graves	Y	Y	N	Y	Y	N
10 Broun	Y	Y	N	Y	Y	N
11 Gingrey	+	Y	N	Y	Y	N
12 Barrow	Y	Y	Y	Y	Y	Y
13 Scott, D.	N	Y	Y	Y	Y	N
HAWAII						
1 Hanabusa	N	Y	Y	Y	N	Y
2 Hirono	N	Y	Y	Y	N	Y
IDAHO						
1 Labrador	?	Y	N	N	Y	N
2 Simpson	Y	Y	N	Y	Y	Y
ILLINOIS						
1 Rush	N	Y	Y	N	N	Y
2 Jackson	N	Y	Y	N	N	Y
3 Lipinski	N	Y	Y	Y	Y	Y
4 Gutierrez	Y	Y	N	N	N	Y
5 Quigley	N	Y	Y	N	N	?
6 Roskam	Y	Y	N	Y	Y	N
7 Davis	N	Y	Y	N	N	Y
8 Walsh	Y	N	Y	Y	Y	N
9 Schakowsky	N	Y	Y	N	N	Y
10 Dold	Y	Y	N	Y	Y	Y
11 Kinzinger	Y	Y	N	Y	Y	N
12 Costello	?	?	?	?	?	?
13 Biggert	Y	Y	N	Y	Y	N
14 Hultgren	Y	Y	N	Y	Y	N
15 Johnson	Y	Y	N	N	Y	?

KEY   **Republicans**   Democrats

Y Voted for (yea)	**X** Paired against	**C** Voted "present" to avoid possible conflict of interest
# Paired for	**–** Announced against	
+ Announced for	**P** Voted "present"	**?** Did not vote or otherwise make a position known
N Voted against (nay)		

	288	289	290	291	292	293
16 **Manzullo**	Y	Y	N	Y	Y	N
17 **Schilling**	+	Y	N	Y	Y	N
18 **Schock**	?	Y	N	Y	Y	N
19 **Shimkus**	Y	Y	N	Y	Y	N
INDIANA						
1 Visclosky	N	Y	Y	Y	N	Y
2 Donnelly	Y	Y	Y	Y	Y	Y
3 **Stutzman**	Y	Y	N	Y	Y	N
4 **Rokita**	?	Y	N	Y	Y	N
5 **Burton**	Y	Y	N	Y	Y	N
6 **Pence**	Y	Y	N	Y	Y	N
7 Carson	N	N	Y	N	N	Y
8 **Bucshon**	Y	Y	N	Y	Y	N
9 **Young**	Y	Y	N	Y	Y	N
IOWA						
1 Braley	?	?	?	?	?	?
2 Loebsack	N	Y	Y	Y	Y	Y
3 Boswell	N	Y	Y	Y	Y	Y
4 **Latham**	Y	Y	N	Y	Y	Y
5 **King**	Y	Y	N	Y	Y	N
KANSAS						
1 **Huelskamp**	Y	Y	N	N	Y	N
2 **Jenkins**	Y	Y	N	Y	Y	N
3 **Yoder**	Y	Y	N	Y	Y	Y
4 **Pompeo**	Y	Y	N	Y	Y	N
KENTUCKY						
1 **Whitfield**	Y	Y	N	Y	Y	Y
2 **Guthrie**	Y	Y	N	Y	Y	Y
3 Yarmuth	N	Y	Y	N	N	Y
4 **Davis**	Y	Y	N	Y	Y	N
5 **Rogers**	Y	Y	N	Y	Y	Y
6 Chandler	Y	Y	Y	Y	Y	Y
LOUISIANA						
1 **Scalise**	Y	Y	N	Y	Y	N
2 Richmond	N	Y	Y	N	N	Y
3 **Landry**	Y	Y	N	Y	?	?
4 **Fleming**	Y	Y	N	Y	Y	N
5 **Alexander**	Y	Y	N	Y	Y	N
6 **Cassidy**	Y	Y	N	Y	Y	N
7 **Boustany**	Y	Y	N	Y	Y	N
MAINE						
1 Pingree	N	Y	Y	N	N	Y
2 Michaud	N	Y	Y	N	N	Y
MARYLAND						
1 **Harris**	Y	Y	N	Y	Y	N
2 Ruppersberger	N	Y	Y	Y	Y	Y
3 Sarbanes	N	Y	Y	N	N	Y
4 Edwards	N	N	Y	N	N	Y
5 Hoyer	N	Y	Y	Y	N	Y
6 **Bartlett**	Y	Y	N	Y	Y	N
7 Cummings	N	Y	Y	Y	?	?
8 Van Hollen	N	Y	Y	N	N	Y
MASSACHUSETTS						
1 Olver	?	N	Y	N	N	Y
2 Neal	N	Y	Y	N	N	Y
3 McGovern	N	Y	Y	N	N	Y
4 Frank	?	?	Y	N	N	Y
5 Tsongas	N	Y	Y	Y	?	?
6 Tierney	N	Y	Y	N	N	Y
7 Markey	N	Y	Y	N	N	Y
8 Capuano	N	Y	Y	N	?	Y
9 Lynch	N	Y	Y	N	Y	Y
10 Keating	N	Y	Y	N	N	Y
MICHIGAN						
1 **Benishek**	Y	Y	N	Y	Y	N
2 **Huizenga**	Y	Y	N	Y	Y	N
3 **Amash**	N	Y	N	N	Y	N
4 **Camp**	Y	Y	N	Y	Y	N
5 Kildee	N	Y	Y	Y	N	Y
6 **Upton**	Y	Y	N	Y	Y	Y
7 **Walberg**	Y	Y	N	Y	Y	N
8 **Rogers**	Y	Y	N	Y	Y	N
9 Peters	N	Y	Y	N	N	Y
10 **Miller**	Y	Y	N	Y	Y	Y
11 **McCotter**	Y	Y	N	Y	Y	N
12 Levin	N	Y	Y	Y	N	Y
13 Clarke	N	Y	Y	N	N	Y
14 Conyers	N	Y	Y	N	N	Y
15 Dingell	N	Y	Y	Y	Y	Y
MINNESOTA						
1 Walz	N	Y	Y	Y	Y	Y
2 **Kline**	Y	Y	N	Y	Y	N
3 **Paulsen**	Y	Y	N	Y	Y	N
4 McCollum	N	N	Y	N	N	Y

	288	289	290	291	292	293
5 Ellison	N	N	Y	N	N	Y
6 **Bachmann**	Y	Y	N	Y	Y	N
7 Peterson	Y	N	Y	Y	Y	Y
8 **Cravaack**	Y	Y	N	Y	Y	Y
MISSISSIPPI						
1 **Nunnelee**	?	Y	N	Y	Y	N
2 Thompson	N	N	Y	N	N	Y
3 **Harper**	Y	Y	N	Y	Y	N
4 **Palazzo**	Y	Y	N	Y	Y	N
MISSOURI						
1 Clay	N	Y	Y	N	N	Y
2 **Akin**	Y	Y	N	Y	Y	N
3 Carnahan	N	Y	Y	Y	N	Y
4 **Hartzler**	Y	Y	N	Y	Y	N
5 Cleaver	N	Y	Y	N	N	Y
6 **Graves**	Y	Y	N	Y	Y	N
7 **Long**	Y	Y	N	Y	Y	N
8 **Emerson**	Y	Y	N	Y	Y	Y
9 **Luetkemeyer**	Y	Y	N	Y	Y	N
MONTANA						
AL **Rehberg**	Y	Y	N	Y	Y	N
NEBRASKA						
1 **Fortenberry**	Y	Y	N	Y	Y	Y
2 **Terry**	Y	Y	N	Y	Y	N
3 **Smith**	Y	Y	N	Y	Y	N
NEVADA						
1 Berkley	N	Y	Y	Y	N	Y
2 **Amodei**	?	?	?	?	?	?
3 **Heck**	Y	Y	N	Y	Y	N
NEW HAMPSHIRE						
1 **Guinta**	Y	Y	N	Y	Y	N
2 **Bass**	Y	Y	N	Y	N	N
NEW JERSEY						
1 Andrews	N	N	Y	Y	N	Y
2 **LoBiondo**	Y	Y	N	Y	Y	Y
3 **Runyan**	Y	Y	N	Y	Y	Y
4 **Smith**	Y	Y	N	Y	Y	Y
5 **Garrett**	Y	Y	N	Y	Y	N
6 Pallone	N	Y	Y	N	N	Y
7 **Lance**	Y	Y	N	Y	Y	N
8 Pascrell	–	+	+	–	+	+
9 Rothman	N	Y	Y	N	N	Y
10 Vacant						
11 **Frelinghuysen**	Y	Y	N	Y	Y	N
12 Holt	N	N	Y	N	N	Y
13 Sires	N	Y	Y	Y	Y	Y
NEW MEXICO						
1 Heinrich	N	Y	Y	Y	N	Y
2 **Pearce**	Y	Y	N	Y	Y	N
3 Luján	N	Y	Y	N	N	Y
NEW YORK						
1 Bishop	N	Y	Y	Y	N	Y
2 Israel	N	Y	Y	Y	N	Y
3 **King**	Y	Y	N	Y	Y	N
4 McCarthy	N	Y	Y	Y	N	Y
5 Ackerman	N	N	Y	Y	N	Y
6 Meeks	N	Y	Y	Y	N	Y
7 Crowley	N	Y	Y	N	N	Y
8 Nadler	N	Y	Y	N	N	Y
9 **Turner**	Y	Y	N	Y	Y	N
10 Towns	N	N	Y	Y	N	Y
11 Clarke	N	N	Y	N	N	Y
12 Velázquez	N	Y	Y	N	N	Y
13 **Grimm**	?	Y	N	Y	Y	N
14 Maloney	N	Y	Y	N	N	Y
15 Rangel	N	N	Y	N	N	Y
16 Serrano	N	Y	Y	N	N	Y
17 Engel	N	Y	Y	Y	N	Y
18 Lowey	N	Y	Y	N	N	Y
19 **Hayworth**	Y	Y	N	Y	Y	N
20 **Gibson**	N	Y	N	N	Y	Y
21 Tonko	–	Y	Y	N	N	Y
22 Hinchey	N	Y	Y	N	N	Y
23 Owens	N	Y	Y	Y	Y	N
24 **Hanna**	Y	Y	N	Y	Y	N
25 **Buerkle**	Y	Y	N	Y	Y	N
26 Hochul	N	Y	Y	Y	Y	Y
27 Higgins	?	Y	Y	Y	N	Y
28 Slaughter	?	?	?	?	?	?
29 **Reed**	Y	Y	N	Y	Y	N
NORTH CAROLINA						
1 Butterfield	N	N	Y	N	N	Y
2 **Ellmers**	Y	Y	N	Y	Y	N
3 **Jones**	Y	Y	Y	N	Y	Y
4 Price	N	Y	Y	N	N	Y

	288	289	290	291	292	293
5 **Foxx**	Y	Y	N	Y	Y	N
6 **Coble**	Y	Y	N	Y	Y	Y
7 McIntyre	Y	Y	Y	Y	Y	Y
8 Kissell	Y	Y	Y	Y	Y	Y
9 **Myrick**	Y	Y	N	Y	Y	Y
10 **McHenry**	Y	Y	N	Y	Y	Y
11 Shuler	Y	Y	Y	Y	Y	Y
12 Watt	N	N	Y	N	N	Y
13 Miller	N	Y	Y	N	N	Y
NORTH DAKOTA						
AL **Berg**	Y	Y	N	Y	Y	N
OHIO						
1 **Chabot**	Y	Y	N	Y	Y	Y
2 **Schmidt**	Y	Y	N	Y	Y	Y
3 **Turner**	Y	Y	N	Y	Y	N
4 **Jordan**	Y	Y	N	Y	Y	N
5 **Latta**	Y	Y	N	Y	Y	Y
6 **Johnson**	Y	Y	N	Y	Y	Y
7 **Austria**	Y	Y	N	Y	Y	N
8 **Boehner**						
9 Kaptur	N	Y	Y	Y	?	Y
10 Kucinich	N	N	Y	N	N	Y
11 Fudge	N	N	Y	N	N	Y
12 **Tiberi**	Y	Y	N	Y	Y	N
13 Sutton	N	Y	Y	Y	N	Y
14 **LaTourette**	?	Y	N	Y	Y	Y
15 **Stivers**	Y	Y	N	Y	Y	N
16 **Renacci**	Y	Y	N	Y	Y	Y
17 Ryan	N	Y	+	–	N	Y
18 **Gibbs**	Y	Y	N	Y	Y	N
OKLAHOMA						
1 **Sullivan**	?	?	?	?	?	?
2 Boren	N	Y	Y	Y	Y	Y
3 **Lucas**	Y	Y	N	Y	Y	N
4 **Cole**	Y	Y	N	Y	Y	N
5 **Lankford**	Y	Y	N	Y	Y	N
OREGON						
1 Bonamici	N	N	Y	N	N	Y
2 **Walden**	Y	Y	N	Y	Y	N
3 Blumenauer	N	N	Y	N	N	Y
4 DeFazio	N	N	Y	N	N	Y
5 Schrader	N	Y	Y	N	N	Y
PENNSYLVANIA						
1 Brady	N	Y	Y	Y	N	Y
2 Fattah	N	Y	Y	N	N	Y
3 **Kelly**	Y	Y	N	Y	Y	N
4 Altmire	Y	Y	Y	Y	Y	Y
5 **Thompson**	Y	Y	N	Y	Y	N
6 **Gerlach**	Y	Y	N	Y	Y	Y
7 **Meehan**	Y	Y	N	Y	Y	Y
8 **Fitzpatrick**	Y	Y	N	Y	Y	Y
9 **Shuster**	Y	Y	N	Y	Y	Y
10 **Marino**	Y	Y	N	Y	Y	N
11 **Barletta**	Y	Y	N	Y	Y	N
12 Critz	N	Y	Y	Y	N	Y
13 Schwartz	N	Y	Y	N	N	Y
14 Doyle	N	Y	Y	N	N	Y
15 **Dent**	Y	Y	N	Y	Y	Y
16 **Pitts**	Y	Y	N	Y	Y	Y
17 Holden	N	Y	Y	Y	N	Y
18 **Murphy**	Y	Y	N	Y	Y	Y
19 **Platts**	Y	Y	N	Y	Y	Y
RHODE ISLAND						
1 Cicilline	N	Y	Y	N	N	Y
2 Langevin	N	Y	Y	Y	N	Y
SOUTH CAROLINA						
1 **Scott**	Y	Y	N	Y	Y	N
2 **Wilson**	Y	Y	N	Y	Y	N
3 **Duncan**	Y	Y	N	Y	Y	N
4 **Gowdy**	Y	Y	N	Y	Y	N
5 **Mulvaney**	Y	Y	N	Y	Y	N
6 Clyburn	N	N	Y	N	N	Y
SOUTH DAKOTA						
AL **Noem**	Y	Y	N	Y	Y	N
TENNESSEE						
1 **Roe**	Y	Y	N	N	Y	N
2 **Duncan**	Y	Y	N	N	Y	Y
3 **Fleischmann**	Y	Y	N	Y	Y	N
4 **DesJarlais**	Y	Y	N	Y	Y	Y
5 Cooper	Y	N	Y	Y	Y	Y
6 **Black**	Y	Y	N	Y	Y	N
7 **Blackburn**	Y	Y	N	Y	Y	N
8 **Fincher**	Y	Y	N	Y	Y	N
9 Cohen	N	Y	Y	N	N	Y

	288	289	290	291	292	293
TEXAS						
1 **Gohmert**	Y	Y	N	Y	Y	?
2 **Poe**	Y	Y	N	Y	Y	Y
3 **Johnson, S.**	Y	Y	N	Y	Y	N
4 **Hall**	Y	Y	N	Y	Y	Y
5 **Hensarling**	Y	Y	N	Y	Y	N
6 **Barton**	Y	Y	N	Y	Y	Y
7 **Culberson**	Y	Y	N	Y	Y	Y
8 **Brady**	Y	Y	N	Y	Y	N
9 Green, A.	N	Y	Y	Y	N	Y
10 **McCaul**	Y	Y	N	Y	Y	N
11 **Conaway**	Y	Y	N	Y	Y	N
12 **Granger**	Y	Y	N	Y	Y	N
13 **Thornberry**	Y	Y	N	Y	Y	N
14 **Paul**	N	N	Y	N	Y	N
15 Hinojosa	N	Y	Y	Y	N	Y
16 Reyes	N	Y	Y	Y	N	Y
17 **Flores**	Y	Y	N	Y	Y	N
18 Jackson Lee	N	Y	Y	Y	N	Y
19 **Neugebauer**	Y	Y	N	Y	Y	N
20 Gonzalez	N	Y	Y	Y	N	Y
21 **Smith**	Y	Y	N	Y	Y	N
22 **Olson**	Y	Y	N	Y	Y	N
23 **Canseco**	Y	Y	N	Y	Y	N
24 **Marchant**	Y	Y	N	Y	Y	N
25 Doggett	N	Y	Y	Y	N	Y
26 **Burgess**	Y	Y	N	N	Y	Y
27 **Farenthold**	Y	Y	N	Y	Y	N
28 Cuellar	Y	Y	Y	Y	Y	Y
29 Green, G.	N	Y	Y	Y	N	Y
30 Johnson, E.	N	Y	Y	Y	N	Y
31 **Carter**	Y	Y	N	Y	Y	N
32 **Sessions**	Y	Y	N	Y	Y	N
UTAH						
1 **Bishop**	Y	Y	N	Y	?	Y
2 Matheson	Y	Y	Y	Y	Y	N
3 **Chaffetz**	Y	Y	N	Y	Y	N
VERMONT						
AL Welch	?	Y	Y	N	N	Y
VIRGINIA						
1 **Wittman**	Y	Y	N	Y	Y	Y
2 **Rigell**	Y	Y	N	Y	Y	N
3 Scott	N	Y	Y	N	N	Y
4 **Forbes**	Y	Y	N	Y	Y	N
5 **Hurt**	Y	Y	N	Y	Y	Y
6 **Goodlatte**	Y	Y	N	Y	Y	Y
7 **Cantor**	Y	Y	N	Y	Y	N
8 Moran	N	Y	Y	N	N	Y
9 **Griffith**	Y	Y	N	N	Y	Y
10 **Wolf**	Y	?	N	Y	Y	Y
11 Connolly	N	Y	Y	Y	N	Y
WASHINGTON						
1 Vacant						
2 Larsen	N	Y	Y	N	N	Y
3 **Herrera Beutler**	Y	Y	N	Y	Y	Y
4 **Hastings**	Y	Y	N	Y	Y	N
5 **McMorris Rodgers**	Y	Y	N	Y	Y	Y
6 Dicks	N	Y	Y	Y	N	Y
7 McDermott	N	Y	Y	N	N	Y
8 **Reichert**	Y	Y	N	Y	Y	N
9 Smith	N	Y	Y	Y	N	Y
WEST VIRGINIA						
1 **McKinley**	Y	Y	N	Y	Y	Y
2 **Capito**	Y	Y	N	Y	Y	Y
3 Rahall	N	N	Y	N	N	Y
WISCONSIN						
1 **Ryan**	Y	Y	N	Y	Y	N
2 Baldwin	N	Y	Y	N	N	Y
3 Kind	N	Y	Y	N	N	Y
4 Moore	N	Y	Y	N	N	Y
5 **Sensenbrenner**	Y	Y	N	Y	Y	N
6 **Petri**	Y	Y	N	Y	Y	Y
7 **Duffy**	Y	Y	N	Y	Y	Y
8 **Ribble**	Y	Y	N	Y	Y	N
WYOMING						
AL **Lummis**	Y	Y	N	Y	Y	N

IN THE HOUSE | By Vote Number

294. **HR 5651. FDA User Fees/Passage.** Upton, R-Mich., motion to suspend the rules and pass the bill that would reauthorize Food and Drug Administration (FDA) user fee programs through fiscal 2017 to pay for pre-market approval of prescription drugs and medical devices. The bill also would authorize new user fee programs for generic drugs and biosimilar biological products. It would require drugmakers to notify the FDA of expected shortages of certain critical drugs and the FDA to inform health care providers of the potential drug shortage. Motion agreed to 387-5: R 219-4; D 168-1. A two-thirds majority of those present and voting (262 in this case) is required for passage under suspension of the rules. May 30, 2012.

295. **HR 4201. Servicemember Custody Protections/Passage.** Stearns, R-Fla., motion to suspend the rules and pass the bill that would require courts to reinstate custody arrangements approved before a servicemember was deployed unless a court determines the arrangement is no longer in the child's best interest. Motion agreed to 390-2: R 220-2; D 170-0. A two-thirds majority of those present and voting (262 in this case) is required for passage under suspension of the rules. May 30, 2012.

296. **HR 915. Border Enforcement Security/Passage.** King, R-N.Y., motion to suspend the rules and pass the bill that would establish a Border Enforcement Security Task Force program within the Homeland Security Department's Immigration and Customs Enforcement bureau. It would coordinate federal, state and local efforts by border and law enforcement officials to combat crime along and across U.S. borders. Motion agreed to 391-2: R 220-2; D 171-0. A two-thirds majority of those present and voting (262 in this case) is required for passage under suspension of the rules. May 30, 2012.

297. **HR 5743, HR 5325, HR 5855, HR 5854. Intelligence Authorization and Fiscal 2013 Spending Bills/Previous Question.** Nugent, R-Fla., motion to order the previous question (thus ending debate and possibility of amendment) on the rule (H Res 667) that would provide for House floor consideration of the fiscal 2013 intelligence authorization bill (HR 5743) as well as the fiscal 2013 Energy-Water (HR 5325), Homeland Security (HR 5855) and Military Construction-VA (HR 5854) spending bills. Motion agreed to 233-180: R 231-0; D 2-180. May 31, 2012.

298. **HR 5743, HR 5325, HR 5855, HR 5854. Intelligence Authorization and Fiscal 2013 Spending Bills/Rule.** Adoption of the rule (H Res 667) that would provide for House floor consideration of the fiscal 2013 intelligence authorization bill (HR 5743) as well as the fiscal 2013 Energy-Water (HR 5325), Homeland Security (HR 5855) and Military Construction-VA (HR 5854) spending bills. Adopted 246-166: R 232-0; D 14-166. May 31, 2012.

299. **HR 3541. Sex-Selection Abortion Ban/Passage.** Franks, R-Ariz., motion to suspend the rules and pass the bill that would impose fines or a maximum five-year sentence, or both, on individuals who perform an abortion knowing the abortion is sought based on the sex of the fetus. The same penalties would apply to individuals who transport a woman into the United States or across state lines for the purpose of terminating a pregnancy based on the sex of the fetus or to anyone who solicits or accepts payment for performing an abortion based solely on the sex of the fetus. Motion rejected 246-168: R 226-7; D 20-161. A two-thirds majority of those present and voting (276 in this case) is required for passage under suspension of the rules. May 31, 2012.

	294	295	296	297	298	299
ALABAMA						
1 Bonner	Y	Y	Y	Y	Y	Y
2 Roby	?	?	?	?	?	?
3 Rogers	Y	Y	Y	Y	Y	Y
4 Aderholt	Y	Y	Y	?	Y	Y
5 Brooks	Y	Y	Y	Y	Y	
6 Bachus	Y	Y	Y	Y	Y	Y
7 Sewell	Y	Y	Y	N	N	N
ALASKA						
AL Young	Y	Y	Y	Y	Y	Y
ARIZONA						
1 Gosar	Y	Y	Y	Y	Y	Y
2 Franks	Y	Y	Y	Y	Y	Y
3 Quayle	Y	Y	Y	Y	Y	Y
4 Pastor	Y	Y	Y	N	N	N
5 Schweikert	Y	Y	Y	Y	Y	Y
6 Flake	Y	Y	Y	Y	Y	Y
7 Grijalva	Y	Y	Y	N	N	N
8 Vacant						
ARKANSAS						
1 Crawford	Y	Y	Y	Y	Y	Y
2 Griffin	Y	Y	Y	Y	Y	Y
3 Womack	Y	Y	Y	Y	Y	Y
4 Ross	Y	Y	Y	N	Y	Y
CALIFORNIA						
1 Thompson	Y	Y	Y	N	N	N
2 Herger	Y	Y	Y	Y	Y	Y
3 Lungren	Y	Y	Y	Y	Y	Y
4 McClintock	N	Y	Y	Y	Y	Y
5 Matsui	Y	Y	Y	N	N	N
6 Woolsey	Y	Y	Y	N	N	N
7 Miller, George	Y	Y	Y	N	N	N
8 Pelosi	Y	Y	N	?	?	N
9 Lee	Y	Y	Y	N	N	N
10 Garamendi	Y	Y	Y	N	N	Y
11 McNerney	Y	Y	Y	N	N	N
12 Speier	Y	Y	Y	N	N	N
13 Stark	Y	Y	Y	N	N	N
14 Eshoo	Y	Y	Y	N	N	N
15 Honda	Y	Y	Y	N	N	N
16 Lofgren	Y	Y	Y	N	N	N
17 Farr	Y	Y	Y	N	N	N
18 Cardoza	Y	Y	Y	N	N	N
19 Denham	Y	Y	Y	Y	Y	Y
20 Costa	?	?	?	N	N	N
21 Nunes	Y	Y	Y	Y	Y	Y
22 McCarthy	?	?	?	?	?	?
23 Capps	Y	Y	Y	N	N	N
24 Gallegly	Y	Y	Y	Y	Y	Y
25 McKeon	Y	Y	Y	Y	Y	Y
26 Dreier	Y	Y	Y	Y	Y	Y
27 Sherman	Y	Y	Y	N	N	N
28 Berman	Y	Y	Y	N	N	N
29 Schiff	Y	Y	Y	N	N	N
30 Waxman	Y	Y	Y	N	N	N
31 Becerra	Y	Y	Y	N	N	N
32 Chu	Y	Y	Y	N	N	N
33 Bass	Y	Y	Y	N	N	N
34 Roybal-Allard	Y	Y	Y	N	N	N
35 Waters	Y	Y	Y	N	N	N
36 Hahn	?	?	?	N	N	N
37 Richardson	Y	Y	Y	N	N	N
38 Napolitano	Y	Y	Y	N	N	?
39 Sánchez, Linda	Y	?	Y	N	N	N
40 Royce	Y	Y	Y	Y	Y	Y
41 Lewis	?	?	?	?	?	?
42 Miller, Gary	Y	Y	Y	Y	Y	Y
43 Baca	Y	Y	Y	N	N	N
44 Calvert	Y	Y	Y	Y	Y	Y
45 Bono Mack	Y	Y	Y	Y	Y	Y
46 Rohrabacher	?	?	?	Y	Y	Y
47 Sanchez, Loretta	Y	Y	Y	N	N	N
48 Campbell	Y	Y	Y	Y	Y	Y
49 Issa	Y	Y	Y	Y	Y	Y
50 Bilbray	Y	Y	Y	Y	Y	Y
51 Filner	+	+	+	N	N	N
52 Hunter	Y	Y	Y	Y	Y	Y
53 Davis	Y	Y	Y	N	N	N

	294	295	296	297	298	299
COLORADO						
1 DeGette	Y	Y	Y	N	N	N
2 Polis	Y	Y	Y	N	N	N
3 Tipton	Y	Y	Y	Y	Y	Y
4 Gardner	Y	Y	Y	Y	Y	Y
5 Lamborn	Y	Y	Y	Y	Y	Y
6 Coffman	Y	Y	Y	Y	Y	Y
7 Perlmutter	Y	Y	Y	N	N	N
CONNECTICUT						
1 Larson	Y	Y	Y	N	N	N
2 Courtney	Y	Y	Y	N	N	N
3 DeLauro	Y	Y	Y	N	N	N
4 Himes	Y	Y	Y	N	N	N
5 Murphy	Y	Y	Y	N	Y	N
DELAWARE						
AL Carney	Y	Y	Y	N	Y	N
FLORIDA						
1 Miller	Y	Y	Y	Y	Y	Y
2 Southerland	Y	Y	Y	Y	Y	Y
3 Brown	Y	Y	Y	N	N	N
4 Crenshaw	Y	Y	Y	Y	Y	Y
5 Nugent	Y	Y	Y	Y	Y	Y
6 Stearns	Y	Y	Y	Y	Y	Y
7 Mica	Y	Y	Y	Y	Y	Y
8 Webster	Y	Y	Y	Y	Y	Y
9 Bilirakis	Y	Y	Y	Y	Y	Y
10 Young	?	?	?	?	?	?
11 Castor	Y	Y	Y	N	N	N
12 Ross	Y	Y	Y	Y	Y	Y
13 Buchanan	Y	Y	Y	Y	Y	Y
14 Mack	?	?	?	?	?	?
15 Posey	Y	Y	Y	Y	Y	Y
16 Rooney	Y	Y	Y	Y	Y	Y
17 Wilson	Y	Y	Y	N	N	N
18 Ros-Lehtinen	Y	Y	Y	Y	Y	Y
19 Deutch	Y	Y	Y	N	N	N
20 Wasserman Schultz	Y	Y	Y	N	N	N
21 Diaz-Balart	Y	Y	Y	Y	Y	Y
22 West	Y	Y	Y	Y	Y	Y
23 Hastings	Y	Y	Y	N	N	N
24 Adams	Y	Y	Y	Y	Y	Y
25 Rivera	Y	Y	Y	Y	Y	Y
GEORGIA						
1 Kingston	Y	Y	Y	Y	Y	Y
2 Bishop	Y	Y	Y	N	N	N
3 Westmoreland	Y	Y	Y	Y	Y	Y
4 Johnson	Y	Y	N	N	?	N
5 Lewis	Y	Y	Y	?	?	N
6 Price	Y	Y	Y	Y	Y	Y
7 Woodall	Y	Y	Y	Y	Y	Y
8 Scott, A.	Y	Y	Y	Y	Y	Y
9 Graves	Y	Y	Y	Y	Y	Y
10 Broun	Y	Y	Y	Y	Y	Y
11 Gingrey	Y	Y	Y	Y	Y	Y
12 Barrow	Y	Y	Y	N	N	Y
13 Scott, D.	Y	Y	Y	N	N	N
HAWAII						
1 Hanabusa	Y	Y	Y	N	N	N
2 Hirono	+	+	+	N	N	N
IDAHO						
1 Labrador	N	Y	Y	Y	Y	Y
2 Simpson	Y	Y	Y	Y	Y	Y
ILLINOIS						
1 Rush	?	?	?	N	N	N
2 Jackson	Y	Y	Y	N	N	N
3 Lipinski	Y	Y	Y	N	N	Y
4 Gutierrez	?	?	?	N	N	N
5 Quigley	Y	Y	Y	N	N	N
6 Roskam	Y	Y	Y	Y	Y	Y
7 Davis	Y	Y	Y	N	N	N
8 Walsh	Y	Y	Y	Y	Y	Y
9 Schakowsky	Y	Y	Y	N	N	N
10 Dold	Y	Y	Y	Y	Y	N
11 Kinzinger	Y	Y	Y	Y	Y	Y
12 Costello	Y	Y	Y	N	N	Y
13 Biggert	Y	Y	Y	Y	Y	Y
14 Hultgren	Y	Y	Y	Y	Y	Y
15 Johnson	Y	Y	Y	Y	Y	Y

KEY   **Republicans**   Democrats

Y Voted for (yea)	**X** Paired against	**C** Voted "present" to avoid possible conflict of interest
# Paired for	**–** Announced against	
+ Announced for	**P** Voted "present"	**?** Did not vote or otherwise make a position known
N Voted against (nay)		

	294	295	296	297	298	299
16 **Manzullo**	Y	Y	Y	Y	Y	Y
17 **Schilling**	Y	Y	Y	Y	Y	Y
18 **Schock**	Y	Y	Y	Y	Y	Y
19 **Shimkus**	Y	Y	Y	Y	Y	Y
INDIANA						
1 Visclosky	Y	Y	Y	N	N	N
2 Donnelly	Y	Y	Y	N	Y	Y
3 **Stutzman**	Y	Y	Y	Y	Y	Y
4 **Rokita**	Y	Y	Y	Y	Y	Y
5 **Burton**	?	?	?	?	?	?
6 **Pence**	Y	Y	Y	Y	Y	Y
7 Carson	Y	Y	Y	N	N	N
8 **Bucshon**	Y	Y	Y	Y	Y	Y
9 **Young**	Y	Y	Y	Y	Y	Y
IOWA						
1 Braley	Y	Y	Y	N	N	N
2 Loebsack	Y	Y	Y	N	N	N
3 Boswell	Y	Y	Y	N	N	N
4 **Latham**	Y	Y	Y	Y	Y	Y
5 **King**	Y	Y	Y	Y	Y	Y
KANSAS						
1 **Huelskamp**	Y	Y	Y	Y	Y	Y
2 **Jenkins**	Y	Y	Y	Y	Y	Y
3 **Yoder**	Y	Y	Y	Y	Y	Y
4 **Pompeo**	Y	Y	Y	Y	Y	Y
KENTUCKY						
1 **Whitfield**	Y	Y	Y	Y	Y	Y
2 **Guthrie**	Y	Y	Y	Y	Y	Y
3 Yarmuth	Y	Y	Y	N	N	N
4 **Davis**	Y	Y	Y	?	?	Y
5 **Rogers**	Y	Y	Y	Y	Y	Y
6 Chandler	Y	Y	Y	N	Y	?
LOUISIANA						
1 **Scalise**	Y	Y	Y	Y	Y	Y
2 Richmond	Y	Y	Y	N	N	N
3 **Landry**	?	?	?	Y	Y	Y
4 **Fleming**	Y	Y	Y	Y	Y	Y
5 **Alexander**	Y	Y	Y	Y	Y	Y
6 **Cassidy**	Y	Y	Y	Y	Y	Y
7 **Boustany**	Y	Y	Y	Y	Y	Y
MAINE						
1 Pingree	Y	Y	Y	N	N	N
2 Michaud	Y	Y	Y	N	N	N
MARYLAND						
1 **Harris**	Y	Y	Y	Y	Y	Y
2 Ruppersberger	Y	Y	Y	N	N	N
3 Sarbanes	Y	Y	Y	N	N	N
4 Edwards	Y	Y	Y	N	N	N
5 Hoyer	Y	Y	Y	N	N	N
6 **Bartlett**	Y	Y	Y	Y	Y	Y
7 Cummings	Y	Y	Y	N	N	N
8 Van Hollen	Y	Y	Y	N	N	N
MASSACHUSETTS						
1 Olver	Y	Y	Y	N	N	N
2 Neal	Y	Y	Y	N	N	N
3 McGovern	Y	Y	Y	N	N	N
4 Frank	?	Y	Y	N	N	N
5 Tsongas	Y	Y	Y	N	N	N
6 Tierney	Y	Y	Y	N	N	N
7 Markey	Y	Y	Y	N	N	N
8 Capuano	Y	Y	Y	N	N	N
9 Lynch	Y	Y	Y	N	N	Y
10 Keating	Y	Y	Y	N	N	N
MICHIGAN						
1 **Benishek**	Y	Y	?	Y	Y	Y
2 **Huizenga**	Y	Y	Y	Y	Y	Y
3 **Amash**	N	N	N	Y	Y	N
4 **Camp**	Y	Y	Y	Y	Y	Y
5 Kildee	Y	Y	Y	N	N	N
6 **Upton**	Y	Y	Y	Y	Y	Y
7 **Walberg**	Y	Y	Y	Y	Y	Y
8 **Rogers**	Y	Y	Y	Y	Y	Y
9 Peters	Y	Y	Y	N	N	N
10 **Miller**	Y	Y	Y	Y	Y	Y
11 **McCotter**	Y	Y	Y	Y	Y	Y
12 Levin	Y	Y	Y	N	N	N
13 Clarke	Y	Y	Y	N	N	N
14 Conyers	Y	Y	Y	N	N	N
15 Dingell	Y	Y	Y	N	N	N
MINNESOTA						
1 Walz	Y	Y	Y	N	N	N
2 **Kline**	Y	Y	Y	Y	Y	Y
3 **Paulsen**	Y	Y	Y	Y	Y	Y
4 McCollum	Y	Y	Y	N	N	N

	294	295	296	297	298	299
5 Ellison	Y	Y	Y	?	?	?
6 **Bachmann**	+	+	+	Y	Y	Y
7 Peterson	Y	Y	Y	N	N	Y
8 **Cravaack**	Y	Y	Y	Y	Y	Y
MISSISSIPPI						
1 **Nunnelee**	Y	Y	Y	Y	Y	Y
2 Thompson	Y	Y	Y	N	N	N
3 **Harper**	Y	Y	Y	Y	Y	Y
4 **Palazzo**	+	+	?	Y	Y	Y
MISSOURI						
1 Clay	Y	Y	Y	N	N	N
2 **Akin**	Y	Y	Y	Y	Y	Y
3 Carnahan	Y	Y	Y	N	N	N
4 **Hartzler**	Y	Y	Y	Y	Y	Y
5 Cleaver	Y	Y	Y	N	N	N
6 **Graves**	Y	Y	Y	Y	Y	Y
7 **Long**	Y	Y	Y	Y	Y	Y
8 **Emerson**	Y	Y	Y	Y	Y	Y
9 **Luetkemeyer**	Y	Y	Y	Y	Y	Y
MONTANA						
AL **Rehberg**	Y	Y	Y	Y	Y	Y
NEBRASKA						
1 **Fortenberry**	?	?	?	?	?	?
2 **Terry**	Y	Y	Y	Y	Y	Y
3 **Smith**	Y	Y	Y	Y	Y	Y
NEVADA						
1 Berkley	Y	Y	Y	N	N	N
2 **Amodei**	Y	Y	Y	Y	Y	Y
3 **Heck**	Y	Y	Y	Y	Y	Y
NEW HAMPSHIRE						
1 **Guinta**	?	?	?	?	?	?
2 **Bass**	Y	Y	Y	Y	Y	N
NEW JERSEY						
1 Andrews	Y	Y	Y	N	N	N
2 **LoBiondo**	Y	Y	Y	Y	Y	Y
3 **Runyan**	Y	Y	Y	Y	Y	Y
4 **Smith**	Y	?	Y	Y	Y	Y
5 **Garrett**	Y	Y	Y	Y	Y	Y
6 Pallone	Y	Y	Y	N	N	N
7 **Lance**	Y	Y	Y	Y	Y	Y
8 Pascrell	+	+	+	–	–	–
9 Rothman	?	?	?	N	N	N
10 Vacant						
11 **Frelinghuysen**	Y	Y	Y	Y	Y	Y
12 Holt	Y	Y	Y	N	N	N
13 Sires	?	?	?	N	N	N
NEW MEXICO						
1 Heinrich	?	?	?	?	?	?
2 **Pearce**	Y	Y	Y	Y	Y	Y
3 Luján	?	Y	Y	N	N	N
NEW YORK						
1 Bishop	Y	Y	Y	N	N	N
2 Israel	Y	Y	Y	N	N	N
3 **King**	Y	Y	Y	Y	Y	Y
4 McCarthy	Y	Y	Y	N	N	N
5 Ackerman	Y	Y	Y	N	N	N
6 Meeks	?	–	?	N	N	N
7 Crowley	Y	Y	Y	N	N	N
8 Nadler	Y	Y	Y	N	N	N
9 **Turner**	?	+	+	Y	Y	Y
10 Towns	?	?	?	N	N	N
11 Clarke	Y	Y	Y	N	N	N
12 Velázquez	?	?	?	?	?	?
13 **Grimm**	Y	Y	Y	Y	Y	Y
14 Maloney	+	+	+	N	N	N
15 Rangel	Y	Y	Y	?	?	?
16 Serrano	Y	Y	Y	N	N	N
17 Engel	Y	Y	Y	N	N	N
18 Lowey	Y	Y	Y	N	N	N
19 **Hayworth**	Y	Y	Y	Y	Y	N
20 **Gibson**	Y	Y	Y	Y	Y	Y
21 Tonko	Y	Y	Y	N	N	N
22 Hinchey	N	Y	Y	N	N	N
23 Owens	Y	Y	Y	N	Y	N
24 **Hanna**	Y	Y	Y	Y	Y	N
25 **Buerkle**	Y	Y	Y	Y	Y	Y
26 Hochul	Y	Y	Y	N	N	N
27 Higgins	Y	Y	Y	N	N	N
28 Slaughter	+	+	+	?	?	?
29 **Reed**	Y	Y	Y	Y	Y	Y
NORTH CAROLINA						
1 Butterfield	Y	Y	Y	N	N	N
2 **Ellmers**	Y	Y	Y	Y	Y	Y
3 **Jones**	Y	Y	Y	Y	Y	Y
4 Price	Y	Y	Y	N	N	N

	294	295	296	297	298	299
5 **Foxx**	Y	Y	Y	Y	Y	Y
6 **Coble**	Y	Y	Y	Y	Y	Y
7 McIntyre	Y	Y	Y	N	N	Y
8 Kissell	Y	Y	Y	N	Y	Y
9 **Myrick**	Y	Y	Y	Y	Y	Y
10 **McHenry**	Y	Y	Y	Y	Y	Y
11 Shuler	Y	Y	Y	Y	Y	Y
12 Watt	Y	Y	Y	N	N	N
13 Miller	Y	Y	Y	N	N	N
NORTH DAKOTA						
AL **Berg**	Y	Y	Y	Y	Y	Y
OHIO						
1 **Chabot**	Y	Y	Y	Y	Y	Y
2 **Schmidt**	Y	Y	Y	Y	Y	Y
3 **Turner**	Y	Y	Y	Y	Y	Y
4 **Jordan**	+	+	+	Y	Y	Y
5 **Latta**	Y	Y	Y	Y	Y	Y
6 **Johnson**	Y	Y	Y	Y	Y	Y
7 **Austria**	Y	Y	Y	Y	Y	Y
8 **Boehner**						
9 Kaptur	Y	Y	Y	N	N	N
10 Kucinich	Y	Y	Y	N	N	N
11 Fudge	Y	Y	Y	N	N	N
12 **Tiberi**	Y	Y	Y	Y	Y	Y
13 Sutton	Y	Y	Y	N	N	N
14 **LaTourette**	Y	Y	Y	Y	Y	Y
15 **Stivers**	Y	Y	Y	Y	Y	Y
16 **Renacci**	Y	Y	Y	Y	Y	Y
17 Ryan	Y	Y	Y	N	N	N
18 **Gibbs**	Y	Y	Y	Y	Y	Y
OKLAHOMA						
1 **Sullivan**	Y	Y	Y	Y	Y	Y
2 Boren	Y	Y	Y	N	Y	Y
3 **Lucas**	Y	Y	Y	Y	Y	Y
4 **Cole**	Y	Y	Y	Y	Y	Y
5 **Lankford**	Y	Y	Y	Y	Y	Y
OREGON						
1 Bonamici	Y	Y	Y	N	N	N
2 **Walden**	Y	Y	Y	Y	Y	Y
3 Blumenauer	Y	Y	Y	N	N	N
4 DeFazio	Y	Y	Y	N	N	N
5 Schrader	Y	Y	Y	N	N	N
PENNSYLVANIA						
1 Brady	Y	Y	Y	N	N	N
2 Fattah	Y	Y	Y	N	N	N
3 **Kelly**	Y	Y	Y	Y	Y	Y
4 Altmire	Y	Y	Y	N	N	Y
5 **Thompson**	Y	Y	Y	Y	Y	Y
6 **Gerlach**	Y	Y	Y	Y	Y	Y
7 **Meehan**	Y	Y	Y	Y	Y	Y
8 **Fitzpatrick**	Y	Y	Y	Y	Y	Y
9 **Shuster**	Y	Y	Y	Y	Y	Y
10 **Marino**	Y	Y	Y	Y	Y	Y
11 **Barletta**	Y	Y	Y	Y	Y	Y
12 Critz	Y	Y	Y	N	N	Y
13 Schwartz	Y	Y	Y	N	N	N
14 Doyle	?	?	?	?	?	?
15 **Dent**	Y	Y	Y	Y	Y	Y
16 **Pitts**	Y	Y	Y	Y	Y	Y
17 Holden	Y	Y	Y	N	N	Y
18 **Murphy**	Y	Y	Y	Y	Y	Y
19 **Platts**	Y	Y	Y	Y	Y	Y
RHODE ISLAND						
1 Cicilline	Y	Y	Y	N	N	N
2 Langevin	+	+	Y	N	N	N
SOUTH CAROLINA						
1 **Scott**	Y	Y	Y	Y	Y	Y
2 **Wilson**	Y	Y	Y	Y	Y	Y
3 **Duncan**	Y	Y	Y	Y	Y	Y
4 **Gowdy**	Y	Y	Y	Y	Y	Y
5 **Mulvaney**	Y	Y	Y	Y	Y	Y
6 Clyburn	Y	Y	Y	N	N	N
SOUTH DAKOTA						
AL **Noem**	Y	Y	Y	Y	Y	Y
TENNESSEE						
1 **Roe**	Y	Y	Y	Y	Y	Y
2 **Duncan**	Y	Y	Y	Y	Y	Y
3 **Fleischmann**	Y	Y	Y	Y	Y	Y
4 **DesJarlais**	Y	Y	Y	Y	Y	Y
5 Cooper	Y	Y	Y	N	N	Y
6 **Black**	Y	Y	Y	Y	Y	Y
7 **Blackburn**	Y	Y	Y	Y	Y	Y
8 **Fincher**	Y	Y	Y	Y	Y	Y
9 Cohen	Y	Y	Y	N	N	N

	294	295	296	297	298	299
TEXAS						
1 **Gohmert**	Y	Y	Y	Y	Y	Y
2 **Poe**	Y	Y	Y	Y	Y	Y
3 **Johnson, S.**	?	?	?	Y	Y	Y
4 **Hall**	Y	Y	Y	Y	Y	Y
5 **Hensarling**	Y	Y	Y	Y	Y	Y
6 **Barton**	Y	Y	Y	Y	Y	Y
7 **Culberson**	Y	Y	Y	Y	Y	Y
8 **Brady**	?	?	?	Y	Y	Y
9 Green, A.	Y	Y	Y	N	N	N
10 **McCaul**	Y	Y	Y	Y	Y	Y
11 **Conaway**	Y	Y	Y	Y	Y	Y
12 **Granger**	Y	Y	Y	Y	Y	Y
13 **Thornberry**	Y	Y	Y	Y	Y	Y
14 **Paul**	N	N	N	Y	Y	N
15 Hinojosa	?	?	?	N	N	N
16 Reyes	Y	Y	Y	N	N	Y
17 **Flores**	Y	Y	Y	Y	Y	Y
18 Jackson Lee	Y	Y	Y	N	N	N
19 **Neugebauer**	?	?	?	Y	Y	Y
20 Gonzalez	Y	Y	Y	N	N	N
21 **Smith**	Y	Y	Y	Y	Y	Y
22 **Olson**	Y	Y	Y	Y	Y	Y
23 **Canseco**	Y	Y	Y	Y	Y	Y
24 **Marchant**	?	?	?	Y	Y	Y
25 Doggett	Y	Y	Y	N	N	N
26 **Burgess**	Y	Y	Y	Y	Y	Y
27 **Farenthold**	Y	Y	Y	Y	Y	Y
28 Cuellar	Y	Y	Y	N	Y	Y
29 Green, G.	Y	Y	Y	N	N	N
30 Johnson, E.	Y	Y	Y	N	N	N
31 **Carter**	Y	Y	Y	Y	Y	Y
32 **Sessions**	Y	Y	Y	Y	Y	Y
UTAH						
1 **Bishop**	Y	Y	Y	Y	Y	Y
2 Matheson	Y	Y	Y	Y	Y	Y
3 **Chaffetz**	Y	Y	Y	Y	Y	Y
VERMONT						
AL Welch	Y	Y	Y	N	N	N
VIRGINIA						
1 **Wittman**	Y	Y	Y	Y	Y	Y
2 **Rigell**	Y	Y	Y	Y	Y	Y
3 Scott	Y	Y	Y	N	N	N
4 **Forbes**	Y	Y	Y	Y	Y	Y
5 **Hurt**	Y	Y	Y	Y	Y	Y
6 **Goodlatte**	Y	Y	Y	Y	Y	Y
7 **Cantor**	Y	Y	Y	Y	Y	Y
8 Moran	Y	Y	Y	N	Y	N
9 **Griffith**	Y	Y	Y	Y	Y	Y
10 **Wolf**	Y	Y	Y	Y	Y	Y
11 Connolly	Y	Y	Y	N	N	N
WASHINGTON						
1 Vacant						
2 Larsen	Y	Y	Y	N	N	N
3 **Herrera Beutler**	Y	Y	Y	Y	Y	Y
4 **Hastings**	Y	Y	Y	Y	Y	Y
5 **McMorris Rodgers**	Y	Y	Y	Y	Y	Y
6 Dicks	Y	Y	Y	N	N	N
7 McDermott	Y	Y	Y	N	N	N
8 **Reichert**	Y	Y	Y	Y	Y	Y
9 Smith	+	+	+	N	N	N
WEST VIRGINIA						
1 **McKinley**	Y	Y	Y	Y	Y	Y
2 **Capito**	Y	Y	Y	Y	Y	Y
3 Rahall	Y	Y	Y	N	N	Y
WISCONSIN						
1 **Ryan**	Y	Y	Y	Y	Y	Y
2 Baldwin	Y	Y	Y	N	N	N
3 Kind	Y	Y	Y	N	N	N
4 Moore	Y	Y	?	N	N	N
5 **Sensenbrenner**	Y	Y	Y	Y	Y	Y
6 **Petri**	Y	Y	Y	Y	Y	Y
7 **Duffy**	Y	Y	Y	Y	Y	Y
8 **Ribble**	Y	Y	Y	Y	Y	Y
WYOMING						
AL **Lummis**	Y	Y	Y	Y	Y	Y

IN THE HOUSE | By Vote Number

300. HR 5743. Fiscal 2013 Intelligence Authorization/Recommit.
Critz, D-Pa., motion to recommit the bill to the House Select Intelligence Committee and report it back immediately with an amendment that would require the heads of the intelligence community to prevent intelligence and information about U.S. military capability from being stolen by or improperly transferred to a foreign state or state sponsor of terror. It also would require intelligence community leaders to protect U.S. capabilities and sensitive economic, financial and consumer information from cyberattacks and prohibit the outsourcing of intelligence contracts to foreign-owned companies unless the director of national intelligence determines that it would be in the interests of national security. Motion rejected 180-235: R 1-231; D 179-4. May 31, 2012.

301. HR 5743. Fiscal 2013 Intelligence Authorization/Passage.
Passage of the bill that would authorize classified amounts in fiscal 2013 for 16 intelligence agencies, including the Office of the Director of National Intelligence, the CIA and the National Security Agency and for intelligence activities of the Defense Department, the FBI, the Homeland Security Department and other agencies. It would authorize covert action programs, research and development and projects to improve information dissemination. The bill would direct the president to develop a strategy and timeline for carrying out current requirements regarding reciprocity of security clearances among intelligence, executive and defense agencies. Passed 386-28: R 224-7; D 162-21. May 31, 2012.

302. HR 5854. Fiscal 2013 Military Construction-VA Appropriations/Project Labor Agreements. Grimm, R-N.Y., amendment that would strike language from the bill that would prohibit federal government construction contracts funded by the bill from requiring or prohibiting project labor agreements. Adopted in Committee of the Whole 218-198: R 34-197; D 184-1. May 31, 2012.

303. HR 5854. Fiscal 2013 Military Construction-VA Appropriations/Wage Requirements. Franks, R-Ariz., amendment that would bar the use of funds in the bill to enforce the Davis Bacon Act prevailing wage requirements. Rejected in Committee of the Whole 180-237: R 180-52; D 0-185. May 31, 2012.

304. HR 5854. Fiscal 2013 Military Construction-VA Appropriations/Recommit. Barrow, D-Ga., motion to recommit the bill to the House Appropriations Committee and report it back immediately with an amendment that would reduce by $56.7 million the amount provided in the bill for the Defense Base Closure Account and increase by $28.3 million the amount provided for medical and prosthetic research and development. Motion rejected 188-230: R 3-230; D 185-0. May 31, 2012.

305. HR 5854. Fiscal 2013 Military Construction-VA Appropriations/Passage. Passage of the bill that would provide $146.4 billion in fiscal 2013 for the Department of Veterans Affairs (VA), military construction and military housing. It would provide $71.7 billion in discretionary funds, including $55.7 billion for veterans' health programs. The bill would provide $74.6 billion in mandatory spending for veterans' service-connected compensation, benefits and pensions. The total funding in the bill also includes $10.6 billion for military construction, including $1.7 billion for military family housing, and $476 million for base realignment and closure. The bill would provide $54.5 billion in advance appropriations for certain VA medical care accounts for fiscal 2014. Passed 407-12: R 226-8; D 181-4. A "nay" was a vote in support of the president's position. May 31, 2012.

	300	301	302	303	304	305
ALABAMA						
1 Bonner	N	Y	N	Y	N	Y
2 Roby	?	?	N	Y	N	Y
3 Rogers	N	Y	N	Y	N	Y
4 Aderholt	N	Y	N	Y	?	Y
5 Brooks	N	Y	N	Y	N	Y
6 Bachus	N	Y	N	Y	N	Y
7 Sewell	Y	Y	Y	N	Y	Y
ALASKA						
AL Young	N	N	Y	N	N	Y
ARIZONA						
1 Gosar	N	Y	N	Y	N	Y
2 Franks	N	Y	N	Y	N	Y
3 Quayle	N	Y	N	Y	N	Y
4 Pastor	Y	Y	Y	N	Y	Y
5 Schweikert	N	Y	N	Y	N	Y
6 Flake	N	Y	N	Y	N	N
7 Grijalva	Y	Y	Y	N	Y	Y
8 Vacant						
ARKANSAS						
1 Crawford	N	Y	N	Y	N	Y
2 Griffin	N	Y	N	Y	N	Y
3 Womack	N	Y	N	Y	N	Y
4 Ross	Y	Y	Y	N	Y	Y
CALIFORNIA						
1 Thompson	Y	Y	Y	N	Y	Y
2 Herger	N	Y	N	Y	N	Y
3 Lungren	N	Y	N	Y	N	Y
4 McClintock	N	Y	N	Y	N	Y
5 Matsui	Y	Y	Y	N	Y	Y
6 Woolsey	Y	N	Y	N	Y	Y
7 Miller, George	Y	N	Y	N	Y	Y
8 Pelosi	Y	Y	Y	N	Y	Y
9 Lee	Y	N	Y	N	Y	Y
10 Garamendi	Y	Y	Y	N	Y	Y
11 McNerney	Y	Y	Y	N	Y	Y
12 Speier	Y	Y	Y	N	Y	Y
13 Stark	Y	N	Y	N	Y	N
14 Eshoo	Y	Y	Y	N	Y	Y
15 Honda	Y	Y	Y	N	Y	Y
16 Lofgren	Y	N	Y	N	Y	Y
17 Farr	Y	Y	Y	N	Y	Y
18 Cardoza	Y	Y	Y	N	Y	Y
19 Denham	N	Y	N	Y	N	Y
20 Costa	N	Y	Y	N	Y	Y
21 Nunes	N	Y	N	Y	N	Y
22 McCarthy	?	?	?	?	?	?
23 Capps	Y	Y	Y	N	Y	Y
24 Gallegly	N	Y	N	Y	N	Y
25 McKeon	N	Y	N	Y	N	Y
26 Dreier	N	Y	N	Y	N	Y
27 Sherman	Y	Y	Y	N	Y	Y
28 Berman	Y	Y	Y	N	Y	Y
29 Schiff	Y	Y	Y	N	Y	Y
30 Waxman	Y	Y	Y	N	Y	Y
31 Becerra	Y	Y	Y	N	Y	Y
32 Chu	Y	Y	Y	N	Y	Y
33 Bass	Y	Y	Y	N	Y	Y
34 Roybal-Allard	Y	Y	Y	N	Y	Y
35 Waters	Y	Y	Y	N	Y	Y
36 Hahn	Y	Y	Y	N	Y	Y
37 Richardson	Y	Y	Y	N	Y	Y
38 Napolitano	Y	Y	Y	N	Y	Y
39 Sánchez, Linda	Y	Y	Y	N	Y	Y
40 Royce	N	Y	N	Y	N	Y
41 Lewis	?	?	?	?	?	?
42 Miller, Gary	N	Y	N	Y	N	Y
43 Baca	Y	Y	Y	N	Y	Y
44 Calvert	N	Y	N	Y	N	Y
45 Bono Mack	N	Y	N	N	N	Y
46 Rohrabacher	N	Y	N	Y	N	Y
47 Sanchez, Loretta	Y	Y	Y	N	Y	Y
48 Campbell	N	Y	N	Y	N	N
49 Issa	N	Y	N	Y	N	Y
50 Bilbray	N	Y	N	Y	N	Y
51 Filner	Y	N	Y	N	Y	Y
52 Hunter	N	Y	N	Y	N	Y
53 Davis	Y	Y	Y	N	Y	Y

	300	301	302	303	304	305
COLORADO						
1 DeGette	Y	Y	Y	N	Y	Y
2 Polis	Y	N	Y	N	Y	Y
3 Tipton	N	Y	N	Y	N	Y
4 Gardner	N	Y	N	Y	N	Y
5 Lamborn	N	Y	N	Y	N	Y
6 Coffman	N	Y	N	Y	N	Y
7 Perlmutter	Y	Y	Y	N	Y	Y
CONNECTICUT						
1 Larson	Y	Y	Y	N	Y	Y
2 Courtney	Y	Y	Y	N	Y	Y
3 DeLauro	Y	Y	Y	N	Y	Y
4 Himes	Y	Y	Y	N	Y	Y
5 Murphy	Y	Y	Y	N	Y	Y
DELAWARE						
AL Carney	Y	Y	Y	N	Y	Y
FLORIDA						
1 Miller	N	Y	N	Y	N	Y
2 Southerland	N	Y	N	Y	N	Y
3 Brown	Y	Y	Y	N	Y	Y
4 Crenshaw	N	Y	N	Y	N	Y
5 Nugent	N	Y	N	Y	N	Y
6 Stearns	N	Y	N	Y	N	Y
7 Mica	N	Y	N	Y	N	Y
8 Webster	N	Y	N	Y	N	Y
9 Bilirakis	N	Y	N	Y	N	Y
10 Young	?	?	?	?	?	?
11 Castor	Y	Y	Y	N	Y	Y
12 Ross	N	Y	N	Y	N	Y
13 Buchanan	N	Y	Y	Y	N	Y
14 Mack	?	?	?	?	?	?
15 Posey	N	Y	N	Y	N	Y
16 Rooney	N	Y	N	Y	N	Y
17 Wilson	Y	Y	Y	N	Y	Y
18 Ros-Lehtinen	N	Y	Y	N	Y	Y
19 Deutch	Y	Y	Y	N	Y	Y
20 Wasserman Schultz	Y	Y	Y	N	Y	Y
21 Diaz-Balart	N	Y	N	Y	N	Y
22 West	N	Y	N	Y	N	Y
23 Hastings	Y	Y	Y	N	Y	Y
24 Adams	N	Y	N	Y	N	Y
25 Rivera	N	Y	N	N	N	Y
GEORGIA						
1 Kingston	N	Y	N	Y	N	Y
2 Bishop	Y	Y	Y	N	Y	Y
3 Westmoreland	N	Y	N	Y	N	Y
4 Johnson	Y	Y	Y	N	Y	Y
5 Lewis	Y	N	Y	N	Y	Y
6 Price	N	Y	N	Y	N	Y
7 Woodall	N	Y	N	Y	N	Y
8 Scott, A.	N	Y	N	Y	N	Y
9 Graves	N	Y	N	Y	N	Y
10 Broun	N	Y	N	Y	N	Y
11 Gingrey	N	Y	N	Y	N	Y
12 Barrow	Y	Y	Y	N	Y	Y
13 Scott, D.	Y	Y	Y	N	Y	Y
HAWAII						
1 Hanabusa	Y	Y	Y	N	Y	Y
2 Hirono	Y	Y	Y	N	Y	Y
IDAHO						
1 Labrador	N	Y	N	Y	N	Y
2 Simpson	N	Y	N	Y	N	Y
ILLINOIS						
1 Rush	Y	N	Y	N	Y	Y
2 Jackson	Y	N	Y	N	Y	Y
3 Lipinski	Y	Y	Y	N	Y	Y
4 Gutierrez	Y	Y	Y	N	Y	Y
5 Quigley	Y	Y	Y	N	Y	Y
6 Roskam	N	Y	N	Y	N	Y
7 Davis	Y	Y	Y	N	Y	Y
8 Walsh	N	Y	N	Y	N	Y
9 Schakowsky	Y	Y	Y	N	Y	Y
10 Dold	N	Y	Y	N	Y	Y
11 Kinzinger	N	Y	Y	N	Y	Y
12 Costello	Y	Y	Y	N	Y	Y
13 Biggert	N	Y	Y	N	Y	Y
14 Hultgren	N	Y	N	N	N	Y
15 Johnson	N	N	Y	N	N	Y

KEY Republicans   Democrats

Y Voted for (yea)	X Paired against	C Voted "present" to avoid possible conflict of interest
# Paired for	– Announced against	
+ Announced for	P Voted "present"	? Did not vote or otherwise make a position known
N Voted against (nay)		

	300	301	302	303	304	305
16 **Manzullo**	N	Y	N	Y	N	Y
17 **Schilling**	N	Y	N	N	N	Y
18 **Schock**	N	Y	Y	N	N	Y
19 **Shimkus**	N	Y	Y	N	N	Y
INDIANA						
1 Visclosky	Y	Y	Y	N	Y	Y
2 Donnelly	Y	Y	Y	N	Y	Y
3 **Stutzman**	N	Y	?	?	N	Y
4 **Rokita**	N	Y	N	Y	N	Y
5 **Burton**	?	?	?	?	?	?
6 **Pence**	N	Y	N	Y	N	Y
7 Carson	Y	Y	Y	N	Y	Y
8 **Bucshon**	N	Y	N	Y	N	Y
9 **Young**	N	Y	N	Y	N	Y
IOWA						
1 Braley	Y	Y	Y	N	Y	Y
2 Loebsack	Y	Y	Y	N	Y	Y
3 Boswell	Y	Y	Y	N	Y	Y
4 **Latham**	N	Y	N	Y	Y	Y
5 **King**	N	Y	N	Y	N	Y
KANSAS						
1 **Huelskamp**	N	Y	Y	Y	N	Y
2 **Jenkins**	N	Y	N	Y	N	Y
3 **Yoder**	N	Y	N	Y	N	Y
4 **Pompeo**	N	Y	N	Y	N	Y
KENTUCKY						
1 **Whitfield**	N	Y	N	N	N	Y
2 **Guthrie**	N	Y	N	Y	N	Y
3 Yarmuth	Y	Y	Y	N	Y	Y
4 **Davis**	N	Y	N	Y	N	Y
5 **Rogers**	N	Y	N	Y	N	Y
6 Chandler	Y	Y	Y	N	Y	Y
LOUISIANA						
1 **Scalise**	N	Y	N	Y	N	Y
2 Richmond	Y	Y	Y	N	Y	Y
3 **Landry**	N	Y	N	Y	N	Y
4 **Fleming**	N	Y	N	Y	N	Y
5 **Alexander**	N	Y	N	N	N	Y
6 **Cassidy**	N	Y	N	Y	N	Y
7 **Boustany**	N	Y	N	Y	N	Y
MAINE						
1 Pingree	Y	Y	Y	N	Y	Y
2 Michaud	Y	Y	Y	N	Y	Y
MARYLAND						
1 **Harris**	N	Y	N	Y	N	Y
2 Ruppersberger	Y	Y	Y	N	Y	Y
3 Sarbanes	Y	Y	Y	N	Y	Y
4 Edwards	Y	Y	Y	N	Y	Y
5 Hoyer	Y	Y	Y	N	Y	Y
6 **Bartlett**	N	Y	N	Y	N	Y
7 Cummings	Y	Y	Y	N	Y	Y
8 Van Hollen	Y	Y	Y	N	Y	Y
MASSACHUSETTS						
1 Olver	Y	N	Y	N	Y	Y
2 Neal	Y	Y	Y	N	Y	Y
3 McGovern	Y	N	Y	N	Y	Y
4 Frank	Y	N	Y	N	Y	Y
5 Tsongas	Y	Y	Y	N	Y	Y
6 Tierney	Y	Y	Y	N	Y	Y
7 Markey	Y	N	Y	N	Y	Y
8 Capuano	Y	N	Y	N	Y	N
9 Lynch	Y	Y	Y	N	Y	Y
10 Keating	Y	Y	Y	N	Y	Y
MICHIGAN						
1 **Benishek**	N	Y	N	Y	N	Y
2 **Huizenga**	N	Y	N	Y	N	Y
3 **Amash**	N	N	N	Y	N	N
4 **Camp**	N	Y	N	Y	N	Y
5 Kildee	Y	Y	Y	N	Y	Y
6 **Upton**	N	Y	N	N	N	Y
7 **Walberg**	N	Y	N	Y	N	Y
8 **Rogers**	N	Y	N	Y	N	Y
9 Peters	Y	Y	Y	N	Y	Y
10 **Miller**	N	Y	N	N	N	Y
11 **McCotter**	N	Y	Y	N	N	Y
12 Levin	Y	Y	Y	N	Y	Y
13 Clarke	Y	Y	Y	N	Y	Y
14 Conyers	N	Y	Y	N	Y	Y
15 Dingell	Y	Y	Y	N	Y	Y
MINNESOTA						
1 Walz	Y	Y	Y	N	Y	Y
2 **Kline**	N	Y	N	Y	N	Y
3 **Paulsen**	N	Y	N	Y	N	Y
4 McCollum	Y	Y	Y	N	Y	Y

	300	301	302	303	304	305
5 Ellison	?	?	?	?	?	?
6 **Bachmann**	N	Y	N	Y	N	Y
7 Peterson	Y	Y	Y	N	Y	Y
8 **Cravaack**	N	Y	Y	N	N	Y
MISSISSIPPI						
1 **Nunnelee**	N	Y	N	Y	N	Y
2 Thompson	Y	Y	Y	N	Y	Y
3 **Harper**	N	Y	N	Y	N	Y
4 **Palazzo**	N	Y	N	Y	N	Y
MISSOURI						
1 Clay	?	?	?	?	?	?
2 **Akin**	N	Y	N	Y	N	Y
3 Carnahan	Y	Y	Y	N	Y	Y
4 **Hartzler**	N	Y	N	Y	N	Y
5 Cleaver	Y	?	Y	N	Y	Y
6 **Graves**	N	Y	N	Y	N	Y
7 **Long**	N	Y	N	Y	N	Y
8 **Emerson**	N	Y	Y	N	N	Y
9 **Luetkemeyer**	N	Y	N	Y	N	Y
MONTANA						
AL **Rehberg**	N	Y	N	N	N	Y
NEBRASKA						
1 **Fortenberry**	?	?	?	?	?	?
2 **Terry**	N	Y	Y	Y	N	Y
3 **Smith**	N	Y	N	Y	N	Y
NEVADA						
1 Berkley	Y	Y	Y	N	Y	Y
2 **Amodei**	N	Y	N	Y	N	Y
3 **Heck**	N	Y	N	N	N	Y
NEW HAMPSHIRE						
1 **Guinta**	?	?	?	?	?	?
2 **Bass**	N	Y	N	Y	N	Y
NEW JERSEY						
1 Andrews	Y	Y	Y	N	Y	Y
2 **LoBiondo**	N	Y	Y	N	N	Y
3 **Runyan**	N	Y	Y	N	N	Y
4 **Smith**	N	Y	Y	N	N	Y
5 **Garrett**	N	Y	N	Y	N	Y
6 Pallone	Y	Y	Y	N	Y	Y
7 **Lance**	N	Y	Y	N	N	Y
8 Pascrell	Y	Y	Y	N	Y	Y
9 Rothman	Y	Y	Y	N	Y	Y
10 Vacant						
11 **Frelinghuysen**	N	Y	N	Y	N	Y
12 Holt	Y	N	Y	N	Y	Y
13 Sires	Y	Y	Y	N	Y	Y
NEW MEXICO						
1 Heinrich	Y	Y	Y	N	Y	Y
2 **Pearce**	N	Y	N	Y	N	Y
3 Luján	Y	Y	Y	N	Y	Y
NEW YORK						
1 Bishop	Y	Y	Y	N	Y	Y
2 Israel	Y	Y	Y	N	Y	Y
3 **King**	N	Y	Y	N	N	Y
4 McCarthy	N	Y	Y	N	Y	Y
5 Ackerman	Y	Y	Y	N	Y	Y
6 Meeks	Y	Y	Y	N	Y	Y
7 Crowley	Y	Y	Y	N	Y	Y
8 Nadler	Y	Y	Y	N	Y	Y
9 **Turner**	N	Y	N	Y	N	Y
10 Towns	Y	Y	Y	N	Y	Y
11 Clarke	Y	N	Y	N	Y	Y
12 Velázquez	?	?	?	?	?	?
13 **Grimm**	N	Y	Y	N	N	Y
14 Maloney	?	Y	Y	N	Y	Y
15 Rangel	?	?	Y	N	Y	Y
16 Serrano	Y	Y	Y	N	Y	Y
17 Engel	Y	Y	Y	N	Y	Y
18 Lowey	Y	Y	Y	N	Y	Y
19 **Hayworth**	N	Y	N	Y	N	Y
20 **Gibson**	N	N	Y	N	N	Y
21 Tonko	Y	Y	Y	N	Y	Y
22 Hinchey	Y	Y	Y	N	Y	Y
23 Owens	Y	Y	Y	N	Y	Y
24 **Hanna**	N	Y	N	N	N	Y
25 **Buerkle**	N	Y	N	Y	N	Y
26 Hochul	Y	Y	Y	N	Y	Y
27 Higgins	Y	Y	Y	N	Y	Y
28 Slaughter	?	?	?	?	?	?
29 **Reed**	N	Y	N	Y	N	Y
NORTH CAROLINA						
1 Butterfield	Y	Y	Y	N	Y	Y
2 **Ellmers**	N	Y	N	Y	N	Y
3 **Jones**	Y	N	N	Y	Y	Y
4 Price	Y	Y	Y	N	Y	Y

	300	301	302	303	304	305
5 **Foxx**	N	Y	N	Y	N	Y
6 **Coble**	N	Y	N	Y	N	Y
7 McIntyre	Y	Y	Y	N	Y	Y
8 Kissell	Y	Y	Y	N	Y	Y
9 **Myrick**	N	Y	N	Y	N	Y
10 **McHenry**	N	Y	N	Y	N	Y
11 Shuler	N	Y	Y	N	Y	Y
12 Watt	Y	Y	Y	N	Y	Y
13 Miller	Y	Y	Y	N	Y	Y
NORTH DAKOTA						
AL **Berg**	N	Y	N	Y	N	Y
OHIO						
1 **Chabot**	N	Y	N	Y	N	Y
2 **Schmidt**	N	Y	Y	N	N	Y
3 **Turner**	N	Y	Y	N	N	Y
4 **Jordan**	N	Y	N	Y	N	Y
5 **Latta**	N	Y	N	Y	N	Y
6 **Johnson**	N	Y	N	Y	N	Y
7 **Austria**	N	Y	N	Y	N	Y
8 **Boehner**						
9 Kaptur	Y	Y	Y	N	Y	Y
10 Kucinich	Y	N	Y	N	Y	N
11 Fudge	Y	Y	Y	N	Y	Y
12 **Tiberi**	N	?	N	N	N	Y
13 Sutton	Y	Y	Y	N	Y	Y
14 **LaTourette**	N	?	Y	N	N	Y
15 **Stivers**	N	Y	N	N	N	Y
16 **Renacci**	N	Y	Y	Y	N	Y
17 Ryan	Y	Y	Y	N	Y	Y
18 **Gibbs**	N	Y	N	Y	N	Y
OKLAHOMA						
1 **Sullivan**	N	Y	N	Y	N	Y
2 Boren	Y	Y	N	N	Y	Y
3 **Lucas**	N	Y	N	Y	N	Y
4 **Cole**	N	Y	N	Y	N	Y
5 **Lankford**	N	Y	N	Y	N	Y
OREGON						
1 Bonamici	Y	Y	Y	N	Y	Y
2 **Walden**	N	Y	N	N	N	Y
3 Blumenauer	Y	N	Y	N	Y	Y
4 DeFazio	Y	Y	Y	N	Y	Y
5 Schrader	Y	Y	Y	N	Y	Y
PENNSYLVANIA						
1 Brady	Y	Y	Y	N	Y	Y
2 Fattah	Y	Y	Y	N	Y	Y
3 **Kelly**	N	Y	N	N	N	Y
4 Altmire	Y	Y	Y	N	Y	Y
5 **Thompson**	N	Y	N	N	N	Y
6 **Gerlach**	N	Y	N	N	N	Y
7 **Meehan**	N	Y	Y	N	N	Y
8 **Fitzpatrick**	N	Y	N	N	N	Y
9 **Shuster**	N	Y	N	N	N	Y
10 **Marino**	N	Y	N	N	N	Y
11 **Barletta**	N	Y	N	N	N	Y
12 Critz	Y	Y	Y	N	Y	Y
13 Schwartz	Y	Y	Y	N	Y	Y
14 Doyle	?	?	?	?	?	?
15 **Dent**	N	Y	N	Y	N	Y
16 **Pitts**	N	Y	N	Y	N	Y
17 Holden	Y	Y	Y	N	Y	Y
18 **Murphy**	N	Y	Y	N	N	Y
19 **Platts**	N	Y	N	Y	N	Y
RHODE ISLAND						
1 Cicilline	Y	Y	Y	N	Y	Y
2 Langevin	Y	Y	Y	N	Y	Y
SOUTH CAROLINA						
1 **Scott**	N	Y	N	Y	N	Y
2 **Wilson**	N	Y	N	Y	N	Y
3 **Duncan**	N	Y	N	Y	N	Y
4 **Gowdy**	N	Y	N	Y	N	Y
5 **Mulvaney**	N	Y	N	Y	N	Y
6 Clyburn	Y	Y	Y	N	Y	Y
SOUTH DAKOTA						
AL **Noem**	N	Y	N	Y	N	Y
TENNESSEE						
1 **Roe**	N	Y	N	N	N	Y
2 **Duncan**	N	N	N	Y	N	N
3 **Fleischmann**	N	Y	N	Y	N	Y
4 **DesJarlais**	N	Y	N	Y	N	Y
5 Cooper	Y	Y	Y	N	Y	Y
6 **Black**	N	Y	N	Y	N	Y
7 **Blackburn**	N	Y	N	Y	N	Y
8 **Fincher**	N	Y	N	Y	N	Y
9 Cohen	Y	Y	Y	N	Y	Y

	300	301	302	303	304	305
TEXAS						
1 **Gohmert**	N	Y	N	Y	N	Y
2 **Poe**	N	Y	N	Y	N	Y
3 **Johnson, S.**	N	Y	N	Y	N	Y
4 **Hall**	N	Y	N	Y	N	Y
5 **Hensarling**	N	Y	N	Y	N	Y
6 **Barton**	N	Y	N	Y	N	Y
7 **Culberson**	N	Y	N	Y	N	Y
8 **Brady**	N	Y	N	Y	N	Y
9 Green, A.	Y	Y	Y	N	Y	Y
10 **McCaul**	N	Y	N	Y	N	Y
11 **Conaway**	N	Y	N	Y	N	Y
12 **Granger**	?	Y	N	Y	N	Y
13 **Thornberry**	N	Y	N	Y	N	Y
14 **Paul**	N	N	N	Y	Y	N
15 Hinojosa	Y	Y	Y	N	Y	Y
16 Reyes	Y	Y	Y	N	Y	Y
17 **Flores**	N	Y	N	Y	N	Y
18 Jackson Lee	Y	Y	Y	N	Y	Y
19 **Neugebauer**	N	Y	N	Y	N	Y
20 Gonzalez	Y	Y	Y	N	Y	Y
21 **Smith**	N	Y	N	Y	N	Y
22 **Olson**	N	Y	?	Y	N	Y
23 **Canseco**	N	Y	N	Y	N	Y
24 **Marchant**	N	Y	N	Y	N	Y
25 Doggett	Y	Y	Y	N	Y	Y
26 **Burgess**	N	Y	N	Y	N	Y
27 **Farenthold**	N	Y	N	Y	N	Y
28 Cuellar	Y	Y	Y	N	Y	Y
29 Green, G.	Y	Y	Y	N	Y	Y
30 Johnson, E.	Y	Y	Y	N	Y	Y
31 **Carter**	N	Y	N	Y	N	Y
32 **Sessions**	N	Y	N	Y	N	Y
UTAH						
1 **Bishop**	N	Y	N	Y	N	Y
2 Matheson	Y	Y	Y	N	Y	Y
3 **Chaffetz**	N	Y	N	Y	N	Y
VERMONT						
AL Welch	Y	Y	Y	N	Y	Y
VIRGINIA						
1 **Wittman**	N	Y	N	Y	N	Y
2 **Rigell**	N	Y	N	Y	N	Y
3 Scott	Y	Y	Y	N	Y	Y
4 **Forbes**	N	Y	N	Y	N	Y
5 **Hurt**	N	Y	?	?	N	Y
6 **Goodlatte**	N	Y	N	Y	N	Y
7 **Cantor**	N	Y	N	Y	N	Y
8 Moran	Y	Y	Y	N	Y	Y
9 **Griffith**	N	Y	N	Y	N	Y
10 **Wolf**	N	Y	N	Y	N	N
11 Connolly	Y	Y	Y	N	Y	Y
WASHINGTON						
1 Vacant						
2 Larsen	Y	Y	Y	N	Y	Y
3 **Herrera Beutler**	N	Y	N	Y	N	Y
4 **Hastings**	N	Y	N	Y	N	Y
5 **McMorris Rodgers**	N	Y	N	Y	N	Y
6 Dicks	Y	Y	Y	N	Y	Y
7 McDermott	Y	N	Y	N	Y	Y
8 **Reichert**	N	Y	Y	N	N	Y
9 Smith	Y	Y	Y	N	Y	Y
WEST VIRGINIA						
1 **McKinley**	N	Y	Y	N	N	Y
2 **Capito**	N	Y	Y	N	N	Y
3 Rahall	Y	Y	Y	N	Y	Y
WISCONSIN						
1 **Ryan**	N	Y	N	N	N	Y
2 Baldwin	Y	Y	Y	N	Y	Y
3 Kind	Y	N	Y	N	Y	Y
4 Moore	Y	Y	Y	N	Y	Y
5 **Sensenbrenner**	N	Y	N	Y	N	N
6 **Petri**	N	Y	Y	N	N	Y
7 **Duffy**	N	Y	N	N	N	Y
8 **Ribble**	N	Y	N	Y	N	Y
WYOMING						
AL **Lummis**	N	Y	N	Y	N	N

IN THE HOUSE | By Vote Number

306. HR 5325. Fiscal 2013 Energy-Water Appropriations/Army Corps of Engineers Construction. Scalise, R-La., amendment that would increase by $10 million the amount provided for Army Corps of Engineers harbor and river construction, flood and storm damage reduction, shore protection, and aquatic ecosystem restoration projects. It would reduce by the same amount funding provided for Energy Department salaries and expenses. Adopted in Committee of the Whole 216-177: R 139-85; D 77-92. A "yea" was a vote in support of the president's position. June 1, 2012.

307. HR 5325. Fiscal 2013 Energy-Water Appropriations/Army Corps of Engineers Construction. King, R-Iowa, amendment that would reduce by $1 million the amount provided for Army Corps of Engineers harbor and river construction, flood and storm damage reduction, shore protection, and aquatic ecosystem restoration projects. It would increase by $571,000 funding for the operation, maintenance and care of existing river and harbor, flood and storm damage reduction, and aquatic ecosystem restoration projects. Adopted in Committee of the Whole 203-185: R 188-33; D 15-152. June 1, 2012.

308. HR 5325. Fiscal 2013 Energy-Water Appropriations/Clean-Water Guidance. Moran, D-Va., amendment that would strike language that would bar the use of funds in the bill for the Army Corps of Engineers to develop, adopt, implement, administer or enforce changes to rules pertaining to the definition of navigable waters under the Clean Water Act. Rejected in Committee of the Whole 152-237: R 6-214; D 146-23. A "yea" was a vote in support of the president's position. June 1, 2012.

309. HR 5325. Fiscal 2013 Energy-Water Appropriations/Energy Department Science Programs. Hultgren, R-Ill., amendment that would increase by $15 million the amount provided for Energy Department science activities and reduce by $30 million funding for energy efficiency and renewable-energy activities. Rejected in Committee of the Whole 130-256: R 125-93; D 5-163. June 1, 2012.

310. HR 5325. Fiscal 2013 Energy-Water Appropriations/Energy Efficiency and Renewable-Energy Funding. Chaffetz, R-Utah, amendment that would reduce by $74 million the amount provided for energy efficiency and renewable-energy activities and direct the same amount to the bill's spending reduction account. Rejected in Committee of the Whole 140-245: R 139-81; D 1-164. June 1, 2012.

311. HR 5325. Fiscal 2013 Energy-Water Appropriations/Energy Efficiency and Renewable-Energy Funding. McClintock, R-Calif., amendment that would eliminate all funding provided in the bill for energy efficiency and renewable-energy programs. The $1.5 billion total includes an appropriation of $115 million that would remain available through fiscal 2014. It would transfer $1.5 billion to the bill's spending-reduction account. Rejected in Committee of the Whole 113-275: R 113-107; D 0-168. June 1, 2012.

312. HR 5325. Fiscal 2013 Energy-Water Appropriations/Energy Efficiency and Renewable-Energy Funding. Kaptur, D-Ohio, amendment that would increase by $10 million the amount provided for energy efficiency and renewable-energy activities and reduce by the same amount funding for the Energy Department salaries and expenses account. Rejected in Committee of the Whole 183-200: R 26-191; D 157-9. June 1, 2012.

Member	306	307	308	309	310	311	312
ALABAMA							
1 Bonner	N	Y	N	N	N	N	N
2 Roby	N	Y	N	N	N	N	N
3 Rogers	N	Y	N	N	N	N	N
4 Aderholt	N	Y	N	Y	N	Y	N
5 Brooks	N	Y	N	Y	Y	Y	N
6 Bachus	N	Y	N	Y	Y	Y	N
7 Sewell	Y	N	Y	N	N	N	Y
ALASKA							
AL Young	Y	Y	N	Y	Y	Y	N
ARIZONA							
1 Gosar	Y	Y	N	Y	Y	Y	N
2 Franks	Y	Y	N	Y	Y	Y	N
3 Quayle	Y	Y	N	Y	Y	Y	N
4 Pastor	Y	N	Y	N	N	N	Y
5 Schweikert	Y	Y	N	Y	Y	Y	N
6 Flake	Y	Y	N	Y	Y	Y	N
7 Grijalva	N	N	Y	N	N	N	Y
8 Vacant							
ARKANSAS							
1 Crawford	Y	N	N	N	N	N	N
2 Griffin	Y	N	N	N	N	N	N
3 Womack	N	N	N	N	N	N	N
4 Ross	N	N	N	N	N	N	Y
CALIFORNIA							
1 Thompson	N	N	Y	N	N	N	Y
2 Herger	?	?	?	?	?	?	?
3 Lungren	Y	Y	N	Y	Y	N	N
4 McClintock	Y	Y	N	Y	Y	Y	N
5 Matsui	N	N	Y	N	N	N	Y
6 Woolsey	N	N	Y	N	N	N	Y
7 Miller, George	N	N	Y	N	N	N	Y
8 Pelosi	Y	N	Y	N	N	N	Y
9 Lee	Y	N	Y	N	N	N	Y
10 Garamendi	N	N	Y	N	N	N	Y
11 McNerney	N	N	Y	N	N	N	Y
12 Speier	N	N	Y	N	N	N	Y
13 Stark	N	N	Y	N	N	N	Y
14 Eshoo	N	N	Y	N	N	N	?
15 Honda	N	N	Y	N	N	N	Y
16 Lofgren	N	N	Y	Y	N	N	Y
17 Farr	N	N	Y	N	N	N	Y
18 Cardoza	?	?	?	?	?	?	?
19 Denham	Y	Y	N	N	N	N	N
20 Costa	?	?	?	?	?	?	?
21 Nunes	N	Y	N	N	Y	Y	N
22 McCarthy	?	?	?	?	?	?	?
23 Capps	N	N	Y	N	N	N	Y
24 Gallegly	?	?	?	?	?	?	?
25 McKeon	?	?	?	?	?	?	?
26 Dreier	N	Y	N	N	N	N	N
27 Sherman	Y	N	Y	N	N	N	Y
28 Berman	N	N	Y	N	N	N	Y
29 Schiff	N	N	Y	N	N	N	Y
30 Waxman	N	N	Y	N	N	N	Y
31 Becerra	Y	N	Y	N	N	N	Y
32 Chu	N	Y	Y	N	N	N	Y
33 Bass	Y	?	Y	N	?	N	Y
34 Roybal-Allard	N	N	Y	N	N	N	Y
35 Waters	?	?	?	?	?	?	?
36 Hahn	N	N	Y	N	N	N	Y
37 Richardson	Y	N	Y	N	N	N	Y
38 Napolitano	N	N	Y	N	N	N	Y
39 Sánchez, Linda	N	N	Y	N	N	N	Y
40 Royce	Y	Y	N	Y	Y	Y	N
41 Lewis	?	?	?	?	?	?	?
42 Miller, Gary	?	?	?	?	?	?	?
43 Baca	?	?	?	?	?	?	?
44 Calvert	Y	N	Y	N	Y	Y	N
45 Bono Mack	N	N	N	N	Y	N	Y
46 Rohrabacher	N	Y	N	Y	Y	Y	N
47 Sanchez, Loretta	N	N	Y	N	N	N	Y
48 Campbell	Y	N	N	Y	Y	Y	N
49 Issa	N	Y	N	Y	N	Y	N
50 Bilbray	N	N	Y	N	N	N	Y
51 Filner	N	N	Y	N	N	N	Y
52 Hunter	N	Y	N	Y	Y	Y	N
53 Davis	N	N	Y	N	N	N	Y
COLORADO							
1 DeGette	Y	N	Y	N	N	N	Y
2 Polis	Y	N	Y	N	N	N	Y
3 Tipton	Y	N	N	N	N	N	Y
4 Gardner	N	N	N	N	N	N	N
5 Lamborn	Y	Y	N	Y	Y	?	N
6 Coffman	Y	Y	N	N	N	Y	N
7 Perlmutter	N	N	Y	N	N	N	Y
CONNECTICUT							
1 Larson	Y	N	Y	N	N	N	Y
2 Courtney	Y	N	Y	N	N	N	Y
3 DeLauro	N	N	Y	N	N	N	Y
4 Himes	N	N	Y	N	N	N	Y
5 Murphy	N	N	Y	N	?	N	Y
DELAWARE							
AL Carney	Y	N	Y	N	N	N	Y
FLORIDA							
1 Miller	Y	Y	N	Y	Y	Y	N
2 Southerland	Y	Y	N	Y	Y	Y	N
3 Brown	Y	N	Y	N	N	N	Y
4 Crenshaw	N	N	N	N	N	N	N
5 Nugent	Y	Y	N	Y	Y	Y	N
6 Stearns	Y	Y	N	Y	Y	Y	N
7 Mica	Y	Y	N	Y	Y	Y	N
8 Webster	N	Y	N	Y	Y	Y	N
9 Bilirakis	Y	Y	N	Y	Y	Y	N
10 Young	?	?	?	?	?	?	?
11 Castor	N	N	N	N	N	N	Y
12 Ross	Y	Y	N	Y	Y	Y	N
13 Buchanan	Y	Y	N	Y	Y	Y	N
14 Mack	?	?	?	?	?	?	?
15 Posey	Y	Y	N	Y	Y	Y	N
16 Rooney	Y	Y	N	Y	Y	Y	N
17 Wilson	Y	N	Y	N	N	N	Y
18 Ros-Lehtinen	Y	Y	N	Y	Y	Y	N
19 Deutch	Y	N	Y	N	N	N	Y
20 Wasserman Schultz	Y	N	Y	N	N	N	Y
21 Diaz-Balart	N	N	N	N	N	N	Y
22 West	Y	Y	N	Y	Y	Y	N
23 Hastings	Y	N	Y	N	N	N	Y
24 Adams	Y	Y	N	Y	Y	Y	N
25 Rivera	N	Y	N	N	N	N	N
GEORGIA							
1 Kingston	N	Y	N	N	N	N	N
2 Bishop	Y	N	N	N	N	N	Y
3 Westmoreland	Y	Y	N	Y	Y	Y	N
4 Johnson	N	N	Y	N	N	N	Y
5 Lewis	Y	N	Y	N	N	N	Y
6 Price	Y	Y	N	Y	Y	Y	N
7 Woodall	Y	Y	N	Y	Y	Y	N
8 Scott, A.	Y	Y	N	Y	Y	Y	Y
9 Graves	Y	Y	N	?	Y	Y	N
10 Broun	N	Y	Y	N	Y	Y	N
11 Gingrey	Y	Y	N	Y	Y	Y	Y
12 Barrow	Y	N	N	N	N	N	Y
13 Scott, D.	?	?	?	?	?	?	?
HAWAII							
1 Hanabusa	Y	N	Y	N	N	N	Y
2 Hirono	N	N	Y	N	N	N	Y
IDAHO							
1 Labrador	N	Y	N	Y	Y	Y	N
2 Simpson	N	N	N	N	N	N	N
ILLINOIS							
1 Rush	N	N	Y	N	N	N	Y
2 Jackson	Y	N	Y	N	N	N	Y
3 Lipinski	N	Y	Y	N	N	N	Y
4 Gutierrez	N	N	Y	N	N	N	Y
5 Quigley	N	N	Y	N	N	N	Y
6 Roskam	N	Y	N	N	N	N	N
7 Davis	Y	N	Y	N	N	N	Y
8 Walsh	?	?	?	?	?	?	?
9 Schakowsky	Y	N	Y	N	N	N	Y
10 Dold	N	Y	Y	N	N	N	Y
11 Kinzinger	Y	Y	N	Y	N	N	N
12 Costello	Y	N	Y	N	N	N	Y
13 Biggert	N	N	N	N	Y	N	Y
14 Hultgren	Y	Y	N	Y	Y	Y	N
15 Johnson	Y	Y	N	Y	Y	N	N

KEY   Republicans   Democrats

Y Voted for (yea)	**X** Paired against	**C** Voted "present" to avoid possible conflict of interest
# Paired for	**–** Announced against	
+ Announced for	**P** Voted "present"	**?** Did not vote or otherwise make a position known
N Voted against (nay)		

	306	307	308	309	310	311	312
16 **Manzullo**	Y	Y	N	Y	Y	Y	N
17 **Schilling**	+	+	–	+	+	–	–
18 **Schock**	Y	Y	N	Y	Y	N	N
19 **Shimkus**	Y	Y	N	Y	N	N	N
INDIANA							
1 Visclosky	N	Y	Y	N	N	N	Y
2 Donnelly	N	N	N	N	N	N	Y
3 **Stutzman**	N	Y	N	Y	?	Y	N
4 **Rokita**	Y	Y	N	Y	Y	Y	N
5 **Burton**	–	+	–	+	+	+	–
6 **Pence**	Y	Y	N	Y	Y	Y	N
7 Carson	Y	N	Y	N	N	N	Y
8 **Bucshon**	N	Y	N	?	Y	N	N
9 **Young**	N	Y	N	Y	Y	Y	N
IOWA							
1 Braley	N	Y	Y	N	N	N	Y
2 Loebsack	N	Y	N	N	N	N	Y
3 Boswell	N	Y	N	N	N	N	Y
4 **Latham**	N	Y	N	N	N	N	Y
5 **King**	Y	Y	N	N	Y	N	Y
KANSAS							
1 **Huelskamp**	Y	Y	N	Y	Y	Y	N
2 **Jenkins**	Y	Y	N	Y	Y	Y	N
3 **Yoder**	N	Y	N	N	Y	Y	N
4 **Pompeo**	N	Y	N	Y	Y	Y	N
KENTUCKY							
1 **Whitfield**	Y	N	N	N	N	Y	N
2 **Guthrie**	N	Y	N	N	Y	N	N
3 Yarmuth	Y	N	Y	N	N	N	Y
4 **Davis**	N	Y	N	N	N	N	N
5 **Rogers**	N	Y	N	N	N	N	N
6 Chandler	N	N	N	N	N	N	Y
LOUISIANA							
1 **Scalise**	Y	Y	N	Y	Y	Y	N
2 Richmond	Y	N	Y	N	N	N	Y
3 **Landry**	Y	?	N	Y	Y	Y	N
4 **Fleming**	Y	Y	N	Y	Y	Y	N
5 **Alexander**	Y	?	?	?	?	?	?
6 **Cassidy**	Y	Y	N	Y	Y	Y	N
7 **Boustany**	Y	Y	N	Y	Y	Y	N
MAINE							
1 Pingree	Y	N	Y	N	N	N	Y
2 Michaud	Y	Y	Y	N	N	N	Y
MARYLAND							
1 **Harris**	N	Y	N	N	Y	Y	N
2 Ruppersberger	N	N	Y	N	N	N	Y
3 Sarbanes	N	N	Y	N	N	N	Y
4 Edwards	Y	N	Y	N	N	N	Y
5 Hoyer	N	N	Y	N	N	N	N
6 **Bartlett**	N	Y	N	N	N	N	Y
7 Cummings	Y	N	Y	N	N	N	Y
8 Van Hollen	N	?	Y	N	N	N	Y
MASSACHUSETTS							
1 Olver	N	N	Y	N	N	N	Y
2 Neal	?	?	?	?	?	?	?
3 McGovern	N	N	Y	N	N	N	Y
4 Frank	N	N	Y	N	N	N	Y
5 Tsongas	?	?	?	?	?	?	?
6 Tierney	N	N	Y	N	N	N	Y
7 Markey	Y	N	Y	N	N	N	Y
8 Capuano	N	N	Y	N	N	N	Y
9 Lynch	N	N	Y	N	N	N	Y
10 Keating	Y	N	Y	N	N	N	Y
MICHIGAN							
1 **Benishek**	Y	Y	N	Y	Y	Y	N
2 **Huizenga**	N	?	?	?	?	?	?
3 **Amash**	Y	Y	N	Y	Y	Y	N
4 **Camp**	N	Y	N	N	Y	N	N
5 Kildee	Y	N	Y	N	N	N	Y
6 **Upton**	Y	N	N	N	N	Y	N
7 **Walberg**	Y	Y	N	Y	Y	Y	N
8 **Rogers**	Y	Y	N	Y	N	N	N
9 Peters	Y	N	Y	N	N	N	Y
10 **Miller**	Y	Y	N	N	Y	Y	N
11 **McCotter**	Y	N	N	Y	N	N	N
12 Levin	N	N	Y	N	N	N	Y
13 Clarke	Y	N	Y	N	N	N	Y
14 Conyers	Y	N	Y	N	N	N	Y
15 Dingell	Y	N	Y	N	N	N	Y
MINNESOTA							
1 Walz	?	?	?	?	?	?	?
2 **Kline**	Y	Y	N	Y	Y	Y	N
3 **Paulsen**	Y	Y	N	Y	Y	Y	N
4 McCollum	?	?	?	?	?	?	?

	306	307	308	309	310	311	312
5 Ellison	?	?	?	?	?	?	?
6 **Bachmann**	Y	Y	N	Y	Y	Y	N
7 Peterson	N	Y	N	N	N	N	Y
8 **Cravaack**	Y	Y	N	Y	Y	N	N
MISSISSIPPI							
1 **Nunnelee**	Y	Y	N	N	Y	Y	N
2 Thompson	Y	N	Y	N	N	N	N
3 **Harper**	Y	Y	N	N	N	N	N
4 **Palazzo**	N	Y	N	N	N	N	N
MISSOURI							
1 Clay	?	?	?	?	?	?	?
2 **Akin**	Y	Y	N	Y	Y	Y	?
3 Carnahan	N	N	Y	N	N	N	Y
4 **Hartzler**	N	Y	N	Y	N	Y	N
5 Cleaver	Y	N	Y	N	N	N	Y
6 **Graves**	Y	Y	N	Y	Y	Y	N
7 **Long**	N	N	N	N	Y	Y	N
8 **Emerson**	N	Y	?	N	N	N	N
9 **Luetkemeyer**	Y	Y	N	Y	Y	N	N
MONTANA							
AL **Rehberg**	N	Y	N	N	N	N	N
NEBRASKA							
1 **Fortenberry**	?	?	?	?	?	?	?
2 **Terry**	N	Y	N	N	Y	N	N
3 **Smith**	N	Y	N	Y	Y	N	N
NEVADA							
1 Berkley	N	N	Y	N	N	N	Y
2 **Amodei**	Y	Y	N	Y	Y	Y	N
3 **Heck**	Y	Y	N	N	N	N	N
NEW HAMPSHIRE							
1 **Guinta**	–	+	–	–	–	–	–
2 **Bass**	N	N	Y	N	N	N	Y
NEW JERSEY							
1 Andrews	N	N	Y	N	N	N	Y
2 **LoBiondo**	N	N	N	N	N	N	Y
3 **Runyan**	Y	Y	N	N	N	N	Y
4 **Smith**	N	Y	N	N	N	N	Y
5 **Garrett**	Y	Y	N	Y	Y	Y	N
6 Pallone	N	N	Y	N	N	N	Y
7 **Lance**	N	Y	N	N	Y	N	Y
8 Pascrell	?	?	?	?	?	?	?
9 Rothman	?	?	?	?	?	?	?
10 Vacant							
11 **Frelinghuysen**	N	Y	N	N	N	N	N
12 Holt	N	N	Y	N	N	N	Y
13 Sires	N	N	Y	N	N	N	Y
NEW MEXICO							
1 Heinrich	+	–	+	–	–	–	+
2 **Pearce**	Y	Y	N	Y	Y	Y	N
3 Luján	Y	N	Y	N	N	N	Y
NEW YORK							
1 Bishop	N	N	Y	N	N	N	Y
2 Israel	Y	N	Y	N	N	N	Y
3 **King**	N	Y	N	N	N	N	N
4 McCarthy	Y	N	Y	N	N	N	Y
5 Ackerman	N	N	Y	?	?	?	?
6 Meeks	Y	N	Y	N	N	N	Y
7 Crowley	N	N	Y	N	?	N	Y
8 Nadler	N	N	Y	N	N	N	Y
9 **Turner**	Y	Y	N	Y	Y	Y	N
10 Towns	Y	N	Y	N	N	N	Y
11 Clarke	Y	N	Y	N	N	N	Y
12 Velázquez	+	–	+	–	–	–	+
13 **Grimm**	Y	N	N	Y	N	N	N
14 Maloney	N	N	Y	N	N	N	Y
15 Rangel	Y	N	Y	N	N	N	Y
16 Serrano	Y	N	Y	N	N	N	Y
17 Engel	N	N	Y	N	N	N	Y
18 Lowey	Y	N	Y	N	N	N	Y
19 **Hayworth**	Y	Y	Y	N	Y	N	N
20 **Gibson**	Y	N	N	N	N	N	Y
21 Tonko	Y	N	Y	N	N	N	Y
22 Hinchey	N	N	Y	N	N	N	Y
23 Owens	N	Y	N	N	N	N	Y
24 **Hanna**	Y	N	N	N	N	N	N
25 **Buerkle**	Y	Y	N	Y	Y	Y	N
26 Hochul	Y	Y	N	Y	N	N	N
27 Higgins	N	Y	Y	N	N	N	Y
28 Slaughter	–	–	+	–	–	–	+
29 **Reed**	Y	Y	N	N	N	N	N
NORTH CAROLINA							
1 Butterfield	Y	N	Y	N	N	N	Y
2 **Ellmers**	Y	Y	N	Y	N	N	N
3 **Jones**	Y	N	N	N	Y	Y	Y
4 Price	N	N	Y	N	N	N	Y

	306	307	308	309	310	311	312
5 **Foxx**	N	N	N	N	Y	Y	N
6 **Coble**	?	?	?	?	?	?	?
7 McIntyre	N	Y	N	N	N	N	Y
8 Kissell	Y	Y	N	N	N	N	N
9 **Myrick**	N	Y	N	Y	Y	Y	N
10 **McHenry**	Y	Y	N	Y	N	Y	N
11 Shuler	?	?	?	?	?	?	?
12 Watt	Y	N	Y	N	N	N	Y
13 Miller	N	N	Y	N	N	N	Y
NORTH DAKOTA							
AL **Berg**	N	Y	N	Y	N	N	N
OHIO							
1 **Chabot**	Y	Y	N	Y	Y	Y	N
2 **Schmidt**	Y	Y	N	Y	Y	Y	N
3 **Turner**	N	Y	N	N	N	N	N
4 **Jordan**	Y	Y	N	Y	Y	Y	N
5 **Latta**	N	N	N	N	Y	N	N
6 **Johnson**	Y	Y	N	N	Y	N	N
7 **Austria**	N	Y	N	N	N	N	N
8 **Boehner**							
9 Kaptur	N	N	Y	N	N	N	Y
10 Kucinich	Y	N	Y	N	N	N	Y
11 Fudge	Y	N	Y	N	N	N	Y
12 **Tiberi**	N	N	N	N	N	N	N
13 Sutton	Y	N	Y	N	N	N	Y
14 **LaTourette**	?	?	?	?	?	?	?
15 **Stivers**	N	N	?	N	N	N	N
16 **Renacci**	Y	Y	N	N	N	N	N
17 Ryan	N	N	Y	N	N	N	Y
18 **Gibbs**	Y	Y	N	N	Y	N	N
OKLAHOMA							
1 **Sullivan**	Y	Y	N	N	N	N	N
2 Boren	Y	N	N	N	N	N	Y
3 **Lucas**	Y	Y	N	N	N	N	N
4 **Cole**	Y	Y	N	N	N	N	N
5 **Lankford**	N	Y	N	N	Y	N	N
OREGON							
1 Bonamici	N	N	Y	N	N	N	Y
2 **Walden**	N	N	N	N	Y	N	N
3 Blumenauer	N	N	Y	N	N	N	Y
4 DeFazio	Y	N	Y	N	N	N	?
5 Schrader	N	N	N	N	N	N	Y
PENNSYLVANIA							
1 Brady	N	N	Y	N	N	N	Y
2 Fattah	N	N	Y	N	N	N	Y
3 **Kelly**	Y	Y	N	Y	N	N	N
4 Altmire	Y	N	N	N	N	N	N
5 **Thompson**	N	Y	N	N	N	N	N
6 **Gerlach**	N	Y	N	N	N	N	Y
7 **Meehan**	Y	N	N	N	N	N	N
8 **Fitzpatrick**	Y	Y	Y	N	N	N	Y
9 **Shuster**	N	N	N	N	N	N	N
10 **Marino**	N	Y	N	N	N	N	N
11 **Barletta**	Y	Y	N	N	N	N	N
12 Critz	Y	N	N	N	N	N	Y
13 Schwartz	N	N	Y	N	N	N	Y
14 Doyle	?	?	?	?	?	?	?
15 **Dent**	N	N	N	Y	N	N	Y
16 **Pitts**	Y	Y	N	N	Y	N	N
17 Holden	Y	N	N	N	N	N	N
18 **Murphy**	N	N	N	N	N	N	N
19 **Platts**	Y	Y	Y	N	N	N	Y
RHODE ISLAND							
1 Cicilline	Y	N	Y	N	N	N	Y
2 Langevin	Y	N	Y	N	N	N	Y
SOUTH CAROLINA							
1 **Scott**	Y	Y	N	Y	Y	Y	N
2 **Wilson**	Y	Y	N	Y	Y	Y	N
3 **Duncan**	Y	Y	N	Y	Y	Y	N
4 **Gowdy**	Y	Y	N	Y	Y	Y	N
5 **Mulvaney**	Y	Y	N	Y	Y	Y	N
6 Clyburn	?	?	?	?	?	?	?
SOUTH DAKOTA							
AL **Noem**	N	Y	N	Y	N	N	N
TENNESSEE							
1 **Roe**	Y	Y	N	Y	Y	Y	N
2 **Duncan**	Y	Y	N	Y	Y	Y	N
3 **Fleischmann**	N	Y	N	N	N	N	N
4 **DesJarlais**	N	Y	N	Y	Y	Y	N
5 Cooper	N	N	Y	N	N	N	Y
6 **Black**	N	Y	N	Y	Y	N	N
7 **Blackburn**	N	Y	N	Y	Y	Y	N
8 **Fincher**	N	Y	N	Y	Y	Y	N
9 Cohen	Y	N	Y	N	N	N	Y

	306	307	308	309	310	311	312
TEXAS							
1 **Gohmert**	Y	Y	N	Y	Y	Y	N
2 **Poe**	N	Y	N	Y	Y	Y	N
3 **Johnson, S.**	Y	Y	N	?	?	?	?
4 **Hall**	Y	Y	N	Y	Y	N	N
5 **Hensarling**	Y	Y	N	Y	Y	Y	N
6 **Barton**	Y	Y	N	N	Y	N	N
7 **Culberson**	Y	Y	N	N	N	Y	N
8 **Brady**	Y	Y	N	Y	Y	Y	N
9 Green, A.	Y	N	Y	N	N	N	Y
10 **McCaul**	Y	Y	N	?	Y	N	N
11 **Conaway**	Y	Y	N	Y	Y	Y	N
12 **Granger**	N	Y	N	N	N	N	N
13 **Thornberry**	Y	Y	N	Y	Y	Y	N
14 **Paul**	?	?	?	?	?	?	?
15 Hinojosa	Y	Y	Y	N	N	N	Y
16 Reyes	Y	N	Y	N	N	N	Y
17 **Flores**	N	Y	N	Y	Y	Y	N
18 Jackson Lee	Y	N	Y	N	N	N	Y
19 **Neugebauer**	N	Y	N	Y	Y	Y	N
20 Gonzalez	Y	N	Y	N	N	N	Y
21 **Smith**	Y	Y	N	Y	Y	N	N
22 **Olson**	Y	Y	N	Y	Y	Y	N
23 **Canseco**	Y	Y	N	Y	Y	N	N
24 **Marchant**	Y	Y	N	Y	Y	Y	N
25 Doggett	N	N	Y	N	N	N	Y
26 **Burgess**	Y	Y	N	Y	Y	Y	?
27 **Farenthold**	Y	Y	N	Y	Y	Y	N
28 Cuellar	Y	N	N	N	N	N	Y
29 Green, G.	N	N	Y	N	N	N	Y
30 Johnson, E.	Y	N	Y	N	N	N	Y
31 **Carter**	N	Y	N	N	N	N	?
32 **Sessions**	Y	Y	N	Y	Y	Y	N
UTAH							
1 **Bishop**	Y	Y	N	N	Y	Y	N
2 Matheson	N	N	N	Y	Y	N	N
3 **Chaffetz**	Y	Y	N	N	Y	Y	?
VERMONT							
AL Welch	Y	N	Y	N	N	N	Y
VIRGINIA							
1 **Wittman**	Y	Y	Y	Y	N	N	N
2 **Rigell**	Y	Y	N	Y	Y	N	N
3 Scott	Y	N	Y	N	N	N	Y
4 **Forbes**	Y	Y	N	Y	Y	N	N
5 **Hurt**	Y	Y	N	Y	Y	Y	N
6 **Goodlatte**	Y	Y	N	Y	Y	Y	Y
7 **Cantor**	Y	Y	N	Y	Y	Y	N
8 Moran	N	N	Y	N	N	N	N
9 **Griffith**	Y	Y	N	Y	N	N	Y
10 **Wolf**	N	Y	N	N	Y	N	N
11 Connolly	N	N	Y	N	N	N	N
WASHINGTON							
1 Vacant							
2 Larsen	N	N	Y	N	N	N	Y
3 **Herrera Beutler**	Y	Y	N	N	N	N	N
4 **Hastings**	N	Y	N	N	N	N	N
5 **McMorris Rodgers**	Y	Y	N	N	Y	Y	N
6 Dicks	N	N	Y	N	N	N	Y
7 McDermott	N	N	Y	N	N	N	Y
8 **Reichert**	N	Y	N	N	N	N	Y
9 Smith	Y	N	Y	N	N	N	Y
WEST VIRGINIA							
1 **McKinley**	N	N	N	Y	N	N	N
2 **Capito**	N	Y	N	N	N	N	N
3 Rahall	Y	Y	N	N	N	N	Y
WISCONSIN							
1 **Ryan**	N	Y	N	Y	Y	Y	N
2 Baldwin	N	N	Y	N	N	N	Y
3 Kind	?	?	?	?	?	?	?
4 Moore	?	?	?	?	?	?	?
5 **Sensenbrenner**	Y	N	N	Y	Y	Y	Y
6 **Petri**	Y	Y	N	Y	Y	Y	N
7 **Duffy**	N	Y	N	Y	Y	Y	N
8 **Ribble**	N	Y	N	Y	Y	Y	N
WYOMING							
AL **Lummis**	Y	Y	N	Y	Y	Y	N

IN THE HOUSE | By Vote Number

313. HR 5325. Fiscal 2013 Energy-Water Appropriations/Atomic Energy Defense Weapons Activities. Tonko, D-N.Y., amendment that would decrease by $180 million the amount provided for Energy Department atomic energy defense weapons activities and increase by the same amount funding for energy efficiency and renewable-energy activities. Rejected in Committee of the Whole 148-236: R 7-210; D 141-26. June 1, 2012.

314. HR 5325. Fiscal 2013 Energy-Water Appropriations/Energy Efficiency Funding. Hahn, D-Calif., amendment that would reduce by $100 million the amount provided for Energy Department fossil energy research and development activities and increase by $50 million funding for energy efficiency and renewable-energy activities. Rejected in Committee of the Whole 139-245: R 6-210; D 133-35. June 1, 2012.

315. HR 5325. Fiscal 2013 Energy-Water Appropriations/Nuclear-Energy Programs. McClintock, R-Calif., amendment that would reduce by $514 million the amount provided in the bill for nuclear energy activities and direct the same amount to the bill's spending reduction account. Rejected in Committee of the Whole 106-281: R 91-134; D 15-147. June 5, 2012.

316. HR 5325. Fiscal 2013 Energy-Water Appropriations/Energy Research Projects. Hirono, D-Hawaii, amendment that would reduce the amount in the bill provided for fossil energy research and development activities by $133.4 million and increase funding for Advanced Research Projects Agency-Energy projects by the same amount. Rejected in Committee of the Whole 131-257: R 5-221; D 126-36. June 5, 2012.

317. HR 5325. Fiscal 2013 Energy-Water Appropriations/Fossil Fuel Programs. McClintock, R-Calif., amendment that would eliminate the $554 million funding in the bill provided for fossil fuel programs, which includes an appropriation of $116 million that would remain available through fiscal 2014. The measure would direct an equivalent amount to the bill's spending reduction account. Rejected in Committee of the Whole 138-249: R 102-123; D 36-126. June 5, 2012.

318. HR 5325. Fiscal 2013 Energy-Water Appropriations/Environmental Cleanup. Matheson, D-Utah, amendment that would increase by $9.6 million the amount provided in the bill for non-defense environmental cleanup activities and reduce by the same amount funding for atomic energy defense weapons activities. Rejected in Committee of the Whole 152-235: R 6-219; D 146-16. June 5, 2012.

319. HR 5325. Fiscal 2013 Energy-Water Appropriations/U.S.-China Clean Energy Resource Center. Rohrabacher, R-Calif., amendment that would bar the use of funds in the bill for the U.S.-China Clean Energy Resource Center. Rejected in Committee of the Whole 181-229: R 161-73; D 20-156. June 6, 2012.

	313	314	315	316	317	318	319
ALABAMA							
1 Bonner	N	N	N	N	N	N	N
2 Roby	N	N	N	N	N	N	N
3 Rogers	N	N	N	N	N	N	N
4 Aderholt	N	N	N	N	N	N	N
5 Brooks	N	N	Y	N	Y	N	Y
6 Bachus	N	N	N	N	N	N	N
7 Sewell	Y	N	N	N	N	Y	N
ALASKA							
AL Young	N	N	N	N	N	N	N
ARIZONA							
1 Gosar	N	N	Y	N	Y	N	Y
2 Franks	N	N	Y	N	Y	N	Y
3 Quayle	N	N	Y	N	Y	N	Y
4 Pastor	N	Y	N	Y	N	Y	N
5 Schweikert	N	N	Y	N	Y	N	Y
6 Flake	N	N	Y	N	Y	N	Y
7 Grijalva	Y	Y	N	Y	N	Y	N
8 Vacant							
ARKANSAS							
1 Crawford	N	N	N	N	N	N	Y
2 Griffin	N	N	N	N	N	N	Y
3 Womack	N	N	N	N	N	N	N
4 Ross	N	N	N	N	N	Y	Y
CALIFORNIA							
1 Thompson	N	Y	N	Y	Y	Y	N
2 Herger	?	?	Y	N	Y	N	Y
3 Lungren	N	N	N	N	N	N	Y
4 McClintock	N	N	Y	N	Y	N	Y
5 Matsui	Y	Y	N	Y	N	Y	N
6 Woolsey	Y	Y	N	Y	Y	Y	N
7 Miller, George	Y	Y	N	Y	Y	Y	N
8 Pelosi	Y	Y	N	Y	N	Y	N
9 Lee	Y	Y	N	Y	N	Y	N
10 Garamendi	Y	Y	?	?	?	?	N
11 McNerney	Y	Y	N	Y	N	Y	N
12 Speier	Y	Y	N	Y	N	Y	N
13 Stark	Y	Y	N	Y	Y	Y	N
14 Eshoo	Y	Y	N	Y	N	Y	N
15 Honda	?	Y	N	Y	Y	Y	N
16 Lofgren	N	Y	N	Y	Y	Y	N
17 Farr	Y	Y	N	Y	N	Y	N
18 Cardoza	?	?	N	N	N	N	N
19 Denham	N	N	?	?	?	?	N
20 Costa	?	?	N	N	N	N	N
21 Nunes	N	N	N	N	Y	N	Y
22 McCarthy	?	?	N	N	N	N	Y
23 Capps	Y	Y	N	Y	Y	Y	N
24 Gallegly	?	?	N	N	N	N	N
25 McKeon	?	?	?	?	?	?	?
26 Dreier	N	N	N	N	N	N	N
27 Sherman	Y	Y	–	+	–	+	Y
28 Berman	N	Y	?	?	?	?	?
29 Schiff	N	Y	N	Y	N	Y	N
30 Waxman	Y	Y	N	Y	N	Y	N
31 Becerra	Y	Y	?	?	?	?	N
32 Chu	Y	Y	?	?	?	?	?
33 Bass	Y	Y	?	?	?	?	N
34 Roybal-Allard	Y	Y	N	Y	N	Y	N
35 Waters	?	?	?	?	?	?	N
36 Hahn	Y	Y	?	?	?	?	?
37 Richardson	Y	N	?	?	?	?	?
38 Napolitano	Y	Y	–	+	–	+	?
39 Sánchez, Linda	Y	Y	?	?	?	?	N
40 Royce	N	N	Y	N	Y	N	Y
41 Lewis	?	?	?	?	?	?	?
42 Miller, Gary	?	?	?	?	?	?	?
43 Baca	?	?	?	?	?	?	?
44 Calvert	?	?	N	N	N	N	N
45 Bono Mack	N	N	N	N	N	N	N
46 Rohrabacher	N	N	Y	N	Y	N	Y
47 Sanchez, Loretta	Y	Y	N	Y	N	Y	N
48 Campbell	N	N	Y	N	Y	N	Y
49 Issa	N	N	N	N	Y	N	Y
50 Bilbray	N	Y	N	N	N	N	Y
51 Filner	Y	Y	–	–	+	+	–
52 Hunter	N	N	?	?	?	?	Y
53 Davis	Y	Y	N	Y	N	Y	N

	313	314	315	316	317	318	319
COLORADO							
1 DeGette	Y	Y	N	Y	N	Y	N
2 Polis	Y	Y	N	Y	Y	Y	N
3 Tipton	N	N	Y	N	Y	N	N
4 Gardner	N	N	Y	N	Y	N	Y
5 Lamborn	N	N	Y	N	Y	N	Y
6 Coffman	N	N	N	Y	N	Y	N
7 Perlmutter	Y	Y	N	N	N	N	N
CONNECTICUT							
1 Larson	Y	N	–	–	–	+	N
2 Courtney	Y	N	N	N	N	Y	N
3 DeLauro	Y	N	N	N	N	Y	N
4 Himes	Y	Y	N	Y	N	Y	N
5 Murphy	Y	N	N	N	N	Y	N
DELAWARE							
AL Carney	Y	Y	N	Y	Y	Y	N
FLORIDA							
1 Miller	N	N	Y	N	Y	N	Y
2 Southerland	N	N	Y	N	Y	N	Y
3 Brown	Y	Y	N	N	N	Y	N
4 Crenshaw	N	N	Y	N	Y	N	N
5 Nugent	N	N	N	N	N	N	Y
6 Stearns	?	N	Y	N	Y	N	Y
7 Mica	N	N	N	N	N	N	N
8 Webster	N	N	N	N	N	N	N
9 Bilirakis	N	N	Y	N	Y	N	Y
10 Young	?	?	Y	N	N	N	Y
11 Castor	Y	Y	N	Y	N	Y	?
12 Ross	N	N	Y	N	Y	N	Y
13 Buchanan	N	N	Y	N	Y	N	Y
14 Mack	?	?	?	?	?	?	?
15 Posey	N	N	Y	N	Y	N	Y
16 Rooney	N	N	N	N	Y	N	Y
17 Wilson	Y	Y	N	Y	N	Y	N
18 Ros-Lehtinen	N	N	N	N	N	N	N
19 Deutch	Y	Y	N	Y	N	Y	N
20 Wasserman Schultz	Y	Y	N	Y	N	Y	N
21 Diaz-Balart	N	N	N	N	N	N	Y
22 West	N	N	N	Y	N	Y	N
23 Hastings	Y	Y	N	Y	N	Y	N
24 Adams	N	N	Y	N	Y	N	Y
25 Rivera	N	N	N	N	N	N	Y
GEORGIA							
1 Kingston	N	N	N	N	N	N	N
2 Bishop	Y	Y	N	N	N	Y	N
3 Westmoreland	N	N	Y	N	Y	N	Y
4 Johnson	Y	N	N	Y	N	Y	N
5 Lewis	Y	Y	N	Y	N	Y	N
6 Price	N	N	Y	N	Y	N	Y
7 Woodall	N	N	Y	N	Y	N	Y
8 Scott, A.	N	N	Y	N	N	N	Y
9 Graves	N	N	Y	N	N	N	Y
10 Broun	N	N	?	?	?	?	Y
11 Gingrey	N	N	N	N	Y	N	Y
12 Barrow	N	N	N	N	N	Y	Y
13 Scott, D.	?	?	N	Y	N	Y	N
HAWAII							
1 Hanabusa	Y	Y	N	Y	N	Y	N
2 Hirono	Y	Y	N	Y	N	Y	N
IDAHO							
1 Labrador	N	N	Y	N	Y	N	Y
2 Simpson	N	N	N	N	N	N	N
ILLINOIS							
1 Rush	Y	Y	Y	Y	Y	Y	N
2 Jackson	Y	Y	N	Y	N	Y	N
3 Lipinski	Y	N	N	Y	N	Y	N
4 Gutierrez	Y	Y	Y	Y	Y	Y	N
5 Quigley	Y	Y	N	Y	Y	Y	N
6 Roskam	N	N	N	N	N	N	N
7 Davis	Y	Y	N	Y	N	Y	N
8 Walsh	?	?	Y	N	Y	N	N
9 Schakowsky	Y	Y	Y	Y	Y	Y	N
10 Dold	N	N	N	N	N	N	N
11 Kinzinger	N	N	N	N	N	N	Y
12 Costello	Y	N	N	N	N	Y	N
13 Biggert	N	N	N	N	N	N	N
14 Hultgren	N	N	Y	N	Y	N	Y
15 Johnson	Y	Y	N	Y	Y	Y	N

KEY   **Republicans**   Democrats

Y	Voted for (yea)
#	Paired for
+	Announced for
N	Voted against (nay)

X	Paired against
–	Announced against
P	Voted "present"

C	Voted "present" to avoid possible conflict of interest
?	Did not vote or otherwise make a position known

	313	314	315	316	317	318	319
16 **Manzullo**	N	N	N	N	N	N	Y
17 **Schilling**	–	–	N	N	Y	N	Y
18 **Schock**	N	N	N	N	N	N	N
19 **Shimkus**	N	N	N	N	N	N	N
INDIANA							
1 Visclosky	N	N	N	N	N	Y	Y
2 Donnelly	N	N	?	?	?	?	Y
3 **Stutzman**	N	N	Y	N	Y	N	Y
4 **Rokita**	N	N	Y	N	Y	N	Y
5 **Burton**	–	–	Y	N	Y	N	Y
6 **Pence**	N	N	Y	N	Y	N	Y
7 Carson	Y	Y	Y	N	N	Y	N
8 **Bucshon**	N	N	N	N	N	N	Y
9 **Young**	N	N	N	N	N	N	Y
IOWA							
1 Braley	Y	Y	N	Y	N	Y	N
2 Loebsack	Y	Y	?	?	?	?	N
3 Boswell	Y	Y	N	Y	N	N	Y
4 **Latham**	N	N	N	N	N	N	Y
5 **King**	N	N	N	N	Y	N	Y
KANSAS							
1 **Huelskamp**	N	N	Y	N	Y	N	Y
2 **Jenkins**	N	N	Y	N	Y	N	Y
3 **Yoder**	N	N	Y	N	Y	N	Y
4 **Pompeo**	N	N	Y	N	Y	N	Y
KENTUCKY							
1 **Whitfield**	N	N	N	N	N	N	N
2 **Guthrie**	N	N	N	N	N	N	N
3 Yarmuth	Y	Y	N	Y	N	Y	N
4 **Davis**	N	N	N	N	N	N	N
5 **Rogers**	N	N	N	N	N	N	N
6 Chandler	N	N	N	N	N	Y	N
LOUISIANA							
1 **Scalise**	N	N	Y	N	Y	N	Y
2 Richmond	Y	N	N	Y	N	Y	N
3 **Landry**	N	N	Y	N	Y	N	Y
4 **Fleming**	N	N	Y	N	Y	N	Y
5 **Alexander**	?	?	N	N	N	N	N
6 **Cassidy**	N	N	N	N	N	N	Y
7 **Boustany**	N	N	Y	N	N	N	Y
MAINE							
1 Pingree	Y	Y	N	Y	Y	Y	N
2 Michaud	Y	Y	N	Y	N	Y	Y
MARYLAND							
1 **Harris**	N	N	Y	N	N	N	Y
2 Ruppersberger	Y	Y	N	Y	N	Y	N
3 Sarbanes	Y	Y	N	Y	N	Y	N
4 Edwards	Y	Y	N	Y	N	Y	N
5 Hoyer	Y	Y	N	Y	N	Y	N
6 **Bartlett**	N	N	N	N	N	N	N
7 Cummings	Y	Y	N	Y	N	Y	N
8 Van Hollen	Y	Y	N	Y	N	Y	N
MASSACHUSETTS							
1 Olver	Y	Y	?	?	?	?	N
2 Neal	?	?	N	Y	N	Y	N
3 McGovern	Y	Y	Y	Y	Y	Y	N
4 Frank	Y	Y	N	Y	N	Y	N
5 Tsongas	?	?	N	Y	Y	Y	N
6 Tierney	Y	Y	Y	Y	Y	Y	N
7 Markey	Y	Y	Y	Y	Y	Y	N
8 Capuano	Y	Y	N	Y	N	Y	N
9 Lynch	Y	Y	N	Y	N	N	N
10 Keating	Y	Y	N	Y	Y	Y	N
MICHIGAN							
1 **Benishek**	N	N	Y	N	Y	N	Y
2 **Huizenga**	?	?	Y	N	Y	N	Y
3 **Amash**	N	Y	Y	N	Y	Y	Y
4 **Camp**	N	N	N	N	N	N	N
5 Kildee	Y	Y	N	Y	N	Y	N
6 **Upton**	N	N	N	N	N	N	Y
7 **Walberg**	N	N	N	N	N	N	Y
8 **Rogers**	N	N	N	N	N	N	Y
9 Peters	Y	Y	N	Y	Y	Y	N
10 **Miller**	N	N	Y	N	Y	N	Y
11 **McCotter**	N	N	?	?	?	?	Y
12 Levin	Y	Y	N	Y	N	Y	N
13 Clarke	Y	Y	N	Y	N	Y	N
14 Conyers	Y	Y	Y	Y	Y	Y	N
15 Dingell	Y	Y	N	Y	N	Y	N
MINNESOTA							
1 Walz	?	?	N	N	N	Y	N
2 **Kline**	N	N	N	N	N	N	Y
3 **Paulsen**	N	N	N	N	N	N	Y
4 McCollum	?	?	N	Y	N	Y	N
5 Ellison	?	?	N	Y	N	Y	N
6 **Bachmann**	N	N	Y	N	Y	N	Y
7 Peterson	Y	N	N	N	N	N	Y
8 **Cravaack**	N	N	N	N	N	N	Y
MISSISSIPPI							
1 **Nunnelee**	N	N	N	N	N	N	N
2 Thompson	Y	N	N	Y	N	Y	N
3 **Harper**	N	N	N	N	N	N	N
4 **Palazzo**	N	N	N	N	N	N	Y
MISSOURI							
1 Clay	?	?	N	Y	Y	Y	N
2 **Akin**	N	N	N	N	Y	N	Y
3 Carnahan	Y	Y	N	Y	Y	Y	N
4 **Hartzler**	N	N	N	N	N	N	Y
5 Cleaver	Y	Y	–	+	–	+	N
6 **Graves**	N	N	N	N	N	N	N
7 **Long**	N	N	Y	N	Y	N	Y
8 **Emerson**	N	N	N	N	N	N	N
9 **Luetkemeyer**	N	N	N	N	N	N	Y
MONTANA							
AL **Rehberg**	N	N	N	N	N	N	N
NEBRASKA							
1 **Fortenberry**	?	?	N	N	N	N	Y
2 **Terry**	N	N	N	N	N	N	N
3 **Smith**	N	N	N	N	Y	N	Y
NEVADA							
1 Berkley	N	Y	Y	Y	Y	N	N
2 **Amodei**	N	N	Y	N	Y	N	Y
3 **Heck**	N	N	Y	N	Y	N	Y
NEW HAMPSHIRE							
1 **Guinta**	–	–	N	N	N	N	N
2 **Bass**	Y	Y	N	Y	N	N	N
NEW JERSEY							
1 Andrews	N	Y	N	Y	Y	N	N
2 **LoBiondo**	N	N	N	N	N	N	Y
3 **Runyan**	N	N	N	N	N	N	N
4 **Smith**	N	N	Y	N	N	N	Y
5 **Garrett**	N	N	Y	N	Y	N	Y
6 Pallone	Y	Y	N	Y	N	Y	N
7 **Lance**	N	N	Y	N	Y	N	Y
8 Pascrell	?	?	?	?	?	?	?
9 Rothman	?	?	?	?	?	?	?
10 Vacant							
11 **Frelinghuysen**	N	N	N	N	N	N	N
12 Holt	Y	Y	N	Y	N	Y	N
13 Sires	Y	Y	?	?	?	?	N
NEW MEXICO							
1 Heinrich	–	+	+	+	–	+	N
2 **Pearce**	N	N	N	N	N	N	Y
3 Luján	N	Y	N	Y	N	N	N
NEW YORK							
1 Bishop	Y	Y	N	Y	N	Y	N
2 Israel	Y	Y	N	Y	N	Y	N
3 **King**	N	N	N	N	N	N	N
4 McCarthy	Y	N	N	Y	N	Y	N
5 Ackerman	?	?	N	Y	N	Y	N
6 Meeks	Y	Y	N	Y	N	Y	Y
7 Crowley	Y	Y	N	Y	N	Y	N
8 Nadler	Y	Y	Y	Y	Y	Y	N
9 **Turner**	Y	N	N	N	N	N	N
10 Towns	Y	N	N	Y	N	Y	N
11 Clarke	Y	Y	N	Y	N	Y	N
12 Velázquez	+	+	Y	Y	Y	Y	N
13 **Grimm**	N	N	N	N	N	N	N
14 Maloney	Y	Y	–	+	–	+	N
15 Rangel	Y	Y	N	Y	N	Y	N
16 Serrano	Y	Y	Y	Y	Y	Y	N
17 Engel	Y	N	N	Y	N	Y	?
18 Lowey	Y	Y	N	Y	N	Y	N
19 **Hayworth**	N	N	N	N	N	N	N
20 **Gibson**	Y	Y	N	Y	N	Y	N
21 Tonko	Y	Y	N	Y	N	Y	N
22 Hinchey	Y	Y	N	Y	N	Y	N
23 Owens	N	N	N	Y	N	N	N
24 **Hanna**	Y	N	?	?	?	?	?
25 **Buerkle**	N	N	?	?	?	?	Y
26 Hochul	Y	Y	N	Y	N	Y	N
27 Higgins	Y	Y	N	Y	N	Y	N
28 Slaughter	+	–	–	–	–	–	–
29 **Reed**	N	N	N	N	N	N	Y
NORTH CAROLINA							
1 Butterfield	Y	Y	N	Y	N	Y	N
2 **Ellmers**	N	N	Y	N	Y	N	Y
3 **Jones**	Y	Y	Y	Y	Y	Y	Y
4 Price	Y	Y	N	Y	N	Y	N
5 **Foxx**	N	N	Y	N	Y	N	Y
6 **Coble**	?	?	Y	N	Y	N	?
7 McIntyre	N	N	–	–	–	+	Y
8 Kissell	N	Y	N	N	N	Y	Y
9 **Myrick**	N	N	–	–	–	–	Y
10 **McHenry**	N	N	Y	N	Y	N	Y
11 Shuler	?	?	?	?	?	?	?
12 Watt	Y	Y	?	?	?	?	N
13 Miller	Y	Y	N	Y	N	Y	N
NORTH DAKOTA							
AL **Berg**	N	N	N	N	N	N	N
OHIO							
1 **Chabot**	N	N	Y	N	Y	N	Y
2 **Schmidt**	N	N	N	N	N	N	Y
3 **Turner**	N	N	N	N	N	N	N
4 **Jordan**	N	N	Y	N	Y	N	Y
5 **Latta**	N	N	N	N	N	N	Y
6 **Johnson**	N	N	N	N	N	N	Y
7 **Austria**	N	N	N	N	N	N	N
8 **Boehner**							
9 Kaptur	Y	Y	N	N	N	Y	N
10 Kucinich	Y	Y	Y	Y	Y	Y	Y
11 Fudge	Y	N	N	Y	N	Y	N
12 **Tiberi**	N	N	N	N	Y	N	N
13 Sutton	Y	N	N	N	N	Y	Y
14 **LaTourette**	?	?	N	N	N	N	N
15 **Stivers**	N	N	N	N	N	N	N
16 **Renacci**	N	N	N	N	N	N	N
17 Ryan	Y	N	N	N	N	Y	N
18 **Gibbs**	N	N	N	N	N	N	Y
OKLAHOMA							
1 **Sullivan**	N	N	Y	N	Y	N	Y
2 Boren	N	N	N	N	N	Y	Y
3 **Lucas**	N	N	N	N	N	N	N
4 **Cole**	N	N	N	N	N	N	N
5 **Lankford**	N	N	N	N	N	N	N
OREGON							
1 Bonamici	Y	Y	N	Y	N	Y	N
2 **Walden**	N	N	Y	N	Y	N	N
3 Blumenauer	Y	Y	N	Y	Y	Y	N
4 DeFazio	Y	Y	N	Y	Y	Y	Y
5 Schrader	Y	Y	N	Y	N	Y	N
PENNSYLVANIA							
1 Brady	Y	Y	N	Y	N	Y	N
2 Fattah	Y	Y	N	Y	N	N	N
3 **Kelly**	N	N	N	N	N	N	N
4 Altmire	N	N	N	N	N	Y	N
5 **Thompson**	N	N	N	N	N	N	N
6 **Gerlach**	N	N	N	N	N	N	Y
7 **Meehan**	N	N	N	N	N	N	Y
8 **Fitzpatrick**	Y	N	N	N	N	N	Y
9 **Shuster**	N	N	?	N	N	?	N
10 **Marino**	N	N	?	?	?	?	N
11 **Barletta**	N	N	N	N	N	N	N
12 Critz	N	N	N	N	N	Y	N
13 Schwartz	Y	Y	N	Y	N	Y	N
14 Doyle	?	?	N	N	N	Y	N
15 **Dent**	N	N	N	Y	N	N	Y
16 **Pitts**	N	N	N	N	N	N	Y
17 Holden	Y	N	N	N	N	Y	N
18 **Murphy**	N	N	N	N	N	N	Y
19 **Platts**	N	N	N	N	N	N	?
RHODE ISLAND							
1 Cicilline	Y	Y	N	Y	N	Y	N
2 Langevin	Y	Y	N	Y	N	Y	N
SOUTH CAROLINA							
1 **Scott**	N	N	N	N	Y	N	Y
2 **Wilson**	N	N	N	N	Y	N	Y
3 **Duncan**	N	N	N	N	Y	N	Y
4 **Gowdy**	N	N	N	N	Y	N	Y
5 **Mulvaney**	N	N	Y	N	Y	N	Y
6 Clyburn	?	?	N	Y	N	Y	N
SOUTH DAKOTA							
AL **Noem**	N	N	N	N	N	N	Y
TENNESSEE							
1 **Roe**	N	N	N	N	N	N	Y
2 **Duncan**	N	?	Y	N	Y	N	Y
3 **Fleischmann**	N	N	N	N	N	N	N
4 **DesJarlais**	N	N	N	N	N	N	Y
5 Cooper	Y	Y	N	Y	N	N	N
6 **Black**	N	N	Y	N	Y	N	Y
7 **Blackburn**	N	N	Y	N	Y	N	Y
8 **Fincher**	N	N	N	N	Y	N	Y
9 Cohen	Y	Y	Y	Y	Y	Y	N
TEXAS							
1 **Gohmert**	N	N	Y	N	Y	N	Y
2 **Poe**	N	N	Y	N	Y	N	Y
3 **Johnson, S.**	?	?	N	N	N	N	Y
4 **Hall**	N	N	?	?	?	?	N
5 **Hensarling**	N	N	Y	N	Y	N	Y
6 **Barton**	N	N	N	N	N	N	Y
7 **Culberson**	N	N	Y	N	Y	N	Y
8 **Brady**	N	N	Y	N	Y	N	Y
9 Green, A.	Y	N	N	N	N	Y	N
10 **McCaul**	N	N	N	N	N	N	Y
11 **Conaway**	N	N	Y	N	Y	N	Y
12 **Granger**	N	?	?	?	?	?	N
13 **Thornberry**	N	N	N	N	N	N	Y
14 **Paul**	?	?	?	?	?	?	?
15 Hinojosa	Y	Y	N	N	N	Y	N
16 Reyes	N	Y	N	Y	N	Y	N
17 **Flores**	N	N	N	N	Y	N	Y
18 Jackson Lee	Y	N	N	N	N	Y	N
19 **Neugebauer**	N	N	Y	N	Y	N	Y
20 Gonzalez	N	N	N	N	N	Y	N
21 **Smith**	N	N	N	N	N	N	Y
22 **Olson**	N	N	N	N	N	N	Y
23 **Canseco**	N	N	Y	N	Y	N	Y
24 **Marchant**	N	N	Y	N	N	Y	Y
25 Doggett	Y	Y	Y	Y	Y	N	N
26 **Burgess**	?	?	Y	N	Y	N	Y
27 **Farenthold**	N	N	Y	N	Y	N	Y
28 Cuellar	N	N	N	N	N	Y	Y
29 Green, G.	Y	N	N	N	N	N	N
30 Johnson, E.	Y	Y	N	Y	N	Y	N
31 **Carter**	?	?	N	N	N	N	Y
32 **Sessions**	N	N	Y	N	N	N	Y
UTAH							
1 **Bishop**	N	N	Y	N	Y	N	N
2 Matheson	N	N	N	N	N	Y	Y
3 **Chaffetz**	?	?	Y	N	Y	Y	Y
VERMONT							
AL Welch	Y	Y	N	Y	N	Y	N
VIRGINIA							
1 **Wittman**	N	N	N	N	N	N	Y
2 **Rigell**	N	N	Y	N	Y	N	Y
3 Scott	Y	Y	N	Y	N	Y	N
4 **Forbes**	N	N	N	N	N	N	Y
5 **Hurt**	N	N	N	N	N	N	Y
6 **Goodlatte**	N	N	N	N	N	N	N
7 **Cantor**	N	N	N	N	N	N	Y
8 Moran	Y	Y	N	Y	N	Y	N
9 **Griffith**	N	N	N	N	N	N	N
10 **Wolf**	N	N	N	N	N	N	Y
11 Connolly	Y	Y	N	Y	N	Y	N
WASHINGTON							
1 Vacant							
2 Larsen	N	N	N	N	N	N	N
3 **Herrera Beutler**	N	N	Y	N	Y	N	Y
4 **Hastings**	N	N	N	N	N	N	Y
5 **McMorris Rodgers**	N	N	N	N	N	Y	Y
6 Dicks	N	Y	N	N	N	Y	N
7 McDermott	Y	Y	N	Y	Y	Y	N
8 **Reichert**	N	N	N	N	N	N	N
9 Smith	N	Y	N	Y	N	Y	N
WEST VIRGINIA							
1 **McKinley**	N	N	N	N	N	N	N
2 **Capito**	N	N	N	N	N	N	N
3 Rahall	Y	N	N	N	N	N	N
WISCONSIN							
1 **Ryan**	N	N	Y	N	Y	N	Y
2 Baldwin	Y	Y	N	Y	Y	Y	N
3 Kind	?	?	N	Y	N	Y	N
4 Moore	?	?	?	?	?	?	?
5 **Sensenbrenner**	N	N	Y	N	Y	N	Y
6 **Petri**	N	N	Y	N	Y	N	Y
7 **Duffy**	N	N	Y	N	+	N	Y
8 **Ribble**	N	N	Y	N	Y	N	Y
WYOMING							
AL **Lummis**	N	N	Y	N	Y	N	N

IN THE HOUSE | By Vote Number

320. HR 5325. Fiscal 2013 Energy-Water Appropriations/Loan Guarantees. Stearns, R-Fla., amendment that would bar the use of funds in the bill to subordinate any loan obligation, guaranteed obligation or other financing provided under the demonstration project title of the Energy Policy Act of 2005 and accompanying regulations. Adopted in Committee of the Whole 348-60: R 234-0; D 114-60. June 6, 2012.

321. HR 5325. Fiscal 2013 Energy-Water Appropriations/Nuclear Regulatory Commission Funding. Shimkus, R-Ill., amendment that would increase by $10 million the amount provided in the bill for salaries and expenses of the Nuclear Regulatory Commission and reduce by the same amount funding for Energy Department salaries and expenses. Adopted in Committee of the Whole 326-81: R 228-5; D 98-76. June 6, 2012.

322. HR 5325. Fiscal 2013 Energy-Water Appropriations/Paid Surveys. Tipton, R-Colo., amendment that would bar the use of funds in the bill to pay for any survey in which money is included for the benefit of the respondent. Adopted in Committee of the Whole 355-51: R 232-0; D 123-51. June 6, 2012.

323. HR 5325. Fiscal 2013 Energy-Water Appropriations/Missouri River Projects Study. Luetkemeyer, R-Mo., amendment that would bar the use of funds in the bill for a study of the Missouri River, pursuant to the Water Resources Development Act of 2007. Adopted in Committee of the Whole 242-168: R 225-7; D 17-161. June 6, 2012.

324. HR 5325. Fiscal 2013 Energy-Water Appropriations/Army Corps of Engineers Construction Projects. Jackson Lee, D-Texas, amendment that would increase by $10 million the amount provided for Army Corps of Engineers construction projects and reduce by the same amount funding for atomic energy defense weapons activities. Rejected in Committee of the Whole 150-260: R 7-226; D 143-34. June 6, 2012.

325. HR 5325. Fiscal 2013 Energy-Water Appropriations/Global Threat Reduction Initiative. Fortenberry, R-Neb., amendment that would shift $17 million within the Defense Nuclear Nonproliferation account, with the aim of increasing funding for the Global Threat Reduction Initiative. Adopted in Committee of the Whole 328-89: R 192-44; D 136-45. June 6, 2012.

326. HR 5325. Fiscal 2013 Energy-Water Appropriations/Energy Efficiency and Renewable-Energy Research. Jackson Lee, D-Texas, amendment that would increase by $10 million the amount provided for energy efficiency and renewable-energy research construction projects and reduce by the same amount funding for atomic energy defense weapons activities. Rejected in Committee of the Whole 157-260: R 4-231; D 153-29. June 6, 2012.

	320	321	322	323	324	325	326
ALABAMA							
1 Bonner	Y	Y	Y	Y	N	Y	N
2 Roby	Y	Y	Y	Y	N	Y	N
3 Rogers	Y	Y	Y	Y	N	Y	N
4 Aderholt	Y	Y	Y	Y	N	Y	N
5 Brooks	Y	Y	Y	Y	N	Y	N
6 Bachus	Y	Y	Y	Y	N	N	N
7 Sewell	Y	Y	Y	N	Y	Y	Y
ALASKA							
AL Young	Y	Y	Y	Y	N	Y	N
ARIZONA							
1 Gosar	Y	Y	Y	Y	N	N	N
2 Franks	Y	Y	Y	Y	N	Y	N
3 Quayle	Y	Y	Y	Y	N	Y	N
4 Pastor	Y	N	N	N	N	Y	N
5 Schweikert	Y	Y	Y	Y	N	Y	N
6 Flake	Y	Y	Y	Y	N	Y	N
7 Grijalva	N	N	N	N	Y	N	N
8 Vacant							
ARKANSAS							
1 Crawford	Y	Y	Y	Y	N	Y	N
2 Griffin	Y	Y	Y	Y	N	Y	N
3 Womack	Y	Y	Y	Y	N	Y	N
4 Ross	Y	Y	Y	Y	N	Y	N
CALIFORNIA							
1 Thompson	N	Y	Y	N	Y	Y	Y
2 Herger	Y	Y	Y	Y	N	Y	N
3 Lungren	Y	Y	Y	N	Y	Y	N
4 McClintock	Y	Y	Y	Y	N	Y	N
5 Matsui	Y	N	Y	N	Y	Y	Y
6 Woolsey	N	N	N	N	Y	Y	Y
7 Miller, George	Y	Y	N	N	Y	Y	Y
8 Pelosi	Y	N	N	N	Y	Y	Y
9 Lee	N	N	N	N	Y	Y	Y
10 Garamendi	N	N	N	N	Y	Y	Y
11 McNerney	Y	Y	Y	N	Y	Y	N
12 Speier	Y	Y	N	N	Y	Y	Y
13 Stark	N	N	N	N	N	Y	Y
14 Eshoo	Y	Y	Y	N	Y	Y	Y
15 Honda	N	N	N	N	Y	Y	Y
16 Lofgren	Y	N	N	N	Y	Y	N
17 Farr	Y	?	N	N	Y	Y	Y
18 Cardoza	Y	Y	N	N	N	Y	N
19 Denham	Y	Y	Y	N	Y	Y	N
20 Costa	Y	Y	N	N	N	Y	N
21 Nunes	Y	Y	Y	Y	N	Y	N
22 McCarthy	Y	Y	Y	Y	N	Y	N
23 Capps	Y	N	Y	N	Y	Y	Y
24 Gallegly	Y	Y	Y	Y	N	Y	N
25 McKeon	?	?	?	?	?	?	?
26 Dreier	Y	Y	Y	Y	N	Y	N
27 Sherman	Y	Y	Y	N	Y	Y	Y
28 Berman	?	?	?	?	?	?	?
29 Schiff	Y	Y	Y	N	Y	Y	Y
30 Waxman	Y	N	N	N	Y	Y	Y
31 Becerra	Y	N	N	N	Y	Y	Y
32 Chu	?	?	?	?	?	N	Y
33 Bass	N	N	N	N	Y	Y	Y
34 Roybal-Allard	Y	N	N	N	Y	Y	Y
35 Waters	Y	N	?	N	Y	Y	Y
36 Hahn	?	?	?	?	?	?	?
37 Richardson	?	?	?	?	?	N	Y
38 Napolitano	?	?	?	?	?	?	?
39 Sánchez, Linda	Y	N	Y	N	N	Y	Y
40 Royce	Y	Y	Y	Y	N	Y	N
41 Lewis	?	?	?	?	?	?	?
42 Miller, Gary	?	?	?	?	?	?	?
43 Baca	?	?	?	?	?	?	?
44 Calvert	Y	Y	Y	Y	N	Y	N
45 Bono Mack	Y	Y	Y	Y	N	Y	N
46 Rohrabacher	Y	Y	Y	Y	N	Y	N
47 Sanchez, Loretta	Y	N	Y	N	Y	Y	Y
48 Campbell	Y	Y	Y	Y	N	Y	N
49 Issa	Y	Y	Y	Y	N	Y	N
50 Bilbray	Y	Y	Y	Y	Y	Y	Y
51 Filner	–	–	+	+	+	+	+
52 Hunter	Y	Y	Y	Y	N	N	N
53 Davis	Y	N	Y	N	Y	Y	Y
COLORADO							
1 DeGette	N	Y	Y	N	Y	Y	Y
2 Polis	Y	N	N	Y	Y	Y	Y
3 Tipton	Y	Y	Y	Y	N	Y	N
4 Gardner	Y	Y	Y	Y	N	Y	N
5 Lamborn	Y	Y	Y	Y	N	N	N
6 Coffman	Y	Y	Y	Y	N	Y	N
7 Perlmutter	N	N	Y	N	Y	N	Y
CONNECTICUT							
1 Larson	N	N	Y	N	Y	N	Y
2 Courtney	N	Y	Y	Y	Y	Y	Y
3 DeLauro	N	N	Y	Y	Y	Y	Y
4 Himes	N	Y	Y	Y	Y	Y	Y
5 Murphy	Y	Y	Y	N	Y	N	Y
DELAWARE							
AL Carney	Y	Y	Y	N	Y	Y	Y
FLORIDA							
1 Miller	Y	Y	Y	Y	N	Y	N
2 Southerland	Y	Y	Y	Y	N	Y	N
3 Brown	Y	N	Y	N	Y	Y	Y
4 Crenshaw	Y	Y	Y	Y	N	Y	N
5 Nugent	Y	Y	Y	Y	N	Y	N
6 Stearns	Y	Y	Y	Y	N	Y	N
7 Mica	Y	Y	Y	Y	N	Y	N
8 Webster	Y	Y	Y	Y	N	Y	N
9 Bilirakis	Y	Y	Y	Y	N	Y	N
10 Young	Y	Y	Y	N	N	Y	N
11 Castor	?	?	?	?	?	Y	Y
12 Ross	Y	Y	Y	Y	N	Y	N
13 Buchanan	Y	Y	Y	Y	N	Y	N
14 Mack	Y	Y	Y	Y	N	Y	N
15 Posey	Y	Y	Y	Y	N	Y	N
16 Rooney	Y	Y	Y	Y	N	Y	N
17 Wilson	N	Y	Y	N	Y	Y	Y
18 Ros-Lehtinen	Y	Y	Y	Y	N	Y	N
19 Deutch	N	Y	Y	N	Y	Y	Y
20 Wasserman Schultz	N	N	Y	N	Y	Y	Y
21 Diaz-Balart	Y	Y	Y	Y	N	Y	N
22 West	Y	Y	Y	Y	N	Y	N
23 Hastings	N	N	Y	N	Y	Y	Y
24 Adams	Y	Y	Y	Y	N	Y	N
25 Rivera	Y	Y	Y	Y	N	Y	N
GEORGIA							
1 Kingston	Y	Y	Y	Y	N	N	N
2 Bishop	Y	Y	Y	Y	N	Y	N
3 Westmoreland	Y	Y	Y	Y	N	Y	N
4 Johnson	?	?	Y	Y	Y	Y	Y
5 Lewis	N	N	Y	N	Y	Y	Y
6 Price	Y	Y	Y	Y	N	Y	N
7 Woodall	Y	Y	Y	Y	N	Y	N
8 Scott, A.	Y	Y	Y	Y	N	N	N
9 Graves	Y	Y	Y	Y	N	Y	N
10 Broun	Y	Y	Y	Y	N	Y	N
11 Gingrey	Y	Y	Y	Y	N	Y	N
12 Barrow	Y	Y	Y	N	N	N	N
13 Scott, D.	N	Y	Y	N	Y	N	Y
HAWAII							
1 Hanabusa	Y	Y	Y	N	Y	Y	Y
2 Hirono	Y	N	Y	N	Y	Y	Y
IDAHO							
1 Labrador	Y	Y	Y	Y	N	Y	N
2 Simpson	Y	Y	Y	Y	N	N	N
ILLINOIS							
1 Rush	N	N	N	N	Y	Y	Y
2 Jackson	N	N	N	N	Y	N	Y
3 Lipinski	Y	Y	Y	Y	N	Y	Y
4 Gutierrez	N	N	N	N	?	?	Y
5 Quigley	Y	Y	N	N	Y	Y	Y
6 Roskam	Y	Y	Y	Y	N	Y	N
7 Davis	N	N	N	N	N	Y	Y
8 Walsh	Y	Y	Y	Y	N	Y	N
9 Schakowsky	Y	N	N	N	Y	Y	N
10 Dold	Y	Y	Y	N	Y	Y	N
11 Kinzinger	Y	Y	Y	Y	N	Y	N
12 Costello	Y	Y	Y	Y	N	Y	Y
13 Biggert	Y	Y	Y	Y	N	N	N
14 Hultgren	Y	Y	Y	Y	N	N	N
15 Johnson	Y	N	Y	Y	Y	Y	Y

KEY   Republicans   Democrats

Y Voted for (yea)	X Paired against
# Paired for	– Announced against
+ Announced for	P Voted "present"
N Voted against (nay)	

C Voted "present" to avoid possible conflict of interest

? Did not vote or otherwise make a position known

	320	321	322	323	324	325	326
16 **Manzullo**	Y	Y	Y	N	N	Y	N
17 **Schilling**	Y	Y	Y	Y	N	Y	N
18 **Schock**	Y	Y	Y	Y	N	N	N
19 **Shimkus**	Y	Y	Y	Y	N	Y	N
INDIANA							
1 Visclosky	Y	Y	Y	N	N	Y	Y
2 Donnelly	Y	Y	Y	Y	N	Y	N
3 **Stutzman**	Y	Y	Y	Y	N	Y	?
4 **Rokita**	Y	Y	Y	Y	N	Y	N
5 **Burton**	Y	Y	Y	Y	N	Y	N
6 **Pence**	Y	Y	Y	Y	N	Y	N
7 Carson	N	N	?	N	Y	Y	Y
8 **Bucshon**	Y	Y	Y	Y	N	Y	N
9 **Young**	Y	Y	Y	Y	N	Y	N
IOWA							
1 Braley	Y	Y	Y	Y	Y	+	Y
2 Loebsack	Y	Y	Y	Y	Y	Y	Y
3 Boswell	Y	Y	Y	Y	Y	Y	Y
4 **Latham**	Y	Y	Y	Y	Y	Y	Y
5 **King**	Y	Y	Y	Y	N	Y	N
KANSAS							
1 **Huelskamp**	Y	Y	Y	Y	N	Y	N
2 **Jenkins**	Y	Y	Y	Y	N	Y	N
3 **Yoder**	Y	Y	Y	Y	N	Y	N
4 **Pompeo**	Y	Y	Y	Y	N	Y	N
KENTUCKY							
1 **Whitfield**	Y	Y	Y	Y	N	N	N
2 **Guthrie**	Y	Y	Y	Y	N	Y	N
3 Yarmuth	Y	Y	Y	N	Y	Y	Y
4 **Davis**	Y	Y	Y	Y	N	Y	N
5 **Rogers**	Y	Y	Y	Y	N	Y	N
6 Chandler	Y	Y	Y	N	N	Y	N
LOUISIANA							
1 **Scalise**	Y	Y	Y	Y	N	Y	N
2 Richmond	N	N	N	N	Y	N	Y
3 **Landry**	Y	Y	Y	Y	N	Y	N
4 **Fleming**	Y	Y	Y	Y	N	N	N
5 **Alexander**	Y	Y	Y	Y	N	N	N
6 **Cassidy**	Y	Y	Y	Y	N	N	N
7 **Boustany**	Y	Y	Y	Y	N	N	N
MAINE							
1 Pingree	Y	N	Y	N	Y	Y	Y
2 Michaud	Y	Y	Y	Y	Y	Y	Y
MARYLAND							
1 **Harris**	Y	Y	Y	Y	N	Y	N
2 Ruppersberger	N	Y	Y	N	Y	N	N
3 Sarbanes	Y	Y	Y	N	Y	Y	Y
4 Edwards	N	N	N	N	Y	N	Y
5 Hoyer	Y	N	Y	N	Y	Y	Y
6 **Bartlett**	Y	Y	Y	Y	N	Y	N
7 Cummings	Y	N	N	N	Y	N	Y
8 Van Hollen	Y	Y	Y	N	Y	Y	Y
MASSACHUSETTS							
1 Olver	Y	N	N	N	Y	Y	Y
2 Neal	Y	Y	Y	N	Y	Y	Y
3 McGovern	Y	N	Y	N	Y	Y	Y
4 Frank	N	N	Y	N	Y	Y	Y
5 Tsongas	Y	N	Y	N	Y	Y	Y
6 Tierney	Y	Y	Y	N	Y	Y	Y
7 Markey	Y	N	Y	N	Y	Y	Y
8 Capuano	Y	N	Y	N	Y	Y	Y
9 Lynch	Y	Y	Y	N	Y	Y	N
10 Keating	Y	Y	Y	N	Y	Y	Y
MICHIGAN							
1 **Benishek**	Y	Y	Y	Y	N	Y	N
2 **Huizenga**	Y	Y	Y	Y	N	Y	N
3 **Amash**	Y	Y	Y	Y	N	Y	N
4 **Camp**	Y	Y	Y	Y	N	Y	N
5 Kildee	N	Y	Y	N	Y	Y	Y
6 **Upton**	Y	Y	Y	Y	N	Y	N
7 **Walberg**	Y	Y	Y	Y	N	Y	N
8 **Rogers**	Y	Y	Y	Y	N	Y	N
9 Peters	N	Y	Y	N	Y	N	Y
10 **Miller**	Y	Y	Y	Y	N	Y	N
11 **McCotter**	Y	N	Y	Y	N	Y	N
12 Levin	Y	N	Y	N	Y	Y	Y
13 Clarke	N	N	Y	N	Y	Y	Y
14 Conyers	N	N	N	N	Y	Y	Y
15 Dingell	N	Y	Y	N	Y	Y	Y
MINNESOTA							
1 Walz	N	Y	Y	N	Y	Y	Y
2 **Kline**	Y	Y	Y	Y	N	N	N
3 **Paulsen**	Y	Y	Y	Y	N	Y	N
4 McCollum	N	Y	N	N	Y	N	Y

	320	321	322	323	324	325	326
5 Ellison	N	N	N	N	Y	Y	Y
6 **Bachmann**	Y	Y	Y	Y	N	Y	N
7 Peterson	Y	Y	Y	Y	N	N	N
8 **Cravaack**	Y	Y	Y	Y	N	Y	N
MISSISSIPPI							
1 **Nunnelee**	Y	Y	Y	Y	N	Y	N
2 Thompson	N	N	N	N	Y	N	Y
3 **Harper**	Y	Y	Y	Y	N	Y	N
4 **Palazzo**	Y	Y	Y	Y	N	Y	N
MISSOURI							
1 Clay	N	Y	N	N	Y	N	Y
2 **Akin**	Y	Y	Y	Y	N	Y	N
3 Carnahan	N	N	N	N	Y	Y	Y
4 **Hartzler**	Y	Y	Y	Y	N	Y	N
5 Cleaver	N	Y	?	N	Y	N	Y
6 **Graves**	Y	Y	Y	Y	N	Y	N
7 **Long**	Y	Y	Y	Y	N	N	N
8 **Emerson**	Y	Y	Y	Y	N	Y	N
9 **Luetkemeyer**	Y	Y	Y	Y	N	Y	N
MONTANA							
AL **Rehberg**	Y	Y	Y	N	N	N	N
NEBRASKA							
1 **Fortenberry**	Y	Y	Y	N	N	Y	N
2 **Terry**	Y	Y	Y	Y	N	Y	N
3 **Smith**	Y	Y	Y	Y	N	Y	N
NEVADA							
1 Berkley	N	N	Y	N	N	Y	Y
2 **Amodei**	Y	N	Y	Y	N	Y	N
3 **Heck**	Y	N	Y	Y	N	N	N
NEW HAMPSHIRE							
1 **Guinta**	Y	Y	Y	Y	N	N	N
2 **Bass**	Y	Y	Y	N	N	N	N
NEW JERSEY							
1 Andrews	N	Y	Y	N	N	Y	N
2 **LoBiondo**	Y	Y	Y	Y	N	Y	N
3 **Runyan**	Y	Y	Y	Y	N	N	N
4 **Smith**	Y	?	Y	Y	N	Y	N
5 **Garrett**	Y	Y	Y	Y	N	Y	N
6 Pallone	Y	N	Y	N	Y	Y	Y
7 **Lance**	Y	Y	Y	Y	N	Y	N
8 Pascrell	?	?	Y	N	Y	Y	Y
9 Rothman	?	?	?	?	?	?	?
10 Vacant							
11 **Frelinghuysen**	Y	Y	Y	Y	N	Y	N
12 Holt	Y	N	N	N	Y	Y	Y
13 Sires	N	Y	N	N	Y	N	Y
NEW MEXICO							
1 Heinrich	Y	Y	Y	N	N	Y	N
2 **Pearce**	Y	Y	Y	Y	N	Y	N
3 Luján	Y	N	Y	N	N	N	N
NEW YORK							
1 Bishop	Y	Y	Y	N	Y	N	Y
2 Israel	Y	N	Y	N	Y	N	Y
3 **King**	Y	Y	Y	Y	N	Y	N
4 McCarthy	Y	Y	Y	N	Y	Y	N
5 Ackerman	Y	N	N	N	Y	N	Y
6 Meeks	N	Y	N	N	N	N	Y
7 Crowley	Y	N	N	N	Y	N	Y
8 Nadler	Y	N	N	N	Y	Y	Y
9 **Turner**	Y	Y	Y	Y	N	Y	N
10 Towns	N	Y	N	N	N	N	Y
11 Clarke	N	N	N	N	Y	N	Y
12 Velázquez	N	N	N	N	Y	Y	Y
13 **Grimm**	Y	Y	Y	Y	N	Y	N
14 Maloney	Y	N	Y	N	N	Y	Y
15 Rangel	N	N	Y	N	Y	N	Y
16 Serrano	N	N	N	N	Y	N	Y
17 Engel	?	?	?	?	Y	N	Y
18 Lowey	Y	Y	Y	N	Y	Y	Y
19 **Hayworth**	Y	Y	Y	Y	N	N	N
20 **Gibson**	Y	Y	Y	Y	Y	Y	Y
21 Tonko	Y	Y	Y	N	Y	Y	Y
22 Hinchey	N	N	N	N	Y	N	Y
23 Owens	Y	Y	Y	Y	N	Y	N
24 **Hanna**	?	?	?	?	?	Y	N
25 **Buerkle**	Y	Y	Y	Y	N	Y	N
26 Hochul	Y	Y	Y	Y	Y	Y	Y
27 Higgins	Y	Y	Y	N	Y	Y	Y
28 Slaughter	+	+	–	–	–	+	–
29 **Reed**	Y	Y	Y	Y	N	Y	N
NORTH CAROLINA							
1 Butterfield	Y	Y	Y	N	Y	Y	Y
2 **Ellmers**	Y	Y	Y	Y	N	Y	N
3 **Jones**	Y	Y	Y	Y	Y	N	Y
4 Price	Y	Y	Y	N	Y	Y	Y

	320	321	322	323	324	325	326
5 **Foxx**	Y	Y	Y	Y	N	N	N
6 **Coble**	?	?	?	?	?	?	?
7 McIntyre	Y	Y	Y	Y	Y	Y	N
8 Kissell	Y	N	Y	N	N	N	N
9 **Myrick**	Y	Y	Y	Y	N	Y	N
10 **McHenry**	Y	Y	Y	Y	N	Y	N
11 Shuler	?	?	?	?	?	?	?
12 Watt	N	N	N	N	Y	N	Y
13 Miller	Y	Y	N	N	N	Y	N
NORTH DAKOTA							
AL **Berg**	Y	Y	Y	N	N	N	N
OHIO							
1 **Chabot**	Y	Y	Y	Y	N	Y	N
2 **Schmidt**	Y	Y	Y	Y	N	Y	N
3 **Turner**	Y	Y	Y	Y	N	N	N
4 **Jordan**	Y	Y	Y	Y	N	Y	N
5 **Latta**	Y	Y	Y	Y	N	Y	N
6 **Johnson**	Y	Y	Y	Y	N	Y	N
7 **Austria**	Y	Y	Y	Y	N	Y	N
8 **Boehner**							
9 Kaptur	Y	Y	Y	N	Y	Y	Y
10 Kucinich	Y	Y	N	N	Y	Y	Y
11 Fudge	N	N	N	N	Y	N	Y
12 **Tiberi**	Y	Y	Y	Y	N	Y	N
13 Sutton	Y	Y	Y	N	Y	Y	Y
14 **LaTourette**	Y	Y	Y	Y	N	Y	N
15 **Stivers**	Y	Y	Y	Y	N	Y	N
16 **Renacci**	Y	Y	Y	Y	N	Y	N
17 Ryan	N	Y	Y	N	Y	Y	Y
18 **Gibbs**	Y	Y	Y	Y	N	Y	N
OKLAHOMA							
1 **Sullivan**	Y	Y	?	Y	N	Y	N
2 Boren	Y	Y	Y	N	N	N	N
3 **Lucas**	Y	Y	Y	Y	N	N	N
4 **Cole**	Y	Y	Y	Y	N	Y	N
5 **Lankford**	Y	Y	Y	Y	N	Y	N
OREGON							
1 Bonamici	Y	Y	Y	N	Y	Y	Y
2 **Walden**	Y	Y	Y	Y	N	Y	N
3 Blumenauer	Y	Y	N	N	Y	Y	Y
4 DeFazio	Y	Y	Y	N	Y	Y	Y
5 Schrader	Y	Y	Y	N	Y	Y	Y
PENNSYLVANIA							
1 Brady	Y	Y	Y	N	Y	Y	Y
2 Fattah	Y	N	N	N	?	Y	Y
3 **Kelly**	Y	Y	Y	Y	N	Y	N
4 Altmire	Y	Y	Y	Y	N	N	N
5 **Thompson**	Y	Y	Y	Y	N	Y	N
6 **Gerlach**	Y	Y	Y	Y	N	Y	N
7 **Meehan**	Y	Y	Y	Y	N	Y	N
8 **Fitzpatrick**	Y	Y	Y	Y	N	Y	N
9 **Shuster**	Y	Y	Y	Y	N	Y	N
10 **Marino**	Y	Y	Y	Y	N	Y	N
11 **Barletta**	Y	Y	Y	Y	N	Y	N
12 Critz	Y	Y	Y	N	Y	N	N
13 Schwartz	Y	Y	Y	N	N	Y	Y
14 Doyle	Y	Y	Y	N	Y	N	Y
15 **Dent**	Y	Y	Y	Y	N	Y	N
16 **Pitts**	Y	Y	Y	Y	N	Y	N
17 Holden	Y	Y	Y	Y	Y	N	N
18 **Murphy**	Y	Y	Y	Y	N	N	N
19 **Platts**	?	?	?	?	?	Y	N
RHODE ISLAND							
1 Cicilline	Y	N	Y	N	N	Y	Y
2 Langevin	Y	N	Y	N	N	Y	Y
SOUTH CAROLINA							
1 **Scott**	Y	Y	Y	Y	N	N	N
2 **Wilson**	Y	Y	Y	Y	N	N	N
3 **Duncan**	Y	Y	Y	Y	N	N	N
4 **Gowdy**	Y	Y	Y	Y	N	N	N
5 **Mulvaney**	Y	Y	Y	Y	N	N	N
6 Clyburn	N	Y	N	N	Y	N	Y
SOUTH DAKOTA							
AL **Noem**	Y	Y	Y	N	N	Y	N
TENNESSEE							
1 **Roe**	Y	Y	Y	Y	N	Y	N
2 **Duncan**	Y	Y	Y	Y	Y	Y	N
3 **Fleischmann**	Y	Y	Y	Y	N	N	N
4 **DesJarlais**	Y	Y	Y	Y	N	Y	N
5 Cooper	Y	Y	Y	N	Y	Y	Y
6 **Black**	Y	Y	Y	Y	N	Y	N
7 **Blackburn**	Y	Y	Y	Y	N	N	N
8 **Fincher**	Y	Y	Y	Y	N	Y	N
9 Cohen	Y	Y	N	N	Y	Y	Y

	320	321	322	323	324	325	326
TEXAS							
1 **Gohmert**	Y	Y	?	?	N	Y	N
2 **Poe**	Y	Y	Y	Y	N	Y	N
3 **Johnson, S.**	Y	Y	Y	Y	N	Y	N
4 **Hall**	Y	Y	Y	Y	N	Y	N
5 **Hensarling**	Y	Y	Y	Y	N	Y	N
6 **Barton**	Y	Y	Y	Y	N	Y	N
7 **Culberson**	Y	Y	Y	Y	N	N	N
8 **Brady**	Y	Y	Y	Y	N	Y	N
9 Green, A.	Y	Y	Y	N	Y	N	Y
10 **McCaul**	Y	Y	Y	Y	N	Y	N
11 **Conaway**	Y	Y	Y	Y	N	N	N
12 **Granger**	Y	Y	Y	Y	N	Y	N
13 **Thornberry**	Y	Y	Y	Y	N	N	N
14 **Paul**	?	?	?	?	?	?	?
15 Hinojosa	Y	Y	Y	N	Y	Y	Y
16 Reyes	Y	Y	Y	N	N	N	Y
17 **Flores**	Y	Y	Y	Y	N	Y	N
18 Jackson Lee	Y	N	N	N	Y	N	Y
19 **Neugebauer**	Y	Y	Y	Y	N	Y	N
20 Gonzalez	Y	Y	Y	N	N	Y	Y
21 **Smith**	Y	Y	Y	Y	N	Y	N
22 **Olson**	Y	Y	Y	Y	N	Y	N
23 **Canseco**	Y	Y	Y	Y	N	N	N
24 **Marchant**	Y	Y	Y	?	?	Y	N
25 Doggett	Y	N	Y	N	Y	Y	Y
26 **Burgess**	Y	Y	Y	Y	N	Y	N
27 **Farenthold**	Y	Y	Y	Y	N	Y	N
28 Cuellar	Y	Y	Y	N	Y	N	N
29 Green, G.	Y	Y	Y	N	Y	Y	Y
30 Johnson, E.	N	N	Y	N	Y	N	Y
31 **Carter**	Y	Y	Y	Y	N	Y	N
32 **Sessions**	Y	Y	Y	Y	N	Y	N
UTAH							
1 **Bishop**	Y	Y	Y	Y	N	Y	N
2 Matheson	Y	N	Y	Y	Y	Y	N
3 **Chaffetz**	Y	N	Y	Y	N	Y	N
VERMONT							
AL Welch	Y	Y	Y	N	Y	Y	Y
VIRGINIA							
1 **Wittman**	Y	Y	Y	Y	N	Y	N
2 **Rigell**	Y	Y	Y	Y	N	Y	N
3 Scott	N	Y	N	N	Y	Y	Y
4 **Forbes**	Y	Y	Y	Y	N	Y	N
5 **Hurt**	Y	Y	Y	Y	N	N	N
6 **Goodlatte**	Y	Y	Y	Y	N	N	N
7 **Cantor**	Y	Y	Y	Y	N	Y	N
8 Moran	?	Y	N	N	Y	Y	Y
9 **Griffith**	Y	Y	Y	Y	N	N	N
10 **Wolf**	Y	Y	Y	Y	N	Y	N
11 Connolly	Y	Y	Y	N	N	Y	Y
WASHINGTON							
1 Vacant							
2 Larsen	Y	Y	N	N	N	Y	N
3 **Herrera Beutler**	Y	Y	Y	Y	N	Y	N
4 **Hastings**	Y	Y	Y	Y	N	Y	N
5 **McMorris Rodgers**	Y	Y	Y	Y	N	Y	N
6 Dicks	Y	Y	Y	N	N	Y	Y
7 McDermott	N	N	N	N	Y	Y	Y
8 **Reichert**	Y	Y	Y	Y	N	Y	N
9 Smith	N	Y	Y	N	Y	Y	Y
WEST VIRGINIA							
1 **McKinley**	Y	Y	Y	Y	N	Y	N
2 **Capito**	Y	Y	Y	Y	N	Y	N
3 Rahall	Y	Y	Y	N	Y	Y	Y
WISCONSIN							
1 **Ryan**	Y	Y	Y	Y	N	Y	N
2 Baldwin	Y	Y	Y	N	Y	Y	Y
3 Kind	Y	Y	Y	N	Y	Y	Y
4 Moore	?	?	?	N	Y	Y	Y
5 **Sensenbrenner**	Y	Y	Y	Y	N	Y	N
6 **Petri**	Y	Y	Y	Y	N	Y	N
7 **Duffy**	Y	Y	Y	Y	N	Y	N
8 **Ribble**	Y	Y	Y	Y	N	Y	N
WYOMING							
AL **Lummis**	Y	Y	Y	Y	N	Y	N

IN THE HOUSE | By Vote Number

327. Vote proceedings vacated (not included in chart at right).

328. HR 5325. Fiscal 2013 Energy-Water Appropriations/Loan Guarantee Program. Kucinich, D-Ohio, amendment that would bar the use of funds in the bill to provide new loan guarantees under the demonstration project title of the Energy Policy Act of 2005, which authorizes loans for fossil fuel, nuclear and other demonstration projects. The amendment also would reduce funding for the Innovative Loan Guarantee Program by $33 million. Rejected in Committee of the Whole 136-282: R 109-127; D 27-155. June 6, 2012.

329. HR 5325. Fiscal 2013 Energy-Water Appropriations/Defense Nuclear Non-Proliferation Activities. Burgess, R-Texas, amendment that would reduce by $100 million the amount provided for defense nuclear non-proliferation activities and direct the same amount to the bill's spending reduction account. Rejected in Committee of the Whole 168-249: R 60-175; D 108-74. June 6, 2012.

330. HR 5325. Fiscal 2013 Energy-Water Appropriations/Non-Defense Environmental Cleanup Programs. Reed, R-N.Y., amendment that would increase by $36 million the amount provided in the bill for non-defense environmental cleanup programs, offset by reducing funds provided for Energy Department administrative expenses and the Administrator's Office of the National Nuclear Security Administration each by $18 million. Adopted in Committee of the Whole 223-195: R 94-142; D 129-53. June 6, 2012.

331. HR 5325. Fiscal 2013 Energy-Water Appropriations/Defense Nuclear Non-Proliferation Activities. Loretta Sanchez, D-Calif., amendment that would increase by $16 million the amount provided for defense nuclear non-proliferation activities and reduce by the same amount funding for Energy Department salaries and expenses. Rejected in Committee of the Whole 182-237: R 8-228; D 174-9. June 6, 2012.

332. HR 5325. Fiscal 2013 Energy-Water Appropriations/Nuclear-Weapons Funding. Polis, D-Colo., amendment that would reduce by $298.2 million the amount provided for atomic energy defense weapons activities and direct the same amount to the bill's spending reduction account. Rejected in Committee of the Whole 138-281: R 8-228; D 130-53. June 6, 2012.

333. HR 5325. Fiscal 2013 Energy-Water Appropriations/Atomic Energy Defense Environmental Cleanup. Luján, D-N.M., amendment that would increase by $21.9 million the amount provided for atomic energy defense environmental cleanup activities and reduce by the same amount funding for the administrator of the National Nuclear Security Administration. Rejected in Committee of the Whole 174-244: R 23-212; D 151-32. June 6, 2012.

334. HR 5325. Fiscal 2013 Energy-Water Appropriations/Economic Development Funding. Chabot, R-Ohio, amendment that would eliminate funding in the bill for the Appalachian Regional Commission, Delta Regional Authority, Denali Commission, Northern Border Regional Commission and Southeast Crescent Regional Commission and direct $99.3 million to the bill's spending reduction account. Rejected in Committee of the Whole 141-276: R 135-100; D 6-176. June 6, 2012.

	328	329	330	331	332	333	334
ALABAMA							
1 Bonner	N	N	N	N	N	N	N
2 Roby	N	N	N	N	N	N	N
3 Rogers	N	N	N	N	N	N	N
4 Aderholt	N	N	N	N	N	N	N
5 Brooks	Y	N	N	N	N	N	N
6 Bachus	N	N	N	N	N	N	N
7 Sewell	N	N	N	Y	N	N	N
ALASKA							
AL Young	Y	N	N	N	N	N	N
ARIZONA							
1 Gosar	Y	Y	N	N	N	N	Y
2 Franks	Y	Y	N	N	N	N	Y
3 Quayle	Y	N	N	N	N	N	Y
4 Pastor	N	N	N	N	N	N	N
5 Schweikert	Y	N	N	N	N	N	Y
6 Flake	Y	Y	Y	N	N	Y	Y
7 Grijalva	N	Y	Y	Y	Y	Y	N
8 Vacant							
ARKANSAS							
1 Crawford	N	N	N	N	N	N	N
2 Griffin	Y	N	N	N	N	N	N
3 Womack	N	N	N	N	N	N	N
4 Ross	N	N	Y	Y	N	Y	N
CALIFORNIA							
1 Thompson	N	Y	Y	Y	Y	Y	N
2 Herger	Y	Y	N	N	N	N	Y
3 Lungren	N	N	N	N	N	N	Y
4 McClintock	Y	Y	Y	N	N	Y	Y
5 Matsui	N	Y	Y	Y	Y	Y	N
6 Woolsey	N	Y	Y	Y	Y	Y	N
7 Miller, George	N	Y	Y	Y	Y	Y	N
8 Pelosi	N	Y	Y	Y	Y	Y	N
9 Lee	N	N	N	Y	Y	Y	N
10 Garamendi	N	Y	Y	Y	Y	Y	N
11 McNerney	N	Y	Y	N	Y	Y	N
12 Speier	Y	Y	Y	Y	Y	Y	N
13 Stark	Y	Y	Y	Y	Y	Y	N
14 Eshoo	N	Y	Y	Y	Y	Y	N
15 Honda	N	Y	Y	Y	Y	Y	N
16 Lofgren	N	N	N	Y	N	N	N
17 Farr	N	Y	Y	Y	Y	Y	N
18 Cardoza	N	N	N	Y	N	Y	N
19 Denham	N	N	Y	N	N	N	N
20 Costa	N	N	N	N	N	N	N
21 Nunes	N	N	N	N	N	N	N
22 McCarthy	N	Y	Y	N	N	N	Y
23 Capps	N	Y	Y	Y	Y	Y	N
24 Gallegly	N	N	N	N	N	N	N
25 McKeon	?	?	?	?	?	?	?
26 Dreier	N	N	Y	N	N	N	N
27 Sherman	Y	Y	Y	Y	Y	Y	N
28 Berman	?	?	?	?	?	?	?
29 Schiff	N	Y	Y	Y	Y	Y	N
30 Waxman	N	Y	Y	Y	Y	Y	N
31 Becerra	N	Y	Y	Y	Y	Y	N
32 Chu	N	Y	Y	Y	Y	Y	N
33 Bass	N	Y	Y	Y	Y	Y	N
34 Roybal-Allard	N	Y	Y	Y	Y	Y	N
35 Waters	N	N	Y	Y	N	Y	N
36 Hahn	?	?	?	?	?	?	?
37 Richardson	N	Y	Y	Y	Y	Y	N
38 Napolitano	?	?	?	?	?	?	?
39 Sánchez, Linda	N	N	N	Y	Y	Y	N
40 Royce	Y	Y	Y	N	N	Y	Y
41 Lewis	?	?	?	?	?	?	?
42 Miller, Gary	?	?	?	?	?	?	?
43 Baca	?	?	?	?	?	?	?
44 Calvert	N	N	N	N	N	N	N
45 Bono Mack	N	N	N	N	N	N	N
46 Rohrabacher	Y	Y	N	N	N	N	Y
47 Sanchez, Loretta	N	Y	Y	Y	Y	Y	N
48 Campbell	Y	Y	N	N	N	N	Y
49 Issa	N	N	N	N	N	N	Y
50 Bilbray	N	N	N	N	N	N	Y
51 Filner	–	+	–	+	+	+	–
52 Hunter	Y	N	N	N	N	Y	Y
53 Davis	N	Y	N	Y	Y	N	N

	328	329	330	331	332	333	334
COLORADO							
1 DeGette	N	Y	Y	Y	Y	Y	N
2 Polis	Y	Y	Y	Y	Y	Y	N
3 Tipton	N	N	Y	N	N	Y	Y
4 Gardner	Y	Y	Y	N	N	Y	Y
5 Lamborn	Y	N	N	N	N	N	Y
6 Coffman	Y	N	N	N	N	N	Y
7 Perlmutter	N	N	N	Y	Y	N	Y
CONNECTICUT							
1 Larson	N	N	Y	Y	Y	Y	N
2 Courtney	N	Y	Y	Y	N	Y	N
3 DeLauro	N	Y	Y	Y	Y	Y	N
4 Himes	N	Y	Y	Y	Y	Y	N
5 Murphy	N	N	Y	Y	Y	Y	N
DELAWARE							
AL Carney	N	N	Y	Y	N	Y	N
FLORIDA							
1 Miller	Y	N	N	N	N	N	N
2 Southerland	Y	N	N	N	N	N	N
3 Brown	N	N	Y	N	Y	N	N
4 Crenshaw	N	N	N	N	N	N	N
5 Nugent	N	N	Y	N	N	N	N
6 Stearns	N	Y	N	N	N	Y	N
7 Mica	N	Y	N	N	N	N	N
8 Webster	N	Y	Y	N	N	N	N
9 Bilirakis	N	Y	N	N	N	N	N
10 Young	Y	N	N	N	N	N	N
11 Castor	N	Y	N	Y	Y	Y	N
12 Ross	Y	Y	Y	N	N	N	Y
13 Buchanan	N	N	Y	N	N	N	N
14 Mack	Y	N	N	N	N	N	N
15 Posey	Y	Y	Y	N	N	N	Y
16 Rooney	Y	N	N	N	N	N	N
17 Wilson	Y	N	N	Y	Y	Y	N
18 Ros-Lehtinen	N	N	N	N	N	N	N
19 Deutch	N	Y	Y	Y	Y	Y	N
20 Wasserman Schultz	N	Y	Y	Y	Y	Y	N
21 Diaz-Balart	N	N	N	N	N	N	N
22 West	Y	N	N	N	N	N	N
23 Hastings	N	Y	Y	Y	Y	Y	N
24 Adams	Y	N	N	N	N	N	Y
25 Rivera	N	N	N	N	N	N	N
GEORGIA							
1 Kingston	N	N	N	N	N	N	N
2 Bishop	N	N	Y	N	Y	N	N
3 Westmoreland	Y	N	N	N	N	N	N
4 Johnson	Y	Y	Y	Y	Y	Y	N
5 Lewis	N	Y	Y	Y	Y	Y	N
6 Price	Y	N	N	N	N	N	Y
7 Woodall	N	N	N	N	N	N	Y
8 Scott, A.	N	N	N	N	N	N	N
9 Graves	Y	N	N	N	N	N	Y
10 Broun	Y	Y	N	N	N	N	Y
11 Gingrey	Y	N	N	N	N	N	Y
12 Barrow	N	N	Y	N	Y	Y	N
13 Scott, D.	Y	N	Y	Y	Y	Y	N
HAWAII							
1 Hanabusa	N	N	Y	Y	Y	Y	N
2 Hirono	N	Y	N	Y	Y	Y	N
IDAHO							
1 Labrador	Y	N	N	N	N	N	Y
2 Simpson	N	N	N	N	N	N	N
ILLINOIS							
1 Rush	N	Y	Y	Y	Y	Y	N
2 Jackson	Y	Y	N	Y	Y	Y	N
3 Lipinski	N	N	Y	N	Y	Y	N
4 Gutierrez	Y	N	Y	N	Y	Y	N
5 Quigley	Y	Y	Y	Y	Y	Y	N
6 Roskam	N	Y	N	N	N	N	Y
7 Davis	N	N	Y	N	Y	N	N
8 Walsh	N	N	N	N	N	N	Y
9 Schakowsky	Y	Y	Y	Y	Y	Y	N
10 Dold	N	N	Y	N	N	N	N
11 Kinzinger	N	Y	N	N	N	N	Y
12 Costello	N	Y	Y	N	Y	Y	N
13 Biggert	N	N	N	N	N	N	N
14 Hultgren	Y	N	N	N	N	N	Y
15 Johnson	N	Y	Y	Y	Y	N	N

KEY   Republicans   Democrats

Y Voted for (yea)	**X** Paired against	**C** Voted "present" to avoid possible conflict of interest
# Paired for	**–** Announced against	
+ Announced for	**P** Voted "present"	**?** Did not vote or otherwise make a position known
N Voted against (nay)		

	328	329	330	331	332	333	334
16 **Manzullo**	Y	N	Y	N	N	N	Y
17 **Schilling**	N	N	Y	N	N	N	Y
18 **Schock**	N	N	Y	N	N	N	N
19 **Shimkus**	N	Y	N	N	N	N	N
INDIANA							
1 Visclosky	N	Y	N	Y	N	N	N
2 Donnelly	N	N	N	Y	N	N	N
3 **Stutzman**	Y	Y	Y	N	N	N	Y
4 **Rokita**	Y	Y	N	N	N	N	Y
5 **Burton**	Y	N	N	N	N	N	Y
6 **Pence**	Y	N	N	N	N	N	Y
7 Carson	N	Y	N	Y	N	N	N
8 **Bucshon**	N	N	Y	N	N	N	Y
9 **Young**	Y	N	Y	N	N	?	?
IOWA							
1 Braley	N	N	Y	Y	Y	Y	N
2 Loebsack	N	N	Y	Y	Y	Y	N
3 Boswell	N	N	Y	Y	Y	Y	N
4 **Latham**	N	N	N	N	N	N	N
5 **King**	Y	?	N	N	N	N	Y
KANSAS							
1 **Huelskamp**	Y	Y	N	N	N	N	Y
2 **Jenkins**	Y	N	N	N	N	N	Y
3 **Yoder**	Y	N	Y	N	N	N	Y
4 **Pompeo**	Y	N	N	N	N	N	Y
KENTUCKY							
1 **Whitfield**	N	N	N	N	N	N	N
2 **Guthrie**	N	N	N	N	N	N	N
3 Yarmuth	N	N	Y	Y	Y	Y	N
4 **Davis**	N	N	N	N	N	N	N
5 **Rogers**	N	N	N	N	N	N	N
6 Chandler	N	N	N	Y	N	N	N
LOUISIANA							
1 **Scalise**	Y	N	N	N	N	N	Y
2 Richmond	N	N	N	Y	Y	Y	N
3 **Landry**	Y	N	Y	N	N	N	Y
4 **Fleming**	Y	N	N	N	N	N	Y
5 **Alexander**	N	N	N	N	N	N	N
6 **Cassidy**	N	Y	N	N	N	N	N
7 **Boustany**	Y	N	N	N	N	N	N
MAINE							
1 Pingree	Y	Y	Y	Y	Y	Y	N
2 Michaud	Y	Y	Y	Y	Y	Y	N
MARYLAND							
1 **Harris**	Y	N	N	N	N	N	Y
2 Ruppersberger	N	N	Y	Y	N	Y	N
3 Sarbanes	N	Y	Y	Y	N	Y	N
4 Edwards	Y	Y	Y	Y	Y	Y	N
5 Hoyer	N	N	N	N	Y	Y	N
6 **Bartlett**	Y	N	N	N	N	N	N
7 Cummings	N	Y	N	Y	Y	Y	N
8 Van Hollen	N	N	Y	Y	Y	Y	N
MASSACHUSETTS							
1 Olver	N	N	Y	Y	Y	Y	N
2 Neal	N	Y	Y	Y	Y	Y	N
3 McGovern	N	Y	Y	Y	Y	Y	N
4 Frank	N	Y	N	Y	Y	Y	N
5 Tsongas	N	Y	Y	Y	Y	Y	N
6 Tierney	N	Y	Y	Y	Y	Y	N
7 Markey	Y	Y	N	Y	Y	Y	N
8 Capuano	N	Y	Y	Y	Y	Y	N
9 Lynch	N	Y	Y	Y	Y	N	N
10 Keating	N	Y	N	Y	Y	Y	N
MICHIGAN							
1 **Benishek**	Y	N	Y	N	N	N	Y
2 **Huizenga**	Y	Y	N	N	N	N	Y
3 **Amash**	Y	N	N	N	Y	N	Y
4 **Camp**	Y	N	Y	N	N	N	Y
5 Kildee	N	Y	N	Y	Y	Y	N
6 **Upton**	N	N	Y	N	N	N	Y
7 **Walberg**	Y	Y	N	N	N	N	Y
8 **Rogers**	N	N	N	N	N	N	N
9 Peters	N	N	Y	Y	Y	Y	N
10 **Miller**	Y	N	Y	N	N	N	Y
11 **McCotter**	N	N	N	N	N	N	N
12 Levin	N	Y	Y	Y	Y	Y	N
13 Clarke	N	N	Y	Y	Y	Y	N
14 Conyers	Y	Y	Y	Y	Y	Y	N
15 Dingell	N	Y	Y	Y	Y	Y	N
MINNESOTA							
1 Walz	N	Y	Y	Y	Y	Y	N
2 **Kline**	Y	N	N	N	N	N	Y
3 **Paulsen**	Y	Y	Y	N	N	N	Y
4 McCollum	N	N	Y	N	Y	Y	N

	328	329	330	331	332	333	334
5 Ellison	N	Y	Y	Y	Y	Y	N
6 **Bachmann**	Y	N	Y	N	N	N	Y
7 Peterson	N	N	N	Y	N	N	N
8 **Cravaack**	N	N	N	N	N	N	N
MISSISSIPPI							
1 **Nunnelee**	Y	N	N	N	N	N	N
2 Thompson	N	N	N	Y	N	Y	N
3 **Harper**	N	N	N	N	N	N	N
4 **Palazzo**	N	N	N	N	N	N	N
MISSOURI							
1 Clay	N	N	Y	Y	Y	Y	N
2 **Akin**	N	N	N	N	N	Y	Y
3 Carnahan	Y	N	Y	Y	Y	Y	N
4 **Hartzler**	Y	N	N	N	N	N	Y
5 Cleaver	N	N	Y	Y	Y	Y	N
6 **Graves**	N	N	N	N	N	N	Y
7 **Long**	N	Y	N	N	Y	N	Y
8 **Emerson**	N	N	N	N	N	N	N
9 **Luetkemeyer**	N	N	N	N	N	N	Y
MONTANA							
AL **Rehberg**	N	N	N	N	N	N	N
NEBRASKA							
1 **Fortenberry**	N	N	N	N	N	N	N
2 **Terry**	N	N	N	N	N	N	Y
3 **Smith**	N	Y	N	N	N	N	Y
NEVADA							
1 Berkley	Y	Y	N	Y	N	N	N
2 **Amodei**	N	N	N	N	N	N	Y
3 **Heck**	N	N	N	N	N	N	Y
NEW HAMPSHIRE							
1 **Guinta**	Y	N	N	N	N	N	N
2 **Bass**	N	N	Y	N	N	N	N
NEW JERSEY							
1 Andrews	N	Y	N	Y	Y	N	Y
2 **LoBiondo**	Y	N	N	N	N	N	N
3 **Runyan**	N	N	N	N	N	N	N
4 **Smith**	N	Y	N	N	N	N	N
5 **Garrett**	Y	Y	N	N	N	N	Y
6 Pallone	N	Y	Y	Y	Y	Y	N
7 **Lance**	Y	Y	Y	N	Y	N	Y
8 Pascrell	N	N	Y	Y	N	Y	N
9 Rothman	?	?	?	Y	Y	Y	N
10 Vacant							
11 **Frelinghuysen**	N	N	N	N	N	N	N
12 Holt	N	Y	Y	Y	Y	Y	N
13 Sires	N	N	N	Y	N	Y	N
NEW MEXICO							
1 Heinrich	N	Y	Y	Y	N	Y	Y
2 **Pearce**	Y	Y	Y	N	N	Y	Y
3 Luján	N	Y	Y	Y	N	Y	N
NEW YORK							
1 Bishop	N	N	Y	Y	Y	Y	N
2 Israel	N	Y	Y	Y	N	Y	N
3 **King**	N	N	N	N	N	N	N
4 McCarthy	N	N	Y	Y	N	Y	N
5 Ackerman	N	Y	Y	Y	Y	Y	N
6 Meeks	N	N	Y	Y	Y	Y	N
7 Crowley	N	N	Y	Y	Y	Y	N
8 Nadler	Y	Y	Y	Y	Y	Y	N
9 **Turner**	N	N	Y	N	N	N	N
10 Towns	N	Y	N	Y	Y	Y	N
11 Clarke	N	Y	Y	Y	Y	Y	N
12 Velázquez	N	Y	Y	Y	Y	Y	N
13 **Grimm**	N	N	N	N	N	N	N
14 Maloney	N	Y	Y	Y	Y	Y	N
15 Rangel	Y	Y	Y	Y	N	Y	N
16 Serrano	N	Y	Y	Y	Y	Y	N
17 Engel	N	N	N	N	Y	Y	N
18 Lowey	N	Y	Y	Y	Y	Y	N
19 **Hayworth**	Y	N	Y	N	N	N	N
20 **Gibson**	N	N	Y	Y	Y	Y	N
21 Tonko	Y	Y	Y	Y	Y	Y	N
22 Hinchey	N	Y	Y	Y	Y	Y	N
23 Owens	N	N	Y	Y	N	N	N
24 **Hanna**	N	N	Y	N	N	N	N
25 **Buerkle**	N	N	Y	N	N	N	Y
26 Hochul	N	N	Y	Y	Y	Y	N
27 Higgins	N	Y	Y	Y	Y	Y	N
28 Slaughter	–	+	+	+	–	–	–
29 **Reed**	Y	N	Y	N	N	N	N
NORTH CAROLINA							
1 Butterfield	N	N	Y	Y	Y	Y	N
2 **Ellmers**	N	N	N	N	N	N	Y
3 **Jones**	Y	Y	Y	Y	Y	Y	Y
4 Price	N	Y	Y	Y	Y	N	N

	328	329	330	331	332	333	334
5 **Foxx**	N	N	N	N	N	N	Y
6 **Coble**	?	?	?	?	?	?	?
7 McIntyre	N	N	Y	N	N	Y	N
8 Kissell	N	N	N	Y	N	Y	N
9 **Myrick**	Y	N	N	N	N	N	Y
10 **McHenry**	Y	N	Y	N	N	N	N
11 Shuler	?	?	?	?	?	?	?
12 Watt	N	Y	Y	Y	Y	Y	N
13 Miller	N	N	N	Y	N	Y	N
NORTH DAKOTA							
AL **Berg**	N	N	N	N	N	N	N
OHIO							
1 **Chabot**	N	N	Y	N	N	N	Y
2 **Schmidt**	N	N	Y	N	N	N	N
3 **Turner**	N	N	N	N	N	N	N
4 **Jordan**	Y	N	Y	N	N	N	Y
5 **Latta**	N	N	N	N	N	N	N
6 **Johnson**	N	N	Y	N	N	N	N
7 **Austria**	N	N	N	N	N	N	N
8 **Boehner**							
9 Kaptur	N	N	N	Y	Y	Y	N
10 Kucinich	Y	Y	Y	Y	Y	Y	N
11 Fudge	N	N	N	Y	Y	Y	N
12 **Tiberi**	N	N	N	N	N	N	N
13 Sutton	N	N	Y	Y	N	Y	N
14 **LaTourette**	N	N	N	N	N	N	N
15 **Stivers**	N	N	Y	N	N	N	N
16 **Renacci**	N	N	N	N	N	N	Y
17 Ryan	N	N	N	Y	N	N	N
18 **Gibbs**	N	N	N	N	N	N	N
OKLAHOMA							
1 **Sullivan**	Y	N	N	N	N	N	Y
2 Boren	N	N	Y	Y	N	Y	N
3 **Lucas**	N	N	N	N	N	N	N
4 **Cole**	N	N	N	N	N	N	N
5 **Lankford**	Y	Y	N	N	N	N	Y
OREGON							
1 Bonamici	N	Y	Y	Y	Y	Y	N
2 **Walden**	Y	N	Y	N	N	Y	Y
3 Blumenauer	N	Y	Y	Y	Y	Y	N
4 DeFazio	Y	Y	Y	Y	Y	Y	N
5 Schrader	N	N	Y	Y	Y	Y	N
PENNSYLVANIA							
1 Brady	N	Y	Y	Y	Y	Y	N
2 Fattah	N	N	N	Y	N	N	?
3 **Kelly**	N	N	N	N	N	N	N
4 Altmire	N	N	N	N	N	N	N
5 **Thompson**	N	Y	N	N	N	N	N
6 **Gerlach**	N	N	Y	N	N	N	N
7 **Meehan**	N	N	Y	N	N	N	N
8 **Fitzpatrick**	Y	N	Y	Y	N	Y	N
9 **Shuster**	N	N	N	N	N	N	N
10 **Marino**	N	N	N	N	N	N	N
11 **Barletta**	N	N	N	N	N	N	N
12 Critz	N	N	Y	Y	N	Y	N
13 Schwartz	N	Y	Y	Y	N	Y	N
14 Doyle	N	N	Y	Y	Y	Y	N
15 **Dent**	N	N	Y	N	N	N	N
16 **Pitts**	N	N	Y	N	N	N	Y
17 Holden	N	N	Y	Y	N	N	N
18 **Murphy**	N	N	N	N	N	N	N
19 **Platts**	N	N	Y	N	N	N	N
RHODE ISLAND							
1 Cicilline	N	Y	Y	Y	Y	Y	N
2 Langevin	N	N	Y	Y	N	N	N
SOUTH CAROLINA							
1 **Scott**	Y	N	Y	N	N	N	Y
2 **Wilson**	N	N	Y	N	N	N	Y
3 **Duncan**	Y	N	Y	N	N	N	Y
4 **Gowdy**	Y	N	Y	N	N	N	Y
5 **Mulvaney**	Y	Y	Y	N	N	N	Y
6 Clyburn	N	N	Y	Y	N	Y	N
SOUTH DAKOTA							
AL **Noem**	Y	N	N	N	N	N	Y
TENNESSEE							
1 **Roe**	N	N	Y	N	N	N	N
2 **Duncan**	Y	Y	N	N	Y	N	N
3 **Fleischmann**	Y	N	N	N	N	N	N
4 **DesJarlais**	Y	N	N	N	N	N	N
5 Cooper	N	N	N	Y	Y	N	N
6 **Black**	Y	N	Y	N	N	N	Y
7 **Blackburn**	Y	N	N	N	N	N	N
8 **Fincher**	Y	N	Y	N	N	Y	N
9 Cohen	N	Y	Y	Y	Y	Y	N

	328	329	330	331	332	333	334
TEXAS							
1 **Gohmert**	Y	Y	Y	Y	N	Y	Y
2 **Poe**	Y	N	N	N	N	N	Y
3 **Johnson, S.**	N	N	Y	N	N	N	Y
4 **Hall**	Y	N	N	N	N	N	Y
5 **Hensarling**	Y	Y	N	N	N	N	Y
6 **Barton**	N	Y	Y	N	N	N	Y
7 **Culberson**	Y	Y	N	N	N	N	Y
8 **Brady**	Y	N	N	N	N	N	Y
9 Green, A.	N	N	Y	Y	Y	Y	N
10 **McCaul**	N	N	N	N	N	N	Y
11 **Conaway**	Y	Y	N	N	N	N	Y
12 **Granger**	N	N	N	N	N	N	N
13 **Thornberry**	Y	N	N	Y	N	N	Y
14 **Paul**	?	?	?	?	?	?	?
15 Hinojosa	N	Y	Y	Y	Y	Y	N
16 Reyes	N	Y	N	Y	Y	Y	N
17 **Flores**	N	N	N	N	N	N	Y
18 Jackson Lee	N	Y	N	Y	Y	Y	N
19 **Neugebauer**	Y	Y	N	N	N	N	Y
20 Gonzalez	N	N	N	Y	N	N	N
21 **Smith**	Y	N	N	N	N	N	Y
22 **Olson**	Y	N	N	N	N	N	Y
23 **Canseco**	Y	Y	Y	N	N	N	Y
24 **Marchant**	N	Y	Y	N	N	N	Y
25 Doggett	Y	Y	Y	Y	Y	Y	Y
26 **Burgess**	Y	Y	Y	N	N	N	Y
27 **Farenthold**	Y	Y	N	N	N	N	Y
28 Cuellar	N	Y	Y	Y	N	Y	N
29 Green, G.	N	Y	N	Y	Y	Y	Y
30 Johnson, E.	Y	N	N	N	Y	N	N
31 **Carter**	N	N	N	N	N	N	N
32 **Sessions**	N	Y	N	N	N	N	Y
UTAH							
1 **Bishop**	N	Y	Y	N	N	Y	Y
2 Matheson	Y	N	Y	Y	N	Y	Y
3 **Chaffetz**	Y	Y	Y	N	N	N	Y
VERMONT							
AL Welch	N	Y	Y	Y	Y	Y	N
VIRGINIA							
1 **Wittman**	N	N	N	N	N	N	Y
2 **Rigell**	Y	N	N	N	N	N	Y
3 Scott	N	Y	Y	Y	Y	Y	N
4 **Forbes**	N	N	N	N	N	N	Y
5 **Hurt**	N	N	Y	N	N	N	Y
6 **Goodlatte**	N	N	Y	N	N	N	N
7 **Cantor**	N	N	N	N	N	N	N
8 Moran	N	N	N	N	Y	Y	N
9 **Griffith**	N	N	Y	N	N	N	N
10 **Wolf**	N	N	N	N	N	N	N
11 Connolly	N	Y	Y	Y	N	Y	N
WASHINGTON							
1 Vacant							
2 Larsen	N	Y	N	Y	Y	N	N
3 **Herrera Beutler**	Y	N	Y	N	N	Y	N
4 **Hastings**	N	N	N	N	N	Y	N
5 **McMorris Rodgers**	N	Y	Y	N	N	N	Y
6 Dicks	N	Y	N	Y	N	N	N
7 McDermott	N	Y	Y	Y	Y	Y	N
8 **Reichert**	N	N	Y	N	N	Y	N
9 Smith	Y	Y	Y	Y	N	Y	N
WEST VIRGINIA							
1 **McKinley**	N	N	N	N	N	N	N
2 **Capito**	N	N	N	N	N	N	N
3 Rahall	N	Y	N	Y	Y	Y	N
WISCONSIN							
1 **Ryan**	Y	N	Y	N	N	N	Y
2 Baldwin	N	Y	Y	Y	Y	Y	N
3 Kind	N	N	Y	Y	Y	Y	N
4 Moore	N	Y	Y	Y	Y	Y	N
5 **Sensenbrenner**	Y	Y	Y	Y	N	Y	Y
6 **Petri**	Y	N	Y	N	N	Y	Y
7 **Duffy**	Y	N	Y	N	N	N	Y
8 **Ribble**	Y	N	Y	N	Y	N	Y
WYOMING							
AL **Lummis**	N	Y	N	N	N	N	Y

IN THE HOUSE | By Vote Number

335. HR 5325. Fiscal 2013 Energy-Water Appropriations/
Funding Reduction. Blackburn, R-Tenn., amendment that would make
an across-the-board cut of 1 percent in the bill's discretionary spending. Rejected in Committee of the Whole 157-261: R 152-84; D 5-177.
June 6, 2012.

336. HR 5325. Fiscal 2013 Energy-Water Appropriations/
Funding Reductions. Mulvaney, R-S.C., amendment that would reduce
the amounts made available by the bill by 24 percent. The funding reduction would not apply to Army Corps of Engineers construction projects,
Energy Department defense-related activities and several nuclear-related
initiatives dealing with research, safety, weapons activities and waste disposal. Rejected in Committee of the Whole 125-293: R 125-110; D 0-183.
June 6, 2012.

337. HR 5325. Fiscal 2013 Energy-Water Appropriations/
Funding Reduction. Flake, R-Ariz., amendment that would make an
across-the-board reduction of 0.27 percent in the bill's discretionary
spending. Rejected in Committee of the Whole 144-274: R 140-95;
D 4-179. June 6, 2012.

338. HR 5325. Fiscal 2013 Energy-Water Appropriations/
Prevailing Wages. King, R-Iowa, amendment that would bar the use of
funds in the bill to implement, administer or enforce prevailing wage
requirements under the Davis-Bacon Act when awarding federal contracts. Rejected in Committee of the Whole 184-235: R 184-52; D 0-183.
June 6, 2012.

339. HR 5325. Fiscal 2013 Energy-Water Appropriations/
Uranium Sales. Lummis, R-Wyo., amendment that would bar the use
of funds in the bill for the Energy Department to plan or undertake the
transfer or sale of low-enriched uranium that exceeds a total of 1,917 met-
ric tons of uranium as uranium hexafluoride equivalent in fiscal 2013.
Rejected in Committee of the Whole 114-302: R 70-164; D 44-138.
June 6, 2012.

340. HR 5325. Fiscal 2013 Energy-Water Appropriations/
Fossil Fuels Programs. Connolly, D-Va., amendment that would reduce
by $25 million the amount provided for fossil energy research and
development programs and direct the same amount to the bill's spending reduction account. Adopted in Committee of the Whole 208-207:
R 60-172; D 148-35. (By unanimous consent, the House agreed to vacate
proceedings for roll call vote 327 on the Connolly amendment, and the
Committee of the Whole proceeded to take a re-vote on the amendment.)
June 6, 2012.

341. HR 5325. Fiscal 2013 Energy-Water Appropriations/Recommit.
Boswell, D-Iowa, motion to recommit the bill to the House Appropriations Committee and report it back immediately with an amendment
that would increase by $31.6 million the amount provided for flood
and natural-disaster emergency spending offset by a reduction of the
same amount for the Army Corps of Engineers expenses account. It also
would shift $1 million within the energy efficiency and renewable-energy
account to accommodate U.S.-Israeli non-military energy cooperation
activities. Motion rejected 185-233: R 2-233; D 183-0. June 6, 2012.

	335	336	337	338	339	340	341
ALABAMA							
1 Bonner	N	N	N	Y	N	N	N
2 Roby	N	N	N	Y	N	N	N
3 Rogers	N	N	N	Y	N	N	N
4 Aderholt	N	N	N	Y	N	N	N
5 Brooks	Y	Y	Y	Y	Y	Y	N
6 Bachus	N	N	N	Y	N	N	N
7 Sewell	N	N	N	N	N	Y	Y
ALASKA							
AL Young	N	N	N	N	Y	N	N
ARIZONA							
1 Gosar	Y	N	Y	Y	Y	N	N
2 Franks	Y	Y	Y	Y	Y	N	N
3 Quayle	Y	Y	Y	Y	Y	N	N
4 Pastor	N	N	N	N	N	Y	N
5 Schweikert	Y	Y	Y	Y	Y	Y	N
6 Flake	Y	Y	Y	Y	Y	Y	N
7 Grijalva	N	N	N	N	Y	Y	Y
8 Vacant							
ARKANSAS							
1 Crawford	N	N	N	Y	N	N	N
2 Griffin	Y	Y	Y	Y	N	N	N
3 Womack	N	N	N	Y	N	N	N
4 Ross	N	N	N	N	N	N	Y
CALIFORNIA							
1 Thompson	N	N	N	N	N	Y	Y
2 Herger	Y	Y	Y	Y	Y	Y	N
3 Lungren	N	N	N	Y	N	N	N
4 McClintock	Y	Y	Y	Y	Y	N	N
5 Matsui	N	N	N	N	N	Y	Y
6 Woolsey	N	N	N	N	N	Y	Y
7 Miller, George	N	N	N	N	N	Y	Y
8 Pelosi	N	N	N	N	Y	Y	Y
9 Lee	N	N	N	N	N	Y	Y
10 Garamendi	N	N	N	N	N	Y	Y
11 McNerney	N	N	N	N	N	Y	Y
12 Speier	N	N	N	N	N	Y	Y
13 Stark	N	N	N	N	N	Y	Y
14 Eshoo	N	N	N	N	N	Y	Y
15 Honda	N	N	N	N	Y	Y	Y
16 Lofgren	N	N	N	N	N	Y	Y
17 Farr	N	N	N	N	N	Y	Y
18 Cardoza	N	N	N	N	N	N	Y
19 Denham	Y	N	N	Y	Y	N	N
20 Costa	N	N	N	N	N	Y	N
21 Nunes	N	N	Y	Y	Y	N	N
22 McCarthy	Y	N	N	Y	Y	N	N
23 Capps	N	N	N	N	N	Y	Y
24 Gallegly	N	N	Y	Y	Y	N	N
25 McKeon	?	?	?	?	?	?	?
26 Dreier	N	N	N	N	N	N	N
27 Sherman	N	N	N	N	N	Y	Y
28 Berman	?	?	?	?	?	?	?
29 Schiff	N	N	N	N	N	Y	Y
30 Waxman	N	N	N	N	N	Y	Y
31 Becerra	N	N	N	N	N	Y	Y
32 Chu	N	N	N	N	Y	Y	Y
33 Bass	N	N	N	N	N	Y	Y
34 Roybal-Allard	N	N	N	N	N	Y	Y
35 Waters	N	N	N	N	N	Y	Y
36 Hahn	?	?	?	?	?	?	?
37 Richardson	N	N	N	N	N	Y	Y
38 Napolitano	?	?	?	?	?	?	?
39 Sánchez, Linda	?	?	?	?	?	?	?
40 Royce	Y	Y	Y	N	Y	N	N
41 Lewis	?	?	?	?	?	?	?
42 Miller, Gary	?	?	?	?	?	?	?
43 Baca	?	?	?	?	?	?	?
44 Calvert	N	N	N	Y	N	N	N
45 Bono Mack	Y	N	N	Y	N	N	N
46 Rohrabacher	Y	Y	Y	Y	N	N	N
47 Sanchez, Loretta	N	N	N	N	Y	Y	Y
48 Campbell	Y	Y	Y	Y	Y	Y	N
49 Issa	Y	Y	Y	Y	N	N	N
50 Bilbray	N	N	N	Y	N	N	N
51 Filner	–	–	–	+	+	+	+
52 Hunter	Y	Y	Y	Y	Y	N	N
53 Davis	N	N	N	N	N	Y	Y

	335	336	337	338	339	340	341
COLORADO							
1 DeGette	N	N	N	N	Y	Y	Y
2 Polis	N	N	N	N	Y	Y	Y
3 Tipton	Y	N	N	Y	Y	N	N
4 Gardner	Y	N	Y	Y	Y	N	N
5 Lamborn	Y	Y	Y	Y	?	N	N
6 Coffman	N	N	Y	Y	Y	N	N
7 Perlmutter	N	N	N	N	N	Y	Y
CONNECTICUT							
1 Larson	N	N	N	N	N	Y	Y
2 Courtney	N	N	N	N	N	Y	Y
3 DeLauro	N	N	N	N	N	Y	Y
4 Himes	N	N	N	N	N	Y	Y
5 Murphy	N	N	N	N	N	Y	Y
DELAWARE							
AL Carney	N	N	N	N	N	Y	Y
FLORIDA							
1 Miller	Y	Y	Y	Y	N	Y	N
2 Southerland	Y	Y	Y	Y	N	Y	?
3 Brown	N	N	N	N	N	Y	Y
4 Crenshaw	N	N	Y	N	N	N	N
5 Nugent	Y	N	N	Y	N	N	N
6 Stearns	Y	Y	Y	Y	N	N	N
7 Mica	Y	N	N	Y	N	N	N
8 Webster	N	N	N	Y	N	N	N
9 Bilirakis	Y	Y	Y	Y	N	N	N
10 Young	Y	Y	Y	N	N	N	N
11 Castor	N	N	N	N	N	Y	Y
12 Ross	Y	Y	Y	Y	N	N	N
13 Buchanan	Y	Y	Y	Y	Y	N	N
14 Mack	Y	Y	Y	Y	Y	N	N
15 Posey	N	N	Y	Y	Y	N	N
16 Rooney	Y	Y	Y	Y	Y	N	N
17 Wilson	N	N	N	N	N	Y	Y
18 Ros-Lehtinen	N	N	N	N	Y	Y	Y
19 Deutch	N	N	N	N	Y	Y	Y
20 Wasserman Schultz	N	N	N	N	N	Y	Y
21 Diaz-Balart	N	N	N	N	Y	Y	Y
22 West	N	Y	N	Y	Y	N	N
23 Hastings	N	N	N	N	N	Y	Y
24 Adams	Y	Y	N	Y	N	N	N
25 Rivera	N	N	N	N	N	N	N
GEORGIA							
1 Kingston	N	N	N	Y	N	N	N
2 Bishop	N	N	N	N	N	Y	Y
3 Westmoreland	N	Y	N	Y	N	N	N
4 Johnson	N	N	N	N	N	Y	Y
5 Lewis	N	N	N	N	N	Y	Y
6 Price	Y	Y	Y	Y	Y	N	N
7 Woodall	Y	Y	Y	Y	Y	N	N
8 Scott, A.	Y	Y	Y	Y	Y	N	N
9 Graves	Y	Y	Y	Y	Y	N	N
10 Broun	Y	Y	Y	Y	Y	N	N
11 Gingrey	Y	Y	Y	Y	Y	N	N
12 Barrow	N	N	N	N	N	N	Y
13 Scott, D.	N	N	N	N	N	Y	Y
HAWAII							
1 Hanabusa	N	N	N	N	N	Y	Y
2 Hirono	N	N	N	N	N	Y	Y
IDAHO							
1 Labrador	Y	Y	Y	Y	N	N	N
2 Simpson	N	N	N	Y	N	N	N
ILLINOIS							
1 Rush	N	N	N	N	N	Y	Y
2 Jackson	N	N	N	N	N	Y	Y
3 Lipinski	N	N	N	N	N	N	Y
4 Gutierrez	N	N	N	N	N	Y	Y
5 Quigley	N	N	N	N	N	Y	Y
6 Roskam	N	N	N	Y	N	N	N
7 Davis	N	N	N	N	N	Y	Y
8 Walsh	Y	Y	Y	Y	N	Y	N
9 Schakowsky	N	N	N	N	N	Y	Y
10 Dold	N	N	N	Y	N	N	N
11 Kinzinger	N	N	N	N	N	Y	Y
12 Costello	N	N	N	N	N	Y	Y
13 Biggert	Y	N	N	Y	N	N	N
14 Hultgren	N	N	N	Y	N	N	N
15 Johnson	Y	Y	N	N	Y	P	N

KEY **Republicans** Democrats

Y Voted for (yea)	**X** Paired against	**C** Voted "present" to avoid possible conflict of interest
# Paired for	**–** Announced against	
+ Announced for	**P** Voted "present"	**?** Did not vote or otherwise make a position known
N Voted against (nay)		

	335	336	337	338	339	340	341
16 **Manzullo**	Y	Y	Y	Y	Y	N	N
17 **Schilling**	Y	N	Y	N	N	N	N
18 **Schock**	N	N	N	N	N	N	N
19 **Shimkus**	N	N	N	N	Y	N	N
INDIANA							
1 Visclosky	N	N	N	N	N	Y	Y
2 Donnelly	N	N	N	N	N	N	Y
3 **Stutzman**	Y	Y	Y	Y	Y	Y	N
4 **Rokita**	Y	Y	Y	Y	Y	Y	N
5 **Burton**	Y	Y	N	Y	N	N	N
6 **Pence**	Y	Y	Y	Y	Y	N	N
7 Carson	N	N	N	N	N	N	Y
8 **Bucshon**	N	N	N	Y	N	N	N
9 **Young**	Y	Y	Y	Y	N	N	N
IOWA							
1 Braley	N	N	N	N	N	Y	Y
2 Loebsack	N	N	N	N	N	N	Y
3 Boswell	N	N	N	N	N	N	Y
4 **Latham**	N	N	N	Y	N	N	Y
5 **King**	Y	Y	Y	Y	Y	N	Y
KANSAS							
1 **Huelskamp**	Y	Y	Y	Y	Y	Y	N
2 **Jenkins**	Y	Y	Y	Y	N	N	N
3 **Yoder**	Y	Y	Y	Y	N	N	N
4 **Pompeo**	Y	Y	Y	Y	N	Y	N
KENTUCKY							
1 **Whitfield**	N	N	N	N	N	N	N
2 **Guthrie**	Y	Y	Y	Y	N	N	N
3 Yarmuth	N	N	N	N	N	Y	Y
4 **Davis**	Y	N	Y	Y	N	N	N
5 **Rogers**	N	N	N	Y	N	N	N
6 Chandler	N	N	N	N	N	N	Y
LOUISIANA							
1 **Scalise**	Y	Y	Y	Y	N	Y	N
2 Richmond	N	N	N	N	N	Y	Y
3 **Landry**	Y	Y	Y	Y	Y	N	N
4 **Fleming**	Y	Y	Y	Y	Y	Y	N
5 **Alexander**	N	N	N	N	N	N	N
6 **Cassidy**	Y	N	Y	Y	Y	N	N
7 **Boustany**	N	N	N	Y	N	N	N
MAINE							
1 Pingree	N	N	N	N	N	Y	Y
2 Michaud	N	N	N	N	Y	Y	Y
MARYLAND							
1 **Harris**	Y	Y	Y	Y	Y	N	N
2 Ruppersberger	?	N	N	N	N	Y	Y
3 Sarbanes	N	N	N	N	N	Y	Y
4 Edwards	N	N	N	N	N	Y	Y
5 Hoyer	N	N	N	N	N	Y	Y
6 **Bartlett**	Y	N	Y	Y	N	N	N
7 Cummings	N	N	N	N	N	Y	Y
8 Van Hollen	N	N	N	N	N	Y	Y
MASSACHUSETTS							
1 Olver	N	N	N	N	N	Y	Y
2 Neal	N	N	N	N	N	Y	Y
3 McGovern	N	N	N	N	Y	Y	Y
4 Frank	N	N	N	N	Y	Y	Y
5 Tsongas	N	N	N	N	N	Y	Y
6 Tierney	N	N	N	N	N	Y	Y
7 Markey	N	N	N	N	Y	Y	Y
8 Capuano	N	N	N	N	N	Y	Y
9 Lynch	Y	N	N	N	N	Y	Y
10 Keating	N	N	N	N	N	Y	Y
MICHIGAN							
1 **Benishek**	N	Y	Y	Y	Y	Y	N
2 **Huizenga**	Y	Y	Y	Y	Y	Y	N
3 **Amash**	Y	Y	Y	Y	Y	Y	N
4 **Camp**	Y	N	Y	Y	N	N	N
5 Kildee	N	N	N	N	N	Y	Y
6 **Upton**	Y	Y	Y	N	N	N	N
7 **Walberg**	Y	Y	Y	Y	Y	N	N
8 **Rogers**	Y	N	N	Y	N	N	N
9 Peters	N	N	N	N	N	Y	Y
10 **Miller**	Y	Y	Y	N	N	Y	N
11 **McCotter**	Y	Y	Y	N	N	N	N
12 Levin	N	N	N	N	N	Y	Y
13 Clarke	N	N	N	N	N	Y	Y
14 Conyers	N	N	N	N	N	Y	Y
15 Dingell	N	N	N	N	Y	N	Y
MINNESOTA							
1 Walz	N	N	N	N	N	Y	Y
2 **Kline**	Y	Y	Y	Y	Y	N	N
3 **Paulsen**	Y	N	Y	Y	Y	N	N
4 McCollum	N	N	N	N	N	Y	Y

	335	336	337	338	339	340	341
5 Ellison	N	N	N	N	N	Y	Y
6 **Bachmann**	Y	Y	Y	Y	Y	?	N
7 Peterson	N	N	N	N	N	N	Y
8 **Cravaack**	N	N	N	N	N	N	N
MISSISSIPPI							
1 **Nunnelee**	Y	N	N	Y	N	N	N
2 Thompson	N	N	N	N	N	N	Y
3 **Harper**	N	N	N	Y	N	N	N
4 **Palazzo**	N	N	N	Y	N	N	N
MISSOURI							
1 Clay	N	N	N	N	Y	Y	Y
2 **Akin**	Y	Y	Y	Y	N	N	N
3 Carnahan	N	N	N	N	Y	Y	Y
4 **Hartzler**	Y	Y	Y	Y	N	N	N
5 Cleaver	N	N	N	N	N	Y	Y
6 **Graves**	Y	Y	Y	Y	N	N	N
7 **Long**	Y	Y	Y	Y	N	Y	N
8 **Emerson**	N	N	N	N	N	N	N
9 **Luetkemeyer**	Y	Y	Y	Y	N	N	N
MONTANA							
AL **Rehberg**	N	N	N	N	N	N	N
NEBRASKA							
1 **Fortenberry**	Y	N	Y	Y	N	N	N
2 **Terry**	Y	N	Y	N	N	N	N
3 **Smith**	Y	Y	Y	Y	Y	N	N
NEVADA							
1 Berkley	N	N	N	N	Y	Y	Y
2 **Amodei**	Y	Y	Y	Y	Y	Y	N
3 **Heck**	N	N	N	N	Y	Y	N
NEW HAMPSHIRE							
1 **Guinta**	Y	Y	Y	Y	N	N	N
2 **Bass**	N	?	N	N	N	N	N
NEW JERSEY							
1 Andrews	N	N	N	N	N	Y	Y
2 **LoBiondo**	N	N	N	N	N	N	N
3 **Runyan**	N	N	N	N	N	N	N
4 **Smith**	N	N	N	N	N	N	N
5 **Garrett**	Y	Y	Y	Y	Y	Y	N
6 Pallone	N	N	N	N	Y	Y	Y
7 **Lance**	Y	Y	Y	N	Y	Y	N
8 Pascrell	N	N	N	N	N	Y	Y
9 Rothman	N	N	N	N	N	Y	Y
10 Vacant							
11 **Frelinghuysen**	N	N	N	Y	N	N	N
12 Holt	N	N	N	N	N	Y	Y
13 Sires	N	N	N	N	Y	Y	Y
NEW MEXICO							
1 Heinrich	N	N	N	N	Y	Y	Y
2 **Pearce**	Y	N	Y	Y	Y	N	N
3 Luján	N	N	N	N	Y	Y	Y
NEW YORK							
1 Bishop	N	N	N	N	N	Y	Y
2 Israel	N	N	N	N	N	Y	Y
3 **King**	N	N	N	N	N	N	N
4 McCarthy	N	N	N	N	N	Y	Y
5 Ackerman	N	N	N	N	N	Y	Y
6 Meeks	N	N	N	N	N	Y	Y
7 Crowley	N	N	N	N	Y	Y	Y
8 Nadler	N	N	N	N	Y	Y	Y
9 **Turner**	N	N	N	Y	N	N	N
10 Towns	N	N	N	N	?	Y	Y
11 Clarke	N	N	N	N	N	Y	Y
12 Velázquez	N	N	N	N	N	Y	Y
13 **Grimm**	N	N	N	N	N	N	N
14 Maloney	N	N	N	N	Y	Y	Y
15 Rangel	N	N	N	N	N	Y	Y
16 Serrano	N	N	N	N	N	Y	Y
17 Engel	N	N	N	N	N	N	Y
18 Lowey	N	N	N	N	N	Y	Y
19 **Hayworth**	N	N	N	Y	N	Y	N
20 **Gibson**	N	N	N	N	N	Y	N
21 Tonko	N	N	N	N	N	Y	Y
22 Hinchey	N	N	N	N	N	Y	Y
23 Owens	N	N	N	N	N	N	Y
24 **Hanna**	N	N	N	N	N	N	N
25 **Buerkle**	Y	Y	Y	Y	N	N	N
26 Hochul	Y	N	N	N	N	N	Y
27 Higgins	N	N	N	N	N	Y	Y
28 Slaughter	–	–	–	–	–	+	+
29 **Reed**	Y	N	N	Y	N	N	N
NORTH CAROLINA							
1 Butterfield	N	N	N	N	N	Y	Y
2 **Ellmers**	N	N	N	Y	N	N	N
3 **Jones**	Y	Y	Y	Y	N	Y	N
4 Price	N	N	N	N	N	Y	Y

	335	336	337	338	339	340	341
5 **Foxx**	Y	Y	Y	Y	N	N	N
6 **Coble**	?	?	?	?	?	?	?
7 McIntyre	N	N	N	N	N	N	Y
8 Kissell	N	N	N	N	N	N	Y
9 **Myrick**	Y	Y	Y	Y	N	N	N
10 **McHenry**	Y	Y	Y	Y	Y	N	N
11 Shuler	?	?	?	?	?	?	?
12 Watt	N	N	N	N	N	Y	Y
13 Miller	N	N	N	N	Y	Y	Y
NORTH DAKOTA							
AL **Berg**	N	N	N	Y	N	N	N
OHIO							
1 **Chabot**	Y	Y	Y	Y	N	N	N
2 **Schmidt**	Y	Y	Y	N	N	N	N
3 **Turner**	N	N	N	N	N	N	N
4 **Jordan**	Y	Y	Y	Y	N	Y	N
5 **Latta**	Y	Y	Y	Y	N	N	N
6 **Johnson**	Y	N	Y	Y	N	N	N
7 **Austria**	N	N	N	Y	N	N	N
8 **Boehner**							
9 Kaptur	N	N	N	N	Y	N	Y
10 Kucinich	N	N	N	N	Y	Y	Y
11 Fudge	N	N	N	N	N	N	Y
12 **Tiberi**	N	Y	N	N	N	N	N
13 Sutton	N	N	N	N	N	Y	Y
14 **LaTourette**	N	N	N	N	N	N	N
15 **Stivers**	N	N	N	N	N	N	N
16 **Renacci**	N	N	N	Y	N	N	N
17 Ryan	N	N	N	N	N	N	Y
18 **Gibbs**	N	N	N	Y	N	N	N
OKLAHOMA							
1 **Sullivan**	Y	Y	Y	Y	Y	N	N
2 Boren	N	N	N	N	N	N	Y
3 **Lucas**	N	N	N	Y	N	N	N
4 **Cole**	N	N	N	Y	N	N	N
5 **Lankford**	Y	Y	N	Y	Y	N	N
OREGON							
1 Bonamici	N	N	N	N	N	Y	Y
2 **Walden**	Y	Y	Y	N	N	N	N
3 Blumenauer	N	N	N	N	N	Y	Y
4 DeFazio	N	N	N	N	Y	Y	Y
5 Schrader	N	N	N	N	Y	Y	Y
PENNSYLVANIA							
1 Brady	N	N	N	N	N	Y	Y
2 Fattah	N	N	N	N	N	Y	Y
3 **Kelly**	N	N	N	N	N	N	N
4 Altmire	N	N	N	N	N	N	Y
5 **Thompson**	N	N	N	Y	N	N	N
6 **Gerlach**	N	N	N	N	N	N	N
7 **Meehan**	N	N	N	N	N	N	N
8 **Fitzpatrick**	Y	N	N	N	N	N	N
9 **Shuster**	Y	N	N	N	N	N	N
10 **Marino**	N	N	N	Y	N	N	N
11 **Barletta**	N	N	N	N	N	N	N
12 Critz	N	N	N	N	N	N	Y
13 Schwartz	N	N	N	N	Y	Y	Y
14 Doyle	N	N	N	N	N	Y	Y
15 **Dent**	N	N	N	Y	N	N	N
16 **Pitts**	Y	Y	Y	Y	N	N	N
17 Holden	N	N	N	N	N	N	Y
18 **Murphy**	Y	N	Y	N	N	N	N
19 **Platts**	Y	N	Y	Y	N	N	N
RHODE ISLAND							
1 Cicilline	N	N	N	N	N	Y	Y
2 Langevin	N	N	N	N	N	Y	Y
SOUTH CAROLINA							
1 **Scott**	Y	Y	Y	Y	N	Y	N
2 **Wilson**	Y	Y	Y	Y	N	N	N
3 **Duncan**	Y	Y	Y	Y	N	N	N
4 **Gowdy**	Y	Y	Y	Y	N	N	N
5 **Mulvaney**	Y	Y	Y	Y	N	Y	N
6 Clyburn	N	N	N	N	N	Y	Y
SOUTH DAKOTA							
AL **Noem**	N	N	N	Y	N	N	N
TENNESSEE							
1 **Roe**	Y	Y	Y	Y	N	N	N
2 **Duncan**	Y	Y	Y	Y	N	Y	N
3 **Fleischmann**	N	N	N	Y	N	N	N
4 **DesJarlais**	Y	Y	Y	Y	N	N	N
5 Cooper	Y	N	Y	N	N	N	Y
6 **Black**	Y	Y	Y	Y	N	N	N
7 **Blackburn**	Y	Y	Y	Y	N	N	N
8 **Fincher**	Y	Y	Y	Y	N	Y	N
9 Cohen	N	N	N	N	N	Y	Y

	335	336	337	338	339	340	341
TEXAS							
1 **Gohmert**	Y	Y	Y	Y	Y	Y	N
2 **Poe**	Y	Y	Y	Y	Y	N	N
3 **Johnson, S.**	Y	Y	Y	Y	N	Y	N
4 **Hall**	Y	N	N	Y	N	N	N
5 **Hensarling**	Y	Y	Y	Y	Y	Y	N
6 **Barton**	Y	N	Y	Y	Y	N	N
7 **Culberson**	N	N	N	Y	N	Y	N
8 **Brady**	Y	Y	Y	Y	?	?	N
9 Green, A.	N	N	N	N	Y	N	Y
10 **McCaul**	Y	Y	Y	Y	Y	N	N
11 **Conaway**	Y	Y	Y	Y	N	Y	N
12 **Granger**	N	N	N	Y	N	N	N
13 **Thornberry**	Y	Y	N	Y	N	N	N
14 **Paul**	?	?	?	?	?	?	?
15 Hinojosa	N	N	N	N	Y	Y	Y
16 Reyes	N	N	N	N	Y	Y	Y
17 **Flores**	Y	Y	Y	Y	N	N	N
18 Jackson Lee	N	N	N	N	Y	N	Y
19 **Neugebauer**	Y	Y	Y	Y	Y	Y	N
20 Gonzalez	N	N	N	N	N	Y	Y
21 **Smith**	N	N	N	Y	Y	N	N
22 **Olson**	Y	Y	Y	Y	Y	N	N
23 **Canseco**	Y	Y	Y	Y	Y	N	N
24 **Marchant**	Y	Y	Y	Y	Y	N	N
25 Doggett	N	N	N	N	N	Y	Y
26 **Burgess**	Y	Y	Y	Y	Y	Y	N
27 **Farenthold**	Y	Y	Y	Y	Y	Y	N
28 Cuellar	Y	N	N	N	Y	N	Y
29 Green, G.	N	N	N	N	Y	N	Y
30 Johnson, E.	N	N	N	N	N	Y	Y
31 **Carter**	N	N	N	Y	N	N	N
32 **Sessions**	Y	Y	Y	Y	N	N	N
UTAH							
1 **Bishop**	N	Y	Y	Y	Y	N	N
2 Matheson	Y	N	Y	N	Y	N	Y
3 **Chaffetz**	Y	Y	Y	Y	Y	Y	N
VERMONT							
AL Welch	N	N	N	N	Y	Y	Y
VIRGINIA							
1 **Wittman**	Y	N	Y	Y	N	N	N
2 **Rigell**	Y	Y	N	Y	N	Y	N
3 Scott	N	N	N	N	N	Y	Y
4 **Forbes**	Y	Y	N	Y	N	N	N
5 **Hurt**	Y	Y	Y	Y	N	N	N
6 **Goodlatte**	Y	Y	Y	Y	N	?	N
7 **Cantor**	Y	N	Y	Y	N	N	N
8 Moran	N	N	N	N	N	Y	Y
9 **Griffith**	Y	Y	Y	Y	N	N	N
10 **Wolf**	N	N	N	Y	N	N	N
11 Connolly	N	N	N	N	N	Y	Y
WASHINGTON							
1 Vacant							
2 Larsen	N	N	N	N	N	N	Y
3 **Herrera Beutler**	N	N	Y	Y	N	Y	N
4 **Hastings**	N	N	N	Y	N	N	N
5 **McMorris Rodgers**	Y	Y	Y	Y	Y	N	N
6 Dicks	N	N	N	N	N	Y	Y
7 McDermott	N	N	N	N	Y	Y	Y
8 **Reichert**	N	N	N	Y	N	N	N
9 Smith	N	N	N	N	Y	Y	Y
WEST VIRGINIA							
1 **McKinley**	N	N	N	N	N	N	N
2 **Capito**	N	N	N	N	N	N	N
3 Rahall	N	N	N	N	N	N	Y
WISCONSIN							
1 **Ryan**	Y	Y	Y	N	N	Y	N
2 Baldwin	N	N	N	N	N	N	Y
3 Kind	N	N	Y	N	N	Y	Y
4 Moore	N	N	N	N	N	Y	Y
5 **Sensenbrenner**	Y	Y	Y	Y	N	Y	N
6 **Petri**	Y	Y	?	N	N	Y	N
7 **Duffy**	Y	Y	Y	N	N	Y	N
8 **Ribble**	Y	Y	Y	Y	Y	Y	N
WYOMING							
AL **Lummis**	Y	Y	Y	Y	Y	N	N

IN THE HOUSE | By Vote Number

342. HR 5325. Fiscal 2013 Energy-Water Appropriations/Passage.
Passage of the bill that would provide $32.1 billion in fiscal 2013 to fund the Energy Department, the Army Corps of Engineers, the Interior Department's Bureau of Reclamation and several regional water and power authorities. In total, the bill would provide the Energy Department with $26.1 billion, of which $11.3 billion would be designated for the National Nuclear Security Administration. It would provide $4.8 billion for the Army Corps of Engineers and $967 million for the Interior Department's Bureau of Reclamation. Passed 255-165: R 207-29; D 48-136. A "nay" was a vote in support of the president's position. June 6, 2012.

343. HR 4348. Surface Transportation Extension/Motion to Instruct. Flake, R-Ariz., motion to instruct conferees to agree to Senate-passed provision that would guarantee that states receive a return of at least 95 percent on the tax funds they deposit into the Highway Trust Fund. Motion agreed to 259-154: R 192-43; D 67-111. June 6, 2012.

344. HR 4348. Surface Transportation Extension/Motion to Instruct. Doggett, D-Texas, motion to instruct conferees to agree to a Senate-passed provision that would expand restrictions that the Treasury Department can currently impose on foreign governments and financial institutions that launder money. The language would allow such restrictions to be used on foreign governments and financial institutions that impede U.S. tax enforcement. Motion rejected 192-226: R 14-222; D 178-4. June 6, 2012.

345. HR 5855. Fiscal 2013 Homeland Security Appropriations/ Homeland Security Secretary Expenses. Moore, D-Wis., amendment that would increase by $3 million the amount provided for the Office of the Secretary of Homeland Security and reduce by $4.8 million the funding for automated systems expenses at U.S. Customs and Border Protection. Rejected in Committee of the Whole 154-260: R 0-235; D 154-25. June 6, 2012.

346. HR 5855. Fiscal 2013 Homeland Security Appropriations/ Funding Reduction. Broun, R-Ga., amendment that would reduce funding for all of the administrative expense accounts in the bill by 3 percent, except for the Coast Guard. Rejected in Committee of the Whole 140-273: R 135-101; D 5-172. June 6, 2012.

347. HR 5855. Fiscal 2013 Homeland Security Appropriations/ Homeland Security Grant Programs. Holt, D-N.J., amendment that would increase by $50 million the amount provided for state and local grants, contracts and cooperative agreements for homeland security activities, offset by a $10 million reduction for the Office of the Secretary of Homeland Security, a $25 million cut for intelligence analysis and operations coordination, a $15 million decrease for the Transportation Security Administration's civil aviation security services and a $15 million cut for aviation security direction and enforcement activities. Rejected in Committee of the Whole 173-240: R 24-211; D 149-29. June 6, 2012.

348. HR 5855. Fiscal 2013 Homeland Security Appropriations/ Homeland Security Grant Programs. Clarke, D-Mich., amendment that would increase by $10 million the amount for state and local grants, contracts and cooperative agreements for homeland security activities, offset by a $10 million reduction for the Office of the Undersecretary for Management. Adopted in Committee of the Whole 211-202: R 51-185; D 160-17. June 6, 2012.

	342	343	344	345	346	347	348
ALABAMA							
1 Bonner	Y	Y	N	N	N	N	N
2 Roby	Y	Y	N	N	N	N	N
3 Rogers	Y	Y	N	N	N	N	N
4 Aderholt	Y	Y	N	N	N	N	Y
5 Brooks	Y	?	N	N	N	N	N
6 Bachus	Y	?	N	N	N	N	N
7 Sewell	N	N	Y	Y	N	Y	Y
ALASKA							
AL Young	Y	N	N	N	N	N	N
ARIZONA							
1 Gosar	Y	Y	N	N	Y	N	N
2 Franks	Y	Y	N	N	Y	N	N
3 Quayle	Y	Y	N	N	Y	N	N
4 Pastor	Y	Y	Y	Y	N	N	N
5 Schweikert	N	Y	N	N	Y	N	N
6 Flake	N	Y	N	N	Y	N	N
7 Grijalva	N	Y	Y	Y	?	?	Y
8 Vacant							
ARKANSAS							
1 Crawford	Y	Y	N	N	N	N	N
2 Griffin	Y	Y	N	N	Y	N	N
3 Womack	Y	Y	N	N	N	N	N
4 Ross	Y	Y	Y	N	N	N	Y
CALIFORNIA							
1 Thompson	N	Y	Y	Y	N	Y	Y
2 Herger	Y	Y	N	N	Y	N	N
3 Lungren	Y	Y	N	N	N	N	N
4 McClintock	N	Y	N	N	Y	N	N
5 Matsui	Y	Y	Y	Y	N	Y	Y
6 Woolsey	N	Y	Y	Y	N	Y	Y
7 Miller, George	N	Y	Y	Y	N	Y	Y
8 Pelosi	N	N	Y	Y	N	Y	Y
9 Lee	N	N	Y	Y	N	Y	Y
10 Garamendi	Y	Y	Y	Y	N	Y	Y
11 McNerney	Y	Y	Y	Y	N	Y	Y
12 Speier	Y	Y	Y	?	Y	Y	Y
13 Stark	N	N	Y	?	?	?	?
14 Eshoo	N	Y	Y	Y	Y	Y	Y
15 Honda	N	Y	Y	?	Y	Y	Y
16 Lofgren	Y	Y	Y	Y	Y	Y	Y
17 Farr	Y	Y	Y	Y	Y	Y	Y
18 Cardoza	Y	Y	Y	?	?	?	?
19 Denham	Y	Y	N	?	N	Y	Y
20 Costa	Y	Y	Y	Y	N	N	N
21 Nunes	Y	Y	N	N	N	N	N
22 McCarthy	Y	Y	N	N	N	N	N
23 Capps	N	Y	Y	Y	N	Y	Y
24 Gallegly	Y	Y	N	N	N	N	N
25 McKeon	?	?	?	N	Y	N	N
26 Dreier	Y	Y	N	N	N	N	N
27 Sherman	N	Y	Y	Y	N	Y	Y
28 Berman	?	?	?	Y	Y	Y	Y
29 Schiff	N	Y	Y	Y	N	Y	Y
30 Waxman	N	N	Y	Y	N	Y	Y
31 Becerra	N	Y	Y	Y	N	Y	N
32 Chu	N	Y	Y	Y	N	Y	Y
33 Bass	N	N	Y	?	?	?	?
34 Roybal-Allard	N	Y	Y	Y	N	Y	Y
35 Waters	N	N	Y	Y	N	Y	?
36 Hahn	?	?	Y	Y	Y	Y	Y
37 Richardson	N	Y	Y	Y	N	Y	Y
38 Napolitano	?	?	?	?	?	?	?
39 Sánchez, Linda	N	Y	Y	Y	N	Y	N
40 Royce	N	Y	Y	N	Y	N	N
41 Lewis	?	?	?	?	?	?	?
42 Miller, Gary	?	?	?	N	N	N	N
43 Baca	N	Y	Y	Y	N	Y	Y
44 Calvert	Y	Y	N	N	N	N	N
45 Bono Mack	Y	Y	N	N	N	N	N
46 Rohrabacher	N	Y	Y	N	Y	N	N
47 Sanchez, Loretta	Y	Y	Y	Y	N	Y	Y
48 Campbell	N	Y	N	N	N	N	N
49 Issa	Y	Y	N	N	N	N	N
50 Bilbray	Y	Y	Y	N	N	N	N
51 Filner	−	−	+	+	−	+	+
52 Hunter	Y	Y	N	N	N	N	N
53 Davis	N	Y	Y	Y	N	Y	Y

	342	343	344	345	346	347	348
COLORADO							
1 DeGette	N	N	Y	Y	N	Y	Y
2 Polis	N	?	Y	Y	Y	Y	Y
3 Tipton	Y	Y	N	N	Y	N	N
4 Gardner	Y	Y	Y	N	Y	N	N
5 Lamborn	Y	Y	N	N	Y	N	N
6 Coffman	Y	Y	Y	N	N	N	N
7 Perlmutter	N	Y	Y	N	N	Y	Y
CONNECTICUT							
1 Larson	N	N	Y	Y	N	Y	Y
2 Courtney	N	N	Y	Y	N	Y	Y
3 DeLauro	N	N	Y	Y	N	Y	Y
4 Himes	Y	N	Y	Y	N	Y	Y
5 Murphy	N	N	Y	Y	N	Y	Y
DELAWARE							
AL Carney	N	N	Y	Y	N	Y	Y
FLORIDA							
1 Miller	Y	Y	N	N	Y	N	N
2 Southerland	Y	Y	N	N	Y	N	Y
3 Brown	Y	N	Y	N	Y	N	Y
4 Crenshaw	Y	Y	N	N	Y	N	N
5 Nugent	Y	Y	N	N	Y	N	N
6 Stearns	Y	Y	N	N	Y	N	N
7 Mica	Y	Y	N	N	Y	Y	Y
8 Webster	Y	Y	N	N	Y	N	N
9 Bilirakis	Y	Y	N	N	N	N	N
10 Young	Y	Y	N	N	Y	N	N
11 Castor	Y	N	Y	Y	N	Y	Y
12 Ross	Y	Y	N	N	Y	N	N
13 Buchanan	Y	Y	N	N	Y	Y	N
14 Mack	Y	Y	N	N	Y	Y	N
15 Posey	Y	Y	N	N	Y	Y	N
16 Rooney	Y	Y	N	N	Y	Y	Y
17 Wilson	N	N	Y	Y	N	Y	Y
18 Ros-Lehtinen	Y	Y	N	N	N	Y	N
19 Deutch	N	N	Y	Y	N	Y	Y
20 Wasserman Schultz	N	N	Y	Y	N	Y	Y
21 Diaz-Balart	Y	Y	N	N	N	?	?
22 West	Y	Y	N	N	N	N	N
23 Hastings	N	N	Y	Y	N	Y	Y
24 Adams	Y	Y	N	Y	N	N	N
25 Rivera	Y	Y	N	N	N	N	Y
GEORGIA							
1 Kingston	Y	Y	N	N	N	N	N
2 Bishop	Y	Y	Y	Y	N	Y	?
3 Westmoreland	Y	Y	N	N	N	N	N
4 Johnson	N	N	Y	N	N	Y	Y
5 Lewis	N	N	Y	Y	N	Y	Y
6 Price	Y	Y	N	N	Y	N	N
7 Woodall	Y	Y	N	N	Y	N	N
8 Scott, A.	Y	Y	N	N	Y	N	N
9 Graves	Y	Y	N	N	N	N	N
10 Broun	N	Y	N	N	Y	N	N
11 Gingrey	Y	Y	N	N	Y	N	N
12 Barrow	Y	Y	Y	N	N	N	Y
13 Scott, D.	N	N	Y	?	?	Y	Y
HAWAII							
1 Hanabusa	N	N	Y	Y	N	Y	Y
2 Hirono	N	N	Y	Y	N	?	Y
IDAHO							
1 Labrador	Y	Y	N	N	Y	N	N
2 Simpson	Y	N	N	N	N	N	N
ILLINOIS							
1 Rush	N	N	Y	Y	N	Y	Y
2 Jackson	N	N	Y	Y	N	Y	Y
3 Lipinski	Y	N	Y	Y	N	Y	Y
4 Gutierrez	N	N	Y	Y	N	Y	Y
5 Quigley	N	N	Y	Y	N	Y	Y
6 Roskam	Y	Y	N	N	N	N	N
7 Davis	N	?	Y	Y	N	Y	Y
8 Walsh	N	N	Y	N	Y	N	N
9 Schakowsky	N	N	Y	Y	N	Y	Y
10 Dold	Y	Y	N	N	N	N	N
11 Kinzinger	Y	N	Y	N	Y	N	N
12 Costello	Y	N	Y	Y	N	Y	Y
13 Biggert	Y	Y	N	N	N	N	N
14 Hultgren	Y	N	Y	N	Y	N	N
15 Johnson	N	Y	N	N	N	N	N

KEY   Republicans   Democrats

Y Voted for (yea)	**X** Paired against	**C** Voted "present" to avoid possible conflict of interest
# Paired for	**−** Announced against	
+ Announced for	**P** Voted "present"	**?** Did not vote or otherwise make a position known
N Voted against (nay)		

	342	343	344	345	346	347	348
16 **Manzullo**	Y	Y	N	N	Y	N	N
17 **Schilling**	Y	Y	N	N	N	N	N
18 **Schock**	Y	Y	N	N	N	N	N
19 **Shimkus**	Y	Y	N	N	Y	N	N
INDIANA							
1 Visclosky	Y	Y	Y	Y	N	N	N
2 Donnelly	Y	Y	Y	N	N	N	Y
3 **Stutzman**	Y	Y	N	N	Y	N	Y
4 **Rokita**	Y	Y	N	N	Y	N	N
5 **Burton**	Y	Y	N	N	Y	N	N
6 **Pence**	Y	Y	N	N	Y	Y	N
7 Carson	N	Y	Y	Y	N	Y	Y
8 **Bucshon**	Y	Y	N	N	N	N	N
9 **Young**	Y	Y	N	N	N	N	N
IOWA							
1 Braley	N	Y	Y	Y	N	Y	Y
2 Loebsack	Y	Y	Y	N	N	Y	Y
3 Boswell	Y	Y	Y	N	N	Y	Y
4 **Latham**	Y	N	Y	N	N	N	Y
5 **King**	Y	Y	N	N	Y	N	N
KANSAS							
1 **Huelskamp**	Y	Y	N	N	Y	N	N
2 **Jenkins**	Y	Y	N	N	Y	N	N
3 **Yoder**	Y	Y	N	N	Y	N	N
4 **Pompeo**	Y	Y	N	N	Y	N	N
KENTUCKY							
1 **Whitfield**	Y	Y	N	N	N	N	Y
2 **Guthrie**	Y	N	N	N	Y	N	Y
3 Yarmuth	N	N	Y	Y	N	Y	Y
4 **Davis**	Y	N	N	N	N	N	N
5 **Rogers**	Y	N	N	N	N	N	N
6 Chandler	Y	N	Y	N	N	Y	Y
LOUISIANA							
1 **Scalise**	Y	Y	N	N	Y	Y	Y
2 Richmond	N	N	Y	Y	N	Y	Y
3 **Landry**	Y	Y	N	N	Y	Y	Y
4 **Fleming**	Y	Y	N	N	Y	N	N
5 **Alexander**	Y	Y	N	N	N	N	N
6 **Cassidy**	N	Y	N	N	Y	N	N
7 **Boustany**	N	Y	N	N	N	Y	N
MAINE							
1 Pingree	N	N	Y	Y	N	Y	Y
2 Michaud	N	N	Y	Y	N	Y	Y
MARYLAND							
1 **Harris**	Y	Y	N	N	Y	N	N
2 Ruppersberger	Y	Y	Y	Y	N	Y	N
3 Sarbanes	N	Y	Y	Y	N	Y	Y
4 Edwards	N	N	Y	Y	N	Y	Y
5 Hoyer	N	N	Y	Y	N	N	N
6 **Bartlett**	Y	Y	N	N	Y	N	N
7 Cummings	N	Y	Y	Y	N	Y	Y
8 Van Hollen	N	N	Y	Y	N	Y	Y
MASSACHUSETTS							
1 Olver	N	N	Y	?	?	?	?
2 Neal	N	N	Y	Y	N	Y	Y
3 McGovern	N	N	Y	Y	N	Y	Y
4 Frank	N	?	?	Y	N	Y	N
5 Tsongas	N	N	Y	Y	N	Y	Y
6 Tierney	N	N	Y	Y	N	Y	Y
7 Markey	N	N	Y	Y	N	Y	Y
8 Capuano	N	N	Y	Y	N	Y	Y
9 Lynch	N	N	Y	Y	N	Y	N
10 Keating	N	N	Y	Y	N	Y	Y
MICHIGAN							
1 **Benishek**	Y	Y	N	N	Y	N	Y
2 **Huizenga**	N	Y	N	N	Y	N	Y
3 **Amash**	N	Y	N	N	Y	N	N
4 **Camp**	Y	N	N	N	Y	N	Y
5 Kildee	N	Y	Y	Y	N	Y	Y
6 **Upton**	Y	Y	N	N	Y	N	Y
7 **Walberg**	Y	Y	N	N	Y	N	N
8 **Rogers**	Y	Y	N	N	Y	N	Y
9 Peters	N	Y	Y	Y	N	Y	Y
10 **Miller**	Y	Y	N	N	Y	N	Y
11 **McCotter**	Y	Y	N	N	Y	N	Y
12 Levin	N	Y	Y	Y	N	Y	Y
13 Clarke	N	N	Y	Y	N	Y	Y
14 Conyers	N	?	Y	?	?	?	?
15 Dingell	N	Y	Y	Y	N	Y	Y
MINNESOTA							
1 Walz	N	N	Y	N	N	Y	Y
2 **Kline**	Y	Y	N	N	Y	N	N
3 **Paulsen**	Y	Y	N	N	Y	N	N
4 McCollum	Y	N	Y	Y	N	Y	Y

	342	343	344	345	346	347	348
5 Ellison	N	N	Y	Y	N	Y	Y
6 **Bachmann**	N	Y	N	N	Y	N	Y
7 Peterson	Y	Y	Y	N	N	N	Y
8 **Cravaack**	Y	Y	N	N	Y	N	N
MISSISSIPPI							
1 **Nunnelee**	Y	Y	N	N	Y	N	N
2 Thompson	N	N	Y	Y	N	Y	Y
3 **Harper**	Y	Y	N	N	N	N	N
4 **Palazzo**	Y	Y	N	N	N	N	N
MISSOURI							
1 Clay	N	N	Y	Y	N	Y	Y
2 **Akin**	Y	Y	N	N	Y	N	N
3 Carnahan	N	N	Y	Y	N	Y	Y
4 **Hartzler**	Y	Y	N	N	Y	N	N
5 Cleaver	N	N	Y	Y	N	Y	Y
6 **Graves**	Y	Y	N	N	Y	N	Y
7 **Long**	Y	Y	N	N	Y	N	N
8 **Emerson**	Y	N	N	N	N	N	Y
9 **Luetkemeyer**	Y	Y	N	N	Y	N	Y
MONTANA							
AL **Rehberg**	Y	N	N	N	N	N	N
NEBRASKA							
1 **Fortenberry**	Y	Y	Y	N	Y	N	N
2 **Terry**	Y	Y	N	N	Y	N	N
3 **Smith**	Y	Y	N	N	Y	N	N
NEVADA							
1 Berkley	N	Y	Y	Y	N	Y	Y
2 **Amodei**	N	Y	N	N	N	N	N
3 **Heck**	N	Y	N	N	N	N	N
NEW HAMPSHIRE							
1 **Guinta**	Y	Y	N	N	N	N	N
2 **Bass**	Y	Y	N	N	N	Y	Y
NEW JERSEY							
1 Andrews	N	Y	Y	Y	N	Y	Y
2 **LoBiondo**	Y	Y	N	N	N	N	Y
3 **Runyan**	Y	Y	N	N	N	N	Y
4 **Smith**	Y	Y	N	N	N	N	Y
5 **Garrett**	Y	Y	N	N	Y	N	N
6 Pallone	N	N	Y	Y	N	Y	Y
7 **Lance**	Y	Y	N	N	Y	N	N
8 Pascrell	N	N	Y	Y	N	Y	Y
9 Rothman	N	N	Y	Y	N	Y	Y
10 Vacant							
11 **Frelinghuysen**	Y	Y	N	N	N	N	N
12 Holt	N	N	Y	Y	N	Y	Y
13 Sires	N	N	Y	Y	N	Y	Y
NEW MEXICO							
1 Heinrich	Y	N	Y	Y	N	Y	Y
2 **Pearce**	Y	Y	N	N	N	N	N
3 Luján	Y	N	Y	Y	N	Y	Y
NEW YORK							
1 Bishop	N	N	N	N	N	Y	Y
2 Israel	N	N	Y	N	N	Y	Y
3 **King**	Y	N	N	N	N	N	N
4 McCarthy	N	N	Y	N	N	Y	Y
5 Ackerman	N	N	N	Y	N	Y	Y
6 Meeks	N	N	Y	Y	N	Y	Y
7 Crowley	N	N	Y	Y	N	Y	Y
8 Nadler	N	N	Y	Y	N	Y	Y
9 **Turner**	Y	N	N	N	N	N	N
10 Towns	N	N	Y	Y	N	Y	Y
11 Clarke	N	N	Y	Y	N	Y	Y
12 Velázquez	N	N	Y	Y	N	N	N
13 **Grimm**	Y	N	N	N	N	Y	N
14 Maloney	N	N	Y	Y	N	Y	Y
15 Rangel	N	N	Y	Y	N	Y	Y
16 Serrano	N	N	Y	Y	N	Y	Y
17 Engel	N	N	Y	Y	Y	Y	N
18 Lowey	N	N	Y	N	N	Y	Y
19 **Hayworth**	Y	N	N	N	N	Y	Y
20 **Gibson**	N	N	N	N	N	Y	Y
21 Tonko	N	N	Y	Y	N	Y	Y
22 Hinchey	N	N	Y	Y	N	Y	Y
23 Owens	Y	N	Y	N	N	Y	Y
24 **Hanna**	Y	N	N	N	N	Y	Y
25 **Buerkle**	N	N	N	N	Y	N	Y
26 Hochul	N	N	Y	N	N	N	Y
27 Higgins	N	N	Y	Y	N	Y	Y
28 Slaughter	–	–	+	+	–	+	+
29 **Reed**	Y	N	N	N	N	N	N
NORTH CAROLINA							
1 Butterfield	N	Y	Y	Y	N	Y	Y
2 **Ellmers**	Y	Y	N	N	N	N	N
3 **Jones**	N	Y	Y	N	N	Y	N
4 Price	N	Y	Y	Y	N	N	N

	342	343	344	345	346	347	348
5 **Foxx**	Y	Y	N	N	N	N	N
6 **Coble**	?	?	?	?	?	?	?
7 McIntyre	Y	Y	Y	N	N	N	Y
8 Kissell	Y	Y	Y	N	N	Y	Y
9 **Myrick**	Y	Y	N	–	–	–	–
10 **McHenry**	Y	Y	N	N	Y	N	N
11 Shuler	?	?	?	?	?	?	?
12 Watt	N	Y	Y	Y	N	Y	Y
13 Miller	N	Y	Y	Y	N	Y	Y
NORTH DAKOTA							
AL **Berg**	Y	N	N	N	N	N	N
OHIO							
1 **Chabot**	Y	Y	N	N	Y	N	Y
2 **Schmidt**	Y	Y	N	N	Y	N	N
3 **Turner**	Y	Y	N	N	N	N	N
4 **Jordan**	Y	Y	N	N	Y	N	Y
5 **Latta**	Y	Y	N	N	Y	N	N
6 **Johnson**	Y	Y	Y	N	N	N	N
7 **Austria**	Y	Y	N	N	N	N	N
8 **Boehner**							
9 Kaptur	Y	Y	Y	Y	N	Y	Y
10 Kucinich	N	Y	Y	Y	N	Y	Y
11 Fudge	N	Y	Y	Y	N	Y	Y
12 **Tiberi**	Y	Y	N	N	N	N	N
13 Sutton	N	Y	Y	Y	N	Y	Y
14 **LaTourette**	Y	Y	N	N	N	N	N
15 **Stivers**	Y	Y	N	N	N	N	Y
16 **Renacci**	Y	Y	N	N	N	N	N
17 Ryan	N	N	Y	Y	N	Y	?
18 **Gibbs**	Y	Y	N	N	N	N	N
OKLAHOMA							
1 **Sullivan**	Y	Y	N	N	Y	N	N
2 Boren	Y	Y	N	N	N	N	Y
3 **Lucas**	Y	Y	N	N	N	N	N
4 **Cole**	Y	Y	N	N	N	N	N
5 **Lankford**	Y	Y	N	N	Y	N	N
OREGON							
1 Bonamici	N	N	Y	Y	N	Y	Y
2 **Walden**	Y	N	N	N	Y	Y	N
3 Blumenauer	N	N	Y	Y	N	Y	Y
4 DeFazio	N	N	Y	Y	N	Y	Y
5 Schrader	N	N	Y	Y	N	Y	Y
PENNSYLVANIA							
1 Brady	Y	N	Y	Y	N	Y	Y
2 Fattah	Y	N	Y	Y	N	Y	Y
3 **Kelly**	Y	N	N	N	N	N	N
4 Altmire	Y	N	Y	N	N	N	N
5 **Thompson**	Y	N	N	N	N	N	N
6 **Gerlach**	Y	N	N	N	N	N	N
7 **Meehan**	Y	N	N	N	N	N	Y
8 **Fitzpatrick**	Y	N	N	N	Y	Y	Y
9 **Shuster**	Y	N	N	N	N	N	N
10 **Marino**	Y	N	N	N	N	Y	Y
11 **Barletta**	Y	N	N	N	N	Y	Y
12 Critz	Y	N	Y	N	N	N	Y
13 Schwartz	N	N	Y	Y	N	Y	Y
14 Doyle	N	N	Y	Y	N	Y	Y
15 **Dent**	Y	N	N	N	N	N	N
16 **Pitts**	Y	N	N	N	N	N	N
17 Holden	Y	N	Y	?	?	?	?
18 **Murphy**	Y	N	N	N	N	N	N
19 **Platts**	Y	N	N	N	N	N	N
RHODE ISLAND							
1 Cicilline	N	N	Y	Y	N	Y	Y
2 Langevin	N	N	Y	Y	N	Y	N
SOUTH CAROLINA							
1 **Scott**	Y	Y	N	N	Y	N	N
2 **Wilson**	Y	Y	N	N	Y	N	N
3 **Duncan**	Y	Y	N	N	Y	N	N
4 **Gowdy**	Y	Y	N	N	Y	N	N
5 **Mulvaney**	N	Y	N	N	Y	N	Y
6 Clyburn	N	N	Y	Y	N	Y	Y
SOUTH DAKOTA							
AL **Noem**	Y	N	N	N	N	N	N
TENNESSEE							
1 **Roe**	Y	Y	N	N	Y	N	N
2 **Duncan**	N	Y	Y	N	Y	Y	N
3 **Fleischmann**	Y	Y	N	N	Y	N	N
4 **DesJarlais**	Y	Y	N	N	Y	N	N
5 Cooper	N	Y	Y	Y	N	Y	Y
6 **Black**	Y	Y	N	N	Y	N	N
7 **Blackburn**	Y	Y	N	N	Y	N	N
8 **Fincher**	Y	Y	N	N	Y	N	N
9 Cohen	N	Y	Y	Y	N	Y	Y

	342	343	344	345	346	347	348
TEXAS							
1 **Gohmert**	N	Y	N	N	Y	N	N
2 **Poe**	N	Y	N	N	Y	N	N
3 **Johnson, S.**	Y	Y	N	N	Y	N	N
4 **Hall**	Y	N	N	N	Y	N	N
5 **Hensarling**	Y	Y	N	N	Y	N	N
6 **Barton**	Y	Y	N	N	Y	N	N
7 **Culberson**	Y	Y	N	?	?	?	?
8 **Brady**	Y	Y	N	N	Y	N	N
9 Green, A.	Y	Y	Y	Y	N	Y	Y
10 **McCaul**	Y	Y	N	N	Y	N	N
11 **Conaway**	Y	Y	N	N	Y	N	N
12 **Granger**	Y	Y	N	N	N	N	N
13 **Thornberry**	Y	Y	N	N	Y	N	N
14 **Paul**	?	?	?	?	?	?	?
15 Hinojosa	Y	N	Y	Y	N	Y	Y
16 Reyes	Y	N	Y	N	N	Y	Y
17 **Flores**	Y	Y	N	N	Y	N	N
18 Jackson Lee	Y	Y	Y	Y	N	Y	Y
19 **Neugebauer**	Y	Y	N	N	Y	N	N
20 Gonzalez	Y	N	Y	Y	N	N	Y
21 **Smith**	Y	Y	N	N	N	N	N
22 **Olson**	Y	Y	N	N	Y	N	N
23 **Canseco**	Y	Y	N	N	Y	N	N
24 **Marchant**	Y	Y	N	N	Y	N	N
25 Doggett	N	?	Y	Y	N	Y	Y
26 **Burgess**	N	Y	N	N	Y	Y	N
27 **Farenthold**	Y	Y	N	N	Y	N	N
28 Cuellar	Y	Y	Y	N	N	N	Y
29 Green, G.	Y	Y	Y	N	N	N	Y
30 Johnson, E.	N	N	Y	Y	N	Y	Y
31 **Carter**	Y	Y	N	N	Y	N	N
32 **Sessions**	Y	Y	N	N	Y	N	N
UTAH							
1 **Bishop**	Y	Y	N	N	Y	N	N
2 Matheson	N	Y	N	N	N	Y	Y
3 **Chaffetz**	Y	Y	N	N	Y	N	N
VERMONT							
AL Welch	N	N	Y	Y	N	Y	Y
VIRGINIA							
1 **Wittman**	Y	Y	N	N	N	N	N
2 **Rigell**	Y	Y	Y	N	N	N	Y
3 Scott	Y	Y	Y	Y	N	Y	Y
4 **Forbes**	Y	Y	N	N	N	N	N
5 **Hurt**	Y	Y	N	N	Y	N	N
6 **Goodlatte**	N	Y	N	N	Y	Y	Y
7 **Cantor**	Y	Y	N	N	Y	N	N
8 Moran	N	Y	Y	Y	N	Y	N
9 **Griffith**	N	Y	N	N	Y	Y	Y
10 **Wolf**	Y	Y	N	N	N	N	N
11 Connolly	N	Y	Y	Y	N	Y	Y
WASHINGTON							
1 Vacant							
2 Larsen	Y	N	Y	Y	N	N	Y
3 **Herrera Beutler**	Y	N	N	N	Y	N	N
4 **Hastings**	Y	N	N	N	Y	N	N
5 **McMorris Rodgers**	Y	N	N	N	Y	N	N
6 Dicks	Y	?	?	Y	N	N	N
7 McDermott	N	N	Y	Y	N	Y	Y
8 **Reichert**	Y	N	N	N	N	N	Y
9 Smith	N	N	Y	Y	N	N	N
WEST VIRGINIA							
1 **McKinley**	Y	N	N	N	N	N	N
2 **Capito**	Y	N	N	N	N	N	N
3 Rahall	Y	N	Y	N	N	Y	Y
WISCONSIN							
1 **Ryan**	Y	Y	N	N	Y	N	N
2 Baldwin	N	N	Y	Y	N	Y	Y
3 Kind	N	N	Y	Y	N	Y	Y
4 Moore	N	N	Y	Y	N	Y	Y
5 **Sensenbrenner**	N	Y	N	N	Y	Y	Y
6 **Petri**	Y	N	N	N	Y	Y	Y
7 **Duffy**	Y	Y	N	N	Y	N	N
8 **Ribble**	Y	Y	N	N	Y	N	N
WYOMING							
AL **Lummis**	N	N	N	N	Y	N	N

IN THE HOUSE | By Vote Number

349. **HR 5855. Fiscal 2013 Homeland Security Appropriations/ Homeland Security Grant Programs.** Clarke, D-Mich., amendment that would increase by $10 million the amount for state and local grants, contracts, and cooperative agreements for homeland security activities. It would cut $10 million from immigration and customs law enforcement activities, detention and removal, and investigations as well as $10 million from activities to form agreements to allow state and local law enforcement officials to investigate, apprehend or detain immigrants. Rejected in Committee of the Whole 159-254: R 4-231; D 155-23. June 6, 2012.

350. **HR 5855. Fiscal 2013 Homeland Security Appropriations/ U.S. Customs and Border Protection.** Hahn, D-Calif., amendment that would increase by $10 million the amount provided in the bill for U.S. Customs and Border Protection salaries and expenses. It would cut $24.3 million from Science and Technology Directorate research and $24.3 million from the directorate's operation and construction of laboratory facilities. Rejected in Committee of the Whole 156-261: R 8-228; D 148-33. June 6, 2012.

351. **HR 5855. Fiscal 2013 Homeland Security Appropriations/ Homeland Security Grant Programs.** Hahn, D-Calif., amendment that would increase by $75 million the amount for state and local grants, contracts, and cooperative agreements for homeland security activities. It would decrease by $75 million funding for the purchase or lease of vehicles and by $75 million funding for the Science and Technology Directorate's operation and construction of laboratory facilities. Rejected in Committee of the Whole 144-273: R 7-229; D 137-44. June 6, 2012.

352. **HR 5855. Fiscal 2013 Homeland Security Appropriations/ Border Security Funding.** Poe, R-Texas, amendment that would increase by $10 million the amount for border security fencing, infrastructure and technology expenses and reduce by the same amount funding for expenses for the Office of the Undersecretary for Management. Adopted in Committee of the Whole 302-113: R 221-14; D 81-99. June 6, 2012.

353. **HR 5855. Fiscal 2013 Homeland Security Appropriations/ Emergency Humanitarian Efforts.** Bishop, R-Utah, amendment that would increase by $624,000 the amount provided for assistance to state and local law enforcement for emergency humanitarian efforts, and decrease by $3 million funding for border security fencing, infrastructure and technology expenses. Adopted in Committee of the Whole 230-186: R 209-26; D 21-160. June 6, 2012.

354. **HR 5855. Fiscal 2013 Homeland Security Appropriations/Child Exploitation.** Sanchez, Loretta, D-Calif., amendment that would redirect $40 million in funding within Immigration and Customs Enforcement for activities to combat child exploitation. Rejected in Committee of the Whole 167-249: R 1-235; D 166-14. June 6, 2012.

355. **HR 5855. Fiscal 2013 Homeland Security Appropriations/ Federal Air Marshals Funding.** Jackson Lee, D-Texas, amendment that would increase by $50 million the amount provided for Federal Air Marshals expenses and reduce by $61 million funding for Transportation Security Administration civil aviation security services. Rejected in Committee of the Whole 60-355: R 15-221; D 45-134. June 6, 2012.

	349	350	351	352	353	354	355
ALABAMA							
1 Bonner	N	N	N	Y	Y	N	N
2 Roby	N	N	N	Y	Y	N	N
3 Rogers	N	N	N	Y	Y	N	N
4 Aderholt	N	N	N	N	Y	N	N
5 Brooks	N	N	N	Y	Y	N	N
6 Bachus	N	N	N	Y	Y	N	N
7 Sewell	Y	Y	Y	N	N	N	N
ALASKA							
AL Young	N	N	N	Y	Y	N	N
ARIZONA							
1 Gosar	N	N	N	Y	Y	N	N
2 Franks	N	N	N	Y	Y	N	N
3 Quayle	N	N	N	Y	Y	N	Y
4 Pastor	Y	Y	N	N	N	Y	N
5 Schweikert	N	N	N	Y	Y	N	Y
6 Flake	N	N	N	Y	Y	N	N
7 Grijalva	Y	Y	Y	N	N	Y	Y
8 Vacant							
ARKANSAS							
1 Crawford	N	N	N	Y	Y	N	N
2 Griffin	N	N	N	Y	Y	N	N
3 Womack	N	N	N	Y	Y	N	N
4 Ross	N	N	N	Y	Y	N	N
CALIFORNIA							
1 Thompson	Y	N	N	N	Y	N	N
2 Herger	N	N	N	Y	Y	N	N
3 Lungren	N	N	N	Y	N	N	N
4 McClintock	N	Y	N	Y	Y	N	N
5 Matsui	Y	Y	N	N	N	Y	N
6 Woolsey	Y	Y	Y	N	N	Y	N
7 Miller, George	Y	Y	Y	N	N	Y	N
8 Pelosi	Y	Y	Y	N	N	Y	N
9 Lee	Y	Y	Y	N	N	Y	Y
10 Garamendi	Y	N	N	N	Y	N	N
11 McNerney	N	Y	Y	Y	N	Y	N
12 Speier	Y	Y	N	N	N	Y	N
13 Stark	?	?	?	?	?	?	?
14 Eshoo	Y	Y	Y	N	N	Y	Y
15 Honda	Y	Y	Y	N	N	Y	Y
16 Lofgren	Y	N	Y	N	N	Y	N
17 Farr	Y	N	N	N	N	Y	N
18 Cardoza	?	?	?	?	?	?	?
19 Denham	N	N	N	Y	Y	N	N
20 Costa	N	N	N	Y	Y	N	N
21 Nunes	N	N	N	Y	Y	N	N
22 McCarthy	N	N	N	Y	Y	N	N
23 Capps	Y	Y	Y	Y	N	Y	N
24 Gallegly	N	Y	N	Y	Y	N	N
25 McKeon	N	N	N	Y	Y	N	N
26 Dreier	N	N	N	Y	Y	N	N
27 Sherman	Y	Y	Y	N	N	Y	N
28 Berman	Y	Y	Y	N	N	Y	N
29 Schiff	Y	Y	Y	N	N	Y	N
30 Waxman	Y	Y	Y	N	N	Y	N
31 Becerra	Y	Y	Y	N	N	Y	N
32 Chu	Y	Y	Y	N	N	Y	N
33 Bass	?	?	?	?	?	?	?
34 Roybal-Allard	Y	Y	Y	N	N	Y	N
35 Waters	?	N	Y	N	N	Y	N
36 Hahn	Y	Y	Y	Y	N	Y	N
37 Richardson	Y	Y	Y	N	N	Y	N
38 Napolitano	?	?	?	?	?	?	?
39 Sánchez, Linda	Y	Y	Y	N	Y	Y	Y
40 Royce	N	Y	N	N	N	N	N
41 Lewis	?	?	?	?	?	?	?
42 Miller, Gary	N	Y	N	Y	Y	N	N
43 Baca	N	Y	Y	N	N	Y	N
44 Calvert	N	N	N	Y	Y	N	N
45 Bono Mack	N	N	N	Y	Y	N	N
46 Rohrabacher	N	Y	N	Y	Y	N	N
47 Sanchez, Loretta	Y	Y	Y	N	N	Y	N
48 Campbell	N	N	N	Y	Y	N	N
49 Issa	N	N	N	Y	Y	N	N
50 Bilbray	N	N	N	Y	Y	N	N
51 Filner	+	+	+	−	−	+	−
52 Hunter	N	N	N	Y	N	N	N
53 Davis	Y	Y	Y	Y	Y	Y	N
COLORADO							
1 DeGette	Y	Y	Y	N	N	Y	N
2 Polis	Y	Y	N	N	N	Y	Y
3 Tipton	N	N	N	Y	Y	N	N
4 Gardner	N	N	N	Y	Y	N	N
5 Lamborn	N	N	N	Y	Y	N	N
6 Coffman	N	N	N	Y	Y	N	N
7 Perlmutter	N	N	N	Y	N	Y	N
CONNECTICUT							
1 Larson	Y	Y	Y	Y	N	Y	N
2 Courtney	Y	Y	Y	Y	N	Y	N
3 DeLauro	Y	Y	Y	Y	N	Y	N
4 Himes	Y	Y	Y	Y	N	Y	N
5 Murphy	Y	Y	Y	N	N	Y	N
DELAWARE							
AL Carney	Y	Y	Y	Y	N	Y	N
FLORIDA							
1 Miller	N	N	N	Y	Y	N	N
2 Southerland	N	N	N	Y	Y	N	Y
3 Brown	Y	Y	N	N	Y	Y	N
4 Crenshaw	N	N	N	N	Y	N	N
5 Nugent	N	N	N	Y	Y	N	N
6 Stearns	N	N	N	Y	Y	N	N
7 Mica	N	N	N	Y	Y	N	Y
8 Webster	N	N	N	Y	Y	N	N
9 Bilirakis	N	N	N	Y	Y	N	N
10 Young	N	N	N	Y	Y	N	Y
11 Castor	Y	Y	Y	N	N	Y	Y
12 Ross	N	N	N	Y	Y	N	N
13 Buchanan	N	N	N	Y	Y	N	N
14 Mack	N	N	N	Y	Y	N	N
15 Posey	N	N	N	Y	Y	N	N
16 Rooney	N	N	N	Y	Y	N	N
17 Wilson	Y	Y	Y	N	N	Y	N
18 Ros-Lehtinen	N	N	N	Y	Y	N	N
19 Deutch	Y	Y	Y	N	N	Y	N
20 Wasserman Schultz	Y	Y	Y	N	N	Y	N
21 Diaz-Balart	N	N	N	Y	Y	N	N
22 West	N	N	Y	Y	Y	N	N
23 Hastings	Y	Y	Y	N	N	Y	Y
24 Adams	N	N	N	Y	Y	N	N
25 Rivera	N	N	N	Y	Y	N	N
GEORGIA							
1 Kingston	N	N	N	Y	Y	N	N
2 Bishop	N	Y	Y	N	Y	Y	Y
3 Westmoreland	N	N	N	Y	Y	N	N
4 Johnson	Y	Y	Y	N	N	Y	Y
5 Lewis	Y	Y	Y	N	N	Y	N
6 Price	N	N	N	Y	Y	N	N
7 Woodall	N	N	N	Y	Y	N	N
8 Scott, A.	N	N	N	Y	Y	N	N
9 Graves	N	N	N	Y	Y	N	N
10 Broun	N	N	N	Y	Y	N	N
11 Gingrey	N	N	N	Y	Y	N	N
12 Barrow	N	Y	Y	Y	Y	N	N
13 Scott, D.	Y	Y	Y	Y	Y	Y	N
HAWAII							
1 Hanabusa	Y	Y	Y	N	N	Y	N
2 Hirono	Y	Y	Y	N	N	Y	N
IDAHO							
1 Labrador	N	N	N	Y	Y	N	N
2 Simpson	N	N	N	Y	Y	N	N
ILLINOIS							
1 Rush	Y	Y	Y	N	N	Y	N
2 Jackson	Y	Y	N	N	N	Y	Y
3 Lipinski	N	N	N	Y	Y	N	N
4 Gutierrez	Y	Y	Y	N	N	Y	Y
5 Quigley	Y	Y	Y	N	N	Y	Y
6 Roskam	N	N	N	Y	Y	N	N
7 Davis	Y	Y	Y	N	N	Y	Y
8 Walsh	N	N	N	Y	Y	N	N
9 Schakowsky	Y	Y	Y	N	N	Y	N
10 Dold	N	N	N	Y	Y	N	N
11 Kinzinger	N	N	N	Y	Y	N	N
12 Costello	Y	N	N	Y	Y	N	N
13 Biggert	N	N	N	Y	Y	N	N
14 Hultgren	N	N	N	Y	Y	N	N
15 Johnson	N	N	N	Y	Y	N	N

KEY   **Republicans**   Democrats

Y Voted for (yea)	X Paired against	C Voted "present" to avoid possible conflict of interest
# Paired for	− Announced against	
+ Announced for	P Voted "present"	? Did not vote or otherwise make a position known
N Voted against (nay)		

	349	350	351	352	353	354	355
16 **Manzullo**	Y	N	N	Y	Y	N	N
17 **Schilling**	N	N	N	Y	Y	N	N
18 **Schock**	N	N	N	Y	Y	N	N
19 **Shimkus**	N	N	N	Y	Y	N	N
INDIANA							
1 Visclosky	Y	N	N	N	N	Y	N
2 Donnelly	N	Y	Y	Y	Y	N	N
3 **Stutzman**	N	N	N	Y	Y	N	Y
4 **Rokita**	N	N	N	Y	Y	N	N
5 **Burton**	N	N	N	Y	Y	N	N
6 **Pence**	N	N	N	Y	Y	N	N
7 Carson	Y	Y	Y	N	N	Y	Y
8 **Bucshon**	N	N	N	Y	Y	N	N
9 **Young**	N	N	N	Y	Y	N	N
IOWA							
1 Braley	Y	Y	Y	Y	N	Y	Y
2 Loebsack	Y	N	Y	Y	N	Y	N
3 Boswell	Y	N	N	Y	N	Y	N
4 **Latham**	N	N	N	Y	Y	N	N
5 **King**	N	N	N	Y	N	N	N
KANSAS							
1 **Huelskamp**	N	N	N	Y	N	N	N
2 **Jenkins**	N	N	N	Y	N	N	N
3 **Yoder**	N	N	N	Y	Y	N	N
4 **Pompeo**	N	N	N	Y	Y	N	N
KENTUCKY							
1 **Whitfield**	N	N	N	Y	Y	N	N
2 **Guthrie**	N	N	N	Y	Y	N	N
3 Yarmuth	Y	Y	Y	N	N	Y	N
4 **Davis**	N	N	N	Y	Y	N	N
5 **Rogers**	N	N	N	Y	Y	N	N
6 Chandler	N	Y	N	Y	N	N	N
LOUISIANA							
1 **Scalise**	N	N	N	Y	N	N	N
2 Richmond	Y	Y	Y	N	N	Y	Y
3 **Landry**	N	N	N	Y	Y	N	N
4 **Fleming**	N	N	N	Y	Y	N	N
5 **Alexander**	N	N	N	Y	Y	N	N
6 **Cassidy**	N	N	N	N	Y	N	N
7 **Boustany**	N	N	N	Y	Y	N	N
MAINE							
1 Pingree	Y	Y	Y	Y	N	Y	N
2 Michaud	Y	Y	Y	Y	N	Y	Y
MARYLAND							
1 **Harris**	N	N	N	Y	Y	N	Y
2 Ruppersberger	N	Y	Y	Y	Y	Y	N
3 Sarbanes	Y	N	Y	N	N	Y	N
4 Edwards	Y	N	N	N	Y	Y	N
5 Hoyer	Y	Y	Y	N	N	Y	N
6 **Bartlett**	N	N	N	Y	Y	N	N
7 Cummings	Y	Y	Y	Y	Y	Y	?
8 Van Hollen	Y	Y	Y	N	N	Y	N
MASSACHUSETTS							
1 Olver	?	?	?	?	?	?	?
2 Neal	Y	Y	Y	N	N	Y	N
3 McGovern	Y	Y	Y	N	N	Y	N
4 Frank	Y	Y	Y	N	N	Y	N
5 Tsongas	Y	Y	Y	Y	N	Y	N
6 Tierney	Y	Y	Y	N	N	Y	N
7 Markey	Y	Y	Y	Y	N	Y	Y
8 Capuano	Y	Y	Y	N	N	Y	N
9 Lynch	Y	Y	N	Y	N	N	N
10 Keating	Y	Y	Y	Y	N	Y	N
MICHIGAN							
1 **Benishek**	N	N	N	Y	Y	N	N
2 **Huizenga**	N	N	N	Y	Y	N	N
3 **Amash**	N	Y	N	N	Y	N	Y
4 **Camp**	N	N	N	Y	Y	N	N
5 Kildee	Y	Y	Y	N	N	Y	N
6 **Upton**	N	N	N	Y	Y	N	N
7 **Walberg**	N	N	N	Y	Y	N	N
8 **Rogers**	N	N	N	Y	Y	N	N
9 Peters	Y	Y	Y	Y	N	Y	N
10 **Miller**	N	N	Y	Y	Y	N	N
11 **McCotter**	N	N	N	Y	Y	N	N
12 Levin	Y	Y	Y	N	N	Y	Y
13 Clarke	Y	Y	Y	N	N	Y	N
14 Conyers	Y	Y	Y	Y	N	Y	Y
15 Dingell	Y	Y	N	N	N	Y	N
MINNESOTA							
1 Walz	Y	N	N	Y	N	Y	N
2 **Kline**	N	N	N	Y	Y	N	N
3 **Paulsen**	N	N	N	Y	Y	N	N
4 McCollum	Y	N	N	?	N	Y	N

	349	350	351	352	353	354	355
5 Ellison	Y	Y	Y	N	N	Y	Y
6 **Bachmann**	N	N	N	Y	Y	N	N
7 Peterson	N	N	N	Y	Y	N	N
8 **Cravaack**	N	N	N	Y	Y	N	N
MISSISSIPPI							
1 **Nunnelee**	N	N	N	Y	Y	N	N
2 Thompson	Y	Y	Y	N	N	Y	Y
3 **Harper**	N	N	N	Y	Y	N	N
4 **Palazzo**	N	N	N	Y	Y	N	N
MISSOURI							
1 Clay	Y	Y	Y	N	N	Y	Y
2 **Akin**	N	N	N	Y	Y	N	N
3 Carnahan	Y	Y	Y	N	N	Y	N
4 **Hartzler**	N	N	N	Y	Y	N	N
5 Cleaver	Y	N	N	N	N	Y	Y
6 **Graves**	N	N	N	Y	Y	N	N
7 **Long**	N	N	N	N	N	N	N
8 **Emerson**	N	N	N	Y	Y	N	N
9 **Luetkemeyer**	N	N	N	Y	Y	N	N
MONTANA							
AL **Rehberg**	N	N	N	Y	N	N	N
NEBRASKA							
1 **Fortenberry**	N	N	N	Y	N	N	N
2 **Terry**	N	N	N	Y	Y	N	N
3 **Smith**	N	N	N	N	Y	N	N
NEVADA							
1 Berkley	Y	Y	Y	Y	N	Y	N
2 **Amodei**	N	N	N	Y	Y	N	N
3 **Heck**	N	N	N	Y	N	N	N
NEW HAMPSHIRE							
1 **Guinta**	N	N	N	Y	Y	N	N
2 **Bass**	Y	N	N	Y	N	N	N
NEW JERSEY							
1 Andrews	Y	N	N	N	N	Y	N
2 **LoBiondo**	N	N	N	Y	Y	N	N
3 **Runyan**	N	N	N	Y	Y	N	N
4 **Smith**	N	N	N	Y	Y	N	N
5 **Garrett**	N	N	N	Y	Y	N	Y
6 Pallone	Y	Y	Y	N	N	Y	N
7 **Lance**	N	N	Y	N	Y	N	N
8 Pascrell	Y	Y	Y	Y	N	Y	N
9 Rothman	Y	N	Y	N	N	Y	N
10 Vacant							
11 **Frelinghuysen**	N	N	Y	N	Y	N	N
12 Holt	Y	Y	Y	Y	N	Y	Y
13 Sires	Y	Y	Y	Y	N	Y	N
NEW MEXICO							
1 Heinrich	Y	Y	N	Y	N	Y	Y
2 **Pearce**	N	N	N	Y	Y	N	N
3 Luján	Y	Y	N	Y	N	Y	N
NEW YORK							
1 Bishop	Y	Y	Y	Y	N	Y	N
2 Israel	Y	Y	Y	N	N	Y	N
3 **King**	N	N	N	Y	Y	N	N
4 McCarthy	Y	Y	Y	Y	N	Y	N
5 Ackerman	Y	Y	N	N	N	Y	Y
6 Meeks	Y	Y	Y	N	N	Y	Y
7 Crowley	Y	Y	N	N	N	Y	N
8 Nadler	Y	Y	Y	Y	N	Y	Y
9 **Turner**	N	N	N	Y	Y	N	N
10 Towns	Y	Y	Y	N	N	Y	Y
11 Clarke	?	Y	N	N	N	Y	Y
12 Velázquez	Y	Y	Y	N	N	Y	N
13 **Grimm**	N	N	N	Y	Y	N	N
14 Maloney	Y	Y	Y	N	N	Y	Y
15 Rangel	Y	Y	N	N	N	Y	Y
16 Serrano	Y	Y	Y	N	N	Y	N
17 Engel	Y	Y	N	Y	N	Y	Y
18 Lowey	Y	Y	Y	N	N	Y	N
19 **Hayworth**	Y	N	N	Y	Y	N	N
20 **Gibson**	Y	N	N	Y	Y	N	N
21 Tonko	Y	Y	Y	Y	N	Y	N
22 Hinchey	Y	Y	Y	N	N	Y	Y
23 Owens	N	Y	Y	Y	N	Y	N
24 **Hanna**	N	N	N	Y	Y	N	N
25 **Buerkle**	N	N	N	Y	Y	N	N
26 Hochul	Y	Y	Y	Y	N	Y	N
27 Higgins	Y	Y	Y	Y	N	Y	N
28 Slaughter	+	+	+	–	–	+	–
29 **Reed**	N	N	N	N	Y	N	N
NORTH CAROLINA							
1 Butterfield	?	Y	Y	N	N	Y	N
2 **Ellmers**	N	N	N	Y	Y	N	N
3 **Jones**	N	N	N	Y	Y	N	N
4 Price	Y	N	N	N	N	Y	N

	349	350	351	352	353	354	355
5 **Foxx**	N	N	N	N	Y	N	N
6 **Coble**	?	?	?	?	?	?	?
7 McIntyre	N	N	N	Y	Y	N	N
8 Kissell	N	N	N	Y	N	N	N
9 **Myrick**	–	–	–	+	+	–	–
10 **McHenry**	N	N	N	Y	Y	N	N
11 Shuler	?	?	?	?	?	?	?
12 Watt	Y	N	N	N	N	Y	N
13 Miller	Y	Y	Y	Y	N	Y	Y
NORTH DAKOTA							
AL **Berg**	N	N	N	Y	Y	N	N
OHIO							
1 **Chabot**	N	N	N	Y	Y	N	N
2 **Schmidt**	N	N	N	Y	Y	N	N
3 **Turner**	N	N	N	Y	Y	N	N
4 **Jordan**	N	N	N	Y	Y	N	Y
5 **Latta**	N	N	N	Y	Y	N	N
6 **Johnson**	N	N	N	Y	Y	N	N
7 **Austria**	N	N	N	Y	Y	N	N
8 **Boehner**							
9 Kaptur	Y	Y	N	Y	N	Y	N
10 Kucinich	Y	Y	Y	N	N	Y	Y
11 Fudge	Y	Y	N	N	N	Y	Y
12 **Tiberi**	N	N	N	Y	Y	N	N
13 Sutton	Y	Y	Y	Y	N	Y	Y
14 **LaTourette**	N	N	N	Y	N	N	N
15 **Stivers**	N	N	N	Y	Y	N	N
16 **Renacci**	N	N	N	Y	Y	N	N
17 Ryan	Y	Y	Y	Y	N	Y	N
18 **Gibbs**	N	N	N	Y	Y	N	N
OKLAHOMA							
1 **Sullivan**	N	N	N	Y	Y	N	N
2 Boren	N	N	N	Y	Y	N	N
3 **Lucas**	N	N	N	Y	Y	N	N
4 **Cole**	N	N	N	Y	Y	N	N
5 **Lankford**	N	N	N	Y	Y	N	N
OREGON							
1 Bonamici	Y	Y	Y	Y	N	Y	N
2 **Walden**	N	N	N	Y	Y	N	N
3 Blumenauer	Y	Y	Y	N	N	Y	N
4 DeFazio	N	Y	Y	Y	N	N	N
5 Schrader	N	Y	Y	N	N	Y	N
PENNSYLVANIA							
1 Brady	Y	Y	Y	Y	N	Y	N
2 Fattah	Y	Y	Y	N	N	Y	N
3 **Kelly**	N	N	N	Y	Y	N	N
4 Altmire	N	Y	Y	Y	Y	N	N
5 **Thompson**	N	N	N	N	N	N	N
6 **Gerlach**	N	N	N	Y	Y	N	N
7 **Meehan**	N	Y	N	Y	Y	N	N
8 **Fitzpatrick**	N	N	Y	Y	N	N	Y
9 **Shuster**	N	N	N	Y	Y	N	N
10 **Marino**	N	N	N	Y	Y	N	N
11 **Barletta**	N	N	N	Y	N	N	N
12 Critz	Y	N	N	Y	N	Y	N
13 Schwartz	Y	Y	Y	Y	N	Y	N
14 Doyle	Y	Y	Y	Y	N	Y	N
15 **Dent**	N	N	Y	Y	Y	N	N
16 **Pitts**	N	N	N	Y	Y	N	N
17 Holden	?	?	?	?	?	?	?
18 **Murphy**	N	N	N	Y	Y	N	N
19 **Platts**	N	N	N	Y	Y	N	N
RHODE ISLAND							
1 Cicilline	Y	Y	Y	N	N	Y	N
2 Langevin	Y	Y	Y	N	N	Y	N
SOUTH CAROLINA							
1 **Scott**	N	N	N	Y	Y	N	N
2 **Wilson**	N	N	N	Y	Y	N	N
3 **Duncan**	N	N	N	Y	Y	N	N
4 **Gowdy**	N	N	N	Y	Y	N	N
5 **Mulvaney**	N	N	N	Y	Y	N	Y
6 Clyburn	Y	N	N	N	N	Y	N
SOUTH DAKOTA							
AL **Noem**	N	N	N	Y	Y	N	N
TENNESSEE							
1 **Roe**	N	N	N	Y	Y	N	N
2 **Duncan**	N	N	N	Y	Y	N	N
3 **Fleischmann**	N	N	N	Y	Y	N	N
4 **DesJarlais**	N	N	N	Y	N	N	N
5 Cooper	N	N	N	Y	N	Y	N
6 **Black**	N	N	N	Y	Y	N	N
7 **Blackburn**	N	N	N	Y	Y	N	N
8 **Fincher**	N	N	N	Y	Y	N	N
9 Cohen	Y	Y	Y	N	N	Y	N

	349	350	351	352	353	354	355
TEXAS							
1 **Gohmert**	N	Y	N	Y	Y	N	N
2 **Poe**	N	N	N	Y	N	N	N
3 **Johnson, S.**	N	N	N	Y	Y	N	N
4 **Hall**	N	N	N	Y	Y	N	N
5 **Hensarling**	N	N	N	Y	Y	N	N
6 **Barton**	?	N	N	Y	N	N	N
7 **Culberson**	?	?	?	?	?	?	?
8 **Brady**	N	N	N	Y	N	N	N
9 Green, A.	Y	Y	Y	Y	N	Y	Y
10 **McCaul**	N	N	Y	Y	?	N	N
11 **Conaway**	N	N	N	Y	Y	N	N
12 **Granger**	N	N	N	Y	Y	N	N
13 **Thornberry**	N	N	N	Y	Y	N	N
14 **Paul**	?	?	?	?	?	?	?
15 Hinojosa	Y	Y	Y	N	N	Y	N
16 Reyes	Y	Y	Y	Y	Y	Y	N
17 **Flores**	N	N	N	Y	Y	N	N
18 Jackson Lee	Y	Y	Y	N	N	Y	Y
19 **Neugebauer**	N	N	N	Y	Y	N	N
20 Gonzalez	Y	Y	Y	N	N	Y	N
21 **Smith**	N	N	N	Y	Y	N	N
22 **Olson**	N	N	N	Y	Y	N	N
23 **Canseco**	N	N	N	Y	Y	N	N
24 **Marchant**	N	N	N	Y	Y	N	N
25 Doggett	Y	Y	Y	Y	N	Y	N
26 **Burgess**	N	N	N	Y	N	N	N
27 **Farenthold**	N	N	N	Y	Y	N	N
28 Cuellar	N	Y	Y	Y	Y	Y	N
29 Green, G.	Y	Y	Y	Y	Y	Y	N
30 Johnson, E.	Y	N	N	N	N	Y	N
31 **Carter**	N	N	N	Y	Y	N	N
32 **Sessions**	N	N	N	Y	Y	N	N
UTAH							
1 **Bishop**	N	N	N	Y	Y	N	N
2 Matheson	N	Y	Y	Y	Y	N	N
3 **Chaffetz**	N	N	N	Y	Y	N	N
VERMONT							
AL Welch	Y	N	N	Y	N	Y	Y
VIRGINIA							
1 **Wittman**	N	N	N	Y	Y	N	N
2 **Rigell**	N	N	N	Y	Y	N	N
3 Scott	Y	Y	Y	N	N	Y	Y
4 **Forbes**	N	N	N	Y	Y	N	N
5 **Hurt**	N	N	N	Y	Y	N	N
6 **Goodlatte**	N	N	N	Y	Y	N	N
7 **Cantor**	N	N	N	Y	Y	N	N
8 Moran	Y	Y	Y	N	N	Y	N
9 **Griffith**	N	N	N	Y	Y	N	Y
10 **Wolf**	N	N	N	Y	Y	N	N
11 Connolly	N	Y	Y	Y	N	Y	N
WASHINGTON							
1 Vacant							
2 Larsen	Y	Y	N	N	N	?	?
3 **Herrera Beutler**	N	N	N	Y	Y	N	N
4 **Hastings**	N	N	N	Y	Y	N	N
5 **McMorris Rodgers**	N	N	N	?	Y	N	N
6 Dicks	Y	Y	Y	N	N	Y	N
7 McDermott	Y	Y	Y	N	N	Y	N
8 **Reichert**	N	N	N	Y	Y	N	N
9 Smith	Y	N	Y	Y	N	Y	N
WEST VIRGINIA							
1 **McKinley**	N	N	N	Y	Y	N	N
2 **Capito**	N	N	N	Y	Y	N	N
3 Rahall	Y	Y	Y	Y	N	N	N
WISCONSIN							
1 **Ryan**	N	N	N	Y	Y	N	N
2 Baldwin	Y	Y	Y	Y	N	Y	Y
3 Kind	Y	Y	Y	Y	N	Y	N
4 Moore	Y	Y	Y	N	N	Y	N
5 **Sensenbrenner**	N	N	N	Y	Y	N	N
6 **Petri**	N	N	N	Y	Y	N	N
7 **Duffy**	N	N	N	Y	Y	N	N
8 **Ribble**	N	N	N	Y	Y	N	N
WYOMING							
AL **Lummis**	N	N	N	Y	Y	N	N

IN THE HOUSE | By Vote Number

356. HR 5855. Fiscal 2013 Homeland Security Appropriations/ **Homeland Security Grant Program.** Higgins, D-N.Y., amendment that would increase by $58 million the amount provided for state and local grants, contracts and cooperative agreements for homeland security activities and reduce by the same amount funding for the purchase or lease of vehicles and Science and Technology operation and construction of laboratory facilities. Rejected in Committee of the Whole 150-266: R 18-218; D 132-48. June 6, 2012.

357. HR 5855. Fiscal 2013 Homeland Security Appropriations/ **Science and Technology Funding.** Bishop, D-N.Y., amendment that would reduce by $75 million the amount provided for Science and Technology construction of laboratory facilities and increase by the same amount funding for Science and Technology research activities. Rejected in Committee of the Whole 166-245: R 9-225; D 157-20. June 6, 2012.

358. HR 436, HR 5882. Medical-Device Tax Repeal and Fiscal 2013 **Legislative Branch Appropriations/Previous Question.** Scott, R-S.C., motion to order the previous question (thus ending debate and the possibility of amendment) on the rule (H Res 679) that would provide for House floor consideration of a bill (HR 436) that would repeal an excise tax of 2.3 percent on medical devices and the fiscal 2013 Legislative Branch spending bill (HR 5882). Motion agreed to 240-179: R 235-1; D 5-178. June 7, 2012.

359. HR 436, HR 5882. Medical-Device Tax Repeal and Fiscal **2013 Legislative Branch Appropriations/Rule.** Adoption of the rule (H Res 679) that would provide for House floor consideration of a bill (HR 436) that would repeal an excise tax of 2.3 percent on medical devices and the fiscal 2013 Legislative Branch spending bill (HR 5882). Adopted 241-173: R 233-0; D 8-173. June 7, 2012.

360. HR 436. Medical-Device Tax Repeal/Recommit. Bishop, D-N.Y., motion to recommit the bill to the House Ways and Means Committee and report it back immediately with an amendment that would prohibit tax benefits to a medical-device manufacturer, producer or importer that outsourced American jobs during the calendar year in which the sale occurred. Motion rejected 179-239: R 2-233; D 177-6. June 7, 2012.

	356	357	358	359	360
ALABAMA					
1 Bonner	N	N	Y	Y	N
2 Roby	N	N	Y	Y	N
3 Rogers	N	N	Y	Y	N
4 Aderholt	N	N	Y	Y	N
5 Brooks	N	N	Y	Y	N
6 Bachus	N	N	Y	Y	N
7 Sewell	Y	Y	N	N	Y
ALASKA					
AL Young	N	N	Y	Y	N
ARIZONA					
1 Gosar	N	N	Y	Y	N
2 Franks	N	N	Y	Y	N
3 Quayle	N	N	Y	Y	N
4 Pastor	Y	Y	N	N	Y
5 Schweikert	N	N	Y	Y	N
6 Flake	N	N	Y	Y	N
7 Grijalva	Y	Y	N	N	Y
8 Vacant					
ARKANSAS					
1 Crawford	N	N	Y	Y	N
2 Griffin	N	N	Y	Y	N
3 Womack	N	N	Y	Y	N
4 Ross	N	N	N	Y	N
CALIFORNIA					
1 Thompson	Y	Y	N	N	Y
2 Herger	N	N	Y	Y	N
3 Lungren	N	N	Y	Y	N
4 McClintock	N	N	Y	Y	N
5 Matsui	Y	Y	N	N	Y
6 Woolsey	N	Y	N	N	Y
7 Miller, George	N	Y	N	N	Y
8 Pelosi	Y	Y	N	N	Y
9 Lee	N	Y	N	N	Y
10 Garamendi	N	N	N	N	Y
11 McNerney	N	Y	N	N	Y
12 Speier	Y	Y	N	N	Y
13 Stark	?	?	N	N	Y
14 Eshoo	N	Y	N	N	Y
15 Honda	Y	Y	N	N	Y
16 Lofgren	N	Y	N	N	Y
17 Farr	Y	N	N	N	Y
18 Cardoza	?	?	?	?	Y
19 Denham	N	N	Y	Y	N
20 Costa	N	?	N	N	Y
21 Nunes	N	N	Y	Y	N
22 McCarthy	N	N	Y	Y	N
23 Capps	Y	Y	N	N	Y
24 Gallegly	N	N	Y	Y	N
25 McKeon	N	N	Y	Y	N
26 Dreier	N	N	Y	Y	N
27 Sherman	Y	Y	N	N	Y
28 Berman	Y	Y	N	?	Y
29 Schiff	N	Y	N	N	Y
30 Waxman	N	Y	N	N	Y
31 Becerra	Y	Y	N	N	Y
32 Chu	Y	Y	N	N	Y
33 Bass	?	?	?	?	?
34 Roybal-Allard	N	Y	N	N	Y
35 Waters	Y	?	N	?	Y
36 Hahn	Y	Y	N	N	Y
37 Richardson	Y	N	N	N	Y
38 Napolitano	?	?	N	N	Y
39 Sánchez, Linda	Y	Y	N	N	Y
40 Royce	N	N	Y	Y	N
41 Lewis	?	?	?	?	?
42 Miller, Gary	N	N	Y	Y	N
43 Baca	Y	Y	N	N	Y
44 Calvert	N	N	Y	Y	N
45 Bono Mack	N	N	Y	Y	N
46 Rohrabacher	N	N	Y	Y	N
47 Sanchez, Loretta	Y	Y	N	N	Y
48 Campbell	N	N	Y	Y	N
49 Issa	N	N	Y	Y	N
50 Bilbray	N	N	Y	Y	N
51 Filner	+	+	–	–	+
52 Hunter	N	N	Y	Y	N
53 Davis	N	Y	N	N	Y
COLORADO					
1 DeGette	Y	Y	N	N	Y
2 Polis	N	Y	N	N	Y
3 Tipton	N	N	Y	Y	N
4 Gardner	N	N	Y	Y	N
5 Lamborn	N	N	Y	Y	N
6 Coffman	N	N	Y	Y	N
7 Perlmutter	Y	N	N	N	Y
CONNECTICUT					
1 Larson	Y	Y	N	N	Y
2 Courtney	Y	Y	N	N	Y
3 DeLauro	Y	Y	N	N	Y
4 Himes	Y	Y	N	N	Y
5 Murphy	Y	Y	N	N	Y
DELAWARE					
AL Carney	N	Y	N	N	Y
FLORIDA					
1 Miller	N	–	Y	Y	N
2 Southerland	N	N	Y	Y	N
3 Brown	Y	Y	N	N	Y
4 Crenshaw	N	N	Y	Y	N
5 Nugent	N	N	Y	Y	N
6 Stearns	N	N	Y	Y	N
7 Mica	N	N	Y	Y	N
8 Webster	N	N	Y	Y	N
9 Bilirakis	N	N	?	?	?
10 Young	N	N	Y	Y	N
11 Castor	Y	Y	N	N	Y
12 Ross	N	N	Y	Y	N
13 Buchanan	N	N	Y	Y	N
14 Mack	N	N	Y	Y	N
15 Posey	N	N	Y	Y	N
16 Rooney	N	N	Y	Y	N
17 Wilson	Y	Y	N	N	Y
18 Ros-Lehtinen	N	N	Y	Y	N
19 Deutch	Y	Y	N	N	Y
20 Wasserman Schultz	Y	Y	N	N	Y
21 Diaz-Balart	N	N	Y	Y	N
22 West	N	N	Y	Y	N
23 Hastings	Y	Y	N	N	?
24 Adams	N	N	Y	Y	N
25 Rivera	N	N	Y	Y	N
GEORGIA					
1 Kingston	N	N	Y	Y	N
2 Bishop	Y	Y	N	Y	Y
3 Westmoreland	N	N	Y	Y	N
4 Johnson	Y	Y	N	N	Y
5 Lewis	Y	Y	N	N	Y
6 Price	N	N	Y	Y	N
7 Woodall	N	N	Y	Y	N
8 Scott, A.	N	N	Y	Y	N
9 Graves	N	N	Y	Y	N
10 Broun	N	N	Y	Y	N
11 Gingrey	N	N	Y	Y	N
12 Barrow	Y	Y	N	N	Y
13 Scott, D.	Y	Y	N	N	Y
HAWAII					
1 Hanabusa	Y	Y	N	N	Y
2 Hirono	Y	Y	N	N	Y
IDAHO					
1 Labrador	N	N	Y	Y	N
2 Simpson	N	N	Y	Y	N
ILLINOIS					
1 Rush	Y	Y	N	N	Y
2 Jackson	Y	Y	N	N	Y
3 Lipinski	N	Y	N	N	Y
4 Gutierrez	Y	Y	N	N	Y
5 Quigley	Y	Y	N	N	Y
6 Roskam	N	N	Y	Y	N
7 Davis	Y	Y	N	N	Y
8 Walsh	N	N	Y	Y	N
9 Schakowsky	Y	Y	N	N	Y
10 Dold	N	N	Y	Y	N
11 Kinzinger	N	N	Y	Y	N
12 Costello	N	Y	N	N	Y
13 Biggert	N	N	Y	Y	N
14 Hultgren	N	N	Y	Y	N
15 Johnson	N	N	Y	Y	N

KEY   **Republicans**   Democrats

Y Voted for (yea)	**X** Paired against	**C** Voted "present" to avoid possible conflict of interest
# Paired for	**–** Announced against	
+ Announced for	**P** Voted "present"	**?** Did not vote or otherwise make a position known
N Voted against (nay)		

	356	357	358	359	360
16 Manzullo	Y	Y	Y	Y	N
17 Schilling	N	N	Y	Y	N
18 Schock	N	N	Y	Y	N
19 Shimkus	N	Y	Y	Y	N
INDIANA					
1 Visclosky	Y	Y	N	N	Y
2 Donnelly	Y	Y	N	Y	N
3 Stutzman	N	N	Y	Y	N
4 Rokita	N	N	Y	Y	N
5 Burton	N	N	Y	Y	N
6 Pence	N	N	Y	Y	N
7 Carson	Y	N	N	N	Y
8 Bucshon	N	N	Y	Y	N
9 Young	N	N	Y	Y	N
IOWA					
1 Braley	Y	Y	N	N	Y
2 Loebsack	N	N	N	N	Y
3 Boswell	N	N	N	N	Y
4 Latham	N	N	Y	Y	N
5 King	N	N	N	Y	N
KANSAS					
1 Huelskamp	N	N	Y	Y	N
2 Jenkins	N	N	Y	Y	N
3 Yoder	N	N	Y	Y	N
4 Pompeo	N	N	Y	Y	N
KENTUCKY					
1 Whitfield	N	N	Y	Y	N
2 Guthrie	N	N	Y	Y	N
3 Yarmuth	Y	Y	N	N	N
4 Davis	N	N	Y	Y	N
5 Rogers	N	N	Y	Y	N
6 Chandler	N	N	N	N	Y
LOUISIANA					
1 Scalise	N	N	Y	Y	N
2 Richmond	Y	Y	N	N	Y
3 Landry	N	N	Y	Y	N
4 Fleming	N	N	Y	Y	N
5 Alexander	N	N	Y	Y	N
6 Cassidy	N	N	Y	Y	N
7 Boustany	N	N	Y	Y	N
MAINE					
1 Pingree	Y	Y	N	N	Y
2 Michaud	Y	Y	N	N	Y
MARYLAND					
1 Harris	N	N	Y	Y	N
2 Ruppersberger	Y	Y	N	N	Y
3 Sarbanes	Y	Y	N	N	Y
4 Edwards	N	Y	N	N	Y
5 Hoyer	N	Y	N	N	Y
6 Bartlett	N	N	Y	Y	N
7 Cummings	Y	Y	N	N	Y
8 Van Hollen	N	Y	N	N	Y
MASSACHUSETTS					
1 Olver	?	?	N	N	Y
2 Neal	Y	Y	N	N	Y
3 McGovern	Y	Y	N	N	Y
4 Frank	Y	Y	N	N	Y
5 Tsongas	Y	Y	N	N	Y
6 Tierney	Y	Y	N	N	Y
7 Markey	Y	Y	N	N	Y
8 Capuano	Y	Y	N	N	Y
9 Lynch	Y	Y	N	N	Y
10 Keating	Y	Y	N	N	Y
MICHIGAN					
1 Benishek	N	N	Y	Y	N
2 Huizenga	N	N	Y	Y	N
3 Amash	N	N	Y	Y	N
4 Camp	N	N	Y	Y	N
5 Kildee	Y	Y	N	N	Y
6 Upton	Y	N	Y	Y	N
7 Walberg	N	N	Y	Y	N
8 Rogers	N	N	Y	Y	N
9 Peters	Y	Y	N	N	Y
10 Miller	Y	N	Y	Y	N
11 McCotter	N	N	Y	Y	N
12 Levin	Y	Y	N	N	Y
13 Clarke	Y	Y	N	N	Y
14 Conyers	Y	Y	N	N	Y
15 Dingell	Y	Y	N	N	Y
MINNESOTA					
1 Walz	Y	N	N	N	Y
2 Kline	Y	N	Y	Y	N
3 Paulsen	Y	N	Y	Y	N
4 McCollum	Y	N	N	N	Y

	356	357	358	359	360
5 Ellison	Y	Y	N	N	Y
6 Bachmann	N	N	Y	Y	N
7 Peterson	N	N	Y	N	Y
8 Cravaack	Y	N	Y	Y	N
MISSISSIPPI					
1 Nunnelee	N	N	Y	Y	N
2 Thompson	Y	Y	N	N	Y
3 Harper	N	N	Y	Y	N
4 Palazzo	N	N	Y	Y	N
MISSOURI					
1 Clay	Y	N	N	N	Y
2 Akin	N	N	Y	+	−
3 Carnahan	Y	Y	N	N	Y
4 Hartzler	N	N	Y	Y	N
5 Cleaver	Y	N	N	N	Y
6 Graves	Y	N	Y	Y	N
7 Long	N	N	Y	Y	N
8 Emerson	N	N	Y	Y	N
9 Luetkemeyer	N	N	Y	Y	N
MONTANA					
AL Rehberg	N	N	Y	Y	N
NEBRASKA					
1 Fortenberry	N	N	Y	Y	N
2 Terry	N	N	Y	Y	N
3 Smith	N	N	Y	Y	N
NEVADA					
1 Berkley	Y	Y	N	N	Y
2 Amodei	N	Y	Y	Y	N
3 Heck	N	N	Y	Y	N
NEW HAMPSHIRE					
1 Guinta	N	N	Y	Y	N
2 Bass	Y	N	Y	Y	N
NEW JERSEY					
1 Andrews	Y	Y	N	N	Y
2 LoBiondo	N	N	Y	Y	N
3 Runyan	N	N	Y	Y	N
4 Smith	N	N	Y	Y	N
5 Garrett	N	N	Y	Y	N
6 Pallone	Y	Y	N	N	Y
7 Lance	N	N	Y	Y	N
8 Pascrell	Y	Y	N	N	Y
9 Rothman	Y	Y	N	N	Y
10 Vacant					
11 Frelinghuysen	N	N	Y	Y	N
12 Holt	Y	Y	N	N	Y
13 Sires	Y	Y	N	N	Y
NEW MEXICO					
1 Heinrich	N	N	N	N	Y
2 Pearce	N	N	Y	Y	N
3 Luján	Y	Y	N	N	Y
NEW YORK					
1 Bishop	Y	Y	N	N	Y
2 Israel	N	Y	N	N	Y
3 King	N	Y	Y	Y	N
4 McCarthy	N	Y	N	N	Y
5 Ackerman	Y	Y	N	N	Y
6 Meeks	Y	Y	N	N	Y
7 Crowley	Y	Y	N	N	Y
8 Nadler	Y	Y	N	N	Y
9 Turner	N	Y	Y	Y	N
10 Towns	Y	Y	N	N	Y
11 Clarke	Y	Y	N	N	Y
12 Velázquez	Y	Y	N	N	Y
13 Grimm	N	Y	Y	Y	N
14 Maloney	Y	Y	N	N	Y
15 Rangel	N	Y	N	N	Y
16 Serrano	Y	Y	N	N	Y
17 Engel	Y	Y	N	N	Y
18 Lowey	Y	Y	N	N	Y
19 Hayworth	N	N	Y	Y	N
20 Gibson	N	N	Y	Y	N
21 Tonko	Y	Y	N	N	Y
22 Hinchey	Y	Y	N	N	Y
23 Owens	Y	Y	N	Y	Y
24 Buerkle	N	N	Y	Y	N
25 Hochul	Y	Y	N	N	Y
26 Higgins	Y	Y	N	N	Y
27 Slaughter	+	+	−	−	+
28 Reed	N	N	Y	Y	N
NORTH CAROLINA					
1 Butterfield	N	Y	N	N	Y
2 Ellmers	N	N	Y	Y	N
3 Jones	N	Y	Y	Y	Y
4 Price	N	Y	N	N	Y

	356	357	358	359	360
5 Foxx	N	Y	Y	Y	N
6 Coble	?	?	?	?	?
7 McIntyre	Y	Y	Y	Y	Y
8 Kissell	N	N	Y	Y	Y
9 Myrick	−	−	Y	Y	N
10 McHenry	N	N	Y	Y	N
11 Shuler	?	?	?	?	?
12 Watt	Y	N	N	N	Y
13 Miller	Y	Y	N	N	Y
NORTH DAKOTA					
AL Berg	N	N	Y	Y	N
OHIO					
1 Chabot	N	N	Y	Y	N
2 Schmidt	N	N	Y	Y	N
3 Turner	N	N	Y	Y	N
4 Jordan	N	N	Y	Y	N
5 Latta	N	N	Y	Y	N
6 Johnson	N	N	Y	Y	N
7 Austria	N	N	Y	Y	N
8 Boehner					
9 Kaptur	Y	?	N	N	Y
10 Kucinich	Y	Y	?	?	?
11 Fudge	N	Y	N	N	Y
12 Tiberi	N	N	Y	Y	N
13 Sutton	Y	N	N	N	Y
14 LaTourette	N	N	Y	Y	N
15 Stivers	Y	N	Y	Y	N
16 Renacci	N	N	Y	Y	N
17 Ryan	Y	Y	N	N	Y
18 Gibbs	N	N	Y	Y	N
OKLAHOMA					
1 Sullivan	N	N	Y	Y	N
2 Boren	N	N	Y	Y	N
3 Lucas	N	N	Y	Y	N
4 Cole	N	N	Y	Y	N
5 Lankford	N	N	Y	Y	N
OREGON					
1 Bonamici	Y	Y	N	N	Y
2 Walden	N	N	Y	Y	N
3 Blumenauer	N	Y	N	N	Y
4 DeFazio	Y	Y	N	N	Y
5 Schrader	Y	Y	N	N	Y
PENNSYLVANIA					
1 Brady	Y	Y	N	N	Y
2 Fattah	N	Y	N	N	Y
3 Kelly	N	N	Y	Y	N
4 Altmire	Y	N	N	N	Y
5 Thompson	N	N	Y	Y	N
6 Gerlach	N	N	Y	Y	N
7 Meehan	N	N	Y	Y	N
8 Fitzpatrick	Y	N	Y	Y	N
9 Shuster	N	N	Y	Y	N
10 Marino	N	N	?	?	?
11 Barletta	N	N	Y	Y	N
12 Critz	Y	Y	N	N	Y
13 Schwartz	N	Y	N	N	Y
14 Doyle	Y	Y	N	N	Y
15 Dent	N	N	Y	Y	N
16 Pitts	N	N	Y	Y	N
17 Holden	?	?	N	N	Y
18 Murphy	N	N	Y	Y	N
19 Platts	N	N	Y	Y	N
RHODE ISLAND					
1 Cicilline	Y	Y	N	N	Y
2 Langevin	Y	Y	N	N	Y
SOUTH CAROLINA					
1 Scott	N	N	Y	Y	N
2 Wilson	N	N	Y	Y	N
3 Duncan	N	N	Y	?	N
4 Gowdy	N	N	Y	Y	N
5 Mulvaney	N	N	Y	Y	N
6 Clyburn	N	Y	N	N	Y
SOUTH DAKOTA					
AL Noem	N	N	Y	Y	N
TENNESSEE					
1 Roe	N	N	Y	Y	N
2 Duncan	N	N	Y	Y	Y
3 Fleischmann	N	N	Y	Y	N
4 DesJarlais	N	N	Y	Y	N
5 Cooper	Y	N	N	N	Y
6 Black	N	N	Y	Y	N
7 Blackburn	Y	N	Y	Y	N
8 Fincher	Y	N	Y	Y	N
9 Cohen	Y	Y	N	N	Y

	356	357	358	359	360
TEXAS					
1 Gohmert	N	N	Y	Y	N
2 Poe	N	N	Y	Y	N
3 Johnson, S.	N	N	Y	Y	N
4 Hall	N	N	Y	Y	N
5 Hensarling	N	N	Y	Y	N
6 Barton	N	N	Y	?	N
7 Culberson	?	?	Y	Y	N
8 Brady	N	N	Y	Y	N
9 Green, A.	Y	Y	N	N	Y
10 McCaul	Y	N	Y	Y	N
11 Conaway	N	N	Y	Y	N
12 Granger	N	N	Y	Y	N
13 Thornberry	N	N	Y	Y	N
14 Paul	?	?	?	?	?
15 Hinojosa	Y	Y	N	N	Y
16 Reyes	N	Y	N	N	Y
17 Flores	N	N	Y	Y	N
18 Jackson Lee	Y	Y	N	N	Y
19 Neugebauer	N	N	Y	Y	N
20 Gonzalez	N	Y	N	N	Y
21 Smith	N	N	Y	Y	N
22 Olson	N	N	Y	Y	N
23 Canseco	N	N	Y	Y	N
24 Marchant	N	N	Y	Y	N
25 Doggett	Y	Y	N	N	N
26 Burgess	N	N	Y	Y	N
27 Farenthold	N	N	Y	Y	N
28 Cuellar	Y	Y	N	N	Y
29 Green, G.	Y	Y	N	N	Y
30 Johnson, E.	N	Y	N	N	Y
31 Carter	N	?	Y	Y	N
32 Sessions	N	N	Y	Y	N
UTAH					
1 Bishop	N	N	Y	Y	N
2 Matheson	Y	Y	Y	Y	N
3 Chaffetz	N	N	Y	Y	N
VERMONT					
AL Welch	Y	N	N	N	Y
VIRGINIA					
1 Wittman	N	N	Y	Y	N
2 Rigell	Y	N	Y	Y	N
3 Scott	N	Y	N	N	Y
4 Forbes	N	N	Y	Y	N
5 Hurt	N	N	Y	Y	N
6 Goodlatte	N	N	Y	Y	N
7 Cantor	N	N	Y	Y	N
8 Moran	N	Y	N	N	Y
9 Griffith	N	N	Y	Y	N
10 Wolf	N	N	Y	Y	N
11 Connolly	Y	Y	N	N	Y
WASHINGTON					
1 Vacant					
2 Larsen	?	?	N	N	Y
3 Herrera Beutler	N	N	Y	Y	N
4 Hastings	N	N	Y	Y	N
5 McMorris Rodgers	N	N	Y	Y	N
6 Dicks	N	Y	N	N	Y
7 McDermott	N	Y	N	N	Y
8 Reichert	Y	N	Y	Y	N
9 Smith	N	Y	N	N	Y
WEST VIRGINIA					
1 McKinley	N	N	Y	Y	N
2 Capito	N	N	Y	Y	N
3 Rahall	Y	Y	N	N	Y
WISCONSIN					
1 Ryan	N	N	Y	Y	N
2 Baldwin	Y	Y	?	?	?
3 Kind	Y	Y	N	N	Y
4 Moore	Y	Y	N	N	Y
5 Sensenbrenner	Y	N	Y	Y	N
6 Petri	N	N	Y	Y	N
7 Duffy	N	N	Y	Y	N
8 Ribble	N	N	Y	Y	N
WYOMING					
AL Lummis	N	N	Y	Y	N

IN THE HOUSE | By Vote Number

361. HR 436. **Medical-Device Tax Repeal/Passage.** Passage of the bill that would repeal an excise tax of 2.3 percent on medical devices created under the 2010 health care overhaul. It also would repeal the overhaul law's restrictions on using tax-preferred accounts to pay for over-the-counter drugs and allow individuals to recoup up to $500 of unused funds that are left in their flexible-spending arrangements after the end of a plan year. It would make individuals who receive subsidies to help buy coverage in the state insurance exchanges liable for the full amount of any overpayments. Passed 270-146: R 233-0; D 37-146. A "nay" was a vote in support of the president's position. June 7, 2012.

362. HR 5855. **Fiscal 2013 Homeland Security Appropriations/ Limited English Proficiency.** King, R-Iowa, amendment that would bar the use of funds in the bill to enforce an executive order requiring federal agencies to prepare a plan to improve access to federal services for people with limited English proficiency. Adopted in Committee of the Whole 224-189: R 217-15; D 7-174. June 7, 2012.

363. HR 5855. **Fiscal 2013 Homeland Security Appropriations/ Immigration and Customs Enforcement Memos.** King, R-Iowa, amendment that would bar the use of funds in the bill to finalize, implement, administer or enforce Immigration and Customs Enforcement memos regarding prosecutorial discretion to prioritize the removal of certain illegal immigrants. Adopted in Committee of the Whole 238-175: R 228-4; D 10-171. A "nay" was a vote in support of the president's position. June 7, 2012.

364. HR 5855. **Fiscal 2013 Homeland Security Appropriations/ TSA Uniforms and Badges.** Blackburn, R-Tenn., amendment that would bar the use of funds in the bill to provide a transportation security officer, behavior detection officer or any other TSA employee with a badge, shield, or uniform with epaulets or a badge. Rejected in Committee of the Whole 131-282: R 131-101; D 0-181. June 7, 2012.

365. HR 5855. **Fiscal 2013 Homeland Security Appropriations/ TSA Officers.** Blackburn, R-Tenn., amendment that would bar the use of funds in the bill for Transportation Security Administration security or behavior detection officers on duty outside an airport. Rejected in Committee of the Whole 204-210: R 187-46; D 17-164. June 7, 2012.

	361	362	363	364	365
ALABAMA					
1 **Bonner**	Y	Y	Y	N	Y
2 **Roby**	Y	Y	Y	Y	Y
3 **Rogers**	Y	Y	Y	N	Y
4 **Aderholt**	Y	Y	Y	N	Y
5 **Brooks**	Y	Y	Y	N	Y
6 **Bachus**	Y	Y	Y	Y	Y
7 Sewell	Y	N	N	N	N
ALASKA					
AL **Young**	Y	Y	Y	Y	Y
ARIZONA					
1 **Gosar**	Y	Y	Y	Y	Y
2 **Franks**	Y	Y	Y	Y	Y
3 **Quayle**	Y	Y	Y	Y	Y
4 Pastor	N	N	N	N	N
5 **Schweikert**	Y	Y	Y	Y	Y
6 **Flake**	Y	N	Y	Y	Y
7 Grijalva	N	N	N	N	N
8 Vacant					
ARKANSAS					
1 **Crawford**	Y	Y	Y	N	Y
2 **Griffin**	Y	?	Y	Y	N
3 **Womack**	Y	Y	Y	N	Y
4 Ross	Y	N	N	N	N
CALIFORNIA					
1 Thompson	N	N	N	N	N
2 **Herger**	Y	Y	Y	N	Y
3 **Lungren**	Y	Y	Y	N	N
4 **McClintock**	Y	Y	Y	Y	Y
5 Matsui	N	N	N	N	N
6 Woolsey	N	N	N	N	N
7 Miller, George	N	N	N	N	Y
8 Pelosi	N	N	N	N	N
9 Lee	N	N	N	N	N
10 Garamendi	N	N	N	N	N
11 McNerney	Y	N	N	N	N
12 Speier	Y	N	N	N	Y
13 Stark	N	N	N	N	N
14 Eshoo	N	N	N	N	Y
15 Honda	N	N	N	N	N
16 Lofgren	N	N	N	N	N
17 Farr	N	N	N	N	Y
18 Cardoza	Y	N	N	N	N
19 **Denham**	Y	Y	Y	N	N
20 Costa	Y	N	N	N	N
21 **Nunes**	Y	Y	Y	N	Y
22 **McCarthy**	Y	Y	Y	Y	Y
23 Capps	N	N	N	N	N
24 **Gallegly**	Y	Y	Y	N	Y
25 **McKeon**	Y	Y	Y	N	Y
26 **Dreier**	Y	Y	Y	N	N
27 Sherman	N	N	N	N	N
28 Berman	N	N	N	N	N
29 Schiff	N	N	N	N	N
30 Waxman	N	N	N	N	N
31 Becerra	N	N	N	N	N
32 Chu	N	N	N	N	N
33 Bass	?	?	?	?	?
34 Roybal-Allard	N	N	N	N	N
35 Waters	N	N	N	N	N
36 Hahn	N	N	N	N	N
37 Richardson	N	N	N	N	N
38 Napolitano	N	N	N	N	N
39 Sánchez, Linda	N	N	N	N	N
40 **Royce**	Y	N	Y	N	Y
41 **Lewis**	?	?	?	?	?
42 **Miller, Gary**	Y	Y	Y	Y	Y
43 Baca	N	N	N	N	N
44 **Calvert**	Y	Y	Y	N	Y
45 **Bono Mack**	Y	N	Y	N	Y
46 **Rohrabacher**	Y	N	Y	N	Y
47 Sanchez, Loretta	N	N	N	N	Y
48 **Campbell**	Y	Y	Y	Y	Y
49 **Issa**	Y	Y	Y	Y	Y
50 **Bilbray**	Y	Y	Y	Y	N
51 Filner	–	–	–	–	–
52 **Hunter**	Y	Y	Y	Y	Y
53 Davis	Y	N	N	N	Y

	361	362	363	364	365
COLORADO					
1 DeGette	N	N	N	N	N
2 Polis	N	N	N	N	Y
3 **Tipton**	Y	N	Y	Y	N
4 **Gardner**	Y	Y	Y	Y	Y
5 **Lamborn**	Y	Y	Y	Y	Y
6 **Coffman**	Y	Y	Y	N	Y
7 Perlmutter	N	N	N	N	N
CONNECTICUT					
1 Larson	N	N	N	N	N
2 Courtney	N	N	N	N	N
3 DeLauro	N	N	N	N	N
4 Himes	N	N	N	N	Y
5 Murphy	N	N	N	N	N
DELAWARE					
AL Carney	N	N	N	N	N
FLORIDA					
1 **Miller**	Y	Y	Y	Y	Y
2 **Southerland**	Y	Y	Y	Y	Y
3 Brown	N	N	N	N	N
4 **Crenshaw**	Y	Y	Y	N	N
5 **Nugent**	Y	Y	Y	Y	Y
6 **Stearns**	Y	Y	Y	Y	Y
7 **Mica**	Y	Y	Y	Y	Y
8 **Webster**	Y	Y	Y	Y	Y
9 **Bilirakis**	?	?	?	?	?
10 **Young**	Y	Y	Y	N	N
11 Castor	N	N	N	N	N
12 **Ross**	Y	Y	Y	Y	Y
13 **Buchanan**	Y	Y	Y	Y	Y
14 **Mack**	Y	Y	Y	Y	Y
15 **Posey**	Y	Y	Y	Y	Y
16 **Rooney**	Y	Y	Y	Y	Y
17 Wilson	N	N	N	N	N
18 **Ros-Lehtinen**	N	N	N	N	N
19 Deutch	N	N	N	N	N
20 Wasserman Schultz	N	N	N	N	N
21 **Diaz-Balart**	Y	N	N	N	N
22 **West**	Y	Y	Y	N	Y
23 Hastings	?	N	N	N	N
24 **Adams**	Y	Y	Y	Y	Y
25 **Rivera**	Y	N	N	N	N
GEORGIA					
1 **Kingston**	Y	Y	Y	N	Y
2 Bishop	Y	N	N	N	N
3 **Westmoreland**	Y	Y	Y	Y	Y
4 Johnson	N	N	N	N	N
5 Lewis	N	N	N	N	N
6 **Price**	Y	Y	Y	Y	Y
7 **Woodall**	Y	N	Y	Y	Y
8 **Scott, A.**	Y	Y	Y	Y	Y
9 **Graves**	Y	Y	Y	Y	Y
10 **Broun**	Y	Y	Y	N	Y
11 **Gingrey**	Y	Y	Y	Y	Y
12 **Barrow**	Y	Y	Y	N	N
13 Scott, D.	N	N	N	N	N
HAWAII					
1 Hanabusa	N	N	N	N	N
2 Hirono	N	N	N	N	N
IDAHO					
1 **Labrador**	Y	Y	Y	Y	Y
2 **Simpson**	Y	Y	Y	N	N
ILLINOIS					
1 Rush	N	N	N	N	N
2 Jackson	N	N	N	N	N
3 Lipinski	Y	Y	Y	N	N
4 Gutierrez	N	N	N	N	N
5 Quigley	N	N	N	N	N
6 **Roskam**	Y	Y	Y	Y	N
7 Davis	N	N	N	N	N
8 **Walsh**	Y	Y	Y	Y	Y
9 Schakowsky	N	N	N	N	N
10 **Dold**	Y	N	Y	N	N
11 **Kinzinger**	Y	Y	Y	Y	Y
12 Costello	N	N	N	N	N
13 **Biggert**	Y	N	Y	N	Y
14 **Hultgren**	Y	Y	Y	Y	Y
15 **Johnson**	Y	Y	Y	Y	Y

KEY   **Republicans**   Democrats

Y	Voted for (yea)	X	Paired against
#	Paired for	–	Announced against
+	Announced for	P	Voted "present"
N	Voted against (nay)		

C   Voted "present" to avoid possible conflict of interest

?   Did not vote or otherwise make a position known

	361	362	363	364	365
16 Manzullo	Y	Y	Y	Y	Y
17 Schilling	Y	Y	Y	N	Y
18 Schock	Y	Y	Y	N	Y
19 Shimkus	Y	Y	Y	Y	Y
INDIANA					
1 Visclosky	N	N	N	N	N
2 Donnelly	Y	N	N	N	N
3 Stutzman	Y	Y	Y	Y	Y
4 Rokita	Y	Y	Y	Y	Y
5 Burton	Y	Y	Y	Y	Y
6 Pence	Y	Y	Y	Y	Y
7 Carson	N	N	N	N	N
8 Bucshon	Y	Y	Y	N	Y
9 Young	Y	N	Y	N	Y
IOWA					
1 Braley	N	N	N	N	N
2 Loebsack	Y	N	N	N	Y
3 Boswell	Y	N	N	N	N
4 Latham	Y	Y	Y	N	Y
5 King	Y	Y	Y	?	Y
KANSAS					
1 Huelskamp	Y	Y	Y	Y	Y
2 Jenkins	Y	Y	Y	Y	Y
3 Yoder	Y	Y	Y	Y	Y
4 Pompeo	Y	Y	Y	Y	Y
KENTUCKY					
1 Whitfield	Y	Y	Y	N	N
2 Guthrie	Y	Y	Y	Y	Y
3 Yarmuth	N	N	N	N	N
4 Davis	Y	Y	Y	Y	Y
5 Rogers	Y	Y	Y	N	N
6 Chandler	Y	N	Y	N	N
LOUISIANA					
1 Scalise	Y	Y	Y	Y	Y
2 Richmond	N	N	N	N	N
3 Landry	Y	Y	Y	Y	Y
4 Fleming	Y	Y	Y	Y	Y
5 Alexander	Y	Y	Y	Y	Y
6 Cassidy	Y	Y	Y	N	Y
7 Boustany	Y	Y	Y	Y	Y
MAINE					
1 Pingree	N	N	N	N	N
2 Michaud	N	N	N	N	N
MARYLAND					
1 Harris	Y	Y	Y	Y	Y
2 Ruppersberger	N	N	N	N	N
3 Sarbanes	N	N	N	N	N
4 Edwards	N	N	N	N	N
5 Hoyer	N	N	N	N	N
6 Bartlett	Y	Y	Y	N	Y
7 Cummings	N	N	N	N	N
8 Van Hollen	N	N	N	N	N
MASSACHUSETTS					
1 Olver	N	N	N	N	N
2 Neal	N	?	?	?	?
3 McGovern	N	N	N	N	N
4 Frank	N	N	N	N	N
5 Tsongas	Y	N	N	N	N
6 Tierney	N	N	N	N	N
7 Markey	N	N	N	N	N
8 Capuano	N	N	N	N	N
9 Lynch	N	N	N	N	N
10 Keating	Y	N	N	N	N
MICHIGAN					
1 Benishek	Y	Y	Y	Y	Y
2 Huizenga	Y	Y	Y	Y	Y
3 Amash	Y	Y	Y	Y	Y
4 Camp	Y	Y	Y	Y	Y
5 Kildee	N	N	N	N	N
6 Upton	Y	Y	Y	N	N
7 Walberg	Y	Y	Y	Y	Y
8 Rogers	Y	Y	Y	Y	N
9 Peters	N	N	N	N	N
10 Miller	Y	Y	Y	N	N
11 McCotter	Y	Y	Y	N	N
12 Levin	N	N	N	N	N
13 Clarke	N	N	N	N	N
14 Conyers	N	?	?	?	?
15 Dingell	N	N	N	N	N
MINNESOTA					
1 Walz	Y	N	Y	N	N
2 Kline	Y	Y	Y	Y	Y
3 Paulsen	Y	Y	Y	Y	Y
4 McCollum	Y	N	N	N	N

	361	362	363	364	365
5 Ellison	Y	N	N	N	N
6 Bachmann	Y	Y	Y	Y	Y
7 Peterson	Y	Y	Y	N	N
8 Cravaack	Y	Y	Y	Y	Y
MISSISSIPPI					
1 Nunnelee	Y	Y	Y	Y	Y
2 Thompson	N	N	N	N	N
3 Harper	Y	Y	Y	Y	Y
4 Palazzo	Y	Y	Y	N	Y
MISSOURI					
1 Clay	N	N	N	N	N
2 Akin	+	?	?	?	?
3 Carnahan	N	N	N	N	N
4 Hartzler	Y	Y	Y	Y	Y
5 Cleaver	N	N	N	N	N
6 Graves	Y	Y	Y	Y	Y
7 Long	Y	Y	Y	Y	Y
8 Emerson	Y	Y	Y	N	Y
9 Luetkemeyer	Y	Y	Y	Y	Y
MONTANA					
AL Rehberg	Y	Y	Y	Y	Y
NEBRASKA					
1 Fortenberry	Y	Y	Y	Y	Y
2 Terry	Y	Y	Y	Y	Y
3 Smith	Y	Y	Y	Y	Y
NEVADA					
1 Berkley	N	N	N	N	N
2 Amodei	Y	N	Y	Y	Y
3 Heck	Y	N	Y	Y	Y
NEW HAMPSHIRE					
1 Guinta	Y	Y	Y	Y	Y
2 Bass	Y	Y	Y	N	N
NEW JERSEY					
1 Andrews	N	N	N	N	N
2 LoBiondo	Y	Y	Y	N	N
3 Runyan	Y	?	?	?	?
4 Smith	Y	Y	Y	N	N
5 Garrett	Y	Y	Y	Y	Y
6 Pallone	N	N	N	N	N
7 Lance	Y	Y	Y	N	Y
8 Pascrell	N	N	N	N	N
9 Rothman	N	N	N	N	N
10 Vacant					
11 Frelinghuysen	Y	N	Y	N	Y
12 Holt	N	N	N	N	N
13 Sires	N	N	N	N	N
NEW MEXICO					
1 Heinrich	N	N	N	N	Y
2 Pearce	Y	Y	Y	Y	Y
3 Luján	N	N	N	N	N
NEW YORK					
1 Bishop	Y	N	N	N	N
2 Israel	N	N	N	N	N
3 King	Y	Y	Y	N	N
4 McCarthy	Y	N	N	N	N
5 Ackerman	N	N	N	N	N
6 Meeks	N	N	N	N	N
7 Crowley	N	N	N	N	N
8 Nadler	N	N	N	N	N
9 Turner	Y	Y	Y	N	N
10 Towns	N	?	?	?	?
11 Clarke	N	N	N	N	N
12 Velázquez	N	N	N	N	N
13 Grimm	Y	Y	Y	Y	N
14 Maloney	N	N	N	N	N
15 Rangel	N	N	N	N	N
16 Serrano	N	N	N	N	N
17 Engel	N	N	N	N	N
18 Lowey	N	N	N	N	N
19 Hayworth	Y	Y	Y	N	N
20 Gibson	Y	Y	Y	N	Y
21 Tonko	N	N	N	N	N
22 Hinchey	N	N	N	N	N
23 Owens	Y	N	N	N	N
24 Hanna	Y	Y	Y	N	Y
25 Buerkle	Y	Y	Y	N	N
26 Hochul	Y	N	N	N	N
27 Higgins	Y	N	N	N	N
28 Slaughter	–	–	–	–	–
29 Reed	Y	Y	Y	N	N
NORTH CAROLINA					
1 Butterfield	N	N	N	N	N
2 Ellmers	Y	Y	Y	Y	Y
3 Jones	Y	Y	Y	Y	Y
4 Price	N	N	N	N	N

	361	362	363	364	365
5 Foxx	Y	Y	Y	Y	Y
6 Coble	?	?	?	?	?
7 McIntyre	Y	Y	Y	N	N
8 Kissell	Y	Y	Y	N	N
9 Myrick	Y	?	?	?	?
10 McHenry	Y	Y	Y	Y	Y
11 Shuler	?	?	?	?	?
12 Watt	N	N	N	N	N
13 Miller	N	N	N	N	N
NORTH DAKOTA					
AL Berg	Y	Y	Y	N	Y
OHIO					
1 Chabot	Y	Y	Y	Y	Y
2 Schmidt	?	Y	Y	Y	Y
3 Turner	Y	Y	Y	N	N
4 Jordan	Y	Y	Y	Y	Y
5 Latta	Y	Y	Y	N	N
6 Johnson	Y	Y	Y	N	N
7 Austria	Y	Y	Y	N	Y
8 Boehner					
9 Kaptur	N	N	N	N	N
10 Kucinich	?	?	?	?	?
11 Fudge	N	N	N	N	N
12 Tiberi	Y	Y	Y	N	Y
13 Sutton	N	N	N	N	N
14 LaTourette	Y	?	Y	N	N
15 Stivers	Y	Y	Y	N	Y
16 Renacci	Y	Y	Y	N	N
17 Ryan	N	N	N	N	N
18 Gibbs	Y	Y	Y	N	Y
OKLAHOMA					
1 Sullivan	Y	Y	Y	Y	Y
2 Boren	Y	Y	Y	N	N
3 Lucas	Y	Y	Y	N	Y
4 Cole	Y	Y	Y	N	N
5 Lankford	Y	Y	Y	Y	Y
OREGON					
1 Bonamici	N	N	N	N	N
2 Walden	Y	Y	Y	N	Y
3 Blumenauer	N	N	N	N	N
4 DeFazio	N	N	N	N	Y
5 Schrader	N	N	N	N	Y
PENNSYLVANIA					
1 Brady	N	N	N	N	N
2 Fattah	N	N	N	N	N
3 Kelly	Y	Y	Y	N	Y
4 Altmire	Y	Y	Y	N	N
5 Thompson	Y	Y	Y	N	N
6 Gerlach	Y	Y	Y	N	N
7 Meehan	Y	Y	Y	N	N
8 Fitzpatrick	Y	Y	Y	Y	Y
9 Shuster	Y	Y	Y	N	N
10 Marino	?	?	?	?	?
11 Barletta	Y	Y	Y	N	Y
12 Critz	Y	N	Y	Y	N
13 Schwartz	N	N	N	N	N
14 Doyle	N	N	N	N	N
15 Dent	Y	Y	Y	N	N
16 Pitts	Y	Y	Y	Y	Y
17 Holden	Y	N	N	N	N
18 Murphy	Y	Y	Y	N	Y
19 Platts	Y	Y	Y	N	N
RHODE ISLAND					
1 Cicilline	N	N	N	N	N
2 Langevin	N	N	N	N	N
SOUTH CAROLINA					
1 Scott	Y	Y	Y	Y	Y
2 Wilson	Y	Y	Y	Y	Y
3 Duncan	Y	Y	Y	Y	Y
4 Gowdy	Y	Y	Y	Y	Y
5 Mulvaney	Y	Y	Y	Y	Y
6 Clyburn	N	N	N	N	N
SOUTH DAKOTA					
AL Noem	Y	Y	Y	N	Y
TENNESSEE					
1 Roe	Y	Y	Y	N	Y
2 Duncan	Y	Y	Y	Y	Y
3 Fleischmann	Y	Y	Y	Y	Y
4 DesJarlais	Y	Y	Y	Y	Y
5 Cooper	N	N	N	N	N
6 Black	Y	Y	Y	Y	Y
7 Blackburn	Y	Y	Y	Y	Y
8 Fincher	Y	Y	Y	Y	Y
9 Cohen	N	N	N	N	N

	361	362	363	364	365
TEXAS					
1 Gohmert	?	Y	Y	Y	Y
2 Poe	Y	Y	Y	Y	Y
3 Johnson, S.	Y	Y	Y	Y	Y
4 Hall	Y	Y	Y	N	N
5 Hensarling	Y	Y	Y	Y	Y
6 Barton	Y	Y	Y	Y	Y
7 Culberson	Y	Y	Y	Y	Y
8 Brady	Y	Y	Y	Y	N
9 Green, A.	N	N	N	N	N
10 McCaul	Y	Y	Y	N	Y
11 Conaway	Y	Y	Y	Y	Y
12 Granger	Y	Y	Y	N	N
13 Thornberry	Y	Y	Y	N	N
14 Paul	?	?	?	?	?
15 Hinojosa	N	N	N	N	N
16 Reyes	N	N	N	N	N
17 Flores	Y	Y	Y	Y	Y
18 Jackson Lee	N	N	N	N	N
19 Neugebauer	Y	Y	Y	Y	Y
20 Gonzalez	N	N	N	N	N
21 Smith	Y	Y	Y	N	Y
22 Olson	Y	Y	Y	Y	Y
23 Canseco	Y	Y	Y	Y	Y
24 Marchant	Y	Y	Y	Y	Y
25 Doggett	N	N	N	N	N
26 Burgess	Y	Y	Y	Y	Y
27 Farenthold	Y	Y	Y	Y	Y
28 Cuellar	Y	N	N	N	N
29 Green, G.	N	N	N	N	N
30 Johnson, E.	N	N	N	N	N
31 Carter	Y	Y	Y	N	N
32 Sessions	Y	Y	Y	Y	Y
UTAH					
1 Bishop	Y	Y	Y	Y	N
2 Matheson	Y	N	N	N	N
3 Chaffetz	Y	Y	Y	N	N
VERMONT					
AL Welch	N	N	N	N	N
VIRGINIA					
1 Wittman	Y	Y	Y	Y	Y
2 Rigell	Y	Y	Y	Y	Y
3 Scott	N	N	N	N	N
4 Forbes	Y	Y	Y	Y	Y
5 Hurt	Y	Y	Y	Y	Y
6 Goodlatte	Y	Y	Y	Y	Y
7 Cantor	Y	Y	Y	Y	Y
8 Moran	N	N	N	N	N
9 Griffith	Y	Y	Y	Y	Y
10 Wolf	Y	Y	Y	N	Y
11 Connolly	N	N	N	N	N
WASHINGTON					
1 Vacant					
2 Larsen	N	N	N	N	N
3 Herrera Beutler	Y	Y	Y	Y	Y
4 Hastings	Y	Y	Y	N	Y
5 McMorris Rodgers	Y	Y	Y	N	Y
6 Dicks	N	N	N	N	N
7 McDermott	N	N	N	N	Y
8 Reichert	Y	Y	Y	N	N
9 Smith	N	N	N	N	N
WEST VIRGINIA					
1 McKinley	Y	Y	Y	Y	Y
2 Capito	Y	Y	Y	N	Y
3 Rahall	N	N	Y	N	N
WISCONSIN					
1 Ryan	Y	Y	Y	N	Y
2 Baldwin	?	?	?	?	?
3 Kind	Y	N	Y	N	N
4 Moore	N	N	N	N	N
5 Sensenbrenner	Y	Y	Y	Y	Y
6 Petri	Y	Y	Y	Y	Y
7 Duffy	Y	Y	Y	N	Y
8 Ribble	Y	Y	Y	N	Y
WYOMING					
AL Lummis	Y	Y	Y	Y	Y

IN THE HOUSE | By Vote Number

366. HR 5855. Fiscal 2013 Homeland Security Appropriations/ **Immigration Enforcement Authority.** Sullivan, R-Okla., amendment that would bar the use of funds in the bill to terminate an agreement under an Immigration and Customs Enforcement program to delegate authority for immigration enforcement activities to state and local law enforcement entities. Adopted in Committee of the Whole 250-164: R 232-1; D 18-163. June 7, 2012.

367. HR 5855. Fiscal 2013 Homeland Security Appropriations/ **Surface Transportation Security Inspectors.** Turner, R-N.Y., amendment that would limit funding in the bill for surface transportation security inspectors to $20 million. Both National Explosives Detection Canine Training and Visible Intermodal Prevention and Response teams would be exempt from the funding limitation. Rejected in Committee of the Whole 101-314: R 99-134; D 2-180. June 7, 2012.

368. HR 5855. Fiscal 2013 Homeland Security Appropriations/ **Funding Reductions.** Polis, D-Colo., amendment that would make an across-the-board reduction of 2 percent in the bill's discretionary spending. It would exclude the analysis and operations account, U.S. Secret Service, Domestic Nuclear Detection Office and the bill's protection, preparedness, response and recovery accounts from the reduction. Rejected in Committee of the Whole 99-316: R 79-154; D 20-162. June 7, 2012.

369. HR 5855. Fiscal 2013 Homeland Security Appropriations/ **Recommit.** Tierney, D-Mass., motion to recommit the bill to the House Appropriations Committee and report it back immediately with an amendment that would increase by $16.6 million the amount provided in the bill for the National Protection and Programs Directorate for infrastructure protection and information security programs and activities. The amendment would reduce funding in the bill for the Transportation Security Administration's administrative account by the same amount. It also would increase by $340.3 million the amount for Federal Emergency Management Agency grants for areas at highest risk of a terrorist attack. Motion rejected 165-251: R 0-233; D 165-18. June 7, 2012.

370. HR 5855. Fiscal 2013 Homeland Security Appropriations/ **Passage.** Passage of the bill that would provide $46 billion in fiscal 2013 for the Homeland Security Department and related activities. The bill includes $10.2 billion for Customs and Border Protection; $5.5 billion for Immigration and Customs Enforcement; $7.5 billion for the Transportation Security Administration, including fees; $10 billion for the Coast Guard; $1.6 billion for the Secret Service; and $9.9 billion for the Federal Emergency Management Agency. It also would prohibit federal funding for ICE to provide for abortions, except in cases where the life of the woman would be endangered or in the case of rape or incest. Passed 234-182: R 217-16; D 17-166. A "nay" was a vote in support of the president's position. June 7, 2012.

	366	367	368	369	370
ALABAMA					
1 Bonner	Y	N	N	N	Y
2 Roby	Y	N	N	N	Y
3 Rogers	Y	N	N	N	Y
4 Aderholt	Y	N	N	N	Y
5 Brooks	Y	N	Y	N	Y
6 Bachus	Y	N	N	N	Y
7 Sewell	N	N	N	Y	N
ALASKA					
AL Young	Y	Y	N	N	Y
ARIZONA					
1 Gosar	Y	Y	Y	N	Y
2 Franks	Y	Y	Y	N	Y
3 Quayle	Y	Y	Y	N	Y
4 Pastor	N	N	Y	Y	N
5 Schweikert	Y	Y	Y	N	Y
6 Flake	Y	Y	Y	N	N
7 Grijalva	N	N	Y	Y	N
8 Vacant					
ARKANSAS					
1 Crawford	Y	N	N	N	Y
2 Griffin	Y	N	N	N	Y
3 Womack	Y	N	N	N	Y
4 Ross	Y	N	N	N	Y
CALIFORNIA					
1 Thompson	N	N	N	Y	N
2 Herger	Y	N	Y	N	Y
3 Lungren	Y	N	N	N	Y
4 McClintock	Y	Y	Y	N	N
5 Matsui	N	N	N	Y	N
6 Woolsey	N	N	N	Y	N
7 Miller, George	N	N	N	Y	N
8 Pelosi	N	N	N	Y	N
9 Lee	N	N	Y	Y	N
10 Garamendi	N	N	N	Y	N
11 McNerney	N	N	N	Y	N
12 Speier	N	N	Y	Y	N
13 Stark	N	N	N	Y	N
14 Eshoo	N	N	Y	Y	N
15 Honda	N	N	Y	Y	N
16 Lofgren	N	N	Y	Y	N
17 Farr	N	N	N	Y	N
18 Cardoza	N	N	N	Y	N
19 Denham	Y	N	N	N	Y
20 Costa	N	N	N	Y	N
21 Nunes	Y	N	N	N	Y
22 McCarthy	Y	N	N	N	Y
23 Capps	N	N	N	Y	N
24 Gallegly	Y	N	N	N	Y
25 McKeon	Y	N	N	N	Y
26 Dreier	Y	N	N	N	Y
27 Sherman	N	N	N	Y	N
28 Berman	N	N	N	Y	N
29 Schiff	N	N	N	Y	N
30 Waxman	N	N	N	Y	N
31 Becerra	N	N	Y	Y	N
32 Chu	N	N	N	Y	N
33 Bass	?	?	?	Y	N
34 Roybal-Allard	N	N	N	Y	N
35 Waters	N	N	N	Y	N
36 Hahn	N	N	Y	Y	N
37 Richardson	N	N	N	Y	N
38 Napolitano	N	N	Y	Y	N
39 Sánchez, Linda	N	N	N	Y	N
40 Royce	Y	Y	Y	N	N
41 Lewis	?	?	?	?	?
42 Miller, Gary	Y	N	N	N	Y
43 Baca	N	N	N	Y	N
44 Calvert	Y	N	N	N	Y
45 Bono Mack	Y	N	N	N	Y
46 Rohrabacher	Y	Y	Y	N	Y
47 Sanchez, Loretta	N	N	N	Y	N
48 Campbell	Y	Y	Y	N	N
49 Issa	Y	Y	Y	N	Y
50 Bilbray	Y	N	N	N	Y
51 Filner	-	-	-	+	-
52 Hunter	Y	N	N	N	Y
53 Davis	N	N	N	Y	N

	366	367	368	369	370
COLORADO					
1 DeGette	N	N	N	Y	N
2 Polis	N	N	Y	N	N
3 Tipton	Y	N	N	N	Y
4 Gardner	Y	N	N	N	Y
5 Lamborn	Y	N	Y	N	Y
6 Coffman	Y	N	N	N	Y
7 Perlmutter	N	N	N	Y	N
CONNECTICUT					
1 Larson	N	N	N	Y	N
2 Courtney	N	N	N	Y	N
3 DeLauro	N	N	N	Y	N
4 Himes	N	N	N	Y	N
5 Murphy	N	N	N	Y	N
DELAWARE					
AL Carney	N	N	N	N	N
FLORIDA					
1 Miller	Y	Y	N	N	Y
2 Southerland	Y	Y	N	N	Y
3 Brown	N	N	N	Y	N
4 Crenshaw	Y	N	N	N	Y
5 Nugent	Y	N	N	N	Y
6 Stearns	Y	Y	Y	N	N
7 Mica	Y	Y	N	N	Y
8 Webster	Y	N	N	N	Y
9 Bilirakis	?	?	?	?	?
10 Young	N	N	N	Y	N
11 Castor	N	N	N	Y	N
12 Ross	Y	N	N	N	Y
13 Buchanan	Y	Y	N	N	Y
14 Mack	Y	Y	Y	N	Y
15 Posey	Y	Y	N	N	Y
16 Rooney	Y	N	N	N	Y
17 Wilson	N	N	N	Y	N
18 Ros-Lehtinen	Y	N	N	N	Y
19 Deutch	N	N	Y	Y	N
20 Wasserman Schultz	N	N	N	Y	N
21 Diaz-Balart	Y	N	N	N	Y
22 West	Y	Y	N	N	Y
23 Hastings	N	N	Y	Y	N
24 Adams	Y	Y	Y	N	Y
25 Rivera	Y	N	N	N	Y
GEORGIA					
1 Kingston	Y	Y	N	N	Y
2 Bishop	N	N	Y	N	Y
3 Westmoreland	Y	Y	N	N	Y
4 Johnson	N	N	N	Y	N
5 Lewis	N	N	N	Y	N
6 Price	Y	Y	Y	N	Y
7 Woodall	Y	Y	Y	N	Y
8 Scott, A.	Y	Y	Y	N	Y
9 Graves	Y	Y	Y	N	Y
10 Broun	Y	Y	Y	N	Y
11 Gingrey	Y	Y	N	N	Y
12 Barrow	Y	N	N	N	Y
13 Scott, D.	N	N	N	Y	N
HAWAII					
1 Hanabusa	N	N	N	Y	N
2 Hirono	N	N	N	Y	N
IDAHO					
1 Labrador	Y	Y	Y	N	Y
2 Simpson	Y	N	N	N	Y
ILLINOIS					
1 Rush	N	N	N	Y	N
2 Jackson	N	N	N	Y	N
3 Lipinski	Y	N	N	N	Y
4 Gutierrez	N	N	Y	Y	N
5 Quigley	N	N	N	Y	N
6 Roskam	Y	N	N	N	Y
7 Davis	N	N	N	Y	N
8 Walsh	Y	Y	Y	N	N
9 Schakowsky	N	N	N	Y	N
10 Dold	Y	N	N	N	Y
11 Kinzinger	Y	N	N	N	Y
12 Costello	N	N	N	Y	N
13 Biggert	Y	N	N	N	Y
14 Hultgren	Y	Y	N	N	Y
15 Johnson	Y	Y	Y	N	N

KEY   **Republicans**   Democrats

Y	Voted for (yea)
#	Paired for
+	Announced for
N	Voted against (nay)

X	Paired against
-	Announced against
P	Voted "present"

C	Voted "present" to avoid possible conflict of interest
?	Did not vote or otherwise make a position known

	366	367	368	369	370
16 Manzullo	Y	N	Y	N	Y
17 Schilling	Y	N	Y	N	Y
18 Schock	Y	N	N	N	Y
19 Shimkus	Y	Y	N	N	Y
INDIANA					
1 Visclosky	N	N	N	Y	N
2 Donnelly	Y	N	N	N	Y
3 Stutzman	Y	Y	Y	N	Y
4 Rokita	Y	N	N	N	Y
5 Burton	Y	Y	Y	N	Y
6 Pence	Y	Y	Y	N	Y
7 Carson	N	N	N	Y	N
8 Bucshon	Y	N	N	N	Y
9 Young	Y	N	N	N	Y
IOWA					
1 Braley	N	N	N	N	N
2 Loebsack	N	N	N	N	N
3 Boswell	N	N	N	N	Y
4 Latham	Y	N	N	N	Y
5 King	Y	Y	Y	N	Y
KANSAS					
1 Huelskamp	Y	Y	Y	N	N
2 Jenkins	Y	N	Y	N	Y
3 Yoder	Y	N	N	N	Y
4 Pompeo	Y	N	Y	N	Y
KENTUCKY					
1 Whitfield	Y	N	N	N	Y
2 Guthrie	Y	N	N	N	Y
3 Yarmuth	N	N	N	Y	N
4 Davis	Y	N	N	N	Y
5 Rogers	Y	N	N	N	Y
6 Chandler	Y	N	N	N	Y
LOUISIANA					
1 Scalise	Y	Y	N	N	Y
2 Richmond	N	N	N	Y	N
3 Landry	Y	N	N	N	Y
4 Fleming	Y	N	N	N	Y
5 Alexander	Y	N	N	N	Y
6 Cassidy	Y	Y	N	N	Y
7 Boustany	Y	N	N	N	Y
MAINE					
1 Pingree	N	N	N	Y	N
2 Michaud	N	N	N	N	N
MARYLAND					
1 Harris	Y	Y	N	N	Y
2 Ruppersberger	N	Y	N	Y	N
3 Sarbanes	N	N	N	Y	N
4 Edwards	N	N	N	Y	N
5 Hoyer	N	N	N	Y	N
6 Bartlett	Y	N	N	N	Y
7 Cummings	N	N	N	Y	N
8 Van Hollen	N	N	N	Y	N
MASSACHUSETTS					
1 Olver	N	N	N	Y	N
2 Neal	?	?	?	?	?
3 McGovern	N	N	N	Y	N
4 Frank	N	N	N	Y	N
5 Tsongas	N	N	N	Y	N
6 Tierney	N	N	N	Y	N
7 Markey	N	N	N	Y	N
8 Capuano	N	N	N	Y	N
9 Lynch	N	N	Y	Y	N
10 Keating	N	N	N	Y	Y
MICHIGAN					
1 Benishek	Y	Y	Y	N	Y
2 Huizenga	Y	Y	Y	N	Y
3 Amash	Y	Y	N	N	N
4 Camp	Y	N	Y	N	Y
5 Kildee	N	N	N	Y	N
6 Upton	Y	N	Y	N	Y
7 Walberg	Y	Y	Y	N	Y
8 Rogers	Y	N	N	N	Y
9 Peters	N	N	N	Y	N
10 Miller	Y	N	Y	N	Y
11 McCotter	Y	N	N	N	Y
12 Levin	N	N	N	Y	N
13 Clarke	N	N	N	Y	N
14 Conyers	?	N	N	Y	N
15 Dingell	N	N	N	Y	N
MINNESOTA					
1 Walz	N	N	N	N	N
2 Kline	Y	N	N	N	Y
3 Paulsen	Y	N	N	N	Y
4 McCollum	N	N	N	Y	N

	366	367	368	369	370
5 Ellison	N	N	N	Y	N
6 Bachmann	Y	Y	N	N	Y
7 Peterson	Y	N	N	N	Y
8 Cravaack	Y	Y	N	N	Y
MISSISSIPPI					
1 Nunnelee	Y	Y	Y	N	Y
2 Thompson	N	N	N	Y	N
3 Harper	Y	N	N	N	Y
4 Palazzo	Y	N	N	N	Y
MISSOURI					
1 Clay	N	N	N	Y	N
2 Akin	?	?	?	?	?
3 Carnahan	N	N	N	Y	N
4 Hartzler	Y	Y	Y	N	Y
5 Cleaver	N	N	N	Y	N
6 Graves	Y	Y	N	N	Y
7 Long	Y	Y	N	N	Y
8 Emerson	Y	Y	N	N	Y
9 Luetkemeyer	Y	Y	N	N	Y
MONTANA					
AL Rehberg	Y	N	N	N	Y
NEBRASKA					
1 Fortenberry	Y	N	N	N	Y
2 Terry	Y	N	N	N	Y
3 Smith	Y	Y	N	N	Y
NEVADA					
1 Berkley	N	N	N	Y	Y
2 Amodei	Y	N	N	N	Y
3 Heck	Y	N	N	N	Y
NEW HAMPSHIRE					
1 Guinta	Y	Y	N	N	Y
2 Bass	Y	N	N	N	Y
NEW JERSEY					
1 Andrews	N	N	N	Y	N
2 LoBiondo	Y	N	N	N	Y
3 Runyan	?	?	?	?	?
4 Smith	Y	N	N	N	Y
5 Garrett	Y	Y	Y	N	Y
6 Pallone	N	N	N	Y	N
7 Lance	Y	N	Y	N	Y
8 Pascrell	N	N	N	Y	N
9 Rothman	N	N	N	Y	N
10 Vacant					
11 Frelinghuysen	Y	N	N	N	Y
12 Holt	N	N	N	Y	N
13 Sires	N	N	N	Y	N
NEW MEXICO					
1 Heinrich	N	N	N	N	Y
2 Pearce	Y	N	N	N	Y
3 Luján	N	N	N	N	N
NEW YORK					
1 Bishop	N	N	N	Y	N
2 Israel	N	N	N	Y	N
3 King	Y	N	N	N	Y
4 McCarthy	N	N	N	Y	Y
5 Ackerman	N	N	N	Y	N
6 Meeks	N	N	N	Y	N
7 Crowley	N	N	N	Y	N
8 Nadler	N	N	N	Y	N
9 Turner	Y	Y	N	N	Y
10 Towns	?	?	?	?	?
11 Clarke	N	N	N	Y	N
12 Velázquez	N	N	N	Y	N
13 Grimm	Y	N	N	N	Y
14 Maloney	N	N	N	Y	N
15 Rangel	N	N	N	Y	N
16 Serrano	N	N	Y	Y	N
17 Engel	N	N	N	Y	N
18 Lowey	N	N	N	Y	N
19 Hayworth	Y	N	N	N	Y
20 Gibson	Y	N	N	N	Y
21 Tonko	N	N	N	Y	N
22 Hinchey	N	N	N	Y	N
23 Owens	N	N	N	Y	N
24 Hanna	Y	N	N	N	Y
25 Buerkle	Y	N	Y	N	Y
26 Hochul	N	N	N	Y	N
27 Higgins	N	N	N	Y	N
28 Slaughter	–	–	–	+	–
29 Reed	Y	N	N	N	Y
NORTH CAROLINA					
1 Butterfield	N	N	N	Y	N
2 Ellmers	Y	N	N	N	Y
3 Jones	Y	N	N	N	N
4 Price	N	N	N	Y	N

	366	367	368	369	370
5 Foxx	Y	Y	N	N	Y
6 Coble	?	?	?	?	?
7 McIntyre	Y	N	N	Y	Y
8 Kissell	N	N	N	N	Y
9 Myrick	?	?	?	?	?
10 McHenry	Y	N	N	N	Y
11 Shuler	?	?	?	?	?
12 Watt	N	N	N	Y	N
13 Miller	N	N	N	N	Y
NORTH DAKOTA					
AL Berg	Y	N	N	N	Y
OHIO					
1 Chabot	Y	Y	N	N	Y
2 Schmidt	Y	N	N	N	Y
3 Turner	Y	N	N	N	Y
4 Jordan	Y	Y	N	N	Y
5 Latta	Y	Y	N	N	Y
6 Johnson	Y	N	N	N	Y
7 Austria	Y	N	N	N	Y
8 Boehner					
9 Kaptur	N	N	N	Y	N
10 Kucinich	?	?	?	?	?
11 Fudge	N	N	N	Y	N
12 Tiberi	Y	N	Y	N	Y
13 Sutton	N	N	N	Y	N
14 LaTourette	Y	N	N	N	Y
15 Stivers	Y	N	N	N	Y
16 Renacci	Y	N	N	N	Y
17 Ryan	N	N	N	Y	N
18 Gibbs	Y	N	N	N	Y
OKLAHOMA					
1 Sullivan	Y	N	N	N	Y
2 Boren	Y	N	N	N	Y
3 Lucas	Y	N	N	N	Y
4 Cole	Y	N	N	N	Y
5 Lankford	Y	Y	Y	N	Y
OREGON					
1 Bonamici	N	N	N	Y	N
2 Walden	Y	N	N	N	Y
3 Blumenauer	N	N	N	Y	N
4 DeFazio	N	Y	N	Y	N
5 Schrader	N	N	N	N	N
PENNSYLVANIA					
1 Brady	N	N	N	Y	N
2 Fattah	N	N	N	Y	N
3 Kelly	Y	Y	N	N	Y
4 Altmire	Y	N	N	Y	Y
5 Thompson	N	N	N	N	Y
6 Gerlach	Y	N	N	N	Y
7 Meehan	Y	Y	N	N	Y
8 Fitzpatrick	Y	N	N	N	Y
9 Shuster	Y	N	N	N	Y
10 Marino	?	?	?	?	?
11 Barletta	Y	Y	N	N	Y
12 Critz	Y	N	N	N	Y
13 Schwartz	N	N	N	Y	N
14 Doyle	N	N	N	Y	N
15 Dent	Y	N	N	N	Y
16 Pitts	Y	Y	Y	N	Y
17 Holden	Y	N	N	Y	N
18 Murphy	Y	N	N	N	Y
19 Platts	Y	N	N	N	Y
RHODE ISLAND					
1 Cicilline	N	N	N	Y	N
2 Langevin	N	N	N	Y	N
SOUTH CAROLINA					
1 Scott	Y	Y	Y	N	Y
2 Wilson	Y	Y	Y	N	Y
3 Duncan	Y	Y	Y	N	Y
4 Gowdy	Y	Y	Y	N	Y
5 Mulvaney	Y	Y	Y	N	N
6 Clyburn	N	N	N	Y	N
SOUTH DAKOTA					
AL Noem	Y	N	N	N	Y
TENNESSEE					
1 Roe	Y	N	N	N	Y
2 Duncan	Y	Y	Y	N	N
3 Fleischmann	Y	N	N	N	Y
4 DesJarlais	Y	N	N	N	Y
5 Cooper	N	Y	N	Y	N
6 Black	Y	Y	Y	N	Y
7 Blackburn	Y	Y	Y	N	Y
8 Fincher	Y	Y	Y	N	Y
9 Cohen	N	N	N	Y	N

	366	367	368	369	370
TEXAS					
1 Gohmert	Y	Y	N	N	Y
2 Poe	Y	Y	Y	N	Y
3 Johnson, S.	Y	Y	N	N	Y
4 Hall	Y	N	N	N	Y
5 Hensarling	Y	Y	Y	N	Y
6 Barton	Y	Y	Y	N	Y
7 Culberson	Y	N	N	N	Y
8 Brady	Y	Y	N	N	Y
9 Green, A.	N	N	N	Y	N
10 McCaul	Y	N	N	N	Y
11 Conaway	Y	N	N	N	Y
12 Granger	Y	N	N	N	Y
13 Thornberry	Y	N	N	N	Y
14 Paul	?	?	?	?	?
15 Hinojosa	N	N	N	Y	N
16 Reyes	N	N	N	Y	N
17 Flores	Y	N	N	N	Y
18 Jackson Lee	N	N	N	Y	N
19 Neugebauer	Y	Y	N	N	Y
20 Gonzalez	N	N	N	Y	N
21 Smith	Y	N	N	N	Y
22 Olson	Y	N	N	N	Y
23 Canseco	Y	N	N	N	Y
24 Marchant	Y	Y	N	N	Y
25 Doggett	N	N	N	Y	N
26 Burgess	Y	Y	Y	N	Y
27 Farenthold	Y	N	N	N	Y
28 Cuellar	Y	N	N	N	Y
29 Green, G.	N	N	N	Y	N
30 Johnson, E.	N	N	N	Y	N
31 Carter	Y	N	N	N	Y
32 Sessions	Y	Y	Y	N	Y
UTAH					
1 Bishop	Y	Y	N	N	Y
2 Matheson	Y	N	N	N	Y
3 Chaffetz	Y	Y	Y	N	Y
VERMONT					
AL Welch	N	N	N	Y	N
VIRGINIA					
1 Wittman	Y	N	N	N	Y
2 Rigell	Y	N	Y	N	Y
3 Scott	N	N	N	Y	N
4 Forbes	Y	N	N	N	Y
5 Hurt	Y	N	Y	N	Y
6 Goodlatte	Y	Y	Y	N	Y
7 Cantor	Y	Y	N	N	Y
8 Moran	N	N	N	Y	N
9 Griffith	Y	Y	Y	N	Y
10 Wolf	Y	N	N	N	Y
11 Connolly	N	N	N	Y	N
WASHINGTON					
1 Vacant					
2 Larsen	N	N	Y	Y	N
3 Herrera Beutler	Y	Y	N	N	Y
4 Hastings	Y	N	N	N	Y
5 McMorris Rodgers	Y	N	N	N	Y
6 Dicks	N	N	N	Y	N
7 McDermott	N	N	N	Y	N
8 Reichert	Y	N	N	N	Y
9 Smith	N	N	N	Y	N
WEST VIRGINIA					
1 McKinley	Y	Y	N	N	Y
2 Capito	Y	N	N	N	Y
3 Rahall	Y	N	N	Y	Y
WISCONSIN					
1 Ryan	Y	N	Y	N	N
2 Baldwin	?	?	?	?	?
3 Kind	N	N	N	Y	N
4 Moore	N	N	N	Y	N
5 Sensenbrenner	Y	Y	N	N	N
6 Petri	Y	N	Y	N	Y
7 Duffy	Y	N	Y	N	Y
8 Ribble	Y	Y	Y	N	Y
WYOMING					
AL Lummis	Y	Y	Y	N	N

IN THE HOUSE | By Vote Number

371. **HR 5882. Fiscal 2013 Legislative Branch Appropriations/ Botanic Garden Funding.** Gosar, R-Ariz., amendment that would reduce by $1.2 million the amount provided for the maintenance, care and operation of the Botanic Garden and direct the same amount to the bill's spending reduction account. Adopted in Committee of the Whole 213-193: R 188-41; D 25-152. June 8, 2012.

372. **HR 5882. Fiscal 2013 Legislative Branch Appropriations/ Congressional Research Service Funding.** Broun, R-Ga., amendment that would cut $878,000 from the amount provided for the Congressional Research Service and direct the same amount to the bill's spending reduction account. Adopted in Committee of the Whole 214-189: R 206-25; D 8-164. June 8, 2012.

373. **HR 5882. Fiscal 2013 Legislative Branch Appropriations/ Open World Leadership Center.** Scalise, R-La., amendment that would eliminate funding in the bill for the Open World Leadership Center and direct $1 million to the bill's spending reduction account. Adopted in Committee of the Whole 204-203: R 190-41; D 14-162. June 8, 2012.

374. **HR 5882. Fiscal 2013 Legislative Branch Appropriations/ Polystyrene Products.** Moran, D-Va., amendment that would bar the use of funds in the bill to obtain polystyrene products for use in food service facilities of the House of Representatives. Rejected in Committee of the Whole 178-229: R 10-219; D 168-10. June 8, 2012.

	371	372	373	374
ALABAMA				
1 Bonner	N	N	Y	N
2 Roby	Y	Y	Y	N
3 Rogers	N	Y	Y	N
4 Aderholt	N	N	N	N
5 Brooks	Y	Y	Y	N
6 Bachus	N	N	Y	N
7 Sewell	N	N	N	Y
ALASKA				
AL Young	N	N	N	Y
ARIZONA				
1 Gosar	Y	Y	N	N
2 Franks	Y	Y	Y	N
3 Quayle	Y	Y	Y	N
4 Pastor	N	N	Y	Y
5 Schweikert	Y	Y	Y	N
6 Flake	Y	Y	Y	N
7 Grijalva	N	N	N	Y
8 Vacant				
ARKANSAS				
1 Crawford	N	Y	Y	N
2 Griffin	Y	Y	Y	N
3 Womack	N	Y	N	N
4 Ross	N	N	N	N
CALIFORNIA				
1 Thompson	N	N	N	Y
2 Herger	Y	Y	Y	N
3 Lungren	N	N	N	N
4 McClintock	Y	Y	Y	N
5 Matsui	N	N	N	Y
6 Woolsey	N	N	N	Y
7 Miller, George	N	N	N	Y
8 Pelosi	N	N	N	Y
9 Lee	N	N	N	Y
10 Garamendi	N	N	N	Y
11 McNerney	N	N	N	N
12 Speier	N	N	N	Y
13 Stark	N	N	N	Y
14 Eshoo	N	N	N	Y
15 Honda	N	N	N	Y
16 Lofgren	N	N	N	Y
17 Farr	N	N	N	Y
18 Cardoza	?	?	?	?
19 Denham	?	Y	Y	N
20 Costa	Y	Y	Y	N
21 Nunes	Y	Y	Y	N
22 McCarthy	Y	Y	Y	N
23 Capps	N	N	N	Y
24 Gallegly	Y	Y	Y	?
25 McKeon	Y	Y	N	N
26 Dreier	N	Y	N	N
27 Sherman	N	N	N	Y
28 Berman	N	N	N	Y
29 Schiff	N	N	N	Y
30 Waxman	N	N	N	Y
31 Becerra	N	N	N	Y
32 Chu	N	N	N	Y
33 Bass	?	?	?	?
34 Roybal-Allard	N	N	N	Y
35 Waters	N	N	N	Y
36 Hahn	N	N	N	Y
37 Richardson	N	?	N	Y
38 Napolitano	N	N	N	Y
39 Sánchez, Linda	N	N	N	Y
40 Royce	Y	Y	Y	N
41 Lewis	?	?	?	?
42 Miller, Gary	Y	Y	Y	N
43 Baca	N	N	N	Y
44 Calvert	N	Y	N	N
45 Bono Mack	Y	Y	Y	N
46 Rohrabacher	Y	Y	Y	N
47 Sanchez, Loretta	N	N	N	Y
48 Campbell	Y	Y	Y	N
49 Issa	Y	Y	Y	N
50 Bilbray	Y	Y	Y	N
51 Filner	–	–	–	+
52 Hunter	Y	N	Y	N
53 Davis	N	N	N	Y

	371	372	373	374
COLORADO				
1 DeGette	N	N	N	Y
2 Polis	Y	N	N	Y
3 Tipton	Y	Y	Y	N
4 Gardner	Y	Y	Y	N
5 Lamborn	Y	Y	Y	N
6 Coffman	Y	Y	Y	N
7 Perlmutter	N	N	N	Y
CONNECTICUT				
1 Larson	N	N	N	Y
2 Courtney	N	N	N	Y
3 DeLauro	N	N	N	Y
4 Himes	Y	N	N	Y
5 Murphy	N	N	N	Y
DELAWARE				
AL Carney	Y	N	N	Y
FLORIDA				
1 Miller	+	Y	Y	N
2 Southerland	Y	Y	Y	N
3 Brown	N	N	N	Y
4 Crenshaw	N	Y	N	N
5 Nugent	Y	Y	Y	N
6 Stearns	Y	Y	Y	N
7 Mica	Y	Y	Y	N
8 Webster	Y	Y	Y	N
9 Bilirakis	+	+	+	–
10 Young	Y	Y	Y	N
11 Castor	N	N	N	Y
12 Ross	Y	Y	Y	N
13 Buchanan	Y	Y	Y	N
14 Mack	?	?	?	?
15 Posey	Y	Y	Y	N
16 Rooney	Y	Y	Y	N
17 Wilson	N	N	N	Y
18 Ros-Lehtinen	Y	N	Y	N
19 Deutch	N	?	N	Y
20 Wasserman Schultz	N	N	Y	Y
21 Diaz-Balart	N	Y	N	N
22 West	Y	Y	Y	N
23 Hastings	N	N	N	Y
24 Adams	Y	Y	Y	N
25 Rivera	Y	Y	Y	N
GEORGIA				
1 Kingston	Y	Y	Y	N
2 Bishop	N	N	N	Y
3 Westmoreland	Y	Y	Y	N
4 Johnson	N	N	N	Y
5 Lewis	N	N	N	Y
6 Price	Y	Y	N	N
7 Woodall	Y	Y	Y	N
8 Scott, A.	Y	Y	Y	N
9 Graves	Y	Y	Y	N
10 Broun	Y	Y	Y	N
11 Gingrey	Y	Y	Y	–
12 Barrow	Y	Y	Y	N
13 Scott, D.	N	N	N	Y
HAWAII				
1 Hanabusa	N	N	N	Y
2 Hirono	?	?	?	?
IDAHO				
1 Labrador	?	?	?	?
2 Simpson	N	N	Y	N
ILLINOIS				
1 Rush	N	N	N	Y
2 Jackson	N	N	N	Y
3 Lipinski	N	Y	Y	Y
4 Gutierrez	N	N	N	Y
5 Quigley	N	N	N	Y
6 Roskam	N	Y	Y	N
7 Davis	N	N	?	Y
8 Walsh	Y	Y	Y	N
9 Schakowsky	N	N	N	Y
10 Dold	N	Y	N	N
11 Kinzinger	Y	Y	Y	N
12 Costello	N	N	N	Y
13 Biggert	Y	Y	N	N
14 Hultgren	Y	Y	Y	N
15 Johnson	Y	Y	Y	Y

	371	372	373	374
16 Manzullo	Y	Y	Y	N
17 Schilling	Y	Y	Y	N
18 Schock	N	Y	N	N
19 Shimkus	N	Y	N	N
INDIANA				
1 Visclosky	N	N	N	Y
2 Donnelly	Y	N	N	N
3 Stutzman	Y	Y	Y	N
4 Rokita	Y	Y	Y	N
5 Burton	Y	Y	Y	N
6 Pence	Y	Y	Y	N
7 Carson	N	N	N	Y
8 Bucshon	Y	Y	Y	N
9 Young	Y	Y	Y	N
IOWA				
1 Braley	Y	N	N	Y
2 Loebsack	Y	N	Y	Y
3 Boswell	N	N	Y	Y
4 Latham	N	Y	Y	N
5 King	Y	Y	Y	N
KANSAS				
1 Huelskamp	Y	Y	Y	N
2 Jenkins	Y	Y	Y	N
3 Yoder	Y	Y	Y	N
4 Pompeo	Y	Y	Y	N
KENTUCKY				
1 Whitfield	Y	Y	Y	N
2 Guthrie	Y	Y	Y	N
3 Yarmuth	N	N	N	Y
4 Davis	Y	Y	N	N
5 Rogers	N	Y	N	N
6 Chandler	Y	N	N	Y
LOUISIANA				
1 Scalise	Y	Y	Y	N
2 Richmond	N	N	N	Y
3 Landry	Y	Y	Y	N
4 Fleming	Y	Y	Y	N
5 Alexander	N	Y	Y	N
6 Cassidy	Y	Y	Y	N
7 Boustany	Y	Y	Y	N
MAINE				
1 Pingree	N	N	N	Y
2 Michaud	N	N	N	Y
MARYLAND				
1 Harris	Y	Y	Y	N
2 Ruppersberger	N	N	N	Y
3 Sarbanes	N	N	N	Y
4 Edwards	N	N	N	Y
5 Hoyer	N	N	N	Y
6 Bartlett	Y	Y	Y	N
7 Cummings	N	N	N	Y
8 Van Hollen	N	N	N	Y
MASSACHUSETTS				
1 Olver	N	N	N	Y
2 Neal	?	?	?	?
3 McGovern	N	N	N	Y
4 Frank	N	N	N	Y
5 Tsongas	N	N	N	Y
6 Tierney	N	N	N	Y
7 Markey	N	N	N	Y
8 Capuano	N	N	N	Y
9 Lynch	N	N	N	Y
10 Keating	Y	N	N	Y
MICHIGAN				
1 Benishek	Y	Y	Y	Y
2 Huizenga	Y	Y	Y	N
3 Amash	Y	Y	N	N
4 Camp	Y	N	Y	N
5 Kildee	N	N	N	Y
6 Upton	Y	Y	Y	N
7 Walberg	Y	Y	Y	N
8 Rogers	Y	Y	Y	N
9 Peters	N	N	N	Y
10 Miller	Y	Y	Y	N
11 McCotter	Y	Y	Y	N
12 Levin	N	N	N	Y
13 Clarke	N	N	N	Y
14 Conyers	N	N	N	Y
15 Dingell	N	N	N	Y
MINNESOTA				
1 Walz	N	N	N	Y
2 Kline	Y	Y	Y	N
3 Paulsen	Y	Y	Y	N
4 McCollum	N	N	N	Y

	371	372	373	374
5 Ellison	N	N	N	Y
6 Bachmann	Y	Y	Y	N
7 Peterson	N	Y	Y	N
8 Cravaack	Y	Y	Y	N
MISSISSIPPI				
1 Nunnelee	Y	Y	Y	N
2 Thompson	N	N	N	Y
3 Harper	N	Y	N	N
4 Palazzo	Y	Y	Y	N
MISSOURI				
1 Clay	N	N	N	Y
2 Akin	+	+	+	−
3 Carnahan	N	N	N	Y
4 Hartzler	Y	Y	Y	N
5 Cleaver	N	?	N	Y
6 Graves	Y	Y	Y	N
7 Long	Y	Y	Y	N
8 Emerson	N	Y	N	N
9 Luetkemeyer	Y	Y	Y	N
MONTANA				
AL Rehberg	Y	Y	Y	N
NEBRASKA				
1 Fortenberry	N	Y	Y	N
2 Terry	Y	Y	Y	N
3 Smith	Y	Y	Y	N
NEVADA				
1 Berkley	N	N	N	Y
2 Amodei	Y	N	Y	N
3 Heck	Y	Y	N	N
NEW HAMPSHIRE				
1 Guinta	Y	Y	Y	N
2 Bass	N	Y	Y	Y
NEW JERSEY				
1 Andrews	?	?	N	N
2 LoBiondo	Y	Y	N	N
3 Runyan	N	N	N	N
4 Smith	Y	N	Y	Y
5 Garrett	Y	Y	Y	N
6 Pallone	N	N	N	Y
7 Lance	N	Y	Y	N
8 Pascrell	N	N	N	Y
9 Rothman	N	N	N	Y
10 Vacant				
11 Frelinghuysen	N	Y	N	N
12 Holt	N	N	N	Y
13 Sires	N	N	N	Y
NEW MEXICO				
1 Heinrich	N	N	N	Y
2 Pearce	Y	N	Y	N
3 Luján	N	N	N	Y
NEW YORK				
1 Bishop	Y	N	N	Y
2 Israel	Y	Y	N	Y
3 King	N	N	N	N
4 McCarthy	Y	N	N	Y
5 Ackerman	N	N	N	Y
6 Meeks	N	N	N	Y
7 Crowley	N	N	N	Y
8 Nadler	N	N	N	Y
9 Turner	Y	Y	N	N
10 Towns	?	?	?	?
11 Clarke	N	N	N	Y
12 Velázquez	N	N	N	Y
13 Grimm	N	N	N	N
14 Maloney	N	N	N	Y
15 Rangel	N	N	N	Y
16 Serrano	N	N	N	Y
17 Engel	N	N	N	Y
18 Lowey	N	N	N	Y
19 Hayworth	N	Y	N	N
20 Gibson	Y	Y	N	N
21 Tonko	N	N	N	Y
22 Hinchey	N	N	N	Y
23 Owens	Y	N	Y	Y
24 Hanna	Y	Y	Y	N
25 Buerkle	Y	Y	Y	N
26 Hochul	Y	N	Y	Y
27 Higgins	N	N	N	Y
28 Slaughter	−	−	−	+
29 Reed	Y	Y	Y	N
NORTH CAROLINA				
1 Butterfield	N	N	N	Y
2 Ellmers	Y	Y	Y	N
3 Jones	Y	Y	Y	N
4 Price	N	N	N	Y

	371	372	373	374
5 Foxx	Y	Y	Y	N
6 Coble	?	?	?	?
7 McIntyre	Y	Y	Y	Y
8 Kissell	Y	Y	Y	N
9 Myrick	Y	Y	Y	N
10 McHenry	Y	Y	Y	N
11 Shuler	?	?	?	?
12 Watt	N	N	N	Y
13 Miller	N	N	N	Y
NORTH DAKOTA				
AL Berg	Y	Y	N	N
OHIO				
1 Chabot	Y	Y	Y	N
2 Schmidt	Y	Y	Y	N
3 Turner	Y	Y	N	N
4 Jordan	Y	Y	Y	N
5 Latta	Y	N	Y	N
6 Johnson	Y	Y	Y	N
7 Austria	Y	Y	Y	N
8 Boehner				
9 Kaptur	N	N	N	Y
10 Kucinich	?	?	?	?
11 Fudge	N	N	N	Y
12 Tiberi	N	Y	Y	N
13 Sutton	N	N	N	Y
14 LaTourette	N	N	N	Y
15 Stivers	Y	Y	Y	N
16 Renacci	Y	N	Y	N
17 Ryan	N	N	N	Y
18 Gibbs	Y	Y	Y	N
OKLAHOMA				
1 Sullivan	Y	Y	Y	N
2 Boren	Y	N	N	N
3 Lucas	N	N	N	N
4 Cole	N	Y	N	N
5 Lankford	Y	N	Y	N
OREGON				
1 Bonamici	N	N	N	Y
2 Walden	Y	N	Y	N
3 Blumenauer	N	N	N	Y
4 DeFazio	Y	N	Y	N
5 Schrader	Y	Y	N	N
PENNSYLVANIA				
1 Brady	N	N	N	Y
2 Fattah	N	N	N	Y
3 Kelly	Y	Y	Y	N
4 Altmire	N	N	N	Y
5 Thompson	N	Y	N	N
6 Gerlach	N	N	N	N
7 Meehan	?	?	?	?
8 Fitzpatrick	Y	Y	Y	N
9 Shuster	Y	N	Y	N
10 Marino	Y	Y	Y	N
11 Barletta	Y	Y	Y	N
12 Critz	Y	N	Y	N
13 Schwartz	N	N	N	Y
14 Doyle	N	N	N	Y
15 Dent	Y	Y	N	N
16 Pitts	Y	Y	Y	N
17 Holden	?	?	?	Y
18 Murphy	Y	Y	Y	N
19 Platts	?	?	?	?
RHODE ISLAND				
1 Cicilline	N	?	?	?
2 Langevin	N	N	N	Y
SOUTH CAROLINA				
1 Scott	Y	Y	Y	N
2 Wilson	Y	Y	Y	N
3 Duncan	Y	Y	Y	N
4 Gowdy	Y	Y	Y	N
5 Mulvaney	Y	Y	Y	N
6 Clyburn	N	?	N	Y
SOUTH DAKOTA				
AL Noem	Y	Y	Y	N
TENNESSEE				
1 Roe	Y	Y	Y	N
2 Duncan	Y	Y	Y	N
3 Fleischmann	Y	Y	Y	N
4 DesJarlais	Y	Y	Y	N
5 Cooper	Y	N	Y	N
6 Black	Y	Y	Y	N
7 Blackburn	Y	Y	Y	N
8 Fincher	Y	Y	Y	N
9 Cohen	N	N	N	Y

	371	372	373	374
TEXAS				
1 Gohmert	?	?	?	?
2 Poe	Y	Y	Y	N
3 Johnson, S.	Y	Y	Y	N
4 Hall	Y	Y	Y	N
5 Hensarling	Y	Y	Y	N
6 Barton	Y	Y	Y	N
7 Culberson	N	Y	Y	N
8 Brady	Y	Y	Y	N
9 Green, A.	N	N	N	Y
10 McCaul	Y	Y	Y	N
11 Conaway	Y	Y	Y	N
12 Granger	N	Y	N	N
13 Thornberry	Y	Y	Y	N
14 Paul	?	?	?	?
15 Hinojosa	N	N	N	Y
16 Reyes	N	N	N	Y
17 Flores	Y	Y	Y	N
18 Jackson Lee	N	N	N	Y
19 Neugebauer	Y	Y	Y	N
20 Gonzalez	N	N	N	Y
21 Smith	Y	Y	Y	N
22 Olson	Y	Y	Y	N
23 Canseco	Y	Y	Y	N
24 Marchant	Y	Y	Y	N
25 Doggett	N	N	N	Y
26 Burgess	Y	Y	Y	N
27 Farenthold	Y	Y	Y	N
28 Cuellar	N	N	N	Y
29 Green, G.	?	?	?	?
30 Johnson, E.	N	N	N	Y
31 Carter	N	Y	N	N
32 Sessions	Y	Y	Y	N
UTAH				
1 Bishop	Y	Y	Y	N
2 Matheson	Y	N	N	Y
3 Chaffetz	Y	Y	Y	N
VERMONT				
AL Welch	N	N	N	Y
VIRGINIA				
1 Wittman	Y	N	Y	N
2 Rigell	Y	Y	Y	Y
3 Scott	N	N	N	Y
4 Forbes	Y	N	Y	N
5 Hurt	Y	Y	Y	N
6 Goodlatte	Y	Y	Y	N
7 Cantor	Y	Y	Y	N
8 Moran	N	N	N	Y
9 Griffith	Y	Y	Y	N
10 Wolf	N	Y	N	N
11 Connolly	Y	N	N	Y
WASHINGTON				
1 Vacant				
2 Larsen	N	N	N	Y
3 Herrera Beutler	Y	Y	Y	N
4 Hastings	Y	Y	Y	N
5 McMorris Rodgers	Y	Y	Y	N
6 Dicks	N	N	N	Y
7 McDermott	N	N	N	Y
8 Reichert	Y	Y	Y	Y
9 Smith	N	N	N	Y
WEST VIRGINIA				
1 McKinley	Y	Y	Y	N
2 Capito	N	Y	N	N
3 Rahall	N	N	N	Y
WISCONSIN				
1 Ryan	Y	Y	Y	N
2 Baldwin	?	?	?	?
3 Kind	Y	N	Y	N
4 Moore	N	N	N	Y
5 Sensenbrenner	Y	Y	Y	N
6 Petri	Y	Y	Y	N
7 Duffy	Y	Y	Y	N
8 Ribble	Y	Y	Y	N
WYOMING				
AL Lummis	Y	Y	Y	N

IN THE HOUSE | By Vote Number

375. HR 5882. **Fiscal 2013 Legislative Branch Appropriations/ Online Advertising.** Flake, R-Ariz., amendment that would bar the use of funds in the bill for members, committees and leadership offices to purchase online advertisements on websites outside of their own official sites. Rejected in Committee of the Whole 148-261: R 94-137; D 54-124. June 8, 2012.

376. HR 5882. **Fiscal 2013 Legislative Branch Appropriations/ Recommit.** Pingree, D-Maine, motion to recommit the bill to the House Appropriations Committee and report it back immediately with an amendment that would reduce by $3.1 million the amount provided for salaries and expenses of the House of Representatives. It also would cut $3.1 million from the amount provided for members' representational allowances, including clerk hire, official expenses and official mail. Motion rejected 101-309: R 1-230; D 100-79. June 8, 2012.

377. HR 5882. **Fiscal 2013 Legislative Branch Appropriations/ Passage.** Passage of the bill that would provide $3.3 billion for legislative branch operations, excluding Senate operations, in fiscal 2013. The total would include $1.2 billion for House operations, $593 million for the Library of Congress, $520 million for the Government Accountability Office, $444 million for the Architect of the Capitol and $360 million for the Capitol Police. Passed 307-102: R 211-19; D 96-83. June 8, 2012.

378. HR 4348. **Surface Transportation Extension/Motion to Instruct.** Broun, R-Ga., motion to instruct conferees to limit funding out of the Highway Trust Fund, including the Mass Transit Account, to $37.5 billion for fiscal 2013. Motion rejected 82-323: R 82-145; D 0-178. June 8, 2012.

	375	376	377	378
ALABAMA				
1 Bonner	N	N	Y	N
2 Roby	N	N	Y	N
3 Rogers	N	N	Y	N
4 Aderholt	N	N	Y	N
5 Brooks	N	N	Y	Y
6 Bachus	Y	N	Y	N
7 Sewell	N	N	Y	N
ALASKA				
AL Young	N	N	Y	N
ARIZONA				
1 Gosar	N	?	+	N
2 Franks	Y	N	N	Y
3 Quayle	Y	N	Y	Y
4 Pastor	Y	N	Y	N
5 Schweikert	Y	N	N	Y
6 Flake	Y	N	N	Y
7 Grijalva	N	N	N	N
8 Vacant				
ARKANSAS				
1 Crawford	N	N	Y	N
2 Griffin	Y	N	Y	N
3 Womack	Y	N	Y	N
4 Ross	Y	N	Y	N
CALIFORNIA				
1 Thompson	Y	Y	Y	N
2 Herger	N	N	Y	N
3 Lungren	N	N	Y	N
4 McClintock	Y	N	Y	Y
5 Matsui	Y	Y	Y	N
6 Woolsey	N	N	N	N
7 Miller, George	Y	Y	N	N
8 Pelosi	N	Y	Y	N
9 Lee	N	N	N	N
10 Garamendi	N	Y	Y	N
11 McNerney	Y	Y	Y	N
12 Speier	Y	Y	Y	N
13 Stark	N	Y	N	N
14 Eshoo	Y	Y	Y	N
15 Honda	N	N	N	N
16 Lofgren	Y	Y	N	N
17 Farr	N	Y	N	N
18 Cardoza	?	?	?	?
19 Denham	N	N	Y	N
20 Costa	N	Y	Y	N
21 Nunes	N	N	Y	N
22 McCarthy	N	N	Y	N
23 Capps	N	Y	Y	N
24 Gallegly	Y	N	Y	N
25 McKeon	N	N	Y	N
26 Dreier	N	N	Y	N
27 Sherman	N	Y	N	N
28 Berman	N	Y	Y	N
29 Schiff	N	Y	N	N
30 Waxman	N	Y	Y	N
31 Becerra	N	N	N	N
32 Chu	N	N	N	N
33 Bass	?	Y	Y	N
34 Roybal-Allard	N	N	N	?
35 Waters	N	N	N	N
36 Hahn	N	Y	Y	N
37 Richardson	N	N	Y	N
38 Napolitano	N	N	N	N
39 Sánchez, Linda	N	N	N	N
40 Royce	Y	N	N	Y
41 Lewis	?	?	?	?
42 Miller, Gary	Y	N	Y	N
43 Baca	N	Y	Y	N
44 Calvert	N	N	Y	N
45 Bono Mack	N	N	Y	N
46 Rohrabacher	Y	N	Y	Y
47 Sanchez, Loretta	N	N	N	N
48 Campbell	Y	N	N	Y
49 Issa	N	N	Y	Y
50 Bilbray	N	N	Y	N
51 Filner	-	+	-	-
52 Hunter	N	N	Y	N
53 Davis	N	Y	Y	N

	375	376	377	378
COLORADO				
1 DeGette	Y	N	Y	N
2 Polis	Y	Y	N	N
3 Tipton	Y	N	Y	N
4 Gardner	Y	N	Y	N
5 Lamborn	Y	N	Y	Y
6 Coffman	Y	N	Y	N
7 Perlmutter	Y	Y	Y	N
CONNECTICUT				
1 Larson	N	N	Y	N
2 Courtney	N	N	Y	N
3 DeLauro	N	N	Y	N
4 Himes	N	N	Y	N
5 Murphy	N	Y	Y	N
DELAWARE				
AL Carney	Y	Y	N	N
FLORIDA				
1 Miller	Y	N	Y	Y
2 Southerland	Y	N	Y	Y
3 Brown	N	N	Y	N
4 Crenshaw	N	N	Y	N
5 Nugent	N	N	Y	N
6 Stearns	Y	N	N	N
7 Mica	Y	N	Y	N
8 Webster	N	N	Y	N
9 Bilirakis	-	-	+	-
10 Young	Y	N	Y	N
11 Castor	Y	Y	Y	N
12 Ross	Y	N	Y	Y
13 Buchanan	Y	N	Y	N
14 Mack	?	?	?	?
15 Posey	Y	N	Y	Y
16 Rooney	Y	N	Y	Y
17 Wilson	N	Y	N	N
18 Ros-Lehtinen	N	N	Y	N
19 Deutch	N	Y	Y	N
20 Wasserman Schultz	N	N	Y	N
21 Diaz-Balart	N	N	Y	N
22 West	N	N	Y	Y
23 Hastings	N	Y	Y	N
24 Adams	Y	N	Y	Y
25 Rivera	N	N	Y	N
GEORGIA				
1 Kingston	N	N	Y	N
2 Bishop	N	N	Y	N
3 Westmoreland	N	N	Y	Y
4 Johnson	N	N	Y	N
5 Lewis	N	N	Y	N
6 Price	N	N	N	Y
7 Woodall	N	N	Y	Y
8 Scott, A.	N	N	Y	Y
9 Graves	N	N	Y	Y
10 Broun	N	N	N	Y
11 Gingrey	N	N	Y	Y
12 Barrow	N	N	Y	N
13 Scott, D.	N	N	Y	N
HAWAII				
1 Hanabusa	N	Y	Y	N
2 Hirono	?	?	?	?
IDAHO				
1 Labrador	?	?	?	?
2 Simpson	N	N	Y	N
ILLINOIS				
1 Rush	N	N	N	N
2 Jackson	N	N	N	N
3 Lipinski	N	N	Y	N
4 Gutierrez	N	N	N	N
5 Quigley	Y	Y	Y	N
6 Roskam	N	N	Y	N
7 Davis	N	N	N	N
8 Walsh	Y	N	Y	Y
9 Schakowsky	N	N	N	N
10 Dold	N	N	Y	N
11 Kinzinger	N	N	Y	N
12 Costello	N	Y	N	N
13 Biggert	N	N	Y	N
14 Hultgren	N	N	Y	N
15 Johnson	Y	N	N	N

KEY   **Republicans**   Democrats

Y Voted for (yea)	X Paired against
# Paired for	- Announced against
+ Announced for	P Voted "present"
N Voted against (nay)	

C Voted "present" to avoid possible conflict of interest

? Did not vote or otherwise make a position known

	375	376	377	378
16 Manzullo	N	N	Y	Y
17 Schilling	Y	N	N	N
18 Schock	N	N	Y	N
19 Shimkus	N	N	Y	N
INDIANA				
1 Visclosky	N	N	Y	N
2 Donnelly	Y	Y	Y	N
3 Stutzman	Y	N	Y	Y
4 Rokita	N	N	Y	Y
5 Burton	Y	N	Y	Y
6 Pence	Y	N	Y	Y
7 Carson	N	N	N	N
8 Bucshon	N	N	Y	N
9 Young	N	N	Y	N
IOWA				
1 Braley	Y	N	Y	N
2 Loebsack	Y	Y	N	N
3 Boswell	Y	Y	Y	N
4 Latham	Y	N	Y	N
5 King	Y	N	Y	Y
KANSAS				
1 Huelskamp	N	N	Y	Y
2 Jenkins	Y	N	Y	Y
3 Yoder	N	N	Y	Y
4 Pompeo	N	N	Y	Y
KENTUCKY				
1 Whitfield	N	N	Y	?
2 Guthrie	Y	N	Y	N
3 Yarmuth	N	Y	N	N
4 Davis	N	N	Y	N
5 Rogers	N	N	Y	N
6 Chandler	Y	Y	N	N
LOUISIANA				
1 Scalise	Y	N	Y	Y
2 Richmond	N	N	N	N
3 Landry	N	N	Y	N
4 Fleming	N	N	Y	Y
5 Alexander	N	N	Y	N
6 Cassidy	N	N	Y	N
7 Boustany	N	N	Y	N
MAINE				
1 Pingree	N	Y	N	N
2 Michaud	Y	Y	Y	N
MARYLAND				
1 Harris	Y	N	Y	N
2 Ruppersberger	Y	N	Y	N
3 Sarbanes	N	N	Y	N
4 Edwards	N	N	N	N
5 Hoyer	N	N	Y	N
6 Bartlett	Y	N	Y	N
7 Cummings	N	N	N	N
8 Van Hollen	Y	Y	Y	N
MASSACHUSETTS				
1 Olver	N	N	N	N
2 Neal	?	?	?	?
3 McGovern	Y	Y	N	N
4 Frank	Y	N	N	N
5 Tsongas	N	Y	N	N
6 Tierney	N	Y	N	N
7 Markey	Y	Y	N	N
8 Capuano	N	N	N	N
9 Lynch	N	Y	N	N
10 Keating	N	Y	N	N
MICHIGAN				
1 Benishek	Y	N	Y	N
2 Huizenga	N	N	Y	Y
3 Amash	N	N	N	Y
4 Camp	N	N	Y	N
5 Kildee	Y	Y	Y	N
6 Upton	N	N	Y	N
7 Walberg	N	N	Y	N
8 Rogers	N	N	Y	N
9 Peters	Y	Y	N	N
10 Miller	N	N	Y	N
11 McCotter	N	N	Y	N
12 Levin	N	N	Y	N
13 Clarke	N	Y	N	N
14 Conyers	N	N	N	N
15 Dingell	Y	N	Y	N
MINNESOTA				
1 Walz	Y	Y	Y	N
2 Kline	Y	N	Y	N
3 Paulsen	N	N	Y	N
4 McCollum	Y	Y	Y	N

	375	376	377	378
5 Ellison	N	N	N	N
6 Bachmann	N	N	Y	Y
7 Peterson	Y	Y	Y	N
8 Cravaack	Y	N	Y	N
MISSISSIPPI				
1 Nunnelee	N	N	Y	N
2 Thompson	N	N	N	N
3 Harper	N	N	Y	N
4 Palazzo	Y	N	Y	N
MISSOURI				
1 Clay	N	N	N	N
2 Akin	+	-	+	+
3 Carnahan	N	N	N	N
4 Hartzler	Y	N	Y	N
5 Cleaver	N	N	N	N
6 Graves	Y	N	+	Y
7 Long	Y	N	Y	N
8 Emerson	Y	N	Y	N
9 Luetkemeyer	Y	N	Y	N
MONTANA				
AL Rehberg	Y	N	Y	N
NEBRASKA				
1 Fortenberry	N	N	Y	N
2 Terry	Y	N	Y	N
3 Smith	N	N	Y	N
NEVADA				
1 Berkley	Y	Y	Y	N
2 Amodei	N	N	Y	N
3 Heck	N	N	N	Y
NEW HAMPSHIRE				
1 Guinta	Y	N	Y	N
2 Bass	Y	N	Y	N
NEW JERSEY				
1 Andrews	N	Y	Y	N
2 LoBiondo	Y	N	Y	N
3 Runyan	N	N	Y	N
4 Smith	Y	N	Y	N
5 Garrett	Y	N	Y	Y
6 Pallone	N	Y	N	N
7 Lance	N	N	Y	N
8 Pascrell	Y	N	Y	N
9 Rothman	N	N	Y	N
10 Vacant				
11 Frelinghuysen	N	N	Y	N
12 Holt	N	N	N	N
13 Sires	N	N	Y	N
NEW MEXICO				
1 Heinrich	N	N	Y	N
2 Pearce	N	N	Y	N
3 Luján	N	N	Y	N
NEW YORK				
1 Bishop	Y	Y	N	N
2 Israel	Y	Y	N	N
3 King	N	N	Y	N
4 McCarthy	Y	Y	Y	N
5 Ackerman	Y	Y	Y	N
6 Meeks	N	N	Y	N
7 Crowley	N	N	Y	N
8 Nadler	N	Y	N	N
9 Turner	Y	N	Y	N
10 Towns	?	?	?	?
11 Clarke	N	N	N	N
12 Velázquez	N	Y	N	N
13 Grimm	N	N	Y	N
14 Maloney	N	Y	N	N
15 Rangel	N	Y	N	N
16 Serrano	N	N	Y	N
17 Engel	N	Y	N	N
18 Lowey	N	Y	N	N
19 Hayworth	N	N	Y	N
20 Gibson	Y	N	Y	N
21 Tonko	N	Y	N	N
22 Hinchey	N	N	N	N
23 Owens	Y	Y	N	N
24 Hanna	N	N	Y	N
25 Buerkle	N	N	Y	Y
26 Hochul	Y	Y	Y	N
27 Higgins	Y	Y	Y	N
28 Slaughter	-	+	+	-
29 Reed	N	N	Y	N
NORTH CAROLINA				
1 Butterfield	N	N	N	N
2 Ellmers	N	N	Y	N
3 Jones	Y	Y	N	Y
4 Price	N	N	N	N

	375	376	377	378
5 Foxx	N	N	Y	Y
6 Coble	?	?	?	?
7 McIntyre	Y	Y	N	N
8 Kissell	Y	Y	Y	N
9 Myrick	Y	N	Y	Y
10 McHenry	N	N	Y	Y
11 Shuler	?	?	?	?
12 Watt	N	N	N	N
13 Miller	N	Y	N	N
NORTH DAKOTA				
AL Berg	N	N	Y	N
OHIO				
1 Chabot	Y	N	Y	Y
2 Schmidt	Y	N	Y	N
3 Turner	N	N	Y	N
4 Jordan	Y	N	Y	Y
5 Latta	N	N	Y	Y
6 Johnson	Y	N	Y	N
7 Austria	Y	N	Y	N
8 Boehner				
9 Kaptur	Y	Y	Y	N
10 Kucinich	?	?	?	?
11 Fudge	N	N	N	N
12 Tiberi	Y	N	Y	?
13 Sutton	Y	Y	N	N
14 LaTourette	N	N	Y	N
15 Stivers	N	N	Y	N
16 Renacci	N	N	Y	N
17 Ryan	N	N	N	N
18 Gibbs	Y	N	Y	N
OKLAHOMA				
1 Sullivan	Y	N	Y	Y
2 Boren	N	N	Y	N
3 Lucas	N	N	Y	N
4 Cole	N	N	Y	N
5 Lankford	N	N	Y	N
OREGON				
1 Bonamici	N	Y	Y	N
2 Walden	N	N	Y	N
3 Blumenauer	N	Y	N	N
4 DeFazio	Y	Y	Y	N
5 Schrader	Y	Y	Y	N
PENNSYLVANIA				
1 Brady	N	Y	Y	N
2 Fattah	N	Y	Y	N
3 Kelly	N	N	Y	N
4 Altmire	Y	Y	Y	N
5 Thompson	Y	N	Y	N
6 Gerlach	N	N	Y	N
7 Meehan	?	?	?	?
8 Fitzpatrick	N	N	Y	?
9 Shuster	N	N	Y	N
10 Marino	N	N	Y	N
11 Barletta	N	N	Y	N
12 Critz	N	Y	Y	N
13 Schwartz	N	Y	N	N
14 Doyle	N	N	N	N
15 Dent	Y	N	Y	N
16 Pitts	N	N	Y	N
17 Holden	N	Y	N	N
18 Murphy	N	N	Y	N
19 Platts	?	N	Y	N
RHODE ISLAND				
1 Cicilline	?	?	?	?
2 Langevin	N	Y	N	N
SOUTH CAROLINA				
1 Scott	N	N	Y	Y
2 Wilson	Y	N	Y	Y
3 Duncan	N	N	Y	Y
4 Gowdy	Y	N	Y	Y
5 Mulvaney	Y	N	Y	N
6 Clyburn	N	Y	N	N
SOUTH DAKOTA				
AL Noem	Y	N	Y	N
TENNESSEE				
1 Roe	Y	N	Y	N
2 Duncan	Y	N	N	N
3 Fleischmann	N	N	Y	N
4 DesJarlais	N	N	Y	N
5 Cooper	Y	Y	N	N
6 Black	N	N	Y	Y
7 Blackburn	Y	N	Y	Y
8 Fincher	N	N	Y	Y
9 Cohen	N	Y	N	N

	375	376	377	378
TEXAS				
1 Gohmert	?	?	?	?
2 Poe	N	N	Y	Y
3 Johnson, S.	N	N	Y	?
4 Hall	Y	N	Y	N
5 Hensarling	N	N	Y	Y
6 Barton	N	N	Y	N
7 Culberson	N	N	Y	Y
8 Brady	Y	N	Y	N
9 Green, A.	N	Y	Y	N
10 McCaul	Y	N	Y	Y
11 Conaway	N	N	Y	Y
12 Granger	N	N	Y	Y
13 Thornberry	N	N	Y	Y
14 Paul	?	?	?	?
15 Hinojosa	N	Y	N	N
16 Reyes	N	N	N	N
17 Flores	N	N	Y	N
18 Jackson Lee	N	N	N	N
19 Neugebauer	N	N	Y	Y
20 Gonzalez	N	Y	N	N
21 Smith	Y	N	Y	N
22 Olson	N	N	Y	Y
23 Canseco	N	N	Y	N
24 Marchant	Y	N	Y	N
25 Doggett	Y	Y	N	N
26 Burgess	Y	N	N	Y
27 Farenthold	N	N	Y	N
28 Cuellar	N	Y	N	N
29 Green, G.	?	?	?	?
30 Johnson, E.	N	Y	N	N
31 Carter	N	N	Y	Y
32 Sessions	Y	N	Y	N
UTAH				
1 Bishop	Y	N	Y	?
2 Matheson	N	Y	N	N
3 Chaffetz	Y	N	Y	Y
VERMONT				
AL Welch	N	N	N	N
VIRGINIA				
1 Wittman	N	N	N	N
2 Rigell	N	N	Y	N
3 Scott	Y	N	Y	N
4 Forbes	N	N	Y	N
5 Hurt	N	N	Y	Y
6 Goodlatte	N	N	Y	N
7 Cantor	N	N	Y	N
8 Moran	N	N	Y	N
9 Griffith	Y	N	Y	N
10 Wolf	N	N	Y	N
11 Connolly	N	N	Y	N
WASHINGTON				
1 Vacant				
2 Larsen	N	N	Y	N
3 Herrera Beutler	N	N	Y	N
4 Hastings	N	N	Y	Y
5 McMorris Rodgers	N	N	Y	N
6 Dicks	N	N	Y	N
7 McDermott	Y	N	N	N
8 Reichert	Y	N	N	N
9 Smith	Y	Y	Y	N
WEST VIRGINIA				
1 McKinley	N	N	Y	N
2 Capito	N	N	Y	N
3 Rahall	N	Y	Y	N
WISCONSIN				
1 Ryan	Y	N	Y	Y
2 Baldwin	?	?	?	?
3 Kind	Y	Y	N	N
4 Moore	N	N	Y	N
5 Sensenbrenner	N	N	Y	N
6 Petri	Y	N	Y	N
7 Duffy	N	N	Y	N
8 Ribble	Y	N	Y	N
WYOMING				
AL Lummis	Y	N	N	N

IN THE HOUSE | By Vote Number

379. **S 684. Utah Land Conveyance/Passage.** Hastings, R-Wash., motion to suspend the rules and pass the bill that would convey to the town of Alta, Utah, a maximum area of two acres from the Wasatch-Cache National Forest in Salt Lake County for public purposes. If the land is used for something other than a public purpose, it would revert back to the National Forest System. Motion agreed to 383-3: R 216-3; D 167-0. A two-thirds vote of those present and voting (258 in this case) is required for passage under suspension of the rules. June 18, 2012.

380. **S 404. Michigan Land Grant/Passage.** Hastings, R-Wash., motion to suspend the rules and pass the bill that would amend the land patent issued to the Great Lakes Shipwreck Historical Society regarding Whitefish Point in Chippewa County, Mich., to effectuate the Human Use/Natural Resource Plan for Whitefish Point. Motion agreed to 380-0: R 217-0; D 163-0. A two-thirds vote of those present and voting (254 in this case) is required for passage under suspension of the rules. June 18, 2012.

381. **HR 2578. Federal Lands and Water Projects/Previous Question.** Bishop, R-Utah, motion to order the previous question (thus ending debate and the possibility of amendment) on the rule (H Res 688) that would provide for House floor consideration of a package of federal lands and water project measures. Motion agreed to 238-178: R 233-1; D 5-177. June 19, 2012.

382. **HR 2578. Federal Lands and Water Projects/Rule.** Adoption of the rule (H Res 688) that would provide for House floor consideration of a package of federal lands and water project measures. Adopted 240-175: R 235-1; D 5-174. June 19, 2012.

383. **HR 2578. Federal Lands and Water Projects/Lumber Exports.** DeFazio, D-Ore., amendment that would apply export restrictions regarding the removal of unprocessed lumber from national forests to lumber removed from the Tongass National Forest. Rejected in Committee of the Whole 184-236: R 8-226; D 176-10. June 19, 2012.

384. **HR 2578. Federal Lands and Water Projects/Federal Grazing Fees.** Markey, D-Mass., amendment that would authorize a pilot program to collect a fee to offset the cost for federal grazing permits. It would set the fee at $1 per animal unit month to be imposed from fiscal 2013 through fiscal 2016. Rejected in Committee of the Whole 156-268: R 1-236; D 155-32. June 19, 2012.

385. **HR 2578. Federal Lands and Water Projects/Border Security Environmental Waivers.** Grijalva, D-Ariz., amendment that would strike language from the bill exempting Homeland Security Department border security activities from a wide variety of environmental and land use laws. Rejected in Committee of the Whole 177-247: R 4-233; D 173-14. June 19, 2012.

*Rep. Ron Barber, D-Ariz., was sworn in June 19, 2012, to fill the vacancy created by the Jan. 25 resignation of fellow Democrat Gabrielle Giffords. The first vote for which Barber was eligible was vote 382.

	379	380	381	382	383	384	385
ALABAMA							
1 Bonner	Y	Y	Y	Y	N	N	N
2 Roby	Y	Y	Y	Y	N	N	N
3 Rogers	Y	Y	Y	Y	N	N	N
4 Aderholt	Y	Y	Y	Y	N	N	N
5 Brooks	N	Y	Y	N	Y	N	N
6 Bachus	Y	Y	?	Y	N	N	N
7 Sewell	Y	Y	N	N	Y	Y	Y
ALASKA							
AL Young	Y	Y	Y	Y	N	N	N
ARIZONA							
1 Gosar	Y	Y	Y	Y	N	N	N
2 Franks	Y	Y	Y	Y	N	N	N
3 Quayle	Y	Y	Y	Y	N	N	N
4 Pastor	Y	Y	N	N	Y	Y	Y
5 Schweikert	Y	Y	Y	Y	N	N	N
6 Flake	Y	Y	Y	Y	N	N	N
7 Grijalva	Y	Y	N	N	Y	Y	Y
8 Barber*			N	Y	N	Y	Y
ARKANSAS							
1 Crawford	Y	Y	Y	Y	N	N	N
2 Griffin	+	+	+	+	N	N	N
3 Womack	Y	Y	Y	Y	N	N	N
4 Ross	?	?	N	Y	N	N	N
CALIFORNIA							
1 Thompson	Y	N	N	N	Y	Y	Y
2 Herger	Y	Y	Y	Y	N	N	N
3 Lungren	Y	Y	Y	Y	N	N	N
4 McClintock	Y	Y	Y	Y	N	N	N
5 Matsui	Y	N	N	N	Y	Y	Y
6 Woolsey	Y	N	N	N	Y	Y	Y
7 Miller, George	Y	N	N	N	Y	Y	Y
8 Pelosi	?	?	N	N	Y	Y	Y
9 Lee	Y	?	N	N	Y	Y	Y
10 Garamendi	Y	N	N	N	Y	Y	Y
11 McNerney	Y	Y	N	N	Y	N	Y
12 Speier	?	?	N	N	Y	Y	Y
13 Stark	Y	N	N	N	Y	Y	Y
14 Eshoo	Y	N	N	N	Y	Y	Y
15 Honda	Y	N	N	N	N	Y	Y
16 Lofgren	Y	N	N	N	Y	Y	Y
17 Farr	Y	N	N	N	Y	Y	Y
18 Cardoza	Y	Y	?	?	N	Y	Y
19 Denham	Y	Y	Y	Y	N	N	N
20 Costa	Y	Y	N	N	Y	N	Y
21 Nunes	Y	Y	Y	Y	N	N	N
22 McCarthy	Y	Y	Y	Y	N	N	N
23 Capps	Y	Y	N	N	Y	Y	Y
24 Gallegly	Y	Y	Y	Y	N	N	N
25 McKeon	Y	Y	Y	Y	N	N	N
26 Dreier	Y	Y	Y	Y	N	N	N
27 Sherman	Y	N	N	N	Y	Y	Y
28 Berman	Y	N	N	N	Y	Y	Y
29 Schiff	Y	N	N	N	Y	Y	Y
30 Waxman	Y	N	N	N	Y	Y	Y
31 Becerra	Y	N	N	N	Y	Y	Y
32 Chu	Y	N	N	N	Y	Y	Y
33 Bass	Y	N	N	N	Y	Y	Y
34 Roybal-Allard	Y	N	N	N	Y	Y	Y
35 Waters	Y	N	N	N	Y	Y	Y
36 Hahn	Y	N	N	N	Y	Y	Y
37 Richardson	Y	N	N	N	Y	Y	Y
38 Napolitano	Y	N	N	N	Y	Y	Y
39 Sánchez, Linda	?	?	?	?	?	?	?
40 Royce	Y	Y	Y	Y	N	N	N
41 Lewis	?	?	?	?	?	?	?
42 Miller, Gary	Y	Y	Y	Y	N	N	N
43 Baca	Y	N	N	N	N	N	Y
44 Calvert	Y	Y	Y	Y	N	N	N
45 Bono Mack	Y	Y	Y	Y	N	N	N
46 Rohrabacher	?	?	Y	Y	N	N	N
47 Sanchez, Loretta	Y	Y	N	?	Y	Y	Y
48 Campbell	?	?	Y	Y	N	N	N
49 Issa	Y	Y	Y	Y	N	N	N
50 Bilbray	Y	Y	Y	Y	N	N	N
51 Filner	Y	Y	N	N	Y	Y	Y
52 Hunter	Y	Y	Y	Y	N	N	N
53 Davis	Y	N	N	N	Y	Y	Y

	379	380	381	382	383	384	385
COLORADO							
1 DeGette	Y	Y	N	N	Y	Y	Y
2 Polis	Y	Y	N	N	Y	Y	Y
3 Tipton	Y	Y	Y	Y	N	N	N
4 Gardner	Y	Y	Y	Y	N	N	N
5 Lamborn	Y	Y	Y	Y	N	N	N
6 Coffman	Y	Y	Y	Y	N	N	N
7 Perlmutter	Y	Y	N	N	Y	Y	Y
CONNECTICUT							
1 Larson	Y	Y	N	N	Y	Y	Y
2 Courtney	Y	Y	N	N	Y	Y	Y
3 DeLauro	Y	Y	N	N	Y	Y	Y
4 Himes	Y	Y	N	N	Y	Y	Y
5 Murphy	?	?	N	N	Y	Y	Y
DELAWARE							
AL Carney	Y	Y	N	N	Y	Y	Y
FLORIDA							
1 Miller	?	?	?	?	?	?	?
2 Southerland	Y	Y	Y	Y	N	N	N
3 Brown	Y	Y	N	N	Y	Y	Y
4 Crenshaw	Y	Y	Y	Y	N	N	N
5 Nugent	Y	Y	?	Y	N	N	N
6 Stearns	Y	Y	Y	Y	N	N	N
7 Mica	Y	Y	Y	Y	N	N	N
8 Webster	Y	Y	Y	Y	N	N	N
9 Bilirakis	Y	Y	Y	Y	N	N	N
10 Young	?	?	?	?	?	?	?
11 Castor	Y	Y	N	N	Y	Y	Y
12 Ross	Y	Y	Y	Y	N	N	N
13 Buchanan	Y	Y	Y	Y	N	N	N
14 Mack	Y	Y	Y	Y	N	N	N
15 Posey	Y	Y	Y	Y	N	N	N
16 Rooney	Y	Y	Y	Y	N	N	N
17 Wilson	Y	Y	N	N	Y	Y	Y
18 Ros-Lehtinen	Y	Y	N	N	Y	Y	Y
19 Deutch	Y	Y	N	N	Y	Y	Y
20 Wasserman Schultz	?	?	N	N	Y	Y	Y
21 Diaz-Balart	Y	Y	N	N	Y	Y	Y
22 West	Y	Y	Y	Y	N	N	N
23 Hastings	Y	Y	N	N	Y	Y	Y
24 Adams	Y	Y	Y	Y	N	N	N
25 Rivera	Y	Y	Y	Y	N	N	N
GEORGIA							
1 Kingston	Y	Y	Y	Y	N	N	N
2 Bishop	Y	Y	N	N	Y	N	N
3 Westmoreland	Y	Y	Y	Y	N	N	N
4 Johnson	Y	Y	N	N	Y	Y	Y
5 Lewis	Y	Y	?	N	Y	Y	Y
6 Price	Y	Y	Y	Y	N	N	N
7 Woodall	N	Y	Y	Y	N	N	N
8 Scott, A.	Y	Y	Y	Y	N	N	N
9 Graves	Y	Y	Y	Y	N	N	N
10 Broun	Y	Y	Y	Y	N	N	N
11 Gingrey	?	?	Y	Y	N	N	N
12 Barrow	Y	Y	N	N	Y	N	N
13 Scott, D.	Y	Y	N	N	Y	Y	Y
HAWAII							
1 Hanabusa	Y	Y	N	N	N	Y	Y
2 Hirono	Y	Y	N	N	N	Y	Y
IDAHO							
1 Labrador	Y	Y	Y	Y	N	N	N
2 Simpson	Y	Y	Y	Y	N	N	N
ILLINOIS							
1 Rush	?	?	N	N	Y	Y	Y
2 Jackson	?	?	?	?	?	?	?
3 Lipinski	Y	Y	N	N	Y	Y	Y
4 Gutierrez	+	+	N	N	Y	Y	Y
5 Quigley	Y	Y	N	N	Y	Y	Y
6 Roskam	Y	Y	Y	Y	N	N	N
7 Davis	Y	Y	N	N	Y	Y	Y
8 Walsh	Y	Y	Y	Y	N	N	N
9 Schakowsky	Y	Y	N	N	Y	Y	Y
10 Dold	Y	Y	Y	Y	N	N	N
11 Kinzinger	Y	Y	Y	Y	N	N	N
12 Costello	Y	Y	N	N	Y	N	Y
13 Biggert	Y	Y	Y	Y	N	N	N
14 Hultgren	Y	Y	Y	Y	N	N	N
15 Johnson	+	+	Y	Y	Y	N	N

KEY **Republicans**   Democrats

Y Voted for (yea)	**X** Paired against	**C** Voted "present" to avoid possible conflict of interest
# Paired for	**–** Announced against	
+ Announced for	**P** Voted "present"	**?** Did not vote or otherwise make a position known
N Voted against (nay)		

	379	380	381	382	383	384	385
16 **Manzullo**	Y	Y	Y	Y	N	N	N
17 **Schilling**	?	?	Y	Y	N	N	N
18 **Schock**	Y	Y	Y	Y	N	N	N
19 **Shimkus**	Y	Y	Y	Y	N	N	N
INDIANA							
1 Visclosky	Y	Y	N	N	Y	Y	Y
2 Donnelly	?	?	N	Y	N	N	N
3 **Stutzman**	Y	Y	Y	Y	N	N	N
4 **Rokita**	?	?	Y	Y	N	N	N
5 **Burton**	Y	Y	Y	Y	N	N	N
6 **Pence**	Y	Y	Y	Y	N	N	N
7 Carson	Y	Y	?	N	Y	Y	Y
8 **Bucshon**	Y	Y	Y	Y	N	N	N
9 **Young**	Y	Y	Y	Y	N	N	N
IOWA							
1 Braley	Y	Y	N	N	Y	N	Y
2 Loebsack	Y	Y	N	N	Y	Y	Y
3 Boswell	Y	Y	N	N	Y	N	N
4 **Latham**	Y	Y	Y	Y	N	N	N
5 **King**	Y	Y	Y	N	N	N	N
KANSAS							
1 **Huelskamp**	Y	Y	Y	Y	N	N	N
2 **Jenkins**	Y	Y	Y	Y	N	N	N
3 **Yoder**	Y	Y	Y	Y	N	N	N
4 **Pompeo**	Y	Y	Y	Y	N	N	N
KENTUCKY							
1 **Whitfield**	Y	Y	Y	Y	N	N	N
2 **Guthrie**	Y	Y	Y	Y	N	N	N
3 Yarmuth	Y	Y	N	N	Y	Y	Y
4 **Davis**	+	+	Y	Y	?	N	N
5 **Rogers**	Y	Y	Y	Y	N	N	N
6 Chandler	Y	?	N	N	Y	N	N
LOUISIANA							
1 **Scalise**	Y	Y	Y	Y	N	N	N
2 Richmond	Y	Y	N	N	Y	Y	Y
3 **Landry**	Y	Y	Y	Y	N	N	N
4 **Fleming**	Y	Y	Y	Y	N	N	N
5 **Alexander**	Y	Y	Y	Y	N	N	N
6 **Cassidy**	Y	Y	Y	Y	N	N	N
7 **Boustany**	Y	Y	Y	Y	N	N	N
MAINE							
1 Pingree	Y	Y	N	?	Y	Y	Y
2 Michaud	Y	Y	N	N	Y	Y	Y
MARYLAND							
1 **Harris**	Y	Y	Y	Y	N	N	N
2 Ruppersberger	Y	Y	N	N	Y	Y	Y
3 Sarbanes	Y	Y	N	N	Y	Y	Y
4 Edwards	Y	Y	N	N	Y	Y	Y
5 Hoyer	Y	Y	N	N	Y	Y	Y
6 **Bartlett**	Y	Y	Y	Y	Y	N	N
7 Cummings	Y	Y	N	N	Y	Y	Y
8 Van Hollen	Y	Y	N	N	Y	Y	Y
MASSACHUSETTS							
1 Olver	Y	Y	N	N	Y	Y	Y
2 Neal	Y	Y	N	N	Y	Y	Y
3 McGovern	Y	Y	N	N	Y	Y	Y
4 Frank	Y	Y	N	?	Y	Y	Y
5 Tsongas	Y	Y	N	N	Y	Y	Y
6 Tierney	?	?	N	N	Y	Y	Y
7 Markey	Y	Y	N	N	Y	Y	Y
8 Capuano	Y	Y	N	N	Y	Y	Y
9 Lynch	Y	Y	N	N	Y	Y	Y
10 Keating	Y	Y	N	N	Y	Y	Y
MICHIGAN							
1 **Benishek**	Y	Y	Y	Y	N	N	N
2 **Huizenga**	Y	Y	?	?	?	?	?
3 **Amash**	Y	Y	Y	Y	N	N	N
4 **Camp**	Y	Y	Y	Y	N	N	N
5 Kildee	Y	Y	N	N	Y	Y	Y
6 **Upton**	Y	Y	Y	Y	N	N	N
7 **Walberg**	Y	Y	Y	Y	N	N	N
8 **Rogers**	Y	Y	Y	Y	N	N	N
9 Peters	Y	Y	N	N	Y	Y	Y
10 **Miller**	Y	Y	Y	Y	N	N	N
11 **McCotter**	Y	Y	Y	Y	N	N	N
12 Levin	Y	Y	N	N	Y	Y	Y
13 Clarke	Y	Y	N	N	Y	Y	Y
14 Conyers	Y	Y	N	N	Y	Y	Y
15 Dingell	Y	Y	N	N	?	?	?
MINNESOTA							
1 Walz	Y	Y	N	N	Y	N	Y
2 **Kline**	Y	Y	Y	Y	N	N	N
3 **Paulsen**	Y	Y	Y	Y	N	N	N
4 McCollum	Y	Y	N	N	Y	Y	Y

	379	380	381	382	383	384	385
5 Ellison	Y	Y	N	N	Y	Y	Y
6 **Bachmann**	Y	Y	Y	Y	N	N	N
7 Peterson	Y	Y	N	N	N	N	N
8 **Cravaack**	Y	Y	Y	Y	N	N	N
MISSISSIPPI							
1 **Nunnelee**	Y	Y	Y	Y	N	N	N
2 Thompson	?	?	N	N	Y	Y	Y
3 **Harper**	+	Y	Y	Y	N	N	N
4 **Palazzo**	Y	Y	Y	Y	N	N	N
MISSOURI							
1 Clay	Y	Y	N	N	Y	Y	Y
2 **Akin**	Y	Y	Y	Y	N	N	N
3 Carnahan	Y	Y	N	N	Y	Y	Y
4 **Hartzler**	+	+	Y	Y	N	N	N
5 Cleaver	Y	Y	N	N	Y	Y	Y
6 **Graves**	Y	Y	Y	Y	N	N	N
7 **Long**	Y	Y	Y	Y	N	N	N
8 **Emerson**	Y	Y	Y	Y	N	N	N
9 **Luetkemeyer**	Y	Y	Y	Y	N	N	N
MONTANA							
AL **Rehberg**	Y	Y	Y	Y	N	N	N
NEBRASKA							
1 **Fortenberry**	Y	?	Y	Y	N	N	N
2 **Terry**	Y	Y	Y	Y	N	N	N
3 **Smith**	Y	Y	Y	Y	N	N	N
NEVADA							
1 Berkley	?	?	N	N	Y	N	Y
2 **Amodei**	Y	Y	Y	Y	N	N	N
3 **Heck**	Y	Y	Y	Y	N	N	N
NEW HAMPSHIRE							
1 **Guinta**	Y	Y	Y	Y	N	N	N
2 **Bass**	Y	Y	Y	Y	N	Y	Y
NEW JERSEY							
1 Andrews	Y	Y	N	?	Y	Y	Y
2 **LoBiondo**	Y	Y	Y	Y	Y	N	N
3 **Runyan**	Y	Y	Y	Y	N	N	N
4 **Smith**	Y	Y	Y	Y	Y	N	N
5 **Garrett**	Y	Y	Y	Y	N	N	N
6 Pallone	Y	Y	N	N	Y	Y	Y
7 **Lance**	Y	Y	Y	Y	N	N	N
8 Pascrell	Y	Y	N	N	Y	Y	Y
9 Rothman	Y	Y	N	N	Y	Y	Y
10 Vacant							
11 **Frelinghuysen**	Y	Y	Y	Y	N	N	N
12 Holt	Y	Y	N	N	Y	Y	Y
13 Sires	Y	Y	N	N	Y	Y	Y
NEW MEXICO							
1 Heinrich	Y	Y	N	N	Y	Y	Y
2 **Pearce**	Y	Y	Y	Y	N	N	N
3 Luján	Y	Y	N	N	Y	Y	Y
NEW YORK							
1 Bishop	Y	Y	N	N	Y	Y	Y
2 Israel	?	?	N	N	Y	Y	Y
3 **King**	Y	Y	Y	Y	N	N	N
4 McCarthy	+	+	N	N	Y	Y	Y
5 Ackerman	?	?	N	N	Y	Y	Y
6 Meeks	Y	Y	N	N	Y	Y	Y
7 Crowley	Y	Y	?	?	Y	Y	Y
8 Nadler	Y	Y	N	N	Y	Y	Y
9 **Turner**	Y	Y	Y	Y	N	N	N
10 Towns	?	?	?	?	Y	Y	Y
11 Clarke	Y	Y	N	N	Y	Y	Y
12 Velázquez	Y	Y	N	?	Y	Y	Y
13 **Grimm**	Y	Y	Y	Y	N	N	N
14 Maloney	Y	Y	N	N	Y	Y	Y
15 Rangel	Y	Y	N	N	Y	Y	Y
16 Serrano	Y	Y	N	N	Y	Y	Y
17 Engel	Y	Y	N	N	Y	Y	Y
18 Lowey	?	?	N	N	Y	Y	Y
19 **Hayworth**	Y	Y	Y	Y	?	N	N
20 **Gibson**	Y	Y	Y	Y	N	N	N
21 Tonko	Y	Y	N	N	Y	Y	Y
22 Hinchey	Y	Y	N	N	Y	Y	Y
23 Owens	?	?	N	N	Y	N	Y
24 **Hanna**	Y	Y	Y	Y	N	N	N
25 **Buerkle**	?	?	Y	Y	N	N	N
26 Hochul	Y	Y	N	N	Y	N	N
27 Higgins	Y	Y	N	N	Y	Y	Y
28 Slaughter	Y	Y	N	N	Y	Y	Y
29 **Reed**	Y	Y	Y	Y	N	N	N
NORTH CAROLINA							
1 Butterfield	?	?	N	N	Y	Y	Y
2 **Ellmers**	Y	Y	Y	Y	N	N	N
3 **Jones**	Y	Y	N	Y	Y	N	N
4 Price	Y	Y	N	N	Y	Y	Y

	379	380	381	382	383	384	385
5 **Foxx**	Y	Y	Y	Y	N	N	N
6 **Coble**	?	?	Y	Y	N	N	N
7 McIntyre	Y	Y	N	N	Y	N	N
8 Kissell	Y	Y	N	Y	N	N	N
9 **Myrick**	Y	Y	Y	Y	N	N	N
10 **McHenry**	Y	Y	Y	Y	N	N	N
11 Shuler	Y	Y	Y	Y	Y	N	Y
12 Watt	Y	Y	N	N	Y	Y	Y
13 Miller	Y	Y	N	N	Y	Y	Y
NORTH DAKOTA							
AL **Berg**	Y	Y	Y	Y	N	N	N
OHIO							
1 **Chabot**	Y	Y	Y	Y	N	N	N
2 **Schmidt**	Y	Y	Y	Y	N	N	N
3 **Turner**	Y	+	Y	Y	N	N	N
4 **Jordan**	Y	Y	Y	Y	N	N	N
5 **Latta**	Y	Y	Y	Y	N	N	N
6 **Johnson**	Y	Y	Y	Y	N	N	N
7 **Austria**	?	?	Y	Y	N	N	N
8 **Boehner**							
9 Kaptur	Y	Y	N	?	Y	N	Y
10 Kucinich	Y	Y	N	N	Y	Y	Y
11 Fudge	?	?	N	N	Y	Y	Y
12 **Tiberi**	?	?	Y	Y	N	N	N
13 Sutton	Y	Y	N	N	Y	Y	Y
14 **LaTourette**	Y	Y	Y	Y	N	N	N
15 **Stivers**	Y	Y	Y	Y	N	N	N
16 **Renacci**	Y	Y	Y	Y	N	N	N
17 Ryan	Y	Y	N	N	?	Y	Y
18 **Gibbs**	Y	Y	Y	Y	N	N	N
OKLAHOMA							
1 **Sullivan**	Y	Y	Y	Y	N	N	N
2 Boren	Y	Y	Y	N	N	N	N
3 **Lucas**	Y	?	Y	Y	N	N	N
4 **Cole**	Y	Y	Y	Y	N	N	N
5 **Lankford**	Y	Y	Y	Y	N	N	N
OREGON							
1 Bonamici	Y	Y	N	N	Y	Y	Y
2 **Walden**	Y	Y	Y	Y	N	N	N
3 Blumenauer	?	?	N	N	Y	Y	Y
4 DeFazio	Y	Y	N	N	Y	N	Y
5 Schrader	Y	Y	Y	N	Y	N	Y
PENNSYLVANIA							
1 Brady	Y	Y	N	N	Y	Y	Y
2 Fattah	Y	Y	N	N	Y	Y	Y
3 **Kelly**	Y	Y	Y	Y	N	N	N
4 Altmire	Y	Y	Y	N	?	?	?
5 **Thompson**	Y	Y	Y	Y	N	N	N
6 **Gerlach**	Y	Y	Y	Y	N	N	N
7 **Meehan**	Y	Y	Y	Y	N	N	N
8 **Fitzpatrick**	Y	Y	Y	Y	Y	N	Y
9 **Shuster**	Y	Y	Y	Y	N	N	N
10 **Marino**	Y	Y	Y	Y	N	N	N
11 **Barletta**	Y	Y	Y	Y	N	N	N
12 Critz	Y	Y	N	N	Y	N	Y
13 Schwartz	Y	Y	N	N	Y	Y	Y
14 Doyle	Y	Y	N	N	Y	Y	Y
15 **Dent**	Y	Y	Y	Y	N	N	N
16 **Pitts**	Y	Y	Y	Y	N	N	N
17 Holden	Y	Y	?	?	Y	N	N
18 **Murphy**	Y	Y	Y	Y	N	N	N
19 **Platts**	Y	Y	Y	Y	N	N	N
RHODE ISLAND							
1 Cicilline	Y	?	N	N	Y	Y	Y
2 Langevin	Y	Y	N	N	Y	Y	Y
SOUTH CAROLINA							
1 **Scott**	Y	Y	Y	Y	N	N	N
2 **Wilson**	Y	Y	Y	Y	N	N	N
3 **Duncan**	Y	Y	Y	Y	N	N	N
4 **Gowdy**	Y	Y	Y	Y	N	N	N
5 **Mulvaney**	Y	Y	Y	Y	N	N	N
6 Clyburn	Y	Y	N	N	Y	Y	Y
SOUTH DAKOTA							
AL **Noem**	Y	Y	Y	Y	N	N	N
TENNESSEE							
1 **Roe**	+	+	Y	Y	N	N	N
2 **Duncan**	Y	Y	Y	Y	N	N	N
3 **Fleischmann**	Y	Y	Y	Y	N	N	N
4 **DesJarlais**	Y	Y	Y	Y	N	N	N
5 Cooper	Y	Y	N	N	Y	Y	Y
6 **Black**	Y	Y	Y	Y	N	N	N
7 **Blackburn**	Y	Y	Y	Y	N	N	N
8 **Fincher**	Y	Y	Y	Y	N	N	N
9 Cohen	Y	Y	N	N	Y	Y	Y

	379	380	381	382	383	384	385
TEXAS							
1 **Gohmert**	?	?	Y	Y	N	N	N
2 **Poe**	Y	Y	Y	Y	N	N	N
3 **Johnson, S.**	Y	Y	Y	Y	N	N	N
4 **Hall**	Y	Y	Y	Y	N	N	N
5 **Hensarling**	Y	Y	Y	Y	N	N	N
6 **Barton**	Y	Y	Y	Y	N	N	N
7 **Culberson**	Y	Y	Y	Y	N	N	N
8 **Brady**	Y	Y	Y	Y	N	N	N
9 Green, A.	Y	Y	N	N	Y	Y	Y
10 **McCaul**	Y	Y	Y	Y	N	N	N
11 **Conaway**	Y	Y	Y	Y	N	N	N
12 **Granger**	Y	Y	Y	Y	N	N	N
13 **Thornberry**	Y	Y	Y	Y	N	N	N
14 **Paul**	Y	Y	Y	Y	N	N	Y
15 Hinojosa	Y	Y	N	N	Y	Y	Y
16 Reyes	Y	Y	N	N	Y	Y	Y
17 **Flores**	?	?	Y	Y	N	N	N
18 Jackson Lee	Y	Y	N	N	Y	Y	Y
19 **Neugebauer**	Y	Y	Y	Y	N	N	N
20 Gonzalez	Y	Y	N	N	Y	Y	Y
21 **Smith**	Y	Y	Y	Y	N	N	N
22 **Olson**	Y	Y	Y	Y	N	N	N
23 **Canseco**	Y	Y	Y	Y	N	N	N
24 **Marchant**	?	?	Y	Y	N	N	N
25 Doggett	Y	Y	N	N	Y	Y	Y
26 **Burgess**	Y	Y	Y	Y	N	N	N
27 **Farenthold**	Y	Y	Y	Y	N	N	N
28 Cuellar	Y	Y	N	N	Y	N	Y
29 Green, G.	Y	Y	N	N	Y	Y	Y
30 Johnson, E.	Y	Y	N	N	Y	Y	Y
31 **Carter**	?	?	Y	Y	N	N	N
32 **Sessions**	Y	Y	Y	Y	N	N	N
UTAH							
1 **Bishop**	Y	Y	Y	Y	N	N	N
2 Matheson	Y	Y	Y	Y	N	N	N
3 **Chaffetz**	Y	Y	Y	Y	N	N	N
VERMONT							
AL Welch	Y	Y	N	N	Y	Y	Y
VIRGINIA							
1 **Wittman**	Y	Y	Y	Y	N	N	N
2 **Rigell**	Y	Y	Y	Y	N	N	N
3 Scott	?	?	N	N	Y	Y	Y
4 **Forbes**	Y	Y	Y	Y	N	N	N
5 **Hurt**	Y	Y	Y	Y	–	N	N
6 **Goodlatte**	Y	Y	Y	Y	N	N	N
7 **Cantor**	Y	Y	Y	Y	N	N	N
8 Moran	Y	Y	N	N	Y	Y	Y
9 **Griffith**	N	Y	Y	Y	N	N	N
10 **Wolf**	Y	Y	Y	Y	N	N	N
11 Connolly	Y	Y	N	N	Y	Y	Y
WASHINGTON							
1 Vacant							
2 Larsen	Y	Y	N	N	Y	N	Y
3 **Herrera Beutler**	Y	Y	Y	Y	N	N	N
4 **Hastings**	Y	Y	Y	Y	N	N	N
5 **McMorris Rodgers**	Y	Y	Y	Y	N	N	N
6 Dicks	Y	?	N	N	Y	Y	Y
7 McDermott	Y	Y	N	N	Y	Y	Y
8 **Reichert**	Y	Y	Y	Y	N	N	N
9 Smith	Y	Y	N	N	Y	Y	Y
WEST VIRGINIA							
1 **McKinley**	Y	Y	Y	Y	N	N	N
2 **Capito**	Y	Y	Y	Y	N	N	N
3 Rahall	Y	Y	N	N	Y	Y	Y
WISCONSIN							
1 **Ryan**	Y	Y	Y	Y	N	N	N
2 Baldwin	Y	Y	N	N	Y	Y	Y
3 Kind	Y	Y	N	N	Y	Y	Y
4 Moore	Y	Y	N	N	Y	Y	Y
5 **Sensenbrenner**	Y	Y	Y	Y	N	N	N
6 **Petri**	Y	Y	Y	Y	Y	N	N
7 **Duffy**	Y	Y	Y	Y	N	N	N
8 **Ribble**	Y	Y	Y	Y	N	N	N
WYOMING							
AL **Lummis**	Y	Y	Y	Y	N	N	N

IN THE HOUSE | By Vote Number

386. HR 2578. Federal Lands and Water Projects/Recommit.
Perlmutter, D-Colo., motion to recommit the bill to the House Natural Resources Committee and report it back immediately with an amendment that would allow the Agriculture and Interior departments to enter into contracts with a state to treat insect-infected trees and remove hazardous fuels to reduce the risk of wildfires. It would clarify that nothing in the bill would override Native American tribal sovereignty. It also would require the Interior secretary to ensure that all items offered for sale in National Park gift shops or visitor centers are made in the United States. Motion rejected 188-234: R 2-234; D 186-0. June 19, 2012.

387. HR 2578. Federal Lands and Water Projects/Passage. Passage of the bill that would modify existing water projects, address land conveyances and transfers, allow the hunting of sea lions near the Columbia River in the Pacific Northwest, and repeal restrictions on off-road vehicle use in North Carolina's Cape Hatteras Seashore Recreational Area. It also would waive environmental and other laws to provide U.S. Customs and Border Protection access to federal land along U.S. borders to conduct border security activities, including setting up monitoring equipment, constructing roads or fences, or building temporary bases and facilities. Passed 232-188: R 216-19; D 16-169. A "nay" was a vote in support of the president's position. June 19, 2012.

388. HR 2938. Gila Bend Indian Reservation Gaming/Passage.
Young, R-Alaska, motion to suspend the rules and pass the bill that would prohibit certain gaming activities on Gila Bend Indian Reservation Lands in Arizona, including bingo, slot machines, blackjack, craps and roulette. The bill would not stop the tribe from opening a casino on lands acquired for its benefit south of Phoenix (provided such lands meet other criteria set forth in applicable law), nor does it change the tribe's ability to seek land for gaming under another act of Congress. Motion agreed to 343-78: R 232-4; D 111-74. A two-thirds vote of those present and voting (281 in this case) is required for passage under suspension of the rules. June 19, 2012.

389. HR 4480. Domestic Energy Production/Previous Question.
Bishop, R-Utah, motion to order the previous question (thus ending debate and the possibility of amendment) on the rule (H Res 691) that would provide for House floor consideration of a package of measures related to domestic energy production. Motion agreed to 242-183: R 236-0; D 6-183. June 20, 2012.

390. HR 4480. Domestic Energy Production/Rule. Adoption of the rule (H Res 691) to provide for House floor consideration of a package of measures related to domestic energy production. Adopted 245-178: R 235-0; D 10-178. June 20, 2012.

391. HR 4348. Surface Transportation Extension/Motion to Instruct.
Walz, D-Minn., motion to instruct conferees to resolve all disagreements regarding the surface transportation bill and file a conference report by June 22, 2012. Motion agreed to 386-34: R 198-34; D 188-0. June 20, 2012.

392. HR 4480. Domestic Energy Production/Manager's Amendment. Hastings, R-Wash., amendment that would require the Interior secretary to approve right-of-way corridors for the construction of two separate bridges and pipeline rights of way to help facilitate oil and gas development of the Alaska National Petroleum Reserve. It also would remove the EPA designation of the Colville River Delta as an Aquatic Resource of National Importance. Adopted in Committee of the Whole 253-163: R 234-0; D 19-163. June 21, 2012.

	386	387	388	389	390	391	392
ALABAMA							
1 Bonner	N	Y	Y	Y	Y	Y	Y
2 Roby	N	Y	Y	Y	Y	Y	Y
3 Rogers	N	Y	Y	Y	Y	Y	Y
4 Aderholt	N	Y	Y	Y	Y	Y	Y
5 Brooks	N	Y	Y	Y	Y	Y	Y
6 Bachus	N	Y	Y	?	?	?	Y
7 Sewell	Y	N	N	N	N	Y	N
ALASKA							
AL Young	N	Y	Y	Y	Y	N	Y
ARIZONA							
1 Gosar	N	Y	Y	Y	Y	Y	Y
2 Franks	N	Y	Y	Y	Y	Y	Y
3 Quayle	N	Y	Y	Y	Y	N	Y
4 Pastor	Y	N	N	N	N	Y	N
5 Schweikert	N	Y	Y	Y	Y	Y	Y
6 Flake	N	Y	Y	Y	Y	Y	Y
7 Grijalva	Y	N	N	N	N	N	Y
8 Barber	Y	Y	N	N	N	Y	N
ARKANSAS							
1 Crawford	N	Y	Y	Y	Y	Y	Y
2 Griffin	N	Y	Y	Y	Y	Y	Y
3 Womack	N	Y	Y	Y	Y	Y	Y
4 Ross	Y	Y	N	Y	Y	Y	Y
CALIFORNIA							
1 Thompson	Y	N	N	N	N	Y	N
2 Herger	N	Y	Y	Y	Y	Y	Y
3 Lungren	N	Y	Y	Y	Y	Y	Y
4 McClintock	N	Y	N	Y	Y	N	Y
5 Matsui	Y	N	N	N	N	Y	N
6 Woolsey	Y	N	Y	N	N	Y	N
7 Miller, George	Y	N	N	N	N	Y	N
8 Pelosi	Y	N	N	N	N	Y	N
9 Lee	Y	N	N	N	N	Y	N
10 Garamendi	Y	N	N	N	N	Y	N
11 McNerney	Y	N	N	N	N	Y	N
12 Speier	Y	N	N	N	N	Y	N
13 Stark	Y	N	N	N	N	Y	N
14 Eshoo	Y	N	N	N	N	Y	N
15 Honda	Y	N	N	N	N	Y	N
16 Lofgren	Y	N	N	N	N	Y	N
17 Farr	Y	N	N	N	N	Y	N
18 Cardoza	Y	Y	N	N	Y	Y	Y
19 Denham	N	Y	Y	Y	Y	Y	Y
20 Costa	Y	Y	N	N	Y	Y	Y
21 Nunes	N	Y	Y	Y	Y	Y	Y
22 McCarthy	N	Y	Y	Y	Y	Y	Y
23 Capps	Y	N	Y	N	N	Y	N
24 Gallegly	N	Y	Y	Y	Y	Y	?
25 McKeon	N	Y	Y	Y	Y	Y	Y
26 Dreier	N	Y	Y	Y	?	?	Y
27 Sherman	Y	N	N	N	N	Y	N
28 Berman	Y	N	N	N	N	Y	N
29 Schiff	Y	N	N	N	N	Y	N
30 Waxman	Y	N	N	N	N	Y	N
31 Becerra	Y	N	N	N	+	Y	N
32 Chu	Y	N	P	N	N	Y	N
33 Bass	Y	N	N	N	N	?	N
34 Roybal-Allard	Y	N	N	N	N	Y	N
35 Waters	Y	N	N	N	N	Y	N
36 Hahn	Y	N	N	N	N	Y	N
37 Richardson	Y	N	N	N	N	Y	N
38 Napolitano	Y	N	N	N	N	Y	N
39 Sánchez, Linda	?	?	?	?	?	?	?
40 Royce	N	Y	Y	Y	Y	Y	Y
41 Lewis	?	?	?	?	?	?	?
42 Miller, Gary	N	Y	Y	?	?	?	?
43 Baca	Y	N	Y	N	N	Y	N
44 Calvert	N	Y	Y	Y	Y	Y	Y
45 Bono Mack	N	Y	Y	Y	Y	Y	Y
46 Rohrabacher	N	Y	Y	Y	Y	Y	Y
47 Sanchez, Loretta	Y	N	N	N	N	Y	N
48 Campbell	N	Y	Y	Y	Y	N	Y
49 Issa	?	?	Y	Y	Y	Y	Y
50 Bilbray	N	Y	Y	Y	Y	Y	Y
51 Filner	Y	N	N	N	N	Y	–
52 Hunter	N	Y	Y	Y	Y	Y	Y
53 Davis	Y	N	N	N	N	Y	N

	386	387	388	389	390	391	392
COLORADO							
1 DeGette	Y	N	N	N	N	Y	N
2 Polis	Y	N	N	N	N	Y	N
3 Tipton	N	Y	Y	Y	Y	Y	Y
4 Gardner	N	Y	Y	Y	Y	Y	Y
5 Lamborn	N	Y	Y	Y	Y	Y	Y
6 Coffman	N	Y	Y	Y	Y	Y	Y
7 Perlmutter	Y	N	N	N	N	Y	N
CONNECTICUT							
1 Larson	Y	N	N	N	N	Y	N
2 Courtney	Y	N	N	N	N	Y	N
3 DeLauro	Y	N	N	N	N	Y	N
4 Himes	Y	N	N	N	N	Y	N
5 Murphy	Y	N	N	N	N	Y	N
DELAWARE							
AL Carney	Y	N	N	N	N	Y	N
FLORIDA							
1 Miller	?	?	?	?	?	?	?
2 Southerland	N	Y	Y	Y	Y	Y	Y
3 Brown	Y	N	N	N	N	Y	N
4 Crenshaw	N	Y	Y	Y	Y	Y	Y
5 Nugent	N	Y	Y	Y	Y	Y	Y
6 Stearns	N	Y	Y	Y	Y	N	Y
7 Mica	N	Y	Y	Y	Y	Y	Y
8 Webster	N	Y	Y	Y	Y	N	Y
9 Bilirakis	N	Y	Y	Y	Y	Y	Y
10 Young	?	?	?	Y	Y	Y	Y
11 Castor	Y	N	N	N	N	Y	N
12 Ross	N	Y	Y	Y	Y	Y	Y
13 Buchanan	N	Y	Y	Y	Y	Y	Y
14 Mack	N	Y	Y	Y	Y	Y	?
15 Posey	N	Y	Y	Y	Y	N	Y
16 Rooney	N	Y	Y	Y	Y	N	Y
17 Wilson	Y	N	N	N	N	Y	N
18 Ros-Lehtinen	N	Y	Y	Y	Y	Y	Y
19 Deutch	Y	N	N	N	N	Y	N
20 Wasserman Schultz	Y	N	N	N	N	Y	N
21 Diaz-Balart	N	Y	Y	Y	Y	Y	Y
22 West	N	Y	Y	Y	Y	Y	Y
23 Hastings	Y	N	N	N	N	Y	N
24 Adams	N	Y	Y	Y	Y	Y	Y
25 Rivera	N	Y	Y	Y	Y	Y	Y
GEORGIA							
1 Kingston	N	Y	Y	Y	Y	Y	Y
2 Bishop	Y	Y	N	N	N	Y	N
3 Westmoreland	N	Y	Y	Y	Y	N	Y
4 Johnson	Y	N	N	N	N	Y	N
5 Lewis	Y	N	N	N	N	Y	?
6 Price	N	Y	Y	Y	Y	Y	Y
7 Woodall	N	Y	Y	Y	Y	Y	Y
8 Scott, A.	N	Y	Y	Y	Y	Y	Y
9 Graves	N	Y	Y	Y	Y	Y	Y
10 Broun	N	Y	Y	Y	Y	N	Y
11 Gingrey	N	Y	Y	Y	Y	N	Y
12 Barrow	Y	Y	N	N	Y	Y	Y
13 Scott, D.	Y	N	N	N	N	Y	N
HAWAII							
1 Hanabusa	Y	N	Y	N	N	Y	N
2 Hirono	Y	N	+	N	N	Y	N
IDAHO							
1 Labrador	N	Y	Y	Y	Y	Y	Y
2 Simpson	N	Y	Y	Y	Y	Y	Y
ILLINOIS							
1 Rush	Y	N	N	N	Y	N	N
2 Jackson	?	?	?	?	?	?	?
3 Lipinski	Y	N	Y	N	N	Y	N
4 Gutierrez	Y	N	N	N	N	Y	N
5 Quigley	Y	N	N	N	N	Y	N
6 Roskam	N	Y	Y	Y	Y	Y	Y
7 Davis	Y	N	N	N	N	Y	N
8 Walsh	N	Y	Y	Y	Y	?	Y
9 Schakowsky	Y	N	N	N	N	Y	N
10 Dold	N	Y	Y	Y	Y	Y	Y
11 Kinzinger	N	Y	Y	Y	Y	Y	Y
12 Costello	Y	N	N	N	N	Y	N
13 Biggert	N	Y	Y	Y	Y	Y	Y
14 Hultgren	N	Y	Y	Y	Y	Y	Y
15 Johnson	N	N	Y	Y	Y	Y	Y

KEY	Republicans	Democrats		
Y	Voted for (yea)	X	Paired against	C Voted "present" to avoid possible conflict of interest
#	Paired for	–	Announced against	
+	Announced for	P	Voted "present"	? Did not vote or otherwise make a position known
N	Voted against (nay)			

	386	387	388	389	390	391	392
16 **Manzullo**	N	Y	Y	Y	Y	Y	Y
17 **Schilling**	N	Y	Y	Y	Y	Y	Y
18 **Schock**	N	?	Y	Y	Y	?	Y
19 **Shimkus**	N	Y	Y	Y	Y	Y	Y
INDIANA							
1 Visclosky	Y	N	N	N	N	Y	N
2 Donnelly	Y	Y	N	N	Y	Y	Y
3 **Stutzman**	N	Y	Y	Y	Y	Y	Y
4 **Rokita**	N	Y	Y	Y	Y	Y	Y
5 **Burton**	N	Y	Y	Y	Y	Y	?
6 **Pence**	N	Y	Y	Y	Y	Y	Y
7 Carson	Y	N	Y	N	N	Y	N
8 **Bucshon**	N	Y	Y	Y	Y	Y	Y
9 **Young**	N	Y	Y	Y	Y	Y	Y
IOWA							
1 Braley	Y	N	N	N	N	Y	N
2 Loebsack	Y	N	Y	N	N	Y	N
3 Boswell	Y	Y	Y	N	N	Y	Y
4 **Latham**	N	Y	Y	Y	Y	Y	Y
5 **King**	N	Y	Y	Y	Y	Y	Y
KANSAS							
1 **Huelskamp**	N	N	Y	Y	Y	Y	Y
2 **Jenkins**	N	Y	Y	Y	Y	Y	Y
3 **Yoder**	N	Y	Y	Y	Y	Y	Y
4 **Pompeo**	N	Y	Y	Y	Y	N	Y
KENTUCKY							
1 **Whitfield**	N	Y	Y	Y	Y	Y	Y
2 **Guthrie**	N	Y	Y	Y	Y	Y	Y
3 Yarmuth	Y	N	N	N	N	Y	N
4 **Davis**	N	Y	Y	Y	Y	Y	Y
5 **Rogers**	N	Y	Y	Y	Y	Y	Y
6 Chandler	Y	N	Y	Y	Y	Y	N
LOUISIANA							
1 **Scalise**	N	Y	Y	Y	Y	Y	Y
2 Richmond	Y	N	Y	N	N	Y	N
3 **Landry**	N	Y	Y	Y	Y	Y	Y
4 **Fleming**	N	Y	Y	Y	Y	Y	Y
5 **Alexander**	N	Y	Y	Y	Y	Y	Y
6 **Cassidy**	N	Y	Y	Y	Y	Y	Y
7 **Boustany**	N	Y	Y	Y	Y	Y	Y
MAINE							
1 Pingree	Y	N	N	N	N	Y	N
2 Michaud	Y	N	Y	N	N	Y	N
MARYLAND							
1 **Harris**	N	Y	Y	Y	Y	Y	Y
2 Ruppersberger	Y	N	Y	N	N	Y	N
3 Sarbanes	Y	N	N	N	N	Y	N
4 Edwards	Y	N	N	N	N	Y	N
5 Hoyer	Y	N	N	N	N	Y	N
6 **Bartlett**	N	N	Y	Y	Y	Y	Y
7 Cummings	?	?	Y	N	N	Y	N
8 Van Hollen	Y	N	N	N	N	Y	N
MASSACHUSETTS							
1 Olver	Y	N	Y	N	N	Y	N
2 Neal	Y	N	Y	N	N	Y	N
3 McGovern	Y	N	Y	N	N	Y	N
4 Frank	Y	N	N	N	N	Y	N
5 Tsongas	Y	N	N	N	N	Y	N
6 Tierney	Y	N	N	N	N	Y	N
7 Markey	Y	N	N	N	N	Y	N
8 Capuano	Y	N	Y	N	N	Y	N
9 Lynch	Y	N	N	N	N	Y	N
10 Keating	Y	N	N	N	N	Y	N
MICHIGAN							
1 **Benishek**	N	Y	Y	Y	Y	Y	Y
2 **Huizenga**	?	?	?	Y	Y	N	Y
3 **Amash**	N	N	N	Y	Y	N	Y
4 **Camp**	N	Y	Y	Y	Y	N	Y
5 Kildee	Y	N	Y	N	N	Y	N
6 **Upton**	N	Y	Y	Y	Y	Y	Y
7 **Walberg**	N	Y	Y	Y	Y	Y	Y
8 **Rogers**	N	Y	Y	Y	Y	Y	Y
9 Peters	Y	N	Y	N	N	Y	N
10 **Miller**	N	Y	Y	Y	Y	Y	Y
11 **McCotter**	N	Y	Y	Y	Y	Y	Y
12 Levin	Y	N	N	N	N	Y	N
13 Clarke	Y	N	Y	N	N	Y	N
14 Conyers	Y	N	Y	N	N	Y	N
15 Dingell	?	?	?	N	N	Y	N
MINNESOTA							
1 Walz	Y	N	Y	N	N	Y	N
2 **Kline**	N	Y	Y	Y	Y	Y	Y
3 **Paulsen**	N	Y	Y	Y	Y	Y	Y
4 McCollum	Y	N	Y	N	N	Y	N

	386	387	388	389	390	391	392
5 Ellison	Y	N	Y	N	N	Y	N
6 **Bachmann**	N	Y	Y	Y	Y	Y	Y
7 Peterson	Y	Y	Y	N	N	Y	Y
8 **Cravaack**	N	Y	Y	Y	Y	Y	Y
MISSISSIPPI							
1 **Nunnelee**	N	Y	Y	Y	Y	Y	Y
2 Thompson	Y	N	Y	N	N	Y	N
3 **Harper**	N	Y	Y	Y	Y	Y	Y
4 **Palazzo**	N	Y	Y	Y	Y	Y	Y
MISSOURI							
1 Clay	Y	N	Y	N	N	Y	N
2 **Akin**	N	Y	Y	Y	Y	Y	Y
3 Carnahan	Y	N	Y	N	N	Y	N
4 **Hartzler**	N	Y	Y	Y	Y	Y	Y
5 Cleaver	Y	N	Y	N	N	Y	N
6 **Graves**	N	Y	Y	Y	Y	Y	Y
7 **Long**	N	Y	Y	Y	Y	N	Y
8 **Emerson**	N	Y	Y	Y	Y	Y	Y
9 **Luetkemeyer**	N	Y	Y	Y	Y	Y	Y
MONTANA							
AL **Rehberg**	N	Y	Y	Y	Y	Y	Y
NEBRASKA							
1 **Fortenberry**	N	Y	Y	Y	Y	Y	Y
2 **Terry**	N	Y	Y	Y	Y	Y	Y
3 **Smith**	N	Y	Y	Y	Y	Y	Y
NEVADA							
1 Berkley	Y	N	Y	N	N	Y	N
2 **Amodei**	N	Y	Y	Y	Y	Y	Y
3 **Heck**	N	Y	Y	Y	Y	Y	Y
NEW HAMPSHIRE							
1 **Guinta**	N	N	Y	Y	Y	Y	Y
2 **Bass**	N	N	Y	Y	Y	Y	Y
NEW JERSEY							
1 Andrews	Y	N	Y	N	N	Y	N
2 **LoBiondo**	N	N	Y	Y	Y	Y	Y
3 **Runyan**	N	Y	Y	Y	Y	Y	Y
4 **Smith**	N	N	Y	Y	Y	Y	Y
5 **Garrett**	N	Y	Y	Y	Y	N	Y
6 Pallone	Y	N	Y	N	N	Y	N
7 **Lance**	N	Y	Y	Y	Y	Y	Y
8 Pascrell	Y	N	Y	N	N	Y	N
9 Rothman	Y	N	Y	N	N	Y	N
10 Vacant							
11 **Frelinghuysen**	N	N	Y	Y	Y	Y	Y
12 Holt	Y	N	N	N	N	Y	N
13 Sires	Y	N	Y	N	N	Y	N
NEW MEXICO							
1 Heinrich	Y	N	Y	N	N	Y	–
2 **Pearce**	N	Y	Y	Y	Y	N	Y
3 Luján	Y	N	Y	N	N	Y	N
NEW YORK							
1 Bishop	Y	N	N	N	N	Y	–
2 Israel	Y	N	Y	N	N	Y	N
3 **King**	N	Y	Y	Y	Y	Y	Y
4 McCarthy	Y	N	N	N	N	Y	N
5 Ackerman	Y	N	Y	N	N	Y	N
6 Meeks	Y	N	Y	N	N	Y	N
7 Crowley	Y	N	Y	N	N	Y	N
8 Nadler	Y	N	N	N	N	Y	N
9 **Turner**	N	Y	Y	Y	Y	Y	Y
10 Towns	Y	N	Y	N	N	Y	N
11 Clarke	Y	N	Y	N	N	Y	–
12 Velázquez	Y	N	N	N	N	Y	?
13 **Grimm**	N	Y	Y	Y	Y	Y	Y
14 Maloney	Y	N	Y	N	N	Y	N
15 Rangel	Y	N	Y	N	N	Y	N
16 Serrano	Y	N	N	N	N	Y	N
17 Engel	Y	N	Y	N	N	Y	N
18 Lowey	Y	N	Y	N	N	Y	N
19 **Hayworth**	N	N	Y	Y	Y	Y	Y
20 **Gibson**	N	Y	Y	Y	Y	Y	Y
21 Tonko	Y	N	N	N	N	Y	N
22 Hinchey	Y	N	N	N	N	Y	N
23 Owens	Y	N	N	N	Y	Y	Y
24 **Hanna**	N	Y	Y	Y	Y	Y	Y
25 **Buerkle**	N	Y	Y	Y	Y	Y	Y
26 Hochul	Y	Y	N	N	Y	Y	Y
27 Higgins	Y	N	N	N	N	Y	N
28 Slaughter	Y	N	N	N	N	Y	N
29 **Reed**	N	Y	Y	?	?	?	Y
NORTH CAROLINA							
1 Butterfield	Y	N	Y	N	N	Y	N
2 **Ellmers**	N	Y	Y	Y	Y	Y	Y
3 **Jones**	Y	Y	Y	Y	Y	Y	Y
4 Price	Y	N	N	N	N	Y	N

	386	387	388	389	390	391	392
5 **Foxx**	N	Y	Y	Y	Y	N	Y
6 **Coble**	N	Y	Y	Y	Y	Y	Y
7 McIntyre	Y	Y	Y	Y	Y	Y	N
8 Kissell	Y	Y	N	N	Y	Y	Y
9 **Myrick**	N	Y	Y	Y	Y	Y	Y
10 **McHenry**	N	Y	Y	Y	Y	Y	Y
11 Shuler	Y	Y	Y	Y	Y	Y	N
12 Watt	Y	N	Y	N	N	Y	N
13 Miller	Y	N	N	N	N	Y	N
NORTH DAKOTA							
AL **Berg**	N	Y	Y	Y	Y	Y	Y
OHIO							
1 **Chabot**	N	N	Y	Y	Y	Y	Y
2 **Schmidt**	N	Y	Y	Y	Y	Y	Y
3 **Turner**	N	Y	Y	Y	Y	Y	Y
4 **Jordan**	N	Y	Y	Y	Y	Y	Y
5 **Latta**	N	Y	Y	Y	Y	Y	Y
6 **Johnson**	N	Y	Y	Y	Y	Y	Y
7 **Austria**	N	Y	Y	Y	Y	Y	Y
8 **Boehner**							
9 Kaptur	Y	N	Y	N	N	Y	N
10 Kucinich	Y	N	N	N	N	Y	N
11 Fudge	Y	N	Y	N	N	Y	N
12 **Tiberi**	N	Y	Y	Y	Y	Y	Y
13 Sutton	Y	N	N	N	N	Y	N
14 **LaTourette**	N	Y	P	Y	Y	Y	Y
15 **Stivers**	N	Y	Y	Y	Y	Y	Y
16 **Renacci**	N	Y	Y	Y	Y	Y	Y
17 Ryan	Y	N	N	N	N	Y	N
18 **Gibbs**	N	Y	Y	Y	Y	Y	Y
OKLAHOMA							
1 **Sullivan**	N	Y	Y	Y	Y	Y	Y
2 Boren	Y	Y	Y	Y	Y	Y	Y
3 **Lucas**	N	Y	Y	Y	Y	Y	Y
4 **Cole**	N	Y	Y	Y	Y	Y	Y
5 **Lankford**	N	Y	Y	Y	Y	Y	Y
OREGON							
1 Bonamici	Y	N	N	N	N	Y	N
2 **Walden**	N	Y	Y	Y	Y	Y	Y
3 Blumenauer	Y	N	N	N	N	Y	N
4 DeFazio	Y	N	N	N	N	Y	N
5 Schrader	Y	N	Y	N	N	Y	N
PENNSYLVANIA							
1 Brady	Y	N	Y	N	N	Y	N
2 Fattah	Y	N	Y	N	N	Y	N
3 **Kelly**	N	Y	Y	Y	Y	Y	Y
4 Altmire	?	?	?	N	N	Y	Y
5 **Thompson**	N	Y	Y	Y	Y	N	Y
6 **Gerlach**	N	Y	Y	Y	Y	Y	Y
7 **Meehan**	N	Y	Y	Y	Y	Y	Y
8 **Fitzpatrick**	N	N	Y	Y	Y	Y	Y
9 **Shuster**	N	Y	Y	Y	Y	Y	Y
10 **Marino**	N	Y	Y	Y	Y	Y	Y
11 **Barletta**	N	Y	Y	Y	Y	Y	Y
12 Critz	Y	N	N	N	N	Y	Y
13 Schwartz	Y	–	Y	N	N	Y	N
14 Doyle	Y	N	N	N	N	Y	N
15 **Dent**	N	Y	Y	Y	Y	Y	Y
16 **Pitts**	N	Y	Y	Y	Y	Y	Y
17 Holden	Y	Y	Y	N	N	Y	Y
18 **Murphy**	N	Y	Y	Y	Y	Y	+
19 **Platts**	N	Y	Y	Y	Y	Y	Y
RHODE ISLAND							
1 Cicilline	Y	N	N	N	N	Y	N
2 Langevin	Y	N	N	N	N	Y	N
SOUTH CAROLINA							
1 **Scott**	N	Y	Y	Y	Y	Y	Y
2 **Wilson**	N	Y	Y	Y	Y	Y	Y
3 **Duncan**	N	Y	Y	Y	Y	Y	Y
4 **Gowdy**	N	Y	Y	Y	Y	Y	Y
5 **Mulvaney**	N	N	Y	Y	Y	Y	Y
6 Clyburn	Y	N	Y	N	N	Y	N
SOUTH DAKOTA							
AL **Noem**	N	Y	Y	Y	Y	Y	Y
TENNESSEE							
1 **Roe**	N	Y	Y	Y	Y	Y	Y
2 **Duncan**	Y	Y	Y	Y	Y	Y	Y
3 **Fleischmann**	N	Y	Y	Y	Y	Y	Y
4 **DesJarlais**	N	Y	Y	Y	Y	Y	Y
5 Cooper	Y	N	Y	N	N	Y	N
6 **Black**	N	Y	Y	Y	Y	Y	Y
7 **Blackburn**	N	Y	Y	Y	Y	Y	Y
8 **Fincher**	N	Y	Y	Y	Y	N	Y
9 Cohen	Y	N	Y	N	N	Y	N

	386	387	388	389	390	391	392
TEXAS							
1 **Gohmert**	N	Y	Y	Y	Y	N	Y
2 **Poe**	N	Y	Y	Y	Y	N	Y
3 **Johnson, S.**	N	Y	Y	Y	Y	Y	Y
4 **Hall**	N	Y	Y	Y	Y	Y	Y
5 **Hensarling**	N	Y	Y	Y	Y	Y	Y
6 **Barton**	N	Y	Y	Y	Y	Y	Y
7 **Culberson**	N	Y	Y	Y	Y	N	Y
8 **Brady**	N	Y	Y	Y	Y	N	Y
9 Green, A.	Y	N	Y	N	N	Y	Y
10 **McCaul**	N	Y	Y	Y	Y	Y	Y
11 **Conaway**	N	Y	Y	Y	Y	N	Y
12 **Granger**	N	N	Y	Y	Y	N	Y
13 **Thornberry**	N	Y	Y	Y	Y	N	Y
14 **Paul**	N	N	N	Y	Y	Y	Y
15 Hinojosa	Y	N	Y	N	N	Y	N
16 Reyes	Y	N	Y	N	N	Y	N
17 **Flores**	N	Y	Y	Y	Y	N	Y
18 Jackson Lee	Y	N	Y	N	N	Y	?
19 **Neugebauer**	N	Y	Y	Y	Y	N	Y
20 Gonzalez	Y	N	Y	N	N	Y	N
21 **Smith**	N	Y	Y	Y	Y	Y	Y
22 **Olson**	N	Y	Y	Y	Y	Y	Y
23 **Canseco**	N	Y	Y	Y	Y	N	Y
24 **Marchant**	N	Y	Y	Y	Y	Y	Y
25 Doggett	Y	N	N	N	N	Y	N
26 **Burgess**	N	Y	Y	Y	Y	Y	Y
27 **Farenthold**	N	Y	Y	Y	Y	Y	Y
28 Cuellar	Y	N	Y	N	N	Y	Y
29 Green, G.	Y	N	Y	Y	N	Y	Y
30 Johnson, E.	Y	N	N	N	N	Y	N
31 **Carter**	N	N	Y	Y	Y	N	Y
32 **Sessions**	N	Y	Y	Y	Y	N	Y
UTAH							
1 **Bishop**	N	Y	Y	Y	Y	N	Y
2 Matheson	Y	Y	Y	Y	Y	Y	Y
3 **Chaffetz**	N	Y	Y	Y	Y	Y	Y
VERMONT							
AL Welch	Y	N	N	N	N	Y	N
VIRGINIA							
1 **Wittman**	N	Y	Y	Y	Y	Y	Y
2 **Rigell**	N	Y	Y	Y	Y	Y	Y
3 Scott	Y	N	N	N	N	Y	N
4 **Forbes**	N	Y	Y	Y	Y	Y	Y
5 **Hurt**	N	Y	Y	Y	Y	Y	Y
6 **Goodlatte**	N	Y	Y	Y	Y	Y	Y
7 **Cantor**	N	Y	Y	Y	Y	Y	Y
8 Moran	Y	N	N	N	N	Y	N
9 **Griffith**	N	Y	Y	Y	Y	Y	Y
10 **Wolf**	N	Y	Y	Y	Y	Y	Y
11 Connolly	Y	N	Y	N	N	Y	N
WASHINGTON							
1 Vacant							
2 Larsen	Y	N	N	N	N	Y	N
3 **Herrera Beutler**	N	Y	Y	Y	Y	Y	Y
4 **Hastings**	N	Y	Y	Y	Y	Y	Y
5 **McMorris Rodgers**	N	Y	Y	Y	Y	Y	Y
6 Dicks	Y	N	Y	N	N	Y	N
7 McDermott	Y	N	N	N	N	Y	N
8 **Reichert**	N	N	Y	Y	Y	Y	Y
9 Smith	Y	N	N	N	N	Y	N
WEST VIRGINIA							
1 **McKinley**	N	Y	Y	Y	Y	Y	Y
2 **Capito**	N	Y	Y	Y	Y	Y	Y
3 Rahall	Y	N	Y	N	N	Y	N
WISCONSIN							
1 **Ryan**	N	Y	Y	Y	Y	Y	Y
2 Baldwin	Y	N	Y	N	N	Y	N
3 Kind	Y	N	Y	N	N	Y	N
4 Moore	Y	N	Y	N	N	Y	N
5 **Sensenbrenner**	N	Y	Y	Y	Y	Y	Y
6 **Petri**	N	Y	Y	Y	Y	Y	Y
7 **Duffy**	N	Y	Y	Y	Y	Y	Y
8 **Ribble**	N	Y	Y	Y	Y	P	Y
WYOMING							
AL **Lummis**	N	Y	N	Y	Y	Y	Y

IN THE HOUSE | By Vote Number

393. **HR 4480. Domestic Energy Production/Harmful Pollution.** Waxman, D-Calif., amendment that would prohibit the EPA administrator from delaying the finalization of any rules to establish standards for clean air and pollution reduction if the pollution is contributing to asthma attacks, bronchitis, heart attacks, cancer, birth defects, neurological damage, premature death or other serious harm to human health. Rejected in Committee of the Whole 164-249: R 2-231; D 162-18. June 21, 2012.

394. **HR 4480. Domestic Energy Production/Public Health.** Connolly, D-Va., amendment that would define the term "public health" as the health of members of the species Homo sapiens and not "the health of corporations or any other non-living entities." Rejected in Committee of the Whole 177-242: R 4-231; D 173-11. June 21, 2012.

395. **HR 4480. Domestic Energy Production/Cost Consideration for Air Standards.** Green, D-Texas, amendment that would strike a provision in the bill to require the EPA to consider cost and feasibility when proposing modifications to the national ambient air quality standards for ozone. Rejected in Committee of the Whole 174-244: R 7-229; D 167-15. June 21, 2012.

396. **HR 4480. Domestic Energy Production/Gasoline Prices and Jobs.** Rush, D-Ill., amendment that would prevent the delay of EPA rules and cost analysis requirements associated with modifying national ambient air quality standards from taking effect if it is determined that the provisions would not lower gas prices and create jobs within 10 years of the bill's enactment. Rejected in Committee of the Whole 164-255: R 0-235; D 164-20. June 21, 2012.

397. **HR 4480. Domestic Energy Production/Onshore Oil and Gas Leases.** Holt, D-N.J., amendment that would require a national energy production strategy proposed under the bill to seek a reduction in the number of onshore leases where no exploration or extraction activities are occurring. Rejected in Committee of the Whole 164-256: R 7-229; D 157-27. June 21, 2012.

398. **HR 4480. Domestic Energy Production/Protest Fee.** Connolly, D-Va., amendment that would clarify that the section of the bill requiring a documentation fee for filing a protest against a lease sale or drilling permit would not infringe upon the constitutional protections under the First Amendment to petition for the redress of grievances. Rejected in Committee of the Whole 190-230: R 8-228; D 182-2. June 21, 2012.

399. **HR 4480. Domestic Energy Production/Solid-Minerals Program.** Amodei, R-Nev., amendment that would bar the Interior Department from transferring any part of the solid-minerals program administered by the Bureau of Land Management to the Office of Surface Mining, Reclamation and Enforcement. Adopted in Committee of the Whole 257-162: R 231-4; D 26-158. June 21, 2012.

Member	393	394	395	396	397	398	399
ALABAMA							
1 Bonner	N	N	N	N	N	N	Y
2 Roby	N	N	N	N	N	N	Y
3 Rogers	N	N	N	N	N	N	Y
4 Aderholt	N	N	N	N	N	N	Y
5 Brooks	N	N	N	N	N	N	Y
6 Bachus	N	N	N	?	N	N	Y
7 Sewell	Y	Y	Y	Y	Y	Y	N
ALASKA							
AL Young	N	N	N	N	N	N	Y
ARIZONA							
1 Gosar	N	N	N	N	N	N	Y
2 Franks	N	N	N	N	N	N	Y
3 Quayle	N	N	N	N	N	N	Y
4 Pastor	Y	Y	Y	Y	Y	Y	N
5 Schweikert	N	N	N	N	N	N	Y
6 Flake	N	N	N	N	N	N	Y
7 Grijalva	Y	Y	Y	Y	Y	Y	N
8 Barber	Y	Y	Y	Y	Y	Y	N
ARKANSAS							
1 Crawford	N	N	N	N	N	N	Y
2 Griffin	N	N	N	N	N	N	Y
3 Womack	N	N	N	N	N	N	Y
4 Ross	N	N	Y	N	N	N	Y
CALIFORNIA							
1 Thompson	Y	Y	Y	Y	Y	Y	N
2 Herger	N	N	N	N	N	N	Y
3 Lungren	N	N	N	N	N	N	Y
4 McClintock	N	N	N	N	N	N	Y
5 Matsui	Y	Y	Y	Y	Y	Y	N
6 Woolsey	Y	Y	Y	Y	Y	Y	N
7 Miller, George	Y	Y	Y	Y	Y	Y	N
8 Pelosi	Y	Y	Y	Y	Y	Y	N
9 Lee	Y	Y	Y	Y	Y	Y	N
10 Garamendi	Y	Y	Y	Y	Y	Y	N
11 McNerney	Y	Y	Y	Y	Y	Y	N
12 Speier	Y	Y	Y	Y	Y	Y	N
13 Stark	Y	Y	Y	Y	Y	Y	N
14 Eshoo	Y	Y	Y	Y	Y	Y	N
15 Honda	Y	Y	Y	Y	Y	Y	N
16 Lofgren	Y	Y	Y	Y	Y	Y	N
17 Farr	Y	Y	Y	Y	Y	Y	N
18 Cardoza	N	Y	N	Y	N	N	Y
19 Denham	N	N	N	N	N	N	Y
20 Costa	N	Y	Y	Y	Y	Y	N
21 Nunes	N	N	N	N	N	N	Y
22 McCarthy	N	N	N	N	N	N	Y
23 Capps	Y	Y	Y	Y	Y	Y	N
24 Gallegly	?	?	?	?	?	?	?
25 McKeon	N	N	N	N	N	N	Y
26 Dreier	N	N	N	N	N	N	Y
27 Sherman	Y	Y	Y	Y	Y	Y	N
28 Berman	Y	Y	Y	Y	Y	Y	N
29 Schiff	Y	Y	Y	Y	Y	Y	N
30 Waxman	Y	Y	Y	Y	Y	Y	N
31 Becerra	Y	Y	Y	Y	Y	Y	N
32 Chu	Y	Y	Y	Y	Y	Y	N
33 Bass	Y	Y	Y	Y	Y	Y	N
34 Roybal-Allard	Y	Y	Y	Y	Y	Y	N
35 Waters	Y	Y	Y	Y	Y	Y	N
36 Hahn	Y	Y	Y	Y	Y	Y	N
37 Richardson	Y	Y	Y	Y	Y	Y	N
38 Napolitano	Y	Y	Y	Y	Y	Y	N
39 Sánchez, Linda	?	?	?	?	?	?	?
40 Royce	N	N	N	N	N	N	Y
41 Lewis	?	?	?	?	?	?	?
42 Miller, Gary	?	?	?	?	?	?	?
43 Baca	Y	Y	Y	Y	Y	Y	N
44 Calvert	N	N	N	N	N	N	Y
45 Bono Mack	N	N	N	N	N	N	Y
46 Rohrabacher	N	N	N	N	N	N	Y
47 Sanchez, Loretta	Y	Y	Y	Y	Y	Y	N
48 Campbell	N	N	N	N	N	N	Y
49 Issa	N	N	N	N	N	N	Y
50 Bilbray	N	N	N	N	N	N	Y
51 Filner	+	+	+	+	+	+	–
52 Hunter	N	N	N	N	N	N	Y
53 Davis	Y	Y	Y	Y	Y	Y	N

Member	393	394	395	396	397	398	399
COLORADO							
1 DeGette	Y	Y	Y	Y	Y	Y	N
2 Polis	Y	Y	Y	Y	Y	Y	N
3 Tipton	N	N	N	N	N	N	Y
4 Gardner	N	N	N	N	N	N	Y
5 Lamborn	N	N	N	N	N	N	Y
6 Coffman	N	N	N	N	N	N	Y
7 Perlmutter	Y	Y	Y	N	N	Y	N
CONNECTICUT							
1 Larson	Y	Y	Y	Y	Y	Y	N
2 Courtney	Y	Y	Y	Y	Y	Y	N
3 DeLauro	Y	Y	Y	Y	Y	Y	N
4 Himes	Y	Y	Y	Y	Y	Y	N
5 Murphy	Y	Y	Y	Y	Y	Y	N
DELAWARE							
AL Carney	Y	Y	Y	Y	N	Y	N
FLORIDA							
1 Miller	?	?	?	?	?	?	?
2 Southerland	N	N	N	N	N	N	Y
3 Brown	N	N	Y	Y	N	Y	N
4 Crenshaw	N	N	N	N	N	N	Y
5 Nugent	N	N	N	N	N	N	Y
6 Stearns	N	N	N	N	N	N	Y
7 Mica	N	N	N	N	N	N	Y
8 Webster	N	N	N	N	N	N	Y
9 Bilirakis	N	N	N	N	N	N	Y
10 Young	N	N	N	N	N	N	Y
11 Castor	Y	Y	Y	Y	Y	Y	N
12 Ross	N	N	N	N	N	N	Y
13 Buchanan	N	N	N	N	N	N	Y
14 Mack	?	?	?	?	?	?	?
15 Posey	N	N	N	N	N	N	Y
16 Rooney	N	N	N	N	N	N	Y
17 Wilson	Y	Y	Y	Y	Y	Y	N
18 Ros-Lehtinen	N	N	N	N	N	N	Y
19 Deutch	Y	Y	Y	Y	Y	Y	N
20 Wasserman Schultz	Y	Y	Y	Y	Y	Y	N
21 Diaz-Balart	N	N	N	N	N	N	Y
22 West	N	N	N	N	N	N	Y
23 Hastings	Y	Y	Y	Y	Y	Y	N
24 Adams	N	N	N	N	N	N	Y
25 Rivera	?	N	N	N	N	N	Y
GEORGIA							
1 Kingston	N	N	N	N	N	N	Y
2 Bishop	N	Y	Y	N	N	Y	N
3 Westmoreland	N	N	N	N	N	N	Y
4 Johnson	?	Y	Y	Y	Y	Y	N
5 Lewis	?	Y	Y	Y	Y	Y	N
6 Price	N	N	N	N	N	N	Y
7 Woodall	N	N	N	N	N	N	Y
8 Scott, A.	N	N	N	N	N	N	Y
9 Graves	N	N	N	N	N	N	Y
10 Broun	N	N	N	N	N	N	Y
11 Gingrey	N	N	N	N	N	N	Y
12 Barrow	N	Y	N	N	Y	Y	Y
13 Scott, D.	?	Y	Y	Y	Y	Y	N
HAWAII							
1 Hanabusa	Y	Y	Y	Y	Y	Y	N
2 Hirono	Y	Y	Y	Y	Y	Y	N
IDAHO							
1 Labrador	N	N	N	N	N	N	Y
2 Simpson	N	N	N	N	N	N	Y
ILLINOIS							
1 Rush	Y	Y	Y	Y	Y	Y	N
2 Jackson	?	?	?	?	?	?	?
3 Lipinski	Y	Y	Y	Y	Y	Y	N
4 Gutierrez	Y	Y	Y	Y	Y	Y	Y
5 Quigley	Y	Y	Y	Y	Y	Y	N
6 Roskam	N	N	N	N	N	N	Y
7 Davis	Y	Y	Y	Y	Y	Y	N
8 Walsh	N	N	N	N	N	N	Y
9 Schakowsky	Y	Y	Y	Y	Y	Y	N
10 Dold	N	Y	N	Y	N	N	Y
11 Kinzinger	N	N	N	N	N	N	Y
12 Costello	Y	N	N	Y	N	Y	Y
13 Biggert	N	N	N	N	N	N	Y
14 Hultgren	N	N	N	N	N	N	Y
15 Johnson	Y	Y	Y	N	N	Y	N

KEY	Republicans	Democrats	
Y Voted for (yea)	**X** Paired against	**C** Voted "present" to avoid possible conflict of interest
# Paired for	**–** Announced against	
+ Announced for	**P** Voted "present"	**?** Did not vote or otherwise make a position known
N Voted against (nay)		

	393	394	395	396	397	398	399
16 **Manzullo**	N	N	N	N	N	N	Y
17 **Schilling**	N	N	N	N	N	N	Y
18 **Schock**	N	N	N	N	N	N	Y
19 **Shimkus**	N	N	N	N	N	N	Y
INDIANA							
1 Visclosky	Y	Y	Y	Y	Y	Y	N
2 Donnelly	N	N	N	N	N	Y	Y
3 **Stutzman**	N	N	N	N	N	N	Y
4 **Rokita**	N	N	N	N	N	N	Y
5 **Burton**	?	?	N	N	N	N	?
6 **Pence**	N	N	N	N	N	N	Y
7 Carson	Y	Y	Y	Y	Y	Y	Y
8 **Bucshon**	N	N	N	N	N	N	Y
9 **Young**	N	N	N	N	N	N	Y
IOWA							
1 Braley	Y	Y	Y	Y	Y	Y	N
2 Loebsack	Y	Y	Y	Y	Y	Y	N
3 Boswell	Y	Y	Y	Y	N	Y	N
4 **Latham**	N	N	N	N	N	N	Y
5 **King**	N	N	N	N	N	N	Y
KANSAS							
1 **Huelskamp**	N	N	N	N	N	N	Y
2 **Jenkins**	N	N	N	N	N	N	Y
3 **Yoder**	N	N	N	N	N	N	Y
4 **Pompeo**	N	N	N	N	N	N	Y
KENTUCKY							
1 **Whitfield**	N	N	N	N	N	N	Y
2 **Guthrie**	N	N	N	N	N	N	Y
3 Yarmuth	Y	Y	Y	Y	Y	Y	N
4 **Davis**	N	N	N	N	N	N	Y
5 **Rogers**	N	N	N	N	N	N	Y
6 Chandler	Y	Y	Y	Y	N	Y	Y
LOUISIANA							
1 **Scalise**	N	N	N	N	N	N	Y
2 Richmond	Y	Y	Y	Y	Y	Y	N
3 **Landry**	N	N	N	N	N	N	Y
4 **Fleming**	N	N	N	N	N	N	Y
5 **Alexander**	N	N	N	N	N	N	Y
6 **Cassidy**	N	N	N	N	N	N	Y
7 **Boustany**	N	N	N	N	N	N	Y
MAINE							
1 Pingree	Y	Y	Y	Y	Y	Y	N
2 Michaud	Y	Y	Y	Y	Y	Y	N
MARYLAND							
1 **Harris**	N	N	N	N	N	N	Y
2 Ruppersberger	Y	Y	Y	Y	Y	Y	N
3 Sarbanes	Y	Y	Y	Y	Y	Y	N
4 Edwards	Y	Y	Y	Y	Y	Y	N
5 Hoyer	Y	Y	Y	Y	Y	Y	N
6 **Bartlett**	N	N	N	N	N	N	Y
7 Cummings	Y	Y	Y	Y	Y	Y	N
8 Van Hollen	Y	Y	Y	Y	Y	Y	N
MASSACHUSETTS							
1 Olver	Y	Y	Y	Y	Y	Y	N
2 Neal	Y	Y	Y	Y	Y	Y	Y
3 McGovern	Y	Y	Y	Y	Y	Y	N
4 Frank	Y	Y	Y	Y	Y	Y	N
5 Tsongas	Y	Y	Y	Y	Y	Y	N
6 Tierney	Y	Y	Y	Y	Y	Y	N
7 Markey	Y	Y	Y	Y	Y	Y	N
8 Capuano	Y	Y	Y	Y	Y	Y	Y
9 Lynch	Y	Y	Y	Y	Y	Y	N
10 Keating	Y	Y	Y	Y	Y	Y	N
MICHIGAN							
1 **Benishek**	N	N	N	N	N	N	Y
2 **Huizenga**	N	N	N	N	N	N	Y
3 **Amash**	N	N	N	N	N	N	Y
4 **Camp**	N	N	N	N	N	N	Y
5 Kildee	Y	Y	Y	Y	Y	Y	N
6 **Upton**	N	N	N	N	N	N	Y
7 **Walberg**	N	N	N	N	N	N	Y
8 **Rogers**	N	N	N	N	N	N	Y
9 Peters	Y	Y	Y	Y	Y	Y	N
10 **Miller**	N	N	N	N	N	N	Y
11 **McCotter**	N	N	N	N	N	N	Y
12 Levin	Y	Y	Y	Y	Y	Y	N
13 Clarke	Y	Y	Y	Y	Y	Y	N
14 Conyers	Y	Y	Y	Y	Y	Y	N
15 Dingell	Y	N	Y	Y	Y	Y	N
MINNESOTA							
1 Walz	Y	Y	N	Y	Y	Y	Y
2 **Kline**	N	N	N	N	N	N	Y
3 **Paulsen**	N	N	N	N	N	N	Y
4 McCollum	Y	Y	Y	Y	Y	Y	N

	393	394	395	396	397	398	399
5 Ellison	Y	Y	Y	Y	Y	Y	N
6 **Bachmann**	N	N	N	N	N	N	Y
7 Peterson	N	N	N	N	N	Y	Y
8 **Cravaack**	N	N	N	N	N	N	Y
MISSISSIPPI							
1 **Nunnelee**	N	N	N	N	N	N	Y
2 Thompson	Y	Y	N	Y	Y	Y	N
3 **Harper**	N	N	N	N	N	N	Y
4 **Palazzo**	N	N	N	N	N	N	Y
MISSOURI							
1 Clay	Y	Y	Y	Y	Y	Y	N
2 **Akin**	N	N	N	N	N	N	Y
3 Carnahan	Y	Y	Y	Y	Y	Y	N
4 **Hartzler**	N	N	N	N	N	N	N
5 Cleaver	Y	Y	Y	Y	Y	Y	N
6 **Graves**	N	N	N	N	N	N	Y
7 **Long**	N	N	N	N	N	N	Y
8 **Emerson**	N	N	N	N	N	N	Y
9 **Luetkemeyer**	N	N	N	N	N	N	Y
MONTANA							
AL **Rehberg**	N	N	N	N	N	N	Y
NEBRASKA							
1 **Fortenberry**	N	N	N	N	N	N	Y
2 **Terry**	N	N	N	N	N	Y	Y
3 **Smith**	N	N	N	N	N	N	Y
NEVADA							
1 Berkley	Y	Y	Y	Y	Y	Y	Y
2 **Amodei**	N	N	N	N	N	N	Y
3 **Heck**	N	N	N	N	N	N	Y
NEW HAMPSHIRE							
1 **Guinta**	N	N	N	N	N	N	Y
2 **Bass**	N	N	Y	N	Y	N	Y
NEW JERSEY							
1 Andrews	Y	Y	N	Y	Y	Y	N
2 **LoBiondo**	N	N	N	N	Y	N	Y
3 **Runyan**	N	N	N	N	N	N	Y
4 **Smith**	N	N	N	N	Y	N	N
5 **Garrett**	N	N	N	N	N	N	Y
6 Pallone	Y	Y	Y	Y	Y	Y	N
7 **Lance**	N	N	N	N	N	Y	Y
8 Pascrell	Y	Y	Y	Y	Y	Y	N
9 Rothman	Y	Y	Y	Y	Y	Y	N
10 Vacant							
11 **Frelinghuysen**	N	N	Y	N	N	N	Y
12 Holt	Y	Y	Y	Y	Y	Y	N
13 Sires	Y	Y	Y	Y	Y	Y	N
NEW MEXICO							
1 Heinrich	Y	Y	Y	Y	Y	Y	N
2 **Pearce**	N	N	N	N	N	N	Y
3 Luján	Y	Y	Y	Y	Y	Y	N
NEW YORK							
1 Bishop	+	+	+	+	+	+	–
2 Israel	Y	Y	Y	Y	Y	Y	N
3 **King**	N	N	N	N	N	N	Y
4 McCarthy	Y	Y	Y	Y	Y	Y	N
5 Ackerman	Y	Y	Y	Y	Y	Y	N
6 Meeks	Y	Y	Y	Y	Y	Y	N
7 Crowley	Y	Y	Y	Y	Y	Y	N
8 Nadler	Y	Y	Y	Y	Y	Y	N
9 **Turner**	N	N	N	N	N	N	Y
10 Towns	Y	Y	Y	Y	Y	Y	N
11 Clarke	+	+	+	+	+	+	–
12 Velázquez	?	?	?	?	?	?	?
13 **Grimm**	N	N	N	N	N	N	Y
14 Maloney	Y	Y	Y	Y	Y	Y	N
15 Rangel	Y	Y	Y	Y	Y	Y	N
16 Serrano	Y	Y	Y	Y	Y	Y	N
17 Engel	Y	Y	Y	Y	Y	Y	N
18 Lowey	Y	Y	Y	Y	Y	Y	N
19 **Hayworth**	N	N	Y	N	N	N	Y
20 **Gibson**	Y	Y	N	N	N	Y	Y
21 Tonko	Y	Y	Y	Y	Y	Y	N
22 Hinchey	Y	Y	Y	Y	Y	Y	N
23 Owens	Y	N	N	N	Y	Y	Y
24 **Hanna**	N	N	N	N	N	Y	Y
25 **Buerkle**	N	N	N	N	N	N	Y
26 Hochul	Y	Y	N	N	Y	Y	Y
27 Higgins	Y	Y	Y	Y	Y	Y	N
28 Slaughter	Y	Y	Y	Y	Y	Y	N
29 **Reed**	N	N	N	N	N	N	Y
NORTH CAROLINA							
1 Butterfield	Y	Y	Y	Y	Y	Y	N
2 **Ellmers**	N	N	N	N	N	N	Y
3 **Jones**	N	N	N	N	Y	N	Y
4 Price	Y	Y	Y	Y	Y	Y	N

	393	394	395	396	397	398	399
5 **Foxx**	N	N	N	N	N	N	Y
6 **Coble**	N	N	N	N	N	N	Y
7 McIntyre	N	N	N	N	N	Y	Y
8 Kissell	N	N	Y	N	N	Y	Y
9 **Myrick**	N	N	N	N	N	N	Y
10 **McHenry**	N	N	N	N	N	N	Y
11 Shuler	N	Y	Y	Y	N	Y	Y
12 Watt	Y	Y	Y	Y	Y	Y	N
13 Miller	Y	Y	Y	Y	Y	Y	N
NORTH DAKOTA							
AL **Berg**	N	N	N	N	N	N	Y
OHIO							
1 **Chabot**	N	N	N	N	N	N	Y
2 **Schmidt**	N	N	N	N	N	N	Y
3 **Turner**	N	N	N	N	N	N	Y
4 **Jordan**	N	N	N	N	N	N	Y
5 **Latta**	N	N	N	N	N	N	Y
6 **Johnson**	N	N	N	N	N	N	Y
7 **Austria**	N	N	N	N	N	N	Y
8 **Boehner**							
9 Kaptur	N	Y	Y	Y	Y	Y	N
10 Kucinich	Y	Y	Y	Y	Y	Y	N
11 Fudge	Y	Y	Y	Y	Y	Y	N
12 **Tiberi**	N	N	N	N	N	N	Y
13 Sutton	Y	Y	Y	Y	Y	Y	N
14 **LaTourette**	N	N	N	N	N	N	Y
15 **Stivers**	N	N	N	N	N	N	Y
16 **Renacci**	N	N	N	N	N	N	Y
17 Ryan	Y	Y	Y	Y	Y	Y	N
18 **Gibbs**	N	N	N	N	N	N	Y
OKLAHOMA							
1 **Sullivan**	N	N	N	N	N	N	Y
2 Boren	N	N	N	N	N	N	Y
3 **Lucas**	N	N	N	N	N	N	Y
4 **Cole**	N	N	N	N	N	N	Y
5 **Lankford**	N	N	N	N	N	N	Y
OREGON							
1 Bonamici	Y	Y	Y	Y	Y	Y	N
2 **Walden**	N	N	N	N	N	N	Y
3 Blumenauer	Y	Y	Y	Y	Y	Y	N
4 DeFazio	Y	Y	Y	Y	Y	Y	N
5 Schrader	N	Y	Y	Y	N	Y	N
PENNSYLVANIA							
1 Brady	Y	Y	Y	Y	Y	Y	N
2 Fattah	Y	Y	Y	Y	Y	Y	N
3 **Kelly**	N	N	N	N	N	N	Y
4 Altmire	N	N	N	N	N	Y	Y
5 **Thompson**	N	N	N	N	N	N	Y
6 **Gerlach**	N	N	N	N	N	N	Y
7 **Meehan**	N	N	N	N	N	N	Y
8 **Fitzpatrick**	N	Y	N	N	Y	N	Y
9 **Shuster**	N	N	N	N	N	N	Y
10 **Marino**	N	N	N	N	N	N	Y
11 **Barletta**	N	N	N	N	N	N	Y
12 Critz	N	Y	Y	N	N	Y	Y
13 Schwartz	Y	Y	Y	Y	Y	Y	N
14 Doyle	Y	Y	Y	Y	Y	Y	N
15 **Dent**	N	Y	N	N	N	N	Y
16 **Pitts**	N	N	N	N	N	N	Y
17 Holden	N	Y	Y	N	N	Y	Y
18 **Murphy**	N	N	N	N	N	N	Y
19 **Platts**	N	N	N	N	Y	N	Y
RHODE ISLAND							
1 Cicilline	Y	Y	Y	Y	Y	Y	N
2 Langevin	Y	Y	Y	Y	Y	Y	N
SOUTH CAROLINA							
1 **Scott**	N	N	N	N	N	N	Y
2 **Wilson**	N	N	N	N	N	N	Y
3 **Duncan**	N	N	N	N	N	N	Y
4 **Gowdy**	N	N	N	N	N	N	Y
5 **Mulvaney**	N	N	N	N	N	N	Y
6 Clyburn	Y	Y	N	Y	Y	Y	N
SOUTH DAKOTA							
AL **Noem**	N	N	N	N	N	N	Y
TENNESSEE							
1 **Roe**	N	N	N	N	N	N	Y
2 **Duncan**	N	N	N	N	N	N	Y
3 **Fleischmann**	N	N	N	N	N	N	Y
4 **DesJarlais**	N	N	N	N	N	N	Y
5 Cooper	Y	Y	Y	Y	N	Y	N
6 **Black**	N	N	N	N	N	N	Y
7 **Blackburn**	N	N	N	N	N	N	Y
8 **Fincher**	N	N	N	N	N	N	Y
9 Cohen	Y	Y	Y	Y	Y	Y	N

	393	394	395	396	397	398	399
TEXAS							
1 **Gohmert**	N	N	N	N	N	N	Y
2 **Poe**	?	N	N	N	N	N	Y
3 **Johnson, S.**	N	N	N	N	N	N	Y
4 **Hall**	N	N	N	N	N	N	Y
5 **Hensarling**	N	N	N	N	N	N	Y
6 **Barton**	N	N	N	N	N	N	Y
7 **Culberson**	N	N	N	N	N	N	Y
8 **Brady**	N	N	N	N	N	N	Y
9 Green, A.	Y	Y	Y	N	N	Y	N
10 **McCaul**	N	N	N	N	N	N	Y
11 **Conaway**	N	N	N	N	N	N	Y
12 **Granger**	N	N	N	N	N	N	Y
13 **Thornberry**	N	N	N	N	N	N	Y
14 **Paul**	N	N	N	N	N	N	Y
15 Hinojosa	Y	Y	Y	Y	N	Y	N
16 Reyes	Y	Y	Y	Y	Y	Y	N
17 **Flores**	N	N	N	N	N	N	Y
18 Jackson Lee	?	?	?	?	?	?	?
19 **Neugebauer**	N	N	N	N	N	N	Y
20 Gonzalez	Y	Y	Y	Y	N	Y	N
21 **Smith**	N	N	N	N	N	N	Y
22 **Olson**	N	N	N	N	N	N	Y
23 **Canseco**	N	N	N	N	N	N	Y
24 **Marchant**	N	N	N	N	N	N	Y
25 Doggett	?	Y	?	Y	N	Y	N
26 **Burgess**	N	N	N	N	N	Y	Y
27 **Farenthold**	N	N	N	N	N	N	Y
28 Cuellar	Y	Y	Y	N	N	Y	Y
29 Green, G.	N	Y	Y	N	N	Y	N
30 Johnson, E.	Y	Y	N	Y	Y	Y	N
31 **Carter**	N	N	N	N	N	N	Y
32 **Sessions**	N	N	N	N	N	N	Y
UTAH							
1 **Bishop**	N	N	N	N	N	N	Y
2 Matheson	N	N	Y	N	N	Y	Y
3 **Chaffetz**	N	N	N	N	N	N	Y
VERMONT							
AL Welch	Y	Y	Y	Y	Y	Y	Y
VIRGINIA							
1 **Wittman**	N	N	N	N	N	N	Y
2 **Rigell**	N	N	N	N	N	N	Y
3 Scott	Y	Y	Y	Y	Y	Y	N
4 **Forbes**	N	N	N	N	N	N	Y
5 **Hurt**	N	N	N	N	N	N	Y
6 **Goodlatte**	N	N	N	N	N	N	Y
7 **Cantor**	N	N	N	N	N	N	Y
8 Moran	Y	Y	Y	Y	Y	Y	N
9 **Griffith**	N	N	N	N	N	N	Y
10 **Wolf**	N	N	Y	N	N	N	Y
11 Connolly	Y	Y	Y	Y	Y	Y	N
WASHINGTON							
1 Vacant							
2 Larsen	Y	Y	Y	N	Y	Y	N
3 **Herrera Beutler**	N	N	N	N	N	N	N
4 **Hastings**	N	N	N	N	N	N	Y
5 **McMorris Rodgers**	N	N	N	N	N	N	Y
6 Dicks	Y	Y	Y	Y	Y	Y	N
7 McDermott	Y	Y	Y	Y	Y	Y	N
8 **Reichert**	N	N	Y	N	Y	N	Y
9 Smith	Y	Y	Y	Y	Y	Y	N
WEST VIRGINIA							
1 **McKinley**	N	N	N	N	N	N	Y
2 **Capito**	N	N	N	N	N	N	Y
3 Rahall	Y	Y	N	Y	Y	Y	Y
WISCONSIN							
1 **Ryan**	N	N	N	N	N	N	Y
2 Baldwin	Y	Y	Y	Y	Y	Y	N
3 Kind	Y	Y	Y	Y	Y	Y	N
4 Moore	Y	Y	?	Y	Y	Y	N
5 **Sensenbrenner**	N	N	N	N	N	N	Y
6 **Petri**	N	N	N	N	N	N	Y
7 **Duffy**	N	N	N	N	N	N	Y
8 **Ribble**	N	N	N	N	N	N	Y
WYOMING							
AL **Lummis**	N	N	N	N	N	N	Y

IN THE HOUSE | By Vote Number

400. HR 4480. Domestic Energy Production/Oil and Gas
Exportation. Markey, D-Mass., amendment that would bar the export of oil and gas produced as a result of the requirements imposed by the bill. Rejected in Committee of the Whole 161-256: R 9-225; D 152-31. June 21, 2012.

401. HR 4480. Domestic Energy Production/Revenue Cap.
Landry, R-La., amendment that would raise the cap on annual revenue shared among the Gulf states with energy-producing leases from $500 million to $750 million starting in fiscal 2023. Adopted in Committee of the Whole 244-173: R 221-13; D 23-160. June 21, 2012.

402. HR 4480. Domestic Energy Production/Virginia Outer
Continental Shelf Lease. Rigell, R-Va., amendment that would require the Interior Department to make specific outer continental shelf lands off the coast of Virginia available for leasing within one year of the bill's enactment. It would bar any lease-related activity from interfering with military operations within the area and provide the federal government with the authority to declare portions of the lease as "national defense areas" and withdraw them from energy-related activities. Adopted in Committee of the Whole 263-146: R 230-1; D 33-145. June 21, 2012.

403. HR 4480. Domestic Energy Production/Gulf of Mexico Drilling.
Holt, D-N.J., amendment that would prevent lessees of certain outer continental shelf lands located within the Gulf of Mexico who were granted royalty relief under the terms of a 1994 law from receiving new leases under the provisions of the underlying bill unless they renegotiate their current leases to require royalty payments if the price of oil or natural gas achieves certain thresholds. Rejected in Committee of the Whole 168-250: R 7-228; D 161-22. June 21, 2012.

404. HR 4480. Domestic Energy Production/Meteorological
Permits. Wittman, R-Va., amendment that would require the Interior Department to complete review of offshore meteorological permits within 30 days of receiving the application. It would waive the environmental review requirements of the National Environmental Policy Act regarding the issuance of such permits. Adopted in Committee of the Whole 256-161: R 232-4; D 24-157. June 21, 2012.

405. HR 4480. Domestic Energy Production/Gas Price Analysis.
Bass, D-Calif., amendment that would require the interagency committee created by the bill to include an analysis of how to limit gasoline price fluctuations and supply disruptions in the oil market through reducing U.S. dependence on oil. Rejected in Committee of the Whole 186-233: R 8-228; D 178-5. June 21, 2012.

	400	401	402	403	404	405
ALABAMA						
1 Bonner	N	Y	Y	N	Y	N
2 Roby	N	Y	Y	N	Y	N
3 Rogers	N	Y	Y	N	Y	N
4 Aderholt	N	Y	Y	N	Y	N
5 Brooks	N	Y	Y	N	Y	N
6 Bachus	N	?	Y	N	Y	N
7 Sewell	Y	Y	N	Y	N	Y
ALASKA						
AL Young	N	Y	Y	N	Y	N
ARIZONA						
1 Gosar	N	Y	Y	N	Y	N
2 Franks	N	Y	Y	N	Y	N
3 Quayle	N	Y	Y	N	Y	N
4 Pastor	Y	N	N	Y	N	Y
5 Schweikert	N	Y	Y	N	Y	N
6 Flake	N	Y	Y	N	Y	N
7 Grijalva	Y	N	N	Y	N	Y
8 Barber	Y	N	N	Y	N	Y
ARKANSAS						
1 Crawford	N	Y	Y	N	Y	N
2 Griffin	N	Y	Y	N	Y	N
3 Womack	N	Y	Y	N	Y	N
4 Ross	N	Y	Y	N	Y	N
CALIFORNIA						
1 Thompson	Y	N	N	Y	N	Y
2 Herger	N	Y	Y	N	Y	N
3 Lungren	N	Y	Y	N	Y	N
4 McClintock	N	N	Y	N	Y	N
5 Matsui	Y	N	N	Y	N	Y
6 Woolsey	Y	N	N	Y	N	Y
7 Miller, George	Y	N	N	Y	N	Y
8 Pelosi	Y	N	N	Y	N	Y
9 Lee	Y	N	N	Y	N	Y
10 Garamendi	Y	N	N	Y	Y	Y
11 McNerney	Y	N	Y	Y	N	Y
12 Speier	Y	N	N	Y	N	Y
13 Stark	Y	N	N	Y	N	Y
14 Eshoo	Y	N	N	Y	N	Y
15 Honda	Y	N	N	Y	N	Y
16 Lofgren	Y	N	N	Y	N	Y
17 Farr	Y	N	N	Y	N	Y
18 Cardoza	Y	N	Y	N	Y	Y
19 Denham	N	Y	Y	N	Y	N
20 Costa	Y	N	Y	N	Y	Y
21 Nunes	N	Y	Y	N	Y	N
22 McCarthy	N	Y	Y	N	Y	N
23 Capps	Y	N	N	Y	N	Y
24 Gallegly	?	?	?	?	?	?
25 McKeon	N	Y	Y	N	Y	N
26 Dreier	N	Y	Y	N	Y	N
27 Sherman	Y	N	N	Y	N	Y
28 Berman	Y	N	N	Y	N	Y
29 Schiff	Y	N	N	Y	N	Y
30 Waxman	Y	N	N	Y	N	Y
31 Becerra	Y	N	?	Y	N	Y
32 Chu	Y	N	N	Y	N	Y
33 Bass	Y	N	?	Y	N	Y
34 Roybal-Allard	Y	N	N	Y	N	Y
35 Waters	Y	N	N	Y	N	Y
36 Hahn	Y	N	N	Y	N	Y
37 Richardson	Y	N	N	N	N	Y
38 Napolitano	Y	N	N	Y	–	Y
39 Sánchez, Linda	?	?	?	?	?	?
40 Royce	N	N	Y	N	Y	N
41 Lewis	?	?	?	?	?	?
42 Miller, Gary	?	?	?	?	?	?
43 Baca	Y	N	N	Y	N	Y
44 Calvert	N	Y	Y	N	Y	N
45 Bono Mack	N	Y	Y	N	Y	N
46 Rohrabacher	N	Y	Y	N	Y	N
47 Sanchez, Loretta	Y	N	N	Y	N	Y
48 Campbell	N	N	Y	N	Y	N
49 Issa	N	Y	Y	N	Y	N
50 Bilbray	N	Y	?	N	Y	N
51 Filner	+	–	–	+	–	+
52 Hunter	N	Y	Y	N	Y	N
53 Davis	Y	N	N	Y	N	Y

	400	401	402	403	404	405
COLORADO						
1 DeGette	Y	N	N	Y	N	Y
2 Polis	N	N	N	Y	N	Y
3 Tipton	N	Y	Y	N	Y	N
4 Gardner	N	Y	Y	N	Y	N
5 Lamborn	N	Y	Y	N	Y	N
6 Coffman	N	Y	Y	N	Y	N
7 Perlmutter	N	N	Y	Y	Y	Y
CONNECTICUT						
1 Larson	Y	Y	N	Y	N	Y
2 Courtney	Y	N	N	Y	N	Y
3 DeLauro	Y	N	N	Y	N	Y
4 Himes	N	N	N	Y	N	Y
5 Murphy	Y	N	N	Y	N	Y
DELAWARE						
AL Carney	Y	N	N	Y	N	Y
FLORIDA						
1 Miller	?	?	?	?	?	?
2 Southerland	N	Y	Y	N	Y	N
3 Brown	N	Y	N	Y	N	Y
4 Crenshaw	N	Y	Y	N	Y	N
5 Nugent	N	Y	Y	N	Y	N
6 Stearns	N	Y	Y	N	Y	N
7 Mica	N	Y	Y	N	Y	N
8 Webster	N	Y	Y	N	Y	N
9 Bilirakis	N	Y	Y	N	Y	N
10 Young	N	Y	Y	Y	Y	N
11 Castor	Y	N	N	Y	N	Y
12 Ross	N	Y	Y	N	Y	N
13 Buchanan	N	Y	Y	Y	Y	N
14 Mack	?	?	?	?	?	?
15 Posey	N	Y	Y	N	Y	N
16 Rooney	N	Y	Y	N	Y	N
17 Wilson	Y	N	N	Y	N	Y
18 Ros-Lehtinen	N	Y	Y	N	Y	N
19 Deutch	Y	N	N	Y	N	Y
20 Wasserman Schultz	Y	N	N	Y	N	Y
21 Diaz-Balart	N	Y	Y	N	Y	N
22 West	N	Y	Y	N	Y	N
23 Hastings	Y	N	N	Y	N	Y
24 Adams	N	Y	Y	N	Y	N
25 Rivera	N	Y	Y	N	Y	N
GEORGIA						
1 Kingston	N	Y	Y	N	Y	N
2 Bishop	N	N	Y	N	Y	Y
3 Westmoreland	N	Y	Y	N	Y	N
4 Johnson	Y	N	N	Y	N	Y
5 Lewis	Y	N	N	Y	N	Y
6 Price	N	Y	Y	N	Y	N
7 Woodall	N	Y	Y	N	Y	N
8 Scott, A.	N	Y	Y	N	Y	N
9 Graves	N	Y	Y	N	Y	N
10 Broun	N	Y	Y	N	Y	N
11 Gingrey	N	Y	Y	N	Y	N
12 Barrow	Y	N	Y	N	Y	Y
13 Scott, D.	Y	N	Y	N	Y	N
HAWAII						
1 Hanabusa	Y	Y	N	Y	N	Y
2 Hirono	Y	N	N	Y	N	Y
IDAHO						
1 Labrador	N	Y	Y	N	Y	N
2 Simpson	N	Y	?	N	Y	N
ILLINOIS						
1 Rush	Y	N	N	Y	N	Y
2 Jackson	?	?	?	?	?	?
3 Lipinski	Y	N	Y	N	Y	N
4 Gutierrez	Y	N	N	Y	N	Y
5 Quigley	Y	N	N	Y	N	Y
6 Roskam	N	Y	Y	N	Y	N
7 Davis	Y	Y	N	Y	N	Y
8 Walsh	N	Y	Y	N	Y	N
9 Schakowsky	Y	N	N	Y	N	Y
10 Dold	N	Y	Y	N	Y	N
11 Kinzinger	N	Y	Y	N	Y	N
12 Costello	N	N	Y	Y	Y	Y
13 Biggert	N	Y	Y	N	Y	N
14 Hultgren	N	Y	Y	N	Y	N
15 Johnson	N	Y	Y	N	Y	N

	400	401	402	403	404	405
16 **Manzullo**	N	Y	Y	N	Y	N
17 **Schilling**	N	N	Y	N	Y	Y
18 **Schock**	N	Y	Y	N	Y	N
19 **Shimkus**	N	Y	Y	N	Y	N
INDIANA						
1 Visclosky	N	N	N	Y	N	Y
2 Donnelly	N	N	Y	N	N	Y
3 **Stutzman**	N	Y	Y	N	Y	N
4 **Rokita**	N	Y	Y	N	Y	N
5 **Burton**	?	?	?	?	Y	N
6 **Pence**	N	Y	Y	N	Y	N
7 Carson	Y	N	N	Y	N	Y
8 **Bucshon**	N	Y	Y	N	Y	N
9 **Young**	N	N	Y	N	Y	N
IOWA						
1 Braley	Y	N	N	Y	?	Y
2 Loebsack	Y	N	Y	Y	Y	Y
3 Boswell	Y	N	Y	Y	Y	Y
4 **Latham**	N	Y	Y	N	Y	N
5 **King**	N	Y	Y	N	Y	N
KANSAS						
1 **Huelskamp**	N	Y	Y	N	Y	N
2 **Jenkins**	N	Y	Y	N	Y	N
3 **Yoder**	N	Y	Y	N	Y	N
4 **Pompeo**	N	Y	Y	N	Y	N
KENTUCKY						
1 **Whitfield**	N	Y	Y	N	N	N
2 **Guthrie**	N	Y	Y	N	Y	N
3 Yarmuth	Y	N	N	Y	N	Y
4 **Davis**	N	Y	Y	N	Y	N
5 **Rogers**	N	Y	Y	N	Y	N
6 Chandler	Y	N	Y	N	Y	Y
LOUISIANA						
1 **Scalise**	N	Y	Y	N	Y	N
2 Richmond	N	Y	Y	Y	Y	Y
3 **Landry**	N	Y	Y	N	Y	N
4 **Fleming**	N	Y	Y	N	Y	N
5 **Alexander**	N	Y	Y	N	Y	N
6 **Cassidy**	N	Y	Y	N	Y	N
7 **Boustany**	N	Y	Y	N	Y	N
MAINE						
1 Pingree	Y	N	N	Y	N	Y
2 Michaud	Y	N	N	Y	N	Y
MARYLAND						
1 **Harris**	N	Y	Y	N	N	N
2 Ruppersberger	Y	N	N	Y	N	Y
3 Sarbanes	Y	N	N	Y	N	Y
4 Edwards	Y	N	N	Y	N	Y
5 Hoyer	Y	N	N	Y	N	Y
6 **Bartlett**	N	Y	Y	N	Y	Y
7 Cummings	Y	Y	N	Y	N	Y
8 Van Hollen	Y	N	N	Y	N	Y
MASSACHUSETTS						
1 Olver	Y	N	N	Y	N	Y
2 Neal	Y	N	N	Y	N	Y
3 McGovern	Y	N	N	Y	N	Y
4 Frank	N	N	N	Y	N	Y
5 Tsongas	Y	N	N	Y	N	Y
6 Tierney	Y	N	N	Y	N	Y
7 Markey	Y	N	N	Y	N	Y
8 Capuano	Y	N	N	Y	N	Y
9 Lynch	Y	N	N	Y	N	Y
10 Keating	Y	N	N	Y	N	Y
MICHIGAN						
1 **Benishek**	N	Y	Y	N	Y	N
2 **Huizenga**	N	Y	Y	N	Y	N
3 **Amash**	N	Y	Y	N	Y	N
4 **Camp**	N	Y	Y	N	Y	N
5 Kildee	Y	N	N	Y	N	Y
6 **Upton**	N	Y	Y	N	Y	N
7 **Walberg**	N	Y	Y	N	Y	N
8 **Rogers**	N	Y	Y	N	Y	N
9 Peters	Y	N	N	Y	N	Y
10 **Miller**	N	Y	Y	N	Y	N
11 **McCotter**	N	Y	Y	N	Y	N
12 Levin	Y	N	N	Y	N	Y
13 Clarke	Y	N	N	Y	N	Y
14 Conyers	Y	N	N	Y	N	Y
15 Dingell	N	Y	N	Y	N	Y
MINNESOTA						
1 Walz	Y	Y	N	Y	N	Y
2 **Kline**	N	Y	Y	N	Y	N
3 **Paulsen**	N	Y	Y	N	Y	N
4 McCollum	Y	N	N	Y	N	Y

	400	401	402	403	404	405
5 Ellison	Y	N	N	Y	N	Y
6 **Bachmann**	N	Y	Y	N	Y	N
7 Peterson	N	N	Y	N	Y	N
8 **Cravaack**	N	Y	Y	N	Y	N
MISSISSIPPI						
1 **Nunnelee**	N	Y	Y	N	Y	N
2 Thompson	N	Y	Y	Y	N	Y
3 **Harper**	N	Y	Y	N	Y	N
4 **Palazzo**	N	Y	Y	N	Y	N
MISSOURI						
1 Clay	Y	N	N	Y	N	Y
2 **Akin**	N	Y	Y	N	Y	N
3 Carnahan	Y	N	N	Y	N	Y
4 **Hartzler**	N	Y	Y	N	Y	N
5 Cleaver	Y	N	Y	Y	Y	Y
6 **Graves**	N	Y	Y	N	Y	N
7 **Long**	N	N	Y	N	Y	N
8 **Emerson**	N	Y	Y	N	Y	N
9 **Luetkemeyer**	N	Y	Y	N	Y	N
MONTANA						
AL **Rehberg**	N	Y	Y	N	Y	N
NEBRASKA						
1 **Fortenberry**	Y	Y	Y	Y	Y	Y
2 **Terry**	N	Y	Y	N	Y	N
3 **Smith**	N	Y	Y	N	Y	N
NEVADA						
1 Berkley	Y	N	N	Y	N	Y
2 **Amodei**	N	Y	Y	N	Y	N
3 **Heck**	N	Y	Y	N	Y	N
NEW HAMPSHIRE						
1 **Guinta**	N	Y	Y	N	Y	N
2 **Bass**	N	N	Y	N	Y	N
NEW JERSEY						
1 Andrews	Y	N	N	Y	N	Y
2 **LoBiondo**	Y	N	Y	Y	Y	N
3 **Runyan**	N	Y	Y	N	Y	N
4 **Smith**	Y	N	Y	N	Y	N
5 **Garrett**	N	Y	Y	N	Y	N
6 Pallone	Y	N	N	Y	N	Y
7 **Lance**	N	Y	Y	N	Y	N
8 Pascrell	Y	N	N	Y	N	Y
9 Rothman	Y	N	N	Y	N	Y
10 Vacant						
11 **Frelinghuysen**	N	Y	Y	N	Y	N
12 Holt	Y	N	N	Y	N	Y
13 Sires	Y	N	N	Y	N	Y
NEW MEXICO						
1 Heinrich	N	N	Y	Y	N	Y
2 **Pearce**	N	Y	Y	N	Y	N
3 Luján	N	N	?	Y	N	Y
NEW YORK						
1 Bishop	+	–	–	+	?	+
2 Israel	Y	N	N	Y	N	Y
3 **King**	N	Y	Y	N	Y	N
4 McCarthy	Y	N	N	Y	N	Y
5 Ackerman	Y	N	N	Y	N	Y
6 Meeks	Y	N	N	Y	N	Y
7 Crowley	Y	N	N	Y	N	Y
8 Nadler	Y	N	N	Y	N	Y
9 **Turner**	N	Y	?	N	Y	N
10 Towns	Y	N	N	Y	N	Y
11 Clarke	+	–	–	+	–	+
12 Velázquez	?	?	?	?	?	?
13 **Grimm**	N	Y	Y	N	Y	N
14 Maloney	Y	N	N	Y	N	Y
15 Rangel	Y	?	?	?	N	Y
16 Serrano	Y	N	?	Y	N	Y
17 Engel	Y	N	N	Y	N	Y
18 Lowey	Y	N	N	Y	N	Y
19 **Hayworth**	N	Y	Y	N	Y	N
20 **Gibson**	Y	N	Y	N	Y	Y
21 Tonko	Y	N	N	Y	N	Y
22 Hinchey	Y	N	N	Y	N	Y
23 Owens	Y	N	Y	Y	N	Y
24 **Hanna**	N	N	Y	N	Y	N
25 **Buerkle**	N	Y	Y	N	Y	N
26 Hochul	Y	N	Y	N	Y	Y
27 Higgins	Y	N	N	Y	N	Y
28 Slaughter	Y	N	N	Y	N	Y
29 **Reed**	N	Y	Y	N	Y	N
NORTH CAROLINA						
1 Butterfield	N	N	N	Y	N	Y
2 **Ellmers**	N	Y	Y	N	Y	N
3 **Jones**	Y	Y	N	Y	N	N
4 Price	Y	N	N	Y	N	Y

	400	401	402	403	404	405
5 **Foxx**	N	Y	Y	N	Y	N
6 **Coble**	N	Y	Y	N	Y	N
7 McIntyre	Y	Y	N	N	N	Y
8 Kissell	Y	N	N	N	N	Y
9 **Myrick**	N	Y	Y	N	Y	N
10 **McHenry**	N	Y	Y	N	Y	N
11 Shuler	N	N	Y	N	Y	N
12 Watt	?	N	N	Y	N	?
13 Miller	Y	N	N	Y	N	Y
NORTH DAKOTA						
AL **Berg**	N	Y	Y	N	Y	N
OHIO						
1 **Chabot**	N	Y	Y	N	Y	Y
2 **Schmidt**	N	Y	Y	N	Y	N
3 **Turner**	N	Y	Y	N	Y	N
4 **Jordan**	N	Y	Y	N	Y	N
5 **Latta**	N	Y	Y	N	Y	N
6 **Johnson**	N	Y	Y	N	Y	N
7 **Austria**	N	Y	Y	N	Y	N
8 **Boehner**						
9 Kaptur	Y	N	N	Y	N	Y
10 Kucinich	Y	N	N	Y	N	Y
11 Fudge	Y	N	N	Y	N	Y
12 **Tiberi**	N	Y	Y	N	Y	N
13 Sutton	Y	N	N	Y	N	Y
14 **LaTourette**	N	Y	Y	N	Y	N
15 **Stivers**	N	Y	Y	N	Y	N
16 **Renacci**	N	Y	Y	N	Y	N
17 Ryan	N	N	N	Y	N	Y
18 **Gibbs**	N	Y	Y	N	Y	N
OKLAHOMA						
1 **Sullivan**	N	Y	Y	N	Y	N
2 Boren	N	Y	Y	N	Y	N
3 **Lucas**	N	Y	Y	N	Y	N
4 **Cole**	N	Y	Y	N	Y	N
5 **Lankford**	N	Y	Y	N	Y	N
OREGON						
1 Bonamici	Y	N	N	Y	N	Y
2 **Walden**	N	Y	Y	N	Y	N
3 Blumenauer	Y	N	N	Y	N	Y
4 DeFazio	Y	N	N	Y	N	Y
5 Schrader	Y	N	N	Y	N	Y
PENNSYLVANIA						
1 Brady	Y	N	N	Y	N	Y
2 Fattah	Y	N	N	Y	N	Y
3 **Kelly**	N	Y	Y	N	Y	N
4 Altmire	Y	Y	Y	N	Y	Y
5 **Thompson**	N	Y	Y	N	Y	N
6 **Gerlach**	Y	Y	Y	N	Y	N
7 **Meehan**	N	Y	Y	N	Y	N
8 **Fitzpatrick**	Y	Y	Y	Y	Y	Y
9 **Shuster**	N	Y	Y	N	Y	N
10 **Marino**	N	Y	Y	N	Y	N
11 **Barletta**	N	Y	Y	N	Y	N
12 Critz	N	N	Y	N	Y	Y
13 Schwartz	Y	N	N	Y	N	Y
14 Doyle	N	N	N	Y	N	Y
15 **Dent**	Y	Y	Y	N	Y	N
16 **Pitts**	N	Y	Y	N	Y	N
17 Holden	N	N	Y	Y	Y	Y
18 **Murphy**	N	Y	Y	N	Y	N
19 **Platts**	Y	Y	Y	Y	Y	N
RHODE ISLAND						
1 Cicilline	Y	N	N	Y	N	Y
2 Langevin	Y	N	N	Y	N	Y
SOUTH CAROLINA						
1 **Scott**	N	Y	Y	N	Y	N
2 **Wilson**	N	Y	Y	N	Y	N
3 **Duncan**	N	Y	Y	N	Y	N
4 **Gowdy**	N	Y	Y	N	Y	N
5 **Mulvaney**	N	Y	Y	N	Y	N
6 Clyburn	Y	Y	N	Y	N	Y
SOUTH DAKOTA						
AL **Noem**	N	Y	Y	N	Y	N
TENNESSEE						
1 **Roe**	N	Y	Y	N	Y	N
2 **Duncan**	N	Y	Y	N	Y	N
3 **Fleischmann**	N	Y	Y	N	Y	N
4 **DesJarlais**	N	Y	Y	N	Y	N
5 Cooper	N	N	N	Y	N	Y
6 **Black**	N	Y	Y	N	Y	N
7 **Blackburn**	N	Y	Y	N	Y	N
8 **Fincher**	N	Y	Y	N	Y	N
9 Cohen	Y	N	N	Y	N	Y

	400	401	402	403	404	405
TEXAS						
1 **Gohmert**	N	Y	Y	N	Y	N
2 **Poe**	N	Y	Y	N	Y	N
3 **Johnson, S.**	N	Y	Y	N	Y	N
4 **Hall**	N	Y	Y	N	Y	N
5 **Hensarling**	N	Y	Y	N	Y	N
6 **Barton**	N	Y	Y	N	Y	N
7 **Culberson**	N	Y	Y	N	Y	N
8 **Brady**	N	Y	Y	N	Y	N
9 Green, A.	N	Y	Y	N	N	Y
10 **McCaul**	N	Y	Y	N	Y	N
11 **Conaway**	N	Y	Y	N	Y	N
12 **Granger**	N	Y	Y	N	Y	N
13 **Thornberry**	N	Y	Y	N	Y	N
14 **Paul**	N	N	Y	N	Y	N
15 Hinojosa	Y	Y	Y	N	Y	Y
16 Reyes	Y	N	N	Y	N	Y
17 **Flores**	N	Y	Y	N	Y	N
18 Jackson Lee	?	?	?	?	?	?
19 **Neugebauer**	N	Y	Y	N	Y	N
20 Gonzalez	N	Y	Y	N	N	Y
21 **Smith**	N	Y	Y	N	Y	N
22 **Olson**	N	Y	Y	N	Y	N
23 **Canseco**	N	Y	Y	N	Y	N
24 **Marchant**	N	Y	Y	N	Y	N
25 Doggett	Y	Y	N	Y	N	Y
26 **Burgess**	N	Y	Y	N	Y	N
27 **Farenthold**	N	Y	Y	N	Y	N
28 Cuellar	N	Y	Y	N	Y	Y
29 Green, G.	N	Y	Y	N	Y	Y
30 Johnson, E.	N	Y	Y	Y	N	Y
31 **Carter**	N	Y	Y	N	Y	N
32 **Sessions**	N	Y	Y	N	Y	N
UTAH						
1 **Bishop**	N	Y	Y	N	Y	N
2 Matheson	N	Y	Y	N	Y	N
3 **Chaffetz**	N	Y	Y	N	Y	N
VERMONT						
AL Welch	Y	N	N	Y	N	Y
VIRGINIA						
1 **Wittman**	N	Y	Y	N	Y	N
2 **Rigell**	N	Y	Y	N	Y	N
3 Scott	Y	N	N	Y	N	Y
4 **Forbes**	N	Y	Y	N	Y	N
5 **Hurt**	N	Y	Y	N	Y	N
6 **Goodlatte**	N	Y	Y	N	Y	N
7 **Cantor**	N	Y	Y	N	Y	N
8 Moran	Y	N	N	Y	N	Y
9 **Griffith**	N	Y	Y	N	Y	N
10 **Wolf**	N	Y	Y	N	Y	N
11 Connolly	Y	N	N	Y	N	Y
WASHINGTON						
1 Vacant						
2 Larsen	N	N	N	N	N	Y
3 **Herrera Beutler**	?	Y	Y	N	Y	N
4 **Hastings**	N	Y	Y	N	Y	N
5 **McMorris Rodgers**	N	Y	Y	N	Y	N
6 Dicks	Y	N	?	Y	?	Y
7 McDermott	Y	N	N	Y	N	Y
8 **Reichert**	N	Y	Y	N	N	Y
9 Smith	Y	N	N	Y	N	Y
WEST VIRGINIA						
1 **McKinley**	N	Y	Y	N	Y	N
2 **Capito**	N	Y	Y	N	Y	N
3 Rahall	Y	N	N	Y	N	Y
WISCONSIN						
1 **Ryan**	N	Y	Y	N	Y	N
2 Baldwin	Y	N	N	Y	N	Y
3 Kind	Y	N	N	Y	N	Y
4 Moore	Y	N	N	Y	N	Y
5 **Sensenbrenner**	N	Y	Y	N	Y	N
6 **Petri**	N	Y	Y	N	Y	N
7 **Duffy**	N	Y	Y	N	Y	N
8 **Ribble**	N	Y	Y	N	Y	N
WYOMING						
AL **Lummis**	N	Y	?	N	Y	N

IN THE HOUSE | By Vote Number

406. HR 4480. **Domestic Energy Production/Feasibility Assessment.** Capps, D-Calif., amendment that would require a feasibility assessment of the bill's provisions regarding the interagency cost analysis of regulations. If it is determined that the analysis is infeasible, the six-month delay of EPA rules would not go into effect. Rejected in Committee of the Whole 162-254: R 1-234; D 161-20. June 21, 2012.

407. HR 4480. **Domestic Energy Production/Permit Approval Deadline.** Speier, D-Calif., amendment that would strike language in the bill to require that drilling permits be deemed approved after 60 days. Rejected in Committee of the Whole 162-255: R 1-234; D 161-21. June 21, 2012.

408. HR 4480. **Domestic Energy Production/CFTC Funding.** DeLauro, D-Conn., amendment that would require $128 million received from the sale of energy leases to be directed to the Commodity Futures Trading Commission to facilitate efforts to reduce speculation in energy markets. Rejected in Committee of the Whole 180-235: R 3-231; D 177-4. June 21, 2012.

409. HR 4480. **Domestic Energy Production/Recommit.** Slaughter, D-N.Y., motion to recommit the bill to the House Natural Resources Committee and report it back immediately with an amendment that would prohibit the major integrated oil companies from receiving new drilling leases authorized under the bill unless they agree to not claim certain tax benefits, including the percentage depletion allowance. Motion rejected 166-243: R 1-230; D 165-13. June 21, 2012.

410. HR 4480. **Domestic Energy Production/Passage.** Passage of the bill that would delay the implementation of certain EPA regulations and create an interagency committee to review the impact of EPA rules on energy prices and the broader economy. The Interior Department would be required to develop a strategic plan for the nation's energy needs over 30 years and set domestic production goals to meet demand. It would require the department to ensure that at least 25 percent of eligible federal land is available for leasing each year. It also would increase the amount of federal land available for energy production and streamline the process for approving drilling permits. It would mandate an increase in oil and gas production equivalent to any release from the Strategic Petroleum Reserve and set new standards for judicial review of civil actions filed against energy lease sales or drilling permits. It also would impose new fees associated with filing a protest against a lease sale or permit. Passed 248-163: R 229-5; D 19-158. A "nay" was a vote in support of the president's position. June 21, 2012.

411. HR 4348. **Surface Transportation Extension/Motion to Instruct.** McKinley, R-W.Va., motion to instruct conferees to insist on House-passed provisions that would explicitly allow states to create permitting programs to regulate how waste from coal combustion is managed and disposed. Motion agreed to 260-138: R 221-9; D 39-129. June 21, 2012.

	406	407	408	409	410	411
ALABAMA						
1 Bonner	N	N	N	N	Y	Y
2 Roby	N	N	N	N	Y	Y
3 Rogers	N	N	N	N	N	Y
4 Aderholt	N	N	N	N	Y	Y
5 Brooks	N	N	N	N	Y	Y
6 Bachus	N	N	N	N	Y	Y
7 Sewell	Y	Y	Y	?	–	N
ALASKA						
AL Young	N	N	N	N	Y	N
ARIZONA						
1 Gosar	N	N	N	N	Y	Y
2 Franks	N	N	N	N	Y	Y
3 Quayle	N	N	N	N	Y	Y
4 Pastor	Y	Y	Y	Y	N	Y
5 Schweikert	N	N	N	?	Y	Y
6 Flake	N	N	N	N	Y	Y
7 Grijalva	Y	Y	Y	Y	N	N
8 Barber	Y	Y	Y	Y	N	Y
ARKANSAS						
1 Crawford	N	N	N	N	Y	Y
2 Griffin	N	N	N	N	Y	Y
3 Womack	N	N	N	N	Y	Y
4 Ross	N	N	N	N	Y	Y
CALIFORNIA						
1 Thompson	Y	Y	Y	Y	N	N
2 Herger	?	?	?	N	Y	Y
3 Lungren	N	N	N	N	Y	Y
4 McClintock	N	N	N	N	Y	Y
5 Matsui	Y	Y	Y	Y	N	N
6 Woolsey	Y	Y	Y	Y	N	N
7 Miller, George	Y	Y	?	?	?	?
8 Pelosi	Y	Y	Y	Y	N	N
9 Lee	Y	Y	Y	Y	N	N
10 Garamendi	Y	Y	Y	Y	N	N
11 McNerney	Y	Y	Y	Y	N	N
12 Speier	Y	Y	Y	Y	–	–
13 Stark	Y	Y	Y	Y	N	N
14 Eshoo	Y	Y	Y	Y	N	?
15 Honda	Y	Y	Y	Y	N	N
16 Lofgren	Y	Y	Y	Y	N	?
17 Farr	Y	Y	Y	Y	N	N
18 Cardoza	N	N	Y	?	?	?
19 Denham	N	N	N	N	Y	N
20 Costa	N	N	Y	N	Y	N
21 Nunes	N	N	N	N	Y	Y
22 McCarthy	N	N	N	N	Y	Y
23 Capps	Y	Y	Y	Y	N	N
24 Gallegly	?	?	?	?	?	?
25 McKeon	N	N	N	N	Y	Y
26 Dreier	N	N	N	N	Y	Y
27 Sherman	Y	Y	Y	Y	N	N
28 Berman	Y	Y	Y	Y	N	N
29 Schiff	Y	Y	Y	Y	N	N
30 Waxman	Y	Y	Y	Y	N	N
31 Becerra	Y	Y	Y	Y	N	N
32 Chu	Y	Y	Y	Y	N	N
33 Bass	Y	Y	Y	Y	N	N
34 Roybal-Allard	Y	Y	Y	Y	N	N
35 Waters	Y	Y	Y	Y	N	N
36 Hahn	Y	Y	Y	Y	N	N
37 Richardson	Y	Y	Y	Y	N	N
38 Napolitano	?	Y	Y	Y	N	N
39 Sánchez, Linda	?	?	?	?	?	?
40 Royce	N	N	N	N	Y	Y
41 Lewis	?	?	?	?	?	?
42 Miller, Gary	?	?	?	?	?	?
43 Baca	Y	Y	Y	Y	N	Y
44 Calvert	N	N	N	N	Y	Y
45 Bono Mack	N	N	N	N	Y	Y
46 Rohrabacher	N	N	N	N	Y	Y
47 Sanchez, Loretta	Y	Y	Y	Y	N	N
48 Campbell	N	N	N	N	Y	Y
49 Issa	N	N	N	N	Y	Y
50 Bilbray	N	N	N	N	Y	Y
51 Filner	+	+	+	+	–	–
52 Hunter	N	N	N	N	Y	Y
53 Davis	Y	Y	Y	Y	N	N
COLORADO						
1 DeGette	Y	Y	Y	Y	N	N
2 Polis	Y	Y	N	Y	N	N
3 Tipton	N	N	N	N	Y	Y
4 Gardner	N	N	N	N	Y	Y
5 Lamborn	N	N	N	N	Y	Y
6 Coffman	N	N	N	N	Y	Y
7 Perlmutter	Y	Y	Y	Y	N	Y
CONNECTICUT						
1 Larson	Y	Y	Y	Y	N	N
2 Courtney	Y	Y	Y	Y	N	N
3 DeLauro	Y	Y	Y	Y	N	N
4 Himes	Y	Y	Y	Y	N	N
5 Murphy	Y	Y	Y	Y	N	N
DELAWARE						
AL Carney	Y	Y	Y	Y	N	N
FLORIDA						
1 Miller	?	?	?	?	?	?
2 Southerland	N	N	N	N	Y	Y
3 Brown	Y	Y	Y	Y	N	Y
4 Crenshaw	N	N	N	N	Y	Y
5 Nugent	N	N	N	N	Y	Y
6 Stearns	N	N	N	N	Y	Y
7 Mica	N	N	N	N	Y	Y
8 Webster	N	N	N	N	Y	?
9 Bilirakis	N	N	N	N	Y	Y
10 Young	N	N	N	N	Y	Y
11 Castor	Y	Y	Y	Y	N	N
12 Ross	N	N	N	?	Y	Y
13 Buchanan	N	N	N	N	Y	Y
14 Mack	?	?	?	?	?	?
15 Posey	N	N	N	N	Y	Y
16 Rooney	N	N	N	N	Y	Y
17 Wilson	Y	Y	Y	Y	N	N
18 Ros-Lehtinen	N	N	N	N	Y	Y
19 Deutch	Y	Y	Y	Y	N	N
20 Wasserman Schultz	Y	Y	Y	Y	N	N
21 Diaz-Balart	N	N	N	N	Y	Y
22 West	N	N	N	N	Y	Y
23 Hastings	Y	Y	Y	Y	N	N
24 Adams	N	N	N	N	Y	Y
25 Rivera	N	N	N	N	Y	Y
GEORGIA						
1 Kingston	N	N	N	?	Y	Y
2 Bishop	N	N	Y	N	Y	Y
3 Westmoreland	N	N	N	N	Y	Y
4 Johnson	Y	Y	Y	Y	N	N
5 Lewis	Y	Y	Y	Y	N	N
6 Price	N	N	N	N	Y	Y
7 Woodall	N	N	N	N	Y	Y
8 Scott, A.	N	N	N	N	Y	Y
9 Graves	N	N	N	N	Y	Y
10 Broun	N	N	N	N	Y	Y
11 Gingrey	N	N	N	N	Y	Y
12 Barrow	N	N	N	Y	N	Y
13 Scott, D.	Y	Y	Y	Y	N	N
HAWAII						
1 Hanabusa	Y	Y	Y	Y	N	N
2 Hirono	Y	Y	Y	Y	N	N
IDAHO						
1 Labrador	N	N	N	Y	Y	Y
2 Simpson	N	N	N	Y	Y	Y
ILLINOIS						
1 Rush	Y	Y	Y	Y	N	N
2 Jackson	?	?	?	?	?	?
3 Lipinski	Y	Y	Y	Y	N	N
4 Gutierrez	Y	Y	Y	Y	N	?
5 Quigley	Y	Y	Y	Y	N	N
6 Roskam	N	N	N	N	Y	Y
7 Davis	Y	Y	Y	Y	N	N
8 Walsh	N	N	N	N	Y	Y
9 Schakowsky	Y	Y	Y	Y	N	N
10 Dold	N	N	N	N	Y	Y
11 Kinzinger	N	N	N	N	Y	Y
12 Costello	N	Y	Y	Y	Y	Y
13 Biggert	N	N	N	N	Y	Y
14 Hultgren	N	N	N	N	Y	Y
15 Johnson	Y	Y	N	N	Y	N

	406	407	408	409	410	411
16 **Manzullo**	N	N	N	N	Y	Y
17 **Schilling**	N	N	N	N	Y	Y
18 **Schock**	N	N	N	N	Y	Y
19 **Shimkus**	N	N	N	N	Y	Y
INDIANA						
1 Visclosky	Y	Y	Y	Y	N	Y
2 Donnelly	N	N	Y	N	Y	Y
3 **Stutzman**	N	N	N	N	Y	Y
4 **Rokita**	N	N	N	N	Y	Y
5 **Burton**	N	N	N	N	Y	Y
6 **Pence**	N	N	N	N	Y	Y
7 Carson	Y	Y	Y	Y	N	N
8 **Bucshon**	N	N	N	N	Y	Y
9 **Young**	N	N	N	N	Y	Y
IOWA						
1 Braley	Y	Y	Y	Y	N	N
2 Loebsack	Y	Y	Y	Y	N	Y
3 Boswell	Y	N	Y	Y	Y	Y
4 **Latham**	N	N	N	N	Y	?
5 **King**	N	N	N	N	Y	Y
KANSAS						
1 **Huelskamp**	N	N	N	N	Y	Y
2 **Jenkins**	N	N	N	N	Y	Y
3 **Yoder**	N	N	N	N	Y	Y
4 **Pompeo**	N	N	N	N	Y	Y
KENTUCKY						
1 **Whitfield**	N	N	N	N	Y	Y
2 **Guthrie**	N	N	N	N	Y	Y
3 Yarmuth	Y	Y	Y	Y	N	N
4 **Davis**	N	N	N	N	Y	Y
5 **Rogers**	N	N	N	N	Y	Y
6 Chandler	N	Y	Y	Y	Y	Y
LOUISIANA						
1 **Scalise**	N	N	N	N	Y	Y
2 Richmond	Y	Y	Y	N	N	Y
3 **Landry**	N	N	N	N	Y	Y
4 **Fleming**	N	N	N	N	Y	Y
5 **Alexander**	N	N	N	N	Y	Y
6 **Cassidy**	N	N	N	N	Y	Y
7 **Boustany**	N	N	N	N	Y	Y
MAINE						
1 Pingree	Y	Y	Y	Y	N	N
2 Michaud	Y	Y	Y	Y	N	N
MARYLAND						
1 **Harris**	N	N	N	N	Y	Y
2 Ruppersberger	Y	Y	Y	Y	N	N
3 Sarbanes	Y	Y	Y	Y	N	N
4 Edwards	Y	Y	Y	Y	N	N
5 Hoyer	Y	Y	Y	?	N	N
6 **Bartlett**	N	N	N	N	N	Y
7 Cummings	Y	Y	Y	Y	N	N
8 Van Hollen	Y	Y	Y	Y	N	N
MASSACHUSETTS						
1 Olver	Y	Y	Y	Y	N	N
2 Neal	Y	Y	Y	Y	N	N
3 McGovern	Y	Y	Y	Y	N	N
4 Frank	Y	Y	Y	Y	N	N
5 Tsongas	Y	Y	Y	Y	N	N
6 Tierney	Y	Y	Y	Y	N	?
7 Markey	Y	Y	Y	Y	N	N
8 Capuano	Y	Y	Y	Y	N	N
9 Lynch	Y	Y	Y	Y	N	N
10 Keating	Y	Y	Y	Y	N	N
MICHIGAN						
1 **Benishek**	N	N	N	N	Y	Y
2 **Huizenga**	N	N	N	N	Y	Y
3 **Amash**	N	N	N	N	Y	Y
4 **Camp**	N	N	N	N	Y	N
5 Kildee	Y	Y	Y	Y	N	N
6 **Upton**	N	N	N	N	Y	Y
7 **Walberg**	N	N	N	N	Y	Y
8 **Rogers**	N	N	N	N	Y	Y
9 Peters	Y	Y	Y	Y	N	N
10 **Miller**	N	N	N	N	Y	Y
11 **McCotter**	N	N	N	N	Y	?
12 Levin	Y	Y	Y	Y	N	N
13 Clarke	Y	Y	Y	Y	N	N
14 Conyers	Y	Y	Y	Y	N	N
15 Dingell	Y	Y	Y	Y	?	N
MINNESOTA						
1 Walz	Y	Y	Y	Y	N	Y
2 **Kline**	N	N	N	N	Y	Y
3 **Paulsen**	N	N	N	N	Y	Y
4 McCollum	Y	Y	Y	Y	N	N
5 Ellison	Y	Y	Y	Y	N	N
6 **Bachmann**	N	N	N	N	Y	Y
7 Peterson	N	N	Y	N	Y	Y
8 **Cravaack**	N	N	N	N	Y	Y
MISSISSIPPI						
1 **Nunnelee**	N	N	N	N	Y	Y
2 Thompson	Y	Y	Y	Y	N	Y
3 **Harper**	N	N	N	N	Y	Y
4 **Palazzo**	N	N	N	N	Y	Y
MISSOURI						
1 Clay	Y	Y	Y	Y	N	N
2 **Akin**	N	N	N	N	Y	Y
3 Carnahan	Y	Y	Y	Y	N	N
4 **Hartzler**	N	N	N	N	Y	Y
5 Cleaver	Y	N	Y	Y	N	N
6 **Graves**	N	N	N	N	Y	Y
7 **Long**	N	N	N	N	Y	Y
8 **Emerson**	N	N	N	N	Y	Y
9 **Luetkemeyer**	N	N	N	N	Y	Y
MONTANA						
AL **Rehberg**	N	N	N	N	Y	Y
NEBRASKA						
1 **Fortenberry**	N	N	N	N	Y	Y
2 **Terry**	N	N	N	N	Y	Y
3 **Smith**	N	N	N	N	Y	Y
NEVADA						
1 Berkley	Y	Y	Y	Y	N	N
2 **Amodei**	N	N	N	N	Y	Y
3 **Heck**	N	N	N	N	Y	Y
NEW HAMPSHIRE						
1 **Guinta**	N	N	N	N	Y	Y
2 **Bass**	N	N	N	N	N	Y
NEW JERSEY						
1 Andrews	Y	Y	Y	Y	N	N
2 **LoBiondo**	N	N	N	N	Y	N
3 **Runyan**	N	N	N	N	Y	Y
4 **Smith**	N	N	N	?	?	N
5 **Garrett**	N	N	N	N	Y	Y
6 Pallone	Y	Y	Y	Y	N	N
7 **Lance**	N	N	N	N	Y	Y
8 Pascrell	Y	Y	Y	Y	N	N
9 Rothman	Y	Y	Y	Y	N	N
10 Vacant						
11 **Frelinghuysen**	N	N	N	N	Y	Y
12 Holt	Y	Y	Y	Y	N	N
13 Sires	Y	Y	Y	Y	N	?
NEW MEXICO						
1 Heinrich	Y	Y	Y	Y	N	N
2 **Pearce**	N	N	N	N	Y	Y
3 Luján	Y	Y	Y	Y	N	N
NEW YORK						
1 Bishop	+	+	+	+	−	−
2 Israel	Y	Y	Y	Y	N	N
3 **King**	N	N	N	N	Y	Y
4 McCarthy	Y	Y	Y	Y	N	N
5 Ackerman	Y	Y	Y	Y	N	?
6 Meeks	?	?	?	?	?	?
7 Crowley	Y	Y	Y	Y	N	N
8 Nadler	Y	Y	Y	Y	N	N
9 **Turner**	N	N	N	N	Y	?
10 Towns	Y	Y	Y	Y	N	N
11 Clarke	+	+	+	+	−	−
12 Velázquez	?	?	?	?	?	?
13 **Grimm**	N	N	N	N	Y	Y
14 Maloney	Y	Y	Y	Y	N	N
15 Rangel	?	?	?	?	?	?
16 Serrano	Y	N	Y	Y	N	Y
17 Engel	Y	Y	Y	Y	N	N
18 Lowey	Y	Y	Y	Y	N	N
19 **Hayworth**	N	N	N	N	N	N
20 **Gibson**	N	N	Y	N	Y	N
21 Tonko	Y	Y	Y	Y	N	N
22 Hinchey	Y	Y	Y	Y	N	N
23 Owens	N	N	Y	Y	Y	Y
24 **Hanna**	N	N	?	N	Y	Y
25 **Buerkle**	N	N	N	N	Y	Y
26 Hochul	N	N	Y	Y	Y	N
27 Higgins	Y	Y	Y	Y	N	?
28 Slaughter	Y	Y	Y	Y	N	N
29 **Reed**	N	N	N	N	Y	Y
NORTH CAROLINA						
1 Butterfield	Y	Y	Y	Y	N	N
2 **Ellmers**	N	N	N	N	Y	Y
3 **Jones**	N	N	Y	Y	Y	Y
4 Price	Y	Y	Y	Y	N	N
5 **Foxx**	N	N	N	N	Y	Y
6 **Coble**	N	N	N	N	Y	Y
7 McIntyre	N	N	Y	Y	Y	Y
8 Kissell	N	Y	Y	Y	Y	Y
9 **Myrick**	N	N	N	N	Y	Y
10 **McHenry**	N	N	N	N	Y	Y
11 Shuler	Y	Y	Y	Y	N	Y
12 Watt	Y	Y	Y	Y	N	N
13 Miller	Y	Y	Y	Y	N	N
NORTH DAKOTA						
AL **Berg**	N	N	N	N	Y	Y
OHIO						
1 **Chabot**	N	N	N	N	Y	Y
2 **Schmidt**	N	N	N	N	Y	Y
3 **Turner**	N	N	N	N	Y	Y
4 **Jordan**	N	N	N	N	Y	Y
5 **Latta**	N	N	N	N	Y	Y
6 **Johnson**	N	N	N	N	Y	Y
7 **Austria**	N	N	N	N	Y	Y
8 **Boehner**						
9 Kaptur	Y	Y	Y	Y	N	N
10 Kucinich	Y	Y	Y	Y	N	N
11 Fudge	Y	Y	Y	Y	N	Y
12 **Tiberi**	N	N	N	N	Y	Y
13 Sutton	Y	Y	Y	Y	N	Y
14 **LaTourette**	N	N	N	N	Y	Y
15 **Stivers**	N	N	N	N	Y	Y
16 **Renacci**	N	N	N	N	Y	Y
17 Ryan	Y	Y	Y	Y	N	Y
18 **Gibbs**	N	N	N	N	Y	Y
OKLAHOMA						
1 **Sullivan**	N	N	N	N	+	Y
2 Boren	N	N	N	N	Y	Y
3 **Lucas**	N	N	N	N	Y	Y
4 **Cole**	N	N	N	N	Y	Y
5 **Lankford**	N	N	N	N	Y	Y
OREGON						
1 Bonamici	Y	Y	Y	Y	N	N
2 **Walden**	N	N	N	N	Y	Y
3 Blumenauer	Y	Y	Y	Y	N	N
4 DeFazio	Y	Y	Y	Y	N	Y
5 Schrader	Y	Y	Y	N	N	N
PENNSYLVANIA						
1 Brady	Y	Y	Y	Y	N	N
2 Fattah	Y	Y	Y	Y	N	N
3 **Kelly**	N	N	N	N	Y	Y
4 Altmire	N	N	Y	N	Y	Y
5 **Thompson**	N	N	N	N	Y	Y
6 **Gerlach**	N	N	N	N	Y	Y
7 **Meehan**	N	N	N	N	Y	Y
8 **Fitzpatrick**	N	N	Y	N	Y	Y
9 **Shuster**	N	N	N	N	Y	Y
10 **Marino**	N	N	N	N	Y	Y
11 **Barletta**	N	N	N	N	Y	Y
12 Critz	N	N	Y	N	Y	Y
13 Schwartz	Y	Y	Y	Y	N	N
14 Doyle	Y	Y	Y	Y	N	Y
15 **Dent**	N	N	N	N	Y	Y
16 **Pitts**	N	N	N	N	Y	Y
17 Holden	N	N	Y	Y	Y	Y
18 **Murphy**	N	N	N	N	Y	Y
19 **Platts**	N	N	N	N	Y	Y
RHODE ISLAND						
1 Cicilline	Y	Y	Y	Y	N	N
2 Langevin	Y	Y	Y	Y	N	N
SOUTH CAROLINA						
1 **Scott**	N	N	N	N	Y	Y
2 **Wilson**	N	N	N	N	Y	Y
3 **Duncan**	N	N	N	N	Y	Y
4 **Gowdy**	N	N	N	N	Y	Y
5 **Mulvaney**	N	N	N	N	Y	Y
6 Clyburn	Y	Y	Y	Y	N	Y
SOUTH DAKOTA						
AL **Noem**	N	N	N	N	Y	Y
TENNESSEE						
1 **Roe**	N	N	N	N	Y	Y
2 **Duncan**	N	N	N	N	Y	?
3 **Fleischmann**	N	N	N	N	Y	Y
4 **DesJarlais**	N	N	N	N	Y	+
5 Cooper	Y	Y	N	Y	N	N
6 **Black**	N	N	N	N	Y	Y
7 **Blackburn**	N	N	N	N	Y	Y
8 **Fincher**	N	N	N	N	Y	Y
9 Cohen	Y	Y	Y	Y	N	N
TEXAS						
1 **Gohmert**	N	N	N	N	Y	Y
2 **Poe**	N	N	N	N	Y	Y
3 **Johnson, S.**	N	N	N	N	Y	Y
4 **Hall**	N	N	N	N	Y	Y
5 **Hensarling**	N	N	N	N	Y	Y
6 **Barton**	N	N	N	N	Y	Y
7 **Culberson**	N	N	N	N	Y	Y
8 **Brady**	N	N	N	N	Y	Y
9 Green, A.	Y	Y	Y	Y	N	N
10 **McCaul**	N	N	N	N	Y	Y
11 **Conaway**	N	N	N	N	Y	Y
12 **Granger**	N	N	N	N	Y	Y
13 **Thornberry**	N	N	N	N	Y	Y
14 **Paul**	N	N	N	N	Y	Y
15 Hinojosa	Y	Y	Y	Y	N	?
16 Reyes	Y	Y	Y	Y	N	N
17 **Flores**	N	N	N	?	Y	Y
18 Jackson Lee	?	?	?	?	?	?
19 **Neugebauer**	N	N	N	N	Y	Y
20 Gonzalez	Y	Y	Y	Y	N	Y
21 **Smith**	N	N	N	N	Y	Y
22 **Olson**	N	N	N	N	Y	Y
23 **Canseco**	N	N	N	N	Y	Y
24 **Marchant**	N	N	N	N	Y	Y
25 Doggett	Y	Y	Y	Y	N	N
26 **Burgess**	N	N	N	N	Y	Y
27 **Farenthold**	N	N	N	N	Y	Y
28 Cuellar	N	N	Y	N	Y	Y
29 Green, G.	N	N	Y	N	N	+
30 Johnson, E.	Y	Y	Y	Y	N	N
31 **Carter**	N	N	N	N	Y	Y
32 **Sessions**	N	N	N	N	Y	Y
UTAH						
1 **Bishop**	N	N	N	N	Y	Y
2 Matheson	N	N	Y	N	Y	Y
3 **Chaffetz**	N	N	N	N	Y	Y
VERMONT						
AL Welch	Y	Y	Y	Y	N	N
VIRGINIA						
1 **Wittman**	N	N	N	N	Y	Y
2 **Rigell**	N	N	N	N	Y	Y
3 Scott	Y	Y	Y	Y	N	N
4 **Forbes**	N	N	N	N	Y	Y
5 **Hurt**	N	N	N	N	Y	Y
6 **Goodlatte**	N	N	N	N	Y	Y
7 **Cantor**	N	N	N	N	Y	Y
8 Moran	Y	Y	Y	Y	N	N
9 **Griffith**	N	N	N	N	Y	Y
10 **Wolf**	N	N	N	N	Y	N
11 Connolly	Y	Y	Y	Y	N	N
WASHINGTON						
1 Vacant						
2 Larsen	Y	Y	Y	Y	N	N
3 **Herrera Beutler**	N	N	N	N	Y	Y
4 **Hastings**	N	N	N	N	Y	Y
5 **McMorris Rodgers**	N	N	N	N	Y	Y
6 Dicks	Y	Y	Y	Y	N	?
7 McDermott	Y	Y	Y	Y	N	N
8 **Reichert**	N	N	N	N	Y	Y
9 Smith	Y	Y	Y	Y	N	N
WEST VIRGINIA						
1 **McKinley**	N	N	N	N	Y	Y
2 **Capito**	N	N	N	N	Y	Y
3 Rahall	Y	N	Y	Y	N	Y
WISCONSIN						
1 **Ryan**	N	N	N	N	Y	Y
2 Baldwin	Y	Y	Y	Y	N	Y
3 Kind	Y	Y	Y	Y	N	Y
4 Moore	Y	Y	Y	Y	N	?
5 **Sensenbrenner**	N	N	N	N	Y	Y
6 **Petri**	N	N	N	N	Y	Y
7 **Duffy**	N	N	N	N	Y	Y
8 **Ribble**	N	N	N	N	Y	Y
WYOMING						
AL **Lummis**	N	N	N	N	Y	Y

IN THE HOUSE | By Vote Number

412. **HR 5972, HR 5973. Fiscal 2013 Transportation-HUD and Agriculture Appropriations/Previous Question.** Foxx, R-N.C., motion to order the previous question (thus ending debate and the possibility of amendment) on the rule (H Res 697) that would provide for House floor consideration of the fiscal 2013 Agriculture (HR 5973) and Transportation-HUD (HR 5972) spending bills. Motion agreed to 226-168: R 225-0; D 1-168. June 26, 2012.

413. **HR 5972, HR 5973. Fiscal 2013 Transportation-HUD and Agriculture Appropriations/Rule.** Adoption of the rule (H Res 697) that would provide for House floor consideration of the fiscal 2013 Agriculture (HR 5973) and Transportation-HUD (HR 5972) spending bills. Adopted 229-166: R 225-0; D 4-166. June 26, 2012.

414. **HR 4348. Surface Transportation Extension/Motion to Instruct.** Hoyer, D-Md., motion to instruct conferees to recede from the House's disagreement with a Senate-passed version of the measure that would authorize federal highway, highway safety and public transit programs at $109 billion over two years. Motion rejected 172-225: R 6-222; D 166-3. June 26, 2012.

415. **HR 4348. Surface Transportation Extension/Motion to Instruct.** Black, R-Tenn., motion to instruct House conferees to reject provisions in the Senate-passed measure that would provide grants to prevent and reduce instances of distracted driving, with the exception of provisions calling for a study of distracted driving. Motion agreed to 201-194; R 201-25; D 0-169. June 26, 2012.

416. **HR 5972. Fiscal 2013 Transportation-HUD Appropriations/ Distracted Driving.** Connolly, D-Va., amendment that would increase by $5 million the amount provided for the National Highway Traffic Safety Administration Operations and Research account to combat distracted driving and reduce by $5 million the amount provided for upgrading and enhancing the Transportation Department's financial systems and re-engineering business processes. Rejected in Committee of the Whole 175-222: R 10-219; D 165-3. June 26, 2012.

417. **HR 5972. Fiscal 2013 Transportation-HUD Appropriations/ Essential Air Service Funding.** McClintock, R-Calif., amendment that would eliminate the $114 million funding to carry out the Essential Air Services (EAS) program. Rejected in Committee of the Whole 164-238: R 154-77; D 10-161. June 26, 2012.

418. **HR 5972. Fiscal 2013 Transportation-HUD Appropriations/ Washington Metropolitan Area Transit Authority Grants.** Garrett, R-N.J., amendment that would eliminate $150 million in funding provided for grants to the Washington Metropolitan Area Transit Authority. Rejected in Committee of the Whole 160-243: R 156-76; D 4-167. June 26, 2012.

	412	413	414	415	416	417	418
ALABAMA							
1 **Bonner**	Y	Y	N	Y	N	N	Y
2 **Roby**	Y	Y	N	Y	N	N	N
3 **Rogers**	Y	Y	N	Y	N	N	N
4 **Aderholt**	Y	Y	N	Y	N	N	N
5 **Brooks**	Y	Y	N	N	N	N	N
6 **Bachus**	Y	Y	N	?	N	Y	N
7 Sewell	N	N	Y	N	Y	N	N
ALASKA							
AL **Young**	Y	Y	N	Y	?	?	?
ARIZONA							
1 **Gosar**	Y	Y	N	Y	N	N	Y
2 **Franks**	Y	Y	N	Y	N	Y	Y
3 **Quayle**	Y	Y	N	Y	N	Y	Y
4 Pastor	N	N	Y	N	Y	N	N
5 **Schweikert**	Y	Y	N	N	Y	Y	Y
6 **Flake**	?	?	?	?	N	Y	Y
7 Grijalva	N	N	Y	N	Y	N	N
8 Barber	N	N	Y	N	Y	Y	N
ARKANSAS							
1 **Crawford**	Y	Y	N	Y	N	N	N
2 **Griffin**	Y	Y	N	Y	N	N	Y
3 **Womack**	Y	Y	N	Y	N	N	N
4 Ross	N	N	Y	N	Y	N	N
CALIFORNIA							
1 Thompson	N	N	Y	N	Y	N	N
2 **Herger**	Y	?	N	Y	N	Y	Y
3 **Lungren**	Y	Y	N	Y	N	Y	Y
4 **McClintock**	Y	Y	N	Y	N	Y	Y
5 Matsui	N	N	Y	N	Y	N	N
6 Woolsey	?	?	?	?	?	?	?
7 Miller, George	N	N	Y	N	Y	N	N
8 Pelosi	N	N	Y	N	?	N	N
9 Lee	N	N	Y	N	Y	N	N
10 Garamendi	N	N	Y	N	Y	N	N
11 McNerney	N	N	Y	N	Y	N	N
12 Speier	N	N	Y	N	Y	N	N
13 Stark	N	N	Y	N	Y	N	N
14 Eshoo	N	N	Y	N	Y	N	N
15 Honda	N	N	Y	N	Y	N	N
16 Lofgren	?	?	?	?	?	?	?
17 Farr	N	N	Y	N	Y	N	N
18 Cardoza	N	N	Y	N	Y	N	N
19 **Denham**	Y	Y	N	Y	N	Y	Y
20 Costa	N	N	Y	N	Y	N	Y
21 **Nunes**	Y	Y	N	Y	N	Y	Y
22 **McCarthy**	Y	Y	N	Y	N	Y	Y
23 Capps	N	N	Y	N	Y	N	N
24 **Gallegly**	Y	Y	N	Y	N	N	N
25 **McKeon**	Y	Y	N	Y	N	N	N
26 **Dreier**	Y	Y	N	Y	N	Y	N
27 Sherman	N	N	Y	N	Y	N	N
28 Berman	N	N	Y	N	Y	N	N
29 Schiff	N	N	Y	N	Y	N	N
30 Waxman	N	N	Y	N	Y	N	N
31 Becerra	N	N	Y	N	Y	N	N
32 Chu	N	N	Y	N	Y	N	N
33 Bass	N	N	Y	N	Y	N	N
34 Roybal-Allard	N	N	Y	?	Y	N	N
35 Waters	N	N	Y	N	Y	N	N
36 Hahn	N	N	Y	N	Y	N	N
37 Richardson	N	N	Y	N	Y	N	N
38 Napolitano	N	N	Y	N	Y	N	N
39 Sánchez, Linda	?	?	?	?	?	?	?
40 **Royce**	Y	Y	N	Y	N	Y	Y
41 **Lewis**	?	?	?	?	?	?	?
42 **Miller, Gary**	Y	Y	N	Y	N	Y	N
43 Baca	N	N	Y	N	Y	N	N
44 **Calvert**	Y	Y	N	Y	N	N	N
45 **Bono Mack**	Y	Y	N	Y	N	N	Y
46 **Rohrabacher**	Y	Y	N	Y	N	Y	Y
47 Sanchez, Loretta	N	N	Y	N	Y	N	N
48 **Campbell**	?	?	?	?	N	Y	Y
49 **Issa**	Y	Y	N	Y	N	Y	N
50 **Bilbray**	Y	Y	N	Y	N	Y	Y
51 Filner	N	N	Y	N	Y	N	N
52 **Hunter**	Y	Y	N	Y	N	Y	Y
53 Davis	N	N	Y	N	Y	N	N

	412	413	414	415	416	417	418
COLORADO							
1 DeGette	N	N	Y	N	Y	N	N
2 Polis	N	N	Y	N	Y	N	N
3 **Tipton**	Y	Y	N	Y	N	N	N
4 **Gardner**	Y	Y	N	Y	N	Y	Y
5 **Lamborn**	?	?	?	?	?	?	?
6 **Coffman**	Y	Y	N	Y	N	Y	Y
7 Perlmutter	N	N	Y	N	Y	N	N
CONNECTICUT							
1 Larson	N	N	Y	N	Y	N	N
2 Courtney	N	N	Y	N	Y	N	N
3 DeLauro	N	N	Y	N	Y	N	N
4 Himes	N	N	Y	N	Y	Y	N
5 Murphy	N	N	Y	N	Y	N	N
DELAWARE							
AL Carney	N	N	Y	N	Y	N	N
FLORIDA							
1 **Miller**	Y	Y	N	Y	N	Y	Y
2 **Southerland**	Y	Y	N	Y	N	N	N
3 Brown	N	N	Y	N	Y	N	N
4 **Crenshaw**	Y	Y	N	Y	N	N	N
5 **Nugent**	Y	Y	N	Y	N	Y	Y
6 **Stearns**	Y	Y	N	Y	N	Y	Y
7 **Mica**	Y	Y	N	Y	N	Y	Y
8 **Webster**	Y	Y	N	Y	N	Y	Y
9 **Bilirakis**	Y	Y	N	N	—	Y	N
10 **Young**	?	Y	N	Y	N	Y	N
11 Castor	N	N	Y	N	Y	N	N
12 **Ross**	Y	Y	N	Y	N	Y	Y
13 **Buchanan**	Y	Y	N	Y	N	Y	Y
14 **Mack**	Y	Y	N	Y	N	Y	Y
15 **Posey**	Y	Y	N	Y	N	Y	Y
16 **Rooney**	Y	Y	N	Y	N	Y	Y
17 Wilson	?	?	?	?	Y	N	N
18 **Ros-Lehtinen**	Y	Y	N	Y	N	N	N
19 Deutch	N	N	Y	N	Y	N	N
20 Wasserman Schultz	?	?	?	?	?	?	?
21 **Diaz-Balart**	+	+	−	+	N	N	N
22 **West**	Y	Y	N	N	N	Y	Y
23 Hastings	?	N	Y	N	Y	N	N
24 **Adams**	Y	Y	N	Y	N	Y	Y
25 **Rivera**	Y	Y	N	Y	N	N	N
GEORGIA							
1 **Kingston**	Y	Y	N	Y	N	Y	Y
2 Bishop	N	N	Y	N	Y	N	N
3 **Westmoreland**	Y	Y	N	Y	N	Y	Y
4 Johnson	N	N	Y	N	Y	N	N
5 Lewis	−	−	+	−	+	−	−
6 **Price**	Y	Y	N	Y	N	Y	Y
7 **Woodall**	Y	Y	N	Y	N	Y	Y
8 **Scott, A.**	Y	Y	N	Y	N	Y	Y
9 **Graves**	Y	Y	N	Y	N	Y	Y
10 **Broun**	Y	Y	N	Y	N	Y	Y
11 **Gingrey**	Y	Y	N	Y	?	Y	Y
12 **Barrow**	N	N	Y	N	Y	Y	Y
13 Scott, D.	N	N	Y	N	Y	N	N
HAWAII							
1 Hanabusa	N	N	Y	N	Y	N	N
2 Hirono	N	N	Y	N	Y	N	N
IDAHO							
1 **Labrador**	Y	Y	N	Y	N	Y	Y
2 **Simpson**	Y	Y	N	Y	N	N	N
ILLINOIS							
1 Rush	N	N	Y	N	Y	Y	N
2 Jackson	?	?	?	?	?	?	?
3 Lipinski	N	N	Y	N	Y	N	N
4 Gutierrez	−	−	+	−	?	?	?
5 Quigley	N	N	Y	N	Y	N	N
6 **Roskam**	Y	Y	N	Y	N	Y	Y
7 Davis	N	N	Y	N	Y	N	N
8 **Walsh**	Y	Y	N	Y	N	Y	Y
9 Schakowsky	N	N	Y	N	Y	N	N
10 **Dold**	Y	Y	N	Y	N	Y	N
11 **Kinzinger**	Y	Y	N	N	N	Y	Y
12 Costello	N	N	Y	N	Y	N	N
13 **Biggert**	Y	Y	N	Y	N	Y	Y
14 **Hultgren**	Y	Y	N	N	N	Y	Y
15 Johnson	+	+	−	+	?	?	?

	412	413	414	415	416	417	418
16 **Manzullo**	Y	Y	N	Y	N	Y	Y
17 **Schilling**	Y	Y	Y	Y	N	N	N
18 **Schock**	Y	Y	N	N	N	N	N
19 **Shimkus**	Y	Y	N	Y	N	N	N
INDIANA							
1 Visclosky	N	N	N	N	Y	N	N
2 Donnelly	N	Y	N	N	Y	N	N
3 **Stutzman**	Y	Y	N	Y	N	Y	Y
4 **Rokita**	Y	Y	N	Y	N	Y	Y
5 **Burton**	?	?	?	?	N	Y	Y
6 **Pence**	?	?	N	Y	N	Y	Y
7 Carson	N	N	N	N	Y	N	N
8 **Bucshon**	Y	Y	N	Y	N	Y	Y
9 **Young**	Y	Y	N	Y	N	Y	Y
IOWA							
1 Braley	N	N	Y	N	Y	N	N
2 Loebsack	N	N	Y	N	Y	N	N
3 Boswell	N	N	Y	N	Y	N	N
4 **Latham**	Y	Y	N	Y	N	N	N
5 **King**	Y	Y	N	Y	N	N	Y
KANSAS							
1 **Huelskamp**	Y	Y	N	Y	N	N	Y
2 **Jenkins**	Y	Y	N	Y	N	Y	Y
3 **Yoder**	Y	Y	N	Y	N	Y	Y
4 **Pompeo**	Y	Y	N	Y	N	Y	Y
KENTUCKY							
1 **Whitfield**	Y	Y	N	Y	N	Y	N
2 **Guthrie**	Y	Y	N	Y	N	N	Y
3 Yarmuth	N	N	Y	N	Y	N	N
4 **Davis**	Y	Y	N	Y	N	Y	N
5 **Rogers**	Y	Y	N	Y	N	N	N
6 Chandler	N	Y	Y	N	Y	N	N
LOUISIANA							
1 **Scalise**	Y	Y	N	Y	N	Y	Y
2 Richmond	N	N	Y	N	Y	N	N
3 **Landry**	?	?	?	?	N	Y	Y
4 **Fleming**	Y	Y	N	Y	N	Y	Y
5 **Alexander**	Y	Y	N	?	N	N	Y
6 **Cassidy**	Y	Y	N	Y	N	Y	Y
7 **Boustany**	Y	Y	N	Y	N	Y	Y
MAINE							
1 Pingree	N	N	Y	N	Y	N	N
2 Michaud	N	N	Y	N	Y	N	N
MARYLAND							
1 **Harris**	Y	Y	N	Y	N	Y	Y
2 Ruppersberger	N	N	Y	N	Y	N	N
3 Sarbanes	N	N	Y	N	Y	N	N
4 Edwards	N	N	Y	N	Y	N	N
5 Hoyer	N	N	Y	N	Y	N	N
6 **Bartlett**	Y	Y	N	Y	N	N	N
7 Cummings	N	N	Y	N	?	?	?
8 Van Hollen	N	N	Y	N	Y	N	N
MASSACHUSETTS							
1 Olver	N	N	Y	N	Y	N	N
2 Neal	?	?	?	?	Y	N	N
3 McGovern	N	N	Y	N	Y	N	N
4 Frank	N	N	?	?	Y	N	N
5 Tsongas	?	?	?	?	?	?	?
6 Tierney	N	N	Y	N	Y	N	N
7 Markey	N	N	Y	N	?	?	?
8 Capuano	N	N	Y	N	Y	N	N
9 Lynch	N	N	Y	N	Y	N	N
10 Keating	N	N	Y	N	Y	N	N
MICHIGAN							
1 **Benishek**	Y	Y	N	Y	N	N	Y
2 **Huizenga**	?	?	N	Y	N	Y	Y
3 **Amash**	Y	Y	N	Y	N	Y	Y
4 **Camp**	Y	Y	N	N	N	Y	Y
5 Kildee	N	N	Y	N	Y	N	N
6 **Upton**	Y	Y	N	Y	N	Y	Y
7 **Walberg**	Y	Y	N	Y	N	Y	Y
8 **Rogers**	Y	Y	N	Y	N	N	Y
9 Peters	N	N	Y	N	Y	N	N
10 **Miller**	Y	Y	N	Y	N	Y	Y
11 **McCotter**	Y	Y	N	Y	N	Y	Y
12 Levin	N	N	Y	N	Y	N	N
13 Clarke	N	N	Y	N	Y	N	N
14 Conyers	N	N	Y	N	?	N	N
15 Dingell	N	N	Y	N	Y	N	N
MINNESOTA							
1 Walz	N	N	Y	N	Y	N	N
2 **Kline**	Y	Y	N	Y	N	Y	Y
3 **Paulsen**	Y	Y	N	Y	N	Y	Y
4 McCollum	N	N	Y	N	Y	N	N

	412	413	414	415	416	417	418
5 Ellison	N	N	Y	N	Y	N	N
6 **Bachmann**	Y	Y	N	Y	N	Y	Y
7 Peterson	N	N	Y	N	?	?	?
8 **Cravaack**	Y	Y	N	Y	N	N	Y
MISSISSIPPI							
1 **Nunnelee**	Y	Y	N	Y	N	Y	Y
2 Thompson	N	N	Y	N	Y	N	N
3 **Harper**	Y	Y	N	N	N	N	N
4 **Palazzo**	Y	Y	N	Y	N	N	Y
MISSOURI							
1 Clay	N	N	Y	N	Y	N	N
2 **Akin**	?	?	?	?	?	?	?
3 Carnahan	N	N	Y	N	Y	N	N
4 **Hartzler**	Y	Y	N	Y	N	N	Y
5 Cleaver	N	N	Y	N	Y	N	N
6 **Graves**	Y	Y	N	Y	N	N	Y
7 **Long**	Y	Y	N	Y	N	Y	Y
8 **Emerson**	Y	Y	N	Y	N	N	Y
9 **Luetkemeyer**	Y	Y	N	Y	N	N	Y
MONTANA							
AL **Rehberg**	Y	Y	N	Y	N	N	N
NEBRASKA							
1 **Fortenberry**	Y	Y	N	Y	N	N	N
2 **Terry**	Y	Y	N	Y	N	Y	Y
3 **Smith**	Y	Y	N	Y	N	N	Y
NEVADA							
1 Berkley	N	N	Y	N	Y	N	N
2 **Amodei**	Y	Y	N	Y	N	N	N
3 **Heck**	Y	Y	N	Y	N	N	N
NEW HAMPSHIRE							
1 **Guinta**	Y	Y	N	Y	N	Y	Y
2 **Bass**	Y	Y	Y	Y	N	N	N
NEW JERSEY							
1 Andrews	N	N	Y	N	Y	N	N
2 **LoBiondo**	Y	Y	N	Y	N	Y	Y
3 **Runyan**	Y	Y	N	N	Y	N	N
4 **Smith**	Y	Y	N	N	N	Y	N
5 **Garrett**	Y	Y	N	Y	N	Y	Y
6 Pallone	N	N	Y	N	Y	N	N
7 **Lance**	Y	Y	N	Y	N	Y	Y
8 Pascrell	N	N	Y	N	Y	N	N
9 Rothman	N	N	Y	N	Y	N	N
10 Vacant							
11 **Frelinghuysen**	Y	Y	N	Y	N	Y	N
12 Holt	N	N	Y	N	Y	N	N
13 Sires	N	N	Y	N	Y	N	N
NEW MEXICO							
1 Heinrich	N	N	Y	N	Y	N	N
2 **Pearce**	Y	Y	N	Y	N	N	Y
3 Luján	N	N	Y	N	Y	N	N
NEW YORK							
1 Bishop	N	N	Y	N	Y	N	N
2 Israel	N	N	Y	N	Y	N	N
3 **King**	Y	Y	N	N	N	N	N
4 McCarthy	N	N	Y	N	?	N	N
5 Ackerman	?	?	?	?	?	?	?
6 Meeks	?	?	?	?	?	?	?
7 Crowley	–	–	+	–	+	–	–
8 Nadler	N	N	Y	N	Y	N	N
9 **Turner**	?	?	?	?	?	?	?
10 Towns	?	?	?	?	?	?	?
11 Clarke	–	–	+	–	+	–	–
12 Velázquez	?	?	?	?	?	?	?
13 **Grimm**	Y	Y	N	Y	N	Y	N
14 Maloney	N	N	Y	N	Y	N	N
15 Rangel	?	?	?	?	?	?	?
16 Serrano	N	N	Y	N	Y	N	N
17 Engel	?	?	?	?	?	?	?
18 Lowey	N	N	Y	N	Y	N	N
19 **Hayworth**	Y	Y	N	Y	N	N	N
20 **Gibson**	Y	Y	N	Y	N	N	N
21 Tonko	N	N	Y	N	Y	N	N
22 Hinchey	N	N	Y	N	Y	N	N
23 Owens	N	N	Y	N	Y	N	N
24 **Hanna**	Y	Y	N	N	N	Y	N
25 **Buerkle**	Y	Y	N	Y	N	Y	Y
26 Hochul	N	N	Y	N	Y	N	N
27 Higgins	N	N	Y	N	Y	N	N
28 Slaughter	N	N	Y	N	Y	N	N
29 **Reed**	Y	Y	N	Y	N	Y	N
NORTH CAROLINA							
1 Butterfield	N	N	Y	N	Y	N	N
2 **Ellmers**	Y	Y	N	Y	N	N	N
3 **Jones**	Y	Y	Y	N	Y	Y	Y
4 Price	N	N	Y	N	Y	N	N

	412	413	414	415	416	417	418
5 **Foxx**	Y	Y	N	Y	N	Y	Y
6 **Coble**	Y	Y	N	Y	N	Y	Y
7 McIntyre	N	N	Y	N	Y	Y	Y
8 Kissell	N	N	Y	N	Y	N	N
9 **Myrick**	Y	Y	N	Y	?	?	?
10 **McHenry**	Y	Y	N	Y	N	Y	Y
11 Shuler	Y	Y	Y	N	Y	N	N
12 Watt	N	N	Y	N	Y	N	N
13 Miller	N	N	Y	N	Y	N	N
NORTH DAKOTA							
AL **Berg**	Y	Y	N	Y	N	N	N
OHIO							
1 **Chabot**	Y	Y	N	Y	N	Y	Y
2 **Schmidt**	Y	Y	N	Y	N	Y	Y
3 **Turner**	Y	Y	N	Y	N	Y	N
4 **Jordan**	+	+	–	+	N	Y	Y
5 **Latta**	Y	Y	N	Y	N	Y	Y
6 **Johnson**	Y	Y	N	Y	N	N	Y
7 **Austria**	Y	Y	N	Y	N	Y	N
8 **Boehner**							
9 Kaptur	N	N	Y	N	Y	N	N
10 Kucinich	N	N	Y	N	Y	N	N
11 Fudge	N	N	Y	N	Y	N	N
12 **Tiberi**	Y	Y	N	Y	N	Y	Y
13 Sutton	N	N	Y	N	Y	N	N
14 **LaTourette**	Y	Y	N	N	N	N	N
15 **Stivers**	?	?	?	?	?	?	?
16 **Renacci**	Y	Y	N	Y	N	Y	Y
17 Ryan	N	N	Y	N	Y	N	N
18 **Gibbs**	Y	Y	N	Y	N	N	Y
OKLAHOMA							
1 **Sullivan**	?	?	?	?	?	?	?
2 Boren	N	N	Y	N	N	N	N
3 **Lucas**	Y	Y	N	Y	N	N	N
4 **Cole**	Y	Y	N	Y	N	N	N
5 **Lankford**	Y	Y	N	Y	N	Y	Y
OREGON							
1 Bonamici	N	N	Y	N	Y	N	N
2 **Walden**	Y	Y	N	Y	N	Y	N
3 Blumenauer	?	?	?	?	Y	N	N
4 DeFazio	N	N	P	N	Y	N	N
5 Schrader	N	N	Y	N	N	N	N
PENNSYLVANIA							
1 Brady	N	N	Y	N	Y	N	N
2 Fattah	N	N	Y	N	Y	N	N
3 **Kelly**	Y	Y	N	Y	N	N	Y
4 Altmire	?	?	Y	N	Y	N	N
5 **Thompson**	Y	Y	N	Y	N	N	N
6 **Gerlach**	Y	Y	N	N	Y	Y	N
7 **Meehan**	Y	Y	N	N	N	Y	N
8 **Fitzpatrick**	Y	Y	N	N	Y	N	N
9 **Shuster**	Y	Y	N	Y	N	N	N
10 **Marino**	Y	Y	N	Y	N	N	Y
11 **Barletta**	Y	Y	N	Y	N	N	Y
12 Critz	N	N	Y	N	N	N	N
13 Schwartz	N	N	Y	N	Y	N	N
14 Doyle	N	N	Y	N	Y	N	N
15 **Dent**	Y	Y	N	N	Y	Y	N
16 **Pitts**	Y	Y	N	N	N	N	N
17 Holden	?	?	?	?	?	?	?
18 **Murphy**	Y	Y	N	Y	N	Y	Y
19 **Platts**	Y	Y	N	N	Y	N	N
RHODE ISLAND							
1 Cicilline	N	N	Y	N	Y	N	N
2 Langevin	N	N	Y	N	Y	N	N
SOUTH CAROLINA							
1 **Scott**	Y	Y	N	Y	N	Y	Y
2 **Wilson**	Y	Y	N	Y	N	Y	Y
3 **Duncan**	Y	Y	N	Y	N	Y	Y
4 **Gowdy**	Y	Y	N	Y	N	Y	Y
5 **Mulvaney**	Y	Y	N	Y	N	Y	Y
6 Clyburn	N	N	Y	N	Y	N	N
SOUTH DAKOTA							
AL **Noem**	Y	Y	N	N	N	N	Y
TENNESSEE							
1 **Roe**	Y	Y	N	Y	N	Y	Y
2 **Duncan**	Y	Y	N	N	Y	Y	Y
3 **Fleischmann**	Y	Y	N	Y	N	Y	Y
4 **DesJarlais**	Y	Y	N	Y	N	Y	Y
5 Cooper	N	N	Y	N	Y	N	N
6 **Black**	Y	Y	N	Y	N	Y	Y
7 **Blackburn**	Y	Y	N	Y	N	Y	Y
8 **Fincher**	Y	Y	N	Y	N	Y	Y
9 Cohen	N	N	Y	N	Y	N	N

	412	413	414	415	416	417	418
TEXAS							
1 **Gohmert**	Y	Y	N	Y	N	Y	Y
2 **Poe**	Y	Y	N	Y	N	Y	Y
3 **Johnson, S.**	Y	Y	N	Y	N	Y	Y
4 **Hall**	Y	Y	N	Y	N	N	Y
5 **Hensarling**	Y	Y	N	Y	N	Y	Y
6 **Barton**	Y	Y	N	Y	N	Y	Y
7 **Culberson**	Y	Y	N	Y	N	Y	N
8 **Brady**	Y	Y	N	Y	N	Y	Y
9 Green, A.	N	N	Y	N	Y	N	N
10 **McCaul**	Y	Y	N	Y	N	Y	N
11 **Conaway**	Y	Y	N	Y	N	Y	Y
12 **Granger**	Y	Y	N	Y	N	N	N
13 **Thornberry**	Y	Y	N	Y	N	Y	N
14 **Paul**	Y	Y	N	Y	N	Y	Y
15 Hinojosa	N	N	Y	N	Y	N	N
16 Reyes	N	N	Y	N	Y	N	N
17 **Flores**	Y	Y	N	Y	?	Y	Y
18 Jackson Lee	N	N	Y	N	Y	N	N
19 **Neugebauer**	Y	Y	N	Y	N	Y	Y
20 Gonzalez	N	N	Y	N	Y	N	N
21 **Smith**	Y	Y	N	Y	N	Y	Y
22 **Olson**	Y	Y	N	Y	N	Y	Y
23 **Canseco**	Y	Y	N	Y	N	Y	Y
24 **Marchant**	Y	Y	N	Y	N	Y	Y
25 Doggett	N	N	Y	N	Y	Y	N
26 **Burgess**	Y	Y	N	N	N	?	Y
27 **Farenthold**	Y	Y	N	Y	N	N	Y
28 Cuellar	N	N	Y	N	Y	N	N
29 Green, G.	N	N	Y	N	Y	Y	N
30 Johnson, E.	N	N	Y	N	Y	N	N
31 **Carter**	Y	Y	N	Y	N	N	N
32 **Sessions**	Y	Y	N	Y	N	Y	Y
UTAH							
1 **Bishop**	Y	Y	N	Y	N	Y	Y
2 Matheson	N	Y	Y	N	Y	N	Y
3 **Chaffetz**	Y	Y	N	Y	N	Y	Y
VERMONT							
AL Welch	N	N	Y	N	Y	N	N
VIRGINIA							
1 **Wittman**	Y	Y	N	Y	N	Y	N
2 **Rigell**	Y	Y	N	Y	N	Y	N
3 Scott	N	N	Y	N	Y	N	N
4 **Forbes**	Y	Y	N	Y	N	Y	N
5 **Hurt**	Y	Y	N	N	N	Y	Y
6 **Goodlatte**	Y	Y	N	Y	N	Y	N
7 **Cantor**	Y	Y	N	Y	N	Y	N
8 Moran	N	N	Y	N	Y	N	N
9 **Griffith**	Y	Y	N	Y	N	Y	N
10 **Wolf**	Y	Y	N	N	N	N	N
11 Connolly	N	N	Y	N	Y	Y	N
WASHINGTON							
1 Vacant							
2 Larsen	N	N	Y	N	Y	N	N
3 **Herrera Beutler**	Y	Y	N	Y	N	Y	N
4 **Hastings**	Y	Y	N	Y	N	Y	N
5 **McMorris Rodgers**	Y	Y	N	Y	N	N	Y
6 Dicks	N	N	Y	N	Y	N	N
7 McDermott	N	N	Y	N	Y	N	N
8 **Reichert**	Y	Y	N	Y	N	Y	N
9 Smith	N	N	Y	N	Y	N	N
WEST VIRGINIA							
1 **McKinley**	Y	Y	N	Y	N	N	Y
2 **Capito**	Y	Y	N	Y	N	N	N
3 Rahall	N	N	Y	N	Y	N	N
WISCONSIN							
1 **Ryan**	Y	Y	N	Y	N	Y	Y
2 Baldwin	N	N	Y	N	Y	N	N
3 Kind	N	N	Y	N	Y	N	N
4 Moore	N	N	Y	N	Y	N	N
5 **Sensenbrenner**	Y	Y	N	Y	N	Y	Y
6 **Petri**	Y	Y	N	Y	N	Y	Y
7 **Duffy**	Y	Y	N	Y	N	N	Y
8 **Ribble**	Y	Y	N	Y	N	Y	Y
WYOMING							
AL **Lummis**	Y	Y	N	Y	N	N	Y

IN THE HOUSE | By Vote Number

419. **HR 5972. Fiscal 2013 Transportation-HUD Appropriations/ Housing Counseling Assistance.** Capps, D-Calif., amendment that would increase by $10 million the amount provided for housing counseling assistance. The amendment would reduce by the same amount the funding provided for salaries and expenses for administration, management and operations of the Department of Housing and Urban Development (HUD). Rejected in Committee of the Whole 184-218: R 14-217; D 170-1. June 26, 2012.

420. **HR 5972. Fiscal 2013 Transportation-HUD Appropriations/HUD Salaries and Expenses.** Gosar, R-Ariz., amendment that would reduce by $24.4 million the amount provided for salaries and expenses of administration, management and operations of HUD. Rejected in Committee of the Whole 179-224: R 174-58; D 5-166. June 26, 2012.

421. **HR 5972. Fiscal 2013 Transportation-HUD Appropriations/ Federal Railroad Administration Expenses.** Broun, R-Ga., amendment that would reduce by $5.4 million the amount provided for expenses of the Federal Railroad Administration. Rejected in Committee of the Whole 173-230: R 170-62; D 3-168. June 26, 2012.

422. **HR 5972. Fiscal 2013 Transportation-HUD Appropriations/ Federal Transit Administration Expenses.** Broun, R-Ga., amendment that would reduce by $1.3 million the amount provided for administrative expenses of the Federal Transit Administration's programs. Rejected in Committee of the Whole 188-215: R 183-49; D 5-166. June 26, 2012.

423. **HR 5972. Fiscal 2013 Transportation-HUD Appropriations/ Pipeline and Hazardous Materials Safety Administration Expenses.** Broun, R-Ga., amendment that would reduce by $1.67 million the amount provided for operational expenses of the Pipeline and Hazardous Materials Safety Administration. Rejected in Committee of the Whole 138-265: R 137-95; D 1-170. June 26, 2012.

424. **HR 5972. Fiscal 2013 Transportation-HUD Appropriations/HUD Office of Public and Indian Housing Expenses.** Broun, R-Ga., amendment that would reduce by $6.5 million the amount provided for salaries and expenses of the Office of Public and Indian Housing at HUD. Rejected in Committee of the Whole 168-256: R 166-71; D 2-185. June 27, 2012.

425. **HR 5972. Fiscal 2013 Transportation-HUD Appropriations/ HUD Office of Community Planning and Development Expenses.** Broun, R-Ga., amendment that would reduce by $3.5 million the amount provided for salaries and expenses of the Office of Community Planning and Development at HUD. Rejected in Committee of the Whole 178-240: R 175-59; D 3-181. June 27, 2012.

	419	420	421	422	423	424	425
ALABAMA							
1 Bonner	N	Y	N	Y	N	N	Y
2 Roby	N	Y	N	N	N	N	N
3 Rogers	N	N	N	N	N	N	N
4 Aderholt	N	N	N	N	N	N	N
5 Brooks	N	Y	Y	Y	Y	Y	Y
6 Bachus	N	Y	N	Y	N	N	N
7 Sewell	Y	N	N	N	N	N	N
ALASKA							
AL Young	?	?	?	?	?	N	N
ARIZONA							
1 Gosar	N	Y	Y	Y	Y	Y	Y
2 Franks	N	Y	Y	Y	Y	Y	Y
3 Quayle	N	Y	Y	Y	Y	Y	Y
4 Pastor	Y	N	N	N	N	N	N
5 Schweikert	N	Y	Y	Y	Y	Y	Y
6 Flake	N	Y	Y	Y	Y	Y	Y
7 Grijalva	Y	N	N	N	N	N	N
8 Barber	Y	N	N	N	N	N	N
ARKANSAS							
1 Crawford	N	N	N	Y	N	N	N
2 Griffin	N	Y	Y	Y	Y	Y	Y
3 Womack	N	N	N	N	N	N	N
4 Ross	Y	N	N	N	N	N	N
CALIFORNIA							
1 Thompson	Y	N	N	N	N	N	N
2 Herger	N	Y	Y	Y	Y	Y	Y
3 Lungren	N	Y	N	Y	N	N	Y
4 McClintock	N	Y	Y	Y	Y	Y	Y
5 Matsui	Y	N	N	N	N	N	N
6 Woolsey	?	?	?	?	?	N	N
7 Miller, George	Y	N	N	N	N	N	N
8 Pelosi	Y	N	N	N	N	N	N
9 Lee	Y	N	N	N	N	N	N
10 Garamendi	Y	N	N	N	N	N	N
11 McNerney	Y	N	N	N	N	N	N
12 Speier	Y	N	N	N	N	N	N
13 Stark	Y	N	N	N	N	N	N
14 Eshoo	Y	N	N	N	N	N	N
15 Honda	Y	N	N	N	N	N	N
16 Lofgren	?	?	?	?	?	N	N
17 Farr	Y	N	N	N	N	N	N
18 Cardoza	Y	Y	N	N	N	N	N
19 Denham	N	Y	Y	Y	N	Y	Y
20 Costa	Y	N	N	N	N	N	N
21 Nunes	N	Y	Y	Y	Y	N	N
22 McCarthy	N	Y	N	Y	N	Y	Y
23 Capps	Y	N	N	N	N	N	N
24 Gallegly	N	Y	N	N	N	N	N
25 McKeon	N	N	N	N	N	N	N
26 Dreier	N	Y	Y	Y	N	Y	Y
27 Sherman	Y	N	N	N	N	N	N
28 Berman	Y	N	N	N	N	N	N
29 Schiff	Y	N	N	N	N	N	N
30 Waxman	Y	N	N	N	N	N	N
31 Becerra	Y	N	N	N	N	N	N
32 Chu	Y	N	N	N	N	N	N
33 Bass	Y	N	N	N	N	N	?
34 Roybal-Allard	Y	N	N	N	N	N	N
35 Waters	Y	N	N	N	N	N	N
36 Hahn	Y	N	N	N	N	N	N
37 Richardson	Y	N	N	N	N	N	N
38 Napolitano	Y	N	N	N	N	N	N
39 Sánchez, Linda	?	?	?	?	?	N	N
40 Royce	N	Y	Y	Y	Y	Y	Y
41 Lewis	?	?	?	?	?	?	?
42 Miller, Gary	N	Y	Y	Y	N	N	N
43 Baca	Y	N	N	N	N	N	N
44 Calvert	N	N	N	N	N	N	N
45 Bono Mack	N	Y	Y	Y	N	Y	N
46 Rohrabacher	N	Y	Y	Y	Y	Y	Y
47 Sanchez, Loretta	Y	N	N	N	N	N	N
48 Campbell	N	Y	Y	Y	Y	Y	Y
49 Issa	N	Y	Y	Y	Y	Y	Y
50 Bilbray	N	Y	Y	Y	N	Y	N
51 Filner	Y	N	N	N	N	N	N
52 Hunter	N	Y	Y	Y	Y	N	Y
53 Davis	Y	N	N	N	N	N	N

	419	420	421	422	423	424	425
COLORADO							
1 DeGette	Y	N	N	N	N	N	N
2 Polis	Y	N	N	Y	N	N	N
3 Tipton	N	Y	Y	Y	N	Y	Y
4 Gardner	N	Y	Y	Y	N	Y	Y
5 Lamborn	?	?	?	?	?	Y	Y
6 Coffman	Y	Y	Y	Y	N	N	Y
7 Perlmutter	Y	N	N	N	N	N	N
CONNECTICUT							
1 Larson	Y	N	N	N	N	N	N
2 Courtney	Y	N	N	N	N	N	N
3 DeLauro	Y	N	N	N	N	N	N
4 Himes	Y	N	N	N	N	N	N
5 Murphy	Y	N	N	N	N	N	N
DELAWARE							
AL Carney	Y	N	N	N	N	N	N
FLORIDA							
1 Miller	N	Y	Y	Y	Y	Y	Y
2 Southerland	N	Y	Y	Y	Y	Y	Y
3 Brown	Y	N	N	N	N	N	N
4 Crenshaw	N	N	N	N	N	N	N
5 Nugent	N	Y	Y	Y	Y	Y	Y
6 Stearns	-	Y	Y	Y	Y	Y	Y
7 Mica	N	Y	Y	Y	Y	Y	Y
8 Webster	N	Y	Y	Y	N	Y	Y
9 Bilirakis	N	Y	Y	Y	N	Y	Y
10 Young	N	Y	Y	Y	N	Y	Y
11 Castor	Y	N	N	N	N	N	N
12 Ross	N	Y	Y	Y	Y	Y	Y
13 Buchanan	N	Y	Y	Y	N	Y	Y
14 Mack	N	Y	Y	Y	Y	?	?
15 Posey	N	Y	Y	Y	Y	Y	Y
16 Rooney	Y	Y	Y	Y	Y	Y	Y
17 Wilson	Y	N	N	N	N	N	N
18 Ros-Lehtinen	N	N	N	N	N	N	N
19 Deutch	Y	N	N	N	N	N	N
20 Wasserman Schultz	?	?	?	?	?	N	N
21 Diaz-Balart	N	N	N	N	N	N	N
22 West	N	Y	Y	Y	N	Y	Y
23 Hastings	Y	N	N	N	N	N	N
24 Adams	N	Y	Y	Y	Y	Y	Y
25 Rivera	N	N	N	N	N	N	N
GEORGIA							
1 Kingston	N	Y	Y	Y	Y	Y	Y
2 Bishop	Y	N	N	N	N	N	N
3 Westmoreland	N	Y	Y	Y	Y	Y	Y
4 Johnson	Y	N	N	N	N	N	N
5 Lewis	+	-	-	-	-	N	N
6 Price	N	Y	Y	Y	Y	Y	Y
7 Woodall	N	Y	Y	Y	Y	Y	Y
8 Scott, A.	N	Y	Y	Y	Y	Y	Y
9 Graves	N	Y	Y	Y	Y	Y	Y
10 Broun	N	Y	Y	Y	Y	Y	Y
11 Gingrey	N	Y	Y	Y	Y	Y	Y
12 Barrow	Y	Y	Y	Y	Y	Y	Y
13 Scott, D.	Y	N	N	N	N	N	N
HAWAII							
1 Hanabusa	Y	N	N	N	N	N	N
2 Hirono	Y	N	N	N	N	N	N
IDAHO							
1 Labrador	N	Y	Y	Y	Y	Y	Y
2 Simpson	N	N	N	N	N	N	N
ILLINOIS							
1 Rush	Y	N	Y	N	N	N	N
2 Jackson	?	?	?	?	?	?	?
3 Lipinski	Y	N	N	N	N	N	N
4 Gutierrez	?	?	?	?	?	N	N
5 Quigley	Y	N	N	N	N	N	N
6 Roskam	N	Y	Y	Y	Y	Y	Y
7 Davis	Y	N	N	N	N	N	N
8 Walsh	N	Y	Y	Y	Y	Y	Y
9 Schakowsky	Y	N	N	N	N	N	N
10 Dold	N	N	N	Y	N	N	N
11 Kinzinger	N	N	N	Y	N	N	N
12 Costello	Y	N	N	N	N	N	N
13 Biggert	Y	N	N	N	N	N	N
14 Hultgren	N	Y	Y	Y	Y	Y	Y
15 Johnson	?	?	?	?	?	Y	Y

KEY   **Republicans**   Democrats

Y Voted for (yea)	**X** Paired against	**C** Voted "present" to avoid possible conflict of interest
# Paired for	**–** Announced against	**?** Did not vote or otherwise make a position known
+ Announced for	**P** Voted "present"	
N Voted against (nay)		

	419	420	421	422	423	424	425
16 **Manzullo**	N	Y	Y	Y	Y	Y	Y
17 **Schilling**	N	N	Y	Y	Y	Y	Y
18 **Schock**	N	N	N	N	N	N	N
19 **Shimkus**	N	Y	Y	Y	N	N	N
INDIANA							
1 Visclosky	Y	N	N	N	N	N	N
2 Donnelly	Y	N	N	N	N	N	N
3 **Stutzman**	N	Y	Y	Y	Y	Y	Y
4 **Rokita**	N	Y	Y	Y	Y	Y	Y
5 **Burton**	N	Y	Y	Y	Y	Y	Y
6 **Pence**	N	Y	Y	Y	Y	Y	?
7 Carson	Y	N	N	N	N	N	N
8 **Bucshon**	N	Y	Y	Y	Y	Y	Y
9 **Young**	N	Y	Y	Y	Y	Y	Y
IOWA							
1 Braley	Y	N	N	N	N	N	N
2 Loebsack	Y	N	N	N	N	N	N
3 Boswell	Y	N	N	N	N	N	N
4 **Latham**	N	N	N	N	N	N	N
5 **King**	N	Y	Y	Y	Y	Y	Y
KANSAS							
1 **Huelskamp**	N	Y	Y	Y	Y	Y	Y
2 **Jenkins**	N	Y	Y	Y	N	Y	Y
3 **Yoder**	N	Y	Y	Y	Y	Y	Y
4 **Pompeo**	N	Y	Y	Y	Y	Y	Y
KENTUCKY							
1 **Whitfield**	N	N	N	Y	N	Y	Y
2 **Guthrie**	N	N	Y	Y	N	Y	Y
3 Yarmuth	Y	N	N	N	N	N	N
4 **Davis**	N	N	N	N	N	N	N
5 **Rogers**	N	N	N	N	N	N	N
6 Chandler	Y	N	N	N	N	N	N
LOUISIANA							
1 **Scalise**	N	Y	Y	Y	Y	Y	Y
2 Richmond	Y	N	N	N	N	N	N
3 **Landry**	N	Y	Y	Y	Y	Y	Y
4 **Fleming**	N	Y	Y	Y	Y	Y	Y
5 **Alexander**	N	Y	Y	Y	N	N	N
6 **Cassidy**	N	Y	Y	Y	N	Y	Y
7 **Boustany**	N	Y	Y	Y	Y	Y	Y
MAINE							
1 Pingree	Y	N	N	N	N	N	N
2 Michaud	Y	N	N	Y	N	N	N
MARYLAND							
1 **Harris**	N	Y	N	Y	N	Y	Y
2 Ruppersberger	Y	N	N	N	N	N	N
3 Sarbanes	Y	N	N	N	N	N	N
4 Edwards	Y	N	N	N	N	N	N
5 Hoyer	Y	N	N	N	N	N	N
6 **Bartlett**	N	Y	Y	Y	Y	Y	Y
7 Cummings	?	?	?	?	?	N	N
8 Van Hollen	Y	N	N	N	N	N	N
MASSACHUSETTS							
1 Olver	Y	N	N	N	N	N	N
2 Neal	Y	N	N	N	N	N	N
3 McGovern	Y	N	N	N	N	N	N
4 Frank	Y	N	N	N	N	N	N
5 Tsongas	?	?	?	?	?	N	N
6 Tierney	Y	N	N	N	N	N	N
7 Markey	?	?	?	?	?	N	N
8 Capuano	Y	N	N	N	N	N	N
9 Lynch	Y	N	N	N	N	N	N
10 Keating	Y	N	N	N	N	N	N
MICHIGAN							
1 **Benishek**	N	Y	Y	Y	Y	Y	Y
2 **Huizenga**	N	Y	Y	Y	Y	Y	Y
3 **Amash**	N	Y	Y	Y	Y	Y	Y
4 **Camp**	N	Y	Y	Y	N	Y	Y
5 Kildee	Y	N	N	N	N	N	N
6 **Upton**	N	Y	Y	Y	N	Y	Y
7 **Walberg**	N	Y	Y	Y	Y	Y	Y
8 **Rogers**	N	Y	Y	Y	Y	Y	Y
9 Peters	Y	N	N	N	N	N	N
10 **Miller**	N	Y	Y	Y	Y	Y	Y
11 **McCotter**	N	Y	Y	Y	Y	Y	Y
12 Levin	Y	N	N	N	N	N	N
13 Clarke	Y	N	N	N	N	N	N
14 Conyers	Y	N	N	N	N	N	N
15 Dingell	Y	N	N	N	N	N	N
MINNESOTA							
1 Walz	Y	N	N	N	N	N	N
2 **Kline**	N	Y	Y	Y	Y	Y	Y
3 **Paulsen**	N	Y	Y	Y	Y	Y	Y
4 McCollum	Y	N	N	N	N	N	N

	419	420	421	422	423	424	425
5 Ellison	Y	N	N	N	N	N	N
6 **Bachmann**	Y	Y	Y	Y	Y	Y	Y
7 Peterson	?	?	?	?	?	N	N
8 **Cravaack**	N	N	Y	Y	N	Y	N
MISSISSIPPI							
1 **Nunnelee**	N	Y	Y	Y	Y	Y	Y
2 Thompson	Y	N	N	N	N	?	?
3 **Harper**	N	Y	N	Y	N	N	N
4 **Palazzo**	N	Y	Y	Y	Y	Y	Y
MISSOURI							
1 Clay	Y	N	N	N	N	N	N
2 **Akin**	?	?	?	?	?	Y	Y
3 Carnahan	Y	N	N	N	N	N	N
4 **Hartzler**	N	Y	Y	Y	Y	Y	Y
5 Cleaver	Y	N	N	N	N	N	N
6 **Graves**	N	Y	Y	Y	Y	Y	Y
7 **Long**	N	Y	Y	Y	Y	Y	Y
8 **Emerson**	N	Y	Y	Y	Y	Y	Y
9 **Luetkemeyer**	N	Y	Y	Y	Y	Y	Y
MONTANA							
AL **Rehberg**	N	N	N	N	N	N	N
NEBRASKA							
1 **Fortenberry**	N	Y	Y	Y	N	Y	Y
2 **Terry**	N	N	N	Y	N	Y	Y
3 **Smith**	N	Y	Y	Y	Y	Y	Y
NEVADA							
1 Berkley	Y	N	N	N	N	N	N
2 **Amodei**	N	N	N	N	N	N	Y
3 **Heck**	Y	N	Y	Y	Y	N	N
NEW HAMPSHIRE							
1 **Guinta**	N	N	Y	Y	N	Y	Y
2 **Bass**	N	N	Y	Y	Y	N	N
NEW JERSEY							
1 Andrews	Y	N	N	N	N	N	?
2 **LoBiondo**	N	N	Y	Y	N	Y	Y
3 **Runyan**	Y	Y	N	N	N	N	N
4 **Smith**	N	Y	Y	Y	N	Y	Y
5 **Garrett**	N	Y	Y	Y	Y	Y	Y
6 Pallone	Y	N	N	N	N	N	N
7 **Lance**	N	Y	Y	Y	Y	Y	Y
8 Pascrell	Y	N	N	N	N	N	N
9 Rothman	Y	N	N	N	N	N	N
10 Vacant							
11 **Frelinghuysen**	N	N	N	N	N	N	N
12 Holt	Y	N	N	N	N	N	N
13 Sires	Y	N	N	N	N	N	N
NEW MEXICO							
1 Heinrich	Y	N	N	N	N	N	N
2 **Pearce**	N	N	N	Y	N	N	N
3 Luján	Y	N	N	N	N	N	N
NEW YORK							
1 Bishop	Y	N	N	N	N	N	N
2 Israel	Y	N	N	N	N	N	N
3 **King**	N	N	N	N	N	N	N
4 McCarthy	Y	N	N	N	N	N	N
5 Ackerman	?	?	?	?	?	N	N
6 Meeks	?	?	?	?	?	N	N
7 Crowley	+	–	–	–	–	N	N
8 Nadler	Y	N	N	N	N	N	N
9 **Turner**	?	?	?	?	?	N	N
10 Towns	?	?	?	?	?	N	N
11 Clarke	+	–	–	–	–	N	N
12 Velázquez	?	?	?	?	?	N	N
13 **Grimm**	N	N	N	N	N	Y	Y
14 Maloney	Y	N	N	N	N	N	N
15 Rangel	?	?	?	?	?	N	N
16 Serrano	Y	N	N	N	N	N	N
17 Engel	?	?	?	?	?	?	?
18 Lowey	Y	N	N	N	N	N	N
19 **Hayworth**	N	N	N	N	N	N	N
20 **Gibson**	N	N	N	N	N	N	Y
21 Tonko	Y	N	N	N	N	N	N
22 Hinchey	Y	N	N	N	N	N	N
23 Owens	Y	N	N	N	N	N	N
24 **Hanna**	N	Y	Y	Y	Y	Y	Y
25 **Buerkle**	N	Y	Y	Y	Y	Y	Y
26 Hochul	Y	N	N	N	N	N	N
27 Higgins	Y	N	N	N	N	N	N
28 Slaughter	Y	N	N	N	N	N	N
29 **Reed**	N	N	N	N	N	N	N
NORTH CAROLINA							
1 Butterfield	Y	N	N	N	N	N	N
2 **Ellmers**	N	Y	Y	Y	Y	Y	Y
3 **Jones**	Y	Y	Y	Y	Y	Y	Y
4 Price	Y	N	N	N	N	N	N

	419	420	421	422	423	424	425
5 **Foxx**	N	Y	Y	Y	Y	Y	Y
6 **Coble**	Y	Y	Y	Y	Y	Y	Y
7 McIntyre	Y	Y	N	Y	N	N	Y
8 Kissell	Y	N	N	N	N	N	N
9 **Myrick**	?	?	?	?	?	Y	Y
10 **McHenry**	N	Y	Y	Y	Y	Y	Y
11 Shuler	Y	N	N	N	N	N	N
12 Watt	Y	N	N	N	N	N	N
13 Miller	Y	N	N	N	N	N	N
NORTH DAKOTA							
AL **Berg**	N	N	N	Y	N	N	N
OHIO							
1 **Chabot**	N	Y	Y	Y	Y	Y	Y
2 **Schmidt**	N	Y	Y	Y	Y	Y	Y
3 **Turner**	Y	N	N	N	N	N	N
4 **Jordan**	N	Y	Y	Y	Y	Y	Y
5 **Latta**	N	Y	Y	Y	Y	Y	Y
6 **Johnson**	N	Y	Y	Y	Y	Y	Y
7 **Austria**	N	Y	N	N	N	N	N
8 **Boehner**							
9 Kaptur	Y	N	N	N	N	N	N
10 Kucinich	Y	N	N	N	N	N	N
11 Fudge	Y	N	N	N	N	N	N
12 **Tiberi**	N	N	Y	N	N	Y	N
13 Sutton	Y	N	N	N	N	N	N
14 **LaTourette**	N	N	N	N	N	N	N
15 **Stivers**	?	?	?	?	?	?	?
16 **Renacci**	N	Y	Y	Y	Y	Y	Y
17 Ryan	Y	N	N	N	N	N	N
18 **Gibbs**	N	Y	Y	Y	Y	Y	Y
OKLAHOMA							
1 **Sullivan**	?	?	?	?	?	Y	?
2 Boren	Y	N	N	N	N	N	N
3 **Lucas**	N	N	N	N	N	N	N
4 **Cole**	N	N	N	N	N	N	N
5 **Lankford**	N	Y	Y	Y	Y	Y	Y
OREGON							
1 Bonamici	Y	N	N	N	N	N	N
2 **Walden**	N	Y	Y	Y	Y	N	Y
3 Blumenauer	Y	N	N	N	N	N	N
4 DeFazio	Y	N	N	N	N	N	N
5 Schrader	Y	N	N	N	N	N	?
PENNSYLVANIA							
1 Brady	Y	N	N	N	N	N	N
2 Fattah	Y	N	N	N	N	N	N
3 **Kelly**	N	Y	N	N	N	N	N
4 Altmire	N	N	N	N	N	N	N
5 **Thompson**	N	N	N	N	N	N	N
6 **Gerlach**	Y	N	N	N	N	N	N
7 **Meehan**	N	N	N	N	N	N	N
8 **Fitzpatrick**	Y	N	N	N	N	N	Y
9 **Shuster**	N	Y	N	N	N	N	Y
10 **Marino**	N	Y	Y	Y	N	Y	Y
11 **Barletta**	N	N	N	N	N	N	N
12 Critz	Y	N	N	N	N	N	N
13 Schwartz	Y	N	N	N	N	N	N
14 Doyle	Y	N	N	N	N	N	N
15 **Dent**	Y	N	N	N	N	N	N
16 **Pitts**	N	Y	Y	Y	N	Y	Y
17 Holden	?	?	?	?	?	N	N
18 **Murphy**	N	Y	Y	Y	N	N	Y
19 **Platts**	N	N	N	N	N	N	N
RHODE ISLAND							
1 Cicilline	Y	N	N	N	N	N	N
2 Langevin	Y	N	N	N	N	N	N
SOUTH CAROLINA							
1 **Scott**	N	Y	Y	Y	Y	Y	Y
2 **Wilson**	N	Y	Y	Y	Y	Y	Y
3 **Duncan**	N	Y	Y	Y	Y	Y	Y
4 **Gowdy**	N	Y	Y	Y	Y	Y	Y
5 **Mulvaney**	N	Y	Y	Y	Y	Y	Y
6 Clyburn	Y	N	N	N	N	N	N
SOUTH DAKOTA							
AL **Noem**	N	N	Y	Y	Y	N	Y
TENNESSEE							
1 **Roe**	N	Y	Y	Y	Y	Y	Y
2 **Duncan**	N	Y	Y	Y	Y	Y	Y
3 **Fleischmann**	N	Y	Y	Y	Y	Y	Y
4 **DesJarlais**	N	Y	Y	Y	Y	Y	Y
5 Cooper	Y	N	N	N	N	N	N
6 **Black**	N	Y	Y	Y	Y	Y	Y
7 **Blackburn**	N	Y	Y	Y	Y	Y	Y
8 **Fincher**	N	Y	Y	Y	Y	Y	Y
9 Cohen	Y	N	N	N	N	N	N

	419	420	421	422	423	424	425
TEXAS							
1 **Gohmert**	N	Y	Y	Y	Y	?	?
2 **Poe**	N	Y	Y	Y	Y	Y	Y
3 **Johnson, S.**	N	Y	Y	Y	Y	Y	Y
4 **Hall**	N	N	N	Y	Y	Y	Y
5 **Hensarling**	N	Y	Y	Y	Y	Y	Y
6 **Barton**	Y	Y	Y	Y	Y	Y	Y
7 **Culberson**	N	Y	Y	Y	Y	Y	Y
8 **Brady**	N	Y	Y	Y	Y	Y	Y
9 Green, A.	Y	N	N	N	N	N	N
10 **McCaul**	N	Y	N	N	N	Y	Y
11 **Conaway**	N	Y	Y	Y	Y	Y	Y
12 **Granger**	N	N	N	N	N	N	N
13 **Thornberry**	N	Y	Y	Y	Y	Y	Y
14 **Paul**	N	Y	Y	Y	Y	Y	Y
15 Hinojosa	Y	N	N	N	N	N	N
16 Reyes	Y	N	N	N	N	N	N
17 **Flores**	N	Y	Y	Y	N	Y	Y
18 Jackson Lee	Y	N	N	N	N	N	N
19 **Neugebauer**	N	Y	Y	Y	Y	Y	Y
20 Gonzalez	Y	N	N	N	N	N	N
21 **Smith**	N	Y	Y	Y	Y	Y	Y
22 **Olson**	N	Y	Y	Y	N	Y	Y
23 **Canseco**	N	Y	Y	Y	Y	Y	Y
24 **Marchant**	N	Y	Y	Y	Y	Y	Y
25 Doggett	Y	N	N	N	N	N	N
26 **Burgess**	N	Y	Y	Y	N	Y	Y
27 **Farenthold**	N	Y	Y	Y	Y	Y	Y
28 Cuellar	Y	N	N	N	N	N	N
29 Green, G.	Y	N	N	N	N	N	N
30 Johnson, E.	Y	N	N	N	N	?	?
31 **Carter**	N	N	N	N	N	N	N
32 **Sessions**	N	Y	Y	Y	Y	Y	Y
UTAH							
1 **Bishop**	N	N	Y	Y	Y	N	Y
2 Matheson	Y	Y	Y	Y	N	Y	Y
3 **Chaffetz**	N	Y	Y	Y	Y	Y	Y
VERMONT							
AL Welch	Y	N	N	N	N	N	N
VIRGINIA							
1 **Wittman**	N	Y	Y	Y	N	Y	Y
2 **Rigell**	N	Y	Y	Y	Y	Y	Y
3 Scott	Y	N	N	N	N	N	N
4 **Forbes**	N	Y	Y	Y	N	Y	Y
5 **Hurt**	N	Y	Y	Y	Y	Y	Y
6 **Goodlatte**	N	Y	Y	Y	Y	Y	Y
7 **Cantor**	N	Y	N	Y	N	Y	?
8 Moran	Y	N	N	N	N	N	N
9 **Griffith**	N	Y	Y	Y	Y	Y	Y
10 **Wolf**	N	N	N	N	N	N	N
11 Connolly	Y	N	N	N	N	N	N
WASHINGTON							
1 Vacant							
2 Larsen	Y	N	N	N	N	N	N
3 **Herrera Beutler**	N	Y	Y	Y	Y	Y	Y
4 **Hastings**	N	N	N	N	N	N	N
5 **McMorris Rodgers**	N	Y	Y	Y	Y	Y	Y
6 Dicks	Y	N	N	N	N	N	N
7 McDermott	Y	N	N	N	N	N	N
8 **Reichert**	N	Y	Y	Y	N	Y	Y
9 Smith	Y	N	N	N	N	N	N
WEST VIRGINIA							
1 **McKinley**	N	N	N	N	N	N	N
2 **Capito**	N	N	N	N	N	N	N
3 Rahall	Y	N	N	N	N	N	N
WISCONSIN							
1 **Ryan**	N	Y	Y	Y	Y	Y	Y
2 Baldwin	Y	N	N	N	N	N	N
3 Kind	Y	N	N	N	N	N	N
4 Moore	Y	N	N	N	N	N	N
5 **Sensenbrenner**	N	Y	Y	Y	Y	Y	Y
6 **Petri**	N	Y	Y	Y	Y	Y	Y
7 **Duffy**	N	Y	Y	Y	Y	Y	Y
8 **Ribble**	N	Y	Y	Y	Y	Y	Y
WYOMING							
AL **Lummis**	N	Y	Y	Y	Y	Y	Y

IN THE HOUSE | By Vote Number

426. HR 5972. Fiscal 2013 Transportation-HUD Appropriations/ **HUD Office of Housing Expenses.** Broun, R-Ga., amendment that would reduce by $5 million the amount provided for salaries and expenses of HUD's Office of Housing. Rejected in Committee of the Whole 174-248: R 171-65; D 3-183. June 27, 2012.

427. HR 5972. Fiscal 2013 Transportation-HUD Appropriations/ **HUD Office of Policy Development and Research Expenses.** Broun, R-Ga., amendment that would reduce by $115,000 the amount provided for salaries and expenses of HUD's Office of Policy Development and Research. Rejected in Committee of the Whole 193-229: R 184-50; D 9-179. June 27, 2012.

428. HR 5972. Fiscal 2013 Transportation-HUD Appropriations/HUD **Office of Fair Housing and Equal Opportunity Expenses.** Broun, R-Ga., amendment that would reduce by $304,000 the amount provided for salaries and expenses of HUD's Office of Fair Housing and Equal Opportunity. Rejected in Committee of the Whole 178-247: R 174-63; D 4-184. June 27, 2012.

429. HR 5972. Fiscal 2013 Transportation-HUD Appropriations/ **HUD Public Housing Capital Fund.** Broun, R-Ga., amendment that would reduce by $110 million the amount provided for capital and management activities of public housing agencies under HUD's Public Housing Capital Fund Program. Rejected in Committee of the Whole 169-250: R 167-70; D 2-180. June 27, 2012.

430. HR 5972. Fiscal 2013 Transportation-HUD Appropriations/ **HUD Public Housing Operating Fund.** Broun, R-Ga., amendment that would reduce by $562.2 million the amount provided for payments in 2013 to public housing agencies for the operation and management of public housing. Rejected in Committee of the Whole 160-264: R 157-79; D 3-185. June 27, 2012.

431. HR 5972. Fiscal 2013 Transportation-HUD Appropriations/ **Federal Maritime Commission Expenses.** Broun, R-Ga., amendment that would reduce by $900,000 the amount provided for salaries and expenses of the Federal Maritime Commission. Rejected in Committee of the Whole 172-249: R 168-68; D 4-181. June 27, 2012.

432. HR 5972. Fiscal 2013 Transportation-HUD Appropriations/ **Neighborhood Reinvestment Corporation.** Broun, R-Ga., amendment that would reduce by $12.3 million the amount provided for payment to the Neighborhood Reinvestment Corporation for use in neighborhood reinvestment activities. Rejected in Committee of the Whole 172-250: R 170-65; D 2-185. June 27, 2012.

	426	427	428	429	430	431	432
ALABAMA							
1 **Bonner**	N	Y	Y	N	N	N	Y
2 **Roby**	N	N	N	N	N	N	N
3 **Rogers**	N	N	N	N	N	N	N
4 **Aderholt**	N	N	N	N	N	N	N
5 **Brooks**	Y	Y	Y	Y	Y	Y	Y
6 **Bachus**	N	N	N	N	N	N	N
7 Sewell	N	N	N	N	N	N	N
ALASKA							
AL **Young**	N	N	N	N	N	N	N
ARIZONA							
1 **Gosar**	Y	Y	Y	Y	Y	Y	Y
2 **Franks**	Y	Y	Y	Y	Y	Y	Y
3 **Quayle**	Y	Y	Y	Y	Y	Y	Y
4 Pastor	N	N	N	N	N	N	N
5 **Schweikert**	Y	Y	Y	Y	Y	Y	Y
6 **Flake**	Y	Y	Y	Y	Y	Y	Y
7 Grijalva	N	N	N	N	N	N	N
8 **Barber**	N	N	N	N	N	N	N
ARKANSAS							
1 **Crawford**	N	N	N	N	N	N	N
2 **Griffin**	Y	Y	Y	Y	Y	Y	Y
3 **Womack**	N	N	N	N	N	N	N
4 Ross	N	N	N	N	N	N	N
CALIFORNIA							
1 Thompson	N	N	N	N	N	N	N
2 Herger	Y	Y	Y	Y	Y	Y	Y
3 Lungren	N	Y	N	N	Y	Y	N
4 McClintock	Y	Y	Y	Y	Y	Y	Y
5 Matsui	N	N	N	N	N	N	N
6 Woolsey	N	N	N	N	N	N	N
7 Miller, George	N	N	N	N	N	N	N
8 Pelosi	N	N	N	N	N	N	N
9 Lee	N	N	N	N	N	N	N
10 Garamendi	N	N	N	N	N	N	N
11 McNerney	N	Y	N	N	N	N	N
12 Speier	N	N	N	N	N	N	N
13 Stark	N	N	N	N	N	N	N
14 Eshoo	N	N	N	N	N	N	N
15 Honda	N	N	N	N	N	N	N
16 Lofgren	N	N	N	N	N	N	N
17 Farr	N	N	N	N	N	N	N
18 Cardoza	N	N	N	N	N	N	N
19 **Denham**	Y	Y	Y	Y	Y	Y	Y
20 Costa	N	N	N	N	N	N	N
21 **Nunes**	N	N	N	N	N	N	N
22 **McCarthy**	Y	Y	Y	N	Y	Y	Y
23 Capps	N	N	N	N	N	N	N
24 **Gallegly**	N	Y	N	N	N	N	N
25 **McKeon**	N	N	N	N	N	N	N
26 **Dreier**	Y	Y	Y	Y	Y	Y	Y
27 Sherman	N	N	N	N	N	N	N
28 Berman	N	N	N	N	N	N	N
29 Schiff	N	N	N	N	N	N	N
30 Waxman	N	N	N	N	N	N	N
31 Becerra	N	N	N	N	N	N	N
32 Chu	N	N	N	N	N	N	N
33 Bass	N	N	N	?	N	N	N
34 Roybal-Allard	N	N	N	N	N	N	N
35 Waters	N	N	N	?	N	N	N
36 Hahn	N	N	N	N	N	N	N
37 Richardson	N	N	N	N	N	N	N
38 Napolitano	N	N	N	N	N	N	N
39 Sánchez, Linda	N	N	N	N	N	N	N
40 **Royce**	Y	Y	Y	Y	Y	Y	Y
41 **Lewis**	?	?	?	?	?	?	?
42 **Miller, Gary**	N	Y	N	N	N	N	N
43 Baca	N	N	N	N	N	N	N
44 **Calvert**	N	Y	N	N	N	N	N
45 **Bono Mack**	Y	Y	Y	N	Y	Y	Y
46 **Rohrabacher**	Y	Y	Y	Y	Y	Y	Y
47 Sanchez, Loretta	N	N	N	N	N	N	N
48 **Campbell**	Y	Y	Y	Y	Y	Y	Y
49 **Issa**	Y	Y	Y	Y	Y	Y	Y
50 **Bilbray**	Y	Y	Y	Y	Y	Y	Y
51 Filner	N	N	N	N	N	N	N
52 **Hunter**	Y	Y	Y	Y	Y	Y	Y
53 Davis	N	N	N	N	N	N	N

	426	427	428	429	430	431	432
COLORADO							
1 DeGette	N	N	N	N	N	N	N
2 Polis	N	Y	N	N	Y	N	N
3 **Tipton**	Y	Y	Y	Y	Y	Y	Y
4 **Gardner**	Y	Y	Y	Y	Y	Y	Y
5 **Lamborn**	Y	Y	Y	Y	Y	Y	Y
6 **Coffman**	Y	Y	N	N	N	N	Y
7 Perlmutter	N	Y	N	N	Y	N	N
CONNECTICUT							
1 Larson	N	N	N	N	N	N	N
2 Courtney	N	N	N	N	N	N	N
3 DeLauro	N	N	N	N	N	N	N
4 Himes	N	N	N	N	N	N	N
5 Murphy	N	N	N	N	N	N	N
DELAWARE							
AL Carney	N	N	N	N	N	N	N
FLORIDA							
1 **Miller**	Y	Y	Y	Y	Y	Y	Y
2 **Southerland**	N	Y	Y	N	N	Y	Y
3 Brown	N	N	N	N	N	N	N
4 **Crenshaw**	N	N	N	N	N	N	N
5 **Nugent**	Y	Y	Y	Y	Y	Y	Y
6 **Stearns**	Y	Y	Y	Y	Y	Y	Y
7 **Mica**	Y	Y	Y	Y	Y	Y	Y
8 **Webster**	Y	Y	Y	N	N	Y	N
9 **Bilirakis**	Y	Y	Y	N	Y	Y	?
10 **Young**	Y	Y	Y	Y	Y	Y	Y
11 Castor	N	N	N	N	N	N	N
12 **Ross**	Y	Y	Y	Y	Y	Y	Y
13 **Buchanan**	Y	Y	Y	Y	Y	Y	Y
14 **Mack**	?	?	?	?	?	?	?
15 **Posey**	Y	Y	Y	Y	Y	Y	Y
16 **Rooney**	Y	Y	Y	Y	Y	Y	Y
17 Wilson	N	N	N	N	N	N	N
18 **Ros-Lehtinen**	N	N	N	N	N	N	N
19 Deutch	N	N	N	N	N	N	N
20 Wasserman Schultz	N	N	N	N	N	N	N
21 **Diaz-Balart**	N	N	N	N	N	N	N
22 **West**	Y	Y	Y	Y	Y	Y	Y
23 Hastings	N	N	N	N	N	N	N
24 **Adams**	Y	Y	Y	Y	Y	Y	Y
25 **Rivera**	N	N	N	N	N	N	N
GEORGIA							
1 **Kingston**	Y	Y	Y	Y	Y	Y	Y
2 Bishop	N	N	N	N	N	N	N
3 **Westmoreland**	Y	Y	Y	Y	Y	Y	Y
4 Johnson	N	N	N	N	N	N	N
5 Lewis	N	N	N	N	N	N	N
6 **Price**	Y	Y	Y	Y	Y	Y	Y
7 **Woodall**	Y	Y	Y	Y	Y	Y	Y
8 **Scott, A.**	Y	Y	Y	Y	Y	Y	Y
9 **Graves**	Y	Y	Y	Y	Y	Y	Y
10 **Broun**	Y	Y	Y	Y	Y	Y	Y
11 **Gingrey**	Y	Y	Y	Y	Y	Y	Y
12 Barrow	Y	Y	Y	Y	Y	Y	Y
13 Scott, D.	N	N	N	N	N	N	N
HAWAII							
1 Hanabusa	N	N	N	N	N	N	N
2 Hirono	N	N	N	N	N	N	N
IDAHO							
1 **Labrador**	Y	Y	Y	Y	Y	Y	Y
2 **Simpson**	N	N	N	N	N	N	N
ILLINOIS							
1 Rush	N	N	N	N	N	N	N
2 Jackson	?	?	?	?	?	?	?
3 Lipinski	N	N	N	N	N	N	N
4 Gutierrez	N	N	N	N	N	N	N
5 Quigley	N	N	N	N	N	N	N
6 **Roskam**	Y	Y	Y	Y	Y	Y	Y
7 Davis	N	N	N	N	N	N	N
8 **Walsh**	Y	Y	Y	N	Y	Y	Y
9 Schakowsky	N	N	–	N	N	N	N
10 **Dold**	N	N	N	N	N	N	N
11 **Kinzinger**	N	Y	Y	Y	Y	N	N
12 Costello	N	N	N	N	N	N	N
13 **Biggert**	N	N	N	N	N	N	N
14 **Hultgren**	Y	Y	Y	Y	Y	Y	Y
15 **Johnson**	Y	Y	Y	Y	Y	Y	?

	426	427	428	429	430	431	432
16 **Manzullo**	Y	Y	Y	Y	Y	Y	Y
17 **Schilling**	Y	Y	Y	Y	Y	Y	Y
18 **Schock**	N	N	N	N	N	N	N
19 **Shimkus**	N	Y	N	N	N	N	Y
INDIANA							
1 Visclosky	N	N	N	N	N	N	N
2 Donnelly	N	N	N	N	N	N	N
3 **Stutzman**	Y	Y	Y	Y	Y	Y	Y
4 **Rokita**	Y	Y	Y	Y	Y	Y	Y
5 **Burton**	Y	?	Y	Y	Y	Y	Y
6 **Pence**	Y	Y	Y	Y	Y	Y	Y
7 Carson	N	N	N	N	N	?	N
8 **Bucshon**	Y	Y	Y	Y	N	Y	Y
9 **Young**	Y	Y	Y	Y	Y	Y	Y
IOWA							
1 Braley	N	N	N	N	N	N	N
2 Loebsack	N	N	N	N	N	N	N
3 Boswell	N	N	N	N	N	N	N
4 **Latham**	N	N	N	N	N	N	N
5 **King**	Y	Y	Y	Y	Y	Y	Y
KANSAS							
1 **Huelskamp**	Y	Y	Y	Y	Y	Y	Y
2 **Jenkins**	Y	Y	Y	Y	Y	Y	Y
3 **Yoder**	Y	Y	Y	Y	Y	Y	Y
4 **Pompeo**	Y	Y	Y	Y	Y	Y	Y
KENTUCKY							
1 **Whitfield**	Y	Y	Y	Y	Y	Y	N
2 **Guthrie**	Y	Y	Y	Y	Y	Y	Y
3 Yarmuth	N	N	N	N	N	N	N
4 **Davis**	N	N	N	N	N	N	N
5 **Rogers**	N	N	N	N	N	N	N
6 Chandler	N	N	N	N	N	N	N
LOUISIANA							
1 **Scalise**	Y	Y	Y	Y	Y	Y	Y
2 Richmond	N	N	N	N	N	N	N
3 **Landry**	Y	Y	Y	Y	Y	Y	Y
4 **Fleming**	Y	Y	Y	Y	Y	Y	Y
5 **Alexander**	N	N	N	N	N	N	N
6 **Cassidy**	Y	Y	Y	Y	Y	Y	Y
7 **Boustany**	Y	Y	Y	Y	Y	Y	Y
MAINE							
1 Pingree	N	N	N	N	N	N	N
2 Michaud	N	N	N	N	N	N	N
MARYLAND							
1 **Harris**	Y	Y	Y	Y	?	N	Y
2 Ruppersberger	N	N	N	N	N	N	N
3 Sarbanes	N	N	N	N	N	N	N
4 Edwards	N	N	N	N	N	N	N
5 Hoyer	N	N	N	N	N	N	N
6 **Bartlett**	Y	Y	Y	Y	Y	N	Y
7 Cummings	N	N	N	N	N	N	N
8 Van Hollen	N	N	N	N	N	N	N
MASSACHUSETTS							
1 Olver	N	N	N	N	N	N	N
2 Neal	N	N	N	N	N	N	N
3 McGovern	N	N	N	N	N	N	N
4 Frank	N	N	N	N	N	N	?
5 Tsongas	N	N	N	N	N	N	N
6 Tierney	N	N	N	N	N	N	N
7 Markey	N	N	N	N	N	N	N
8 Capuano	N	N	N	N	N	N	N
9 Lynch	N	Y	N	N	N	N	N
10 Keating	N	N	N	N	N	N	N
MICHIGAN							
1 **Benishek**	Y	Y	Y	Y	Y	Y	Y
2 **Huizenga**	Y	Y	Y	Y	Y	Y	Y
3 **Amash**	Y	Y	Y	Y	Y	Y	Y
4 **Camp**	Y	Y	Y	Y	Y	Y	Y
5 Kildee	N	N	N	N	N	N	N
6 **Upton**	Y	Y	Y	Y	Y	Y	Y
7 **Walberg**	Y	Y	Y	Y	Y	Y	Y
8 **Rogers**	Y	Y	Y	Y	Y	Y	Y
9 Peters	N	N	N	N	N	N	N
10 **Miller**	Y	Y	Y	Y	Y	Y	Y
11 **McCotter**	Y	Y	Y	Y	Y	Y	Y
12 Levin	N	N	N	N	N	N	N
13 Clarke	N	N	N	N	N	N	N
14 Conyers	?	N	N	?	N	N	N
15 Dingell	N	N	N	N	N	N	N
MINNESOTA							
1 Walz	N	N	N	N	N	N	N
2 **Kline**	Y	Y	Y	Y	Y	Y	Y
3 **Paulsen**	Y	Y	Y	Y	Y	Y	Y
4 McCollum	N	N	N	N	N	N	N

	426	427	428	429	430	431	432
5 Ellison	N	N	N	N	N	N	N
6 **Bachmann**	Y	Y	Y	Y	Y	Y	Y
7 Peterson	N	N	N	N	N	N	N
8 **Cravaack**	N	Y	Y	Y	N	N	Y
MISSISSIPPI							
1 **Nunnelee**	Y	Y	Y	Y	Y	Y	Y
2 Thompson	?	?	?	?	?	?	?
3 **Harper**	N	N	N	N	N	N	N
4 **Palazzo**	Y	Y	Y	Y	Y	Y	Y
MISSOURI							
1 Clay	N	N	N	N	N	N	N
2 **Akin**	Y	Y	Y	Y	Y	?	Y
3 Carnahan	N	N	N	N	N	N	N
4 **Hartzler**	Y	Y	Y	Y	Y	Y	Y
5 Cleaver	N	N	N	N	N	N	N
6 **Graves**	Y	Y	Y	Y	Y	Y	Y
7 **Long**	Y	Y	Y	Y	Y	Y	Y
8 **Emerson**	Y	Y	Y	Y	Y	Y	Y
9 **Luetkemeyer**	Y	Y	Y	Y	Y	Y	Y
MONTANA							
AL **Rehberg**	N	N	N	N	N	N	N
NEBRASKA							
1 **Fortenberry**	Y	Y	Y	Y	Y	Y	N
2 **Terry**	Y	Y	Y	Y	Y	N	Y
3 **Smith**	Y	Y	Y	Y	Y	Y	Y
NEVADA							
1 Berkley	N	N	N	N	N	N	N
2 **Amodei**	Y	Y	Y	Y	N	Y	Y
3 **Heck**	N	N	N	N	N	Y	N
NEW HAMPSHIRE							
1 **Guinta**	Y	Y	Y	Y	Y	Y	Y
2 **Bass**	N	N	N	N	N	N	N
NEW JERSEY							
1 Andrews	?	N	N	N	N	N	N
2 **LoBiondo**	Y	Y	Y	N	N	Y	N
3 **Runyan**	N	N	N	N	N	N	N
4 **Smith**	Y	Y	Y	N	N	Y	Y
5 **Garrett**	Y	Y	Y	Y	Y	Y	Y
6 Pallone	N	N	N	N	N	N	N
7 **Lance**	Y	Y	Y	Y	Y	Y	Y
8 Pascrell	N	N	N	N	N	N	N
9 Rothman	N	N	N	N	N	N	N
10 Vacant							
11 **Frelinghuysen**	N	N	N	N	N	N	N
12 Holt	N	N	N	N	N	N	N
13 Sires	N	N	N	N	N	N	N
NEW MEXICO							
1 Heinrich	N	N	N	N	N	N	N
2 **Pearce**	N	Y	Y	Y	Y	Y	Y
3 Luján	N	N	N	N	N	N	N
NEW YORK							
1 Bishop	N	N	N	N	N	N	N
2 Israel	N	N	N	N	N	N	N
3 **King**	N	N	N	N	N	N	N
4 McCarthy	N	N	N	N	N	?	N
5 Ackerman	N	N	N	N	N	N	N
6 Meeks	N	N	N	?	N	N	N
7 Crowley	N	N	N	N	N	N	N
8 Nadler	N	N	N	N	N	N	N
9 **Turner**	N	N	N	N	N	N	N
10 Towns	N	N	N	N	N	N	N
11 Clarke	N	N	N	N	N	N	N
12 Velázquez	N	N	N	N	N	N	N
13 **Grimm**	Y	Y	Y	Y	Y	Y	Y
14 Maloney	N	N	N	N	N	N	N
15 Rangel	N	N	N	N	N	N	N
16 Serrano	N	N	N	N	N	N	N
17 Engel	N	N	N	N	N	N	N
18 Lowey	N	N	N	N	N	N	N
19 **Hayworth**	N	N	N	N	N	N	N
20 **Gibson**	N	N	N	N	N	N	N
21 Tonko	N	N	N	N	N	N	N
22 Hinchey	N	N	N	N	N	N	N
23 Owens	N	N	N	N	N	N	N
24 **Hanna**	Y	Y	Y	N	N	Y	N
25 **Buerkle**	Y	Y	Y	Y	Y	Y	Y
26 Hochul	N	N	N	N	N	N	N
27 Higgins	N	N	N	N	N	N	N
28 Slaughter	N	N	N	N	N	N	N
29 **Reed**	N	N	N	N	N	N	N
NORTH CAROLINA							
1 Butterfield	N	N	N	N	N	N	N
2 **Ellmers**	Y	Y	Y	Y	Y	Y	Y
3 **Jones**	Y	Y	Y	Y	Y	Y	Y
4 Price	N	N	N	N	N	N	N

	426	427	428	429	430	431	432
5 **Foxx**	Y	Y	Y	Y	Y	Y	Y
6 **Coble**	Y	Y	Y	Y	Y	N	Y
7 McIntyre	Y	Y	Y	N	Y	Y	N
8 Kissell	N	Y	N	N	N	N	N
9 **Myrick**	Y	Y	Y	Y	Y	Y	Y
10 **McHenry**	Y	Y	Y	Y	Y	Y	Y
11 Shuler	N	N	N	N	N	N	N
12 Watt	N	N	N	N	N	N	N
13 Miller	N	N	N	N	N	N	N
NORTH DAKOTA							
AL **Berg**	N	N	N	N	N	Y	N
OHIO							
1 **Chabot**	Y	Y	Y	Y	Y	Y	Y
2 **Schmidt**	Y	?	Y	Y	Y	Y	Y
3 **Turner**	N	N	N	N	N	N	N
4 **Jordan**	Y	Y	Y	Y	Y	Y	Y
5 **Latta**	Y	Y	Y	Y	Y	N	Y
6 **Johnson**	Y	Y	Y	Y	Y	Y	Y
7 **Austria**	N	N	N	Y	N	Y	Y
8 **Boehner**							
9 Kaptur	N	N	N	N	N	N	N
10 Kucinich	N	N	N	N	N	N	N
11 Fudge	N	N	N	N	N	N	N
12 **Tiberi**	N	N	N	N	N	N	N
13 Sutton	N	N	N	N	N	N	N
14 **LaTourette**	N	N	N	N	N	N	N
15 **Stivers**	?	?	?	?	?	?	?
16 **Renacci**	Y	Y	Y	Y	N	Y	Y
17 Ryan	N	N	N	N	N	N	N
18 **Gibbs**	Y	Y	Y	Y	N	Y	Y
OKLAHOMA							
1 **Sullivan**	N	Y	Y	Y	Y	Y	Y
2 Boren	N	N	N	N	N	N	N
3 **Lucas**	N	N	N	N	N	N	N
4 **Cole**	N	Y	N	N	N	N	N
5 **Lankford**	Y	Y	Y	Y	Y	Y	Y
OREGON							
1 Bonamici	N	N	N	N	N	N	N
2 **Walden**	Y	Y	N	N	N	Y	Y
3 Blumenauer	N	N	N	N	N	N	N
4 DeFazio	N	Y	N	N	N	?	N
5 Schrader	N	N	N	N	N	N	N
PENNSYLVANIA							
1 Brady	N	N	N	N	N	N	N
2 Fattah	N	N	N	N	N	N	N
3 **Kelly**	N	N	N	N	N	N	N
4 Altmire	N	N	N	N	N	N	N
5 **Thompson**	N	N	N	N	N	N	N
6 **Gerlach**	N	N	N	N	N	N	N
7 **Meehan**	N	Y	N	N	N	Y	N
8 **Fitzpatrick**	Y	Y	Y	N	N	Y	Y
9 **Shuster**	Y	Y	Y	N	N	N	N
10 **Marino**	Y	Y	Y	Y	Y	Y	Y
11 **Barletta**	N	N	N	N	N	N	N
12 Critz	N	N	N	N	N	N	N
13 Schwartz	N	N	N	N	N	N	N
14 Doyle	N	N	N	N	N	N	N
15 **Dent**	N	Y	N	N	N	N	N
16 **Pitts**	Y	Y	Y	Y	Y	Y	Y
17 Holden	N	N	N	N	N	N	N
18 **Murphy**	Y	Y	N	N	N	N	Y
19 **Platts**	N	N	N	N	N	N	N
RHODE ISLAND							
1 Cicilline	N	N	N	N	N	N	N
2 Langevin	N	N	N	N	N	N	N
SOUTH CAROLINA							
1 **Scott**	Y	Y	Y	Y	Y	Y	Y
2 **Wilson**	Y	Y	Y	Y	Y	Y	Y
3 **Duncan**	Y	Y	Y	Y	Y	Y	Y
4 **Gowdy**	Y	Y	Y	Y	Y	Y	Y
5 **Mulvaney**	Y	Y	Y	Y	Y	Y	Y
6 Clyburn	N	N	N	N	N	N	N
SOUTH DAKOTA							
AL **Noem**	Y	Y	Y	Y	Y	Y	Y
TENNESSEE							
1 **Roe**	Y	Y	Y	Y	Y	Y	Y
2 **Duncan**	Y	Y	Y	Y	Y	Y	Y
3 **Fleischmann**	Y	Y	Y	Y	Y	Y	Y
4 **DesJarlais**	Y	Y	Y	Y	Y	Y	Y
5 Cooper	N	N	N	N	N	N	N
6 **Black**	Y	Y	Y	Y	Y	Y	Y
7 **Blackburn**	Y	Y	Y	Y	Y	Y	Y
8 **Fincher**	Y	Y	Y	Y	Y	Y	Y
9 Cohen	N	N	N	N	N	N	N

	426	427	428	429	430	431	432
TEXAS							
1 **Gohmert**	?	?	?	?	?	?	?
2 **Poe**	Y	Y	Y	Y	Y	Y	Y
3 **Johnson, S.**	Y	Y	Y	Y	Y	Y	Y
4 **Hall**	?	?	Y	Y	Y	Y	Y
5 **Hensarling**	Y	Y	Y	Y	Y	Y	Y
6 **Barton**	Y	Y	Y	Y	Y	Y	N
7 **Culberson**	Y	Y	Y	Y	Y	Y	Y
8 **Brady**	Y	Y	Y	Y	Y	Y	Y
9 Green, A.	N	N	N	N	N	N	N
10 **McCaul**	Y	Y	Y	Y	Y	Y	Y
11 **Conaway**	Y	Y	Y	Y	Y	Y	Y
12 **Granger**	N	N	N	N	N	N	N
13 **Thornberry**	Y	Y	Y	Y	Y	Y	Y
14 **Paul**	Y	Y	Y	Y	Y	Y	Y
15 Hinojosa	N	N	N	N	N	N	N
16 Reyes	N	N	N	N	N	N	N
17 **Flores**	Y	Y	Y	Y	Y	Y	Y
18 Jackson Lee	N	N	N	N	N	N	N
19 **Neugebauer**	Y	Y	Y	Y	Y	Y	Y
20 Gonzalez	N	N	N	?	N	N	N
21 **Smith**	Y	Y	Y	Y	Y	Y	Y
22 **Olson**	Y	Y	Y	Y	Y	Y	Y
23 **Canseco**	Y	Y	Y	Y	Y	Y	Y
24 **Marchant**	Y	Y	Y	Y	Y	Y	Y
25 Doggett	N	N	N	N	N	N	N
26 **Burgess**	Y	Y	Y	Y	Y	Y	Y
27 **Farenthold**	Y	Y	Y	Y	Y	Y	Y
28 Cuellar	N	N	N	N	N	N	N
29 Green, G.	N	N	N	N	N	N	N
30 Johnson, E.	?	?	?	?	?	?	?
31 **Carter**	N	N	N	N	N	N	N
32 **Sessions**	Y	Y	Y	Y	Y	Y	Y
UTAH							
1 **Bishop**	Y	Y	Y	Y	Y	Y	Y
2 Matheson	Y	Y	Y	Y	N	Y	Y
3 **Chaffetz**	Y	Y	Y	Y	Y	Y	Y
VERMONT							
AL Welch	N	N	N	N	N	N	N
VIRGINIA							
1 **Wittman**	Y	Y	Y	Y	Y	N	Y
2 **Rigell**	Y	Y	Y	Y	Y	N	Y
3 Scott	N	N	N	N	N	N	N
4 **Forbes**	Y	Y	Y	Y	Y	N	Y
5 **Hurt**	Y	Y	Y	Y	Y	Y	Y
6 **Goodlatte**	Y	Y	Y	Y	Y	Y	Y
7 **Cantor**	Y	Y	N	Y	Y	Y	Y
8 Moran	N	N	N	N	N	N	N
9 **Griffith**	Y	Y	Y	Y	Y	Y	Y
10 **Wolf**	N	N	N	N	N	N	N
11 Connolly	N	N	N	N	N	N	N
WASHINGTON							
1 Vacant							
2 Larsen	N	N	N	N	N	N	N
3 **Herrera Beutler**	N	Y	Y	N	N	Y	N
4 **Hastings**	N	N	N	N	N	N	N
5 **McMorris Rodgers**	Y	Y	Y	Y	Y	Y	Y
6 Dicks	N	N	N	N	N	N	N
7 McDermott	N	N	N	N	N	N	N
8 **Reichert**	Y	Y	N	Y	N	Y	N
9 Smith	N	N	N	N	N	N	N
WEST VIRGINIA							
1 **McKinley**	N	N	N	N	N	N	N
2 **Capito**	N	N	N	N	N	N	Y
3 Rahall	N	N	N	N	N	N	N
WISCONSIN							
1 **Ryan**	Y	Y	Y	Y	Y	Y	Y
2 Baldwin	N	N	N	N	N	N	N
3 Kind	N	N	N	N	N	N	N
4 Moore	N	N	N	N	N	N	N
5 **Sensenbrenner**	Y	Y	Y	Y	Y	Y	Y
6 **Petri**	Y	Y	Y	Y	Y	Y	Y
7 **Duffy**	Y	Y	Y	Y	Y	Y	Y
8 **Ribble**	Y	Y	Y	Y	Y	Y	Y
WYOMING							
AL **Lummis**	Y	Y	Y	Y	Y	Y	Y

IN THE HOUSE | By Vote Number

433. **HR 5972. Fiscal 2013 Transportation-HUD Appropriations/ Community Development Fund.** Chaffetz, R-Utah, amendment that would cut $396 million from the amount provided for assistance to state and local governments for economic and community development activities. Rejected in Committee of the Whole 157-267: R 157-80; D 0-187. June 27, 2012.

434. **HR 5972. Fiscal 2013 Transportation-HUD Appropriations/ Community Development Block Grants.** McClintock, R-Calif., amendment that would eliminate all funding for the Community Development Fund for assistance to state and local governments, a total of $3.4 billion, including $3.34 billion for the Community Development Block Grant program and $60 million in grants to Indian tribes. Rejected in Committee of the Whole 80-342: R 80-156; D 0-186. June 27, 2012.

435. **HR 5972. Fiscal 2013 Transportation-HUD Appropriations/ Community Development Loan Guarantees.** McClintock, R-Calif., amendment that would eliminate all funding for the Community Development Loan Guarantees, a total of $6 million. Rejected in Committee of the Whole 123-300: R 123-114; D 0-186. June 27, 2012.

436. **HR 5972. Fiscal 2013 Transportation-HUD Appropriations/ HOME Investment Partnerships Program.** Flake, R-Ariz., amendment that would reduce the amount provided for the HOME investment partnerships program by $200 million. Rejected in Committee of the Whole 178-242: R 174-59; D 4-183. June 27, 2012.

437. **H Res 706, H Res 711. Holder Contempt Resolutions/Rule.** Adoption of the rule (H Res 708) that would provide for House floor consideration of the resolution (H Res 711) holding Attorney General Eric H. Holder Jr. in contempt for failing to turn over certain documents related to the Justice Department's "Operation Fast and Furious" gun-tracking program. It also would provide for House floor consideration of a resolution (H Res 706) that would authorize the House Oversight and Government Reform Committee to initiate or intervene in judicial proceedings to enforce its subpoena for documents. Adopted 254-173: R 239-0; D 15-173. June 28, 2012.

	433	434	435	436	437
ALABAMA					
1 **Bonner**	N	N	N	N	Y
2 **Roby**	Y	N	Y	Y	Y
3 **Rogers**	N	N	N	N	Y
4 **Aderholt**	N	N	N	N	Y
5 **Brooks**	Y	N	Y	Y	Y
6 **Bachus**	N	N	N	Y	Y
7 Sewell	N	N	N	N	N
ALASKA					
AL **Young**	N	N	N	N	Y
ARIZONA					
1 **Gosar**	Y	Y	Y	Y	Y
2 **Franks**	Y	Y	Y	Y	Y
3 **Quayle**	Y	Y	Y	Y	Y
4 Pastor	N	N	N	N	N
5 **Schweikert**	Y	Y	Y	Y	Y
6 **Flake**	Y	Y	Y	Y	Y
7 Grijalva	N	N	N	N	N
8 Barber	N	N	N	N	N
ARKANSAS					
1 **Crawford**	N	N	N	Y	Y
2 **Griffin**	Y	N	N	Y	Y
3 **Womack**	N	N	N	N	Y
4 Ross	N	N	N	N	Y
CALIFORNIA					
1 Thompson	N	N	N	N	N
2 **Herger**	Y	Y	Y	Y	Y
3 **Lungren**	Y	N	N	Y	Y
4 **McClintock**	Y	Y	Y	Y	Y
5 Matsui	N	N	N	N	N
6 Woolsey	N	N	N	N	N
7 Miller, George	N	N	N	N	N
8 Pelosi	N	N	N	N	N
9 Lee	N	N	N	N	N
10 Garamendi	N	N	N	N	N
11 McNerney	N	N	N	N	N
12 Speier	N	N	N	N	N
13 Stark	N	N	N	N	N
14 Eshoo	N	N	N	N	N
15 Honda	N	N	N	N	N
16 Lofgren	N	N	N	N	N
17 Farr	N	N	N	N	N
18 Cardoza	N	N	N	N	?
19 **Denham**	Y	Y	N	Y	Y
20 Costa	N	N	N	N	N
21 **Nunes**	Y	Y	Y	Y	Y
22 **McCarthy**	Y	N	Y	Y	Y
23 Capps	N	N	N	N	N
24 **Gallegly**	N	N	N	N	Y
25 **McKeon**	N	N	N	N	Y
26 **Dreier**	Y	N	N	Y	Y
27 Sherman	N	N	N	N	N
28 Berman	N	N	N	N	N
29 Schiff	N	N	N	N	N
30 Waxman	N	N	N	N	N
31 Becerra	N	N	N	N	N
32 Chu	N	N	N	N	N
33 Bass	N	N	?	N	N
34 Roybal-Allard	N	N	N	N	N
35 Waters	N	N	N	N	N
36 Hahn	N	N	N	N	N
37 Richardson	N	N	N	N	N
38 Napolitano	N	N	N	N	N
39 Sánchez, Linda	N	N	N	N	N
40 **Royce**	Y	Y	Y	Y	Y
41 **Lewis**	?	?	?	?	?
42 **Miller, Gary**	N	N	N	N	Y
43 Baca	N	N	N	N	N
44 **Calvert**	N	N	N	N	Y
45 **Bono Mack**	Y	N	Y	Y	Y
46 **Rohrabacher**	Y	Y	Y	Y	Y
47 Sanchez, Loretta	N	N	N	N	N
48 **Campbell**	Y	Y	Y	Y	Y
49 **Issa**	Y	Y	Y	Y	Y
50 **Bilbray**	Y	N	N	Y	Y
51 Filner	N	N	N	N	N
52 **Hunter**	Y	Y	Y	Y	Y
53 Davis	N	N	N	N	N

	433	434	435	436	437
COLORADO					
1 DeGette	N	N	N	N	N
2 Polis	N	N	N	N	N
3 **Tipton**	N	N	N	N	Y
4 **Gardner**	Y	N	Y	Y	Y
5 **Lamborn**	Y	Y	Y	Y	Y
6 **Coffman**	Y	N	Y	Y	Y
7 Perlmutter	N	N	N	N	N
CONNECTICUT					
1 Larson	N	N	N	N	N
2 Courtney	N	N	N	N	N
3 DeLauro	N	N	N	N	N
4 Himes	N	N	N	N	N
5 Murphy	N	N	N	N	N
DELAWARE					
AL Carney	N	N	N	N	N
FLORIDA					
1 **Miller**	Y	+	Y	Y	Y
2 **Southerland**	N	N	Y	Y	Y
3 Brown	N	N	N	N	N
4 **Crenshaw**	N	N	N	N	Y
5 **Nugent**	N	N	N	Y	Y
6 **Stearns**	Y	Y	Y	Y	Y
7 **Mica**	Y	N	Y	Y	Y
8 **Webster**	Y	Y	Y	Y	Y
9 **Bilirakis**	N	N	N	Y	Y
10 **Young**	N	N	N	Y	Y
11 Castor	N	N	N	N	N
12 **Ross**	Y	N	N	Y	Y
13 **Buchanan**	Y	N	Y	Y	Y
14 **Mack**	?	?	?	?	Y
15 **Posey**	Y	Y	Y	Y	Y
16 **Rooney**	Y	N	Y	Y	Y
17 Wilson	N	N	N	N	N
18 **Ros-Lehtinen**	N	N	N	Y	Y
19 Deutch	N	N	N	N	N
20 Wasserman Schultz	N	N	N	N	N
21 **Diaz-Balart**	N	N	N	Y	Y
22 **West**	N	N	N	Y	Y
23 Hastings	N	N	N	N	N
24 **Adams**	Y	N	Y	Y	Y
25 **Rivera**	N	N	N	N	Y
GEORGIA					
1 **Kingston**	Y	N	Y	Y	Y
2 Bishop	N	N	N	N	N
3 **Westmoreland**	Y	Y	Y	Y	Y
4 Johnson	N	N	N	N	N
5 Lewis	N	N	N	N	N
6 **Price**	Y	Y	Y	Y	Y
7 **Woodall**	Y	Y	Y	Y	Y
8 **Scott, A.**	Y	Y	Y	Y	Y
9 **Graves**	Y	Y	Y	Y	Y
10 **Broun**	Y	Y	Y	Y	Y
11 **Gingrey**	Y	N	Y	Y	Y
12 Barrow	N	N	N	N	Y
13 Scott, D.	N	N	N	N	N
HAWAII					
1 Hanabusa	N	N	N	N	N
2 Hirono	N	N	N	N	N
IDAHO					
1 **Labrador**	Y	Y	Y	Y	Y
2 **Simpson**	Y	N	N	Y	Y
ILLINOIS					
1 Rush	N	N	N	N	N
2 Jackson	?	?	?	?	?
3 Lipinski	N	N	N	Y	N
4 Gutierrez	N	?	N	N	N
5 Quigley	N	N	N	N	N
6 **Roskam**	N	N	N	N	Y
7 Davis	N	N	N	N	N
8 **Walsh**	Y	Y	Y	Y	Y
9 Schakowsky	N	N	N	N	N
10 **Dold**	N	N	N	N	Y
11 **Kinzinger**	N	N	N	N	Y
12 Costello	N	N	N	N	N
13 **Biggert**	N	N	N	N	Y
14 **Hultgren**	Y	N	Y	Y	Y
15 **Johnson**	Y	Y	Y	Y	Y

KEY   Republicans   Democrats

Y Voted for (yea)	**X** Paired against	**C** Voted "present" to avoid possible conflict of interest
# Paired for	**–** Announced against	**?** Did not vote or otherwise make a position known
+ Announced for	**P** Voted "present"	
N Voted against (nay)		

	433	434	435	436	437
16 Manzullo	Y	Y	Y	Y	Y
17 Schilling	N	N	N	N	Y
18 Schock	N	N	N	N	Y
19 Shimkus	N	N	N	Y	Y
INDIANA					
1 Visclosky	N	N	N	N	N
2 Donnelly	N	N	N	N	Y
3 Stutzman	Y	Y	Y	Y	Y
4 Rokita	Y	Y	Y	Y	Y
5 Burton	Y	Y	Y	Y	Y
6 Pence	Y	Y	Y	Y	Y
7 Carson	N	N	N	N	N
8 Bucshon	Y	N	N	?	Y
9 Young	Y	N	Y	Y	Y
IOWA					
1 Braley	N	N	N	N	N
2 Loebsack	N	N	N	N	N
3 Boswell	N	N	N	N	Y
4 Latham	N	N	N	N	Y
5 King	Y	N	Y	Y	Y
KANSAS					
1 Huelskamp	Y	Y	Y	Y	Y
2 Jenkins	Y	Y	Y	Y	Y
3 Yoder	Y	Y	Y	Y	Y
4 Pompeo	Y	Y	Y	Y	Y
KENTUCKY					
1 Whitfield	N	N	N	N	Y
2 Guthrie	Y	N	N	Y	Y
3 Yarmuth	N	N	N	N	N
4 Davis	N	N	N	N	Y
5 Rogers	N	N	N	N	Y
6 Chandler	N	N	N	N	Y
LOUISIANA					
1 Scalise	Y	Y	Y	Y	Y
2 Richmond	N	N	N	N	N
3 Landry	Y	Y	Y	Y	Y
4 Fleming	Y	Y	Y	Y	Y
5 Alexander	N	N	N	N	Y
6 Cassidy	Y	Y	Y	Y	Y
7 Boustany	Y	N	Y	Y	Y
MAINE					
1 Pingree	N	N	N	N	N
2 Michaud	N	N	N	N	N
MARYLAND					
1 Harris	Y	Y	Y	Y	Y
2 Ruppersberger	N	N	N	N	N
3 Sarbanes	N	N	N	N	N
4 Edwards	N	N	N	N	N
5 Hoyer	N	N	N	N	N
6 Bartlett	Y	Y	Y	Y	Y
7 Cummings	N	N	N	N	N
8 Van Hollen	N	N	N	N	N
MASSACHUSETTS					
1 Olver	N	N	N	N	N
2 Neal	N	N	N	N	N
3 McGovern	N	N	N	N	N
4 Frank	?	?	?	?	N
5 Tsongas	N	N	N	N	N
6 Tierney	N	N	N	N	N
7 Markey	N	N	N	N	N
8 Capuano	N	N	N	N	N
9 Lynch	N	N	N	N	N
10 Keating	N	N	N	N	N
MICHIGAN					
1 Benishek	Y	N	Y	Y	Y
2 Huizenga	Y	Y	Y	Y	Y
3 Amash	Y	Y	Y	Y	Y
4 Camp	Y	N	N	Y	Y
5 Kildee	N	N	N	N	N
6 Upton	Y	N	Y	Y	Y
7 Walberg	N	N	Y	Y	Y
8 Rogers	Y	N	Y	Y	Y
9 Peters	N	N	N	N	N
10 Miller	Y	N	Y	Y	Y
11 McCotter	N	N	N	N	Y
12 Levin	N	N	N	N	N
13 Clarke	N	N	N	N	N
14 Conyers	N	N	N	N	N
15 Dingell	N	N	N	N	N
MINNESOTA					
1 Walz	N	N	N	N	Y
2 Kline	Y	N	Y	Y	Y
3 Paulsen	Y	N	N	Y	Y
4 McCollum	N	N	N	N	N

	433	434	435	436	437
5 Ellison	N	N	N	N	N
6 Bachmann	Y	Y	Y	Y	Y
7 Peterson	N	N	N	N	Y
8 Cravaack	N	N	N	Y	Y
MISSISSIPPI					
1 Nunnelee	Y	Y	Y	Y	Y
2 Thompson	?	?	?	?	N
3 Harper	N	N	N	N	Y
4 Palazzo	Y	N	N	Y	Y
MISSOURI					
1 Clay	N	N	N	N	N
2 Akin	Y	Y	Y	Y	Y
3 Carnahan	N	N	N	N	N
4 Hartzler	Y	N	Y	Y	Y
5 Cleaver	N	N	N	N	N
6 Graves	Y	N	Y	Y	Y
7 Long	Y	Y	Y	Y	Y
8 Emerson	Y	N	Y	Y	Y
9 Luetkemeyer	Y	N	N	Y	Y
MONTANA					
AL Rehberg	N	N	N	?	Y
NEBRASKA					
1 Fortenberry	Y	N	N	Y	Y
2 Terry	N	N	N	Y	Y
3 Smith	Y	N	N	Y	Y
NEVADA					
1 Berkley	N	N	N	N	N
2 Amodei	Y	N	Y	Y	Y
3 Heck	N	N	N	N	N
NEW HAMPSHIRE					
1 Guinta	Y	N	Y	Y	Y
2 Bass	N	N	N	N	Y
NEW JERSEY					
1 Andrews	N	N	N	N	N
2 LoBiondo	N	N	N	N	Y
3 Runyan	N	N	N	N	Y
4 Smith	N	N	N	N	Y
5 Garrett	Y	Y	Y	Y	Y
6 Pallone	N	N	N	N	N
7 Lance	Y	N	Y	Y	Y
8 Pascrell	N	N	N	N	N
9 Rothman	N	N	N	N	N
10 Vacant					
11 Frelinghuysen	N	N	N	N	Y
12 Holt	N	N	N	N	N
13 Sires	N	N	N	N	N
NEW MEXICO					
1 Heinrich	N	N	N	N	N
2 Pearce	N	N	N	Y	Y
3 Luján	N	N	N	N	N
NEW YORK					
1 Bishop	N	N	N	N	N
2 Israel	N	N	N	N	N
3 King	N	N	N	N	Y
4 McCarthy	N	N	N	N	N
5 Ackerman	N	N	N	N	N
6 Meeks	N	N	N	N	N
7 Crowley	N	N	N	N	N
8 Nadler	N	N	N	N	N
9 Turner	N	N	N	N	Y
10 Towns	N	N	N	N	N
11 Clarke	N	N	N	N	N
12 Velázquez	N	N	N	N	N
13 Grimm	Y	N	N	Y	Y
14 Maloney	N	N	N	N	N
15 Rangel	N	N	N	N	N
16 Serrano	N	N	N	N	N
17 Engel	N	N	N	N	N
18 Lowey	N	N	N	N	N
19 Hayworth	Y	N	N	N	Y
20 Gibson	N	N	N	N	Y
21 Tonko	N	N	N	N	N
22 Hinchey	N	N	N	N	N
23 Owens	N	N	N	N	Y
24 Hanna	N	N	N	N	Y
25 Buerkle	Y	N	Y	Y	Y
26 Hochul	N	N	N	Y	Y
27 Higgins	N	N	N	N	N
28 Slaughter	N	N	N	N	N
29 Reed	N	N	N	N	Y
NORTH CAROLINA					
1 Butterfield	N	N	N	N	N
2 Ellmers	Y	N	N	Y	Y
3 Jones	Y	N	N	Y	Y
4 Price	N	N	N	N	N

	433	434	435	436	437
5 Foxx	Y	Y	Y	Y	Y
6 Coble	Y	Y	Y	Y	Y
7 McIntyre	N	N	N	N	Y
8 Kissell	N	N	N	N	Y
9 Myrick	Y	N	N	Y	Y
10 McHenry	Y	Y	Y	Y	Y
11 Shuler	N	N	N	N	N
12 Watt	N	N	N	N	N
13 Miller	N	N	N	N	N
NORTH DAKOTA					
AL Berg	N	N	N	?	Y
OHIO					
1 Chabot	Y	Y	Y	Y	Y
2 Schmidt	Y	N	N	Y	Y
3 Turner	N	N	N	N	Y
4 Jordan	Y	Y	Y	Y	Y
5 Latta	N	N	N	Y	Y
6 Johnson	Y	N	N	Y	Y
7 Austria	N	N	N	N	Y
8 Boehner					
9 Kaptur	N	N	N	N	N
10 Kucinich	N	N	N	N	N
11 Fudge	N	N	N	N	N
12 Tiberi	N	N	N	N	Y
13 Sutton	N	N	N	N	N
14 LaTourette	N	N	N	N	Y
15 Stivers	?	?	?	?	Y
16 Renacci	Y	N	N	Y	Y
17 Ryan	N	N	N	N	N
18 Gibbs	Y	N	N	Y	Y
OKLAHOMA					
1 Sullivan	Y	Y	N	N	Y
2 Boren	N	N	N	N	Y
3 Lucas	N	N	N	N	Y
4 Cole	N	N	N	N	Y
5 Lankford	Y	N	Y	Y	Y
OREGON					
1 Bonamici	N	N	N	N	N
2 Walden	Y	N	Y	Y	Y
3 Blumenauer	N	N	N	N	N
4 DeFazio	N	N	N	N	N
5 Schrader	N	N	N	N	N
PENNSYLVANIA					
1 Brady	N	N	N	N	N
2 Fattah	N	N	N	N	N
3 Kelly	N	N	N	N	Y
4 Altmire	N	N	N	N	N
5 Thompson	N	N	N	N	Y
6 Gerlach	N	N	N	N	Y
7 Meehan	N	N	N	N	Y
8 Fitzpatrick	N	N	N	Y	Y
9 Shuster	N	N	N	N	Y
10 Marino	Y	N	N	Y	Y
11 Barletta	N	N	N	N	Y
12 Critz	N	N	N	N	N
13 Schwartz	N	N	N	N	N
14 Doyle	N	N	N	N	N
15 Dent	N	N	N	N	Y
16 Pitts	Y	N	N	Y	Y
17 Holden	N	N	N	N	N
18 Murphy	Y	N	Y	Y	Y
19 Platts	N	N	N	N	Y
RHODE ISLAND					
1 Cicilline	N	N	N	N	N
2 Langevin	N	N	N	N	N
SOUTH CAROLINA					
1 Scott	Y	Y	Y	Y	Y
2 Wilson	Y	Y	Y	Y	Y
3 Duncan	Y	Y	Y	Y	Y
4 Gowdy	Y	Y	Y	Y	Y
5 Mulvaney	Y	Y	Y	Y	Y
6 Clyburn	N	N	N	N	N
SOUTH DAKOTA					
AL Noem	N	N	N	Y	Y
TENNESSEE					
1 Roe	N	N	Y	Y	Y
2 Duncan	Y	Y	Y	Y	Y
3 Fleischmann	Y	Y	Y	Y	Y
4 DesJarlais	N	N	N	Y	Y
5 Cooper	N	N	N	N	N
6 Black	Y	Y	Y	Y	Y
7 Blackburn	Y	Y	Y	Y	Y
8 Fincher	Y	N	Y	Y	Y
9 Cohen	N	N	N	N	N

	433	434	435	436	437
TEXAS					
1 Gohmert	?	?	?	?	Y
2 Poe	Y	N	Y	Y	Y
3 Johnson, S.	Y	Y	Y	Y	Y
4 Hall	Y	N	Y	Y	Y
5 Hensarling	Y	Y	Y	Y	Y
6 Barton	Y	N	Y	Y	Y
7 Culberson	Y	Y	Y	Y	Y
8 Brady	Y	N	N	Y	Y
9 Green, A.	N	N	N	N	N
10 McCaul	Y	Y	Y	Y	Y
11 Conaway	Y	Y	Y	Y	Y
12 Granger	N	N	N	Y	Y
13 Thornberry	Y	N	Y	Y	Y
14 Paul	Y	Y	Y	?	Y
15 Hinojosa	N	N	N	N	N
16 Reyes	N	N	N	N	N
17 Flores	Y	Y	Y	Y	Y
18 Jackson Lee	N	N	N	N	N
19 Neugebauer	Y	Y	Y	Y	Y
20 Gonzalez	N	N	N	N	N
21 Smith	Y	N	N	Y	Y
22 Olson	Y	Y	Y	Y	Y
23 Canseco	Y	N	N	Y	Y
24 Marchant	Y	N	Y	Y	Y
25 Doggett	N	N	N	N	N
26 Burgess	Y	Y	Y	Y	Y
27 Farenthold	Y	N	N	Y	Y
28 Cuellar	N	N	N	N	N
29 Green, G.	N	N	N	N	N
30 Johnson, E.	?	?	?	?	?
31 Carter	N	N	N	Y	Y
32 Sessions	Y	Y	Y	Y	Y
UTAH					
1 Bishop	Y	N	Y	Y	Y
2 Matheson	N	N	N	Y	Y
3 Chaffetz	Y	Y	Y	Y	Y
VERMONT					
AL Welch	N	N	N	N	N
VIRGINIA					
1 Wittman	Y	N	N	Y	Y
2 Rigell	Y	N	Y	Y	Y
3 Scott	N	N	N	N	N
4 Forbes	Y	N	Y	Y	?
5 Hurt	Y	N	Y	Y	Y
6 Goodlatte	Y	N	Y	Y	Y
7 Cantor	Y	Y	Y	Y	Y
8 Moran	N	N	N	N	N
9 Griffith	Y	N	N	Y	Y
10 Wolf	N	N	N	N	Y
11 Connolly	N	N	N	N	N
WASHINGTON					
1 Vacant					
2 Larsen	N	N	N	N	N
3 Herrera Beutler	N	N	N	Y	Y
4 Hastings	N	N	N	N	Y
5 McMorris Rodgers	Y	N	Y	Y	Y
6 Dicks	N	N	N	N	N
7 McDermott	N	N	N	N	N
8 Reichert	N	N	N	N	N
9 Smith	N	N	N	N	N
WEST VIRGINIA					
1 McKinley	N	N	N	N	Y
2 Capito	N	N	N	N	Y
3 Rahall	N	N	N	N	Y
WISCONSIN					
1 Ryan	Y	N	Y	Y	Y
2 Baldwin	N	N	N	N	N
3 Kind	N	N	N	N	Y
4 Moore	N	N	N	N	N
5 Sensenbrenner	Y	Y	Y	Y	Y
6 Petri	Y	Y	Y	Y	Y
7 Duffy	Y	N	N	Y	Y
8 Ribble	Y	N	Y	Y	Y
WYOMING					
AL Lummis	Y	Y	Y	Y	Y

IN THE HOUSE | By Vote Number

438. **HR 4251. Maritime Security Programs/Passage.** King, R-N.Y., motion to suspend the rules and pass the bill, as amended, that would require the Department of Homeland Security (DHS), by July 1, 2014, to update its Maritime Operations Coordination Plan to better coordinate the maritime security efforts of its agencies, as well as to integrate their work with other government entities, the private sector, and state and local partners. It would require the department to update the plan again on July 1, 2019. The bill also would direct DHS to overhaul procedures for issuing Transportation Worker Identification Credentials. Motion agreed to 402-21: R 220-18; D 182-3. A two-thirds majority of those present and voting (282 in this case) is required for passage under suspension of the rules. June 28, 2012.

439. **HR 4005. Port Security Study/Passage.** King, R-N.Y., motion to suspend the rules and pass the bill, as amended, that would require the Homeland Security Department, within one year of enactment, to conduct a study of the remaining gaps in port security in the United States. It also would require the department to submit a classified report to Congress prioritizing these gaps and a plan to address them. Motion agreed to 411-9: R 228-8; D 183-1. A two-thirds majority of those present and voting (280 in this case) is required for passage under suspension of the rules. June 28, 2012.

440. **H Res 711. Holder Contempt Resolution/Motion to Refer.** Dingell, D-Mich., motion to refer the measure back to the House Committee on Oversight and Government Reform with the requirement that the committee hold new hearings and conduct a more complete investigation. Motion rejected 172-251: R 0-237; D 172-14. June 28, 2012.

441. **H Res 711. Holder Contempt Resolution/Adoption.** Adoption of the resolution that would cite Attorney General Eric H. Holder Jr. for contempt of Congress for refusing to comply with the subpoena issued by the House Oversight and Government Reform Committee to provide documents to the committee regarding the "Operation Fast and Furious" gun-tracking program. Adopted 255-67: R 238-2; D 17-65. A "nay" was a vote in support of the president's position. June 28, 2012.

442. **H Res 706. Judicial Proceedings on Holder Subpoena/Adoption.** Adoption of the resolution that would authorize the House Oversight and Government Reform Committee to initiate or intervene in judicial proceedings to enforce its subpoena for documents related to the Justice Department's "Operation Fast and Furious" gun-tracking program and seek declaratory judgment affirming the duty of Attorney General Eric H. Holder Jr. to comply with the committee's subpoena. Adopted 258-95: R 237-0; D 21-95. A "nay" was a vote in support of the president's position. June 28, 2012.

	438	439	440	441	442
ALABAMA					
1 Bonner	Y	Y	N	Y	Y
2 Roby	Y	Y	N	Y	Y
3 Rogers	Y	Y	N	Y	Y
4 Aderholt	Y	Y	N	Y	Y
5 Brooks	Y	Y	N	Y	Y
6 Bachus	Y	Y	N	Y	Y
7 Sewell	Y	Y	Y	?	?
ALASKA					
AL Young	Y	Y	N	Y	Y
ARIZONA					
1 Gosar	Y	Y	N	Y	Y
2 Franks	Y	Y	N	Y	Y
3 Quayle	Y	Y	N	Y	Y
4 Pastor	Y	Y	Y	N	N
5 Schweikert	Y	Y	N	Y	Y
6 Flake	N	N	N	Y	Y
7 Grijalva	Y	Y	Y	?	?
8 Barber	Y	Y	Y	N	Y
ARKANSAS					
1 Crawford	Y	Y	N	Y	Y
2 Griffin	Y	Y	N	Y	Y
3 Womack	Y	Y	N	Y	Y
4 Ross	Y	Y	N	Y	Y
CALIFORNIA					
1 Thompson	Y	Y	Y	N	N
2 Herger	Y	Y	N	Y	Y
3 Lungren	Y	Y	N	Y	Y
4 McClintock	Y	Y	N	Y	Y
5 Matsui	Y	Y	Y	?	N
6 Woolsey	?	Y	Y	?	?
7 Miller, George	Y	Y	Y	N	N
8 Pelosi	Y	Y	Y	?	?
9 Lee	Y	Y	Y	?	?
10 Garamendi	Y	Y	Y	?	N
11 McNerney	Y	Y	Y	N	N
12 Speier	Y	Y	Y	N	N
13 Stark	Y	Y	Y	?	N
14 Eshoo	Y	Y	Y	N	N
15 Honda	Y	Y	Y	?	?
16 Lofgren	Y	Y	Y	N	N
17 Farr	Y	Y	Y	N	N
18 Cardoza	?	?	?	?	?
19 Denham	Y	Y	N	Y	Y
20 Costa	Y	Y	Y	?	P
21 Nunes	Y	Y	N	Y	Y
22 McCarthy	Y	Y	N	Y	Y
23 Capps	Y	Y	Y	N	N
24 Gallegly	Y	Y	N	Y	Y
25 McKeon	Y	Y	N	Y	Y
26 Dreier	Y	Y	N	Y	Y
27 Sherman	Y	Y	Y	N	N
28 Berman	Y	Y	Y	N	N
29 Schiff	Y	Y	Y	?	N
30 Waxman	Y	Y	Y	N	N
31 Becerra	+	Y	Y	?	?
32 Chu	Y	Y	Y	?	?
33 Bass	Y	Y	Y	?	?
34 Roybal-Allard	Y	Y	Y	?	?
35 Waters	Y	Y	Y	?	?
36 Hahn	Y	Y	Y	?	?
37 Richardson	Y	Y	Y	?	?
38 Napolitano	Y	Y	?	?	?
39 Sánchez, Linda	Y	Y	Y	?	N
40 Royce	Y	Y	N	Y	Y
41 Lewis	?	?	?	?	?
42 Miller, Gary	Y	Y	N	Y	Y
43 Baca	Y	Y	Y	?	?
44 Calvert	Y	Y	N	Y	Y
45 Bono Mack	Y	Y	N	Y	Y
46 Rohrabacher	Y	Y	N	Y	Y
47 Sanchez, Loretta	Y	Y	Y	N	N
48 Campbell	Y	Y	N	Y	Y
49 Issa	Y	Y	N	Y	Y
50 Bilbray	Y	Y	N	Y	Y
51 Filner	Y	Y	Y	?	N
52 Hunter	Y	Y	N	Y	Y
53 Davis	Y	Y	Y	?	N

	438	439	440	441	442
COLORADO					
1 DeGette	Y	Y	Y	?	N
2 Polis	N	Y	Y	?	N
3 Tipton	Y	Y	N	Y	Y
4 Gardner	Y	Y	N	Y	Y
5 Lamborn	Y	Y	N	Y	Y
6 Coffman	Y	Y	N	Y	Y
7 Perlmutter	Y	Y	Y	N	N
CONNECTICUT					
1 Larson	Y	Y	Y	?	?
2 Courtney	Y	Y	Y	N	N
3 DeLauro	Y	Y	Y	N	N
4 Himes	Y	Y	Y	N	N
5 Murphy	Y	Y	Y	N	N
DELAWARE					
AL Carney	Y	Y	Y	?	N
FLORIDA					
1 Miller	Y	Y	N	Y	Y
2 Southerland	Y	Y	N	Y	Y
3 Brown	Y	Y	Y	?	?
4 Crenshaw	Y	Y	N	Y	Y
5 Nugent	Y	Y	N	Y	Y
6 Stearns	Y	Y	N	Y	Y
7 Mica	Y	Y	N	Y	Y
8 Webster	Y	Y	N	Y	Y
9 Bilirakis	Y	Y	N	Y	Y
10 Young	Y	Y	N	Y	Y
11 Castor	Y	Y	Y	?	N
12 Ross	Y	Y	N	Y	Y
13 Buchanan	Y	Y	N	Y	Y
14 Mack	Y	Y	N	Y	Y
15 Posey	N	Y	Y	N	Y
16 Rooney	Y	Y	N	Y	Y
17 Wilson	Y	Y	Y	?	?
18 Ros-Lehtinen	Y	Y	N	Y	Y
19 Deutch	Y	Y	Y	N	N
20 Wasserman Schultz	Y	Y	Y	N	N
21 Diaz-Balart	Y	Y	N	Y	Y
22 West	N	Y	Y	N	Y
23 Hastings	Y	Y	Y	?	?
24 Adams	Y	Y	N	Y	Y
25 Rivera	Y	Y	N	Y	Y
GEORGIA					
1 Kingston	N	Y	N	Y	Y
2 Bishop	Y	Y	Y	?	?
3 Westmoreland	N	Y	N	Y	Y
4 Johnson	Y	Y	Y	?	?
5 Lewis	Y	Y	Y	?	?
6 Price	Y	Y	N	Y	Y
7 Woodall	N	Y	N	Y	Y
8 Scott, A.	Y	Y	N	Y	Y
9 Graves	Y	Y	N	Y	Y
10 Broun	N	Y	N	Y	Y
11 Gingrey	Y	Y	N	Y	Y
12 Barrow	Y	Y	N	Y	Y
13 Scott, D.	Y	Y	Y	?	?
HAWAII					
1 Hanabusa	Y	Y	Y	?	N
2 Hirono	Y	Y	Y	N	N
IDAHO					
1 Labrador	N	Y	N	Y	Y
2 Simpson	Y	Y	N	Y	Y
ILLINOIS					
1 Rush	Y	Y	Y	?	?
2 Jackson	?	?	?	?	?
3 Lipinski	Y	Y	Y	P	P
4 Gutierrez	Y	Y	Y	?	?
5 Quigley	Y	Y	Y	N	N
6 Roskam	Y	Y	N	Y	Y
7 Davis	Y	Y	Y	?	?
8 Walsh	N	N	N	Y	Y
9 Schakowsky	Y	Y	Y	?	?
10 Dold	Y	Y	N	Y	Y
11 Kinzinger	Y	Y	N	Y	Y
12 Costello	Y	Y	Y	N	N
13 Biggert	Y	Y	N	Y	Y
14 Hultgren	Y	Y	N	Y	Y
15 Johnson	Y	Y	N	Y	Y

KEY Republicans   Democrats

Y Voted for (yea)
Paired for
+ Announced for
N Voted against (nay)

X Paired against
− Announced against
P Voted "present"

C Voted "present" to avoid possible conflict of interest
? Did not vote or otherwise make a position known

	438	439	440	441	442
16 Manzullo	?	?	N	Y	Y
17 Schilling	Y	Y	N	Y	Y
18 Schock	Y	Y	N	Y	Y
19 Shimkus	Y	Y	N	Y	Y
INDIANA					
1 Visclosky	Y	Y	Y	N	N
2 Donnelly	Y	Y	N	Y	Y
3 Stutzman	Y	Y	?	Y	Y
4 Rokita	Y	Y	N	Y	Y
5 Burton	Y	Y	N	Y	Y
6 Pence	Y	Y	N	Y	Y
7 Carson	Y	Y	Y	?	?
8 Bucshon	Y	Y	N	Y	Y
9 Young	Y	Y	N	Y	Y
IOWA					
1 Braley	Y	Y	Y	N	N
2 Loebsack	Y	Y	Y	N	N
3 Boswell	Y	Y	Y	Y	Y
4 Latham	Y	Y	N	Y	Y
5 King	Y	Y	N	Y	Y
KANSAS					
1 Huelskamp	N	Y	N	Y	Y
2 Jenkins	Y	Y	N	Y	Y
3 Yoder	Y	Y	N	Y	Y
4 Pompeo	Y	Y	N	Y	Y
KENTUCKY					
1 Whitfield	Y	?	N	Y	Y
2 Guthrie	Y	Y	N	Y	Y
3 Yarmuth	Y	Y	Y	?	?
4 Davis	Y	Y	N	Y	Y
5 Rogers	Y	Y	N	Y	Y
6 Chandler	Y	Y	N	Y	Y
LOUISIANA					
1 Scalise	Y	Y	N	Y	Y
2 Richmond	Y	Y	Y	?	?
3 Landry	Y	Y	N	Y	Y
4 Fleming	Y	Y	N	Y	Y
5 Alexander	Y	Y	N	Y	Y
6 Cassidy	Y	Y	N	Y	Y
7 Boustany	Y	Y	N	Y	Y
MAINE					
1 Pingree	Y	Y	Y	?	N
2 Michaud	Y	Y	Y	N	Y
MARYLAND					
1 Harris	Y	Y	N	Y	?
2 Ruppersberger	Y	Y	Y	?	N
3 Sarbanes	Y	Y	Y	?	?
4 Edwards	Y	Y	Y	?	?
5 Hoyer	Y	Y	Y	?	N
6 Bartlett	Y	Y	N	Y	Y
7 Cummings	Y	Y	Y	?	?
8 Van Hollen	Y	Y	Y	?	?
MASSACHUSETTS					
1 Olver	Y	Y	Y	?	N
2 Neal	Y	Y	Y	?	N
3 McGovern	Y	Y	Y	?	N
4 Frank	Y	?	Y	?	?
5 Tsongas	Y	Y	Y	N	N
6 Tierney	Y	Y	Y	N	N
7 Markey	Y	Y	Y	?	?
8 Capuano	Y	Y	Y	?	?
9 Lynch	Y	Y	Y	N	N
10 Keating	Y	Y	Y	?	N
MICHIGAN					
1 Benishek	Y	Y	N	Y	Y
2 Huizenga	Y	Y	N	Y	Y
3 Amash	N	N	N	Y	Y
4 Camp	Y	Y	N	Y	Y
5 Kildee	Y	Y	Y	?	N
6 Upton	Y	Y	N	Y	Y
7 Walberg	Y	Y	N	Y	Y
8 Rogers	Y	Y	N	Y	Y
9 Peters	Y	Y	Y	?	N
10 Miller	Y	Y	N	Y	Y
11 McCotter	Y	Y	N	Y	Y
12 Levin	Y	Y	Y	?	?
13 Clarke	Y	Y	Y	?	?
14 Conyers	Y	Y	Y	?	?
15 Dingell	Y	Y	Y	N	N
MINNESOTA					
1 Walz	Y	Y	N	Y	Y
2 Kline	Y	Y	N	Y	Y
3 Paulsen	Y	Y	N	Y	Y
4 McCollum	Y	Y	Y	?	N

	438	439	440	441	442
5 Ellison	Y	Y	Y	?	?
6 Bachmann	Y	Y	N	Y	Y
7 Peterson	Y	Y	N	Y	Y
8 Cravaack	Y	Y	N	Y	Y
MISSISSIPPI					
1 Nunnelee	Y	Y	N	Y	Y
2 Thompson	Y	Y	Y	?	?
3 Harper	Y	Y	N	Y	Y
4 Palazzo	Y	Y	N	Y	Y
MISSOURI					
1 Clay	Y	Y	Y	?	?
2 Akin	Y	Y	N	Y	Y
3 Carnahan	Y	Y	Y	?	N
4 Hartzler	Y	Y	N	Y	?
5 Cleaver	Y	Y	Y	?	?
6 Graves	Y	Y	N	Y	Y
7 Long	Y	Y	N	Y	Y
8 Emerson	N	Y	N	Y	Y
9 Luetkemeyer	Y	Y	N	Y	Y
MONTANA					
AL Rehberg	Y	Y	N	Y	Y
NEBRASKA					
1 Fortenberry	Y	Y	N	Y	?
2 Terry	Y	N	N	Y	Y
3 Smith	Y	Y	N	Y	Y
NEVADA					
1 Berkley	Y	Y	Y	N	N
2 Amodei	Y	Y	N	Y	Y
3 Heck	Y	Y	N	Y	Y
NEW HAMPSHIRE					
1 Guinta	Y	Y	N	Y	Y
2 Bass	Y	Y	N	Y	Y
NEW JERSEY					
1 Andrews	Y	Y	Y	?	N
2 LoBiondo	Y	Y	N	Y	Y
3 Runyan	Y	Y	N	Y	Y
4 Smith	Y	Y	N	Y	Y
5 Garrett	Y	Y	N	Y	Y
6 Pallone	Y	Y	Y	?	N
7 Lance	Y	Y	N	Y	Y
8 Pascrell	Y	Y	Y	?	N
9 Rothman	Y	Y	Y	N	N
10 Vacant					
11 Frelinghuysen	Y	Y	N	Y	Y
12 Holt	Y	Y	Y	N	N
13 Sires	Y	Y	Y	?	?
NEW MEXICO					
1 Heinrich	Y	Y	Y	N	N
2 Pearce	Y	Y	N	Y	Y
3 Luján	Y	?	Y	N	N
NEW YORK					
1 Bishop	Y	Y	Y	N	N
2 Israel	Y	Y	Y	?	?
3 King	Y	Y	N	Y	Y
4 McCarthy	Y	Y	Y	?	N
5 Ackerman	Y	Y	Y	?	?
6 Meeks	Y	Y	Y	?	?
7 Crowley	Y	Y	Y	?	N
8 Nadler	Y	Y	Y	N	?
9 Turner	Y	Y	N	Y	Y
10 Towns	Y	Y	Y	?	P
11 Clarke	Y	Y	Y	?	?
12 Velázquez	Y	Y	Y	?	N
13 Grimm	Y	Y	N	Y	Y
14 Maloney	Y	Y	Y	?	N
15 Rangel	Y	?	Y	?	?
16 Serrano	Y	Y	Y	?	?
17 Engel	Y	Y	Y	?	?
18 Lowey	Y	Y	Y	?	?
19 Hayworth	Y	Y	?	Y	Y
20 Gibson	Y	Y	N	Y	Y
21 Tonko	Y	Y	Y	?	N
22 Hinchey	Y	Y	Y	?	N
23 Owens	Y	Y	Y	N	Y
24 Hanna	Y	Y	N	Y	Y
25 Buerkle	Y	Y	N	Y	Y
26 Hochul	Y	Y	N	Y	Y
27 Higgins	Y	Y	Y	N	N
28 Slaughter	Y	Y	Y	N	N
29 Reed	Y	Y	N	Y	Y
NORTH CAROLINA					
1 Butterfield	Y	Y	Y	?	?
2 Ellmers	Y	Y	N	Y	Y
3 Jones	N	Y	N	Y	Y
4 Price	Y	Y	Y	?	N

	438	439	440	441	442
5 Foxx	Y	Y	N	Y	Y
6 Coble	Y	Y	N	Y	Y
7 McIntyre	Y	Y	N	Y	Y
8 Kissell	Y	Y	N	Y	Y
9 Myrick	Y	Y	N	Y	Y
10 McHenry	Y	Y	N	Y	Y
11 Shuler	Y	Y	Y	N	N
12 Watt	Y	Y	Y	?	?
13 Miller	Y	Y	Y	N	Y
NORTH DAKOTA					
AL Berg	Y	Y	N	Y	Y
OHIO					
1 Chabot	Y	Y	N	Y	Y
2 Schmidt	Y	Y	N	Y	Y
3 Turner	Y	Y	N	Y	Y
4 Jordan	Y	Y	N	Y	Y
5 Latta	Y	Y	N	Y	Y
6 Johnson	Y	Y	N	Y	Y
7 Austria	Y	Y	N	Y	Y
8 Boehner					
9 Kaptur	?	?	Y	?	P
10 Kucinich	N	N	Y	?	?
11 Fudge	Y	Y	Y	?	?
12 Tiberi	Y	Y	N	Y	Y
13 Sutton	Y	Y	Y	N	N
14 LaTourette	Y	?	N	N	Y
15 Stivers	Y	Y	N	Y	Y
16 Renacci	Y	Y	N	Y	Y
17 Ryan	Y	Y	?	N	N
18 Gibbs	Y	Y	N	Y	Y
OKLAHOMA					
1 Sullivan	Y	Y	N	Y	Y
2 Boren	Y	Y	N	Y	Y
3 Lucas	Y	Y	N	Y	Y
4 Cole	Y	Y	N	Y	Y
5 Lankford	Y	Y	N	Y	Y
OREGON					
1 Bonamici	Y	Y	Y	N	N
2 Walden	Y	Y	N	Y	Y
3 Blumenauer	Y	Y	Y	N	N
4 DeFazio	Y	Y	Y	N	N
5 Schrader	Y	Y	Y	N	N
PENNSYLVANIA					
1 Brady	Y	Y	Y	?	?
2 Fattah	Y	Y	Y	?	?
3 Kelly	Y	Y	N	Y	Y
4 Altmire	Y	Y	N	Y	Y
5 Thompson	Y	Y	N	Y	Y
6 Gerlach	Y	Y	N	Y	Y
7 Meehan	Y	Y	N	Y	Y
8 Fitzpatrick	Y	Y	N	Y	Y
9 Shuster	Y	Y	N	Y	Y
10 Marino	Y	Y	N	Y	Y
11 Barletta	Y	Y	N	Y	Y
12 Critz	Y	Y	Y	Y	Y
13 Schwartz	Y	Y	Y	N	N
14 Doyle	Y	Y	Y	?	N
15 Dent	Y	Y	N	Y	Y
16 Pitts	Y	Y	N	Y	Y
17 Holden	Y	Y	Y	N	N
18 Murphy	Y	Y	N	Y	Y
19 Platts	Y	Y	N	Y	Y
RHODE ISLAND					
1 Cicilline	Y	Y	Y	?	?
2 Langevin	Y	Y	Y	N	N
SOUTH CAROLINA					
1 Scott	Y	Y	N	Y	Y
2 Wilson	Y	Y	N	Y	Y
3 Duncan	N	Y	N	Y	Y
4 Gowdy	Y	Y	N	Y	Y
5 Mulvaney	Y	Y	N	Y	Y
6 Clyburn	Y	Y	Y	?	?
SOUTH DAKOTA					
AL Noem	Y	Y	N	Y	Y
TENNESSEE					
1 Roe	Y	Y	N	Y	Y
2 Duncan	N	Y	N	Y	Y
3 Fleischmann	+	Y	N	Y	Y
4 DesJarlais	Y	Y	N	Y	Y
5 Cooper	Y	Y	N	Y	N
6 Black	Y	Y	N	Y	Y
7 Blackburn	Y	N	N	Y	Y
8 Fincher	Y	Y	N	Y	Y
9 Cohen	Y	Y	Y	N	N

	438	439	440	441	442
TEXAS					
1 Gohmert	Y	Y	N	Y	Y
2 Poe	Y	Y	N	Y	Y
3 Johnson, S.	Y	Y	N	Y	Y
4 Hall	Y	Y	N	Y	Y
5 Hensarling	Y	Y	N	Y	Y
6 Barton	Y	Y	N	Y	Y
7 Culberson	Y	Y	N	Y	Y
8 Brady	Y	?	N	Y	Y
9 Green, A.	Y	Y	Y	?	?
10 McCaul	Y	Y	N	Y	Y
11 Conaway	Y	Y	N	Y	Y
12 Granger	Y	Y	N	Y	Y
13 Thornberry	Y	Y	N	Y	Y
14 Paul	N	N	N	Y	Y
15 Hinojosa	Y	Y	Y	?	?
16 Reyes	Y	Y	Y	?	N
17 Flores	Y	Y	N	Y	Y
18 Jackson Lee	Y	Y	Y	?	?
19 Neugebauer	Y	Y	N	Y	Y
20 Gonzalez	Y	Y	Y	?	?
21 Smith	Y	Y	N	Y	Y
22 Olson	Y	Y	N	Y	Y
23 Canseco	Y	Y	N	Y	Y
24 Marchant	Y	Y	N	Y	Y
25 Doggett	Y	Y	N	Y	N
26 Burgess	Y	Y	N	Y	Y
27 Farenthold	Y	Y	N	Y	Y
28 Cuellar	Y	Y	N	Y	N
29 Green, G.	Y	Y	N	Y	N
30 Johnson, E.	?	?	?	?	?
31 Carter	Y	Y	N	Y	Y
32 Sessions	Y	Y	N	Y	Y
UTAH					
1 Bishop	Y	Y	?	Y	Y
2 Matheson	Y	Y	N	Y	Y
3 Chaffetz	Y	Y	N	Y	Y
VERMONT					
AL Welch	N	Y	Y	N	N
VIRGINIA					
1 Wittman	Y	Y	N	Y	Y
2 Rigell	Y	Y	N	N	Y
3 Scott	Y	Y	Y	?	?
4 Forbes	Y	Y	N	Y	Y
5 Hurt	Y	Y	N	Y	Y
6 Goodlatte	Y	Y	N	Y	Y
7 Cantor	Y	Y	N	Y	Y
8 Moran	Y	Y	Y	N	N
9 Griffith	Y	Y	N	Y	Y
10 Wolf	Y	Y	N	Y	Y
11 Connolly	Y	Y	Y	N	N
WASHINGTON					
1 Vacant					
2 Larsen	Y	Y	Y	N	N
3 Herrera Beutler	Y	Y	N	Y	Y
4 Hastings	Y	Y	N	Y	Y
5 McMorris Rodgers	Y	Y	N	Y	Y
6 Dicks	Y	Y	Y	N	N
7 McDermott	Y	Y	Y	N	N
8 Reichert	Y	Y	N	Y	Y
9 Smith	Y	Y	Y	N	N
WEST VIRGINIA					
1 McKinley	Y	Y	N	Y	Y
2 Capito	Y	Y	N	Y	Y
3 Rahall	Y	Y	N	Y	Y
WISCONSIN					
1 Ryan	Y	Y	N	Y	Y
2 Baldwin	Y	Y	Y	N	N
3 Kind	Y	Y	Y	Y	Y
4 Moore	Y	Y	Y	?	?
5 Sensenbrenner	Y	Y	N	Y	Y
6 Petri	Y	Y	N	Y	Y
7 Duffy	Y	Y	N	Y	Y
8 Ribble	N	N	N	Y	Y
WYOMING					
AL Lummis	N	N	N	Y	Y

IN THE HOUSE | By Vote Number

443. **H Res 718. Disapproval of Oversight Chairman's Behavior/ Motion to Table.** Webster, R-Fla., motion to table (kill) the resolution that would disapprove of the behavior of the chairman of the House Oversight and Government Reform Committee for interfering with on-going criminal investigations, insisting on a personal attack against the attorney general of the United States and for calling the attorney general a liar on national television without corroborating evidence, thereby discrediting the integrity of the House. Motion agreed to 259-161: R 235-0; D 24-161. June 29, 2012.

444. **HR 4348, HR 5856, HR 6020. Surface Transportation Authorization and Fiscal 2013 Defense and Financial Services Appropriations/Rule.** Adoption of the rule (H Res 717) that would provide for House floor consideration of the conference report on the bill (HR 4348) that would authorize federal highway, mass transit and safety programs through fiscal 2014, extend the 3.4 percent interest rate on subsidized federal student loans for one year and reauthorize the National Flood Insurance Program for five years. The rule would waive through the legislative day of June 29, 2012, the two-thirds requirement to consider a rule on the same day it is reported from the Rules Committee. The waiver would only apply to measures related to surface transportation. It also would provide suspension authority on June 29, 2012, for measures related to surface transportation. The rule also would provide for House floor consideration of the fiscal 2013 Defense (HR 5856) and Financial Services (HR 6020) spending bills. Adopted 244-176: R 232-2; D 12-174. June 29, 2012.

445. **HR 5972. Fiscal 2013 Transportation-HUD Appropriations/ Funding Reductions.** Blackburn, R-Tenn., amendment that would reduce the amounts made available by the bill by 1 percent. Rejected in Committee of the Whole 166-254: R 160-75; D 6-179. June 29, 2012.

446. **HR 5972. Fiscal 2013 Transportation-HUD Appropriations/ California Subway Project.** McClintock, R-Calif., amendment that would bar the use of funds for an expansion of San Francisco's metro rail, called the Third Street Light Rail Phase 2 Central Subway project. Adopted in Committee of the Whole 235-186: R 230-6; D 5-180. June 29, 2012.

447. **HR 5972. Fiscal 2013 Transportation-HUD Appropriations/ Migratory Birds.** Lankford, R-Okla., amendment that would prohibit the Federal Highway Administration from using funds for an analysis required under the National Environmental Protection Act of 1969 to enforce a 1918 protection agreement between the U.S. and Great Britain known as the Migratory Bird Treaty Act or a related 2001 presidential order, Executive Order No. 13186, with respect to the cliff swallow or barn swallow. Adopted in Committee of the Whole 234-191: R 222-16; D 12-175. June 29, 2012.

	443	444	445	446	447
ALABAMA					
1 **Bonner**	Y	Y	N	Y	Y
2 **Roby**	Y	Y	N	Y	Y
3 **Rogers**	Y	Y	N	Y	Y
4 **Aderholt**	Y	Y	N	Y	Y
5 **Brooks**	Y	Y	Y	Y	Y
6 **Bachus**	Y	Y	N	Y	Y
7 Sewell	N	N	N	N	N
ALASKA					
AL **Young**	Y	Y	N	Y	Y
ARIZONA					
1 **Gosar**	Y	Y	Y	Y	Y
2 **Franks**	Y	Y	Y	Y	Y
3 **Quayle**	Y	Y	Y	Y	Y
4 Pastor	N	N	N	N	N
5 **Schweikert**	Y	Y	Y	Y	Y
6 **Flake**	Y	Y	Y	Y	Y
7 Grijalva	N	N	N	N	N
8 Barber	N	N	N	N	N
ARKANSAS					
1 **Crawford**	Y	Y	Y	Y	Y
2 **Griffin**	Y	Y	Y	Y	Y
3 **Womack**	Y	Y	N	Y	Y
4 Ross	Y	Y	N	N	Y
CALIFORNIA					
1 Thompson	N	N	N	N	N
2 **Herger**	Y	Y	Y	Y	Y
3 **Lungren**	Y	Y	Y	Y	Y
4 **McClintock**	Y	Y	Y	Y	Y
5 Matsui	N	N	N	N	N
6 Woolsey	N	N	N	N	N
7 Miller, George	N	N	N	N	N
8 Pelosi	N	N	N	N	N
9 Lee	N	N	N	N	N
10 Garamendi	N	N	N	N	N
11 McNerney	N	N	N	N	N
12 Speier	N	N	N	N	N
13 Stark	N	N	N	N	N
14 Eshoo	N	N	N	N	N
15 Honda	N	N	N	N	N
16 Lofgren	N	N	N	N	N
17 Farr	N	N	N	N	N
18 Cardoza	Y	N	N	N	N
19 **Denham**	Y	Y	N	Y	Y
20 Costa	Y	N	N	N	N
21 **Nunes**	Y	Y	Y	Y	Y
22 **McCarthy**	Y	Y	Y	Y	Y
23 Capps	N	N	N	N	N
24 **Gallegly**	Y	Y	N	Y	Y
25 **McKeon**	Y	Y	N	Y	Y
26 **Dreier**	Y	Y	N	Y	Y
27 Sherman	N	N	N	N	N
28 Berman	N	N	N	N	N
29 Schiff	N	N	N	N	N
30 Waxman	N	N	N	N	N
31 Becerra	N	N	N	N	N
32 Chu	N	N	N	N	N
33 Bass	N	N	N	N	N
34 Roybal-Allard	N	N	N	N	N
35 Waters	N	N	N	N	N
36 Hahn	N	N	N	N	N
37 Richardson	N	Y	N	N	N
38 Napolitano	N	N	N	N	N
39 Sánchez, Linda	N	N	N	N	N
40 **Royce**	Y	Y	Y	Y	Y
41 **Lewis**	?	?	?	?	?
42 **Miller, Gary**	Y	Y	Y	Y	Y
43 Baca	N	N	N	N	N
44 **Calvert**	Y	Y	N	Y	Y
45 **Bono Mack**	Y	Y	Y	Y	Y
46 **Rohrabacher**	Y	Y	Y	Y	Y
47 Sanchez, Loretta	N	N	N	N	N
48 **Campbell**	Y	Y	Y	Y	Y
49 **Issa**	Y	Y	Y	Y	Y
50 **Bilbray**	Y	Y	N	Y	N
51 Filner	–	–	–	–	–
52 **Hunter**	Y	Y	Y	Y	Y
53 Davis	N	N	N	N	N

	443	444	445	446	447
COLORADO					
1 DeGette	N	N	N	N	N
2 Polis	N	N	N	N	N
3 **Tipton**	Y	Y	Y	Y	Y
4 **Gardner**	Y	Y	Y	Y	Y
5 **Lamborn**	?	?	?	?	?
6 **Coffman**	Y	Y	Y	Y	Y
7 Perlmutter	N	Y	N	N	N
CONNECTICUT					
1 Larson	N	N	N	N	N
2 Courtney	N	N	N	N	N
3 DeLauro	N	N	N	N	N
4 Himes	N	N	N	N	N
5 Murphy	N	N	N	N	N
DELAWARE					
AL Carney	N	N	?	?	N
FLORIDA					
1 **Miller**	Y	Y	Y	Y	Y
2 **Southerland**	Y	Y	Y	Y	Y
3 Brown	N	N	N	N	N
4 **Crenshaw**	Y	Y	N	Y	Y
5 **Nugent**	Y	Y	N	Y	Y
6 **Stearns**	Y	Y	Y	Y	Y
7 **Mica**	Y	Y	N	Y	Y
8 **Webster**	Y	Y	N	Y	Y
9 **Bilirakis**	Y	Y	Y	Y	Y
10 **Young**	Y	Y	Y	Y	Y
11 Castor	N	N	N	N	N
12 **Ross**	Y	Y	Y	Y	Y
13 **Buchanan**	Y	Y	Y	Y	Y
14 **Mack**	Y	Y	Y	Y	Y
15 **Posey**	Y	Y	N	Y	Y
16 **Rooney**	Y	Y	N	Y	Y
17 Wilson	N	N	N	N	N
18 **Ros-Lehtinen**	Y	Y	N	Y	Y
19 Deutch	N	N	N	N	N
20 Wasserman Schultz	N	N	N	N	N
21 **Diaz-Balart**	Y	Y	N	Y	Y
22 **West**	Y	Y	Y	Y	Y
23 Hastings	N	N	N	N	N
24 **Adams**	Y	Y	Y	Y	Y
25 **Rivera**	Y	Y	N	Y	Y
GEORGIA					
1 **Kingston**	Y	Y	Y	Y	Y
2 Bishop	N	N	N	N	N
3 **Westmoreland**	Y	Y	Y	Y	Y
4 Johnson	N	N	N	N	N
5 Lewis	N	N	N	N	N
6 **Price**	Y	Y	Y	Y	Y
7 **Woodall**	Y	Y	Y	Y	Y
8 **Scott, A.**	Y	Y	Y	Y	Y
9 **Graves**	Y	Y	?	Y	Y
10 **Broun**	Y	Y	Y	Y	Y
11 **Gingrey**	Y	Y	Y	Y	Y
12 **Barrow**	Y	N	Y	Y	Y
13 Scott, D.	N	N	N	N	N
HAWAII					
1 Hanabusa	N	N	N	N	N
2 Hirono	N	N	N	N	N
IDAHO					
1 **Labrador**	Y	Y	Y	Y	Y
2 **Simpson**	Y	Y	N	Y	Y
ILLINOIS					
1 Rush	N	N	N	N	N
2 Jackson	?	?	?	?	?
3 Lipinski	N	N	N	N	N
4 Gutierrez	N	N	N	N	N
5 Quigley	N	N	N	N	N
6 **Roskam**	Y	Y	Y	Y	Y
7 Davis	N	N	N	N	N
8 **Walsh**	Y	Y	Y	Y	Y
9 Schakowsky	N	N	N	N	N
10 **Dold**	Y	Y	N	N	Y
11 **Kinzinger**	Y	Y	N	Y	Y
12 Costello	N	N	N	N	N
13 **Biggert**	Y	Y	Y	N	Y
14 **Hultgren**	Y	Y	Y	Y	Y
15 **Johnson**	Y	Y	Y	N	Y

Member	443	444	445	446	447
16 Manzullo	Y	Y	Y	Y	Y
17 Schilling	Y	Y	N	Y	Y
18 Schock	Y	Y	N	Y	Y
19 Shimkus	Y	Y	N	Y	Y
INDIANA					
1 Visclosky	N	N	N	N	N
2 Donnelly	Y	Y	Y	Y	Y
3 Stutzman	Y	Y	Y	Y	Y
4 Rokita	Y	Y	Y	Y	Y
5 Burton	Y	Y	Y	Y	Y
6 Pence	Y	Y	Y	Y	Y
7 Carson	N	N	N	N	N
8 Bucshon	Y	Y	N	Y	Y
9 Young	Y	Y	Y	Y	Y
IOWA					
1 Braley	N	N	N	N	N
2 Loebsack	N	N	N	N	N
3 Boswell	Y	N	N	N	N
4 Latham	Y	Y	N	Y	Y
5 King	Y	Y	Y	Y	Y
KANSAS					
1 Huelskamp	Y	Y	Y	Y	Y
2 Jenkins	Y	Y	Y	Y	Y
3 Yoder	Y	Y	Y	Y	Y
4 Pompeo	Y	Y	Y	Y	Y
KENTUCKY					
1 Whitfield	Y	Y	Y	Y	N
2 Guthrie	Y	Y	Y	Y	Y
3 Yarmuth	N	N	N	N	N
4 Davis	Y	Y	Y	Y	Y
5 Rogers	Y	Y	N	Y	Y
6 Chandler	Y	Y	N	N	N
LOUISIANA					
1 Scalise	Y	Y	Y	Y	Y
2 Richmond	N	N	N	N	N
3 Landry	Y	Y	Y	Y	Y
4 Fleming	Y	Y	Y	Y	Y
5 Alexander	Y	Y	N	Y	Y
6 Cassidy	Y	Y	Y	Y	Y
7 Boustany	Y	Y	Y	Y	Y
MAINE					
1 Pingree	N	N	N	N	N
2 Michaud	Y	N	N	N	N
MARYLAND					
1 Harris	Y	?	Y	Y	Y
2 Ruppersberger	N	N	N	N	N
3 Sarbanes	N	N	N	N	N
4 Edwards	N	N	N	N	N
5 Hoyer	N	N	N	N	N
6 Bartlett	Y	Y	Y	Y	N
7 Cummings	N	N	N	N	N
8 Van Hollen	N	N	N	N	N
MASSACHUSETTS					
1 Olver	N	N	N	N	N
2 Neal	N	N	?	?	N
3 McGovern	N	N	N	N	N
4 Frank	N	N	N	N	N
5 Tsongas	N	N	N	N	N
6 Tierney	N	N	N	N	N
7 Markey	N	N	N	N	N
8 Capuano	N	N	N	N	N
9 Lynch	N	N	Y	N	N
10 Keating	N	N	N	N	N
MICHIGAN					
1 Benishek	Y	Y	Y	Y	Y
2 Huizenga	Y	Y	Y	Y	Y
3 Amash	Y	Y	Y	Y	Y
4 Camp	Y	Y	Y	Y	Y
5 Kildee	N	N	N	N	N
6 Upton	Y	Y	Y	Y	Y
7 Walberg	Y	Y	Y	Y	Y
8 Rogers	Y	Y	Y	Y	Y
9 Peters	N	N	N	N	N
10 Miller	Y	Y	Y	Y	Y
11 McCotter	Y	Y	Y	Y	Y
12 Levin	N	N	N	N	N
13 Clarke	N	N	N	N	N
14 Conyers	–	–	N	N	N
15 Dingell	N	N	N	N	N
MINNESOTA					
1 Walz	Y	N	N	N	N
2 Kline	Y	Y	Y	Y	Y
3 Paulsen	Y	Y	Y	Y	Y
4 McCollum	N	N	N	N	N
5 Ellison	N	N	N	N	N
6 Bachmann	Y	Y	Y	Y	Y
7 Peterson	Y	N	N	N	Y
8 Cravaack	Y	Y	N	Y	Y
MISSISSIPPI					
1 Nunnelee	Y	Y	Y	Y	Y
2 Thompson	N	N	N	N	N
3 Harper	Y	Y	Y	Y	Y
4 Palazzo	Y	Y	Y	Y	Y
MISSOURI					
1 Clay	N	N	N	N	N
2 Akin	+	+	?	?	?
3 Carnahan	Y	Y	Y	Y	Y
4 Hartzler	Y	Y	Y	Y	Y
5 Cleaver	N	N	N	N	N
6 Graves	Y	Y	Y	Y	Y
7 Long	Y	Y	Y	Y	Y
8 Emerson	Y	Y	Y	Y	Y
9 Luetkemeyer	Y	Y	Y	Y	Y
MONTANA					
AL Rehberg	Y	Y	N	Y	Y
NEBRASKA					
1 Fortenberry	?	Y	Y	Y	Y
2 Terry	Y	Y	Y	Y	Y
3 Smith	Y	Y	Y	Y	Y
NEVADA					
1 Berkley	N	N	N	N	N
2 Amodei	Y	Y	Y	Y	Y
3 Heck	Y	Y	N	Y	Y
NEW HAMPSHIRE					
1 Guinta	Y	Y	Y	Y	Y
2 Bass	Y	Y	N	Y	N
NEW JERSEY					
1 Andrews	N	N	N	N	N
2 LoBiondo	Y	Y	N	Y	N
3 Runyan	Y	Y	N	Y	Y
4 Smith	Y	Y	N	N	N
5 Garrett	Y	Y	Y	Y	Y
6 Pallone	N	N	N	N	N
7 Lance	Y	Y	Y	Y	Y
8 Pascrell	N	N	N	N	N
9 Rothman	N	N	N	N	N
10 Vacant					
11 Frelinghuysen	Y	Y	Y	Y	Y
12 Holt	N	N	N	N	N
13 Sires	N	N	N	N	N
NEW MEXICO					
1 Heinrich	N	N	N	N	N
2 Pearce	Y	Y	N	Y	Y
3 Luján	N	N	N	N	N
NEW YORK					
1 Bishop	N	N	N	N	N
2 Israel	N	N	N	N	N
3 King	Y	Y	N	Y	Y
4 McCarthy	N	N	N	N	N
5 Ackerman	N	N	N	N	N
6 Meeks	N	Y	N	N	N
7 Crowley	?	N	N	N	N
8 Nadler	N	N	N	N	N
9 Turner	Y	Y	Y	Y	Y
10 Towns	N	N	N	N	N
11 Clarke	N	N	N	N	N
12 Velázquez	N	N	N	N	N
13 Grimm	Y	Y	N	N	Y
14 Maloney	N	N	N	N	N
15 Rangel	N	N	N	N	N
16 Serrano	N	N	N	N	N
17 Engel	N	N	N	N	N
18 Lowey	N	N	N	N	N
19 Hayworth	Y	Y	N	Y	Y
20 Gibson	Y	Y	Y	Y	Y
21 Tonko	N	N	N	N	N
22 Hinchey	N	N	N	N	N
23 Owens	Y	Y	N	N	N
24 Hanna	Y	Y	N	Y	Y
25 Buerkle	Y	Y	Y	Y	Y
26 Hochul	Y	N	N	N	N
27 Higgins	N	N	N	N	N
28 Slaughter	N	N	N	N	N
29 Reed	Y	Y	N	Y	Y
NORTH CAROLINA					
1 Butterfield	N	N	N	N	N
2 Ellmers	Y	Y	Y	Y	Y
3 Jones	Y	Y	Y	Y	Y
4 Price	N	N	N	N	N
5 Foxx	Y	Y	Y	Y	Y
6 Coble	Y	Y	Y	Y	Y
7 McIntyre	Y	Y	Y	Y	Y
8 Kissell	Y	Y	N	Y	Y
9 Myrick	Y	Y	Y	Y	Y
10 McHenry	Y	Y	Y	Y	Y
11 Shuler	Y	Y	Y	N	Y
12 Watt	Y	N	N	N	N
13 Miller	N	N	N	N	N
NORTH DAKOTA					
AL Berg	Y	Y	N	Y	Y
OHIO					
1 Chabot	Y	Y	Y	Y	Y
2 Schmidt	Y	Y	Y	Y	Y
3 Turner	Y	Y	N	Y	Y
4 Jordan	Y	Y	Y	Y	Y
5 Latta	Y	Y	Y	Y	Y
6 Johnson	Y	Y	Y	Y	Y
7 Austria	Y	Y	N	Y	Y
8 Boehner					
9 Kaptur	N	N	N	N	N
10 Kucinich	Y	N	N	N	N
11 Fudge	N	N	N	N	N
12 Tiberi	Y	Y	Y	Y	Y
13 Sutton	N	N	N	N	N
14 LaTourette	Y	Y	N	Y	Y
15 Stivers	Y	Y	Y	Y	Y
16 Renacci	Y	Y	Y	Y	Y
17 Ryan	N	N	N	N	N
18 Gibbs	Y	Y	N	Y	Y
OKLAHOMA					
1 Sullivan	Y	Y	Y	?	Y
2 Boren	Y	N	N	Y	Y
3 Lucas	Y	Y	N	Y	Y
4 Cole	Y	Y	N	Y	Y
5 Lankford	Y	Y	Y	Y	Y
OREGON					
1 Bonamici	N	N	N	N	N
2 Walden	Y	Y	Y	Y	Y
3 Blumenauer	N	N	N	N	N
4 DeFazio	N	N	N	N	N
5 Schrader	Y	Y	N	N	N
PENNSYLVANIA					
1 Brady	N	N	N	N	N
2 Fattah	N	N	N	N	N
3 Kelly	Y	Y	N	Y	Y
4 Altmire	Y	N	N	N	Y
5 Thompson	Y	Y	N	Y	Y
6 Gerlach	Y	Y	N	Y	Y
7 Meehan	Y	Y	N	Y	Y
8 Fitzpatrick	Y	Y	Y	Y	N
9 Shuster	Y	Y	Y	Y	Y
10 Marino	Y	Y	Y	Y	Y
11 Barletta	Y	Y	N	Y	Y
12 Critz	Y	N	N	N	Y
13 Schwartz	N	N	N	N	N
14 Doyle	N	N	N	N	N
15 Dent	Y	Y	N	Y	Y
16 Pitts	Y	Y	Y	Y	Y
17 Holden	N	N	N	N	Y
18 Murphy	Y	Y	N	Y	Y
19 Platts	?	?	N	Y	Y
RHODE ISLAND					
1 Cicilline	N	N	N	N	N
2 Langevin	N	N	N	N	N
SOUTH CAROLINA					
1 Scott	Y	Y	Y	Y	Y
2 Wilson	Y	Y	Y	Y	Y
3 Duncan	Y	Y	Y	Y	Y
4 Gowdy	Y	Y	Y	Y	Y
5 Mulvaney	Y	Y	Y	Y	Y
6 Clyburn	?	?	?	?	?
SOUTH DAKOTA					
AL Noem	Y	Y	N	Y	Y
TENNESSEE					
1 Roe	Y	Y	Y	Y	Y
2 Duncan	Y	Y	?	?	Y
3 Fleischmann	Y	Y	Y	Y	Y
4 DesJarlais	Y	Y	Y	Y	Y
5 Cooper	N	N	Y	N	N
6 Black	Y	Y	Y	Y	Y
7 Blackburn	Y	Y	Y	Y	Y
8 Fincher	Y	Y	Y	Y	Y
9 Cohen	N	N	N	N	N
TEXAS					
1 Gohmert	Y	?	Y	Y	Y
2 Poe	Y	Y	Y	Y	Y
3 Johnson, S.	Y	Y	Y	Y	Y
4 Hall	Y	Y	N	Y	Y
5 Hensarling	Y	Y	Y	Y	Y
6 Barton	?	?	Y	Y	Y
7 Culberson	Y	Y	Y	Y	Y
8 Brady	Y	Y	Y	Y	Y
9 Green, A.	N	N	N	N	N
10 McCaul	Y	Y	Y	Y	Y
11 Conaway	Y	Y	Y	Y	Y
12 Granger	Y	Y	N	N	N
13 Thornberry	Y	Y	Y	Y	Y
14 Paul	Y	Y	Y	Y	Y
15 Hinojosa	N	N	N	N	N
16 Reyes	N	N	N	N	N
17 Flores	Y	Y	Y	Y	Y
18 Jackson Lee	N	N	N	N	N
19 Neugebauer	Y	Y	Y	Y	Y
20 Gonzalez	N	N	N	N	N
21 Smith	Y	Y	N	Y	Y
22 Olson	Y	Y	Y	Y	Y
23 Canseco	Y	Y	Y	Y	Y
24 Marchant	Y	Y	Y	Y	Y
25 Doggett	N	N	N	N	N
26 Burgess	Y	Y	Y	Y	Y
27 Farenthold	Y	Y	Y	Y	Y
28 Cuellar	N	Y	N	N	N
29 Green, G.	N	N	N	N	N
30 Johnson, E.	?	?	?	?	?
31 Carter	Y	Y	N	Y	N
32 Sessions	Y	Y	Y	Y	Y
UTAH					
1 Bishop	Y	Y	N	Y	Y
2 Matheson	Y	Y	Y	Y	Y
3 Chaffetz	Y	Y	Y	Y	Y
VERMONT					
AL Welch	N	N	N	N	N
VIRGINIA					
1 Wittman	Y	Y	Y	Y	Y
2 Rigell	Y	Y	Y	Y	Y
3 Scott	Y	N	N	N	N
4 Forbes	Y	Y	Y	Y	Y
5 Hurt	Y	Y	Y	Y	Y
6 Goodlatte	Y	Y	Y	Y	Y
7 Cantor	Y	Y	?	Y	Y
8 Moran	N	N	N	N	N
9 Griffith	Y	Y	Y	Y	Y
10 Wolf	Y	Y	N	Y	Y
11 Connolly	N	N	N	N	N
WASHINGTON					
1 Vacant					
2 Larsen	N	N	N	N	N
3 Herrera Beutler	Y	Y	N	Y	Y
4 Hastings	Y	Y	N	Y	Y
5 McMorris Rodgers	Y	Y	Y	Y	Y
6 Dicks	N	N	N	N	N
7 McDermott	N	N	N	N	N
8 Reichert	Y	Y	N	Y	Y
9 Smith	N	N	N	N	N
WEST VIRGINIA					
1 McKinley	Y	Y	N	Y	Y
2 Capito	Y	Y	N	Y	Y
3 Rahall	N	N	N	N	N
WISCONSIN					
1 Ryan	Y	Y	Y	Y	Y
2 Baldwin	N	N	N	N	N
3 Kind	Y	N	N	N	N
4 Moore	N	N	N	N	N
5 Sensenbrenner	Y	Y	Y	Y	Y
6 Petri	Y	Y	Y	Y	Y
7 Duffy	Y	Y	Y	Y	Y
8 Ribble	Y	Y	Y	Y	Y
WYOMING					
AL Lummis	Y	Y	Y	Y	Y

IN THE HOUSE | By Vote Number

448. HR 5972. Fiscal 2013 Transportation-HUD Appropriations/ **California High-Speed Rail.** Denham, R-Calif., amendment that would bar the use of funds for high-speed rail in California or for the California High-Speed Rail Authority. Adopted in Committee of the Whole 239-185: R 235-2; D 4-183. June 29, 2012.

449. HR 5972. Fiscal 2013 Transportation-HUD Appropriations/ **Recommit.** Barber, D-Ariz., motion to recommit the bill to the House Appropriations Committee and report it back immediately with provisions that would increase the amount for tenant-based rental assistance and veteran rental voucher assistance each by $75 million. It also would reduce the funding level for Housing and Urban Development salaries and expenses accounts by $86 million. Motion rejected 188-233: R 3-233; D 185-0. June 29, 2012.

450. HR 5972. Fiscal 2013 Transportation-HUD Appropriations/ **Passage.** Passage of the bill that would appropriate $103.6 billion in fiscal 2013 for the departments of Transportation and Housing and Urban Development and related agencies. It would provide $69.7 billion for the Transportation Department, including $16 billion for the Federal Aviation Administration, $39.9 billion for highway programs and $10.4 billion for transit programs. It also would provide $33.6 billion for HUD, including $19.1 billion for the tenant-based Section 8 rental assistance program. Passed 261-163: R 182-55; D 79-108. A "nay" was a vote in support of the president's position. June 29, 2012.

451. HR 4348. Surface Transportation Authorization/Conference **Report.** Adoption of the conference report on the bill that would authorize federal highway, mass transit and safety programs through fiscal 2014 at current levels with inflationary increases for certain programs. It would provide $21.2 billion for the Highway Trust Fund, $80 billion in contract authority for programs administered by the Federal Highway Administration in fiscal 2013 and fiscal 2014, and $21.3 billion for programs administered by the Federal Transit Administration. It also would extend the 3.4 percent interest rate on subsidized federal student loans through July 1, 2013, reauthorize the National Flood Insurance Program through Sept. 30, 2017, and provide for the distribution of penalties paid by those responsible for the 2010 Gulf of Mexico oil spill to Gulf Coast states for environmental restoration activities. Adopted (thus sent to the Senate) 373-52: R 186-52; D 187-0. June 29, 2012.

	448	449	450	451
ALABAMA				
1 Bonner	Y	N	Y	Y
2 Roby	Y	N	Y	Y
3 Rogers	Y	N	Y	Y
4 Aderholt	Y	N	Y	Y
5 Brooks	Y	N	N	N
6 Bachus	Y	N	Y	Y
7 Sewell	N	Y	Y	Y
ALASKA				
AL Young	Y	N	Y	Y
ARIZONA				
1 Gosar	Y	N	N	N
2 Franks	Y	N	N	N
3 Quayle	Y	N	N	N
4 Pastor	N	Y	Y	Y
5 Schweikert	Y	N	N	N
6 Flake	Y	N	N	N
7 Grijalva	N	Y	N	Y
8 Barber	N	Y	Y	Y
ARKANSAS				
1 Crawford	Y	N	Y	Y
2 Griffin	Y	N	Y	Y
3 Womack	Y	N	Y	Y
4 Ross	N	Y	Y	Y
CALIFORNIA				
1 Thompson	N	Y	N	Y
2 Herger	Y	N	Y	Y
3 Lungren	Y	N	Y	Y
4 McClintock	Y	N	N	N
5 Matsui	N	Y	N	Y
6 Woolsey	N	Y	N	Y
7 Miller, George	N	Y	Y	Y
8 Pelosi	N	?	N	Y
9 Lee	N	Y	N	Y
10 Garamendi	N	Y	N	Y
11 McNerney	N	Y	N	Y
12 Speier	N	Y	N	Y
13 Stark	N	Y	Y	Y
14 Eshoo	N	Y	N	Y
15 Honda	N	Y	N	Y
16 Lofgren	N	Y	N	Y
17 Farr	N	Y	N	Y
18 Cardoza	N	Y	Y	Y
19 Denham	Y	N	Y	Y
20 Costa	N	Y	Y	Y
21 Nunes	Y	N	Y	Y
22 McCarthy	Y	N	Y	Y
23 Capps	N	Y	N	Y
24 Gallegly	Y	N	Y	Y
25 McKeon	Y	N	Y	Y
26 Dreier	Y	N	Y	Y
27 Sherman	N	Y	N	Y
28 Berman	N	Y	N	Y
29 Schiff	N	Y	N	Y
30 Waxman	N	Y	N	Y
31 Becerra	N	Y	N	Y
32 Chu	N	Y	N	Y
33 Bass	N	Y	N	Y
34 Roybal-Allard	N	Y	N	Y
35 Waters	N	Y	N	Y
36 Hahn	N	Y	N	Y
37 Richardson	N	Y	Y	Y
38 Napolitano	N	Y	N	Y
39 Sánchez, Linda	N	Y	N	Y
40 Royce	Y	N	N	Y
41 Lewis	?	?	?	?
42 Miller, Gary	Y	N	Y	Y
43 Baca	N	Y	Y	Y
44 Calvert	Y	N	Y	Y
45 Bono Mack	Y	N	Y	Y
46 Rohrabacher	Y	N	Y	Y
47 Sanchez, Loretta	N	Y	N	Y
48 Campbell	Y	N	N	N
49 Issa	Y	N	?	Y
50 Bilbray	Y	N	Y	Y
51 Filner	–	+	–	+
52 Hunter	Y	N	Y	Y
53 Davis	N	Y	Y	Y

	448	449	450	451
COLORADO				
1 DeGette	N	Y	N	Y
2 Polis	N	Y	N	Y
3 Tipton	Y	N	N	Y
4 Gardner	Y	N	N	Y
5 Lamborn	?	?	?	?
6 Coffman	Y	N	Y	Y
7 Perlmutter	N	Y	N	Y
CONNECTICUT				
1 Larson	N	Y	N	Y
2 Courtney	N	Y	N	Y
3 DeLauro	N	Y	N	Y
4 Himes	N	Y	Y	Y
5 Murphy	N	Y	N	Y
DELAWARE				
AL Carney	N	Y	Y	Y
FLORIDA				
1 Miller	Y	N	N	Y
2 Southerland	Y	N	N	Y
3 Brown	N	Y	N	Y
4 Crenshaw	Y	N	Y	Y
5 Nugent	Y	N	Y	N
6 Stearns	Y	N	N	Y
7 Mica	Y	N	Y	Y
8 Webster	Y	N	Y	Y
9 Bilirakis	Y	N	Y	Y
10 Young	Y	N	Y	Y
11 Castor	N	?	N	Y
12 Ross	Y	N	N	N
13 Buchanan	Y	N	N	Y
14 Mack	Y	N	N	N
15 Posey	Y	N	N	N
16 Rooney	Y	N	Y	Y
17 Wilson	N	Y	N	Y
18 Ros-Lehtinen	Y	N	Y	Y
19 Deutch	N	Y	N	Y
20 Wasserman Schultz	N	Y	N	Y
21 Diaz-Balart	Y	N	Y	Y
22 West	Y	N	Y	Y
23 Hastings	N	Y	N	Y
24 Adams	Y	N	N	N
25 Rivera	Y	N	Y	Y
GEORGIA				
1 Kingston	Y	N	Y	Y
2 Bishop	N	Y	Y	Y
3 Westmoreland	Y	N	N	N
4 Johnson	N	Y	N	Y
5 Lewis	N	Y	N	Y
6 Price	Y	N	N	Y
7 Woodall	Y	N	Y	N
8 Scott, A.	Y	N	N	N
9 Graves	Y	N	N	N
10 Broun	Y	N	N	N
11 Gingrey	Y	N	N	Y
12 Barrow	Y	Y	Y	Y
13 Scott, D.	N	Y	N	Y
HAWAII				
1 Hanabusa	N	Y	N	Y
2 Hirono	N	Y	N	Y
IDAHO				
1 Labrador	Y	N	N	N
2 Simpson	Y	N	Y	Y
ILLINOIS				
1 Rush	N	Y	N	Y
2 Jackson	?	?	?	?
3 Lipinski	N	Y	Y	Y
4 Gutierrez	N	Y	N	Y
5 Quigley	N	Y	N	Y
6 Roskam	Y	N	Y	Y
7 Davis	N	Y	N	Y
8 Walsh	Y	Y	N	N
9 Schakowsky	N	Y	N	Y
10 Dold	Y	N	Y	Y
11 Kinzinger	Y	N	Y	Y
12 Costello	N	Y	N	Y
13 Biggert	Y	N	Y	Y
14 Hultgren	Y	N	Y	Y
15 Johnson	Y	N	N	Y

KEY   **Republicans**   Democrats

Y Voted for (yea)	X Paired against	C Voted "present" to avoid possible conflict of interest
# Paired for	– Announced against	
+ Announced for	P Voted "present"	? Did not vote or otherwise make a position known
N Voted against (nay)		

		448	449	450	451
16	Manzullo	Y	N	Y	Y
17	Schilling	Y	N	Y	Y
18	Schock	Y	?	Y	Y
19	Shimkus	Y	N	Y	Y
INDIANA					
1	Visclosky	N	Y	Y	Y
2	Donnelly	N	Y	Y	Y
3	Stutzman	Y	N	N	Y
4	Rokita	Y	N	Y	Y
5	Burton	Y	N	Y	Y
6	Pence	Y	N	Y	Y
7	Carson	N	Y	N	Y
8	Bucshon	Y	N	Y	Y
9	Young	Y	?	Y	Y
IOWA					
1	Braley	N	Y	Y	Y
2	Loebsack	N	Y	Y	Y
3	Boswell	N	Y	Y	Y
4	Latham	Y	N	Y	Y
5	King	Y	Y	Y	Y
KANSAS					
1	Huelskamp	Y	N	N	N
2	Jenkins	Y	N	Y	N
3	Yoder	Y	N	Y	N
4	Pompeo	Y	N	N	N
KENTUCKY					
1	Whitfield	Y	N	Y	Y
2	Guthrie	Y	N	Y	Y
3	Yarmuth	N	Y	N	Y
4	Davis	Y	N	Y	Y
5	Rogers	Y	N	Y	Y
6	Chandler	N	Y	Y	Y
LOUISIANA					
1	Scalise	Y	N	Y	Y
2	Richmond	N	Y	N	Y
3	Landry	Y	N	N	Y
4	Fleming	Y	N	N	Y
5	Alexander	Y	N	Y	Y
6	Cassidy	Y	N	Y	Y
7	Boustany	Y	N	N	Y
MAINE					
1	Pingree	N	Y	N	Y
2	Michaud	N	Y	Y	Y
MARYLAND					
1	Harris	Y	N	Y	N
2	Ruppersberger	N	Y	Y	Y
3	Sarbanes	N	Y	N	Y
4	Edwards	N	Y	N	Y
5	Hoyer	N	Y	Y	Y
6	Bartlett	Y	N	Y	Y
7	Cummings	N	Y	N	Y
8	Van Hollen	N	Y	N	Y
MASSACHUSETTS					
1	Olver	N	Y	Y	Y
2	Neal	N	Y	N	Y
3	McGovern	N	Y	N	Y
4	Frank	N	Y	N	Y
5	Tsongas	N	Y	N	Y
6	Tierney	N	Y	N	Y
7	Markey	N	Y	N	Y
8	Capuano	N	Y	N	Y
9	Lynch	N	Y	Y	Y
10	Keating	N	Y	Y	Y
MICHIGAN					
1	Benishek	Y	N	Y	Y
2	Huizenga	Y	N	Y	N
3	Amash	Y	N	N	N
4	Camp	Y	N	Y	Y
5	Kildee	N	Y	Y	Y
6	Upton	Y	N	Y	Y
7	Walberg	Y	N	Y	N
8	Rogers	Y	N	Y	Y
9	Peters	N	Y	Y	Y
10	Miller	Y	N	Y	Y
11	McCotter	Y	N	Y	Y
12	Levin	N	Y	Y	Y
13	Clarke	N	Y	Y	Y
14	Conyers	N	Y	Y	Y
15	Dingell	N	Y	Y	Y
MINNESOTA					
1	Walz	N	Y	Y	Y
2	Kline	Y	N	Y	Y
3	Paulsen	Y	N	Y	Y
4	McCollum	N	Y	N	Y

		448	449	450	451
5	Ellison	N	Y	N	Y
6	Bachmann	Y	N	N	N
7	Peterson	N	Y	Y	Y
8	Cravaack	Y	N	Y	Y
MISSISSIPPI					
1	Nunnelee	Y	N	Y	Y
2	Thompson	N	Y	N	Y
3	Harper	Y	N	Y	Y
4	Palazzo	Y	N	Y	Y
MISSOURI					
1	Clay	N	Y	Y	Y
2	Akin	?	?	?	?
3	Carnahan	N	Y	Y	Y
4	Hartzler	Y	N	Y	Y
5	Cleaver	N	Y	Y	Y
6	Graves	Y	N	Y	Y
7	Long	Y	N	Y	Y
8	Emerson	Y	N	N	Y
9	Luetkemeyer	Y	N	Y	Y
MONTANA					
AL	Rehberg	Y	N	Y	Y
NEBRASKA					
1	Fortenberry	Y	N	Y	Y
2	Terry	Y	N	Y	Y
3	Smith	Y	N	Y	Y
NEVADA					
1	Berkley	N	Y	Y	Y
2	Amodei	Y	N	Y	Y
3	Heck	Y	N	Y	Y
NEW HAMPSHIRE					
1	Guinta	Y	N	Y	Y
2	Bass	Y	N	Y	Y
NEW JERSEY					
1	Andrews	N	Y	Y	Y
2	LoBiondo	Y	N	Y	Y
3	Runyan	Y	N	Y	Y
4	Smith	Y	N	Y	N
5	Garrett	Y	N	Y	N
6	Pallone	N	Y	N	Y
7	Lance	Y	N	Y	Y
8	Pascrell	N	Y	N	Y
9	Rothman	N	Y	Y	Y
10	Vacant				
11	Frelinghuysen	Y	N	Y	Y
12	Holt	N	Y	N	Y
13	Sires	N	Y	N	Y
NEW MEXICO					
1	Heinrich	N	Y	N	Y
2	Pearce	Y	N	N	Y
3	Luján	Y	Y	Y	Y
NEW YORK					
1	Bishop	N	Y	N	Y
2	Israel	N	Y	Y	Y
3	King	Y	N	Y	Y
4	McCarthy	N	Y	Y	Y
5	Ackerman	N	Y	Y	Y
6	Meeks	N	Y	N	Y
7	Crowley	N	Y	N	Y
8	Nadler	N	Y	N	Y
9	Turner	Y	N	Y	Y
10	Towns	N	Y	Y	Y
11	Clarke	N	Y	N	Y
12	Velázquez	N	Y	N	Y
13	Grimm	N	Y	Y	Y
14	Maloney	N	Y	Y	Y
15	Rangel	N	Y	Y	Y
16	Serrano	N	Y	N	Y
17	Engel	N	Y	Y	Y
18	Lowey	N	Y	N	Y
19	Hayworth	Y	N	Y	Y
20	Gibson	Y	N	Y	Y
21	Tonko	N	Y	Y	Y
22	Hinchey	N	Y	N	Y
23	Owens	N	Y	Y	Y
24	Hanna	Y	N	Y	Y
25	Buerkle	Y	N	Y	Y
26	Hochul	N	Y	Y	Y
27	Higgins	N	Y	N	Y
28	Slaughter	N	Y	N	Y
29	Reed	N	N	Y	Y
NORTH CAROLINA					
1	Butterfield	N	Y	N	Y
2	Ellmers	Y	N	Y	Y
3	Jones	Y	Y	Y	Y
4	Price	N	Y	Y	Y

		448	449	450	451
5	Foxx	Y	N	Y	N
6	Coble	Y	N	Y	Y
7	McIntyre	Y	Y	Y	Y
8	Kissell	N	Y	Y	Y
9	Myrick	Y	N	Y	Y
10	McHenry	Y	N	Y	N
11	Shuler	N	Y	Y	Y
12	Watt	N	Y	N	Y
13	Miller	N	Y	N	Y
NORTH DAKOTA					
AL	Berg	Y	N	Y	Y
OHIO					
1	Chabot	Y	N	N	N
2	Schmidt	Y	N	N	N
3	Turner	Y	N	Y	Y
4	Jordan	Y	N	N	N
5	Latta	Y	N	N	Y
6	Johnson	Y	N	Y	Y
7	Austria	Y	N	Y	Y
8	Boehner				
9	Kaptur	N	Y	Y	Y
10	Kucinich	N	Y	N	Y
11	Fudge	N	Y	N	Y
12	Tiberi	Y	N	Y	Y
13	Sutton	N	Y	N	Y
14	LaTourette	Y	N	Y	Y
15	Stivers	Y	N	Y	Y
16	Renacci	Y	N	Y	Y
17	Ryan	N	Y	N	Y
18	Gibbs	Y	N	Y	Y
OKLAHOMA					
1	Sullivan	Y	N	Y	Y
2	Boren	N	Y	Y	Y
3	Lucas	Y	N	Y	Y
4	Cole	Y	N	Y	Y
5	Lankford	Y	N	Y	Y
OREGON					
1	Bonamici	N	Y	N	Y
2	Walden	Y	N	Y	Y
3	Blumenauer	N	Y	N	Y
4	DeFazio	N	Y	N	Y
5	Schrader	N	Y	Y	Y
PENNSYLVANIA					
1	Brady	N	Y	N	Y
2	Fattah	N	Y	N	Y
3	Kelly	Y	N	Y	Y
4	Altmire	N	Y	Y	Y
5	Thompson	Y	N	Y	Y
6	Gerlach	Y	N	Y	Y
7	Meehan	Y	N	Y	Y
8	Fitzpatrick	?	N	Y	Y
9	Shuster	Y	N	Y	Y
10	Marino	Y	N	Y	Y
11	Barletta	Y	N	Y	Y
12	Critz	N	Y	Y	Y
13	Schwartz	N	Y	N	Y
14	Doyle	N	Y	N	Y
15	Dent	Y	N	Y	Y
16	Pitts	Y	N	N	Y
17	Holden	N	Y	Y	Y
18	Murphy	Y	N	Y	Y
19	Platts	Y	N	Y	Y
RHODE ISLAND					
1	Cicilline	N	Y	N	Y
2	Langevin	N	Y	N	Y
SOUTH CAROLINA					
1	Scott	Y	N	N	N
2	Wilson	Y	N	N	N
3	Duncan	Y	N	N	N
4	Gowdy	Y	N	N	N
5	Mulvaney	Y	N	N	N
6	Clyburn	?	?	?	?
SOUTH DAKOTA					
AL	Noem	Y	N	Y	Y
TENNESSEE					
1	Roe	Y	N	Y	Y
2	Duncan	Y	N	Y	Y
3	Fleischmann	Y	N	Y	Y
4	DesJarlais	Y	N	Y	Y
5	Cooper	N	Y	N	Y
6	Black	Y	N	Y	N
7	Blackburn	Y	N	Y	Y
8	Fincher	Y	N	N	Y
9	Cohen	N	Y	N	Y

		448	449	450	451
TEXAS					
1	Gohmert	Y	N	N	N
2	Poe	Y	N	Y	Y
3	Johnson, S.	Y	N	Y	Y
4	Hall	Y	N	Y	Y
5	Hensarling	Y	N	Y	Y
6	Barton	Y	N	Y	Y
7	Culberson	Y	N	Y	Y
8	Brady	Y	N	Y	Y
9	Green, A.	N	Y	Y	Y
10	McCaul	Y	N	Y	Y
11	Conaway	Y	N	Y	N
12	Granger	Y	N	Y	Y
13	Thornberry	Y	N	Y	Y
14	Paul	Y	N	N	N
15	Hinojosa	N	Y	Y	Y
16	Reyes	N	Y	N	Y
17	Flores	Y	N	Y	Y
18	Jackson Lee	N	Y	Y	Y
19	Neugebauer	Y	N	N	N
20	Gonzalez	N	Y	Y	Y
21	Smith	Y	N	Y	Y
22	Olson	Y	N	Y	N
23	Canseco	Y	N	Y	Y
24	Marchant	Y	N	Y	Y
25	Doggett	N	Y	Y	Y
26	Burgess	Y	N	N	N
27	Farenthold	Y	N	Y	Y
28	Cuellar	N	Y	Y	Y
29	Green, G.	N	Y	Y	Y
30	Johnson, E.	?	?	?	?
31	Carter	Y	N	Y	Y
32	Sessions	Y	N	Y	Y
UTAH					
1	Bishop	Y	N	Y	Y
2	Matheson	Y	Y	N	Y
3	Chaffetz	Y	N	N	Y
VERMONT					
AL	Welch	N	Y	N	Y
VIRGINIA					
1	Wittman	Y	N	Y	Y
2	Rigell	Y	N	Y	Y
3	Scott	N	Y	N	Y
4	Forbes	Y	N	Y	Y
5	Hurt	Y	N	Y	N
6	Goodlatte	Y	N	Y	N
7	Cantor	Y	N	Y	Y
8	Moran	N	Y	Y	Y
9	Griffith	Y	N	Y	Y
10	Wolf	Y	N	Y	Y
11	Connolly	N	Y	Y	Y
WASHINGTON					
1	Vacant				
2	Larsen	N	Y	Y	Y
3	Herrera Beutler	Y	N	Y	Y
4	Hastings	Y	N	Y	Y
5	McMorris Rodgers	Y	N	Y	Y
6	Dicks	N	Y	Y	Y
7	McDermott	N	Y	Y	Y
8	Reichert	Y	N	Y	Y
9	Smith	N	Y	Y	Y
WEST VIRGINIA					
1	McKinley	Y	N	Y	Y
2	Capito	Y	N	Y	Y
3	Rahall	N	Y	Y	Y
WISCONSIN					
1	Ryan	Y	N	Y	Y
2	Baldwin	N	Y	N	Y
3	Kind	N	Y	N	Y
4	Moore	N	Y	N	Y
5	Sensenbrenner	Y	N	Y	Y
6	Petri	Y	N	Y	Y
7	Duffy	Y	N	Y	Y
8	Ribble	Y	N	Y	Y
WYOMING					
AL	Lummis	Y	N	N	N

IN THE HOUSE | By Vote Number

452. **HR 4155. Veterans Licensing/Passage.** Chaffetz, R-Utah, motion to suspend the rules and pass the bill that would direct the heads of federal licensing authorities to consider and apply any relevant training received by members of the armed forces toward training or certification requirements for federal licenses. Motion agreed to 369-0: R 206-0; D 163-0. A two-thirds majority of those present and voting (246 in this case) is required for passage under suspension of the rules. July 9, 2012.

453. **HR 4367. ATM Fee Disclosures/Passage.** Luetkemeyer, R-Mo., motion to suspend the rules and pass the bill that would repeal the requirement that banks and credit unions maintain physical placards on automated teller machines warning that customers may be assessed fees for use of an ATM if they are not account holders at that financial institution. Motion agreed to 371-0: R 211-0; D 160-0. A two-thirds majority of those present and voting (248 in this case) is required for passage under suspension of the rules. July 9, 2012.

454. **HR 5892. Hydropower Facility Permits/Passage.** McMorris Rodgers, R-Wash., motion to suspend the rules and pass the bill that would modify the permitting process for hydropower facilities by imposing deadlines on licensing authorities and exempting small-generating units. The bill would extend the period provided for preliminary project permits by two years in certain cases. Motion agreed to 372-0: R 208-0; D 164-0. A two-thirds majority of those present and voting (248 in this case) is required for passage under suspension of the rules. July 9, 2012.

455. **Procedural Motion/Motion to Adjourn.** Ellison, D-Minn., motion to adjourn. Motion rejected 75-318: R 0-227; D 75-91. July 10, 2012.

456. **HR 6079. Repeal of Health Care Overhaul/Previous Question.** Sessions, R-Texas, motion to order the previous question (thus ending debate and the possibility of amendment) on the rule (H Res 724) that would provide for House floor consideration of the bill to repeal the 2010 health care law. Motion agreed to 238-184: R 235-0; D 3-184. July 10, 2012.

457. **H Res 724. Repeal of Health Care Overhaul/Rule.** Adoption of the rule (H Res 724) that would provide for House floor consideration of the bill to repeal the 2010 health care law. Adopted 240-182: R 236-0; D 4-182. July 10, 2012.

	452	453	454	455	456	457
ALABAMA						
1 **Bonner**	?	?	?	?	?	?
2 **Roby**	Y	Y	Y	N	Y	Y
3 **Rogers**	Y	Y	Y	N	Y	Y
4 **Aderholt**	Y	Y	Y	?	Y	Y
5 **Brooks**	?	?	?	N	Y	Y
6 **Bachus**	Y	Y	Y	N	Y	Y
7 **Sewell**	Y	Y	Y	Y	N	N
ALASKA						
AL **Young**	?	?	?	N	Y	Y
ARIZONA						
1 **Gosar**	?	?	?	?	Y	Y
2 **Franks**	Y	Y	Y	N	Y	Y
3 **Quayle**	Y	Y	Y	N	Y	Y
4 **Pastor**	Y	Y	Y	N	N	N
5 **Schweikert**	Y	Y	Y	N	Y	Y
6 **Flake**	?	?	?	N	Y	Y
7 **Grijalva**	Y	Y	Y	N	N	N
8 **Barber**	Y	Y	Y	N	N	N
ARKANSAS						
1 **Crawford**	Y	Y	Y	N	Y	Y
2 **Griffin**	Y	Y	Y	N	Y	Y
3 **Womack**	Y	Y	Y	N	Y	Y
4 **Ross**	Y	Y	Y	N	N	Y
CALIFORNIA						
1 **Thompson**	Y	Y	Y	N	N	N
2 **Herger**	Y	Y	Y	N	Y	Y
3 **Lungren**	Y	Y	Y	N	Y	Y
4 **McClintock**	Y	Y	Y	N	Y	Y
5 **Matsui**	Y	Y	Y	N	N	N
6 **Woolsey**	Y	Y	Y	N	N	N
7 **Miller, George**	+	+	+	+	–	–
8 **Pelosi**	Y	Y	Y	?	N	N
9 **Lee**	?	?	?	Y	N	N
10 **Garamendi**	Y	Y	Y	N	N	N
11 **McNerney**	Y	Y	Y	N	N	N
12 **Speier**	Y	Y	Y	N	N	N
13 **Stark**	Y	Y	Y	N	N	N
14 **Eshoo**	Y	Y	Y	N	N	N
15 **Honda**	Y	Y	Y	N	N	N
16 **Lofgren**	Y	Y	Y	N	N	N
17 **Farr**	Y	Y	Y	N	N	N
18 **Cardoza**	?	?	?	N	N	N
19 **Denham**	Y	Y	Y	N	Y	Y
20 **Costa**	Y	Y	Y	?	N	N
21 **Nunes**	Y	Y	Y	N	Y	Y
22 **McCarthy**	Y	Y	Y	N	Y	Y
23 **Capps**	Y	Y	Y	N	N	N
24 **Gallegly**	Y	Y	Y	N	Y	Y
25 **McKeon**	Y	Y	Y	N	Y	Y
26 **Dreier**	Y	Y	Y	N	Y	Y
27 Sherman	Y	Y	Y	N	N	N
28 Berman	Y	Y	Y	N	N	N
29 Schiff	Y	Y	Y	N	N	N
30 Waxman	Y	Y	Y	N	N	N
31 Becerra	Y	Y	Y	?	N	N
32 Chu	Y	Y	Y	N	N	N
33 Bass	Y	Y	Y	N	N	N
34 Roybal-Allard	Y	Y	Y	N	N	N
35 Waters	Y	Y	Y	N	N	N
36 Hahn	Y	Y	Y	N	N	N
37 Richardson	Y	Y	Y	N	N	N
38 Napolitano	Y	Y	Y	N	N	N
39 Sánchez, Linda	Y	?	Y	Y	N	N
40 **Royce**	Y	Y	Y	N	Y	Y
41 **Lewis**	?	?	?	N	Y	Y
42 **Miller, Gary**	Y	Y	Y	N	Y	Y
43 Baca	Y	Y	Y	N	N	N
44 **Calvert**	Y	Y	Y	N	Y	Y
45 **Bono Mack**	Y	Y	Y	N	Y	Y
46 **Rohrabacher**	?	?	?	N	Y	Y
47 Sanchez, Loretta	Y	Y	Y	N	N	N
48 **Campbell**	?	?	?	N	Y	Y
49 **Issa**	Y	Y	Y	N	Y	Y
50 **Bilbray**	Y	Y	Y	N	Y	Y
51 Filner	+	+	+	Y	N	N
52 **Hunter**	Y	Y	?	N	Y	Y
53 Davis	Y	Y	Y	N	N	N

	452	453	454	455	456	457
COLORADO						
1 DeGette	Y	Y	Y	N	N	N
2 Polis	Y	Y	Y	N	N	N
3 **Tipton**	Y	Y	Y	N	Y	Y
4 **Gardner**	Y	Y	Y	N	Y	Y
5 **Lamborn**	Y	Y	Y	N	Y	Y
6 **Coffman**	Y	Y	Y	N	Y	Y
7 Perlmutter	Y	Y	Y	N	N	N
CONNECTICUT						
1 Larson	Y	Y	Y	?	N	N
2 Courtney	Y	Y	Y	N	N	N
3 DeLauro	Y	Y	Y	N	N	N
4 Himes	Y	Y	Y	N	N	N
5 Murphy	?	?	?	N	N	N
DELAWARE						
AL Carney	Y	Y	Y	N	N	N
FLORIDA						
1 **Miller**	Y	Y	Y	N	Y	Y
2 **Southerland**	Y	Y	Y	N	Y	Y
3 Brown	Y	Y	Y	N	N	N
4 **Crenshaw**	Y	Y	Y	N	Y	Y
5 **Nugent**	Y	Y	Y	N	Y	Y
6 **Stearns**	Y	Y	Y	N	Y	Y
7 **Mica**	Y	Y	Y	N	Y	Y
8 **Webster**	Y	Y	Y	N	Y	Y
9 **Bilirakis**	Y	Y	Y	N	Y	Y
10 **Young**	Y	Y	Y	N	Y	Y
11 Castor	Y	Y	Y	?	N	N
12 **Ross**	Y	Y	Y	N	Y	Y
13 **Buchanan**	Y	Y	Y	N	Y	Y
14 **Mack**	Y	Y	Y	N	Y	Y
15 **Posey**	Y	Y	Y	N	Y	Y
16 **Rooney**	Y	Y	Y	N	Y	Y
17 Wilson	Y	Y	Y	N	N	N
18 **Ros-Lehtinen**	Y	Y	Y	N	Y	Y
19 Deutch	?	?	?	?	N	N
20 Wasserman Schultz	?	?	?	N	N	N
21 **Diaz-Balart**	?	Y	Y	N	Y	Y
22 **West**	Y	Y	Y	N	Y	Y
23 Hastings	Y	Y	Y	N	N	N
24 **Adams**	Y	Y	Y	N	Y	Y
25 **Rivera**	Y	Y	Y	N	Y	Y
GEORGIA						
1 **Kingston**	Y	Y	Y	N	Y	Y
2 Bishop	Y	?	Y	Y	N	N
3 **Westmoreland**	Y	Y	Y	N	Y	Y
4 Johnson	Y	Y	Y	N	N	N
5 Lewis	Y	Y	Y	N	N	N
6 **Price**	Y	Y	Y	N	Y	Y
7 **Woodall**	Y	Y	Y	N	Y	?
8 **Scott, A.**	Y	Y	Y	N	Y	Y
9 **Graves**	Y	Y	Y	N	Y	Y
10 **Broun**	Y	Y	Y	N	Y	Y
11 **Gingrey**	?	Y	Y	N	Y	Y
12 Barrow	Y	Y	Y	N	N	N
13 Scott, D.	Y	Y	Y	N	N	N
HAWAII						
1 Hanabusa	Y	Y	Y	N	N	N
2 Hirono	?	?	?	?	?	?
IDAHO						
1 **Labrador**	Y	Y	Y	N	Y	Y
2 **Simpson**	?	?	?	N	Y	Y
ILLINOIS						
1 Rush	?	?	?	Y	N	N
2 Jackson	?	?	?	?	?	?
3 Lipinski	?	?	?	N	N	N
4 Gutierrez	+	+	+	+	–	–
5 Quigley	Y	Y	Y	N	N	N
6 **Roskam**	Y	Y	Y	N	Y	Y
7 Davis	Y	Y	Y	N	N	N
8 **Walsh**	Y	Y	Y	N	Y	Y
9 Schakowsky	Y	Y	Y	N	N	N
10 **Dold**	Y	Y	Y	N	Y	Y
11 **Kinzinger**	Y	Y	Y	N	Y	Y
12 Costello	Y	Y	Y	N	N	N
13 **Biggert**	Y	Y	Y	N	Y	Y
14 **Hultgren**	Y	Y	Y	N	Y	Y
15 **Johnson**	+	+	+	?	Y	Y

KEY   **Republicans**   Democrats

Y	Voted for (yea)	X Paired against
#	Paired for	– Announced against
+	Announced for	P Voted "present"
N	Voted against (nay)	
	C	Voted "present" to avoid possible conflict of interest
	?	Did not vote or otherwise make a position known

*Rep. Thaddeus McCotter, R-Mich., resigned effective July 6, 2012. The last vote for which he was eligible was vote 451.

	452	453	454	455	456	457
16 **Manzullo**	+	+	+	N	Y	Y
17 **Schilling**	Y	Y	Y	N	Y	Y
18 **Schock**	?	?	?	?	Y	Y
19 **Shimkus**	Y	Y	Y	?	Y	Y
INDIANA						
1 Visclosky	Y	Y	Y	N	N	N
2 Donnelly	Y	Y	Y	N	N	N
3 **Stutzman**	?	?	?	N	Y	Y
4 **Rokita**	Y	Y	Y	N	Y	Y
5 **Burton**	Y	Y	Y	N	Y	Y
6 **Pence**	?	?	?	?	Y	Y
7 Carson	Y	Y	Y	Y	N	N
8 **Bucshon**	Y	Y	Y	N	Y	Y
9 **Young**	Y	Y	Y	N	Y	Y
IOWA						
1 Braley	Y	Y	Y	Y	N	N
2 Loebsack	Y	Y	Y	N	N	N
3 Boswell	Y	Y	Y	N	N	N
4 **Latham**	Y	Y	Y	N	Y	Y
5 **King**	Y	Y	Y	N	?	?
KANSAS						
1 **Huelskamp**	Y	Y	Y	N	Y	Y
2 **Jenkins**	Y	Y	Y	N	Y	Y
3 **Yoder**	Y	Y	Y	N	Y	Y
4 **Pompeo**	Y	Y	Y	N	Y	Y
KENTUCKY						
1 **Whitfield**	?	?	?	N	Y	Y
2 **Guthrie**	Y	Y	Y	N	Y	Y
3 Yarmuth	Y	Y	Y	N	N	N
4 **Davis**	Y	Y	Y	N	Y	Y
5 **Rogers**	Y	Y	Y	N	Y	Y
6 Chandler	?	?	?	?	N	N
LOUISIANA						
1 **Scalise**	Y	Y	Y	N	Y	Y
2 Richmond	Y	Y	Y	Y	N	N
3 **Landry**	?	?	?	N	Y	Y
4 **Fleming**	Y	Y	Y	N	Y	Y
5 **Alexander**	Y	Y	Y	N	Y	Y
6 **Cassidy**	+	Y	Y	N	Y	Y
7 **Boustany**	Y	Y	Y	N	Y	Y
MAINE						
1 Pingree	Y	Y	Y	Y	N	N
2 Michaud	Y	Y	Y	N	N	N
MARYLAND						
1 **Harris**	Y	Y	Y	N	Y	Y
2 Ruppersberger	?	?	?	N	N	N
3 Sarbanes	Y	Y	Y	Y	N	N
4 Edwards	Y	?	Y	Y	N	N
5 Hoyer	Y	Y	Y	N	N	N
6 **Bartlett**	Y	Y	Y	N	Y	Y
7 Cummings	Y	Y	Y	Y	N	N
8 Van Hollen	Y	Y	Y	Y	N	N
MASSACHUSETTS						
1 Olver	Y	Y	Y	Y	N	N
2 Neal	?	?	?	N	N	N
3 McGovern	Y	Y	Y	Y	N	N
4 Frank	?	?	?	?	N	N
5 Tsongas	Y	Y	Y	N	N	N
6 Tierney	Y	Y	Y	N	N	N
7 Markey	Y	Y	Y	N	N	N
8 Capuano	Y	Y	Y	?	N	N
9 Lynch	+	?	?	N	N	N
10 Keating	Y	Y	Y	Y	N	N
MICHIGAN						
1 **Benishek**	?	?	?	N	Y	Y
2 **Huizenga**	Y	Y	Y	N	Y	Y
3 **Amash**	Y	Y	Y	N	Y	Y
4 **Camp**	Y	Y	Y	N	Y	Y
5 Kildee	Y	Y	Y	Y	N	N
6 **Upton**	Y	Y	Y	N	Y	Y
7 **Walberg**	Y	Y	Y	N	Y	Y
8 **Rogers**	Y	Y	Y	N	Y	Y
9 Peters	?	?	?	Y	N	N
10 **Miller**	Y	Y	Y	N	Y	Y
11 Vacant*						
12 Levin	Y	Y	Y	N	N	N
13 Clarke	Y	Y	Y	N	N	N
14 Conyers	+	+	+	N	N	N
15 Dingell	Y	Y	Y	?	N	N
MINNESOTA						
1 Walz	Y	Y	Y	N	N	N
2 **Kline**	Y	Y	Y	N	Y	Y
3 **Paulsen**	Y	Y	Y	N	Y	Y
4 McCollum	Y	Y	Y	N	N	N

	452	453	454	455	456	457
5 Ellison	+	+	+	Y	N	N
6 **Bachmann**	Y	Y	Y	N	Y	Y
7 Peterson	Y	Y	Y	N	N	N
8 **Cravaack**	Y	Y	?	N	Y	Y
MISSISSIPPI						
1 **Nunnelee**	Y	Y	Y	N	Y	Y
2 Thompson	Y	Y	Y	Y	N	N
3 **Harper**	Y	Y	Y	N	Y	Y
4 **Palazzo**	Y	Y	Y	N	Y	Y
MISSOURI						
1 Clay	Y	Y	Y	Y	N	N
2 **Akin**	+	+	+	–	+	+
3 Carnahan	Y	Y	Y	N	N	N
4 **Hartzler**	Y	Y	Y	N	Y	Y
5 Cleaver	?	?	?	Y	N	N
6 **Graves**	Y	Y	Y	N	Y	Y
7 **Long**	Y	Y	Y	N	Y	Y
8 **Emerson**	Y	Y	Y	N	Y	Y
9 **Luetkemeyer**	Y	Y	Y	N	Y	Y
MONTANA						
AL **Rehberg**	Y	Y	Y	N	Y	Y
NEBRASKA						
1 **Fortenberry**	Y	Y	Y	N	Y	Y
2 **Terry**	Y	Y	Y	N	Y	Y
3 **Smith**	Y	Y	Y	N	Y	Y
NEVADA						
1 Berkley	Y	Y	Y	N	N	N
2 **Amodei**	Y	Y	Y	N	Y	Y
3 **Heck**	Y	Y	Y	N	Y	Y
NEW HAMPSHIRE						
1 **Guinta**	Y	Y	Y	N	Y	Y
2 **Bass**	Y	Y	Y	N	Y	Y
NEW JERSEY						
1 Andrews	Y	Y	Y	Y	N	N
2 **LoBiondo**	Y	Y	Y	N	Y	Y
3 **Runyan**	Y	Y	Y	N	Y	Y
4 **Smith**	Y	Y	Y	N	Y	Y
5 **Garrett**	Y	Y	Y	N	Y	Y
6 Pallone	Y	Y	Y	Y	N	N
7 **Lance**	Y	Y	Y	N	Y	Y
8 Pascrell	+	+	+	?	N	N
9 Rothman	Y	Y	Y	?	N	N
10 Vacant						
11 **Frelinghuysen**	Y	Y	Y	N	Y	Y
12 Holt	Y	Y	Y	N	N	N
13 Sires	Y	Y	Y	?	N	N
NEW MEXICO						
1 Heinrich	Y	Y	Y	N	N	N
2 **Pearce**	Y	Y	Y	N	Y	Y
3 Luján	Y	Y	Y	N	N	N
NEW YORK						
1 Bishop	Y	Y	Y	N	N	?
2 Israel	Y	Y	Y	Y	N	N
3 **King**	Y	Y	Y	N	Y	Y
4 McCarthy	Y	Y	Y	N	N	N
5 Ackerman	Y	Y	Y	N	N	N
6 Meeks	?	?	?	Y	N	N
7 Crowley	Y	Y	Y	Y	N	N
8 Nadler	Y	Y	Y	Y	N	N
9 **Turner**	Y	Y	Y	N	Y	Y
10 Towns	Y	Y	Y	?	N	N
11 Clarke	+	+	Y	Y	N	N
12 Velázquez	Y	Y	Y	Y	N	N
13 **Grimm**	Y	Y	Y	N	Y	Y
14 Maloney	Y	Y	Y	Y	N	N
15 Rangel	Y	Y	Y	N	N	N
16 Serrano	Y	Y	Y	N	N	N
17 Engel	Y	Y	Y	N	N	N
18 Lowey	Y	Y	Y	Y	N	N
19 **Hayworth**	Y	Y	Y	N	Y	Y
20 **Gibson**	Y	Y	Y	N	Y	Y
21 Tonko	Y	Y	Y	Y	N	N
22 Hinchey	Y	Y	Y	Y	N	N
23 Owens	Y	Y	Y	Y	N	N
24 **Hanna**	Y	Y	Y	N	Y	Y
25 **Buerkle**	Y	Y	Y	N	Y	Y
26 Hochul	Y	Y	Y	N	N	N
27 Higgins	Y	Y	Y	Y	N	N
28 Slaughter	Y	Y	Y	Y	N	N
29 **Reed**	Y	Y	Y	N	Y	Y
NORTH CAROLINA						
1 Butterfield	?	?	?	N	N	N
2 **Ellmers**	Y	Y	Y	N	Y	Y
3 **Jones**	Y	Y	Y	N	Y	Y
4 Price	Y	Y	Y	N	N	N

	452	453	454	455	456	457
5 **Foxx**	Y	Y	Y	N	Y	Y
6 **Coble**	?	?	?	N	Y	Y
7 McIntyre	Y	Y	Y	?	Y	Y
8 Kissell	Y	Y	Y	?	N	Y
9 **Myrick**	+	+	+	N	Y	Y
10 **McHenry**	Y	Y	Y	N	Y	Y
11 Shuler	?	?	?	?	Y	N
12 Watt	Y	Y	Y	N	N	N
13 Miller	Y	Y	Y	?	N	N
NORTH DAKOTA						
AL **Berg**	Y	Y	Y	N	Y	Y
OHIO						
1 **Chabot**	Y	Y	Y	N	Y	Y
2 **Schmidt**	?	?	?	N	Y	Y
3 **Turner**	Y	Y	Y	–	Y	Y
4 **Jordan**	Y	Y	Y	N	Y	Y
5 **Latta**	Y	Y	Y	N	Y	Y
6 **Johnson**	Y	Y	Y	N	Y	Y
7 **Austria**	?	?	?	N	Y	Y
8 **Boehner**						
9 Kaptur	Y	Y	Y	Y	N	N
10 Kucinich	Y	Y	Y	Y	N	N
11 Fudge	Y	Y	Y	Y	N	N
12 **Tiberi**	Y	Y	Y	N	Y	Y
13 Sutton	Y	Y	Y	N	N	N
14 **LaTourette**	Y	Y	Y	N	Y	Y
15 **Stivers**	Y	Y	Y	N	Y	Y
16 **Renacci**	Y	Y	Y	N	Y	Y
17 Ryan	Y	Y	Y	N	N	N
18 **Gibbs**	Y	Y	Y	N	Y	Y
OKLAHOMA						
1 **Sullivan**	Y	Y	Y	?	?	Y
2 Boren	Y	Y	Y	N	Y	Y
3 **Lucas**	Y	Y	Y	N	Y	Y
4 **Cole**	Y	Y	Y	N	Y	Y
5 **Lankford**	Y	Y	Y	N	Y	Y
OREGON						
1 Bonamici	Y	Y	Y	N	N	N
2 **Walden**	Y	Y	Y	N	Y	Y
3 Blumenauer	Y	Y	Y	N	N	N
4 DeFazio	Y	Y	Y	N	N	N
5 Schrader	Y	Y	Y	N	N	N
PENNSYLVANIA						
1 Brady	Y	Y	Y	Y	N	N
2 Fattah	Y	Y	Y	?	N	N
3 **Kelly**	Y	Y	Y	N	Y	Y
4 Altmire	Y	Y	Y	?	N	N
5 **Thompson**	Y	Y	Y	N	Y	Y
6 **Gerlach**	Y	Y	Y	N	Y	Y
7 **Meehan**	Y	Y	Y	N	Y	Y
8 **Fitzpatrick**	Y	Y	Y	N	Y	Y
9 **Shuster**	Y	Y	Y	N	Y	Y
10 **Marino**	Y	Y	Y	N	Y	Y
11 **Barletta**	Y	Y	Y	N	Y	Y
12 Critz	Y	Y	Y	N	N	N
13 Schwartz	Y	Y	Y	Y	N	N
14 Doyle	Y	Y	Y	N	N	N
15 **Dent**	Y	Y	Y	N	Y	Y
16 **Pitts**	Y	Y	Y	N	Y	Y
17 Holden	Y	Y	Y	N	N	N
18 **Murphy**	Y	Y	Y	N	Y	Y
19 **Platts**	Y	Y	Y	N	?	Y
RHODE ISLAND						
1 Cicilline	Y	Y	Y	N	N	N
2 Langevin	Y	Y	Y	N	N	N
SOUTH CAROLINA						
1 **Scott**	Y	Y	Y	N	Y	Y
2 **Wilson**	+	Y	Y	N	Y	Y
3 **Duncan**	Y	Y	Y	N	Y	Y
4 **Gowdy**	Y	Y	Y	N	Y	Y
5 **Mulvaney**	Y	Y	Y	N	Y	Y
6 Clyburn	Y	Y	Y	N	N	N
SOUTH DAKOTA						
AL **Noem**	Y	Y	Y	N	Y	Y
TENNESSEE						
1 **Roe**	Y	Y	Y	N	Y	Y
2 **Duncan**	Y	Y	Y	N	Y	Y
3 **Fleischmann**	?	?	?	N	Y	Y
4 **DesJarlais**	+	+	+	N	Y	Y
5 Cooper	Y	Y	Y	N	N	N
6 **Black**	Y	Y	Y	N	Y	Y
7 **Blackburn**	Y	Y	Y	N	Y	Y
8 **Fincher**	Y	Y	Y	N	Y	Y
9 Cohen	Y	Y	Y	N	N	N

	452	453	454	455	456	457
TEXAS						
1 **Gohmert**	Y	Y	Y	N	Y	Y
2 **Poe**	Y	Y	Y	N	Y	Y
3 **Johnson, S.**	Y	Y	Y	N	Y	Y
4 **Hall**	Y	Y	Y	N	Y	Y
5 **Hensarling**	Y	Y	Y	N	Y	Y
6 **Barton**	Y	Y	Y	N	Y	Y
7 **Culberson**	?	?	?	N	Y	Y
8 **Brady**	Y	Y	Y	N	Y	Y
9 Green, A.	+	+	+	N	N	N
10 **McCaul**	Y	Y	?	N	Y	Y
11 **Conaway**	Y	Y	Y	N	Y	Y
12 **Granger**	Y	Y	Y	N	Y	Y
13 **Thornberry**	Y	Y	Y	N	Y	Y
14 **Paul**	?	?	?	N	Y	Y
15 Hinojosa	Y	Y	Y	N	N	N
16 Reyes	Y	Y	Y	Y	N	N
17 **Flores**	Y	Y	Y	?	Y	Y
18 Jackson Lee	?	?	?	N	N	N
19 **Neugebauer**	Y	Y	Y	N	Y	Y
20 Gonzalez	Y	Y	Y	N	N	N
21 **Smith**	Y	Y	Y	N	Y	Y
22 **Olson**	+	+	+	N	Y	Y
23 **Canseco**	Y	Y	Y	N	Y	Y
24 **Marchant**	Y	Y	Y	N	Y	Y
25 Doggett	Y	Y	Y	N	N	N
26 **Burgess**	Y	Y	Y	N	Y	Y
27 **Farenthold**	?	?	?	N	Y	Y
28 Cuellar	Y	Y	Y	Y	N	N
29 Green, G.	Y	Y	Y	–	N	N
30 Johnson, E.	Y	Y	Y	Y	N	N
31 **Carter**	?	?	?	N	Y	Y
32 **Sessions**	Y	Y	Y	N	Y	Y
UTAH						
1 **Bishop**	Y	Y	Y	N	Y	Y
2 Matheson	Y	Y	Y	N	N	N
3 **Chaffetz**	Y	Y	Y	N	Y	Y
VERMONT						
AL Welch	Y	Y	Y	Y	N	N
VIRGINIA						
1 **Wittman**	Y	Y	Y	N	Y	Y
2 **Rigell**	Y	Y	Y	N	Y	Y
3 Scott	?	?	?	N	N	N
4 **Forbes**	Y	Y	Y	N	Y	Y
5 **Hurt**	Y	Y	Y	N	Y	Y
6 **Goodlatte**	Y	Y	Y	N	Y	Y
7 **Cantor**	Y	Y	Y	N	Y	Y
8 Moran	Y	Y	Y	N	N	N
9 **Griffith**	Y	Y	Y	N	Y	Y
10 **Wolf**	Y	Y	Y	N	Y	Y
11 Connolly	Y	Y	Y	N	N	N
WASHINGTON						
1 Vacant						
2 Larsen	Y	Y	Y	N	N	N
3 **Herrera Beutler**	Y	Y	Y	N	Y	Y
4 **Hastings**	Y	Y	Y	N	Y	Y
5 **McMorris Rodgers**	Y	Y	Y	N	Y	Y
6 Dicks	Y	Y	Y	Y	N	N
7 McDermott	Y	Y	Y	Y	N	N
8 **Reichert**	Y	Y	Y	N	Y	Y
9 Smith	Y	Y	Y	N	N	N
WEST VIRGINIA						
1 **McKinley**	Y	Y	Y	N	Y	Y
2 **Capito**	Y	Y	Y	?	Y	Y
3 Rahall	Y	Y	Y	N	N	N
WISCONSIN						
1 **Ryan**	+	Y	Y	N	Y	Y
2 Baldwin	Y	Y	Y	N	N	N
3 Kind	Y	Y	Y	N	N	N
4 Moore	Y	Y	Y	Y	N	N
5 **Sensenbrenner**	Y	Y	Y	N	Y	Y
6 **Petri**	Y	Y	Y	N	Y	Y
7 **Duffy**	Y	Y	Y	N	Y	Y
8 **Ribble**	Y	Y	Y	P	Y	Y
WYOMING						
AL **Lummis**	Y	Y	Y	N	Y	Y

IN THE HOUSE | By Vote Number

458. **Procedural Motion/Journal.** Approval of the House Journal of Monday July 9, 2012. Approved 312-105: R 185-49; D 127-56. July 10, 2012.

459. **HR 6079. Repeal of Health Care Overhaul/Recommit.** Andrews, D-N.J., motion to recommit the bill to the House Energy and Commerce, Ways and Means and Education and the Workforce committees and report it back immediately with language that would make any member of the House of Representatives who votes in favor of the bill to repeal the 2010 health care overhaul law ineligible for the Federal Employees Health Benefits Program. Motion rejected 180-248: R 0-239; D 180-9. July 11, 2012.

460. **HR 6079. Repeal of Health Care Overhaul/Passage.** Passage of the bill that would repeal the 2010 health care overhaul law, which requires most individuals to buy health insurance by 2014, makes changes to government health care programs and sets new requirements for health insurers. The bill would restore the provisions of law amended or repealed by the health care overhaul, and repeal certain provisions of the health care reconciliation law. Passed 244-185: R 239-0; D 5-185. A "nay" was a vote in support of the president's position. July 11, 2012.

461. **HR 4402. Mineral Mining Projects/Rule.** Adoption of the rule (H Res 726) that would provide for House floor consideration of a bill that would expedite environmental review of critical mineral mining projects. Adopted 245-180: R 235-0; D 10-180. July 11, 2012.

462. **HR 4402. Mineral Mining Projects/Strategic and Critical Minerals Definition.** Tonko, D-N.Y., amendment that would limit the scope of the bill by modifying the definition of "strategic and critical minerals" to minerals specifically identified in the National Research Council's 2008 report on critical minerals or other minerals identified by the council. The amendment would make clay, sand and gravel mines ineligible for the expedited permitting and review process created by the bill. Rejected in Committee of the Whole 162-251: R 0-233; D 162-18. July 12, 2012.

		458	459	460	461	462
ALABAMA						
1	Bonner	?	?	?	?	N
2	Roby	Y	N	Y	Y	N
3	Rogers	Y	N	Y	Y	N
4	Aderholt	Y	N	Y	Y	N
5	Brooks	Y	N	Y	Y	N
6	Bachus	Y	N	Y	Y	N
7	Sewell	Y	Y	N	N	Y
ALASKA						
AL	Young	N	N	Y	Y	N
ARIZONA						
1	Gosar	Y	N	Y	Y	N
2	Franks	Y	N	Y	Y	N
3	Quayle	N	N	Y	Y	N
4	Pastor	N	Y	N	N	Y
5	Schweikert	Y	N	Y	Y	N
6	Flake	Y	N	Y	Y	N
7	Grijalva	?	Y	N	N	Y
8	Barber	Y	Y	N	N	Y
ARKANSAS						
1	Crawford	Y	N	Y	Y	N
2	Griffin	N	N	Y	Y	N
3	Womack	Y	N	Y	Y	N
4	Ross	Y	N	Y	Y	N
CALIFORNIA						
1	Thompson	N	Y	N	N	Y
2	Herger	Y	N	Y	Y	N
3	Lungren	Y	N	Y	Y	N
4	McClintock	Y	N	Y	Y	N
5	Matsui	Y	Y	N	N	Y
6	Woolsey	Y	Y	N	N	Y
7	Miller, George	–	Y	N	N	Y
8	Pelosi	N	Y	N	N	Y
9	Lee	N	Y	N	N	Y
10	Garamendi	Y	Y	N	N	Y
11	McNerney	Y	Y	N	N	Y
12	Speier	Y	Y	N	N	Y
13	Stark	Y	Y	N	N	Y
14	Eshoo	Y	Y	N	N	Y
15	Honda	Y	Y	N	N	Y
16	Lofgren	Y	Y	N	N	Y
17	Farr	Y	Y	N	N	Y
18	Cardoza	N	Y	N	N	?
19	Denham	N	N	Y	Y	N
20	Costa	N	Y	N	N	?
21	Nunes	Y	N	Y	Y	N
22	McCarthy	Y	N	Y	Y	N
23	Capps	Y	Y	N	N	Y
24	Gallegly	Y	N	Y	?	?
25	McKeon	Y	N	Y	Y	N
26	Dreier	Y	N	Y	Y	N
27	Sherman	Y	Y	N	N	Y
28	Berman	Y	Y	N	N	Y
29	Schiff	Y	Y	N	N	Y
30	Waxman	Y	Y	N	N	Y
31	Becerra	Y	Y	N	N	Y
32	Chu	Y	Y	N	N	Y
33	Bass	N	Y	N	N	Y
34	Roybal-Allard	Y	Y	N	N	Y
35	Waters	Y	Y	N	N	Y
36	Hahn	Y	Y	N	N	Y
37	Richardson	Y	Y	N	N	Y
38	Napolitano	Y	Y	N	N	Y
39	Sánchez, Linda	N	Y	N	N	Y
40	Royce	Y	N	Y	Y	N
41	Lewis	Y	N	Y	Y	N
42	Miller, Gary	Y	N	Y	Y	N
43	Baca	Y	Y	N	N	Y
44	Calvert	Y	N	Y	Y	N
45	Bono Mack	Y	N	Y	Y	N
46	Rohrabacher	Y	N	Y	Y	N
47	Sanchez, Loretta	N	Y	N	N	Y
48	Campbell	Y	N	Y	Y	N
49	Issa	Y	N	Y	Y	N
50	Bilbray	Y	N	Y	Y	N
51	Filner	N	Y	N	N	Y
52	Hunter	Y	N	Y	Y	N
53	Davis	Y	Y	N	N	Y

		458	459	460	461	462
COLORADO						
1	DeGette	Y	Y	N	N	Y
2	Polis	Y	Y	N	N	Y
3	Tipton	N	N	Y	Y	N
4	Gardner	N	N	Y	Y	N
5	Lamborn	Y	N	Y	Y	N
6	Coffman	N	N	Y	Y	N
7	Perlmutter	Y	Y	N	N	Y
CONNECTICUT						
1	Larson	N	Y	N	N	Y
2	Courtney	Y	Y	N	N	Y
3	DeLauro	Y	Y	N	N	Y
4	Himes	Y	Y	N	N	Y
5	Murphy	Y	Y	N	N	Y
DELAWARE						
AL	Carney	Y	Y	N	Y	Y
FLORIDA						
1	Miller	Y	N	Y	Y	N
2	Southerland	Y	N	Y	Y	N
3	Brown	N	Y	N	N	Y
4	Crenshaw	Y	N	Y	Y	N
5	Nugent	N	N	Y	Y	N
6	Stearns	Y	N	Y	Y	N
7	Mica	Y	N	Y	Y	N
8	Webster	Y	N	Y	Y	N
9	Bilirakis	Y	N	Y	Y	N
10	Young	Y	N	Y	Y	N
11	Castor	Y	Y	N	N	Y
12	Ross	Y	N	Y	Y	N
13	Buchanan	Y	N	Y	Y	N
14	Mack	Y	N	Y	Y	N
15	Posey	Y	N	Y	Y	N
16	Rooney	N	N	Y	Y	N
17	Wilson	Y	Y	N	N	Y
18	Ros-Lehtinen	Y	N	Y	Y	N
19	Deutch	Y	Y	N	N	Y
20	Wasserman Schultz	Y	Y	N	N	Y
21	Diaz-Balart	Y	N	Y	Y	N
22	West	Y	N	Y	Y	N
23	Hastings	N	Y	N	N	Y
24	Adams	N	N	Y	Y	N
25	Rivera	Y	N	Y	Y	N
GEORGIA						
1	Kingston	Y	N	Y	Y	N
2	Bishop	Y	Y	N	N	N
3	Westmoreland	Y	N	Y	Y	N
4	Johnson	Y	Y	N	N	Y
5	Lewis	?	Y	N	N	Y
6	Price	Y	N	Y	Y	N
7	Woodall	N	N	Y	Y	N
8	Scott, A.	Y	N	Y	Y	N
9	Graves	Y	N	Y	Y	N
10	Broun	Y	N	Y	Y	N
11	Gingrey	Y	N	Y	Y	N
12	Barrow	N	N	N	N	N
13	Scott, D.	Y	Y	N	N	Y
HAWAII						
1	Hanabusa	Y	Y	N	N	Y
2	Hirono	?	Y	N	N	Y
IDAHO						
1	Labrador	Y	N	Y	Y	N
2	Simpson	Y	N	Y	Y	N
ILLINOIS						
1	Rush	Y	Y	N	N	?
2	Jackson	?	?	?	?	?
3	Lipinski	Y	Y	N	N	Y
4	Gutierrez	–	Y	N	N	?
5	Quigley	Y	Y	N	N	Y
6	Roskam	Y	N	Y	Y	N
7	Davis	Y	Y	N	N	Y
8	Walsh	N	N	Y	Y	N
9	Schakowsky	N	Y	N	N	Y
10	Dold	N	N	Y	Y	N
11	Kinzinger	N	N	Y	Y	N
12	Costello	N	Y	N	N	N
13	Biggert	Y	N	Y	Y	N
14	Hultgren	Y	N	Y	Y	N
15	Johnson	Y	N	Y	Y	N

KEY   **Republicans**   Democrats

Y	Voted for (yea)	X	Paired against	C	Voted "present" to avoid possible conflict of interest
#	Paired for	–	Announced against		
+	Announced for	P	Voted "present"	?	Did not vote or otherwise make a position known
N	Voted against (nay)				

	458	459	460	461	462
16 Manzullo	Y	N	Y	Y	N
17 Schilling	N	N	Y	Y	N
18 Schock	Y	N	Y	Y	N
19 Shimkus	Y	N	Y	Y	N
INDIANA					
1 Visclosky	N	Y	N	N	Y
2 Donnelly	N	Y	N	Y	N
3 Stutzman	Y	N	Y	Y	N
4 Rokita	Y	N	Y	Y	N
5 Burton	Y	N	Y	Y	N
6 Pence	Y	N	Y	Y	N
7 Carson	Y	Y	N	N	Y
8 Bucshon	Y	N	Y	Y	N
9 Young	Y	N	Y	Y	N
IOWA					
1 Braley	Y	Y	N	N	Y
2 Loebsack	Y	Y	N	N	Y
3 Boswell	N	Y	N	N	N
4 Latham	N	N	Y	Y	N
5 King	?	N	Y	Y	N
KANSAS					
1 Huelskamp	Y	N	Y	Y	N
2 Jenkins	Y	N	Y	Y	?
3 Yoder	N	N	Y	Y	N
4 Pompeo	Y	N	Y	Y	N
KENTUCKY					
1 Whitfield	Y	N	Y	Y	N
2 Guthrie	Y	N	Y	Y	N
3 Yarmuth	Y	Y	N	N	Y
4 Davis	Y	N	Y	N	N
5 Rogers	Y	N	Y	Y	N
6 Chandler	N	Y	N	N	N
LOUISIANA					
1 Scalise	Y	N	Y	Y	N
2 Richmond	Y	Y	N	N	Y
3 Landry	?	N	Y	Y	N
4 Fleming	Y	N	Y	Y	N
5 Alexander	Y	N	Y	Y	N
6 Cassidy	Y	N	Y	Y	N
7 Boustany	Y	N	Y	Y	N
MAINE					
1 Pingree	Y	Y	N	N	Y
2 Michaud	Y	Y	N	N	Y
MARYLAND					
1 Harris	Y	N	Y	Y	N
2 Ruppersberger	Y	Y	N	N	Y
3 Sarbanes	Y	Y	N	N	Y
4 Edwards	Y	Y	N	N	Y
5 Hoyer	N	N	N	N	Y
6 Bartlett	Y	N	Y	Y	N
7 Cummings	Y	Y	N	N	Y
8 Van Hollen	Y	+	N	N	Y
MASSACHUSETTS					
1 Olver	N	Y	N	N	Y
2 Neal	Y	Y	N	N	Y
3 McGovern	N	Y	N	N	Y
4 Frank	Y	Y	N	N	Y
5 Tsongas	Y	Y	N	N	Y
6 Tierney	Y	Y	N	N	Y
7 Markey	Y	Y	N	N	Y
8 Capuano	N	Y	N	N	Y
9 Lynch	N	Y	N	N	Y
10 Keating	N	Y	N	N	Y
MICHIGAN					
1 Benishek	N	N	Y	Y	N
2 Huizenga	Y	N	Y	Y	N
3 Amash	P	N	Y	Y	N
4 Camp	Y	N	Y	Y	N
5 Kildee	Y	Y	N	N	Y
6 Upton	Y	N	Y	Y	N
7 Walberg	N	N	Y	Y	N
8 Rogers	Y	N	Y	Y	N
9 Peters	N	Y	N	N	Y
10 Miller	Y	N	Y	Y	N
11 Vacant					
12 Levin	Y	Y	N	N	Y
13 Clarke	N	Y	N	N	Y
14 Conyers	N	Y	N	N	Y
15 Dingell	Y	Y	N	N	Y
MINNESOTA					
1 Walz	Y	Y	N	N	Y
2 Kline	Y	N	Y	Y	N
3 Paulsen	N	N	Y	Y	N
4 McCollum	Y	Y	N	N	Y

	458	459	460	461	462
5 Ellison	N	Y	N	N	Y
6 Bachmann	Y	N	Y	Y	N
7 Peterson	N	Y	N	N	N
8 Cravaack	N	N	Y	Y	N
MISSISSIPPI					
1 Nunnelee	Y	N	Y	Y	N
2 Thompson	N	Y	N	N	Y
3 Harper	Y	N	Y	Y	N
4 Palazzo	Y	N	Y	Y	N
MISSOURI					
1 Clay	Y	Y	N	N	Y
2 Akin	+	N	Y	Y	?
3 Carnahan	Y	Y	N	N	Y
4 Hartzler	Y	N	Y	Y	N
5 Cleaver	Y	Y	N	N	Y
6 Graves	N	N	Y	Y	N
7 Long	Y	N	Y	Y	N
8 Emerson	Y	N	Y	Y	N
9 Luetkemeyer	Y	N	Y	Y	N
MONTANA					
AL Rehberg	Y	N	Y	Y	N
NEBRASKA					
1 Fortenberry	Y	N	Y	Y	N
2 Terry	N	N	Y	Y	N
3 Smith	Y	N	Y	Y	N
NEVADA					
1 Berkley	Y	Y	N	N	Y
2 Amodei	Y	N	Y	Y	N
3 Heck	N	N	Y	Y	N
NEW HAMPSHIRE					
1 Guinta	N	N	Y	Y	N
2 Bass	Y	N	Y	Y	N
NEW JERSEY					
1 Andrews	N	Y	N	N	Y
2 LoBiondo	N	N	Y	Y	N
3 Runyan	Y	N	Y	Y	N
4 Smith	Y	N	Y	Y	N
5 Garrett	Y	N	Y	Y	N
6 Pallone	N	Y	N	N	Y
7 Lance	Y	N	Y	Y	N
8 Pascrell	Y	Y	N	N	Y
9 Rothman	Y	Y	N	N	Y
10 Vacant					
11 Frelinghuysen	Y	N	Y	Y	N
12 Holt	N	Y	N	N	Y
13 Sires	N	Y	N	N	Y
NEW MEXICO					
1 Heinrich	Y	Y	N	N	Y
2 Pearce	Y	Y	Y	Y	N
3 Luján	Y	Y	N	N	Y
NEW YORK					
1 Bishop	?	Y	N	N	Y
2 Israel	N	Y	N	N	Y
3 King	Y	N	Y	Y	N
4 McCarthy	Y	Y	N	N	Y
5 Ackerman	Y	Y	N	N	?
6 Meeks	Y	Y	N	N	Y
7 Crowley	Y	Y	N	N	Y
8 Nadler	Y	Y	N	N	Y
9 Turner	Y	N	Y	Y	N
10 Towns	N	Y	N	N	Y
11 Clarke	Y	Y	N	N	Y
12 Velázquez	N	Y	N	N	Y
13 Grimm	Y	N	Y	Y	N
14 Maloney	Y	Y	N	N	Y
15 Rangel	Y	Y	N	N	Y
16 Serrano	N	Y	N	N	Y
17 Engel	Y	Y	N	N	Y
18 Lowey	N	Y	N	N	?
19 Hayworth	Y	N	Y	Y	N
20 Gibson	N	N	Y	Y	N
21 Tonko	Y	Y	N	N	Y
22 Hinchey	N	Y	N	N	Y
23 Owens	P	N	Y	Y	N
24 Hanna	N	N	Y	Y	N
25 Buerkle	Y	N	Y	Y	N
26 Hochul	Y	Y	N	N	Y
27 Higgins	Y	Y	N	N	Y
28 Slaughter	N	Y	N	N	Y
29 Reed	N	N	Y	?	N
NORTH CAROLINA					
1 Butterfield	Y	Y	N	N	Y
2 Ellmers	Y	N	Y	Y	N
3 Jones	Y	N	Y	Y	N
4 Price	Y	Y	N	N	Y

	458	459	460	461	462
5 Foxx	Y	N	Y	Y	N
6 Coble	Y	N	Y	Y	?
7 McIntyre	Y	Y	N	Y	N
8 Kissell	Y	N	Y	Y	N
9 Myrick	Y	N	Y	Y	N
10 McHenry	Y	N	Y	Y	N
11 Shuler	Y	N	N	Y	Y
12 Watt	Y	Y	N	N	Y
13 Miller	Y	Y	N	N	Y
NORTH DAKOTA					
AL Berg	Y	N	Y	Y	N
OHIO					
1 Chabot	Y	N	Y	Y	N
2 Schmidt	Y	N	Y	Y	N
3 Turner	Y	N	Y	Y	N
4 Jordan	Y	N	Y	Y	N
5 Latta	Y	N	Y	Y	N
6 Johnson	N	N	Y	Y	N
7 Austria	Y	N	Y	Y	N
8 Boehner					
9 Kaptur	Y	Y	N	N	Y
10 Kucinich	N	Y	N	N	Y
11 Fudge	Y	Y	N	N	Y
12 Tiberi	Y	N	Y	Y	N
13 Sutton	Y	N	Y	N	Y
14 LaTourette	Y	N	Y	Y	N
15 Stivers	N	N	Y	Y	N
16 Renacci	N	N	Y	Y	N
17 Ryan	N	Y	N	N	Y
18 Gibbs	Y	N	Y	Y	N
OKLAHOMA					
1 Sullivan	Y	N	Y	Y	N
2 Boren	Y	N	Y	Y	N
3 Lucas	Y	N	Y	Y	N
4 Cole	Y	N	Y	Y	N
5 Lankford	Y	N	Y	Y	N
OREGON					
1 Bonamici	Y	Y	N	N	Y
2 Walden	N	N	Y	Y	N
3 Blumenauer	Y	Y	N	N	Y
4 DeFazio	N	Y	N	N	Y
5 Schrader	Y	Y	N	N	Y
PENNSYLVANIA					
1 Brady	N	Y	N	N	Y
2 Fattah	Y	Y	N	N	Y
3 Kelly	Y	N	Y	Y	N
4 Altmire	Y	N	Y	Y	N
5 Thompson	Y	N	Y	Y	N
6 Gerlach	N	N	Y	Y	N
7 Meehan	N	N	Y	Y	N
8 Fitzpatrick	N	N	Y	Y	N
9 Shuster	Y	N	Y	Y	N
10 Marino	Y	N	Y	Y	N
11 Barletta	Y	N	Y	Y	N
12 Critz	N	Y	N	N	N
13 Schwartz	Y	Y	N	N	Y
14 Doyle	N	Y	N	N	Y
15 Dent	N	N	Y	Y	N
16 Pitts	Y	N	Y	Y	N
17 Holden	Y	Y	N	N	N
18 Murphy	N	N	Y	Y	?
19 Platts	Y	N	Y	Y	N
RHODE ISLAND					
1 Cicilline	Y	Y	N	N	Y
2 Langevin	Y	Y	N	N	Y
SOUTH CAROLINA					
1 Scott	Y	N	Y	Y	N
2 Wilson	Y	N	Y	Y	N
3 Duncan	Y	N	Y	Y	N
4 Gowdy	Y	N	Y	Y	N
5 Mulvaney	Y	N	Y	Y	N
6 Clyburn	Y	Y	N	N	Y
SOUTH DAKOTA					
AL Noem	Y	N	Y	Y	N
TENNESSEE					
1 Roe	N	N	Y	Y	N
2 Duncan	Y	N	Y	Y	N
3 Fleischmann	Y	N	Y	Y	N
4 DesJarlais	Y	N	Y	Y	N
5 Cooper	Y	N	Y	N	Y
6 Black	Y	N	Y	Y	N
7 Blackburn	Y	N	Y	Y	N
8 Fincher	Y	N	Y	Y	N
9 Cohen	Y	N	N	N	Y

	458	459	460	461	462
TEXAS					
1 Gohmert	P	N	Y	Y	N
2 Poe	Y	N	Y	Y	N
3 Johnson, S.	Y	N	Y	Y	N
4 Hall	Y	N	Y	Y	N
5 Hensarling	Y	N	Y	Y	N
6 Barton	Y	N	Y	Y	N
7 Culberson	Y	N	Y	Y	N
8 Brady	Y	N	Y	Y	N
9 Green, A.	Y	Y	N	N	Y
10 McCaul	Y	N	Y	Y	N
11 Conaway	N	N	Y	Y	N
12 Granger	Y	N	Y	Y	N
13 Thornberry	Y	N	Y	Y	N
14 Paul	Y	N	Y	Y	N
15 Hinojosa	Y	Y	N	N	Y
16 Reyes	Y	Y	N	N	Y
17 Flores	Y	N	Y	Y	N
18 Jackson Lee	Y	Y	N	N	?
19 Neugebauer	Y	N	Y	Y	N
20 Gonzalez	Y	Y	N	N	Y
21 Smith	Y	N	Y	Y	N
22 Olson	Y	N	Y	Y	N
23 Canseco	Y	N	Y	Y	N
24 Marchant	Y	N	Y	Y	N
25 Doggett	Y	Y	N	N	Y
26 Burgess	N	N	Y	Y	N
27 Farenthold	Y	N	Y	Y	N
28 Cuellar	Y	N	Y	Y	N
29 Green, G.	N	Y	N	N	Y
30 Johnson, E.	Y	Y	N	N	Y
31 Carter	Y	N	Y	Y	N
32 Sessions	Y	N	Y	Y	N
UTAH					
1 Bishop	Y	N	Y	?	?
2 Matheson	N	N	Y	Y	N
3 Chaffetz	Y	N	Y	Y	N
VERMONT					
AL Welch	N	Y	N	N	?
VIRGINIA					
1 Wittman	N	N	Y	Y	N
2 Rigell	N	N	Y	Y	N
3 Scott	Y	Y	N	N	Y
4 Forbes	N	N	Y	Y	N
5 Hurt	Y	N	Y	Y	N
6 Goodlatte	Y	N	Y	Y	N
7 Cantor	Y	N	Y	Y	N
8 Moran	Y	Y	N	N	Y
9 Griffith	Y	N	Y	Y	N
10 Wolf	Y	N	Y	Y	N
11 Connolly	Y	Y	N	N	?
WASHINGTON					
1 Vacant					
2 Larsen	Y	Y	N	N	Y
3 Herrera Beutler	N	N	Y	Y	N
4 Hastings	Y	N	Y	Y	N
5 McMorris Rodgers	Y	N	Y	Y	N
6 Dicks	Y	Y	N	N	?
7 McDermott	N	Y	N	N	Y
8 Reichert	Y	N	Y	Y	N
9 Smith	Y	N	N	N	Y
WEST VIRGINIA					
1 McKinley	Y	N	Y	Y	N
2 Capito	Y	N	Y	Y	N
3 Rahall	N	Y	N	N	Y
WISCONSIN					
1 Ryan	Y	N	Y	Y	N
2 Baldwin	N	Y	N	N	Y
3 Kind	N	Y	N	N	Y
4 Moore	N	Y	N	N	Y
5 Sensenbrenner	Y	N	Y	Y	N
6 Petri	Y	N	Y	Y	N
7 Duffy	N	N	Y	Y	N
8 Ribble	N	N	Y	Y	N
WYOMING					
AL Lummis	Y	N	Y	?	?

IN THE HOUSE | By Vote Number

463. HR 4402. **Mineral Mining Projects/Application Review Extension.** Hastings, D-Fla., amendment that would permit the lead agency responsible for issuing a mineral exploration or mine permit to extend the bill's 30-month time limit for permit application reviews by up to 12 months. Rejected in Committee of the Whole 162-252: R 0-233; D 162-19. July 12, 2012.

464. HR 4402. **Mineral Mining Projects/Royalty Payments.** Markey, D-Mass., amendment that would require the lead agency responsible for issuing a mineral exploration or mine permit to require royalty payments of 12.5 percent of the value of minerals extracted from federal lands. The funds would be dedicated, subject to appropriation, to the reclamation of abandoned hard-rock mines. Rejected in Committee of the Whole 163-253: R 3-230; D 160-23. July 12, 2012.

465. HR 4402. **Mineral Mining Projects/Permit Approvals.** Young, R-Alaska, amendment that would exempt existing mineral prescriptions for strategic minerals in national forests from certain regulations in order to facilitate mining permit approval and extraction activities. The amendment also would exempt areas within national forests that would be used for infrastructure to access mining facilities or mineral deposits. Adopted in Committee of the Whole 238-178: R 225-8; D 13-170. July 12, 2012.

466. HR 4402. **Mineral Mining Projects/Expedited Permit and Review Exemptions.** Grijalva, D-Ariz., amendment that would prevent the bill's expedited permitting or environmental review processes from applying to mining permits that are determined to diminish hunting, fishing, grazing and other recreational activities on federal lands. Rejected in Committee of the Whole 167-248: R 2-232; D 165-16. July 12, 2012.

467. HR 4402. **Mineral Mining Projects/Recommit.** Slaughter, D-N.Y., motion to recommit the bill to the House Natural Resources Committee and report it back immediately with language that would prohibit the issuance of mining permits to individuals, corporations or their subsidiaries that have failed to pay state or federal taxes. It also would add language to require federal mineral exploration or mining permits issued under the bill to include language that would prohibit the export of strategic and critical minerals to China and Iran. Permits issued under the bill would have to require, to the extent practicable, that all mining equipment used be made in the United States. It also would prohibit permit holders from outsourcing U.S. jobs. Motion rejected 181-231: R 1-228; D 180-3. July 12, 2012.

468. HR 4402. **Mineral Mining Projects/Passage.** Passage of the bill that would reclassify certain mining operations as "infrastructure projects" in order to streamline the permitting process for mining on federal lands. It would require federal agencies to expedite the environmental review process for such mining projects, and limit the judicial review process for challenges to approved mining permits or associated environmental reviews. Passed 256-160: R 234-0; D 22-160. A "nay" was a vote in support of the president's position. July 12, 2012.

	463	464	465	466	467	468
ALABAMA						
1 Bonner	N	N	Y	N	N	Y
2 Roby	N	N	Y	N	N	Y
3 Rogers	N	N	Y	N	N	Y
4 Aderholt	N	N	Y	N	N	Y
5 Brooks	N	N	Y	N	N	Y
6 Bachus	N	N	Y	N	N	Y
7 Sewell	Y	Y	N	Y	Y	Y
ALASKA						
AL Young	N	N	Y	N	N	Y
ARIZONA						
1 Gosar	N	N	Y	N	N	Y
2 Franks	N	N	Y	N	N	Y
3 Quayle	N	N	Y	N	N	Y
4 Pastor	Y	Y	N	Y	Y	N
5 Schweikert	N	N	Y	N	N	Y
6 Flake	N	N	Y	N	N	Y
7 Grijalva	Y	Y	N	Y	Y	N
8 Barber	Y	Y	N	Y	Y	N
ARKANSAS						
1 Crawford	N	N	Y	N	N	Y
2 Griffin	N	N	Y	N	N	Y
3 Womack	N	N	Y	N	N	Y
4 Ross	N	N	Y	N	N	Y
CALIFORNIA						
1 Thompson	Y	Y	N	Y	Y	N
2 Herger	N	N	Y	N	N	Y
3 Lungren	N	N	Y	N	N	Y
4 McClintock	N	N	Y	N	N	Y
5 Matsui	Y	Y	N	Y	Y	N
6 Woolsey	Y	Y	N	Y	Y	N
7 Miller, George	Y	Y	N	Y	Y	N
8 Pelosi	Y	Y	N	Y	Y	N
9 Lee	Y	Y	N	Y	Y	N
10 Garamendi	Y	Y	N	Y	Y	N
11 McNerney	Y	Y	N	Y	Y	N
12 Speier	Y	Y	N	Y	Y	N
13 Stark	Y	Y	N	Y	Y	N
14 Eshoo	Y	Y	N	Y	Y	N
15 Honda	Y	Y	N	Y	Y	N
16 Lofgren	Y	Y	N	Y	Y	N
17 Farr	Y	Y	N	Y	Y	N
18 Cardoza	?	?	?	?	?	?
19 Denham	N	N	Y	N	N	Y
20 Costa	?	Y	Y	Y	Y	N
21 Nunes	N	N	Y	N	N	Y
22 McCarthy	N	N	Y	N	N	Y
23 Capps	Y	Y	N	Y	Y	N
24 Gallegly	?	?	?	?	?	?
25 McKeon	N	N	Y	N	N	Y
26 Dreier	N	N	Y	N	N	Y
27 Sherman	Y	Y	N	Y	Y	N
28 Berman	Y	Y	N	Y	Y	N
29 Schiff	Y	Y	N	Y	Y	N
30 Waxman	Y	Y	N	Y	Y	N
31 Becerra	Y	Y	N	Y	Y	N
32 Chu	Y	Y	N	Y	Y	N
33 Bass	Y	Y	N	Y	Y	N
34 Roybal-Allard	Y	Y	N	Y	Y	N
35 Waters	Y	Y	N	Y	Y	N
36 Hahn	Y	Y	N	Y	Y	N
37 Richardson	Y	Y	N	Y	Y	N
38 Napolitano	Y	Y	N	Y	Y	N
39 Sánchez, Linda	Y	Y	N	Y	Y	N
40 Royce	N	N	Y	N	N	Y
41 Lewis	N	N	Y	N	N	Y
42 Miller, Gary	N	N	Y	N	N	Y
43 Baca	Y	Y	N	Y	Y	N
44 Calvert	N	N	Y	N	N	Y
45 Bono Mack	N	N	Y	N	N	Y
46 Rohrabacher	N	N	Y	N	N	Y
47 Sanchez, Loretta	Y	Y	N	Y	Y	N
48 Campbell	N	N	Y	N	N	Y
49 Issa	N	N	Y	N	N	Y
50 Bilbray	N	N	Y	N	Y	N
51 Filner	Y	Y	N	Y	Y	N
52 Hunter	N	N	Y	N	N	Y
53 Davis	Y	Y	N	Y	Y	N
COLORADO						
1 DeGette	Y	Y	N	Y	Y	N
2 Polis	Y	Y	N	Y	Y	N
3 Tipton	N	N	Y	N	N	Y
4 Gardner	N	N	Y	N	N	Y
5 Lamborn	N	N	Y	N	N	Y
6 Coffman	N	N	Y	N	N	Y
7 Perlmutter	Y	N	N	Y	Y	N
CONNECTICUT						
1 Larson	Y	Y	N	Y	Y	N
2 Courtney	Y	Y	N	Y	Y	N
3 DeLauro	Y	Y	N	Y	Y	N
4 Himes	Y	Y	N	Y	Y	N
5 Murphy	Y	Y	N	Y	Y	N
DELAWARE						
AL Carney	Y	Y	Y	Y	Y	N
FLORIDA						
1 Miller	N	N	Y	N	N	Y
2 Southerland	N	N	Y	N	N	Y
3 Brown	Y	Y	N	Y	Y	N
4 Crenshaw	N	N	Y	N	N	Y
5 Nugent	N	N	Y	N	N	Y
6 Stearns	N	N	Y	N	N	Y
7 Mica	N	N	Y	N	N	Y
8 Webster	N	N	N	N	N	Y
9 Bilirakis	N	N	Y	N	N	Y
10 Young	N	N	Y	N	N	Y
11 Castor	Y	Y	N	Y	Y	N
12 Ross	N	N	Y	N	N	Y
13 Buchanan	N	N	Y	N	N	Y
14 Mack	N	N	Y	N	N	Y
15 Posey	N	N	Y	N	N	Y
16 Rooney	N	N	Y	N	N	Y
17 Wilson	Y	Y	N	Y	Y	N
18 Ros-Lehtinen	N	N	Y	N	N	Y
19 Deutch	Y	Y	N	Y	Y	N
20 Wasserman Schultz	Y	Y	N	Y	Y	N
21 Diaz-Balart	N	N	Y	N	N	Y
22 West	N	N	Y	N	N	Y
23 Hastings	Y	Y	N	Y	Y	N
24 Adams	N	N	Y	N	N	Y
25 Rivera	N	N	Y	N	N	Y
GEORGIA						
1 Kingston	N	N	Y	N	N	Y
2 Bishop	N	N	Y	N	Y	Y
3 Westmoreland	N	N	Y	N	N	Y
4 Johnson	Y	Y	N	Y	Y	N
5 Lewis	Y	Y	N	Y	Y	N
6 Price	N	N	Y	N	N	Y
7 Woodall	N	N	Y	N	?	Y
8 Scott, A.	N	N	Y	N	+	Y
9 Graves	N	N	Y	N	N	Y
10 Broun	N	N	Y	N	N	Y
11 Gingrey	N	N	Y	N	N	Y
12 Barrow	N	N	N	Y	Y	Y
13 Scott, D.	Y	Y	N	Y	Y	N
HAWAII						
1 Hanabusa	Y	Y	N	Y	Y	N
2 Hirono	Y	+	Y	Y	Y	N
IDAHO						
1 Labrador	N	N	Y	N	N	Y
2 Simpson	N	N	Y	N	N	Y
ILLINOIS						
1 Rush	?	?	?	?	?	?
2 Jackson	?	?	?	?	?	?
3 Lipinski	Y	Y	N	N	Y	N
4 Gutierrez	?	Y	N	Y	Y	N
5 Quigley	Y	Y	N	Y	Y	N
6 Roskam	N	N	Y	N	N	Y
7 Davis	Y	Y	?	Y	Y	N
8 Walsh	N	N	Y	N	N	Y
9 Schakowsky	Y	Y	N	Y	Y	N
10 Dold	N	N	Y	N	N	Y
11 Kinzinger	N	N	Y	N	N	Y
12 Costello	N	N	Y	N	Y	Y
13 Biggert	N	N	Y	N	N	Y
14 Hultgren	N	N	Y	N	N	Y
15 Johnson	N	N	Y	Y	N	Y

KEY	Republicans	Democrats	
Y Voted for (yea)		X Paired against	C Voted "present" to avoid possible conflict of interest
# Paired for		– Announced against	
+ Announced for		P Voted "present"	? Did not vote or otherwise make a position known
N Voted against (nay)			

	463	464	465	466	467	468
16 **Manzullo**	N	N	Y	N	N	Y
17 **Schilling**	N	N	Y	N	N	Y
18 **Schock**	N	N	Y	N	N	Y
19 **Shimkus**	N	N	Y	N	N	Y
INDIANA						
1 Visclosky	Y	Y	N	Y	Y	N
2 Donnelly	N	N	N	N	Y	Y
3 **Stutzman**	N	N	Y	N	N	Y
4 **Rokita**	N	N	Y	N	N	Y
5 **Burton**	N	N	Y	N	N	Y
6 **Pence**	N	N	Y	N	N	Y
7 Carson	Y	Y	N	N	Y	N
8 **Bucshon**	N	N	Y	N	N	Y
9 **Young**	N	N	Y	N	N	Y
IOWA						
1 Braley	Y	Y	N	Y	Y	N
2 Loebsack	Y	Y	N	Y	Y	N
3 Boswell	N	Y	Y	Y	Y	Y
4 **Latham**	N	N	Y	N	N	Y
5 **King**	N	N	Y	N	N	Y
KANSAS						
1 **Huelskamp**	N	N	Y	N	N	Y
2 **Jenkins**	?	?	?	?	?	?
3 **Yoder**	N	N	Y	N	N	Y
4 **Pompeo**	N	N	Y	N	N	Y
KENTUCKY						
1 **Whitfield**	N	N	Y	N	N	Y
2 **Guthrie**	N	N	Y	N	N	Y
3 Yarmuth	Y	Y	N	Y	Y	N
4 **Davis**	N	N	Y	N	N	Y
5 **Rogers**	N	N	Y	N	N	Y
6 Chandler	Y	N	N	Y	Y	Y
LOUISIANA						
1 **Scalise**	N	N	Y	N	N	Y
2 Richmond	Y	Y	N	Y	Y	N
3 **Landry**	N	N	Y	N	N	Y
4 **Fleming**	N	N	Y	N	N	Y
5 **Alexander**	N	N	Y	N	N	Y
6 **Cassidy**	N	N	Y	N	N	Y
7 **Boustany**	N	N	Y	N	N	Y
MAINE						
1 Pingree	Y	Y	N	Y	Y	N
2 Michaud	Y	Y	N	Y	Y	N
MARYLAND						
1 **Harris**	N	N	Y	N	N	Y
2 Ruppersberger	Y	Y	N	Y	Y	N
3 Sarbanes	Y	Y	N	Y	Y	N
4 Edwards	Y	Y	N	Y	Y	N
5 Hoyer	Y	Y	N	Y	Y	N
6 **Bartlett**	N	N	Y	N	N	Y
7 Cummings	Y	Y	N	Y	Y	N
8 Van Hollen	Y	Y	N	Y	Y	N
MASSACHUSETTS						
1 Olver	Y	Y	N	Y	Y	N
2 Neal	Y	Y	N	Y	Y	N
3 McGovern	Y	Y	N	Y	Y	N
4 Frank	Y	Y	N	Y	Y	N
5 Tsongas	Y	Y	N	Y	Y	N
6 Tierney	Y	Y	N	Y	Y	N
7 Markey	Y	Y	N	Y	Y	N
8 Capuano	Y	Y	N	Y	Y	N
9 Lynch	Y	Y	N	Y	Y	N
10 Keating	Y	Y	N	Y	Y	N
MICHIGAN						
1 **Benishek**	N	N	Y	N	N	Y
2 **Huizenga**	N	N	Y	N	N	Y
3 **Amash**	N	N	Y	N	N	Y
4 **Camp**	N	N	Y	N	N	Y
5 Kildee	Y	Y	N	Y	Y	N
6 **Upton**	N	N	Y	N	N	Y
7 **Walberg**	N	N	Y	N	N	Y
8 **Rogers**	N	N	Y	N	N	Y
9 Peters	Y	Y	N	Y	Y	N
10 **Miller**	N	N	Y	N	N	Y
11 Vacant						
12 Levin	Y	Y	N	Y	Y	N
13 Clarke	Y	Y	N	Y	Y	N
14 Conyers	Y	Y	N	Y	Y	N
15 Dingell	Y	Y	N	Y	Y	N
MINNESOTA						
1 Walz	Y	Y	N	Y	Y	N
2 **Kline**	N	N	Y	N	N	Y
3 **Paulsen**	N	N	Y	N	N	Y
4 McCollum	Y	Y	N	Y	Y	N

	463	464	465	466	467	468
5 Ellison	Y	Y	N	Y	Y	N
6 **Bachmann**	N	Y	Y	N	N	Y
7 Peterson	N	N	Y	N	Y	Y
8 **Cravaack**	N	N	Y	N	N	Y
MISSISSIPPI						
1 **Nunnelee**	N	N	Y	N	N	Y
2 Thompson	Y	Y	N	Y	Y	N
3 **Harper**	N	N	Y	N	N	Y
4 **Palazzo**	N	N	Y	N	N	Y
MISSOURI						
1 Clay	Y	Y	N	Y	Y	N
2 **Akin**	?	?	?	?	?	+
3 Carnahan	Y	Y	N	Y	Y	N
4 **Hartzler**	N	N	Y	N	N	Y
5 Cleaver	Y	Y	N	Y	Y	N
6 **Graves**	N	N	Y	N	N	Y
7 **Long**	N	N	Y	N	N	Y
8 **Emerson**	N	N	Y	N	N	Y
9 **Luetkemeyer**	N	N	Y	N	N	Y
MONTANA						
AL **Rehberg**	N	N	Y	Y	N	Y
NEBRASKA						
1 **Fortenberry**	N	N	Y	N	N	Y
2 **Terry**	N	N	Y	N	N	Y
3 **Smith**	N	N	Y	N	N	Y
NEVADA						
1 Berkley	Y	N	N	Y	Y	Y
2 **Amodei**	N	N	Y	N	N	Y
3 **Heck**	N	N	Y	N	N	Y
NEW HAMPSHIRE						
1 **Guinta**	N	N	Y	N	N	Y
2 **Bass**	N	N	Y	N	N	Y
NEW JERSEY						
1 Andrews	Y	Y	N	Y	Y	N
2 **LoBiondo**	N	N	Y	N	N	Y
3 **Runyan**	N	N	Y	N	N	Y
4 **Smith**	N	N	Y	N	N	Y
5 **Garrett**	N	N	Y	N	N	Y
6 Pallone	Y	Y	N	Y	Y	N
7 **Lance**	N	N	Y	N	N	Y
8 Pascrell	Y	Y	N	Y	Y	N
9 Rothman	Y	Y	N	Y	Y	N
10 Vacant						
11 **Frelinghuysen**	N	N	Y	N	N	Y
12 Holt	Y	Y	N	Y	Y	N
13 Sires	Y	Y	N	Y	Y	N
NEW MEXICO						
1 Heinrich	Y	Y	N	Y	Y	N
2 **Pearce**	N	N	Y	N	N	Y
3 Luján	Y	Y	N	Y	Y	N
NEW YORK						
1 Bishop	Y	Y	N	Y	Y	N
2 Israel	Y	Y	N	Y	Y	N
3 **King**	N	N	Y	N	N	Y
4 McCarthy	Y	Y	N	Y	Y	N
5 Ackerman	?	?	?	?	?	?
6 Meeks	Y	Y	N	Y	Y	N
7 Crowley	Y	Y	N	Y	Y	N
8 Nadler	Y	Y	N	Y	Y	N
9 **Turner**	N	N	Y	N	N	Y
10 Towns	Y	Y	N	Y	?	N
11 Clarke	Y	Y	N	Y	Y	N
12 Velázquez	?	Y	N	Y	Y	N
13 **Grimm**	N	N	Y	N	N	Y
14 Maloney	Y	Y	N	Y	Y	N
15 Rangel	Y	Y	N	Y	Y	N
16 Serrano	Y	Y	N	Y	Y	?
17 Engel	Y	Y	N	Y	Y	N
18 Lowey	?	?	?	?	?	?
19 **Hayworth**	N	N	Y	N	N	Y
20 **Gibson**	N	Y	N	N	N	Y
21 Tonko	Y	Y	N	Y	Y	N
22 Hinchey	Y	Y	N	Y	Y	N
23 Owens	N	N	N	N	Y	Y
24 **Hanna**	?	N	Y	N	N	Y
25 **Buerkle**	N	N	Y	N	N	Y
26 Hochul	N	N	N	N	Y	Y
27 Higgins	N	N	N	Y	Y	N
28 Slaughter	Y	Y	N	Y	Y	N
29 **Reed**	N	N	Y	N	N	Y
NORTH CAROLINA						
1 Butterfield	Y	Y	N	Y	Y	N
2 **Ellmers**	N	N	Y	N	N	Y
3 **Jones**	N	N	Y	N	Y	Y
4 Price	Y	Y	N	Y	Y	N

	463	464	465	466	467	468
5 **Foxx**	N	N	Y	N	N	Y
6 **Coble**	?	?	?	?	?	?
7 McIntyre	N	N	N	N	Y	Y
8 Kissell	Y	N	N	N	Y	Y
9 **Myrick**	N	N	Y	N	N	Y
10 **McHenry**	N	N	Y	N	N	Y
11 Shuler	N	N	N	Y	Y	Y
12 Watt	Y	Y	N	Y	Y	N
13 Miller	Y	Y	N	Y	Y	N
NORTH DAKOTA						
AL **Berg**	N	N	Y	N	N	Y
OHIO						
1 **Chabot**	N	N	N	N	N	Y
2 **Schmidt**	N	N	N	N	N	Y
3 **Turner**	N	N	Y	N	N	Y
4 **Jordan**	N	N	Y	N	N	Y
5 **Latta**	N	N	Y	N	N	Y
6 **Johnson**	N	N	Y	N	N	Y
7 **Austria**	N	N	Y	N	N	Y
8 **Boehner**						
9 Kaptur	Y	Y	N	Y	Y	N
10 Kucinich	Y	Y	N	Y	Y	N
11 Fudge	Y	Y	N	Y	Y	N
12 **Tiberi**	N	N	Y	N	N	Y
13 Sutton	Y	Y	N	Y	Y	N
14 **LaTourette**	N	N	Y	N	N	Y
15 **Stivers**	N	N	Y	N	N	Y
16 **Renacci**	N	N	Y	N	N	Y
17 Ryan	Y	Y	N	?	Y	N
18 **Gibbs**	N	N	Y	N	N	Y
OKLAHOMA						
1 **Sullivan**	N	N	Y	N	N	Y
2 Boren	N	N	Y	N	Y	Y
3 **Lucas**	N	N	Y	N	N	Y
4 **Cole**	N	N	Y	N	N	Y
5 **Lankford**	N	N	Y	N	N	Y
OREGON						
1 Bonamici	Y	Y	N	Y	Y	N
2 **Walden**	N	N	Y	N	N	Y
3 Blumenauer	Y	Y	N	Y	Y	N
4 DeFazio	Y	N	N	Y	Y	N
5 Schrader	N	Y	N	Y	Y	N
PENNSYLVANIA						
1 Brady	Y	Y	N	Y	Y	N
2 Fattah	Y	Y	N	Y	Y	N
3 **Kelly**	N	N	Y	N	N	Y
4 Altmire	N	N	Y	N	Y	Y
5 **Thompson**	N	N	Y	N	N	Y
6 **Gerlach**	N	N	N	N	N	Y
7 **Meehan**	N	N	Y	N	N	Y
8 **Fitzpatrick**	N	N	N	N	N	Y
9 **Shuster**	N	N	Y	N	N	Y
10 **Marino**	N	N	Y	N	N	Y
11 **Barletta**	N	N	Y	N	N	Y
12 Critz	N	N	Y	N	N	Y
13 Schwartz	Y	Y	N	Y	Y	N
14 Doyle	Y	Y	N	Y	Y	N
15 **Dent**	N	N	Y	N	N	Y
16 **Pitts**	N	N	Y	N	N	Y
17 Holden	N	N	Y	N	Y	Y
18 **Murphy**	N	N	Y	N	N	Y
19 **Platts**	N	N	Y	N	N	Y
RHODE ISLAND						
1 Cicilline	Y	Y	N	Y	Y	N
2 Langevin	Y	Y	N	Y	Y	N
SOUTH CAROLINA						
1 **Scott**	N	N	Y	N	N	Y
2 **Wilson**	N	N	Y	N	N	Y
3 **Duncan**	N	N	Y	N	N	Y
4 **Gowdy**	N	N	Y	N	N	Y
5 **Mulvaney**	N	N	Y	N	N	Y
6 Clyburn	Y	Y	N	Y	Y	N
SOUTH DAKOTA						
AL **Noem**	N	N	Y	N	N	Y
TENNESSEE						
1 **Roe**	N	N	Y	N	N	Y
2 **Duncan**	N	N	Y	N	N	Y
3 **Fleischmann**	N	N	Y	N	N	Y
4 **DesJarlais**	N	N	Y	N	N	Y
5 Cooper	Y	Y	N	Y	Y	N
6 **Black**	N	N	Y	N	N	Y
7 **Blackburn**	N	N	Y	N	N	Y
8 **Fincher**	N	N	Y	N	N	Y
9 Cohen	Y	Y	N	Y	Y	N

	463	464	465	466	467	468
TEXAS						
1 **Gohmert**	N	N	Y	N	N	Y
2 **Poe**	N	N	Y	N	N	Y
3 **Johnson, S.**	N	N	Y	N	N	Y
4 **Hall**	N	N	Y	N	N	Y
5 **Hensarling**	N	N	Y	N	N	Y
6 **Barton**	N	N	Y	N	N	Y
7 **Culberson**	N	N	Y	N	N	Y
8 **Brady**	N	N	Y	N	N	Y
9 Green, A.	Y	Y	N	Y	Y	N
10 **McCaul**	N	N	Y	N	N	Y
11 **Conaway**	N	N	Y	N	N	Y
12 **Granger**	N	N	Y	N	N	Y
13 **Thornberry**	N	N	Y	N	N	Y
14 **Paul**	N	N	Y	N	N	Y
15 Hinojosa	Y	N	N	?	Y	N
16 Reyes	Y	Y	N	Y	Y	?
17 **Flores**	N	N	Y	N	?	Y
18 Jackson Lee	?	?	?	?	?	?
19 **Neugebauer**	N	N	Y	N	N	Y
20 Gonzalez	Y	Y	N	Y	Y	N
21 **Smith**	N	N	Y	N	N	Y
22 **Olson**	N	N	Y	N	N	Y
23 **Canseco**	N	N	Y	N	N	Y
24 **Marchant**	N	N	Y	N	?	Y
25 Doggett	Y	Y	N	Y	Y	N
26 **Burgess**	N	N	Y	N	N	Y
27 **Farenthold**	N	N	Y	N	N	Y
28 Cuellar	N	N	Y	Y	Y	Y
29 Green, G.	Y	Y	Y	Y	Y	N
30 Johnson, E.	Y	Y	N	Y	Y	N
31 **Carter**	N	N	Y	N	?	Y
32 **Sessions**	N	N	Y	N	N	Y
UTAH						
1 **Bishop**	?	?	?	?	?	?
2 Matheson	N	N	Y	N	N	Y
3 **Chaffetz**	N	N	Y	N	N	Y
VERMONT						
AL Welch	Y	Y	N	Y	Y	N
VIRGINIA						
1 **Wittman**	N	N	Y	N	N	Y
2 **Rigell**	N	N	Y	N	N	Y
3 Scott	Y	Y	N	Y	Y	N
4 **Forbes**	N	N	Y	N	N	Y
5 **Hurt**	N	N	Y	N	N	Y
6 **Goodlatte**	N	N	Y	N	N	Y
7 **Cantor**	N	N	Y	N	N	Y
8 Moran	Y	Y	N	Y	Y	N
9 **Griffith**	N	N	Y	N	N	Y
10 **Wolf**	N	N	N	N	N	Y
11 Connolly	Y	Y	N	Y	Y	N
WASHINGTON						
1 Vacant						
2 Larsen	Y	Y	N	Y	Y	N
3 **Herrera Beutler**	N	N	N	N	N	Y
4 **Hastings**	N	N	Y	N	N	Y
5 **McMorris Rodgers**	N	N	Y	N	N	Y
6 Dicks	?	?	?	?	?	?
7 McDermott	Y	Y	N	Y	Y	N
8 **Reichert**	N	N	Y	N	N	Y
9 Smith	Y	Y	N	?	Y	N
WEST VIRGINIA						
1 **McKinley**	N	N	Y	N	N	Y
2 **Capito**	N	N	Y	N	N	Y
3 Rahall	Y	Y	N	Y	Y	N
WISCONSIN						
1 **Ryan**	N	N	Y	N	N	Y
2 Baldwin	Y	Y	N	Y	Y	N
3 Kind	Y	Y	N	Y	Y	N
4 Moore	Y	Y	N	Y	Y	N
5 **Sensenbrenner**	N	N	Y	N	N	Y
6 **Petri**	N	Y	Y	N	N	Y
7 **Duffy**	N	N	Y	N	N	Y
8 **Ribble**	N	?	?	N	N	Y
WYOMING						
AL **Lummis**	?	?	?	?	?	?

IN THE HOUSE | By Vote Number

469. HR 6018. Fiscal 2013 Foreign Relations Authorization/Passage. Ros-Lehtinen, R-Fla., motion to suspend the rules and pass the bill that would authorize fiscal 2013 funding for the State Department and certain international organizations. The measure would authorize $9 billion for the State Department's diplomatic and consular programs, $1.6 billion for dues to international organizations and $1.8 billion for contributions for international peacekeeping activities. Motion agreed to 333-61: R 166-60; D 167-1. A two-thirds majority of those present and voting (263 in this case) is required for passage under suspension of the rules. July 17, 2012.

470. S 2009. American Samoa Minimum Wage/Passage. Ros-Lehtinen, R-Fla., motion to suspend the rules and pass the bill that would delay a required 50-cent minimum wage increase for American Samoa until Sept. 30, 2015. It also would require the Energy Department to conduct radiochemical analyses of the groundwater surrounding the Cactus Crater containment structure on the Marshall Islands. Motion agreed to 378-11: R 212-11; D 166-0. A two-thirds majority of those present and voting (260 in this case) is required for passage under suspension of the rules. July 17, 2012.

471. HR 5872. Sequestration Study/Passage. Ryan, R-Wis., motion to suspend the rules and pass the bill that would require the White House to produce within 30 days of the bill's enactment a report explaining how the automatic spending cuts scheduled to go into effect in January 2013 would affect domestic and defense programs. Motion agreed to 414-2: R 237-0; D 177-2. A two-thirds majority of those present and voting (278 in this case) is required for passage under suspension of the rules. July 18, 2012.

472. HR 5856. Fiscal 2013 Defense Appropriations/Military Bands. McCollum, D-Minn., amendment that would reduce the military personnel account for military bands by $188 million and transfer the savings to a spending-reduction account. Rejected in Committee of the Whole 166-250: R 84-154; D 82-96. July 18, 2012.

473. HR 5856. Fiscal 2013 Defense Appropriations/NASCAR Sponsorship. Kingston, R-Ga., amendment that would reduce various operations and maintenance accounts by $72.3 million to restrict NASCAR sponsorship and transfer the savings to a spending-reduction account. Rejected in Committee of the Whole 202-216: R 81-156; D 121-60. July 18, 2012.

474. HR 5856. Fiscal 2013 Defense Appropriations/Destroyer Funding Reduction. Quigley, D-Ill., amendment that would reduce funding for one DDG-151 Destroyer by $998 million and transfer the savings to a spending-reduction account. Rejected in Committee of the Whole 60-359: R 24-214; D 36-145. July 18, 2012.

	469	470	471	472	473	474
ALABAMA						
1 Bonner	Y	Y	Y	Y	Y	N
2 Roby	Y	Y	Y	Y	Y	N
3 Rogers	Y	Y	Y	N	N	N
4 Aderholt	Y	Y	Y	N	N	N
5 Brooks	N	Y	Y	N	Y	N
6 Bachus	Y	Y	Y	N	N	N
7 Sewell	+	+	+	–	+	–
ALASKA						
AL Young	Y	Y	Y	N	N	N
ARIZONA						
1 Gosar	?	?	?	Y	Y	N
2 Franks	N	Y	Y	Y	N	N
3 Quayle	N	Y	Y	Y	Y	N
4 Pastor	Y	Y	Y	N	N	N
5 Schweikert	N	Y	Y	Y	Y	N
6 Flake	?	?	Y	Y	Y	Y
7 Grijalva	Y	Y	Y	N	N	Y
8 Barber	Y	Y	Y	N	N	N
ARKANSAS						
1 Crawford	Y	Y	Y	N	N	N
2 Griffin	Y	Y	Y	N	Y	N
3 Womack	Y	Y	Y	N	N	N
4 Ross	Y	Y	Y	N	N	N
CALIFORNIA						
1 Thompson	Y	Y	Y	N	N	N
2 Herger	Y	?	Y	N	N	N
3 Lungren	Y	Y	Y	N	Y	N
4 McClintock	N	Y	Y	Y	Y	Y
5 Matsui	Y	Y	Y	N	N	N
6 Woolsey	Y	Y	Y	N	Y	N
7 Miller, George	Y	Y	Y	N	Y	N
8 Pelosi	Y	Y	Y	Y	Y	N
9 Lee	Y	Y	Y	N	Y	Y
10 Garamendi	Y	Y	Y	N	N	Y
11 McNerney	Y	Y	Y	Y	Y	N
12 Speier	Y	Y	Y	Y	Y	Y
13 Stark	Y	Y	Y	N	Y	Y
14 Eshoo	Y	Y	Y	Y	Y	N
15 Honda	Y	Y	Y	Y	Y	N
16 Lofgren	Y	Y	Y	N	Y	N
17 Farr	Y	Y	Y	Y	Y	N
18 Cardoza	Y	?	Y	?	?	?
19 Denham	Y	Y	Y	N	N	N
20 Costa	Y	Y	Y	N	N	N
21 Nunes	Y	Y	Y	N	N	N
22 McCarthy	Y	Y	Y	N	N	N
23 Capps	Y	Y	Y	N	Y	N
24 Gallegly	Y	Y	Y	N	N	N
25 McKeon	Y	Y	Y	N	N	N
26 Dreier	Y	Y	Y	N	Y	N
27 Sherman	Y	Y	Y	Y	Y	N
28 Berman	Y	Y	Y	N	Y	N
29 Schiff	Y	Y	Y	N	Y	N
30 Waxman	Y	Y	Y	Y	Y	N
31 Becerra	Y	Y	Y	+	Y	Y
32 Chu	Y	Y	Y	N	Y	Y
33 Bass	Y	?	Y	Y	Y	Y
34 Roybal-Allard	Y	Y	Y	N	Y	N
35 Waters	Y	Y	Y	Y	Y	N
36 Hahn	?	?	?	?	?	?
37 Richardson	Y	Y	Y	N	N	N
38 Napolitano	+	Y	Y	Y	N	Y
39 Sánchez, Linda	Y	Y	Y	Y	Y	Y
40 Royce	Y	Y	Y	Y	Y	N
41 Lewis	Y	Y	Y	N	N	N
42 Miller, Gary	Y	Y	Y	Y	Y	N
43 Baca	Y	Y	Y	N	N	N
44 Calvert	Y	Y	Y	N	N	N
45 Bono Mack	Y	Y	Y	N	Y	N
46 Rohrabacher	Y	Y	Y	Y	Y	Y
47 Sanchez, Loretta	Y	Y	Y	N	Y	N
48 Campbell	?	?	Y	Y	N	Y
49 Issa	Y	Y	Y	N	N	N
50 Bilbray	Y	Y	Y	Y	Y	N
51 Filner	+	+	+	+	+	–
52 Hunter	Y	Y	Y	N	N	N
53 Davis	Y	Y	Y	N	Y	N

	469	470	471	472	473	474
COLORADO						
1 DeGette	Y	Y	Y	N	Y	Y
2 Polis	?	?	?	?	?	?
3 Tipton	N	Y	Y	Y	Y	Y
4 Gardner	N	Y	Y	Y	N	N
5 Lamborn	N	Y	Y	N	N	N
6 Coffman	Y	Y	Y	Y	N	N
7 Perlmutter	Y	Y	Y	Y	N	N
CONNECTICUT						
1 Larson	Y	Y	Y	N	Y	N
2 Courtney	Y	Y	Y	Y	Y	N
3 DeLauro	Y	Y	Y	Y	Y	N
4 Himes	Y	Y	Y	Y	Y	N
5 Murphy	?	?	Y	Y	N	N
DELAWARE						
AL Carney	Y	Y	Y	Y	Y	N
FLORIDA						
1 Miller	Y	Y	Y	N	N	N
2 Southerland	Y	Y	Y	Y	Y	N
3 Brown	Y	Y	Y	N	N	N
4 Crenshaw	Y	Y	Y	N	N	N
5 Nugent	Y	Y	Y	N	N	N
6 Stearns	N	Y	Y	Y	Y	N
7 Mica	Y	Y	Y	Y	Y	N
8 Webster	Y	Y	Y	Y	Y	N
9 Bilirakis	Y	Y	Y	N	N	N
10 Young	Y	Y	Y	N	N	N
11 Castor	Y	Y	Y	N	N	N
12 Ross	N	Y	Y	N	N	N
13 Buchanan	?	?	Y	Y	Y	N
14 Mack	?	?	Y	Y	N	N
15 Posey	N	Y	Y	N	N	N
16 Rooney	N	Y	Y	N	N	N
17 Wilson	Y	Y	Y	Y	Y	N
18 Ros-Lehtinen	Y	Y	Y	N	N	N
19 Deutch	Y	Y	Y	Y	Y	N
20 Wasserman Schultz	Y	Y	Y	N	N	N
21 Diaz-Balart	Y	Y	Y	N	N	N
22 West	Y	Y	Y	N	N	N
23 Hastings	Y	Y	Y	N	Y	N
24 Adams	N	Y	Y	N	N	N
25 Rivera	Y	Y	Y	N	N	N
GEORGIA						
1 Kingston	?	?	Y	Y	Y	N
2 Bishop	Y	Y	Y	N	N	N
3 Westmoreland	N	N	Y	N	N	N
4 Johnson	Y	Y	Y	N	N	N
5 Lewis	Y	Y	?	N	Y	N
6 Price	N	Y	Y	N	N	N
7 Woodall	Y	N	Y	N	N	N
8 Scott, A.	N	Y	Y	N	N	N
9 Graves	N	Y	Y	Y	N	N
10 Broun	N	N	Y	N	Y	N
11 Gingrey	N	Y	Y	N	N	N
12 Barrow	Y	Y	Y	Y	Y	N
13 Scott, D.	Y	Y	Y	N	N	N
HAWAII						
1 Hanabusa	Y	Y	Y	N	N	N
2 Hirono	?	?	?	?	?	?
IDAHO						
1 Labrador	?	?	Y	Y	Y	Y
2 Simpson	Y	Y	Y	N	N	N
ILLINOIS						
1 Rush	Y	Y	Y	N	N	N
2 Jackson	?	?	?	?	?	?
3 Lipinski	Y	Y	Y	N	N	N
4 Gutierrez	+	+	Y	Y	Y	N
5 Quigley	Y	Y	Y	N	Y	Y
6 Roskam	Y	Y	Y	N	N	N
7 Davis	Y	Y	Y	N	Y	Y
8 Walsh	N	Y	Y	Y	Y	N
9 Schakowsky	Y	Y	Y	N	Y	N
10 Dold	Y	Y	Y	N	Y	N
11 Kinzinger	Y	Y	Y	N	N	N
12 Costello	Y	Y	Y	N	Y	N
13 Biggert	Y	Y	Y	N	Y	N
14 Hultgren	Y	Y	Y	N	Y	N
15 Johnson	?	?	Y	Y	N	Y

KEY   Republicans   Democrats

Y Voted for (yea)	X Paired against	C Voted "present" to avoid possible conflict of interest
# Paired for	– Announced against	
+ Announced for	P Voted "present"	? Did not vote or otherwise make a position known
N Voted against (nay)		

	469	470	471	472	473	474
16 **Manzullo**	Y	Y	Y	N	N	N
17 **Schilling**	Y	Y	Y	Y	Y	N
18 **Schock**	Y	Y	Y	N	N	N
19 **Shimkus**	Y	Y	Y	N	N	N
INDIANA						
1 Visclosky	Y	Y	Y	N	N	N
2 Donnelly	Y	Y	Y	Y	N	N
3 **Stutzman**	N	N	Y	N	N	N
4 **Rokita**	Y	Y	Y	N	Y	N
5 **Burton**	Y	Y	Y	N	N	N
6 **Pence**	Y	Y	Y	N	N	N
7 Carson	Y	Y	Y	N	N	Y
8 **Bucshon**	Y	Y	Y	N	N	N
9 **Young**	Y	Y	Y	Y	N	N
IOWA						
1 Braley	Y	Y	Y	Y	Y	N
2 Loebsack	Y	Y	Y	Y	N	N
3 Boswell	Y	Y	Y	N	N	N
4 **Latham**	Y	Y	Y	Y	N	N
5 **King**	Y	Y	Y	N	Y	N
KANSAS						
1 **Huelskamp**	Y	N	Y	Y	Y	Y
2 **Jenkins**	Y	Y	Y	Y	N	N
3 **Yoder**	Y	Y	Y	N	N	N
4 **Pompeo**	Y	Y	Y	Y	N	N
KENTUCKY						
1 **Whitfield**	Y	Y	Y	N	N	N
2 **Guthrie**	Y	Y	Y	N	N	N
3 Yarmuth	Y	Y	Y	N	N	N
4 **Davis**	Y	Y	Y	N	N	N
5 **Rogers**	Y	Y	Y	N	N	N
6 Chandler	Y	Y	Y	Y	N	N
LOUISIANA						
1 **Scalise**	Y	Y	Y	N	N	N
2 Richmond	?	?	Y	N	Y	Y
3 **Landry**	?	?	Y	N	N	N
4 **Fleming**	N	Y	Y	N	N	N
5 **Alexander**	Y	Y	Y	N	Y	N
6 **Cassidy**	Y	Y	Y	Y	Y	N
7 **Boustany**	Y	Y	Y	N	Y	N
MAINE						
1 Pingree	Y	Y	Y	Y	Y	N
2 Michaud	Y	Y	Y	Y	Y	N
MARYLAND						
1 **Harris**	N	Y	Y	N	N	N
2 Ruppersberger	Y	Y	?	Y	N	N
3 Sarbanes	Y	Y	Y	Y	Y	N
4 Edwards	Y	Y	Y	N	Y	N
5 Hoyer	Y	Y	Y	N	Y	N
6 **Bartlett**	Y	Y	Y	N	N	N
7 Cummings	Y	Y	Y	N	Y	N
8 Van Hollen	Y	Y	Y	Y	Y	Y
MASSACHUSETTS						
1 Olver	Y	Y	Y	Y	Y	N
2 Neal	Y	Y	Y	Y	Y	N
3 McGovern	Y	Y	Y	N	Y	N
4 Frank	Y	Y	Y	Y	Y	Y
5 Tsongas	Y	Y	Y	Y	Y	N
6 Tierney	Y	Y	Y	Y	Y	N
7 Markey	Y	Y	Y	Y	Y	Y
8 Capuano	Y	Y	Y	N	Y	N
9 Lynch	Y	Y	Y	Y	Y	N
10 Keating	Y	Y	Y	Y	Y	N
MICHIGAN						
1 **Benishek**	Y	Y	Y	Y	Y	Y
2 **Huizenga**	N	N	Y	Y	Y	Y
3 **Amash**	N	Y	Y	Y	Y	Y
4 **Camp**	Y	Y	Y	N	Y	N
5 Kildee	Y	Y	Y	N	Y	N
6 **Upton**	Y	Y	Y	N	Y	Y
7 **Walberg**	N	Y	Y	N	N	N
8 **Rogers**	Y	Y	Y	N	N	N
9 Peters	Y	Y	Y	Y	Y	Y
10 **Miller**	Y	Y	Y	N	N	N
11 Vacant						
12 Levin	Y	Y	Y	Y	Y	N
13 Clarke	Y	Y	Y	N	Y	N
14 Conyers	Y	Y	Y	?	Y	Y
15 Dingell	Y	Y	Y	Y	Y	N
MINNESOTA						
1 Walz	Y	Y	Y	N	N	N
2 **Kline**	Y	Y	Y	N	N	N
3 **Paulsen**	Y	Y	Y	Y	N	N
4 McCollum	Y	Y	Y	Y	Y	Y
5 Ellison	Y	Y	Y	Y	Y	N
6 **Bachmann**	N	Y	Y	N	?	N
7 Peterson	Y	Y	Y	N	N	Y
8 **Cravaack**	N	Y	Y	N	N	N
MISSISSIPPI						
1 **Nunnelee**	Y	Y	Y	N	N	N
2 Thompson	Y	Y	Y	N	Y	N
3 **Harper**	Y	Y	Y	N	N	N
4 **Palazzo**	N	Y	Y	N	N	N
MISSOURI						
1 Clay	Y	Y	Y	Y	Y	N
2 **Akin**	−	+	+	−	+	−
3 Carnahan	Y	Y	Y	Y	Y	N
4 **Hartzler**	Y	Y	Y	Y	N	N
5 Cleaver	Y	?	Y	N	Y	N
6 **Graves**	Y	Y	Y	N	N	N
7 **Long**	Y	Y	Y	N	N	N
8 **Emerson**	N	Y	Y	N	Y	N
9 **Luetkemeyer**	Y	Y	Y	Y	N	N
MONTANA						
AL **Rehberg**	Y	Y	Y	N	Y	N
NEBRASKA						
1 **Fortenberry**	Y	Y	Y	N	N	N
2 **Terry**	Y	Y	Y	N	Y	N
3 **Smith**	Y	Y	Y	N	N	N
NEVADA						
1 Berkley	Y	Y	Y	N	N	N
2 **Amodei**	Y	Y	Y	N	N	N
3 **Heck**	Y	Y	Y	N	N	N
NEW HAMPSHIRE						
1 **Guinta**	Y	Y	Y	N	N	N
2 **Bass**	Y	Y	Y	Y	N	N
NEW JERSEY						
1 Andrews	Y	Y	Y	N	Y	N
2 **LoBiondo**	Y	Y	Y	Y	Y	N
3 **Runyan**	Y	Y	Y	N	N	N
4 **Smith**	Y	Y	Y	N	Y	N
5 **Garrett**	N	Y	Y	Y	Y	N
6 Pallone	Y	Y	Y	N	N	N
7 **Lance**	Y	Y	Y	Y	Y	N
8 Pascrell	Y	Y	Y	N	Y	N
9 Rothman	Y	Y	Y	N	Y	N
10 Vacant						
11 **Frelinghuysen**	Y	Y	Y	N	N	N
12 Holt	Y	Y	Y	N	Y	N
13 Sires	Y	Y	Y	N	N	N
NEW MEXICO						
1 Heinrich	Y	Y	Y	Y	Y	N
2 **Pearce**	Y	Y	Y	N	N	N
3 Luján	Y	Y	Y	Y	Y	N
NEW YORK						
1 Bishop	Y	Y	Y	N	Y	N
2 Israel	?	?	Y	Y	Y	N
3 **King**	Y	Y	Y	N	N	N
4 McCarthy	Y	Y	Y	N	Y	N
5 Ackerman	?	?	Y	Y	Y	N
6 Meeks	Y	Y	Y	Y	Y	N
7 Crowley	Y	Y	Y	N	Y	N
8 Nadler	Y	Y	Y	Y	Y	N
9 **Turner**	Y	Y	Y	N	N	N
10 Towns	Y	Y	Y	Y	Y	N
11 Clarke	Y	Y	Y	N	Y	N
12 Velázquez	Y	Y	Y	Y	Y	Y
13 **Grimm**	Y	Y	Y	N	N	N
14 Maloney	Y	Y	Y	Y	Y	N
15 Rangel	Y	Y	Y	N	N	N
16 Serrano	Y	Y	Y	Y	N	Y
17 Engel	Y	Y	N	N	N	N
18 Lowey	Y	Y	Y	Y	Y	Y
19 **Hayworth**	Y	Y	Y	N	N	N
20 **Gibson**	N	Y	Y	Y	Y	N
21 Tonko	N	Y	Y	Y	Y	N
22 Hinchey	Y	Y	N	Y	Y	N
23 Owens	Y	Y	Y	N	Y	N
24 **Hanna**	Y	Y	Y	Y	N	N
25 **Buerkle**	Y	Y	Y	N	N	N
26 Hochul	Y	Y	Y	N	Y	N
27 Higgins	Y	Y	Y	Y	Y	Y
28 Slaughter	Y	Y	Y	N	Y	N
29 **Reed**	Y	Y	Y	Y	N	N
NORTH CAROLINA						
1 Butterfield	?	?	Y	N	N	N
2 **Ellmers**	Y	Y	Y	N	N	N
3 **Jones**	N	Y	Y	N	Y	Y
4 Price	Y	Y	Y	Y	Y	Y
5 **Foxx**	N	Y	Y	N	N	N
6 **Coble**	Y	Y	Y	N	N	N
7 McIntyre	Y	Y	Y	N	N	N
8 Kissell	Y	Y	Y	Y	N	N
9 **Myrick**	Y	Y	Y	N	N	N
10 **McHenry**	Y	Y	Y	N	N	N
11 Shuler	Y	Y	Y	N	N	N
12 Watt	Y	Y	Y	N	N	N
13 Miller	Y	Y	Y	N	N	Y
NORTH DAKOTA						
AL **Berg**	Y	Y	Y	N	N	N
OHIO						
1 **Chabot**	Y	Y	Y	Y	Y	N
2 **Schmidt**	N	N	Y	Y	Y	N
3 **Turner**	Y	Y	Y	N	N	N
4 **Jordan**	N	Y	Y	Y	Y	N
5 **Latta**	Y	Y	Y	N	N	N
6 **Johnson**	Y	Y	Y	N	N	N
7 **Austria**	Y	Y	Y	N	N	N
8 **Boehner**						
9 Kaptur	Y	Y	Y	N	Y	N
10 Kucinich	Y	Y	Y	Y	Y	Y
11 Fudge	Y	Y	Y	N	Y	N
12 **Tiberi**	Y	Y	Y	N	Y	N
13 Sutton	Y	Y	Y	Y	Y	N
14 **LaTourette**	Y	Y	Y	N	N	N
15 **Stivers**	?	?	?	?	?	?
16 **Renacci**	Y	Y	Y	Y	N	N
17 Ryan	Y	Y	Y	N	N	N
18 **Gibbs**	N	Y	Y	Y	N	N
OKLAHOMA						
1 **Sullivan**	Y	Y	Y	N	N	N
2 Boren	?	?	?	?	?	?
3 **Lucas**	Y	Y	Y	N	N	N
4 **Cole**	Y	Y	Y	N	N	N
5 **Lankford**	Y	Y	Y	N	N	N
OREGON						
1 Bonamici	Y	Y	Y	N	Y	Y
2 **Walden**	Y	Y	Y	Y	Y	Y
3 Blumenauer	Y	Y	Y	N	Y	Y
4 DeFazio	?	?	Y	Y	Y	Y
5 Schrader	?	?	Y	Y	Y	Y
PENNSYLVANIA						
1 Brady	Y	Y	Y	Y	N	N
2 Fattah	Y	Y	Y	N	Y	N
3 **Kelly**	Y	Y	Y	N	N	N
4 Altmire	Y	Y	Y	Y	N	N
5 **Thompson**	Y	Y	Y	N	N	N
6 **Gerlach**	Y	Y	Y	N	N	N
7 **Meehan**	Y	Y	Y	Y	N	N
8 **Fitzpatrick**	Y	Y	Y	Y	N	N
9 **Shuster**	Y	Y	Y	N	N	N
10 **Marino**	Y	Y	Y	N	N	N
11 **Barletta**	Y	Y	Y	N	N	N
12 Critz	Y	Y	Y	N	N	N
13 Schwartz	Y	Y	Y	Y	Y	N
14 Doyle	Y	Y	Y	N	Y	N
15 **Dent**	Y	Y	Y	Y	Y	N
16 **Pitts**	Y	Y	Y	N	Y	N
17 Holden	Y	Y	Y	N	N	N
18 **Murphy**	N	Y	Y	N	N	N
19 **Platts**	?	?	Y	N	N	N
RHODE ISLAND						
1 Cicilline	Y	Y	Y	Y	Y	N
2 Langevin	Y	Y	Y	Y	Y	N
SOUTH CAROLINA						
1 **Scott**	N	Y	Y	N	N	N
2 **Wilson**	Y	Y	Y	N	Y	N
3 **Duncan**	Y	Y	Y	Y	N	N
4 **Gowdy**	N	Y	Y	N	N	N
5 **Mulvaney**	Y	N	Y	Y	Y	N
6 Clyburn	Y	Y	Y	N	Y	N
SOUTH DAKOTA						
AL **Noem**	Y	Y	Y	Y	Y	N
TENNESSEE						
1 **Roe**	N	Y	Y	N	N	N
2 **Duncan**	N	Y	Y	Y	Y	Y
3 **Fleischmann**	N	Y	Y	N	N	N
4 **DesJarlais**	N	Y	Y	N	N	N
5 Cooper	Y	Y	Y	Y	N	Y
6 **Black**	N	Y	Y	Y	N	N
7 **Blackburn**	N	Y	Y	N	N	N
8 **Fincher**	N	Y	Y	N	N	N
9 Cohen	Y	Y	Y	N	Y	N
TEXAS						
1 **Gohmert**	N	N	Y	Y	N	N
2 **Poe**	?	?	Y	N	N	N
3 **Johnson, S.**	Y	Y	Y	N	N	N
4 **Hall**	Y	Y	Y	N	N	N
5 **Hensarling**	Y	Y	Y	N	N	N
6 **Barton**	Y	Y	Y	N	N	N
7 **Culberson**	Y	Y	Y	N	Y	N
8 **Brady**	Y	Y	Y	Y	Y	N
9 Green, A.	+	+	Y	N	N	N
10 **McCaul**	Y	Y	Y	N	N	N
11 **Conaway**	N	Y	Y	N	N	N
12 **Granger**	Y	Y	Y	N	N	N
13 **Thornberry**	Y	Y	Y	N	N	N
14 **Paul**	?	?	Y	Y	Y	Y
15 Hinojosa	Y	Y	Y	N	N	Y
16 Reyes	?	?	?	?	?	?
17 **Flores**	N	Y	Y	N	N	N
18 Jackson Lee	+	+	?	?	?	?
19 **Neugebauer**	N	Y	Y	Y	Y	N
20 Gonzalez	?	?	?	N	N	N
21 **Smith**	Y	?	Y	N	N	N
22 **Olson**	Y	Y	Y	N	N	N
23 **Canseco**	Y	Y	Y	N	N	N
24 **Marchant**	N	Y	Y	N	Y	N
25 Doggett	?	?	Y	N	Y	N
26 **Burgess**	N	Y	Y	N	Y	N
27 **Farenthold**	Y	Y	Y	Y	N	N
28 Cuellar	Y	Y	Y	N	N	N
29 Green, G.	Y	Y	Y	N	N	Y
30 Johnson, E.	Y	Y	Y	N	N	N
31 **Carter**	Y	Y	Y	N	N	N
32 **Sessions**	Y	Y	Y	N	N	N
UTAH						
1 **Bishop**	N	Y	Y	N	Y	N
2 Matheson	Y	Y	Y	Y	Y	N
3 **Chaffetz**	Y	Y	Y	Y	N	N
VERMONT						
AL Welch	Y	Y	Y	?	N	N
VIRGINIA						
1 **Wittman**	Y	Y	Y	N	N	N
2 **Rigell**	N	Y	Y	N	N	N
3 Scott	?	?	Y	N	Y	N
4 **Forbes**	Y	Y	Y	N	N	N
5 **Hurt**	N	Y	Y	Y	Y	N
6 **Goodlatte**	N	Y	Y	Y	Y	N
7 **Cantor**	Y	Y	Y	Y	N	N
8 Moran	Y	Y	Y	Y	Y	N
9 **Griffith**	N	Y	Y	Y	Y	Y
10 **Wolf**	Y	Y	Y	N	Y	N
11 Connolly	Y	Y	Y	Y	Y	N
WASHINGTON						
1 Vacant						
2 Larsen	Y	Y	Y	Y	Y	N
3 **Herrera Beutler**	Y	Y	Y	Y	Y	Y
4 **Hastings**	Y	Y	Y	N	N	N
5 **McMorris Rodgers**	Y	?	Y	N	N	N
6 Dicks	?	?	Y	N	Y	N
7 McDermott	Y	Y	Y	Y	Y	N
8 **Reichert**	Y	Y	Y	N	Y	N
9 Smith	Y	Y	Y	N	N	N
WEST VIRGINIA						
1 **McKinley**	Y	Y	Y	Y	Y	N
2 **Capito**	Y	Y	Y	N	N	N
3 Rahall	Y	Y	Y	N	N	N
WISCONSIN						
1 **Ryan**	Y	Y	Y	Y	Y	N
2 Baldwin	Y	Y	Y	Y	Y	N
3 Kind	Y	Y	Y	Y	Y	N
4 Moore	Y	Y	Y	N	N	N
5 **Sensenbrenner**	Y	Y	Y	Y	Y	Y
6 **Petri**	Y	Y	Y	Y	Y	Y
7 **Duffy**	Y	Y	Y	Y	Y	Y
8 **Ribble**	N	N	Y	Y	Y	Y
WYOMING						
AL **Lummis**	Y	N	Y	Y	Y	Y

IN THE HOUSE | By Vote Number

475. **HR 5856. Fiscal 2013 Defense Appropriations/Navy Procurement Reduction.** Cohen, D-Tenn., amendment that would reduce Navy procurement by $506 million and increase Defense Health Programs by $235 million. The remainder of the savings would go toward deficit reduction. Rejected in the Committee of the Whole 145-273: R 16-221; D: 129-52. July 18, 2012.

476. **HR 5856. Fiscal 2013 Defense Appropriations/Rapid Innovation Fund.** Pompeo, R-Kan., amendment that would remove $250 million for the Rapid Innovation Fund and transfer the savings to a spending-reduction account. Rejected in Committee of the Whole 137-282: R 120-118; D 17-164. July 18, 2012.

477. **HR 5856. Fiscal 2013 Defense Appropriations/Ground-Based Missile Defense.** Markey, D-Mass., amendment that would reduce ground-based missile defense by $75 million and transfer the savings to a spending-reduction account. Rejected in Committee of the Whole 150-268: R 12-226; D 138-42. July 18, 2012.

478. **HR 5856. Fiscal 2013 Defense Appropriations/Commercial Contracting.** Amash, R-Mich., amendment that would strike the section in the bill that prohibits the Defense Department from contracting out any commercial function unless it would save the Defense Department at least $10 million or 10 percent of its performance costs. Rejected in Committee of the Whole 186-233: R 185-53; D 1-180. July 18, 2012.

479. **HR 5856. Fiscal 2013 Defense Appropriations/Afghanistan Infrastructure Fund.** Cohen, D-Tenn., amendment that would reduce the Afghanistan Infrastructure Fund by $175 million and transfer the savings to a spending-reduction account. Adopted in Committee of the Whole 228-191: R 68-170; D 160-21. July 18, 2012.

480. **HR 5856. Fiscal 2013 Defense Appropriations/Afghanistan Infrastructure Fund.** Cicilline, D-R.I., amendment that would eliminate $375 million for the Afghanistan Infrastructure Fund and transfer the savings to a spending-reduction account. Rejected in Committee of the Whole 149-270: R 48-190; D 101-80. July 18, 2012.

	475	476	477	478	479	480
ALABAMA						
1 Bonner	N	Y	N	Y	N	N
2 Roby	N	Y	N	Y	N	N
3 Rogers	N	Y	N	Y	N	N
4 Aderholt	N	N	N	Y	N	N
5 Brooks	N	Y	N	Y	Y	Y
6 Bachus	N	Y	N	Y	N	N
7 Sewell	–	–	–	–	–	–
ALASKA						
AL Young	N	N	N	N	N	N
ARIZONA						
1 Gosar	N	Y	N	Y	N	N
2 Franks	N	N	N	Y	N	N
3 Quayle	N	Y	N	Y	N	N
4 Pastor	N	N	N	N	Y	N
5 Schweikert	N	Y	N	Y	N	N
6 Flake	N	Y	N	Y	N	N
7 Grijalva	Y	N	Y	N	Y	Y
8 Barber	N	N	N	N	N	N
ARKANSAS						
1 Crawford	N	N	N	Y	N	N
2 Griffin	N	N	N	Y	N	N
3 Womack	N	N	N	Y	N	N
4 Ross	N	N	N	N	Y	N
CALIFORNIA						
1 Thompson	Y	N	Y	N	Y	Y
2 Herger	N	N	N	Y	N	N
3 Lungren	N	N	N	Y	N	N
4 McClintock	N	Y	N	Y	Y	Y
5 Matsui	Y	N	Y	N	Y	Y
6 Woolsey	Y	N	Y	N	Y	Y
7 Miller, George	Y	N	Y	N	Y	Y
8 Pelosi	Y	N	Y	N	Y	N
9 Lee	Y	N	Y	N	Y	Y
10 Garamendi	Y	N	Y	N	Y	Y
11 McNerney	Y	N	N	N	Y	N
12 Speier	Y	Y	Y	N	Y	Y
13 Stark	Y	N	Y	N	Y	Y
14 Eshoo	Y	N	Y	N	Y	Y
15 Honda	Y	N	Y	N	Y	Y
16 Lofgren	Y	N	Y	N	Y	Y
17 Farr	Y	N	Y	N	Y	N
18 Cardoza	?	?	?	?	?	?
19 Denham	N	Y	N	Y	N	N
20 Costa	N	N	N	N	Y	N
21 Nunes	N	N	N	N	N	N
22 McCarthy	N	N	N	Y	N	N
23 Capps	Y	N	Y	N	Y	Y
24 Gallegly	N	N	N	Y	N	N
25 McKeon	N	N	N	Y	N	N
26 Dreier	N	N	N	Y	N	N
27 Sherman	Y	N	Y	N	Y	Y
28 Berman	Y	N	Y	N	Y	Y
29 Schiff	N	N	Y	N	N	N
30 Waxman	Y	N	Y	N	Y	N
31 Becerra	Y	N	Y	N	Y	Y
32 Chu	Y	N	Y	N	Y	Y
33 Bass	Y	N	Y	N	Y	Y
34 Roybal-Allard	Y	N	Y	N	Y	Y
35 Waters	Y	N	Y	N	Y	Y
36 Hahn	?	?	?	?	?	?
37 Richardson	N	N	N	N	Y	Y
38 Napolitano	Y	N	Y	N	Y	Y
39 Sánchez, Linda	Y	N	Y	N	Y	Y
40 Royce	N	Y	N	Y	Y	Y
41 Lewis	N	N	N	N	N	N
42 Miller, Gary	N	Y	N	Y	N	N
43 Baca	N	N	N	N	Y	N
44 Calvert	N	N	N	Y	N	N
45 Bono Mack	N	N	N	Y	N	N
46 Rohrabacher	N	Y	N	Y	Y	Y
47 Sanchez, Loretta	N	N	Y	N	Y	Y
48 Campbell	N	Y	N	Y	Y	Y
49 Issa	N	N	N	Y	N	N
50 Bilbray	N	N	N	N	N	N
51 Filner	+	+	+	–	+	+
52 Hunter	N	N	N	Y	N	N
53 Davis	N	N	Y	N	Y	N
COLORADO						
1 DeGette	Y	N	Y	N	Y	N
2 Polis	?	?	?	?	?	?
3 Tipton	N	N	N	Y	N	N
4 Gardner	N	Y	N	Y	N	N
5 Lamborn	N	Y	N	Y	N	N
6 Coffman	N	N	N	N	N	N
7 Perlmutter	Y	N	N	N	Y	N
CONNECTICUT						
1 Larson	Y	N	Y	N	Y	Y
2 Courtney	N	N	Y	N	Y	Y
3 DeLauro	Y	N	Y	N	Y	Y
4 Himes	Y	Y	Y	N	Y	Y
5 Murphy	Y	Y	Y	N	Y	Y
DELAWARE						
AL Carney	Y	N	Y	N	Y	N
FLORIDA						
1 Miller	N	N	N	Y	N	N
2 Southerland	N	N	N	Y	N	N
3 Brown	N	N	N	N	N	N
4 Crenshaw	N	N	N	Y	N	N
5 Nugent	N	Y	N	Y	N	N
6 Stearns	N	Y	N	Y	Y	Y
7 Mica	N	N	N	Y	N	N
8 Webster	N	Y	N	Y	Y	Y
9 Bilirakis	N	N	N	Y	N	N
10 Young	N	N	N	Y	N	N
11 Castor	Y	N	N	N	Y	N
12 Ross	N	Y	N	Y	Y	Y
13 Buchanan	Y	Y	N	Y	Y	Y
14 Mack	N	Y	N	Y	N	N
15 Posey	N	Y	N	Y	Y	Y
16 Rooney	N	N	N	N	N	N
17 Wilson	N	Y	N	Y	N	Y
18 Ros-Lehtinen	Y	N	Y	N	Y	Y
19 Deutch	Y	N	Y	N	Y	Y
20 Wasserman Schultz	Y	N	Y	N	Y	Y
21 Diaz-Balart	N	N	N	N	N	N
22 West	N	N	N	N	N	N
23 Hastings	N	N	N	N	N	N
24 Adams	N	Y	N	Y	Y	Y
25 Rivera	N	N	N	Y	N	N
GEORGIA						
1 Kingston	N	N	N	Y	N	N
2 Bishop	N	N	N	N	N	N
3 Westmoreland	N	Y	N	Y	N	N
4 Johnson	Y	N	Y	N	Y	Y
5 Lewis	Y	N	Y	N	Y	Y
6 Price	N	Y	N	Y	Y	Y
7 Woodall	N	Y	N	Y	N	N
8 Scott, A.	N	Y	N	N	N	N
9 Graves	N	Y	N	Y	Y	Y
10 Broun	N	Y	N	Y	Y	Y
11 Gingrey	N	Y	N	Y	N	N
12 Barrow	N	N	N	N	N	N
13 Scott, D.	N	N	N	Y	N	N
HAWAII						
1 Hanabusa	N	N	N	N	Y	Y
2 Hirono	?	?	?	?	?	?
IDAHO						
1 Labrador	N	Y	Y	Y	Y	Y
2 Simpson	N	N	N	Y	N	N
ILLINOIS						
1 Rush	Y	N	N	Y	Y	Y
2 Jackson	?	?	?	?	?	?
3 Lipinski	N	N	N	N	N	N
4 Gutierrez	Y	Y	Y	N	Y	Y
5 Quigley	Y	Y	Y	N	Y	Y
6 Roskam	N	N	N	Y	N	N
7 Davis	Y	N	Y	N	Y	N
8 Walsh	N	Y	N	Y	Y	Y
9 Schakowsky	Y	N	Y	N	Y	Y
10 Dold	N	N	N	Y	N	N
11 Kinzinger	N	N	N	Y	N	N
12 Costello	N	N	N	Y	Y	Y
13 Biggert	N	Y	N	Y	N	N
14 Hultgren	N	Y	N	Y	N	N
15 Johnson	Y	Y	N	N	Y	Y

KEY	Republicans	Democrats

Y Voted for (yea)	X Paired against	C Voted "present" to avoid possible conflict of interest
# Paired for	– Announced against	
+ Announced for	P Voted "present"	? Did not vote or otherwise make a position known
N Voted against (nay)		

	475	476	477	478	479	480
16 **Manzullo**	N	Y	N	Y	Y	Y
17 **Schilling**	N	N	N	N	N	N
18 **Schock**	N	N	N	Y	N	N
19 **Shimkus**	N	N	N	N	N	N
INDIANA						
1 Visclosky	N	N	N	N	Y	Y
2 Donnelly	N	N	N	N	Y	N
3 **Stutzman**	N	Y	N	Y	Y	N
4 **Rokita**	N	Y	N	Y	Y	N
5 **Burton**	N	Y	N	Y	N	N
6 **Pence**	N	Y	N	Y	N	N
7 Carson	Y	N	N	N	Y	Y
8 **Bucshon**	N	Y	N	Y	N	N
9 **Young**	N	Y	N	Y	N	N
IOWA						
1 Braley	Y	N	Y	N	Y	Y
2 Loebsack	Y	N	Y	N	Y	Y
3 Boswell	Y	N	Y	N	Y	Y
4 **Latham**	Y	N	N	N	N	N
5 **King**	N	Y	N	Y	N	N
KANSAS						
1 **Huelskamp**	N	Y	N	Y	Y	N
2 **Jenkins**	N	Y	N	Y	N	N
3 **Yoder**	Y	Y	N	Y	Y	Y
4 **Pompeo**	N	Y	N	Y	N	N
KENTUCKY						
1 **Whitfield**	N	N	N	N	Y	N
2 **Guthrie**	N	N	N	Y	N	N
3 Yarmuth	Y	N	Y	N	Y	Y
4 **Davis**	N	N	N	Y	N	N
5 **Rogers**	N	N	N	Y	N	N
6 Chandler	N	N	N	N	Y	N
LOUISIANA						
1 **Scalise**	N	Y	N	Y	N	N
2 Richmond	Y	N	N	N	Y	Y
3 **Landry**	N	Y	N	Y	N	Y
4 **Fleming**	N	N	N	Y	N	N
5 **Alexander**	N	N	N	Y	N	N
6 **Cassidy**	N	Y	N	Y	N	N
7 **Boustany**	N	Y	N	Y	N	N
MAINE						
1 Pingree	Y	N	Y	N	Y	Y
2 Michaud	Y	Y	Y	N	Y	Y
MARYLAND						
1 **Harris**	N	N	N	Y	N	N
2 Ruppersberger	N	N	N	N	N	N
3 Sarbanes	Y	N	Y	N	Y	N
4 Edwards	Y	Y	Y	N	Y	Y
5 Hoyer	N	N	Y	N	Y	N
6 **Bartlett**	N	N	N	Y	Y	Y
7 Cummings	Y	N	Y	N	Y	Y
8 Van Hollen	N	N	Y	N	N	N
MASSACHUSETTS						
1 Olver	Y	N	Y	N	Y	Y
2 Neal	Y	N	Y	N	Y	Y
3 McGovern	Y	N	Y	N	Y	Y
4 Frank	Y	N	Y	N	Y	Y
5 Tsongas	Y	N	?	N	Y	N
6 Tierney	Y	N	Y	N	Y	Y
7 Markey	Y	N	Y	N	Y	Y
8 Capuano	Y	N	Y	N	Y	Y
9 Lynch	Y	N	Y	N	Y	N
10 Keating	Y	N	Y	N	Y	Y
MICHIGAN						
1 **Benishek**	N	Y	N	Y	Y	Y
2 **Huizenga**	N	Y	Y	Y	Y	N
3 **Amash**	N	Y	Y	Y	Y	Y
4 **Camp**	N	Y	N	Y	Y	N
5 Kildee	Y	N	Y	N	N	N
6 **Upton**	N	Y	Y	N	Y	Y
7 **Walberg**	N	Y	N	Y	Y	Y
8 **Rogers**	N	N	N	N	N	N
9 Peters	Y	Y	Y	N	Y	Y
10 **Miller**	N	Y	N	N	Y	Y
11 Vacant						
12 Levin	Y	N	Y	N	Y	N
13 Clarke	Y	N	Y	N	Y	Y
14 Conyers	Y	N	Y	N	Y	Y
15 Dingell	Y	N	Y	N	N	N
MINNESOTA						
1 Walz	N	Y	Y	N	Y	N
2 **Kline**	N	N	N	Y	N	N
3 **Paulsen**	Y	Y	N	Y	N	N
4 McCollum	Y	N	Y	N	Y	Y

	475	476	477	478	479	480
5 Ellison	Y	Y	Y	N	Y	Y
6 **Bachmann**	N	Y	Y	Y	N	N
7 Peterson	N	Y	N	Y	Y	Y
8 **Cravaack**	N	Y	N	Y	N	N
MISSISSIPPI						
1 **Nunnelee**	N	N	N	N	N	N
2 Thompson	N	N	N	N	Y	N
3 **Harper**	N	N	N	Y	N	N
4 **Palazzo**	N	N	N	Y	N	N
MISSOURI						
1 Clay	Y	N	Y	N	Y	Y
2 **Akin**	–	+	–	+	–	–
3 Carnahan	Y	N	Y	N	Y	Y
4 **Hartzler**	N	N	N	N	N	N
5 Cleaver	Y	N	Y	N	Y	N
6 **Graves**	N	Y	N	Y	N	N
7 **Long**	N	N	N	Y	N	N
8 **Emerson**	N	N	N	N	Y	N
9 **Luetkemeyer**	N	Y	N	Y	N	N
MONTANA						
AL **Rehberg**	Y	N	N	Y	N	N
NEBRASKA						
1 **Fortenberry**	N	Y	N	N	Y	N
2 **Terry**	N	Y	N	N	N	N
3 **Smith**	N	N	N	Y	N	N
NEVADA						
1 Berkley	Y	N	N	N	N	N
2 **Amodei**	N	Y	N	Y	N	N
3 **Heck**	N	N	N	N	N	N
NEW HAMPSHIRE						
1 **Guinta**	N	N	N	Y	N	N
2 **Bass**	N	Y	N	Y	Y	Y
NEW JERSEY						
1 Andrews	N	N	Y	N	Y	N
2 **LoBiondo**	N	N	N	N	N	N
3 **Runyan**	N	N	N	N	N	N
4 **Smith**	N	N	N	N	N	N
5 **Garrett**	N	Y	N	Y	N	N
6 Pallone	Y	N	Y	N	Y	Y
7 **Lance**	Y	Y	N	N	Y	N
8 Pascrell	Y	N	Y	N	Y	Y
9 Rothman	N	N	Y	N	Y	N
10 Vacant						
11 **Frelinghuysen**	N	N	N	Y	N	N
12 Holt	Y	N	Y	N	Y	Y
13 Sires	Y	N	Y	N	Y	Y
NEW MEXICO						
1 Heinrich	Y	N	Y	N	Y	N
2 **Pearce**	N	N	N	Y	N	N
3 Luján	Y	N	Y	N	Y	N
NEW YORK						
1 Bishop	Y	N	Y	N	Y	Y
2 Israel	Y	N	Y	N	Y	N
3 **King**	N	N	N	N	N	N
4 McCarthy	Y	N	N	N	Y	N
5 Ackerman	N	N	Y	N	Y	Y
6 Meeks	Y	N	N	N	Y	N
7 Crowley	Y	N	Y	N	Y	Y
8 Nadler	Y	N	Y	N	Y	Y
9 **Turner**	N	N	N	N	N	N
10 Towns	Y	N	Y	N	Y	Y
11 Clarke	Y	N	Y	N	Y	Y
12 Velázquez	Y	N	Y	N	Y	Y
13 **Grimm**	N	N	N	N	N	N
14 Maloney	Y	N	Y	N	Y	N
15 Rangel	N	N	Y	N	N	Y
16 Serrano	Y	N	Y	N	Y	Y
17 Engel	Y	N	N	N	Y	N
18 Lowey	Y	N	Y	N	Y	N
19 **Hayworth**	N	N	N	Y	N	N
20 **Gibson**	N	N	N	N	Y	Y
21 Tonko	Y	N	Y	N	Y	N
22 Hinchey	Y	N	Y	N	Y	N
23 Owens	N	N	Y	N	Y	N
24 **Hanna**	Y	N	N	Y	Y	Y
25 **Buerkle**	N	Y	N	Y	N	N
26 Hochul	Y	N	Y	N	Y	Y
27 Higgins	Y	N	Y	N	Y	Y
28 Slaughter	N	N	Y	N	Y	Y
29 **Reed**	Y	Y	N	Y	Y	N
NORTH CAROLINA						
1 Butterfield	Y	N	N	N	N	N
2 **Ellmers**	N	Y	N	Y	N	N
3 **Jones**	Y	Y	Y	Y	Y	Y
4 Price	Y	N	Y	N	Y	N

	475	476	477	478	479	480
5 **Foxx**	N	Y	N	Y	Y	Y
6 **Coble**	N	Y	N	Y	Y	Y
7 McIntyre	N	N	N	N	Y	Y
8 Kissell	N	N	N	N	Y	N
9 **Myrick**	N	N	N	N	N	N
10 **McHenry**	N	Y	N	Y	N	N
11 Shuler	N	N	N	N	Y	N
12 Watt	Y	N	Y	N	Y	N
13 Miller	Y	N	Y	N	Y	N
NORTH DAKOTA						
AL **Berg**	N	N	N	Y	N	N
OHIO						
1 **Chabot**	N	Y	N	Y	N	N
2 **Schmidt**	N	Y	N	Y	N	N
3 **Turner**	N	N	N	Y	N	N
4 **Jordan**	N	Y	N	Y	N	N
5 **Latta**	N	Y	N	Y	N	N
6 **Johnson**	N	N	N	N	N	N
7 **Austria**	N	N	N	Y	N	N
8 **Boehner**						
9 Kaptur	N	N	N	N	Y	N
10 Kucinich	Y	Y	Y	N	Y	Y
11 Fudge	Y	N	Y	N	Y	Y
12 **Tiberi**	N	N	N	N	N	N
13 Sutton	N	N	Y	N	Y	N
14 **LaTourette**	N	N	N	N	N	N
15 **Stivers**	?	?	?	?	?	?
16 **Renacci**	N	Y	N	Y	N	N
17 Ryan	N	N	N	N	N	N
18 **Gibbs**	N	Y	N	Y	N	N
OKLAHOMA						
1 **Sullivan**	?	N	N	N	N	N
2 Boren	?	?	?	?	?	?
3 **Lucas**	N	N	N	Y	N	N
4 **Cole**	N	N	N	Y	N	N
5 **Lankford**	N	Y	N	Y	N	N
OREGON						
1 Bonamici	Y	N	Y	N	Y	Y
2 **Walden**	N	Y	Y	Y	Y	Y
3 Blumenauer	Y	N	Y	Y	Y	Y
4 DeFazio	Y	Y	Y	N	Y	Y
5 Schrader	N	N	Y	N	Y	Y
PENNSYLVANIA						
1 Brady	Y	N	Y	N	Y	N
2 Fattah	Y	N	Y	N	Y	Y
3 **Kelly**	N	N	N	Y	N	N
4 Altmire	Y	N	N	N	N	N
5 **Thompson**	N	N	N	Y	N	N
6 **Gerlach**	N	N	N	Y	N	N
7 **Meehan**	N	N	N	N	Y	N
8 **Fitzpatrick**	N	N	N	N	Y	N
9 **Shuster**	N	N	N	N	N	N
10 **Marino**	N	N	N	Y	N	N
11 **Barletta**	N	N	N	Y	N	N
12 Critz	N	N	Y	N	Y	N
13 Schwartz	Y	N	Y	N	N	N
14 Doyle	Y	N	Y	N	Y	N
15 **Dent**	Y	N	N	Y	N	N
16 **Pitts**	N	Y	N	N	N	N
17 Holden	N	N	Y	N	Y	N
18 **Murphy**	N	N	N	Y	N	N
19 **Platts**	N	N	N	N	N	N
RHODE ISLAND						
1 Cicilline	N	N	Y	N	Y	Y
2 Langevin	N	N	Y	N	Y	Y
SOUTH CAROLINA						
1 **Scott**	N	Y	N	Y	Y	N
2 **Wilson**	N	N	N	Y	N	N
3 **Duncan**	N	Y	N	Y	N	N
4 **Gowdy**	N	Y	N	Y	N	N
5 **Mulvaney**	N	Y	Y	Y	Y	Y
6 Clyburn	N	N	N	N	Y	N
SOUTH DAKOTA						
AL **Noem**	N	N	N	Y	N	N
TENNESSEE						
1 **Roe**	N	N	N	Y	N	N
2 **Duncan**	Y	Y	Y	Y	Y	Y
3 **Fleischmann**	N	Y	N	Y	N	N
4 **DesJarlais**	N	N	N	Y	Y	Y
5 Cooper	Y	N	Y	N	Y	N
6 **Black**	N	Y	N	Y	N	N
7 **Blackburn**	N	N	N	Y	N	N
8 **Fincher**	N	Y	N	Y	N	N
9 Cohen	Y	Y	Y	N	Y	N

	475	476	477	478	479	480
TEXAS						
1 **Gohmert**	N	Y	N	Y	Y	Y
2 **Poe**	N	Y	N	Y	Y	N
3 **Johnson, S.**	N	N	N	N	N	N
4 **Hall**	N	N	N	Y	N	N
5 **Hensarling**	N	Y	N	Y	N	N
6 **Barton**	N	Y	N	N	Y	N
7 **Culberson**	N	N	N	N	N	N
8 **Brady**	N	Y	N	Y	N	N
9 Green, A.	Y	N	N	N	Y	Y
10 **McCaul**	N	N	N	Y	N	N
11 **Conaway**	N	Y	N	Y	N	N
12 **Granger**	N	N	N	N	N	N
13 **Thornberry**	N	N	N	N	N	N
14 **Paul**	Y	Y	Y	Y	Y	Y
15 Hinojosa	Y	Y	Y	N	Y	Y
16 Reyes	?	?	?	?	?	?
17 **Flores**	N	N	N	N	N	N
18 Jackson Lee	?	?	?	?	?	?
19 **Neugebauer**	N	Y	N	Y	Y	Y
20 Gonzalez	Y	N	Y	N	N	N
21 **Smith**	N	N	N	Y	N	N
22 **Olson**	N	N	N	Y	N	N
23 **Canseco**	N	Y	N	Y	N	N
24 **Marchant**	N	Y	N	Y	N	N
25 Doggett	Y	Y	Y	N	Y	Y
26 **Burgess**	N	Y	N	Y	Y	N
27 **Farenthold**	N	Y	N	Y	N	N
28 Cuellar	N	N	N	N	N	N
29 Green, G.	Y	N	N	N	Y	Y
30 Johnson, E.	Y	N	N	N	N	Y
31 **Carter**	N	N	N	N	N	N
32 **Sessions**	N	N	N	Y	N	N
UTAH						
1 **Bishop**	N	N	N	N	N	N
2 Matheson	N	N	Y	N	N	N
3 **Chaffetz**	N	Y	N	Y	N	N
VERMONT						
AL Welch	Y	N	Y	N	Y	Y
VIRGINIA						
1 **Wittman**	N	N	N	Y	N	N
2 **Rigell**	N	N	N	Y	Y	Y
3 Scott	N	N	Y	N	Y	N
4 **Forbes**	N	N	N	N	N	N
5 **Hurt**	N	Y	N	Y	Y	Y
6 **Goodlatte**	N	Y	N	Y	Y	Y
7 **Cantor**	N	Y	N	Y	N	N
8 Moran	N	N	N	N	Y	Y
9 **Griffith**	N	Y	N	Y	Y	Y
10 **Wolf**	N	N	N	N	N	N
11 Connolly	N	N	Y	N	Y	N
WASHINGTON						
1 Vacant						
2 Larsen	Y	N	N	N	Y	Y
3 **Herrera Beutler**	Y	N	Y	Y	Y	N
4 **Hastings**	N	N	N	Y	N	N
5 **McMorris Rodgers**	N	Y	N	Y	N	N
6 Dicks	N	N	N	N	Y	N
7 McDermott	Y	N	Y	N	Y	N
8 **Reichert**	N	N	N	Y	N	N
9 Smith	N	N	N	Y	N	N
WEST VIRGINIA						
1 **McKinley**	Y	Y	N	N	Y	Y
2 **Capito**	N	N	N	N	N	N
3 Rahall	Y	N	Y	N	Y	Y
WISCONSIN						
1 **Ryan**	N	Y	N	Y	N	N
2 Baldwin	Y	N	Y	N	Y	Y
3 Kind	Y	Y	Y	N	Y	Y
4 Moore	Y	N	Y	N	Y	Y
5 **Sensenbrenner**	N	Y	N	Y	Y	Y
6 **Petri**	N	Y	N	Y	Y	Y
7 **Duffy**	N	Y	N	Y	Y	Y
8 **Ribble**	N	Y	N	Y	Y	Y
WYOMING						
AL **Lummis**	Y	Y	N	Y	Y	Y

IN THE HOUSE | By Vote Number

481. HR 5856. Fiscal 2013 Defense Appropriations/Funding Reductions. Woolsey, D-Calif., amendment that would reduce overall spending in the bill by $181 million. Rejected in Committee of the Whole 114-302: R 28-209; D 86-93. July 18, 2012.

482. HR 5856. Fiscal 2013 Defense Appropriations/Intercontinental Ballistic Missile Limits. Markey, D-Mass., amendment that would prohibit funds in the bill from being used to operate or maintain more than 300 land-based intercontinental ballistic missiles. Rejected in Committee of the Whole 136-283: R 3-235; D 133-48. July 18, 2012.

483. HR 5856. Fiscal 2013 Defense Appropriations/Funding Reductions. Woolsey, D-Calif., amendment that would reduce overall spending in the bill by $294 million. Rejected in Committee of the Whole 106-311: R 19-217; D 87-94. July 18, 2012.

484. HR 5856. Fiscal 2013 Defense Appropriations/Funding Reductions. Woolsey, D-Calif., amendment that would reduce overall spending in the bill by $1.7 billion. Rejected in Committee of the Whole 91-328: R 14-224; D 77-104. July 18, 2012.

485. HR 5856. Fiscal 2013 Defense Appropriations/Afghanistan Withdrawal Funding. Lee, D-Calif., amendment that would reduce the budget for overseas contingency operations by $20.8 billion and limit the use of funds provided for operations in Afghanistan to the purpose of conducting a safe and orderly withdrawal. Rejected in Committee of the Whole 107-312: R 8-230; D 99-82. July 18, 2012.

486. HR 5856. Fiscal 2013 Defense Appropriations/Wage Requirements. King, R-Iowa, amendment that would prohibit funds in the bill from being used to enforce or implement prevailing wage requirements of the labor law known as the Davis-Bacon Act (PL 71-798). Rejected in Committee of the Whole 182-235: R 182-54; D 0-181. July 18, 2012.

	481	482	483	484	485	486
ALABAMA						
1 Bonner	N	N	N	N	N	Y
2 Roby	N	N	N	N	N	Y
3 Rogers	N	N	N	N	N	Y
4 Aderholt	N	N	N	N	N	+
5 Brooks	N	N	N	N	N	Y
6 Bachus	N	N	N	N	N	Y
7 Sewell	–	–	–	–	–	–
ALASKA						
AL Young	N	N	N	N	N	N
ARIZONA						
1 Gosar	N	N	N	N	N	Y
2 Franks	N	N	N	N	N	Y
3 Quayle	N	N	N	N	N	Y
4 Pastor	Y	N	N	N	N	N
5 Schweikert	N	N	N	N	N	Y
6 Flake	N	N	N	N	N	Y
7 Grijalva	Y	Y	Y	Y	Y	N
8 Barber	N	N	N	N	N	N
ARKANSAS						
1 Crawford	N	N	N	N	N	Y
2 Griffin	N	N	N	N	N	Y
3 Womack	N	N	N	N	N	Y
4 Ross	N	N	N	N	N	N
CALIFORNIA						
1 Thompson	Y	Y	Y	Y	Y	N
2 Herger	N	N	N	N	N	Y
3 Lungren	N	N	N	N	N	Y
4 McClintock	Y	N	Y	N	Y	Y
5 Matsui	Y	Y	Y	Y	Y	N
6 Woolsey	Y	Y	Y	Y	Y	N
7 Miller, George	Y	Y	Y	Y	Y	N
8 Pelosi	N	Y	Y	N	N	N
9 Lee	Y	Y	Y	Y	Y	N
10 Garamendi	Y	Y	Y	N	N	N
11 McNerney	N	Y	N	N	N	N
12 Speier	Y	Y	Y	Y	Y	N
13 Stark	Y	Y	Y	Y	Y	N
14 Eshoo	Y	Y	Y	Y	Y	N
15 Honda	Y	Y	Y	Y	Y	N
16 Lofgren	Y	Y	Y	Y	Y	N
17 Farr	Y	Y	Y	Y	Y	N
18 Cardoza	?	?	?	?	?	?
19 Denham	N	N	N	N	N	Y
20 Costa	N	N	N	N	N	N
21 Nunes	N	N	N	N	N	Y
22 McCarthy	N	N	N	N	N	Y
23 Capps	N	Y	N	N	Y	N
24 Gallegly	N	N	N	N	N	Y
25 McKeon	N	N	N	N	N	Y
26 Dreier	N	N	N	N	N	Y
27 Sherman	N	N	N	N	N	N
28 Berman	N	Y	N	N	N	N
29 Schiff	N	Y	N	N	N	N
30 Waxman	N	Y	N	N	N	N
31 Becerra	Y	Y	Y	Y	Y	N
32 Chu	Y	Y	Y	Y	Y	N
33 Bass	Y	Y	Y	Y	Y	N
34 Roybal-Allard	Y	Y	Y	Y	Y	N
35 Waters	Y	Y	Y	Y	Y	N
36 Hahn	?	?	?	?	?	?
37 Richardson	N	N	N	N	Y	N
38 Napolitano	Y	Y	Y	Y	Y	N
39 Sánchez, Linda	Y	Y	Y	Y	Y	N
40 Royce	Y	N	Y	N	Y	Y
41 Lewis	N	N	N	N	N	Y
42 Miller, Gary	N	N	N	N	N	Y
43 Baca	N	N	N	N	N	N
44 Calvert	N	N	N	N	N	Y
45 Bono Mack	N	N	N	N	N	Y
46 Rohrabacher	Y	Y	Y	Y	Y	Y
47 Sanchez, Loretta	N	Y	N	N	N	N
48 Campbell	Y	N	Y	Y	Y	Y
49 Issa	N	N	N	N	N	Y
50 Bilbray	N	N	N	N	N	Y
51 Filner	+	+	+	+	+	–
52 Hunter	N	N	N	N	N	?
53 Davis	N	Y	N	N	N	N

	481	482	483	484	485	486
COLORADO						
1 DeGette	Y	Y	Y	Y	Y	N
2 Polis	?	?	?	?	?	Y
3 Tipton	N	N	N	N	N	Y
4 Gardner	N	N	N	N	N	Y
5 Lamborn	N	N	N	N	N	Y
6 Coffman	N	N	N	N	N	Y
7 Perlmutter	N	N	N	N	N	N
CONNECTICUT						
1 Larson	N	Y	N	N	Y	N
2 Courtney	N	Y	N	N	N	N
3 DeLauro	N	Y	N	N	Y	N
4 Himes	Y	Y	Y	N	Y	N
5 Murphy	Y	Y	Y	N	Y	N
DELAWARE						
AL Carney	N	N	N	N	N	N
FLORIDA						
1 Miller	N	N	N	N	N	Y
2 Southerland	N	N	N	N	N	Y
3 Brown	N	Y	N	N	N	N
4 Crenshaw	N	N	N	N	N	Y
5 Nugent	N	N	N	N	N	Y
6 Stearns	Y	N	Y	N	N	Y
7 Mica	N	N	N	N	N	Y
8 Webster	N	N	N	N	N	Y
9 Bilirakis	N	N	N	N	N	Y
10 Young	N	N	N	N	N	Y
11 Castor	Y	Y	Y	Y	N	N
12 Ross	N	N	N	N	N	Y
13 Buchanan	Y	N	N	N	N	Y
14 Mack	N	N	N	N	N	Y
15 Posey	N	N	N	N	N	Y
16 Rooney	N	N	N	N	N	Y
17 Wilson	Y	Y	Y	Y	Y	N
18 Ros-Lehtinen	N	N	N	N	N	N
19 Deutch	Y	Y	Y	Y	Y	N
20 Wasserman Schultz	N	Y	N	N	N	N
21 Diaz-Balart	N	N	N	N	N	Y
22 West	N	N	N	N	N	Y
23 Hastings	N	Y	N	N	N	N
24 Adams	N	N	N	N	N	Y
25 Rivera	N	N	N	N	N	N
GEORGIA						
1 Kingston	N	N	N	N	N	Y
2 Bishop	N	N	N	N	N	N
3 Westmoreland	N	N	N	N	N	Y
4 Johnson	Y	Y	Y	Y	N	N
5 Lewis	Y	Y	Y	Y	Y	N
6 Price	N	N	N	N	N	Y
7 Woodall	N	N	N	N	N	Y
8 Scott, A.	N	N	N	N	N	Y
9 Graves	Y	N	N	N	N	Y
10 Broun	N	N	N	N	N	Y
11 Gingrey	N	N	N	N	N	Y
12 Barrow	N	N	N	N	N	N
13 Scott, D.	N	N	N	N	N	N
HAWAII						
1 Hanabusa	N	N	N	N	Y	N
2 Hirono	?	?	?	?	?	?
IDAHO						
1 Labrador	Y	N	Y	Y	N	Y
2 Simpson	N	N	N	N	N	Y
ILLINOIS						
1 Rush	Y	Y	Y	Y	Y	N
2 Jackson	?	?	?	?	?	?
3 Lipinski	N	N	N	N	N	N
4 Gutierrez	Y	Y	Y	Y	Y	N
5 Quigley	Y	Y	Y	Y	Y	N
6 Roskam	N	N	N	N	N	Y
7 Davis	N	Y	Y	Y	Y	N
8 Walsh	N	N	N	N	N	N
9 Schakowsky	Y	Y	Y	Y	Y	N
10 Dold	N	N	N	N	N	N
11 Kinzinger	N	N	N	N	N	N
12 Costello	N	N	N	N	N	N
13 Biggert	N	N	N	N	N	N
14 Hultgren	N	N	N	N	N	N
15 Johnson	Y	N	Y	Y	Y	N

	481	482	483	484	485	486
16 **Manzullo**	N	N	N	N	N	Y
17 **Schilling**	N	N	N	N	N	N
18 **Schock**	N	N	N	N	N	N
19 **Shimkus**	N	N	N	N	N	N
INDIANA						
1 Visclosky	–	Y	N	N	Y	N
2 Donnelly	N	N	N	N	N	N
3 **Stutzman**	Y	N	N	N	N	Y
4 **Rokita**	N	N	?	N	N	Y
5 **Burton**	N	N	N	N	N	N
6 **Pence**	N	N	N	N	N	Y
7 Carson	N	N	Y	Y	Y	N
8 **Bucshon**	N	N	N	N	N	Y
9 **Young**	N	N	N	N	N	Y
IOWA						
1 Braley	?	Y	Y	Y	Y	N
2 Loebsack	N	Y	N	N	Y	N
3 Boswell	N	Y	N	N	Y	N
4 **Latham**	N	N	N	N	N	Y
5 **King**	N	N	N	N	N	Y
KANSAS						
1 **Huelskamp**	N	N	N	N	N	Y
2 **Jenkins**	N	N	N	N	N	Y
3 **Yoder**	Y	N	N	N	N	Y
4 **Pompeo**	N	N	N	N	N	Y
KENTUCKY						
1 **Whitfield**	N	N	N	N	N	N
2 **Guthrie**	N	N	N	N	N	Y
3 Yarmuth	Y	Y	Y	Y	Y	N
4 **Davis**	N	N	N	N	N	Y
5 **Rogers**	N	N	N	N	N	Y
6 Chandler	N	N	N	N	N	N
LOUISIANA						
1 **Scalise**	N	N	N	N	N	Y
2 Richmond	N	Y	N	N	Y	N
3 **Landry**	N	N	N	N	N	Y
4 **Fleming**	N	N	N	N	N	Y
5 **Alexander**	N	N	N	N	N	N
6 **Cassidy**	N	N	N	N	N	Y
7 **Boustany**	N	N	N	N	N	Y
MAINE						
1 Pingree	Y	Y	Y	N	Y	N
2 Michaud	Y	Y	Y	Y	Y	N
MARYLAND						
1 **Harris**	N	N	N	N	N	Y
2 Ruppersberger	N	N	N	N	N	N
3 Sarbanes	Y	Y	Y	Y	N	N
4 Edwards	Y	Y	Y	Y	Y	N
5 Hoyer	N	Y	N	N	N	N
6 **Bartlett**	N	N	N	N	N	Y
7 Cummings	N	Y	Y	Y	Y	N
8 Van Hollen	N	Y	N	N	N	N
MASSACHUSETTS						
1 Olver	Y	Y	Y	Y	Y	N
2 Neal	Y	Y	Y	Y	Y	N
3 McGovern	Y	Y	Y	Y	Y	N
4 Frank	Y	Y	Y	Y	Y	N
5 Tsongas	Y	Y	Y	Y	Y	N
6 Tierney	Y	Y	Y	Y	Y	N
7 Markey	Y	Y	Y	Y	Y	N
8 Capuano	Y	Y	Y	Y	Y	N
9 Lynch	N	Y	N	N	N	N
10 Keating	Y	Y	Y	Y	Y	N
MICHIGAN						
1 **Benishek**	Y	N	Y	Y	Y	Y
2 **Huizenga**	N	N	N	N	N	Y
3 **Amash**	Y	N	Y	Y	Y	Y
4 **Camp**	N	N	N	N	N	Y
5 Kildee	N	Y	N	N	N	N
6 **Upton**	N	N	N	N	N	N
7 **Walberg**	N	N	N	N	N	Y
8 **Rogers**	N	N	N	N	N	Y
9 Peters	Y	Y	Y	Y	N	N
10 **Miller**	Y	N	Y	Y	N	N
11 Vacant						
12 Levin	N	Y	N	N	N	N
13 Clarke	Y	Y	Y	Y	Y	N
14 Conyers	Y	Y	Y	Y	Y	N
15 Dingell	N	N	N	N	N	N
MINNESOTA						
1 Walz	N	Y	N	N	N	N
2 **Kline**	N	N	N	N	N	Y
3 **Paulsen**	N	N	N	N	N	Y
4 McCollum	Y	Y	Y	Y	Y	N

	481	482	483	484	485	486
5 Ellison	Y	Y	Y	Y	Y	N
6 **Bachmann**	N	N	N	N	N	Y
7 Peterson	Y	N	Y	N	N	N
8 **Cravaack**	N	N	N	N	N	N
MISSISSIPPI						
1 **Nunnelee**	N	N	N	N	N	Y
2 Thompson	N	Y	N	N	Y	N
3 **Harper**	N	N	N	N	N	Y
4 **Palazzo**	N	N	N	N	N	Y
MISSOURI						
1 Clay	Y	Y	Y	Y	Y	N
2 **Akin**	–	–	–	–	–	?
3 Carnahan	Y	Y	Y	Y	N	N
4 **Hartzler**	N	N	N	N	N	Y
5 Cleaver	Y	Y	N	N	Y	N
6 **Graves**	N	N	N	N	N	Y
7 **Long**	N	N	N	N	N	Y
8 **Emerson**	N	N	N	N	N	N
9 **Luetkemeyer**	N	N	N	N	N	Y
MONTANA						
AL **Rehberg**	N	N	N	N	N	N
NEBRASKA						
1 **Fortenberry**	N	N	N	N	N	Y
2 **Terry**	N	N	N	N	N	N
3 **Smith**	N	N	N	N	N	Y
NEVADA						
1 Berkley	N	N	N	N	N	N
2 **Amodei**	N	N	N	N	N	Y
3 **Heck**	N	N	N	N	N	N
NEW HAMPSHIRE						
1 **Guinta**	N	N	N	N	N	Y
2 **Bass**	N	N	N	N	N	Y
NEW JERSEY						
1 Andrews	N	N	N	N	N	N
2 **LoBiondo**	N	N	N	N	N	N
3 **Runyan**	N	N	N	N	N	N
4 **Smith**	N	N	N	N	N	N
5 **Garrett**	N	N	N	N	N	Y
6 Pallone	Y	Y	Y	Y	Y	N
7 **Lance**	Y	N	N	N	N	N
8 Pascrell	Y	Y	Y	Y	N	N
9 Rothman	N	N	N	N	N	N
10 Vacant						
11 **Frelinghuysen**	N	N	N	N	N	N
12 Holt	Y	Y	Y	Y	Y	N
13 Sires	N	Y	N	N	N	N
NEW MEXICO						
1 Heinrich	N	Y	N	N	N	N
2 **Pearce**	N	N	N	N	N	Y
3 Luján	N	Y	N	N	N	N
NEW YORK						
1 Bishop	N	Y	N	N	N	N
2 Israel	N	Y	N	N	N	N
3 **King**	N	N	N	N	N	N
4 McCarthy	N	N	N	N	N	N
5 Ackerman	N	N	N	N	N	N
6 Meeks	N	Y	N	N	Y	N
7 Crowley	Y	Y	N	N	Y	N
8 Nadler	Y	Y	Y	Y	Y	N
9 **Turner**	?	N	N	N	N	N
10 Towns	Y	Y	Y	Y	Y	N
11 Clarke	Y	Y	Y	Y	Y	N
12 Velázquez	Y	Y	Y	Y	Y	N
13 **Grimm**	N	N	N	N	N	N
14 Maloney	Y	Y	N	Y	Y	N
15 Rangel	Y	Y	Y	Y	Y	N
16 Serrano	Y	Y	Y	Y	Y	N
17 Engel	N	N	N	N	N	N
18 Lowey	N	Y	N	N	N	N
19 **Hayworth**	N	N	N	N	N	Y
20 **Gibson**	Y	N	N	N	N	N
21 Tonko	N	Y	N	N	Y	N
22 Hinchey	N	Y	Y	N	Y	N
23 Owens	N	N	N	N	N	N
24 **Hanna**	N	N	N	N	N	N
25 **Buerkle**	N	N	N	N	N	Y
26 Hochul	N	N	N	N	N	N
27 Higgins	N	Y	N	N	Y	N
28 Slaughter	Y	Y	Y	Y	Y	N
29 **Reed**	N	N	N	N	N	Y
NORTH CAROLINA						
1 Butterfield	N	N	N	N	N	N
2 **Ellmers**	N	N	N	N	N	Y
3 **Jones**	Y	Y	Y	Y	Y	Y
4 Price	N	Y	N	N	Y	N

	481	482	483	484	485	486
5 **Foxx**	N	N	N	N	N	Y
6 **Coble**	Y	N	N	N	N	Y
7 McIntyre	N	N	N	N	N	N
8 Kissell	N	N	N	N	N	N
9 **Myrick**	N	N	N	N	N	Y
10 **McHenry**	N	N	N	N	N	Y
11 Shuler	N	N	N	N	N	N
12 Watt	Y	Y	Y	N	Y	N
13 Miller	N	Y	N	N	N	N
NORTH DAKOTA						
AL **Berg**	N	N	N	N	N	Y
OHIO						
1 **Chabot**	N	N	N	N	N	Y
2 **Schmidt**	N	N	N	N	N	N
3 **Turner**	N	N	N	N	N	N
4 **Jordan**	N	N	N	N	N	Y
5 **Latta**	N	N	N	N	N	Y
6 **Johnson**	N	N	N	N	N	Y
7 **Austria**	N	N	N	N	N	Y
8 **Boehner**						
9 Kaptur	N	Y	N	N	N	N
10 Kucinich	Y	Y	Y	Y	Y	N
11 Fudge	Y	Y	Y	Y	Y	N
12 **Tiberi**	N	N	N	N	N	N
13 Sutton	N	Y	N	N	N	N
14 **LaTourette**	N	N	N	N	N	N
15 **Stivers**	?	?	?	?	?	?
16 **Renacci**	N	N	N	N	N	Y
17 Ryan	N	Y	N	N	N	N
18 **Gibbs**	N	N	N	N	N	Y
OKLAHOMA						
1 **Sullivan**	N	N	N	N	N	N
2 Boren	?	?	?	?	?	?
3 **Lucas**	N	N	N	N	N	Y
4 **Cole**	N	N	N	N	N	Y
5 **Lankford**	N	N	N	N	N	Y
OREGON						
1 Bonamici	Y	Y	Y	Y	Y	N
2 **Walden**	N	N	N	N	N	N
3 Blumenauer	Y	Y	Y	Y	Y	N
4 DeFazio	Y	Y	Y	Y	Y	N
5 Schrader	Y	N	Y	N	Y	N
PENNSYLVANIA						
1 Brady	N	Y	N	N	N	N
2 Fattah	N	N	N	N	Y	N
3 **Kelly**	N	N	N	N	N	N
4 Altmire	N	N	N	N	N	N
5 **Thompson**	N	N	N	N	N	Y
6 **Gerlach**	N	N	N	N	N	N
7 **Meehan**	N	N	N	N	N	N
8 **Fitzpatrick**	N	N	N	N	N	N
9 **Shuster**	N	N	N	N	N	N
10 **Marino**	N	N	N	N	N	Y
11 **Barletta**	N	N	N	N	N	N
12 Critz	N	N	N	N	N	N
13 Schwartz	Y	Y	N	N	N	N
14 Doyle	Y	Y	Y	Y	Y	N
15 **Dent**	N	N	N	N	N	Y
16 **Pitts**	N	N	N	N	N	Y
17 Holden	N	N	N	N	N	N
18 **Murphy**	N	N	N	N	N	N
19 **Platts**	N	N	N	N	N	Y
RHODE ISLAND						
1 Cicilline	N	Y	N	N	Y	N
2 Langevin	N	Y	N	N	N	N
SOUTH CAROLINA						
1 **Scott**	N	N	N	N	N	Y
2 **Wilson**	N	N	N	N	N	Y
3 **Duncan**	N	N	N	N	N	Y
4 **Gowdy**	N	N	N	N	N	Y
5 **Mulvaney**	Y	N	Y	Y	N	Y
6 Clyburn	N	N	N	N	Y	N
SOUTH DAKOTA						
AL **Noem**	N	N	N	N	N	Y
TENNESSEE						
1 **Roe**	N	N	N	N	N	Y
2 **Duncan**	Y	N	Y	Y	Y	Y
3 **Fleischmann**	N	N	N	N	N	Y
4 **DesJarlais**	N	N	N	N	N	Y
5 Cooper	Y	N	Y	Y	N	N
6 **Black**	N	N	N	N	N	Y
7 **Blackburn**	N	N	N	N	N	Y
8 **Fincher**	N	N	N	N	N	Y
9 Cohen	N	Y	Y	Y	Y	N

	481	482	483	484	485	486
TEXAS						
1 **Gohmert**	N	N	N	N	N	Y
2 **Poe**	N	N	N	N	N	Y
3 **Johnson, S.**	N	N	N	N	N	Y
4 **Hall**	N	N	N	N	N	Y
5 **Hensarling**	N	N	N	N	N	Y
6 **Barton**	Y	N	N	N	N	Y
7 **Culberson**	N	N	N	N	N	Y
8 **Brady**	N	N	N	N	N	Y
9 Green, A.	N	N	N	N	N	N
10 **McCaul**	N	N	?	N	N	Y
11 **Conaway**	N	N	N	N	N	Y
12 **Granger**	N	N	N	N	N	Y
13 **Thornberry**	N	N	N	N	N	Y
14 **Paul**	Y	Y	Y	Y	Y	Y
15 Hinojosa	Y	Y	Y	Y	Y	N
16 Reyes	?	?	?	?	?	?
17 **Flores**	N	N	N	N	N	Y
18 Jackson Lee	?	?	?	?	?	?
19 **Neugebauer**	N	N	N	N	N	Y
20 Gonzalez	N	N	N	N	N	N
21 **Smith**	N	N	N	N	N	Y
22 **Olson**	N	N	N	N	N	Y
23 **Canseco**	N	N	N	N	N	Y
24 **Marchant**	N	N	N	N	N	Y
25 Doggett	N	Y	N	N	N	N
26 **Burgess**	N	N	N	N	N	Y
27 **Farenthold**	N	N	N	N	N	Y
28 Cuellar	N	N	N	N	N	N
29 Green, G.	Y	N	N	N	N	N
30 Johnson, E.	N	N	N	N	Y	N
31 **Carter**	N	N	N	N	N	Y
32 **Sessions**	N	N	N	N	N	Y
UTAH						
1 **Bishop**	N	N	N	N	N	Y
2 Matheson	N	N	N	N	N	N
3 **Chaffetz**	N	N	N	N	N	Y
VERMONT						
AL Welch	Y	Y	Y	Y	Y	N
VIRGINIA						
1 **Wittman**	N	N	N	N	N	Y
2 **Rigell**	N	N	N	N	N	Y
3 Scott	N	Y	N	N	Y	N
4 **Forbes**	N	N	N	N	N	Y
5 **Hurt**	N	N	N	N	N	Y
6 **Goodlatte**	Y	N	Y	N	N	Y
7 **Cantor**	N	N	N	N	N	Y
8 Moran	N	Y	N	N	Y	N
9 **Griffith**	Y	N	Y	N	N	Y
10 **Wolf**	N	N	N	N	N	Y
11 Connolly	N	N	N	N	N	N
WASHINGTON						
1 Vacant						
2 Larsen	Y	N	N	Y	Y	N
3 **Herrera Beutler**	N	N	N	N	N	N
4 **Hastings**	N	N	N	N	N	Y
5 **McMorris Rodgers**	N	N	N	N	N	Y
6 Dicks	N	Y	N	N	N	N
7 McDermott	Y	Y	Y	N	Y	N
8 **Reichert**	N	N	N	N	N	N
9 Smith	N	Y	N	N	N	N
WEST VIRGINIA						
1 **McKinley**	N	N	N	N	N	N
2 **Capito**	N	N	N	N	N	N
3 Rahall	Y	Y	Y	Y	N	N
WISCONSIN						
1 **Ryan**	N	N	N	N	N	N
2 Baldwin	Y	Y	Y	Y	Y	N
3 Kind	N	Y	N	N	N	N
4 Moore	Y	Y	Y	Y	Y	N
5 **Sensenbrenner**	Y	N	Y	Y	N	Y
6 **Petri**	Y	N	Y	N	N	N
7 **Duffy**	Y	N	N	N	N	N
8 **Ribble**	Y	N	Y	N	N	Y
WYOMING						
AL **Lummis**	N	N	N	N	N	Y

IN THE HOUSE | By Vote Number

487. HR 5856. Fiscal 2013 Defense Appropriations/Defense of Marriage Act. King, R-Iowa, amendment that would bar funds in the bill from being used in contravention of current law that defines marriage as a legal union between a man and a woman. Adopted in Committee of the Whole 247-166: R 230-5; D 17-161. A "nay" was a vote in support of the president's position. July 19, 2012.

488. HR 5856. Fiscal 2013 Defense Appropriations/Spending Reduction. Lee, D-Calif., amendment that would reduce total appropriations by $19.2 billion, which would bring the bill's total to $500 billion. The amendment would exempt from the reduction funding for military personnel and the Defense Health Program as well as for these two activities within overseas contingency operations. Rejected in Committee of the Whole 87-326: R 7-228; D 80-98. July 19, 2012.

489. HR 5856. Fiscal 2013 Defense Appropriations/Debt Limit Law Funding Level. Lee, D-Calif., amendment that would reduce appropriations in the bill by $7.6 billion, which would bring the total to the amount authorized under the Budget Control Act (PL 112-25). The amendment would exempt funding for military personnel, health care and overseas contingency operations from the reduction. Rejected in Committee of the Whole 171-243: R 24-212; D 147-31. A "yea" was a vote in support of the president's position. July 19, 2012.

490. HR 5856. Fiscal 2013 Defense Appropriations/Russian Loan Guarantees. Moran, D-Va., amendment that would bar the use of funds in the bill to enter into contracts or cooperative agreements or provide grants, loans or loan guarantees to Rosoboronexport, Russia's official weapons exporter. Adopted in Committee of the Whole 407-5: R 231-4; D 176-1. July 19, 2012.

491. HR 5856. Fiscal 2013 Defense Appropriations/Nuclear Forces. Turner, R-Ohio, amendment that would bar the use of funds in the bill to reduce U.S. nuclear forces, implement the Nuclear Posture Review Implementation Study or change parts of the Secretary of Defense Guidance for Employment of Force or the Joint Strategic Capabilities Plan. Adopted in Committee of the Whole 235-178: R 227-8; D 8-170. A "nay" was a vote in support of the president's position. July 19, 2012.

492. HR 5856. Fiscal 2013 Defense Appropriations/NATO Infantry Withdrawal. Coffman, R-Colo., amendment that would bar the use of funds in the bill for the deployment of the 170th and 172nd infantry brigade after fiscal 2013. The Army plans to withdraw the two brigade combat teams from Europe, unless there is an emergency sanctioned by NATO. Rejected in Committee of the Whole 123-292: R 46-190; D 77-102. July 19, 2012.

	487	488	489	490	491	492
ALABAMA						
1 Bonner	Y	N	N	Y	Y	N
2 Roby	Y	N	N	Y	Y	N
3 Rogers	Y	N	N	Y	Y	N
4 Aderholt	Y	N	N	Y	Y	N
5 Brooks	Y	N	N	Y	Y	N
6 Bachus	Y	N	N	Y	Y	N
7 Sewell	N	N	N	Y	N	N
ALASKA						
AL Young	Y	N	N	Y	Y	N
ARIZONA						
1 Gosar	Y	N	N	Y	Y	N
2 Franks	Y	N	N	Y	Y	N
3 Quayle	Y	N	N	Y	Y	N
4 Pastor	N	N	Y	Y	N	N
5 Schweikert	Y	N	N	Y	Y	N
6 Flake	Y	N	Y	Y	N	N
7 Grijalva	N	Y	Y	Y	N	Y
8 Barber	N	N	N	Y	N	N
ARKANSAS						
1 Crawford	Y	N	N	Y	Y	N
2 Griffin	Y	N	N	Y	Y	N
3 Womack	Y	N	N	Y	Y	N
4 Ross	Y	N	N	Y	N	N
CALIFORNIA						
1 Thompson	N	Y	Y	Y	N	N
2 Herger	Y	N	N	Y	Y	N
3 Lungren	Y	N	N	Y	Y	N
4 McClintock	Y	N	Y	Y	Y	Y
5 Matsui	N	Y	Y	Y	N	N
6 Woolsey	N	Y	Y	Y	N	Y
7 Miller, George	N	Y	Y	Y	N	Y
8 Pelosi	N	N	Y	Y	N	N
9 Lee	N	Y	Y	Y	N	Y
10 Garamendi	N	N	Y	Y	N	N
11 McNerney	N	N	N	Y	N	N
12 Speier	N	Y	Y	Y	N	N
13 Stark	?	Y	Y	Y	N	Y
14 Eshoo	N	Y	Y	Y	N	N
15 Honda	N	Y	Y	Y	N	Y
16 Lofgren	N	Y	Y	Y	N	Y
17 Farr	N	Y	Y	Y	N	Y
18 Cardoza	N	N	Y	Y	N	N
19 Denham	Y	N	N	Y	Y	N
20 Costa	N	N	Y	Y	N	N
21 Nunes	Y	N	N	Y	Y	Y
22 McCarthy	Y	N	N	Y	Y	N
23 Capps	N	N	Y	Y	N	N
24 Gallegly	Y	N	N	Y	Y	N
25 McKeon	Y	N	N	Y	Y	N
26 Dreier	Y	N	N	Y	Y	N
27 Sherman	N	N	Y	Y	N	Y
28 Berman	N	N	Y	Y	N	Y
29 Schiff	N	N	Y	Y	N	Y
30 Waxman	N	N	Y	Y	N	Y
31 Becerra	N	Y	Y	Y	N	Y
32 Chu	N	Y	Y	Y	N	Y
33 Bass	N	Y	Y	Y	N	Y
34 Roybal-Allard	N	Y	Y	Y	N	Y
35 Waters	N	Y	Y	Y	N	Y
36 Hahn	N	Y	Y	Y	N	Y
37 Richardson	N	Y	Y	Y	N	Y
38 Napolitano	N	Y	Y	Y	N	Y
39 Sánchez, Linda	N	Y	Y	Y	N	Y
40 Royce	Y	N	Y	Y	Y	Y
41 Lewis	Y	N	N	Y	Y	N
42 Miller, Gary	Y	N	N	Y	Y	N
43 Baca	N	N	Y	Y	N	Y
44 Calvert	Y	N	N	Y	Y	N
45 Bono Mack	Y	N	N	Y	Y	N
46 Rohrabacher	Y	N	Y	Y	Y	Y
47 Sanchez, Loretta	N	N	Y	Y	N	N
48 Campbell	Y	Y	Y	Y	N	N
49 Issa	Y	N	Y	Y	Y	N
50 Bilbray	Y	N	N	Y	Y	N
51 Filner	–	+	+	+	–	+
52 Hunter	Y	N	N	Y	Y	N
53 Davis	N	N	N	Y	N	Y

	487	488	489	490	491	492
COLORADO						
1 DeGette	N	Y	Y	Y	N	Y
2 Polis	?	?	?	?	?	?
3 Tipton	Y	N	N	Y	Y	N
4 Gardner	Y	N	N	Y	Y	N
5 Lamborn	Y	N	N	Y	Y	N
6 Coffman	Y	N	N	Y	Y	Y
7 Perlmutter	N	N	Y	Y	N	Y
CONNECTICUT						
1 Larson	N	N	N	Y	N	N
2 Courtney	N	N	N	Y	N	N
3 DeLauro	N	N	Y	Y	N	N
4 Himes	N	N	Y	Y	N	N
5 Murphy	N	Y	Y	Y	N	Y
DELAWARE						
AL Carney	N	N	Y	Y	N	Y
FLORIDA						
1 Miller	Y	N	N	Y	Y	N
2 Southerland	Y	N	N	Y	Y	N
3 Brown	?	?	?	?	?	?
4 Crenshaw	Y	N	N	Y	Y	N
5 Nugent	Y	N	N	Y	Y	N
6 Stearns	Y	N	Y	Y	Y	Y
7 Mica	Y	N	N	Y	Y	N
8 Webster	Y	N	N	Y	Y	N
9 Bilirakis	Y	N	N	Y	Y	N
10 Young	Y	N	N	Y	Y	N
11 Castor	N	Y	Y	Y	N	N
12 Ross	Y	N	N	Y	Y	N
13 Buchanan	N	N	N	Y	Y	N
14 Mack	Y	N	N	Y	Y	N
15 Posey	Y	N	Y	Y	Y	N
16 Rooney	Y	N	N	Y	Y	N
17 Wilson	N	Y	Y	Y	N	N
18 Ros-Lehtinen	N	N	N	Y	Y	N
19 Deutch	?	?	?	?	?	?
20 Wasserman Schultz	?	?	?	?	?	?
21 Diaz-Balart	N	N	N	Y	Y	N
22 West	Y	N	N	Y	Y	N
23 Hastings	N	Y	Y	Y	N	N
24 Adams	Y	N	N	Y	Y	N
25 Rivera	Y	N	N	Y	Y	N
GEORGIA						
1 Kingston	Y	N	N	Y	Y	Y
2 Bishop	Y	N	N	Y	Y	N
3 Westmoreland	Y	N	N	Y	Y	N
4 Johnson	N	N	N	Y	N	N
5 Lewis	N	Y	Y	Y	N	N
6 Price	Y	N	N	Y	Y	N
7 Woodall	Y	N	N	Y	Y	Y
8 Scott, A.	Y	N	N	Y	Y	N
9 Graves	Y	N	N	Y	Y	N
10 Broun	Y	N	N	Y	Y	N
11 Gingrey	Y	N	N	Y	Y	N
12 Barrow	Y	N	N	Y	Y	N
13 Scott, D.	N	N	Y	Y	N	N
HAWAII						
1 Hanabusa	N	N	N	Y	N	N
2 Hirono	?	?	?	?	?	?
IDAHO						
1 Labrador	Y	N	N	Y	N	Y
2 Simpson	Y	N	N	Y	Y	N
ILLINOIS						
1 Rush	N	Y	Y	Y	N	N
2 Jackson	?	?	?	?	?	?
3 Lipinski	Y	N	N	Y	N	N
4 Gutierrez	N	Y	Y	Y	?	Y
5 Quigley	N	Y	Y	Y	N	Y
6 Roskam	Y	N	N	Y	N	N
7 Davis	?	Y	Y	Y	N	N
8 Walsh	Y	N	N	Y	Y	Y
9 Schakowsky	N	Y	Y	Y	N	Y
10 Dold	Y	N	N	Y	Y	N
11 Kinzinger	Y	N	N	Y	Y	N
12 Costello	N	Y	N	Y	Y	N
13 Biggert	N	N	N	Y	Y	N
14 Hultgren	Y	N	N	Y	Y	N
15 Johnson	Y	Y	Y	?	Y	Y

KEY   **Republicans**   Democrats

Y Voted for (yea)	X Paired against
# Paired for	– Announced against
+ Announced for	P Voted "present"
N Voted against (nay)	

C Voted "present" to avoid possible conflict of interest

? Did not vote or otherwise make a position known

	487	488	489	490	491	492
16 **Manzullo**	Y	N	N	Y	Y	N
17 **Schilling**	Y	N	N	Y	Y	N
18 **Schock**	Y	N	N	Y	Y	Y
19 **Shimkus**	Y	N	N	Y	Y	N
INDIANA						
1 Visclosky	N	N	Y	Y	N	N
2 Donnelly	Y	N	N	Y	N	N
3 **Stutzman**	Y	N	N	Y	Y	N
4 **Rokita**	Y	N	N	Y	Y	Y
5 **Burton**	Y	N	N	Y	Y	N
6 **Pence**	Y	N	N	Y	Y	N
7 Carson	N	Y	Y	Y	N	N
8 **Bucshon**	Y	N	N	Y	Y	N
9 **Young**	Y	N	N	Y	Y	N
IOWA						
1 Braley	N	Y	Y	Y	N	Y
2 Loebsack	N	N	N	Y	N	Y
3 Boswell	N	N	Y	Y	N	N
4 **Latham**	Y	N	N	Y	Y	N
5 **King**	Y	N	N	Y	Y	N
KANSAS						
1 **Huelskamp**	Y	N	Y	Y	Y	Y
2 **Jenkins**	Y	N	N	Y	Y	N
3 **Yoder**	Y	N	N	Y	Y	N
4 **Pompeo**	Y	N	N	Y	Y	N
KENTUCKY						
1 **Whitfield**	Y	N	N	Y	Y	N
2 **Guthrie**	Y	N	N	Y	Y	N
3 Yarmuth	N	N	Y	Y	N	Y
4 **Davis**	Y	N	N	Y	Y	N
5 **Rogers**	Y	N	N	Y	Y	N
6 Chandler	Y	N	N	Y	N	Y
LOUISIANA						
1 **Scalise**	Y	N	N	Y	Y	N
2 Richmond	N	N	Y	Y	N	N
3 **Landry**	Y	N	N	Y	Y	Y
4 **Fleming**	Y	N	N	Y	Y	N
5 **Alexander**	Y	N	N	Y	Y	N
6 **Cassidy**	Y	N	N	Y	Y	N
7 **Boustany**	Y	N	N	Y	Y	N
MAINE						
1 Pingree	N	Y	Y	Y	N	Y
2 Michaud	N	Y	Y	Y	N	Y
MARYLAND						
1 **Harris**	Y	N	N	Y	Y	Y
2 Ruppersberger	N	N	N	Y	N	N
3 Sarbanes	N	N	Y	Y	N	N
4 Edwards	N	Y	Y	Y	N	Y
5 Hoyer	N	N	Y	Y	N	N
6 **Bartlett**	Y	N	N	Y	Y	N
7 Cummings	N	Y	Y	Y	N	Y
8 Van Hollen	N	N	Y	Y	N	Y
MASSACHUSETTS						
1 Olver	N	Y	Y	?	N	Y
2 Neal	N	Y	Y	Y	N	Y
3 McGovern	N	Y	Y	Y	N	Y
4 Frank	N	Y	Y	Y	N	Y
5 Tsongas	N	Y	Y	Y	N	N
6 Tierney	N	Y	Y	Y	N	Y
7 Markey	N	Y	Y	Y	N	Y
8 Capuano	N	Y	Y	Y	N	Y
9 Lynch	N	N	Y	Y	N	N
10 Keating	N	Y	Y	Y	N	Y
MICHIGAN						
1 **Benishek**	Y	N	N	Y	Y	Y
2 **Huizenga**	Y	N	N	Y	Y	Y
3 **Amash**	Y	Y	Y	Y	N	Y
4 **Camp**	Y	N	N	Y	Y	Y
5 Kildee	N	N	Y	Y	N	N
6 **Upton**	Y	N	N	Y	Y	Y
7 **Walberg**	Y	N	N	Y	Y	N
8 **Rogers**	Y	N	N	Y	Y	N
9 Peters	N	N	Y	Y	Y	Y
10 **Miller**	Y	N	N	Y	Y	Y
11 Vacant						
12 Levin	N	N	Y	Y	N	N
13 Clarke	N	Y	Y	Y	N	Y
14 Conyers	N	N	Y	Y	N	Y
15 Dingell	N	N	Y	Y	N	N
MINNESOTA						
1 Walz	N	N	Y	Y	N	N
2 **Kline**	Y	N	N	Y	Y	N
3 **Paulsen**	Y	N	N	Y	Y	N
4 McCollum	N	Y	Y	Y	N	N

	487	488	489	490	491	492
5 Ellison	N	Y	Y	Y	N	N
6 **Bachmann**	Y	N	N	Y	Y	Y
7 Peterson	Y	N	Y	Y	Y	N
8 **Cravaack**	Y	N	N	Y	Y	N
MISSISSIPPI						
1 **Nunnelee**	Y	N	N	Y	Y	N
2 Thompson	N	Y	Y	Y	N	N
3 **Harper**	Y	N	N	Y	Y	N
4 **Palazzo**	Y	N	N	Y	Y	N
MISSOURI						
1 Clay	N	Y	Y	Y	N	Y
2 **Akin**	+	–	–	+	+	–
3 Carnahan	N	Y	Y	Y	N	N
4 **Hartzler**	Y	N	N	Y	Y	N
5 Cleaver	N	Y	Y	Y	N	N
6 **Graves**	Y	N	N	Y	Y	N
7 **Long**	Y	N	N	N	Y	N
8 **Emerson**	Y	N	N	Y	Y	N
9 **Luetkemeyer**	Y	N	N	Y	Y	N
MONTANA						
AL **Rehberg**	Y	N	N	Y	Y	N
NEBRASKA						
1 **Fortenberry**	Y	N	N	Y	Y	N
2 **Terry**	Y	N	N	Y	Y	N
3 **Smith**	Y	N	N	Y	Y	N
NEVADA						
1 Berkley	N	N	N	Y	N	N
2 **Amodei**	Y	N	N	Y	Y	N
3 **Heck**	Y	N	N	Y	Y	N
NEW HAMPSHIRE						
1 **Guinta**	Y	N	N	Y	Y	N
2 **Bass**	Y	N	N	Y	Y	Y
NEW JERSEY						
1 Andrews	N	N	Y	Y	N	N
2 **LoBiondo**	Y	N	N	Y	Y	N
3 **Runyan**	Y	N	N	Y	Y	N
4 **Smith**	Y	N	N	Y	Y	N
5 **Garrett**	Y	N	N	Y	Y	N
6 Pallone	N	Y	Y	Y	N	Y
7 **Lance**	Y	N	N	Y	Y	N
8 Pascrell	N	N	Y	Y	N	N
9 Rothman	N	N	Y	Y	N	N
10 Vacant						
11 **Frelinghuysen**	Y	N	N	Y	Y	N
12 Holt	N	Y	Y	Y	N	Y
13 Sires	N	N	Y	Y	N	N
NEW MEXICO						
1 Heinrich	N	N	N	Y	N	Y
2 **Pearce**	Y	N	N	Y	Y	N
3 Luján	N	N	Y	Y	N	Y
NEW YORK						
1 Bishop	?	?	?	?	?	?
2 Israel	N	N	?	Y	N	N
3 **King**	Y	N	N	Y	Y	N
4 McCarthy	N	N	Y	Y	N	N
5 Ackerman	N	N	Y	Y	N	N
6 Meeks	N	N	Y	Y	N	N
7 Crowley	N	Y	Y	Y	N	N
8 Nadler	N	Y	Y	Y	N	Y
9 **Turner**	Y	N	N	Y	Y	N
10 Towns	N	Y	Y	Y	N	N
11 Clarke	N	Y	Y	Y	N	N
12 Velázquez	N	Y	Y	Y	N	Y
13 **Grimm**	Y	N	N	Y	Y	N
14 Maloney	N	N	Y	Y	N	N
15 Rangel	N	Y	Y	Y	N	N
16 Serrano	N	Y	Y	Y	N	Y
17 Engel	N	N	Y	Y	N	N
18 Lowey	N	?	?	?	?	?
19 **Hayworth**	N	?	N	N	Y	N
20 **Gibson**	Y	N	N	Y	N	Y
21 Tonko	N	N	Y	Y	N	Y
22 Hinchey	N	N	Y	Y	N	N
23 Owens	N	N	N	Y	N	N
24 **Hanna**	N	N	N	Y	Y	N
25 **Buerkle**	?	?	?	?	?	?
26 Hochul	N	N	N	Y	N	N
27 Higgins	N	Y	Y	Y	N	N
28 Slaughter	N	Y	Y	Y	N	Y
29 **Reed**	Y	N	N	Y	Y	N
NORTH CAROLINA						
1 Butterfield	N	N	N	Y	N	N
2 **Ellmers**	Y	N	N	Y	Y	N
3 **Jones**	Y	Y	Y	Y	N	Y
4 Price	N	N	Y	Y	N	N

	487	488	489	490	491	492
5 **Foxx**	Y	N	N	Y	Y	N
6 **Coble**	Y	Y	Y	Y	Y	Y
7 McIntyre	Y	N	N	Y	Y	N
8 Kissell	Y	N	N	Y	Y	N
9 **Myrick**	Y	N	N	Y	Y	N
10 **McHenry**	Y	N	N	Y	Y	N
11 Shuler	Y	N	N	Y	Y	N
12 Watt	N	Y	Y	Y	N	N
13 Miller	N	N	Y	Y	N	N
NORTH DAKOTA						
AL **Berg**	Y	N	N	Y	Y	N
OHIO						
1 **Chabot**	Y	N	N	Y	Y	Y
2 **Schmidt**	Y	N	N	Y	Y	N
3 **Turner**	Y	N	N	Y	Y	N
4 **Jordan**	Y	N	N	Y	Y	N
5 **Latta**	Y	N	N	Y	Y	N
6 **Johnson**	Y	N	N	Y	Y	N
7 **Austria**	Y	N	N	Y	Y	N
8 **Boehner**						
9 Kaptur	N	N	Y	Y	N	N
10 Kucinich	N	Y	Y	Y	N	Y
11 Fudge	N	Y	Y	Y	N	N
12 **Tiberi**	Y	N	N	Y	Y	Y
13 Sutton	N	N	Y	Y	N	Y
14 **LaTourette**	Y	N	N	Y	Y	N
15 **Stivers**	?	?	?	?	?	?
16 **Renacci**	Y	N	Y	Y	Y	N
17 Ryan	N	N	Y	Y	N	Y
18 **Gibbs**	Y	N	N	Y	Y	N
OKLAHOMA						
1 **Sullivan**	Y	N	N	Y	?	N
2 Boren	?	?	?	?	?	?
3 **Lucas**	Y	N	N	Y	Y	N
4 **Cole**	Y	N	N	Y	Y	N
5 **Lankford**	Y	N	N	Y	Y	N
OREGON						
1 Bonamici	N	Y	Y	Y	N	Y
2 **Walden**	Y	N	N	Y	Y	Y
3 Blumenauer	N	Y	Y	?	N	Y
4 DeFazio	N	Y	Y	Y	N	Y
5 Schrader	N	N	Y	Y	Y	Y
PENNSYLVANIA						
1 Brady	N	N	Y	Y	N	N
2 Fattah	N	Y	Y	Y	N	N
3 **Kelly**	Y	N	N	Y	Y	N
4 Altmire	N	N	N	Y	N	N
5 **Thompson**	Y	N	N	Y	Y	N
6 **Gerlach**	Y	N	N	Y	Y	N
7 **Meehan**	Y	N	N	Y	Y	Y
8 **Fitzpatrick**	Y	N	N	Y	Y	N
9 **Shuster**	Y	N	N	Y	Y	N
10 **Marino**	Y	N	N	Y	Y	N
11 **Barletta**	Y	N	N	Y	Y	N
12 Critz	Y	N	N	Y	N	N
13 Schwartz	N	N	Y	Y	N	N
14 Doyle	N	Y	Y	Y	N	Y
15 **Dent**	Y	N	N	Y	Y	N
16 **Pitts**	Y	N	N	Y	Y	N
17 Holden	Y	N	N	Y	N	N
18 **Murphy**	Y	N	N	Y	Y	N
19 **Platts**	Y	N	N	Y	Y	N
RHODE ISLAND						
1 Cicilline	N	N	Y	Y	N	Y
2 Langevin	N	N	Y	Y	N	Y
SOUTH CAROLINA						
1 **Scott**	Y	N	N	Y	Y	N
2 **Wilson**	Y	N	N	Y	Y	N
3 **Duncan**	Y	N	N	Y	Y	N
4 **Gowdy**	Y	N	N	Y	Y	N
5 **Mulvaney**	Y	N	N	Y	Y	Y
6 Clyburn	N	N	Y	Y	N	N
SOUTH DAKOTA						
AL **Noem**	Y	N	N	Y	Y	N
TENNESSEE						
1 **Roe**	Y	N	N	Y	Y	N
2 **Duncan**	Y	Y	Y	Y	Y	Y
3 **Fleischmann**	?	?	?	?	?	?
4 **DesJarlais**	Y	N	N	Y	Y	N
5 Cooper	N	N	N	Y	N	Y
6 **Black**	Y	N	N	Y	Y	N
7 **Blackburn**	Y	N	N	Y	Y	N
8 **Fincher**	Y	N	N	Y	Y	N
9 Cohen	N	N	Y	Y	N	Y

	487	488	489	490	491	492
TEXAS						
1 **Gohmert**	Y	N	N	Y	Y	Y
2 **Poe**	Y	N	N	Y	Y	N
3 **Johnson, S.**	Y	N	N	Y	Y	N
4 **Hall**	Y	N	N	Y	Y	N
5 **Hensarling**	Y	N	N	Y	Y	N
6 **Barton**	Y	N	N	N	Y	N
7 **Culberson**	Y	N	N	Y	Y	N
8 **Brady**	Y	N	N	Y	Y	N
9 Green, A.	N	N	Y	Y	N	N
10 **McCaul**	Y	N	N	Y	Y	N
11 **Conaway**	Y	N	N	Y	Y	N
12 **Granger**	Y	N	N	Y	Y	N
13 **Thornberry**	Y	N	N	Y	Y	N
14 **Paul**	Y	Y	Y	N	N	Y
15 Hinojosa	N	Y	Y	Y	N	N
16 Reyes	?	?	?	?	?	?
17 **Flores**	Y	N	N	Y	Y	Y
18 Jackson Lee	?	?	?	?	?	?
19 **Neugebauer**	Y	N	N	Y	Y	N
20 Gonzalez	N	N	Y	Y	N	N
21 **Smith**	Y	N	N	Y	Y	N
22 **Olson**	Y	N	N	Y	Y	N
23 **Canseco**	Y	N	N	Y	Y	N
24 **Marchant**	Y	N	N	Y	Y	N
25 Doggett	N	N	N	Y	N	Y
26 **Burgess**	Y	N	N	Y	Y	N
27 **Farenthold**	Y	N	N	Y	Y	N
28 Cuellar	Y	?	N	Y	N	N
29 Green, G.	Y	N	Y	Y	N	N
30 Johnson, E.	N	Y	Y	Y	N	N
31 **Carter**	Y	N	N	Y	Y	N
32 **Sessions**	Y	N	N	Y	Y	N
UTAH						
1 **Bishop**	Y	N	N	Y	Y	N
2 Matheson	Y	N	N	Y	N	N
3 **Chaffetz**	Y	N	Y	Y	Y	N
VERMONT						
AL Welch	N	Y	Y	Y	N	Y
VIRGINIA						
1 **Wittman**	Y	N	N	Y	Y	N
2 **Rigell**	Y	N	N	Y	Y	N
3 Scott	N	N	Y	Y	N	N
4 **Forbes**	Y	N	N	Y	Y	N
5 **Hurt**	Y	N	N	Y	Y	N
6 **Goodlatte**	Y	N	Y	Y	Y	Y
7 **Cantor**	?	N	N	Y	Y	N
8 Moran	N	Y	Y	Y	N	N
9 **Griffith**	Y	N	Y	Y	Y	Y
10 **Wolf**	Y	N	N	Y	Y	N
11 Connolly	N	N	Y	Y	N	N
WASHINGTON						
1 Vacant						
2 Larsen	N	N	Y	Y	N	Y
3 **Herrera Beutler**	Y	N	N	Y	Y	N
4 **Hastings**	Y	N	N	Y	Y	N
5 **McMorris Rodgers**	Y	N	N	Y	Y	Y
6 Dicks	N	N	Y	Y	N	N
7 McDermott	N	Y	Y	Y	N	Y
8 **Reichert**	Y	N	N	Y	Y	N
9 Smith	N	N	Y	N	N	N
WEST VIRGINIA						
1 **McKinley**	Y	N	N	Y	Y	N
2 **Capito**	Y	N	N	Y	Y	N
3 Rahall	Y	N	Y	Y	N	N
WISCONSIN						
1 **Ryan**	Y	N	N	Y	Y	Y
2 Baldwin	N	Y	Y	Y	N	Y
3 Kind	N	N	Y	Y	N	Y
4 Moore	N	Y	Y	Y	N	Y
5 **Sensenbrenner**	Y	N	Y	Y	Y	N
6 **Petri**	Y	N	Y	Y	Y	Y
7 **Duffy**	Y	N	Y	Y	Y	Y
8 **Ribble**	Y	N	Y	Y	Y	Y
WYOMING						
AL **Lummis**	Y	N	N	Y	Y	Y

IN THE HOUSE | By Vote Number

493. **HR 5856. Fiscal 2013 Defense Appropriations/Nuclear Weapons.** Berg, R-N.D., amendment that would bar the use of funds in the bill to reduce the number of nuclear weapons delivery vehicles. These include heavy bomber aircraft, air-launched cruise missiles, nuclear-powered ballistic missile submarines, submarine-launched ballistic missiles and intercontinental ballistic missiles. Adopted in Committee of the Whole 232-183: R 220-16; D 12-167. A "nay" was a vote in support of the president's position. July 19, 2012.

494. **HR 5856. Fiscal 2013 Defense Appropriations/Overseas Contingency Operations.** Garamendi, D-Calif., amendment that would reduce funding provided in the Overseas Contingency Operations account by $12.7 billion. The reduction would not apply to: the Afghanistan Security Forces Fund; the Defense Health Program; Drug Interdiction and Counter-Drug Activities, Defense; Joint Improvised Explosive Device Defeat Fund; or the Office of the Inspector General. Rejected in Committee of the Whole 137-278: R 8-228; D 129-50. July 19, 2012.

495. **HR 5856. Fiscal 2013 Defense Appropriations/Maintain Current Spending Level.** Mulvaney, R-S.C., amendment that would decrease spending in the bill by $1.1 billion. The reduction would not apply to military personnel, the Defense Health Program or overseas contingency operations. Adopted in Committee of the Whole 247-167: R 89-146; D 158-21. July 19, 2012.

496. **HR 5856. Fiscal 2013 Defense Appropriations/Overseas Contingency Funding.** Mulvaney, R-S.C., amendment that would increase, and then decrease, overseas contingency funding for Army personnel by $4.4 billion. It also would increase, and then decrease, overseas contingency funding for Marine Corps personnel by $1.2 billion. Adopted in Committee of the Whole 238-178: R 154-82; D 84-96. July 19, 2012.

497. **HR 5856. Fiscal 2013 Defense Appropriations/TRICARE.** Stearns, R-Fla., amendment that would bar the use of funds in the bill for the Defense Department to implement new TRICARE for Life enrollment fees. Adopted in Committee of the Whole 399-17: R 236-0; D 163-17. A "nay" was a vote in support of the president's position. July 19, 2012.

498. **HR 5856. Fiscal 2013 Defense Appropriations/Passage.** Passage of the bill that would provide $605.8 billion for the Defense Department in fiscal 2013. The total includes $518.1 billion in base discretionary funding and an additional $87.7 billion for overseas contingency operations, including those in Afghanistan. Of the combined funding, about $239 billion would be for operations and maintenance, $110 billion for procurement, and $70 billion for research and development. The bill would provide $33.9 billion for the Defense Health Program and about $142 billion for military personnel, including a 1.7 percent pay raise. Passed 326-90: R 225-11; D 101-79. A "nay" was a vote in support of the president's position. July 19, 2012.

	493	494	495	496	497	498
ALABAMA						
1 Bonner	Y	N	N	Y	Y	Y
2 Roby	Y	N	N	Y	Y	Y
3 Rogers	Y	N	N	Y	Y	Y
4 Aderholt	Y	N	N	Y	Y	Y
5 Brooks	N	N	N	Y	Y	Y
6 Bachus	Y	N	N	Y	Y	Y
7 Sewell	N	Y	N	N	Y	Y
ALASKA						
AL Young	Y	N	N	N	Y	Y
ARIZONA						
1 Gosar	Y	N	Y	Y	Y	Y
2 Franks	Y	N	N	N	Y	Y
3 Quayle	Y	N	N	Y	Y	Y
4 Pastor	N	N	Y	Y	Y	Y
5 Schweikert	Y	N	Y	Y	Y	Y
6 Flake	Y	N	Y	Y	Y	Y
7 Grijalva	N	Y	N	Y	N	Y
8 Barber	N	N	N	N	Y	Y
ARKANSAS						
1 Crawford	Y	N	N	Y	Y	Y
2 Griffin	Y	N	Y	Y	Y	Y
3 Womack	Y	N	N	Y	Y	Y
4 Ross	Y	N	N	N	Y	Y
CALIFORNIA						
1 Thompson	N	Y	Y	Y	Y	N
2 Herger	Y	N	N	N	Y	Y
3 Lungren	Y	N	N	N	Y	Y
4 McClintock	Y	N	Y	Y	Y	N
5 Matsui	N	Y	Y	Y	Y	N
6 Woolsey	N	Y	Y	Y	N	N
7 Miller, George	N	Y	Y	Y	N	N
8 Pelosi	N	N	Y	N	Y	Y
9 Lee	N	Y	Y	Y	Y	N
10 Garamendi	N	Y	Y	N	Y	Y
11 McNerney	N	N	N	N	Y	Y
12 Speier	N	Y	Y	Y	Y	N
13 Stark	N	Y	Y	N	N	N
14 Eshoo	N	Y	Y	Y	Y	N
15 Honda	N	Y	?	Y	N	N
16 Lofgren	N	Y	Y	N	Y	N
17 Farr	N	Y	Y	N	Y	N
18 Cardoza	N	N	Y	Y	Y	Y
19 Denham	Y	N	N	Y	Y	Y
20 Costa	N	N	Y	Y	Y	Y
21 Nunes	Y	N	N	Y	Y	Y
22 McCarthy	Y	N	N	Y	Y	Y
23 Capps	N	Y	Y	Y	Y	N
24 Gallegly	Y	N	N	N	Y	Y
25 McKeon	Y	N	N	N	Y	Y
26 Dreier	Y	N	N	Y	Y	Y
27 Sherman	N	Y	Y	Y	Y	Y
28 Berman	N	Y	Y	Y	Y	Y
29 Schiff	N	Y	Y	Y	Y	Y
30 Waxman	N	Y	Y	N	Y	Y
31 Becerra	N	Y	Y	N	Y	N
32 Chu	N	Y	Y	Y	Y	N
33 Bass	N	Y	Y	Y	Y	N
34 Roybal-Allard	N	Y	Y	Y	Y	N
35 Waters	N	Y	Y	Y	Y	N
36 Hahn	Y	Y	Y	Y	Y	N
37 Richardson	Y	Y	Y	Y	Y	Y
38 Napolitano	N	Y	Y	Y	Y	N
39 Sánchez, Linda	N	Y	Y	Y	N	N
40 Royce	Y	N	Y	N	Y	N
41 Lewis	Y	N	N	N	Y	Y
42 Miller, Gary	Y	N	N	Y	Y	Y
43 Baca	N	N	Y	N	Y	Y
44 Calvert	Y	N	N	Y	Y	Y
45 Bono Mack	Y	N	?	N	Y	Y
46 Rohrabacher	N	N	Y	Y	Y	N
47 Sanchez, Loretta	N	Y	N	N	Y	Y
48 Campbell	N	N	Y	Y	Y	N
49 Issa	Y	N	N	Y	Y	Y
50 Bilbray	N	N	N	N	Y	Y
51 Filner	–	+	+	+	+	–
52 Hunter	Y	N	N	N	Y	Y
53 Davis	N	Y	Y	Y	Y	Y
COLORADO						
1 DeGette	N	Y	Y	Y	Y	N
2 Polis	?	?	Y	?	?	?
3 Tipton	Y	N	N	Y	Y	Y
4 Gardner	Y	N	N	Y	Y	Y
5 Lamborn	Y	N	N	Y	Y	Y
6 Coffman	Y	N	Y	Y	Y	Y
7 Perlmutter	N	Y	Y	Y	N	Y
CONNECTICUT						
1 Larson	N	Y	Y	N	Y	Y
2 Courtney	N	Y	Y	N	Y	Y
3 DeLauro	N	Y	Y	N	Y	Y
4 Himes	N	Y	Y	Y	Y	Y
5 Murphy	N	Y	Y	Y	Y	N
DELAWARE						
AL Carney	N	Y	Y	Y	Y	N
FLORIDA						
1 Miller	Y	N	N	N	Y	Y
2 Southerland	Y	N	Y	Y	Y	Y
3 Brown	?	?	?	?	?	?
4 Crenshaw	Y	N	N	Y	Y	Y
5 Nugent	Y	N	N	N	Y	Y
6 Stearns	Y	N	Y	Y	Y	Y
7 Mica	Y	N	Y	Y	Y	Y
8 Webster	Y	N	Y	Y	Y	Y
9 Bilirakis	Y	N	N	Y	Y	Y
10 Young	Y	N	N	N	Y	Y
11 Castor	N	Y	Y	N	Y	Y
12 Ross	Y	N	Y	Y	Y	Y
13 Buchanan	N	N	Y	Y	Y	Y
14 Mack	Y	N	Y	Y	Y	Y
15 Posey	Y	N	Y	Y	Y	Y
16 Rooney	Y	N	N	N	Y	Y
17 Wilson	N	Y	Y	N	Y	Y
18 Ros-Lehtinen	Y	N	N	Y	Y	Y
19 Deutch	?	?	?	?	?	?
20 Wasserman Schultz	?	?	?	?	?	?
21 Diaz-Balart	Y	N	N	N	Y	Y
22 West	Y	N	N	Y	Y	Y
23 Hastings	N	Y	Y	Y	Y	Y
24 Adams	Y	N	N	Y	Y	Y
25 Rivera	Y	N	N	Y	Y	Y
GEORGIA						
1 Kingston	Y	N	Y	Y	Y	Y
2 Bishop	Y	N	N	Y	Y	Y
3 Westmoreland	Y	N	Y	Y	Y	Y
4 Johnson	N	N	N	N	Y	N
5 Lewis	N	Y	Y	N	Y	N
6 Price	Y	N	Y	Y	Y	Y
7 Woodall	N	N	Y	Y	Y	Y
8 Scott, A.	Y	N	N	Y	Y	Y
9 Graves	Y	N	Y	Y	Y	Y
10 Broun	Y	N	Y	Y	Y	N
11 Gingrey	Y	N	N	Y	Y	Y
12 Barrow	Y	N	N	N	Y	Y
13 Scott, D.	N	N	Y	N	Y	Y
HAWAII						
1 Hanabusa	N	Y	Y	N	Y	Y
2 Hirono	?	?	?	?	?	?
IDAHO						
1 Labrador	N	N	Y	Y	Y	Y
2 Simpson	Y	N	N	N	Y	Y
ILLINOIS						
1 Rush	N	Y	Y	Y	Y	N
2 Jackson	?	?	?	?	?	?
3 Lipinski	N	N	Y	Y	Y	N
4 Gutierrez	N	Y	Y	N	Y	N
5 Quigley	N	Y	Y	N	Y	N
6 Roskam	Y	N	N	Y	Y	Y
7 Davis	N	Y	Y	Y	Y	N
8 Walsh	N	Y	Y	Y	Y	Y
9 Schakowsky	N	Y	Y	Y	Y	N
10 Dold	Y	N	N	Y	Y	Y
11 Kinzinger	Y	N	N	N	Y	Y
12 Costello	N	Y	Y	N	Y	Y
13 Biggert	Y	N	N	Y	Y	Y
14 Hultgren	Y	N	Y	Y	Y	Y
15 Johnson	Y	Y	Y	Y	Y	N

KEY   Republicans   Democrats

Y Voted for (yea)	**X** Paired against
# Paired for	**–** Announced against
+ Announced for	**P** Voted "present"
N Voted against (nay)	

C Voted "present" to avoid possible conflict of interest

? Did not vote or otherwise make a position known

	493	494	495	496	497	498
16 **Manzullo**	Y	N	Y	Y	Y	Y
17 **Schilling**	Y	N	N	Y	Y	Y
18 **Schock**	Y	N	N	N	Y	Y
19 **Shimkus**	Y	N	N	N	Y	Y
INDIANA						
1 Visclosky	N	N	Y	N	N	Y
2 Donnelly	N	N	N	N	Y	Y
3 **Stutzman**	Y	N	Y	Y	Y	Y
4 **Rokita**	Y	Y	Y	Y	Y	Y
5 **Burton**	Y	N	N	Y	Y	Y
6 **Pence**	Y	N	Y	Y	Y	Y
7 Carson	N	Y	Y	Y	Y	Y
8 **Bucshon**	Y	N	Y	Y	Y	Y
9 **Young**	Y	N	N	Y	Y	Y
IOWA						
1 Braley	N	Y	Y	N	Y	N
2 Loebsack	N	Y	Y	Y	Y	Y
3 Boswell	N	Y	Y	Y	Y	Y
4 **Latham**	Y	N	Y	Y	Y	Y
5 **King**	Y	N	N	Y	Y	Y
KANSAS						
1 **Huelskamp**	Y	N	Y	Y	Y	N
2 **Jenkins**	Y	N	N	Y	Y	Y
3 **Yoder**	Y	N	Y	Y	Y	Y
4 **Pompeo**	Y	N	Y	Y	Y	Y
KENTUCKY						
1 **Whitfield**	Y	N	N	N	Y	Y
2 **Guthrie**	Y	N	N	Y	Y	Y
3 Yarmuth	N	Y	Y	Y	Y	N
4 **Davis**	Y	N	N	N	Y	Y
5 **Rogers**	Y	N	N	N	Y	Y
6 Chandler	N	N	N	N	Y	Y
LOUISIANA						
1 **Scalise**	Y	N	Y	Y	Y	Y
2 Richmond	N	Y	Y	Y	Y	Y
3 **Landry**	Y	N	Y	Y	Y	Y
4 **Fleming**	Y	N	N	N	Y	Y
5 **Alexander**	Y	N	N	N	Y	Y
6 **Cassidy**	Y	N	N	Y	Y	Y
7 **Boustany**	Y	N	N	Y	Y	Y
MAINE						
1 Pingree	N	Y	Y	Y	Y	N
2 Michaud	N	Y	Y	Y	Y	N
MARYLAND						
1 **Harris**	Y	N	Y	N	Y	Y
2 Ruppersberger	N	N	N	N	N	Y
3 Sarbanes	N	Y	Y	N	Y	Y
4 Edwards	N	Y	Y	N	Y	N
5 Hoyer	N	N	Y	N	N	Y
6 **Bartlett**	Y	N	N	Y	Y	Y
7 Cummings	N	Y	Y	Y	Y	Y
8 Van Hollen	N	N	Y	Y	Y	N
MASSACHUSETTS						
1 Olver	N	Y	Y	N	N	N
2 Neal	N	Y	Y	N	Y	N
3 McGovern	N	Y	Y	Y	Y	N
4 Frank	N	Y	Y	Y	Y	N
5 Tsongas	N	Y	Y	Y	Y	Y
6 Tierney	N	Y	Y	N	Y	N
7 Markey	N	Y	Y	Y	Y	N
8 Capuano	N	Y	Y	N	Y	N
9 Lynch	N	Y	Y	N	Y	Y
10 Keating	N	Y	Y	Y	Y	N
MICHIGAN						
1 **Benishek**	Y	Y	Y	Y	Y	Y
2 **Huizenga**	Y	N	Y	Y	Y	Y
3 **Amash**	N	Y	Y	Y	Y	N
4 **Camp**	Y	N	N	N	Y	Y
5 Kildee	N	Y	Y	N	Y	Y
6 **Upton**	Y	N	N	N	Y	Y
7 **Walberg**	Y	N	Y	Y	Y	Y
8 **Rogers**	Y	N	N	N	Y	Y
9 Peters	N	Y	Y	Y	Y	Y
10 **Miller**	Y	N	Y	Y	Y	Y
11 Vacant						
12 Levin	N	N	Y	N	Y	N
13 Clarke	N	Y	Y	N	Y	N
14 Conyers	N	Y	Y	Y	Y	N
15 Dingell	N	N	Y	N	Y	Y
MINNESOTA						
1 Walz	N	N	N	N	Y	Y
2 **Kline**	Y	N	N	Y	Y	Y
3 **Paulsen**	Y	N	N	Y	Y	Y
4 McCollum	N	Y	Y	N	Y	N
5 Ellison	N	Y	Y	N	Y	N
6 **Bachmann**	Y	N	N	N	Y	Y
7 Peterson	Y	N	Y	Y	Y	Y
8 **Cravaack**	Y	N	N	Y	Y	Y
MISSISSIPPI						
1 **Nunnelee**	Y	N	N	Y	Y	Y
2 Thompson	N	Y	Y	Y	Y	Y
3 **Harper**	Y	N	N	Y	Y	Y
4 **Palazzo**	Y	N	N	Y	Y	Y
MISSOURI						
1 Clay	N	Y	Y	N	Y	N
2 **Akin**	+	–	–	+	+	+
3 Carnahan	N	Y	Y	N	Y	Y
4 **Hartzler**	Y	N	N	N	Y	Y
5 Cleaver	N	Y	Y	N	Y	N
6 **Graves**	Y	N	N	Y	Y	Y
7 **Long**	Y	N	N	Y	Y	Y
8 **Emerson**	Y	N	N	N	Y	Y
9 **Luetkemeyer**	Y	N	N	Y	Y	Y
MONTANA						
AL **Rehberg**	Y	N	N	N	Y	Y
NEBRASKA						
1 **Fortenberry**	N	N	Y	N	Y	Y
2 **Terry**	Y	N	Y	Y	Y	Y
3 **Smith**	Y	N	N	Y	Y	Y
NEVADA						
1 Berkley	N	N	Y	Y	Y	Y
2 **Amodei**	Y	N	Y	Y	Y	Y
3 **Heck**	Y	N	N	N	Y	Y
NEW HAMPSHIRE						
1 **Guinta**	Y	N	Y	Y	Y	Y
2 **Bass**	Y	N	Y	Y	Y	Y
NEW JERSEY						
1 Andrews	N	Y	Y	N	Y	Y
2 **LoBiondo**	Y	N	N	N	Y	Y
3 **Runyan**	Y	N	N	Y	Y	Y
4 **Smith**	Y	N	N	N	Y	Y
5 **Garrett**	Y	N	Y	Y	Y	Y
6 Pallone	N	Y	Y	Y	Y	N
7 **Lance**	Y	N	Y	Y	Y	Y
8 Pascrell	N	Y	Y	Y	Y	Y
9 Rothman	N	N	Y	N	Y	Y
10 Vacant						
11 **Frelinghuysen**	Y	N	N	N	Y	Y
12 Holt	N	Y	Y	Y	Y	N
13 Sires	N	Y	Y	Y	Y	Y
NEW MEXICO						
1 Heinrich	N	Y	Y	Y	Y	Y
2 **Pearce**	Y	N	N	Y	Y	Y
3 Luján	N	N	Y	N	Y	Y
NEW YORK						
1 Bishop	?	?	?	?	?	?
2 Israel	N	N	N	N	Y	Y
3 **King**	Y	N	N	N	Y	Y
4 McCarthy	Y	N	Y	Y	Y	Y
5 Ackerman	N	N	N	N	Y	Y
6 Meeks	N	Y	Y	Y	Y	Y
7 Crowley	N	Y	Y	Y	Y	Y
8 Nadler	N	Y	Y	Y	Y	N
9 **Turner**	Y	N	N	N	Y	Y
10 Towns	N	Y	N	Y	Y	N
11 Clarke	N	Y	Y	N	Y	N
12 Velázquez	N	Y	Y	Y	Y	N
13 **Grimm**	Y	N	N	Y	Y	Y
14 Maloney	N	Y	Y	N	Y	Y
15 Rangel	N	Y	Y	Y	Y	N
16 Serrano	N	Y	Y	Y	Y	N
17 Engel	N	Y	N	N	Y	Y
18 Lowey	?	?	Y	N	Y	Y
19 **Hayworth**	Y	N	N	N	Y	Y
20 **Gibson**	N	N	Y	Y	Y	Y
21 Tonko	N	Y	Y	N	Y	N
22 Hinchey	N	Y	Y	N	Y	N
23 Owens	N	N	N	N	Y	Y
24 **Hanna**	Y	N	N	N	Y	Y
25 **Buerkle**	?	?	?	?	?	?
26 Hochul	N	N	N	N	Y	Y
27 Higgins	N	Y	N	Y	Y	Y
28 Slaughter	N	Y	Y	N	Y	N
29 **Reed**	Y	N	Y	Y	Y	Y
NORTH CAROLINA						
1 Butterfield	N	Y	Y	N	Y	Y
2 **Ellmers**	Y	N	N	N	Y	Y
3 **Jones**	N	Y	Y	Y	Y	N
4 Price	N	Y	Y	N	Y	N
5 **Foxx**	Y	N	N	N	Y	Y
6 **Coble**	Y	N	Y	Y	Y	Y
7 McIntyre	Y	N	N	N	Y	Y
8 Kissell	Y	N	N	N	Y	Y
9 **Myrick**	Y	N	N	N	Y	Y
10 **McHenry**	Y	N	Y	N	Y	Y
11 Shuler	Y	N	Y	Y	N	Y
12 Watt	N	Y	Y	N	Y	N
13 Miller	N	Y	Y	N	Y	Y
NORTH DAKOTA						
AL **Berg**	Y	N	N	Y	Y	Y
OHIO						
1 **Chabot**	Y	N	Y	Y	Y	Y
2 **Schmidt**	Y	N	N	Y	Y	Y
3 **Turner**	Y	N	N	N	Y	Y
4 **Jordan**	Y	N	Y	Y	Y	Y
5 **Latta**	Y	N	N	Y	Y	Y
6 **Johnson**	Y	N	N	Y	Y	Y
7 **Austria**	Y	N	N	N	Y	Y
8 **Boehner**						
9 Kaptur	N	N	Y	N	Y	Y
10 Kucinich	N	Y	Y	Y	Y	N
11 Fudge	N	Y	Y	N	Y	N
12 **Tiberi**	Y	N	N	N	Y	Y
13 Sutton	N	Y	Y	Y	Y	Y
14 **LaTourette**	Y	N	Y	Y	Y	Y
15 **Stivers**	?	?	?	?	?	?
16 **Renacci**	N	N	Y	Y	Y	Y
17 Ryan	N	N	Y	N	Y	N
18 **Gibbs**	Y	N	Y	Y	Y	Y
OKLAHOMA						
1 **Sullivan**	Y	N	N	Y	Y	Y
2 Boren	?	?	?	?	?	?
3 **Lucas**	Y	N	N	N	Y	Y
4 **Cole**	Y	N	N	N	Y	Y
5 **Lankford**	Y	N	N	Y	Y	Y
OREGON						
1 Bonamici	N	Y	Y	Y	Y	N
2 **Walden**	Y	N	N	Y	Y	Y
3 Blumenauer	N	Y	Y	N	N	N
4 DeFazio	N	Y	Y	Y	Y	N
5 Schrader	N	Y	Y	Y	Y	N
PENNSYLVANIA						
1 Brady	N	Y	Y	Y	Y	Y
2 Fattah	N	Y	Y	N	Y	Y
3 **Kelly**	Y	N	N	N	Y	Y
4 Altmire	N	N	N	N	Y	Y
5 **Thompson**	N	N	N	Y	Y	Y
6 **Gerlach**	Y	N	N	Y	Y	Y
7 **Meehan**	Y	N	N	N	Y	Y
8 **Fitzpatrick**	Y	N	Y	N	Y	Y
9 **Shuster**	Y	N	Y	Y	Y	Y
10 **Marino**	Y	N	N	Y	Y	Y
11 **Barletta**	Y	N	N	Y	Y	Y
12 Critz	N	N	Y	N	Y	Y
13 Schwartz	N	N	Y	N	Y	N
14 Doyle	N	Y	Y	N	Y	N
15 **Dent**	N	N	N	N	Y	Y
16 **Pitts**	Y	N	N	Y	Y	Y
17 Holden	N	N	Y	N	Y	Y
18 **Murphy**	Y	N	N	Y	Y	Y
19 **Platts**	Y	N	N	N	Y	Y
RHODE ISLAND						
1 Cicilline	N	Y	Y	N	Y	Y
2 Langevin	N	N	Y	N	Y	Y
SOUTH CAROLINA						
1 **Scott**	Y	N	Y	Y	Y	Y
2 **Wilson**	Y	N	N	N	Y	Y
3 **Duncan**	Y	N	Y	Y	Y	Y
4 **Gowdy**	Y	N	Y	Y	Y	Y
5 **Mulvaney**	Y	N	Y	Y	Y	Y
6 Clyburn	Y	Y	Y	N	Y	Y
SOUTH DAKOTA						
AL **Noem**	Y	N	N	Y	Y	Y
TENNESSEE						
1 **Roe**	Y	N	Y	Y	Y	Y
2 **Duncan**	N	Y	Y	Y	Y	N
3 **Fleischmann**	?	?	?	?	?	?
4 **DesJarlais**	Y	N	N	Y	Y	Y
5 Cooper	N	N	Y	N	N	Y
6 **Black**	Y	N	Y	Y	Y	Y
7 **Blackburn**	Y	N	N	Y	Y	Y
8 **Fincher**	Y	N	Y	Y	Y	Y
9 Cohen	N	Y	Y	Y	Y	N
TEXAS						
1 **Gohmert**	Y	N	Y	Y	Y	Y
2 **Poe**	Y	N	N	Y	Y	Y
3 **Johnson, S.**	Y	N	N	N	Y	Y
4 **Hall**	Y	N	N	N	Y	Y
5 **Hensarling**	Y	N	Y	Y	Y	Y
6 **Barton**	Y	N	Y	Y	Y	Y
7 **Culberson**	Y	N	N	N	Y	Y
8 **Brady**	Y	N	Y	Y	Y	Y
9 Green, A.	N	N	Y	N	Y	Y
10 **McCaul**	Y	N	N	N	Y	Y
11 **Conaway**	Y	N	N	N	Y	Y
12 **Granger**	Y	N	N	N	Y	Y
13 **Thornberry**	Y	N	N	N	Y	Y
14 **Paul**	N	Y	Y	Y	Y	N
15 Hinojosa	N	Y	Y	Y	Y	Y
16 Reyes	?	?	?	?	?	?
17 **Flores**	Y	N	Y	Y	Y	Y
18 Jackson Lee	?	?	?	?	?	?
19 **Neugebauer**	Y	N	Y	Y	Y	Y
20 Gonzalez	N	N	Y	Y	Y	Y
21 **Smith**	Y	N	N	N	Y	Y
22 **Olson**	Y	N	N	N	Y	Y
23 **Canseco**	Y	N	N	N	Y	Y
24 **Marchant**	Y	N	Y	N	Y	Y
25 Doggett	N	Y	Y	Y	Y	Y
26 **Burgess**	Y	N	Y	Y	Y	Y
27 **Farenthold**	Y	N	N	Y	Y	Y
28 Cuellar	Y	N	Y	Y	Y	Y
29 Green, G.	N	N	Y	N	Y	Y
30 Johnson, E.	N	Y	Y	N	N	Y
31 **Carter**	Y	N	N	N	Y	Y
32 **Sessions**	Y	N	Y	Y	Y	Y
UTAH						
1 **Bishop**	Y	N	N	N	Y	Y
2 Matheson	N	N	Y	Y	Y	Y
3 **Chaffetz**	Y	N	Y	Y	Y	Y
VERMONT						
AL Welch	N	Y	Y	Y	Y	N
VIRGINIA						
1 **Wittman**	Y	N	N	N	Y	Y
2 **Rigell**	Y	N	N	N	Y	Y
3 Scott	N	Y	Y	N	Y	Y
4 **Forbes**	Y	N	N	N	Y	Y
5 **Hurt**	Y	N	Y	Y	Y	Y
6 **Goodlatte**	Y	N	Y	Y	Y	Y
7 **Cantor**	Y	N	N	Y	Y	Y
8 Moran	N	Y	Y	Y	N	Y
9 **Griffith**	Y	N	Y	Y	Y	Y
10 **Wolf**	Y	N	N	N	Y	Y
11 Connolly	N	N	Y	N	Y	Y
WASHINGTON						
1 Vacant						
2 Larsen	N	Y	Y	N	N	Y
3 **Herrera Beutler**	Y	N	Y	Y	Y	Y
4 **Hastings**	Y	N	N	N	Y	Y
5 **McMorris Rodgers**	Y	N	N	N	Y	Y
6 Dicks	N	N	Y	N	N	Y
7 McDermott	N	Y	Y	N	N	N
8 **Reichert**	Y	N	N	N	Y	Y
9 Smith	N	N	Y	Y	N	Y
WEST VIRGINIA						
1 **McKinley**	Y	N	N	N	Y	Y
2 **Capito**	Y	N	N	Y	Y	Y
3 Rahall	N	Y	Y	Y	Y	Y
WISCONSIN						
1 **Ryan**	Y	N	N	Y	Y	Y
2 Baldwin	N	Y	Y	Y	Y	N
3 Kind	N	Y	Y	Y	Y	N
4 Moore	N	Y	Y	Y	Y	N
5 **Sensenbrenner**	Y	N	Y	Y	Y	Y
6 **Petri**	Y	Y	Y	Y	Y	Y
7 **Duffy**	Y	N	Y	Y	Y	Y
8 **Ribble**	Y	N	Y	Y	Y	Y
WYOMING						
AL **Lummis**	Y	N	Y	Y	Y	Y

IN THE HOUSE | By Vote Number

499. HR 2362. **Tribal-Land Leases/Passage.** Cole, R-Okla., motion to suspend the rules and pass the bill that would allow up to six tribes to participate in a demonstration project in which they could lease tribal lands held in trust by the federal government to private entities from Turkey and other World Trade Organization countries without having to get approval from the Interior secretary. Motion rejected 222-160: R 179-42; D 43-118. A two-thirds majority of those present and voting (255 in this case) is required for passage under suspension of the rules. July 23, 2012.

500. S 2039. **Levee Construction/Passage.** Young, R-Alaska, motion to suspend the rules and pass the bill that would allow state, local or tribal governments in North Dakota that participate in the National Flood Insurance Program to construct levees on certain properties otherwise designated as open space land. It would require a government that builds a levee to submit an annual maintenance plan to the Federal Emergency Management Agency and the Army Corps of Engineers. Motion rejected 126-254: R 117-103; D 9-151. A two-thirds majority of those present and voting (254 in this case) is required for passage under suspension of the rules. July 23, 2012.

501. HR 3477. **David McNerney Post Office/Passage.** Poe, R-Texas, motion to suspend the rules and pass the bill that would designate a post office in Crosby, Texas, as the "Army 1st Sgt. David McNerney Post Office Building." Motion agreed to 379-0: R 219-0; D 160-0. A two-thirds majority of those present and voting (253 in this case) is required for passage under suspension of the rules. July 23, 2012.

502. HR 4078, HR 6082. **Regulatory Revisions and Offshore Oil and Gas Leasing /Previous Question.** Foxx, R-N.C., motion to order the previous question (thus ending debate and the possibility of amendment) on the rule (H Res 738) that would provide for House floor consideration of a package (HR 4078) of regulatory measures and a bill (HR 6082) that would replace the administration's offshore leasing plan and open additional areas to oil and gas drilling. Motion agreed to 238-177: R 235-0; D 3-177. July 24, 2012.

503. HR 4078, HR 6082. **Regulatory Revisions and Offshore Oil and Gas Leasing/Rule.** Adoption of the rule (H Res 738) that would provide for House floor consideration of a package (HR 4078) of regulatory measures and a bill (HR 6082) that would replace the administration's offshore leasing plan and open additional areas to oil and gas drilling. Adopted 244-170: R 235-0; D 9-170. July 24, 2012.

504. HR 6082. **Republican Offshore Oil and Gas Drilling Plan/ Environmental-Impact Statement.** Holt, D-N.J., amendment that would strike the provision that would require the Interior secretary to provide an environmental impact statement for all new drilling areas under the bill. Rejected in Committee of the Whole 163-253: R 8-230; D 155-23. July 25, 2012.

505. HR 6082. **Republican Offshore Oil and Gas Drilling Plan/Gas Exportation Ban.** Markey, D-Mass., amendment that would prohibit the exportation of any gas resources produced as a result of lease sales required under the bill. Rejected in Committee of the Whole 158-262: R 6-232; D 152-30. July 25, 2012.

	499	500	501	502	503	504	505
ALABAMA							
1 Bonner	Y	N	Y	Y	Y	N	N
2 Roby	Y	N	Y	Y	Y	N	N
3 Rogers	Y	Y	Y	Y	Y	N	N
4 Aderholt	Y	N	Y	Y	Y	N	N
5 Brooks	Y	N	Y	Y	Y	N	N
6 Bachus	Y	Y	Y	Y	Y	N	N
7 Sewell	N	N	Y	N	N	Y	N
ALASKA							
AL Young	Y	Y	Y	?	Y	N	N
ARIZONA							
1 Gosar	?	?	?	Y	Y	N	N
2 Franks	Y	N	Y	Y	Y	N	N
3 Quayle	Y	N	Y	Y	Y	N	N
4 Pastor	Y	N	Y	N	N	Y	Y
5 Schweikert	Y	N	Y	Y	Y	N	N
6 Flake	?	?	?	Y	Y	N	N
7 Grijalva	N	N	Y	?	N	Y	?
8 Barber	N	N	Y	N	N	Y	Y
ARKANSAS							
1 Crawford	Y	Y	Y	Y	Y	N	N
2 Griffin	Y	N	Y	Y	Y	N	N
3 Womack	Y	Y	Y	Y	Y	N	N
4 Ross	Y	Y	Y	Y	Y	N	N
CALIFORNIA							
1 Thompson	N	N	Y	N	N	Y	Y
2 Herger	Y	Y	Y	Y	Y	N	N
3 Lungren	Y	Y	Y	Y	Y	N	N
4 McClintock	Y	N	Y	Y	Y	N	N
5 Matsui	N	N	Y	N	N	Y	Y
6 Woolsey	N	N	Y	N	N	+	Y
7 Miller, George	–	–	+	N	N	Y	Y
8 Pelosi	N	?	?	N	N	Y	Y
9 Lee	–	–	+	–	–	Y	Y
10 Garamendi	Y	N	Y	N	N	?	?
11 McNerney	Y	N	N	N	N	Y	Y
12 Speier	?	?	?	N	N	N	?
13 Stark	N	N	Y	N	N	Y	Y
14 Eshoo	N	N	Y	N	N	Y	Y
15 Honda	?	?	?	N	N	N	Y
16 Lofgren	N	N	Y	N	N	Y	Y
17 Farr	?	?	?	N	N	Y	Y
18 Cardoza	?	?	?	N	N	N	N
19 Denham	N	N	Y	Y	Y	N	N
20 Costa	N	N	Y	N	N	?	N
21 Nunes	N	N	Y	Y	Y	N	N
22 McCarthy	N	Y	Y	Y	Y	N	N
23 Capps	N	N	Y	N	N	Y	Y
24 Gallegly	Y	Y	Y	Y	Y	N	N
25 McKeon	Y	N	Y	Y	Y	N	N
26 Dreier	Y	Y	Y	Y	Y	N	N
27 Sherman	N	N	Y	N	N	Y	Y
28 Berman	?	?	?	N	N	Y	Y
29 Schiff	N	N	Y	N	N	Y	Y
30 Waxman	N	N	Y	N	N	Y	Y
31 Becerra	–	–	?	N	N	Y	Y
32 Chu	N	N	Y	N	N	Y	Y
33 Bass	Y	N	Y	?	?	N	Y
34 Roybal-Allard	N	N	Y	N	N	Y	Y
35 Waters	?	?	?	N	N	Y	Y
36 Hahn	N	N	Y	N	N	Y	Y
37 Richardson	Y	N	Y	N	N	Y	Y
38 Napolitano	N	N	Y	N	N	Y	Y
39 Sánchez, Linda	N	N	Y	N	N	Y	Y
40 Royce	N	N	Y	Y	Y	N	N
41 Lewis	Y	Y	Y	Y	Y	N	N
42 Miller, Gary	?	?	?	Y	Y	N	N
43 Baca	N	N	Y	N	N	Y	Y
44 Calvert	Y	N	Y	Y	Y	N	N
45 Bono Mack	Y	Y	Y	Y	Y	N	N
46 Rohrabacher	?	?	?	Y	Y	N	N
47 Sanchez, Loretta	N	N	Y	N	N	Y	Y
48 Campbell	N	N	Y	Y	Y	N	N
49 Issa	Y	Y	Y	Y	Y	N	N
50 Bilbray	N	N	Y	Y	Y	N	N
51 Filner	–	–	+	N	N	Y	Y
52 Hunter	Y	Y	Y	Y	Y	N	N
53 Davis	N	N	Y	N	N	Y	Y
COLORADO							
1 DeGette	N	N	Y	N	N	Y	Y
2 Polis	Y	N	Y	N	N	Y	N
3 Tipton	Y	Y	Y	Y	Y	N	N
4 Gardner	Y	Y	Y	Y	Y	N	N
5 Lamborn	Y	N	Y	Y	Y	N	N
6 Coffman	N	Y	Y	Y	Y	N	N
7 Perlmutter	?	?	?	N	N	Y	N
CONNECTICUT							
1 Larson	Y	N	Y	N	N	Y	Y
2 Courtney	N	N	Y	N	N	Y	N
3 DeLauro	N	N	Y	N	N	Y	Y
4 Himes	N	N	Y	N	N	Y	Y
5 Murphy	?	?	?	N	N	Y	Y
DELAWARE							
AL Carney	N	N	Y	N	N	Y	Y
FLORIDA							
1 Miller	N	N	Y	Y	Y	N	N
2 Southerland	N	Y	Y	Y	Y	N	N
3 Brown	N	N	Y	N	N	Y	Y
4 Crenshaw	Y	Y	Y	Y	Y	N	N
5 Nugent	N	N	Y	Y	Y	N	N
6 Stearns	Y	N	Y	Y	Y	N	N
7 Mica	Y	N	Y	Y	Y	N	N
8 Webster	Y	N	Y	Y	Y	N	N
9 Bilirakis	N	Y	Y	Y	Y	N	N
10 Young	N	N	Y	Y	Y	N	N
11 Castor	N	N	Y	N	N	Y	Y
12 Ross	N	Y	Y	Y	Y	N	N
13 Buchanan	Y	Y	Y	Y	Y	N	N
14 Mack	?	?	?	Y	Y	N	N
15 Posey	Y	Y	Y	Y	Y	N	N
16 Rooney	N	N	Y	Y	Y	N	–
17 Wilson	N	N	Y	N	N	Y	Y
18 Ros-Lehtinen	Y	Y	Y	Y	Y	N	N
19 Deutch	N	N	Y	N	N	Y	Y
20 Wasserman Schultz	N	N	Y	N	N	Y	Y
21 Diaz-Balart	N	N	Y	Y	Y	N	N
22 West	N	N	Y	Y	Y	N	N
23 Hastings	Y	N	Y	N	?	Y	Y
24 Adams	N	N	Y	Y	Y	N	N
25 Rivera	N	Y	Y	Y	Y	N	N
GEORGIA							
1 Kingston	Y	Y	Y	Y	Y	N	N
2 Bishop	Y	N	Y	N	N	N	Y
3 Westmoreland	N	Y	Y	N	N	Y	Y
4 Johnson	Y	N	Y	N	N	Y	Y
5 Lewis	N	N	Y	N	N	Y	Y
6 Price	Y	N	Y	Y	Y	N	N
7 Woodall	N	N	Y	Y	Y	N	N
8 Scott, A.	Y	Y	Y	Y	Y	N	N
9 Graves	N	Y	Y	Y	Y	?	N
10 Broun	Y	N	Y	Y	Y	N	N
11 Gingrey	?	?	?	Y	Y	N	N
12 Barrow	N	N	Y	N	N	Y	Y
13 Scott, D.	N	N	Y	N	N	Y	Y
HAWAII							
1 Hanabusa	Y	N	Y	N	N	Y	Y
2 Hirono	?	?	?	?	?	?	?
IDAHO							
1 Labrador	?	N	Y	Y	Y	N	N
2 Simpson	Y	N	Y	Y	Y	N	N
ILLINOIS							
1 Rush	N	N	Y	N	N	Y	Y
2 Jackson	?	?	?	?	?	?	?
3 Lipinski	N	N	Y	N	N	Y	Y
4 Gutierrez	?	?	?	N	N	Y	Y
5 Quigley	N	N	Y	N	N	Y	Y
6 Roskam	Y	Y	Y	Y	Y	N	N
7 Davis	N	N	Y	N	N	Y	Y
8 Walsh	N	N	Y	Y	Y	N	N
9 Schakowsky	N	N	Y	N	–	Y	Y
10 Dold	N	N	Y	Y	Y	N	N
11 Kinzinger	Y	N	Y	Y	Y	N	N
12 Costello	N	N	Y	N	N	N	Y
13 Biggert	Y	N	Y	Y	Y	N	N
14 Hultgren	Y	N	Y	Y	Y	N	N
15 Johnson	+	–	+	Y	Y	Y	N

KEY **Republicans** Democrats

Y Voted for (yea)	**X** Paired against	**C** Voted "present" to avoid possible conflict of interest
# Paired for	**–** Announced against	
+ Announced for	**P** Voted "present"	**?** Did not vote or otherwise make a position known
N Voted against (nay)		

	499	500	501	502	503	504	505
16 **Manzullo**	Y	N	Y	Y	Y	N	N
17 **Schilling**	Y	N	Y	Y	Y	N	N
18 **Schock**	Y	?	Y	Y	Y	N	N
19 **Shimkus**	Y	Y	Y	Y	Y	N	N
INDIANA							
1 Visclosky	N	N	Y	N	N	Y	N
2 Donnelly	?	?	?	N	Y	N	N
3 **Stutzman**	Y	N	Y	Y	Y	N	N
4 **Rokita**	?	N	Y	Y	Y	N	N
5 **Burton**	?	?	?	Y	Y	N	N
6 **Pence**	Y	N	Y	Y	Y	N	N
7 Carson	N	N	Y	N	N	Y	Y
8 **Bucshon**	Y	N	?	Y	Y	N	N
9 **Young**	Y	N	Y	Y	Y	N	N
IOWA							
1 Braley	N	Y	Y	N	N	Y	Y
2 Loebsack	N	N	Y	N	N	Y	Y
3 Boswell	N	N	Y	N	N	Y	Y
4 **Latham**	Y	N	Y	Y	Y	N	N
5 **King**	Y	Y	Y	Y	Y	N	N
KANSAS							
1 **Huelskamp**	N	Y	Y	Y	Y	N	N
2 **Jenkins**	Y	Y	Y	Y	Y	N	N
3 **Yoder**	Y	Y	Y	Y	Y	N	N
4 **Pompeo**	Y	Y	Y	Y	Y	N	N
KENTUCKY							
1 **Whitfield**	Y	Y	Y	Y	Y	N	N
2 **Guthrie**	Y	Y	Y	Y	Y	N	N
3 Yarmuth	N	N	Y	N	N	Y	Y
4 **Davis**	Y	Y	Y	Y	Y	N	N
5 **Rogers**	?	?	?	Y	Y	N	N
6 Chandler	Y	N	Y	N	N	Y	Y
LOUISIANA							
1 **Scalise**	Y	Y	Y	Y	Y	N	N
2 Richmond	N	N	Y	N	?	?	?
3 **Landry**	Y	Y	Y	Y	Y	N	N
4 **Fleming**	Y	N	Y	Y	Y	N	N
5 **Alexander**	Y	N	Y	Y	Y	N	N
6 **Cassidy**	Y	N	Y	Y	Y	N	N
7 **Boustany**	Y	N	Y	Y	Y	N	N
MAINE							
1 Pingree	N	N	Y	N	N	Y	Y
2 Michaud	N	N	Y	N	N	Y	Y
MARYLAND							
1 **Harris**	Y	Y	Y	Y	Y	N	N
2 Ruppersberger	Y	N	Y	N	N	Y	Y
3 Sarbanes	N	N	Y	N	N	Y	Y
4 Edwards	Y	N	Y	–	–	Y	Y
5 Hoyer	N	N	Y	N	N	?	N
6 **Bartlett**	Y	N	Y	Y	Y	N	N
7 Cummings	N	N	Y	N	N	Y	Y
8 Van Hollen	N	N	Y	N	N	Y	Y
MASSACHUSETTS							
1 Olver	?	?	?	N	N	Y	Y
2 Neal	N	N	Y	N	N	Y	Y
3 McGovern	N	N	Y	N	N	Y	Y
4 Frank	N	N	Y	N	N	Y	Y
5 Tsongas	N	N	Y	N	N	Y	Y
6 Tierney	N	N	Y	N	N	Y	Y
7 Markey	N	N	Y	N	N	Y	Y
8 Capuano	N	N	Y	N	N	Y	Y
9 Lynch	N	N	Y	N	N	Y	Y
10 Keating	N	N	Y	N	N	Y	Y
MICHIGAN							
1 **Benishek**	Y	Y	Y	Y	Y	N	N
2 **Huizenga**	Y	N	Y	Y	Y	N	N
3 **Amash**	N	N	Y	Y	Y	N	N
4 **Camp**	Y	Y	Y	Y	Y	N	N
5 Kildee	N	N	Y	N	N	Y	Y
6 **Upton**	N	N	Y	Y	Y	N	N
7 **Walberg**	Y	Y	Y	Y	Y	N	N
8 **Rogers**	Y	N	Y	Y	Y	N	N
9 Peters	–	–	Y	N	N	Y	Y
10 **Miller**	Y	N	Y	Y	Y	N	N
11 Vacant							
12 Levin	N	N	Y	N	N	Y	Y
13 Clarke	N	N	Y	N	N	Y	Y
14 Conyers	–	–	+	N	N	Y	Y
15 Dingell	N	N	Y	N	N	Y	N
MINNESOTA							
1 Walz	N	N	Y	N	N	Y	Y
2 **Kline**	Y	Y	Y	Y	Y	N	N
3 **Paulsen**	Y	Y	+	Y	Y	N	N
4 McCollum	Y	N	Y	N	N	Y	Y

	499	500	501	502	503	504	505
5 Ellison	–	–	+	N	N	Y	Y
6 **Bachmann**	Y	Y	Y	Y	Y	N	N
7 Peterson	Y	Y	Y	N	N	N	N
8 **Cravaack**	Y	Y	Y	Y	Y	N	N
MISSISSIPPI							
1 **Nunnelee**	Y	N	Y	Y	Y	N	N
2 Thompson	N	N	Y	N	N	Y	Y
3 **Harper**	Y	Y	Y	Y	Y	N	N
4 **Palazzo**	N	N	Y	Y	Y	N	N
MISSOURI							
1 Clay	N	N	Y	N	N	Y	Y
2 **Akin**	?	?	?	+	+	N	N
3 Carnahan	Y	N	Y	N	N	Y	Y
4 **Hartzler**	Y	+	Y	Y	Y	N	N
5 Cleaver	N	N	Y	?	N	Y	Y
6 **Graves**	+	+	+	Y	Y	N	N
7 **Long**	Y	Y	Y	Y	Y	N	N
8 **Emerson**	Y	Y	Y	Y	Y	N	N
9 **Luetkemeyer**	Y	Y	Y	Y	Y	N	N
MONTANA							
AL **Rehberg**	Y	Y	Y	Y	Y	N	N
NEBRASKA							
1 **Fortenberry**	N	Y	Y	Y	Y	N	Y
2 **Terry**	Y	Y	Y	Y	Y	N	N
3 **Smith**	Y	Y	Y	Y	Y	N	N
NEVADA							
1 Berkley	N	N	Y	N	N	Y	Y
2 **Amodei**	Y	Y	Y	Y	Y	N	N
3 **Heck**	Y	Y	Y	Y	Y	N	N
NEW HAMPSHIRE							
1 **Guinta**	Y	N	Y	Y	Y	N	N
2 **Bass**	Y	N	Y	Y	Y	Y	N
NEW JERSEY							
1 Andrews	N	N	Y	N	N	Y	Y
2 **LoBiondo**	N	N	Y	Y	Y	Y	Y
3 **Runyan**	Y	N	Y	Y	Y	N	N
4 **Smith**	N	N	Y	Y	Y	Y	Y
5 **Garrett**	Y	Y	Y	Y	Y	N	N
6 Pallone	N	N	Y	N	N	Y	Y
7 **Lance**	Y	N	Y	Y	Y	N	N
8 Pascrell	Y	N	Y	N	N	Y	Y
9 Rothman	N	N	Y	N	N	Y	Y
10 Vacant							
11 **Frelinghuysen**	N	Y	Y	Y	Y	N	N
12 Holt	N	N	Y	N	N	Y	Y
13 Sires	N	N	Y	N	N	Y	Y
NEW MEXICO							
1 Heinrich	Y	N	Y	N	N	Y	N
2 **Pearce**	Y	Y	Y	Y	Y	N	N
3 Luján	Y	N	Y	N	N	Y	N
NEW YORK							
1 Bishop	N	N	Y	N	N	Y	Y
2 Israel	N	N	Y	N	N	Y	Y
3 **King**	N	Y	Y	Y	Y	N	N
4 McCarthy	N	N	Y	N	N	Y	Y
5 Ackerman	?	?	?	N	N	Y	Y
6 Meeks	Y	N	Y	N	N	?	Y
7 Crowley	N	N	Y	N	N	Y	Y
8 Nadler	N	N	Y	N	N	?	Y
9 **Turner**	Y	Y	Y	Y	Y	N	N
10 Towns	Y	N	Y	N	N	Y	Y
11 Clarke	N	N	Y	N	N	Y	Y
12 Velázquez	N	N	Y	N	N	Y	Y
13 **Grimm**	N	Y	Y	Y	Y	N	N
14 Maloney	N	N	Y	N	N	Y	Y
15 Rangel	N	N	Y	N	N	Y	Y
16 Serrano	N	N	Y	N	N	Y	Y
17 Engel	N	N	Y	N	N	?	Y
18 Lowey	N	N	Y	N	N	N	Y
19 **Hayworth**	Y	N	Y	Y	Y	N	N
20 **Gibson**	Y	Y	Y	Y	Y	N	Y
21 Tonko	N	N	Y	N	N	Y	Y
22 Hinchey	N	N	Y	N	N	Y	Y
23 Owens	Y	N	Y	Y	Y	N	Y
24 **Hanna**	Y	N	Y	Y	Y	N	N
25 **Buerkle**	N	N	Y	Y	Y	N	N
26 Hochul	Y	N	Y	N	N	Y	Y
27 Higgins	N	N	Y	N	N	Y	Y
28 Slaughter	N	N	Y	N	N	Y	Y
29 **Reed**	Y	Y	Y	Y	Y	N	N
NORTH CAROLINA							
1 Butterfield	N	N	?	N	N	Y	N
2 **Ellmers**	Y	Y	Y	Y	Y	N	N
3 **Jones**	Y	N	Y	Y	Y	Y	Y
4 Price	N	N	Y	N	N	Y	Y

	499	500	501	502	503	504	505
5 **Foxx**	Y	Y	Y	Y	Y	N	N
6 **Coble**	Y	Y	Y	Y	Y	N	N
7 McIntyre	?	?	?	N	Y	N	Y
8 Kissell	?	?	?	N	Y	Y	Y
9 **Myrick**	Y	N	Y	Y	Y	N	N
10 **McHenry**	Y	Y	Y	Y	Y	N	N
11 Shuler	Y	N	Y	Y	Y	N	N
12 Watt	N	N	Y	N	N	Y	Y
13 Miller	N	N	Y	N	N	Y	Y
NORTH DAKOTA							
AL **Berg**	Y	Y	Y	Y	Y	N	N
OHIO							
1 **Chabot**	Y	N	Y	?	?	N	N
2 **Schmidt**	Y	N	Y	Y	Y	N	N
3 **Turner**	Y	N	Y	Y	Y	N	N
4 **Jordan**	N	N	Y	Y	Y	N	N
5 **Latta**	Y	N	Y	Y	Y	N	N
6 **Johnson**	Y	Y	Y	Y	Y	N	N
7 **Austria**	?	?	?	Y	Y	N	N
8 **Boehner**							
9 Kaptur	N	N	Y	N	N	Y	Y
10 Kucinich	N	N	Y	N	N	Y	Y
11 Fudge	Y	N	Y	N	N	Y	Y
12 **Tiberi**	N	N	Y	Y	Y	N	N
13 Sutton	N	N	Y	N	N	Y	Y
14 **LaTourette**	N	N	Y	Y	Y	N	N
15 **Stivers**	?	?	?	?	?	?	?
16 **Renacci**	Y	N	Y	Y	Y	N	N
17 Ryan	N	N	Y	N	N	Y	N
18 **Gibbs**	Y	N	Y	Y	Y	N	N
OKLAHOMA							
1 **Sullivan**	Y	?	Y	Y	Y	N	N
2 Boren	Y	Y	Y	Y	Y	N	N
3 **Lucas**	Y	Y	Y	Y	Y	N	N
4 **Cole**	Y	Y	Y	Y	Y	N	N
5 **Lankford**	Y	Y	Y	Y	Y	N	N
OREGON							
1 Bonamici	Y	N	Y	N	N	Y	Y
2 **Walden**	Y	Y	Y	Y	Y	N	N
3 Blumenauer	Y	N	Y	N	N	Y	Y
4 DeFazio	N	N	Y	N	N	Y	Y
5 Schrader	?	?	?	N	N	Y	N
PENNSYLVANIA							
1 Brady	Y	Y	Y	N	N	Y	Y
2 Fattah	Y	Y	Y	N	N	Y	Y
3 **Kelly**	Y	Y	Y	Y	Y	N	N
4 Altmire	N	Y	Y	N	N	N	N
5 **Thompson**	Y	Y	Y	Y	Y	N	N
6 **Gerlach**	Y	N	Y	Y	Y	N	N
7 **Meehan**	N	N	Y	Y	Y	N	N
8 **Fitzpatrick**	Y	N	Y	Y	Y	N	Y
9 **Shuster**	Y	N	Y	Y	Y	N	N
10 **Marino**	Y	Y	Y	Y	Y	N	N
11 **Barletta**	Y	Y	Y	Y	Y	N	N
12 Critz	?	?	?	N	N	N	N
13 Schwartz	N	N	Y	N	N	Y	Y
14 Doyle	Y	N	Y	N	N	Y	N
15 **Dent**	Y	Y	Y	Y	Y	N	N
16 **Pitts**	Y	Y	?	Y	Y	N	N
17 Holden	Y	Y	Y	N	N	Y	N
18 **Murphy**	N	Y	Y	Y	Y	N	N
19 **Platts**	Y	Y	Y	Y	Y	N	N
RHODE ISLAND							
1 Cicilline	N	N	Y	N	N	Y	Y
2 Langevin	N	N	Y	N	N	Y	Y
SOUTH CAROLINA							
1 **Scott**	Y	Y	Y	Y	Y	N	N
2 **Wilson**	Y	Y	Y	Y	Y	N	N
3 **Duncan**	Y	Y	Y	Y	Y	N	N
4 **Gowdy**	Y	Y	Y	Y	Y	N	N
5 **Mulvaney**	Y	Y	Y	Y	Y	N	N
6 Clyburn	Y	N	Y	?	N	Y	Y
SOUTH DAKOTA							
AL **Noem**	Y	Y	Y	Y	Y	N	N
TENNESSEE							
1 **Roe**	Y	Y	Y	Y	Y	N	N
2 **Duncan**	N	N	Y	Y	Y	N	N
3 **Fleischmann**	?	?	?	Y	Y	N	N
4 **DesJarlais**	Y	Y	Y	Y	Y	N	N
5 Cooper	N	N	Y	N	N	Y	N
6 **Black**	Y	Y	Y	Y	Y	N	N
7 **Blackburn**	Y	Y	Y	Y	Y	N	N
8 **Fincher**	Y	N	Y	Y	Y	N	N
9 Cohen	Y	N	Y	N	N	Y	Y

	499	500	501	502	503	504	505
TEXAS							
1 **Gohmert**	?	?	?	Y	Y	N	N
2 **Poe**	Y	N	Y	Y	Y	N	N
3 **Johnson, S.**	Y	Y	Y	Y	Y	N	N
4 **Hall**	Y	N	Y	Y	Y	N	N
5 **Hensarling**	Y	N	Y	Y	Y	N	N
6 **Barton**	Y	Y	Y	Y	Y	N	N
7 **Culberson**	Y	N	Y	Y	Y	N	N
8 **Brady**	Y	Y	Y	Y	Y	N	N
9 Green, A.	N	N	Y	N	N	N	N
10 **McCaul**	Y	N	Y	Y	Y	N	N
11 **Conaway**	Y	N	Y	Y	Y	N	N
12 **Granger**	Y	N	?	Y	Y	N	N
13 **Thornberry**	Y	N	Y	Y	Y	N	N
14 **Paul**	Y	N	Y	Y	Y	N	N
15 Hinojosa	?	?	?	N	N	?	?
16 Reyes	?	?	?	?	?	Y	Y
17 **Flores**	Y	Y	Y	Y	Y	N	N
18 Jackson Lee	N	N	Y	?	?	?	?
19 **Neugebauer**	Y	N	Y	Y	Y	N	N
20 Gonzalez	N	N	Y	N	N	N	N
21 **Smith**	Y	Y	Y	Y	Y	N	N
22 **Olson**	Y	Y	Y	Y	Y	N	N
23 **Canseco**	Y	N	Y	Y	Y	N	N
24 **Marchant**	Y	N	Y	Y	?	N	N
25 Doggett	Y	N	Y	N	N	Y	Y
26 **Burgess**	Y	N	Y	Y	Y	N	N
27 **Farenthold**	Y	Y	Y	Y	Y	N	N
28 Cuellar	Y	N	Y	N	N	N	N
29 Green, G.	N	N	Y	N	Y	N	N
30 Johnson, E.	Y	N	Y	N	N	Y	Y
31 **Carter**	Y	N	Y	Y	Y	N	N
32 **Sessions**	Y	N	Y	Y	Y	N	N
UTAH							
1 **Bishop**	?	?	?	?	?	N	N
2 Matheson	Y	N	Y	N	Y	N	N
3 **Chaffetz**	Y	N	Y	Y	Y	N	N
VERMONT							
AL Welch	N	Y	Y	N	N	Y	Y
VIRGINIA							
1 **Wittman**	Y	N	Y	Y	Y	N	N
2 **Rigell**	Y	Y	Y	Y	Y	N	N
3 Scott	N	N	Y	N	N	Y	Y
4 **Forbes**	N	N	Y	Y	Y	N	N
5 **Hurt**	Y	Y	Y	Y	Y	N	N
6 **Goodlatte**	Y	Y	Y	Y	Y	N	N
7 **Cantor**	Y	Y	Y	Y	Y	N	N
8 Moran	Y	N	Y	N	N	Y	Y
9 **Griffith**	Y	Y	Y	Y	Y	N	N
10 **Wolf**	N	N	Y	Y	Y	N	N
11 Connolly	Y	N	Y	N	N	Y	Y
WASHINGTON							
1 Vacant							
2 Larsen	?	?	?	N	N	N	N
3 **Herrera Beutler**	Y	Y	Y	Y	Y	N	N
4 **Hastings**	Y	Y	Y	Y	Y	N	N
5 **McMorris Rodgers**	Y	Y	Y	Y	Y	N	N
6 Dicks	?	?	?	N	N	Y	Y
7 McDermott	N	N	Y	N	+	+	+
8 **Reichert**	Y	N	Y	Y	Y	Y	N
9 Smith	–	–	+	–	–	Y	Y
WEST VIRGINIA							
1 **McKinley**	Y	Y	Y	Y	Y	N	N
2 **Capito**	?	?	?	Y	Y	N	N
3 Rahall	Y	N	Y	N	N	Y	Y
WISCONSIN							
1 **Ryan**	Y	Y	Y	Y	Y	N	N
2 Baldwin	N	N	Y	N	N	Y	Y
3 Kind	N	N	Y	N	N	Y	Y
4 Moore	N	N	Y	N	N	Y	Y
5 **Sensenbrenner**	N	N	Y	Y	Y	N	N
6 **Petri**	Y	N	Y	Y	Y	N	N
7 **Duffy**	Y	Y	Y	Y	Y	N	N
8 **Ribble**	Y	Y	Y	Y	Y	N	N
WYOMING							
AL **Lummis**	Y	Y	Y	Y	Y	N	N

IN THE HOUSE | By Vote Number

506. HR 6082. Republican Offshore Oil and Gas Drilling Plan/ **Drilling Safety Changes.** Markey, D-Mass., amendment that would require leases offered under the bill to include new safety requirements such as third-party verification of safety systems, blowout preventer performance standards and implementing technologies that would limit the risk of hydrocarbon ignition. Rejected in Committee of the Whole 189-232: R 15-224; D 174-8. July 25, 2012.

507. HR 6082. Republican Offshore Oil and Gas Drilling Plan/ **Leasing Royalty Rates.** Holt, D-N.J., amendment that would prevent lessees of certain outer continental shelf lands located within the Gulf of Mexico who were granted royalty relief under the terms of a 1994 law from receiving new leases under the bill unless they renegotiate their current leases to require the payment of royalties if the price of oil or natural gas reaches certain thresholds. Rejected in Committee of the Whole 177-247: R 10-229; D 167-18. July 25, 2012.

508. HR 6082. Republican Offshore Oil and Gas Drilling Plan/ **Impact on Gas Prices.** Hastings, D-Fla., amendment that would require drilling permit applications for wells to include an estimate of the potential impact on gas prices resulting from oil and gas developed on leased land. Rejected in Committee of the Whole 158-266: R 1-237; D 157-29. July 25, 2012.

509. HR 6082. Republican Offshore Oil and Gas Drilling Plan/ **Climate Change.** Hastings, D-Fla., amendment that would require drilling permit applications for wells to include an estimate of the impact that consumption of oil and gas resources discovered under the lease would have on climate change. Rejected in Committee of the Whole 150-275: R 1-238; D 149-37. July 25, 2012.

510. HR 6082. Republican Offshore Oil and Gas Drilling Plan/ **Recommit.** Slaughter, D-N.Y., motion to recommit the bill to the House Natural Resources Committee and report it back immediately with an amendment that would prohibit the issuing of a drilling lease to any person in violation of current sanctions on Iran or Syria. Motion rejected in Committee of the Whole 179-240: R 0-239; D 179-1. July 25, 2012.

511. HR 6082. Republican Offshore Oil and Gas Drilling Plan/ **Passage.** Passage of the bill that would replace the Interior Department's current offshore oil and gas drilling plan with one that would establish a timeline for 29 specific leases, up from the current 15. Certain leases would be conducted under a 2009 draft regulation rather than the 2012 plan. The bill also would require the Interior Department to prepare a multilease environmental impact statement for any leases required under the bill not in the June 2012 plan. Passed 253-170: R 228-9; D 25-161. A "nay" was a vote in support of the president's position. July 25, 2012.

512. HR 6168. Administration Offshore Oil and Gas Drilling Plan/ **Passage.** Hastings, R-Wash., motion to suspend the rules and pass the bill that would direct the Interior secretary to implement the administration's Proposed Final Outer Continental Shelf Oil and Gas Leasing Program. It would authorize 12 oil and gas drilling leases in the Gulf of Mexico, as well as three leases near Alaska through 2017. The plan would require the Bureau of Ocean Energy Management to study the fair market value of leasing areas and not sell any area for less than the determined value. Motion rejected 164-261: R 1-238; D 163-23. A two-thirds majority of those present and voting (284 in this case) is required for passage under suspension of the rules. A "yea" was a vote in support of the president's position. July 25, 2012.

	506	507	508	509	510	511	512
ALABAMA							
1 Bonner	N	N	N	N	N	Y	N
2 Roby	N	N	N	N	N	Y	N
3 Rogers	N	N	N	N	N	Y	N
4 Aderholt	N	N	N	N	N	Y	N
5 Brooks	N	N	N	N	N	Y	N
6 Bachus	N	N	N	N	N	Y	N
7 Sewell	Y	Y	Y	Y	Y	N	N
ALASKA							
AL Young	N	N	N	N	N	Y	N
ARIZONA							
1 Gosar	N	N	N	N	N	Y	N
2 Franks	N	N	N	N	N	Y	N
3 Quayle	N	N	N	N	N	Y	N
4 Pastor	Y	Y	Y	Y	Y	N	Y
5 Schweikert	N	N	N	N	N	Y	N
6 Flake	N	N	N	N	N	Y	N
7 Grijalva	Y	Y	Y	Y	Y	N	Y
8 Barber	Y	Y	Y	Y	Y	N	Y
ARKANSAS							
1 Crawford	N	N	N	N	N	Y	N
2 Griffin	N	N	N	N	N	Y	N
3 Womack	N	N	N	N	N	Y	N
4 Ross	N	N	N	N	Y	Y	N
CALIFORNIA							
1 Thompson	Y	Y	Y	Y	Y	N	Y
2 Herger	N	N	N	N	N	Y	N
3 Lungren	N	N	N	N	N	Y	N
4 McClintock	N	N	N	N	N	Y	N
5 Matsui	Y	Y	Y	Y	Y	N	Y
6 Woolsey	Y	Y	Y	Y	Y	N	Y
7 Miller, George	Y	Y	Y	N	Y	N	Y
8 Pelosi	Y	Y	Y	Y	Y	N	Y
9 Lee	Y	Y	Y	Y	Y	N	Y
10 Garamendi	?	?	?	?	?	–	+
11 McNerney	Y	Y	Y	Y	Y	N	Y
12 Speier	Y	Y	Y	Y	Y	N	Y
13 Stark	Y	Y	Y	Y	Y	N	Y
14 Eshoo	Y	Y	Y	Y	Y	N	Y
15 Honda	Y	Y	Y	Y	Y	N	Y
16 Lofgren	Y	Y	Y	Y	Y	N	Y
17 Farr	Y	Y	Y	Y	Y	N	Y
18 Cardoza	Y	Y	N	Y	Y	N	N
19 Denham	N	N	N	N	N	Y	N
20 Costa	N	N	N	N	Y	Y	N
21 Nunes	N	N	N	N	N	Y	N
22 McCarthy	N	N	N	N	N	Y	N
23 Capps	Y	Y	Y	Y	Y	N	Y
24 Gallegly	N	N	N	N	N	Y	N
25 McKeon	N	N	N	N	N	Y	N
26 Dreier	N	N	N	N	N	Y	N
27 Sherman	Y	Y	Y	Y	Y	N	Y
28 Berman	Y	Y	Y	Y	Y	N	Y
29 Schiff	Y	Y	Y	Y	Y	N	Y
30 Waxman	Y	Y	Y	Y	Y	N	Y
31 Becerra	Y	Y	Y	Y	Y	N	Y
32 Chu	Y	Y	Y	Y	Y	N	Y
33 Bass	Y	Y	Y	Y	Y	N	Y
34 Roybal-Allard	Y	Y	Y	Y	Y	N	Y
35 Waters	?	Y	Y	Y	Y	N	Y
36 Hahn	Y	Y	Y	Y	Y	N	Y
37 Richardson	Y	Y	Y	Y	Y	N	Y
38 Napolitano	Y	Y	Y	Y	Y	N	Y
39 Sánchez, Linda	Y	Y	Y	Y	Y	N	Y
40 Royce	N	N	N	N	N	Y	N
41 Lewis	N	N	N	N	N	Y	N
42 Miller, Gary	N	N	N	N	N	Y	N
43 Baca	Y	Y	Y	Y	Y	Y	Y
44 Calvert	N	N	N	N	N	Y	N
45 Bono Mack	N	N	N	N	N	Y	N
46 Rohrabacher	N	N	N	N	N	Y	N
47 Sanchez, Loretta	Y	Y	Y	Y	Y	N	Y
48 Campbell	N	N	N	N	N	Y	N
49 Issa	N	N	N	N	N	Y	N
50 Bilbray	Y	N	N	N	N	N	N
51 Filner	Y	Y	Y	Y	Y	N	Y
52 Hunter	N	N	N	N	N	Y	N
53 Davis	Y	Y	Y	Y	Y	N	Y
COLORADO							
1 DeGette	Y	Y	Y	Y	Y	N	Y
2 Polis	Y	Y	N	Y	N	Y	Y
3 Tipton	N	N	N	N	N	Y	N
4 Gardner	N	N	N	N	N	Y	N
5 Lamborn	N	N	N	N	N	Y	N
6 Coffman	N	N	N	N	N	Y	N
7 Perlmutter	Y	Y	Y	N	Y	N	Y
CONNECTICUT							
1 Larson	Y	Y	Y	Y	Y	N	Y
2 Courtney	Y	Y	Y	Y	Y	N	Y
3 DeLauro	Y	Y	Y	Y	Y	N	Y
4 Himes	Y	Y	Y	Y	Y	N	Y
5 Murphy	Y	Y	Y	Y	Y	N	Y
DELAWARE							
AL Carney	Y	Y	Y	Y	Y	N	Y
FLORIDA							
1 Miller	N	N	N	N	N	Y	N
2 Southerland	N	N	N	N	N	Y	N
3 Brown	Y	Y	Y	Y	Y	N	Y
4 Crenshaw	N	N	N	N	N	Y	N
5 Nugent	N	N	N	N	N	Y	N
6 Stearns	N	N	N	N	N	Y	N
7 Mica	N	N	N	N	N	Y	N
8 Webster	N	N	N	N	N	Y	N
9 Bilirakis	N	N	N	N	N	Y	N
10 Young	Y	Y	N	N	N	Y	N
11 Castor	Y	Y	Y	Y	Y	N	Y
12 Ross	N	N	N	N	N	Y	N
13 Buchanan	Y	Y	N	N	N	Y	N
14 Mack	N	N	N	N	N	Y	N
15 Posey	N	N	N	N	N	Y	N
16 Rooney	N	N	N	N	N	Y	N
17 Wilson	Y	Y	Y	Y	Y	N	Y
18 Ros-Lehtinen	Y	N	N	N	N	Y	N
19 Deutch	Y	Y	Y	Y	Y	N	Y
20 Wasserman Schultz	Y	Y	Y	Y	Y	N	Y
21 Diaz-Balart	N	N	N	N	N	Y	N
22 West	N	N	N	N	N	Y	N
23 Hastings	Y	Y	Y	Y	Y	N	Y
24 Adams	N	N	N	N	N	Y	N
25 Rivera	N	N	N	N	N	Y	N
GEORGIA							
1 Kingston	N	N	N	N	N	Y	N
2 Bishop	N	N	N	N	Y	Y	N
3 Westmoreland	N	N	N	N	N	Y	N
4 Johnson	Y	Y	Y	Y	Y	N	Y
5 Lewis	Y	Y	Y	Y	Y	N	Y
6 Price	N	N	N	N	N	Y	N
7 Woodall	N	N	N	N	N	Y	N
8 Scott, A.	N	N	N	N	N	Y	N
9 Graves	N	N	N	N	N	Y	N
10 Broun	N	N	N	N	N	Y	N
11 Gingrey	N	N	N	N	N	Y	N
12 Barrow	N	N	N	N	Y	Y	N
13 Scott, D.	Y	Y	Y	Y	Y	N	Y
HAWAII							
1 Hanabusa	Y	Y	Y	Y	Y	N	Y
2 Hirono	?	?	?	?	?	?	?
IDAHO							
1 Labrador	N	N	N	N	N	Y	N
2 Simpson	N	N	N	N	N	Y	N
ILLINOIS							
1 Rush	Y	N	Y	Y	Y	N	Y
2 Jackson	?	?	?	?	?	?	?
3 Lipinski	Y	Y	N	Y	Y	N	Y
4 Gutierrez	Y	Y	Y	Y	Y	N	Y
5 Quigley	Y	Y	Y	Y	Y	N	Y
6 Roskam	N	N	N	N	N	Y	N
7 Davis	Y	Y	Y	Y	Y	N	Y
8 Walsh	N	N	N	N	N	Y	N
9 Schakowsky	Y	Y	Y	Y	Y	N	Y
10 Dold	Y	N	N	N	N	Y	N
11 Kinzinger	N	N	N	N	N	Y	N
12 Costello	Y	Y	N	N	?	Y	Y
13 Biggert	N	N	N	N	N	Y	N
14 Hultgren	N	N	N	N	N	Y	N
15 Johnson	Y	N	N	N	N	Y	N

KEY | **Republicans** | Democrats

Y Voted for (yea)	**X** Paired against	**C** Voted "present" to avoid possible conflict of interest
# Paired for	**–** Announced against	
+ Announced for	**P** Voted "present"	**?** Did not vote or otherwise make a position known
N Voted against (nay)		

	506	507	508	509	510	511	512
16 **Manzullo**	N	N	N	N	N	Y	N
17 **Schilling**	N	N	N	N	N	Y	N
18 **Schock**	N	N	N	N	N	Y	N
19 **Shimkus**	N	N	N	N	N	Y	N
INDIANA							
1 Visclosky	Y	Y	Y	Y	Y	N	Y
2 Donnelly	Y	N	N	N	Y	Y	N
3 **Stutzman**	N	N	N	N	N	Y	N
4 **Rokita**	N	N	N	N	N	Y	N
5 **Burton**	N	N	N	N	N	Y	N
6 **Pence**	N	N	N	N	N	Y	N
7 Carson	Y	Y	Y	Y	Y	N	Y
8 **Bucshon**	N	N	N	N	N	Y	N
9 **Young**	N	N	N	N	N	Y	N
IOWA							
1 Braley	Y	Y	Y	Y	Y	N	Y
2 Loebsack	Y	Y	Y	Y	Y	Y	Y
3 Boswell	Y	Y	Y	N	Y	Y	Y
4 **Latham**	N	N	N	N	N	Y	N
5 **King**	N	N	N	N	N	Y	N
KANSAS							
1 **Huelskamp**	N	N	N	N	N	Y	N
2 **Jenkins**	N	N	N	N	N	Y	N
3 **Yoder**	N	N	N	N	N	Y	N
4 **Pompeo**	N	N	N	N	N	Y	N
KENTUCKY							
1 **Whitfield**	N	N	N	N	N	Y	N
2 **Guthrie**	N	N	N	N	N	Y	N
3 Yarmuth	Y	Y	Y	Y	Y	N	Y
4 **Davis**	N	N	N	N	N	Y	N
5 **Rogers**	N	N	N	N	N	Y	N
6 Chandler	Y	N	Y	Y	Y	Y	Y
LOUISIANA							
1 **Scalise**	N	N	N	N	N	Y	N
2 Richmond	?	?	?	?	?	?	?
3 **Landry**	N	N	N	N	N	Y	N
4 **Fleming**	N	N	N	N	N	Y	N
5 **Alexander**	N	N	N	N	N	Y	N
6 **Cassidy**	N	N	N	N	N	Y	N
7 **Boustany**	N	N	N	N	N	Y	N
MAINE							
1 Pingree	Y	Y	Y	Y	Y	N	Y
2 Michaud	Y	Y	Y	Y	Y	N	Y
MARYLAND							
1 **Harris**	N	N	N	N	N	Y	N
2 Ruppersberger	Y	Y	Y	Y	Y	N	Y
3 Sarbanes	Y	Y	Y	Y	Y	N	Y
4 Edwards	Y	Y	Y	Y	Y	N	Y
5 Hoyer	Y	Y	Y	Y	Y	N	Y
6 **Bartlett**	N	N	N	N	N	Y	N
7 Cummings	Y	Y	Y	Y	?	N	Y
8 Van Hollen	Y	Y	Y	Y	Y	N	Y
MASSACHUSETTS							
1 Olver	Y	Y	Y	Y	Y	N	Y
2 Neal	Y	Y	Y	Y	Y	N	Y
3 McGovern	Y	Y	Y	Y	Y	N	Y
4 Frank	Y	Y	Y	Y	Y	N	Y
5 Tsongas	?	Y	Y	Y	Y	N	Y
6 Tierney	Y	Y	Y	N	Y	N	Y
7 Markey	Y	Y	Y	Y	Y	N	Y
8 Capuano	Y	Y	Y	Y	Y	N	Y
9 Lynch	Y	Y	N	N	Y	N	Y
10 Keating	Y	Y	Y	Y	Y	N	Y
MICHIGAN							
1 **Benishek**	N	N	N	N	N	Y	N
2 **Huizenga**	N	N	N	N	N	Y	N
3 **Amash**	N	N	N	N	N	Y	N
4 **Camp**	N	N	N	N	N	Y	N
5 Kildee	Y	Y	Y	Y	Y	N	Y
6 **Upton**	N	N	N	N	N	Y	N
7 **Walberg**	N	N	N	N	N	Y	N
8 **Rogers**	N	N	N	N	N	Y	N
9 Peters	Y	Y	Y	Y	Y	N	Y
10 **Miller**	N	N	N	N	N	Y	N
11 Vacant							
12 Levin	Y	Y	Y	Y	Y	N	Y
13 Clarke	Y	Y	Y	Y	Y	N	Y
14 Conyers	Y	Y	Y	Y	?	N	Y
15 Dingell	Y	Y	N	N	?	N	Y
MINNESOTA							
1 Walz	Y	Y	Y	Y	Y	N	Y
2 **Kline**	N	N	N	N	N	Y	N
3 **Paulsen**	N	N	N	N	N	Y	N
4 McCollum	Y	Y	Y	Y	Y	N	Y

	506	507	508	509	510	511	512
5 Ellison	Y	Y	Y	Y	Y	N	Y
6 **Bachmann**	N	N	N	N	N	Y	N
7 Peterson	N	N	N	N	Y	Y	N
8 **Cravaack**	N	N	N	N	N	Y	N
MISSISSIPPI							
1 **Nunnelee**	N	N	N	N	N	Y	N
2 Thompson	Y	Y	Y	Y	Y	N	Y
3 **Harper**	N	N	N	N	N	Y	N
4 **Palazzo**	N	N	N	N	N	Y	N
MISSOURI							
1 Clay	Y	Y	Y	Y	Y	N	Y
2 **Akin**	N	N	?	N	N	Y	N
3 Carnahan	Y	Y	Y	Y	Y	N	Y
4 **Hartzler**	N	N	N	N	N	Y	N
5 Cleaver	Y	Y	Y	Y	Y	N	Y
6 **Graves**	N	N	N	N	N	Y	N
7 **Long**	N	N	N	N	N	Y	N
8 **Emerson**	N	N	N	N	N	Y	N
9 **Luetkemeyer**	N	N	N	N	N	Y	N
MONTANA							
AL **Rehberg**	N	N	N	N	N	Y	N
NEBRASKA							
1 **Fortenberry**	N	Y	N	N	N	Y	N
2 **Terry**	N	N	N	N	N	Y	N
3 **Smith**	N	N	N	N	N	Y	N
NEVADA							
1 Berkley	Y	Y	Y	Y	Y	N	Y
2 **Amodei**	N	N	N	N	N	Y	N
3 **Heck**	N	N	N	N	N	Y	N
NEW HAMPSHIRE							
1 **Guinta**	N	N	N	N	N	Y	N
2 **Bass**	N	N	N	N	N	N	N
NEW JERSEY							
1 Andrews	Y	Y	Y	Y	Y	N	Y
2 **LoBiondo**	Y	Y	N	N	N	N	N
3 **Runyan**	N	N	N	N	N	N	N
4 **Smith**	Y	Y	N	N	N	N	N
5 **Garrett**	N	N	N	N	N	Y	N
6 Pallone	Y	Y	Y	Y	Y	N	N
7 **Lance**	Y	N	N	N	N	N	N
8 Pascrell	Y	Y	Y	Y	Y	N	N
9 Rothman	Y	Y	Y	Y	Y	N	Y
10 Vacant							
11 **Frelinghuysen**	N	N	N	N	N	N	N
12 Holt	Y	Y	Y	Y	Y	N	Y
13 Sires	Y	Y	Y	Y	Y	N	Y
NEW MEXICO							
1 Heinrich	Y	Y	Y	Y	Y	N	Y
2 **Pearce**	N	N	N	N	N	Y	N
3 Luján	Y	Y	Y	Y	Y	N	Y
NEW YORK							
1 Bishop	Y	Y	Y	Y	Y	N	Y
2 Israel	Y	Y	Y	Y	Y	N	Y
3 **King**	N	N	N	N	N	Y	N
4 McCarthy	Y	Y	Y	Y	?	N	Y
5 Ackerman	Y	Y	Y	Y	Y	N	Y
6 Meeks	Y	Y	Y	Y	Y	N	Y
7 Crowley	Y	Y	Y	Y	Y	N	Y
8 Nadler	Y	Y	Y	Y	Y	N	Y
9 **Turner**	N	N	N	N	N	Y	N
10 Towns	Y	Y	Y	Y	Y	N	Y
11 Clarke	Y	Y	Y	Y	Y	N	Y
12 Velázquez	Y	?	Y	Y	Y	N	Y
13 **Grimm**	N	N	N	N	N	Y	N
14 Maloney	Y	Y	Y	Y	Y	N	Y
15 Rangel	Y	Y	Y	Y	Y	N	Y
16 Serrano	Y	Y	Y	Y	Y	N	Y
17 Engel	Y	Y	Y	Y	Y	N	Y
18 Lowey	Y	Y	Y	Y	Y	N	Y
19 **Hayworth**	N	N	N	N	N	Y	N
20 **Gibson**	Y	Y	Y	Y	N	Y	N
21 Tonko	Y	Y	Y	Y	Y	N	Y
22 Hinchey	Y	Y	Y	Y	Y	N	Y
23 Owens	Y	Y	N	N	Y	Y	N
24 **Hanna**	Y	N	N	N	N	Y	N
25 **Buerkle**	N	N	N	N	N	?	N
26 Hochul	Y	Y	Y	N	Y	Y	N
27 Higgins	Y	Y	Y	Y	Y	N	Y
28 Slaughter	Y	Y	Y	Y	Y	N	Y
29 **Reed**	N	N	N	N	N	Y	N
NORTH CAROLINA							
1 Butterfield	Y	Y	Y	Y	Y	N	Y
2 **Ellmers**	N	N	N	N	N	Y	N
3 **Jones**	Y	Y	N	N	N	N	N
4 Price	Y	Y	Y	Y	Y	N	Y

	506	507	508	509	510	511	512
5 **Foxx**	N	N	N	N	N	Y	N
6 **Coble**	N	N	N	N	N	Y	N
7 McIntyre	Y	N	N	N	Y	Y	N
8 Kissell	Y	Y	N	N	Y	N	Y
9 **Myrick**	N	N	N	N	N	Y	N
10 **McHenry**	N	N	N	N	N	Y	N
11 Shuler	Y	N	Y	N	Y	Y	Y
12 Watt	Y	Y	Y	Y	Y	N	Y
13 Miller	Y	Y	Y	Y	Y	N	Y
NORTH DAKOTA							
AL **Berg**	N	N	N	N	N	Y	N
OHIO							
1 **Chabot**	N	N	N	N	N	Y	N
2 **Schmidt**	N	N	N	N	N	Y	N
3 **Turner**	N	N	N	N	N	Y	N
4 **Jordan**	N	N	N	N	N	Y	N
5 **Latta**	N	N	N	N	N	Y	N
6 **Johnson**	N	N	N	N	N	Y	N
7 **Austria**	N	N	N	N	N	Y	N
8 **Boehner**							
9 Kaptur	Y	Y	Y	Y	Y	N	Y
10 Kucinich	Y	Y	Y	Y	N	N	N
11 Fudge	Y	Y	Y	Y	Y	N	Y
12 **Tiberi**	N	N	N	N	N	Y	N
13 Sutton	Y	Y	Y	N	Y	N	Y
14 **LaTourette**	N	N	N	N	N	Y	N
15 **Stivers**	?	?	?	?	?	?	?
16 **Renacci**	N	N	N	N	N	Y	N
17 Ryan	Y	Y	N	N	Y	N	Y
18 **Gibbs**	N	N	N	N	N	Y	N
OKLAHOMA							
1 **Sullivan**	N	N	N	N	N	Y	N
2 Boren	N	N	N	N	Y	Y	N
3 **Lucas**	N	N	N	N	N	Y	N
4 **Cole**	N	N	N	N	N	Y	N
5 **Lankford**	N	N	N	N	N	Y	N
OREGON							
1 Bonamici	Y	Y	Y	Y	Y	N	Y
2 **Walden**	N	N	N	N	N	Y	N
3 Blumenauer	Y	Y	Y	Y	Y	N	Y
4 DeFazio	Y	Y	Y	Y	Y	N	Y
5 Schrader	Y	Y	Y	Y	Y	N	Y
PENNSYLVANIA							
1 Brady	Y	Y	Y	Y	Y	N	Y
2 Fattah	Y	Y	Y	Y	Y	N	N
3 **Kelly**	N	N	N	N	N	Y	N
4 Altmire	Y	N	N	N	Y	Y	N
5 **Thompson**	N	N	N	N	N	Y	N
6 **Gerlach**	N	N	N	N	N	Y	N
7 **Meehan**	N	N	N	N	N	Y	N
8 **Fitzpatrick**	Y	Y	N	N	N	Y	N
9 **Shuster**	N	N	N	N	N	Y	N
10 **Marino**	N	N	N	N	N	Y	N
11 **Barletta**	N	N	N	N	N	Y	N
12 Critz	N	N	N	N	?	Y	N
13 Schwartz	Y	Y	Y	Y	Y	N	Y
14 Doyle	Y	Y	Y	Y	Y	N	Y
15 **Dent**	Y	Y	N	N	N	Y	N
16 **Pitts**	N	N	N	N	N	Y	N
17 Holden	Y	Y	Y	N	Y	Y	N
18 **Murphy**	N	N	N	N	N	Y	N
19 **Platts**	N	Y	N	N	N	Y	N
RHODE ISLAND							
1 Cicilline	Y	Y	Y	Y	Y	N	Y
2 Langevin	Y	Y	Y	Y	Y	N	Y
SOUTH CAROLINA							
1 **Scott**	N	N	N	N	N	Y	N
2 **Wilson**	N	N	N	N	N	Y	N
3 **Duncan**	N	N	N	N	N	Y	N
4 **Gowdy**	N	N	N	N	N	Y	N
5 **Mulvaney**	N	N	N	N	N	Y	N
6 Clyburn	Y	Y	Y	Y	Y	N	Y
SOUTH DAKOTA							
AL **Noem**	N	N	N	N	N	Y	N
TENNESSEE							
1 **Roe**	N	N	N	N	N	Y	N
2 **Duncan**	N	N	N	N	N	Y	N
3 **Fleischmann**	N	N	N	N	N	Y	N
4 **DesJarlais**	N	N	N	N	N	Y	N
5 Cooper	Y	Y	N	Y	Y	Y	Y
6 **Black**	N	N	N	N	N	Y	N
7 **Blackburn**	N	N	N	N	N	Y	N
8 **Fincher**	N	N	N	N	N	Y	N
9 Cohen	Y	Y	N	N	Y	N	Y

	506	507	508	509	510	511	512
TEXAS							
1 **Gohmert**	N	N	N	N	N	Y	N
2 **Poe**	N	N	N	N	N	Y	N
3 **Johnson, S.**	N	N	N	N	N	Y	N
4 **Hall**	N	N	N	N	N	Y	N
5 **Hensarling**	N	N	N	N	N	Y	N
6 **Barton**	N	N	N	N	N	Y	N
7 **Culberson**	N	N	N	N	N	Y	N
8 **Brady**	N	N	N	N	N	Y	N
9 Green, A.	Y	N	N	N	Y	Y	Y
10 **McCaul**	N	N	N	N	N	Y	N
11 **Conaway**	N	N	N	N	N	Y	N
12 **Granger**	N	N	N	N	N	Y	N
13 **Thornberry**	N	N	N	N	N	Y	N
14 **Paul**	N	N	N	N	N	Y	N
15 Hinojosa	?	Y	N	N	Y	N	Y
16 Reyes	Y	Y	Y	Y	Y	N	Y
17 **Flores**	N	N	N	N	N	Y	N
18 Jackson Lee	?	?	?	?	?	?	?
19 **Neugebauer**	N	N	N	N	N	Y	N
20 Gonzalez	Y	N	Y	N	Y	N	Y
21 **Smith**	N	N	N	N	N	Y	N
22 **Olson**	N	N	N	N	N	Y	N
23 **Canseco**	N	N	N	N	N	Y	N
24 **Marchant**	N	N	N	N	N	Y	N
25 Doggett	Y	Y	Y	Y	Y	N	Y
26 **Burgess**	N	N	N	N	N	Y	N
27 **Farenthold**	N	N	N	N	N	Y	N
28 Cuellar	Y	N	Y	Y	Y	Y	Y
29 Green, G.	Y	N	N	N	Y	Y	Y
30 Johnson, E.	Y	Y	Y	Y	Y	N	Y
31 **Carter**	N	N	N	N	N	Y	N
32 **Sessions**	N	N	N	N	N	?	N
UTAH							
1 **Bishop**	N	N	N	N	N	Y	N
2 Matheson	N	N	N	N	Y	Y	N
3 **Chaffetz**	N	N	N	N	N	Y	N
VERMONT							
AL Welch	Y	Y	Y	Y	Y	N	Y
VIRGINIA							
1 **Wittman**	N	N	N	N	N	Y	N
2 **Rigell**	N	N	N	N	N	Y	N
3 Scott	Y	Y	Y	Y	Y	N	N
4 **Forbes**	N	N	N	N	N	Y	N
5 **Hurt**	N	N	N	N	N	Y	N
6 **Goodlatte**	N	N	N	N	N	Y	N
7 **Cantor**	N	N	N	N	N	Y	N
8 Moran	Y	Y	Y	Y	Y	N	Y
9 **Griffith**	N	N	N	N	N	Y	N
10 **Wolf**	N	N	N	N	N	Y	N
11 Connolly	Y	Y	N	N	Y	N	Y
WASHINGTON							
1 Vacant							
2 Larsen	Y	Y	N	N	Y	N	Y
3 **Herrera Beutler**	N	N	N	N	N	Y	N
4 **Hastings**	N	N	N	N	N	Y	N
5 **McMorris Rodgers**	N	N	N	N	N	Y	N
6 Dicks	Y	Y	Y	Y	Y	N	Y
7 McDermott	+	Y	Y	Y	Y	N	Y
8 **Reichert**	Y	N	N	N	N	Y	N
9 Smith	Y	Y	N	N	Y	N	Y
WEST VIRGINIA							
1 **McKinley**	N	N	N	N	N	Y	N
2 **Capito**	N	N	N	N	N	Y	N
3 Rahall	Y	Y	Y	N	Y	Y	N
WISCONSIN							
1 **Ryan**	N	N	N	N	N	Y	N
2 Baldwin	Y	Y	Y	Y	Y	N	Y
3 Kind	Y	Y	Y	Y	Y	N	Y
4 Moore	Y	Y	Y	Y	Y	N	Y
5 **Sensenbrenner**	N	N	N	N	N	Y	N
6 **Petri**	N	N	N	N	N	Y	N
7 **Duffy**	N	N	N	N	N	Y	N
8 **Ribble**	N	N	N	N	N	Y	N
WYOMING							
AL **Lummis**	N	N	N	N	N	Y	N

IN THE HOUSE | By Vote Number

513. HR 459. Federal Reserve Audit/Passage. Issa, R-Calif., motion to suspend the rules and pass the bill that would direct the Government Accountability Office to audit all actions of the Federal Reserve and issue a report to Congress within 12 months of enactment. Motion agreed to 327-98: R 238-1; D 89-97. A two-thirds majority of those present and voting (284 in this case) is required for passage under suspension of the rules. July 25, 2012.

514. HR 4078. Regulatory Revisions/Drinking-Water Regulations. Hastings, D-Fla., amendment that would exempt regulatory proposals directed at maintaining or enhancing the safety of drinking water from the moratorium on "significant regulatory actions." Rejected in Committee of the Whole 188-231: R 14-222; D 174-9. July 25, 2012.

515. HR 4078. Regulatory Revisions/Consent Decrees and Settlements. Johnson, D-Ga., amendment that would exempt consent decrees and settlement agreements pertaining to the health care overhaul from the bill's provisions to change the settlement process. Rejected in Committee of the Whole 159-259: R 2-234; D 157-25. July 25, 2012.

516. HR 4078. Regulatory Revisions/Oil Speculation Regulations. Kucinich, D-Ohio, amendment that would exempt regulations designed to limit oil speculation from the moratorium on "significant regulatory actions." Rejected in Committee of the Whole 173-245: R 6-231; D 167-14. July 25, 2012.

517. HR 4078. Regulatory Revisions/Energy Efficiency Regulations. Welch, D-Vt., amendment that would exempt regulations designed to increase or promote energy efficiency from the restrictions relating to consent decrees and settlement agreements, "significant regulatory actions" and "midnight rules." Rejected in Committee of the Whole 174-242: R 3-232; D 171-10. July 25, 2012.

518. HR 4078. Regulatory Revisions/Extreme-Weather Regulations. Markey, D-Mass., amendment that would exempt regulations to protect the public from extreme weather events, such as droughts, flooding and catastrophic wildfires, from the restrictions on "significant regulatory actions" and "midnight rules." Rejected in Committee of the Whole 177-240: R 7-230; D 170-10. July 25, 2012.

	513	514	515	516	517	518
ALABAMA						
1 Bonner	Y	N	N	N	N	N
2 Roby	Y	N	N	N	N	N
3 Rogers	Y	N	N	N	N	N
4 Aderholt	Y	N	N	N	N	N
5 Brooks	Y	N	N	N	N	N
6 Bachus	Y	N	N	N	N	N
7 Sewell	N	Y	Y	Y	Y	Y
ALASKA						
AL Young	Y	N	N	N	N	N
ARIZONA						
1 Gosar	Y	N	N	N	N	N
2 Franks	Y	N	N	N	N	N
3 Quayle	Y	N	N	N	N	N
4 Pastor	Y	Y	Y	Y	Y	Y
5 Schweikert	Y	N	N	N	N	N
6 Flake	Y	N	N	N	N	N
7 Grijalva	Y	Y	Y	Y	Y	Y
8 Barber	Y	Y	Y	Y	Y	Y
ARKANSAS						
1 Crawford	Y	N	N	N	N	N
2 Griffin	Y	N	N	N	N	N
3 Womack	Y	N	N	N	N	N
4 Ross	Y	N	N	N	N	N
CALIFORNIA						
1 Thompson	Y	Y	Y	Y	Y	Y
2 Herger	Y	N	N	N	N	N
3 Lungren	Y	N	N	N	N	N
4 McClintock	Y	N	Y	N	N	N
5 Matsui	N	Y	Y	Y	Y	Y
6 Woolsey	N	Y	Y	Y	Y	Y
7 Miller, George	N	Y	Y	Y	Y	Y
8 Pelosi	N	Y	Y	Y	Y	Y
9 Lee	N	Y	Y	Y	Y	Y
10 Garamendi	+	?	?	?	?	?
11 McNerney	Y	Y	Y	Y	Y	Y
12 Speier	Y	Y	Y	Y	Y	Y
13 Stark	N	Y	Y	Y	Y	Y
14 Eshoo	N	Y	Y	Y	Y	Y
15 Honda	Y	Y	Y	Y	Y	Y
16 Lofgren	Y	Y	Y	Y	Y	Y
17 Farr	Y	Y	Y	Y	Y	Y
18 Cardoza	N	Y	Y	Y	Y	Y
19 Denham	Y	N	N	N	N	N
20 Costa	Y	Y	Y	Y	Y	Y
21 Nunes	Y	N	N	N	N	N
22 McCarthy	Y	N	N	N	N	N
23 Capps	N	Y	Y	Y	Y	Y
24 Gallegly	Y	N	N	N	N	N
25 McKeon	Y	N	N	N	N	N
26 Dreier	Y	N	N	N	N	N
27 Sherman	Y	Y	Y	Y	Y	Y
28 Berman	Y	Y	Y	Y	Y	Y
29 Schiff	Y	Y	Y	Y	Y	Y
30 Waxman	N	Y	Y	Y	Y	Y
31 Becerra	N	Y	Y	Y	Y	Y
32 Chu	N	Y	Y	Y	Y	Y
33 Bass	N	Y	Y	Y	Y	Y
34 Roybal-Allard	N	Y	Y	Y	Y	Y
35 Waters	Y	Y	Y	Y	Y	Y
36 Hahn	Y	Y	Y	Y	Y	Y
37 Richardson	Y	Y	Y	Y	Y	Y
38 Napolitano	N	Y	Y	Y	Y	Y
39 Sánchez, Linda	N	Y	Y	Y	Y	Y
40 Royce	Y	N	N	N	N	N
41 Lewis	Y	?	?	?	?	?
42 Miller, Gary	Y	N	N	N	N	N
43 Baca	Y	Y	Y	Y	Y	Y
44 Calvert	Y	N	N	N	N	N
45 Bono Mack	Y	N	N	N	N	N
46 Rohrabacher	Y	N	N	N	N	N
47 Sanchez, Loretta	Y	Y	Y	Y	Y	Y
48 Campbell	Y	N	N	N	N	N
49 Issa	Y	N	N	N	N	N
50 Bilbray	Y	N	N	Y	Y	N
51 Filner	Y	Y	Y	Y	Y	Y
52 Hunter	Y	N	N	N	N	N
53 Davis	N	Y	Y	Y	Y	Y

	513	514	515	516	517	518
COLORADO						
1 DeGette	N	Y	Y	Y	Y	Y
2 Polis	Y	Y	Y	Y	Y	Y
3 Tipton	Y	N	N	N	Y	N
4 Gardner	Y	N	N	N	N	N
5 Lamborn	Y	N	N	N	N	N
6 Coffman	Y	N	N	N	N	N
7 Perlmutter	Y	Y	Y	Y	Y	Y
CONNECTICUT						
1 Larson	N	Y	Y	Y	Y	Y
2 Courtney	Y	Y	Y	Y	Y	Y
3 DeLauro	N	Y	Y	Y	Y	Y
4 Himes	N	Y	Y	Y	Y	Y
5 Murphy	Y	Y	Y	Y	Y	Y
DELAWARE						
AL Carney	N	Y	Y	Y	Y	Y
FLORIDA						
1 Miller	Y	N	N	N	N	N
2 Southerland	Y	N	N	N	N	N
3 Brown	N	Y	N	Y	Y	Y
4 Crenshaw	Y	N	N	N	N	N
5 Nugent	Y	N	N	N	N	N
6 Stearns	Y	N	–	N	N	N
7 Mica	Y	N	N	N	N	N
8 Webster	Y	N	N	N	N	N
9 Bilirakis	Y	N	N	N	N	N
10 Young	Y	Y	N	N	N	N
11 Castor	N	Y	Y	Y	Y	Y
12 Ross	Y	N	N	N	N	N
13 Buchanan	Y	N	N	N	Y	N
14 Mack	Y	N	N	N	N	N
15 Posey	Y	N	N	N	N	N
16 Rooney	Y	N	N	N	N	N
17 Wilson	N	Y	Y	Y	Y	Y
18 Ros-Lehtinen	Y	N	N	N	N	N
19 Deutch	N	Y	Y	Y	Y	Y
20 Wasserman Schultz	N	Y	Y	Y	Y	Y
21 Diaz-Balart	Y	N	N	N	N	N
22 West	Y	N	N	N	N	N
23 Hastings	N	Y	Y	Y	Y	Y
24 Adams	Y	N	N	N	N	N
25 Rivera	Y	N	N	N	N	N
GEORGIA						
1 Kingston	Y	N	N	N	N	N
2 Bishop	Y	Y	N	N	N	N
3 Westmoreland	Y	N	N	N	N	N
4 Johnson	N	Y	Y	Y	Y	Y
5 Lewis	N	Y	Y	Y	Y	?
6 Price	Y	N	N	N	N	N
7 Woodall	Y	N	N	N	N	N
8 Scott, A.	Y	N	N	N	N	N
9 Graves	Y	N	N	N	N	N
10 Broun	Y	N	N	N	N	N
11 Gingrey	Y	N	N	N	N	N
12 Barrow	Y	N	N	N	N	N
13 Scott, D.	Y	Y	Y	Y	Y	Y
HAWAII						
1 Hanabusa	N	Y	Y	Y	Y	Y
2 Hirono	?	?	?	?	?	?
IDAHO						
1 Labrador	Y	N	N	N	N	N
2 Simpson	Y	N	N	N	N	N
ILLINOIS						
1 Rush	N	Y	Y	Y	Y	Y
2 Jackson	?	?	?	?	?	?
3 Lipinski	Y	Y	Y	Y	Y	Y
4 Gutierrez	N	Y	Y	Y	Y	Y
5 Quigley	Y	Y	Y	Y	Y	Y
6 Roskam	Y	N	N	N	N	N
7 Davis	N	Y	Y	Y	Y	Y
8 Walsh	Y	N	N	N	N	N
9 Schakowsky	N	Y	Y	Y	Y	Y
10 Dold	Y	Y	N	N	N	N
11 Kinzinger	Y	N	N	N	N	N
12 Costello	Y	Y	Y	Y	Y	Y
13 Biggert	Y	N	N	N	N	N
14 Hultgren	Y	N	N	N	N	N
15 Johnson	Y	Y	N	N	Y	N

KEY **Republicans** Democrats

Y	Voted for (yea)	X	Paired against	C	Voted "present" to avoid possible conflict of interest
#	Paired for	–	Announced against		
+	Announced for	P	Voted "present"	?	Did not vote or otherwise make a position known
N	Voted against (nay)				

	513	514	515	516	517	518
16 **Manzullo**	Y	N	N	N	N	N
17 **Schilling**	Y	N	N	N	N	N
18 **Schock**	Y	N	N	N	N	N
19 **Shimkus**	Y	N	N	N	N	N
INDIANA						
1 Visclosky	Y	Y	Y	Y	Y	Y
2 Donnelly	Y	Y	Y	Y	Y	Y
3 **Stutzman**	Y	N	N	N	N	N
4 **Rokita**	Y	N	N	N	N	N
5 **Burton**	Y	N	N	N	N	N
6 **Pence**	Y	N	N	N	N	N
7 Carson	N	Y	Y	Y	Y	Y
8 **Bucshon**	Y	N	N	N	N	N
9 **Young**	Y	N	N	N	N	N
IOWA						
1 Braley	Y	Y	Y	Y	Y	Y
2 Loebsack	Y	Y	Y	Y	Y	Y
3 Boswell	Y	Y	Y	Y	Y	Y
4 **Latham**	Y	N	N	N	N	N
5 **King**	Y	N	N	N	N	N
KANSAS						
1 **Huelskamp**	Y	N	N	N	N	N
2 **Jenkins**	Y	N	N	N	N	N
3 **Yoder**	Y	N	N	N	N	N
4 **Pompeo**	Y	N	N	N	N	N
KENTUCKY						
1 **Whitfield**	Y	N	N	N	N	N
2 **Guthrie**	Y	N	N	N	N	N
3 Yarmuth	Y	Y	Y	Y	Y	Y
4 **Davis**	Y	N	N	N	N	N
5 **Rogers**	Y	N	N	N	N	N
6 Chandler	Y	Y	N	Y	Y	Y
LOUISIANA						
1 **Scalise**	Y	N	N	N	N	N
2 Richmond	?	?	?	?	?	?
3 **Landry**	Y	N	N	N	N	N
4 **Fleming**	Y	N	N	N	N	N
5 **Alexander**	Y	N	N	N	N	N
6 **Cassidy**	Y	N	N	N	N	N
7 **Boustany**	Y	N	N	N	N	N
MAINE						
1 Pingree	Y	Y	Y	Y	Y	Y
2 Michaud	Y	Y	Y	Y	Y	Y
MARYLAND						
1 **Harris**	Y	N	N	N	N	N
2 Ruppersberger	Y	Y	Y	Y	Y	Y
3 Sarbanes	N	Y	Y	Y	Y	Y
4 Edwards	N	Y	Y	Y	Y	Y
5 Hoyer	N	Y	Y	Y	Y	Y
6 **Bartlett**	Y	N	N	N	N	N
7 Cummings	N	Y	Y	Y	Y	Y
8 Van Hollen	N	Y	Y	Y	Y	Y
MASSACHUSETTS						
1 Olver	N	Y	Y	Y	Y	Y
2 Neal	N	Y	Y	Y	Y	Y
3 McGovern	Y	Y	Y	Y	Y	Y
4 Frank	N	Y	Y	Y	Y	Y
5 Tsongas	Y	Y	Y	Y	Y	Y
6 Tierney	Y	Y	Y	Y	Y	Y
7 Markey	N	Y	Y	Y	Y	Y
8 Capuano	N	Y	Y	Y	Y	Y
9 Lynch	Y	Y	Y	?	Y	Y
10 Keating	N	Y	Y	Y	Y	Y
MICHIGAN						
1 **Benishek**	Y	N	N	N	N	N
2 **Huizenga**	Y	N	N	N	N	N
3 **Amash**	Y	N	N	N	N	N
4 **Camp**	Y	N	N	N	N	N
5 Kildee	Y	Y	Y	Y	Y	Y
6 **Upton**	Y	N	N	N	N	N
7 **Walberg**	Y	N	N	N	N	N
8 **Rogers**	Y	N	N	N	N	N
9 Peters	N	Y	Y	Y	Y	Y
10 **Miller**	Y	N	N	N	N	N
11 Vacant						
12 Levin	N	Y	Y	Y	Y	Y
13 Clarke	Y	Y	Y	Y	Y	Y
14 Conyers	N	Y	Y	Y	Y	Y
15 Dingell	N	Y	Y	Y	Y	Y
MINNESOTA						
1 Walz	Y	Y	Y	Y	Y	Y
2 **Kline**	Y	N	N	N	N	N
3 **Paulsen**	Y	N	N	N	N	N
4 McCollum	N	Y	Y	Y	Y	Y

	513	514	515	516	517	518
5 Ellison	N	Y	Y	Y	Y	Y
6 **Bachmann**	Y	N	N	N	N	N
7 Peterson	Y	N	N	N	N	N
8 **Cravaack**	Y	N	N	N	N	N
MISSISSIPPI						
1 **Nunnelee**	Y	N	N	N	N	N
2 Thompson	N	Y	N	Y	Y	Y
3 **Harper**	Y	N	N	N	N	N
4 **Palazzo**	Y	N	N	N	N	N
MISSOURI						
1 Clay	Y	Y	N	Y	Y	Y
2 **Akin**	Y	N	N	N	?	N
3 Carnahan	Y	Y	Y	Y	Y	Y
4 **Hartzler**	Y	N	N	N	N	N
5 Cleaver	N	Y	N	Y	Y	Y
6 **Graves**	Y	N	N	N	N	N
7 **Long**	Y	N	N	N	N	N
8 **Emerson**	Y	N	N	N	N	N
9 **Luetkemeyer**	Y	N	N	N	N	N
MONTANA						
AL **Rehberg**	Y	N	N	N	N	N
NEBRASKA						
1 **Fortenberry**	Y	Y	N	Y	N	N
2 **Terry**	Y	N	N	N	N	N
3 **Smith**	Y	N	N	N	N	N
NEVADA						
1 Berkley	Y	Y	Y	Y	Y	Y
2 **Amodei**	Y	N	N	N	N	N
3 **Heck**	Y	N	N	N	N	N
NEW HAMPSHIRE						
1 **Guinta**	Y	N	N	N	N	N
2 **Bass**	Y	N	N	N	N	N
NEW JERSEY						
1 Andrews	N	Y	Y	Y	Y	Y
2 **LoBiondo**	Y	Y	N	Y	N	N
3 **Runyan**	Y	Y	N	N	N	N
4 **Smith**	Y	Y	N	N	N	N
5 **Garrett**	Y	N	N	N	N	N
6 Pallone	N	Y	Y	Y	Y	Y
7 **Lance**	Y	N	N	N	N	N
8 Pascrell	Y	Y	Y	Y	Y	Y
9 Rothman	N	Y	Y	Y	Y	Y
10 Vacant						
11 **Frelinghuysen**	Y	N	N	N	N	N
12 Holt	N	Y	Y	Y	Y	Y
13 Sires	N	Y	Y	Y	Y	Y
NEW MEXICO						
1 Heinrich	Y	Y	Y	Y	Y	Y
2 **Pearce**	Y	N	N	N	N	N
3 Luján	Y	Y	Y	Y	Y	Y
NEW YORK						
1 Bishop	Y	Y	?	?	?	?
2 Israel	N	Y	Y	Y	Y	Y
3 **King**	Y	N	N	N	N	N
4 McCarthy	Y	Y	Y	Y	Y	Y
5 Ackerman	N	Y	Y	Y	Y	Y
6 Meeks	N	Y	N	Y	?	?
7 Crowley	N	Y	Y	Y	Y	Y
8 Nadler	Y	Y	Y	Y	Y	Y
9 **Turner**	N	N	N	N	N	N
10 Towns	N	Y	Y	Y	Y	Y
11 Clarke	Y	Y	Y	Y	Y	Y
12 Velázquez	N	Y	Y	Y	Y	Y
13 **Grimm**	Y	N	N	N	N	N
14 Maloney	N	Y	Y	Y	Y	Y
15 Rangel	N	Y	Y	Y	Y	Y
16 Serrano	N	Y	Y	Y	Y	Y
17 Engel	N	Y	Y	Y	Y	Y
18 Lowey	N	Y	Y	Y	Y	Y
19 **Hayworth**	Y	N	N	N	N	N
20 **Gibson**	Y	Y	N	Y	N	Y
21 Tonko	Y	Y	Y	Y	Y	Y
22 Hinchey	N	Y	Y	Y	Y	Y
23 Owens	Y	N	N	N	Y	Y
24 **Hanna**	Y	N	N	N	N	N
25 **Buerkle**	Y	N	N	N	N	N
26 Hochul	Y	Y	Y	Y	Y	Y
27 Higgins	Y	Y	Y	Y	Y	Y
28 Slaughter	N	Y	Y	Y	Y	Y
29 **Reed**	Y	N	N	N	N	N
NORTH CAROLINA						
1 Butterfield	N	Y	N	Y	Y	Y
2 **Ellmers**	Y	N	N	N	N	N
3 **Jones**	Y	N	N	Y	Y	Y
4 Price	N	Y	Y	Y	Y	Y

	513	514	515	516	517	518
5 **Foxx**	Y	N	N	N	N	N
6 **Coble**	Y	N	N	N	N	N
7 McIntyre	Y	Y	N	N	N	Y
8 Kissell	Y	Y	N	Y	Y	Y
9 **Myrick**	Y	N	N	N	N	N
10 **McHenry**	Y	N	N	N	N	N
11 Shuler	N	N	N	N	N	N
12 Watt	N	Y	Y	Y	Y	Y
13 Miller	N	Y	Y	Y	Y	Y
NORTH DAKOTA						
AL **Berg**	Y	N	N	N	N	N
OHIO						
1 **Chabot**	Y	N	N	N	N	N
2 **Schmidt**	Y	N	N	N	N	N
3 **Turner**	Y	N	N	N	N	N
4 **Jordan**	Y	N	N	N	N	N
5 **Latta**	Y	N	N	N	N	N
6 **Johnson**	Y	N	N	N	N	N
7 **Austria**	Y	N	N	N	N	N
8 **Boehner**						
9 Kaptur	N	Y	Y	Y	Y	Y
10 Kucinich	Y	Y	Y	Y	Y	Y
11 Fudge	N	Y	N	Y	Y	Y
12 **Tiberi**	Y	N	N	N	N	N
13 Sutton	Y	+	+	+	+	+
14 **LaTourette**	Y	N	N	N	N	N
15 **Stivers**	?	?	?	?	?	?
16 **Renacci**	Y	N	N	N	N	N
17 Ryan	N	Y	Y	Y	Y	Y
18 **Gibbs**	Y	N	N	N	N	N
OKLAHOMA						
1 **Sullivan**	Y	N	N	N	N	N
2 Boren	Y	N	N	N	N	N
3 **Lucas**	Y	N	N	N	N	N
4 **Cole**	Y	N	N	N	N	N
5 **Lankford**	Y	N	N	N	N	N
OREGON						
1 Bonamici	N	Y	Y	Y	Y	Y
2 **Walden**	Y	N	N	N	N	N
3 Blumenauer	N	Y	Y	Y	Y	Y
4 DeFazio	Y	Y	Y	Y	Y	Y
5 Schrader	Y	Y	Y	N	Y	N
PENNSYLVANIA						
1 Brady	N	Y	Y	Y	Y	Y
2 Fattah	N	Y	Y	Y	Y	Y
3 **Kelly**	Y	N	N	N	N	N
4 Altmire	Y	Y	N	Y	Y	Y
5 **Thompson**	Y	N	N	N	N	N
6 **Gerlach**	Y	Y	N	N	N	N
7 **Meehan**	Y	Y	N	N	N	N
8 **Fitzpatrick**	Y	Y	N	Y	N	N
9 **Shuster**	Y	N	N	N	N	N
10 **Marino**	Y	N	N	N	N	N
11 **Barletta**	Y	N	N	N	N	N
12 Critz	Y	Y	Y	Y	Y	Y
13 Schwartz	N	Y	Y	Y	Y	Y
14 Doyle	Y	Y	Y	Y	Y	Y
15 **Dent**	Y	Y	N	N	N	N
16 **Pitts**	Y	N	N	N	N	N
17 Holden	Y	N	N	N	N	N
18 **Murphy**	Y	N	N	N	N	N
19 **Platts**	Y	Y	N	N	N	Y
RHODE ISLAND						
1 Cicilline	Y	Y	Y	Y	Y	Y
2 Langevin	Y	Y	Y	Y	Y	Y
SOUTH CAROLINA						
1 **Scott**	Y	N	N	N	N	N
2 **Wilson**	Y	N	N	N	N	N
3 **Duncan**	Y	N	N	N	N	N
4 **Gowdy**	Y	N	N	N	N	N
5 **Mulvaney**	Y	N	N	N	N	N
6 Clyburn	N	Y	N	Y	Y	Y
SOUTH DAKOTA						
AL **Noem**	Y	?	N	N	N	N
TENNESSEE						
1 **Roe**	Y	N	N	N	N	N
2 **Duncan**	Y	N	N	N	N	N
3 **Fleischmann**	Y	N	N	N	N	N
4 **DesJarlais**	Y	N	N	N	N	N
5 Cooper	N	Y	Y	N	Y	Y
6 **Black**	Y	N	N	N	N	N
7 **Blackburn**	Y	N	N	N	N	N
8 **Fincher**	Y	N	N	N	N	N
9 Cohen	Y	Y	Y	Y	Y	Y

	513	514	515	516	517	518
TEXAS						
1 **Gohmert**	Y	N	N	N	N	N
2 **Poe**	Y	N	N	N	N	N
3 **Johnson, S.**	Y	N	N	N	N	N
4 **Hall**	Y	N	N	N	N	N
5 **Hensarling**	Y	N	N	N	N	N
6 **Barton**	Y	N	N	N	N	N
7 **Culberson**	Y	?	?	?	?	?
8 **Brady**	Y	N	N	N	N	N
9 Green, A.	Y	Y	N	Y	Y	Y
10 **McCaul**	Y	N	N	N	N	N
11 **Conaway**	Y	N	N	N	N	N
12 **Granger**	Y	N	N	N	N	N
13 **Thornberry**	Y	N	N	N	N	N
14 **Paul**	Y	N	N	N	N	N
15 Hinojosa	Y	Y	Y	Y	Y	Y
16 Reyes	N	?	?	?	?	?
17 **Flores**	Y	N	N	N	N	N
18 Jackson Lee	?	?	?	?	?	?
19 **Neugebauer**	Y	N	N	N	N	N
20 Gonzalez	N	Y	Y	Y	Y	Y
21 **Smith**	Y	N	N	N	N	N
22 **Olson**	Y	N	N	N	N	N
23 **Canseco**	Y	N	N	N	N	N
24 **Marchant**	Y	N	N	N	N	N
25 Doggett	Y	Y	Y	Y	Y	Y
26 **Burgess**	Y	N	N	N	N	N
27 **Farenthold**	Y	N	N	N	N	N
28 Cuellar	Y	Y	Y	N	Y	Y
29 Green, G.	Y	Y	N	Y	Y	Y
30 Johnson, E.	N	Y	N	Y	Y	Y
31 **Carter**	Y	N	N	N	N	N
32 **Sessions**	Y	N	N	N	N	N
UTAH						
1 **Bishop**	Y	N	N	N	N	N
2 Matheson	Y	N	N	N	N	N
3 **Chaffetz**	Y	N	N	N	N	N
VERMONT						
AL Welch	Y	Y	Y	Y	Y	Y
VIRGINIA						
1 **Wittman**	Y	N	N	N	N	N
2 **Rigell**	Y	N	N	N	N	N
3 Scott	Y	Y	Y	Y	Y	Y
4 **Forbes**	Y	N	N	N	N	N
5 **Hurt**	Y	N	N	N	N	N
6 **Goodlatte**	Y	N	N	N	N	N
7 **Cantor**	Y	N	N	N	N	N
8 Moran	Y	Y	Y	Y	Y	Y
9 **Griffith**	Y	N	N	N	N	N
10 **Wolf**	Y	N	N	N	N	N
11 Connolly	Y	Y	Y	Y	Y	Y
WASHINGTON						
1 Vacant						
2 Larsen	N	Y	Y	Y	Y	Y
3 **Herrera Beutler**	Y	N	N	N	?	N
4 **Hastings**	Y	N	N	N	N	N
5 **McMorris Rodgers**	Y	N	N	N	N	N
6 Dicks	N	?	?	?	?	?
7 McDermott	N	Y	Y	Y	Y	Y
8 **Reichert**	Y	Y	Y	N	N	Y
9 Smith	Y	Y	Y	Y	Y	Y
WEST VIRGINIA						
1 **McKinley**	Y	N	N	N	N	N
2 **Capito**	Y	N	N	N	N	N
3 Rahall	Y	N	N	N	N	N
WISCONSIN						
1 **Ryan**	Y	N	N	N	N	N
2 Baldwin	Y	Y	Y	Y	Y	Y
3 Kind	N	Y	Y	Y	Y	Y
4 Moore	N	Y	Y	Y	Y	Y
5 **Sensenbrenner**	Y	N	N	N	N	N
6 **Petri**	Y	N	N	N	N	N
7 **Duffy**	Y	N	N	N	N	N
8 **Ribble**	Y	N	N	N	N	N
WYOMING						
AL **Lummis**	Y	N	N	N	N	N

IN THE HOUSE | By Vote Number

519. **HR 4078. Regulatory Revisions/Previous Question.** Foxx, R-N.C., motion to order the previous question (thus ending debate and the possibility of amendment) on the rule (H Res 741) that would provide for further House floor consideration of a package (HR 4078) of regulatory measures. Motion agreed to 235-183: R 232-2; D 3-181. (Subsequently, the rule was adopted by voice vote.) July 26, 2012.

520. **HR 4078. Regulatory Revisions/Patent and Trademark Regulations.** Watt, D-N.C., amendment that would exempt regulations intended to increase efficiency within the patent and trademark process from the restrictions in the bill relating to consent decrees and settlement agreements, "midnight rules" and "significant regulatory actions." Rejected in Committee of the Whole 177-244: R 0-237; D 177-7. July 26, 2012.

521. **HR 4078. Regulatory Revisions/Fuel Price Regulations.** Loebsack, D-Iowa, amendment that would exempt regulations designed to lower fuel prices from the moratorium on "significant regulatory actions" in the bill. Rejected in Committee of the Whole 177-238: R 3-232; D 174-6. July 26, 2012.

522. **HR 4078. Regulatory Revisions/Health Care Overhaul Implementation.** Richardson, D-Calif., amendment that would make regulations and rules proposed to implement the health care overhaul law eligible for a presidential waiver from the moratorium on "significant regulatory actions" in the bill. Rejected in Committee of the Whole 170-247: R 1-234; D 169-13. July 26, 2012.

523. **HR 4078. Regulatory Revisions/Credit Reporting Regulations.** Richardson, D-Calif., amendment that would make regulations pertaining to the Fair Credit Reporting Act eligible for a presidential waiver from the moratorium on "significant regulatory actions" in the bill. Rejected in Committee of the Whole 173-246: R 0-237; D 173-9. July 26, 2012.

524. **HR 4078. Regulatory Revisions/Presidential Exemption Requests.** Connolly, D-Va., amendment that would require Congress to review any presidential request for a waiver from the moratorium on "significant regulatory actions" in the bill within seven days of its submission, and allow the waiver to take effect absent such a review. Rejected in Committee of the Whole 179-234: R 3-230; D 176-4. July 26, 2012.

	519	520	521	522	523	524
ALABAMA						
1 Bonner	Y	N	N	N	N	N
2 Roby	Y	N	N	N	N	N
3 Rogers	Y	N	N	N	N	N
4 Aderholt	Y	N	N	N	N	N
5 Brooks	Y	N	N	N	N	N
6 Bachus	Y	N	N	N	N	?
7 Sewell	N	Y	Y	Y	Y	Y
ALASKA						
AL Young	Y	N	N	N	N	N
ARIZONA						
1 Gosar	Y	N	N	N	N	N
2 Franks	Y	N	N	N	N	N
3 Quayle	Y	N	N	N	N	N
4 Pastor	N	Y	Y	Y	Y	Y
5 Schweikert	Y	N	N	N	N	N
6 Flake	Y	N	N	N	N	N
7 Grijalva	N	Y	Y	Y	Y	Y
8 Barber	N	Y	Y	Y	Y	Y
ARKANSAS						
1 Crawford	Y	N	N	N	N	N
2 Griffin	Y	N	N	N	N	N
3 Womack	Y	N	N	N	N	N
4 Ross	N	N	N	N	N	Y
CALIFORNIA						
1 Thompson	N	Y	Y	Y	Y	Y
2 Herger	Y	N	N	N	N	N
3 Lungren	Y	N	N	N	N	N
4 McClintock	Y	N	N	N	N	N
5 Matsui	N	Y	Y	Y	Y	Y
6 Woolsey	N	Y	Y	Y	Y	Y
7 Miller, George	N	Y	Y	Y	Y	Y
8 Pelosi	N	Y	Y	Y	Y	Y
9 Lee	N	Y	Y	Y	Y	Y
10 Garamendi	N	Y	Y	Y	Y	Y
11 McNerney	N	Y	Y	Y	Y	Y
12 Speier	N	Y	?	Y	Y	Y
13 Stark	N	Y	Y	Y	Y	Y
14 Eshoo	N	Y	Y	Y	Y	Y
15 Honda	N	Y	Y	Y	Y	Y
16 Lofgren	N	Y	Y	Y	Y	Y
17 Farr	N	Y	Y	Y	Y	Y
18 Cardoza	?	?	?	?	?	?
19 Denham	Y	N	N	N	N	N
20 Costa	N	Y	Y	Y	Y	Y
21 Nunes	Y	N	N	N	N	N
22 McCarthy	Y	N	N	N	N	N
23 Capps	N	Y	Y	Y	Y	Y
24 Gallegly	Y	N	N	N	N	N
25 McKeon	N	N	N	N	N	N
26 Dreier	Y	N	N	N	N	N
27 Sherman	N	Y	Y	Y	Y	Y
28 Berman	N	Y	Y	Y	Y	Y
29 Schiff	N	Y	Y	Y	Y	Y
30 Waxman	N	Y	Y	Y	Y	Y
31 Becerra	N	Y	Y	Y	Y	Y
32 Chu	N	Y	Y	Y	Y	Y
33 Bass	N	Y	Y	?	?	Y
34 Roybal-Allard	N	Y	Y	Y	Y	Y
35 Waters	N	Y	Y	Y	Y	Y
36 Hahn	N	Y	Y	Y	Y	Y
37 Richardson	N	Y	Y	Y	Y	Y
38 Napolitano	N	Y	Y	Y	Y	Y
39 Sánchez, Linda	N	Y	Y	N	Y	Y
40 Royce	Y	N	N	N	N	N
41 Lewis	Y	N	N	N	N	N
42 Miller, Gary	Y	N	N	N	N	N
43 Baca	N	Y	Y	Y	Y	Y
44 Calvert	Y	N	N	N	N	N
45 Bono Mack	Y	N	N	N	N	N
46 Rohrabacher	Y	N	?	N	N	N
47 Sanchez, Loretta	N	Y	Y	Y	Y	Y
48 Campbell	Y	N	N	N	N	N
49 Issa	Y	N	N	N	N	N
50 Bilbray	Y	N	N	N	N	N
51 Filner	N	Y	Y	Y	Y	Y
52 Hunter	Y	N	N	N	N	N
53 Davis	N	Y	Y	Y	Y	Y

	519	520	521	522	523	524
COLORADO						
1 DeGette	N	Y	Y	Y	Y	Y
2 Polis	N	Y	Y	Y	Y	Y
3 Tipton	Y	N	N	N	N	N
4 Gardner	Y	N	N	N	N	N
5 Lamborn	Y	N	N	N	N	N
6 Coffman	Y	N	N	N	N	N
7 Perlmutter	N	Y	Y	Y	Y	Y
CONNECTICUT						
1 Larson	N	Y	Y	Y	Y	Y
2 Courtney	N	Y	Y	Y	Y	Y
3 DeLauro	N	Y	Y	Y	Y	Y
4 Himes	N	Y	Y	Y	Y	Y
5 Murphy	N	?	?	?	?	?
DELAWARE						
AL Carney	N	Y	Y	Y	Y	Y
FLORIDA						
1 Miller	Y	N	N	N	N	N
2 Southerland	Y	N	N	N	N	N
3 Brown	N	Y	Y	Y	Y	Y
4 Crenshaw	Y	N	N	N	N	N
5 Nugent	Y	N	N	N	N	N
6 Stearns	Y	N	N	N	N	N
7 Mica	Y	N	N	N	N	N
8 Webster	Y	N	N	N	N	N
9 Bilirakis	Y	N	N	N	N	N
10 Young	Y	N	N	N	N	N
11 Castor	N	Y	Y	Y	Y	Y
12 Ross	Y	N	N	N	N	N
13 Buchanan	Y	N	N	N	N	N
14 Mack	Y	N	N	N	N	?
15 Posey	Y	N	N	N	N	N
16 Rooney	Y	N	N	N	N	N
17 Wilson	N	Y	Y	Y	Y	Y
18 Ros-Lehtinen	Y	N	N	N	N	N
19 Deutch	N	Y	Y	Y	Y	Y
20 Wasserman Schultz	N	Y	Y	Y	Y	Y
21 Diaz-Balart	Y	N	N	N	N	N
22 West	Y	N	N	N	N	N
23 Hastings	N	Y	Y	Y	Y	Y
24 Adams	Y	N	N	N	N	N
25 Rivera	Y	N	N	N	N	N
GEORGIA						
1 Kingston	Y	N	N	N	N	N
2 Bishop	N	Y	?	Y	Y	Y
3 Westmoreland	Y	N	N	N	N	N
4 Johnson	N	Y	Y	Y	Y	Y
5 Lewis	N	Y	Y	Y	Y	Y
6 Price	Y	N	N	N	N	N
7 Woodall	Y	N	N	N	N	N
8 Scott, A.	Y	N	N	N	N	N
9 Graves	Y	N	N	N	N	N
10 Broun	Y	N	N	N	N	N
11 Gingrey	Y	N	N	N	N	N
12 Barrow	N	N	N	N	N	N
13 Scott, D.	N	Y	Y	Y	Y	Y
HAWAII						
1 Hanabusa	N	Y	Y	Y	Y	Y
2 Hirono	?	?	?	?	?	?
IDAHO						
1 Labrador	Y	N	N	N	N	N
2 Simpson	Y	N	N	N	N	N
ILLINOIS						
1 Rush	N	Y	Y	Y	Y	Y
2 Jackson	?	?	?	?	?	?
3 Lipinski	N	Y	Y	N	Y	Y
4 Gutierrez	N	Y	Y	Y	Y	Y
5 Quigley	N	Y	Y	Y	Y	Y
6 Roskam	Y	N	N	N	N	N
7 Davis	N	Y	Y	?	Y	?
8 Walsh	Y	N	N	N	N	N
9 Schakowsky	N	Y	Y	Y	Y	?
10 Dold	Y	N	N	N	N	N
11 Kinzinger	Y	N	N	N	N	N
12 Costello	N	Y	Y	Y	Y	Y
13 Biggert	Y	N	N	N	N	N
14 Hultgren	Y	N	N	N	N	N
15 Johnson	Y	N	N	N	N	Y

KEY   **Republicans**   Democrats

Y	Voted for (yea)	X	Paired against
#	Paired for	−	Announced against
+	Announced for	P	Voted "present"
N	Voted against (nay)		

C   Voted "present" to avoid possible conflict of interest

?   Did not vote or otherwise make a position known

	519	520	521	522	523	524
16 **Manzullo**	Y	N	N	N	N	N
17 **Schilling**	Y	N	N	N	N	N
18 **Schock**	Y	N	N	N	N	N
19 **Shimkus**	Y	N	N	N	N	N
INDIANA						
1 Visclosky	N	Y	Y	Y	Y	Y
2 Donnelly	N	Y	Y	Y	Y	Y
3 **Stutzman**	Y	N	N	N	N	N
4 **Rokita**	Y	N	N	N	N	N
5 **Burton**	Y	N	N	N	N	N
6 **Pence**	Y	N	N	N	N	N
7 Carson	N	Y	Y	Y	Y	Y
8 **Bucshon**	Y	N	N	N	N	N
9 **Young**	Y	N	N	N	N	N
IOWA						
1 Braley	N	Y	Y	Y	Y	Y
2 Loebsack	N	Y	Y	Y	Y	Y
3 Boswell	N	Y	Y	Y	Y	Y
4 **Latham**	Y	N	N	N	N	N
5 **King**	Y	N	N	N	N	N
KANSAS						
1 **Huelskamp**	Y	N	N	N	N	N
2 **Jenkins**	Y	N	N	N	N	N
3 **Yoder**	Y	N	N	N	N	N
4 **Pompeo**	Y	N	N	N	N	N
KENTUCKY						
1 **Whitfield**	Y	N	N	N	N	N
2 **Guthrie**	Y	N	N	N	N	N
3 Yarmuth	N	Y	Y	Y	Y	Y
4 **Davis**	Y	N	N	N	N	N
5 **Rogers**	Y	N	N	N	N	N
6 Chandler	N	Y	Y	N	Y	Y
LOUISIANA						
1 **Scalise**	Y	N	N	N	N	N
2 Richmond	N	Y	Y	Y	Y	?
3 **Landry**	Y	N	N	N	N	N
4 **Fleming**	Y	N	N	N	N	N
5 **Alexander**	Y	N	N	N	N	N
6 **Cassidy**	Y	N	N	N	N	N
7 **Boustany**	Y	N	N	N	N	N
MAINE						
1 Pingree	N	Y	Y	Y	Y	Y
2 Michaud	N	Y	Y	Y	Y	Y
MARYLAND						
1 **Harris**	Y	N	N	N	N	N
2 Ruppersberger	N	Y	Y	Y	Y	Y
3 Sarbanes	N	Y	Y	Y	Y	Y
4 Edwards	N	Y	Y	Y	Y	Y
5 Hoyer	N	Y	Y	Y	Y	Y
6 **Bartlett**	Y	N	N	N	N	N
7 Cummings	N	Y	Y	Y	Y	Y
8 Van Hollen	N	Y	Y	Y	Y	Y
MASSACHUSETTS						
1 Olver	N	Y	Y	Y	Y	Y
2 Neal	N	Y	Y	Y	Y	Y
3 McGovern	N	Y	Y	Y	Y	Y
4 Frank	N	Y	Y	Y	Y	Y
5 Tsongas	N	Y	Y	Y	Y	Y
6 Tierney	N	Y	Y	Y	Y	Y
7 Markey	N	Y	Y	Y	Y	Y
8 Capuano	N	Y	Y	Y	Y	Y
9 Lynch	N	Y	Y	Y	Y	Y
10 Keating	?	Y	Y	Y	Y	Y
MICHIGAN						
1 **Benishek**	Y	N	N	N	N	N
2 **Huizenga**	Y	N	N	N	N	N
3 **Amash**	Y	N	N	N	N	N
4 **Camp**	Y	N	N	N	N	N
5 Kildee	N	Y	Y	Y	Y	Y
6 **Upton**	Y	N	N	N	N	N
7 **Walberg**	Y	N	N	N	N	N
8 **Rogers**	Y	N	N	N	N	N
9 Peters	N	Y	Y	Y	Y	Y
10 **Miller**	Y	N	N	N	N	N
11 Vacant						
12 Levin	N	Y	Y	Y	Y	Y
13 Clarke	N	Y	Y	Y	Y	Y
14 Conyers	N	Y	Y	Y	Y	Y
15 Dingell	N	Y	Y	Y	Y	Y
MINNESOTA						
1 Walz	N	Y	Y	Y	Y	Y
2 **Kline**	Y	N	N	N	N	N
3 **Paulsen**	Y	N	N	N	N	N
4 McCollum	N	Y	Y	Y	Y	Y

	519	520	521	522	523	524
5 Ellison	N	Y	Y	Y	Y	Y
6 **Bachmann**	Y	N	N	N	N	N
7 Peterson	N	N	N	N	N	N
8 **Cravaack**	Y	N	N	N	N	N
MISSISSIPPI						
1 **Nunnelee**	Y	N	N	N	N	N
2 Thompson	N	Y	Y	Y	Y	Y
3 **Harper**	Y	N	N	N	N	N
4 **Palazzo**	Y	N	N	N	N	N
MISSOURI						
1 Clay	N	Y	Y	Y	Y	Y
2 **Akin**	+	−	−	−	−	−
3 Carnahan	N	Y	Y	Y	Y	?
4 **Hartzler**	Y	N	N	N	N	N
5 Cleaver	N	Y	Y	Y	Y	Y
6 **Graves**	Y	N	N	N	N	N
7 **Long**	Y	N	N	N	N	N
8 **Emerson**	Y	N	N	N	N	N
9 **Luetkemeyer**	Y	N	N	N	N	N
MONTANA						
AL **Rehberg**	Y	N	N	N	N	N
NEBRASKA						
1 **Fortenberry**	?	N	N	N	N	N
2 **Terry**	Y	N	N	N	N	N
3 **Smith**	Y	N	N	N	N	N
NEVADA						
1 Berkley	N	Y	Y	Y	Y	Y
2 **Amodei**	Y	N	N	N	N	N
3 **Heck**	Y	N	N	N	N	N
NEW HAMPSHIRE						
1 **Guinta**	Y	N	N	N	N	N
2 **Bass**	Y	N	N	N	N	N
NEW JERSEY						
1 Andrews	N	Y	Y	Y	Y	Y
2 **LoBiondo**	Y	N	N	N	N	N
3 **Runyan**	Y	N	N	N	N	N
4 **Smith**	Y	N	N	N	N	N
5 **Garrett**	?	N	N	N	N	N
6 Pallone	N	Y	Y	Y	Y	Y
7 **Lance**	Y	N	N	N	N	N
8 Pascrell	N	Y	Y	Y	Y	Y
9 Rothman	N	Y	Y	Y	Y	Y
10 Vacant						
11 **Frelinghuysen**	N	N	N	N	N	N
12 Holt	N	Y	Y	Y	Y	Y
13 Sires	N	Y	Y	Y	Y	Y
NEW MEXICO						
1 Heinrich	N	Y	Y	Y	Y	Y
2 **Pearce**	Y	N	N	N	N	N
3 Luján	N	Y	Y	Y	Y	Y
NEW YORK						
1 Bishop	N	Y	Y	Y	Y	Y
2 Israel	N	Y	Y	Y	Y	Y
3 **King**	Y	N	N	N	N	N
4 McCarthy	N	Y	Y	Y	Y	Y
5 Ackerman	?	?	?	?	?	?
6 Meeks	?	?	?	?	?	?
7 Crowley	N	Y	Y	Y	Y	Y
8 Nadler	N	Y	Y	Y	Y	Y
9 **Turner**	Y	N	N	N	N	N
10 Towns	N	Y	Y	Y	Y	Y
11 Clarke	N	Y	Y	Y	Y	Y
12 Velázquez	N	Y	Y	Y	Y	Y
13 **Grimm**	Y	N	N	N	N	N
14 Maloney	N	Y	Y	Y	Y	Y
15 Rangel	N	Y	Y	Y	?	Y
16 Serrano	N	Y	Y	Y	Y	Y
17 Engel	N	Y	Y	Y	Y	Y
18 Lowey	N	Y	Y	Y	Y	Y
19 **Hayworth**	Y	N	N	N	N	N
20 **Gibson**	Y	N	Y	N	N	Y
21 Tonko	N	Y	Y	Y	Y	Y
22 Hinchey	N	Y	Y	Y	Y	Y
23 Owens	N	Y	Y	Y	Y	Y
24 **Hanna**	Y	N	N	N	N	N
25 **Buerkle**	Y	N	N	N	N	N
26 Hochul	N	Y	Y	Y	Y	Y
27 Higgins	N	Y	Y	Y	Y	Y
28 Slaughter	N	Y	Y	Y	Y	Y
29 **Reed**	Y	N	N	N	N	N
NORTH CAROLINA						
1 Butterfield	N	Y	Y	Y	Y	Y
2 **Ellmers**	Y	N	N	N	N	N
3 **Jones**	Y	N	Y	N	N	N
4 Price	N	Y	Y	Y	Y	Y

	519	520	521	522	523	524
5 **Foxx**	Y	N	N	N	N	N
6 **Coble**	Y	N	N	N	N	N
7 McIntyre	N	Y	+	N	N	N
8 Kissell	N	Y	Y	N	Y	Y
9 **Myrick**	Y	N	N	N	N	N
10 **McHenry**	Y	N	N	N	N	N
11 Shuler	Y	Y	N	N	N	Y
12 Watt	N	Y	Y	Y	Y	Y
13 Miller	N	Y	Y	Y	Y	Y
NORTH DAKOTA						
AL **Berg**	Y	N	N	N	N	N
OHIO						
1 **Chabot**	Y	N	N	N	N	N
2 **Schmidt**	Y	N	N	N	N	N
3 **Turner**	Y	N	N	N	N	N
4 **Jordan**	Y	N	N	N	N	N
5 **Latta**	Y	N	N	N	N	N
6 **Johnson**	Y	N	N	N	N	N
7 **Austria**	Y	N	N	N	N	N
8 **Boehner**						
9 Kaptur	N	Y	Y	Y	Y	Y
10 Kucinich	N	N	Y	Y	Y	Y
11 Fudge	N	Y	Y	Y	Y	Y
12 **Tiberi**	Y	N	N	N	N	N
13 Sutton	N	Y	Y	Y	Y	Y
14 **LaTourette**	Y	N	N	N	N	N
15 **Stivers**	?	?	?	?	?	?
16 **Renacci**	Y	N	N	N	N	N
17 Ryan	N	Y	Y	Y	Y	Y
18 **Gibbs**	Y	N	N	N	N	N
OKLAHOMA						
1 **Sullivan**	Y	N	N	N	N	N
2 Boren	Y	N	N	N	N	Y
3 **Lucas**	Y	N	N	N	N	N
4 **Cole**	Y	N	N	N	N	N
5 **Lankford**	Y	N	N	N	N	N
OREGON						
1 Bonamici	N	Y	Y	Y	Y	Y
2 **Walden**	Y	N	N	N	N	N
3 Blumenauer	N	Y	Y	Y	Y	Y
4 DeFazio	N	Y	Y	Y	Y	Y
5 Schrader	N	Y	Y	N	N	N
PENNSYLVANIA						
1 Brady	N	Y	Y	Y	Y	Y
2 Fattah	N	Y	Y	Y	Y	Y
3 **Kelly**	Y	N	N	N	N	N
4 Altmire	N	Y	Y	Y	Y	Y
5 **Thompson**	Y	N	N	N	N	N
6 **Gerlach**	Y	N	N	N	N	N
7 **Meehan**	Y	N	N	N	N	N
8 **Fitzpatrick**	Y	N	N	N	N	N
9 **Shuster**	Y	N	N	N	N	N
10 **Marino**	Y	N	N	N	N	N
11 **Barletta**	Y	N	N	N	N	N
12 Critz	N	Y	Y	Y	Y	Y
13 Schwartz	N	Y	Y	Y	Y	Y
14 Doyle	N	Y	Y	Y	Y	Y
15 **Dent**	Y	N	N	N	N	N
16 **Pitts**	Y	N	N	N	N	N
17 Holden	N	Y	Y	Y	Y	Y
18 **Murphy**	Y	N	N	N	N	N
19 **Platts**	Y	N	?	?	N	N
RHODE ISLAND						
1 Cicilline	N	Y	Y	Y	Y	Y
2 Langevin	N	Y	Y	Y	Y	Y
SOUTH CAROLINA						
1 **Scott**	Y	N	N	N	N	N
2 **Wilson**	Y	N	N	N	N	N
3 **Duncan**	Y	N	N	N	N	?
4 **Gowdy**	Y	N	N	N	N	N
5 **Mulvaney**	Y	N	N	N	N	N
6 Clyburn	N	Y	Y	Y	Y	Y
SOUTH DAKOTA						
AL **Noem**	Y	N	N	N	N	N
TENNESSEE						
1 **Roe**	Y	N	N	N	N	N
2 **Duncan**	Y	N	N	N	N	N
3 **Fleischmann**	Y	N	N	N	N	N
4 **DesJarlais**	Y	N	N	N	N	N
5 Cooper	N	Y	Y	Y	Y	Y
6 **Black**	Y	N	N	N	N	N
7 **Blackburn**	Y	N	N	N	N	N
8 **Fincher**	Y	N	N	N	N	N
9 Cohen	N	Y	Y	Y	Y	Y

	519	520	521	522	523	524
TEXAS						
1 **Gohmert**	Y	N	N	N	N	N
2 **Poe**	Y	N	N	N	N	N
3 **Johnson, S.**	Y	N	N	N	N	N
4 **Hall**	Y	N	N	N	N	N
5 **Hensarling**	Y	N	N	N	N	N
6 **Barton**	Y	N	N	N	N	N
7 **Culberson**	?	?	?	?	?	?
8 **Brady**	Y	N	N	?	N	N
9 Green, A.	N	Y	Y	Y	Y	Y
10 **McCaul**	Y	N	N	N	N	N
11 **Conaway**	Y	N	N	N	N	N
12 **Granger**	Y	N	N	N	N	N
13 **Thornberry**	Y	N	N	N	N	N
14 **Paul**	Y	N	N	N	N	N
15 Hinojosa	N	Y	Y	Y	Y	Y
16 Reyes	N	Y	Y	Y	Y	Y
17 **Flores**	Y	N	N	N	N	N
18 Jackson Lee	?	?	?	?	?	?
19 **Neugebauer**	Y	N	N	N	N	N
20 Gonzalez	N	Y	Y	Y	Y	Y
21 **Smith**	Y	N	N	N	N	N
22 **Olson**	Y	N	N	N	N	N
23 **Canseco**	Y	N	N	N	N	N
24 **Marchant**	Y	N	N	N	N	?
25 Doggett	N	Y	Y	Y	Y	Y
26 **Burgess**	Y	N	N	N	N	N
27 **Farenthold**	Y	N	N	N	N	N
28 Cuellar	N	Y	Y	Y	Y	Y
29 Green, G.	N	Y	Y	Y	Y	Y
30 Johnson, E.	N	Y	Y	Y	Y	Y
31 **Carter**	Y	N	N	N	N	N
32 **Sessions**	Y	N	N	N	N	N
UTAH						
1 **Bishop**	?	N	N	N	N	N
2 Matheson	Y	N	N	N	N	Y
3 **Chaffetz**	Y	N	N	N	N	N
VERMONT						
AL Welch	N	Y	Y	Y	Y	Y
VIRGINIA						
1 **Wittman**	Y	N	N	N	N	N
2 **Rigell**	Y	N	N	N	N	Y
3 Scott	N	Y	Y	Y	Y	Y
4 **Forbes**	Y	N	N	N	N	N
5 **Hurt**	Y	N	N	N	N	N
6 **Goodlatte**	Y	N	N	N	N	N
7 **Cantor**	Y	N	N	N	N	N
8 Moran	N	Y	Y	Y	Y	Y
9 **Griffith**	Y	N	N	N	N	N
10 **Wolf**	Y	N	N	N	N	N
11 Connolly	N	Y	Y	Y	Y	Y
WASHINGTON						
1 Vacant						
2 Larsen	N	Y	Y	Y	Y	Y
3 **Herrera Beutler**	Y	N	N	N	N	N
4 **Hastings**	Y	N	N	N	N	N
5 **McMorris Rodgers**	Y	N	N	N	N	N
6 Dicks	N	Y	Y	Y	Y	Y
7 McDermott	N	Y	Y	Y	Y	Y
8 **Reichert**	Y	N	N	N	N	N
9 Smith	N	Y	?	Y	Y	Y
WEST VIRGINIA						
1 **McKinley**	Y	N	N	N	N	N
2 **Capito**	Y	N	N	N	N	N
3 Rahall	N	N	Y	N	N	Y
WISCONSIN						
1 **Ryan**	Y	N	N	N	N	N
2 Baldwin	N	Y	Y	Y	Y	Y
3 Kind	N	Y	Y	Y	Y	Y
4 Moore	N	Y	Y	Y	Y	Y
5 **Sensenbrenner**	Y	N	N	N	N	N
6 **Petri**	Y	N	N	N	N	N
7 **Duffy**	Y	N	N	N	N	N
8 **Ribble**	Y	N	N	N	N	N
WYOMING						
AL **Lummis**	Y	N	N	N	N	N

IN THE HOUSE | By Vote Number

525. HR 4078. Regulatory Revisions/Attorney Fees. Posey, R-Fla., amendment that would require any attorney fees paid as a result of federal agency violations of the bill's moratorium on "significant regulatory actions" to be paid out of the offending agency's administrative budget. Adopted in Committee of the Whole 248-171: R 230-6; D 18-165. July 26, 2012.

526. HR 4078. Regulatory Revisions/Nuclear-Power and Environmental-Review Regulations. Nadler, D-N.Y., amendment that would exempt regulations related to nuclear power plant safety from the definition of "significant regulatory actions" and from provisions related to consent decrees, settlement agreements and environmental review requirements. Rejected in Committee of the Whole 176-243: R 9-227; D 167-16. July 26, 2012.

527. HR 4078. Regulatory Revisions/'Significant Regulatory Action' Definition. McKinley, R-W.Va., amendment that would reduce the economic cost threshold for the definition of "significant regulatory action" from $100 million to $50 million. Adopted in Committee of the Whole 240-178: R 226-10; D 14-168. July 26, 2012.

528. HR 4078. Regulatory Revisions/Workplace Injuries and Flammable-Dust Regulations. Miller, D-Calif., amendment that would exempt regulations designed to prevent workplace injuries or deaths resulting from the ignition of flammable dust from the definition of "significant regulatory actions" and the restrictions on "midnight rules." Rejected in Committee of the Whole 174-239: R 2-231; D 172-8. July 26, 2012.

529. HR 4078. Regulatory Revisions/Workplace Injuries and High-Voltage Regulations. Woolsey, D-Calif., amendment that would exempt regulations designed to reduce the number of electrocutions or fatalities resulting from working with high-voltage transmission and distribution lines from the definition of "significant regulatory actions" and the restrictions on "midnight rules." Rejected in Committee of the Whole 178-236: R 5-229; D 173-7. July 26, 2012.

530. HR 4078. Regulatory Revisions/SEC Cost-Benefit Analysis. Waters, D-Calif., amendment that would authorize the appropriation of such sums as necessary for the Securities and Exchange Commission to carry out the cost-benefit analysis requirements of the bill. Rejected in Committee of the Whole 171-247: R 1-235; D 170-12. July 26, 2012.

	525	526	527	528	529	530
ALABAMA						
1 **Bonner**	Y	N	Y	N	N	N
2 **Roby**	Y	N	Y	N	N	N
3 **Rogers**	Y	N	Y	N	N	N
4 **Aderholt**	Y	N	Y	N	N	N
5 **Brooks**	Y	N	Y	N	N	N
6 **Bachus**	N	N	Y	N	N	N
7 Sewell	N	Y	N	Y	Y	Y
ALASKA						
AL **Young**	Y	N	Y	N	N	N
ARIZONA						
1 **Gosar**	Y	N	Y	N	N	N
2 **Franks**	Y	N	Y	N	N	N
3 **Quayle**	Y	N	Y	N	N	N
4 Pastor	Y	Y	N	Y	Y	Y
5 **Schweikert**	Y	N	Y	N	N	N
6 **Flake**	Y	N	Y	N	N	N
7 Grijalva	N	Y	N	Y	Y	Y
8 Barber	N	Y	N	Y	Y	Y
ARKANSAS						
1 **Crawford**	Y	N	Y	N	N	N
2 **Griffin**	Y	N	Y	N	N	N
3 **Womack**	Y	N	Y	N	N	N
4 Ross	Y	N	Y	N	Y	N
CALIFORNIA						
1 Thompson	N	Y	N	Y	Y	Y
2 **Herger**	Y	N	Y	N	N	N
3 **Lungren**	Y	N	Y	N	N	N
4 **McClintock**	Y	N	Y	N	N	N
5 Matsui	N	Y	N	Y	Y	Y
6 Woolsey	N	Y	N	Y	Y	Y
7 Miller, George	N	Y	N	Y	Y	Y
8 Pelosi	N	Y	N	Y	Y	Y
9 Lee	N	Y	N	Y	Y	Y
10 Garamendi	N	Y	N	Y	Y	Y
11 McNerney	N	Y	N	Y	Y	Y
12 Speier	N	Y	N	Y	Y	Y
13 Stark	N	Y	N	Y	Y	Y
14 Eshoo	N	Y	N	Y	Y	Y
15 Honda	N	Y	N	Y	Y	Y
16 Lofgren	N	Y	N	Y	Y	Y
17 Farr	N	Y	N	Y	Y	Y
18 Cardoza	?	?	?	?	?	?
19 **Denham**	Y	N	Y	N	N	N
20 Costa	Y	N	N	N	N	Y
21 **Nunes**	Y	N	Y	N	N	N
22 **McCarthy**	Y	N	Y	N	N	N
23 Capps	N	Y	N	Y	Y	Y
24 **Gallegly**	Y	N	Y	N	N	N
25 **McKeon**	Y	N	Y	N	N	N
26 **Dreier**	Y	N	Y	N	N	N
27 Sherman	N	Y	Y	Y	Y	Y
28 Berman	N	Y	N	Y	Y	Y
29 Schiff	N	Y	N	Y	Y	Y
30 Waxman	N	Y	?	Y	Y	Y
31 Becerra	N	Y	N	Y	Y	Y
32 Chu	N	Y	N	Y	Y	Y
33 Bass	Y	Y	N	?	Y	Y
34 Roybal-Allard	N	Y	N	Y	Y	Y
35 Waters	N	Y	N	Y	Y	Y
36 Hahn	N	Y	N	Y	Y	Y
37 Richardson	N	Y	N	Y	Y	Y
38 Napolitano	N	Y	N	Y	Y	Y
39 Sánchez, Linda	N	Y	N	Y	Y	Y
40 **Royce**	Y	N	Y	N	N	N
41 **Lewis**	Y	N	Y	N	N	N
42 **Miller, Gary**	Y	N	Y	N	N	N
43 Baca	N	Y	N	Y	Y	Y
44 **Calvert**	Y	N	Y	N	N	N
45 **Bono Mack**	Y	N	Y	N	N	N
46 **Rohrabacher**	Y	N	Y	N	N	N
47 Sanchez, Loretta	N	Y	N	Y	Y	Y
48 **Campbell**	Y	N	Y	N	N	N
49 **Issa**	Y	N	Y	N	N	N
50 **Bilbray**	Y	N	N	N	N	N
51 Filner	N	Y	N	Y	Y	Y
52 **Hunter**	Y	N	Y	N	N	N
53 Davis	N	Y	N	Y	Y	Y

	525	526	527	528	529	530
COLORADO						
1 DeGette	N	Y	N	Y	Y	Y
2 Polis	N	Y	N	Y	Y	Y
3 **Tipton**	Y	N	Y	N	N	N
4 **Gardner**	Y	N	Y	N	N	N
5 **Lamborn**	Y	N	Y	N	N	N
6 **Coffman**	Y	N	Y	N	N	N
7 Perlmutter	N	Y	N	Y	Y	Y
CONNECTICUT						
1 Larson	N	Y	N	Y	Y	Y
2 Courtney	N	Y	N	Y	?	Y
3 DeLauro	N	Y	N	Y	Y	Y
4 Himes	N	Y	N	Y	Y	Y
5 Murphy	?	?	?	?	?	?
DELAWARE						
AL Carney	N	Y	N	Y	Y	Y
FLORIDA						
1 **Miller**	Y	N	Y	N	N	N
2 **Southerland**	Y	N	Y	N	N	N
3 Brown	N	Y	N	Y	Y	Y
4 **Crenshaw**	Y	N	Y	N	N	N
5 **Nugent**	Y	N	Y	N	N	N
6 **Stearns**	Y	N	Y	N	N	N
7 **Mica**	Y	N	Y	N	N	N
8 **Webster**	Y	N	Y	N	N	N
9 **Bilirakis**	Y	N	Y	N	N	N
10 **Young**	Y	N	Y	N	N	N
11 Castor	N	Y	N	Y	Y	Y
12 **Ross**	Y	N	Y	N	N	N
13 **Buchanan**	Y	N	Y	N	N	N
14 **Mack**	?	?	?	?	?	?
15 **Posey**	Y	N	Y	N	N	N
16 **Rooney**	Y	N	Y	N	N	N
17 Wilson	N	Y	N	Y	Y	Y
18 **Ros-Lehtinen**	Y	N	Y	N	N	N
19 Deutch	N	Y	N	Y	Y	Y
20 Wasserman Schultz	N	Y	N	Y	Y	Y
21 **Diaz-Balart**	Y	N	Y	N	N	N
22 **West**	Y	N	Y	N	N	N
23 Hastings	N	Y	N	Y	Y	Y
24 **Adams**	Y	N	Y	N	N	N
25 **Rivera**	Y	N	Y	N	N	N
GEORGIA						
1 **Kingston**	Y	N	Y	N	N	N
2 Bishop	N	Y	N	Y	Y	Y
3 **Westmoreland**	Y	N	Y	N	N	N
4 Johnson	N	Y	N	Y	Y	Y
5 Lewis	N	Y	N	Y	Y	Y
6 **Price**	Y	N	Y	N	N	N
7 **Woodall**	Y	N	Y	N	N	N
8 **Scott, A.**	Y	N	Y	N	N	N
9 **Graves**	Y	N	Y	N	N	N
10 **Broun**	Y	N	Y	N	N	N
11 **Gingrey**	Y	N	Y	N	N	N
12 Barrow	Y	N	Y	N	Y	N
13 Scott, D.	N	Y	N	Y	Y	Y
HAWAII						
1 Hanabusa	N	Y	N	Y	Y	Y
2 Hirono	?	?	?	?	?	?
IDAHO						
1 **Labrador**	Y	N	Y	N	N	N
2 **Simpson**	Y	N	Y	N	N	N
ILLINOIS						
1 Rush	N	Y	N	Y	Y	Y
2 Jackson	?	?	?	?	?	?
3 Lipinski	N	N	N	Y	Y	Y
4 Gutierrez	N	Y	N	?	Y	Y
5 Quigley	N	Y	N	Y	Y	Y
6 **Roskam**	Y	N	Y	N	N	N
7 Davis	?	?	?	?	?	?
8 **Walsh**	Y	N	Y	N	N	N
9 Schakowsky	N	Y	N	Y	Y	Y
10 **Dold**	Y	N	N	N	N	N
11 **Kinzinger**	Y	N	Y	N	N	N
12 Costello	N	N	Y	Y	Y	Y
13 **Biggert**	N	N	Y	N	N	N
14 **Hultgren**	Y	N	Y	N	N	N
15 **Johnson**	N	Y	N	N	Y	N

KEY   Republicans   Democrats

Y Voted for (yea)	X Paired against	C Voted "present" to avoid possible conflict of interest
# Paired for	– Announced against	
+ Announced for	P Voted "present"	? Did not vote or otherwise make a position known
N Voted against (nay)		

	525	526	527	528	529	530
16 **Manzullo**	Y	N	Y	N	N	N
17 **Schilling**	Y	N	Y	N	N	N
18 **Schock**	Y	N	Y	N	N	N
19 **Shimkus**	Y	N	Y	N	N	N
INDIANA						
1 Visclosky	N	Y	N	Y	Y	Y
2 Donnelly	N	Y	Y	Y	Y	Y
3 **Stutzman**	Y	N	Y	N	N	N
4 **Rokita**	Y	N	Y	N	N	N
5 **Burton**	Y	N	Y	N	N	N
6 **Pence**	Y	N	Y	N	N	N
7 Carson	N	Y	N	Y	Y	Y
8 **Bucshon**	Y	N	Y	N	N	N
9 **Young**	Y	N	Y	N	N	N
IOWA						
1 Braley	N	Y	N	Y	Y	Y
2 Loebsack	Y	Y	N	Y	Y	Y
3 Boswell	Y	Y	N	Y	Y	Y
4 **Latham**	Y	N	Y	N	N	N
5 **King**	Y	N	Y	N	N	N
KANSAS						
1 **Huelskamp**	Y	N	Y	N	N	N
2 **Jenkins**	Y	N	Y	N	N	N
3 **Yoder**	Y	N	Y	N	N	N
4 **Pompeo**	Y	N	Y	N	N	N
KENTUCKY						
1 **Whitfield**	Y	N	Y	N	N	N
2 **Guthrie**	Y	N	Y	N	N	N
3 Yarmuth	N	Y	N	Y	Y	Y
4 **Davis**	Y	N	Y	N	N	N
5 **Rogers**	Y	N	Y	N	N	N
6 Chandler	Y	Y	N	Y	Y	N
LOUISIANA						
1 **Scalise**	Y	N	Y	N	N	N
2 Richmond	N	Y	N	Y	Y	Y
3 **Landry**	Y	N	Y	N	N	N
4 **Fleming**	Y	N	Y	N	N	N
5 **Alexander**	Y	N	Y	N	N	N
6 **Cassidy**	Y	N	Y	N	N	N
7 **Boustany**	Y	N	Y	N	N	N
MAINE						
1 Pingree	N	Y	N	Y	Y	Y
2 Michaud	N	Y	N	N	Y	Y
MARYLAND						
1 **Harris**	Y	N	Y	N	N	N
2 Ruppersberger	N	Y	N	Y	Y	Y
3 Sarbanes	N	Y	N	Y	Y	Y
4 Edwards	N	Y	N	Y	Y	Y
5 Hoyer	N	Y	N	Y	Y	Y
6 **Bartlett**	Y	N	Y	N	N	N
7 Cummings	N	Y	N	Y	Y	Y
8 Van Hollen	N	Y	N	Y	Y	Y
MASSACHUSETTS						
1 Olver	N	Y	N	Y	Y	Y
2 Neal	N	Y	N	Y	Y	Y
3 McGovern	N	Y	N	Y	Y	Y
4 Frank	N	Y	N	Y	Y	Y
5 Tsongas	N	Y	N	Y	Y	Y
6 Tierney	N	Y	N	Y	Y	Y
7 Markey	N	Y	N	Y	Y	Y
8 Capuano	N	Y	N	Y	Y	Y
9 Lynch	N	Y	Y	Y	Y	Y
10 Keating	N	Y	N	Y	Y	Y
MICHIGAN						
1 **Benishek**	Y	N	Y	N	N	N
2 **Huizenga**	Y	N	Y	N	N	N
3 **Amash**	Y	N	Y	N	N	N
4 **Camp**	Y	N	Y	N	N	N
5 Kildee	N	Y	N	Y	Y	Y
6 **Upton**	Y	N	Y	N	N	N
7 **Walberg**	Y	N	Y	N	N	N
8 **Rogers**	Y	N	Y	?	N	N
9 Peters	N	Y	N	Y	Y	Y
10 **Miller**	Y	N	Y	N	N	N
11 Vacant						
12 Levin	N	Y	N	Y	Y	Y
13 Clarke	N	Y	N	Y	Y	Y
14 Conyers	N	Y	N	Y	Y	Y
15 Dingell	N	Y	N	Y	Y	Y
MINNESOTA						
1 Walz	N	Y	N	Y	Y	Y
2 **Kline**	Y	N	Y	N	N	N
3 **Paulsen**	Y	N	Y	N	N	N
4 McCollum	N	Y	N	Y	Y	Y
5 Ellison	N	Y	N	Y	Y	Y
6 **Bachmann**	Y	N	Y	N	N	N
7 Peterson	Y	N	N	N	N	N
8 **Cravaack**	Y	N	Y	N	N	N
MISSISSIPPI						
1 **Nunnelee**	Y	N	Y	N	N	N
2 Thompson	N	Y	N	Y	Y	Y
3 **Harper**	Y	N	Y	N	N	N
4 **Palazzo**	Y	N	Y	N	N	N
MISSOURI						
1 Clay	N	Y	N	Y	Y	Y
2 **Akin**	+	–	+	–	–	–
3 Carnahan	N	Y	N	Y	Y	Y
4 **Hartzler**	Y	N	Y	N	N	N
5 Cleaver	N	Y	N	Y	Y	Y
6 **Graves**	Y	N	Y	N	N	N
7 **Long**	N	N	Y	N	N	N
8 **Emerson**	Y	N	Y	N	N	N
9 **Luetkemeyer**	Y	N	Y	N	N	N
MONTANA						
AL **Rehberg**	Y	N	Y	N	N	N
NEBRASKA						
1 **Fortenberry**	Y	N	Y	N	N	N
2 **Terry**	Y	N	Y	N	N	N
3 **Smith**	Y	N	Y	N	N	N
NEVADA						
1 Berkley	N	Y	N	Y	Y	Y
2 **Amodei**	Y	N	Y	N	N	N
3 **Heck**	Y	N	Y	N	N	N
NEW HAMPSHIRE						
1 **Guinta**	Y	N	Y	N	N	N
2 **Bass**	N	N	N	N	N	N
NEW JERSEY						
1 Andrews	N	Y	N	Y	Y	Y
2 **LoBiondo**	Y	N	N	N	Y	N
3 **Runyan**	Y	N	Y	N	Y	N
4 **Smith**	Y	N	Y	N	N	N
5 **Garrett**	Y	N	Y	N	N	N
6 Pallone	N	Y	N	Y	Y	Y
7 **Lance**	Y	N	Y	N	N	N
8 Pascrell	N	Y	N	Y	?	Y
9 Rothman	N	Y	N	Y	Y	Y
10 Vacant						
11 **Frelinghuysen**	Y	N	Y	N	N	N
12 Holt	N	Y	N	Y	Y	Y
13 Sires	N	Y	N	Y	Y	Y
NEW MEXICO						
1 Heinrich	N	Y	N	Y	Y	Y
2 **Pearce**	Y	N	Y	N	N	N
3 Luján	N	Y	N	Y	Y	Y
NEW YORK						
1 Bishop	N	Y	N	Y	Y	Y
2 Israel	N	N	N	Y	Y	Y
3 **King**	Y	N	Y	N	N	N
4 McCarthy	N	Y	N	Y	Y	Y
5 Ackerman	?	?	?	?	?	?
6 Meeks	?	?	?	?	?	?
7 Crowley	N	Y	N	Y	Y	Y
8 Nadler	N	Y	N	Y	Y	Y
9 **Turner**	Y	N	Y	N	N	N
10 Towns	N	Y	N	Y	Y	Y
11 Clarke	N	Y	N	Y	Y	Y
12 Velázquez	N	Y	N	Y	Y	Y
13 **Grimm**	Y	N	Y	N	N	N
14 Maloney	N	Y	N	Y	Y	Y
15 Rangel	N	Y	N	Y	Y	Y
16 Serrano	N	Y	N	Y	Y	Y
17 Engel	N	Y	N	Y	Y	Y
18 Lowey	N	Y	N	Y	Y	Y
19 **Hayworth**	Y	Y	N	N	N	N
20 **Gibson**	Y	Y	N	Y	Y	N
21 Tonko	N	Y	N	Y	Y	Y
22 Hinchey	N	Y	N	Y	Y	Y
23 Owens	Y	N	N	N	N	Y
24 **Hanna**	Y	N	Y	N	N	N
25 **Buerkle**	Y	N	Y	N	N	N
26 Hochul	N	Y	N	Y	Y	N
27 Higgins	N	Y	N	Y	Y	Y
28 Slaughter	N	Y	N	Y	Y	Y
29 **Reed**	Y	N	Y	N	N	N
NORTH CAROLINA						
1 Butterfield	N	Y	N	Y	Y	Y
2 **Ellmers**	Y	N	Y	N	N	N
3 **Jones**	Y	Y	Y	N	N	Y
4 Price	N	Y	N	Y	Y	Y
5 **Foxx**	Y	N	N	N	N	N
6 **Coble**	Y	N	Y	N	N	N
7 McIntyre	Y	Y	Y	Y	Y	N
8 Kissell	N	Y	Y	Y	Y	Y
9 **Myrick**	Y	N	Y	N	N	N
10 **McHenry**	Y	N	Y	N	N	N
11 Shuler	N	N	N	N	N	N
12 Watt	N	Y	N	Y	Y	Y
13 Miller	N	Y	N	Y	Y	Y
NORTH DAKOTA						
AL **Berg**	Y	N	Y	N	N	N
OHIO						
1 **Chabot**	Y	N	Y	N	N	N
2 **Schmidt**	Y	N	Y	N	N	N
3 **Turner**	Y	N	Y	N	N	N
4 **Jordan**	Y	N	Y	N	N	N
5 **Latta**	Y	N	Y	N	N	N
6 **Johnson**	Y	N	Y	N	N	N
7 **Austria**	Y	N	Y	N	N	N
8 **Boehner**		?				
9 Kaptur	N	N	Y	Y	Y	Y
10 Kucinich	N	Y	N	Y	Y	Y
11 Fudge	N	Y	N	Y	Y	Y
12 **Tiberi**	Y	N	Y	N	N	N
13 Sutton	N	Y	N	Y	Y	Y
14 **LaTourette**	Y	N	N	N	N	N
15 **Stivers**	?	?	?	?	?	?
16 **Renacci**	Y	N	Y	N	N	N
17 Ryan	N	Y	N	Y	Y	Y
18 **Gibbs**	Y	N	Y	N	N	N
OKLAHOMA						
1 **Sullivan**	Y	N	Y	?	N	N
2 Boren	Y	N	Y	N	N	N
3 **Lucas**	Y	N	N	N	N	N
4 **Cole**	Y	N	Y	N	N	N
5 **Lankford**	Y	N	Y	N	N	N
OREGON						
1 Bonamici	N	Y	N	Y	Y	Y
2 **Walden**	Y	N	Y	N	N	N
3 Blumenauer	N	Y	N	Y	Y	Y
4 DeFazio	N	Y	N	Y	Y	Y
5 Schrader	N	Y	N	Y	Y	N
PENNSYLVANIA						
1 Brady	N	Y	N	Y	Y	Y
2 Fattah	N	Y	N	?	?	?
3 **Kelly**	Y	N	Y	N	N	N
4 Altmire	Y	N	N	Y	Y	N
5 **Thompson**	Y	N	Y	N	N	N
6 **Gerlach**	Y	Y	Y	N	N	N
7 **Meehan**	Y	N	Y	N	N	N
8 **Fitzpatrick**	Y	Y	Y	N	N	N
9 **Shuster**	Y	N	Y	N	N	N
10 **Marino**	Y	N	Y	N	N	N
11 **Barletta**	Y	N	Y	N	N	N
12 Critz	N	Y	N	Y	Y	Y
13 Schwartz	N	Y	N	Y	Y	Y
14 Doyle	N	Y	N	Y	Y	Y
15 **Dent**	Y	Y	Y	N	N	N
16 **Pitts**	Y	N	Y	N	N	N
17 Holden	Y	N	N	Y	Y	Y
18 **Murphy**	Y	N	Y	N	N	N
19 **Platts**	Y	Y	Y	N	N	N
RHODE ISLAND						
1 Cicilline	N	Y	N	Y	Y	Y
2 Langevin	N	Y	N	Y	Y	Y
SOUTH CAROLINA						
1 **Scott**	Y	N	Y	N	N	N
2 **Wilson**	Y	N	Y	N	N	N
3 **Duncan**	Y	N	Y	N	N	N
4 **Gowdy**	Y	N	Y	N	N	N
5 **Mulvaney**	Y	N	Y	N	N	N
6 Clyburn	N	Y	N	Y	Y	Y
SOUTH DAKOTA						
AL **Noem**	Y	N	Y	N	N	N
TENNESSEE						
1 **Roe**	Y	N	Y	N	N	N
2 **Duncan**	Y	N	Y	N	N	N
3 **Fleischmann**	Y	N	Y	N	N	N
4 **DesJarlais**	Y	N	Y	N	N	N
5 Cooper	N	Y	N	Y	Y	Y
6 **Black**	Y	N	Y	N	N	N
7 **Blackburn**	Y	N	Y	N	N	N
8 **Fincher**	Y	N	Y	N	N	N
9 Cohen	N	Y	N	Y	Y	Y
TEXAS						
1 **Gohmert**	Y	N	Y	N	N	N
2 **Poe**	Y	N	Y	N	N	N
3 **Johnson, S.**	Y	N	Y	N	N	N
4 **Hall**	Y	N	Y	N	N	N
5 **Hensarling**	Y	N	Y	N	N	N
6 **Barton**	Y	N	Y	N	N	N
7 **Culberson**	?	?	?	?	?	?
8 **Brady**	Y	N	Y	N	N	N
9 Green, A.	N	Y	N	Y	Y	Y
10 **McCaul**	Y	N	Y	N	N	N
11 **Conaway**	Y	N	Y	N	N	N
12 **Granger**	Y	N	Y	N	N	N
13 **Thornberry**	Y	N	Y	N	N	N
14 **Paul**	Y	N	Y	N	N	N
15 Hinojosa	N	Y	N	Y	Y	Y
16 Reyes	N	Y	N	Y	Y	Y
17 **Flores**	Y	N	Y	N	N	N
18 Jackson Lee	?	?	?	?	?	?
19 **Neugebauer**	Y	N	Y	N	N	N
20 Gonzalez	N	Y	N	Y	Y	Y
21 **Smith**	Y	N	Y	N	?	N
22 **Olson**	Y	N	Y	N	N	N
23 **Canseco**	Y	N	Y	N	N	N
24 **Marchant**	Y	N	Y	?	N	N
25 Doggett	N	Y	N	Y	Y	Y
26 **Burgess**	Y	N	Y	N	N	N
27 **Farenthold**	Y	N	Y	N	N	N
28 Cuellar	Y	Y	Y	Y	Y	Y
29 Green, G.	Y	N	Y	Y	Y	N
30 Johnson, E.	N	Y	N	Y	Y	Y
31 **Carter**	Y	N	Y	N	N	N
32 **Sessions**	Y	N	Y	N	N	N
UTAH						
1 **Bishop**	Y	N	Y	N	?	N
2 Matheson	Y	N	Y	N	N	N
3 **Chaffetz**	Y	N	Y	N	N	N
VERMONT						
AL Welch	N	Y	N	Y	Y	Y
VIRGINIA						
1 **Wittman**	Y	N	Y	N	N	N
2 **Rigell**	Y	N	Y	N	N	N
3 Scott	N	Y	N	Y	Y	Y
4 **Forbes**	Y	N	Y	N	N	N
5 **Hurt**	Y	N	Y	N	N	N
6 **Goodlatte**	Y	N	Y	N	N	N
7 **Cantor**	Y	N	Y	N	N	N
8 Moran	N	Y	N	Y	Y	Y
9 **Griffith**	Y	N	Y	N	N	N
10 **Wolf**	N	N	Y	N	N	N
11 Connolly	N	Y	N	Y	Y	Y
WASHINGTON						
1 Vacant						
2 Larsen	N	Y	N	Y	Y	Y
3 **Herrera Beutler**	Y	N	Y	N	N	N
4 **Hastings**	Y	N	Y	N	N	N
5 **McMorris Rodgers**	Y	N	Y	N	N	N
6 Dicks	N	Y	N	Y	Y	Y
7 McDermott	N	Y	N	Y	Y	Y
8 **Reichert**	Y	Y	Y	Y	Y	N
9 Smith	N	Y	N	Y	Y	Y
WEST VIRGINIA						
1 **McKinley**	Y	N	Y	N	N	N
2 **Capito**	Y	N	Y	N	N	N
3 Rahall	Y	N	Y	Y	Y	Y
WISCONSIN						
1 **Ryan**	Y	N	Y	N	N	N
2 Baldwin	N	Y	N	Y	Y	Y
3 Kind	N	Y	N	Y	Y	Y
4 Moore	N	Y	N	Y	Y	Y
5 **Sensenbrenner**	Y	N	Y	N	N	N
6 **Petri**	Y	N	Y	N	N	N
7 **Duffy**	Y	N	Y	N	N	N
8 **Ribble**	Y	N	Y	N	N	N
WYOMING						
AL **Lummis**	Y	N	Y	N	N	N

IN THE HOUSE | By Vote Number

531. HR 4078. Regulatory Revisions/Financial Reporting Requirements. Fitzpatrick, R-Pa., amendment that would direct the Securities and Exchange Commission to conduct a cost-benefit analysis on financial reporting requirements for companies with $250 million or less in outstanding shares controlled by public investors, referred to as a "public float." Adopted in Committee of the Whole 251-166: R 233-3; D 18-163. July 26, 2012.

532. HR 4078. Regulatory Revisions/Climate Change Regulations. Posey, R-Fla., amendment that would bar the Securities and Exchange Commission from issuing or enforcing interpretive guidance designed to address climate change. Adopted in Committee of the Whole 245-171: R 231-5; D 14-166. July 26, 2012.

533. HR 4078. Regulatory Revisions/SEC Provisions. Maloney, D-N.Y., amendment that would delay the implementation of the bill's provisions related to the Securities and Exchange Commission until the SEC certifies that the requirements for a cost-benefit analysis would not divert resources from the agency's core mission. Rejected in Committee of the Whole 173-243: R 2-234; D 171-9. July 26, 2012.

534. HR 4078. Regulatory Revisions/Non-Resident Aliens. Posey, R-Fla., amendment that would bar the Treasury Department from issuing regulations regarding bank deposits of foreign citizens. Adopted in Committee of the Whole 251-165: R 233-3; D 18-162. July 26, 2012.

535. HR 4078. Regulatory Revisions/Recommit. Sutton, D-Ohio, motion to recommit the bill to the House Oversight and Government Reform Committee and report it back immediately with an amendment that would provide exemptions from the bill's moratorium on regulations for laws dealing with offshore bank account disclosures, middle-income tax relief, consumer protections, invasive species, prescription drug safety, home foreclosure relief or predatory lending. Motion rejected 181-234: R 1-233; D 180-1. July 26, 2012.

536. HR 4078. Regulatory Revisions/Passage. Passage of the bill that would prohibit federal agencies from issuing new rules that have an annual economic cost of more than $50 million until the unemployment rate drops to or below 6 percent. It also would prevent outgoing administrations from proposing or finalizing so-called "midnight rules" after Election Day. The measure would permit third-party intervention in litigation between private parties and government agencies that could result in legal settlements compelling agencies to take regulatory actions. It also would require most independent regulatory agencies to assess the effects of significant regulations that are exempted under current law and it would change the environmental review process for permits. Passed 245-172: R 232-2; D 13-170. A "nay" was a vote in support of the president's position. July 26, 2012.

	531	532	533	534	535	536
ALABAMA						
1 Bonner	Y	Y	N	Y	N	Y
2 Roby	Y	Y	N	Y	N	Y
3 Rogers	Y	Y	N	Y	N	Y
4 Aderholt	Y	Y	N	Y	N	Y
5 Brooks	Y	Y	N	Y	N	Y
6 Bachus	Y	Y	N	Y	N	Y
7 Sewell	N	N	Y	N	?	N
ALASKA						
AL Young	Y	Y	N	Y	N	Y
ARIZONA						
1 Gosar	Y	Y	N	Y	N	Y
2 Franks	Y	Y	N	Y	N	Y
3 Quayle	Y	Y	N	Y	N	Y
4 Pastor	N	N	Y	N	Y	N
5 Schweikert	Y	Y	N	Y	N	Y
6 Flake	Y	Y	N	Y	N	Y
7 Grijalva	N	N	Y	N	Y	N
8 Barber	N	N	Y	N	Y	N
ARKANSAS						
1 Crawford	Y	Y	N	Y	N	Y
2 Griffin	Y	Y	N	Y	N	Y
3 Womack	Y	Y	N	Y	N	Y
4 Ross	Y	Y	N	Y	Y	Y
CALIFORNIA						
1 Thompson	N	N	Y	N	Y	N
2 Herger	Y	Y	N	Y	N	Y
3 Lungren	Y	Y	N	Y	N	Y
4 McClintock	Y	Y	N	Y	N	Y
5 Matsui	N	N	Y	N	Y	N
6 Woolsey	N	N	Y	N	Y	N
7 Miller, George	N	N	Y	N	Y	N
8 Pelosi	N	N	Y	N	Y	N
9 Lee	N	N	Y	N	Y	N
10 Garamendi	N	N	Y	N	Y	N
11 McNerney	N	N	Y	N	Y	N
12 Speier	N	N	Y	N	Y	N
13 Stark	N	N	Y	N	Y	N
14 Eshoo	N	N	Y	N	Y	N
15 Honda	N	N	Y	N	Y	N
16 Lofgren	N	N	Y	N	Y	N
17 Farr	N	N	Y	N	Y	N
18 Cardoza	?	?	?	?	?	?
19 Denham	Y	Y	N	Y	N	Y
20 Costa	N	N	Y	N	Y	Y
21 Nunes	Y	Y	N	Y	N	Y
22 McCarthy	Y	Y	N	Y	N	Y
23 Capps	N	N	Y	N	Y	N
24 Gallegly	Y	Y	N	Y	N	Y
25 McKeon	Y	Y	N	Y	N	Y
26 Dreier	Y	Y	N	Y	N	Y
27 Sherman	N	N	Y	N	Y	N
28 Berman	N	N	Y	N	Y	N
29 Schiff	N	N	Y	N	Y	N
30 Waxman	N	N	Y	N	Y	N
31 Becerra	N	N	Y	N	Y	N
32 Chu	N	N	Y	N	Y	N
33 Bass	N	N	Y	N	Y	N
34 Roybal-Allard	N	N	Y	N	Y	N
35 Waters	?	N	?	?	Y	N
36 Hahn	N	N	Y	N	Y	N
37 Richardson	N	N	Y	N	Y	N
38 Napolitano	N	N	Y	N	Y	N
39 Sánchez, Linda	N	N	Y	N	Y	N
40 Royce	Y	Y	N	Y	N	Y
41 Lewis	Y	Y	N	Y	N	Y
42 Miller, Gary	Y	Y	N	Y	N	Y
43 Baca	N	N	Y	N	Y	N
44 Calvert	Y	Y	N	Y	N	Y
45 Bono Mack	Y	Y	N	Y	N	Y
46 Rohrabacher	Y	Y	N	Y	N	Y
47 Sanchez, Loretta	N	N	Y	N	Y	N
48 Campbell	N	Y	N	Y	N	Y
49 Issa	Y	Y	N	Y	N	Y
50 Bilbray	Y	Y	N	Y	?	?
51 Filner	N	N	Y	N	Y	N
52 Hunter	Y	Y	N	Y	N	Y
53 Davis	N	N	Y	N	Y	N
COLORADO						
1 DeGette	N	N	Y	N	Y	N
2 Polis	N	N	Y	N	Y	N
3 Tipton	Y	Y	N	Y	N	Y
4 Gardner	Y	Y	N	Y	N	Y
5 Lamborn	Y	Y	N	Y	N	Y
6 Coffman	Y	Y	N	Y	N	?
7 Perlmutter	N	N	Y	N	Y	N
CONNECTICUT						
1 Larson	N	N	Y	N	Y	N
2 Courtney	N	N	Y	N	Y	N
3 DeLauro	N	N	Y	N	Y	N
4 Himes	N	N	Y	Y	Y	N
5 Murphy	?	?	?	?	?	?
DELAWARE						
AL Carney	N	N	Y	N	Y	N
FLORIDA						
1 Miller	Y	Y	N	Y	N	Y
2 Southerland	Y	Y	N	Y	N	Y
3 Brown	N	N	Y	N	Y	N
4 Crenshaw	Y	Y	N	Y	N	Y
5 Nugent	Y	Y	N	Y	N	Y
6 Stearns	Y	Y	N	Y	N	Y
7 Mica	Y	Y	N	Y	N	Y
8 Webster	Y	Y	N	Y	N	Y
9 Bilirakis	Y	Y	N	Y	N	Y
10 Young	Y	Y	N	Y	N	Y
11 Castor	N	N	Y	Y	Y	N
12 Ross	Y	Y	N	Y	N	Y
13 Buchanan	Y	Y	N	Y	N	Y
14 Mack	?	?	?	?	?	?
15 Posey	Y	Y	N	Y	N	Y
16 Rooney	Y	Y	N	Y	N	Y
17 Wilson	N	N	Y	N	Y	N
18 Ros-Lehtinen	Y	Y	N	Y	N	Y
19 Deutch	N	N	Y	Y	Y	N
20 Wasserman Schultz	N	N	Y	Y	Y	N
21 Diaz-Balart	Y	Y	N	Y	N	Y
22 West	Y	Y	N	Y	N	Y
23 Hastings	N	N	Y	Y	Y	N
24 Adams	Y	Y	N	Y	N	Y
25 Rivera	Y	Y	N	Y	N	Y
GEORGIA						
1 Kingston	Y	Y	N	Y	N	Y
2 Bishop	N	Y	N	Y	N	N
3 Westmoreland	Y	Y	N	Y	N	Y
4 Johnson	N	N	Y	N	Y	N
5 Lewis	N	N	Y	N	Y	N
6 Price	Y	Y	N	Y	N	Y
7 Woodall	Y	Y	N	Y	N	Y
8 Scott, A.	Y	Y	N	Y	N	Y
9 Graves	Y	Y	N	Y	N	Y
10 Broun	Y	Y	N	N	N	Y
11 Gingrey	Y	Y	N	Y	N	Y
12 Barrow	Y	Y	N	Y	N	Y
13 Scott, D.	N	N	Y	N	Y	N
HAWAII						
1 Hanabusa	N	N	Y	N	Y	N
2 Hirono	?	?	?	?	?	?
IDAHO						
1 Labrador	Y	Y	N	Y	N	Y
2 Simpson	Y	Y	N	Y	N	Y
ILLINOIS						
1 Rush	N	N	Y	N	Y	N
2 Jackson	?	?	?	?	?	?
3 Lipinski	N	N	Y	N	Y	N
4 Gutierrez	N	N	Y	N	Y	N
5 Quigley	N	N	Y	N	Y	N
6 Roskam	Y	Y	N	Y	N	Y
7 Davis	?	?	?	?	?	?
8 Walsh	Y	Y	N	Y	N	Y
9 Schakowsky	N	N	Y	N	Y	N
10 Dold	Y	Y	N	Y	N	N
11 Kinzinger	Y	Y	N	Y	N	Y
12 Costello	N	N	Y	N	Y	N
13 Biggert	Y	Y	N	Y	N	Y
14 Hultgren	Y	Y	N	Y	N	Y
15 Johnson	Y	N	Y	N	Y	Y

	531	532	533	534	535	536
16 **Manzullo**	Y	Y	N	Y	N	Y
17 **Schilling**	Y	Y	N	Y	N	Y
18 **Schock**	Y	Y	N	Y	N	Y
19 **Shimkus**	Y	Y	N	Y	N	Y
INDIANA						
1 Visclosky	N	N	Y	N	Y	N
2 Donnelly	N	N	Y	Y	Y	N
3 **Stutzman**	Y	Y	N	Y	N	Y
4 **Rokita**	Y	Y	N	Y	N	Y
5 **Burton**	Y	Y	N	Y	N	Y
6 **Pence**	Y	Y	N	Y	N	Y
7 Carson	N	N	Y	N	Y	N
8 **Bucshon**	Y	Y	N	Y	N	Y
9 **Young**	Y	Y	N	Y	N	Y
IOWA						
1 Braley	N	N	Y	N	Y	N
2 Loebsack	Y	N	Y	N	Y	N
3 Boswell	Y	N	Y	N	Y	N
4 **Latham**	Y	Y	N	Y	N	Y
5 **King**	Y	Y	N	Y	N	Y
KANSAS						
1 **Huelskamp**	Y	Y	N	Y	N	Y
2 **Jenkins**	Y	Y	N	Y	N	Y
3 **Yoder**	Y	Y	N	Y	N	Y
4 **Pompeo**	Y	Y	N	Y	N	Y
KENTUCKY						
1 **Whitfield**	Y	Y	N	Y	N	Y
2 **Guthrie**	Y	Y	N	Y	N	Y
3 Yarmuth	N	N	Y	N	Y	N
4 **Davis**	Y	Y	N	Y	N	Y
5 **Rogers**	Y	Y	N	Y	N	Y
6 Chandler	N	N	Y	Y	Y	Y
LOUISIANA						
1 **Scalise**	Y	Y	N	Y	N	Y
2 Richmond	N	N	Y	N	Y	N
3 **Landry**	Y	Y	N	Y	N	Y
4 **Fleming**	Y	Y	N	Y	N	Y
5 **Alexander**	Y	Y	N	Y	N	Y
6 **Cassidy**	Y	Y	N	Y	N	Y
7 **Boustany**	Y	Y	N	Y	N	Y
MAINE						
1 Pingree	N	Y	Y	N	Y	N
2 Michaud	N	N	Y	N	Y	N
MARYLAND						
1 **Harris**	Y	Y	N	Y	N	Y
2 Ruppersberger	N	N	Y	N	Y	N
3 Sarbanes	N	N	Y	N	Y	N
4 Edwards	N	N	Y	N	Y	N
5 Hoyer	N	N	Y	N	Y	N
6 **Bartlett**	Y	Y	N	Y	N	Y
7 Cummings	N	N	Y	N	Y	N
8 Van Hollen	N	N	Y	N	Y	N
MASSACHUSETTS						
1 Olver	N	N	Y	N	Y	N
2 Neal	N	N	Y	N	Y	N
3 McGovern	N	N	Y	N	Y	N
4 Frank	N	N	Y	N	Y	N
5 Tsongas	N	N	Y	N	Y	N
6 Tierney	N	N	Y	N	Y	N
7 Markey	N	N	Y	N	Y	N
8 Capuano	N	N	Y	N	Y	N
9 Lynch	N	N	Y	N	Y	N
10 Keating	N	N	Y	N	?	N
MICHIGAN						
1 **Benishek**	Y	Y	N	Y	N	Y
2 **Huizenga**	Y	Y	N	Y	N	Y
3 **Amash**	Y	N	N	Y	N	Y
4 **Camp**	Y	Y	N	Y	N	Y
5 Kildee	N	N	Y	N	Y	N
6 **Upton**	Y	Y	N	Y	N	Y
7 **Walberg**	Y	Y	N	Y	N	Y
8 **Rogers**	Y	Y	N	Y	N	Y
9 Peters	N	N	Y	N	Y	N
10 **Miller**	Y	Y	N	Y	N	Y
11 Vacant						
12 Levin	N	N	Y	N	Y	N
13 Clarke	N	N	Y	N	Y	N
14 Conyers	N	N	Y	N	Y	N
15 Dingell	N	N	Y	N	Y	N
MINNESOTA						
1 Walz	N	N	Y	N	Y	N
2 **Kline**	Y	Y	N	Y	N	Y
3 **Paulsen**	Y	Y	N	Y	N	Y
4 McCollum	N	N	Y	N	Y	N

	531	532	533	534	535	536
5 Ellison	N	N	Y	N	Y	N
6 **Bachmann**	Y	Y	N	Y	N	Y
7 Peterson	Y	N	N	N	Y	Y
8 **Cravaack**	Y	Y	N	Y	N	Y
MISSISSIPPI						
1 **Nunnelee**	Y	Y	N	Y	N	Y
2 Thompson	N	N	Y	N	Y	N
3 **Harper**	Y	Y	N	Y	N	Y
4 **Palazzo**	Y	Y	N	Y	N	Y
MISSOURI						
1 Clay	N	N	Y	N	Y	N
2 **Akin**	+	+	–	+	–	+
3 Carnahan	N	N	Y	N	Y	N
4 **Hartzler**	Y	Y	N	Y	N	Y
5 Cleaver	N	N	Y	N	Y	N
6 **Graves**	Y	Y	N	Y	N	Y
7 **Long**	Y	Y	N	Y	N	Y
8 **Emerson**	Y	Y	N	Y	N	Y
9 **Luetkemeyer**	Y	Y	N	Y	N	Y
MONTANA						
AL **Rehberg**	Y	Y	N	Y	N	Y
NEBRASKA						
1 **Fortenberry**	Y	Y	N	Y	N	Y
2 **Terry**	Y	Y	N	Y	N	Y
3 **Smith**	Y	Y	N	Y	N	Y
NEVADA						
1 Berkley	N	N	Y	N	Y	N
2 **Amodei**	Y	Y	N	Y	N	Y
3 **Heck**	Y	Y	N	Y	N	Y
NEW HAMPSHIRE						
1 **Guinta**	Y	Y	N	Y	N	Y
2 **Bass**	N	N	N	N	N	N
NEW JERSEY						
1 Andrews	N	N	Y	N	Y	N
2 **LoBiondo**	Y	Y	N	Y	N	Y
3 **Runyan**	Y	Y	N	Y	N	Y
4 **Smith**	Y	Y	N	Y	N	Y
5 **Garrett**	Y	Y	N	Y	N	Y
6 Pallone	N	N	Y	N	Y	N
7 **Lance**	Y	Y	N	Y	N	Y
8 Pascrell	N	N	Y	N	Y	N
9 Rothman	N	?	Y	N	Y	N
10 Vacant						
11 **Frelinghuysen**	Y	Y	N	Y	N	Y
12 Holt	N	N	Y	N	Y	N
13 Sires	N	N	Y	N	Y	N
NEW MEXICO						
1 Heinrich	N	N	Y	N	Y	N
2 **Pearce**	Y	Y	N	Y	N	Y
3 Luján	N	N	Y	N	Y	N
NEW YORK						
1 Bishop	N	N	Y	N	Y	N
2 Israel	N	N	Y	N	Y	N
3 **King**	Y	Y	N	Y	N	Y
4 McCarthy	N	N	Y	N	Y	N
5 Ackerman	?	?	?	?	?	?
6 Meeks	?	?	?	?	?	?
7 Crowley	N	N	Y	N	Y	N
8 Nadler	N	N	Y	N	Y	N
9 **Turner**	Y	Y	N	Y	N	Y
10 Towns	N	N	Y	N	Y	N
11 Clarke	N	N	Y	N	Y	N
12 Velázquez	N	N	Y	N	Y	N
13 **Grimm**	Y	Y	N	Y	N	Y
14 Maloney	N	N	Y	N	Y	N
15 Rangel	N	N	Y	N	Y	N
16 Serrano	Y	N	Y	N	Y	N
17 Engel	N	N	Y	N	Y	N
18 Lowey	N	N	Y	N	Y	N
19 **Hayworth**	Y	Y	N	Y	N	Y
20 **Gibson**	Y	N	Y	Y	N	Y
21 Tonko	N	N	Y	N	Y	N
22 Hinchey	N	N	Y	N	Y	N
23 Owens	Y	N	N	Y	N	Y
24 **Hanna**	Y	Y	N	Y	N	Y
25 **Buerkle**	Y	Y	N	Y	N	Y
26 Hochul	N	N	Y	N	Y	N
27 Higgins	N	N	Y	N	Y	N
28 Slaughter	N	N	Y	N	Y	N
29 **Reed**	Y	Y	N	Y	N	Y
NORTH CAROLINA						
1 Butterfield	N	N	?	?	Y	N
2 **Ellmers**	Y	Y	N	Y	N	Y
3 **Jones**	Y	Y	Y	Y	Y	Y
4 Price	N	N	Y	N	Y	N

	531	532	533	534	535	536
5 **Foxx**	Y	Y	N	Y	N	Y
6 **Coble**	Y	Y	N	Y	N	Y
7 McIntyre	Y	Y	Y	Y	Y	Y
8 Kissell	Y	Y	Y	Y	Y	Y
9 **Myrick**	Y	Y	N	Y	?	Y
10 **McHenry**	Y	Y	N	Y	N	Y
11 Shuler	N	N	N	N	Y	N
12 Watt	N	N	Y	N	Y	N
13 Miller	N	?	Y	N	Y	N
NORTH DAKOTA						
AL **Berg**	Y	Y	N	Y	N	Y
OHIO						
1 **Chabot**	Y	Y	N	Y	N	Y
2 **Schmidt**	Y	Y	N	Y	N	Y
3 **Turner**	Y	Y	N	Y	N	Y
4 **Jordan**	Y	Y	N	Y	N	Y
5 **Latta**	Y	Y	N	Y	N	Y
6 **Johnson**	Y	Y	N	Y	N	Y
7 **Austria**	Y	Y	N	Y	N	Y
8 **Boehner**						
9 Kaptur	N	N	Y	N	Y	N
10 Kucinich	N	N	Y	N	Y	N
11 Fudge	N	N	Y	N	Y	N
12 **Tiberi**	Y	Y	N	Y	N	Y
13 Sutton	N	N	Y	N	Y	N
14 **LaTourette**	Y	Y	N	N	N	Y
15 **Stivers**	?	?	?	?	?	?
16 **Renacci**	Y	Y	N	Y	N	Y
17 Ryan	N	N	Y	N	Y	N
18 **Gibbs**	Y	Y	N	Y	N	Y
OKLAHOMA						
1 **Sullivan**	Y	Y	N	Y	N	Y
2 Boren	Y	Y	N	Y	Y	Y
3 **Lucas**	Y	Y	N	Y	N	Y
4 **Cole**	Y	Y	N	Y	N	Y
5 **Lankford**	Y	Y	N	Y	N	Y
OREGON						
1 Bonamici	N	N	Y	N	Y	N
2 **Walden**	Y	Y	N	Y	N	Y
3 Blumenauer	N	N	Y	N	Y	N
4 DeFazio	N	N	Y	N	Y	N
5 Schrader	Y	N	N	Y	Y	N
PENNSYLVANIA						
1 Brady	N	N	Y	N	Y	N
2 Fattah	?	?	?	?	Y	N
3 **Kelly**	Y	Y	N	Y	N	Y
4 Altmire	N	Y	Y	N	Y	N
5 **Thompson**	Y	Y	N	Y	N	Y
6 **Gerlach**	Y	Y	N	Y	N	Y
7 **Meehan**	Y	Y	N	Y	N	Y
8 **Fitzpatrick**	Y	Y	N	Y	N	Y
9 **Shuster**	Y	Y	N	Y	N	Y
10 **Marino**	Y	Y	N	Y	N	Y
11 **Barletta**	Y	Y	N	Y	N	Y
12 Critz	Y	Y	Y	N	Y	N
13 Schwartz	N	N	Y	N	Y	N
14 Doyle	N	N	Y	N	Y	N
15 **Dent**	Y	Y	N	Y	N	Y
16 **Pitts**	Y	Y	N	Y	N	Y
17 Holden	Y	Y	Y	N	Y	N
18 **Murphy**	Y	Y	N	Y	N	Y
19 **Platts**	Y	Y	N	Y	N	Y
RHODE ISLAND						
1 Cicilline	N	N	Y	N	Y	N
2 Langevin	N	N	Y	N	Y	N
SOUTH CAROLINA						
1 **Scott**	Y	Y	N	Y	N	Y
2 **Wilson**	Y	Y	N	Y	N	Y
3 **Duncan**	Y	Y	N	Y	N	Y
4 **Gowdy**	Y	Y	N	Y	N	Y
5 **Mulvaney**	Y	Y	N	Y	N	Y
6 Clyburn	N	N	Y	N	Y	N
SOUTH DAKOTA						
AL **Noem**	Y	Y	N	Y	N	Y
TENNESSEE						
1 **Roe**	Y	Y	N	Y	N	Y
2 **Duncan**	Y	Y	N	Y	N	Y
3 **Fleischmann**	Y	Y	N	Y	N	Y
4 **DesJarlais**	Y	Y	N	Y	N	Y
5 Cooper	N	N	Y	N	Y	N
6 **Black**	Y	Y	N	Y	N	Y
7 **Blackburn**	Y	Y	N	Y	N	Y
8 **Fincher**	Y	Y	N	Y	N	Y
9 Cohen	N	N	Y	N	Y	N

	531	532	533	534	535	536
TEXAS						
1 **Gohmert**	Y	Y	N	Y	N	Y
2 **Poe**	Y	Y	N	Y	N	Y
3 **Johnson, S.**	Y	Y	N	Y	N	Y
4 **Hall**	Y	Y	N	Y	N	Y
5 **Hensarling**	Y	Y	N	Y	N	Y
6 **Barton**	Y	Y	N	Y	N	Y
7 **Culberson**	?	?	?	?	?	?
8 **Brady**	N	Y	N	Y	N	Y
9 Green, A.	N	N	Y	Y	Y	N
10 **McCaul**	Y	Y	N	Y	N	Y
11 **Conaway**	Y	Y	N	Y	N	Y
12 **Granger**	Y	Y	N	Y	N	Y
13 **Thornberry**	Y	Y	N	Y	N	Y
14 **Paul**	Y	Y	N	Y	N	Y
15 Hinojosa	N	N	Y	Y	Y	N
16 Reyes	N	N	Y	N	Y	N
17 **Flores**	Y	Y	N	Y	N	Y
18 Jackson Lee	?	?	?	?	?	?
19 **Neugebauer**	Y	Y	N	Y	N	Y
20 Gonzalez	N	N	Y	N	Y	N
21 **Smith**	Y	Y	N	Y	N	Y
22 **Olson**	Y	Y	N	Y	N	Y
23 **Canseco**	Y	Y	N	Y	N	Y
24 **Marchant**	Y	Y	N	Y	N	Y
25 Doggett	N	N	Y	N	Y	N
26 **Burgess**	Y	Y	N	Y	N	Y
27 **Farenthold**	Y	Y	N	Y	N	Y
28 Cuellar	Y	N	Y	Y	Y	Y
29 Green, G.	N	Y	Y	N	Y	N
30 Johnson, E.	N	N	Y	N	Y	N
31 **Carter**	Y	Y	N	Y	N	Y
32 **Sessions**	Y	Y	N	Y	N	Y
UTAH						
1 **Bishop**	Y	Y	N	Y	N	Y
2 Matheson	Y	Y	N	Y	Y	Y
3 **Chaffetz**	Y	Y	N	Y	N	Y
VERMONT						
AL Welch	N	N	Y	N	Y	N
VIRGINIA						
1 **Wittman**	Y	Y	N	Y	N	Y
2 **Rigell**	Y	Y	N	Y	N	Y
3 Scott	N	N	Y	N	Y	N
4 **Forbes**	Y	Y	N	Y	N	Y
5 **Hurt**	Y	Y	N	Y	N	Y
6 **Goodlatte**	Y	Y	N	Y	N	Y
7 **Cantor**	Y	Y	N	Y	N	Y
8 Moran	N	N	Y	N	Y	N
9 **Griffith**	Y	Y	N	Y	N	Y
10 **Wolf**	Y	Y	N	Y	N	Y
11 Connolly	Y	N	Y	N	Y	N
WASHINGTON						
1 Vacant						
2 Larsen	N	N	Y	N	Y	N
3 **Herrera Beutler**	Y	Y	N	Y	N	Y
4 **Hastings**	Y	Y	N	Y	N	Y
5 **McMorris Rodgers**	Y	Y	N	Y	N	Y
6 Dicks	N	N	Y	N	Y	N
7 McDermott	N	N	Y	N	Y	N
8 **Reichert**	Y	N	N	Y	N	Y
9 Smith	N	N	Y	N	Y	N
WEST VIRGINIA						
1 **McKinley**	Y	Y	N	Y	N	Y
2 **Capito**	Y	Y	N	Y	N	Y
3 Rahall	Y	Y	N	Y	Y	Y
WISCONSIN						
1 **Ryan**	Y	Y	N	Y	N	Y
2 Baldwin	N	N	Y	N	Y	N
3 Kind	Y	N	Y	N	Y	N
4 Moore	N	N	Y	N	Y	N
5 **Sensenbrenner**	Y	Y	N	Y	N	Y
6 **Petri**	Y	Y	N	Y	N	Y
7 **Duffy**	Y	Y	N	Y	N	Y
8 **Ribble**	Y	Y	N	Y	N	Y
WYOMING						
AL **Lummis**	Y	Y	N	Y	N	Y

IN THE HOUSE | By Vote Number

537. S 679. Senate Confirmation Requirement/Passage. Chaffetz, R-Utah, motion to suspend the rules and pass the bill that would eliminate the requirement for Senate confirmation for 169 executive branch positions and establish an executive branch working group to study and report on streamlining the paperwork required for executive nominations and the impact of background investigations on the appointments process. Motion agreed to 261-116: R 95-115; D 166-1. A two-thirds majority of those present and voting (251 in this case) is required for passage under suspension of the rules. July 31, 2012.

538. HR 828. Tax Debts/Passage. Chaffetz, R-Utah, motion to suspend the rules and pass the bill that would make individuals with seriously delinquent tax debts, including current federal employees, ineligible for federal employment, effective nine months after the date of enactment. Motion agreed to 263-114: R 204-6; D 59-108. A two-thirds majority of those present and voting (252 in this case) is required for passage under suspension of the rules. July 31, 2012.

539. HR 3803. D.C. Abortion Ban/Passage. Franks, R-Ariz., motion to suspend the rules and pass the bill that would prohibit abortions in the District of Columbia after 20 weeks of pregnancy, except when the woman's life is endangered. The bill would impose reporting requirements for any abortions performed prior to the 20-week threshold. Violators would be subject to fines or imprisonment, with a maximum two-year sentence. The measure would prohibit the prosecution of the woman obtaining the abortion. Motion rejected 220-154: R 203-6; D 17-148. A two-thirds majority of those present and voting (250 in this case) is required for passage under suspension of the rules. July 31, 2012.

540. HR 8, HR 6169. Tax Rate Extension and Tax Code Overhaul/ Previous Question. Scott, R-S.C., motion to order the previous question (thus ending debate and the possibility of amendment) on the rule (H Res 747) that would provide for House floor consideration of a bill (HR 8) that would extend expiring 2001 and 2003 tax cuts and a bill (HR 6169) that would expedite the legislative process for an overhaul of the tax code in the 113th Congress. Motion agreed to 240-183: R 236-0; D 4-183. Aug. 1, 2012.

541. HR 8, HR 6169. Tax Rate Extension and Tax Code Overhaul/ Legislative Engrossment. Scott, R-S.C., amendment that would instruct the House clerk, upon passage of both bills, to add the text of the bill (HR 6169) that would expedite the legislative process for an overhaul of the tax code in the 113th Congress to a measure (HR 8) that would extend expiring 2001 and 2003 tax cuts. Adopted 238-186: R 237-0; D 1-186. Aug. 1, 2012.

542. HR 8, HR 6169. Tax Rate Extension and Tax Code Overhaul/ Rule. Adoption of the rule (H Res 747) that would provide for House floor consideration of a bill (HR 8) that would extend expiring 2001 and 2003 tax cuts and a bill (HR 6169) that would expedite the legislative process for an overhaul of the tax code in the 113th Congress. The rule also would waive, through the legislative day of Aug. 2, 2012, the two-thirds majority vote requirement to consider a rule on the same day it is reported from the Rules Committee. It would permit the Speaker to entertain motions to suspend the rules on Aug. 2, 2012. As amended, the rule would add the text of the tax code overhaul bill to the bill that would extend expiring tax cuts upon passage of both bills. Adopted 240-184: R 237-0; D 3-184. Aug. 1, 2012.

*Republican Geoff Davis of Kentucky resigned effective July 31, 2012. The last vote for which he was eligible was vote 539.

	537	538	539	540	541	542
ALABAMA						
1 **Bonner**	Y	Y	Y	Y	Y	Y
2 **Roby**	Y	Y	Y	Y	Y	Y
3 **Rogers**	Y	Y	Y	Y	Y	Y
4 **Aderholt**	N	Y	Y	Y	Y	Y
5 **Brooks**	N	Y	Y	Y	Y	Y
6 **Bachus**	Y	Y	Y	Y	Y	Y
7 Sewell	Y	N	N	N	N	N
ALASKA						
AL **Young**	Y	N	Y	Y	Y	Y
ARIZONA						
1 **Gosar**	N	Y	Y	Y	Y	Y
2 **Franks**	Y	Y	Y	Y	Y	Y
3 **Quayle**	N	Y	Y	Y	Y	Y
4 Pastor	?	?	?	N	N	N
5 **Schweikert**	N	Y	Y	Y	Y	Y
6 **Flake**	Y	Y	Y	Y	Y	Y
7 Grijalva	Y	N	N	N	N	N
8 Barber	Y	N	N	N	N	N
ARKANSAS						
1 **Crawford**	N	Y	Y	Y	Y	Y
2 **Griffin**	N	Y	Y	Y	Y	Y
3 **Womack**	N	Y	Y	Y	Y	Y
4 Ross	Y	Y	Y	N	N	N
CALIFORNIA						
1 Thompson	Y	Y	N	N	N	N
2 **Herger**	Y	Y	Y	Y	Y	Y
3 **Lungren**	Y	Y	Y	Y	Y	Y
4 **McClintock**	N	Y	Y	Y	Y	Y
5 Matsui	Y	Y	N	N	N	N
6 Woolsey	Y	N	N	N	N	N
7 Miller, George	Y	Y	N	N	N	N
8 Pelosi	Y	N	N	N	N	N
9 Lee	Y	N	N	N	N	N
10 Garamendi	Y	Y	N	N	N	N
11 McNerney	Y	Y	N	N	N	N
12 Speier	Y	Y	N	N	N	N
13 Stark	Y	Y	N	N	N	N
14 Eshoo	Y	Y	N	N	?	N
15 Honda	Y	N	N	N	N	N
16 Lofgren	Y	Y	N	N	N	N
17 Farr	Y	Y	N	N	N	N
18 Cardoza	?	?	?	?	?	?
19 **Denham**	N	Y	Y	Y	Y	Y
20 Costa	Y	Y	N	N	N	N
21 **Nunes**	Y	Y	Y	Y	Y	Y
22 **McCarthy**	Y	Y	Y	Y	Y	Y
23 Capps	Y	Y	N	N	N	N
24 **Gallegly**	Y	Y	Y	Y	Y	Y
25 **McKeon**	Y	Y	Y	Y	Y	Y
26 **Dreier**	Y	Y	N	Y	Y	Y
27 Sherman	Y	N	N	N	N	N
28 Berman	Y	Y	N	N	N	N
29 Schiff	Y	Y	N	N	N	N
30 Waxman	Y	N	N	N	N	N
31 Becerra	Y	N	N	N	N	N
32 Chu	Y	N	N	N	N	N
33 Bass	Y	N	N	N	N	N
34 Roybal-Allard	Y	N	N	N	N	N
35 Waters	Y	N	N	N	N	N
36 Hahn	Y	N	N	N	N	N
37 Richardson	Y	N	N	N	N	N
38 Napolitano	Y	N	N	N	N	N
39 Sánchez, Linda	Y	N	N	N	N	N
40 **Royce**	N	Y	Y	Y	Y	Y
41 **Lewis**	Y	Y	Y	Y	Y	Y
42 **Miller, Gary**	N	Y	Y	Y	Y	Y
43 Baca	Y	N	N	N	N	N
44 **Calvert**	Y	Y	Y	Y	Y	Y
45 **Bono Mack**	Y	Y	Y	Y	Y	Y
46 Rohrabacher	?	?	?	Y	Y	Y
47 Sanchez, Loretta	Y	Y	N	N	N	N
48 **Campbell**	?	?	?	Y	Y	Y
49 **Issa**	Y	Y	Y	Y	Y	Y
50 **Bilbray**	Y	Y	Y	Y	Y	Y
51 Filner	+	–	–	N	N	N
52 **Hunter**	Y	Y	Y	Y	Y	Y
53 Davis	Y	Y	N	N	N	N

	537	538	539	540	541	542
COLORADO						
1 DeGette	?	?	?	N	N	N
2 Polis	Y	Y	N	N	N	N
3 **Tipton**	Y	Y	Y	Y	Y	Y
4 **Gardner**	N	Y	Y	Y	Y	Y
5 **Lamborn**	N	Y	Y	Y	Y	Y
6 **Coffman**	N	Y	Y	Y	Y	Y
7 Perlmutter	Y	N	N	N	N	N
CONNECTICUT						
1 Larson	Y	N	N	N	N	N
2 Courtney	Y	N	N	N	N	N
3 DeLauro	Y	N	N	N	N	N
4 Himes	Y	Y	N	N	N	N
5 Murphy	Y	Y	N	N	N	N
DELAWARE						
AL Carney	Y	Y	N	N	N	N
FLORIDA						
1 **Miller**	N	Y	Y	Y	Y	Y
2 **Southerland**	N	Y	Y	Y	Y	Y
3 Brown	Y	N	N	N	N	N
4 **Crenshaw**	?	?	?	Y	Y	Y
5 **Nugent**	N	Y	Y	Y	Y	Y
6 **Stearns**	N	Y	Y	Y	Y	Y
7 **Mica**	N	Y	Y	Y	Y	Y
8 **Webster**	N	Y	Y	Y	Y	Y
9 **Bilirakis**	N	Y	Y	Y	Y	Y
10 **Young**	N	Y	Y	Y	Y	Y
11 Castor	Y	N	N	N	N	N
12 **Ross**	N	Y	Y	Y	Y	Y
13 **Buchanan**	N	Y	Y	Y	Y	Y
14 **Mack**	?	?	?	Y	Y	Y
15 **Posey**	N	Y	Y	Y	Y	Y
16 **Rooney**	N	Y	Y	Y	Y	Y
17 Wilson	Y	Y	N	N	N	N
18 **Ros-Lehtinen**	Y	Y	Y	Y	Y	Y
19 Deutch	Y	N	N	N	N	N
20 Wasserman Schultz	Y	N	N	N	N	N
21 **Diaz-Balart**	Y	Y	Y	Y	Y	Y
22 **West**	N	Y	Y	Y	Y	Y
23 Hastings	Y	N	N	N	N	N
24 **Adams**	N	Y	Y	Y	Y	Y
25 **Rivera**	Y	Y	Y	Y	Y	Y
GEORGIA						
1 **Kingston**	Y	Y	Y	Y	Y	Y
2 Bishop	?	?	?	N	N	N
3 **Westmoreland**	?	?	?	Y	Y	Y
4 Johnson	?	?	?	N	N	N
5 Lewis	?	?	?	N	N	N
6 **Price**	Y	Y	Y	Y	Y	Y
7 **Woodall**	N	Y	Y	Y	Y	Y
8 **Scott, A.**	–	+	+	Y	Y	Y
9 **Graves**	N	Y	?	Y	Y	Y
10 **Broun**	?	?	?	Y	Y	Y
11 **Gingrey**	–	+	+	Y	Y	Y
12 Barrow	Y	Y	N	N	N	N
13 Scott, D.	Y	N	N	N	N	N
HAWAII						
1 Hanabusa	Y	N	N	N	N	N
2 Hirono	?	?	?	N	N	N
IDAHO						
1 **Labrador**	?	?	?	Y	Y	Y
2 **Simpson**	Y	Y	Y	Y	Y	Y
ILLINOIS						
1 Rush	?	?	?	N	N	N
2 Jackson	?	?	?	?	?	?
3 Lipinski	Y	Y	N	N	N	N
4 Gutierrez	Y	N	N	N	N	?
5 Quigley	Y	N	N	N	N	N
6 **Roskam**	Y	Y	Y	Y	Y	Y
7 Davis	Y	N	N	N	N	N
8 **Walsh**	N	Y	Y	Y	Y	Y
9 Schakowsky	Y	N	N	N	N	N
10 **Dold**	Y	Y	N	Y	Y	Y
11 **Kinzinger**	Y	Y	Y	Y	Y	Y
12 Costello	Y	Y	N	N	N	N
13 **Biggert**	Y	Y	N	Y	Y	Y
14 **Hultgren**	Y	Y	Y	Y	Y	Y
15 Johnson	+	+	+	Y	Y	Y

KEY **Republicans**   Democrats

Y Voted for (yea)	**X** Paired against	**C** Voted "present" to avoid possible conflict of interest
# Paired for	**–** Announced against	
+ Announced for	**P** Voted "present"	**?** Did not vote or otherwise make a position known
N Voted against (nay)		

	537	538	539	540	541	542
16 **Manzullo**	N	Y	Y	Y	Y	Y
17 **Schilling**	N	Y	Y	Y	Y	Y
18 **Schock**	Y	Y	Y	Y	Y	Y
19 **Shimkus**	Y	Y	Y	Y	Y	Y
INDIANA						
1 Visclosky	Y	Y	N	N	N	N
2 Donnelly	Y	Y	Y	N	N	N
3 **Stutzman**	N	Y	Y	Y	Y	Y
4 **Rokita**	Y	Y	Y	Y	Y	Y
5 **Burton**	N	Y	Y	Y	Y	Y
6 **Pence**	?	?	?	Y	Y	Y
7 Carson	Y	N	N	N	N	N
8 **Bucshon**	N	Y	Y	Y	Y	Y
9 **Young**	?	?	?	Y	Y	Y
IOWA						
1 Braley	Y	N	N	N	N	N
2 Loebsack	Y	Y	N	N	N	N
3 Boswell	Y	N	N	N	N	N
4 **Latham**	Y	Y	Y	Y	Y	Y
5 **King**	N	Y	Y	Y	Y	Y
KANSAS						
1 **Huelskamp**	N	Y	Y	Y	Y	Y
2 **Jenkins**	N	Y	Y	Y	Y	Y
3 **Yoder**	N	Y	Y	Y	Y	Y
4 **Pompeo**	N	Y	Y	Y	Y	Y
KENTUCKY						
1 **Whitfield**	Y	Y	Y	Y	Y	Y
2 **Guthrie**	Y	Y	Y	Y	Y	Y
3 Yarmuth	Y	Y	N	N	N	N
4 Davis*	Y	Y	Y			
5 **Rogers**	?	?	?	Y	Y	Y
6 Chandler	Y	Y	N	N	N	N
LOUISIANA						
1 **Scalise**	N	Y	Y	Y	Y	Y
2 Richmond	?	?	?	N	N	N
3 **Landry**	N	Y	Y	Y	Y	Y
4 **Fleming**	–	+	Y	Y	Y	Y
5 **Alexander**	?	?	?	Y	Y	Y
6 **Cassidy**	?	?	?	Y	Y	Y
7 **Boustany**	N	Y	Y	Y	Y	Y
MAINE						
1 Pingree	Y	N	N	N	N	N
2 Michaud	Y	N	N	N	N	N
MARYLAND						
1 **Harris**	N	Y	Y	Y	Y	Y
2 Ruppersberger	Y	N	N	N	N	N
3 Sarbanes	Y	N	N	N	N	N
4 Edwards	Y	N	N	N	N	N
5 Hoyer	Y	N	N	?	N	N
6 **Bartlett**	N	Y	Y	Y	Y	Y
7 Cummings	Y	N	N	N	N	N
8 Van Hollen	Y	N	N	N	N	N
MASSACHUSETTS						
1 Olver	Y	N	N	N	N	N
2 Neal	Y	N	N	N	N	N
3 McGovern	Y	N	N	N	N	N
4 Frank	Y	N	?	N	N	N
5 Tsongas	Y	Y	N	N	N	N
6 Tierney	Y	Y	N	N	N	N
7 Markey	Y	N	N	N	N	N
8 Capuano	Y	N	N	N	N	N
9 Lynch	Y	N	N	N	N	N
10 Keating	Y	N	N	N	N	N
MICHIGAN						
1 **Benishek**	?	?	?	Y	Y	Y
2 **Huizenga**	?	?	?	Y	Y	Y
3 **Amash**	N	Y	Y	Y	Y	Y
4 **Camp**	Y	Y	Y	Y	Y	Y
5 Kildee	Y	N	Y	N	N	N
6 **Upton**	Y	Y	Y	Y	Y	Y
7 **Walberg**	?	?	?	Y	Y	Y
8 **Rogers**	Y	Y	Y	Y	Y	Y
9 Peters	Y	Y	N	N	N	N
10 **Miller**	Y	Y	Y	Y	Y	Y
11 Vacant						
12 Levin	Y	N	N	N	N	N
13 Clarke	Y	N	N	N	N	N
14 Conyers	Y	N	N	N	N	N
15 Dingell	Y	Y	N	?	?	?
MINNESOTA						
1 Walz	Y	N	N	N	N	N
2 **Kline**	N	Y	Y	Y	Y	Y
3 **Paulsen**	N	Y	Y	Y	Y	Y
4 McCollum	Y	Y	N	N	N	N

	537	538	539	540	541	542
5 Ellison	Y	N	N	N	N	N
6 **Bachmann**	N	Y	Y	Y	Y	Y
7 Peterson	N	Y	Y	N	N	N
8 **Cravaack**	Y	Y	Y	?	Y	Y
MISSISSIPPI						
1 **Nunnelee**	N	Y	Y	Y	Y	Y
2 Thompson	Y	N	N	N	N	N
3 **Harper**	Y	Y	Y	Y	Y	Y
4 **Palazzo**	N	Y	Y	Y	Y	Y
MISSOURI						
1 Clay	Y	N	N	N	N	N
2 **Akin**	?	?	?	?	?	?
3 Carnahan	+	–	–	N	N	N
4 **Hartzler**	N	Y	Y	Y	Y	Y
5 Cleaver	Y	N	N	N	N	N
6 **Graves**	Y	Y	Y	Y	Y	Y
7 **Long**	Y	Y	Y	Y	Y	Y
8 **Emerson**	N	Y	Y	Y	Y	Y
9 **Luetkemeyer**	N	Y	Y	Y	Y	Y
MONTANA						
AL **Rehberg**	N	Y	Y	Y	Y	Y
NEBRASKA						
1 **Fortenberry**	N	Y	Y	Y	Y	Y
2 **Terry**	N	Y	Y	Y	Y	Y
3 **Smith**	Y	Y	Y	Y	Y	Y
NEVADA						
1 Berkley	?	?	?	N	N	N
2 **Amodei**	Y	Y	Y	Y	Y	Y
3 **Heck**	Y	Y	Y	Y	Y	Y
NEW HAMPSHIRE						
1 **Guinta**	Y	Y	Y	Y	Y	Y
2 **Bass**	Y	Y	N	Y	Y	Y
NEW JERSEY						
1 Andrews	Y	N	N	N	N	N
2 **LoBiondo**	Y	N	Y	Y	Y	Y
3 **Runyan**	Y	Y	Y	Y	Y	Y
4 **Smith**	Y	N	Y	Y	Y	Y
5 **Garrett**	N	Y	Y	Y	Y	Y
6 Pallone	Y	N	N	N	N	N
7 **Lance**	N	Y	Y	Y	Y	Y
8 Pascrell	Y	N	N	N	N	N
9 Rothman	Y	Y	N	N	N	N
10 Vacant						
11 **Frelinghuysen**	Y	Y	Y	Y	Y	Y
12 Holt	Y	N	N	N	N	N
13 Sires	Y	N	N	N	N	N
NEW MEXICO						
1 Heinrich	?	?	?	N	N	N
2 **Pearce**	N	Y	Y	Y	Y	Y
3 Luján	Y	N	?	N	N	N
NEW YORK						
1 Bishop	Y	N	N	N	N	N
2 Israel	Y	N	N	N	N	N
3 **King**	Y	N	Y	Y	Y	Y
4 McCarthy	Y	N	N	N	N	N
5 Ackerman	Y	N	N	N	N	N
6 Meeks	Y	N	N	N	N	N
7 Crowley	Y	N	N	N	N	N
8 Nadler	Y	N	N	N	N	N
9 **Turner**	Y	Y	Y	Y	Y	Y
10 Towns	?	?	?	N	N	N
11 Clarke	Y	N	N	N	N	N
12 Velázquez	Y	N	N	N	N	N
13 **Grimm**	Y	N	Y	Y	Y	Y
14 Maloney	Y	Y	N	N	N	N
15 Rangel	Y	N	N	N	N	N
16 Serrano	Y	N	N	N	N	N
17 Engel	Y	N	N	N	N	N
18 Lowey	Y	N	N	N	N	N
19 **Hayworth**	?	Y	P	Y	Y	Y
20 **Gibson**	N	Y	Y	Y	Y	Y
21 Tonko	Y	N	N	N	N	N
22 Hinchey	Y	N	N	N	N	N
23 Owens	Y	Y	N	N	N	N
24 **Hanna**	+	+	–	Y	Y	Y
25 **Buerkle**	N	Y	Y	Y	Y	Y
26 Hochul	Y	Y	N	N	N	N
27 Higgins	?	?	?	N	N	N
28 Slaughter	Y	N	N	N	N	N
29 **Reed**	Y	Y	Y	Y	Y	Y
NORTH CAROLINA						
1 Butterfield	Y	N	N	N	N	N
2 **Ellmers**	N	Y	Y	Y	Y	Y
3 **Jones**	N	Y	Y	Y	Y	Y
4 Price	Y	N	N	N	N	N

	537	538	539	540	541	542
5 **Foxx**	N	Y	Y	Y	Y	Y
6 **Coble**	N	Y	Y	Y	Y	Y
7 McIntyre	Y	Y	Y	Y	Y	Y
8 Kissell	Y	Y	Y	N	N	N
9 **Myrick**	Y	Y	Y	Y	Y	Y
10 **McHenry**	Y	Y	Y	Y	Y	Y
11 Shuler	Y	Y	Y	Y	N	N
12 Watt	Y	N	N	N	N	N
13 Miller	Y	Y	N	N	N	N
NORTH DAKOTA						
AL **Berg**	N	Y	Y	Y	Y	Y
OHIO						
1 **Chabot**	N	Y	Y	Y	Y	Y
2 **Schmidt**	N	Y	Y	Y	Y	Y
3 **Turner**	N	Y	Y	Y	Y	Y
4 **Jordan**	–	+	+	Y	?	Y
5 **Latta**	N	Y	Y	Y	Y	Y
6 **Johnson**	N	Y	Y	Y	Y	Y
7 **Austria**	N	Y	Y	Y	Y	Y
8 **Boehner**						
9 Kaptur	?	?	?	N	N	N
10 Kucinich	?	?	?	N	N	N
11 Fudge	Y	N	N	N	N	N
12 **Tiberi**	Y	Y	Y	Y	Y	Y
13 Sutton	+	+	–	N	N	N
14 **LaTourette**	Y	N	P	Y	Y	Y
15 **Stivers**	Y	?	Y	Y	Y	Y
16 **Renacci**	?	?	?	Y	Y	Y
17 Ryan	Y	Y	N	N	N	N
18 **Gibbs**	N	Y	Y	Y	Y	Y
OKLAHOMA						
1 **Sullivan**	Y	Y	Y	?	Y	Y
2 Boren	Y	Y	Y	Y	N	Y
3 **Lucas**	N	Y	Y	Y	Y	Y
4 **Cole**	N	Y	Y	Y	Y	Y
5 **Lankford**	N	Y	Y	Y	Y	Y
OREGON						
1 Bonamici	Y	N	N	N	N	N
2 **Walden**	Y	Y	Y	Y	Y	Y
3 Blumenauer	Y	Y	N	N	N	N
4 DeFazio	Y	Y	N	N	N	N
5 Schrader	Y	N	N	N	N	N
PENNSYLVANIA						
1 Brady	Y	N	N	N	N	N
2 Fattah	Y	N	N	N	N	N
3 **Kelly**	N	Y	Y	Y	Y	Y
4 Altmire	Y	N	Y	N	N	N
5 **Thompson**	Y	Y	Y	Y	Y	Y
6 **Gerlach**	N	Y	Y	Y	Y	Y
7 **Meehan**	Y	Y	Y	Y	Y	Y
8 **Fitzpatrick**	N	Y	Y	Y	Y	Y
9 **Shuster**	Y	Y	Y	Y	Y	Y
10 **Marino**	N	Y	Y	Y	Y	Y
11 **Barletta**	N	Y	Y	Y	Y	Y
12 Critz	Y	Y	Y	N	N	N
13 Schwartz	Y	Y	N	N	N	N
14 Doyle	Y	N	N	N	N	N
15 **Dent**	Y	Y	N	Y	Y	Y
16 **Pitts**	N	Y	Y	Y	Y	Y
17 Holden	Y	N	Y	N	N	N
18 **Murphy**	N	Y	Y	Y	Y	Y
19 **Platts**	Y	Y	Y	Y	Y	Y
RHODE ISLAND						
1 Cicilline	Y	N	N	N	N	N
2 Langevin	Y	N	Y	N	N	N
SOUTH CAROLINA						
1 **Scott**	Y	Y	Y	Y	Y	Y
2 **Wilson**	N	Y	Y	Y	Y	Y
3 **Duncan**	N	Y	Y	Y	Y	Y
4 **Gowdy**	?	?	?	Y	Y	Y
5 **Mulvaney**	N	Y	Y	Y	Y	Y
6 Clyburn	Y	N	N	N	N	N
SOUTH DAKOTA						
AL **Noem**	?	?	?	Y	Y	Y
TENNESSEE						
1 **Roe**	N	Y	Y	Y	Y	Y
2 **Duncan**	N	Y	Y	Y	Y	Y
3 **Fleischmann**	N	Y	Y	Y	Y	Y
4 **DesJarlais**	–	+	+	Y	Y	Y
5 Cooper	Y	Y	N	N	N	N
6 **Black**	N	Y	Y	Y	Y	Y
7 **Blackburn**	N	Y	Y	Y	Y	Y
8 **Fincher**	Y	Y	Y	Y	Y	Y
9 Cohen	Y	N	N	N	N	N

	537	538	539	540	541	542
TEXAS						
1 **Gohmert**	N	Y	Y	Y	Y	Y
2 **Poe**	N	Y	Y	Y	Y	Y
3 **Johnson, S.**	Y	Y	Y	Y	Y	Y
4 **Hall**	N	Y	Y	Y	Y	Y
5 **Hensarling**	Y	Y	Y	Y	Y	Y
6 **Barton**	N	Y	Y	Y	Y	Y
7 **Culberson**	N	Y	Y	Y	Y	Y
8 **Brady**	Y	Y	Y	Y	Y	Y
9 Green, A.	Y	Y	N	N	N	N
10 **McCaul**	?	?	?	Y	Y	Y
11 **Conaway**	N	Y	Y	Y	Y	Y
12 **Granger**	Y	Y	Y	Y	Y	Y
13 **Thornberry**	Y	Y	Y	Y	Y	Y
14 **Paul**	?	?	?	Y	Y	Y
15 Hinojosa	Y	N	N	N	N	N
16 Reyes	Y	N	N	N	N	N
17 **Flores**	N	Y	Y	Y	Y	Y
18 Jackson Lee	?	?	?	N	N	N
19 **Neugebauer**	N	Y	Y	Y	Y	Y
20 Gonzalez	Y	Y	N	N	N	N
21 **Smith**	Y	Y	Y	Y	Y	Y
22 **Olson**	N	Y	Y	Y	Y	Y
23 **Canseco**	N	Y	Y	Y	Y	Y
24 **Marchant**	N	Y	Y	Y	Y	Y
25 Doggett	?	?	?	N	N	N
26 **Burgess**	N	Y	Y	Y	Y	Y
27 **Farenthold**	N	Y	Y	Y	Y	Y
28 Cuellar	Y	Y	Y	N	N	N
29 Green, G.	Y	Y	N	N	N	N
30 Johnson, E.	Y	N	N	N	N	N
31 **Carter**	Y	Y	Y	Y	Y	Y
32 **Sessions**	Y	Y	Y	Y	Y	Y
UTAH						
1 **Bishop**	N	Y	Y	Y	Y	Y
2 Matheson	Y	Y	Y	Y	N	Y
3 **Chaffetz**	Y	Y	Y	Y	Y	Y
VERMONT						
AL Welch	Y	N	N	N	N	N
VIRGINIA						
1 **Wittman**	N	Y	Y	Y	Y	Y
2 **Rigell**	N	Y	Y	Y	Y	Y
3 Scott	Y	N	N	N	N	N
4 **Forbes**	N	Y	Y	Y	Y	Y
5 **Hurt**	Y	Y	Y	Y	Y	Y
6 **Goodlatte**	Y	Y	Y	Y	Y	Y
7 **Cantor**	Y	Y	Y	Y	Y	Y
8 Moran	Y	N	N	N	N	N
9 **Griffith**	Y	Y	Y	Y	Y	Y
10 **Wolf**	N	Y	Y	Y	Y	Y
11 Connolly	Y	N	N	N	N	N
WASHINGTON						
1 Vacant						
2 Larsen	Y	N	N	N	N	N
3 **Herrera Beutler**	N	Y	Y	Y	Y	Y
4 **Hastings**	Y	Y	Y	Y	Y	Y
5 **McMorris Rodgers**	Y	Y	Y	Y	Y	Y
6 Dicks	?	?	?	N	N	N
7 McDermott	Y	N	N	N	N	N
8 **Reichert**	Y	Y	Y	Y	Y	Y
9 Smith	Y	N	N	N	N	N
WEST VIRGINIA						
1 **McKinley**	N	Y	Y	Y	Y	?
2 **Capito**	Y	Y	Y	Y	Y	Y
3 Rahall	Y	Y	Y	N	N	N
WISCONSIN						
1 **Ryan**	Y	Y	Y	Y	Y	Y
2 Baldwin	?	?	?	N	N	N
3 Kind	Y	Y	N	N	N	N
4 Moore	+	–	–	N	N	N
5 **Sensenbrenner**	Y	Y	Y	Y	Y	Y
6 **Petri**	Y	Y	Y	Y	Y	Y
7 **Duffy**	?	?	?	Y	Y	Y
8 **Ribble**	N	Y	Y	Y	Y	Y
WYOMING						
AL **Lummis**	N	Y	Y	Y	Y	Y

IN THE HOUSE | By Vote Number

543. **HR 8. Tax Rate Extension/Democratic Tax Rate Extension Plan.** Levin, D-Mich., amendment that would extend the 2001 and 2003 tax cuts for one year on taxable income up to $200,000 for single filers and $250,000 for joint filers. It would tax adjusted gross income above $250,000 at 36 percent and AGI above $400,000 at 39.6 percent. It also would expand the child tax credit and extend the college tuition tax credit and the earned income tax credit. It would set the maximum tax rate for long-term capital gains and dividends at 20 percent, allow a business property deduction of $250,000 and increase the alternative minimum tax exemption for 2012 income. Rejected in Committee of the Whole 170-257: R 0-238; D 170-19. Aug. 1, 2012.

544. **HR 8. Tax Rate Extension/Recommit.** DeFazio, D-Ore., motion to recommit the bill to the House Ways and Means Committee and report it back immediately with provisions that would extend, for one year, current tax rates for income under $1 million. It would tax income over $1 million at 39.6 percent. The additional revenue would be used to increase the expensable amount for small businesses for new U.S.-made equipment from $100,000 to $1 million. Motion rejected 181-246: R 2-236; D 179-10. Aug. 1, 2012.

545. **HR 8. Tax Rate Extension/Passage.** Passage of the bill that would extend all expiring 2001 and 2003 tax rates for one year. The bill would effectively tie alternative minimum tax exemption amounts to inflation in 2012 and 2013. The bill would extend the so-called marriage-penalty-tax relief, the $1,000 child tax credit and the 15 percent top rate on dividends and capital gains. It would keep the estate tax at its current levels. Passed 256-171: R 237-1; D 19-170. A "nay" was a vote in support of the president's position. Aug. 1, 2012.

546. **HR 1905. Iran and Syria Sanctions/Adoption.** Ros-Lehtinen, R-Fla., motion to suspend the rules and adopt the resolution (H Res 750) that would provide for the concurrence by the House in the Senate amendment to the bill with an amendment. The measure would expand the list of activities that could trigger sanctions against third parties doing business with Iran. Sanctionable activities would include providing insurance for vessels that ship Iranian oil, purchasing Iranian debt and supporting Iranian port-facility construction and management. Motion agreed to 421-6: R 233-5; D 188-1. A two-thirds majority of those present and voting (285 in this case) is required for adoption under suspension of the rules. Aug. 1, 2012.

547. **HR 4365. Retirement Savings Accounts/Passage.** Chaffetz, R-Utah, motion to suspend the rules and pass the bill that would clarify that federal employee retirement savings accounts in the Thrift Savings Fund are subject to IRS tax levies. Motion agreed to 414-6: R 232-3; D 182-3. A two-thirds majority of those present and voting (280 in this case) is required for passage under suspension of the rules. Aug. 1, 2012.

548. **HR 6233. Drought Assistance/Previous Question.** Foxx, R-N.C., motion to order the previous question (thus ending debate and the possibility of amendment) on the rule (H Res 752) that would provide for House floor consideration of a bill that would authorize $383 million in supplemental agricultural disaster assistance for fiscal 2012. Motion agreed to 236-182: R 233-0; D 3-182. Aug. 2, 2012.

549. **HR 6233. Drought Assistance/Rule.** Adoption of the rule (H Res 752) that would provide for House floor consideration of a bill that would authorize $383 million in supplemental agricultural disaster assistance for fiscal 2012. Adopted 235-181: R 233-0; D 2-181. Aug. 2, 2012.

	543	544	545	546	547	548	549
ALABAMA							
1 Bonner	N	N	Y	Y	Y	Y	Y
2 Roby	N	N	Y	Y	Y	Y	Y
3 Rogers	N	N	Y	Y	Y	Y	Y
4 Aderholt	N	Y	Y	Y	Y	Y	Y
5 Brooks	N	N	Y	Y	Y	Y	Y
6 Bachus	N	N	Y	Y	Y	Y	Y
7 Sewell	Y	Y	N	Y	Y	N	N
ALASKA							
AL Young	N	N	Y	Y	N	Y	Y
ARIZONA							
1 Gosar	N	N	Y	Y	Y	Y	Y
2 Franks	N	N	Y	Y	Y	Y	Y
3 Quayle	N	N	Y	Y	Y	Y	Y
4 Pastor	Y	Y	N	Y	Y	N	N
5 Schweikert	N	N	Y	Y	Y	Y	Y
6 Flake	N	N	Y	Y	Y	Y	Y
7 Grijalva	Y	Y	N	Y	Y	N	N
8 Barber	Y	Y	N	Y	Y	N	N
ARKANSAS							
1 Crawford	N	N	Y	Y	Y	Y	Y
2 Griffin	N	N	Y	Y	Y	Y	Y
3 Womack	N	N	Y	Y	Y	Y	Y
4 Ross	N	N	Y	Y	Y	N	N
CALIFORNIA							
1 Thompson	N	Y	N	Y	Y	N	N
2 Herger	N	N	Y	Y	Y	Y	Y
3 Lungren	N	N	Y	Y	Y	Y	Y
4 McClintock	N	N	Y	Y	Y	Y	Y
5 Matsui	Y	Y	N	Y	Y	N	N
6 Woolsey	Y	Y	N	Y	Y	N	N
7 Miller, George	Y	Y	N	Y	Y	N	N
8 Pelosi	Y	Y	N	Y	Y	N	N
9 Lee	Y	Y	N	Y	Y	N	N
10 Garamendi	Y	Y	N	Y	Y	N	N
11 McNerney	N	Y	Y	Y	Y	N	N
12 Speier	Y	Y	N	Y	Y	N	N
13 Stark	Y	Y	N	Y	Y	N	N
14 Eshoo	Y	Y	N	Y	Y	N	N
15 Honda	Y	Y	N	Y	Y	N	N
16 Lofgren	Y	Y	N	Y	Y	N	N
17 Farr	Y	Y	N	Y	Y	N	N
18 Cardoza	?	?	?	?	?	?	?
19 Denham	N	N	Y	Y	Y	Y	Y
20 Costa	Y	Y	Y	Y	Y	N	N
21 Nunes	N	N	Y	Y	Y	Y	Y
22 McCarthy	N	N	Y	Y	Y	Y	Y
23 Capps	Y	Y	N	Y	Y	N	N
24 Gallegly	N	N	Y	Y	Y	Y	Y
25 McKeon	N	N	Y	Y	Y	Y	Y
26 Dreier	N	N	Y	Y	Y	Y	Y
27 Sherman	Y	Y	N	Y	Y	N	N
28 Berman	Y	Y	N	Y	Y	N	N
29 Schiff	Y	Y	N	Y	Y	N	N
30 Waxman	Y	Y	N	Y	Y	N	N
31 Becerra	Y	Y	N	Y	Y	N	N
32 Chu	Y	Y	N	Y	Y	N	N
33 Bass	Y	Y	N	Y	N	N	N
34 Roybal-Allard	Y	Y	N	Y	Y	N	N
35 Waters	Y	Y	N	Y	Y	N	N
36 Hahn	Y	Y	N	Y	Y	N	N
37 Richardson	Y	Y	N	Y	Y	N	N
38 Napolitano	Y	Y	N	Y	Y	N	N
39 Sánchez, Linda	Y	Y	N	Y	Y	N	N
40 Royce	N	N	Y	Y	Y	Y	Y
41 Lewis	N	N	Y	Y	Y	Y	Y
42 Miller, Gary	N	N	Y	Y	Y	Y	Y
43 Baca	Y	Y	N	Y	Y	N	N
44 Calvert	N	N	Y	Y	Y	Y	Y
45 Bono Mack	N	N	Y	Y	Y	Y	Y
46 Rohrabacher	N	N	Y	Y	Y	Y	Y
47 Sanchez, Loretta	Y	Y	N	Y	Y	N	N
48 Campbell	N	N	Y	Y	Y	Y	Y
49 Issa	N	N	Y	Y	Y	Y	Y
50 Bilbray	N	N	Y	Y	Y	Y	Y
51 Filner	Y	Y	N	Y	Y	N	N
52 Hunter	N	N	Y	Y	Y	Y	Y
53 Davis	Y	Y	N	Y	Y	N	N

	543	544	545	546	547	548	549
COLORADO							
1 DeGette	Y	Y	N	Y	Y	N	N
2 Polis	Y	Y	N	Y	Y	N	N
3 Tipton	N	N	Y	Y	Y	Y	Y
4 Gardner	N	N	Y	Y	Y	Y	Y
5 Lamborn	N	N	Y	Y	?	Y	Y
6 Coffman	N	N	Y	Y	Y	Y	Y
7 Perlmutter	Y	Y	N	Y	Y	N	N
CONNECTICUT							
1 Larson	Y	Y	N	Y	Y	N	N
2 Courtney	Y	Y	N	Y	Y	N	N
3 DeLauro	Y	Y	N	Y	Y	N	N
4 Himes	Y	Y	N	Y	Y	N	N
5 Murphy	Y	Y	N	Y	Y	N	N
DELAWARE							
AL Carney	Y	Y	N	Y	Y	N	N
FLORIDA							
1 Miller	N	N	Y	Y	Y	Y	Y
2 Southerland	N	N	Y	Y	?	Y	Y
3 Brown	Y	Y	N	Y	Y	N	N
4 Crenshaw	N	N	Y	Y	Y	Y	Y
5 Nugent	N	N	Y	Y	Y	Y	Y
6 Stearns	N	N	Y	Y	Y	Y	Y
7 Mica	N	N	Y	Y	Y	Y	Y
8 Webster	N	N	Y	Y	Y	Y	Y
9 Bilirakis	N	N	Y	Y	Y	Y	Y
10 Young	N	N	Y	Y	Y	Y	Y
11 Castor	Y	Y	N	Y	Y	N	N
12 Ross	N	N	Y	Y	Y	Y	Y
13 Buchanan	N	N	Y	Y	Y	Y	Y
14 Mack	N	N	Y	Y	Y	Y	Y
15 Posey	N	N	Y	Y	Y	Y	Y
16 Rooney	N	N	Y	Y	Y	Y	Y
17 Wilson	Y	Y	N	Y	Y	N	N
18 Ros-Lehtinen	N	N	Y	Y	Y	Y	Y
19 Deutch	Y	Y	N	Y	Y	N	N
20 Wasserman Schultz	Y	Y	N	Y	?	N	N
21 Diaz-Balart	N	N	Y	Y	Y	Y	Y
22 West	N	N	Y	Y	Y	Y	Y
23 Hastings	Y	Y	N	Y	?	N	N
24 Adams	N	N	Y	Y	Y	Y	Y
25 Rivera	N	N	Y	Y	Y	Y	Y
GEORGIA							
1 Kingston	N	N	Y	Y	Y	Y	Y
2 Bishop	Y	Y	Y	Y	Y	N	N
3 Westmoreland	N	N	Y	Y	Y	Y	Y
4 Johnson	Y	Y	N	Y	?	?	?
5 Lewis	Y	Y	N	Y	Y	N	N
6 Price	N	N	Y	Y	Y	Y	Y
7 Woodall	N	N	Y	Y	Y	Y	Y
8 Scott, A.	N	N	Y	Y	Y	Y	Y
9 Graves	N	N	Y	Y	Y	Y	Y
10 Broun	N	N	Y	Y	Y	Y	Y
11 Gingrey	N	N	Y	Y	Y	Y	Y
12 Barrow	N	N	Y	Y	Y	N	N
13 Scott, D.	Y	Y	N	Y	Y	N	N
HAWAII							
1 Hanabusa	Y	Y	N	Y	Y	N	N
2 Hirono	Y	Y	N	Y	Y	N	N
IDAHO							
1 Labrador	N	N	Y	Y	Y	Y	Y
2 Simpson	N	N	Y	Y	Y	Y	Y
ILLINOIS							
1 Rush	Y	Y	N	Y	Y	N	N
2 Jackson	?	?	?	?	?	?	?
3 Lipinski	Y	Y	N	Y	Y	N	N
4 Gutierrez	Y	Y	N	Y	Y	N	N
5 Quigley	Y	Y	N	Y	Y	N	N
6 Roskam	N	N	Y	Y	Y	Y	Y
7 Davis	Y	Y	N	Y	Y	N	N
8 Walsh	N	N	Y	Y	Y	Y	Y
9 Schakowsky	Y	Y	N	Y	Y	N	N
10 Dold	N	N	Y	Y	Y	Y	Y
11 Kinzinger	N	N	Y	Y	Y	Y	Y
12 Costello	Y	Y	N	Y	Y	?	?
13 Biggert	N	N	Y	Y	Y	Y	Y
14 Hultgren	N	N	Y	Y	Y	Y	Y
15 Johnson	N	N	N	Y	P	Y	Y

KEY   **Republicans**   Democrats

Y Voted for (yea)	X Paired against	C Voted "present" to avoid possible conflict of interest
# Paired for	– Announced against	
+ Announced for	P Voted "present"	? Did not vote or otherwise make a position known
N Voted against (nay)		

	543	544	545	546	547	548	549
16 **Manzullo**	N	N	Y	Y	Y	Y	Y
17 **Schilling**	N	N	Y	Y	Y	Y	Y
18 **Schock**	N	N	Y	Y	Y	Y	Y
19 **Shimkus**	N	N	Y	Y	Y	Y	Y
INDIANA							
1 Visclosky	Y	Y	N	Y	Y	N	N
2 Donnelly	N	N	Y	Y	Y	N	Y
3 **Stutzman**	N	N	Y	Y	Y	Y	Y
4 **Rokita**	N	N	Y	Y	Y	Y	Y
5 **Burton**	N	N	Y	Y	Y	?	?
6 **Pence**	N	N	Y	Y	Y	Y	Y
7 Carson	Y	Y	N	Y	Y	N	N
8 **Bucshon**	N	N	Y	Y	Y	Y	Y
9 **Young**	N	N	Y	Y	Y	Y	Y
IOWA							
1 Braley	Y	Y	N	Y	Y	N	N
2 Loebsack	Y	Y	Y	Y	Y	N	N
3 Boswell	Y	Y	Y	Y	Y	N	N
4 **Latham**	N	N	Y	Y	Y	Y	Y
5 **King**	N	N	Y	Y	Y	Y	Y
KANSAS							
1 **Huelskamp**	N	N	Y	Y	Y	Y	Y
2 **Jenkins**	N	N	Y	Y	Y	Y	Y
3 **Yoder**	N	N	Y	Y	Y	?	?
4 **Pompeo**	N	N	Y	Y	Y	Y	Y
KENTUCKY							
1 **Whitfield**	N	N	Y	Y	Y	Y	Y
2 **Guthrie**	N	N	Y	Y	Y	Y	Y
3 Yarmuth	Y	Y	N	Y	Y	N	N
4 Vacant							
5 **Rogers**	N	N	Y	Y	Y	Y	Y
6 Chandler	N	Y	Y	Y	Y	N	N
LOUISIANA							
1 **Scalise**	N	N	Y	Y	Y	Y	Y
2 Richmond	Y	Y	N	Y	Y	N	N
3 **Landry**	N	N	Y	Y	Y	Y	Y
4 **Fleming**	N	N	Y	Y	Y	Y	Y
5 **Alexander**	N	N	Y	Y	Y	Y	Y
6 **Cassidy**	N	N	Y	Y	Y	Y	Y
7 **Boustany**	N	N	Y	Y	Y	Y	Y
MAINE							
1 Pingree	Y	Y	N	Y	Y	N	N
2 Michaud	Y	Y	N	Y	Y	N	N
MARYLAND							
1 **Harris**	N	N	Y	Y	Y	Y	Y
2 Ruppersberger	Y	Y	N	Y	Y	N	N
3 Sarbanes	Y	Y	N	Y	Y	N	N
4 Edwards	Y	Y	N	Y	Y	N	N
5 Hoyer	Y	Y	N	Y	Y	N	N
6 **Bartlett**	N	N	Y	Y	Y	Y	Y
7 Cummings	Y	Y	N	Y	Y	N	N
8 Van Hollen	Y	Y	N	Y	Y	N	N
MASSACHUSETTS							
1 Olver	Y	Y	N	Y	Y	N	N
2 Neal	Y	Y	N	Y	Y	N	N
3 McGovern	Y	Y	N	Y	Y	N	N
4 Frank	Y	Y	N	Y	Y	N	N
5 Tsongas	Y	Y	N	Y	Y	N	N
6 Tierney	Y	Y	N	Y	Y	N	N
7 Markey	Y	Y	N	Y	Y	N	N
8 Capuano	Y	Y	N	Y	Y	N	N
9 Lynch	Y	Y	N	Y	Y	N	N
10 Keating	Y	Y	N	Y	Y	N	N
MICHIGAN							
1 **Benishek**	N	N	Y	Y	Y	Y	Y
2 **Huizenga**	N	N	Y	Y	Y	Y	Y
3 **Amash**	N	N	Y	N	Y	Y	Y
4 **Camp**	N	N	Y	Y	Y	Y	Y
5 Kildee	Y	Y	N	Y	Y	N	N
6 **Upton**	N	N	Y	Y	Y	Y	Y
7 **Walberg**	N	N	Y	Y	Y	Y	Y
8 **Rogers**	N	N	Y	Y	Y	Y	Y
9 Peters	Y	Y	N	Y	Y	N	N
10 **Miller**	N	N	Y	Y	Y	Y	Y
11 Vacant							
12 Levin	Y	Y	N	Y	Y	N	N
13 Clarke	Y	Y	N	Y	Y	N	N
14 Conyers	Y	Y	N	Y	Y	N	N
15 Dingell	Y	Y	N	Y	Y	N	N
MINNESOTA							
1 Walz	N	Y	Y	Y	Y	N	N
2 **Kline**	N	N	Y	Y	Y	Y	Y
3 **Paulsen**	N	N	Y	Y	Y	Y	Y
4 McCollum	Y	Y	N	Y	Y	N	N

	543	544	545	546	547	548	549
5 Ellison	Y	Y	N	Y	Y	N	N
6 **Bachmann**	N	N	Y	Y	Y	Y	Y
7 Peterson	N	N	Y	Y	Y	N	N
8 **Cravaack**	N	N	Y	Y	Y	Y	Y
MISSISSIPPI							
1 **Nunnelee**	N	N	Y	Y	Y	Y	Y
2 Thompson	Y	Y	N	Y	Y	N	N
3 **Harper**	N	N	Y	Y	Y	Y	Y
4 **Palazzo**	N	N	Y	Y	Y	Y	Y
MISSOURI							
1 Clay	Y	Y	N	Y	Y	N	N
2 **Akin**	?	?	?	?	?	?	?
3 Carnahan	Y	Y	N	Y	Y	N	N
4 **Hartzler**	N	N	Y	Y	Y	Y	Y
5 Cleaver	Y	Y	N	Y	Y	N	N
6 **Graves**	N	N	Y	Y	Y	?	?
7 **Long**	N	N	Y	Y	Y	Y	Y
8 **Emerson**	N	N	Y	Y	Y	Y	Y
9 **Luetkemeyer**	N	N	Y	Y	Y	Y	Y
MONTANA							
AL **Rehberg**	N	N	Y	Y	Y	Y	Y
NEBRASKA							
1 **Fortenberry**	N	N	Y	Y	Y	Y	Y
2 **Terry**	N	N	Y	Y	Y	Y	Y
3 **Smith**	N	N	Y	Y	Y	Y	Y
NEVADA							
1 Berkley	Y	Y	N	Y	Y	N	N
2 **Amodei**	N	N	Y	Y	Y	Y	Y
3 **Heck**	N	N	Y	Y	Y	Y	Y
NEW HAMPSHIRE							
1 **Guinta**	N	N	Y	Y	Y	Y	Y
2 **Bass**	N	N	Y	Y	Y	Y	Y
NEW JERSEY							
1 Andrews	Y	Y	N	Y	Y	N	N
2 **LoBiondo**	N	N	Y	Y	Y	Y	Y
3 **Runyan**	N	N	Y	Y	Y	Y	Y
4 **Smith**	N	N	Y	Y	Y	Y	Y
5 **Garrett**	N	N	Y	Y	Y	Y	Y
6 Pallone	Y	Y	N	Y	Y	N	N
7 **Lance**	N	N	Y	Y	Y	Y	Y
8 Pascrell	Y	Y	N	Y	Y	N	N
9 Rothman	Y	Y	N	Y	Y	N	N
10 Vacant							
11 **Frelinghuysen**	N	N	Y	Y	Y	Y	Y
12 Holt	Y	Y	N	Y	Y	N	N
13 Sires	Y	Y	N	Y	Y	N	N
NEW MEXICO							
1 Heinrich	Y	Y	N	Y	Y	N	N
2 **Pearce**	N	N	Y	Y	Y	Y	Y
3 Luján	Y	Y	N	Y	Y	N	N
NEW YORK							
1 Bishop	Y	Y	N	Y	Y	N	N
2 Israel	Y	Y	N	Y	Y	N	N
3 **King**	N	N	Y	Y	Y	Y	Y
4 McCarthy	Y	Y	N	Y	Y	N	N
5 Ackerman	Y	Y	N	Y	N	N	N
6 Meeks	Y	Y	N	Y	N	N	N
7 Crowley	Y	Y	N	Y	Y	N	N
8 Nadler	Y	Y	N	Y	Y	N	N
9 **Turner**	N	N	Y	Y	Y	Y	Y
10 Towns	Y	Y	N	Y	Y	N	N
11 Clarke	Y	Y	N	Y	Y	N	N
12 Velázquez	Y	Y	N	Y	Y	N	N
13 **Grimm**	N	N	Y	Y	Y	Y	Y
14 Maloney	Y	Y	N	Y	Y	N	N
15 Rangel	Y	Y	N	Y	Y	N	N
16 Serrano	Y	Y	N	Y	Y	N	N
17 Engel	Y	Y	N	Y	Y	N	N
18 Lowey	Y	Y	N	Y	Y	N	N
19 **Hayworth**	N	N	Y	Y	Y	Y	Y
20 **Gibson**	N	N	Y	Y	Y	Y	Y
21 Tonko	Y	Y	N	Y	Y	N	N
22 Hinchey	Y	Y	N	Y	Y	N	N
23 Owens	N	Y	Y	Y	Y	N	N
24 **Hanna**	N	N	Y	Y	Y	Y	Y
25 **Buerkle**	N	N	Y	Y	Y	Y	Y
26 Hochul	Y	Y	N	Y	Y	N	N
27 Higgins	Y	Y	N	Y	Y	N	N
28 Slaughter	Y	Y	N	Y	Y	N	N
29 **Reed**	N	N	Y	Y	Y	Y	Y
NORTH CAROLINA							
1 Butterfield	Y	Y	N	Y	Y	N	?
2 **Ellmers**	N	N	Y	Y	Y	Y	Y
3 **Jones**	N	Y	Y	N	N	Y	Y
4 Price	Y	Y	N	Y	Y	N	N

	543	544	545	546	547	548	549
5 **Foxx**	N	N	Y	Y	Y	Y	Y
6 **Coble**	N	N	Y	Y	Y	Y	Y
7 McIntyre	N	N	Y	Y	Y	Y	N
8 Kissell	N	Y	Y	Y	Y	N	?
9 **Myrick**	N	N	Y	Y	Y	Y	Y
10 **McHenry**	N	N	Y	Y	Y	Y	Y
11 Shuler	N	N	N	Y	Y	Y	Y
12 Watt	Y	Y	N	Y	Y	N	N
13 Miller	Y	Y	N	Y	Y	N	N
NORTH DAKOTA							
AL **Berg**	N	N	Y	Y	Y	Y	Y
OHIO							
1 **Chabot**	N	N	Y	Y	Y	Y	Y
2 **Schmidt**	N	N	Y	Y	Y	Y	Y
3 **Turner**	N	N	Y	Y	Y	Y	Y
4 **Jordan**	N	N	Y	Y	Y	Y	Y
5 **Latta**	N	N	Y	Y	Y	Y	Y
6 **Johnson**	N	N	Y	Y	Y	Y	Y
7 **Austria**	N	N	Y	Y	Y	Y	Y
8 **Boehner**							
9 Kaptur	Y	Y	N	Y	?	N	N
10 Kucinich	Y	Y	N	N	Y	N	N
11 Fudge	Y	Y	N	Y	Y	N	N
12 **Tiberi**	N	N	Y	Y	Y	Y	Y
13 Sutton	Y	Y	N	Y	Y	N	N
14 **LaTourette**	N	N	Y	Y	Y	Y	Y
15 **Stivers**	N	N	Y	Y	Y	Y	Y
16 **Renacci**	N	N	Y	Y	Y	Y	Y
17 Ryan	Y	Y	N	Y	Y	N	N
18 **Gibbs**	N	N	Y	Y	Y	Y	Y
OKLAHOMA							
1 **Sullivan**	N	N	Y	Y	Y	Y	Y
2 Boren	N	N	Y	Y	Y	N	N
3 **Lucas**	N	N	Y	Y	Y	Y	Y
4 **Cole**	N	N	Y	Y	Y	Y	Y
5 **Lankford**	N	N	Y	Y	Y	Y	Y
OREGON							
1 Bonamici	Y	Y	N	Y	Y	N	N
2 **Walden**	N	N	Y	Y	Y	Y	Y
3 Blumenauer	Y	Y	N	Y	Y	N	N
4 DeFazio	Y	Y	N	Y	Y	N	N
5 Schrader	N	N	N	Y	Y	N	N
PENNSYLVANIA							
1 Brady	Y	Y	N	Y	Y	N	N
2 Fattah	Y	Y	N	Y	Y	N	N
3 **Kelly**	N	N	Y	Y	Y	Y	Y
4 Altmire	N	N	N	Y	Y	N	N
5 **Thompson**	N	N	Y	Y	Y	Y	Y
6 **Gerlach**	N	N	Y	Y	Y	Y	Y
7 **Meehan**	N	N	Y	Y	Y	Y	Y
8 **Fitzpatrick**	N	N	Y	Y	Y	Y	Y
9 **Shuster**	N	N	Y	Y	Y	Y	Y
10 **Marino**	N	N	Y	Y	Y	Y	Y
11 **Barletta**	N	N	Y	Y	Y	Y	Y
12 Critz	Y	Y	Y	Y	Y	N	N
13 Schwartz	Y	Y	N	Y	Y	N	N
14 Doyle	Y	Y	N	Y	Y	N	N
15 **Dent**	N	N	Y	Y	Y	Y	Y
16 **Pitts**	N	N	Y	Y	Y	Y	Y
17 Holden	Y	Y	N	Y	Y	N	N
18 **Murphy**	N	N	Y	Y	Y	Y	Y
19 **Platts**	N	N	Y	Y	Y	Y	Y
RHODE ISLAND							
1 Cicilline	Y	Y	N	Y	Y	N	N
2 Langevin	Y	Y	N	Y	Y	N	N
SOUTH CAROLINA							
1 **Scott**	N	N	Y	Y	Y	Y	Y
2 **Wilson**	N	N	Y	Y	Y	Y	Y
3 **Duncan**	N	N	Y	Y	Y	Y	Y
4 **Gowdy**	N	N	Y	Y	Y	Y	Y
5 **Mulvaney**	N	N	Y	Y	Y	Y	Y
6 Clyburn	Y	Y	N	Y	Y	N	N
SOUTH DAKOTA							
AL **Noem**	N	N	Y	Y	Y	Y	Y
TENNESSEE							
1 **Roe**	N	N	Y	Y	Y	Y	Y
2 **Duncan**	N	Y	Y	N	Y	Y	Y
3 **Fleischmann**	N	N	Y	Y	Y	?	?
4 **DesJarlais**	N	N	Y	Y	Y	Y	Y
5 Cooper	N	Y	N	Y	Y	N	N
6 **Black**	N	N	Y	Y	Y	?	?
7 **Blackburn**	N	N	Y	Y	Y	Y	Y
8 **Fincher**	N	N	Y	Y	Y	Y	Y
9 Cohen	Y	Y	N	Y	Y	?	?

	543	544	545	546	547	548	549
TEXAS							
1 **Gohmert**	N	N	Y	Y	Y	Y	Y
2 **Poe**	N	N	Y	Y	Y	Y	Y
3 **Johnson, S.**	N	N	Y	Y	Y	Y	Y
4 **Hall**	N	N	Y	Y	Y	Y	Y
5 **Hensarling**	N	N	Y	Y	Y	Y	Y
6 **Barton**	N	N	Y	Y	Y	Y	Y
7 **Culberson**	N	N	Y	Y	Y	Y	Y
8 **Brady**	N	N	Y	Y	Y	Y	Y
9 Green, A.	Y	Y	N	Y	Y	N	N
10 **McCaul**	N	N	Y	Y	Y	Y	Y
11 **Conaway**	N	N	Y	Y	Y	Y	Y
12 **Granger**	N	N	Y	Y	Y	Y	Y
13 **Thornberry**	N	N	Y	Y	Y	Y	Y
14 **Paul**	N	N	Y	N	N	Y	Y
15 Hinojosa	Y	Y	N	Y	Y	N	N
16 Reyes	Y	Y	N	Y	Y	N	N
17 **Flores**	N	N	Y	Y	Y	Y	Y
18 Jackson Lee	Y	Y	N	Y	Y	?	?
19 **Neugebauer**	N	N	Y	Y	Y	Y	Y
20 Gonzalez	Y	Y	N	Y	Y	N	N
21 **Smith**	N	N	Y	Y	Y	Y	Y
22 **Olson**	N	N	Y	Y	Y	Y	Y
23 **Canseco**	N	N	Y	Y	Y	Y	Y
24 **Marchant**	N	N	Y	Y	Y	Y	Y
25 Doggett	Y	Y	N	Y	Y	N	N
26 **Burgess**	N	N	Y	Y	Y	Y	Y
27 **Farenthold**	N	N	Y	Y	Y	Y	Y
28 Cuellar	N	Y	Y	Y	Y	N	N
29 Green, G.	Y	Y	N	Y	Y	N	N
30 Johnson, E.	Y	Y	N	Y	Y	N	N
31 **Carter**	N	N	Y	Y	Y	Y	Y
32 **Sessions**	N	N	Y	Y	Y	Y	Y
UTAH							
1 **Bishop**	N	N	Y	Y	Y	Y	Y
2 Matheson	N	N	Y	Y	Y	Y	N
3 **Chaffetz**	N	N	Y	Y	Y	Y	Y
VERMONT							
AL Welch	Y	Y	N	Y	Y	N	N
VIRGINIA							
1 **Wittman**	N	N	Y	Y	Y	Y	Y
2 **Rigell**	N	N	Y	Y	Y	Y	Y
3 Scott	Y	Y	N	Y	Y	N	N
4 **Forbes**	N	N	Y	Y	Y	Y	Y
5 **Hurt**	N	N	Y	Y	Y	Y	Y
6 **Goodlatte**	N	N	Y	Y	Y	Y	Y
7 **Cantor**	N	N	Y	Y	Y	Y	Y
8 Moran	Y	Y	N	Y	Y	N	N
9 **Griffith**	N	N	Y	Y	Y	Y	Y
10 **Wolf**	N	N	Y	Y	Y	Y	Y
11 Connolly	Y	Y	Y	Y	Y	N	N
WASHINGTON							
1 Vacant							
2 Larsen	Y	Y	N	Y	Y	N	N
3 **Herrera Beutler**	N	N	Y	Y	Y	Y	Y
4 **Hastings**	N	N	Y	Y	Y	Y	Y
5 **McMorris Rodgers**	N	N	Y	Y	Y	Y	Y
6 Dicks	Y	Y	N	Y	?	N	N
7 McDermott	Y	Y	N	Y	Y	N	N
8 **Reichert**	N	N	Y	Y	Y	Y	Y
9 Smith	Y	Y	N	Y	Y	N	N
WEST VIRGINIA							
1 **McKinley**	N	N	Y	Y	Y	Y	Y
2 **Capito**	N	N	Y	Y	Y	Y	Y
3 Rahall	Y	Y	N	Y	Y	N	N
WISCONSIN							
1 **Ryan**	N	N	Y	Y	Y	Y	Y
2 Baldwin	Y	Y	N	Y	Y	N	N
3 Kind	Y	Y	N	Y	Y	N	N
4 Moore	Y	Y	N	Y	Y	N	N
5 **Sensenbrenner**	N	N	Y	Y	Y	Y	Y
6 **Petri**	N	N	Y	Y	Y	Y	Y
7 **Duffy**	N	N	Y	Y	Y	Y	Y
8 **Ribble**	N	N	Y	Y	Y	Y	Y
WYOMING							
AL **Lummis**	N	N	Y	Y	Y	Y	Y

IN THE HOUSE | By Vote Number

550. HR 6169. Tax Code Overhaul/Democratic Substitute. Slaughter, D-N.Y., substitute amendment that would strike the text of the bill and insert congressional findings stating that the House should proceed to a tax overhaul measure that includes a progressive tax rate structure, the repeal of the alternative minimum tax, the elimination of tax breaks for companies that move jobs and profits overseas and incentives for small-business investment and growth. Rejected in Committee of the Whole 176-246: R 0-236; D 176-10. Aug. 2, 2012.

551. HR 6169. Tax Code Overhaul/Recommit. Bishop, D-N.Y., motion to recommit the bill to the House Ways and Means Committee and report it back immediately with language that would require that, to be eligible for the special legislative protections provided in the bill, a tax overhaul bill could not repeal, reduce or eliminate the existing deductions for mortgage interest or charitable contributions. Motion rejected 188-235: R 3-233; D 185-2. Aug. 2, 2012.

552. HR 6169. Tax Code Overhaul/Passage. Passage of the bill that would establish rules in the House and Senate for the expedited consideration of a tax overhaul measure in the 113th Congress. The bill would outline principles that a tax measure would need to meet to receive the expedited consideration, including the consolidation of the six current tax brackets into two brackets, one at 10 percent and the other at no more than 25 percent; the reduction of the corporate tax rate to no greater than 25 percent; the repeal of the alternative minimum tax; and the expansion of the tax base to maintain revenue between 18 percent and 19 percent of the economy. Passed 232-189: R 232-3; D 0-186. A "nay" was a vote in support of the president's position. Aug. 2, 2012.

553. HR 6233. Drought Assistance/Recommit. Costa, D-Calif., motion to recommit the bill to the House Agriculture Committee and report it back immediately with language that would express the sense of the House that a five-year farm bill would provide greater certainty and stability for U.S. farm families than extending farm policy for one year or authorizing short-term disaster assistance. Motion rejected 189-232: R 2-232; D 187-0. Aug. 2, 2012.

554. HR 6233. Drought Assistance/Passage. Passage of the bill that would authorize $383 million in supplemental agricultural disaster assistance for losses in fiscal 2012. The bill would authorize the Agriculture Department to use such sums as necessary to make livestock indemnity payments for farms that have incurred livestock deaths in excess of the normal mortality rate due to adverse weather. It would offset the cost of the supplemental assistance by making reductions to the Conservation Stewardship Program and the Environmental Quality Incentives Program. Passed 223-197: R 188-46; D 35-151. Aug. 2, 2012.

555. H Con Res 127. Internet Openness/Adoption. Walden, R-Ore., motion to suspend the rules and adopt the concurrent resolution that would express the sense of Congress that the U.S. delegation to the International Telecommunication Union should promote a global Internet free from government control and should preserve the multistakeholder model that governs the Internet today. Motion agreed to 414-0: R 229-0; D 185-0. A two-thirds majority of those present and voting (276 in this case) is required for adoption under suspension of the rules. Aug. 2, 2012.

556. S Con Res 56. Adjournment/Adoption. Adoption of the concurrent resolution that would provide for the conditional adjournment of the Senate and the adjournment of the House until Sept. 10, 2012. Rejected 150-265: R 150-78; D 0-187. Aug. 2, 2012.

	550	551	552	553	554	555	556
ALABAMA							
1 Bonner	N	N	Y	N	Y	Y	N
2 Roby	N	N	Y	N	Y	Y	Y
3 Rogers	N	N	Y	N	Y	Y	Y
4 Aderholt	N	N	Y	N	Y	Y	N
5 Brooks	N	N	Y	N	N	Y	N
6 Bachus	N	N	Y	N	Y	Y	Y
7 Sewell	Y	Y	N	Y	Y	Y	N
ALASKA							
AL Young	N	N	Y	N	Y	Y	Y
ARIZONA							
1 Gosar	N	N	Y	N	N	Y	N
2 Franks	N	N	Y	N	N	Y	Y
3 Quayle	N	N	Y	N	N	Y	N
4 Pastor	Y	Y	N	Y	N	Y	N
5 Schweikert	N	N	Y	N	N	Y	Y
6 Flake	N	N	Y	N	N	Y	Y
7 Grijalva	Y	Y	N	Y	N	Y	N
8 Barber	Y	Y	N	Y	N	Y	N
ARKANSAS							
1 Crawford	N	N	Y	N	Y	Y	Y
2 Griffin	N	N	Y	N	Y	Y	Y
3 Womack	N	N	Y	N	Y	Y	Y
4 Ross	Y	Y	N	Y	Y	Y	N
CALIFORNIA							
1 Thompson	Y	Y	N	Y	N	Y	N
2 Herger	N	N	Y	N	Y	Y	Y
3 Lungren	N	N	Y	N	Y	Y	Y
4 McClintock	N	N	Y	N	N	Y	Y
5 Matsui	Y	Y	N	Y	N	Y	N
6 Woolsey	Y	Y	N	Y	N	Y	N
7 Miller, George	Y	Y	N	Y	N	Y	N
8 Pelosi	Y	Y	N	Y	N	Y	N
9 Lee	Y	Y	N	Y	N	Y	N
10 Garamendi	Y	Y	N	Y	N	Y	N
11 McNerney	Y	Y	N	Y	Y	Y	N
12 Speier	Y	Y	N	Y	N	Y	N
13 Stark	Y	Y	N	Y	N	Y	N
14 Eshoo	Y	Y	N	Y	N	Y	N
15 Honda	Y	Y	N	Y	N	Y	N
16 Lofgren	Y	Y	N	Y	N	Y	N
17 Farr	Y	Y	N	Y	N	Y	N
18 Cardoza	?	?	?	?	?	?	?
19 Denham	N	N	Y	N	Y	Y	N
20 Costa	N	Y	N	Y	N	Y	N
21 Nunes	N	N	Y	N	Y	Y	Y
22 McCarthy	N	N	Y	N	Y	Y	Y
23 Capps	Y	Y	N	Y	N	Y	N
24 Gallegly	N	N	Y	N	Y	Y	Y
25 McKeon	N	N	Y	N	Y	Y	Y
26 Dreier	N	N	Y	N	Y	Y	Y
27 Sherman	Y	Y	N	Y	N	Y	N
28 Berman	Y	Y	N	Y	N	Y	N
29 Schiff	N	Y	N	Y	N	Y	N
30 Waxman	?	Y	N	Y	N	Y	N
31 Becerra	Y	Y	N	Y	N	Y	N
32 Chu	Y	Y	N	Y	N	Y	N
33 Bass	Y	Y	N	Y	N	Y	N
34 Roybal-Allard	Y	Y	N	Y	N	Y	N
35 Waters	Y	Y	N	Y	N	Y	N
36 Hahn	Y	Y	N	Y	N	Y	N
37 Richardson	Y	Y	N	Y	N	?	N
38 Napolitano	Y	Y	N	Y	N	Y	N
39 Sánchez, Linda	Y	Y	N	Y	N	Y	N
40 Royce	N	N	Y	N	N	Y	Y
41 Lewis	N	N	Y	N	N	Y	Y
42 Miller, Gary	N	N	Y	N	N	Y	Y
43 Baca	Y	Y	N	Y	N	Y	N
44 Calvert	N	N	Y	N	N	Y	Y
45 Bono Mack	N	N	Y	N	N	Y	N
46 Rohrabacher	N	N	Y	N	Y	Y	N
47 Sanchez, Loretta	Y	Y	N	Y	N	Y	N
48 Campbell	N	N	?	?	?	?	?
49 Issa	N	N	Y	N	Y	Y	N
50 Bilbray	N	N	Y	N	Y	Y	N
51 Filner	Y	Y	N	Y	N	Y	N
52 Hunter	N	N	Y	N	Y	Y	Y
53 Davis	Y	Y	N	Y	N	Y	N

	550	551	552	553	554	555	556
COLORADO							
1 DeGette	Y	Y	N	Y	N	Y	N
2 Polis	Y	Y	N	Y	N	Y	N
3 Tipton	N	N	Y	N	Y	Y	N
4 Gardner	N	N	Y	N	Y	Y	Y
5 Lamborn	N	N	Y	N	Y	Y	Y
6 Coffman	N	N	Y	N	Y	Y	N
7 Perlmutter	Y	Y	N	Y	N	Y	N
CONNECTICUT							
1 Larson	Y	Y	N	Y	N	Y	N
2 Courtney	Y	Y	N	Y	N	Y	N
3 DeLauro	Y	Y	N	Y	N	Y	N
4 Himes	Y	N	Y	N	Y	Y	N
5 Murphy	Y	Y	N	Y	N	Y	N
DELAWARE							
AL Carney	Y	Y	N	Y	N	Y	N
FLORIDA							
1 Miller	N	N	Y	N	N	Y	N
2 Southerland	N	N	Y	N	Y	Y	N
3 Brown	Y	Y	N	Y	Y	Y	N
4 Crenshaw	N	N	Y	N	Y	Y	Y
5 Nugent	N	N	Y	N	Y	Y	Y
6 Stearns	N	N	Y	N	Y	Y	Y
7 Mica	N	N	Y	N	Y	Y	Y
8 Webster	N	N	Y	N	Y	Y	Y
9 Bilirakis	N	N	Y	N	Y	Y	Y
10 Young	N	N	Y	N	Y	Y	Y
11 Castor	Y	Y	N	Y	N	Y	N
12 Ross	N	N	Y	N	Y	Y	Y
13 Buchanan	N	N	Y	N	Y	Y	?
14 Mack	N	N	Y	N	N	Y	N
15 Posey	N	N	Y	N	N	Y	N
16 Rooney	N	N	Y	N	Y	Y	Y
17 Wilson	Y	Y	N	Y	N	Y	N
18 Ros-Lehtinen	N	N	Y	N	Y	Y	Y
19 Deutch	Y	Y	N	Y	N	Y	N
20 Wasserman Schultz	Y	Y	N	Y	N	Y	N
21 Diaz-Balart	N	N	Y	N	Y	Y	Y
22 West	N	N	Y	N	Y	Y	N
23 Hastings	Y	Y	N	Y	N	Y	N
24 Adams	N	N	Y	N	Y	Y	N
25 Rivera	N	N	Y	N	Y	Y	Y
GEORGIA							
1 Kingston	N	N	Y	N	Y	Y	Y
2 Bishop	Y	Y	N	Y	Y	Y	N
3 Westmoreland	N	N	Y	N	Y	Y	N
4 Johnson	Y	Y	N	Y	?	Y	N
5 Lewis	Y	Y	N	Y	N	Y	N
6 Price	N	N	Y	N	Y	Y	N
7 Woodall	N	N	Y	N	Y	Y	Y
8 Scott, A.	N	N	Y	N	Y	Y	Y
9 Graves	N	N	Y	N	N	Y	Y
10 Broun	N	N	Y	N	N	Y	Y
11 Gingrey	N	N	Y	N	Y	Y	Y
12 Barrow	Y	Y	N	Y	Y	Y	N
13 Scott, D.	Y	Y	N	Y	Y	Y	N
HAWAII							
1 Hanabusa	Y	Y	N	Y	N	Y	N
2 Hirono	Y	Y	N	Y	N	Y	N
IDAHO							
1 Labrador	N	N	Y	N	Y	Y	N
2 Simpson	N	N	Y	N	Y	Y	Y
ILLINOIS							
1 Rush	Y	Y	N	Y	N	Y	N
2 Jackson	?	?	?	?	?	?	?
3 Lipinski	N	Y	N	Y	N	Y	N
4 Gutierrez	Y	Y	N	Y	N	Y	N
5 Quigley	Y	Y	N	Y	N	Y	N
6 Roskam	N	N	Y	N	Y	Y	Y
7 Davis	Y	Y	N	Y	N	Y	N
8 Walsh	N	N	Y	N	Y	Y	Y
9 Schakowsky	Y	Y	N	Y	N	Y	N
10 Dold	N	N	Y	N	Y	Y	N
11 Kinzinger	N	N	Y	N	Y	Y	Y
12 Costello	Y	Y	N	Y	Y	Y	Y
13 Biggert	N	N	Y	N	Y	Y	Y
14 Hultgren	N	N	Y	N	Y	Y	Y
15 Johnson	N	N	Y	N	Y	Y	N

KEY	**Republicans**	Democrats		
Y Voted for (yea)		**X** Paired against		**C** Voted "present" to avoid possible conflict of interest
# Paired for		**–** Announced against		**?** Did not vote or otherwise make a position known
+ Announced for		**P** Voted "present"		
N Voted against (nay)				

	550	551	552	553	554	555	556
16 **Manzullo**	N	N	Y	N	Y	Y	Y
17 **Schilling**	N	N	Y	N	Y	Y	N
18 **Schock**	N	N	Y	N	Y	Y	Y
19 **Shimkus**	N	N	Y	N	Y	Y	Y
INDIANA							
1 Visclosky	Y	Y	N	Y	N	Y	N
2 Donnelly	N	Y	N	Y	Y	Y	N
3 **Stutzman**	N	N	Y	N	Y	Y	N
4 **Rokita**	N	N	Y	N	Y	Y	Y
5 **Burton**	N	N	Y	?	Y	Y	?
6 **Pence**	N	N	Y	N	Y	Y	Y
7 Carson	Y	Y	N	Y	Y	Y	N
8 **Bucshon**	N	N	Y	N	Y	Y	Y
9 **Young**	N	N	Y	N	Y	Y	Y
IOWA							
1 Braley	Y	Y	N	Y	Y	Y	N
2 Loebsack	Y	Y	N	Y	Y	Y	N
3 Boswell	Y	Y	N	Y	Y	Y	N
4 **Latham**	N	N	Y	Y	Y	Y	Y
5 **King**	N	N	Y	N	Y	Y	N
KANSAS							
1 **Huelskamp**	N	N	Y	N	Y	Y	Y
2 **Jenkins**	N	N	Y	N	Y	Y	N
3 **Yoder**	N	N	Y	N	N	Y	Y
4 **Pompeo**	N	N	Y	N	Y	Y	Y
KENTUCKY							
1 **Whitfield**	N	N	Y	N	Y	Y	Y
2 **Guthrie**	N	N	Y	N	Y	Y	Y
3 Yarmuth	Y	Y	N	Y	N	Y	N
4 Vacant							
5 **Rogers**	N	N	Y	N	Y	Y	Y
6 Chandler	Y	Y	N	Y	Y	Y	N
LOUISIANA							
1 **Scalise**	N	N	Y	N	N	Y	N
2 Richmond	Y	Y	N	Y	Y	Y	N
3 **Landry**	N	N	Y	N	Y	Y	Y
4 **Fleming**	N	N	Y	N	N	Y	N
5 **Alexander**	N	N	Y	N	Y	Y	Y
6 **Cassidy**	N	N	Y	N	Y	Y	N
7 **Boustany**	N	N	Y	N	Y	Y	N
MAINE							
1 Pingree	Y	Y	N	Y	N	Y	N
2 Michaud	Y	Y	N	Y	N	Y	N
MARYLAND							
1 **Harris**	N	N	Y	N	N	Y	N
2 Ruppersberger	Y	Y	N	Y	N	Y	N
3 Sarbanes	Y	Y	N	Y	N	Y	N
4 Edwards	Y	Y	N	Y	N	Y	N
5 Hoyer	Y	Y	N	Y	N	Y	N
6 **Bartlett**	N	N	Y	N	N	Y	Y
7 Cummings	Y	Y	N	Y	N	Y	N
8 Van Hollen	Y	Y	N	Y	N	Y	N
MASSACHUSETTS							
1 Olver	Y	Y	N	Y	N	Y	N
2 Neal	Y	Y	N	Y	N	Y	N
3 McGovern	Y	Y	N	Y	N	Y	N
4 Frank	Y	Y	N	Y	N	Y	N
5 Tsongas	Y	Y	N	Y	N	Y	N
6 Tierney	Y	Y	N	Y	N	Y	N
7 Markey	Y	Y	N	Y	N	Y	N
8 Capuano	Y	Y	N	Y	N	Y	N
9 Lynch	Y	Y	N	Y	N	Y	N
10 Keating	Y	Y	N	Y	N	Y	N
MICHIGAN							
1 **Benishek**	N	N	Y	N	N	Y	Y
2 **Huizenga**	N	N	Y	N	N	Y	N
3 **Amash**	N	N	Y	N	N	Y	N
4 **Camp**	N	N	Y	N	Y	Y	Y
5 Kildee	Y	Y	N	Y	Y	Y	N
6 **Upton**	N	N	Y	N	Y	Y	N
7 **Walberg**	N	N	Y	N	N	Y	N
8 **Rogers**	N	N	Y	N	Y	Y	N
9 Peters	Y	Y	N	Y	N	Y	N
10 **Miller**	N	N	Y	N	Y	Y	N
11 Vacant							
12 Levin	Y	Y	N	Y	N	Y	N
13 Clarke	Y	Y	N	Y	N	Y	N
14 Conyers	Y	Y	N	Y	N	Y	N
15 Dingell	Y	Y	N	Y	N	Y	N
MINNESOTA							
1 Walz	Y	Y	N	Y	N	Y	N
2 **Kline**	N	N	Y	N	Y	Y	Y
3 **Paulsen**	N	N	Y	N	Y	Y	Y
4 McCollum	Y	Y	N	Y	N	Y	N

	550	551	552	553	554	555	556
5 Ellison	Y	Y	N	Y	N	Y	N
6 **Bachmann**	N	N	Y	N	N	Y	N
7 Peterson	Y	Y	N	Y	Y	Y	N
8 **Cravaack**	N	N	Y	N	Y	Y	Y
MISSISSIPPI							
1 **Nunnelee**	N	N	Y	N	Y	Y	Y
2 Thompson	Y	Y	N	Y	Y	Y	N
3 **Harper**	N	N	Y	N	Y	Y	Y
4 **Palazzo**	N	N	Y	N	Y	Y	Y
MISSOURI							
1 Clay	Y	Y	N	Y	Y	Y	N
2 **Akin**	?	?	?	?	?	?	?
3 Carnahan	Y	Y	N	Y	N	Y	N
4 **Hartzler**	N	N	Y	N	Y	Y	Y
5 Cleaver	Y	Y	N	Y	Y	?	N
6 **Graves**	N	N	Y	N	+	Y	Y
7 **Long**	N	N	Y	N	Y	Y	Y
8 **Emerson**	N	N	Y	N	Y	Y	N
9 **Luetkemeyer**	N	N	Y	N	Y	Y	Y
MONTANA							
AL **Rehberg**	N	N	Y	N	Y	Y	Y
NEBRASKA							
1 **Fortenberry**	N	N	Y	N	Y	Y	Y
2 **Terry**	N	N	Y	N	Y	Y	N
3 **Smith**	N	N	Y	N	Y	Y	Y
NEVADA							
1 Berkley	Y	Y	N	Y	Y	Y	N
2 **Amodei**	N	N	Y	N	Y	Y	N
3 **Heck**	N	N	Y	N	Y	Y	N
NEW HAMPSHIRE							
1 **Guinta**	N	N	Y	N	N	Y	Y
2 **Bass**	N	N	Y	N	N	Y	Y
NEW JERSEY							
1 Andrews	Y	Y	N	Y	N	Y	N
2 **LoBiondo**	N	N	Y	N	N	Y	N
3 **Runyan**	N	N	Y	N	N	Y	Y
4 **Smith**	N	N	Y	N	N	Y	Y
5 **Garrett**	N	N	Y	N	N	Y	Y
6 Pallone	Y	Y	N	Y	N	Y	N
7 **Lance**	N	N	Y	N	N	Y	Y
8 Pascrell	Y	Y	N	Y	N	Y	N
9 Rothman	Y	Y	N	Y	N	Y	N
10 Vacant							
11 **Frelinghuysen**	N	N	Y	N	N	Y	N
12 Holt	Y	Y	N	Y	N	Y	N
13 Sires	Y	Y	N	Y	N	Y	N
NEW MEXICO							
1 Heinrich	Y	Y	N	Y	N	Y	N
2 **Pearce**	N	N	Y	N	Y	Y	N
3 Luján	Y	Y	N	Y	N	Y	N
NEW YORK							
1 Bishop	Y	Y	N	Y	N	Y	N
2 Israel	Y	Y	N	Y	N	Y	N
3 **King**	N	N	Y	N	Y	Y	Y
4 McCarthy	Y	Y	N	Y	N	Y	N
5 Ackerman	Y	Y	N	Y	N	Y	N
6 Meeks	Y	Y	N	Y	N	Y	N
7 Crowley	Y	Y	N	Y	N	Y	N
8 Nadler	Y	Y	N	Y	N	Y	N
9 **Turner**	N	N	Y	N	Y	Y	Y
10 Towns	Y	Y	N	Y	N	Y	N
11 Clarke	Y	Y	N	Y	N	Y	N
12 Velázquez	Y	Y	N	Y	N	Y	N
13 **Grimm**	N	N	Y	N	Y	Y	Y
14 Maloney	Y	Y	N	Y	N	Y	N
15 Rangel	Y	Y	N	Y	N	Y	N
16 Serrano	Y	Y	N	Y	N	Y	N
17 Engel	Y	Y	N	Y	N	Y	N
18 Lowey	Y	Y	N	Y	N	Y	N
19 **Hayworth**	N	N	Y	N	Y	Y	Y
20 **Gibson**	N	N	N	N	N	Y	N
21 Tonko	Y	Y	N	Y	N	Y	N
22 Hinchey	Y	Y	N	Y	N	Y	N
23 Owens	Y	Y	N	Y	N	Y	N
24 **Hanna**	N	N	Y	N	Y	Y	Y
25 **Buerkle**	N	N	Y	N	Y	Y	Y
26 Hochul	Y	Y	N	Y	N	Y	N
27 Higgins	Y	Y	N	Y	N	Y	N
28 Slaughter	Y	Y	N	Y	N	Y	N
29 **Reed**	N	N	Y	N	Y	Y	Y
NORTH CAROLINA							
1 Butterfield	Y	Y	N	Y	N	Y	N
2 **Ellmers**	N	N	Y	N	Y	Y	Y
3 **Jones**	N	Y	N	Y	N	Y	Y
4 Price	Y	Y	N	Y	N	Y	N

	550	551	552	553	554	555	556
5 **Foxx**	N	N	Y	N	N	Y	Y
6 **Coble**	N	N	Y	N	Y	Y	Y
7 McIntyre	N	Y	N	Y	Y	Y	N
8 Kissell	N	Y	N	Y	Y	Y	N
9 **Myrick**	N	N	Y	N	Y	Y	Y
10 **McHenry**	N	N	Y	N	Y	Y	Y
11 Shuler	N	Y	N	Y	Y	Y	N
12 Watt	Y	Y	N	Y	N	Y	N
13 Miller	Y	Y	N	Y	N	Y	N
NORTH DAKOTA							
AL **Berg**	N	N	Y	N	Y	Y	N
OHIO							
1 **Chabot**	N	N	Y	N	N	Y	Y
2 **Schmidt**	N	Y	Y	N	N	Y	N
3 **Turner**	N	N	Y	N	Y	Y	N
4 **Jordan**	N	N	Y	N	N	Y	N
5 **Latta**	N	N	Y	N	Y	Y	N
6 **Johnson**	N	N	Y	N	Y	Y	Y
7 **Austria**	N	N	Y	N	Y	Y	Y
8 **Boehner**							
9 Kaptur	Y	Y	N	Y	N	Y	N
10 Kucinich	Y	Y	N	Y	N	Y	N
11 Fudge	Y	Y	N	Y	Y	Y	N
12 **Tiberi**	N	N	Y	N	Y	Y	Y
13 Sutton	Y	Y	N	Y	N	Y	N
14 **LaTourette**	N	N	Y	N	Y	Y	Y
15 **Stivers**	N	N	Y	N	Y	Y	Y
16 **Renacci**	N	N	Y	N	Y	Y	Y
17 Ryan	Y	Y	N	Y	N	Y	N
18 **Gibbs**	N	N	Y	N	Y	Y	Y
OKLAHOMA							
1 **Sullivan**	N	N	Y	N	Y	?	?
2 Boren	N	Y	N	Y	Y	Y	N
3 **Lucas**	N	N	Y	N	Y	Y	Y
4 **Cole**	N	N	Y	N	Y	Y	Y
5 **Lankford**	N	N	Y	N	Y	Y	N
OREGON							
1 Bonamici	Y	Y	N	Y	N	Y	N
2 **Walden**	N	N	Y	N	Y	Y	Y
3 Blumenauer	Y	N	–	Y	N	Y	N
4 DeFazio	Y	Y	N	Y	N	Y	N
5 Schrader	Y	Y	N	Y	N	Y	N
PENNSYLVANIA							
1 Brady	Y	Y	N	Y	N	Y	N
2 Fattah	Y	Y	N	Y	N	Y	N
3 **Kelly**	N	N	Y	N	Y	Y	Y
4 Altmire	Y	Y	N	Y	Y	Y	N
5 **Thompson**	N	N	Y	N	Y	Y	Y
6 **Gerlach**	N	N	Y	N	Y	Y	Y
7 **Meehan**	N	N	Y	N	Y	Y	N
8 **Fitzpatrick**	N	N	Y	N	Y	Y	N
9 **Shuster**	N	N	Y	N	Y	Y	Y
10 **Marino**	N	N	Y	N	Y	Y	Y
11 **Barletta**	N	N	Y	N	Y	Y	Y
12 Critz	Y	Y	N	Y	Y	Y	N
13 Schwartz	Y	Y	N	Y	N	Y	N
14 Doyle	Y	Y	N	Y	N	Y	N
15 **Dent**	N	N	Y	N	Y	Y	Y
16 **Pitts**	N	N	Y	N	N	Y	?
17 Holden	Y	Y	N	Y	Y	Y	N
18 **Murphy**	N	N	Y	N	Y	+	Y
19 **Platts**	N	N	Y	N	Y	Y	Y
RHODE ISLAND							
1 Cicilline	Y	Y	N	Y	N	Y	N
2 Langevin	Y	Y	N	Y	N	Y	N
SOUTH CAROLINA							
1 **Scott**	N	N	Y	N	Y	Y	Y
2 **Wilson**	N	N	Y	N	Y	Y	Y
3 **Duncan**	N	N	Y	N	Y	Y	N
4 **Gowdy**	N	N	Y	N	Y	Y	Y
5 **Mulvaney**	N	N	Y	N	Y	Y	N
6 Clyburn	Y	Y	N	Y	Y	Y	N
SOUTH DAKOTA							
AL **Noem**	N	N	Y	N	Y	Y	N
TENNESSEE							
1 **Roe**	N	N	Y	N	Y	Y	Y
2 **Duncan**	N	Y	Y	N	Y	Y	N
3 **Fleischmann**	?	?	?	?	?	?	?
4 **DesJarlais**	N	N	Y	N	Y	Y	N
5 Cooper	N	Y	N	Y	N	Y	N
6 **Black**	?	?	+	?	?	?	?
7 **Blackburn**	N	N	Y	N	Y	Y	Y
8 **Fincher**	N	N	Y	N	Y	?	?
9 Cohen	?	?	?	?	?	?	?

	550	551	552	553	554	555	556
TEXAS							
1 **Gohmert**	N	N	Y	N	N	Y	N
2 **Poe**	N	N	Y	N	Y	Y	N
3 **Johnson, S.**	N	N	Y	N	Y	Y	Y
4 **Hall**	N	N	Y	N	Y	Y	N
5 **Hensarling**	N	N	Y	N	Y	Y	Y
6 **Barton**	N	N	Y	N	Y	?	?
7 **Culberson**	N	N	Y	N	Y	Y	N
8 **Brady**	N	N	Y	N	Y	Y	Y
9 Green, A.	Y	Y	N	Y	N	Y	N
10 **McCaul**	N	N	Y	N	Y	Y	N
11 **Conaway**	N	N	Y	N	Y	Y	Y
12 **Granger**	N	N	Y	N	Y	Y	Y
13 **Thornberry**	N	N	Y	N	Y	Y	Y
14 **Paul**	N	N	N	N	N	Y	Y
15 Hinojosa	Y	Y	N	Y	N	Y	N
16 Reyes	Y	Y	N	Y	N	Y	N
17 **Flores**	N	N	Y	N	Y	Y	N
18 Jackson Lee	?	?	?	?	?	?	?
19 **Neugebauer**	N	N	Y	N	Y	Y	Y
20 Gonzalez	Y	Y	N	Y	N	Y	N
21 **Smith**	N	N	Y	N	Y	Y	Y
22 **Olson**	N	N	Y	N	Y	Y	Y
23 **Canseco**	N	N	Y	N	Y	Y	N
24 **Marchant**	N	N	Y	N	Y	Y	Y
25 Doggett	Y	Y	N	Y	N	Y	N
26 **Burgess**	N	N	Y	N	Y	Y	Y
27 **Farenthold**	N	N	Y	N	Y	Y	N
28 Cuellar	Y	Y	N	Y	Y	Y	N
29 Green, G.	Y	Y	N	Y	N	Y	N
30 Johnson, E.	Y	Y	N	Y	N	Y	N
31 **Carter**	N	N	Y	N	Y	Y	Y
32 **Sessions**	N	N	Y	N	Y	Y	Y
UTAH							
1 **Bishop**	N	N	Y	N	Y	Y	Y
2 Matheson	N	Y	N	Y	N	Y	N
3 **Chaffetz**	N	N	Y	N	Y	Y	Y
VERMONT							
AL Welch	Y	Y	N	Y	N	Y	N
VIRGINIA							
1 **Wittman**	N	N	Y	N	N	Y	N
2 **Rigell**	N	N	Y	N	N	?	N
3 Scott	Y	Y	N	Y	N	Y	N
4 **Forbes**	N	N	Y	N	Y	Y	Y
5 **Hurt**	N	N	Y	N	Y	Y	N
6 **Goodlatte**	N	N	Y	N	Y	Y	N
7 **Cantor**	N	N	Y	N	Y	Y	Y
8 Moran	Y	Y	N	Y	N	Y	N
9 **Griffith**	N	N	Y	N	Y	Y	N
10 **Wolf**	N	N	Y	N	N	Y	Y
11 Connolly	Y	Y	N	Y	N	Y	N
WASHINGTON							
1 Vacant							
2 Larsen	Y	Y	N	Y	N	Y	N
3 **Herrera Beutler**	N	N	Y	N	Y	Y	N
4 **Hastings**	N	N	Y	N	Y	Y	Y
5 **McMorris Rodgers**	N	N	Y	N	Y	Y	Y
6 Dicks	Y	Y	N	Y	N	Y	N
7 McDermott	Y	Y	N	Y	N	Y	N
8 **Reichert**	N	N	Y	N	Y	Y	Y
9 Smith	Y	Y	N	Y	N	Y	N
WEST VIRGINIA							
1 **McKinley**	N	N	Y	N	Y	Y	N
2 **Capito**	N	N	Y	N	Y	Y	Y
3 Rahall	Y	Y	N	Y	Y	Y	N
WISCONSIN							
1 **Ryan**	N	N	Y	N	Y	Y	Y
2 Baldwin	Y	Y	N	Y	N	Y	N
3 Kind	Y	Y	N	Y	N	Y	N
4 Moore	Y	Y	N	Y	N	Y	N
5 **Sensenbrenner**	N	N	Y	N	N	Y	Y
6 **Petri**	N	N	Y	N	Y	Y	Y
7 **Duffy**	N	N	Y	N	Y	?	?
8 **Ribble**	N	N	Y	N	Y	Y	Y
WYOMING							
AL **Lummis**	N	N	Y	N	Y	Y	Y

IN THE HOUSE | By Vote Number

557. HR 6122. Library of Congress Gifts/Passage. Lungren, R-Calif., motion to suspend the rules and pass the bill that would allow the librarian of Congress to accept gifts of securities, personal property less than $25,000, non-personal services and voluntary and uncompensated personal services. The librarian would need to sell gifts of securities and provide the donor with a receipt. Motion agreed to 377-0: R 214 0; D 163-0. A two-thirds majority of those present and voting (252 in this case) is required for passage under suspension of the rules. Sept. 10, 2012.

558. HR 2139. Lions Club Commemorative Coins/Passage. Dold, R-Ill., motion to suspend the rules and pass the bill that would require the Treasury to mint and issue $1 coins to commemorate the centennial of Lions Club International. It would authorize the surcharge on sales of the coins to be distributed to the Lions Club International Foundation. Motion agreed to 376-2: R 213-2; D 163-0. A two-thirds majority of those present and voting (252 in this case) is required for passage under suspension of the rules. Sept. 10, 2012.

559. HR 6186. Flood Insurance Study/Passage. Biggert, R-Ill., motion to suspend the rules and pass the bill that would require the Federal Emergency Management Agency to conduct a study on options, methods and strategies for making voluntary community-based flood insurance policies available through the National Flood Insurance Program. A report with recommendations would need to be submitted to Congress. Motion agreed to 364-11: R 204-11; D 160-0. A two-thirds majority of those present and voting (250 in this case) is required for passage under suspension of the rules. Sept. 10, 2012.

560. HR 5544, HR 5949. Foreign Intelligence Surveillance and Minnesota Land Exchange/Previous Question. Nugent, R-Fla., motion to order the previous question (thus ending debate and the possibility of amendment) on the rule (H Res 773) that would provide for House floor consideration of a five-year extension (HR 5949) of foreign intelligence surveillance powers and a bill (HR 5544) that would direct the Agriculture Department to exchange certain Minnesota federal lands. Motion agreed to 232-177: R 227-2; D 5-175. Sept. 11, 2012.

561. HR 5544, HR 5949. Foreign Intelligence Surveillance and Minnesota Land Exchange/Rule. Adoption of the rule (H Res 773) that would provide for House floor consideration of a five-year extension (HR 5949) of foreign intelligence surveillance powers and a bill (HR 5544) that would direct the Agriculture Department to exchange certain Minnesota federal lands. Adopted 233-179: R 227-3; D 6-176. Sept. 11, 2012.

562. HR 4264. FHA Mortgage Insurance/Passage. Biggert, R-Ill., motion to suspend the rules and pass the bill that would establish minimum annual premiums for mortgage insurance from the Federal Housing Administration(FHA) and create an indemnification process in the event of insurance fraud or misrepresentation. The bill would allow the Housing and Urban Affairs Department to bar lenders with high rates of early default or insurance claims from originating or underwriting FHA-insured loans. Motion agreed to 402-7: R 223-7; D 179-0. A two-thirds majority of those present and voting (273 in this case) is required for passage under suspension of the rules. Sept. 11, 2012.

563. HR 5544. Minnesota Land Exchange/Tribal Consultation. McCollum, D-Minn., amendment that would require the Agriculture Department to consult with tribal governments that may be potentially affected by the land exchange. Rejected in Committee of the Whole 201-213: R 19-213; D 182-0. Sept. 12, 2012.

	557	558	559	560	561	562	563
ALABAMA							
1 Bonner	Y	Y	Y	Y	Y	Y	N
2 Roby	Y	Y	Y	Y	Y	Y	N
3 Rogers	Y	Y	Y	Y	Y	Y	N
4 Aderholt	Y	Y	Y	Y	Y	Y	N
5 Brooks	Y	Y	Y	Y	Y	Y	N
6 Bachus	Y	Y	Y	Y	Y	Y	N
7 Sewell	Y	Y	Y	N	Y	Y	Y
ALASKA							
AL Young	Y	Y	Y	Y	Y	Y	N
ARIZONA							
1 Gosar	Y	Y	Y	Y	Y	Y	N
2 Franks	Y	Y	Y	Y	Y	Y	N
3 Quayle	Y	Y	N	Y	Y	Y	N
4 Pastor	?	?	?	N	N	Y	Y
5 Schweikert	Y	Y	Y	Y	Y	Y	N
6 Flake	?	?	?	Y	N	N	N
7 Grijalva	Y	Y	Y	N	N	Y	Y
8 Barber	Y	Y	Y	N	N	Y	Y
ARKANSAS							
1 Crawford	Y	Y	Y	Y	Y	Y	N
2 Griffin	Y	Y	Y	Y	Y	Y	N
3 Womack	Y	Y	Y	Y	Y	Y	N
4 Ross	Y	Y	Y	N	Y	Y	Y
CALIFORNIA							
1 Thompson	Y	Y	Y	N	N	Y	Y
2 Herger	?	?	?	?	?	?	?
3 Lungren	Y	Y	Y	Y	Y	Y	Y
4 McClintock	Y	Y	Y	Y	Y	Y	N
5 Matsui	Y	Y	Y	N	N	Y	Y
6 Woolsey	Y	Y	Y	N	N	Y	Y
7 Miller, George	+	+	+	N	N	Y	Y
8 Pelosi	Y	Y	Y	N	N	Y	Y
9 Lee	+	+	+	N	N	Y	Y
10 Garamendi	Y	Y	Y	N	Y	Y	Y
11 McNerney	Y	Y	Y	N	N	Y	Y
12 Speier	?	?	?	?	?	?	Y
13 Stark	Y	Y	Y	N	N	Y	Y
14 Eshoo	Y	Y	Y	N	N	Y	Y
15 Honda	Y	Y	Y	N	N	Y	Y
16 Lofgren	Y	Y	Y	N	N	Y	Y
17 Farr	Y	Y	Y	N	N	Y	Y
18 Vacant							
19 Denham	Y	Y	Y	Y	Y	Y	N
20 Costa	Y	Y	Y	N	N	Y	Y
21 Nunes	Y	Y	Y	Y	Y	Y	N
22 McCarthy	Y	Y	Y	Y	Y	Y	N
23 Capps	Y	Y	Y	N	N	Y	Y
24 Gallegly	?	?	?	?	?	?	N
25 McKeon	Y	Y	Y	Y	Y	Y	N
26 Dreier	Y	Y	Y	Y	Y	Y	N
27 Sherman	Y	Y	Y	N	N	Y	Y
28 Berman	?	?	?	N	N	Y	Y
29 Schiff	Y	Y	Y	N	N	Y	Y
30 Waxman	Y	Y	Y	N	N	Y	Y
31 Becerra	Y	Y	Y	N	N	Y	Y
32 Chu	Y	Y	Y	N	N	Y	Y
33 Bass	?	Y	?	N	N	Y	Y
34 Roybal-Allard	Y	Y	Y	N	N	Y	Y
35 Waters	Y	Y	Y	N	N	Y	Y
36 Hahn	Y	Y	Y	N	N	Y	Y
37 Richardson	Y	Y	Y	N	N	Y	Y
38 Napolitano	?	?	?	?	?	?	Y
39 Sánchez, Linda	Y	Y	Y	N	N	Y	Y
40 Royce	Y	Y	Y	Y	Y	Y	N
41 Lewis	?	?	?	?	?	?	N
42 Miller, Gary	Y	Y	Y	Y	Y	Y	N
43 Baca	Y	Y	Y	N	N	Y	Y
44 Calvert	Y	Y	Y	Y	Y	Y	N
45 Bono Mack	Y	Y	Y	Y	Y	Y	N
46 Rohrabacher	Y	Y	Y	Y	Y	Y	N
47 Sanchez, Loretta	Y	Y	Y	N	N	Y	Y
48 Campbell	Y	Y	Y	Y	Y	Y	N
49 Issa	Y	Y	Y	Y	Y	Y	N
50 Bilbray	Y	Y	Y	Y	Y	Y	N
51 Filner	+	+	+	N	N	Y	Y
52 Hunter	Y	Y	Y	Y	Y	Y	N
53 Davis	Y	Y	Y	N	N	Y	Y

	557	558	559	560	561	562	563
COLORADO							
1 DeGette	Y	Y	Y	N	N	Y	Y
2 Polis	Y	Y	Y	N	N	Y	Y
3 Tipton	Y	Y	Y	Y	Y	Y	Y
4 Gardner	Y	Y	Y	Y	Y	Y	N
5 Lamborn	Y	Y	Y	Y	Y	Y	N
6 Coffman	Y	Y	Y	Y	Y	Y	N
7 Perlmutter	Y	Y	Y	N	N	Y	Y
CONNECTICUT							
1 Larson	Y	Y	Y	N	N	Y	Y
2 Courtney	Y	Y	Y	N	N	Y	Y
3 DeLauro	Y	Y	Y	N	N	Y	Y
4 Himes	Y	Y	Y	N	N	Y	Y
5 Murphy	Y	Y	Y	N	N	Y	Y
DELAWARE							
AL Carney	Y	Y	Y	N	N	Y	Y
FLORIDA							
1 Miller	Y	Y	Y	Y	Y	Y	N
2 Southerland	Y	Y	Y	Y	Y	Y	N
3 Brown	Y	?	Y	N	N	Y	Y
4 Crenshaw	Y	Y	Y	Y	Y	Y	N
5 Nugent	Y	Y	Y	Y	Y	Y	N
6 Stearns	Y	Y	Y	Y	Y	Y	N
7 Mica	Y	Y	Y	Y	Y	Y	N
8 Webster	Y	Y	Y	Y	Y	Y	N
9 Bilirakis	Y	Y	Y	Y	Y	Y	N
10 Young	Y	Y	Y	?	Y	Y	N
11 Castor	Y	Y	Y	N	N	Y	Y
12 Ross	Y	Y	N	Y	Y	Y	N
13 Buchanan	Y	Y	Y	Y	Y	Y	N
14 Mack	Y	Y	Y	Y	Y	Y	N
15 Posey	Y	Y	Y	Y	Y	Y	N
16 Rooney	Y	Y	N	Y	Y	Y	N
17 Wilson	?	Y	?	N	N	Y	Y
18 Ros-Lehtinen	Y	Y	Y	Y	Y	Y	N
19 Deutch	Y	Y	Y	N	N	Y	Y
20 Wasserman Schultz	Y	Y	Y	N	N	Y	Y
21 Diaz-Balart	Y	Y	Y	Y	Y	Y	N
22 West	Y	Y	Y	Y	Y	Y	N
23 Hastings	Y	Y	Y	N	N	Y	Y
24 Adams	Y	Y	N	Y	Y	Y	N
25 Rivera	?	?	?	Y	Y	Y	N
GEORGIA							
1 Kingston	Y	Y	Y	Y	Y	Y	N
2 Bishop	Y	Y	Y	N	N	Y	Y
3 Westmoreland	Y	Y	Y	Y	Y	N	N
4 Johnson	Y	Y	Y	N	N	Y	Y
5 Lewis	Y	Y	?	N	N	Y	Y
6 Price	Y	Y	Y	Y	Y	N	N
7 Woodall	Y	Y	Y	Y	Y	Y	N
8 Scott, A.	Y	Y	Y	Y	Y	Y	N
9 Graves	Y	Y	Y	Y	Y	Y	N
10 Broun	?	?	?	?	?	?	?
11 Gingrey	Y	Y	Y	Y	Y	Y	?
12 Barrow	Y	Y	Y	N	N	Y	Y
13 Scott, D.	Y	Y	Y	N	N	Y	Y
HAWAII							
1 Hanabusa	Y	Y	Y	N	N	Y	Y
2 Hirono	?	?	?	?	?	?	?
IDAHO							
1 Labrador	Y	Y	Y	Y	Y	Y	N
2 Simpson	Y	Y	Y	Y	Y	Y	N
ILLINOIS							
1 Rush	?	?	?	N	N	Y	Y
2 Jackson	?	?	?	?	?	?	?
3 Lipinski	Y	Y	Y	N	N	Y	Y
4 Gutierrez	?	?	?	N	N	?	Y
5 Quigley	Y	Y	Y	N	N	Y	Y
6 Roskam	Y	Y	Y	Y	Y	Y	N
7 Davis	Y	Y	Y	N	N	Y	Y
8 Walsh	Y	Y	Y	Y	Y	Y	N
9 Schakowsky	Y	Y	Y	N	N	Y	Y
10 Dold	Y	Y	Y	Y	Y	Y	N
11 Kinzinger	+	+	+	Y	Y	Y	N
12 Costello	Y	Y	Y	N	N	Y	Y
13 Biggert	Y	Y	Y	Y	Y	Y	N
14 Hultgren	Y	Y	Y	Y	Y	Y	N
15 Johnson	+	+	+	Y	N	N	Y

KEY   **Republicans**   Democrats

Y Voted for (yea)	X Paired against	C Voted "present" to avoid possible conflict of interest
# Paired for	– Announced against	
+ Announced for	P Voted "present"	? Did not vote or otherwise make a position known
N Voted against (nay)		

	557	558	559	560	561	562	563
16 **Manzullo**	+	+	+	Y	Y	Y	N
17 **Schilling**	Y	Y	Y	Y	Y	Y	N
18 **Schock**	?	?	?	Y	Y	Y	N
19 **Shimkus**	Y	Y	Y	Y	Y	Y	N
INDIANA							
1 Visclosky	Y	Y	Y	N	N	Y	Y
2 Donnelly	?	?	?	Y	Y	Y	Y
3 **Stutzman**	?	Y	Y	Y	Y	Y	N
4 **Rokita**	Y	Y	Y	Y	Y	Y	N
5 **Burton**	?	?	?	Y	Y	Y	?
6 **Pence**	Y	Y	Y	Y	Y	Y	N
7 Carson	Y	Y	Y	N	N	Y	Y
8 **Bucshon**	Y	Y	Y	Y	Y	Y	N
9 **Young**	Y	Y	Y	Y	Y	Y	N
IOWA							
1 Braley	Y	Y	Y	N	N	Y	Y
2 Loebsack	Y	Y	Y	N	N	Y	Y
3 Boswell	?	Y	Y	N	N	Y	Y
4 **Latham**	Y	Y	Y	Y	Y	Y	N
5 **King**	Y	Y	Y	Y	Y	Y	N
KANSAS							
1 **Huelskamp**	Y	Y	Y	Y	Y	Y	N
2 **Jenkins**	Y	Y	Y	Y	Y	Y	N
3 **Yoder**	Y	Y	Y	Y	Y	Y	N
4 **Pompeo**	Y	Y	Y	Y	Y	Y	N
KENTUCKY							
1 **Whitfield**	Y	Y	Y	Y	Y	Y	N
2 **Guthrie**	Y	Y	Y	Y	Y	Y	N
3 Yarmuth	Y	Y	Y	N	N	Y	Y
4 Vacant							
5 **Rogers**	Y	Y	Y	Y	Y	Y	N
6 Chandler	Y	Y	Y	N	N	Y	Y
LOUISIANA							
1 **Scalise**	Y	Y	Y	Y	Y	Y	N
2 Richmond	?	?	?	N	N	Y	Y
3 **Landry**	Y	Y	Y	Y	Y	Y	N
4 **Fleming**	Y	Y	Y	Y	Y	Y	N
5 **Alexander**	?	?	?	Y	Y	Y	N
6 **Cassidy**	Y	Y	Y	Y	Y	Y	N
7 **Boustany**	Y	Y	Y	Y	Y	Y	N
MAINE							
1 Pingree	Y	Y	Y	N	N	Y	Y
2 Michaud	Y	Y	Y	N	N	Y	Y
MARYLAND							
1 **Harris**	Y	Y	Y	Y	Y	Y	N
2 Ruppersberger	Y	Y	?	N	N	Y	Y
3 Sarbanes	Y	Y	Y	N	N	Y	Y
4 Edwards	Y	Y	Y	N	N	Y	Y
5 Hoyer	Y	Y	Y	N	N	Y	Y
6 **Bartlett**	Y	Y	Y	Y	Y	Y	N
7 Cummings	Y	Y	Y	N	N	Y	Y
8 Van Hollen	Y	Y	Y	N	N	Y	Y
MASSACHUSETTS							
1 Olver	Y	Y	Y	N	N	Y	Y
2 Neal	Y	Y	Y	N	N	Y	Y
3 McGovern	Y	Y	Y	N	N	Y	Y
4 Frank	Y	Y	Y	N	N	Y	Y
5 Tsongas	Y	Y	Y	N	N	Y	Y
6 Tierney	?	?	?	N	N	Y	Y
7 Markey	Y	Y	Y	N	N	Y	Y
8 Capuano	Y	Y	Y	N	N	Y	Y
9 Lynch	Y	Y	Y	N	N	Y	Y
10 Keating	Y	Y	Y	N	N	Y	Y
MICHIGAN							
1 **Benishek**	Y	Y	N	Y	Y	Y	N
2 **Huizenga**	Y	Y	Y	Y	Y	Y	N
3 **Amash**	Y	N	N	Y	Y	N	N
4 **Camp**	Y	Y	Y	Y	Y	Y	Y
5 Kildee	Y	Y	Y	N	N	Y	Y
6 **Upton**	Y	Y	Y	Y	Y	Y	N
7 **Walberg**	Y	Y	N	Y	Y	Y	N
8 **Rogers**	Y	Y	Y	Y	Y	Y	N
9 Peters	Y	Y	Y	N	N	Y	Y
10 **Miller**	Y	Y	N	Y	Y	Y	N
11 Vacant							
12 Levin	Y	Y	Y	N	N	Y	Y
13 Clarke	Y	Y	Y	N	N	Y	Y
14 Conyers	Y	Y	Y	N	N	Y	Y
15 Dingell	Y	Y	Y	N	N	Y	Y
MINNESOTA							
1 Walz	Y	Y	Y	N	N	Y	Y
2 **Kline**	Y	Y	Y	Y	Y	Y	Y
3 **Paulsen**	Y	Y	Y	Y	Y	Y	Y
4 McCollum	Y	Y	Y	N	N	Y	Y

	557	558	559	560	561	562	563
5 Ellison	Y	Y	Y	N	N	Y	Y
6 **Bachmann**	?	?	?	Y	Y	Y	N
7 Peterson	Y	Y	Y	N	N	Y	Y
8 **Cravaack**	Y	Y	Y	Y	Y	Y	N
MISSISSIPPI							
1 **Nunnelee**	Y	Y	Y	Y	Y	Y	N
2 Thompson	Y	Y	Y	N	N	Y	Y
3 **Harper**	?	?	?	?	?	?	N
4 **Palazzo**	Y	Y	Y	Y	Y	Y	N
MISSOURI							
1 Clay	Y	Y	Y	N	N	Y	Y
2 **Akin**	Y	Y	Y	?	?	?	?
3 Carnahan	Y	Y	Y	N	N	Y	Y
4 **Hartzler**	Y	Y	Y	Y	Y	Y	N
5 Cleaver	Y	Y	?	N	N	Y	Y
6 **Graves**	Y	Y	Y	Y	Y	Y	N
7 **Long**	Y	Y	Y	Y	Y	Y	N
8 **Emerson**	Y	Y	Y	Y	Y	Y	N
9 **Luetkemeyer**	Y	Y	Y	Y	Y	Y	N
MONTANA							
AL **Rehberg**	Y	Y	Y	Y	Y	Y	Y
NEBRASKA							
1 **Fortenberry**	Y	Y	Y	Y	Y	Y	N
2 **Terry**	Y	Y	?	Y	Y	Y	N
3 **Smith**	Y	Y	Y	Y	Y	Y	N
NEVADA							
1 Berkley	Y	Y	Y	N	N	Y	Y
2 **Amodei**	Y	Y	Y	Y	Y	Y	N
3 **Heck**	Y	Y	Y	Y	Y	Y	N
NEW HAMPSHIRE							
1 **Guinta**	Y	Y	Y	Y	Y	Y	N
2 **Bass**	Y	Y	Y	Y	Y	Y	N
NEW JERSEY							
1 Andrews	Y	+	+	N	N	Y	Y
2 **LoBiondo**	Y	Y	Y	Y	Y	Y	Y
3 **Runyan**	Y	Y	Y	Y	Y	Y	N
4 **Smith**	Y	Y	Y	Y	Y	Y	N
5 **Garrett**	Y	Y	Y	Y	Y	Y	N
6 Pallone	Y	Y	Y	N	N	Y	Y
7 **Lance**	Y	Y	Y	Y	Y	Y	N
8 Pascrell	Y	Y	Y	N	N	Y	Y
9 Rothman	Y	Y	Y	N	N	Y	Y
10 Vacant							
11 **Frelinghuysen**	Y	Y	Y	Y	Y	Y	N
12 Holt	Y	Y	Y	N	N	Y	Y
13 Sires	Y	Y	Y	N	N	Y	Y
NEW MEXICO							
1 Heinrich	+	+	+	N	N	Y	Y
2 **Pearce**	Y	Y	Y	Y	Y	Y	N
3 Luján	Y	Y	Y	N	N	Y	Y
NEW YORK							
1 Bishop	Y	Y	Y	N	N	Y	Y
2 Israel	Y	Y	Y	?	?	?	Y
3 **King**	?	?	?	?	?	?	N
4 McCarthy	Y	Y	Y	N	N	Y	Y
5 Ackerman	?	?	?	N	N	Y	Y
6 Meeks	Y	Y	Y	N	N	Y	Y
7 Crowley	Y	Y	Y	N	N	?	Y
8 Nadler	?	?	?	N	N	Y	Y
9 **Turner**	Y	Y	Y	Y	Y	Y	N
10 Towns	?	?	?	?	?	?	?
11 Clarke	Y	Y	Y	N	N	Y	Y
12 Velázquez	Y	?	Y	N	N	Y	Y
13 **Grimm**	Y	Y	Y	Y	Y	Y	N
14 Maloney	?	?	?	N	N	Y	Y
15 Rangel	?	?	?	N	N	Y	Y
16 Serrano	Y	Y	Y	N	N	Y	Y
17 Engel	Y	Y	Y	N	N	Y	Y
18 Lowey	?	?	?	?	?	?	Y
19 **Hayworth**	Y	Y	Y	?	?	?	N
20 **Gibson**	Y	Y	Y	Y	Y	Y	Y
21 Tonko	Y	Y	Y	N	N	Y	Y
22 Hinchey	Y	Y	Y	N	N	Y	Y
23 Owens	Y	Y	Y	N	N	Y	Y
24 **Hanna**	Y	Y	Y	Y	Y	Y	Y
25 **Buerkle**	Y	Y	Y	Y	Y	Y	N
26 Hochul	Y	Y	Y	N	Y	+	Y
27 Higgins	Y	Y	Y	N	N	Y	Y
28 Slaughter	Y	Y	Y	N	N	Y	Y
29 **Reed**	Y	Y	Y	Y	Y	Y	N
NORTH CAROLINA							
1 Butterfield	Y	Y	Y	N	N	Y	?
2 **Ellmers**	Y	Y	Y	Y	Y	Y	N
3 **Jones**	Y	Y	Y	N	N	Y	Y
4 Price	Y	Y	Y	N	N	Y	Y

	557	558	559	560	561	562	563
5 **Foxx**	Y	Y	Y	Y	Y	N	N
6 **Coble**	?	?	?	Y	Y	Y	N
7 McIntyre	Y	Y	Y	Y	Y	Y	Y
8 Kissell	Y	Y	Y	N	Y	Y	Y
9 **Myrick**	Y	Y	?	Y	Y	Y	N
10 **McHenry**	Y	Y	Y	Y	Y	Y	N
11 Shuler	?	?	?	Y	Y	Y	Y
12 Watt	Y	Y	Y	N	N	Y	Y
13 Miller	Y	Y	Y	N	N	Y	Y
NORTH DAKOTA							
AL **Berg**	Y	Y	Y	Y	Y	Y	Y
OHIO							
1 **Chabot**	Y	Y	Y	Y	Y	Y	N
2 **Schmidt**	Y	Y	Y	Y	Y	Y	N
3 **Turner**	+	Y	Y	Y	Y	Y	N
4 **Jordan**	Y	Y	Y	Y	Y	Y	N
5 **Latta**	Y	Y	Y	Y	Y	Y	N
6 **Johnson**	Y	Y	Y	Y	Y	Y	N
7 **Austria**	Y	Y	Y	Y	Y	Y	N
8 **Boehner**							
9 Kaptur	Y	Y	Y	N	N	Y	Y
10 Kucinich	Y	Y	Y	N	N	Y	Y
11 Fudge	Y	Y	Y	N	N	Y	Y
12 **Tiberi**	Y	Y	N	Y	Y	Y	N
13 Sutton	Y	Y	Y	N	N	Y	Y
14 **LaTourette**	Y	Y	Y	Y	Y	Y	N
15 **Stivers**	Y	Y	Y	Y	Y	Y	N
16 **Renacci**	Y	Y	Y	Y	Y	Y	N
17 Ryan	Y	Y	Y	N	N	Y	Y
18 **Gibbs**	?	?	?	Y	Y	Y	N
OKLAHOMA							
1 **Sullivan**	Y	Y	Y	Y	Y	Y	N
2 Boren	Y	Y	Y	Y	N	Y	Y
3 **Lucas**	Y	Y	Y	Y	Y	Y	N
4 **Cole**	Y	Y	Y	Y	Y	Y	Y
5 **Lankford**	Y	Y	Y	Y	Y	Y	N
OREGON							
1 Bonamici	Y	Y	Y	N	N	Y	Y
2 **Walden**	?	?	?	Y	Y	Y	N
3 Blumenauer	Y	Y	Y	N	N	Y	Y
4 DeFazio	Y	Y	Y	N	N	Y	Y
5 Schrader	Y	Y	Y	N	N	Y	Y
PENNSYLVANIA							
1 Brady	Y	Y	Y	N	N	Y	Y
2 Fattah	Y	Y	Y	N	N	Y	Y
3 **Kelly**	Y	Y	Y	Y	Y	Y	N
4 Altmire	Y	Y	Y	N	N	Y	Y
5 **Thompson**	Y	Y	Y	Y	Y	Y	N
6 **Gerlach**	Y	Y	Y	Y	Y	Y	N
7 **Meehan**	Y	Y	Y	Y	Y	Y	N
8 **Fitzpatrick**	Y	Y	Y	Y	Y	Y	Y
9 **Shuster**	Y	Y	Y	Y	Y	Y	N
10 **Marino**	Y	Y	Y	Y	Y	Y	N
11 **Barletta**	Y	Y	Y	Y	Y	Y	N
12 Critz	Y	Y	Y	N	N	Y	Y
13 Schwartz	Y	Y	Y	N	N	Y	Y
14 Doyle	Y	Y	Y	N	N	Y	Y
15 **Dent**	Y	Y	Y	Y	Y	Y	N
16 **Pitts**	Y	Y	Y	Y	Y	Y	N
17 Holden	Y	Y	?	N	N	Y	?
18 **Murphy**	Y	Y	Y	Y	Y	Y	N
19 **Platts**	?	?	Y	Y	Y	Y	N
RHODE ISLAND							
1 Cicilline	+	+	+	–	–	+	Y
2 Langevin	Y	Y	Y	N	N	Y	Y
SOUTH CAROLINA							
1 **Scott**	Y	Y	Y	Y	Y	Y	N
2 **Wilson**	Y	Y	Y	Y	Y	Y	N
3 **Duncan**	Y	Y	Y	Y	Y	Y	N
4 **Gowdy**	Y	Y	Y	Y	Y	Y	N
5 **Mulvaney**	Y	P	Y	Y	Y	Y	N
6 Clyburn	Y	Y	Y	N	N	Y	Y
SOUTH DAKOTA							
AL **Noem**	Y	Y	Y	Y	Y	Y	Y
TENNESSEE							
1 **Roe**	Y	Y	Y	Y	Y	Y	N
2 **Duncan**	Y	Y	Y	Y	Y	Y	N
3 **Fleischmann**	Y	Y	Y	Y	Y	Y	N
4 **DesJarlais**	Y	Y	Y	Y	Y	Y	N
5 Cooper	Y	Y	Y	N	N	Y	Y
6 **Black**	Y	Y	Y	Y	Y	Y	N
7 **Blackburn**	Y	Y	Y	Y	Y	Y	N
8 **Fincher**	Y	Y	Y	Y	Y	Y	N
9 Cohen	Y	Y	Y	N	N	Y	Y

	557	558	559	560	561	562	563
TEXAS							
1 **Gohmert**	?	Y	N	Y	Y	Y	N
2 **Poe**	Y	Y	Y	Y	Y	Y	N
3 **Johnson, S.**	Y	Y	Y	Y	Y	Y	Y
4 **Hall**	Y	Y	Y	Y	Y	Y	N
5 **Hensarling**	Y	Y	Y	Y	Y	Y	N
6 **Barton**	Y	Y	Y	Y	Y	Y	N
7 **Culberson**	Y	Y	Y	Y	Y	Y	?
8 **Brady**	Y	N	Y	Y	Y	Y	N
9 Green, A.	Y	Y	Y	N	N	Y	Y
10 **McCaul**	Y	Y	Y	Y	Y	Y	N
11 **Conaway**	Y	Y	Y	Y	Y	Y	N
12 **Granger**	Y	Y	Y	Y	Y	Y	N
13 **Thornberry**	Y	Y	Y	Y	Y	Y	N
14 **Paul**	?	?	?	N	N	N	Y
15 Hinojosa	Y	Y	Y	?	N	Y	Y
16 Reyes	Y	Y	Y	N	N	Y	Y
17 **Flores**	?	?	?	Y	Y	Y	N
18 Jackson Lee	Y	Y	Y	N	N	Y	Y
19 **Neugebauer**	Y	Y	Y	Y	Y	Y	N
20 Gonzalez	Y	Y	Y	?	N	Y	Y
21 **Smith**	Y	Y	Y	Y	Y	Y	N
22 **Olson**	Y	Y	Y	Y	Y	Y	N
23 **Canseco**	Y	Y	?	Y	Y	Y	N
24 **Marchant**	Y	Y	Y	Y	Y	Y	N
25 Doggett	Y	Y	Y	N	N	Y	Y
26 **Burgess**	Y	Y	Y	Y	Y	Y	N
27 **Farenthold**	Y	Y	Y	Y	Y	Y	N
28 Cuellar	Y	Y	Y	N	N	Y	Y
29 Green, G.	Y	Y	Y	N	N	Y	Y
30 Johnson, E.	Y	Y	Y	N	N	Y	Y
31 **Carter**	Y	Y	Y	Y	Y	Y	N
32 **Sessions**	Y	Y	Y	Y	Y	Y	N
UTAH							
1 **Bishop**	Y	Y	Y	Y	Y	Y	N
2 Matheson	Y	Y	Y	Y	N	Y	Y
3 **Chaffetz**	Y	Y	Y	Y	Y	Y	N
VERMONT							
AL Welch	Y	Y	Y	N	N	Y	?
VIRGINIA							
1 **Wittman**	Y	Y	Y	Y	Y	Y	N
2 **Rigell**	Y	Y	Y	Y	Y	Y	N
3 Scott	Y	Y	Y	N	N	Y	Y
4 **Forbes**	Y	Y	Y	Y	Y	Y	N
5 **Hurt**	Y	Y	Y	Y	Y	Y	N
6 **Goodlatte**	Y	Y	Y	Y	Y	Y	N
7 **Cantor**	Y	Y	Y	Y	Y	Y	N
8 Moran	Y	Y	Y	N	N	Y	Y
9 **Griffith**	Y	Y	Y	Y	Y	Y	N
10 **Wolf**	Y	Y	Y	Y	Y	Y	N
11 Connolly	Y	Y	Y	N	N	Y	Y
WASHINGTON							
1 Vacant							
2 Larsen	Y	Y	Y	N	N	Y	Y
3 **Herrera Beutler**	Y	Y	Y	Y	Y	Y	N
4 **Hastings**	Y	Y	Y	Y	Y	Y	N
5 **McMorris Rodgers**	Y	Y	Y	Y	Y	Y	N
6 Dicks	Y	Y	Y	N	N	Y	Y
7 McDermott	Y	Y	Y	N	N	Y	Y
8 **Reichert**	Y	Y	Y	Y	Y	Y	N
9 Smith	Y	Y	Y	N	N	Y	Y
WEST VIRGINIA							
1 **McKinley**	Y	Y	Y	Y	Y	Y	N
2 **Capito**	Y	Y	Y	Y	Y	Y	N
3 Rahall	Y	Y	Y	N	N	Y	Y
WISCONSIN							
1 **Ryan**	?	?	?	?	?	?	?
2 Baldwin	?	?	?	N	N	Y	?
3 Kind	Y	Y	Y	N	N	Y	Y
4 Moore	Y	Y	Y	N	N	Y	Y
5 **Sensenbrenner**	Y	Y	Y	Y	Y	N	N
6 **Petri**	Y	Y	Y	Y	Y	Y	N
7 **Duffy**	Y	Y	Y	Y	Y	Y	N
8 **Ribble**	Y	Y	N	Y	Y	Y	N
WYOMING							
AL **Lummis**	Y	?	Y	Y	Y	Y	N

IN THE HOUSE | By Vote Number

564. HR 5544. Minnesota Land Exchange/NEPA Requirements.
Holt, D-N.J., amendment that would strike the bill's waiver provisions regarding environmental assessment requirements under the National Environmental Policy Act. It also would make the land exchange mandated by the bill voluntary. Rejected in Committee of the Whole 177-236: R 2-227; D 175-9. Sept. 12, 2012.

565. HR 5544. Minnesota Land Exchange/National Forest System Prohibition. Ellison, D-Minn., amendment that would bar the inclusion of National Forest System lands within the designated land exchange when the inclusion of such lands would have a negative impact on private property values and small businesses. Rejected in Committee of the Whole 190-225: R 7-223; D 183-2. Sept. 12, 2012.

566. HR 5544. Minnesota Land Exchange/Appraisal Process.
Grijalva, D-Ariz., amendment that would strike the appraisal provisions in the bill, which would defer to state law, and replace it with language that would conform to standard land exchange appraisal practices. Rejected in Committee of the Whole 191-223: R 7-222; D 184-1. Sept. 12, 2012.

567. HR 5544. Minnesota Land Exchange/Recommit. Ellison, D-Minn., motion to recommit the bill to the Natural Resources Committee and report it back immediately with an amendment that would add a provision barring the Interior secretary from including in the exchange any land used for hunting, fishing or motorized recreation, including snowmobiling in season. Motion rejected 183-233: R 0-232; D 183-1. Sept. 12, 2012.

568. HR 5544. Minnesota Land Exchange/Passage. Passage of the bill that would direct the Agriculture Department to exchange unspecified federal lands with the state of Minnesota for roughly 90,000 acres of state-held land within the Boundary Water Canoe Area Wilderness. The Agriculture Department would decide which federal lands to exchange and Minnesota would be required to pay the costs of all appraisals or land surveys. The bill would waive federal environmental review requirements and would prevent the Forest Service from barring hunting and fishing activities, which are currently permitted on state land. Passed 225-189: R 223-8; D 2-181. Sept. 12, 2012.

569. HR 5949. FISA Reauthorization/Passage. Passage of the bill that would reauthorize for five years, through 2017, the Foreign Intelligence Surveillance Act (FISA), which governs electronic surveillance of foreign terrorism suspects. The law allows warrantless surveillance of foreign targets who may be communicating with people in the United States provided that the secret FISA court approves surveillance procedures. Passed 301-118: R 227-7; D 74-111. A "yea" was a vote in support of the president's position. Sept. 12, 2012.

570. HR 3857. Transit Security Grant Funds/Passage. Turner, R-N.Y., motion to suspend the rules and pass the bill that would authorize $400 million per year from fiscal 2012 to 2013 for the Transit Security Grant Program and specify that the funds can be used by local transit systems for specialized operational teams. Fiscal year limitations would not apply as long as the local agency submits a sustainment plan. Motion agreed to 355-62: R 176-57; D 179-5. A two-thirds majority of those present and voting (278 in this case) is required for passage under suspension of the rules. Sept. 12, 2012.

	564	565	566	567	568	569	570
ALABAMA							
1 Bonner	N	N	N	N	Y	Y	Y
2 Roby	N	N	N	N	Y	Y	Y
3 Rogers	N	N	N	N	Y	Y	Y
4 Aderholt	N	N	N	N	Y	Y	Y
5 Brooks	N	N	N	N	Y	Y	N
6 Bachus	N	N	N	N	Y	Y	Y
7 Sewell	Y	Y	Y	Y	N	Y	Y
ALASKA							
AL Young	N	N	N	N	Y	?	Y
ARIZONA							
1 Gosar	N	N	N	N	Y	Y	Y
2 Franks	N	–	N	N	Y	Y	Y
3 Quayle	N	N	N	N	Y	Y	N
4 Pastor	Y	Y	Y	N	N	N	Y
5 Schweikert	N	N	N	N	Y	Y	N
6 Flake	N	N	N	N	Y	Y	N
7 Grijalva	Y	Y	Y	N	N	N	Y
8 Barber	Y	Y	Y	N	Y	N	Y
ARKANSAS							
1 Crawford	N	N	N	N	Y	Y	Y
2 Griffin	N	N	N	N	Y	Y	Y
3 Womack	N	N	N	N	Y	Y	Y
4 Ross	N	Y	Y	Y	N	Y	Y
CALIFORNIA							
1 Thompson	Y	Y	Y	N	N	Y	Y
2 Herger	?	?	?	?	?	?	?
3 Lungren	N	N	N	N	Y	N	Y
4 McClintock	N	N	N	N	Y	N	N
5 Matsui	Y	Y	Y	N	N	N	Y
6 Woolsey	Y	Y	Y	N	N	N	Y
7 Miller, George	Y	Y	Y	N	N	N	N
8 Pelosi	Y	Y	Y	N	N	N	Y
9 Lee	Y	Y	Y	N	N	N	Y
10 Garamendi	Y	Y	Y	N	N	N	Y
11 McNerney	Y	Y	Y	N	N	N	Y
12 Speier	Y	Y	Y	N	N	N	Y
13 Stark	Y	Y	Y	N	N	N	Y
14 Eshoo	Y	Y	Y	N	N	N	Y
15 Honda	Y	Y	Y	N	N	N	Y
16 Lofgren	Y	Y	Y	N	N	N	N
17 Farr	Y	Y	Y	N	N	N	N
18 Vacant							
19 Denham	N	N	N	N	Y	Y	Y
20 Costa	N	Y	Y	N	Y	Y	Y
21 Nunes	N	N	N	N	Y	Y	Y
22 McCarthy	?	?	?	N	Y	Y	Y
23 Capps	Y	Y	Y	N	N	Y	Y
24 Gallegly	N	N	N	N	Y	Y	Y
25 McKeon	N	N	N	N	Y	Y	Y
26 Dreier	N	N	N	N	Y	Y	Y
27 Sherman	Y	Y	Y	N	N	Y	Y
28 Berman	Y	Y	Y	N	N	Y	Y
29 Schiff	Y	Y	Y	N	N	Y	Y
30 Waxman	Y	Y	Y	N	N	N	Y
31 Becerra	Y	Y	Y	N	N	N	Y
32 Chu	Y	Y	Y	N	N	N	Y
33 Bass	Y	Y	Y	N	N	N	Y
34 Roybal-Allard	Y	Y	Y	N	N	N	Y
35 Waters	Y	Y	Y	N	N	N	Y
36 Hahn	Y	Y	Y	N	N	N	Y
37 Richardson	Y	Y	Y	N	N	N	Y
38 Napolitano	Y	Y	Y	N	N	N	Y
39 Sánchez, Linda	Y	Y	Y	N	N	N	Y
40 Royce	N	N	N	N	Y	Y	Y
41 Lewis	N	N	N	N	Y	Y	Y
42 Miller, Gary	N	N	N	N	Y	Y	Y
43 Baca	Y	Y	Y	N	Y	N	Y
44 Calvert	N	N	N	N	Y	Y	Y
45 Bono Mack	N	N	N	N	Y	Y	Y
46 Rohrabacher	N	N	N	N	Y	Y	Y
47 Sanchez, Loretta	Y	Y	Y	N	N	Y	Y
48 Campbell	N	N	N	N	Y	Y	Y
49 Issa	N	N	N	N	Y	Y	Y
50 Bilbray	N	N	N	N	Y	Y	Y
51 Filner	Y	Y	Y	N	N	N	Y
52 Hunter	N	N	N	N	Y	Y	Y
53 Davis	Y	Y	Y	N	N	Y	Y

	564	565	566	567	568	569	570
COLORADO							
1 DeGette	Y	Y	Y	N	N	N	Y
2 Polis	Y	Y	Y	N	Y	N	Y
3 Tipton	N	Y	N	N	Y	Y	Y
4 Gardner	N	N	N	N	Y	Y	N
5 Lamborn	N	N	N	N	Y	Y	N
6 Coffman	N	N	N	N	Y	Y	N
7 Perlmutter	Y	Y	Y	N	Y	N	Y
CONNECTICUT							
1 Larson	Y	Y	Y	N	N	N	Y
2 Courtney	Y	Y	Y	N	N	N	Y
3 DeLauro	Y	Y	Y	N	N	N	Y
4 Himes	Y	Y	Y	N	N	N	Y
5 Murphy	Y	Y	Y	N	N	N	Y
DELAWARE							
AL Carney	Y	Y	Y	N	N	N	Y
FLORIDA							
1 Miller	N	N	N	N	Y	Y	N
2 Southerland	N	N	N	N	Y	Y	N
3 Brown	?	?	?	?	?	?	?
4 Crenshaw	N	N	N	N	Y	Y	Y
5 Nugent	N	N	N	N	Y	Y	Y
6 Stearns	N	N	N	N	Y	Y	Y
7 Mica	N	N	N	N	Y	Y	Y
8 Webster	N	N	N	N	Y	Y	Y
9 Bilirakis	N	N	N	N	Y	Y	Y
10 Young	N	Y	N	N	Y	N	Y
11 Castor	Y	Y	Y	N	Y	N	Y
12 Ross	N	N	N	N	Y	Y	Y
13 Buchanan	N	N	N	N	Y	Y	Y
14 Mack	N	N	N	N	Y	Y	Y
15 Posey	N	N	N	N	Y	Y	Y
16 Rooney	N	N	N	N	Y	Y	N
17 Wilson	Y	Y	Y	N	N	N	Y
18 Ros-Lehtinen	N	N	N	N	Y	Y	Y
19 Deutch	Y	Y	Y	N	N	N	Y
20 Wasserman Schultz	Y	Y	Y	N	N	N	Y
21 Diaz-Balart	N	N	N	N	Y	Y	Y
22 West	N	N	?	N	Y	Y	Y
23 Hastings	Y	Y	Y	N	N	Y	Y
24 Adams	N	N	N	N	Y	Y	Y
25 Rivera	N	N	N	N	Y	Y	Y
GEORGIA							
1 Kingston	N	N	N	N	Y	Y	N
2 Bishop	N	Y	Y	N	Y	Y	Y
3 Westmoreland	N	N	N	N	Y	Y	N
4 Johnson	Y	Y	Y	N	N	N	Y
5 Lewis	Y	Y	Y	N	N	N	Y
6 Price	N	N	N	N	Y	Y	N
7 Woodall	N	N	N	N	Y	Y	N
8 Scott, A.	N	N	N	N	Y	Y	N
9 Graves	N	N	N	N	Y	Y	N
10 Broun	?	?	?	?	?	?	?
11 Gingrey	?	?	?	?	?	Y	N
12 Barrow	Y	Y	Y	N	Y	Y	Y
13 Scott, D.	Y	Y	Y	N	Y	Y	Y
HAWAII							
1 Hanabusa	Y	Y	Y	N	N	Y	Y
2 Hirono	?	?	?	?	?	?	?
IDAHO							
1 Labrador	N	N	N	N	Y	Y	Y
2 Simpson	N	N	N	N	Y	Y	Y
ILLINOIS							
1 Rush	Y	Y	Y	N	N	N	Y
2 Jackson	?	?	?	?	?	?	?
3 Lipinski	Y	Y	Y	N	N	Y	Y
4 Gutierrez	Y	Y	Y	N	N	Y	Y
5 Quigley	Y	Y	Y	N	N	Y	Y
6 Roskam	N	N	N	N	Y	Y	Y
7 Davis	Y	Y	Y	N	N	N	Y
8 Walsh	N	N	N	N	Y	Y	N
9 Schakowsky	Y	Y	Y	N	N	N	Y
10 Dold	N	Y	N	N	Y	Y	Y
11 Kinzinger	N	N	N	N	Y	Y	Y
12 Costello	Y	Y	Y	N	N	Y	Y
13 Biggert	N	N	N	N	Y	Y	Y
14 Hultgren	N	N	N	N	Y	Y	Y
15 Johnson	Y	Y	Y	N	N	N	Y

KEY   **Republicans**   Democrats

Y Voted for (yea)	X Paired against	C Voted "present" to avoid possible conflict of interest
# Paired for	– Announced against	
+ Announced for	P Voted "present"	? Did not vote or otherwise make a position known
N Voted against (nay)		

	564	565	566	567	568	569	570
16 **Manzullo**	N	N	N	N	Y	Y	Y
17 **Schilling**	N	N	N	N	Y	Y	Y
18 **Schock**	?	N	N	N	Y	Y	Y
19 **Shimkus**	N	N	N	N	Y	Y	Y
INDIANA							
1 Visclosky	Y	Y	Y	Y	N	N	Y
2 Donnelly	Y	N	Y	Y	N	Y	Y
3 **Stutzman**	N	N	N	N	Y	Y	N
4 **Rokita**	N	N	N	N	Y	Y	Y
5 **Burton**	?	N	N	N	Y	Y	N
6 **Pence**	N	N	N	N	Y	Y	N
7 Carson	Y	Y	Y	Y	N	N	Y
8 **Bucshon**	N	N	N	N	Y	Y	Y
9 **Young**	N	N	N	N	Y	Y	Y
IOWA							
1 Braley	Y	Y	Y	Y	N	N	Y
2 Loebsack	Y	Y	Y	Y	N	Y	Y
3 Boswell	Y	Y	Y	Y	N	Y	Y
4 **Latham**	N	N	N	N	Y	Y	Y
5 **King**	N	N	N	N	Y	Y	Y
KANSAS							
1 **Huelskamp**	N	N	N	N	Y	Y	Y
2 **Jenkins**	N	N	N	N	Y	Y	Y
3 **Yoder**	N	N	N	N	Y	Y	Y
4 **Pompeo**	N	N	N	N	Y	Y	Y
KENTUCKY							
1 **Whitfield**	N	N	N	N	?	Y	Y
2 **Guthrie**	N	N	N	N	Y	Y	Y
3 Yarmuth	Y	Y	Y	Y	N	Y	Y
4 Vacant							
5 **Rogers**	N	N	N	N	Y	Y	Y
6 Chandler	Y	Y	Y	Y	?	Y	Y
LOUISIANA							
1 **Scalise**	N	N	N	N	Y	Y	Y
2 Richmond	Y	Y	Y	Y	N	Y	Y
3 **Landry**	N	N	?	N	Y	Y	N
4 **Fleming**	N	N	N	N	Y	Y	N
5 **Alexander**	N	N	N	N	Y	Y	Y
6 **Cassidy**	N	N	N	N	Y	Y	N
7 **Boustany**	N	N	N	N	Y	Y	Y
MAINE							
1 Pingree	Y	Y	Y	Y	N	N	Y
2 Michaud	Y	Y	Y	Y	N	N	Y
MARYLAND							
1 **Harris**	N	N	N	N	Y	Y	Y
2 Ruppersberger	Y	Y	Y	Y	N	Y	Y
3 Sarbanes	Y	Y	Y	Y	N	N	Y
4 Edwards	Y	Y	Y	Y	N	N	Y
5 Hoyer	Y	Y	Y	Y	N	Y	Y
6 **Bartlett**	N	N	N	N	N	Y	Y
7 Cummings	Y	Y	Y	Y	N	N	Y
8 Van Hollen	Y	Y	Y	Y	N	N	Y
MASSACHUSETTS							
1 Olver	Y	Y	Y	Y	N	N	Y
2 Neal	Y	Y	Y	Y	N	N	Y
3 McGovern	Y	Y	Y	Y	N	N	Y
4 Frank	Y	Y	Y	Y	N	N	Y
5 Tsongas	Y	Y	Y	Y	N	N	Y
6 Tierney	Y	Y	Y	Y	N	N	Y
7 Markey	Y	Y	Y	Y	N	N	Y
8 Capuano	Y	Y	Y	Y	N	N	Y
9 Lynch	Y	Y	Y	Y	N	Y	Y
10 Keating	Y	Y	Y	Y	N	N	Y
MICHIGAN							
1 **Benishek**	N	N	N	N	Y	Y	Y
2 **Huizenga**	N	N	N	N	Y	Y	N
3 **Amash**	N	N	N	N	Y	N	N
4 **Camp**	N	N	N	N	Y	Y	Y
5 Kildee	Y	Y	Y	Y	N	N	Y
6 **Upton**	N	N	N	N	Y	Y	Y
7 **Walberg**	N	N	N	N	Y	Y	Y
8 **Rogers**	N	N	N	N	Y	Y	Y
9 Peters	Y	Y	Y	Y	N	Y	Y
10 **Miller**	N	N	N	N	Y	Y	Y
11 Vacant							
12 Levin	Y	Y	Y	Y	N	Y	Y
13 Clarke	Y	Y	Y	Y	N	N	Y
14 Conyers	Y	Y	Y	Y	N	N	Y
15 Dingell	Y	Y	Y	Y	N	N	Y
MINNESOTA							
1 Walz	N	Y	Y	Y	N	N	Y
2 **Kline**	N	N	N	N	Y	Y	Y
3 **Paulsen**	N	Y	N	N	Y	Y	Y
4 McCollum	Y	Y	Y	Y	N	N	Y

	564	565	566	567	568	569	570
5 Ellison	Y	Y	Y	Y	N	N	Y
6 **Bachmann**	N	N	N	N	Y	Y	Y
7 Peterson	N	Y	Y	Y	N	Y	Y
8 **Cravaack**	N	N	N	N	Y	Y	Y
MISSISSIPPI							
1 **Nunnelee**	N	N	N	N	Y	Y	N
2 Thompson	Y	Y	Y	Y	N	N	Y
3 **Harper**	N	N	N	N	Y	Y	Y
4 **Palazzo**	N	N	N	N	Y	Y	N
MISSOURI							
1 Clay	Y	Y	Y	Y	N	N	Y
2 **Akin**	?	?	?	?	?	?	?
3 Carnahan	Y	Y	Y	Y	N	Y	Y
4 **Hartzler**	N	N	N	N	Y	Y	?
5 Cleaver	Y	Y	Y	Y	N	N	Y
6 **Graves**	N	N	N	N	Y	Y	Y
7 **Long**	N	N	N	N	Y	Y	N
8 **Emerson**	N	N	N	N	Y	Y	Y
9 **Luetkemeyer**	N	N	N	N	Y	Y	Y
MONTANA							
AL **Rehberg**	N	N	N	N	Y	Y	Y
NEBRASKA							
1 **Fortenberry**	N	N	?	N	Y	Y	Y
2 **Terry**	N	N	N	N	Y	Y	Y
3 **Smith**	N	N	N	N	Y	Y	Y
NEVADA							
1 Berkley	Y	Y	Y	Y	N	Y	Y
2 **Amodei**	N	N	N	N	Y	Y	Y
3 **Heck**	N	N	N	N	Y	Y	Y
NEW HAMPSHIRE							
1 **Guinta**	N	N	N	N	Y	Y	Y
2 **Bass**	Y	N	N	N	N	Y	Y
NEW JERSEY							
1 Andrews	Y	Y	Y	Y	N	N	Y
2 **LoBiondo**	N	N	N	N	Y	Y	Y
3 **Runyan**	N	N	N	N	Y	Y	Y
4 **Smith**	N	N	N	N	Y	Y	Y
5 **Garrett**	N	N	N	N	Y	Y	Y
6 Pallone	Y	Y	Y	Y	N	N	Y
7 **Lance**	N	N	N	N	Y	Y	Y
8 Pascrell	Y	Y	Y	Y	N	N	Y
9 Rothman	Y	Y	Y	Y	N	Y	Y
10 Vacant							
11 **Frelinghuysen**	N	N	N	N	Y	Y	Y
12 Holt	Y	Y	Y	Y	N	N	Y
13 Sires	Y	Y	Y	Y	N	Y	Y
NEW MEXICO							
1 Heinrich	Y	Y	Y	Y	N	Y	Y
2 **Pearce**	N	N	N	N	Y	Y	N
3 Luján	Y	Y	Y	Y	N	Y	Y
NEW YORK							
1 Bishop	Y	Y	Y	Y	N	Y	Y
2 Israel	Y	Y	Y	Y	N	N	Y
3 **King**	N	N	N	N	Y	Y	Y
4 McCarthy	Y	Y	Y	Y	N	Y	Y
5 Ackerman	Y	Y	Y	Y	N	Y	Y
6 Meeks	Y	Y	Y	Y	N	N	Y
7 Crowley	Y	Y	Y	Y	N	N	Y
8 Nadler	Y	Y	Y	Y	N	N	Y
9 **Turner**	N	N	N	N	Y	Y	Y
10 Towns	Y	Y	Y	Y	N	?	?
11 Clarke	Y	Y	Y	Y	N	N	Y
12 Velázquez	Y	Y	Y	Y	N	N	?
13 **Grimm**	N	N	N	N	Y	Y	Y
14 Maloney	Y	Y	Y	Y	N	N	Y
15 Rangel	Y	Y	Y	Y	N	N	Y
16 Serrano	Y	Y	Y	Y	N	N	Y
17 Engel	Y	Y	Y	Y	N	N	Y
18 Lowey	Y	Y	Y	Y	N	Y	Y
19 **Hayworth**	N	N	N	N	N	Y	Y
20 **Gibson**	N	Y	Y	N	N	N	Y
21 Tonko	Y	Y	Y	Y	N	N	Y
22 Hinchey	Y	Y	Y	Y	N	N	Y
23 Owens	Y	Y	Y	Y	N	N	Y
24 **Hanna**	N	N	N	N	Y	Y	Y
25 **Buerkle**	N	N	N	N	Y	Y	N
26 Hochul	Y	Y	Y	Y	N	Y	Y
27 Higgins	Y	Y	Y	Y	N	Y	Y
28 Slaughter	Y	Y	Y	Y	N	N	Y
29 **Reed**	N	N	N	N	Y	Y	Y
NORTH CAROLINA							
1 Butterfield	?	?	?	?	?	?	?
2 **Ellmers**	N	N	N	N	Y	Y	Y
3 **Jones**	N	N	Y	N	Y	N	N
4 Price	Y	Y	Y	Y	N	N	Y

	564	565	566	567	568	569	570
5 **Foxx**	N	N	N	N	Y	Y	N
6 **Coble**	N	N	N	N	Y	Y	N
7 McIntyre	Y	Y	Y	Y	N	Y	Y
8 Kissell	N	Y	Y	Y	N	Y	Y
9 **Myrick**	N	?	N	N	Y	Y	Y
10 **McHenry**	N	N	N	N	Y	Y	Y
11 Shuler	Y	Y	Y	Y	N	Y	Y
12 Watt	Y	Y	Y	Y	N	N	Y
13 Miller	Y	Y	Y	Y	N	Y	Y
NORTH DAKOTA							
AL **Berg**	N	N	N	N	Y	Y	Y
OHIO							
1 **Chabot**	N	N	N	N	Y	Y	Y
2 **Schmidt**	N	N	N	N	Y	Y	Y
3 **Turner**	N	N	N	N	Y	Y	Y
4 **Jordan**	N	N	N	N	Y	Y	N
5 **Latta**	N	N	N	N	Y	Y	Y
6 **Johnson**	N	N	N	N	Y	Y	Y
7 **Austria**	N	N	N	N	Y	Y	Y
8 **Boehner**							
9 Kaptur	Y	Y	Y	Y	N	Y	Y
10 Kucinich	Y	Y	Y	Y	N	N	N
11 Fudge	Y	Y	Y	Y	N	N	Y
12 **Tiberi**	N	N	N	N	Y	Y	Y
13 Sutton	Y	Y	Y	Y	N	N	Y
14 **LaTourette**	?	N	N	N	Y	Y	Y
15 **Stivers**	N	N	N	N	Y	Y	Y
16 **Renacci**	N	N	N	N	Y	Y	Y
17 Ryan	Y	Y	Y	Y	N	Y	Y
18 **Gibbs**	N	N	N	N	Y	Y	Y
OKLAHOMA							
1 **Sullivan**	N	N	N	N	Y	Y	Y
2 Boren	N	Y	Y	Y	N	Y	Y
3 **Lucas**	N	N	N	N	Y	Y	Y
4 **Cole**	N	N	N	N	Y	Y	Y
5 **Lankford**	N	N	N	N	Y	Y	Y
OREGON							
1 Bonamici	Y	Y	Y	Y	N	N	Y
2 **Walden**	N	N	N	N	Y	Y	Y
3 Blumenauer	Y	Y	Y	Y	N	N	Y
4 DeFazio	Y	Y	Y	Y	N	N	Y
5 Schrader	N	Y	Y	Y	N	N	Y
PENNSYLVANIA							
1 Brady	Y	Y	Y	Y	N	N	Y
2 Fattah	Y	Y	Y	Y	N	Y	Y
3 **Kelly**	N	N	N	N	Y	Y	Y
4 Altmire	Y	Y	Y	Y	N	Y	Y
5 **Thompson**	N	N	N	N	Y	Y	Y
6 **Gerlach**	N	N	Y	N	N	Y	Y
7 **Meehan**	N	N	N	N	Y	Y	Y
8 **Fitzpatrick**	N	Y	Y	N	N	Y	Y
9 **Shuster**	N	N	N	N	Y	Y	Y
10 **Marino**	N	N	N	N	Y	Y	Y
11 **Barletta**	N	N	N	N	Y	Y	Y
12 Critz	Y	Y	Y	Y	N	Y	Y
13 Schwartz	Y	Y	Y	Y	N	Y	Y
14 Doyle	Y	Y	Y	Y	N	N	Y
15 **Dent**	N	N	N	N	Y	Y	Y
16 **Pitts**	N	N	N	N	Y	Y	Y
17 Holden	?	?	?	?	?	Y	Y
18 **Murphy**	N	N	N	N	Y	Y	Y
19 **Platts**	N	N	N	N	Y	Y	Y
RHODE ISLAND							
1 Cicilline	Y	Y	Y	Y	N	Y	Y
2 Langevin	Y	Y	Y	Y	N	Y	Y
SOUTH CAROLINA							
1 **Scott**	N	N	N	N	Y	Y	Y
2 **Wilson**	N	N	N	N	Y	Y	Y
3 **Duncan**	N	N	N	N	Y	Y	Y
4 **Gowdy**	N	N	N	N	Y	Y	N
5 **Mulvaney**	N	Y	N	N	Y	Y	N
6 Clyburn	Y	Y	Y	Y	N	Y	Y
SOUTH DAKOTA							
AL **Noem**	N	N	N	N	Y	Y	Y
TENNESSEE							
1 **Roe**	N	N	N	N	Y	Y	N
2 **Duncan**	N	N	N	N	Y	N	N
3 **Fleischmann**	N	N	N	N	Y	Y	Y
4 **DesJarlais**	N	N	N	N	Y	Y	N
5 Cooper	Y	Y	Y	Y	N	Y	Y
6 **Black**	N	N	N	N	Y	Y	Y
7 **Blackburn**	N	N	N	N	Y	Y	Y
8 **Fincher**	N	N	N	N	Y	Y	Y
9 Cohen	Y	Y	Y	Y	N	N	Y

	564	565	566	567	568	569	570
TEXAS							
1 **Gohmert**	N	N	N	N	Y	Y	N
2 **Poe**	N	N	N	N	Y	Y	N
3 **Johnson, S.**	N	N	N	?	?	Y	Y
4 **Hall**	N	N	N	N	Y	Y	Y
5 **Hensarling**	N	N	N	N	Y	Y	N
6 **Barton**	N	N	N	N	Y	Y	N
7 **Culberson**	?	?	?	?	?	Y	N
8 **Brady**	N	N	N	N	Y	Y	N
9 Green, A.	Y	Y	Y	Y	N	Y	Y
10 **McCaul**	N	N	N	N	Y	Y	Y
11 **Conaway**	N	N	N	N	Y	Y	Y
12 **Granger**	N	N	N	N	Y	Y	Y
13 **Thornberry**	N	N	N	N	Y	Y	Y
14 **Paul**	N	N	N	N	Y	N	?
15 Hinojosa	Y	Y	Y	Y	N	Y	Y
16 Reyes	Y	Y	Y	Y	N	Y	Y
17 **Flores**	N	N	N	N	Y	Y	Y
18 Jackson Lee	Y	Y	Y	Y	N	N	Y
19 **Neugebauer**	N	N	N	N	Y	Y	N
20 Gonzalez	Y	Y	Y	Y	N	Y	Y
21 **Smith**	N	N	N	N	Y	Y	Y
22 **Olson**	N	N	N	N	Y	Y	Y
23 **Canseco**	N	N	N	N	Y	Y	Y
24 **Marchant**	N	N	N	N	Y	Y	N
25 Doggett	Y	Y	Y	Y	N	N	Y
26 **Burgess**	N	N	N	N	Y	Y	N
27 **Farenthold**	N	N	N	N	Y	Y	Y
28 Cuellar	Y	Y	Y	Y	N	Y	Y
29 Green, G.	Y	Y	Y	Y	N	Y	Y
30 Johnson, E.	Y	Y	Y	Y	N	N	Y
31 **Carter**	N	N	N	N	Y	Y	Y
32 **Sessions**	N	N	N	N	Y	Y	Y
UTAH							
1 **Bishop**	N	N	N	N	Y	Y	Y
2 Matheson	N	N	N	N	Y	Y	Y
3 **Chaffetz**	N	N	N	N	Y	Y	Y
VERMONT							
AL Welch	Y	Y	Y	Y	N	N	Y
VIRGINIA							
1 **Wittman**	N	N	N	N	Y	Y	Y
2 **Rigell**	N	N	N	N	Y	Y	Y
3 Scott	Y	Y	Y	Y	N	N	Y
4 **Forbes**	N	N	N	N	Y	Y	Y
5 **Hurt**	N	N	N	N	Y	Y	N
6 **Goodlatte**	N	N	N	N	Y	Y	N
7 **Cantor**	N	N	N	N	Y	Y	Y
8 Moran	Y	Y	Y	?	?	N	Y
9 **Griffith**	N	N	N	N	Y	Y	N
10 **Wolf**	N	N	N	N	Y	Y	Y
11 Connolly	Y	Y	Y	Y	N	Y	Y
WASHINGTON							
1 Vacant							
2 Larsen	Y	Y	Y	Y	N	N	Y
3 **Herrera Beutler**	N	N	N	N	Y	Y	Y
4 **Hastings**	N	N	N	N	Y	Y	Y
5 **McMorris Rodgers**	N	N	N	N	Y	Y	Y
6 Dicks	Y	Y	Y	Y	N	Y	Y
7 McDermott	Y	Y	Y	Y	N	N	Y
8 **Reichert**	N	N	N	N	Y	Y	Y
9 Smith	Y	Y	Y	Y	N	Y	Y
WEST VIRGINIA							
1 **McKinley**	N	N	N	N	Y	Y	Y
2 **Capito**	N	N	N	N	Y	Y	Y
3 Rahall	Y	Y	Y	Y	N	Y	Y
WISCONSIN							
1 **Ryan**	?	?	?	?	?	?	?
2 Baldwin	?	Y	Y	Y	N	N	Y
3 Kind	Y	Y	Y	Y	N	N	Y
4 Moore	Y	Y	Y	Y	N	N	Y
5 **Sensenbrenner**	N	N	N	N	Y	Y	N
6 **Petri**	N	N	N	N	Y	Y	N
7 **Duffy**	N	N	N	N	Y	Y	Y
8 **Ribble**	N	N	N	N	Y	Y	N
WYOMING							
AL **Lummis**	N	N	N	N	Y	Y	N

IN THE HOUSE | By Vote Number

571. HR 5865. Manufacturing Growth Strategy/Passage.
Bono Mack, R-Calif., motion to suspend the rules and pass the bill that would require the president to publish a comprehensive growth strategy in 2014 and 2018 to bolster the nation's manufacturing sector. The bill would establish the American Manufacturing Competitiveness Board to advise the president, who would have to include the board's recommendations when developing the annual budget request. Motion agreed to 339-77: R 157-76; D 182-1. A two-thirds majority of those present and voting (278 in this case) is required for passage under suspension of the rules. Sept. 12, 2012.

572. H J Res 117, HR 6365. Continuing Resolution and Sequestration Replacement/Previous Question.
Woodall, R-Ga., motion to order the previous question (thus ending debate and the possibility of amendment) on the rule (H Res 778) to provide for House floor consideration of a continuing resolution (H J Res 117) that would fund fiscal 2013 government operations for six months and a bill (HR 6365) that would direct the president to send to Congress by Oct. 15, 2012, legislation that would replace the automatic discretionary spending cuts under the sequester and mandatory defense spending cuts scheduled to take effect on Jan. 2, 2013. Motion agreed to 235-178: R 229-2; D 6-176. Sept. 13, 2012.

573. H J Res 117, HR 6365. Continuing Resolution and Sequestration Replacement/Rule.
Adoption of the rule (H Res 778) that would provide for House floor consideration of a continuing resolution (H J Res 117) that would fund fiscal 2013 government operations for six months and a bill (HR 6365) that would direct the president to send to Congress by Oct. 15, 2012, legislation that would replace the automatic discretionary spending cuts under the sequester and mandatory defense spending cuts scheduled to take effect on Jan. 2, 2013. Adopted 232-182: R 230-2; D 2-180. Sept. 13, 2012.

574. HR 6213. Energy Department Loans/Rule.
Adoption of the rule (H Res 779) that would provide for House floor consideration of the bill that would prohibit the Energy Department from issuing new loan guarantees for energy project applications submitted after Dec. 31, 2011. Adopted 232-182: R 228-2; D 4-180. Sept. 13, 2012.

575. HR 1775. Military Service Fraud/Passage.
Smith, R-Texas, motion to suspend the rules and pass the bill that would establish penalties against individuals who fraudulently claim to be recipients of military honors or decoration with the intent to obtain compensation. Violators would be subject to fines or imprisonment of no more than a year, or both. Motion agreed to 410-3: R 229-2; D 181-1. A two-thirds majority of those present and voting (276 in this case) is required for passage under suspension of the rules. Sept. 13, 2012.

	571	572	573	574	575
ALABAMA					
1 Bonner	Y	Y	Y	Y	Y
2 Roby	Y	Y	Y	Y	Y
3 Rogers	Y	Y	Y	Y	Y
4 Aderholt	Y	Y	Y	Y	Y
5 Brooks	N	Y	Y	Y	Y
6 Bachus	Y	Y	Y	Y	Y
7 Sewell	Y	N	N	N	Y
ALASKA					
AL Young	Y	Y	Y	?	Y
ARIZONA					
1 Gosar	Y	Y	Y	Y	Y
2 Franks	N	Y	Y	Y	Y
3 Quayle	N	Y	Y	Y	Y
4 Pastor	Y	N	N	N	Y
5 Schweikert	Y	?	Y	Y	Y
6 Flake	N	Y	Y	Y	Y
7 Grijalva	Y	N	N	N	Y
8 Barber	Y	N	N	N	Y
ARKANSAS					
1 Crawford	Y	Y	Y	Y	Y
2 Griffin	Y	Y	Y	Y	Y
3 Womack	Y	Y	Y	Y	Y
4 Ross	Y	?	?	?	?
CALIFORNIA					
1 Thompson	Y	?	N	N	Y
2 Herger	?	?	?	?	?
3 Lungren	Y	Y	Y	Y	Y
4 McClintock	N	Y	Y	Y	Y
5 Matsui	Y	N	N	N	Y
6 Woolsey	Y	N	N	N	Y
7 Miller, George	Y	N	?	N	N
8 Pelosi	Y	N	N	N	?
9 Lee	Y	N	N	N	Y
10 Garamendi	Y	N	N	N	Y
11 McNerney	Y	N	N	N	Y
12 Speier	Y	N	N	N	Y
13 Stark	Y	N	N	N	Y
14 Eshoo	Y	N	N	N	Y
15 Honda	Y	N	N	N	Y
16 Lofgren	Y	N	N	N	Y
17 Farr	Y	N	N	N	Y
18 Vacant					
19 Denham	Y	Y	Y	Y	Y
20 Costa	Y	Y	N	Y	Y
21 Nunes	Y	Y	Y	Y	Y
22 McCarthy	Y	Y	Y	Y	Y
23 Capps	Y	N	N	N	Y
24 Gallegly	Y	Y	Y	Y	Y
25 McKeon	Y	Y	Y	Y	Y
26 Dreier	Y	Y	Y	Y	Y
27 Sherman	Y	N	N	N	Y
28 Berman	Y	N	N	N	Y
29 Schiff	Y	N	N	N	Y
30 Waxman	Y	N	N	N	Y
31 Becerra	Y	N	N	N	Y
32 Chu	Y	N	N	N	Y
33 Bass	Y	N	N	N	Y
34 Roybal-Allard	Y	N	N	N	Y
35 Waters	Y	N	N	N	Y
36 Hahn	Y	N	N	N	Y
37 Richardson	Y	N	N	N	Y
38 Napolitano	Y	N	N	N	Y
39 Sánchez, Linda	Y	N	N	N	Y
40 Royce	Y	Y	Y	Y	Y
41 Lewis	Y	Y	Y	Y	Y
42 Miller, Gary	Y	Y	Y	Y	Y
43 Baca	Y	N	N	N	Y
44 Calvert	Y	Y	Y	Y	Y
45 Bono Mack	Y	Y	Y	Y	Y
46 Rohrabacher	N	Y	Y	Y	Y
47 Sanchez, Loretta	Y	N	N	N	Y
48 Campbell	N	Y	Y	Y	Y
49 Issa	Y	Y	Y	Y	Y
50 Bilbray	Y	Y	Y	Y	Y
51 Filner	Y	N	N	N	Y
52 Hunter	Y	Y	Y	Y	Y
53 Davis	Y	N	N	N	Y

	571	572	573	574	575
COLORADO					
1 DeGette	Y	N	N	N	Y
2 Polis	N	N	N	N	Y
3 Tipton	Y	Y	Y	Y	Y
4 Gardner	N	Y	Y	Y	Y
5 Lamborn	N	Y	Y	Y	Y
6 Coffman	Y	Y	Y	Y	Y
7 Perlmutter	Y	N	N	N	Y
CONNECTICUT					
1 Larson	Y	N	N	N	Y
2 Courtney	Y	N	N	N	Y
3 DeLauro	Y	N	N	N	Y
4 Himes	Y	N	N	N	Y
5 Murphy	Y	N	N	N	Y
DELAWARE					
AL Carney	Y	N	N	N	Y
FLORIDA					
1 Miller	N	Y	Y	Y	Y
2 Southerland	N	Y	Y	Y	Y
3 Brown	?	N	N	N	Y
4 Crenshaw	Y	Y	Y	Y	Y
5 Nugent	Y	Y	Y	Y	Y
6 Stearns	Y	Y	Y	Y	Y
7 Mica	N	Y	Y	Y	Y
8 Webster	N	Y	Y	Y	Y
9 Bilirakis	Y	Y	Y	Y	Y
10 Young	Y	Y	Y	Y	Y
11 Castor	Y	N	N	N	Y
12 Ross	N	Y	Y	Y	Y
13 Buchanan	Y	Y	Y	?	Y
14 Mack	N	Y	Y	Y	Y
15 Posey	N	Y	Y	Y	Y
16 Rooney	N	Y	Y	Y	Y
17 Wilson	Y	N	N	N	Y
18 Ros-Lehtinen	Y	Y	Y	Y	Y
19 Deutch	Y	N	N	N	Y
20 Wasserman Schultz	Y	N	N	N	Y
21 Diaz-Balart	Y	?	?	Y	Y
22 West	Y	Y	Y	Y	Y
23 Hastings	Y	N	N	N	Y
24 Adams	N	Y	Y	Y	Y
25 Rivera	Y	Y	Y	Y	Y
GEORGIA					
1 Kingston	N	Y	Y	Y	Y
2 Bishop	Y	N	N	N	Y
3 Westmoreland	Y	Y	Y	Y	Y
4 Johnson	Y	N	N	N	Y
5 Lewis	Y	N	N	N	Y
6 Price	N	Y	Y	Y	Y
7 Woodall	N	Y	Y	Y	Y
8 Scott, A.	N	Y	Y	Y	Y
9 Graves	N	Y	Y	Y	Y
10 Broun	?	?	?	?	?
11 Gingrey	Y	Y	Y	Y	Y
12 Barrow	Y	N	N	N	Y
13 Scott, D.	Y	N	N	N	Y
HAWAII					
1 Hanabusa	Y	N	N	N	Y
2 Hirono	?	N	N	N	Y
IDAHO					
1 Labrador	N	Y	Y	Y	Y
2 Simpson	Y	Y	Y	Y	Y
ILLINOIS					
1 Rush	Y	N	N	N	Y
2 Jackson	?	?	?	?	?
3 Lipinski	Y	N	N	N	Y
4 Gutierrez	Y	N	N	N	Y
5 Quigley	Y	N	N	N	Y
6 Roskam	Y	Y	Y	Y	Y
7 Davis	Y	N	N	N	Y
8 Walsh	Y	Y	Y	Y	Y
9 Schakowsky	Y	N	N	N	Y
10 Dold	Y	Y	Y	Y	Y
11 Kinzinger	Y	Y	Y	Y	Y
12 Costello	Y	N	N	N	Y
13 Biggert	Y	Y	Y	Y	Y
14 Hultgren	Y	Y	Y	Y	Y
15 Johnson	N	Y	Y	Y	Y

	571	572	573	574	575
16 Manzullo	Y	Y	Y	Y	Y
17 Schilling	Y	Y	Y	Y	Y
18 Schock	Y	Y	Y	Y	Y
19 Shimkus	Y	Y	Y	Y	Y
INDIANA					
1 Visclosky	Y	N	N	N	Y
2 Donnelly	Y	Y	N	N	Y
3 Stutzman	N	Y	Y	Y	Y
4 Rokita	Y	Y	Y	Y	Y
5 Burton	N	Y	Y	Y	Y
6 Pence	Y	Y	Y	Y	Y
7 Carson	Y	N	N	N	Y
8 Bucshon	Y	Y	Y	Y	Y
9 Young	Y	Y	Y	Y	Y
IOWA					
1 Braley	Y	N	N	N	Y
2 Loebsack	Y	N	N	N	Y
3 Boswell	Y	N	N	N	Y
4 Latham	Y	Y	Y	Y	Y
5 King	Y	Y	Y	Y	Y
KANSAS					
1 Huelskamp	N	Y	Y	Y	Y
2 Jenkins	N	Y	Y	Y	Y
3 Yoder	N	Y	Y	Y	Y
4 Pompeo	Y	Y	Y	Y	Y
KENTUCKY					
1 Whitfield	Y	Y	Y	Y	Y
2 Guthrie	Y	Y	Y	Y	Y
3 Yarmuth	Y	N	N	N	Y
4 Vacant					
5 Rogers	Y	Y	Y	Y	Y
6 Chandler	Y	N	N	N	Y
LOUISIANA					
1 Scalise	N	Y	Y	Y	Y
2 Richmond	Y	N	N	N	Y
3 Landry	N	Y	Y	Y	Y
4 Fleming	N	Y	Y	Y	Y
5 Alexander	Y	Y	Y	Y	Y
6 Cassidy	N	Y	Y	Y	Y
7 Boustany	Y	Y	Y	Y	Y
MAINE					
1 Pingree	Y	N	N	N	Y
2 Michaud	Y	?	?	?	?
MARYLAND					
1 Harris	Y	Y	Y	Y	Y
2 Ruppersberger	Y	N	N	N	Y
3 Sarbanes	Y	N	N	N	Y
4 Edwards	Y	N	N	N	Y
5 Hoyer	Y	N	N	N	Y
6 Bartlett	Y	Y	Y	Y	Y
7 Cummings	Y	N	N	N	Y
8 Van Hollen	Y	N	N	N	Y
MASSACHUSETTS					
1 Olver	Y	N	N	N	Y
2 Neal	Y	N	N	N	?
3 McGovern	Y	N	N	N	Y
4 Frank	Y	N	N	N	Y
5 Tsongas	Y	N	N	N	Y
6 Tierney	Y	N	N	N	Y
7 Markey	Y	N	N	N	Y
8 Capuano	Y	N	N	N	Y
9 Lynch	Y	N	N	N	Y
10 Keating	Y	N	N	N	Y
MICHIGAN					
1 Benishek	Y	Y	Y	Y	Y
2 Huizenga	N	Y	Y	Y	Y
3 Amash	N	Y	Y	Y	N
4 Camp	Y	Y	Y	Y	Y
5 Kildee	Y	N	N	N	Y
6 Upton	Y	Y	Y	Y	Y
7 Walberg	N	Y	Y	Y	Y
8 Rogers	Y	Y	Y	Y	Y
9 Peters	Y	N	N	N	Y
10 Miller	N	Y	Y	Y	Y
11 Vacant					
12 Levin	Y	N	N	N	Y
13 Clarke	Y	N	N	N	Y
14 Conyers	Y	N	N	N	Y
15 Dingell	Y	N	N	N	Y
MINNESOTA					
1 Walz	Y	N	N	N	Y
2 Kline	N	Y	Y	Y	Y
3 Paulsen	Y	Y	Y	Y	Y
4 McCollum	Y	N	N	N	Y

	571	572	573	574	575
5 Ellison	Y	N	N	N	Y
6 Bachmann	Y	Y	Y	Y	Y
7 Peterson	Y	N	N	N	Y
8 Cravaack	Y	Y	Y	Y	Y
MISSISSIPPI					
1 Nunnelee	Y	Y	Y	Y	Y
2 Thompson	Y	N	N	N	Y
3 Harper	Y	Y	Y	Y	Y
4 Palazzo	N	Y	Y	Y	Y
MISSOURI					
1 Clay	Y	N	N	N	Y
2 Akin	?	?	?	?	?
3 Carnahan	Y	N	N	N	Y
4 Hartzler	Y	Y	Y	Y	Y
5 Cleaver	Y	?	?	?	?
6 Graves	Y	Y	Y	Y	Y
7 Long	N	Y	Y	Y	Y
8 Emerson	Y	Y	Y	?	Y
9 Luetkemeyer	N	Y	Y	Y	Y
MONTANA					
AL Rehberg	Y	Y	Y	Y	Y
NEBRASKA					
1 Fortenberry	Y	Y	Y	Y	Y
2 Terry	Y	Y	Y	Y	Y
3 Smith	N	Y	Y	Y	?
NEVADA					
1 Berkley	Y	N	N	N	Y
2 Amodei	Y	Y	Y	Y	Y
3 Heck	N	Y	Y	Y	Y
NEW HAMPSHIRE					
1 Guinta	Y	Y	Y	Y	Y
2 Bass	Y	Y	Y	Y	Y
NEW JERSEY					
1 Andrews	Y	N	N	N	Y
2 LoBiondo	Y	Y	Y	Y	Y
3 Runyan	Y	Y	Y	Y	Y
4 Smith	Y	Y	Y	Y	Y
5 Garrett	N	Y	Y	Y	Y
6 Pallone	Y	N	N	N	Y
7 Lance	Y	Y	Y	Y	Y
8 Pascrell	Y	N	N	N	Y
9 Rothman	Y	N	N	N	Y
10 Vacant					
11 Frelinghuysen	Y	Y	Y	Y	Y
12 Holt	Y	N	N	N	Y
13 Sires	Y	?	N	N	Y
NEW MEXICO					
1 Heinrich	Y	N	N	N	Y
2 Pearce	N	Y	Y	N	Y
3 Luján	Y	N	N	N	Y
NEW YORK					
1 Bishop	Y	N	N	N	Y
2 Israel	Y	N	N	N	Y
3 King	Y	?	?	?	?
4 McCarthy	Y	N	N	N	Y
5 Ackerman	Y	N	N	N	Y
6 Meeks	Y	N	N	N	Y
7 Crowley	Y	N	N	N	Y
8 Nadler	Y	?	?	?	Y
9 Turner	Y	Y	Y	Y	Y
10 Towns	?	?	?	?	?
11 Clarke	Y	N	N	N	Y
12 Velázquez	?	N	N	N	Y
13 Grimm	Y	Y	Y	Y	Y
14 Maloney	Y	N	N	N	Y
15 Rangel	Y	N	N	N	Y
16 Serrano	Y	N	N	N	Y
17 Engel	Y	N	N	N	Y
18 Lowey	Y	N	N	N	Y
19 Hayworth	Y	Y	Y	Y	Y
20 Gibson	Y	Y	Y	Y	Y
21 Tonko	Y	N	N	N	Y
22 Hinchey	Y	N	N	N	Y
23 Owens	Y	N	N	N	Y
24 Hanna	N	Y	Y	Y	Y
25 Buerkle	Y	Y	Y	Y	Y
26 Hochul	Y	N	N	N	Y
27 Higgins	Y	N	N	N	Y
28 Slaughter	Y	N	N	N	Y
29 Reed	Y	Y	Y	Y	Y
NORTH CAROLINA					
1 Butterfield	?	N	N	N	Y
2 Ellmers	Y	Y	Y	Y	Y
3 Jones	Y	N	N	N	Y
4 Price	Y	N	N	N	Y

	571	572	573	574	575
5 Foxx	Y	Y	Y	Y	Y
6 Coble	Y	Y	Y	Y	Y
7 McIntyre	Y	Y	N	Y	Y
8 Kissell	Y	N	Y	N	Y
9 Myrick	Y	Y	Y	Y	?
10 McHenry	Y	Y	Y	Y	Y
11 Shuler	Y	Y	Y	Y	Y
12 Watt	Y	N	N	N	Y
13 Miller	Y	N	N	N	Y
NORTH DAKOTA					
AL Berg	Y	?	?	?	?
OHIO					
1 Chabot	Y	Y	Y	Y	Y
2 Schmidt	Y	Y	Y	Y	Y
3 Turner	Y	Y	Y	Y	Y
4 Jordan	N	Y	Y	Y	Y
5 Latta	Y	Y	Y	Y	Y
6 Johnson	Y	Y	Y	Y	Y
7 Austria	Y	Y	Y	Y	Y
8 Boehner					
9 Kaptur	Y	N	N	N	Y
10 Kucinich	Y	N	N	N	Y
11 Fudge	Y	N	N	N	Y
12 Tiberi	Y	Y	Y	Y	Y
13 Sutton	Y	N	N	N	Y
14 LaTourette	Y	Y	Y	Y	Y
15 Stivers	Y	Y	Y	Y	Y
16 Renacci	Y	Y	Y	Y	Y
17 Ryan	Y	N	N	N	Y
18 Gibbs	Y	Y	Y	Y	Y
OKLAHOMA					
1 Sullivan	?	Y	Y	Y	Y
2 Boren	Y	Y	N	N	Y
3 Lucas	Y	Y	Y	Y	Y
4 Cole	Y	Y	Y	Y	Y
5 Lankford	N	Y	Y	Y	Y
OREGON					
1 Bonamici	Y	N	N	N	Y
2 Walden	Y	Y	Y	Y	Y
3 Blumenauer	Y	N	N	N	Y
4 DeFazio	Y	N	N	N	Y
5 Schrader	Y	N	N	N	Y
PENNSYLVANIA					
1 Brady	Y	N	N	N	Y
2 Fattah	Y	N	N	N	Y
3 Kelly	Y	Y	Y	Y	Y
4 Altmire	Y	N	N	N	Y
5 Thompson	Y	Y	Y	Y	Y
6 Gerlach	Y	Y	Y	Y	Y
7 Meehan	Y	Y	Y	Y	Y
8 Fitzpatrick	Y	Y	Y	Y	Y
9 Shuster	Y	Y	Y	Y	Y
10 Marino	Y	Y	Y	Y	Y
11 Barletta	Y	Y	Y	Y	Y
12 Critz	Y	N	N	N	Y
13 Schwartz	Y	N	N	N	Y
14 Doyle	Y	N	N	N	Y
15 Dent	Y	Y	Y	Y	Y
16 Pitts	N	Y	Y	Y	Y
17 Holden	Y	N	N	N	Y
18 Murphy	Y	Y	Y	Y	Y
19 Platts	Y	Y	Y	Y	Y
RHODE ISLAND					
1 Cicilline	Y	N	N	N	Y
2 Langevin	Y	N	N	N	Y
SOUTH CAROLINA					
1 Scott	N	Y	Y	Y	Y
2 Wilson	N	Y	Y	Y	Y
3 Duncan	N	Y	Y	Y	Y
4 Gowdy	N	Y	Y	Y	Y
5 Mulvaney	N	Y	Y	Y	Y
6 Clyburn	Y	N	N	N	Y
SOUTH DAKOTA					
AL Noem	Y	Y	Y	Y	Y
TENNESSEE					
1 Roe	Y	Y	Y	Y	Y
2 Duncan	Y	Y	Y	Y	Y
3 Fleischmann	Y	Y	Y	Y	Y
4 DesJarlais	Y	Y	Y	Y	Y
5 Cooper	Y	N	N	N	Y
6 Black	Y	Y	Y	Y	Y
7 Blackburn	Y	Y	Y	Y	Y
8 Fincher	Y	Y	Y	Y	Y
9 Cohen	Y	N	N	N	Y

	571	572	573	574	575
TEXAS					
1 Gohmert	N	N	N	Y	Y
2 Poe	N	Y	Y	Y	Y
3 Johnson, S.	Y	Y	Y	Y	Y
4 Hall	N	Y	Y	Y	Y
5 Hensarling	N	Y	Y	Y	Y
6 Barton	Y	Y	Y	Y	Y
7 Culberson	N	Y	Y	Y	Y
8 Brady	N	Y	Y	Y	Y
9 Green, A.	Y	N	N	N	Y
10 McCaul	Y	Y	Y	Y	Y
11 Conaway	N	Y	Y	Y	Y
12 Granger	N	Y	Y	Y	Y
13 Thornberry	N	Y	Y	Y	Y
14 Paul	?	Y	Y	Y	N
15 Hinojosa	Y	N	N	N	Y
16 Reyes	Y	N	N	N	Y
17 Flores	N	Y	Y	Y	Y
18 Jackson Lee	Y	N	N	N	Y
19 Neugebauer	N	Y	Y	Y	Y
20 Gonzalez	Y	N	N	N	Y
21 Smith	Y	Y	Y	Y	Y
22 Olson	Y	Y	Y	Y	Y
23 Canseco	N	Y	Y	Y	Y
24 Marchant	N	Y	Y	Y	Y
25 Doggett	Y	N	N	N	Y
26 Burgess	N	Y	Y	Y	Y
27 Farenthold	N	Y	Y	Y	Y
28 Cuellar	Y	N	N	N	Y
29 Green, G.	Y	N	N	N	Y
30 Johnson, E.	Y	N	N	N	Y
31 Carter	N	Y	Y	Y	Y
32 Sessions	N	Y	Y	Y	Y
UTAH					
1 Bishop	N	Y	Y	Y	Y
2 Matheson	Y	Y	N	N	Y
3 Chaffetz	Y	Y	Y	Y	Y
VERMONT					
AL Welch	Y	N	?	N	Y
VIRGINIA					
1 Wittman	Y	Y	Y	Y	Y
2 Rigell	Y	Y	Y	Y	Y
3 Scott	Y	N	N	N	Y
4 Forbes	Y	Y	Y	Y	Y
5 Hurt	Y	Y	Y	Y	Y
6 Goodlatte	Y	Y	Y	Y	Y
7 Cantor	Y	Y	Y	Y	Y
8 Moran	Y	N	N	N	Y
9 Griffith	Y	Y	Y	Y	Y
10 Wolf	Y	Y	Y	Y	Y
11 Connolly	Y	N	N	N	Y
WASHINGTON					
1 Vacant					
2 Larsen	Y	N	N	N	Y
3 Herrera Beutler	Y	Y	Y	Y	Y
4 Hastings	Y	Y	Y	Y	Y
5 McMorris Rodgers	Y	Y	Y	Y	Y
6 Dicks	?	N	N	N	Y
7 McDermott	Y	N	N	N	Y
8 Reichert	Y	Y	Y	Y	Y
9 Smith	Y	N	N	N	Y
WEST VIRGINIA					
1 McKinley	Y	Y	Y	Y	Y
2 Capito	Y	Y	Y	Y	Y
3 Rahall	Y	N	N	N	Y
WISCONSIN					
1 Ryan	?	?	?	?	?
2 Baldwin	Y	N	N	N	Y
3 Kind	Y	N	N	N	Y
4 Moore	Y	N	N	N	?
5 Sensenbrenner	N	Y	Y	Y	Y
6 Petri	Y	Y	Y	Y	Y
7 Duffy	Y	Y	Y	Y	Y
8 Ribble	Y	Y	Y	Y	Y
WYOMING					
AL Lummis	N	Y	Y	Y	Y

IN THE HOUSE | By Vote Number

576. **HR 6365. Sequestration Replacement/Recommit.** Van Hollen, D-Md., motion to recommit the bill to the House Budget Committee and report it back immediately with an amendment that would nullify automatic spending reductions required by the 2011 debt limit law, provided that subsequent deficit reduction is enacted that equals or exceeds the sequestration's deficit reduction over 10 years and that would allow upper-income tax cuts to expire. Motion rejected 170-247: R 0-234; D 170-13. Sept. 13, 2012.

577. **HR 6365. Sequestration Replacement/Passage.** Passage of the bill that would direct the president to send to Congress by Oct. 15, 2012, legislation that would replace the automatic discretionary spending cuts under the sequester currently scheduled to take effect Jan. 2, 2013. The measure would specify that the president's plan replace the automatic cuts with other spending cuts, and not with revenues. Once replacement cuts are enacted, it would reduce the cap on discretionary spending for fiscal 2013 by $19 billion and eliminate the separate caps for defense and non-defense discretionary spending, which would allow Congress to approve higher levels of defense spending. Passed 223-196: R 222-12; D 1-184. A "nay" was a vote in support of the president's position. Sept. 13, 2012.

578. **H J Res 117. Continuing Resolution/Recommit.** Barber, D-Ariz., motion to recommit the bill to the House Appropriations Committee and report it back immediately with an amendment that would add a provision to fully fund military, Reserve and National Guard personnel for the full fiscal year. The motion would also extend coverage of disability examinations and the treatment of and additional services for homeless and mentally ill veterans. Motion rejected 189-232: R 3-232; D 186-0. Sept. 13, 2012.

579. **H J Res 117. Continuing Resolution/Passage.** Passage of the joint resolution that would provide continuing appropriations for the federal government through March 27, 2013, at an annualized rate of $1.047 trillion in discretionary spending for regular appropriations. The measure would increase funding for most federal programs and agencies by 0.6 percent, with higher levels for certain programs, such as cybersecurity and wildfire suppression. It also would provide nearly $88.5 billion in war funding and $6.4 billion in advance disaster relief funds. Passed 329-91: R 165-70; D 164-21. A "yea" was a vote in support of the president's position. Sept. 13, 2012.

580. **S 3245. Immigration and Visa Program Renewal/Passage.** Smith, R-Texas, motion to suspend the rules and pass the bill that would renew for three years expiring immigration and visa programs, including E-Verify, an online workplace verification system used to determine a job applicant's immigration status. Motion agreed to 412-3: R 228-3; D 184-0. A two-thirds majority of those present and voting (277 in this case) is required for passage under suspension of the rules. Sept. 13, 2012.

	576	577	578	579	580
ALABAMA					
1 **Bonner**	N	Y	N	Y	Y
2 **Roby**	N	Y	N	Y	Y
3 **Rogers**	N	Y	N	Y	Y
4 **Aderholt**	N	Y	N	Y	Y
5 **Brooks**	N	Y	N	N	Y
6 **Bachus**	?	Y	N	Y	Y
7 Sewell	Y	N	Y	Y	Y
ALASKA					
AL **Young**	N	Y	N	Y	Y
ARIZONA					
1 **Gosar**	N	Y	N	N	Y
2 **Franks**	N	Y	N	N	Y
3 **Quayle**	N	Y	N	N	Y
4 Pastor	Y	N	Y	Y	Y
5 **Schweikert**	N	Y	N	N	Y
6 **Flake**	N	Y	N	N	Y
7 Grijalva	Y	N	Y	Y	Y
8 Barber	Y	N	Y	Y	Y
ARKANSAS					
1 **Crawford**	N	Y	N	Y	Y
2 **Griffin**	N	Y	N	Y	Y
3 **Womack**	N	Y	N	Y	Y
4 Ross	?	?	?	?	?
CALIFORNIA					
1 Thompson	Y	N	Y	Y	Y
2 **Herger**	?	?	?	?	?
3 **Lungren**	N	Y	N	Y	Y
4 **McClintock**	N	N	N	N	Y
5 Matsui	Y	N	Y	Y	Y
6 Woolsey	Y	N	Y	N	Y
7 Miller, George	Y	N	Y	?	Y
8 Pelosi	Y	N	Y	Y	Y
9 Lee	Y	N	Y	N	Y
10 Garamendi	?	?	Y	Y	Y
11 McNerney	Y	N	Y	Y	Y
12 Speier	Y	N	Y	Y	Y
13 Stark	Y	N	Y	N	Y
14 Eshoo	Y	N	Y	Y	?
15 Honda	Y	N	Y	Y	Y
16 Lofgren	Y	N	Y	Y	Y
17 Farr	Y	N	Y	Y	Y
18 Vacant					
19 **Denham**	N	Y	N	Y	Y
20 Costa	Y	N	Y	Y	Y
21 **Nunes**	N	Y	N	Y	Y
22 **McCarthy**	N	Y	N	Y	Y
23 Capps	Y	N	Y	Y	Y
24 **Gallegly**	N	Y	N	Y	Y
25 **McKeon**	N	Y	N	N	Y
26 **Dreier**	N	Y	N	Y	Y
27 Sherman	Y	N	Y	Y	Y
28 Berman	Y	N	Y	Y	Y
29 Schiff	Y	N	Y	Y	Y
30 Waxman	Y	N	Y	Y	Y
31 Becerra	Y	N	Y	Y	Y
32 Chu	Y	N	Y	Y	Y
33 Bass	Y	N	Y	Y	Y
34 Roybal-Allard	Y	N	Y	Y	Y
35 Waters	Y	N	Y	Y	Y
36 Hahn	Y	N	Y	Y	Y
37 Richardson	Y	N	Y	Y	Y
38 Napolitano	Y	N	Y	Y	Y
39 Sánchez, Linda	Y	N	Y	Y	Y
40 **Royce**	N	Y	N	Y	Y
41 **Lewis**	N	Y	N	Y	Y
42 **Miller, Gary**	N	Y	N	N	Y
43 Baca	Y	N	Y	Y	Y
44 **Calvert**	N	Y	N	Y	Y
45 **Bono Mack**	N	Y	N	N	Y
46 **Rohrabacher**	N	Y	N	Y	Y
47 Sanchez, Loretta	Y	N	Y	Y	Y
48 **Campbell**	N	Y	N	Y	Y
49 **Issa**	N	Y	N	Y	Y
50 **Bilbray**	N	Y	N	Y	Y
51 Filner	Y	N	Y	Y	Y
52 **Hunter**	N	Y	N	Y	Y
53 Davis	Y	N	Y	Y	Y

	576	577	578	579	580
COLORADO					
1 DeGette	Y	N	Y	Y	Y
2 Polis	Y	N	Y	Y	Y
3 **Tipton**	N	Y	N	Y	Y
4 **Gardner**	N	Y	N	N	Y
5 **Lamborn**	N	Y	N	N	Y
6 **Coffman**	N	Y	N	Y	Y
7 Perlmutter	Y	N	Y	Y	Y
CONNECTICUT					
1 Larson	Y	N	Y	Y	Y
2 Courtney	Y	N	Y	Y	Y
3 DeLauro	Y	N	Y	Y	Y
4 Himes	Y	N	Y	Y	Y
5 Murphy	Y	N	Y	Y	Y
DELAWARE					
AL Carney	Y	N	Y	Y	Y
FLORIDA					
1 **Miller**	N	Y	N	N	Y
2 **Southerland**	N	Y	N	Y	Y
3 Brown	Y	N	Y	Y	Y
4 **Crenshaw**	N	Y	N	N	Y
5 **Nugent**	N	Y	N	Y	Y
6 **Stearns**	N	Y	N	N	Y
7 **Mica**	N	Y	N	Y	Y
8 **Webster**	N	Y	N	Y	Y
9 **Bilirakis**	N	Y	N	Y	Y
10 **Young**	N	Y	N	Y	Y
11 Castor	Y	N	Y	Y	Y
12 **Ross**	N	Y	N	N	Y
13 **Buchanan**	N	Y	N	Y	Y
14 **Mack**	N	Y	N	N	Y
15 **Posey**	N	Y	N	N	Y
16 **Rooney**	N	Y	N	Y	Y
17 Wilson	Y	N	Y	Y	Y
18 **Ros-Lehtinen**	N	Y	N	Y	Y
19 Deutch	Y	N	Y	Y	Y
20 Wasserman Schultz	Y	N	Y	Y	Y
21 **Diaz-Balart**	N	Y	N	Y	Y
22 **West**	N	Y	N	Y	Y
23 Hastings	Y	N	Y	Y	Y
24 **Adams**	N	Y	N	N	Y
25 **Rivera**	N	Y	N	Y	Y
GEORGIA					
1 **Kingston**	N	Y	N	Y	Y
2 Bishop	Y	N	Y	Y	Y
3 **Westmoreland**	N	Y	N	Y	Y
4 Johnson	?	N	Y	Y	Y
5 Lewis	Y	N	Y	Y	Y
6 **Price**	N	Y	N	Y	Y
7 **Woodall**	N	Y	N	Y	Y
8 **Scott, A.**	N	Y	N	Y	Y
9 **Graves**	N	Y	N	Y	Y
10 **Broun**	?	?	?	?	?
11 **Gingrey**	N	Y	N	N	Y
12 Barrow	N	N	Y	Y	Y
13 Scott, D.	Y	N	Y	Y	Y
HAWAII					
1 Hanabusa	Y	N	Y	Y	Y
2 Hirono	Y	N	Y	Y	Y
IDAHO					
1 **Labrador**	N	N	N	N	Y
2 **Simpson**	N	Y	N	N	Y
ILLINOIS					
1 Rush	Y	N	Y	N	Y
2 Jackson	?	?	?	?	?
3 Lipinski	N	N	Y	Y	Y
4 Gutierrez	Y	N	Y	Y	Y
5 Quigley	Y	N	Y	Y	Y
6 **Roskam**	N	Y	N	Y	Y
7 Davis	Y	N	Y	N	Y
8 **Walsh**	N	Y	N	N	Y
9 Schakowsky	Y	N	Y	Y	Y
10 **Dold**	N	Y	N	Y	Y
11 **Kinzinger**	N	Y	N	Y	Y
12 Costello	Y	N	Y	N	Y
13 **Biggert**	N	Y	N	Y	Y
14 **Hultgren**	N	Y	N	Y	Y
15 Johnson	N	N	N	N	Y

	576	577	578	579	580
16 Manzullo	N	Y	N	Y	Y
17 Schilling	N	Y	N	N	Y
18 Schock	N	Y	N	Y	Y
19 Shimkus	N	Y	N	Y	Y
INDIANA					
1 Visclosky	Y	N	Y	Y	Y
2 Donnelly	N	Y	Y	Y	Y
3 Stutzman	N	Y	N	N	Y
4 Rokita	N	Y	N	Y	Y
5 Burton	N	?	N	N	Y
6 Pence	N	Y	N	Y	Y
7 Carson	Y	N	Y	Y	Y
8 Bucshon	N	Y	N	Y	Y
9 Young	N	Y	N	Y	Y
IOWA					
1 Braley	Y	N	Y	Y	Y
2 Loebsack	Y	N	Y	Y	Y
3 Boswell	Y	N	Y	Y	Y
4 Latham	N	Y	N	Y	Y
5 King	N	Y	N	Y	Y
KANSAS					
1 Huelskamp	N	Y	N	N	Y
2 Jenkins	N	Y	N	Y	Y
3 Yoder	N	Y	N	N	Y
4 Pompeo	N	Y	N	Y	Y
KENTUCKY					
1 Whitfield	N	Y	N	Y	Y
2 Guthrie	N	Y	N	Y	Y
3 Yarmuth	Y	N	Y	Y	Y
4 Vacant					
5 Rogers	N	Y	N	Y	Y
6 Chandler	N	N	Y	Y	?
LOUISIANA					
1 Scalise	N	Y	N	Y	Y
2 Richmond	Y	N	Y	Y	Y
3 Landry	N	Y	N	N	Y
4 Fleming	N	Y	N	N	Y
5 Alexander	N	Y	N	Y	Y
6 Cassidy	N	Y	N	Y	Y
7 Boustany	N	Y	N	N	Y
MAINE					
1 Pingree	N	N	Y	Y	Y
2 Michaud	Y	N	Y	Y	Y
MARYLAND					
1 Harris	N	Y	N	Y	Y
2 Ruppersberger	Y	N	Y	Y	Y
3 Sarbanes	Y	N	Y	Y	Y
4 Edwards	Y	N	Y	Y	Y
5 Hoyer	Y	N	Y	Y	Y
6 Bartlett	N	Y	N	Y	Y
7 Cummings	Y	N	Y	Y	Y
8 Van Hollen	Y	N	Y	Y	Y
MASSACHUSETTS					
1 Olver	Y	N	Y	N	Y
2 Neal	Y	N	Y	Y	Y
3 McGovern	Y	N	Y	Y	Y
4 Frank	Y	N	Y	N	Y
5 Tsongas	Y	N	Y	N	Y
6 Tierney	Y	N	Y	Y	Y
7 Markey	Y	N	Y	Y	Y
8 Capuano	Y	N	Y	N	Y
9 Lynch	Y	N	Y	Y	Y
10 Keating	Y	N	Y	Y	Y
MICHIGAN					
1 Benishek	N	Y	N	Y	Y
2 Huizenga	N	Y	N	Y	Y
3 Amash	N	N	N	N	N
4 Camp	N	Y	N	Y	Y
5 Kildee	Y	N	Y	Y	Y
6 Upton	N	Y	N	Y	Y
7 Walberg	N	Y	N	Y	Y
8 Rogers	N	Y	N	Y	Y
9 Peters	N	N	Y	Y	Y
10 Miller	N	Y	N	Y	Y
11 Vacant					
12 Levin	Y	N	Y	Y	Y
13 Clarke	Y	N	Y	Y	Y
14 Conyers	Y	N	Y	N	Y
15 Dingell	Y	N	Y	Y	Y
MINNESOTA					
1 Walz	Y	N	Y	Y	Y
2 Kline	N	Y	N	Y	Y
3 Paulsen	N	Y	N	Y	Y
4 McCollum	Y	N	Y	Y	Y

	576	577	578	579	580
5 Ellison	Y	N	Y	Y	Y
6 Bachmann	N	Y	N	N	Y
7 Peterson	N	N	Y	N	Y
8 Cravaack	N	Y	N	Y	Y
MISSISSIPPI					
1 Nunnelee	N	Y	N	Y	Y
2 Thompson	Y	N	Y	Y	Y
3 Harper	N	Y	N	Y	Y
4 Palazzo	N	Y	N	Y	Y
MISSOURI					
1 Clay	Y	N	Y	Y	Y
2 Akin	?	?	?	?	?
3 Carnahan	Y	N	Y	Y	Y
4 Hartzler	N	Y	N	N	Y
5 Cleaver	Y	N	Y	Y	Y
6 Graves	N	Y	N	N	Y
7 Long	N	Y	N	Y	Y
8 Emerson	N	Y	N	N	Y
9 Luetkemeyer	N	Y	N	Y	Y
MONTANA					
AL Rehberg	N	Y	N	N	Y
NEBRASKA					
1 Fortenberry	N	Y	N	Y	Y
2 Terry	N	Y	N	Y	Y
3 Smith	N	Y	N	Y	Y
NEVADA					
1 Berkley	Y	N	Y	Y	Y
2 Amodei	N	Y	N	Y	Y
3 Heck	N	Y	N	Y	Y
NEW HAMPSHIRE					
1 Guinta	N	Y	N	Y	Y
2 Bass	N	N	N	Y	Y
NEW JERSEY					
1 Andrews	Y	N	Y	Y	Y
2 LoBiondo	N	Y	N	Y	Y
3 Runyan	N	Y	N	Y	Y
4 Smith	N	Y	N	Y	Y
5 Garrett	N	Y	N	Y	Y
6 Pallone	Y	N	Y	Y	Y
7 Lance	N	Y	N	Y	Y
8 Pascrell	Y	N	Y	Y	Y
9 Rothman	Y	N	Y	Y	Y
10 Vacant					
11 Frelinghuysen	N	Y	N	Y	Y
12 Holt	Y	N	Y	Y	Y
13 Sires	Y	N	Y	Y	Y
NEW MEXICO					
1 Heinrich	Y	N	Y	Y	Y
2 Pearce	N	Y	N	Y	Y
3 Luján	Y	N	Y	Y	Y
NEW YORK					
1 Bishop	Y	N	Y	Y	Y
2 Israel	Y	N	Y	Y	Y
3 King	?	?	?	?	?
4 McCarthy	Y	N	Y	Y	Y
5 Ackerman	Y	N	Y	Y	Y
6 Meeks	Y	N	Y	Y	Y
7 Crowley	Y	N	Y	Y	Y
8 Nadler	Y	N	Y	Y	Y
9 Turner	N	Y	N	Y	Y
10 Towns	?	?	?	?	?
11 Clarke	Y	N	Y	Y	Y
12 Velázquez	Y	N	Y	Y	Y
13 Grimm	N	Y	N	Y	?
14 Maloney	Y	N	Y	Y	Y
15 Rangel	Y	N	Y	Y	Y
16 Serrano	Y	N	Y	Y	Y
17 Engel	Y	N	Y	Y	Y
18 Lowey	Y	N	Y	Y	Y
19 Hayworth	N	Y	N	Y	Y
20 Gibson	N	Y	N	Y	Y
21 Tonko	Y	N	Y	Y	Y
22 Hinchey	Y	N	Y	Y	Y
23 Owens	Y	N	Y	Y	Y
24 Hanna	N	Y	N	Y	Y
25 Buerkle	N	Y	N	Y	?
26 Hochul	Y	N	Y	Y	Y
27 Higgins	Y	N	Y	Y	Y
28 Slaughter	Y	N	Y	Y	Y
29 Reed	N	Y	N	Y	Y
NORTH CAROLINA					
1 Butterfield	Y	N	Y	Y	Y
2 Ellmers	N	Y	N	Y	Y
3 Jones	N	N	Y	N	Y
4 Price	Y	N	Y	Y	Y

	576	577	578	579	580
5 Foxx	N	Y	N	N	Y
6 Coble	N	Y	N	Y	Y
7 McIntyre	N	N	Y	N	Y
8 Kissell	N	N	Y	N	Y
9 Myrick	N	Y	N	Y	Y
10 McHenry	N	Y	N	Y	Y
11 Shuler	N	N	Y	N	Y
12 Watt	Y	N	Y	Y	Y
13 Miller	Y	N	Y	Y	Y
NORTH DAKOTA					
AL Berg	N	Y	N	N	Y
OHIO					
1 Chabot	N	Y	N	N	Y
2 Schmidt	N	Y	N	N	Y
3 Turner	N	Y	N	N	Y
4 Jordan	N	Y	N	N	Y
5 Latta	N	Y	N	Y	Y
6 Johnson	N	Y	N	Y	Y
7 Austria	N	Y	N	Y	Y
8 Boehner					
9 Kaptur	Y	N	Y	Y	Y
10 Kucinich	Y	N	Y	N	Y
11 Fudge	Y	N	Y	Y	Y
12 Tiberi	N	Y	N	Y	Y
13 Sutton	Y	N	Y	Y	Y
14 LaTourette	N	N	N	Y	Y
15 Stivers	N	Y	N	Y	Y
16 Renacci	N	Y	N	Y	Y
17 Ryan	Y	N	Y	Y	Y
18 Gibbs	N	Y	N	Y	Y
OKLAHOMA					
1 Sullivan	N	Y	N	Y	Y
2 Boren	N	N	Y	Y	Y
3 Lucas	N	Y	N	Y	Y
4 Cole	N	Y	N	Y	?
5 Lankford	N	Y	N	Y	Y
OREGON					
1 Bonamici	Y	N	Y	Y	Y
2 Walden	N	Y	N	Y	Y
3 Blumenauer	?	?	?	?	?
4 DeFazio	Y	N	Y	Y	Y
5 Schrader	Y	N	Y	N	Y
PENNSYLVANIA					
1 Brady	Y	N	Y	Y	Y
2 Fattah	Y	N	Y	Y	Y
3 Kelly	N	Y	N	Y	Y
4 Altmire	N	N	Y	N	Y
5 Thompson	N	Y	N	Y	Y
6 Gerlach	N	Y	N	Y	Y
7 Meehan	N	Y	N	Y	Y
8 Fitzpatrick	N	Y	N	Y	Y
9 Shuster	N	Y	N	Y	Y
10 Marino	N	Y	N	Y	Y
11 Barletta	N	Y	N	Y	Y
12 Critz	?	N	Y	Y	Y
13 Schwartz	Y	N	Y	Y	Y
14 Doyle	Y	N	Y	Y	Y
15 Dent	N	Y	N	Y	Y
16 Pitts	N	Y	N	Y	Y
17 Holden	N	Y	N	Y	Y
18 Murphy	N	Y	N	Y	Y
19 Platts	N	Y	Y	Y	Y
RHODE ISLAND					
1 Cicilline	Y	N	Y	Y	Y
2 Langevin	Y	N	Y	Y	Y
SOUTH CAROLINA					
1 Scott	N	Y	N	N	Y
2 Wilson	N	Y	N	N	Y
3 Duncan	N	Y	N	N	Y
4 Gowdy	N	Y	N	N	Y
5 Mulvaney	N	Y	N	N	Y
6 Clyburn	Y	N	Y	Y	Y
SOUTH DAKOTA					
AL Noem	N	Y	N	N	Y
TENNESSEE					
1 Roe	N	Y	N	Y	Y
2 Duncan	N	N	N	Y	Y
3 Fleischmann	N	Y	N	Y	Y
4 DesJarlais	N	Y	N	N	Y
5 Cooper	Y	N	Y	Y	Y
6 Black	N	Y	N	Y	Y
7 Blackburn	N	Y	N	Y	Y
8 Fincher	N	Y	N	N	Y
9 Cohen	Y	N	Y	Y	Y

	576	577	578	579	580
TEXAS					
1 Gohmert	N	Y	N	N	N
2 Poe	N	Y	N	N	Y
3 Johnson, S.	N	Y	N	Y	Y
4 Hall	N	Y	N	N	Y
5 Hensarling	N	Y	N	Y	Y
6 Barton	N	N	N	N	Y
7 Culberson	N	Y	N	Y	Y
8 Brady	N	Y	N	Y	Y
9 Green, A.	Y	N	Y	Y	Y
10 McCaul	N	Y	N	Y	Y
11 Conaway	N	Y	N	Y	Y
12 Granger	N	Y	N	Y	Y
13 Thornberry	N	Y	N	Y	Y
14 Paul	N	N	N	N	N
15 Hinojosa	Y	N	Y	Y	Y
16 Reyes	Y	N	Y	Y	Y
17 Flores	N	Y	N	N	Y
18 Jackson Lee	Y	N	Y	Y	Y
19 Neugebauer	N	Y	N	N	Y
20 Gonzalez	Y	N	Y	Y	Y
21 Smith	N	Y	N	Y	Y
22 Olson	N	Y	N	Y	Y
23 Canseco	N	Y	N	N	Y
24 Marchant	N	Y	N	N	Y
25 Doggett	Y	N	Y	Y	Y
26 Burgess	N	Y	N	Y	Y
27 Farenthold	N	Y	N	Y	Y
28 Cuellar	Y	N	Y	Y	Y
29 Green, G.	Y	N	Y	Y	Y
30 Johnson, E.	Y	N	Y	Y	Y
31 Carter	N	Y	N	Y	Y
32 Sessions	N	Y	N	Y	Y
UTAH					
1 Bishop	N	Y	N	Y	Y
2 Matheson	N	N	Y	N	Y
3 Chaffetz	N	Y	N	Y	Y
VERMONT					
AL Welch	Y	N	Y	Y	Y
VIRGINIA					
1 Wittman	N	Y	N	N	Y
2 Rigell	N	Y	N	N	Y
3 Scott	Y	N	Y	Y	Y
4 Forbes	N	Y	N	N	Y
5 Hurt	N	Y	N	Y	Y
6 Goodlatte	N	Y	N	Y	Y
7 Cantor	N	Y	N	Y	Y
8 Moran	Y	N	Y	Y	Y
9 Griffith	N	Y	N	N	Y
10 Wolf	N	N	N	N	Y
11 Connolly	Y	N	Y	Y	Y
WASHINGTON					
1 Vacant					
2 Larsen	Y	N	Y	Y	Y
3 Herrera Beutler	N	N	N	Y	Y
4 Hastings	N	Y	N	Y	Y
5 McMorris Rodgers	N	Y	N	Y	Y
6 Dicks	Y	N	Y	Y	Y
7 McDermott	Y	N	Y	N	Y
8 Reichert	N	Y	N	Y	Y
9 Smith	Y	N	Y	Y	Y
WEST VIRGINIA					
1 McKinley	N	Y	N	Y	Y
2 Capito	N	Y	N	Y	Y
3 Rahall	Y	N	Y	Y	Y
WISCONSIN					
1 Ryan	N	Y	N	Y	?
2 Baldwin	Y	N	Y	Y	Y
3 Kind	Y	N	Y	Y	Y
4 Moore	Y	N	Y	Y	Y
5 Sensenbrenner	N	Y	N	Y	Y
6 Petri	N	Y	N	N	Y
7 Duffy	N	Y	N	Y	Y
8 Ribble	N	Y	N	Y	Y
WYOMING					
AL Lummis	N	Y	N	N	Y

IN THE HOUSE | By Vote Number

581. HR 6213. Energy Department Loan Guarantees/Including Administration Testimony. DeGette, D-Colo., amendment that would modify the findings language in the bill to reflect testimony provided by administration officials regarding the decision-making process surrounding the Solyndra loan guarantee. The amendment would also add a section on the estimated number of jobs created by the loan guarantee program. Rejected in Committee of the Whole 169-238: R 0-228; D 169-10. Sept. 14, 2012.

582. HR 6213. Energy Department Loan Guarantees/New Loan Guarantees. Waxman, D-Calif., amendment that would strike language prohibiting the Energy Department from issuing new loan guarantees after Dec. 31, 2011. Rejected in Committee of the Whole 170-231: R 5-219; D 165-12. Sept. 14, 2012.

583. HR 6213. Energy Department Loan Guarantees/Recommit. Markey, D-Mass., motion to recommit the bill to the Energy and Commerce Committee and report it back immediately with an amendment that would prohibit loan guarantees unless the Energy Department certifies that at least 75 percent of the materials used for the construction of new energy loan projects are produced in the United States, unless it is not feasible to obtain them domestically. Any such project would also have to be located in the United States. The amendment also would make the bill's prohibition on new loan guarantees contingent on extension of the wind energy production tax credit. Motion rejected 175-234: R 0-228; D 175-6. Sept. 14, 2012.

584. HR 6213. Energy Department Loan Guarantees/Passage. Passage of the bill that would prohibit the Energy Department from issuing new loan guarantees for energy projects. Applications submitted before Dec. 31, 2011, would still be eligible for loans. For any pending loan guarantee applications submitted prior to that date, the Treasury Department would be required to review the loan's financial terms and conditions, and the Energy Department would be required to report to Congress within 60 days of issuing the guarantee. Passed 245-161: R 223-4; D 22-157. Sept. 14, 2012.

585. HR 5044. Deceased-Veterans Loan Exemption/Passage. Johnson, R-Texas, motion to suspend the rules and pass the bill that would exclude forgiven student loans held by deceased veterans from taxable income. The exclusion would apply to forgiven loans occurring after Oct. 7, 2001, and families would have up to one year after enactment to file refunds. The bill would clarify that federal employee retirement savings in the Thrift Savings Fund would remain taxable and collected revenue would go towards deficit reduction. Motion agreed to 400-0: R 226-0; D 174-0. A two-thirds majority of those present and voting (267 in this case) is required for passage under suspension of the rules. Sept. 19, 2012.

586. HR 5912. Political-Convention Funding/Passage. Lungren, R-Calif., motion to suspend the rules and pass the bill that would prohibit the use of the Presidential Election Campaign Fund for party conventions for elections held after 2012. Motion agreed to 310-95: R 225-0; D 85-95. A two-thirds majority of those present and voting (270 in this case) is required for passage under suspension of the rules. Sept. 19, 2012.

	581	582	583	584	585	586
ALABAMA						
1 Bonner	N	N	N	Y	Y	Y
2 Roby	N	N	N	Y	Y	Y
3 Rogers	N	N	N	Y	Y	Y
4 Aderholt	N	N	N	Y	Y	Y
5 Brooks	N	N	N	Y	Y	Y
6 Bachus	N	N	N	Y	Y	Y
7 Sewell	Y	Y	Y	N	Y	Y
ALASKA						
AL Young	N	N	N	Y	Y	Y
ARIZONA						
1 Gosar	N	N	N	Y	Y	Y
2 Franks	N	N	N	Y	Y	Y
3 Quayle	N	N	N	Y	Y	Y
4 Pastor	Y	Y	Y	N	Y	Y
5 Schweikert	N	N	N	Y	Y	Y
6 Flake	N	N	N	Y	Y	Y
7 Grijalva	Y	Y	Y	N	Y	N
8 Barber	Y	Y	Y	N	Y	Y
ARKANSAS						
1 Crawford	N	N	N	Y	Y	Y
2 Griffin	N	N	N	Y	Y	Y
3 Womack	N	N	N	Y	Y	Y
4 Ross	–	–	+	+	?	?
CALIFORNIA						
1 Thompson	Y	Y	Y	N	?	N
2 Herger	?	?	?	?	?	Y
3 Lungren	N	N	N	Y	Y	Y
4 McClintock	N	N	N	Y	Y	Y
5 Matsui	Y	Y	Y	N	Y	N
6 Woolsey	Y	Y	Y	N	Y	N
7 Miller, George	Y	Y	Y	N	Y	Y
8 Pelosi	Y	Y	Y	N	Y	N
9 Lee	Y	Y	Y	N	+	–
10 Garamendi	Y	Y	Y	Y	Y	Y
11 McNerney	Y	Y	Y	Y	Y	Y
12 Speier	?	?	?	?	?	?
13 Stark	Y	Y	Y	N	Y	N
14 Eshoo	Y	Y	Y	N	Y	N
15 Honda	Y	Y	Y	N	Y	N
16 Lofgren	Y	Y	Y	N	Y	Y
17 Farr	Y	Y	Y	N	Y	N
18 Vacant						
19 Denham	N	N	N	Y	Y	Y
20 Costa	Y	Y	Y	N	Y	Y
21 Nunes	N	N	N	Y	Y	Y
22 McCarthy	N	N	N	Y	Y	Y
23 Capps	Y	Y	Y	N	Y	N
24 Gallegly	N	N	N	Y	?	?
25 McKeon	N	N	N	Y	Y	Y
26 Dreier	N	N	N	Y	Y	Y
27 Sherman	Y	Y	Y	N	Y	Y
28 Berman	Y	Y	Y	N	Y	Y
29 Schiff	Y	Y	Y	N	Y	Y
30 Waxman	Y	Y	Y	N	Y	N
31 Becerra	Y	Y	Y	N	Y	N
32 Chu	Y	Y	Y	N	Y	N
33 Bass	Y	Y	Y	N	Y	N
34 Roybal-Allard	Y	Y	Y	N	?	N
35 Waters	Y	Y	Y	N	Y	N
36 Hahn	Y	Y	Y	N	Y	N
37 Richardson	Y	Y	Y	N	Y	N
38 Napolitano	Y	?	Y	N	Y	N
39 Sánchez, Linda	Y	Y	Y	N	Y	N
40 Royce	N	N	N	Y	Y	Y
41 Lewis	N	N	N	Y	Y	?
42 Miller, Gary	N	N	N	Y	Y	Y
43 Baca	Y	Y	Y	N	Y	N
44 Calvert	N	N	N	Y	Y	Y
45 Bono Mack	N	N	N	Y	Y	Y
46 Rohrabacher	N	N	N	Y	Y	Y
47 Sanchez, Loretta	?	?	?	?	Y	Y
48 Campbell	N	N	N	Y	?	?
49 Issa	N	N	N	Y	Y	Y
50 Bilbray	N	Y	N	N	Y	Y
51 Filner	Y	Y	Y	N	?	–
52 Hunter	N	N	N	Y	Y	Y
53 Davis	Y	Y	Y	N	Y	Y

	581	582	583	584	585	586
COLORADO						
1 DeGette	Y	Y	Y	N	Y	N
2 Polis	Y	Y	N	N	Y	N
3 Tipton	N	N	N	Y	Y	Y
4 Gardner	N	N	N	Y	Y	Y
5 Lamborn	N	Y	N	Y	Y	Y
6 Coffman	N	N	N	Y	Y	Y
7 Perlmutter	Y	Y	Y	N	Y	Y
CONNECTICUT						
1 Larson	Y	Y	Y	N	Y	N
2 Courtney	Y	Y	Y	N	Y	N
3 DeLauro	Y	Y	Y	N	?	N
4 Himes	Y	Y	Y	N	Y	Y
5 Murphy	Y	Y	Y	N	Y	Y
DELAWARE						
AL Carney	Y	Y	Y	N	Y	Y
FLORIDA						
1 Miller	N	N	N	Y	Y	Y
2 Southerland	N	N	N	Y	Y	Y
3 Brown	Y	Y	Y	N	Y	N
4 Crenshaw	N	N	N	Y	Y	Y
5 Nugent	N	N	N	Y	Y	Y
6 Stearns	N	N	N	Y	Y	Y
7 Mica	N	N	N	Y	Y	Y
8 Webster	N	N	N	Y	Y	Y
9 Bilirakis	N	N	N	Y	Y	Y
10 Young	N	N	N	Y	Y	Y
11 Castor	Y	Y	Y	N	Y	Y
12 Ross	N	N	N	Y	Y	Y
13 Buchanan	N	N	N	Y	Y	Y
14 Mack	?	?	?	?	Y	Y
15 Posey	N	N	N	Y	Y	Y
16 Rooney	N	N	N	Y	Y	Y
17 Wilson	Y	Y	Y	N	Y	Y
18 Ros-Lehtinen	?	?	N	Y	Y	Y
19 Deutch	Y	Y	Y	N	Y	Y
20 Wasserman Schultz	Y	Y	Y	N	Y	N
21 Diaz-Balart	N	N	N	Y	Y	Y
22 West	N	N	N	Y	Y	Y
23 Hastings	Y	Y	Y	N	Y	Y
24 Adams	N	N	N	Y	Y	Y
25 Rivera	N	N	N	Y	?	?
GEORGIA						
1 Kingston	N	N	N	Y	Y	Y
2 Bishop	Y	Y	Y	Y	Y	Y
3 Westmoreland	N	N	N	Y	Y	Y
4 Johnson	Y	Y	Y	N	Y	N
5 Lewis	Y	Y	Y	N	Y	Y
6 Price	N	N	N	Y	Y	Y
7 Woodall	N	N	N	Y	Y	Y
8 Scott, A.	N	N	N	Y	Y	Y
9 Graves	N	N	N	Y	Y	Y
10 Broun	?	?	?	?	Y	Y
11 Gingrey	N	N	N	Y	Y	Y
12 Barrow	N	N	N	Y	Y	Y
13 Scott, D.	Y	Y	Y	N	Y	N
HAWAII						
1 Hanabusa	Y	Y	Y	N	Y	Y
2 Hirono	Y	Y	Y	N	?	?
IDAHO						
1 Labrador	N	N	N	Y	?	?
2 Simpson	N	N	N	Y	Y	Y
ILLINOIS						
1 Rush	Y	Y	Y	N	Y	N
2 Jackson	?	?	?	?	?	?
3 Lipinski	N	Y	Y	Y	Y	Y
4 Gutierrez	?	?	Y	N	Y	N
5 Quigley	Y	Y	Y	N	Y	Y
6 Roskam	N	N	N	Y	Y	Y
7 Davis	Y	Y	Y	N	Y	N
8 Walsh	N	N	N	Y	Y	Y
9 Schakowsky	Y	Y	Y	N	Y	N
10 Dold	N	Y	N	Y	Y	Y
11 Kinzinger	N	N	N	Y	Y	Y
12 Costello	Y	Y	Y	N	Y	Y
13 Biggert	N	N	N	Y	Y	Y
14 Hultgren	N	N	N	Y	Y	Y
15 Johnson	N	N	N	Y	+	+

KEY   **Republicans**   Democrats

Y	Voted for (yea)	X	Paired against
#	Paired for	–	Announced against
+	Announced for	P	Voted "present"
N	Voted against (nay)		

C   Voted "present" to avoid possible conflict of interest

?   Did not vote or otherwise make a position known

	581	582	583	584	585	586
16 **Manzullo**	N	N	N	Y	Y	Y
17 **Schilling**	N	N	N	Y	Y	Y
18 **Schock**	N	N	N	Y	Y	Y
19 **Shimkus**	N	N	N	Y	Y	Y
INDIANA						
1 Visclosky	Y	Y	Y	N	Y	N
2 Donnelly	N	N	Y	Y	Y	Y
3 **Stutzman**	N	N	N	Y	Y	Y
4 **Rokita**	N	N	N	Y	Y	Y
5 **Burton**	N	N	N	Y	Y	Y
6 **Pence**	N	N	N	Y	Y	Y
7 Carson	Y	Y	Y	N	Y	Y
8 **Bucshon**	N	N	N	Y	Y	Y
9 **Young**	N	N	N	Y	Y	Y
IOWA						
1 Braley	Y	Y	Y	N	Y	Y
2 Loebsack	Y	Y	Y	Y	Y	Y
3 Boswell	Y	N	Y	Y	Y	Y
4 **Latham**	N	?	N	Y	Y	Y
5 **King**	N	N	N	Y	Y	Y
KANSAS						
1 **Huelskamp**	N	N	N	Y	Y	Y
2 **Jenkins**	N	N	N	Y	Y	Y
3 **Yoder**	N	N	N	Y	Y	Y
4 **Pompeo**	N	N	N	Y	Y	Y
KENTUCKY						
1 **Whitfield**	N	N	N	Y	Y	Y
2 **Guthrie**	N	N	N	Y	Y	Y
3 Yarmuth	Y	Y	Y	N	Y	N
4 Vacant						
5 **Rogers**	N	N	N	Y	Y	Y
6 Chandler	N	N	Y	Y	Y	Y
LOUISIANA						
1 **Scalise**	N	N	N	Y	Y	Y
2 Richmond	Y	Y	Y	N	Y	N
3 **Landry**	N	N	N	Y	Y	Y
4 **Fleming**	N	N	N	Y	Y	Y
5 **Alexander**	N	N	N	Y	Y	Y
6 **Cassidy**	N	N	N	Y	Y	Y
7 **Boustany**	N	N	N	Y	Y	Y
MAINE						
1 Pingree	Y	Y	Y	N	Y	N
2 Michaud	Y	Y	Y	N	Y	Y
MARYLAND						
1 **Harris**	N	N	N	Y	Y	Y
2 Ruppersberger	Y	Y	Y	N	Y	Y
3 Sarbanes	Y	Y	Y	N	Y	N
4 Edwards	Y	Y	Y	N	Y	N
5 Hoyer	Y	Y	Y	N	Y	N
6 **Bartlett**	N	N	N	Y	Y	Y
7 Cummings	Y	Y	Y	N	Y	Y
8 Van Hollen	Y	Y	Y	N	Y	N
MASSACHUSETTS						
1 Olver	Y	Y	Y	N	Y	N
2 Neal	Y	Y	Y	N	Y	N
3 McGovern	Y	Y	Y	N	Y	N
4 Frank	Y	Y	Y	N	Y	N
5 Tsongas	Y	Y	Y	N	?	?
6 Tierney	Y	Y	Y	N	Y	Y
7 Markey	Y	Y	Y	N	Y	N
8 Capuano	Y	Y	Y	N	Y	Y
9 Lynch	N	Y	Y	Y	?	?
10 Keating	Y	Y	Y	N	Y	Y
MICHIGAN						
1 **Benishek**	N	N	N	Y	Y	Y
2 **Huizenga**	N	N	N	Y	Y	Y
3 **Amash**	N	N	N	Y	Y	Y
4 **Camp**	N	N	N	Y	Y	Y
5 Kildee	Y	Y	Y	N	Y	N
6 **Upton**	N	N	N	Y	Y	Y
7 **Walberg**	N	N	N	Y	Y	Y
8 **Rogers**	N	N	N	Y	Y	Y
9 Peters	Y	Y	Y	N	Y	N
10 **Miller**	N	N	N	Y	Y	Y
11 Vacant						
12 Levin	Y	Y	Y	N	Y	N
13 Clarke	Y	Y	Y	N	?	N
14 Conyers	Y	Y	Y	N	Y	N
15 Dingell	Y	Y	Y	N	Y	N
MINNESOTA						
1 Walz	Y	N	Y	Y	Y	Y
2 **Kline**	N	N	N	Y	Y	Y
3 **Paulsen**	N	N	N	Y	Y	Y
4 McCollum	Y	Y	Y	N	Y	N

	581	582	583	584	585	586
5 Ellison	Y	Y	Y	N	Y	N
6 **Bachmann**	N	N	N	Y	Y	Y
7 Peterson	N	?	Y	Y	Y	Y
8 **Cravaack**	N	N	N	Y	Y	Y
MISSISSIPPI						
1 **Nunnelee**	N	N	N	Y	Y	Y
2 Thompson	Y	Y	Y	N	Y	N
3 **Harper**	N	N	N	Y	Y	Y
4 **Palazzo**	N	N	N	Y	Y	Y
MISSOURI						
1 Clay	Y	Y	Y	N	Y	N
2 **Akin**	?	?	?	?	?	?
3 Carnahan	Y	Y	Y	N	Y	Y
4 **Hartzler**	N	N	N	Y	Y	Y
5 Cleaver	Y	Y	Y	N	Y	N
6 **Graves**	N	N	N	+	Y	Y
7 **Long**	N	N	N	Y	Y	Y
8 **Emerson**	N	N	N	Y	Y	Y
9 **Luetkemeyer**	N	N	N	Y	Y	Y
MONTANA						
AL **Rehberg**	N	N	N	Y	Y	Y
NEBRASKA						
1 **Fortenberry**	N	N	N	Y	Y	Y
2 **Terry**	N	N	N	Y	Y	Y
3 **Smith**	N	N	N	Y	Y	Y
NEVADA						
1 Berkley	Y	Y	Y	N	Y	Y
2 **Amodei**	N	N	N	Y	Y	Y
3 **Heck**	N	N	N	Y	Y	Y
NEW HAMPSHIRE						
1 **Guinta**	N	N	N	Y	Y	Y
2 **Bass**	N	Y	N	N	Y	Y
NEW JERSEY						
1 Andrews	Y	Y	Y	N	Y	N
2 **LoBiondo**	N	N	N	Y	Y	Y
3 **Runyan**	N	N	N	Y	Y	Y
4 **Smith**	N	N	N	Y	Y	Y
5 **Garrett**	N	N	N	Y	Y	Y
6 Pallone	Y	Y	Y	N	Y	N
7 **Lance**	N	N	N	Y	Y	Y
8 Pascrell	Y	Y	Y	N	Y	N
9 Rothman	Y	Y	Y	N	Y	Y
10 Vacant						
11 **Frelinghuysen**	N	N	N	Y	Y	Y
12 Holt	Y	Y	Y	N	Y	N
13 Sires	Y	Y	Y	N	Y	N
NEW MEXICO						
1 Heinrich	?	?	?	?	Y	Y
2 **Pearce**	N	N	N	Y	Y	Y
3 Luján	Y	Y	Y	N	Y	N
NEW YORK						
1 Bishop	Y	Y	Y	N	Y	Y
2 Israel	Y	Y	Y	N	Y	Y
3 **King**	N	N	N	Y	Y	Y
4 McCarthy	Y	Y	Y	N	Y	Y
5 Ackerman	?	?	?	?	Y	N
6 Meeks	Y	Y	Y	?	Y	N
7 Crowley	Y	Y	Y	N	Y	N
8 Nadler	Y	Y	Y	N	Y	N
9 **Turner**	N	N	N	Y	Y	Y
10 Towns	?	?	?	?	Y	N
11 Clarke	Y	Y	Y	N	Y	N
12 Velázquez	Y	Y	Y	N	Y	N
13 **Grimm**	N	N	N	Y	Y	Y
14 Maloney	Y	Y	Y	N	?	Y
15 Rangel	Y	Y	Y	N	Y	N
16 Serrano	Y	Y	Y	N	Y	N
17 Engel	Y	Y	Y	N	Y	N
18 Lowey	Y	Y	Y	N	Y	Y
19 **Hayworth**	N	N	N	Y	Y	Y
20 **Gibson**	N	Y	N	N	Y	Y
21 Tonko	Y	Y	Y	N	Y	Y
22 Hinchey	Y	Y	Y	N	Y	N
23 Owens	Y	N	N	Y	Y	Y
24 **Hanna**	N	N	N	Y	Y	Y
25 **Buerkle**	N	N	N	Y	Y	Y
26 Hochul	N	N	N	Y	Y	Y
27 Higgins	Y	Y	Y	–	Y	Y
28 Slaughter	Y	Y	Y	N	Y	Y
29 **Reed**	N	N	N	Y	Y	Y
NORTH CAROLINA						
1 Butterfield	Y	Y	Y	N	Y	Y
2 **Ellmers**	N	N	N	Y	Y	Y
3 **Jones**	N	?	?	?	Y	Y
4 Price	Y	Y	Y	N	Y	N

	581	582	583	584	585	586
5 **Foxx**	N	N	N	Y	Y	Y
6 **Coble**	?	?	?	?	Y	Y
7 McIntyre	Y	N	Y	Y	Y	Y
8 Kissell	Y	Y	Y	Y	Y	Y
9 **Myrick**	N	N	N	Y	Y	Y
10 **McHenry**	N	N	N	Y	Y	Y
11 Shuler	Y	N	N	Y	?	?
12 Watt	Y	Y	Y	N	Y	N
13 Miller	Y	Y	Y	N	Y	N
NORTH DAKOTA						
AL **Berg**	N	N	N	Y	Y	Y
OHIO						
1 **Chabot**	N	N	N	Y	Y	Y
2 **Schmidt**	N	N	N	Y	Y	Y
3 **Turner**	N	N	N	Y	Y	Y
4 **Jordan**	N	N	N	Y	Y	Y
5 **Latta**	N	N	N	Y	Y	Y
6 **Johnson**	N	N	N	Y	Y	Y
7 **Austria**	N	N	N	Y	Y	Y
8 **Boehner**						
9 Kaptur	Y	Y	Y	N	Y	N
10 Kucinich	Y	Y	Y	N	Y	Y
11 Fudge	Y	Y	Y	N	Y	N
12 **Tiberi**	N	N	N	Y	Y	?
13 Sutton	Y	Y	Y	N	Y	Y
14 **LaTourette**	?	?	?	?	Y	Y
15 **Stivers**	N	N	N	Y	Y	Y
16 **Renacci**	N	N	N	Y	Y	Y
17 Ryan	Y	Y	Y	N	Y	Y
18 **Gibbs**	N	N	N	Y	Y	Y
OKLAHOMA						
1 **Sullivan**	?	?	N	Y	Y	Y
2 Boren	N	N	Y	Y	Y	Y
3 **Lucas**	N	N	N	Y	Y	Y
4 **Cole**	N	N	N	Y	Y	Y
5 **Lankford**	N	N	N	Y	Y	Y
OREGON						
1 Bonamici	Y	Y	Y	N	Y	Y
2 **Walden**	N	N	N	Y	Y	Y
3 Blumenauer	+	+	+	–	Y	Y
4 DeFazio	Y	Y	Y	Y	Y	Y
5 Schrader	Y	Y	Y	N	Y	Y
PENNSYLVANIA						
1 Brady	Y	Y	Y	N	Y	N
2 Fattah	Y	Y	Y	N	Y	N
3 **Kelly**	N	N	N	Y	Y	Y
4 Altmire	N	Y	Y	N	Y	Y
5 **Thompson**	N	N	N	Y	Y	Y
6 **Gerlach**	N	?	N	Y	Y	Y
7 **Meehan**	N	N	N	Y	Y	Y
8 **Fitzpatrick**	N	N	N	Y	Y	Y
9 **Shuster**	N	N	N	Y	Y	Y
10 **Marino**	N	N	N	Y	Y	Y
11 **Barletta**	N	N	N	Y	Y	Y
12 Critz	Y	Y	Y	Y	Y	Y
13 Schwartz	Y	Y	Y	N	Y	N
14 Doyle	Y	Y	Y	N	Y	N
15 **Dent**	N	N	N	Y	Y	Y
16 **Pitts**	N	N	N	Y	Y	Y
17 Holden	Y	Y	Y	N	Y	Y
18 **Murphy**	N	N	N	Y	Y	Y
19 **Platts**	N	N	N	Y	?	?
RHODE ISLAND						
1 Cicilline	Y	Y	Y	N	Y	Y
2 Langevin	Y	Y	Y	N	Y	Y
SOUTH CAROLINA						
1 **Scott**	N	N	N	Y	Y	Y
2 **Wilson**	N	N	N	Y	Y	Y
3 **Duncan**	N	N	N	Y	Y	Y
4 **Gowdy**	N	N	N	Y	Y	Y
5 **Mulvaney**	N	N	N	Y	Y	Y
6 Clyburn	Y	Y	Y	N	Y	N
SOUTH DAKOTA						
AL **Noem**	N	N	N	Y	Y	Y
TENNESSEE						
1 **Roe**	N	N	N	Y	Y	Y
2 **Duncan**	N	N	N	Y	Y	Y
3 **Fleischmann**	N	N	N	Y	Y	Y
4 **DesJarlais**	N	N	N	Y	Y	Y
5 Cooper	Y	Y	Y	N	Y	N
6 **Black**	N	N	N	Y	Y	Y
7 **Blackburn**	?	?	?	?	Y	Y
8 **Fincher**	N	N	N	Y	Y	Y
9 Cohen	Y	Y	Y	N	Y	N

	581	582	583	584	585	586
TEXAS						
1 **Gohmert**	N	?	N	Y	Y	Y
2 **Poe**	?	?	?	?	Y	Y
3 **Johnson, S.**	N	N	N	Y	?	?
4 **Hall**	N	N	N	Y	Y	Y
5 **Hensarling**	N	N	N	Y	Y	Y
6 **Barton**	N	N	N	Y	Y	Y
7 **Culberson**	N	N	N	Y	Y	Y
8 **Brady**	N	N	N	Y	?	+
9 Green, A.	Y	Y	Y	N	?	?
10 **McCaul**	N	N	N	Y	Y	Y
11 **Conaway**	N	N	N	Y	Y	Y
12 **Granger**	N	N	N	Y	?	?
13 **Thornberry**	N	N	N	Y	Y	Y
14 **Paul**	N	N	N	Y	Y	Y
15 Hinojosa	Y	Y	Y	N	Y	N
16 Reyes	?	?	Y	N	Y	N
17 **Flores**	N	N	N	Y	Y	Y
18 Jackson Lee	Y	Y	Y	N	Y	N
19 **Neugebauer**	N	N	N	Y	Y	Y
20 Gonzalez	Y	Y	Y	N	Y	N
21 **Smith**	N	N	N	Y	Y	Y
22 **Olson**	N	N	N	Y	Y	Y
23 **Canseco**	N	N	N	Y	Y	Y
24 **Marchant**	N	N	N	Y	Y	Y
25 Doggett	Y	Y	Y	N	Y	Y
26 **Burgess**	N	N	N	Y	Y	Y
27 **Farenthold**	N	N	N	Y	Y	Y
28 Cuellar	Y	Y	Y	N	Y	Y
29 Green, G.	Y	Y	Y	N	?	Y
30 Johnson, E.	?	?	?	?	Y	N
31 **Carter**	N	N	N	Y	Y	Y
32 **Sessions**	N	N	N	Y	Y	Y
UTAH						
1 **Bishop**	N	N	N	Y	Y	Y
2 Matheson	N	N	N	Y	Y	Y
3 **Chaffetz**	N	N	N	Y	Y	Y
VERMONT						
AL Welch	Y	Y	Y	N	Y	Y
VIRGINIA						
1 **Wittman**	N	N	N	Y	Y	Y
2 **Rigell**	N	N	N	Y	Y	Y
3 Scott	Y	Y	Y	N	Y	N
4 **Forbes**	N	N	N	Y	?	?
5 **Hurt**	N	N	N	Y	Y	Y
6 **Goodlatte**	N	N	–	+	Y	Y
7 **Cantor**	N	N	N	Y	Y	Y
8 Moran	Y	Y	Y	N	Y	Y
9 **Griffith**	N	N	N	Y	Y	Y
10 **Wolf**	N	N	N	Y	Y	Y
11 Connolly	Y	Y	Y	N	Y	N
WASHINGTON						
1 Vacant						
2 Larsen	Y	Y	Y	N	Y	N
3 **Herrera Beutler**	N	N	N	Y	Y	Y
4 **Hastings**	N	N	N	Y	Y	Y
5 **McMorris Rodgers**	N	N	N	Y	Y	Y
6 Dicks	Y	Y	Y	N	Y	Y
7 McDermott	Y	Y	Y	N	Y	N
8 **Reichert**	N	N	N	Y	Y	Y
9 Smith	Y	Y	Y	N	Y	N
WEST VIRGINIA						
1 **McKinley**	N	N	N	Y	Y	Y
2 **Capito**	N	N	N	Y	Y	Y
3 Rahall	Y	N	Y	Y	Y	Y
WISCONSIN						
1 **Ryan**	–	–	–	+	?	?
2 Baldwin	Y	Y	Y	N	Y	Y
3 Kind	Y	Y	Y	N	Y	Y
4 Moore	Y	Y	Y	N	Y	N
5 **Sensenbrenner**	N	N	N	Y	Y	Y
6 **Petri**	N	N	N	Y	Y	Y
7 **Duffy**	N	N	N	Y	Y	Y
8 **Ribble**	N	N	N	Y	Y	Y
WYOMING						
AL **Lummis**	N	N	N	Y	Y	Y

IN THE HOUSE | By Vote Number

587. **H J Res 118, HR 3409. TANF Work Requirements Disapproval and Energy Regulatory Revisions/Previous Question.** Slaughter, D-N.Y., motion to order the previous question (thus ending debate and the possibility of amendment) on the rule (H Res 788) that would provide for House floor consideration of a joint resolution (H J Res 118) that would nullify the Health and Human Services Department's decision to allow states to waive the work requirements set by the Temporary Assistance for Needy Families program and a package (HR 3409) of energy regulatory measures. Motion agreed to 238-179: R 231-0; D 7-179. Sept. 20, 2012.

588. **H J Res 118, HR 3409. TANF Work Requirements Disapproval and Energy Regulatory Revisions/Rule.** Adoption of the rule (H Res 788) that would provide for House floor consideration of a joint resolution (H J Res 118) that would nullify the Health and Human Services Department's decision to allow states to waive the work requirements set by the TANF program and a package (HR 3409) of energy regulatory measures. Adopted 233-182: R 229-1; D 4-181. Sept. 20, 2012.

589. **H J Res 118. TANF Work Requirements Disapproval/Passage.** Passage of the joint resolution that would nullify a rule proposed by the Health and Human Services Department to allow states to waive the work requirements set by the TANF program. Passed 250-164: R 231-0; D 19-164. Sept. 20, 2012.

590. **HR 6429. STEM Visa Program/Passage.** Smith, R-Texas, motion to suspend the rules and pass the bill that would create a new visa program under which foreign students earning advanced degrees in science, technology, engineering and mathematics (STEM) at eligible U.S. colleges and universities could remain in the United States to work in those fields. The bill would eliminate the Diversity Visa Program and reallocate those visas to the new STEM visa program. A two-thirds majority of those present and voting (277 in this case) is required for passage under suspension of the rules. Motion rejected 257-158: R 227-5; D 30-153. A "nay" was a vote in support of the president's position. Sept. 20, 2012.

591. **HR 5987. Manhattan Project National Park/Passage.** Hastings, R-Wash., motion to suspend the rules and pass the bill that would establish a Manhattan Project National Historical Park and specify that areas in Los Alamos, N.M., Oak Ridge, Tenn., and Hanford, Wash., may be included in the park. Motion rejected 237-180: R 121-112; D 116-68. A two-thirds majority of those present and voting (278 in this case) is required for passage under suspension of the rules. Sept. 20, 2012.

	587	588	589	590	591
ALABAMA					
1 Bonner	Y	Y	Y	Y	Y
2 Roby	Y	Y	Y	Y	Y
3 Rogers	Y	Y	Y	Y	Y
4 Aderholt	Y	Y	Y	Y	Y
5 Brooks	Y	Y	Y	Y	N
6 Bachus	Y	Y	Y	Y	Y
7 Sewell	N	N	N	N	N
ALASKA					
AL Young	Y	Y	Y	Y	N
ARIZONA					
1 Gosar	Y	Y	Y	Y	Y
2 Franks	Y	Y	Y	Y	N
3 Quayle	Y	Y	Y	Y	N
4 Pastor	N	N	N	N	Y
5 Schweikert	Y	Y	Y	Y	N
6 Flake	Y	Y	Y	Y	N
7 Grijalva	N	N	N	N	Y
8 Barber	N	N	Y	Y	Y
ARKANSAS					
1 Crawford	Y	Y	Y	Y	Y
2 Griffin	Y	Y	Y	Y	N
3 Womack	Y	Y	Y	Y	Y
4 Ross	?	?	?	?	?
CALIFORNIA					
1 Thompson	N	N	N	N	N
2 Herger	Y	Y	Y	Y	N
3 Lungren	Y	Y	Y	Y	Y
4 McClintock	Y	Y	Y	Y	Y
5 Matsui	N	N	N	N	N
6 Woolsey	N	N	N	N	N
7 Miller, George	N	N	N	N	Y
8 Pelosi	N	N	N	N	N
9 Lee	N	N	N	N	N
10 Garamendi	N	N	Y	N	Y
11 McNerney	N	N	Y	Y	Y
12 Speier	?	?	?	?	?
13 Stark	N	N	N	N	N
14 Eshoo	N	N	N	N	Y
15 Honda	N	N	N	N	N
16 Lofgren	N	N	N	N	N
17 Farr	N	N	N	N	Y
18 Vacant					
19 Denham	Y	Y	Y	N	Y
20 Costa	N	N	N	N	Y
21 Nunes	Y	Y	Y	Y	N
22 McCarthy	Y	Y	Y	Y	N
23 Capps	N	N	N	N	Y
24 Gallegly	?	?	?	?	?
25 McKeon	Y	Y	Y	Y	N
26 Dreier	Y	Y	Y	Y	Y
27 Sherman	N	N	N	N	N
28 Berman	N	N	N	Y	N
29 Schiff	N	N	N	N	Y
30 Waxman	N	N	N	N	Y
31 Becerra	N	N	N	N	Y
32 Chu	N	N	N	N	N
33 Bass	N	N	N	N	N
34 Roybal-Allard	N	N	N	N	Y
35 Waters	N	N	N	?	N
36 Hahn	N	N	N	N	Y
37 Richardson	N	N	N	N	N
38 Napolitano	N	N	N	N	N
39 Sánchez, Linda	N	N	N	N	Y
40 Royce	Y	Y	Y	Y	N
41 Lewis	Y	Y	Y	Y	Y
42 Miller, Gary	Y	Y	Y	Y	Y
43 Baca	N	N	N	N	Y
44 Calvert	Y	Y	Y	Y	Y
45 Bono Mack	Y	Y	Y	Y	Y
46 Rohrabacher	Y	Y	Y	Y	N
47 Sanchez, Loretta	N	N	N	N	N
48 Campbell	Y	Y	Y	Y	Y
49 Issa	Y	Y	Y	Y	Y
50 Bilbray	Y	Y	Y	Y	Y
51 Filner	–	–	–	?	+
52 Hunter	Y	Y	Y	Y	Y
53 Davis	N	N	N	N	N

	587	588	589	590	591
COLORADO					
1 DeGette	N	N	N	N	N
2 Polis	N	N	N	N	N
3 Tipton	Y	Y	Y	Y	Y
4 Gardner	Y	Y	Y	Y	Y
5 Lamborn	Y	Y	Y	Y	Y
6 Coffman	Y	Y	Y	Y	N
7 Perlmutter	N	N	N	N	Y
CONNECTICUT					
1 Larson	N	N	N	N	Y
2 Courtney	N	N	N	N	Y
3 DeLauro	N	N	N	N	Y
4 Himes	N	N	N	N	Y
5 Murphy	N	N	N	N	Y
DELAWARE					
AL Carney	Y	N	N	Y	Y
FLORIDA					
1 Miller	Y	Y	Y	Y	N
2 Southerland	Y	Y	Y	Y	N
3 Brown	N	N	N	N	N
4 Crenshaw	Y	Y	Y	Y	Y
5 Nugent	Y	Y	Y	Y	N
6 Stearns	Y	Y	Y	Y	N
7 Mica	Y	Y	Y	Y	Y
8 Webster	Y	Y	Y	Y	N
9 Bilirakis	Y	Y	Y	Y	Y
10 Young	Y	Y	Y	Y	Y
11 Castor	N	N	N	N	Y
12 Ross	Y	Y	Y	Y	N
13 Buchanan	Y	Y	Y	Y	Y
14 Mack	Y	Y	+	Y	N
15 Posey	Y	?	Y	Y	N
16 Rooney	Y	Y	Y	Y	N
17 Wilson	N	N	N	N	Y
18 Ros-Lehtinen	Y	Y	Y	Y	N
19 Deutch	N	N	N	N	Y
20 Wasserman Schultz	N	N	N	N	Y
21 Diaz-Balart	Y	Y	Y	Y	Y
22 West	Y	Y	Y	Y	N
23 Hastings	N	N	N	N	N
24 Adams	Y	Y	Y	Y	N
25 Rivera	Y	Y	Y	Y	Y
GEORGIA					
1 Kingston	Y	Y	Y	Y	N
2 Bishop	N	N	N	N	Y
3 Westmoreland	Y	Y	Y	Y	N
4 Johnson	N	N	N	N	?
5 Lewis	N	N	N	N	N
6 Price	Y	Y	Y	Y	N
7 Woodall	Y	Y	Y	Y	Y
8 Scott, A.	Y	Y	Y	Y	N
9 Graves	Y	Y	Y	Y	N
10 Broun	Y	Y	Y	Y	N
11 Gingrey	Y	Y	Y	Y	Y
12 Barrow	N	N	Y	Y	Y
13 Scott, D.	N	N	N	N	N
HAWAII					
1 Hanabusa	N	N	N	N	N
2 Hirono	N	N	N	N	N
IDAHO					
1 Labrador	Y	Y	Y	Y	N
2 Simpson	Y	Y	Y	?	Y
ILLINOIS					
1 Rush	N	N	N	N	N
2 Jackson	?	?	?	?	?
3 Lipinski	N	N	Y	Y	Y
4 Gutierrez	N	N	N	N	N
5 Quigley	N	N	N	N	Y
6 Roskam	Y	Y	Y	Y	Y
7 Davis	N	N	?	N	?
8 Walsh	Y	Y	Y	Y	N
9 Schakowsky	N	N	N	N	N
10 Dold	Y	Y	Y	N	Y
11 Kinzinger	Y	Y	Y	Y	Y
12 Costello	N	N	N	N	Y
13 Biggert	Y	Y	Y	N	Y
14 Hultgren	Y	Y	Y	?	N
15 Johnson	+	+	Y	Y	Y

KEY   **Republicans**   Democrats

Y Voted for (yea)	**X** Paired against	**C** Voted "present" to avoid possible conflict of interest
# Paired for	**–** Announced against	
+ Announced for	**P** Voted "present"	**?** Did not vote or otherwise make a position known
N Voted against (nay)		

	587	588	589	590	591
16 Manzullo	Y	Y	Y	Y	N
17 Schilling	Y	Y	Y	Y	Y
18 Schock	Y	Y	Y	Y	Y
19 Shimkus	Y	Y	Y	Y	Y
INDIANA					
1 Visclosky	N	N	N	N	N
2 Donnelly	Y	N	Y	Y	Y
3 Stutzman	Y	Y	Y	Y	N
4 Rokita	Y	Y	Y	Y	N
5 Burton	Y	Y	Y	Y	N
6 Pence	Y	Y	Y	Y	N
7 Carson	N	N	N	N	Y
8 Bucshon	Y	Y	Y	Y	N
9 Young	Y	Y	Y	Y	N
IOWA					
1 Braley	N	N	N	N	Y
2 Loebsack	N	N	Y	N	Y
3 Boswell	N	N	Y	Y	Y
4 Latham	Y	Y	Y	Y	Y
5 King	Y	Y	Y	Y	Y
KANSAS					
1 Huelskamp	Y	Y	Y	Y	N
2 Jenkins	?	?	?	?	?
3 Yoder	Y	Y	Y	Y	N
4 Pompeo	Y	Y	Y	Y	N
KENTUCKY					
1 Whitfield	Y	Y	Y	Y	N
2 Guthrie	Y	Y	Y	Y	Y
3 Yarmuth	N	N	N	N	N
4 Vacant					
5 Rogers	Y	Y	Y	N	Y
6 Chandler	N	Y	Y	Y	Y
LOUISIANA					
1 Scalise	Y	Y	Y	Y	N
2 Richmond	N	N	?	N	N
3 Landry	Y	Y	Y	Y	N
4 Fleming	Y	Y	Y	Y	Y
5 Alexander	Y	Y	Y	Y	N
6 Cassidy	Y	Y	Y	Y	N
7 Boustany	Y	Y	Y	Y	N
MAINE					
1 Pingree	N	N	N	N	N
2 Michaud	N	N	Y	Y	Y
MARYLAND					
1 Harris	Y	Y	Y	Y	Y
2 Ruppersberger	N	N	N	Y	Y
3 Sarbanes	N	N	N	N	Y
4 Edwards	N	N	N	N	N
5 Hoyer	N	N	N	N	Y
6 Bartlett	Y	Y	Y	Y	N
7 Cummings	N	N	N	N	N
8 Van Hollen	N	N	N	N	Y
MASSACHUSETTS					
1 Olver	N	N	N	N	N
2 Neal	N	N	N	N	N
3 McGovern	N	N	N	N	N
4 Frank	N	N	N	N	Y
5 Tsongas	N	N	N	N	N
6 Tierney	N	N	N	N	N
7 Markey	N	N	N	N	Y
8 Capuano	N	N	N	N	Y
9 Lynch	N	N	Y	N	Y
10 Keating	N	N	N	N	Y
MICHIGAN					
1 Benishek	Y	Y	Y	Y	N
2 Huizenga	Y	Y	Y	Y	N
3 Amash	Y	Y	Y	Y	N
4 Camp	Y	Y	Y	Y	N
5 Kildee	N	N	N	N	Y
6 Upton	Y	Y	Y	Y	N
7 Walberg	Y	Y	Y	Y	N
8 Rogers	Y	Y	Y	Y	N
9 Peters	N	N	N	N	Y
10 Miller	Y	Y	Y	Y	Y
11 Vacant					
12 Levin	N	N	N	N	Y
13 Clarke	N	N	N	N	Y
14 Conyers	N	N	N	N	Y
15 Dingell	N	N	N	N	Y
MINNESOTA					
1 Walz	N	N	N	N	Y
2 Kline	Y	Y	Y	Y	Y
3 Paulsen	Y	Y	Y	Y	Y
4 McCollum	N	N	N	N	N

	587	588	589	590	591
5 Ellison	N	N	N	N	N
6 Bachmann	Y	Y	Y	Y	Y
7 Peterson	N	N	Y	Y	Y
8 Cravaack	Y	Y	Y	Y	Y
MISSISSIPPI					
1 Nunnelee	Y	Y	Y	Y	Y
2 Thompson	N	N	N	N	N
3 Harper	Y	Y	Y	Y	Y
4 Palazzo	Y	Y	Y	Y	N
MISSOURI					
1 Clay	N	N	N	N	N
2 Akin	?	?	?	?	?
3 Carnahan	N	N	N	N	Y
4 Hartzler	Y	Y	Y	Y	N
5 Cleaver	N	N	N	N	N
6 Graves	Y	Y	Y	Y	Y
7 Long	Y	Y	Y	Y	N
8 Emerson	Y	Y	Y	Y	N
9 Luetkemeyer	Y	Y	Y	Y	Y
MONTANA					
AL Rehberg	Y	Y	Y	Y	Y
NEBRASKA					
1 Fortenberry	Y	Y	Y	Y	Y
2 Terry	Y	Y	Y	Y	Y
3 Smith	Y	Y	Y	Y	Y
NEVADA					
1 Berkley	N	N	N	N	Y
2 Amodei	Y	Y	Y	Y	Y
3 Heck	Y	Y	Y	Y	Y
NEW HAMPSHIRE					
1 Guinta	Y	Y	Y	Y	Y
2 Bass	Y	Y	Y	Y	Y
NEW JERSEY					
1 Andrews	N	N	N	N	N
2 LoBiondo	Y	Y	Y	Y	N
3 Runyan	Y	Y	Y	Y	N
4 Smith	Y	Y	Y	Y	N
5 Garrett	Y	Y	Y	Y	Y
6 Pallone	N	N	N	N	Y
7 Lance	Y	Y	Y	Y	N
8 Pascrell	N	N	N	N	Y
9 Rothman	N	N	N	N	Y
10 Vacant					
11 Frelinghuysen	Y	Y	Y	Y	Y
12 Holt	N	N	N	N	Y
13 Sires	N	N	N	N	Y
NEW MEXICO					
1 Heinrich	N	?	N	N	Y
2 Pearce	Y	Y	Y	Y	Y
3 Luján	N	N	N	N	Y
NEW YORK					
1 Bishop	N	N	N	N	N
2 Israel	N	N	N	N	Y
3 King	Y	Y	Y	Y	N
4 McCarthy	N	N	N	N	Y
5 Ackerman	N	N	N	N	Y
6 Meeks	N	N	N	N	Y
7 Crowley	N	N	N	N	Y
8 Nadler	N	N	N	N	Y
9 Turner	Y	Y	Y	Y	N
10 Towns	N	N	?	?	?
11 Clarke	N	N	N	N	N
12 Velázquez	N	N	N	N	Y
13 Grimm	Y	Y	Y	Y	Y
14 Maloney	N	N	N	N	Y
15 Rangel	N	N	N	N	Y
16 Serrano	N	N	N	N	Y
17 Engel	N	N	N	N	Y
18 Lowey	N	N	N	N	Y
19 Hayworth	Y	Y	Y	Y	Y
20 Gibson	Y	Y	Y	Y	N
21 Tonko	N	N	N	N	Y
22 Hinchey	N	N	N	N	N
23 Owens	Y	Y	Y	N	Y
24 Hanna	Y	Y	Y	Y	N
25 Buerkle	Y	Y	Y	Y	Y
26 Hochul	N	Y	Y	Y	Y
27 Higgins	N	N	N	N	Y
28 Slaughter	N	N	N	N	Y
29 Reed	Y	Y	Y	Y	Y
NORTH CAROLINA					
1 Butterfield	N	N	N	N	Y
2 Ellmers	Y	Y	Y	Y	Y
3 Jones	Y	Y	N	Y	?
4 Price	N	N	N	N	Y

	587	588	589	590	591
5 Foxx	Y	Y	Y	Y	N
6 Coble	Y	Y	Y	Y	Y
7 McIntyre	Y	Y	Y	Y	Y
8 Kissell	N	N	Y	Y	Y
9 Myrick	Y	Y	Y	Y	Y
10 McHenry	Y	Y	Y	Y	Y
11 Shuler	Y	Y	Y	Y	Y
12 Watt	N	N	N	N	N
13 Miller	N	N	N	N	Y
NORTH DAKOTA					
AL Berg	Y	Y	Y	Y	Y
OHIO					
1 Chabot	Y	Y	Y	Y	N
2 Schmidt	Y	Y	?	Y	N
3 Turner	Y	Y	Y	Y	N
4 Jordan	Y	Y	Y	Y	N
5 Latta	Y	Y	Y	Y	N
6 Johnson	Y	Y	Y	Y	N
7 Austria	Y	Y	Y	Y	N
8 Boehner					
9 Kaptur	N	N	N	N	N
10 Kucinich	N	N	N	N	N
11 Fudge	N	N	N	N	Y
12 Tiberi	Y	Y	Y	Y	N
13 Sutton	N	N	N	N	Y
14 LaTourette	Y	Y	Y	Y	Y
15 Stivers	Y	Y	Y	Y	N
16 Renacci	?	?	Y	Y	N
17 Ryan	N	N	N	N	N
18 Gibbs	Y	Y	Y	Y	N
OKLAHOMA					
1 Sullivan	?	?	?	Y	N
2 Boren	Y	N	Y	Y	Y
3 Lucas	Y	Y	Y	Y	Y
4 Cole	Y	Y	Y	Y	Y
5 Lankford	Y	Y	Y	Y	N
OREGON					
1 Bonamici	N	N	N	N	Y
2 Walden	Y	Y	Y	Y	N
3 Blumenauer	N	N	N	N	N
4 DeFazio	N	N	N	Y	N
5 Schrader	N	N	N	N	Y
PENNSYLVANIA					
1 Brady	N	N	N	N	Y
2 Fattah	N	N	N	N	Y
3 Kelly	Y	Y	Y	Y	N
4 Altmire	N	N	N	N	Y
5 Thompson	Y	Y	Y	Y	N
6 Gerlach	Y	Y	Y	Y	N
7 Meehan	Y	Y	Y	Y	N
8 Fitzpatrick	Y	Y	Y	Y	Y
9 Shuster	Y	Y	?	Y	N
10 Marino	Y	Y	Y	Y	N
11 Barletta	Y	Y	Y	Y	N
12 Critz	N	N	N	Y	Y
13 Schwartz	N	N	N	N	Y
14 Doyle	N	N	N	N	N
15 Dent	Y	Y	Y	Y	N
16 Pitts	Y	Y	Y	Y	Y
17 Holden	N	N	N	Y	Y
18 Murphy	Y	Y	Y	Y	N
19 Platts	Y	Y	+	Y	Y
RHODE ISLAND					
1 Cicilline	N	N	N	N	Y
2 Langevin	N	N	N	N	Y
SOUTH CAROLINA					
1 Scott	Y	Y	Y	Y	N
2 Wilson	Y	Y	Y	Y	Y
3 Duncan	Y	Y	Y	Y	N
4 Gowdy	Y	Y	Y	Y	N
5 Mulvaney	Y	Y	Y	Y	N
6 Clyburn	N	N	N	N	N
SOUTH DAKOTA					
AL Noem	Y	Y	Y	Y	Y
TENNESSEE					
1 Roe	Y	Y	Y	Y	N
2 Duncan	Y	Y	Y	Y	N
3 Fleischmann	Y	Y	Y	Y	Y
4 DesJarlais	Y	Y	Y	Y	Y
5 Cooper	N	N	N	N	Y
6 Black	Y	Y	Y	Y	N
7 Blackburn	Y	Y	Y	Y	Y
8 Fincher	Y	Y	Y	Y	N
9 Cohen	N	N	N	N	Y

	587	588	589	590	591
TEXAS					
1 Gohmert	Y	Y	Y	Y	N
2 Poe	Y	Y	Y	Y	N
3 Johnson, S.	Y	Y	Y	Y	Y
4 Hall	Y	Y	Y	Y	Y
5 Hensarling	Y	Y	Y	Y	N
6 Barton	Y	Y	Y	Y	Y
7 Culberson	Y	Y	Y	Y	Y
8 Brady	Y	Y	Y	Y	N
9 Green, A.	N	N	N	N	N
10 McCaul	Y	Y	Y	Y	Y
11 Conaway	Y	Y	Y	Y	Y
12 Granger	?	?	?	?	?
13 Thornberry	Y	Y	Y	Y	Y
14 Paul	Y	Y	Y	Y	Y
15 Hinojosa	N	N	N	N	Y
16 Reyes	N	N	N	N	Y
17 Flores	Y	Y	Y	Y	Y
18 Jackson Lee	N	N	N	N	N
19 Neugebauer	Y	Y	Y	Y	Y
20 Gonzalez	N	N	N	N	Y
21 Smith	Y	Y	Y	Y	Y
22 Olson	Y	Y	Y	Y	N
23 Canseco	Y	Y	Y	Y	Y
24 Marchant	Y	Y	Y	Y	N
25 Doggett	N	N	N	N	Y
26 Burgess	Y	Y	Y	Y	N
27 Farenthold	Y	Y	Y	Y	N
28 Cuellar	N	N	N	N	Y
29 Green, G.	N	N	N	N	Y
30 Johnson, E.	N	N	N	N	N
31 Carter	Y	Y	Y	Y	Y
32 Sessions	Y	Y	Y	Y	Y
UTAH					
1 Bishop	Y	Y	Y	Y	Y
2 Matheson	Y	N	Y	Y	Y
3 Chaffetz	Y	Y	Y	Y	N
VERMONT					
AL Welch	N	N	N	N	Y
VIRGINIA					
1 Wittman	Y	N	Y	Y	N
2 Rigell	Y	Y	Y	Y	Y
3 Scott	N	N	N	N	N
4 Forbes	Y	Y	Y	Y	N
5 Hurt	Y	Y	Y	Y	N
6 Goodlatte	Y	Y	Y	Y	N
7 Cantor	Y	Y	Y	Y	Y
8 Moran	N	N	N	Y	Y
9 Griffith	Y	Y	Y	Y	N
10 Wolf	Y	Y	Y	Y	Y
11 Connolly	N	N	N	N	Y
WASHINGTON					
1 Vacant					
2 Larsen	N	N	N	N	Y
3 Herrera Beutler	Y	Y	Y	Y	N
4 Hastings	Y	Y	Y	Y	Y
5 McMorris Rodgers	Y	Y	Y	Y	Y
6 Dicks	N	N	N	N	Y
7 McDermott	N	N	N	N	N
8 Reichert	Y	Y	Y	Y	Y
9 Smith	N	N	N	N	Y
WEST VIRGINIA					
1 McKinley	Y	Y	Y	Y	Y
2 Capito	Y	Y	Y	Y	Y
3 Rahall	N	N	N	N	Y
WISCONSIN					
1 Ryan	?	?	Y	Y	?
2 Baldwin	N	N	N	N	N
3 Kind	N	N	N	N	Y
4 Moore	N	N	N	N	N
5 Sensenbrenner	Y	Y	Y	Y	N
6 Petri	Y	Y	Y	Y	Y
7 Duffy	Y	Y	Y	Y	N
8 Ribble	Y	Y	Y	Y	N
WYOMING					
AL Lummis	Y	Y	Y	Y	N

IN THE HOUSE | By Vote Number

592. HR 3409. **Energy Regulatory Revisions/Human Health Rules.**
Markey, D-Mass., amendment that would allow the Interior Department to issue mining regulations that reduce pulmonary diseases, lung cancer, cardiovascular disease or birth defects. Rejected in Committee of the Whole 174-229: R 9-216; D 165-13. Sept. 21, 2012.

593. HR 3409. **Energy Regulatory Revisions/EPA Findings.** Waxman, D-Calif., amendment that would strike language to repeal EPA findings on the harmful effects of carbon pollution. Rejected in Committee of the Whole 178-229: R 5-221; D 173-8. Sept. 21, 2012.

594. HR 3409. **Energy Regulatory Revisions/Transportation Department Report.** Kelly, R-Pa., amendment that would require the Transportation Department to report on the number of jobs lost, fatalities and economic costs as a result of new emissions standards for vehicles manufactured after 2017. It would also bar the department from consulting with the EPA or California Air Resource Board beyond what is necessary to compile the report. Adopted in Committee of the Whole 242-168: R 222-6; D 20-162. Sept. 21, 2012.

595. HR 3409. **Energy Regulatory Revisions/Rules to Reduce Oil Demand.** Markey, D-Mass., amendment that would allow the EPA to issue regulations otherwise barred by the bill if the proposals would reduce the U.S. demand for oil. Rejected in Committee of the Whole 164-246: R 0-228; D 164-18. Sept. 21, 2012.

596. HR 3409. **Energy Regulatory Revisions/Commenting Deadlines.**
Jackson Lee, D-Texas, amendment that would strike language from the bill to maintain current commenting deadlines under the Clean Water Act. Rejected in Committee of the Whole 164-247: R 2-227; D 162-20. Sept. 21, 2012.

597. HR 3409. **Energy Regulatory Revisions/Retroactive Vetoes.**
McKinley, R-W.Va., amendment that would bar the EPA from retroactively vetoing discharge permits provided under the Clean Water Act. Adopted in Committee of the Whole 247-163: R 224-4; D 23-159. Sept. 21, 2012.

	592	593	594	595	596	597
ALABAMA						
1 Bonner	N	N	Y	N	N	Y
2 Roby	N	N	Y	N	N	Y
3 Rogers	N	N	Y	N	N	Y
4 Aderholt	N	N	Y	N	N	Y
5 Brooks	N	N	Y	N	N	Y
6 Bachus	N	N	Y	N	N	Y
7 Sewell	Y	Y	N	Y	Y	N
ALASKA						
AL Young	N	N	Y	N	N	Y
ARIZONA						
1 Gosar	N	N	Y	N	N	Y
2 Franks	N	N	Y	N	N	Y
3 Quayle	N	N	Y	N	N	Y
4 Pastor	Y	Y	N	Y	Y	N
5 Schweikert	N	N	Y	N	N	Y
6 Flake	N	N	Y	N	N	Y
7 Grijalva	Y	Y	N	Y	Y	N
8 Barber	Y	Y	N	Y	Y	N
ARKANSAS						
1 Crawford	N	N	Y	N	N	Y
2 Griffin	N	N	Y	N	N	Y
3 Womack	N	N	Y	N	N	Y
4 Ross	–	+	+	–	–	+
CALIFORNIA						
1 Thompson	Y	Y	N	Y	Y	N
2 Herger	N	N	Y	N	N	Y
3 Lungren	N	N	Y	N	N	Y
4 McClintock	N	N	Y	N	N	Y
5 Matsui	Y	Y	N	Y	Y	N
6 Woolsey	Y	Y	N	Y	Y	N
7 Miller, George	Y	Y	N	Y	Y	N
8 Pelosi	Y	Y	N	Y	Y	N
9 Lee	Y	Y	N	Y	Y	N
10 Garamendi	Y	Y	N	Y	Y	N
11 McNerney	Y	Y	N	Y	Y	N
12 Speier	?	?	?	?	?	?
13 Stark	Y	Y	N	Y	Y	N
14 Eshoo	Y	Y	N	Y	Y	N
15 Honda	Y	Y	N	Y	Y	N
16 Lofgren	Y	Y	N	Y	Y	N
17 Farr	Y	Y	N	Y	Y	N
18 Vacant						
19 Denham	N	N	Y	N	N	Y
20 Costa	Y	Y	Y	Y	N	Y
21 Nunes	N	N	Y	N	N	Y
22 McCarthy	N	N	Y	N	N	Y
23 Capps	Y	Y	N	Y	Y	N
24 Gallegly	?	?	?	?	?	?
25 McKeon	Y	N	Y	N	N	Y
26 Dreier	N	N	Y	N	N	Y
27 Sherman	Y	Y	N	Y	Y	N
28 Berman	?	?	?	?	?	?
29 Schiff	Y	Y	N	Y	Y	N
30 Waxman	Y	Y	N	Y	Y	N
31 Becerra	Y	Y	N	Y	Y	N
32 Chu	Y	Y	N	Y	Y	N
33 Bass	?	?	?	?	?	?
34 Roybal-Allard	Y	Y	N	Y	Y	N
35 Waters	Y	Y	N	Y	Y	N
36 Hahn	Y	Y	N	Y	Y	N
37 Richardson	Y	Y	N	Y	Y	N
38 Napolitano	Y	Y	N	Y	Y	N
39 Sánchez, Linda	Y	Y	N	Y	Y	N
40 Royce	N	N	Y	N	N	Y
41 Lewis	N	N	Y	N	N	Y
42 Miller, Gary	N	N	Y	N	N	Y
43 Baca	Y	Y	N	Y	Y	N
44 Calvert	N	N	Y	N	N	Y
45 Bono Mack	N	N	Y	N	N	Y
46 Rohrabacher	N	N	Y	N	N	Y
47 Sanchez, Loretta	Y	Y	N	Y	Y	N
48 Campbell	N	N	Y	N	N	Y
49 Issa	N	N	Y	N	N	Y
50 Bilbray	N	N	N	N	Y	Y
51 Filner	+	+	–	+	+	–
52 Hunter	N	N	Y	N	N	Y
53 Davis	Y	Y	N	Y	Y	N

	592	593	594	595	596	597
COLORADO						
1 DeGette	Y	Y	N	Y	Y	N
2 Polis	Y	Y	N	Y	Y	N
3 Tipton	N	N	Y	N	N	Y
4 Gardner	N	N	Y	N	N	Y
5 Lamborn	Y	N	Y	N	N	Y
6 Coffman	N	N	Y	N	N	Y
7 Perlmutter	Y	Y	Y	Y	Y	N
CONNECTICUT						
1 Larson	Y	Y	N	Y	Y	N
2 Courtney	Y	Y	N	Y	Y	N
3 DeLauro	Y	Y	N	Y	Y	N
4 Himes	?	Y	N	Y	Y	N
5 Murphy	Y	Y	N	Y	Y	N
DELAWARE						
AL Carney	Y	Y	N	Y	Y	N
FLORIDA						
1 Miller	N	N	Y	N	N	Y
2 Southerland	N	N	Y	N	N	Y
3 Brown	Y	Y	N	Y	Y	N
4 Crenshaw	N	N	Y	N	N	Y
5 Nugent	N	N	Y	N	N	Y
6 Stearns	N	N	Y	N	N	Y
7 Mica	N	N	Y	N	N	Y
8 Webster	N	N	Y	N	N	Y
9 Bilirakis	N	N	Y	?	N	Y
10 Young	N	N	N	N	N	Y
11 Castor	?	Y	N	Y	Y	N
12 Ross	N	N	Y	N	N	Y
13 Buchanan	N	N	Y	N	N	Y
14 Mack	?	?	?	?	?	?
15 Posey	N	N	Y	N	N	Y
16 Rooney	N	N	Y	N	N	Y
17 Wilson	Y	Y	N	Y	Y	N
18 Ros-Lehtinen	N	N	Y	N	N	Y
19 Deutch	Y	Y	N	Y	Y	N
20 Wasserman Schultz	Y	Y	N	Y	Y	N
21 Diaz-Balart	N	N	Y	N	N	Y
22 West	N	N	Y	N	N	Y
23 Hastings	Y	Y	N	Y	Y	N
24 Adams	N	N	Y	N	N	Y
25 Rivera	N	N	Y	N	N	Y
GEORGIA						
1 Kingston	N	N	Y	N	N	Y
2 Bishop	N	Y	N	N	N	Y
3 Westmoreland	N	N	Y	N	N	Y
4 Johnson	Y	?	N	Y	Y	N
5 Lewis	Y	Y	N	Y	Y	N
6 Price	N	N	Y	N	N	Y
7 Woodall	N	N	Y	N	N	Y
8 Scott, A.	N	N	Y	N	N	Y
9 Graves	N	N	Y	N	N	Y
10 Broun	N	N	Y	N	N	Y
11 Gingrey	N	N	Y	N	N	Y
12 Barrow	N	Y	N	N	N	Y
13 Scott, D.	Y	Y	N	Y	Y	N
HAWAII						
1 Hanabusa	Y	Y	N	Y	Y	N
2 Hirono	Y	Y	N	Y	Y	N
IDAHO						
1 Labrador	N	N	N	N	N	Y
2 Simpson	N	N	Y	N	N	Y
ILLINOIS						
1 Rush	Y	Y	N	Y	Y	N
2 Jackson	?	?	?	?	?	?
3 Lipinski	Y	Y	N	Y	Y	N
4 Gutierrez	Y	Y	N	Y	Y	N
5 Quigley	Y	Y	N	Y	Y	N
6 Roskam	N	N	Y	N	N	Y
7 Davis	Y	Y	N	Y	Y	N
8 Walsh	N	N	Y	N	N	Y
9 Schakowsky	Y	Y	N	Y	Y	N
10 Dold	N	Y	Y	N	N	Y
11 Kinzinger	N	N	Y	N	N	Y
12 Costello	N	N	Y	N	N	Y
13 Biggert	N	N	Y	N	N	Y
14 Hultgren	N	N	Y	N	N	Y
15 Johnson	Y	Y	Y	N	Y	?

KEY	**Republicans**		Democrats		
Y Voted for (yea)			**X** Paired against		**C** Voted "present" to avoid possible conflict of interest
# Paired for			**–** Announced against		
+ Announced for			**P** Voted "present"		**?** Did not vote or otherwise make a position known
N Voted against (nay)					

	592	593	594	595	596	597
16 **Manzullo**	N	N	Y	N	N	N
17 **Schilling**	N	N	Y	N	N	Y
18 **Schock**	N	N	Y	N	N	Y
19 **Shimkus**	?	?	?	?	?	?
INDIANA						
1 Visclosky	Y	Y	N	Y	Y	N
2 Donnelly	N	Y	Y	N	N	Y
3 **Stutzman**	N	N	Y	N	N	Y
4 **Rokita**	N	N	Y	N	N	Y
5 **Burton**	N	N	Y	N	N	Y
6 **Pence**	N	N	Y	N	N	Y
7 Carson	Y	Y	N	Y	Y	N
8 **Bucshon**	N	N	Y	N	N	Y
9 **Young**	N	N	Y	N	N	Y
IOWA						
1 Braley	Y	Y	N	Y	Y	N
2 Loebsack	Y	Y	Y	Y	Y	N
3 Boswell	Y	Y	Y	N	Y	Y
4 **Latham**	N	N	Y	N	N	Y
5 **King**	N	N	Y	N	N	Y
KANSAS						
1 **Huelskamp**	N	N	Y	N	N	Y
2 **Jenkins**	?	?	?	?	?	?
3 **Yoder**	N	N	Y	N	N	Y
4 **Pompeo**	N	N	Y	N	N	Y
KENTUCKY						
1 **Whitfield**	N	N	Y	N	N	Y
2 **Guthrie**	N	N	Y	N	N	Y
3 Yarmuth	Y	Y	N	Y	Y	N
4 Vacant						
5 **Rogers**	N	N	Y	N	N	Y
6 Chandler	N	Y	Y	N	N	Y
LOUISIANA						
1 **Scalise**	N	N	Y	N	N	Y
2 Richmond	Y	Y	N	Y	Y	N
3 **Landry**	?	?	?	?	?	?
4 **Fleming**	N	N	Y	N	N	Y
5 **Alexander**	N	N	Y	N	N	Y
6 **Cassidy**	N	N	Y	N	N	Y
7 **Boustany**	N	N	Y	N	N	Y
MAINE						
1 Pingree	Y	Y	N	Y	Y	N
2 Michaud	Y	Y	N	Y	Y	N
MARYLAND						
1 **Harris**	N	N	Y	N	N	Y
2 Ruppersberger	?	?	?	?	?	?
3 Sarbanes	Y	Y	N	Y	Y	N
4 Edwards	Y	Y	N	Y	Y	N
5 Hoyer	Y	Y	N	Y	Y	N
6 **Bartlett**	N	N	Y	N	N	Y
7 Cummings	Y	Y	N	Y	Y	N
8 Van Hollen	Y	Y	N	Y	Y	N
MASSACHUSETTS						
1 Olver	Y	Y	N	Y	Y	N
2 Neal	Y	Y	N	Y	Y	N
3 McGovern	Y	Y	N	Y	Y	N
4 Frank	Y	Y	N	Y	Y	Y
5 Tsongas	Y	Y	N	Y	Y	N
6 Tierney	Y	Y	N	Y	Y	N
7 Markey	Y	Y	N	Y	Y	N
8 Capuano	Y	Y	N	Y	Y	N
9 Lynch	Y	Y	N	Y	Y	N
10 Keating	Y	Y	N	Y	Y	N
MICHIGAN						
1 **Benishek**	N	N	Y	N	N	Y
2 **Huizenga**	N	N	Y	N	N	Y
3 **Amash**	N	N	Y	N	N	Y
4 **Camp**	N	N	Y	N	N	Y
5 Kildee	Y	Y	N	Y	Y	N
6 **Upton**	N	N	Y	N	N	Y
7 **Walberg**	N	N	Y	N	N	Y
8 **Rogers**	N	N	Y	N	N	Y
9 Peters	Y	Y	Y	Y	Y	N
10 **Miller**	N	N	Y	N	N	Y
11 Vacant						
12 Levin	Y	Y	N	Y	Y	N
13 Clarke	Y	Y	N	Y	Y	N
14 Conyers	Y	Y	N	Y	Y	N
15 Dingell	Y	Y	N	N	Y	N
MINNESOTA						
1 Walz	Y	Y	N	Y	N	Y
2 **Kline**	N	N	Y	N	N	Y
3 **Paulsen**	N	N	Y	N	N	Y
4 McCollum	Y	Y	N	Y	Y	N

	592	593	594	595	596	597
5 Ellison	?	Y	N	Y	Y	N
6 **Bachmann**	N	N	Y	N	N	Y
7 Peterson	N	N	Y	N	N	Y
8 **Cravaack**	N	N	Y	N	N	Y
MISSISSIPPI						
1 **Nunnelee**	N	N	Y	N	N	Y
2 Thompson	Y	Y	N	Y	Y	N
3 **Harper**	N	N	Y	N	N	Y
4 **Palazzo**	N	N	Y	N	N	Y
MISSOURI						
1 Clay	Y	Y	N	Y	Y	N
2 **Akin**	?	?	?	?	?	?
3 Carnahan	Y	Y	N	Y	Y	N
4 **Hartzler**	N	N	Y	N	N	Y
5 Cleaver	Y	Y	N	Y	Y	N
6 **Graves**	N	N	Y	N	N	Y
7 **Long**	N	N	Y	N	N	Y
8 **Emerson**	N	N	Y	N	N	Y
9 **Luetkemeyer**	N	N	Y	N	N	Y
MONTANA						
AL **Rehberg**	N	N	Y	N	N	Y
NEBRASKA						
1 **Fortenberry**	N	N	Y	N	N	Y
2 **Terry**	N	N	Y	N	N	Y
3 **Smith**	N	N	Y	N	N	Y
NEVADA						
1 Berkley	Y	Y	N	Y	Y	N
2 **Amodei**	N	N	Y	N	N	Y
3 **Heck**	N	N	Y	N	N	Y
NEW HAMPSHIRE						
1 **Guinta**	N	N	Y	N	N	Y
2 **Bass**	N	Y	Y	N	N	N
NEW JERSEY						
1 Andrews	Y	Y	N	Y	Y	N
2 **LoBiondo**	Y	N	Y	N	N	Y
3 **Runyan**	N	N	Y	N	N	Y
4 **Smith**	Y	N	Y	N	N	Y
5 **Garrett**	–	–	+	–	–	+
6 Pallone	Y	Y	N	Y	Y	N
7 **Lance**	N	N	Y	N	N	Y
8 Pascrell	Y	Y	N	Y	Y	N
9 Rothman	Y	Y	N	Y	Y	N
10 Vacant						
11 **Frelinghuysen**	N	N	Y	N	N	Y
12 Holt	Y	Y	N	Y	N	N
13 Sires	Y	Y	N	Y	Y	N
NEW MEXICO						
1 Heinrich	Y	Y	N	Y	Y	N
2 **Pearce**	?	?	?	?	?	?
3 Luján	Y	Y	N	Y	Y	N
NEW YORK						
1 Bishop	Y	Y	N	Y	Y	N
2 Israel	Y	Y	N	Y	Y	N
3 **King**	N	N	Y	N	N	Y
4 McCarthy	Y	Y	N	Y	Y	N
5 Ackerman	?	?	?	?	?	?
6 Meeks	Y	Y	N	Y	Y	N
7 Crowley	Y	Y	N	Y	Y	N
8 Nadler	Y	Y	N	Y	Y	N
9 **Turner**	N	N	Y	N	N	Y
10 Towns	Y	Y	Y	Y	Y	N
11 Clarke	Y	Y	N	Y	Y	N
12 Velázquez	Y	Y	N	Y	Y	N
13 **Grimm**	N	N	Y	N	N	Y
14 Maloney	Y	Y	N	Y	Y	N
15 Rangel	Y	Y	N	Y	Y	N
16 Serrano	Y	Y	N	Y	Y	N
17 Engel	Y	Y	N	Y	Y	N
18 Lowey	Y	Y	N	Y	Y	N
19 **Hayworth**	N	N	Y	N	N	Y
20 **Gibson**	Y	Y	Y	N	N	Y
21 Tonko	Y	Y	N	Y	Y	N
22 Hinchey	Y	Y	N	Y	Y	N
23 Owens	Y	Y	Y	Y	Y	Y
24 **Hanna**	N	N	Y	N	N	Y
25 **Buerkle**	N	N	Y	N	N	Y
26 Hochul	Y	Y	N	Y	Y	Y
27 Higgins	Y	Y	N	Y	Y	N
28 Slaughter	Y	Y	N	Y	Y	N
29 **Reed**	N	N	Y	N	N	Y
NORTH CAROLINA						
1 Butterfield	Y	Y	N	Y	Y	N
2 **Ellmers**	N	N	Y	N	N	Y
3 **Jones**	Y	N	Y	N	N	Y
4 Price	Y	Y	N	Y	Y	N

	592	593	594	595	596	597
5 **Foxx**	N	N	Y	N	N	Y
6 **Coble**	N	N	Y	N	N	Y
7 McIntyre	Y	Y	Y	N	N	Y
8 Kissell	Y	N	Y	Y	N	Y
9 **Myrick**	N	N	Y	N	N	Y
10 **McHenry**	N	N	Y	N	N	Y
11 Shuler	N	N	N	N	N	N
12 Watt	Y	Y	N	Y	Y	N
13 Miller	Y	Y	N	Y	Y	N
NORTH DAKOTA						
AL **Berg**	N	N	Y	N	N	Y
OHIO						
1 **Chabot**	N	N	Y	N	N	Y
2 **Schmidt**	N	N	Y	N	N	Y
3 **Turner**	Y	N	Y	N	N	Y
4 **Jordan**	N	N	Y	N	N	Y
5 **Latta**	N	N	Y	N	N	Y
6 **Johnson**	N	N	Y	N	N	Y
7 **Austria**	N	N	Y	N	N	Y
8 **Boehner**						
9 Kaptur	Y	Y	N	Y	Y	N
10 Kucinich	Y	Y	N	Y	Y	N
11 Fudge	Y	Y	N	Y	Y	N
12 **Tiberi**	N	N	Y	N	N	Y
13 Sutton	Y	Y	N	Y	Y	N
14 **LaTourette**	N	N	Y	N	N	Y
15 **Stivers**	N	N	Y	N	N	Y
16 **Renacci**	N	N	Y	N	N	Y
17 Ryan	Y	Y	N	Y	Y	N
18 **Gibbs**	N	N	Y	N	N	Y
OKLAHOMA						
1 **Sullivan**	?	?	?	N	N	Y
2 Boren	N	N	Y	N	N	Y
3 **Lucas**	N	?	Y	N	N	Y
4 **Cole**	N	N	Y	N	N	Y
5 **Lankford**	N	N	Y	N	N	Y
OREGON						
1 Bonamici	Y	Y	N	Y	Y	N
2 **Walden**	N	N	Y	N	N	Y
3 Blumenauer	Y	Y	N	Y	Y	N
4 DeFazio	Y	Y	N	Y	Y	Y
5 Schrader	Y	Y	Y	N	Y	Y
PENNSYLVANIA						
1 Brady	Y	Y	N	Y	Y	N
2 Fattah	Y	Y	N	Y	Y	N
3 **Kelly**	N	N	Y	N	N	Y
4 Altmire	N	N	N	N	N	Y
5 **Thompson**	N	N	Y	N	N	Y
6 **Gerlach**	N	N	Y	N	N	Y
7 **Meehan**	N	N	Y	N	N	Y
8 **Fitzpatrick**	Y	N	Y	N	Y	N
9 **Shuster**	N	N	Y	N	N	Y
10 **Marino**	N	N	Y	N	N	Y
11 **Barletta**	N	N	Y	N	N	Y
12 Critz	N	Y	Y	N	N	Y
13 Schwartz	Y	Y	N	Y	Y	N
14 Doyle	Y	Y	N	Y	Y	N
15 **Dent**	N	N	Y	N	N	Y
16 **Pitts**	N	N	Y	N	N	Y
17 Holden	N	N	Y	N	N	Y
18 **Murphy**	N	N	Y	N	N	Y
19 **Platts**	N	N	N	N	N	Y
RHODE ISLAND						
1 Cicilline	Y	Y	N	Y	Y	N
2 Langevin	Y	Y	N	Y	Y	N
SOUTH CAROLINA						
1 **Scott**	N	N	Y	N	N	Y
2 **Wilson**	N	N	Y	N	N	Y
3 **Duncan**	N	N	Y	N	N	Y
4 **Gowdy**	N	N	Y	N	N	Y
5 **Mulvaney**	N	N	Y	N	N	Y
6 Clyburn	Y	Y	N	Y	Y	N
SOUTH DAKOTA						
AL **Noem**	N	N	Y	N	N	Y
TENNESSEE						
1 **Roe**	N	N	Y	N	N	Y
2 **Duncan**	N	Y	Y	N	N	Y
3 **Fleischmann**	N	N	Y	N	N	Y
4 **DesJarlais**	N	N	Y	N	N	Y
5 Cooper	Y	Y	N	Y	Y	N
6 **Black**	N	N	Y	N	N	Y
7 **Blackburn**	N	N	Y	N	N	Y
8 **Fincher**	N	N	Y	N	N	Y
9 Cohen	Y	Y	N	Y	Y	N

	592	593	594	595	596	597
TEXAS						
1 **Gohmert**	N	N	Y	N	N	Y
2 **Poe**	N	N	Y	N	N	Y
3 **Johnson, S.**	N	N	Y	N	N	Y
4 **Hall**	N	N	Y	N	N	Y
5 **Hensarling**	N	N	Y	N	N	Y
6 **Barton**	N	N	N	N	N	Y
7 **Culberson**	N	N	Y	N	N	Y
8 **Brady**	N	N	Y	N	N	Y
9 Green, A.	Y	Y	N	Y	Y	N
10 **McCaul**	N	N	Y	N	N	Y
11 **Conaway**	N	N	Y	N	N	Y
12 **Granger**	?	?	?	?	?	?
13 **Thornberry**	N	N	Y	N	N	Y
14 **Paul**	N	N	Y	N	N	Y
15 Hinojosa	Y	Y	N	Y	Y	N
16 Reyes	Y	Y	N	Y	Y	N
17 **Flores**	N	N	Y	N	N	Y
18 Jackson Lee	Y	Y	N	Y	Y	N
19 **Neugebauer**	N	N	Y	N	N	Y
20 Gonzalez	Y	Y	N	Y	Y	N
21 **Smith**	N	N	Y	N	N	Y
22 **Olson**	N	N	Y	N	N	Y
23 **Canseco**	N	N	Y	N	N	Y
24 **Marchant**	?	N	Y	N	N	Y
25 Doggett	Y	Y	N	Y	Y	N
26 **Burgess**	N	N	Y	N	N	Y
27 **Farenthold**	?	N	Y	N	N	Y
28 Cuellar	Y	Y	Y	N	N	N
29 Green, G.	Y	Y	N	Y	Y	Y
30 Johnson, E.	Y	Y	N	Y	Y	N
31 **Carter**	N	N	Y	N	N	Y
32 **Sessions**	N	?	Y	N	N	Y
UTAH						
1 **Bishop**	?	N	Y	N	N	Y
2 Matheson	N	Y	Y	N	N	Y
3 **Chaffetz**	N	N	Y	N	N	Y
VERMONT						
AL Welch	Y	Y	N	Y	Y	N
VIRGINIA						
1 **Wittman**	N	N	Y	N	N	Y
2 **Rigell**	N	N	Y	N	N	Y
3 Scott	Y	Y	N	Y	Y	N
4 **Forbes**	N	N	Y	N	N	Y
5 **Hurt**	N	N	Y	N	N	Y
6 **Goodlatte**	N	N	Y	N	N	Y
7 **Cantor**	N	N	Y	N	N	Y
8 Moran	Y	Y	N	Y	Y	N
9 **Griffith**	N	N	Y	N	N	Y
10 **Wolf**	N	N	Y	N	N	Y
11 Connolly	Y	Y	N	Y	Y	N
WASHINGTON						
1 Vacant						
2 Larsen	Y	Y	N	Y	Y	N
3 **Herrera Beutler**	N	N	Y	N	N	Y
4 **Hastings**	N	N	Y	N	N	Y
5 **McMorris Rodgers**	N	N	Y	N	N	Y
6 Dicks	Y	Y	N	Y	Y	N
7 McDermott	Y	Y	N	Y	Y	N
8 **Reichert**	N	N	Y	N	N	N
9 Smith	Y	Y	N	Y	Y	N
WEST VIRGINIA						
1 **McKinley**	N	N	Y	N	N	Y
2 **Capito**	N	N	Y	N	N	Y
3 Rahall	N	N	Y	N	N	Y
WISCONSIN						
1 **Ryan**	–	–	+	–	–	+
2 Baldwin	Y	Y	N	Y	Y	N
3 Kind	Y	Y	N	Y	Y	N
4 Moore	+	Y	N	Y	Y	N
5 **Sensenbrenner**	N	N	Y	N	N	Y
6 **Petri**	N	N	Y	N	N	Y
7 **Duffy**	N	N	Y	N	N	Y
8 **Ribble**	N	N	Y	N	N	Y
WYOMING						
AL **Lummis**	N	N	Y	N	N	Y

IN THE HOUSE | By Vote Number

598. **HR 3409. Energy Regulatory Revisions/National Standard for Renewable Energy.** Markey, D-Mass., amendment that would create a national standard for electricity and energy efficiency and require 50 percent of generated electricity to come from renewable sources by 2035. The rate would be adjusted if it is determined that it is not economically or technically feasible. Rejected in Committee of the Whole 160-250: R 3-225; D 157-25. Sept. 21, 2012.

599. **HR 3409. Energy Regulatory Revisions/Coal Dust Report.** DeFazio, D-Ore., amendment that would require the EPA and Transportation Department to report to Congress within six months on the health effects of dust generated by transporting coal. Rejected in Committee of the Whole 168-243: R 7-222; D 161-21. Sept. 21, 2012.

600. **HR 3409. Energy Regulatory Revisions/Visibility Standards.** Flake, R-Ariz., amendment that would allow states to opt out of current visibility standards and implement new standards within two years using altered criteria. It would mandate that EPA approve or reject state plans in their entirety and give states five years to comply with any EPA-mandated plan if a state plan were rejected. With regard to visibility standards in national parks, monuments and similarly protected areas, implementation would be at the discretion of the states in which the protected areas are located. Adopted in Committee of the Whole 228-183: R 218-11; D 10-172. Sept. 21, 2012.

601. **HR 3409. Energy Regulatory Revisions/Visibility Regulations on Native American Reservations.** Gosar, R-Ariz., amendment that would bar the EPA from issuing visibility regulations affecting the Navajo Generating Station if the regulations would result in reduced employment, revenues or the amount of coal available on Navajo and Hopi reservation lands. Adopted in Committee of the Whole 226-181: R 215-10; D 11-171. Sept. 21, 2012.

602. **HR 3409. Energy Regulatory Revisions/Recommit.** Capps, D-Calif., motion to recommit the bill to the Energy and Commerce Committee and report it back immediately with language that would describe the effects of a national fuel efficiency program on the U.S. economy and consumers. The motion also would prohibit the legislation from overturning EPA and Transportation Department rules on fuel efficiency and pollution controls for 2017 through 2025 model year vehicles if the bill's provisions result in consumers paying more for gasoline over the vehicles' lifetimes, a loss of jobs in the U.S. auto manufacturing industry or a negative impact on the U.S. economy. Motion rejected 173-233: R 0-227; D 173-6. Sept. 21, 2012.

603. **HR 3409. Energy Regulatory Revisions/Passage.** Passage of the bill that would prevent the Interior Department from issuing new rules that would limit surface mining and reclamation operations or adversely affect coal-mining revenue, employment or production. It also would create an interagency committee to review federal regulations and create a regulatory framework for the establishment of state-level permitting programs for the storage of coal combustion residuals. The bill would transfer authority from the EPA to the states to allow them to make determinations on water quality standards and bar the EPA from issuing regulations on greenhouse gas emissions in association with efforts to reduce climate change. Passed 233-175: R 214-13; D 19-162. A "nay" was a vote in support of the president's position. Sept. 21, 2012.

	598	599	600	601	602	603
ALABAMA						
1 Bonner	N	N	Y	Y	N	Y
2 Roby	N	N	Y	Y	N	Y
3 Rogers	N	N	Y	Y	N	Y
4 Aderholt	N	N	Y	Y	N	Y
5 Brooks	N	N	Y	Y	N	Y
6 Bachus	N	N	Y	Y	N	Y
7 Sewell	Y	Y	N	N	Y	N
ALASKA						
AL Young	N	N	Y	Y	N	Y
ARIZONA						
1 Gosar	N	N	Y	Y	N	Y
2 Franks	N	N	Y	Y	N	Y
3 Quayle	N	N	Y	Y	N	Y
4 Pastor	Y	Y	N	N	Y	N
5 Schweikert	N	N	Y	Y	N	Y
6 Flake	N	N	Y	Y	N	Y
7 Grijalva	Y	Y	N	N	Y	N
8 Barber	Y	N	N	N	Y	N
ARKANSAS						
1 Crawford	N	N	Y	Y	N	Y
2 Griffin	N	N	Y	Y	N	Y
3 Womack	N	N	Y	Y	N	Y
4 Ross	–	–	+	+	+	+
CALIFORNIA						
1 Thompson	Y	Y	N	N	Y	N
2 Herger	N	N	Y	?	N	Y
3 Lungren	N	N	Y	Y	N	Y
4 McClintock	N	N	Y	Y	N	Y
5 Matsui	Y	Y	N	N	Y	N
6 Woolsey	Y	Y	N	N	Y	N
7 Miller, George	Y	Y	N	N	Y	N
8 Pelosi	Y	Y	N	N	Y	N
9 Lee	Y	Y	N	N	Y	N
10 Garamendi	Y	Y	N	N	Y	N
11 McNerney	Y	Y	N	N	Y	N
12 Speier	?	?	?	?	?	?
13 Stark	Y	Y	N	N	Y	N
14 Eshoo	Y	Y	N	N	Y	N
15 Honda	Y	Y	N	N	Y	N
16 Lofgren	Y	Y	N	N	Y	N
17 Farr	Y	Y	N	N	Y	N
18 Vacant						
19 Denham	N	N	Y	Y	N	Y
20 Costa	N	N	Y	N	Y	Y
21 Nunes	N	N	Y	Y	N	Y
22 McCarthy	N	N	Y	Y	N	Y
23 Capps	Y	Y	N	N	Y	N
24 Gallegly	?	?	?	?	?	?
25 McKeon	N	N	Y	Y	N	Y
26 Dreier	N	N	Y	Y	N	Y
27 Sherman	Y	Y	N	N	Y	N
28 Berman	?	?	?	?	?	?
29 Schiff	Y	Y	N	N	Y	N
30 Waxman	Y	Y	N	N	Y	N
31 Becerra	Y	Y	N	N	Y	N
32 Chu	Y	Y	N	N	Y	N
33 Bass	?	?	?	?	?	?
34 Roybal-Allard	Y	Y	N	N	Y	N
35 Waters	Y	Y	N	N	Y	N
36 Hahn	Y	Y	N	N	Y	N
37 Richardson	Y	Y	N	N	Y	N
38 Napolitano	Y	Y	N	N	Y	N
39 Sánchez, Linda	Y	Y	N	N	Y	N
40 Royce	N	N	Y	Y	N	Y
41 Lewis	N	N	N	N	N	Y
42 Miller, Gary	N	N	Y	Y	N	?
43 Baca	Y	Y	N	N	Y	N
44 Calvert	N	N	Y	Y	N	Y
45 Bono Mack	N	N	Y	Y	N	Y
46 Rohrabacher	N	N	Y	Y	N	Y
47 Sanchez, Loretta	Y	Y	N	N	Y	N
48 Campbell	N	N	Y	Y	N	Y
49 Issa	N	N	Y	Y	?	Y
50 Bilbray	Y	N	Y	Y	N	N
51 Filner	+	+	–	–	+	–
52 Hunter	N	N	Y	Y	N	Y
53 Davis	Y	Y	N	N	Y	N
COLORADO						
1 DeGette	Y	Y	N	N	Y	N
2 Polis	Y	Y	N	N	Y	N
3 Tipton	N	N	Y	Y	N	Y
4 Gardner	N	N	Y	Y	N	Y
5 Lamborn	N	N	Y	Y	N	Y
6 Coffman	N	N	Y	Y	N	Y
7 Perlmutter	Y	Y	N	N	Y	N
CONNECTICUT						
1 Larson	Y	Y	N	N	Y	N
2 Courtney	Y	Y	N	N	Y	N
3 DeLauro	Y	Y	N	N	Y	N
4 Himes	Y	Y	N	N	Y	N
5 Murphy	Y	Y	N	N	Y	?
DELAWARE						
AL Carney	Y	Y	N	N	Y	N
FLORIDA						
1 Miller	N	N	Y	Y	N	Y
2 Southerland	N	N	Y	Y	N	Y
3 Brown	Y	Y	N	N	Y	N
4 Crenshaw	N	N	Y	Y	N	Y
5 Nugent	N	N	Y	Y	N	Y
6 Stearns	N	N	Y	Y	N	Y
7 Mica	N	N	Y	Y	N	Y
8 Webster	N	N	Y	Y	N	Y
9 Bilirakis	N	N	Y	Y	N	Y
10 Young	N	N	Y	Y	N	Y
11 Castor	Y	Y	N	N	Y	N
12 Ross	N	N	Y	Y	N	Y
13 Buchanan	N	N	Y	Y	N	Y
14 Mack	?	?	?	?	?	?
15 Posey	N	N	Y	Y	N	Y
16 Rooney	N	N	Y	Y	N	Y
17 Wilson	Y	Y	N	N	Y	N
18 Ros-Lehtinen	N	N	Y	Y	N	Y
19 Deutch	Y	Y	N	N	Y	N
20 Wasserman Schultz	Y	Y	N	N	Y	N
21 Diaz-Balart	N	N	Y	Y	N	Y
22 West	N	N	Y	Y	N	Y
23 Hastings	Y	Y	N	N	Y	N
24 Adams	N	N	Y	Y	N	Y
25 Rivera	N	N	Y	Y	N	Y
GEORGIA						
1 Kingston	N	N	Y	Y	N	Y
2 Bishop	N	N	N	N	Y	Y
3 Westmoreland	N	N	Y	Y	N	Y
4 Johnson	Y	Y	N	N	Y	N
5 Lewis	Y	Y	N	N	Y	N
6 Price	N	N	Y	Y	N	Y
7 Woodall	N	N	Y	Y	N	Y
8 Scott, A.	N	N	Y	Y	N	Y
9 Graves	N	N	Y	Y	N	Y
10 Broun	N	N	Y	Y	N	Y
11 Gingrey	N	N	Y	Y	N	Y
12 Barrow	N	N	Y	N	Y	Y
13 Scott, D.	Y	Y	N	N	Y	N
HAWAII						
1 Hanabusa	Y	Y	N	N	Y	N
2 Hirono	Y	Y	N	N	Y	N
IDAHO						
1 Labrador	N	N	Y	Y	N	Y
2 Simpson	N	N	Y	Y	N	Y
ILLINOIS						
1 Rush	Y	Y	N	N	Y	N
2 Jackson	?	?	?	?	?	?
3 Lipinski	Y	Y	N	N	Y	N
4 Gutierrez	Y	Y	N	N	Y	N
5 Quigley	Y	Y	N	N	Y	N
6 Roskam	N	N	Y	Y	N	Y
7 Davis	Y	Y	N	N	Y	N
8 Walsh	N	N	Y	Y	N	Y
9 Schakowsky	Y	Y	N	N	Y	N
10 Dold	N	N	N	N	N	N
11 Kinzinger	N	N	Y	Y	N	Y
12 Costello	N	N	Y	Y	Y	Y
13 Biggert	N	N	Y	Y	N	Y
14 Hultgren	N	N	Y	Y	N	Y
15 Johnson	N	N	Y	Y	N	N

KEY **Republicans** Democrats

Y Voted for (yea)	X Paired against
# Paired for	– Announced against
+ Announced for	P Voted "present"
N Voted against (nay)	

C Voted "present" to avoid possible conflict of interest

? Did not vote or otherwise make a position known

	598	599	600	601	602	603
16 **Manzullo**	N	N	Y	Y	N	Y
17 **Schilling**	N	N	Y	Y	N	Y
18 **Schock**	N	N	Y	Y	N	Y
19 **Shimkus**	?	?	?	?	?	?
INDIANA						
1 Visclosky	Y	Y	N	N	Y	N
2 Donnelly	N	N	N	N	N	Y
3 **Stutzman**	N	N	Y	Y	N	Y
4 **Rokita**	N	N	Y	Y	N	Y
5 **Burton**	N	N	Y	N	N	Y
6 **Pence**	N	N	Y	Y	N	Y
7 Carson	Y	Y	N	N	Y	N
8 **Bucshon**	N	N	Y	Y	N	Y
9 **Young**	N	N	Y	Y	N	Y
IOWA						
1 Braley	Y	Y	N	N	Y	N
2 Loebsack	Y	Y	N	N	Y	Y
3 Boswell	N	N	N	N	Y	Y
4 **Latham**	N	N	Y	Y	N	Y
5 **King**	N	N	Y	Y	N	Y
KANSAS						
1 **Huelskamp**	N	N	Y	Y	N	Y
2 **Jenkins**	?	?	?	?	?	?
3 **Yoder**	N	N	Y	Y	N	Y
4 **Pompeo**	N	N	Y	Y	N	Y
KENTUCKY						
1 **Whitfield**	N	N	Y	Y	N	Y
2 **Guthrie**	N	N	Y	Y	N	Y
3 Yarmuth	Y	Y	N	N	Y	N
4 Vacant						
5 **Rogers**	N	N	Y	Y	N	Y
6 Chandler	N	N	N	Y	Y	Y
LOUISIANA						
1 **Scalise**	N	N	Y	Y	N	Y
2 Richmond	Y	Y	N	N	Y	N
3 **Landry**	?	?	?	?	?	?
4 **Fleming**	N	N	Y	Y	N	Y
5 **Alexander**	N	N	Y	Y	N	Y
6 **Cassidy**	N	N	Y	Y	N	Y
7 **Boustany**	N	N	Y	Y	N	Y
MAINE						
1 Pingree	Y	Y	N	N	Y	N
2 Michaud	Y	Y	N	N	Y	N
MARYLAND						
1 **Harris**	N	N	Y	?	N	Y
2 Ruppersberger	?	?	?	?	?	?
3 Sarbanes	Y	Y	N	N	Y	N
4 Edwards	Y	Y	N	N	Y	N
5 Hoyer	Y	Y	N	N	Y	N
6 **Bartlett**	N	N	Y	Y	N	Y
7 Cummings	Y	Y	N	N	Y	N
8 Van Hollen	Y	Y	N	N	Y	N
MASSACHUSETTS						
1 Olver	Y	Y	N	N	Y	N
2 Neal	Y	Y	N	N	Y	N
3 McGovern	Y	Y	N	N	?	N
4 Frank	Y	Y	N	N	Y	N
5 Tsongas	Y	Y	N	N	Y	N
6 Tierney	Y	Y	N	N	Y	N
7 Markey	Y	Y	N	N	Y	N
8 Capuano	Y	Y	N	N	Y	N
9 Lynch	Y	Y	N	N	Y	N
10 Keating	Y	Y	N	N	Y	N
MICHIGAN						
1 **Benishek**	N	N	Y	Y	N	Y
2 **Huizenga**	N	N	Y	Y	N	Y
3 **Amash**	N	N	Y	N	N	Y
4 **Camp**	N	N	Y	Y	N	Y
5 Kildee	Y	Y	N	N	Y	N
6 **Upton**	N	N	Y	Y	N	Y
7 **Walberg**	N	N	Y	Y	N	Y
8 **Rogers**	N	N	Y	Y	N	Y
9 Peters	Y	Y	N	N	Y	N
10 **Miller**	N	N	Y	Y	N	Y
11 Vacant						
12 Levin	Y	Y	N	N	Y	N
13 Clarke	Y	Y	N	N	Y	N
14 Conyers	Y	Y	N	N	Y	N
15 Dingell	Y	Y	N	N	Y	N
MINNESOTA						
1 Walz	N	N	N	N	Y	N
2 **Kline**	N	N	Y	Y	N	Y
3 **Paulsen**	N	N	Y	Y	N	Y
4 McCollum	Y	Y	N	N	Y	N

	598	599	600	601	602	603
5 Ellison	Y	Y	N	N	Y	N
6 **Bachmann**	N	N	Y	Y	N	Y
7 Peterson	N	N	Y	Y	N	Y
8 **Cravaack**	N	N	Y	Y	N	Y
MISSISSIPPI						
1 **Nunnelee**	N	N	Y	Y	N	Y
2 Thompson	N	Y	N	N	Y	N
3 **Harper**	N	N	Y	Y	N	Y
4 **Palazzo**	N	N	Y	Y	N	Y
MISSOURI						
1 Clay	Y	Y	N	N	Y	N
2 **Akin**	?	?	?	?	?	?
3 Carnahan	Y	Y	N	N	Y	N
4 **Hartzler**	N	N	Y	Y	N	Y
5 Cleaver	Y	Y	N	N	Y	N
6 **Graves**	N	N	Y	Y	N	Y
7 **Long**	N	N	Y	Y	N	Y
8 **Emerson**	N	N	Y	Y	N	Y
9 **Luetkemeyer**	N	N	Y	Y	N	Y
MONTANA						
AL **Rehberg**	N	N	Y	Y	N	Y
NEBRASKA						
1 **Fortenberry**	N	N	Y	Y	N	Y
2 **Terry**	N	Y	Y	Y	N	Y
3 **Smith**	N	N	Y	Y	N	Y
NEVADA						
1 Berkley	Y	Y	N	N	Y	Y
2 **Amodei**	N	N	Y	Y	N	Y
3 **Heck**	N	N	Y	Y	N	Y
NEW HAMPSHIRE						
1 **Guinta**	N	N	Y	Y	N	Y
2 **Bass**	Y	N	N	Y	N	N
NEW JERSEY						
1 Andrews	Y	Y	N	N	Y	N
2 **LoBiondo**	N	Y	N	N	N	N
3 **Runyan**	N	N	N	Y	N	Y
4 **Smith**	N	Y	N	Y	N	N
5 **Garrett**	–	–	+	+	–	+
6 Pallone	Y	Y	N	N	Y	N
7 **Lance**	N	N	Y	Y	N	Y
8 Pascrell	Y	Y	N	N	Y	N
9 Rothman	Y	Y	N	N	Y	N
10 Vacant						
11 **Frelinghuysen**	N	N	N	N	N	Y
12 Holt	Y	Y	N	N	Y	N
13 Sires	Y	Y	N	N	Y	N
NEW MEXICO						
1 Heinrich	Y	Y	N	N	Y	N
2 **Pearce**	?	?	?	?	?	?
3 Luján	Y	Y	N	N	?	N
NEW YORK						
1 Bishop	Y	Y	N	N	Y	N
2 Israel	Y	Y	N	N	Y	N
3 **King**	N	N	Y	Y	N	Y
4 McCarthy	Y	Y	N	N	Y	N
5 Ackerman	?	?	?	?	?	?
6 Meeks	Y	Y	N	N	Y	N
7 Crowley	Y	Y	N	N	Y	N
8 Nadler	Y	Y	N	N	Y	N
9 **Turner**	N	N	Y	Y	N	Y
10 Towns	Y	Y	N	N	Y	N
11 Clarke	Y	Y	N	N	Y	N
12 Velázquez	Y	Y	N	N	Y	N
13 **Grimm**	N	N	Y	Y	N	Y
14 Maloney	N	Y	N	N	Y	N
15 Rangel	Y	Y	N	N	Y	N
16 Serrano	Y	Y	N	N	Y	N
17 Engel	Y	Y	N	N	Y	N
18 Lowey	Y	Y	N	N	Y	N
19 **Hayworth**	N	N	N	Y	N	N
20 **Gibson**	N	N	N	N	N	N
21 Tonko	Y	Y	N	N	Y	N
22 Hinchey	Y	Y	N	N	Y	N
23 Owens	N	N	N	N	Y	N
24 **Hanna**	N	N	N	Y	N	Y
25 **Buerkle**	N	N	Y	Y	N	Y
26 Hochul	Y	Y	N	N	Y	N
27 Higgins	Y	Y	N	N	Y	N
28 Slaughter	Y	Y	N	N	Y	N
29 **Reed**	N	N	Y	Y	N	Y
NORTH CAROLINA						
1 Butterfield	Y	Y	N	N	Y	N
2 **Ellmers**	N	N	Y	Y	N	Y
3 **Jones**	N	Y	Y	Y	N	Y
4 Price	Y	Y	N	N	Y	N

	598	599	600	601	602	603
5 **Foxx**	N	N	Y	Y	N	Y
6 **Coble**	N	N	Y	Y	N	Y
7 McIntyre	N	N	Y	Y	Y	Y
8 Kissell	N	N	Y	Y	Y	Y
9 **Myrick**	N	N	Y	Y	N	Y
10 **McHenry**	N	N	Y	Y	N	Y
11 Shuler	Y	N	N	N	Y	N
12 Watt	Y	Y	N	N	Y	N
13 Miller	Y	Y	N	N	Y	N
NORTH DAKOTA						
AL **Berg**	N	N	Y	Y	N	Y
OHIO						
1 **Chabot**	N	N	Y	Y	N	Y
2 **Schmidt**	N	N	Y	Y	N	Y
3 **Turner**	N	N	Y	Y	N	Y
4 **Jordan**	N	N	Y	Y	N	Y
5 **Latta**	N	N	Y	Y	N	Y
6 **Johnson**	N	N	Y	Y	N	Y
7 **Austria**	N	N	Y	Y	N	Y
8 **Boehner**						
9 Kaptur	Y	Y	N	N	Y	N
10 Kucinich	Y	Y	N	N	Y	N
11 Fudge	Y	Y	N	N	Y	N
12 **Tiberi**	N	N	Y	N	N	Y
13 Sutton	N	Y	N	N	Y	N
14 **LaTourette**	N	N	Y	N	N	Y
15 **Stivers**	N	N	Y	Y	N	Y
16 **Renacci**	N	N	Y	Y	N	Y
17 Ryan	Y	Y	N	N	Y	N
18 **Gibbs**	N	N	Y	Y	N	Y
OKLAHOMA						
1 **Sullivan**	N	N	Y	Y	N	Y
2 Boren	N	N	Y	Y	Y	Y
3 **Lucas**	N	N	Y	Y	N	Y
4 **Cole**	N	N	Y	Y	N	Y
5 **Lankford**	N	N	Y	Y	N	Y
OREGON						
1 Bonamici	Y	Y	N	N	Y	N
2 **Walden**	N	N	Y	Y	N	Y
3 Blumenauer	Y	Y	N	N	Y	N
4 DeFazio	Y	Y	N	N	Y	N
5 Schrader	Y	Y	N	N	Y	N
PENNSYLVANIA						
1 Brady	Y	Y	N	N	Y	N
2 Fattah	Y	Y	N	N	Y	N
3 **Kelly**	N	N	Y	Y	N	Y
4 Altmire	N	N	N	N	Y	Y
5 **Thompson**	N	N	Y	Y	N	Y
6 **Gerlach**	N	Y	N	N	N	Y
7 **Meehan**	N	N	Y	Y	N	Y
8 **Fitzpatrick**	N	N	Y	Y	N	N
9 **Shuster**	N	N	Y	Y	N	Y
10 **Marino**	N	N	Y	Y	N	Y
11 **Barletta**	N	N	Y	Y	N	Y
12 Critz	N	N	N	Y	Y	Y
13 Schwartz	Y	Y	N	N	Y	N
14 Doyle	Y	Y	N	N	Y	N
15 **Dent**	N	N	Y	Y	N	Y
16 **Pitts**	N	N	Y	Y	N	Y
17 Holden	N	N	Y	Y	N	Y
18 **Murphy**	N	N	Y	Y	N	Y
19 **Platts**	Y	N	N	N	N	Y
RHODE ISLAND						
1 Cicilline	Y	Y	N	N	Y	N
2 Langevin	Y	Y	N	N	Y	N
SOUTH CAROLINA						
1 **Scott**	N	N	Y	Y	N	Y
2 **Wilson**	N	N	Y	?	N	Y
3 **Duncan**	N	N	Y	Y	N	Y
4 **Gowdy**	N	N	Y	Y	N	Y
5 **Mulvaney**	N	N	Y	Y	N	Y
6 Clyburn	N	Y	N	N	Y	N
SOUTH DAKOTA						
AL **Noem**	N	N	Y	Y	N	Y
TENNESSEE						
1 **Roe**	N	N	Y	Y	N	Y
2 **Duncan**	N	N	Y	Y	N	Y
3 **Fleischmann**	N	N	Y	Y	N	Y
4 **DesJarlais**	N	N	Y	Y	N	Y
5 Cooper	Y	Y	N	N	Y	N
6 **Black**	N	N	Y	?	N	Y
7 **Blackburn**	N	N	Y	Y	N	Y
8 **Fincher**	N	N	Y	Y	N	Y
9 Cohen	Y	Y	N	N	?	N

	598	599	600	601	602	603
TEXAS						
1 **Gohmert**	?	N	Y	Y	N	Y
2 **Poe**	N	N	Y	Y	N	Y
3 **Johnson, S.**	N	N	Y	Y	N	Y
4 **Hall**	N	N	Y	Y	N	Y
5 **Hensarling**	N	N	Y	Y	N	Y
6 **Barton**	N	N	Y	Y	N	Y
7 **Culberson**	N	N	Y	Y	N	Y
8 **Brady**	N	N	Y	Y	N	Y
9 Green, A.	Y	Y	N	N	Y	N
10 **McCaul**	N	N	Y	Y	N	Y
11 **Conaway**	N	N	Y	Y	N	Y
12 **Granger**	?	?	?	?	?	?
13 **Thornberry**	N	N	Y	Y	N	Y
14 **Paul**	N	N	Y	Y	N	Y
15 Hinojosa	N	Y	N	N	Y	N
16 Reyes	Y	Y	N	N	Y	N
17 **Flores**	N	N	Y	Y	N	Y
18 Jackson Lee	Y	Y	N	N	Y	N
19 **Neugebauer**	N	N	Y	Y	N	Y
20 Gonzalez	N	Y	N	N	Y	N
21 **Smith**	N	N	Y	Y	?	Y
22 **Olson**	N	N	Y	Y	N	Y
23 **Canseco**	N	N	Y	Y	N	Y
24 **Marchant**	N	N	Y	Y	N	Y
25 Doggett	Y	Y	N	N	Y	N
26 **Burgess**	N	N	Y	Y	N	Y
27 **Farenthold**	N	N	Y	Y	N	Y
28 Cuellar	Y	Y	N	N	Y	Y
29 Green, G.	N	Y	N	N	Y	N
30 Johnson, E.	Y	Y	N	N	Y	N
31 **Carter**	N	N	Y	Y	N	Y
32 **Sessions**	N	N	Y	Y	N	?
UTAH						
1 **Bishop**	N	N	Y	Y	N	Y
2 Matheson	N	N	Y	Y	N	Y
3 **Chaffetz**	N	N	Y	Y	N	Y
VERMONT						
AL Welch	Y	Y	N	N	Y	N
VIRGINIA						
1 **Wittman**	N	N	Y	Y	N	N
2 **Rigell**	N	N	Y	Y	N	N
3 Scott	Y	Y	N	N	Y	N
4 **Forbes**	N	N	Y	Y	N	Y
5 **Hurt**	N	N	Y	Y	N	Y
6 **Goodlatte**	N	N	Y	Y	N	Y
7 **Cantor**	N	N	Y	Y	N	Y
8 Moran	Y	Y	N	N	Y	N
9 **Griffith**	N	N	Y	Y	N	Y
10 **Wolf**	N	N	Y	Y	N	N
11 Connolly	Y	Y	N	N	Y	N
WASHINGTON						
1 Vacant						
2 Larsen	Y	N	N	N	Y	N
3 **Herrera Beutler**	N	N	Y	Y	N	Y
4 **Hastings**	N	N	Y	Y	N	Y
5 **McMorris Rodgers**	N	N	Y	Y	N	Y
6 Dicks	Y	Y	N	N	Y	N
7 McDermott	Y	Y	N	N	Y	N
8 **Reichert**	N	N	Y	Y	N	N
9 Smith	Y	Y	N	N	Y	N
WEST VIRGINIA						
1 **McKinley**	N	N	Y	Y	N	Y
2 **Capito**	N	N	Y	Y	N	Y
3 Rahall	N	N	Y	Y	N	Y
WISCONSIN						
1 **Ryan**	–	–	+	+	–	+
2 Baldwin	Y	Y	N	N	Y	N
3 Kind	Y	Y	N	N	Y	N
4 Moore	Y	Y	N	N	Y	N
5 **Sensenbrenner**	N	N	Y	Y	N	Y
6 **Petri**	N	N	Y	Y	N	Y
7 **Duffy**	N	N	Y	Y	N	Y
8 **Ribble**	N	N	Y	Y	N	Y
WYOMING						
AL **Lummis**	N	N	Y	Y	N	Y

IN THE HOUSE | By Vote Number

604. **HR 6371. Federal Contractor Employee Claims/Passage.**
Walberg, R-Mich., motion to suspend the rules and pass the bill that would transfer from the Government Accountability Office to the Labor Department the authority to process unpaid wage claims of workers hired by federal contractors. Motion agreed to 361-3: R 212-3; D 149-0. A two-thirds majority of those present and voting (243 in this case) is required for passage under suspension of the rules. Nov. 13, 2012.

605. **HR 6156. Russia Trade Relations/Previous Question.** Dreier, R-Calif., motion to order the previous question (thus ending debate and the possibility of amendment) on the rule (H Res 808) that would provide for House floor consideration of a bill that would establish permanent normal trade relations with Russia and Moldova and end Jackson-Vanik restrictions on both economies. Motion agreed to 243-164: R 230-2; D 13-162. Nov. 15, 2012.

606. **HR 6156. Russia Trade Relations/Rule.** Adoption of the rule (H Res 808) that would provide for House floor consideration of the bill that would establish permanent normal trade relations with Russia and Moldova and end Jackson-Vanik restrictions on both economies. Adopted 253-150: R 229-2; D 24-148. Nov. 15, 2012.

607. **HR 2453. Mark Twain Commemorative Coin/Motion to Concur.** Luetkemeyer, R-Mo., motion to suspend the rules and concur in the Senate amendments to the bill that would direct the Treasury Department to issue $5 and $1 coins commemorating author Mark Twain for one year. Motion agreed to 370-19: R 207-18; D 163-1. A two-thirds majority of those present and voting (260 in this case) is required for passage under suspension of the rules. Nov. 15, 2012.

608. **HR 6156. Russia Trade Relations/Passage.** Passage of the bill that would establish permanent normal trade relations with Russia and Moldova and end Jackson-Vanik restrictions on both economies. The bill also would provide sanctions against persons involved in human rights violations in Russia. Passed 365-43: R 227-6; D 138-37. A "yea" was a vote in support of the president's position. Nov. 16, 2012.

[1]Rep. Thomas Massie, R-Ky., was sworn in Nov. 13, 2012, to fill the seat left vacant by fellow Republican Geoff Davis, who resigned July 31.

[2]Rep. David A. Curson, D-Mich., was sworn in Nov. 13, 2012, to fill the seat left vacant by Republican Thaddeus McCotter, who resigned July 6.

[3]Rep. Donald M. Payne Jr., D-N.J., was sworn in Nov. 15, 2012, to fill the seat left vacant by his father, fellow Democrat Donald M. Payne, who died March 6.

[4]Rep. Suzan DelBene, D-Wash., was sworn in Nov. 13, 2012, to fill the seat left vacant by fellow Democrat Jay Inslee, who resigned March 20 to run for governor.

	604	605	606	607	608
ALABAMA					
1 Bonner	Y	Y	Y	Y	Y
2 Roby	Y	Y	Y	Y	Y
3 Rogers	?	Y	Y	Y	Y
4 Aderholt	Y	Y	Y	Y	Y
5 Brooks	Y	Y	Y	N	Y
6 Bachus	?	Y	Y	Y	Y
7 Sewell	Y	N	N	Y	Y
ALASKA					
AL Young	Y	Y	Y	Y	Y
ARIZONA					
1 Gosar	Y	Y	Y	Y	Y
2 Franks	Y	Y	Y	N	Y
3 Quayle	Y	Y	Y	Y	Y
4 Pastor	Y	N	N	Y	Y
5 Schweikert	Y	Y	Y	N	Y
6 Flake	Y	Y	Y	Y	Y
7 Grijalva	Y	?	?	?	N
8 Barber	Y	N	N	Y	Y
ARKANSAS					
1 Crawford	Y	Y	Y	Y	Y
2 Griffin	Y	Y	Y	Y	Y
3 Womack	Y	Y	Y	Y	Y
4 Ross	Y	N	Y	Y	Y
CALIFORNIA					
1 Thompson	Y	N	N	Y	Y
2 Herger	Y	Y	Y	?	Y
3 Lungren	Y	Y	Y	Y	Y
4 McClintock	N	Y	Y	Y	Y
5 Matsui	Y	N	N	Y	Y
6 Woolsey	Y	?	?	?	?
7 Miller, George	+	?	?	?	?
8 Pelosi	?	N	N	Y	Y
9 Lee	Y	N	N	Y	N
10 Garamendi	Y	N	N	Y	Y
11 McNerney	Y	N	N	Y	Y
12 Speier	Y	N	N	Y	Y
13 Stark	Y	Y	N	Y	N
14 Eshoo	Y	Y	Y	Y	Y
15 Honda	Y	N	N	Y	Y
16 Lofgren	Y	N	N	Y	N
17 Farr	Y	N	N	Y	Y
18 Vacant					
19 Denham	Y	Y	Y	Y	Y
20 Costa	Y	Y	Y	Y	Y
21 Nunes	Y	Y	Y	Y	Y
22 McCarthy	Y	Y	Y	Y	Y
23 Capps	+	N	N	Y	Y
24 Gallegly	?	?	?	?	?
25 McKeon	Y	Y	Y	Y	Y
26 Dreier	Y	Y	Y	Y	Y
27 Sherman	Y	N	N	Y	Y
28 Berman	Y	N	Y	?	Y
29 Schiff	Y	N	N	Y	Y
30 Waxman	Y	N	N	Y	Y
31 Becerra	+	N	N	Y	Y
32 Chu	Y	N	N	Y	N
33 Bass	Y	N	N	?	Y
34 Roybal-Allard	Y	N	N	Y	Y
35 Waters	?	N	N	Y	Y
36 Hahn	Y	N	N	Y	N
37 Richardson	Y	N	N	Y	N
38 Napolitano	Y	N	N	Y	N
39 Sánchez, Linda	Y	N	?	?	Y
40 Royce	Y	Y	Y	?	Y
41 Lewis	Y	Y	?	?	Y
42 Miller, Gary	Y	Y	Y	Y	Y
43 Baca	Y	N	N	Y	N
44 Calvert	Y	Y	N	Y	Y
45 Bono Mack	?	Y	Y	Y	Y
46 Rohrabacher	Y	Y	Y	Y	Y
47 Sanchez, Loretta	Y	?	?	?	Y
48 Campbell	N	Y	Y	Y	Y
49 Issa	Y	Y	Y	Y	Y
50 Bilbray	Y	Y	Y	Y	Y
51 Filner	+	-	-	+	?
52 Hunter	Y	Y	Y	Y	Y
53 Davis	Y	N	N	Y	Y

	604	605	606	607	608
COLORADO					
1 DeGette	Y	Y	?	?	Y
2 Polis	Y	N	N	Y	Y
3 Tipton	Y	Y	Y	Y	Y
4 Gardner	Y	Y	Y	Y	Y
5 Lamborn	?	Y	Y	Y	Y
6 Coffman	Y	Y	Y	Y	Y
7 Perlmutter	Y	N	N	Y	Y
CONNECTICUT					
1 Larson	?	N	N	Y	Y
2 Courtney	Y	N	N	Y	Y
3 DeLauro	+	N	N	Y	N
4 Himes	Y	Y	N	Y	Y
5 Murphy	Y	N	N	Y	Y
DELAWARE					
AL Carney	Y	N	Y	?	Y
FLORIDA					
1 Miller	Y	Y	Y	Y	Y
2 Southerland	Y	Y	Y	Y	Y
3 Brown	Y	Y	Y	Y	Y
4 Crenshaw	Y	Y	Y	Y	Y
5 Nugent	Y	Y	Y	Y	Y
6 Stearns	Y	Y	Y	Y	Y
7 Mica	Y	Y	Y	Y	Y
8 Webster	Y	Y	Y	Y	Y
9 Bilirakis	Y	Y	Y	Y	Y
10 Young	Y	Y	Y	Y	Y
11 Castor	Y	N	N	Y	Y
12 Ross	Y	Y	Y	N	Y
13 Buchanan	Y	?	?	?	Y
14 Mack	?	Y	Y	Y	Y
15 Posey	Y	Y	Y	Y	Y
16 Rooney	Y	Y	Y	Y	Y
17 Wilson	Y	N	N	Y	N
18 Ros-Lehtinen	Y	Y	Y	Y	Y
19 Deutch	Y	N	N	Y	Y
20 Wasserman Schultz	Y	N	N	Y	Y
21 Diaz-Balart	Y	Y	Y	Y	Y
22 West	Y	Y	Y	Y	Y
23 Hastings	Y	N	N	Y	Y
24 Adams	Y	Y	Y	Y	Y
25 Rivera	Y	Y	Y	Y	Y
GEORGIA					
1 Kingston	Y	Y	Y	Y	Y
2 Bishop	Y	N	N	Y	?
3 Westmoreland	Y	Y	Y	Y	Y
4 Johnson	Y	N	N	Y	Y
5 Lewis	?	?	?	?	?
6 Price	Y	Y	Y	Y	Y
7 Woodall	Y	Y	Y	Y	Y
8 Scott, A.	Y	Y	Y	Y	Y
9 Graves	Y	Y	Y	N	Y
10 Broun	N	Y	Y	Y	Y
11 Gingrey	Y	Y	Y	Y	Y
12 Barrow	Y	N	N	Y	Y
13 Scott, D.	Y	N	N	Y	Y
HAWAII					
1 Hanabusa	Y	N	N	Y	Y
2 Hirono	Y	N	N	Y	Y
IDAHO					
1 Labrador	Y	Y	Y	Y	Y
2 Simpson	Y	Y	Y	Y	Y
ILLINOIS					
1 Rush	?	?	?	?	?
2 Jackson	?	?	?	?	?
3 Lipinski	?	N	N	Y	N
4 Gutierrez	?	N	N	Y	Y
5 Quigley	Y	N	N	Y	Y
6 Roskam	Y	Y	Y	Y	Y
7 Davis	Y	N	N	Y	Y
8 Walsh	?	Y	Y	Y	Y
9 Schakowsky	Y	N	N	Y	Y
10 Dold	Y	Y	Y	Y	Y
11 Kinzinger	Y	Y	Y	Y	Y
12 Costello	Y	N	?	?	?
13 Biggert	Y	Y	Y	Y	Y
14 Hultgren	Y	Y	Y	Y	Y
15 Johnson	+	Y	Y	Y	Y

KEY   **Republicans**   Democrats

Y Voted for (yea)	X Paired against	C Voted "present" to avoid possible conflict of interest
# Paired for	– Announced against	
+ Announced for	P Voted "present"	? Did not vote or otherwise make a position known
N Voted against (nay)		

	604	605	606	607	608
16 Manzullo	?	?	?	?	Y
17 Schilling	Y	Y	Y	Y	Y
18 Schock	Y	Y	Y	Y	Y
19 Shimkus	Y	Y	Y	Y	Y
INDIANA					
1 Visclosky	Y	N	N	Y	N
2 Donnelly	Y	Y	Y	Y	Y
3 Stutzman	Y	Y	Y	?	Y
4 Rokita	Y	Y	Y	Y	Y
5 Burton	?	Y	Y	Y	Y
6 Pence	+	?	?	?	?
7 Carson	Y	N	N	Y	Y
8 Bucshon	Y	Y	Y	Y	Y
9 Young	Y	Y	Y	Y	Y
IOWA					
1 Braley	Y	N	N	Y	Y
2 Loebsack	Y	N	N	?	Y
3 Boswell	Y	N	N	Y	Y
4 Latham	Y	Y	Y	Y	Y
5 King	Y	Y	Y	Y	Y
KANSAS					
1 Huelskamp	Y	Y	Y	N	Y
2 Jenkins	Y	Y	Y	Y	Y
3 Yoder	Y	Y	Y	Y	Y
4 Pompeo	Y	Y	Y	Y	Y
KENTUCKY					
1 Whitfield	Y	Y	Y	Y	Y
2 Guthrie	Y	Y	Y	Y	Y
3 Yarmuth	Y	?	?	?	?
4 Massie[1]		Y	Y	N	Y
5 Rogers	Y	Y	Y	?	Y
6 Chandler	Y	N	N	?	Y
LOUISIANA					
1 Scalise	Y	Y	Y	Y	Y
2 Richmond	Y	N	N	Y	Y
3 Landry	Y	Y	Y	Y	Y
4 Fleming	Y	Y	Y	Y	Y
5 Alexander	Y	Y	Y	Y	Y
6 Cassidy	Y	Y	Y	Y	Y
7 Boustany	Y	Y	Y	Y	Y
MAINE					
1 Pingree	Y	N	N	Y	N
2 Michaud	Y	N	N	Y	Y
MARYLAND					
1 Harris	Y	Y	Y	Y	Y
2 Ruppersberger	?	N	N	?	Y
3 Sarbanes	Y	N	N	Y	Y
4 Edwards	Y	N	N	Y	Y
5 Hoyer	?	N	N	Y	Y
6 Bartlett	?	?	?	?	?
7 Cummings	Y	N	N	Y	Y
8 Van Hollen	?	N	N	Y	Y
MASSACHUSETTS					
1 Olver	Y	N	N	Y	Y
2 Neal	?	N	N	Y	Y
3 McGovern	?	N	N	Y	Y
4 Frank	Y	Y	?	?	Y
5 Tsongas	Y	N	N	Y	Y
6 Tierney	Y	N	N	Y	N
7 Markey	?	N	N	Y	Y
8 Capuano	Y	N	N	Y	N
9 Lynch	?	N	Y	Y	Y
10 Keating	Y	N	N	?	N
MICHIGAN					
1 Benishek	Y	Y	Y	Y	Y
2 Huizenga	Y	Y	Y	Y	Y
3 Amash	Y	Y	Y	N	Y
4 Camp	Y	Y	Y	Y	Y
5 Kildee	Y	N	N	Y	N
6 Upton	Y	Y	Y	N	Y
7 Walberg	Y	Y	Y	Y	Y
8 Rogers	?	Y	Y	Y	N
9 Peters	Y	N	N	Y	Y
10 Miller	Y	Y	Y	Y	Y
11 Curson[2]		N	N	Y	Y
12 Levin	Y	N	N	Y	Y
13 Clarke	Y	N	N	Y	N
14 Conyers	Y	N	N	Y	Y
15 Dingell	Y	N	N	Y	Y
MINNESOTA					
1 Walz	?	N	N	Y	Y
2 Kline	Y	Y	Y	Y	Y
3 Paulsen	Y	Y	Y	Y	Y
4 McCollum	Y	N	N	Y	N

	604	605	606	607	608
5 Ellison	Y	N	N	Y	Y
6 Bachmann	?	Y	Y	Y	Y
7 Peterson	Y	N	Y	Y	Y
8 Cravaack	Y	Y	Y	Y	Y
MISSISSIPPI					
1 Nunnelee	Y	Y	Y	Y	Y
2 Thompson	Y	N	N	Y	N
3 Harper	Y	Y	Y	Y	Y
4 Palazzo	Y	Y	Y	Y	Y
MISSOURI					
1 Clay	?	N	N	Y	Y
2 Akin	?	?	?	?	Y
3 Carnahan	?	N	N	Y	Y
4 Hartzler	Y	Y	Y	Y	Y
5 Cleaver	?	N	N	Y	Y
6 Graves	Y	Y	Y	Y	Y
7 Long	Y	Y	Y	Y	Y
8 Emerson	Y	Y	Y	Y	Y
9 Luetkemeyer	Y	Y	Y	Y	Y
MONTANA					
AL Rehberg	Y	Y	Y	Y	Y
NEBRASKA					
1 Fortenberry	Y	Y	Y	Y	Y
2 Terry	Y	Y	Y	Y	Y
3 Smith	Y	Y	Y	Y	Y
NEVADA					
1 Berkley	Y	N	N	Y	Y
2 Amodei	Y	Y	Y	Y	Y
3 Heck	Y	Y	Y	Y	Y
NEW HAMPSHIRE					
1 Guinta	Y	Y	Y	Y	Y
2 Bass	Y	Y	Y	Y	Y
NEW JERSEY					
1 Andrews	?	N	?	?	Y
2 LoBiondo	Y	Y	Y	Y	N
3 Runyan	Y	Y	Y	Y	Y
4 Smith	Y	Y	Y	Y	Y
5 Garrett	Y	Y	Y	N	Y
6 Pallone	?	N	N	Y	N
7 Lance	Y	Y	Y	Y	Y
8 Pascrell	Y	N	N	Y	Y
9 Rothman					
10 Payne[3]				Y	Y
11 Frelinghuysen	Y	Y	Y	Y	Y
12 Holt	Y	?	?	?	?
13 Sires	?	N	N	Y	Y
NEW MEXICO					
1 Heinrich	Y	?	?	?	?
2 Pearce	Y	Y	Y	Y	Y
3 Luján	Y	N	N	Y	Y
NEW YORK					
1 Bishop	Y	N	N	Y	Y
2 Israel	?	N	N	Y	Y
3 King	Y	Y	Y	Y	Y
4 McCarthy	Y	N	N	Y	Y
5 Ackerman	Y	N	N	Y	Y
6 Meeks	Y	?	?	?	Y
7 Crowley	Y	N	Y	Y	Y
8 Nadler	Y	N	N	Y	N
9 Turner	Y	Y	Y	Y	Y
10 Towns	?	?	?	?	?
11 Clarke	+	N	N	Y	Y
12 Velázquez	Y	N	N	Y	N
13 Grimm	Y	?	?	?	Y
14 Maloney	?	N	N	Y	?
15 Rangel	Y	N	N	Y	Y
16 Serrano	Y	N	N	Y	N
17 Engel	Y	N	N	Y	Y
18 Lowey	Y	N	N	Y	Y
19 Hayworth	Y	Y	Y	Y	Y
20 Gibson	Y	Y	Y	Y	Y
21 Tonko	Y	N	N	Y	Y
22 Hinchey	Y	N	N	Y	Y
23 Owens	Y	N	N	Y	Y
24 Hanna	Y	Y	Y	Y	Y
25 Buerkle	Y	Y	Y	Y	Y
26 Hochul	Y	N	N	Y	Y
27 Higgins	Y	N	N	Y	Y
28 Slaughter	+	N	N	Y	Y
29 Reed	?	Y	Y	Y	Y
NORTH CAROLINA					
1 Butterfield	Y	N	N	Y	Y
2 Ellmers	Y	Y	Y	Y	Y
3 Jones	Y	N	N	Y	N
4 Price	Y	N	N	Y	Y

	604	605	606	607	608
5 Foxx	Y	Y	Y	Y	Y
6 Coble	Y	Y	Y	Y	Y
7 McIntyre	Y	Y	Y	Y	Y
8 Kissell	Y	N	Y	Y	Y
9 Myrick	Y	Y	Y	Y	Y
10 McHenry	Y	Y	Y	Y	Y
11 Shuler	?	?	Y	Y	?
12 Watt	Y	N	N	Y	Y
13 Miller	Y	N	N	Y	Y
NORTH DAKOTA					
AL Berg	Y	Y	Y	Y	Y
OHIO					
1 Chabot	Y	Y	Y	Y	Y
2 Schmidt	Y	Y	Y	Y	Y
3 Turner	Y	Y	Y	?	Y
4 Jordan	Y	Y	Y	Y	Y
5 Latta	Y	Y	Y	Y	Y
6 Johnson	+	Y	Y	Y	Y
7 Austria	Y	Y	Y	Y	Y
8 Boehner					
9 Kaptur	Y	N	N	Y	N
10 Kucinich	Y	N	N	N	N
11 Fudge	Y	N	N	Y	N
12 Tiberi	?	Y	Y	Y	Y
13 Sutton	Y	N	N	Y	N
14 LaTourette	Y	Y	Y	Y	N
15 Stivers	Y	Y	Y	Y	Y
16 Renacci	Y	Y	Y	Y	Y
17 Ryan	Y	N	N	Y	N
18 Gibbs	Y	Y	Y	Y	Y
OKLAHOMA					
1 Sullivan	Y	Y	Y	?	?
2 Boren	?	?	?	?	?
3 Lucas	?	Y	Y	Y	Y
4 Cole	Y	Y	Y	Y	Y
5 Lankford	Y	Y	Y	Y	Y
OREGON					
1 Bonamici	Y	N	N	Y	Y
2 Walden	Y	Y	Y	Y	Y
3 Blumenauer	Y	N	N	Y	Y
4 DeFazio	Y	N	N	Y	N
5 Schrader	Y	N	N	Y	Y
PENNSYLVANIA					
1 Brady	Y	N	N	Y	?
2 Fattah	Y	N	N	Y	Y
3 Kelly	Y	Y	Y	Y	Y
4 Altmire	Y	N	N	Y	Y
5 Thompson	Y	Y	Y	Y	Y
6 Gerlach	Y	Y	Y	Y	Y
7 Meehan	Y	Y	Y	Y	Y
8 Fitzpatrick	Y	Y	Y	Y	?
9 Shuster	Y	Y	Y	Y	Y
10 Marino	Y	Y	Y	Y	Y
11 Barletta	Y	Y	Y	Y	Y
12 Critz	Y	N	N	Y	Y
13 Schwartz	Y	N	N	Y	Y
14 Doyle	Y	N	N	Y	N
15 Dent	Y	Y	Y	Y	Y
16 Pitts	Y	Y	Y	Y	Y
17 Holden	?	N	N	Y	Y
18 Murphy	Y	Y	Y	Y	Y
19 Platts	?	Y	Y	Y	Y
RHODE ISLAND					
1 Cicilline	?	N	N	Y	N
2 Langevin	+	N	N	Y	Y
SOUTH CAROLINA					
1 Scott	Y	Y	Y	Y	Y
2 Wilson	Y	Y	Y	Y	Y
3 Duncan	Y	Y	Y	Y	Y
4 Gowdy	?	Y	Y	Y	Y
5 Mulvaney	Y	Y	Y	N	Y
6 Clyburn	Y	N	N	Y	Y
SOUTH DAKOTA					
AL Noem	Y	Y	Y	Y	Y
TENNESSEE					
1 Roe	Y	Y	Y	Y	Y
2 Duncan	Y	Y	Y	Y	Y
3 Fleischmann	Y	Y	Y	Y	Y
4 DesJarlais	Y	Y	Y	Y	Y
5 Cooper	Y	N	Y	Y	Y
6 Black	Y	Y	Y	Y	Y
7 Blackburn	Y	Y	Y	N	Y
8 Fincher	Y	Y	Y	Y	Y
9 Cohen	Y	N	N	Y	Y

	604	605	606	607	608
TEXAS					
1 Gohmert	Y	Y	Y	Y	Y
2 Poe	Y	Y	Y	N	Y
3 Johnson, S.	Y	Y	Y	Y	Y
4 Hall	Y	Y	Y	Y	Y
5 Hensarling	Y	Y	Y	Y	Y
6 Barton	Y	Y	Y	Y	Y
7 Culberson	Y	Y	Y	Y	Y
8 Brady	?	Y	Y	N	Y
9 Green, A.	Y	N	N	Y	Y
10 McCaul	Y	Y	Y	Y	Y
11 Conaway	Y	Y	Y	Y	Y
12 Granger	Y	Y	Y	Y	Y
13 Thornberry	Y	Y	Y	N	Y
14 Paul	Y	N	N	N	N
15 Hinojosa	Y	N	N	Y	Y
16 Reyes	Y	N	N	Y	Y
17 Flores	Y	Y	Y	Y	Y
18 Jackson Lee	Y	?	?	?	?
19 Neugebauer	Y	Y	Y	Y	Y
20 Gonzalez	Y	N	N	Y	Y
21 Smith	Y	Y	Y	Y	Y
22 Olson	Y	Y	Y	Y	Y
23 Canseco	Y	Y	Y	Y	Y
24 Marchant	Y	Y	Y	Y	Y
25 Doggett	?	N	N	Y	Y
26 Burgess	Y	Y	Y	Y	Y
27 Farenthold	Y	Y	Y	Y	Y
28 Cuellar	?	N	N	Y	Y
29 Green, G.	Y	N	N	Y	N
30 Johnson, E.	Y	N	N	Y	Y
31 Carter	Y	Y	Y	Y	Y
32 Sessions	Y	Y	Y	Y	Y
UTAH					
1 Bishop	Y	Y	Y	Y	Y
2 Matheson	Y	Y	Y	Y	Y
3 Chaffetz	Y	Y	Y	Y	Y
VERMONT					
AL Welch	Y	N	N	Y	Y
VIRGINIA					
1 Wittman	Y	Y	Y	Y	Y
2 Rigell	Y	Y	Y	N	Y
3 Scott	Y	N	N	Y	Y
4 Forbes	?	?	?	?	?
5 Hurt	Y	Y	Y	Y	Y
6 Goodlatte	Y	Y	Y	Y	Y
7 Cantor	Y	Y	Y	Y	Y
8 Moran	Y	N	Y	Y	Y
9 Griffith	Y	Y	Y	Y	Y
10 Wolf	Y	Y	Y	Y	?
11 Connolly	Y	Y	Y	Y	Y
WASHINGTON					
1 DelBene[4]		N	N	Y	Y
2 Larsen	Y	N	N	Y	Y
3 Herrera Beutler	Y	Y	Y	Y	Y
4 Hastings	Y	Y	Y	Y	Y
5 McMorris Rodgers	Y	Y	Y	Y	Y
6 Dicks	Y	N	N	Y	Y
7 McDermott	Y	N	N	Y	Y
8 Reichert	Y	Y	Y	Y	Y
9 Smith	Y	N	N	Y	Y
WEST VIRGINIA					
1 McKinley	Y	Y	Y	Y	Y
2 Capito	?	Y	Y	Y	Y
3 Rahall	Y	N	N	Y	N
WISCONSIN					
1 Ryan	Y	Y	Y	Y	Y
2 Baldwin	Y	N	N	Y	Y
3 Kind	Y	Y	Y	Y	Y
4 Moore	Y	N	N	Y	Y
5 Sensenbrenner	Y	Y	Y	Y	Y
6 Petri	Y	Y	Y	Y	Y
7 Duffy	Y	Y	Y	Y	Y
8 Ribble	Y	Y	Y	N	Y
WYOMING					
AL Lummis	Y	Y	Y	Y	Y

IN THE HOUSE | By Vote Number

609. **HR 5997. Medical Preparedness Grants/Passage.** Bilirakis, R-Fla., motion to suspend the rules and pass the bill that would expand existing authorization of the Homeland Security Department's Urban Area Security Initiative and State Homeland Security Grant Program to allow funds to be used for local general emergency medical preparedness programs. Motion agreed to 397-1: R 223-1; D 174-0. A two-thirds majority of those present and voting (266 in this case) is required for passage under suspension of the rules. Nov. 27, 2012.

610. **HR 915. Border Security Task Force/Motion to Concur.** McCaul, R-Texas, motion to suspend the rules and concur in the Senate amendment to the bill that would establish a Border Enforcement Security Task Force within the Homeland Security Department to coordinate federal, state and local efforts to protect U.S. border communities from violence associated with transnational crime. Motion agreed to 397-4: R 222-3; D 175-1. A two-thirds majority of those present and voting (268 in this case) is required for passage under suspension of the rules. Nov. 27, 2012.

611. **HR 6429. STEM Visa Program/Rule.** Adoption of the rule (H Res 821) that would provide for House floor consideration of the bill that would create a new visa program under which foreign students earning advanced degrees in science, technology, engineering and mathematics at eligible U.S. colleges and universities could remain in the United States to work in those fields. Adopted 243-170: R 233-0; D 10-170. Nov. 29, 2012.

612. **HR 6429. STEM Visa Program/Recommit.** Lofgren, D-Calif., motion to recommit the bill to the House Judiciary Committee and report it back immediately with an amendment that would preserve the Diversity Visa Program while also allocating 55,000 high-tech visas for foreign students who graduate with advanced degrees in science, technology, engineering or mathematics from U.S. universities. The motion also would require that STEM visa workers receive pay comparable to U.S. workers. Motion rejected 157-231: R 0-226; D 157-5. Nov. 30, 2012.

613. **HR 6429. STEM Visa Program/Passage.** Passage of the bill that would create a new visa program under which foreign students earning advanced degrees in science, technology, engineering or mathematics at eligible U.S. colleges and universities could remain in the United States to work in those fields. The bill would eliminate the Diversity Visa Program and would reallocate 55,000 visas to the new STEM visa program. It would allow spouses and children of a STEM graduate to reside in the United States without work authorization after a one-year waiting period. Passed 245-139: R 218-5; D 27-134. A "nay" was a vote in support of the president's position. Nov. 30, 2012.

614. **HR 6582. Heating and Cooling Equipment Energy Efficiency Standards/Passage.** Whitfield, R-Ky., motion to suspend the rules and pass the bill that would clarify federal energy efficiency standards for water heaters, air conditioners, residential-ventilation units and commercial refrigerators. The bill would exempt walk-in refrigeration units and would direct the Energy Department to establish research partnerships. Motion agreed to 398-2: R 218-2; D 180-0. A two-thirds majority of those present and voting (267 in this case) is required for passage under suspension of the rules. Dec. 4, 2012.

615. **Procedural Motion/Journal.** Approval of the House Journal of Dec. 3, 2012. Approved 290-106: R 164-53; D 126-53. Dec. 4, 2012.

	609	610	611	612	613	614	615
ALABAMA							
1 Bonner	Y	Y	Y	?	?	?	?
2 Roby	Y	Y	Y	N	Y	Y	Y
3 Rogers	Y	Y	Y	N	Y	Y	Y
4 Aderholt	Y	Y	Y	N	Y	Y	Y
5 Brooks	Y	Y	Y	N	Y	Y	Y
6 Bachus	Y	Y	Y	N	Y	Y	Y
7 Sewell	Y	Y	N	Y	N	Y	Y
ALASKA							
AL Young	Y	Y	Y	?	?	Y	N
ARIZONA							
1 Gosar	?	?	Y	N	Y	Y	Y
2 Franks	Y	Y	Y	N	Y	Y	Y
3 Quayle	Y	Y	Y	N	Y	Y	Y
4 Pastor	Y	Y	N	Y	N	Y	N
5 Schweikert	Y	Y	Y	N	?	Y	Y
6 Flake	Y	Y	Y	N	Y	Y	Y
7 Grijalva	Y	Y	N	Y	N	?	?
8 Barber	+	+	–	+	+	Y	Y
ARKANSAS							
1 Crawford	Y	Y	Y	N	Y	N	Y
2 Griffin	Y	Y	Y	N	Y	Y	N
3 Womack	Y	Y	Y	N	Y	Y	N
4 Ross	?	?	Y	Y	Y	Y	Y
CALIFORNIA							
1 Thompson	Y	Y	N	Y	N	Y	N
2 Herger	Y	Y	Y	–	+	Y	Y
3 Lungren	Y	Y	Y	N	Y	Y	Y
4 McClintock	Y	Y	Y	?	?	N	Y
5 Matsui	Y	Y	N	Y	N	Y	N
6 Woolsey	Y	Y	N	Y	N	Y	N
7 Miller, George	Y	Y	N	Y	N	Y	N
8 Pelosi	Y	Y	N	Y	N	Y	N
9 Lee	Y	Y	?	Y	N	Y	N
10 Garamendi	Y	Y	N	Y	N	Y	Y
11 McNerney	Y	Y	N	Y	Y	Y	Y
12 Speier	Y	Y	N	?	?	Y	Y
13 Stark	?	?	?	?	?	Y	Y
14 Eshoo	Y	Y	N	Y	N	Y	N
15 Honda	Y	Y	N	Y	N	Y	N
16 Lofgren	Y	Y	N	Y	N	Y	N
17 Farr	Y	Y	N	Y	N	Y	Y
18 Vacant							
19 Denham	Y	Y	Y	N	N	Y	N
20 Costa	Y	Y	N	?	N	Y	N
21 Nunes	Y	Y	Y	N	Y	?	?
22 McCarthy	Y	Y	Y	N	Y	Y	Y
23 Capps	Y	Y	N	Y	N	Y	Y
24 Gallegly	?	?	?	?	?	Y	Y
25 McKeon	Y	Y	Y	N	Y	Y	Y
26 Dreier	Y	Y	Y	N	Y	Y	Y
27 Sherman	Y	Y	N	N	N	Y	Y
28 Berman	Y	Y	N	?	?	Y	Y
29 Schiff	Y	Y	N	Y	N	Y	Y
30 Waxman	Y	Y	N	Y	N	Y	Y
31 Becerra	Y	Y	N	Y	N	Y	Y
32 Chu	Y	Y	N	Y	N	Y	Y
33 Bass	Y	Y	N	Y	N	Y	N
34 Roybal-Allard	+	+	?	+	–	Y	Y
35 Waters	Y	Y	N	?	N	Y	N
36 Hahn	Y	Y	N	Y	N	Y	Y
37 Richardson	Y	Y	N	?	?	Y	Y
38 Napolitano	Y	Y	N	Y	N	Y	Y
39 Sánchez, Linda	Y	Y	N	Y	N	Y	N
40 Royce	Y	Y	Y	N	Y	Y	Y
41 Lewis	Y	Y	Y	N	Y	Y	Y
42 Miller, Gary	Y	Y	Y	N	Y	?	?
43 Baca	Y	Y	N	Y	N	?	?
44 Calvert	Y	Y	Y	N	Y	Y	Y
45 Bono Mack	?	?	Y	N	Y	?	?
46 Rohrabacher	Y	Y	Y	N	Y	Y	Y
47 Sanchez, Loretta	?	?	N	Y	N	Y	Y
48 Campbell	?	?	Y	N	Y	Y	Y
49 Issa	Y	Y	Y	N	Y	Y	Y
50 Bilbray	Y	Y	Y	N	?	?	Y
51 Filner*	+	+	–	+	–		
52 Hunter	Y	Y	Y	N	Y	Y	N
53 Davis	Y	Y	N	Y	N	Y	Y

	609	610	611	612	613	614	615
COLORADO							
1 DeGette	Y	Y	N	?	?	Y	Y
2 Polis	Y	Y	N	Y	N	Y	Y
3 Tipton	Y	Y	Y	N	Y	Y	N
4 Gardner	Y	Y	Y	N	Y	Y	N
5 Lamborn	Y	Y	Y	N	Y	Y	N
6 Coffman	Y	Y	Y	N	Y	Y	N
7 Perlmutter	Y	Y	N	Y	N	Y	Y
CONNECTICUT							
1 Larson	Y	Y	N	Y	N	Y	Y
2 Courtney	Y	Y	N	Y	N	Y	Y
3 DeLauro	Y	Y	N	Y	N	Y	Y
4 Himes	Y	Y	N	Y	Y	Y	Y
5 Murphy	?	?	?	?	?	Y	Y
DELAWARE							
AL Carney	Y	Y	N	Y	Y	Y	Y
FLORIDA							
1 Miller	Y	Y	Y	N	Y	Y	Y
2 Southerland	Y	Y	Y	N	Y	Y	N
3 Brown	?	?	N	Y	N	Y	Y
4 Crenshaw	Y	Y	Y	N	Y	Y	Y
5 Nugent	Y	Y	Y	N	Y	Y	N
6 Stearns	Y	Y	Y	N	Y	Y	N
7 Mica	Y	Y	Y	N	Y	Y	Y
8 Webster	Y	Y	Y	N	Y	Y	Y
9 Bilirakis	Y	Y	Y	N	Y	Y	N
10 Young	?	?	N	Y	N	Y	Y
11 Castor	Y	Y	N	Y	N	Y	Y
12 Ross	Y	Y	Y	N	Y	Y	N
13 Buchanan	Y	Y	Y	N	Y	Y	N
14 Mack	?	?	N	Y	?	?	?
15 Posey	Y	Y	Y	N	Y	Y	Y
16 Rooney	Y	Y	Y	N	Y	Y	N
17 Wilson	Y	Y	N	Y	N	Y	Y
18 Ros-Lehtinen	Y	Y	Y	N	Y	Y	Y
19 Deutch	Y	Y	N	Y	N	Y	Y
20 Wasserman Schultz	Y	Y	N	Y	N	Y	Y
21 Diaz-Balart	Y	Y	N	Y	Y	Y	Y
22 West	Y	Y	Y	N	Y	Y	Y
23 Hastings	Y	Y	N	?	?	Y	?
24 Adams	Y	Y	Y	N	Y	Y	N
25 Rivera	?	?	Y	N	Y	Y	Y
GEORGIA							
1 Kingston	Y	Y	Y	N	Y	Y	Y
2 Bishop	Y	Y	N	Y	N	Y	Y
3 Westmoreland	Y	Y	N	Y	N	Y	Y
4 Johnson	Y	Y	N	Y	N	Y	Y
5 Lewis	Y	Y	N	?	?	Y	Y
6 Price	Y	Y	Y	N	Y	Y	N
7 Woodall	Y	Y	Y	N	Y	Y	N
8 Scott, A.	Y	Y	Y	N	Y	Y	Y
9 Graves	Y	Y	Y	N	Y	Y	N
10 Broun	Y	Y	Y	N	Y	Y	N
11 Gingrey	Y	Y	Y	N	Y	?	?
12 Barrow	Y	Y	N	Y	N	Y	Y
13 Scott, D.	Y	Y	N	Y	N	Y	Y
HAWAII							
1 Hanabusa	Y	Y	N	Y	N	Y	Y
2 Hirono	Y	Y	N	Y	N	Y	Y
IDAHO							
1 Labrador	Y	Y	Y	N	Y	Y	Y
2 Simpson	Y	Y	Y	N	+	Y	Y
ILLINOIS							
1 Rush	Y	Y	N	Y	?	Y	Y
2 Vacant							
3 Lipinski	?	?	N	Y	Y	Y	Y
4 Gutierrez	?	?	N	Y	N	Y	Y
5 Quigley	Y	Y	N	Y	N	Y	Y
6 Roskam	Y	Y	Y	N	Y	Y	Y
7 Davis, D.	Y	Y	N	Y	N	?	?
8 Walsh	Y	Y	Y	N	Y	Y	Y
9 Schakowsky	Y	Y	N	Y	N	Y	N
10 Dold	Y	Y	N	Y	N	Y	N
11 Kinzinger	Y	Y	Y	N	Y	Y	N
12 Costello	Y	Y	?	?	?	Y	N
13 Biggert	Y	Y	Y	N	Y	Y	Y
14 Hultgren	Y	Y	Y	N	Y	Y	Y
15 Johnson	?	?	Y	N	Y	+	+

KEY Republicans Democrats

Y Voted for (yea)	X Paired against	C Voted "present" to avoid possible conflict of interest
# Paired for	– Announced against	
+ Announced for	P Voted "present"	? Did not vote or otherwise make a position known
N Voted against (nay)		

* Rep. Bob Filner, D-Calif., resigned effective Dec. 3, 2012. The last vote for which he was eligible was vote 613.

	609	610	611	612	613	614	615
16 **Manzullo**	+	+	+	–	+	Y	Y
17 **Schilling**	Y	Y	Y	N	Y	?	?
18 **Schock**	Y	Y	Y	N	Y	Y	N
19 **Shimkus**	Y	Y	Y	N	Y	Y	Y
INDIANA							
1 Visclosky	Y	Y	N	Y	–	Y	N
2 Donnelly	Y	Y	Y	N	Y	Y	N
3 **Stutzman**	Y	Y	Y	N	Y	Y	Y
4 **Rokita**	Y	Y	Y	N	Y	Y	Y
5 **Burton**	Y	Y	Y	?	?	Y	Y
6 **Pence**	?	?	+	–	–	+	+
7 Carson	Y	Y	N	Y	N	Y	Y
8 **Bucshon**	Y	Y	Y	N	Y	Y	Y
9 **Young**	Y	Y	Y	N	Y	Y	Y
IOWA							
1 Braley	Y	Y	N	Y	N	Y	Y
2 Loebsack	Y	Y	N	Y	N	Y	Y
3 Boswell	Y	Y	Y	Y	Y	Y	N
4 **Latham**	Y	Y	Y	N	Y	Y	N
5 **King**	Y	Y	Y	N	Y	Y	Y
KANSAS							
1 **Huelskamp**	Y	Y	Y	N	Y	Y	Y
2 **Jenkins**	Y	Y	Y	N	Y	Y	Y
3 **Yoder**	Y	Y	Y	N	Y	Y	N
4 **Pompeo**	Y	Y	Y	N	Y	Y	Y
KENTUCKY							
1 **Whitfield**	Y	Y	Y	N	Y	Y	Y
2 **Guthrie**	Y	Y	Y	N	Y	Y	Y
3 Yarmuth	Y	Y	N	Y	N	Y	Y
4 **Massie**	Y	Y	Y	N	Y	Y	Y
5 **Rogers**	Y	Y	Y	N	Y	Y	Y
6 Chandler	Y	Y	N	?	?	Y	Y
LOUISIANA							
1 **Scalise**	Y	Y	Y	N	Y	Y	Y
2 Richmond	Y	Y	N	Y	N	Y	Y
3 **Landry**	Y	Y	Y	N	Y	Y	N
4 **Fleming**	Y	Y	Y	N	Y	Y	Y
5 **Alexander**	Y	Y	Y	N	Y	Y	Y
6 **Cassidy**	Y	Y	Y	N	Y	Y	Y
7 **Boustany**	Y	Y	Y	N	Y	Y	Y
MAINE							
1 Pingree	Y	Y	N	Y	N	Y	Y
2 Michaud	Y	Y	N	Y	Y	Y	Y
MARYLAND							
1 **Harris**	Y	Y	Y	N	Y	Y	Y
2 Ruppersberger	Y	Y	N	Y	Y	Y	Y
3 Sarbanes	Y	Y	N	Y	N	Y	N
4 Edwards	Y	Y	N	+	–	Y	Y
5 Hoyer	Y	Y	N	Y	N	Y	N
6 **Bartlett**	?	?	Y	N	Y	?	?
7 Cummings	Y	Y	N	Y	N	Y	Y
8 Van Hollen	Y	Y	N	Y	N	Y	Y
MASSACHUSETTS							
1 Olver	Y	Y	N	Y	N	Y	N
2 Neal	Y	Y	N	Y	N	Y	Y
3 McGovern	Y	Y	N	Y	N	Y	N
4 Frank	Y	Y	?	Y	N	Y	?
5 Tsongas	Y	Y	N	Y	N	Y	Y
6 Tierney	Y	Y	N	Y	N	Y	Y
7 Markey	Y	Y	N	Y	N	Y	Y
8 Capuano	Y	Y	N	Y	N	Y	N
9 Lynch	Y	Y	N	Y	N	Y	N
10 Keating	Y	Y	N	Y	N	Y	Y
MICHIGAN							
1 **Benishek**	Y	Y	Y	N	Y	Y	N
2 **Huizenga**	Y	Y	Y	N	Y	Y	Y
3 **Amash**	N	N	Y	N	Y	N	P
4 **Camp**	Y	Y	Y	N	Y	Y	Y
5 Kildee	Y	Y	N	Y	N	Y	N
6 **Upton**	Y	Y	Y	N	Y	Y	Y
7 **Walberg**	Y	Y	Y	N	Y	Y	?
8 **Rogers**	Y	Y	Y	N	Y	Y	Y
9 Peters	Y	Y	N	Y	N	Y	N
10 **Miller**	Y	Y	Y	N	Y	Y	Y
11 Curson	Y	Y	N	Y	N	Y	N
12 Levin	Y	Y	N	Y	N	Y	Y
13 Clarke	Y	Y	N	Y	N	Y	Y
14 Conyers	Y	Y	N	Y	N	Y	Y
15 Dingell	?	?	N	Y	N	Y	N
MINNESOTA							
1 Walz	Y	Y	N	Y	N	Y	Y
2 **Kline**	Y	Y	Y	N	Y	?	?
3 **Paulsen**	Y	Y	Y	N	Y	Y	N
4 McCollum	Y	Y	N	Y	N	Y	Y

	609	610	611	612	613	614	615
5 Ellison	Y	Y	N	Y	N	Y	N
6 **Bachmann**	Y	Y	Y	N	Y	?	?
7 Peterson	Y	Y	Y	Y	Y	Y	N
8 **Cravaack**	Y	Y	Y	N	Y	Y	Y
MISSISSIPPI							
1 **Nunnelee**	Y	Y	Y	N	Y	Y	Y
2 Thompson	Y	Y	N	Y	N	Y	N
3 **Harper**	Y	Y	Y	N	Y	Y	Y
4 **Palazzo**	Y	Y	Y	N	Y	Y	Y
MISSOURI							
1 Clay	Y	Y	N	Y	N	Y	Y
2 **Akin**	Y	Y	Y	?	?	?	?
3 Carnahan	Y	Y	N	?	?	Y	Y
4 **Hartzler**	Y	Y	Y	N	Y	Y	N
5 Cleaver	Y	Y	N	Y	N	Y	Y
6 **Graves**	Y	Y	Y	N	Y	Y	N
7 **Long**	Y	Y	Y	N	Y	Y	Y
8 **Emerson**	Y	Y	Y	N	Y	P	Y
9 **Luetkemeyer**	Y	Y	Y	N	Y	Y	Y
MONTANA							
AL **Rehberg**	?	Y	Y	N	Y	Y	Y
NEBRASKA							
1 **Fortenberry**	Y	Y	Y	N	Y	?	?
2 **Terry**	Y	Y	Y	N	Y	Y	N
3 **Smith**	Y	Y	Y	N	Y	Y	Y
NEVADA							
1 Berkley	Y	Y	N	Y	N	Y	Y
2 **Amodei**	Y	Y	Y	N	Y	Y	Y
3 **Heck**	Y	Y	Y	N	Y	Y	N
NEW HAMPSHIRE							
1 **Guinta**	Y	Y	Y	N	Y	Y	N
2 **Bass**	Y	Y	Y	N	Y	+	+
NEW JERSEY							
1 Andrews	Y	Y	N	Y	N	Y	N
2 **LoBiondo**	Y	Y	Y	N	Y	Y	N
3 **Runyan**	Y	Y	Y	N	Y	Y	Y
4 **Smith**	Y	Y	Y	N	Y	Y	Y
5 **Garrett**	Y	Y	Y	N	Y	Y	N
6 Pallone	Y	Y	N	Y	N	Y	N
7 **Lance**	Y	Y	Y	N	Y	Y	N
8 Pascrell	Y	Y	N	Y	N	Y	Y
9 Rothman	Y	Y	N	?	?	?	?
10 Payne	Y	Y	?	Y	N	Y	Y
11 **Frelinghuysen**	+	+	Y	N	+	Y	Y
12 Holt	Y	Y	N	Y	N	Y	N
13 Sires	Y	Y	N	Y	N	Y	Y
NEW MEXICO							
1 Heinrich	Y	Y	N	Y	N	?	?
2 **Pearce**	Y	Y	Y	N	Y	Y	Y
3 Luján	Y	Y	N	Y	N	Y	Y
NEW YORK							
1 Bishop	?	Y	N	Y	N	Y	N
2 Israel	Y	Y	N	Y	N	Y	N
3 **King**	Y	Y	Y	N	Y	Y	Y
4 McCarthy	Y	Y	N	Y	N	Y	Y
5 Ackerman	Y	Y	?	Y	N	?	?
6 Meeks	Y	Y	N	Y	N	Y	Y
7 Crowley	Y	Y	N	Y	N	Y	N
8 Nadler	Y	Y	N	Y	N	Y	Y
9 **Turner**	Y	Y	Y	N	Y	Y	Y
10 Towns	?	?	?	?	?	?	?
11 Clarke	Y	Y	N	Y	N	Y	N
12 Velázquez	Y	Y	N	Y	–	Y	N
13 **Grimm**	Y	Y	Y	N	Y	Y	Y
14 Maloney, C.	Y	Y	N	Y	N	Y	Y
15 Rangel	Y	Y	N	Y	N	Y	Y
16 Serrano	Y	Y	N	Y	N	Y	Y
17 Engel	Y	Y	N	Y	N	Y	Y
18 Lowey	Y	Y	N	Y	N	Y	Y
19 **Hayworth**	Y	Y	Y	N	Y	Y	Y
20 **Gibson**	Y	Y	Y	N	Y	Y	N
21 Tonko	Y	Y	N	Y	Y	Y	Y
22 Hinchey	Y	Y	N	Y	N	?	?
23 Owens	Y	Y	–	+	–	Y	P
24 **Hanna**	Y	Y	Y	N	Y	Y	N
24 Maffei							
25 **Buerkle**	Y	Y	Y	N	Y	Y	Y
26 Hochul	Y	+	N	Y	Y	Y	Y
27 Higgins	Y	Y	N	Y	N	?	?
28 Slaughter	Y	Y	N	+	–	Y	Y
29 **Reed**	Y	Y	Y	N	Y	Y	N
NORTH CAROLINA							
1 Butterfield	Y	Y	N	Y	N	Y	Y
2 **Ellmers**	Y	Y	Y	N	Y	Y	Y
3 **Jones**	Y	Y	Y	N	N	Y	Y
4 Price	Y	Y	N	Y	N	Y	Y

	609	610	611	612	613	614	615
5 **Foxx**	Y	Y	Y	N	Y	Y	N
6 **Coble**	Y	Y	Y	N	Y	Y	Y
7 McIntyre	Y	Y	Y	Y	Y	Y	Y
8 Kissell	Y	Y	Y	Y	Y	Y	Y
9 **Myrick**	Y	Y	Y	N	Y	Y	Y
10 **McHenry**	Y	Y	Y	N	Y	Y	Y
11 Shuler	Y	Y	Y	?	?	Y	Y
12 Watt	?	?	N	?	?	Y	Y
13 Miller	Y	Y	N	Y	N	Y	Y
NORTH DAKOTA							
AL **Berg**	Y	Y	Y	N	Y	Y	Y
OHIO							
1 **Chabot**	Y	Y	Y	N	Y	Y	Y
2 **Schmidt**	Y	Y	?	?	?	Y	Y
3 **Turner**	Y	Y	+	N	Y	Y	Y
4 **Jordan**	Y	Y	Y	N	Y	Y	Y
5 **Latta**	Y	Y	Y	N	Y	Y	N
6 **Johnson**	Y	Y	Y	N	Y	Y	N
7 **Austria**	?	?	?	N	Y	Y	Y
8 **Boehner**							
9 Kaptur	Y	Y	N	Y	N	Y	Y
10 Kucinich	Y	N	N	Y	N	Y	N
11 Fudge	Y	Y	N	Y	N	Y	Y
12 **Tiberi**	Y	Y	Y	N	Y	Y	Y
13 Sutton	Y	Y	N	?	?	Y	Y
14 **LaTourette**	Y	Y	Y	N	Y	Y	Y
15 **Stivers**	Y	Y	Y	N	Y	Y	Y
16 **Renacci**	Y	Y	Y	N	Y	Y	N
17 Ryan	Y	Y	N	Y	N	Y	Y
18 **Gibbs**	Y	Y	Y	N	Y	Y	Y
OKLAHOMA							
1 **Sullivan**	Y	Y	?	N	Y	?	?
2 Boren	Y	Y	Y	?	?	Y	Y
3 **Lucas**	Y	Y	Y	N	Y	Y	Y
4 **Cole**	Y	Y	Y	N	Y	Y	Y
5 **Lankford**	Y	Y	Y	N	Y	Y	Y
OREGON							
1 Bonamici	Y	Y	N	Y	N	Y	Y
2 **Walden**	Y	Y	Y	N	Y	Y	Y
3 Blumenauer	Y	Y	N	Y	Y	Y	Y
4 DeFazio	Y	Y	N	N	Y	Y	N
5 Schrader	Y	Y	N	Y	Y	Y	Y
PENNSYLVANIA							
1 Brady	Y	Y	N	Y	N	Y	N
2 Fattah	?	Y	N	?	?	Y	Y
3 **Kelly**	Y	Y	Y	N	Y	Y	Y
4 Altmire	Y	Y	N	Y	Y	Y	Y
5 **Thompson**	Y	Y	Y	N	Y	Y	Y
6 **Gerlach**	Y	Y	Y	N	Y	Y	Y
7 **Meehan**	Y	Y	Y	N	Y	Y	N
8 **Fitzpatrick**	Y	Y	Y	N	Y	Y	N
9 **Shuster**	Y	Y	Y	N	Y	Y	Y
10 **Marino**	?	?	Y	N	Y	?	?
11 **Barletta**	Y	Y	Y	N	N	Y	Y
12 Critz	Y	Y	N	Y	N	Y	N
13 Schwartz	Y	Y	N	–	+	Y	Y
14 Doyle	Y	Y	N	Y	N	Y	Y
15 **Dent**	Y	Y	Y	N	Y	Y	Y
16 **Pitts**	Y	Y	Y	N	Y	Y	Y
17 Holden	?	?	N	Y	N	Y	Y
18 **Murphy**	Y	Y	Y	N	Y	Y	Y
19 **Platts**	Y	Y	Y	N	Y	+	+
RHODE ISLAND							
1 Cicilline	Y	Y	N	Y	N	Y	Y
2 Langevin	+	Y	N	Y	N	Y	Y
SOUTH CAROLINA							
1 **Scott**	Y	Y	Y	N	Y	Y	Y
2 **Wilson**	Y	Y	Y	N	Y	Y	Y
3 **Duncan**	Y	Y	Y	N	Y	Y	Y
4 **Gowdy**	Y	Y	Y	N	Y	Y	Y
5 **Mulvaney**	Y	Y	Y	N	Y	Y	N
6 Clyburn	Y	Y	N	Y	N	Y	Y
SOUTH DAKOTA							
AL **Noem**	Y	Y	Y	N	Y	Y	Y
TENNESSEE							
1 **Roe**	Y	Y	Y	N	Y	Y	N
2 **Duncan**	Y	Y	Y	N	Y	Y	Y
3 **Fleischmann**	Y	Y	Y	N	Y	Y	Y
4 **DesJarlais**	Y	Y	Y	N	Y	Y	N
5 Cooper	Y	Y	N	Y	Y	Y	Y
6 **Black**	Y	Y	Y	N	+	Y	Y
7 **Blackburn**	Y	Y	Y	N	Y	Y	Y
8 **Fincher**	Y	Y	Y	N	Y	Y	Y
9 Cohen	Y	Y	N	Y	Y	Y	Y

	609	610	611	612	613	614	615
TEXAS							
1 **Gohmert**	Y	N	Y	N	Y	Y	?
2 **Poe**	Y	Y	Y	N	Y	Y	N
3 **Johnson, S.**	Y	Y	Y	N	Y	Y	Y
4 **Hall**	Y	Y	Y	N	Y	Y	Y
5 **Hensarling**	Y	Y	Y	N	Y	Y	Y
6 **Barton**	Y	Y	Y	N	Y	Y	Y
7 **Culberson**	Y	Y	Y	?	?	Y	Y
8 **Brady**	Y	Y	Y	N	Y	Y	Y
9 Green, A.	Y	Y	N	Y	N	Y	Y
10 **McCaul**	?	Y	Y	N	Y	Y	Y
11 **Conaway**	Y	Y	Y	N	Y	Y	N
12 **Granger**	Y	Y	Y	N	Y	Y	?
13 **Thornberry**	Y	Y	Y	N	Y	Y	Y
14 **Paul**	Y	N	Y	N	Y	?	?
15 Hinojosa	Y	Y	N	Y	N	Y	Y
16 Reyes	Y	Y	N	?	?	Y	Y
17 **Flores**	Y	Y	Y	N	Y	Y	Y
18 Jackson Lee	Y	Y	N	Y	N	Y	N
19 **Neugebauer**	Y	Y	Y	N	Y	Y	N
20 Gonzalez	Y	Y	N	Y	N	Y	Y
21 **Smith**	Y	Y	Y	?	?	Y	Y
22 **Olson**	Y	Y	Y	N	Y	Y	Y
23 **Canseco**	Y	Y	Y	N	Y	Y	Y
24 **Marchant**	Y	Y	Y	N	Y	Y	N
25 Doggett	Y	Y	N	Y	N	Y	Y
26 **Burgess**	Y	Y	Y	N	Y	Y	N
27 **Farenthold**	Y	Y	Y	N	Y	Y	N
28 Cuellar	Y	Y	N	Y	Y	Y	Y
29 Green, G.	Y	Y	N	Y	N	Y	N
30 Johnson, E.	Y	Y	N	Y	N	Y	N
31 **Carter**	Y	Y	Y	?	Y	Y	Y
32 **Sessions**	Y	Y	Y	N	Y	Y	Y
UTAH							
1 **Bishop**	Y	Y	Y	N	Y	Y	Y
2 Matheson	Y	Y	Y	N	Y	Y	N
3 **Chaffetz**	Y	Y	Y	N	Y	Y	Y
VERMONT							
AL Welch	Y	Y	N	Y	N	?	Y
VIRGINIA							
1 **Wittman**	Y	Y	Y	N	Y	Y	Y
2 **Rigell**	Y	?	Y	N	Y	Y	N
3 Scott	Y	Y	N	Y	N	Y	Y
4 **Forbes**	Y	Y	Y	N	Y	Y	Y
5 **Hurt**	Y	Y	Y	N	Y	Y	Y
6 **Goodlatte**	Y	Y	Y	N	Y	Y	Y
7 **Cantor**	Y	Y	Y	N	Y	Y	Y
8 Moran	Y	Y	Y	Y	Y	Y	Y
9 **Griffith**	Y	Y	Y	N	Y	Y	Y
10 **Wolf**	Y	Y	Y	N	Y	Y	Y
11 Connolly	Y	Y	N	Y	N	Y	Y
WASHINGTON							
1 DelBene	Y	Y	N	Y	N	Y	Y
2 Larsen	Y	Y	N	Y	N	Y	Y
3 **Herrera Beutler**	Y	Y	Y	N	Y	Y	N
4 **Hastings**	Y	Y	Y	N	N	Y	Y
5 **McMorris Rodgers**	Y	Y	Y	N	Y	Y	Y
6 Dicks	?	?	N	Y	N	Y	Y
7 McDermott	Y	Y	N	Y	N	Y	N
8 **Reichert**	Y	Y	Y	N	Y	Y	Y
9 Smith	Y	Y	N	+	–	Y	Y
WEST VIRGINIA							
1 **McKinley**	Y	Y	Y	N	Y	Y	N
2 **Capito**	Y	Y	Y	N	Y	Y	Y
3 Rahall	Y	Y	N	Y	N	Y	N
WISCONSIN							
1 **Ryan**	Y	Y	Y	N	Y	Y	Y
2 Baldwin	Y	Y	N	?	?	Y	N
3 Kind	Y	Y	N	Y	Y	Y	N
4 Moore	Y	Y	N	Y	N	Y	N
5 **Sensenbrenner**	Y	Y	Y	N	Y	Y	Y
6 **Petri**	Y	Y	Y	N	Y	Y	Y
7 **Duffy**	Y	Y	Y	N	Y	Y	N
8 **Ribble**	Y	Y	Y	N	Y	Y	Y
WYOMING							
AL **Lummis**	Y	Y	Y	N	Y	Y	Y

IN THE HOUSE | By Vote Number

616. **Procedural Motion/Motion to Adjourn.** Ellison, D-Minn., motion to adjourn. Motion rejected 3-393: R 1-217; D 2-176. Dec. 4, 2012.

617. **S Con Res 50. Global Internet Regulations/Adoption.**
Blackburn, R-Tenn., motion to suspend the rules and adopt the concurrent resolution that would express the sense of Congress that the secretary of State should work to preserve an open and free Internet as part of the U.S. delegation to the International Telecommunication Union and advance the current multistakeholder model that governs the Internet. Motion agreed to 397-0: R 218-0; D 179-0. A two-thirds majority of those present and voting (265 in this case) is required for adoption under suspension of the rules. Dec. 5, 2012.

618. **HR 6602. National Observances and Ceremonies/Passage.**
Smith, R-Texas, motion to suspend the rules and pass the bill that would make technical and clarifying changes to provisions in U.S. code that relate to patriotic national observances, ceremonies and organizations. Motion agreed to 392-0: R 216-0; D 176-0. A two-thirds majority of those present and voting (262 in this case) is required for passage under suspension of the rules. Dec. 5, 2012.

619. **S 2367. Language in Federal Law/Passage.** Smith, R-Texas, motion to suspend the rules and pass the bill that would strike the word "lunatic" from federal law and portions of U.S. code dealing with banking. Motion agreed to 398-1: R 217-1; D 181-0. A two-thirds majority of those present and voting (266 in this case) is required for passage under suspension of the rules. Dec. 5, 2012.

	616	617	618	619
ALABAMA				
1 Bonner	?	?	?	?
2 Roby	N	Y	Y	Y
3 Rogers	N	Y	Y	Y
4 Aderholt	N	Y	Y	Y
5 Brooks	N	Y	Y	Y
6 Bachus	N	Y	Y	Y
7 Sewell	N	Y	Y	Y
ALASKA				
AL Young	N	Y	Y	Y
ARIZONA				
1 Gosar	N	Y	Y	Y
2 Franks	N	Y	Y	Y
3 Quayle	N	Y	Y	Y
4 Pastor	N	Y	Y	Y
5 Schweikert	N	Y	Y	Y
6 Flake	N	Y	Y	Y
7 Grijalva	?	Y	?	Y
8 Barber	N	Y	?	Y
ARKANSAS				
1 Crawford	N	Y	Y	Y
2 Griffin	N	Y	Y	Y
3 Womack	N	Y	Y	Y
4 Ross	N	Y	Y	Y
CALIFORNIA				
1 Thompson	N	Y	Y	Y
2 Herger	N	Y	Y	Y
3 Lungren	N	Y	Y	Y
4 McClintock	N	Y	Y	Y
5 Matsui	N	?	?	?
6 Woolsey	N	Y	Y	Y
7 Miller, George	N	Y	Y	Y
8 Pelosi	N	Y	Y	Y
9 Lee	N	Y	Y	Y
10 Garamendi	N	Y	Y	Y
11 McNerney	N	Y	Y	Y
12 Speier	N	?	?	?
13 Stark	N	Y	Y	Y
14 Eshoo	N	Y	Y	Y
15 Honda	N	Y	Y	Y
16 Lofgren	N	Y	Y	Y
17 Farr	N	Y	Y	Y
18 Vacant				
19 Denham	N	Y	Y	Y
20 Costa	N	Y	Y	Y
21 Nunes	?	Y	Y	Y
22 McCarthy	N	Y	Y	Y
23 Capps	N	Y	Y	Y
24 Gallegly	N	Y	Y	Y
25 McKeon	N	?	?	?
26 Dreier	N	Y	Y	Y
27 Sherman	N	Y	Y	Y
28 Berman	N	Y	?	Y
29 Schiff	N	Y	Y	Y
30 Waxman	N	Y	Y	Y
31 Becerra	N	Y	Y	Y
32 Chu	N	Y	Y	Y
33 Bass	N	Y	Y	Y
34 Roybal-Allard	N	Y	Y	Y
35 Waters	?	Y	Y	Y
36 Hahn	N	Y	Y	Y
37 Richardson	N	Y	Y	Y
38 Napolitano	N	Y	Y	Y
39 Sánchez, Linda	N	Y	Y	Y
40 Royce	N	Y	Y	Y
41 Lewis	N	Y	Y	Y
42 Miller, Gary	?	?	?	?
43 Baca	?	?	?	?
44 Calvert	N	?	?	?
45 Bono Mack	?	?	?	?
46 Rohrabacher	N	Y	Y	Y
47 Sanchez, Loretta	N	Y	Y	Y
48 Campbell	N	Y	Y	Y
49 Issa	N	Y	Y	Y
50 Bilbray	?	?	?	?
51 Vacant				
52 Hunter	N	Y	Y	Y
53 Davis	N	Y	Y	Y

	616	617	618	619
COLORADO				
1 DeGette	N	Y	Y	Y
2 Polis	N	Y	Y	Y
3 Tipton	N	Y	Y	Y
4 Gardner	N	Y	Y	Y
5 Lamborn	N	Y	Y	Y
6 Coffman	N	Y	Y	Y
7 Perlmutter	N	Y	Y	Y
CONNECTICUT				
1 Larson	N	Y	Y	Y
2 Courtney	N	Y	Y	Y
3 DeLauro	N	Y	Y	Y
4 Himes	N	Y	Y	Y
5 Murphy	N	Y	Y	Y
DELAWARE				
AL Carney	N	Y	Y	Y
FLORIDA				
1 Miller	N	Y	Y	Y
2 Southerland	N	Y	Y	Y
3 Brown	N	Y	Y	Y
4 Crenshaw	N	Y	Y	Y
5 Nugent	N	Y	Y	Y
6 Stearns	N	Y	Y	Y
7 Mica	N	Y	Y	Y
8 Webster	N	Y	Y	Y
9 Bilirakis	N	Y	Y	Y
10 Young	N	Y	Y	Y
11 Castor	N	Y	Y	Y
12 Ross	N	Y	Y	Y
13 Buchanan	N	Y	Y	Y
14 Mack	?	?	?	?
15 Posey	N	Y	Y	Y
16 Rooney	N	Y	Y	Y
17 Wilson	N	Y	Y	Y
18 Ros-Lehtinen	N	Y	Y	Y
19 Deutch	N	Y	Y	Y
20 Wasserman Schultz	N	Y	Y	Y
21 Diaz-Balart	N	Y	Y	Y
22 West	N	Y	Y	Y
23 Hastings	?	?	?	?
24 Adams	N	Y	Y	Y
25 Rivera	N	Y	Y	Y
GEORGIA				
1 Kingston	N	Y	Y	Y
2 Bishop	N	Y	Y	Y
3 Westmoreland	N	Y	Y	Y
4 Johnson	N	Y	Y	Y
5 Lewis	N	Y	Y	Y
6 Price	N	Y	Y	Y
7 Woodall	N	Y	Y	Y
8 Scott, A.	N	Y	Y	Y
9 Graves	N	Y	Y	Y
10 Broun	N	Y	Y	Y
11 Gingrey	?	Y	Y	Y
12 Barrow	N	Y	Y	Y
13 Scott, D.	N	Y	Y	Y
HAWAII				
1 Hanabusa	N	Y	Y	Y
2 Hirono	N	Y	Y	Y
IDAHO				
1 Labrador	N	Y	Y	Y
2 Simpson	N	Y	Y	Y
ILLINOIS				
1 Rush	N	Y	Y	Y
2 Vacant				
3 Lipinski	N	Y	Y	Y
4 Gutierrez	N	Y	Y	Y
5 Quigley	N	Y	?	?
6 Roskam	N	Y	Y	Y
7 Davis	?	Y	Y	Y
8 Walsh	N	Y	Y	Y
9 Schakowsky	N	Y	Y	Y
10 Dold	N	Y	Y	Y
11 Kinzinger	N	Y	Y	Y
12 Costello	N	?	?	?
13 Biggert	N	Y	Y	Y
14 Hultgren	N	Y	Y	Y
15 Johnson	?	?	?	?

KEY   **Republicans**   Democrats

Y Voted for (yea)	**X** Paired against
# Paired for	**–** Announced against
+ Announced for	**P** Voted "present"
N Voted against (nay)	

C Voted "present" to avoid possible conflict of interest

? Did not vote or otherwise make a position known

	616	617	618	619
16 Manzullo	N	Y	Y	Y
17 Schilling	?	?	?	?
18 Schock	N	Y	Y	Y
19 Shimkus	N	Y	Y	Y
INDIANA				
1 Visclosky	N	?	?	?
2 Donnelly	N	Y	Y	Y
3 Stutzman	N	Y	Y	Y
4 Rokita	N	Y	Y	Y
5 Burton	N	?	?	?
6 Pence	?	?	?	?
7 Carson	N	Y	Y	Y
8 Bucshon	N	Y	Y	Y
9 Young	N	Y	Y	Y
IOWA				
1 Braley	N	Y	Y	Y
2 Loebsack	N	Y	Y	Y
3 Boswell	N	Y	Y	Y
4 Latham	N	Y	Y	Y
5 King	N	Y	Y	Y
KANSAS				
1 Huelskamp	N	Y	Y	Y
2 Jenkins	N	Y	Y	Y
3 Yoder	N	Y	Y	Y
4 Pompeo	N	Y	Y	Y
KENTUCKY				
1 Whitfield	N	Y	?	Y
2 Guthrie	N	Y	Y	Y
3 Yarmuth	N	Y	Y	Y
4 Massie	N	Y	Y	Y
5 Rogers	N	Y	Y	Y
6 Chandler	N	Y	Y	Y
LOUISIANA				
1 Scalise	N	Y	Y	Y
2 Richmond	N	Y	Y	Y
3 Landry	N	Y	Y	Y
4 Fleming	N	Y	?	Y
5 Alexander	N	Y	Y	Y
6 Cassidy	N	Y	Y	Y
7 Boustany	N	Y	Y	Y
MAINE				
1 Pingree	N	Y	Y	Y
2 Michaud	N	Y	Y	Y
MARYLAND				
1 Harris	N	Y	Y	Y
2 Ruppersberger	N	?	Y	Y
3 Sarbanes	N	Y	Y	Y
4 Edwards	N	Y	Y	Y
5 Hoyer	N	Y	Y	Y
6 Bartlett	?	?	?	?
7 Cummings	N	Y	Y	Y
8 Van Hollen	N	Y	Y	Y
MASSACHUSETTS				
1 Olver	N	Y	Y	Y
2 Neal	?	Y	Y	Y
3 McGovern	N	Y	Y	Y
4 Frank	N	Y	Y	Y
5 Tsongas	N	Y	Y	Y
6 Tierney	N	Y	Y	Y
7 Markey	N	Y	Y	Y
8 Capuano	N	Y	Y	Y
9 Lynch	N	Y	Y	Y
10 Keating	N	Y	Y	Y
MICHIGAN				
1 Benishek	N	Y	Y	Y
2 Huizenga	N	Y	Y	Y
3 Amash	N	Y	Y	Y
4 Camp	N	Y	Y	Y
5 Kildee	N	Y	Y	Y
6 Upton	N	Y	Y	Y
7 Walberg	N	Y	Y	Y
8 Rogers	N	Y	Y	Y
9 Peters	N	Y	Y	Y
10 Miller	N	Y	Y	+
11 Curson	N	Y	Y	Y
12 Levin	N	Y	Y	Y
13 Clarke	N	Y	Y	Y
14 Conyers	Y	Y	Y	Y
15 Dingell	N	Y	Y	Y
MINNESOTA				
1 Walz	N	Y	Y	Y
2 Kline	?	?	?	?
3 Paulsen	N	Y	Y	Y
4 McCollum	N	Y	Y	Y

	616	617	618	619
5 Ellison	N	Y	Y	Y
6 Bachmann	?	?	?	?
7 Peterson	N	Y	Y	Y
8 Cravaack	Y	Y	Y	Y
MISSISSIPPI				
1 Nunnelee	N	Y	Y	Y
2 Thompson	N	Y	Y	Y
3 Harper	N	Y	Y	Y
4 Palazzo	N	Y	Y	Y
MISSOURI				
1 Clay	N	Y	Y	Y
2 Akin	?	?	?	?
3 Carnahan	N	Y	Y	Y
4 Hartzler	N	Y	Y	Y
5 Cleaver	N	Y	Y	Y
6 Graves	N	Y	Y	Y
7 Long	N	Y	Y	Y
8 Emerson	N	Y	Y	Y
9 Luetkemeyer	N	Y	Y	Y
MONTANA				
AL Rehberg	N	Y	Y	Y
NEBRASKA				
1 Fortenberry	?	Y	Y	Y
2 Terry	N	Y	Y	Y
3 Smith	N	Y	Y	Y
NEVADA				
1 Berkley	N	Y	Y	Y
2 Amodei	N	Y	Y	Y
3 Heck	N	Y	Y	Y
NEW HAMPSHIRE				
1 Guinta	N	Y	Y	Y
2 Bass	–	+	+	+
NEW JERSEY				
1 Andrews	N	Y	Y	Y
2 LoBiondo	N	Y	Y	Y
3 Runyan	N	Y	Y	Y
4 Smith	N	Y	Y	Y
5 Garrett	N	Y	Y	Y
6 Pallone	N	Y	Y	Y
7 Lance	N	Y	Y	Y
8 Pascrell	N	Y	Y	Y
9 Rothman	?	Y	Y	Y
10 Payne, Jr.	N	Y	Y	Y
11 Frelinghuysen	N	Y	Y	Y
12 Holt	N	Y	Y	Y
13 Sires	N	Y	Y	Y
NEW MEXICO				
1 Heinrich	?	Y	Y	Y
2 Pearce	N	Y	Y	Y
3 Luján	N	Y	Y	Y
NEW YORK				
1 Bishop	N	Y	Y	Y
2 Israel	N	Y	Y	Y
3 King	N	Y	Y	Y
4 McCarthy	N	Y	Y	Y
5 Ackerman	?	?	?	?
6 Meeks	N	Y	Y	Y
7 Crowley	N	Y	Y	Y
8 Nadler	N	?	Y	Y
9 Turner	N	Y	Y	Y
10 Towns	?	?	?	Y
11 Clarke	N	Y	Y	Y
12 Velázquez	N	?	?	?
13 Grimm	N	Y	Y	Y
14 Maloney	N	Y	Y	Y
15 Rangel	Y	Y	Y	Y
16 Serrano	N	Y	Y	Y
17 Engel	N	Y	Y	Y
18 Lowey	N	Y	Y	Y
19 Hayworth	N	Y	Y	Y
20 Gibson	N	Y	Y	Y
21 Tonko	N	Y	Y	Y
22 Hinchey	?	Y	Y	Y
23 Owens	N	Y	Y	Y
24 Hanna	N	Y	Y	Y
25 Buerkle	N	Y	Y	Y
26 Hochul	N	Y	Y	Y
27 Higgins	?	Y	Y	Y
28 Slaughter	N	Y	Y	Y
29 Reed	N	Y	Y	Y
NORTH CAROLINA				
1 Butterfield	N	Y	Y	Y
2 Ellmers	N	Y	Y	Y
3 Jones	N	Y	Y	Y
4 Price	N	Y	Y	Y

	616	617	618	619
5 Foxx	N	Y	Y	Y
6 Coble	N	Y	Y	Y
7 McIntyre	N	Y	Y	Y
8 Kissell	N	Y	Y	Y
9 Myrick	N	Y	Y	Y
10 McHenry	N	Y	Y	Y
11 Shuler	N	?	?	?
12 Watt	N	Y	Y	Y
13 Miller	N	Y	Y	Y
NORTH DAKOTA				
AL Berg	N	Y	Y	Y
OHIO				
1 Chabot	N	Y	Y	Y
2 Schmidt	N	Y	Y	Y
3 Turner	N	Y	Y	Y
4 Jordan	N	Y	Y	Y
5 Latta	N	Y	Y	Y
6 Johnson	N	Y	Y	Y
7 Austria	?	?	?	?
8 Boehner				
9 Kaptur	N	Y	Y	Y
10 Kucinich	N	Y	Y	Y
11 Fudge	N	Y	Y	Y
12 Tiberi	N	Y	Y	Y
13 Sutton	N	Y	Y	Y
14 LaTourette	N	Y	Y	Y
15 Stivers	N	Y	Y	Y
16 Renacci	N	Y	Y	Y
17 Ryan	N	Y	Y	Y
18 Gibbs	N	Y	Y	Y
OKLAHOMA				
1 Sullivan	?	?	?	?
2 Boren	N	Y	Y	Y
3 Lucas	N	Y	Y	Y
4 Cole	N	Y	Y	Y
5 Lankford	N	Y	Y	Y
OREGON				
1 Bonamici	N	Y	Y	Y
2 Walden	N	Y	Y	Y
3 Blumenauer	N	Y	Y	Y
4 DeFazio	N	Y	Y	Y
5 Schrader	N	Y	Y	Y
PENNSYLVANIA				
1 Brady	N	Y	Y	Y
2 Fattah	N	Y	Y	Y
3 Kelly	N	Y	Y	Y
4 Altmire	N	Y	Y	Y
5 Thompson	N	Y	Y	Y
6 Gerlach	N	Y	Y	Y
7 Meehan	N	Y	Y	Y
8 Fitzpatrick	N	Y	Y	Y
9 Shuster	N	Y	Y	?
10 Marino	?	?	?	?
11 Barletta	N	Y	Y	Y
12 Critz	?	Y	Y	Y
13 Schwartz	N	Y	Y	Y
14 Doyle	N	Y	Y	Y
15 Dent	N	Y	Y	Y
16 Pitts	N	Y	Y	Y
17 Holden	N	Y	Y	Y
18 Murphy	N	Y	Y	?
19 Platts	–	Y	Y	Y
RHODE ISLAND				
1 Cicilline	N	Y	Y	Y
2 Langevin	N	Y	Y	Y
SOUTH CAROLINA				
1 Scott	N	Y	Y	Y
2 Wilson	N	Y	Y	Y
3 Duncan	N	Y	Y	Y
4 Gowdy	N	Y	Y	Y
5 Mulvaney	N	Y	Y	Y
6 Clyburn	N	Y	Y	Y
SOUTH DAKOTA				
AL Noem	N	Y	Y	Y
TENNESSEE				
1 Roe	N	Y	Y	Y
2 Duncan	N	Y	Y	Y
3 Fleischmann	N	Y	Y	Y
4 DesJarlais	N	Y	Y	Y
5 Cooper	N	Y	Y	Y
6 Black	N	?	Y	Y
7 Blackburn	N	Y	Y	Y
8 Fincher	N	Y	Y	Y
9 Cohen	N	Y	Y	Y

	616	617	618	619
TEXAS				
1 Gohmert	?	Y	Y	N
2 Poe	N	Y	Y	Y
3 Johnson, S.	N	Y	Y	Y
4 Hall	N	Y	Y	Y
5 Hensarling	N	Y	Y	Y
6 Barton	N	Y	Y	Y
7 Culberson	N	Y	Y	Y
8 Brady	N	Y	Y	Y
9 Green, A.	N	Y	Y	Y
10 McCaul	N	Y	Y	Y
11 Conaway	N	Y	Y	Y
12 Granger	N	Y	Y	Y
13 Thornberry	N	?	Y	?
14 Paul	?	?	?	?
15 Hinojosa	N	Y	Y	Y
16 Reyes	N	Y	Y	Y
17 Flores	N	Y	Y	Y
18 Jackson Lee	N	Y	Y	Y
19 Neugebauer	N	Y	Y	Y
20 Gonzalez	N	Y	Y	Y
21 Smith	N	Y	?	Y
22 Olson	N	Y	Y	Y
23 Canseco	N	Y	Y	Y
24 Marchant	N	Y	Y	Y
25 Doggett	N	Y	Y	Y
26 Burgess	N	Y	Y	Y
27 Farenthold	N	Y	Y	Y
28 Cuellar	N	Y	Y	Y
29 Green, G.	N	Y	Y	Y
30 Johnson, E.	N	Y	Y	Y
31 Carter	N	Y	Y	Y
32 Sessions	N	Y	Y	Y
UTAH				
1 Bishop	N	Y	Y	Y
2 Matheson	N	Y	Y	Y
3 Chaffetz	N	Y	Y	Y
VERMONT				
AL Welch	N	Y	Y	Y
VIRGINIA				
1 Wittman	N	Y	Y	Y
2 Rigell	N	Y	Y	Y
3 Scott	N	Y	Y	Y
4 Forbes	N	Y	Y	Y
5 Hurt	N	Y	Y	Y
6 Goodlatte	N	Y	Y	Y
7 Cantor	N	Y	Y	Y
8 Moran	N	Y	Y	Y
9 Griffith	N	Y	Y	Y
10 Wolf	N	Y	Y	Y
11 Connolly	N	Y	Y	Y
WASHINGTON				
1 DelBene	N	Y	Y	Y
2 Larsen	N	Y	Y	Y
3 Herrera Beutler	N	Y	Y	Y
4 Hastings	N	Y	Y	Y
5 McMorris Rodgers	N	Y	?	Y
6 Dicks	N	Y	?	Y
7 McDermott	N	Y	Y	Y
8 Reichert	N	Y	Y	Y
9 Smith	N	Y	Y	Y
WEST VIRGINIA				
1 McKinley	N	Y	Y	Y
2 Capito	N	Y	Y	Y
3 Rahall	N	Y	Y	Y
WISCONSIN				
1 Ryan	N	Y	Y	Y
2 Baldwin	N	Y	Y	Y
3 Kind	N	Y	Y	Y
4 Moore	N	Y	Y	Y
5 Sensenbrenner	N	Y	Y	Y
6 Petri	N	Y	Y	Y
7 Duffy	N	Y	Y	Y
8 Ribble	N	Y	Y	Y
WYOMING				
AL Lummis	N	Y	Y	Y

IN THE HOUSE | By Vote Number

620. Procedural Motion/Journal. Approval of the House Journal of Friday, Dec. 7, 2012. Approved 272-102: R 162-50; D 110-52. Dec. 11, 2012.

621. H Res 827. Suspension Authority/Previous Question. Sessions, R-Texas, motion to order the previous question (thus ending debate and the possibility of amendment) on the rule that would provide for House floor consideration of bills under suspension of the rules at any time through the legislative day of Friday, Dec. 28, 2012. Motion agreed to 224-183: R 224-0; D 0-183. Dec. 12, 2012.

622. H Res 827. Suspension Authority/Rule. Adoption of the rule that would provide for House floor consideration of bills under suspension of the rules at any time through the legislative day of Friday, Dec. 28, 2012. Adopted 226-178: R 222-3; D 4-175. Dec. 12, 2012.

623. HR 6190. Sale of Epinephrine Inhalers/Passage. Burgess, R-Texas, motion to suspend the rules and pass the bill that would permit the sale, distribution and consumption of remaining inventories of epinephrine inhalers through Aug. 1, 2013. It also would prevent the EPA from initiating any enforcement action to restrict such distribution or sale. Motion rejected 229-182: R 198-29; D 31-153. A two-thirds majority of those present and voting (274 in this case) is required for passage under suspension of the rules. Dec. 12, 2012.

624. HR 4310. Fiscal 2013 Defense Authorization/Motion to Instruct. Davis, D-Calif., motion to instruct conferees to agree to Senate-passed provisions that would require a report to Congress on a plan to promote the security of Afghan women and girls in the transition from U.S. to Afghan-led security in Afghanistan. Motion agreed to 399-4: R 218-4; D 181-0. Dec. 13, 2012.

625. HR 4310. Fiscal 2013 Defense Authorization/Motion to Close Conference. McKeon, R-Calif., motion to close portions of the conference on the bill that would authorize funding for defense programs for fiscal 2013. Motion agreed to 351-53: R 185-37; D 166-16. Dec. 13, 2012.

626. HR 4053. Payment Eligibility Verification/Passage. Chaffetz, R-Utah, motion to suspend the rules and pass the bill that would require the Office of Management and Budget to identify and report on federal programs at high risk for improper payments and to create a standardized methodology for estimating improper payments. It would allow for data sharing between agencies and require the OMB to establish a plan for curbing improper payments to deceased individuals. Motion agreed to 402-0: R 222-0; D 180-0. A two-thirds majority of those present and voting (268 in this case) is required for passage under suspension of the rules. Dec. 13, 2012.

	620	621	622	623	624	625	626
ALABAMA							
1 Bonner	Y	Y	Y	Y	Y	Y	Y
2 Roby	Y	Y	Y	N	Y	Y	Y
3 Rogers	Y	Y	Y	Y	Y	Y	Y
4 Aderholt	Y	Y	Y	Y	Y	Y	Y
5 Brooks	Y	Y	Y	Y	Y	Y	Y
6 Bachus	Y	Y	Y	Y	Y	Y	Y
7 Sewell	N	N	N	N	Y	Y	Y
ALASKA							
AL Young	N	Y	Y	Y	Y	Y	Y
ARIZONA							
1 Gosar	?	Y	Y	Y	Y	Y	Y
2 Franks	Y	Y	Y	Y	Y	Y	Y
3 Quayle	N	Y	Y	Y	Y	Y	Y
4 Pastor	?	N	N	Y	Y	Y	Y
5 Schweikert	Y	Y	Y	Y	Y	Y	Y
6 Flake	Y	Y	Y	Y	Y	Y	Y
7 Grijalva	?	N	N	N	Y	Y	Y
8 Barber	Y	N	N	N	Y	Y	Y
ARKANSAS							
1 Crawford	N	Y	Y	Y	Y	Y	Y
2 Griffin	?	?	?	?	?	?	?
3 Womack	Y	Y	Y	Y	Y	Y	Y
4 Ross	?	?	?	?	Y	Y	Y
CALIFORNIA							
1 Thompson	N	N	N	N	Y	Y	Y
2 Herger	Y	Y	Y	Y	Y	Y	Y
3 Lungren	Y	Y	Y	Y	Y	Y	Y
4 McClintock	Y	Y	Y	Y	Y	Y	Y
5 Matsui	N	N	N	N	Y	Y	Y
6 Woolsey	+	N	N	N	Y	N	Y
7 Miller, George	N	N	N	N	Y	Y	Y
8 Pelosi	Y	N	N	N	Y	Y	Y
9 Lee	N	N	N	N	Y	N	Y
10 Garamendi	Y	N	N	N	Y	Y	Y
11 McNerney	Y	N	N	N	Y	Y	Y
12 Speier	Y	N	N	N	Y	Y	Y
13 Stark	?	N	N	N	?	?	?
14 Eshoo	Y	N	N	?	Y	Y	Y
15 Honda	?	N	N	N	Y	N	Y
16 Lofgren	Y	N	N	N	Y	Y	Y
17 Farr	Y	N	N	N	Y	N	Y
18 Vacant							
19 Denham	N	Y	Y	Y	Y	Y	Y
20 Costa	N	N	N	Y	Y	Y	Y
21 Nunes	Y	Y	Y	Y	Y	Y	Y
22 McCarthy	Y	?	?	?	?	?	?
23 Capps	Y	N	N	N	Y	Y	Y
24 Gallegly	?	?	?	?	?	?	?
25 McKeon	Y	Y	Y	Y	Y	Y	Y
26 Dreier	Y	Y	Y	Y	Y	Y	Y
27 Sherman	Y	N	N	N	Y	Y	Y
28 Berman	Y	N	N	N	Y	Y	Y
29 Schiff	Y	N	N	N	Y	Y	Y
30 Waxman	Y	N	N	N	Y	Y	Y
31 Becerra	Y	N	N	N	Y	Y	Y
32 Chu	Y	N	N	N	Y	Y	Y
33 Bass	N	N	N	N	Y	Y	Y
34 Roybal-Allard	Y	N	N	N	Y	Y	Y
35 Waters	Y	?	?	?	Y	N	Y
36 Hahn	Y	N	N	N	Y	N	Y
37 Richardson	Y	N	N	N	Y	Y	Y
38 Napolitano	Y	N	N	N	Y	Y	Y
39 Sánchez, Linda	N	N	N	N	Y	Y	Y
40 Royce	?	Y	Y	Y	Y	Y	Y
41 Lewis	Y	Y	Y	Y	Y	Y	Y
42 Miller, Gary	Y	Y	Y	Y	Y	Y	Y
43 Baca	?	N	N	N	Y	Y	Y
44 Calvert	Y	Y	?	Y	Y	Y	Y
45 Bono Mack	Y	?	?	?	?	?	?
46 Rohrabacher	Y	Y	Y	Y	Y	Y	Y
47 Sanchez, Loretta	Y	N	N	Y	?	?	?
48 Campbell	Y	Y	Y	Y	Y	Y	Y
49 Issa	Y	Y	Y	Y	Y	?	?
50 Bilbray	N	Y	Y	Y	Y	Y	Y
51 Vacant							
52 Hunter	Y	Y	Y	Y	Y	Y	Y
53 Davis	Y	N	N	N	Y	Y	Y

	620	621	622	623	624	625	626
COLORADO							
1 DeGette	Y	?	?	N	Y	Y	Y
2 Polis	Y	N	N	N	Y	N	Y
3 Tipton	N	Y	Y	Y	Y	Y	Y
4 Gardner	N	Y	Y	Y	Y	Y	Y
5 Lamborn	Y	Y	Y	Y	Y	Y	Y
6 Coffman	N	Y	Y	Y	Y	Y	Y
7 Perlmutter	Y	N	N	N	Y	Y	Y
CONNECTICUT							
1 Larson	Y	N	N	Y	Y	Y	Y
2 Courtney	Y	N	N	N	Y	Y	Y
3 DeLauro	Y	N	N	N	Y	Y	Y
4 Himes	Y	N	N	N	Y	Y	Y
5 Murphy	Y	N	N	N	Y	Y	Y
DELAWARE							
AL Carney	Y	N	N	N	?	Y	Y
FLORIDA							
1 Miller	N	Y	Y	N	Y	Y	Y
2 Southerland	Y	Y	Y	Y	Y	Y	Y
3 Brown	Y	N	N	N	Y	Y	Y
4 Crenshaw	Y	Y	Y	N	Y	Y	Y
5 Nugent	N	Y	Y	N	Y	Y	Y
6 Stearns	Y	Y	Y	Y	Y	Y	Y
7 Mica	Y	Y	Y	Y	Y	Y	Y
8 Webster	Y	Y	Y	Y	Y	Y	Y
9 Bilirakis	Y	Y	Y	Y	Y	Y	Y
10 Young	Y	Y	Y	N	Y	Y	Y
11 Castor	Y	N	N	N	Y	Y	Y
12 Ross	Y	Y	Y	N	?	?	?
13 Buchanan	Y	Y	Y	Y	Y	Y	Y
14 Mack	Y	?	?	?	?	?	?
15 Posey	Y	Y	Y	Y	Y	N	Y
16 Rooney	Y	Y	Y	N	Y	Y	Y
17 Wilson	?	N	N	N	Y	Y	Y
18 Ros-Lehtinen	Y	Y	Y	Y	?	?	?
19 Deutch	?	N	N	N	Y	Y	Y
20 Wasserman Schultz	Y	N	N	N	Y	Y	Y
21 Diaz-Balart	Y	Y	Y	Y	Y	Y	Y
22 West	Y	Y	Y	Y	Y	Y	Y
23 Hastings	N	N	N	N	Y	Y	Y
24 Adams	N	Y	Y	N	Y	N	Y
25 Rivera	Y	Y	Y	Y	Y	Y	Y
GEORGIA							
1 Kingston	Y	Y	Y	Y	Y	Y	Y
2 Bishop	Y	N	N	N	Y	Y	Y
3 Westmoreland	Y	Y	Y	N	Y	Y	Y
4 Johnson	N	N	N	N	Y	Y	Y
5 Lewis	?	N	N	N	?	?	?
6 Price	N	Y	Y	Y	Y	N	Y
7 Woodall	N	Y	Y	Y	Y	Y	Y
8 Scott, A.	Y	Y	Y	Y	Y	Y	Y
9 Graves	N	Y	Y	Y	Y	Y	Y
10 Broun	Y	Y	Y	Y	Y	N	Y
11 Gingrey	?	Y	Y	Y	Y	Y	Y
12 Barrow	Y	N	N	Y	Y	Y	Y
13 Scott, D.	Y	N	N	N	Y	Y	Y
HAWAII							
1 Hanabusa	Y	N	N	N	Y	Y	Y
2 Hirono	Y	N	N	N	Y	Y	Y
IDAHO							
1 Labrador	Y	Y	Y	N	Y	N	Y
2 Simpson	?	Y	Y	Y	Y	Y	Y
ILLINOIS							
1 Rush	Y	N	N	N	Y	Y	Y
2 Vacant							
3 Lipinski	?	N	N	N	Y	Y	Y
4 Gutierrez	?	N	N	N	Y	Y	Y
5 Quigley	Y	N	N	N	Y	Y	Y
6 Roskam	Y	Y	Y	Y	Y	Y	Y
7 Davis	Y	N	N	N	Y	Y	Y
8 Walsh	?	Y	Y	N	Y	N	Y
9 Schakowsky	N	N	N	N	Y	Y	Y
10 Dold	N	Y	Y	N	Y	Y	Y
11 Kinzinger	N	Y	Y	Y	Y	Y	Y
12 Costello	?	?	?	?	?	?	?
13 Biggert	Y	Y	Y	Y	Y	Y	Y
14 Hultgren	Y	Y	Y	Y	Y	Y	Y
15 Johnson	?	?	?	?	?	?	?

KEY Republicans Democrats

Y Voted for (yea)	**X** Paired against	**C** Voted "present" to avoid possible conflict of interest
# Paired for	**–** Announced against	
+ Announced for	**P** Voted "present"	**?** Did not vote or otherwise make a position known
N Voted against (nay)		

	620	621	622	623	624	625	626
16 **Manzullo**	N	Y	Y	Y	Y	Y	Y
17 **Schilling**	?	Y	Y	Y	Y	Y	Y
18 **Schock**	?	Y	Y	Y	Y	Y	Y
19 **Shimkus**	Y	Y	Y	Y	Y	Y	Y
INDIANA							
1 Visclosky	N	N	N	N	Y	Y	Y
2 Donnelly	N	N	Y	Y	Y	Y	Y
3 **Stutzman**	Y	?	Y	Y	Y	Y	Y
4 **Rokita**	Y	Y	Y	Y	Y	Y	Y
5 **Burton**	?	?	?	?	Y	N	Y
6 **Pence**	Y	?	?	?	?	?	?
7 Carson	Y	N	?	N	Y	Y	Y
8 **Bucshon**	Y	Y	Y	Y	Y	Y	Y
9 **Young**	Y	Y	Y	Y	Y	Y	Y
IOWA							
1 Braley	Y	N	N	N	Y	Y	Y
2 Loebsack	N	N	N	N	Y	Y	Y
3 Boswell	Y	N	N	N	Y	Y	Y
4 **Latham**	N	Y	Y	Y	Y	Y	Y
5 **King**	Y	?	Y	Y	Y	Y	Y
KANSAS							
1 **Huelskamp**	Y	Y	Y	Y	Y	N	Y
2 **Jenkins**	Y	Y	Y	Y	Y	Y	Y
3 **Yoder**	N	Y	Y	Y	Y	Y	Y
4 **Pompeo**	Y	Y	Y	Y	Y	Y	Y
KENTUCKY							
1 **Whitfield**	Y	Y	Y	Y	Y	Y	Y
2 **Guthrie**	Y	Y	Y	Y	Y	Y	Y
3 Yarmuth	Y	N	N	N	Y	Y	Y
4 **Massie**	N	Y	Y	Y	N	N	Y
5 **Rogers**	Y	Y	Y	Y	Y	Y	Y
6 Chandler	?	N	N	N	Y	Y	Y
LOUISIANA							
1 **Scalise**	Y	Y	Y	Y	Y	Y	Y
2 Richmond	Y	N	N	Y	Y	Y	Y
3 **Landry**	N	Y	N	Y	Y	Y	Y
4 **Fleming**	Y	Y	Y	Y	Y	Y	Y
5 **Alexander**	Y	Y	Y	Y	Y	Y	Y
6 **Cassidy**	Y	Y	Y	N	Y	Y	Y
7 **Boustany**	Y	Y	Y	Y	Y	Y	Y
MAINE							
1 Pingree	Y	N	N	N	Y	Y	Y
2 Michaud	Y	N	N	N	Y	Y	Y
MARYLAND							
1 **Harris**	Y	Y	Y	Y	Y	Y	?
2 Ruppersberger	Y	N	N	N	Y	Y	Y
3 Sarbanes	N	N	N	N	Y	Y	Y
4 Edwards	Y	N	N	N	Y	Y	Y
5 Hoyer	N	N	N	N	Y	Y	Y
6 **Bartlett**	?	?	?	?	?	?	?
7 Cummings	N	N	N	N	Y	Y	Y
8 Van Hollen	Y	N	N	N	Y	Y	Y
MASSACHUSETTS							
1 Olver	?	N	N	N	Y	Y	Y
2 Neal	N	N	N	N	Y	Y	Y
3 McGovern	N	N	N	N	Y	Y	Y
4 Frank	?	N	N	N	Y	Y	Y
5 Tsongas	Y	N	N	N	Y	Y	Y
6 Tierney	?	N	N	N	Y	Y	Y
7 Markey	N	N	N	N	Y	Y	Y
8 Capuano	N	N	N	Y	Y	Y	Y
9 Lynch	N	N	N	Y	Y	Y	Y
10 Keating	Y	N	N	N	Y	Y	Y
MICHIGAN							
1 **Benishek**	N	Y	Y	Y	Y	Y	Y
2 **Huizenga**	Y	Y	Y	Y	Y	Y	Y
3 **Amash**	P	Y	Y	N	N	N	Y
4 **Camp**	Y	Y	Y	Y	Y	Y	Y
5 Kildee	Y	N	N	Y	Y	Y	Y
6 **Upton**	Y	Y	Y	Y	Y	Y	Y
7 **Walberg**	N	Y	Y	Y	Y	Y	Y
8 **Rogers**	Y	Y	Y	Y	Y	Y	Y
9 Peters	N	N	N	Y	Y	Y	Y
10 **Miller**	Y	Y	Y	Y	Y	Y	Y
11 Curson	N	N	N	Y	Y	Y	Y
12 Levin	Y	N	N	N	Y	Y	Y
13 Clarke	Y	N	N	N	Y	Y	Y
14 Conyers	?	?	?	N	Y	Y	Y
15 Dingell	Y	N	N	Y	Y	Y	Y
MINNESOTA							
1 Walz	Y	N	N	N	Y	Y	Y
2 **Kline**	Y	Y	Y	Y	Y	Y	Y
3 **Paulsen**	N	Y	Y	N	Y	Y	Y
4 McCollum	Y	N	N	N	Y	Y	Y

	620	621	622	623	624	625	626
5 Ellison	?	N	N	N	Y	N	Y
6 **Bachmann**	?	Y	Y	Y	Y	Y	Y
7 Peterson	N	N	?	Y	Y	Y	Y
8 **Cravaack**	?	Y	Y	Y	Y	Y	Y
MISSISSIPPI							
1 **Nunnelee**	?	?	?	?	?	?	?
2 Thompson	N	N	N	N	Y	Y	Y
3 **Harper**	Y	Y	Y	Y	Y	Y	Y
4 **Palazzo**	Y	Y	Y	Y	Y	Y	Y
MISSOURI							
1 Clay	Y	N	N	Y	Y	Y	Y
2 **Akin**	?	?	?	?	?	?	?
3 Carnahan	Y	N	N	N	Y	Y	Y
4 **Hartzler**	Y	Y	Y	Y	Y	Y	Y
5 Cleaver	Y	N	N	Y	Y	Y	Y
6 **Graves**	?	Y	Y	Y	Y	Y	Y
7 **Long**	Y	Y	Y	Y	Y	Y	Y
8 **Emerson**	Y	Y	Y	Y	Y	Y	Y
9 **Luetkemeyer**	Y	Y	Y	N	Y	Y	Y
MONTANA							
AL **Rehberg**	Y	Y	Y	Y	Y	Y	Y
NEBRASKA							
1 **Fortenberry**	Y	Y	Y	Y	Y	Y	Y
2 **Terry**	N	Y	Y	Y	Y	Y	Y
3 **Smith**	Y	Y	Y	Y	Y	Y	Y
NEVADA							
1 Berkley	Y	N	N	N	Y	Y	Y
2 **Amodei**	Y	Y	Y	N	Y	N	Y
3 **Heck**	N	Y	Y	N	Y	Y	Y
NEW HAMPSHIRE							
1 **Guinta**	N	Y	Y	Y	Y	Y	Y
2 **Bass**	Y	Y	Y	Y	Y	Y	Y
NEW JERSEY							
1 Andrews	N	N	N	N	Y	Y	Y
2 **LoBiondo**	N	Y	Y	Y	Y	Y	Y
3 **Runyan**	Y	Y	Y	Y	Y	Y	Y
4 **Smith**	Y	Y	Y	Y	Y	Y	Y
5 **Garrett**	N	Y	Y	Y	Y	Y	Y
6 Pallone	N	N	N	N	Y	Y	Y
7 **Lance**	N	Y	Y	Y	Y	Y	Y
8 Pascrell	N	N	N	N	Y	Y	Y
9 Rothman	Y	N	N	N	Y	Y	Y
10 Payne, Jr.	Y	N	N	N	Y	Y	Y
11 **Frelinghuysen**	Y	Y	Y	Y	Y	Y	Y
12 Holt	Y	N	N	N	Y	Y	Y
13 Sires	?	N	N	N	Y	Y	Y
NEW MEXICO							
1 Heinrich	Y	N	N	N	Y	Y	Y
2 **Pearce**	Y	Y	N	Y	Y	N	Y
3 Luján	Y	N	?	N	Y	Y	Y
NEW YORK							
1 Bishop	N	N	N	N	Y	Y	Y
2 Israel	Y	N	N	N	Y	Y	Y
3 **King**	Y	Y	Y	Y	Y	Y	Y
4 McCarthy	?	N	N	N	Y	Y	Y
5 Ackerman	Y	N	N	N	?	?	?
6 Meeks	Y	N	N	N	Y	Y	Y
7 Crowley	Y	N	N	N	Y	Y	Y
8 Nadler	Y	N	N	N	Y	Y	Y
9 **Turner**	Y	Y	Y	Y	Y	Y	Y
10 Towns	?	N	N	Y	Y	Y	Y
11 Clarke	Y	N	N	N	Y	N	Y
12 Velázquez	N	N	N	N	Y	Y	Y
13 **Grimm**	Y	Y	Y	Y	Y	Y	Y
14 Maloney	Y	N	N	N	Y	Y	Y
15 Rangel	N	N	?	N	Y	Y	Y
16 Serrano	Y	N	N	N	Y	Y	Y
17 Engel	Y	N	N	Y	Y	Y	Y
18 Lowey	Y	N	N	N	Y	Y	Y
19 **Hayworth**	Y	Y	Y	N	?	Y	Y
20 **Gibson**	N	Y	Y	N	Y	Y	Y
21 Tonko	Y	N	N	N	Y	Y	Y
22 Hinchey	Y	N	N	N	Y	Y	Y
23 Owens	P	N	N	N	Y	Y	Y
24 **Hanna**	N	Y	Y	Y	Y	Y	Y
25 **Buerkle**	Y	Y	Y	Y	Y	N	Y
26 Hochul	Y	N	Y	N	Y	Y	Y
27 Higgins	Y	N	N	N	Y	Y	?
28 Slaughter	N	N	N	N	Y	Y	Y
29 **Reed**	N	Y	Y	Y	Y	Y	Y
NORTH CAROLINA							
1 Butterfield	Y	N	N	N	Y	Y	Y
2 **Ellmers**	Y	Y	Y	Y	Y	Y	Y
3 **Jones**	N	Y	Y	Y	N	N	Y
4 Price	Y	N	N	N	Y	Y	Y

	620	621	622	623	624	625	626
5 **Foxx**	N	Y	Y	Y	Y	Y	Y
6 **Coble**	Y	Y	Y	Y	Y	Y	Y
7 McIntyre	Y	N	N	Y	Y	Y	Y
8 Kissell	Y	N	N	Y	Y	Y	Y
9 **Myrick**	Y	Y	Y	Y	Y	Y	Y
10 **McHenry**	Y	Y	Y	Y	Y	Y	Y
11 Shuler	N	N	N	Y	Y	Y	Y
12 Watt	Y	N	N	N	Y	Y	Y
13 Miller	?	N	N	N	Y	Y	Y
NORTH DAKOTA							
AL **Berg**	Y	Y	Y	Y	Y	Y	Y
OHIO							
1 **Chabot**	Y	Y	Y	Y	Y	Y	Y
2 **Schmidt**	Y	?	Y	Y	Y	Y	Y
3 **Turner**	Y	Y	Y	Y	Y	Y	Y
4 **Jordan**	Y	Y	Y	N	Y	N	Y
5 **Latta**	Y	Y	Y	Y	Y	Y	Y
6 **Johnson**	N	Y	Y	Y	Y	Y	Y
7 **Austria**	Y	?	?	?	Y	Y	Y
8 **Boehner**							
9 Kaptur	Y	N	N	N	Y	Y	Y
10 Kucinich	N	N	N	N	Y	N	Y
11 Fudge	Y	N	N	N	Y	Y	Y
12 **Tiberi**	Y	Y	Y	Y	Y	Y	Y
13 Sutton	N	N	N	N	Y	Y	Y
14 **LaTourette**	Y	Y	Y	Y	?	?	?
15 **Stivers**	N	Y	Y	Y	Y	Y	Y
16 **Renacci**	N	Y	Y	Y	Y	Y	Y
17 Ryan	N	N	N	Y	Y	Y	Y
18 **Gibbs**	N	Y	Y	Y	Y	Y	Y
OKLAHOMA							
1 **Sullivan**	Y	Y	Y	Y	Y	Y	Y
2 Boren	?	N	N	Y	Y	Y	Y
3 **Lucas**	Y	Y	Y	Y	Y	Y	Y
4 **Cole**	Y	Y	Y	Y	+	+	+
5 **Lankford**	Y	Y	Y	Y	Y	Y	Y
OREGON							
1 Bonamici	Y	N	N	N	Y	Y	Y
2 **Walden**	Y	Y	Y	Y	Y	Y	Y
3 Blumenauer	Y	N	N	N	Y	N	Y
4 DeFazio	N	N	N	Y	Y	N	Y
5 Schrader	N	N	N	N	Y	Y	Y
PENNSYLVANIA							
1 Brady	N	N	N	N	Y	Y	Y
2 Fattah	Y	N	N	N	Y	Y	Y
3 **Kelly**	Y	Y	Y	Y	Y	Y	Y
4 Altmire	N	N	N	Y	Y	Y	Y
5 **Thompson**	Y	Y	Y	Y	Y	Y	Y
6 **Gerlach**	Y	Y	Y	N	Y	Y	Y
7 **Meehan**	Y	Y	Y	N	Y	Y	Y
8 **Fitzpatrick**	N	Y	Y	N	Y	Y	Y
9 **Shuster**	Y	Y	Y	Y	Y	Y	Y
10 **Marino**	Y	Y	Y	Y	Y	Y	Y
11 **Barletta**	Y	Y	Y	Y	Y	Y	Y
12 Critz	N	N	N	Y	Y	Y	Y
13 Schwartz	Y	N	N	N	Y	Y	Y
14 Doyle	N	N	N	Y	Y	Y	Y
15 **Dent**	Y	Y	Y	Y	Y	Y	Y
16 **Pitts**	?	?	?	?	?	?	?
17 Holden	N	?	?	?	?	?	?
18 **Murphy**	Y	Y	Y	Y	Y	Y	Y
19 **Platts**	Y	Y	Y	Y	Y	Y	Y
RHODE ISLAND							
1 Cicilline	Y	N	N	N	Y	Y	Y
2 Langevin	N	N	N	N	Y	Y	Y
SOUTH CAROLINA							
1 **Scott**	Y	Y	Y	Y	Y	Y	Y
2 **Wilson**	Y	Y	Y	Y	Y	Y	Y
3 **Duncan**	Y	Y	Y	Y	Y	Y	Y
4 **Gowdy**	Y	Y	Y	Y	Y	Y	Y
5 **Mulvaney**	N	Y	Y	Y	Y	N	Y
6 Clyburn	Y	N	N	Y	Y	Y	Y
SOUTH DAKOTA							
AL **Noem**	Y	Y	Y	Y	?	?	?
TENNESSEE							
1 **Roe**	Y	Y	Y	Y	Y	Y	Y
2 **Duncan**	Y	Y	Y	Y	Y	Y	Y
3 **Fleischmann**	Y	Y	Y	Y	Y	Y	Y
4 **DesJarlais**	Y	Y	Y	Y	Y	Y	Y
5 Cooper	Y	N	N	N	Y	Y	Y
6 **Black**	?	Y	Y	Y	Y	Y	Y
7 **Blackburn**	Y	Y	Y	Y	Y	Y	Y
8 **Fincher**	Y	Y	Y	Y	Y	Y	Y
9 Cohen	Y	N	N	N	Y	Y	Y

	620	621	622	623	624	625	626
TEXAS							
1 **Gohmert**	P	Y	Y	Y	Y	N	Y
2 **Poe**	N	Y	Y	Y	Y	N	Y
3 **Johnson, S.**	Y	Y	Y	Y	Y	N	Y
4 **Hall**	Y	Y	Y	Y	Y	Y	Y
5 **Hensarling**	Y	Y	Y	Y	Y	N	Y
6 **Barton**	Y	Y	Y	Y	Y	N	Y
7 **Culberson**	?	Y	Y	Y	Y	N	Y
8 **Brady**	Y	Y	Y	Y	Y	N	Y
9 Green, A.	Y	N	N	N	Y	N	Y
10 **McCaul**	Y	Y	Y	Y	Y	Y	Y
11 **Conaway**	Y	Y	Y	Y	Y	N	Y
12 **Granger**	Y	Y	Y	Y	Y	N	Y
13 **Thornberry**	Y	Y	Y	Y	Y	Y	Y
14 **Paul**	?	Y	Y	Y	N	N	Y
15 Hinojosa	Y	N	N	N	Y	Y	Y
16 Reyes	?	?	?	?	?	?	?
17 **Flores**	?	Y	Y	Y	Y	N	Y
18 Jackson Lee	Y	N	Y	N	Y	N	Y
19 **Neugebauer**	Y	Y	Y	Y	Y	N	Y
20 Gonzalez	?	N	N	N	Y	Y	Y
21 **Smith**	Y	Y	Y	Y	Y	Y	Y
22 **Olson**	Y	Y	Y	Y	Y	N	Y
23 **Canseco**	Y	Y	Y	Y	Y	N	Y
24 **Marchant**	?	Y	Y	Y	Y	N	Y
25 Doggett	Y	N	N	N	?	?	?
26 **Burgess**	N	Y	Y	Y	Y	N	Y
27 **Farenthold**	N	Y	Y	Y	Y	N	Y
28 Cuellar	Y	N	N	Y	Y	N	Y
29 Green, G.	N	N	N	Y	Y	Y	?
30 Johnson, E.	Y	N	N	N	Y	Y	Y
31 **Carter**	Y	Y	Y	Y	Y	N	Y
32 **Sessions**	Y	Y	Y	Y	Y	Y	Y
UTAH							
1 **Bishop**	Y	Y	Y	Y	Y	Y	Y
2 Matheson	N	N	N	Y	Y	Y	Y
3 **Chaffetz**	Y	Y	Y	N	Y	Y	Y
VERMONT							
AL Welch	Y	N	N	N	Y	Y	Y
VIRGINIA							
1 **Wittman**	N	Y	Y	Y	Y	Y	Y
2 **Rigell**	N	Y	Y	Y	Y	Y	Y
3 Scott	Y	N	N	N	Y	Y	Y
4 **Forbes**	Y	Y	Y	Y	Y	Y	Y
5 **Hurt**	Y	Y	Y	N	Y	Y	Y
6 **Goodlatte**	Y	Y	Y	Y	Y	Y	Y
7 **Cantor**	Y	Y	Y	Y	?	?	Y
8 Moran	?	N	N	N	Y	Y	Y
9 **Griffith**	?	Y	Y	Y	Y	Y	Y
10 **Wolf**	?	Y	Y	Y	Y	Y	Y
11 Connolly	Y	N	N	N	Y	Y	Y
WASHINGTON							
1 DelBene	Y	N	N	N	Y	Y	Y
2 Larsen	Y	N	N	N	Y	Y	Y
3 **Herrera Beutler**	N	Y	Y	Y	Y	N	Y
4 **Hastings**	?	Y	Y	Y	Y	Y	Y
5 **McMorris Rodgers**	Y	Y	Y	Y	Y	Y	Y
6 Dicks	?	?	?	?	?	?	?
7 McDermott	N	N	N	N	Y	Y	Y
8 **Reichert**	N	Y	Y	Y	Y	Y	Y
9 Smith	Y	N	N	N	Y	Y	Y
WEST VIRGINIA							
1 **McKinley**	Y	Y	Y	Y	Y	Y	Y
2 **Capito**	Y	Y	Y	N	Y	Y	Y
3 Rahall	N	N	N	Y	Y	Y	Y
WISCONSIN							
1 **Ryan**	Y	Y	Y	Y	Y	Y	Y
2 Baldwin	N	N	N	N	Y	Y	Y
3 Kind	N	N	N	N	Y	Y	Y
4 Moore	N	N	N	N	Y	Y	Y
5 **Sensenbrenner**	Y	Y	Y	Y	Y	Y	Y
6 **Petri**	Y	Y	Y	Y	Y	Y	Y
7 **Duffy**	N	Y	?	Y	Y	Y	Y
8 **Ribble**	N	Y	Y	N	Y	N	Y
WYOMING							
AL **Lummis**	Y	Y	Y	N	Y	N	Y

IN THE HOUSE | By Vote Number

627. **HR 4606. Pipeline Right-of-Way/Passage.** Bishop, R-Utah, motion to suspend the rules and pass the bill that would authorize the National Park Service to grant a right-of-way permit for an existing natural-gas pipeline located in Glacier National Park. Motion agreed to 286-10: R 177-0; D 109-10. A two-thirds majority of those present and voting (258 in this case) is required for passage under suspension of the rules. Dec. 17, 2012.

628. **S 3193. Barona Band Land Exchange/Passage.** Bishop, R-Utah, motion to suspend the rules and pass the bill that would revise the description of land held in trust for the Barona Band of Mission Indians in California and clarify that a parcel of private land was not intended to be tribal land. Motion agreed to 306-0: R 178-0; D 128-0. A two-thirds majority of those present and voting (204 in this case) is required for passage under suspension of the rules. Dec. 17, 2012.

629. **HR 6504. Small-Business Leverage/Passage.** Chabot, R-Ohio, motion to suspend the rules and pass the bill that would increase the maximum amount of leverage that can be made available to two or more Small Business Investment Companies under common control from $225 million to $350 million. Motion agreed to 359-36: R 187-36; D 172-0. A two-thirds majority of those present and voting (264 in this case) is required for passage under suspension of the rules. Dec. 18, 2012.

630. **HR 3783. Iran Policy/Passage.** Ros-Lehtinen, R-Fla., motion to suspend the rules and concur in the Senate amendment to the bill that would state that the United States shall use a governmentwide strategy to counter Iran's presence in the Western Hemisphere and would direct the secretary of State to assess the threats posed by Iran and submit to Congress a strategy to counter Iran's increased activity. Motion agreed to (thus clearing the bill for the president) 386-6: R 217-5; D 169-1. A two-thirds majority of those present and voting (262 in this case) is required for passage under suspension of the rules. Dec. 18, 2012.

631. **HR 6621. Patent Overhaul Revisions/Passage.** Smith, R-Texas, motion to suspend the rules and pass the bill that would make several changes to the 2011 patent overhaul law, among them clarifying that parties have the right to seek the advice of legal counsel in the federal appeals process and specifying that decisions on whether to begin a derivation proceeding may not be appealed. Motion agreed to 308-89: R 157-70; D 151-19. A two-thirds majority of those present and voting (265 in this case) is required for passage under suspension of the rules. Dec. 18, 2012.

632. **S 3642. Definition of Trade-Secrets Theft/Passage.** Smith, R-Texas, motion to suspend the rules and pass the bill that would clarify that the definition of trade-secrets theft applies to anything that is a product or service used, or intended for use, in interstate or foreign commerce. Motion agreed to 388-4: R 221-4; D 167-0. A two-thirds majority of those present and voting (262 in this case) is required for passage under suspension of the rules. Dec. 18, 2012.

	627	628	629	630	631	632
ALABAMA						
1 Bonner	Y	Y	Y	Y	Y	Y
2 Roby	Y	Y	Y	Y	Y	Y
3 Rogers	?	Y	Y	Y	Y	Y
4 Aderholt	Y	Y	Y	Y	Y	Y
5 Brooks	Y	Y	Y	Y	N	Y
6 Bachus	Y	Y	Y	Y	Y	Y
7 Sewell	Y	Y	Y	Y	Y	Y
ALASKA						
AL Young	?	Y	Y	Y	N	N
ARIZONA						
1 Gosar	Y	Y	Y	Y	Y	Y
2 Franks	?	?	Y	Y	Y	Y
3 Quayle	Y	Y	Y	Y	Y	Y
4 Pastor	?	?	Y	Y	N	Y
5 Schweikert	Y	Y	Y	Y	Y	Y
6 Flake	?	?	N	Y	N	Y
7 Grijalva	?	?	?	?	?	?
8 Barber	?	Y	Y	Y	Y	Y
ARKANSAS						
1 Crawford	Y	Y	Y	Y	Y	Y
2 Griffin	?	?	Y	Y	Y	Y
3 Womack	Y	Y	Y	Y	Y	Y
4 Ross	?	?	?	?	?	?
CALIFORNIA						
1 Thompson	?	Y	Y	Y	Y	Y
2 Herger	Y	Y	Y	Y	Y	Y
3 Lungren	Y	Y	Y	Y	N	Y
4 McClintock	Y	Y	N	Y	N	Y
5 Matsui	?	Y	Y	Y	Y	Y
6 Woolsey	Y	Y	Y	Y	Y	Y
7 Miller, George	Y	Y	Y	Y	Y	Y
8 Pelosi	?	?	Y	Y	Y	Y
9 Lee	Y	Y	Y	Y	Y	Y
10 Garamendi	Y	Y	Y	Y	N	Y
11 McNerney	?	Y	Y	Y	Y	Y
12 Speier	?	?	Y	Y	Y	Y
13 Stark	?	?	?	?	?	?
14 Eshoo	Y	Y	Y	Y	Y	Y
15 Honda	Y	Y	Y	Y	Y	Y
16 Lofgren	Y	Y	Y	Y	Y	Y
17 Farr	N	Y	Y	Y	Y	?
18 Vacant						
19 Denham	Y	Y	Y	Y	N	Y
20 Costa	?	?	Y	Y	Y	Y
21 Nunes	?	?	?	?	?	?
22 McCarthy	Y	Y	Y	Y	Y	Y
23 Capps	+	+	Y	Y	Y	Y
24 Gallegly	?	?	Y	Y	Y	Y
25 McKeon	Y	Y	Y	Y	Y	Y
26 Dreier	Y	Y	Y	Y	Y	Y
27 Sherman	Y	Y	Y	Y	N	Y
28 Berman	?	?	?	?	?	?
29 Schiff	Y	Y	Y	Y	Y	Y
30 Waxman	Y	Y	Y	Y	Y	Y
31 Becerra	Y	Y	Y	Y	Y	Y
32 Chu	Y	Y	Y	Y	Y	Y
33 Bass	Y	Y	Y	Y	Y	Y
34 Roybal-Allard	Y	Y	Y	Y	Y	Y
35 Waters	?	Y	Y	Y	Y	Y
36 Hahn	Y	Y	Y	Y	Y	Y
37 Richardson	Y	Y	Y	Y	Y	Y
38 Napolitano	Y	Y	Y	Y	Y	Y
39 Sánchez, Linda	Y	?	Y	Y	Y	Y
40 Royce	Y	Y	N	Y	N	Y
41 Lewis	Y	Y	Y	Y	Y	Y
42 Miller, Gary	Y	Y	Y	Y	Y	Y
43 Baca	?	?	?	?	?	?
44 Calvert	Y	Y	Y	Y	Y	Y
45 Bono Mack	Y	Y	?	?	?	?
46 Rohrabacher	?	?	Y	Y	N	Y
47 Sanchez, Loretta	?	?	?	?	?	?
48 Campbell	?	?	N	Y	Y	Y
49 Issa	Y	Y	Y	Y	Y	Y
50 Bilbray	Y	Y	Y	Y	Y	Y
51 Vacant						
52 Hunter	Y	Y	Y	Y	N	Y
53 Davis	Y	Y	Y	Y	Y	Y

	627	628	629	630	631	632
COLORADO						
1 DeGette	Y	Y	Y	Y	Y	Y
2 Polis	Y	Y	Y	Y	N	Y
3 Tipton	Y	Y	Y	N	Y	Y
4 Gardner	Y	Y	Y	N	Y	Y
5 Lamborn	Y	N	N	N	Y	Y
6 Coffman	Y	Y	Y	N	Y	Y
7 Perlmutter	Y	Y	Y	Y	Y	Y
CONNECTICUT						
1 Larson	+	Y	Y	Y	Y	Y
2 Courtney	?	Y	Y	Y	Y	Y
3 DeLauro	?	Y	Y	Y	Y	Y
4 Himes	?	Y	Y	Y	Y	Y
5 Murphy	Y	Y	Y	Y	Y	Y
DELAWARE						
AL Carney	Y	Y	Y	Y	Y	Y
FLORIDA						
1 Miller	Y	Y	Y	Y	N	Y
2 Southerland	Y	Y	N	Y	N	Y
3 Brown	Y	Y	Y	Y	Y	Y
4 Crenshaw	?	?	Y	Y	Y	Y
5 Nugent	Y	Y	Y	Y	N	Y
6 Stearns	Y	Y	N	Y	N	Y
7 Mica	Y	Y	Y	Y	N	Y
8 Webster	Y	Y	Y	Y	N	Y
9 Bilirakis	Y	Y	Y	Y	Y	Y
10 Young	?	?	Y	Y	Y	Y
11 Castor	Y	Y	Y	Y	Y	Y
12 Ross	Y	Y	Y	Y	Y	Y
13 Buchanan	?	?	Y	Y	Y	Y
14 Mack	Y	Y	?	?	?	?
15 Posey	Y	Y	Y	Y	N	Y
16 Rooney	Y	Y	Y	Y	N	Y
17 Wilson	?	?	Y	Y	Y	Y
18 Ros-Lehtinen	Y	Y	Y	Y	Y	Y
19 Deutch	Y	Y	Y	Y	Y	Y
20 Wasserman Schultz	Y	Y	Y	Y	Y	Y
21 Diaz-Balart	Y	Y	Y	Y	Y	Y
22 West	?	?	Y	Y	N	Y
23 Hastings	Y	Y	Y	Y	Y	Y
24 Adams	Y	Y	Y	Y	Y	Y
25 Rivera	?	?	Y	Y	Y	Y
GEORGIA						
1 Kingston	Y	Y	N	Y	N	Y
2 Bishop	Y	Y	Y	Y	Y	Y
3 Westmoreland	?	?	N	Y	N	Y
4 Johnson	Y	Y	Y	Y	Y	Y
5 Lewis	N	Y	Y	Y	Y	Y
6 Price	Y	Y	N	Y	N	Y
7 Woodall	Y	Y	N	Y	N	Y
8 Scott, A.	Y	Y	Y	Y	Y	Y
9 Graves	Y	Y	N	Y	N	Y
10 Broun	Y	Y	N	Y	N	Y
11 Gingrey	Y	Y	Y	Y	Y	Y
12 Barrow	Y	Y	Y	Y	Y	Y
13 Scott, D.	Y	Y	Y	Y	Y	Y
HAWAII						
1 Hanabusa	?	?	Y	Y	N	Y
2 Hirono	?	?	Y	Y	Y	Y
IDAHO						
1 Labrador	Y	Y	Y	Y	N	Y
2 Simpson	?	?	Y	Y	Y	Y
ILLINOIS						
1 Rush	?	?	Y	Y	Y	Y
2 Vacant						
3 Lipinski	?	?	Y	Y	Y	Y
4 Gutierrez	?	?	Y	Y	Y	?
5 Quigley	Y	Y	Y	Y	Y	Y
6 Roskam	Y	Y	Y	Y	Y	Y
7 Davis	?	?	Y	Y	Y	Y
8 Walsh	?	?	N	Y	N	Y
9 Schakowsky	+	Y	Y	Y	Y	Y
10 Dold	Y	Y	Y	Y	Y	Y
11 Kinzinger	Y	Y	Y	Y	Y	Y
12 Costello	?	?	?	?	?	?
13 Biggert	Y	Y	Y	Y	N	Y
14 Hultgren	Y	Y	Y	Y	Y	Y
15 Johnson	?	?	?	?	?	?

KEY **Republicans** Democrats

Y Voted for (yea)	**X** Paired against	**C** Voted "present" to avoid possible conflict of interest
# Paired for	**–** Announced against	
+ Announced for	**P** Voted "present"	**?** Did not vote or otherwise make a position known
N Voted against (nay)		

	627	628	629	630	631	632
16 **Manzullo**	?	?	Y	Y	N	Y
17 **Schilling**	?	?	Y	Y	N	Y
18 **Schock**	?	?	Y	Y	N	Y
19 **Shimkus**	?	?	Y	Y	Y	Y
INDIANA						
1 Visclosky	Y	Y	Y	Y	Y	Y
2 Donnelly	Y	Y	Y	Y	Y	Y
3 **Stutzman**	Y	Y	N	Y	Y	Y
4 **Rokita**	?	?	Y	Y	Y	Y
5 **Burton**	?	?	N	Y	N	Y
6 **Pence**	?	?	?	?	?	?
7 Carson	Y	Y	Y	Y	Y	Y
8 **Bucshon**	Y	Y	Y	Y	Y	Y
9 **Young**	Y	Y	Y	Y	Y	Y
IOWA						
1 Braley	Y	Y	Y	Y	Y	Y
2 Loebsack	Y	Y	Y	Y	Y	Y
3 Boswell	?	?	Y	Y	Y	Y
4 **Latham**	Y	Y	Y	Y	Y	Y
5 **King**	Y	Y	Y	?	Y	Y
KANSAS						
1 **Huelskamp**	Y	Y	N	Y	N	Y
2 **Jenkins**	Y	Y	Y	Y	Y	Y
3 **Yoder**	Y	Y	Y	Y	Y	Y
4 **Pompeo**	Y	Y	N	Y	Y	Y
KENTUCKY						
1 **Whitfield**	?	?	Y	Y	Y	Y
2 **Guthrie**	Y	Y	Y	Y	Y	Y
3 Yarmuth	Y	Y	?	?	?	?
4 **Massie**	Y	Y	N	N	N	N
5 **Rogers**	Y	Y	Y	Y	Y	Y
6 Chandler	Y	Y	Y	Y	Y	Y
LOUISIANA						
1 **Scalise**	Y	Y	Y	Y	N	Y
2 Richmond	?	?	Y	Y	Y	Y
3 **Landry**	?	?	?	?	?	?
4 **Fleming**	?	?	?	Y	Y	Y
5 **Alexander**	Y	Y	Y	Y	Y	Y
6 **Cassidy**	Y	Y	Y	Y	Y	Y
7 **Boustany**	Y	Y	Y	Y	Y	Y
MAINE						
1 Pingree	Y	Y	Y	Y	Y	Y
2 Michaud	Y	Y	Y	Y	Y	Y
MARYLAND						
1 **Harris**	?	?	N	Y	N	Y
2 Ruppersberger	Y	?	Y	Y	Y	Y
3 Sarbanes	?	Y	Y	Y	Y	Y
4 Edwards	N	Y	Y	Y	N	Y
5 Hoyer	Y	Y	Y	Y	Y	Y
6 **Bartlett**	?	?	?	?	?	?
7 Cummings	Y	Y	Y	Y	N	Y
8 Van Hollen	Y	Y	Y	Y	Y	Y
MASSACHUSETTS						
1 Olver	?	?	Y	Y	Y	Y
2 Neal	?	?	Y	Y	Y	Y
3 McGovern	?	Y	Y	Y	Y	Y
4 Frank	Y	Y	?	?	Y	Y
5 Tsongas	Y	Y	Y	Y	Y	Y
6 Tierney	Y	Y	Y	Y	Y	Y
7 Markey	?	?	Y	Y	?	?
8 Capuano	?	?	Y	Y	Y	Y
9 Lynch	N	?	?	?	?	?
10 Keating	Y	Y	Y	Y	Y	Y
MICHIGAN						
1 **Benishek**	Y	Y	Y	Y	N	Y
2 **Huizenga**	Y	Y	N	Y	Y	Y
3 **Amash**	Y	Y	N	N	N	N
4 **Camp**	Y	Y	Y	Y	Y	Y
5 Kildee	Y	Y	Y	Y	Y	Y
6 **Upton**	Y	Y	Y	Y	Y	Y
7 **Walberg**	Y	Y	Y	Y	Y	Y
8 **Rogers**	Y	Y	Y	Y	Y	Y
9 Peters	Y	Y	Y	Y	Y	Y
10 **Miller**	Y	Y	Y	Y	Y	Y
11 Curson	Y	Y	Y	Y	Y	Y
12 Levin	Y	Y	Y	Y	Y	Y
13 Clarke	Y	Y	Y	Y	Y	Y
14 Conyers	N	Y	Y	Y	Y	Y
15 Dingell	?	?	?	?	?	?
MINNESOTA						
1 Walz	Y	Y	Y	Y	Y	Y
2 **Kline**	Y	Y	Y	Y	Y	Y
3 **Paulsen**	Y	Y	Y	Y	Y	Y
4 McCollum	Y	Y	Y	Y	Y	Y
5 Ellison	Y	Y	Y	?	Y	Y
6 **Bachmann**	?	?	Y	Y	Y	Y
7 Peterson	Y	Y	Y	Y	N	Y
8 **Cravaack**	?	?	?	?	?	?
MISSISSIPPI						
1 **Nunnelee**	?	?	?	?	?	?
2 Thompson	Y	Y	Y	Y	Y	Y
3 **Harper**	Y	Y	Y	Y	Y	Y
4 **Palazzo**	Y	Y	Y	Y	N	Y
MISSOURI						
1 Clay	N	Y	Y	Y	Y	Y
2 **Akin**	?	?	?	?	?	?
3 Carnahan	?	?	Y	Y	Y	Y
4 **Hartzler**	+	+	Y	Y	N	Y
5 Cleaver	Y	Y	Y	Y	Y	Y
6 **Graves**	Y	Y	Y	Y	Y	Y
7 **Long**	Y	Y	Y	Y	Y	Y
8 **Emerson**	Y	Y	Y	Y	N	Y
9 **Luetkemeyer**	Y	Y	Y	Y	Y	Y
MONTANA						
AL **Rehberg**	Y	Y	Y	Y	Y	Y
NEBRASKA						
1 **Fortenberry**	?	?	Y	Y	Y	Y
2 **Terry**	+	+	Y	Y	Y	Y
3 **Smith**	Y	Y	Y	Y	N	Y
NEVADA						
1 Berkley	Y	Y	Y	Y	Y	Y
2 **Amodei**	Y	Y	Y	Y	Y	Y
3 **Heck**	Y	Y	Y	Y	Y	Y
NEW HAMPSHIRE						
1 **Guinta**	?	?	Y	Y	Y	Y
2 **Bass**	?	?	Y	Y	Y	Y
NEW JERSEY						
1 Andrews	Y	Y	Y	Y	N	Y
2 **LoBiondo**	Y	Y	Y	Y	Y	Y
3 **Runyan**	Y	Y	Y	Y	Y	Y
4 **Smith**	?	?	Y	Y	Y	Y
5 **Garrett**	Y	Y	N	Y	Y	Y
6 Pallone	Y	Y	Y	Y	Y	Y
7 **Lance**	Y	Y	Y	Y	Y	Y
8 Pascrell	Y	Y	Y	Y	Y	Y
9 Rothman	?	?	Y	Y	Y	Y
10 Payne, Jr.	Y	Y	Y	Y	Y	Y
11 **Frelinghuysen**	Y	Y	Y	Y	Y	Y
12 Holt	+	+	Y	Y	Y	Y
13 Sires	Y	Y	Y	Y	Y	Y
NEW MEXICO						
1 Heinrich	?	?	Y	Y	Y	Y
2 **Pearce**	Y	Y	N	Y	N	Y
3 Luján	?	?	?	?	?	?
NEW YORK						
1 Bishop	?	?	Y	Y	Y	Y
2 Israel	Y	Y	Y	Y	Y	Y
3 **King**	Y	Y	Y	Y	Y	?
4 McCarthy	Y	?	Y	Y	Y	Y
5 Ackerman	?	?	?	?	?	?
6 Meeks	?	?	Y	Y	Y	?
7 Crowley	Y	Y	Y	Y	Y	Y
8 Nadler	Y	Y	Y	Y	Y	Y
9 **Turner**	Y	Y	Y	Y	N	Y
10 Towns	?	?	Y	Y	Y	Y
11 Clarke	N	Y	Y	Y	Y	Y
12 Velázquez	Y	Y	Y	Y	Y	Y
13 **Grimm**	Y	Y	Y	Y	Y	Y
14 Maloney	Y	Y	Y	Y	Y	Y
15 Rangel	Y	Y	Y	Y	Y	Y
16 Serrano	N	Y	Y	Y	Y	Y
17 Engel	Y	Y	Y	Y	Y	Y
18 Lowey	Y	Y	Y	Y	Y	Y
19 **Hayworth**	Y	Y	Y	Y	Y	Y
20 **Gibson**	?	?	Y	Y	N	Y
21 Tonko	Y	Y	Y	Y	Y	Y
22 Hinchey	?	?	Y	Y	Y	Y
23 Owens	?	?	Y	Y	Y	Y
24 **Hanna**	?	?	Y	Y	Y	Y
25 **Buerkle**	Y	Y	Y	Y	Y	Y
26 Hochul	Y	Y	Y	Y	Y	Y
27 Higgins	?	?	Y	Y	Y	Y
28 Slaughter	+	+	Y	Y	Y	Y
29 **Reed**	Y	Y	Y	Y	Y	Y
NORTH CAROLINA						
1 Butterfield	?	?	Y	Y	Y	Y
2 **Ellmers**	Y	Y	Y	Y	Y	Y
3 **Jones**	?	?	Y	N	N	Y
4 Price	Y	Y	Y	Y	Y	Y
5 **Foxx**	Y	Y	Y	Y	Y	Y
6 **Coble**	?	?	Y	Y	Y	Y
7 McIntyre	?	?	Y	Y	Y	Y
8 Kissell	?	?	?	?	?	?
9 **Myrick**	Y	Y	Y	Y	N	Y
10 **McHenry**	Y	Y	Y	Y	Y	Y
11 Shuler	?	?	?	?	?	?
12 Watt	Y	Y	Y	Y	Y	Y
13 Miller	Y	Y	Y	Y	Y	Y
NORTH DAKOTA						
AL **Berg**	Y	Y	Y	Y	Y	Y
OHIO						
1 **Chabot**	Y	Y	Y	Y	Y	Y
2 **Schmidt**	Y	Y	Y	Y	N	Y
3 **Turner**	Y	Y	Y	Y	Y	Y
4 **Jordan**	Y	Y	N	Y	N	Y
5 **Latta**	Y	Y	Y	Y	Y	Y
6 **Johnson**	Y	Y	Y	Y	Y	Y
7 **Austria**	?	?	?	?	?	?
8 **Boehner**						
9 Kaptur	Y	Y	Y	Y	N	Y
10 Kucinich	N	Y	Y	N	N	Y
11 Fudge	Y	Y	Y	Y	Y	Y
12 **Tiberi**	?	?	Y	Y	Y	Y
13 Sutton	?	?	Y	Y	Y	Y
14 **LaTourette**	Y	Y	Y	Y	Y	Y
15 **Stivers**	?	?	Y	Y	Y	Y
16 **Renacci**	Y	?	Y	Y	Y	Y
17 Ryan	Y	Y	Y	Y	Y	Y
18 **Gibbs**	Y	Y	Y	Y	Y	Y
OKLAHOMA						
1 **Sullivan**	?	?	?	?	?	?
2 Boren	Y	Y	?	?	?	?
3 **Lucas**	Y	Y	Y	?	Y	Y
4 **Cole**	Y	Y	Y	Y	N	Y
5 **Lankford**	Y	Y	N	Y	Y	Y
OREGON						
1 Bonamici	Y	Y	Y	Y	Y	Y
2 **Walden**	Y	Y	Y	Y	Y	Y
3 Blumenauer	Y	Y	Y	Y	?	Y
4 DeFazio	Y	Y	Y	Y	Y	Y
5 Schrader	Y	Y	Y	Y	Y	Y
PENNSYLVANIA						
1 Brady	?	?	Y	Y	Y	Y
2 Fattah	Y	Y	Y	Y	Y	Y
3 **Kelly**	Y	Y	Y	Y	N	Y
4 Altmire	Y	Y	Y	Y	Y	Y
5 **Thompson**	Y	Y	Y	Y	N	Y
6 **Gerlach**	+	+	Y	Y	Y	Y
7 **Meehan**	Y	Y	Y	Y	Y	Y
8 **Fitzpatrick**	Y	Y	Y	Y	Y	Y
9 **Shuster**	Y	Y	Y	Y	Y	Y
10 **Marino**	Y	Y	Y	Y	Y	Y
11 **Barletta**	Y	Y	Y	Y	Y	Y
12 Critz	?	?	Y	Y	N	Y
13 Schwartz	Y	Y	Y	Y	N	Y
14 Doyle	Y	Y	Y	Y	N	Y
15 **Dent**	Y	Y	Y	Y	Y	Y
16 **Pitts**	Y	Y	Y	Y	Y	Y
17 Holden	?	?	Y	Y	N	Y
18 **Murphy**	Y	Y	Y	Y	Y	Y
19 **Platts**	Y	Y	Y	Y	N	Y
RHODE ISLAND						
1 Cicilline	?	Y	Y	Y	Y	Y
2 Langevin	?	?	Y	Y	N	Y
SOUTH CAROLINA						
1 **Scott**	?	?	N	Y	Y	Y
2 **Wilson**	Y	Y	Y	Y	Y	Y
3 **Duncan**	Y	Y	N	Y	N	Y
4 **Gowdy**	?	?	Y	Y	Y	Y
5 **Mulvaney**	Y	Y	P	Y	Y	Y
6 Clyburn	?	?	Y	Y	Y	Y
SOUTH DAKOTA						
AL **Noem**	Y	Y	Y	Y	Y	Y
TENNESSEE						
1 **Roe**	Y	Y	Y	Y	N	Y
2 **Duncan**	Y	Y	N	N	N	Y
3 **Fleischmann**	Y	Y	Y	Y	N	Y
4 **DesJarlais**	Y	Y	N	Y	N	Y
5 Cooper	Y	Y	Y	Y	Y	Y
6 **Black**	Y	Y	Y	?	N	Y
7 **Blackburn**	Y	Y	Y	Y	N	Y
8 **Fincher**	?	?	Y	Y	N	Y
9 Cohen	+	+	Y	Y	Y	Y
TEXAS						
1 **Gohmert**	?	?	Y	Y	N	Y
2 **Poe**	Y	Y	N	Y	N	Y
3 **Johnson, S.**	?	?	Y	?	Y	Y
4 **Hall**	Y	Y	Y	Y	Y	Y
5 **Hensarling**	Y	Y	N	Y	Y	Y
6 **Barton**	?	?	N	Y	Y	Y
7 **Culberson**	?	?	Y	Y	Y	Y
8 **Brady**	?	?	Y	Y	Y	Y
9 Green, A.	Y	Y	Y	?	?	?
10 **McCaul**	Y	Y	Y	Y	Y	Y
11 **Conaway**	Y	Y	Y	Y	Y	Y
12 **Granger**	?	?	?	?	?	?
13 **Thornberry**	Y	Y	Y	Y	Y	Y
14 **Paul**	Y	Y	N	N	N	N
15 Hinojosa	Y	Y	Y	Y	Y	Y
16 Reyes	?	?	?	?	?	?
17 **Flores**	Y	Y	Y	Y	Y	?
18 Jackson Lee	?	?	Y	Y	Y	Y
19 **Neugebauer**	Y	Y	N	Y	Y	Y
20 Gonzalez	?	?	?	?	?	?
21 **Smith**	Y	Y	Y	Y	Y	Y
22 **Olson**	Y	Y	Y	Y	Y	Y
23 **Canseco**	Y	Y	Y	Y	Y	Y
24 **Marchant**	?	?	Y	Y	Y	Y
25 Doggett	Y	Y	Y	Y	Y	Y
26 **Burgess**	?	?	Y	Y	N	Y
27 **Farenthold**	Y	Y	Y	Y	Y	Y
28 Cuellar	Y	Y	Y	Y	Y	Y
29 Green, G.	Y	Y	Y	Y	N	Y
30 Johnson, E.	Y	Y	Y	Y	N	Y
31 **Carter**	Y	Y	Y	Y	Y	Y
32 **Sessions**	Y	Y	Y	Y	Y	Y
UTAH						
1 **Bishop**	Y	Y	Y	Y	Y	Y
2 Matheson	Y	Y	Y	Y	Y	Y
3 **Chaffetz**	Y	Y	Y	Y	Y	Y
VERMONT						
AL Welch	?	?	Y	Y	Y	Y
VIRGINIA						
1 **Wittman**	Y	Y	Y	Y	Y	Y
2 **Rigell**	Y	Y	Y	Y	Y	Y
3 Scott	Y	Y	Y	Y	Y	Y
4 **Forbes**	?	?	Y	Y	Y	Y
5 **Hurt**	Y	Y	Y	Y	Y	Y
6 **Goodlatte**	+	+	Y	Y	Y	Y
7 **Cantor**	Y	Y	Y	Y	Y	Y
8 Moran	?	?	?	?	?	?
9 **Griffith**	Y	Y	Y	Y	Y	Y
10 **Wolf**	Y	Y	Y	Y	N	Y
11 Connolly	Y	Y	Y	Y	Y	Y
WASHINGTON						
1 DelBene	Y	Y	Y	Y	Y	Y
2 Larsen	Y	Y	Y	Y	Y	Y
3 **Herrera Beutler**	?	?	Y	Y	Y	Y
4 **Hastings**	Y	Y	Y	Y	Y	Y
5 **McMorris Rodgers**	Y	Y	Y	Y	Y	Y
6 Dicks	?	?	Y	Y	Y	?
7 McDermott	N	Y	Y	Y	Y	Y
8 **Reichert**	Y	Y	Y	Y	Y	Y
9 Smith	+	+	Y	Y	Y	Y
WEST VIRGINIA						
1 **McKinley**	Y	Y	Y	Y	Y	Y
2 **Capito**	Y	Y	Y	Y	Y	Y
3 Rahall	Y	Y	Y	Y	Y	Y
WISCONSIN						
1 **Ryan**	Y	Y	+	+	Y	Y
2 Baldwin	Y	Y	Y	Y	Y	Y
3 Kind	?	?	Y	Y	Y	Y
4 Moore	?	?	Y	Y	N	Y
5 **Sensenbrenner**	Y	Y	Y	Y	N	Y
6 **Petri**	Y	Y	Y	Y	N	Y
7 **Duffy**	Y	Y	Y	Y	Y	Y
8 **Ribble**	Y	Y	N	Y	N	Y
WYOMING						
AL **Lummis**	Y	Y	N	Y	N	Y

IN THE HOUSE | By Vote Number

633. **HR 6672. Medical-Response Reauthorization/Passage.** Rogers, R-Mich., motion to suspend the rules and pass the bill that would reauthorize medical-disaster and emergency-response programs that develop medical countermeasures to chemical, biological, radioactive and nuclear agents. The bill also would create an interagency National Advisory Committee on Children and Disasters. Motion agreed to 383-16: R 205-16; D 178-0. A two-thirds majority of those present and voting (266 in this case) is required for passage under suspension of the rules. Dec. 19, 2012.

634. **HR 1845. Medicare IVIG Coverage/Passage.** Brady, R-Texas, motion to suspend the rules and pass the bill that would establish a demonstration project to evaluate the benefits of allowing Medicare to cover in-home intravenous immune globin treatments and require the Department of Health and Human Services to report on any access and reimbursement issues. Motion agreed to 401-3: R 223-3; D 178-0. A two-thirds majority of those present and voting (270 in this case) is required for passage under suspension of the rules. Dec. 19, 2012.

635. **H Res 668. Quapaw Trust Claim/Adoption.** Smith, R-Texas, motion to suspend the rules and adopt the resolution that would facilitate legal proceedings relating to the Quapaw Tribe of Oklahoma's trust claim against the U.S. government in the U.S. Court of Federal Claims. Motion agreed to 398-5: R 222-4; D 176-1. A two-thirds majority of those present and voting (267 in this case) is required for adoption under suspension of the rules. Dec. 19, 2012.

636. **HR 6655. Child Abuse Commission/Passage.** Camp, R-Mich., motion to suspend the rules and pass the bill that would create a Commission to Eliminate Child Abuse and Neglect Fatalities tasked with crafting a national strategy for reducing child abuse and examining the effectiveness of federally funded child welfare services. Motion agreed to 330-77: R 151-77; D 179-0. A two-thirds majority of those present and voting (272 in this case) is required for passage under suspension of the rules. Dec. 19, 2012.

637. **S 3564. Public Interest Declassification Board/Passage.** Farenthold, R-Texas, motion to suspend the rules and pass the bill that would extend the 2000 law that established the Public Interest Declassification Board to advise the president on matters regarding declassification, through 2014, and clarify that reappointed board members serve a three-year term from the date of reappointment. Motion agreed to 409-1: R 227-1; D 182-0. A two-thirds majority of those present and voting (274 in this case) is required for passage under suspension of the rules. Dec. 19, 2012.

638. **HR 6016. Senior Executive Service Employee Termination/Passage.** Farenthold, R-Texas, motion to suspend the rules and pass the bill that would expand options to discipline Senior Executive Service employees, including allowing the termination of such employees for misappropriation of funds and allowing them to be placed on unpaid leave. Motion agreed to 402-2: R 224-0; D 178-2. A two-thirds majority of those present and voting (270 in this case) is required for passage under suspension of the rules. Dec. 19, 2012.

	633	634	635	636	637	638
ALABAMA						
1 Bonner	Y	Y	Y	Y	Y	Y
2 Roby	Y	Y	Y	Y	Y	Y
3 Rogers	Y	Y	Y	Y	Y	Y
4 Aderholt	Y	Y	Y	Y	Y	Y
5 Brooks	Y	Y	Y	N	Y	?
6 Bachus	Y	Y	Y	Y	Y	Y
7 Sewell	Y	Y	Y	Y	Y	Y
ALASKA						
AL Young	Y	Y	Y	N	N	Y
ARIZONA						
1 Gosar	Y	Y	Y	N	Y	Y
2 Franks	Y	Y	Y	Y	Y	Y
3 Quayle	Y	Y	Y	N	Y	Y
4 Pastor	Y	Y	Y	Y	Y	Y
5 Schweikert	Y	Y	Y	N	Y	Y
6 Flake	N	Y	Y	N	Y	Y
7 Grijalva	Y	Y	Y	Y	Y	Y
8 Barber	Y	Y	Y	Y	Y	Y
ARKANSAS						
1 Crawford	Y	Y	Y	Y	Y	Y
2 Griffin	Y	Y	Y	Y	Y	Y
3 Womack	Y	Y	Y	Y	Y	Y
4 Ross	Y	Y	Y	Y	Y	?
CALIFORNIA						
1 Thompson	Y	Y	Y	Y	Y	Y
2 Herger	Y	Y	Y	Y	Y	Y
3 Lungren	Y	Y	Y	Y	Y	Y
4 McClintock	Y	N	N	N	Y	Y
5 Matsui	Y	Y	Y	Y	Y	N
6 Woolsey	Y	Y	Y	Y	Y	Y
7 Miller, George	Y	Y	Y	Y	Y	Y
8 Pelosi	Y	Y	Y	Y	Y	Y
9 Lee	Y	Y	Y	Y	Y	Y
10 Garamendi	Y	Y	?	Y	Y	Y
11 McNerney	Y	Y	Y	Y	Y	Y
12 Speier	Y	Y	Y	Y	Y	Y
13 Stark	?	?	?	?	?	?
14 Eshoo	Y	Y	Y	Y	Y	Y
15 Honda	Y	Y	Y	Y	Y	Y
16 Lofgren	Y	Y	Y	Y	Y	Y
17 Farr	Y	Y	Y	Y	Y	Y
18 Vacant						
19 Denham	Y	Y	Y	Y	Y	Y
20 Costa	Y	Y	Y	Y	Y	Y
21 Nunes	Y	Y	Y	Y	Y	Y
22 McCarthy	Y	Y	Y	Y	Y	Y
23 Capps	Y	Y	Y	Y	Y	Y
24 Gallegly	Y	Y	Y	Y	Y	Y
25 McKeon	Y	Y	Y	Y	Y	Y
26 Dreier	Y	Y	Y	Y	Y	Y
27 Sherman	Y	Y	Y	Y	Y	Y
28 Berman	?	?	?	Y	Y	Y
29 Schiff	Y	Y	Y	Y	Y	Y
30 Waxman	Y	Y	Y	?	?	?
31 Becerra	Y	Y	Y	Y	Y	Y
32 Chu	Y	Y	Y	Y	Y	Y
33 Bass	?	Y	Y	Y	Y	Y
34 Roybal-Allard	Y	Y	Y	Y	Y	Y
35 Waters	Y	Y	Y	Y	Y	Y
36 Hahn	Y	Y	Y	Y	Y	Y
37 Richardson	Y	Y	Y	?	Y	Y
38 Napolitano	Y	Y	Y	Y	Y	Y
39 Sánchez, Linda	Y	Y	Y	Y	Y	Y
40 Royce	Y	Y	Y	Y	Y	Y
41 Lewis	Y	Y	Y	Y	Y	Y
42 Miller, Gary	Y	Y	Y	Y	Y	Y
43 Baca	?	?	Y	?	Y	?
44 Calvert	Y	Y	Y	Y	Y	Y
45 Bono Mack	?	?	?	?	?	?
46 Rohrabacher	Y	Y	Y	N	Y	Y
47 Sanchez, Loretta	Y	Y	Y	Y	Y	Y
48 Campbell	N	Y	N	N	Y	Y
49 Issa	Y	Y	Y	Y	Y	Y
50 Bilbray	?	?	?	?	?	?
51 Vacant						
52 Hunter	Y	Y	Y	N	Y	Y
53 Davis	Y	Y	Y	Y	Y	Y
COLORADO						
1 DeGette	Y	Y	?	Y	Y	Y
2 Polis	Y	Y	Y	Y	Y	Y
3 Tipton	Y	Y	Y	Y	Y	Y
4 Gardner	Y	Y	Y	N	Y	Y
5 Lamborn	Y	Y	Y	N	Y	Y
6 Coffman	+	Y	Y	Y	Y	Y
7 Perlmutter	Y	Y	Y	Y	Y	Y
CONNECTICUT						
1 Larson	Y	Y	Y	Y	Y	Y
2 Courtney	Y	Y	Y	Y	Y	Y
3 DeLauro	Y	Y	Y	Y	Y	Y
4 Himes	Y	Y	Y	Y	Y	Y
5 Murphy	?	?	?	?	?	?
DELAWARE						
AL Carney	Y	Y	Y	Y	Y	Y
FLORIDA						
1 Miller	Y	Y	Y	N	Y	Y
2 Southerland	Y	Y	Y	N	Y	Y
3 Brown	Y	Y	Y	Y	Y	Y
4 Crenshaw	Y	Y	Y	Y	Y	Y
5 Nugent	Y	Y	Y	Y	Y	Y
6 Stearns	Y	Y	Y	N	Y	Y
7 Mica	Y	Y	Y	Y	+	+
8 Webster	Y	Y	Y	Y	Y	Y
9 Bilirakis	Y	Y	Y	Y	Y	Y
10 Young	?	Y	Y	Y	Y	Y
11 Castor	Y	Y	Y	Y	Y	Y
12 Ross	Y	Y	Y	N	Y	Y
13 Buchanan	Y	Y	Y	Y	Y	Y
14 Mack	?	?	?	?	?	?
15 Posey	Y	Y	Y	Y	Y	Y
16 Rooney	Y	Y	Y	Y	Y	Y
17 Wilson	Y	Y	Y	Y	Y	Y
18 Ros-Lehtinen	Y	Y	Y	Y	Y	Y
19 Deutch	Y	Y	Y	Y	Y	Y
20 Wasserman Schultz	Y	Y	Y	Y	Y	Y
21 Diaz-Balart	Y	Y	Y	Y	Y	Y
22 West	Y	Y	Y	Y	Y	Y
23 Hastings	Y	Y	Y	Y	Y	Y
24 Adams	Y	Y	Y	Y	Y	Y
25 Rivera	Y	Y	Y	Y	Y	Y
GEORGIA						
1 Kingston	N	Y	Y	N	Y	Y
2 Bishop	Y	Y	Y	Y	Y	Y
3 Westmoreland	Y	Y	Y	N	Y	Y
4 Johnson	Y	Y	Y	Y	Y	Y
5 Lewis	Y	Y	Y	Y	Y	Y
6 Price	Y	Y	Y	N	Y	Y
7 Woodall	N	Y	Y	N	Y	Y
8 Scott, A.	Y	Y	Y	N	Y	Y
9 Graves	N	Y	Y	N	Y	Y
10 Broun	N	Y	Y	N	Y	Y
11 Gingrey	Y	Y	Y	?	Y	Y
12 Barrow	Y	Y	Y	Y	Y	Y
13 Scott, D.	Y	Y	Y	Y	Y	Y
HAWAII						
1 Hanabusa	Y	Y	Y	Y	Y	Y
2 Hirono	Y	Y	Y	Y	Y	Y
IDAHO						
1 Labrador	N	Y	Y	N	Y	Y
2 Simpson	Y	Y	Y	Y	Y	Y
ILLINOIS						
1 Rush	Y	Y	Y	Y	Y	Y
2 Vacant						
3 Lipinski	Y	Y	Y	Y	Y	Y
4 Gutierrez	Y	Y	?	Y	Y	Y
5 Quigley	Y	Y	Y	Y	Y	Y
6 Roskam	Y	Y	Y	Y	Y	Y
7 Davis	Y	Y	Y	Y	Y	Y
8 Walsh	N	Y	Y	N	Y	Y
9 Schakowsky	Y	Y	Y	Y	Y	Y
10 Dold	Y	Y	Y	Y	Y	Y
11 Kinzinger	Y	Y	Y	Y	Y	Y
12 Costello	?	?	?	Y	Y	Y
13 Biggert	Y	Y	Y	Y	Y	Y
14 Hultgren	Y	Y	Y	Y	Y	Y
15 Johnson	?	?	?	?	?	?

KEY **Republicans** Democrats

Y Voted for (yea)	**X** Paired against	**C** Voted "present" to avoid possible conflict of interest
# Paired for	**–** Announced against	
+ Announced for	**P** Voted "present"	**?** Did not vote or otherwise make a position known
N Voted against (nay)		

	633	634	635	636	637	638
16 **Manzullo**	Y	Y	Y	N	Y	Y
17 **Schilling**	Y	Y	Y	N	Y	Y
18 **Schock**	Y	Y	Y	Y	Y	Y
19 **Shimkus**	Y	Y	Y	Y	Y	?
INDIANA						
1 Visclosky	Y	Y	Y	Y	Y	Y
2 Donnelly	Y	Y	Y	Y	Y	Y
3 **Stutzman**	N	Y	Y	N	Y	Y
4 **Rokita**	Y	Y	Y	N	Y	Y
5 **Burton**	Y	Y	Y	Y	Y	?
6 **Pence**	?	?	?	?	?	?
7 Carson	Y	Y	Y	Y	Y	Y
8 **Bucshon**	Y	Y	Y	Y	Y	Y
9 **Young**	Y	Y	Y	Y	Y	Y
IOWA						
1 Braley	Y	Y	Y	Y	Y	Y
2 Loebsack	Y	Y	Y	Y	Y	Y
3 Boswell	Y	Y	Y	?	?	?
4 **Latham**	Y	Y	Y	Y	Y	Y
5 **King**	Y	Y	Y	?	Y	Y
KANSAS						
1 **Huelskamp**	Y	Y	Y	N	Y	Y
2 **Jenkins**	Y	Y	Y	Y	Y	Y
3 **Yoder**	Y	Y	Y	Y	Y	Y
4 **Pompeo**	Y	Y	Y	N	Y	Y
KENTUCKY						
1 **Whitfield**	Y	Y	Y	Y	Y	?
2 **Guthrie**	Y	Y	Y	Y	Y	Y
3 Yarmuth	Y	Y	Y	Y	Y	Y
4 **Massie**	N	Y	Y	N	Y	Y
5 **Rogers**	Y	Y	Y	Y	Y	Y
6 Chandler	Y	Y	Y	Y	Y	Y
LOUISIANA						
1 **Scalise**	Y	Y	Y	N	Y	Y
2 Richmond	Y	Y	Y	Y	Y	Y
3 **Landry**	?	?	?	N	Y	Y
4 **Fleming**	Y	Y	?	N	Y	Y
5 **Alexander**	Y	Y	Y	Y	Y	Y
6 **Cassidy**	Y	Y	Y	Y	Y	Y
7 **Boustany**	Y	Y	Y	Y	Y	Y
MAINE						
1 Pingree	Y	Y	Y	Y	Y	Y
2 Michaud	Y	Y	Y	Y	Y	Y
MARYLAND						
1 **Harris**	N	Y	Y	N	Y	Y
2 Ruppersberger	Y	Y	Y	Y	Y	Y
3 Sarbanes	Y	Y	Y	Y	Y	Y
4 Edwards	Y	Y	Y	Y	Y	Y
5 Hoyer	Y	Y	Y	Y	Y	Y
6 **Bartlett**	?	?	?	?	?	?
7 Cummings	Y	Y	Y	Y	Y	Y
8 Van Hollen	Y	Y	Y	Y	Y	Y
MASSACHUSETTS						
1 Olver	Y	Y	Y	Y	Y	Y
2 Neal	Y	Y	Y	Y	Y	Y
3 McGovern	Y	Y	Y	Y	Y	Y
4 Frank	Y	Y	Y	Y	Y	Y
5 Tsongas	Y	Y	Y	Y	Y	Y
6 Tierney	Y	Y	Y	Y	Y	Y
7 Markey	Y	Y	N	Y	Y	Y
8 Capuano	Y	Y	Y	Y	Y	Y
9 Lynch	Y	Y	Y	Y	Y	Y
10 Keating	Y	Y	Y	Y	Y	Y
MICHIGAN						
1 **Benishek**	Y	Y	Y	N	Y	Y
2 **Huizenga**	Y	Y	Y	N	Y	Y
3 **Amash**	N	N	N	N	Y	Y
4 **Camp**	Y	Y	Y	Y	Y	Y
5 Kildee	Y	Y	Y	Y	Y	Y
6 **Upton**	Y	Y	Y	Y	Y	Y
7 **Walberg**	Y	Y	Y	Y	Y	Y
8 **Rogers**	Y	Y	Y	Y	Y	Y
9 Peters	Y	Y	Y	Y	Y	Y
10 **Miller**	Y	Y	Y	Y	Y	Y
11 Curson	Y	Y	Y	Y	Y	Y
12 Levin	Y	Y	Y	Y	Y	Y
13 Clarke	Y	Y	Y	Y	Y	Y
14 Conyers	Y	Y	Y	Y	Y	Y
15 Dingell	?	Y	Y	Y	Y	Y
MINNESOTA						
1 Walz	Y	Y	Y	Y	Y	Y
2 **Kline**	Y	Y	Y	Y	Y	Y
3 **Paulsen**	Y	Y	Y	Y	Y	Y
4 McCollum	Y	Y	Y	Y	Y	Y

	633	634	635	636	637	638
5 Ellison	Y	Y	Y	Y	Y	Y
6 **Bachmann**	Y	Y	Y	Y	Y	Y
7 Peterson	Y	?	Y	Y	Y	Y
8 **Cravaack**	Y	Y	Y	N	Y	Y
MISSISSIPPI						
1 **Nunnelee**	?	?	?	?	?	?
2 Thompson	Y	Y	Y	Y	Y	Y
3 **Harper**	Y	Y	Y	Y	Y	Y
4 **Palazzo**	Y	Y	Y	N	Y	Y
MISSOURI						
1 Clay	Y	Y	Y	Y	Y	Y
2 **Akin**	?	?	?	N	Y	Y
3 Carnahan	Y	Y	Y	Y	Y	Y
4 **Hartzler**	Y	Y	Y	Y	Y	Y
5 Cleaver	Y	Y	Y	Y	Y	Y
6 **Graves**	Y	Y	Y	N	Y	Y
7 **Long**	Y	Y	Y	Y	Y	Y
8 **Emerson**	Y	Y	Y	Y	Y	Y
9 **Luetkemeyer**	Y	Y	Y	Y	Y	Y
MONTANA						
AL **Rehberg**	Y	Y	Y	Y	Y	Y
NEBRASKA						
1 **Fortenberry**	Y	Y	Y	Y	Y	Y
2 **Terry**	Y	Y	Y	Y	Y	Y
3 **Smith**	Y	Y	Y	Y	Y	Y
NEVADA						
1 Berkley	Y	Y	Y	Y	Y	Y
2 **Amodei**	Y	Y	Y	Y	Y	Y
3 **Heck**	Y	Y	Y	Y	Y	Y
NEW HAMPSHIRE						
1 **Guinta**	Y	Y	Y	Y	Y	Y
2 **Bass**	Y	Y	Y	Y	Y	Y
NEW JERSEY						
1 Andrews	Y	Y	Y	Y	Y	Y
2 **LoBiondo**	Y	Y	Y	Y	Y	Y
3 **Runyan**	Y	Y	Y	Y	Y	Y
4 **Smith**	Y	Y	Y	Y	Y	Y
5 **Garrett**	Y	Y	Y	N	Y	Y
6 Pallone	Y	Y	Y	Y	Y	Y
7 **Lance**	Y	Y	Y	Y	Y	Y
8 Pascrell	Y	?	Y	Y	Y	Y
9 Rothman	Y	Y	Y	Y	Y	Y
10 Payne, Jr.	Y	Y	Y	Y	Y	Y
11 **Frelinghuysen**	Y	Y	Y	Y	Y	Y
12 Holt	Y	Y	Y	Y	Y	Y
13 Sires	Y	Y	Y	Y	Y	Y
NEW MEXICO						
1 Heinrich	Y	Y	Y	Y	Y	Y
2 **Pearce**	Y	Y	Y	Y	Y	Y
3 Luján	?	?	?	?	?	?
NEW YORK						
1 Bishop	Y	Y	Y	Y	Y	Y
2 Israel	Y	Y	Y	Y	Y	Y
3 **King**	?	?	?	Y	Y	Y
4 McCarthy	Y	Y	Y	Y	Y	Y
5 Ackerman	Y	Y	Y	Y	Y	Y
6 Meeks	Y	Y	Y	Y	Y	Y
7 Crowley	Y	Y	Y	Y	Y	Y
8 Nadler	Y	Y	Y	Y	Y	Y
9 **Turner**	Y	Y	Y	Y	Y	?
10 Towns	?	?	?	Y	Y	Y
11 Clarke	Y	Y	Y	Y	Y	Y
12 Velázquez	Y	Y	Y	Y	Y	Y
13 **Grimm**	Y	Y	Y	Y	Y	Y
14 Maloney	Y	Y	Y	Y	Y	Y
15 Rangel	Y	Y	Y	Y	Y	Y
16 Serrano	Y	Y	Y	Y	Y	Y
17 Engel	Y	Y	Y	Y	Y	Y
18 Lowey	Y	Y	Y	Y	Y	Y
19 **Hayworth**	Y	Y	Y	Y	Y	Y
20 **Gibson**	Y	Y	Y	Y	Y	Y
21 Tonko	Y	Y	Y	Y	Y	Y
22 Hinchey	Y	Y	Y	Y	Y	Y
23 Owens	Y	Y	Y	Y	Y	Y
24 **Hanna**	Y	Y	Y	Y	Y	Y
25 **Buerkle**	Y	Y	Y	N	Y	Y
26 Hochul	Y	Y	Y	Y	Y	Y
27 Higgins	Y	Y	Y	Y	Y	Y
28 Slaughter	Y	Y	Y	Y	Y	Y
29 **Reed**	Y	Y	Y	Y	Y	Y
NORTH CAROLINA						
1 Butterfield	Y	Y	Y	Y	Y	Y
2 **Ellmers**	Y	Y	Y	Y	Y	Y
3 **Jones**	Y	Y	Y	Y	Y	Y
4 Price	Y	Y	Y	Y	Y	Y

	633	634	635	636	637	638
5 **Foxx**	N	N	Y	N	Y	Y
6 **Coble**	Y	Y	Y	Y	Y	Y
7 McIntyre	Y	Y	Y	Y	Y	Y
8 Kissell	Y	Y	Y	Y	Y	Y
9 **Myrick**	Y	Y	Y	N	Y	Y
10 **McHenry**	Y	Y	Y	N	Y	Y
11 Shuler	?	?	?	?	?	?
12 Watt	Y	Y	Y	Y	Y	Y
13 Miller	Y	Y	Y	Y	Y	Y
NORTH DAKOTA						
AL **Berg**	Y	Y	Y	Y	Y	Y
OHIO						
1 **Chabot**	Y	Y	Y	N	Y	Y
2 **Schmidt**	?	Y	Y	Y	Y	Y
3 **Turner**	Y	Y	Y	Y	Y	Y
4 **Jordan**	Y	Y	Y	N	Y	Y
5 **Latta**	Y	Y	Y	Y	Y	Y
6 **Johnson**	Y	Y	Y	Y	Y	Y
7 **Austria**	Y	Y	Y	Y	Y	Y
8 **Boehner**						
9 Kaptur	Y	Y	Y	Y	Y	Y
10 Kucinich	Y	Y	Y	Y	Y	Y
11 Fudge	Y	Y	Y	Y	Y	Y
12 **Tiberi**	Y	Y	Y	Y	Y	Y
13 Sutton	Y	Y	Y	Y	Y	Y
14 **LaTourette**	Y	Y	Y	?	?	?
15 **Stivers**	Y	Y	Y	Y	Y	Y
16 **Renacci**	Y	Y	Y	Y	Y	Y
17 Ryan	Y	Y	Y	Y	Y	Y
18 **Gibbs**	Y	Y	Y	Y	Y	Y
OKLAHOMA						
1 **Sullivan**	?	?	?	Y	Y	Y
2 Boren	Y	Y	Y	Y	Y	Y
3 **Lucas**	Y	Y	Y	Y	Y	Y
4 **Cole**	Y	Y	Y	Y	?	Y
5 **Lankford**	Y	Y	Y	N	Y	Y
OREGON						
1 Bonamici	Y	Y	Y	Y	Y	Y
2 **Walden**	Y	Y	Y	Y	Y	Y
3 Blumenauer	Y	Y	Y	Y	Y	Y
4 DeFazio	Y	Y	Y	Y	Y	Y
5 Schrader	Y	Y	Y	Y	Y	Y
PENNSYLVANIA						
1 Brady	Y	Y	Y	Y	Y	Y
2 Fattah	Y	Y	Y	Y	Y	Y
3 **Kelly**	Y	Y	Y	Y	Y	Y
4 Altmire	Y	Y	Y	Y	Y	Y
5 **Thompson**	Y	Y	Y	Y	Y	Y
6 **Gerlach**	Y	Y	Y	Y	Y	Y
7 **Meehan**	Y	Y	Y	Y	Y	Y
8 **Fitzpatrick**	Y	Y	Y	Y	Y	Y
9 **Shuster**	Y	Y	Y	Y	Y	Y
10 **Marino**	Y	Y	Y	Y	Y	Y
11 **Barletta**	Y	Y	Y	Y	Y	Y
12 Critz	Y	Y	Y	Y	Y	Y
13 Schwartz	Y	Y	Y	Y	Y	Y
14 Doyle	Y	Y	Y	Y	Y	Y
15 **Dent**	Y	Y	Y	Y	Y	Y
16 **Pitts**	Y	Y	Y	Y	Y	Y
17 Holden	Y	Y	Y	?	Y	Y
18 **Murphy**	Y	Y	Y	Y	Y	Y
19 **Platts**	+	+	+	Y	Y	Y
RHODE ISLAND						
1 Cicilline	Y	Y	Y	Y	Y	Y
2 Langevin	Y	Y	Y	Y	Y	Y
SOUTH CAROLINA						
1 **Scott**	Y	Y	Y	N	Y	Y
2 **Wilson**	Y	Y	Y	Y	Y	Y
3 **Duncan**	N	Y	Y	N	Y	Y
4 **Gowdy**	Y	Y	Y	N	Y	Y
5 **Mulvaney**	Y	Y	Y	N	Y	Y
6 Clyburn	Y	Y	Y	Y	Y	Y
SOUTH DAKOTA						
AL **Noem**	Y	Y	Y	Y	Y	Y
TENNESSEE						
1 **Roe**	Y	Y	Y	Y	Y	Y
2 **Duncan**	N	Y	Y	N	Y	Y
3 **Fleischmann**	Y	Y	Y	N	Y	Y
4 **DesJarlais**	Y	Y	Y	N	Y	Y
5 Cooper	Y	Y	Y	Y	Y	Y
6 **Black**	Y	Y	Y	Y	Y	Y
7 **Blackburn**	Y	Y	Y	N	Y	Y
8 **Fincher**	Y	Y	Y	Y	Y	Y
9 Cohen	Y	Y	Y	Y	Y	Y

	633	634	635	636	637	638
TEXAS						
1 **Gohmert**	Y	Y	Y	?	?	Y
2 **Poe**	N	Y	Y	Y	Y	Y
3 **Johnson, S.**	Y	Y	Y	Y	Y	Y
4 **Hall**	?	Y	Y	Y	Y	Y
5 **Hensarling**	Y	Y	Y	N	Y	Y
6 **Barton**	Y	Y	Y	Y	Y	Y
7 **Culberson**	Y	Y	Y	N	Y	Y
8 **Brady**	Y	Y	Y	Y	Y	Y
9 Green, A.	+	+	+	Y	Y	Y
10 **McCaul**	Y	Y	Y	Y	Y	Y
11 **Conaway**	Y	Y	Y	N	Y	Y
12 **Granger**	Y	Y	Y	Y	Y	Y
13 **Thornberry**	Y	Y	Y	N	Y	Y
14 **Paul**	?	?	Y	N	Y	Y
15 Hinojosa	Y	Y	Y	Y	Y	Y
16 Reyes	?	?	?	?	?	?
17 **Flores**	Y	Y	Y	N	Y	Y
18 Jackson Lee	Y	Y	Y	Y	Y	Y
19 **Neugebauer**	Y	Y	Y	N	Y	Y
20 Gonzalez	?	?	?	?	?	?
21 **Smith**	Y	Y	Y	Y	Y	Y
22 **Olson**	Y	Y	Y	N	Y	Y
23 **Canseco**	Y	Y	Y	Y	Y	Y
24 **Marchant**	Y	Y	Y	N	Y	Y
25 Doggett	Y	Y	Y	Y	Y	Y
26 **Burgess**	Y	Y	Y	N	Y	Y
27 **Farenthold**	Y	Y	Y	N	Y	Y
28 Cuellar	Y	Y	Y	Y	Y	Y
29 Green, G.	Y	Y	Y	Y	Y	Y
30 Johnson, E.	Y	Y	Y	Y	Y	Y
31 **Carter**	Y	Y	Y	N	Y	Y
32 **Sessions**	Y	Y	Y	N	Y	Y
UTAH						
1 **Bishop**	Y	Y	Y	N	Y	Y
2 Matheson	Y	Y	Y	Y	Y	Y
3 **Chaffetz**	Y	Y	Y	N	Y	Y
VERMONT						
AL Welch	Y	Y	Y	Y	Y	Y
VIRGINIA						
1 **Wittman**	Y	Y	Y	Y	Y	Y
2 **Rigell**	Y	Y	Y	Y	Y	Y
3 Scott	Y	Y	Y	?	Y	Y
4 **Forbes**	Y	Y	Y	Y	Y	Y
5 **Hurt**	Y	Y	Y	Y	Y	Y
6 **Goodlatte**	Y	Y	Y	Y	Y	Y
7 **Cantor**	Y	Y	Y	Y	Y	?
8 Moran	Y	Y	Y	Y	Y	N
9 **Griffith**	Y	Y	Y	Y	Y	Y
10 **Wolf**	Y	Y	Y	Y	Y	Y
11 Connolly	Y	Y	Y	Y	Y	Y
WASHINGTON						
1 DelBene	Y	Y	Y	Y	Y	Y
2 Larsen	Y	Y	Y	Y	Y	Y
3 **Herrera Beutler**	Y	Y	Y	Y	Y	Y
4 **Hastings**	Y	Y	N	Y	Y	Y
5 **McMorris Rodgers**	Y	Y	Y	Y	Y	Y
6 Dicks	Y	Y	Y	Y	Y	?
7 McDermott	Y	Y	Y	Y	Y	Y
8 **Reichert**	Y	Y	Y	Y	Y	Y
9 Smith	Y	Y	Y	Y	Y	Y
WEST VIRGINIA						
1 **McKinley**	?	?	?	?	?	?
2 **Capito**	Y	Y	Y	Y	Y	Y
3 Rahall	Y	Y	Y	Y	Y	Y
WISCONSIN						
1 **Ryan**	Y	Y	Y	Y	Y	Y
2 Baldwin	Y	Y	Y	Y	Y	Y
3 Kind	Y	Y	Y	Y	Y	Y
4 Moore	Y	Y	Y	Y	Y	Y
5 **Sensenbrenner**	Y	Y	Y	N	Y	Y
6 **Petri**	Y	Y	Y	Y	Y	Y
7 **Duffy**	Y	Y	Y	N	Y	Y
8 **Ribble**	Y	Y	Y	Y	Y	Y
WYOMING						
AL **Lummis**	?	Y	Y	N	Y	Y

IN THE HOUSE | By Vote Number

639. **H J Res 66, HR 6648. Sequester Replacement and Tax Cut Extension/Previous Question.** Dreier, R-Calif., motion to order the previous question (thus ending debate and the possibility of amendment) on the rule (H Res 841) that would provide for House floor consideration of a joint resolution (H J Res 66) that would permanently extend the 2001 and 2003 tax cuts for taxable income levels of up to $1 million and a bill (HR 6648) that would cancel the across-the-board cuts scheduled for Jan. 2, 2013. Motion agreed to 233-184: R 233-1; D 0-183. Dec. 20, 2012.

640. **H J Res 66, HR 6648. Sequester Replacement and Tax Cut Extension/Rule.** Adoption of the rule (H Res 841) that would provide for House floor consideration of a joint resolution (H J Res 66) that would permanently extend the 2001 and 2003 tax cuts for taxable income levels of up to $1 million and a bill (HR 6648) that would cancel the across-the-board cuts scheduled for Jan. 2, 2013. Adopted 219-197: R 219-13; D 0-184. Dec. 20, 2012.

641. **HR 4310. Fiscal 2013 Defense Authorization/Previous Question.** Bishop, R-Utah, motion to order the previous question (thus ending debate and the possibility of amendment) on the rule (H Res 840) that would provide for House floor consideration of the conference report on the bill that would authorize $648.7 billion for defense programs in fiscal 2013. Motion agreed to 233-186: R 233-1; D 0-185. Dec. 20, 2012.

642. **HR 4310. Fiscal 2013 Defense Authorization/Rule.** Adoption of the rule (H Res 840) that would provide for House floor consideration of the conference report on the bill that would authorize $648.7 billion for defense programs in fiscal 2013. Adopted 243-177: R 232-2; D 11-175. Dec. 20, 2012.

643. **HR 6684. Sequester Replacement/Recommit.** Van Hollen, D-Md., motion to recommit the bill to the Ways and Means Committee and report it back immediately with an amendment that would require the Health and Human Services secretary to provide a public report on the number of Medicare, Medicaid and Children's Health Insurance Program beneficiaries in each congressional district who would lose coverage or experience premium increases as a result of the bill. Motion rejected 179-243: R 1-234; D 178-9. Dec. 20, 2012.

	639	640	641	642	643
ALABAMA					
1 **Bonner**	Y	Y	Y	Y	N
2 **Roby**	Y	Y	Y	Y	N
3 **Rogers**	Y	Y	Y	Y	N
4 **Aderholt**	Y	Y	Y	Y	N
5 **Brooks**	Y	Y	Y	Y	N
6 **Bachus**	Y	Y	Y	Y	N
7 Sewell	N	N	N	N	Y
ALASKA					
AL **Young**	Y	Y	Y	Y	N
ARIZONA					
1 **Gosar**	Y	Y	Y	Y	N
2 **Franks**	Y	N	Y	Y	N
3 **Quayle**	Y	Y	Y	Y	N
4 Pastor	N	N	N	N	Y
5 **Schweikert**	Y	Y	Y	Y	N
6 **Flake**	Y	Y	Y	Y	N
7 Grijalva	N	N	N	N	Y
8 Barber	N	N	N	N	Y
ARKANSAS					
1 **Crawford**	Y	Y	Y	Y	N
2 **Griffin**	Y	Y	Y	Y	N
3 **Womack**	Y	Y	Y	Y	N
4 Ross	N	N	?	Y	Y
CALIFORNIA					
1 Thompson	N	N	N	N	Y
2 **Herger**	Y	Y	Y	Y	N
3 **Lungren**	Y	Y	Y	Y	N
4 **McClintock**	Y	Y	Y	Y	N
5 Matsui	N	N	N	N	Y
6 Woolsey	?	N	N	N	Y
7 Miller, George	N	N	N	Y	Y
8 Pelosi	N	N	N	N	?
9 Lee	N	N	N	N	Y
10 Garamendi	N	N	N	N	Y
11 McNerney	N	N	N	N	Y
12 Speier	N	N	N	N	Y
13 Stark	N	N	N	N	?
14 Eshoo	N	N	N	Y	Y
15 Honda	N	N	N	N	Y
16 Lofgren	N	N	N	N	Y
17 Farr	N	N	N	N	Y
18 Vacant					
19 **Denham**	Y	Y	Y	Y	N
20 Costa	N	N	N	N	N
21 **Nunes**	Y	Y	Y	Y	N
22 **McCarthy**	Y	Y	Y	Y	N
23 Capps	N	N	N	N	Y
24 **Gallegly**	Y	Y	Y	Y	N
25 **McKeon**	Y	Y	Y	Y	N
26 **Dreier**	Y	Y	Y	N	N
27 Sherman	N	N	N	N	Y
28 Berman	N	N	N	N	Y
29 Schiff	N	N	N	N	Y
30 Waxman	N	N	N	N	Y
31 Becerra	N	N	N	N	Y
32 Chu	N	N	N	N	Y
33 Bass	N	N	N	N	Y
34 Roybal-Allard	N	N	N	N	Y
35 Waters	N	N	?	N	Y
36 Hahn	N	N	N	N	Y
37 Richardson	?	?	?	?	Y
38 Napolitano	N	N	N	N	Y
39 Sánchez, Linda	N	N	N	N	Y
40 **Royce**	Y	Y	Y	Y	N
41 **Lewis**	Y	Y	Y	Y	N
42 **Miller, Gary**	Y	Y	Y	Y	N
43 Baca	N	N	N	N	Y
44 **Calvert**	Y	Y	Y	Y	N
45 **Bono Mack**	Y	Y	Y	Y	N
46 **Rohrabacher**	Y	Y	Y	Y	N
47 Sanchez, Loretta	N	N	N	N	Y
48 **Campbell**	Y	Y	Y	Y	N
49 **Issa**	Y	Y	Y	Y	N
50 **Bilbray**	Y	Y	Y	Y	N
51 Vacant					
52 **Hunter**	Y	Y	Y	Y	N
53 Davis	N	N	N	N	Y

	639	640	641	642	643
COLORADO					
1 DeGette	N	N	N	N	Y
2 Polis	N	N	N	N	Y
3 **Tipton**	Y	Y	Y	Y	N
4 **Gardner**	Y	Y	Y	Y	N
5 **Lamborn**	Y	?	Y	Y	N
6 **Coffman**	Y	Y	Y	Y	N
7 Perlmutter	N	N	N	N	Y
CONNECTICUT					
1 Larson	+	N	N	N	Y
2 Courtney	N	N	N	N	Y
3 DeLauro	N	N	N	N	Y
4 Himes	N	N	N	N	Y
5 Murphy	N	N	N	N	Y
DELAWARE					
AL Carney	N	N	N	N	Y
FLORIDA					
1 **Miller**	Y	Y	Y	Y	N
2 **Southerland**	Y	Y	Y	Y	N
3 Brown	N	N	N	N	Y
4 **Crenshaw**	Y	Y	Y	Y	N
5 **Nugent**	Y	Y	Y	Y	N
6 **Stearns**	Y	Y	Y	Y	N
7 Mica	+	+	+	+	Y
8 **Webster**	Y	Y	?	Y	N
9 **Bilirakis**	Y	Y	Y	Y	N
10 **Young**	Y	Y	Y	Y	N
11 Castor	N	N	N	N	Y
12 **Ross**	Y	Y	Y	Y	N
13 **Buchanan**	Y	Y	Y	Y	N
14 **Mack**	Y	Y	Y	Y	N
15 **Posey**	Y	Y	Y	Y	N
16 **Rooney**	Y	Y	Y	Y	N
17 Wilson	N	N	N	N	Y
18 **Ros-Lehtinen**	Y	Y	Y	Y	N
19 Deutch	N	N	N	N	Y
20 Wasserman Schultz	N	N	N	N	Y
21 **Diaz-Balart**	Y	Y	Y	Y	N
22 **West**	Y	Y	Y	Y	N
23 Hastings	N	N	N	N	Y
24 **Adams**	Y	Y	Y	Y	N
25 Rivera	?	?	?	?	?
GEORGIA					
1 **Kingston**	Y	Y	Y	Y	N
2 Bishop	N	N	N	N	Y
3 **Westmoreland**	Y	Y	Y	Y	N
4 Johnson	N	N	N	N	Y
5 Lewis	N	N	N	N	Y
6 **Price**	Y	Y	Y	Y	N
7 **Woodall**	Y	Y	Y	Y	N
8 **Scott, A.**	Y	Y	Y	Y	N
9 **Graves**	Y	Y	Y	Y	N
10 **Broun**	Y	N	Y	Y	N
11 **Gingrey**	Y	Y	Y	Y	N
12 Barrow	N	N	N	N	Y
13 Scott, D.	N	N	N	N	Y
HAWAII					
1 Hanabusa	N	N	N	N	Y
2 Hirono	N	N	N	N	Y
IDAHO					
1 **Labrador**	Y	Y	Y	Y	N
2 **Simpson**	Y	Y	Y	Y	N
ILLINOIS					
1 Rush	N	N	N	N	Y
2 Vacant					
3 Lipinski	N	N	N	N	Y
4 Gutierrez	N	N	N	N	Y
5 Quigley	N	N	N	N	Y
6 **Roskam**	Y	Y	Y	Y	N
7 Davis	N	N	N	N	Y
8 **Walsh**	Y	N	Y	Y	N
9 Schakowsky	N	N	N	N	Y
10 **Dold**	Y	Y	Y	Y	N
11 **Kinzinger**	Y	Y	Y	Y	N
12 Costello	N	N	N	N	Y
13 **Biggert**	Y	Y	Y	Y	N
14 **Hultgren**	Y	Y	Y	Y	N
15 **Johnson**	Y	Y	Y	Y	N

	639	640	641	642	643
16 Manzullo	Y	Y	Y	Y	N
17 Schilling	Y	Y	Y	Y	N
18 Schock	Y	Y	Y	Y	N
19 Shimkus	Y	Y	Y	Y	N
INDIANA					
1 Visclosky	N	N	N	N	Y
2 Donnelly	N	N	N	Y	Y
3 Stutzman	Y	Y	Y	Y	N
4 Rokita	Y	Y	Y	Y	N
5 Burton	Y	?	Y	Y	N
6 Pence	Y	Y	Y	Y	N
7 Carson	N	N	N	N	Y
8 Bucshon	Y	Y	Y	Y	N
9 Young	Y	Y	Y	Y	N
IOWA					
1 Braley	N	N	N	N	Y
2 Loebsack	N	N	N	N	Y
3 Boswell	N	N	N	N	Y
4 Latham	Y	Y	Y	Y	N
5 King	Y	Y	Y	Y	N
KANSAS					
1 Huelskamp	Y	N	Y	Y	N
2 Jenkins	Y	Y	Y	Y	N
3 Yoder	Y	Y	Y	Y	N
4 Pompeo	Y	Y	Y	Y	N
KENTUCKY					
1 Whitfield	Y	Y	Y	Y	N
2 Guthrie	Y	Y	Y	Y	N
3 Yarmuth	?	N	N	N	Y
4 Massie	Y	N	Y	N	Y
5 Rogers	Y	Y	Y	Y	N
6 Chandler	N	N	N	N	Y
LOUISIANA					
1 Scalise	Y	Y	Y	Y	N
2 Richmond	N	N	N	?	Y
3 Landry	Y	N	Y	Y	N
4 Fleming	Y	Y	Y	Y	N
5 Alexander	Y	Y	Y	Y	N
6 Cassidy	Y	Y	Y	Y	N
7 Boustany	Y	Y	Y	Y	N
MAINE					
1 Pingree	N	N	N	N	Y
2 Michaud	N	N	N	N	Y
MARYLAND					
1 Harris	Y	N	Y	Y	N
2 Ruppersberger	N	N	N	N	Y
3 Sarbanes	N	N	N	N	Y
4 Edwards	N	N	N	N	Y
5 Hoyer	N	N	N	N	Y
6 Bartlett	Y	Y	Y	Y	N
7 Cummings	N	N	N	N	Y
8 Van Hollen	N	N	N	N	Y
MASSACHUSETTS					
1 Olver	N	N	N	N	?
2 Neal	N	N	N	N	Y
3 McGovern	N	N	N	N	Y
4 Frank	N	N	N	N	Y
5 Tsongas	N	N	N	N	Y
6 Tierney	N	N	N	N	Y
7 Markey	N	N	N	N	Y
8 Capuano	N	N	N	N	Y
9 Lynch	N	?	N	N	Y
10 Keating	N	N	N	N	Y
MICHIGAN					
1 Benishek	Y	Y	Y	Y	N
2 Huizenga	Y	Y	Y	Y	N
3 Amash	Y	N	Y	Y	N
4 Camp	Y	Y	Y	Y	N
5 Kildee	N	N	N	N	Y
6 Upton	Y	Y	Y	Y	N
7 Walberg	Y	Y	Y	Y	N
8 Rogers	Y	Y	Y	Y	N
9 Peters	N	N	N	N	Y
10 Miller	Y	Y	Y	Y	N
11 Curson	N	N	N	N	Y
12 Levin	N	N	N	N	Y
13 Clarke	N	N	N	N	Y
14 Conyers	N	N	N	N	Y
15 Dingell	N	N	N	N	Y
MINNESOTA					
1 Walz	N	N	N	Y	Y
2 Kline	Y	Y	Y	Y	N
3 Paulsen	Y	Y	Y	?	N
4 McCollum	N	N	N	N	Y

	639	640	641	642	643
5 Ellison	N	N	N	N	Y
6 Bachmann	Y	Y	Y	Y	N
7 Peterson	N	N	N	N	Y
8 Cravaack	Y	Y	Y	Y	N
MISSISSIPPI					
1 Nunnelee	Y	Y	Y	Y	?
2 Thompson	N	N	N	N	Y
3 Harper	Y	Y	Y	Y	N
4 Palazzo	Y	Y	Y	Y	N
MISSOURI					
1 Clay	N	?	N	N	Y
2 Akin	Y	Y	Y	Y	N
3 Carnahan	N	?	N	N	Y
4 Hartzler	Y	Y	Y	Y	N
5 Cleaver	N	N	N	N	Y
6 Graves	Y	Y	Y	Y	N
7 Long	Y	Y	Y	Y	N
8 Emerson	Y	Y	Y	Y	N
9 Luetkemeyer	Y	Y	Y	Y	N
MONTANA					
AL Rehberg	Y	Y	Y	Y	N
NEBRASKA					
1 Fortenberry	Y	Y	Y	Y	N
2 Terry	Y	Y	Y	Y	N
3 Smith	Y	Y	Y	Y	N
NEVADA					
1 Berkley	N	N	N	N	Y
2 Amodei	Y	Y	Y	Y	N
3 Heck	Y	Y	Y	Y	N
NEW HAMPSHIRE					
1 Guinta	Y	Y	Y	Y	N
2 Bass	Y	Y	Y	Y	N
NEW JERSEY					
1 Andrews	N	N	N	N	Y
2 LoBiondo	Y	Y	Y	Y	N
3 Runyan	Y	Y	Y	Y	N
4 Smith	Y	Y	Y	Y	N
5 Garrett	Y	Y	Y	Y	N
6 Pallone	N	N	N	N	Y
7 Lance	Y	Y	Y	Y	N
8 Pascrell	N	N	N	N	Y
9 Rothman	N	N	N	N	Y
10 Payne, Jr.	N	N	N	N	Y
11 Frelinghuysen	Y	Y	Y	Y	N
12 Holt	N	N	N	N	Y
13 Sires	N	N	N	N	Y
NEW MEXICO					
1 Heinrich	N	N	N	N	Y
2 Pearce	Y	Y	Y	Y	N
3 Luján	N	N	N	N	Y
NEW YORK					
1 Bishop	N	N	N	N	Y
2 Israel	N	N	N	N	Y
3 King	Y	Y	Y	Y	N
4 McCarthy	N	N	N	N	Y
5 Ackerman	N	N	N	N	Y
6 Meeks	N	N	N	N	Y
7 Crowley	N	N	N	N	Y
8 Nadler	N	N	N	N	Y
9 Turner	Y	Y	Y	Y	N
10 Towns	N	N	N	N	Y
11 Clarke	N	N	N	N	Y
12 Velázquez	N	N	N	N	Y
13 Grimm	?	?	?	?	N
14 Maloney	N	N	N	N	Y
15 Rangel	N	N	N	N	Y
16 Serrano	N	N	N	N	Y
17 Engel	N	N	N	N	Y
18 Lowey	?	N	N	N	Y
19 Hayworth	Y	Y	Y	Y	N
20 Gibson	Y	Y	Y	Y	N
21 Tonko	N	N	N	N	Y
22 Hinchey	?	?	?	?	Y
23 Owens	N	N	N	Y	Y
24 Hanna	Y	Y	Y	Y	N
25 Buerkle	Y	Y	Y	Y	?
26 Hochul	N	N	N	Y	Y
27 Higgins	N	N	N	Y	Y
28 Slaughter	N	N	N	N	Y
29 Reed	Y	Y	Y	Y	N
NORTH CAROLINA					
1 Butterfield	N	N	N	N	Y
2 Ellmers	Y	Y	Y	Y	N
3 Jones	?	N	Y	N	Y
4 Price	N	N	N	N	Y

	639	640	641	642	643
5 Foxx	Y	Y	Y	Y	N
6 Coble	Y	Y	Y	Y	N
7 McIntyre	N	N	N	Y	Y
8 Kissell	N	N	N	N	Y
9 Myrick	Y	Y	Y	Y	N
10 McHenry	Y	Y	Y	Y	N
11 Shuler	?	?	?	?	Y
12 Watt	N	N	N	N	Y
13 Miller	N	N	N	N	Y
NORTH DAKOTA					
AL Berg	Y	Y	Y	Y	N
OHIO					
1 Chabot	Y	Y	Y	Y	N
2 Schmidt	Y	N	Y	Y	N
3 Turner	Y	Y	Y	Y	N
4 Jordan	Y	N	Y	Y	N
5 Latta	Y	Y	Y	Y	N
6 Johnson	Y	Y	Y	Y	N
7 Austria	Y	Y	Y	Y	N
8 Boehner					
9 Kaptur	N	N	N	N	Y
10 Kucinich	N	N	N	N	Y
11 Fudge	N	N	N	N	Y
12 Tiberi	Y	Y	Y	Y	N
13 Sutton	N	N	N	N	Y
14 LaTourette	Y	Y	Y	Y	N
15 Stivers	Y	Y	Y	Y	N
16 Renacci	Y	Y	Y	Y	N
17 Ryan	N	N	N	N	Y
18 Gibbs	Y	Y	Y	Y	N
OKLAHOMA					
1 Sullivan	Y	Y	Y	Y	N
2 Boren	N	N	N	Y	Y
3 Lucas	Y	Y	Y	Y	N
4 Cole	Y	Y	Y	Y	N
5 Lankford	Y	Y	Y	Y	N
OREGON					
1 Bonamici	N	N	N	N	Y
2 Walden	Y	Y	Y	Y	N
3 Blumenauer	N	N	N	N	Y
4 DeFazio	N	N	N	N	Y
5 Schrader	N	N	N	N	Y
PENNSYLVANIA					
1 Brady	N	N	N	N	Y
2 Fattah	N	N	N	N	Y
3 Kelly	Y	Y	Y	Y	N
4 Altmire	N	N	N	N	Y
5 Thompson	Y	Y	Y	Y	N
6 Gerlach	Y	Y	Y	Y	N
7 Meehan	Y	Y	Y	Y	N
8 Fitzpatrick	Y	Y	Y	Y	N
9 Shuster	Y	Y	Y	Y	N
10 Marino	Y	Y	Y	Y	N
11 Barletta	Y	Y	Y	Y	N
12 Critz	N	N	N	N	Y
13 Schwartz	N	N	N	N	Y
14 Doyle	N	N	N	N	Y
15 Dent	Y	Y	Y	Y	N
16 Pitts	Y	Y	Y	Y	N
17 Holden	N	N	N	N	Y
18 Murphy	Y	Y	Y	Y	N
19 Platts	Y	Y	Y	Y	N
RHODE ISLAND					
1 Cicilline	N	N	N	N	Y
2 Langevin	N	N	N	N	Y
SOUTH CAROLINA					
1 Scott	Y	Y	Y	Y	N
2 Wilson	Y	Y	Y	Y	N
3 Duncan	Y	Y	Y	Y	N
4 Gowdy	Y	Y	Y	Y	N
5 Mulvaney	Y	Y	Y	Y	N
6 Clyburn	N	N	N	N	Y
SOUTH DAKOTA					
AL Noem	Y	Y	Y	Y	N
TENNESSEE					
1 Roe	Y	Y	Y	Y	N
2 Duncan	Y	Y	Y	Y	N
3 Fleischmann	Y	Y	Y	Y	N
4 DesJarlais	Y	Y	Y	Y	N
5 Cooper	N	N	N	N	Y
6 Black	Y	Y	Y	Y	N
7 Blackburn	Y	Y	Y	Y	N
8 Fincher	Y	Y	Y	Y	N
9 Cohen	N	N	N	N	Y

	639	640	641	642	643
TEXAS					
1 Gohmert	Y	N	Y	Y	N
2 Poe	Y	Y	Y	Y	N
3 Johnson, S.	?	?	?	?	?
4 Hall	Y	Y	Y	Y	N
5 Hensarling	Y	Y	Y	Y	N
6 Barton	N	Y	N	Y	N
7 Culberson	?	?	?	?	?
8 Brady	Y	Y	Y	Y	N
9 Green, A.	N	N	N	N	N
10 McCaul	Y	Y	Y	Y	N
11 Conaway	Y	Y	Y	Y	N
12 Granger	Y	Y	Y	Y	N
13 Thornberry	Y	Y	Y	Y	N
14 Paul	Y	N	Y	N	N
15 Hinojosa	N	N	N	N	Y
16 Reyes	?	?	?	?	?
17 Flores	Y	Y	Y	Y	N
18 Jackson Lee	N	N	N	N	N
19 Neugebauer	Y	Y	Y	Y	N
20 Gonzalez	N	N	N	N	Y
21 Smith	Y	Y	Y	Y	N
22 Olson	Y	Y	Y	Y	N
23 Canseco	Y	Y	Y	Y	N
24 Marchant	Y	Y	Y	Y	N
25 Doggett	N	N	N	N	Y
26 Burgess	Y	Y	Y	Y	N
27 Farenthold	Y	Y	Y	Y	N
28 Cuellar	N	N	N	N	Y
29 Green, G.	N	N	N	N	N
30 Johnson, E.	N	N	N	N	Y
31 Carter	Y	Y	Y	Y	N
32 Sessions	Y	Y	Y	Y	N
UTAH					
1 Bishop	Y	Y	Y	Y	N
2 Matheson	N	N	N	Y	N
3 Chaffetz	Y	?	Y	Y	N
VERMONT					
AL Welch	N	N	N	N	Y
VIRGINIA					
1 Wittman	Y	Y	Y	Y	N
2 Rigell	Y	Y	Y	Y	N
3 Scott	N	N	N	N	Y
4 Forbes	Y	Y	Y	Y	N
5 Hurt	Y	Y	Y	Y	N
6 Goodlatte	Y	Y	Y	Y	N
7 Cantor	Y	Y	Y	Y	N
8 Moran	N	N	N	N	Y
9 Griffith	Y	Y	Y	Y	N
10 Wolf	Y	Y	Y	Y	N
11 Connolly	N	N	N	N	Y
WASHINGTON					
1 DelBene	N	N	N	N	Y
2 Larsen	N	N	N	N	Y
3 Herrera Beutler	Y	Y	Y	Y	N
4 Hastings	Y	Y	Y	Y	N
5 McMorris Rodgers	Y	Y	Y	Y	N
6 Dicks	N	N	N	N	Y
7 McDermott	N	N	N	N	Y
8 Reichert	Y	Y	Y	Y	N
9 Smith	N	N	N	N	Y
WEST VIRGINIA					
1 McKinley	Y	Y	Y	Y	N
2 Capito	Y	Y	Y	Y	N
3 Rahall	N	N	N	N	Y
WISCONSIN					
1 Ryan	Y	Y	Y	Y	N
2 Baldwin	N	N	N	N	Y
3 Kind	N	N	N	N	Y
4 Moore	N	N	N	N	Y
5 Sensenbrenner	Y	Y	Y	Y	N
6 Petri	Y	Y	Y	Y	N
7 Duffy	Y	Y	Y	Y	N
8 Ribble	Y	Y	Y	Y	N
WYOMING					
AL Lummis	Y	Y	Y	Y	N

IN THE HOUSE | By Vote Number

644. **HR 6684. Sequester Replacement/Passage.** Passage of the bill that would cancel the automatic cuts from discretionary programs set to occur in January 2013 and replace the sequester with a $19 billion reduction in the discretionary cap for fiscal 2013 and savings from mandatory programs totaling more than $300 billion over 10 years. It also would eliminate the separate cap on defense spending for the year to allow for higher spending levels. Passed 215-209: R 215-21; D 0-188. A "nay" was a vote in support of the president's position. Dec. 20, 2012.

645. **HR 4310. Fiscal 2013 Defense Authorization/Conference Report.** Adoption of the conference report on the bill that would authorize $648.7 billion for defense programs in fiscal 2013, including $85.5 billion for overseas military operations. It would authorize $237.7 billion for operations and maintenance and $149.8 billion for military personnel. It would authorize $10.8 billion for military construction and family housing projects but prohibit funds to start another round of base closures. It would authorize $33.6 billion for the Defense Health Program as well as a 1.7 percent pay raise for military personnel. The measure would block the use of Defense Department funds for one year to transfer or release prisoners at the Guantánamo Bay, Cuba, detention center into the United States and its territories or possessions. It also would clarify that suspected U.S. terrorists detained inside the United States be tried only in federal civilian courts. It would authorize the use of Defense Department funds for abortion for military personnel in cases of rape or incest. Adopted (thus sent to the Senate) 315-107: R 205-30; D 110-77. Dec. 20, 2012.

646. **HR 3197. Mann-Grandstaff Medical Center/Passage.** Miller, R-Fla., motion to suspend the rules and pass the bill that would designate the Veterans Affairs Department medical center in Spokane, Wash., as the "Mann-Grandstaff Department of Veterans Affairs Medical Center." Motion agreed to 421-1: R 234-1; D 187-0. A two-thirds majority of those present and voting (282 in this case) is required for passage under suspension of the rules. Dec. 20, 2012.

647. **HR 6443. William 'Bill' Kling VA Clinic/Passage.** Miller, R-Fla., motion to suspend the rules and pass the bill that would name the Veterans Affairs Department facility in Sunrise, Fla., the "William 'Bill' Kling VA Clinic." Motion agreed to 422-0: R 236-0; D 186-0. A two-thirds majority of those present and voting (282 in this case) is required for passage under suspension of the rules. Dec. 20, 2012.

648. **S 925. Mt. Andrea Lawrence Peak/Passage.** Hastings, R-Wash., motion to suspend the rules and pass the bill that would name a peak located in the northern border of the Ansel Adams Wilderness and Yosemite National Park as Mt. Andrea Lawrence. Motion agreed to 408-7: R 228-6; D 180-1. A two-thirds majority of those present and voting (277 in this case) is required for passage under suspension of the rules. Dec. 20, 2012.

	644	645	646	647	648
ALABAMA					
1 Bonner	Y	Y	Y	Y	Y
2 Roby	Y	Y	Y	Y	Y
3 Rogers	Y	Y	Y	Y	Y
4 Aderholt	Y	Y	Y	Y	Y
5 Brooks	Y	Y	Y	Y	Y
6 Bachus	Y	Y	Y	Y	Y
7 Sewell	N	Y	Y	Y	Y
ALASKA					
AL Young	Y	Y	Y	Y	N
ARIZONA					
1 Gosar	Y	N	Y	Y	Y
2 Franks	Y	Y	Y	Y	Y
3 Quayle	Y	Y	Y	Y	Y
4 Pastor	N	Y	Y	Y	Y
5 Schweikert	N	N	Y	Y	Y
6 Flake	Y	Y	Y	Y	Y
7 Grijalva	N	N	Y	Y	?
8 Barber	N	Y	Y	Y	Y
ARKANSAS					
1 Crawford	Y	Y	Y	Y	Y
2 Griffin	Y	Y	Y	Y	Y
3 Womack	Y	Y	Y	Y	Y
4 Ross	N	Y	Y	Y	Y
CALIFORNIA					
1 Thompson	N	N	Y	Y	Y
2 Herger	Y	Y	Y	Y	Y
3 Lungren	Y	Y	Y	Y	Y
4 McClintock	Y	N	Y	Y	Y
5 Matsui	N	N	Y	Y	Y
6 Woolsey	N	N	Y	Y	Y
7 Miller, George	N	N	Y	Y	Y
8 Pelosi	N	N	Y	Y	Y
9 Lee	N	N	Y	Y	Y
10 Garamendi	N	Y	Y	Y	Y
11 McNerney	N	Y	Y	Y	Y
12 Speier	N	Y	Y	Y	Y
13 Stark	?	?	?	?	?
14 Eshoo	N	Y	Y	Y	Y
15 Honda	N	N	Y	Y	?
16 Lofgren	N	N	Y	Y	Y
17 Farr	N	N	Y	Y	Y
18 Vacant					
19 Denham	Y	Y	Y	Y	Y
20 Costa	N	Y	Y	Y	Y
21 Nunes	Y	Y	Y	Y	Y
22 McCarthy	Y	Y	Y	Y	Y
23 Capps	N	Y	Y	Y	Y
24 Gallegly	Y	Y	Y	Y	Y
25 McKeon	Y	Y	Y	Y	Y
26 Dreier	Y	Y	Y	Y	Y
27 Sherman	N	Y	Y	Y	Y
28 Berman	N	Y	Y	Y	Y
29 Schiff	N	Y	Y	Y	Y
30 Waxman	N	Y	Y	?	Y
31 Becerra	N	N	Y	Y	Y
32 Chu	N	N	Y	Y	Y
33 Bass	N	N	Y	Y	?
34 Roybal-Allard	N	?	Y	Y	Y
35 Waters	N	N	Y	N	N
36 Hahn	N	N	Y	Y	Y
37 Richardson	N	Y	Y	Y	Y
38 Napolitano	N	N	Y	Y	Y
39 Sánchez, Linda	N	Y	Y	Y	Y
40 Royce	Y	Y	Y	Y	Y
41 Lewis	Y	Y	Y	Y	Y
42 Miller, Gary	Y	Y	Y	Y	Y
43 Baca	N	Y	Y	Y	Y
44 Calvert	Y	Y	Y	Y	Y
45 Bono Mack	Y	Y	Y	Y	Y
46 Rohrabacher	Y	Y	Y	Y	Y
47 Sanchez, Loretta	N	Y	Y	Y	Y
48 Campbell	Y	N	Y	Y	N
49 Issa	Y	Y	Y	Y	Y
50 Bilbray	Y	Y	Y	Y	Y
51 Vacant					
52 Hunter	Y	Y	Y	Y	Y
53 Davis	N	Y	Y	Y	Y

	644	645	646	647	648
COLORADO					
1 DeGette	N	N	Y	Y	Y
2 Polis	N	N	Y	Y	Y
3 Tipton	Y	Y	Y	Y	Y
4 Gardner	Y	Y	Y	Y	Y
5 Lamborn	Y	Y	Y	Y	Y
6 Coffman	Y	Y	Y	Y	Y
7 Perlmutter	N	Y	Y	Y	Y
CONNECTICUT					
1 Larson	N	Y	Y	Y	Y
2 Courtney	N	Y	?	?	?
3 DeLauro	N	N	Y	Y	Y
4 Himes	N	N	Y	Y	Y
5 Murphy	N	N	Y	Y	Y
DELAWARE					
AL Carney	N	N	Y	Y	Y
FLORIDA					
1 Miller	Y	Y	Y	Y	Y
2 Southerland	Y	Y	Y	Y	Y
3 Brown	N	Y	Y	Y	Y
4 Crenshaw	Y	Y	Y	Y	Y
5 Nugent	Y	N	Y	Y	Y
6 Stearns	Y	Y	Y	Y	Y
7 Mica	Y	Y	Y	Y	Y
8 Webster	Y	Y	Y	Y	Y
9 Bilirakis	Y	Y	Y	Y	Y
10 Young	Y	Y	Y	Y	Y
11 Castor	N	Y	Y	Y	Y
12 Ross	Y	Y	Y	Y	Y
13 Buchanan	Y	Y	Y	Y	Y
14 Mack	Y	N	Y	Y	Y
15 Posey	Y	Y	Y	Y	Y
16 Rooney	Y	Y	Y	Y	Y
17 Wilson	N	Y	Y	Y	Y
18 Ros-Lehtinen	Y	Y	Y	Y	Y
19 Deutch	N	Y	Y	Y	Y
20 Wasserman Schultz	N	Y	Y	Y	Y
21 Diaz-Balart	Y	Y	Y	Y	Y
22 West	Y	Y	Y	Y	Y
23 Hastings	N	Y	Y	Y	Y
24 Adams	Y	Y	Y	Y	Y
25 Rivera	?	?	?	?	?
GEORGIA					
1 Kingston	Y	Y	Y	Y	Y
2 Bishop	N	Y	Y	Y	Y
3 Westmoreland	Y	Y	Y	Y	Y
4 Johnson	N	N	Y	Y	Y
5 Lewis	N	N	Y	Y	Y
6 Price	Y	Y	Y	Y	Y
7 Woodall	Y	Y	Y	Y	Y
8 Scott, A.	Y	Y	Y	Y	?
9 Graves	Y	N	Y	Y	Y
10 Broun	N	Y	Y	Y	Y
11 Gingrey	Y	Y	Y	Y	Y
12 Barrow	N	Y	Y	Y	Y
13 Scott, D.	N	Y	Y	Y	Y
HAWAII					
1 Hanabusa	N	Y	Y	Y	Y
2 Hirono	N	Y	Y	Y	Y
IDAHO					
1 Labrador	N	N	Y	Y	Y
2 Simpson	Y	Y	Y	Y	Y
ILLINOIS					
1 Rush	N	N	Y	Y	?
2 Vacant					
3 Lipinski	N	Y	Y	Y	Y
4 Gutierrez	N	N	Y	Y	Y
5 Quigley	N	N	Y	Y	Y
6 Roskam	Y	Y	Y	Y	Y
7 Davis	N	N	Y	Y	Y
8 Walsh	N	N	Y	Y	N
9 Schakowsky	N	N	Y	Y	Y
10 Dold	Y	Y	Y	Y	Y
11 Kinzinger	Y	Y	Y	Y	Y
12 Costello	?	Y	Y	Y	Y
13 Biggert	Y	Y	Y	Y	Y
14 Hultgren	Y	Y	Y	Y	Y
15 Johnson	N	N	Y	Y	Y

KEY **Republicans** Democrats

Y Voted for (yea)	X Paired against	C Voted "present" to avoid possible conflict of interest
# Paired for	- Announced against	
+ Announced for	P Voted "present"	? Did not vote or otherwise make a position known
N Voted against (nay)		

	644	645	646	647	648
16 Manzullo	Y	Y	?	Y	Y
17 Schilling	Y	Y	Y	Y	Y
18 Schock	Y	Y	Y	Y	?
19 Shimkus	Y	Y	Y	Y	Y
INDIANA					
1 Visclosky	N	Y	Y	Y	Y
2 Donnelly	N	Y	Y	Y	Y
3 Stutzman	Y	Y	Y	Y	Y
4 Rokita	Y	Y	Y	Y	Y
5 Burton	Y	?	Y	Y	Y
6 Pence	Y	Y	Y	Y	Y
7 Carson	N	N	Y	Y	Y
8 Bucshon	Y	Y	Y	Y	Y
9 Young	Y	Y	Y	Y	Y
IOWA					
1 Braley	N	N	Y	Y	Y
2 Loebsack	N	N	Y	Y	Y
3 Boswell	N	N	Y	Y	Y
4 Latham	Y	N	Y	Y	Y
5 King	Y	N	Y	Y	Y
KANSAS					
1 Huelskamp	N	N	Y	Y	Y
2 Jenkins	Y	Y	Y	Y	Y
3 Yoder	Y	Y	Y	Y	Y
4 Pompeo	Y	Y	Y	Y	Y
KENTUCKY					
1 Whitfield	N	Y	Y	Y	Y
2 Guthrie	Y	Y	Y	Y	Y
3 Yarmuth	N	N	Y	Y	Y
4 Massie	N	N	Y	Y	Y
5 Rogers	Y	Y	Y	Y	Y
6 Chandler	N	Y	Y	Y	Y
LOUISIANA					
1 Scalise	Y	Y	Y	Y	Y
2 Richmond	N	N	Y	Y	Y
3 Landry	N	N	Y	Y	Y
4 Fleming	Y	Y	Y	Y	Y
5 Alexander	Y	Y	Y	Y	Y
6 Cassidy	N	Y	Y	Y	Y
7 Boustany	Y	Y	Y	Y	Y
MAINE					
1 Pingree	N	N	Y	Y	Y
2 Michaud	N	N	Y	Y	Y
MARYLAND					
1 Harris	Y	N	Y	Y	Y
2 Ruppersberger	N	Y	Y	Y	Y
3 Sarbanes	N	N	Y	Y	Y
4 Edwards	N	N	Y	Y	Y
5 Hoyer	N	Y	Y	Y	Y
6 Bartlett	Y	Y	Y	Y	Y
7 Cummings	N	Y	Y	Y	Y
8 Van Hollen	N	N	Y	Y	Y
MASSACHUSETTS					
1 Olver	N	N	Y	Y	Y
2 Neal	N	N	Y	Y	Y
3 McGovern	N	N	Y	Y	Y
4 Frank	N	N	Y	Y	Y
5 Tsongas	N	Y	Y	Y	Y
6 Tierney	N	N	Y	Y	Y
7 Markey	N	N	Y	Y	?
8 Capuano	N	N	Y	Y	Y
9 Lynch	N	N	Y	Y	Y
10 Keating	N	Y	Y	Y	Y
MICHIGAN					
1 Benishek	Y	Y	Y	Y	Y
2 Huizenga	Y	Y	Y	Y	Y
3 Amash	N	N	Y	Y	N
4 Camp	Y	Y	Y	Y	Y
5 Kildee	N	Y	Y	Y	Y
6 Upton	Y	Y	Y	Y	Y
7 Walberg	Y	N	Y	Y	Y
8 Rogers	Y	Y	Y	Y	Y
9 Peters	N	N	Y	Y	Y
10 Miller	Y	Y	Y	Y	Y
11 Curson	N	Y	Y	Y	Y
12 Levin	N	Y	Y	Y	Y
13 Clarke	N	N	Y	Y	Y
14 Conyers	N	N	Y	Y	Y
15 Dingell	N	Y	Y	Y	Y
MINNESOTA					
1 Walz	N	Y	Y	Y	Y
2 Kline	Y	Y	Y	Y	Y
3 Paulsen	Y	Y	Y	Y	Y
4 McCollum	N	N	Y	Y	Y
5 Ellison	N	N	Y	Y	Y
6 Bachmann	Y	N	Y	Y	Y
7 Peterson	N	Y	Y	Y	Y
8 Cravaack	Y	Y	Y	Y	Y
MISSISSIPPI					
1 Nunnelee	Y	Y	Y	Y	Y
2 Thompson	N	Y	Y	Y	Y
3 Harper	Y	Y	Y	Y	Y
4 Palazzo	Y	Y	Y	Y	Y
MISSOURI					
1 Clay	N	Y	Y	Y	Y
2 Akin	Y	Y	Y	Y	Y
3 Carnahan	N	Y	Y	Y	Y
4 Hartzler	Y	Y	Y	Y	Y
5 Cleaver	N	Y	Y	Y	Y
6 Graves	Y	Y	Y	Y	Y
7 Long	Y	Y	Y	Y	Y
8 Emerson	Y	Y	?	?	?
9 Luetkemeyer	Y	Y	Y	Y	Y
MONTANA					
AL Rehberg	Y	Y	Y	Y	Y
NEBRASKA					
1 Fortenberry	Y	?	Y	Y	Y
2 Terry	Y	Y	Y	Y	Y
3 Smith	Y	Y	Y	Y	Y
NEVADA					
1 Berkley	N	?	Y	Y	Y
2 Amodei	Y	Y	Y	Y	Y
3 Heck	Y	Y	Y	Y	Y
NEW HAMPSHIRE					
1 Guinta	Y	Y	Y	Y	Y
2 Bass	Y	Y	Y	Y	Y
NEW JERSEY					
1 Andrews	N	Y	Y	Y	Y
2 LoBiondo	N	Y	Y	Y	Y
3 Runyan	Y	Y	Y	Y	Y
4 Smith	Y	Y	Y	Y	Y
5 Garrett	Y	Y	Y	Y	Y
6 Pallone	N	N	Y	Y	Y
7 Lance	Y	Y	Y	Y	Y
8 Pascrell	N	Y	Y	Y	Y
9 Rothman	N	Y	Y	Y	Y
10 Payne, Jr.	N	N	Y	Y	Y
11 Frelinghuysen	Y	Y	Y	Y	Y
12 Holt	N	Y	Y	Y	Y
13 Sires	N	Y	Y	Y	Y
NEW MEXICO					
1 Heinrich	N	Y	Y	Y	Y
2 Pearce	Y	Y	Y	Y	Y
3 Luján	N	Y	Y	Y	Y
NEW YORK					
1 Bishop	N	Y	Y	Y	Y
2 Israel	N	Y	Y	Y	Y
3 King	Y	Y	Y	Y	Y
4 McCarthy	N	Y	Y	Y	Y
5 Ackerman	N	N	Y	Y	Y
6 Meeks	N	Y	Y	Y	Y
7 Crowley	N	Y	Y	Y	Y
8 Nadler	N	N	Y	Y	Y
9 Turner	Y	Y	Y	Y	Y
10 Towns	N	Y	Y	Y	Y
11 Clarke	N	N	Y	Y	Y
12 Velázquez	N	N	Y	Y	Y
13 Grimm	Y	Y	Y	Y	Y
14 Maloney	N	Y	Y	Y	Y
15 Rangel	N	N	Y	Y	Y
16 Serrano	N	N	Y	Y	?
17 Engel	N	Y	Y	Y	Y
18 Lowey	N	Y	Y	Y	Y
19 Hayworth	Y	Y	Y	Y	Y
20 Gibson	N	Y	Y	Y	Y
21 Tonko	N	N	Y	Y	Y
22 Hinchey	N	N	Y	Y	Y
23 Owens	N	Y	Y	Y	Y
24 Hanna	Y	Y	Y	Y	Y
25 Buerkle	Y	Y	Y	Y	Y
26 Hochul	N	Y	Y	Y	Y
27 Higgins	N	Y	Y	Y	Y
28 Slaughter	N	N	Y	Y	Y
29 Reed	Y	Y	Y	Y	N
NORTH CAROLINA					
1 Butterfield	N	Y	Y	Y	Y
2 Ellmers	Y	Y	Y	Y	Y
3 Jones	N	N	Y	Y	Y
4 Price	N	Y	Y	Y	Y
5 Foxx	Y	Y	Y	Y	Y
6 Coble	Y	Y	Y	Y	Y
7 McIntyre	N	Y	Y	Y	Y
8 Kissell	N	Y	Y	Y	Y
9 Myrick	Y	Y	Y	Y	Y
10 McHenry	Y	Y	Y	Y	Y
11 Shuler	N	Y	Y	Y	Y
12 Watt	N	N	Y	Y	Y
13 Miller	N	N	Y	Y	Y
NORTH DAKOTA					
AL Berg	Y	Y	Y	Y	Y
OHIO					
1 Chabot	Y	Y	Y	Y	Y
2 Schmidt	Y	Y	Y	Y	Y
3 Turner	Y	Y	Y	Y	Y
4 Jordan	Y	Y	Y	Y	Y
5 Latta	Y	Y	Y	Y	Y
6 Johnson	Y	Y	Y	Y	Y
7 Austria	Y	Y	Y	Y	Y
8 Boehner					
9 Kaptur	N	N	Y	Y	Y
10 Kucinich	N	N	Y	Y	Y
11 Fudge	N	N	Y	Y	Y
12 Tiberi	Y	Y	Y	Y	Y
13 Sutton	N	Y	Y	Y	Y
14 LaTourette	Y	Y	Y	Y	Y
15 Stivers	Y	Y	Y	Y	Y
16 Renacci	Y	Y	Y	Y	Y
17 Ryan	N	Y	Y	Y	Y
18 Gibbs	Y	Y	Y	Y	Y
OKLAHOMA					
1 Sullivan	Y	Y	Y	Y	Y
2 Boren	N	Y	Y	Y	Y
3 Lucas	Y	Y	Y	Y	Y
4 Cole	Y	Y	Y	Y	Y
5 Lankford	Y	Y	Y	Y	Y
OREGON					
1 Bonamici	N	Y	Y	Y	Y
2 Walden	Y	Y	Y	Y	Y
3 Blumenauer	N	N	Y	Y	Y
4 DeFazio	N	Y	Y	Y	Y
5 Schrader	N	Y	Y	Y	Y
PENNSYLVANIA					
1 Brady	N	Y	Y	Y	Y
2 Fattah	N	N	Y	Y	Y
3 Kelly	Y	Y	Y	Y	Y
4 Altmire	N	Y	Y	Y	Y
5 Thompson	Y	Y	Y	Y	Y
6 Gerlach	Y	Y	Y	Y	Y
7 Meehan	Y	Y	Y	Y	Y
8 Fitzpatrick	N	Y	Y	Y	Y
9 Shuster	Y	Y	Y	Y	Y
10 Marino	Y	Y	Y	Y	Y
11 Barletta	Y	Y	Y	Y	Y
12 Critz	N	Y	Y	Y	Y
13 Schwartz	N	Y	Y	Y	Y
14 Doyle	N	N	Y	Y	Y
15 Dent	Y	Y	Y	Y	Y
16 Pitts	Y	Y	Y	Y	Y
17 Holden	N	Y	Y	Y	Y
18 Murphy	Y	Y	Y	Y	Y
19 Platts	N	Y	Y	Y	Y
RHODE ISLAND					
1 Cicilline	N	Y	Y	Y	Y
2 Langevin	N	Y	Y	Y	Y
SOUTH CAROLINA					
1 Scott	Y	Y	Y	Y	Y
2 Wilson	Y	Y	Y	Y	Y
3 Duncan	Y	Y	Y	Y	Y
4 Gowdy	Y	Y	Y	Y	Y
5 Mulvaney	Y	Y	Y	Y	Y
6 Clyburn	N	Y	Y	Y	Y
SOUTH DAKOTA					
AL Noem	Y	Y	Y	Y	Y
TENNESSEE					
1 Roe	Y	N	Y	Y	Y
2 Duncan	N	N	Y	Y	Y
3 Fleischmann	Y	Y	Y	Y	Y
4 DesJarlais	Y	N	Y	Y	Y
5 Cooper	N	Y	Y	Y	Y
6 Black	Y	Y	Y	Y	Y
7 Blackburn	Y	Y	Y	Y	Y
8 Fincher	Y	Y	Y	Y	Y
9 Cohen	N	N	Y	Y	Y
TEXAS					
1 Gohmert	N	Y	Y	Y	Y
2 Poe	Y	Y	Y	Y	Y
3 Johnson, S.	?	?	?	?	?
4 Hall	Y	N	Y	Y	Y
5 Hensarling	Y	Y	Y	Y	Y
6 Barton	Y	Y	Y	Y	Y
7 Culberson	?	?	?	?	?
8 Brady	Y	Y	Y	Y	Y
9 Green, A.	N	Y	Y	Y	Y
10 McCaul	Y	Y	Y	Y	Y
11 Conaway	Y	Y	Y	Y	Y
12 Granger	Y	Y	Y	Y	Y
13 Thornberry	Y	Y	Y	Y	Y
14 Paul	N	N	Y	Y	Y
15 Hinojosa	N	Y	Y	Y	Y
16 Reyes	?	?	?	?	?
17 Flores	Y	Y	Y	Y	N
18 Jackson Lee	N	Y	Y	Y	Y
19 Neugebauer	Y	Y	Y	Y	Y
20 Gonzalez	N	Y	Y	Y	Y
21 Smith	Y	Y	Y	Y	Y
22 Olson	Y	Y	Y	Y	Y
23 Canseco	Y	Y	Y	Y	Y
24 Marchant	Y	N	Y	Y	Y
25 Doggett	N	Y	Y	Y	Y
26 Burgess	Y	Y	Y	Y	Y
27 Farenthold	Y	Y	Y	Y	Y
28 Cuellar	N	Y	Y	Y	Y
29 Green, G.	N	Y	Y	Y	Y
30 Johnson, E.	N	Y	Y	Y	Y
31 Carter	Y	Y	Y	Y	Y
32 Sessions	Y	Y	Y	Y	Y
UTAH					
1 Bishop	P	Y	Y	Y	Y
2 Matheson	N	Y	Y	Y	Y
3 Chaffetz	Y	Y	Y	Y	Y
VERMONT					
AL Welch	N	N	Y	Y	Y
VIRGINIA					
1 Wittman	Y	Y	Y	Y	Y
2 Rigell	Y	Y	N	Y	Y
3 Scott	N	Y	Y	Y	Y
4 Forbes	Y	Y	Y	Y	Y
5 Hurt	Y	Y	Y	Y	Y
6 Goodlatte	Y	Y	Y	Y	Y
7 Cantor	Y	Y	Y	Y	Y
8 Moran	N	Y	Y	Y	Y
9 Griffith	Y	N	Y	Y	Y
10 Wolf	N	Y	Y	Y	Y
11 Connolly	N	Y	Y	Y	Y
WASHINGTON					
1 DelBene	N	Y	Y	Y	Y
2 Larsen	N	Y	Y	Y	Y
3 Herrera Beutler	N	Y	Y	Y	Y
4 Hastings	Y	Y	Y	Y	Y
5 McMorris Rodgers	Y	Y	Y	Y	Y
6 Dicks	N	Y	?	?	?
7 McDermott	N	N	Y	Y	Y
8 Reichert	Y	Y	Y	Y	?
9 Smith	N	Y	Y	Y	Y
WEST VIRGINIA					
1 McKinley	Y	Y	Y	Y	Y
2 Capito	Y	Y	Y	Y	Y
3 Rahall	N	Y	Y	Y	Y
WISCONSIN					
1 Ryan	Y	Y	Y	Y	Y
2 Baldwin	N	N	Y	Y	Y
3 Kind	N	N	Y	Y	Y
4 Moore	N	N	Y	Y	Y
5 Sensenbrenner	Y	Y	Y	Y	Y
6 Petri	Y	Y	Y	Y	Y
7 Duffy	Y	Y	Y	Y	Y
8 Ribble	Y	N	Y	Y	Y
WYOMING					
AL Lummis	Y	N	Y	Y	Y

IN THE HOUSE | By Vote Number

649. HR 3159. Foreign Aid Transparency/Passage. Ros-Lehtinen, R-Fla., motion to suspend the rules and pass the bill that would require the president to establish guidelines for federal agencies regarding performance metrics, goals and progress monitoring for projects funded by U.S. foreign development aid. The bill would require the creation of a publicly available website where information regarding project efficiency and goals will be available and updated. Motion agreed to 390-0: R 221-0; D 169-0. A two-thirds majority of those present and voting (260 in this case) is required for passage under suspension of the rules. Dec. 30, 2012.

650. HR 4057. Education Information for Veterans/Motion to Concur. Miller, R-Fla., motion to suspend the rules and concur in the Senate amendment to the bill that would require the Veterans Affairs Department to provide information on educational institutions to veterans and servicemembers. It also would place restrictions on bonuses and incentives paid by the VA and institutions of postsecondary education. Motion agreed to (thus clearing the bill for the president) 392-3: R 220-3; D 172-0. A two-thirds majority of those present and voting (264 in this case) is required for passage under suspension of the rules. Dec. 30, 2012.

651. S 3202. Veterans Burial Arrangements/Passage. Miller, R-Fla., motion to suspend the rules and pass the bill that would authorize the Veterans Affairs Department to provide caskets and urns for deceased veterans who don't have identified next of kin. It would require the VA to establish a registry for veterans injured or exposed to toxic chemicals created by open burn pits. It also would provide for an off-base transitional assistance program. Motion agreed to 393-0: R 220-0; D 173-0. A two-thirds majority of those present and voting (262 in this case) is required for passage under suspension of the rules. Dec. 30, 2012.

652. S 3454. Fiscal 2013 Intelligence Authorization/Passage. Rogers, R-Mich., motion to suspend the rules and pass the bill that would authorize classified amounts in fiscal 2013 for 16 U.S. intelligence agencies, including the Office of the Director of National Intelligence, the CIA and the National Security Agency, and other intelligence-related activities of the U.S. government. It would authorize covert-action programs and research and development. The bill would require government officials responsible for authorized disclosures of national intelligence or intelligence related to national security to notify congressional Intelligence committees "on a timely basis" of such disclosures. It would direct the president to develop a strategy and timeline for carrying out current requirements regarding reciprocity of security clearances among government agencies. Motion agreed to (thus clearing the bill for the president) 373-29: R 222-5; D 151-24. A two-thirds majority of those present and voting (268 in this case) is required for passage under suspension of the rules. Dec. 31, 2012.

653. HR 6612. Research Center and Test Range Redesignation/Passage. Hall, R-Texas, motion to suspend the rules and pass the bill that would redesignate the Dryden Flight Research Center at Edwards Air Force Base in California as the "Neil A. Armstrong Flight Research Center" and the Western Aeronautical Test Range within the center as the "Hugh L. Dryden Aeronautical Test Range." Motion agreed to 404-0: R 227-0; D 177-0. A two-thirds majority of those present and voting (270 in this case) is required for passage under suspension of the rules. Dec. 31, 2012.

654. HR 6364. WWI Commemoration/Motion to Concur. Chaffetz, R-Utah, motion to suspend the rules and concur in the Senate amendment to the bill that would create a commission to oversee preparations for the U.S. centennial commemoration of World War I. Motion agreed to (thus clearing the bill for the president) 401-5: R 223-5; D 178-0. A two-thirds majority of those present and voting (271 in this case) is required for passage under suspension of the rules. Dec. 31, 2012.

	649	650	651	652	653	654
ALABAMA						
1 Bonner	Y	Y	Y	Y	Y	Y
2 Roby	Y	Y	Y	Y	Y	Y
3 Rogers	Y	Y	Y	Y	Y	Y
4 Aderholt	Y	Y	Y	Y	Y	Y
5 Brooks	Y	N	Y	Y	Y	Y
6 Bachus	Y	Y	Y	Y	Y	Y
7 Sewell	Y	Y	Y	Y	Y	Y
ALASKA						
AL Young	Y	Y	Y	Y	Y	Y
ARIZONA						
1 Gosar	Y	Y	Y	Y	Y	Y
2 Franks	Y	Y	Y	Y	Y	Y
3 Quayle	Y	Y	Y	Y	Y	Y
4 Pastor	?	?	?	?	?	?
5 Schweikert	Y	Y	Y	Y	Y	N
6 Flake	Y	Y	Y	Y	Y	Y
7 Grijalva	Y	Y	Y	N	Y	Y
8 Barber	Y	Y	Y	Y	Y	Y
ARKANSAS						
1 Crawford	Y	Y	Y	?	Y	Y
2 Griffin	Y	Y	Y	Y	Y	Y
3 Womack	Y	Y	Y	Y	Y	Y
4 Ross	Y	Y	Y	Y	Y	Y
CALIFORNIA						
1 Thompson	Y	Y	Y	Y	Y	Y
2 Herger	Y	Y	Y	Y	Y	Y
3 Lungren	Y	Y	Y	Y	Y	Y
4 McClintock	Y	Y	Y	Y	Y	Y
5 Matsui	Y	Y	Y	Y	Y	Y
6 Woolsey	?	?	?	?	?	?
7 Miller, George	Y	Y	Y	N	Y	Y
8 Pelosi	Y	Y	Y	?	Y	Y
9 Lee	Y	Y	Y	N	Y	Y
10 Garamendi	Y	?	Y	Y	Y	Y
11 McNerney	Y	Y	Y	Y	Y	Y
12 Speier	Y	Y	Y	N	Y	Y
13 Stark	?	?	?	?	?	?
14 Eshoo	Y	Y	Y	Y	Y	Y
15 Honda	Y	Y	Y	N	Y	Y
16 Lofgren	Y	Y	Y	N	Y	Y
17 Farr	Y	Y	Y	Y	Y	Y
18 Vacant						
19 Denham	Y	Y	Y	Y	Y	Y
20 Costa	Y	Y	Y	Y	Y	Y
21 Nunes	Y	Y	Y	Y	Y	Y
22 McCarthy	Y	Y	Y	Y	Y	Y
23 Capps	Y	Y	Y	Y	Y	Y
24 Gallegly	?	?	?	?	?	?
25 McKeon	Y	Y	Y	Y	Y	Y
26 Dreier	Y	Y	Y	Y	Y	Y
27 Sherman	Y	Y	Y	Y	Y	Y
28 Berman	Y	Y	Y	Y	Y	Y
29 Schiff	Y	Y	Y	Y	Y	Y
30 Waxman	Y	Y	Y	?	?	?
31 Becerra	?	Y	Y	Y	Y	Y
32 Chu	Y	Y	Y	Y	Y	Y
33 Bass	Y	Y	Y	Y	?	Y
34 Roybal-Allard	?	?	?	?	?	?
35 Waters	Y	Y	Y	N	Y	Y
36 Hahn	Y	Y	Y	N	Y	Y
37 Richardson	Y	Y	Y	Y	Y	Y
38 Napolitano	Y	Y	Y	Y	Y	Y
39 Sánchez, Linda	Y	Y	Y	Y	Y	Y
40 Royce	Y	Y	Y	Y	Y	Y
41 Lewis	?	?	?	?	?	?
42 Miller, Gary	Y	Y	Y	Y	Y	Y
43 Baca	Y	Y	Y	Y	Y	Y
44 Calvert	Y	Y	Y	Y	Y	Y
45 Bono Mack	?	?	?	?	?	?
46 Rohrabacher	?	?	?	?	?	?
47 Sanchez, Loretta	Y	Y	Y	Y	Y	Y
48 Campbell	Y	Y	Y	Y	Y	Y
49 Issa	Y	Y	Y	Y	Y	Y
50 Bilbray	Y	Y	Y	Y	Y	Y
51 Vacant						
52 Hunter	Y	Y	Y	Y	Y	Y
53 Davis	Y	Y	Y	Y	Y	Y

	649	650	651	652	653	654
COLORADO						
1 DeGette	?	?	?	N	Y	Y
2 Polis	Y	Y	Y	N	Y	Y
3 Tipton	Y	Y	Y	Y	Y	Y
4 Gardner	Y	Y	Y	Y	Y	Y
5 Lamborn	Y	Y	Y	Y	Y	Y
6 Coffman	Y	Y	Y	Y	Y	Y
7 Perlmutter	Y	Y	Y	Y	Y	Y
CONNECTICUT						
1 Larson	?	Y	Y	Y	Y	Y
2 Courtney	Y	Y	Y	Y	Y	Y
3 DeLauro	Y	Y	Y	Y	Y	Y
4 Himes	Y	Y	Y	Y	Y	Y
5 Murphy	Y	Y	Y	Y	Y	Y
DELAWARE						
AL Carney	Y	Y	Y	Y	Y	Y
FLORIDA						
1 Miller	Y	Y	Y	Y	Y	Y
2 Southerland	Y	Y	Y	Y	Y	Y
3 Brown	Y	Y	Y	Y	Y	Y
4 Crenshaw	Y	Y	Y	Y	Y	Y
5 Nugent	Y	Y	Y	Y	Y	Y
6 Stearns	Y	Y	?	Y	Y	Y
7 Mica	Y	Y	Y	Y	Y	Y
8 Webster	Y	Y	Y	Y	Y	Y
9 Bilirakis	Y	Y	Y	Y	Y	Y
10 Young	Y	Y	Y	Y	Y	Y
11 Castor	Y	Y	Y	?	Y	Y
12 Ross	Y	Y	Y	?	?	Y
13 Buchanan	Y	Y	Y	Y	Y	Y
14 Mack	?	?	?	?	?	?
15 Posey	Y	Y	Y	Y	Y	Y
16 Rooney	Y	Y	Y	Y	Y	Y
17 Wilson	Y	Y	Y	Y	Y	Y
18 Ros-Lehtinen	Y	Y	Y	Y	Y	Y
19 Deutch	Y	Y	Y	Y	Y	Y
20 Wasserman Schultz	Y	Y	Y	Y	Y	Y
21 Diaz-Balart	Y	Y	Y	Y	Y	Y
22 West	Y	Y	Y	Y	Y	Y
23 Hastings	Y	Y	Y	Y	Y	Y
24 Adams	Y	Y	Y	Y	Y	Y
25 Rivera	Y	Y	Y	Y	Y	Y
GEORGIA						
1 Kingston	Y	Y	Y	Y	Y	Y
2 Bishop	Y	Y	Y	Y	Y	Y
3 Westmoreland	Y	Y	Y	Y	Y	Y
4 Johnson	Y	Y	Y	Y	Y	Y
5 Lewis	Y	Y	Y	?	?	?
6 Price	Y	Y	Y	Y	Y	Y
7 Woodall	Y	Y	Y	Y	Y	Y
8 Scott, A.	Y	Y	Y	Y	Y	Y
9 Graves	Y	Y	Y	Y	Y	Y
10 Broun	Y	Y	Y	Y	Y	Y
11 Gingrey	?	Y	Y	Y	Y	Y
12 Barrow	Y	Y	Y	Y	Y	Y
13 Scott, D.	Y	Y	Y	Y	Y	Y
HAWAII						
1 Hanabusa	Y	Y	Y	N	Y	Y
2 Hirono	Y	Y	Y	Y	Y	Y
IDAHO						
1 Labrador	Y	Y	Y	Y	Y	Y
2 Simpson	Y	Y	Y	?	?	Y
ILLINOIS						
1 Rush	Y	Y	Y	Y	Y	Y
2 Vacant						
3 Lipinski	?	?	?	Y	Y	Y
4 Gutierrez	?	?	?	N	Y	Y
5 Quigley	Y	Y	Y	Y	Y	Y
6 Roskam	Y	Y	Y	Y	Y	Y
7 Davis	Y	Y	Y	N	Y	Y
8 Walsh	Y	Y	Y	Y	Y	Y
9 Schakowsky	Y	Y	Y	Y	Y	Y
10 Dold	Y	Y	Y	Y	Y	Y
11 Kinzinger	Y	Y	Y	Y	Y	Y
12 Costello	?	?	?	?	?	?
13 Biggert	Y	Y	Y	Y	Y	Y
14 Hultgren	Y	Y	Y	Y	Y	Y
15 Johnson	?	?	?	?	?	?

	649	650	651	652	653	654
16 **Manzullo**	Y	Y	Y	Y	Y	Y
17 **Schilling**	Y	Y	Y	Y	Y	Y
18 **Schock**	?	?	?	Y	Y	Y
19 **Shimkus**	Y	Y	Y	Y	Y	Y
INDIANA						
1 Visclosky	?	?	?	Y	Y	Y
2 Donnelly	Y	Y	Y	Y	Y	Y
3 **Stutzman**	Y	Y	Y	Y	Y	Y
4 **Rokita**	Y	Y	Y	Y	Y	Y
5 **Burton**	?	?	?	?	?	?
6 **Pence**	?	?	?	Y	Y	Y
7 Carson	Y	Y	Y	Y	Y	Y
8 **Bucshon**	Y	Y	Y	Y	Y	Y
9 **Young**	Y	Y	Y	Y	Y	Y
IOWA						
1 Braley	Y	Y	Y	Y	Y	Y
2 Loebsack	Y	Y	Y	Y	Y	Y
3 Boswell	Y	Y	Y	Y	Y	Y
4 **Latham**	Y	Y	Y	Y	Y	Y
5 **King**	Y	Y	Y	Y	Y	Y
KANSAS						
1 **Huelskamp**	Y	Y	Y	Y	Y	Y
2 **Jenkins**	Y	Y	Y	Y	Y	Y
3 **Yoder**	Y	Y	Y	Y	Y	Y
4 **Pompeo**	Y	Y	Y	Y	Y	Y
KENTUCKY						
1 **Whitfield**	Y	Y	Y	Y	Y	Y
2 **Guthrie**	Y	Y	Y	Y	Y	Y
3 Yarmuth	Y	Y	Y	Y	Y	Y
4 **Massie**	Y	Y	Y	N	Y	N
5 **Rogers**	Y	Y	Y	Y	Y	Y
6 Chandler	?	?	?	Y	Y	Y
LOUISIANA						
1 **Scalise**	Y	Y	Y	Y	Y	Y
2 Richmond	Y	Y	Y	Y	Y	Y
3 **Landry**	?	?	?	Y	Y	Y
4 **Fleming**	Y	Y	Y	Y	Y	Y
5 **Alexander**	Y	Y	Y	Y	Y	Y
6 **Cassidy**	Y	Y	Y	Y	Y	Y
7 **Boustany**	Y	Y	Y	Y	Y	Y
MAINE						
1 Pingree	Y	Y	Y	N	Y	Y
2 Michaud	Y	Y	Y	Y	Y	Y
MARYLAND						
1 **Harris**	Y	Y	Y	Y	Y	Y
2 Ruppersberger	Y	Y	Y	Y	Y	Y
3 Sarbanes	Y	Y	Y	Y	Y	Y
4 Edwards	Y	Y	Y	Y	Y	Y
5 Hoyer	Y	Y	Y	Y	Y	Y
6 **Bartlett**	Y	Y	Y	Y	Y	Y
7 Cummings	Y	Y	Y	N	Y	Y
8 Van Hollen	Y	Y	Y	Y	Y	Y
MASSACHUSETTS						
1 Olver	Y	Y	Y	N	Y	Y
2 Neal	Y	Y	Y	Y	Y	Y
3 McGovern	Y	Y	Y	N	Y	Y
4 Frank	Y	Y	Y	Y	Y	Y
5 Tsongas	Y	Y	Y	Y	Y	Y
6 Tierney	Y	Y	Y	Y	Y	Y
7 Markey	Y	Y	Y	Y	Y	Y
8 Capuano	Y	Y	Y	N	Y	Y
9 Lynch	Y	Y	Y	Y	Y	Y
10 Keating	?	Y	Y	Y	Y	Y
MICHIGAN						
1 **Benishek**	Y	Y	Y	Y	Y	Y
2 **Huizenga**	Y	Y	Y	Y	Y	Y
3 **Amash**	Y	N	Y	N	Y	N
4 **Camp**	Y	Y	Y	Y	Y	Y
5 Kildee	Y	Y	Y	Y	Y	Y
6 **Upton**	Y	Y	Y	Y	Y	Y
7 **Walberg**	Y	Y	Y	Y	?	Y
8 **Rogers**	Y	Y	Y	Y	Y	Y
9 Peters	Y	Y	Y	Y	Y	Y
10 **Miller**	Y	Y	Y	Y	Y	Y
11 Curson	Y	Y	Y	Y	Y	Y
12 Levin	Y	Y	Y	Y	Y	Y
13 Clarke	Y	Y	Y	Y	Y	Y
14 Conyers	Y	Y	Y	N	Y	Y
15 Dingell	Y	Y	Y	Y	Y	Y
MINNESOTA						
1 Walz	Y	Y	Y	Y	Y	Y
2 **Kline**	Y	Y	Y	Y	Y	Y
3 **Paulsen**	Y	Y	Y	Y	Y	Y
4 McCollum	Y	Y	Y	Y	Y	Y

	649	650	651	652	653	654
5 Ellison	Y	Y	Y	N	Y	Y
6 **Bachmann**	Y	Y	Y	Y	Y	Y
7 Peterson	Y	Y	Y	Y	Y	Y
8 **Cravaack**	Y	Y	Y	Y	Y	Y
MISSISSIPPI						
1 **Nunnelee**	Y	Y	Y	Y	Y	Y
2 Thompson	Y	Y	Y	Y	Y	Y
3 **Harper**	Y	Y	Y	Y	Y	Y
4 **Palazzo**	Y	Y	Y	Y	Y	Y
MISSOURI						
1 Clay	?	Y	Y	Y	Y	Y
2 **Akin**	Y	Y	Y	Y	Y	Y
3 Carnahan	Y	Y	Y	Y	Y	Y
4 **Hartzler**	Y	Y	Y	Y	Y	Y
5 Cleaver	?	?	?	Y	Y	Y
6 **Graves**	?	?	?	Y	Y	Y
7 **Long**	Y	Y	Y	Y	Y	Y
8 **Emerson**	Y	Y	Y	Y	Y	Y
9 **Luetkemeyer**	Y	Y	Y	Y	Y	Y
MONTANA						
AL **Rehberg**	Y	Y	Y	Y	Y	Y
NEBRASKA						
1 **Fortenberry**	Y	Y	Y	Y	Y	Y
2 **Terry**	Y	Y	Y	Y	Y	Y
3 **Smith**	Y	Y	Y	Y	Y	Y
NEVADA						
1 Berkley	Y	Y	Y	Y	Y	Y
2 **Amodei**	Y	Y	Y	Y	Y	Y
3 **Heck**	Y	Y	Y	Y	Y	Y
NEW HAMPSHIRE						
1 **Guinta**	Y	Y	Y	Y	Y	Y
2 **Bass**	?	?	?	?	?	?
NEW JERSEY						
1 Andrews	Y	Y	Y	Y	Y	Y
2 **LoBiondo**	Y	Y	Y	Y	Y	Y
3 **Runyan**	Y	Y	Y	Y	Y	Y
4 **Smith**	Y	Y	Y	Y	Y	Y
5 **Garrett**	Y	Y	Y	Y	Y	Y
6 Pallone	Y	Y	Y	Y	Y	Y
7 **Lance**	Y	Y	Y	Y	Y	Y
8 Pascrell	Y	Y	Y	?	Y	Y
9 Rothman	Y	Y	Y	Y	Y	Y
10 Payne, Jr.	Y	Y	Y	Y	Y	Y
11 **Frelinghuysen**	Y	Y	Y	Y	Y	Y
12 Holt	Y	Y	Y	N	Y	Y
13 Sires	Y	Y	Y	Y	Y	Y
NEW MEXICO						
1 Heinrich	Y	Y	Y	Y	Y	Y
2 **Pearce**	Y	Y	Y	Y	Y	Y
3 Luján	Y	Y	Y	Y	Y	Y
NEW YORK						
1 Bishop	Y	Y	Y	Y	Y	Y
2 Israel	Y	Y	Y	Y	Y	Y
3 **King**	Y	Y	Y	Y	Y	Y
4 McCarthy	Y	Y	Y	?	?	?
5 Ackerman	Y	Y	?	?	?	?
6 Meeks	Y	Y	Y	Y	Y	Y
7 Crowley	?	Y	Y	Y	Y	Y
8 Nadler	?	?	?	Y	Y	Y
9 **Turner**	Y	Y	Y	Y	Y	Y
10 Towns	Y	Y	Y	?	?	?
11 Clarke	Y	Y	Y	Y	Y	Y
12 Velázquez	Y	?	Y	Y	Y	Y
13 **Grimm**	Y	Y	Y	Y	Y	Y
14 Maloney	Y	Y	Y	?	?	?
15 Rangel	Y	Y	Y	Y	Y	Y
16 Serrano	Y	Y	Y	Y	Y	Y
17 Engel	Y	Y	Y	Y	Y	Y
18 Lowey	Y	Y	Y	Y	Y	Y
19 **Hayworth**	Y	Y	Y	Y	Y	Y
20 **Gibson**	Y	Y	Y	N	Y	Y
21 Tonko	Y	Y	Y	Y	Y	Y
22 Hinchey	Y	Y	Y	Y	Y	Y
23 Owens	Y	Y	Y	Y	Y	Y
24 **Hanna**	Y	Y	Y	Y	Y	Y
25 **Buerkle**	Y	Y	Y	Y	Y	Y
26 Hochul	Y	Y	Y	Y	Y	Y
27 Higgins	Y	Y	Y	Y	Y	Y
28 Slaughter	Y	Y	Y	Y	Y	Y
29 **Reed**	Y	Y	Y	Y	Y	Y
NORTH CAROLINA						
1 Butterfield	Y	Y	Y	Y	Y	Y
2 **Ellmers**	Y	Y	Y	Y	Y	Y
3 **Jones**	?	?	?	N	Y	Y
4 Price	Y	Y	Y	Y	Y	Y

	649	650	651	652	653	654
5 **Foxx**	Y	Y	Y	Y	Y	Y
6 **Coble**	Y	Y	Y	Y	Y	Y
7 McIntyre	Y	Y	Y	Y	Y	Y
8 Kissell	?	?	?	Y	Y	Y
9 **Myrick**	Y	Y	Y	Y	Y	Y
10 **McHenry**	Y	Y	Y	Y	Y	Y
11 Shuler	?	?	?	?	?	?
12 Watt	Y	Y	Y	Y	Y	Y
13 Miller	Y	Y	Y	Y	Y	Y
NORTH DAKOTA						
AL **Berg**	Y	Y	Y	Y	Y	Y
OHIO						
1 **Chabot**	Y	Y	Y	Y	Y	Y
2 **Schmidt**	Y	Y	Y	?	?	?
3 **Turner**	Y	Y	Y	Y	Y	Y
4 **Jordan**	Y	Y	Y	Y	Y	Y
5 **Latta**	Y	Y	Y	Y	Y	Y
6 **Johnson**	Y	Y	Y	Y	Y	Y
7 **Austria**	Y	Y	Y	Y	Y	Y
8 **Boehner**						
9 Kaptur	Y	Y	Y	Y	Y	Y
10 Kucinich	Y	Y	Y	N	Y	Y
11 Fudge	Y	Y	Y	Y	Y	Y
12 **Tiberi**	Y	Y	Y	Y	Y	Y
13 Sutton	Y	Y	Y	Y	Y	Y
14 **LaTourette**	Y	Y	Y	Y	Y	Y
15 **Stivers**	Y	Y	Y	Y	Y	Y
16 **Renacci**	Y	Y	Y	Y	Y	Y
17 Ryan	Y	Y	Y	Y	Y	Y
18 **Gibbs**	Y	Y	Y	Y	Y	Y
OKLAHOMA						
1 **Sullivan**	Y	Y	Y	Y	Y	Y
2 Boren	Y	Y	Y	Y	Y	Y
3 **Lucas**	Y	Y	Y	Y	Y	Y
4 **Cole**	Y	Y	Y	Y	Y	Y
5 **Lankford**	Y	Y	Y	Y	Y	Y
OREGON						
1 Bonamici	Y	Y	Y	Y	Y	Y
2 **Walden**	Y	Y	Y	Y	Y	Y
3 Blumenauer	Y	Y	Y	N	Y	Y
4 DeFazio	Y	Y	Y	Y	Y	Y
5 Schrader	Y	Y	Y	Y	Y	Y
PENNSYLVANIA						
1 Brady	Y	Y	Y	Y	Y	Y
2 Fattah	Y	Y	Y	Y	Y	Y
3 **Kelly**	Y	Y	Y	Y	Y	Y
4 Altmire	Y	Y	Y	Y	Y	Y
5 **Thompson**	Y	Y	Y	Y	Y	Y
6 **Gerlach**	?	?	?	Y	Y	Y
7 **Meehan**	Y	Y	Y	Y	Y	Y
8 **Fitzpatrick**	Y	Y	Y	Y	Y	Y
9 **Shuster**	Y	Y	Y	Y	Y	Y
10 **Marino**	Y	Y	Y	Y	Y	Y
11 **Barletta**	Y	Y	Y	Y	Y	Y
12 Critz	Y	Y	Y	Y	Y	Y
13 Schwartz	Y	Y	Y	Y	Y	Y
14 Doyle	Y	Y	Y	Y	Y	Y
15 **Dent**	Y	Y	Y	Y	Y	Y
16 **Pitts**	Y	Y	Y	Y	Y	Y
17 Holden	Y	Y	Y	Y	Y	Y
18 **Murphy**	Y	Y	Y	Y	Y	Y
19 **Platts**	Y	Y	Y	Y	Y	Y
RHODE ISLAND						
1 Cicilline	Y	Y	Y	Y	Y	Y
2 Langevin	Y	Y	Y	Y	Y	Y
SOUTH CAROLINA						
1 **Scott**	Y	Y	Y	Y	Y	Y
2 **Wilson**	Y	Y	?	Y	Y	Y
3 **Duncan**	Y	Y	Y	Y	Y	Y
4 **Gowdy**	Y	Y	Y	Y	Y	Y
5 **Mulvaney**	Y	Y	Y	Y	Y	Y
6 Clyburn	Y	Y	Y	Y	Y	Y
SOUTH DAKOTA						
AL **Noem**	Y	Y	Y	Y	Y	Y
TENNESSEE						
1 **Roe**	Y	Y	Y	Y	Y	Y
2 **Duncan**	Y	Y	Y	N	Y	Y
3 **Fleischmann**	Y	Y	Y	Y	Y	Y
4 **DesJarlais**	Y	Y	Y	Y	Y	Y
5 Cooper	Y	Y	Y	Y	Y	Y
6 **Black**	Y	Y	Y	Y	Y	Y
7 **Blackburn**	Y	Y	Y	Y	Y	Y
8 **Fincher**	Y	Y	Y	Y	Y	Y
9 Cohen	Y	Y	Y	N	Y	Y

	649	650	651	652	653	654
TEXAS						
1 **Gohmert**	Y	Y	Y	Y	Y	Y
2 **Poe**	Y	Y	Y	Y	Y	Y
3 **Johnson, S.**	?	?	?	Y	Y	Y
4 **Hall**	Y	Y	Y	Y	Y	Y
5 **Hensarling**	Y	Y	Y	Y	Y	Y
6 **Barton**	Y	Y	Y	Y	Y	Y
7 **Culberson**	Y	Y	Y	Y	Y	Y
8 **Brady**	Y	Y	Y	Y	Y	Y
9 Green, A.	Y	Y	Y	Y	Y	Y
10 **McCaul**	Y	Y	Y	Y	Y	Y
11 **Conaway**	Y	Y	Y	Y	Y	Y
12 **Granger**	Y	Y	Y	Y	Y	Y
13 **Thornberry**	?	?	?	Y	Y	Y
14 **Paul**	?	?	?	?	?	?
15 Hinojosa	Y	Y	Y	?	?	?
16 Reyes	?	?	?	Y	Y	Y
17 **Flores**	Y	Y	Y	Y	Y	N
18 Jackson Lee	Y	Y	Y	Y	Y	Y
19 **Neugebauer**	Y	Y	Y	Y	Y	Y
20 Gonzalez	Y	Y	Y	Y	Y	Y
21 **Smith**	Y	Y	?	Y	Y	Y
22 **Olson**	Y	Y	Y	Y	Y	Y
23 **Canseco**	Y	Y	Y	Y	Y	Y
24 **Marchant**	Y	Y	Y	Y	Y	Y
25 Doggett	Y	Y	Y	N	Y	Y
26 **Burgess**	Y	Y	Y	Y	Y	Y
27 **Farenthold**	Y	Y	Y	Y	Y	Y
28 Cuellar	Y	Y	Y	Y	Y	Y
29 Green, G.	Y	Y	Y	Y	Y	Y
30 Johnson, E.	Y	Y	Y	Y	Y	Y
31 **Carter**	Y	Y	Y	Y	Y	Y
32 **Sessions**	Y	Y	Y	Y	Y	Y
UTAH						
1 **Bishop**	Y	Y	Y	Y	Y	Y
2 Matheson	Y	Y	Y	Y	Y	Y
3 **Chaffetz**	Y	Y	Y	Y	Y	Y
VERMONT						
AL Welch	?	?	?	Y	Y	Y
VIRGINIA						
1 **Wittman**	Y	Y	Y	Y	Y	Y
2 **Rigell**	Y	Y	Y	Y	Y	Y
3 Scott	Y	Y	Y	Y	Y	Y
4 **Forbes**	?	Y	Y	Y	Y	Y
5 **Hurt**	Y	Y	Y	Y	Y	Y
6 **Goodlatte**	Y	Y	Y	Y	Y	Y
7 **Cantor**	Y	Y	Y	Y	Y	Y
8 Moran	Y	Y	Y	Y	Y	Y
9 **Griffith**	Y	Y	Y	Y	Y	Y
10 **Wolf**	Y	Y	Y	Y	Y	Y
11 Connolly	Y	Y	Y	Y	Y	Y
WASHINGTON						
1 DelBene	Y	Y	Y	Y	Y	Y
2 Larsen	Y	Y	Y	Y	Y	Y
3 **Herrera Beutler**	Y	Y	Y	Y	Y	Y
4 **Hastings**	Y	Y	Y	Y	Y	Y
5 **McMorris Rodgers**	Y	Y	Y	Y	Y	Y
6 Dicks	Y	Y	Y	Y	Y	Y
7 McDermott	Y	Y	Y	Y	Y	Y
8 **Reichert**	Y	Y	Y	Y	Y	Y
9 Smith	?	?	?	Y	Y	Y
WEST VIRGINIA						
1 **McKinley**	Y	Y	Y	Y	Y	Y
2 **Capito**	Y	Y	Y	Y	Y	Y
3 Rahall	Y	Y	Y	Y	Y	Y
WISCONSIN						
1 **Ryan**	Y	Y	Y	Y	Y	Y
2 Baldwin	Y	Y	Y	Y	Y	Y
3 Kind	Y	Y	Y	Y	Y	Y
4 Moore	Y	Y	Y	Y	Y	Y
5 **Sensenbrenner**	Y	Y	Y	Y	Y	Y
6 **Petri**	Y	Y	Y	Y	Y	Y
7 **Duffy**	Y	Y	Y	Y	Y	Y
8 **Ribble**	Y	Y	Y	Y	Y	N
WYOMING						
AL **Lummis**	Y	N	Y	Y	Y	Y

IN THE HOUSE | By Vote Number

655. HR 6726. Federal Employee Pay Freeze/Passage. Issa, R-Calif., motion to suspend the rules and pass a bill that would extend the current statutory pay freeze for federal civilian employees, including members of Congress, through Dec. 31, 2013. Motion agreed to 287-129: R 232-2; D 55-127. A two-thirds majority of those present and voting (278 in this case) is required for passage under suspension of the rules. A "nay" was a vote in support of the president's position. Jan. 1, 2013.

656. HR 443. Alaska Land Conveyance/Motion to Concur. Young, R-Alaska, motion to suspend the rules and concur in the Senate amendment to the bill that would authorize the Health and Human Services Department to convey three adjacent parcels of federal land totaling 14.6 acres to the Maniilaq Association, a nonprofit organization founded by 12 American Indian tribes in Alaska. Motion agreed to 410-5: R 229-3; D 181-2. A two-thirds majority of those present and voting (277 in this case) is required for passage under suspension of the rules. Jan. 1, 2013.

657. HR 4212. Drywall-Labeling Regulations/Motion to Concur. Terry, R-Neb., motion to suspend the rules and concur in the Senate amendment to the bill that would create labeling and regulatory standards for drywall. The bill would direct the Consumer Product Safety Commission to set drywall-labeling regulations according to standards issued by ASTM International. It also would require the commission to issue a regulation limiting the sulfur content of drywall. Motion agreed to 378-37: R 195-37; D 183-0. A two-thirds majority of those present and voting (277 in this case) is required for passage under suspension of the rules. Jan. 1, 2013.

658. HR 8. Tax Rates Extensions/Rule. Adoption of the rule (H Res 844) that would provide for House floor consideration of the bill that would permanently extend the 2001 and 2003 tax rates for individual income below $400,000 and joint-filer income below $450,000 and would delay the automatic, across-the-board cuts known as sequester for two months. Adopted 408-10: R 232-2; D 176-8. Jan. 1, 2013.

659. HR 8. Tax Rates Extensions/Motion to Concur. Camp, R-Mich., motion to concur in the Senate amendments to the bill that would permanently extend the 2001 and 2003 tax rates for individual income below $400,000 and joint-filer income below $450,000. Rates for income above those thresholds would rise from 35 percent to 39.6 percent. It also would permanently extend the tax rates on dividends and capital gains for individual income below $400,000 and joint-filer income below $450,000. Rates for the dividends and capital gains taxes would rise to 20 percent for income above those thresholds. The measure would delay the automatic, across-the-board cuts known as sequester for two months. Half of the sequester delay would be offset by discretionary cuts, split between defense and non-defense, and the other half offset by revenue raised through the voluntary transfer of traditional IRAs to Roth IRAs, which would tax retirement savings when transferred. The measure also would tax individual estates valued at more than $5 million and joint estates valued at more than $10 million at 40 percent. It would permanently "patch" the alternative minimum tax to account for inflation. Unemployment insurance would be extended through 2013. The bill would block scheduled cuts to Medicare physician payment rates and extend for five years tax credits included in the 2009 stimulus law including the child tax credit and the earned income tax credit. It would allow the 2 percent payroll tax holiday to expire. It also would extend the Milk Income Loss Contract program at current rates. Motion agreed to (thus clearing the bill for the president) 257-167: R 85-151; D 172-16. A "yea" was a vote in support of the president's position. Jan. 1, 2013.

	655	656	657	658	659
ALABAMA					
1 Bonner	Y	Y	Y	Y	N
2 Roby	Y	Y	Y	Y	N
3 Rogers	Y	Y	Y	Y	N
4 Aderholt	Y	Y	Y	Y	N
5 Brooks	Y	Y	Y	Y	N
6 Bachus	Y	Y	Y	Y	N
7 Sewell	N	Y	Y	Y	Y
ALASKA					
AL Young	Y	Y	Y	Y	Y
ARIZONA					
1 Gosar	Y	Y	Y	Y	N
2 Franks	Y	Y	Y	Y	N
3 Quayle	Y	Y	N	Y	N
4 Pastor	N	Y	Y	Y	Y
5 Schweikert	Y	Y	Y	Y	N
6 Flake	Y	Y	N	Y	N
7 Grijalva	?	?	?	?	Y
8 Barber	Y	Y	Y	Y	Y
ARKANSAS					
1 Crawford	Y	Y	Y	Y	N
2 Griffin	Y	Y	Y	Y	N
3 Womack	Y	Y	Y	Y	N
4 Ross	Y	Y	Y	Y	Y
CALIFORNIA					
1 Thompson	N	Y	Y	Y	Y
2 Herger	Y	Y	Y	Y	Y
3 Lungren	Y	Y	Y	Y	Y
4 McClintock	Y	Y	N	Y	N
5 Matsui	N	Y	Y	Y	Y
6 Woolsey	?	?	?	?	?
7 Miller, George	?	Y	Y	Y	Y
8 Pelosi	N	Y	Y	Y	Y
9 Lee	N	Y	Y	Y	Y
10 Garamendi	Y	Y	Y	Y	Y
11 McNerney	Y	Y	Y	Y	Y
12 Speier	N	Y	Y	Y	Y
13 Stark	?	?	?	?	?
14 Eshoo	Y	Y	Y	Y	Y
15 Honda	N	Y	Y	Y	Y
16 Lofgren	Y	Y	Y	Y	Y
17 Farr	N	Y	Y	Y	Y
18 Vacant					
19 Denham	Y	Y	Y	Y	Y
20 Costa	N	Y	Y	Y	Y
21 Nunes	Y	Y	Y	Y	N
22 McCarthy	Y	Y	N	Y	N
23 Capps	Y	Y	Y	Y	Y
24 Gallegly	Y	Y	Y	Y	Y
25 McKeon	Y	Y	Y	Y	Y
26 Dreier	Y	Y	Y	Y	Y
27 Sherman	N	Y	Y	Y	Y
28 Berman	N	Y	Y	Y	Y
29 Schiff	N	Y	Y	Y	Y
30 Waxman	N	Y	Y	Y	Y
31 Becerra	N	Y	Y	Y	N
32 Chu	N	Y	Y	Y	Y
33 Bass	N	Y	Y	Y	Y
34 Roybal-Allard	N	Y	Y	Y	Y
35 Waters	N	Y	Y	Y	Y
36 Hahn	Y	Y	Y	Y	Y
37 Richardson	N	Y	Y	Y	Y
38 Napolitano	N	Y	Y	Y	Y
39 Sánchez, Linda	N	Y	Y	Y	Y
40 Royce	Y	Y	Y	Y	Y
41 Lewis	?	?	?	?	?
42 Miller, Gary	Y	Y	Y	Y	Y
43 Baca	N	Y	Y	Y	Y
44 Calvert	Y	Y	Y	Y	Y
45 Bono Mack	?	?	?	Y	Y
46 Rohrabacher	Y	Y	Y	Y	N
47 Sanchez, Loretta	N	Y	Y	Y	Y
48 Campbell	Y	Y	N	?	N
49 Issa	Y	Y	Y	Y	N
50 Bilbray	Y	Y	Y	Y	Y
51 Vacant					
52 Hunter	Y	Y	Y	Y	N
53 Davis	N	Y	Y	Y	Y

	655	656	657	658	659
COLORADO					
1 DeGette	N	Y	Y	Y	Y
2 Polis	Y	Y	Y	Y	Y
3 Tipton	Y	Y	Y	Y	N
4 Gardner	Y	Y	N	Y	N
5 Lamborn	Y	Y	N	Y	N
6 Coffman	Y	Y	Y	Y	N
7 Perlmutter	N	?	Y	Y	Y
CONNECTICUT					
1 Larson	N	Y	Y	Y	Y
2 Courtney	N	Y	Y	Y	Y
3 DeLauro	N	Y	Y	Y	N
4 Himes	N	Y	Y	Y	Y
5 Murphy	N	Y	Y	Y	Y
DELAWARE					
AL Carney	Y	Y	Y	Y	Y
FLORIDA					
1 Miller	Y	Y	Y	Y	N
2 Southerland	Y	Y	N	Y	N
3 Brown	N	Y	Y	Y	Y
4 Crenshaw	Y	Y	Y	Y	N
5 Nugent	Y	Y	Y	Y	N
6 Stearns	Y	Y	Y	Y	N
7 Mica	Y	Y	?	Y	N
8 Webster	Y	Y	Y	Y	N
9 Bilirakis	Y	Y	Y	Y	N
10 Young	Y	Y	Y	Y	Y
11 Castor	N	Y	Y	Y	Y
12 Ross	Y	Y	Y	Y	N
13 Buchanan	Y	Y	Y	Y	Y
14 Mack	?	?	?	Y	N
15 Posey	Y	Y	Y	N	N
16 Rooney	Y	Y	Y	Y	N
17 Wilson	N	Y	Y	Y	Y
18 Ros-Lehtinen	Y	Y	Y	Y	Y
19 Deutch	Y	Y	Y	Y	Y
20 Wasserman Schultz	Y	Y	Y	Y	Y
21 Diaz-Balart	Y	Y	Y	Y	Y
22 West	Y	Y	Y	Y	N
23 Hastings	N	Y	Y	Y	Y
24 Adams	Y	Y	Y	Y	N
25 Rivera	Y	Y	Y	Y	N
GEORGIA					
1 Kingston	Y	Y	N	Y	N
2 Bishop	N	Y	Y	Y	Y
3 Westmoreland	Y	Y	N	Y	N
4 Johnson	N	Y	Y	Y	Y
5 Lewis	?	?	?	?	?
6 Price	Y	Y	N	Y	N
7 Woodall	Y	Y	N	Y	N
8 Scott, A.	Y	Y	Y	Y	N
9 Graves	Y	Y	N	Y	N
10 Broun	Y	Y	N	Y	N
11 Gingrey	Y	Y	Y	Y	N
12 Barrow	Y	Y	Y	N	N
13 Scott, D.	N	Y	Y	Y	Y
HAWAII					
1 Hanabusa	N	Y	Y	Y	Y
2 Hirono	N	Y	Y	?	Y
IDAHO					
1 Labrador	Y	Y	N	Y	N
2 Simpson	Y	Y	Y	Y	Y
ILLINOIS					
1 Rush	N	Y	Y	Y	Y
2 Vacant					
3 Lipinski	Y	Y	Y	Y	Y
4 Gutierrez	N	Y	Y	Y	Y
5 Quigley	Y	Y	Y	Y	Y
6 Roskam	Y	Y	Y	Y	N
7 Davis	N	Y	Y	Y	Y
8 Walsh	Y	N	N	Y	N
9 Schakowsky	N	Y	Y	Y	Y
10 Dold	Y	Y	Y	Y	Y
11 Kinzinger	Y	Y	Y	Y	Y
12 Costello	N	Y	Y	Y	Y
13 Biggert	Y	Y	Y	Y	Y
14 Hultgren	Y	Y	Y	Y	N
15 Johnson	Y	Y	Y	Y	Y

KEY   **Republicans**   Democrats

Y	Voted for (yea)	X Paired against
#	Paired for	– Announced against
+	Announced for	P Voted "present"
N	Voted against (nay)	

C Voted "present" to avoid possible conflict of interest

? Did not vote or otherwise make a position known

	655	656	657	658	659
16 Manzullo	Y	Y	Y	Y	Y
17 Schilling	Y	Y	Y	Y	N
18 Schock	Y	Y	Y	Y	Y
19 Shimkus	Y	Y	Y	Y	Y
INDIANA					
1 Visclosky	N	Y	Y	N	N
2 Donnelly	Y	Y	Y	Y	Y
3 Stutzman	Y	Y	N	Y	N
4 Rokita	Y	?	Y	Y	N
5 Burton	?	?	?	?	?
6 Pence	Y	Y	N	Y	N
7 Carson	N	Y	Y	Y	Y
8 Bucshon	Y	Y	Y	Y	N
9 Young	Y	Y	Y	Y	N
IOWA					
1 Braley	Y	N	Y	Y	Y
2 Loebsack	Y	Y	Y	Y	Y
3 Boswell	Y	Y	Y	Y	Y
4 Latham	Y	Y	Y	Y	N
5 King	Y	Y	Y	Y	N
KANSAS					
1 Huelskamp	Y	Y	Y	Y	N
2 Jenkins	Y	Y	Y	Y	N
3 Yoder	Y	Y	Y	Y	N
4 Pompeo	Y	Y	N	Y	N
KENTUCKY					
1 Whitfield	Y	Y	Y	?	N
2 Guthrie	Y	Y	Y	Y	N
3 Yarmuth	N	Y	Y	Y	Y
4 Massie	Y	Y	N	Y	N
5 Rogers	Y	Y	Y	Y	Y
6 Chandler	Y	Y	Y	Y	Y
LOUISIANA					
1 Scalise	Y	Y	Y	Y	N
2 Richmond	N	Y	?	Y	Y
3 Landry	Y	Y	N	Y	N
4 Fleming	Y	Y	Y	Y	N
5 Alexander	Y	Y	Y	Y	Y
6 Cassidy	Y	Y	Y	Y	N
7 Boustany	Y	Y	Y	Y	N
MAINE					
1 Pingree	N	Y	Y	Y	Y
2 Michaud	Y	Y	Y	Y	Y
MARYLAND					
1 Harris	Y	Y	Y	Y	N
2 Ruppersberger	Y	Y	Y	Y	Y
3 Sarbanes	N	Y	Y	Y	Y
4 Edwards	N	Y	Y	Y	Y
5 Hoyer	N	Y	Y	Y	Y
6 Bartlett	?	?	?	Y	N
7 Cummings	N	Y	Y	Y	Y
8 Van Hollen	N	Y	Y	Y	Y
MASSACHUSETTS					
1 Olver	N	Y	Y	Y	Y
2 Neal	N	Y	Y	Y	Y
3 McGovern	N	Y	Y	Y	Y
4 Frank	?	?	?	Y	Y
5 Tsongas	N	Y	Y	Y	Y
6 Tierney	Y	Y	Y	Y	Y
7 Markey	N	Y	Y	Y	Y
8 Capuano	N	Y	Y	Y	Y
9 Lynch	N	Y	Y	Y	Y
10 Keating	Y	Y	Y	Y	Y
MICHIGAN					
1 Benishek	Y	Y	Y	Y	Y
2 Huizenga	Y	Y	Y	Y	N
3 Amash	Y	N	N	Y	N
4 Camp	Y	Y	Y	Y	Y
5 Kildee	N	Y	Y	Y	Y
6 Upton	Y	Y	Y	Y	Y
7 Walberg	Y	Y	Y	Y	N
8 Rogers	Y	Y	Y	Y	Y
9 Peters	N	Y	Y	Y	Y
10 Miller	Y	Y	Y	Y	Y
11 Curson	N	Y	Y	Y	Y
12 Levin	N	Y	Y	Y	Y
13 Clarke	N	Y	Y	Y	Y
14 Conyers	N	Y	Y	?	Y
15 Dingell	N	Y	Y	Y	Y
MINNESOTA					
1 Walz	Y	Y	Y	Y	Y
2 Kline	Y	Y	Y	Y	Y
3 Paulsen	Y	Y	Y	Y	N
4 McCollum	–	+	+	Y	Y

	655	656	657	658	659
5 Ellison	N	Y	Y	Y	Y
6 Bachmann	Y	Y	?	Y	N
7 Peterson	Y	Y	Y	N	N
8 Cravaack	Y	Y	Y	Y	N
MISSISSIPPI					
1 Nunnelee	Y	Y	Y	?	N
2 Thompson	N	N	Y	Y	Y
3 Harper	Y	Y	Y	Y	N
4 Palazzo	Y	Y	Y	Y	N
MISSOURI					
1 Clay	N	Y	Y	?	Y
2 Akin	Y	Y	Y	Y	N
3 Carnahan	Y	Y	Y	Y	Y
4 Hartzler	Y	Y	Y	Y	N
5 Cleaver	N	Y	Y	Y	Y
6 Graves	Y	Y	Y	Y	–
7 Long	Y	Y	Y	Y	N
8 Emerson	Y	Y	Y	Y	Y
9 Luetkemeyer	Y	Y	Y	Y	Y
MONTANA					
AL Rehberg	Y	Y	Y	Y	N
NEBRASKA					
1 Fortenberry	Y	Y	Y	Y	Y
2 Terry	Y	Y	Y	Y	N
3 Smith	Y	Y	Y	Y	N
NEVADA					
1 Berkley	N	Y	Y	Y	Y
2 Amodei	Y	Y	Y	Y	N
3 Heck	Y	Y	Y	Y	Y
NEW HAMPSHIRE					
1 Guinta	Y	Y	Y	Y	N
2 Bass	Y	Y	Y	?	Y
NEW JERSEY					
1 Andrews	Y	Y	Y	Y	Y
2 LoBiondo	Y	Y	Y	Y	Y
3 Runyan	Y	Y	Y	Y	Y
4 Smith	Y	Y	Y	Y	Y
5 Garrett	Y	Y	Y	Y	N
6 Pallone	N	Y	Y	Y	Y
7 Lance	Y	Y	Y	Y	Y
8 Pascrell	N	Y	Y	Y	Y
9 Rothman	N	Y	Y	Y	Y
10 Payne, Jr.	N	Y	Y	Y	Y
11 Frelinghuysen	Y	Y	Y	Y	Y
12 Holt	N	Y	Y	Y	Y
13 Sires	N	Y	Y	Y	Y
NEW MEXICO					
1 Heinrich	Y	Y	Y	Y	Y
2 Pearce	Y	Y	Y	Y	N
3 Luján	Y	Y	Y	Y	Y
NEW YORK					
1 Bishop	Y	Y	Y	Y	Y
2 Israel	Y	Y	Y	Y	Y
3 King	Y	Y	Y	Y	Y
4 McCarthy	?	?	?	Y	Y
5 Ackerman	N	Y	Y	Y	Y
6 Meeks	N	Y	Y	Y	Y
7 Crowley	N	Y	Y	Y	Y
8 Nadler	N	Y	Y	Y	Y
9 Turner	Y	Y	Y	Y	Y
10 Towns	N	Y	Y	Y	Y
11 Clarke	N	Y	Y	Y	Y
12 Velázquez	N	Y	Y	Y	Y
13 Grimm	Y	Y	Y	Y	Y
14 Maloney	N	Y	Y	Y	Y
15 Rangel	Y	Y	Y	Y	Y
16 Serrano	N	Y	Y	Y	Y
17 Engel	N	Y	Y	Y	Y
18 Lowey	Y	Y	Y	Y	Y
19 Hayworth	Y	Y	Y	Y	Y
20 Gibson	Y	Y	Y	Y	Y
21 Tonko	N	Y	Y	Y	Y
22 Hinchey	N	Y	Y	Y	Y
23 Owens	Y	Y	Y	Y	Y
24 Hanna	Y	Y	Y	Y	Y
25 Buerkle	Y	Y	N	Y	–
26 Hochul	Y	Y	Y	Y	Y
27 Higgins	N	Y	Y	Y	Y
28 Slaughter	N	Y	Y	Y	Y
29 Reed	Y	Y	N	Y	Y
NORTH CAROLINA					
1 Butterfield	N	Y	Y	Y	Y
2 Ellmers	Y	Y	Y	Y	N
3 Jones	Y	Y	N	Y	N
4 Price	N	Y	Y	Y	Y

	655	656	657	658	659
5 Foxx	Y	Y	Y	Y	N
6 Coble	Y	Y	Y	Y	Y
7 McIntyre	Y	Y	Y	Y	N
8 Kissell	Y	Y	Y	Y	N
9 Myrick	Y	Y	Y	Y	N
10 McHenry	Y	Y	Y	Y	N
11 Shuler	N	Y	Y	Y	Y
12 Watt	N	Y	Y	Y	Y
13 Miller	N	Y	Y	Y	N
NORTH DAKOTA					
AL Berg	Y	Y	Y	Y	N
OHIO					
1 Chabot	Y	Y	Y	Y	N
2 Schmidt	Y	Y	N	N	N
3 Turner	Y	Y	Y	Y	Y
4 Jordan	Y	Y	N	Y	N
5 Latta	Y	Y	Y	Y	Y
6 Johnson	Y	Y	Y	Y	Y
7 Austria	Y	Y	Y	Y	N
8 Boehner			Y	Y	Y
9 Kaptur	N	Y	Y	Y	Y
10 Kucinich	N	Y	Y	Y	Y
11 Fudge	N	Y	Y	Y	Y
12 Tiberi	Y	Y	Y	Y	Y
13 Sutton	?	Y	Y	Y	Y
14 LaTourette	Y	Y	Y	Y	Y
15 Stivers	Y	Y	Y	Y	Y
16 Renacci	Y	Y	Y	Y	N
17 Ryan	Y	Y	Y	Y	Y
18 Gibbs	Y	Y	Y	Y	N
OKLAHOMA					
1 Sullivan	Y	Y	Y	Y	Y
2 Boren	Y	Y	Y	Y	Y
3 Lucas	Y	Y	Y	Y	Y
4 Cole	Y	Y	Y	Y	Y
5 Lankford	Y	Y	Y	Y	N
OREGON					
1 Bonamici	N	Y	Y	Y	Y
2 Walden	Y	Y	Y	Y	Y
3 Blumenauer	N	Y	Y	N	N
4 DeFazio	Y	Y	Y	N	N
5 Schrader	N	Y	Y	Y	N
PENNSYLVANIA					
1 Brady	N	Y	Y	Y	Y
2 Fattah	N	Y	Y	Y	Y
3 Kelly	Y	Y	Y	Y	Y
4 Altmire	Y	Y	Y	Y	Y
5 Thompson	Y	Y	Y	Y	Y
6 Gerlach	Y	Y	Y	Y	Y
7 Meehan	Y	Y	Y	Y	Y
8 Fitzpatrick	Y	Y	Y	Y	Y
9 Shuster	Y	Y	Y	Y	Y
10 Marino	Y	Y	Y	Y	Y
11 Barletta	Y	Y	Y	Y	Y
12 Critz	N	Y	Y	Y	Y
13 Schwartz	Y	Y	Y	Y	Y
14 Doyle	N	Y	Y	Y	Y
15 Dent	Y	Y	Y	Y	Y
16 Pitts	Y	Y	Y	Y	Y
17 Holden	N	Y	Y	Y	Y
18 Murphy	Y	Y	Y	Y	Y
19 Platts	Y	Y	Y	Y	Y
RHODE ISLAND					
1 Cicilline	Y	Y	Y	Y	Y
2 Langevin	Y	Y	Y	Y	Y
SOUTH CAROLINA					
1 Scott	Y	Y	Y	Y	N
2 Wilson	Y	Y	Y	Y	N
3 Duncan	Y	Y	N	Y	N
4 Gowdy	Y	Y	Y	Y	N
5 Mulvaney	Y	N	N	Y	N
6 Clyburn	N	Y	Y	Y	Y
SOUTH DAKOTA					
AL Noem	Y	Y	Y	Y	Y
TENNESSEE					
1 Roe	Y	Y	Y	Y	N
2 Duncan	Y	Y	Y	Y	N
3 Fleischmann	Y	Y	Y	Y	N
4 DesJarlais	Y	Y	Y	Y	N
5 Cooper	Y	Y	Y	Y	Y
6 Black	Y	Y	Y	Y	N
7 Blackburn	Y	Y	Y	Y	N
8 Fincher	Y	Y	Y	Y	N
9 Cohen	N	Y	Y	Y	Y

	655	656	657	658	659
TEXAS					
1 Gohmert	Y	Y	N	Y	N
2 Poe	Y	Y	N	Y	N
3 Johnson, S.	Y	Y	Y	Y	N
4 Hall	Y	Y	Y	Y	Y
5 Hensarling	Y	Y	N	Y	N
6 Barton	Y	Y	Y	Y	N
7 Culberson	Y	Y	Y	Y	N
8 Brady	Y	?	Y	Y	Y
9 Green, A.	N	Y	Y	Y	Y
10 McCaul	Y	Y	Y	Y	N
11 Conaway	Y	Y	Y	Y	N
12 Granger	Y	Y	Y	Y	N
13 Thornberry	Y	Y	Y	Y	Y
14 Paul	?	?	?	?	?
15 Hinojosa	N	Y	Y	Y	Y
16 Reyes	N	Y	Y	Y	Y
17 Flores	Y	Y	Y	Y	N
18 Jackson Lee	N	Y	Y	Y	Y
19 Neugebauer	N	Y	Y	Y	Y
20 Gonzalez	N	Y	Y	Y	Y
21 Smith	Y	Y	Y	Y	N
22 Olson	Y	Y	Y	Y	N
23 Canseco	Y	Y	Y	Y	N
24 Marchant	Y	Y	N	Y	N
25 Doggett	N	Y	Y	Y	Y
26 Burgess	Y	Y	Y	Y	N
27 Farenthold	Y	Y	Y	Y	N
28 Cuellar	Y	Y	Y	Y	Y
29 Green, G.	N	Y	Y	Y	Y
30 Johnson, E.	N	Y	Y	Y	Y
31 Carter	Y	Y	Y	Y	N
32 Sessions	Y	Y	Y	Y	N
UTAH					
1 Bishop	Y	N	N	Y	N
2 Matheson	Y	Y	Y	Y	N
3 Chaffetz	Y	N	N	Y	N
VERMONT					
AL Welch	N	Y	Y	Y	Y
VIRGINIA					
1 Wittman	N	Y	Y	Y	N
2 Rigell	Y	Y	Y	Y	N
3 Scott	N	Y	N	N	N
4 Forbes	Y	Y	Y	Y	N
5 Hurt	Y	Y	Y	Y	N
6 Goodlatte	Y	Y	N	Y	N
7 Cantor	Y	Y	Y	Y	N
8 Moran	N	Y	Y	N	N
9 Griffith	Y	Y	Y	Y	N
10 Wolf	Y	Y	Y	Y	N
11 Connolly	N	Y	Y	Y	Y
WASHINGTON					
1 DelBene	Y	Y	Y	Y	Y
2 Larsen	N	Y	Y	Y	Y
3 Herrera Beutler	Y	Y	Y	Y	Y
4 Hastings	Y	Y	Y	Y	Y
5 McMorris Rodgers	Y	Y	Y	Y	Y
6 Dicks	N	Y	Y	Y	Y
7 McDermott	N	Y	Y	N	N
8 Reichert	Y	Y	Y	Y	Y
9 Smith	N	Y	Y	Y	N
WEST VIRGINIA					
1 McKinley	Y	Y	Y	Y	Y
2 Capito	Y	Y	Y	Y	N
3 Rahall	Y	Y	Y	Y	Y
WISCONSIN					
1 Ryan	Y	Y	Y	Y	Y
2 Baldwin	Y	Y	Y	Y	Y
3 Kind	Y	Y	Y	Y	Y
4 Moore	N	Y	Y	Y	Y
5 Sensenbrenner	Y	Y	N	Y	N
6 Petri	Y	Y	Y	Y	Y
7 Duffy	Y	Y	Y	Y	Y
8 Ribble	Y	Y	Y	Y	Y
WYOMING					
AL Lummis	Y	Y	N	Y	N

House Roll Call Index by Subject

SENATE VOTES

Senate Roll Call Index By Bill Number

IN THE SENATE | By Vote Number

1. Gerrard Nomination/Confirmation. Confirmation of President Obama's nomination of John M. Gerrard of Nebraska to be a judge for the U.S. District Court for the District of Nebraska. Confirmed 74-16: D 48-0; R 26-16. A "yea" was a vote in support of the president's position. Jan. 23, 2012.

2. H J Res 98. Debt Limit Disapproval/Motion to Proceed. McConnell, R-Ky., motion to proceed to the joint resolution that would disapprove of a request by the president for a $1.2 trillion debt limit increase. Current law provides for a $1.2 trillion increase in the debt limit upon certification from the president that the debt is within $100 billion of the debt limit unless a disapproval measure is enacted. Motion rejected 44-52: D 2-49; R 42-1; I 0-2. A "nay" was a vote in support of the president's position. Jan. 26, 2012.

3. S 2038. Congressional Insider-Trading Ban/Cloture. Motion to invoke cloture (thus limiting debate) on the Reid, D-Nev., motion to proceed to the bill that would prohibit stock trading by members of Congress and aides using information obtained in the course of their duties. Motion agreed to 93-2 : D 49-0; R 42-2; I 2-0. Three-fifths of the total Senate (60) is required to invoke cloture. Jan. 30, 2012.

4. S 2038. Congressional Insider-Trading Ban/Certification. Paul, R-Ky., substitute amendment that would require senators to sign a statement each year to certify that they have not violated existing laws and regulations against insider trading. Rejected 37-61: D 7-44; R 30-15; I 0-2. Feb. 2, 2012.

5. S 2038. Congressional Insider-Trading Ban/Executive Branch. Paul, R-Ky., amendment to the Reid, D-Nev., substitute amendment. The Paul amendment would extend stock-trading disclosure requirements to executive branch officials in addition to lawmakers. It would prohibit executive branch appointees or staff from holding positions giving them oversight, rule-making, loan or grant-making abilities over industries or companies in which they or their spouse have a significant financial interest. The substitute would clarify that members of Congress and their aides are covered by current Securities and Exchange Commission regulations barring the use of non-public information for trading stocks and bonds. Rejected 48-51: D 10-41; R 38-8; I 0-2. (By unanimous consent, the Senate agreed to raise the majority requirement for adoption of the Paul amendment to 60 votes.) Feb. 2, 2012.

6. S 2038. Congressional Insider-Trading Ban/Senior Executive Branch Officials. Lieberman, I-Conn., amendment to the Reid, D-Nev., substitute amendment. The Lieberman amendment would extend reporting provisions of the substitute to many executive branch officials subject to Senate confirmation and some other senior officials. It would prohibit executive branch appointees or staff from holding positions giving them oversight, rule-making, loan or grant-making abilities over industries or companies in which they or their spouse have a significant financial interest. Adopted 81-18: D 50-1; R 29-17; I 2-0. Feb. 2, 2012.

State / Senator	1	2	3	4	5	6
ALABAMA						
Shelby	N	Y	Y	Y	Y	N
Sessions	N	Y	Y	?	Y	N
ALASKA						
Murkowski	Y	Y	Y	N	N	Y
Begich	Y	N	Y	N	N	Y
ARIZONA						
McCain	Y	?	Y	N	Y	Y
Kyl	Y	Y	Y	Y	Y	Y
ARKANSAS						
Pryor	Y	N	Y	N	N	Y
Boozman	N	Y	Y	N	Y	Y
CALIFORNIA						
Feinstein	Y	N	Y	N	N	Y
Boxer	Y	N	Y	N	N	Y
COLORADO						
Udall	Y	N	Y	N	N	Y
Bennet	Y	N	Y	N	N	Y
CONNECTICUT						
Lieberman	?	N	Y	N	N	Y
Blumenthal	Y	N	Y	N	N	Y
DELAWARE						
Carper	Y	N	Y	N	Y	Y
Coons	Y	N	Y	N	N	Y
FLORIDA						
Nelson	Y	N	Y	N	Y	Y
Rubio	N	Y	Y	N	Y	Y
GEORGIA						
Chambliss	?	?	Y	Y	Y	N
Isakson	N	Y	+	N	Y	Y
HAWAII						
Inouye	Y	N	Y	N	N	Y
Akaka	Y	N	Y	N	N	Y
IDAHO						
Crapo	Y	Y	Y	Y	Y	Y
Risch	N	Y	Y	Y	Y	Y
ILLINOIS						
Durbin	Y	N	Y	N	N	Y
Kirk	?	?	?	?	?	?
INDIANA						
Lugar	Y	Y	Y	Y	Y	N
Coats	Y	Y	Y	Y	Y	Y
IOWA						
Grassley	Y	Y	Y	N	Y	Y
Harkin	Y	N	Y	N	N	Y
KANSAS						
Roberts	Y	Y	Y	Y	Y	Y
Moran	Y	Y	Y	Y	Y	N
KENTUCKY						
McConnell	Y	Y	Y	Y	Y	N
Paul	N	Y	Y	Y	Y	Y
LOUISIANA						
Landrieu	Y	N	?	N	N	Y
Vitter	N	Y	Y	N	Y	N
MAINE						
Snowe	Y	Y	Y	N	Y	Y
Collins	Y	Y	Y	N	N	Y
MARYLAND						
Mikulski	?	N	Y	N	N	Y
Cardin	Y	N	Y	N	N	Y
MASSACHUSETTS						
Kerry	Y	N	Y	N	N	Y
Brown	Y	N	Y	N	N	Y
MICHIGAN						
Levin	Y	N	Y	N	Y	Y
Stabenow	Y	N	Y	N	Y	Y
MINNESOTA						
Klobuchar	Y	N	Y	N	Y	Y
Franken	Y	N	Y	N	N	Y
MISSISSIPPI						
Cochran	Y	Y	Y	Y	N	Y
Wicker	N	Y	?	Y	N	N
MISSOURI						
McCaskill	Y	N	Y	N	N	Y
Blunt	Y	Y	Y	Y	Y	Y

State / Senator	1	2	3	4	5	6
MONTANA						
Baucus	Y	N	Y	N	N	Y
Tester	Y	N	Y	N	N	Y
NEBRASKA						
Nelson	Y	Y	Y	Y	Y	Y
Johanns	Y	Y	Y	N	N	Y
NEVADA						
Reid	Y	N	Y	N	N	Y
Heller	Y	Y	Y	N	Y	Y
NEW HAMPSHIRE						
Shaheen	Y	N	Y	N	N	Y
Ayotte	Y	Y	Y	Y	Y	Y
NEW JERSEY						
Lautenberg	?	N	Y	N	N	Y
Menendez	Y	N	+	N	Y	Y
NEW MEXICO						
Bingaman	Y	N	Y	N	N	N
Udall	Y	N	Y	N	N	Y
NEW YORK						
Schumer	Y	N	Y	N	N	Y
Gillibrand	Y	N	Y	N	N	Y
NORTH CAROLINA						
Burr	Y	Y	N	Y	Y	Y
Hagan	?	N	Y	N	N	Y
NORTH DAKOTA						
Conrad	Y	N	Y	N	Y	Y
Hoeven	?	Y	Y	Y	N	Y
OHIO						
Brown	Y	N	Y	N	N	Y
Portman	Y	Y	Y	N	N	N
OKLAHOMA						
Inhofe	N	Y	Y	N	Y	Y
Coburn	N	Y	N	Y	Y	N
OREGON						
Wyden	Y	N	Y	N	N	Y
Merkley	Y	N	Y	N	N	Y
PENNSYLVANIA						
Casey	Y	N	Y	N	Y	Y
Toomey	N	Y	Y	Y	Y	N
RHODE ISLAND						
Reed	Y	N	Y	N	N	Y
Whitehouse	Y	N	Y	N	N	Y
SOUTH CAROLINA						
Graham	?	Y	Y	Y	Y	Y
DeMint	N	Y	Y	Y	Y	N
SOUTH DAKOTA						
Johnson	Y	N	Y	N	N	Y
Thune	Y	Y	Y	Y	Y	Y
TENNESSEE						
Alexander	Y	Y	Y	Y	Y	Y
Corker	Y	+	Y	Y	Y	Y
TEXAS						
Hutchison	Y	Y	Y	N	Y	Y
Cornyn	N	Y	Y	Y	Y	Y
UTAH						
Hatch	+	Y	Y	Y	Y	Y
Lee	N	Y	Y	Y	Y	N
VERMONT						
Leahy	Y	N	Y	Y	N	Y
Sanders	?	N	Y	N	N	Y
VIRGINIA						
Webb	Y	N	Y	N	Y	Y
Warner	Y	N	Y	N	Y	Y
WASHINGTON						
Murray	Y	N	Y	N	N	Y
Cantwell	Y	N	Y	N	N	Y
WEST VIRGINIA						
Rockefeller	Y	N	Y	N	N	Y
Manchin	Y	Y	Y	N	N	Y
WISCONSIN						
Kohl	Y	N	Y	N	N	Y
Johnson	N	Y	Y	Y	Y	Y
WYOMING						
Enzi	Y	Y	Y	Y	Y	N
Barrasso	Y	Y	Y	Y	Y	N

KEY — **Republicans**   Democrats   *Independents*

Y Voted for (yea)	X Paired against	C Voted "present" to avoid possible conflict of interest
# Paired for	– Announced against	
+ Announced for	P Voted "present"	? Did not vote or otherwise make a position known
N Voted against (nay)		

IN THE SENATE | By Vote Number

7. S 2038. Congressional Insider-Trading Ban/Executive Branch.
Shelby, R-Ala., amendment to the Reid, D-Nev., substitute amendment. The Shelby amendment would extend reporting provisions of the substitute to executive branch employees in addition to lawmakers. It would prohibit executive branch appointees or staff from holding positions giving them oversight, rule-making, loan or grant-making abilities over industries or companies in which they or their spouse have a significant financial interest. Adopted 58-41: D 12-39; R 46-0; I 0-2. Feb. 2, 2012.

8. S 2038. Congressional Insider-Trading Ban/Earmark Prohibition.
Toomey, R-Pa., amendment to the Reid, D-Nev., substitute amendment. The Toomey amendment would prohibit the congressional practice of targeting money to individual projects in spending and authorization bills, known as earmarking, by establishing points of order in the House and Senate against the practice. Rejected 40-59: D 7-44; R 33-13; I 0-2. (By unanimous consent, the Senate agreed to raise the majority requirement for adoption of the Toomey amendment to 60 votes.) Feb. 2, 2012.

9. Congressional Insider-Trading Ban/Unauthorized Earmark Prohibition.
Inhofe, R-Okla., amendment to the Reid, D-Nev., substitute amendment. The Inhofe amendment would prohibit earmarks that have not been included in authorizing legislation from being included in bills, amendments, joint resolutions and other legislative vehicles. The prohibition could be waived only by the vote of three-fourths of the Senate. Rejected 26-73: D 6-45; R 20-26; I 0-2. (By unanimous consent, the Senate agreed to raise the majority requirement for adoption of the Inhofe amendment to 60 votes.) Feb. 2, 2012.

10. S 2038. Congressional Insider-Trading Ban/CRS Reporting Requirements.
Coburn, R-Okla., amendment to the Reid, D-Nev., substitute amendment. The Coburn amendment would amend Senate rules to require the Congressional Research Service to conduct an analysis of legislation before it reaches the Senate floor to determine if the bill would create duplicative government programs. Rejected 60-39: D 14-37; R 46-0; I 0-2. (By unanimous consent, the Senate agreed to raise the majority requirement for adoption of the Coburn amendment to two-thirds of senators present and voting [66 in this case].) Feb. 2, 2012.

	7	8	9	10			7	8	9	10
ALABAMA						**MONTANA**				
Shelby	Y	N	Y	Y		Baucus	N	N	N	N
Sessions	Y	N	Y	Y		Tester	N	N	N	Y
ALASKA						**NEBRASKA**				
Murkowski	Y	N	Y	Y		Nelson	Y	N	N	Y
Begich	N	N	Y	Y		**Johanns**	Y	Y	N	Y
ARIZONA						**NEVADA**				
McCain	Y	Y	N	Y		Reid	N	N	N	N
Kyl	Y	Y	Y	Y		**Heller**	Y	Y	N	Y
ARKANSAS						**NEW HAMPSHIRE**				
Pryor	Y	N	N	Y		Shaheen	Y	N	N	N
Boozman	Y	Y	N	Y		**Ayotte**	Y	Y	N	Y
CALIFORNIA						**NEW JERSEY**				
Feinstein	N	N	N	N		Lautenberg	N	N	N	N
Boxer	N	N	Y	N		Menendez	N	N	N	N
COLORADO						**NEW MEXICO**				
Udall	N	Y	N	Y		Bingaman	N	N	N	N
Bennet	N	Y	N	Y		Udall	N	N	N	N
CONNECTICUT						**NEW YORK**				
Lieberman	N	N	N	N		Schumer	N	N	N	N
Blumenthal	N	N	N	N		Gillibrand	N	N	N	N
DELAWARE						**NORTH CAROLINA**				
Carper	N	N	N	N		**Burr**	Y	Y	N	Y
Coons	N	N	N	N		Hagan	N	Y	N	N
FLORIDA						**NORTH DAKOTA**				
Nelson	Y	Y	Y	Y		Conrad	N	N	N	N
Rubio	Y	Y	N	Y		**Hoeven**	Y	N	N	Y
GEORGIA						**OHIO**				
Chambliss	Y	Y	Y	Y		Brown	N	N	N	N
Isakson	Y	Y	Y	Y		**Portman**	Y	Y	Y	Y
HAWAII						**OKLAHOMA**				
Inouye	N	N	N	N		**Inhofe**	Y	N	Y	Y
Akaka	N	N	N	N		**Coburn**	Y	Y	N	Y
IDAHO						**OREGON**				
Crapo	Y	Y	N	Y		Wyden	Y	N	N	N
Risch	Y	Y	N	Y		Merkley	Y	N	N	Y
ILLINOIS						**PENNSYLVANIA**				
Durbin	N	N	N	N		Casey	N	N	Y	Y
Kirk	?	?	?	?		**Toomey**	Y	Y	N	Y
INDIANA						**RHODE ISLAND**				
Lugar	Y	N	N	Y		Reed	N	N	N	N
Coats	Y	Y	N	Y		Whitehouse	N	N	N	N
IOWA						**SOUTH CAROLINA**				
Grassley	Y	Y	N	Y		**Graham**	Y	Y	Y	Y
Harkin	N	N	N	N		**DeMint**	Y	Y	N	Y
KANSAS						**SOUTH DAKOTA**				
Roberts	Y	N	Y	Y		Johnson	N	N	N	N
Moran	Y	Y	N	Y		**Thune**	Y	Y	Y	Y
KENTUCKY						**TENNESSEE**				
McConnell	Y	Y	N	Y		**Alexander**	Y	N	Y	N
Paul	Y	Y	N	Y		**Corker**	Y	Y	Y	Y
LOUISIANA						**TEXAS**				
Landrieu	N	N	N	N		**Hutchison**	Y	N	Y	Y
Vitter	Y	N	Y	Y		**Cornyn**	Y	Y	N	Y
MAINE						**UTAH**				
Snowe	Y	Y	Y	Y		**Hatch**	Y	Y	N	Y
Collins	Y	N	Y	Y		**Lee**	Y	Y	N	Y
MARYLAND						**VERMONT**				
Mikulski	N	N	N	N		Leahy	N	N	N	N
Cardin	N	N	N	N		*Sanders*	N	N	N	N
MASSACHUSETTS						**VIRGINIA**				
Kerry	Y	N	N	N		Webb	N	N	N	N
Brown	Y	Y	Y	Y		Warner	N	Y	N	Y
MICHIGAN						**WASHINGTON**				
Levin	N	N	N	N		Murray	N	N	N	N
Stabenow	Y	Y	Y	Y		Cantwell	Y	N	N	N
MINNESOTA						**WEST VIRGINIA**				
Klobuchar	Y	N	N	Y		Rockefeller	N	N	N	N
Franken	N	N	N	N		Manchin	Y	N	N	Y
MISSISSIPPI						**WISCONSIN**				
Cochran	Y	N	Y	Y		Kohl	N	N	Y	N
Wicker	Y	N	Y	Y		**Johnson**	Y	Y	N	Y
MISSOURI						**WYOMING**				
McCaskill	Y	Y	N	Y		**Enzi**	Y	Y	N	Y
Blunt	Y	N	Y	Y		**Barrasso**	Y	Y	N	Y

KEY	**Republicans**	Democrats	*Independents*		
Y	Voted for (yea)	X	Paired against	C	Voted "present" to avoid possible conflict of interest
#	Paired for	−	Announced against		
+	Announced for	P	Voted "present"	?	Did not vote or otherwise make a position known
N	Voted against (nay)				

IN THE SENATE | By Vote Number

11. **S 2038. Congressional Insider-Trading Ban/Congressional Term Limits.** DeMint, R-S.C., amendment to the Reid, D-Nev., substitute amendment. The DeMint amendment would express the sense of the Senate in support of amending the Constitution to provide for congressional term limits. Rejected 24-75: D 1-50; R 23-23; I 0-2. (By unanimous consent, the Senate agreed to raise the majority requirement for adoption of the DeMint amendment to 60 votes.) Feb. 2, 2012.

12. **S 2038. Congressional Insider-Trading Ban/Political Intelligence Registration.** Grassley, R-Iowa, amendment to the Reid, D-Nev., substitute amendment. The Grassley amendment would require a new category, "political intelligence" consultants, to register in a manner similar to lobbyists. Adopted 60-39: D 27-24; R 32-14; I 1-1. (By unanimous consent, the Senate agreed to raise the majority requirement for adoption of the Grassley amendment to 60 votes.) Feb. 2, 2012.

13. **S 2038. Congressional Insider-Trading Ban/Investment Prohibition.** Brown, D-Ohio, amendment to the Reid, D-Nev., substitute amendment that would require lawmakers to either divest of stock and security holdings in industries they have jurisdiction over through their congressional work, or place them in blind trusts. Rejected 26-73: D 20-31; R 5-41; I 1-1. (By unanimous consent, the Senate agreed to raise the majority requirement for adoption of the Brown amendment to 60 votes.) Feb. 2, 2012.

14. **S 2038. Congressional Insider-Trading Ban/Passage.** Passage of the bill that would clarify that members of Congress and their aides are covered by current Securities and Exchange Commission regulations that bar the use of non-public information for trading stocks and bonds. The bill would state that existing House and Senate ethics rules bar lawmakers from voting on legislation on which they have a conflict of interest. It would require lawmakers and congressional aides who already file annual financial disclosure statements to report stock and bond transactions within 30 days of the transaction. The information would be posted on a publicly available website. The bill would require lawmakers to disclose more financial data on their home mortgages and would prohibit the payment of bonuses to Fannie Mae and Freddie Mac executives while the two mortgage giants are under government conservatorship. Passed 96-3: D 50-1; R 44-2; I 2-0. A "yea" was a vote in support of the president's position. Feb. 2, 2012.

	11	12	13	14		11	12	13	14
ALABAMA					**MONTANA**				
Shelby	N	Y	N	Y	Baucus	N	N	N	Y
Sessions	Y	Y	N	Y	Tester	N	Y	N	Y
ALASKA					**NEBRASKA**				
Murkowski	N	Y	Y	Y	Nelson	N	N	N	Y
Begich	N	Y	N	Y	**Johanns**	Y	N	N	Y
ARIZONA					**NEVADA**				
McCain	N	Y	N	Y	Reid	N	N	N	Y
Kyl	N	N	N	Y	**Heller**	Y	Y	Y	Y
ARKANSAS					**NEW HAMPSHIRE**				
Pryor	N	N	Y	Y	Shaheen	N	N	Y	Y
Boozman	Y	Y	N	Y	**Ayotte**	Y	Y	N	Y
CALIFORNIA					**NEW JERSEY**				
Feinstein	N	Y	N	Y	Lautenberg	N	Y	N	Y
Boxer	N	N	N	Y	Menendez	N	Y	Y	Y
COLORADO					**NEW MEXICO**				
Udall	N	Y	Y	Y	Bingaman	N	N	N	N
Bennet	N	Y	N	Y	Udall	N	N	Y	Y
CONNECTICUT					**NEW YORK**				
Lieberman	N	N	N	Y	Schumer	N	N	N	Y
Blumenthal	N	N	Y	Y	Gillibrand	N	Y	N	Y
DELAWARE					**NORTH CAROLINA**				
Carper	N	Y	Y	Y	**Burr**	N	N	N	N
Coons	N	N	N	Y	Hagan	N	N	N	Y
FLORIDA					**NORTH DAKOTA**				
Nelson	N	Y	N	Y	Conrad	N	N	N	Y
Rubio	Y	Y	N	Y	**Hoeven**	N	Y	N	Y
GEORGIA					**OHIO**				
Chambliss	N	Y	N	Y	Brown	N	Y	Y	Y
Isakson	N	Y	N	Y	**Portman**	Y	Y	N	Y
HAWAII					**OKLAHOMA**				
Inouye	N	N	N	Y	**Inhofe**	N	Y	N	Y
Akaka	N	N	N	Y	**Coburn**	Y	Y	N	N
IDAHO					**OREGON**				
Crapo	N	N	N	Y	Wyden	N	Y	Y	Y
Risch	N	N	N	Y	Merkley	N	Y	Y	Y
ILLINOIS					**PENNSYLVANIA**				
Durbin	N	N	N	Y	Casey	N	Y	Y	Y
Kirk	?	?	?	?	**Toomey**	Y	N	N	Y
INDIANA					**RHODE ISLAND**				
Lugar	N	Y	N	Y	Reed	N	Y	Y	Y
Coats	N	Y	N	Y	Whitehouse	N	Y	Y	Y
IOWA					**SOUTH CAROLINA**				
Grassley	Y	Y	N	Y	**Graham**	Y	Y	N	Y
Harkin	N	N	N	Y	**DeMint**	Y	Y	N	Y
KANSAS					**SOUTH DAKOTA**				
Roberts	N	Y	N	Y	Johnson	N	N	N	Y
Moran	Y	Y	N	Y	**Thune**	Y	Y	N	Y
KENTUCKY					**TENNESSEE**				
McConnell	N	N	N	Y	**Alexander**	N	N	N	Y
Paul	Y	Y	N	Y	**Corker**	Y	Y	N	Y
LOUISIANA					**TEXAS**				
Landrieu	N	N	N	Y	**Hutchison**	Y	Y	Y	Y
Vitter	Y	N	N	Y	**Cornyn**	N	N	N	Y
MAINE					**UTAH**				
Snowe	N	Y	Y	Y	**Hatch**	Y	Y	N	Y
Collins	N	N	N	Y	**Lee**	Y	Y	N	Y
MARYLAND					**VERMONT**				
Mikulski	N	N	N	Y	Leahy	N	Y	N	Y
Cardin	N	Y	N	Y	*Sanders*	N	Y	Y	Y
MASSACHUSETTS					**VIRGINIA**				
Kerry	N	Y	Y	Y	Webb	N	N	N	Y
Brown	Y	N	Y	Y	Warner	N	N	N	Y
MICHIGAN					**WASHINGTON**				
Levin	N	N	Y	Y	Murray	N	Y	N	Y
Stabenow	N	Y	Y	Y	Cantwell	N	Y	N	Y
MINNESOTA					**WEST VIRGINIA**				
Klobuchar	N	Y	Y	Y	Rockefeller	N	N	N	Y
Franken	N	Y	Y	Y	Manchin	Y	Y	Y	Y
MISSISSIPPI					**WISCONSIN**				
Cochran	N	N	N	Y	Kohl	N	Y	N	Y
Wicker	N	Y	N	Y	**Johnson**	Y	Y	N	Y
MISSOURI					**WYOMING**				
McCaskill	N	Y	Y	Y	**Enzi**	N	Y	N	Y
Blunt	Y	Y	N	Y	**Barrasso**	N	Y	N	Y

KEY   **Republicans**   Democrats   *Independents*

Y	Voted for (yea)	X	Paired against
#	Paired for	–	Announced against
+	Announced for	P	Voted "present"
N	Voted against (nay)	C	Voted "present" to avoid possible conflict of interest
		?	Did not vote or otherwise make a position known

IN THE SENATE | By Vote Number

15. **HR 658. FAA Reauthorization/Conference Report.** Adoption of the conference report on the bill that would authorize $15.9 billion annually for federal aviation programs through fiscal 2015. The measure would increase the proportion of eligible members of the National Mediation Board needed to petition for new union elections from 35 percent to 50 percent. It would increase by 16 the number of slots permitted for long-distance flights in and out of Ronald Reagan Washington National Airport. Adopted (thus cleared for the president) 75-20: D 36-14; R 38-5; I 1-1. (By unanimous consent, the Senate agreed to raise the majority requirement for adoption of the conference report to 60 votes.) Feb. 6, 2012.

16. **Bencivengo Nomination/Confirmation.** Confirmation of President Obama's nomination of Cathy Ann Bencivengo of California to be a judge for the U.S. District Court for the Southern District of California. Confirmed 90-6: D 51-0; R 37-6; I 2-0. A "yea" was a vote in support of the president's position. Feb. 9, 2012.

17. **S 1813. Surface Transportation Authorization/Cloture.** Motion to invoke cloture (thus limiting debate) on the Reid, D-Nev., motion to proceed to the bill that would authorize $109 billion for surface transportation programs through fiscal 2013. Motion agreed to 85-11: D 49-2; R 34-9; I 2-0. Three-fifths of the total Senate (60) is required to invoke cloture. Feb. 9, 2012.

18. **Jordan Nomination/Cloture.** Motion to invoke cloture (thus limiting debate) on President Obama's nomination of Adalberto Jose Jordan of Florida to be a judge for the 11th U.S. Circuit Court of Appeals. Motion agreed to 89-5: D 50-0; R 38-5; I 1-0. Three-fifths of the total Senate (60) is required to invoke cloture. Feb. 13, 2012.

19. **Jordan Nomination/Confirmation.** Confirmation of President Obama's nomination of Adalberto Jose Jordan of Florida to be a judge for the 11th U.S. Circuit Court of Appeals. Confirmed 94-5: D 51-0; R 41-5; I 2-0. A "yea" was a vote in support of the president's position. Feb. 15, 2012.

	15	16	17	18	19
ALABAMA					
Shelby	Y	N	Y	Y	Y
Sessions	Y	Y	Y	Y	Y
ALASKA					
Murkowski	Y	Y	N	Y	Y
Begich	Y	Y	N	Y	Y
ARIZONA					
McCain	Y	Y	Y	Y	Y
Kyl	Y	Y	Y	Y	Y
ARKANSAS					
Pryor	Y	Y	Y	Y	Y
Boozman	Y	Y	Y	Y	Y
CALIFORNIA					
Feinstein	Y	Y	Y	Y	Y
Boxer	Y	Y	Y	Y	Y
COLORADO					
Udall	Y	Y	Y	Y	Y
Bennet	Y	Y	Y	Y	Y
CONNECTICUT					
Lieberman	Y	Y	Y	?	Y
Blumenthal	N	Y	Y	Y	Y
DELAWARE					
Carper	Y	Y	Y	Y	Y
Coons	Y	Y	Y	Y	Y
FLORIDA					
Nelson	Y	Y	Y	Y	Y
Rubio	Y	Y	N	Y	Y
GEORGIA					
Chambliss	Y	Y	Y	Y	Y
Isakson	Y	Y	Y	Y	Y
HAWAII					
Inouye	Y	Y	Y	Y	Y
Akaka	N	Y	Y	Y	Y
IDAHO					
Crapo	N	N	Y	Y	Y
Risch	N	N	N	Y	Y
ILLINOIS					
Durbin	Y	Y	Y	Y	Y
Kirk	?	?	?	?	?
INDIANA					
Lugar	Y	Y	Y	Y	Y
Coats	Y	Y	Y	Y	Y
IOWA					
Grassley	Y	Y	Y	Y	Y
Harkin	N	Y	Y	Y	Y
KANSAS					
Roberts	Y	?	?	Y	Y
Moran	Y	?	?	Y	Y
KENTUCKY					
McConnell	Y	Y	Y	Y	Y
Paul	N	N	N	N	Y
LOUISIANA					
Landrieu	Y	Y	Y	?	Y
Vitter	?	Y	N	N	N
MAINE					
Snowe	Y	Y	Y	Y	Y
Collins	Y	Y	Y	Y	Y
MARYLAND					
Mikulski	N	Y	Y	Y	Y
Cardin	N	Y	Y	Y	Y
MASSACHUSETTS					
Kerry	Y	Y	Y	Y	Y
Brown	Y	Y	Y	Y	Y
MICHIGAN					
Levin	Y	Y	Y	Y	Y
Stabenow	N	Y	Y	Y	Y
MINNESOTA					
Klobuchar	N	Y	Y	Y	Y
Franken	N	Y	Y	Y	Y
MISSISSIPPI					
Cochran	Y	Y	Y	Y	Y
Wicker	Y	?	?	Y	Y
MISSOURI					
McCaskill	N	Y	Y	Y	Y
Blunt	Y	Y	N	N	N
MONTANA					
Baucus	Y	Y	Y	Y	Y
Tester	Y	Y	Y	Y	Y
NEBRASKA					
Nelson	Y	Y	Y	Y	Y
Johanns	Y	Y	N	Y	Y
NEVADA					
Reid	Y	Y	Y	Y	Y
Heller	Y	Y	Y	Y	Y
NEW HAMPSHIRE					
Shaheen	Y	Y	Y	Y	Y
Ayotte	Y	Y	Y	Y	Y
NEW JERSEY					
Lautenberg	Y	Y	Y	Y	Y
Menendez	Y	Y	Y	Y	Y
NEW MEXICO					
Bingaman	Y	Y	Y	Y	Y
Udall	Y	Y	Y	Y	Y
NEW YORK					
Schumer	Y	Y	Y	Y	Y
Gillibrand	N	Y	Y	Y	Y
NORTH CAROLINA					
Burr	Y	Y	Y	Y	Y
Hagan	Y	Y	Y	Y	Y
NORTH DAKOTA					
Conrad	?	Y	Y	Y	Y
Hoeven	Y	Y	Y	Y	Y
OHIO					
Brown	N	Y	Y	Y	Y
Portman	Y	Y	Y	Y	Y
OKLAHOMA					
Inhofe	Y	Y	Y	Y	Y
Coburn	Y	Y	Y	Y	Y
OREGON					
Wyden	Y	Y	Y	Y	Y
Merkley	N	Y	Y	Y	Y
PENNSYLVANIA					
Casey	N	Y	Y	Y	Y
Toomey	Y	Y	Y	N	N
RHODE ISLAND					
Reed	Y	Y	Y	Y	Y
Whitehouse	Y	Y	Y	Y	Y
SOUTH CAROLINA					
Graham	Y	Y	Y	Y	Y
DeMint	N	N	N	–	N
SOUTH DAKOTA					
Johnson	Y	Y	Y	Y	Y
Thune	Y	Y	Y	Y	Y
TENNESSEE					
Alexander	Y	Y	Y	Y	Y
Corker	Y	Y	Y	Y	Y
TEXAS					
Hutchison	Y	Y	Y	?	Y
Cornyn	Y	Y	Y	Y	Y
UTAH					
Hatch	–	Y	N	+	Y
Lee	N	N	N	N	N
VERMONT					
Leahy	N	Y	Y	Y	Y
Sanders	N	Y	Y	Y	Y
VIRGINIA					
Webb	Y	Y	Y	Y	Y
Warner	Y	Y	Y	Y	Y
WASHINGTON					
Murray	Y	Y	Y	Y	Y
Cantwell	Y	Y	N	Y	Y
WEST VIRGINIA					
Rockefeller	Y	Y	Y	Y	Y
Manchin	Y	Y	Y	Y	Y
WISCONSIN					
Kohl	Y	Y	Y	Y	Y
Johnson	Y	Y	N	Y	Y
WYOMING					
Enzi	Y	Y	Y	Y	Y
Barrasso	?	Y	Y	Y	Y

KEY **Republicans** Democrats *Independents*

Y Voted for (yea)	X Paired against	C Voted "present" to avoid possible conflict of interest
# Paired for	– Announced against	
+ Announced for	P Voted "present"	? Did not vote or otherwise make a position known
N Voted against (nay)		

IN THE SENATE | By Vote Number

20. **S 1813. Surface Transportation Authorization/Cloture.** Motion to invoke cloture (thus limiting debate) on the Reid, D-Nev., amendment that would add safety, revenue and public transit titles to a bill that would authorize federal highway programs for two years. Motion rejected 54-42: D 50-0; R 2-42; I 2-0. Three-fifths of the total Senate (60) is required to invoke cloture. Feb. 17, 2012.

21. **Furman Nomination/Confirmation.** Confirmation of President Obama's nomination of Jesse M. Furman of New York to be a judge for the U.S. District Court for the Southern District of New York. Confirmed 62-34: D 50-0; R 10-34; I 2-0. A "yea" was a vote in support of the president's position. Feb. 17, 2012.

22. **HR 3630. Payroll Tax Relief Extension/Conference Report.** Adoption of the conference report on the bill that would extend the 4.2 percent employee payroll tax rate through 2012. It also would renew long-term unemployment benefits into January 2013, with three stages of reductions. The current Medicare reimbursement rate for physicians would be preserved through 2012, preventing a scheduled 27.4 percent payment cut. The cost of the legislation would be partially offset by requiring larger pension payments from newly hired federal employees and from lawmakers, by auctioning blocks of electromagnetic spectrum used by television broadcasters, and by reducing funds for certain programs tied to the 2010 health care overhaul. Adopted (thus cleared for the president) 60-36: D 45-5; R 14-30; I 1-1. A "yea" was a vote in support of the president's position. Feb. 17, 2012.

23. **Brodie Nomination/Confirmation.** Confirmation of President Obama's nomination of Margo Kitsy Brodie of New York to be a judge for the U.S. District Court for the Eastern District of New York. Confirmed 86-2: D 45-0; R 39-2; I 2-0. A "yea" was a vote in support of the president's position. Feb. 27, 2012.

24. **S 1813. Surface Transportation Authorization/Religious Exemptions for Health Care.** Murray, D-Wash., motion to table (kill) the Blunt, R-Mo., amendment to the Reid, D-Nev., amendment. The Blunt amendment would allow health insurance plans to deny coverage for medical services that run counter to the plan sponsor's or employer's religious beliefs. It also would establish a private right of legal action for enforcement of the coverage exemptions. The Reid amendment would add safety, revenue and public-transit titles to a bill that would authorize federal highway programs for two years. Motion agreed to 51-48: D 48-3; R 1-45; I 2-0. A "yea" was a vote in support of the president's position. March 1, 2012.

	20	21	22	23	24		20	21	22	23	24
ALABAMA						**MONTANA**					
Shelby	N	N	N	Y	N	Baucus	Y	Y	Y	Y	Y
Sessions	N	Y	N	Y	N	Tester	Y	Y	Y	Y	Y
ALASKA						**NEBRASKA**					
Murkowski	N	Y	Y	Y	N	Nelson	Y	Y	Y	Y	N
Begich	Y	Y	Y	Y	Y	Johanns	N	N	N	Y	N
ARIZONA						**NEVADA**					
McCain	N	Y	N	?	N	Reid	Y	Y	Y	Y	Y
Kyl	N	Y	N	Y	N	Heller	Y	N	Y	Y	N
ARKANSAS						**NEW HAMPSHIRE**					
Pryor	Y	Y	Y	Y	Y	Shaheen	Y	Y	Y	Y	Y
Boozman	N	N	N	Y	N	Ayotte	N	N	Y	Y	N
CALIFORNIA						**NEW JERSEY**					
Feinstein	Y	Y	Y	Y	Y	Lautenberg	Y	Y	Y	?	Y
Boxer	Y	Y	Y	Y	Y	Menendez	Y	Y	Y	Y	Y
COLORADO						**NEW MEXICO**					
Udall	Y	Y	Y	Y	Y	Bingaman	?	?	?	Y	Y
Bennet	Y	Y	Y	Y	Y	Udall	Y	Y	Y	Y	Y
CONNECTICUT						**NEW YORK**					
Lieberman	Y	Y	Y	Y	Y	Schumer	Y	Y	Y	Y	Y
Blumenthal	Y	Y	Y	Y	Y	Gillibrand	Y	Y	Y	Y	Y
DELAWARE						**NORTH CAROLINA**					
Carper	Y	Y	Y	Y	Y	Burr	N	N	N	Y	N
Coons	Y	Y	Y	Y	Y	Hagan	Y	Y	Y	Y	Y
FLORIDA						**NORTH DAKOTA**					
Nelson	Y	Y	Y	Y	Y	Conrad	Y	Y	Y	Y	Y
Rubio	N	N	N	Y	N	Hoeven	N	N	Y	Y	N
GEORGIA						**OHIO**					
Chambliss	N	N	N	Y	N	Brown	Y	Y	Y	Y	Y
Isakson	N	N	N	Y	N	Portman	N	N	N	?	N
HAWAII						**OKLAHOMA**					
Inouye	Y	Y	Y	?	Y	Inhofe	N	N	N	?	N
Akaka	Y	Y	Y	Y	Y	Coburn	N	N	N	?	N
IDAHO						**OREGON**					
Crapo	N	N	N	Y	N	Wyden	Y	Y	Y	Y	Y
Risch	N	N	N	Y	N	Merkley	Y	Y	Y	Y	Y
ILLINOIS						**PENNSYLVANIA**					
Durbin	Y	Y	Y	Y	Y	Casey	Y	Y	Y	Y	Y
Kirk	?	?	?	?	?	Toomey	N	N	N	Y	N
INDIANA						**RHODE ISLAND**					
Lugar	N	N	Y	Y	N	Reed	Y	Y	Y	Y	Y
Coats	N	N	N	Y	N	Whitehouse	Y	Y	Y	Y	Y
IOWA						**SOUTH CAROLINA**					
Grassley	N	N	Y	Y	N	Graham	N	Y	Y	Y	N
Harkin	Y	Y	N	?	Y	DeMint	N	N	N	N	N
KANSAS						**SOUTH DAKOTA**					
Roberts	?	?	?	Y	N	Johnson	Y	Y	Y	Y	Y
Moran	N	N	N	Y	N	Thune	N	N	N	Y	N
KENTUCKY						**TENNESSEE**					
McConnell	N	N	Y	Y	N	Alexander	N	Y	N	Y	N
Paul	N	N	N	Y	N	Corker	N	Y	N	Y	N
LOUISIANA						**TEXAS**					
Landrieu	Y	Y	Y	?	Y	Hutchison	N	N	N	Y	N
Vitter	?	?	?	?	N	Cornyn	N	N	N	Y	N
MAINE						**UTAH**					
Snowe	N	Y	Y	Y	Y	Hatch	N	N	N	Y	N
Collins	N	Y	Y	Y	N	Lee	N	N	N	N	N
MARYLAND						**VERMONT**					
Mikulski	Y	Y	N	Y	Y	Leahy	Y	Y	Y	Y	Y
Cardin	Y	Y	N	Y	Y	Sanders	Y	Y	N	Y	Y
MASSACHUSETTS						**VIRGINIA**					
Kerry	Y	Y	Y	Y	Y	Webb	Y	Y	Y	Y	Y
Brown	Y	Y	Y	Y	N	Warner	Y	Y	N	Y	Y
MICHIGAN						**WASHINGTON**					
Levin	Y	Y	Y	Y	Y	Murray	Y	Y	Y	Y	Y
Stabenow	Y	Y	Y	?	Y	Cantwell	Y	Y	Y	Y	Y
MINNESOTA						**WEST VIRGINIA**					
Klobuchar	Y	Y	Y	Y	Y	Rockefeller	Y	Y	Y	Y	Y
Franken	Y	Y	Y	Y	Y	Manchin	Y	Y	N	Y	N
MISSISSIPPI						**WISCONSIN**					
Cochran	N	N	Y	Y	N	Kohl	Y	Y	Y	Y	Y
Wicker	N	N	Y	Y	N	Johnson	N	N	N	Y	N
MISSOURI						**WYOMING**					
McCaskill	Y	Y	Y	?	Y	Enzi	N	N	N	Y	N
Blunt	N	N	N	Y	N	Barrasso	N	N	N	Y	N

KEY **Republicans**   Democrats   *Independents*

Y Voted for (yea)	X Paired against	C Voted "present" to avoid possible conflict of interest
# Paired for	– Announced against	
+ Announced for	P Voted "present"	? Did not vote or otherwise make a position known
N Voted against (nay)		

IN THE SENATE | By Vote Number

25. **S 1813. Surface Transportation Reauthorization/Cloture.**
Motion to invoke cloture (thus limiting debate) on the Reid, D-Nev., substitute amendment that would authorize federal highway, highway safety and public transit programs for $109 billion over two years. The amendment would consolidate existing functions of the Interstate Maintenance, National Highway System and Highway Bridge programs into a new National Highway Performance Program. Motion rejected 52-44: D 48-1; R 2-43; I 2-0. Three-fifths of the total Senate (60) is required to invoke cloture. (Subsequently, the substitute amendment was adopted by unanimous consent.) March 6, 2012.

26. **Phillips Nomination/Confirmation.** Confirmation of President Obama's nomination of Mary Elizabeth Phillips of Missouri to be a judge for the U.S. District Court for the Western District of Missouri. Confirmed 95-2: D 50-0; R 43-2; I 2-0. A "yea" was a vote in support of the president's position. March 6, 2012.

27. **Rice Nomination/Confirmation.** Confirmation of President Obama's nomination of Thomas Owen Rice of Washington to be a judge for the U.S. District Court for the Eastern District of Washington. Confirmed 93-4: D 50-0; R 41-4; I 2-0. A "yea" was a vote in support of the president's position. March 6, 2012.

28. **S 1813. Surface Transportation Authorization/Outer Continental Shelf Leases.** Vitter, R-La., amendment that would provide for implementation of a 2008 offshore drilling plan. It would allow new oil and gas leases throughout the outer continental shelf. Rejected 44-54: D 3-48; R 41-4; I 0-2. (By unanimous consent, the Senate agreed to raise the majority requirement for adoption of the Vitter amendment to 60 votes.) March 8, 2012.

29. **S 1813. Surface Transportation Authorization/Secure Rural Schools.** Baucus, D-Mont., amendment that would reauthorize, for one year, payments in lieu of taxes made to rural communities and the Secure Rural Schools program. The programs fund rural schools and other local government services in areas with large amounts of federal land that cannot be taxed to support those services. The amendment would be offset with changes to federal employee retirement regulations and other tax provisions. Adopted 82-16: D 45-6; R 36-9; I 1-1. (By unanimous consent, the Senate agreed to raise the majority requirement for adoption of the Baucus amendment to 60 votes.) March 8, 2012.

30. **S 1813. Surface Transportation Authorization/Boiler Emission Standards.** Collins, R-Maine, amendment that would delay the implementation of EPA emission standards for industrial and commercial boilers, known as Maximum Achievable Control Technology standards, and grant the agency 15 months to propose new rules. It would delay the compliance date for the new rules by five years. Rejected 52-46: D 8-43; R 44-1; I 0-2. (By unanimous consent, the Senate agreed to raise the majority requirement for adoption of the Collins amendment to 60 votes.) A "nay" was a vote in support of the president's position. March 8, 2012.

	25	26	27	28	29	30
ALABAMA						
Shelby	N	Y	Y	Y	Y	Y
Sessions	N	Y	Y	Y	Y	Y
ALASKA						
Murkowski	N	Y	Y	N	Y	Y
Begich	?	?	?	N	Y	N
ARIZONA						
McCain	N	Y	Y	Y	N	Y
Kyl	N	Y	Y	Y	N	Y
ARKANSAS						
Pryor	Y	Y	Y	N	Y	Y
Boozman	N	Y	Y	Y	Y	Y
CALIFORNIA						
Feinstein	Y	Y	Y	N	Y	N
Boxer	Y	Y	Y	N	Y	N
COLORADO						
Udall	Y	Y	Y	N	Y	N
Bennet	Y	Y	Y	N	Y	N
CONNECTICUT						
Lieberman	Y	Y	Y	N	N	N
Blumenthal	Y	Y	Y	N	Y	N
DELAWARE						
Carper	Y	Y	Y	N	Y	N
Coons	Y	Y	Y	N	Y	N
FLORIDA						
Nelson	Y	Y	Y	N	Y	N
Rubio	N	Y	Y	Y	Y	Y
GEORGIA						
Chambliss	N	Y	N	Y	Y	Y
Isakson	N	Y	N	Y	Y	Y
HAWAII						
Inouye	Y	Y	Y	N	Y	N
Akaka	Y	Y	Y	N	N	N
IDAHO						
Crapo	N	Y	Y	Y	Y	Y
Risch	N	Y	Y	Y	Y	Y
ILLINOIS						
Durbin	Y	Y	Y	N	Y	N
Kirk	?	?	?	?	?	?
INDIANA						
Lugar	N	Y	Y	Y	Y	Y
Coats	N	Y	Y	Y	Y	Y
IOWA						
Grassley	N	Y	Y	Y	Y	Y
Harkin	Y	Y	Y	N	N	N
KANSAS						
Roberts	N	Y	Y	Y	Y	Y
Moran	N	Y	Y	Y	N	Y
KENTUCKY						
McConnell	N	Y	Y	Y	Y	Y
Paul	N	Y	Y	Y	N	Y
LOUISIANA						
Landrieu	Y	Y	Y	Y	Y	Y
Vitter	N	Y	Y	Y	Y	Y
MAINE						
Snowe	N	Y	Y	N	Y	Y
Collins	Y	Y	Y	N	Y	Y
MARYLAND						
Mikulski	Y	Y	Y	N	N	N
Cardin	Y	Y	Y	N	N	N
MASSACHUSETTS						
Kerry	Y	Y	Y	N	Y	N
Brown	Y	Y	Y	N	Y	N
MICHIGAN						
Levin	Y	Y	Y	N	Y	N
Stabenow	Y	Y	Y	N	Y	Y
MINNESOTA						
Klobuchar	Y	Y	Y	N	Y	N
Franken	Y	Y	Y	N	Y	N
MISSISSIPPI						
Cochran	N	Y	Y	Y	Y	Y
Wicker	N	Y	Y	Y	Y	Y
MISSOURI						
McCaskill	Y	Y	Y	N	Y	Y
Blunt	N	Y	Y	Y	Y	Y

	25	26	27	28	29	30
MONTANA						
Baucus	Y	Y	Y	N	Y	N
Tester	Y	Y	Y	N	Y	N
NEBRASKA						
Nelson	Y	Y	Y	N	Y	Y
Johanns	N	Y	Y	Y	Y	Y
NEVADA						
Reid	N	Y	Y	N	Y	N
Heller	?	?	?	Y	Y	Y
NEW HAMPSHIRE						
Shaheen	Y	Y	Y	N	Y	N
Ayotte	N	Y	Y	Y	Y	Y
NEW JERSEY						
Lautenberg	Y	Y	Y	N	Y	N
Menendez	Y	Y	Y	N	Y	N
NEW MEXICO						
Bingaman	Y	Y	Y	N	Y	N
Udall	Y	Y	Y	N	Y	N
NEW YORK						
Schumer	Y	Y	Y	N	Y	N
Gillibrand	Y	Y	Y	N	Y	N
NORTH CAROLINA						
Burr	N	Y	Y	Y	Y	Y
Hagan	Y	Y	Y	N	Y	N
NORTH DAKOTA						
Conrad	Y	Y	Y	N	Y	N
Hoeven	N	Y	Y	Y	Y	Y
OHIO						
Brown	Y	Y	Y	N	N	N
Portman	N	Y	Y	Y	Y	Y
OKLAHOMA						
Inhofe	N	Y	Y	Y	Y	Y
Coburn	N	Y	Y	Y	N	Y
OREGON						
Wyden	Y	Y	Y	N	Y	N
Merkley	Y	Y	Y	N	Y	N
PENNSYLVANIA						
Casey	Y	Y	Y	N	Y	N
Toomey	N	Y	Y	Y	N	Y
RHODE ISLAND						
Reed	Y	Y	Y	N	Y	N
Whitehouse	Y	Y	Y	N	Y	N
SOUTH CAROLINA						
Graham	N	Y	Y	Y	Y	Y
DeMint	N	N	N	Y	N	Y
SOUTH DAKOTA						
Johnson	Y	Y	Y	N	Y	N
Thune	N	Y	Y	?	?	?
TENNESSEE						
Alexander	N	Y	Y	Y	Y	Y
Corker	N	Y	Y	Y	N	Y
TEXAS						
Hutchison	N	Y	Y	Y	Y	Y
Cornyn	N	Y	Y	Y	Y	Y
UTAH						
Hatch	N	Y	Y	Y	Y	Y
Lee	N	N	N	Y	Y	Y
VERMONT						
Leahy	+	Y	Y	N	Y	N
Sanders	Y	Y	Y	N	Y	N
VIRGINIA						
Webb	Y	Y	Y	N	Y	N
Warner	Y	Y	Y	N	Y	N
WASHINGTON						
Murray	Y	Y	Y	N	Y	N
Cantwell	Y	Y	Y	N	Y	N
WEST VIRGINIA						
Rockefeller	Y	Y	Y	N	Y	N
Manchin	Y	Y	Y	Y	Y	Y
WISCONSIN						
Kohl	Y	Y	Y	N	Y	N
Johnson	N	Y	Y	Y	N	Y
WYOMING						
Enzi	N	Y	Y	Y	Y	Y
Barrasso	N	Y	Y	Y	Y	Y

KEY **Republicans** Democrats *Independents*

Y Voted for (yea)
Paired for
+ Announced for
N Voted against (nay)

X Paired against
– Announced against
P Voted "present"

C Voted "present" to avoid possible conflict of interest
? Did not vote or otherwise make a position known

IN THE SENATE | By Vote Number

31. **S 1813. Surface Transportation Authorization/Duplicative Government Programs.** Coburn, R-Okla., amendment that would direct the Office of Management and Budget to coordinate, within 150 days, with department and agency officials to eliminate and consolidate duplicative government programs identified in two Government Accountability Office Reports. OMB would be required to find at least $10 billion in spending rescissions. Rejected 52-46: D 7-44; R 45-0; I 0-2. (By unanimous consent, the Senate agreed to raise the majority requirement for adoption of the Coburn amendment to 60 votes.) March 8, 2012.

32. **S 1813. Surface Transportation Authorization/Gulf Coast Restoration.** Nelson, D-Fla., amendment that would direct 80 percent of Clean Water Act penalties stemming from the Deepwater Horizon oil spill to a trust fund for Gulf Coast restoration. It also would authorize $1.4 billion for the Land and Water Conservation Fund over two years. The amendment would be offset by delaying for one year the implementation of a rule that gives multinational corporations more flexibility in accounting for interest costs. Adopted 76-22: D 51-0; R 23-22; I 2-0. (By unanimous consent, the Senate agreed to raise the majority requirement for adoption of the Nelson amendment to 60 votes.) March 8, 2012.

33. **S 1813. Surface Transportation Authorization/Keystone XL Pipeline.** Wyden, D-Ore., amendment that would prohibit the export of crude oil transported by the Keystone XL pipeline and related facilities, unless the prohibition is waived by the president, and require the use of U.S. iron, steel and manufactured goods in the construction of the pipeline with certain exceptions. Rejected 33-65: D 32-19; R 0-45; I 1-1. (By unanimous consent, the Senate agreed to raise the majority requirement for adoption of the Wyden amendment to 60 votes.) March 8, 2012.

34. **S 1813. Surface Transportation Authorization/Keystone XL Pipeline.** Hoeven, R-N.D., amendment that would provide for approval of the Keystone XL pipeline between Canada and the United States. It would require that the route for the pipeline in Nebraska be submitted by the state of Nebraska. It also would provide for certain environmental protections. Rejected 56-42: D 11-40; R 45-0; I 0-2. (By unanimous consent, the Senate agreed to raise the majority requirement for adoption of the Hoeven amendment to 60 votes.) A "nay" was a vote in support of the president's position. March 8, 2012.

35. **S 1813. Surface Transportation Authorization/Motion to Waive.** Boxer, D-Calif., motion to waive all applicable budget laws with respect to the Corker, R-Tenn., point of order against the bill that would authorize federal highway, highway safety and public transit programs at $109 billion over two years. Motion agreed to 66-31: D 50-1; R 14-30; I 2-0. (A three-fifths majority vote of the total Senate (60) is required to waive the applicable budget laws.) March 8, 2012.

	31	32	33	34	35
ALABAMA					
Shelby	Y	Y	N	Y	Y
Sessions	Y	Y	N	Y	N
ALASKA					
Murkowski	Y	Y	N	N	Y
Begich	N	Y	N	Y	Y
ARIZONA					
McCain	Y	N	N	Y	N
Kyl	Y	N	N	Y	N
ARKANSAS					
Pryor	N	Y	N	Y	Y
Boozman	Y	Y	N	Y	Y
CALIFORNIA					
Feinstein	N	Y	Y	N	Y
Boxer	N	Y	Y	N	Y
COLORADO					
Udall	N	Y	N	N	Y
Bennet	N	Y	N	N	Y
CONNECTICUT					
Lieberman	N	Y	Y	N	Y
Blumenthal	N	Y	Y	N	Y
DELAWARE					
Carper	N	Y	Y	N	Y
Coons	N	Y	Y	N	Y
FLORIDA					
Nelson	N	Y	Y	N	Y
Rubio	Y	N	N	Y	N
GEORGIA					
Chambliss	Y	Y	N	Y	N
Isakson	Y	Y	N	Y	N
HAWAII					
Inouye	N	Y	Y	N	Y
Akaka	N	Y	N	N	Y
IDAHO					
Crapo	Y	Y	N	Y	N
Risch	Y	N	N	Y	N
ILLINOIS					
Durbin	N	Y	Y	N	Y
Kirk	?	?	?	?	?
INDIANA					
Lugar	Y	N	N	Y	N
Coats	Y	N	N	Y	N
IOWA					
Grassley	Y	N	N	Y	N
Harkin	N	Y	Y	N	Y
KANSAS					
Roberts	Y	Y	N	Y	N
Moran	Y	Y	N	Y	N
KENTUCKY					
McConnell	Y	N	N	Y	N
Paul	Y	N	N	Y	?
LOUISIANA					
Landrieu	N	Y	N	Y	Y
Vitter	Y	Y	N	Y	Y
MAINE					
Snowe	Y	Y	N	Y	Y
Collins	Y	Y	N	Y	Y
MARYLAND					
Mikulski	N	Y	Y	N	Y
Cardin	N	Y	Y	N	Y
MASSACHUSETTS					
Kerry	N	Y	N	N	Y
Brown	Y	Y	N	Y	Y
MICHIGAN					
Levin	N	Y	Y	N	Y
Stabenow	Y	Y	Y	N	Y
MINNESOTA					
Klobuchar	Y	Y	Y	N	Y
Franken	N	Y	Y	N	Y
MISSISSIPPI					
Cochran	Y	Y	N	Y	Y
Wicker	Y	Y	N	Y	Y
MISSOURI					
McCaskill	Y	Y	Y	Y	Y
Blunt	Y	Y	Y	Y	Y
MONTANA					
Baucus	Y	Y	N	Y	Y
Tester	Y	Y	Y	Y	Y
NEBRASKA					
Nelson	Y	Y	N	N	Y
Johanns	Y	N	N	Y	N
NEVADA					
Reid	N	Y	Y	N	Y
Heller	Y	N	N	Y	Y
NEW HAMPSHIRE					
Shaheen	N	Y	N	N	Y
Ayotte	Y	Y	N	Y	N
NEW JERSEY					
Lautenberg	N	Y	Y	N	Y
Menendez	N	Y	Y	N	Y
NEW MEXICO					
Bingaman	N	Y	Y	N	Y
Udall	N	Y	Y	N	Y
NEW YORK					
Schumer	N	Y	Y	N	Y
Gillibrand	N	Y	N	N	Y
NORTH CAROLINA					
Burr	Y	N	N	Y	N
Hagan	N	Y	N	Y	Y
NORTH DAKOTA					
Conrad	N	Y	Y	Y	Y
Hoeven	Y	Y	N	Y	Y
OHIO					
Brown	N	Y	Y	N	Y
Portman	Y	Y	N	Y	N
OKLAHOMA					
Inhofe	Y	Y	N	Y	Y
Coburn	Y	N	N	Y	N
OREGON					
Wyden	N	Y	Y	N	Y
Merkley	N	Y	Y	N	Y
PENNSYLVANIA					
Casey	N	Y	N	Y	Y
Toomey	Y	N	N	Y	N
RHODE ISLAND					
Reed	N	Y	N	N	Y
Whitehouse	N	Y	N	N	Y
SOUTH CAROLINA					
Graham	Y	N	N	Y	N
DeMint	Y	N	N	Y	N
SOUTH DAKOTA					
Johnson	N	Y	Y	N	Y
Thune	?	?	?	?	?
TENNESSEE					
Alexander	Y	Y	Y	Y	Y
Corker	Y	N	N	Y	N
TEXAS					
Hutchison	Y	Y	Y	Y	Y
Cornyn	Y	Y	N	Y	N
UTAH					
Hatch	Y	N	N	Y	N
Lee	Y	N	N	Y	N
VERMONT					
Leahy	N	Y	N	N	Y
Sanders	N	Y	N	N	Y
VIRGINIA					
Webb	N	Y	N	Y	Y
Warner	N	Y	N	N	N
WASHINGTON					
Murray	N	Y	Y	N	Y
Cantwell	N	Y	Y	N	Y
WEST VIRGINIA					
Rockefeller	N	Y	N	N	Y
Manchin	Y	Y	N	Y	Y
WISCONSIN					
Kohl	N	Y	Y	N	Y
Johnson	Y	N	N	Y	N
WYOMING					
Enzi	Y	N	N	Y	N
Barrasso	Y	N	N	Y	N

KEY   **Republicans**   Democrats   *Independents*

Y Voted for (yea)	X Paired against	C Voted "present" to avoid possible conflict of interest
# Paired for	– Announced against	
+ Announced for	P Voted "present"	? Did not vote or otherwise make a position known
N Voted against (nay)		

IN THE SENATE | By Vote Number

36. **S 1813. Surface Transportation Authorization/State Discretionary Authority.** DeMint, R-S.C., substitute amendment that would provide additional flexibility for state surface transportation projects and reauthorize certain core highway programs through fiscal 2018. It would specify that only projects funded by the federal government would be considered federal-aid highways. It also would reduce the federal tax rates for gasoline and other fuels that fund the Highway Trust Fund. Rejected 30-67: D 0-50; R 30-15; I 0-2. March 13, 2012.

37. **S 1813. Surface Transportation Authorization/Privatized Highways.** Bingaman, D-N.M., amendment that would require the amount of federal highway funds that states receive under prescribed formulas to be reduced based on the portion of the National Highway System in a state that has leased tolled highways to private operators. Adopted 50-47: D 42-8; R 6-39; I 2-0. March 13, 2012.

38. **S 1813. Surface Transportation Authorization/Drilling Approval and Energy Tax Extensions.** Roberts, R-Kan., amendment that would extend energy tax credit programs, excluding the production credit and the stimulus grant program that expired in 2011. It also would approve the Keystone XL pipeline and expand oil and gas drilling in new areas, including the Arctic National Wildlife Refuge in Alaska. Provisions would be partially offset by extending the federal employee pay freeze through 2013. Rejected 41-57: D 3-48; R 38-7; I 0-2. (By unanimous consent, the Senate agreed to raise the majority requirement for adoption of the Roberts amendment to 60 votes.) March 13, 2012.

39. **S 1813. Surface Transportation Authorization/Energy Tax Extensions.** Stabenow, D-Mich., amendment that would extend a number of lapsed and soon-to-expire energy tax benefits, including the production tax credit for wind energy producers and a program from the 2009 economic stimulus law allowing businesses to opt for grants instead of tax credits for renewable-energy projects. Rejected 49-49: D 47-4; R 0-45; I 2-0. (By unanimous consent, the Senate agreed to raise the majority requirement for adoption of the Stabenow amendment to 60 votes.) March 13, 2012.

40. **S 1813. Surface Transportation Authorization/Energy Tax Subsidy Termination.** DeMint, R-S.C., amendment that would eliminate certain tax preferences for certain energy producers and repeal tax benefits for several energy-efficient technologies, including electric vehicles. The increased revenue would be applied to a reduction in the corporate income tax rate. Rejected 26-72: D 0-51; R 26-19; I 0-2. (By unanimous consent, the Senate agreed to raise the majority requirement for adoption of the DeMint amendment to 60 votes.) March 13, 2012.

	36	37	38	39	40
ALABAMA					
Shelby	N	N	Y	N	Y
Sessions	Y	N	Y	N	Y
ALASKA					
Murkowski	N	Y	Y	N	N
Begich	N	Y	Y	Y	N
ARIZONA					
McCain	Y	N	Y	N	Y
Kyl	Y	N	Y	N	Y
ARKANSAS					
Pryor	N	Y	N	Y	N
Boozman	Y	N	Y	N	N
CALIFORNIA					
Feinstein	N	N	N	Y	N
Boxer	N	N	N	Y	N
COLORADO					
Udall	N	Y	N	Y	N
Bennet	N	Y	N	Y	N
CONNECTICUT					
Lieberman	N	Y	N	Y	N
Blumenthal	N	Y	N	Y	N
DELAWARE					
Carper	N	N	N	Y	N
Coons	N	N	N	Y	N
FLORIDA					
Nelson	N	Y	N	Y	N
Rubio	Y	N	N	N	Y
GEORGIA					
Chambliss	Y	N	Y	N	Y
Isakson	Y	N	Y	N	N
HAWAII					
Inouye	N	Y	N	Y	N
Akaka	N	Y	N	Y	N
IDAHO					
Crapo	Y	N	Y	N	Y
Risch	Y	N	Y	N	Y
ILLINOIS					
Durbin	N	Y	N	Y	N
Kirk	?	?	?	?	?
INDIANA					
Lugar	Y	N	Y	N	N
Coats	Y	N	Y	N	Y
IOWA					
Grassley	Y	Y	Y	N	N
Harkin	N	Y	N	Y	N
KANSAS					
Roberts	Y	N	Y	N	N
Moran	Y	N	Y	N	N
KENTUCKY					
McConnell	N	N	Y	N	Y
Paul	Y	N	Y	N	Y
LOUISIANA					
Landrieu	N	Y	N	Y	N
Vitter	Y	N	Y	N	Y
MAINE					
Snowe	N	N	N	N	N
Collins	N	N	N	N	N
MARYLAND					
Mikulski	N	Y	N	Y	N
Cardin	N	Y	N	Y	N
MASSACHUSETTS					
Kerry	N	N	N	Y	N
Brown	N	N	N	N	N
MICHIGAN					
Levin	N	Y	N	Y	N
Stabenow	N	Y	N	Y	N
MINNESOTA					
Klobuchar	N	Y	N	Y	N
Franken	N	Y	N	Y	N
MISSISSIPPI					
Cochran	N	Y	Y	N	N
Wicker	Y	N	Y	N	Y
MISSOURI					
McCaskill	N	Y	Y	N	N
Blunt	N	N	Y	N	Y
MONTANA					
Baucus	N	N	Y	N	N
Tester	N	Y	N	Y	N
NEBRASKA					
Nelson	N	Y	N	Y	N
Johanns	N	N	Y	N	Y
NEVADA					
Reid	N	Y	N	Y	N
Heller	N	Y	Y	N	N
NEW HAMPSHIRE					
Shaheen	N	Y	N	Y	N
Ayotte	Y	N	Y	N	Y
NEW JERSEY					
Lautenberg	?	?	N	Y	N
Menendez	N	Y	N	Y	N
NEW MEXICO					
Bingaman	N	Y	N	Y	N
Udall	N	Y	N	Y	N
NEW YORK					
Schumer	N	Y	N	Y	N
Gillibrand	N	Y	N	Y	N
NORTH CAROLINA					
Burr	Y	N	Y	N	Y
Hagan	N	Y	N	Y	N
NORTH DAKOTA					
Conrad	N	Y	N	Y	N
Hoeven	N	Y	Y	N	N
OHIO					
Brown	N	Y	N	Y	N
Portman	Y	N	Y	N	Y
OKLAHOMA					
Inhofe	Y	N	Y	N	Y
Coburn	Y	N	Y	N	Y
OREGON					
Wyden	N	Y	N	Y	N
Merkley	N	Y	N	Y	N
PENNSYLVANIA					
Casey	N	Y	N	Y	N
Toomey	Y	N	Y	N	Y
RHODE ISLAND					
Reed	N	Y	N	Y	N
Whitehouse	N	Y	N	Y	N
SOUTH CAROLINA					
Graham	Y	N	Y	N	Y
DeMint	Y	N	N	N	Y
SOUTH DAKOTA					
Johnson	N	Y	N	Y	N
Thune	N	N	Y	N	N
TENNESSEE					
Alexander	N	N	Y	N	N
Corker	Y	N	N	N	Y
TEXAS					
Hutchison	Y	Y	Y	N	N
Cornyn	Y	N	Y	N	N
UTAH					
Hatch	+	–	?	–	+
Lee	Y	N	N	N	Y
VERMONT					
Leahy	N	Y	N	Y	N
Sanders	N	Y	N	Y	N
VIRGINIA					
Webb	N	N	N	N	N
Warner	N	N	N	N	N
WASHINGTON					
Murray	N	Y	N	Y	N
Cantwell	N	Y	N	Y	N
WEST VIRGINIA					
Rockefeller	N	Y	N	Y	N
Manchin	N	Y	N	Y	N
WISCONSIN					
Kohl	N	Y	N	Y	N
Johnson	Y	N	Y	N	Y
WYOMING					
Enzi	N	N	Y	N	N
Barrasso	N	N	Y	N	N

KEY **Republicans** Democrats *Independents*

Y Voted for (yea)	X Paired against	C Voted "present" to avoid possible conflict of interest
# Paired for	– Announced against	
+ Announced for	P Voted "present"	? Did not vote or otherwise make a position known
N Voted against (nay)		

IN THE SENATE | By Vote Number

41. **S 1813. Surface Transportation Authorization/Natural-Gas Incentives.** Menendez, D-N.J., amendment that would provide tax incentives to promote natural gas as a fuel for cars, trucks and heavy-duty fleets. Rejected 51-47: D 44-7; R 6-39; I 1-1. (By unanimous consent, the Senate agreed to raise the majority requirement for adoption of the Menendez amendment to 60 votes.) March 13, 2012.

42. **S 1813. Surface Transportation Authorization/Federal-Aid Apportionment.** Coats, R-Ind., amendment that would modify the apportionment formula so that states would receive funds based on the percentage of gas taxes paid. Rejected 28-70: D 4-47; R 24-21; I 0-2. March 13, 2012.

43. **S 1813. Surface Transportation Authorization/Federal Highway Program Opt-Out.** Portman, R-Ohio, amendment that would allow states to opt out of receiving apportioned or allocated funding and instead receive the amount they paid in taxes to the Highway Trust Fund, reduced by a pro-rated amount withheld by the Transportation secretary to fund certain programs. Rejected 30-68: D 0-51; R 30-15; I 0-2. March 13, 2012.

44. **S 1813. Surface Transportation Authorization/Spending-Cap Reduction.** Corker, R-Tenn., motion to waive all applicable budget laws with respect to the Inouye, D-Hawaii, point of order against the Corker amendment. The amendment would reduce the non-defense discretionary spending cap set in the 2011 budget law to offset the cost of mandatory spending in the surface transportation bill. Motion rejected 40-58: D 0-51; R 40-5; I 0-2. A three-fifths majority vote of the total Senate (60) is required to waive the applicable budget laws. (Subsequently, the point of order was sustained and the amendment fell.) March 13, 2012.

45. **S 1813. Surface Transportation Authorization/Uses of Highway Rest Areas.** Portman, R-Ohio, amendment that would eliminate restrictions in current law that generally prohibit states from building commercialized rest areas along federally funded interstate highways. It would effectively let states open restaurants, gas stations or other commercial businesses at interstate rest areas, thus allowing states to get revenue from concessions. Rejected 12-86: D 2-49; R 9-36; I 1-1. March 13, 2012.

	41	42	43	44	45
ALABAMA					
Shelby	N	N	N	Y	N
Sessions	N	N	N	Y	N
ALASKA					
Murkowski	N	N	N	Y	Y
Begich	Y	N	N	N	N
ARIZONA					
McCain	N	Y	Y	Y	Y
Kyl	N	Y	Y	Y	Y
ARKANSAS					
Pryor	N	N	N	N	N
Boozman	N	N	Y	Y	N
CALIFORNIA					
Feinstein	Y	N	N	N	N
Boxer	Y	N	N	N	N
COLORADO					
Udall	Y	N	N	N	N
Bennet	Y	N	N	N	N
CONNECTICUT					
Lieberman	Y	N	N	N	Y
Blumenthal	Y	N	N	N	N
DELAWARE					
Carper	Y	N	N	N	Y
Coons	Y	N	N	N	Y
FLORIDA					
Nelson	Y	N	N	N	N
Rubio	N	Y	Y	Y	N
GEORGIA					
Chambliss	Y	Y	Y	Y	N
Isakson	Y	Y	Y	Y	N
HAWAII					
Inouye	Y	N	N	N	N
Akaka	Y	N	N	N	N
IDAHO					
Crapo	N	N	N	Y	Y
Risch	N	N	N	Y	Y
ILLINOIS					
Durbin	Y	N	N	N	N
Kirk	?	?	?	?	?
INDIANA					
Lugar	N	Y	Y	Y	N
Coats	N	Y	Y	Y	Y
IOWA					
Grassley	N	Y	Y	Y	N
Harkin	N	N	N	N	N
KANSAS					
Roberts	N	Y	Y	Y	N
Moran	N	Y	Y	Y	N
KENTUCKY					
McConnell	N	Y	Y	Y	N
Paul	N	Y	Y	Y	N
LOUISIANA					
Landrieu	Y	N	N	N	N
Vitter	N	N	Y	Y	N
MAINE					
Snowe	Y	N	N	N	N
Collins	Y	N	N	N	N
MARYLAND					
Mikulski	Y	N	N	N	N
Cardin	Y	N	N	N	N
MASSACHUSETTS					
Kerry	Y	N	N	N	N
Brown	N	N	N	N	N
MICHIGAN					
Levin	N	Y	N	N	N
Stabenow	N	Y	N	N	N
MINNESOTA					
Klobuchar	Y	N	N	N	N
Franken	Y	N	N	N	N
MISSISSIPPI					
Cochran	N	N	Y	Y	N
Wicker	N	N	Y	Y	N
MISSOURI					
McCaskill	Y	N	N	N	N
Blunt	N	N	N	Y	N

	41	42	43	44	45
MONTANA					
Baucus	Y	N	N	N	N
Tester	Y	N	N	N	N
NEBRASKA					
Nelson	N	N	N	N	N
Johanns	N	Y	Y	Y	N
NEVADA					
Reid	Y	N	N	N	N
Heller	N	Y	N	N	N
NEW HAMPSHIRE					
Shaheen	Y	N	N	N	N
Ayotte	N	N	Y	Y	Y
NEW JERSEY					
Lautenberg	Y	N	N	N	N
Menendez	Y	N	N	N	N
NEW MEXICO					
Bingaman	Y	N	N	N	N
Udall	Y	N	N	N	N
NEW YORK					
Schumer	Y	N	N	N	N
Gillibrand	Y	N	N	N	N
NORTH CAROLINA					
Burr	Y	Y	Y	Y	N
Hagan	Y	N	N	N	N
NORTH DAKOTA					
Conrad	Y	N	N	N	N
Hoeven	N	N	N	Y	N
OHIO					
Brown	Y	Y	N	N	N
Portman	N	Y	Y	Y	Y
OKLAHOMA					
Inhofe	N	N	N	Y	N
Coburn	Y	N	Y	Y	N
OREGON					
Wyden	Y	N	N	N	N
Merkley	Y	N	N	N	N
PENNSYLVANIA					
Casey	Y	N	N	N	N
Toomey	N	Y	Y	Y	Y
RHODE ISLAND					
Reed	Y	N	N	N	N
Whitehouse	Y	N	N	N	N
SOUTH CAROLINA					
Graham	N	Y	Y	Y	N
DeMint	N	Y	Y	Y	N
SOUTH DAKOTA					
Johnson	Y	N	N	N	N
Thune	N	N	N	Y	N
TENNESSEE					
Alexander	N	Y	Y	Y	N
Corker	N	Y	Y	Y	N
TEXAS					
Hutchison	N	Y	N	Y	N
Cornyn	N	Y	Y	Y	N
UTAH					
Hatch	+	+	+	+	+
Lee	N	Y	Y	Y	N
VERMONT					
Leahy	N	N	N	N	N
Sanders	N	N	N	N	N
VIRGINIA					
Webb	N	N	N	N	N
Warner	Y	N	N	N	N
WASHINGTON					
Murray	Y	N	N	N	N
Cantwell	Y	N	N	N	N
WEST VIRGINIA					
Rockefeller	Y	N	N	N	N
Manchin	Y	N	N	N	N
WISCONSIN					
Kohl	Y	N	N	N	N
Johnson	N	Y	N	Y	N
WYOMING					
Enzi	N	N	N	Y	N
Barrasso	N	N	N	Y	N

KEY   **Republicans**   Democrats   *Independents*

Y Voted for (yea)	X Paired against
# Paired for	− Announced against
+ Announced for	P Voted "present"
N Voted against (nay)	

C Voted "present" to avoid possible conflict of interest

? Did not vote or otherwise make a position known

IN THE SENATE | By Vote Number

46. S 1813. Surface Transportation Authorization/Expedited Reviews.
Boxer, D-Calif., amendment that would express the sense of the Senate in support of expedited environmental reviews, approvals and licensing for transportation construction projects after disasters. Adopted 76-20: D 50-0; R 24-20; I 2-0. March 14, 2012.

47. S 1813. Surface Transportation Authorization/Emergency Exemptions.
Paul, R-Ky., motion to waive all applicable budget laws with respect to the Boxer, D-Calif., point of order against the Paul amendment that would exempt reconstruction of roads, highways or bridges for safety reasons from relevant environmental regulations. Motion rejected 42-54: D 1-49; R 41-3; I 0-2. A three-fifths majority vote of the total Senate (60) is required to waive the applicable budget laws. (Subsequently, the point of order was sustained and the amendment fell.) March 14, 2012.

48. S 1813. Surface Transportation Authorization/Passage.
Passage of the bill that would authorize federal highway, highway safety and public transit programs at $109 billion over two years. It would consolidate the functions of the Interstate Maintenance, National Highway System and Highway Bridge programs into a new National Highway Performance Program. The bill would authorize $1 billion annually for fiscal 2012 and 2013 for a transportation financing program. The cost of the measure would be offset through continued collection of vehicle fuel taxes and other revenue provisions. As amended, the bill also would direct 80 percent of Clean Water Act penalties stemming from the Deepwater Horizon oil spill to a trust fund for Gulf Coast restoration. It would authorize $1.4 billion for the Land and Water Conservation Fund over two years. Passed 74-22: D 50-0; R 22-22; I 2-0. A "yea" was a vote in support of the president's position. March 14, 2012.

49. Groh Nomination/Confirmation.
Confirmation of President Obama's nomination of Gina Marie Groh of West Virginia to be a judge for the U.S. District Court for the Northern District of West Virginia. Confirmed 95-2: D 51-0; R 42-2; I 2-0. A "yea" was a vote in support of the president's position. March 15, 2012.

50. Fitzgerald Nomination/Confirmation.
Confirmation of President Obama's nomination of Michael Walter Fitzgerald of California to be a judge for the U.S. District Court of the Central District of California. Confirmed 91-6: D 51-0; R 38-6; I 2-0. A "yea" was a vote in support of the president's position. March 15, 2012.

	46	47	48	49	50
ALABAMA					
Shelby	Y	Y	Y	Y	Y
Sessions	Y	Y	Y	Y	Y
ALASKA					
Murkowski	Y	Y	Y	Y	Y
Begich	Y	N	Y	Y	Y
ARIZONA					
McCain	N	Y	N	Y	Y
Kyl	N	Y	N	Y	Y
ARKANSAS					
Pryor	Y	N	Y	Y	Y
Boozman	Y	Y	Y	Y	Y
CALIFORNIA					
Feinstein	Y	N	Y	Y	Y
Boxer	Y	N	Y	Y	Y
COLORADO					
Udall	Y	N	Y	Y	Y
Bennet	Y	N	Y	Y	Y
CONNECTICUT					
Lieberman	Y	N	Y	Y	Y
Blumenthal	Y	N	Y	Y	Y
DELAWARE					
Carper	Y	N	Y	Y	Y
Coons	Y	N	Y	Y	Y
FLORIDA					
Nelson	Y	N	Y	Y	Y
Rubio	Y	Y	N	Y	Y
GEORGIA					
Chambliss	Y	Y	Y	Y	Y
Isakson	Y	Y	Y	Y	Y
HAWAII					
Inouye	Y	N	Y	Y	Y
Akaka	Y	N	Y	Y	Y
IDAHO					
Crapo	?	?	?	Y	Y
Risch	N	Y	N	Y	Y
ILLINOIS					
Durbin	Y	N	Y	Y	Y
Kirk	?	?	?	?	?
INDIANA					
Lugar	N	Y	N	Y	Y
Coats	N	Y	N	Y	Y
IOWA					
Grassley	N	Y	Y	Y	Y
Harkin	Y	N	Y	Y	Y
KANSAS					
Roberts	N	Y	Y	Y	Y
Moran	N	Y	Y	Y	Y
KENTUCKY					
McConnell	N	Y	N	Y	Y
Paul	N	Y	N	Y	N
LOUISIANA					
Landrieu	Y	Y	Y	Y	Y
Vitter	Y	Y	Y	Y	N
MAINE					
Snowe	Y	N	Y	Y	Y
Collins	Y	N	Y	Y	Y
MARYLAND					
Mikulski	Y	N	Y	Y	Y
Cardin	Y	N	Y	Y	Y
MASSACHUSETTS					
Kerry	Y	N	Y	Y	Y
Brown	Y	N	Y	Y	Y
MICHIGAN					
Levin	Y	N	Y	Y	Y
Stabenow	Y	N	Y	Y	Y
MINNESOTA					
Klobuchar	Y	N	Y	Y	Y
Franken	Y	N	Y	Y	Y
MISSISSIPPI					
Cochran	Y	Y	Y	Y	Y
Wicker	N	Y	Y	Y	Y
MISSOURI					
McCaskill	Y	N	Y	Y	Y
Blunt	N	Y	Y	Y	N
MONTANA					
Baucus	Y	N	Y	Y	Y
Tester	Y	N	Y	Y	Y
NEBRASKA					
Nelson	Y	N	Y	Y	Y
Johanns	N	Y	N	Y	Y
NEVADA					
Reid	Y	N	Y	Y	Y
Heller	Y	Y	Y	Y	Y
NEW HAMPSHIRE					
Shaheen	Y	N	Y	Y	Y
Ayotte	Y	Y	N	Y	Y
NEW JERSEY					
Lautenberg	?	?	?	Y	Y
Menendez	Y	N	Y	Y	Y
NEW MEXICO					
Bingaman	Y	N	Y	Y	Y
Udall	Y	N	Y	Y	Y
NEW YORK					
Schumer	Y	N	Y	Y	Y
Gillibrand	Y	N	Y	Y	Y
NORTH CAROLINA					
Burr	N	Y	N	Y	Y
Hagan	Y	N	Y	Y	Y
NORTH DAKOTA					
Conrad	Y	N	Y	Y	Y
Hoeven	Y	Y	Y	Y	Y
OHIO					
Brown	Y	N	Y	Y	Y
Portman	Y	Y	N	Y	Y
OKLAHOMA					
Inhofe	Y	Y	Y	Y	N
Coburn	Y	Y	N	Y	Y
OREGON					
Wyden	Y	N	Y	Y	Y
Merkley	Y	N	Y	Y	Y
PENNSYLVANIA					
Casey	Y	N	Y	Y	Y
Toomey	Y	Y	N	Y	Y
RHODE ISLAND					
Reed	Y	N	Y	Y	Y
Whitehouse	Y	N	Y	Y	Y
SOUTH CAROLINA					
Graham	Y	Y	N	Y	Y
DeMint	N	Y	N	N	N
SOUTH DAKOTA					
Johnson	Y	N	Y	Y	Y
Thune	N	Y	Y	Y	Y
TENNESSEE					
Alexander	N	Y	Y	+	+
Corker	N	Y	N	Y	Y
TEXAS					
Hutchison	Y	Y	Y	Y	Y
Cornyn	N	Y	N	Y	Y
UTAH					
Hatch	+	+	–	?	?
Lee	N	Y	N	N	N
VERMONT					
Leahy	Y	N	Y	Y	Y
Sanders	Y	N	Y	Y	Y
VIRGINIA					
Webb	Y	N	Y	Y	Y
Warner	Y	N	Y	Y	Y
WASHINGTON					
Murray	Y	N	Y	Y	Y
Cantwell	Y	N	Y	Y	Y
WEST VIRGINIA					
Rockefeller	Y	N	Y	Y	Y
Manchin	Y	N	Y	Y	Y
WISCONSIN					
Kohl	Y	N	Y	Y	Y
Johnson	Y	Y	N	Y	Y
WYOMING					
Enzi	Y	Y	N	Y	Y
Barrasso	Y	Y	N	Y	Y

KEY   Republicans   Democrats   *Independents*

Y Voted for (yea)	X Paired against	C Voted "present" to avoid possible conflict of interest
# Paired for	– Announced against	
+ Announced for	P Voted "present"	? Did not vote or otherwise make a position known
N Voted against (nay)		

IN THE SENATE | By Vote Number

51. **HR 3606. Small-Business Startups/Cloture.** Motion to invoke cloture (thus limiting debate) on the Reed, D-R.I., substitute amendment that would ease certain Securities and Exchange Commission regulations for small businesses. It would exempt certain companies with less than $350 million in revenue from some federal audit requirements. Motion rejected 54-45: D 51-0; R 1-45; I 2-0. Three-fifths of the total Senate (60) is required to invoke cloture. March 20, 2012.

52. **HR 3606. Small-Business Startups/Cloture.** Motion to invoke cloture (thus limiting debate) on the Cantwell, D-Wash., amendment that would reauthorize the charter for the Export-Import bank for four years and increase its lending cap by $40 billion. Motion rejected 55-44: D 51-0; R 3-43; I 1-1. Three-fifths of the total Senate (60) is required to invoke cloture. March 20, 2012.

53. **HR 3606. Small-Business Startups/Cloture.** Motion to invoke cloture (thus limiting debate) on the bill that would define "emerging growth companies" and exempt them from certain independent auditing requirements. It would lift a Securities and Exchange Commission ban that prevents small, privately held companies from using advertisements to solicit investors. Motion agreed to 76-22: D 30-21; R 45-0; I 1-1. Three-fifths of the total Senate (60) is required to invoke cloture. March 21, 2012.

54. **HR 3606. Small-Business Startups/'Crowdfunding' Restrictions.** Merkley, D-Ore., amendment that would strike provisions in the underlying bill on "crowdfunding," which involves pooling money, usually via the Internet. The amendment would replace them with more restrictive conditions under which security issuers could advertise to potential investors and businesses could use crowdfunding. It would require anyone acting as a crowdfunding intermediary to register with securities regulators. Adopted 64-35: D 50-1; R 12-34; I 2-0. March 22, 2012.

	51	52	53	54		51	52	53	54
ALABAMA					**MONTANA**				
Shelby	N	N	Y	N	Baucus	Y	Y	N	Y
Sessions	N	N	Y	N	Tester	Y	Y	Y	Y
ALASKA					**NEBRASKA**				
Murkowski	N	N	Y	Y	Nelson	Y	Y	Y	Y
Begich	Y	Y	Y	Y	Johanns	N	N	Y	N
ARIZONA					**NEVADA**				
McCain	N	N	Y	N	Reid	Y	Y	Y	Y
Kyl	N	N	Y	N	Heller	N	Y	Y	N
ARKANSAS					**NEW HAMPSHIRE**				
Pryor	Y	Y	Y	Y	Shaheen	Y	Y	Y	Y
Boozman	N	N	Y	N	Ayotte	N	N	Y	N
CALIFORNIA					**NEW JERSEY**				
Feinstein	Y	Y	N	Y	Lautenberg	Y	Y	N	Y
Boxer	Y	Y	N	Y	Menendez	Y	Y	N	Y
COLORADO					**NEW MEXICO**				
Udall	Y	Y	Y	Y	Bingaman	Y	Y	Y	Y
Bennet	Y	Y	Y	Y	Udall	Y	Y	Y	Y
CONNECTICUT					**NEW YORK**				
Lieberman	Y	Y	Y	Y	Schumer	Y	Y	Y	Y
Blumenthal	Y	Y	N	Y	Gillibrand	Y	Y	N	Y
DELAWARE					**NORTH CAROLINA**				
Carper	Y	Y	Y	Y	Burr	N	N	Y	N
Coons	Y	Y	Y	Y	Hagan	Y	Y	Y	Y
FLORIDA					**NORTH DAKOTA**				
Nelson	Y	Y	Y	Y	Conrad	Y	Y	N	Y
Rubio	N	N	Y	N	Hoeven	N	N	Y	N
GEORGIA					**OHIO**				
Chambliss	N	N	Y	N	Brown	Y	Y	N	Y
Isakson	N	N	Y	N	Portman	N	N	Y	N
HAWAII					**OKLAHOMA**				
Inouye	Y	Y	Y	Y	Inhofe	N	N	Y	N
Akaka	Y	Y	N	Y	Coburn	N	N	Y	N
IDAHO					**OREGON**				
Crapo	N	N	?	N	Wyden	Y	Y	Y	Y
Risch	N	N	Y	N	Merkley	Y	Y	N	Y
ILLINOIS					**PENNSYLVANIA**				
Durbin	Y	Y	Y	Y	Casey	Y	Y	Y	Y
Kirk	?	?	?	?	Toomey	N	N	Y	N
INDIANA					**RHODE ISLAND**				
Lugar	N	N	Y	N	Reed	Y	Y	N	Y
Coats	N	N	Y	Y	Whitehouse	Y	Y	N	Y
IOWA					**SOUTH CAROLINA**				
Grassley	N	N	Y	Y	Graham	N	N	Y	N
Harkin	Y	Y	N	Y	DeMint	N	N	Y	N
KANSAS					**SOUTH DAKOTA**				
Roberts	N	N	Y	N	Johnson	Y	Y	Y	Y
Moran	N	N	Y	Y	Thune	N	N	Y	N
KENTUCKY					**TENNESSEE**				
McConnell	N	N	Y	N	Alexander	N	N	Y	N
Paul	N	N	Y	N	Corker	N	N	Y	N
LOUISIANA					**TEXAS**				
Landrieu	Y	Y	N	Y	Hutchison	N	N	Y	Y
Vitter	N	N	Y	N	Cornyn	N	N	Y	Y
MAINE					**UTAH**				
Snowe	N	N	Y	Y	Hatch	N	N	Y	N
Collins	N	Y	Y	Y	Lee	N	N	Y	N
MARYLAND					**VERMONT**				
Mikulski	Y	Y	N	Y	Leahy	Y	Y	N	Y
Cardin	Y	Y	N	Y	*Sanders*	Y	N	N	Y
MASSACHUSETTS					**VIRGINIA**				
Kerry	Y	Y	Y	Y	Webb	Y	Y	N	N
Brown	Y	Y	Y	Y	Warner	Y	Y	Y	Y
MICHIGAN					**WASHINGTON**				
Levin	Y	Y	N	Y	Murray	Y	Y	Y	Y
Stabenow	Y	Y	Y	Y	Cantwell	Y	Y	Y	Y
MINNESOTA					**WEST VIRGINIA**				
Klobuchar	Y	Y	Y	Y	Rockefeller	Y	Y	Y	Y
Franken	Y	Y	N	Y	Manchin	Y	Y	Y	Y
MISSISSIPPI					**WISCONSIN**				
Cochran	N	N	Y	Y	Kohl	Y	Y	Y	Y
Wicker	N	N	Y	Y	Johnson	N	N	Y	N
MISSOURI					**WYOMING**				
McCaskill	Y	Y	Y	Y	Enzi	N	N	Y	N
Blunt	N	N	Y	Y	Barrasso	N	N	Y	N

KEY	**Republicans**	Democrats	*Independents*	
Y	Voted for (yea)	X	Paired against	C Voted "present" to avoid possible conflict of interest
#	Paired for	–	Announced against	
+	Announced for	P	Voted "present"	? Did not vote or otherwise make a position known
N	Voted against (nay)			

IN THE SENATE | By Vote Number

55. **HR 3606. Small-Business Startups/Passage.** Passage of the bill that would define "emerging growth companies" and exempt them from certain independent auditing requirements. It would increase from $5 million to $50 million the annual public offering threshold for companies to be exempt from full Securities and Exchange Commission filing requirements and raise the number of shareholders that would trigger mandatory SEC registration from 750 to 2,000. It also would raise to 2,000 the number of shareholders that would trigger a requirement for SEC registration for a bank. The bill would lift an SEC ban that prevents small, privately-held companies from using advertisements to solicit investors and allow companies to sell up to $1 million worth of securities. As amended, it also would require anyone acting as a "crowdfunding" intermediary to register with securities regulators. Passed 73-26: D 26-25; R 46-0; I 1-1. A "yea" was a vote in support of the president's position. March 22, 2012.

56. **S 2038. Congressional Insider Trading Ban/Cloture.** Motion to invoke cloture (thus limiting debate) on the Reid, D-Nev., motion to concur in the House amendment to the bill that would clarify that members of Congress as well as officials and senior staff of the legislative, executive and judicial branches of the U.S. government are covered by current regulations that bar the use of non-public information for trading stocks and bonds. It would require lawmakers and other covered officials to publicly report any stock or securities transaction within 45 days of when the transaction occurs. It would bar lawmakers and other covered officials from participating in initial stock offerings on a favored basis. Motion agreed to 96-3: D 51-0; R 43-3; I 2-0. Three-fifths of the total Senate (60) is required to invoke cloture. (Subsequently, the motion to concur in the House amendment was agreed to by unanimous consent, thus clearing the bill for the president.) A "yea" was a vote in support of the president's position. March 22, 2012.

57. **Nuffer Nomination/Confirmation.** Confirmation of President Obama's nomination of David Nuffer of Utah to be a judge for the U.S. District Court for the District of Utah. Confirmed 96-2: D 51-0; R 43-2; I 2-0. A "yea" was a vote in support of the president's position. March 22, 2012.

58. **Abrams Nomination/Confirmation.** Confirmation of President Obama's nomination of Ronnie Abrams of New York to be a judge for the U.S. District Court for the Southern District of New York. Confirmed 96-2: D 51-0; R 43-2; I 2-0. A "yea" was a vote in support of the president's position. March 22, 2012.

	55	56	57	58			55	56	57	58
ALABAMA						**MONTANA**				
Shelby	Y	Y	Y	Y		Baucus	N	Y	Y	Y
Sessions	Y	Y	Y	Y		Tester	Y	Y	Y	Y
ALASKA						**NEBRASKA**				
Murkowski	Y	Y	Y	Y		Nelson	Y	Y	Y	Y
Begich	N	Y	Y	Y		**Johanns**	Y	Y	Y	Y
ARIZONA						**NEVADA**				
McCain	Y	Y	Y	Y		Reid	Y	Y	Y	Y
Kyl	Y	Y	Y	Y		**Heller**	Y	Y	?	?
ARKANSAS						**NEW HAMPSHIRE**				
Pryor	Y	Y	Y	Y		Shaheen	Y	Y	Y	Y
Boozman	Y	Y	Y	Y		**Ayotte**	Y	Y	Y	Y
CALIFORNIA						**NEW JERSEY**				
Feinstein	N	Y	Y	Y		Lautenberg	N	Y	Y	Y
Boxer	N	Y	Y	Y		Menendez	Y	Y	Y	Y
COLORADO						**NEW MEXICO**				
Udall	Y	Y	Y	Y		Bingaman	Y	Y	Y	Y
Bennet	Y	Y	Y	Y		Udall	N	Y	Y	Y
CONNECTICUT						**NEW YORK**				
Lieberman	Y	Y	Y	Y		Schumer	Y	Y	Y	Y
Blumenthal	N	Y	Y	Y		Gillibrand	N	Y	Y	Y
DELAWARE						**NORTH CAROLINA**				
Carper	Y	Y	Y	Y		**Burr**	Y	N	Y	Y
Coons	Y	Y	Y	Y		Hagan	Y	Y	Y	Y
FLORIDA						**NORTH DAKOTA**				
Nelson	Y	Y	Y	Y		Conrad	N	Y	Y	Y
Rubio	Y	Y	Y	Y		**Hoeven**	Y	Y	Y	Y
GEORGIA						**OHIO**				
Chambliss	Y	Y	Y	Y		Brown	N	Y	Y	Y
Isakson	Y	Y	Y	Y		**Portman**	Y	Y	Y	Y
HAWAII						**OKLAHOMA**				
Inouye	Y	Y	Y	Y		**Inhofe**	Y	Y	Y	Y
Akaka	N	Y	Y	Y		**Coburn**	Y	N	Y	Y
IDAHO						**OREGON**				
Crapo	Y	Y	Y	Y		Wyden	Y	Y	Y	Y
Risch	Y	Y	Y	Y		Merkley	N	Y	Y	Y
ILLINOIS						**PENNSYLVANIA**				
Durbin	N	Y	Y	Y		Casey	Y	Y	Y	Y
Kirk	?	?	?	?		**Toomey**	Y	Y	Y	Y
INDIANA						**RHODE ISLAND**				
Lugar	Y	Y	Y	Y		Reed	N	Y	Y	Y
Coats	Y	Y	Y	Y		Whitehouse	N	Y	Y	Y
IOWA						**SOUTH CAROLINA**				
Grassley	Y	N	Y	Y		**Graham**	Y	Y	Y	Y
Harkin	N	Y	Y	Y		**DeMint**	Y	Y	N	N
KANSAS						**SOUTH DAKOTA**				
Roberts	Y	Y	Y	Y		Johnson	Y	Y	Y	Y
Moran	Y	Y	Y	Y		**Thune**	Y	Y	Y	Y
KENTUCKY						**TENNESSEE**				
McConnell	Y	Y	Y	Y		**Alexander**	Y	Y	Y	Y
Paul	Y	Y	Y	Y		**Corker**	Y	Y	Y	Y
LOUISIANA						**TEXAS**				
Landrieu	N	Y	Y	Y		**Hutchison**	Y	Y	Y	Y
Vitter	Y	Y	Y	Y		**Cornyn**	Y	Y	Y	Y
MAINE						**UTAH**				
Snowe	Y	Y	Y	Y		**Hatch**	Y	Y	Y	Y
Collins	Y	Y	Y	Y		**Lee**	Y	Y	N	N
MARYLAND						**VERMONT**				
Mikulski	N	Y	Y	Y		Leahy	N	Y	Y	Y
Cardin	N	Y	Y	Y		*Sanders*	N	Y	Y	Y
MASSACHUSETTS						**VIRGINIA**				
Kerry	Y	Y	Y	Y		Webb	N	Y	Y	Y
Brown	Y	Y	Y	Y		Warner	Y	Y	Y	Y
MICHIGAN						**WASHINGTON**				
Levin	N	Y	Y	Y		Murray	N	Y	Y	Y
Stabenow	Y	Y	Y	Y		Cantwell	Y	Y	Y	Y
MINNESOTA						**WEST VIRGINIA**				
Klobuchar	Y	Y	Y	Y		Rockefeller	N	Y	Y	Y
Franken	N	Y	Y	Y		Manchin	Y	Y	Y	Y
MISSISSIPPI						**WISCONSIN**				
Cochran	Y	Y	Y	Y		Kohl	Y	Y	Y	Y
Wicker	Y	Y	Y	Y		**Johnson**	Y	Y	Y	Y
MISSOURI						**WYOMING**				
McCaskill	Y	Y	Y	Y		**Enzi**	Y	Y	Y	Y
Blunt	Y	Y	Y	Y		**Barrasso**	Y	Y	Y	Y

KEY   **Republicans**   Democrats   *Independents*

Y	Voted for (yea)	X	Paired against	C	Voted "present" to avoid possible conflict of interest
#	Paired for	–	Announced against	
+	Announced for	P	Voted "present"	?	Did not vote or otherwise make a position known
N	Voted against (nay)			

IN THE SENATE | By Vote Number

59. **S 2204. Oil and Gas Tax Breaks/Cloture.** Motion to invoke cloture (thus limiting debate) on the Reid, D-Nev., motion to proceed to the bill that would roll back certain tax preferences for large oil and gas companies. Motion agreed to 92-4: D 47-3; R 43-1; I 2-0. Three-fifths of the total Senate (60) is required to invoke cloture. March 26, 2012.

60. **S 1789. Postal Service Overhaul/Cloture.** Motion to invoke cloture (thus limiting debate) on the Reid, D-Nev., motion to proceed to the bill that would allow the Postal Service to recoup about $11 billion in overpayments to a retirement account and use the money to provide to some 100,000 employees financial incentives to retire. It also would delay for two years a cost-savings plan to eliminate Saturday postal deliveries. Motion rejected 51-46: D 44-7; R 5-39; I 2-0. Three-fifths of the total Senate (60) is required to invoke cloture. (Subsequently, Reid entered a motion to reconsider the vote.). March 27, 2012.

61. **Du Nomination/Confirmation.** Confirmation of President Obama's nomination of Miranda Du of Nevada to be a judge for the U.S. District Court for the District of Nevada. Confirmed 59-39: D 51-0; R 6-39; I 2-0. A "yea" was a vote in support of the president's position. March 28, 2012.

62. **Morgan Nomination/Confirmation.** Confirmation of President Obama's nomination of Susie Morgan of Louisiana to be a judge for the U.S. District Court for the Eastern District of Louisiana. Confirmed 96-1: D 51-0; R 43-1; I 2-0. A "yea" was a vote in support of the president's position. March 28, 2012.

63. **S 2204. Oil and Gas Tax Breaks/Cloture.** Motion to invoke cloture (thus limiting debate) on the bill that would roll back certain tax preferences for large oil and gas companies. The bill would use revenue generated from eliminating certain oil and gas tax incentives to pay for an extension of some renewable-energy tax credits and incentives. Motion rejected 51-47: D 47-4; R 2-43; I 2-0. Three-fifths of the total Senate (60) is required to invoke cloture. A "yea" was a vote in support of the president's position. March 29, 2012.

	59	60	61	62	63
ALABAMA					
Shelby	Y	N	N	Y	N
Sessions	Y	?	N	Y	N
ALASKA					
Murkowski	Y	N	Y	Y	N
Begich	N	Y	Y	Y	N
ARIZONA					
McCain	Y	N	Y	Y	N
Kyl	Y	N	N	Y	N
ARKANSAS					
Pryor	Y	Y	Y	Y	Y
Boozman	Y	N	N	Y	N
CALIFORNIA					
Feinstein	Y	Y	Y	Y	Y
Boxer	+	Y	Y	Y	Y
COLORADO					
Udall	Y	Y	Y	Y	Y
Bennet	Y	Y	Y	Y	Y
CONNECTICUT					
Lieberman	Y	Y	Y	Y	Y
Blumenthal	Y	Y	Y	Y	Y
DELAWARE					
Carper	Y	Y	Y	Y	Y
Coons	Y	Y	Y	Y	Y
FLORIDA					
Nelson	Y	Y	Y	Y	Y
Rubio	Y	N	N	Y	N
GEORGIA					
Chambliss	Y	N	N	Y	N
Isakson	Y	N	N	Y	N
HAWAII					
Inouye	Y	Y	Y	Y	Y
Akaka	Y	Y	Y	Y	Y
IDAHO					
Crapo	Y	N	N	Y	N
Risch	Y	N	N	Y	N
ILLINOIS					
Durbin	Y	Y	Y	Y	Y
Kirk	?	?	?	?	?
INDIANA					
Lugar	Y	N	N	Y	N
Coats	Y	N	N	Y	N
IOWA					
Grassley	Y	N	N	Y	N
Harkin	Y	Y	Y	Y	Y
KANSAS					
Roberts	Y	N	N	Y	N
Moran	Y	Y	N	Y	N
KENTUCKY					
McConnell	Y	N	N	Y	N
Paul	Y	N	N	Y	N
LOUISIANA					
Landrieu	N	Y	Y	Y	N
Vitter	Y	N	N	Y	N
MAINE					
Snowe	Y	Y	N	Y	Y
Collins	Y	Y	Y	Y	Y
MARYLAND					
Mikulski	Y	N	Y	Y	Y
Cardin	Y	N	Y	Y	Y
MASSACHUSETTS					
Kerry	Y	Y	Y	Y	Y
Brown	Y	Y	N	Y	N
MICHIGAN					
Levin	Y	Y	Y	Y	Y
Stabenow	Y	Y	Y	Y	Y
MINNESOTA					
Klobuchar	Y	Y	Y	Y	Y
Franken	Y	Y	Y	Y	Y
MISSISSIPPI					
Cochran	Y	N	N	Y	N
Wicker	Y	N	N	Y	N
MISSOURI					
McCaskill	Y	Y	Y	Y	Y
Blunt	Y	N	N	Y	N

	59	60	61	62	63
MONTANA					
Baucus	Y	N	Y	Y	Y
Tester	Y	Y	Y	Y	Y
NEBRASKA					
Nelson	N	Y	Y	Y	N
Johanns	Y	N	N	Y	N
NEVADA					
Reid	Y	N	Y	Y	Y
Heller	Y	N	Y	Y	N
NEW HAMPSHIRE					
Shaheen	Y	Y	Y	Y	Y
Ayotte	Y	N	N	Y	N
NEW JERSEY					
Lautenberg	Y	Y	Y	Y	Y
Menendez	Y	Y	Y	Y	Y
NEW MEXICO					
Bingaman	Y	Y	Y	Y	Y
Udall	Y	Y	Y	Y	Y
NEW YORK					
Schumer	Y	Y	Y	Y	Y
Gillibrand	Y	Y	Y	Y	Y
NORTH CAROLINA					
Burr	Y	N	N	Y	N
Hagan	Y	Y	Y	Y	Y
NORTH DAKOTA					
Conrad	Y	Y	Y	Y	Y
Hoeven	Y	Y	N	Y	N
OHIO					
Brown	Y	Y	Y	Y	Y
Portman	Y	N	N	Y	N
OKLAHOMA					
Inhofe	N	N	N	Y	N
Coburn	Y	N	N	Y	N
OREGON					
Wyden	Y	Y	Y	Y	Y
Merkley	Y	N	Y	Y	Y
PENNSYLVANIA					
Casey	Y	Y	Y	Y	Y
Toomey	Y	N	N	Y	N
RHODE ISLAND					
Reed	Y	Y	Y	Y	Y
Whitehouse	Y	Y	Y	Y	Y
SOUTH CAROLINA					
Graham	Y	N	Y	Y	N
DeMint	Y	N	N	N	N
SOUTH DAKOTA					
Johnson	Y	Y	Y	Y	Y
Thune	Y	N	N	Y	N
TENNESSEE					
Alexander	Y	N	Y	Y	N
Corker	Y	N	N	Y	N
TEXAS					
Hutchison	Y	N	N	Y	N
Cornyn	Y	N	N	Y	N
UTAH					
Hatch	?	?	−	+	−
Lee	?	N	N	?	N
VERMONT					
Leahy	Y	Y	Y	Y	Y
Sanders	Y	Y	Y	Y	Y
VIRGINIA					
Webb	Y	Y	Y	N	Y
Warner	Y	Y	Y	Y	Y
WASHINGTON					
Murray	Y	Y	Y	Y	Y
Cantwell	Y	Y	Y	Y	Y
WEST VIRGINIA					
Rockefeller	Y	N	Y	Y	Y
Manchin	Y	N	Y	Y	Y
WISCONSIN					
Kohl	Y	Y	Y	Y	Y
Johnson	Y	N	N	Y	N
WYOMING					
Enzi	Y	N	N	Y	N
Barrasso	Y	N	N	Y	N

KEY   **Republicans**   Democrats   *Independents*

Y Voted for (yea)	X Paired against	C Voted "present" to avoid possible conflict of interest
# Paired for	− Announced against	
+ Announced for	P Voted "present"	? Did not vote or otherwise make a position known
N Voted against (nay)		

IN THE SENATE | By Vote Number

64. Thacker Nomination/Confirmation. Confirmation of President Obama's nomination of Stephanie Dawn Thacker of West Virginia to be a judge for the 4th U.S. Circuit Court of Appeals. Confirmed 91-3: D 49-0; R 41-3; I 1-0. A "yea" was a vote in support of the president's position. April 16, 2012.

65. S 2230. Minimum Tax Rates/Cloture. Motion to invoke cloture (thus limiting debate) on the Reid, D-Nev., motion to proceed to the bill that would require taxpayers with more than $2 million in income to pay an alternative minimum of 30 percent in federal taxes, with a phase-in of the higher rate starting at the $1 million level. Motion rejected 51-45: D 49-1; R 1-44; I 1-0. Three-fifths of the total Senate (60) is required to invoke cloture. A "yea" was a vote in support of the president's position. April 16, 2012.

66. S 1789. Postal Service Overhaul/Cloture. Motion to invoke cloture (thus limiting debate) on the Reid, D-Nev., motion to proceed to the bill that would allow the Postal Service to recoup about $11 billion in overpayments to a retirement account and use the money to provide financial incentives to some 100,000 employees to retire. It also would delay for two years a cost-savings plan to eliminate Saturday postal deliveries. Motion agreed to 74-22: D 45-4; R 27-18; I 2-0. Three-fifths of the total Senate (60) is required to invoke cloture. (Previously, the Senate adopted a motion to reconsider the vote by unanimous consent.) April 17, 2012.

67. Wimes Nomination/Confirmation. Confirmation of President Obama's nomination of Brian C. Wimes of Missouri to be a judge for the U.S. District Courts for the Eastern and Western Districts of Missouri. Confirmed 92-1: D 49-0; R 41-1; I 2-0. A "yea" was a vote in support of the president's position. April 23, 2012.

68. S J Res 36. Union Election Rules/Motion to Proceed. Enzi, R-Wyo., motion to proceed to the joint resolution that would disapprove of a National Labor Relations Board rule regarding union elections. Motion rejected 45-54: D 0-51; R 45-1; I 0-2. A "nay" was a vote in support of the president's position. April 24, 2012.

69. S 1789. Postal Service Overhaul/Motion to Waive. Lieberman, I-Conn., motion to waive all applicable budget laws and budget resolutions with respect to the Sessions, R-Ala., point of order against the bill that would allow the Postal Service to recoup about $11 billion in overpayments to a retirement account and use the money to provide financial incentives to some 100,000 employees to retire. Motion agreed to 62-37: D 51-0; R 9-37; I 2-0. A three-fifths majority vote of the total Senate (60) is required to waive the applicable budget laws. April 24, 2012.

	64	65	66	67	68	69		64	65	66	67	68	69
ALABAMA							**MONTANA**						
Shelby	Y	N	Y	Y	Y	N	Baucus	Y	Y	N	Y	N	Y
Sessions	Y	N	Y	Y	Y	N	Tester	Y	Y	Y	Y	N	Y
ALASKA							**NEBRASKA**						
Murkowski	Y	N	Y	Y	N	Y	Nelson	Y	Y	Y	Y	N	Y
Begich	Y	Y	Y	Y	N	Y	**Johanns**	Y	N	N	Y	N	Y
ARIZONA							**NEVADA**						
McCain	Y	N	N	?	Y	N	Reid	Y	Y	Y	Y	N	Y
Kyl	Y	N	Y	Y	Y	N	**Heller**	Y	N	N	Y	Y	N
ARKANSAS							**NEW HAMPSHIRE**						
Pryor	Y	N	Y	Y	N	Y	Shaheen	Y	Y	Y	Y	N	Y
Boozman	Y	N	Y	Y	Y	N	**Ayotte**	Y	N	Y	Y	Y	N
CALIFORNIA							**NEW JERSEY**						
Feinstein	Y	Y	Y	Y	N	Y	Lautenberg	Y	Y	Y	Y	N	Y
Boxer	Y	Y	Y	Y	N	Y	Menendez	Y	Y	Y	Y	N	Y
COLORADO							**NEW MEXICO**						
Udall	Y	Y	Y	Y	N	Y	Bingaman	Y	Y	Y	Y	N	Y
Bennet	?	Y	Y	Y	N	Y	Udall	Y	Y	Y	Y	N	Y
CONNECTICUT							**NEW YORK**						
Lieberman	?	?	Y	Y	N	Y	Schumer	Y	Y	Y	Y	N	Y
Blumenthal	Y	Y	Y	Y	N	Y	Gillibrand	Y	Y	Y	Y	N	Y
DELAWARE							**NORTH CAROLINA**						
Carper	Y	Y	Y	Y	N	Y	**Burr**	Y	N	N	Y	Y	N
Coons	Y	Y	Y	Y	N	Y	Hagan	Y	Y	Y	Y	N	Y
FLORIDA							**NORTH DAKOTA**						
Nelson	Y	Y	Y	Y	N	Y	Conrad	Y	Y	Y	Y	N	Y
Rubio	Y	N	N	Y	Y	N	**Hoeven**	Y	N	Y	Y	Y	Y
GEORGIA							**OHIO**						
Chambliss	Y	N	N	Y	Y	N	Brown	Y	Y	Y	Y	N	Y
Isakson	Y	N	Y	Y	Y	N	**Portman**	Y	N	Y	Y	Y	N
HAWAII							**OKLAHOMA**						
Inouye	Y	Y	Y	?	N	Y	**Inhofe**	Y	N	N	Y	Y	N
Akaka	?	?	?	Y	N	Y	**Coburn**	Y	N	N	Y	Y	N
IDAHO							**OREGON**						
Crapo	Y	N	N	Y	Y	N	Wyden	Y	Y	Y	Y	N	Y
Risch	Y	N	N	Y	Y	N	Merkley	Y	Y	Y	Y	N	Y
ILLINOIS							**PENNSYLVANIA**						
Durbin	Y	Y	Y	Y	N	Y	Casey	Y	Y	Y	?	N	Y
Kirk	?	?	?	?	?	?	**Toomey**	Y	N	N	?	Y	N
INDIANA							**RHODE ISLAND**						
Lugar	Y	N	Y	Y	Y	N	Reed	Y	Y	Y	Y	N	Y
Coats	Y	N	Y	Y	Y	N	Whitehouse	Y	Y	Y	Y	N	Y
IOWA							**SOUTH CAROLINA**						
Grassley	Y	N	Y	Y	Y	Y	**Graham**	Y	N	Y	Y	Y	N
Harkin	Y	Y	Y	Y	N	Y	**DeMint**	N	N	N	?	Y	N
KANSAS							**SOUTH DAKOTA**						
Roberts	Y	N	Y	Y	Y	Y	Johnson	Y	Y	Y	Y	N	Y
Moran	Y	N	Y	Y	Y	Y	**Thune**	Y	N	Y	Y	Y	N
KENTUCKY							**TENNESSEE**						
McConnell	Y	N	Y	Y	Y	N	**Alexander**	Y	N	Y	Y	Y	N
Paul	Y	N	N	Y	Y	N	**Corker**	Y	N	Y	Y	Y	N
LOUISIANA							**TEXAS**						
Landrieu	Y	Y	Y	Y	N	Y	**Hutchison**	Y	N	Y	Y	Y	N
Vitter	N	N	N	?	Y	N	**Cornyn**	Y	N	Y	Y	Y	N
MAINE							**UTAH**						
Snowe	Y	N	Y	Y	Y	Y	**Hatch**	+	−	?	Y	Y	N
Collins	Y	Y	Y	Y	Y	Y	**Lee**	N	N	N	N	Y	N
MARYLAND							**VERMONT**						
Mikulski	Y	Y	N	Y	N	Y	Leahy	Y	Y	+	Y	N	Y
Cardin	Y	Y	N	Y	N	Y	*Sanders*	Y	Y	Y	Y	N	Y
MASSACHUSETTS							**VIRGINIA**						
Kerry	Y	Y	Y	Y	N	Y	Webb	Y	Y	Y	Y	N	Y
Brown	Y	N	Y	Y	Y	Y	Warner	Y	Y	Y	Y	N	Y
MICHIGAN							**WASHINGTON**						
Levin	Y	Y	Y	Y	N	Y	Murray	Y	Y	Y	Y	N	Y
Stabenow	Y	Y	Y	Y	N	Y	Cantwell	Y	Y	Y	Y	N	Y
MINNESOTA							**WEST VIRGINIA**						
Klobuchar	Y	Y	Y	Y	N	Y	Rockefeller	Y	Y	Y	Y	N	Y
Franken	Y	Y	Y	Y	N	Y	Manchin	Y	Y	N	Y	N	Y
MISSISSIPPI							**WISCONSIN**						
Cochran	Y	N	Y	Y	Y	Y	Kohl	Y	Y	Y	Y	N	Y
Wicker	Y	N	Y	Y	Y	N	**Johnson**	Y	N	N	Y	Y	N
MISSOURI							**WYOMING**						
McCaskill	Y	Y	Y	Y	N	Y	**Enzi**	?	N	Y	Y	Y	N
Blunt	Y	N	Y	Y	Y	Y	**Barrasso**	Y	N	Y	Y	Y	N

KEY **Republicans** Democrats *Independents*

Y	Voted for (yea)	X	Paired against
#	Paired for	−	Announced against
+	Announced for	P	Voted "present"
N	Voted against (nay)		

C Voted "present" to avoid possible conflict of interest

? Did not vote or otherwise make a position known

IN THE SENATE | By Vote Number

70. **S 1789. Postal Service Overhaul/Postal Reorganization.** McCain, R-Ariz., amendment to the Lieberman, I-Conn., substitute amendment. The McCain amendment would establish a new Commission on Postal Reorganization responsible for providing recommendations for postal facility closures and consolidations. Rejected 30-69: D 0-51; R 30-16; I 0-2. (By unanimous consent, the Senate agreed to raise the majority requirement for adoption of the McCain amendment to 60 votes.) April 24, 2012.

71. **S 1789. Postal Service Overhaul/Mandatory Retirement.** Coburn, R-Okla., amendment to the Lieberman, I-Conn., substitute amendment. The Coburn amendment would allow the U.S. postmaster general to require employees of the postal service eligible for retirement to retire, beginning two years after enactment of the bill. Rejected 33-65: D 0-51; R 33-12; I 0-2. (By unanimous consent, the Senate agreed to raise the majority requirement for adoption of the Coburn amendment to 60 votes.) April 24, 2012.

72. **S 1789. Postal Service Overhaul/Delivery Service.** Udall, D-N.M., amendment to the Lieberman, I-Conn., substitute amendment. The Udall amendment would strike provisions in the bill that would allow for reducing delivery service to five days a week starting two years from the date of the bill's enactment. Rejected 43-56: D 41-10; R 1-45; I 1-1. (By unanimous consent, the Senate agreed to raise the majority requirement for adoption of the Udall amendment to 60 votes.) April 24, 2012.

73. **S 1789. Postal Service Overhaul/Workers' Compensation.** Akaka, D-Hawaii, amendment to the Lieberman, I-Conn., substitute amendment. The Akaka amendment would strike provisions in the bill restricting workers' compensation and replace them with adjustments to laws governing federal employees. It would allow payments of certain benefits in the event of terrorism incidents and allow payments of up to $6,000 for funeral expenses in the event of death of certain federal employees. Rejected 46-53: D 44-7; R 1-45; I 1-1. (By unanimous consent, the Senate agreed to raise the majority requirement for adoption of the Akaka amendment to 60 votes.) April 24, 2012.

74. **S 1789. Postal Service Overhaul/Delivery Service.** Corker, R-Tenn., amendment to the Lieberman, I-Conn., substitute amendment. The Corker amendment would allow the Postal Service to transition immediately to a delivery service of five days per week. Rejected 29-70: D 0-51; R 29-17; I 0-2. (By unanimous consent, the Senate agreed to raise the majority requirement for adoption of the Corker amendment to 60 votes.) April 24, 2012.

75. **S 1789. Postal Service Overhaul/Supervisory Organizations.** Akaka, D-Hawaii, amendment to the Lieberman, I-Conn., substitute amendment. The Akaka amendment would allow supervisory organizations to participate in planning Postal Service pay policies, certain benefits and other policies. Rejected 57-42: D 51-0; R 4-42; I 2-0. (By unanimous consent, the Senate agreed to raise the majority requirement for adoption of the Akaka amendment to 60 votes.) April 24, 2012.

	70	71	72	73	74	75		70	71	72	73	74	75
ALABAMA							**MONTANA**						
Shelby	Y	Y	N	N	Y	N	Baucus	N	N	Y	Y	N	Y
Sessions	Y	Y	N	N	Y	N	Tester	N	N	Y	Y	N	Y
ALASKA							**NEBRASKA**						
Murkowski	N	Y	N	N	N	Y	Nelson	N	N	Y	Y	N	Y
Begich	N	N	Y	Y	N	Y	Johanns	Y	Y	N	N	Y	N
ARIZONA							**NEVADA**						
McCain	Y	Y	N	N	Y	N	Reid	N	N	Y	Y	N	Y
Kyl	Y	Y	N	N	Y	N	Heller	N	N	N	Y	N	N
ARKANSAS							**NEW HAMPSHIRE**						
Pryor	N	N	N	Y	N	Y	Shaheen	N	N	Y	Y	N	Y
Boozman	N	N	N	N	N	N	Ayotte	N	N	N	N	Y	N
CALIFORNIA							**NEW JERSEY**						
Feinstein	N	N	N	Y	N	Y	Lautenberg	N	N	Y	Y	N	Y
Boxer	N	N	Y	Y	N	Y	Menendez	N	N	Y	Y	N	Y
COLORADO							**NEW MEXICO**						
Udall	N	N	Y	N	N	Y	Bingaman	N	N	Y	Y	N	Y
Bennet	N	N	Y	N	N	Y	Udall	N	N	Y	Y	N	Y
CONNECTICUT							**NEW YORK**						
Lieberman	N	N	N	N	N	Y	Schumer	N	N	Y	Y	N	Y
Blumenthal	N	N	Y	N	N	Y	Gillibrand	N	N	Y	Y	N	Y
DELAWARE							**NORTH CAROLINA**						
Carper	N	N	N	N	N	Y	Burr	Y	Y	N	N	Y	N
Coons	N	N	Y	Y	N	Y	Hagan	N	N	N	N	N	Y
FLORIDA							**NORTH DAKOTA**						
Nelson	N	N	Y	Y	N	Y	Conrad	N	N	Y	Y	N	Y
Rubio	Y	N	N	N	Y	N	Hoeven	N	N	N	N	N	N
GEORGIA							**OHIO**						
Chambliss	Y	Y	N	N	Y	N	Brown	N	N	Y	Y	N	Y
Isakson	Y	Y	N	N	Y	N	Portman	Y	Y	N	N	N	N
HAWAII							**OKLAHOMA**						
Inouye	N	N	Y	Y	N	Y	Inhofe	Y	Y	N	N	Y	N
Akaka	N	N	N	Y	N	Y	Coburn	Y	Y	N	N	Y	N
IDAHO							**OREGON**						
Crapo	Y	Y	N	N	Y	N	Wyden	N	N	Y	Y	N	Y
Risch	Y	Y	N	N	Y	N	Merkley	N	N	Y	Y	N	Y
ILLINOIS							**PENNSYLVANIA**						
Durbin	N	N	Y	Y	N	Y	Casey	N	N	Y	Y	N	Y
Kirk	?	?	?	?	?	?	Toomey	Y	Y	N	N	Y	N
INDIANA							**RHODE ISLAND**						
Lugar	Y	N	N	N	Y	N	Reed	N	N	Y	Y	N	Y
Coats	Y	Y	N	N	Y	N	Whitehouse	N	N	Y	Y	N	Y
IOWA							**SOUTH CAROLINA**						
Grassley	N	N	N	N	N	N	Graham	Y	Y	N	N	Y	N
Harkin	N	N	Y	Y	N	Y	DeMint	Y	?	N	N	Y	N
KANSAS							**SOUTH DAKOTA**						
Roberts	N	Y	N	N	Y	N	Johnson	N	N	Y	Y	N	Y
Moran	N	Y	N	N	N	N	Thune	N	Y	N	N	N	N
KENTUCKY							**TENNESSEE**						
McConnell	Y	Y	N	N	Y	N	Alexander	Y	Y	N	N	Y	N
Paul	Y	Y	N	N	Y	N	Corker	N	N	N	N	Y	N
LOUISIANA							**TEXAS**						
Landrieu	N	N	N	N	N	Y	Hutchison	Y	Y	N	N	Y	N
Vitter	Y	Y	N	N	Y	N	Cornyn	Y	Y	N	N	Y	N
MAINE							**UTAH**						
Snowe	N	N	Y	N	N	Y	Hatch	Y	Y	N	N	Y	N
Collins	N	N	N	N	N	Y	Lee	Y	Y	N	N	Y	N
MARYLAND							**VERMONT**						
Mikulski	N	N	Y	Y	N	Y	Leahy	N	N	Y	Y	N	Y
Cardin	N	N	Y	Y	N	Y	Sanders	N	N	Y	Y	N	Y
MASSACHUSETTS							**VIRGINIA**						
Kerry	N	N	Y	Y	N	Y	Webb	N	N	Y	Y	N	Y
Brown	N	N	N	N	N	Y	Warner	N	N	N	N	N	Y
MICHIGAN							**WASHINGTON**						
Levin	N	N	Y	Y	N	Y	Murray	N	N	Y	Y	N	Y
Stabenow	N	N	Y	Y	N	Y	Cantwell	N	N	Y	Y	N	Y
MINNESOTA							**WEST VIRGINIA**						
Klobuchar	N	N	Y	Y	N	Y	Rockefeller	N	N	Y	Y	N	Y
Franken	N	N	Y	Y	N	Y	Manchin	N	N	Y	Y	N	Y
MISSISSIPPI							**WISCONSIN**						
Cochran	N	Y	N	N	N	N	Kohl	N	N	Y	Y	N	Y
Wicker	Y	Y	N	N	N	N	Johnson	Y	Y	N	N	Y	N
MISSOURI							**WYOMING**						
McCaskill	N	N	Y	N	N	Y	Enzi	N	Y	N	N	N	N
Blunt	Y	Y	N	N	N	N	Barrasso	N	Y	N	N	N	N

KEY   **Republicans**   Democrats   *Independents*

Y Voted for (yea)	**X** Paired against	**C** Voted "present" to avoid possible conflict of interest
# Paired for	**–** Announced against	
+ Announced for	**P** Voted "present"	**?** Did not vote or otherwise make a position known
N Voted against (nay)		

IN THE SENATE | By Vote Number

76. **S 1789. Postal Service Overhaul/Mailbox Usage.** Paul, R-Ky., amendment to the Lieberman, I-Conn., substitute amendment. The Paul amendment would allow mailbox owners to determine whether to allow organizations or entities other than the Postal Service to put things in their mailboxes. Rejected 35-64: D 0-51; R 35-11; I 0-2. (By unanimous consent, the Senate agreed to raise the majority requirement for adoption of the Paul amendment to 60 votes.) April 24, 2012.

77. **S 1789. Postal Service Overhaul/Closure Moratorium.** Manchin, D-W.Va., amendment to the Lieberman, I-Conn., substitute amendment. The Manchin amendment would place a two-year moratorium on the closure of post offices and mail processing facilities. Rejected 43-53: D 38-12; R 4-40; I 1-1. (By unanimous consent, the Senate agreed to raise the majority requirement for adoption of the Manchin amendment to 60 votes.) April 25, 2012.

78. **S 1789. Postal Service Overhaul/Local Mail Delivery Pilot Program.** Paul, R-Ky., amendment to the Lieberman, I-Conn., substitute amendment. The Paul amendment would establish a pilot program to allow local postmasters to determine the best ways to process and deliver mail within their jurisdictions, with approval of the Postal Regulatory Commission. Rejected 35-64: D 0-51; R 35-11; I 0-2. (By unanimous consent, the Senate agreed to raise the majority requirement for adoption of the Paul amendment to 60 votes.) April 25, 2012.

79. **S 1789. Postal Service Overhaul/Collective Bargaining.** Paul, R-Ky., amendment to the Lieberman, I-Conn., substitute amendment. The Paul amendment would prohibit collective bargaining by Postal Service employees. Rejected 23-76: D 0-51; R 23-23; I 0-2. (By unanimous consent, the Senate agreed to raise the majority requirement for adoption of the Paul amendment to 60 votes.) April 25, 2012.

	76	77	78	79			76	77	78	79
ALABAMA						**MONTANA**				
Shelby	Y	N	Y	Y		Baucus	N	Y	N	N
Sessions	Y	N	Y	Y		Tester	N	Y	N	N
ALASKA						**NEBRASKA**				
Murkowski	N	N	N	N		Nelson	N	Y	N	N
Begich	N	Y	N	N		Johanns	Y	N	Y	N
ARIZONA						**NEVADA**				
McCain	Y	N	Y	Y		Reid	N	Y	N	N
Kyl	Y	N	Y	Y		Heller	Y	Y	Y	Y
ARKANSAS						**NEW HAMPSHIRE**				
Pryor	N	Y	N	N		Shaheen	N	Y	N	N
Boozman	Y	N	N	N		Ayotte	Y	N	Y	N
CALIFORNIA						**NEW JERSEY**				
Feinstein	N	?	N	N		Lautenberg	N	Y	N	N
Boxer	N	Y	N	N		Menendez	N	Y	N	N
COLORADO						**NEW MEXICO**				
Udall	N	N	N	N		Bingaman	N	N	N	N
Bennet	N	N	N	N		Udall	N	Y	N	N
CONNECTICUT						**NEW YORK**				
Lieberman	N	N	N	N		Schumer	N	Y	N	N
Blumenthal	N	Y	N	N		Gillibrand	N	Y	N	N
DELAWARE						**NORTH CAROLINA**				
Carper	N	N	N	N		**Burr**	N	N	Y	Y
Coons	N	N	N	N		Hagan	N	Y	N	N
FLORIDA						**NORTH DAKOTA**				
Nelson	N	Y	N	N		Conrad	N	N	N	N
Rubio	Y	N	Y	N		**Hoeven**	N	N	N	N
GEORGIA						**OHIO**				
Chambliss	Y	?	Y	Y		Brown	N	Y	N	N
Isakson	Y	N	N	N		**Portman**	N	N	N	N
HAWAII						**OKLAHOMA**				
Inouye	N	Y	N	N		**Inhofe**	N	N	Y	Y
Akaka	N	Y	N	N		**Coburn**	Y	N	N	N
IDAHO						**OREGON**				
Crapo	Y	N	Y	Y		Wyden	N	Y	N	N
Risch	Y	N	Y	Y		Merkley	N	Y	N	N
ILLINOIS						**PENNSYLVANIA**				
Durbin	N	Y	N	N		Casey	N	Y	N	N
Kirk	?	?	?	?		**Toomey**	Y	N	Y	Y
INDIANA						**RHODE ISLAND**				
Lugar	N	N	Y	N		Reed	N	Y	N	N
Coats	N	N	Y	N		Whitehouse	N	Y	N	N
IOWA						**SOUTH CAROLINA**				
Grassley	Y	N	Y	N		**Graham**	Y	N	Y	Y
Harkin	N	Y	N	N		**DeMint**	Y	N	Y	Y
KANSAS						**SOUTH DAKOTA**				
Roberts	Y	N	Y	N		Johnson	N	Y	N	N
Moran	Y	N	Y	N		**Thune**	Y	N	Y	Y
KENTUCKY						**TENNESSEE**				
McConnell	Y	N	Y	Y		**Alexander**	Y	N	Y	N
Paul	Y	N	Y	Y		**Corker**	Y	N	Y	Y
LOUISIANA						**TEXAS**				
Landrieu	N	Y	N	N		**Hutchison**	N	N	N	N
Vitter	Y	N	Y	Y		**Cornyn**	Y	N	Y	Y
MAINE						**UTAH**				
Snowe	N	N	N	N		**Hatch**	Y	?	Y	Y
Collins	N	N	N	N		**Lee**	Y	N	Y	Y
MARYLAND						**VERMONT**				
Mikulski	N	Y	N	N		Leahy	N	Y	N	N
Cardin	N	Y	N	N		*Sanders*	N	Y	N	N
MASSACHUSETTS						**VIRGINIA**				
Kerry	N	Y	N	N		Webb	N	N	N	N
Brown	N	N	N	N		Warner	N	N	N	N
MICHIGAN						**WASHINGTON**				
Levin	N	Y	N	N		Murray	N	N	N	N
Stabenow	N	Y	N	N		Cantwell	N	N	N	N
MINNESOTA						**WEST VIRGINIA**				
Klobuchar	N	N	N	N		Rockefeller	N	Y	N	N
Franken	N	N	N	N		Manchin	N	Y	N	N
MISSISSIPPI						**WISCONSIN**				
Cochran	Y	N	N	N		Kohl	N	Y	N	N
Wicker	Y	Y	Y	N		**Johnson**	Y	N	Y	N
MISSOURI						**WYOMING**				
McCaskill	N	Y	N	N		**Enzi**	Y	Y	Y	Y
Blunt	Y	N	N	N		**Barrasso**	Y	Y	Y	Y

KEY	**Republicans**		Democrats	*Independents*			
Y	Voted for (yea)		X	Paired against		C	Voted "present" to avoid possible conflict of interest
#	Paired for		–	Announced against			
+	Announced for		P	Voted "present"		?	Did not vote or otherwise make a position known
N	Voted against (nay)						

IN THE SENATE | By Vote Number

80. **S 1789. Postal Service Overhaul/Delivery Times.** Casey, D-Pa., amendment to the Lieberman, I-Conn., substitute amendment. The Casey amendment would prohibit the Postal Service from extending the standard delivery time for certain products, including periodicals and other bound printed matter. Rejected 44-54: D 41-9; R 2-44; I 1-1. (By unanimous consent, the Senate agreed to raise the majority requirement for adoption of the Casey amendment to 60 votes.) April 25, 2012.

81. **S 1789. Postal Service Overhaul/Union Dues.** DeMint, R-S.C., amendment to the Lieberman, I-Conn., substitute amendment. The De-Mint amendment would bar the use of union dues paid by Postal Service employees for purposes other than collective bargaining and similar activities without an annual certification. Rejected 46-53: D 0-51; R 46-0; I 0-2. (By unanimous consent, the Senate agreed to raise the majority requirement for adoption of the DeMint amendment to 60 votes.) April 25, 2012.

82. **S 1789. Postal Service Overhaul/Passage.** Passage of the bill that would allow the Postal Service to recoup about $11 billion in overpayments to a retirement account and use the money to provide financial incentives to some 100,000 employees to retire. It also would delay for two years a cost savings plan to eliminate Saturday postal deliveries. It would establish limits on the compensation of executives of the Postal Service. It would direct the postmaster general to maintain overnight delivery for some first-class mail for the next three years. It also would allow the operation of only one post office on each side of the Capitol complex. Passed 62-37: D 47-4; R 13-33; I 2-0. (By unanimous consent, the Senate agreed to raise the majority requirement for passage of the bill to 60 votes.) April 25, 2012.

83. **Costa Nomination/Confirmation.** Confirmation of President Obama's nomination of Gregg Jeffrey Costa to be a judge for the U.S. District Court for the Southern District of Texas. Confirmed 97-2: D 51-0; R 44-2; I 2-0. A "yea" was a vote in support of the president's position. April 26, 2012.

	80	81	82	83		80	81	82	83
ALABAMA					**MONTANA**				
Shelby	N	Y	N	Y	Baucus	Y	N	Y	Y
Sessions	N	Y	N	Y	Tester	Y	N	Y	Y
ALASKA					**NEBRASKA**				
Murkowski	N	Y	Y	Y	Nelson	Y	N	Y	Y
Begich	Y	N	Y	Y	**Johanns**	N	Y	N	Y
ARIZONA					**NEVADA**				
McCain	N	Y	N	Y	Reid	N	N	Y	Y
Kyl	N	Y	N	Y	**Heller**	Y	Y	N	Y
ARKANSAS					**NEW HAMPSHIRE**				
Pryor	Y	N	Y	Y	Shaheen	Y	N	Y	Y
Boozman	N	Y	Y	Y	**Ayotte**	N	Y	N	Y
CALIFORNIA					**NEW JERSEY**				
Feinstein	N	N	Y	Y	Lautenberg	Y	N	Y	Y
Boxer	Y	N	Y	Y	Menendez	Y	N	N	Y
COLORADO					**NEW MEXICO**				
Udall	Y	N	Y	Y	Bingaman	N	N	Y	Y
Bennet	Y	N	Y	Y	Udall	Y	N	Y	Y
CONNECTICUT					**NEW YORK**				
Lieberman	N	N	Y	Y	Schumer	Y	N	Y	Y
Blumenthal	Y	N	Y	Y	Gillibrand	Y	N	Y	Y
DELAWARE					**NORTH CAROLINA**				
Carper	N	N	Y	Y	**Burr**	N	Y	N	Y
Coons	N	N	Y	Y	Hagan	N	N	Y	Y
FLORIDA					**NORTH DAKOTA**				
Nelson	N	N	Y	Y	Conrad	?	N	Y	Y
Rubio	N	Y	N	Y	**Hoeven**	N	Y	Y	Y
GEORGIA					**OHIO**				
Chambliss	N	Y	N	Y	Brown	Y	N	Y	Y
Isakson	N	Y	N	Y	**Portman**	N	Y	N	Y
HAWAII					**OKLAHOMA**				
Inouye	Y	N	Y	Y	**Inhofe**	N	Y	N	Y
Akaka	Y	N	N	Y	**Coburn**	N	Y	N	Y
IDAHO					**OREGON**				
Crapo	N	Y	N	Y	Wyden	Y	N	Y	Y
Risch	N	Y	N	Y	Merkley	Y	N	Y	Y
ILLINOIS					**PENNSYLVANIA**				
Durbin	Y	N	Y	Y	Casey	Y	N	Y	Y
Kirk	?	?	?	?	**Toomey**	N	Y	N	Y
INDIANA					**RHODE ISLAND**				
Lugar	N	Y	N	Y	Reed	Y	N	Y	Y
Coats	N	Y	N	Y	Whitehouse	Y	N	Y	Y
IOWA					**SOUTH CAROLINA**				
Grassley	N	Y	Y	Y	**Graham**	N	Y	N	Y
Harkin	Y	N	Y	Y	**DeMint**	N	Y	N	N
KANSAS					**SOUTH DAKOTA**				
Roberts	N	Y	Y	Y	Johnson	Y	N	Y	Y
Moran	N	Y	Y	Y	**Thune**	N	Y	N	Y
KENTUCKY					**TENNESSEE**				
McConnell	N	Y	N	Y	**Alexander**	N	Y	Y	Y
Paul	N	Y	N	Y	**Corker**	N	Y	N	Y
LOUISIANA					**TEXAS**				
Landrieu	N	N	Y	Y	**Hutchison**	N	Y	N	Y
Vitter	N	Y	N	Y	**Cornyn**	N	Y	N	Y
MAINE					**UTAH**				
Snowe	Y	Y	Y	Y	**Hatch**	N	Y	N	Y
Collins	N	Y	Y	Y	**Lee**	N	Y	N	N
MARYLAND					**VERMONT**				
Mikulski	Y	N	Y	Y	Leahy	Y	N	Y	Y
Cardin	Y	N	Y	Y	*Sanders*	Y	N	Y	Y
MASSACHUSETTS					**VIRGINIA**				
Kerry	Y	N	Y	Y	Webb	Y	N	Y	Y
Brown	N	Y	Y	Y	Warner	N	N	Y	Y
MICHIGAN					**WASHINGTON**				
Levin	Y	N	Y	Y	Murray	Y	N	Y	Y
Stabenow	Y	N	Y	Y	Cantwell	Y	N	Y	Y
MINNESOTA					**WEST VIRGINIA**				
Klobuchar	Y	N	Y	Y	Rockefeller	Y	N	N	Y
Franken	Y	N	Y	Y	Manchin	Y	N	N	Y
MISSISSIPPI					**WISCONSIN**				
Cochran	N	Y	Y	Y	Kohl	Y	N	Y	Y
Wicker	N	Y	Y	Y	**Johnson**	N	Y	N	Y
MISSOURI					**WYOMING**				
McCaskill	Y	N	Y	Y	**Enzi**	N	Y	N	Y
Blunt	N	Y	Y	Y	**Barrasso**	N	Y	N	Y

KEY	**Republicans**	Democrats	*Independents*
Y Voted for (yea)	**X** Paired against		**C** Voted "present" to avoid possible conflict of interest
# Paired for	**–** Announced against		
+ Announced for	**P** Voted "present"		**?** Did not vote or otherwise make a position known
N Voted against (nay)			

IN THE SENATE | By Vote Number

84. **S 1925. Violence Against Women Reauthorization/DNA Backlog Grants.** Klobuchar, D-Minn., amendment that would authorize $151 million in Debbie Smith grants for DNA backlog testing in each of fiscal years 2013 through 2017, with provisions made for allowing the Justice Department to award grants for backlog audits. Rejected 57-41: D 50-0; R 5-41; I 2-0. (By unanimous consent, the Senate agreed to raise the majority requirement amendment for adoption of the Klobuchar amendment to 60 votes.) April 26, 2012.

85. **S 1925. Violence Against Women Reauthorization/DNA Backlog.** Cornyn, R-Texas, amendment that would require the Justice Department to use more than 70 percent of funds authorized under a 2006 law to help reduce a backlog of rape kits for DNA tests and conduct audits to account for stored rape test kits. Rejected 50-48: D 3-47; R 46-0; I 1-1. (By unanimous consent, the Senate agreed to raise the majority requirement for adoption of the Cornyn amendment to 60 votes.) April 26, 2012.

86. **S 1925. Violence Against Women Reauthorization/Republican Substitute.** Hutchison, R-Texas, substitute amendment that would reauthorize the Violence Against Women Act for five years. It would use gender-neutral terms in references to gender bias crimes in the underlying law. It would establish new mandatory minimum sentences of up to 15 years for certain domestic violence crimes. It would grant the U.S. Marshals Service the authority to issue administrative subpoenas to locate unregistered sex offenders. It would strike from the bill provisions to grant tribal law enforcement certain new powers to enforce restraining orders. Rejected 37-62: D 0-51; R 37-9; I 0-2. (By unanimous consent, the Senate agreed to raise the majority requirement for adoption of the Hutchison amendment to 60 votes.) April 26, 2012.

87. **S 1925. Violence Against Women Reauthorization/Passage.** Passage of the bill that would reauthorize the Violence Against Women Act for five years. It would provide for a special category of temporary visas for immigrant women who have been victims of domestic violence. It also would ban organizations that receive federal grants from discriminating on the basis of sexual orientation or gender identity. The bill would provide new authorities to tribal courts for enforcing restraining orders. It would add the terms "gender identity" and "sexual orientation" to existing provisions that condition grant money for victim services organizations on their compliance with non-discrimination practices. Passed 68-31: D 51-0; R 15-31; I 2-0. A "yea" was a vote in support of the president's position. April 26, 2012.

88. **Nguyen Nomination/Confirmation.** Confirmation of President Obama's nomination of Jacqueline H. Nguyen of California to be a judge for the 9th U.S. Circuit Court of Appeals. Confirmed 91-3: D 50-0; R 39-3; I 2-0. A "yea" was a vote in support of the president's position. May 7, 2012.

89. **S 2343. Student Loans/Cloture.** Motion to invoke cloture (thus limiting debate) on the Reid, D-Nev., motion to proceed to the bill that would extend, for one year, a 3.4 interest rate on certain federally backed student loans. It would be offset by eliminating a tax preference for S corporations, which are companies that pass their income, losses, deductions and credits through to shareholders for federal tax purposes. Rejected 52-45: D 50-1; R 0-44; I 2-0. Three-fifths of the total Senate (60) is required to invoke cloture. A "yea" was a vote in support of the president's position. May 8, 2012.

Senator	84	85	86	87	88	89
ALABAMA						
Shelby	N	Y	Y	N	Y	N
Sessions	N	Y	Y	N	Y	N
ALASKA						
Murkowski	Y	Y	N	Y	?	N
Begich	Y	N	N	Y	Y	Y
ARIZONA						
McCain	N	Y	Y	Y	Y	N
Kyl	N	Y	Y	N	Y	N
ARKANSAS						
Pryor	Y	N	N	Y	Y	Y
Boozman	N	Y	N	Y	N	N
CALIFORNIA						
Feinstein	Y	N	N	Y	Y	Y
Boxer	Y	N	N	Y	Y	Y
COLORADO						
Udall	Y	N	N	Y	Y	Y
Bennet	Y	Y	N	Y	Y	Y
CONNECTICUT						
Lieberman	Y	Y	N	Y	Y	Y
Blumenthal	Y	N	N	Y	Y	Y
DELAWARE						
Carper	Y	N	N	Y	Y	Y
Coons	Y	N	N	Y	Y	Y
FLORIDA						
Nelson	Y	N	N	Y	Y	Y
Rubio	N	Y	N	N	Y	N
GEORGIA						
Chambliss	N	Y	Y	N	Y	N
Isakson	N	Y	Y	N	Y	N
HAWAII						
Inouye	Y	N	N	Y	?	Y
Akaka	Y	N	N	Y	Y	Y
IDAHO						
Crapo	N	Y	Y	N	Y	N
Risch	N	Y	Y	N	Y	N
ILLINOIS						
Durbin	Y	N	N	Y	Y	Y
Kirk	?	?	?	?	?	?
INDIANA						
Lugar	N	Y	Y	N	?	?
Coats	N	Y	Y	Y	Y	N
IOWA						
Grassley	N	Y	Y	N	Y	N
Harkin	Y	N	N	Y	Y	Y
KANSAS						
Roberts	N	Y	Y	N	Y	N
Moran	N	Y	Y	N	Y	N
KENTUCKY						
McConnell	N	Y	Y	N	Y	N
Paul	N	Y	N	N	Y	N
LOUISIANA						
Landrieu	Y	N	N	Y	Y	Y
Vitter	N	Y	Y	Y	N	N
MAINE						
Snowe	Y	Y	N	Y	Y	P
Collins	Y	Y	N	Y	Y	N
MARYLAND						
Mikulski	Y	N	N	Y	Y	Y
Cardin	Y	N	N	Y	Y	Y
MASSACHUSETTS						
Kerry	Y	N	N	Y	Y	Y
Brown	Y	Y	N	Y	Y	N
MICHIGAN						
Levin	Y	N	N	Y	Y	Y
Stabenow	Y	N	N	Y	Y	Y
MINNESOTA						
Klobuchar	Y	N	N	Y	Y	Y
Franken	Y	N	N	Y	Y	Y
MISSISSIPPI						
Cochran	N	Y	Y	N	Y	N
Wicker	N	Y	Y	N	Y	N
MISSOURI						
McCaskill	Y	Y	N	Y	Y	Y
Blunt	N	Y	Y	N	Y	N

Senator	84	85	86	87	88	89
MONTANA						
Baucus	Y	N	N	Y	Y	Y
Tester	Y	Y	N	Y	Y	Y
NEBRASKA						
Nelson	Y	N	N	Y	Y	Y
Johanns	N	Y	Y	Y	Y	N
NEVADA						
Reid	Y	N	N	Y	Y	N
Heller	Y	N	Y	Y	Y	N
NEW HAMPSHIRE						
Shaheen	Y	N	N	Y	Y	Y
Ayotte	N	Y	Y	Y	Y	N
NEW JERSEY						
Lautenberg	Y	N	N	Y	Y	Y
Menendez	Y	N	N	Y	Y	Y
NEW MEXICO						
Bingaman	Y	N	N	Y	Y	Y
Udall	Y	N	N	Y	Y	Y
NEW YORK						
Schumer	Y	N	N	Y	Y	Y
Gillibrand	Y	N	N	Y	Y	Y
NORTH CAROLINA						
Burr	N	Y	Y	N	Y	N
Hagan	N	N	N	Y	Y	Y
NORTH DAKOTA						
Conrad	Y	N	N	Y	Y	Y
Hoeven	N	Y	Y	Y	Y	N
OHIO						
Brown	Y	N	N	Y	Y	Y
Portman	N	Y	Y	Y	Y	N
OKLAHOMA						
Inhofe	N	Y	Y	N	Y	N
Coburn	N	Y	N	N	Y	N
OREGON						
Wyden	Y	N	N	Y	Y	Y
Merkley	Y	N	N	Y	Y	Y
PENNSYLVANIA						
Casey	Y	N	N	Y	Y	Y
Toomey	N	Y	N	N	N	N
RHODE ISLAND						
Reed	Y	N	N	Y	Y	Y
Whitehouse	Y	N	N	Y	Y	Y
SOUTH CAROLINA						
Graham	N	Y	Y	N	?	N
DeMint	N	Y	N	N	?	N
SOUTH DAKOTA						
Johnson	Y	N	N	Y	Y	Y
Thune	N	Y	Y	N	Y	N
TENNESSEE						
Alexander	N	Y	Y	Y	Y	N
Corker	N	Y	Y	Y	Y	N
TEXAS						
Hutchison	N	Y	Y	Y	N	N
Cornyn	N	Y	Y	N	Y	N
UTAH						
Hatch	N	Y	N	Y	N	N
Lee	N	Y	N	N	N	N
VERMONT						
Leahy	Y	N	N	Y	Y	Y
Sanders	Y	N	N	Y	Y	Y
VIRGINIA						
Webb	?	?	N	Y	Y	Y
Warner	Y	N	N	Y	Y	Y
WASHINGTON						
Murray	Y	N	N	Y	Y	Y
Cantwell	Y	N	N	Y	Y	Y
WEST VIRGINIA						
Rockefeller	Y	N	N	Y	Y	Y
Manchin	Y	N	N	Y	Y	Y
WISCONSIN						
Kohl	Y	N	N	Y	Y	Y
Johnson	N	Y	Y	N	Y	N
WYOMING						
Enzi	N	Y	Y	N	Y	N
Barrasso	N	Y	Y	N	Y	N

KEY **Republicans**   Democrats   *Independents*

Y Voted for (yea)	X Paired against	C Voted "present" to avoid possible conflict of interest
# Paired for	- Announced against	
+ Announced for	P Voted "present"	? Did not vote or otherwise make a position known
N Voted against (nay)		

IN THE SENATE | By Vote Number

90. Tharp Nomination/Confirmation. Confirmation of President Obama's nomination of John J. Tharp Jr. of Illinois to be a judge for the U.S. District Court for the Northern District of Illinois. Confirmed 86-1: D 48-0; R 36-1; I 2-0. A "yea" was a vote in support of the president's position. May 14, 2012.

91. HR 2072. Export-Import Bank/Termination. Lee, R-Utah, amendment that would terminate the Export-Import Bank one year after reauthorization and direct the president to pursue negotiations with other countries to end export subsidies. Rejected 12-86: D 0-50; R 12-34; I 0-2. (By unanimous consent, the Senate agreed to raise the majority requirement for adoption of the Lee amendment to 60 votes.) May 15, 2012.

92. HR 2072. Export-Import Bank/U.S. Security Holdings. Paul, R-Ky., amendment that would prohibit the Export-Import Bank from making loans in countries that hold U.S. Treasury securities. Rejected 9-89: D 0-50; R 9-37; I 0-2. (By unanimous consent, the Senate agreed to raise the majority requirement for adoption of the Paul amendment to 60 votes.) May 15, 2012.

93. HR 2072. Export-Import Bank/Capital Requirements. Corker, R-Tenn., amendment that would allow the Export-Import Bank to provide financing only for transactions subsidized by export credit agencies of other countries or for which private sector financing is unavailable or prohibitively expensive. It also would require the bank to maintain a ratio of capital to the outstanding principal balance of loans and loan guarantees of not less than 10 percent. Rejected 36-62: D 0-50; R 36-10; I 0-2. (By unanimous consent, the Senate agreed to raise the majority requirement for adoption of the Corker amendment to 60 votes.) May 15, 2012.

94. HR 2072. Export-Import Bank/Renewable-Energy Projects. Vitter, R-La., amendment that would prohibit the Export-Import Bank from financing foreign fossil fuel projects that are similar to projects in the United States. It also would prohibit the bank from financing foreign manufacturing of renewable energy products. Rejected 37-61: D 0-50; R 37-9; I 0-2. (By unanimous consent, the Senate agreed to raise the majority requirement for adoption of the Vitter amendment to 60 votes.) May 15, 2012.

95. HR 2072. Export-Import Bank/Multilateral Negotiations. Toomey, R-Pa., amendment that would place conditions on the Export-Import Bank's lending until progress is made on multilateral negotiations to end export-financing programs. Rejected 35-63: D 0-50; R 35-11; I 0-2. (By unanimous consent, the Senate agreed to raise the majority requirement for adoption of the Toomey amendment to 60 votes.) May 15, 2012.

96. HR 2072. Export-Import Bank/Passage. Passage of the bill that would reauthorize through Sept. 30, 2014, the charter for the U.S. Export-Import Bank. It would incrementally increase to $140 billion, from $100 billion, the cap on outstanding loans, guarantees and insurance that the bank is authorized to have at any given time. Passed (thus cleared for the president) 78-20: D 50-0; R 27-19; I 1-1. (By unanimous consent, the Senate agreed to raise the majority requirement for passage of the bill to 60 votes.) A "yea" was a vote in support of the president's position. May 15, 2012.

	90	91	92	93	94	95	96
ALABAMA							
Shelby	Y	N	N	Y	Y	Y	Y
Sessions	Y	N	N	Y	Y	Y	Y
ALASKA							
Murkowski	?	N	N	Y	Y	N	Y
Begich	Y	N	N	N	N	N	Y
ARIZONA							
McCain	Y	Y	N	Y	Y	Y	N
Kyl	Y	Y	N	Y	Y	Y	N
ARKANSAS							
Pryor	Y	N	N	N	N	N	Y
Boozman	Y	N	N	Y	Y	Y	Y
CALIFORNIA							
Feinstein	Y	N	N	N	N	N	Y
Boxer	Y	N	N	N	N	N	Y
COLORADO							
Udall	Y	N	N	N	N	N	Y
Bennet	Y	N	N	N	N	N	Y
CONNECTICUT							
Lieberman	Y	N	N	N	N	N	Y
Blumenthal	Y	N	N	N	N	N	Y
DELAWARE							
Carper	Y	N	N	N	N	N	Y
Coons	Y	N	N	N	N	N	Y
FLORIDA							
Nelson	?	N	N	N	N	N	Y
Rubio	Y	Y	Y	Y	Y	Y	N
GEORGIA							
Chambliss	Y	N	N	Y	Y	Y	Y
Isakson	Y	N	N	Y	Y	Y	Y
HAWAII							
Inouye	Y	N	N	N	N	N	Y
Akaka	Y	N	N	N	N	N	Y
IDAHO							
Crapo	Y	Y	N	Y	Y	Y	N
Risch	Y	Y	Y	Y	Y	Y	N
ILLINOIS							
Durbin	Y	N	N	N	N	N	Y
Kirk	?	?	?	?	?	?	?
INDIANA							
Lugar	Y	N	N	N	N	N	Y
Coats	Y	N	N	Y	Y	Y	Y
IOWA							
Grassley	Y	Y	N	Y	Y	Y	N
Harkin	Y	N	N	N	N	N	Y
KANSAS							
Roberts	Y	N	N	N	N	N	Y
Moran	?	N	Y	Y	N	Y	Y
KENTUCKY							
McConnell	Y	N	N	Y	Y	Y	N
Paul	?	Y	Y	Y	Y	Y	N
LOUISIANA							
Landrieu	Y	N	N	N	N	N	Y
Vitter	Y	Y	Y	Y	Y	Y	N
MAINE							
Snowe	Y	N	N	Y	Y	Y	Y
Collins	Y	N	N	Y	N	N	Y
MARYLAND							
Mikulski	Y	N	N	N	N	N	Y
Cardin	Y	N	N	N	N	N	Y
MASSACHUSETTS							
Kerry	Y	N	N	N	N	N	Y
Brown	Y	N	N	N	N	N	Y
MICHIGAN							
Levin	Y	N	N	N	N	N	Y
Stabenow	Y	N	N	N	N	N	Y
MINNESOTA							
Klobuchar	Y	N	N	N	N	N	Y
Franken	Y	N	N	N	N	N	Y
MISSISSIPPI							
Cochran	Y	N	N	Y	Y	Y	Y
Wicker	?	N	N	Y	Y	Y	Y
MISSOURI							
McCaskill	Y	N	N	N	N	N	Y
Blunt	?	N	N	N	N	N	Y
MONTANA							
Baucus	Y	N	N	N	N	N	Y
Tester	Y	N	N	N	N	N	Y
NEBRASKA							
Nelson	Y	N	N	N	N	N	Y
Johanns	Y	N	N	N	Y	N	Y
NEVADA							
Reid	Y	N	N	N	N	N	Y
Heller	Y	N	N	N	N	N	Y
NEW HAMPSHIRE							
Shaheen	Y	N	N	N	N	N	Y
Ayotte	Y	N	N	Y	Y	Y	Y
NEW JERSEY							
Lautenberg	Y	N	N	N	N	N	Y
Menendez	Y	N	N	N	N	N	Y
NEW MEXICO							
Bingaman	Y	N	N	N	N	N	Y
Udall	Y	N	N	N	N	N	Y
NEW YORK							
Schumer	Y	N	N	N	N	N	Y
Gillibrand	Y	N	N	N	N	N	Y
NORTH CAROLINA							
Burr	?	N	N	Y	Y	Y	Y
Hagan	?	N	N	N	N	N	Y
NORTH DAKOTA							
Conrad	Y	N	N	N	N	N	Y
Hoeven	Y	N	N	N	N	N	Y
OHIO							
Brown	Y	N	N	N	N	N	Y
Portman	Y	N	N	N	N	Y	Y
OKLAHOMA							
Inhofe	Y	N	N	Y	Y	Y	N
Coburn	Y	N	Y	Y	Y	Y	Y
OREGON							
Wyden	Y	N	N	N	N	N	Y
Merkley	Y	N	N	N	N	N	Y
PENNSYLVANIA							
Casey	?	N	N	N	N	N	Y
Toomey	Y	N	N	Y	Y	Y	N
RHODE ISLAND							
Reed	Y	N	N	N	N	N	Y
Whitehouse	Y	N	N	N	N	N	Y
SOUTH CAROLINA							
Graham	Y	N	N	N	N	N	Y
DeMint	-	Y	Y	Y	Y	Y	N
SOUTH DAKOTA							
Johnson	Y	N	N	N	N	N	Y
Thune	?	N	Y	Y	Y	Y	Y
TENNESSEE							
Alexander	Y	N	N	Y	Y	Y	Y
Corker	Y	N	N	Y	Y	Y	N
TEXAS							
Hutchison	Y	N	N	Y	Y	Y	N
Cornyn	+	Y	N	Y	Y	Y	N
UTAH							
Hatch	Y	Y	Y	N	Y	Y	N
Lee	N	Y	Y	Y	Y	Y	N
VERMONT							
Leahy	Y	N	N	N	N	N	Y
Sanders	Y	N	N	N	N	N	Y
VIRGINIA							
Webb	Y	N	N	N	N	N	Y
Warner	Y	N	N	N	N	N	Y
WASHINGTON							
Murray	Y	N	N	N	N	N	Y
Cantwell	Y	N	N	N	N	N	Y
WEST VIRGINIA							
Rockefeller	Y	?	?	?	?	?	?
Manchin	Y	N	N	N	N	N	Y
WISCONSIN							
Kohl	Y	N	N	N	N	N	Y
Johnson	Y	N	N	Y	Y	Y	Y
WYOMING							
Enzi	Y	N	N	Y	Y	Y	N
Barrasso	Y	N	N	Y	Y	Y	N

KEY   **Republicans**   Democrats   *Independents*

Y Voted for (yea)	X Paired against	C Voted "present" to avoid possible conflict of interest
# Paired for	- Announced against	
+ Announced for	P Voted "present"	? Did not vote or otherwise make a position known
N Voted against (nay)		

IN THE SENATE | By Vote Number

97. **S Con Res 41. President's Fiscal 2013 Budget Resolution/Motion to Proceed.** Conrad, D-N.D., motion to proceed to the concurrent resolution that would allow $2.982 trillion in new budget authority for fiscal 2013, not including off-budget accounts. Motion rejected 0-99: D 0-51; R 0-46; I 0-2. May 16, 2012.

98. **H Con Res 112. House Fiscal 2013 Budget Resolution/Motion to Proceed.** Conrad, D-N.D., motion to proceed to the concurrent resolution that would allow $2.794 trillion in new budget authority for fiscal 2013, not including off-budget accounts. Motion rejected 41-58: D 0-51; R 41-5; I 0-2. May 16, 2012.

99. **S Con Res 37. Toomey Fiscal 2013 Budget Resolution/Motion to Proceed.** Conrad, D-N.D., motion to proceed to the concurrent resolution that would allow $2.843 trillion in new budget authority for fiscal 2013, not including off-budget accounts. Motion rejected 42-57: D 0-51; R 42-4; I 0-2. May 16, 2012.

100. **S Con Res 42. Paul Fiscal 2013 Budget Resolution/Motion to Proceed.** Conrad, D-N.D., motion to proceed to the concurrent resolution that would allow $3.084 trillion in new budget authority for fiscal 2013, not including off-budget accounts. Motion rejected 16-83: D 0-51; R 16-30; I 0-2. May 16, 2012.

101. **S Con Res 44. Lee Fiscal 2013 Budget Resolution/Motion to Proceed.** Conrad, D-N.D., motion to proceed to the concurrent resolution that would allow $3.269 trillion in new budget authority for fiscal 2013, not including off-budget accounts. Motion rejected 17-82: D 0-51; R 17-29; I 0-2. May 16, 2012.

102. **Stein Nomination/Confirmation.** Confirmation of President Obama's nomination of Jeremy C. Stein of Massachusetts to be a member of the Board of Governors of the Federal Reserve System. Confirmed 70-24: D 47-0; R 21-24; I 2-0. (By unanimous consent, the Senate agreed to raise the majority requirement for confirmation of the Stein nomination to 60 votes.) A "yea" was a vote in support of the president's position. May 17, 2012.

103. **Powell Nomination/Confirmation.** Confirmation of President Obama's nomination of Jerome H. Powell of Maryland to be a member of the Board of Governors of the Federal Reserve System. Confirmed 74-21: D 48-0; R 25-20; I 1-1. (By unanimous consent, the Senate agreed to raise the majority requirement for confirmation of the Powell nomination to 60 votes.) A "yea" was a vote in support of the president's position. May 17, 2012.

	97	98	99	100	101	102	103
ALABAMA							
Shelby	N	Y	Y	Y	N	Y	Y
Sessions	N	Y	Y	Y	Y	N	N
ALASKA							
Murkowski	N	Y	Y	N	N	Y	Y
Begich	N	N	N	N	N	Y	Y
ARIZONA							
McCain	N	Y	Y	N	N	N	Y
Kyl	N	Y	Y	N	N	Y	Y
ARKANSAS							
Pryor	N	N	N	N	N	Y	Y
Boozman	N	Y	Y	N	N	N	Y
CALIFORNIA							
Feinstein	N	N	N	N	N	Y	Y
Boxer	N	N	N	N	N	Y	Y
COLORADO							
Udall	N	N	N	N	N	Y	Y
Bennet	N	N	N	N	N	Y	Y
CONNECTICUT							
Lieberman	N	N	N	N	N	Y	Y
Blumenthal	N	N	N	N	N	Y	Y
DELAWARE							
Carper	N	N	N	N	N	Y	Y
Coons	N	N	N	N	N	Y	Y
FLORIDA							
Nelson	N	N	N	N	N	Y	Y
Rubio	N	Y	Y	N	N	N	N
GEORGIA							
Chambliss	N	Y	Y	N	N	N	N
Isakson	N	Y	Y	N	N	N	N
HAWAII							
Inouye	N	N	N	N	N	?	?
Akaka	N	N	N	N	N	Y	Y
IDAHO							
Crapo	N	Y	Y	Y	Y	Y	Y
Risch	N	Y	Y	Y	Y	N	N
ILLINOIS							
Durbin	N	N	N	N	N	Y	Y
Kirk	?	?	?	?	?	?	?
INDIANA							
Lugar	N	Y	Y	N	N	Y	Y
Coats	N	Y	Y	N	Y	Y	Y
IOWA							
Grassley	N	Y	Y	N	Y	Y	Y
Harkin	N	N	N	N	N	Y	Y
KANSAS							
Roberts	N	Y	Y	N	N	N	N
Moran	N	Y	Y	Y	N	N	N
KENTUCKY							
McConnell	N	Y	Y	Y	N	Y	Y
Paul	N	N	Y	Y	Y	N	N
LOUISIANA							
Landrieu	N	N	N	N	N	Y	Y
Vitter	N	Y	Y	Y	Y	N	N
MAINE							
Snowe	N	N	N	N	N	Y	Y
Collins	N	N	N	N	N	Y	Y
MARYLAND							
Mikulski	N	N	N	N	N	Y	?
Cardin	N	N	N	N	N	Y	Y
MASSACHUSETTS							
Kerry	N	N	N	N	N	Y	Y
Brown	N	N	N	N	N	Y	Y
MICHIGAN							
Levin	N	N	N	N	N	Y	Y
Stabenow	N	N	N	N	N	Y	Y
MINNESOTA							
Klobuchar	N	N	N	N	N	Y	Y
Franken	N	N	N	N	N	Y	Y
MISSISSIPPI							
Cochran	N	Y	Y	N	N	Y	Y
Wicker	N	Y	Y	N	N	Y	Y
MISSOURI							
McCaskill	N	N	N	N	N	?	?
Blunt	N	Y	Y	N	N	N	N
MONTANA							
Baucus	N	N	N	N	N	Y	Y
Tester	N	N	N	N	N	Y	Y
NEBRASKA							
Nelson	N	N	N	N	N	Y	Y
Johanns	N	Y	Y	N	N	Y	Y
NEVADA							
Reid	N	N	N	N	N	Y	Y
Heller	N	N	N	N	N	N	N
NEW HAMPSHIRE							
Shaheen	N	N	N	N	N	Y	Y
Ayotte	N	Y	Y	N	N	N	N
NEW JERSEY							
Lautenberg	N	N	N	N	N	Y	Y
Menendez	N	N	N	N	N	Y	Y
NEW MEXICO							
Bingaman	N	N	N	N	N	Y	Y
Udall	N	N	N	N	N	Y	Y
NEW YORK							
Schumer	N	N	N	N	N	Y	Y
Gillibrand	N	N	N	N	N	Y	Y
NORTH CAROLINA							
Burr	N	Y	Y	N	N	Y	Y
Hagan	N	N	N	N	N	Y	Y
NORTH DAKOTA							
Conrad	N	N	N	N	N	Y	Y
Hoeven	N	Y	Y	N	N	Y	Y
OHIO							
Brown	N	N	N	N	N	Y	Y
Portman	N	Y	Y	N	N	N	Y
OKLAHOMA							
Inhofe	N	Y	Y	N	Y	N	N
Coburn	N	Y	Y	Y	Y	N	N
OREGON							
Wyden	N	N	N	N	N	Y	Y
Merkley	N	N	N	N	N	?	Y
PENNSYLVANIA							
Casey	N	N	N	N	N	Y	Y
Toomey	N	Y	Y	N	N	N	N
RHODE ISLAND							
Reed	N	N	N	N	N	Y	Y
Whitehouse	N	N	N	N	N	+	Y
SOUTH CAROLINA							
Graham	N	Y	Y	N	N	N	N
DeMint	N	Y	Y	Y	Y	?	?
SOUTH DAKOTA							
Johnson	N	N	N	N	N	Y	Y
Thune	N	Y	Y	Y	N	N	N
TENNESSEE							
Alexander	N	Y	Y	N	N	Y	Y
Corker	N	Y	Y	N	N	Y	Y
TEXAS							
Hutchison	N	Y	Y	N	N	Y	Y
Cornyn	N	Y	Y	N	N	N	N
UTAH							
Hatch	N	Y	Y	Y	Y	N	N
Lee	N	Y	Y	Y	Y	N	N
VERMONT							
Leahy	N	N	N	N	N	Y	Y
Sanders	N	N	N	N	N	Y	N
VIRGINIA							
Webb	N	N	N	N	N	Y	Y
Warner	N	N	N	N	N	Y	Y
WASHINGTON							
Murray	N	N	N	N	N	Y	Y
Cantwell	N	N	N	N	N	Y	Y
WEST VIRGINIA							
Rockefeller	N	N	N	N	N	Y	Y
Manchin	N	N	N	N	N	Y	Y
WISCONSIN							
Kohl	N	N	N	N	N	Y	Y
Johnson	N	Y	Y	Y	Y	Y	N
WYOMING							
Enzi	N	Y	Y	Y	Y	Y	Y
Barrasso	N	Y	Y	Y	Y	Y	Y

KEY   **Republicans**   Democrats   *Independents*

Y Voted for (yea)	X Paired against	C Voted "present" to avoid possible conflict of interest
# Paired for	– Announced against	
+ Announced for	P Voted "present"	? Did not vote or otherwise make a position known
N Voted against (nay)		

IN THE SENATE | By Vote Number

104. Watford Nomination/Confirmation. Confirmation of President Obama's nomination of Paul J. Watford of California to be a judge for the 9th U.S. Circuit Court of Appeals. Confirmed 61-34: D 50-0; R 9-34; I 2-0. A "yea" was a vote in support of the president's position. May 21, 2012.

105. S 3187. FDA User Fees/Generic-Drug Delays. Bingaman, D-N.M., amendment that would allow companies that produce generic drugs to share some of the 180-day marketing exclusivity period given to the original generic patent holder if that holder enters into a delay agreement. Rejected 28-67: D 24-25; R 3-41; I 1-1. (By unanimous consent, the Senate agreed to raise the majority requirement for adoption of the Bingaman amendment to 60 votes.) May 24, 2012.

106. S 3187. FDA User Fees/Genetically Engineered Salmon. Murkowski, R-Alaska, amendment that would require the National Oceanic and Atmospheric Administration to analyze the effects of genetically engineered salmon on the economy and the environment before the Food and Drug Administration could declare the salmon fit for human consumption. Rejected 46-50: D 35-15; R 9-35; I 2-0. (By unanimous consent, the Senate agreed to raise the majority requirement for adoption of the Murkowski amendment to 60 votes.) May 24, 2012.

107. S 3187. FDA User Fees/Restrictions on FDA Authorities. Harkin, D-Iowa, motion to table (kill) the Paul, R-Ky., amendment that would prevent the Food and Drug Administration from classifying and regulating food or dietary supplements as drugs on the basis that the products make certain health claims. It would prohibit the FDA from regulating the health claims made by any such products unless a federal court finds the claim false and misleading. Motion agreed to 78-15: D 47-0; R 29-15; I 2-0. May 24, 2012.

108. S 3187. FDA User Fees/Canadian Drug Importation. McCain, R-Ariz., amendment that would allow the importation by individuals of drugs from approved Canadian online pharmacies. It would require the Health and Human Services secretary to publish on the Food and Drug Administration website a list of approved Canadian pharmacies, including their website addresses. Rejected 43-54: D 26-24; R 16-29; I 1-1. (By unanimous consent, the Senate agreed to raise the majority requirement for adoption of the McCain amendment to 60 votes.) May 24, 2012.

109. S 3187. FDA User Fees/Exclusivity. Sanders, I-Vt., amendment that would terminate any period of exclusivity granted to a company that commits a drug violation or fails to report the violation. Rejected 9-88: D 7-43; R 1-44; I 1-1. (By unanimous consent, the Senate agreed to raise the majority requirement for adoption of the Sanders amendment to 60 votes.) May 24, 2012.

110. S 3187. FDA User Fees/Dietary-Supplement Registration. Harkin, D-Iowa, motion to table (kill) the Durbin, D-Ill., amendment that would require a facility engaged in the manufacturing, processing, packing or holding of dietary supplements to register with the Food and Drug Administration. This would include energy drinks designated as dietary supplements. Motion agreed to 77-20: D 31-19; R 45-0; I 1-1. May 24, 2012.

	104	105	106	107	108	109	110
ALABAMA							
Shelby	N	N	N	Y	Y	N	Y
Sessions	N	N	N	Y	Y	N	Y
ALASKA							
Murkowski	Y	N	Y	Y	Y	Y	Y
Begich	Y	N	Y	Y	Y	N	Y
ARIZONA							
McCain	Y	Y	N	Y	Y	Y	Y
Kyl	Y	N	N	N	Y	N	Y
ARKANSAS							
Pryor	Y	Y	N	Y	Y	N	N
Boozman	N	N	N	N	Y	N	Y
CALIFORNIA							
Feinstein	Y	Y	Y	Y	Y	N	N
Boxer	Y	Y	Y	?	Y	N	N
COLORADO							
Udall	Y	Y	Y	Y	N	N	Y
Bennet	Y	N	Y	Y	N	Y	Y
CONNECTICUT							
Lieberman	Y	N	Y	Y	N	N	Y
Blumenthal	Y	?	?	?	?	?	?
DELAWARE							
Carper	Y	N	N	Y	N	N	Y
Coons	Y	N	N	Y	N	N	Y
FLORIDA							
Nelson	Y	N	Y	Y	Y	N	Y
Rubio	N	N	N	N	Y	N	Y
GEORGIA							
Chambliss	N	N	N	Y	N	Y	Y
Isakson	N	N	N	Y	N	N	Y
HAWAII							
Inouye	Y	Y	N	Y	N	N	Y
Akaka	Y	Y	Y	?	N	N	Y
IDAHO							
Crapo	N	?	?	N	N	N	Y
Risch	N	N	N	N	N	N	Y
ILLINOIS							
Durbin	Y	Y	Y	Y	N	Y	N
Kirk	?	?	?	?	?	?	?
INDIANA							
Lugar	Y	N	N	Y	N	N	Y
Coats	N	N	N	Y	N	N	Y
IOWA							
Grassley	N	N	N	Y	Y	N	Y
Harkin	Y	N	N	Y	N	N	Y
KANSAS							
Roberts	N	N	N	Y	N	N	Y
Moran	N	N	N	Y	N	N	Y
KENTUCKY							
McConnell	N	N	N	Y	N	N	Y
Paul	N	N	N	N	Y	N	Y
LOUISIANA							
Landrieu	Y	N	Y	Y	N	N	Y
Vitter	?	Y	N	N	Y	N	Y
MAINE							
Snowe	Y	Y	Y	Y	Y	N	Y
Collins	Y	N	Y	Y	Y	N	Y
MARYLAND							
Mikulski	Y	?	Y	Y	N	N	Y
Cardin	Y	Y	Y	Y	N	Y	N
MASSACHUSETTS							
Kerry	Y	N	N	Y	N	N	Y
Brown	Y	N	N	Y	N	N	Y
MICHIGAN							
Levin	Y	Y	Y	Y	Y	Y	Y
Stabenow	Y	N	Y	?	Y	N	Y
MINNESOTA							
Klobuchar	Y	Y	N	Y	Y	N	N
Franken	Y	Y	N	Y	Y	Y	N
MISSISSIPPI							
Cochran	N	N	Y	N	Y	N	Y
Wicker	N	N	Y	N	N	N	Y
MISSOURI							
McCaskill	?	N	N	Y	Y	N	N
Blunt	N	N	N	Y	N	N	Y

	104	105	106	107	108	109	110
MONTANA							
Baucus	Y	N	Y	Y	N	N	N
Tester	Y	N	Y	Y	N	N	Y
NEBRASKA							
Nelson	Y	N	N	Y	Y	N	Y
Johanns	N	N	N	N	N	N	Y
NEVADA							
Reid	Y	N	Y	Y	N	N	Y
Heller	?	N	N	?	Y	N	Y
NEW HAMPSHIRE							
Shaheen	Y	Y	Y	Y	N	Y	N
Ayotte	N	N	Y	N	N	N	Y
NEW JERSEY							
Lautenberg	Y	N	Y	Y	N	N	N
Menendez	Y	N	Y	Y	N	N	Y
NEW MEXICO							
Bingaman	Y	Y	Y	Y	N	N	N
Udall	Y	Y	Y	Y	N	Y	N
NEW YORK							
Schumer	Y	Y	Y	Y	N	Y	N
Gillibrand	Y	Y	Y	Y	N	N	N
NORTH CAROLINA							
Burr	N	N	N	Y	N	N	Y
Hagan	N	N	N	Y	N	Y	Y
NORTH DAKOTA							
Conrad	Y	Y	Y	Y	N	N	N
Hoeven	N	N	Y	N	N	N	Y
OHIO							
Brown	Y	Y	Y	Y	Y	Y	Y
Portman	N	N	N	Y	N	N	Y
OKLAHOMA							
Inhofe	N	N	N	Y	N	N	Y
Coburn	N	N	Y	N	N	N	Y
OREGON							
Wyden	Y	N	Y	Y	N	N	Y
Merkley	Y	Y	Y	Y	Y	N	Y
PENNSYLVANIA							
Casey	Y	N	N	Y	N	N	Y
Toomey	N	N	N	N	Y	N	Y
RHODE ISLAND							
Reed	Y	Y	Y	Y	N	N	N
Whitehouse	Y	Y	Y	Y	Y	Y	Y
SOUTH CAROLINA							
Graham	Y	N	Y	Y	N	Y	Y
DeMint	?	N	N	N	N	N	Y
SOUTH DAKOTA							
Johnson	Y	Y	Y	Y	N	Y	N
Thune	N	N	N	Y	N	N	Y
TENNESSEE							
Alexander	Y	N	Y	N	N	Y	Y
Corker	N	N	N	Y	N	N	Y
TEXAS							
Hutchison	N	?	?	?	?	?	?
Cornyn	N	N	N	Y	N	N	Y
UTAH							
Hatch	N	N	N	Y	N	N	Y
Lee	N	N	N	N	Y	N	Y
VERMONT							
Leahy	Y	N	Y	Y	N	N	N
Sanders	Y	Y	Y	Y	Y	N	Y
VIRGINIA							
Webb	Y	Y	Y	Y	Y	N	N
Warner	Y	N	Y	Y	N	N	Y
WASHINGTON							
Murray	Y	N	Y	Y	N	N	Y
Cantwell	Y	N	Y	Y	N	N	Y
WEST VIRGINIA							
Rockefeller	Y	Y	Y	Y	Y	N	N
Manchin	Y	N	Y	Y	N	N	Y
WISCONSIN							
Kohl	Y	Y	Y	Y	N	Y	Y
Johnson	N	N	N	N	N	N	Y
WYOMING							
Enzi	N	N	N	Y	N	N	Y
Barrasso	N	N	N	Y	N	N	Y

KEY — Republicans Democrats *Independents*

Y Voted for (yea)	X Paired against	C Voted "present" to avoid possible conflict of interest
# Paired for	– Announced against	
+ Announced for	P Voted "present"	? Did not vote or otherwise make a position known
N Voted against (nay)		

IN THE SENATE | By Vote Number

111. **S 3187. FDA User Fees/Passage.** Passage of the bill that would grant a five-year reauthorization of the Food and Drug Administration's user fees programs, which help fund reviews of prescription drugs and medical devices. The measure also would create user fee programs for generic drugs and generic biologic drugs. As amended, the bill also would require the Health and Human Services Department to develop uniform standards for exchange of prescription drug information. It would designate a variety of synthetic drugs, including those marketed as "bath salts," as Schedule I controlled substances. Passed 96-1: D 50-0; R 45-0; I 1-1. A "yea" was a vote in support of the president's position. May 24, 2012.

112. **S 2343. Student Loans/Republican Substitute.** Alexander, R-Tenn., substitute amendment that would extend, for one year, a 3.4 percent interest rate on certain federally subsidized undergraduate student loans. It would be offset by repealing the Prevention and Public Health Fund established by the 2010 health care overhaul law and rescinding unobligated amounts in the fund. Rejected 34-62: D 0-50; R 34-10; I 0-2. (By unanimous consent, the Senate agreed to raise the majority requirement for adoption of the Alexander amendment to 60 votes.). A "nay" was a vote in support of the president's position. May 24, 2012.

113. **S 2343. Student Loans/Passage.** Passage of the bill that would extend, for one year, a 3.4 percent interest rate on certain federally subsidized, undergraduate student loans. It would be offset by eliminating a tax preference for S corporations, which are companies that pass their income, losses, deductions and credits through to shareholders for federal tax purposes. Rejected 51-43: D 49-1; R 0-42; I 2-0. (By unanimous consent, the Senate agreed to raise the majority requirement for passage of the bill to 60 votes.). A "yea" was a vote in support of the president's position. May 24, 2012.

114. **Hillman Nomination/Confirmation.** Confirmation of President Obama's nomination of Timothy S. Hillman of Massachusetts to be a judge for the U.S. District Court for the District of Massachusetts. Confirmed 88-1: D 48-0; R 38-1; I 2-0. A "yea" was a vote in support of the president's position. June 4, 2012.

115. **S 3220. Wage Discrimination/Cloture.** Motion to invoke cloture (thus limiting debate) on the Reid, D-Nev., motion to proceed to the bill that would require that employers show that any pay disparity is job-related and not based on gender. Motion rejected 52-47: D 50-1; R 0-46; I 2-0. Three-fifths of the total Senate (60) is required to invoke cloture. A "yea" was a vote in support of the president's position. June 5, 2012.

116. **Helmick Nomination/Confirmation.** Confirmation of President Obama's nomination of Jeffrey J. Helmick of Ohio to be a judge for the U.S. District Court for the Northern District of Ohio. Confirmed 62-36: D 51-0; R 9-36; I 2-0. A "yea" was a vote in support of the president's position. June 6, 2012.

117. **S 3240. Farm Programs/Cloture.** Motion to invoke cloture (thus limiting debate) on the Reid, D-Nev., motion to proceed to the bill that would reauthorize farm, food, nutrition and conservation programs for five years, through Sept. 30, 2017. The bill would overhaul the federal crop insurance program. Motion agreed to 90-8: D 51-0; R 37-8; I 2-0. Three-fifths of the total Senate (60) is required to invoke cloture. June 7, 2012.

	111	112	113	114	115	116	117
ALABAMA							
Shelby	Y	Y	N	Y	N	N	Y
Sessions	Y	Y	N	Y	N	N	Y
ALASKA							
Murkowski	Y	Y	N	Y	N	Y	Y
Begich	Y	Y	Y	Y	Y	Y	Y
ARIZONA							
McCain	Y	Y	N	Y	N	N	Y
Kyl	Y	Y	?	Y	N	N	Y
ARKANSAS							
Pryor	Y	N	Y	Y	Y	Y	Y
Boozman	Y	Y	N	Y	N	N	Y
CALIFORNIA							
Feinstein	Y	N	Y	Y	Y	Y	Y
Boxer	Y	N	Y	Y	Y	Y	Y
COLORADO							
Udall	Y	N	Y	Y	Y	Y	Y
Bennet	Y	N	Y	Y	Y	Y	Y
CONNECTICUT							
Lieberman	Y	N	Y	Y	Y	Y	Y
Blumenthal	?	?	?	Y	Y	Y	Y
DELAWARE							
Carper	Y	N	Y	Y	Y	Y	Y
Coons	Y	N	Y	Y	Y	Y	Y
FLORIDA							
Nelson	Y	N	Y	Y	Y	Y	Y
Rubio	Y	Y	N	?	N	N	Y
GEORGIA							
Chambliss	Y	Y	N	?	N	N	Y
Isakson	Y	Y	N	Y	N	N	Y
HAWAII							
Inouye	Y	N	Y	Y	Y	Y	Y
Akaka	Y	N	Y	Y	Y	Y	Y
IDAHO							
Crapo	Y	Y	N	Y	N	N	Y
Risch	Y	Y	N	Y	N	N	Y
ILLINOIS							
Durbin	Y	N	Y	Y	Y	Y	Y
Kirk	?	?	?	?	?	?	?
INDIANA							
Lugar	Y	Y	N	Y	N	Y	Y
Coats	Y	Y	N	?	N	N	Y
IOWA							
Grassley	Y	Y	N	Y	N	N	Y
Harkin	Y	N	Y	?	Y	Y	Y
KANSAS							
Roberts	Y	Y	N	Y	N	N	Y
Moran	Y	N	N	Y	N	N	Y
KENTUCKY							
McConnell	Y	Y	N	Y	N	N	Y
Paul	Y	N	N	Y	N	N	Y
LOUISIANA							
Landrieu	Y	N	Y	Y	Y	Y	Y
Vitter	Y	Y	N	Y	N	?	?
MAINE							
Snowe	Y	P	P	Y	N	Y	Y
Collins	Y	Y	N	Y	N	Y	Y
MARYLAND							
Mikulski	Y	N	Y	Y	Y	Y	Y
Cardin	Y	N	Y	Y	Y	Y	Y
MASSACHUSETTS							
Kerry	Y	N	Y	Y	Y	Y	Y
Brown	Y	Y	N	Y	N	Y	Y
MICHIGAN							
Levin	Y	N	Y	Y	Y	Y	Y
Stabenow	Y	N	Y	Y	Y	Y	Y
MINNESOTA							
Klobuchar	Y	N	Y	Y	Y	Y	Y
Franken	Y	N	Y	Y	Y	Y	Y
MISSISSIPPI							
Cochran	Y	Y	N	Y	N	N	Y
Wicker	Y	Y	N	Y	N	N	Y
MISSOURI							
McCaskill	Y	N	Y	Y	Y	Y	Y
Blunt	Y	Y	N	Y	N	N	Y
MONTANA							
Baucus	Y	N	Y	Y	Y	Y	Y
Tester	Y	N	Y	Y	Y	Y	Y
NEBRASKA							
Nelson	Y	N	Y	Y	Y	Y	Y
Johanns	Y	Y	N	Y	N	N	Y
NEVADA							
Reid	Y	N	Y	Y	N	Y	Y
Heller	Y	Y	N	?	N	N	N
NEW HAMPSHIRE							
Shaheen	Y	N	Y	Y	Y	Y	Y
Ayotte	Y	Y	N	Y	N	N	Y
NEW JERSEY							
Lautenberg	Y	N	Y	?	Y	Y	Y
Menendez	Y	N	Y	?	Y	Y	Y
NEW MEXICO							
Bingaman	Y	N	Y	Y	Y	Y	Y
Udall	Y	N	Y	Y	Y	Y	Y
NEW YORK							
Schumer	Y	N	Y	Y	Y	Y	Y
Gillibrand	Y	N	Y	Y	Y	Y	Y
NORTH CAROLINA							
Burr	Y	N	N	?	N	N	Y
Hagan	Y	N	Y	Y	Y	Y	Y
NORTH DAKOTA							
Conrad	Y	N	Y	Y	Y	Y	Y
Hoeven	Y	Y	N	Y	N	N	Y
OHIO							
Brown	Y	N	Y	Y	Y	Y	Y
Portman	Y	Y	N	?	N	Y	Y
OKLAHOMA							
Inhofe	Y	N	N	Y	N	N	N
Coburn	Y	N	N	Y	N	N	N
OREGON							
Wyden	Y	N	Y	Y	Y	Y	Y
Merkley	Y	N	Y	Y	Y	Y	Y
PENNSYLVANIA							
Casey	Y	N	Y	Y	Y	Y	Y
Toomey	Y	N	Y	N	N	N	Y
RHODE ISLAND							
Reed	Y	N	Y	Y	Y	Y	Y
Whitehouse	Y	N	Y	Y	Y	Y	Y
SOUTH CAROLINA							
Graham	Y	Y	N	Y	N	Y	Y
DeMint	Y	N	N	?	N	N	N
SOUTH DAKOTA							
Johnson	Y	N	Y	Y	Y	Y	Y
Thune	Y	Y	N	Y	N	N	Y
TENNESSEE							
Alexander	Y	Y	N	Y	N	Y	Y
Corker	Y	N	Y	N	Y	N	Y
TEXAS							
Hutchison	?	?	?	Y	N	N	Y
Cornyn	Y	Y	N	Y	N	N	Y
UTAH							
Hatch	Y	Y	N	Y	N	N	Y
Lee	Y	N	N	N	N	N	N
VERMONT							
Leahy	Y	N	Y	Y	Y	Y	Y
Sanders	N	N	Y	Y	Y	Y	Y
VIRGINIA							
Webb	Y	N	Y	Y	Y	Y	Y
Warner	Y	N	Y	Y	Y	Y	Y
WASHINGTON							
Murray	Y	N	Y	Y	Y	Y	Y
Cantwell	Y	N	Y	Y	Y	Y	Y
WEST VIRGINIA							
Rockefeller	Y	N	Y	Y	Y	Y	Y
Manchin	Y	N	Y	Y	Y	Y	Y
WISCONSIN							
Kohl	Y	N	Y	Y	Y	Y	Y
Johnson	Y	N	N	Y	N	N	N
WYOMING							
Enzi	Y	Y	?	Y	N	N	Y
Barrasso	Y	Y	N	Y	N	N	Y

KEY **Republicans**   Democrats   *Independents*

Y Voted for (yea)	**X** Paired against	**C** Voted "present" to avoid possible conflict of interest
# Paired for	**–** Announced against	
+ Announced for	**P** Voted "present"	**?** Did not vote or otherwise make a position known
N Voted against (nay)		

IN THE SENATE | By Vote Number

118. **Hurwitz Nomination/Cloture.** Motion to invoke cloture (thus limiting debate) on President Obama's nomination of Andrew D. Hurwitz of Arizona to be a judge for the 9th U.S. Circuit Court of Appeals. Motion agreed to 60-31: D 50-1; R 8-30; I 2-0. Three-fifths of the total Senate (60) is required to invoke cloture. A "yea" was a vote in support of the president's position. June 11, 2012.

119. **S 3240. Farm Programs/Sugar Program Repeal.** Reid, D-Nev., motion to table (kill) the Reid amendment to the Reid amendment to the motion to recommit the bill to the Agriculture, Nutrition and Forestry Committee. The Reid amendment would phase out the federal price support program for sugar, eliminating the funding entirely for crop year 2015. The underlying Reid amendment would replace the Supplemental Nutrition Assistance Program with block grants to states to provide nutrition assistance. The motion would recommit the bill to the committee with instruction to report it back immediately with a third Reid amendment, a perfecting amendment, that would replace the Supplemental Nutrition Assistance Program with block grants to states to provide nutrition assistance. Motion agreed to 50-46: D 32-16; R 16-30; I 2-0. June 13, 2012.

120. **S 3240. Farm Programs/Nutrition Assistance Block Grants.** Reid, D-Nev., motion to table (kill) the Reid amendment to the motion to recommit the bill to the Agriculture, Nutrition and Forestry Committee. The Reid amendment would replace the Supplemental Nutrition Assistance Program with block grants to states to provide nutrition assistance. The motion would recommit the bill to the committee with instructions to report the bill back immediately with a Reid perfecting amendment that would replace the Supplemental Nutrition Assistance Program with block grants to states to provide nutrition assistance. Motion agreed to 65-33: D 50-0; R 13-33; I 2-0. June 13, 2012.

121. **Aponte Nomination/Cloture.** Motion to invoke cloture (thus limiting debate) on President Obama's nomination of Mari Carmen Aponte of the District of Columbia to be U.S. ambassador to the Republic of El Salvador. Motion agreed to 62-37: D 51-0; R 9-37; I 2-0. Three-fifths of the total Senate (60) is required to invoke cloture. A "yea" was a vote in support of the president's position. (Subsequently, the Aponte nomination was confirmed by voice vote.) June 14, 2012.

	118	119	120	121			118	119	120	121
ALABAMA						**MONTANA**				
Shelby	N	N	N	N		Baucus	Y	Y	Y	Y
Sessions	N	N	N	N		Tester	Y	Y	Y	Y
ALASKA						**NEBRASKA**				
Murkowski	Y	N	Y	Y		Nelson	Y	Y	Y	Y
Begich	Y	Y	Y	Y		Johanns	N	Y	Y	N
ARIZONA						**NEVADA**				
McCain	Y	N	N	Y		Reid	Y	Y	Y	Y
Kyl	Y	N	N	N		Heller	N	N	N	N
ARKANSAS						**NEW HAMPSHIRE**				
Pryor	Y	Y	Y	Y		Shaheen	Y	N	Y	Y
Boozman	N	N	Y	N		Ayotte	N	N	N	Y
CALIFORNIA						**NEW JERSEY**				
Feinstein	Y	Y	Y	Y		Lautenberg	Y	N	Y	Y
Boxer	Y	Y	Y	Y		Menendez	Y	Y	Y	Y
COLORADO						**NEW MEXICO**				
Udall	Y	Y	Y	Y		Bingaman	Y	Y	Y	Y
Bennet	Y	Y	Y	Y		Udall	Y	Y	Y	Y
CONNECTICUT						**NEW YORK**				
Lieberman	Y	Y	Y	Y		Schumer	Y	Y	Y	Y
Blumenthal	Y	N	Y	Y		Gillibrand	Y	Y	Y	Y
DELAWARE						**NORTH CAROLINA**				
Carper	Y	N	Y	Y		Burr	?	N	N	N
Coons	Y	N	Y	Y		Hagan	Y	N	Y	Y
FLORIDA						**NORTH DAKOTA**				
Nelson	Y	Y	Y	Y		Conrad	Y	Y	Y	Y
Rubio	N	Y	N	Y		Hoeven	N	Y	N	N
GEORGIA						**OHIO**				
Chambliss	?	Y	N	N		Brown	Y	N	Y	Y
Isakson	?	Y	N	N		Portman	N	N	Y	N
HAWAII						**OKLAHOMA**				
Inouye	Y	Y	Y	Y		Inhofe	N	N	N	N
Akaka	Y	Y	Y	Y		Coburn	?	N	N	N
IDAHO						**OREGON**				
Crapo	N	Y	N	N		Wyden	Y	N	Y	Y
Risch	N	Y	N	N		Merkley	Y	N	Y	Y
ILLINOIS						**PENNSYLVANIA**				
Durbin	Y	N	Y	Y		Casey	Y	N	Y	Y
Kirk	?	?	?	?		Toomey	?	N	N	N
INDIANA						**RHODE ISLAND**				
Lugar	Y	N	Y	Y		Reed	Y	N	Y	Y
Coats	N	N	N	N		Whitehouse	Y	N	Y	Y
IOWA						**SOUTH CAROLINA**				
Grassley	N	N	N	N		Graham	N	N	N	Y
Harkin	Y	Y	Y	Y		DeMint	N	N	N	N
KANSAS						**SOUTH DAKOTA**				
Roberts	N	Y	N	Y		Johnson	Y	Y	Y	Y
Moran	N	Y	N	N		Thune	N	Y	N	N
KENTUCKY						**TENNESSEE**				
McConnell	N	N	N	N		Alexander	Y	N	Y	Y
Paul	N	N	N	N		Corker	N	N	Y	N
LOUISIANA						**TEXAS**				
Landrieu	Y	Y	Y	Y		Hutchison	N	N	N	N
Vitter	?	Y	N	N		Cornyn	N	N	N	N
MAINE						**UTAH**				
Snowe	Y	N	Y	Y		Hatch	?	N	N	N
Collins	Y	N	Y	Y		Lee	N	N	N	N
MARYLAND						**VERMONT**				
Mikulski	Y	Y	Y	Y		Leahy	Y	Y	Y	Y
Cardin	Y	Y	Y	Y		Sanders	Y	Y	Y	Y
MASSACHUSETTS						**VIRGINIA**				
Kerry	Y	Y	Y	Y		Webb	Y	N	Y	Y
Brown	Y	N	Y	Y		Warner	Y	?	?	Y
MICHIGAN						**WASHINGTON**				
Levin	Y	Y	Y	Y		Murray	Y	Y	Y	Y
Stabenow	Y	Y	Y	Y		Cantwell	Y	Y	Y	Y
MINNESOTA						**WEST VIRGINIA**				
Klobuchar	Y	Y	Y	Y		Rockefeller	Y	?	Y	Y
Franken	Y	Y	Y	Y		Manchin	N	N	Y	N
MISSISSIPPI						**WISCONSIN**				
Cochran	N	Y	Y	N		Kohl	Y	N	Y	Y
Wicker	N	Y	N	N		Johnson	N	N	N	N
MISSOURI						**WYOMING**				
McCaskill	Y	?	Y	Y		Enzi	?	Y	N	N
Blunt	N	Y	N	N		Barrasso	N	Y	N	N

KEY   **Republicans**   Democrats   *Independents*

Y Voted for (yea)	X Paired against	C Voted "present" to avoid possible conflict of interest
# Paired for	– Announced against	? Did not vote or otherwise make a position known
+ Announced for	P Voted "present"	
N Voted against (nay)		

IN THE SENATE | By Vote Number

122. Lewis Nomination/Confirmation. Confirmation of President Obama's nomination of Mary Geiger Lewis of South Carolina to be a judge for the U.S. District Court for the District of South Carolina. Confirmed 64-27: D 48-0; R 14-27; I 2-0. A "yea" was a vote in support of the president's position. June 18, 2012.

123. S 3240. Farm Programs/Value-Added Agricultural Products. Ayotte, R-N.H., amendment that would overhaul a grant program for producers of value-added agricultural products, which are products that are modified to expand the customer base and increase the revenue share of produce. Grants could not be provided to producers of alcoholic beverages. Rejected 38-61: D 1-50; R 37-9; I 0-2. June 19, 2012.

124. S 3240. Farm Programs/Milk Prices. Snowe, R-Maine, amendment that would direct the Agriculture secretary to eliminate end-product price formulas in setting certain milk prices. It also would overhaul the process of amending federal milk marketing orders. Adopted 66-33: D 42-9; R 22-24; I 2-0. June 19, 2012.

125. S 3240. Farm Programs/Loan Marketing Payment Limits. Grassley, R-Iowa, amendment that would set payment limits for marketing loan gains and loan deficiency payments on certain agricultural commodities. The payment limit for peanuts and other covered commodities would be $75,000. Adopted 75-24: D 45-6; R 29-17; I 1-1. June 19, 2012.

126. S 3240. Farm Programs/Rural Development. Brown, D-Ohio, amendment that would provide $150 million for various rural development programs administered by the Commodity Credit Corporation, as well as $50 million in funding for water and sewer projects in small rural communities. Adopted 55-44: D 50-1; R 3-43; I 2-0. June 19, 2012.

127. S 3240. Farm Programs/SNAP Eligibility. Sessions, R-Ala., amendment that would restrict categorical eligibility for the Supplemental Nutrition Assistance Program, formerly known as food stamps, to recipients of cash assistance from other state and federal aid programs. Rejected 43-56: D 1-50; R 42-4; I 0-2. June 19, 2012.

128. S 3240. Farm Programs/Pulse Crops for School Meals. Cantwell, D-Wash., amendment that would direct the Agriculture secretary to purchase pulse crop products, derived from dry beans, dry peas, lentils and chickpeas, for school meal programs. Adopted 58-41: D 50-1; R 6-40; I 2-0. June 19, 2012.

	122	123	124	125	126	127	128
ALABAMA							
Shelby	N	Y	Y	N	N	Y	N
Sessions	N	Y	Y	N	N	Y	N
ALASKA							
Murkowski	Y	Y	Y	Y	N	Y	N
Begich	Y	N	Y	Y	Y	N	Y
ARIZONA							
McCain	Y	Y	Y	Y	N	Y	N
Kyl	N	Y	N	Y	N	Y	N
ARKANSAS							
Pryor	Y	N	Y	N	Y	N	Y
Boozman	N	Y	N	N	N	Y	N
CALIFORNIA							
Feinstein	Y	N	N	Y	Y	N	Y
Boxer	Y	N	N	Y	Y	N	Y
COLORADO							
Udall	Y	N	N	Y	Y	N	Y
Bennet	Y	N	N	Y	Y	N	Y
CONNECTICUT							
Lieberman	Y	N	Y	Y	Y	N	Y
Blumenthal	Y	N	Y	Y	Y	N	Y
DELAWARE							
Carper	Y	N	Y	Y	Y	N	Y
Coons	Y	N	Y	Y	Y	N	Y
FLORIDA							
Nelson	Y	N	Y	Y	Y	N	Y
Rubio	?	Y	Y	Y	N	Y	N
GEORGIA							
Chambliss	N	Y	N	N	N	Y	N
Isakson	N	Y	N	N	N	Y	N
HAWAII							
Inouye	Y	N	Y	Y	Y	N	Y
Akaka	Y	N	Y	Y	Y	N	Y
IDAHO							
Crapo	N	Y	N	Y	N	Y	Y
Risch	N	Y	N	Y	N	Y	Y
ILLINOIS							
Durbin	Y	N	N	Y	Y	N	Y
Kirk	?	?	?	?	?	?	?
INDIANA							
Lugar	Y	N	N	Y	N	Y	Y
Coats	N	Y	N	Y	N	Y	N
IOWA							
Grassley	N	N	Y	Y	N	Y	N
Harkin	?	N	Y	Y	Y	N	Y
KANSAS							
Roberts	N	N	Y	Y	N	Y	N
Moran	?	N	Y	N	N	Y	N
KENTUCKY							
McConnell	N	Y	Y	Y	N	Y	N
Paul	N	Y	N	Y	N	Y	N
LOUISIANA							
Landrieu	Y	N	Y	N	Y	N	Y
Vitter	?	Y	N	N	Y	N	Y
MAINE							
Snowe	Y	Y	Y	Y	N	N	N
Collins	Y	N	Y	Y	Y	N	N
MARYLAND							
Mikulski	Y	N	Y	Y	Y	N	Y
Cardin	Y	N	Y	Y	Y	N	Y
MASSACHUSETTS							
Kerry	Y	N	Y	Y	Y	N	Y
Brown	Y	Y	Y	Y	Y	N	N
MICHIGAN							
Levin	Y	N	Y	Y	Y	N	Y
Stabenow	Y	N	Y	Y	Y	N	Y
MINNESOTA							
Klobuchar	Y	N	Y	Y	Y	N	Y
Franken	Y	N	Y	Y	Y	N	Y
MISSISSIPPI							
Cochran	Y	N	Y	N	N	Y	N
Wicker	Y	Y	N	N	N	Y	N
MISSOURI							
McCaskill	?	N	Y	Y	N	Y	Y
Blunt	N	N	N	N	Y	N	Y
MONTANA							
Baucus	Y	N	Y	Y	Y	N	Y
Tester	Y	N	Y	Y	Y	N	Y
NEBRASKA							
Nelson	Y	N	N	Y	Y	N	Y
Johanns	N	N	N	Y	N	Y	Y
NEVADA							
Reid	Y	N	Y	Y	Y	N	Y
Heller	Y	N	Y	Y	Y	N	N
NEW HAMPSHIRE							
Shaheen	Y	N	Y	Y	Y	N	Y
Ayotte	Y	Y	Y	Y	N	Y	N
NEW JERSEY							
Lautenberg	Y	N	Y	Y	Y	N	Y
Menendez	Y	N	Y	Y	Y	N	Y
NEW MEXICO							
Bingaman	Y	N	Y	Y	Y	N	Y
Udall	Y	N	Y	Y	Y	N	Y
NEW YORK							
Schumer	Y	N	Y	Y	Y	N	Y
Gillibrand	Y	N	Y	Y	Y	N	Y
NORTH CAROLINA							
Burr	N	Y	N	N	N	Y	N
Hagan	Y	N	Y	N	Y	N	Y
NORTH DAKOTA							
Conrad	Y	N	Y	N	Y	N	Y
Hoeven	Y	N	N	N	N	Y	Y
OHIO							
Brown	Y	N	Y	Y	Y	N	Y
Portman	N	Y	Y	Y	N	Y	N
OKLAHOMA							
Inhofe	N	Y	Y	N	N	Y	N
Coburn	N	Y	Y	Y	N	Y	N
OREGON							
Wyden	Y	N	Y	Y	Y	N	Y
Merkley	Y	N	Y	Y	Y	N	Y
PENNSYLVANIA							
Casey	?	N	Y	Y	Y	N	Y
Toomey	?	Y	Y	.	Y	N	Y
RHODE ISLAND							
Reed	Y	N	Y	Y	Y	N	Y
Whitehouse	Y	N	Y	Y	Y	N	Y
SOUTH CAROLINA							
Graham	Y	Y	Y	N	N	Y	N
DeMint	N	Y	N	N	N	Y	N
SOUTH DAKOTA							
Johnson	Y	N	Y	Y	Y	N	Y
Thune	N	Y	N	Y	N	Y	N
TENNESSEE							
Alexander	Y	Y	Y	Y	N	Y	N
Corker	Y	Y	Y	Y	N	Y	N
TEXAS							
Hutchison	Y	Y	N	N	N	Y	N
Cornyn	N	Y	N	N	N	Y	N
UTAH							
Hatch	N	Y	Y	Y	N	Y	N
Lee	N	Y	Y	Y	N	Y	N
VERMONT							
Leahy	Y	N	Y	N	Y	N	Y
Sanders	Y	N	Y	N	Y	N	Y
VIRGINIA							
Webb	Y	N	Y	Y	Y	N	Y
Warner	Y	N	Y	N	Y	N	Y
WASHINGTON							
Murray	Y	N	Y	Y	Y	N	Y
Cantwell	Y	N	Y	Y	Y	N	Y
WEST VIRGINIA							
Rockefeller	Y	N	Y	Y	Y	N	Y
Manchin	Y	Y	Y	Y	Y	N	Y
WISCONSIN							
Kohl	Y	N	Y	Y	Y	N	Y
Johnson	?	Y	N	N	N	Y	N
WYOMING							
Enzi	N	Y	N	Y	N	Y	N
Barrasso	N	Y	N	Y	N	Y	N

KEY   **Republicans**   *Democrats*   *Independents*

Y Voted for (yea)	X Paired against	C Voted "present" to avoid possible conflict of interest
# Paired for	– Announced against	
+ Announced for	P Voted "present"	? Did not vote or otherwise make a position known
N Voted against (nay)		

IN THE SENATE | By Vote Number

129. **S 3240. Farm Programs/SNAP Bonus Payments.** Sessions, R-Ala., amendment that would repeal provisions allowing bonus payments to states under the Supplemental Nutrition Assistance Program, formerly known as food stamps. Rejected 41-58: D 0-51; R 41-5; I 0-2. June 19, 2012.

130. **S 3240. Farm Programs/Dairy Price Reporting.** Casey, D-Pa., amendment that would require more frequent reporting on the price of dairy products by manufacturers. It also would require the Agriculture secretary to study the feasibility of establishing two classes of milk, a fluid class and a manufacturing class, to replace the four-class system currently in effect. Adopted 73-26: D 49-2; R 22-24; I 2-0. June 19, 2012.

131. **S 3240. Farm Programs/Income Limit on Beneficiaries.** Paul, R-Ky., amendment that would establish a $250,000 limit on adjusted gross income for recipients of benefits provided under the bill. Rejected 15-84: D 1-50; R 14-32; I 0-2. June 19, 2012.

132. **S 3240. Farm Programs/Wind Energy Loans.** Alexander, R-Tenn., amendment that would prohibit entities that receive wind energy loans and loan guarantees under the bill from receiving other federal benefits for the same project. Rejected 33-66: D 0-51; R 33-13; I 0-2. June 19, 2012.

133. **S 3240. Farm Programs/Study on Food Safety Insurance.** Feinstein, D-Calif., amendment that would direct the Federal Crop Insurance Corporation to study the feasibility of establishing a food safety insurance program. Adopted 76-23: D 51-0; R 23-23; I 2-0. June 19, 2012.

134. **S 3240. Farm Programs/Organic Certification Cost Share Assistance.** Toomey, R-Pa., amendment that would eliminate the Agriculture Department's National Organic Certification Cost Share Program and Agriculture Management Assistance Program, which reimburse producers for costs associated with certifying organic agricultural products. Rejected 42-57: D 1-50; R 41-5; I 0-0. June 19, 2012.

135. **S 3240. Farm Programs/SNAP Funding.** Gillibrand, D-N.Y., amendment that would strike the bill's proposed cuts to the Supplemental Nutrition Assistance Program, formerly known as food stamps, and replace it with $4.5 billion in cuts to subsidies for the federal crop insurance program over 10 years. It also would increase mandatory funding by $50 million per year for the Fresh Fruit and Vegetable Program. Rejected 33-66: D 27-24; R 4-42; I 2-0. June 19, 2012.

State / Senator	129	130	131	132	133	134	135
ALABAMA							
Shelby	Y	N	N	Y	N	Y	N
Sessions	Y	N	N	Y	N	Y	N
ALASKA							
Murkowski	N	Y	Y	Y	Y	Y	Y
Begich	N	Y	N	N	Y	N	Y
ARIZONA							
McCain	Y	N	Y	Y	N	Y	N
Kyl	Y	N	Y	Y	N	Y	N
ARKANSAS							
Pryor	N	Y	N	N	Y	N	N
Boozman	Y	Y	N	N	Y	Y	N
CALIFORNIA							
Feinstein	N	N	N	N	Y	N	Y
Boxer	N	N	N	N	Y	N	Y
COLORADO							
Udall	N	Y	N	Y	N	N	N
Bennet	N	Y	N	N	Y	N	N
CONNECTICUT							
Lieberman	N	Y	N	N	Y	N	Y
Blumenthal	N	Y	N	N	Y	N	Y
DELAWARE							
Carper	N	Y	N	N	Y	N	N
Coons	N	Y	N	N	Y	N	Y
FLORIDA							
Nelson	N	Y	N	N	Y	N	N
Rubio	Y	N	Y	Y	N	Y	N
GEORGIA							
Chambliss	Y	Y	N	Y	Y	Y	N
Isakson	Y	Y	N	Y	Y	Y	N
HAWAII							
Inouye	N	Y	N	N	Y	N	N
Akaka	N	Y	N	N	Y	N	Y
IDAHO							
Crapo	Y	Y	N	Y	Y	Y	N
Risch	Y	Y	N	Y	Y	Y	N
ILLINOIS							
Durbin	N	Y	N	N	Y	N	N
Kirk	?	?	?	?	?	?	?
INDIANA							
Lugar	Y	Y	N	N	Y	Y	N
Coats	Y	Y	N	Y	N	Y	N
IOWA							
Grassley	Y	Y	N	N	Y	Y	N
Harkin	N	Y	N	N	Y	N	N
KANSAS							
Roberts	Y	Y	N	N	Y	Y	N
Moran	Y	N	N	N	Y	Y	N
KENTUCKY							
McConnell	Y	N	N	Y	N	Y	N
Paul	Y	N	Y	Y	N	Y	N
LOUISIANA							
Landrieu	N	Y	N	N	Y	N	N
Vitter	Y	Y	N	Y	Y	Y	N
MAINE							
Snowe	N	Y	N	Y	Y	N	Y
Collins	N	Y	N	N	Y	N	N
MARYLAND							
Mikulski	N	Y	N	N	Y	N	Y
Cardin	N	Y	N	N	Y	N	Y
MASSACHUSETTS							
Kerry	N	Y	N	N	Y	N	Y
Brown	N	N	N	N	Y	N	Y
MICHIGAN							
Levin	N	Y	N	N	Y	N	Y
Stabenow	N	Y	N	N	Y	N	N
MINNESOTA							
Klobuchar	N	Y	N	N	Y	N	N
Franken	N	Y	N	N	Y	N	N
MISSISSIPPI							
Cochran	Y	N	N	Y	Y	Y	N
Wicker	Y	N	N	Y	Y	Y	N
MISSOURI							
McCaskill	N	Y	N	N	Y	N	N
Blunt	Y	Y	N	Y	Y	Y	N

State / Senator	129	130	131	132	133	134	135
MONTANA							
Baucus	N	Y	N	N	Y	N	N
Tester	N	Y	N	N	Y	N	N
NEBRASKA							
Nelson	N	Y	N	N	Y	N	N
Johanns	Y	Y	N	N	Y	Y	N
NEVADA							
Reid	N	Y	N	N	Y	N	Y
Heller	N	Y	Y	N	N	Y	Y
NEW HAMPSHIRE							
Shaheen	N	Y	N	N	Y	N	Y
Ayotte	Y	Y	Y	Y	Y	Y	N
NEW JERSEY							
Lautenberg	N	Y	N	N	Y	N	Y
Menendez	N	Y	N	N	Y	N	Y
NEW MEXICO							
Bingaman	N	Y	N	N	Y	N	N
Udall	N	Y	N	N	Y	N	Y
NEW YORK							
Schumer	N	Y	N	N	Y	N	Y
Gillibrand	N	Y	N	N	Y	N	Y
NORTH CAROLINA							
Burr	Y	N	Y	Y	Y	Y	N
Hagan	N	Y	N	N	Y	N	N
NORTH DAKOTA							
Conrad	N	Y	N	N	Y	N	N
Hoeven	Y	N	N	N	N	N	N
OHIO							
Brown	N	Y	N	N	Y	N	Y
Portman	Y	Y	Y	Y	Y	Y	N
OKLAHOMA							
Inhofe	Y	N	N	N	Y	N	N
Coburn	Y	N	N	Y	N	Y	N
OREGON							
Wyden	N	Y	N	N	Y	N	Y
Merkley	N	Y	N	N	Y	N	Y
PENNSYLVANIA							
Casey	N	Y	N	N	Y	N	Y
Toomey	Y	Y	Y	Y	N	Y	N
RHODE ISLAND							
Reed	N	Y	N	N	Y	N	Y
Whitehouse	N	Y	N	N	Y	N	Y
SOUTH CAROLINA							
Graham	Y	N	Y	N	Y	N	N
DeMint	Y	N	Y	Y	Y	Y	N
SOUTH DAKOTA							
Johnson	N	Y	N	N	Y	N	N
Thune	Y	N	N	N	N	Y	N
TENNESSEE							
Alexander	Y	Y	N	Y	N	Y	N
Corker	Y	Y	N	Y	N	Y	N
TEXAS							
Hutchison	Y	Y	N	Y	Y	Y	N
Cornyn	Y	N	N	Y	Y	Y	N
UTAH							
Hatch	Y	N	Y	Y	N	Y	N
Lee	Y	N	Y	Y	N	Y	N
VERMONT							
Leahy	N	Y	N	N	Y	N	Y
Sanders	N	Y	N	N	Y	N	Y
VIRGINIA							
Webb	N	Y	N	N	Y	N	N
Warner	N	Y	N	N	Y	N	N
WASHINGTON							
Murray	N	Y	N	N	Y	N	Y
Cantwell	N	Y	N	N	Y	N	Y
WEST VIRGINIA							
Rockefeller	N	Y	N	N	Y	N	Y
Manchin	N	Y	N	N	Y	Y	N
WISCONSIN							
Kohl	N	Y	N	N	Y	N	Y
Johnson	Y	N	Y	Y	N	Y	N
WYOMING							
Enzi	Y	N	Y	N	Y	N	N
Barrasso	Y	N	Y	N	Y	N	N

KEY   **Republicans**   Democrats   *Independents*

Y Voted for (yea)	X Paired against	C Voted "present" to avoid possible conflict of interest
# Paired for	– Announced against	
+ Announced for	P Voted "present"	? Did not vote or otherwise make a position known
N Voted against (nay)		

IN THE SENATE | By Vote Number

136. **S 3240. Farm Programs/Broadband Access Funding.** DeMint, R-S.C., amendment that would maintain funding at current levels for programs that provide access to broadband telecommunications services in rural areas. Rejected 45-54: D 0-51; R 45-1; I 0-2. June 19, 2012.

137. **S 3240. Farm Programs/Loan Guarantees.** DeMint, R-S.C., amendment that would prohibit the Agriculture secretary from making loan guarantees. Rejected 14-84: D 0-50; R 14-32; I 0-2. June 19, 2012.

138. **S 3240. Farm Programs/Mandatory Check-Off Programs.** DeMint, R-S.C., amendment that would prohibit mandatory or compulsory "check-off" programs, which promote or provide research and information for a particular agricultural commodity without reference to specific producers or brands. Rejected 20-79: D 0-51; R 20-26; I 0-2. June 19, 2012.

139. **S J Res 37. Utility MACT Disapproval/Motion to Proceed.** McConnell, R-Ky., motion to proceed to the joint resolution that would nullify the EPA rule regarding the establishment of Mercury and Air Toxics Standards for certain utilities. Motion rejected 46-53: D 5-46; R 41-5; I 0-2. A "nay" was a vote in support of the president's position. June 20, 2012.

140. **S 3240. Farm Programs/Organic Crop Insurance.** Merkley, D-Ore., amendment that would require the Federal Crop Insurance Corporation to provide insurance for organic crops that reflects the retail or wholesale prices received by producers of other crops. Adopted 63-36: D 51-0; R 10-36; I 2-0. June 20, 2012.

141. **S 3240. Farm Programs/Rural Broadband.** DeMint, R-S.C., amendment that would eliminate the authority of the Agriculture Department to increase the federal share of certain new grants for rural broadband development beyond 50 percent. Rejected 44-55: D 1-50; R 43-3; I 0-2. June 20, 2012.

142. **S 3240. Farm Programs/Market Access Program.** Coburn, R-Okla., amendment that would reduce by 20 percent the amount provided in the bill in each of the next five fiscal years for the Agriculture Department's Market Access Program, which provides funding to help producers and trade associations finance promotional campaigns. The amendment would prohibit funding for wine tastings, reality television programs, animal spa products and food for cats and dogs. Rejected 30-69: D 2-49; R 28-18; I 0-2. June 20, 2012.

	136	137	138	139	140	141	142
ALABAMA							
Shelby	Y	N	N	Y	N	Y	Y
Sessions	Y	N	Y	Y	N	Y	Y
ALASKA							
Murkowski	N	N	Y	Y	Y	N	N
Begich	N	N	N	N	Y	N	N
ARIZONA							
McCain	Y	Y	Y	Y	N	Y	Y
Kyl	Y	Y	Y	Y	N	Y	Y
ARKANSAS							
Pryor	N	N	N	N	Y	N	N
Boozman	Y	N	N	Y	N	Y	N
CALIFORNIA							
Feinstein	N	N	N	N	Y	N	N
Boxer	N	N	N	N	Y	N	N
COLORADO							
Udall	N	N	N	N	Y	N	N
Bennet	N	N	N	N	Y	N	N
CONNECTICUT							
Lieberman	N	N	N	N	Y	N	N
Blumenthal	N	N	N	N	Y	N	N
DELAWARE							
Carper	N	N	N	N	Y	N	N
Coons	N	N	N	N	Y	N	N
FLORIDA							
Nelson	N	N	N	N	Y	N	N
Rubio	Y	Y	Y	N	Y	N	Y
GEORGIA							
Chambliss	Y	N	N	Y	N	Y	N
Isakson	Y	N	N	Y	N	Y	N
HAWAII							
Inouye	N	N	N	N	Y	N	N
Akaka	N	N	N	N	Y	N	N
IDAHO							
Crapo	Y	N	N	Y	N	Y	Y
Risch	Y	N	N	Y	N	Y	Y
ILLINOIS							
Durbin	N	N	N	N	Y	N	N
Kirk	?	?	?	?	?	?	?
INDIANA							
Lugar	Y	N	N	Y	Y	N	N
Coats	Y	N	Y	Y	Y	Y	Y
IOWA							
Grassley	Y	N	N	Y	Y	Y	Y
Harkin	N	?	N	N	Y	N	N
KANSAS							
Roberts	Y	N	N	Y	N	Y	N
Moran	Y	N	N	Y	Y	N	N
KENTUCKY							
McConnell	Y	N	Y	Y	N	Y	Y
Paul	Y	Y	Y	Y	N	Y	Y
LOUISIANA							
Landrieu	N	N	N	Y	Y	N	N
Vitter	Y	N	N	Y	N	Y	Y
MAINE							
Snowe	Y	N	N	N	Y	Y	N
Collins	Y	N	N	N	Y	Y	N
MARYLAND							
Mikulski	N	N	N	N	Y	N	N
Cardin	N	N	N	N	Y	N	N
MASSACHUSETTS							
Kerry	N	N	N	N	Y	N	N
Brown	Y	N	Y	N	Y	Y	N
MICHIGAN							
Levin	N	N	N	N	Y	N	N
Stabenow	N	N	N	N	Y	N	N
MINNESOTA							
Klobuchar	N	N	N	N	Y	N	N
Franken	N	N	N	N	Y	N	N
MISSISSIPPI							
Cochran	Y	N	N	Y	N	Y	N
Wicker	Y	N	N	Y	N	Y	Y
MISSOURI							
McCaskill	N	N	N	N	Y	Y	Y
Blunt	Y	N	N	Y	N	Y	N
MONTANA							
Baucus	N	N	N	N	Y	N	N
Tester	N	N	N	N	Y	N	Y
NEBRASKA							
Nelson	N	N	N	Y	Y	N	N
Johanns	Y	N	N	Y	N	Y	N
NEVADA							
Reid	N	N	N	N	Y	N	N
Heller	Y	N	Y	Y	N	Y	Y
NEW HAMPSHIRE							
Shaheen	N	N	N	N	Y	N	N
Ayotte	Y	Y	Y	N	N	Y	Y
NEW JERSEY							
Lautenberg	N	N	N	N	Y	N	N
Menendez	N	N	N	N	Y	N	N
NEW MEXICO							
Bingaman	N	N	N	N	Y	N	N
Udall	N	N	N	N	Y	N	N
NEW YORK							
Schumer	N	N	N	N	Y	N	N
Gillibrand	N	N	N	N	Y	N	N
NORTH CAROLINA							
Burr	Y	Y	Y	Y	N	Y	Y
Hagan	N	N	N	N	Y	N	N
NORTH DAKOTA							
Conrad	N	N	N	N	Y	N	N
Hoeven	Y	N	N	Y	Y	N	N
OHIO							
Brown	N	N	N	N	Y	N	N
Portman	Y	N	N	Y	N	Y	Y
OKLAHOMA							
Inhofe	Y	Y	N	Y	N	Y	Y
Coburn	Y	Y	Y	Y	N	Y	Y
OREGON							
Wyden	N	N	N	N	Y	N	N
Merkley	N	N	N	N	Y	N	N
PENNSYLVANIA							
Casey	N	N	N	N	Y	N	N
Toomey	Y	Y	Y	Y	N	Y	Y
RHODE ISLAND							
Reed	N	N	N	N	Y	N	N
Whitehouse	N	N	N	N	Y	N	N
SOUTH CAROLINA							
Graham	Y	Y	Y	Y	N	Y	Y
DeMint	Y	Y	Y	Y	N	Y	Y
SOUTH DAKOTA							
Johnson	N	N	N	N	Y	N	N
Thune	Y	N	N	Y	N	Y	N
TENNESSEE							
Alexander	Y	N	N	N	Y	N	Y
Corker	Y	Y	N	Y	Y	Y	Y
TEXAS							
Hutchison	Y	N	N	Y	N	Y	N
Cornyn	Y	N	Y	Y	N	Y	Y
UTAH							
Hatch	Y	N	Y	Y	N	Y	Y
Lee	Y	Y	Y	Y	N	Y	Y
VERMONT							
Leahy	N	N	N	N	Y	N	N
Sanders	N	N	N	N	Y	N	N
VIRGINIA							
Webb	N	N	Y	Y	Y	N	N
Warner	N	N	N	Y	Y	N	N
WASHINGTON							
Murray	N	N	N	N	Y	N	N
Cantwell	N	N	N	N	Y	N	N
WEST VIRGINIA							
Rockefeller	N	N	N	N	Y	N	N
Manchin	N	N	N	Y	Y	N	N
WISCONSIN							
Kohl	N	N	N	N	Y	N	N
Johnson	Y	Y	Y	Y	N	Y	Y
WYOMING							
Enzi	Y	N	N	Y	N	Y	N
Barrasso	Y	N	N	Y	N	Y	N

KEY   Republicans   Democrats   *Independents*

Y Voted for (yea)	**X** Paired against
# Paired for	**–** Announced against
+ Announced for	**P** Voted "present"
N Voted against (nay)	

C Voted "present" to avoid possible conflict of interest

? Did not vote or otherwise make a position known

IN THE SENATE | By Vote Number

143. **S 3240. Farm Programs/Conservation Income Limits.** Coburn, R-Okla., amendment that would rescind the authority of the Agriculture secretary to grant waivers to allow individuals with non-farm adjusted gross income in excess of $1 million to receive payments for conservation programs. Adopted 62-37: D 15-36; R 46-0; I 1-1. June 20, 2012.

144. **S 3240. Farm Programs/Aid to North Korea.** Kerry, D-Mass., amendment that would prohibit federal food assistance to North Korea, subject to a waiver if the president certified that providing the aid was in the national interest. Adopted 59-40: D 51-0; R 7-39; I 1-1. June 20, 2012.

145. **S 3240. Farm Programs/Aid to North Korea.** Kyl, R-Ariz., amendment that would place a prohibition on federal food assistance to North Korea. Rejected 43-56: D 0-51; R 42-4; I 1-1. June 20, 2012.

146. **S 3240. Farm Programs/Insect and Disease Infestation.** Udall, D-Colo., amendment that would increase the authorization level for the designation of treatment areas to address insect or disease infestation from $100 million to $200 million per year through fiscal 2017. Adopted 77-22: D 49-2; R 26-20; I 2-0. June 20, 2012.

147. **S 3240. Farm Programs/Forest Legacy Program.** Lee, R-Utah, amendment that would repeal the Forest Service's Forest Legacy Program. The program provides funds in support of local-, regional- and state-level efforts to preserve privately owned forest land and prevent development. Rejected 21-77: D 0-50; R 21-25; I 0-2. June 20, 2012.

148. **S 3240. Farm Programs/Conservation Programs.** Lee, R-Utah, amendment that would repeal the Agriculture Department's Conservation Stewardship Program, a voluntary program available on tribal, private agricultural and non-industrial private forest land, and Conservation Reserve Program, a voluntary program for agricultural landowners. Rejected 15-84: D 0-51; R 15-31; I 0-2. June 20, 2012.

149. **S 3240. Farm Programs/Food Assistance.** Boozman, R-Ark., amendment that would authorize an additional $43 million per year for emergency food assistance through fiscal 2017. The cost would be paid for by repealing bonus payments to states that reduce error rates in the Supplemental Nutrition Assistance Program, formerly known as food stamps. Rejected 35-63: D 3-48; R 32-13; I 0-2. June 20, 2012.

	143	144	145	146	147	148	149
ALABAMA							
Shelby	Y	N	Y	Y	N	N	Y
Sessions	Y	N	Y	Y	N	N	Y
ALASKA							
Murkowski	Y	Y	N	Y	Y	Y	N
Begich	N	Y	N	Y	N	N	N
ARIZONA							
McCain	Y	N	Y	Y	Y	Y	N
Kyl	Y	N	Y	Y	Y	Y	Y
ARKANSAS							
Pryor	N	Y	N	Y	N	N	Y
Boozman	Y	N	Y	Y	N	N	Y
CALIFORNIA							
Feinstein	N	Y	N	Y	N	N	N
Boxer	N	Y	N	Y	N	N	N
COLORADO							
Udall	N	Y	N	Y	N	N	N
Bennet	Y	Y	N	Y	N	N	N
CONNECTICUT							
Lieberman	Y	N	Y	Y	N	N	N
Blumenthal	N	Y	N	Y	N	N	N
DELAWARE							
Carper	N	Y	N	Y	N	N	N
Coons	N	Y	N	Y	N	N	N
FLORIDA							
Nelson	N	Y	N	Y	N	N	Y
Rubio	Y	N	Y	N	Y	Y	Y
GEORGIA							
Chambliss	Y	N	Y	N	N	N	Y
Isakson	Y	N	Y	Y	N	N	Y
HAWAII							
Inouye	N	Y	N	Y	N	N	N
Akaka	N	Y	N	Y	N	N	N
IDAHO							
Crapo	Y	N	Y	Y	N	N	Y
Risch	Y	N	Y	Y	N	N	Y
ILLINOIS							
Durbin	N	Y	N	Y	N	N	N
Kirk	?	?	?	?	?	?	?
INDIANA							
Lugar	Y	Y	N	Y	N	N	Y
Coats	Y	N	Y	N	Y	Y	Y
IOWA							
Grassley	Y	N	Y	N	N	N	Y
Harkin	N	Y	N	Y	N	N	N
KANSAS							
Roberts	Y	N	Y	N	N	N	Y
Moran	Y	N	Y	N	Y	N	Y
KENTUCKY							
McConnell	Y	N	Y	Y	Y	N	Y
Paul	Y	N	Y	N	Y	Y	P
LOUISIANA							
Landrieu	N	Y	N	Y	N	N	N
Vitter	Y	N	Y	N	Y	Y	Y
MAINE							
Snowe	Y	Y	Y	Y	N	N	N
Collins	Y	Y	Y	Y	N	N	N
MARYLAND							
Mikulski	Y	Y	N	Y	?	N	N
Cardin	N	Y	N	Y	N	N	N
MASSACHUSETTS							
Kerry	Y	Y	N	Y	N	N	N
Brown	Y	Y	N	N	N	N	N
MICHIGAN							
Levin	Y	Y	N	Y	N	N	N
Stabenow	Y	Y	N	Y	N	N	N
MINNESOTA							
Klobuchar	N	Y	N	Y	N	N	N
Franken	N	Y	N	Y	N	N	N
MISSISSIPPI							
Cochran	Y	N	Y	Y	N	N	Y
Wicker	Y	N	Y	Y	N	N	Y
MISSOURI							
McCaskill	Y	Y	N	N	N	N	N
Blunt	Y	Y	N	Y	N	Y	N

	143	144	145	146	147	148	149
MONTANA							
Baucus	N	Y	N	Y	N	N	N
Tester	N	Y	N	Y	N	N	N
NEBRASKA							
Nelson	Y	Y	N	Y	N	N	N
Johanns	Y	N	Y	Y	Y	N	Y
NEVADA							
Reid	N	Y	N	Y	N	N	N
Heller	Y	N	Y	Y	N	N	N
NEW HAMPSHIRE							
Shaheen	N	Y	N	Y	N	N	N
Ayotte	Y	N	Y	N	N	Y	N
NEW JERSEY							
Lautenberg	N	Y	N	Y	N	N	N
Menendez	Y	Y	N	Y	N	N	N
NEW MEXICO							
Bingaman	Y	Y	N	Y	N	N	N
Udall	N	Y	N	Y	N	N	N
NEW YORK							
Schumer	N	Y	N	Y	N	N	N
Gillibrand	N	Y	N	Y	N	N	N
NORTH CAROLINA							
Burr	Y	N	Y	N	N	N	Y
Hagan	N	Y	N	Y	N	N	N
NORTH DAKOTA							
Conrad	Y	Y	N	Y	N	N	N
Hoeven	Y	N	Y	Y	N	N	Y
OHIO							
Brown	Y	Y	N	Y	N	N	N
Portman	Y	Y	Y	N	N	N	N
OKLAHOMA							
Inhofe	Y	N	Y	N	Y	N	Y
Coburn	Y	N	Y	Y	Y	Y	N
OREGON							
Wyden	Y	Y	N	N	N	N	N
Merkley	Y	Y	N	Y	N	N	N
PENNSYLVANIA							
Casey	N	Y	N	Y	N	N	N
Toomey	Y	N	Y	N	Y	Y	Y
RHODE ISLAND							
Reed	N	Y	N	Y	N	N	N
Whitehouse	N	Y	N	Y	N	N	N
SOUTH CAROLINA							
Graham	Y	N	Y	Y	N	N	Y
DeMint	Y	N	Y	N	Y	N	Y
SOUTH DAKOTA							
Johnson	N	Y	N	Y	N	N	N
Thune	Y	N	Y	Y	N	N	Y
TENNESSEE							
Alexander	Y	N	Y	N	N	N	Y
Corker	Y	N	Y	N	N	Y	N
TEXAS							
Hutchison	Y	N	Y	N	N	N	Y
Cornyn	Y	N	Y	N	Y	N	Y
UTAH							
Hatch	Y	N	Y	N	Y	Y	N
Lee	Y	N	Y	N	Y	Y	N
VERMONT							
Leahy	N	Y	N	Y	N	N	N
Sanders	N	Y	N	Y	N	N	N
VIRGINIA							
Webb	N	Y	N	Y	N	N	Y
Warner	N	Y	N	Y	N	N	N
WASHINGTON							
Murray	N	Y	N	Y	N	N	N
Cantwell	N	Y	N	Y	N	N	N
WEST VIRGINIA							
Rockefeller	Y	Y	N	Y	N	N	N
Manchin	Y	Y	N	Y	N	N	N
WISCONSIN							
Kohl	N	Y	N	Y	N	N	N
Johnson	Y	N	Y	N	Y	Y	N
WYOMING							
Enzi	Y	N	Y	Y	Y	N	Y
Barrasso	Y	N	Y	Y	Y	N	Y

KEY   **Republicans**   Democrats   *Independents*

Y Voted for (yea)	X Paired against
# Paired for	– Announced against
+ Announced for	P Voted "present"
N Voted against (nay)	

C Voted "present" to avoid possible conflict of interest

? Did not vote or otherwise make a position known

IN THE SENATE | By Vote Number

150. S 3240. **Farm Programs/Biorefinery Funding.** Toomey, R-Pa., amendment that would strike aid for the manufacture of biorefineries, renewable chemicals and biological products from the bill, including language to provide mandatory funding for loan guarantees of the Commodity Credit Corporation. Rejected 36-63: D 1-50; R 35-11; I 0-2. June 20, 2012.

151. S 3240. **Farm Programs/Sugar Policy.** Toomey, R-Pa., amendment that would rescind increases in price support levels and requirements for government sugar purchases enacted as part of the 2008 farm law. It also would repeal restrictions on import quotas for sugar. Rejected 46-53: D 18-33; R 28-18; I 0-2. June 20, 2012.

152. S 3240. **Farm Programs/Recommit.** Lee, R-Utah, motion to recommit the bill to the Agriculture, Nutrition and Forestry Committee with instructions that it be reported back with an amendment that would reduce authorization levels to $714.2 billion, matching 2008 levels. Motion rejected 29-70: D 0-51; R 29-17; I 0-2. June 20, 2012.

153. S 3240. **Farm Programs/Recommit.** Johnson, R-Wis., motion to recommit the bill to the Agriculture, Nutrition and Forestry Committee with instructions that it be reported back as two separate bills. One would contain the nutrition title of the bill, including provisions regarding the Supplemental Nutrition Assistance Program, formerly known as food stamps. The other would contain all other provisions of the original bill. Motion rejected 40-59: D 0-51; R 40-6; I 0-2. June 20, 2012.

154. S 3240. **Farm Programs/Pet Regulations.** Vitter, R-La., amendment that would exclude individual pet owners from being subject to regulations designed primarily for circus animals if they use their pets in movies or other entertainment ventures. It also would amend federal criminal law to prohibit individuals from knowingly attending animal fights. Adopted 88-11: D 50-1; R 36-10; I 2-0. (By unanimous consent, the Senate agreed to raise the majority requirement for adoption of the Vitter amendment to 60 votes.) June 20, 2012.

155. S 3240. **Farm Programs/Wetland Conservation.** Chambliss, R-Ga., amendment that would make an individual who produces an agricultural commodity on highly-erodible or converted wetland ineligible for certain benefits from federal crop insurance programs. It would require crop insurance policy holders to comply with highly erodible land and wetland conservation standards. Adopted 52-47: D 38-13; R 12-34; I 2-0. June 20, 2012.

156. S 3240. **Farm Programs/Crop Insurance Companies.** Thune, R-S.D., amendment that would require the Agriculture Department to consult with crop insurance companies before reducing premium subsidies on crop insurance policies for policyholders with adjusted gross incomes in excess of $750,000. Rejected 44-55: D 16-35; R 27-19; I 1-1. June 20, 2012.

	150	151	152	153	154	155	156
ALABAMA							
Shelby	Y	N	Y	Y	Y	N	Y
Sessions	Y	Y	Y	Y	N	N	N
ALASKA							
Murkowski	Y	N	Y	Y	Y	Y	Y
Begich	Y	N	N	N	Y	N	Y
ARIZONA							
McCain	Y	Y	Y	Y	Y	N	N
Kyl	Y	Y	Y	Y	Y	Y	N
ARKANSAS							
Pryor	N	N	N	N	Y	Y	N
Boozman	Y	Y	N	Y	Y	Y	N
CALIFORNIA							
Feinstein	N	Y	N	Y	Y	Y	Y
Boxer	N	N	N	N	Y	Y	N
COLORADO							
Udall	N	N	N	N	Y	Y	N
Bennet	N	N	N	N	Y	Y	N
CONNECTICUT							
Lieberman	N	N	N	N	Y	Y	N
Blumenthal	N	Y	N	N	Y	N	N
DELAWARE							
Carper	N	Y	N	N	Y	Y	N
Coons	N	Y	N	N	Y	Y	N
FLORIDA							
Nelson	N	N	N	N	Y	N	Y
Rubio	Y	N	Y	Y	N	Y	N
GEORGIA							
Chambliss	Y	N	N	Y	Y	Y	Y
Isakson	Y	N	N	Y	Y	Y	Y
HAWAII							
Inouye	N	N	N	N	Y	N	N
Akaka	N	N	N	N	Y	N	N
IDAHO							
Crapo	N	N	Y	Y	Y	N	Y
Risch	N	N	Y	Y	Y	N	Y
ILLINOIS							
Durbin	N	Y	N	N	Y	Y	N
Kirk	?	?	?	?	?	?	?
INDIANA							
Lugar	N	Y	N	N	Y	N	Y
Coats	Y	Y	N	Y	Y	N	Y
IOWA							
Grassley	N	Y	N	Y	Y	N	N
Harkin	N	N	N	N	Y	Y	N
KANSAS							
Roberts	Y	N	Y	Y	Y	N	Y
Moran	Y	N	Y	Y	Y	N	Y
KENTUCKY							
McConnell	Y	Y	Y	Y	Y	N	Y
Paul	Y	Y	Y	Y	N	N	N
LOUISIANA							
Landrieu	N	N	N	N	Y	Y	Y
Vitter	Y	N	Y	Y	Y	N	Y
MAINE							
Snowe	Y	Y	N	Y	Y	Y	Y
Collins	N	Y	N	N	Y	Y	Y
MARYLAND							
Mikulski	N	N	N	N	Y	Y	N
Cardin	N	N	N	N	Y	Y	N
MASSACHUSETTS							
Kerry	N	N	N	N	Y	Y	N
Brown	N	Y	N	N	Y	Y	N
MICHIGAN							
Levin	N	N	N	N	Y	Y	N
Stabenow	N	N	N	N	Y	N	Y
MINNESOTA							
Klobuchar	N	N	N	N	Y	Y	Y
Franken	N	N	N	N	Y	Y	N
MISSISSIPPI							
Cochran	N	N	N	N	Y	N	N
Wicker	N	N	Y	Y	Y	N	Y
MISSOURI							
McCaskill	N	Y	N	N	Y	N	Y
Blunt	Y	Y	Y	Y	Y	N	Y
MONTANA							
Baucus	N	N	N	N	Y	N	N
Tester	N	N	N	N	Y	N	Y
NEBRASKA							
Nelson	N	N	N	N	Y	N	Y
Johanns	N	N	N	Y	Y	N	N
NEVADA							
Reid	N	N	N	N	Y	Y	Y
Heller	Y	Y	N	Y	Y	N	Y
NEW HAMPSHIRE							
Shaheen	N	Y	N	N	Y	Y	N
Ayotte	Y	Y	Y	Y	Y	N	N
NEW JERSEY							
Lautenberg	N	N	N	N	Y	Y	N
Menendez	N	Y	N	N	Y	Y	N
NEW MEXICO							
Bingaman	N	N	N	N	N	Y	N
Udall	N	N	N	N	Y	Y	N
NEW YORK							
Schumer	N	N	N	N	Y	Y	Y
Gillibrand	N	N	N	N	Y	N	Y
NORTH CAROLINA							
Burr	Y	N	Y	Y	N	Y	N
Hagan	N	N	N	N	Y	Y	Y
NORTH DAKOTA							
Conrad	N	N	N	Y	Y	N	N
Hoeven	N	N	N	N	Y	N	Y
OHIO							
Brown	N	Y	N	N	Y	Y	N
Portman	Y	Y	N	Y	Y	N	N
OKLAHOMA							
Inhofe	Y	Y	Y	Y	N	N	Y
Coburn	Y	Y	Y	Y	N	N	N
OREGON							
Wyden	N	Y	N	N	Y	Y	N
Merkley	N	Y	N	N	Y	Y	N
PENNSYLVANIA							
Casey	N	Y	N	N	Y	Y	Y
Toomey	Y	Y	Y	Y	N	N	N
RHODE ISLAND							
Reed	N	Y	N	N	Y	Y	N
Whitehouse	N	Y	N	N	Y	Y	N
SOUTH CAROLINA							
Graham	Y	Y	Y	Y	N	Y	N
DeMint	Y	Y	Y	Y	N	N	N
SOUTH DAKOTA							
Johnson	N	N	N	Y	Y	N	N
Thune	N	N	N	Y	Y	N	Y
TENNESSEE							
Alexander	Y	Y	N	Y	N	N	Y
Corker	Y	Y	Y	Y	Y	N	N
TEXAS							
Hutchison	Y	Y	N	Y	Y	N	Y
Cornyn	Y	Y	Y	Y	Y	N	Y
UTAH							
Hatch	Y	Y	N	Y	Y	Y	Y
Lee	Y	Y	Y	Y	N	N	N
VERMONT							
Leahy	N	N	N	N	Y	Y	Y
Sanders	N	N	N	N	Y	Y	Y
VIRGINIA							
Webb	N	Y	N	N	Y	Y	N
Warner	N	Y	N	N	Y	Y	N
WASHINGTON							
Murray	N	N	N	N	Y	N	N
Cantwell	N	N	N	N	Y	N	N
WEST VIRGINIA							
Rockefeller	N	N	N	N	Y	Y	N
Manchin	N	N	N	N	Y	Y	N
WISCONSIN							
Kohl	N	Y	N	N	Y	Y	N
Johnson	Y	Y	Y	Y	Y	N	N
WYOMING							
Enzi	Y	N	Y	Y	Y	N	Y
Barrasso	Y	N	Y	Y	Y	N	Y

KEY   **Republicans**   Democrats   *Independents*

Y Voted for (yea)	X Paired against	C Voted "present" to avoid possible conflict of interest
# Paired for	– Announced against	
+ Announced for	P Voted "present"	? Did not vote or otherwise make a position known
N Voted against (nay)		

IN THE SENATE | By Vote Number

157. **S 3240. Farm Programs/Crop Insurance.** Durbin, D-Ill., amendment that would raise subsidized crop insurance premiums for policyholders with an adjusted gross income of more than $750,000 a year. The higher premiums would not take effect until the Agriculture Department conducted a study, in consultation with the Government Accountability Office, to determine whether the increase would significantly raise premiums for other farmers or increase the overall costs of the program. Adopted 66-33: D 41-10; R 24-22; I 1-1. June 20, 2012.

158. **S 3240. Farm Programs/Aerial Inspections.** Boxer, D-Calif., amendment that would allow the EPA administrator to conduct aerial overflights to inspect agricultural operations only if it was deemed more cost-effective than ground inspections and the EPA had notified state officials of such flights. Rejected 47-48: D 45-4; R 0-44; I 2-0 (By unanimous consent, the Senate agreed to raise the majority requirement for adoption of the Boxer amendment to 60 votes.) June 21, 2012.

159. **S 3240. Farm Programs/Aerial Inspections.** Johanns, R-Neb., amendment that would prohibit the EPA from conducting aerial surveillance to inspect agricultural operations or to record images of agricultural operations. Rejected 56-43: D 10-41; R 46-0; I 0-2 (By unanimous consent, the Senate agreed to raise the majority requirement for adoption of the Johanns amendment to 60 votes.) June 21, 2012.

160. **S 3240. Farm Programs/Consumer Confidence Reports.** Toomey, R-Pa., amendment that would modify requirements for community water systems to send annual reports to customers. The reports would have to be transmitted by mail only when the water supply exceeded allowable contaminant levels. The report could be provided through the Internet if the water supply did not exceed allowable limits. Rejected 58-41: D 12-39; R 46-0; I 0-2 (By unanimous consent, the Senate agreed to raise the majority requirement for adoption of the Toomey amendment to 60 votes.) June 21, 2012.

161. **S 3240. Farm Programs/Labels for Genetically Engineered Food.** Sanders, I-Vt., amendment that would allow states to require the labeling of any food, beverage or other edible product that contains a genetically engineered ingredient. Rejected 26-73: D 23-28; R 1-45; I 2-0. (By unanimous consent, the Senate agreed to raise the majority requirement for adoption of the Sanders amendment to 60 votes.) June 21, 2012.

	157	158	159	160	161			157	158	159	160	161
ALABAMA							**MONTANA**					
Shelby	Y	?	Y	Y	N		Baucus	N	Y	Y	N	N
Sessions	Y	N	Y	Y	N		Tester	N	Y	Y	N	N
ALASKA							**NEBRASKA**					
Murkowski	Y	N	Y	Y	Y		Nelson	N	N	Y	Y	N
Begich	Y	Y	Y	N	Y		Johanns	N	N	Y	Y	N
ARIZONA							**NEVADA**					
McCain	Y	N	Y	Y	N		Reid	Y	Y	N	N	N
Kyl	Y	N	Y	Y	N		Heller	Y	N	Y	Y	N
ARKANSAS							**NEW HAMPSHIRE**					
Pryor	N	Y	Y	Y	N		Shaheen	Y	Y	N	N	N
Boozman	N	N	Y	Y	N		Ayotte	Y	N	Y	Y	N
CALIFORNIA							**NEW JERSEY**					
Feinstein	Y	Y	N	N	Y		Lautenberg	Y	Y	N	N	Y
Boxer	Y	Y	N	N	Y		Menendez	Y	?	N	N	N
COLORADO							**NEW MEXICO**					
Udall	Y	Y	N	Y	N		Bingaman	Y	Y	N	N	N
Bennet	Y	Y	N	N	Y		Udall	Y	Y	N	N	N
CONNECTICUT							**NEW YORK**					
Lieberman	Y	Y	N	N	Y		Schumer	Y	Y	Y	N	N
Blumenthal	Y	Y	N	N	Y		Gillibrand	N	Y	N	N	N
DELAWARE							**NORTH CAROLINA**					
Carper	Y	Y	N	N	N		Burr	Y	N	Y	Y	N
Coons	Y	Y	N	N	N		Hagan	N	Y	Y	Y	N
FLORIDA							**NORTH DAKOTA**					
Nelson	Y	Y	N	Y	N		Conrad	Y	N	Y	Y	N
Rubio	Y	N	Y	Y	N		Hoeven	N	N	Y	Y	N
GEORGIA							**OHIO**					
Chambliss	N	N	Y	Y	N		Brown	Y	Y	N	Y	N
Isakson	N	N	Y	Y	N		Portman	Y	N	Y	Y	N
HAWAII							**OKLAHOMA**					
Inouye	Y	Y	N	N	Y		Inhofe	N	N	Y	Y	N
Akaka	Y	Y	N	N	Y		Coburn	Y	N	Y	Y	N
IDAHO							**OREGON**					
Crapo	N	N	Y	Y	N		Wyden	Y	Y	N	N	Y
Risch	N	N	Y	Y	N		Merkley	Y	Y	N	N	Y
ILLINOIS							**PENNSYLVANIA**					
Durbin	Y	Y	N	N	N		Casey	Y	Y	N	Y	N
Kirk	?	?	?	?	?		Toomey	Y	?	Y	Y	N
INDIANA							**RHODE ISLAND**					
Lugar	N	N	Y	Y	N		Reed	Y	Y	N	N	Y
Coats	N	N	Y	Y	N		Whitehouse	Y	Y	N	N	Y
IOWA							**SOUTH CAROLINA**					
Grassley	Y	N	Y	Y	N		Graham	Y	N	Y	Y	N
Harkin	Y	Y	N	N	N		DeMint	Y	N	Y	Y	N
KANSAS							**SOUTH DAKOTA**					
Roberts	N	N	Y	Y	N		Johnson	Y	+	N	N	Y
Moran	N	N	Y	Y	N		Thune	N	N	Y	Y	N
KENTUCKY							**TENNESSEE**					
McConnell	N	N	Y	Y	N		Alexander	Y	N	Y	Y	N
Paul	Y	N	Y	Y	N		Corker	Y	N	Y	Y	N
LOUISIANA							**TEXAS**					
Landrieu	N	N	Y	N	N		Hutchison	N	N	Y	Y	N
Vitter	N	N	Y	Y	N		Cornyn	N	N	Y	Y	N
MAINE							**UTAH**					
Snowe	Y	N	Y	Y	N		Hatch	Y	N	Y	Y	N
Collins	Y	N	Y	Y	N		Lee	Y	N	Y	Y	N
MARYLAND							**VERMONT**					
Mikulski	Y	Y	N	N	Y		Leahy	N	Y	N	Y	Y
Cardin	Y	Y	N	N	Y		Sanders	N	Y	N	N	Y
MASSACHUSETTS							**VIRGINIA**					
Kerry	Y	Y	N	N	Y		Webb	Y	Y	N	N	N
Brown	Y	N	Y	Y	N		Warner	Y	Y	N	N	N
MICHIGAN							**WASHINGTON**					
Levin	Y	Y	N	N	N		Murray	Y	Y	N	N	Y
Stabenow	N	Y	N	N	N		Cantwell	Y	Y	N	N	Y
MINNESOTA							**WEST VIRGINIA**					
Klobuchar	Y	Y	N	N	N		Rockefeller	Y	Y	N	N	Y
Franken	Y	Y	N	N	N		Manchin	Y	Y	N	Y	Y
MISSISSIPPI							**WISCONSIN**					
Cochran	N	N	Y	Y	N		Kohl	Y	Y	N	Y	N
Wicker	N	N	Y	Y	N		Johnson	Y	N	Y	Y	N
MISSOURI							**WYOMING**					
McCaskill	N	N	Y	Y	N		Enzi	N	N	Y	Y	N
Blunt	N	N	Y	Y	N		Barrasso	N	N	Y	Y	N

KEY	**Republicans**	Democrats	*Independents*	
Y	Voted for (yea)	X	Paired against	C	Voted "present" to avoid possible conflict of interest
#	Paired for	–	Announced against	
+	Announced for	P	Voted "present"	?	Did not vote or otherwise make a position known
N	Voted against (nay)			

IN THE SENATE | By Vote Number

162. **S 3240. Farm Programs/Political-Convention Funding.** Coburn, R-Okla., amendment that would bar the use of federal money from the Presidential Election Campaign Fund for party conventions. Adopted 95-4: D 47-4; R 46-0; I 2-0. (By unanimous consent, the Senate agreed to raise the majority requirement for adoption of the Coburn amendment to 60 votes.) June 21, 2012.

163. **S 3240. Farm Programs/Employee Wages.** Rubio, R-Fla., amendment that would allow employers to pay higher wages to their employees, even if those wage increases were not agreed to under a collective bargaining agreement. Rejected 45-54: D 0-51; R 45-1; I 0-2. (By unanimous consent, the Senate agreed to raise the majority requirement for adoption of the Rubio amendment to 60 votes.) June 21, 2012.

164. **S 3240. Farm Programs/Passage.** Passage of the bill that would reauthorize federal farm and nutrition programs for five years, including crop subsidies, food stamps, conservation, rural development and foreign food aid programs, for a total projected cost of roughly $969 billion over the next decade. It would reauthorize the Supplemental Nutrition Assistance Program. The bill would eliminate direct and counter-cyclical payments and replace them with a new supplemental coverage option that would allow producers to purchase additional crop insurance coverage. The bill would make any person with a non-farm adjusted gross income of more than $750,000 ineligible for payments from commodity programs, currently capped at $50,000, pending a study to determine the impact on costs. Passed 64-35: D 46-5; R 16-30; I 2-0. (By unanimous consent, the Senate agreed to raise the majority requirement for passage of the bill to 60 votes.) A "yea" was a vote in support of the president's position. June 21, 2012.

165. **S 1940. Flood Insurance Reauthorization/Cloture.** Motion to invoke cloture (thus limiting debate) on the Reid, D-Nev., motion to proceed to the bill that would reauthorize the National Flood Insurance Program for five years. Motion agreed to 96-2: D 49-1; R 45-1; I 2-0. Three-fifths of the total Senate (60) is required to invoke cloture. June 21, 2012.

166. **S 3187. FDA User Fees/Cloture.** Motion to invoke cloture (thus limiting debate) on the Reid, D-Nev., motion to concur in the House amendment to the bill that would grant a five-year reauthorization of the Food and Drug Administration's user fees programs, which help fund reviews of prescription drugs and medical devices. Motion agreed to 89-3: D 49-0; R 39-2; I 1-1. Three-fifths of the total Senate (60) is required to invoke cloture. June 25, 2012.

167. **Rosenbaum Nomination/Confirmation.** Confirmation of President Obama's nomination of Robin S. Rosenbaum of Florida to be a judge for the U.S. District Court for the Southern District of Florida. Confirmed 92-3: D 48-0; R 42-3; I 2-0. A "yea" was a vote in support of the president's position. June 26, 2012.

168. **S 3187. FDA User Fees/Motion to Concur.** Reid, D-Nev., motion to concur in the House amendment to the bill that would grant a five-year reauthorization of the Food and Drug Administration's user fee programs, which help fund reviews of prescription drugs and medical devices. The measure also would create new user fee programs for generic drugs and generic biologic drugs. It also would require drugmakers to notify the FDA six months in advance of expected shortages of certain critical drugs and the FDA to inform health care providers of the potential drug shortage. Motion agreed to, thus clearing the bill for the president, 92-4: D 50-0; R 41-3; I 1-1. A "yea" was a vote in support of the president's position. June 26, 2012.

State / Senator	162	163	164	165	166	167	168
ALABAMA							
Shelby	Y	Y	N	Y	Y	Y	Y
Sessions	Y	Y	N	Y	Y	Y	Y
ALASKA							
Murkowski	Y	N	N	Y	?	Y	Y
Begich	Y	N	Y	Y	Y	Y	Y
ARIZONA							
McCain	Y	Y	N	Y	Y	Y	?
Kyl	Y	Y	N	Y	?	Y	Y
ARKANSAS							
Pryor	Y	N	N	N	Y	Y	Y
Boozman	Y	Y	N	Y	Y	Y	Y
CALIFORNIA							
Feinstein	Y	N	Y	Y	Y	Y	Y
Boxer	N	N	Y	?	Y	Y	Y
COLORADO							
Udall	Y	N	Y	Y	?	?	?
Bennet	Y	N	Y	Y	Y	Y	Y
CONNECTICUT							
Lieberman	Y	N	Y	Y	Y	Y	Y
Blumenthal	Y	N	Y	Y	Y	Y	Y
DELAWARE							
Carper	Y	N	Y	Y	Y	Y	Y
Coons	Y	N	Y	Y	Y	Y	Y
FLORIDA							
Nelson	Y	N	Y	Y	Y	Y	Y
Rubio	Y	Y	N	Y	?	Y	Y
GEORGIA							
Chambliss	Y	Y	N	Y	Y	Y	Y
Isakson	Y	Y	N	Y	Y	Y	Y
HAWAII							
Inouye	Y	N	Y	Y	Y	Y	Y
Akaka	Y	N	Y	Y	Y	Y	Y
IDAHO							
Crapo	Y	Y	N	Y	Y	Y	Y
Risch	Y	Y	N	Y	Y	Y	Y
ILLINOIS							
Durbin	Y	N	Y	Y	Y	Y	Y
Kirk	?	?	?	?	?	?	?
INDIANA							
Lugar	Y	Y	Y	Y	Y	Y	Y
Coats	Y	Y	Y	Y	Y	Y	Y
IOWA							
Grassley	Y	Y	Y	Y	Y	Y	Y
Harkin	Y	N	Y	Y	Y	Y	Y
KANSAS							
Roberts	Y	Y	Y	Y	Y	Y	Y
Moran	Y	Y	Y	Y	Y	Y	Y
KENTUCKY							
McConnell	Y	Y	N	Y	Y	Y	Y
Paul	Y	Y	N	N	N	N	N
LOUISIANA							
Landrieu	N	N	N	Y	Y	Y	Y
Vitter	Y	Y	N	Y	Y	Y	Y
MAINE							
Snowe	Y	Y	Y	Y	Y	Y	Y
Collins	Y	Y	Y	Y	Y	Y	Y
MARYLAND							
Mikulski	N	N	Y	Y	Y	Y	Y
Cardin	Y	N	Y	Y	Y	Y	Y
MASSACHUSETTS							
Kerry	Y	N	Y	Y	Y	Y	Y
Brown	Y	Y	Y	Y	Y	Y	Y
MICHIGAN							
Levin	Y	N	Y	Y	Y	Y	Y
Stabenow	Y	N	Y	Y	Y	Y	Y
MINNESOTA							
Klobuchar	Y	N	Y	Y	Y	Y	Y
Franken	Y	N	Y	Y	Y	Y	Y
MISSISSIPPI							
Cochran	Y	Y	N	Y	Y	Y	Y
Wicker	Y	Y	N	Y	Y	Y	Y
MISSOURI							
McCaskill	Y	N	Y	Y	Y	Y	Y
Blunt	Y	Y	Y	Y	Y	Y	Y
MONTANA							
Baucus	Y	N	Y	Y	Y	Y	Y
Tester	Y	N	Y	Y	Y	Y	Y
NEBRASKA							
Nelson	Y	N	Y	Y	Y	Y	Y
Johanns	Y	Y	Y	Y	Y	Y	Y
NEVADA							
Reid	Y	N	Y	Y	Y	Y	Y
Heller	Y	Y	N	Y	Y	Y	Y
NEW HAMPSHIRE							
Shaheen	Y	N	Y	Y	?	Y	Y
Ayotte	Y	Y	N	Y	Y	Y	Y
NEW JERSEY							
Lautenberg	Y	N	N	Y	Y	Y	Y
Menendez	Y	N	Y	Y	Y	Y	Y
NEW MEXICO							
Bingaman	Y	N	Y	Y	Y	Y	Y
Udall	Y	N	Y	Y	Y	Y	Y
NEW YORK							
Schumer	Y	N	Y	Y	Y	Y	Y
Gillibrand	Y	N	Y	Y	Y	Y	Y
NORTH CAROLINA							
Burr	Y	Y	N	Y	N	Y	N
Hagan	Y	N	Y	Y	Y	Y	Y
NORTH DAKOTA							
Conrad	Y	N	Y	Y	Y	Y	Y
Hoeven	Y	Y	Y	Y	Y	Y	Y
OHIO							
Brown	Y	N	Y	Y	Y	Y	Y
Portman	Y	Y	N	Y	Y	Y	Y
OKLAHOMA							
Inhofe	Y	Y	Y	N	Y	Y	Y
Coburn	Y	Y	N	Y	?	Y	N
OREGON							
Wyden	Y	N	Y	Y	Y	Y	Y
Merkley	Y	N	Y	Y	Y	Y	Y
PENNSYLVANIA							
Casey	Y	N	Y	Y	Y	Y	Y
Toomey	Y	Y	N	Y	Y	Y	Y
RHODE ISLAND							
Reed	Y	N	N	Y	Y	Y	Y
Whitehouse	Y	N	N	Y	Y	Y	Y
SOUTH CAROLINA							
Graham	Y	Y	Y	Y	Y	Y	Y
DeMint	Y	Y	N	Y	Y	N	Y
SOUTH DAKOTA							
Johnson	Y	N	Y	Y	Y	Y	Y
Thune	Y	Y	Y	Y	Y	Y	Y
TENNESSEE							
Alexander	Y	Y	N	Y	Y	Y	Y
Corker	Y	N	Y	Y	Y	Y	Y
TEXAS							
Hutchison	Y	Y	Y	Y	Y	Y	Y
Cornyn	Y	Y	Y	Y	Y	Y	Y
UTAH							
Hatch	Y	Y	N	Y	+	?	+
Lee	Y	Y	N	Y	N	Y	Y
VERMONT							
Leahy	Y	N	Y	Y	Y	Y	Y
Sanders	Y	N	Y	Y	N	Y	N
VIRGINIA							
Webb	Y	N	Y	Y	Y	?	Y
Warner	Y	N	Y	Y	Y	Y	Y
WASHINGTON							
Murray	Y	N	Y	Y	Y	Y	Y
Cantwell	Y	N	Y	Y	Y	Y	Y
WEST VIRGINIA							
Rockefeller	N	N	Y	Y	Y	?	Y
Manchin	Y	N	Y	Y	Y	Y	Y
WISCONSIN							
Kohl	Y	N	Y	Y	Y	Y	Y
Johnson	Y	Y	N	Y	Y	Y	Y
WYOMING							
Enzi	Y	Y	Y	Y	Y	Y	Y
Barrasso	Y	Y	Y	Y	Y	Y	Y

KEY — Republicans   Democrats   *Independents*

Y Voted for (yea)	X Paired against	C Voted "present" to avoid possible conflict of interest
# Paired for	− Announced against	? Did not vote or otherwise make a position known
+ Announced for	P Voted "present"	
N Voted against (nay)		

IN THE SENATE | By Vote Number

169. HR 4348. Surface Transportation Authorization/Motion to Waive.
Reid, D-Nev., motion to waive provisions of Rule XXVIII regarding the availability of conference report text with respect to the McConnell, R-Ky., point of order against the bill that would authorize federal highway, mass transit and safety programs through fiscal 2014 at current levels, with inflationary increases for certain programs. Motion agreed to 72-22: D 48-0; R 22-22; I 2-0. A three-fifths majority vote of the total Senate (60) is required to waive Rule XXVIII. June 29, 2012.

170. HR 4348. Surface Transportation Authorization/Motion to Waive.
Reid, D-Nev., motion to waive provisions of Rule XXVIII regarding the inclusion of material outside the scope of a conference committee with respect to the Coats, R-Ind., point of order against the bill that would authorize federal highway, mass transit and safety programs through fiscal 2014 at current levels with inflationary increases for certain programs. Motion agreed to 66-28: D 48-0; R 16-28; I 2-0. A three-fifths majority vote of the total Senate (60) is required to waive Rule XXVIII. June 29, 2012.

171. HR 4348. Surface Transportation Authorization/Motion to Waive.
Reid, D-Nev., motion to waive all applicable budget laws and budget resolutions with respect to the Corker, R-Tenn., point of order against the conference report on the bill that would authorize federal highway, mass transit and safety programs through fiscal 2014 at current levels, with inflationary increases for certain programs. Motion agreed to 63-30: D 48-0; R 13-30; I 2-0. A three-fifths majority vote of the total Senate (60) is required to waive the applicable budget laws. June 29, 2012.

172. HR 4348. Surface Transportation Authorization/Adoption.
Adoption of the conference report on the bill that would authorize federal highway, mass transit and safety programs through fiscal 2014 at current levels, with inflationary increases for certain programs. It would provide $21.2 billion for the Highway Trust Fund, $80 billion in contract authority for programs administered by the Federal Highway Administration in fiscal 2013 and 2014 and $21.3 billion for programs administered by the Federal Transit Administration. It also would extend the 3.4 percent interest rate on subsidized federal student loans through July 1, 2013; reauthorize the National Flood Insurance Program through Sept. 30, 2017; and provide for the distribution of penalties, paid by those responsible for the 2010 Gulf of Mexico oil spill, to Gulf Coast states for environmental restoration activities. Adopted (thus cleared for the president) 74-19: D 48-0; R 24-19; I 2-0. By unanimous consent, the Senate agreed to raise the majority requirement for adoption of the conference report to 60 votes. June 29, 2012.

	169	170	171	172
ALABAMA				
Shelby	Y	Y	Y	Y
Sessions	N	Y	N	Y
ALASKA				
Murkowski	Y	Y	Y	Y
Begich	Y	Y	Y	Y
ARIZONA				
McCain	N	N	N	N
Kyl	N	N	N	Y
ARKANSAS				
Pryor	Y	Y	Y	Y
Boozman	Y	Y	N	Y
CALIFORNIA				
Feinstein	Y	Y	Y	Y
Boxer	Y	Y	Y	Y
COLORADO				
Udall	?	?	?	?
Bennet	?	?	?	+
CONNECTICUT				
Lieberman	Y	Y	Y	Y
Blumenthal	Y	Y	Y	Y
DELAWARE				
Carper	Y	Y	Y	Y
Coons	Y	Y	Y	Y
FLORIDA				
Nelson	Y	Y	Y	Y
Rubio	N	N	N	N
GEORGIA				
Chambliss	Y	N	N	Y
Isakson	Y	N	N	Y
HAWAII				
Inouye	?	?	?	?
Akaka	Y	Y	Y	Y
IDAHO				
Crapo	N	N	N	N
Risch	N	N	N	N
ILLINOIS				
Durbin	Y	Y	Y	Y
Kirk	?	?	?	?
INDIANA				
Lugar	Y	Y	Y	Y
Coats	N	N	N	N
IOWA				
Grassley	N	N	Y	Y
Harkin	Y	Y	Y	Y
KANSAS				
Roberts	N	N	Y	Y
Moran	N	N	N	N
KENTUCKY				
McConnell	Y	N	N	Y
Paul	N	N	N	N
LOUISIANA				
Landrieu	Y	Y	Y	Y
Vitter	Y	Y	Y	Y
MAINE				
Snowe	N	N	P	P
Collins	Y	Y	Y	Y
MARYLAND				
Mikulski	Y	Y	Y	Y
Cardin	Y	Y	Y	Y
MASSACHUSETTS				
Kerry	Y	Y	Y	Y
Brown	Y	Y	Y	Y
MICHIGAN				
Levin	Y	Y	Y	Y
Stabenow	Y	Y	Y	Y
MINNESOTA				
Klobuchar	Y	Y	Y	Y
Franken	Y	Y	Y	Y
MISSISSIPPI				
Cochran	Y	Y	Y	Y
Wicker	Y	Y	Y	Y
MISSOURI				
McCaskill	Y	Y	Y	Y
Blunt	Y	Y	Y	Y
MONTANA				
Baucus	Y	Y	Y	Y
Tester	Y	Y	Y	Y
NEBRASKA				
Nelson	Y	Y	Y	Y
Johanns	Y	Y	Y	Y
NEVADA				
Reid	Y	Y	Y	Y
Heller	Y	Y	Y	Y
NEW HAMPSHIRE				
Shaheen	Y	Y	Y	Y
Ayotte	N	N	N	N
NEW JERSEY				
Lautenberg	Y	Y	Y	Y
Menendez	Y	Y	Y	Y
NEW MEXICO				
Bingaman	Y	Y	Y	Y
Udall	Y	Y	Y	Y
NEW YORK				
Schumer	Y	Y	Y	Y
Gillibrand	Y	Y	Y	Y
NORTH CAROLINA				
Burr	N	N	N	Y
Hagan	Y	Y	Y	Y
NORTH DAKOTA				
Conrad	Y	Y	Y	Y
Hoeven	Y	Y	Y	Y
OHIO				
Brown	Y	Y	Y	Y
Portman	N	Y	N	N
OKLAHOMA				
Inhofe	Y	Y	Y	Y
Coburn	?	?	?	?
OREGON				
Wyden	Y	Y	Y	Y
Merkley	Y	Y	Y	Y
PENNSYLVANIA				
Casey	Y	Y	Y	Y
Toomey	N	N	N	N
RHODE ISLAND				
Reed	Y	Y	Y	Y
Whitehouse	Y	Y	Y	Y
SOUTH CAROLINA				
Graham	Y	N	N	N
DeMint	N	N	N	N
SOUTH DAKOTA				
Johnson	Y	Y	Y	Y
Thune	Y	N	N	Y
TENNESSEE				
Alexander	–	–	–	–
Corker	N	N	N	N
TEXAS				
Hutchison	Y	N	N	Y
Cornyn	N	N	N	N
UTAH				
Hatch	N	N	N	N
Lee	N	N	N	N
VERMONT				
Leahy	Y	Y	Y	Y
Sanders	Y	Y	Y	Y
VIRGINIA				
Webb	Y	Y	Y	Y
Warner	Y	Y	Y	Y
WASHINGTON				
Murray	Y	Y	Y	Y
Cantwell	Y	Y	Y	Y
WEST VIRGINIA				
Rockefeller	Y	Y	Y	Y
Manchin	Y	Y	Y	Y
WISCONSIN				
Kohl	Y	Y	Y	Y
Johnson	N	N	N	N
WYOMING				
Enzi	Y	N	N	N
Barrasso	Y	N	N	N

KEY   **Republicans**   Democrats   *Independents*

Y Voted for (yea)	X Paired against	C Voted "present" to avoid possible conflict of interest
# Paired for	– Announced against	
+ Announced for	P Voted "present"	? Did not vote or otherwise make a position known
N Voted against (nay)		

IN THE SENATE | By Vote Number

173. Fowlkes Nomination/Confirmation. Confirmation of President Obama's nomination of John Thomas Fowlkes Jr. to be a judge for the U.S. District Court of the Western District of Tennessee. Confirmed 94-2: D 51-0; R 42-2; I 1-0. A "yea" was a vote in support of the president's position. July 10, 2012.

174. S 2237. Small-Business Tax Cuts/Cloture. Motion to invoke cloture (thus limiting debate) on the Reid, D-Nev., motion to proceed to the bill that would give employers a credit of up to $500,000 to offset 10 percent of the amount they spend to expand their payroll in 2012 compared with 2011. It also would allow businesses to deduct the full cost of equipment purchased this year. Motion agreed to 80-14: D 48-1; R 30-13; I 2-0. Three-fifths of the total Senate (60) is required to invoke cloture. July 10, 2012.

175. S 2237. Small-Business Tax Cuts/Motion to Table. Baucus, D-Mont., motion to table (kill) the Reid, D-Nev., amendment, which would strike the text of the bill and replace it with provisions to allow businesses with fewer than 500 employees a 20 percent deduction on their taxable income in 2012. A business would be eligible for the deduction in calendar year 2010 or 2011. If the business was not in existence in those years, then the threshold would be applied in 2012. The amendment would limit the deduction to 50 percent of certain W-2 wages paid by the business. Motion agreed to 73-24: D 50-0; R 21-24; I 2-0. July 12, 2012.

176. S 2237. Small-Business Tax Cuts/Cloture. Motion to invoke cloture (thus limiting debate) on the Landrieu, D-La., substitute amendment that would extend certain tax benefits for small businesses, including the elimination of capital gains taxes for certain small-business stock, expanded carry-back of credits to recover prior taxes, expanded expensing for certain capital investments and higher deduction allowances for start-up costs. Motion rejected 57-41: D 50-1; R 5-40; I 2-0. Three-fifths of the total Senate (60) is required to invoke cloture. July 12, 2012.

177. S 2237. Small-Business Tax Cuts/Cloture. Motion to invoke cloture (thus limiting debate) on the bill that would give employers a credit of up to $500,000 to offset 10 percent of the amount they spend to expand their payroll in 2012 compared with 2011. It also would allow businesses to deduct the full cost of equipment purchased this year. Motion rejected 53-44: D 49-1; R 2-43; I 2-0. Three-fifths of the total Senate (60) is required to invoke cloture. A "yea" was a vote in support of the president's position. July 12, 2012.

State / Senator	173	174	175	176	177
ALABAMA					
Shelby	Y	N	N	N	N
Sessions	Y	N	Y	N	N
ALASKA					
Murkowski	Y	Y	Y	N	N
Begich	Y	Y	Y	Y	Y
ARIZONA					
McCain	Y	N	N	N	N
Kyl	Y	Y	N	N	N
ARKANSAS					
Pryor	Y	Y	Y	Y	Y
Boozman	Y	Y	N	N	N
CALIFORNIA					
Feinstein	Y	Y	Y	Y	Y
Boxer	Y	Y	Y	Y	?
COLORADO					
Udall	Y	Y	Y	Y	Y
Bennet	Y	Y	Y	Y	Y
CONNECTICUT					
Lieberman	Y	Y	Y	Y	Y
Blumenthal	Y	Y	Y	Y	Y
DELAWARE					
Carper	Y	Y	Y	Y	Y
Coons	Y	Y	Y	Y	Y
FLORIDA					
Nelson	Y	Y	Y	Y	Y
Rubio	Y	Y	Y	N	N
GEORGIA					
Chambliss	?	?	Y	N	N
Isakson	Y	Y	N	N	N
HAWAII					
Inouye	Y	Y	Y	Y	Y
Akaka	Y	Y	Y	Y	Y
IDAHO					
Crapo	Y	N	Y	N	N
Risch	Y	N	Y	N	N
ILLINOIS					
Durbin	Y	Y	Y	Y	Y
Kirk	?	?	?	?	?
INDIANA					
Lugar	Y	Y	N	N	N
Coats	Y	Y	Y	N	N
IOWA					
Grassley	Y	Y	N	N	N
Harkin	Y	Y	Y	Y	Y
KANSAS					
Roberts	Y	Y	N	N	N
Moran	Y	Y	?	?	?
KENTUCKY					
McConnell	Y	Y	N	N	N
Paul	Y	Y	N	N	N
LOUISIANA					
Landrieu	Y	Y	Y	Y	Y
Vitter	Y	?	Y	Y	N
MAINE					
Snowe	Y	Y	N	Y	N
Collins	Y	Y	N	Y	N
MARYLAND					
Mikulski	Y	Y	Y	Y	Y
Cardin	Y	?	Y	Y	Y
MASSACHUSETTS					
Kerry	Y	Y	Y	Y	Y
Brown	Y	Y	N	Y	Y
MICHIGAN					
Levin	Y	Y	Y	Y	Y
Stabenow	Y	Y	Y	Y	Y
MINNESOTA					
Klobuchar	Y	Y	Y	Y	Y
Franken	Y	Y	Y	Y	Y
MISSISSIPPI					
Cochran	Y	Y	N	N	N
Wicker	Y	N	N	N	N
MISSOURI					
McCaskill	Y	Y	Y	Y	Y
Blunt	Y	Y	N	N	N
MONTANA					
Baucus	Y	Y	Y	Y	Y
Tester	Y	Y	Y	Y	Y
NEBRASKA					
Nelson	Y	Y	Y	Y	Y
Johanns	Y	N	N	N	N
NEVADA					
Reid	Y	Y	Y	Y	Y
Heller	Y	Y	N	Y	Y
NEW HAMPSHIRE					
Shaheen	Y	Y	Y	Y	Y
Ayotte	Y	N	Y	N	N
NEW JERSEY					
Lautenberg	Y	Y	Y	Y	Y
Menendez	Y	Y	Y	Y	Y
NEW MEXICO					
Bingaman	Y	Y	Y	Y	Y
Udall	Y	Y	+	Y	Y
NEW YORK					
Schumer	Y	Y	Y	Y	Y
Gillibrand	Y	Y	Y	Y	Y
NORTH CAROLINA					
Burr	?	Y	N	N	N
Hagan	Y	Y	Y	Y	Y
NORTH DAKOTA					
Conrad	Y	Y	Y	Y	Y
Hoeven	Y	N	N	N	N
OHIO					
Brown	Y	Y	Y	Y	Y
Portman	Y	Y	Y	N	N
OKLAHOMA					
Inhofe	Y	N	N	N	N
Coburn	Y	Y	Y	N	N
OREGON					
Wyden	Y	Y	Y	Y	Y
Merkley	Y	Y	Y	Y	Y
PENNSYLVANIA					
Casey	Y	Y	Y	Y	Y
Toomey	Y	Y	Y	N	N
RHODE ISLAND					
Reed	Y	Y	Y	Y	Y
Whitehouse	Y	Y	Y	Y	Y
SOUTH CAROLINA					
Graham	Y	N	Y	N	N
DeMint	N	N	Y	N	N
SOUTH DAKOTA					
Johnson	Y	Y	Y	Y	Y
Thune	Y	Y	N	Y	N
TENNESSEE					
Alexander	Y	Y	Y	N	N
Corker	Y	Y	N	Y	N
TEXAS					
Hutchison	Y	Y	N	N	N
Cornyn	Y	N	Y	N	N
UTAH					
Hatch	Y	Y	N	N	N
Lee	N	?	N	N	N
VERMONT					
Leahy	Y	Y	Y	Y	Y
Sanders	+	Y	Y	Y	Y
VIRGINIA					
Webb	Y	Y	Y	Y	Y
Warner	Y	Y	Y	Y	Y
WASHINGTON					
Murray	Y	Y	Y	Y	Y
Cantwell	Y	Y	Y	Y	Y
WEST VIRGINIA					
Rockefeller	Y	?	Y	Y	Y
Manchin	Y	N	Y	N	N
WISCONSIN					
Kohl	Y	Y	Y	Y	Y
Johnson	Y	N	Y	N	N
WYOMING					
Enzi	Y	Y	Y	N	N
Barrasso	Y	Y	Y	N	N

KEY — Republicans · Democrats · *Independents*

Y Voted for (yea)	X Paired against	C Voted "present" to avoid possible conflict of interest
# Paired for	– Announced against	? Did not vote or otherwise make a position known
+ Announced for	P Voted "present"	
N Voted against (nay)		

IN THE SENATE | By Vote Number

178. McNulty Nomination /Confirmation. Confirmation of President Obama's nomination of Kevin McNulty of New Jersey to be a judge for the U.S. District Court for the District of New Jersey. Confirmed 91-3: D 49-0; R 40-3; I 2-0. A "yea" was a vote in support of the president's position. July 16, 2012.

179. S 3369. Campaign Financial Disclosures/Cloture. Motion to invoke cloture (thus limiting debate) on the Reid, D-Nev., motion to proceed to the bill that would require groups and companies to disclose independent campaign expenditures and donations to independent groups over $10,000. Motion rejected 51-44: D 49-1; R 0-43; I 2-0. Three-fifths of the total Senate (60) is required to invoke cloture. A "yea" was a vote in support of the president's position. July 16, 2012.

180. S 3369. Campaign Financial Disclosures/Cloture. Motion to invoke cloture (thus limiting debate) on the Reid, D-Nev., motion to proceed to the bill that would require groups and companies to disclose independent campaign expenditures and donations to independent groups over $10,000. Motion rejected 53-45: D 51-0; R 0-45; I 2-0. Three-fifths of the total Senate (60) is required to invoke cloture. A "yea" was a vote in support of the president's position. July 17, 2012.

181. S 3364. Outsourcing Tax Credits/Cloture. Motion to invoke cloture (thus limiting debate) on the Reid, D-Nev., motion to proceed to the bill that would provide a 20 percent business tax credit to cover the cost of shifting overseas jobs back to the United States and eliminate tax credits for expenses related to moving operations abroad. Motion rejected 56-42: D 50-0; R 4-42; I 2-0. Three-fifths of the total Senate (60) is required to invoke cloture. A "yea" was a vote in support of the president's position. July 19, 2012.

	178	179	180	181			178	179	180	181
ALABAMA						**MONTANA**				
Shelby	Y	N	–	N		Baucus	Y	Y	Y	Y
Sessions	Y	N	N	N		Tester	?	Y	Y	Y
ALASKA						**NEBRASKA**				
Murkowski	?	?	N	N		Nelson	Y	Y	Y	Y
Begich	Y	Y	Y	Y		Johanns	Y	N	N	N
ARIZONA						**NEVADA**				
McCain	Y	N	N	N		Reid	Y	N	Y	Y
Kyl	Y	N	N	N		Heller	?	?	N	Y
ARKANSAS						**NEW HAMPSHIRE**				
Pryor	Y	Y	Y	Y		Shaheen	Y	Y	Y	Y
Boozman	Y	N	N	N		Ayotte	Y	N	N	N
CALIFORNIA						**NEW JERSEY**				
Feinstein	Y	Y	Y	Y		Lautenberg	Y	Y	Y	Y
Boxer	Y	Y	Y	Y		Menendez	Y	Y	Y	Y
COLORADO						**NEW MEXICO**				
Udall	Y	Y	Y	Y		Bingaman	Y	Y	Y	Y
Bennet	Y	Y	Y	Y		Udall	Y	Y	Y	Y
CONNECTICUT						**NEW YORK**				
Lieberman	Y	Y	Y	Y		Schumer	P	Y	Y	Y
Blumenthal	Y	Y	Y	Y		Gillibrand	Y	Y	Y	Y
DELAWARE						**NORTH CAROLINA**				
Carper	Y	Y	Y	Y		Burr	Y	N	N	N
Coons	Y	Y	Y	Y		Hagan	Y	Y	Y	Y
FLORIDA						**NORTH DAKOTA**				
Nelson	Y	Y	Y	Y		Conrad	Y	Y	Y	Y
Rubio	Y	N	N	N		Hoeven	Y	N	N	N
GEORGIA						**OHIO**				
Chambliss	Y	N	N	N		Brown	Y	Y	Y	Y
Isakson	Y	N	N	N		Portman	Y	N	N	N
HAWAII						**OKLAHOMA**				
Inouye	Y	Y	Y	Y		Inhofe	Y	N	N	N
Akaka	Y	Y	Y	Y		Coburn	Y	N	N	N
IDAHO						**OREGON**				
Crapo	Y	N	N	N		Wyden	Y	Y	Y	Y
Risch	Y	N	N	N		Merkley	Y	Y	Y	Y
ILLINOIS						**PENNSYLVANIA**				
Durbin	Y	Y	Y	Y		Casey	Y	Y	Y	Y
Kirk	?	?	?	?		Toomey	Y	N	N	N
INDIANA						**RHODE ISLAND**				
Lugar	Y	N	N	N		Reed	Y	Y	Y	Y
Coats	Y	N	N	N		Whitehouse	Y	Y	Y	Y
IOWA						**SOUTH CAROLINA**				
Grassley	Y	N	N	N		Graham	Y	N	N	N
Harkin	Y	Y	Y	Y		DeMint	N	N	N	N
KANSAS						**SOUTH DAKOTA**				
Roberts	Y	N	N	N		Johnson	Y	Y	Y	Y
Moran	Y	N	N	N		Thune	Y	N	N	N
KENTUCKY						**TENNESSEE**				
McConnell	Y	N	N	N		Alexander	Y	N	N	N
Paul	N	N	N	N		Corker	Y	N	N	N
LOUISIANA						**TEXAS**				
Landrieu	Y	?	Y	Y		Hutchison	Y	N	N	N
Vitter	Y	N	N	N		Cornyn	Y	N	N	N
MAINE						**UTAH**				
Snowe	Y	N	N	Y		Hatch	Y	N	N	N
Collins	Y	N	N	Y		Lee	N	N	N	N
MARYLAND						**VERMONT**				
Mikulski	Y	Y	Y	Y		Leahy	Y	Y	Y	Y
Cardin	Y	Y	Y	Y		*Sanders*	Y	Y	Y	Y
MASSACHUSETTS						**VIRGINIA**				
Kerry	Y	Y	Y	Y		Webb	Y	Y	Y	Y
Brown	Y	N	N	Y		Warner	Y	Y	Y	Y
MICHIGAN						**WASHINGTON**				
Levin	Y	Y	Y	Y		Murray	Y	Y	Y	Y
Stabenow	Y	Y	Y	Y		Cantwell	Y	Y	Y	Y
MINNESOTA						**WEST VIRGINIA**				
Klobuchar	Y	Y	Y	Y		Rockefeller	Y	Y	Y	Y
Franken	Y	Y	Y	Y		Manchin	Y	Y	Y	Y
MISSISSIPPI						**WISCONSIN**				
Cochran	Y	N	N	N		Kohl	Y	Y	Y	?
Wicker	?	?	N	N		Johnson	Y	N	N	N
MISSOURI						**WYOMING**				
McCaskill	Y	Y	Y	Y		Enzi	Y	N	N	N
Blunt	Y	N	N	N		Barrasso	Y	N	N	N

KEY   Republicans   Democrats   *Independents*

Y	Voted for (yea)	X	Paired against	C Voted "present" to avoid possible conflict of interest
#	Paired for	–	Announced against	
+	Announced for	P	Voted "present"	? Did not vote or otherwise make a position known
N	Voted against (nay)			

IN THE SENATE | By Vote Number

182. Shipp Nomination/Confirmation. Confirmation of President Obama's nomination of Michael A. Shipp of New Jersey to be a judge for the U.S. District Court for the District of New Jersey. Confirmed 91-1: D 46-0; R 43-1; I 2-0. A "yea" was a vote in support of the president's position. July 23, 2012.

183. S 3412. Tax Rates Extensions/Republican Substitute. McConnell, R-Ky., substitute amendment that would extend the 2001 and 2003 tax cuts for all income levels for one year. It also would extend estate tax levels, with a 35 percent on estates worth more than $5 million. The substitute also would extend alternative minimum tax provisions through 2013. Rejected 45-54: D 1-50; R 44-2; I 0-2. July 25, 2012.

184. S 3412. Tax Rates Extensions/Passage. Passage of the bill that would extend the 2001 and 2003 tax cuts for one year on taxable income of up to $200,000 for single filers or up to $250,000 for joint filers. The bill would set the tax rate for adjusted gross income above $250,000 at 36 percent and for adjusted gross income above $400,000 at 39.6 percent. It also would expand the child tax credit and extend the college tuition tax credit and the earned-income tax credit. It would set tax rates for long-term capital gains and dividends at 20 percent. The bill also would allow a business property deduction of up to $250,000 and extend the alternative minimum tax provisions for 2012 income. Passed 51-48: D 50-1; R 0-46; I 1-1. A "yea" was a vote in support of the president's position. July 25, 2012.

185. S 3414. Cybersecurity Standards/Cloture. Motion to invoke cloture (thus limiting debate) on the Reid, D-Nev., motion to proceed to the bill that would create voluntary security standards for critical digital infrastructure. Motion agreed to 84-11: D 48-2; R 34-9; I 2-0. Three-fifths of the total Senate (60) is required to invoke cloture. A "yea" was a vote in support of the president's position. July 26, 2012.

	182	183	184	185
ALABAMA				
Shelby	Y	Y	N	Y
Sessions	Y	Y	N	Y
ALASKA				
Murkowski	Y	Y	N	Y
Begich	?	N	Y	Y
ARIZONA				
McCain	Y	Y	N	Y
Kyl	Y	Y	N	Y
ARKANSAS				
Pryor	Y	Y	Y	Y
Boozman	Y	Y	N	Y
CALIFORNIA				
Feinstein	Y	N	Y	Y
Boxer	?	N	Y	Y
COLORADO				
Udall	+	N	Y	Y
Bennet	Y	N	Y	Y
CONNECTICUT				
Lieberman	Y	N	N	Y
Blumenthal	Y	N	Y	Y
DELAWARE				
Carper	Y	N	Y	Y
Coons	Y	N	Y	Y
FLORIDA				
Nelson	Y	N	Y	Y
Rubio	Y	Y	N	N
GEORGIA				
Chambliss	Y	Y	N	Y
Isakson	Y	Y	N	Y
HAWAII				
Inouye	Y	N	Y	Y
Akaka	Y	N	Y	Y
IDAHO				
Crapo	Y	Y	N	Y
Risch	Y	Y	N	Y
ILLINOIS				
Durbin	Y	N	Y	Y
Kirk	?	?	?	?
INDIANA				
Lugar	Y	Y	N	Y
Coats	Y	Y	N	Y
IOWA				
Grassley	Y	Y	N	Y
Harkin	?	N	Y	Y
KANSAS				
Roberts	Y	Y	N	N
Moran	Y	Y	N	N
KENTUCKY				
McConnell	Y	Y	N	Y
Paul	Y	Y	N	N
LOUISIANA				
Landrieu	Y	N	Y	Y
Vitter	Y	Y	N	Y
MAINE				
Snowe	Y	Y	N	Y
Collins	Y	N	N	Y
MARYLAND				
Mikulski	Y	N	Y	Y
Cardin	Y	N	Y	Y
MASSACHUSETTS				
Kerry	Y	N	Y	Y
Brown	Y	N	N	Y
MICHIGAN				
Levin	Y	N	Y	Y
Stabenow	Y	N	Y	Y
MINNESOTA				
Klobuchar	Y	N	Y	Y
Franken	Y	N	Y	Y
MISSISSIPPI				
Cochran	Y	Y	N	Y
Wicker	Y	Y	N	Y
MISSOURI				
McCaskill	Y	N	Y	Y
Blunt	Y	Y	N	Y

	182	183	184	185
MONTANA				
Baucus	Y	N	Y	N
Tester	Y	N	Y	N
NEBRASKA				
Nelson	Y	N	Y	Y
Johanns	Y	Y	N	N
NEVADA				
Reid	Y	N	Y	Y
Heller	Y	Y	N	N
NEW HAMPSHIRE				
Shaheen	Y	N	Y	Y
Ayotte	Y	Y	N	Y
NEW JERSEY				
Lautenberg	Y	N	Y	Y
Menendez	Y	N	Y	Y
NEW MEXICO				
Bingaman	Y	N	Y	Y
Udall	Y	N	Y	Y
NEW YORK				
Schumer	Y	N	Y	Y
Gillibrand	Y	N	Y	Y
NORTH CAROLINA				
Burr	Y	Y	N	Y
Hagan	Y	N	Y	Y
NORTH DAKOTA				
Conrad	Y	N	Y	?
Hoeven	Y	Y	N	Y
OHIO				
Brown	Y	N	Y	Y
Portman	Y	Y	N	Y
OKLAHOMA				
Inhofe	Y	Y	N	?
Coburn	Y	Y	N	Y
OREGON				
Wyden	Y	N	Y	Y
Merkley	Y	N	Y	Y
PENNSYLVANIA				
Casey	?	N	Y	Y
Toomey	Y	Y	N	Y
RHODE ISLAND				
Reed	Y	N	Y	Y
Whitehouse	Y	N	Y	Y
SOUTH CAROLINA				
Graham	Y	Y	N	Y
DeMint	?	Y	N	-
SOUTH DAKOTA				
Johnson	Y	N	Y	Y
Thune	Y	Y	N	Y
TENNESSEE				
Alexander	Y	Y	N	Y
Corker	Y	Y	N	Y
TEXAS				
Hutchison	Y	Y	N	Y
Cornyn	Y	Y	N	Y
UTAH				
Hatch	+	Y	N	Y
Lee	N	Y	N	?
VERMONT				
Leahy	Y	N	Y	Y
Sanders	Y	N	Y	Y
VIRGINIA				
Webb	Y	N	Y	Y
Warner	Y	N	Y	Y
WASHINGTON				
Murray	Y	N	Y	Y
Cantwell	Y	N	Y	Y
WEST VIRGINIA				
Rockefeller	Y	N	Y	Y
Manchin	Y	N	Y	Y
WISCONSIN				
Kohl	Y	N	Y	Y
Johnson	Y	Y	N	N
WYOMING				
Enzi	Y	Y	N	N
Barrasso	Y	Y	N	N

KEY   Republicans   Democrats   *Independents*

Y	Voted for (yea)
#	Paired for
+	Announced for
N	Voted against (nay)
X	Paired against
-	Announced against
P	Voted "present"
C	Voted "present" to avoid possible conflict of interest
?	Did not vote or otherwise make a position known

IN THE SENATE | By Vote Number

186. Bacharach Nomination/Cloture. Motion to invoke cloture (thus limiting debate) on President Obama's nomination of Robert E. Bacharach of Oklahoma to be a judge for the 10th U.S. Circuit Court of Appeals. Motion rejected 56-34: D 51-0; R 3-34; I 2-0. Three-fifths of the total Senate (60) is required to invoke cloture. A "yea" was a vote in support of the president's position. July 30, 2012.

187. S 3414. Cybersecurity Standards/Cloture. Motion to invoke cloture (thus limiting debate) on the bill that would create voluntary security standards for vital digital infrastructure. Three-fifths of the total Senate (60) is required to invoke cloture. Motion rejected 52-46: D 45-6; R 5-40; I 2-0. A "yea" was a vote in support of the president's position. Aug. 2, 2012.

188. S 3326. African Trade and Myanmar Sanctions/Substitute Amendment. Coburn, R-Okla., substitute amendment that would strike provisions in the bill modifying textile and apparel rules of origin for the Dominican Republic-Central America-United States free-trade agreement and extend Myanmar sanctions. It also would offset the cost of the bill by reducing spending on certain trade programs by $192 million over two years. Rejected 40-58: D 3-48; R 37-8; I 0-2. Aug. 2, 2012.

189. Drain Nomination/Confirmation. Confirmation of President Obama's nomination of Gershwin A. Drain of Michigan to be a judge for the U.S. District Court for the Eastern District of Michigan. Confirmed 55-41: D 50-1; R 3-40; I 2-0. A "yea" was a vote in support of the president's position. Aug. 2, 2012.

190. Rose Nomination/Confirmation. Confirmation of President Obama's nomination of Stephanie Marie Rose of Iowa to be a judge for the U.S. District Court for the Southern District of Iowa. Confirmed 89-1: D 48-0; R 39-1; I 2-0. A "yea" was a vote in support of the president's position. Sept. 10, 2012.

191. S 3457. Veterans Job Training/Cloture. Motion to invoke cloture (thus limiting debate) on the motion to proceed to the bill that would give veterans priority for certain federal jobs and provide training for servicemembers in search of civilian work. Motion agreed to 95-1: D 49-0; R 44-1; I 2-0. Three-fifths of the total Senate (60) is required to invoke cloture. Sept. 11, 2012.

192. S 3457. Veterans Jobs Training/Motion to Proceed. Reid, D-Nev., motion to proceed to the bill that would give veterans priority for certain federal jobs and provide training for servicemembers in search of civilian work. Motion agreed to 84-8: D 47-0; R 35-8; I 2-0. Sept. 12, 2012.

	186	187	188	189	190	191	192
ALABAMA							
Shelby	N	N	Y	N	Y	Y	Y
Sessions	N	N	Y	Y	Y	Y	N
ALASKA							
Murkowski	?	N	Y	N	?	Y	Y
Begich	Y	Y	N	Y	Y	Y	Y
ARIZONA							
McCain	?	N	Y	N	Y	Y	Y
Kyl	N	N	Y	N	Y	Y	Y
ARKANSAS							
Pryor	Y	N	N	Y	Y	Y	Y
Boozman	N	N	N	Y	Y	Y	Y
CALIFORNIA							
Feinstein	Y	Y	N	Y	Y	Y	Y
Boxer	Y	Y	N	Y	Y	Y	Y
COLORADO							
Udall	Y	Y	N	Y	Y	Y	Y
Bennet	Y	Y	N	Y	Y	Y	Y
CONNECTICUT							
Lieberman	Y	Y	N	Y	Y	Y	Y
Blumenthal	Y	Y	N	Y	Y	Y	Y
DELAWARE							
Carper	Y	Y	N	Y	Y	Y	Y
Coons	Y	Y	N	Y	Y	Y	Y
FLORIDA							
Nelson	Y	Y	N	Y	Y	Y	Y
Rubio	N	?	?	?	?	?	?
GEORGIA							
Chambliss	N	N	Y	N	Y	Y	Y
Isakson	N	N	Y	N	Y	Y	Y
HAWAII							
Inouye	Y	Y	N	Y	Y	Y	?
Akaka	Y	Y	N	Y	Y	Y	Y
IDAHO							
Crapo	N	N	Y	N	Y	Y	Y
Risch	N	N	Y	N	Y	Y	Y
ILLINOIS							
Durbin	Y	Y	N	Y	Y	Y	Y
Kirk	?	?	?	?	?	?	?
INDIANA							
Lugar	N	Y	N	N	Y	Y	Y
Coats	N	Y	N	Y	Y	Y	Y
IOWA							
Grassley	N	N	N	N	Y	Y	Y
Harkin	Y	Y	N	Y	Y	Y	Y
KANSAS							
Roberts	N	N	N	N	Y	Y	Y
Moran	N	N	Y	?	Y	Y	Y
KENTUCKY							
McConnell	N	N	N	N	Y	Y	Y
Paul	N	N	Y	N	?	N	N
LOUISIANA							
Landrieu	Y	Y	N	Y	Y	Y	?
Vitter	N	N	Y	?	?	Y	Y
MAINE							
Snowe	Y	Y	N	N	Y	Y	Y
Collins	Y	Y	N	N	Y	Y	Y
MARYLAND							
Mikulski	Y	Y	N	Y	Y	Y	Y
Cardin	Y	Y	N	Y	Y	Y	Y
MASSACHUSETTS							
Kerry	Y	Y	N	Y	Y	Y	Y
Brown	Y	Y	N	Y	Y	Y	Y
MICHIGAN							
Levin	Y	Y	N	Y	Y	Y	Y
Stabenow	Y	Y	N	Y	Y	Y	Y
MINNESOTA							
Klobuchar	Y	Y	N	Y	Y	Y	Y
Franken	Y	Y	N	Y	Y	Y	Y
MISSISSIPPI							
Cochran	N	N	N	N	Y	Y	Y
Wicker	N	N	Y	N	Y	Y	Y
MISSOURI							
McCaskill	Y	Y	N	Y	Y	Y	Y
Blunt	N	N	Y	N	Y	Y	N

	186	187	188	189	190	191	192
MONTANA							
Baucus	Y	N	N	Y	Y	Y	Y
Tester	Y	N	N	Y	Y	Y	Y
NEBRASKA							
Nelson	Y	Y	N	N	Y	Y	Y
Johanns	N	N	N	N	Y	Y	?
NEVADA							
Reid	Y	N	N	Y	Y	Y	Y
Heller	N	N	N	N	Y	Y	Y
NEW HAMPSHIRE							
Shaheen	Y	Y	N	Y	?	Y	Y
Ayotte	?	N	Y	N	Y	Y	Y
NEW JERSEY							
Lautenberg	Y	Y	N	A	?	Y	Y
Menendez	Y	Y	N	Y	Y	Y	Y
NEW MEXICO							
Bingaman	Y	Y	N	Y	Y	Y	Y
Udall	Y	Y	N	Y	Y	Y	Y
NEW YORK							
Schumer	Y	Y	N	Y	Y	Y	Y
Gillibrand	Y	Y	N	Y	Y	Y	Y
NORTH CAROLINA							
Burr	N	N	Y	N	Y	Y	Y
Hagan	Y	Y	N	Y	Y	Y	Y
NORTH DAKOTA							
Conrad	Y	Y	N	Y	Y	Y	Y
Hoeven	N	N	N	N	Y	Y	Y
OHIO							
Brown	Y	Y	N	Y	Y	Y	Y
Portman	N	N	Y	N	?	Y	Y
OKLAHOMA							
Inhofe	P	N	Y	N	Y	Y	N
Coburn	P	N	Y	N	?	Y	N
OREGON							
Wyden	Y	N	N	Y	Y	Y	Y
Merkley	Y	N	N	Y	Y	Y	Y
PENNSYLVANIA							
Casey	Y	Y	N	Y	Y	Y	Y
Toomey	N	N	Y	N	Y	Y	Y
RHODE ISLAND							
Reed	Y	Y	N	Y	Y	Y	Y
Whitehouse	Y	Y	N	Y	?	Y	Y
SOUTH CAROLINA							
Graham	?	N	Y	N	Y	Y	Y
DeMint	?	N	Y	N	N	Y	N
SOUTH DAKOTA							
Johnson	Y	Y	N	Y	Y	?	?
Thune	N	N	Y	N	Y	Y	Y
TENNESSEE							
Alexander	N	N	Y	N	Y	Y	Y
Corker	N	N	Y	N	Y	Y	Y
TEXAS							
Hutchison	N	N	Y	N	Y	Y	Y
Cornyn	N	N	Y	N	Y	Y	+
UTAH							
Hatch	P	N	N	N	Y	Y	N
Lee	?	N	Y	N	Y	N	N
VERMONT							
Leahy	Y	Y	N	Y	Y	Y	Y
Sanders	Y	Y	N	Y	Y	Y	Y
VIRGINIA							
Webb	Y	Y	Y	Y	Y	Y	?
Warner	Y	Y	N	Y	Y	?	Y
WASHINGTON							
Murray	Y	Y	N	Y	Y	Y	Y
Cantwell	Y	Y	N	Y	Y	Y	Y
WEST VIRGINIA							
Rockefeller	Y	Y	N	Y	Y	Y	Y
Manchin	Y	Y	Y	Y	Y	Y	Y
WISCONSIN							
Kohl	Y	Y	N	Y	Y	Y	Y
Johnson	N	N	Y	N	Y	Y	N
WYOMING							
Enzi	N	N	Y	N	Y	Y	Y
Barrasso	N	N	Y	N	Y	Y	Y

KEY — **Republicans** (bold) — Democrats — *Independents* (italic)

Y	Voted for (yea)
#	Paired for
+	Announced for
N	Voted against (nay)
X	Paired against
–	Announced against
P	Voted "present"
C	Voted "present" to avoid possible conflict of interest
?	Did not vote or otherwise make a position known

IN THE SENATE | By Vote Number

193. S 3457. Veterans Jobs Training/Motion to Waive.

Reid, D-Nev., motion to waive all applicable budget laws with respect to the Sessions, R-Ala., point of order against the Murray, D-Wash., substitute amendment that would require states to issue certain licenses for trade jobs such as plumbing or truck driving to veterans without requiring training or apprenticeships if the veterans pass examinations and have at least 10 years of experience in related military occupations. Motion rejected 58-40: D 51-0; R 5-40; I 2-0. A three-fifths majority vote of the total Senate (60) is required to waive the applicable budget laws. A "yea" was a vote in support of the president's position. Sept. 19, 2012.

194. H J Res 117. Continuing Resolution/Cloture.

Reid, D-Nev., motion to invoke cloture (thus limiting debate) on the motion to proceed to the joint resolution that would provide continuing appropriations for the federal government through March 27, 2013. Motion agreed to 76-22: D 50-1; R 24-21; I 2-0. Three-fifths of the total Senate (60) is required to invoke cloture. Sept. 19, 2012.

195. H J Res 117. Continuing Resolution/Motion to Proceed.

Reid, D-Nev., motion to proceed to the joint resolution that would provide continuing appropriations for the federal government through March 27, 2013. Motion agreed to 67-31: D 50-1; R 15-30; I 2-0. Sept. 19, 2012.

196. S 3576. Foreign Aid/Passage.

Passage of the bill that would cut off foreign aid to Pakistan, Egypt, Libya and any other country where U.S. diplomatic facilities are attacked, trespassed on or breached. The bill also would allow the president to request the restoration of aid to Pakistan if Dr. Shakil Afridi is released from prison with no criminal charges and allowed to leave Pakistan alive. The measure would provide for expedited consideration of such a presidential request. Rejected 10-81: D 0-49; R 10-30; I 0-2. Sept. 22, 2012 (in the session that began and the Congressional Record dated Sept. 21, 2012).

	193	194	195	196			193	194	195	196
ALABAMA						**MONTANA**				
Shelby	N	N	N	Y		Baucus	Y	Y	Y	N
Sessions	N	N	N	N		Tester	Y	Y	Y	N
ALASKA						**NEBRASKA**				
Murkowski	Y	Y	Y	N		Nelson	Y	Y	Y	N
Begich	Y	Y	Y	N		Johanns	N	Y	Y	N
ARIZONA						**NEVADA**				
McCain	N	N	N	N		Reid	Y	Y	Y	N
Kyl	N	Y	Y	N		Heller	Y	Y	Y	+
ARKANSAS						**NEW HAMPSHIRE**				
Pryor	Y	Y	Y	N		Shaheen	Y	Y	Y	N
Boozman	N	N	N	?		Ayotte	N	Y	N	N
CALIFORNIA						**NEW JERSEY**				
Feinstein	Y	Y	Y	N		Lautenberg	Y	Y	Y	N
Boxer	Y	Y	Y	–		Menendez	Y	Y	Y	N
COLORADO						**NEW MEXICO**				
Udall	Y	Y	Y	N		Bingaman	Y	Y	Y	N
Bennet	Y	Y	Y	N		Udall	Y	Y	Y	N
CONNECTICUT						**NEW YORK**				
Lieberman	Y	Y	Y	N		Schumer	Y	Y	Y	N
Blumenthal	Y	Y	Y	N		Gillibrand	Y	Y	Y	N
DELAWARE						**NORTH CAROLINA**				
Carper	Y	Y	Y	N		Burr	N	Y	N	?
Coons	Y	Y	Y	N		Hagan	Y	Y	Y	N
FLORIDA						**NORTH DAKOTA**				
Nelson	Y	Y	Y	N		Conrad	Y	Y	Y	N
Rubio	N	N	N	?		Hoeven	N	Y	Y	N
GEORGIA						**OHIO**				
Chambliss	N	Y	N	N		Brown	Y	Y	Y	N
Isakson	N	Y	N	N		Portman	N	Y	N	N
HAWAII						**OKLAHOMA**				
Inouye	Y	Y	Y	N		Inhofe	?	?	?	?
Akaka	Y	Y	Y	N		Coburn	N	N	N	N
IDAHO						**OREGON**				
Crapo	N	N	N	Y		Wyden	Y	Y	Y	N
Risch	N	N	N	Y		Merkley	Y	Y	Y	N
ILLINOIS						**PENNSYLVANIA**				
Durbin	Y	Y	Y	N		Casey	Y	Y	Y	N
Kirk	?	?	?	?		Toomey	N	N	N	Y
INDIANA						**RHODE ISLAND**				
Lugar	N	Y	Y	N		Reed	Y	Y	Y	N
Coats	N	Y	Y	N		Whitehouse	Y	Y	Y	N
IOWA						**SOUTH CAROLINA**				
Grassley	N	N	N	Y		Graham	N	N	N	N
Harkin	Y	Y	Y	N		DeMint	N	N	N	Y
KANSAS						**SOUTH DAKOTA**				
Roberts	N	Y	N	Y		Johnson	Y	Y	Y	N
Moran	N	N	N	Y		Thune	N	Y	N	N
KENTUCKY						**TENNESSEE**				
McConnell	N	Y	Y	N		Alexander	N	Y	Y	N
Paul	N	N	N	Y		Corker	N	N	N	N
LOUISIANA						**TEXAS**				
Landrieu	Y	Y	Y	N		Hutchison	N	Y	Y	N
Vitter	N	N	N	?		Cornyn	N	Y	N	N
MAINE						**UTAH**				
Snowe	Y	N	N	N		Hatch	N	Y	N	N
Collins	Y	N	N	N		Lee	N	N	N	Y
MARYLAND						**VERMONT**				
Mikulski	Y	Y	Y	N		Leahy	Y	Y	Y	N
Cardin	Y	Y	Y	N		Sanders	Y	Y	Y	N
MASSACHUSETTS						**VIRGINIA**				
Kerry	Y	Y	Y	N		Webb	Y	Y	Y	N
Brown	Y	Y	Y	N		Warner	Y	Y	Y	N
MICHIGAN						**WASHINGTON**				
Levin	Y	Y	Y	N		Murray	Y	Y	Y	?
Stabenow	Y	Y	Y	N		Cantwell	Y	Y	Y	N
MINNESOTA						**WEST VIRGINIA**				
Klobuchar	Y	Y	Y	N		Rockefeller	Y	Y	Y	N
Franken	Y	Y	Y	N		Manchin	Y	N	N	N
MISSISSIPPI						**WISCONSIN**				
Cochran	N	Y	Y	N		Kohl	Y	Y	Y	N
Wicker	N	Y	Y	N		Johnson	N	Y	N	N
MISSOURI						**WYOMING**				
McCaskill	Y	Y	Y	N		Enzi	N	N	N	N
Blunt	N	Y	Y	N		Barrasso	N	N	N	N

KEY	**Republicans**	Democrats	*Independents*		
Y	Voted for (yea)		X Paired against		C Voted "present" to avoid possible conflict of interest
#	Paired for		– Announced against		
+	Announced for		P Voted "present"		? Did not vote or otherwise make a position known
N	Voted against (nay)				

IN THE SENATE | By Vote Number

197. S J Res 41. Iran Nuclear Containment/Passage. Passage of the joint resolution that would urge for "diplomatic and economic" pressure to deter Iran from developing nuclear weapons capability. The measure would express that Congress strongly supports U.S. policy to prevent Iran from acquiring nuclear weapons capability and rejects any policy that would rely on efforts to contain a nuclear-weapons-capable Iran. Passed 90-1: D 49-0; R 39-1; I 2-0. Sept. 22, 2012 (in the session that began and the Congressional Record dated Sept. 21, 2012).

198. H J Res 117. Continuing Appropriations/Cloture. Motion to invoke cloture (thus limiting debate) on the joint resolution that would provide continuing appropriations for the federal government through March 27, 2013. Motion agreed to 62-30: D 48-1; R 12-29; I 2-0. Three-fifths of the total Senate (60) is required to invoke cloture. Sept. 22, 2012 (in the session that began and the Congressional Record dated Sept. 21, 2012).

199. H J Res 117. Continuing Appropriations/Passage. Passage of the joint resolution that would provide continuing appropriations for the federal government through March 27, 2013, at an annualized rate of $1.047 trillion in discretionary spending for regular appropriations. The measure would increase funding for most federal programs and agencies by 0.6 percent, with higher levels for certain programs, such as cybersecurity and wildfire suppression. It also would provide nearly $100 billion in war funding and $6.4 billion in advance disaster-relief funds. Passed (thus cleared for the president) 62-30: D 48-1; R 12-29; I 2-0. A "yea" was a vote in support of the president's position. Sept. 22, 2012 (in the session that began and the Congressional Record dated Sept. 21, 2012).

200. S 3525. Hunting and Sporting Access to Federal Land/Cloture. Motion to invoke cloture (thus limiting debate) on the Reid, D-Nev., motion to proceed to the bill that would provide additional recreational access to specified public lands for hunting and fishing. The bill also would exclude ammunition and fish tackle from EPA regulations, ease a ban on importing polar bear remains and reauthorize several conservation measures, including a grant program for wetlands conservation projects for birds and other wildlife. Motion agreed to 84-7: D 46-3; R 36-4; I 2-0. Three-fifths of the total Senate (60) is required to invoke cloture. Sept. 22, 2012 (in the session that began and the Congressional Record dated Sept. 21, 2012).

	197	198	199	200			197	198	199	200
ALABAMA						**MONTANA**				
Shelby	Y	N	N	Y		Baucus	Y	Y	Y	Y
Sessions	Y	N	N	Y		Tester	Y	Y	Y	Y
ALASKA						**NEBRASKA**				
Murkowski	Y	Y	Y	Y		Nelson	Y	Y	Y	Y
Begich	Y	Y	Y	Y		Johanns	Y	Y	Y	Y
ARIZONA						**NEVADA**				
McCain	Y	N	N	N		Reid	Y	Y	Y	Y
Kyl	Y	Y	Y	N		Heller	+	+	+	+
ARKANSAS						**NEW HAMPSHIRE**				
Pryor	Y	Y	Y	Y		Shaheen	Y	Y	Y	Y
Boozman	?	?	?	?		Ayotte	Y	N	N	Y
CALIFORNIA						**NEW JERSEY**				
Feinstein	Y	Y	Y	Y		Lautenberg	Y	Y	Y	Y
Boxer	+	?	+	-		Menendez	Y	Y	Y	N
COLORADO						**NEW MEXICO**				
Udall	Y	Y	Y	Y		Bingaman	Y	Y	Y	Y
Bennet	Y	Y	Y	Y		Udall	Y	Y	Y	Y
CONNECTICUT						**NEW YORK**				
Lieberman	Y	Y	Y	Y		Schumer	Y	Y	Y	Y
Blumenthal	Y	Y	Y	N		Gillibrand	Y	Y	Y	Y
DELAWARE						**NORTH CAROLINA**				
Carper	Y	Y	Y	Y		Burr	?	?	?	?
Coons	Y	Y	Y	Y		Hagan	Y	Y	Y	Y
FLORIDA						**NORTH DAKOTA**				
Nelson	Y	Y	Y	Y		Conrad	Y	Y	Y	Y
Rubio	?	N	N	Y		Hoeven	Y	Y	Y	Y
GEORGIA						**OHIO**				
Chambliss	Y	N	N	Y		Brown	Y	Y	Y	Y
Isakson	Y	N	N	Y		Portman	Y	N	N	Y
HAWAII						**OKLAHOMA**				
Inouye	Y	Y	Y	Y		Inhofe	?	?	?	?
Akaka	Y	Y	Y	Y		Coburn	Y	N	N	?
IDAHO						**OREGON**				
Crapo	Y	N	N	Y		Wyden	Y	Y	Y	Y
Risch	Y	N	N	Y		Merkley	Y	Y	Y	Y
ILLINOIS						**PENNSYLVANIA**				
Durbin	Y	Y	Y	Y		Casey	Y	Y	Y	Y
Kirk	?	?	?	?		Toomey	Y	N	N	Y
INDIANA						**RHODE ISLAND**				
Lugar	Y	Y	Y	Y		Reed	Y	Y	Y	N
Coats	Y	N	N	Y		Whitehouse	Y	Y	Y	Y
IOWA						**SOUTH CAROLINA**				
Grassley	Y	N	N	Y		Graham	Y	N	N	Y
Harkin	Y	Y	Y	Y		DeMint	Y	N	N	N
KANSAS						**SOUTH DAKOTA**				
Roberts	Y	N	N	Y		Johnson	Y	Y	Y	Y
Moran	Y	N	N	Y		Thune	Y	N	N	Y
KENTUCKY						**TENNESSEE**				
McConnell	Y	Y	Y	Y		Alexander	Y	Y	Y	Y
Paul	N	N	N	N		Corker	Y	N	N	Y
LOUISIANA						**TEXAS**				
Landrieu	Y	Y	Y	Y		Hutchison	Y	Y	Y	Y
Vitter	?	?	?	?		Cornyn	Y	N	N	Y
MAINE						**UTAH**				
Snowe	Y	N	N	Y		Hatch	Y	N	N	Y
Collins	Y	N	N	Y		Lee	Y	N	N	Y
MARYLAND						**VERMONT**				
Mikulski	Y	Y	Y	Y		Leahy	Y	Y	Y	Y
Cardin	Y	Y	Y	Y		Sanders	Y	Y	Y	Y
MASSACHUSETTS						**VIRGINIA**				
Kerry	Y	Y	Y	Y		Webb	Y	Y	Y	Y
Brown	Y	Y	Y	Y		Warner	Y	Y	Y	Y
MICHIGAN						**WASHINGTON**				
Levin	Y	Y	Y	Y		Murray	?	?	?	?
Stabenow	Y	Y	Y	Y		Cantwell	Y	Y	Y	Y
MINNESOTA						**WEST VIRGINIA**				
Klobuchar	Y	Y	Y	Y		Rockefeller	Y	Y	Y	Y
Franken	Y	Y	Y	Y		Manchin	Y	N	N	Y
MISSISSIPPI						**WISCONSIN**				
Cochran	Y	Y	Y	Y		Kohl	Y	Y	Y	Y
Wicker	Y	Y	Y	Y		Johnson	Y	N	N	Y
MISSOURI						**WYOMING**				
McCaskill	Y	Y	Y	Y		Enzi	Y	N	N	Y
Blunt	Y	Y	Y	Y		Barrasso	Y	N	N	Y

KEY   **Republicans**   Democrats   *Independents*

Y Voted for (yea)	X Paired against	C Voted "present" to avoid possible conflict of interest
# Paired for	- Announced against	
+ Announced for	P Voted "present"	? Did not vote or otherwise make a position known
N Voted against (nay)		

IN THE SENATE | By Vote Number

201. **S 3525. Hunting and Sporting Access to Federal Land/Motion to Proceed.** Reid, D-Nev., motion to proceed to the bill that would provide additional recreational access to certain public lands for hunters. The bill also would exclude ammunition and fish tackle from EPA regulations; ease a ban on importing polar bear remains; and reauthorize several conservation measures, including a grant program for wetlands conservation projects for birds and other wildlife. Motion agreed to 92-5: D 48-1; R 42-4; I 2-0. Nov. 13, 2012.

202. **S 3414. Cybersecurity Standards/Cloture.** Motion to invoke cloture (thus limiting debate) on the bill that would create voluntary security standards for vital digital infrastructure. Motion rejected 51-47: D 45-5; R 4-42; I 2-0. Three-fifths of the total Senate (60) is required to invoke cloture. Nov. 14, 2012.

203. **S 3525. Hunting and Sporting Access to Federal Land/Cloture.** Motion to invoke cloture (thus limiting debate) on the bill that would provide additional recreational access to certain public lands for hunters. The bill also would exclude ammunition and fish tackle from EPA regulations; ease a ban on importing polar bear remains; and reauthorize several conservation measures, including a grant program for wetlands conservation projects for birds and other wildlife. Motion agreed to 84-12: D 44-4; R 38-8; I 2-0. Three-fifths of the total Senate (60) is required to invoke cloture. Nov. 15, 2012.

	201	202	203
ALABAMA			
Shelby	Y	N	Y
Sessions	N	N	N
ALASKA			
Murkowski	Y	N	Y
Begich	?	Y	Y
ARIZONA			
McCain	Y	N	Y
Kyl	Y	N	N
ARKANSAS			
Pryor	Y	N	Y
Boozman	Y	N	Y
CALIFORNIA			
Feinstein	Y	Y	Y
Boxer	N	Y	N
COLORADO			
Udall	Y	Y	Y
Bennet	Y	Y	Y
CONNECTICUT			
Lieberman	Y	Y	Y
Blumenthal	Y	Y	Y
DELAWARE			
Carper	Y	Y	Y
Coons	Y	Y	Y
FLORIDA			
Nelson	Y	Y	Y
Rubio	Y	N	Y
GEORGIA			
Chambliss	Y	N	Y
Isakson	Y	N	Y
HAWAII			
Inouye	Y	?	?
Akaka	Y	Y	Y
IDAHO			
Crapo	Y	N	Y
Risch	Y	N	Y
ILLINOIS			
Durbin	Y	Y	Y
Kirk	?	?	?
INDIANA			
Lugar	Y	Y	Y
Coats	Y	N	Y
IOWA			
Grassley	Y	N	Y
Harkin	Y	Y	Y
KANSAS			
Roberts	Y	N	Y
Moran	Y	N	Y
KENTUCKY			
McConnell	Y	N	Y
Paul	N	N	N
LOUISIANA			
Landrieu	Y	Y	Y
Vitter	Y	N	Y
MAINE			
Snowe	Y	Y	Y
Collins	Y	Y	Y
MARYLAND			
Mikulski	Y	Y	Y
Cardin	Y	Y	Y
MASSACHUSETTS			
Kerry	Y	Y	+
Brown	Y	Y	Y
MICHIGAN			
Levin	Y	Y	Y
Stabenow	Y	Y	Y
MINNESOTA			
Klobuchar	Y	Y	Y
Franken	Y	Y	Y
MISSISSIPPI			
Cochran	Y	N	Y
Wicker	Y	N	Y
MISSOURI			
McCaskill	Y	Y	Y
Blunt	Y	N	Y

	201	202	203
MONTANA			
Baucus	Y	N	Y
Tester	Y	N	Y
NEBRASKA			
Nelson	Y	Y	Y
Johanns	Y	N	Y
NEVADA			
Reid	Y	Y	Y
Heller	Y	N	Y
NEW HAMPSHIRE			
Shaheen	Y	Y	Y
Ayotte	Y	N	Y
NEW JERSEY			
Lautenberg	Y	Y	N
Menendez	Y	Y	N
NEW MEXICO			
Bingaman	Y	Y	Y
Udall	Y	Y	Y
NEW YORK			
Schumer	Y	Y	Y
Gillibrand	Y	Y	Y
NORTH CAROLINA			
Burr	Y	N	Y
Hagan	Y	Y	Y
NORTH DAKOTA			
Conrad	Y	Y	Y
Hoeven	Y	N	Y
OHIO			
Brown	Y	Y	Y
Portman	Y	N	Y
OKLAHOMA			
Inhofe	Y	N	Y
Coburn	N	N	N
OREGON			
Wyden	Y	N	Y
Merkley	Y	N	Y
PENNSYLVANIA			
Casey	Y	Y	Y
Toomey	Y	N	N
RHODE ISLAND			
Reed	–	Y	N
Whitehouse	Y	Y	Y
SOUTH CAROLINA			
Graham	Y	N	Y
DeMint	N	N	N
SOUTH DAKOTA			
Johnson	Y	Y	Y
Thune	Y	N	Y
TENNESSEE			
Alexander	Y	N	Y
Corker	Y	N	Y
TEXAS			
Hutchison	Y	N	Y
Cornyn	Y	N	N
UTAH			
Hatch	Y	N	Y
Lee	Y	N	N
VERMONT			
Leahy	Y	Y	Y
Sanders	Y	Y	Y
VIRGINIA			
Webb	Y	Y	Y
Warner	Y	Y	Y
WASHINGTON			
Murray	Y	Y	Y
Cantwell	Y	Y	Y
WEST VIRGINIA			
Rockefeller	Y	Y	?
Manchin	Y	Y	Y
WISCONSIN			
Kohl	Y	Y	Y
Johnson	Y	N	Y
WYOMING			
Enzi	Y	N	Y
Barrasso	Y	N	Y

KEY   **Republicans**   Democrats   *Independents*

Y Voted for (yea)	X Paired against	C Voted "present" to avoid possible conflict of interest
# Paired for	– Announced against	
+ Announced for	P Voted "present"	? Did not vote or otherwise make a position known
N Voted against (nay)		

IN THE SENATE | By Vote Number

204. S 3525. Hunting and Sporting Access to Federal Land/ Motion to Waive. Tester, D-Mont., motion to waive all applicable budget laws with respect to the Sessions, R-Ala., point of order against the Tester substitute amendment that would provide additional recreational access to certain public lands for hunters. It would exclude ammunition and fish tackle from EPA regulations; ease a ban on importing polar bear remains; reauthorize several conservation measures; and allow the Interior Department to increase fees for duck stamps, a federal migratory-bird hunting license that also helps fund conservation efforts. The substitute would strike provisions in the bill to prohibit the sale of billfish and require a report on artificial reefs in the Gulf of Mexico. Motion rejected 50-44: D 47-1; R 1-43; I 2-0. A three-fifths majority vote of the total Senate (60) is required to waive the applicable budget laws. A "yea" was a vote in support of the president's position. Nov. 26, 2012.

205. Treaty Doc 112-7. Convention on the Rights of Persons with Disabilities/Motion to Proceed. Reid, D-Nev., motion to proceed to executive session to consider the Convention on the Rights of Persons with Disabilities, which would establish global standards for the treatment of people with disabilities. Motion agreed to 61-36: D 50-0; R 9-36; I 2-0. Nov. 27, 2012.

206. S 3254. Fiscal 2013 Defense Authorization/Alternative Fuels. Udall, D-Colo., amendment that would strike the section of the bill that would limit Defense Department procurement and production of alternative fuels to those that do not exceed the cost of traditional fossil fuels. Adopted 62-37: D 49-2; R 11-35; I 2-0. A "yea" was a vote in support of the president's position. Nov. 28, 2012.

207. S 3254. Fiscal 2013 Defense Authorization/Public Safety Officers Benefit Program. Leahy, D-Vt., amendment that would extend federal benefits to the surviving families of emergency medical workers from nonprofit ambulance services who are killed or disabled in the line of duty. Adopted 85-11: D 49-0; R 34-11; I 2-0. Nov. 28, 2012.

208. S 3254. Fiscal 2013 Defense Authorization/Veterans Claims Backlog. Cornyn, R-Texas, amendment that would require the Veterans Affairs secretary to submit a plan to reduce the backlog of pending claims for veterans benefits. Adopted 95-0: D 49-0; R 44-0; I 2-0. Nov. 29, 2012.

	204	205	206	207	208			204	205	206	207	208
ALABAMA							**MONTANA**					
Shelby	N	N	N	Y	Y		Baucus	Y	Y	Y	Y	Y
Sessions	N	N	N	Y	Y		Tester	Y	Y	Y	Y	Y
ALASKA							**NEBRASKA**					
Murkowski	N	Y	Y	Y	Y		Nelson	Y	Y	Y	Y	Y
Begich	?	Y	Y	Y	Y		Johanns	N	N	Y	Y	Y
ARIZONA							**NEVADA**					
McCain	N	Y	N	N	Y		Reid	Y	Y	Y	Y	Y
Kyl	N	N	N	N	Y		Heller	N	N	N	Y	?
ARKANSAS							**NEW HAMPSHIRE**					
Pryor	Y	Y	Y	Y	Y		Shaheen	Y	Y	Y	Y	Y
Boozman	N	N	N	Y	Y		Ayotte	N	Y	N	Y	Y
CALIFORNIA							**NEW JERSEY**					
Feinstein	Y	Y	Y	Y	Y		Lautenberg	Y	Y	Y	Y	Y
Boxer	N	Y	Y	Y	Y		Menendez	Y	Y	Y	Y	Y
COLORADO							**NEW MEXICO**					
Udall	Y	Y	Y	Y	Y		Bingaman	Y	Y	Y	?	Y
Bennet	Y	Y	Y	Y	Y		Udall	Y	Y	Y	Y	Y
CONNECTICUT							**NEW YORK**					
Lieberman	Y	Y	Y	Y	Y		Schumer	Y	Y	Y	Y	Y
Blumenthal	Y	+	Y	Y	Y		Gillibrand	Y	Y	Y	Y	Y
DELAWARE							**NORTH CAROLINA**					
Carper	Y	Y	Y	Y	Y		Burr	N	N	N	Y	Y
Coons	Y	Y	Y	Y	Y		Hagan	Y	Y	Y	Y	Y
FLORIDA							**NORTH DAKOTA**					
Nelson	Y	Y	Y	Y	Y		Conrad	Y	Y	Y	Y	Y
Rubio	N	N	N	Y	Y		Hoeven	?	N	Y	Y	Y
GEORGIA							**OHIO**					
Chambliss	N	N	N	Y	Y		Brown	Y	Y	Y	Y	Y
Isakson	?	N	N	Y	Y		Portman	N	N	N	Y	Y
HAWAII							**OKLAHOMA**					
Inouye	Y	Y	Y	Y	Y		Inhofe	N	N	N	N	Y
Akaka	Y	Y	Y	Y	Y		Coburn	N	N	N	N	Y
IDAHO							**OREGON**					
Crapo	N	N	N	Y	Y		Wyden	Y	Y	Y	?	?
Risch	N	N	N	Y	Y		Merkley	Y	Y	Y	Y	Y
ILLINOIS							**PENNSYLVANIA**					
Durbin	Y	Y	Y	Y	Y		Casey	Y	Y	Y	Y	Y
Kirk	?	?	?	?	?		Toomey	N	N	N	Y	Y
INDIANA							**RHODE ISLAND**					
Lugar	N	Y	Y	Y	Y		Reed	Y	Y	Y	Y	Y
Coats	N	N	N	N	Y		Whitehouse	Y	Y	Y	Y	Y
IOWA							**SOUTH CAROLINA**					
Grassley	N	N	Y	Y	Y		Graham	N	N	N	N	Y
Harkin	?	Y	Y	Y	Y		DeMint	N	N	N	N	?
KANSAS							**SOUTH DAKOTA**					
Roberts	N	?	N	Y	Y		Johnson	Y	Y	Y	Y	Y
Moran	N	N	Y	Y	Y		Thune	N	Y	Y	Y	Y
KENTUCKY							**TENNESSEE**					
McConnell	N	N	N	Y	Y		Alexander	N	N	N	Y	Y
Paul	N	N	N	?	Y		Corker	N	N	N	N	Y
LOUISIANA							**TEXAS**					
Landrieu	?	Y	Y	Y	Y		Hutchison	N	N	N	Y	Y
Vitter	N	N	N	Y	Y		Cornyn	N	N	N	N	Y
MAINE							**UTAH**					
Snowe	Y	Y	Y	Y	Y		Hatch	N	Y	N	Y	Y
Collins	N	Y	Y	Y	Y		Lee	N	N	N	N	Y
MARYLAND							**VERMONT**					
Mikulski	Y	Y	Y	Y	Y		Leahy	Y	Y	Y	Y	Y
Cardin	Y	Y	Y	Y	Y		Sanders	Y	Y	Y	Y	Y
MASSACHUSETTS							**VIRGINIA**					
Kerry	Y	Y	-Y	Y	Y		Webb	Y	N	N	Y	Y
Brown	N	Y	N	Y	Y		Warner	Y	Y	Y	Y	Y
MICHIGAN							**WASHINGTON**					
Levin	Y	Y	Y	Y	Y		Murray	Y	Y	Y	Y	Y
Stabenow	Y	Y	Y	Y	Y		Cantwell	Y	Y	Y	Y	Y
MINNESOTA							**WEST VIRGINIA**					
Klobuchar	Y	Y	Y	Y	Y		Rockefeller	Y	Y	Y	Y	Y
Franken	Y	Y	Y	Y	Y		Manchin	Y	N	Y	Y	Y
MISSISSIPPI							**WISCONSIN**					
Cochran	N	N	Y	Y	Y		Kohl	Y	Y	Y	Y	Y
Wicker	N	N	N	Y	Y		Johnson	N	N	N	N	Y
MISSOURI							**WYOMING**					
McCaskill	Y	Y	Y	Y	?		Enzi	N	N	N	Y	Y
Blunt	N	N	Y	Y	Y		Barrasso	N	Y	N	Y	Y

KEY   **Republicans**   Democrats   *Independents*

Y Voted for (yea)	X Paired against	C Voted "present" to avoid possible conflict of interest
# Paired for	– Announced against	
+ Announced for	P Voted "present"	? Did not vote or otherwise make a position known
N Voted against (nay)		

IN THE SENATE | By Vote Number

209. **S 3254. Fiscal 2013 Defense Authorization/Biofuel Refineries.**
Hagan, D-N.C., amendment that would strike a section of the bill that would prohibit the Defense Department from entering into a contract to plan, refurbish or construct a biofuel refinery or similar facility unless authorized by law. Adopted 54-41: D 48-1; R 4-40; I 2-0. Nov. 29, 2012.

210. **S 3254. Fiscal 2013 Defense Authorization/Afghanistan Withdrawal.** Merkley, D-Ore., amendment that would express the sense of Congress that security operations in Afghanistan should be transferred to the Afghanistan government by midsummer 2013 and combat operations by U.S. troops should end no later than Dec. 31, 2014. Adopted 62-33: D 48-1; R 13-31; I 1-1. Nov. 29, 2012.

211. **S 3254. Fiscal 2013 Defense Authorization/Tricare Coverage.**
Gillibrand, D-N.Y., amendment that would expand coverage of the military health insurance program Tricare to include behavioral health treatment for autism spectrum disorders when prescribed by a doctor. Adopted 66-29: D 48-1; R 16-28; I 2-0. Nov. 29, 2012.

212. **S 3254. Fiscal 2013 Defense Authorization/Guantánamo Bay Detainees.** Ayotte, R-N.H., amendment that would prohibit the transfer of detainees from Guantánamo Bay military facilities to the United States. Adopted 54-41: D 9-40; R 44-0; I 1-1. A "nay" was a vote in support of the president's position. Nov. 29, 2012.

213. **S 3254. Fiscal 2013 Defense Authorization/Indefinite Detention.** Feinstein, D-Calif., amendment that would make it unlawful to detain a U.S. citizen or permanent resident apprehended in the United States without charge or trial. Adopted 67-29: D 46-3; R 20-25; I 1-1. Nov. 29, 2012.

	209	210	211	212	213
ALABAMA					
Shelby	N	N	N	Y	N
Sessions	N	N	N	Y	N
ALASKA					
Murkowski	N	N	Y	Y	Y
Begich	Y	Y	Y	N	Y
ARIZONA					
McCain	N	N	N	Y	Y
Kyl	N	N	N	Y	N
ARKANSAS					
Pryor	Y	N	Y	Y	N
Boozman	N	N	N	Y	Y
CALIFORNIA					
Feinstein	Y	Y	Y	N	Y
Boxer	Y	Y	Y	N	Y
COLORADO					
Udall	Y	Y	Y	N	Y
Bennet	Y	Y	Y	N	Y
CONNECTICUT					
Lieberman	Y	N	Y	Y	N
Blumenthal	Y	Y	Y	N	Y
DELAWARE					
Carper	Y	Y	Y	N	Y
Coons	Y	Y	Y	N	Y
FLORIDA					
Nelson	Y	Y	Y	N	Y
Rubio	N	N	Y	Y	N
GEORGIA					
Chambliss	N	N	Y	Y	N
Isakson	N	N	Y	Y	N
HAWAII					
Inouye	Y	Y	Y	Y	Y
Akaka	Y	Y	Y	N	Y
IDAHO					
Crapo	N	N	N	Y	Y
Risch	N	N	N	Y	Y
ILLINOIS					
Durbin	Y	Y	Y	N	Y
Kirk	?	?	?	?	?
INDIANA					
Lugar	Y	Y	Y	Y	N
Coats	N	N	Y	Y	Y
IOWA					
Grassley	Y	Y	Y	Y	N
Harkin	Y	Y	Y	N	Y
KANSAS					
Roberts	N	N	Y	Y	N
Moran	N	Y	Y	Y	Y
KENTUCKY					
McConnell	N	N	Y	Y	N
Paul	N	Y	N	Y	Y
LOUISIANA					
Landrieu	Y	Y	Y	Y	Y
Vitter	N	N	N	Y	N
MAINE					
Snowe	N	Y	Y	Y	Y
Collins	Y	Y	Y	Y	Y
MARYLAND					
Mikulski	Y	Y	Y	N	Y
Cardin	Y	Y	Y	N	Y
MASSACHUSETTS					
Kerry	Y	Y	Y	N	Y
Brown	N	Y	Y	Y	N
MICHIGAN					
Levin	Y	Y	Y	N	Y
Stabenow	Y	Y	Y	Y	Y
MINNESOTA					
Klobuchar	Y	Y	Y	N	Y
Franken	Y	Y	Y	N	Y
MISSISSIPPI					
Cochran	N	Y	N	Y	N
Wicker	N	N	N	Y	N
MISSOURI					
McCaskill	?	?	Y	N	Y
Blunt	N	N	N	Y	Y

	209	210	211	212	213
MONTANA					
Baucus	Y	Y	Y	Y	Y
Tester	Y	Y	Y	N	Y
NEBRASKA					
Nelson	Y	Y	N	Y	N
Johanns	Y	N	N	Y	N
NEVADA					
Reid	Y	Y	Y	N	Y
Heller	?	?	?	?	+
NEW HAMPSHIRE					
Shaheen	Y	Y	Y	N	Y
Ayotte	N	N	Y	Y	N
NEW JERSEY					
Lautenberg	Y	Y	?	N	Y
Menendez	Y	Y	Y	N	Y
NEW MEXICO					
Bingaman	Y	Y	Y	N	Y
Udall	Y	Y	Y	N	Y
NEW YORK					
Schumer	Y	Y	Y	N	Y
Gillibrand	Y	Y	Y	N	Y
NORTH CAROLINA					
Burr	N	N	N	Y	N
Hagan	Y	Y	Y	Y	Y
NORTH DAKOTA					
Conrad	Y	Y	Y	N	Y
Hoeven	N	Y	N	Y	Y
OHIO					
Brown	Y	Y	Y	N	Y
Portman	N	N	N	Y	N
OKLAHOMA					
Inhofe	N	N	N	Y	N
Coburn	N	N	N	Y	Y
OREGON					
Wyden	?	?	?	?	?
Merkley	Y	Y	Y	N	Y
PENNSYLVANIA					
Casey	Y	Y	Y	N	Y
Toomey	N	Y	N	Y	N
RHODE ISLAND					
Reed	Y	Y	Y	N	Y
Whitehouse	Y	Y	Y	N	Y
SOUTH CAROLINA					
Graham	N	N	Y	Y	Y
DeMint	?	?	?	?	Y
SOUTH DAKOTA					
Johnson	Y	Y	Y	N	Y
Thune	N	Y	N	Y	N
TENNESSEE					
Alexander	N	N	N	Y	Y
Corker	N	Y	N	Y	Y
TEXAS					
Hutchison	N	N	Y	Y	N
Cornyn	N	N	N	Y	N
UTAH					
Hatch	N	N	Y	Y	N
Lee	N	Y	N	Y	Y
VERMONT					
Leahy	Y	Y	Y	N	Y
Sanders	Y	Y	Y	N	Y
VIRGINIA					
Webb	N	Y	Y	Y	Y
Warner	Y	Y	Y	N	Y
WASHINGTON					
Murray	Y	Y	Y	N	Y
Cantwell	Y	Y	Y	N	Y
WEST VIRGINIA					
Rockefeller	Y	Y	Y	?	?
Manchin	Y	Y	Y	N	Y
WISCONSIN					
Kohl	Y	Y	Y	N	Y
Johnson	N	N	N	Y	N
WYOMING					
Enzi	N	N	N	Y	Y
Barrasso	N	N	N	Y	Y

KEY   **Republicans**   Democrats   *Independents*

Y Voted for (yea)	**X** Paired against
# Paired for	**–** Announced against
+ Announced for	**P** Voted "present"
N Voted against (nay)	

C Voted "present" to avoid possible conflict of interest

? Did not vote or otherwise make a position known

IN THE SENATE | By Vote Number

214. S 3254. **Fiscal 2013 Defense Authorization/Civilian and Contractor Workforces.** Cardin, D-Md., amendment that would direct the Defense secretary to ensure that civilian and contract services workforces are sufficiently sized. Rejected 41-53: D 37-12; R 2-41; I 2-0. Nov. 30, 2012.

215. S 3254. **Fiscal 2013 Defense Authorization/Iran Sanctions.** Menendez, D-N.J., amendment that would bar all transactions with Iran's energy, shipping and shipbuilding sectors and its ports. It would ban the sale to Iran of certain metals, including graphite, aluminum, steel and metallurgical coal, which are used in those sectors and in other industrial processes. Adopted 94-0: D 49-0; R 43-0; I 2-0. Nov. 30, 2012.

216. S 3254. **Fiscal 2013 Defense Authorization/Motion to Waive.** Nelson, D-Fla., motion to waive all applicable budget laws and budget resolutions with respect to the Corker, R-Tenn., point of order against the Nelson amendment that would repeal a provision to reduce annuities paid to the surviving spouses of military personnel by the amount of dependency and indemnity compensation to which the spouses are entitled. Motion rejected 58-34: D 47-1; R 9-33; I 2-0. A three-fifths majority vote of the total Senate (60) is required to waive the applicable budget laws. Nov. 30, 2012.

217. **Grimm Nomination/Confirmation.** Confirmation of President Obama's nomination of Paul William Grimm of Maryland to be a judge for the U.S. District Court for the District of Maryland. Confirmed 92-1: D 47-0; R 44-1; I 1-0. A "yea" was a vote in support of the president's position. Dec. 3, 2012.

218. S 3254. **Fiscal 2013 Defense Authorization/Cloture.** Motion to invoke cloture (thus limiting debate) on the bill that would authorize $525.8 billion for the base Defense Department budget and $88.2 billion for the overseas contingency operations, which include military activities in Afghanistan. The bill also would authorize $17.4 billion for defense programs in the Energy Department. Motion agreed to 93-0: D 47-0; R 45-0; I 1-0. Three-fifths of the total Senate (60) is required to invoke cloture. Dec. 3, 2012.

219. Treaty Doc 112-7. **Convention on the Rights of Persons with Disabilities/Adoption.** Adoption of the resolution of ratification of the Convention on the Rights of Persons with Disabilities, which would establish global standards for the treatment of people with disabilities. The resolution would state that current U.S. law fulfills or exceeds the obligations of the treaty. Rejected 61-38: D 51-0; R 8-38; I 2-0. A two-thirds majority of those present and voting, 66 in this case, is required for adoption of resolutions of ratification. A "yea" was a vote in support of the president's position. Dec. 4, 2012.

	214	215	216	217	218	219
ALABAMA						
Shelby	N	Y	N	Y	Y	N
Sessions	N	Y	N	Y	Y	N
ALASKA						
Murkowski	Y	Y	Y	Y	Y	Y
Begich	Y	Y	Y	Y	Y	Y
ARIZONA						
McCain	N	Y	N	Y	Y	Y
Kyl	N	Y	N	Y	Y	N
ARKANSAS						
Pryor	Y	Y	Y	Y	Y	Y
Boozman	N	Y	Y	Y	Y	N
CALIFORNIA						
Feinstein	N	Y	Y	Y	Y	Y
Boxer	Y	Y	Y	Y	Y	Y
COLORADO						
Udall	Y	Y	Y	Y	Y	Y
Bennet	N	Y	Y	Y	Y	Y
CONNECTICUT						
Lieberman	Y	Y	Y	Y	Y	Y
Blumenthal	Y	Y	Y	Y	Y	Y
DELAWARE						
Carper	N	Y	N	Y	Y	Y
Coons	Y	Y	Y	Y	Y	Y
FLORIDA						
Nelson	Y	Y	Y	Y	Y	Y
Rubio	N	Y	Y	Y	Y	Y
GEORGIA						
Chambliss	N	Y	N	Y	Y	N
Isakson	N	Y	N	Y	Y	N
HAWAII						
Inouye	Y	Y	Y	Y	Y	Y
Akaka	Y	Y	Y	Y	Y	Y
IDAHO						
Crapo	N	Y	N	Y	Y	N
Risch	N	Y	N	Y	Y	N
ILLINOIS						
Durbin	Y	Y	Y	Y	Y	Y
Kirk	?	?	?	?	?	?
INDIANA						
Lugar	N	Y	N	Y	Y	Y
Coats	N	Y	N	Y	Y	N
IOWA						
Grassley	N	Y	N	Y	Y	N
Harkin	Y	Y	Y	Y	Y	Y
KANSAS						
Roberts	N	Y	N	Y	Y	N
Moran	N	Y	Y	Y	Y	N
KENTUCKY						
McConnell	N	Y	N	Y	Y	N
Paul	N	Y	N	Y	Y	N
LOUISIANA						
Landrieu	Y	Y	Y	Y	Y	Y
Vitter	N	Y	N	?	?	N
MAINE						
Snowe	Y	Y	Y	Y	Y	Y
Collins	N	Y	Y	Y	Y	Y
MARYLAND						
Mikulski	Y	Y	Y	Y	Y	Y
Cardin	Y	Y	Y	Y	Y	Y
MASSACHUSETTS						
Kerry	Y	Y	Y	Y	Y	Y
Brown	N	Y	Y	Y	Y	Y
MICHIGAN						
Levin	N	Y	Y	Y	Y	Y
Stabenow	Y	Y	Y	Y	Y	Y
MINNESOTA						
Klobuchar	N	Y	Y	Y	Y	Y
Franken	Y	Y	Y	?	?	Y
MISSISSIPPI						
Cochran	N	Y	N	Y	Y	N
Wicker	N	Y	Y	Y	Y	N
MISSOURI						
McCaskill	Y	Y	Y	Y	Y	Y
Blunt	N	Y	Y	N	Y	N

	214	215	216	217	218	219
MONTANA						
Baucus	N	Y	Y	Y	Y	Y
Tester	Y	Y	Y	Y	Y	Y
NEBRASKA						
Nelson	Y	Y	Y	Y	Y	Y
Johanns	N	Y	N	Y	Y	N
NEVADA						
Reid	Y	Y	Y	Y	Y	Y
Heller	?	+	?	Y	Y	N
NEW HAMPSHIRE						
Shaheen	Y	Y	Y	Y	Y	Y
Ayotte	N	Y	N	Y	Y	Y
NEW JERSEY						
Lautenberg	Y	Y	Y	Y	Y	Y
Menendez	Y	Y	Y	Y	Y	Y
NEW MEXICO						
Bingaman	N	Y	Y	Y	Y	Y
Udall	Y	Y	Y	Y	Y	Y
NEW YORK						
Schumer	Y	Y	Y	Y	Y	Y
Gillibrand	Y	Y	Y	Y	Y	Y
NORTH CAROLINA						
Burr	N	Y	N	Y	Y	N
Hagan	Y	Y	Y	Y	Y	Y
NORTH DAKOTA						
Conrad	N	Y	Y	Y	Y	Y
Hoeven	N	Y	N	Y	Y	N
OHIO						
Brown	Y	Y	Y	Y	Y	Y
Portman	N	Y	N	Y	Y	N
OKLAHOMA						
Inhofe	N	Y	N	Y	Y	N
Coburn	N	Y	N	Y	Y	N
OREGON						
Wyden	?	?	?	?	?	Y
Merkley	Y	Y	Y	+	+	Y
PENNSYLVANIA						
Casey	Y	Y	Y	Y	Y	Y
Toomey	N	Y	N	Y	Y	N
RHODE ISLAND						
Reed	Y	Y	Y	Y	Y	Y
Whitehouse	N	Y	Y	Y	Y	Y
SOUTH CAROLINA						
Graham	N	Y	N	Y	Y	N
DeMint	N	Y	N	Y	Y	N
SOUTH DAKOTA						
Johnson	N	Y	Y	Y	Y	Y
Thune	N	Y	N	Y	Y	N
TENNESSEE						
Alexander	–	+	–	Y	Y	N
Corker	N	Y	N	Y	Y	N
TEXAS						
Hutchison	N	Y	?	Y	Y	N
Cornyn	N	Y	N	Y	Y	N
UTAH						
Hatch	?	?	+	Y	Y	N
Lee	N	Y	N	Y	Y	N
VERMONT						
Leahy	Y	Y	Y	Y	Y	Y
Sanders	Y	Y	Y	?	?	Y
VIRGINIA						
Webb	Y	Y	Y	Y	Y	Y
Warner	Y	Y	Y	Y	Y	Y
WASHINGTON						
Murray	Y	Y	?	Y	Y	Y
Cantwell	Y	Y	Y	Y	Y	Y
WEST VIRGINIA						
Rockefeller	?	?	?	?	?	Y
Manchin	N	Y	Y	Y	Y	Y
WISCONSIN						
Kohl	N	Y	Y	Y	Y	Y
Johnson	N	Y	N	Y	Y	N
WYOMING						
Enzi	N	Y	N	Y	Y	N
Barrasso	N	Y	N	Y	Y	Y

KEY **Republicans** Democrats *Independents*

Y Voted for (yea)	**X** Paired against
# Paired for	**–** Announced against
+ Announced for	**P** Voted "present"
N Voted against (nay)	

C Voted "present" to avoid possible conflict of interest

? Did not vote or otherwise make a position known

IN THE SENATE | By Vote Number

220. S 3254. Fiscal 2013 Defense Authorization/Syria Study.

McCain, R-Ariz., amendment that would require a classified Pentagon report on the possibility of limited U.S. military action against Syria's air force, including an assessment of possible airstrikes, the deployment of air defense systems in neighboring countries and the imposition of no-fly zones over population centers. Adopted 92-6: D 49-1; R 41-5; I 2-0. Dec. 4, 2012.

221. S 3254. Fiscal 2013 Defense Authorization/Passage.

Passage of the bill that would authorize $631.4 billion for defense programs in fiscal 2013, including $88.2 billion for overseas contingency operations. Excluding the war funding, it would authorize $174.8 billion for operations and maintenance; $97 billion for procurement; $135.1 billion for military personnel; $10.6 billion for military construction, family housing and base closure; $69.3 billion for research, development, testing and evaluation; $9.7 billion for missile defense; and $32.9 billion for the Defense Health Program. The bill would authorize a 1.7 percent pay increase for military personnel. As amended, it would bar all transactions with Iran's energy, shipping and shipbuilding sectors and its ports. It also would make it unlawful to detain a U.S. citizen or permanent resident apprehended in the United States without charge or trial and would prohibit the transfer of detainees from military facilities in Guantánamo Bay, Cuba, to the United States. Passed 98-0: D 50-0; R 46-0; I 2-0. A "nay" was a vote in support of the president's position. Dec. 4, 2012.

222. Shea Nomination/Confirmation.

Confirmation of President Obama's nomination of Michael P. Shea of Connecticut to be a judge for the U.S. District Court for the District of Connecticut. Confirmed 72-23: D 49-0; R 21-23; I 2-0. A "yea" was a vote in support of the president's position. Dec. 5, 2012.

223. HR 6156. Russia Trade Relations/Passage.

Passage of the bill that would establish permanent normal trade relations with Russia and Moldova and end Jackson-Vanik restrictions on both economies. The bill also would provide sanctions against persons involved in human rights violations in Russia. Passed (thus cleared for the president) 92-4: D 45-3; R 46-0; I 1-1. A "yea" was a vote in support of the president's position. Dec. 6, 2012.

224. Walker Nomination/Confirmation.

Confirmation of President Obama's nomination of Mark E. Walker to be a judge for the U.S. District Court for the Northern District of Florida. Confirmed 94-0: D 48-0; R 44-0; I 2-0. A "yea" was a vote in support of the president's position. Dec. 6, 2012.

	220	221	222	223	224		220	221	222	223	224
ALABAMA						**MONTANA**					
Shelby	Y	Y	Y	Y	Y	Baucus	Y	Y	Y	Y	Y
Sessions	Y	Y	Y	Y	Y	Tester	Y	Y	Y	Y	Y
ALASKA						**NEBRASKA**					
Murkowski	Y	Y	Y	Y	Y	Nelson	Y	Y	Y	Y	Y
Begich	Y	Y	Y	Y	Y	Johanns	Y	Y	Y	Y	Y
ARIZONA						**NEVADA**					
McCain	Y	Y	Y	Y	Y	Reid	Y	Y	Y	Y	Y
Kyl	Y	Y	Y	Y	Y	Heller	Y	Y	N	Y	Y
ARKANSAS						**NEW HAMPSHIRE**					
Pryor	Y	Y	Y	Y	Y	Shaheen	Y	Y	Y	Y	Y
Boozman	Y	Y	N	Y	Y	Ayotte	Y	Y	Y	Y	Y
CALIFORNIA						**NEW JERSEY**					
Feinstein	Y	Y	Y	Y	Y	Lautenberg	Y	Y	Y	Y	Y
Boxer	Y	Y	Y	Y	Y	Menendez	Y	Y	Y	Y	Y
COLORADO						**NEW MEXICO**					
Udall	Y	Y	Y	Y	Y	Bingaman	Y	Y	Y	Y	Y
Bennet	Y	Y	Y	Y	Y	Udall	Y	Y	Y	Y	Y
CONNECTICUT						**NEW YORK**					
Lieberman	Y	Y	Y	Y	Y	Schumer	Y	Y	Y	Y	Y
Blumenthal	Y	Y	Y	Y	Y	Gillibrand	Y	Y	Y	Y	Y
DELAWARE						**NORTH CAROLINA**					
Carper	Y	Y	Y	Y	Y	Burr	Y	Y	Y	Y	?
Coons	Y	Y	Y	Y	Y	Hagan	Y	Y	Y	Y	Y
FLORIDA						**NORTH DAKOTA**					
Nelson	Y	Y	Y	Y	Y	Conrad	Y	Y	Y	+	?
Rubio	Y	Y	N	Y	Y	Hoeven	Y	Y	Y	Y	Y
GEORGIA						**OHIO**					
Chambliss	Y	Y	N	Y	Y	Brown	Y	Y	Y	Y	Y
Isakson	Y	Y	N	Y	Y	Portman	Y	Y	Y	Y	Y
HAWAII						**OKLAHOMA**					
Inouye	Y	Y	Y	?	?	Inhofe	Y	Y	N	Y	Y
Akaka	Y	Y	Y	Y	Y	Coburn	Y	Y	N	Y	Y
IDAHO						**OREGON**					
Crapo	Y	Y	N	Y	Y	Wyden	Y	Y	Y	Y	Y
Risch	Y	Y	N	Y	Y	Merkley	Y	Y	Y	Y	Y
ILLINOIS						**PENNSYLVANIA**					
Durbin	N	Y	Y	Y	Y	Casey	Y	Y	Y	Y	Y
Kirk	?	?	?	?	?	Toomey	Y	Y	N	Y	Y
INDIANA						**RHODE ISLAND**					
Lugar	Y	Y	Y	Y	Y	Reed	Y	Y	Y	N	Y
Coats	Y	Y	Y	Y	Y	Whitehouse	Y	Y	Y	N	Y
IOWA						**SOUTH CAROLINA**					
Grassley	Y	Y	Y	Y	Y	Graham	Y	Y	Y	Y	Y
Harkin	Y	Y	Y	Y	Y	DeMint	N	Y	-	Y	?
KANSAS						**SOUTH DAKOTA**					
Roberts	Y	Y	N	Y	Y	Johnson	Y	Y	Y	Y	Y
Moran	Y	Y	Y	Y	Y	Thune	Y	Y	N	Y	Y
KENTUCKY						**TENNESSEE**					
McConnell	Y	Y	N	Y	Y	Alexander	N	Y	-	Y	Y
Paul	N	Y	N	Y	Y	Corker	Y	Y	Y	Y	Y
LOUISIANA						**TEXAS**					
Landrieu	Y	Y	Y	Y	Y	Hutchison	N	Y	N	Y	Y
Vitter	Y	Y	N	Y	Y	Cornyn	Y	Y	N	Y	Y
MAINE						**UTAH**					
Snowe	Y	Y	Y	Y	Y	Hatch	Y	Y	Y	Y	Y
Collins	Y	Y	Y	Y	Y	Lee	N	Y	N	Y	Y
MARYLAND						**VERMONT**					
Mikulski	Y	Y	Y	Y	Y	Leahy	Y	Y	Y	Y	Y
Cardin	Y	Y	Y	Y	Y	Sanders	Y	Y	Y	N	Y
MASSACHUSETTS						**VIRGINIA**					
Kerry	Y	Y	Y	Y	Y	Webb	Y	Y	?	Y	Y
Brown	Y	Y	Y	Y	Y	Warner	Y	Y	Y	Y	Y
MICHIGAN						**WASHINGTON**					
Levin	Y	Y	Y	N	Y	Murray	Y	Y	Y	Y	Y
Stabenow	Y	Y	Y	Y	Y	Cantwell	Y	Y	Y	Y	Y
MINNESOTA						**WEST VIRGINIA**					
Klobuchar	Y	Y	Y	Y	Y	Rockefeller	?	?	?	?	?
Franken	Y	Y	Y	Y	Y	Manchin	Y	Y	Y	Y	Y
MISSISSIPPI						**WISCONSIN**					
Cochran	Y	Y	N	Y	Y	Kohl	Y	Y	Y	Y	Y
Wicker	Y	Y	N	Y	Y	Johnson	Y	Y	Y	Y	Y
MISSOURI						**WYOMING**					
McCaskill	Y	Y	Y	Y	Y	Enzi	Y	Y	N	Y	Y
Blunt	Y	Y	N	Y	Y	Barrasso	Y	Y	N	Y	Y

KEY	**Republicans**		Democrats	*Independents*	
Y	Voted for (yea)	X	Paired against	C	Voted "present" to avoid possible conflict of interest
#	Paired for	-	Announced against		
+	Announced for	P	Voted "present"	?	Did not vote or otherwise make a position known
N	Voted against (nay)				

IN THE SENATE | By Vote Number

225. **S 3637. TAG Program Extension/Cloture.** Motion to invoke cloture (thus limiting debate) on the motion to proceed to consideration of a bill that would extend the Federal Deposit Insurance Corporation's Transaction Account Guarantee program until Dec. 31, 2014. The program provides unlimited deposit insurance for non-interest-bearing transaction accounts. Motion agreed to 76-20: D 49-0; R 25-20; I 2-0. Three-fifths of the total Senate (60) is required to invoke cloture. Dec. 11, 2012.

226. **Dowdell Nomination/Confirmation.** Confirmation on President Obama's nomination of John E. Dowdell of Oklahoma to be a judge for the U.S. District Court for the Northern District of Oklahoma. Confirmed 95-0: D 47-0; R 46-0; I 2-0. A "yea" was a vote in support of the president's position. Dec. 11, 2012.

227. **S 3637. TAG Program Extension/Motion to Waive.** Reid, D-Nev., motion to waive all applicable budget laws with respect to the Toomey, R-Pa., point of order against the bill that would extend the Federal Deposit Insurance Corporation's Transaction Account Guarantee program until Dec. 31, 2014. The program provides unlimited deposit insurance for non-interest-bearing transaction accounts. Motion rejected 50-42: D 46-1; R 2-41; I 2-0. A three-fifths majority vote of the total Senate (60) is required to waive the applicable budget laws. A "yea" was a vote in support of the president's position. Dec. 13, 2012.

228. **Schofield Nomination/Confirmation.** Confirmation on President Obama's nomination of Lorna G. Schofield of New York to be a judge for the U.S. District Court for the Southern District of New York. Confirmed 91-0: D 48-0; R 41-0; I 2-0. A "yea" was a vote in support of the president's position. Dec. 13, 2012.

	225	226	227	228		225	226	227	228
ALABAMA					**MONTANA**				
Shelby	N	Y	N	Y	Baucus	Y	Y	Y	Y
Sessions	N	Y	N	Y	Tester	Y	Y	Y	Y
ALASKA					**NEBRASKA**				
Murkowski	Y	Y	N	Y	Nelson	Y	?	Y	Y
Begich	Y	Y	Y	Y	Johanns	Y	Y	N	Y
ARIZONA					**NEVADA**				
McCain	Y	Y	?	?	Reid	Y	Y	Y	Y
Kyl	Y	Y	N	Y	Heller	N	Y	N	Y
ARKANSAS					**NEW HAMPSHIRE**				
Pryor	Y	Y	Y	Y	Shaheen	Y	Y	Y	Y
Boozman	Y	Y	N	Y	Ayotte	N	Y	N	Y
CALIFORNIA					**NEW JERSEY**				
Feinstein	Y	Y	Y	Y	Lautenberg	?	?	?	?
Boxer	Y	Y	?	?	Menendez	Y	Y	Y	Y
COLORADO					**NEW MEXICO**				
Udall	Y	Y	Y	Y	Bingaman	Y	Y	Y	Y
Bennet	Y	Y	Y	Y	Udall	Y	Y	Y	Y
CONNECTICUT					**NEW YORK**				
Lieberman	Y	Y	Y	Y	Schumer	Y	Y	Y	Y
Blumenthal	Y	Y	Y	Y	Gillibrand	Y	Y	Y	Y
DELAWARE					**NORTH CAROLINA**				
Carper	Y	Y	Y	Y	Burr	Y	Y	N	Y
Coons	Y	Y	Y	Y	Hagan	Y	Y	Y	Y
FLORIDA					**NORTH DAKOTA**				
Nelson	Y	Y	Y	Y	Conrad	Y	Y	Y	Y
Rubio	N	Y	N	Y	Hoeven	Y	Y	?	?
GEORGIA					**OHIO**				
Chambliss	?	Y	N	Y	Brown	Y	Y	Y	Y
Isakson	Y	Y	N	Y	Portman	Y	Y	N	Y
HAWAII					**OKLAHOMA**				
Inouye	?	?	?	?	Inhofe	N	Y	?	?
Akaka	Y	Y	Y	Y	Coburn	N	Y	N	Y
IDAHO					**OREGON**				
Crapo	N	Y	N	Y	Wyden	Y	Y	Y	Y
Risch	N	Y	N	Y	Merkley	Y	Y	Y	Y
ILLINOIS					**PENNSYLVANIA**				
Durbin	Y	Y	Y	Y	Casey	Y	Y	Y	Y
Kirk	?	?	?	?	Toomey	N	Y	N	Y
INDIANA					**RHODE ISLAND**				
Lugar	Y	Y	N	Y	Reed	Y	Y	Y	Y
Coats	Y	Y	N	Y	Whitehouse	Y	Y	Y	Y
IOWA					**SOUTH CAROLINA**				
Grassley	Y	Y	N	Y	Graham	N	Y	N	Y
Harkin	Y	Y	Y	Y	DeMint	N	Y	N	Y
KANSAS					**SOUTH DAKOTA**				
Roberts	N	Y	N	Y	Johnson	Y	Y	Y	Y
Moran	Y	Y	N	?	Thune	N	Y	N	Y
KENTUCKY					**TENNESSEE**				
McConnell	Y	Y	N	Y	Alexander	Y	Y	N	Y
Paul	N	Y	N	Y	Corker	N	Y	N	Y
LOUISIANA					**TEXAS**				
Landrieu	Y	Y	Y	Y	Hutchison	Y	Y	Y	Y
Vitter	Y	Y	N	?	Cornyn	Y	Y	N	Y
MAINE					**UTAH**				
Snowe	Y	Y	N	Y	Hatch	N	Y	N	Y
Collins	Y	Y	Y	Y	Lee	N	Y	N	Y
MARYLAND					**VERMONT**				
Mikulski	Y	Y	N	Y	Leahy	Y	Y	?	Y
Cardin	Y	Y	Y	Y	Sanders	Y	Y	Y	Y
MASSACHUSETTS					**VIRGINIA**				
Kerry	Y	Y	Y	Y	Webb	Y	Y	Y	Y
Brown	Y	Y	N	Y	Warner	Y	Y	Y	Y
MICHIGAN					**WASHINGTON**				
Levin	Y	Y	Y	Y	Murray	Y	Y	Y	Y
Stabenow	Y	Y	Y	Y	Cantwell	Y	Y	Y	Y
MINNESOTA					**WEST VIRGINIA**				
Klobuchar	Y	Y	Y	Y	Rockefeller	Y	Y	Y	Y
Franken	Y	Y	Y	Y	Manchin	Y	Y	Y	Y
MISSISSIPPI					**WISCONSIN**				
Cochran	Y	Y	N	Y	Kohl	Y	Y	Y	Y
Wicker	Y	Y	N	Y	Johnson	N	Y	N	Y
MISSOURI					**WYOMING**				
McCaskill	Y	?	Y	Y	Enzi	Y	Y	N	Y
Blunt	Y	Y	N	Y	Barrasso	N	Y	N	Y

KEY   **Republicans**   Democrats   *Independents*

Y	Voted for (yea)	X	Paired against
#	Paired for	–	Announced against
+	Announced for	P	Voted "present"
N	Voted against (nay)		

C   Voted "present" to avoid possible conflict of interest

?   Did not vote or otherwise make a position known

IN THE SENATE | By Vote Number

229. HR 4310. Fiscal 2013 Defense Authorization/Conference Report.
Adoption of the conference report on the bill that would authorize $648.7 billion for defense programs in fiscal 2013, including $85.5 billion for overseas military operations. It would authorize $237.7 billion for operations and maintenance and $149.8 billion for military personnel. It would authorize $10.8 billion for military construction and family housing projects but prohibit funds to start another round of base closures. It would authorize $33.6 billion for the Defense Health Program as well as a 1.7 percent pay raise for military personnel. The measure would block the use of Defense Department funds for one year to transfer or release prisoners at the Guantánamo Bay, Cuba, detention center into the United States and its territories or possessions. It also would clarify that suspected U.S. terrorists detained inside the United States be tried only in federal civilian courts. It would authorize the use of Defense Department funds for abortion for military personnel in cases of rape or incest. Adopted (thus cleared for the president) 81-14: D 44-6; R 36-7; I 1-1. Dec. 21, 2012.

230. HR 1. Superstorm Supplemental/Cloture.
Motion to invoke cloture (thus limiting debate) on the Reid, D-Nev., substitute amendment that would provide $60.4 billion in emergency spending for communities hit by Superstorm Sandy, including an additional $9.7 billion in borrowing authority of the National Flood Insurance Program, $13 billion for mitigation projects, $11.5 billion for the Federal Emergency Management Agency's Disaster Relief Fund and $10.8 billion to the Federal Transit Administration to rebuild public transit systems. Motion agreed to 91-1: D 50-0; R 39-1; I 2-0. A three-fifths majority vote of the total Senate (60) is required to invoke cloture. Dec. 21, 2012.

231. HR 1. Superstorm Supplemental/Motion to Waive.
Mikulski, D-Md., motion to waive the Budget Act with respect to the Toomey, R-Pa., point of order against the Reid, D-Nev., substitute amendment that would provide $60.4 billion in emergency spending for communities hit by Superstorm Sandy. Motion rejected 57-34: D 50-0; R 5-34; I 2-0. A three-fifths majority vote of the total Senate (60) is required to waive the Budget Act. Dec. 21, 2012.

232. HR 5949. FISA Reauthorization/Substitute Amendment.
Leahy, D-Vt., substitute amendment that would reauthorize until June 2015, the Foreign Intelligence Surveillance Act, which governs electronic surveillance of foreign terrorism suspects. It also would require the intelligence community inspector general to review the implementation of surveillance authorities and report findings to Congress no later than Dec. 31, 2014. Rejected 38-52: D 36-10; R 2-41; I 0-1. (By unanimous consent, the Senate agreed to raise the majority requirement for adoption of the Leahy amendment to 60 votes.) Dec. 27, 2012.

233. HR 5949. FISA Reauthorization/Intelligence Surveillance Court Disclosures.
Merkley, D-Ore., amendment that would require the government to disclose Foreign Intelligence Surveillance Court decisions, orders or opinions on surveillance requests unless such a disclosure is not in the interest of U.S. national security. Rejected 37-54: D 34-13; R 3-40; I 0-1. (By unanimous consent, the Senate agreed to raise the majority requirement for adoption of the Merkley amendment to 60 votes.) Dec. 27, 2012.

234. HR 5949. FISA Reauthorization/Third-Party Information.
Paul, R-Ky., amendment that would require the government to either get a warrant or express consent to obtain information given to third parties. Rejected 12-79: D 9-38; R 3-40; I 0-1. (By unanimous consent, the Senate agreed to raise the majority requirement for adoption of the Paul amendment to 60 votes.) Dec. 27, 2012.

* Sen. Brian Schatz, D-Hawaii, was sworn in Dec. 27, 2012, to fill the seat vacated by the Dec. 17 death of fellow Democrat Daniel K. Inouye. The last vote for which Inouye was eligible was vote 228; the first vote for which Schatz was eligible was vote 232.

	229	230	231	232	233	234
ALABAMA						
Shelby	Y	Y	Y	N	N	N
Sessions	Y	Y	N	N	N	N
ALASKA						
Murkowski	Y	Y	N	?	?	?
Begich	Y	Y	Y	Y	Y	Y
ARIZONA						
McCain	Y	Y	N	N	N	N
Kyl	Y	N	N	N	N	N
ARKANSAS						
Pryor	Y	Y	Y	N	Y	N
Boozman	Y	Y	N	N	N	N
CALIFORNIA						
Feinstein	Y	Y	Y	N	N	N
Boxer	Y	Y	Y	?	?	?
COLORADO						
Udall	Y	Y	Y	Y	N	N
Bennet	Y	Y	Y	Y	Y	N
CONNECTICUT						
Lieberman	Y	Y	N	N	N	N
Blumenthal	Y	Y	Y	Y	N	N
DELAWARE						
Carper	Y	Y	Y	Y	Y	N
Coons	Y	Y	Y	Y	Y	N
FLORIDA						
Nelson	Y	Y	Y	N	N	N
Rubio	Y	N	N	N	N	N
GEORGIA						
Chambliss	Y	Y	N	N	N	N
Isakson	Y	Y	N	N	N	N
HAWAII						
Akaka	Y	Y	Y	Y	Y	N
Schatz*				Y	Y	N
IDAHO						
Crapo	N	Y	N	N	N	N
Risch	N	Y	N	N	N	N
ILLINOIS						
Durbin	N	Y	Y	Y	Y	N
Kirk	?	?	?	?	?	?
INDIANA						
Lugar	Y	Y	N	N	N	N
Coats	Y	Y	N	N	N	N
IOWA						
Grassley	N	Y	N	N	N	N
Harkin	N	Y	Y	?	?	?
KANSAS						
Roberts	Y	Y	N	N	N	N
Moran	?	?	?	N	N	N
KENTUCKY						
McConnell	Y	Y	N	N	N	N
Paul	N	Y	N	Y	Y	Y
LOUISIANA						
Landrieu	Y	Y	Y	N	N	N
Vitter	Y	Y	Y	N	N	N
MAINE						
Snowe	Y	Y	Y	N	N	N
Collins	Y	Y	N	N	N	N
MARYLAND						
Mikulski	Y	Y	Y	N	N	N
Cardin	Y	Y	Y	Y	N	N
MASSACHUSETTS						
Kerry	Y	Y	Y	N	N	N
Brown	+	+	–	N	N	N
MICHIGAN						
Levin	Y	Y	Y	Y	Y	N
Stabenow	Y	Y	Y	Y	Y	Y
MINNESOTA						
Klobuchar	Y	Y	Y	Y	Y	N
Franken	N	Y	Y	Y	Y	N
MISSISSIPPI						
Cochran	Y	Y	Y	N	N	N
Wicker	Y	Y	N	N	N	N
MISSOURI						
McCaskill	Y	Y	Y	N	N	N
Blunt	Y	Y	Y	N	N	N

	229	230	231	232	233	234
MONTANA						
Baucus	Y	Y	Y	Y	Y	Y
Tester	Y	Y	Y	Y	Y	Y
NEBRASKA						
Nelson	Y	Y	Y	Y	Y	N
Johanns	Y	Y	N	N	N	N
NEVADA						
Reid	Y	Y	Y	Y	Y	N
Heller	Y	Y	N	N	Y	Y
NEW HAMPSHIRE						
Shaheen	Y	Y	Y	Y	Y	N
Ayotte	Y	Y	N	N	N	N
NEW JERSEY						
Lautenberg	Y	Y	Y	?	?	?
Menendez	Y	Y	Y	Y	Y	N
NEW MEXICO						
Bingaman	Y	Y	Y	Y	Y	Y
Udall	Y	Y	Y	Y	Y	Y
NEW YORK						
Schumer	Y	Y	Y	Y	Y	N
Gillibrand	Y	Y	Y	?	Y	N
NORTH CAROLINA						
Burr	Y	?	?	N	N	N
Hagan	Y	Y	Y	N	N	N
NORTH DAKOTA						
Conrad	Y	Y	Y	Y	Y	N
Hoeven	Y	Y	N	N	N	N
OHIO						
Brown	Y	Y	Y	?	?	?
Portman	Y	Y	N	N	N	N
OKLAHOMA						
Inhofe	Y	?	?	?	?	?
Coburn	Y	?	?	N	N	N
OREGON						
Wyden	N	Y	Y	Y	Y	Y
Merkley	N	Y	Y	Y	Y	Y
PENNSYLVANIA						
Casey	Y	Y	Y	Y	N	N
Toomey	Y	N	N	N	N	N
RHODE ISLAND						
Reed	Y	Y	Y	Y	N	N
Whitehouse	Y	Y	Y	Y	N	N
SOUTH CAROLINA						
Graham	Y	Y	N	N	N	N
DeMint	?	?	?	?	?	?
SOUTH DAKOTA						
Johnson	Y	Y	Y	N	N	N
Thune	Y	Y	N	N	N	N
TENNESSEE						
Alexander	Y	Y	N	N	N	N
Corker	Y	Y	N	N	N	N
TEXAS						
Hutchison	Y	Y	N	N	N	N
Cornyn	Y	Y	N	N	N	N
UTAH						
Hatch	Y	Y	N	N	N	N
Lee	N	Y	?	Y	Y	Y
VERMONT						
Leahy	N	Y	Y	Y	Y	N
Sanders	N	Y	Y	?	?	?
VIRGINIA						
Webb	Y	Y	Y	Y	Y	N
Warner	Y	Y	Y	N	N	N
WASHINGTON						
Murray	Y	Y	Y	Y	Y	N
Cantwell	Y	Y	Y	Y	Y	Y
WEST VIRGINIA						
Rockefeller	Y	Y	Y	N	N	N
Manchin	Y	Y	Y	N	N	N
WISCONSIN						
Kohl	Y	Y	Y	Y	N	N
Johnson	Y	Y	N	N	N	N
WYOMING						
Enzi	N	Y	N	N	N	N
Barrasso	N	Y	N	N	N	N

KEY	**Republicans**	Democrats	*Independents*		
Y	Voted for (yea)	X	Paired against	C	Voted "present" to avoid possible conflict of interest
#	Paired for	–	Announced against		
+	Announced for	P	Voted "present"	?	Did not vote or otherwise make a position known
N	Voted against (nay)				

IN THE SENATE | By Vote Number

235. HR 5949. FISA Reauthorization/Domestic-Communications Report.
Wyden, D-Ore., amendment that would require the director of national intelligence to report to Congress on how many domestic communications the government has collected under the 2008 foreign surveillance law. Rejected 43-52: D 36-12; R 6-39; I 1-1. (By unanimous consent, the Senate agreed to raise the majority requirement for adoption of the Wyden amendment to 60 votes.) Dec. 28, 2012.

236. HR 5949. FISA Reauthorization/Passage.
Passage of the bill that would reauthorize for five years, through 2017, the Foreign Intelligence Surveillance Act, which governs electronic surveillance of foreign terrorism suspects. The law allows surveillance of foreign targets who may be communicating with people in the United States provided that the secret FISA court approves surveillance procedures. Passed (thus cleared for the president) 73-23: D 30-19; R 42-3; I 1-1. (By unanimous consent, the Senate agreed to raise the majority requirement for passage of the bill to 60 votes.) A "yea" was a vote in support of the president's position. Dec. 28, 2012.

237. HR 1. Superstorm Supplemental/Palau Typhoon Agreement.
Bingaman, D-N.M., amendment to the Reid, D-Nev., substitute amendment. The Bingaman amendment would allow for the approval of an agreement between the United States and Palau in response to Super Typhoon Bopha. The substitute would provide $60.4 billion in emergency spending for communities hit by Superstorm Sandy, including an additional $9.7 billion in borrowing authority for the National Flood Insurance Program, $13 billion for mitigation projects and $11.5 billion for the Federal Emergency Management Agency's Disaster Relief Fund. Rejected 52-43: D 46-2; R 4-41; I 2-0. (By unanimous consent, the Senate agreed to raise the majority requirement for adoption of the Bingaman amendment to 60 votes.) Dec. 28, 2012.

238. HR 1. Superstorm Supplemental/Motion to Waive.
Tester, D-Mont., motion to waive all applicable budget laws with respect to the Sessions, R-Ala., point of order against the Tester amendment to the Reid, D-Nev., substitute amendment. The Tester amendment would provide $653 million for wildfire management and require a Government Accountability Office study by Dec. 31, 2013, on how to better project future wildfire suppression costs. Motion rejected 51-44: D 47-1; R 2-43; I 2-0. A three-fifths majority vote of the total Senate (60) is required to waive the applicable budget laws. Dec. 28, 2012.

239. HR 1. Superstorm Supplemental/Federal Cost Share.
Coburn, R-Okla., amendment to the Reid, D-Nev., substitute amendment. The Coburn amendment would decrease the federal cost requirements for rebuilding certain damaged maritime assets such as harbors and locks to 65 percent of the Army Corps of Engineers costs rather than 90 percent. Rejected 44-51: D 0-48; R 44-1; I 0-2. (By unanimous consent, the Senate agreed to raise the majority requirement for adoption of the Coburn amendment to 60 votes.) Dec. 28, 2012.

240. HR 1. Superstorm Supplemental/Limitations on Fisheries Aid.
Division II of the Coburn, R-Okla., amendment to the Reid, D-Nev., substitute amendment. Division II would prohibit supplemental funds from being used for commercial fisheries located more than 50 miles outside the boundaries of the designated disaster area. Rejected 35-60: D 2-46; R 33-12; I 0-2. (By unanimous consent, the Senate agreed to divide the question on the Coburn amendment and to raise the majority requirement for adoption of each division of the amendment to 60 votes.) Dec. 28, 2012.

	235	236	237	238	239	240
ALABAMA						
Shelby	N	Y	N	N	Y	N
Sessions	N	Y	N	N	Y	Y
ALASKA						
Murkowski	Y	N	Y	N	Y	N
Begich	Y	N	Y	Y	N	N
ARIZONA						
McCain	N	Y	Y	N	Y	Y
Kyl	N	Y	N	N	Y	Y
ARKANSAS						
Pryor	N	Y	Y	Y	N	N
Boozman	N	Y	N	N	Y	N
CALIFORNIA						
Feinstein	N	Y	Y	Y	N	N
Boxer	?	?	?	?	?	?
COLORADO						
Udall	Y	N	Y	Y	N	N
Bennet	Y	Y	Y	Y	N	N
CONNECTICUT						
Lieberman	N	Y	Y	Y	N	N
Blumenthal	Y	Y	Y	Y	N	N
DELAWARE						
Carper	Y	Y	Y	N	N	Y
Coons	Y	N	Y	Y	N	N
FLORIDA						
Nelson	N	Y	Y	Y	N	N
Rubio	N	Y	N	N	Y	Y
GEORGIA						
Chambliss	N	Y	N	N	Y	Y
Isakson	N	Y	N	N	Y	Y
HAWAII						
Akaka	Y	N	Y	Y	N	N
Schatz	Y	N	Y	Y	N	N
IDAHO						
Crapo	N	Y	N	N	Y	Y
Risch	N	Y	N	N	Y	Y
ILLINOIS						
Durbin	Y	N	Y	Y	N	N
Kirk	?	?	?	?	?	?
INDIANA						
Lugar	N	Y	N	N	Y	Y
Coats	N	Y	N	N	Y	N
IOWA						
Grassley	Y	Y	N	N	Y	Y
Harkin	Y	N	Y	Y	N	N
KANSAS						
Roberts	N	Y	N	N	Y	Y
Moran	N	Y	N	N	Y	N
KENTUCKY						
McConnell	N	Y	N	N	Y	Y
Paul	Y	N	N	N	Y	Y
LOUISIANA						
Landrieu	Y	Y	Y	Y	N	N
Vitter	N	Y	N	N	N	N
MAINE						
Snowe	N	Y	N	N	Y	N
Collins	N	Y	N	Y	Y	N
MARYLAND						
Mikulski	N	Y	Y	Y	N	N
Cardin	Y	Y	Y	Y	N	N
MASSACHUSETTS						
Kerry	N	Y	Y	Y	N	N
Brown	N	Y	N	N	Y	N
MICHIGAN						
Levin	Y	Y	Y	Y	N	N
Stabenow	Y	Y	Y	Y	N	N
MINNESOTA						
Klobuchar	Y	Y	Y	Y	N	N
Franken	Y	N	Y	Y	N	N
MISSISSIPPI						
Cochran	N	Y	N	N	Y	N
Wicker	N	Y	N	N	Y	N
MISSOURI						
McCaskill	?	Y	Y	Y	N	Y
Blunt	N	Y	N	N	Y	Y

	235	236	237	238	239	240
MONTANA						
Baucus	Y	N	Y	Y	N	N
Tester	Y	N	Y	Y	N	N
NEBRASKA						
Nelson	Y	Y	Y	Y	N	N
Johanns	N	Y	N	Y	N	Y
NEVADA						
Reid	Y	Y	Y	Y	N	N
Heller	Y	Y	Y	Y	Y	Y
NEW HAMPSHIRE						
Shaheen	Y	Y	Y	Y	N	N
Ayotte	N	Y	N	N	Y	N
NEW JERSEY						
Lautenberg	?	?	?	?	?	?
Menendez	Y	N	Y	Y	N	N
NEW MEXICO						
Bingaman	Y	N	Y	Y	N	N
Udall	Y	N	Y	Y	N	N
NEW YORK						
Schumer	N	Y	Y	Y	N	N
Gillibrand	Y	Y	Y	Y	N	N
NORTH CAROLINA						
Burr	N	Y	N	N	Y	Y
Hagan	N	Y	N	N	Y	N
NORTH DAKOTA						
Conrad	Y	Y	Y	Y	N	N
Hoeven	N	Y	N	N	Y	Y
OHIO						
Brown	Y	N	Y	Y	N	N
Portman	N	Y	N	N	Y	Y
OKLAHOMA						
Inhofe	N	Y	N	N	Y	Y
Coburn	N	Y	N	N	Y	Y
OREGON						
Wyden	Y	N	Y	Y	N	N
Merkley	Y	N	Y	Y	N	N
PENNSYLVANIA						
Casey	Y	Y	Y	Y	N	N
Toomey	Y	Y	N	N	Y	Y
RHODE ISLAND						
Reed	Y	Y	Y	Y	N	N
Whitehouse	N	Y	Y	Y	N	N
SOUTH CAROLINA						
Graham	N	Y	N	N	Y	N
DeMint	?	?	?	?	?	?
SOUTH DAKOTA						
Johnson	N	Y	Y	Y	N	N
Thune	N	Y	N	N	Y	N
TENNESSEE						
Alexander	N	Y	N	N	Y	N
Corker	N	Y	N	N	Y	Y
TEXAS						
Hutchison	N	Y	N	N	Y	N
Cornyn	N	Y	N	N	Y	Y
UTAH						
Hatch	N	Y	N	N	Y	N
Lee	Y	N	N	N	Y	N
VERMONT						
Leahy	Y	N	Y	Y	N	N
Sanders	Y	N	Y	Y	N	N
VIRGINIA						
Webb	Y	Y	Y	Y	N	N
Warner	N	Y	?	?	?	?
WASHINGTON						
Murray	Y	N	Y	Y	N	N
Cantwell	Y	N	Y	Y	N	N
WEST VIRGINIA						
Rockefeller	N	Y	Y	Y	N	N
Manchin	Y	Y	N	Y	N	N
WISCONSIN						
Kohl	N	Y	Y	Y	N	N
Johnson	N	Y	N	Y	N	Y
WYOMING						
Enzi	N	Y	N	N	Y	Y
Barrasso	N	Y	N	N	Y	Y

KEY   Republicans   Democrats   *Independents*

Y Voted for (yea)
Paired for
+ Announced for
N Voted against (nay)

X Paired against
– Announced against
P Voted "present"

C Voted "present" to avoid possible conflict of interest
? Did not vote or otherwise make a position known

IN THE SENATE | By Vote Number

241. **HR 1. Superstorm Supplemental/Per Capita Damage Indicators.** Coburn, R-Okla., amendment to the Reid, D-Nev., substitute amendment. The Coburn amendment would require the Federal Emergency Management Agency to begin the rule-making process for indexing to inflation the per capita damage indicators used to determine whether federal disaster assistance is necessary. Rejected 40-55: D 6-42; R 34-11; I 0-2. (By unanimous consent, the Senate agreed to raise the majority requirement for adoption of the Coburn amendment to 60 votes.) Dec. 28, 2012.

242. **HR 1. Superstorm Supplemental/Competitive Disaster Recovery Contracts.** Coburn, R-Okla., amendment to the Reid, D-Nev., substitute amendment that would require merit-based and competitive awards of disaster recovery contracts. Rejected 48-47: D 9-39; R 39-6; I 0-2. (By unanimous consent, the Senate agreed to raise the majority requirement for adoption of the Coburn amendment to 60 votes.) Dec. 28, 2012.

243. **HR 1. Superstorm Supplemental/Prevailing Wages.** Paul, R-Ky., amendment to the Reid, D-Nev., substitute amendment that would bar the use of funds in the bill to administer or enforce prevailing wage requirements under the Davis-Bacon Act for public works projects. Rejected 42-52: D 0-47; R 42-3; I 0-2. (By unanimous consent, the Senate agreed to raise the majority requirement for adoption of the Paul amendment to 60 votes.) Dec. 28, 2012.

244. **HR 1. Superstorm Supplemental/Spending Offsets.** Paul, R-Ky., amendment to the Reid, D-Nev., substitute amendment that would strip spending provisions of their emergency designation and rescind $8.97 billion in certain fiscal 2013 unobligated spending. Rejected 3-91: D 0-47; R 3-42; I 0-2. (By unanimous consent, the Senate agreed to raise the majority requirement for adoption of the Paul amendment to 60 votes.) Dec. 28, 2012.

245. **HR 1. Superstorm Supplemental/Forest Restoration Funding.** McCain, R-Ariz., amendment to the Reid, D-Nev., substitute amendment that would strike funding for an emergency forest restoration fund. Rejected 46-49: D 3-45; R 43-2; I 0-2. (By unanimous consent, the Senate agreed to raise the majority requirement for adoption of the McCain amendment to 60 votes.) Dec. 28, 2012.

246. **HR 1. Superstorm Supplemental/Motion to Waive.** Merkley, D-Ore., motion to waive all applicable budget laws with respect to the Sessions, R-Ala., point of order on the Merkley amendment to the Reid, D-Nev., substitute amendment. The Merkley amendment would reimburse ranchers, fruit growers and farmers for lost crops, livestock and damaged land caused by drought or certain other natural disasters in the 2012 crop year. Rejected 55-40: D 48-0; R 5-40; I 2-0. A three-fifths majority vote of the total Senate (60) is required to waive the applicable budget laws. Dec. 28, 2012.

247. **HR 1. Superstorm Supplemental/Republican Substitute.** Coats, R-Ind., substitute amendment to the Reid, D-Nev., substitute amendment. The Coats amendment would provide $23.8 billion in emergency funding for communities hit by Superstorm Sandy. It would eliminate $13 billion in mitigation funds and spending on a variety of programs outside of the North Atlantic coastal region. Rejected 41-54: D 0-48; R 41-4; I 0-2. (By unanimous consent, the Senate agreed to raise the majority requirement for adoption of the Coats amendment to 60 votes.) Dec. 28, 2012.

State / Senator	241	242	243	244	245	246	247
ALABAMA							
Shelby	Y	Y	Y	N	Y	N	Y
Sessions	Y	Y	Y	N	Y	N	Y
ALASKA							
Murkowski	N	N	N	N	Y	N	Y
Begich	N	N	N	?	N	Y	N
ARIZONA							
McCain	Y	Y	Y	N	Y	N	Y
Kyl	Y	Y	Y	N	Y	N	Y
ARKANSAS							
Pryor	N	N	N	N	N	Y	N
Boozman	Y	Y	Y	N	Y	N	Y
CALIFORNIA							
Feinstein	N	N	N	N	N	Y	N
Boxer	?	?	?	?	?	?	?
COLORADO							
Udall	N	Y	N	N	N	Y	N
Bennet	N	Y	N	N	N	Y	N
CONNECTICUT							
Lieberman	N	N	N	N	N	Y	N
Blumenthal	N	N	N	N	N	Y	N
DELAWARE							
Carper	Y	N	N	N	Y	Y	N
Coons	Y	N	N	N	N	Y	N
FLORIDA							
Nelson	N	N	N	N	N	Y	N
Rubio	Y	N	Y	N	Y	N	Y
GEORGIA							
Chambliss	Y	Y	Y	N	Y	N	Y
Isakson	Y	Y	Y	N	Y	N	Y
HAWAII							
Akaka	N	N	N	N	N	Y	N
Schatz	N	N	N	N	N	Y	N
IDAHO							
Crapo	Y	Y	Y	N	Y	N	Y
Risch	Y	Y	Y	N	Y	N	Y
ILLINOIS							
Durbin	N	N	N	N	N	Y	N
Kirk	?	?	?	?	?	?	?
INDIANA							
Lugar	Y	Y	Y	N	Y	N	Y
Coats	Y	Y	Y	N	Y	N	Y
IOWA							
Grassley	Y	Y	Y	N	Y	N	Y
Harkin	N	N	N	N	N	Y	N
KANSAS							
Roberts	N	Y	Y	N	Y	N	Y
Moran	N	Y	Y	N	Y	Y	Y
KENTUCKY							
McConnell	N	Y	Y	N	Y	N	Y
Paul	Y	Y	Y	N	Y	N	N
LOUISIANA							
Landrieu	N	N	N	N	N	Y	N
Vitter	Y	Y	Y	N	Y	N	Y
MAINE							
Snowe	N	Y	Y	N	N	Y	N
Collins	N	N	Y	N	Y	N	N
MARYLAND							
Mikulski	N	N	N	N	N	Y	N
Cardin	N	N	N	N	N	Y	N
MASSACHUSETTS							
Kerry	N	N	N	N	Y	Y	N
Brown	N	Y	N	N	Y	Y	N
MICHIGAN							
Levin	N	N	N	N	N	Y	N
Stabenow	N	N	N	N	N	Y	N
MINNESOTA							
Klobuchar	Y	Y	N	N	N	Y	N
Franken	N	N	N	N	N	Y	N
MISSISSIPPI							
Cochran	Y	N	Y	N	N	N	Y
Wicker	Y	Y	Y	N	Y	N	Y
MISSOURI							
McCaskill	Y	Y	N	N	Y	Y	N
Blunt	Y	N	Y	N	Y	Y	Y

State / Senator	241	242	243	244	245	246	247
MONTANA							
Baucus	N	Y	N	N	N	Y	N
Tester	N	Y	N	N	N	Y	N
NEBRASKA							
Nelson	N	N	N	N	N	Y	N
Johanns	Y	Y	N	N	N	Y	N
NEVADA							
Reid	N	N	?	N	N	Y	N
Heller	N	Y	Y	Y	Y	N	Y
NEW HAMPSHIRE							
Shaheen	N	N	N	N	N	Y	N
Ayotte	N	Y	Y	N	Y	N	Y
NEW JERSEY							
Lautenberg	?	?	?	?	?	?	?
Menendez	N	N	N	N	N	Y	N
NEW MEXICO							
Bingaman	N	N	N	N	N	Y	N
Udall	N	N	N	N	N	Y	N
NEW YORK							
Schumer	N	N	N	N	N	Y	N
Gillibrand	N	N	N	N	N	Y	N
NORTH CAROLINA							
Burr	Y	Y	Y	N	Y	N	Y
Hagan	N	N	N	N	N	Y	N
NORTH DAKOTA							
Conrad	N	N	N	N	N	Y	N
Hoeven	N	N	Y	N	Y	Y	Y
OHIO							
Brown	N	N	N	N	N	Y	N
Portman	Y	Y	Y	N	Y	N	Y
OKLAHOMA							
Inhofe	Y	Y	Y	N	Y	N	Y
Coburn	Y	Y	Y	N	Y	N	Y
OREGON							
Wyden	N	N	N	N	N	Y	N
Merkley	N	N	N	N	N	Y	N
PENNSYLVANIA							
Casey	N	N	N	N	N	Y	N
Toomey	Y	Y	Y	N	Y	N	Y
RHODE ISLAND							
Reed	N	N	N	N	N	Y	N
Whitehouse	N	N	N	N	N	Y	N
SOUTH CAROLINA							
Graham	Y	Y	Y	N	Y	N	Y
DeMint	?	?	?	?	?	?	?
SOUTH DAKOTA							
Johnson	N	N	N	N	N	Y	N
Thune	Y	Y	Y	N	Y	N	Y
TENNESSEE							
Alexander	Y	Y	Y	N	Y	N	Y
Corker	Y	Y	Y	N	Y	N	Y
TEXAS							
Hutchison	Y	Y	Y	N	Y	N	Y
Cornyn	Y	Y	Y	N	Y	N	Y
UTAH							
Hatch	N	Y	Y	N	Y	N	Y
Lee	Y	Y	Y	N	Y	N	Y
VERMONT							
Leahy	N	N	N	N	N	Y	N
Sanders	N	N	N	N	N	Y	N
VIRGINIA							
Webb	Y	Y	N	N	N	Y	N
Warner	?	?	?	?	?	?	?
WASHINGTON							
Murray	N	N	N	N	N	Y	N
Cantwell	N	N	N	N	N	Y	N
WEST VIRGINIA							
Rockefeller	N	N	N	N	N	Y	N
Manchin	N	Y	N	N	Y	Y	N
WISCONSIN							
Kohl	Y	Y	N	N	N	Y	N
Johnson	Y	Y	Y	N	Y	N	Y
WYOMING							
Enzi	Y	Y	Y	N	Y	N	Y
Barrasso	Y	Y	Y	N	Y	N	Y

KEY   **Republicans**   Democrats   *Independents*

Y	Voted for (yea)	X Paired against	C Voted "present" to avoid possible conflict of interest
#	Paired for	– Announced against	
+	Announced for	P Voted "present"	? Did not vote or otherwise make a position known
N	Voted against (nay)		

IN THE SENATE | By Vote Number

248. **HR 1. Superstorm Supplemental/Passage.** Passage of the bill that would provide $60.4 billion in emergency spending for communities hit by Superstorm Sandy, including an additional $9.7 billion in borrowing authority for the National Flood Insurance Program, $13 billion for mitigation projects, $11.5 billion for the Federal Emergency Management Agency's Disaster Relief Fund and $10.8 billion to the Federal Transit Administration to rebuild public transit systems. As amended, the bill would provide $17 billion for the Community Development Fund, with $500 million designated for regions that suffered major disasters or for "small, economically distressed areas" with less-severe calamities in 2011 and 2012. It would allow the transfer of previously appropriated foreign affairs funds to pay for increased security at U.S. embassies and other overseas posts. Passed 62-32: D 48-0; R 12-32; I 2-0. (Prior to passage, the Reid, D-Nev., substitute amendment was adopted by voice vote.) A "yea" was a vote in support of the president's position. Dec. 28, 2012.

249. **Baer Nomination/Confirmation.** Confirmation of President Obama's nomination of William Joseph Baer to be assistant attorney general for antitrust at the Justice Department. Confirmed 64-26: D 48-0; R 14-26; I 2-0. A "yea" was a vote in support of the president's position. Dec. 30, 2012.

250. **Galante Nomination/Confirmation.** Confirmation of President Obama's nomination of Carol J. Galante of California to be assistant secretary of Housing and Urban Development and commissioner of the Federal Housing Administration. Confirmed 69-24: D 49-0; R 18-24; I 2-0. (By unanimous consent, the Senate agreed to raise the majority requirement for confirmation to 60 votes.) A "yea" was a vote in support of the president's position. Dec. 30, 2012.

251. **HR 8. Tax Rates Extensions/Passage.** Passage of the bill that would permanently extend the 2001 and 2003 tax rates for individual income below $400,000 and joint-filer income below $450,000. Rates for income above those thresholds would rise to 39.6 percent from 35 percent. It also would permanently extend the tax rates on dividends and capital gains for individual income below $400,000 and joint-filer income below $450,000. Rates for the dividends and capital gains taxes would rise to 20 percent for income above those thresholds. The measure would delay the automatic, across-the-board cuts known as "sequester" for two months. Half of the sequester delay would be offset by discretionary cuts, split between defense and non-defense, and the other half offset by revenue raised through the voluntary transfer of traditional IRAs to Roth IRAs, which would tax retirement savings when transferred. It also would tax individual estates valued at more than $5 million and joint estates valued at more than $10 million at 40 percent. It would permanently "patch" the alternative minimum tax to account for inflation. Unemployment insurance would be extended through 2013. The bill would block scheduled cuts to Medicare physician payment rates and extend for five years tax credits included in the 2009 stimulus law including the child tax credit and the earned income tax credit. It would allow the 2 percent payroll tax holiday to expire. It would also extend the Milk Income Loss Contract program at current rates. Passed 89-8: D 47-3; R 40-5; I 2-0. (By unanimous consent, the Senate agreed to raise the majority requirement for passage of the bill to 60 votes.) A "yea" was a vote in support of the president's position. Jan. 1, 2013 (in the session that began and the Congressional Record dated Dec. 31, 2012).

	248	249	250	251
ALABAMA				
Shelby	Y	N	N	N
Sessions	N	N	N	Y
ALASKA				
Murkowski	Y	Y	Y	Y
Begich	Y	Y	Y	Y
ARIZONA				
McCain	N	N	Y	Y
Kyl	N	N	N	Y
ARKANSAS				
Pryor	Y	Y	Y	Y
Boozman	N	N	N	Y
CALIFORNIA				
Feinstein	Y	Y	Y	Y
Boxer	?	Y	Y	Y
COLORADO				
Udall	Y	Y	Y	Y
Bennet	Y	Y	N	N
CONNECTICUT				
Lieberman	Y	Y	Y	Y
Blumenthal	Y	Y	Y	Y
DELAWARE				
Carper	Y	Y	Y	N
Coons	Y	Y	Y	Y
FLORIDA				
Nelson	Y	Y	Y	Y
Rubio	N	?	N	N
GEORGIA				
Chambliss	N	?	?	Y
Isakson	N	N	Y	Y
HAWAII				
Akaka	Y	Y	Y	Y
Schatz	Y	Y	Y	Y
IDAHO				
Crapo	N	N	N	Y
Risch	?	N	N	Y
ILLINOIS				
Durbin	Y	Y	Y	Y
Kirk	?	?	?	?
INDIANA				
Lugar	Y	Y	Y	Y
Coats	N	N	Y	Y
IOWA				
Grassley	N	N	N	N
Harkin	Y	Y	Y	N
KANSAS				
Roberts	N	N	N	Y
Moran	N	Y	N	Y
KENTUCKY				
McConnell	N	N	N	Y
Paul	N	Y	N	N
LOUISIANA				
Landrieu	Y	Y	Y	Y
Vitter	Y	N	N	Y
MAINE				
Snowe	Y	Y	Y	Y
Collins	Y	Y	Y	Y
MARYLAND				
Mikulski	Y	Y	Y	Y
Cardin	Y	Y	Y	Y
MASSACHUSETTS				
Kerry	Y	?	?	Y
Brown	Y	Y	Y	Y
MICHIGAN				
Levin	Y	Y	Y	Y
Stabenow	Y	Y	Y	Y
MINNESOTA				
Klobuchar	Y	Y	Y	Y
Franken	Y	Y	Y	Y
MISSISSIPPI				
Cochran	Y	N	N	Y
Wicker	Y	N	N	Y
MISSOURI				
McCaskill	Y	Y	Y	Y
Blunt	N	N	Y	Y
MONTANA				
Baucus	Y	Y	Y	Y
Tester	Y	Y	Y	Y
NEBRASKA				
Nelson	Y	Y	Y	Y
Johanns	N	?	N	Y
NEVADA				
Reid	Y	Y	Y	Y
Heller	Y	Y	N	Y
NEW HAMPSHIRE				
Shaheen	Y	Y	Y	Y
Ayotte	N	Y	N	Y
NEW JERSEY				
Lautenberg	?	?	?	?
Menendez	Y	Y	Y	Y
NEW MEXICO				
Bingaman	Y	Y	Y	Y
Udall	Y	Y	Y	Y
NEW YORK				
Schumer	Y	Y	Y	Y
Gillibrand	Y	Y	Y	Y
NORTH CAROLINA				
Burr	N	N	Y	Y
Hagan	Y	Y	Y	Y
NORTH DAKOTA				
Conrad	Y	Y	Y	Y
Hoeven	Y	N	Y	Y
OHIO				
Brown	Y	Y	Y	Y
Portman	N	?	?	Y
OKLAHOMA				
Inhofe	N	N	N	Y
Coburn	N	N	Y	Y
OREGON				
Wyden	Y	Y	Y	Y
Merkley	Y	Y	Y	Y
PENNSYLVANIA				
Casey	Y	Y	Y	Y
Toomey	N	Y	N	Y
RHODE ISLAND				
Reed	Y	Y	Y	Y
Whitehouse	Y	Y	Y	Y
SOUTH CAROLINA				
Graham	N	Y	Y	Y
DeMint	?	?	?	?
SOUTH DAKOTA				
Johnson	Y	Y	Y	Y
Thune	N	N	Y	Y
TENNESSEE				
Alexander	N	?	?	Y
Corker	N	Y	Y	Y
TEXAS				
Hutchison	Y	N	Y	Y
Cornyn	N	N	N	Y
UTAH				
Hatch	N	N	N	Y
Lee	N	Y	N	N
VERMONT				
Leahy	Y	?	Y	Y
Sanders	Y	Y	Y	Y
VIRGINIA				
Webb	?	Y	Y	Y
Warner	Y	Y	Y	Y
WASHINGTON				
Murray	Y	Y	Y	Y
Cantwell	Y	Y	Y	Y
WEST VIRGINIA				
Rockefeller	Y	Y	Y	Y
Manchin	Y	Y	Y	Y
WISCONSIN				
Kohl	Y	Y	Y	Y
Johnson	N	Y	Y	Y
WYOMING				
Enzi	N	N	N	Y
Barrasso	N	N	N	Y

KEY   Republicans   Democrats   *Independents*

Y Voted for (yea)	X Paired against
# Paired for	− Announced against
+ Announced for	P Voted "present"
N Voted against (nay)	

C Voted "present" to avoid possible conflict of interest

? Did not vote or otherwise make a position known

Senate Roll Call Index by Subject